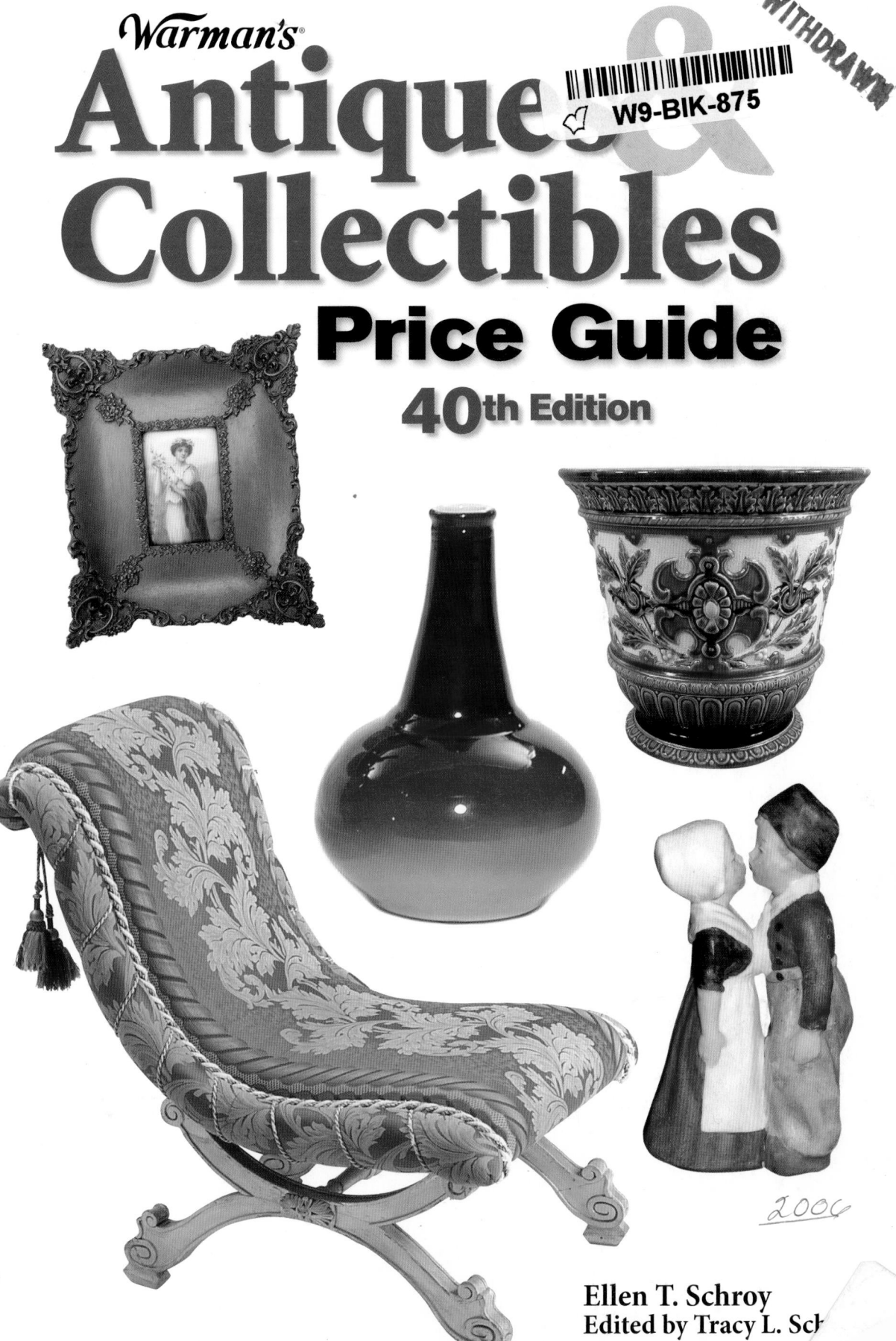

Warman's
Antiques & Collectibles
Price Guide
40th Edition

W9-BIK-875

2006

Ellen T. Schroy
Edited by Tracy L. Sch

©2006 Krause Publications

Published by

krause publications

An Imprint of F+W Publications

700 East State Street • Iola, WI 54990-0001
715-445-2214 • 888-457-2873

Our toll-free number to place an order or obtain
a free catalog is (800) 258-0929.

As condition, regional fluctuations, and other factors influence market pricing, the prices
contained in this book are intended to serve only as a guide. The publisher recommends
users research price trends in their regions before buying and selling items.

On the front cover:
Turtle brooch, $25; Cranberry Glass opalescent vase, Fenton, $229; wooden shelf, $1,000.

Library of Congress Catalog Number: 2005932127

ISBN-13: 978-089689-317-7

ISBN-10: 0-89689-317-0

Designed by Wendy Wendt

Edited by Tracy L. Schmidt

Printed in China

CONTENTS

DEDICATION

To Ann Marie Schroy with love from grandma Ellen.

To Dan, my stability; Taylor Grace, my shooting star, and to Emily Claire, who inspires me to be stronger—Tracy

Introduction

WARMAN'S: SERVING THE TRADE FOR MORE THAN 50 YEARS

In 1994, *Warman's Antiques and Their Prices* became *Warman's Antiques and Collectibles Price Guide.* Longtime Warman's users will find new changes to this edition. The biggest change is the book has been reorganized for enhanced ease of use.

Individuals in the trade refer to this book simply as Warman's, a fitting tribute to E. G. Warman and the product he created. Warman's has been around for more than 50 years. We are proud as peacocks that Warman's continues to establish the standards for general antiques and collectibles price guides in 2005, just as it did in 1972 when its first rival appeared on the scene.

Warman's, the antiques and collectibles "bible," covers objects made between 1700 and the present. Because it reflects market trends, Warman's has added more and more 20th-century material to each edition. Remember, 1900 was more than 100 years ago—the distant past to the new generation of 20-something and 30-something collectors. The general "antiques" market consists of antiques (for the purposes of this book, objects made before 1945), collectibles (objects of the post-World War II era that enjoy an established secondary market), and desirables (contemporary objects that are collected, but speculative in price). Although Warman's contains information on all three market segments, its greatest emphasis is on antiques and collectibles. In fact, this book is the essential field guide to the antiques and collectibles marketplace, which indicates that Warman's is much more than a list of object descriptions and prices. It is a basic guide to the field as a whole, providing you with the key information you need every time you encounter a new object or collecting category.

'Warman's is the Key'

Warman's provides the keys needed by auctioneers, collectors, dealers, and others to understand and deal with the complexities of the antiques and collectibles market. A price list is only one of many keys needed today. Warman's 40th edition contains histories, marks, reproductions and useful buying and collecting hints. Used properly, there are few doors these keys will not open. Warman's is designed to be your first key to the exciting world of antiques and collectibles. As you use the keys this book provides to advance further in your specialized collecting areas, Warman's hopes you will remember with fondness where you received your start. When you encounter items outside your area of specialty, remember Warman's remains your key to unlocking the information you need, just as it has in the past.

HOW DO YOU LIKE YOUR WARMAN'S®?

The editorial staff at Krause Publications would like to get your feedback and suggestions to further grow and improve *Warman's® Antiques & Collectibles.* Your feedback will make a difference. Please email your responses for the following questions to: tracy.schmidt@fwpubs.com

1. As the book continues to expand, would you prefer an emphasis on adding photos or listings?
2. What categories should we expand?
3. What categories should we add to the book that are not currently covered?
4. Would you be interested in being a category advisor or be able to provide other information?
5. How do you like the changes we have made to the 40th edition?

Organization

Listings: Objects are listed alphabetically. The major collecting areas have been compiled into individual areas at the front of the book and have been color coded. The lisitngs contain some harder-to-find objects that are included to demonstrate market spread—useful information worth considering when you have not traded actively in a category recently. Each year as the market changes, we carefully review our categories—adding, dropping, and combining to provide the most comprehensive coverage possible. Warman's quick response to developing trends in the marketplace is one of the prime reasons for its continued leadership in the field.

History: Collectors and dealers enhance their appreciation of objects by knowing something about their history. We present a capsule history for each category. In many cases, this history contains collecting hints or other useful information.

References: Krause Publications also publishes other Warman's titles. Each concentrates on a specific collecting group, e.g., American pottery and porcelain, Americana and collectibles, glass, and jewelry. Several are second or subsequent editions. They have been included in each section. There are also several good publications collectors and dealers should be aware of to be knowledgeable about antiques and collectibles in general. Space does not permit listing all of the national and regional publications in the antiques and collectibles field; this is a sampling:

- **Antique & The Arts Weekly**, Bee Publishing Company, 5 Church Hill Road, Newton, CT 06470; http://www.thebee.com/aweb
- **Antique Review**, P.O. Box 538, Worthington, OH 43085
- **Antique Trader Weekly**, published by Krause Publications, Iola, WI.
- **AntiqueWeek**, P.O. Box 90, Knightstown, IN 46148; http://www.antiqueweek.com
- **Maine Antique Digest**, P.O. Box 358, Waldoboro, ME 04572; http:// www.maineantiquedigest.com
- **New England Antiques Journal**, 4 Church St., Ware, MA 01082

Reproductions: Reproductions are a major concern to all collectors and dealers. Throughout this edition, boxes will alert you to known reproductions and keys to recognizing them. Most reproductions are unmarked; the newness of their appearance is often the best clue to uncovering them. Specific objects known to be reproduced are marked within the listings with an asterisk (*). The information is designed to serve as a reminder of past reproductions and prevent you from buying them, believing them to be period. We strongly recommend subscribing to *Antique & Collectors Reproduction News,* a monthly newsletter that reports on past and present reproductions, copycats, fantasies, and fakes. Send $32 for 12 issues to: ACRN, Box 12130, Des Moines, IA 50312-9403; (www.repronews.com). This newsletter has been published for many years. Consider buying all available back issues. The information they contain will be of service long into the future.

Price notes

In assigning prices, we assume the object is in very good condition; if otherwise, we note this in our description. It would be ideal to suggest that mint, or unused, examples of all objects exist. The reality is that objects from the past were used, whether they are glass, china, dolls, or toys. Because of this, some normal wear must be expected. In fact, if an object such as a piece of furniture does not show wear, its origins may be more suspect than if it does show wear. Whenever possible, we have tried to provide a broad listing of prices within a category so you have a "feel" for the market. We emphasize the middle range of prices within a category, while also listing some objects of high and low value to show market spread. We do not use ranges because they tend to confuse, rather than help, the collector and dealer. How do you determine if your object is at the high or low end of the range? There is a high degree of flexibility in pricing in the antiques field. If you want to set ranges, add or subtract 10 percent from our prices.

Price research

Everyone asks, "Where do you get your prices?"

They come from many sources. First, we rely on auctions. Auction houses and auctioneers do not always command the highest prices. If they did, why do so many dealers buy from them? The key to understanding auction prices is to know when a price is high or low in the range. We think we do this and do it well. The 40th edition represents a concentrated effort to contact more regional auction houses, both large and small. The cooperation has been outstanding and has resulted in an ever-growing pool of auction prices and trends to help us determine the most up-to-date auction prices.

Second, we work closely with dealers. We screen our contacts to make certain they have full knowledge of the market. Dealers make their living from selling antiques; they cannot afford to have a price guide that is not in touch with the market. More than 50 antiques and collectibles magazines, newspapers, and journals come into our office regularly. They are excellent barometers of what is moving and what is not. We don't hesitate to call an advertiser and ask if his listed merchandise sold. When the editorial staff is doing fieldwork, we identify ourselves. Our conversations with dealers and collectors around the country have enhanced this book. Teams from Warman's are in the field at antiques shows, malls, flea markets, and auctions recording prices and taking photographs. Collectors work closely with us. They are specialists whose devotion to research and accurate information is inspiring. Generally, they are not dealers. Whenever we have asked them for help, they have responded willingly and admirably.

Board of advisers

Our board of advisers is made up of specialists, both dealers and collectors, who feel a commitment to accurate information. You'll find their names listed in the front of the book. Several have authored a major reference work on their subject. Our esteemed board of advisers has increased in number and scope. Participants have all provided detailed information regarding the history and reference section of their particular area of expertise, as well as preparing price listings. Many have furnished photographs and even shared with us their thoughts on the state of the market. We are delighted to include those who are valuable members, officers, and founders of collectors' clubs. They are authors of books and articles, and many frequently lecture to groups about their specialties. Most of our advisers have been involved with antiques and collectibles for more than 20 years. Several are retired, and the antiques and collectibles business is a hobby that encompasses most of their free time. Others are a bit younger and either work full time or part time in the antiques and collectibles profession. One thing they all have in common is their enthusiasm for the antiques and collectibles marketplace. They are eager to share their knowledge with collectors. Many have developed wonderful friendships through their efforts and are enriched by them. If you wish to buy or sell an object in the field of expertise of any of our advisers, drop them a note along with a SASE. If time permits, they will respond.

Buyer's guide, not seller's guide

Warman's is designed to be a buyer's guide, suggesting what you would have to pay to purchase an object on the open market from a dealer or collector. It is not a seller's guide to prices. People frequently make this mistake. In doing so, they deceive themselves. If you have an object listed in this book and wish to sell it to a dealer, you should expect to receive approximately 50 percent of the listed value. If the object will not resell quickly, expect to receive even less. Private collectors may pay more, perhaps 70 to 80 percent of our listed price, if your object is something needed for their collection. If you have an extremely rare object or an object of exceptionally high value, these guidelines do not apply. Examine your piece as objectively as possible. As an antiques and collectibles appraiser, I spend a great deal of time telling people their treasures are not "rare" at all, but items readily available in the marketplace. In respect to buying and selling, a simple philosophy is that a good purchase occurs when the buyer and seller are happy with the price. Don't look back. Hindsight has little value in the antiques and collectibles field. Given time, things tend to balance out.

Always improving

Warman's is always trying to improve. Space is freely given to long price descriptions to help you understand what the piece looks like, and perhaps what's special about it. With this edition, we've arranged some old formats, Many times, identifying what you've got is the hardest part. Well, the first place to start is how big—grab that ruler and see what you can find that's a comparable size. You are still going to have to make a determination about what the object is made of, be it china, glass, porcelain, wood, or other materials. Use all your senses to discover what you've got. Ask questions about your object, who made it, and why, how was it used, where, and when. As you find answers to these questions, you'll be helping yourself figure out just what the treasure is all about.

Eager to hear from readers

At Warman's and Krause Publications, we're always eager to hear what you think about this book and how we can improve it. Write to either

Ellen Schroy
Warman's Editor
135 S. Main St.,
Quakertown, PA 18951-1119
schroy@voicenet.com

or

Tracy Schmidt
Krause Publications
700 E. State St.
Iola, WI 54990
tracy.schmidt@fwpubs.com

It's our goal to continue in the Warman's tradition and make it the best price guide available.

Saturday Evening Girls, perpetual calendar, tree and river landscape, marked, 3-1/2" x 2", **$800.**
Photo courtesy of David Rago Auctions Inc.

Saturday Evening Girls, bowl, painted hen and chick on bright orange band, mottled gray ground, signed "SEG," opposing hairlines, 2-1/4" x 4-1/4", **$650.**
Photo courtesy of David Rago Auctions Inc.

Cloisonné, vase, oxblood wireless enamel, silver fittings, Hawakawa Komejiro, Japanese, sgd on base, 4-3/4" h, **$500.**
Photo courtesy of David Rago Auctions Inc.

Statue, marble, Venus de Milo, placed on stop-fluted pedestal with Greek key decoration, white, 66" x 14" x 14", **$1,300.**
Photo courtesy of David Rago Auctions Inc.

Whirligig, horse jumping over well, painted tin, Frederick Metzinger, Elizabeth, New Jersey, turn of century, 23" x 14", **$700.**
Photo courtesy of David Rago Auctions Inc.

STATE OF THE MARKET
WARMAN'S ANTIQUES & COLLECTIBLES PRICE GUIDE
40TH EDITION

While having one of our weekly editorial chats, F+W editor Tracy Schmidt mentioned that "life has many seasons" as she told me she as much as she treasured the cranberry glass she had inherited from her grandmother, having a toddler in the house meant that it might not be the best time to have it displayed or add to her collection. Her phrase "many seasons" seemed to rattle around in my brain all evening long. Truly, the antiques world has seasons too, but what is the present season?

If you read the antiques trade papers faithfully, you will see how many auctions are achieving record prices; how many antique shows and flea markets are well attended; or you may see which ones fell victim to outside forces, such as bad weather and rising gas prices. The 2005 antiques season was one of highs and lows, external influences brought some new buyers into the market and sadly some long time collectors said their goodbyes.

Noted majolica-specialist auctioneer Michael G. Strawser dispersed the extensive collection of the late Marilyn G. Karmason in December of 2005. Mrs. Karmason's family chose to keep a very small portion of her extensive collection and collectors and dealers were eager to add a piece with such an excellent provenance to their bulging shelves. Many of the pieces included in the auction had been featured in Mrs. Karmason's well done reference books, adding yet another layer to their perceived value. Buyers came in anticipation of finding unique items and they were not disappointed. Some of the records set for that auction include a Minton cheese keeper in the shape of a beehive with a twig base. The hammer price was $74,750, far above the $35,000 to $42,500 pre-bid estimate placed by Strawser. A covered quail game dish by maker George Jones in turquoise brought a record price of $57,500, despite the repaired hairline on the cover. Another large piece, a figural Egyptian garden seat made by T. C. Brown-Westhead, Moore & Co., sold for $19,550. At 22" high, that's a lot of colorful majolica.

In an after-the-auction interview, Mr. Strawser commented that he was encouraged by all the new faces in the crowd, who were buying low to mid-range pieces. They sat elbow-to-elbow with the seasoned collectors who were bidding fiercely on some of the more expensive pieces. Anytime an auctioneer brings both young and seasoned collectors together, there is a successful auction.

Other auctioneers all around the country experienced this same phenomena all season long. Many auctioneers are finding themselves competing more aggressively for the large collections that come up during the year. As a result of this competition, collectors are often treated to articles about an upcoming auction as the auction house tries to promote what they are selling weeks in advance to make sure they get the word out to the collecting world. As the cost of advertising, renting a hall, transporting auction contents continue to rise, the importance of communication between auctioneers, dealers, and collectors is becoming even more keen.

To help solve this, many auctioneers are resorting to e-mails, postcards, or flyers to good customers to make sure they mark the calendar and attend previews and the auction. One such example would be that Bertoia Auction of Vineland, NJ, thought its upcoming Toy Feast auction was important enough for them to go to Atlantique City to promote the auction and their services. One of the toys Jeanne Bertoia took to illustrate the high quality of their auction was a Rogelio Sanchez Minnie Mouse nanny pushing baby Felix in a pram. This wonderful tin wind-up sold at their Toy Feast auction for $20,900.

Many of the big antique shows this season, including the fabulous Atlantique City Megafair, saw a less than record attendance. When considering why, it's a hard question to answer. Some outdoor shows had weather issues, Mother Nature just wasn't going to cooperate and kept dealers and collectors from meeting on the fields that had often yielded marvelous treasures in the past. Some shows found their very fields being bought up and sold to developers, forcing them to find another location, which is getting harder and harder to do. Some dealers felt they could no longer travel as far to sell their wares as in the past, due to record setting gas prices.

Spatterware purple and blue rainbow-paneled pitcher and wash bowl, pitcher 10-1/2" h, bowl 12" d, **$2,300.**
Photo courtesy of Pook & Pook Inc.

Sports, croquet set, Abercrombie & Fitch, four maple mallets with brass bands, six wrought iron wickets, four turned balls, contained in orig green enamel box, stenciled "Made in England for Abercrombie & Fitch Co., New York," 10-3/4" x 43-1/2" x 10", **$400.**
Photo courtesy of David Rago Auctions, Inc.

Collectors too felt the pinch at the pump as they traveled less to shows and flea markets. However, for those who could get out and do some antiquing, they were often rewarded with dealers who were eager to sell and good buys could be found.

Collectors who journeyed to Atlantique City in either March or October were treated to a show filled with international dealers, who had brought fresh merchandise and were also eager to sell. The October Atlantique City featured stunning Halloween exhibits utilizing the collections of Pamela Apkarian-Russell and Claire Lavin. Showcases filled with black and orange delighted the visitors as both ladies eagerly explained the fine points of this fast-growing collector area. It gave interested collectors a wonderful chance to meet and talk with Warman's adviser Lavin, something that certainly adds to the fabric of a great show.

If you analyze the seasons of life of the antiques world, perhaps we are now in the autumn of the hobby. The spring season might consist of the time when an antique or collectible is "new" and enjoying its first life. Its "summer" season may be that lazy hazy time of life an object spends resting in the back of a cupboard or tucked in a box in a dusty attic, waiting for its reintroduction to the world. The "autumn" season would find the object coming to the welcoming hands of new collectors where it can be appreciated for it's special attributes.

As you may be noticing, this edition of *Warman's Antiques and Collectibles,* has undergone a significant face lift. Perhaps it too is rejoicing in the seasons of life. Founder E. G. Warman gave it life and nurtured it through its tough growing years. Former editors Harry Rinker and I took turns caring for it during the summer season and now it is bursting with colors and a new format. One of my favorite songs is Bette Midler's *The Rose* where she croons about how a rose blossoms after resting under the winter snow. Perhaps the 40th edition will be that rose. What will the 2006 antiques season bring for collectors and dealers? Hopefully a renewed interest in a hobby that has lots of room to grow and is wonderful in that it continually perpetuates itself.

ACKNOWLEDGMENTS

We at Warman's would like to thank the following people for their contributions to the new 40th edition of *Warman's Antiques & Collectibles Price Guide*:

Bill and Sliv Carlson; photographer Maurice Childs; Heritage Galleries & Auctioneers; Larry and Debbie Hicklin of Middle Tenessee Relics; photographer Paul Goodwin; Leigh Leshner; Cathy and Jamie Melton of Wytheville, Va.; Karen O'Brien; Gerald and Louise Schleich of Lincoln Neb.; Carol Seman and Dan Eggent of Brecksville, Ohio; Majolica Auctions by Michael G. Strawser; The Dane's Home Antiques of Waupaca, Wis.; Jim and Jan Van Hoven; Peggy Whiteneck; the Wisconsin Veterans Museum, and Karen and Lorie Wuttke of Remember When Antiques, Delavan, Wis.

Chinese Export, Chinese, figural horse and cart, ideograms on base, late 19th C, 5" l, 2-1/4" h, tail missing, **$150.**

Portrait, George Washington, oil on canvas, signed, "Washington by D. Ellinger 1932," 9-1/4" x 7-3/4", **$2,300.**
Photo courtesy of Pook & Pook Inc.

Lavabo, French pewter, dolphin form, shell form bowl, later wood bracket, 19th C, 32" h, **$550.**
Photo courtesy of Sloans & Kenyon Auctioneers and Appraisers

Royal Flemish, banquet lamp, font and globe blue and turquoise sections, dividing gold lineage, gold griffin and lion with shield, reticulated metal base, original font and base, reproduction globe, **$1,800.**
Photo courtesy of The Early Auction Company, LLC.

BOARD OF ADVISERS

Bob Armstrong
15 Monadnock Road
Worcester, MA 01609
(508) 799-0644
Puzzles

Ayers Auction Service
P.O. Box 320
Tremont, IL 61566-0520
(309) 925-3115
Web site: www.ayerauction.com

Al Bagdade
The Country Peasants
1325 N. State Parkway, Apt 15A
Chicago, IL 60610
(312) 397-1321
Quimper

Brunk Auctions
117 Tunnel Road
Asheville, North Carolina 28805
(828) 254-6846
Web site: www.brunkauctions.com

Burns Auction Service
P.O. Box 608
Bath, NY 14810
(607) 776-7932
Web site: www.tomburnsauction.
   com

Estate Traders, LLC
7393 West 44th Ave.
Wheat Ridge, CO 80033
(303) 425-0607
Web site: www.estate- traders.com

Guyette & Schmidt
P.O. Box 522
West Farmington, Maine 04992
(207) 778-6256
Web site:
   www.guyetteandschmidt.com

Ted Hake
Hake's Americana & Collectibles
   Auctions
P.O. Box 1444
York, PA 17405
(717) 848-1333
e-mail: auction@hakes.com
Disneyana, Political

I.M. Chait Gallery Auctioneers
9330 Civic Center Drive
Beverly Hills, CA 90210
(310) 285-0182
Web site: www.chait.com

Mary Harris
221 Scarborough Lane
Millersville, PA 17551
(717) 872-8288
e-mail: marymaj@dejazzd.com
Majolica

Leslie Hindman, Inc.
122 N. Aberdeen St.
Chicago, IL 60607
(312) 280-1212
Web site: www.lesliehindman.com

Joan Hull
1376 Nevada
Huron, SD 57350
(605) 352-1685
Hull Pottery

David Irons
Irons Antiques
223 Covered Bridge Road
Northampton, PA 18067
(610) 262-9335
e-mail: Dave@ironsantiques.com
Irons

Michael Ivankovich
Auction Co.
P.O. Box 1536
Doylestown, PA 18901
(215) 345-6094
Web site:http:// www.wnutting.
   com
*Wallace Nutting,
Wallace Nutting
Look-Alikes
American Hand-Painted Porcelain,
American Hand-
Painted Jewelry*

W.D. and M. J. Keagy
*P.O. Box 106
Bloomfield, IN 47424
(812) 384-3471
Yard-Long Prints*

Ellen G. King
King's Antiques
359 Peaceful Valley Rd.
Hilliards, PA 16040-1926
(724) 894-2596
e-mail: ellenk2@earthlink.net
*Flow Blue
Mulberry China*

Michael Krumme
P.O. Box 48225
Los Angeles, CA 90048-0225
Paden City

Claire Lavin
P.O. Box 354
Cheltenham, PA 19019
(215) 663-9523
e-mail: clavin9036@aol.com
Halloween

Robert Levy
The Unique One
2802 Centre St.
Pennsauken, NJ 08109
(856) 663-2554
Web site: Antiqueslotmachines.
   com
e-mail: theuniqueone@worldnet.
   att.net
Coin-Operated Items

Clarence and Betty Maier
The Burmese Cruet
P.O. Box 432
Montgomeryville, PA 18936
(215) 855-5388
e-mail: burmesecruet@erols.com
*Burmese Glass
Crown Milano
Royal Flemish*

James S. Maxwell, Jr.
P.O. Box 367
Lampeter, PA 17537
(717) 464-5573
Banks, Mechanical

Parker-Braden Auctions
Carlsbad, NM
(800) 748-3946
Web site: www.parkerbraden.com

Suzanne Perrault
Perrault Rago Gallery
333 North Main Street
Lambertville, NJ 08530
phone: 609.397.1802
fax: 609.397.9377
email: suzanne@ragoarts.com
Ceramics

Bob Perzel
505 Rt. 579
Ringoes, NJ 08551
(908) 782-9361
Stangl Birds

Evalene Pulati
National Valentine Collectors Assoc.
P.O. Box 1404
Santa Ana, CA 92702
Valentines

John D. Querry
RD 2, Box 137B
Martinsburg, PA 16662
(814) 793-3185
Gaudy Dutch

Quinn's Auction Galleries
431 N. Maple Ave.
Falls Church, VA 22046
(703) 532-5632
Web site: www.quinnsauction.com

David Rago
David Rago Auctions, Inc.
333 N. Main St.
Lambertville, NJ 8530
(609) 397-9374
e-mail: http://www.ragoarts.com
Art Pottery
Arts & Crafts
Fulper
Furniture
Grueby
Newcomb

Remmen Auctions &
  Appraisal Services
P.O. Box 301398
Portland, OR 97294
(503) 256-1226
Web site: www.remmenauction.
  com

Charles and Joan Rhoden
8693 N. 1950 East Road
Georgetown, IL 61846-6254
(217) 662-8046
e-mail: rhoden@soltec.net
Yard-Long Prints

Julie P. Robards
P.O. Box 117
Upper Jay, NY 12987
(518) 946-7753
Celluloid

Jerry Rosen
15 Hampden St.
Swampscott, MA 01907
Piano Babies

Kenneth E. Schneringer
157 Holly Mill Village Drive
Canton, GA 30114
(707) 704-9913
e-mail: trademan68@aol.com
Catalogs

Susan Scott
882 Queen St. West
Toronto, Ontario Canada
M6K 1Q3
e-mail: SusanScottCA@aol.com
Chintz

George Sparacio
P.O. Box 791
Malaga, NJ 08328-0791
(856) 694-4167
e-mail: mrvesta1@aol.com
Match Safes

Henry A. Taron
Tradewinds Antiques
P.O. Box 249
Manchester By-The-Sea, MA
  01944-0249
(978) 526-4085
e-mail:
  taron@tradewindsantiques.com
Canes

Lewis S. Walters
143 Lincoln Lane
Berlin, NJ 08009
(856) 719-1513
e-mail: lew69@erols.com
Phonographs
Radios

Peggy Whiteneck
allwritealready2000@yahoo.com
  Lladró

Crown Milano, bulbouse stick vase, enameled pink and white roses, applied snake around neck, 11" h, $1,650.
Photo courtesy of The Early Auction Company, LLC.

ABBREVIATIONS

The following are standard abbreviations, which we have used throughout this edition of Warman's.

ABP	-	American Brilliant Period	ll	-	lower left
ADS	-	Autograph Document Signed	lr	-	lower right
adv	-	advertising	ls	-	low standard
ah	-	applied handle	LS	-	Letter Signed
ALS	-	Autograph Letter Signed	mfg	-	manufactured
AQS	-	Autograph Quotation Signed	MIB	-	mint in box
C	-	century	MOP	-	mother-of-pearl
c	-	circa	n/c	-	no closure
Cal.	-	caliber	ND	-	no date
circ	-	circular	NE	-	New England
cyl.	-	cylinder	No.	-	number
cov	-	cover	NRFB	-	never removed from box
CS	-	Card Signed	ns	-	no stopper
d	-	diameter or depth	r/c	-	reproduction closure
dec	-	decorated	o/c	-	original closure
dj	-	dust jacket	opal	-	opalescent
DQ	-	Diamond Quilted	orig	-	original
DS	-	Document Signed	os	-	orig stopper
ed	-	edition	oz	-	ounce
emb	-	embossed	pcs	-	pieces
ext.	-	exterior	pgs	-	pages
eyep.	-	eyepiece	PUG	-	printed under the glaze
Folio	-	12" x 16"	pr	-	pair
ftd	-	footed	PS	-	Photograph Signed
ga	-	gauge	pt	-	pint
gal	-	gallon	qt	-	quart
ground	-	background	RM	-	red mark
h	-	height	rect	-	rectangular
horiz.	-	horizontal	sgd	-	signed
hp	-	hand painted	S. N.	-	Serial Number
hs	-	high standard	SP	-	silver plated
illus	-	illustrated, illustration	SS	-	Sterling silver
imp	-	impressed	sq	-	square
int.	-	interior	TLS	-	Typed Letter Signed
irid	-	iridescent	unp	-	unpaged
IVT	-	inverted thumbprint	vert.	-	vertical
j	-	jewels	vol	-	volume
K	-	karat	w	-	width
l	-	length	yg	-	yellow gold
lb	-	pound	#	-	numbered
litho	-	lithograph			

Grading Condition. The following numbers represent the standard grading system used by dealers, collectors, and auctioneers:

C.10	Mint
C.9	Near Mint
C.8.5	Outstanding
C.8	Excellent
C.7.5	Fine+
C.7	Fine
C.6.5	Fine - (good)
C.6	Poor

Ceramics

STATE OF THE POTTERY MARKET

by Suzanne Perrault of the Perrault-Rago Gallery

The pottery market has ended another year with a good health report, with more ups than downs. As with other aspects of American Decorative Arts, the high-end of the market has remained strong, while some middle-range areas seem to have stagnated for now.

Hot on people's minds is what's happening with the Gulf Coast potteries as collectibles, post-Katrina. We've not seen any movement up or down for Newcomb College, George Ohr, or Shearwater due to that tragedy. Newcomb College had been cooling a little for some time prior to that, especially the carved matte pieces made in great number over several decades (knowing that, please bear in mind that only few are available below $2,000).

The early, glossy vessels remain a cornerstone of any serious pottery collection, and have recently brought up to $75,000. Matte vases over 12" tall with the staple Spanish moss and live oak tree with full moon still bring into five figures.

Shearwater items remain extremely collectible, especially those from their earlier period made by brothers Peter, Walter, and James Anderson. The annihilation of the pottery will be a loss to Shearwater collectors, as well as to the city of Ocean Springs, Mississippi.

Lastly, the works of master potter George Ohr, whose museum is being built in Biloxi, Miss., by top architect Frank Gehry, are still out of the reach of most. Probably because of the important museum's project, and the expectation of a spike in prices once it opens, Ohr pottery prices have been climbing steadily for several years. Some sections of the architecture were severely damaged in the storm, and the projected opening date is now unknown. However, the onsite pottery was moved to a safe location at the Mobile Museum of Art. The only pieces which were lost were displayed at the Beau Rivage Casino. The Ohr-O'Keefe Museum is gratefully accepting donations for their project.

A cornerstone of the American art pottery market, Grueby, which has been at the top of the list for over twenty years, has finally started to cool. The quality of the wares is unassailable, but perhaps due to the number of pieces being brought out by the stellar prices, the demand finally had to start flattening out. Grueby tiles, an important part of that company's output, remain very collectible, especially its rare designs in large formats. The more commonly seen patterns have been placed in many collections by now, and demand for them is slightly less aggressive.

Other important potteries such as Van Briggle, Tiffany, and Teco, are all doing quite well. Early Van Briggle still brings a premium, especially pieces made before its founder's death in 1904. Look for strong molds showing clay through active, multi-colored glazes. The next breakpoint is 1912, when the widow Anna left the business. Tiffany's glazed, molded wares have been gathering momentum for some time, although nowhere as much as the glass. Bronzed and green glazes are still favorites, while bisques are still less desirable. Architectural Teco, especially in larger sizes, still brings really strong prices. Damage, however slight, will affect the price by a good bit, except on the best of pieces. Matte green glazes still bring the strongest prices, especially when coupled with some charcoaling effect along edges and handles.

Along the same lines, the very best Fulper vessels and early table lamps still bring in the four and five figures respectively. Run-of-the-mill vases produced during the 1920s and 30s, are less in demand these days. Anything with damage suffers.

Rookwood pottery prices have been surprisingly healthy, especially on some of their later lines. While the early glazes such as Standard, Cameo, and Limoges-Style have been dismissed as Victorian and dated for some time, modern wares by Jens Jensen, Elizabeth Barrett, William Hentschel, and even later Shirayamadanis are now commanding a premium. Fine Iris glazes and Vellums, especially uncrazed, continue to be at the top of the market, in both hollowares and plaques. Rookwood tiles made by their Faience division are also performing well, especially in larger sizes with lush landscapes or whimsical animals.

Lastly, Zanesville pottery buyers know that, while middle-range lines have been less regarded than in previous times, the higher end items are still very much in demand. Hand-decorated lines by Weller such as Hudson (early), Etna, and the Rhead lines are finding their way into the best collections, but Sicard is surprisingly depressed (and we can't figure out why). Coppertone is still very strong, collected by people who enjoy the antique bronze look and whimsical frogs.

Good Roseville lines still bring records: A Tourist wall-pocket just brought over $18,000 + 17.5% buyer's premium; Della Robbia (especially in several colors) is still a top-of-the-line product; Baneda, Ferrella, and Sunflower are as popular as ever. 1940s lines have flat-lined for the time being.

So, all in all, American art pottery is still a good place to put one's money. As we've always recommended, however, one should buy what one likes, and not look at it with the detached eye of an investor. Due to circumstances beyond anyone's control, prices and demand fluctuate. So far, though, the pottery is holding its own.

RESOURCES

Magazines

Antique Trader, published by Krause Publications, Iola, WI.

Books

Antique Trader® American & European Art Pottery Price Guide, 2nd Ed., by Kyle Husfloen, Krause Publications, Iola, WI.

Antique Trader® Pottery & Porcelain Ceramics Price Guide, 4th Ed., by Kyle Husfloen, Krause Publications, Iola, WI.

Antique Trader® Stoneware and Blue & White Pottery Price Guide, by Kyle Husfloen, Krause Publications, Iola, WI.

Antique Trader® Teapots Price Guide, by Kyle Husfloen, Krause Publications, Iola, WI.

Collecting Lladró®, 2nd Ed., by Peggy Whiteneck, Krause Publications, Iola, WI.

Luckey´s Hummel® Figurines & Plates, by Carl F. Luckey, updated by Dean Genth, 12th Ed., Krause Publications, Iola, WI.

Price Guide to Contemporary Collectibles and Limited Editions, 9th Ed., by Mary L. Sieber, Krause Publications, Iola, WI.

Warman's® American Pottery & Porcelain, 2nd Ed., by Susan and Al Bagdade, Krause Publications, Iola, WI.

Warman's® Cookie Jars, by Mark F. Moran, Krause Publications, Iola, WI.

Warman's® English & Continental Pottery & Porcelain, by Al Bagdade, Krause Publications, Iola, WI.

Warman's® Fiesta Ware, by Mark F. Moran, Krause Publications, Iola, WI.

Warman's® Flea Market Price Guide, by Ellen T. Schroy, Krause Publications, Iola, WI.

Warman's® Hummel® Field Guide, by Carl F. Luckey, updated by Dean Genth, Krause Publications, Iola, WI.

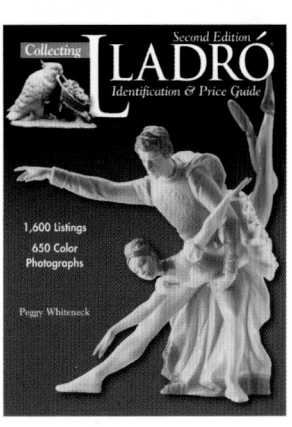

Warman's® McCoy Pottery, by Mark F. Moran, Krause Publications, Iola, WI.

Warman's® Red Wing Pottery, by Mark F. Moran, Krause Publications, Iola, WI.

Warman's® Roseville Pottery, by Mark F. Moran, Krause Publications, Iola, WI.

GALLERY

Jervis (Oyster Bay), vase, flaring, enamel dec, green and white mistletoe, teal blue ground, incised "Jervis," short and tight opposing hairlines, 6" x 6", **$1,600.**
Photo courtesy of David Rago Auctions, Inc.

Overbeck vase, decorated by Elizabeth and Hannah Overbeck, heavily stylized Queen Anne's lace blossoms in mottled brown, cherry red, and turquoise, brown and mauve ground, incised "OBK/E/H," restoration to hairlines at base and small rim chip, 8-1/2" x 4-1/2", **$21,000.**
Photo courtesy of David Rago Auctions, Inc.

Grueby humidor, cylindrical, decorated by Wilhemina Post, band of ivory and yellow five-petaled tobacco blossoms, thick curdled matte green ground, stamped pottery mark, WP, paper label, three hairlines from rim, restoration to lid, 4-1/2" d, 7-1/2" h, **$4,600.**
Photo courtesy of David Rago Auctions, Inc.

Fulper vase, Vasekraft, tapering, long cut-out buttressed handles, Leopard's Skin crystalline glaze, vertical mark, 11" x 5", **$1,000.**
Photo courtesy of David Rago Auctions, Inc.

Minton vase, ovoid, designed by Louis Mark Solon, decorated in trail-slip, swags and medallions in bright polychrome, stamped "MINTONS Ltd. No. 1, 3707," 12" x 5", **$1,600.**
Photo courtesy of David Rago Auctions, Inc.

Newcomb College pottery bud vase, carved by A. F. Simpson, white and yellow daffodils, blue ground, corseted, 1921, NC/JM/170/AFS/LU18, 7-1/2" x 3-1/4", **$2,500.**
Photo courtesy of David Rago Auctions, Inc.

AMERICAN HAND-PAINTED CHINA JEWELRY AND BUTTONS

History: The American china painting movement began in 1876, about the time the mass production of jewelry also occurred. Porcelain manufacturers and distributors offered a variety of porcelain shapes and settings for brooches, pendants, cuff links, and shirt-waist buttons. Thousands of artisans painted flowers, people, landscapes and conventions (geometric) motifs. The category of hand-painted porcelain jewelry comprises a unique category, separate from costume and fine jewelry. While the materials were inexpensive to produce, the painted decoration was a work of fine art.

Marks: American painted porcelain jewelry bears no factory marks, and is usually unsigned.

Notes: The quality of the artwork, the amount of detail, and technical excellence—not the amount of gilding—are the key pricing factors. Uncommon shapes also influence value.

Belt buckle brooch
Dec with white pansy, accented with white enamel, burnished gold ground, gold-plated bezel, 1900-1917, oval, 1-11/16" x 2-1/4" **$75**
Oval, dec with horse chestnuts, baby blue ground, gold-plated bezel, 1900-1917, 2" x 2-1/2" **$100**

Brooch
Crescent shape, dec with dark pink roses, burnished gold tips, brass bezel, 1900-20, 1-7/8" w **$45**
Cross-shape, dec with pink and ruby roses, polychrome ground, tips dec with raised paste dots, gold-plated bezel with tubular hinge, 1" x 1" **$80**
Diamond shape, dec with waterscape with water lilies, white enamel highlights, burnished with gold border, brass bezel, c1920-1940, 7/8" sq **$35**
Dec with Colonial dame, burnished gold rim, brass bezel, c1890-1910, 1" d **$40**
Dec with woman's portrait surrounded by forget-me-nots, ivory ground, white enamel highlights, framed by burnished gold, raised paste scrolls and dots, gold-plated bezel, oval, 1-1/4" x 1-7/8" **$80**
Dec with pink roses, burnished gold border, sgd "Albrecht," brass bezel, oval, 1-7/16" x 1-7/8" **$65**
Dec with Art Nouveau-style woman's head and neck, poppies in her hair, gold-plated bezel, oval, 1-1/4" x 1-7/8"...**$90**
Dec with stained glass-like conventional design in polychrome colors and burnished gold, gold-plated bezel, oval, 1905-15, 1-1/2" x 2" **$65**

Dec with daisy, burnished gold border, brass bezel, c1900-10, 1-3/4" d **$45**
Dec with columbine and greenery, polychrome ground, burnished gold trim, gold-plated bezel, oval, 1-13/16" x 2-3/16" **$75**
Dec with pink roses and greenery on light blue and yellow, burnished gold ground, scrolls, and dots, sgd "E. GARDE," 1920s, gold-plated setting, 1-9/16" x 1-7/8"...................**$50**
Dec with a tropical landscape, burnished gold rim, sgd "OC" (Olive Commons, St. John's Island, FL, 1908-1920), gold-plated bezel, 1-11/16" x 2-1/8" **$105**
Dec with Art Nouveau-style poppies, burnished gold border, brass bezel, oval, 1856-1915, 2" x 1-5/8".......**$75**
Dec with pink and ruby roses, solid dark blue ground, white enamel highlights, burnished gold border, brass bezel, c1940, oval, 2" x 1-1/2" **$65**
Dec with violets, burnished gold rim, brass bezel, 1900-1920, 2-1/16" d **$65**
Florida landscape in white on platinum ground, sterling silver bezel, rectangle, c1920-40, 1" x 3/4" **$75**
Horseshoe shape, dec with violets, burnished gold tips, brass bezel, 2-1/2" l.......................................**$100**
Pink and ruby rose, leaves, polychrome ground, burnished gold rim, gold-plated bezels, 7/8" d, price for pr **$50**
Cuff buttons, pr, dec with lavender flowers, border of burnished gold dots and apple green jewels, burnished gold rims, c1890-1920, ovals, 3/4" x 1" **$40**

Dress set
Five pieces: belt buckle brooch, oval brass bezel, 2" x 2-5/8"; pr shirt waist buttons with shanks 1" d; pr shirt waist buttons with sew-through backs 1" d; dec with forget-me-nots, black green scalloped borders rimmed in burnished gold, c1900-17...............................**$400**
Four pieces: shirt waist collar button, 3/4" d; three shirt waist buttons, 5/8" d; dec with pink roses, white enamel highlights, burnished gold rims, shank backs......................**$60**
Flapper pin, dec with stylized woman, burnished gold border, brass bezel, oval, 1924-28, 1-5/8" x 2-1/8".......**$75**
Hat pin, dec with four-leaf clover on burnished gold ground, brass bezel, 1900-20, 3/4" wide by 1" oval medallion, 6" l shaft.............................**$115**
Pendant
Dec with violets, burnished gold border, brass bezel, oval, c1880-1914, 1-5/8" x 2-1/8" **$60**
Dec with forget-me-nots, white enamel highlights, burnished gold rim, brass bezel, c1900-20, oval, 1-3/4" x 1-3/4" **$50**
Shirt-waist button
Set, with shanks, dec with maidenhair fern, pastel polychrome ground, burnished gold borders, two 7/8" d, three 5/8" d, price for five-pc set **$80**
With eye, dec with single daisy, burnished gold ground, 1-3/16" d...**$20**
With shank, dec with conventional floral design, burnished gold ground, 1-3/16" d......................**$35**
With shank, dec with violets entwined around burnished gold fancy letter "J," burnished gold border, sgd with illegible cipher, 7/8" sq.............**$20**

AMPHORA

Amphora vessel, covered, squatty, Art Deco-style enamel polychrome decoration with birds and leaves, stamped mark "15449/30," 4-1/2" x 6-1/4", $300.
Photo courtesy of David Rago Auctions, Inc.

Amphora vase, applied pinecone decoration, 6-1/2" x 6", $1,200.
Photo courtesy of David Rago Auctions, Inc.

History: The Amphora Porcelain Works was one of several pottery companies located in the Teplitz-Turn region of Bohemia in the late 19th and early 20th centuries. It is best known for art pottery, especially Art Nouveau and Art-Deco pieces.

Marks: Several markings were used, including the name and location of the pottery and the Imperial mark, which included a crown. Prior to World War I, Bohemia was part of the Austro-Hungarian Empire, so the word "Austria" may appear as part of the mark. After World War I, the word "Czechoslovakia" may be part of the mark.

Additional Listings: Teplitz.

Center bowl, incised dec outlined in black, enameled blue-green and pink cabochons, mottled tan matte ground, four legs, circular base, 2-1/8" h **$200**

Ewer, pink, gold, and green floral dec, gold accents, salamander entwined handle, c1900, 14-1/2" h **$575**

Lamp base, stoneware, double handles ending in dragons, straw-colored glaze, China, T'ang period (618-920), drilled, 12-1/2" h **$650**

Umbrella stand, emb gleaners, stylized indigo trees, lustered amber glaze, stamped "Amphora (crown) Austria," restoration to base, 26-1/2" h, 15" d **$2,200**

Vase
Flattened spherical form, shoulder dec with alternating large and small moths in shades of blue, pink, and yellow, raised gilt outline, relief spider webs and enameled disk centers, gilt highlights on green and blue ground, imp "Amphora" in oval, printed "R. S. & K. Turn-Teplitz Bohemia" with maker's device on base, 6" h **$900**

Painted with portrait of Joan of Arc, eagle helmet, enameled garb, mkd "Amphora 1K" and red ink stamp mark, 6-1/4" h, 4" d **$2,600**

Pear shape, extended neck, two tri-part handles, mottled matte green and brown glaze, inscribed cipher, R. S. & K, Teplitz, Bohemia, c1900, crazing, base chip, 11-1/8" h **$1,035**

Three buttressed handles dec with naturalistic leafy rose vines, rose hip clusters, matte green rose on mottled brown round, gilt highlights, imp mark and stamp on base, 5-1/4" h **$250**

Wall plaque, Moorish man and woman in relief, red ground, gilt molded frames, marked "Amphora," 18-1/2" d, price for pr **$900**

ART POTTERY (GENERAL)

Art Pottery, Jugtown, vessel, ovoid, flaring rim, two handles, mottled brown glaze, 20th C, 9-1/2" x 7-1/2", $175.
Photo courtesy of David Rago Auctions, Inc.

History: America's interest in art pottery can be traced to the Centennial Exposition in Philadelphia in 1877, where Europe's finest producers of decorative art displayed an impressive selection of their wares. America's artists rose to the challenge immediately, and by 1900, native artisans were winning gold medals for decorative ceramics here and abroad.

The Art Pottery "Movement" in America lasted from about 1880 until the first World War. During this time, more than 200 companies, in most states, produced decorative ceramics ranging from borderline production ware to intricately decorated, labor intensive artware establishing America as a decorative art powerhouse. Listed here is the work by various factories and studios, with pricing, from a number of these companies.

Additional Listings: See Clifton, Cowan, Dedham, Fulper, Grueby, Jugtown, Marblehead, Moorcroft, Newcomb, North Dakota School of Mines, Ohr, Paul Revere, Peters and Reed, Rookwood, Roseville, Van Briggle, Weller, and Zanesville.

Notes: Condition, design, size, execution, and glaze quality are the key considerations when buying art pottery. This category includes only companies not found elsewhere in this book.

Adviser: David Rago.

*Art Pottery, Markham, vase, ovoid, two low buttressed handles, green and orange dead matte glaze, incised "Markham 2923," few minor nicks, 7-1/4" x 7-1/2", **$700.***
Photo courtesy of David Rago Auctions, Inc.

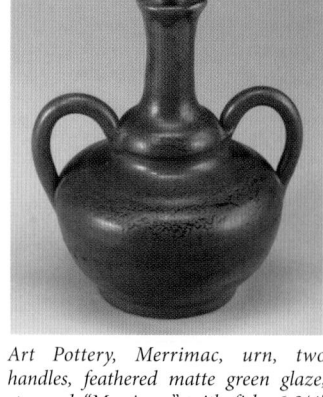

*Art Pottery, Merrimac, urn, two handles, feathered matte green glaze, stamped "Merrimac" with fish, 6-3/4" x 6", **$815.***
Photo courtesy of David Rago Auctions, Inc.

*Art Pottery, Jervis (Oyster Bay), mug, enamel dec, repeating pattern of rabbit crouched in front of full moon, gray, yellow, and brown, teal blue ground, incised "Jervis," couple of short rim lines, few glaze chips at base, 4-1/4" x 5-1/4", **$1,400.***
Photo courtesy of David Rago Auctions, Inc.

*Art Pottery, Clewell, vase, bulbous, copper-clad, bronze patina, incised "Clewell 292-4," 9-1/2" x 4", **$650.***
Photo courtesy of David Rago Auctions, Inc.

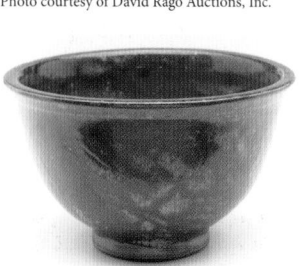

*Art Pottery, Jugtown, bowl, hemispherical, Chinese Blue glaze, Jugtown Ware stamp, 4-1/2" x 8", **$750.***
Photo courtesy of David Rago Auctions, Inc.

Arequipa

Bowl, closed-in, emb eucalyptus branches, matte green and dark blue glaze, stamped mark, incised "KH/11," 6-1/2" d, 2-1/4" h **$800**

Vase, baluster, purple and brown mottled semi-matte glaze, incised "Arequipa California/ 404/JG/JJ," 10-1/2" h, 7-1/2" d **$1,600**

Vase, baluster, carved foliate design, sheer green and turquoise glaze, incised "G.B. Arequipa California," 13-1/2" h, 6-1/4" d **$2,500**

Vessel, squat, carved swirls, matte green and indigo glaze, stamped "Arequipa California" with potter, 4-1/4" h, 4-1/4" d **$1,500**

Avon, Vance, vase, designed by Frederick Rhead, squeezebag stylized trees, orange and green ground, incised "Avon/WPTS.CO./174-1241," 5" d, 5-1/2" h...........................**$920**

Bachelder, O. L., vase, bulbous, cobalt blue and teal sheer glossy glaze, incised "OLB/R," ink cipher, 5" h, 3-3/4" d..............................**$500**

Bennett, Edwin, vase, flat, Albion, painted squirrels on stonewall, pine bough above, "E. Bennett Pottery/1895/AHB/Albion, " 1895, 8" h, 8-1/2" w **$2,400**

Bennett, John

Charger, dec with polychrome daisies and poppies enc within hearts, cobalt blue ground, black scroll design, sgd "J. Bennett/ 412 E24/NY/Oct 9/79," added inscription "Wed last 100 degs in shade," 14-1/2" d **$4,600**

Vase, bulbous, painted burgundy phlox and honeybee, ivory ground, min-

ute rim fleck, marked "BENNETT/ W2E24/NJ/artist's cipher," 3-3/4" d, 7-1/2" h **$2,870**

Binns, Charles F., ovoid, amber, ochre, and chocolate brown hare's fur mirrored glaze, 1931, mkd "C.F.B. 1931," 7" h, 5-1/2" h.................**$3,250**

Cole, A. R., urn, hand-thrown, three fanciful twisted handles, mirror black glaze, unmarked, shallow scratches, 18-1/2" h, 9-1/2" d **$400**

Denaura, Denver, vase, squat top, small opening, molded poppies, matte green vellum glaze, stamped "Denaura/ Denver/169," 5-1/2" h, 5" d **$2,700**

Grand Feu, vase, corseted bulbous, purple and verdigris semi-matte crystalline glaze, stamped "Grand Feu Pottery, L.A. Cal, TT 154," 7" h, 4-1/4" d..................................**$11,000**

Jervis, goblet, enameled green and white mistletoe, teal blue ground, vertical mark, few minute glaze flecks, 4" h, 3" d **$2,000**

Kenton Hills, vase

Cylindrical, white prunts cov in mirrored umber glaze, incised "Hentschel" for William Hentschel, imp "KH/124," 4-3/4" d, 7-1/4" h **$775**

Four-sided, aventurine glaze, imp "KH/ 171," 6" d, 7-1/2" h.........**$650**

Norse, vase, applied salamander, verdigris and bronze glaze, stamped "Norse 25," 11-1/2" h, 7" d **$850**

Pewabic

Bookends, pr, emb animal, lustered blue and green glaze, stamped "Pewabic," repair to small edge chip, 4" w, 4-3/4" h **$415**

Art Pottery, Teco, vase, architectural, four-sided, four short buttressed handles at top, matte green glaze, stamped "Teco," 4-1/4" w, 9" h, **$3,500.**
Photo courtesy of David Rago Auctions, Inc.

Art Pottery, Teco, wall pocket, embossed with tall slender leaves, smooth matte green glaze, stamped "Teco" and two paper labels, tight short line between hanging hole and rim, 6-3/4" w, 14-1/2" l, **$1,400.**
Photo courtesy of David Rago Auctions, Inc.

Art Pottery, Teco, pitcher, twisted handle, smooth matte green glaze, no visible mark, 4" d, 13" h, **$1,700.**
Photo courtesy of David Rago Auctions, Inc.

Miniature, vase, crackled turquoise glaze, blue plumes, sgd "Pewabic/ Detroit/PP," 2" h **$265**

Plate, white crackleware, rim dec with squeezebag yellow and red roosters on green field, stamped "Pewabic," some loss of glaze, chips on back, 9-1/4" d **$920**

Vase, cylindrical with squatty base, mottled and lustered purple and turquoise glaze, paper label, hand written "Anne/ 1942," small glaze scale at rim, 3" d, 3-3/4" h **$265**

Vessel, bulbous, ribbed, glossy teal glaze, stamped "Pewabic/ Detroit," 5-1/4" d, 5-1/2" h **$520**

Pisgah Forest
Tea set, Cameo Ware, wagon and landscape dec, dark matte green ground, raised mark and date 1943, 5-1/4" h teapot **$950**

Vase, bulbous, white, blue, and yellow crystalline glaze, unmarked, 4-3/4" d, 6-1/4" h **$460**

Vessel, spherical, amber glaze, white and blue crystals, raised potter's mark and date 1947, 5" h, 5-3/4" d **$350**

Poillon, Clara, pitcher, bulbous, medium green glaze, incised CPI monogram, 5" d, 4-1/2" h **$365**

San Jose, charger, cuerda seca dec, polychrome wagon train scene, green semi-matte ground, unmarked, small rim fleck, 15-1/2" d **$435**

Robineau, Adelaide, vessel, hemispherical, café-au-lait and verdigris crystalline glaze, carved "AB/184/5," opposing lines to rim, 3" h, 4-1/4" d **$2,500**

Teco
Vase, cylindrical, organic buttressed handles, matte buff glaze, stamped "Teco," few base flakes, 10-3/4" h, 3-1/2" d **$3,000**

Vase, buttressed handles, smooth matte green glaze, stamped "Teco," restored chip on handle, 11-1/4" h, 5" d **$1,300**

Vase, ribbed flaring neck surrounded by individual narrow leaves forming handles, matte green and charcoal glaze, stamped "Teco," restoration to two leaves, rim touch-ups, 11-1/2" h, 4-1/2" d **$5,000**

Vessel, three handles, smooth matte green glaze, stamped "Teco," touch-up to rim bruise, 4-3/4" d, 3-1/4" h **$490**

Vessel, corseted, four handles, smooth matte green glaze with charcoal highlights, stamped "Teco," incised 172, restoration, 10" d, 14-1/2" h **$5,175**

Tiffany Pottery
Bud vase, emb tulips, Old Ivory glaze, incised "LCT," 7" h, 2-1/2" d .. **$4,250**

Lamp base, collar rim, brown and gunmetal flambé glaze, incised "LCT," 7" h, 8" d **$2,400**

Art Pottery, Wheatley, floor vase, full-height buttressed handles, tall molded leaves alternating with buds, frothy matte green glaze, mkd "WP 623," restoration to 5" handle, 10-1/2" d, 19-1/2" h, **$2,100.**
Photo courtesy of David Rago Auctions, Inc.

Art Pottery, Pewabic, vase, bulbous, applied blossoms on swirling stems, smooth matte green glaze, mark obscured by glaze, 6-1/4" x 4-1/2", **$4,320.**
Photo courtesy of David Rago Auctions, Inc.

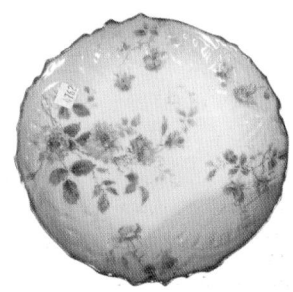

Austrian Ware plate, yellow and pink flowers, green leaves, brown twigs, gold trim, embossed swirls, **$25.**

Volkmar, pitcher, bulbous, collared neck, cucumber green matte glaze, incised illegible inscription, 4" d, 4-1/2" h **$265**

Walley, W. J., vase, bottle shape, sheer light green and gunmetal glaze, imp "W.J.W.," 6-1/2" h **$535**

Walrath
Cider set, pitcher, five cups, painted with cherries on green and brown ground, incised Walrath Pottery, orig Handicraft Guild label on pitcher, 6-1/2" x 8" pitcher **$4,250**

Vase, matte-painted green foliage trees, brown trunks, dark green ground, incised "Walrath Pottery," 6-3/4" h, 4-1/2" d **$4,250**

Wheatley
Lamp base, emb poppy pods, frothy

matte green glaze, new hammered copper fittings, Japanese split-bamboo shade lined with new coral silk, stamped mark, 14" d, 23" h **$1,380**

Sand jar, high relief sculpted grape leaves and vines from rim, feathered medium green matte glaze, incised mark/722, several glaze nicks restored, 15" d, 24" h **$2,415**

Vase, bulbous, three climbing lizards, feathered medium matte green glaze, remnant of paper label, restoration to drill hole on side, 6-3/4" d, 12-1/4" h **$1,380**

White, Denver, vase, squatty, smooth matte gold and green glaze, incised "Denver/1916," small bruise under rim, 6-1/2" d, 3-3/4" h **$210**

AUSTRIAN WARE

History: More than 100 potteries were located in the Austro-Hungarian Empire in the late 19th and early 20th centuries. Although Carlsbad was the center of the industry, the factories spread as far as the modern-day Czech Republic.

Many of the factories were either owned or supported by Americans; hence, their wares were produced mainly for export to the United States.

Marks: Many wares do not have a factory mark but only the word "Austrian" in response to the 1891 law specifying that the country of origin had to be marked on imported products.

Additional Listings: Amphora, Carlsbad, Royal Dux, and Royal Vienna.

Biscuit jar, cov, two handles, small pink roses dec, mkd "MZ Austria," 6-1/2" h **$200**

Bowl, handles, marked "Imperial H&C Carlsbad Austria," numbers "2552" and "18," wear to gold edge, repaired chip, 14" d **$50**

Celery tray, scalloped border, pink roses, green leaves, gold trim, 12" l **$75**

Ewer, rococo gold scroll, hp pink and yellow wild roses, gold outlines, four ftd, 11-3/4" h, 6" d **$125**

Figural group, bronze, cold painted, realistically modeled as small songbird perched on wide leaf in front of tall iris flowers, twig base, late 19th/early 20th C, 13-1/2" w, 14-1/2" h **$1,840**

Luncheon plates
Carlsbad, "Austrian Plaque," oval, portrait of Pope Leo XIII, c1900, imp "Karl Knoll, Carlsbad," 7" h **$150**

Gilt, bead-molded shaped rim, body with cartouches of turquoise faux jewels on gilt ground, gilt scroll-

work and quatrefoils with white jeweled points and mauve enameled centers, late 19th/early 20th C, set of 12, 9-3/8" d **$1,300**

Oyster plate, porcelain, shell-shaped wells to center, scalloped rim, blue and gilt enamel flowers, fish, and birds dec, 19th C, 9-7/8" d **$175**

Perfume set, orange cut glass finials, angular opaque black glass vessels, metal mounts, enameled fan motif, all imp "Austria" on metal, two acid-etched "Austria," 6-1/8" h atomizer, 5-3/8" h perfume, 5" h cov box, imperfections **$500**

Pin tray, irregular scalloped shape, roses, green leaves, white ground, marked "Victoria Carlsbad Austria," 8-1/2" l **$40**

Pokal, glass
Green, detailed enameled cavalier holding empty stein, c1890, 17-1/2" h **$400**

Green, detailed enameled scene of knight on horseback, colorful scrolled

acanthus dec, c1890, 18-1/2" h ... **$400**

Table lamp, attributed to Wiener Werkstatte, in the manner of Susi Singer, ceramic, ovoid, flanked by two mermaid figures in high relief, fish, octopus, and starfish in relief, glossy aqua, orange, white, and irid glazes, textured mottled green and brown ground, gilt highlights, four patinated metal dolphins on stepped metal base, 22-1/4" h **$375**

Trinket box, cov, oval, the gilt metal box stamped with continuous bands of anthemion and torches, porcelain set lid with printed scene of two classical beauties on cobalt blue ground, velveteen lining, early 20th C, 4-1/4" l .. **$450**

Urn, rose bouquet, shaded ivory ground, marked "Carlsbad Austria," 14-1/2" h **$155**

Vase, charcoal gray iridescent pottery body relief-decorated with iridescent green branches, orange wash glaze int., Turn-Teplitz, Austria, numbered 3517, 7-1/4" d **$825**

BAVARIAN CHINA

History: Bavaria, Germany, was an important porcelain production center, similar to the Staffordshire district in England. The phrase "Bavarian China" refers to the products of companies operating in Bavaria, among which were Hutschenreuther, Thomas, and Zeh, Scherzer & Co. (Z. S. & Co.). Very little of the production from this area was imported into the United States prior to 1870.

Bavarian coffee set, coffeepot, two cups and saucers, white and pink shaded roses, green foliage, gold tracery and borders, marked, **$145.**

Bowl, ovoid, reticulated sides, beaded rim, center and sides painted with scenic roundels en grisaille, blue ribbon cartouches with gilt detailing, scenes titled on underside "Badenburg," "Apolloscumpeil," and "Schloss Nymphenburg," late 19th C, 7-3/8" l, 6" w **$325**

Celery tray, center with basket of fruit, luster edge, c1900, 11" l **$45**

Chocolate set, cov chocolate pot, six cups and saucers, shaded blue and white, large white leaves, pink, red, and white roses, crown mark **$295**

Creamer and sugar, purple and white pansy dec, marked "Meschendorf, Bavaria" **$65**

Cup and saucer, roses and foliage, gold handle **$30**

Dinner service, King Cedric, service for eight, plus two platters **$150**

Fish set, 13 plates, matching sauce boat, artist sgd **$295**

Pitcher, bulbous, blackberry dec, shaded ground, burnished gold lizard handle, sgd "D. Churchill," 9" h **$125**

Portrait vase, gold enameled flowers and leaves, hp portrait of Naomi, blue beehive mark and "TG Bavaria" mark, 10" h **$520**

Ramekin, underplate, ruffled, small red roses with green foliage, gold rim **$45**

Salt and pepper shakers, pr, pink apple blossom sprays, white ground, reticulated gold tops, pr **$35**

Shaving mug, hp, two colorful ducks at water's edge, mkd "J. & C Bavaria," 3-5/8" x 3-5/8" **$100**

Vase, hp, red poppies, gold enamel dec, marked "Classic Bavaria," 12" h **$260**

Bavarian dinner set, gilt edges, bread and butter plates, dinner plates, luncheon plates, finger bowls, soup bowls, teacups and saucers, platters, mkd "Bavaria," service for 11, **$300.**

Photo courtesy of David Rago Auctions, Inc.

BELLEEK

History: Belleek, a thin, ivory-colored, almost-iridescent porcelain, was first made in 1857 in county Fermanagh, Ireland. Production continued until World War I, was discontinued for a period of time, and then resumed. The Shamrock pattern is most familiar, but many patterns were made, including Limpet, Tridacna, and Grasses.

There is an Irish saying: If a newly married couple receives a gift of Belleek, their marriage will be blessed with lasting happiness.

Several American firms made a Belleek-type porcelain. The first was Ott and Brewer Co. of Trenton, New Jersey, in 1884, followed by Willets. Other firms producing this ware included The Ceramic Art Co. (1889), American Art China Works (1892), Columbian Art Co. (1893), and Lenox, Inc. (1904).

Marks: The European Belleek company used specific marks during given time periods, which makes it relatively easy to date a piece of Irish Belleek. Variations in mark color are important, as well as the symbols and words.

First mark: Black Harp, Hound, and Castle, 1863-1890.

Second mark: Black Harp, Hound, and Castle and the words "Co. Fermanagh, Ireland," 1891-1826.

Third mark: Black, "Deanta in Eirinn" added, 1926-1946.

Fourth mark: Green, same as third mark except for color, 1946-1955.

Fifth mark: Green, "R" inside a circle added, 1955-1965.

Sixth mark: Green, "Co. Fermanagh" omitted, 1965-March 1980.

Seventh mark: Gold, "Deanta in Eirinn" omitted, April 1980-Dec. 1992.

Eighth mark: Blue, Blue version of the second mark with "R" inside a circle added, Jan. 1993-present.

Additional Listings: Lenox.

Belleek beer set, 12" h beer pitcher with silver hinged lid, six mugs painted by Sturgis Laurence in the Delft style, different male characters drinking spirits, each signed "FWR Sturgis Laurence, Trenton, NJ, Dec 8 '94," 1894, **$2,200.**
Photo courtesy of David Rago Auctions, Inc.

Belleek urn, spherical, two upright handles, four reticulated feet, red Oriental poppies decoration, light wear to gilting around rim, red O&B crown stamp, 8" x 6", **$1,725.**
Photo courtesy of David Rago Auctions, Inc.

American

Bowl

Double handles, ruffled rim, gilt trim and handles, gilt and rose-colored flowers dec, brown Willets mark, 7" d, 4-1/4" h **$275**

Green ext., wide gilt textured border, int. with hp floral design, artist sgd "MS" on base, brown Willets mark, 7-1/2" d **$100**

Candy dish, shell form, ivory ground, hp floral dec, ruffled gilt rim, marked "Columbia Art Co., Trenton, NJ," 8" x 6" **$80**

Chocolate pot, ivory ground, Art Deco rose design, pale green and yellow wide borders, gilt accents, green Lenox pallet mark, 10-1/4" h **$135**

Cider jug, hp, fruit dec, gilt handle, green Lenox pallet mark, 6" h **$50**

Cup and saucer, hp, pale pink and green beaded dec, gilt borders, brown Willets mark, 2" cup, 5-3/4" d saucer **$60**

Jug, hp, pale yellow ground, floral dec, gilt rim and handle, green CAC pallet mark, 5-1/2" h **$110**

Mug, pink luster and enamel dec, continuous scene of drunken taverners, artist sgd "EMS '04," printed Ceramic Art Co. mark, Trenton, New Jersey, c1904, 4-1/2" h **$150**

Pitcher, hp, white ground, geometric blue floral design, gilt trim, artist sgd "G. L. Urban," green Willets mark, 7" h **$85**

Plate

Gilt foliate rim, blue enamel beads, red Willets mark, price for pr, 7-1/4" d **$45**

Swan, ivory, open back, green Lenox wreath mark, 8-1/2" h **$90**

Salt, 1-1/2" d

Gilt, ruffled edge, marked "CAC," price for set of six **$45**

Pale green, hp pink enamel dec, artist sgd "E.S.M.," Lenox pallet mark, price for set of six **$135**

Tankard, hand painted, 5-3/4" h

Brown and blue painted ground, poppy dec, sgd "LM '06," green CAC pallet mark **$135**

Multicolored ground, foliage dec, sgd "B.M.A.," brown Willets mark **$125**

Teapot, blue glazed ground, gilt dec, brown Willets mark, 6" h **$135**

Vase

Baluster, hp pine cone dec, artist sgd "A.E.G.," green Lenox pallet mark, 15" h **$450**

Cylindrical, hand painted, egrets in landscape, artist sgd "A.MacM.F.," printed mark, Trenton, NJ, c1900, 10" h **$215**

Irish

Basket, four strand, applied flowers, Belleek Co. Fermangh Ireland pad mark, some repairs, petal missing, 6-1/2" x 4-1/2" **$80**

Bread plate, Shamrock pattern, double handle, third green mark, 10-1/2" l, 9-1/4" w **$80**

Bowl, Imperial Shell, modeled shell supported on shell adorned coral base, third black mark, c1930, 4-1/2" h **$565**

Butter dish, cov, Limpet pattern, first black mark, 6-1/2" d top, 8-1/2" d base **$475**

Cake plate, mask with grape leaves pattern, four looped handles, pale yellow edge, third black mark, 10-1/2" d **$155**

Compote, shell modeled dish, triangular base set with three dolphin, first black mark, c1880, dish restored, slight rim chips, 6-3/4" h **$470**

Creamer

Lifford pattern, third green mark, 3-1/4" h **$60**

Ribbon pattern, third green mark, 3-1/4" h **$40**

Cleary pattern, first green mark, 3-1/2" h **$50**

Rathmore pattern, third green mark, 4" h **$40**

Undine pattern, third black mark, 4-1/2" h **$55**

Creamer and sugar, 3-1/2" h creamer, 2" h sugar, Lotus pattern, third black mark, rim chip **$70**

Cream jug, Thorn Tea Ware, pale yellow relief dec, first mark, c1880, 5-1/2" h **$300**

Belleek vase, applied flowers and leaves; black mark, 8" h, bowl, green mark, 4-3/4" d; vase, tree trunk shape, 6-1/4" h, **$150.**
Photo courtesy of Joy Luke Auctions.

Belleek basket, openwork, decorated with delicate floral details on rims and handles, marked, 5" x 11" x 8-1/2", **$650.**
Photo courtesy of David Rago Auctions, Inc.

Cup and saucer, Tea Ware, hexagon, pink tint, second black mark, early 20th C, 5-3/8" d saucer, price for pr **$460**

Figure

Pig, third green mark, 2-1/2" h **$90**

Harp, third green mark, 6" h **$70**

Flowerpot, naturalistically modeled shell body, applied flowers and foliage, second black mark, chips to leaves, c1900, 7" h **$940**

Font, Sacred Heart, cross form, shaped font, second green mark, 7" h **$50**

Lithophane, rect shape with arched top, modeled as two ladies with bird, no visible mark, mounted in electrified shadow box, 19th C, 5-1/2" l **$715**

Mint tray, shell form, pink highlights on rim, brown mark, 8-1/2" l **$70**

Mustache cup and saucer, Tridacna, pink rim, first black mark, 2-1/2" h cup, 6" d saucer **$495**

Night light, figural, lighthouse, pierced cover and insert pot, modeled rocky base, second black mark, restored rim on insert pot, c1900, 10-3/4" h **$1,410**

Pitcher, Aberdeen, applied with flowers and leaves, second black mark, chips to leaves, c1900, 9" h **$300**

Plate, scalloped edge, woven, three strands, pad mark, 10-1/2" d **$200**

Spill vase

Shamrock, second green mark, 5" h **$50**

Shamrock Daisy, third green mark, 5-1/2" h **$65**

Owl, second green mark, 8" h **$55**

Sugar bowl, Shell, pink tinted edge and coral, first black mark, c1880, foot-rim chips, 4" h **$575**

Swan, open back, yellow wings and head, brown mark, 4" h............... **$55**

Tea kettle, cov, Thorn Tea Ware, pale yellow relief dec, first mark, c1880, 7" h... **$350**

Tea set

Grass tea ware, 4" h covered teapot; 3-3/4" h cov sugar bowl; cream jug; first black marks, c1880........ **$1,175**

Tridacna, 5-1/2" h cov teapot; 4-1/4" h cov sugar bowl; 3-1/4" h cream jug; 3" h waste bowl, each with third black mark; 15-1/2" l rect tray with second black mark, c1920-30............. **$1,120**

Tea urn, cov, gilt, bronze and enamel dec, China man finial, first black mark, c1880, cover with hairline and chip, stand missing, 6-1/2" h ... **$4,410**

Tray, Thorn tea ware, scalloped rim, molded floral border, web interior with central spider, second black mark, c1900, 14-1/2" sq **$1,175**

Vase

Six-sided pot, third green mark, 4-1/4" h **$45**

Cardium, shell form, coral and shell base, second black mark, 4-3/4" h, 5-3/4" d **$80**

Coral, pink tinted coral and shell int., first black mark, c1880, 8" h ... **$1,150**

Dolphin, first black mark, chip on tail, 8-1/4" h **$775**

Two scrolled and pierced handles, delicate applied bouquet of flowers, 1891 mark, 9" h, price for pr ... **$690**

Tree trunk with three lower and three upper vase spouts, applied with flowers and leaves, bird perched atop arched branches above another bird in nest, second black mark, c1900, chips to leaves, hairline repair to lower trunk, 12" h ... **$1,175**

Belleek dessert set, clover design, black marks, 9" d platter, **$400.**
Photo courtesy of David Rago Auctions, Inc.

Belleek Irish cup and saucer, Nautilus shape, green handle, **$265.**

Bennington inkwell, unsigned, five holes, formed column design, applied flint Bennington glaze, c1850, 3" d, 2" h, **$200.**
Photo courtesy of Bruce and Vicki Wassdorp.

Bennington stoneare jug, two gallons, ovoid, strap handle, ornate cobalt blue floral sprig dec, impressed maker's marks, "J.NORTON & CO BENNING-TON VT," 1839-43, 14" h, **$600.**
Photo courtesy of Skinner, Inc.

Bennington-type dog, seated, molded base, Rockingham glaze, 8" w, 11" h, **$350.**
Photo courtesy of Dotta Auction Co., Inc.

BENNINGTON AND BENNINGTON- TYPE POTTERY

History: In 1845, Christopher Webber Fenton joined Julius Norton, his brother-in-law, in the manufacturing of stoneware pottery in Bennington, Vermont. Fenton sought to expand the company's products and glazes; Norton wanted to concentrate solely on stoneware. In 1847, Fenton broke away and established his own factory.

Fenton introduced to America the famous Rockingham glaze, developed in England and named after the Marquis of Rockingham. In 1849, he patented a flint enamel glaze, "Fenton's Enamel," which added flecks, spots, or streaks of color (usually blues, greens, yellows, and oranges) to the brown Rockingham glaze. Forms included candlesticks, coachman bottles, cow creamers, poodles, sugar bowls, and toby pitchers.

Fenton produced the little-known scroddled ware, commonly called lava or agate ware. Scroddled ware is composed of differently colored clays, which are mixed with cream-colored clay, molded, turned on a potter's wheel, coated with feldspar and flint, and fired. It was not produced in quantity, as there was little demand for it.

Fenton also introduced Parian ware to America. Parian was developed in England in 1842 and known as "Statuary ware." Parian is translucent porcelain that has no glaze and resembles marble. Bennington made the blue and white variety in the form of vases, cologne bottles, and trinkets.

The hound-handled pitcher is probably the best-known Bennington piece. Hound-handled pitchers were made by about 30 different potteries in more than 55 variations. Rockingham glaze was used by more than 150 potteries in 11 states, mainly in the Midwest, between 1830 and 1900.

Marks: Five different marks were used, with many variations. Only about 20 percent of the pieces carried any mark; some forms were almost always marked, others never. Marks include:

1849 mark (four variations) for flint enamel and Rockingham

E. Fenton's Works, 1845-1847, on Parian and occasionally on scroddled ware

U. S. Pottery Co., ribbon mark, 1852-1858, on Parian and blue and white porcelain

U. S. Pottery Co., lozenge mark, 1852-1858, on Parian

U. S. Pottery, oval mark, 1853- 1858, mainly on scroddled ware

Additional Listings: Stoneware.

Bowl, shallow, brown and yellow Rockingham glaze, Fenton's 1849 mark, 7-1/8" d..........................**$775**

Candlestick, flint enamel glaze, 8-1/4" h..........................**$875**

Curtain tiebacks, pr, Barrett plate 200, one chipped, 1849-58, 4-1/2" l **$185**

Figure, poodle, standing, basket in mouth, Barrett plate 367, repairs to tail and hind quarters, 8-1/2" h, 9" l **$2,500**

Flask, book, Barrett plate 411, flint enamel, title imp on spine, 1849-58

"Bennington Battle" on spine, brown and blue flint enamel glaze, 5-3/4" w, 2-5/8" d, 7-3/4" h ..**$3,300**
Titled "Hermit's Life & Suffering," 6" h **$980**
Titled "Ladies Companion," 7" h ..**$690**

Flowerpot, molded shells, imp "Bennington Aug 16, 1877 Centennial," shallow flake, 3-1/8" h..................**$200**

Jug, stoneware, cobalt blue leaf dec, imp mark "E. Norton & Co., Bennington, VT, 4," strap handle, stains, base flakes, 17-3/4" h..........................**$300**

Marble, blue, some wear, 1-1/2" d ..**$90**

Paperweight, spaniel, 1849-58, Barrett plate 407, 3" h, 4-1/2" h **$815**

Picture frame, oval, Barrett plate VIII, chips and repairs, pr, 1948-58, 9-1/2" h **$230**

Pitcher, hunting scene, Barrett pate 26, chips, 8" h **$175**

Spittoon, flint enamel glaze, rare 1849 mark, 9-1/2" d **$450**

Sugar bowl, cov, Parian, blue and white, Repeated Oak Leaves pattern, raised grapevine dec on lid, 3-3/4" h **$150**

Teapot, cov, flint enamel, Alternate Rib pattern, pierced pouring spout **$425**

Wash bowl and pitcher, flint enamel glaze **$1,100**

Bennington-Type

Bank, chest of drawers shape, Rockingham glaze, Barrett plate 428, small chip to front top edge, 3-1/4" h, 3-3/4" h **$150**

Creamer, figural, cow, Rockingham glaze, Barrett plate 378, chipped cov, repairs, 5-1/2" h, 6-3/4" l **$115**

Flask, boot, laced up one side, daubed Rockingham glaze, rare removable spout included, lip repaired, 7-1/4" l, 7" h **$450**

Spittoon, scallop shell form, Rockingham glaze, 19th C, 8-1/2" d **$175**

Toby bottle, barrel, Rockingham glaze, rim and base chips, mid-19th C, 9" h **$175**

BISCUIT JARS

History: The biscuit or cracker jar was the forerunner of the cookie jar. Biscuit jars were made of various materials by leading glassworks and potteries of the late 19th and early 20th centuries.

Note: All items listed have silver-plated (SP) mountings unless otherwise noted.

Biscuit Jar, Carlton Ware, Peony pattern, flowers decoration, silver-plated lid, **$295.**

Photo courtesy of Joy Luke Auctions.

Biscuit Jar, English, dark cobalt blue transfer of morning glories, brass lid with shaped finial, elaborately shaped handle, **$495.**

Crown Milano

Jeweled body, starfish dec, rust and cream colored body, Mt. Washington, non- matching lid, 6" w **$550**

Rect, raised gold tracery and large chrysanthemums, emb metal lid with seashell design, stamped "M.W. 4413," 10" h **$400**

Earthenware, Crown Ford, scenic dec, desert scene with figures and camels, 9" h **$200**

Nippon China, sq, white, multicolored floral bands, gold outlines and trim, 7-1/2" h, 4-1/2" w **$110**

Porcelain

Art Nouveau floral dec, silver plated lid and handle, 10" h **$230**

Blue flowers on molded panels, four-footed, 5-1/2" h **$125**

Crown Devon, molded panels, flowers dec, silver plated lid and handle, 10" h **$145**

Fruit dec, minor rim chips, 7-1/2" h **$90**

German, cityscape panel dec, 7-1/2" h **$175**

Panels of small pink flowers, cobalt blue border, gilding, ftd, 7" h .. **$150**

Portrait panels and flowers, Tirchenreuth dec, 7" h **$175**

Roses and leaves dec, 7-1/2" h **$120**

Scenic panels dec, blue beehive mark, silver plated lid and handle, 8" h . **$175**

Unmarked, oriental landscape panels, silver plated lid and handle, 9" h **$145**

Pottery, blue morning glory flowers and leaves, silver plated lid and handle, 9" h **$150**

Royal Bayreuth, Poppy, blue mark **$650**

Wedgwood, jasper

Central dark blue ground bordered in light blue, applied white Muses in relief, banded laurel border, SP rim, handle and cover, imp mark, slight relief loss, c1900, 5-3/4" h **$650**

Central dark blue ground bordered in light blue ground, applied white classical relief, SP footrim, rim, handle and cover, imp mark, slight firing lines to relief, c1900, 6" h **$600**

Green dip ground, applied white classical figure groups above acanthus leafs, SP rim, handle and cover, imp Wedgwood mark, footrim nick, late 19th C, 5" h **$400**

Yellow ground, applied black relief of Muses below fruiting grapevine festoons terminating in lion masks with rings, grapevine border to foot, SP rim, handle and cover, imp mark, c1930, 5-3/4" h **$800**

Bisque court figure, white ground, gold trim, black and peach accents, painted facial features including blue eyes, $195.
Photo courtesy of Dotta Auction Co., Inc.

Bisque figure, semi-nude child seated on a stone plinth, mold incised "H. Dopping," German, early 20th C, 17-5/8" h, $250.
Photo courtesy of Skinner, Inc.

Bisque hen on nest with basketweave, naturalistic colors, English, 8-1/2" h, 9-1/2" l, $275.
Photo courtesy of Joy Luke Auctions.

BISQUE

History: Bisque or biscuit china is the name given to wares that have been fired once and have not been glazed.

Bisque figurines and busts, which were popular during the Victorian era, were used on fireplace mantels, dining room buffets, and end tables. Manufacturing was centered in the United States and Europe. By the mid-20th century, Japan was the principal source of bisque items, especially character-related items.

Bust, female holding flower, green ribbons in hair, Cybis #471, 12" h ... **$435**

Dish, cov, dog, brown, and white, green blanket, white and gilt basketweave base, 9" x 6-1/2" x 5-1/2" **$500**

Figure
Hunters, dressed in Indian attire, riding on elephants, shooting attacking tigers, polychrome enameling, facing pair, 7-1/2" h **$350**
Woman seated in chair, Cybis #298, issued 1968, 11-1/2" h **$380**
Young man and woman, each with light green bicycling attire, holding metal bicycle, Heubach Brothers, Thuringia, Germany, early 20th C, 14" h, price for pr **$1,175**

Match holder, figural, Dutch girl, copper and gold trim **$45**

Planter, carriage, four wheels, pale blue and pink, white ground, gold dots, royal markings.................... **$165**

Salt, figural, walnut, cream, branch base, matching spoon, 3" d.......... **$75**

Wall plaque, light green, scrolled and pierced scallop, white relief figures in center, man playing mandolin, lady wearing hat, c1900, pr, 10-1/4" d .. **$275**

Bisque box, covered, oval, two lambs on lid, applied coleslaw type grass and flowers, applied flowers on base, minor damage, 5" l, 4-1/2" h, $95.
Photo courtesy of Joy Luke Auctions.

BUFFALO POTTERY

History: Buffalo Pottery Co., Buffalo, New York, was chartered in 1901. The first kiln was fired in October 1903. Larkin Soap Company established Buffalo Pottery to produce premiums for its extensive mail-order business. Wares also were sold to the public by better department and jewelry stores. Elbert Hubbard and Frank Lloyd Wright, who designed the Larkin Administration Building in Buffalo in 1904, were two prominent names associated with the Larkin Company.

Early Buffalo Pottery production consisted mainly of semi-vitreous china dinner sets. Buffalo was the first pottery in the United States to produce successfully the Blue Willow pattern. Buffalo also made a line of hand-decorated, multicolored willow ware, called Gaudy Willow. Other early items include a series of game, fowl, and fish sets, pitchers, jugs, and a line of commemorative, historical, and advertising plates and mugs.

From 1908 to 1909 and again from 1921 to 1923, Buffalo Pottery produced the line for which it is most famous—Deldare Ware. The earliest of this olive green, semi-vitreous china displays hand-decorated scenes from English artist Cecil Aldin's *Fallowfield Hunt*. Hunt scenes were done only from 1908 to 1909. English village scenes also were characteristic of the ware and were used during both periods. Most pieces are artist signed.

In 1911, Buffalo Pottery produced Emerald Deldare, which used scenes from Goldsmith's *The Three Tours of Dr. Syntax* and an Art Nouveau-type border. Completely decorated Art Nouveau pieces also were made.

Abino, which was introduced in 1912, had a Deldare body and displayed scenes of sailboats, windmills, or the sea. Rust was the main color used, and all pieces were signed by the artist and numbered.

In 1915, the manufacturing process was modernized, giving the company the ability to produce vitrified china. Consequently, hotel and institutional ware became the main production items, with hand-decorated ware de-emphasized. The Buffalo firm became a leader in producing and designing the most-famous railroad, hotel, and restaurant patterns.

In the early 1920s, fine china was made for home use. Bluebird is one of the patterns from this era. In 1950, Buffalo made its first Christmas plate. These were given away to customers and employees primarily from 1950 to 1960. However, it is known that Hample Equipment Co. ordered some as late as 1962. The Christmas plates are very scarce in today's resale market.

The Buffalo China Company made "Buffalo Pottery" and "Buffalo China"—the difference being that one is semi-vitreous ware and the other vitrified. In 1956, the company was reorganized, and Buffalo China became the corporate name. Today, Buffalo China is owned by Oneida Silver Company.

Marks: Blue Willow pattern is marked "First Old Willow Ware Mfg. in America."

Buffalo pitcher, George Washington on horseback, blue and white decoration, some staining and crazing, 7-1/2" h, **$160.**
Photo courtesy of Joy Luke Auctions.

Canton plate, marked "China," 6", **$115.**
Photo courtesy of Alderfer Auction Co.

Abino Ware

Candlestick, sailing ships, 1913, 9" h **$475**

Pitcher, Portland Head Light, 7" h..**$700**

Tankard, sailing scene, 10-1/2" h...**$900**

Advertising Ware

Jug, blue and green transfer print, inscribed "The Whaling City Souvenir of New Bedford, Mass.," whaling motifs, staining, 6-1/4" h **$325**

Mug, Calumet Club, 4-1/2" h..........**$90**

Plate, Indian Head Pontiac, 9-3/4" d..**$55**

Platter, US Army Medical Dept., 1943, 13-1/2" l...**$60**

Deldare

Calling card tray, street scene ..**$395**

Cereal bowl, Fallowfield Hunt, 6" d **$295**

Chop plate, Fallowfield Hunt, 14" d **$795**

Cup and saucer, street scene **$225**

Hair receiver, street scene **$465**

Jardinière, street scene..............**$975**

Mug
  Fallowfield Hunt, 3-1/2" h **$395**
  Three Pigeons, 4-1/2" h..............**$350**

Pitcher, The Great Controversy, sgd "W. Fozter," stamped mark, 12" h, 7" w **$320**

Powder jar, street scene.............**$395**

Punch cup, Fallowfield Hunt......**$375**

Soup plate, street scene, 9" d **$425**

Tankard, Three Pigeons............**$1,175**

Tea tile, Fallowfield Hunt............**$395**

Tea tray, street scene...................**$650**

Vase, King Fisher, green and white dec, olive ground, stamped mark, artist signature, 7-3/4" h, 6-1/2" d **$1,380**

Emerald Deldare

Creamer **$450**

Fruit bowl....................................**$1,450**

Mug, 4-1/2" h................................**$475**

Vase, stylized foliate motif, shades of green and white, olive ground, stamp mark, 8-1/2" h, 6-1/2" h **$810**

CANTON CHINA

History: Canton china is a type of Oriental porcelain made in the Canton region of China from the late 18th century to the present. It was produced largely for export. Canton china has a hand-decorated light- to dark-blue underglaze on white ground. Design motifs include houses, mountains, trees, boats, and bridges. A design similar to willow pattern is the most common.

Borders on early Canton feature a rain-and-cloud motif (a thick band of diagonal lines with a scalloped bottom). Later pieces usually have a straight-line border.

Early, c1790-1840, plates are very heavy and often have an unfinished bottom, while serving pieces have an overall "orange-peel" bottom. Early covered pieces, such as tureens, vegetable dishes, and sugars, have strawberry finials and twisted handles. Later ones have round finials and a straight, single handle.

Marks: The markings "Made in China" and "China" indicate wares that date after 1891.

Canton platter, octagonal, cut corners, blue underglaze landscape, white ground, Chinese Export, 13" l, 10-1/4" w, minor roughness on rim, **$250.**
Photo courtesy of Alderfer Auction Co.

Reproduction Alert. Several museum gift shops and private manufacturers are issuing reproductions of Canton china.

Bowl, cut corner, minor int. glaze imperfections, 19th C, 9-1/2" d **$900**

Box, cov, sq, domed top, cloud-and-rain border on lids, early 19th C, pr **$6,270**

Coffeepot, mismatched cover, 7-1/4" h **$750**

Cup, cov, handle, repaired lid, 4" l, 3-1/2" h..........................**$165**

Dish, leaf shape, 19th C, chips
6-3/4" l **$145**
8-1/2" l **$165**

Fruit basket
Minor chips, 9-1/4" d **$690**
Reticulated, with undertray, 10-1/2" l **$1,100**

Milk pitcher, very minor chips, 6-1/8" h..**$575**

Miniature, tureen, underplate, 6-1/2" l, 5" w, 4" h...................................**$300**

Plate, early, c1820-30
Bread and butter, 6" d **$65**
Dessert, 8" d................................**$95**
Dinner, set of six, one with rim chips, 19th C, 10-3/8" d, price for set..**$360**
Lunch, 9" d **$115**
Salad, 7-1/2" d **$85**

Platter
Dark blue, finely detailed scene with figure inside pagoda, bridge, trees, mountains, small sailboat, bas-

ketweave design around rim, glaze flakes, 14" x 17" **$460**
Octagonal, oblong, China, small chip underside of rim, 19th C, 14-3/8" x 17-1/4"................................**$350**
Octagonal, oblong, China, minor glaze imperfections, 19th C, 14-3/4" x 18" **$450**
Octagonal, oblong, well and tree, Chinese Export, rim chip and glaze wear, 19th C, 17-1/4" x 20-1/4"..........**$390**

Salt, trench, chips, three-pc set, 3-3/4" l...................................**$550**

Sauce boat, lobed, applied bifurcated handles, rim chips, one handle cracked, 6-7/8" w, 8" l, 3-3/8" h, price for pr....................................**$850**

Serving dish, octagonal, 19th C, 15-1/4" x 18-1/4"....................**$650**

Shrimp dish, minor edge roughness, 10-1/4" d, pr...........................**$690**

Tea caddy, cov, octagonal, 19th C, 5-1/2" h..............................**$2,645**

Tray, lobed lozenge form, 19th C, 11-1/4" l, 8-1/4" w....................**$875**

Tureen, cov, stem finial, oval, ftd, hog snout handles, 14" l, 9-3/4" w, 7-3/4" h **$1,265**

Vegetable dish, cov, diamond shape, scalloped edges, fruit finial, orange peel glaze, unglazed bottom, 9-1/2" w, 8" d, 3-1/4" h **$225**

CAPO-DI-MONTE

Capo-di-Monte basket, yellow, pink, and white roses, green foliage, tan basketweave base, marked with crown and "Capo-di-Monte, Made in Italy," **$75.**

History: In 1743, King Charles of Naples established a soft-paste porcelain factory near Naples. The firm made figurines and dinnerware. In 1760, many of the workmen and most of the molds were moved to Buen Retiro, near Madrid, Spain. A new factory, which also made hard-paste porcelains, opened in Naples in 1771. In 1834, the Doccia factory in Florence purchased the molds and continued production in Italy.

Capo-di-Monte was copied heavily by other factories in Hungary, Germany, France, and Italy.

Reproduction Alert. Many of the pieces in today's market are of recent vintage. Do not be fooled by the crown over the "N" mark; it also was copied.

Box, cov, round, domed lid molded with low relief figures of cherubs with flower baskets, sides similarly molded with cherubs at various artistic pursuits, gilt-metal rim mounts, int. painted with floral sprigs, late 19th C, 8" d, 4-1/4" h **$475**

Casket, molded opal body, cherubs in relief, detailed polychrome floral dec, gilt highlights, underglaze blue crown "N" mark, 19th C, 13" l, 8" w, 5-1/2" h **$2,400**

Creamer and sugar, mythological raised scene, dragon handles, claw feet, lion finial, 5-1/2" x 6" creamer, 6-1/4" x 6" cov sugar...................**$250**

Dresser set, mythological raised scene, pair of 4" d, 7" h perfume bottles with figural stoppers, 5" d, 4" h cov powder jar, 30" l x 15" w tray **$500**

Ferner, oval, relief molded and enameled allegorical figures, full relief female mask eat each end, 11" l ...**$120**

Lamp, table, figural Bacchus, female, and grapes, 25" h **$1,300**

Plate, each with Capo-di-Monte crest at top, pair of swans, pair of cranes, crimson, blue, yellow, and burntorange flowers on border, gold trim, minor wear, price for eight-pc set, 8-3/8" d.....................................**$1,100**

Snuffbox, hinged lid, cartouche shape, molded basketweave and flower-head ext., painted int. with court lady and page examining portrait of gentlemen, gold mountings, minor restoration, c1740, 3-1/4" d **$1,650**

Stein, lion-hunt scene, lion on lid, elephant-trunk handle, 7-1/2" h **$400**

Table decoration, 8-3/4" h figural group of three female dancers on hexagonal base, 6-3/4" l four individual dancers, 6-1/4" l four kidney-shaped flower wells, gilt dec, 20th C, price for nine pcs **$365**

Urn, cov, ovoid, central-molded frieze of Nerieds and putti, molded floral garlands, gadroon upper section, acanthus-molded lower section, socle foot with putti, sq plinth base, applied ram's-head handles, domed cov, acorn finial, underglaze crowned "N" mark, minor chips and losses, 21-1/8" h, pr **$1,650**

Capo-di-Monte plaques, pair, colored relief of Adam and Eve and The Adoration, conforming ebonized frames, mounted with gilt-bronze strapwork cartouche scrolls and marble medallions, blue crowned N marks, 20th C, 19-1/2" h, **$1,065.**
Photo courtesy of Sloans & Kenyon Auctioneers and Appraisers.

CELADON

History: The term "celadon," meaning a pale grayish-green color, is derived from the theatrical character Celadon, who wore costumes of varying shades of grayish green in Honore d'Urfe's 17th-century pastoral romance, L'Astree. French Jesuits living in China used the name to refer to a specific type of Chinese porcelain.

Celadon divides into two types. Northern celadon, made during the Sung Dynasty up to the 1120s, has a gray-to-brownish body, relief decoration, and monochromatic olive-green glaze. Southern (Lung-ch'uan) celadon, made during the Sung Dynasty and much later, is paint-decorated with floral and other scenic designs and is found in forms that appeal to the European-and American-export market. Many of the southern pieces date from 1825 to 1885. A blue square with Chinese or pseudo-Chinese characters appears on pieces after 1850. Later pieces also have a larger and sparser decorative patterning.

Celadon bowl, large, deep, lightly embossed pattern, hairlines, **$165.**
Photo courtesy of Wiederseim Associates, Inc.

Reproduction Alert.

Bowl

Cut corner shape, Rose Canton dec, hardwood stand, repaired, 9-1/2" d, 4-1/2" h **$385**

Exterior carved with lotus petals, China, 14th C, 6-1/4" d **$365**

Lung Chuan ware, interior with kylin and waves, China, 14th C, 15-1/4" d **$1,450**

Scalloped rim, dec with exotic birds, butterflies, and flowers, repairs and gilt losses to edge, 10-1/2" d **$245**

Sea green color, inlaid in Sangam technique with branches and sprigs of flowers, Korea, Koryo period, 12th/13th C, 7-1/2" d **$475**

Sea green color, inlaid in Sangam technique with clouds and phoenix, Korea, Koryo period, 12th C, 7-1/2" d **$875**

Wide flaring form, dark gray-green color, traces of three spurs on base, surface entirely glazed, Korea, Koryo period, 12th C, 5-3/4" d **$600**

Brush box, cov, dec in Rose Medallion palette, 7-1/2" w, 3-1/4" d, 2-1/2" h **$400**

Center dish, diamond shape, conforming foot, court scenes, central scene contained in vasiform device, Rose Canton pattern, China, gilt wear, 19th C, 11-1/4" l..........................**$530**

Charger

Mandarin warrior, One Hundred Antiques border, China, 19th C, 10" d **$210**

Rose Medallion, court scene within medallion, Famille Rose border, minor glaze wear, 13-1/2" d **$725**

Ice cream tray, rect, flange handles, Rose Canton motif, China, minor gilt wear, 19th C, 7" x 13-1/4" **$600**

Celadon vase, porcelain, celadon crackled glaze over blue underglaze, Buddhist wheel designs in concentric circles on shoulder and lower body, Chinese, pieced wooden lid and base, 19th C, 9" x 7", **$1,000.**
Photo courtesy of David Rago Auctions, Inc.

Celadon Canton plate, multicolored floral and butterflies decoration, gold rim, Chinese, 10" d, $150.

Incense burner, lid surmounted by Buddhist, lion base with lion mask feet, sea-green color, Korea, 12th C **$8,000**

Plate

Hexagonal, Lung Chuan ware, lattice-work center and floral rim, China, Ming period (15th-16th C), 11" d **$1,175**

River scene, butterfly and floral border, minor gilt and glaze wear, 10-1/4" d **$150**

Rose Canton dec, China, 19th C, 5-1/4" d **$90**

Rose Canton motif, bird and butterflies around tree peony, underglaze blue sq mark, wear, some in-painting, 10-1/4" h **$210**

Platter, oval, Rose Canton dec, 13-1/4" x 15-3/4" **$650**

Rice bowl, cov, underplate, dec with various animals, figures, and flowers, 7-1/2" d, 5-3/4" h **$390**

Sauce tureen, cov, undertray, gilt floriform finial, gilt handles, bird, butterfly, and floral motifs, China, minor edge wear, 19th C **$600**

Serving dish, cov, domed lid, single handle, Rose Canton dec, imperfections, 10" d, 6-1/2" h..................**$300**

Shrimp dish, bird, butterfly, and floral motif, China, minor glaze wear, 19th C, 10-1/4" x 9-3/4" **$650**

Soap dish, three part, figures in garden on lid, Rose Medallion border, minor edge wear, 4-1/8" l, 5-1/4" w, 2-1/2" h..................**$265**

Vase

Hexagonal paneled form, two handles, bird and floral dec, handle chip, gilt wear, 12-3/4" h **$385**

Maebyong form, carved floral sprigs on body and lotus petals at base, deep sea-green color, Korea, Koryo period, old repair to mouth, 12th/13th C, 10-3/4" h **$1,800**

CHINTZ CHINA

History: Chintz china has been produced since the 17th century. The brightly colored exotic patterns produced on fabric imported from India to England were then recreated on ceramics. Early chintz patterns were hand painted and featured large flowers, fantastical birds, and widely spaced patterns. The advent of transfer printing resulted in the development of chintz dishes, which could be produced cheaply enough to sell to the masses. By the 1830s, a number of Staffordshire potteries were producing chintzware for everyday use. These early patterns are now starting to attract the interest of some chintz collectors.

Collectors typically want the patterns dating from roughly 1920 until the 1950s although some of the earlier un-named Royal Winton patterns are starting to become popular with longtime collectors. In 1920, A.G. Richardson "Crown Ducal" produced a range of all-over-transfer chintz patterns that proved to be very popular in North America, particularly the East Coast. Florida was the most popular of the Crown Ducal patterns in North America for collectors, but Pink Chintz and Peony have become increasingly popular.

From the late 1920s until the mid-1950s, Royal Winton produced more than 80 chintz patterns. In some cases, the background color was varied and the name changed: Hazel, Spring, and Welbeck is the same pattern in different colorways. After World War II, Royal Winton created more than 15 new patterns, many of which were more modern looking with large flowers and rich dark burgundy, blue or black backgrounds—patterns such as May Festival, Spring Glory and Peony. These patterns have not been as popular with collectors as 1930s patterns, although other 1950s patterns such as Florence and Stratford have become almost as popular as Julia and Welbeck. Some of the more widely spaced patterns, like Victorian Rose and Cotswold, are now attracting collectors.

The 1930s were hard times in the potteries and factories struggled to survive. They copied any successful patterns from any other factories. James Kent Ltd. produced chintzes such as DuBarry, Apple Blossom and Rosalynde. The most popular pattern for collectors is the white Hydrangea, although Apple Blossom seems to be more and more sought after. Elijah Cotton "Lord Nelson" was another factory that produced large amounts of chintz. The workers at Elijah Cotton were never as skilled as the Grimwades' workers, and usually the handles and spouts of teapots and coffeepots were left undecorated. Collectors love the Nelson Ware stacking teapots, especially in Black Beauty and Green Tulip.

Although a number of factories produced bone china after World War II, only Shelley Pottery seems to be highly desired by today's collector.

By the late 1950s, young brides didn't want the dishes of their mothers and grandmothers, but preferred the clean lines of modern Scandinavian furniture and dishes. Chintz gradually died out by the early 1960s, and it was not until the 1990s that collectors began to search for the dishes their mothers had scorned.

Notes: A newsletter devoted to Chintz is available, *Crazed Collector*, P.O. Box 2635, Dublin, CA 94568, CrazedCollctr@aol.com, www.crazedcollector.net. For those who prefer on-line information, there is a free Chintz chat group: chintz-subscribe@yahoogroups.com.

Adviser: Susan Scott.

Reproduction Alert. Both Royal Winton and James Kent reproduced some of their more popular patterns. Royal Winton is reproducing Welbeck, Florence, Summertime and Julia; in 1999 it added Joyce-Lynn, Marion, Majestic, Royalty and Richmond, Old Cottage Chintz and Stratford. The company added several new chintz patterns such as Blue Cottage and Christmas Chintz. James Kent reproduced Du Barry, Hydrangea, and Rosalynde, as well as creating several new colorways of old patterns. James Kent has discontinued the production of chintz ware. Elijah Cotton backstamp was purchased and as well as reproducing Rosetime chintz the factory has issued a number of new chintzes with the new backstamp. Wade recently produced three chintz patterns— Butterfly, Thistle and Sweet Pea. Two's Company and Godinger have also copied some of the Royal Winton patterns. Prices for vintage chintz seem to be rising again as new collectors have been attracted to the market but they are still well below the very high prices of the late 1990s. Inexperienced collectors often pay high prices for brand new pieces so check backstamps carefully.

Warning: Before you buy chintz, ask whether it is new or vintage. Ask to see a photograph of the backstamps if not examining the piece in person. The "1995" on the RW backstamp refers to the year the company was bought, and not the year the chintz was made. Compare old and new backstamps on www.chintz.net. com or in Susan Scott's *Charlton Standard Catalogue of Chintz*, 3rd edition, New Chintz Section.

Elijah Cotton "Lord Nelson"

Bud vase, Marina pattern, 5" h **$65**
Creamer and sugar, Briar Rose pattern **$75**
Cup and saucer, Rosetime **$50**
Jug, Bute shape, Pansy pattern, 6" h .. **$150**
Plate, Briar Rose pattern, 8" **$50**
Sauce boat, undertray, Country Lane pattern **$95**

Teapot, stacking, totally patterned, Marina **$250**

Grimwades "Royal Winton"

Biscuit barrel, Rheims shape, Hazel pattern **$600**
Breakfast set, Somerset pattern **$700**
Bud vase, Royalty pattern **$115**
Candy dish, covered, Gordon shape, Cotswold pattern **$175**
Cake stand, three-tier Sweet Pea pattern **$195**
Coffeepot, Albans shape, Julia pattern **$400**

Cup and saucer, Chelsea pattern **$75**
Eggcup, footed, Bedale pattern **$90**
Hot water pot, Albans shape, Royalty pattern **$300**
Jug, Duval shape, Majestic pattern, 5" h **$175**
Plate, Ascot shape, Beeston pattern, 10" **$165**
Salt and pepper shakers on tray, Hazel pattern **$115**
Teapot
  Albans shape, Esther pattern **$350**
  Stacking, Pekin pattern **$225**
  Stacking, Stratford pattern **$875**
Toastrack, Stafford shape, Summertime pattern **$200**
Tray, June Roses pattern, 10" Ascot shape **$175**

James Kent Ltd.

Coffeepot, Granville shape, Du Barry pattern **$300**
Dish
  Octagonal, Milles Fleur pattern, 12" l **$95**
  Ruffled, Chelsea Rose pattern, 12" x 8" **$75**
Plate
  Crazy Paving pattern, 9" d **$95**
  Hydrangea pattern, 10" d **$75**
Tray, Apple Blossom pattern, 8" by 5" **$55**
Teapot, Square Diamond shape, Mille Fleur pattern **$200**
Vase, Hydrangea pattern, 2" h **$105**

A. G. Richardson "Crown Ducal"

Cake plate, Peony pattern, 10" .. **$150**
Plate, Blue Chintz pattern, 9" sq **$65**
Sugar shaker, Primula pattern **$95**
Teapot, Georgian shape, Roseland pattern **$350**
Teapot and trivet, Primula pattern **$295**

Chintz, Royal Winton, bud vases, left: Floral Feast, **$125;** *right: Old Cottage,* **$65.**

Chintz, Royal Winton, June, creamer and sugar on tray, **$225.**

Chintz, Royal Winton, Evesham, stacking creamer, sugar and teapot, **$450.**

Vase
  Florida pattern, 8" h **$145**
  Ivory Chintz pattern, 6" h **$125**

Shelley Potteries Ltd.

Biscuit barrel, Blue Pansy pattern **$235**
Cup and saucer
  Henley shape, Countryside pattern **$165**
  Henley shape, Summer Glory pattern **$125**
  Miniature, Blue Pansy pattern .. **$1,860**
  Oleander shape, Rock Garden pattern **$105**
  Ripon shape, Briar Rose pattern **$160**
Plate, Oleander shape, Primrose pattern, 7" round **50.00**
Teapot, Henley shape, Summer Glory pattern **$375**
Toast rack, 5 bar Melody pattern .. **$115**

Clifton Pottery, Crystal patina squat covered teapot, squat two-handled organically shaped vase covered in matte green glaze, both marked, 6-1/4" h, **$300.**
Photo courtesy of David Rago Auctions, Inc.

CLIFTON POTTERY

History: The Clifton Art Pottery, Newark, New Jersey, was established by William A. Long, once associated with Lonhuda Pottery, and Fred Tschirner, a chemist.

Production consisted of two major lines: Crystal Patina, which resembled true porcelain with a subdued crystal-like glaze, and Indian Ware or Western Influence, an adaptation of the American Indians' unglazed and decorated pottery with a high-glazed black interior. Other lines included Robin's-Egg Blue and Tirrube. Robin's-Egg Blue is a variation of the crystal patina line, but in blue-green instead of straw-colored hues and with a less-prominent crushed-crystal effect in the glaze. Tirrube, which is often artist signed, features brightly colored, slip-decorated flowers on a terra-cotta ground.

Marks: Marks are incised or impressed. Early pieces may be dated and impressed with a shape number. Indian wares are identified by tribes.

Clifton Pottery, vase, Indian Ware, bulbous, tan, brown and terra cotta rounded panel design, incised "Clifton/231" and "Middle Mississippi Valley" around base, several glaze nicks around rim, 12-1/4" x 8-1/2", **$445.**
Photo courtesy of David Rago Auctions, Inc.

Biscuit jar, cov, gray-brown ground, enameled running ostrich and stork, florals, bail handle, 7" h, 4-1/4" d **$300**
Bowl, Indian, black glazed dec, marked, minor rim flake, 9" d **$150**
Creamer, Crystal Patina, incised "Clifton," dated **$225**
Decanter, rose shading to deep rose, purple flowers, gilt butterfly on neck, applied handle, marbleized rose and white stopper, 11-1/2" h **$150**
Jardinière, Four Mile Ruin, Arizona, incised and painted motif, buff and black on brown ground, imp mark and incised inscription, hairline to rim, 8-1/2" h, 11" d **$400**
Pedestal, Indian, unmarked, small chip to top and glaze, 20" h **$690**
Sweetmeat jar, hp ducks and cranes, robin's egg blue ground, cow finial, 4" h **$375**

Teapot, brown and black geometric design, 6" h **$200**
Vase
　Angular handles, Crystal Patina, incised "Clifton," 10" h, 7" d **$450**
　Bottle shape, Crystal Patina, incised "Clifton/158," 9-1/2" h, 4-1/2" d **$350**
　Bulbous, Indian, collared rim, geometric chain pattern, "Homolobi, #233," marked, few shallow scratches, 7-1/2" x 10" **$925**
　Bulbous, Indian, dark birds in flight, "Homolobi, #235," marked, 8" x 9" **$975**
　Spherical, Crystal Patina, green and mirrored caramel glaze, sgd and dated 1906, 6-1/2" d, 5-1/2" h ...**$575**
Vessel
　Gourd shape, Indian, swirl pattern, Arkansas, #216, marked, 5-1/4" **$380**

French, Paris, urns, pair with scene of Arabian figures and ruins on green ground with gold highlights, sold together with smaller example with sailing ship, c1850, 8-1/2" h, **$500.**
Photo courtesy of Pook & Pook, Inc.

CONTINENTAL CHINA AND PORCELAIN (GENERAL)

History: By 1700, porcelain factories existed in large numbers throughout Europe. In the mid-18th century, the German factories at Meissen and Nymphenburg were dominant. As the century ended, French potteries assumed the leadership role. The 1740s to the 1840s were the golden age of Continental china and porcelains.

Americans living in the last half of the 19th century eagerly sought the masterpieces of the European porcelain factories. In the early 20th century, this style of china and porcelain was considered "blue chip" by antiques collectors.

Additional Listings: French— Haviland, Limoges, Sarreguemines, and Sevres; German—Austrian Ware, Bavarian China, Dresden/Meissen, Rosenthal, Royal Bayreuth, Royal Bonn, Royal Rudolstadt, Royal Vienna, Schlegelmilch, and Villeroy and Boch; Italian—Capo-di-Monte.

French

Choisy, plate, earthenware transfer printed and hand enameled, each with different numbered scene relating to story of soldier's courtship and military life, naïve enamel accenting, mid-19th C, 8-1/4" d, price for set of 12 .... **$500**

Creil

Jug, transfer printed, canary ground, imp "CREIL" **$300**

Pitcher, 10-3/4" h, glazed pottery, ewer-form, central beige band dec with trees, cream ground, imp "CREIL," 5-1/4" h **$420**

Faience

Bulb pot, sq, molded acanthus-capped scroll feet, conforming handles, front with scene of courting couple, verso landscape, each side with floral sprays, sq form insert, gilt highlights, attributed to Marseilles, last quarter 18th C, 3-1/8" d, pr **$900**

Inkstand, figural, cartouche-shaped base molded with scrolls, front painted with harbor scene flanked by tower and knight-shaped inkpots, back sections support large figure of lion with raised paw resting on shield with armorial, 13-1/2" l **$650**

Plate, blue and white floral dec, foliate border, 9" d **$115**

Sugar caster, brightly polychrome scene of courting couple in landscape, floral sprays borders, dec band of fleur-de-lis border, pierced cov with conforming dec, early 19th C, 8-1/2" h **$450**

H.A. Balleroy Bros., attributed to, late 19th C, charger, 22-1/4" d, painted with scene of gentlemen studying drawings at trestle table, inscribed lower left "Le Portrait de L'Hote faience d'apres Brillouin par Pascault," gilt rim, mounted in 34" sq Aesthetic Movement gilt and copper frame with round inner surround **$1,100**

Lessore, Emile, platter, oval, earthenware, polychrome figural landscape with putti, artist signed, printed factory mark for Hautin and Boulenger, France, rim chip, c1855, 14-1/4" l **$450**

Paris

Cache pot, ovoid, apple-green ground, floral roundels in leaf surround, two gilt lion's head masks on sides, narrow undertray, late 19th C, 6" h **$115**

Candlesticks, pr, everted sconce, column-form standard, shaped base with man and woman among rocaille leaves, 9" h **$200**

Dessert plate, hand painted, four with flower centers, two with fruit centers, all with peach borders, gilt scrolls, maroon band at molded rim, late 19th C, 9-1/8" d **$750**

Lamp base, egg-shaped bodies, enamel dec multicolored floral sprays and gilt vines on lavender ground, drilled and electrified, late 19th C, 10-3/4" h, price for pr **$250**

Urn, Gilding, hand-painted scene, two oval reserves, one with church near lake, other with courting couple, double handles with faintly molded heads, wear, lid missing, 10-5/8" h **$375**

Vase garniture, three vases, each with aqua ground, floral bouquet roundels in gilt surrounds, short scroll handles, domed foot molded with scallop shells, late 19th C, 8" h, 8-1/4" h, 9-1/2" h **$500**

Veilleuse, hand painted, small pot with black and pink bands, over enameled with gilt scrolls, short gilt spout, angular handle, octagonal pagoda-form stand hp with scenes titled "acqueduque de Buc," showing elevated aqueduct, and "a Bonnebose (Calvados)," showing village, base missing, 20th C, 4-1/2" h pot, 9" h overall **$475**

Samson & Co.

Character figure, three figures in masks and caps, two wielding swords, other dagger, bearded figure with guitar, each by vine-covered tree trunk, rect base, guilloche borders, 20th C, 6-3/8" to 7-5/8" h, price for four-pc set **$450**

Figure, Neptune, upraised hands standing on scallop shell, dolphin at feet, rocaille base encrusted with shells and seaweed, gilt accents, late 19th C, 12-1/4" h **$230**

Perfume bottle, figural, boy with vessel seated on dolphin, enamel detailing, boy's head as stopper, late 19th C, 2-7/8" l **$230**

Unknown maker

Plate, centers painted with pastoral scenes, tooled gilt border, white ground, pink rim with three scenes within gilt cartouches, mid-19th C, 10" d, price for pr **$815**

Tray, painted in Oriental manner to resemble cloisonné, parrot and fish

Paris china, two-tier serving dish, salmon border bands, gold trim, ornate porcelain standards and ring handle, **$150.**
Photo courtesy of Wiederseim Associates, Inc.

on turquoise ground gold geometric design, cast bronze frame with bamboo and scroll Oriental designs with trace of gilding, some areas of verdigris, unmarked, 12-3/4" x 18-1/2" **$575**

Germany

Böttger, tea cup and saucer, red stoneware, black lacquered ground, stylized auricular handles, c1715, 3-1/8" h, 5-7/8" d saucer **$31,070**

Herend, dinner service, partial, Indian Basket pattern, puce dec on white ground, 10 dinner plates, six salad plates, five bread and butter plates, six bone dishes, five soup bowls, four serving trays of various size and form, gravy boat, four cups and six saucers, early 20th C **$1,450**

Hutschenreuther

Plaque, oval, Madonna and Child, giltwood frame, late 19th C, 5-1/8" x 6-7/8" **$600**

Service plate, central dec, summer flowers within heavily gilt cavetto, rim worked with scrolling acanthus, textured ground, under-glaze green factory marks, minor rubbing, 12-pc set, 10-7/8" d **$1,600**

Vase, mehlem, detailed painted birds, irises, and foliage, bronze patinated handles and base, imp marks, "Franz Anton Mehlem Bonn," c1900, 13-1/2" h, price for pr **$1,380**

Nymphenburg

Dinner service, each hand painted in enamels and trimmed in gilt with cartouches of landscapes in blue bead pattern, titles on reverse, 12, 10" d dinner plates; 11, 8-1/4" d plates; 8-1/4" d cov soup tureen with undertray; two coffee cups and saucers; 12 tea cups; 16 saucers; 7-1/2" h cov water pitcher; 2-5/8" h cream jug; 3-5/8" h cov sugar bowl; 18-1/2" l oval tea tray; two 6-5/8" d cov vegetable dishes; two 7" h fruit coolers with inserts; 8-7/8" square serving dish; 10-3/4" l triangular serving dish; two 9-1/2" d serving dishes; printed marks, mid-10th C **$28,200**

Vase, wide baluster form, enamel dec, continuous landscape scene, titled on underside "Vorfrohling in Ober-bayorn," signed "R. Sieck," 20th C, 10-1/2" d **$750**

Unknown maker

Cup and saucer, bucket-shaped cup, cerulean blue band over horizontal gilt beaded band above landscape scene, short gilt acanthus scroll handle, three gilt paw feet, similarly beaded and gilded saucer, 3-5/8" h **$1,035**

Plaque, girl with candle, titled "Guten Nahct," oval, reeded giltwood frame, late 19th/early 20th C, 5" l **$1,035**

Italian

Pattarino, mask, Bacchus, finely mold-ed, polychrome glaze, sprigged hair adjorned with applied grape clusters and vines, inscribed "Prof. E. Pat-tarino, Italy," 11-1/2" h **$2,645**

COOKIE JARS

History: Cookie jars, colorful and often whimsical, are popular with collectors. They were made by almost every manufacturer, in all types of materials. Figural character cookie jars are the most popular with collectors.

Cookie jars often were redesigned to reflect newer tastes. Hence, the same jar may be found in several different variations and these variations can affect the price.

Marks: Many cookie-jar shapes were manufactured by more than one company and, as a result, can be found with different marks. This often happened because of mergers or separations, e.g., Brush-McCoy, which became Nelson McCoy. Molds also were traded and sold among companies.

Cookie Bucket, McCoy **$75.**

Jack-o'-Lantern cookie jar by Abingdon, ink-stamped on bottom, "Abingdon U.S.A.," and impressed "674," c1950, 7-7/8" h, **$550.**

Abingdon Pottery

Bo Peep, No. 694D, 12" h **$425**

Choo Choo, No. 561D, 7-1/2" h **$120**

Daisy, No. 677, 8" h **$50**

Pumpkin, No. 674D, 8" h **$550**

Three Bears, No. 696D, 8-3/4" h **$245**

Windmill, No. 678, 10-1/2" h **$500**

Brayton Laguna Pottery

Partridges, Model No. V-12, 7-1/4" h **$200**

Provincial Lady, high-gloss white apron and scarf, red, green and yellow flowers and hearts, marked "Brayton Laguna Calif. K-27," 13" h **$455**

Swedish Maid, incised mark, 1941, 11" h **$600**

Hull Pottery

Barefoot Boy **$320**

Duck **$60**

Gingerbread Boy, blue and white trim **$400**

Gingerbread Man, 12" h **$550**

Little Red Riding Hood, open basket, gold stars on apron **$375**

Metlox Pottery

Bear, blue sweater **$100**

Chef Pierre **$100**

Pine Cone, gray squirrel finial, Model No. 509, 11" h **$115**

Rex Dinosaur, white **$120**

Tulip, yellow and green **$425**

Red Wing Pottery

French Chef, blue glaze **$250**

Grapes, yellow, marked "Red Wing USA," 10" h **$125**

Rooster, green glaze **$165**

Shawnee Pottery

Cinderella, unmarked **$125**

Dutch Boy, striped pants, marked "USA," 11" h **$190**

Dutch Girl, marked "USA," 11-1/2" h **$175**

Great Northern Boy, marked "Great Northern USA 1025," 9-3/4" h **$425**

Jo-Jo the Clown, marked "Shawnee USA, 12," 9" h **$300**

Little Chef **$95**

Muggsy Dog, blue bow, gold trim and decals, marked "Patented Muggsy U.S.A.," 11-3/4" h **$850**

Smiley Pig, clover blossom dec, marked "Patented Smiley USA," 11-1/2" h **$550**

Winnie Pig, clover blossom dec, marked "Patented Winnie USA," 12" h **$575**

Stoneware, cobalt blue dec, unknown maker

Basketweave and Morning Glory, marked "Put Your Fist In," 7-1/2" h **$625**

Flying Bird, 9" h **$1,250**

Watt Pottery

Apple, No. 21, 7-1/2" h **$400**

Cookie Barrel, wood grain, 10-1/2" h **$50**

Goodies, No. 76, 6-1/2" h **$150**

Happy/Sad Face, No. 34, wooden lid **$165**

Starflower, No. 503, 8" h **$350**

Drummer Boy cookie jar by Red Wing, all original, faint mark, early 1960s, 9" h, **$800.**

Bluebird on Pine Cone cookie jar by Metlox, marked on bottom, "Made in USA," and gold and brown foil label, "Metlox Manufacturing Co.," 11-1/2" h, **$350.**

Owl cookie jar by Shawnee, gold trim, impressed mark, "U.S.A.," late 1940s, 11-1/2" h, **$500.**

Watt Policeman cookie jar, unmarked, date unknown, **$900.**

Wedding Ring Granny cookie jar by Brayton Laguna, hand inscribed on bottom, "Brayton Laguna Pottery," 1940s, 11-3/4" h, **$500.**

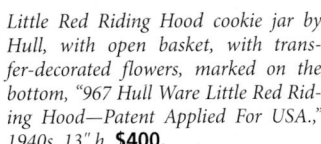

Left: Stoneware cookie jar , "spool" form, by Red Wing, with hand-painted flowers and "Cookies" in raised lettering, ink-stamped, "Red Wing Saffron Ware." 1930s, 9-1/4" h, **$200.**

Little Red Riding Hood cookie jar by Hull, with open basket, with transfer-decorated flowers, marked on the bottom, "967 Hull Ware Little Red Riding Hood—Patent Applied For USA.," 1940s, 13" h, **$400.**

COPELAND AND SPODE

History: In 1749, Josiah Spode was apprenticed to Thomas Whieldon and in 1754 worked for William Banks in Stoke-on-Trent. In the early 1760s, Spode started his own pottery, making cream-colored earthenware and blue-printed whiteware. In 1770, he returned to Banks' factory as master, purchasing it in 1776.

Spode pioneered the use of steam-powered pottery-making machinery and mastered the art of transfer printing from copper plates. Spode opened a London shop in 1778 and sent William Copeland there about 1784. A number of larger London locations followed. At the turn of the century, Spode introduced bone china. In 1805, Josiah Spode II and William Copeland entered into a partnership for the London business. A series of partnerships between Josiah Spode II, Josiah Spode III and William Taylor Copeland resulted.

In 1833, Copeland acquired Spode's London operations and seven years later, the Stoke plants. William Taylor Copeland managed the business until his death in 1868. The firm remained in the hands of Copeland heirs. In 1923, the plant was electrified; other modernization followed.

In 1976, Spode merged with Worcester Royal Porcelain to become Royal Worcester Spode, Ltd.

Copeland Spode dinner plate, red rose center, blue border with white floral decoration, gold rim, **$20.**

Copeland Spode dinner set, transferware dec, floral and geometric pattern, gilt highlights, three cov dishes, large soup tureen, two large trays, gravy bowl, perforated plate, bowl, nine luncheon plates, 13, 10" d dinner plates, **$400.**
Photo courtesy of David Rago Auctions, Inc.

Copeland Spode Cup and saucer, Gainsborough pattern, **$65.**
Photo courtesy of Joy Luke Auctions.

Bust, Una, by John Hancock, traces of printed verse on back, short socle, late 19th C, 11-1/2" h **$300**

Cabinet plate, artist sgd "Samuel Alcock," 1-3/4" jeweled border, intricate gold, beading, pearl and turquoise jeweling, c1889, 9-1/2" d **$750**

Coffee cup and saucer, 2-1/4" h cylindrical cup with allover maroon and gilt scrolled dec, 5" d saucer, retained by Tiffany & Co., late 19th C, price for set of 12 .... **$325**

Dinner service
Indian Tree, service for 10, serving pcs, 46 pcs **$500**
Maritime Rose pattern, service for 12, serving pieces, some repairs **$1,100**

Figure, parian
Chastity, standing female figure modeled holding some lilies, impressed "J. Durham, sc," title and manufacturer, England, c1865, 25" h **$1,530**
Ophelia, standing female figure modeled clenching flowers in her cloak, impressed "W. Calder Marshall RA," publishing date and manufacture, England, missing a leaf of one floret, c1863, 16-1/2" h **$500**

Fish plate, artist sgd "H. C. Lea," four-part gold-swirled design, hp fly in each section, c1891, 9-3/4" d **$175**

Jug, orange, teal green and gold dec, matte cream ground, ornate handle with two mythological characters, c1847 .... **$450**

Plate, blue and white, hunting scenes, 9-1/2" d **$225**

Platter, Blue Willow pattern, oval, deep, shaped edge, marked "Copeland & Garrett/Late Spode," 18" x 23-1/4" d **$375**

Service plate, Brompton pattern, floral border, central design of birds and foliage, retailed by Wright, Tyndale & Van Roden, Inc., Philadelphia, marked "Rd. No. 608584," price for set of 10, 10-1/4" d **$335**

Spill vase, flared rim, pale lilac, gilt octagonal panels with portrait of bearded man, band of pearls on rims and bases, Spode, c1920, 4-3/4" h **$425**

Tea set, Blue Willow, retailed by Tiffany & Co., pattern registered January 1879, printed at rim with quotation from Robert Burns "Auld Lang Syne," 5" h cov hexagonal teapot, creamer, cov sugar, seven cups, six saucers, 20-3/4" d round tray with scalloped gilt rim, gilt handles, gilt foo dog lid finials, price for 17-pc set **$950**

Tray, black transfer, passion flowers, grape vines border, emb grapes, vines, and leaves on tab handles, c1900, 8-1/2" l **$200**

Tureen, cov, white, gold and blue accents, marked "Spode New Stone," 13" w x 11" h **$1,470**

Urn, cov, Louis XVI style, cobalt blue ground, medallions on each side with bouquet of roses, majolica, repair to one handle, nick to one lid, pr, 15" h **$900**

Water pitcher, bulbous, tan acanthus leaf handle and spout, green field dec with white relief classical figures of dancing women, white relief banded floral garland dec at neck, marked "Rd. No. 180288," 8-1/4" h **$250**

DEDHAM POTTERY

History: Alexander W. Robertson established a pottery in Chelsea, Massachusetts, about 1866. After his brother, Hugh Cornwall Robertson, joined him in 1868, the firm was called A. W. & H. C. Robertson. Their father, James Robertson, joined his sons in 1872, and the name Chelsea Keramic Art Works Robertson and Sons was used.

The pottery's initial products were simple flower and bean pots, but the firm quickly expanded its output to include a wide variety of artistic pottery. It produced a very fine redware body used in classical forms, some with black backgrounds imitating ancient Greek and Apulian works. It experimented with underglaze slip decoration on vases. The Chelsea Keramic Art Works Pottery also produced high-glazed vases, pitchers and plaques with a buff clay body, with either sculpted or molded applied decoration.

James Robertson died in 1880 and Alexander moved to California in 1884, leaving Hugh C. Robertson alone in Chelsea, where his tireless experiments eventually yielded a stunning imitation of the prized Chinese Ming-era blood-red glaze. Hugh's vases with that glaze were marked with an impressed "CKAW." Creating these red-glazed vases was very expensive, and even though they received great critical acclaim, the company declared bankruptcy in 1889.

Recapitalized by a circle of Boston art patrons in 1891, Hugh started the Chelsea Pottery U.S., which produced gray crackle-glazed dinnerware with cobalt-blue decorations, the rabbit pattern being the most popular.

The business moved to new facilities in Dedham, Massachusetts, and began production in 1896 under the name Dedham Pottery. Hugh's son and grandson operated the business until it closed in 1943, by which time between 50 and 80 patterns had been produced, some very briefly.

Marks: The following marks help determine the approximate age of items:

• "Chelsea Keramic Art Works Robertson and Sons," impressed, 1874-1880

• "CKAW," impressed, 1875-1889

• "CPUS," impressed in a cloverleaf, 1891-1895

• Foreshortened rabbit only, impressed, 1894-1896

• Conventional rabbit with "Dedham Pottery" in square blue stamped mark along with one impressed foreshortened rabbit, 1896-1928

• Blue rabbit stamped mark with "registered" beneath, along with two impressed foreshortened rabbit marks, 1929-1943

Bowl
Rabbit pattern, reg. stamp, 8-1/2" sq
.... **$600**
Swan pattern, reg. stamp, 8-1/2" sq
.... **$725**
Bowl, Poppy pattern, cut edge rim, Oriental-type, sloping poppies, registered blue ink stamp, "D" in red, minor glaze miss near base edge, 9-3/8" d, 3-3/4" h........ **$1,035**
Breakfast plate
Crab pattern, blue ink stamp, glaze imperfections, 8-3/4" d **$375**
Rabbit pattern, assembled set, marks include blue registered stamp, imp foreshortened rabbit, and 1931 stamp, set of six, one with rim chip, 8-3/4" d.. **$635**
Butter plate, Swan pattern, registered blue ink stamp, 4-3/8" d.. **$260**

Dedham Pottery pitcher, "Oak Block" style, blue registered stamp, 1.5 pints, 5.5", **$975.**
Photo courtesy of Jim Kaufman.

Dedham Pottery plate, Dolphin, or "Upside Down Dolphin" variation, CPUS cloverleaf mark, 8.5" d, **$675.**
Photo courtesy of Jim Kaufman.

Dedham Pottery butter pat, Rabbit pattern, **$125.**

Dedham Pottery teapot, Rabbit pattern, 6 cup size, blue stamp, 8.125" h, **$875.**
Photo courtesy of Jim Kaufman.

Dedham Pottery vase, bulbous, experimental, by Hugh Robertson, fine, frothy, dripping green, brown, and amber glazes, incised "Dedham Pottery/HCR/ tr/B.W.," ink mark "DP7/A#53," 8" x 6-3/4", **$1,000.**
Photo courtesy of David Rago Auctions, Inc.

Dedham Pottery vase, bulbous, experimental, by Hugh Robertson, fine, frothy, dripping green glaze, incised "Dedham Pottery/HCR/B.W.," ink mark "DP8B/ #41A," 8" x 6-3/4", **$1,200.**
Photo courtesy of David Rago Auctions, Inc.

Dedham Pottery vase, bulbous, experimental, by Hugh Robertson, fine, thick mottled amber and blue-green glaze, incised "Dedham Pottery," ink mark "DP88A," 8" x 6", **$1,500.**
Photo courtesy of David Rago Auctions, Inc.

Candlesticks, pr
   Elephant pattern, reg. blue stamp
   .... **$525**
   Rabbit pattern, reg. blue stamp.. **$32**
Creamer and sugar, Rabbit pattern, blue stamp and "1931" on creamer, blue registered stamp on sugar, 3-1/4" and 4".......................... **$350**
Cup and saucer, Rabbit pattern, 3-7/8" d cup, 6" d saucers with rabbit borders, blue registered stamps, set of six **$700**
Knife rest, Rabbit form, blue reg. stamp **$575**
Paperweight, Rabbit form, blue reg. stamp **$495**
Pickle dish, Elephant pattern, blue reg. stamp, 10-1/2" l **$750**
Pitcher
   Chickens pattern, blue stamp, 5-1/8" h **$2,300**
   Rabbit pattern, 3-1/4" h **$175**
   Rabbit pattern, blue stamp, 9" h
   .... **$700**
   Style of 1850, blue reg. stamp.. **$975**
   Turkey pattern, blue stamp, 7" h
   .... **$585**
Plate, 6" d
   Clover pattern, reg. stamp **$625**
   Iris pattern, blue stamp, Maude Davenport's "O" rebus **$280**
   Rabbit pattern, registered blue ink stamp, set of four, foot chips on two **$290**
Plate, 6-1/8" d
   Horse Chestnut pattern, one impressed rabbit mark **$150**

   Magnolia pattern, blue ink stamp mark **$115**
Plate, Lobster pattern, registered blue ink stamp, two imp rabbits, 7-1/2" d.................................. **$290**
Plate, Rabbit pattern, glaze burst, 8-1/4" d.................................. **$125**
Plate, 8-1/2" d
   Crab pattern, blue stamp **$550**
   Elephant pattern, blue reg. stamp
   .... **$650**
   Oriental Poppy, single rabbit and blue ink stamp mark, in-the-making glaze bursts **$265**
   Rabbit pattern, blue stamp **$175**
   Rabbit pattern, blue stamp, Maude Davenport's "O" rebus **$235**
   Snow Tree pattern, blue stamp
   .... **$210**
   Upside down dolphin, CPUS .. **$900**
Plate, 10" d
   Dolphin pattern, blue reg. stamp
   .... **$875**
   Elephant pattern, blue reg. stamp
   .... **$900**
   Pine Apple pattern, CPUS **$775**
   Turkey pattern, blue stamp, Maude Davenport's "O" rebus **$475**
Plate, Rabbit pattern, registered blue ink stamp, one imp rabbit, 10-1/4" d **$150**
Platter, Rabbit pattern, rect, blue ink stamp, two imp rabbits, 9-7/8" l, 6-3/8" w **$260**
Salt and pepper shakers, pr, Rabbit pattern, glaze miss, 3-1/2" h
   .... **$200**

Sherbet, two handles, Rabbit pattern, blue stamp **$350**
Tea cup and saucer
   Azalea pattern, reg. stamp **$130**
   Butterfly pattern, blue stamp
   .... **$345**
   Duck pattern, reg. stamp **$190**
   Turtle pattern, reg. stamp **$680**
   Water Lily pattern, reg. stamp.. **$130**
Tea set, 8-1/2" h teapot, creamer, cov sugar, five 4" d cups, five saucers, waste bowl, small plate, Rabbit pattern, ink stamps on base, glaze voids and bubble bursts **$1,000**
Tea tile, Rabbit, round form with projections at ears and feet, white crackle glaze with outline of long-eared rabbit in blue, glaze missing to depict eyes against a blue-green ground, white clay body, base chip, 6-1/4" d **$390**
Vase
   Bulbous body, long neck, mottled green glossy glaze, incised "Dedham Pottery," William Robertson's initials, c1900, 9-1/4" h
   .... **$2,650**
   Experimental, by Hugh Robertson, thick glossy emerald green glaze dripping over indigo, pink, brown, and green volcanic base, incised "Dedham Pottery HCR," 6-1/2" h, 4-1/2" d **$4,500**
   Ovoid, mottled green glossy glaze, incised "Dedham Pottery" with Hugh Robertson's initials, c1900, 9-1/8" h **$2,500**

DELFTWARE

History: Delftware is pottery with a soft, red-clay body and tin-enamel glaze. The white, dense, opaque color came from adding tin ash to lead glaze. The first examples had blue designs on a white ground. Polychrome examples followed.

The name originally applied to pottery made in the region around Delft, Holland, beginning in the 16th century and ending in the late 18th century. The tin used came from the Cornish mines in England. By the 17th and 18th centuries, English potters in London, Bristol, and Liverpool were copying the glaze and designs. Some designs unique to English potters also developed.

In Germany and France, the ware is known as Faience, and in Italy as Majolica.

Reproduction Alert. Since the late 19th century, much Delft-type souvenir material has been produced to appeal to the foreign traveler. Don't confuse these modern pieces with the older examples.

Bowl, interior and exterior painted with polychrome orange, yellow, and blue flowers, hairline, late 18th C, 9" d, 3-3/4" h $900

Charger

Blue and white, foliate devices, chips, glass wear, restoration, 19th C, 13-5/8" d $320

Blue and white, foliate devices, Dutch, chips, glaze wear, 19th C, 13-1/8" d $410

Center branch with fruiting blossoms, two birds, conforming florals on wide rim, sgd "G. A. Kleynoven," c1655, 16-1/2" d **$2,250**

Floral design, building scene, manganese and blue, edge chips, 13" d $615

Dish

Fluted oval, blue and white floral design, attributed to Lambeth, chips, 12-3/8" l $440

Molded rim, blue and white, stylized landscape and floral design, edge chips, 8-1/4" d $315

Flower brick, blue and white, Chinese figures in landscape, Dutch, chips, cracks, 18th C, 4-5/8" l, 2-1/2" h $375

Garniture, three bulbous 17-1/4" h cov urns, two octagonal tapered 12-3/4" h vases, polychrome dec foliage surrounding central blue figural panels, Dutch, late 18th/early 19th C $8,625

Inkwell, heart shape, blue and white floral dec, wear and edge chips, 4-1/2" h................................ $495

Jar, blue and white, chips, pr, 5" h $715

Lamp base, octagonal bottle form with continuous blue and white Oriental figural landscape design, England, foot rim chips, drilled, 18th C $690

Model, tall case clock, blue dec white ground, panels of figural and architectural landscapes between scrolled foliate borders, slight glaze wear, 19th C, 17-1/2" h $320

Mug, blue and white, armorial surrounded by exotic landscape, palm trees, marked on base, Dutch, minor chips, glaze wear, 19th C, 6-3/8" h $490

Plate

Painted in polychrome manganese, blue, green and red with stylized flowers, few glaze chips around rims, late 18th C, 8-1/2" d $950

Tin-glazed earthenware, blue Chinoiserie motifs, manganese purple cracked-ice pattern border, England, chips, 18th C, 9-1/4" d $295

Tin glazed earthenware, central blue rosette, England, chips, 18th C, 7-7/8" d................... $125

Tin glazed earthenware, flowers, bird in birdbath in center, minor damage, 8-7/8" d $150

Tin glazed earthenware, Oriental fence and chrysanthemum dec, yellow rim, axe and "X" mark, minor damage, 9" d $150

White tin glazed earthenware, two-tone blue flowers, wavy border, "6" mark, edge flakes, old repairs, 9-1/8" d.................... $115

Posset pot, blue and white, birds among foliage, England, minor chips and cracks, 19th C, 4-3/4" h $920

Sauce boat, applied scrolled handles, fluted flaring lip, blue and white Oriental design, edge chips and hairline, later added yellow enamel rim, 8-1/4" l $440

Saucer, table ring, blue, iron-red, yellow and manganese bowl of flowers dec, 8-3/4" d $825

Strainer bowl, blue and white floral design, three short feet, chips, 9-1/8" d........................... $520

Tankard, tin glazed earthenware, pewter mounts, polychrome floral sprays, "IK 1793," indistinct signature inscribed on pewter top, England, cracks, 18th C, 9" h .. $400

Tea caddy, blue and white floral dec, scalloped bottom edge, marked "MVS 1750," cork closure, wear, edge flakes, old filled in chip on lid, 5-7/8" h $550

Tile, Fazackerly, polychrome dec of floral bouquets, price for pr, one with edge nicks, other with edge flaking and chips, c1760, 5" sq .. $350

Delft tile frieze, Dutch landscape with windmills, signed "Delft Blauw/ Handpainted/Made in Holland," framed, splintering to two edges of frame, 11-1/2" x 17-1/4", $245.
Photo courtesy of David Rago Auctions, Inc.

DRESDEN/MEISSEN

Dresden bowl, floral form, hand-painted floral decoration, hand-painted gilt design on border, impressed "D" mark, 10" d, 4" h, **$135.**

Photo courtesy of Alderfer Auction Co.

History: Augustus II, Elector of Saxony and King of Poland, founded the Royal Saxon Porcelain Manufactory in the Albrechtsburg, Meissen, in 1710. Johann Frederick Boettger, an alchemist, and Tschirnhaus, a nobleman, experimented with kaolin from the Dresden area to produce porcelain. By 1720, the factory produced a whiter hard-paste porcelain than that from the Far East. The factory experienced its golden age from the 1730s to the 1750s under the leadership of Samuel Stolzel, kiln master, and Johann Gregor Herold, enameler.

The Meissen factory was destroyed and looted by forces of Frederick the Great during the Seven Years' War (1756-1763). It was reopened, but never achieved its former greatness.

In the 19th century, the factory reissued some of its earlier forms. These later wares are called "Dresden" to differentiate them from the earlier examples. Further, there were several other porcelain factories in the Dresden region and their products also are grouped under the "Dresden" designation.

Marks: Many marks were used by the Meissen factory. The first was a pseudo-Oriental mark in a square. The famous crossed swords mark was adopted in 1724. A small dot between the hilts was used from 1763 to 1774, and a star between the hilts from 1774 to 1814. Two modern marks are swords with a hammer and sickle and swords with a crown.

Meissen stemmed compote, reticulated basket with two handles, raised polychrome flowers, stem of two cherubs, signed with blue cross swords under glaze, minor flower restorations, 12" h, **$775.**

Photo courtesy of The Early Auction Company, LLC.

Meissen cup and saucer, historical view of Washington and Franklin in profile and spread-winged eagle, cobalt blue ground, gilt dec, chip to rim of cup, 7" d, 5" x 4", **$225.**

Photo courtesy of David Rago Auctions, Inc.

Dresden

Cabinet vase, cylindrical, ruby, gold scrolling hand-painted scene of children playing, sgd "Dresden," 4-3/4" h **$800**

Compote, figural, shaped pierced oval bowl with applied florets, support stems mounted with two figures of children, printed marks, pr, late 19th/early 20th C, 14-1/4" h **$350**

Cup and saucer, hp medallion, marked "GLC Dresden" **$150**

Dessert plate in frame, set of four, 8" d printed and tinted plate, scenes of courting couples, insets, and floral sprigs, gilt details, early 20th C, 15-3/4" sq giltwood shadowbox frame **$175**

Figural group
Putti charting the heavens, putto seated at table, peering through telescope, another putto studying celestial globe, ovoid base, loss, crazing, late 19th/early 20th C, 5-3/4" h, 5-1/2" w **$375**
Two ladies, modeled as mischievous maidens in 18th C dress, ovoid base, early 20th C, 11" h **$460**

Loving cup, three handles, woodland scene with nymph, gold trim, 6-1/2" h **$475**

Plaque, molded relief of two partially nude women, flowing gowns, gilt florals, mounted in 22" x 16" glazed shadow box frame, price for pr, mid 20th C, 13-1/2" x 11" **$435**

Portrait vase, front with oval roundel printed with portrait bust of 18th C lady, gilt floral surround, central band of beaded landscape cartouches and foliate scrolls, faux jeweled diapered ground, two short gilt flying-loop handles, 6" h **$635**

Urn, cov, domed lid with fruit finial, body with two gilt flying-loop handles, trumpet foot on sq base, rose Pompadour ground, painted scenes of courting couples and floral bouquets, price for pr, one damaged, late 19th/early 20th C, 14-1/2" h **$700**

Vase
Alternating panels of lowers and turquoise ground floral bouquets, minor damage, cov, pr, c1900, 14" h **$375**
Alternating panels of figures and yellow floral bouquets, Thieme factory, late 19th C, 13-1/4" h **$115**

Meissen

Basket, leaf form, entwined branch handle, gilt dec, over flowing polychrome porcelain blossoms, underglaze blue crossed swords mark, incised "Y5," some losses, c1847 .... **$1,725**

Meissen figural group, porcelain, drunken silenus on donkey, underglaze blue cancelled crossed swords, incised 2724, 137, late 19th C, 7-3/4" l x 9" h, **$950.**
Photo courtesy of Sloans & Kenyon Auctioneers and Appraisers.

Meissen plate, wide reticulated border with polychrome decorated flowers, center with hand-painted courting scene on cobalt blue ground, crossed swords Meissen mark, 9-1/2" d, **$1,650.**
Photo courtesy of Alderfer Auction Co.

Cabinet plate, enameled center with cupid and female in wooded landscape, gilt dec pink and burgundy border, titled on reverse "Lei Wiedergut," 9-5/8" d **$490**

Chandelier, baluster-form shaft with hand-painted flower and leaf motifs, similar applied motifs on white ground, six S-scroll arms with conforming applied floral dec, candle cups, suspending tassels with applied floral bouquets, 23" h **$900**

Clock, Rococo style, clock face surrounded by applied floral dec, four fully molded figures representing four seasons, 18-3/4" h **$3,400**

Compote, stemmed, reticulated two handle basket, raised polychrome flowers, porcelain stem of two semi-nude cherubs, blue cross swords mark under glad, some restoration to flowers, 12" h............................. **$775**

Cup and saucer, flower-filled basket dec **$90**

Demitasse cup and saucer set, six cups and saucers with different designs, including oriental dragons, phoenix birds, and assorted flowers, each with blue underglaze blue swords mark, faux alligator box with crossed swords mark, box worn and damaged, 18-1/4" w, 10-1/4" d, 3-3/4" h.. **$500**

Dessert service, partial, pink floral dec, gilt trim, five 8" d plates with pierced rims, two 11-1/2" h compotes with figures of boy and girl flower sellers in center of dish, pierced rims, 20th C **$1,850**

Dinner service, partial, Deutsche Blumen, molded New Dulong border, gilt highlights, two oval serving platters,

circular platter, fish platter, 8-1/2" cov tureen with figural finial, two sauce boats with attached underplates, two serving spoons, sq serving dish, two small oval dishes, cov jam pot with attached underplate and spoon, 20 dinner plates, 11 teacups and saucers, nine salad plates, 10 bread plates, 10 soups, 74-pc set **$8,500**

Dish, cov, female blackamoor, beside covered dish with molded basketweave and rope edge, modeled on freeform oval base with applied florets, incised #328, 20th C, 6-5/8" h **$575**

Figure
Cockatoo, perched on tree stump, flower and leaves at base, early 20th C, 14-1/4" h **$2,300**
Continental woman holding basket of flowers, crossed swords mark, 5" h **$350**
Cupid dressed as blacksmith, heart on anvil, shell base, hand painted polychrome, gilt accents, underglaze blue crossed swords mark, 5" h **$875**
Five children at play with dog and lamb, hand painted polychrome, gilt accents, underglaze blue crossed swords mark, minor edge damage, repairs, 7" h, 5-3/4" d **$1,610**
Monkey band, all in 18th C dress, figure carrying drums, bag piper, clarinet player, harpsichordist riding another monkey, conductor, ovoid gilt accented bases, losses, late 19th/early 20th C, 5" h to 5-3/4" h **$5,300**
Seated man holding basket of flowers and rooster, blue cross swords mark, 4-1/4" h **$450**

Young girl with basket of flowers, hand painted polychrome, gilt accents, underglaze blue crossed swords mark, 4-1/4" h............. **$675**

Mirror, oval, heavily applied with leaves and flowers, top adorned with two cherubs supporting floral garland, Germany, c1900, 9-1/2" l **$1,380**

Nodder, Oriental gentleman, seated cross legged, nodding head, moving hands and tongue, white robe patterned with indianische blumen, gilt collar, blue slippers, underglaze blue crossed swords mark, incised "157," gilt painter's numerals "36," mid/late 19th C, 7-1/8" h **$5,750**

Plate, molded with four cartouches of bunches of fruit, shaped edge with C-scroll and wings, gilt dec, price for pr, late 19th C, 9" d..................... **$250**

Stand, top painted and encrusted with flowers, pierced apron dec with floral garlands, scrolled legs, underglaze blue crossed swords mark, 5-1/2" d, 3" h.. **$250**

Tea set, partial, brown, pink, green, blue, gray, purple and orange enameled birds in center, dragons on rim, gilt accents, seven teacups, seven 6" d saucers, nine 7" plates, 23 pcs **$700**

Tray, oval, enameled floral sprays, gilt trim, 20th C, 17-3/8" l **$400**

Urn on pedestal, figural cartouches, scattered floral dec, two handles in form of pair of entwined snakes, mounted as lamps, pr, 21" h **$4,000**

Vase, cov
Facial form body, plinth of applied scrolled acanthus borders, similar dec domed lid with encrusted floral bouquets, bolted, crossed swords underglaze with star and numeral II, some losses, 13-1/2" h **$1,380**
Schnellball, thistle shaped bodies with domed lids, encrusted with small white flowerheads, applied with flowerhead spherules, branches and birds, lid with bird and branch finials, Meissen, price for pr, 20th C, 8-1/4" h **$7,100**

Vase, scrolled snake handles, cobalt blue ground, gold and silver floral dec, new gold trim to handles, 19th C, 15-1/2" h **$2,300**

Wall garniture, 12-5/8" w, 19" l two-light girandole in rococo-style frame topped by putto figure, two figures of children among flowers on sides, brackets for two serpentine candle arms, two 15-1/2" w, 15-3/4" h scenic plaques with center painted scenes of bustling harbor, similar styled frames, sockets for candle arms, two 15-3/4" w, 15-3/4" h rococo-style three-light wall sconces, framed as rocaille scroll with three floral-encrusted serpentine candle arms, 19th C **$3,100**

Wine cooler, exterior boldly painted with sprays of deutsche Blumen, interior with fish, insects, and vegetation, gilt-edged scalloped rim set with two handles, underglaze blue

crossed swords mark, 25" d, 9-1/2" h **$10,160**

Tobacco jar, blue and white, Indians and "Siville," older brass stepped lid, chips, 10" h **$1,870**

Vase, urn shape, ftd, cherub framed with applied fruit wreath, two figure centaurs on each side, mkd with hand painted rooster and "22", 18" h **$350**

Vase, cov, Delft blue and white, oval paneled sides with Chinese style dec alternating with female figures in courtyard setting, flowers and fence design, hexagonal form rim,

foot and cov, cat finial, unidentified mark, Holland, rim damage, footrim chips, chips to cat's ears, typical edge flaking of tin glaze, 18th C, 23" h **$815**

Wall plaque, cartouche shape, blue enamel dec, windmill shoreline scene, Dutch, early 20th C, 23-1/2" l **$530**

Wall pocket, vasiform, ogee backplate, pierced grillwork, blue and white scenes of figures at harbor, scrollwork borders, applied flower buds on sides, price for pr, 20th C, 6-1/4" w, 4-1/2" d, 7" h **$350**

ENGLISH CHINA AND PORCELAIN (GENERAL)

English fish platter, center farm scene with pheasant and other game birds flying above, shaped floral border, marked "Brownfield & Son, Trademark, Woodland," registry diamond reads "Rd. No. 14058," **$125.**

History: By the 19th century, more than 1,000 china and porcelain manufacturers were scattered throughout England, with the majority of the factories located in the Staffordshire district.

By the 19th century, English china and porcelain had achieved a worldwide reputation for excellence. American stores imported large quantities for their customers. The special-production English pieces of the 18th and early 19th centuries held a position of great importance among early American antiques collectors.

English Caughley jug, molded cabbage leaves, mask spout, transfer-printed blue floral decoration, underglaze blue crescent mark, c1785, 8-1/2" h, **$800.**
Photo courtesy of Sloans & Kenyon Auctioneers and Appraisers.

Bow

Bowl, blue trailing vine, white ground, c1770, 4-1/2" d **$175**

Candlesticks, pr, two birds on flowering branches, dog and sheep on grassy base, wood stand, c1755 .... **$1,200**

Egg cup, two half-flower panels, powder blue ground, pseudo Oriental mark, c1760, 2-1/2" h **$900**

Plate, Turk's Cap Lily, dragonfly and moths, c1755, 9" d **$850**

Bradley Pottery

Jug, stoneware, applied in high relief with fruiting grapevine band above individually applied designs including windmill, cottage, manor house, farming implements, wheelbarrow and wagon, all surrounding central British coat of arms, impressed to one side of shoulder "MRS. ROBERTS" and "BARRELL INN" on other side, "BAGWORTH 1849" impressed below coat of arms, inscribed under the base "Made By John Bacon At Bradley Pottery 1849" inscribed under base, hairlines, rim chip, 15-3/4" h... **$1,300**

Chelsea

Candlesticks, pr, figural, draped putti, sitting on tree stump holding flower,

scroll-molded base, encircled in puce, gilt, wax pan, 7-1/2" h **$850**

Cup and saucer, multicolored exotic birds, white ground, gold anchor mark, c1765 .... **$750**

Plate, multicolored floral design, scalloped rim, gold anchor mark, 8-1/2" d **$475**

Davenport

Cup plate, Teaberry pattern, pink luster **$40**

Jug, Jardiniere pattern, blue, orange, green, peach and gold, peach luster rim, c1805-20, 5-1/2" h **$450**

Plate, Oriental style design similar to Gaudy Welsh Grapes pattern, orange, blue, fuchsia, green and gilt, transfer labels on back, minor wear, set of four, 8-1/4" d **$350**

Serving bowl, cov, Chinoiserie Bridgeless pattern, internal bowl with steam holes, c1810, 7" w, 9-3/4" l **$700**

Tea service, Imari pattern, teapot, creamer, cov sugar, four cups and saucers, 18" l tray **$850**

Derby

Beaker, two short shell-shaped handles, two painted landscape roundels in gilt borders, scenes titled "Near Spondon" and "Near Breadshall," both Derbyshire scenes, pale yellow ground, late 18th/early 19th C, 3-1/8" h..........................**$1,265**

Dessert dishes, underglaze blue and iron red dec of trees and flowering vines, gilt enamel accenting, mid-19th C, two 9-3/4" l heart-shaped dishes; 11-1/4" l navette-shaped dish......**$400**

Figure, pastoral, boy resting against tree stump playing bagpipe, black hat, bleu-do-roi jacket, gilt trim, yellow breeches, girl with green hat, bleu-du-roi bodice, pink skirt, white apron with iron-red flowerheads, gilt centers, leaves, scroll molded mound base, crown and incised iron-red D mark, pr, 8" h, 8-1/2" h...........**$2,200**

Jar, cov, octagonal, iron-red, bottle green and leaf green, alternating cobalt blue and white grounds, gilding, grotesque sea-serpent handles, now fitted as lamp with carved base, pr, 19th C, 22" h **$10,000**

Plate, enamel dec, stylized Imari-type designs of birds in three, shaped molded rim, Bloor mark, price for set of seven, second quarter 19th C, 10-1/8" d...............................**$300**

Devon Art Pottery

Jug, pottery, slip dec, brown and yellow glazed sgraffito designs, late 19th C, 8-1/4" h...................................**$1,530**

Earthenware

Stirrup mug, fox head, polychrome, small losses to ear tips, early 19th C, 5" l..................................**$715**

Flight, Barr & Barr

Crocus pot, D-form, molded columns and architrave, peach-ground panels, ruined abbey landscape reserve, gilding, 9" w, 4" d, 6-1/4" h............**$2,400**

Pastille burner, cottage, four open chimneys, marked, c1815, 3-1/2" h **$425**

Tea service, gilt foliate, orange ground banded border, 9-1/2" h cov teapot (finial restoration), 7" l teapot stand, 4-3/4" h creamer, 4-1/2" h sugar bowl, 6-5/8" d waste bowl, two 8" deep dishes, 10 coffee cans, 11 teacups, 11 saucers, minor chips to cups and saucers, incised "B" mark, light wear to gilt at rim throughout, c1792-1804.....**$1,320**

Grainger

Punch bowl, ext. enamel dec with

large floral bouquets on either side of clipper ship titled above "City of Poonah," gilt inscription "Presented by Captain James Wilson to John Carr Esq. 1839," int. with central crest of stag, floral and foliate border in green, buff and gold, int. glaze stains, c1839, 13-5/8" d.....................**$3,525**

Herculaneum

Jug, creamware, black transfer printed, obverse "Washington," oval design with medallion portrait on monument surmounted by wreath, birth and death dates below, flanked by eagle and grieving woman, upper ribbon inscribed "Washington in Glory," lower ribbon "America In Tears," reverse transfer of American sailing vessel, American eagle beneath spout, inscription "Herculaneum Pottery Liverpool," incised mark on base, imperfections, 10" h **$1,100**

Jackfield

Cheese dish, dome cover, black glaze, white, yellow, pink and blue flowers, gilding, 7-1/2" h..........................**$125**

Creamer, bulbous, emb grapes design, leaves, and tendrils, gilt highlights, three pr paw feet, ear-shaped handle, 4-1/4" h..................................**$185**

Pitcher, applied handle, black, traces of enameling, bird, initials and "1763," wear, small flakes, 6-1/2" h **$125**

Sugar bowl, cov, scalloped SS rims, SS-mounted cov and ornate pierced finial, 4-1/2" h, 3-3/4" d **$250**

Lowestoft

Teapot, cov, fluted globular body, polychrome enamel dec Chinese figural courtyard scenes, cover with small chips, hairline to interior collar, 18th C, 5-1/4" h **$4,150**

Masons

Creamer, Oriental-style shape, marked "Mason's Patent Ironstone," 4" h **$85**

Jug, octagonal, Hydra pattern, waisted straight neck, green-enameled handle, lion-head terminal, underglaze blue and iron-red flowers and vase, two imp marks and printed rounded crown mark, c1813-30, 8" h.......**$320**

Platter, Double-Landscape pattern, Oriental motif, deep green and brick red, c1883, 13-1/2" x 10-3/4" **$265**

Potpourri vase, cov, hexagonal body, cobalt blue, large gold stylized peony blossom, chrysanthemums, prunus and butterflies, gold and blue dragon handles and knobs, trellis diaper-rim border, c1820-25, 25-1/4" h **$1,750**

New Hall

Bowl, Pattern 425, Window pattern, over-glaze polychrome enamels, late 18th C, 5" d **$350**

Coffeepot, cov, Pattern 425, Window pattern, pear shape, over-glaze polychrome enamels, late 18th C, 9-5/8" h..................................**$1,950**

Dessert dishes, set of six, each with wide pale blue ground, floral and vine relief, gilt trim, polychrome enamel dec centers, 9-1/8" l oval with basket of fruit; five 9-1/4" l ovals with landscapes; four 7-7/8" strawberry shaped, each with gilt rim wear, c1825 ...**$940**

Dinner service, partial, landscape transfer dec, six shaped dishes, six plates, cup, two saucers, cov sauce tureen with ladle.....................**$1,100**

Miniature, tea set, Pattern 2720, over-glaze enamel floral bands, consisting of a 3-3/4" h cov teapot; 3-1/4" h cov sugar bowl; 2-3/8" h cream jug; four tea cups with 2-3/4" d saucers, 19th C **$1,000**

Punch bowl, Pattern 425, Window pattern, overglaze polychrome enamel dec, late 18th C, 11-1/8" d.....**$1,800**

Teapot, cov, Pattern 425, Window pattern, oval shape, overglaze polychrome enamels, late 18th C, 5-1/4" h ..**$1,750**

Teapot stand, Pattern 425, Window pattern, overglaze polychrome enamels, late 18th C, 6-5/8" l...............**$750**

Tea service, partial
Pattern 264, gilt decorated with foliage, 6-1/2" h oval-shaped cov teapot and cover; 6-3/4" l oval teapot stand; 5-5/8" h oval shaped cov sugar bowl; 4" h cream jug; 4-3/4" cov tea canister; 7-7/8" d serving dish; 8-3/8" serving dish; eight 3-1/4" d tea bowls; 10 coffee cups; seven 5" d saucers, hairlines, late 18th C.............**$1,775**
Pattern 1064, polychrome enamel dec, two 5-3/4" h cov teapots; two 7-1/2" l teapot stands; two 3-5/8" h cream jugs; 4-1/2" h rect cov sugar bowl, 5" h oval cov sugar bowl, three 6-1/2" d bowls; three 7-7/8" d shallow bowls; nine coffee cups, three tea bowls, 17 assorted teacups, 29 assorted saucers, chips, hairlines on many pcs, early 19th C **$1,410**

Rockingham

Tea set, rococo-style, each with central pale buff band, enamel decorated landscape cartouche, gilt scrolled foliate trim, 10-1/2" l cov teapot with scrolled foliate handle and serpent-form spout, rim hairline, light gilt wear to spout and handle; 4-3/8" h creamer, slight chip to side of handle; 6" h cov sugar bowl; 7-1/8" d waste bowl, c1820 ....**$220**

Swansea

Tea set, floral pattern, underglaze blue, black transfer, gilt trim, 12 8" d plates; 11 each teacups, coffee cups, saucers; teapot; creamer; three trays; 7-1/2" d bowl, some professional repair, worn gilt, several pcs with chips and hairlines **$590**

Ralph Wood

Figure, pearlware
9-1/8" h shepherd and 8-3/4" h shepherdess, mounted to lamp bases, restoration, losses, 18th C **$1,000**
Seated herding couple, man playing pipe, lamb, goat, and dog at their feet, mounted to a lamp base, losses, restoration, 18th C, 11-1/2" h
..................................**$235**

Woods

Cup and saucer, handleless, Woods Rose **$65**
Dish, dark blue transfer of castle, imp "Wood," 8" l, 6" w **$165**
Jug, ovoid, cameos of Queen Caroline, pink luster ground, beaded edge, molded and painted floral border, c1820, 5-3/4" h **$425**
Plate, Woods Rose, scalloped edge, 9" d
..................................**$125**
Stirrup cup, modeled hound's head, translucent shades of brown, c1760, 5-1/2" l **$2,200**
Whistle, modeled as seated sphinx, blue accents, oval green base, c1770, 3-7/8" h **$600**

Worcester, Chamberlain's, armorial

Sauce tureen, cov, stand, pr, finial in form of bull's head and crown, modeled on the crest of the Marquis of Abergavenny, painted Japan pattern of flowering Oriental plants, reserves painted with arms of Admiral Lord Nevill, Marquis of Abergavenny above the motto Ne Vile Velis; red script mark, c1813, 15" l, 10-1/2" h
..................................**$8,365**
Soup tureen, cov, stand, finial in form of bull's head and crown, modeled on the crest of the Marquis of Abergavenny, painted Japan pattern of flowering Oriental plants, reserves painted with arms of Admiral Lord Nevill, Marquis of Abergavenny above the motto Ne Vile Velis; red script mark, c1813, 15" l, 10-1/2" h **$11,355**

Worcester, Dr. Wall

Cup and saucer, oriental design, flowers, mythical animals, oriental mark in underglaze blue **$950**
Plate, scalloped edge, Oriental design, flowers, mythical animals, oriental mark in underglaze blue, 7-1/2" d
..................................**$850**

ENGLISH SOFT PASTE

English soft paste pearlware figure, crying boy in white smock, square base, chips, restoration to hands, late 18th/early 19th C, 8" h, **$350.**
Photo courtesy of Sloans & Kenyon Auctions.

History: Between 1820 and 1860, a large number of potteries in England's Staffordshire district produced decorative wares with a soft earthenware (creamware) base and a plain white or yellow glazed ground.

Design or "stick" spatterware was created by a cut sponge (stamp), hand painting, or transfers. Blue was the predominant color. The earliest patterns were carefully arranged geometrics that generally covered the entire piece. Later pieces had a decorative border with a central motif, usually a tulip. In the 1850s, Elsmore and Foster developed the Holly Leaf pattern.

King's Rose features a large, cabbage-type rose in red, pale red, or pink. The pink rose often is called "Queen's Rose." Secondary colors are pastels—yellow, pink, and, occasionally, green. The borders vary: a solid band, vined, lined, or sectional. The King's Rose exists in an oyster motif.

Strawberry Chinaware comes in three types: strawberries and strawberry leaves (often called strawberry luster), green featherlike leaves with pink flowers (often called cut-strawberry, primrose, or old strawberry), and relief decoration. The first two types are characterized by rust-red moldings. Most pieces have a cream ground. Davenport was only one of the many potteries that made this ware.

Yellow-glazed earthenware (canary luster) has a canary yellow ground, a transfer design that is usually in black, and occasional luster decoration. The earliest pieces date from the 1780s and have a fine creamware base. A few hand-painted pieces are known. Not every piece has luster decoration.

Because the base material is soft paste, the ware is subject to cracking and chipping. Enamel colors and other types of decoration do not hold well. It is not unusual to see a piece with the decoration worn off.

Marks: Marked pieces are uncommon.

Additional Listings: Gaudy Dutch, Staffordshire Items.

Creamware

Basket, green trim, open sides, woven bottom, undertray with conforming pattern, reticulated border, green trim, hairline on basket side, wear on sides of underplate, 7-1/2" x 6-1/2", 9-1/2" x 7-1/2" undertray **$950**

Coffeepot, cov, pear shape, polychrome dec black transfer of Tea Party and Shepherd prints, leaf-molded spout, chips, restoration to body, attributed to Wedgwood, c1775, 10" h **$350**

Jug, reeded lapped handle, emb floral applications, sides dec with red and green floral sprays, glaze wear, small rim nicks, 19th C, 5-1/8" h **$260**

Mug, Orange Institution, red transfer printed symbols with verse above "Holiness to the Lord" and verse below "May the Orange Institution stand as firm as the Oak and the Enemies fall off like the leaves in October," England, early 19th C, 3-1/3" h **$300**

Pitcher, two oval reserves with black transfer printed scenes of naval engagements, "The Wasp Boarding the Frolic," sgd "Bentley, Wear, and Bourne Engravers and Printers Shelton, Staffordshire," reverse depicting "The Constitution taking the Cyane and Livant," light green ground, luster embellishments, imperfections, 6-1/4" h **$2,760**

Plate, shaped edge, cutout floral design, unmarked, flakes on rim, price for pr, 9-1/2" d **$715**

Platter, oval, scallop dec rim, chips, restorations, 18" l, 14-1/2" w **$300**

Sugar bowl, int. with red and green enamel floral dec, purple luster and underglaze blue, ext. marked "Be Canny with the Sugar" flanked by small flowers, 5-1/8" d, 2-3/4" h **$385**

Teapot
Flower knop, floral dec entwined reeded handle with touches of gilt, rim chip, restored spout, gilt loss, 19th C, 6-1/2" h **$230**
Molded acanthus spout, ribbed handle, small flakes, 4-3/4" h **$385**

King's Rose

Bowl, Rose, broken solid border, flakes, 7-3/4" d **$55**

Cup and saucer, handleless
Oyster pattern, hairline cracks **$40**
Rose, vine border **$150**

Plate
Pink border, wear, 5-5/8" d **$55**
Scalloped border, four pcs, 9-3/4" d **$220**
Some flaking, 7-3/8" d **$90**
Vine border, three pcs, 8-1/4" d ... **$255**
Pitcher, dark red rose, blue and yellow flowers, green leaves, some wear, 5-5/8" h **$220**
Soup plate, broken solid border, scalloped edges, some flakes, three pcs, 9-1/2" d **$360**
Teapot, broken solid border, some flakes, 5-3/4" h **$140**

Pearlware
Bowl
Black and brown slip-filled rouletted band at rim, field of rust with blue, black, and white scroddled dots, repaired, early 19th C, 4-3/4" d **$940**
Cream top band, rust, dark brown, and buff marbling, repaired, 8-1/2" d **$825**
Coffeepot, cov, baluster form, dome lid, ochre, green, brown and blue floral dec, imperfections, early 19th C, 13" h **$200**
Creamer, cup shape, straight sides, applied handle, light brown stripes, yellow band, gilt and light brown foliage band, slight bubbles to yellow, minor spout rim flake **$125**
Cup and saucer, handleless, black transfer scene of horse-drawn chariot, flying putti set of six, 3-1/2" d cup, 5" d saucer **$525**

Figure
Sheep, brown, blue, and yellow ochre sponging, small edge flakes, 3" l **$275**
Squirrel, nut and collar with ring, polychrome, orange coat, attributed to Derby, minor wear and small flakes on base, 3-1/4" h **$635**

English soft paste cups and saucers, handleless, Strawberry pattern, pink luster strawberries, green leaves, copper luster vines, set of five, **$650.**
Photo courtesy of Alderfer Auction Co.

FAMILLE ROSE

Famille Verte decoration, covered jar, painted with Kilin within round medallions, framed by band of ruyi, overall floral decoration, round pommel lid, China, 18th C, 10" d, chips on lid rim, **$1,250.**

History: Famille Rose is Chinese export enameled porcelain on which the pink color predominates. It was made primarily in the 18th and 19th centuries. Other porcelains in the same group are Famille Jaune (yellow), Famille Noire (black), and Famille Verte (green).

Decorations include courtyard and home scenes, birds, and insects. Secondary colors are yellow, green, blue, aubergine, and black.

Rose Canton, Rose Mandarin, and Rose Medallion are mid-to late-19th century Chinese-export wares, which are similar to Famille Rose.

Bowl, shallow, polychrome birds and butterflies, pink flowers, fruit, and vegetables, gilt rims, few rim chips, 8" d, price for set of six **$395**

Brush washer, sprays of peonies, cicada, and grass hopper on side, chi dragon in iron red and gold slithering around rim and peering into well, four-character mark in iron red on recessed base, "Jerentang Zhi," China, early 20th C, 2-7/8" h, 3-5/8" d **$1,035**

Cache pot, stand, 11" l, 7-1/4" w, 6" h, clusters of flowers on plain ground, 10-1/2" l, 7-1/2" w, 1-1/2" h stand, repaired, reglued foot **$1,100**

Charger, central figural dec, brocade border, 12" d **$265**

Dish, cov, figural dec, Qing dynasty, 11" d **$200**

Figure

Cockerels, 16" h, pr **$550**

Peacocks, 13" h, pr **$275**

Garden set, hexagonal, pictorial double panels, flanked and bordered by floral devices, blue ground, minor glaze loss, 19th C, 18-1/2" h **$1,100**

Jar, cov, baluster form, domed lid, ovoid finial, birds on rocky outcrop, flowering branches dec, early 20th C, 19" h, price for pr **$500**

Jardinierè, flowering branches dec, Jiaqing, 9-3/4" h **$700**

Lamp base, made from ginger jar, pink, orange, and purple roses and other flowers, green foliage, on base, electrified, 12-1/2" h.................. **$320**

Mug, Mandarin palette, Qianlong, 1790, 5" h **$425**

Plate, floral dec, ribbed body, Tongzhi mark, 10" d, pr **$275**

Platter, ogee form, export, China, 18th C, 19" l **$1,100**

Pot, cov, iron-red and gilt "JHS," cross, three swords in scalloped cartouche, "Jesus Hominum Salvator," phoenix standing on pierced rock among flowers and ducks, blue key fret base border, ruyi band on shoulder, iron-

Famille Rose Chinese vase, cabbage leaf, porcelain, insect decoration, 19th C, **$1,300.**
Photo courtesy of Sloans & Kenyon Auctioneers and Appraisers.

Famille Rose Chinese, tureen, boar form, 15-1/2" l, **$750.**
Photo courtesy of Sloans & Kenyon Auctioneers and Appraisers.

red seal on base, six-character mark, "Daoguang," China, minor scratches, carved wooden lid, wear to gilding, c1821-50, 4-1/2" h **$700**

Tray, oval, multicolored center armorial crest, underglaze blue diaper and trefoil borders, reticulated rim, late 18th C, 8" l.................................. **$550**

Tureen, pink roses, polychrome butterflies, birds, fruits, and gourds in shades of orange, blue, green, yellow, foliage finial, twig handles, gilt accents, orange peel glaze, minor wear to gilt, hairline in base, 15-1/2" l, 10-1/2" h **$815**

Vase

Baluster, pr, 9-7/8" h................. **$450**

Birds and flowers dec, 19th C, 23-1/2" h **$450**

Diamond shape with flanged edges, landscapes and flowers, six-character Ch'ien Lung mark in red on the base, China, 19th C, 10-1/2" h **$1,120**

Flat pear shape with pointed sides, two raised panels outlined in iron-red and gold, molded horizontal lines on body, iron-red four-character mark on base, "Shen de Tang Zhi," China, 19th C, 5-1/4" h **$200**

Pair, flowering peony and butterflies, mkd on base in square "Hongxian Nian Zhi," Chinese, early 20th C, 9-1/4" h **$1,750**

Underglaze blue with enameled landscape, early 20th C, 9" h **$1,000**

Vase, cov, shouldered ovoid, large cartouches with scenes of warriors on horseback, dignitaries holding court, molded fu-dog handles, conforming cartouches on lid, fu-dog finial, c1850-70, 26" h, pr **$2,400**

Water dropper, molded as lotus flowers, stem forming spout, inscribed in stems with commemorative inscriptions, Guangxu, China, 7-1/8" l, pr **$3,150**

Famille Rose porcelain figure of bird, electrified, 19th C, 17-1/2" h, **$400.**
Photo courtesy of Sloans & Kenyon Auctioneers and Appraisers.

Famille Rose plaque, lobed, enameled cicada perched on yellow flower, China, early 20th C, 9-1/8" l, 8" w, **$125.**

Famille Verte

Bottle, porcelain, enameled flowering peonies and birds, Chinese, replaced wooden lids, 19th C, price for pr, 7-3/4" h **$1,495**

Figure, pair of cockerels, China, 19th C, 17" h **$1,880**

Ginger jar, cov, ovoid, foo dog beside sea reserve, floral and butterfly patterned ground, Kangxi, 10-1/2" h **$420**

Vase

High relief dec, warrior on horseback riding under pine tree in mountainous landscape, base with incised Qianlong four-character mark in sq reserve, China, 18th or 19th C, 9-1/8" h, 4-7/8" d **$425**

Dec with magpies flying among prunus trees, black ground, Rouleau, China, 17-1/4" h, pr **$1,920**

Famille Verte Chinese vase, porcelain, figural decoration, electrified, Qing Dynasty, 19th C, 16" h, **$400.**
Photo courtesy of Sloans & Kenyon Auctioneers and Appraisers.

Left: Famille Rose Meiping painted peaches, flowers, scrolling foliage, and calligraphy, yellow ground, Chinese Jiaqing mark, Republic period, 9-1/2" h, **$3,500.**
Photo courtesy of Sloans & Kenyon Auctioneers and Appraisers.

FIESTA

Fiesta Ware, footed salad bowl, red, 11-3/8" x 5-1/2", **$585.**

Fiesta Ware, carafe, turquiose, 9-1/4" x 7-1/8" x 6-1/8", **$275.**

Fiesta Ware, covered casserole, red, 9-3/4" x 7-7/8" x 5-3/4", **$275.**

Fiesta Ware, coffeepot, turquoise, with lid, 10-3/8" x 8", **$170.**

History: The Homer Laughlin China Company introduced Fiesta dinnerware in January 1936 at the Pottery and Glass Show in Pittsburgh, Pennsylvania. Frederick Rhead designed the pattern; Arthur Kraft and Bill Bensford molded it. Dr. A. V. Bleininger and H. W. Thiemecke developed the glazes.

The original five colors were red, dark blue, light green (with a trace of blue), brilliant yellow, and ivory. A vigorous marketing campaign took place between 1939 and 1943. In mid-1937, turquoise was added. Red was removed in 1943 because some of the chemicals used to produce it were essential to the war effort; it did not reappear until 1959. In 1951, light green, dark blue, and ivory were retired and forest green, rose, chartreuse, and gray were added to the line. Other color changes took place in the late 1950s, including the addition of a medium green.

Fiesta ware was redesigned in 1969 and discontinued about 1972. In 1986, Homer Laughlin China Company reintroduced Fiesta. The new china body shrinks more than the old semi-vitreous and ironstone pieces, thus making the new pieces slightly smaller than the earlier pieces. The modern colors are also different in tone or hue, e.g., the cobalt blue is darker than the old blue.

Color Guide

Color Name	Color palette	Years of Production
Red	Reddish-orange	1936-43, 1959-72
Blue	Cobalt blue	1936-51
Ivory	Creamy yellow-white	1936-51
Yellow	Golden yellow	1936-69
Green	Light green	1936-51
Turquoise	Sky blue	1937-69
Rose	Dark dusky rose	1951-59
Chartreuse	Yellow-green	1951-59
Forest green	Dark hunter green	1951-59
Gray	Light gray	1951-59
Medium green	Deep bright green	1959-69
Antique gold	Dark butterscotch	1969-72
Turf green	Olive green	1969-72
Cobalt blue	Very dark blue, almost black	1986-
Rose	Bubblegum pink	1986-
White	Pearly white	1986-
Black	High gloss black	1986-
Apricot	Peach-beige	1986-98
Turquoise	Greenish-blue	1988-
Yellow	Pale yellow	1987-2002
Periwinkle blue	Pastel gray-blue	1989-
Sea mist green	Pastel light green	1991-
Lilac	Pastel violet	1993-95
Persimmon	Coral	1995-
Sapphire (Bloomingdale's exclusive)	Blue	1996-97
Chartreuse	More yellow than green	1997-99
Pearl gray	Similar to vintage gray, more transparent	1999-2001
Juniper green	Dark blue-green	1999-2001
Cinnabar	Brown-maroon	2000-
Sunflower	Bright yellow	2001-
Plum	Rich purple	2002-
Shamrock	Grassy green	2002-
Tangerine	Bright orange	2003-

Fiesta Ware, fruit bowl, chartreuse, 5-1/2", **$35.**

Fiesta Ware, ashtray, cobalt blue, 6-1/4" x 1-1-4", **$55.**

Fiesta Ware, dessert bowl, medium green, 6-1/4" x 1-1/4", **$750.**

Ashtray
Ivory	$55
Red	$60
Turquoise	$50
Yellow	$48

Bowl, green, 5-1/2" d $60
Cake plate, green $1,950

Candlesticks, pr, bulb
Cobalt blue	$125
Ivory	$125
Red	$120
Turquoise	$110
Candlesticks, pr, tripod, yellow	$550

Carafe
Cobalt blue	$495
Ivory	$385

Casserole, cov, two handles, 10" d
Ivory	$195
Yellow	$160

Chop plate, gray, 13" d $95

Coffeepot
Cobalt blue	$235
Ivory	$390
Red	$250
Turquoise	$250
Yellow	$185

Compote, low, ftd, 12" d
Cobalt blue	$175
Ivory	$165
Red	$185
Yellow	$165

Creamer
Cobalt blue	$35
Ivory	$30
Red	$65
Yellow	$30

Creamer and sugar, figure-eight server, yellow creamer and sugar, cobalt blue gray $315

Cream soup bowl
Cobalt blue	$60
Ivory	$55
Red	$65
Turquoise	$48
Yellow	$45

Cup, ring handle
Cobalt blue	$35
Ivory	$30
Red	$30

Turquoise	$25
Yellow	$25

Demitasse cup, stick handle
Cobalt blue	$75
Ivory	$80
Red	$85
Turquoise	$75
Yellow	$65

Demitasse pot, cov, stick handle
Cobalt blue	$650
Ivory	$535
Red	$575
Turquoise	$650
Yellow	$465

Dessert bowl, 6" d
Cobalt blue	$50
Ivory	$45
Turquoise	$40
Yellow	$40

Egg cup
Cobalt blue	$75
Ivory	$72
Red	$80
Turquoise	$55
Yellow	$70

Fruit bowl, 5-1/2" d
Ivory	$33
Turquoise	$25
Yellow	$25

Fruit bowl, 11-3/4" d, cobalt blue ... $485

Gravy boat
Cobalt blue	$75
Ivory	$65
Red	$85
Turquoise	$45
Yellow	$50

Juice tumbler
Cobalt blue	$40
Rose	$65
Yellow	$40

Marmalade jar, cov
Cobalt blue	$335
Red	$345
Turquoise	$325
Yellow	$250

Mixing bowl
#1, red, 5" d	$375
#2, cobalt blue	$195
#2, yellow	$140

Fiesta Ware, cream soup bowl, turquoise, 6-5/8" x 5-1/16" x 2-1/4", **$60.**

Fiesta Ware, demitasse coffeepot, green, with lid, 7-5/8" x 6-7/8", **$700.**

Fiesta Ware, Tom & Jerry mug, medium green, 3-1/8" x 3-1/8" x 4-3/8", **$120.**

Fiesta Ware, teapot, rose, 8-1/2" x 5-5/8" with lid, **$275.**

Fiesta Ware, mixing bowl #6, red, 6-1/4" x 9-3/4", **$340.**

Fiesta Ware, oval platter, yellow, **$55.**

Fiesta Ware, ivory nappy, 8-1/2", **$55.**

Fiesta Ware, disk pitcher, rose, 7-1/2" x 8-3/4" x 5", **$300.**

Fiesta Ware, individual salad bowl, red, 7-5/8" x 2-3/8", **$125.**

Fiesta Ware, salt and pepper shakers, cobalt blue, 2-3/8" x 2-3/4", **$35.**

Fiesta Ware, sugar bowl, with lid, turquoise, **$50.**

Fiesta Ware, plate, medium green, 9" d, **$75.**

#4, green	$195
#5, ivory	$275
#7, ivory	$580

Mixing bowl lid, #1, red ... $1,100

Mug

Dark green	$90
Ivory, marked	$125
Rose	$95

Mustard, cov

Cobalt blue	$325
Turquoise	$275

Nappy, 8-1/2" d

Cobalt blue	$55
Red	$55
Turquoise	$42
Yellow	$45

Nappy, 9-1/2" d

Cobalt blue	$65
Ivory	$65
Red	$70
Turquoise	$55
Yellow	$60

Onion soup, cov, turquoise ... $8,000

Pitcher, disk

Chartreuse	$275
Turquoise	$110

Pitcher, ice lip

Green	$135
Turquoise	$195

Plate, deep

Gray	$42
Rose	$42

Plate, 6" d

Dark green	$15
Ivory	$7
Light green	$9
Turquoise	$8
Yellow	$5

Plate, 7" d

Chartreuse	$12
Ivory	$10
Light green	$9
Medium green	$30
Rose	$14
Turquoise	$9

Plate, 9" d

Cobalt blue	$15
Ivory	$14
Red	$15
Yellow	$13

Plate, dinner, 10" d

Gray	$42
Light green	$28
Medium green	$125
Red	$35
Turquoise	$30

Platter, oval

Gray	$35
Ivory	$25
Red	$45

Relish

Ivory base and center, turquoise inserts	$285
Red, base and inserts	$425

Salad bowl, large, ftd

Cobalt blue	$375
Red	$460
Turquoise	$335
Yellow	$400

Salt and pepper shakers, pr

Red	$24
Turquoise	$135

Saucer

Light green	$5
Turquoise	$5

Soup plate

Ivory	$36
Turquoise	$29

Sugar bowl, cov

Chartreuse	$65
Gray	$75
Rose	$75

Syrup

Green	$450
Ivory	$600
Red	$695

Sweetmeat compote, high standard

Cobalt blue	$95
Ivory	$85
Red	$100
Turquoise	$125
Yellow	$400

Tea cup, flat bottom, cobalt blue ... $100

Teapot, cov

Cobalt blue, large	$335
Red, large	$245
Rose, medium	$350

Tumbler, cobalt blue ... $75

FLOW BLUE

History: Flow blue, or flown blue, is the name applied to china of cobalt blue and white, whose color, when fired in a kiln, produced a flowing or blurred effect. The blue varies from dark royal cobalt blue to navy or steel blue. The flow may be very slight to a heavy blur, where the pattern cannot be easily recognized. The blue color does not permeate through the body of the china. The amount of flow on the back of a piece is determined by the position of the item in the sagger during firing.

Known patterns of flow blue were first produced around 1830 in the Staffordshire area of England. Credit is generally given to Josiah Wedgwood, who worked in that area. Many other potters followed, including Alcock, Davenport, Grindley, Johnson Brothers, Meakin, Meigh and New Wharf. They were attempting to imitate the blue and white wares brought back by the ship captains of the tea trade. Early flow blue, 1830s to 1870s, was usually of the pearl ware or ironstone variety. The later patterns, 1880s to 1900s, and the modern patterns after 1910, were of the more delicate semi-porcelains. Most flow blue was made in England but it was made in many other countries as well. Germany, Holland, France, Spain, Wales and Scotland are also known locations. Many patterns were made in the United States by several companies, Mercer, Warwick, Sterling and the Wheeling Pottery to name a few.

Adviser: Ellen G. King.

Educational Alert. The Flow Blue International Collectors' Club, Inc. has been studying and discussing new versus reproduction flow blue and mulberry. There are still areas of personal judgment as yet undetermined. The general rule accepted has been "new" indicates recent or contemporary manufacture and "reproduction" is a copy of an older pattern. Problems arise when either of these fields is sold at "old" flow blue prices.

In an effort to help educate its membership, the club continues to inform of all known changes through its conventions, newsletters and the Web site: www.flowblue.org.

Warman's is working to those ends also. The following is a listing of "new" flow blue, produced since the 1960s.

Blossom: Ashworth Bros., Hanley, 1962. Wash bowl and pitcher made for many years now, in several items.

Iris: by Dunn, Bennett, Burslem, has been reproduced in a full chamber set.

Romantic Flow Blue: Blakeney Pottery, 1970s. Resembles Watteau, but not exact. The old patterns never had the words "flow blue" written on them.

Touraine: by Stanley, by far the most prolific reproduction made recently, in 2002. Again, the "England" is missing from the mark, and it is made in China. Nearly the entire dinnerware set has been made and is being sold on the market.

Victoria Ware: mark is of lion and uniform, but has paper label "Made in China," 1990s. Made in various patterns and design, but the give-away is the roughness on the bottoms, and much of it has a pea green background. Some of this line is also being made in Mulberry.

Vinranka: Upsala-Ekeby, Sweden, 1967-1968. Now discontinued and highly collectible, a full dinnerware set.

Waldorf: by New Wharf cups and saucers are out, but missing "England" from their mark and are made in China.

Floral pitchers (jugs) and teapots bearing a copied "T. Rathbone England" swan mark.

Williams-Sonoma and Cracker Barrel are also each releasing a vivid blue and white line. Both are made in China. One line is a simplified dahlia flower on white; the other has summer bouquets. Both are well made and readily available, just not old. The reproductions are more of a threat to collectors.

In all cases, regarding new pieces and reproductions, be aware of unglazed areas on the bottoms. The footpads are rough and just too white. The reproductions, particularly the Touraine, are heavier in weight, having a distinctive thick feel. The embossing isn't as crisp and the pieces are frequently slightly smaller in overall size than the originals.

Check the Flow Blue International Collectors' Club, Inc., Web site and also www.repronews.com. Join the club, study the books available, and always, always, KNOW your dealer! Good dealers guarantee their merchandise and protect their customers.

Flow Blue Acme, Hancock, covered butter dish, 1880, **$350.**

Flow Blue Crawford, Upper Hanley, creamer, 1898, 5", **$150.**

Flow Blue Dresden, unknown maker, polychrome low compote with lid, 1880, **$400.**

Flow Blue La Belle, Wheeling, orange bowl, 1890, **$2,550.**

Flow Blue Marble, maker unknown, pitcher, mark Henry Framer, 1845, **$495.**

Abbey, Jones, 1900
Double inkwell, pewter lids **$295**
Small 8" open oval vegetable bowl, 1900 .... **$100**

Alaska, Grindley, 1891
Butter dish, no insert **$375**
Butter pat **$48**
Creamer **$165**
Gravy boat with undertray **$195**
Pitcher, 8" **$185**
Plate, 9" **$75**
Rimmed soup **$85**
Sugar bowl with lid **$155**

Amoy, Davenport, 1844
Cake plate, square, tab handle.... **$450**
Child's creamer, restoration to spout **$550**
Child's cup and plate **$600**
Child's punch bowl, rim chip restored **$795**
Child's teapot, restoration to rim **$3,000**
Compote, low foot **$375**
Cup plate, 4-1/4" **$100**
Gravy boat **$225**
Honey dish **$185**
Pitcher, spout restoration, 7" **$150**
Plate, 10-1/2" d **$175**
Platter, 18" l **$550**
Soup bowl, 10-1/2" d **$150**
Sugar bowl with lid, restoration to cover **$300**
Teapot with lid **$650**

Arabesque, Mayer, 1845
Sugar bowl with lid **$175**

Arcadia, Wilkenson, 1900
Creamer and sugar, with lid, as set **$175**

Argyle, Grindley, 1890
Butter pat **$55**
Gravy boat with undertray **$150**
Platter, 17" l **$395**
Soup ladle **$425**
Soup tureen with lid **$495**

Art Nouveau, 1890, no maker mark
Candle sticks, poppy pattern **$350**
Toothbrush/comb holder with lid **$275**

Astral Grindley, 1891, Grindley, 14" platter **$175**

Babes in Woods, Doulton, 1890
Jardeniere, 11-1/2" x 12" **$500**
Vase **$350**

Beaufort, Grindley, 1903
Butter dish with insert and lid ... **$225**
Pitcher, 6" **$120**
Pitcher, 7-1/2" **$145**
Pitcher, 8-3/8" **$250**

Bentick, Cauldon, 1905, soup bowl **$45**

Bisley, Grindley, 1910
Pedestal compote **$245**
Plate, 10" **$85**

Blackberry, maker unknown, 1850
Plate, 10" **$95**
Tea cup and saucer **$110**

Bleeding Heart, unknown maker, 1840
Sugar bowl with lid, nicks under lid **$125**

Bluebell, Ridgway, 1840
Syrup pitcher, 6-3/4" **$250**

Bonita, Wheeling Pottery, 1900
Pitcher, 7" **$275**

Boston, Grindley, 1890
Potty with lid **$200**

Brushstroke, unknown maker
Child's cup and saucer, bell border, 1850 .... **$275**
Creamer, 1850 .... **$400**
Hexagonal creamer, 1840 .... **$385**

Bryonia, Utzschneider, 1891
Pot de Creme set, 4 cups, 4 saucers, and 4 plates **$575**
Teapot with lid **$450**

Butterflies, maker unknown, 1870
Relief pitcher, 7" **$185**

Campion, Grindley, 1894
Chamber pot with lid **$195**

Carlton, Alcock
Cake plate **$150**
Polychromed tea cup and saucer.. **$90**

Cashmere, Ridgway, Morley
Bowl, oval, 8-1/2" l **$200**
Cup plate **$125**
Plate, 6-1/4" d **$100**
Plate, 9" d **$175**
Plate, 10-1/2" d **$250**
Platter, 10-1/2" l **$400**
Platter, 15-1/2" l **$775**
Sauce dish **$100**
Soup bowl **$145**
Soup tureen, cov, undertray **$3200**
Teacup and saucer **$200**
Teapot, cov **$850**
Toddy plate, 5" d **$375**
Vegetable tureen, cov **$975**

Casket Japan, unknown, oval drainer, 16" **$350**

Cavendish, Keeling, vase, handled, 13" h **$195**

Chapoo, Wedgwood, 1850
Child's waste bowl **$175**
Creamer **$255**
Ewer, 12" **$450**
Teapot with lid **$575**

Chen-Si, Meir, 1835
Tea cup and saucer, handleless... **$145**
Vegetable tureen with lid **$250**

Chinese, Dimmock, urn with lid, 1840, 15-1/2" **$1,350**

Chinese Sports, Furnival, child's
cup and saucer **$275**

Chusan, Clementson, 1830
Chestnut bowl with base **$500**
Soap dish with insert and lid **$275**
Sugar bowl, with lid **$225**
Tea cup and saucer **$110**
Vegetable tureen, with lid **$275**

Clematis and Star, unknown maker,
wash pitcher with basin, 1855. **$2,200**

Clive, Rathbone, milk jug, 1912, 8"
.... **$225**

Colburg, Edwards, milk pitcher, 1850
.... **$375**

Corey Hill, Ridgway, 1890
Dresser set, 10 pcs. **$350**
Sugar shaker **$200**
Teapot with lid **$250**

Delft, Minton, round open vegetable
bowl, 10" **$225**

Doris, Grindley, platter, 1890, 20-1/4"
.... **$275**

Elsie, New Wharf, 1891
Plate, 9" **$80**
Sauce tureen, lid, base, tray **$225**

Fairy Villas, Adams
Sauce tureen, 4pcs. **$375**
Soup tureen with lid **$450**

Fernwood, Bean, sauce tureen, 4pcs.,
1891 .... **$250**

Festoon, Grindley, 1890
Potty with lid **$250**
Slop jar with lid **$475**

Floral, Burgess and Leigh, jarde-
niere, 1930 .... **$250**

Florida, Johnson Bros., soup ladle,
1898 .... **$450**

Gironde, Grindley, 1891
Cream soup, handles **$55**
Platter, 15" **$185**

Grace, Grindley, 1891
Butter dish with insert and lid ... **$325**
Butter pat **$55**
Fruit compote **$350**
Gravy boat **$175**

Heaths Flower, Heath, plate, 6" .. **$65**

Hindustan, Maddock, vegetable
bowl, 1855, 11" **$355**

Holland, Johnson Bros., vegetable
tureen with lid, 1891 .... **$225**

Hong Kong, Meigh, 1850
Milk pitcher **$350**
Pitcher, inverted loop shape, 9" .. **$350**
Sauce tureen, lid, base, undertray
.... **$195**
Soup ladle with staple repair **$325**
Soup tureen with lid **$450**

Hong, Broughham & Mayer, plate,
1853, 8-1/2" **$75**

Idris, Grindley, plate, 1890, 10"
.... **$95**

Indian, Pratt, soup bowl with rimmed
edge, 1840 .... **$165**

Indian Stone, Walley, plate, 1850,
9-1/2" **$145**

Japan, Fell, stemmed compote, 1860
.... **$350**

Japanese Cranes, unknown maker,
jardiniere and pedestal, 1870, 37"
.... **$1,550**

Janette, Grindley, 1890
Platter, 15" **$175**
Sugar bowl with lid **$125**

Java, B & T, soup tureen with lid and
undertray, 1880 .... **$550**

Kyber, Adams, 1890
Platter, 10" **$125**
Platter, 17" **$250**
Vegetable tureen with lid **$275**

La Belle, Wheeling, 1890
Biscuit jar with lid **$450**
Charger, 15" d **$275**
Creamer **$450**
Footed helmet bowl **$350**
Punch cup **$425**
Ramikin with plate **$375**
Round tray, 13" **$250**
Sugar bowl, with lid **$225**
Tea cup and saucer **$175**
Vegetable bowl, oval, 9-1/2" **$150**
Water pitcher **$450**

Lancaster, New Wharf, 1891
Creamer **$155**
Plate, 10" **$110**
Tea cup and saucer **$95**

Lilac, Wedgwood, 1891
Slop jar with lid, 13" **$325**

Lily, Kaolin Ware, Dimmock, plat-
ter, 1860, 21-1/2" **$375**

Linda, Maddock, 1898
Egg cup **$110**
Creamer **$125**
Plate, 10" **$95**

Lonsdale, Ridgway, 1910
Pedestal bowl with lid **$200**
Sugar bowl with lid **$175**

Lorne, Grindley, 1900
Milk pitcher **$350**
Vegetable tureen with lid **$275**

Lugano, Ridgway, 1900
Bone dish **$55**
Dessert dish, individual **$40**

Madras, Doulton, 1900
Soup bowl **$60**
Teapot with lid, 2 cup size **$195**

Manilla, Podmore Walker, 1850
Soup tureen with lid **$695**
Teapot with lid **$350**
Vegetable bowl, oval **$150**

Marechal Neil, Grindley, 1890
Oyster bowl **$125**
Plate, 10" **$110**

*Flow Blue Astoria, Upper Hanley, round
vegetable bowl, 10",* **$225.**

*Flow Blue Brushstroke, unknown maker,
bowl, Scotland, 1860s, 8" d,* **$150.**

*Flow Blue pitcher, John Westwood, Low
Toryburn, 1866,* **$575.**

*Flow Blue Buccleuch, maker unknown,
teapot with lid, 1850,* **$550.**

Flow Blue, unknown pattern, unknown maker, polychromed tea caddy with lid, 1875, **$450.**

Flow Blue Water Lily, Adams, milk pitcher, 1879 10", **$450.**

Flow Blue, unknown pattern, K & G, France, tea cup and saucer, 1880, **$110.**

Marguerite, Grindley, 1895
Coffee cup and saucer $125
Sauce tureen, 4pcs. $475
Sugar bowl with lid $150
Teapot with lid $450
Tea cup and saucer $95

Melbourne, Grindley, 1890
Plate, 9" $80
Sauce tureen, lid, base, undertray
....$325
Vegetable tureen with lid $295

Milan, Ford, soup tureen with lid, 1908 ....$250

Monterey, Heath, teapot with lid
....$185

Nankin, Doulton, Well and Tree platter, 1900, 22" l $425

Neopolitan, Johnson Brothers, 1900
Plate, 10" $90
Teapot with lid $275

Non Pariel, Burgess & Leigh, 1891
Bone dish $55
Platter, 13-1/2" d $150
Soup bowl $45
Teapot with lid $550

Oriental, Alcock, 1840
Plate, 9" $65
Plate, polychromed green, 9-1/4" ..$225
Platter, 17" $375
Underplate, 13" $185

Oriental, Ridgway, 1891
Butter dish with lid $275
Sauce tureen with lid $300

Osaka, Kent, biscuit jar, cov $250

Peach, Johnson Bros., 1890
Dessert dish, individual $35
Vegetable tureen with lid $250

Pelew, Challinor, teapot with lid, 1845 ....$475

Persian Moss, Utzschneider, 1891
Coffee cup and saucer $125
Teapot with lid $255
Vegetable bowl, round, 9" $95

Persian Spray, Doulton, oil lamp, 1855 ....$600

Richmond, Beardmore, 1910
Shaving mug $145
Soap dish with insert and lid $250
Wash pitcher with bowl $450

Richmond, S & B, cheese tray bottom with sponged edge, 1875 ....$350

Rock, Challinor, relish dish, 1845
....$150

Roseville, Maddock
Gravy boat, with attached undertray
....$225
Well and Tree platter with feet, 22"
....$550

Saskia, Ridgway, ladies' spitton, 1905
....$250

Scinde, Alcock, 1840
Covered dish with staple repair ..$450
Milk pitcher, rim restoration $275
Sauce turen with lid and undertray
....$350
Soup bowl, 10-1/2" $195
Teapot with lid, finial restoration ..$575
Vegetable bowl, open 4250
Vegetable bowl, octagon, 11 x 8 ..$325
Wash bowl and pitcher, small hairline to spout $995

Scroll, Davenport, platter, 1840, 16"
....$475

Sevres, unknown maker, cheese dish with lid, 1898 ....$450

Shanghai, Grindley, 1900
Demitasse cup and saucer $65
Honey jar with lid and attached undertray $225
Plate, 9-3/4" $85

Shell, Dimmock, 1844
Sugar bowl with lid $225
Waste bowl $175

Stratford, Burgess & Leigh, wash pitcher and basin, 1891 ....$750

Sunflower, Morley, Well and Tree platter, 1860, 19" $650

Triumph, Grindley, toothbrush holder and mug, 1893 ....$175

Touraine, Alcock, 1898
Creamer $150
Individual oval vegetable bowl $95
Plate, 6-1/2" $45
Waste bowl $150
Water pitcher $375

Touraine, Stanley, 1898
Bone dish $65
Butter base $175
Cereal bowl $45
Teapot and lid $575

Tonquin, Adams, child's mug, 1845
....$350

Turkey Ohio China Co., turkey set, 8 plates, 1 platter, 1880 ....$650

Turkey, Doulton, plate, 1890, 10" ..$145

Tyrolean, Ridgways, charger, 1850, 12-1/4" $235

Unknown pattern, Copeland, polychromed compote, 1858 ......$465

Unknown pattern, Forester, polychromed pink vases, pair, 1868 ..$375

Utopia, Grindley, pedestal fruit bowl, 1890 ....$150

Wagon Wheel, unknown maker, 1880
Child's cup and saucer $75
Child's sugar bowl with lid $125

Waldorf, New Wharf, 1895
Gravy boat $165
Tea cup and saucer $95

Watteau, Doulton, 1900
Lamp $425
Low fruit compote $250

Wild Rose, Warwick, 1900
Bowl, 9" $195
Tray with handles $255

Windsor Scrolls, Forester & Hulme, 1887
Hot water pitcher $295
Soup with rimmed edge $125
Teapot with lid $550

FULPER POTTERY

History: The Fulper Pottery Company of Flemington, New Jersey, made stoneware pottery and utilitarian ware beginning in the early 1800s. It switched to the production of art pottery in 1909 and continued until about 1935.

The company's earliest artware was called the Vasekraft line (1910-1915), featuring intense glazine and rectilinear, Germanic forms. Its middle period (1915-1925) included some of the earlier shapes, but they also incorporated Oriental forms. Their glazing at this time was less consistent but more diverse. The last period (1925-1935) was characterized by watered-down Art-Deco forms with relatively weak glazing.

Pieces were almost always molded, though careful hand glazing distinguished this pottery as one of the premier semi-commercial producers. Pieces from all periods are almost always marked.

Marks: A rectangular mark, FULPER, in a rectangle is known as the "ink mark" and dates from 1910-1915. The second mark, as shown, dates from 1915-1925; it was incised or in black ink. The final mark, FULPER, die-stamped, dates from about 1925 to 1935.

Adviser: David Rago.

Fulper pitcher, promotional type, incised blue line dec of sample designs: male figure; dog treeing cat; dog chasing cat; cat and rat; dog spying on cat around brick wall; inscribed "Ice water" and "Lemonade," mkd "Made at Flemington Pottery" and "Fulper Brothers & Co. Jug," hairline at top, restoration to handle, 19th C, 6" d, 9" h, **$3,500.**
Photo courtesy of David Rago Auctions, Inc.

Bowl, flower holder, blue-green crystalline glaze, rect ink mark, 8" d, 5" h **$110**

Bud vase, baluster, Butterscotch flambé glaze, ink racetrack mark, 9" h **$275**

Chinese urn, two handles, Mirrored Black glaze, vertical mark, few short scratches, 9" h, 9" d **$1,400**

Doorstop, figural bulldog, amber, blue, purple crystalline glaze, unmarked, restoration to tip of ear and one toe, 8" x 10" **$600**

Effigy bowl
Copperdust Crystalline glaze int., Mirrored Black glaze ext., vertical mark, 10-1/4" d, 7-1/4" h **$1,400**
Mahogany and amber glaze int., indigo and matte beige ext., vertical mark, 10-1/2" d, 7-1/2" h **$700**

Ibis bowl, green and blue flambé over Copperdust Crystalline, ink racetrack mark, 10-1/2" d, 5-1/2" h **$815**

Jug, tall handle, Copperdust Crystalline glaze, vertical mark, 11-3/4" h, 7-3/4" d **$1,600**

Lamp, table
Mushroom-shaped lamp shade, covered in strong Leopard Skin Crystalline glaze, inset with leaded slag glass pieces, two orig sockets, rect ink mark on both pcs, hairline between two inset pcs, 15-1/4" d, 18-1/2" h **$5,750**
Mushroom-shaped shade covered in brown, celadon and blue glaze, inset with green and amber slag glass, on

Cucumber Green matte base, rect ink mark on both, possibly married piece, 17" d, 21-1/2" h **$1,610**

Place card vases, covered in matte turquoise to gunmetal green flambé glaze, orig cardboard box which reads "For a dinner most select/These place card vases are quite correct/I know you like all things that's new/Hence I'm sending these to you, Fulper Co., Flemington, NJ," set of 12, 2-1/4" h **$1,600**

Urn
Two handles, fine Mirrored Green, Mahogany and Ivory flambé glazes, rect ink mark, 7-1/2" d, 12" h **$1,200**
Hammered, frothy indigo and light blue glaze, incised racetrack mark, stilt-pull bruise, 11-3/4" d, 11-3/4" h **$865**

Vase
Baluster, Cat's Eye flambé glaze, vertical mark, 16-1/2" h, 9" d **$1,600**
Bullet, frothy Leopard Skin Crystalline glaze, ink racetrack mark, two small opposing bursts at rim, grinding chips on base, 4-3/4" d, 7" h **$520**
Bulbous, double ribbon handles, textured surface, Mission Verde matte green glaze, vertical mark, 9" h, 8-3/4" d **$1,100**
Bulbous, floriform, emb panels, covered in exceptional mirrored Cat's Eye flambé glaze, raised racetrack mark, 11-1/2" h, 9" d **$2,990**

Fulper urn, squat, hammered textured, two double handles, cucumber green matte glaze, vertical mark "587-51," 8-3/4" x 9", **$500.**
Photo courtesy of David Rago Auctions, Inc.

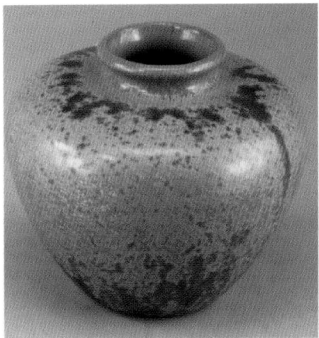

Fulper vase, flat shoulder, covered in fine Leopard Skin Crystalline glaze, vertical mark, 7-1/4" x 8", **$1,150.**

Bulbous, hammered texture, Mirrored Black, cobalt and blue crystalline flambé glaze, vertical mark, grinding chip, 12" h, 11-1/2" d...............**$2,200**

Bulbous, two handles, mottled gray and amber flambé glaze, vertical mark, 6-3/4" h, 7" d....................**$475**

Cattail, covered in Leopard Skin crystalline glaze, rect ink mark, rim minor burst bubble, 11-1/2" h, 7-3/4" d **$2,300**

Moss-to-Rose flambé glaze, vertical mark, 7-1/2" h, 6-1/4" d **$400**

Ovoid, light green crystalline glaze, vertical mark, 8" h, 5-1/4" d **$460**

Pillow, Cat's Eye flambé glaze, ink racetrack mark, 6-1/4" h, 5-3/4" w **$175**

Tear shape, gunmetal to Copperdust Crystalline flambé glaze, vertical mark, restoration to flat chip on foot ring, 13" h, 7-1/2" d **$1,900**

Vessel

Bulbous, four short handles, covered in Leopard Skin Crystalline glaze, incised racetrack mark, restoration to drill hole in bottom, 11-1/2" d, 13-1/4" h **$2,990**

Bulbous, three horn-shaped handles, ivory, blue and Mirror Black flambé glaze, vertical ink mark, 6" d, 6-1/2" h **$860**

Spherical, two buttressed handles, mirrored Cat's Eye flambé glaze, ink racetrack mark, 7-1/2" d, 6-1/4" h **$435**

Squatty, two angular handles, frothy blue flambé glaze, ink racetrack mark, restoration to one handle, 6" d, 5" h..................................**$195**

Fulper pair of bookends, Aztec masks, green and blue flambé glaze, 5-1/4" x 6", **$850.**
Photo courtesy of David Rago Auctions, Inc.

Fulper urn, embossed upright handles, covered in frothy blue-green mirrored glaze, vertical mark, 11-1/2" x 9", **$2,530.**
Photo courtesy of David Rago Auctions, Inc.

Fulper lamp, parrot, porcelain, yellow, and green matte glaze, perched on a stump that separates to expose the bulb, racetrack mark, artist's initials, 9-1/2" x 6-1/2" x 5-1/2", **$800.**
Photo courtesy of David Rago Auctions, Inc.

Fulper vase, baluster, fine, frothy cucumber matte glaze, vertical mark, 6-1/2" d, 13" h, **$950.**
Photo courtesy of David Rago Auctions, Inc.

Fulper low bowl, collar rim, covered in fine, frothy blue mirror glaze dripping over Famille Rose ground, vertical mark, 3-3/4" x 10", **$490.**
Photo courtesy of David Rago Auctions, Inc.

GAUDY DUTCH

History: Gaudy Dutch is an opaque, soft-paste ware made between 1790 and 1825 in England's Staffordshire district.

The wares first were hand decorated in an underglaze blue and fired; then additional decorations were added over the glaze. The over-glaze decoration is extensively worn on many of the antique pieces. Gaudy Dutch found a ready market in the Pennsylvania German community because it was inexpensive and extremely colorful. It had little appeal in England.

Marks: Marks of various potters, including the impressed marks of Riley and Wood, have been found on some pieces, although most are unmarked.

Adviser: John D. Querry.

Gaudy Dutch plate, cobalt blue flowers and leaves, copper luster trim, **$115.**

Reproduction Alert. Cup plates, bearing the impressed mark "CYBRIS," have been reproduced and are collectible in their own right. The Henry Ford Museum has issued pieces in the Single Rose pattern. They are porcelain, rather than soft paste.

Butterfly
Coffeepot, 11" h $9,500
Cup and saucer, handleless, minor enamel flakes, chips on table ring $950
Plate, 7-1/4" d $645
Sugar bowl, cov...........................$900
Teapot, 5" h, squat baluster form $2,400

Carnation
Bowl, 6-1/4" d $925
Creamer, 4-3/4" h $700
Pitcher, 6" h................................$675
Plate, 9-3/4" d $1,265
Saucer, cobalt blue, orange, green and yellow, stains, hairline, minor flake on table ring, 5-1/2" d.............$115
Teapot, cov $2,200
Waste bowl $675

Dahlia
Bowl, 6-1/4" d $1,800
Plate, 8" d $2,800
Tea bowl and saucer $8,000

Double Rose
Bowl, 6-1/4" d $545
Creamer.......................................$650
Gravy boat...................................$950
Plate, 8-1/4" d $675
Sugar bowl, cov............................$750
Tea bowl and saucer $675
Toddy plate, 4-1/2" d $675
Waste bowl, 6-1/2" d, 3" h...........$850

Dove
Creamer.......................................$675
Plate, very worn, scratches, stains, 8-1/8" d $245
Plate, 8-1/2" d $770

Tea bowl and saucer $500
Waste bowl...................................$650
Flower Basket, plate, 6-1/2" d ...$375
Grape
Bowl, lustered rim, 6-1/2" d $475
Plate, cobalt blue, orange, green and yellow, minor stains, 8-1/4" d..$450
Sugar bowl, cov............................$675
Tea bowl and saucer $475
Toddy plate, 5" d.........................$475
Leaf, bowl, shallow, 11-1/2" d....$4,800
No Name
Plate, 8-3/4" d $17,000
Teapot, cov $16,000
Oyster
Bowl, 5-1/2" d $675
Coffeepot, cov, 12" h..............$10,000
Plate, 10" d $1,550
Soup plate, 8-1/2" d $550
Tea bowl and saucer $1,275
Toddy plate, 5-1/2" d $475
Single Rose
Coffeepot, cov $8,500
Cup and saucer, handleless, minor wear and stains........................$330
Plate, 7-1/4" d $550
Plate, 10" d $975
Quill holder, cov.......................$2,500
Sugar bowl, cov............................$700
Teapot, cov $1,200
Toddy plate, 5-1/4" d $250
Sunflower
Bowl, 6-1/2" d $900
Coffeepot, cov, 9-1/2" h............$6,500
Cup and saucer, handleless, wear, chips $575
Plate, 9-3/4" d $825
Urn
Creamer.......................................$475
Cup and saucer, handleless.........$550
Plate, 8-1/4" d $910
Plate, very worn, scratches, stains, rim, chips, 9-7/8" d $225
Sugar bowl, cov, round, tip and base restored, 6-1/2" h....................$295
Teapot...$895

Gaudy Dutch plate, Morning Glory motif, cobalt blue flowers, two-toned green leaves, pink highlights, chips, **$25.**

Gaudy Dutch plate, Morning Glory motif, cobalt blue flowers and leaves, chip, **$35.**

Gaudy Dutch cup and saucer, War Bonnet pattern, **$520.**
Photo courtesy of Pook & Pook, Inc.

War Bonnet
Bowl, cov $225
Coffeepot, cov $9,500
Plate, pinpoint rim flake, minor wear, 8-1/8" d $880
Teapot, cov $4,400
Toddy plate, 4-1/2" d..................$975
Zinna, soup plate, impressed "Riley," 10" d...$4,675

GAUDY IRONSTONE

History: Gaudy Ironstone was made in England around 1850. Ironstone is an opaque, heavy-bodied earthenware which contains large proportions of flint and slag. Gaudy Ironstone is decorated in patterns and colors similar to those of Gaudy Welsh.

Marks: Most pieces are impressed "Ironstone" and bear a registry mark.

Gaudy Ironstone Strawberry pattern, left: covered sugar bowl with paneled sides, applied acanthus leaf handles, small interior rim chip, 8-1/2" h, **$575;** *right: pitcher, paneled sides, cracking in handle, discoloration on rim, small chip, 8-1/2" h,* **$850.**
Photo courtesy of Alderfer Auction Co.

Gaudy Ironstone pitcher, large red rose, blue cornflowers, green leaves, embossed scrolls around top and handle, **$225.**

Biscuit jar, Rococo molded body, polychrome floral, Flow Blue accents, backstamp monogram for "F. J. Emery," Burslem, England, c1890, 7-1/2" h **$195**

Bread plate, marked "Tunstall, England, by Enoch Wedgwood," 10-1/4" l, 5-1/4" w **$65**

Charger

Blue star design, orange-red flowers, blue green detail, wear, 10-7/8" d **$150**

Center yellow daisy-shaped flower surrounded by orange-red flowers, tornado shaped blossoms, cobalt blue leaves, copper luster detail, imp "Emberton" on back, minor scratches, 12-1/8" d **$350**

Red Adams type roses, green leaves, blue feathers, red and yellow border, partial imp label, wear, 14-1/8" d, 2-5/8" h **$250**

Stylized urn, large cobalt blue and orange-red flowers, small green leaves, copper luster highlights, price for pr, 11-3/8" d **$435**

Coffeepot, cov, Strawberry pattern, 10" h **$650**

Creamer and sugar, fruit finial, Blackberry pattern, underglaze blue, yellow, and orange enamel and luster, wear, small flakes, int. chip on sugar, 6-3/4" h **$990**

Cup and saucer, handleless

Blackberry pattern, underglaze blue, yellow, and orange enamel and luster, imp label or registry mark with "E. Walley," price for set of 10 .... **$1,375**

Deep blue and orange flowers, pink and copper luster leaves **$225**

Jug, yellow, red, white, and blue tulips on sides, light blue pebble ground, luster trim, rim outlined, 7-1/2" h **$350**

Pitcher, six-color floral dec, blue, green, burgundy, mauve, black, and yellow, molded serpent handle, dec has been enhanced, then reglazed, spider, 11" h **$320**

Plate

Morning Glories and Strawberries pattern, underglaze blue, polychrome enamel and luster trim, 6-1/4" d **$80**

Blackberry pattern, underglaze blue, yellow, and orange enamel and luster, some wear, set of seven, 9-1/2" d **$1,320**

Platter, recessed tree and well, cobalt blue floral dec, over glaze tomato red detail, imp "Mason's Patent Ironstone," wear, some flowers simply outlined, 18" x 14-1/2" **$250**

Soup plate, Blackberry pattern, underglaze blue, yellow, and orange enamel and luster, one imp "Elsmore & Forster, Tunstall," price for set of three, 9-7/8" d **$650**

Teapot, domed cov, floral finial, paneled body, blue flower, red and green strawberries, gilt highlights, c1850, 9-3/4" h **$2,300**

Wash basin and pitcher, 14" d bowl, 13" h pitcher, hexagonal, blue morning glories and leaves, copper accents, hp red, green, and yellow berries, hairlines **$1,225**

Gaudy Ironstone plates, flow blue underglaze decoration, red, green, and gilt floral decoration painted over glaze, copper luster rims, two 9-1/4" d octagonal plates, six 8-1/2" d round plates, scattered edge chips, **$300.**
Photo courtesy of Alderfer Auction Co.

GAUDY WELSH

History: Gaudy Welsh is a translucent porcelain that was originally made in the Swansea area of England from 1830 to 1845. Although the designs resemble Gaudy Dutch, the body texture and weight differ. One of the characteristics is the gold luster on top of the glaze. In 1890, Allerton made a similar ware from heavier opaque porcelain.

Marks: Allerton pieces usually bear an export mark.

Gaudy Welsh plate, underglaze cobalt blue floral design, **$75.**

Bethesda, pitcher, paneled form, scalloped rims, figural dragon handles, imp "Ironstone, China," some wear, price for pr, 6-3/8" h $300

Chinoiserie, teapot, c1830-40 ..... $750

Columbine

Bowl, ftd, underglaze blue and polychrome enamel floral dec, 10" d, 5-1/2" h $400

Plate, 5-1/2" d $65

Tea set, 17-pc set, c1810 .... $625

Conwys, jug, 9" h $750

Daisy and Chain

Creamer $175

Cup and saucer $95

Sugar, cov $195

Teapot, cov $225

Flower Basket

Bowl, 10-1/2" d $190

Mug, 4" h $90

Plate $65

Sugar, cov, luster trim $195

Grape

Bowl, 5-1/4" d $50

Cup and saucer $75

Mug, 2-1/2" h $65

Plate, 5-1/4" d $65

Grapevine Variant, miniature pitcher and bowl, 4-1/4" h pitcher, 4-1/2" d bowl, cobalt blue, orange, green and luster, scalloped edges $250

Oyster

Bowl, 6" d $80

Creamer, 3" h $100

Jug, c1820, 5-3/4" h $85

Soup plate, flange rim, 10" d $85

Primrose, plate, 8-1/4" d $350

Strawberry

Cup and saucer $75

Mug, 4-1/8" h $125

Plate, 8-1/4" d $150

Tulip

Bowl, 6-1/4" d $50

Cake plate, molded handles, 10" d $120

Creamer, 5-1/4" h $125

Plate, tea size $95

Tea cup and saucer, slight crazing in cup $115

Teapot, 7-1/4" h $225

Wagon Wheel

Cup and saucer $75

Pitcher, 8-1/2" h $195

Plate, 8-3/4" d $85

Platter $125

Gaudy Welsh syrup pitcher, pewter lid, underglaze blue and red floral decoration, gilt highlights, **$325.**

Gaudy Welsh pitcher, green mark "Allertons, Est. 1831, Made in England," **$125.**
Photo courtesy of Dotta Auction Co., Inc.

GOUDA POTTERY

History: Gouda and the surrounding areas of Holland have been principal Dutch pottery centers for centuries. Originally, the potteries produced a simple utilitarian tin-glazed Delft-type earthenware and the famous clay smoker's pipes.

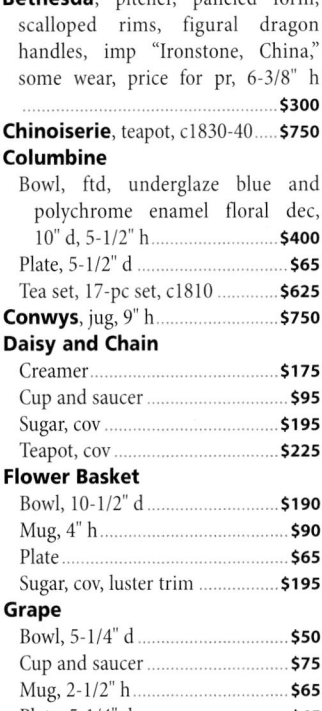
MADE IN
Zuid Holland

When pipe making declined in the early 1900s, the Gouda potteries turned to art pottery. Influenced by the Art Nouveau and Art Deco movements, artists expressed themselves with free-form and stylized designs in bold colors.

Reproduction Alert. With the Art Nouveau and Art Deco revivals of recent years, modern reproductions of Gouda pottery currently are on the market. They are difficult to distinguish from the originals.

Bowl

Art Nouveau scrolled floral and foliage dec, shades of green, brown and blue, cracked white semi-matte glazed ground, black rooster mark on base, Arnhem factory, repairs to rim, c1910, 7" h $100

Gouda tray, scalloped, painted yellow flowers and cobalt blue medallions, stamped "Fanny Gouda," 10" x 13", **$195.**
Photo courtesy of David Rago Auctions, Inc.

Dec with three clusters of flowers in symmetrical pattern, matte glaze, shades of orange, yellow and blue, black ground, blue painted maker's mark, c1927, 10-1/4" d, 2-1/2" h $225

Stylized floral design, matte glaze, yellow, orange, green and blue, black ground, black painted Regina marks, rim repair, c1927, 11-3/4" d, 2-3/4" h $185

Candlesticks and vase set, Art Nouveau style dec, matte glaze blue, orange, turquoise, brown and yellow, painted "Westland (house) Gouda Holland," date and artist's initials, pr 9-1/2" h candlesticks, 10-3/4" h vase $400

Candlesticks, pr, bulbed cup, ruffled rim drop pan, tall ribbed flared standard, Art Nouveau-style motif, high glaze, shades of blue, green, yellow and black, underglaze mark "Gouda Blauw (house)," date mark, artist's

Gouda vase, baluster shape, geometric dec, shades of blue, green, ochre on black ground, signed and numbered, **$250.**

Photo courtesy of David Rago Auctions, Inc.

Grueby tiles, modeled with knight on horseback, indigo on butter yellow ground, stamped "655," price for pair, **$850.**

Photo courtesy of David Rago Auctions, Inc.

initials, and "Made in Holland, 872, 893," dec attributed to Franciscus Ijsselstein, base chip on one, c1926, 18" h..$435

Clock garniture, circular clock mouth with painted ceramic face supported by four ceramic arms on baluster-shaped body and flared base, candlesticks of similar form, all dec with Art Nouveau-style flowers, glossy glaze pink, purple, blue, green and tan, sgd "Zuid Holland" and imp house and "R" on base, repairs to candlesticks, 20-1/2" h clock, 16-3/4" h pr candlesticks $2,875

Charger, multicolored flowers, rope border, black trim, 12" d $150

Compote, black ground, geometric design, multicolored scroll int., 7-5/8" $175

Ewer

Handle, floral and foliage design, high glaze, shades of purple, mauve, green, blue and taupe, base painted "Made in Zuid Holland (house)," and artist's initials, 7" h............$325

Handle, stylized floral and foliage design, high glazes, shades of green, pink and purple on tan and brown ground, painted "Made in Zuid, Holland," 7-5/8" h....................$350

Incense burner, Roba, flowers and geometric designs, green ground, 8" h $120

Jug, Rosalie, cream ground, green handle, turquoise interior, marked "Rosalie, #5155," and "Zuid-Holland, Gouda," c1930, 5-3/4" d $195

Lamp base, flared rim, tapered oval form, butterfly design, matte glaze, shades of green, blue, gold, red and cream, base painted "380 Butterfly (tree, house) AJK Holland," c1920, 11-3/4" h.................................$290

Miniature, vase, floral and foliate design, high glaze, shades of green, purple, red, brown and black, 2-1/4" h................................$125

Pitcher, stylized designs in shades of green, blue, rust and gold on black ground matte glaze, all with maker's marks, crazing, 1923, 8-1/4" h Henley $275

Plate, Unique Metallique, scalloped edge, deep blue-green ground, irid copper luster dec, 8-1/4" d.........$350

Shoe, floral and foliate design, high glaze, shades of green, purple, red, brown and black, 4-7/8" h $125

Urn, stylized designs in shades of green, blue, rust and black

ground matte glaze, all with maker's marks, crazing, 1923, 8-1/8" h Gotton $275

Vase

Art Nouveau style, elongated neck, squat form, stylized flowers and leaves, high glaze, white, green and rust, taupe ground, painted "Holland Utrecht" on base, 6" h $200

Breetvelt double handles, all with stylized designs in shades of green, blue, rust and gold on black ground matte glaze, all with maker's marks, crazing, 9-3/4" h $295

Elongated neck on bulbous body, Art Nouveau stylized lilies, foliage, high glaze purple, green, yellow and black, base painted with wooden shoe "NB Faience du (illegible) Holland 504 Dec A," 13-1/4" h $865

Flared rim, ovoid form, stylized flowers and foliage, matte glaze, shades of yellow, green, blue, orange and brown, painted mark "Del Breetvelt (house) Zuid Holland Gouda," 10-3/4" h $420

Flared, stylized lily dec, high glaze, purple, brown, green, dark blue, yellow and cream, painted mark "Made in Holland (house)," price for pr, c1898, 20-1/4" h $575

Raised rim, squatty form, flower blossoms dec, semi-matte glaze, yellow, brown, blue and cream, black ground, painted and paper labels, 4-1/2" h $200

Tapered oval, flowers and leaves, semi-matte glaze, gold, brown, turquoise, cream and black, painted maker's marks, 10-1/2" h........$200

Two handles, bulbed neck flanked by arched handles on squatty body, tulip and foliate designs, high glaze gray, green, yellow and brown tones, painted "Distel," distel factory, early 20th C, 7-3/4" h $520

Two handles, ftd, bulbous, brown, blue and green butterflies dec, crackled white matte ground, black stamped rooster mark on base, Arnhem factory, c1910, 7-1/4" h $150

Two handles, ovoid, ftd, floral and foliage design, high glaze, shades of purple, mauve, green, blue and taupe, base painted "Made in Zuid Holland (house)", and artist's initials, 10" h $350

GRUEBY POTTERY

History: William Grueby was active in the ceramic industry for several years before he developed his own method of producing matte-glazed pottery and founded the Grueby Faience Company in Boston, Massachusetts, in 1897. The art pottery was hand thrown in natural shapes, hand molded, and hand tooled. A variety of colored glazes, singly or in combinations, was produced, but green was the most popular. In 1908, the firm was divided into the Grueby Pottery Company and the Grueby Faience and Tile Co. The Grueby Faience and Tile Company made art tile until 1917, although its pottery production was phased out about 1910.

Minor damage is acceptable to most collectors of Grueby Pottery.

Adviser: David Rago.

Bowl, flaring, broad molded leaves, cucumber matte green ground, dec by Ruth Erickson, imp circular mark, incised "ER," two very short and shallow opposing lines, 9" d, 5-1/2" h **$1,900**

Jardinière, two-color three rows of curled leaves below nine light blue five-petaled flowers, oatmeal matte green glaze, stamped "Grueby Faience/174" and "EG," couple of minor flecks, 7-1/2" x 9" **$575**

Miniature vase, green-gray glaze, sgd "GRUEBY POTTERY BOSTON USA," in mold, 1899, 3" h **$600**

Paperweight, scarab, blue-gray glaze, sgd "GRUEBY FAIENCE Co. BOSTON. U.S.A.," c1905, 3" l **$650**

Planter, flaring, by Edith R. Felton, modeled leaves, closed-in rim, rich cucumber matte green glaze, circular Faience mark, ERF, three short tight lines at top, use scratches on interior, 4-1/2" h, 12" l **$1,100**

Tile, cuenca dec

Large oak tree against blue sky, puffy white clouds, #28 on reverse, 6" sq **$1,150**

"The Pines," polychrome cuenca, marked "FH," 6" sq **$1,485**

Yellow tulip on matte green ground, mounted in sterling silver trivet base by Karl Leinonen (Boston League of Arts & Crafts), tile unmarked, mount stamped "Sterling" and "L," very light abrasion to surface, 6-1/4" sq... **$2,990**

Vase

Bulbous, rolled rim, alternating rows of tight yellow bunds and broad leaves, rich medium to dark matte green ground, circular mark, 4" h, 4-1/4" d **$2,900**

Cylindrical neck, bulbous bottom, base dec with overlapping modeled leaves, medium green matte glaze, circular mark, 9-1/2" h, 6" d **$2,300**

Five-sided neck, full height tooled and applied leaves alternating with ivory buds, leathery matte brown glaze, by Wilhemina Post, Grueby Pottery stamp mark and "WP/4/10," minute old bruise to one corner, 11-1/4" h, 5-1/2" d **$8,500**

Flaring rim, squat base, tooled and applied blossoms alternating with rounded, curled leaves, leathery matte green glaze, circular pottery stamp 187, 2" bruise to rim, 7-3/4" h, 7-3/4" d **$2,200**

Flat shoulder, tooled and applied rows of leaves, matte green glaze, shaved off mark, 3-1/2" h, 3" d **$2,600**

Ovoid, carved stylized leaves, medium matte green ground, imp circular mark, incised "MEJ," 7-1/4" h, 5-1/2" d **$1,500**

Ovoid, by Marie Seaman, green buds alternating with spade-shaped leaves, rich cucumber matte glaze, die-stamped faience mark, 28 MS, nicks to leaf edges, 11-1/2" h, 5-3/4" d ... **$3,500**

Tapering, crisply modeled with broad flat leaves, flowing ochre matte glaze, circular die-stamp mark, several small flakes to leaf edges, 7-1/4" h, 4-1/2" d **$4,500**

Grueby vase, spherical, by Ruth Erickson, closed-in rim surrounded with tooled and applied full height green leaves on blue-gray ground, circular pottery stamp, paper label, incised "RE-D," 3-3/4" x 4-1/2", **$22,000.**
Photo courtesy of David Rago Auctions, Inc.

Grueby vase, by Ruth Erickson, melon-shape, full height tooled and applied covered leaves, frothy matte green glaze against a glossier ground, circular pottery mark, "RE/10/13," few small nicks to edges, 11" x 8-1/2", **$16,000.**
Photo courtesy of David Rago Auctions, Inc.

Grueby vessel, squat, two rows of footed and applied leaves, curdled rich matte green glaze, circular pottery stamp, artist signature, some scratches to glossy interior, provenance: from estate of Miriam Hubbard Roelofs, Elbert and Alice Hubbard's daughter, 3" x 5-1/2", **$2,400.**
Photo courtesy of David Rago Auctions, Inc.

Grueby vase, by Ruth Erickson, ovoid, full height tooled and applied leaves, veined oatmealed matted green glaze, circular pottery mark, RE/9/1, few minor nicks to edges, 9" x 5-1/2", **$7,000.**
Photo courtesy of David Rago Auctions, Inc.

Teapot, squatty, deep maroon, silver trim, marked, **$85.**

Hall Dripolator, light blue base and lid with gold leaf decoration, marked, **$75.**

Hall pitcher, ball shape, Autumn Leaf, **$70.**

Hall front: batter pitcher, "ear handle," **$90;** *rear: another ball-shaped pitcher, both Autumn Leaf pattern, gold trim,* **$70.**

HALL CHINA COMPANY

History: Robert Hall founded the Hall China Company in 1903 in East Liverpool, Ohio. He died in 1904 and was succeeded by his son, Robert Taggart Hall. After years of experimentation, Robert T. Hall developed a leadless glaze in 1911, opening the way for production of glazed household products.

The Hall China Company made many types of kitchenware, refrigerator sets, and dinnerware in a wide variety of patterns. Some patterns were made exclusively for a particular retailer, such as Heather Rose for Sears.

One of the most popular patterns was Autumn Leaf, a premium designed by Arden Richards in 1933 for the exclusive use by the Jewel Tea Company. Still a Jewel Tea property, Autumn Leaf has not been listed in catalogs since 1978, has been produced on a replacement basis with the date stamped on the back.

Additional Listings: See *Warman's Americana & Collectibles* for more examples.

Cookie jar, cov

Autumn Leaf, Tootsie $265
Blue Blossom, Five-Band shape $275
Chinese Red, Five-Band shape ... $150
Gold Dot, Zeisel $95
Meadow Flower, Five-Band shape $230
Owl, brown glaze $90
Red Poppy $50

Kitchen ware and advertising

Bean pot, New England, #1, Orange Poppy $80
Casserole, cov, Chinese Red, Sundial, #4, 8" w $65
Coffeepot, percolator, ducks and partridge dec $100
Cuspidor, green and white, 7-1/4" d, 4-1/4" h $90
Drip jar, Little Red Riding Hood, 4-1/2" h, 5" w $3,300
Jug, Primrose, rayed $20
Mixing bowl, nested set of three, pink, basketweave and floral dec, gold trim, 6" d, 7-1/2" d, 8-1/2" d $85
Mug, Braniff International Airlines, 4" h, 2" d $18
Refrigerator bowl, Addison Gray and Daffodil, ink stamped "GE Refrigerators, Hall Ovenware China, Made for General Electric," c1938 .... $12
Sauce boat, Quartermasters logo emb near handle on both sides, c1940, 10" l $25

Patterns
Autumn Leaf
Bowl, 5-1/2" d $8
Coffeepot, electric $300
Cup and saucer $18

Juice reamer $250
Pepper shaker, gold trim, 4-1/4" h $20
Pie bird, 5" h $40
Plate, 8" d $15
Teapot, cov, automobile shape, 1993 .... $465
Tidbit tray, three tiers $125
Tumbler, frosted, 5-5/8" h, 2-3/4" d $45
Utensil holder, marked "Utensils," 7-1/4" h $275

Blue Bouquet
Bowl, 7" d, 3" h $30
Creamer, Boston $25
Cup and saucer $28
French baker, round $35
Platter, 13" l $35
Soup, flat $30
Spoon $100
Teapot, Aladdin infuser $165

Cameo Rose
Bowl, 5-1/4" d $3
Butter dish, 3/4 lb. $30
Casserole $25
Creamer and sugar $10
Cream soup, 6" d $7
Cup and saucer $9
Plate, 8" d $2.50
Teapot, cov, six cup $35
Tidbit, three tier $40

Gamebirds
Percolator, electric $140
Teapot, cov, two-cup size, ducks and pheasant $200

Mount Vernon
Coffeepot $125
Creamer $12
Cup $10
Fruit bowl $8
Gravy boat $20
Saucer $4
Soup bowl, flat, 8" d $17

Red Poppy

Bowl, 5-1/2" d $5
Cake plate.......................................$18
Casserole, cov $25
Coffeepot, cov $12
Creamer and sugar $15
Cup and saucer $8
French baker, fluted $15
Jug, Daniel, Radiance..................$28
Plate, 9" d $7
Salad bowl, 9" d $14
Teapot, New York $90

Silhouette

Bean pot $50
Bowl, 7-7/8" d $50

Coffeepot, cov $30
Mug...$35
Pretzel jar $75
Trivet $125

Tulip

Bowl, oval, 10-1/4" l $36
Coffee maker, drip, Kadota, all china
....$115
Condiment jar................................$165
Fruit bowl, 5-1/2" d $10
Mixing bowl, 6" d $27
Plate, luncheon, 9" d....................$16
Platter, oval, 13-1/4" l...................$42
Shakers, bulge-type, price for pr
....$110

Sugar, cov $25

Teapots

Camellia, gold roses, windshield, gold trim on handle, spout, rim, and finial, mkd "Hall 0698 6 cup made in USA"
....$100
Chinese Red, donut, 9-1/2" w, 7-1/2" h
....$500
Cleveland, turquoise and gold
....$165
Lipton Tea, off white stoneware, aluminum cozy, 9-1/2" l, 7-1/2" h
....$30

HAMPSHIRE POTTERY

History: In 1871, James S. Taft founded the Hampshire Pottery Company in Keene, New Hampshire. Production began with redwares and stonewares, followed by majolica in 1879. A semi-porcelain, with the recognizable matte glazes plus the Royal Worcester glaze, was introduced in 1883.

Until World War I, the factory made an extensive line of utilitarian and art wares including souvenir items. After the war, the firm resumed operations, but made only hotel dinnerware and tiles. The company was dissolved in 1923.

Bowl, matte green glaze over foliate-forms, imp "Hampshire, M.O.," 5-1/2" d, 2-1/2" h $320
Chocolate pot, cream, holly dec, 9-1/2" h.....................................$275
Compote, ftd, two handles, Ivory pattern, light green highlights, cream ground, red decal mark, 13-1/4" d
....$175
Inkwell, round, large center well, three pen holes, 4-1/8" d, 2-3/4" h $125
Oil lamp, matte green glaze, price for pr, one handle restored, 3-1/2" x 7"
....$485
Stein, 1/2 liter, transfer printed scene of Pine Grove Springs resort, 7" h......$110
Tankard, band of stylized dec, green matte glaze, imp "Hampshire," 7" h
....$100

Vase

Barrel shape, emb dandelions, feathered matte cobalt blue glaze, Hampshire Pottery 4 64, 6" h, 5-1/4" d $950
Bottle shape, imp leaves, feathered green glaze, blue-gray ground, Hampshire Pottery 124, 9-1/4" h, 6-1/2" d $1,000
Mottled drip glaze, soft clay and blue-green colors on slate blue ground, repeating leaf dec, incised pottery mark, "M" cipher, c1908, 8-3/4" h
....$765
Ovoid, full height leaves, frothy matte blue-green glaze, cobalt blue and apricot shoulder, Hampshire Pottery 98, 7" h, 4-1/2" d...............$700
Soft matte blue-green glaze, modeled

Hampshire Pottery vase, molded full-height leaves, curdled blue-green glaze, stamped "Hampshire Pottery 129," grinding chips inside footring, 5-1/2" x 6-1/2", **$1,000.**
Photo courtesy of David Rago Auctions, Inc.

leaf blades centered by buds and trailing stems, imp pottery mark and "M" cipher, numbered "33" c1908, 6-3/4" h.......................$765
Thick matte green glaze, incised detail at rim, imp pottery mark, cipher, and number "76," spider hairline at base, possibly in-the-making, c1908, 4" h, 5-1/2" d................$325
Wide mouth, glossy blue glaze, broad overlapping leaf dec, incised pottery mark and "M" cipher, Keene, New Hampshire, c1908, 8-1/4" h.....$600

HAVILAND CHINA

History: In 1842, American china importer David Haviland moved to Limoges, France, where he began manufacturing and decorating china specifically for the U.S. market. Haviland is synonymous with fine, white, translucent porcelain, although early hand-painted patterns were generally larger and darker colored on heavier whiteware blanks than were later ones.

David revolutionized French china factories by both manufacturing the whiteware blank and decorating it at the same site. In addition, Haviland and Company pioneered the use of decals in decorating china.

David's sons, Charles Edward and Theodore, split the company in 1892. In 1936, Theodore opened an American division, which still operates today. In 1941, Theodore bought out Charles Edward's heirs and recombined both companies under the original name of H. and Co. The Haviland family sold the firm in 1981.

Haviland plate, multicolored phoenix in center, floral rim border with medallions with phoenix motif, gold trim, marked "Theodore Haviland Limoges France, Rajah," **$45.**

Haviland oyster plate, delicate pink roses, green foliage, gilt trim, five shaped oyster depressions and center round well, marked "Theodore Haviland Limoges, France," **$275.**
Photo courtesy of Wiederseim Associates, Inc.

Haviland oyster plate, scattered green florals, gilt trim, five shaped oyster depressions and center round well, marked "Theodore Haviland Limoges, France, Patent Applied For," **$275.**
Photo courtesy of Wiederseim Associates, Inc.

Haviland Limoges, seafood plates, hand painted in different marine patterns, each stamped "CFH/GDM," 7-1/2" square, price for set of 12, **$300.**
Photo courtesy of David Rago Auctions, Inc.

Charles Field Haviland, cousin of Charles Edward and Theodore, worked for and then, after his marriage in 1857, ran the Casseaux Works until 1882. Items continued to carry his name as decorator until 1941.

Thousands of Haviland patterns were made, but not consistently named until after 1926. The similarities in many of the patterns makes identification difficult. Numbers assigned by Arlene Schleiger and illustrated in her books have become the identification standard.

Bone dish, hp, 8-1/4" l
Crab dec **$60**
Turtle dec **$65**
Bouillon cup and saucer, hp bluebirds, luster ground, gold rims, artist sgd "Poirer," green marks, price for set of 12..**$400**
Bowl, hp, yellow roses, 8" d **$35**
Butter dish, cov, Gold Band, marked "Theo Haviland"............................**$45**
Butter pat, sq, rounded corners, gold trim...**$12**
Cake plate, gold handles and border, 10" d...**$35**
Celery dish, scalloped edge, green flowers, pale pink scroll **$45**
Chocolate pot, cov, Countess pattern, green mark, c1893, 10-1/2" l **$475**
Cream soup, underplate, cranberry and blue scroll border **$30**
Creamer and sugar, small pink flowers, scalloped, gold trim................**$65**
Cup and saucer, Etoile..............**$470**
Dinner set
Forever Spring, service for five...**$165**
Pink roses, 69 pcs **$500**
Violets, gold trim, service for 12, plus serving pcs.............................**$1,295**
Game plate, hp, center scene of shore birds in natural setting, apple green edge, printed gold scrolled rim dec, artist sgd "B. Albert," Theodore Haviland & Co. blanks, price for set of 12, early 20th C, 9-1/4" d **$865**
Gravy boat, attached underplate
Chantilly......................................**$270**
Monteray **$315**
Schleiger #57..............................**$250**
Milk pitcher, pink flowers, green branches, underglaze green Haviland mark, red "Haviland & Co., Limoges for PDG, Indianapolis, Ind.," 8" h, 4-3/4" d.......................................**$450**
Oyster plate, five wells
Rose dec, bright red roses, blue forget-me-nots, hp muscle scars, importer's mark "Warren & Wood, Providence, RI".......................**$700**

Seascape, shellfish, aquatic plants, under glaze mark, CFH/GDM mark **$845**
Seaweed, raised dec, underglaze green mark, importer's mark "J. E. Caldwell Co., Philadelphia, PA," 8-3/4" d **$600**
Wave design, multicolored metallic dec, gold highlights and brushed rim, CFH/GDM mark **$725**
Oyster plate, six wells
Floral transfers, hp muscle marks, told trim, price for set of six, c1881-90...**$1,650**
Hand brushed gold dec, white ground, five oyster wells, center sauce well, underglaze green mark, price for set of four......................................**$760**
Rose pattern, violet rim trim, price for set of six, c1877 ....**$1,350**
Pitcher, Rosalinde, 7-1/2" h **$280**
Plate, dinner
Crowning Fashion, tan...................**$8**
Golden Quail...............................**$275**
Platter
Chantilly......................................**$275**
Golden Quail...............................**$350**
Relish dish, blue and pink flowers **$25**
Sandwich plate, Drop Rose pattern, 11-1/2" d...................................**$275**
Teacup and saucer, small blue flowers, green leaves..........................**$30**
Teapot, Portland **$250**
Tea set, rope and anchor pattern, transfer-printed, hand tinted blossoms, stamped "Haviland-Limoges" mark, restoration to lids, price for three-pc set, 8-1/2" d, 8" h teapot **$200**
Tureen, cov, pink roses, green ivy, 12" l, 6-1/2" h..**$360**
Vase, tan, brown, pink and rose, two oval scenes of lady in large hat, baskets and flower garlands, Charles Field Haviland and GDA Limoges mark, 5-1/2" h, 3-5/8" d **$275**
Vegetable dish, open, Golden Quail, 9-1/2" x 7-1/2"............................**$435**

HOLT-HOWARD COLLECTIBLES

History: Three young entrepreneurs, Grant Holt and brothers John and Robert Howard, started Holt-Howard from their apartment in Manhattan, in 1949. All three of the partners were great salesman, but Robert handled product development, while John managed sales; Grant was in charge of financial affairs and office management. By 1955, operations were large enough to move the company to Connecticut, but it still maintained its New York showroom and later added its final showroom in Los Angeles. Production facilities eventually expanded to Holt-Howard Canada; Holt-Howard West, Holt-Howard International.

The company's first successful product was the Angel-Abra, followed closely by its Christmas line. This early success spurred the partners to expand their wares. Their line of Christmas and kitchen-related giftware was popular with 1950s consumers. Probably the most famous line was Pixieware, which began production in 1958. Production of these whimsical pieces continued until 1962. Other lines, such as Cozy Kittens and Merry Mouse, brought even more smiles as they invaded homes in many forms. Three things that remained constant with all Holt-Howard products were a high quality of materials and workmanship, innovation, and good design.

The founders of this unique company sold their interests to General Housewares Corp. in 1968, where it became part of the giftware group. By 1974, the three original partners had left the firm. By 1990, what remained of Holt-Howard was sold to Kay Dee Designs of Rhode Island.

Holt-Howard pieces were marked with an ink-stamp. Many were also copyright dated. Some pieces were marked only with a foil sticker, especially the small pieces, where a stamp mark was too difficult. Four types of foil stickers have been identified.

Adviser: Walter Dworkin.

Holt-Howard Sam n' Sally salad cruet set, one for oil, other for vinegar, copyrighted 1958, 9" h, each **$185.**

Holt-Howard Pixiewares, liquor decanters, 300 Proof, Whiskey, solid color base, copyrighted 1958, 10-1/2" h, each **$580.**

Holt-Howard Pixiewares, liquor decanters, striped bodies, Devil Brew, 300 Proof, Whiskey, copyrighted 1958, 10-1/2" h, each **$580.**

Christmas

Air freshener, Girl Christmas Tree **$65**

Ashtray, Snow Baby **$35**

Ashtray/cigarette holder, Starry-eyed Santa **$45**

Bells, Elf Girls, pr **$55**

Bottle opener, wooden
Santa **$28**
Snowman **$28**

Candle climbers, Ole Snowy, snowman, set **$48**

Candleholders
Camels **$38**
Carolers trio **$30**
Elf Girls, NOEL, set of four **$38**
Ermine Angels with snowflake rings, set **$48**
Green Holly Elf, pr **$35**
Madonna and Child **$25**
Naughty Choir Boy, set of two **$30**
Reindeer, pr **$38**
Santa driving car candleholders, traffic light candle rings, pr **$55**
Santa riding stage coach, pr **$38**
Santas, NOEL, set of four **$90**
Snow Babies, igloo, set of two **$55**
Three Choir Boy **$60**
Three Snowmen **$50**

Totem Pole, Santa **$25**
Wee Three Kings, set of three **$60**
Cigarette holder with ashtrays, Santa King, stackable **$70**
Coffee mug, Green Holly Elf **$23**

Cookie jar, pop-up, Santa **$150**

Cookie jar/candy jar combination, Santa **$155**

Creamer and sugar
Reindeer **$48**
Winking Santas **$55**
Decanter and glasses, Santa King **$100**
Dish, divided, Green Holly Elf **$50**
Floral ring, Green Holly Elf **$48**

Head vase, My Fair Lady **$75**

Letter and pen holder, Santa **$55**

Napkin holder, Santa, 4" **$25**

Nutmeg shaker, Winking Santa **$55**

Pitcher and mug set, Winking Santa **$75**

Place card holders, Green Holly Elf, set of four **$40**

Planter
Camel **$40**
Elf Girl in Sleigh **$58**
Ermine Angel **$38**
Green Holly Elf, pr **$75**

Punch bowl set, punch bowl and eight mugs, Santa **$145**

Salt and pepper shakers, pr
  Cloud Santa......................................**$38**
  Holly Girls, pr **$23**
  Rock' N' Roll Santas, on springs **$75**

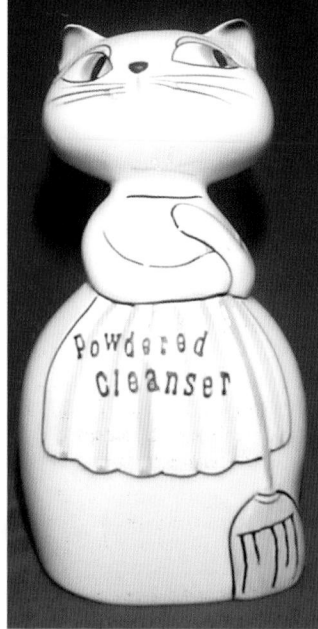

Holt-Howard Cozy Kittens, powdered cleanser, 6-3/4" h, **$70.**

Santa and Rudolph sleeping in bed **$105**
Santa and snowman in NOEL candle-holder **$95**
Snow Babies **$35**

Server, divided tray, Santa King....**$60**

Wall pocket
  Green Holly Elf **$65**
  Santa ornament **$58**

Cozy Kittens

Ashtray, with match holder...........**$55**
Bud vase, pr....................................**$105**
Butter dish, cov **$105**
Condiment jar, Cat
  Instant Coffee.............................**$190**
  Jam 'N' Jelly **$180**
  Ketchup **$180**
  Mustard **$180**
Cookie jar, pop-up......................**$250**
Cottage cheese crock **$60**
Creamer and sugar **$200**
Kitty catch clip..............................**$38**
Letter holder/caddy.....................**$58**
Match dandy **$75**
Memo minder **$90**
Meow milk pitcher **$110**
Meow mug **$35**
Meow oil and vinegar................**$175**
Salt and pepper shakers, pr.....**$20**
Sewing kit, Merry Measure..........**$70**
Spice set of four, with rack **$110**
String holder..................................**$45**
Sugar pour **$85**

Totem pole stacking seasons ... **$65**

Cows

Creamer and sugar **$75**
Milk glass, moo cow **$32**
Salt and pepper shakers, pr
  Heads **$40**
  Moveable tongues.........................**$50**

Easter

Candelabra, three rabbits **$58**
Candle climbers, four-pc set
  Feathered Chicks, cracked egg floral frog bases **$78**
  Honey Bunnies, floral frog bases ...**$78**
Candleholder
  Totem pole, chicks.........................**$38**
  Totem pole, rabbits.......................**$38**
Egg cups, Slick Chick, pr of egg cups with Chick salt and pepper shaker, four-pc set **$50**
Salt and pepper shakers with napkin holder, Winking Wabbits **$60**
Salt and pepper shakers, pr
  Bunnies in baskets.........................**$28**
  Rabbit, pink and yellow **$25**

Jeeves, butler

Ashtray...**$70**
Chip dish **$80**
Liquor decanter **$165**
Martini shaker set.....................**$195**
Olives, condiment jar **$135**

Merry Mouse

Cocktail kibitzers, mice, set of six **$120**
Coaster, ashtray, corner **$55**
Crock, "Stinky Cheese"..................**$50**
Desk pen pal..................................**$85**
Match mouse **$70**
Salt and pepper shakers, pr.....**$35**

Minnie & Moby Mermaids

Ashtray, Moby **$55**
Cotton ball dispenser, Minnie..**$75**
Matchbox holder, Moby **$65**
Pill box, Minnie & Moby **$50**
Planter, seahorse, Minnie & Moby, pr **$85**
Powder jar, Minnie & Moby **$50**

Miscellaneous

Ashtray
  Golfer Image **$110**
  Li'l Old Lace **$50**
Bank, bobbing, Dandy Lion..........**$135**
Bud vase, Daisy Dorable **$70**
Candelabra, Li'l Old Lace, spiral..**$50**

Holt-Howard Jeeves, three pieces, left: olives, **$135;** *liquor decanter,* **$165;** *cherries,* **$135.**

Candle climbers, Honey Bunnies, with bases, set...........**$85**
Candle holder, Market Piggy **$28**
Candle rings, Ballerina, with bases, set...........**$58**
Cookie jar, pop-up, Clown.........**$225**
Desk organizer, Market Piggy.....**$78**
Letter holder, Pheasant...............**$60**
Memo holder, Pheasant **$60**
Napkin doll, Sunbonnet Miss.......**$75**
Peepin' Tom & Tweetie Birds
  Butter dish, cov...............................**$65**
  Candle holder/floral holder **$38**
  Candle food-warmer set, three pcs **$65**
  Creamer, sugar and saccharin holder, 4-1/2"...........**$75**
  Egg cups, thermal salt and pepper tops, 4" h **$60**
  Salt and pepper shakers, set **$35**
  Stackable condiment bowls, set of three **$40**
Pencil holder and sharpener, two-pc set
  Chickadee...........**$65**
  Cock-A-Doodle...........**$60**
  Professor Perch...........**$65**
Planter, Doe & Fawn **$35**
Salt and pepper shakers, with napkin holder, Winking Wabbits **$60**
Salt and pepper shakers, pr
  Bell Bottom Gobs (sailors)...........**$50**
  Chattercoons, Peppy and Salty **$38**
  Daisy Dorables, ponytail girls.......**$35**
  Goose 'N' Golden Egg **$35**
  Pink cat, white poodle **$65**
  Rock 'N' Doll Kids, on springs **$75**
Tape dispenser
  Chickadee...........**$50**
  Pelican Pete...........**$68**
Tea maker, Tea Time Tillie **$38**

Pixiewares, 1958
Bottle bracelets
  Bourbon **$100**
  Gin...........**$100**
  Scotch **$100**
  Whiskey...........**$100**
Child's Pixie spoon
  Carrot nose, flesh-colored Pixie...**$135**
  Green head Pixie **$135**
  Orange head Pixie **$135**
  Yellow chicken beak Pixie...........**$135**
Condiment jar
  Cherries...........**$120**
  Cocktail Cherries **$135**
  Cocktail Olives **$130**
  Cocktail Onions **$155**
  Instant Coffee...........**$255**
  Jam 'N' Jelly...........**$75**

Ketchup **$75**
Mustard **$75**
Olives **$100**
Onions **$145**
L'il sugar and cream crock **$155**
Liquor decanter
  "Devil Brew" **$580**
  "300 Proof" **$580**
  "Whisky" **$580**
Oil cruet, Sally **$185**
Oil cruet, Sam **$185**
Stacking seasons, shakers, set of four **$85**

Pixiewares, 1959
Ashtray Pixie
  Blue stripe **$160**
  Green stripe **$160**
  Pink stripe **$160**
  Red stripe **$160**
Condiment jar
  Chili Sauce **$365**
  Honey **$725**
  Mayonnaise **$185**
  Relish **$225**
Hanging planter, rare...............**$450**
Party Pixies hors d'oeuvre dish
  Green stripe boy pixie...............**$200**
  Orange stripe girl pixie, Australian **$475**
  Pink stripe girl pixie...........**$200**
Salad dressing jar
  Flat head, French Pixie...............**$140**
  Flat head, Italian Pixie **$140**
  Flat head, Russian Pixie **$140**
  Round head, French Pixie...........**$125**
  Round head, Italian Pixie **$125**
  Round head, Russian Pixie **$125**
Salty & Peppy shakers **$350**
Snack Pixie bowl
  Berries **$685**
  Goo **$1,000**
  Ketchup Katie **$675**
  Mustard Max...........**$675**
  Nuts **$600**

Onion Annie **$685**
Oscar Olives **$575**
Peanut Butter Pat...........**$675**
Pickle Pete **$675**
Tartar Tom **$850**
Teapot candleholder hurricane vase, complete with glass globe
  Blue stripe boy **$285**
  Pink stripe girl **$285**
Towel hook
  Brother **$150**
  Dad **$150**
  Mom **$150**
  Sister **$150**

Red Rooster, "Coq Rouge"
Butter dish, cov **$65**
Candleholders, pr...........**$30**
Coffee mug...........**$14**
Coffee server, 36 oz **$65**
Cookie jar **$100**
Creamer and sugar **$55**
Dinner plate **$18**
Electric coffee pot, six cups **$70**
Mustard condiment jar...........**$55**
Pitcher
  12 oz **$45**
  32 oz **$60**
  48 oz **$75**
Salt and pepper shakers, pr, 4-1/2" **$25**
Snack tray...........**$18**
Spoon rest...........**$25**
Wooden
  Canister set, four pcs...........**$85**
  Cigarette carton holder **$45**
  Recipe box...........**$70**
  Salt & pepper shakers, pr.....**$23**

Tigers
Child's cup...........**$15**
Cookie jar...........**$40**
Napkin holder...........**$20**
Salt and pepper shakers, pr **$23**

Holt-Howard Pelican Pete, tape dispenser, 8-3/4" l copyrighted 1958, **$68.**

HULL POTTERY

History: In 1905, Addis E. Hull purchased the Acme Pottery Company, Crooksville, Ohio. In 1917, the A. E. Hull Pottery Company began making art pottery, novelties, stoneware and kitchenware, later including the famous Little Red Riding Hood line. Most items had a matte finish, with shades of pink and blue or brown predominating.

After a disastrous flood and fire in 1950, J. Brandon Hull reopened the factory in 1952 as the Hull Pottery Company. New, more-modern-style pieces, mostly with glossy finish, were produced. The company added dinnerware patterns, and glossy finished pottery. The company closed its doors in 1986.

Marks: Hull pottery molds and patterns are easily identified. Pre-1950 vases are marked "Hull USA" or "Hull Art USA" on the bottom. Many also retain their paper labels. Post-1950 pieces are marked "Hull" in large script or "HULL" in block letters.

Each pattern has a distinctive letter or number, e.g., Wildflower has a "W" and a number; Waterlily, "L" and number; Poppy, numbers in the 600s; Orchid, in the 300s. Early stoneware pieces are marked with an "H."

For more information about these marks and Hull Pottery patterns and history, consult Joan Hull's book, *Hull, The Heavenly Pottery,* 7th ed., 2000, and, *Hull, The Heavenly Pottery Shirt Pocket Price List,* 4th ed., 1999.

Additional Listings: See *Warman's Americana & Collectibles* for more examples.

Adviser: Joan Hull.

Pre-1950 Matte

Bowknot
B-4 vase, 6-1/2" h	**$250**
B-7 cornucopia	**$325**
B-12, basket, 10-1/2" h	**$750**
B-17 candleholders, pr	**$225**

Calla Lily
500-32 bowl	**$200**
520-33, vase, 8" h	**$150**

Dogwood (Wild Rose)
501, basket, 8-1/2" h	**$300**
508 window box, 10-1/2"	**$195**
513, vase, 6-1/2" h	**$125**

Little Red Riding Hood
Creamer and sugar, side pour	**$400**
Dresser or cracker jar	**$800**
Lamp	**$2,500**

Salt and pepper shakers, pr, small	**$120**
Teapot, cov	**$395**

Magnolia
3 vase, 8-1/2" h	**$125**
9 vase, 10-1/2" h	**$200**
14 pitcher, 4-3/4" h	**$75**
20 floor vase, 15"	**$500**

Open Rose/Camellia
106 pitcher, 13-1/2" h	**$650**
119 vase, 8-1/2" h	**$175**
127 vase, 4-3/4" h	**$75**

Orchid
302 vase, 6" h	**$175**
304 vase, 10-1/2" h	**$350**
310 jardinière, 9-1/2"	**$450**

Poppy
601 basket, 9" h	**$800**
610 pitcher, 13"	**$900**
613 vase, 6-1/2" h	**$200**

Rosella
R-2 vase, 5" h	**$35**
R-6 vase, 6-1/2" h	**$45**
R-15 vase, 8-1/2" h	**$75**

Tulip
101-33 vase, 9" h	**$245**
107-33 vase, 6" h	**$125**
109-33 pitcher, 8"	**$235**

Waterlily
L-14, basket, 10-1/2"	**$350**
L-16, vase, 12-1/2"	**$395**

Wild Flower, No. Series
53 vase, 8-1/2" h	**$295**
61 vase, 6-1/2" h	**$175**
66 basket, 10-1/4" h	**$2,000**
71 vase, 12" h	**$450**

Woodland
W9 basket, 8-3/4" h	**$245**
W11 flower pot and saucer, 5-1/2"	**$175**
W13 wall pocket, shell, 7-1/2" l	**$195**
W14 window box, 10-1/2"	**$200**

Post 1950

Blossom Flite
T4 basket, 8-1/2" h	**$125**
T13 pitcher, 12-1/2" h	**$150**

Butterfly
B9 vase, 9" h	**$55**
B13 basket, 8" h	**$150**
B15 pitcher, 13-1/2" h	**$200**

Continental
C29 vase, 12" h	**$95**
C55 basket, 12-1/2"	**$150**
C62 candy dish, 8-1/4"	**$45**

Ebb Tide
E-1 bud vase, 7" h	**$75**
E-8 ashtray with mermaid	**$225**
E-10 pitcher, 13" h	**$275**

Parchment and Pine
S-3 basket, 6" h	**$95**
S-11 and S-12 tea set	**$250**
S-15 coffeepot, 8" h	**$175**

Serenade
S1 vase, 6" h	**$55**
S-15 fruit bowl, ftd, 11-1/2" d	**$125**
S17 teapot, creamer and sugar	**$275**

Sunglow
53 grease jar	**$60**
82 wall pocket, whisk broom	**$75**
85 vase, bird, 8-3/4" h	**$60**

Tokay/Tuscany
3 pitcher, 8" h	**$95**
8 vase, 10" h	**$150**
10 cornucopia, 11" l	**$65**

Tropicana
T53 vase, 8-1/2" h	**$550**
T55, basket, 12-3/4" h	**$750**

Woodland (glossy)
W1 vase, 5-1/2" h	**$45**
W15 vase, double, 8-1/2" h	**$75**
W19 console bowl, 14" d	**$100**

Hull Woodland post glossy basket, No. 22, 12-1/2", **$250.**

Hull Woodland post glossy vases, No. 4, 6-1/2", **$65.**

HUMMEL ITEMS

History: Hummel items are the original creations of Berta Hummel, who was born in 1909 in Massing, Bavaria, Germany. At age 18, she was enrolled in the Academy of Fine Arts in Munich to further her mastery of drawing and the palette.

Berta entered the Convent of Siessen and became Sister Maria Innocentia in 1934. In this Franciscan cloister, she continued drawing and painting images of her childhood friends.

In 1935, W. Goebel Co. in Rodental, Germany, began producing Sister Maria Innocentia's sketches as three-dimensional bisque figurines. The Schmid Brothers of Randolph, Massachusetts, introduced the figurines to America and became Goebel's U.S. distributor.

In 1967, Goebel began distributing Hummel items in the U.S.A. Controversy developed between the two companies, the Hummel family, and the convent. Law suits and counter-suits ensued. The German courts finally effected a compromise: the convent held legal rights to all works produced by Sister Maria Innocentia from 1934 until her death in 1946 and licensed Goebel to reproduce these works; Schmid was to deal directly with the Hummel family for permission to reproduce any pre-convent art.

Marks: All authentic Hummel pieces bear both the signature "M. I. Hummel" and a Goebel trademark. Various trademarks were used to identify the year of production. For purposes of simplification the various trademarks have been abbreviated in the following list. Should you encounter any trouble interpreting the abbreviations, refer to the list below.

Trademark	Abbreviations	Dates
Crown	TMK-1	1934-1950
Full Bee	TMK-2	1940-1959
Stylized Bee	TMK-3	1958-1972
Three Line Mark	TMK-4	1964-1972
Last Bee	TMK-5	1972-1979
Missing Bee	TMK-6	1979-1991
Hummel Mark	TMK-7	1991-1999
Millennium Bee (Current)	TMK-8	2000-present

Additional Listings: See *Warman's Americana & Collectibles* for more examples.

Note: The first seventeen Hummels made are highly prized by collectors. We have included the first five in this book with listings for all of the known marks.

All photos appear courtesy of Goebel of North America unless otherwise indicated.

Hummel, figure, Ring Around the Rosey, no. 348, stylized bee mark, 7-1/4" h, **$750.**
Photo courtesy of David Rago Auctions, Inc.

Hum No. 1 Puppy Love, **$305-$1,000.**

Hum No. 2 Little Fiddler, **$130-$4,000.**

The First Five

Hum No. 1, Book Worm

TMK-1, 5"	**$755-$1,000**
TMK-2, 5"	**$550-$600**
TMK-3, 5"	**$510-$550**
TMK-4, 5"	**$400-$510**
TMK-5, 5"	**$350-$400**
TMK-6, 5"	**$305-$350**

Hum No. 2, Little Fiddler

No. 2/4/0, TMK-6, 3-1/2"	**$130-$140**
No. 2/0, 6"	
TMK-1	**$700-$850**
TMK-2	**$430-$500**
TMK-3	**$350-$400**
TMK-4	**$325-$350**
TMK-5	**$275-$300**
TMK-6	**$260-$275**

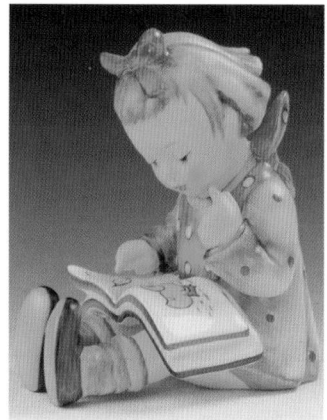

Hum No. 3 Book Worm, **$365-$4,000.**

Hum No. 4 Little Fiddler, **$240-$800.**

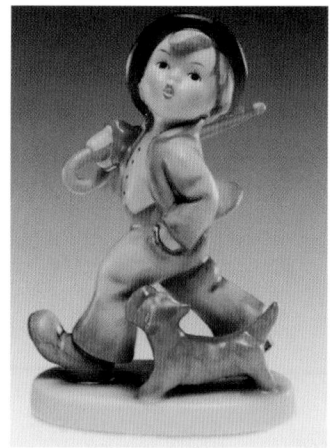

Hum No. 5 Strolling Along, **$275-$950.**

Hum No. 775 Christmas Bell 1989, **$28.**

Hum No. 776 Christmas Bell 1990, **$28.**

Hummel, The Village Bakery, **$50.**

TMK-7	$260-$275
TMK-8	$260

2/I, 7-1/2"

TMK-1	$1,110-$1,500
TMK-2	$650-$930
TMK-3	$565-$650
TMK-4	$460-$560
TMK-5	$425-$435
TMK-6	$415-$420

2/II

TMK-1	$2,500-$3,500
TMK-2	$1,800-$2,300
TMK-3	$1,515-$1,600
TMK-4	$1,300-$1,515
TMK-5	$1,200-$1,300
TMK-6	$1,110-$1,200

2/III

TMK-1, 12-1/4"	$3,500-$4,000
TMK-2, 12-1/4"	$2,310-$2,800
TMK-3, 12-1/4"	$1,600-$1,800
TMK-4, 12-1/4"	$1,400-$1,600
TMK-5, 12-1/4"	$1,300-$1,400
TMK-6, 12-1/4"	$1,205-$1,300
TMK-8, 12-1/4"	$1,550

Hum No. 3, Book Worm

3/I, 5-1/2"

TMK-1	$900-$1,110
TMK-2	$600-$700
TMK-3	$475-$500
TMK-4	$400-$475
TMK-5	$380-$400
TMK-6	$370-$380
TMK-7	$365-$370
TMK-8	$370

3/II, 8"

TMK-1	$2,500-$3,500
TMK-2	$1,800-$2,300
TMK-3	$1,500-$1,600
TMK-4	$1,300-$1,500
TMK-5	$1,200-$1,300
TMK-6	$1,110-$1,200

3/III, 9-1/2"

TMK-1	$3,500-$4,000
TMK-2	$2,300-$2,800
TMK-3	$1,600-$1,800
TMK-4	$1,460-$1,600
TMK-5	$1,360-$1,460
TMK-6	$1,250-$1,360

Hum No. 4, Little Fiddler

4, 4-3/4"

TMK-1	$650-$800
TMK-2	$400-$500
TMK-3	$325-$375
TMK-4	$300-$325
TMK-5	$270-$300
TMK-6	$250-$270
TMK-7	$245-$250
TMK-8	$240

Hum No. 5, Strolling Along

5, 4-3/4"

TMK-1	$700-$950
TMK-2	$500-$600
TMK-3	$450-$500
TMK-4	$350-$450
TMK-5	$300-$350
TMK-6	$275-$300

Bell, Annual

Anniversary Bell, Hum 730, 1985 .... **$1,500-$2,000**

Busy Student, Hum 710, 1988 ..... **$58**

Farewell, Hum 701, 1979 .... **$25**

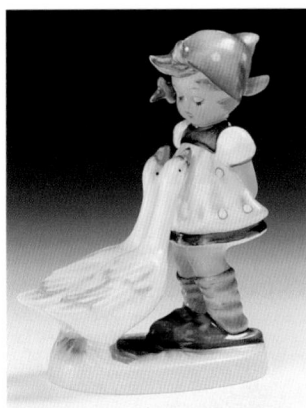

Hum No. 47/0 Goose Girl, **$290-$900.**

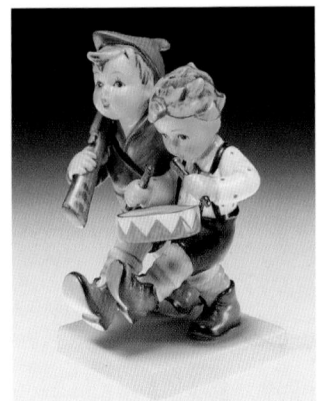

Hum No. 50/0 Volunteers, **$375-$1,100.**

Hum No. 56/A Culprits, **$365-$650.**

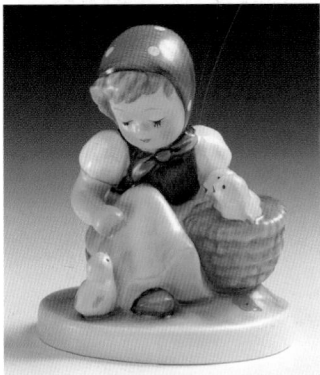

Hum No. 57/2/0 Chick Girl, **$185-$200.**

Hum No. 71/2/0 Stormy Weather, **$365-$380.**

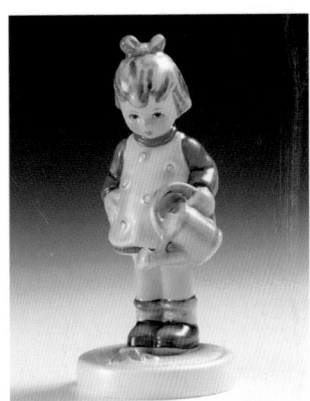

Hum No. 74 Little Gardener, **$150-$550.**

Favorite Pet, Hum 713, 1991 .... $58
Festival Harmony With Flute, Hum 781, 1995 .... $35
In Tune, Hum 703, 1981 .... $38
Knit One, Hum 705, 1983 .... $35
Latest News, Hum 711, 1989 .... $58
Let's Sing, Hum 700, 1978 .... $38
Mountaineer, Hum 706, 1984 ..... $35
She Loves Me, Hum 704, 1982 .... $35
Sing Along, Hum 708, 1986 .... $58
Sweet Song, Hum 707, 1985 .... $35
Thoughtful, Hum 702, 1980 .... $25
What's New?, Hum 712, 1990 ...... $58
Whistler's Duet, Hum 714, 1992
.... $58
With Loving Greetings, Hum 709, 1987 .... $58

Bell, Christmas

Angel With Flute, 1972 .... $45
Angelic Gifts, 1987 .... $48
Angelic Messenger, 1983 .... $58
Angelic Procession, 1982 .... $45
Cheerful Cherubs, 1988 .... $53

Echoes Of Joy, Hum 784, 1998 .... $28
Gift From Heaven, 1984 .... $45
Herald Angel, 1977 .... $45
Nativity, 1973 .... $45
Parade Into Toyland, 1980 .... $45
Sacred Journey, 1976 .... $45
Starlight Angel, 1979 .... $47

Cottages, Bavarian Village

Angel's Duet, 1996 .... $50
Bench & Pine Tree, The/Set, 1996
.... $25
Christmas Mail, 1996 .... $50
Company's Coming, 1996 .... $50
Sled & Pine Tree, The/Set, 1996 .. $25
Village Bridge, The, 1996 .... $25
Winter's Comfort, 1996 .... $50
Wishing Well, The, 1996 .... $25

Dolls and Plush

Anderl 1718 .... $150
Birthday Serenade/Boy, 1984 ... $275
Birthday Serenade/Girl, 1984 .. $275

Brieftrager 1720 .... $175
Carnival, 1985 .... $275
Christl 1715 .... $150
Easter Greetings, 1985 .... $275
Felix 1608 .... $175
Felix 1708 .... $175
Gretel 1501 .... $200
Gretel 1901, 1964 .... $160
Hansel 1504 .... $200
Hansel 1604 .... $175
Konditor 1723 .... $175
Lost Stocking 1926, 1964 .... $125
Mariandl 1713 .... $150
Max 1506 .... $200
Merry Wanderer 1906, 1964 .... $125
On Secret Path 1928, 1964 .... $85
Peterle 1710 .... $150
School Boy 1910, 1964 .... $130
School Girl 1909, 1964 .... $130
Skihaserl 1722 .... $175
Valentine Gift Doll, Hum 524
.... $200-$250
Visiting An Invalid 1927, 1964 .. $130
Wanderbub 1507 .... $200

Figurine, M.I. Hummel

Due to space constraints, a range of pricing has provided. Please consult the 12th edition of *Luckey's Hummel® Figurines & Plates Identification and Price Guide* for individual pricing based upon trademark variations.

Accompanist, The, Hum 453, 1988 .... **$140**

Accordion Boy, Hum 185, 1947 .... **$200-$750**

Adoration With Bird, Hum 105, 1938 .... **$7,000-$8,000**

Angel Duet, Hum 261, 1968 .... **$270-$850**

Angel Lights, Candleholder, Hum 241 .... **$300-$500**

Angel With Accordion, Hum 238 B, 1967 .... **$73-$125**

Angel With Lute, Hum 238 A, 1967 .... **$73-$125**

Angel With Trumpet, Hum 238 C, 1967 .... **$73-$125**

Angel/Accordion, Candleholder, Hum 1/39/0 .... **$80-$200**

Angel/Accordion, Candleholder, Hum 111/39/0 .... **$60-$200**

Angel/Accordion, Candleholder, Hum 111/39/1 .... **$200-$350**

Angel/Lute, Candleholder, Hum 111/38/1 .... **$200-$350**

Angel/Trumpet, Candleholder, Hum 1/40/0 .... **$73-$200**

Angel/Trumpet, Candleholder, Hum 111/40/0 .... **$60-$200**

Angel/Trumpet, Candleholder, Hum 111/40/1 .... **$200-$350**

Angelic Conductor, Hum 2096/A, 2002 .... **$135**

Apple Tree Boy, Hum 142 .... **$650-$950**

Apple Tree Boy, Hum 142/3/0 .... **$180-$550**

Apple Tree Boy, Hum 142/I .... **$350-$800**

Apple Tree Boy, Candleholder, Hum 677 .... **$200-$250**

Apple Tree Boy/Girl-Bookends, Hum 252 A&B .... **$300-$425**

Apple Tree Girl, Hum 141 .... **$650-$950**

Apple Tree Girl, Hum 141/3/0 .... **$180-$550**

Apple Tree Girl, Candleholder, Hum 676 .... **$200-$250**

Ba-Bee-Ring, Hum 30/0 A&B .... **$245-$700**

Band Leader, Hum 129/4/0 .... **$125-$140**

Barnyard Hero, Hum 195/2/0 .... **$205-$450**

Barnyard Hero, Hum 195/I .... **$350-$700**

Chimney Sweep, Hum 12 **$425-$800**

Chimney Sweep, Hum 12/2/0 .... **$145-$325**

Christ Child, Hum 18 .... **$165-$550**

Christmas Gift, 1999 .... **$95**

Christmas Song, Hum 343/4/0, 1996 .... **$135**

Come Back Soon, Hum 545, 1995 .... **$180-$500**

Congratulations, Hum 17/0 .... **$230-$750**

Coquettes, Hum 179, 1948 .... **$325-$1100**

Culprits, Hum 56 .... **$900-$1,100**

Hum No. 88/I Heavenly Protection, **$540-$750.**

Hum No. 94/3/0 Surprise, **$190-$550.**

Hum No. 123 Max and Moritz, **$270-$800.**

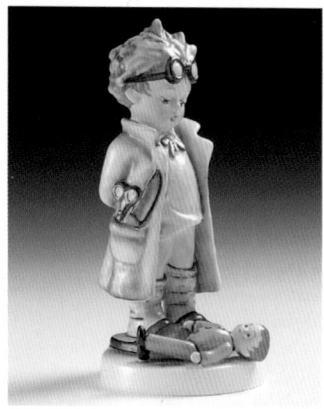

Hum No. 127 Doctor, **$190-$650.**

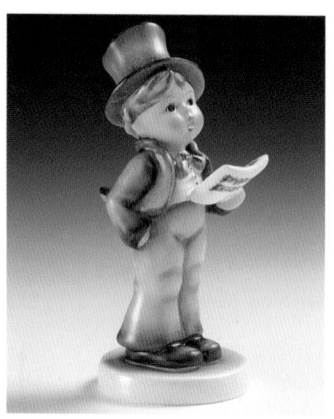

Hum No. 131 Street Singer, **$245-$700.**

Hum No. 152/A/0 Umbrella Boy, **$300.**

Culprits, Hum 56 A .... $365-$650
Dearly Beloved, Hum 2003, 1999 .... $200-$520
Delicious, Hum 435/3/0 ..... $170-$175
Doll Mother, Hum 67 .... $257-$900
Duet, Hum 130 .... $300-$1,000
Evening Prayer, Hum 495, 1991 .... $135
Eventide (Rare), Hum 99 .... $3,000-$3,500
Eventide, Hum 99 .... $360-$1250
Farewell, Hum 65 .... $275-$1,000
Farewell, Hum 65/I .... $325-$1,000
Farewell, Hum 65/0 ..... $5,000-$8,000
Farm Boy, Hum 66 .... $270-$900
Farm Boy/Goose Girl Bookends, Hum 60 A&B .... $400-$1,250
Favorite Pet, Hum 361 .... $335-$5,000
Feeding Time, Hum 199 .... $525-$1,000
Feeding Time, Hum 199/I .... $315-$575
Feeding Time, Hum 199/0 $250-$500

Festival Harmony (Flute), Hum 173/0 .... $350-$650
Festival Harmony (Mandolin), Hum 172 .... $1,000-$3,500
Festival Harmony (Mandolin), Hum 172/4/0 .... $135
Festival Harmony (Mandolin), Hum 172/II .... $450-$800
Festival Harmony (Mandolin), Hum 172/0 .... $350-$650
Flying Angel, Hum 366 .... $150-$275
Flying High, Hum 452, 1984 .... $175-$300
Follow The Leader, Hum 369 .... $1,390-$5,000
For Father, Hum 87 .... $270-$800
Forest Shrine, Hum 183 .... $595-$1,900
Free Flight, Hum 569, 1993 .... $215
Friend Or Foe, Hum 434, 1991 .... $275
Friends, Hum 136/I .... $240-$950
Girl With Doll, Hum 239B .... $73-$200

Girl With Nosegay, Hum 239A .... $73-$200
Girl With Sheet Of Music, Hum 389 .... $110-$275
Girl With Trumpet, Hum 391 .... $110-$275
Globe Trotter, Hum 79 ..... $200-$750
Going To Grandma's, Hum 52 .... $850-$1,600
Good Friends, Hum 182 .... $250-$750
Good Hunting, Hum 307 .... $300-$5,000
Goose Girl, Hum 47, 1996 .... $205-$1,300
Goose Girl, Hum 47 .... $800-$900
Grandma's Girl, Hum 561, 1990 .... $185
Grandpa's Boy, Hum 562, 1990 .... $185
Guardian, The, Hum 455, 1991 ... $205
Guiding Angel, Hum 357 .... $110-$150
Happiness, Hum 86 .... $170-$500

Hum No. 167 Holy Water Font, Angel With Bird, **$300-$325.**

Hum No. 170, The School Boys, stylized bee mark, 9-1/2" x 7-1/4", **$700.**
Photo courtesy of David Rago Auctions, Inc.

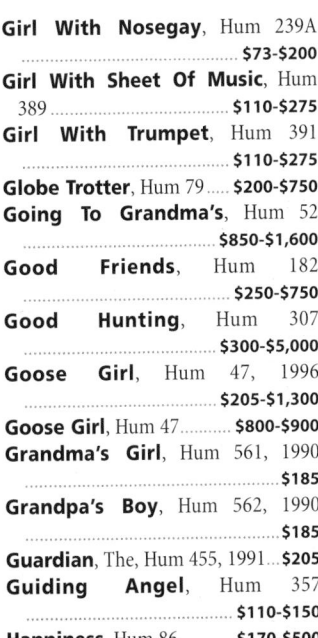

Hum No. 176/0 Happy Birthday, **$280-$500.**

Hum No. 177 The School Girls, stylized bee mark, 9-1/4" x 6-3/4", **$425.**
Photo courtesy of David Rago Auctions, Inc.

Hum No. 186 Sweet Music, **$250-$750.**

Hum No. 257/0 For Mother, **$255.**

Hum No. 311 Kiss Me, **$335-$550.**

Hum No. 375/3/0 Morning Stroll, **$215.**

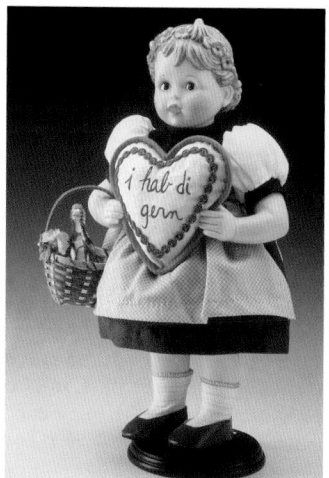

Hum No. 524 Valentine Gift Doll, **$200-$250.**

Hum No. 355 Autumn Harvest, **$250-$3,000.**

Hum No. 364 Supreme Protection, **$3,000-$4,000.**

Happy Days, Hum 150 ... **$900-$1,600**
Happy Days, Hum 150/2/0... **$210-$400**
Happy Pastime, Hum 69.. **$190-$650**
Happy Traveller, Hum 109/II .... **$375-$900**
Happy Traveller, Hum 109/0 .... **$185-$350**
Hear Ye, Hear Ye, Hum 15/2/0 .... **$185-$190**
Hear Ye, Hear Ye, Hum 15/I .... **$280-$900**
Hear Ye, Hear Ye, Hum 15/II .... **$450-$1,500**
Hear Ye, Hear Ye, Hum 15/0 .... **$230-$750**
Heavenly Angel, Hum 21/I .... **$320-$1,000**
Heavenly Angel, Hum 21/0 .... **$160-$500**
Heavenly Angel, Hum 21/0 1/2 .... **$270-$850**
Heavenly Lullaby, Hum 262 .... **$270-$850**
Hello, Hum 124 .... **$450-$1,000**
Hello, Hum 124/I.............. **$275-$1,000**
Hello, Hum 124/0 .... **$255-$450**
Holy Water Font, Angel Cloud, Hum 206 .... **$60-$500**
Holy Water Font, Angel Duet, Hum 146 .... **$60-$225**
Holy Water Font, Angel Joyous News, Hum 241, 1955 .... **$1,500-$2,000**
Holy Water Font, Angel Joyous News, Hum 242, 1955 .... **$1,500-$2,000**
Holy Water Font, Angel Shrine, Hum 147 .... **$68-$275**
Holy Water Font, Angel Sitting, Hum 22 .... **$68-$300**

Home From Market, Hum 198 .... **$375-$800**
Home From Market, Hum 198/2/0 .... **$190-$375**
Home From Market, Hum 198/I .... **$240-$500**
Horse Trainer, Hum 423, 1990 .... **$268-$280**
Hosanna, Hum 480, 1989 .... **$140**
I'll Protect Him, Hum 483, 1989 .... **$115**
I'm Carefree, Hum 633, 1994 .... **$440-$1,000**
I'm Here, Hum 478, 1989............. **$145**
In D Major, Hum 430, 1989 .... **$255**
In The Meadow, Hum 459, 1987 .... **$255**
Joyful, Hum 53.................... **$140-$450**
Joyous News, Hum 27/3 .... **$280-$2,000**
Joyous News, Hum 27/I... **$250-$500**
Joyous News, Hum 27/III **$253**
Jubilee, Hum 416, 1985 ..... **$500-$600**
Just Dozing, Hum 451, 1984 ..... **$265**
Just Resting, Hum 112 ..... **$700-$850**
Just Resting, Hum 112/3/0 .... **$185-$550**
Just Resting, Hum 112/I... **$320-$800**
Kindergartner, Hum 467, 1987 .... **$255**
Knit One, Purl One , Hum 432, 1983 .... **$160**
Knitting Lesson, Hum 256 .... **$535-$1,150**
Latest News, Hum 184 .... **$360-$1,100**
Let's Play, Hum 2051/B, 1999....... **$95**
Let's Sing, Hum 110 .... **$325-$600**

Let's Sing, Hum 110/I........ $195-$375
Let's Sing, Hum 110/0....... $160-$500
Letter To Santa Claus Prototype, Hum 340, 1956 .... $15,000-20,000
Letter To Santa, Hum 340 .... $400-$1,000
Little Architect, The, Hum 410, 1978 .... $3,000-$4,000
Little Band (On Base), Hum 392 .... $275-$450
Little Bookkeeper, Hum 306 .... $335-$1,500
Little Cellist, Hum 89 .... $1,250-$1,600
Little Cellist, Hum 89/I..... $270-$850
Little Cellist, Hum 89/II .... $450-$1,500
Little Fiddler, Hum 2/4/0 .... $130-$140
Little Fiddler, Hum 2/I .... $415-$1,500
Little Fiddler, Hum 2/II .... $1,110-$3,500
Little Fiddler, Hum 2/III .... $1,205-$4,000
Little Fiddler, Hum 2/0..... $325-$850
Little Gabriel, Hum 32, 1935 .... $2,000-$2,500
Little Goat Herder, Hum 200 .... $500-$850
Little Goat Herder, Hum 200/I .... $270-$550
Little Hiker, Hum 16 .... $450-$750
Little Hiker, Hum 16/2/0 .... $140-$450
Little Hiker, Hum 16/I....... $245-$700
Little Sweeper, Hum 171/4/0 .... $130
Little Sweeper, Hum 171/0 .... $185
Little Tailor, Hum 308....... $305-$350
Little Thrifty, Bank, Hum 118 .... $185-$650
Lost Sheep, Hum 68.......... $350-$750
Lost Sheep, Hum 68/2/0 .... $160-$350
Lost Sheep, Hum 68/0 .... $200-$450
Lost Stocking, Hum 374 .... $185-$1500
Madonna Holding Child, Hum 151, 1955 .... $9,000-$12,000
Make A Wish, Hum 475, 1989 .... $240
March Winds, Hum 43...... $180-$600
Meditation, Hum 13 ... $4,000-$5,000
Message Of Love, Hum 2050/A, 1999 .... $95
Mischief Maker, Hum 342 .... $320-$1,000
Mountaineer, Hum 315 .... $250-$1,000

Not For You!, Hum 317 .... $300-$1,000
Old Man Reading Newspaper, Hum 181, 1948 .... $15,000-$20,000
Old Woman Walking To Market, Hum 190, 1948 .....$15,000-$20,000
Ooh, My Tooth, Hum 533, 1995 .... $145
Out Of Danger, Hum 56 B .... $345-$650
Out Of Danger, Table Lamp, Hum 44 B .... $325-$650
Photographer, Hum 178 .. $335-$1,100
Pixie, Hum 768, 1995.................. $145
Playmates, Hum 58 .... $500-$1050
Playmates, Hum 58/2/0 .... $185-$200
Playmates, Hum 58/I ..... $320-$1,000
Postman, Hum 119, 1989 .... $255-$750
Postman, Hum 119/2/0 ....$185
Postman, Hum 119/0.................$250
Prayer Before Battle, Hum 20 .... $195-$650
Puppy Love, Hum 1........ $305-$1,000
Puppy Pause, Hum 2032, 2002 .... $195
Ring Around The Rosie, Hum 348, 1957 .... $3,200-$5,000
Run-A-Way, Hum 327........ $310-$325
Saint George, Hum 55 .... $350-$3000
School Boy, Hum 82.......... $625-$775
School Boy, Hum 82/2/0... $170-$600
School Boy, Hum 82/II .... $500-$1,600
School Boy, Hum 82/0 .... $235-$775
School Girl, Hum 81 .... $350-$750
School Girl, Hum 81/2/0 .... $180-$600
School Girl, Hum 81/0 ..... $225-$700
Sensitive Hunter, Hum 6/2/0 .... $170-$180
Sensitive Hunter, Hum 6/0 .... $250-$800
Seraphim Soprano, Hum 2096/R, 2002 .... $135
Serenade, Hum 85 ..... $775-$1,550
Serenade, Hum 85/4/0 .... $130
Serenade, Hum 85/II..... $500-$1,500
Serenade, Hum 85/0.......... $160-$500
Shepherd Boy, Hum 395, 1996 .... $280-$315
Shepherd's Boy, Hum 64 .... $330-$900
Shining Light, Hum 358 .... $110-$150
Sing Along, Hum 433, 1987 ....$330
Sing With Me, Hum 405, 1985 .... $360-$4,000
Singing Lesson, Ashtray, Hum 34 .... $175-$650

Sister, Hum 98 .... $325-$700
Sister, Hum 98/2/0.............. $180-$250
Sister, Hum 98/0................. $230-$325
Skier, Hum 59................. $250-$900
Soloist, Hum 135............. $180-$550
Soloist, Hum 135/4/0.................$135
Soloist, Hum 135/0.................$175
Spring Cheer, Hum 72..... $200-$650
Standing Boy, Plaque, Hum 168 .... $200-$1100
Standing Madonna With Child, Hum 247, 1955 ....$10,000-$15,000
Star Gazer, Hum 132........ $258-$800
Stitch In Time, Hum 255 .... $325-$800
Stitch In Time, Hum 255/4/0 .... $115-$140
Teacher's Pet, Hum 2125, 2002 .... $175
Telling Her Secret, Hum 196 .... $800-$1,500
Telling Her Secret, Hum 196/I .... $400-$950
Telling Her Secret, Hum 196/II .... $375-$750
To Market, Hum 49/3/0 ..... $195-$650
Trumpet Boy, Hum 97 ..... $150-$525
Tuneful Angel, Hum 359 .... $110-$150
Village Boy, Hum 51 ..... $900-$1,150
Village Boy, Hum 51/2/0 .... $185-$550
Village Boy, Hum 51/3/0 .... $150-$450
Village Boy, Hum 51/I .... $300-$1,100
Village Boy, Hum 51/0 .... $280-$900
Visiting An Invalid, Hum 382 .... $250-$1,500
Wash Day, Hum 321 .... $275-$1,000
Wash Day, Hum 321/I .... $355-$365
Wash Day, Hum 321/4/0 .... $125-$140
Watchful Angel, Hum 194 .... $385-$2,100
Weary Wanderer, Hum 204 .... $280-$900
What's New?, Hum 418, 1990 .... $350-$380
Whitsuntide, Hum 163 .... $330-$1,200
Winter Song, Hum 476, 1988 .... $150
With Loving Greetings, Hum 309, 1983 .... $220-$5000
Wonder Of Christmas, Hum 2015 With Steiff Bear, 1999 .... $575
Worship, Hum 84 .... $475-$1,500
Worship, Hum 84/0........ $200-$600
Worship, Hum 84/V ..... $1,125-$3,000

*Pair of lidded jars, all over orange and blue design, 10" h, **$250**.*
Photo courtesy of Joy Luke Auctions.

*Imari, Japanese, porcelain fish bowl, molded catouches floral and brocade decoration, Meiji period, 8" h x 11" d, **$500**.*
Photo courtesy of Sloans & Kenyon Auctioneers and Appraisers.

*Imari plate, brick red, cobalt blue, green and gold decoration, scalloped edge, blue and brick-red motifs on underside, marked, **$35**.*

*Imari plate, center with butterfly swooping over large peony, rich border with dragon and geometric patterns, back border with Buddhistic emblems, underside marked with Koranska Fukagama mark, Japan, slight wear to gilding, late 19th C, 12-1/8" d, **$550**.*

IMARI

History: Imari derives its name from a Japanese port city. Although Imari ware was manufactured in the 17th century, the pieces most commonly encountered are those made between 1770 and 1900.

Early Imari was decorated simply, quite unlike the later heavily decorated brocade pattern commonly associated with Imari. Most of the decorative patterns are an underglaze blue and overglaze "seal wax" red complimented by turquoise and yellow.

The Chinese copied Imari ware. The Japanese examples can be identified by grayer clay, thicker glaze, runny and darker blue, and deep red opaque hues.

The pattern and colors of Imari inspired many English and European potteries, such as Derby and Meissen, to adopt a similar style of decoration for their wares.

Reproduction Alert. Reproductions abound, and many manufacturers continue to produce pieces in the traditional style.

Bottle vases, lobated form, underglaze blue with red, green, aubergine enamels and gilt, Japan, price for pr, late 19th C, 11" h **$775**

Bowl
Designs of dragons and auspicious emblems, set of 12, 19th C, 6" d **$400**
Gilt floral scrolling, heraldic emblems surrounding central dragon, six-character mark on base, 19th C, 13-3/4" d **$560**
Sq form with ribs, design of various flowers, Wan Li six-character mark on base, 19th C, 9" w ... **$120**

Charger
Fans with warriors and dragons dec, sgd "Koransha," late 19th C, 22" d **$1,645**
Hp, cinnabar red, underglaze dark blue, green and gilt, dragons in clouds circle border, leaves and clouds below, two phoenixes in center, ext. cov with blossoming vines, center base with cinnabar and gilt flower, glued repair to edge, gilt imperfections, 20-1/4" d, 4-3/4" h **$715**
Underglaze blue and enamel dec, central reserve of planter with flowers, grape and brocade borders, Japan, late 19th/early 20th C, 14-1/2" d **$250**

Creamer and sugar, ovoid, dragon form handles, gilt and bright enamels, shaped reserves, dragon-like beasts, stylized animal medallions, brocade ground, high dome lid, knob, cipher mark of Mount Fuji, Fukagama Studio marks, Meiji period, 5-1/2" h creamer, 5-7/8" cov sugar **$500**

Dish
Central scene with fence and flowering tree dec, shaped cartouches enclosing flowers and hares on crackle blue ground at rim, gilt highlights, Meiji period, price for pr, 8-3/8" d **$650**
Gourd shape, flowering tree with checkered design in foreground, brown glaze on rim, underside with underglaze blue tendrils, Fuku mark on base, Japanese, pr, one with rim chip, 18th C, 6-3/4" l **$1,650**

Food box, three section, ext. and lid with phoenix and floral design, underglaze blue, iron-red and gilt enamels, 19th C, 6" h **$400**

Jar, cov, ribbed forms with shishi finials, Japan, price for pr, late 19th C, 26" h **$2,000**

Jardinière, hexagonal, bulbous, short flared foot, alternating bijin figures and immortal symbols, stylized ground, 10" h **$250**

Luncheon set, partial, 12 8" d plates, four 10-1/4" oblong serving dishes, two boat-shaped serving dishes, sq serving dish, coffee van, Spode, 20 pcs, 19th C **$2,820**

Planter and stand, lobed form, floral dec, brocade patterns, Japan, late 19th C, 17" d, 43" h **$460**

Plate
Reserves of dragons and flowers arranged around phoenix roundel, Japan, set of nine, 19th C, 8-1/2" d **$470**
Brocade pattern, set of nine, 19th C, 9" d **$470**

Sq, scalloped edge, central design of basket of flowers, 19th C, 17-1/4".................................. **$1,765**

Platter, alternating panels of figures and foliage, trellis work ground, Japanese, late 19th C, 18" d.... **$475**

Punch bowl, rubbed, c1870, 12" d **$1,650**

Teabowl and saucer, floriform, floral spray dec, gilt highlights on saucer, 5" d **$200**

Tea set, 6-1/8" h teapot; teapot stand; creamer; cov sugar; 8-1/4" d serving plate; two 7-3/4" d serving plates; two 6" d bowls; 16 5-3/8" d saucers; 11 coffee cans, 12 teacups, English,

48 pcs, early 19th C **$2,235**

Umbrella stand, allover hexagonal panels with gold pheasants and orange drawings, flowers and plants, orange, tomato red, yellow, green and cobalt blue, old shield shaped "U.S. Customs" label underneath, 25" h **$550**

Urn, tomato red, light green, mauve, and cobalt blue, dark gold details, floral panels on sides with pheasants and cranes, geometric band of dec around base, minor roughness around rim, 36-1/2" h **$2,100**

Vase, baluster, late Meiji period, c1900, 14-1/2" h **$775**

Imari dish, octagonal, large, blue underglaze decoration, red and green overglaze decoration, **$275.**
Photo courtesy of Wiederseim Associates, Inc.

KPM

History: The "KPM" mark has been used separately and in conjunction with other symbols by many German porcelain manufacturers, among which are the Königliche Porzellan Manufactur in Meissen, 1720s; Königliche Porzellan Manufactur in Berlin, 1832-1847; and Krister Porzellan Manufactur in Waldenburg, mid-19th century.

Collectors now use the term KPM to refer to the high-quality porcelain produced in the Berlin area in the 18th and 19th centuries.

Cheese board, rose and leaf garland border, pierce for hanging, marked **$48**

Cup and saucer, hunting scene, filigree, 19th C **$65**

Dinner service, partial, basketweave molded rim, enamel painted sepia-toned floral sprays, 10 6-3/4" d side plates, nine 9-1/2" d dinner plates, eight 8-3/8" d salad plates, 12" l oval platter, 13-5/8" l oval platter, 8" oblong dish, late 19th/early 20th C, price for 30-pc set **$520**

Figure, young man with cocked hat, long coat, trousers, and boots, young lady in Empire-style dress, fancy hat and fan, white ground, brown details, gold trim, round base, blue underglaze KPM mark, price for pr, 8-1/2" h, 3-1/2" d **$350**

Perfume bottle, rococo-cartouche form, sepia enamel dec of cherub in flight, floral bouquet, gilt detailing, gilt-metal and coral mounted stopper, late 19th C, 3-5/8" l **$230**

Plaque
Monk tasting wine, ornate frame, imp on verso KPM and specter mark, c1900, 9-1/2" x 6-1/2" **$1,840**
First Snowfall, grandfather with two grandchildren standing in door-

way, snowy foreground, 21" w, 18" h elaborate carved wood frame of scrolling acanthus, imp scepter mark and "KPM," artist sgd lower right "F. X. Thallmaier Munchen," 7-1/2" w, 10" h **$4,370**
Ruth, after painting by Bouguereau, late 19th C, 12-3/4" l, 7-7/8" w **$2,300**
Sistine Madonna, after Raphael, finely dec, period gilt frame, verso imp with scepter mark and "KPM," 10" w, 12" h **$1,955**
Titled "Entflohen," two young beauties seated in windswept wood, diaphanous gowns, floral headbands, anthemion and quatrefoil border, irid teal ground, 22-1/4" d giltwood and gesso frame, 13-3/4" d **$10,925**
Young beauty facing right, sgd "Grenier" lower left, verso imp "K.P.M" with scepter, c1900, ornate 14-1/2" frame, 5" x 7" **$2,300**

Punch bowl, cov, domed lid, Dionysian putto figural finial, enamel dec on one side with 18th C wigged gentleman at a drunken meeting of punch society, similar scene of gentleman at table to one side, vignette of couple outside village on other, floral bouquets and

KPM plaque, hand painted, robed girl with sprig of flowers, raised gilt dec, titled "Carers Garland," signed lower right and stamped on reverse "Made in Germany," framed, 3-1/2" x 2-1/2", **$900.**
Photo courtesy of David Rago Auctions, Inc.

KPM plaque, after Guido Reni, young woman in white turban, gilded frame, 11-1/2" x 10", **$2,400.**
Photo courtesy of David Rago Auctions, Inc.

sprigs, imp basketweave rim, gilt edging, underglaze blue mark, late 19th C, 12" d, 14-1/2" h **$2,775**

Teapot, oval, medallion with floral dec, gilt ground, 6" h **$95**

Vase, baluster, two handles, hp multi-colored florals, celery green ground, 8-1/2" h **$200**

KPM plaque, 11" x 9" portrait of mother and child, gold gilt frame with reticulated leaves, stamped KPM with scepter mark, 17" x 1'4" overall, $2,900.
Photo courtesy of The Early Auction Company, LLC.

KPM plaque, "Fm Reiche der Tone," by A. Lesrel, French nobleman playing violin, gilt frame, KPM mark and scepter, Dresden mark with lamb, 4-3/4" x 7-1/2", $1,800.
Photo courtesy of The Early Auction Company, LLC.

KPM three vases, assorted glazes, all with indigo stamps and numbers, tallest (13" h) with post-factory drilled bottom, price for three, $2,200.
Photo courtesy of David Rago Auctions, Inc.

LEEDS CHINA

History: The Leeds Pottery in Yorkshire, England, began production about 1758. Among its products was creamware that was competitive with that of Wedgwood. The original factory closed in 1820, but various subsequent owners continued until 1880. They made exceptional cream-colored wares, either plain, salt glazed, or painted with colored enamels, and glazed and unglazed redware.

Marks: Early wares are unmarked. Later pieces are marked "Leeds Pottery," sometimes followed by "Hartley-Green and Co." or the letters "LP."

Leeds plate, green scalloped edge, blue and yellow flowers, brown and green leaves, 8-3/4" d, $575.
Photo courtesy of Pook & Pook, Inc..

Reproduction Alert. Reproductions have the same marks as the antique pieces.

Bowl, pearlware, shallow, molded basketwork, pierced loop, rim edged in cobalt blue, 18th C, 8" d **$225**

Charger, yellow urn with double handles and brown swag design holds cobalt blue, brown and yellow flowers, green foliage, blue line detail surrounding dec, scalloped blue father edge, in-the-making separation along inner edge, minor glaze flakes, 14-3/8" d **$1,870**

Chop plate, blue and yellow brown polychrome flowers, green foliage, white ground, blue scalloped feather edge, wear, old chip beneath rim, 11-1/4" d **$825**

Creamer, yellow, brown and green tulip, umber and green sprig design on sides, dark brown stripe on rim and applied handle, flakes on table ring **$800**

Cup and saucer, handleless

Blue, yellow, green and goldenrod floral design, underglaze blue brushed crescent mark **$220**

Brown rim stripes, blue, green, shades of gold, and yellow floral swag, flakes, chips on saucer table ring, stains on cup **$150**

Cup plate

Octagonal, green feathered edge, 4-1/4" d **$200**

Round, green feathered edge, 4" d **$150**

Dish, leaf form, green feathered edge, imp "Rogers," 5-3/4" l **$225**

Egg cup, creamware, reticulated, 2-3/4" **$150**

Medallion, set of 12, black basalt, assorted subjects, shapes and sizes, impressed marks, England, late 19th C, 1-3/4" x 2-5/8" d **$530**

Miniature

Creamer and sugar, blue flower, green and brown buds, tooled handle on 2-3/4" h creamer, minor flake on 2-1/2" h sugar **$350**

Cup and saucer, handleless, pearlware, gold flower, green and brown leaves **$275**

Teapot, cov, yellow bands with green, orange, blue and brown sprigs, flakes, 4" h..............................**$450**

Mug, multicolored polychrome floral dec, 5" h..................................**$250**

Mustard pot, cov, pearlware, cobalt blue bands, minor rim chips, 18th C, 3-3/8" h...................................**$425**

Pepper pot, green feathered edge, roughness, loss on rim and near holes, 4-1/2" h **$200**

Plate

Green feathered edge, patterned design, 8" d **$225**

Pearlware, central floral spray surrounded by trailing vine, brown, ochre, green and blue, feathered blue scalloped edge, 18th C, 10" d **$275**

Platter

Oval, blue feathered edge, 17-1/4" x 14".....................................**$1,600**

Elongated octagonal form, green-feathered edge, rim wear, 19" x 14-1/4".................................**$525**

Sauce boat, underplate, 7-1/2" l, 3-3/4" h sauce boat, 6-1/2" x 5-1/4" underplate, green feathered edge, small crack on base, minor edge roughness...................................**$335**

Teapot, cov, creamware, intertwined ribbed handle, molded floral ends and flower finial, polychrome enameled rose, 4-3/4" h....................**$3,025**

Tureen, cov, cov with pierced rim, melon finial, enamel dec, feather edge trim, floral sprays and wreaths, urn designs, slight edge nicks and enamel flaking, late 18th C, 8-1/2" h **$980**

Waste bowl, blue band, green, gold, mustard and black leaves, minor flakes on table ring, 4-1/4" d, 3" h **$110**

LENOX CHINA

History: In 1889, Jonathan Cox and Walter Scott Lenox established The Ceramic Art Co. at Trenton, New Jersey. By 1906, Lenox formed his own company, Lenox, Inc. Using potters lured from Belleek, Lenox began making an American version of the famous Irish ware. The firm is still in business.

Marks: Older Lenox china has one of two marks: a green wreath or a palette. The palette mark appears on blanks supplied to amateurs who hand painted china as a hobby. The Lenox company currently uses a gold stamped mark.

Bouillon cup and saucer, Detroit Yacht Club, palette mark..............**$85**

Candlesticks, pr, Holiday, pillar, 7-1/2" h................................**$140**

Chocolate set, cov chocolate pot, six cups and saucers, Golden Wheat pattern, cobalt blue ground, 13-pc set **$275**

Coffeepot, Lenox Legend **$170**

Cream soup, Tuxedo, green mark **$40**

Cup and saucer, Alden **$25**

Dinner plate, Montclair, two platinum bands, set of four...............**$195**

Dinner service

Golden Wreath, service for 20, serving pcs, 138 pcs **$650**

Imperial pattern, 12 each dinner plates, salad plates, bread plates, cups, saucers, one platter.........**$275**

Gravy boat and underplate

Biltmore Hotel, New York City, Gorham silver plated lid, base mkd "2047 Lexon 12 oz," lid mkd "The Biltmore 1917 Gorham 02702 Electroplate," 7-1/4" d, 4-3/4" h......**$165**

Tuscany, bird and scroll dec, gold rim **$260**

Honey pot, ivory beehive, gold bee and trim, underplate, 5" h, 6-1/4" d **$85**

Jug, hp, grapes and leaves, shaded brown ground, sgd "G. Morley," 4" h **$250**

Perfume lamp, figural, Marie Antoinette, bisque finish, dated 1929, 9" h **$650**

Platter

Castle Garden, coupe shape, gold trim, small **$200**

Plum Blossoms, medium **$240**

Salt, creamy ivory ground, molded seashells and coral, green wreath mark, 3" d..**$35**

Server, Holiday, oval, 16" x 11"...**$155**

Shoe, white, bow trim..................**$190**

Tankard set, 14-1/2" h tankard, four 5-1/2" h steins, hp by W. Clayton, tippling Monk draining vintage bottle on tankard, different monk posed on each stein, ornate handles, shaded green grounds, wear to gilt at rim interiors................................**$995**

Teapot, Weatherly, coupe shape, platinum trim....................................**$215**

Vase, corset shape, pink orchids dec by William Morley, green stamp mark, artist sgd, 11-3/4" h, 4-1/2" d......**$850**

Vegetable dish, cov, Lenox Legend **$260**

LIMOGES

History: Limoges porcelain has been produced in Limoges, France, for more than a century by numerous factories, in addition to the famed Haviland.

Marks: One of the most frequently encountered marks is "T. & V. Limoges," on the wares made by Tressman and Vought. Other identifiable Limoges marks are "A. L." (A. Lanternier), "J. P. L." (J. Pouyat, Limoges), "M. R." (M. Reddon), "Elite," and "Coronet."

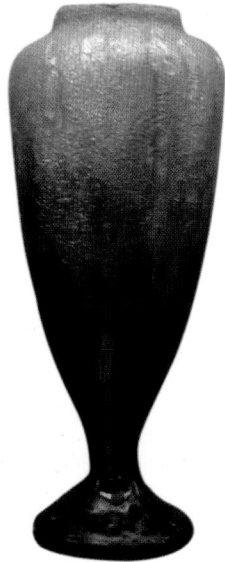

Limoges vase, baluster form, enamel on copper, foil under iridescent glaze graduating from pale pink at neck to dark burgundy at foot, random splotches of yellow on shoulders, glaze on neck and shoulders rough with raised smooth globules giving effect of ice, foot signed "C. Faure, Limoges," restoration to edge of foot, 6" h, **$250.**
Photo courtesy of Alderfer Auction Co.

Limoges punch bowl, grapes and leaves decoration, separate stand with four lion paw feet, 14-3/4" d, 9-3/4" h, **$700.**
Photo courtesy of Joy Luke Auctions.

Limoges fish plate, hand painted, two fish and aquatic plants, gold scrolling border, marked "Souvenir Limoges, T & V France," **$60.**
Photo courtesy of Dotta Auction Co., Inc.

Bowl, ftd, hp, wild roses and leaves, sgd "J. E. Dodge, 1892," 4-1/2" h .. **$85**

Box, cov, cobalt blue and white ground, cupids on lid, pate-sur-pate dec, 4-1/4" sq **$195**

Cache pot, male and female pheasants on front, mountain scene on obverse, gold handles and four ball feet, 7-1/2" w, 9" h.............................. **$225**

Cake plate, ivory ground, brushed gold scalloped rim, gold medallion, marked "Limoges T & V," 11-1/2" d............. **$75**

Candy dish, ftd, two handles, silver overlay, white ground, c1920, 6-1/2" d **$95**

Chocolate pot, purple violets and green leaves, cream-colored ground, gold handle, spout, and base, sgd "Kelly JPL/France," 13" h............. **$350**

Creamer and sugar, cov, purple flowers, white ground, gold handle and trim, 3-1/4" h....................... **$100**

Cup and saucer, hp, roses, gold trim, artist sgd... **$75**

Dessert plates, Laviolette, gilt scalloped rim, printed green husk trim, center violet and grape sprays, retailed by Lewis Straus & Sons, New York, price for 12-pc set, late 19th/early 20th C, 8-1/4" d **$220**

Dresser set, pink flowers, pastel blue, green, and yellow ground, large tray, cov powder, cov rouge, pin tray, talc jar, pr candlesticks, seven-pc set **$425**

Figure, three girls, arms entwined, holding basket of flowers, books and purse, marked "C & V" and "L & L," 25" h, 13" w **$460**

Fish service, 22-3/4" platter, ten 9-1/4" plates, sgd "A. R. Bullock 1894" ..**$1,555**

Hair receiver, blue flowers and white butterflies, ivory ground, gold trim, marked "JPL"........................... **$80**

Lemonade pitcher, matching tray, water lily dec, sgd "Vignard Limoges" **$350**

Nappy, curved gold handle, gold scalloped edges, soft pink blossoms, blue-green ground, 6" d................**$35**

Oyster plate, molded, scalloped edge, gilt rim, enamel dec of poppy sprays, raised gilt detailing, marked "A. Lanternier & Co., Limoges," price for set of eight, early 20th C, 9-1/4" d.......**$1,500**

Panel, enameled, Christ with crown of thorns, framed, 4-1/2" x 3-3/8" ..**$250**

Pitcher, platinum handle, platinum mistletoe berries and leaves, gray and pink ground, Art Deco style, marked "J. P. Limoges, Pouyat," 6" h, 5-1/8" d **$155**

Plaque, enameled, cavalier, after Meissonier, multicolored garb and banner, late 19th C, 7-5/8" x 4-1/2" **$460**

Plate
  Cavalier smoking pipe, marked "Coronet," 9-1/2" d **$90**
  Transfer scene of peacocks and flowers, hp border, 8" d **$290**

Punch bowl, hand painted grapes, marked "T& V Limoges France Depose," minor repairs, 14" d **$320**

Snuff box, cov, hp, wildflowers and gold tracery, pink ground, artist sgd, dated 1800................................ **$200**

Tankard set, five-pc set, hp, grape dec, gold and green ground, 14" h tankard, four mugs **$450**

Tea set, 9-1/2" h cov teapot, two 3" h cups, two 4-1/2" d saucers, 15" d tray, cream ground, floral dec, gold trim, red stamp "L. S. & S. Limoges France," green stamp "Limoges France" on two saucers, slight wear **$500**

Vase, hand painted, sgd "Florence Sladnick," 15" h **$350**

Limoges oyster plate, five oyster-shaped wells, white ground, pink and white roses, green leaves, blue forget-me-not borders, gold trim, signed "GDA France" in black, green wreath mark, **$250.**
Photo courtesy of Wiederseim Associates, Inc.

Limoges oyster plate, five oyster-shaped wells, round center well, white ground, multicolored florals, gold trim, marked "G. D. & Co., Limoges France" in green, "1205" in red, **$195.**

LITHOPHANES

History: Lithophanes are highly translucent porcelain panels with impressed designs. The designs result from differences in the thickness of the plaque; thin parts transmit an abundance of light, while thicker parts represent shadows.

Lithophanes were first made by the Royal Berlin Porcelain Works in 1828. Other factories in Germany, France, and England later produced them. The majority of lithophanes on the market today were made between 1850 and 1900.

Candle shield, panel with scene of two country boys playing with goat, castle in background, 9" h **$275**

Fairy lamp, three panels, lady leaning out of tower, rural romantic scenes, 9" h **$1,250**

Lamp, colored umbrella style shade, four panels of outdoor Victorian scenes, bronze and slate standard, German, 20-3/4" h **$675**

Night lamp, sq, four scenes, irid green porcelain base, gold trim, electrified, 5-1/4" h **$650**

Panel
PPM, view of Paterson Falls, 3-1/4" x 5-1/4" **$190**
PR Sickle, scene of two women in doorway, dog, and two pigeons, sgd, #1320, 4-1/4" x 5" **$100**

Unmarked, Madonna and Child, 6" x 7-1/2" **$175**

Pitcher, puzzle type, Victorian scene, nude on bottom **$175**

Stein, regimental, half liter **$200**

Tea warmer, one-pc cylindrical panel, four seasonal landscapes with children, copper frame, finger grip and molded base, 5-7/8" h **$250**

LIVERPOOL CHINA

History: Liverpool is the name given to products made at several potteries in Liverpool, England, between 1750 and 1840. Seth and James Pennington and Richard Chaffers were among the early potters who made tin-enameled earthenware.

By the 1780s, tin-glazed earthenware gave way to cream-colored wares decorated with cobalt blue, enameled colors, and blue or black transfers.

Bubbles and frequent clouding under the foot rims characterize the Liverpool glaze. By 1800, about 80 potteries were working in the town producing not only creamware, but soft paste, soapstone and bone porcelain.

A transfer of the *Caroline* also was used on a Sunderland bowl about 1936 and reproduction mugs were made bearing the name "James Leech" and an eagle.

The reproduction pieces have a crackled glaze and often age cracks have been artificially produced. When compared to genuine pieces, reproductions are thicker and heavier and have weaker transfers, grayish color (not as crisp and black), ecru or gray body color instead of cream, and crazing that does not spiral upward.

Reproduction Alert. Reproduction Liverpool pieces were documented as early as 1942. One example is a black transfer-decorated jug made in the 1930s. The jugs vary in height from 8-1/2 to 11 inches. On one side is "The Shipwright's Arms"; on the other, the ship Caroline flying the American flag; and under the spout, a wreath with the words "James Leech."

Bowl, creamware
Black transfer printed, polychrome enamel dec, int. with American sailing vessel *Apollo*, border of military devices, ext. with nautical themes, coat of arms, vignette of lovers holding heart, above inscription "J. & S. Appleton," green, yellow, red, white and blue enamels, imperfections, 11-3/8" d **$5,875**

Black transfer printed, polychrome enamel dec, int. with British sailing ship, red, white, blue, gold and green enamels above inscription "James and Sarah Venn Bridgewater, 1796," rim dec with military devices, outside with vignettes of "Poor Jack," and "Billy's Farewell," sea creatures and mermaids, imperfections, 10-7/8" d **$560**

Cup and saucer, handleless, black transfer, bust of Washington and other gentleman on cup, "Washington, His Country's Father" on saucer, hairlines in cup **$330**

Jug, creamware
Black transfer printed and polychrome dec, obverse American Militia, oval scenic reserve with militiaman with flag, ships, and armament, surrounded by inscription, reverse with American sailing vessel above banner inscribed "Success to Trade," American eagle with Jefferson quote, red, blue, green and yellow enamels, yellow highlight around rim, minor imperfections, dated 1802 under spout, 8-3/4" h
.... **$3,525**

Black transfer printed, "L. Insurgent and Constellation, Feb 10, 1799," depicting naval battle with American frigate on left, French frigate on right, inscription beneath each, reverse "Shipbuilding," oval wreath inscribed "Success to the Wooden Walls of America" beneath spout, imperfections, 8-3/4" h **$1,650**

Black transfer printed, obverse with mortally wounded officer surrounded by his aides, successful sharpshooter waves his cap from background, reverse with British Man-of-War, beneath spout and rim dec with floral devices, imperfections, 10-1/2" h **$1,650**

Transfer printed, imperfections, obverse with Commodore Preble, reverse with Commodore Prebles Squadron Attacking the City of Tripoli Aug. 3, 1804, 9-1/8" h, 5" d **$2,185**

Transfer printed, obverse with compass and verse, reverse with The Sailors Adieu, minor imperfections, 7-1/4" h, 3-1/2" d **$750**

Transfer printed, obverse with Salem Shipyard and verse, revere with transfer printed with polychrome enamels of Boston Frigate, transfer "LW" in cartouche above eagle and shield, imperfections, 10-1/4" h, 4-7/8" d **$4,890**

Transfer printed, obverse with ship *Massachusetts*, reverse with map of Newburyport Harbor with "Success to the Commerce of Newburyport" on other, gilt embellishments, circular reserve of Columbia, minor imperfections, 11-3/4" h, 6-5/8" d **$14,950**

Transfer printed, obverse with The Sailor's Return, reverse with courting couple above verse "A Sailor's life's a pleasant life..." on other, motto reserve below spout "From Rocks & Sands and every ill..." imperfections, 8" h, 4" d **$550**

Transfer printed, obverse with three-masted ship, reverse with The Joiners Arms, eagle and shield below spout, repaired, 11-1/2" h, 5-3/4" d **$865**

Transfer printed, obverse with Washington, Liberty, and Franklin viewing map of early 19th C US, reverse with three-masted ship painted with polychrome enamels, eagle and shield, standing figure of Hope below spout, imperfections, 9" h, 4-3/4" d **$990**

Transfer printed and painted with polychrome enamels, imperfections, obverse with Hope, reverse with three-masted ship flying American flag, American eagle below spout with Jefferson quote, dated 1804, 9-1/4" h, 4-5/8" d **$3,740**

Transfer printed and painted with polychrome enamels, obverse with Boston Fusilier, reverse with "United We Stand, Divided We Fall," eagle and shield below spout, imperfections, 9-1/2" h, 4-1/2" d **$17,250**

Transfer printed and painted with polychrome enamels, repaired, obverse with Proscribed Patriots, reverse with "Success to America whose Militia...," eagle and shield with Jefferson quote dated 1802 below spout, 10" h, 5" d **$3,220**

Jug, pearlware, black transfer printed, obverse with American eagle with ribbon in its beak, inscribed "E. Pluribus Unum," 15 scattered stars above its head, reverse with vignette of embracing couple, fleet of sailing vessels below spout, rim dec with scattered blossoms, black enamel highlights on rim, shoulder, and handle edges, minor imperfections, 6-1/4" h **$1,120**

Plate, black transfer printed, ten are dec with sailing vessels, one inscribed "Returning Hopes" with lady waiting for return of her lover's ship, minor imperfections, price for 11 pc set, 10" d **$1,570**

Sauce boat, oval, paneled sides, underglaze blue floral dec, attributed to Pennington & Part, c1780, 5-3/4" l **$460**

Tureen, cov, domed cov with oval handle, round base, black transfer dec on lid, int., and ext. depicting figure flanked by two coat-of-arm shields, two monograms "TF" and "BW" within oval, imperfections, 12-1/4" d, 9-1/2" h **$1,100**

LLADRÓ PORCELAINS

History: Brothers Vicente, Jose, and Juan Lladró formally incorporated themselves as a company in 1953 and, by 1955, were selling their early porcelain creations in their own retail shop in Valencia, Spain. By 1958, they had acquired the land to build a small factory, probably not operational until the early 1960s. The factory underwent at least one major renovation and expansion, which went online in 1969, also the year of first export to the United States. Today, Lladró exports all over the globe. Management of the company has passed to the second generation of the Lladró family, with the aging founders in retirement.

Lladró is entirely hand-made of fine porcelain, with many molds and artisans involved in the production of each item, and using traditional porcelain-making techniques that have changed little in the centuries since the famous Meissen manufactory of Germany first developed them. This intimate connection between artisan and product accounts for why the product is so expensive. Lladró is famous for its flowerwork, in which each stamen, petal, and leaf is separately applied, and items with flowerwork in mint condition command premium prices on the secondary market.

Oldest Lladró items found on today's secondary market would have been fired as early as the mid-1960s, and some of these made their way to the United States in tourist suitcases prior to 1969. Marks of these oldest items are impressed or etched into the porcelain base and include the word "Lladró" as well as the words "Made in Spain" and sometimes "España" (Spanish for "Spain"). The famous Lladró cobalt blue backstamp was first used in the late 1960s to early 1970s, with the accent missing, in this first mark, from the "o" in Lladró. The mark went through several minor changes throughout the 80s and 90s.

"Seconds" are sold at the factory in Spain and in the company's "outlet" stores in the U.S. Seconds are indicated by the scraping off of the logo flower in the backstamp. Serious collectors avoid these, as they are worth only a fraction of the value of a first-quality piece.

As Lladró has grown in popularity and value, the backstamp has also been counterfeited. Counterfeit marks have disproportionately large accent marks over the "o" and are a pale grayish purple in color rather than the deep cobalt blue of the genuine mark.

Other genuine Lladró and Lladró-affiliated brands have included NAO (which is still in production), Zaphir, and Golden Memories. Production of the latter two brands ceased more than a decade ago, but they are still seen on the secondary market. Each can be readily identified by its own unique backstamp. Although NAO is generally considered to be not as valuable as regular Lladró-marked pieces, its secondary market values have heated up as collectors seek a more affordable alternative to Lladró's expensive regular collection. NAO is also found with older, impressed marks.

Lladró has many Valencian competitors who are working "in the Lladró style," but such products have little or no following among serious collectors.

Adviser: Peggy Whiteneck

Listings in the follwoing Lladró section are © Peggy Whiteneck, used with permission.

Note: The letter "G" following the item number indicates the glazed finish. The letter "M" indicates a matte finish. **All photos appear courtesy of Lladró, USA, Inc.**

Core Collection

#311.13, Boy with Bull [small boy with bull calf out in front of him on a tether (Ret. c 1965)...... **$2,000-$2,500**

#323.13, Flirt [small Peke-style dog, considered extremely rare] (Ret. c1971)................. **$1,800-$1,850**

#1006G, Pan with Cymbals [small satyr seated on column and holding cymbals] (Ret. 1975)......... **$500-$650**

#1007G, Pan with Pipes [small satyr seated on column and playing pan flute] (Ret. 1975) .... **$500-$650**

#1008G, Satyr Group [pan with cymbals seated on column, pan with pan flute seated on ground] (Ret. 1975)
.... **$800-$1,000**

#1031G/M, Sancho Panza [sitting on stool, legs out before him, hat on knee] (Ret. 1989)............... **$500-$600**

#1037G, Horseman [considered very rare, man sits on horse with its head lowered to graze; man's upper torso turned to look back] (Ret. 1970)
.... **$1,500-$1,700**

#1038G, Girl with Turkeys [girl with basket on arm, pair of turkeys at feet] (Ret. 1978) .... **$450-$550**

#1040G/M, Girl with Letter [elongated figure holding letter and standing in front of jar] (Ret. 1978)
.... **$400-$450**

#1041G/M, Hen [pecking at ground] (Ret. 1975) .... **$325-$350**

#1042G/M, Hen [alert, head raised] (Ret. 1975) .... **$250-$350**

#1043G/M, Cock [alert rooster, bushier tail than hens] (Ret. 1975)
.... **$300-$350**

#1064G/M, Deer [small, reclining] (Ret. 1986) .... **$325-$425**

#1062G, Bull with Head Down [spotted colorings] (Ret. 1975)
.... **$1,100-$1,250**

#1063G, Bull with Head Up [solid coloring] (Ret. 1975) ...... **$925-$1,100**

#1091G, Girl and Gazelle [young woman feeding baby gazelle as mother-gazelle looks on] (Ret. 1975)
.... **$1,500-$2,000**

#1121G, Pups in a Box [four dogs in a packing crate] (Ret. 1971)
.... **$1,200-$1,800**

#1149G, Dog's Head [head of hound dog] (Ret. 1981)................. **$400-$450**

#1151G, Two Elephants [mother with small baby trailing, both with trunks extended] (Ret. 1999) ...... **$450-$475**

#1163G, Soldier with Saber [child in uniform, saber held up against shoulder; white jacket w/blue piping, blue pants] (Ret. 1978)
.... **$375-$400**

#1164G, Soldier with Gun [blue jacket with gold piping, white pants, rifle standing at side] (Ret. 1978)
.... **$375-$400**

#1165G, Soldier with Flag [flag formed from gun barrel held at side, blue jacket, white pants] (Ret. 1978)
.... **$475-$500**

#1166G, Soldier with Cornet [boy soldier blowing horn, blue jacket, white pants] (Ret. 1978)............. **$475-$500**

#1167G, Soldier with Drum [blue jacket, white pants] (Ret. 1978)
.... **$475-$500**

#1251G/M, Pony Ride [girl and smaller boy riding pony] (Ret. 1979)
.... **$1,200-$1,400**

#1300G, Bird and Butterfly [bird with wings spread looking at butterfly

Lladró, "Illusion" (#1413G), issued in 1982, **$275.**

Lladró, "Platero and Marcellino" (#1181G), issued in 1971 and retired in 1989, **$350-$450.**

Lladró, "Hunters" (#1048G/M), first issued in the late 1960s and retired in 1985, 18" tall, **$1,400 to $1,600.**

Lladró, "Sad Chimney Sweep" (#1253G), issued in 1974 and retired in 1983, 17" tall, **$1,200-$1,300.**

perched on one of two flowers] (Ret. 1985)......................... **$800-$950**

#1341G, Jockey [seated jockey, no horse, holding riding crop, looking left] (Ret. 1979) .... **$600-$625**

#1345G, Sacristan [elderly sacristan in vestments holding lamp on pole] (Ret. 1979) .... **$2,100-$2,300**

#1367G, Playful Dogs [two poodles with tipped-over basket] (Ret. 1982) .... **$750-$800**

#2000, Monkeys [Gres, mother monkey with infant] (Ret. 1975) .... **$500-$600**

#2001, Cat [Gres, brown cat with large eyes, body crouching low to ground] (Ret. 1975) .... **$600-$625**

#2019, Owl [squat, stylized Gres] (Ret. 1973) .... **$425-$450**

#2037, Hedeghog [seldom seen, Gres] (Ret. 1973) .... **$350-$400**

#2044, Horse Head [very large Gres sculpture of horse's head] (Ret. 1975) .... **$500-$600**

#2052, Magistrates [Gres, two Jewish lawyers in ancient garb] (Ret. 1981) .... **$950-$1,200**

#2055, Harlequin [Gres three-quarter figure of harlequin with right hand touching hip] (Ret. 1978) .... **$1,400-$1,500**

#2067, Dogs Bust [Gres, heads of two young dogs with collars] (Ret. 1979) .... **$800-$900**

#2084, Don Quixote Dreaming [Gres, Don Quixote sitting on stack of books, chin resting on right hand, left hand on knee] (Ret. 1985) .... **$1,800-$2,100**

#2087, Big Partridge [Gres, 9" tall] (Ret. 1981) .... **$375-$400**

#2088, Small Partridge [Gres, 5" tall] (Ret. 1981) .... **$225-$300**

#2204, Farmyard Grace [Gres, Franciscan monk in apron feeding small animals at feet] (Ret. 1991) .... **$300-$325**

#3516, Jesus Christ [Gres figure of Christ with arms extended in classic pose] (Ret. 1988) .... **$1,800-$1,975**

#4502G/M, Marketing Day [woman in white apron and shawl, market basket on arm, cloth bundle on head] (Ret. 1985).................. **$375-$400**

#4503G/M, Seated Harlequin [elongated reclining harlequin holding guitar] (Ret. 1975) .... **$400-$550**

#4514G/M, Diana [elongated figure of woman in kerchief standing in front of gazelle-like deer cran-

ing its neck around her] (Ret. 1981) .... **$750-$850**

#4515G/M, Man on Horse [man in formal riding habit and top hat astride a rearing horse] (Ret. 1985) .... **$1,100-$1,300**

#4517G, Boy Student [tall, elongated figure leaning against pile of rocks, reaching from book held in right hand] (Ret. 1978) .... **$475-$500**

#4525G, Turkeys [pair, tom and hen] (Ret. 1972) .... **$450-$475**

#4570G, Girl with Goat [elongated figure of seated shepherdess next to standing goat] (Ret. 1978) .... **$650-$700**

#4571G/M, Resting [shepherd sitting on rock, leaning on right arm, ewe and lamb on knees at his feet] (Ret. 1981).................. **$400-$475**

#4587G, Rooster [rooster with colored plumage, posturing body to ground, tail in air—8" high (Ret. 1979) .... **$375-$450**

#4588G/M, White Cockerel [same as 4587, in white] (Ret. 1979) .... **$300-$325**

#4589G/M, Small Rooster [same as 4588 but smaller—7" high] (Ret. 1981) .... **$275-$300**

#4594G/M, Lady with Greyhound [lady in long dress and hat held on by scarf, holding closed umbrella and standing with greyhound dog] (Ret. 1981).................. **$700-$850**

#4604G, Bread and Water [classic elongated Lladró style, two women walking with arms linked, one holding bread, the other a jug] (Ret. 1972) .... **$650-$675**

#4617G/M, Group of Musicians [seated boy with base drum and standing boy with horn] (Ret. 1979) .... **$500-$550**

#4622G/M, Old Man with Violin [man in long coat and hat, violin under arm] (Ret. 1982) .... **$650-$750**

#4628G, Hen and Chicks [mother hen looking down at chick poking its head out from under her] (Ret. 1972) .... **$900-$950**

#4653G/M, Orchestra Conductor [conductor behind podium, right arm extended forward] (Ret. 1979) .... **$850-$950**

#4660G/M, Shepherdess with Dove [reclining shepherdess, dove next to her on branch] (Ret. 1993) .... **$250-$300**

#4731G, German Shepherd with Pup [reclining in dog basket] (Ret. 1975) .... **$950-$1,000**

#4732G/M, Artist [man walking forward in businesses hat and suit, canvas held under left arm, paint box carried in right hand] (Ret. 1976) .... **$725-$900**

#4755G, Boy with Dog [reclining boy leaning against rock, dog resting paws on leg] (Ret. 1978) .... **$400-$450**

#4756G, Girl with Goat [reclining girl next to reclining goat] (Ret. 1978) .... **$400-$500**

#4762G/M, Dentist [wearing dentist's smock with tools in front pocket, right hand raised at right angle] (Ret. 1978).................................. **$500-$550**

#4798G/M, Female Tennis Player [leaning against wall, ankles crossed, racket under left arm] (Ret. 1981) .... **$350-$450**

#4800G/M, Gypsy with Brother [little girl carrying baby brother on back; baby has finger in mouth] (Ret. 1979)................................ **$425-$550**

#4809M, Going Fishing [matte version] (Ret. 1991) .... **$200-$225**

#4811G/M, Dutch Boy [boy in Dutch clothing and cap, pail in each hand] (Ret. 1988) .... **$350-$400**

#4814G, Little Girl with Turkey [standing, with long hair, holding tom turkey with fanned tail] (Ret. 1981) .... **$450-$475**

#4827G/M, Caressing a Little Calf [kneeling girl caressing reclining calf] (Ret. 1981) .... **$550-$600**

#4829G/M, Swan [stylized swan with head tucked, wings rounded] (Ret. 1983) .... **$400-$450**

#4840G/M, Oriental Girl [kneeling Japanese girl in traditional dress, arranging pot of-flowers on low table] (Ret. 1947)............... **$550-$600**

#4853G, Cobbler [seated man in porkpie cap and workman's apron holds shoe sole up on lap, cobbler's hammer in right hand] (Ret. 1985) .... **$650-$725**

#4856G/M, Waltz Time [two children dancing, she in long skirt and hat leaning away from him as he leans in to steal a kiss] (Ret. 1985) .... **$425-$450**

#4861G, Horse [Percheron horse grooming rear hoof] (Ret. 1978) .... **$500-$550**

#4888G, The Kiss [girl hugging seated fireman in full gear] (Ret. 1983) .... **$700-$775**

#4956G, Tavern Drinkers [three obviously inebriated male revelers hoist a cup, middle figure seated, right figure bent at waist, left figure down on one knee] (Ret. 1985)......... **$3,250-$3,500**

#4965G, Little Red Riding Hood [looking down at crouching wolf] (Ret. 1983).................................. **$500-$575**

#4966G, Tennis Player Puppet [caricature tennis player in visored cap, ball in one hand, racket under other arm] (Ret. 1985) .... **$600-$650**

#4971G, Hunter Puppet [caricature in visored hat holding rifle, reclining dog wrapped around feet] (Ret. 1985).................................. **$675-$800**

#5025G, A Clean Sweep [young girl in long dress and apron, standing with old-fashioned broom, handle leaning on her shoulder as her hands are held as if she were applauding] (Ret. 1985) .... **$350-$400**

#5029G, The Flower Peddler [boy on pedal-powered cart full of flowers] (Ret. 1985) .... **$1,350-$1,500**

#5031G, Girl with Flowers in Tow [girl riding three-wheel bicycle pulling basketful of flowers] (Ret. 1985) .... **$1,700-$1,800**

#5037G, Sleigh Ride [very large figure of two children on sled hitched to dog] (Ret. 1996)........... **$1,400-$1,500**

#5046G, Organ Grinder [old man with white beard, long coat, and hat, carrying monkey on shoulder, man cranking organ hung around neck] (Ret. 1981)............................... **$1650-$1750**

#5049G, At the Pond [boy and girl feeding two swans] (Ret. 1981) .... **$650-$750**

#5057G, Clown with Violin [clown with head down holding violin behind back] (Ret. 1985) .... **$800-$850**

#5058G, Clown with Concertina [clown seated, head in hands, concertina on ground behind feet] (Ret. 1985) .... **$600-$625**

#5059G, Clown with Saxophone [seated clown in pointed hat holding saxophone and looking down at Dalmatian puppy] (Ret. 1985) .... **$700-$725**

#5070G, Napping [little boy asleep in big armchair, feet dangling] (Ret. 1983) .... **$650-$800**

#5078G, Teasing the Dog [little girl in bonnet holding ball on string just out of reach of dog up on hind legs] (Ret. 1985) ... **$500-$600**

#5085G, Angelic Harmon [seated girl angel caressing

Lladró, "A Lady of Taste" (#1495G), issued in 1986, **$1,100.**

Lladró, "Egyptian Cat, Black" (#2130), Gres, issued in 1983 and retired in 1985, 13" tall, **$450-$650.**

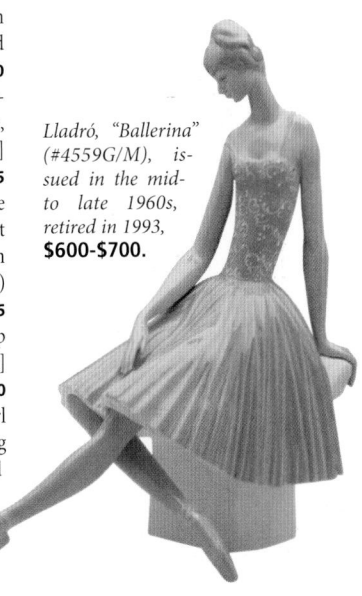

Lladró, "Ballerina" (#4559G/M), issued in the mid-to late 1960s, retired in 1993, **$600-$700.**

Lladró, "Hunter with Dog" (#5002G/M), 1978-1979, **$1,250-$1,300.**

Lladró, "Pottery Seller" (#5079G), issued in 1980, retired in 1985, **$650-$750.**

Lladró, "The Fireman" (#5976G), retired in 1997, **$500-$600.**

puppy in arms while standing girl angel looks on] (Ret. 1997) .... **$600-$650**

#5111G/M, Baffled [seated bloodhound looking confused] (Ret. 1985) .... **$550-$600**

#5116G/M, Young Matador [child matador in full costume, holding cape against body with right hand, left hand raised] (Ret. 1985) .... **$325-$500**

#5132G/M, Miguel de Cervantes [writer in ruffled collar, seated in chair, cape draped over lap and arm, quill held in right hand] (Ret. 1988) .... **$1,200-$1,600**

#5137G/M, Billy Baseball Player [in uniform at bat] (Ret. 1983) .... **$700-$750**

#5138G/M, Billy Golfer [golf club back for a swing] (Ret. 1983) ... **$800-$1,000**

#5147G, "I" Is for Ivy [girl holding dot atop the vowel I] (Ret. 1985) .... **$550-$600**

#5148G, "O" Is for Olivia [girl sitting inside vowel O, chin in hands] (Ret. 1985) .... **$450-$575**

#5149G, "U" Is for Ursula [girl standing inside the vowel U] (Ret. 1985), ... **$525-$550**

#5161G, Old Fashioned Motorist [man on motorcycle, woman in sidecar] (Ret. 1985) ..... **$2,800-$3,000**

#5176G/M, Lady Lying on Divan [reclining woman in 1920s dress, holding long cigarette holder and listening to old-fashioned Victrola with large horn] (Ret. 1985) .... **$1,400-$1,500**

#5178G, Stubborn Donkey [boy pulling bridle of donkey sitting down on job while small dog looks on; saddle bags carry water jars] (Ret. 1993) .... **$500-$525**

#5194G, Roving Photographer [man in porkpie hat and long workman's coat with cloth dangling from right pocket stands carrying old-fashioned camera tripod over shoulder] (Ret. 1985) .... **$1,700-$1,900**

#5288G, Mallard Duck [swimming male] (Ret. 1994) .... **$550-$600**

#5303G/M, Playing with the Ducks [kneeling girl and seated boy feeding ducks at pond] (Ret. 1990) .... **$600-$800**

#5305G, Visit with Granny [toddler sitting on piano bench next to grandmother in shawl] (Ret. 1993) .... **$600-$625**

#5315G, Miniature Dromedary [reclining camel] (Ret. 1990) .... **$150-$175**

#5319G/M, Wistful Centaur Girl [reclining centaur with flowers in hair and holding bouquet] (Ret. 1990) .... **$375-$450**

#5331G, Gymnast with Ring [girl on stomach, working ring with left hand and foot] (Ret. 1988) .... **$300-$425**

#5332G, Gymnast Balancing Ball [gymnast on floor, leaning on left elbow, right leg raised, ball balanced on right hand] (Ret. 1988) .... **$300-$375**

#5336G, Aerobics Scissor Figure [girl in leotard, body to side, supported by right arm, legs scissored] (Ret. 1988) .... **$250-$300**

#5337G, La Giaconda [Mona Lisa, bust] (Ret. 1988) .... **$400-$600**

#5351G, Woe Is Me [seated beagle looking up, one paw raised] (Ret. 1990) .... **$200-$250**

#5356G, Wolfhound [seated, 4" high, very long nose] (Ret. 1990) .... **$200-$250**

#5359G, El Greco [the famed artist in ruffled collar stands before a dais topped by a pot of paint brushes, palette held in his left hand] (Ret. 1990) .... **$750-$825**

#5377G, Can Can [two female dancers swishing skirts, one with leg extended up and out] (Ret. 1990) .... **$1,200-$1,400**

#5380G, Sweet Harvest [three young boys seated surrounded by harvest produce, one on far right is holding up a bunch of grapes from basket at feet while middle boy looks on, boy on far left smokes an illicit cigarette] (Ret. 1990) .... **$850-$875**

#5403G, The Drummer Boy [in uniform, white jacket with red piping, blue pants, white plume on helmet] (Ret. 1990) .... **$400-$450**

#5404G, Cadet Captain [in uniform, saber against shoulder; white jacket with red piping, white plume in helmet] (Ret. 1990) .... **$375-$400**

#5407G, At Attention [cadet standing at attention, white jacket with red piping, white plume in hat] (Ret. 1990) .... **$325-$350**

#5433G, Kangaroo [mother kanga with joey in pouch] (Ret. 1990) .... **$225-$300**

#5436G, Lion [miniature recumbent lion with mane] (Ret. 1990) .... **$200-$250**

#5437G, Rhino [miniature] (Ret. 1990).................... **$175-$200**

#5438G, Elephant [miniature] (Ret. 1990).................... **$250-$275**

#5550G, Serene Moment (Blue) [standing blue-habited nun in white winged veil, holding vase with flower] (Ret. 1993) .... **$250-$275**

#5552G, Morning Chores (Blue) [blue-habited nun in apron, holding bucket and broom] (Ret. 1993) .... **$250-$275**

#5552.3G/M, Morning Chores (White) (Ret. 1991) .... **$250-$275**

#5592G, Male Siamese Dancer [dancer in traditional costume with right hand raised in traditional dance posture] (Ret. 1993) .... **$450-$550**

#5593G, Siamese Dancer [female Siamese dancer in traditional costume, left hand raised, right lowered] (Ret. 1993).................... **$400-$550**

#5595G, Joy in a Basket [girl with puppies in basket] (Ret. 1997)' .... **$300-$350**

#5658G, Venetian Carnival [young couple in carnival costume—hers with huge, double-ruffled collar—lean into each other; masks for comedy and tragedy adorn front of base] (Ret. 1993) .... **$650-$700**

#5679G, In No Hurry [girl on tricycle at rest, puppy at feet] (Ret. 1994) .... **$650-$700**

#5733G, Horticulturist [man in old fashioned clothing, including lace cravat, kneeling to plant a tree] (Ret. 1993).................... **$495-$550**

#5753G, Hold Her Still! [boy milking goat held by girl] (Ret. 1993) .... **$700-$750**

#5795G, Floral Getaway [girl on scooter with sidecar full of flowers] (Ret. 1993).................... **$750-$825**

#5804G/M, Playing Tag [three naked toddlers running] (Ret. 1993) .... **$250-$300**

#5843G, A Quiet Afternoon [elderly couple in old-fashioned garb sitting on park bench feeding pigeons; pigeon is perched on her hand] (Ret. 1995).......................... **$1,200-$1,250**

#5852G, Easter Bonnets [girl in hat with round hat box hanging from one arm, square box on ground beside her] (Ret. 1993) .... **$400-$450**

#6229G, Contented Companion [little girl with brush astride a reclining Saint Bernard] (Ret. 2000) .... **$200-$225**

#6233G/M, Chef's Apprentice [boy chef in tall chef's hat and bowtie, seated on floor getting ready to peel a sack of potatoes] (Ret. 1998) .... **$300-$325**

#6234G/M, The Great Chef [little boy with tall chef's hat carrying huge pot with cover] (Ret. 1998) .... **$225-$235**

#6242G/M, Winged Companions [Pegasus on cloud looking at small bird on upturned hoof] (Ret. 1999) .... **$300-$350**

#6248G, Regatta [racing sailboat tilting over waves] (Ret. 1996) .... **$700-$725**

#6273G, Pharmacist [standing pharmacist in full white apron holding mortar and pestle] (Ret. 2000) .... **$300-$325**

#6286G/M, Tennis Champion [on knees with arms, head, and racket raised in victory] (Ret. 1999) .... **$350-$400**

#6288G/M, Taking Flight [white dove with wings active to take off] (Ret. 1999) .... **$165-$175**

#6299G, Little Bear [toddler girl sitting in high chair holding teddy bear in arms] (Ret. 1999) .... **$300-$325**

#6300G, Rubber Ducky [boy toddler in baseball cap sitting in high chair, rubber ducky on tray] (Ret. 2000) .... **$300-$325**

#6304G, Bass Drummer [boy in band uniform leaning over bass drum, front of which says "Music Band"] (Ret. 1998) .... **$400-$450**

#6318G, Little Distraction [boy with chin in hands sitting before a pile of books, top one open with bird perched on it] (Ret. 1999) .... **$350-$375**

#6319G, Beautiful Rhapsody [girl in long dress playing flute in front of music stand] (Ret. 2001) .... **$475-$500**

#6332G, Concerto [girl in broad-brimmed hat playing cello and reading from music stand] (Ret. 2002) .... **$500-$525**

#6340G, Sweet Country [female Country-Western singer playing banjo] (Ret. 1998) .... **$750-$800**

Lladró, "The Rabbi" (#6209G), 1995-1997, **$400-$425.**

Lladró, "Goya Lady" (#5125G/M), issued in 1982, retired in 1990, **$300-$350.**

LUSTER WARE

History: Lustering on a piece of pottery creates a metallic, sometimes iridescent, appearance. Josiah Wedgwood experimented with the technique in the 1790s. Between 1805 and 1840, lustered earthenware pieces were created in England by makers such as Adams, Bailey and Batkin, Copeland and Garrett, Wedgwood and Enoch Wood.

Luster decorations often were used in conjunction with enamels and transfers. Transfers used for luster decoration covered a wide range of public and domestic subjects. They frequently were accompanied by pious or sentimental doggerel, as well as phrases that reflected on the humors of everyday life.

Copper luster was created by the addition of a copper compound to the glaze. It was very popular in America during the 19th century, and collecting it became a fad from the 1920s to the 1950s. Today it has a limited market.

Using a gold mixture made pink luster. Silver luster pieces were first covered completely with a thin coating of a "steel luster" mixture, containing a small quantity of platinum oxide. An additional coating of platinum, worked in water, was then applied before firing.

Sunderland is a coarse type of cream-colored earthenware with a marbled or spotted pink luster decoration, which shades from pink to purple. A solution of gold compound applied to the white body developed the many shades of pink.

The development of electroplating in 1840 created a sharp decline in the demands for metal-surfaced earthenware.

Reproduction Alert. The market for copper luster has been softened by reproductions, especially creamers and the "polka" jug, which may fool new buyers. Reproductions are heavier in appearance and weight than the earlier pieces.

Luster ware tea set, covered teapot, creamer and sugar, silver luster on white ground, England, **$125.**

Canary

Child's mug, "A Present for Charles," pink luster trim, minor wear, 1-3/4" h **$625**

Miniature, creamer, red and green flowers, pink luster accents and rim, pinpoint flake, 2-3/4" h **$850**

Pitcher, baluster form, low neck and spout, sides printed with scenes titled "Attempt before the guard…," On Guard, Single Stick, Staffordshire, c1810, 6-1/4" l, 6" h **$220**

Copper

Goblet, mauve and green colored band with floral dec around mid section, c1850, 3" d, 3-3/4" h **$85**

Pitcher, blue band with molded flower dec on both sides, copper luster bulbous base, 4" h **$50**

Tea cup and saucer, turquoise blue background, copper luster floral band **$65**

Vase, two handles, stag scene, 7-1/4" w, 6-1/2" h **$70**

Pink

Child's mug, pink luster band, reddish hunter and dogs transfer, green highlighted foliate transfer, 2" h ... **$85**

Creamer, stylized flower band, pink luster highlights and rim, ftd, 4-3/8" h **$75**

Cup and saucer, magenta transfers, Faith, Hope and Charity, applied green enamel highlights, pink luster line borders **$60**

Figure, dogs, white, luster gilt collar, cobalt blue base with gilt trim, Staffordshire, pr, 4-1/2" h **$620**

Pitcher, emb ribs, eagle, and flowers in pink and purple luster, 5-3/4" h **$150**

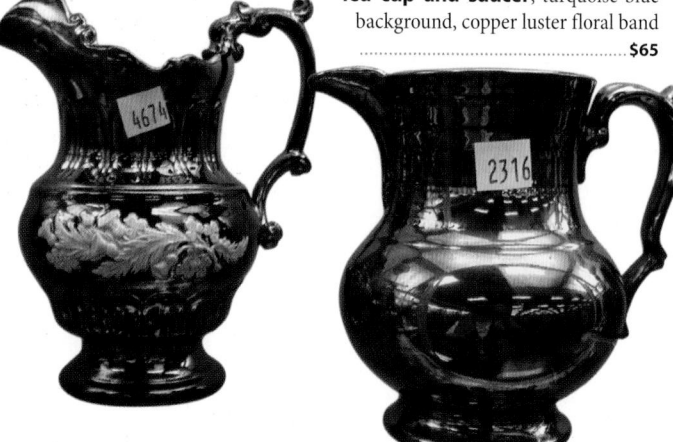

Two copper luster ware pitchers, left: applied blue and white swirled decoration, ornate scrolled handle, **$95;** *right: plain,* **$75.**

Luster ware creamer, copper luster, wide cream-colored band, two panels of rust transfer depicting woman listening to musician, band of magenta and rust leaf garland decoration on cream ground, small spout flake, 6-1/4" w spout to handle, 5-1/2" h, **$80.**

Photo courtesy of Alderfer Auction Co.

MAASTRICHT WARE

History: Petrus Regout founded the De Sphinx Pottery in 1836 in Maastricht, Holland. The firm specialized in transfer-printed earthenwares. Other factories also were established in the area, many employing English workmen and adopting their techniques. Maastricht china was exported to the United States in competition with English products.

Bowl, red, green, and blue agate pattern, "Petrous Regout, Maastricht" and lion mark, 5-3/4" d **$35**

Cup and saucer, Oriental pattern, c1929, 3-1/4" d, 2" h cup **$25**

Pitcher, rooster with iris and leaves, red transfer, marked "Regout & Co. Haan," 5" h **$75**

Plate

Rusty brown border, pink and yellow roses in center, Royal Sphinx mark, c1891, 7-1/2" d **$50**

Timor pattern, 8-1/4" d **$30**

Canton pattern, Geisha girls and man on walkway, marked "Canton, P.

Regout Maastricht," c1836, 8-1/2" d **$40**

Delft, blue and white windmill scene, Royal Sphinx mark, 10" d **$50**

Platter, gaudy polychrome florals, red, yellow, and green white ground, 11-1/2" d **$70**

MAJOLICA

History: Majolica, an opaque, tin-glazed pottery, has been produced in many countries for centuries. It was named after the Spanish island of Majorca, where figuline—a potter's clay—is found. Today, however, the term "majolica" denotes a type of pottery made during the last half of the 19th century in Europe and America.

Majolica frequently depicts elements of nature: leaves, flowers, birds and fish. Designs were painted on the soft-clay body using vitreous colors and fired under a clear lead glaze to impart the rich color and brilliance characteristic of majolica.

Victorian decorative art philosophy dictated that the primary function of design was to attract the eye; usefulness was secondary. Majolica was a welcome and colorful change from the familiar blue and white wares, creamwares and white ironstone of the day.

Marks: Wedgwood, George Jones, Holdcraft and Minton were a few of the English majolica manufacturers who marked their wares. Most of their pieces can be identified through the English Registry mark and/or the potter-designer's mark. Sarreguemines in France and Villeroy and Boch in Baden, Germany, produced majolica that compared favorably with the finer English majolica. Most Continental pieces had an incised number on the base.

Although 600-plus American potteries produced majolica between 1850 and 1900, only a handful chose to identify their wares. Among these manufacturers were George Morely, Edwin Bennett, the Chesapeake Pottery Company, the New Milford-Wannoppee Pottery Company and the firm of Griffen, Smith and Hill. The others hoped their unmarked pieces would be taken for English examples.

Notes: Prices listed here are for pieces with good color and in mint condition. For less-than-perfect pieces, decrease value proportionally according to the degree of damage or restoration. Majolica images depicted appear courtesy of Michael Strawser Auction Group unless otherwise noted.

Reproduction Alert. Majolica-style pieces are a favorite of today's interior decorators. Many exact copies of period pieces are being manufactured. In addition, fantasy pieces incorporating late Victorian-era design motifs have entered the market and confused many novice collectors.

Modern majolica reproductions differ from period pieces in these ways: (1) modern reproductions tend to be lighter in weight than their Victorian ancestors; (2) the glaze on newer pieces may not be as rich or deeply colored as on period pieces; (3) new pieces usually have a plain white bottom, period pieces almost always have colored or mottled bases; (4) a bisque finish either inside or on the bottom generally means the piece is new; and (5) if the design prevents the piece from being functional—e.g., a lip of a pitcher that does not allow proper pouring—it is a new piece made primarily for decorative purposes.

Some reproductions bear old marks. Period marks found on modern pieces include (a) "Etruscan Majolica" (the mark of Griffen, Smith and Hill) and (b) a British registry mark.

Basket

Bird on branch, pink ribbon on handle, 10" x 6-1/2" **$250**

Yellow, angel faces on each side, 8" .. **$200**

Bread tray

Floral, butterflies, pastel colors, "Waste Not Want Not" **$250**

Geranium and basketweave, "Eat thy bread with thankfulness," 12-3/4" **$300**

Bud vase, Minton, yellow, green ribbon, triple holes, 6" **$450**

Butter pat

Cobalt blue, sunflower **$140**

Holdcroft, fan shape, bird in flight **$175**

Wedgwood, chrysanthemum **$150**

Cake stand

Etruscan, morning glory, 8-1/4" .. **$175**

George Jones, leaf on napkin, white ground, 9" w, 6" h **$450**

Majolica bird on branch, low cake stand, 8-3/4" d, **$60.**

Majolica George Jones, table centerpiece with putto riding dolphin atop shell and coral base while holding shell, rim chip to one shell and hairline to another, outstanding color and detail, 15" h, 13-1/2" w, **$3,500.**

Majolica Copeland pansy butter pat, good color, **$150.**

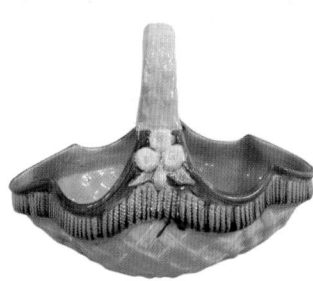

Majolica yellow basketweave basket, with flowers, attributed to Holdcroft, 10" l, **$300.**

Wedgwood, green leaf, green ground, 8" d, 2-1/2" h **$125**

Candlestick, figural
Palmer Cox Brownie, 8-1/2" h **$250**
Wardle, water lily form, all green **$125**

Cheese keeper, cov
Bird on branch, yellow ground, ribbon and bow accents...............**$375**
George Jones, apple blossom and basketweave, 10" d **$1,900**
Mottled brown and green, wedge shape, florals, 12" l **$250**
Turquoise, blackberry and cow, 11-1/2" h **$700**

Compote, Wedgwood, double dolphin, nautilus shell top, 16" **$800**

Cup and saucer
Banks and Thorley, Basketweave and Bamboo, butterfly handle........**$275**
Etruscan, bamboo **$125**
Lovebirds on branch, green and tan **$75**
Shell shape, pink, yellow and brown **$175**

Humidor, cov, figural
Clown head, yellow hat and collar, 6" h **$75**

Majolica floral and basketweave basket with bird perched on twig handle, bird missing beak, 8" h, **$300.**

Majolica large French birds on branch, blackberry, floral and leaves oval jardinière, good detail, 8" h, 15" w, **$500.**

Man, night cape and pipe, 4-1/2" h **$75**
Oriental lady, hat, 5" h **$75**
Policeman, pot bellied, 10-1/2" h . **$150**
Sailor, hat and beard, 5"..............**$50**

Jardinière, Wardle, Bamboo and Fern, 8"...**$550**

Match striker, Continental
Happy Hooligan, hat **$100**
Lady with tambourine, 10-1/2" ..**$100**
Man with violin, 12"....................**$125**
Monk, stein and brick barrels, 8" **$100**
Monkey, cobalt blue cape, 5-1/2" . **$125**

Mug
Etruscan, Water Lily....................**$250**
Samuel Lear, classical urn..........**$100**
Wedgwood, grape and vine **$150**
Mustache cup and saucer, Wild Rose and Rope **$250**

Oyster plate
French Orchies, blue and beige, 10" d **$150**
Minton, pink wells, 9" d..............**$450**
Russian, Imperial eagle, 9-1/2" d.. **$500**
Seaweed and Shell, cobalt blue center, 10" d **$375**

Pitcher
Bird and bird nest, 9" h...............**$225**

Majolica George Jones apple blossom full-size cheese keeper, strong color, hairline to cover, 12-1/2" h, **$2,500.**

Majolica bread tray, George Jones, strawberry blossom dec, impressed registry mark, date code for 1873, 10-1/2" l, 2-3/4" h, **$700.**
Photo courtesy of David Rago Auctions, Inc.

Gnarled tree trunk and florals, 8" h **$150**

Robin, mottled, 9-1/4" h **$100**

Stork in marsh, 11" h **$225**

Water lily, green and yellow, 8" h **$175**

Plate

Bellflowers, cobalt blue, 8-3/4" d **$225**

Bird and Fan, pebbles, cobalt blue, 9" d **$150**

Bird in flight, fern and cattail, white ground, 8-1/2" d **$125**

Blackberry and basketweave, brown, 9" d **$125**

Platter

Dragonfly and leaf, pink border, 11-1/2" l **$200**

Eureka, bird and fan, diamond shaped, 15-1/2" l **$250**

Leaves and ferns, oval, greens and brown, 12" **$250**

Sardine box, cov

English, green and brown mottled **$250**

Fielding, Fan and Scroll, attached underplate, blue and yellow **$500**

Wedgwood, boat shaped anchor finial **$550**

Server, Holdcroft, double leaf, squirrel handle, 13" **$675**

Spittoon, Etruscan, Pineapple, yellow and green **$500**

Syrup, pewter top

Holdcroft, Pond Lily, turquoise, 3-3/4" **$300**

Wedgwood, Caterer jug, turquoise and brown, 7-1/2" **$250**

Wedgwood, Doric, mottled cobalt blue and brown, 7-1/2" h **$125**

Teapot, cov

Basketweave and floral, pink and turquoise, pewter lid, 6-3/4" h **$275**

Bird and Bird's Nest, figural, brown and green, 9" **$225**

Fielding, Fan and Scroll, insect, pebble ground, cream and purple, 7" **$275**

Pyramid shape, brown, yellow and green, 8-1/2" **$250**

Wild Rose, yellow pebble ground, white flowers, 5-1/2" **$225**

Tray, Minton, bird, oak leaf shape, 8" **$500**

Tureen, George Jones, mackerel on bed of ferns, 19" **$4,250**

Majolica Brownfield ewer with putti, leaves and flowers in high relief and putti handle, professional rim and base repair, 16-1/2" h, **$1,200-$1,500.**

Majolica Rorstrand cachepot, hairline, rim and base chip, 8" h, 8-3/4" d, **$25.**

Majolica George Jones, picket fence and daisy full-size cheese keeper, cobalt, outstanding color, minor professional rim repair to underplate, 12" h, 12" d, **$10,000.**

Majolica Wedgwood nautilus centerpiece with double dolphin supports, also marked with impressed "GA," c1880, 16-3/8" h, **$1,800.**
Photo courtesy of Joan Sween.

Majolica Palissy Ware jug with oak leaves, acorns and snake wrapped around jug with frog on spout, professional rim, handle and spout repair, 10" h, **$1,100.**

Majolica Etruscan maple leaf, shallow compote, with early mark for Griffen, Smith and Hill, 9" d, 5-1/2" h, **$250.**
Photo courtesy of Joan Sween.

Majolica wild rose and rope teapot, minor rim nick to pot, 7-1/4" h, **$150.**

Majolica figural parrot pitcher, 10" h, **$225.**

Majolica "B Block" figural Blackamoor with baskets match striker, outstanding color and detail, minor repair to rim of basket, head reattached, 10-1/2" h, **$350.**

Majolica figural fish pitcher, 10-1/4" h, **$175.**

Majolica brown French oyster plate, 9-1/2" d, **$40.**

Majolica Sarreguemines dark green large oyster platter, 15" d, **$70.**

Majolica French figural, horse inkwell, very unusual, ears professionally restored, 10-1/2" w, **$400.**

Majolica Brownfield pink hops and wheat pitcher with lavender ground, minor glaze nick and hairline, Bacall Collection, 6 1/2" h, **$2,300.**

Majolica George Jones turquoise, water lily and iris pitcher, outstanding color and detail, Bacall Collection, 8-1/4" h, **$2,500.**

Majolica George Jones apple blossom and basket weave mug, good color and detail, 5 1/2" h, **$2,000.**

Majolica Wedgwood Classical-style, lion footed compote with floral reticulated top, strong color and detail, professional repair to base, 5-1/2" h, 9" d, **$175.**

Majolica fern and floral plate good color, 8-1/2" d, **$70.**

Majolica George Jones leaf and ferns plate with turquoise ground, surface wear, 8-1/2" d, **$200.**

Majolica Wedgwood chrysanthemum plate, 9" d, **$275.**

Majolica Cobalt floral platter, strong color, 13-1/4" w, **$250.**

Majolica geranium platter with lavender flowers, outstanding color and detail, 12" w, **$550.**

Majolica Etruscan oak leaf tray 12" w, **$175.**

Majolica French placement tray with yellow rope trim and red tassels, 12-1/2" w, **$60.**

Majolica Etruscan, overlapping begonia leaf plate, 9" d, **$100.**

Majolica Royal Worcester, dragon-handled teapot with birds, flowers and vine in relief, strong color and detail, minor professional spout repair, rare, 7-1/2" h, **$3,000.**

Majolica Minton dolphin candlestick, professional repair to top, 8-1/4" h, **$450.**

Majolica Minton vase with basketweave and applied floral motif, hairline, shape no. 1287, good color, date code for 1870, 6-3/4" h, **$700.**

Majolica Minton cobalt and turquoise lily vase, shape no. 293, great detail, professional rim repair and base repair, 6-1/2" h, **$200.**

MARBLEHEAD POTTERY

Marblehead vessel, squat, incised and painted wreath of stylized light green flowers, red berries, indigo leaves, smooth matte indigo ground, stamped ship mark, glaze misses to interior, 2-1/2" x 5-1/2", **$1,300.**

Photo courtesy of David Rago Auctions, Inc.

History: This hand-thrown pottery was first made in 1905 as part of a therapeutic program introduced by Dr. J. Hall for the patients confined to a sanitarium located in Marblehead, Massachusetts. In 1916, production was removed from the hospital to another site. The factory continued under the directorship of Arthur E. Baggs until it closed in 1936.

Most pieces found today are glazed with a smooth, porous, even finish in a single color. The most desirable pieces have a conventional design in one or more subordinate colors.

Centerpiece bowl, flaring, incised lotus leaf design on ext., dark blue matte glaze, imp sip mark, 3-3/4" h, 8-1/4" d.........................**$425**

Chamberstick, bright yellow matte glaze, imp ship mark, 4" h, 4-1/2" d **$275**

Flower pot, terra cotta glaze, imp ship mark, 5" d.........................**$195**

Humidor, lightly modeled stylized dark blue flora, speckled sandy ground, rare large paper label, Arthur Baggs, marked "AEB and MHC/$5.00," 5" h, 4-1/4" d.........................**$4,100**

Tile, cuerda seca, polychrome trees and house, matte gray ground, mounted in period frame, ship mark, remnant of paper label, restoration to Y-shaped crack, 6" sq **$1,725**

Marblehead vessel, bulbous, covered in smooth matte mauve glaze, stamped ship mark, 4-1/2" d, 3-3/4" h, **$435.**

Marblehead vessel, squat, covered in smooth speckled brown glaze, stamped ship mark, 5-1/2" d, 3-3/4" h, **$460.**

Tile frieze, two tiles, incised lake scene, matte yellow, browns and greens, imp mark, paper label, orig price tag on each, orig frame retaining sticker marked "o. 2-64 tiles Poplars with Reflections, Dec by A. E. Baggs, Price $10.00," minor edge nicks, kiln pops, from estate of Dr. Hall, founder of Marblehead Pottery, 7-1/2" sq tiles **$21,850**

Trivet, stylized flowers, matte blue, green, yellow and red, imp mark, paper label, remnant of price label, from estate of Dr. Hall, founder of Marblehead Pottery, 6" sq **$865**

Vase

Barrel shape, blue and gray band of flying geese, speckled gray ground, remnant of imp ship mark, drilled bottom, 6" d, 6-1/4" h **$4,025**

Beaker shape, brown gooseberry leaves, indigo branches, dark blue

Marblehead vase, ovoid, incised wreath of grapevines and leaves, purple and green glaze, entirely covered in matte yellow, ship mark, 5-1/4" x 3-1/4", **$2,200.**

Photo courtesy of David Rago Auctions, Inc.

ground, imp ship mark, 5" d, 6" h **$1,955**

Bulbous, smooth indigo matte glaze, imp ship mark, 3-3/4" h..........**$475**

Cabinet, tapering, designed by Arthur Baggs, dec by Hannah Tutt, incised chevron pattern, two-tone mottled matte green glaze, imp ship mark, artist's cipher, 2-3/4" d, 4-1/4" h **$5,350**

Curved rim, widening at base, mottled lavender semi-matte glaze, imp mark, c1915-36, 6" h.................**$650**

Fan shape, matte blue glaze, imp mark, paper label, 8" d, 6-1/4" h **$320**

Geometric, lightly tooled, stylized light brown trees, matte speckled sand-colored ground, imp ship mark, 4-1/4" d, 6-1/4" h........**$4,750**

Vessel, squatty, incised and painted stylized pattern in dark green on lighter green ground, ship mark, incised "MT", 2-1/4" h, 4-1/2" d **$3,750**

Wall pocket, speckled gray ext., robin's egg blue int., unmarked, 5-1/4" w, 5" h **$295**

Marblehead glaze sample tile, 25 colors on bright yellow ground, stamped ship mark, chips to three corners and one edge, 6" sq, **$1,000.**

Photo courtesy of David Rago Auctions, Inc.

MCCOY POTTERY

History: The J. W. McCoy Pottery Co. was established in Roseville, Ohio, in September 1899. The early McCoy company produced both stoneware and some art pottery lines, including Rosewood. In October 1911, three potteries merged, creating the Brush-McCoy Pottery Co. This firm continued to produce the original McCoy lines and added several new art lines. Much of the early pottery is not marked.

In 1910, Nelson McCoy and his father, J. W. McCoy, founded the Nelson McCoy Sanitary Stoneware Co. In 1925, the McCoy family sold their interest in the Brush-McCoy Pottery Co. and started to expand and improve the Nelson McCoy Co. The new company produced stoneware, earthenware specialties, and artware.

Marks: The Nelson McCoy Co. made Most of the pottery marked "McCoy."

Additional Listings: See *Warman's Americana & Collectibles* for more examples.

McCoy barn jar with cow in door, McCoy USA mark, lid was easily damaged, 1960s, **$350-$400.**

Reproduction Alert. Unfortunately, Nelson McCoy never registered his McCoy trademark, a fact discovered by Roger Jensen of Tennessee. As a result, Jensen began using the McCoy mark on a series of ceramic reproductions made in the early 1990s. While the marks on these recently made pieces copy the original, Jensen made objects that were never produced by the Nelson McCoy Co. The best-known example is the Red Riding Hood cookie jar, originally designed by Hull, and also made by Regal China.

The McCoy fakes are a perfect example of how a mark on a piece can be deceptive. A mark alone is not proof that a piece is period or old. Knowing the proper marks and what was made in respect to forms, shapes and decorative motifs is critical in authenticating a pattern.

McCoy strawberry jar, McCoy USA mark, 1950s, **$125.**

Bean pot, cov, Suburbia Ware, brown, blue lid..$48

Cookie jar, cov
Aunt Jemima..............................$275
Bobby Baker..............................$95
Bugs Bunny, cylinder, 1971-72 ....$185
Chef, "Cookies" on hat band.........$85
Clown, bust, c1943 ....$95
Clown in Barrel, marked "McCoy USA," overall crazing, c1953-56 ....$145
Davy Crocket, c1956, 10" h.........$325
Engine, black $175
Kangaroo with Joey, 12" h...........$525
Little Red Riding Hood, 10-1/2" h $650
Panda, upside down, Avon label in heart logo on paw.....................$150
Rooster, shades of brown, light tan head, green highlights $225
Strawberry $125
Touring Car, marked "McCoy USA," c1962-64, 6-1/2" h.................$155

Creamer and sugar, Sunburst $120

Decanter set, Jupiter 60 Train, Central Pacific locomotive, c1969.....$350

Flower pot, saucer, hobnail and leaf $40

Hanging basket, Pine Cone Rustic $45

Jardinière, green, brown and gold, emb lion's heads and columns, 5-3/4" d, 5-1/4" d $45

Jardinière pedestal, Onyx glaze, sgd "Cusick," c1909, 16-1/4" h...........$400

Lamp base, cowboy boots, c1956, 14" h...$150
Low bowl, turtle flower frog, polychrome squeezebag dec, swastikas on bowl, 9" d, 2-3/4" h $500

Planter
Brown, white drip dec, 7-1/2" l, 4-1/2" w, 3" h $20
Hunting Dog, No Fishing on sign, 12" l $275
Three large pink chrysanthemums, marked "McCoy," 8" h $155

Spoon rest, yellow, foliage, overall crazing, 1940s, 8" l......................$145

Strawberry jar, stoneware, 12" h $150

Tankard pitcher, Buccaneer, green, 8-1/2" h..................................$135

W.F. McCoy 5-gallon crock, salt glaze with stenciled ink lettering: "W.F. McCoy Wholesale Dealer in Stoneware–Zanesville, O.," with impressed "5," late 1800s, 13" h, **$1,200-$1,400.**

McCoy tassel vase in glossy raspberry, stoneware, unmarked, 1930s, 8" h, **$75-$85.**

McCoy strap pitcher in glossy burgundy, McCoy mark, late 1940s, **$75-$85.**

McCoy basketweave horn of plenty wall pocket, McCoy USA mark, 1950s, 8", **$100-$120.**

McCoy urn wall pocket in speckled pink glaze with gold trim, McCoy USA mark, also found in chartreuse, 4-1/2" long, **$75-$85.**

McCoy ivy jardinière in brown and green, unmarked, also found in a brighter glossy tan and green with matching pedestal, early 1950s, 8" h, **$350-$450.**

McCoy jardinière and pedestal, decorated with trees and birds, sheer green glaze, sgd "A. Cusick" in mold, abrasions and several small nicks, 27" h, **$325.**
Photo courtesy of David Rago Auctions, Inc.

Tea set, cov teapot, open creamer and sugar, Pinecone, c1946 .... **$350**
Umbrella stand, maroon, rose and yellow glaze, c1915, 11" d, 22" h **$795**
Valet, eagle **$75**
Vase
  Bulbous, flaring rim, jeweled, pastel Squeezebag dec, green base, mkd "042," 8-3/4" h **$575**
  Cornucopia, green, 7-1/4" h **$125**

Swan, white, gold trim, 9-1/2" h **$250**
Wall pocket
  Bellows **$60**
  Cuckoo Clock, brown, green, white, yellow bird **$225**
  Fan, blue **$65**
  Post Box, green **$70**
  Sunflower, blue **$80**
Window box, Pine Cone Rustic **$40**

METTLACH

History: In 1809, Jean Francis Boch established a pottery at Mettlach in Germany's Moselle Valley. His father had started a pottery at Septfontaines in 1767. Nicholas Villeroy began his pottery career at Wallerfanger in 1789.

In 1841, these three factories merged. They pioneered underglaze printing on earthenware, using transfers from copper plates, and also were among the first companies to use coal-fired kilns. Other factories were developed at Dresden, Wadgassen and Danischburg. Mettlach decorations include relief and etched designs, prints under the glaze, and cameos.

Marks: The castle and Mercury emblems are the two chief marks, although secondary marks are known. The base of each piece also displays a shape mark and usually a decorator's mark.

Additional Listings: Villeroy & Boch.

Note: Prices in this listing are for print-under-glaze pieces (PUG), unless otherwise specified.

Coaster, PUG, drinking scene, marked "Mettlach, Villeroy & Boch," 4-7/8" d **$150**

Jardinière, #2427, expanded bulbous body, fish and flower dec, imp castle mark and number, 16" w, 12" h **$1,100**

Loving cup, three handles, musicians dec, 7-3/8" w, 6-3/4" h **$185**

Plaque

#1044-1067, water wheel on side of building, sgd "F. Reiss," PUG, gold wear on edge, 17" d **$495**

#1168, Cavalier, threading and glaze, sgd "Warth," chip on rear hanging rim, 16-1/2" d **$465**

#2196, Stolzensels Castle on the Rhein, 17" d **$1,100**

#2442, classical scene of Trojan warriors in ship, cameo, white high relief, blue-gray ground, artist sgd "J. Stahl," some professional restoration, 18-1/4" d.......................**$1,200**

Stein

#485, one liter, cameo relief with musicians and dancers, inlaid lid, 9-5/8" h **$365**

#1526, transfer and enameled, Student Society, Amico Pectus Hosti Frontem, roster on either side of crest, pewter lid, slight discoloration to int, dated 1902............**$465**

#1896, 1/4 liter, maiden on one side, cherub face on other, grape dec, pewter lift handle **$350**

#2028, 1/2 liter, etched, men in Gasthaus, inlaid lid.........................**$550**

#2057, 1/2 liter, etched, festive dancing scene, inlaid lid.................**$325**

#2093, 1/2 liter, etched and glazed, suit of cards, inlaid lid............**$700**

#2204, 1/2 liter, etched and relief, Prussian eagle, inlaid lid..........**$780**

#2580, 1/2 liter, etched, Die Kannenburg, conical inlay lid, knight in castle.................................**$695**

#5001, 4.6 liter, faience type, coat of arms, pewter lid **$850**

MINTON CHINA

History: In 1793, Thomas Minton joined other men to form a partnership and build a small pottery at Stoke-on-Trent, Staffordshire, England. Production began in 1798 with blueprinted earthenware, mostly in the Willow pattern. In 1798, cream-colored earthenware and bone china were introduced.

A wide range of styles and wares was produced. Minton introduced porcelain figures in 1826, Parian wares in 1846, encaustic tiles in the late 1840s, and Majolica wares in 1850. Many famous designers and artists in the English pottery industry worked for Minton.

In 1883, the modern company was formed and called Mintons Limited. The "s" was dropped in 1968. Minton still produces bone-china tablewares and some ornamental pieces.

Marks: Many early pieces are unmarked or have a Sevres-type marking. The "ermine" mark was used in the early 19th century. Date codes can be found on tableware and majolica. The mark used between 1873 and 1911 was a small globe with a crown on top and the word "Minton."

Minton plate, enamel decoration, Oriental medallion of peony and prunus, sky blue ground, faint stamp, 1874, light wear to gild on rim, 9" d, **$700.**
Photo courtesy of David Rago Auctions, Inc.

Bud vase and stand, majolica, amphora shape, double handled vase seated in tripod stand, molded ram's heads and hoof feet, impressed mark on base, England, glaze crazing, 1863, 6-7/8" h...................................**$1,175**

Centerpiece, elongated parian vessel, molded scroll handles and feet, pierced rim, two brown reserves, white pate-sur-pate amorini, gilding, dec, attributed to Lawrence Birks, marked "Minton," retailer's marks of Thomas Goode & Co., Ltd., London, c1889, 16" l.............................**$1,400**

Compote, majolica, figural, lobed oval dish and plinth, brown glaze on agate body, dish supported on backs of two cherubs holding laurel wreaths, center lovebirds, impressed mark, c1863, 10-1/2" l....................................**$2,415**

Dinner service, partial, Florentine pattern, 12 10-1/2" d dinner plates; 12 9" d luncheon plates; 12 2-3/8" h teacups; 11 saucers; 10 10-1/2" d soup plates; eight 8" d dessert plates; seven 2-5/8" h coffee cups; six 7" d side plates; five 4-5/8" bowls; three 13", 15", 17" l graduated serving platters; two 10-1/2" l cov serving dishes; two small oval dishes; two pickle dishes; two 5-5/8" d side plates; a sq cov serving dish; cov sugar; creamer; milk jug; sauce boat and undertray; 9-3/4" d serving bowl; open 12" l serving tureen; 15" l cov tureen, 108 pieces total, third quarter 19th C **$2,185**

Figure, putti, yellow basket and grape vine, professional repair at rim of basket, 1867, 10-1/2" h............**$2,750**

Minton vase, designed by Louis Solon, two handles, trail-slip decoration of swags and medallions in bright polychrome, red ground, stamped "Minton Ltd. No. 1,8503," 11-1/2" x 5-1/4", **$900.**
Photo courtesy of David Rago Auctions, Inc.

Floor urn, majolica, Neo-Classical, turquoise, massive foliage handles, 35" h, 18" d **$12,650**

Garden set, earthenware, barrel form, central pierced band of entwined rings between blue printed bands of flowers, scrolled vines, imp mark, glaze wear, price for pr, 19th C, 17-3/4" h **$1,100**

Jardinière, majolica, ftd, bowl with swags of fruit terminating at lion masks, base molded with three partially draped male figures between cornucopia of fruits, impressed mark, England, restored, c1868, 21" h **$3,525**

Nut dish, majolica, leaf-molded dish with squirrel handle, imp mark, restored chips to ears, c1869, 9-3/4" l **$1,840**

Oyster plate, majolica

Mottled **$935**

Turquoise **$495**

Oyster server, four tiers, majolica, green and brown, white wells, turquoise finial, rim damage to six wells, mechanical turning mechanism missing **$3,575**

Plaque, framed, painted scene of Dutch man reading document by row of books, initials "HH" lower right, date mark for 1883, 11-1/2" sq **$290**

Plate, 9" d, hp, polychrome dec, garlands and swags on rims, marked "Mintons/England/Rd. No. 608547/73793/Pat. Apr 1st 1913," price for set of 12 ....**$225**

Portrait plate, 9" d, Duchess de Berri Caroline, Princis Lambelle, Madame Mars, Madame Elizabeth, sgd "A.S.I.," names on reverse, price for set of four **$350**

Sweetmeat dish, majolica, blue titmouse on branch, leaf-shaped dish, imp mark, 1888, 8" d **$675**

Tower pitcher, majolica, castle molded body with relief of dancing villagers in medieval dress, imp marks, chips to cov thumb rest, spout rim, c1873, 12-1/2" h **$1,035**

Vase, celadon green ground, five-spout, fan form, applied white floral relief, fish head feet, imp mark, foot rim chip, c1855, 6-1/4" h **$215**

MOCHA

Mocha creamer, band of decoration in blue and brown on yellow body, hairlines, 4-1/2" h, **$120.**
Photo courtesy of Alderfer Auction Co.

History: Mocha decoration usually is found on utilitarian creamware and stoneware pieces and was produced through a simple chemical action. A color pigment of brown, blue, green or black was made acidic by an infusion of tobacco or hops. When the acidic colorant was applied in blobs to an alkaline ground, it reacted by spreading in feathery designs resembling sea plants. This type of decoration usually was supplemented with bands of light-colored slip.

Types of decoration vary greatly, from those done in a combination of motifs, such as Cat's Eye and Earthworm, to a plain pink mug decorated with green ribbed bands. Most forms of mocha are hollow, e.g., mugs, jugs, bowls and shakers.

English potters made the vast majority of the pieces. Collectors group the wares into three chronological periods: 1780-1820, 1820-1840 and 1840-1880.

Reproduction Alert.

Beaker, pearlware

Dark brown, medium brown and ochre marble decoration on rust field, thin lines of medium brown at rim and base, England, rim chips and glaze wear, early 19th C, 3" h **$2,475**

Rust, dark brown, medium brown and white combed marble slip, England, early 19th C, 3" h **$2,820**

Bowl

Ochre band, black seaweed, crazing, stains, 6-7/8" d, 3-1/2" h **$275**

Aqua band, blue stripes, blue, brown and white earthworm design, faint imp label, stained, small edge flakes, 7-1/4" d, 3-1/4" h **$325**

Chamber pot, two-tone blue bands, black stripes, black and white earthworm, leaf handle, some wear and edge flakes, 8-3/4" d **$125**

Child's mug

Black banding with black and gray earthworm dec on green field, yellow glazed, extruded handle with foliate terminals, impressed partial maker's mark on bottom, England, chips to base edge, glaze wear to rim, early 19th C, 2-5/8" h **$2,990**

Pearlware, green glazed rouletted upper and lower bands flanking rust field with dark brown scroddled dots, with bisecting lines cut through slip to white body, applied handle, England, repaired, early 19th C, 2-1/2" h **$825**

Creamer, black and white checkered band on shoulder medium blue glaze, 5-1/4" h **$215**

Cup, imp border above brown and white earthworm design, blue ground, imperfections, 19th C, 2-7/8" h **$375**

Ink sander, pearlware, two rows of dark brown trailed slip "tendrils" on blue field, England, two small chips, early 19th C, 3-1/4" h **$1,175**

Jug, barrel-form, banded in blue and black, black, white and blue earthworm dec on ocher field, handles with foliate terminals, England, 5/8" rim chip, associated crack, 1/2" chip on spout, c1840, 7-1/2" h **$1,880**

Measure, tankard, blue, black and tan seaweed dec, one with applied white label "Imperial Pint," other with resist label "Quart," minor stains, wear, and crazing, three-pc set, 5", 6" and 6-1/4" h **$440**

Milk pitcher, dark bluish-gray band, black stripes, emb band with green and black seaweed, leaf handle, wear and painted over spout flake, 4-5/8" h **$440**

Mug

Barrel-form, black mocha seaweed

dec on ocher field between black and blue bands, extruded handles with foliate terminals, England, small chip on base edge, c1820, 3-7/8" h **$1,410**

Brown checkerboard design, 19th C, 3" h **$260**

Ftd, pink, blue and black marbling, England, five small hairlines on rim, 19th C, 3-1/2" h, 4-1/8" d **$360**

Quart, banded in dark brown and rust, two rows of blue, dark brown, rust and white earthworm flanked by upper and lower white rouletted bands, extruded handle with foliate terminals, England, circular and spider cracks in the base, three rim chips, early 19th C, 6" h **$1,765**

Mustard pot, cov

Creamware, blue banded lid with blue reeded band, cylindrical body with matching banding, dark brown, rust, gray and white earthworm pattern, extruded handle with foliate handles, creamware, England, chips to the lid, small crack to the body,

discoloration, early 19th C, 2-1/2" h **$1,300**

Pearlware, lid with acorn finial, brown bands with dendritic seaweed on rust field, body decorated in the same manner, extruded handle with foliate terminals, England, finial repair, small rim and base chips, early 19th C, 3-1/2" h **$1,645**

Pearlware, lid with ball finial banded in dark brown and rust, matching banding on the body, unusual band of rust and dark brown slip in finely trailed diamond pattern, extruded handle with foliate terminals, England, crack in the handle, minor glaze wear, early 19th C, 3-1/2" h **$2,585**

Pitcher

Large band of dark brown seaweed and beaded diamonds on ochre ground between bands of dark brown and green stripes, imp chevron bands, 8-1/2" h, some minor glaze loss **$1,725**

Yellowware, brown bands, black

seaweed, glaze flaking, three base chips **$5,250**

Portrait box, transfer and painted dec of Napoleon III and Empress Eugenie, 5" d.. **$150**

Salt, open, chocolate brown band, black seaweed dec, small chip on foot, 2-3/4" d, 1-3/4" h **$520**

Shaker

Blue band, black stripe, brown, black, and white earthworm dec, blue top, repair, 4-7/8" h.......................... **$330**

Tan bands, brown stripes, black seaweed dec, chips, 4-1/8" h **$220**

Tea canister, blue, black and white band on shoulder, white fluted band on bottom, medium blue glaze, 4" h.. **$125**

Teapot, oval shape, medium blue, fluted band on bottom, black and white checkered band on top, acorn finial, 5-7/8" h.. **$500**

Waste bowl, amber band, black seaweed dec separated into five segments by squiggly lines, green molded lip band, stains and hairlines, 4-3/4" d **$275**

MOORCROFT

History: William Moorcroft was first employed as a potter by James Macintyre & Co., Ltd., of Burslem in 1897. He established the Moorcroft pottery in 1913.

The majority of the art pottery wares were hand thrown, resulting in a great variation among similarly styled pieces. Color and marks are keys to determining age.

Walker, William's son, continued the business upon his father's death and made wares in the same style.

Marks: The company initially used an impressed mark, "Moorcroft, Burslem;" a signature mark, "W. Moorcroft" followed. Modern pieces are marked simply "Moorcroft," with export pieces also marked "Made in England."

Bowl, pansy dec, pale green ground, imp maker's mark, 3-5/8" d **$150**

Box, cov, pansy dec on lid, pale green ground, imp maker's mark, crazing, 4-3/4" l, 1-1/2" w, 1-3/4" h **$200**

Compote, Lily motif, yellow and green ground, 7-1/4" d **$150**

Ginger jar, cov, pomegranate dec, 11-1/2" h...................................... **$525**

Jar, cov, Cornflower, ivory ground, coat of arms of Kings College, Oxford, c1911 .... **$1,450**

Lamp base, Anemone, 6-1/4" d, 11-1/4" h.. **$920**

Loving cup, Pomegranate pattern,

stamped mark, minor rim fleck, 1914-16, 6" d, 5-1/2" h **$1,150**

Pitcher, Forget-Me-Not, c1902, 6-1/4" h **$1,350**

Plate, toadstool, blue ground, imp "Moorcroft Claremont," 7-1/4" d **$600**

Vase

Eventide pattern, ovoid, squeezebag green trees, cobalt blue ground, stamped "Moorcroft/Made in England" and signature, rim chip, 2" line, 6-1/2" d, 15" h **$1,840**

Leaf & Berry, matte glaze, William's initials in blue, 7" h **$1,150**

Moorcroft vase, Eventide pattern, yellow background, sgd "W. Moorcroft," numbered RD0397964, extensive restoration, 7-3/4" d, 11-3/4" h, **$650.**
Photo courtesy of David Rago Auctions, Inc.

Moorcroft plate, Pomegranate and Berry pattern, glossy cobalt blue ground, stamped "Made In England," ink signature, mounted in metal plate hanger, small plate ring chip, 8-1/2" d, **$175.**

Photo courtesy of David Rago Auctions, Inc.

Moorfcroft cabinet vase, orchid design, glossy cobalt blue ground, paper label, 2-1/2" d, 3-3/4" h, **$235.**

Photo courtesy of David Rago Auctions, Inc.

Long narrow neck on bulbous base, green poppies, green ground, Moorcroft handmade pottery paper label, painted signature, imp mark, and "made in England," rim restoration, c1918, 12-3/8" h **$1,410**
Orchid, flambé, sgd by William in blue, imp "Potter to HM The Queen," 12" h **$4,350**
Pomegranate, vasiform, blue ground, red pomegranates, purple seeds, imp factory mark with facsimile signature, printed paper Royal Warrant label, 1928-49, 7-3/8" h **$500**

MULBERRY CHINA

History: Mulberry china was made primarily in the Staffordshire district of England between 1830 and 1860. The ware often has a flowing effect similar to flow blue. It is the color of crushed mulberries, a dark purple, sometimes with a gray tinge or bordering almost on black. The potteries that manufactured flow blue also made Mulberry china, and, in fact, frequently made some patterns in both types of wares. To date, there are no known reproductions.

Educational Alert: The Flow Blue International Collectors' Club, Inc., has been discussing new versus reproduction mulberry and flow blue. There are still areas of personal judgment as yet undetermined. The general rule accepted has been "new" indicates recent or contemporary manufacture and "reproduction" is a copy of an older pattern. Problems arise when either of fields is sold at "old" mulberry prices.

In an effort to help educate its membership, the club continues to inform of all known changes through its conventions, newsletters and the Web site: www.flowblue.com.

Warman's is working to those ends also. The following is a listing of "new" mulberry, produced since the 1960s.

Victoria Ware: Mark is of a lion and uniform, but has paper label "Made in China," 1990s. Made in various patterns and design, but the giveaway is the roughness on the bottoms, and much of it has a pea green background. Some of this line is also being made in flow blue.

Check the Flow Blue International Collectors' Club, Inc. Web site www.flowblue.org. Join the club, study the books available, and always, always, KNOW your dealer! Good dealers guarantee their merchandise and protect their customers.

Adviser: Ellen G. King.

Mulberry, Bryonia, Utzschneider, demitasse cup and saucer, **$65.**

Alleghany, Goodfellow, 1840
 Plate, 8" **$85**
 Soup tureen with undertray **$650**
Athens, Adams, child's sugar bowl with lid, 1849 .... **$120**
Beauties of China, Venables, 1845
 Creamer **$100**
 Teapot with lid **$550**
Berry, Ridgway, 1850
 Cake plate with handles **$135**
 Plate, 8" **$75**
Bochara, Edwards, bowl, 1847, 10" **$85**
Bouquet, Wedgwood, 1846

Plate, 9" **$65**
Plate, charger, 12-1/2" **$125**
Bryonia, Utzshneider, footed fruit compote, 1890 .... **$220**
Corea, Clementson, platter, 1840, 16 x 12-1/2" **$225**
Corean, Podmore-Walker, 1849
 Sauce tureen with undertray **$400**
 Teapot with lid **$425**
Cyprus, Davenport, shell relish, mask on handle, 1850 .... **$100**
Flora, Hulme & Booth, vegetable bowl, 1851, 9" **$75**
Flora, Walker, 1848
 Cup plate **$110**

Pitcher, 12" $200

Plate, 8" $75

Foliage, Walley, 1846

Plate, 9" $55

Plate, 10" $80

Genoa, Davenport, platter, 1840, 13-3/4" $200

Hollyhock, Wedgwood, green round low tazza, 1860 ....$145

Hopberry, Meigh, child's sugar with lid, 1845 ....$110

Ivy, unknown maker, child's wash bowl and pitcher, polychrome, 1850 ....$575

Jardinere, U & C, plate, 1860, 8" ..$55

Lily, Dimmock & Smith, pitcher, 1850 ....$125

Marble, Wedgwood, 1850

Bowl, open vegetable, 9-1/2" $90

Platter, 15-1/2" $150

Medina, Furnivals, 1848

Plate, 9" $75

Tea cup and saucer $85

Milan, South Wales Pottery, platter, 1840, 14" $250

Montezuma, Goodwin, plate, 1846, 9-1/2" $80

Moss and Sprig, maker unknown, plate, 1845, 8" $75

Ning Po, R. Hall, 1845

Cup plate $55

Vegetable bowl, oval, 10" $100

Pelew, Challinor, 1840

Creamer $100

Teapot with lid, gothic shape $300

Round, open vegetable bowl, 12-1/2" $250

Peruvian, Wedgwood, sugar bowl with lid, scroll handles, 1849 ....$235

Rhone Scenery, Mayer, 1850

Plate, 9" $65

Plate, 10" $80

Rose, Walker, 1846

Cup plate $110

Milk pitcher $225

Seaweed, Ridgway, 1840

Plate, 9" $75

Tea cup, handless, with saucer $135

Seville, Wood & Sons, plate, 1890, 9-1/4" $50

Shanghae, Furnival, sugar bowl with lid, 1850 ....$75

The Temple, Podmore-Walker, 1850

Creamer, 5-1/4" $195

Sugar bowl with lid $100

Tulip & Fern, unknown maker, brush-stroke pattern, mitten relish, 1840 ....$155

Washington Vase, Podmore-Walker, 1850

Classic gothic creamer $135

Platter, 18-1/4" $300

Mulberry, Marble, unknown maker, milk pitcher, 1850, **$145.**

Mulberry, Coral, Challinor, teapot with lid, polychromed shells, 1845, **$255.**

NEWCOMB COLLEGE POTTERY

History: The Sophie Newcomb Memorial College, an adjunct of Tulane University in New Orleans, LA, was originated as a school to train local women in the decorative arts. While metalworking, painting and embroidery were among the classes taught, the production of fine, handcrafted art pottery remains its most popular and collectible pursuit.

Pottery was made by the Newcomb women for nearly 50 years, with earlier work being the rarest and most valuable. This is characterized by shiny finishes and broad, flat-painted and modeled designs. More common, though still quite valuable, are the matte glaze pieces, often depicting bayou scenes and native flora. All bear the impressed NC mark.

Adviser: David Rago.

Newcomb College pottery bowl, carved by A. F. Simpson, wreath of white and yellow daffodils, blue ground, NC/JM/AFS/56/KV45, 1920, 3-1/4" x 6-1/2", **$1,800.**
Photo courtesy of David Rago Auctions, Inc.

Newcomb College pottery vase, incised by Harriet Joor, ivory and yellow magnolia blossoms, green foliage, pale blue ground, NC/HJ/0024/JM, restoration to two rim chips, 1904, 11-3/4" x 7", **$20,000.**
Photo courtesy of David Rago Auctions, Inc.

Newcomb College pottery charger, incised by Charlotte Payne, clusters of light green fruit, dark green foliage, indigo ground around stylized cross-section of same fruit in blues and greens, NC/JM/CP/TT31, 3" E-shaped hairline from rim, 1904, 9-1/2" d, **$4,000.**

Photo courtesy of David Rago Auctions, Inc.

Bud vase, tapered, high glaze, carved yellow jonquils, green leaves, blue ground, by Anna Frances Simpson, marked "NC/Q/FS/CQ52/JM," 1908, 9" h, 3-1/4" d **$6,900**

Cabinet vase, by Anna F. Simpson, 1926, blue live oak and Spanish moss, gray ground, high glaze, marked "NC/JH/PP56/15/AFS," 2" d, 4-1/2" h **$3,335**

Chocolate set, teal blue pine trees carved by A. F. Simpson, light blue and green glossy ground, two matching cups, four saucers, mkd "NC/AFS/JM/E112/B," some damage, 1911, 10-1/2" h, 6" d chocolate pot **$5,500**

Low bowl, carved pink irises, green leaves, medium blue matte ground, by A. F. Simpson, marked "NC/NF31/313/JM" and artist's cipher, couple of short, tight lines to rim, 1923, 9-1/4" d, 3-1/4" h **$1,610**

Vase

Bulbous, painted by Sara Levy, bright yellow blossom, green stems, pale ground, mkd "NC/S.B.L./JM/Q," c1903, 5-1/2" h, 3-1/2" d **$6,500**

Carved matte, by Sadie Irvine, pink and red loquat fruit and leaves around undulating rim, marked "NC/SK/JM/I47/NP47," small chips to foot ring, short tight line to rim, 1924, 4-1/2" d, 6-1/2" h **$1,150**

Vessel

Matte, squatty, by Sadie Irvine, sharply carved pink Japanese iris, green stems, around undulating top conforming to shape of blossoms, purple and blue ground, marked "NC/SI/JM/213?MV17," 1922, 6-1/2" d, 4-1/2" h **$3,220**

Organically shaped, by Marie De Hoa LeBlanc, three modeled ginkgo leaf handles, semi-matte olive green and gunmetal glaze, marked "NC/Q/JM/MHL," orig price tag, c1905, 7-1/2" d, 6" h **$5,175**

NILOAK POTTERY

Niloak Mission Ware cordial set, four matching tumblers, all marbleized clay, paper labels and stamps, 12" h stoppered bottle, **$900.**

Photo courtesy of David Rago Auctions, Inc.

History: Niloak Pottery was made near Benton, Arkansas. Charles Dean Hyten experimented with native clay, trying to preserve its natural colors. By 1911, he perfected Mission Ware, a marbleized pottery in which the cream and brown colors predominate. The company name is the word "kaolin" spelled backward.

After a devastating fire, the pottery was rebuilt and named Eagle Pottery. This factory included enough space to add a novelty pottery line in 1929. Hyten left the pottery in 1941, and in 1946 operations ceased.

Marks: The early pieces were marked "Niloak." Eagle Pottery products usually were marked "Hywood-Niloak" until 1934, when the "Hywood" was dropped from the mark.

Additional Listings: See *Warman's Americana & Collectibles* for more examples, especially the novelty pieces.

Note: Prices listed here are for Mission Ware pieces.

Niloak Mission Ware vase, ovoid,, marbleized clays, stamped "Niloak," spider line to base, 4" d, 8" h, **$115.**

Photo courtesy of David Rago Auctions, Inc.

Bowl, marbleized swirls, blue, tan, and brown, 4-1/2" d............................. **$65**

Candlesticks, pr, marbleized swirls, blue, cream, terra cotta, and brown, 8" h... **$250**

Flower pot, ruffled rim, green matte glaze, c1930................................. **$155**

Toothpick holder, marbleized swirls, tan and blue **$100**

Urn, marbleized swirls, brown and blue, 4-1/2" h **$45**

Vase

Applied twisted handles, Ozark Dawn glaze, c1930, 6" h...................... **$120**

Early foil label, c1920-30, 3-1/4" h **$95**

Ozark Dawn glaze, c1930, 8-3/4" h, ... **$140**

Second art mark, c1925, 4-1/2" h **$75**

Starved rock mark, c1925, 4-1/2" h **$95**

Swirled colors, first art mark, c1910-24, 8-1/2" h................... **$230**

Swollen baluster with broad rim, brown, rose, blue, and cream, second art mark, 10-1/2" h **$500**

NIPPON CHINA, 1891-1921

Reproduction Alert. Distinguishing old marks from new:

An old leaf mark approximately one-quarter-inch wide, has "Hand" with "Painted" below to the left of the stem and "NIPPO Box N" beneath. The newer mark has the identical lettering, but size is now one-half, rather than one-quarter, inch.

An old mark consisted of "Hand Painted" arched above a solid rising sun logo with "NIPPO Box N" in a straight line beneath. The modern fake mark has the same lettering pattern, but the central logo looks like a mound with a jagged line enclosing a blank space above it.

History: Nippon, Japanese hand-painted porcelain, was made for export between 1891 and 1921. In 1891, when the McKinley Tariff Act proclaimed that all items of foreign manufacture be stamped with their country of origin, Japan chose to use "Nippon." In 1921, the United States decided the word "Nippon" was no longer acceptable and required all Japanese wares to be marked "Japan," ending the Nippon era.

Marks: There are more than 220 recorded Nippon backstamps or marks; the three most popular are the wreath, maple leaf, and rising sun. Wares with variations of all three marks are being reproduced today. A knowledgeable collector can easily spot the reproductions by the mark variances.

The majority of the marks are found in three different colors: green, blue, or magenta. Colors indicate the quality of the porcelain used: green for first-grade porcelain, blue for second-grade, and magenta for third-grade. Marks were applied by two methods: decal stickers under glaze and imprinting directly on the porcelain.

Basket, handle
Allover moriage dec, unmarked, 8-1/2" h **$375**
Hp roses, stippled gilt ground, unmarked, 7-1/2" h **$90**

Berry set, azalea dec, enameled and gilt floral borders, green M in wreath mark, 10-1/4" d master bowl, four 5" d individual bowls **$90**

Bowl
Ftd, grape dec, gilt borders, green M in wreath mark, 9-1/2" d **$175**
Hp, sailing ships with palm tree and ruins, three handles, green wreath mark, 8-1/2" d **$150**

Box, cov, floral dec, green maple leaf mark, 4-1/2" d **$115**

Cake plate, lavender coastal scene, green and gilt borders, blue maple leaf mark, 10-1/2" d **$195**

Chocolate pot
Hp, cottage and lake scene, green wreath mark, 7-1/2" h **$260**
Hp, etched gold panels, jewel trim, green wreath mark, 9-1/2" h .. **$175**

Condensed milk jar, cov, underplate, pink roses, green leaves, gilt accents, unmarked **$295**

Humidor
Blown-out, reclining camel, jeweled saddle, green "M" in wreath mark, 6-1/2" h **$2,300**
Moriage trailings, partial "Imperial Nippon" mark, 7-1/2" h **$320**
Six panel sides, gilt trim, blue "maple leaf" mark, 5-1/2" h **$115**
Water lilies dec, tight hairline in base, unmarked, 5-1/2" h **$70**

Mayonnaise set, ftd bowl, matching underplate, ladle, delicate floral design, green M in wreath mark, blue mark on ladle **$80**

Nut dish, blown-out design, three ftd, green M in wreath mark, 7-1/4" d ... **$55**

Plate
Rose dec, raspberry and gilt border, blue maple leaf mark, 7-1/2" d .. **$220**
Scalloped edge, rose dec, gilt dec, blue maple leaf mark, 10" d **$250**

Portrait plate, raised gilt, enameled jeweled border, blue maple leaf mark, 9" d **$835**

Portrait vase
Lacy gilt ground, blue maple leaf mark, 7" h **$435**
Two handles, portrait of Madame Lebrun, gilt tracery ground, drilled for lamp and later plugged, 9-3/4" h **$245**

Tankard, hp, gold dec rim and base, applied scrolled handle, blue maple leaf mark, minor gold loss, 13" h **$350**

Tea set, hp, powder blue background, swans dec, Paolownia flower mark **$325**

Toothpick holder, Woodland, white, green "M" in wreath mark, 2" h ... **$115**

Tray, hp, scenic center, medallions of roses at ends, green wreath mark, 8" l, 6-1/4" w **$150**

Urn
Scenic, enameled florals, blue maple leaf mark, bolted, lid missing, 11" h **$150**

*Nippon urn, six-sided, hand-painted, scene of trees and lake, marked, some fading of gilt on handles, rim, and base, 14-3/4" h, **$395.***
Photo courtesy of David Rago Auctions, Inc.

Two handles, allover moriage dec, unmarked, 8-1/2" h **$150**

Vase
Coralene, six-ftd base, "Pat. Applied For" mark, 4-3/4" h **$230**
Four panels with cottage scene, concave shoulders, green "M" in wreath mark, 13" h **$700**
Four scenic panels in blown out medallions, green "M" in wreath mark, bolted, 14-1/2" h **$1,350**
Ring handles, floral dec, blue maple leaf mark, chip on one foot, 9-3/4" h **$150**
Snow scene, handles, "M" in wreath mark, minor gilt wear, 5" h **$260**
Two handles, moriage dec bird, blue maple leaf mark, minor professional rim repair, 7-1/2" h **$375**

NORITAKE CHINA

History: Morimura Brothers founded Noritake China in 1904 in Nagoya, Japan. The company made high-quality chinaware for export to the United States and also produced a line of china blanks for hand painting. In 1910, the company perfected a technique for the production of high-quality dinnerware and introduced streamlined production.

During the 1920s, the Larkin Company of Buffalo, New York, was a prime distributor of Noritake China. Larkin offered Azalea, Briarcliff, Linden, Modjeska, Savory, Sheridan, and Tree in the Meadow patterns as part of its premium line.

The factory was heavily damaged during World War II, and production was reduced. Between 1946 and 1948, the company sold its china under the "Rose China" mark, since the quality of production did not match the earlier Noritake China. Expansion in 1948 brought about the resumption of quality production and the use of the Noritake name once again.

Marks: There are close to 100 different marks for Noritake, the careful study of which can determine the date of production. Most pieces are marked "Noritake" with a wreath, "M," "N," or "Nippon." The use of the letter N was registered in 1953.

Bowl, oval, Rosewin #6584 pattern, 10" l **$30**

Cake set, desert scene with tent and man on camel, cobalt blue and gilt border, marked "Noritake/Made in Japan/Hand Painted," 11" d cake plate, six 6-1/4" serving plates **$770**

Noritake Azalea pattern, lemon dish, ring handle, **$30.**

Candlesticks, pr, gold flowers and bird, blue luster ground, wreath with "M" mark, 8-1/4" h **$125**

Console set, 11-3/4" d bowl, pr 8" h candlesticks, amber pearl center, 1" black rim with gold floral dec, green mark **$465**

Creamer and sugar, Art Deco, pink Japanese lanterns, cobalt blue ground, basket type handle on sugar, wreath with "M" mark **$50**

Cup and saucer, Florola **$24**

Demitasse cup and saucer, Tree in the Meadow **$45**

Dinner set, floral motif, gold rimmed, 115-pc set **$375**

Gravy boat, Tree in the Meadow .. **$50**

Hair receiver, Art Deco, geometric designs, gold luster, wreath with "M" mark, 3-1/4" h, 3-1/2" w **$50**

Napkin ring, Art Deco man and woman, wreath with "M" mark, pr **$60**

Place card holder, figural, bluebird with butterfly, gold luster, white stripes, wreath with "M" mark, pr **$35**

Punch bowl set, 12" h two-part punch bowl with three-ftd base, six 2-3/4" h cups, peacock design, cobalt blue and gilt borders, blue ground ext., melon and blue interior, "M" in wreath mark **$600**

Salt, swan, white, orange luster, pr, 3" l **$25**

Salt and pepper shakers, pr, Tree in the Meadow, marked "Made in Japan" **$35**

Tea tile, Tree in the Meadow, green mark, 5" w **$35**

Vegetable bowl, cov, Magnificience, #9736 .... **$350**

Waffle set, handled serving plate, sugar shaker, Art Deco flowers, wreath with "M" mark **$50**

Wall pocket, butterfly, wreath with "M" mark **$75**

NORTH DAKOTA SCHOOL OF MINES

North Dakota School of Mines vase, bulbous, decorated by Julia Mattson, band of leaping bison in matte green on brown ground, ink stamp "JM 111," 5" x 6", **$1,600.**

Photo courtesy of David Rago Auctions, Inc.

History: The North Dakota School of Mines was established in 1890. Earle J. Babcock, a chemistry instructor, was impressed with the high purity level of North Dakota potter's clay. In 1898, Babcock received funds to develop his finds. He tried to interest commercial potteries in the North Dakota clay, but had limited success.

In 1910, Babcock persuaded the school to establish a Ceramics Department. Margaret Cable, who studied under Charles Binns and Frederick H. Rhead, was appointed head. She remained until her retirement in 1949.

Decorative emphasis was placed on native themes, e.g., flowers and animals. Art Nouveau, Art Deco, and fairly plain pieces were made.

Marks: The pottery is marked with a cobalt blue underglaze circle of the words "University of North Dakota/Grand Forks, N.D./Made at School of Mines/N.D. Clay." Some early pieces are marked only "U.N.D." or "U.N.D./Grand Forks, N.D." Most pieces are numbered (they can be dated from University records) and signed by both the instructor and student. Cable-signed pieces are the most desirable.

Bowl, closed-in, incised birds of paradise and cornflowers, blue, ivory, and green, by L. Whiting, circular ink stamp, incised "L. Whiting," minor fleck at shoulder, 7-1/2" d, 4-1/4" h **$1,725**

Charger, carved by Margaret Cable, stylized turquoise flowers, terra cotta ground, incised "67/M Cable," stamped "Prarie Pottery Und Grand Forks," 8-1/4" d **$450**

Figure, Bentonite cowboy, brick-red, black, and gold glaze, incised "JJ/13/ UND," Julia Mattson, 1913, 4-1/2" h, 3-1/4" w **$650**

Vase

Bulbous, polychrome painted band of pioneers and covered wagons, glossy brown ground, by Flora Huckfield, circular stamp mark/72/ Huck, incised H?, 3-1/2" d, 5-1/2" h **$1,850**

Bulbous, emb prairie roses, mottled green crystalline glaze, circular ink mark, incised "Steen-Huck-1100," Huckfield and Steen, 4-1/2" d, 5" h **$1,200**

Bulbous, emb cowboy scene, matte chocolate brown glaze, circular ink stamp, sgd "Flora Huckfield," titled "N. D. Rodeo," 5" d, 7-1/4" h ...**$1,500**

Bulbous, carved narcissus, brown and umber matte glaze, by Margaret Cable, stamped circular mark, incised "M. Cable/223," 5-1/2" d, 7-1/2" h **$1,840**

By Woodward, green semi-matte glaze, circular ink stamp mark, 6" d ...**$200**

Carved mocha brown narcissus, dark brown ground, ink stamp, incised "E. Cunningham/12/6/50," E. Cunningham, 1950, 5" h, 9" d **$1,000**

North Dakota School of Mines vase, conical, by Flora Huckfield and student, glossy celadon and brown glaze, circular ink stamp, incised "Huck and Le Masurier 2371," 3" x 5", **$235.**
Photo courtesy of David Rago Auctions, Inc.

Carved daffodils, mahogany matte glaze, circular ink mark, incised "McCosh '48," 5-1/2" d, 8" h...**$1,100**

Conical, by Flora Huckfield and student, glossy celadon and brown glaze, circular ink stamp, incised "Huck" and "Le Masurier/2371," 5" d, 3" h.................................**$230**

Ovoid, carved sheaves of wheat, purple-brown matte glaze, ink stamped and incised "Huck 30/No. Dak. Wheat," F. Huckfield, 5-1/2" d, 10" h........**$1,300**

Sq tapering, repeating scenes of farmer and horse-drawn plough, green and brown matte glaze, circular ink mark, incised "The Plowman/ Huck/119," F. Huckfield, 6-1/4" d, 4-3/4" h **$1,200**

Vessel

Beaker shape, matte brown glaze, stamped and incised marks, small rim chip, c1915, 3-1/2" h, 3-1/2" d **$115**

Squatty, carved band of cowboys under terra cotta and brown matte glaze, by Julia Mattson, stamped circular mark, incised "Cowboy-54C/J Mattson," 5" d, 3-1/2" h **$980**

North Dakota School of Mines vessel, squat, carved repeating owls under light to dark brown matte glaze, ink stamp "M.O.R. to KSR 34," 3" x 5-1/4", **$1,900.**
Photo courtesy of David Rago Auctions, Inc.

North Dakota School of Mines vase, bulbous, decorated by Julia Mattson, rodeo scenes in olive green and dark brown, circular ink stamp/JM/75, 7" x 4-3/4", **$1,400.**
Photo courtesy of David Rago Auctions, Inc.

Spherical, Covered Wagon, carved frieze of wagons and oxen, sandy brown matte glaze, circular ink mark, incised "M. Cable" and title, by Margaret Cable, 7" d, 6" h **$1,400**

OHR POTTERY

History: Ohr pottery was produced by George E. Ohr in Biloxi, Mississippi. There is a discrepancy as to when he actually established his pottery; some say 1878, but Ohr's autobiography indicates 1883. In 1884, Ohr exhibited 600 pieces of his work, suggesting that he had been a potter for some time.

Ohr's techniques included twisting, crushing, folding, denting, and crinkling thin-walled clay into odd, grotesque, and, sometimes, graceful forms. His later pieces were often left unglazed.

In 1906, Ohr closed the pottery and stored more than 6,000 pieces as a legacy to his family. He had hoped the U.S. government would purchase it, but that never happened. The entire collection remained in storage until it was rediscovered in 1972.

Today Ohr is recognized as one of the leaders in the American art-pottery movement. Some greedy individuals have taken the later unglazed pieces and covered them with poor-quality glazes in hopes of making them more valuable. These pieces do not have stilt marks on the bottom.

Marks: Much of Ohr's early work was signed with an impressed stamp including his name and location in block letters. His later work was often marked with the flowing script designation "G. E. Ohr."

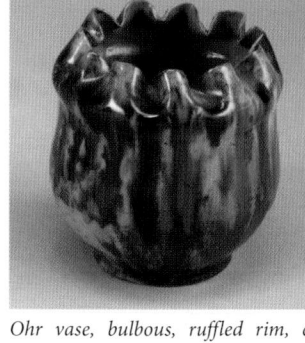

Ohr vase, bulbous, scalloped rim, flori-form dimple on front, green, gunmetal, brown, and amber mottled glaze, mkd "G. E. OHR, Biloxi, Miss," small nicks to rim, 5-1/4" x 6", sold with handwritten letter from George Ohr with poem and signature by George and his six children, dated 1899, and period newspaper clipping concerning Ohr, **$27,500.**
Photo courtesy of David Rago Auctions, Inc.

Ohr cabinet vase, urn shape, pinched and folded rim, bulbous base, black-speckled green glaze, mkd "BILOX, MISS, GEO. E. OHR," 3" x 3", **$8,000.**
Photo courtesy of David Rago Auctions, Inc.

Ohr vase, bulbous, ruffled rim, co-balt blue, pink, yellow and green flambé glaze, marked "5-1-1897, E. Dan Smith, 175 Mobile, Ala-bama," stamped "G.E. OHR, Biloxi, Miss," restoration to small rim chip, 4-1/2" d, 4-1/2" h, **$11,150.**
Photo courtesy of David Rago Auctions, Inc.

Ohr vase, baluster shape, top covered in indigo glaze over green and raspberry mottled base, mkd "G. E. OHR, Biloxi, Miss," 6-3/4" x 3", **$8,500.**
Photo courtesy of David Rago Auctions, Inc.

Bank, acorn shape, lustered brown and mirror black glaze, int. rattle, stamped "G.E.OHR/Biloxi, Miss," 2" d, 4" h **$1,100**

Candleholder, organic, pinched ribbon handle, in-body twist, ribbed base, yellow, green, and raspberry matte mottled glaze, small chip to base, script mark, 6-1/2" h, 4" d....................**$3,300**

Chalice, ovoid cup, flaring base, lus-tered black and umber glaze, script signature, restoration to cup, 3-1/4" d, 6" h..**$805**

Demitasse cup, ext. with rare green, cobalt blue, and raspberry marbleized glaze, int. with sponged cobalt and raspberry volcanic glaze, die-stamped "G. E. Ohr, Biloxi, Miss," 2-1/2" h, 3-3/4" d..**$1,500**

Jar, cov, spherical, gunmetal and green glaze dripping over mottled raspber-ry ground, shallow storage abrasion, die-stamped "G.E. OHR, Biloxi, Miss," 4-1/4" h, 5" d.............................**$1,500**

Jug
Commemorative, molded form, wide mouth and angled handle, President on one side and Ohr's wife on other, decorative star and floral motifs, caramel-colored glaze, artist's mark imp on side and signature on base, 7-1/2" h **$3,820**
Flared cylindrical rim, pinched spout, bulbous body dimpled around middle, angled handle, dark brown matte glaze, imp "G. E. OHR, Biloxi, M...," 4-3/4" h........................**$4,350**

Mug
Cylindrical form, flared base and angled handle, mottled green on yellow glaze ext., yellow glaze and green flecks int., inscription around lower portion of mug reads "Heres your good health and your family's and may they all live long and pros-per, J. Jefferson," base signed and dated "3-18-96," 6" h **$2,820**
Cylindrical waisted form, black mirror glaze, base sgd, c1900, 4-3/4" h **$1,175**

Mustache cup, hand built as a shirt cuff, ribbon handle, sponged blue glaze, die-stamped "GEO. E. OHR/BILOXI, MISS," 2-3/4" h, 4" d **$2,000**

Pitcher, pinched and folded bisque, scroddled terra cotta and buff clays, script sgd, two large sanded rim chips, 4" h, 5-1/4" d **$3,775**

Puzzle mug, mottled green, yellow, and brown glaze on exterior and inte-rior, animal head carved into angled handle, three drinking holes along rim and 16 holes around upper body, base imp "G. E. OHR Biloxi Miss," c1900, 3-1/2" h..........................**$1,775**

Vase
Bottle shape, brown, green, and amber speckled lustered glaze, restora-tion to tiny rim chip, die-stamped "G. E. OHR, Biloxi, Miss," 8-1/2" h **$1,200**
Bottle shape, mottled raspberry, pur-ple, cobalt blue, and green satin glaze, small abrasion ring around widest part from years of storage at production site, die-stamped "G. E. OHR/Biloxi, Miss," 9-1/4" h...**$2,500**

Ohr vessel, corseted, four-lobed rim, deep in-body twist, fine red, green, and blue leathery matted glaze, script signature, restoration to rim chips, 4-1/4" x 4-1/2", **$4,750.**
Photo courtesy of David Rago Auctions, Inc.

Ohr vase, bulbous, lobed rim, carved band, fine pink, green and cobalt blue mottled glaze, stamped "G.E. OHR, Biloxi, Miss," firing line to shoulder, 4-1/2" d, 5" h, **$9,750.**
Photo courtesy of David Rago Auctions, Inc.

Ohr puzzle jug, stepped handle, brown semi-gloss glaze, stamped twice "G.E. OHR, BILOXI," 5" d, 6-1/2" h, **$9,200.**

Cinched middle, folded rim, speckled brown and amber glaze, stamped "G. E. OHR/Biloxi, Miss," 4" d, 3-1/4" h **$3,220**
Cylindrical form expanding at base, caramel-colored glaze with green and black speckles, base incised "GEO E OHR, BILOXI MISS," 3-3/4" h **$2,585**
Tapered, asymmetrically folded

rim, gunmetal and yellow glaze ext., bright orange int., marked "G.E.OHR/Biloxi, miss," few minute rim flecks, 2-3/4" d, 5-1/4" h **$4,875**
Three-sectioned bottle form, glossy olive glaze, top and bottom sponged dark blue, center purple metallic glaze, die-stamped "G. E. OHR/ Biloxi, Miss," 7" h **$1,200**

Vessel
Collared rim, bulbous base, mottled dark brown and gunmetal glaze, incised "Biloxi," 3" d, 4-1/2" h **$2,300**
Dimpled, squatty, floriform top, black-mirrored glaze sponged on amber ground, stamped "G. E. OHR/Biloxi, Miss," 4-1/2" d, 3" h **$4,025**

OLD SLEEPY EYE

History: Sleepy Eye, a Sioux Indian chief who reportedly had a droopy eye, gave his name to Sleepy Eye, Minnesota, and one of its leading flour mills. In the early 1900s, Old Sleepy Eye Flour offered four Flemish-gray heavy stoneware premiums decorated in cobalt blue: a straight-sided butter crock, curved salt bowl, stein, and vase. The premiums were made by Weir Pottery Company, later to become Monmouth Pottery Company, and finally to emerge as the present-day Western Stoneware Company of Monmouth, Illinois.

Additional pottery and stoneware pieces also were issued. Forms included five sizes of pitchers (4, 5-1/2, 6-1/2, 8, and 9 inches), mugs, steins, sugar bowls, and tea tiles (hot plates). Most were cobalt blue on white, but other glaze hues, such as browns, golds, and greens, were used.

Old Sleepy Eye also issued many other items, including bakers' caps, lithographed barrel covers, beanies, fans, multicolored pillow tops, postcards, and trade cards. Regular production of Old Sleepy Eye stoneware ended in 1937.

In 1952, Western Stoneware Company made 22- and 40-ounce steins in chestnut brown glaze with a redesigned Indian's head. From 1961 to 1972, gift editions were made for the board of directors and others within the company. Beginning in 1973, Western Stoneware Company issued an annual limited edition stein for collectors.

Marks: The gift editions made in the 1960s and 1970s were dated and signed with a maple leaf mark. The annual limited edition steins are marked and dated.

Old Sleepy Eye pitcher, cobalt blue, white background, **$195.**

Reproduction Alert. Blue-and-white pitchers, crazed, weighted, and often with a stamp or the word "Ironstone" are the most common reproductions. The stein and salt bowl also have been made. Many reproductions come from Taiwan.

A line of fantasy items, new items which never existed as Old Sleepy Eye originals, includes an advertising pocket mirror with miniature flour-barrel label, small glass plates, fruit jars, toothpick holders, glass and pottery miniature pitchers, and salt and pepper shakers. One mill item has been made, a sack marked as though it were old, but of a size that could not possibly hold the amount of flour indicated.

Mill items

Advertising premium cards, full-color Indian lore illus, Old Sleepy Eye Indian character trademark, 10-pc set, 9-1/4" x 11-1/2" d **$875**

Cookbook, Sleepy Eye Milling Co., loaf of bread shape, portrait of chief **$150**

Label, egg crate, Sleepy Eye Brand, A. J. Pietrus & Sons Co., Sleepy Eye, MN, red, blue, and yellow, 9-1/4" x 11-1/2" d..**$25**

Letter opener, bronze, Indian-head handle, marked "Sleepy Eye Milling Co., Sleepy Eye, MN"..................**$750**

Pinback button, "Old Sleepy Eye for Me," bust portrait of chief..........**$175**

Pottery and stoneware

Bowl, ftd, Bristol glaze, relief profile of Indian on one side, floral design on other, imp "X" on bottom, 4" h...**$360**

Butter crock, cov, blue and gray salt glaze, relief and blue accented Indian profile on one side, trees and teepee on other side, imp "H" on bottom, surface rim chip, 4-3/4" h **$495**

Mug, marked "WS Co. Monmouth, Ill," 3-1/2" d, 4-3/4" h **$395**

Pitcher, #4, 7-3/4" h.....................**$675**

Stein, Bristol glaze, relief and blue accented Indian profile on one side, trees and teepee on other side, 7-1/2" h **$470**

Tile, cobalt blue and white **$850**

ONION MEISSEN

Ashtray, blue crossed swords mark, 5" d...**$75**

Bowl, reticulated, blue crossed swords mark, 19th C, 8-1/2" d **$395**

Box, cov, round, rose finial, 4-1/2" d **$80**

Bread plate, 6-1/2" d....................**$75**

Cake stand, 13-1/2" d, 4-1/2" h **$220**

Candlesticks, pr, 7" h **$90**

Creamer and sugar, gold edge, c1900 ....**$175**

Demitasse cup and saucer, c1890 ....**$95**

Fruit compote, circular, openwork bowl, five oval floral medallions, 9" h **$375**

Fruit knives, six-pc set.................**$75**

Hot plate, handles.......................**$125**

Ladle, wooden handle..................**$115**

Lamp, oil, frosted glass globular form shade, 22" h...............................**$475**

Plate, 10" d..................................**$100**

Platter, crossed swords mark, 13" x 10" **$295**

Pot de creme **$65**

Serving dish, floral design on handle, 9-1/4" w, 11" l............................**$200**

Tray, cartouche shape, gilt edge, 17" l **$425**

Vegetable dish, cov, sq, 10" w **$150**

History: The blue onion or bulb pattern is of Chinese origin and depicts peaches and pomegranates, not onions. It was first made in the 18th century by Meissen, hence the name Onion Meissen.

Factories in Europe, Japan, and elsewhere copied the pattern. Many still have the pattern in production, including the Meissen factory in Germany.

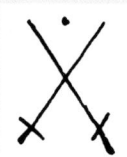

Marks: Many pieces are marked with a company's logo; after 1891, the country of origin is indicated on imported pieces.

Note: Prices given are for pieces produced between 1870 and 1930. Early Meissen examples bring a high premium.

Onion Meissen sardine box, covered, rectangular, fish finial, titled on front in plaque, marked, **$225.**

ORIENTAL CERAMICS

History: The Oriental pottery tradition has existed for thousands of years. By the 16th century, Chinese ceramic wares were being exported to India, Persia, and Egypt. During the Ming dynasty (1368-1643), earthenwares became more highly developed. The Ch'ien Lung period (1736-1795) of the Ch'ing dynasty marked the golden age of interchange with the West.

Trade between the Orient and the West began in the 16th century, when the Portuguese established Macao. The Dutch entered the trade early in the 17th century. With the establishment of the English East India Company, all of Europe sought Oriental influenced pottery and porcelain. Styles, shapes, and colors were developed to suit Western tastes, a tradition which continued until the late 19th century.

Fine Oriental ceramics continued to be made into the 20th century, and modern artists enjoy equal fame with older counterparts.

Additional Listings: Canton, Fitzhugh, Imari, Kutani, Nanking, Orientalia, Rose Medallion, and Satsuma.

Oriental bowl, flowers on side, clusters of butterflies in center, gold, pale blue, green, pink, white, and yellow, scalloped, white exterior with more floral medallions, applied table ring with small feet, red character mark, **$35.**

Bowl

Arita ware, crayfish and citron, floral sprigs on int., Japan, 19th C, 10" d **$360**

Blue and white, central design of deer and pine tree, borders of rocks, tree peonies, and banana plats, ext. of foliate scrolling, five spur marks and fuku character on base, Japan, late 17th/early 18th C, 12" d **$4,410**

Blue and white, cranes enameled on int., Yongzheng mark, China, 3-7/8" d **$360**

Light brown glaze, six-character underglaze blue mark, Xuantong, China, 1909-1911, 5-3/4" d, 3-3/16" d **$1,495**

Stoneware, hare's fur glaze, steep rounded sides, lustrous black glaze radiating off center with unglazed spot, exterior with heavy pooling of glaze towards unglazed base, China, possibly Song Dynasty (960-1279), area of raised glaze blob ground and smoothed, 4-1/2" d, 2-1/2" h **$450**

Thin body, int. with incised dragons among clouds, four-character mark, pale celadon glaze, China, 19th or 20th C, 9-1/8" l, 2-1/2" h **$300**

Box, cov

Cov painted with dragon in famille rose enamels, turquoise ground, squiggly blue line pattern, int. with same pattern without dragon, China, imperfections to glaze, 19th C, 4-1/2" d, 2-1/2" h **$120**

Peach bloom glaze, Qianglong four-character underglaze blue mark within double circle, China, small rim chips, 19th or 20th C, 5-3/8" d **$150**

Brush pot, biscuit porcelain, cylindrical, relief landscape dec, Chen Lung six-character mark on base, Chinese, 18th or 19th C, 5" h, 2-1/4" d **$575**

Brush rest, robin's egg blue glaze, three wild animals perched on rock, turquoise glaze on underside, China, 18th or 19th C, 3-5/8" l, 2-1/8" h **$230**

Brush washer, peach-form, grayish celadon crackle glaze, some areas unglazed gray color base, China, possibly Ming Dynasty, 4-1/2" l, 3-3/8" w, 1-7/8" h **$200**

Charger, blue and white, landscape with scholar on horseback being led over bridge, six-character Cheng Hua honorific mark on base, Japan, 19th C, 19-1/4" d **$765**

Cup

Quatrefoil lobed outline, turquoise glazed int., blue ground ext. with traces of gilt designs, slight flaring foot with iron red Jiaqing seal mark, China, 19th C, 3-3/4" l, 3-1/4" w, 2-3/4" h **$150**

Two medallions painted in rose enamel, underglaze blue ground, gilt highlights, border of flowers and geometric pattern inside rim, Kang Xi six-character mark on base, traces of gilt on rim, China, 18th or 19th C, 3" d, 1-1/2" h **$100**

Cup stand, Wucai dec, two dragons facing in opposite directions chasing flaming pearl, step-down base with underglaze blue band interspersed with iron red circles, deep recessed glazed base with four-character underglaze blue Yu Tang Jia Qi mark, two incised characters to left within double circle, China, 18th C or earlier, 5-5/8" d.................................**$1,100**

Figure

Seated geisha, enveloped in kimono dec with maple leaves, Japanese, small loss to enamel, 19th C, 6-1/4" h **$325**

Sitting hound, mouth slightly open, brown glazed tongue, bell suspended from green glazed collar, China, 18th or 19th C, 6-3/4" h **$375**

Garden seat, painted underglaze blue dec, continuous band of peonies and ruyi designs around top and base, Chinese, hairline crack, 18th C, 9" d, 8" h..**$925**

Incense burner

Ceramic, squat globular body tapering inwards and rising at neck, two loop handles at top of rim, thick black glaze thinning to brown around the rim, int. and base unglazed, three unglazed feet, China, firing cracks around feet, 19th C or earlier **$175**

Wucai style, painted underglaze blue and iron-red dragons on sides, band of waves, green and yellow enamels, elephant handles with attached ring, six-character underglaze blue Wanli mark on base, three feet, China, one foot chipped, cover missing, 18th C or earlier.................................**$325**

Pair of Chinese Famille rose vases, flowering peony and butterfly decoration, marked in square on base "Hongzian Nian Zhi," early 20th C, 9-1/4" h, **$1,750.**
Photo courtesy of Alderfer Auction Co.

Chinese export charger, bird and floral polychrome decoration, scalloped rim, decorated on underside, 12" d, **$200.**
Photo courtesy of Alderfer Auction Co.

Chinese export charger, underglaze blue and white floral decoration, thought to be Kang His, 16-3/4" d, **$875.**
Photo courtesy of Alderfer Auction Co.

Jar, cov, pr, bright turquoise ground, white slip dec of dragons among flowers and tendrils, cov with rose and yellow glazed peach final, base with rose Hong Xian seal mark, China, wear to glaze on finials, early 20th C, 4-3/4" h, 5-1/4" d **$990**

Lamp base, 10-1/2" h double gourd vase, underglaze blue dec, outline painted flowers and horses conforming to raised molded panels, fluted paneled neck, China, 17th C, 23" h **$1,100**

Model, Tabarabune, painted overall with overglaze enamels, sides with birds flying over turbulent waves, waves and spray modeled in relief, int. with scene of people in garden landscape, two standing on side of large fish, dragon as figurehead, Japan, 19th C, 14-1/2" l, 6" h **$1,100**

Plaque, painted, scene of samurai protecting woman and child from pursuers, 14" x 12" **$400**

Plate

Finely painted overglaze dec of bird swooping over flowering peony, two medallions with precious things inset in fence of geometric designs, back with rect Kutani and artist's mark, Japan, Meiji period, 11-7/8" h **$530**

Round, side wall rising sharply, forming deep well, center with painted dragon among clouds within a circle, cavetto with interlocking band of ruyi, band of alternating triangles on outer border, foot rim painted with basketweave design, kiln grit on inside, underglaze blue mark on base, China, Ming Dynasty, 17th C, 7-5/8" d **$320**

Studio porcelain, painted with under-

glaze blue hydrangea with pink highlights, mkd on base, Japanese, c1900, 6-1/4" d **$120**

Platter

Octagonal oblong, gilt-starred cobalt blue oval centered with gilt floral spray, gilt and cobalt blue borders, Chinese Export, glaze and gilt wear to cavetto, late 18th C, 12-1/4" x 15-3/4" **$300**

Oval, blue Fitzhugh border, shield-shaped armorial and motto "SPES INFLEXIBILIS," (hope unbending), Chinese Export, Chien Lung, repaired, c1785, 17-1/2" l **$300**

Sake washer, underglaze blue scrolling tendrils, int. with landscape, Japanese, 19th C, 6" d, 3-1/2" h **$200**

Seal paste box, underglaze blue dec of dragon among clouds, stylized waves on bottom, Kang Xi four-character mark on base, China, 20th C, 2-1/8" d **$100**

Table screen, porcelain, underglaze blue dec, one side painted with flowers, other with mountainous landscape, flat spherical form with geometrical designs on border, Japanese, 19th C, 5-5/16" d, 5-1/2" h **$350**

Tazza, ceramic, in the style of Ogata Kenzan, thick black glaze, stylized flower wheels in bright enamels, Kenzan signature on side of bowl, Japanese, small rip chips, old repairs, 18th or 19th C, 6-1/2" d, 5" h **$500**

Vase

All-around painted landscape dec in grisaille colors, two open work handles on sides of neck, base with four character Chien Lung mark, Chinese, early 20th C, 8-3/4" h **$1,725**

Baluster, blue and white continuous figural scene, Kangxi mark, China, 14-1/4" h **$1,195**

Bottle shape, coral red with a relief dragon with gilt accents, China, six-character Ch'ien Lung mark on base, but probably 19th C, 13-1/2" h **$3,200**

Blue and white dec of dragon, tiger, and pine tree, China, Transitional period (17th C), lines to base, 11-1/2" h **$1,410**

Blue and white, design of peonies and phoenixes, China, 19th C, 25-1/2" h **$450**

Carmine red glaze, incised feather-like spiral dec, interspersed with Buddhist precious things, two gilt stylized elephant handles with loose rings, Jurentang Zhi seal mark on base, China, Hongixan, wear to rim gilt, 1915-16, 7-7/16" h **$875**

Finely painted in black and brown on biscuit ground, dragon among clouds, carp leaping waterfall, dragon and clouds on neck, Xuande six-character mark on recessed base, China, 19th or 20th C, 9" h **$300**

Flat bear shape tapering to rect neck, painted in iron red and overglaze enamels with chi dragons and sacred fungus, elephant handles top with ruyi design and key fret border on base, China, 19th C, 5-3/8" h **$425**

Hexagonal, painted in famille noire enamels, front and back panels with molded relief dec of cranes and gnarled tree trunk, elephant handles, China, 18th or 19th C, 10" h **$350**

Hexagonal, six panels with fluted ridges and aubergine glaze, yellow glazed flaring neck with chi

dragon sculpted in relief in green and aubergine glaze, China, small foot rim chips, 18th C, 4-3/16" h
....**$135**

Hirado, underglaze blue dec of fishing boats moored near gnarled pine tree, flock of cranes flying on large flared neck, loose ring handles on sides, Japanese, old restoration, 18th or 19th C, 20-1/2" h, 10-3/8" d
....**$700**

Molded design of peony blossom, other peony flowers and foliage, underglaze blue mark of Makuzu Kozan within square, Japan, Meiji period (1868-1911), 8-1/2" h **$3,300**

Narrow slender form, tapering body unglazed towards base, mottled green and copper red glazes, underside revealing deep recessed glazed base with underglaze blue six-character Kan Xi mark, China, wooden stand, repairs, 18th C, 6-7/8" h **$260**

Painted famille verte enamels on yellow ground, two stylized dragon handles with aubergine glaze, China, 19th or 20th C, 6-5/8" h
....**$200**

Peach bloom glaze of celadon green running to deep red, Mei Ping, China, 19th C, 16" h **$1,100**

Shibayama, gold lacquer, diamond form, four sides dec with birds among flowering plants, mother-of-pearl, coral, and stained ivory, unsigned, Japanese, Meiji period, small rim chips, 6" h **$1,650**

Slender form, mottled copper red glaze with green splashes, heavy pooling of glaze towards base and partly ground, six-character underglaze blue Kang XI mark on slightly recessed base, China, 18th or 19th C, 5-1/4" h **$250**

Chinese vase, woman and child in rock garden, over-glaze enamels, base marked with square seal "Jurentang Zhi," early 20th C, 9" h, small foot ring chip, **$950.**

Photo courtesy of Alderfer Auction Co.

Stoneware, double gourd, incised floral dec, beige-brown crackled glaze with distinct horizontal banding above base, China, several small fired cracks, glaze chips, 18th or 19th C, 12-3/4" h **$500**

Surface carved with lotus meanders under a mustard yellow glaze, Mei Ping, six character Ch'ien Lung mark and probably of the period, 7-1/2" h **$1,100**

Tall cylindrical neck with two raised rings, mottled green and copper red glaze, underglaze blue six-character Kang Xi mark, China 19th C, 7-7/16" h **$850**

Underglaze blue dec, band of stylized flowers around bulbous body, ruyi and artemesia leaf dec on shoul-

Chinese plates, blue bats on bright yellow incised ground, central Shou type symbol, red six-character mark on underside, Chinese, 9-3/4" d, price for pair, **$200.**

Photo courtesy of Alderfer Auction Co.

der and neck, Kan Xi six-character mark on base, China, 18th or 19th C, 8-3/4" h **$550**

Underglaze blue dec, three friends of winter, prunus, pine, and bamboo, Chinese, transitional period or late Ming, slight fritting to rim, 6" h
....**$750**

Woman and child in rock garden with over-glaze enamels, base with sq seal "Jurentang Zhi," Chinese, small foot ring chip, early 20th C, 9" h.....**$900**

Water dropper, curved fish form, blue enamel glaze, Korean, price for pr, 19th C, 3-1/8" w **$300**

Whistle, modeled as child lying on tummy, pale celadon glaze, green, red, and black enamels, China, 17th or 18th C, 2-1/2" l, 1-1/2" h **$200**

OWENS POTTERY

History: J. B. Owens began making pottery in 1885 near Roseville, Ohio. In 1891, he built a plant in Zanesville and in 1897, began producing art pottery. After 1907, most of the firm's production centered on tiles.

Owens Pottery, employing many of the same artists and designs as its two cross-town rivals, Roseville and Weller, can appear very similar to that of its competitors, e.g., Utopian (brown glaze), Lotus (light glaze), and Aqua Verde (green glaze).

There were a few techniques used exclusively at Owens. These included Red Flame ware (slip decoration under a high red glaze) and Mission (over-glaze, slip decorations in mineral colors) depicting Spanish Missions. Other specialties included Opalesce (semi-gloss designs in lustered gold and orange) and Coralene (small beads affixed to the surface of the decorated vases).

Bud vase, standard glaze, yellow roses, marked "#804," initials for Harry Robinson, 6-1/4" h, 2-1/2" w **$165**

Ewer, brown high glaze, cherry design, 10" h **$200**

Jug, standard glaze, ear of corn dec, marked and sgd "Tot Steele," 8" w, 4-1/2" w **$230**

Lamp base, Utopian, classically shaped, painted yellow daffodils, unmarked, drilled, some glaze bubbles to back, hairline around neck, 11-1/4" h, 5" d **$350**

Mug, standard glaze, cherries, marked "#830," sgd "Henry R. Robinson," hairlines to int., 7-1/2" h **$110**

Tankard, brown high glaze, Indian design, incised signature, restored, 7" h **$325**

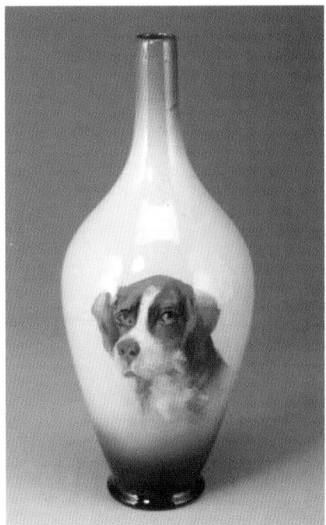

Owens vase, bottle shape, Utopian, by A. Haubrich, dec with portrait of spaniel, shaded blue and gray ground, stamped mark, artist sgd on body, tight rim hairline, 6-1/2" d, 16-1/4" h, **$1,355.**

Owens vase, Henri-Deux, tapered neck, squat base, incised white poppies, gold accents, unmarked, 9" h, **$450.**
Photo courtesy of David Rago Auctions, Inc.

PARIAN WARE

Parian Ware figure, Homer, partially draped adult male and youth figures mounted atop oval base, England, c1870, 13-1/2" h, **$1,000.**
Photos courtesy of Skinner, Inc.

History: Parian ware is a creamy white, translucent porcelain that resembles marble. It originated in England in 1842 and was first called "statuary porcelain." Minton and Copeland have been credited with its development; Wedgwood also made it. In America, parian ware objects were manufactured by Christopher Fenton in Bennington, Vermont.

At first, parian ware was used only for figures and figural groups. By the 1850s, it became so popular that a vast range of items was manufactured.

Bust

Apollo, English, second half 19th C, 9-3/8" h **$295**

Beethoven, titled, mounted on waisted circular socle, England, second half 19th C, 20-3/4" h **$1,880**

Charles Dickens, printed quote from The Old Curiosity Shop on back, short socle, English, late 19th C, 10-1/2" h **$215**

Classical Woman, with impressed "RC" mark at shoulder, English, second half 19th C, 11-3/4" h .. **$275**

Clytie, woman with Romanesque hair and draping bodice, with leaftip surround, England/France, late 19th/early 20th C, after the antique, 12" h **$300**

Maiden with ivy circlet, English, second half 19th C, 8-3/4" h **$250**

Peabody, mounted on waisted circular socle, raised title, England, c1870, 10-1/2" h **$250**

Creamer, 5" h, Tulip pattern, relief dec **$100**

Doll

Countess Dagmar, shoulder head, café au lait molded hair with side-swept wings to comb and curls in back, curls on forehead held by molded band, blue painted eyes, pierced ears, cloth body, brown leather arms, blue plaid wool dress, orig underwear, blue leather shoes, c1870, 18-1/2" h **$250**

Lady, bisque shoulder head, very pale coloring, center part blond hairstyle, 10 vertical curls, painted features, blue eyes, closed mouth, three sew holes, cloth body, kid arms, separate fingers, red cotton print jumper, white blouse with tucking and lace trim, leather slippers, Germany, c1870, 20" h....**$350**

Figure

Comedy modeled as woman adorned with flowers, seated on freeform rocky base, impressed year cipher, Minton, England, second half 19th C, 13-3/4" h **$1,200**

Lady with Lyre, modeled as draped woman, seated on rocky base, England, toe, finger, and lyre repair, c1870, 18-1/4" h **$765**

The Bather, scantily clad female figure modeled standing by tree stump, England, toe repair, footrim chip, c1870, 25-3/4" h **$1,300**

Una and Lion, unmarked, England, second half 19th C, 14-1/2" h......**$1,115**

Vision of the Red Crosse Knight, John Rose & Co. later Coalport China, modeled by Josh Pitts, England, c1851, 18-3/4" h **$2,235**

Plaque, relief, angels, brass frames, orig German labels, Boston retailers label, pr, 6" d **$275**

Sculpture, nude riding back of lion, early registry marks, c1860 ....**$895**

Urn, cov, classical shape, allegorical scene in low relief, three Graces, temples, revelers, and centaur, fish scale pattern on pedestal base, double scrolled handles, fruit finial, base marked with crown with ribbon and "FB," 20" h **$250**

Vase, applied white monkey type figures, grape clusters at shoulders, blue ground, pr, c1850, 10" h.............**$265**

Parian Ware figure, Milton, standing figure, modeled leaning on pedestal topped with stack of books, England, c1870, 14" h, **$600.**

PATE-SUR-PATE

History: Pate-sur-pate, paste-on-paste, is a 19th-century porcelain-decorating method featuring relief designs achieved by painting layers of thin pottery paste one on top of the other.

About 1880, Marc Solon and other Sevres artists, inspired by a Chinese celadon vase in the Ceramic Museum at Sevres, experimented with this process. Solon emigrated to England at the outbreak of the Franco-Prussian War and worked at Minton, where he perfected pate-sur-pate.

Box, cov, round, white female portrait, blue ground, Limoges, France, late 19th C, 5-3/4" d **$690**

Centerpiece, elongated parian vessel, molded scroll handles and feet, pierced rim, two brown reserves, white pate-sur-pate amorini, gilding, dec attributed to Lawrence Birks, marked "Minton," retailer's mark of Thomas Goode & Co., Ltd., London, c1889, 16" l.............................**$1,400**

Dresser jar, ovoid, cobalt blue ground, lid with pate-sure-pate profile bust of classical woman, gilt banding, Meissen, Germany, early 20th C, 3-3/4" d.............................**$1,955**

Lamp base, Chinoiserie-style, black ground moon flask with pate-sur-pate and blue-printed dec of village scenes, mounted on gilt-metal beaded and scroll ftd base, price for pr, 20th C, 10-1/4" h...........................**$490**

Medallion, oval, blue ground, white relief cherub figure, unidentified factory mark on reverse, France, edge ground, 19th C, 2-3/8" x 3-3/8" **$320**

Plaque

Demi-lune shape, green ground, white slip, central figure of Venus holding mirror in each hand, fending off two groups of putti with their reflections, artist sgd Louis Solin, rosewood frame, 15" l............**$9,200**

One with maiden and cupid spinning web, other with maiden seated on bench with whip in one hand, sunflowers stalked with humanistic snail on other, artist sgd "Louis Solin," both marked on back, framed, pr, 7-5/8" d..............**$2,500**

Victoria Ware, Wedgwood, rust ground, gilt florets, applied white figure of Adam, imp mark, rim chip, framed, c1880, 5-1/4" x 11-1/4".................................**$2,200**

Plate, deep brown ground, gilt trim, white dec of nude child behind net supported by two small trees, artist monogram sgd "Henry Saunders," printed and imp Moore Brothers factory marks, c1885, 9-1/8" d **$750**

Tile, sword wielding warrior on horseback, cobalt blue ground, sgd "Limo-ges France" in gold script, mounted in antique frame, 7" l, 5" w..............**$220**

Urn, double handles, pedestal base, portrait medallion, pale green ground, ivory trim, gilt accents, 8" h **$250**

Vase

Brown ground, white slip dec of cherubs flying among foliage, gilt trim rings and stylized foliate band at necks, impressed George Jones marks, c1880, price for pr, one with slight glaze abrasion, 6" h.....**$5,000**

Cov, dark brown ground, white slip of partially draped female figure holding flowering branch, shaped tripod base, gilt dec at rim, artist sgd Louis Solon, printed and imp marks, rim cover damage, minor gilt wear, 1898, 13-3/4" h......**$2,300**

Cov, deep green ground, circular panels dec in white slip, Psyche being carried heavenward by Mercury, maiden figures applied to shoulder, gilt trim, artist sgd Frederick Schenck, imp George Jones factory marks, cov damaged, hairlines to figures, light gilt wear, dated 1880, 16-1/2" h...............**$3,565**

PAUL REVERE POTTERY

Paul Revere Pottery pitcher, blue-gray matte glaze, frothy white glaze around rim, stamped "PAUL REVERE POTTERY," 4-1/2" d, 4-1/2" h, **$95.**
Photo courtesy of David Rago Auctions, Inc.

History: Paul Revere Pottery, Boston, was an out-growth of a club known as The Saturday Evening Girls. The S.E.G. was composed of young female immigrants who met on Saturday nights to read and participate in craft projects, such as ceramics.

Regular pottery production began in 1908, and the name "Paul Revere" was adopted because the pottery was located near the Old North Church. In 1915, the firm moved to Brighton, Massachusetts. Known as the "Bowl Shop," the pottery grew steadily. In spite of popular acceptance and technical advancements, the pottery required continual subsidies. It finally closed in January 1942.

Items produced range from plain and decorated vases to tablewares to illustrated tiles. Many decorated wares were incised and glazed either in an Art Nouveau matte finish or an occasional high glaze.

Marks: In addition to an impressed mark, paper "Bowl Shop" labels were used prior to 1915. Pieces also can be found with a date and "P.R.P." or "S.E.G." painted on the base.

Bookends, pr, night scene of owls, ink marked "S.E.G./11-21," flat chip to one base, 1921, 4" h, 5" w **$1,300**

Bowl
Cuerda seca dec, band of white irises on bright yellow ground, mkd "S.E.G./4-16," restoration to chip, 4" h, 5" w **$900**
Cuerda seca dec, by Fannie Levine, white geese, bright yellow ground, 11-1/2" d, 5" h....................**$35,000**

Cake set, Tree pattern, black outline scene, blue sky, green trees, 10" d cake plate, six 8-1/2" d serving plates, each marked "J.G., S.E.G.," three dated 7/15, three dated 1/4/15, one dated 3/15, price for seven-pc set.....**$1,840**

Candle sconce, cuerda seca dec, mountainous landscape with trees and irises in foreground, mkd "SG/SEG/11-13," two tight lines from center edge, 7-3/4" h, 4-1/4" w.....**$4,250**

Cereal bowl, cuerda seca dec, white swans swimming on blue water, S.E.G./A70.5.11/AS, 5-1/2" d, 2-1/2" h **$1,000**

Child's breakfast set, dec with running rabbits, white, green, and blue, monogrammed "David His Mug," "His Bowl," "His Plate," potter's mark, two chips on mug, 3-1/2" h mug, 5-5/8" d bowl, and 7-3/4" d plate **$1,380**

Fruit set, green glaze with cream-colored border, incised and outlined in black, initialed "F. G." (Fanny Ginsburg) and "S. E. G." stylistic detail,

large 8-1/4" d fruit bowl with artist's initials "I. G.," numbered "239.6.11," and "S. E. G."; and six 3-3/4" d smaller bowls with artist's initials "I. G.," sequentially numbered "196.6.11, 197.6.11, 198.6.11, 199.6.11, 200.6.11, 201.6.11" **$1,880**

Goblet, cuerda seca dec, band of white lotus, bright yellow ground, S.E.G./3.16/FL, 3-3/4" h **$850**

Humidor, cov, spherical, blue matte glaze, pink int., minute int. rim nick, sgd in slip "P.R.P. 3/36," 6-1/4" h, 5-3/4" d.........................**$400**

Lamp base, ovoid, yellow glaze, reticulated wooden base, unmarked, 18-3/4" h........................**$230**

Mug, cuerda seca dec, three fishing boats, sails monogrammed "C.R.S.," green, brown, blue, and ivory, mkd "AM/224-412/S.E.G.," 6" h, 4-3/4" d **$2,300**

Pitcher
Ovoid, applied handle, charcoal gray glaze, partial imp potter's mark, painted "4 26," artist's initials L.S., three rim chips, c1926, 6-3/4" h **$70**
Ovoid, applied handle, green glaze, painted "J.M.D. June 17, 1920 S.E.G. 5-20," by Josephine M. Davis, handle repaired, 7-1/8" h **$115**

Plate
Cuerda seca dec, white and blue geese and water lilies, green matte ground, marked "S.E.G./6-17/AM," 8" d **$1,380**

Incised geese in mottled green on speckled blue ground, painted "S.E.G. 6-13," artist's initials "I.G.," c1913, 7-5/8" d........................**$490**

Incised white mice, celadon and brown band, ink mark "Dorothy Hopkins/Her Plate," 1911, 6-1/2" d **$1,300**

Ring tray, circular, blue-gray and green band of trees, blue-gray ground, marked "S.E.G./J.G.," 4" d **$275**

Teapot, brown and white wavy band of sailboats, yellow sky, restored, 1918, 4-1/2" h, 9" d **$700**

Tile, Washington Street, blue, white, green, and brown, marked "H.S. S4 9/1/10," edge chips, 3-3/4" sq **$420**

Trivet
Medallion of house against setting sun, blue-gray ground, imp P.R.P. mark, 1924, 4-1/4" d **$425**
Medallion of poplar trees in landscape, blue-green ground, imp P.R.P. mark, 1925, 5-1/2" d **$600**

Vase
Band of trees in blue and green glaze outlined in black, charcoal gray glazed body, imp pottery mark at center of base, dated "8-23," Brighton, MA, fine hairline at rim, 10-1/2" h **$1,300**
Ovoid, cuerda seca dec, band of green trees against blue sky, gunmetal black ground, 4-1/4" h, 4" d **$2,400**
Semi-matte ochre glaze, signed "P. R. P.," dated 1926, 9-1/4" h **$265**

PETERS AND REED POTTERY

History: J. D. Peters and Adam Reed founded their pottery company in South Zanesville, Ohio, in 1900. Common flowerpots, jardiniéres, and cooking wares comprised the majority of their early output. Occasionally, art pottery was attempted, but it was not until 1912 that their Moss Aztec line was introduced and widely accepted. Other art wares include Chromal, Landsun, Montene, Pereco, and Persian.

Peters retired in 1921 and Reed changed the name of the firm to Zane Pottery Company.

Marks: Marked pieces of Peters and Reed Pottery are unknown.

Bowl, closed-in rim, round tapering bowl, raised budding branches and berries in relief, matte green glaze, couple of chips on branch, 9" d, 3-1/4" h..................................**$175**

Doorstop, cat, yellow..................**$375**

Ewer, orange and yellow raised grapes dec, brown ground, 11" h.............**$50**

Jardinière, Moss Aztec, unmarked, few small chips to dec, c1925, 9-1/2" d, 9" h, ...**$200**

Mug, blended glaze........................**$40**

Pitcher, green and yellow raised fern leaves, gloss dark brown ground, 4" h **$65**

Vase, Moss Aztec, corseted, stylized flowers and leaves, 4-1/4" d, 10-1/2" h **$230**

Peters and Reed vase, Moss Aztec, jeweled, unmarked, c1925, few small chips to decoration, 9-1/2" d, 9" h, **$250.**
Photo courtesy of David Rago Auctions, Inc.

Peters and Reed vase, Moss Aztec, corseted, stylized flowers and leaves, unmarked, 4-1/4" d, 10-1/2" h, **$235.**
Photo courtesy of David Rago Auctions, Inc.

Peters and Reed vase, Chromal Ware, ovoid, unmarked, 4" d, 9-1/4" h, **$815.**
Photo courtesy of David Rago Auctions, Inc.

PIANO BABIES

History: In the late 1800s, a well-decorated home had a parlor equipped with a piano, which usually was covered by a lovely shawl. To hold the shawl in place, piano babies were used. Piano babies are figures of babies, usually made of unglazed bisque. These "Piano Babies" range in size from three inches to more than 20 inches. They were made in a variety of poses—sitting up, crawling, lying on their tummies and on their backs. Some babies were dressed, while others were nude. The smaller babies were used to decorate miniature pianos.

Most piano babies were produced in Germany, England and France. There were more than 15 factories in Germany that produced this type of bisque ware. Among them Hertwig and Co., Julius Heubach, Royal Rudolstadt, Simon and Halbig, Kling and Co, and Gerbruder Heubach were the most prolific. Ger. Heubach produced most of his wares for export, between 1914 and 1918. The Heubach company often produced several versions or sizes of the same Piano Baby. Many of these manufacturers also made dolls and carried the artistry required for fine doll making to their piano baby creations.

A large number of the piano babies found today were manufactured by the Heubach Brothers (1820-1945) in Germany, whose rising sun mark is well known. However, many pieces left factories with no mark. The Heubach factory is well known also for creating the same baby, but in different sizes. The Heubach babies are well known for their realistic facial features as well as their attention to minute details, such as intaglio eyes, small teeth looking out from lips, blond hair, blue eyes, etc.

Adviser: Jerry Rosen.

Piano Baby holding spoon in hands dressed in white and pink gown, 6-1/2" t, **$175.**

Reproduction Alert. In the 1950s, US companies began importing bisque piano babies from Japan. They seem to be everywhere! Many of these were originally only marked with paper labels. They are not "true reproductions," as they do not truly duplicate earlier styles, but collectors should be aware that they are also not vintage bisque piano babies just because they aren't marked. Generally these types of piano babies will have a different type of painting, especially around the eyes and are usually not as detailed as the original piano babies, the quality of the bisque is usually inferior to that of genuine old bisque babies, and at times have the numbers on the base painted in red. Red mark numbers are not a sure sign of a reproduction as some antique piano babies were also marked in this way. Many reproductions also have a larger bisque-manufacturing hole in the bottom while older ones have a smaller hole. Because these Japanese bisque versions are from the 1950s and not the 1890s, their values should be considerably less than vintage German bisque piano babies.

Piano Baby, boy dressed in blue, wearing Shriners' fez cap with white tassel on back, curly hair, sitting on chair, pince-nez glasses, 9-1/2" h, **$295.**

Piano Baby wearing white dress with tiny white beads and thin green band along the top. Gold buttons at shoulders. Dress has slipped from baby's shoulder and is untied on the left side, Heubach incised Sunburst mark, 10-1/4" t, **$565.**

Piano Baby with left hand on ear, white beaded gown, #8443 incised on back, 5" t, **$125.**

Baby dressed in yellow outfit, lying on stomach with thumb in front of face, 17" l $305

Baby lying on back, with feet in air, 9" l $325

Baby on back, playing with toes, 4-1/4" t, 7-1/2" l $275

Baby seated on wicker stool, holding dress up w/both hands, 12" t $400

Baby sitting on chamber pot, holding two piglets, 7" h $240

Baby sitting up, holding bottle, 4-1/2" t......................................$102

Baby with bonnet, sitting up wearing white dress, 5" h $160

Baby with bonnet, crawling with brown and white dog on his back, 2-1/2" t, 6-1/2" l $150

Baby with dimples on face, open mouth lying on back holding kitten, 5" h, 9" l $225

Baby with flowering dress, with pear in left hand, 10" h $215

Baby with pink jeweled dress, sitting in chair, 9" $75

Bisque baby nodder, with hat taking off socks, 4-1/2" h $100

Bisque baby, standing in boots,

incised number "6751" on back of gown, 9" h $175

Boy holding two pug puppies, one in each arm, 11-1/2" t, 5" w $1300

Boy on swing, holding basket (shelf sitter), 5-1/4" h, 2-3/4" w $175

Boy wearing a green dotted sleeping dress, sitting on potty, 7-1/2" h, 3-1/2" w $125

Child in white and blue dress, with large orange hat, one sock off, 6" h $275

Crawling on hands, with legs raised, 8" l $250

Dutch girl holding egg shells in apron, 7-1/2" t, 3-1/2" w $185

Girl sitting on swing (shelf sitter) hanging with string, 5-1/4" h, 3-3/4" w $120

Girl standing in an egg, 5-3/4" t $175

Heubach, baby sitting up with arms raised, 5-1/2" t $350

Heubach, bisque Dutch girl with hand-painted egg behind her, 4-1/2" t, 6" l $75

Heubach, crawling boy, blond hair, blue bow on back of outfit, blue ink stamp marking with sun rising below imp marks, 7-1/2 to 8" l, 4-1/2" h $450

Heubach, figurine of boy, bare chest standing in tub, 8-1/2" t $250

Heubach, intaglio blue eyed molded baby wearing white gown with mint green trim, white raised dots along ruffling at top gown front, detailed dimples in knees, elbows and back, incised mark on back with Heubach sunburst marking, green #37 on bottom, 8" h...................................$600

Heubach, little boy holding his dog, blond, intaglio eyes, sunburst Heubach mark, model #11160 dep, Germany, 8" l, 4" w $560

Heubach, piano baby lying on tummy fingers in air, 4-3/4" t, 2" l...........$295

Heubach, bicycled figures, man and woman with light green bicycling attire holding metal bicycle, 14" $1,400

Lying on back baby boy, with hat and cherries in hand, 5-1/2" h, 10" $600

Pair of children, sitting on pedestals, 11" t $1,415

Piano Baby lying on her belly with feet in air clutching a stein of beer with pacifier going into stein, 3" t, 7" l, **$75.**

Pouty naked piano baby, fists curled and feet away from body, 5" t $410

Seated baby, wearing white nightshirt with gold beads and blue ribbons removing one of his socks, 6-1/2" h $250

Two Dutch Heubach children sitting, 10" t $400

Unmarked girl with bonnet and pink ribbon, hands raised to cheek, 4-1/2" t..$250

Piano Baby lying on back dressed in white gown with blue dotted collar hands touching raised foot, 5" t, 9" l, **$225.**

PICKARD CHINA

History: The Pickard China Company was founded by Wilder Pickard in Chicago in 1897. Originally the company imported European china blanks, principally from the Havilands at Limoges, which were then hand painted. The firm presently is located in Antioch, Illinois.

Bowl

Autumn Blackberries, sgd "O. Goess" (Otto Goess), 1905-10 mark, 6" d $200

Red and white tulips, gold dec, Limoges blank, 10" d $230

Strawberries, white blossoms, and gooseberries dec, ftd, sgd "E. Challinor" (Edward Challinor), 1905-10 mark, 9-1/2" d, 4-1/2" h $300

Cabinet plate

Heavy gold enameled border, Limoges blank, 8-1/2" d..................$175

Lilies, gold background, artist sgd "Yeschek", 9" d $100

Celery set, two-handled oval dish, five matching salts, allover gold dec, 1925-30 mark...........................$125

Chocolate set, 12" h chocolate pot, creamer, cov sugar, 11" tray, sgd "F. Lind" (Frederick Lindner), Pickard and various French and German back stamps, c1903 ....$1,495

Claret set, claret jug, five tumblers, 11-1/2" d tray, Deserted Garden pattern, sgd "J. Nessy" (John Nessy), 1912-18 mark..........................$2,600

Coffee set, Modern Conventional pattern, coffee pot sgd "Hessler" (Robert Hessler), 1910-12 mark, eight cups and saucers sgd "Hess & RH" (Robert Hessler), 1912-18 mark $1,450

Creamer, Tulip Conventional, sgd "Tomash" (Rudolph Tomascheko), 1903-05 mark, 5-1/4" h $400

Pickard vase, tapered cylindrical form, double gilt handles, rim, and foot, bands below rim in iridescent blue and yellow, decorated with floral motifs, vertical bands of cobalt blue with white floral decoration, textured gold body, mark obscured by paper label inscribed "Pickard China, Arno vase, Eg. G. Linear," Edith Arno, early 1900s, 7-1/4" h, **$325.**

Photo courtesy of Alderfer Auction Co.

Pickard vase, embossed gold decoration, marked, **$65.**

Creamer and sugar
Deserted Garden pattern, sgd "J. Nessy" (John Nessy), 1912-18 mark...... **$200**

White Poppies & Daisy, sgd, 1912-18 mark.. **$250**

Demitasse cup and saucer
Gold Tracery Rose & Daisy pattern, green band, 1925-30 mark....... **$40**

Poppy pattern, sgd "LOH" (John Loh), price for pr, 1910-12................. **$325**

Lemonade pitcher
Encrusted Honeysuckle pattern, 1919-22 mark........................ **$100**

Schoner Lemon pattern, sgd "Schoner" (Otto Schoner), 1903-05 mark
....**$1,700**

Match holder, Rose & Daisy pattern, allover gold, 1925-30.................... **$40**

Pin dish, violets dec........................ **$40**

Plate
Blackberries and leaves, sgd "Beitler" (Joseph Beitler), 1903-15, 8-1/2" d
....**$90**

Calla Lily pattern, sgd "Marker" (Curtis H. Marker), 1905-10 mark, 8-1/2" d **$225**

Florida Moonlight, sgd "E. Challinor" (Edward Challinor), 1912-18 mark, 8-3/4" d **$2,300**

Gibson Narcissus pattern, sgd "E. Gibson" (Edward Gibson), 1903-05 mark, 8-1/2" d **$300**

Lilium Ornatum pattern, sgd "Beulet" (F. Beulet), 1910-12 mark, 8-1/2" d
....**$100**

Yeschek Currants in Gold pattern, sgd "Blaha" (Joseph Blaha), 1905-10 mark, 9" d **$110**

Punch bowl, grape dec, sgd "Coufall" (John Anton Coufall) upper right, "T & V Limoges" and "Pickard" back stamps, c1905, 11" d.................. **$895**

Tankard, red poppies, anonymous artist, "T & V Limoges" and "Pickard" back stamps, c1905, 10-1/4" h **$1,150**

Tea set, cov teapot, creamer, cov sugar, Carnation Garden pattern, each sgd "Yeschek" (Joseph T. Yeschek), 1903-05 marks..............................**$2,600**

Vase
Calla Lily pattern, sgd "Marker" (Curtis H. Marker), 1905-10 mark, 11" h **$550**

Carmen, red poppies, sgd "J. Kiefus" (Jacob Kiefus) lower right, "D & C France" and "Pickard" back stamps, c1905, 13-1/2" h **$595**

Golden Pheasant pattern, sgd "E. Challinor" (Edward Challinor), 1919-22 mark, 8" h **$500**

Scenic, sgd "E. Challinor" (Edward Challinor), 1912-18 mark, 8-1/4" h
....**$425**

PORTRAIT WARE

Portrait plate, Queen Louise, scarf around neck and head, unmarked, 10" d, **$95.**

Dresden porcelain portrait plaque, handpainted portrait of young woman holding candle, c1900, 9-1/4", **$920.**
Photo courtesy of Pook & Pook, Inc.

History: Plates, vases, and other articles with portraits on them were popular in the second half of the 19th century. Although male subjects, such as Napoleon or Louis XVI, were used, the ware usually depicts a beautiful, and often unidentified, woman.

A large number of English and Continental china manufacturers made portrait ware. Because most was hand painted, an artist's signature often is found.

Cabinet plate, classical woman and young girl, dark green border, set into 19" d bronze and gilt metal reticulated surround with six cartouches of cavorting cherubs, German, late 19th/early 20th C, 8-1/4" d
....**$560**

Charger, Elizabethan style figures, polychrome enamel and gilt dec, artist sgd "G. Sieves 79," impressed Worcester Royal Porcelain Works factory marks, England, price for pr, c1879, 18-3/4" d.....................**$4,460**

Dresser box, cov, brass heart-shaped box, inlaid lid with hp portrait on ivory of women in formal dress, Florentine designs on box, portrait sgd "Brun," 4" l, 3-1/4" w, 1-1/2" h
....**$350**

Medallion, Le Pensee, sgd "Wagner," jeweled gilt bronze frame, 3-1/2" d
....**$975**

Plaque
Porcelain, partially nude beauty, sgd "Wagner," ornate 8-1/2" x 9-1/2" gilt shadow box frame, 3-1/2" x 2-3/4"
....**$1,035**

Woman in white gown, pink drape, outstretched hand with flowers, gilt bronze frame, putti and garlands, minor scratches, 6" x 4" **$725**

Plate
Empress Louise, central printed portrait, indistinctly titled and signed "L. Dgt," in gilt surround, paneled rim with scrolls, urns, and griffins, possibly Hutschenreuther, Bavaria, late 19th/early 20th C, 9-1/4" d **$115**

Dark haired mother and child, deep olive green border, gold tracery, marked "Royal Vienna," 9-1/2" d............. **$125**

Napoleon I, sgd "Wagner," cobalt blue and pale blue band, cornucopia and urn ornamentation, inscribed "Made for Mrs. John Doyle" verso, minor gilt loss, 9-1/2" d **$970**

Octagonal shape, hp portrait of Psyche, blue Vienna beehive mark, 9-3/4" d **$490**

Young woman with wreath of flowers in hair, marked "Royal Munich," 10" h **$115**

Young woman, gilt bronze-colored border, mounted in 15" x 17" walnut frame, German, 12" d **$300**

Tray, Napolean I, standing, looking left, left hand behind back exposing dress sword and medals, background of fine furniture and papers, gilt garland border, dark blue-green ground, fitted frame, sgd "Reseh," marked "Vienna, FD, Austria," 9-1/2" sq **$1,320**

Urn, cov, double handles, "Mme de Montesson," central portrait of French woman wearing white wig, floral designs, reverse with floral dec, marked "2912, S-2," illegible ring mark, restored lid, 15-1/2" h **$275**

Vase

Bulbous, titled "Ariadne," sgd "Wagner," maroon ground, gilt floral dec, Austrian beehive mark, 4-3/4" h **$850**

Clementine, sgd "N. Kiesel," Art Nouveau form, green-brown mirrored ground, heavily gilt acanthus leaves and vines, bearing mark of Richard Klemm, 8-1/2" h **$1,690**

Finely dec portrait of young man, natural colors, enameled bronze, tinted silver foil under sparkling crystal glaze, unmarked, attributed to Limoges, early 20th C, 7-1/2" h **$750**

Gold enamel framed portrait of Ruth, violet luster ground, blue beehive mark with "Germany" in script, 5-3/4" h **$435**

Hp portrait of young girl framed in gold enamel, violet luster ground, German, unmarked, 8" h **$375**

Woman holding yellow roses, opalescent ground in shades of green and purple, gilt floral design, Dresden, wear to gilding, 12" h **$1,570**

Young beauty with basket of flowers in garden setting, artist sgd "Garnet," base imp "Made in France," enamel on bronze, c1900, 6-1/2" h **$500**

Young beauty in red dress, red roses in hair, finely enameled on bronze, tinted silver foil cartouche against translucent emerald green ground, French, c1900, 7" h **$865**

Limoges portrait plaque, oval, depicting head and shoulders of maiden, 19th C, 3-3/4" x 5", **$425.**

Photo courtesy of Sloans & Kenyon Auctioneers and Appraisers.

Portrait plaque, hand painted porcelain, young woman draped in gossamer thin veil, accompanied by cherubs with sprig of flowers, raised gilt decoration, stamped "Made in Germany," signed "Springtime, C. Viollemot," 4-1/2" x 7", **$1,400.**

Photo courtesy of David Rago Auctions, Inc.

Knowles, Taylor & Knowles portrait plate, Napolean, dated 1901, 8" d, **$100.**

Photo courtesy of The Early Auction Company, LLC.

PRATT WARE

History: The earliest Pratt earthenware was made in the late 18th century by William Pratt, Lane Delph, Staffordshire, England. From 1810 to 1818, Felix and Robert Pratt, William's sons, ran their own firm, F. & R. Pratt, in Fenton in the Staffordshire district. Potters in Yorkshire, Liverpool, Sunderland, Tyneside, and Scotland copied the products.

The wares consisted of relief-molded jugs, commercial pots and tablewares with transfer decoration, commemorative pieces, and figures and figural groups of both people and animals.

Marks: Much of the early ware is unmarked. The mid-19th century wares bear several different marks in conjunction with the name Pratt, including "& Co."

Pratt dish, multicolored border with white flowers, yellow lilies, blue cornflowers, and green leaves, center with milkmaid and cow, 3-7/8" d, **$45.**

Bank, figural, underglaze enamel dec center chimney house, male and female figure to either side, Yorkshire, damage to chimney and backside of roof, 19th C, 5" h **$275**

Cow creamer, sponge dec, milkmaid dressed in yellow, some edge damage, rebuilt ear, lid missing, 7" l **$350**

Cradle, pearlware

Underglaze polychrome enamels, one molded with baby sleeping, repairs to hood and side of body, c1800, 4" l **$100**

Underglaze polychrome enamels, oval form molded as hooded cradle with sleeping child, restored to lower body and under base, chip and hairline to hood, c1800, 7-3/4" l **$600**

Underglaze polychrome enamel, restored chip, c1800, 5-1/4" l **$100**

Cup plate, Dalmatian, white, black spots, 3-1/8" d **$95**

Figure

Gentleman feeding black bird, sitting on tree stump, chips, restorations, 10" h **$310**

Lady with barrel, pitcher at her feet, chips, restorations, 9-3/4" h **$300**

Flask, pearlware, shell-form, underglaze polychrome enamels, slight glaze blemishes, c1800, 4-1/8" l **$765**

Jar, cov, chromolithograph lid

Rect, milkmaid, damage, undersized lid, 3-1/4" l **$150**

Round, Albert Memorial, mismatched base, stains, flakes, 4-1/8" d **$100**

Round, Dangerous, ice skating man falling, stains, flakes, 4-1/4" d ... **$125**

Round, Dr. Johnson, three men in parlor, flakes, 4" d **$150**

Round, man reading the *Times*, stains, flakes, 4-1/8" d **$115**

Round, mother and children playing hide and seek, stains, flakes, 4" d **$95**

Round, shrimpers filling their nets, flakes and stains, 4-1/4" d **$165**

Jug, molded leaves at neck and base, raised and polychrome painted hunting scene on colored ground, c1800, 8" h **$750**

Mug, colorful tavern scene transfer, 4" h **$95**

Pitcher

Medium blue transfer scene on each side of "Swiss Cottage," by J. & W. Pratt, molded handle with man's face at end, stains, hairline, 12" h **$90**

Molded figures on sides, leaves at rim and base, one side with Toby Philpots, other with classical warrior, green, gold, dark brown, and cobalt blue, flakes on base and handle, short hairline on spout, 5-5/8" h **$675**

Plaque, Louis XVI portrait, oval form, beaded border, polychrome enamels, rim nicks, glaze wear, c1793, 6-1/4" x 7-1/4" **$900**

Plate, Haddon Hall, classical figure border, 9" d **$120**

Pot lid, chromolithograph

Dogs overturning kettle of fish, flakes, 4" d **$100**

View of Windsor Castle, 6-1/2" d **$170**

Village wedding, flakes, 4-1/8" d .. **$100**

Tea caddy, rect, raised figural panels front and back, fluted and yellow trimmed lid, blue, yellow, orange, and green dec, 6-1/4" h **$350**

PRECIOUS MOMENTS

History: Artist Sam Butcher 's artwork was spotted by Enesco Corp. CEO Eugene Freedman at a booksellers' covention in 1975. At that time, Butcher and his business partner, Bill Biel, had a greeting card company. The characters depicted in Butcher's designs were teardrop-eyed children with inspiring messages. Freedman arranged to have a figurine created from one of Butcher's drawings by an Oriental sculptor, Yasuhei Fujioka.

Butcher liked the figurine and agreed to Enesco's creation of 20 others based on his artwork. He was very involved in the creation of the figurine line. The public embraced the original 21 figurines, which were released in 1978 and a collectible legacy was born.

Marks:

1981	Triangle	1989	Bow & Arrow	1997	Sword
1982	Hourglass	1990	Flame	1998	Glasses
1983	Fish	1991	Vessel	1999	Star
1984	Cross	1992	Clef	2000	Cracked Egg
1985	Dove	1993	Butterfly	2001	Sandal
1986	Olive Branch	1994	Trumpet	2002	Cross in Heart
1987	Cedar Tree	1995	Ship	2003	Crown
1988	Flower	1996	Heart		

Images appear courtesy of Enesco Group, Incorporated.

Additional Listings: See *Price Guide To Contemporary Collectibles and Limited Editions*, 9th edition by Mary L. Sieber, KP Books.

Advisor: Mary L. Sieber

...MPER

: Quimper faience, dating back to the 17th century, is named for Quimper, a French
here numerous potteries were located. Several mergers resulted in the evolution of
or houses—the Jules Henriot and Hubaudière-Bousquet factories.

sant design first appeared in the 1860s, and many variations exist. Florals and geo-
equally popular, also were produced in large quantities. During the 1920s, the Hu-
e-Bousquet factory introduced the Odetta line, which utilized a stone body and Art
corations.

major houses merged in 1968, the products retaining the individual characteristics
rks of the originals. The concern suffered from labor problems in the 1980s and was
ed by an American group.

The "HR" and "HR Quimper" marks are found on Henriot pieces prior to 1922. The
t Quimper" mark was used after 1922. The "HB" mark covers a long time span. Numbers or dots and dashes
ded for inventory purposes and are found on later pieces. Most marks are in blue or black. Pieces ordered by
ent stores, such as Macy's and Carson Pirie Scott, carry the store mark along with the factory mark, making
s desirable to collectors. A comprehensive list of marks is found in Bondhus's book.

: Al Bagdade.

nal Terms:

che border decor—single brush stroke to create floral

Broderie decor—stylized blue and gold pattern inspired by a popular embroidery pattern often used on
costumes, dates from the Art Deco era.

e—criss-cross pattern

tiche border—acanthus leaves in two colors

e lys—the symbol of France

triangle shape, raised brown
bust of male peasant in
nd blue bands in center, yel-
ton broderie" enamel band of
s on cobalt ground, starbursts
rs, "HB Quimper" mk, 7" w
..........$120

Biberon, center band of blue, green
and red flowers, yellow collar, blue
striped pedestal base, red single
stroke flowerhead around spout, "HB
Quimper" mk, 4-1/2" h $150

Bowl, male peasant w/sythe over shoulder, ft on rock, fence in bkd, green

acanthus inner and outer border,
repaired corner, Porquier Beau, 7-1/4"
..........$2400

Chamberstick, female peasant on
base, scattered blue, red and green
florals and nozzle, cobalt bobiche,
lobed base, blue dash ring handle,
"HB Quimper" mk, 6-3/4" 4125

Champagne Goblet, figural male
or female peasant bent at waist, blue
striped goblet on back, male in blue-
green jacket, white trousers, woman
in cobalt blouse, pink apron, circ base
with blue stripe, "CH Maillard," "Hen-
Riot Quimper France" mks, pr, 4-1/4"h
..........$475

Cheese Dish, cov, male and female
peasants on cov, w/band of red, green
and blue dot flowers, green serpent
knob, scattered florals on base, shaped
blue outlined base, "HB Quimper"
mk, 9" d $325

Coffeepot, raised arched panel w/
male peasant smoking pipe, band of
red and green stylized leaves on horiz
brown branch, repeat on spout and
cov, dk blue knob, wishbone handle,
hairlines, "HB Quimper" mk, 7-3/4"
..........$250

Cream Pitcher, female peasant under
spout, vert bands of blue sponged

...mper sugar bowl, covered, male peasant with walking stick, **$265.**

Bell, Annual
God Sent His Love, 15873, 1985
..........$40
I'll Play My Drum For Him, E2358,
1982..........$55
Let The Heavens Rejoice, E5622,
1980..........$175
Love Is The Best Gift Of All,
109835, 1987..........$35
May Your Christmas Be Merry,
524182, 1990..........$35
Oh Holy Night, 522821, 1988.......$40
Once Upon A Holy Night, 523828,
1989..........$35
Surrounded With Joy, E-0522,
1983..........$65
Time To Wish/Merry Christmas,
115304, 1988..........$40
Wishing You A Cozy Christmas,
102318, 1985..........$40
Wishing You A Merry Christmas,
E5393, 1984..........$50

Doll
Autumn's Praise, 408808, 1990
..........$155

Figurine, Precious Moments
3 Mini Nativity Houses/Palm Tree,
E2387, 1982..........$60
Animal Collection, Bunny, E 9267c,
1982..........$28
Animal Collection, Dog, E 9267b,
1982..........$28
Animal Collection, Kitty w/Bow,
E 9267d, 1982..........$28
Animal Collection, Lamb w/Bird
E 9267e, 1982..........$28
Animal Collection, Pig w/Patches
E 9267f, 1982..........$28
Animal Collection, Teddy Bear
E 9267a, 1982..........$28
Autumn's Praise Musical, 408751,
1984..........$135
Baby Figurines Six Pc. Set, E 2852,
1983..........$197
Baby's First Christmas, 15539, 1985
..........$27
Baby's First Christmas, 15547, 1985
..........$27
Baby's First Trip, 16012, 1985
..........$303
Be Not Weary In Well Doing,
E 3111, 1979..........$154
Bear Ye One Another's Burdens
E 5200, 1980..........$105
Believe The Impossible, 109487,
1988..........$90
Bless This House, E 7164, 1981
..........$240

Precious Moments, figurines from left to right, I'm So Glad That God Has Blessed Me With A Friend Like You, *523623, 1992,* **$100;** The Lord Giveth, And The Lord Taketh Away, *100226, 1986,* **$75;** A Friend Is Someone Who Cares, *520632, 1988,* **$80;** *and* Puppy Love Is From Above, *106798, 1987,* **$90.**

Bless You Two, E 9255, 1982 .....$53
Blessed Are The Peacemakers,
E 3107, 1979..........$102
Blessed Are The Pure In Heart,
E 3104, 1980..........$52
**Blessings From My House To
Yours**, E0503, 1983..........$85
Bridesmaid, E2831, 1984 ....$25
Bringing God's Blessing To You,
E0509, 1983..........$90
Bundles Of Joy, E 2374, 1982....$104
Bunny, Turtle & Lamb 3 Pc 102296,
1985..........$36
But Love Goes On Forever, E 3115,
1979..........$75
But Love Goes On Forever, E6118,
1981..........$112
But Love Goes On Forever Plaque,
E-0102, 1982..........$103
Camel, E2363, 1982..........$48
Cheers To The Leader, 104035, 1986
..........$75
Christmas Is A Time To Share,
E2802, 1979..........$95
Christmas Joy From Head To Toe,
E2361, 1982..........$81
Christmastime Is For Sharing,
E-0504, 1983..........$96
Clown Balancing Ball, 12238a, 1984
..........$35
Clown Bending Over Ball, 12238c,
1984..........$35
Clown Holding Balloon, 12238b,
1984..........$35
Clown Holding Flower Pot, 12238d,
1984..........$35

Congratulations, Princess 106208,
1986..........$50
Cow With Bell Figurine, E5638, 1980
..........$45
Crown Him Lord Of All, E2803, 1979
..........$97
Donkey Figurine, E5621, 1980...$25
Dropping In For Christmas, E2350,
1982..........$85
Dropping Over For Christmas,
E2375, 1982..........$103
Easter's On Its Way 521892, 1989
..........$75
End Is In Sight, The, E9253, 1982
..........$115
Especially For Ewe, E9282c, 1982
..........$44
First Noel, The, E2365, 1982.......$78
First Noel, The, E2366, 1982.......$80
For God So Loved The World,
E5382, 1984..........$136
Forgiving Is Forgetting E9252,
1981..........$82
Friends Never Drift Apart, 100250,
1985..........$71
Get Into The Habit Of Prayer,
12203, 1984..........$49
Goat Figurine, E2364, 1982 ....$62
God Bless America, 102938, 1985
..........$54
God Bless Our Home, 12319, 1984
..........$77
God Bless Our Years Together,
12440, 1984..........$240
**God Bless The Day We Found
You**, 100145, 1985 ....$115

dots and red/blue stylized foliage, blue outlined borders, "HB Quimper" mk under handle, 4-3/4" h **$185**

Cup and Saucer

Flying orange and blue bird, yellow and green tail, scattered typical flowers, orange sponged borders, "HenRiot Quimper" mk..........**$100**

Paneled, peasant woman holding flowers, panels, of ajonc florals alternating w/red and blue criss-cross designs, blue lined shaped rims, "HB Quimper" mk........**$125**

Dish, mauve or yellow flowers on green leafy stems, multicolored insect, blue Greek key design on molded and pinched ribbon border, Porquier Beau, 8"d **$2400**

Dish, cov, fluted cov w/seated male peasant playing bagpipe, ajonc florals and four blue dot designs, blue dash knob, band of med blue acanthus on lt blue ground between orange stripes on side of cov and base, "HB Quimper" mk, 7-1/4" d **$395**

Egg Dish, peasant woman in center salt well, six blue dash outlined oval wells w/scattered florals in centers, blue lined shaped rim, "HB Quimper" mk, 9-7/8 " d **$225**

Egg Stand, base w/scattered typical florals, overhead handle w/orange zigzag design, six cups w/band of red, green and blue florals, "HB Quimper" mk, 12" l x 8-1/2" w **$650**

Ewer, male peasant on front, vert red, green and blue florals, four blue dot designs, band of same florals on reverse, orange and blue striped ft, band of bluedot and half circles and yellow band w/red dots on shoulder, blue dashed hoop handle w/orange and blue side stripes, "HenRiot Quimper France" mk, 6-1/2" h...............**$95**

Figure, 3-3/4" h

Male peasant carrying flute, green shirt, orange trimmed vest, orange trousers, canted base w/Youenn on front, "HB Quimper" mk..........**$95**

Male peasant in sailor suit, linked arms w/female peasant, dk blue skirt, turquoise apron, orange blouse, "HB Quimper" mk **$125**

Fish Plate, figural fish, female peasant in center flanked by vert florals, ornage-red and blue tail, "HenRiot Quimper France" mk, 10" l.....**$100**

Holy Water Font, blue painted flowerhead on bowl, St. Anne and Mary as child on backplate, blue wavy lines

and dots on shaped border, blue cross at top, 9-1/4" l **$225**

Jam Jar, male peasant on cov, bands of green, red and blue florals, shell knob, border base of blue half circles and dots, "HR Quimper" mk, 4-1/4" h **$375**

Jug, stoneware, dbl spouts, overhead handle, cobalt chevrons, dots and ovals on grey metallic ground, "HB Quimper Odetta" mk, c1920, 6-1/4" h **$250**

Match Holder, blue outlined rect body, male peasant on front, female on rev, green butterfly handles, red dash base, "HR Quimper" mk, 3-3/4" h.................................**$275**

Oyster Plate, yellow center sauce well, red, yellow and blue "Ivoire Corbeille" design of eight inner shell shaped wells, same design on 14 outer wells on border w/busts of female or male peasant in two, yellow rim, "HenRiot Quimper" mk, 16" d **$895**

Plate

Dancing peasant couple, dk blue acanthus or "decor Riche" border on lt blue ground, crest of Britanny at top, orange rim, "HenRiot Quimper" mk, 9-1/4" d.....................**$450**

Female peasant holdoing basket of eggs in center, border of blue outlined red and blue cross hatched design alternating w/ajonc florals, "HB Quimper" mk, 9-1/2" d **$165**

Goose flapping wings, flanked by vert florals, border of red and green single stroke dashes, blue rim, "HenRiot Quimper" mk, 9-1/4 " d **$275**

Male peasant in center, green jacket, cobalt trousers, orange-yellow stockings, red green and blue vert foliage, border of alternating red, blue, green and yellow floral bunches and four blue dot designs, shaped blue lined rim, "HenRiot Quimper France" mk, 9" d **$125**

Platter

Male peasant courting seated female peasant in meadow w/trees, cobalt border w/yellow "Breton Broderie" band of enameled chevrons, cobalt rim, "HB Quimper" mk, 12-3/4" d **$1600**

Male peasants blowing horn or playing bagpipe to theree dancing female peasants in meadow, blue acanthus inner border, blue streaked free form border w/yellow,

green and blue lobes, two small handles, "HB Quimper" mk, 17" h **$2800**

Porringer, yellow and blue bird in center, vert blue, red, and green florals, green sponged inner band and tab handles, "HB Quimper France" mk, 5" h **$175**

Salad bowl, green, yellow, red, and blue exotic bird perched between two large green cabbage roses, inner band of red, yellow, and green single stroke florals, blue outlined multilobed rim, 10" d..............................**$450**

Salt, dbl, two figural swans w/center ring handle, female peasant or single stroke florals on ints, blue spot and feathered bodies, blue dash necks, "HenRiot Quimper" mk, 33/34" l **$110**

Serving Bowl, oct, crest of quimper in center, Rouen style hanging drapes on border, blue twist handles, Porquier Beau, 11" h **$1000**

Strawberry Dish, male peasant between red, green, and blue vert florals, scattered four blue dot designs, cream bowl section w/typical florals, blue outlined shaped rim, "HenRiot Quimper France" mk, 10" w **$220**

Teapot, hex paneled, male peasant in front panel, female on reverse, remaining panels w/red, green and blue florals, blue streaked knob, wishbone handle, "HR Quimper France" mk, 8" h.............................**$275**

Vase

Bullet shaped body, circ ft, vert rect handles, courint couple on front, crest of Brittany or Quimper on reverse, scattered ajonc florals, blue acanthus border on shoulder and ft, mottled blue handles, "HenRiot Quimper France" mks, pr, 5" h **$1850**

Corset shape, painted peasant lady holding knitting between blue acanthus borders, multicolored florals on reverse, "HB" mk, 10-1/4"..........**$250**

Wall Pocket

Bagpipe shape, molded brown pipes and blue ribbon, female peasant w/vert florals, "HB Quimper" mk, 7-1/2" h **$475**

Dbl, overlapped cones, frontal views of male or female peasants, blue ribbon at junction, blue and red dash borders, "HenRiot Quimper France" mk, 10" h **$495**

REDWARE

Redware egg cup, green and orange manganese decoration, attributed to Bell Pottery, 19th C, 2-1/2" h, **$2,185.**

Redware flower pot, attached undertray, green and brown glaze over cream ground, Shenandoah Valley, 19th C, 7-1/2" d, 8" h, **$2,900.**

Redware plate, sgraffito, showing Ben Franklin reading book, framed by Pennsylvania Dutch verse, dated 1779, 12" diameter, 2" deep, 19th C repair to glued crack, **$2,530.**
Photo courtesy of Bruce & Vicki Wassdorp.

History: The availability of clay, the same used to make bricks and roof tiles, accounted for the great production of red earthenware pottery in the American colonies. Redware pieces are mainly utilitarian—bowls, crocks, jugs, etc.

Lead-glazed redware retained its reddish color, but a variety of colored glazes were obtained by the addition of metals to the basic glaze. Streaks and mottled splotches in redware items resulted from impurities in the clay and/or uneven firing temperatures.

Slipware is the term used to describe redwares decorated by the application of slip, a semi-liquid paste made of clay. Slipwares were made in England, Germany, and elsewhere in Europe for decades before becoming popular in the Pennsylvania German region and other areas in colonial America.

Birdhouse, incised banding dec, finial with hanging hole, 8" d, 10-1/2" h **$470**

Bowl, mottled, orange glaze, unglazed exterior, attributed to Miller Pottery, minor chips, usage wear, 6-3/8" d, 1-1/2" h......................................**$440**

Crock
Molded rim, manganese brown int. glaze, 3-1/2" d, 2-1/2" h **$250**
Molded rim, red-orange and green glaze, 6" d, 4" h **$360**

Figure
Chicken on base, orange glaze, attributed to Jesiah Shorb, W Manheim Twp, York County, Pennsylvania, restoration to front edge of base, 2" h, 2-1/4" l, 1-1/2" w...........**$1,320**
Dog carrying basket of fruit, green-orange glazing, base sgd "Ernst Beicher, the 8 1/3 Month 1862," provenance: possibly one of two known sgd examples, Eugene and Dorothy Elgin collection, Conestoga Auction, April 3, 2004, 5-1/2" h, 6-1/2" l, 2-3/4" w **$44,000**

Freestanding hound, yellow glazed, brown raised and incised ears and tail, attributed to Peter Bell, 5" l **$9,000**
Poodle, standing, yellow, green, and brown, coleslaw clay to front half of body, leads and raised head, stepped orange oval base, incised "Anton Audon Ruppert May 1869," 7-1/2" l, 8" w **$20,000**
Rooster on base, orange glaze, attributed to Jesiah Shorb, W Manheim Twp, York County, Pennsylvania, restoration front edge of base, 2-5/8" h, 2-3/4" l, 1-1/2" w **$1,485**
Seated begging dog on base, basket of fruit, incised fur, orange glaze, attributed to Jesiah Shorb, W Manheim Twp, York County, Pennsylvania, 4-1/4" h, 2-3/4" l, 2-1/4" h **$7,150**
Seated begging dog on base, incised, dark glaze, circular banding imp at base, attributed to Elia Swartzbaugh, Jefferson, York County, Pennsylvania, 4-3/4" h, 3-1/2" l, 2" w **$2,970**
Seated dog, reddish-brown glaze, row of incised circles at base, attributed to Peter Bell, Shenandoah Valley, Waynesboro, Pennsylvania, 5" h **$8,500**
Seated squirrel on base, eating nut, orange glaze, attributed to Jesiah Shorb, W Manheim Twp, York County, Pennsylvania, tail restoration, 3-1/2" h, 2-3/4" l, 2" w...........**$1,715**

Finger bowl, orange ground, brown sponge dec, molded base, incised banding to rim, chips, small rim restoration, 4" d, 1-3/4" h................**$385**

Fireplace trivet, scalloped edges, four feet, unglazed, sgd "S. Hiney" on base, wear, 6-1/4" sq, 2-1/2" h **$635**

Flower pot, mottled green and brown glaze, rust ground, crimped rim, attached saucer, attributed to John Bell, 5-5/8" h **$275**

Redware pie plate, yellow slip decoration of three wave lines in center, straight lines on right and left, three branches on top and bottom, lead glaze, southeastern Pennsylvania, early to mid-1800s, 8" d, **$500.**
Photo courtesy of Gamal Amer.

Bell, Annual

God Sent His Love, 15873, 1985
.... **$40**
I'll Play My Drum For Him, E2358,
1982 .... **$55**
Let The Heavens Rejoice, E5622,
1980 .... **$175**
Love Is The Best Gift Of All,
109835, 1987 .... **$35**
May Your Christmas Be Merry,
524182, 1990 .... **$35**
Oh Holy Night, 522821, 1988 ...... **$40**
Once Upon A Holy Night, 523828,
1989 .... **$35**
Surrounded With Joy, E-0522,
1983 .... **$65**
Time To Wish/Merry Christmas,
115304, 1988 .... **$40**
Wishing You A Cozy Christmas,
102318, 1985 .... **$40**
Wishing You A Merry Christmas,
E5393, 1984 .... **$50**

Doll

Autumn's Praise, 408808, 1990
.... **$155**

Figurine, Precious Moments

3 Mini Nativity Houses/Palm Tree,
E2387, 1982 .... **$60**
Animal Collection, Bunny, E 9267c,
1982 .... **$28**
Animal Collection, Dog, E 9267b,
1982 .... **$28**
Animal Collection, Kitty w/Bow,
E 9267d, 1982 .... **$28**
Animal Collection, Lamb w/Bird
E 9267e, 1982 .... **$28**
Animal Collection, Pig w/Patches
E 9267f, 1982 .... **$28**
Animal Collection, Teddy Bear
E 9267a, 1982 .... **$28**
Autumn's Praise Musical, 408751,
1984 .... **$135**
Baby Figurines Six Pc. Set, E 2852,
1983 .... **$197**
Baby's First Christmas, 15539, 1985
.... **$27**
Baby's First Christmas, 15547, 1985
.... **$27**
Baby's First Trip, 16012, 1985
.... **$303**
Be Not Weary In Well Doing,
E 3111, 1979 .... **$154**
Bear Ye One Another's Burdens
E 5200, 1980 .... **$105**
Believe The Impossible, 109487,
1988 .... **$90**
Bless This House, E 7164, 1981
.... **$240**

Precious Moments, figurines from left to right, I'm So Glad That God Has Blessed Me With A Friend Like You, *523623, 1992,* **$100;** The Lord Giveth, And The Lord Taketh Away, *100226, 1986,* **$75;** A Friend Is Someone Who Cares, *520632, 1988,* **$80;** *and* Puppy Love Is From Above, *106798, 1987,* **$90.**

Bless You Two, E 9255, 1982 .... **$53**
Blessed Are The Peacemakers,
E 3107, 1979 .... **$102**
Blessed Are The Pure In Heart,
E 3104, 1980 .... **$52**
Blessings From My House To
Yours, E0503, 1983 .... **$85**
Bridesmaid, E2831, 1984 .... **$25**
Bringing God's Blessing To You,
E0509, 1983 .... **$90**
Bundles Of Joy, E 2374, 1982 .... **$104**
Bunny, Turtle & Lamb 3 Pc 102296,
1985 .... **$36**
But Love Goes On Forever, E 3115,
1979 .... **$75**
But Love Goes On Forever, E6118,
1981 .... **$112**
But Love Goes On Forever Plaque,
E-0102, 1982 .... **$103**
Camel, E2363, 1982 .... **$48**
Cheers To The Leader, 104035, 1986
.... **$75**
Christmas Is A Time To Share,
E2802, 1979 .... **$95**
Christmas Joy From Head To Toe,
E2361, 1982 .... **$81**
Christmastime Is For Sharing,
E-0504, 1983 .... **$96**
Clown Balancing Ball, 12238a, 1984
.... **$35**
Clown Bending Over Ball, 12238c,
1984 .... **$35**
Clown Holding Balloon, 12238b,
1984 .... **$35**
Clown Holding Flower Pot, 12238d,
1984 .... **$35**

Congratulations, Princess 106208,
1986 .... **$50**
Cow With Bell Figurine, E5638, 1980
.... **$45**
Crown Him Lord Of All, E2803, 1979
.... **$97**
Donkey Figurine, E5621, 1980 .... **$25**
Dropping In For Christmas, E2350,
1982 .... **$85**
Dropping Over For Christmas,
E2375, 1982 .... **$103**
Easter's On Its Way 521892, 1989
.... **$75**
End Is In Sight, The, E9253, 1982
.... **$115**
Especially For Ewe, E9282c, 1982
.... **$44**
First Noel, The, E2365, 1982 .... **$78**
First Noel, The, E2366, 1982 .... **$80**
For God So Loved The World,
E5382, 1984 .... **$136**
Forgiving Is Forgetting E9252,
1981 .... **$82**
Friends Never Drift Apart, 100250,
1985 .... **$71**
Get Into The Habit Of Prayer,
12203, 1984 .... **$49**
Goat Figurine, E2364, 1982 .... **$62**
God Bless America, 102938, 1985
.... **$54**
God Bless Our Home, 12319, 1984
.... **$77**
God Bless Our Years Together,
12440, 1984 .... **$240**
God Bless The Day We Found
You, 100145, 1985 .... **$115**

God Bless The Day We Found You, 100153, 1985 ....$107

God Bless This Bride, E2832, 1983 ....$58

God Has Sent His Son, E-0507, 1983 ....$93

God Is Love E5213, 1980 ....$98

God Is Love, Dear Valentine, E7153, 1981 ....$45

God Is Love, Dear Valentine, E7154, 1981 ....$48

God Is Watching Over You, E7163, 1981 ....$104

God Loveth A Cheerful Giver, E1378, 1979 ....$1000

God Sends The Gift Of His Love, E6613, 1984 ....$76

God Sent His Love, 15881, 1985 ....$32

God Understands, E1379b, 1979 ....$122

God's Promises Are Sure, E9260, 1983 ....$83

God's Speed, E3112, 1979 ....$97

Hand That Rocks The Future, The, E3108, 1979 ....$93

He Leadeth Me, E1377a, 1979 .. $124

He Upholdeth Those Who Fall, E-0526, 1983 ....$93

He Watches Over Us All, E3105, 1979 ....$83

Heaven Bless You, 520934, 1989 ....$78

Heavenly Light, The, E5637, 1980 ....$59

His Burden Is Light E1380g, 1979, ...$130

His Name Is Jesus, E5381, 1984 ....$118

His Sheep Am I, E7161, 1981 .....$95

I Believe In Miracles E7156, 1981 ....$98

If God Be For Us...Against Us, E9285, 1982 ....$97

I'll Play My Drum For Him, E2356, 1982 ....$101

I'll Play My Drum For Him, E2360, 1982 ....$42

I'll Play My Drum For Him, E5384, 1984 ....$30

I'm A Possibility, 100188, 1985 .. $79

I'm Sending You A White Christmas, E2829, 1984 ....$78

Isn't He Precious?, E5379, 1984 ....$44

Isn't He Wonderful, E5639, 1980 ....$72

Isn't He Wonderful, E5640, 1980 ....$75

It Is Better To Give...To Receive, 12297, 1984 ....$174

It's No Yolk/I Say I Love You, 522104, 1990 ....$96

It's What's Inside That Counts, E3119, 1979 ....$125

Jesus Is Born, E2012, 1979 ....$138

Jesus Is Born, E2801, 1979 ....$360

Jesus Is The Answer, E1381, 1979 ....$165

Jesus Is The Light, E1373g, 1979 ....$89

Jesus Is The Light That Shines, E-0502, 1983 ....$68

Jesus Loves Me, E1372b, 1979 ... $81

Jesus Loves Me, E1372g, 1979 .... $81

Jesus Loves Me, E9278, 1982 .....$33

Jesus Loves Me, E9279, 1982 ......$32

Join In On The Blessings, E0104, 1984 ....$42

Joy To The World, E2343, 1982... $58

Joy To The World, E2344, 1982, 112

Joy To The World, E5378, 1984... $60

Let Heaven And Nature Sing, E2347, 1982 ....$45

Let Not The Sun Go Down... Wrath, E5203, 1980 ....$180

Let The Whole World Know, E7165, 1981 ....$128

Lord Bless You And Keep You, The, E3114, 1979 ....$75

Lord Bless You And Keep You, The, E4720, 1980 ....$47

Lord Bless You And Keep You, The, E4721, 1980 ....$60

Lord Give Me Patience, E7159, 1981 ....$62

Love Beareth All Things, E7158, 1981 ....$63

Love Cannot Break/True Friendship, E4722, 1980 ....$133

Love Is Kind, E1379a, 1979 ....$121

Love Is Kind, E2847, 1983 ....$45

Love Is Patient, E9251, 1982 ......$89

Love Is Sharing, E7162, 1981 ... $180

Love Lifted Me, E1375a, 1979 ... $125

Love Lifted Me, E5201, 1980 .....$108

Love Never Fails, 12300, 1984 .... $55

Love One Another, E1376, 1979.. $90

Loving Is Sharing, E3110b, 1979 ....$111

Loving Is Sharing, E3110g, 1979 .. $75

Make A Joyful Noise, E1374g, 1979 ....$84

May Your Birthday Be Gigantic, 15970, 1985 ....$24

May Your Christmas Be Blessed, E5376, 1984 ....$78

May Your Christmas Be Cozy, E2345, 1982 ....$87

May Your Christmas Be Delightful, 15482, 1985 ....$61

May Your Christmas Be Warm,

E2348, 1982 ....$132

Mother Sew Dear, E3106, 1979 ....$65

My Guardian Angel, E5207, 1980 ....$223

Nativity Buildings & Tree, E2387, 1982 ....$120

Nativity Set Of 9 Pcs. E2800, 1979 ....$185

Nativity Wall, E5644 (Set Of 2), 1980 ....$143

Nobody's Perfect, E9268, 1982 ....$313

O Come All Ye Faithful, E2353, 1982 ....$93

O Worship The Lord, 102229, 1985 ....$48

Oh Worship The Lord E5385, 1984 ....$58

Oh, Taste & See That The Lord Is Good, E9274, 1982 ....$77

Onward Christian Soldiers, E-0523, 1983 ....$95

Our First Christmas Together, E2377, 1982 ....$95

Part Of Me Wants To Be Good, 12149, 1984 ....$84

Peace Amid The Storm, E4723, 1980 ....$98

Peace On Earth, E2804, 1979 ... $148

Peace On Earth, E4725, 1981 ......$95

Peace On Earth, E9287, 1982 ... $187

Perfect Grandpa, The, E7160, 1981 ....$72

Praise The Lord Anyhow, E1374b, 1979 ....$93

Praise The Lord Anyhow, E9254, 1983 ....$97

Prayer Changes Things, E1375b, 1979 ....$195

Prayer Changes Things, E5214, 1980 ....$141

Precious Memories, E2828, 1983 ....$103

Prepare Ye The Way Of The Lord, E-0508, 1983 ....$165

Press On, E9265, 1983 ....$88

Purr-Fect Grandma, The, E3109, 1979 ....$60

Purr-Fect Grandma, The, E7242, 1982 ....$90

Purr-Fect Grandma, The, Thimble 13307, 1985 ....$30

Rejoice O Earth, E5636, 1980 ......$59

Rejoicing With You, E4724, 1980 ....$83

Serving The Lord, 100293, 1985... $54

Sharing Our Christmas Together, 102490, 1986 ....$89

Sharing Our Joy Together, E2834, 1982 ....$61

Sharing Our Season Together, E-0501, 1983 .... $155
Shepherd Of Love, 102261, 1985 .... $17
Silent Knightl, E5642, 1980 ...... $375
Silent Night, 15814, 1985 .... $99
Smile, God Loves You, E1373b, 1979 .... $85
Summer's Joy Musical, 408743, 1984 .... $200
Surrounded With Joy, E-0506, 1983 .... $85
Tell Me The Story Of Jesus, E2349, 1982 .... $115
Thank You For Coming To My Aide, E5202, 1980 .... $143
Thanking Him For You, E7155, 1981 .... $57
Thee I Love, E3116, 1979 .... $118
There Is Joy In Serving Jesus, E7157, 1981 .... $65
They Followed The Star, E5624, 1980 .... $288
They Followed The Star, E5641, 1980 .... $230
This Is Your Day To Shine, E2822, 1983 .... $102
Thou Art Mine, E3113, 1979 .... $70
To A Special Dad, E5212, 1980 ... $55
To A Very Special Mom, E2824, 1983 .... $51
To A Very Special Sister, E2825, 1983 .... $68
To God Be The Glory, E2823, 1983 110
To My Favorite Paw, 100021, 1985 .... $78
To My Forever Friend, 100072, 1985 .... $88
To Some Bunny Special, E9282a, 1982 .... $53
To Thee W/Love E3120, 1979 ... $83
Trust In The Lord E9289, 1982 .. $77
Tubby's First Christmas, E-0511, 1983 .... $42
Unto Us A Child Is Born, E2013, 1979 .... $120
Voice Of Spring Musical, The, 408735, 1984 .... $205
Walking By Faith, E3117, 1979 .. $109
We Are God's Workmanship, E9258, 1982 .... $50
We Have Seen His Star, E2010, 1979 .... $105
Wee Three Kings, E5635, 1980 ... $118
We're In It Together, E9259, 1982 .... $82
Wishing You A Cozy Christmas, 102342, 1985 .... $50
Wishing You A Merry Christmas, E5383, 1984 .... $43

Wishing You A Yummy Christmas, 109754, 1986 .... $65
Worship The Lord, 100064, 1985 .. $40
You Are My Happiness, 526185, 1990 .... $75
You Can Fly 12335, 1985 .... $70
You Can't Run Away From God, E-0525, 1983 .... $130
You Have Touched So Many Hearts, 527661, 1982 .... $43
You Have Touched So Many Hearts, E2821, 1984 .... $68
You're Worth Your Weight In Gold, E9282b, 1982 .... $40

Figurine, Family Christmas Scene
Christmas Fireplace, 524883, 1990 .... $60
God Gave His Best, 15806, 1985 .. $44
Have A Beary Merry Christmas, 522856, 1989 .... $43
May You Have...Sweetest Christmas, 15776, 1985 .... $48
Sharing Our Christmas Together, 102490, 1986 .... $89
Story Of God's Love, The, 15784, 1985 .... $55
Tell Me A Story, 15792, 1985 ..... $34

Figurine, Nativity
Come Let Us Adore Him, 104000 (Set Of 9), 1986 .... $145
Come Let Us Adore Him, 104523, 1986 .... $465
Come Let Us Adore Him, E2011, 1979 .... $320
Come Let Us Adore Him, E2395 (Set Of 11), 1982 .... $158
Come Let Us Adore Him, E2800 (Set Of 9), 1980 .... $300
Come Let Us Adore Him, E5619, 1980 .... $44

Plate, Christmas Collection
Come Let Us Adore Him, E5646, 1981 .... $55
Let Heaven And Nature Sing, E2347, 1982 .... $45
Unto Us A Child Is Born, E5395, 1984 .... $45
Wee Three Kings, E-0538, 1983 .. $50

Plate, Christmas Love
I'm Sending You A White Christmas, 101834, 1986 .... $50
May Your Christmas Be/Happy Home, 523003, 1989 .... $50
Merry Christmas Deer, 520284, 1988 .... $60

My Peace I Give To Thee, 102954, 1987 .... $70

Plate, Joy Of Christmas
Christmastime Is For Sharing, E-0505, 1983 .... $80
I'll Play My Drum For Him, E2357, 1982 .... $70
Tell Me The Story Of Jesus, 15237, 1984 .... $80
Wonder Of Christmas, The, E5396, 1984 .... $50

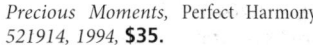

Precious Moments, Perfect Harmony, *521914, 1994,* **$35.**

Precious Moments, You Suit Me To a Tee, *526193,* **$38.**

Precious Moments, Mother's Day, Thinking Of You Is What I Really Like To Do, *1993,* **$55.**

QUIMPER

History: Quimper faience, dating back to the 17th century, is named for Quimper, a French town where numerous potteries were located. Several mergers resulted in the evolution of two major houses—the Jules Henriot and Hubaudière-Bousquet factories.

The peasant design first appeared in the 1860s, and many variations exist. Florals and geometrics, equally popular, also were produced in large quantities. During the 1920s, the Hubaudière-Bousquet factory introduced the Odetta line, which utilized a stone body and Art Deco decorations.

The two major houses merged in 1968, the products retaining the individual characteristics and marks of the originals. The concern suffered from labor problems in the 1980s and was purchased by an American group.

Marks: The "HR" and "HR Quimper" marks are found on Henriot pieces prior to 1922. The "Henriot Quimper" mark was used after 1922. The "HB" mark covers a long time span. Numbers or dots and dashes were added for inventory purposes and are found on later pieces. Most marks are in blue or black. Pieces ordered by department stores, such as Macy's and Carson Pirie Scott, carry the store mark along with the factory mark, making them less desirable to collectors. A comprehensive list of marks is found in Bondhus's book.

Adviser: Al Bagdade.

Additional Terms:

A la touche border decor—single brush stroke to create floral

Breton Broderie decor—stylized blue and gold pattern inspired by a popular embroidery pattern often used on Breton costumes, dates from the Art Deco era.

Croisille—criss-cross pattern

Decor Riche border—acanthus leaves in two colors

Fleur de lys—the symbol of France

Ashtray, triangle shape, raised brown washed bust of male peasant in orange and blue bands in center, yellow "Breton broderie" enamel band of chevrons on cobalt ground, starbursts at corners, "HB Quimper" mk, 7" w **$120**

Biberon, center band of blue, green and red flowers, yellow collar, blue striped pedestal base, red single stroke flowerhead around spout, "HB Quimper" mk, 4-1/2" h **$150**

Bowl, male peasant w/sythe over shoulder, ft on rock, fence in bkd, green acanthus inner and outer border, repaired corner, Porquier Beau, 7-1/4" **$2400**

Chamberstick, female peasant on base, scattered blue, red and green florals and nozzle, cobalt bobiche, lobed base, blue dash ring handle, "HB Quimper" mk, 6-3/4" **4125**

Champagne Goblet, figural male or female peasant bent at waist, blue striped goblet on back, male in blue-green jacket, white trousers, woman in cobalt blouse, pink apron, circ base with blue stripe, "CH Maillard," "Henriot Quimper France" mks, pr, 4-1/4"h **$475**

Cheese Dish, cov, male and female peasants on cov, w/band of red, green and blue dot flowers, green serpent knob, scattered florals on base, shaped blue outlined base, "HB Quimper" mk, 9" d **$325**

Coffeepot, raised arched panel w/ male peasant smoking pipe, band of red and green stylized leaves on horiz brown branch, repeat on spout and cov, dk blue knob, wishbone handle, hairlines, "HB Quimper" mk, 7-3/4" **$250**

Cream Pitcher, female peasant under spout, vert bands of blue sponged

Quimper sugar bowl, covered, male peasant with walking stick, **$265.**

dots and red/blue stylized foliage, blue outlined borders, "HB Quimper" mk under handle, 4-3/4" h **$185**

Cup and Saucer

Flying orange and blue bird, yellow and green tail, scattered typical flowers, orange sponged borders, "HenRiot Quimper" mk **$100**

Paneled, peasant woman holding flowers, panels, of ajonc florals alternating w/red and blue criss-cross designs, blue lined shaped rims, "HB Quimper" mk **$125**

Dish, mauve or yellow flowers on green leafy stems, multicolored insect, blue Greek key design on molded and pinched ribbon border, Porquier Beau, 8"d **$2400**

Dish, cov, fluted cov w/seated male peasant playing bagpipe, ajonc florals and four blue dot designs, blue dash knob, band of med blue acanthus on lt blue ground between orange stripes on side of cov and base, "HB Quimper" mk, 7-1/4" d **$395**

Egg Dish, peasant woman in center salt well, six blue dash outlined oval wells w/scattered florals in centers, blue lined shaped rim, "HB Quimper" mk, 9-7/8" d **$225**

Egg Stand, base w/scattered typical florals, overhead handle w/orange zigzag design, six cups w/band of red, green and blue florals, "HB Quimper" mk, 12" l x 8-1/2" w **$650**

Ewer, male peasant on front, vert red, green and blue florals, four blue dot designs, band of same florals on reverse, orange and blue striped ft, band of bluedot and half circles and yellow band w/red dots on shoulder, blue dashed hoop handle w/orange and blue side stripes, "HenRiot Quimper France" mk, 6-1/2" h **$95**

Figure, 3-3/4" h

Male peasant carrying flute, green shirt, orange trimmed vest, orange trousers, canted base w/Youenn on front, "HB Quimper" mk **$95**

Male peasant in sailor suit, linked arms w/female peasant, dk blue skirt, turquoise apron, orange blouse, "HB Quimper" mk **$125**

Fish Plate, figural fish, female peasant in center flanked by vert florals, ornage-red and blue tail, "HenRiot Quimper France" mk, 10" l **$100**

Holy Water Font, blue painted flowerhead on bowl, St. Anne and Mary as child on backplate, blue wavy lines

and dots on shaped border, blue cross at top, 9-1/4" l **$225**

Jam Jar, male peasant on cov, bands of green, red and blue florals, shell knob, border base of blue half circles and dots, "HR Quimper" mk, 4-1/4" h **$375**

Jug, stoneware, dbl spouts, overhead handle, cobalt chevrons, dots and ovals on grey metallic ground, "HB Quimper Odetta" mk, c1920, 6-1/4" h **$250**

Match Holder, blue outlined rect body, male peasant on front, female on rev, green butterfly handles, red dash base, "HR Quimper" mk, 3-3/4" h **$275**

Oyster Plate, yellow center sauce well, red, yellow and blue "Ivoire Corbeille" design of eight inner shell shaped wells, same design on 14 outer wells on border w/busts of female or male peasant in two, yellow rim, "HenRiot Quimper" mk, 16" d **$895**

Plate

Dancing peasant couple, dk blue acanthus or "decor Riche" border on lt blue ground, crest of Britanny at top, orange rim, "HenRiot Quimper" mk, 9-1/4" d **$450**

Female peasant holdoing basket of eggs in center, border of blue outlined red and blue cross hatched design alternating w/ajonc florals, "HB Quimper" mk, 9-1/2" d **$165**

Goose flapping wings, flanked by vert florals, border of red and green single stroke dashes, blue rim, "HenRiot Quimper" mk, 9-1/4 " d **$275**

Male peasant in center, green jacket, cobalt trousers, orange-yellow stockings, red green and blue vert foliage, border of alternating red, blue, green and yellow floral bunches and four blue dot designs, shaped blue lined rim, "HenRiot Quimper France" mk, 9" d **$125**

Platter

Male peasant courting seated female peasant in meadow w/trees, cobalt border w/yellow "Breton Broderie" band of enameled chevrons, cobalt rim, "HB Quimper" mk, 12-3/4" d **$1600**

Male peasants blowing horn or playing bagpipe to theree dancing female peasants in meadow, blue acanthus inner border, blue streaked free form border w/yellow,

green and blue lobes, two small handles, "HB Quimper" mk, 17" h **$2800**

Porringer, yellow and blue bird in center, vert blue, red, and green florals, green sponged inner band and tab handles, "HB Quimper France" mk, 5" h **$175**

Salad bowl, green, yellow, red, and blue exotic bird perched between two large green cabbage roses, inner band of red, yellow, and green single stroke florals, blue outlined multilobed rim, 10" d **$450**

Salt, dbl, two figural swans w/center ring handle, female peasant or single stroke florals on ints, blue spot and feathered bodies, blue dash necks, "HenRiot Quimper" mk, 33/34" l **$110**

Serving Bowl, oct, crest of quimper in center, Rouen style hanging drapes on border, blue twist handles, Porquier Beau, 11" h **$1000**

Strawberry Dish, male peasant between red, green, and blue vert florals, scattered four blue dot designs, cream bowl section w/typical florals, blue outlined shaped rim, "HenRiot Quimper France" mk, 10" w **$220**

Teapot, hex paneled, male peasant in front panel, female on reverse, remaining panels w/red, green and blue florals, blue streaked knob, wishbone handle, "HR Quimper France" mk, 8" h **$275**

Vase

Bullet shaped body, circ ft, vert rect handles, courint couple on front, crest of Brittany or Quimper on reverse, scattered ajonc florals, blue acanthus border on shoulder and ft, mottled blue handles, "HenRiot Quimper France" mks, pr, 5" h **$1850**

Corset shape, painted peasant lady holding knitting between blue acanthus borders, multicolored florals on reverse, "HB" mk, 10-1/4" **$250**

Wall Pocket

Bagpipe shape, molded brown pipes and blue ribbon, female peasant w/vert florals, "HB Quimper" mk, 7-1/2" h **$475**

Dbl, overlapped cones, frontal views of male or female peasants, blue ribbon at junction, blue and red dash borders, "HenRiot Quimper France" mk, 10" h **$495**

REDWARE

History: The availability of clay, the same used to make bricks and roof tiles, accounted for the great production of red earthenware pottery in the American colonies. Redware pieces are mainly utilitarian—bowls, crocks, jugs, etc.

Lead-glazed redware retained its reddish color, but a variety of colored glazes were obtained by the addition of metals to the basic glaze. Streaks and mottled splotches in redware items resulted from impurities in the clay and/or uneven firing temperatures.

Slipware is the term used to describe redwares decorated by the application of slip, a semi-liquid paste made of clay. Slipwares were made in England, Germany, and elsewhere in Europe for decades before becoming popular in the Pennsylvania German region and other areas in colonial America.

Redware egg cup, green and orange manganese decoration, attributed to Bell Pottery, 19th C, 2-1/2" h, **$2,185.**

Redware flower pot, attached undertray, green and brown glaze over cream ground, Shenandoah Valley, 19th C, 7-1/2" d, 8" h, **$2,900.**

Redware plate, sgraffito, showing Ben Franklin reading book, framed by Pennsylvania Dutch verse, dated 1779, 12" diameter, 2" deep, 19th C repair to glued crack, **$2,530.**
Photo courtesy of Bruce & Vicki Wassdorp.

Redware pie plate, yellow slip decoration of three wave lines in center, straight lines on right and left, three branches on top and bottom, lead glaze, southeastern Pennsylvania, early to mid-1800s, 8" d, **$500.**
Photo courtesy of Gamal Amer.

Birdhouse, incised banding dec, finial with hanging hole, 8" d, 10-1/2" h **$470**

Bowl, mottled, orange glaze, unglazed exterior, attributed to Miller Pottery, minor chips, usage wear, 6-3/8" d, 1-1/2" h **$440**

Crock
Molded rim, manganese brown int. glaze, 3-1/2" d, 2-1/2" h **$250**
Molded rim, red-orange and green glaze, 6" d, 4" h **$360**

Figure
Chicken on base, orange glaze, attributed to Jesiah Shorb, W Manheim Twp, York County, Pennsylvania, restoration to front edge of base, 2" h, 2-1/4" l, 1-1/2" w **$1,320**
Dog carrying basket of fruit, green-orange glazing, base sgd "Ernst Beicher, the 8 1/3 Month 1862," provenance: possibly one of two known sgd examples, Eugene and Dorothy Elgin collection, Conestoga Auction, April 3, 2004, 5-1/2" h, 6-1/2" l, 2-3/4" w **$44,000**

Freestanding hound, yellow glazed, brown raised and incised ears and tail, attributed to Peter Bell, 5" l **$9,000**
Poodle, standing, yellow, green, and brown, coleslaw clay to front half of body, leads and raised head, stepped orange oval base, incised "Anton Audon Ruppert May 1869," 7-1/2" l, 8" w **$20,000**
Rooster on base, orange glaze, attributed to Jesiah Shorb, W Manheim Twp, York County, Pennsylvania, restoration front edge of base, 2-5/8" h, 2-3/4" l, 1-1/2" w **$1,485**
Seated begging dog on base, basket of fruit, incised fur, orange glaze, attributed to Jesiah Shorb, W Manheim Twp, York County, Pennsylvania, 4-1/4" h, 2-3/4" l, 2-1/4" h **$7,150**
Seated begging dog on base, incised, dark glaze, circular banding imp at base, attributed to Elia Swartzbaugh, Jefferson, York County, Pennsylvania, 4-3/4" h, 3-1/2" l, 2" w **$2,970**
Seated dog, reddish-brown glaze, row of incised circles at base, attributed to Peter Bell, Shenandoah Valley, Waynesboro, Pennsylvania, 5" h **$8,500**
Seated squirrel on base, eating nut, orange glaze, attributed to Jesiah Shorb, W Manheim Twp, York County, Pennsylvania, tail restoration, 3-1/2" h, 2-3/4" l, 2" w **$1,715**

Finger bowl, orange ground, brown sponge dec, molded base, incised banding to rim, chips, small rim restoration, 4" d, 1-3/4" h................. **$385**

Fireplace trivet, scalloped edges, four feet, unglazed, sgd "S. Hiney" on base, wear, 6-1/4" sq, 2-1/2" h **$635**

Flower pot, mottled green and brown glaze, rust ground, crimped rim, attached saucer, attributed to John Bell, 5-5/8" h **$275**

Inkwell, three inkwells, sander, two pen compartments, dark manganese glaze, PA, firing line on front, 8" l, 3-1/2" w, 3-3/4" h **$600**

Jar, cov, bear shape, button finial, orange-brown glaze, 7-5/8" h, 6" d **$1,045**

Jar, open

Barrel shaped, splotched dec, four ribbed and incised bands, dated "1766," 7-1/2" h **$5,000**

Bulbous, flared rim, incised banding, red-orange ground, black sponge-dripped highlights, 5-1/4" h, 5" d **$750**

Flared rim, sloped shoulder, brownish-green glaze with lighter spots and dark brown streaks, attributed to New England, minor wear to glaze on rim, late 18th/early 19th C, 7" h **$360**

Flared rim, three color slip dec of village, houses, pine trees, grass, festooned yellow slip border, found in Hanover, Pennsylvania, 6-3/4" h, 6" d **$9,350**

Ovoid, raised rim, lug handles, incised line on shoulder, brown streak deco, CT, minor shallow rim chips, early 19th C, 11" h **$1,530**

Jug

Applied handle, incised banding at center, brown manganese glaze, 5-3/4" d, 6-1/4" h **$200**

Bulbous, applied handle, brown manganese glaze, minor chips, 4-1/2" d, 5" h **$415**

Bulbous, applied handle, incised banding on shoulder, manganese glaze, glaze chips, 5-1/2" d, 6-1/2" h **$440**

Bulbous, applied handle, formed spout, brown manganese glaze, 6-1/2" d, 9" h **$220**

Bulbous, applied handle, molded spout, brown manganese glaze, 6" d, 7-1/8" h **$250**

Bulbous, applied handle, brown manganese glaze, 7" d, 8-3/4" h ..**$275**

Applied handle, brown manganese glaze, usage wear, base chips, 7-1/4" d, 8-1/4" h **$210**

Harvest, spout, mottled glaze, yellow and brown glaze, stamped "G. H. Baker" on side, ("G. H. Baker, Hamilton Twp, Adams County, PA," 9" d **$2,860**

Miniature

Jug, applied handle, brown and black mottled glaze, attributed to Jesiah Shorb, W Manheim Twp, York County, Pennsylvania, handle broken and glued, 2-1/2" w, 3" h ..**$110**

Turk's head, brown-orange glaze, Pennsylvania, 3-3/4" d, 1-1/2" h **$715**

Pie plate, slip dec, orange base glaze int., three double slip squiggle lines, 8-5/8" d, 1-3/4" h **$1,375**

Plate

Orange ground glaze, green and black slip tulip dec, attributed to Dryville Pottery, some discoloration, 8-7/8" d, 1-1/2" h **$2,750**

Serrated rim, yellow slip dec of bird on branch, orange glaze, normal wear, 10-3/4" d, 1-3/4" h **$8,525**

Sgraffito dec, centralized flower, German text banding rim, orange ground, yellow, blue, and green highlights to flower, dated 1846, translation of rim inscription "The Star that Looks Down on the Flask has Destroyed the Luck of Many," minor chips on rim, 10-3/4" d, 1-3/4" h **$11,000**

Mary's Dish, squiggle lines and dots, interior flakes and chips, 11-3/4" d **$4,800**

Pot, incised bands at rim and base, brown glaze, 4-3/4" d, 3-7/8" h ...**$135**

Potter's brick, orange glaze, inscribed "Solomon Miller, Reading Township, Adams Co. May 28," back with date 186?, wear from use as door stop, 4-1/2" l, 3" w, 2" h **$715**

Salt, open, master, incised banding, brown and black glaze, inscribed "Made by Solomon Miller," Adams Co., Pennsylvania, 3-3/4" d, 2" h.......**$2,310**

Shaving mug, reddish-brown glazed slipware, brown splotched dots and lines, two bands of incised lines, c1805-25, small scuttle container **$3,300**

Smoking pipe, orange and brown mottled glaze, 3-1/2" w, 3-1/2" h ..**$750**

Sugar bowl, cov

Open reticulated work on bowl and lid, rope twist handles, yellow-brown glaze, attributed to Jesiah Shorb, W Manheim Twp, York County, Pennsylvania...........**$9,900**

Two applied handles, molded rim, red-brown glaze, drip manganese brown dec, zigzag banding on lid with finial, 6-1/2" w, 5-1/4" h **$1,595**

Vessel, tapered, incised banding, D-shaped cut-out handles, orange and green mottled glaze, Dover, York County, Pennsylvania, 7-3/4" d, 5-3/4" h...**$880**

Redware charger, Pennsylvania, yellow slip decoration, 14" d, **$980.**
Photo courtesy of Pook & Pook, Inc.

Redware charger, Pennsylvania, yellow slip wavy line, 19th C, 14-1/4" d, **$635.**
Photo courtesy of Pook & Pook, Inc.

Redware charger, Pennsylvania, yellow slip wavy line, 19th C, 12" d, **$575.**
Photo courtesy of Pook & Pook, Inc.

Redware plate, yellow slip decoration, Pennsylvania, 19th C, chip, 5-3/4" d, **$415.**

Red Wing ten-gallon crock with Washington advertising that includes crockery, **$1,500.**

Red Wing, two-gallon crock, with tilted birch leaves and oval stamp with "Minnesota Stoneware Company" (spelled out, commonly found as "Co."), 12" t with lid, otherwise unmarked, **$1,500.**

Red Wing two-gallon white stoneware water cooler, small wing and bail handles, 11" h without lid; lid, 9" d, **$2,200.**

Red Wing two-gallon white stoneware churn with birch leaves, and cover, 12-1/2" t without cover, **$500-$700.**

RED WING POTTERY

History: The Red Wing pottery category includes several potteries from Red Wing, Minnesota. In 1868, David Hallem started Red Wing Stoneware Co., the first pottery with stoneware as its primary product. The Minnesota Stoneware Co. started in 1883. The North Star Stoneware Co. was in business from 1892 to 1896.

The Red Wing Stoneware Co. and the Minnesota Stoneware Co. merged in 1892. The new company, the Red Wing Union Stoneware Co., made stoneware until 1920 when it introduced a pottery line that it continued until the 1940s. In 1936, the name was changed to Red Wing Potteries, Inc. During the 1930s, this firm introduced several popular patterns of hand-painted dinnerware, which were distributed through department stores, mail-order catalogs, and gift-stamp centers. Dinnerware production declined in the 1950s and was replaced with hotel and restaurant china in the early 1960s. The plant closed in 1967.

Marks: Red Wing Stoneware Co. was the first firm to mark pieces with a red wing stamped under the glaze. The North Star Stoneware Co. used a raised star and the words "Red Wing" as its mark.

Red Wing six-gallon white stoneware churn with birch leaves called "elephant ears," 17-1/2" t, **$800-$1,000.**

Bean pot, cov, "It Pays to Trade with Shors & Alexander Pocahontas, IA"
.... **$85**

Bowl
Brown shoulder, bottom mkd, 7" d
.... **$45**
Greek Key, 6" d **$115**
Shoulder, mkd, 13" d **$175**
Sponge dec, cap shape, 7" d **$95**
Spongeband, 4" d **$275**
Spongeband, 9" d **$145**
Spongeband, "Merry Christmas from Weigolb & Nordby Stores, Mix With Us," 8" d **$125**

Butter churn, two gallons, 2" wing and oval mark **$250**
Butter crock
One gallon, "Polly Ann Boston Baked Beans" **$175**
Five lbs, "Goodhue County Co-operative Co.," minor nick on top edge
.... **$95**
Three lbs, "Fresh Butter Model Dairy Inc." **$75**
Three lbs, "North American Creameries, Inc., Meadowbrook Butter" .. **$125**
Three lbs, "White & Mathers" adv
.... **$200**

Red Wing four-gallon white stoneware water cooler without gallon mark, lid impressed "3W"; 12-3/4" h without lid; lid, 9-1/2" d, **$800-$1,000.**

Red Wing five-gallon salt-glaze "beehive" jug with cobalt "tornado" decoration, with glaze drippings called "turkey droppings," unmarked, c1890, 17" t, **$2,750-$3,000.**

Red Wing rare five-gallon white stoneware "beehive" two-handle jug with advertising, 17" h, **$4,000.**

Casserole, Spongeband, large **$125**
Casserole, cov, "Merry Christmas Hokah Co-Op Creamery," 8" d **$195**
Chicken water, half gallon, "Oak Leaf Simmon's Hardware Co." **$250**
Churn, four gallons
  Oval mark and 4" wing **$175**
  Oval over birch leaf, hairline in bottom **$145**
  Salt glaze, lazy 8 and target dec ... **$375**
Churn lid, 5/6 gallon **$120**
Crock
  Eight gallons, chip on base, oval mark and 6" wing **$75**
  One gallon, 2" wing **$350**
  Ten gallon, oval mark and 6" wing, "10" and oval in black ink **$125**
  Two gallons, 4" wing mark **$90**
  Three gallons, circle oval mark and 2" wing **$90**
  Three gallon, "Potteries" oval, 2" wing **$65**
  Twenty gallons, oval mark and 6" wing **$125**

Crock, salt glaze
  Five gallons, birchleaf, Union label, chip on handle **$55**
  Six gallons, leaf dec **$175**
  Two gallons, target, bottom mkd .. **$100**
  Ten gallons, leaf, front stamped "Minnesota Stoneware," hairline **$250**
  Three gallons, tornado, front stamped "Red Wing Stoneware Company," large chip at bottom **$250**
  Twenty lbs, butterfly, back stamped, hairlines **$175**
Crock lid
  One-gallon size **$90**

Fifteen gallons, nick where wire handle enters lid **$65**
Two gallons **$225**
Custard, Spongeband
  Large, tight hairline **$65**
  Small **$85**
Funeral vase, Brushware **$65**
Hotplate, Minnesota Centennial, 1958 .... **$45**
Jug
  One-eighth pint, Michigan advertising **$225**
  One gallon, ball top shoulders, bottom mkd **$95**
  One gallon, brown top shoulders, "The Banner Liquor Store, Winona, Minn" **$175**
  One gallon, brown top shoulders, wing mark **$195**
  One gallon, "Fargo Creamery Supply House St. Paul, Minn" in oval, bottom marked **$150**
  One gallon, tomato, brown top, wing mark **$395**
  Five gallons, Imperial, shoulder, 4" wing and oval mark **$125**
  Five gallon, shoulders, "Union" oval and 4" wing **$80**
  Five gallon, shoulder, "The Mason House & Mineral Springs, Colfax Iowa," shield and Union label .. **$775**
  Three gallons, shoulder, no oval mark, 2" wing **$35**
Koverwate
  Fifteen gallons, mkd "15," small nick **$125**
  Three gallons, "3" on side with instructions **$450**

Red Wing four-gallon salt-glaze water cooler, cobalt lazy 8 decoration, original cover, unmarked, c1890, 11" h without lid, **$3,000.**

Red Wing rare "dome top" jug, "bird jug," about 1-1/2 gallons, in Albany slip glaze, c1895, 9-1/4" h, **$150.**

Red Wing two-gallon salt-glaze crock with strong cobalt decoration of "target with tail," marked on bottom, "Minnesota Stoneware Co. Red Wing, Minn.," c1890, **$475.**

Red Wing white stoneware "Koverwates," two sizes, which were placed inside crocks to keep foods submerged in preserving liquid, sizes shown are for three and four gallons, found up to 20-gallon size; three-gallon, 8" d; four-gallon, 9" d, depending on size, **$250-$500.**

Rockingham pitcher, hound handle, Yellowware, relief design of eight columns of hanging game and fowl, relief eagle below spout, minor hairline, c1850, 9-1/2" h, **$125.**
Photo courtesy of Bruce & Vicki Wassdorp.

Red Wing large cherry band pitcher with Marble Rock, Iowa, advertising, 9-1/2", **$1,000.**

Mug
Blue bands, "Certainly" $150
Blue bands, "Good Luck Malt Syrup," hairline $135
Blue bands, "I Came From Atlas Malt Products Co., Janesville, WI," hairline $115
Blue bands, "Souvenir West End Commercial Club, St. Paul June 21-26, 1909" $185
Spongeband $575
Nappy
Blue and white $120
Saffronware, "Compliments of C. A. Habergarten & Co., Waconia, Minn" $195
Pitcher
Blue mottled, large, minor bottom edge chips $200

Cherry band, large $175
Cherry band, small $195
Spongeband, large $195
Sponge, mottled $165
Spongeband, small $335
Refrigerator jar, small size, hairline $65
Salt shaker, Spongeband, white glaze $120
Sewer tile $70
Snuff jar, cov, North Star, Albany slip, minor chip under lid $125
Spittoon, German-style, bottom edge chip $375
Thrashing jug, five gallons, beehive, six-sided spigot hole, oval mark and 4" wing $1,650
Water cooler, five gallons, 4" wing mark $350

ROCKINGHAM AND ROCKINGHAM BROWN-GLAZED WARES

History: Rockingham ware can be divided into two categories. The first consists of the fine china and porcelain pieces made between 1826 and 1842 by the Rockingham Company of Swinton, Yorkshire, England, and its predecessor firms: Swinton, Bingley, Don, Leeds, and Brameld. The Bramelds developed the cadogan, a lidless teapot. Between 1826 and 1842, the Bramelds developed a quality soft-paste product with a warm, silky feel. Elaborate specialty pieces were made. By 1830, the company employed 600 workers and listed 400 designs for dessert sets and 1,000 designs for tea and coffee services in its catalog. Unable to meet its payroll, the company closed in 1842.

The second category of Rockingham ware includes pieces produced in the famous Rockingham brown glaze that became an intense and vivid purple-brown when fired. It had a dark, tortoiseshell appearance. The glaze was copied by many English and American potteries. American manufacturers that used Rockingham glaze include D. & J. Henderson of Jersey City, New Jersey; United States Pottery in Bennington, Vermont; potteries in East Liverpool, Ohio; and several potteries in Indiana and Illinois.

Additional Listings: Bennington and Bennington-Type Pottery.

Bowl, 9-1/2" d, 3-1/4" h **$65**

Casserole, cov, oval, fruit finial, applied handles, 12" l, 10-1/4" h **$275**

Creamer, cow-form, minor chips, 19th C, 6-3/4" h **$260**

Cuspidor, four sides, molded eagles, dark brown Rockingham glaze, 6-5/8", 4" h **$330**

Figure, molded seated spaniel, mottled brown glaze over yellow pottery, chips, flakes, 12-1/2" h **$615**

Flask, molded floral dec, band, 8" h **$45**

Flower pot, emb acanthus leaves, matching saucer, 10-1/4" h **$45**

Inkwell, shoe shape, 4-1/8" l **$60**

Mixing bowl, nested set of three, emb design **$95**

Pie plate, Rockingham glaze, 10" d **$80**

Pitcher, Revolutionary War battle scene with George Washington, 12" h **$2,750**

Plate, painted center with exotic bird in landscape, raised C-scroll border with gilt and painting, puce griffin and green number marks, 9" d **$650**

Potpourri vase, cov, two handles, pink ground borders with central enamel dec floral bouquets, gilt foli-

age and trim, pierced neck, rim, and cov, printed griffin mark, slight gilt rim wear to vase, rim chips and hairline to cover, c1835, 11" h **$290**

Scent bottle, onion shape, applied garden flowers, gilt line rims, printed puce griffin mark, c1831-40, 6" h **$465**

Vase, flared, painted view of Larington Yorkshire, figures and sheep, wide gilt border, dark blue ground, restored, iron-red griffin and painted title, c1826-30, 4-3/8" h **$420**

Washboard, imperfections, 19th C, 24-1/4" h **$350**

ROOKWOOD POTTERY

History: Mrs. Marie Longworth Nicholas Storer, Cincinnati, Ohio, founded Rookwood Pottery in 1880. The name of this outstanding American art pottery came from her family estate, "Rookwood," named for the rooks (crows) that inhabited the wooded grounds.

Though the Rookwood pottery filed for bankruptcy in 1941, it was soon reorganized under new management. Efforts at maintaining the pottery proved futile, and it was sold in 1956 and again in 1959. The pottery was moved to Starkville, Mississippi, in conjunction with the Herschede Clock Co. It finally ceased operating in 1967.

Rookwood wares changed with the times. The variety is endless, in part because of the creativity of the many talented artists responsible for great variations in glazes and designs.

Marks: There are five elements to the Rookwood marking system—the clay or body mark, the size mark, the decorator mark, the date mark, and the factory mark. The best way to date Rookwood art pottery is from factory marks.

From 1880 to 1882, the factory mark was the name "Rookwood" incised or painted on the base. Between 1881 and 1886, the firm name, address, and year appeared in an oval frame. Beginning in 1886, the impressed "RP" monogram appeared and a flame mark was added for each year until 1900. After 1900, a Roman numeral, indicating the last two digits of the year of production, was added at the bottom of the "RP" flame mark. This last mark is the one most often seen on Rookwood pieces in the antiques marketplace.

Rookwood urn, standard glaze, decorated by Matthew Daly, orange chrysanthemums, covered with elaborate silver overlay of putti and organic foliage by Spaulding & Co., flame mark/581C/W/ MAD/Spaulting & Co. Jewelers, Chicago, few breaks and minor loss to silver, repair to hairline on body, couple of small burst glaze bubbles, 1892, 12-1/2" x 12-1/2", **$2,300.**
Photo courtesy of David Rago Auctions, Inc.

Architectural tile, cuenca, tree landscape, blue, green, and tan matte glazes, mounted in Arts & Crafts frame, imp "Rookwood Faience," 17-1/2" sq **$3,450**

Bookend, elephant, semi-matte ivory glaze, production, 1920, flame mark/XX/244C, firing line to back, X'd for glaze drip, 6-1/4" w, 5-3/4" h **$145**

Bowl, Ombroso, carved and inlaid poppy pod dec around top, dec by Charles Todd, 1915, 6-1/2" d **$2,200**

Bud vase, bulbous, flowers on brown to gold ground, flame mark/III/745C/ CCL, by Clara Lindeman, 1903, 5-1/4" h **$360**

Cabinet jug, by N. J. Hirschfeld, dec in Limoges-style, bamboo and butterfly, shaded brown, ivory, and blue-green ground, gilded details, stamped "Rookwood 1883 G 61," artist's cipher, 3-1/2" d, 4-1/2" h **$410**

Cabinet vase, Tiger Eye, flame mark obscured by glaze, two very minor grinding base chips, 3" d, 3" h **$350**

Rookwood vase, Jewel Porcelain, cylindrical, finely painted by Arthur Conant, branches of blossoms in pink, caramel, blue, and green, uncrazed, flame mark/XVIII/1873/P/C, 1928, 3-3/4" d, 5-1/4" h, **$2,300.**
Photo courtesy of David Rago Auctions, Inc.

Rookwood loving cup, standard glaze, decorated by Grace Young, American Indian brave with illegible name beneath portrait, chased silver band, silver medallion of side, de-accessioned from Cincinnati Museum, flame mark/810/GY/title/Stanley Burt's red mark, Y-shaped line to interior of bottom foot ring, 1898, 6-3/4" x 8", **$6,000.**
Photo courtesy of David Rago Auctions, Inc.

Rookwood paperweights, four production figural pieces, including fish, rabbit, cat, and dog, all marked, test 4-3/4" h, **$1,100.**
Photo courtesy of David Rago Auctions, Inc.

Rookwood urn, standard glaze, painted by Matt Daly, branches of yellow dogwood, gently tooled underglaze design encircling collar, flame mark/MAD/L/425/W, 1/2" glaze chip to base, possibly from manufacture, 1888, **$3,250.**
Photo courtesy of David Rago Auctions, Inc.

Rookwood plaque, scenic vellum, painted by Margaret MacDonald, "Summer," brightly colored lakeside landscape, flame mark/XVII/V/MHM, 1917, 5-1/4" x 8-1/4" plaque mounted in orig frame with paper label, **$5,500.**
Photo courtesy of David Rago Auctions, Inc.

Chamberstick, Standard Glaze, painted by Jeannette Swing, yellow violets, flame mark, artist's cipher, 1894, 3" h **$350**

Charger, mauve and ochre galleon center, light blue splashed border, John Wareham, dated 1905, 12-1/2" d **$1,500**

Chocolate pot, standard glaze, oak leaves and across dec, shape #722, Lenore Ashbury, 1904, 10" h **$700**

Ewer, Standard glaze, painted by A. R. Valentien, branches of yellow cherry blossoms, flame mark/387A/S.A.R.V./I., minimal crazing, firing line to handle, 1890, 14" h, 8" d.................**$1,100**

Figure, woman's head, matte white glaze, flame mark/XXIV/2026, 1924, 7-1/2" d, 8" h **$365**

Flower boat, standard glaze, pansies dec, shape #3745, Matt A. Daly, 1890, 16" l **$900**

Flower frog, #2251, 1915 ....**$325**

Humidor, cov, round, Standard Glaze, portrait of American Indian, Pueblo Man, painted by Grace Young, dated 1901, 6" h **$3,750**

Jug, by Albert Humphrys, Limoges style, geese flying over bamboo thicket, stamped "ROOKWOOD 1882 A.H." with anchor, 1882, 3-1/2" d, 5-1/4" h **$490**

Pitcher
Flowers on green to gold ground, flame mark/I/657D/FH, artist's initials FH, 1901, 6" h.................**$270**
Flowers on blue to white ground, flame mark/VI/907F/EN, by Eliza Lawrence, 1906, 7" h **$300**
Standard glaze, Kataro Shirayamadani, flowering tree branch, gold to brown ground, imp maker's and artist's mark on base, 1890, 9-1/2" h **$1,000**

Rookwood plaque, scenic vellum, painted by E. T. Hurley, sheep gracing under apple tree, flame mark/XIV/E.T.H., 1914, 9" x 12-1/4" plaque in orig Arts & Crafts frame, **$22,500.**
Photo courtesy of David Rago Auctions, Inc.

Planter, incised stylized leaves, frothy brown-green matte glaze, flame mark/XI/180C, c1910, 8-3/4" h, 8-1/2" d **$500**

Plaque, scenic vellum
End of the Woods, view of trees and winter scene, frozen lake at twilight, painted by Elizabeth F. McDermott, 1910, 11-1/2" x 9" **$7,500**
Lake bordered by shade trees and mountain, painted by Ed Diers, orig frame, 1919, 14-1/2" x 9-1/2" **$10,000**
Meadow and trees, painted by L. Asbury, orig frame, 1922, 12" x 9-1/2".................................**$7,000**
Ombroso, pr of Rooks flanking bowl and reverse RP symbol, 1915, minor edge flakes, 7-1/2" x 3-1/2" **$6,000**
Penacock Lane, Concord, New Hampshire, view of lake through trees, sgd "ED," Rookwood flame mark and date on reverse, dec by Ed Diers, Cincinnati, Ohio, framed, crazing, 1916, 14-1/4" w, 8-3/4" h.................**$8,625**
Shade trees in foreground, lake and mountain in background, Arts & Crafts oak frame, 2" sq.........**$2,500**
The Morning Hour, Venetian sailboats, painted by Carl Schmidt, 9-1/2" x 11-1/2".................................**$6,500**

Teapot, cov, Turkish, frog fishing with pole and bobber on riverbank, painting attributed to Maria Longworth Nichols, dated 1833, 11" **$1,500**

Vase
Artist sgd with initials for W. E. Hentschel, olive brown mat glaze above emb green, blue, and light gray flowers, dated 1915, 7-3/8" h **$1,775**

Rookwood vase, jewel porcelain, painted by Kataro Shirayamadani, pink and yellow flowers, vermilion ground, uncrazed, flame mark/ XXXIV/S/Japanese cipher, 1934, 6-1/4" x 3-1/4", **$1,800.**
Photo courtesy of David Rago Auctions, Inc.

Rookwood vase, iris glaze, decorated by Sallie Coyne, flaring, delicate branches of white apple blossoms, celadon ground, flame mark/X/1357D/SEC/W, horizontal crazing, few scratches, 1910, 8-3/4" x 4", **$1,300.**
Photo courtesy of David Rago Auctions, Inc.

Rookwood vase, iris glaze, bottle shape, carved and slip-painted golden tulips and long celadon leaves, white ground, orig factory label covers artist's signature, which appears to be Sara Sax, traces of red crayon museum mark, flame mark/S1656/W, 1900, 13-1/4" x 4", **$12,000.**
Photo courtesy of David Rago Auctions, Inc.

Baluster, flowers on green to gold ground, flame mark/V/605E/GH, by Grace Hall, 1905, 5" h **$300**

Bottle shape, sea green, painted blue bells, black to celadon ground, Sally Toohey, flame mark/742D/ST/G, 1899, 12-1/2" h, 3-3/4" d **$5,500**

Bulbous, blue, turquoise, and magenta running glaze, flame mark/XXI/ 915F/LNL, by Elizabeth Lincoln, 1921, 4-3/4" h **$475**

Bulbous, flowers on brown to gold ground, flame mark/VII/654D/LEL, by Laura Lindeman, 1907, 5-1/4" h **$330**

Drip glaze, bulbous body, long neck, imp maker's mark and numbered "6363," 1949, 6" h **$300**

Iris glaze, decorated by Ed Diers, earthtone underglaze color at neck shading to soft greens, mauve carnation with buds and trailing stems, marks include Rookwood logo, date, artist's monogram, "879D," paper label "133," crazing, c1904, 9-1/2" d **$1,530**

Iris glaze, painted by A. R. Valentien, two rooks on pine branch, shading from dark green to celadon to sky blue, flame mark/IV/S1766/A.R. Valentien, uncrazed, 1904, 15" h, 6-1/2" d **$22,500**

Iris glaze, possibly decorated by Rose Fechleimer, 1901, peach-colored underglaze shading to white near base, clusters of pendant flowers with wide green leaves and trailing stem, mkd with Rookwood logo, date, artist's monogram, incised "W" and "786C," paper label "257," crazing, 9-3/4" h **$1,530**

Iris glaze, diaphanous white poppies, pearl gray ground, painted by A. R. Valentien, flame mark/II/922B/ A. R. Valentien, 1902, 10-3/4" h, 5-1/2" d **$2,100**

Jewel Porcelain, Oriental landscape with sailboats and prunus trees on three panels, painted by Arthur Conant, flame mark/XIX/2103/C, uncrazed, 1919, 5-1/4" h, 3-3/4" d **$4,500**

Later Tiger Eye, Empire Green, carved sea horse dec, by E. T. Hurley, 1923, 9-1/2" h **$3,500**

Matt, by O. G. Reed, pink roses with yellow centers, indigo-to-rose ground, flame mark/VI/907DD/O.G.R., 1906, 9-1/2" h, 3-3/4" d **$11,000**

Ovoid, flowers on blue to white ground, flame mark/VI/907F/EN, by Edith Nooan, 1906, 7" h **$800**

Rookwood vase, iris glaze, painted by Carl Schmidt, tapering, diaphanous white irises on black to pink shaded ground, flame mark/W/artist cipher, uncrazed, neatly drilled bottom, 1910, 9" x 5", **$5,000.**
Photo courtesy of David Rago Auctions, Inc.

Rookwood vase, vellum, delicately painted by K. Shiryamadani, buff-colored poppies, teal blue wheat stalks, flame mark/Xxi/951B/V/Japanese cipher, 1921, 12-3/4" x 5", **$1,200.**
Photo courtesy of David Rago Auctions, Inc.

Rookwood tile, faience, modeled with ship in green and purple matte glaze, blue sky, stamped "ROOKWOOD FAIENCE/12378Y," mounted and framed, two lines to sides, two small chips on bottom edge, **$1,500.**
Photo courtesy of David Rago Auctions, Inc.

Scenic vellum, trees by lake, pink and blue sky, painted by Fred Rothenbusch, flame mark/XXIV/926B/FR, uncrazed, 1924, 11" h, 6" d **$6,500**

Scenic vellum, stark landscape at sunset, painted by Sally Coyne, flame mark/XII/SEC/951D/V/G, 1912, 9" h, 3-3/4" h **$3,500**

Scenic vellum, river landscape, blue and apricot sky, painted by E. T. Hurley, flame mark/XXI/892C/E.T.H., uncrazed, 1931, 9" h, 4-1/2" h **$2,700**

Standard glaze, bottle shape, painted by A. R. Valentien, orange nasturtium, flame mark/537B/A.R.V., shallow chip to int. of foot ring, 1897, 17-1/2" h, 11" d **$1,500**

Standard glaze, silver overlay of wild roses, poppies, and lily-of-the-valleys, painted nasturtiums, L. N. Lincoln, c1895, 8" h **$5,750**

Standard glaze, three handles, painted by Artus Van Briggle, woman's portrait, three champagne bottles, flame mark/659/W/AVB/L, 1893, 8" h, 10" d **$1,700**

Vellum glaze, Venetian harbor scene, Carl Schmidt signature stamp, dated 1922, 9-1/2" h **$3,450**

Vellum, bulbous, blue irises, purple ground, painted by Fred Rothenbusch, flame mark/VIII/1659/FR/V, 1908, 11-1/4" h, 5" d **$1,800**

Wax Matte, by Jens Jensen, stylized yellow, red, and purple flowers, pink ground, flame mark/XXIX/2303/artist's cipher, 1929, 6" d, 9-1/2" h..**$1,610**

Rookwood vase, standard glaze, bronze overlay decorated by Kataro Shirayamadani, Japanese scene of fish and sea plants, flame mark/804C/Japanese cipher, 1898, 12-3/4" x 5", **$26,000.**
Photo courtesy of David Rago Auctions, Inc.

Rookwood vase, scenic vellum, painted by Ed Diers, baluster, trees in landscape against yellow sky, flame mark/XXIV/922B/V/ED, 1914, 11" x 5-1/2", **$4,250.**
Photo courtesy of David Rago Auctions, Inc.

Rookwood vase, scenic vellum, painted by Fred Rothenbusch, landscape, cobalt ground, flame mark/XXXI/1664D/FR, 1931, 10-1/2" x 4-3/4", **$3,000.**
Photo courtesy of David Rago Auctions, Inc.

Rookwood vase, vellum, bulbous, by Kataro Shirayamadani, brown crocus and green leaves on shaded yellow ground, flame mark/XXIV/S/X and artist's cipher, seconded mark for small black glaze spots, 1934, 4" d, 5-1/2" h, **$1,610.**
Photo courtesy of David Rago Auctions, Inc.

Rookwood vase, standard glaze, ovoid, painted by Kataro Shirayamadani, branches of yellow dogwood on yellow and amber ground, flame mark/531F/ Japanese cipher, remnants of red crayon museum marks, 1886, 9-1/4" x 8-1/2", **$2,100.**
Photo courtesy of David Rago Auctions, Inc.

Rookwood vase, wax matte, painted by Kataro Shirayamadani, bulbous, orange and blue crocuses on shaded pastel ground, flame mark/XXXV/S/artist cipher, 1935, 6-1/2" x 3-3/4", **$1,200.**
Photo courtesy of David Rago Auctions, Inc.

ROSE CANTON, ROSE MANDARIN, AND ROSE MEDALLION

History: The pink rose color has given its name to three related groups of Chinese export porcelain: Rose Mandarin, Rose Medallion, and Rose Canton.

Rose Mandarin, produced from the late 18th century to approximately 1840, derives its name from the Mandarin figure(s) found in garden scenes with women and children. The women often have gold decorations in their hair. Polychrome enamels and birds separate the scenes.

Rose Medallion, which originated in the early 19th century and was made through the early 20th century, has alternating panels of figures and birds and flowers. The elements are four in number, separated evenly around the center medallion. Peonies and foliage fill voids.

Rose Canton, introduced somewhat later than Rose Mandarin and produced through the first half of the 19th century, is similar to Rose Medallion except the figural panels are replaced by flowers. People are present only if the medallion partitions are absent. Some patterns have been named, e.g., Butterfly and Cabbage and Rooster. Rose Canton actually is a catchall term for any pink enamelware not fitting into the first two groups.

Rose Medallion bowl, scalloped rim, decorated with panels of birds and flowers, 10" d, **$475.**
Photo courtesy of Joy Luke Auctions.

Rose Medallion porcelain platter, Chinese, Qing Dynasty, 19th C, 17-1/2" l, **$500.**
Photo courtesy of Sloans & Kenyon Auctioneers and Appraisers.

> **Reproduction Alert.** Rose Medallion is still made, although the quality does not match the earlier examples.

Rose Canton

Brush pot, scenic, ladies, reticulated, gilt trim, 4-1/2" h........................**$275**

Charger, floral panels, 19th C, 13" d
....**$215**

Platter, enamel and gilt wear, 19th C, 16-1/2" l.......................................**$200**

Puzzle teapot, Cadogan, painted birds and foliage, light blue ground, minor chips, late 19th C, 6" h.....**$150**

Umbrella jar, minor chips, 19th C, 24-1/4" h....................................**$805**

Urn, cov, minor chips, cracks, gilt wear, pr, 19-1/4" h..............................**$2,990**

Vase, four panels of birds and butterflies, rocks and tree peonies, applied molded gilded serpents and animals at neck and shoulder, converted to electric lamp, slight wear, 14" h..**$320**

Rose Mandarin

Bowl, exterior with continuous courtyard scene, multiple figures including

Rose Mandarin, Chinese, bowl, porcelain, figural decoration, Qing Dynasty, Qialong period, 10" d, **$325.**
Photo courtesy of Sloans & Kenyon Auctioneers and Appraisers.

horse and groom, musician, checkers players, scholars, int. with mandarin panels surrounding gilt fretwork, alternating images of fans, scrolls, and vases, rose, bird, and butterfly border, gilt ground, gilt details, orange peel glaze, wooden base, 13-1/4" d, 5-1/2" h **$2,300**

Brush pot, continuous scene of empress on throne, surrounded by court ladies and maids, gilt trim, bright rose and butterfly border, small rim flakes and crow's foot in base, 5-3/8" d, 6-1/4" h **$230**

Rose Medallion, covered jar, four gilt lion masks on shoulders, lion finial (damaged) on cover with stapled repair, body with various hairlines, wooden base, 9-1/2" d, 17" h, **$175.**
Photo courtesy of David Rago Auctions, Inc.

Rose Mandarin, vase, famille rose enamels, dragons, and foo dogs, 19th C, 25" h, **$2,470.**
Photo courtesy of Skinner, Inc.

Creamer, continuous scene with figures indoors and in fenced yard, 100 Antiques border on int., gold accents, 3-1/2" h **$200**

Cup and saucer, courtyard scenes in center, kissing carp border alternating with scrolls and other fish, wear **$350**

Dish, kidney shape, courtyard scenes, bird and flower borders, orange peel glaze, wear, 8-1/4" x 10-1/2" **$200**

Plate

Brilliant blue fretwork borders with pink flowers, flower baskets, dark mustard yellow irid ground, detailed center with women and children in courtyard, man brandishing sword at woman, minor wear, price for pr, 9-3/4" d **$500**

Courtyard scenes, bird and flower borders, 8-5/8" d **$200**

Detailed courtyard scene with fish pond, armored warrior with elaborate pheasant tail headdress, border of gourds, vases, and scrolls, gilt details, some wear, 10" d **$375**

Man and four women seated in courtyard overlooking lake, border of butterflies and birds with two reclining deer, minor wear, 7-3/4" d **$350**

Platter

26 Children, courtiers with large necklaces, man holding scepter, kissing carp border with alternating blue and green scrolls, dark gray silver oxide painted carp, faint orange peel glaze, minor wear, 14" x 17" **$1,955**

Court scene with 16 figures, borders with figures alternating with objects covered in Oriental calligraphy, gilt trim, orange peel glaze, 14-1/2" x 16-1/2" **$2,100**

Multiple figures, scribe, and soldiers, border with birds chasing insects, butterflies, orange peel glaze, 10" x 13" **$600**

Shrimp dish, bright butterflies, flowers, fruit on gilt border, gold trim and hair accents, orange peel glaze, minor wear, shallow rim flake, 10-1/8" x 10-1/4" **$865**

Soup plate, armorial, one with garden scene, other with man holding baby with three women in courtyard, borders with multiple butterflies, birds, tree peonies, and bamboo trees, each with European dolphin above belt with "Avis La Fin," monogram "RAK," gilt trim and accents,

two minor flakes, price for pr, 10" d **$1,840**

Tray, oval, scalloped edge, gilt and rose border, gilt highlighted figures in center, one with gilt robe, orange peel glaze, flake on table ring, 9-1/2" x 11" **$250**

Tureen, cov, matching underplate, continuous courtyard scene, gild accents, pink roses and white trailing flowers borders, gilt finial and intertwined handles, well done professional restoration to lid and underplate, 7-3/4" l, 6" h **$650**

Rose Medallion

Armorial plate, exotic birds, butterflies, marbleized textures, gold hair accents, hand painted orange armorial device in center with belt surrounding sword and laurel wreath, "Fides Praestantior Auro," slight wear, price for pr, 9-5/8" d **$600**

Basket and undertray, two handles, reticulated, China, chips, 19th C, 9-3/4" l, 7-1/4" w, 3-3/4" h **$325**

Boullion cup and saucer, cov, thinly potted, double handles **$200**

Bowl, detailed panels with four figures and man at window alternating with roses and birds, wear, 10" d, 4" h **$260**

Candlesticks, pr, China, one with a couple base edge repairs, 19th C, 7-1/4" h **$600**

Charger

Celadon, court scene within shaped One Hundred Antiques border, textured ground, gilt wear to rim, 10-1/2" d **$275**

Celadon, court scene bordered with animals and floral trophies, textured ground, minor gilt wear, 13" d **$355**

Dish, scalloped rim, 19th C, 9-1/4" d **$275**

Lamp, chi dragons around neck, foo dog handles, mounted on pierced wood stand, China, late 19th C, 18" h vase **$760**

Plate

Alternating panels of men and women, birds and butterflies, faint gold dec, 8" d **$115**

Light blue, yellow, and pink reticulated border, 8-5/8" d **$120**

Alternating panels, gold trim, wear, 9-1/2" d **$90**

Platter

Oval, six alternating panels, orange peel glaze, faded colors, 12" x 15" **$115**

Six alternating panels, orange peel glaze, worn gilt trim, shallow rim flakes, 14" x 18-1/4" **$350**

Punch bowl

Chinese Export, 19th C, 13-1/2" d **$825**

Hp scenes, four with birds, fruits, clouds, and flowers, alternating with panels of village scenes, gilt rim and highlights, 24" d **$3,680**

Saucer, figures dec, gilt, minor rim flakes, price for set of eight, 6-1/4" d **$250**

Serving dish, oval, shaped rim, celadon, mid-19th C, 10-3/4" l, 9-1/4" w, 1-3/4" h........................**$400**

Soup bowl, Mandarin scene, gilding, 8-1/4" d..**$110**

Teapot, domed cov, squatty, gilt floral embellishments on handle and spout, 8" h...**$765**

Tray, landscapes alternating with birds and flowers, hillside fort with multiple flakes, pagodas, fishing boats, orange peel glaze ext., 9-1/8" sq **$250**

Umbrella stand, cylindrical, China, 19th C

23-5/8" h, cylindrical form, repaired cracks **$400**

24-1/4" h..................................**$1,880**

Vase

Four panels with matching mandarin courtyard scenes, scalloped edge rims, applied molded serpents and animals on neck and shoulder with worn gilding, birds and butterflies, wear, wooden stand, price for pr, 14" h **$700**

Truncated, mounted as a lamp, 19th C, 12" h **$400**

Vegetable tureen, cov, oval underplate, figures with gilt trim, blue bats under two intertwined handles, orange peel glaze on base, molded gilt finial, minor wear, 9-3/4" l, 8" h **$920**

ROSENTHAL

History: Rosenthal Porcelain Manufactory began operating at Selb, Bavaria, in 1880. Specialties were tablewares and figurines. The firm is still in operation.

Box, cov, Studio Line, sgd "Peynet" **$175**

Cake plate, grape dec, scalloped ruffled edge, ruffled handles, 12" w **$75**

Candlestick, Art Deco woman holding candlestick, 9-1/2" h **$275**

Chocolate set, San Souci pattern, six cups and saucers, cov pot, creamer and sugar, marked "Selb Bavaria," c1880, 15-pc set **$425**

Creamer and sugar, pate-sur-pate type blue cherries dec **$115**

Cup and saucer, San Souci pattern, white..**$20**

Demitasse cup and saucer, Marie pattern **$25**

Design page, hand rendered, each page showing transfer printed and hand-tinted designs, most numbered or named, some on graph paper, 10 pages, 6" w, 9-1/2" h **$230**

Figure

Band figure, male cello player, 5-1/4" h **$250**

Band figure, male clarinet player **$250**

Band figure, male tuba player ...**$285**

Man taking snuff, 8-1/2" h..........**$295**

Middle Eastern child with scimitar **$250**

Middle Eastern lantern lighter ...**$200**

Middle Eastern man with urn **$200**

Middle Eastern pipe smoker **$230**

Plaque, titled "Die Falknerin," sgd "Hans Makart," 9" x 7-1/2".......**$1,100**

Plate, girl and lamb dec, multicolored, 10" d...**$40**

Portrait plate, bust portrait of lady, pale yellow and white ground, faux green, turquoise, blue, and red hardstone jewels, 9-7/8" d **$350**

Vase, Hp, multicolored roses, 11" h **$125**

Rosenthal dinner set, prototype (never produced), red, blue edging, 13 each: dinner plates, dessert plates, mugs; 12 each: bowls, lunch plates, saucers; coffeepot, creamer, cov sugar, two serving platters, two bowls, **$550.**
Photo courtesy of David Rago Auctions, Inc.

Rosenthal luncheon plates, painted with flowers, gold swag border, 9" d, price for set of 10, **$150.**
Photo courtesy of David Rago Auctions, Inc.

Rosenthal pitcher, creamy ivory body, red rose bud decoration, green foliate, silvered base, marked, **$95.**

ROSEVILLE POTTERY

Roseville jardinière and pedestal, Baneda, green, unmarked, restoration to rim and base of jardinière, minor abrasions to top of pedestal, **$1,300.**
Photo courtesy of David Rago Auctions, Inc.

Roseville vessel, Sunflower, squatty, unmarked, 6-1/4" h, **$850.**
Photo courtesy of David Rago Auctions, Inc.

Roseville wall pocket, Baneda, green, foil sticker, 8-1/4" l, **$2,200.**
Photo courtesy of David Rago Auctions, Inc.

History: In the late 1880s, a group of investors purchased the J. B. Owens Pottery in Roseville, Ohio, and made utilitarian stoneware items. In 1892, the firm was incorporated and joined by George F. Young, who became general manager. Four generations of Youngs controlled Roseville until the early 1950s.

A series of acquisitions began: Midland Pottery of Roseville in 1898, Clark Stoneware Plant in Zanesville (formerly used by Peters and Reed), and Muskingum Stoneware (Mosaic Tile Company) in Zanesville. In 1898, the offices also moved from Roseville to Zanesville.

In 1900, Roseville introduced Rozane, an art pottery. Rozane became a trade name to cover a large series of lines. The art lines were made in limited amounts after 1919.

The success of Roseville depended on its commercial lines, first developed by John J. Herald and Frederick Rhead in the first decades of the 1900s. In 1918, Frank Ferrell became art director and developed more than 80 lines of pottery. The economic depression of the 1930s brought more lines, including Pine Cone.

In the 1940s, a series of high-gloss glazes were tried in an attempt to revive certain lines. In 1952, Raymor dinnerware was produced. None of these changes brought economic success and in November 1954, Roseville was bought by the Mosaic Tile Company.

Basket
Gardenia, green, raised mark, No. 618-15" **$490**
Jonquil, pillow, unmarked, 10-1/2" d, 7-1/2" h **$750**
Ming Tree, white, raised mark, No. 585-14" **$425**
Poppy, green, raised mark, No. 347-10" **$350**
Vista, unmarked, 4-3/4" d, 6-3/4" h **$575**

Basket planter
Apple Blossom, green, asymmetrical rim, raised mark, No. 311-12 ....**$490**
Iris, spherical, pink, imp mark, No. 354-8 ....**$365**

Bookends, pr
Iris, book shape, blue, raised mark, No. 5, 5-1/4" w, 5-1/4" h **$290**
Water Lily, model no. 14, molded open book form, water lily blossoms in relief, walnut brown glaze, raised "Roseville U.S.A." mark, repair, 4-3/4" l, 5-1/4" d, 5-1/2" h **$200**

Bowl
Chloron, buttressed, unmarked, 4" x 8" **$225**
Futura, "Aztec," faceted, unmarked, 4" x 8" **$325**
Futura, "Balloons," unmarked, touchups, 3-1/2" x 8-1/2" **$150**
Imperial II, emb snail-like designs around entire body, pale green dripping glaze over pink ground, unmarked **$2,000**
Mostique, two handles, bands of blue and white flowers, unmarked, 3" x 10" **$350**

Bud vase
Orange blossoms, green ground, model no. 870, double reservoir, raised "Roseville U.S.A." mark, c1940, 6-1/4" h **$100**
Pine Cone, blue, raised mark, minute flake on base, 5" d, 7-1/2" h **$400**

Candlesticks, pr
Blackberry, gold foil label, 4" h, 4-1/2" h **$690**
Imperial II, orange and green mottled glaze, unmarked, 3" x 4-1/4" ...**$350**
Sunflower, black paper label, 3-3/4" d, 4-1/4" h **$800**
Wisteria, brown, unmarked, 4-3/4" d, 4-3/4" h **$460**

Coffee set, cov coffeepot, cov teapot, creamer, cov sugar, Mock Orange, green, raised marks, 10-3/4" h coffeepot, minor spider lines to spout **$490**

Compote, Donatello, 7-1/2" d **$150**

Console bowl
Cremona, oval, pink, unmarked, 11" d, 2-1/4" h **$95**
Ferella, ovoid, brown, black paper label, 13" l, 5-3/4" h **$815**

Moderne, semi-matte ivory glaze, incised mark, No. 301-10 .... **$230**

Console set

Fuchsia, brown, imp marks, No. 1133-5 and No. 350-8" **$490**

Iris, pink, No. 360-10" oval center-bowl, pair of No. 1135-4-1/2 candlesticks, imp marks **$375**

Thorn Apple, pink, low center bowl No. 307-6", pair of No. 1111 candlesticks, imp marks **$290**

Cookie jar, cov

Clematis, No. 3-8, green ground .. **$550**

Magnolia, No. 2-8, tan ground ... **$450**

Water Lily, No. 1-8, gold shading to brown ground **$555**

Zephr Lily, No. 5-8, blue ground .. **$360**

Cornucopia vase

Pine Cone **$140**

White Rose **$95**

Ewer

Apple Blossom, green, raised mark, No. 318-15, minute fleck to body **$630**

Carnelian I, pink and gray glaze, RV ink mark, 7" d, 12-1/4" h **$345**

Freesia, green, raised mark, No. 21-15", two base chips **$290**

Gardenia, brown, raised mark, No. 618-15" **$490**

Mock Orange, No. 918-16, white blossoms, green leaves, pink ground, 16" h **$310**

Pine Cone, brown, raised mark, No. 909-10" **$690**

Floor vase

Fuchsia, brown, raised mark, No. 905-18" **$750**

Pine Cone, brown, incised mark, No. 913-18", repair to rim and base **$815**

Vista, bulbous, 18" h, unmarked, several bruises and chips **$860**

Water Lily, green, raised mark, No. 85-18" **$630**

Flower pot and underplate, Iris, blue, raised marks, No. 648-5", 1" bruise to rim **$365**

Hanging basket, Mock Orange, white blossoms, green leaves **$375**

Jardinière

Baneda, pink, paper label, 4" x 5-1/2", small base nicks **$250**

Cherry Blossom, pink, 6" x 8-1/2" **$500**

Jonquil, spherical, unmarked, 9" d, 6" h, small stilt-pull chips **$2,300**

Velmoss, broad leaves and buds, unmarked, 7" x 9-1/2" **$1,100**

Jardinière on stand

Freesia, No. 669, Delftware blue glaze, creamy yellow and white blossoms, raised "Roseville U.S.A." mark, stand marked "U.S.A.," c1945 .... **$500**

Freesia, No. 669-8, molded florals, blue ground, base emb "Roseville, USA," 669-8, c1935 .... **$865**

Moss, green **$3,250**

Mostique **$900**

Lamp base, Imperial II, bulbous emb band around rim, dripping pale green over pink glaze, factory drilled **$1,400**

Low bowl

Blackberry, unmarked, minor glaze bubbles, 7-3/4" d, 3-1/4" h **$345**

Sunflower, low shoulder, unmarked, burst bubble on one leaf, 7-1/4" d, 4" h **$535**

Mug, Pine Cone, blue, imp mark, price for pr, No. 960-4" **$700**

Pitcher

Fuchsia, brown, imp mark, peppering to body, 8-1/2" d, 8" h **$400**

Pine Cone, No. 415, green glaze, brown, and cream tones, raised "Roseville, U.S.A." mark, c1931, 9-1/4" h **$750**

Rozane Olympic, Ulysees at the Table of Circe, signed and titled, restoration to 5" spider lines, 8-1/2" d, 7" h **$1,495**

White Rose, pink, raised mark, No. 1324, glaze drip around rim, 8" d, 7" h **$275**

Planter

Blackberry, faceted, unmarked, 9-3/4" d, 3-1/2" h **$435**

Florentine, brown, rect, few base chips, 11-1/4" l, 5-1/4" h **$290**

Lily, squeezebag dec with water lilies and waves, orig liner, unmarked, 6" x 7-1/2" **$800**

Persian, fitted liner, unmarked, abrasion to rim, 5" x 6-1/4" **$350**

Primrose, bulbous, pink, incised mark, No. 634-6 ", flecks to flowers and one handle **$85**

Wisteria, blue, unmarked, minor touch-ups, 6-1/4" x 8-3/4" **$475**

Planter bookends, pr, Columbine, blue, raised mark, 5" w, 5" d, 5-1/4" h **$260**

Sand jar, Primrose, blue, base chip and hairline, 15-3/4" h **$575**

Teapot, cov, Rozanne Della Robbia, hearts, cups, saucers, and Japanese fans dec, brown and celadon, Rozane Ware wafer, small lid nicks, 1" clay burst at rim **$1,355**

Roseville vase, Futura, Balloon Globe, multicolored spheres on green ground, unmarked, 8-1/2" h, **$1,000.**
Photo courtesy of David Rago Auctions, Inc.

Roseville pitcher, Pine Cone, blue, ice lip, pinhead size burst or fleck to rim, faint impressed mark, **$475.**
Photo courtesy of David Rago Auctions, Inc.

Roseville vase, Luffa, green, unmarked, strong mold and color, 14-1/2" h, **$700.**
Photo courtesy of David Rago Auctions, Inc.

Roseville basket, Jonquil, paper label, few bursts to body, 9", $750.
Photo courtesy of David Rago Auctions, Inc.

Roseville jardinière, experimental, colorful hand-carved grape leaves and branches on ivory ground, unmarked, 9" x 12-1/2", $2,300.
Photo courtesy of David Rago Auctions, Inc.

Roseville wall pocket, Tourist, few deep crazing lines, unmarked, 10" l, $18,000.
Photo courtesy of David Rago Auctions, Inc.

Tea set, cov teapot, creamer, cov sugar
Freesia, blue, raised marks **$415**
Snowberry, blue, raised marks ... **$750**
White Rose, pink raised marks .. **$490**
Wincraft, brown, raised marks, minor
flaws **$200**

Umbrella stand, Pine Cone, brown, raised mark, No. 777-20", minor scaling area at handle, 1" rim bruise **$2,070**

Urn

Baneda, bulbous, pink, black foil label, 7-3/4" d, 10-1/2" h **$1,355**
Carnelian I, pink and gray glaze, RV ink mark, 8-1/4" d, 9-1/2" h **$375**
Iris, bulbous, pink, imp mark, No. 928-12" **$460**
Moss, bulbous, buttressed base, incised mark, restorations to base and rim **$200**
Pine Cone, blue, imp mark, No. 912-15", restoration to rim chip **$2,185**
Velmoss, orange glaze, foil label, 8-1/4" x 6-3/4" **$675**

Vase

Baneda, bulbous, pink, foil label, 5-1/2" x 6-3/4" **$450**
Blackberry, black paper label, 6-1/2" x 5-3/4" **$550**
Cherry Blossom, two handles, sq base, pink, unmarked, 8-1/2" x 5" **$700**
Earlam, tapering, ribbed, pink, unmarked, 8-1/2" x 6" **$450**
Falline, bulbous, blue, stepped neck, two handles, foil label, 7-1/4" x 6" **$2,300**
Ferella, bulbous, red, unmarked, 8-1/2" x 7", restoration to base **$850**
Ferella, flaring, brown, paper label, 5" x 7" **$500**
Futura, conical form, three stepped rect devices on sides, round disk base, semi-gloss terra cotta, blue, and green glazes, unmarked, c1928, 8" h **$575**
Imperial II, bulbous, band of wave-like designs at rim, bright blue mottled glaze, paper label, tight 2" line from rim **$1,400**
Imperial II, flaring, mottled green and orange glaze, unmarked, 8-1/2" x 7" **$3,250**

Imperial II, tapering, ribbed bands around body, pale green and gray mottled glaze, unmarked, 5-1/2" x 3-3/4" **$300**
Montacello, bulbous, brown, unmarked, 7-1/2" x 6-1/2" **$500**
Morning Glory, pillow shape, two buttresses at base, unmarked, 7" x 3-3/4" **$500**
Orion, cylindrical neck, red, unmarked, 7-1/2" x 4-3/4" **$500**
Rozane Royal Dark, tapering, by Hester Pillsbury, painted yellow wild roses, Roxane Ware wafer, 7" d, 8-3/4" h **$475**
Rozane Woodland, corseted, enamel dec, white blossoms, green leaves, Rozane Ware/Woodland wafer, 3" d, 10" h **$575**
Sunflower, double handles, 9" h **$1,300**
Velmoss, spherical, unmarked, 6-1/2" x 8-1/2" **$350**
Vista, bulbous, unmarked, 7-1/2" d, 17-1/2" h **$1,890**
Wisteria, blue, 10" h **$2,000**

Vessel

Imperial II, squat, yellow and green glaze over matte blue-gray ground, unmarked, 5-1/2" **$1,400**
Montacello, squat, green, unmarked, 4-1/2" x 5" **$300**
Sunflower, squat, unmarked, 4-1/4" x 7-1/2" **$700**
Wisteria, bulbous, blue, partial foil label, 6-3/4" x 8-1/2", tiny fleck to one leaf **$650**
Wisteria, squat, blue, unmarked, 4-1/2" x 6-1/2" **$450**

Wall pocket

Blackberry, flaring, unmarked, 7-3/4" l **$1,610**
Cosmos, double, blue, unmarked, silver foil label **$630**
Earlham, unmarked, 6-1/2" l **$920**
Imperial II, mottled green over lavender glaze, paper label, 6-1/2" x 6-1/2" **$800**
Moss, bucket, pink, unmarked, 10" l, 1/2" chip, small edge nick **$520**
Pine Cone, triple, blue, raised mark, 9" l **$1,725**
Savona, blue, unmarked, 8-1/4" l **$630**
Silhouette, pink, ivy leaves, raised mark No. 766-8" **$290**

ROYAL BAYREUTH

History: In 1794, the Royal Bayreuth factory was founded in Tettau, Bavaria. Royal Bayreuth introduced its figural patterns in 1885. Designs of animals, people, fruits, and vegetables decorated a wide array of tablewares and inexpensive souvenir items.

Tapestry wares, in rose and other patterns, were made in the late 19th century. The surface of the piece feels and looks like woven cloth. Tapestry ware was made by covering the porcelain with a piece of fabric tightly stretched over the surface, decorating the fabric, glazing the piece, and firing.

Royal Bayreuth still manufactures dinnerware. It has not maintained production of earlier wares, particularly the figural items. Since thorough records are unavailable, it is difficult to verify the chronology of production.

Marks: The Royal Bayreuth crest used to mark the wares varied in design and color.

Royal Bayreuth creamer, elk, figural, brown and white, marked, **$125.**

Ashtray, elk **$225**

Bell, Musicians scene, man playing cello and mandolin **$300**

Candleholder, basset hound, dark body, unmarked **$400**

Creamer
Bird of Paradise **$225**
Cat, black and orange **$200**
Crow, brown bill **$200**
Duck **$200**
Eagle **$300**
Frog, green **$225**
Lamplighter, green **$250**
Pear **$295**
Robin **$195**
Water Buffalo, black and orange **$225**

Cup and saucer, yellow and gold, purple and red flowers, green leaves, white ground, green mark **$80**

Hatpin holder, courting couple, cut-out base with gold dec, blue mark **$400**

Milk pitcher, butterfly **$1,200**

Miniature, pitcher, portrait **$95**

Portrait plate, Arab and camel, green back stamp, 9" d **$125**

Ring box, cov, pheasant scene, glossy finish **$85**

Salt and pepper shakers, pr, Elk **$165**

Vase, peasant ladies and sheep scene, silver rim, three handles, blue mark, 3-1/2" h **$60**

Patterns

Conch Shell

Creamer, green, lobster handles **$125**
Match holder, hanging **$225**
Sugar, cov, small flake **$85**

Corinthian

Creamer and sugar, classical figures, black ground **$85**
Pitcher, red ground, pinched spout, 12" h **$225**
Vase, conical, black, blue mark, 8-1/2" h **$225**

Devil and Cards

Ashtray **$650**
Creamer, blue mark, 4" h **$175**
Mug, large **$295**
Salt, master **$325**

Lobster

Ashtray, claw **$145**
Celery tray, figural, blue mark, 12-1/2" l **$245**
Pitcher, figural, orange-red, green handle, 7-3/4" h **$175**
Salt and pepper shakers, pr **$150**

Nursery Rhyme

Bell, Jack and the Beanstalk **$425**
Planter, Jack and the Beanstalk, round, orig liner **$225**
Plate, Little Jack Horner **$125**
Plate, Little Miss Muffet **$100**

Snow Babies

Bowl, 6" d **$325**
Creamer, gold trim **$110**
Jewelry box, cov **$275**
Milk pitcher, corset shape **$185**
Tea tile, blue mark, 6" sq **$100**

Sunbonnet Babies

Bell, babies sewing, unmarked ... **$425**
Cake plate, babies washing, 10-1/4" d **$400**
Cup and saucer, babies fishing ... **$225**
Dish, babies ironing, ruffled edge, blue mark, 8" d **$175**
Mustard pot, cov, babies sweeping, blue mark **$395**
Nappy, Sunbonnet Babies, Wash Day,

blue mark, 6" l **$230**
Plate, Sunbonnet Girls, pair, one washing, other sweeping **$290**

Tomato

Creamer and sugar, blue mark **$190**
Milk pitcher **$165**
Mustard, cov **$125**
Salt and pepper shakers, pr **$85**

Rose tapestry

Basket, reticulated, 5" h **$400**

Bell, American Beauty Rose, pink, 3" h **$500**

Boot **$550**

Bowl, pink and yellow roses, 10-1/2" d **$675**

Creamer **$250**

Dresser tray **$395**

Hairpin box, pink and white **$245**

Nut dish, three-color roses, gold feet, green mark, 3-1/4" d, 1-3/4" h **$175**

Pin tray, three-color roses **$195**

Plate, three-color roses, blue mark, 6" d **$150**

Salt and pepper shakers, pr, pink roses **$375**

Shoe, roses and figures dec **$550**

Tapestry, miscellaneous

Bowl, scenic, wheat, girl, and chickens, 9-1/2" d **$395**

Box, courting couple, multicolored, blue mark, 3-3/4" l, 2" w **$245**

Charger, scenic, boy and donkeys, 13" d **$300**

Dresser tray, goose girl **$495**

Hatpin holder, swimming swans and sunset, saucer base, blue mark **$250**

ROYAL BONN

Royal Bonn vase, tapered vasiform body, sinuous everted rim with short open-work loops, sinuous spreading base with openwork loops, glazed in maroon and green, body hand-painted with roses, gilt accenting, Franz Anton Mehlem Earthenware Factory, Bonn, Germany, early 20th C, 12-3/8" h, $300.
Photo courtesy of Skinner, Inc.

History: In 1836, Franz Anton Mehlem founded a Rhineland factory that produced earthenware and porcelain, including household, decorative, technical, and sanitary items.

The firm reproduced Hochst figures between 1887 and 1903. These figures, in both porcelain and earthenware, were made from the original molds from the defunct Prince-Electoral Mayence Manufactory in Hochst. The factory was purchased by Villeroy and Boch in 1921 and closed in 1931.

Marks: In 1890, the word "Royal" was added to the mark. All items made after 1890 include the "Royal Bonn" mark.

Console set, all over painted scenes on tapestry ground, gilt metal mounts, 14" l oval bowl, pr 13-1/2" h vases **$2,990**

Cup and saucer, relief luster bands, marked **$40**

Ewer, red and pink flowers, raised gold, fancy handle, 10-1/8" h **$75**

Portrait urn, cov, elaborate tooled gilt foliage dec, portrait of woman on one side, burgundy ground, sq plinth, underglaze blue beehive mark, c1900, 35" h **$3,910**

Tea tile, hp, pink, yellow, and purple pansies, white ground, green border, marked "Bonn-Rhein," 7" d **$35**

Urn, cov, hp, multicolored flowers, green, and yellow ground, two gold handles, artist sgd, 13" h **$120**

Vase

Blue ground, gilt and enameled floral designs, scrolled handles, printed and imp marks, late 19th C, 18-3/4" h **$400**

Hp multicolored floral spray with raised gold dec, link handles, ftd, 20" h, 5" d **$240**

ROYAL COPENHAGEN

Royal Copenhagen plaque, oval, beaded rim surmounted by ribbon and bow decoration, depicting Fredensborg Castle, back marked "Prove," 5-3/4" w, 8" h, $615.
Photo courtesy of Alderfer Auction Co.

Royal Copenhagen teaset, teapot, sugar, and creamer, blue and white, floral decoration, $395.
Photo courtesy of Joy Luke Auctions.

History: Franz Mueller established a porcelain factory at Copenhagen in 1775. When bankruptcy threatened in 1779, the Danish king acquired ownership, appointing Mueller manager and selecting the name "Royal Copenhagen." The crown sold its interest in 1867; the company remains privately owned today.

Blue Fluted, Royal Copenhagen's most famous pattern, was created in 1780. It is of Chinese origin and comes in three styles: smooth edge, closed lace edge, and perforated lace edge (full lace). Many other factories copied it.

Flora Danica, named for a famous botanical work, was introduced in 1789 and remained exclusive to Royal Copenhagen. It is identified by its free-hand illustrations of plants and its hand-cut edges and perforations.

Marks: Royal Copenhagen porcelain is marked with three wavy lines, which signify ancient waterways, and a crown, added in 1889. Stoneware does not have the crown mark.

Bowl, reticulated blue and white **$125**

Candlesticks, pr, blue floral design, white ground, bisque lion heads, floral garlands, 9" h **$160**

Cream soup, #1812 .... **$75**

Cup and saucer, 2-1/2" h cylindrical cup with angular handle, 5-1/2" d saucer with molded and gilded rim, hp floral specimen, 20th C **$575**

Dish, reticulated blue and white **$175**

Figure

Girl knitting, No. 1314, 6-3/4" h. **$350**

Dachshund, blue wave mark, 7-1/2" h, 11" l **$375**

Nymph with Satyr, timid satyr kneeling at feet of nude female nymph, on naturalistic ovoid base, 20th C, 15-1/4" h **$1,100**

Royal Copenhagen figure, little girl and boy embracing puppy, **$85.**
Photo courtesy of Joy Luke Auctions.

Royal Copenhagen figure, milkmaid and cow, **$80.**
Photo courtesy of Joy Luke Auctions.

Royal Copenhagen figures, left: girl mending sock, right: boy whittling stick, each **$75.**
Photo courtesy of Joy Luke Auctions.

Fish plate, different fish swimming among marine plants, molded and gilt border, light green highlights, gilt dentil edge, crown circular mark, 10-pc set, 10" d **$8,250**

Inkwell, Blue Fluted pattern, matching tray **$150**

Pickle tray, Half Lace pattern, blue triple wave mark, 9" l **$70**

Plates, each with gilt serrated rim and central hp floral specimen, price for eight-pc set, two 7-5/8" d, six 10" d **$2,990**

Platter, #1556, 14-1/2" l **$140**

Salad bowl, Flora Danica, botanical specimen, molded gilt border, dentil edge, pink highlights, blue triple wave and green crown mark, 9-7/8" d **$825**

Soup tureen, cov, stand, Flora Danica, oval, enamel painted botanical specimens, twin handles, finial, factory marks, botanical identification, modern, 14-1/2" l **$5,750**

Tray, Blue Fluted pattern, 10" l **$65**

Vase, sage green and gray crackled glaze, 7" h **$150**

ROYAL CROWN DERBY

History: Derby Crown Porcelain Co., established in 1875 in Derby, England, had no connection with earlier Derby factories which operated in the late 18th and early 19th centuries. In 1890, the company was appointed "Manufacturers of Porcelain to Her Majesty" (Queen Victoria) and since that date has been known as "Royal Crown Derby."

Most of these porcelains, both tableware and figural, were hand decorated. A variety of printing processes were used for additional adornment. Today, Royal Crown Derby is a part of Royal Doulton Tableware, Ltd.

Marks: Derby porcelains from 1878 to 1890 carry only the standard crown printed mark. After 1891, the mark includes the "Royal Crown Derby" wording. In the 20th century, "Made in England" and "English Bone China" were added to the mark.

Bottle, orig stopper, molded body, two handles, hp flowers, gold accents, 6" h **$150**

Candlesticks, pr, bone china, Imari pattern, paneled baluster form, bulbous toes, brass nozzle **$765**

Cup and saucer, Imari pattern, 20th C, 5" d saucer **$70**

Dessert service, Pattern 1128, Imari pattern, bone china, twelve 8-1/2" d dessert plates; twelve 6-1/2" d bowls; twelve teacups and saucers **$1,880**

Ewer, Oriental-style gold enameled dec, soft coral ground, handle, 6" h **$200**

Luncheon plates, dark Kelly green rim, gilt inner and outer rims, white faux jewelling applied to outer rim, price for set of 12, c1898, 9-1/8" d **$470**

Jug, Imari palette, pink round, gold trim, pr, c1885 .... **$750**

Mug, grapes and vines dec, blue and gold **$125**

Plate, Daisy pattern, blue transfer print, gilt details, price for set of 11, late 19th/early 20th C, 8" d **$260**

Soup plate, inner band of gold jewelling with wide rim of gilt quatrefoils, grapevine, and leaf sprays, some leaves accented with bronze tone, shaped beaded edge, retailed by Tiffany & Co., price for set of 18, early 20th C, 9-7/8" d **$5,750**

Tea and coffee service, bone china, Pattern 1128, Imari dec, 9" h ovoid coffeepot, 7-1/4" h teapot, creamer, cov sugar, modern **$950**

Urn, squatty, double reticulated handles

Royal Crown Derby soup tureen, covered, stand, Kings pattern, oval, c1830, 10" x 17-1/2", **$2,300.**

and finials, birds, butterfly, and floral designs, ivory ground, gilt accents, marked "Bailey, Banks, and Biddle," dripped for lamp, finials replaced, restoration to one handle, price for pr, 12" h **$1,325**

Vase

Enameled floral dec, gold encrusted lip, 7-1/2" h **$320**

Ovoid, narrow neck, flared rim, serpent handle, cobalt blue and iron-red Imari type dec, gilt accents, hp floral panels, minor gilt loss, touchup, price for pr, 13" h **$925**

ROYAL DOULTON

Royal Doulton figure, balloon seller, **$395.**

Royal Doulton figure, man using plane, **$350.**

Royal Doulton pitcher, stoneware, decorated in graffito by Hannah Barlow, mother cat surrounded by kittens, floriform stamp/HBB/AB/2280/MA/782, c1887-1891, 6-1/2" x 6-1/2", **$2,400.**

Photo courtesy of David Rago Auctions, Inc.

History: Doulton pottery began in 1815 under the direction of John Doulton at the Doulton & Watts pottery in Lambeth, England. Early output was limited to salt-glazed industrial stoneware. After John Watts retired in 1854, the firm became Doulton and Company, and production was expanded to include hand-decorated stoneware such as figurines, vases, dinnerware, and flasks.

In 1878, John's son, Sir Henry Doulton, purchased Pinder Bourne & Co. in Burslem. The companies became Doulton & Co., Ltd. in 1882. Decorated porcelain was added to Doulton's earthenware production in 1884.

Most Doulton figurines were produced at the Burslem plants, where they were made continuously from 1890 until 1978. After a short interruption, a new line of Doulton figurines was introduced in 1979.

Dickens ware, in earthenware and porcelain, was introduced in 1908. The pieces were decorated with characters from Dickens' novels. Most of the line was withdrawn in the 1940s, except for plates, which continued to be made until 1974.

Character jugs, a 20th-century revival of early Toby models, were designed by Charles J. Noke for Doulton in the 1930s. Character jugs are limited to bust portraits, while Royal Doulton toby jugs are full figured. The character jugs come in four sizes and feature fictional characters from Dickens, Shakespeare, and other English and American novelists, as well as historical heroes. Marks on both character and toby jugs must be carefully identified to determine dates and values.

Doulton's Rouge Flambé (Veined Sung) is a high-glazed, strong-colored ware noted primarily for the fine modeling and exquisite colorings, especially in the animal items. The process used to produce the vibrant colors is a Doulton secret.

Production of stoneware at Lambeth ceased in 1956; production of porcelain continues today at Burslem.

Marks: Beginning in 1872, the "Royal Doulton" mark was used on all types of wares produced by the company.

Beginning in 1913, an "HN" number was assigned to each new Doulton figurine design. The "HN" numbers, which referred originally to Harry Nixon, a Doulton artist, were chronological until 1940, after which blocks of numbers were assigned to each modeler. From 1928 until 1954, a small number was placed to the right of the crown mark; this number added to 1927 gives the year of manufacture.

Animal

Alsatian, HN117 ....**$175**
Bull terrier, K14 ....**$325**
Dalmatian, HN114 ....**$250**
English bulldog, HN1074............**$175**
Salmon, flambé, printed mark, 12" h
....**$435**
Tiger, flambé, printed mark, 14" l
....**$375**

Biscuit jar, earthenware
Emb scrolled mold, polychrome florals, nickel silver mount, handle, and lid, green "Doulton Burslem England" backstamp, 6-1/2" h
....**$220**

Silver plated lid and handle, floral dec, Doulton Burslem mark, 9" h
....**$200**
Silver plated lid and handle, floral dec, Doulton Burslem mark, 9-1/2" h **$290**
Stoneware, enamel decorated geometric designs in relief, silver plated rim, handle and cover, imp Doulton Lambeth mark, 1882, 6-3/4" h **$265**
Bowl, farm scene, rect, 1932 mark, 9" l, 7-1/2" w **$115**
Cabinet plate, pink and yellow roses painted in center, lower left artist sgd

Royal Doulton biscuit jars, gold and rust colored chrysanthemums, foliage in gray-greens and gold, c1894, **$995;** scrolled motif with white and pink passion flowers, gold trim, Doulton Burslem, 1891, **$895.**

Royal Doulton biscuit jars, peach colored body with multicolored florals, gold foliage, Doulton Burslem, 1891, **$995;** Carlton Ware, tan ground with pink and white flowers, yellow centers, blue forget-me-nots, cobalt blue drapery panels at top alternating with beige, gold trim, c1894, **$1,250.**

Royal Doulton, Walton Ware, four-piece tea set, 5" h teapot with underplate, covered sugar bowl, creamer, all depicting Battle of Hastings, cream-color earthenware ground, stamped mark, chip to spout, hairline to sugar lid, c1910, **$365.**
Photo courtesy of David Rago Auctions, Inc.

"W. Slater," raised gilt border and rim, turquoise faux jewel accents, early 20th C **$325**

Candlesticks, pr, Walton Ware, Battle of Hastings, cream color earthenware ground, stamped mark, small base chip on one, c1910, 6-1/2" h **$290**

Chambersticks, pr, Walton Ware, fishermen dec, ivory earthenware ground, stamped mark, one of pair damaged, c1910, 2" h **$400**

Character jug, large
Cardinal.................................... **$150**
Poacher, D6781 .... **$350**

Character jug, miniature
Blacksmith **$50**
Pickwick **$65**

Character jug, small
Pearly King.............................. **$35**
Toby Philpots **$85**

Charger, hp, allover incised leaf, berry, and vine border, central fruits and leaves, attributed to Frank Bragwyn, printed mark, c1930, 12-5/8" d
.... **$245**

Clock case, King's ware, night watchman, c1905................................. **$450**

Cuspidor, Isaac Walton ware, polychrome dec, transfer printed, fisherman on ext., verses on int. lip, printed mark, 7" h................................... **$325**

Dinner service, Rondelay pattern, service for eight, platter, tea set, 60 pcs
.... **$450**

Figure
Carolyn, HN 2112, 71/4" h, 3-1/2" d
.... **$335**
Fair Lady, coral pink, HN2835 ... **$225**
King Charles I, dark brown gloves, black flora at boots, imp date 1919
.... **$1,312**

Orange Lady, HN1758................ **$245**
Queen Mother's 80th Birthday, HN464, 1980........................... **$750**
Priscilla, pantaloons showing beneath crinoline, HN1380, 1920-40
.... **$288**
Sandra, HN2275 .... **$200**
The Leisure Hour, HN2055......... **$400**
Victorian Lady, HN1208, 1926-38
.... **$355**

Fish plate, swimming fish centers, pale yellow ground, gold bands and rims, sgd "J. Hallmark," 10-pc set, 9" d
.... **$700**

Game plate, bone china, each with gilt trim lines and polychrome enamel painted with shore birds in landscapes, artist sgd "C. Holloway," titled and factory marked on reverse, retailed by Tiffany & Co., set of 12, c1925, 9-1/2" d...................... **$1,300**

Humidor, Walton Ware, Battle of Hastings, cream color earthenware ground, stamped mark, c1910, 7-1/2" h..................................... **$365**

Inkstand, stoneware, tapered cylindrical form molded with floral sprays, blue, ochre, and brown glazes, silver mounts, Doulton Lambeth, hallmarked London, 1901, 3" h
.... **$215**

Jardinière, Walton Ware, Battle of Hastings, cream color earthenware ground, stamped mark, c1910, 4-1/2" h..................................... **$350**

Jug, Regency Coach, limited edition, printed marks, 20th C, 10-1/2" h
.... **$930**

Loving cup
King George V and Queen Mary, 25-year reign anniversary, c1935, 10-1/4" d **$750**

Royal Doulton pitcher, stoneware, carved by Frank Butler, stylized leaves, pods, and whiplash elements, brown and green glaze, floriform stamp/England/FAB/299, three tight firing lines to base, c1891-1902, 7" x 7", **$1,100.**
Photo courtesy of David Rago Auctions, Inc.

Royal Doulton Gibson Girl plate, titled "Some think she has remained in retirement too long, others are surprised she is out so soon," **$95.**
Photo courtesy of Dotta Auction Co., Inc.

Three Musketeers, limited edition, sgd "Noke, H. Fenton," orig certificate, 20th C, 9-3/4" h **$920**

Milk pitcher, sharkskin ground, cobalt blue flowers trimmed in gold, US patent, 7" h **$150**

Mug

Gladiator, #D6553, 4" h **$300**

St. John Falstaff, 8-1/4" h **$125**

Pitcher

Stoneware, dec by Florence Barlow, stippled ground with enameled pate-sur-pate design of birds in flight among marshy grass, incised artist monogram and imp Doulton Lambeth mark, c1884, 7-3/4" h **$1,000**

Walton Ware, fishermen dec, ivory earthenware ground, stamped mark, price for pr, one with bruise and restoration, c1910, 12-1/2" h **$400**

Plate, English Garden series, 8-1/2" d **$115**

Platter, Dr. Johnson at Bootham Bar-York, registered in Australia, 9" l, 7-1/2" w **$120**

Service plate, cream-colored ground, interior band of gilt anthemia, rim with gilt scrollwork over cream-colored ground, apple green reserves, gilt-shaped rim, price for 18-pc set, mold date mark 1910, 10-5/8" d **$5,465**

Spirits barrel, King's Ware, double, silver trim rings and cov, oak stand, c1909, 7" l **$1,200**

Sweet meat, sharkskin ground,

Royal Doulton Toby mug, large, pirate, green and yellow parrot for handle, black hat with white skull and crossbones, brown shirt, $85.

applied flowers, silvered lid and handle, rosette mark artist sgd "Eleanor Tosen," 5" d, 3-1/2" h **$125**

Tankard, hinged pewter lid, incised frieze of herons among reeds, blue slip enamel, imp mark, sgd, c1875, 9-1/2" h **$1,600**

Teacup and saucer, cobalt blue, heavy gold dec **$120**

Tea set, Walton Ware, cov teapot with underplate, creamer, sugar bowl, Battle of Hastings, cream-colored earthenware ground, stamped mark, chip on spout, hairline on sugar lid **$365**

Tobacco jar, incised frieze of cattle, goats, and donkeys, imp mark, sgd, worn SP rim, handle and cover, dated 1880, 8" h **$995**

Toby jug

Beefeater, #D6206, 6" h **$85**

Winston Churchill, #8360 .... **$95**

Royal Doulton Toby jug, large size, Falstaff, marked on base, $245.

Umbrella stand, stoneware, enamel dec, applied floral medallions within diamond formed panels, framed by button motifs, imp mark, glaze crazing, c1910, 23-1/2" h **$550**

Vase

Emb tapestry dec, enameled scrolls, imp mark, Slaters patent, price for pr, early 20th C, 11-3/4" h **$2,250**

Hannah Barlow dec, double handled, wide central panel with incised landscape and horses grazing by sleeping hound, enameled bands of scrolled leaves and stylized stiff leaves to borders, artist signed and imp Doulton Lambeth mark, 1882, 6-1/2" h **$1,765**

Titanium Ware, sq, hand painted enamel dec of birds below sunny sky, titled "Herring Gulls," artist signed Harry Allen, printed mark, c1925, 7-3/4" h **$1,645**

ROYAL DUX

Royal Dux figure, shepherd and shepherdess, lady standing holding staff, man seated playing an instrument, naturalistic ovoid base, indistinct initials OAP?, man lacking item from hands, Czechoslovakia, early 20th C, 22" h, **$825.**

Photo courtesy of Skinner, Inc.

History: Royal Dux porcelain was made in Dux, Bohemia (now the Czech Republic), by E. Eichler at the Duxer Porzellan-Manufaktur, established in 1860. Many items were exported to the United States. By the turn of the century, Royal Dux figurines, vases, and accessories, especially those featuring Art-Nouveau designs, were captivating consumers.

Marks: A raised triangle with an acorn and the letter "E" plus "Dux, Bohemia" was used as a mark between 1900 and 1914.

Bowl, modeled as female tending a fishing net, oval shell-form bowl, imp mark, early 20th C, 17-1/2" l **$490**

Bust, female portrait, raised leaves and berries on base, Czechoslovakia, unmarked, chips, early 20th C, 14" h **$290**

Compote, figural, modeled as female atop shell-form bowl, another figure within the wave modeled free-form base, imp mark, early 20th C, 14-1/2" l **$750**

Figure

Flamenco dancer, cobalt blue and white glaze, gold trim, pink triangle mark, stamped, numbered, 15" x 9-1/2" x 4-1/2" **$1,250**

Pierrot serenading lover, perched on harvest moon, pre-war "E" mark, price for facing pair, 18" x 11" x 6" **$3,500**

Male and female European peasant, sgd on inner side of base, price for facing pr, 21" h.................. **$750**

Floor vase, date palm tree form, Middle Eastern woman and water urn on one, her suitor playing lute on other, matte finish flesh toned skin, cobalt blue clothing against white, gilt rims and highlights, ink labels "Royal Dux Bohemia" with acorn in triangle, glued unstable repairs to man, price for pr, 36-1/2" h, 37-1/4" h......**$5,225**

Tazza, figural, putti and classically draped woman supporting shell, price for pr, one with hairline in base, 19-1/2" h................................. **$880**

Vase, Grecian, "E" mark, 11" h.....**$595**

Royal Dux figure, female bather, nude woman seated on rocky outcrop, drying her foot with gilt enameled cloth, oblong base, Czechoslovakia, early 20th C, 18-1/2" h, **$1,000.**
Photo courtesy of Skinner, Inc.

Royal Dux figurines, pr, male and female, European peasants, signed on base, 21" h, **$750.**
Photo courtesy of The Early Auction Company, LLC.

ROYAL WORCESTER

History: In 1751, the Worcester Porcelain Company, led by Dr. John Wall and William Davis, acquired the Bristol pottery of Benjamin Lund and moved it to Worcester. The first wares were painted blue under the glaze; soon thereafter decorating was accomplished by painting on the glaze in enamel colors. Among the most-famous 18th-century decorators were James Giles and Jefferys Hamet O'Neale. Transfer-print decoration was developed by the 1760s.

A series of partnerships took place after Davis' death in 1783: Flight (1783-1793); Flight & Barr (1793-1807); Barr, Flight, & Barr (1807-1813); and Flight, Barr, & Barr (1813-1840). In 1840, the factory was moved to Chamberlain & Co. in Diglis. Decorative wares were discontinued. In 1852, W. H. Kerr and R. W. Binns formed a new company and revived the production of ornamental wares.

In 1862, the firm became the Royal Worcester Porcelain Co. Among the key modelers of the late 19th century were James Hadley, his three sons, and George Owen, an expert with pierced clay pieces. Royal Worcester absorbed the Grainger factory in 1889 and the James Hadley factory in 1905. Modern designers include Dorothy Doughty and Doris Lindner.

Basket, flaring pierced sides mounted with floral heads, pine cone and floral cluster int., blue and white transfer dec, first period, mid-18th C, 8-1/2" d **$550**

Biscuit jar, cov, fluted body, raised spear head borders surrounding enamel floral design, 7-1/4" h **$550**

Bowl, scalloped border, shell molded boy, fruit and floral spray, blue and white transfer dec, first period, mid-18th C, 10" d **$320**

Butter tub, cov, cylindrical, fully sculpted finial, painted floral sprays below geometric borders, first period, c1765, 4-1/4" d, 3-1/4" h **$450**

Demitasse cups and saucers, 4-3/8" d saucer, hand painted, painted fruits dec, gilt rims and handles, sgd "E. Townsend," retailed by the Goldsmiths and Silversmiths Company, c1936, orig boxed set includes set of six 4" l gold-washed silver spoons, London, 1931, maker's mark HJH **$3,820**

Dessert plate
Bone china, hand painted, center with peach stem and bluettes, sgd lower right "E. Townsend," gilt rocaille inner rim, seafoam green fluted outer rim, set of 12, c1941, 9-1/8" d **$900**

Royal Worcester ewer, white body, gold neck band and handle, multicolored floral decoration, crossed arrows mark, one of pair shown, **$400.**
Photo courtesy of Dotta Auction Co., Inc.

Royal Worcester pitcher, hand-painted polychrome flowers, cream ground with gilded details, purple ink stamp, fully marked, 5-1/4" d, 6-1/2" h, $150.
Photo courtesy of David Rago Auctions, Inc.

Royal Worcester lamp base, tripod, gilt floral decoration and satyr motif, damage to foot, 10" x 9" base, $325.
Photo courtesy of David Rago Auctions, Inc.

Bone china, hand painted, center with flowers, gilt rim, labeled "Designed by A. H. Williamson, Royal Worcester, Made in England," set of 12, 9-1/4" d **$375**

Ewer, pale pink powder horn shape, gold stag horn handle, minor chip, 9" h **$150**

Figure

Cairo water carrier, 1895, 8-3/4" h **$635**

Lady and gentleman, George III costumes, sgd "Hadley," pr, 7-3/4" h and 8-1/4" h **$1,100**

Welsh girl, shot enamel porcelain, sgd "Hadley," late-19th C, 6-1/2" h **$690**

Fish plates, bone china, hp fish, gilt lattice and foliage border, sgd "Harry Ayrton," printed marks, 13-pc set, c1930, 9-1/4" d..........................**$2,300**

Fruit cooler, cylindrical, Royal Lily pattern, stylized floral reserve, stepped circular foot, first period, c1800, 6-1/4" h **$225**

Lamp base, baluster vase form, slender gilt neck, two short Moorish-style gilt handles, hand-painted scene of gilt shipwreck on shore by lighthouse, reverse with small scenic roundel, gilt guilloche foot, electrified, 13-3/4" h **$325**

Mustard pot, cylindrical, blue and white transfer, floral clusters, floral finial, first period, mid-18th C, 4" h **$325**

Pitcher

Cream, gold enamel dec, 5-3/4" h ..**$150**
Floral dec, gold handle, 6" h, 5" d ..**$230**
Indian elephant head handle, 5-3/4" h **$175**
Tri-corner shape, blue and white overlapping circles, gold enameled

pouring lip, c1860, 5-3/4" h **$260**

Plate

Blind Earl pattern, raised rose spray, polychrome floral sprays, scalloped border, first period, mid-18th C, 7-3/4" d **$1,100**

Octagonal, landscape fan form reserves, cobalt blue ground, first period, pr, 18th C, 7" w **$350**

Salad bowl, leaf molded, three handles, printed mark, c1899, 9" d ..**$560**

Sauce boat, geometric band above foliate molded body, painted floral sprays, oval foot, first period, pr, c1765, 4-1/4" h **$275**

Service plate, hand painted, central roundel painted with dense spray of various flowers, sgd "E. Phillips," speckled green inner rim, gilt outer rim etched with laurel wreaths and husk swags, price for set of 12, c1921, 10-1/2" d **$1,530**

Sweetmeat jar, molded swirl base, thistles dec, silverplate lid, bail, and handle, marked "RW" with crown, 6" d **$200**

Tankard, cylindrical, blue and white transfer dec of parrot among fruit, first period, mid-18th C, 6" h **$325**

Teabowl and saucer, painted chinoiserie vignette, blue border, first period, c1865 ....**$185**

Teapot, cov, globular form body, fully sculpted blossom finial, domed top, painted floral sprays, first period, c1765, 6-1/2" h **$375**

Urn, cov, pierced dome top, globular body, painted floral sprays, basketweave molded base, early 20th C, 11-1/2" h **$195**

Vase, double handles, gilt and enamel dec, scene of birds by moonlit sky, printed mark, c1887, 9-5/8" h **$715**

SARREGUEMINES CHINA

Sarreguemines fruit basket, white plate center with cobalt blue floral decoration, wirework frame, $175.

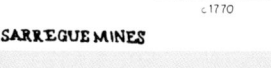
SARREGUEMINES

History: Sarreguemines ware is a faience porcelain, i.e., tin-glazed earthenware. The factory that made it was established in Lorraine, France, in 1770, under the supervision of Utzschneider and Fabry. The factory was regarded as one of the three most prominent manufacturers of French faience. Most of the wares found today were made in the 19th century.

Marks: Later wares are impressed "Sarreguemines" and "Germany" as a result of changes in international boundaries.

Basket, quilted, green, heavy leopard skin crystallization, 9" h **$250**

Centerpiece, bowl with pierced ringlets to sides, supported by center stem flanked by sea nymphs either side, mounted atop circular base on four scrolled feet, polychrome dec, imp marks, chips, restorations, c1875, 14-3/4" h, 14-3/4" d **$900**

Cup and saucer, Orange, majolica, crack to one cup, nicks, set of four **$200**

Dinnerware service, white china, multicolored scenes, six luncheon plates, six bread and butter plates, six demitasse cups, six porringers, two platters, divided dish..................**$150**

Face jug, majolica
Suspicious Eyes, #3320................**$550**
Upward Eyes, #3257 ....**$500**

Garniture, Art Nouveau faience, pr of vases, shouldered trumpet form, shaped oval centerpiece bowl, each with wide gilt band of foliage within diamond borders centered by decorative medallion, verte ground, 10-3/4" h **$350**

Plate, dec with music and characters from French children's songs, 12-pc set, 7-1/2" d **$375**

Tankard, cov, stoneware, continuous country scene of dancing and celebrating villagers, branch handle, pewter lid with porcelain medallion and painted polychrome coat of arms, dated 1869, 11" h **$325**

Urn, gilt metal mounted majolica, baluster form, cobalt blue glazed, mounted with the figure of a crowned lion holding sword, lion and mask handled sides, pierced foliate rim, raised on four scrolling foliate cast feet, imp "Majolica Sarreguemines," second half 19th C, 31-1/4" h ..**$1,800**

SATSUMA

History: Satsuma, named for a war lord who brought skilled Korean potters to Japan in the early 1600s, is a hand-crafted Japanese faience (tinglazed) pottery. It is finely crackled, has a cream, yellow-cream, or gray-cream color, and is decorated with raised enamels in floral, geometric, and figural motifs.

Figural satsuma was made specifically for export in the 19th century. Later satsuma, referred to as satsuma-style ware, is a Japanese porcelain also hand decorated in raised enamels. From 1912 to the present, satsuma-style ware has been mass produced. Much of the ware on today's market is of this later period.

Satsuma vase, ovoid form, scene having many figures, reverse with floral decoration, unmarked, crazed, 7" h, **$100.**
Photo courtesy of Alderfer Auction Co.

Bowl
Lobed body, scalloped rim, overall flowering peonies and chrysanthemums in red and gold, mkd on base, Meiji period, slight wear to gilding, 12-1/4" d, 5-1/4" h **$2,000**
Scene of figures before Mount Fuji, sgd, late 19th C, 10" d **$470**

Cache pot, figural and landscape scene, 6-1/2" h **$120**

Censor
Ovoid, three cabriole legs, two shaped handles rising from shoulder, lid with large shishi seated on top, continual river landscape scene, patterned lappet border above, key fret border below, base sealed "Yabu Meizan," minor loss to one ear on shishi, 3-1/2" h......................**$2,990**
Tapering rect form, lobed base, two squared handles, pierced domed lid, all-over dec or Arhats, Meiji period, 10-1/4" h **$635**

Cup and saucer, bird and floral motif, cobalt blue border, Kinkozan **$115**

Figure
God of Longevity, holding scroll, sgd, 4" h **$360**
Kannon, seated on rock throne holding lotus, repairs, 19th C, 12" h **$765**

Incense burner, two reserves, one with sparrows and flowers, other of Mijo shrine, borders of brocade patterns, butterflies caught in net, and hanging jewels, sgd "Kinkozan," Meiji period, 1868-1911, 5" d **$5,500**

Jar, cov, two cartouche panels, one of Samurai, other with birds, insects, and flowers, one side ring missing, 4" d, 6" h................................**$230**

Koro, pierced lid, hexagonal, six bracket feet, each side with flowers blooming behind garden fences, domed lid, sgd with Shimazu mon, 3" h **$2,185**

Miniature cup, interior painted with Bishamon and Hoi tei, ext. with dancing children, mille fleur borders, sgd with paulownia crest in gold, Meiji period, 1868-1911, 2" d..............**$980**

Plate
One Hundred Birds design, early 20th C, 9-1/4" d **$650**
Samurai design, monogram at top, sgd "Kinkozan" in gold on base, Meiji period (1868-1911), 10-1/2" d **$345**

Seal paste box, cobalt blue, gilt trim, reserve of children flying kites, sgd "Kozan," Meiji period, minor int. chip, 1868-1911, 5" d..................**$320**

Tea bowl, dec with butterflies, powdered gold ground, sgd "Kinkozan," Meiji period, 1868-1911, 4-3/4" d ..**$350**

Tea cup and saucer, colorful groups of flowerheads with scrolling gilt vines, minor gilt wear, sgd "Yabu Meizan," 1-3/4" h cup, 4-3/4" d saucer **$900**

Tea set, paneled designs of courtesans in courtyard settings, c1900, 6-1/2" h teapot, creamer, sugar, six cups and saucers, six 7-1/4" d plates..........**$290**

Tray, rounded form with indented edge, design of scrolls of birds, flowers, and women, cobalt ground with gold bamboo, sgd with imp seal "Kinkozan," Meiji period, 1868-1911, 11-1/2" d **$1,650**

Urn, dragon handles, geishas in landscape, 37-1/2" h **$295**

Vase
Basketweave design with panels of prunus blossoms, sgd "Taizan," 19th C, 12" h **$360**

Satsuma doll tea set, decorated with flowers: tray, teapot, lidded sugar, creamer, two cups and two saucers, **$65.**

Photo courtesy of Joy Luke Auctions.

Cylindrical form, slight neck, mythological scenes with brocade and floral borders, sgd "Hakuzan," Meiji period (1868-1911), 6-1/2" h **$2,235**

Double gourd earthenware body, enameled and gilt battle scenes, upper body with applied sinuous dragon, sgd, price for matched pair, 19th C, 12-3/4" h **$1,000**

Double handles, designs of dragons and various brocade patterns, sgd

"Senzan," 7" x 6" **$1,410**

Double handles, blue ground, pheasants, butterflies, flowers, sgd "Taizan," Meiji period (1868-1911), 12" h **$530**

Samurai on horseback, fighting each other and tigers, price for pr, 4-7/8" h **$500**

Sq, blue and yellow panels, birds, flowers, and butterflies, sgd "Taizan," Meiji period (1868-1911), 12" h **$650**

SCHLEGELMILCH PORCELAINS

History: Erdmann Schlegelmilch founded his porcelain factory in Suhl in the Thuringia region in 1861. Reinhold, his brother, established a porcelain factory at Tillowitz in Upper Silesia in 1869. In the 1860s, Prussia controlled Thuringia and Upper Silesia, both rich in the natural ingredients needed for porcelain.

By the late 19th century, an active export business was conducted with the United States and Canada due to a large supply of porcelain at reasonable costs achieved through industrialization and cheap labor.

The Suhl factory ceased production in 1920, unable to recover from the effects of World War I. The Tillowitz plant, located in an area of changing international boundaries, finally came under Polish socialist government control in 1956.

Marks: Both brothers marked their pieces with the "RSP" mark, a designation honoring Rudolph Schlegelmilch, their father. More than 30 mark variations have been discovered.

Reproduction Alert. Dorothy Hammond in her 1979 book, *Confusing Collectibles,* illustrates an R. S. Prussia decal that was available from a china-decorating supply company for $14 a sheet. This was the first of several fake R. S. Prussia reproduction marks that have caused confusion among collectors. Acquaint yourself with some of the subtle distinctions between fake and authentic marks as described in the following.

The period mark consists of a wreath that is open at the top. A five-pointed star sits in the opening. An "R" and an "S" flank a wreath twig in the center. The word "Prussia" is located beneath. In the period mark, the leg of the letter "P" extends down past the letter "r." In the reproduction mark, it does not. In the period mark, the letter "I" is dotted. It is dotted in some fake marks, but not in others.

The "R" and the "S" in the period mark are in a serif face and uniform in width. One fake mark uses a lettering style that utilizes a thin/thick letter body. The period mark has a period after the word "Prussia." Some fake marks fail to include it. Several fake marks do not include the word "Prussia" at all.

The period mark has a fine center line within each leaf of the wreath. Several fake marks do not.

Schlegelmilch R.S. Prussia, flower form tea set: 8" h green and lavender teapot, 7-1/2" h lidded sugar, 7-1/2" h creamer, 7-1/2" h pink and green teapot, **$300.**
Photo courtesy of Joy Luke Auctions.

Reproduction Alert. Many "fake" Schlegelmilch pieces are appearing on the market. These reproductions have new decal marks, transfers, or recently hand-painted animals on old, authentic R. S. Prussia pieces.

R.S. Germany

Biscuit jar, cov, loop handles, roses dec, satin finish, gold knob, 6" h **$95**

Bonbon dish, pink carnations, gold dec, silver-gray ground, looped inside handle, 7-3/4" l, 4-1/2" w **$40**

Bowl

Emb floral mold, red steeple mark, 10-1/4" d **$100**

Lily mold, "S & T" steeple mark, 10-1/2" d **$165**

Bread plate, iris variant edge mold, blue and white, gold outlined petals and rim, multicolored center flowers, steeple mark.............................. **$115**

Cake plate, deep yellow, two parrots on hanging leaf vine, open handles, green mark................................. **$235**

Celery tray, lily dec, gold rim, open handles, blue label, 11" l, 5-3/4" w **$120**

Chocolate pot, white rose florals, blue mark **$95**

Cup and saucer, plain mold, swan, blue water, mountain and brown castle background, RM................. **$225**

Demitasse cup and saucer, pink roses, gold-stenciled dec, satin finish, blue mark, 3" h **$90**

Dessert plate, yellow and cream roses, green and rich brown shaded ground, six-pc set, 6-1/2" d **$135**

Ewer, mold #640, green mark, 4-3/4" h **$75**

Hatpin holder, Art Deco mold, green mark, 4-1/2" h **$85**

Lemon plate, cutout handle shaped as colorful parrot, white ground, gold trim, artist sgd "B. Hunter" **$60**

Napkin ring, green, pink roses, white snowballs................................. **$55**

Nut bowl, cream, yellow, roses, green scalloped edge, 5-1/4" d, 2-3/4" h **$65**

Pitcher, light blue, chrysanthemums, pink roses, gold trim, 5-3/4" h **$85**

Plate, allegorical scene, sgd "Kaufmann," green mark, 9-1/2" d **$90**

Powder box, cov, green poppies, green mark................................. **$50**

Punch bowl, mahogany shading to pink, polychrome enameled flowers with gilt, imp fleur-de-lis mark with "J. S. Germany," 17-1/4" d, 8" h **$275**

Tea tile, peach and tan, greenish white snowballs, RM over faint blue mark **$165**

Toothpick holder, Art Deco mold, green mark, 2-3/4" h **$80**

Vase, crystalline glaze, orange and white, 6" h **$45**

R. S. Poland

Berry bowl, white and pale orange floral design, green leaves, small orange-

gold border flowers, marked, 4-1/2" sq **$45**

Creamer, soft green, chain of violets, applied fleur-de-lis feet, RM....... **$110**

Dresser set, glossy, pink roses, pr 6-1/4" h candlesticks, 5" h hatpin holder, 13" x 9" tray **$425**

Flower holder, pheasants, brass frog insert **$675**

Vase

Large white and tan roses, shaded brown and green ground, 8-1/2" h, 4-3/4" d **$195**

White poppies, cream shaded to brown ground, pr, 12" h, 6-1/4" d **$750**

R. S. Prussia

Biscuit jar, cov

Clematis florals, red mark, 9" l **$225**

Mold #501, unmarked, 5-1/2" h **$115**

Mold #644, red roses, red mark, 7" h **$300**

Bowl, lily mold #29, ftd, red mark, 10-1/2" h **$275**

Box, cov, rect, detailed floral and gilt highlights, sgd, 4-3/4" h, 1-1/2" h **$150**

Butter dish, cov, porcelain insert, cream and gold shading, pink roses, raised enamel, RM **$715**

Cake plate, reflecting lilies dec, red mark, 11" d.............................. **$165**

Celery dish, mold #207, rose dec, red mark, 12" l.............................. **$85**

Chocolate pot, mold #501, rose dec, red mark, 9-1/2" h **$150**

Creamer and sugar

Iris mold, Winter Portrait, red mark, very minor flake touch-up on creamer **$275**

Mold #605, red mark, sugar lid finial reattached **$125**

Pedestal form, florals, red mark **$185**

Dresser tray, mold #18, red mark, 11-3/4" l.............................. **$165**

Ferner, mold 876, florals on purple and green ground, unsgd, 7" d **$165**

Hair receiver, green lilies of the valley, white ground, RM.................. **$95**

Milk pitcher, Morning Glory mold, pink carnations dec, 5" h **$200**

Mustard, cov, mold #511, red mark, 3-1/4" h.............................. **$50**

Plate

Floral mold, red mark, 8-3/4" d **$115**

Swans in lake, red mark, 9" d **$210**

Portrait bowl, mold #18, dice player variant, red mark, 5-1/2" d **$275**

Portrait plate, mold #32, Springtime, red mark, faint 1" hairline on back, 8-3/4" d.............................. **$375**

Shaving mug, emb floral mold, 3-3/4" h.............................. **$85**

Spoon holder, pink and white roses, 14" l.............................. **$200**

Syrup, cov, underplate, green and yellow luster, pink flowers **$125**

Tankard

Ftd, mold #642, red mark, 10-3/4" h **$275**

Mold #643, reflecting water lilies, red mark, repaired, 14" h **$165**

Striped floral mold #525, red mark, small flake touch-up on lip, 13" h **$325**

Toothpick holder, green shadows, pink and white roses, jeweled, six feet, RM................................. **$250**

Vase, jeweled, rose floral dec, embedded opal jewels, sgd, 6-1/4" h **$275**

R. S. Suhl

Coffee set, coffeepot, creamer, sugar, six cups and saucers, figural scenes dec, some marked "Angelica Kauffmann," 9" h.............................. **$1,750**

Pin tray, round, Nightwatch, 4-1/2" d **$375**

Plate, cherubs dec, 6-3/4" d........... **$90**

Powder dish, cov, Nightwatch, green shading.............................. **$425**

Vase, four pheasants, green mark, 8" h **$275**

R. S. Tillowitz

Bowl, slanted sides, open handles, four leaf-shaped feet, matte finish, pale green ground, roses and violets, gold flowered rim, marked, 7-3/4" d **$125**

Creamer and sugar, soft yellow and salmon roses **$65**

Plate, mixed floral spray, gold beading, emb rim, brown wing mark, 6-1/2" d **$120**

Relish tray, oval, hp, shaded green, white roses, green leaves, center handle, blue mark, 8" l **$45**

Tea set, stacking teapot, creamer, and sugar, yellow, rust, and blue flowers, gold trim, ivory ground, marked "Royal Silesia," green mark in wreath **$95**

Vase, pheasants, brown and yellow, two curved handles, 10" h **$125**

SEVRES

Sevres-style, pair of plates, each painted with scene of youths picking cherries, gilded accents, 16" d, **$1,800.**
Photo courtesy of David Rago Auctions, Inc.

Reproduction Alert.

History: The principal patron of the French porcelain industry in early 18th-century France was Jeanne Antoinette Poisson, Marquise de Pompadour. She supported the Vincennes factory of Gilles and Robert Dubois and their successors in their attempt to make soft-paste porcelain in the 1740s. In 1753, she moved the porcelain operations to Sevres, near her home, Chateau de Bellevue.

The Sevres soft-paste formula used sand from Fontainebleau, salt, saltpeter, soda of alicante, powdered alabaster, clay, and soap. Many famous colors were developed, including a cobalt blue. Such famous decorators as Watteau, La Tour, and Boucher painted the wonderful scenic designs on the ware. In the 18th century, Sevres porcelain was the world's foremost diplomatic gift.

In 1769, kaolin was discovered in France, and a hard-paste formula was developed. The baroque gave way to rococo, a style favored by Jeanne du Barry, Louis XV's next mistress. Louis XVI took little interest in Sevres, and many factories began to turn out counterfeits. In 1876, the factory was moved to St. Cloud and was eventually nationalized.

Marks: Louis XV allowed the firm to use the "double L" in its marks.

Box, cov
Oval, cobalt blue ground, panels of putti dec, sgd "JB," chip on base, 2-1/2" l, 1-1/4" w, 1-1/2" h **$425**
Oval, hp, hinged lid, opalescent cranberry ground, gilt roses and scrolls, lid with painted scene of woman and putti, sgd "E. Carelle," int. dec with polychrome floral panels, 7" l, 4-1/2" w, 3-1/4" h **$650**

Bud vase, gilt ground, enamel Art Nouveau stylized leaf and flower design, printed mark, 6" h **$635**

Bust, Marie Antoinette, bisque bust, gilt highlights, cobalt blue ground, molded porcelain socle with central garland and monogram, 19th C, 13" h **$650**

Café au lait cup and saucer, ftd cup, cobalt blue enameled ground, gilt eagle roundel and torcheres, corresponding molded saucer, early 20th C, 6" h **$200**

Candelabra, pr, painted scenes of winged cherubs, Bleu-celeste ground, foliate gilt border, figural gilt bronze cherubs holding branches of three candle sockets, c1900, 18" h **$2,530**

Centerpiece, int. painted with scene of two lovers, Bleu-celeste ground, scrolled gilt border, bronze plinth, foliate gilt bronze handles, 19th C, 17-1/2" l, 13-1/2" h **$2,990**

Clock, emb metal case, five inset painted porcelain panels, three are scenic,

frontal pc with young lovers, c1900, 17" h **$815**

Compote, int. painted with young beauty and cherub, sgd "Lote," Bleu-celeste ground, dec porcelain pedestal, bronze plinth, 19th C, 11-1/2" d, 9-1/2" h **$2,760**

Cup and saucer, cobalt blue ground, painted roundel depicting an 18th century couple playing with dog, gilt tooled surround, saucer with floral painted center, blue border with floral cartouches, late 19th C, 3" h cup **$815**

Dish, rim dec with flowers, reserve with portrait of lady, turquoise ground, gilt bronze stand with two handles cast with scrollwork, garlands of leaves and grapes, 19th C, 14" d, 7" h **$2,150**

Display tray, round, short gilt handles, cobalt blue rim with rocaille scrolls, center painted with scene of courting couple, sgd E. Roy, early 20th C, 14-5/8" h **$400**

Ecuelle, cov, panel florals, bright enamels, raised gilt cartouches, pink ground, round matching stand, c1860, 8" d **$460**

Figure, pair in Elizabethian dress, royal blue ground, gold accents, early, 8-1/2" h **$640**

Inkwell, scene of winged cherub and florals against Bleu-celeste ground, foliage gilt borders, each ink receptacle supported by gilt bronze sphinxlike young beauty, 19th C, 11-1/2" l, 8-1/2" h **$1,150**

Lamp base, urn shape, cartouches painted with allegorical female depictions of Spring and Autumn, surrounded by cherubs, gilt enamel surrounds, cerulean blue ground, landscape cartouches recto, mounted with vine wrapped reeded handles ending in Demetre masks, trumpet foot topped by turquoise molded beading, rect bronze base molded with swags, corners with swag centered patera, electrified, price for pr, late 19th C, 21-1/2" h **$7,650**

Mantel urns, pr, lidded teal blue tapered vases with horizontal gilt banding, oblong bases set with pair of kneeling bisque figures of semi-nude classical women, base chips, c1919, 18" h **$2,500**

Mantel vase, cov, painted with wide central band of courtiers on verandas in pastoral landscape, white and red faux jeweled borders, body with cobalt blue ground accented with gilt enameling, angular husk-draped ormolu handles, lids with inverted berry finials, price for pr, late 19th C, 19-1/2" h **$9,400**

Monteiths, pr, scalloped rim flanked by two scroll handles, floral garlands and blue ribbon dec, white ground, blue interlaced L's mark, 19th C, 12" w **$960**

Patch box, cov, shaped ovoid, green ground, hinged lid with hand painted scene of Napoleon on horseback, sgd lower right "Morin," 3-1/4" l **$250**

Plaque, 10-1/2" l, 9-5/8" w oval format, Marie Antoniette, mauve gown, blue celeste border with gilt scrollwork, late 19th C, 10-3/4" x 13-5/8" giltwood and crème painted frame **$550**

Portrait plate, Lobelia portrait, surrounded by wreath, cobalt blue band border with gilt dec including Napoleonic crest and crowns, mounted in shadow box frame, gilt loss, 9" d **$150**

Solitaire, 6-1/4" h teapot, cup and saucer, cov sugar, tray, gilt scrollwork, reserves dec with flowers or fetes galantes, turquoise ground, 19th C **$1,135**

Tray, six-sided oblong form, French allegorical park scene, ladies with parasols, Florentine gilt border, sgd "Bertien," 18-1/2" x 13" **$525**

Urn

Campana form, Napoleonic scenes painted reserves, green ground, sgd "L. Loreau," mounted on plastic base, fitted as lamp, 19" h **$1,195**

Light blue body, hp elephant lady framed with gold medallion, overall random amethyst leafy stemmed flowers, gold gilt emb foot, metal handled collar, blue trademark, metal stamped "France," 15" h **$950**

Urn, cov

Dome cov, pine cone finial, neck dec with band of vitruvian scrolls and ram's heads, reserves dec with flowers, fluted socle and octagonal base, gilt metal mounts, 19th C, 14-1/2" h **$1,675**

Finely painted French garden scene by L. Bertren within gilt foliate cartouche, cobalt blue ground, winged anthropomorphic bronze handles, verso with pastoral cottage and stream scene, bronzed acorn finial lid, mkd with Serves style cipher, c1900, 40-1/2" h **$10,120**

Vase, pink ground, oval cartouches with figural landscapes and ornaments, metal mount, pr, 11" h **$1,380**

Sevres wall plaque, portrait of two girls in skirts, gilt trim, signed "E. Furloud, underglaze blue Sevres mark, 17" d, **$1,300.**

Photo courtesy of The Early Auction Company, LLC.

Wine cooler, Louis XVI style, circular tapering form, top section with gilded ram's heads over reeded band, base dec with ribboned garlands and entwined laurel, multicolored, white ground, 10-1/4" h **$2,300**

SHAWNEE POTTERY

History: The Shawnee Pottery Co. was founded in 1937 in Zanesville, Ohio. The company acquired a 650,000-square-foot plant that had previously housed the American Encaustic Tiling Company. Shawnee produced as many as 100,000 pieces of pottery a day until 1961, when the plant closed.

Shawnee limited its production to kitchenware, decorative art pottery, and dinnerware. Distribution was primarily through jobbers and chain stores.

Marks: Shawnee can be marked "Shawnee," "Shawnee U.S.A.," "USA #--," "Kenwood," or with character names, e.g., "Pat. Smiley" and "Pat. Winnie."

Bank, bulldog **$50**
Basket, 9" l, 5-1/2" h at handle, turquoise glaze, relief flowers and leaves, USA 688 .... **$45**
Batter pitcher, Fern **$65**
Casserole, cov, Corn Queen, large **$40**
Cookie jar, cov
Cinderella, unmarked **$125**
Drum major, marked "USA 10," 10" h **$295**
Jo-Jo the Clown, marked "Shawnee USA, 12," 9" h **$300**
Little Chef **$75**
Owl **$110**
Creamer
Elephant **$25**
Puss n' Boots, green and yellow **$65**

Smiley Pig, clover bud **$165**
Figure
Gazelle **$45**
Squirrel **$30**
Rabbit **$40**
Fruit bowl, Corn Queen **$25**
Mug, Corn King **$35**
Paperweight, Muggsy **$65**
Pitcher
Bo Peep, blue bonnet, yellow dress **$125**
Chanticleer **$75**
Planter
Gazelle **$25**
Horse with hat and cart **$20**
Locomotive, black **$60**
Mouse and cheese, pink and yellow **$25**
Wheelbarrow **$20**

Shawnee cookie jar, Smiley Pig, green ruffled color, red roses and green leaves on hat, purse tucked under arm, **$325.**

Shawnee planter, mill scene, olive green glaze, marked "Shawnee, USA, 769," **$65.**

Salt and pepper shakers, pr
Chanticleer, large, orig label **$45**
Dutch Boy and Girl, large **$55**
Milk cans....................................**$30**
Mugsey, small **$65**
Puss n' Boots, small......................**$30**
Smiley, small **$30**
Watering cans **$28**

Teapot
Granny Ann, peach apron **$125**
Horseshoe, blue **$65**
Tom Tom, blue, red, and yellow
....**$175**
Utility jar, Corn King....................**$50**
Wall pocket, bird house **$25**

SPATTERWARE

Spatterware plate, paneled, red, green, and blue rainbow spatter, 9-1/4" d, **$1,150.**
Photo courtesy of Pook & Pook, Inc.

Spatterware pitcher, Peafowl decoration, red spatter, 8" w, 7" h, **$775.**
Photo courtesy of Joy Luke Auctions.

Spatterware plate, Stick spatter, blue cog flowers, green leaves, red petals, English, **$250.**
Photo courtesy of Wiederseim Associates, Inc.

History: Spatterware generally was made of common earthenware, although occasionally creamware was used. The earliest English examples were made about 1780. The peak period of production was from 1810 to 1840. Firms known to have made spatterware are Adams, Barlow, and Harvey and Cotton.

The amount of spatter decoration varies from piece to piece. Some objects simply have decorated borders. These often were decorated with a brush, requiring several hundred touches per square inch to achieve the spatter effect. Other pieces have the entire surface covered with spatter.

Marks: Marked pieces are rare.

Notes: Collectors today focus on the patterns—Cannon, Castle, Fort, Peafowl, Rainbow, Rose, Thistle, Schoolhouse, etc. The decoration on flatware is in the center of the piece; on hollow ware, it occurs on both sides.

Aesthetics and the color of spatter are key to determining value. Blue and red are the most common colors; green, purple, and brown are in a middle group; black and yellow are scarce.

Like any soft paste, spatterware is easily broken or chipped. Prices in this listing are for pieces in very good to mint condition.

Reproduction Alert. Cybis spatter is an increasingly collectible ware in its own right. The pieces, made by the Polishman Boleslaw Cybis in the 1940s, have an Adams-type peafowl design. Many contemporary craftsmen also are reproducing spatterware.

Bowl, Morning Glory flowers, red spatter, purple flowers, light overall crazing, small table rim chip, 5-1/2" d
....**$65**

Charger
Stick spatter, red, blue, green, and purple flowers, purple stick spatter border, 12-1/2" d **$125**
Stick spatter, red and blue flowers, green leaves, purple stick spatter buds, mkd "Adams, England," minor staining, 14-1/2" d **$100**

Creamer
Morning Glory, blue and green flower, red spatter, 3-3/4" h.............**$2,750**
Peafowl, red, green, and blue, paneled, unusual squiggly branches, minor enamel flake in blue, 5-5/8" h
....**$770**
Rainbow Thumbprint, red, yellow, and blue peafowl, red, blue, and green spatter, damage and restoration, 4" h
....**$1,650**
Red and green cockscomb design, blue spatter, paneled, stains on foot, minor flakes, 5" h....................**$860**
Red and green rose, brown and black spatter, rim flake, 3-1/2" h.......**$650**
Cup, blue stick spatter looping pattern, red, green, and blue long tulip **$75**
Cup and saucer, handleless
Dark blue, green, and red pomegranate, yellow dots, blue spatter, light stains, crazed saucer **$800**

Light brown spatter, red and blue spray with green leaves, hairlines **$385**

Peafowl, light blue, mustard yellow, and green dec, red spatter, damage and repair to cup, flake and inpainting in saucer **$150**

Rainbow, Drape pattern, red, yellow, and green, small rim repair on cup, minor stains on saucer **$3,080**

Red, mustard, and green six-pointed star, stains on cup, foot chip **$925**

Red, yellow, green, and blue tulip dec, blue spatter, cup has stained area, filled-in flakes, hairline...........**$110**

Miniature, handleless cup and saucer
Blue spatter, blue, mauve, and green dahlia.................................**$300**

Blue spatter, light green yellow, and red peafowl **$350**

Red spatter....................................**$200**

Pitcher
Acorns, yellow and teal green, green and dark brown leaves, purple spatter, paneled, bubbles in brown and yellow, stains, rim repair, 8-1/2" h **$3,650**

Blue drape with bands on shoulder, rim, and handle, hairlines, some stains, in-the-making separation at handle, 4-3/4" h......................**$460**

Paneled sides, five-color rainbow spatter, handle cracked, 7-1/2" h **$5,500**

Plate
Black Beauty, black floral border, red, blue, and green floral center,

transfer label "Wm. Adams & Co., Tunstall, England," 9-1/8" d.....**$150**

Blue border, blue, red, and green dahlia pattern, 8-3/8" d...........**$350**

Blue border, center red and green flower, light stains, 8-1/2" d **$150**

Blue flowers, red and blue flowers green leaves, 10-3/4" d.............**$150**

Peafowl, dark blue, green, and dark brown, long tail, red spatter, short hairline, in-the-making chip on table ring, 8-1/2" d **$715**

Peafowl, red, yellow, and green, blue spatter border, rim chips, 7-1/2" d **$110**

Rainbow, blue and reddish-purple, red Adams rose in center, stains, rim flake, 9-5/8" d **$450**

Rainbow, light red, blue, and yellow border, rim flake, 8-1/2" d **$3,300**

Rainbow, purple and black, bull's eye center, 9-1/2" d **$1,500**

Rainbow, red, blue, and green border, scalloped edge, imp "Adams," filled-in rim chip, 10-1/2" d.............**$385**

Rainbow, red, yellow, and blue spatter, few minor knife scratches, 8-5/8" d **$3,250**

Red border, red, blue, and green flowers, minor enamel imperfections, minor stains, 8-3/4" d **$110**

Platter
Dark brown eagle and shield transfer center, blue spatter border, octagonal, stains and hairline, 13-3/4" x 17-1/2" **$295**

Light blue borders, rect white cen-

ter panel, oblong, scalloped corners, minor rim flakes, 12-3/8" d, 15-7/8" w....................................**$220**

Peafowl, red, blue, and dark brown, appears to have been scoured, two hairlines, and flake on rim underside, 8-1/4" x 10-3/4"..............**$615**

Red and green rainbow border, large red and blue tulip with green and black foliage, imp anchor mark, restorations, hairline, 10-1/2" x 13-3/4"..............................**$4,510**

Soup plate, blue border, red, green, and yellow stripes, floral center, 8-3/4" d...**$195**

Sugar bowl, cov
Blue, green, and red designs, blue stripes, minor roughness on inside flange, 5" d, 5" h **$250**

Paneled, red schoolhouse, green spatter trees and grass, blue spatter, small crow's foot, restored handles, lid blue transfer replacement, 5-3/4" h **$715**

Teapot
Cockscomb, red and green design, blue spatter, hairlines in base, restored replaced lid, 7-5/8" h **$550**

Peafowl, blue, green, and red, red spatter, small flakes, 9" h **$1,400**

Rainbow, green and yellow with purple loops, black spots, stains, filled-in rim chip, restoration to handle, spout, and lid, 5" h **$5,060**

Waste bowl, brown, red, and black Fort pattern, blue spatter, hairline, 6-1/4" d, 3-1/2" h **$200**

STAFFORDSHIRE, HISTORICAL

History: The Staffordshire district of England is the center of the English pottery industry. There were 80 different potteries operating there in 1786, with the number increasing to 179 by 1802. The district includes Burslem, Cobridge, Etruria, Fenton, Foley, Hanley, Lane, Lane End, Longport, Shelton, Stoke, and Tunstall. Among the many famous potters were Adams, Davenport, Spode, Stevenson, Wedgwood, and Wood.

Notes: The view is the most critical element when establishing the value of historical Staffordshire; American collectors pay much less for non-American views. Dark blue pieces are favored; light views continue to remain under-priced. Among the forms, soup tureens have shown the largest price increases.

Prices listed here are for mint examples, unless otherwise noted. Reduce prices by 20 percent for a hidden chip, a faint hairline, or an invisible professional repair; by 35 percent for knife marks through the glaze and a visible professional repair; by 50 percent for worn glaze and major repairs.

The numbers in parentheses refer to items in the Armans' books, which constitute the most detailed list of American historical views and their forms.

Staffordshire, unknown maker, bowl, "A View Near Philadelphia," titled on back, 9-3/4" d, **$395.**
Photo courtesy of Wiederseim Associates, Inc.

Adams

W. ADAMS & SONS   ADAMS

The Adams family has been associated with ceramics since the mid-17th century. In 1802, William Adams of Stoke-on-Trent produced American views.

In 1819, a fourth William Adams, son of William of Stoke, became a partner with his father and was later joined by his three brothers. The firm became William Adams & Sons. The father died in 1829 and William, the eldest son, became manager.

The company operated four potteries at Stoke and one at Tunstall. American views were produced at Tunstall in black, light blue, sepia, pink, and green in the 1830-40 period. William Adams died in 1865. All operations were moved to Tunstall. The firm continues today under the name of Wm. Adams & Sons, Ltd.

Bowl, English scenes with ruins, dark blue transfer, yellowed repair on back, 11" d, 2-1/2" h **$155**

Creamer, English scene, imp "Adams," dark blue, 5-3/8" d......................**$175**

Pitcher, Eagle, Scroll in Beak, blue and white transfer, illegible imp mark for William Adams, Stoke, glaze scratches, 1827-31, 5-3/4" h...............**$1,320**

Plate, Mitchell & Freeman's China and Glass Warehouse, Chatham St, Boston, blue and white transfer, imp marker's mark and printed title on reverse, 10-1/4" d............................**$500**

Teapot, Log Cabin, medallions of Gen. Harrison on border, pink (458) **$450**

Clews

From sketchy historical accounts that are available, it appears that James Clews took over the closed plant of A. Stevenson in 1819. His brother Ralph entered the business later. The firm continued until about 1836, when James Clews came to America to enter the pottery business at Troy, Indiana. The venture was a failure because of the lack of skilled workmen and the proper type of clay. He returned to England, but did not re-enter the pottery business.

Staffordshire, Clews, plate, America and Independence, States border, imp mark, 10-1/2" d, **$175.**
Photo courtesy of Wiederseim Associates, Inc.

Bowl, Landing of General Lafayette, ext. floral design, rim repair, 9" d **$410**

Cup plate, Landing of General Lafayette at Castle Garden, dark blue **$400**

Pitcher
Welcome General Lafayette the Nation's Guest and Our Country's Glory, blue and white transfer, handle repair, int. staining, 6" h **$2,070**

States Border pattern, scenic country vista with mansion on hill, river in foreground, blue and white transfer dec, minor int. staining, 6-3/4" h **$980**

Plate
America and Independence, States border, America wears Mason's apron, holds portrait of Washington, dark blue transfer, scalloped edge, imp "Clews, Warranted, Staffordshire," 10-1/2" d **$825**

Landing of General Lafayette, blue and white transfer, imp maker's mark for James and Ralph Clews, minor wear, c1819-36, 7-3/4" d **$500**

Landing of General Lafayette, imp "Clews," dark blue, very minor wear, 10" d **$350**

States series, America and Independence, fisherman with net, imp "Clews," dark blue, small rim flake, 10-5/8" d **$440**

Platter
Landing of General Lafayette at Castle Garden New York 16 August 1824, blue and white transfer, imp maker's mark, minor glaze scratches, 11-3/4" x 15-1/4" **$2,200**

States Border, center with vista of river with two swans, two men, rowboat

Staffordshire, Clews, plate, The Landing of General Lafayette at Castle Garden, impressed Clews mark, 10" d, **$375.**
Photo courtesy of Wiederseim Associates, Inc.

on river bank, large country house surrounded by trees in background, blue and white transfer, imp marker's mark of James and Ralph Clews, Cobridge, glaze scratches, 1819-36 ....**$2,530**

Winter View of Pittsfield Massachusetts, blue and white transfer, imp maker's mark, glaze scratches, 14" x 16-1/2"......................................**$3,450**

Soup plate
Picturesque Views, Pittsburgh, Pennsylvania, imp "Clews," steam ships with "Home, Nile, Larch," black transfer, chips on table ring, 10-1/2" d **$330**

Winter View of Pittsfield, Massachusetts, imp "Clews," dark blue, 10-3/8" d **$440**

Saucer, Landing of Gen. Lafayette, dark blue transfer, imp "Clews Warranted Staffordshire"..................**$275**

Toddy plate, Winter View of Pittsfield, Massachusetts, scalloped edge, medium blue transfer, imp "Clews Warranted Staffordshire," 5-3/4" d **$400**

J. & J. Jackson

J. & J. JACKSON

Job and John Jackson began operations at the Churchyard Works, Burslem, about 1830. The works formerly were owned by the Wedgwood family. The firm produced transfer scenes in a variety of colors, such as black, light blue, pink, sepia, green, maroon, and mulberry. More than 40 different American views of Connecticut, Massachusetts, Pennsylvania, New York, and Ohio were issued. The firm is believed to have closed about 1844.

Deep dish, American Beauty Series, Yale College (493) **$125**

Plate, The President's House, Washington, purple transfer, 10-3/8" d **$275**

Platter, American Beauty Series Iron Works at Saugerties (478), 12" l **$275**

View of Newburgh, black transfer (463), 17-1/2" l **$575**

Soup plate, American Beauty Series, Hartford, Connecticut, black transfer (476), 10" d **$150**

Thomas Mayer

In 1829, Thomas Mayer and his brothers, John and Joshua, purchased Stubbs' Dale Hall Works of Burslem. They continued to produce a superior grade of ceramics.

Cream pitcher, Lafayette at Franklin's Tomb, dark blue, 4" h **$550**

Gravy tureen, Arms of the American States, CT, dark blue (498) **$3,800**

Plate, Arms of Rhode Island, blue and white transfer, eagle back stamp, minor glaze scratches, 1829, 8-1/2" d **$790**

Platter

Arms of the American States, New Jersey, dark blue (503), 19" l **$7,200**

Lafayette at Franklin's Tomb, dark blue, 8-1/4" l **$525**

Sugar bowl, cov, Lafayette at Franklin's Tomb, dark blue (510) **$850**

Mellor, Veneables & Co.

Little information is recorded on Mellor, Veneables & Co., except that it was listed as potters in Burslem in 1843. The company's Scenic Views with the Arms of the States Border does include the arms for New Hampshire. This state is missing from the Mayer series.

Plate, Tomb of Washington, Mt. Vernon, Arms of States border, 7-1/2" d **$125**

Platter

European view, light blue and white transfer, imp and printed maker's mark, hairline, light wear, c1843, 14-1/2" x 19-3/4" **$365**

Scenic Views, Arms of States border, Albany, light blue (516), 15" l **$265**

Sugar bowl, cov, Arms of States, Pennsylvania, dark blue **$350**

Teapot, Windsor pattern, dark blue, 9-1/2" h **$200**

J. & W. Ridgway and William Ridgway & Co.

J.W.R.
Stone China

W. RIDGWAY

John and William Ridgway, sons of Job Ridgway and nephews of George Ridgway, who owned Bell Bank Works and Cauldon Place Works, produced the popular Beauties of America series at the Cauldon plant. The partnership between the two brothers was dissolved in 1830. John remained at Cauldon.

William managed the Bell Bank Works until 1854. Two additional series were produced based upon the etchings of Bartlett's American Scenery. The first series had various borders including narrow lace. The second series is known as Catskill Moss. Beauties of America in dark blue. The other series are found in light transfer colors of blue, pink, brown, black, and green.

Plate

American Scenery, Valley of the Shenandoah from Jefferson's Rock, brown (289), 7" d **$120**

Beauties of America, City Hall, New York, dark blue (260), 10" h **$225**

Platter

Beauties of America series, Alms House New York, blue and white transfer, printed title, scratches, scattered minor staining, 12-3/4" x 16-1/2" **$1,265**

Catskill Moss, Boston and Bunker's Hill, imp "William Ridgway Son & Co," medium blue, minor chips, knife marks, edge wear, dated 1844, 19" l **$525**

Relish tray, Savannah Bank, Beauties of America Series, blue and white transfer, printed title, minor imperfections, c1814-30, 5-3/8" x 8-1/4" **$750**

Soup plate, Octagon Church Boston,

imp "Ridgway," dark medium blue, 9-7/8" d **$330**

Wash bowl, American Scenery, Albany (279) **$325**

Rogers

ROGERS

John Rogers and his brother George established a pottery near Longport in 1782. After George's death in 1815, John's son Spencer became a partner, and the firm operated under the name of John Rogers & Sons. John died in 1916. His son continued the use of the name until he dissolved the pottery in 1842.

Basket and undertray, Boston State House, blue and white transfer, imp marker's mark for John Rogers and Son, Longport, hairline cracks, 1815-50, 3" x 6-1/2" x 9-1/4" **$2,760**

Cup and saucer, Boston Harbor, dark blue (441) **$650**

Cup plate, Boston Harbor, dark blue (441) **$1,400**

Deep dish, Boston State House, blue and white transfer, imp marker's mark for John Rogers and Son, Longport, minor glaze scratches, 1815-42, 12-3/4" d **$2,070**

Plate, The Canal at Buffalo, lace border, purple transfer, int. hairline, 9-5/8" d **$55**

Platter, Boston State House, medium dark blue (442), 16-5/8" l **$1,000**

Sauce tureen, cov, undertray, Boston State House, blue and white transfer, imp maker's mark for John Rogers and Son, Longport, 1815-42 .... **$2,900**

Waste bowl, Boston Harbor, dark blue (441) **$850**

Stevenson

R.S.W.

As early as the 17th century, the name Stevenson has been associated with the pottery industry. Andrew Stevenson of Cobridge introduced American scenes with the flower and scroll border. Ralph Stevenson, also of Cobridge, used a vine and leaf border on his dark blue historical views and a lace border on his series in light transfers.

The initials R. S. & W. indicate Ralph Stevenson and Williams are associated with the acorn and leaf border. It has been reported that Williams was Ralph's New York agent and the wares were produced by Ralph alone.

Bowl

Capitol Washington, blue and white transfer, printed mark, Ralph Stevens and Williams, Cobridge, glaze imperfections, 1815-40, 11" d **$2,645**

Park Theater New York, blue and white transfer, printed mark, Ralph Stevens and Williams, Cobridge, minute scratches, 1815-40, 8-3/4" d **$2,530**

Cup and saucer, New Orleans, floral and scroll border **$95**

Jug, dark blue print, 8-1/4" h.........**$750**

Pitcher, Almshouse, Boston, reverse with Esplanade and Castle Garden New York, blue and white transfer, unmarked, 10" h **$2,300**

Plate

Boston Hospital, blue and white transfer, stamped title, maker's initials, imp maker's mark, minor glaze scratches, 9" d **$350**

Catholic Cathedral, New York, floral and scroll border, dark blue (395), 6-1/2" d **$1,650**

Columbia College, portrait medallion of President Washington, inset View of the Aqueduct Bridge at Rochester, blue and white transfer, Ralph Stevens and Williams, Cobridge, minor scratches, 1815-40, 7-1/2" d **$8,625**

New York from Brooklyn Heights, printed title, imp maker's mark,

Staffordshire, unknown maker, coffeepot, dark blue transfer printed decoration, wide floral and scroll border, English landscape scene with old woman and seated man, rim chip, lid broken, 9" h, **$390.**

Photo courtesy of Alderfer Auction Co.

A. Stevenson, Cobridge, 1808-29, 10-1/4" d **$900**

View of Governor's Island, printed title, imp maker's mark, A. Stevenson, Cobridge, 1808-29, 10-1/4" d **$950**

Welcome Lafayette the Nation's Guest, portrait medallion of President Washington, City Hotel, New York, inset "entrance to the Canal into the Hudson at Albany," blue and white transfer, Ralph Stevens and Williams, Cobridge, minor scratches, 1815-40, 8-1/2" d **$4,600**

Welcome LaFayette the Nation's Guest, Jefferson, Washington, Governor Clinton, Park Street Theater New York, vignette of View of Aqueduct Bridge at Little Falls, blue and white transfer, Ralph Stevens and Williams, Cobridge, minor scratches, 1815-40, 10" d **$3,740**

Platter

Battle of Bunker Hill, blue and white transfer, printed title, imp maker's mark, Ralph Stevenson, Cobridge, one scratch, 1815-40, 10-1/4" x 13" **$8,625**

New York Esplanade and Castle Garden, blue and white transfer, printed title, imp maker's mark, Ralph Stevenson, Cobridge, minor glaze scratches, 1815-40, 14-1/2" x 18-1/2" **$5,750**

Troy from Mount Ida, by W. G. Wallogy, landscape scene, floral border, blue and white transfer, back stamped with American eagle, marked "A. Stevenson Warranted Staffordshire," 7-1/4" x 9-1/4" **$1,550**

Soup plate, View on the Road to Lake George, printed title, imp maker's mark, A. Stevenson, Cobridge, 1808-29, 9" d....................**$1,100**

Toddy plate, American Museum, New York, dark blue transfer, mkd "Scudder's American Museum, R.S.W.," impressed Stevenson, 4-7/8" d **$660**

Wash bowl, Riceborough, Georgia, lace border (388) **$375**

Stubbs

In 1790, Stubbs established a pottery works at Burslem, England. He operated it until 1829, when he retired and sold the pottery to the Mayer brothers. He probably produced his American views about 1825. Many of his scenes were from Boston, New York, New Jersey, and Philadelphia.

Gravy boat, Hoboken in New Jersey, Steven's House, blue and white transfer, printed title, Joseph Stubbs, Burslem, minor imperfections, 1790-1829, 4-1/4" h **$550**

Pitcher, Boston State House, reverse with City Hall New York, blue and white transfer, unmarked, small chip on handle, 6" h.................**$980**

Plate

City Hall New York, floral and eagle border, medium blue transfer, unmarked, minor wear and small repair, 6-1/2" h.....................**$225**

Fair Mount near Philadelphia, floral border with eagles, medium blue transfer, imp "Stubbs," 10-1/4" h **$475**

Upper Ferry Bridge of the River Schuylkill, blue and white transfer, printed title, Joseph Stubbs, Burslem, imperfections, 1790-1829, 9" d **$950**

Platter

State House Boston, blue and white transfer, printed title, marked "Joseph Stubbs, Burslem," minor scratches and crazing, 1790-1829, 12" x 14-3/4" **$1,265**

Mendenhall Ferry, blue and white transfer, printed title, minor glaze scratches, 13-3/4" x 16-3/4" **$2,185**

Upper Ferry Bridge over the River Schuylkill, well and tree, printed title on reverse, hairline, 15-1/2" x 18-3/4" **$715**

Salt shaker, Hoboken in New Jersey, spread eagle border, dark blue (326) **$700**

Wash bowl and pitcher, Upper Ferry Bridge Over the River Schuylkill, 12-5/8" d bowl, 10" h pitcher, blue and white, printed title, Joseph Stubbs, Burslem, 1790-1829 ....**$1,840**

Unknown makers

Bowl, Franklin, scene of Ben flying kite, red transfer, minor wear, 11-1/8" d, 3-1/4" d...................................**$495**

Cup, handleless, dark blue transfer, Quadruped series, llama on both

sides, floral border, scalloped rim
.... **$115**

Fruit bowl, undertray, reticulated, blue and white transfer, figures, cows, and manors in rural landscape, floral borders, 10-1/2" l, 5" h **$765**

Jug, pearlware, brown transfer print, commemorating British Admiral Nelson, portrait, ship *Victory,* various nautical devices, orange enamel highlights on rim and edges of handle, minor imperfections, 6-3/4" h
.... **$1,650**

Pitcher, dark blue transfer, View of the Erie Canal, floral borders, transfer slightly blurred, repairs, 5-7/8" h
.... **$715**

Plate

City Hall, New York, dark blue transfer, minor wear, 9-3/4" d
.... **$275**

Court House Baltimore, blue and white transfer, fruit and flower border, printed title on reverse, light wear, hairline, 8-1/2" d **$470**

Exchange Baltimore, blue and white transfer, fruit and floral border, printed title on reverse, 10" d
.... **$390**

Fulton's Steamboat, blue and white transfer, floral border, minor scratches and rim chips, 10-1/4"
.... **$890**

Nahant Hotel near Boston, dark blue transfer, wear, chips on table ring, 8-3/4" d **$200**

The Dam and Waterworks Philadelphia, blue and white transfer, fruit and flower border, printed title on reverse, 9-7/8" d
.... **$650**

The Residence of the late Richard Jordon, New Jersey, brown, minor wear and stains, 9" d **$250**

View from Coenties-slip, scene of Great Fire, City New York, light blue transfer, wear, small edge flakes, 8" d **$385**

Platter, Sandusky, dark blue, very minor scratches, 16-5/8" l **$8,525**

Saucer, scene of early railroad, engine and one car, floral border, dark blue, 5-7/8" d **$275**

Teapot, The Residence of the Late Richard Jordan, New Jersey, brown transfer, small chip, stain and repair to lid, 8-1/4" h **$715**

Tea service, partial, Mount Vernon the Seat of the Late Gen Washington, blue and white transfer, floral border, three teapots, creamer, three cov

sugar bowls, waste bowl, 13 tea bowls, 12 saucers, some with printed titles, imperfections **$8,625**

Wood

Enoch Wood, sometimes referred to as the father of English pottery, began operating a pottery at Fountain Place, Burslem, in 1783. A cousin, Ralph Wood, was associated with him. In 1790, James Caldwell became a partner and the firm was known as Wood and Caldwell. In 1819, Wood and his sons took full control.

Enoch died in 1840. His sons continued under the name of Enoch Wood & Sons. The American views were first made in the mid-1820s and continued through the 1840s.

It is reported that the pottery produced more signed historical views than any other Staffordshire firm. Many of the views attributed to unknown makers probably came from the Woods.

Marks vary, although always include the name Wood. The establishment was sold to Messrs. Pinder, Bourne & Hope in 1846.

Creamer, horse drawn sleigh, imp "Wood," dark blue, minor hairline in base, 5-3/4" h **$550**

Cup and saucer, handleless

Commodore MacDonnough's Victory, imp "Wood & Sons," dark blue, pinpoints on cup table ring........... **$355**

Ship with American flag, Chancellor Livingston, imp "Wood & Sons"
.... **$770**

Gravy boat, Catskill Mountains Hudson River, blue and white transfer, printed title, minor imperfections, 7-1/2" l **$650**

Pitcher and basin, Lafayette at Franklin's Tomb, floral and foliate borders, blue transfer dec, Burslem, England, repair on spout of pitcher, 1819-46, 4-1/2" d x 9-5/8" h pitcher, 12" d basin.............................. **$1,410**

Plate

Boston State House, blue and white transfer, imp maker's mark, 1819-46, 8-1/2" d..................... **$325**

Commodore MacDonnough's Victory, shell border, blue transfer, printed titles on the front and impressed maker's marks on the reverse, c1819-46, 7-5/8" d **$325**

Commodore MacDonnough's Victory, shell border, blue transfer, printed titles on the front and impressed maker's marks on the reverse, c1819-46, 9-1/8" d **$300**

Commodore MacDonnough's Victory, shell border, blue transfer, printed titles on the front and impressed maker's marks on the reverse, c1819-46, 10-1/4" d **$300**

Constitution and Guerriere, imp "Wood," dark blue minor scratches, 10-3/8" d **$1,760**

Cowes Harbour, blue and white transfer, shell border, imp maker's mark on reverse, light wear, 6-1/2" d **$245**

Dartmouth, ships in harbor, irregular shell border, medium blue transfer, unmarked, knife scratches, minor stains, 8-1/4" d......................... **$350**

East Cowes Isle of Wright, shell border, blue and white transfer, 10-1/2" d **$765**

Mount Vernon, the Seat of the Late Gen'l Washington, blue and white transfer, imp maker's mark, 1819-46, 6-1/2" d **$850**

Pine Orchard House, Catskill Mountains, blue and white transfer, printed title, glaze scratches, 10-1/4" d **$575**

The Baltimore & Ohio Railroad, (incline), imp "Enoch Wood," dark blue, 9-1/4" d **$770**

The Baltimore & Ohio Railroad, (straight), imp "Wood," dark blue, minor scratches, 10-1/4" d **$825**

Transylvania University, Kentucky, shell border, dark blue, label with eagle and banner and "E Pluribus Unim," imp "Wood," 6-1/2" d
.... **$775**

View of Liverpool, shell border, blue transfer, printed titles on the front and impressed maker's marks on the reverse, c1819-46, 10" d **$350**

Platter

Christianburg Danish Settlement on the Gold Coast Africa, blue and white transfer, imp maker's mark, minor glaze imperfections, 14-1/2" x 18-3/4"............................... **$3,220**

Highlands Hudson River, blue and white transfer, printed title, imp maker's mark, Enoch Wood & Sons,

Burslem, minor roughness, 1819-46, 10" x 12-3/4" $3,335

Lake George State of New York, blue and white transfer, printed title, partial imp marker's mark, minor glaze imperfections, c1819-46, 12-3/4" x 16-1/2" $2,585

Sugar bowl, cov, Wadsworth Tower, blue and white transfer, scalloped shaped handles, minor imperfections, 7" d, 6" h $265

Tea service, partial, Wadsworth Tower, cov teapot, two large teacups, one large saucer, five teacups, six saucers, 15 plates, imperfections ..$2,645

Toddy plate, dark blue transfer, Catskill House, Hudson, imp "Wood," minor wear and stains, 6-1/2" d $525

Tureen, cov, Passaic Falls, State of New Jersey, blue and white transfer, repairs, glaze wear, 7" h $200

Undertray, Pass in the Catskill Mountains, blue and white transfer, imp maker's mark, printed title, repair to handle, 8-1/8" l $200

Waste bowl, Washington standing at Tomb, scroll in hand, blue and white transfer, unmarked, Enoch Wood & Sons, Burslem, minor imperfections, 1819-40, 6-1/4" d, 3-1/4" h $750

STAFFORDSHIRE ITEMS

History: A wide variety of ornamental pottery items originated in England's Staffordshire district, beginning in the 17th century and still continuing today. The height of production took place from 1820 to 1890.

Many collectors consider these naive pieces folk art. Most items were not made carefully; some even were made and decorated by children.

The types of objects are varied, e.g., animals, cottages, and figurines (chimney ornaments).

Note: The key to price is age and condition. As a general rule, the older the piece, the higher the price.

Reproduction Alert. Early Staffordshire figurines and hollowware forms were molded. Later examples were made using a slip-casting process. Slip casting leaves telltale signs that are easy to spot. Look in the interior. Hand molding created a smooth interior surface. Slip casting produces indentations that conform to the exterior design. Holes occur where handles meet the body of slip-cast pieces. There is not hole in a hand-molded piece.

A checkpoint on figurines is the firing or vent hole, which is a necessary feature on these forms. Early figurines had small holes; modern reproductions feature large holes often the size of a dime or quarter. Vent holes are found on the sides or hidden among the decoration in early Staffordshire figurines; most modern reproductions have them in the base.

These same tips can be used to spot modern reproductions of Flow Blue, Majolica, Old Sleepy Eye, Stoneware, Willow, and other ceramic pieces.

Staffordshire figures of William Wallace and Scottish lass, mounted as lamps, 19th C, 16-1/2", **$625.**
Photo courtesy of Sloans & Kenyon Auctioneers and Appraisers.

Staffordshire figure, milkmaid and cow, polychrome decoration, multicolored oval base, **$125.**

Bank, cottage shape, repairs, 5-1/4" h $195

Bust, Empress Maria Theresa, England, lead glaze creamware, underglaze translucent enamels, half bust mounted atop waisted socle, pierced hole to one shoulder factory made and apparently for holding additional ornament, slight glaze chip, late 18th C, 8-1/4" h $1,175

Cake stand, blue and white transfer, Wild Rose pattern, crazing, 12" d, 2-1/2" h $400

Candlestick, lead glazed creamware

Underglaze translucent colors, free form tree with leaf molded sconce and applied florets, restorations, late 18th C, 11-1/4" h $1,175

Underglaze translucent brown, green, and blue enamels, molded tree form with applied foliage and shells, bird perched on branch, male figure standing on flat platform in center, restorations, late 18th C, 11-3/4" h $650

Cheese dish, cov, figural, cow head, enamel and pink luster detailing, shaped undertray, 9-3/4" l, 7-1/2" h $265

Chimney piece

Castle with two towers, drummer, polychrome enamel dec, gilt, coleslaw foliage, minor edge damage, 7-1/4" h $215

Multistoried house, coleslaw trim, pierced windows, topped with vining strawberries, some wear, hairlines, 9-1/8" h $320

Creamer, cow, blue and dark red splotch polychrome dec, pearlware, early 19th C, 7" l, 2-1/2" h $235

Cup and saucer, handleless, Gaudy floral design, blue, dark green, and gold, saucer imp "Clews Warranted Staffordshire," small rim flake on cup **$250**

Cup plate

Hand dec, polychrome floral wreath border, spring center, imp "TT," 3-3/4" d **$145**

Moral Maxim, red, two border reserves, 4-1/8" d....................**$125**

Moses and the Ten Commandments, red, floral and shell border, indiscernible imp mark, 4" d..........**$180**

Prunus Wreath, medium dark blue, imp "Rogers," 4" d **$165**

Sheltered Peasants, dark blue, flower and fruit border, mkd with title, 3-15/16" d **$110**

Three unidentified vases, light blue, mkd "Smith & Pardee, Kingston, NY," 4-1/4" d **$55**

Two hunters, one seated, hunting dog, light blue, border with gun and bag, imp "D," 3-7/8" d **$100**

Figure, polychrome enamel dec

Antony and Cleopatra, reclining, silver lustered armor, England, possibly Wood and Caldwell, slight footrim chips, price for pr, early 19th C, 12" l **$2,585**

Charles Stewart Parnell, England, c1880, standing, holding shillelagh in one hand, flag bearing the Union Jack and Irish harp in other, raised title on base, Victorian, gilt wear, c1880, 13-7/8" h **$450**

Cow and calf with tree trunk vase, facing pair, Victorian, c1870, 10-7/8" h **$470**

Gordon-Cumming, modeled standing by dead lion, titled "The Lion Slayer," c1860, 16-1/2" h...........**$275**

King John Signing the Magna Carta, King John seated beneath tent, page to either side, Victorian, restored chip at tip of flag, pen chipped, c1865, 12-3/4" h **$300**

Male and female figures arm in arm, seated beneath arbor, Victorian, stained glaze, c1860, 13-3/4" h **$200**

Mary, standing, holding book, peasant garb, Victorian, c1860, 15-1/2" h **$200**

Napoleon III, standing, military uniform, holding cocked hat, base titled "Louis Napoleon," enamel and gilt dec, Victorian, c1855, 15-1/2" h **$200**

Prodigal's Return, two standing figures, raised title on base, gilt highlights, Victorian, c1880, 13-1/4" h **$360**

Scottish couple, matching green feathered caps, man wearing green and orange tartan, holding horn, woman holding basket, 9-1/4" h............**$115**

Spaniels, seated, red and white, yellow collars, hairlines, pr, 7-5/8" h **$320**

Sportsman, orange jacket, mounted on horse, hairlines, 7" h **$350**

St. Patrick, standing, hand to heart, base titled, enamel and gilt dec, Victorian, c1860, 11-3/4" h......**$215**

Templars, modeled as three officials, two women flanking bearded man, raised initials I.O.G.T. (International Order of Good Templars), Victorian, c1870, 11" h **$200**

The Lost Sheep, pearlware, shepherd wearing maroon coat, ochre striped vest and green breeches, carrying sheep with its legs tied to stick over his shoulder, rocky base and square plinth, England, small repair, 1750-85, 8-1/8" h **$530**

Turpin and King, titled bases, late Victorian, price for pr, 11" h....**$400**

Victoria and Victor Emmanuel II, modeled standing figures, man in military attire with hound by his feet, woman in formal dress, base titled "Queen & King of Sardinia," gilt trim, Victorian, crazing, c1855, 13-3/4" h **$200**

Whippet holding rabbit in its mouth, Victorian, price for pr, one with leg damage, 10-3/4" h, second half 19th C **$425**

William Wallace, standing, holding shield in one hand, sword in other, raised title to base, Victorian, c1860, 14-3/4" h **$250**

Fruit basket and underplate, 12" l basket molded and reticulated with central guilloche band, 10" d underplate with matching rim, underglaze blue and pink floral sprays, gilt accenting, mid-19th C...............**$235**

Hen on nest, polychrome, good color, minor edge wear and chips on inner flange of base, 10-1/2" l...............**$715**

Jar, cov, melon shape, alternating yellow and green stripes, cov with molded leaf, lead glaze, hairline to cover, finial and rim chips, 18th C, 3-1/4" h **$4,315**

Jug, Fair Hebe, high relief, modeled as tree trunk, creamware, lead glaze,

attributed to Yoyez, rim chip and repair, c1788, 8-1/2" h **$998**

Miniature, tea set, Gaudy pink and green rose dec, 4-1/4" h teapot, creamer, sugar, waste bowl, two cups and saucers, few flakes, repairs **$425**

Mug, pearlware, black transfer print of Hope in landscape scene, silver luster highlights, minor imperfections, 3-3/4" h............................**$60**

Pitcher, mask, pink luster rim, glaze wear, hairline to spout, 4-7/8" h ...**$175**

Plate

New York, US, medium red, eagle and cornucopia mark, 5-7/8" d.....**$95**

Shannondale Springs, Virginia, US, medium red, eagle and cornucopia mark, 7-7/8" d **$70**

Platter, blue and white transfer, "The Italian Pattern," attributed to Spode, unmarked, glaze wear, scratches, early 19th C, 21" d......................**$575**

Sauce boat, fruit and flowers, molded feet and handle, dark blue, rim chips, 7-7/8" l............................**$330**

Stirrup cup, creamware, modeled as a stag and decorated in translucent brown and yellow enamels, lead glaze, England, restorations, 18th C, 4-3/4" l **$2,585**

Teapot, cov, black basalt, oval form, scalloped rim and classical reliefs centering columns with floral festoons, banded drapery on shoulder, incised brick banded lower body, unmarked, restored spout, early 19th C, 9-3/4" l..........................**$360**

Toddy plate, multicolored view of thatched cottage at foot of hill, surmounted by castle ruins, sepia butterfly border, imp "P," 4-13/16" d...**$90**

Tureen, cov, stoneware, white, salt glazed, oval, press molded dot and diaper, star and diaper and basket pattern, three grotesque mask and paw feet, England, rim line, repaired chips to two feet, c1760, 10-1/4" l **$2,350**

Vegetable dish, cov, domed cover with ornately molded knop and handles, blue transfer flowers, fruit, and shells, sq foot, Longport, England, minor nick to knop and cover rim, early 19th C, 10-3/4" d, 7-1/2" h......................**$1,410**

Waste bowl, Forget Me Not, red transfer, edge roughness, 5-5/8" d..........**$60**

Whistle, overglazed enamel dec, modeled as bird perched on tree trunk, applied florets, tail restored, c1820, 3-1/2" h..**$420**

STAFFORDSHIRE, ROMANTIC

Romantic Staffordshire coffeepot, blue transfer decoration, Oriental-type scene, **$350.**
Photo courtesy of Dotta Auction Co., Inc.

History: In the 1830s, two factors transformed the blue-and-white printed wares of the Staffordshire potters into what is now called "Romantic Staffordshire." Technical innovations expanded the range of transfer-printed colors to light blue, pink, purple, black, green, and brown. There was also a shift from historical to imaginary scenes with less printed detail and more white space, adding to the pastel effect.

Shapes from the 1830s are predominately rococo with rounded forms, scrolled handles, and floral finials. Over time, patterns and shapes became simpler and the earthenware bodies coarser. The late 1840s and 1850s saw angular gothic shapes and pieces with the weight and texture of ironstone.

The most dramatic post-1870 change was the impact of the craze for all things Japanese. Staffordshire designs adopted zigzag border elements and motifs such as bamboo, fans, and cranes. Brown printing dominated this style, sometimes with polychrome enamel highlights.

Marks: Wares are often marked with pattern or potter's names, but marking was inconsistent and many authentic, unmarked examples exist. The addition of "England" as a country of origin mark in 1891 helps to distinguish 20th-century wares made in the romantic style.

Caledonia, Williams Adams, 1830s
Plate, purple transfer, imp "Adams," 9-1/2" d **$60**
Platter, 17" l **$500**
Soup plate, two colors **$175**

Canova, Thomas Mayer, c1835; G. Phillips, c1840
Plate, 10-1/2" d **$95**
Pudding bowl, two colors **$200**
Vegetable, cov **$325**

Cheshire pattern, Burleigh Ware, cheese dish, cov, rect, sloped lid, underglaze blue ovoid finial, rect undertray, transfer printed green and blue, dish 9-1/4" l, 5" h **$115**

Columbia, W. Adams & Sons, 1850
Creamer **$115**
Cup and saucer **$65**
Cup plate **$65**
Plate, 10" d **$60**
Relish **$65**

Dado, Ridgways, 1880s
Creamer, brown **$75**
Cup and saucer, polychrome **$80**
Plate, brown, 7-1/2" d **$35**

Dr. Syntax, James and Ralph Clews, Cobridge, 1819-36
Plate, Dr. Syntax Disputing his Bill with the Landlady, blue and white transfer, 10-1/2" d **$125**
Platter, Dr. Syntax Amused with Pat in the Pond, blue and white transfer, glaze scratches, scattered minor staining, 14-1/4" x 19" **$1,840**
Undertray, Death of Punch, Dr. Syntax

literary series, blue and white transfer, crazing on reverse, 10" x 5-3/4" **$85**

Marmora, William Ridgway & Co., 1830s
Platter, 16-1/2" l **$325**
Sauce tureen, matching tray **$350**
Soup plate **$100**

Millenium, Ralph Stevenson & Son, 1830s, plate, 10-1/2" d **$145**

Palestine, William Adams, 1836
Creamer and sugar **$265**
Cup and saucer, two colors **$135**
Cup plate **$75**
Platter, 13" l **$325**
Vegetable, open, 12" l **$200**

Quadrupeds, John Hall, 1814-32
Plate, central medallion with lion, printed maker's mark, pattern mark in crown, price for pr, 10" d **$865**
Platter, Quadrupeds pattern, central cartouche of elephant, printed maker's mark, pattern mark in crown, minor surface imperfections, 14-3/4" x 19" **$4,315**

Shell pattern, Stubbs and Kent, Longport, 1828-30
Cream jug, blue and white transfer, unmarked, imperfections, 5" h **$1,200**
Milk pitcher, blue and white transfer, unmarked, imperfections, 7" h **$900**

Platter, oval, blue and white transfer, imp maker's mark, repaired rim chip, 18-1/2" l **$1,955**
Soup plate, blue and white transfer, imp maker's mark, wear, price for three, 10" d **$750**
Tea bowl and saucer, blue and white transfer, imp maker's mark, 2-1/2" h **$450**
Vegetable dish, oval, blue and white transfer, imp maker's mark, scratches, wear, 12-1/4" d, 2-1/2" h **$1,150**

Union, William Ridgway Son & Co., 1840s
Plate, 10-1/2" d **$70**
Platter, 15" l **$165**

Unknown pattern
Cup and Saucer, two dogs, flower and leaf border, imp maker's mark for James & Ralph Clews, Cobridge, minor light wear, 1817-34, 2-1/4" h, 5-3/4" h **$150**
Tea Set, partial, blue and white transfer
Bird in oval reverse, floral border, two teapots, creamer, small bowl, waste bowl, imperfections **$1,265**
Three figures in landscape, manor house in distance, teapot, creamer, and two cov sugar bowls **$1,610**
Venus, Podmore, Walker & Co., 1850s, plate, 7-1/2" d **$50**
Yorkshire, soup plate, light blue, slight glaze lines, 10" d **$200**

STANGL POTTERY BIRDS

History: Stangl ceramic birds were produced from 1940 until the Stangl factory closed in 1978. The birds were produced at Stangl's Trenton plant and either decorated there or shipped to its Flemington, New Jersey, outlet for hand painting.

During World War II, the demand for these birds, and other types of Stangl pottery as well, was so great that 40 to 60 decorators could not keep up with the demand. Orders were contracted out to be decorated by individuals in their own homes. These orders then were returned for firing and finishing. Colors used to decorate these birds varied according to the artist.

Marks: As many as 10 different trademarks were used. Almost every bird is numbered; many are artist signed. However, the signatures are used only for dating purposes and add very little to the value of the birds.

Adviser: Bob Perzel.

Note: Several birds were reissued between 1972 and 1977. These reissues are dated on the bottom and are worth approximately same as older birds, if well decorated.

3250, preening duck, natural colors $125
3273, rooster, 5-3/4" h $800
3274, penguin $500
3276, bluebird $90
3281, mother duck $600
3285, rooster, early blue green base, 4-1/2" h...............................$100
3400, lovebird, old, wavy base.....$135
3400, lovebird, revised leaf base.....**$75**
3402, pair of orioles, revised $115
3402, pair of orioles, old $300
3404, pair of lovebirds, old $400
3404, pair of lovebirds, revised $125
3405, pair of cockatoos, revised, open base...$150
3406, pair of kingfishers, blue $165
3407, owl $350
3430, duck, 22" $8,000
3431, duck, standing, brown $850
3432, rooster, 16" h $3,500
3443, flying duck, teal.................$250
3445, rooster, yellow $185
3446, hen, gray $300
3450, passenger pigeon...............$1,800
3451, William Ptarmigan $3,500
3453, mountain bluebird $1,500
3454, Key West quail dove, single wing up...$275

3454, Key West quail dove, both wings up....................................$1,800
3455, shoveler duck.................$2,000
3457, walking pheasant $3,500
3458, quail..............................$2,000
3459, falcon/fish hawk/osprey $6,000
3490, pair of redstarts..................$200
3492, cock pheasant $225
3518, pair of white-headed pigeons $950
3580, cockatoo, medium..............$150
3580, cockatoo, medium, white $600
3581, group of chickadees, black and white $300
3582, pair of green parakeets $225
3582, pair of blue parakeets $250
3584, cockatoo, large..................$275
3590, chat $165
3591, Brewers blackbird..............$160
3595, Bobolink $150
3596, gray cardinal......................$80
3597, Wilson warbler, yellow.........**$55**
3599, pair of hummingbirds.........$325
3625, Bird of Paradise, large, 13-1/2" h $2,500
3634, Allen hummingbird $90
3635, group of goldfinches $215

3717, pair of blue jays $3,500
3746, canary, rose flower $250
3749, scarlet tanager $425
3750, pair of western tanagers $500
3751, red-headed woodpecker, pink glossy $300
3752, pair of red-headed woodpeckers, red matte $550
3754, pair of white-winged crossbills, pink glossy $425
3755, audubon warbler $475
3756, pair of audubon warblers ...$600
3758, magpie jay.....................$1,400
3810, blackpoll warber................$185
3811, chestnut chickadee.............$145
3812, chestnut-sided warbler $150
3813, evening grosbeak $150
3814, blackthroated green warbler $165
3815, western bluebird.................$440
3848, golden crowned kinglet $125
3852, cliff swallow.......................$170
3853, group of golden crowned kingfishers $780
3868, summer tanager $750
3921, yellow-headed verdin.......$1,700
3922, European finch $1,200
3924, yellow-throated warbler $680
Bird sign $2,500

STONEWARE

History: Made from dense kaolin and commonly salt-glazed, stonewares were hand-thrown and high-fired to produce a simple, bold, vitreous pottery. Stoneware crocks, jugs, and jars were made to store products and fill other utilitarian needs. These intended purposes dictated shape and design—solid, thick-walled forms with heavy rims, necks, and handles and with little or no embellishment. Any decorations were simple: brushed cobalt oxide, incised, slip trailed, stamped, or tooled.

Stoneware has been made for centuries. Early American settlers imported stoneware items at first. As English and European potters refined their earthenware, colonists began to produce their own wares. Two major North American traditions emerged based only on location or type of clay. North Jersey and parts of New York comprise the first area; the second was eastern Pennsylvania spreading westward and into Maryland, Virginia, and West Virginia. These two distinct geographical boundaries, style of decoration, and shape are discernible factors in classifying and dating early stoneware.

By the late 18th century, stoneware was manufactured in all sections of the country. This vigorous industry flourished during the 19th century until glass fruit jars appeared and the use of refrigeration became widespread. By 1910, commercial production of salt-glazed stoneware came to an end.

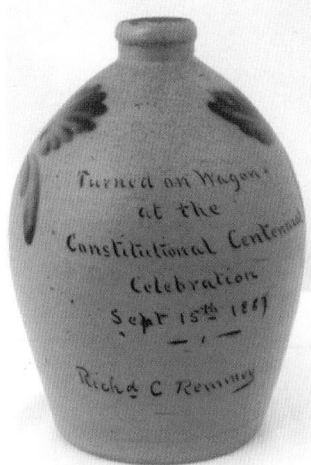

Stoneware jug, Remmey Pottery, PA, inscribed "Turned on wagon at the Constitutional Centennial Celebration Sept. 15th 1889, Richard C. Remmey," cobalt blue floral decoration, 7-3/4" h, **$13,800.**
Photo courtesy of Pook & Pook, Inc.

Stoneware butter churn, five gallons, New York Stoneware Co., Fort Edward, New York, bull's eye stylized flower design, c1880, 17-1/2" h, **$330.**
Photo courtesy of Bruce & Vicki Wassdorp.

Advertising

Butter crock, 1 lb size, "Western Dairy Company Pasture Queen Butter, Chicago, Ill," hairline **$90**

Jug, J. Fisher, Lyons, New York, 1 gal, blue script on front "Collins & Jordan 351 Elk St Buffalo, NY," minor wear and staining from use, c1870, 10-1/2" h **$315**

Jug, unsigned, half gal, Bristol glaze, stenciled under glaze "This Jug Not To be Sold Registered," blue script "Hollander Bros., 1-3-5 Main St, Paterson, NJ," glaze flakes throughout, glaze chipping at spout, c1880, 9" h **$440**

Preserve jar, S. Hart, 3 gal, imp and blue accents, "Crawfords & Murdock, Dealers in Dry Goods Groceries, Clothing Crokery & Hardware, Pulaskie, NY," blue script "3" surrounded by brushed plumes below store mark, professional restoration to rim chip at front, c1875, 12-1/2" h **$385**

Rolling pin, cobalt blue wildflower dec, "John Quast & Son Furniture, Pianos-Undertaking, Buffalo Lake, Minn" **$665**

Rolling pin, "Mix with Us and Save Dough, H. D. Bryam & Son General Mdse & Drugs," blue bands **$485**

Batter jug
Cowden and Wilcox, Harrisburg, Pennsylvania, scrolling floral dec, orig bail handle, tin spout, tin spout cover, 8-1/2" h **$7,000**

Batter pail

N. White & Co., Binghamton, blue brush accents at ears, handle, spout, and impressed name, orig bail handle, surface chip under spout, c1860, 8-1/2" h.......................... **$415**

Unsigned, attributed to Whites, Utica, one gal, cobalt blue slip leaf below spout on front, orig bail handle, c1865, 9" h **$615**

Unsigned, attributed to White's, Utica, six quarts, imp "6," oak leaf design under spout, orig bale handle, short tight hairline, c1865, 6" h **$330**

Unsigned, attributed to Whites, Utica, six quarts, navy blue hollyhock dec, professional restoration to rim chips and lug handle, c1865, 10" h **$360**

Bottle

Imp and blue accented "B. F. Haley California Pop Beer 1889," glaze drip at shoulder to right of imp name, 10" h **$135**

Imp and blue accented "C. F. Washburn," minor crow's foot at shoulder, 9-1/2" h **$35**

Butter churn

H. M. Whitman, Havana, New York, five gal, dasher guide, top to bottom iris dec, blue at name and gallon designation, long in-body thru line that runs thru design on left side, c1860, 18" h **$2,200**

J Burger Jr, Rochester, New York, six gal, dotted bird on stump dec, blue accent at maker's mark, professional restoration, c1885, 20" h **$1,210**

J Norton & Co., Bennington, Vermont, six gal, orig dasher guide, flowering cornucopia of flowers, some very minor staining, 3" very tight lie on side, c1861, 19" h.................. **$8,250**

Joshua J. German, Muskingum County, Ohio, five gal, imp "5" capacity mark, raised initials "JJG" hidden in the mark that was filled in with raised dots, incised owl, stenciled C. C. Rankin, (Newark, OH grocer), badly cracked, wide metal band and wire around rim to stabilize it, ex-Clark Garrett **$4,800**

West Troy New York Pottery, six gal, stoneware guide, blue dec, bird perched in large tree stump, restoration to glaze flaking, c1880, 19" h **$1,020**

White & Wood, Binghamton, New York, five gal, dasher guide, top to bottom paddletail dec, double flower branch, fully filled bird's body, long surface chip at front worn smooth from use, c1885, 17-1/2" h **$8,800**

Whites, Utica, four gal, ribbed orchid dec, possible fire damage on left side, ear missing, c1865, 16" h **$330**

Cake crock, cov

J. & E Norton, Bennington, Vermont, c1855, two gal, dotted reclining deer with fences, pine tree, tree stump, ground cover, two extremely

Stoneware crock, Cowden & Wilcox, Harrisburg, PA, cobalt blue leaf decoration, 8-1/2" d, 7-1/2" h, **$225.**
Photo courtesy of Joy Luke Auctions.

Stoneware cake crock, four gallons, unsigned, attributed to New York state, bold flower and leaf decoration, some staining from use, 2" clay separation the base that occurred in the making, c1870, 9-1/2" h, **$275.**
Photo courtesy of Bruce & Vicki Wassdorp.

Stoneware crock, unsigned, attributed to New York state, brushed and sponge blue horse design below gallon mark, c1870, 8" h, **$4,400.**
Photo courtesy of Bruce & Vicki Wassdorp.

tight hairlines at back of right ear, 12" d, 7-1/2" h **$18,700**

Salt glazed, stamped "John Bell, Waynesboro" under lid and handle, 8" d, 4-3/4" h **$3,850**

Salt glazed, applied handles, stamped under handle, cobalt blue floral dec, attributed to Peter Hermann, Baltimore, 13" d, 7-1/2" h **$1,925**

Canning jar, unsigned, 1 gal, four wide accent stripes across front, stack mark, glaze burns on left side, c1850, 9-1/2" h **$110**

Chicken waterer, unsigned, probably Pennsylvania origin, 1 gal, imp "I" at shoulder, brushed blue accents at button top and inner and out rim of watering hole, c1840, 11" h **$415**

Cream pot

Roberts, Binghamton, New York, 1 gal, bird on branch, ext. rim chip on back, c1860, 7-1/2" h **$770**

Brady & Ryan, Ellenville, New York, 6 quarts, singing bird on dotted branch, imp "6" below maker's name, extensive glaze flaking at rim and spots on back, c1885, 8-1/2" h **$180**

T. Harrington Lyons, two gal, brushed wreath surrounding gallon designation, couple of minor surface chips at rim in back, c1865, 10-1/2" h **$330**

Crock, cov

Four gal, straight sided, two handles, "No. 4" stamped on side, copious cobalt blue floral dec, line repair on side **$2,420**

Three gal, floral cobalt blue banding, "No. 3" stamped on side, two handles, 11" d, 14-1/2" h **$1,155**

Crock

Brady & Ryan, Ellenville, New York, two gal, singing bird on plume,

professional restoration, c1885, 9" h **$550**

D. Mooney, Ithaca, NY, pail shape, brushed blue dec, somewhat overglazed in the firing, c1862, 8" h **$330**

E & L P Norton, Bennington, VT, three gal, bird on plume dec, small stone ping in design, c1880, 10-1/2" h **$360**

F. B. Norton & Co., Worcester, Mass, three gal, chicken pecking corn design, blue at maker's mark and imp gallon designation, thick blue cobalt application, c1870, 10-1/2" h **$3,850**

J. Clark & Co., Troy, two gal, ovoid, simple brushed design, blue at deeply imp maker's mark, blue accents under ears, couple of surface chips at rim, c1826, 9-1/2" h **$360**

J Fisher Lyons NY, five gal, "Lyons" in artistic script across front, some surface roughness at rim, age spider line, c1880, 13" h **$275**

Lyons, two gal, double tulip dec, blue accents at name and ears, stained from use, c1860, 9" h **$165**

N. A. White & Son, Utica, NY, five gal, flying bird dec, floral wreath, artistically shaded tail feathers, professional restoration, c1870, 12-1/2" h **$3,960**

N York Corlears Hook Commeraws, two gal, ovoid, applied open handles, deep incised and blue accented clam shell swag design all along shoulder, deep signature impression, stack mark and kiln burn on one side, minor surface wear at base, c1805 .... **$5,390**

Paul Cushman, Albany, approx 1-1/2 gal, brush blue accents, deep-

ly impressed name, blue accent at handles, three petal lightly brushed flower on back, deeply tooled diamond and leaf pattern all around extended rim, cinnamon clay color in the making, c1807, 9-1/2" h **$2,530**

Paul Cushman Stoneware Factory, 1 gal, deeply impressed unusual maker's mark, blue handles, large stone ping thru name, restoration to full-length hairline on back, c1807, 11" h **$1,980**

Salt glazed, attributed to Pfaltzgraff, York, PA, bulbous, flared rim, incised banding at top, cobalt blue dec tulip, int. brown glaze, small line at top rim, 4-3/4" d, 4-3/4" h **$3,960**

Three gal, Eagle Pottery, eagle stencil **$1,765**

Three gal, ovoid, freehand dec of catlike face **$19,000**

Three gal, America, early 19th C, salt glazed, cylindrical form, brown Albany slip interior, applied lug handles, impressed cow motif filled with cobalt blue, 10" h **$900**

Three gal, Wedding Proposal, NY **$10,450**

Troy NY Pottery, four gal, large dotted and stylized leaf and floral design, some glaze flakes, c1870, 11" h **$360**

Two gal, B. C. Milburn, Alexandra, VA, sunflower and flourishes **$3,520**

Unsigned, attributed to Crolius, NY, three gal, ovoid, thick blue draped design all around shoulder, blue accents at open handles, overall stained from use, old age cracks, c1800, 13" h **$500**

Unsigned, attributed to Macquoid & Co. Pottery Works, New York city, 1 gal, Victorian style woman's profile on front, minor staining, 3" tight hairline, c1870, 7" h **$4,620**

Weston & Gregg, Ellenville, NY, six gal, large bird on detailed plume, blue accent at deeply imp maker's mark, Y-shaped through line extending along bottom, c1869, 12-1/2" h **$1,155**

Whites Utica, three gal, standing stag among ground cover, dry glaze in the making, c1865, 10-1/2" h **$3,190**

Stoneware jug, embossed New York, S & Co., Fort Edward, NY, cobalt blue flourish, strap handle, **$395.**

Stoneware pitcher, maidens carrying water jugs, intricate tooled top and bottom bands, applied handle, unmarked, **$350.**

Face jug, black man, caricatured features, imperfections, 6-1/2" h ..**$4,600**

Flask, unsigned, brushed blue tree dec, design repeated on both sides, incised reeded accents at neck, minor surface wear at base, stack mark, c1810, 6-1/2" h **$2,630**

Jar

Attributed to New York or New Jersey, salt-glazed, wide-mouth ovoid, applied open loop handles, cobalt blue inscriptions around shoulder, (some indistinct) "Mark PBH N???29 1797," minor chips, c1797, 9-1/4" h **$3,100**

N. Clark & Co., Lyons, one gal, ovoid, stoneware lid, brush blue lollipop flower, blue accents at ears and maker's mark, minor surface chip, 10-1/2" h **$690**

Jug

America, imp "2" below top, cobalt blue bird with high comb and long bill perched on large leaf, light staining, early 19th C, 13" h **$420**

America, salt glazed, ovoid, applied strap handle, cobalt blue stylized head of an animal, minor base chip, early 19th C, 13-5/8" h **$1,100**

America, salt-glazed, ovoid, applied strap handle, cobalt blue "1833," few minor rim chips, 1833, 15-3/8" h **$600**

Humiston & Stockwell, S. Amboy, New Jersey three gal, ovoid, large brushed flower design, pin head size flake at top of lip, stack mark on side, c1830, 15" h **$1,890**

J. Clark & Co., Troy, two gal, brushed blue flower dec, blue at marker's mark, stack mark at top, c1827, 14-1/2" h **$220**

J & E Norton, Bennington, Vermont, two gal, peacock dec, minor stone ping at back near handle, c1855, 14"h **$4,950**

J & E Norton, Bennington, Vermont, three gal, compote of flowers, thick glassy cobalt, professional restoration, some staining from use, c1855, 16" h **$550**

J Fisher & Co, Lyons, New York, two gal, bee stinger dec, minor glaze burning, large glaze drips at shoulder and back, c1880, 13-1/2" h **$180**

N. A. White & Son Utica, New York, two gal, paddletail bird, ribbed wings, head, and beak, kiln burn, stone ping, c1870, 14" h **$1,595**

N. Clark Jr., Athens, New York, c1850, five gal, double handled, brushed blue bird with dotted wing perched on flowering branch, blue at maker's mark, very tight jagged hairlines extends down from rim and thru pottery's mark, 18-1/2" h **$935**

Lyons, two gal, large brushed leaf design, some over glazing at shoulder, c1865, 13-1/2" h **$165**

S Hart Fulton, three gal, signature double love birds, staining from use, long J-shaped glued crack on back, c1875, 13-1/2" h **$500**

W. Hart, Ogdensburgh, four gal, horse-head design, blue at name, minor stone pings in the making, c1860, 16" h **$17,325**

Whites, Binghamton, two gal, dotted double poppy dec, professional restoration to tight line, c1860, 12-1/2" h **$275**

Whites, Utica, one gal, long tailed bird, blue at maker's mark, very tight lie in handle, short clay separation line at base, c1865, 11-1/2" h **$880**

Keg, unmarked, ovoid, incised bands, painted cobalt blue pinwheels, stars, and leaves, molded relief dec of man's head, ex-Clark Garrett, 13-3/4" h **$10,000**

Milk pitcher, unsigned, Shenandoah Valley origin, attributed to Remmey factory, three gal, brushed blue floral design fills entire front, professional restoration to handle, partially replaced, c1850, 17" h **$1,210**

Mug, Shenandoah Valley, incised banding, single cobalt blue flower and leaves on each side, bottom initialed "L. B.," attributed to Levi Dice Bell, 4-1/2" h, 4-1/4" d **$2,090**

Pitcher

J. Burger, Rochester, New York, 1 gal, blue accents at handle and imp name, bow tie dec, c1880, 11" h **$615**

Ovoid, applied handle, brushed cobalt blue flower with long leaves, three flourishes around rim at handle, interior with grown glaze, hairline at base, 7" h..............................**$675**

Unsigned, attributed to Lyons, New York, factory, 1 gal, wreath surrounding floral design, blue accent at handle, cobalt blue has bled because of heavy application by potter, surface chip at spout may be in the making, c1860, 10-1/2" h **$330**

Whites Binghamton, incised line around middle, raised rim, cobalt blue polka dot floral dec, 10" h $615

Plaque, emb with Daniel and the lion, 5" x 6" $1,800

Preserve jar

1-1/2 gal, J. Norton & Co., Bennington, Vermont, stylized flower design, blue at deeply imp maker's mark, c1861, 11" h $2,420

1-1/2 gal, Little West, 12th St. N. Pottery Works, double dropping flower design, two short clay separation lines at rim probably occurred in making, c1870, 10" h $495

1-1/2 gal, unknown maker, military general, orig lid $18,700

Two gal, A. O. Whittemore, Havana, New York, squat, blue flower design, blue "2" and blue at maker's mark, couple of short hairlines, c1870, 10" h $310

Two gal, Brady & Ryan, Ellenville, New York, fitted stoneware lid, bushy tailed bird on dotted plume dec in bright blue, surface chip on lid, mottled clay color in the making, c1885, 12" h $470

Two gal, F. Stetzenmeyer & G. Goetzman Rochester, New York, blue dec ribbed leaf and flower bud design, long glaze spider on side, c1857, 11" h $990

Two gal, Harrington & Burger, Rochester, bowed wreath design, script blue in canter of wreath, blue at name, int. short clay separation line at rim occurred in making, c1853, 11" h $330

Two gal, J & E Norton, Bennington, Vermont, peacock on stump design, short clay separation lines that occurring in the making, c1855.........$635

Two gal, John Burger, Rochester, orig stoneware lid, triple fern design surrounds large "2," minor crow's foot glaze spider on side, c1865, 11-1/2" h $580

Two gal, N. Clark & Co., Rochester, New York, stoneware lid, finely executed floral design, int. lime staining, couple of surface chips at rim, stone ping on side, c1850, 11-1/2" d $1,760

Two gal, T. Harrington Lyons, bull's eye wreath design, two blue "2"s, light blue at maker's mark, professional restoration to surface chips

around rim and full-length hairline at back, c1850 ....$415

Two gal, W. Hart Ogendsburg, orig lid, signature horse head design, cinnamon clay color, dry glaze in the making, chips, surface wear, staining from use, hairline at rim at back, c1860 ....$3,300

Three gal, Cortland, brushed plume design, blue accent at name, minor surface chips from use, c1850, 12" h $165

Three gal, J & F Norton, Bennington, antlered and spotted deer in landscape with trees and fences, ex-Clark Garrett, surface edge chip to handle $16,000

Three gal, N. A. White & Son, Utica, New York, wide paddletail bird, very minor design fry to thick blue, c1868, 13-1/2" h $3,520

Four gal, Buffalo, New York, rooster, orig lid, few hairline cracks, c1870 ....$34,100

Five gal, freehand dec of Colonial-era soldier, long coat, broad rimmed hat, holding riffle, handle, 15-3/4" h $14,000

Five gal, freehand dec of standing woman in long dress, tulips on either side, circled "V" $9,000

Five gal, freehand dec of woman holding garment, standing between two trees above standing peacock and two more trees, 15-3/4" h $19,000

Stoneware water cooler, three gallons, Somerset Potters Works, elaborate incised double bird decoration, blue accents at ears, maker's mark, blue dabs and brush blue leaf designs at rim and front, c1870, 15" h, $3,960.
Photo courtesy of Bruce & Vicki Wassdorp.

Water cooler

Gates City, patented May 25, 1886, six quarts, stoneware lid, orig spigot, cobalt blue bird dec, 11" h $935

Henry Dilts, Ohio, 12 gal, two handles, elaborate tree emblem and Masonic compass, incised "12," ex-Clark Garrett, handles and some lip missing $11,000

J & E Norton, Bennington, Vermont, six gal, barrel shape, incised and blue accented horizontal lines frame dotted centerpiece floral design, additional blue dotted accents at bung hole, X-shaped spider line to left of design, c1855, 15-1/2" h $1,760

Somerset Potters Works, three gal, elaborate incised double bird dec, blue accents at ears, maker's mark, blue dabs and brush blue leaf designs at rim and front, brushed, potted, double flower design on back, kiln burn on front, glued crack, chip out of bung hole frame that may have occurred during the making, c1870, 15" h $3,960

Whimsy, slide of watermelon, orig paint, ex-Clark Garrett, c1900, 7" l $5,500

Whistle, figural, Rockingham glaze, c1870

Bird, chips in glaze, 1-1/2" h $90

Owl on stump, 3-1/2" h.............$220

Seated poodle, 3-3/4" h.............$250

TEAPOTS

History: The origins of the teapot have been traced to China in the late 16th century. Early Yixing teapots were no bigger than the tiny cups previously used for drinking tea. By the 17th century, tea had spread to civilized nations of the world. The first recorded advertisement for tea in London is dated 1658 and called a "China drink…call Tcha, by other Nations Tay, alias Tee…" Although coffee houses were already established, they began to add tea to their selections.

From the very first teapots, figural shapes have always been a favorite with tea drinkers. The Victorian era saw a change from more utilitarian teapots toward beautiful, floral, and Rococo designs, yet figural pots continued to be manufactured.

Early American manufacturers mimicked Oriental and British designs. While the new land demanded sturdy teapots in the unsettled land, potteries were established steadily in the Eastern states. Rockingham teapots were produced by many companies, deriving this term from British companies manufacturing a strong, shiny brown glaze on heavy pottery. The best known is from the Bennington, Vermont, potteries.

By the 1800s and the turn-of-the-century, many pottery companies were well established in the U. S., producing a lighter dinnerware and china including teapots. Figural teapots from this era are highly desired by collectors, while others concentrate on collecting all known patterns produced by a company.

The last 20 years has seen a renewed interest in teapots and collectors desire not only older examples, but also high-priced, specialty manufactured teapots or individual artist creations commanding hundreds of dollars.

Reproduction Alert. Teapots and other ware with a blurry mark of a shield and two animals, ironstone, celadon-colored body background, and a design made to look like flow blue, are new products, possibly from China. Yixing teapots have been reproduced or made in similar styles for centuries.

Basalt, black, oval form, scalloped rim and classical relief centering columns with floral festoons, banded drapery on shoulder, incised brick banded lower body, unmarked, England, restored spout, early 19th C, 9-3/4" l **$360**

Cloisonné, panel with butterflies and flowers, Chinese, late 19th C **$450**

Earthenware, brown and green speckled ext., matching lid, c1880, 7" h **$420**

Flow blue, Scinde pattern, Alcock, octagonal, 8-1/2" h **$950**

Graniteware, large teapot with pewter handle, lid and spout, Manning Bowman & Co. Manufacturers, called Perfection Granite Ironware, West Meriden, Connecticut **$325**

Ironstone, Mason's Ironstone, Vista pattern, red and white scenic dec, matching trivet **$195**

Majolica, fish, multicolored, Minton, no mark, late 1800s **$2,000**

Pratt, pearlware, underglaze polychrome enamels on oval forms molded with ribbed bodies and central medallions of classical reliefs, swan finial, slight flake and line to cover, chipped spout, 6" h **$450**

Rockingham glaze, brown glaze, tree trunk form body, molded fruiting vines, branch handle, twig finial, imp Wedgwood, England, mark, chip to cover collar, c1870, 4-3/8" h **$520**

Silver, Hester Bateman, London, oval, domed lid with beaded rim, engraved bands, body with engraved bands and central cartouche, wood ear handle and finial, approx 13 troy oz, 1786, 5-3/4" h **$3,450**

Wedgwood, Rosso Antico, Egyptian, applied black basalt hieroglyphs, crocodile finial, imp mark, slight chips to rim and spout, early 19th C, 7-1/4" l **$1,100**

Yang-Tz-u, enameled, hexagonal, bright polychrome painted mountainous landscapes on each panel, imitation famille rose and jaune dec top and borders, Chinese export, professional repairs on spout, lid, and handle, 19th C, 8-1/4" h **$250**

TERRA-COTTA WARE

History: Terra-cotta is ware made of hard, semi-fired ceramic. The color of the pottery ranges from a light orange-brown to a deep brownish red. It is usually unglazed, but some pieces are partially glazed and have incised, carved, or slip designs. Utilitarian objects, as well as statuettes and large architectural pieces, were made. Fine early Chinese terra-cotta pieces recently have sold for substantial prices.

Architectural element, foo lion, scribed character on sides, fish scale design on bodies, small saddles carry filled bags, flat base, price for pr, base and edge chips, 22" w, 22" h
.... **$425**

Bowl, glazed, 6" d, 2" h **$30**

Bust, good detail, dark red patina, hollow interior, firing separation noticeable from underside, nose restored, 10-1/2" w, 10" h **$125**

Figure
Aphrodite, dressed in tunic, open back, South Italian, third century B.C., 7-1/2" h **$345**

St. Joseph, wearing long loose robes, black hat, polychrome dec, Spanish, 19th C, 11" h **$600**

Reclining male figure with dog, inscribed "Claude Janin," 18-3/4" l
.... **$400**

Pedestal, price for pr, 7" sq top, 24" h **$400**

Planter, garland and mask motif, 10-1/4" h **$100**

Portrait plaque, Benjamin Franklin, circular shape, self-framed with raised title "B. Franklin Americain" surrounding portrait in relief, sgd "Nini" (for Jean Baptiste Nini) dated 1777, unidentified impressed fleur-de-lis mark, France, mounted in ebonized wood frame, shallow rim nicks, 4-1/2" d **$1,410**

Statue, Minera, woman in draped toga, grape and cable head dress, holding wine cup, 55" h **$2,000**

Urn, molded putti and foliage dec, green glaze, waisted neck, two handles, circular base, 29-1/2" h **$395**

Water pitcher, base chip, c1810, 13" h **$325**

TILES

History: The use of decorated tiles peaked during the latter part of the 19th century. More than 100 companies in England alone were producing tiles by 1880. By 1890, companies had opened in Belgium, France, Australia, Germany, and the United States.

Tiles were not used only as fireplace adornments. Many were installed into furniture, such as washstands, hall stands, and folding screens. Since tiles were easily cleaned and, hence, hygienic, they were installed on the floors and walls of entry halls, hospitals, butcher shops, or any place where sanitation was a concern.

Note: Condition is an important factor in determining price. A cracked, badly scuffed and scratched, or heavily chipped tile has very little value. Slight chipping around the outer edges of a tile is, at times, considered acceptable by collectors, especially if a frame can cover these chips.

It is not uncommon for the highly glazed surface of some tiles to have become crazed. Crazing is not considered detrimental as long as it does not detract from the overall appearance of the tile.

Terra-cotta wall relief, three-dimensional head, green and blue matte glazes, incised signature of G. Staindl, 15-1/2" x 10-1/2" x 2-1/2", **$235.**
Photo courtesy of David Rago Auctions, Inc.

Oriental framed tile, white heron on blue ground, 11-1/2" x 10", **$150.**
Photo courtesy of Joy Luke Auctions.

Art pottery, landscape with birds and moose in foreground, dark green high gloss glaze, 6" h, 12" w **$175**

Arts & Crafts, framed, scene of salt marsh landscape, blues, greens, and white, c1907, 10" x 5-1/2" **$2,100**

Batchelder, beige bisque clay with blue engobe, stamped "Batchelder/ Los Angeles," 6" h, 18" l
Bouquet of flowers and birds, slight abrasion to surface **$375**
California desert landscape, abrasion to a few spots **$850**

California Art, scene of California court yard with fountain, restored color and varnish, imp mark, mounted in Arts & Crafts frame, 8" h, 12" l **$1,600**

Cambridge Art Tile, Covington, Kentucky, 6" x 18"
Goddess and Cherub, amber, pr ..**$250**
Night and Morning, pr **$500**

Claycraft
Five tile faience panel, molded landscape of Mediterranean houses by sea, marks hidden by contemporary Arts & Crafts frame, 13-1/4" h, 35" l **$2,400**

Horizontal, English thatched roof cottage next to foot bridge, semi-matte polychrome, mounted in period ebonized Arts and Crafts frame, covered stamp mark, 6" x 12" **$1,610**

Molded lone tree rising over ocean, matte polychrome glazes, stamped "Claycraft," mounted in new Arts & Crafts frame, 7-3/4" x 4" **$815**

Grueby, mottled matte green glaze, mustard yellow blossom, ftd copper frame, raised indecipherable mark on base, 6-1/4" sq **$1,100**

J. & J. G. Low, Chelsea, MA
Putti carrying grapes, blue, pr, 4-1/4" sq **$75**
Circular, yellow, minor edge nicks and glaze wear, 6" d **$35**
Woman wearing hood, brown, 6" sq **$95**

KPM, portrait of monk, titled "Hieronymus of Ferrara sends this image to the prophet to God," small nicks to corners, 5-3/4" x 3-3/8" **$245**

Lowe, Chelsea, Massachusetts, architectural, glossy taupe glaze, including forty-eight undecorated bricks, thirty-four scroll and leaf pattern, two pairs of framed tiles, one depicting winged dragon, the other warriors faces in mottled cream-color and brown glossy glazes, some with pottery marks, late 19th/early 20th C **$360**

Marblehead, ships, blue and white, pr, 4-5/8" sq **$125**

Minton China Works
Aesops Fables, Fox and Crow, black and white, 6" sq **$75**

Rob Roy, Waverly Tales, brown and cream, 8" sq **$95**

Minton Hollins & Co.

Morning, blue and white, 8" sq **$100**

Urn and floral relief, green ground, 6" sq **$45**

Moravian

Autumn, young man picking apples, basket at his feet, stamped "MR," made for Old Wicker Art School, Detroit, Michigan, custom made wrought iron museum stand, 1920s, 18" d, 1-1/2" h **$5,750**

Tempus, Father Time, blue and ivory glaze, red clay showing through, unmarked, small glaze flake on one

edge, 10" x 7-1/4" **$1,150**

Mosaic Tile Co., Zanesville, Ohio

Fortune and the Boy, polychrome, 6" sq **$80**

Delft windmill, blue and white, framed, 8" sq..............**$55**

Pardee, C.

Chick and griffin, blue-green matte, 4-1/4" sq **$175**

Portrait of Grover Cleveland, gray-lavender, 6" sq..............**$125**

Providential Tile Works, Trenton, New Jersey, round, stove type, hold in center, flowered **$20**

Rookwood Faience, emb pink, ochre, and green geometric floral pattern, Arts & Crafts frame, stamped

"RP," chips to corners, 8" h..........**$325**

Sherwin & Cotton

Dog head, brown, artist sgd, 6" sq **$100**

Quiltmaker and Ledger, orange, pr, 6" x 12"..............**$145**

Trent, 6" sq, head of Michelangelo, sea green glaze, sgd by Isaac Broome, imp mark **$115**

U. S. Encaustic Tile Works, Indianapolis, IN, panel, Dawn, green, framed, 6" x 18"..............**$150**

Wedgwood, England

Calendar, November, boy at seashore, peacock blue, 6" sq.............**$95**

Tally Ho, man riding horse, blue and white, 8" sq **$85**

TOBY JUGS

History: Toby jugs are drinking vessels that usually depict a full-figured, robust, genial drinking man. They originated in England in the late 18th century. The term "Toby" probably is related to the character Uncle Toby from Tristram Shandy by Laurence Sterne.

Reproduction Alert. During the last 100 years or more, Tobies have been copiously reproduced by many potteries in the United States and England.

Bennington type, standing, 9-1/2" h **$175**

Delft, man seated on barrel, green hat, green and black sponged coat, blue and yellow pants, old cork stopper, 19th C, 11-1/4" h **$365**

Luster ware, blue coat, spotted vest, 19th C, 6-1/2" h **$175**

Minton, majolica, Quaker man and woman, polychrome dec, imp mark, pr, 11-1/4" h **$4,600**

Portobello pottery, standing, spatter enamel dec, orig cov, c1840, 10" h **$275**

Pratt

Hearty Good Fellow, blue jacket, yellow-green vest, blue and yellow striped pants, blue and ochre sponged base and handle, stopper missing, slight glaze wear, c1770-80, 10-3/4" h **$1,500**

Pearlware glaze, typical blue, brown, and ochre palette, hat inset, small chips, 9-1/4" h..............**$425**

Royal Doulton

Sam Weller, #d6265, "A" mark, 4-1/2" h **$190**

Stoneware, blue coat, double XX, Harry Simson, 6-1/2" h **$395**

The Fortune Teller, 2-3/4" h........**$500**

Winston Churchill, DT6171, 9" h **$175**

Shaker, polychrome dec, standing figure, yellow hat, blue coat, and red breeches with pink luster highlights, England, 19th C, 5" h **$150**

Shorter Son, Ltd., England, Long John Silver, 9-3/4" h..............**$375**

Staffordshire

Cobalt blue coat, red breeches, gilt accented vest, standing on green sponged ground, minor wear to gilding, 9-7/8" h..............**$300**

Martha Gunn, translucent brown and ochre glazes, pearl body, brim repaired at hairline, 9-1/4" h **$1,265**

Pearlware, seated figure, sponged blue jacket, ochre buttons, ochre and lavender speckled vest and trousers, brown hair and hat, green glazed base, shallow flake inside hat rim, attributed to Ralph Wood, c1770-80, 9" h **$1,950**

Seated, holding jug in one hand, glass in other, cobalt blue jacket, plaid vest, orange trousers, yellow hat, c1850, 5-1/4" h, 4-1/4" h **$235**

Whieldon, pearlware, seated figure, yellow greatcoat, green vest, blue trousers, holding brown jug in left hand, raises foaming glass of ale towards mouth, lid missing, c1770-80, 9-1/2" h..............**$1,600**

Wilkinson

Field Marshall Haig, modeled by Sir Francis Carruthers Gould, titled "Push and Go," printed marks, c1917, 10-3/4" h **$460**

Marshall Joffre, modeled by Sir Francis Carruthers Gould, titled "75mm Ce que joffre," printed mark, hat brim restored, c1918, 10" h **$345**

Winston Churchill, multicolored, designed by Clarice Cliff, black printed marks, number and facsimile signature, c1940, 11-3/4" h **$825**

Yorkshire-Type, caryatid form handle, Pratt palette dec, sponged base and hat brim int., 7-3/4" h..........**$750**

Royal Doulton Toby jug, large size, Falstaff, marked on base, **$245.**

VAN BRIGGLE POTTERY

History: Artus Van Briggle, born in 1869, was a talented Ohio artist. He joined Rookwood in 1887 and studied in Paris under Rookwood's sponsorship from 1893 until 1896. In 1899, he moved to Colorado for his health and established his own pottery in Colorado Springs in 1901.

The Art Nouveau schools he had seen in France heavily influenced Van Briggle's work. He produced a great variety of matte-glazed wares in this style. Colors varied.

Artus died in 1904. Anne Van Briggle continued the pottery until 1912.

Marks: The "AA" mark, a date, and "Van Briggle" were incised on all pieces prior to 1907 and on some pieces into the 1920s. After 1920, "Colorado Springs, Colorado" or an abbreviation was added. Dated pieces are the most desirable.

Van Briggle vase, embossed blossoms, unusual lavender to chartreuse matte glaze, marked, 1" line from rim, 1908-1911, 3-3/4", **$250.**

Reproduction Alert. Van Briggle Pottery still is made today. These modern pieces often are mistaken for older examples. Among the glazes used are Moonglo (off white), Turquoise Ming, Russet, and Midnight (black).

Advertising plaque, green and blue matte glaze, emb "VAN BRIGGLE POTTERY/COLORADO CLAY," 1/3" corner chip, few smaller edge chips, 11-1/2" l, 5-3/4" h **$2,300**

Bowl, spade-shaped leaves, frothy green and purple matte glaze, robin's egg blue ground, buff clay showing through, mkd "AA Van Briggle/Colo Spgs/737," 2-1/2" hairline from rim, 1908-11, 5" x 10" **$1,690**

Cabinet vase, emb flowers in curved panels, covered in dark teal matte glaze, incised AA/Van Briggle/190?/186, with XXII/IV/33188 in ink, 1904, 2-1/2" d, 4-1/4" h **$1,610**

Chamberstick, molded-leaf shape, hood over candle socket, green glaze, 5-1/2" h **$115**

Figure, female nude holding shell, matte Persian blue glaze, incised "Van Briggle," 7" h **$250**

Lamp base, emb stylized florals under maroon glaze with blue over-spray, orig factory fittings, incised varnished bottom with logo, name, and Colorado Sprgs, c1920, 9" h **$115**

Low bowl

Dragonfly, closed-in rim, four molded dragonflies around rim, deep mulberry matte glaze, incised cipher, incised Van Briggle U.S.A., c1922-29, 8-3/4" d, 2-3/4" h **$350**

Mug, feathered matte green over blue glaze, overfired, burst bubbles, crack in handle, 1908-11, 6" h **$175**

Shape no. "689," emb arrow root design, under matte green glaze, incised with logo, varnished bottom, Colo Sprgs, c1920, 6-1/2" h **$260**

Night light, figural, stylized owl, bulb cavity, light refracting glass eyes, turquoise blue matte glaze, unsgd, 8-1/2" h **$425**

Tile, six tile frieze, cuenca with stylized trees against blue sky, framed, 18" x 12" **$250**

Vase

Bulbous, crisply emb spade-shaped leaves, covered in mottled purple dripping over green matte glaze, incised AA/Van Briggle/Colo. Spgs./804/18/7, c1907-11, 3/4" rim bruise, 8-1/4" h, 2-3/4" d **$1,100**

Bulbous, crisply molded, spade-shaped leaves, sheer frothy light turquoise glaze, clay showing through, AA Van Briggle, 1908, 4-3/4" h, 4" d **$800**

Bulbous, cupped rim, two loop handles, emb leaves around base, covered in rare purple and green matte glaze, incised AA/Van Briggle/1903/III/232, 9" h, 6" d ... **$3,775**

Bulbous, emb panels of berries and leaves, covered in caramel, amber, and indigo matte glaze, incised AA/Van Briggle/1904/V/164, 8-1/2" h, 7" d **$6,900**

Bulbous, emb panels of stylized flowers and heart-shaped leaves in purple and green, matte blue ground, incised AA/Van Briggle/1905/?09/X, small glaze scale to one stem, 5-1/2" h, 5-1/4" d **$2,760**

Van Briggle vessel, flat shoulder, 1908-1911, yellow and light green matte glaze, marked, 4", **$350.**

Van Briggle vase, gourd shape, embossed with blossoms and leaves, matted raspberry glaze with touch of green, AA/Van Briggle/1903/III, 1903, 10" x 5-1/4", **$3,250.**

Photo courtesy of David Rago Auctions, Inc.

Van Briggle vase, bulbous, embossed trefoils under rich, feathery matte green glaze, AA/Van Briggle/Colo Springs/1906, some burst glaze bubbles from firing, 1906, 7" x 6-1/2", **$2,400.**
Photo courtesy of David Rago Auctions, Inc.

Van Briggle vessel, straight sides, embossed with tulips, covered in fine, frothy brownish-green matte glaze, red clay showing through, AA/VAN BRIG-GLE/COLORADO SPRINGS/19??/06, 4-3/4" x 5", **$1,600.**
Photo courtesy of David Rago Auctions, Inc.

Van Briggle vessel, squat, embossed butterflies, Persian Rose glaze, marked, 4", **$125.**

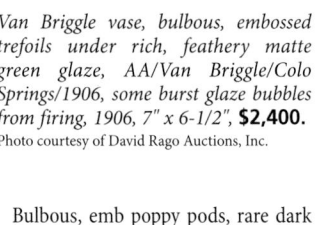

Bulbous, emb poppy pods, rare dark blue-green leathery matte glaze, incised AA/Van Briggle/1903/III/18, 9" h, 6" d **$4,890**
Emb tulips, purple to periwinkle matte glaze, AA/Van Briggle/1903/II/141, 1903, 7-3/4" h, 3" d **$2,000**
Figural, Native American Indian with pottery vase, incised "Van Briggle Col. Spgs D.R.," 8" h **$360**
Incised and molded stylized flowers, under blue/gray glaze with tur-

quoise over-spray, "dirty bottom" incised with logo, name, and date "20," c1920, 6" h **$375**
Shape no. 833, molded stylized flowers, under brown glaze with green over-spray, dirty bottom with incised logo, name and Colo Sprgs, c1920, 5-1/2" h **$230**
Squat, emb spade-shaped leaves, stylized blossoms, mustard and olive green dead matte glaze, 1904, AA/Van Briggle/1904/151, 4-3/4" h, 5-1/4" d **$1,300**

Tapering, emb peacock fathers, covered in charcoal and chartreuse matte glaze, incised AA/Van Briggle/1905/III/174, 11-1/4" h, 4" d **$5,750**
Tapering, emb tobacco leaves, covered in matte ochre and umber glaze, incised AA, die-stamped 1915 and 45, 10-1/4" h, 4-1/4" d **$1,380**
Vessel, bulbous, molded poppies, fine indigo and teal green frothy glaze, AA Van Briggle, Colo Spgs mark, 1908-11, 4-1/4" h, 5-1/2" d **$1,000**

VILLEROY & BOCH

Villeroy & Boch, stein, 1/2 litre, stoneware, dancing figures, King of Hops, #1909, pewter lid, **$100.**
Photo courtesy of Joy Luke Auctions.

History: Pierre Joseph Boch established a pottery near Luxembourg, Germany, in 1767. Jean Francis, his son, introduced the first coal-fired kiln in Europe and perfected a water-power-driven potter's wheel. Pierre's grandson, Eugene Boch, managed a pottery at Mettlach; Nicholas Villeroy also had a pottery nearby.

In 1841, the three potteries merged into the firm of Villeroy & Boch. Early production included a hard-paste earthenware comparable to English ironstone. The factory continues to use this hard-paste formula for its modern tablewares.

Beaker, quarter liter, couple at feast, multicolored, printed underglaze **$115**
Charger, gentleman on horseback, sgd "Stocke," 15-1/2" d **$600**
Dish, cov, triangular, orange and black dec, marked "Villeroy & Boch, Mettlach," and "Made in Saar-Basin," molded "3865," c1880-1900 ....**$125**

Ewer, central frieze of festive beer hall, band playing while couples dance and drink, neck and foot with formal panels between leaf molded borders, subdued tones, imp shape number, production number and date codes, c1884, 17-3/4" h **$900**
Figure, Venus, scantily clad seated figure, ribbon tied headdress, left arm raised across chest, resting on rock,

inscribed "Villeroy & Boch," damage to foot and base, 53" h............**$1,900**

Platter, white basketweave ground, blue fish and aquatic plants dec, marked "Villeroy & Boch, Delphin, Mettlach, Ceschutzt," 9-1/4" l, 8" w
....**$110**

Stein, #2942, half liter, pewter lid, brown ground, beige earthenware cartouche "Braun ist meine Maid,

Schaumt uber jeder-zeit," Jewish Star of David on reverse, marked "Villery & Boch/Mettlach, 7 02"..............**$275**

Tray, metal gallery with geometric cutouts, ceramic base with border and stylized geometric pattern, white ground, soft gray high gloss glaze, blue accents, base marked, 11-1/4" d... **$200**

Tureen, cov, Burgenland, dark pink transfer, white ground, marked

"Mettlach, Made by Villeroy & Boch," 11" w................................**$195**

Vase, bulbous, cylindrical, deep cobalt blue glaze, splashes of drizzled white, three handled SP mount cast with leaves, berries, and blossoms, molded, pierced foot, vase imp "V" & "B," "S" monogram, numbered, price for pr, c1900, 15" h
....**$2,750**

WEDGWOOD

History: In 1754, Josiah Wedgwood and Thomas Whieldon of Fenton Vivian, Staffordshire, England, became partners in a pottery enterprise. Their products included marbled, agate, tortoiseshell, green glaze, and Egyptian black wares. In 1759, Wedgwood opened his own pottery at the Ivy House works, Burslem. In 1764, he moved to the Brick House (Bell Works) at Burslem. The pottery concentrated on utilitarian pieces.

Between 1766 and 1769, Wedgwood built the famous works at Etruria. Among the most-renowned products of this plant were the Empress Catherina of Russia dinner service (1774) and the Portland Vase (1790s). The firm also made caneware, unglazed earthenwares (drabwares), piecrust wares, variegated and marbled wares, black basalt (developed in 1768), Queen's or creamware, and Jasperware (perfected in 1774).

Bone china was produced under the direction of Josiah Wedgwood II between 1812 and 1822 and revived in 1878. Moonlight luster was made from 1805 to 1815. Fairyland luster began in 1920. All luster production ended in 1932.

A museum was established at the Etruria pottery in 1906. When Wedgwood moved to its modern plant at Barlaston, North Staffordshire, the museum was expanded.

Wedgwood, miscellaneous, pitcher, green glaze, mottled grapes and grape leaves, "Made in England" mark, **$65.**
Photo courtesy of Joseph P. Smalley, Jr., Auctioneer.

Agate ware

Candleholder, surface agate, applied creamware drapery swags, black basalt base, wafer Wedgwood & Bentley mark, restored chip to socle, c1775, 6-1/2" h
....**$1,495**

Vase, cov, solid agate, creamware sibyl finials, traces of gilding, black basalt base, imp wafer Wedgwood & Bentley marks, gilt rim wear, covers with rim chips, nicks to bases, pr, c1770, 9-1/2" h................................**$7,500**

Artist designed

Bowl, Norman Wilson "Unique Ware" design, moonstone ground exterior, interior with translucent green glaze shading to blue center, impressed mark, England, 1930-60, 8-1/8" d
....**$400**

Inkstand, Keith Murray design, rect form pen tray with shallow wells and central cov box supporting two inkpots, matte green ground, imp and printed marks, slight chip under cover's rim, c1936, 10-1/8" l..............**$590**

Jug, Keith Murray design, celadon slip, cream colored ground, imp and printed marks, c1940, 8" h..........**$210**

Vase, Keith Murray design
Globular, engine turned banding, imp and printed marks, c1935, 6" h
....**$650**

Straw glaze, horizontally turned body, printed mark, c1940, 7-1/4" h
....**$765**

Basalt

Bough pot, cov, scrolled handles terminating in ram's heads, pierced disc lid with removable candle nozzle, imp

Wedgwood dragon lustre vase, porcelain, magenta ground with gild dragon motif, 9" h, **$450.**
Photo courtesy of Sloans & Kenyon Auctioneers and Appraisers.

Wedgwood Basalt, tea set, Art Deco style, marked, shape no. 225, 8-3/4" h, **$300.**
Photo courtesy of David Rago Auctions, Inc.

mark, restored nozzle and one handle, mid-19th C, 7" h **$1,265**

Bowl, engine turned dec, imp mark, early 20th C, 10-1/8" d **$230**

Bust, Horace, mounted on waisted circular socle, titled on reverse, impressed Wedgwood & Bentley marks to bust and base, c1775, 14" h **$3,100**

Candlestick, Ceres, modeled holding cornucopia form candle sconce and mounted to stepped circular base, imp title and mark, restored candle nozzle, rim nicks to base, 19th C, 11-1/2" h **$1,265**

Canopic jar, cov, bands of hieroglyphs and zodiac symbols in relief on jar, cover modeled as Egyptian head, impressed marks, price for pr, restored, c1867, 10" h **$3,820**

Cream jug, Encaustic dec, green, black and white enamels, leaf and berry swags terminating at ribbon bows, below gilt trimmed band of foliage, impressed mark, early 19th C, 4-3/8" h.......................**$1,800**

Crocus pot and tray, hedgehog shape, imp marks, repaired chips, c1800, 9-3/4" l **$920**

Cup and saucer, iron red and white banded palmette borders, Encaustic dec, imp lower case mark, slight enamel flake to saucer rim, late 18th C, 5" d saucer...................**$1,265**

Figure
Adonis, standing nude male modeled with cloth over his shoulder, impressed mark, 20th C, 12-1/4" h **$2,235**

Rousseau, standing figure modeled holding bunch of flowers in one hand and walking stick in other, impressed upper-lower case mark, chip to end of flower bunch, stick possibly replaced, late 18th C, 11-1/2" h **$4,000**

Venus, standing nude woman modeled by tree trunk on circular base, impressed title and mark, 19th C, 9-1/2" h **$950**

Hanging flower vase, bottle shape, overhead loop handle, impressed mark, early 19th C, 7-3/8" h **$1,765**

Inkstand, relief of classical figures bordered in oak leaves, gilted and bronzed, impressed marks, corner footrim nick, wear to gilt at top rim, c1875, 2-1/4" h sq shaped inkpot with insert **$5,875**

Jug, central putti-relief between bands of engine turning, mask head to handle terminal, metal mounts, imp lower case mark, late 19th C, 7-1/4" h **$2,875**

Lamp, vestal and reading, cov, female figure seated on oval lamps, applied acanthus leaves and bellflowers, imp marks, slight flake to book of reading lamp, ball finial reglued, finial and pitcher missing on vestal lamp, rim chip repair, price for pr, 19th C, 8-3/8" h...**$920**

Miniature, bust, Zeus, half-bust modeled wearing crown, impressed mark, mounted to silver collar with screw thread, 19th C, 1-3/4" h **$500**

Model
Bulldog, glass eyes, by Ernest Light, imp mark, imp nick to ear, c1915, 2-3/4" h **$345**

Sphinx, female figure, lion body, stepped rect base, imp mark, chips to footrim and headdress, early 19th C, 11-1/4" h **$865**

Plaque
Oval, classical figures in relief depicting seasons, impressed marks, price for pr, mounted to velvet lined wood frames, 19th C, 4-1/4" l............**$825**

Oval, relief depicting groups of three Graces, impressed marks, price for pr, 19th C, 6-1/2" x 8-1/2".......**$900**

Self-framed, oval, relief representing Day and Night, impressed marks, mounted in gilt wood frames, price for pr, 19th C, 5" x 6-1/4".........**$765**

Self-framed, oval, relief representing Day and Night, impressed marks, mounted in velvet lined painted wood frames, price for pr, early 19th C, 5" x 6-1/2"...................**$450**

Portrait medallion, oval
Captain Cook, black basalt, relief bust above impressed title, scooped back, self-framed, impressed Wedgwood & Bentley mark, shallow back edge chips, c1779, 3-1/8" x 4" **$4,410**

Martin Heinrich Klaproth, German chemist, black basalt, applied rosso antico bust above an impressed title, impressed mark, c1815, 2-1/2" x 3-1/4"...**$650**

Oliver Cromwell, black basalt, relief bust above impressed title, scooped back, impressed mark, Wedgwood & Bentley mark, slight edge nick, c1779, 3" x 3-3/4" **$650**

Potpourri, cov, globular, upturned loop handles, enamel and gilt dec tropical bird and flowers in famille rose style, impressed mark, finial possibly re-cemented at join, inner disc lid missing, c1820, 13" h **$3,055**

Slave Medallion, oval, slave relief centering verse "Am I not a man and a brother?" imp mark and date, c1891, 1-1/8" x 1-1/4"............................**$635**

Rum kettle, body with bacchanalian boys in relief above engine turned band, shaped bale handle, Sybil finial, imp lower case mark, restored chip on cov rim and finial, late 18th C, 5-3/4" h................................**$600**

Tankard, cylindrical form, applied classical figures in relief, imp mark, restored rim chip, 19th C, 4-1/4" h **$360**

Tea cup and saucer, Iris Kenlock Ware, enamel dec floral design, imp mark, c1895 ....**$815**

Teapot, cov, oval, molded arabesque floral body, sunflower finial, imp mark, rim nick to cover, tip of spout slightly ground, early 19th C, 3-3/4" h **$290**

Carrara

Bust, Stephenson, mounted on waisted circular socle, impressed mark, title, publish date and sculptor, E.W. Wyon. F, c1858, 14-3/4" h **$900**

Figure, Venus Victrix, semi-nude figure modeled standing on freeform base, inscribed title, imp mark, shallow chip and nick to base, mid-19th C, 20-1/4" h.................................**$1,450**

Vase, cov, trophy relief between floral festoons terminating at ram's heads, foliate borders, bronzed and gilt, imp and printed marks, cover restored, c1900, 7-1/2" h.......................**$1,495**

Wedgwood, Jasper cache pot, green, 8-1/4" d, 7-1/4" h, **$200.**
Photo courtesy of The Early Auction Company, LLC.

Wedgwood, Jasper, covered cheese dish, 10" d, 8" h; powdered sugar shaker with silver plate top, **$300.**
Photo courtesy of David Rago Auctions, Inc.

Cane, Wedgwood Jasper, matte finish pale blue, white Neoclassical figures on top of tau handle, three foliate chains, white blossoms with yellow centers at each end of tau handle, thin gold ring collar, maccassar ebony shaft, 1" re-placed brass ferrule, English, c1890, 1-3/4" h x 3" l x 1/2" d handle, 37" l, **$3,500.**
Photo courtesy of Henry A. Taron.

Cream ware

Bowl

Reticulated, molded fiddleback ladle, imp "Wedgwood," stains, edge chip, 8-1/8" l **$160**

Scalloped edge, cut-out design, imp "Wedgwood," 7-1/2" d **$600**

Plate, scenic, little girl and mother buying buns from the Bun Man, back titled "Buns!, Buns!, Buns!," 1863 mark and artist sgd "Lessore," 9-1/8" d **$335**

Vase, molded grape vines and foliage, painted band of strawberries, mid-19th C, 6" h **$250**

Drabware

Club jug, molded body, hunt sub-ject, applied white fruiting grapevine border, imp mark, shallow rim chip, c1830, 7-3/8" h **$490**

Potpourri, cov, upturned loop handles, bulbous middle applied with band of blue foliage, pierced cover, acorn finial, solid insert disc lid, impressed mark, c1825, 10" h **$1,650**

Tea set, 6-1/2" h cov teapot (slight chips to spout and sibyl finial), 4-1/4" h creamer (rim chip), 5" h cov sugar, imp marks, c1830 .... **$575**

Jasper

Barber bottle, three color, solid white body, applied bacchus heads at shoulder, classical relief, green foliate and lilac ground medallions, ram's heads and berries, impressed mark, cover married, mid 19th C, 10" h **$1,775**

Biscuit jar, cov

Three color dip, applied white classi-cal figures in relief on black ground bordered with yellow ground bands, silver plated rim, handle and cover, impressed mark, needs replating, late 19th C, 5-1/4" h **$1,000**

Three color dip, applied white relief with classical figures and floral fes-toons terminating at ram's heads on green ground, bordered in lilac with foliate borders, silver plated rim, handle and cover, impressed mark, footrim nick, repaired chips to trim rings, needs replating, mid 19th C, 5-1/4" h **$600**

Bough pot, solid light blue, sq shape with arched recesses to paneled sides, applied white relief figures represent-ing four seasons within palm framed corners, impressed mark, missing lid, restored foot, late 18th C, 6-3/8" h **$1,175**

Bowl

Black dip, applied white Dancing Hours figures in relief, running laurel and berry and acanthus leaf borders, impressed mark, c1959, 10" d **$720**

Dark blue dip, applied white Dancing Hours relief, imp mark, mid-19th C, 7-1/8" d **$920**

Solid blue, basketweave body, imp mark, early 19th C, 6-5/8" d **$1,380**

Bowl, cov, crimson dip, applied white classical figures in relief within foli-ate framed panels, acanthus leaves on cover, impressed mark, c1920, 5-1/8" d **$1,880**

Brooch, octagonal, three-color, applied white classical relief on green ground, solid light blue medallion, gold mounted frame, imp mark, 19th C, 1" x 1-1/4" **$490**

Cache pot, undertray, dark blue dip, pot with applied white classical relief, band of flowers on tray, impressed

marks, price for pr, 19th C, 5" h **$1,100**

Candlesticks, pr

Black dip, applied white classical relief within bands of foliage and arabesque floral design, impressed mark, one with edge nick, early 20th C, 4-1/4" h **$715**

Yellow dip, applied black classi-cal relief and arabesque floral banded border, impressed marks, stain in drip dish, c1930, 7-3/4" h **$1,100**

Candy dish, cov

Lilac dip, applied white classical relief figures, silver plated rim, handle, and cov, imp mark, imp mark, light crazing, slight pitting to surface, c1877, 2-5/8" h **$690**

Three-color dip, dark blue ground with applied yellow zigzags and white florets, foliage, and diamond border, silver plated rim, handle, and cov, imp mark, slight foot rim chip repaired, c1881, 2-1/4" h **$550**

Goblet, dark blue dip, applied white stiff leaves, impressed mark, 19th C, 5-7/8" h **$500**

Hair receiver, crimson dip, applied white classical relief and foliage designs, imp mark, slight loss to one figure, c1920, 4-3/8" d **$1,265**

Humidor, cov, solid light blue, applied white relief with classical figures and urns framed within palm tree panels, banded arabesque floral dec, engine turned dome cover with Diana fin-ial, limited edition in Masterpiece series, numbered 59 in edition of 200, printed and impressed marks, c1985, 9-3/8" h **$720**

Inkstand, solid pale blue, sarcophagus form supporting two pots, applied white relief with central medallion of The Sacrifice to Hymen within drapery enclosure, impressed mark, missing covers, crazing throughout, old restorations to pots, backside of stand, and scrolled foliate relief, late 18th C, 6-7/8" h **$1,495**

Jam jar, cov, three-color dip, central light green ground band bordered in lilac, applied white classical figures below floral festoons and foliate border, silver plated rim, handle, and cov, imp mark, mid-19th C, 3-3/4" h **$650**

Jardinière

Black dip, applied white classical relief, impressed mark, price for pr, one with rim repair, marks partially removed, early 20th C, 7-1/8" h **$825**

Olive green dip, applied white classical Muses in relief below fruiting grapevine festoon terminating at lion masks and rings, impressed mark, c1920, 8" h **$400**

Three-color, solid white ground, applied green floral festoons and foliate borders, lilac ram's heads and trophy drops, imp mark, 19th C, 5-1/4" h **$1,035**

Jewel box, cov, dark blue dip, oval, classical subject medallion mounted to three of paneled sides, larger medallion set on hinged lid, gilt brass mountings, 19th C, 4-1/2" h **$1,100**

Jug

Crimson dip, barrel shape with applied white classical Muses in relief within foliate framed panels, trophy below spout, impressed mark, c1920, 3-7/8" h...........**$1,530**

Crimson dip, applied white classical relief below border of floral garlands, impressed mark, shallow chip to side of spout, c1920, 6-1/2" h **$940**

Three color, solid white body, applied pale lilac trophies terminating at ram's heads, green floral festoon, oak leaf bands and acanthus leaves, impressed mark, shallow footrim chips, some discoloration to white jasper, mid-19th C, 7-1/4" h **$1,650**

Mustard pot, cov, yellow dip, attached underplate, applied black fruiting grapevine relief, pot with lion masks and rings, silver plated cover, impressed mark, rim chip, stained interior, dish rim restored, c1930, 4" h **$325**

Necklace, lilac dip, 21 assorted beads, each with applied relief, 14 teardrop-shaped with classical subjects, seven oval with stars and stiff leaves, unmarked, 19th C, 21" l **$920**

Oenochoe jug, dark blue dip, applied white classical relief, scrolled handle terminating at female mask head, impressed mark, early 19th C, 11" h **$3,100**

Oil lamp, dark blue dip, applied white classical relief, Zodiac signs border, imp mark, early 19th C, 5-1/4" l **$1,265**

Perfume bottle, solid light blue, applied white relief portraits of George III on one side, reverse with Queen Charlotte, each bordered by floral festoons, unmarked, repair, chips to neck, late 18th/early 19th C, 1-7/8" d..**$490**

Plaque

Black dip, rect, applied white relief depictions of Domestic Employment from design by Lady Templetown, impressed mark, England, painted wood frame, 19th C, 3" x 8-1/4" **$765**

Black dip, rect, applied white relief of children with fruit, reading and playing musical instruments, impressed mark, mid-19th C, 4" x 9"..**$1,300**

Green dip, rect, applied white relief of children at play, impressed mark, England, gilded and ebonized wood frame, 19th C, 2-1/2" x 7-1/4" **$1,120**

Portrait plaque, green dip, Ariadne, oval, applied white relief, inscribed title and impressed mark, giltwood frame, 19th C, 8" d **$650**

Potpourri, cov, solid light blue, squat cylindrical shape, applied white stiff leaves below running laurel border, impressed mark, 19th C, 2-1/2" h **$825**

Salad bowl

Dark blue dip, applied white classical relief below floral festoons terminating in ram's heads, foliate borders, silver plated rim, imp mark, 19th C, 5-3/4" d **$375**

Three-color dip, dark blue ground with applied relief alternating as bands of yellow trellis and white scrolls, silver plated rim, imp mark, old repairs to rim and foot rim chip, c1882, 10-3/8" d......................**$460**

Salad set, 7-1/2" d bowl, dark blue dip, applied white classical relief, silver plated rim, 11" l silver plate fork and spoon servers with dark blue handles, applied foliate relief, late 19th C **$350**

Salt, open, solid light blue, applied white Dancing Hours in relief, imp marks, one with rim chip, other with relief loss to figure, price for pr, 19th C, 2-7/8" d **$750**

Slave medallion, solid white, raised verse surrounding applied black figure in relief, partial impressed mark, lacquered wood and brass frame, late 18th C, 1" x 1-1/4" **$1,765**

Spill vase, three-color dip, light blue ground, engine turned fluting below lilac ground medallions, applied white classical relief above floral festoons terminating at ram's heads, imp mark, mid-19th C, 3" h **$1,035**

Sugar bowl, cov, crimson dip, applied white classical relief, imp mark, restored chip on cover collar and two areas of relief, c1920....................**$290**

Syrup jug

Dark blue dip, applied white birds in relief below oak leaf banded border, silver plated insert cov, imp mark, early 20th C, 6-1/4" h **$550**

Three-color dip, dark blue ground with applied vertical bands of yellow trellis and white scrolls, hinged pewter lid, imp mark, restored, late 19th C, 7-3/4" h **$350**

Tea bowl and saucer, solid pale blue, applied white relief, children playing above band of engine turning on cup, 5" d saucer with acanthus and stiff leaves bordering engine turned center, imp mark, late 18th C **$980**

Tea service, dark blue dip, 4-1/2" h cov teapot, 6" d waste bowl, twelve 6-1/8" d plates, seven 5-1/2" d tea cups, seven saucers, each with applied white grass and foliate border, impressed marks, few rim chips, 19th C......................................**$1,765**

Vase, cov

Crimson dip, upturned loop handles, applied white classical relief and foliate borders, impressed mark, cover with hairlines, restored finial, c1920, 11" h **$3,525**

Dark blue dip, applied white bacchus head handles and Dancing Hours in relief, foliate framed borders, impressed marks, price for pr, one handle simply reglued, late 19th C, 6-1/2" h **$1,880**

Dark blue dip, bottle shape with applied white classical figures in relief within foliate frames, impressed marks, price for pr, early 19th C, 7-1/4" h **$1,765**

Dark blue dip, upturned loop handles, applied white classical relief, acanthus leaf borders, impressed marks, price for pr, mid-19th C, 9-1/2" h **$1,530**

Green dip, applied white relief with Dancing Hours, foliate borders, bacchus head handles, impressed marks, price for pr, one finial reglued, one handle repaired, chip to socle rim, mid-19th C, 8-1/2" h **$2,115**

Vase

Black dip, applied white relief with classical muses below fruiting festoons terminating at lion masks and rings, trophies to shoulder, fruiting grapevine and acanthus leaf borders, impressed mark, late 19th C, 15" h **$2,585**

Light blue dip, bottle shape, applied white classical relief within foliate framed panels, neck with floral festoons terminating at ram's heads, impressed marks, price for pr, c1867, 8" h **$1,000**

Solid light blue, applied white relief with columnar framed panels of floral festoons and classical medallions below band of vine and scrolled ribbon, impressed mark, slight discoloration to foot, 19th C, 6-3/4" h **$825**

Three color dip, green ground, applied lilac medallions, white portraits in relief between drapery swags, imp mark, rim and foot rim chips, 19th C, 3" h..**$435**

Yellow dip, applied blue relief with classical figures within foliate framed panels, fruiting grapevine and stiff leaf borders, impressed mark, missing disc lid, chips restored below base, 19th C, 5-1/2" h **$940**

Lusters

Bough pot, cov, Moonlight, wall pocket modeled as nautilus shell, pierced insert grid, impressed mark, cover repaired, slight chip to spine, c1815, 10" l..................................**$940**

Box, cov, Dragon, pattern Z4829, mottled blue glaze, mother-of-pearl int., printed mark, c1920, 4" x 7" **$1,850**

Bowl

Dragon, octagonal, mottled blue ground ext., mother-of-pearl int., Z4829, printed mark, slight glaze scratches, c1920, 7-1/8" d **$470**

Fairyland Lustre, octagonal, exterior with "Castle on a Road" on deep blue shaded sky, interior with "Fairy in a Cage" with daylight sky, Z5125, printed mark, slight wear to center, c1920, 9" d **$3,820**

Fairyland Lustre, octagonal, exterior with "Moorish" design on black ground, interior with "Smoke Ribbons" on daylight sky, Z5125, printed mark, c1920, 7-3/4" d **$5,875**

Fish dec, mottled blue ext., mother-of-pearl int., printed mark, c1920, 4" d **$350**

Oriental motifs, mottled green/black ext. with dragon, mother-of-pearl int., printed mark, c1920, 3-1/8" d **$400**

Chalice bowl, Fairyland Lustre, exterior with "Twyford Garlands" on flame ground, interior with "Fairy Gondola" on flame sky, Z5360, printed mark, stem restored, hairlines to base, c1920, 10-5/8" d **$6,500**

Coffeepot, cov, Moonlight, imp mark, small chips to spout and cover, c1810, 5-1/2" h......................................**$690**

Cup, three handles, Dragon, blue ext., gilt reptiles, eggshell int. with central dragon, printed mark, c1920, 2" h **$275**

Dish, Dragon, Daisy Makeig Jones marks, Z4831, c1914-31, 4-3/4" d.............**$675**

Imperial bowl

Fairyland Lustre, exterior with firbolg design on red ground, mother-of-pearl interior with Thumbelina center, Z5275, printed mark, light glaze scratches to exterior, c1920, 10-1/2" d **$2,250**

Fairyland Lustre, exterior "Poplar Trees" on night sky, interior "Feather Hat" on daylight sky, Z4968, printed mark, center gilt wear, c1920, 10" d **$5,000**

Malfrey pot, cov, Fairyland Lustre, "Candlemas" pattern, Z5157, printed mark, vase rim regilded, c1920, 8-1/4" h...................................**$3,820**

Punch bowl, Butterfly, ruby lustre exterior with butterflies and insects,

mother-of-pearl interior with butterflies, Z4827, printed mark, c1920, 11" d **$2,820**

Teapot, cov, Moonlight, drum form, imp mark, rim chips restored, nicks to spout rim, c1810, 3" h............**$575**

Vase

Dragon, pattern Z4829, mottled blue ext., mother-of-pearl int., Chinese pagoda panels, printed mark, c1920, 11" h **$1,150**

Fairyland, black, trumpet, shape 2810, Z4968, Butterfly Women, printed marks, pr, c1920, 9-3/4" h **$4,000**

Fairyland, exterior with "Firbolgs" on deep ruby ground, interior rim dec with fish from Thumbelina motifs on mother-of-pearl ground, printed mark, c1920, 8-3/4" h...........**$2,590**

Hummingbird, mottled blue exterior, orange/red mottled interior, Z5294, printed mark, c1920, 8-1/2" h **$1,175**

Paneled Daventry design, pale plum ground, Z5418, printed mark, c1920, 8-1/2" h...........................**$3,300**

Wall pocket, Moonlight, nautilus shell, restorations, pr, c1810, 10" l **$575**

Majolica

Barber bottle, cov, cobalt blue ground, molded body with festooning fruiting grapevines between Bacchus mask heads applied to shoulder bordered in laurel and berries, imp mark, cover collar restored, c1869, 11" h..**$1,840**

Biscuit jar, cov, jar with molded dec of elephants within floral framed cartouches flanked by elephant masks, silver plated rim, bale handle and cover, imp mark, cover possibly married, c1867, 5-1/2" h **$1,250**

Bowl, cauliflower, multicolored, cobalt blue, rim nick on back, 11" d......**$495**

Compote, bowl molded as nautilus shell, base molded as two dolphins with entwined tails, impressed mark, possibly married, base chips, c1866, 16" h..**$1,100**

Crocus pot, hedgehog, oval shaped pierced body, green glaze, impressed mark, missing undertray, slight foot-rim chips, c1865, 6" h.................**$400**

Fish platter, Argenta, oval, scalloped rim, molded in relief with large fish atop vegetation, impressed mark, staining, c1878, 25-1/4" l **$825**

Floor urn, cobalt blue, ladies seated at top of bulbous vase, drapes of laurel wreaths and ladies head at base, turquoise, yellow, white, brown, green, and pink, repair to one base, minor nicks and repair to feet of ladies, pr, 26" h...**$5,500**

Jug, applied central fruiting grapevine band, imp marks, one with slight relief loss, price for pr, c1868, 8-3/4" h **$1,300**

Oyster plate, brown basketweave and shell **$1,210**

Pitcher, sunflower and urn, turquoise, 7" h...**$770**

Plate
Crane, 9" d...**$690**
Mottled, reticulated, 8-3/4" d **$165**

Salt, open, modeled as scantily clad boy holding basket, freeform base, imp mark, slight hairlines to rim, glaze flakes, restored base chips, c1889, 5-1/2" h...**$350**

Sugar, Argenta, bird and fan, repair to lid, hairline in base.............................**$125**

Umbrella stand, Argenta Fan, hairlines, 24" h...**$1,760**

Vase, bottle shape, raised bands of foliage, flowers and fruiting festoons surrounding oval medallions, impressed mark, c1870, 10" h.............................**$900**

Pearlware

Candlesticks, pr, turquoise glaze, modeled as classical female holding cornucopia form base, supporting leafy sconce, imp mark, glaze wear, nicks to glaze surface, c1872 ....**$1,380**

Fruit basket, 10-5/8" on stand, oval, basketweave molded center, pierced gallery, green enamel trim, imp mark, early 19th C, some damage to strapping of basket, glaze wear on stand **$320**

Platter, well and tree, gaudy cobalt blue and rust Chrysanthemum pattern, repaired, c1800 ....**$595**

Potpourri vase, pierced cov, blue ground, white relief floral swags, band above engine-turned fluting, imp mark, body restoration, married cover, c1800 ....**$230**

Tea tray, rect, cut corners, red/pink transfer printed border, c1886, 18-1/8" l...**$200**

Vase, upturned loop handles, red ground with gilt trimmed blue transfer printed floral and bird design, impressed mark, cover missing, repaired handle, mid-19th C, 12-3/4" h...**$500**

Queen's Ware

Basket, oval, twisted overhead handles, molded basketweave body, pierced rim, enamel and gilt dec, impressed marks, price for pr, early 19th C, 9" l **$1,175**

Bidet, fitted mahogany stand with cov, imp mark, 21-1/2" l....................**$425**

Bough pot, cov, sq form, paneled sides, relief alternating with two figures representing Seasons and two urns, foliate molded sq disc lid and center insert, imp mark, old repair to hairline on disc lid, mid-19th C, 6" h **$460**

Box, cov, flat cylindrical form, gilt trim to green transfer printed foliate design, imp mark, light wear, c1882, 3-3/4" d **$500**

Dish, diamond shape, enamel painted Emile Lessore dec cherubs, artist sgd, impressed mark, c1860, 5-1/8" d **$600**

Flemish jug, molded body with majolica glazes, blue incised designs, relief portrait of Queen Victoria below spout, brown banded neck and foot, imp mark, 1877, 8-1/4" h **$375**

Orange bowl, cov, low pedestal foot, wide lobe-fluted flaring rim, high domed pieced cover with long tapering ovals framed by molded scroll lattice and floral designs, imp mark, 20th C, 9-1/2" h **$635**

Plate, molded border, enamel dec center with Cupid and Psyche, artist sgd "E. Lossore," imp mark, c1870, 8-3/4" d...**$635**

Platter, oval, polychrome bird and floral dec in Chelsea style, imp mark, 1871, 15-3/4" x 20-3/8" **$375**

Sauceboat, molded trellis and scroll pattern after 19th C salt glaze stoneware model, imp mark, 19th C, 8" l...**$460**

Soup ladle, bowl with yellow ground banding, black enamel foliate vine dec, imp mark, early 19th C, 11-1/4" l **$320**

Rosso Antico

Bowl
Applied black basalt relief, fern dec, imp mark, early 19th C, 6-3/4" d **$850**

Egyptian, applied black basalt meander band above stylized foliate molded body, imp mark, early 19th C, 7-7/8" d **$1,300**

Box, cov, flat cylindrical form, enamel painted flowers, imp mark, base rim chip, c1860, 3-1/2" d...................**$175**

Bust, Matthew Prior, mounted on raised circular base, imp mark and title, restorations, 7-1/4" h **$420**

Candlesticks, pr, polychrome floral sprays, imp mark, each sconce restored, mid-19th C, 7" h **$415**

Club jug, polychrome floral sprays, imp mark, mid-19th C, 6-1/4" h **$520**

Cream jug, hexagonal form, banded Greek key relief, imp mark, early 19th C, 2-1/4" h **$450**

Inkstand, applied black basalt leaf and berry border on stand, supported by three dolphin feet, central pot insert, imp mark, foot rim restored, early 19th C, 4" h **$550**

Jug, oval, molded lobed body, foliage, stem, and flower relief, imp mark, restored spout rim chip, early 19th C, 5-1/8" l...**$675**

Tray, oval, Egyptian, applied black basalt hieroglyphs in relief, imp mark, early 19th C, 8-1/2" l **$1,100**

Vase, cov, tripod, applied black basalt Egyptian relief with central hieroglyph band, impressed mark, repair to one leg and finial, early 19th C, 8" h **$1,880**

Stoneware

Bough pot, cov, D-shape, mottled green and white relief floral swags, acanthus, stiff leaves, England, impressed mark, chip to pot back corner and interior edge, cover as is, c1785, 4-3/4" h.............................**$775**

Crocus basket, cov, pierced and engine turned body with overhead bow handle, dark blue dip dicing, impressed mark, early 19th C, 6-1/2" h **$2,585**

Dish, leaf form, white, enamel floral sprays, imp mark, very slight rim nick, early 19th C, 9-3/8" l.........**$230**

Mortar and pestle, 7-1/2" d mortar with spout, 10-1/4" l pestle with wood handle, vitrified, impressed marks, early 19th C, wear, chip on head **$360**

Vase, goblet shape, sponged brown and blue underglaze enamels, raised black basalt base, England, wafer Wedgwood & Bentley mark, slight flake to base, missing cover, c1775, 5-7/8" h...**$600**

WELLER POTTERY

History: In 1872, Samuel A. Weller opened a small factory in Fulton-ham, near Zanesville, Ohio. There he produced utilitarian stoneware, such as milk pans and sewer tile. In 1882, he moved his facilities to Zanesville.

Then in 1890 Weller built a new plant in the Putnam section of Zanesville along the tracks of the Cincinnati and Muskingum Railway. Additions followed in 1892 and 1894.

In 1894, Weller entered into an agreement with William A. Long to purchase the Lonhuda Faience Company, which had developed an art pottery line under the guidance of Laura A. Fry, formerly of Rookwood. Long left in 1895, but Weller continued to produce Lonhuda under the new name "Louwelsa." Replacing Long as art director was Charles Babcock Upjohn. He, along with Jacques Sicard, Frederick Hurten Rhead, and Gazo Fudji, developed Weller's art pottery lines.

At the end of World War I, many prestige lines were discontinued and Weller concentrated on commercial wares. Rudolph Lorber joined the staff and designed lines such as Roma, Forest, and Knifewood. In 1920, Weller purchased the plant of the Zanesville Art Pottery and claimed to produce more pottery than anyone else in the country.

Art pottery enjoyed a revival when the Hudson Line was introduced in the early 1920s. The 1930s saw Coppertone and Graystone Garden ware added. However, the Depression forced the closing of the Putnam plant and one on Marietta Street in Zanesville. After World War II, inexpensive Japanese imports took over Weller's market. In 1947, Essex Wire Company of Detroit bought the controlling stock, but early in 1948, operations ceased.

Additional Listings: See *Warman's Americana & Collectibles* for more examples.

*Weller basket, Ardsley, unmarked, 12-1/4", **$750.***
Photo courtesy of David Rago Auctions, Inc.

*Weller bowl and flower frog, Coppertone, figural frog perched on lily pad, stamped mark, small nick on frog's head, 15-1/2" x 10", **$450.***
Photo courtesy of David Rago Auctions, Inc.

*Weller bowl, Muskota turtle, built-in flower frog, unmarked, 9" l, 4" h, **$850.***
Photo courtesy of David Rago Auctions, Inc.

Bowl

Ardsley, flaring, stamped mark **$265**

Coppertone, perched frogs and lily-pads, stamped mark **$550**

Glendale, flaring, birds and waves crashing over rocks dec, stamped mark, few minor firing separations **$350**

Cabinet jug, Louwelsa, small yellow blossoms, silver overlay, imp mark, 3-3/4" x 2-3/4" **$1,000**

Candlestick

Round rim, sq pyramid form, reticulated arches near base, raised flowers and berries on vine, matted brown glaze, pink, blue, and highlights, one imp "Weller" on base, price for pr, late 1920s, 9-3/8" h **$150**

Glendale, owl dec, 13-1/2" h **$520**

Console set, pr candlesticks, green, Tutone, stamped marks, 7" d, 3-1/2" h three-sided bowl **$250**

Ewer, Jap Birdimal, squeezebag trees and geisha dec by Rheadin, incised mark **$3,000**

Figure, turtle, Coppertown, unmarked, 2-1/2" x 6" **$450**

Frog tray, oval, raised edge, frog and water lily on one side, lily pads on other, blotchy semi-gloss green glaze, "Weller Pottery" ink stamp, 15-1/2" l **$635**

Hanging basket

Forest, unmarked, 7-3/4" x 3-1/2" **$300**

Parian, conical, unmarked, 9-1/4" x 5-3/4" **$125**

Garden ornament, swan, ivory glaze, minor flakes, 20" x 18" **$6,500**

Jardinière

Aurelian, brown glaze, painted fruit, sgd "Frank Ferrell" **$1,100**

Sicard, sunflowers, emerald green and gold on deep purple ground **$2,900**

Lamp base

Forest, unmarked, 2" chip next to hole at base, 5" d, 11-1/4" h **$460**

*Weller Jardinière, Burntwood, carved roosters, impressed mark, 2" line from rim, 9-1/2" d, 8-1/2" h, **$225.***
Photo courtesy of David Rago Auctions, Inc.

Weller vase, L'Art Nouveau, embossed orange poppies, impressed "WELLER," 14" h, **$475.**
Photo courtesy of David Rago Auctions, Inc.

Weller umbrella stand, Flemish, decorated with maidens, chains of pink blossoms and ivy, stamped mark, few minor abrasions, 20", **$1,190.**
Photo courtesy of David Rago Auctions, Inc.

Weller vase, Hudson, blue and yellow irises painted on both sides by Pillsbury, stamped mark, artist's signature, 1" blue glaze run next to iris on one side, 7" d, 15-1/2" h, **$1,700.**
Photo courtesy of David Rago Auctions, Inc.

Weller ewer, Jap Birdimal, finely decorated by Rhead in squeezebag, trees and geisha, incised "Weller Faience Rhead G580," 10-3/4" x 7", pinhead size fleck to spout, **$3,000.**
Photo courtesy of David Rago Auctions, Inc.

Louwelsa, by Hattie Mitchell, gourd shape, painted yellow cherry blossoms, stamped "Weller Louwelsa," sgd "H. Mitchell" on body, 10" d, 13-1/4" h **$460**

Mug, Dickensware, dolphin handle and band, sgraffito ducks **$250**

Pitcher
Marvo, pink, unmarked, 8" h, 8" d **$250**
Zona, kingfisher and cattails, imp mark, glaze nick at base, 9" h, 8-1/2" d **$250**

Planter
Rosemont, unmarked, several lines, 7-1/2" x 9-1/2" **$350**
Woodcraft, applied squirrel climbing up tree, 2" tight line **$375**

Vase
Aurelia, singing monk playing the mandolin in earthtone glazes, mkd "Aurelian" on base, numbered, decorator's signature for R. G. Turner on side, crazing, c1904, 19" h **$1,530**
Aurelia, tapering, berries and leaves, imp mark, 9-1/2" h, 4" d **$300**
Baldin, blue, imp mark, glaze nick at rim, 9" h, 9" d **$475**

Burntwood, bulbous, band of flowers, unmarked, 4-1/4" h, 3-3/4" d **$100**
Eocean, short rim on cylindrical form, thistle plants in pink, maroon, and cream, green stems on brown to green to cream-colored ground, incised "Eocean Rose Weller," numbered "547," letter "Y" on base, artist's initials on side for Eugene Roberts, crazing and areas of glaze roughness, c1907, 21" h **$1,880**
Fru Russet, emb flowers, pale blue-gray and green glaze, imp mark, 14" h, 5-3/4" **$2,600**
Greora, flaring, etched mark, 11-1/2" h, 7" d **$450**
Hudson, bulbous, painted band of white blossoms and leaves, Timberlake, stamped mark, artist's signature, 6-3/4" h, 6-1/2" h **$500**
Hudson, bulbous, painted pink tulips, imp mark, 10-1/2" h, 4-3/4" d **$425**
Hudson, trumpet shape, painted berries and leaves, imp mark, 11" h, 4" d **$400**
L'Art Nouveau, pillow, one side with maiden in profile, other with shell, stamped mark partially obscured, 9-1/2" h, 8-1/2" w **$450**

Weller vase, Sicard, pillow shape, curved handles, decorated with nasturtiums, iridescent blue, green, purple, and gold ground, script mark on body, small area of over-firing under base, 9-1/4" h, 6-1/2" w, **$1,200.**
Photo courtesy of David Rago Auctions, Inc.

Zona pitcher, kingfisher and cattails decoration, impressed mark, 8-1/2" x 9", **$275.**
Photo courtesy of David Rago Auctions, Inc.

Weller vase, Coppertone, double vase in the form of two fish, stamped mark, very minor flecks on top of one inside fin, 8-1/2" h, **$2,100.**
Photo courtesy of David Rago Auctions, Inc.

L'Art Nouveau, shell shape, painted maiden and flowers, imp mark, 1" line, two minor glaze flakes, 10" h, 8" d **$450**

Louwelsa, bulbous, orange and yellow carnations, imp mark, few short shallow scratches, 12" h, 3-1/4" h **$100**

Louwelsa, ovoid, gooseberries and leaves, imp mark, fleck to rim, few shallow scratches, 10-1/2" h, 5-1/2" d **$100**

Louwelsa, vasiform body, yellow rose stems on brown ground, decorator's signature on side for

Hattie Mitchell, imp maker's mark on base, numbered "466" and "1," minor glaze loss, c1900, 20-3/4" h **$1,880**

Rosemont, bulbous, flaring rim, imp mark, 10" h, 4-1/2" d **$450**

Silverton, bulbous, pink chrysanthemums, ink stamp mark, 9" h, 5-1/2" h **$395**

Silverton, cylindrical, pink and white flowers, ink stamp mark, 8" h, 3-1/2" d **$300**

Silverton, flaring, calla lilies dec, ink stamp mark, 11-3/4" h, 5" d **$375**

Silverton, gourd shape, twisted handles, yellow flowers, ink stamp mark, 6-1/2" h, 6" d **$275**

Silverton, two angular handles, pink and white flowers, Silverton and Weller paper labels, 10" h, 5-1/2" d **$300**

Warwick, unmarked, 10" h, 4-1/2" d **$200**

Wall pocket

Glendale, imp mark, restoration, 12" h **$250**

Suevo, conical, unmarked, minor wear to glaze, 12-1/4" h **$250**

WHITE-PATTERNED IRONSTONE

History: White-patterned ironstone is a heavy earthenware, first patented under the name "Patent Ironstone China" in 1813 by Charles Mason, Staffordshire, England. Other English potters soon began copying this opaque, feldspathic, white china.

All-white ironstone dishes first became available in the American market in the early 1840s. The first patterns had simple Gothic lines similar to the shapes used in transfer wares. Pattern shapes, such as New York, Union, and Atlantic, were designed to appeal to the American housewife. Motifs, such as wheat, corn, oats, and poppies, were embossed on the pieces as the American prairie influenced design. Eventually, more than 200 shapes and patterns, with variations on finials and handles, were made.

White-patterned ironstone is identified by shape names and pattern names. Many potters only identified the shape in their catalogs. Pattern names usually refer to the decorative motif.

White-patterned ironstone tureen, covered, underplate, small, original ladle, **$125.**

Butter dish, cov, Athens, Podmore Walker, c1857 .... **$95**

Cake plate, Brocade, Mason, handled, 9" d **$180**

Chamber pot, cov, emb Fleur-De-Lis & Daisy on handle, 1883-1913, marked "Johnson Bros." **$165**

Coffeepot, cov
Laurel Wreath **$275**

Wheat and Blackberry, Clementson Bros **$220**

Compote, ftd, Taylor & Davis, 10" d, 6" h **$220**

Creamer
Fig, Davenport **$95**
Wheat in the Meadow, Powell & Bishop, 1870 .... **$85**

Creamer and sugar, Scroll pattern,

E. Walley, repaired finial, luster dec **$170**

Cup and saucer
Acorn and Tiny Oak, Parkhurst ... **$35**
Grape and Medallion, Challinor ... **$40**
Wheat, Brockhurst, handleless, luster dec **$25**

Ewer, Scalloped Decagon, Wedgwood **$150**

Gravy boat
  Bordered Fuchsia, Anthony Shaw.. **$75**
  Wheat & Blackberry, Meakin **$65**
Milk pitcher, Leaf, marked "Royal Ironstone China, Alfred Meakin, England," 9" h **$245**
Nappy, Prairie Flowers, Livesley & Powell **$20**
Pitcher
  Berlin Swirl, Mayer & Elliot........ **$120**
  Japan, Mason, c1915 .... **$275**
  Syndenhaum, T. & R. Boote **$195**
  Thomas Furnival, 9" w, 9-1/2" h ..**$220**
Plate
  Ceres, Elsmore & Forster, 8-1/2" d. **$15**
  Corn, Davenport, 10-1/2" d **$20**
  Fluted Pearl, Wedgwood, 9-1/2" d**$15**
  Laurel Wreath, set of 13, 10"...... **$325**
  Prairie, Clemenston, Hanley, 6-5/8" d
  .... **$15**
  Scroll pattern, E. Walley, 8" d **$55**

Wheat and Clover, Turner & Tomkinson **$24**
Platter
  Columbia, 20" x 15".................... **$125**
  Laurel Wreath, three graduated sizes
  .... **$325**
  Wheat, Meakin, 20-3/4" x 15-3/4" ... **$95**
Punch bowl
  Berry Cluster, J. Furnival **$175**
  Rosettes, handles, Thomas Furnival & Sons, c1851-90, 9-1/2", 6" h..... **$315**
Relish
  Laurel Wreath, diamond shape **$25**
  Wheat, W. E. corn........................ **$30**
Sauce tureen, cov
  Columbia, underplate, Joseph Goodwin, 1855 .... **$315**
  Prize Bloom, T.J. & J. Mayer, Dale Hall Pottery **$320**
  Wheat & Blackberry, Clementson Bros. **$275**

Soap dish, Bordered Hyacinth, cov, insert, W. Baker & Co., 1860s .. **$150**
Sugar bowl, cov
  Hyacinth, Wedgwood................. **$145**
  Fuchsia, Meakin.......................... **$140**
  Livesley Powell & Co., registry mark, 8" h **$295**
Teapot, cov, T & R Boote, Burslem, registry mark for Nov. 26, 1879, 9-1/2" h **$240**
Toothbrush holder
  Bell Flower, Burgess **$50**
  Cable and Ring, Cockson & Seddon
  .... **$40**
Tureen, cov, underplate, Grape, matching ladle, chips **$135**
Vegetable, cov
  Blackberry.................................... **$95**
  Lily of the Valley, pear finial....... **$110**
Vegetable, open, Laurel Wreath, pr..**$200**
Waste bowl, Laurel Wreath.......... **$45**

WILLOW PATTERN CHINA

History: Josiah Spode developed the first "traditional" willow pattern in 1810. The components, all motifs taken from Chinese export china, are a willow tree, "apple" tree, two pagodas, fence, two birds, and three figures crossing a bridge. The legend, in its many versions, is an English invention based on this scenic design.

By 1830, there were more than 200 makers of willow pattern china in England. The pattern has remained in continuous production. Some of the English firms that still produce it are Burleigh, Johnson Bros. (Wedgwood Group), Royal Doulton (continuing production of the Booths' pattern), and Wedgwood.

By the end of the 19th century, production of this pattern spread to France, Germany, Holland, Ireland, Sweden, and the United States. Buffalo Pottery made the first willow pattern in the United States beginning in 1902. Many other companies followed, developing willow variants using rubber-stamp simplified patterns, as well as overglaze decals. The largest American manufacturers of the traditional willow pattern were Royal China and Homer Laughlin, usually preferred because it is dated. Shenango pieces are the most desirable among restaurant-quality wares.

Japan began producing large quantities of willow pattern china in the early 20th century. Noritake began about 1902. Most Japanese pieces are porous earthenware with a dark blue pattern using the traditional willow design, usually with no inner border. Noritake did put the pattern on china bodies. Unusual forms include salt and pepper shakers, one-quarter pound butter dishes, and canisters. The most desirable Japanese willow is the fine quality NKT Co. ironstone with a copy of the old Booths pattern. Recent Japanese willow is a paler shade of blue on a porcelain body.

The most common dinnerware color is blue. However, pieces can also be found in black (with clear glaze or mustard-colored glaze by Royal Doulton), brown, green, mulberry, pink (red), and polychrome.

Marks: Early pieces of Noritake have a Nippon "Royal Sometuke" mark. "Occupied Japan" may add a small percentage to the value of common tablewares. Pieces marked "Maruta" or "Moriyama" are especially valued.

Note: Although colors other than blue are hard to find, there is less demand; thus, pieces may not necessarily be higher priced.

Willow Pattern grill plate, divided sections, marked "Made in Japan," **$24.**

Reproduction Alert. The Scio Pottery, Scio, Ohio, currently manufactures a willow pattern set sold in variety stores. The pieces have no marks or backstamps, and the transfer is of poor quality. The plates are flatter in shape than those of other manufacturers.

Berry bowl, small
  Blue, Homer Laughlin Co. **$6.50**

Pink, marked "Japan".................... **$5**
Bowl, Mason, 9" d **$45**
Cake plate, Newport Pottery Ltd., England, SP base, c1920 .... **$300**
Charger, 13" d............................. **$55**
Coffeepot, cov, 10" h, 3" h warmer stand....................................... **$165**
Creamer, round handle, Royal China Co.. **$12**
Cup and saucer
  Booths **$30**

Buffalo Pottery $25
Homer Laughlin $10
Japanese, decal inside cup, pink... $25
Shenango $15
Dinner plate
Allerton, 10" d.............................. $25
Buffalo Pottery, 9" d $20
Johnson Bros., 10" d $15
Egg, transfer printed pattern on ceramic body, early 20th C
Gray ground, 4-1/2" l $95

Light blue ground, 5-1/2" l $85
White ground, 5" l $90
Platter, marked "Copeland, Made in England," c1940, 19" x 14-1/2" ... $195
Sugar, cov, Allerton $65
Tea cup and saucer, scalloped, Allerton $45
Tea set, 5" h hexagonal teapot, creamer, cov sugar, tray, seven cups, six saucers, 20-3/4" d round tray with scalloped rim, gilt foo dog lid finials,

gilt handles and rims, pattern registered January, 1879, printed at rim with quotation from Robert Burns' "Auld Lang Syne," Spode, retailed by Tiffany & Co., price for 17-pc set, late 19th C $950
Toby jug, overall crazing, 6" d $930
Wash bowl and pitcher, Adderlys Ltd., Staffordshire, age crack in pitcher, c1906, 7-1/2" h pitcher, 12" d bowl... $375

YELLOWWARE

History: Yellowware is a heavy earthenware which varies in color from a rich pumpkin to lighter shades, which are more tan than yellow. The weight and strength varies from piece to piece. Although plates, nappies, and custard cups are found, kitchen bowls and other cooking utensils are most prevalent.

The first American yellowware was produced at Bennington, Vermont. English yellowware has additional ingredients that make its body much harder. Derbyshire and Sharp's were foremost among the English manufacturers.

Bank, house shape, molded detail highlighted in black, roof marked "For My Dear Girl," firing crack at chimney, 3-5/8" h $660
Bean pot, cov, three white slip accent bands, bands repeated on orig matching lid, relief lines on both, Watt pottery logo on base, orig lid has been broken and reglued, bowl has some staining from use, 6-1/2" h $165
Bottle, slip dec attributed to Rudolph Christ, NC Moravian, early 19th C $9,900
Bowl, minor age crazing to glaze, 8-1/2" d, 4" h $35
Butter tub, twist handles, lead and manganese glaze, sgd "John Bell" $6,050
Candleholders, pr, Rockingham glaze, attributed to Bennington, replaced glass chimneys, c1850, 2-1/2" h.................................... $615
Canning jar, relief draped design, some crazing to glaze, rim surface chips, 6-1/2" h.............................. $125
Coffeepot, Rockingham glaze, relief of woman snorting snuff on one side, man smoking pipe on other side, matching lid, c1850, 8-1/2" h $50
Creamer, brown stripes, white band, blue seaweed dec, shallow flake on inside edge of table ring, 4-3/4" h... $440

Figure, recumbent lion, 8" l
Incised "Buck" on front............ $4,000
Plain front, chip $2,600
Flask, book shape, Rockingham glaze, two unglazed spots on one side, c1850, 7-3/4" h.. $275
Food mold
Miniature, Yellow Rock, Phila mark, 3-3/4" d, 1-1/4" h $185
Turk's head, 7-1/2" d, 2-3/4" h $145
Foot warmer, Rockingham glaze, relief scroll design at shoulder, c1850, 9" h... $440
Lamp base, prominent rings, running brown and yellow/green glaze, partial lamp parts, 8-1/2" h.................... $115
Measure, Spearpoint & Trellis, 5-3/4" h, 6-1/2" d $300
Miniature, chamber pot, cream and blue spongeware glaze, c1900, 1-1/2" h $90

Yellowware coffeepot, covered, top pot with pierced holes in base, covered, **$315.**

Yellowware pitcher, white mid band, applied strap handle, **$225.**
Photo courtesy of Joseph P. Smalley, Jr., Auctioneer.

Yellowware mixing bowl, folded rim, green and white stripes, some wear from use, 10" d, **$85.**

Yellowware bowl, rolled rim, three brown stripes, 9" d, **$95.**

ZANE POTTERY

History: In 1921, Adam Reed and Harry McClelland bought the Peters and Reed Pottery in Zanesville, Ohio. The firm continued production of garden wares and introduced several new art lines: Sheen, Powder Blue, Crystalline, and Drip. The factory was sold in 1941 to Lawton Gonder.

Bowl
   Blue, marked "Zanesware," 6-1/2" d
   .... **$35**
   Brown and blue, 5" d **$45**
Figure, cat, black, green eyes, 10-1/8" h
   .... **$500**

Jardinière, green matte glaze, matching pedestal, artist sgd "Frank Ferreu," 34" h **$375**
Vase
   Flowing medium green over dark forest green ground, 7" h **$85**

Green, cobalt blue drip glaze, 5" h
   .... **$30**
Ivory glaze, emb flowers and leaves, 8" h **$75**
Wall pocket, Moss Aztec, 8-1/4" l
   .... **$95**

ZANESVILLE POTTERY

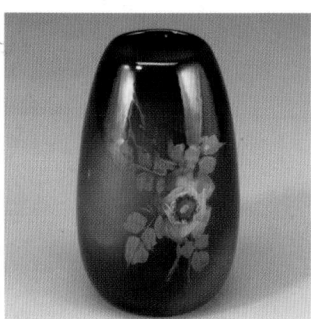

Zanesville vase, Standard Glaze, wild rose decoration, marked "SO," factory-drilled, 4" d, 8-1/4" h, $175.
Photo courtesy of David Rago Auctions, Inc.

Bowl, fluted edge, mottled blue glaze, 6-1/2" d **$65**
Coffeepot, cov, stoneware, Bodine Pottery Co., sand colored, unglazed

History: Zanesville Art Pottery, one of several potteries located in Zanesville, Ohio, began production in 1900. At first, a line of utilitarian products was made; art pottery was introduced shortly thereafter. The major line was La Moro, which was hand painted and decorated under glaze. The firm was bought by S. A. Weller in 1920 and became known as Weller Plant No. 3.

Marks: The impressed block-print mark "La Moro" appears on the high-glazed and matte-glazed decorated ware.

ext., Albany slip int., tin wire straps, handle, spout, lid, and wire bale handle, c1880, 8" h **$1,020**
Jardinière
   Ruffled rim, cream to light amber peony blossoms, shaded brown ground, 8-1/4" h **$75**
   Waisted cylindrical form, landscape scene, blue, green, and maroon matte

glaze, c1908, 7-1/8" h, 8-1/2" d **$175**
Vase
   Cone-shaped top, bulbous base, La Morro, marked "2/802/4," 8-3/4" h
   .... **$350**
   Light gray horse portrait, light olive green to blue-green ground, matte ext., glossy brown int., sgd "R. G. Turner," 10-1/4" h **$825**

ZSOLNAY POTTERY

Zsolnay jardinière, closed-in rim, vermilion enameled tulips, chartreuse whiplash leaves, purple lustered ground, raised castle medallion/644/14, 4-1/2" x 7", $3,250.
Photo courtesy of David Rago Auctions, Inc.

Bowl, sea shell shape, hp florals, gold highlights and edging, blue mark "Zsolnay Pecs," castle mark, "Patent," imp factory mark and numbers, 6-1/2" l, 2-1/2" h **$160**
Cache pot, young girls dance holding hands around stylized tree form, blue, pale silver, and pale lilac glazes, 13" d
   .... **$4,250**
Coffee set, cobalt blue and gold trim, white ground, creamer, sugar, cake plate, six cups, saucers, and dessert plates, 8-1/2" h cov coffeepot **$600**

History: Vilmos Zsolnay (1828-1900) assumed control of his brother's factory in Pécs, Hungary, in the mid-19th century. In 1899, Miklos, Vilmos's son, became manager. The firm still produces ceramic ware.

The early wares are highly ornamental, glazed, and have a cream-colored ground. Eosin glaze, a deep rich play of colors reminiscent of Tiffany's iridescent wares, received a gold medal at the 1900 Paris exhibition. Zsolnay Art Nouveau pieces show great creativity.

Marks: Originally, no trademark was used; but in 1878 the company began to use a blue mark depicting the five towers of the cathedral at Pécs. The initials "TJM" represent the names of Miklos's three children.

Notes: Zsolnay's recent series of iridescent-glazed figurines, which initially were inexpensive, now are being sought by collectors and steadily increasing in value.

Compote, ribbed, four caryatids molded as angels supports, blue-green irid glaze, 11" d **$1,100**
Creamer, fierce dragon handle, 6-1/2" l **$250**
Figure
   Bears, pair, emerald green glaze, 7-1/2" l, 5" h **$695**
   Spaniel, artist sgd, 5" h **$95**
Jardinière, ovoid, multicolored florals, protruding pierced roundels, cream ground, blue steep mark, 16" l
   .... **$450**

Pitcher, form #5064, red/maroon metallic Eosin ground, cream and pale brown flower dec, millennium factory mark, c1898, 7-1/2" h
   .... **$750**
Puzzle jug, pierced roundels, irid dec, cream ground, castle mark, imp "Zsolnay," 6-1/2" h **$195**
Vase
   Classic shape, flaring rim, nacreous chartreuse glaze, stylized suns and flowers, gold stamp mark, 11" h, 5" d
   .... **$495**

Furniture

STATE OF THE FURNITURE MARKET

by David Rago of David Rago Auctions, Inc.

The market for 20th century furniture has undergone vast changes in the last ten years. The emphasis, which had primarily been on either furniture from the Arts and Crafts Period such as Gustav Stickley, or Mid-Century masters, such as Charles Eames and George Nelson, has expanded to encompass designers from across the globe. Arts and Crafts, while part of a continuum of furniture design, had for years staked out its own collector territory. One must consider that such material consisted primarily of pieces made by only a handful of American designers, working for a brief period of time, from about 1895 until about 1915. Collector favorites had, and have, been limited to works by the aforementioned Gustav Stickley, as well as examples by his brothers Leopold and John George, as well as that of the Roycrofters, Charles Rohlfs, and the Limbert furniture company.

Pieces by these producers are still in strong demand, especially rarer and/or earlier works in mostly original condition. What makes selling high-end Mission oak so difficult is that the early fumed finishes, which were considered integral to the production process, must be nearly entirely intact. These dark finishes were induced chemically rather than applied, often resulting in deep brown to charcoal hues. Such intensity fell out of favor shortly after the demise of the Arts and Crafts period and the pieces that weren't outright destroyed were often lightened in color by sanding, dipping, or the simple application of a coat of paint. It is not an exaggeration to say that an early, important piece of Gustav Stickley furniture with its original fumed finish, worth about $50,000, would be very easy to sell. The same piece, with a light overcoat of shellac, or worse, would be hard to sell at $15,000.

Mid-range pieces in good condition remain surprisingly easy to sell, though at price levels of about five years ago. There has been no noticeable appreciation since then, but they have at least retained most of their value. The problem with selling furniture of any sort is that it uses a certain amount of space in a collector's home and, once that dining table is in place, most people are hard pressed to replace it with another. As one astute observer noted, "You can buy one Gustav Stickley bookcase, or 40 pottery vases to put in it." In spite of this conundrum, we are happy to report that people are still avidly buying non-collector level Arts and Crafts furniture, those $1000-$4000 pieces that are handsome additions to the sensitive home.

This is still more counterintuitive considering the frenzied interest in work by more contemporary designers. Interior decorators, designers, and advanced collectors from around the world have shifted their focus to designers and producers working from about 1950 to about 1990. A glance at any of the raft of shelter magazines would confirm this interest in masters as varied as France's Jean Prouve, America's George Nakashima, and Italy's Gio Ponti. Unlike Arts and Crafts furniture, the modern design market can choose from over 50 years of work by hundreds of producers from across the globe. Further, a refinished piece of Nakashima (which, I might add, can be tended to by the Nakashima Studio itself, still operating with the same high standards in New Hope, Pa.) is worth the same as one with the original finish. This variety and quantity has proved enticing to dealers, collectors, and auction houses alike.

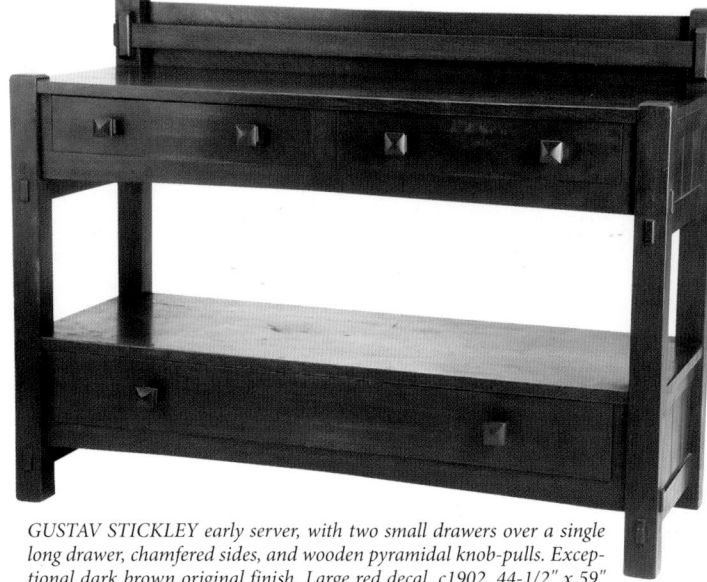

GUSTAV STICKLEY early server, with two small drawers over a single long drawer, chamfered sides, and wooden pyramidal knob-pulls. Exceptional dark brown original finish. Large red decal, c1902, 44-1/2" x 59" x 23-1/2", SOLD FOR $58,750.

GALLERY

GEORGE NAKASHIMA Conoid settee, American black walnut with curved overhanging crestrail, hickory spindles, and webbed seat support with re-upholstered fabric cushions. This unique settee demonstrates Nakashima's architectual background, co-mingling strong modern lines with traditional Japanese craft. The only example of a Conoid settee ever built. We believe this is one of the finest pieces of Nakashima ever to come to the market. (From the original owner, accompanied by copy of original order sheet.) Unmarked, 1963-1964 33-1/2" x 81-3/4" x 31", SOLD FOR **$72,000.**
Photo courtesy of David Rago Auctions, Inc.

PAUL EVANS Sculpture-Front room divider of steel with geometeric elements, covered in treated paint in reds, greens and purples with gold-leaf accents, signed Paul Evans 67/D, 1967, 72-3/4" x 96" x 4", SOLD FOR **$90,000.**

VLADIMIR KAGAN Fine Floating Seat and Back sofa upholstered in royal blue velvet on sculptural walnut legs. Unmarked. 31" x 80" x 48", SOLD FOR **$22,800.**

CHARLES ROHLFS exceptional drop-front desk on pivoting base, with two interior drawers, bookstand, side cabinet with shelves and four drawers on opposite side, elaborately carved with flame finials to top, 1900. Excellent condition, original finish, original green varnish to drawer interiors, two spots reglued, minor chips. Carved R 1900 and tag "This Piece is Guaranteed to be Made by Charles Rohlfs and is Number 847," 55" x 25-3/4" x 20", SOLD FOR **$193,875.**

MARIE ZIMMERMANN carved wooden box on round ivory ball feet with cast bronze handles, hinges and hasp fashioned in Egyptian motifs, studded with cabochon jewels of amethyst and semi-precious quartz. The hand-carved wood surface is painted in green, blue, red and yellow with black outlining and natural brown wood edges. The box is lined in purple silk with small medallion designs in Eastern taste. Some small and unobtrusive areas of paint loss, minute edge chip to back. Unmarked. Provenance: craftsman's family, 10-1/4" x 12-1/2" x 8-5/8", SOLD FOR **$117,500.**
Photo courtesy of David Rago Auctions, Inc.

GUSTAV STICKLEY rare and exceptional four-sided lantern with an overhanging hammered copper top on panels of hammered amber leaded glass, depicting stylized flowers in reds and greens. Original patina, some looseness to corners. Complete with original chain and square ceiling cap. Circular Craftsman stamp. Lantern: 13" x 10-1/4" x 10-1/4", with chain: 37-1/2" h, SOLD FOR **$364,250.**

RESOURCES

Furniture Field Guide, Krause Publications, Iola, WI.

Antique Trunks Identification & Price Guide by Linda Edelstein and Paul Pat Morse, Krause Publications, Iola, WI.

Warman's American Furniture, Ellen T. Schroy ed., Krause Publications, Iola, WI.

Warman's Arts & Crafts Furniture Identification & Price Guide by Mark F. Moran, Krause Publications, Iola, WI.

Antique Trader Furniture Price Guide by Kyle Husfloen, Mark F. Moran contrib. ed., published by Krause Publications, Iola, WI.

Left: TIFFANY STUDIOS exceptional turtle-back hanging chandelier with two rows of glass medallions in lustered blue-green Favrile glass over a six-socket fixture, and topped by a vented Lotus bronze cap with hook. Turtlebacks perfect, two tight lines to white mottled interior glass. Consigned by the family of the original owners. Provenance available). No visible signature, 14-1/2" x 22", new chain 46", SOLD FOR **$129,250.**
Photo courtesy of David Rago Auctions, Inc.

GEORGE NAKASHIMA exceptional coffee table with free-edge Persian walnut top, on Minguren base. (From family of the original owner. Provenance available). 14-1/4" x 67-1/2" x 24-1/4", SOLD FOR **$38,704.**

FURNITURE

History: Two major currents dominate the American furniture marketplace—furniture made in Great Britain and furniture made in the United States. American buyers continue to show a strong prejudice for objects manufactured in the United States. They will pay a premium for such pieces and accept them above technically superior and more aesthetically appealing English examples.

Until the last half of the 19th century, English examples and design books dictated formal American styles. Regional furniture, such as the Hudson River Valley (Dutch) and the Pennsylvania German styles, did develop. Less-formal furniture, often designated as "country" or vernacular style, developed throughout the 19th and early 20th centuries. These country pieces deviated from the accepted formal styles and have a charm that many collectors find irresistible.

America did contribute a number of unique decorative elements to English styles. The American Federal period is a reaction to the English Hepplewhite period. American designers created furniture that influenced, rather than reacted to, world taste in the Gothic-Revival style and Arts and Crafts, Art Deco, and Modern International movements.

Furniture styles

Furniture styles can be determined by careful study and remembering what design elements each one embraces. To help understand what defines each period, here are some of the major design elements for each period.

William and Mary, 1690-1730: The style is named for the English King William of Orange and his consort, Mary. New colonists in America brought their English furniture traditions with them and tried to translate these styles using native woods. Their furniture was practical and sturdy. Lines of this furniture style tend to be crisp, while facades might be decorated with bold grains of walnut or maple veneers, framed by inlaid bands. Moldings and turnings are exaggerated in size. Turnings are baluster-shaped and the use of C-scrolls was quite common, giving some look of movement to a piece of furniture. Feet found in this period generally are round or oval. One exception to this is known as the Spanish foot, which flares to a scroll. Woods tend to be maple, walnut, white pine, or Southern yellow pine. One type of decoration that begins in the William and Mary period and extends through to Queen Anne and Chippendale styles is known as japanning, referring to an imitation lacquering process.

Queen Anne, 1720-1760: Evolution of this design style is from Queen Anne's court, 1702 to 1714, and lasted until the Revolution. This style of furniture is much more delicate than its predecessor. It was one way for the young Colonists to show their own unique style, with each regional area initiating special design elements. Forms tend to be attenuated in New England. Chair rails were more often mortised through the back legs when made in Philadelphia. New England furniture makers preferred pad feet, while the makers in Philadelphia used triffid feet. Makers in Connecticut and New York often preferred slipper and claw and ball feet. The most popular woods were walnut, poplar, cherry, and maple. Japanned decoration tends to be in red, green and gilt, often on a blue-green field. A new furniture form of this period was the tilting tea table.

Chippendale, 1755-1790: This period is named for the famous English cabinetmaker, Thomas Chippendale, who wrote a book of furniture designs, *Gentlemen and Cabinet-Makers Director*, published in 1754, 1755, and 1762. This book gave cabinetmakers real direction and they soon eagerly copied the styles presented. Chippendale was influenced by ancient cultures, such as the Romans, and Gothic influences. Look for Gothic arches, Chinese fretwork, columns, capitals, C-scrolls, S-scrolls, ribbons, flowers, leaves, scallop shells, gadrooning, and acanthus. The most popular wood used in this period was mahogany, with walnut, maple, and cherry also present. Legs become straight

Side chair, Queen Anne, English, walnut and mahogany, shaped crest and splat, pad feet, H-stretcher, replaced seat frame, c1760, 18" h seat, 38-1/2" h back, **$425.**

Photo courtesy of Alderfer Auction Co.

Sideboard, Federal (Hepplewhite), Pennsylvania, cherry, bowfront top over frieze drawer flanked by two short drawers above two cupboard doors flanked by bottle doors, all with line inlaid edges, square tapering legs with bellflower inlay and banded cuffs, c1810, 67" w, 41" h, **$7,475.**
Photo courtesy of Pook & Pook, Inc.

Dining table, Sheraton, Pennsylvania, tiger maple and cherry, two parts, top with rounded corners, conforming skirt supported by turned and reeded legs, c1815, 76" l, 40-1/2" w, 29" h, **$5,300.**
Photo courtesy of Pook & Pook, Inc.

and regional differences still exist in design elements, such as feet. Claw and ball feet become even larger and more decorative. Pennsylvania cabinetmakers used Marlborough feet, while other regions favored ogee bracket feet. The center of furniture manufacturing gradually shifts from New England and Mid-Atlantic city centers to Charleston. One of the most popular forms of this period was a card table that sported five legs instead of the four of Queen Anne designs.

Federal (Hepplewhite), 1790-1815: This period reflects the growing patriotism felt in the young American states. Their desire to develop their own distinctive furniture style was apparent. Stylistically it also reflects the architectural style known as Federal, where balance and symmetry were extremely important. Woods used during this period were first and foremost mahogany and mahogany veneer, but other native woods, such as maple, birch, or satinwood, were used. Reflecting the architectural ornamentation of the period, inlays were popular, as was carving, and even painted highlights. The motifs used for inlay included bellflowers, urns, festoons, acanthus leaves, and pilasters to name but a few. Inlaid bands and lines were also popular and often used in combination with other inlay. Legs of this period tend to be straight or tapered to the foot. The foot might be a simple extension of the leg or bulbous, or spade shaped. Two new furniture forms were created in this period. They are the sideboard and the worktable, reflecting forms that came into favor as they served a very functional use. Expect to find a little more comfort in chairs and sofas, but not very thick cushions or seats.

When a piece of furniture is made in England, or styled after an English example, it may be known as Hepplewhite. The time frame is the same. Robert Adam is credited with creating the style known as Hepplewhite during the 1760s and leading the form. Another English book heavily influenced the designers of the day. This one was by Alice Hepplewhite, and titled *The Cabinet Maker and Upholsterer's Guide,* with publisher dates of 1788, 1789, and 1794.

Sheraton, 1790-1810: The style known as Sheraton closely resembles Federal. The lines are somewhat straighter and the designs plainer than Federal. Sheraton pieces are more closely associated with rural cabinetmakers. Woods would include mahogany, mahogany veneer, maple, and pine, as well as other native woods. This period was heavily influenced by the work of Thomas Sheraton and his series of books, *The Cabinet Maker and Upholster's Drawing Book,* from 1791-1794, and his *The Cabinet Directory,* 1803, and *The Cabinet-Maker, Upholsterer, and General Artist's Encyclopedia* of 1804.

Empire (Classical), 1805-1830: By the beginning of the 19th Century, a new design style was emerging. Known as Empire, it had an emphasis on the classical world of Greece, Egypt, and other ancient European influences. The American craftsmen began to incorporate more flowing patriotic motifs, such as eagles with spread wings. The basic wood used in the Empire period was mahogany. However, during this period, dark woods were so favored that often mahogany was painted black. Inlays were popular when made of ebony or maple veneer. The dark woods offset gilt highlights, as were the brass ormolu mountings often found in this period. The legs of this period are substantial and more flowing than those found in the Federal or Sheraton periods. Feet can be highly ornamental as when they are carved to look like lion feet, or plain when they extend to the floor with a swept leg. Regional differences in this style are very apparent, with New York City being the center of the design style as it was also the center of fashion at the time.

New furniture forms of this period include a bed known as a sleigh bed, with the headboard and footboard forming a graceful arch, similar to that found on a sleigh, hence the name. Several new forms of tables also came into being, especially the sofa table. Because the architectural style of the Empire period used big open rooms, the sofa was now allowed to be in the center of the room, with a table behind it. Former architectural periods found most furniture placed against the outside perimeter of the walls and brought forward to be used.

Victorian, 1830-1890: The Victorian period as it relates to furniture styles can be divided into several distinct styles. However, not every piece of furniture can be dated or definitely identified, so the generic term "Victorian" will apply to those pieces. Queen Victoria's reign affected the design styles of furniture, clothing, and all sorts of items used in daily living. Her love of ornate styles is well known. When thinking of the general term, Victorian, it is best to think of a cluttered environment, full of heavy furniture, and surrounded by plants, heavy fabrics, and lots of china and glassware.

French Restauration, 1830-1850: This is the first sub-category of the Victoria era. This style is best simplified as the plainest of the Victorian styles. Lines tend to be sweeping, undulating curves. It is named for the style that was popular in France as the Bourbons tried to restore their claim to the French throne, from 1814 to 1848. The Empire (Classical) period influence is felt, but French Restauration lacks some of the ornamentation and fussiness of that period. Design motifs continue to reflect an interest in the classics of Greece and Egypt. Chair backs are styled with curved and concave crest rails, making them a little more comfortable than earlier straight back chairs. The use of bolster pillows and more upholstery is starting to emerge. The style was only popular in clusters, but did entice makers from larger metropolitan areas, such as Boston, and New Orleans, to embrace the style.

The Gothic Revival period, 1840-1860: This is one relatively easy to identify for collectors. It is one of the few styles that celebrates elements found in the corresponding architectural style: turrets, pointed arches, and quatrefoils—things found in 12th and 16th centuries that were adapted to this interesting mid-century furniture style. The furniture shelving form known as an étagère is born in this period, allowing Victorians to have more room to display their treasured collections. Furniture that had mechanical parts also was embraced by the Victorians of this era. The woods preferred by makers of this period were walnut and oak, with some use of mahogany and rosewood. The scale used ranged from large and grand to small and petite. Carved details gave dimension and interest.

Rococo Revival, 1845-1870: This design style features the use of scrolls, either in a "C" shape or the more fluid "S" shape. Carved decoration in the form of scallop shells, leaves, and flowers, particularly roses, and acanthus further add to the ornamentation of this style of furniture. Legs and feet of this form are cabriole or scrolling. Other than what might be needed structurally, it is often difficult to find a straight element in Rococo Revival furniture. The use of marble for tabletops was quite popular, but expect to find the corners shaped to conform to the overall scrolling form. To accomplish all this carving, walnut, rosewood, and mahogany were common choices. When lesser woods were used, they were often painted to reflect these more expensive woods. Some cast iron elements can be found on furniture from this period, especially if it was cast as scrolls. The style began in France and England, but eventually migrated to America where it evolved into two other furniture styles, Naturalistic and Renaissance Revival.

Elizabethan, 1850-1915: This sub-category of the Victorian era is probably the most feminine-influenced style. It also makes use of the new machine turned spools and spiral turnings that were fast becoming popular with furniture makers. New technology advancements allowed more machined parts to be generated. By adding flowers, either carved, or painted, the furniture pieces of this era had a softness to them that made them highly suitable. Chair backs tend to be high and narrow, having a slight back tilt. Legs vary from straight to baluster turned types to spindle turned. This period of furniture design saw more usage of needlework upholstery and decoratively painted surfaces.

Louis XVI, 1850-1914: One period of the Victorian era that flies away with straight lines is Louis XVI. However, this furniture style is not austere; it is adorned with ovals, arches, applied medallions, wreaths, garlands, urns, and other Victorian flourishes. As the period aged, more ornamentation became present on the finished furniture styles. Furniture of this time was made from

Bookcases, stacking, Victorian, glass fronts, **$425.**
Photo courtesy of Dotta Auction Co., Inc.

Console table, Victorian, Gothic Revival, carved mahogany, rectangular, Gothic apron and faceted posts joined by turned stretcher, c1850, 39" x 40" x 18-1/2", **$535.**
Photo courtesy of David Rago Auctions, Inc.

Mirror, Renaissance Revival, ebonized and parcel gilt, walnut, molded frame with incised geometric and scrolling decoration, each corner with ebony roundel, gilt framed rect mirror plate, late 19th C, 34" x 30-1/4", **$800.**
Photo courtesy of Sloans & Kenyon Auctioneers and Appraisers.

Magazine stand, Eastlake, ebonized and parcel gilt, two adjustable hinged racks, turned supports, shaped legs, folding easel support, c1880, 19" w, 45" h, **$850.**
Photo courtesy of Skinner, Inc.

Chest of drawers, Arts & Crafts, Gustav Stickley, designed by Harvey Ellis, gallery top, nine drawers, tapered trapezoidal legs, mushroom pulls, arched apron, original finish, red decal inside top right drawer, 36" w, 20" d, 50-1/2" h, **$8,100.**
Photo courtesy of David Rago Auctions, Inc.

more expensive woods, such as ebonized woods or rosewood. Walnut was popular around the 1890s. Other dark woods were featured, often to contrast the lighter ornaments. Expect to find straight legs or fluted and slightly tapered legs.

Naturalistic, 1850-1914: This furniture period takes the scrolling effects of the Rococo Revival designs and adds more flowers and fruits to the styles. More detail is spent on the leaves—so much that one can tell if they are to represent grape, rose, or oak leaves. Technology advances enhanced this design style as manufacturers developed a way of laminating woods together. This layered effect was achieved by gluing thin layers together, with the grains running at right angles on each new layer. The thick panels created were then steamed in molds to create the illusion of carving. The woods used as a basis for the heavy ornamentation were mahogany, walnut, and some rosewood. Upholstery of this period is often tufted, eliminating any large flat surface, as the tufting creates curved peaks and valleys. The name of John Henry Belter is often connected with this period, for it was when he did some of this best design work. John and Joseph W. Meeks also enjoyed success with laminated furniture. Original labels bearing these names are sometimes found on furniture pieces from this period, giving further provenance.

Renaissance Revival, 1850-1880: Furniture made in this style period reflects how cabinetmakers interpreted 16th and 17th century French designs. Their designs range from curvilinear and florid early in the period to angular and almost severe by the end of the period. Dark woods, such as mahogany and walnut, were primary with some use of rosewood and ebony. Walnut veneer panels were a real favorite in the 1870s designs. Upholstery, usually of a more generous nature, was also often incorporated into this design style. Ornamentation and high relief carving included flowers, fruits, game, classical busts, acanthus scrolls, strapwork, tassels, and masks. Architectural motifs, such as pilasters, columns, pediments, balusters, and brackets are another prominent design feature. Legs are usually cabriole or pretty substantial turned legs.

Néo-Greek, 1855-1885: This design style easily merges with both the Louis XVI and Renaissance Revival styles. It is characterized by elements reminiscent of Greek architecture, such as pilasters, flutes, column, acanthus, foliate scrolls, Greek key motifs, and anthemion high relief carving. This style originated with the French, but was embraced by American furniture manufacturers. Woods are dark and often ebonized. Ornamentation may be gilded or bronzed. Legs tend to be curved to scrolled or cloven hoof feet.

Eastlake, 1870-1890: This design style is named for Charles Locke Eastlake who wrote a very popular book in 1872 called *Hints on Household Taste*. It was originally published in London. One of his principles was the relationship between function, form, and craftsmanship. Shapes of furniture from this style tend to be more rectangular. Ornamentation was created through the use of brackets, grooves, chamfers, and geometric designs. American furniture manufacturers were enthusiastic about this style since it was so easy to adapt for mass production. Woods used were again dark, but more native woods, such as maple and pine were incorporated. Legs and chair backs are straighter, often with incised decoration.

Art Furniture, 1880-1914: This design period represents furniture designs gone mad, almost an "anything goes" school of thought. The style embraces both straight and angular with some pieces that are much more fluid, reflecting several earlier design periods. This period sees the wide usage of turned moldings and dark woods, but this time stained to imitate ebony and lacquer. The growing Oriental influence is seen in furniture from this period, including the use of bamboo, which was imported and included in the designs. Legs tend to be straight; feet tend to be small.

Arts and Crafts, 1895-1915: The Arts and Crafts period furniture represents one of the strongest periods for current collectors. Quality period Arts and Crafts furniture is available through most of the major auction houses. And, for those desiring the look, good quality modern furniture is also made in this style. The Arts and Crafts period furniture is generally rectilinear and a definite correlation is seen between form and function. The primary designers of this period were George Stickley, Leopold Stickley, J. George Stickley, George Niedeken, Elbert Hubbard, Frank Lloyd Wright, and the Englishman William Morris. Their furniture designs often overlapped into architectural and interior design including rugs, textiles, and other accessories. Woods used for Arts and Crafts furniture is primarily oak. Finishes were natural, fumed, or painted. Upholstery is leather or of a fabric design also created by the same hand. Hardware was often made in copper. Legs are straight and feet are small, if present at all, as they were often a simple extension of the leg. Some inlay of natural materials was used, such as silver, copper, and abalone shells.

Art Nouveau, 1896-1914: Just as the Art Nouveau period is known for women with long hair, flowers, and curves, so is Art Nouveau furniture. The Paris Exposition of 1900 introduced furniture styles reflecting what was happening in the rest of the design world, such as jewelry and silver. This style of furniture was not warmly embraced, as the sweeping lines were not very conducive to mass production. The few manufacturers that did interpret it for their factories found interest to be slight in America. The French held it in higher esteem. Woods used were dark, stylized lilies, poppies, and other more fluid designs were included. Legs tend to be sweeping or cabriole. Upholstery becomes slimmer.

Art Deco, 1920-1945: Furniture of the Art Deco period reflects the general feel of the period. The Paris *"l Exposition International des Arts Décorative et Industriels Modernes"* became the mantra for designs of everything in this period. Lines are crisp, with some use of controlled curves. The Chrysler Building in New York City remains the finest example of Art Deco architecture and those same straight lines and gentle curves are found in furniture. Furniture makers used expensive materials, such as veneers, lacquered woods, glass, and steel. The cocktail table first enters the furniture scene during this period. Upholstery can be vinyl or smooth fabrics. Legs are straight or slightly tapered; chair backs tend to be either low or extremely high.

International Movement, 1940-present: Furniture designed and produced during this period is distinctive as it represents the usage of some new materials, like plastic, aluminum, and molded laminates. The Bauhaus and also the Museum of Modern Art heavily influenced some designers. In 1940, the museum organized competitions for domestic furnishings. Designers Eero Saarien and Charles Eames won first prize for their designs. A new chair design combined the back, seat, and arms together as one unit. Tables were designed that incorporated the top, pedestal, and base as one. Shelf units were also designed in this manner. These styles could easily be mass-produced in plastic, plywood, or metal.

Additional Listings: Arts and Craft Movement, Art Deco, Art Nouveau, Children's Nursery Items, Orientalia, and Shaker Items.
Notes: Furniture is one of the types of antiques for which regional preferences are a factor in pricing. Victorian furniture is popular in New Orleans and unpopular in New England. Oak is in demand in the Northwest, but not as much so in the middle Atlantic states.

Prices vary considerably on furniture. Shop around. Furniture is plentiful unless you are after a truly rare example. Examine all pieces thoroughly—avoid buying on impulse. Turn items upside down; take them apart. Price is heavily influenced by the amount of repairs and restoration. Make certain you know if any such work has been done to a piece before buying it.

The prices listed here are "average" prices. They are only a guide. High and low prices are given to show market range.

Reproduction Alert. Beware of the large number of reproductions. During the 25 years following the American Centennial of 1876, there was a great revival in copying furniture styles and manufacturing techniques of earlier eras. These centennial pieces now are more than 100 years old. They confuse many dealers, as well as collectors.

Desk, Art Nouveau, made for Boys Lyman St. School, Westborough, MA, mahogany, cast iron mounts, drop front, fitted interior, open shelves, weighted pulleys working sliding panel which opens to reveal drawers and shelves, three drawers, open shelf, paw feet, 33-1/2" w, 17" d, 83-1/2" h, **$3,525.**
Photo courtesy of Skinner, Inc.

Bedside tables, Art Deco style, ebonized supports and plinth bases, pair, 14-1/2" w, 24" d, 24" h, **$750.**
Photo courtesy of Sloans & Kenyon Auctioneers and Appraisers.

Chairs, arm, International Movement, pair of Norman Cherner for Plycraft, molded plywood, walnut veneer, bentwood legs, one has Plycraft label, 24-1/4" w, 17" d, 30-3/4" h, **$1,150.**
Photo courtesy of David Rago Auctions, Inc.

Feet

Ball

Hairy Paw

Claw and Ball

Triffid

Pad

Cut-out

French

Bracket

Ogee Bracket

Marlborough

Spanish

Turned Ball

Spider

Spade

Snake

Legs

English Adam   Round Tapered   Double Tapered with Reeding   Ring-Turned   Straight Tapered   Straight   Cabriole

Split-Spindle

Ring-turned

Spider

Snake

Hardware

Bail Handle

Teardrop Pull

Oval Brass

Brass

Pressed Glass

Eagle Brass

Construction Details

Handmade Dovetail Joint

Machine-made Dovetail Joint

Machine-made Rounded Dovetail Joint

Typical Gateleg Construction

Mortise-and-Tenon Joint

ThroughMortise-and-Tenon Joint

Typical Parts of a Bed

Daybed, Pennsylvania, William and Mary, cherry, scalloped crest rail over three vasiform splats, rush seat, turned baulester legs and stretchers, c1740, 15-/14" h x 22-1/2" w x 67" l, **$2,290.**
Photo courtesy of Pook & Pook, Inc.

Beds

Art Deco, France, single curvilinear bed frame with hanging shelf compartments, price for pr, c1930, 82" l...**$1,410**

Art Nouveau, Emile Galle, French, satin wood and marquetry inlay, mirrored armoire, single size bed, bed stand, floral inlays of iris in walnut, kingwood, and tulipwood, mother-of-pearl accents, headboard sgd in marquetry "Galle," c1890 ....**$3,800**

Arts and Crafts

Limbert, #651, daybed, angled headrest with spade cut-out, orig finish, recovered cushions, branded, numbered, 74" w, 25" d, 23" h.........**$650**

Stickley Bros, attributed to, headboard with narrow vertical slats and panels, tapered feet, orig side rails, orig finish, minor scratches, stenciled "9001-1/2," 80-1/2" l, 56-1/2" w, 30" h.....................**$1,355**

Stickley, Gustav, single size, pyramidal posts, nine spindles to the head and footboard, complete with side rails, branded mark, 79-1/2" l, 43-3/4" w, 49-1/4" h **$8,575**

Baroque, Italian, simulated marble high scrolling headboard dec in patiglia with vacant cartouches and foliage, carved scrolling feet, painted, green and blue marbleized dec, losses to paint and gilt, pr, 45-3/4" w, 84" h **$3,750**

Belle Epoque, French, walnut, each pc mounted with bronze floral wreaths, hardware, and claw feet, three-door armoire, two twin beds, four drawer dresser, two dressing chairs, wall unit with chests, c1910, mounted with 20" x 12" bronze plaque of mother and child..**$4,200**

Biedermeier, figured mahogany veneer, octagonal posts, turned feet

and finials, paneled head and footboards, orig rails, some veneer damage, 38" w, 72" l, 45" h, pr............**$750**

Chippendale, tall post, curly maple, turned posts, scrolled headboard with poplar panel, orig side rails, old mellow refinishing, minor repairs to posts, 60" w, 72" l, 80" h **$3,000**

Classical

Massachusetts, carved mahogany, tall post, scrolled mahogany headboard flanked by reeded, carved, and ring-turned posts, acanthus leaf, beading, gothic arches, and foliage carving, reeded and turned feet, orig rails later fitted for angle irons and bed bolts, orig surface, central finial missing, c1825-35, 59" w, 81" d, 98" h..............................**$6,900**

Middle Atlantic States, carved mahogany veneer, low post, scrolled and paneled headboard, leaf-carved finials flanked by posts with pineapple finials, acanthus leaves above spiral carved and ring-turned posts, orig rails, bed bolts, and covers, refinished, imperfections, 1835-45, 58-1/2" w, 78" d, 56-1/2" h....**$1,100**

New England, painted, turned tall post, turned and tapering head posts flanking shaped headboard, spiral-carved foot post joined by rails fitted for roping, accompanying tester, old red paint, restored, c1820, 54" w, 79" l, 60-1/2" h **$1,400**

Country, American, rope, high post, curly maple, areas of tight curl, evidence of old red wash, turned and tapered legs, boldly turned posts taper toward the top, paneled headboard with scrolled crest, turned top finial, pierced restorations, 53-1/2" w, 70" l rails with orig bolts.........**$1,890**

Country, American, day bed, birch, old red paint, tapered supports on

head and footboards, tapered legs, raised turned feet, casters, contemporary blue and white upholstery, 74" l, 25-1/2" d, 27-1/4" h **$400**

Country, American, trundle, southwestern PA, walnut, mortised joints, turned posts, and finials, shaped corners along top edge of head, foot, and sideboards, refinished, 71-1/2" l, 44" d...**$125**

Edwardian, A. H. Davenport, painted maple, bed, two door side cabinet, two chairs, dressing table, early 20th C **$5,450**

Empire, American

Single, fitted as daybed or sofa, mahogany and mahogany figured veneer, turned and acanthus carved posts, upholstered cushion, 31-1/2" x 80" x 43-3/4" h......................**$825**

Tall post, curly maple posts, poplar scrolled headboard with old soft finish, turned detail, acorn finials, rails and headboard replaced, 57-1/4" w, 72-1/2" l rails, 89" h ..**$1,650**

Empire-style, sleigh, red painted, scrolled ends, bronze mounted foliate and mask mounts, price for pr, 20th C **$1,650**

Federal

American, cherry, tester, three-quarter, rect headboard with concave side edges, footboard lower, baluster-turned posts continuing to turned legs, rails with rope pegs, first half 19th C, 81-1/2" l, 53-1/2" w, 78-1/4" h **$500**

Massachusetts, attributed to Abner Toppan, Newburyport, canopy, cherry, vase and ring-turned, reeded, and swelled foot posts joined to chamfered tapering head posts and arched headboard by an arched canopy frame, old red stained surface, 72" l, 49" w, 83" h; accompanied by chamber stand with sq pierced top on beaded sq legs joined by cutout skirt and medial shelf with incised beaded drawer, refinished, remnants of red stain, also accompanied by orig receipt, 1810, 12" top, 31" h **$9,400**

New England, maple, arched canopy above vase and ring-turned reeded and swelled foot posts, vase and ring-turned legs joined to ring-turned tapering head posts and arched headboard, old red-stained surface, minor imperfections, c1815, 51" w, 70" l, 80" h **$5,000**

New England, tester, maple, vase and ring-turned foot posts continuing to tapering sq legs and molded spade feet joined to sq tapering head posts continuing to sq legs, arched headboard, later arched canopy, refinished, c1810, 51" w, 83-3/4" h ...**$815**

New England, mahogany, turned and carved, tall post tester, arched canopy frame on vase and ring-turned spiral carved fluted tapering foot posts, joined to the turned tapering head posts with shaped headboard, ring-turned tapering feet, c1810-15, 45-1/2" w, 72" d, 61" h **$1,775**

Salem, Massachusetts, mahogany, tall post, vase and ring-turned swelled fluted foot post with leaf carving on fluted plinths continuing to vase and ring-turned legs joined to ring-turned tapering head posts, shaped headboard, old surface, c1810, 51" w, 71" d, 650" h **$3,175**

George III, four poster, carved walnut, brass mounted, circular tapered head posts, shaped mahogany headboard, reeded and acanthus-carved foot posts, ring-turned feet, casters, 9-1/2" h...................**$10,000**

Gothic Revival, American, carved mahogany, tall headboard with three Gothic arch panels, leaf-carved crest rail, flanked by heavy round ribbed posts topped by ring-turned finials, arched and paneled footboard flanked by lower foot posts, heavy bun feet, c1850 ....**$4,750**

Hepplewhite-style, Philadelphia, mahogany, four tall posts each with reeded slender vasiform section over short vasiform turned carved with continuous swag designs, upholstered tester, c1943, 82" l, 62" w, 93" h.......**$1,550**

International Movement, George Nelson for Howard Miller, Thin Edge,

*Bed, attributed to Old Hickory, spindled and reed paneled head and foot boards, orig finish, unmarked, full size, 62" x 54" x 79", **$650**.*
Photo courtesy of David Rago Auctions, Inc.

caned headboard, 34" x 76" x 35" **$1,610**

International Movement, day bed Tugendhat-style, after design by Mies van der Rohe, rect black leather cushion with head rest, webbed wood frame, four cylindrical legs, 77" l, 38" w, 15-1/2" h............**$2,350**

Hans Wegner, Denmark, retailed by Georg Jensen Inc., New York, natural woven backrest, lifts and folds to create upholstered day bed, retail label on base, c1965 teak, 78" l, 33-3/4" d, 28-3/4" h **$2,710**

Queen Anne, Pennsylvania, low poster, turned and painted pine, head and footposts with flattened ball finials, shaped head and footboards, tapered feet, orig rope rails, orig green paint, early 19th C, 48-1/2" w, 74-3/4" h.................**$3,600**

Renaissance Revival, walnut, double, high headboard topped by rounded pediment, pointed finial **$1,700**

Rope
Country, curly maple and cherry, old mellow finish, urn shaped finials, scrolled headboard, large turned foot rail, 68-1/2" l orig rails, 51-1/2" w, 47" h **$200**

Country, pine and poplar, old dark red over orig lighter red paint, short turned finials and feet, 69" l orig rails, 51" w, 31" h headboard...**$250**

Pennsylvania, summer/winter, softwood, painted blue, removable turned posts, arched headboard, replacement canopy support, 50-1/2" w, 77" l, 80-1/2" h **$2,200**

Sheraton, canopy
Carved mahogany, headboard posts simple turned with ring and block turnings, simple headboard, heavily carved footboard posts with

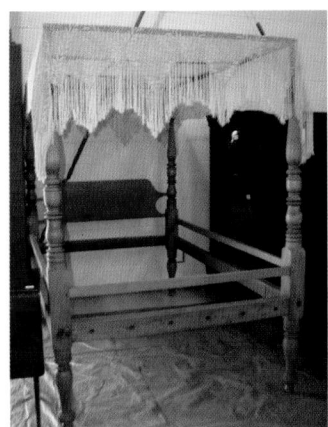

*Bed, Sheraton, tester, maple, carved fluted posts, shaped headboard, **$500**.*
Photo courtesy of Wiederseim Associates, Inc.

*Bed, Modern, Frank Lloyd Wright, paneled 41-1/2" x 62-1/4" head and foot boards, linear detailing, broad side slats, queen size, contemporary vintage, sold with pair of 21-1/2" x 19-3/4" x 19-3/4" two-drawer bedside tables, **$2,400**.*
Photo courtesy of David Rago Auctions, Inc.

spiral turnings and acanthus leaf bell, sq tester with curtains, 58" w, 73-1/2" l, 88" without finials **$3,200**

Painted, headboard with D-type cut outs on side, footboard with reeded and turned posts, canopy frame, painted red, 52" w, 76" l, 68" h **$750**

Sheraton, country, day, pine, old brown finish, ring turned and tapered legs, ball feet, pegged construction, adjustable back, large dovetails at corners, contemporary cushions, 20" d, 70-1/2" l..........................**$900**

Victorian, high headboard
Brass, c1900, four capped corner posts, fine applied brass scroll on headboard and footboard, c1900, 57" w, 78" l, 69" h............................**$1,850**

Brass, straight top rail, curved corners, ring-shaped capitals, cast iron side rails, c1900, 55" w, 61" h **$1,200**

Walnut, plain, 52" w, 50" h..........**$250**

Walnut and burlwood, ornately carved crest, 56" w, 90" h......**$1,150**

Trestle bench, Arts & Crafts, Rose Valley, carved oak, stretcher mortised through flaring plank legs, keyed through-tenons, orig finish, seam separation at top, branded, 18" x 60" x 15-1/2", **$10,000.**
Photo courtesy of David Rago Auctions, Inc.

Benches

Arts & Crafts, settle

Stickley Bros, cube, vertical slats, orig drop-in seat covered in new green leather, excellent orig finish, stenciled number, 50" l, 22-1/2" d, 33" h
....**$2,530**

Stickley, Gustav, No. 208, even arm, vertical slats all around, top rail mortised through legs, drop-in spring seat covered in new green leather, red Gustav decal, light sanding, some color added to orig finish, 76-1/2" l, 32" d, 29-1/4" h **$6,900**

Stickley, tapering posts, tightly spaced canted slats to back and sides, leather upholstered drop-in seat, fine orig finish, red decal, minor veneer chips, 36" x 80" x 32", Gustav, No. 222
....**$11,500**

Stickley, Gustav, No. 225, single board horizontal back panel, vertical side slats, recovered brown leather drop-in seat, over-coated orig finish, unmarked, 59-3/4" l, 31" d, 29-1/4" h **$7,475**

Stickley, L. & J. G., cube, border vertical panels on back and under each arm, brown leather cushion, orig condition and finish, orig upholstery, "The Work of L. and J. G. Stickley" label, 72" l, 27" w, 28" h....................**$3,450**

Stickley, L. & J. G., open arm, cloud lift top rail, horizontal backslat and corbels, new tan leather upholstered seat cushion, new finish, The Work of L & J. G. Stickley label, 53" l, 26" w, 36" h, some looseness .. **$1,650**

Young, J. M., cube, capped top rail, vertical slats all around, fabric cov drop-in spring seat, refinished, unmarked, 78" l, 29-1/2" h, 34" h
....**$2,870**

Bucket

Country, walnut, sq nail construction, shaped ends, four mortised shelves, old dry brown finish, age splits, one shelf notched out in back, 39-1/2" w, 12-1/2" d, 44" h....**$1,700**

Pennsylvania, softwood, mortised construction, shaped cut-out legs, blue-green over earlier red surface, 80" l, 18" d, 29-1/2" h **$2,750**

Pennsylvania, softwood, beaded sides and shelves, stepped lower shelf with shaped cut-out feet, dovetailed, mortised, and nailed construction, old red painted surface, two shelves, 34-1/2" w, 14" d, 47-1/2" h....**$5,225**

Classical, window

Boston, carved mahogany veneer, upholstered seat, veneered rail, leaf-carved cyma curved ends, joined by ring-turned medial stretcher, 1835-45, 48" w, 16-1/4" d, 17-1/2" h........**$2,185**

New York, mahogany veneer, curving upholstered seat flanked by scrolled ends, scrolled base, old refinish, some veneer cracking and loss, 20th C olive green velvet upholstery, 1815-25, 39-1/2" w, 14" d, 23-5/8" h
....**$3,500**

Classical Revival, mahogany, carved paw feet and lion's heads, maroon velvet cushion, old finish, 16-1/2" l, 29-1/4" w, 23" h...........................**$600**

Country

Pennsylvania, softwood, mortised leg, double skirt, shaped cut-out legs, old orange painted surface, 36" l, 13-1/2" d, 15-1/2" h **$3,520**

Pennsylvania, softwood, mortised leg, shaped cut-out legs, double molded skirt and towel bars, old blue-gray painted base, 38" l, 12" d, 20" h
....**$6,600**

Settle bench, Arts & Crafts, Gustav Stickley, No. 208, even arm, vertical back slats, fine orig finish, replaced upholstery, branded signature, 29" x 76" x 32", **$6,900.**
Photo courtesy of David Rago Auctions, Inc.

Settle bench, Arts & Crafts, Gustav Stickley, No. 173, even-arms crib type, canted sides, loose seat cushion, fine orig finish, leather and cane decking, unmarked, tear to leather, small veneer repairs to top right post, 38-3/4" x 70" x 32", **$22,500.**
Photo courtesy of David Rago Auctions, Inc.

Bench, International Movement, George Nelson for Herman Miller, two blond wood slatted benches on ebonized round edged legs, early, unmarked, some finish wear, 48-1/4" l, 18-3/4" w, 14" h, **$1,400.**
Photo courtesy of David Rago Auctions, Inc.

Bench, English, Cornwall, country, pine, high back, shaped sides, 19th C, 61" x 39" x 22", **$950.**
Photo courtesy of David Rago Auctions, Inc.

Lounge chair, Thonet, rocking, cane paneled back and seat. 40" x 26" x 38", **$175.**
Photo courtesy of David Rago Auctions, Inc.

Bentwood child's desk, one piece, **$350.**
Photo courtesy of Dotta Auction Co., Inc.

Bar stool, Thonet, black suede upholstery, ebonized frame with circular stretchers, two have Thonet factory tags, 14-1/4" d, 30-1/4" h, **$525.**
Photo courtesy of David Rago Auctions, Inc.

Pennsylvania, softwood, mortised leg, shaped cut-out legs, reinforcing slats, old red painted surface, 53" l, 11-1/2" d, 17-3/4" h..............**$1,430**

Pine, old worn and weathered green repaint, one board top with rounded front corners, beaded edge apron, cut-out feet mortised through top, age crack in one end of top, 104" l, 13-1/2" w....................................**$325**

Decorated, orig dark green with reddish brown paint, yellow line dec, mortised construction, some sq nails, arched end panels, replaced shoe feet, some later nails added, 33" w, 14" d, 23-1/4" h..**$275**

Federal

New England, window, mahogany, upholstered seat and rolled arms, sq tapering legs, H-form stretchers, refinished, minor repair to one leg, c1810, 39-1/2" l, 16" d, 29" h ...**$900**

New York, window, figured mahogany, each end with rect crotch-fig-ured crest centering removable slip seat, matching seat rail, saber legs, c1825, 40-1/2" l......................**$3,500**

George III, English, window, mahogany, rect seat, scrolling arms, later velvet cov, straight legs, blind fret craved, H-form stretcher, pr, mid-18th C, 38" l **$4,750**

Gothic Revival, American, carved mahogany, angled over-upholstered seat, carved seat rails centering quatrefoil, facet lancet-carved legs, molded faceted feet, c1820-40, 65" l, 20" d, 15-1/2" h.................................**$1,750**

Kneeling, Pennsylvania, walnut, mortised, turned splayed legs, oval cut top, 36" l, 10" d, 9" h....................**$250**

Louis XVI-style, window, carved cherry, overstuffed seat, channeled rails, flanked by molded, overscroll arms carved with be-ribboned foliate sprays, turned, tapered, and leaf-capped legs....................................**$200**

Meeting hall, pine and butternut, old sun bleached finish, tapered pencil post legs mortised through single board seat, narrow crest rail and supports, from Amana Colonies, 93" w, 19" d, 35" h........................**$600**

Piano, Arts & Crafts, Gustav Stickley, cut-out handles on plank sides, plank top, broad up-ended cross-stretcher, orig finish, red decal, 36" l, 12-3/4" w, 22" h..**$4,600**

Victorian-style, chaise lounge, Chesterfield, tufted brown leather, adjustable backrest, casters, early 20th C, 62" l..**$3,000**

Wagon seat, New England, painted, two pairs of arched slats joining three turned stiles, double rush seat flanked by turned arms ending in turned hand-holds, tapering legs, old brown paint over earlier gray, late 18th C, 15" h seat, 30" h........................**$1,200**

Wicker, painted white, hooped crest rail flanked by rows of dec curlicues, spiral wrapped posts and 6 spindles, pressed-in oval seat, dec curlicue apron, wrapped cabriole legs, X-form stretcher, 35" w, 31" h................**$500**

Windsor, settle, 20th C green paint, yellow in turnings, 29 spindles with bamboo turnings across back with turned arms, well-shaped seat with incised rain gutter around back, eight splayed legs joined by cross stretchers, splits in seat, old iron braces added underneath for support, 77-1/2" w, 22" d, 36-3/4" h **$2,100**

Bentwood

In 1856, Michael Thonet of Vienna perfected the process of bending wood using steam. Shortly afterward, Bentwood furniture became popular. Other manufacturers of Bentwood furniture were Jacob and Joseph Kohn, Philip Strobel and Son, Sheboygan Chair Co., and Tidoute Chair Co. Bentwood furniture is still being produced today by the Thonet firm and others.

Box

Circular, blue and white open and closed tulips dec on dry salmon ground, c1780, 5" d **$10,000**

Oval, laced seams on lid and base, old dark green paint on ext., dark red on int., dark red "AKHD Anno 1804" on lid, wear, splits, 12" l, 6" h **$300**

Continuous scene of man, woman, two dogs, tulips, rose trees, bulging crack, no lid, 13" d **$16,000**

Oval, dark green paint, laced seams, replaced lacing, glued edge splits, 17-3/4" w, 9-3/4" d, 7-3/8" h....**$150**

Oval, laced seams, orig blue paint, black and red foliage around borders, initials "F.G.S.B. 1836," sq nails around base, edge damage, age splits, 22" l, 13" d, 8-1/4" h.......**$700**

Chair, Austrian, Vienna Secession-style, side, back splat with three circular perforations, three slender spindles, painted black, set of eight, c1910 ....**$5,500**

Cradle, ivory fittings, 41" l, 39" h .. **$440**

Hall tree, Thonet, bentwood frame, contrasting striped wood inlay, coat hooks with central beveled mirror above one door, metal drip pan, orig label, c1910, 57" w, 13" d, 76" h **$2,750**

Plant stand, Thonet, Austria, round top with black printed classical urn and flower motif, bentwood tripod base, imp "Thonet," paper label, wear, couple of breaks on feet, late 19th C, 18-5/8" d, 30-5/8" h **$210**

Rocker, Thonet, arched twined top rail, cut-velvet fabric fitted back, armrests, and seat, elaborate scrolling frame, curved runners, 53" l.................**$750**

Stool, Thonet, attributed to Marcel Kammerer, Austria, beech, sq seat, four legs, U-shaped braces forming spandrels, shaped bronze sabot feet, 1901, 14-1/4" sq, 18-1/2" h **$1,500**

Table, Josef Hoffman, c1905, circular top, wooden spheres dec below rim, 21-1/4" h....................................**$500**

Blanket chest, Lehigh Valley, Pennsylvania, painted poplar, dower chest, lift lid over case, cartouche inscribed "Elisabeth Schonlisi 1786" above three panels with potted flowers, sides with similar panels over mid molding above two short drawers, straight bracket feet, dated 1786, 47" w, 27-1/2" h, $4,000.
Photo courtesy of Pook & Pook, Inc.

Blanket chest, English, oak, chip carved paneled lid and front, early iron hardware, losses, early hinge replacements, 50-1/2" w, 19" d, 21" h, $600.
Photo courtesy of Alderfer Auction Co.

Dower chest, Northampton County Pennsylvania, inscribed "Magthalena Knaussin," trailing ivnes and tulips, two arched panels with floral trees, two green drawers, straight bracket feet, 28" h x 48" w x 23" d, c1800, $23,000.
Photo courtesy of Pook & Pook, Inc.

Blanket chest, Pennsylvania, possibly Montgomery County, painted, poplar, blue-green stippled painted finish, red details, three drawers, original Sandwich glass knobs, original feet, cast iron hinges, painted panel on front "Johannes Hoffert 1837," old hinge replacement, missing glue blocks, lid of glove box, and crab lock, 51" l, 22" d, 28" h, $12,650.
Photo courtesy of Alderfer Auction Co.

Blanket chests

Chippendale

Country, attributed to southwest PA, cherry, chestnut secondary wood, dovetailed case, cov interior till, dovetailed drawers, molded base, shaped bracket feet with scalloped returns, wrought iron strap hinges, old refinishing, replaced brass pulls, restorations and replacements to feet and lid, 22-3/4" d, 28-1/2" h **$1,050**

Pennsylvania, figured walnut, molded rect hinged top opens to interior with lidded till, dovetailed case inlaid with "17 MM 85" with panel bordered by geometric banding, horizontal applied molding below, two thumb molded half drawers, bracket feet, two orig escutcheons, old surface, minor imperfections, 1785, 47" w, 22" d, 47" h **$14,100**

Decorated

American, poplar, orig black over red sponge dec, one board top, molded trim, arched cut-outs on end aprons, scalloped front apron, int. fitted with covered till, dovetailed drawer, cast iron hinges, minor touch-up, later coat of varnish, 43-1/4" w, 17" d, 21-1/4" h **$495**

New York, Schohaire County, 6 board, painted blue, molded top, dovetailed constructed base with painted diamond and draped frieze with Chinese export punchbowl and ladle, dotted, banded, vine, and diamond border flanked by enamel Stiegel flip glasses with circular borders, minor imperfections, early 19th C, 37" w, 17" d, 15" h **$6,900**

Ohio, pine and poplar, six-board construction, eagle dec, cover with considerable paint wear, restoration, c1820-40, 49-1/2" w, 21" d, 23-3/4" h **$2,300**

Ohio, attributed to Knox County, dovetailed poplar, orig sponged circles and meandering borders, two board top with molding, scalloped base painted black, beveled aprons, fitted int. with covered till, early iron casters, 39" w, 29-1/2" d **$825**

Pennsylvania, Dauphin County, made for Madlen Nafrez, three blue panels on front, center one with name and date, other two panels with six pointed stars, 1808 ....**$35,000**

Pennsylvania, softwood, front panel dec with six arched top panels, potted floral and foliate motif in style of Heinrich Otto, side panels dec with eight-point stars, molded lid and base, wrought iron strap hinges, interior till, 51" w, 23" d, 22-1/2" h **$11,000**

Pennsylvania, three tombstone shaped panels with stylized flowers, unicorns in center, reddish brown ground, loss to paint on lid, c1780 ....**$9,500**

Dowry, Mahantango Valley, Pennsylvania, "Samuel Grebiel 1799," orig paint dec, red, blue, mustard, black, and white, two shaped polygons painted in blue grain painting, identical polygons on each side, two in front with banner above with name and date, int. lidded till, black painted dovetailed bracket base, off-set strap hinges, orig lock, 48-1/2" w, 21" d, 23-1/2" h **$3,000**

Federal, Pennsylvania, pine and cherry, molded lift top, well with till, case with two thumb-molded graduated drawers, dovetailed bracket feet, old refinish, minor imperfections, early 18th C, 40" w, 20-1/2" d, 43" h **$1,880**

Grain painted, New York state, molded hinged lift top, lidded till, molded bracket black painted base, orig fanciful ochre and raw umber graining, c1830, 48" w, 22" d, 29" h **$1,265**

Jacobean, oak, paneled construction with relief carving, drawer and feet replaced, repairs to lid and molding, old dark finish, 44-1/2" w, 19-1/2" d, 31-3/4" h **$825**

Miniature, England, mahogany, molded lift-top with wire hinges, dovetail constructed box base, mid molding trim, heavy molded bracket base, worm holes, wear, early 19th C, 14-1/4" l, 6-3/4" h **$1,035**

Mule, America, pine, thumb-molded top, two overlapping dovetailed drawers, bracket feet, old dark finishing, int. lined with 1875 Boston newspaper, pierced repairs to feet and drawer fronts, 40" w, 18" d, 34-3/4" h **$700**

Painted

Massachusetts, molded hinged top, case of two drawers, tall cut-out feet with valanced skirt, orig red-brown grain paint with contrasting beige grained drawers, orig pulls, first quarter 19th C, 36-3/4" w, 17-1/4" d, 37-3/4" h **$11,750**

Blanket chest, Lane, cedar lined, pre-World War II, applied moldings, turned ball feet with scrolled returns, **$125.**

New England, hinged top, well with till, case with single drawer, cut-out base, orig mustard-brown graining resembling wood, minor imperfections, early 19th C, 39-1/4" w, 18-1/4" d, 40" h **$850**

New England, six-board, rect top, case with two drawer, cut-out feet joined by straight skirt, all-over orig reddish brown and yellow grain paint resembling exotic wood, old brass pulls, minor imperfections, minor paint wear, early 19th C, 41-1/4" w, 18-1/2" d, 32-1/4" h **$2,115**

Ohio, wide poplar boards, orig red paint, traces of silvery white star designs on lid and front, dovetailed case, molded top edge, bracket feet, small scalloped returns, molded base, int. till with lid, hinges and narrow hinge rail old replacements, minor edge wear, 49-1/4" w, 21" d, 26" h **$650**

Pennsylvania, Bucks County, red moldings and base, mottled reddish-brown ground, large triple banded hearts on front and sides, corners with half-hearts, over lozenges with names and date, two lower drawers, molded skirt with central drop, cut-out bracket feet, int. till, secret drawers, orig paint, minor losses, one side foot and back braces replaced, dated 1770, 49" l, 24" d, 29-1/2" h **$18,750**

Queen Anne, New England, marriage chest, pine, hinged lift lid, upper half faced with faux drawer fronts, brown paint, c1750, 35" **$4,000**

Sheraton, country, pine and poplar, orig red paint, molded edge top, paneled front and ends, sq corner posts, mortised and pinned frame, scalloped apron, turned feet, 44" w, 19-1/2" d, 25-1/2" h **$900**

William and Mary, New England, oak and yellow pine, joined, drawer base, old finish, minor imperfections, c1700, 48-1/2" w, 22" d, 32-3/4" h **$4,500**

Bookcases
Arts & Crafts

English, double door, corbelled overhanging top, inlaid pewter, ebony, and fruitwood tulips, leaded glass panels with green tear-shaped inserts, curvilinear backsplash, emb strap handles, orig finish, unmarked, some corbels loose, 46" w, 12-1/2" d, 52-1/2" h **$2,615**

Limbert, Grand Rapids, Michigan, oak, two elongated glass panels on each of two doors, three adjustable shelves on each side, round copper pulls, medium brown finish, branded mark on reverse, imperfections, early 20th C, 40-1/2" l, 14" d, 57-1/2" h **$2,775**

Stickley Bros, quarter-sawn oak, double door, slatted gallery top, single panes of glass, orig medium finish, brass tag, 35-1/2" w, 12" d, 50" h **$4,875**

Stickley, Gustav, quarter sawn oak, double door, eight glass panes to each door, gallery top, hammered copper V-pulls, three int. shelves, top and bottom mortised thru sides, red decal and paper Craftsman label, refinished, 42-3/4" w, 13" d, 56-1/4" h **$5,175**

Stickley, Gustav, quarter sawn oak, double door, 12 panes per door, gallery top, brass V-pulls, mortised top, paper label, refinished, warp in right door, stripped hardware, 54" w, 13" d, 55" h **$5,175**

Stickley, L. & J. G., Fayetteville, New York, oak, No. 641, gallery top with through tenons, Handcraft decal, some stains, door missing, c1912, 30" w, 55" h **$1,300**

Biedermeier-style, inlaid cherry, outset molded cornice with ebonized bead, front with two recessed glazed doors, four shelves, outset molded base raised on black feet, burr poplar panels, ebonized stringing, 53-1/2" w, 21" d, 72" h **$700**

Chippendale

English, two pcs, mahogany, oak and pine secondary woods, top with two doors with geometric mullions and old glass, four adjustable shelves, two dovetailed drawers with beaded edges, short bracket feet, molded base, old replaced oval brasses, old refinishing, restorations to cornice and feet, later backboards, 32-3/8" w, 14" d, 83-1/4" h **$2,300**

Bookcase, Arts & Crafts type, three doors, leaded glass, **$450.**

Bookcase, Arts & Crafts, L. & J. G. Stickley, No. 643, single-door, gallery top, keyed through-tenons, 16 panes, copper hardware, dry orig finish, handcraft decal inside, 55" x 39" x 12", **$3,750.**
Photo courtesy of David Rago Auctions, Inc.

Bookcase, Arts & Crafts, Lifetime, three-doors, six panes per door, gallery top and bottom mortised through sides with keyed through tenons, excellent orig finish, Paine Furn. Co. label, 44" x 59" x 12", **$5,000.**
Photo courtesy of David Rago Auctions, Inc.

Bookcases, Victorian, Globe-Wernicke, stacking, pair, one in six sections, size D-8-1/4, 82" x 34" x 11"; losses to glass on top section; other in five sections, size D-8-1/2", both marked, c1900, **$1,700.**
Photo courtesy of David Rago Auctions, Inc.

New England, southern, mahogany and maple, scroll top, top section with molded scrolled cresting, carved pinwheel terminals centering carved fan and bordered with punchwork flanked by flame urn-turned finials, two thumb-molded recessed panel doors opening to compartmented shelved int., lower section with fall front desk opening to stepped multi-drawer compartmented int. above case of four graduated scratchbeaded drawers, bracket feet, replaced brasses, refinished, imperfections, late 18th C, 39" w, 21" d, 84-3/4" h........... **$7,100**

Chippendale-style, New England, mahogany, broken arch pedestal over two arched-paneled doors, fitted secretary int. with pigeonholes, six small drawers, lower section with fall front, stepped fitted int., straight front, two small and two wide drawers, brass bail handle, escutcheons, lock plates, straight bracket feet, 42" w, 24" d, 93-3/4" h.................................... **$3,200**

Classical, Boston, carved mahogany veneer, cove molded cornice above two glazed doors flanked by columns with leaf carved tops and turned bases, foldout felt lined writing surface, sectioned for writing implements, two small cockbeaded drawers over two long drawers,

flanked by similar columns with carved tops, four reeded and carved bulbous feet, glazed doors open to bird's eye maple veneered int. with two adjustable shelves, valanced open compartments, five small drawers, brasses and wooden pulls appear to be orig, old refinish, imperfections, 1830s, 44-3/4" w, 22-1/4" d, 88" h.......................... **$11,500**

Eastlake
America, ebonized, three glazed doors flanked by turned carved columns, incised and gilt dec, three drawer base, c1785, 58" w, 14" d, 74-1/2" h **$1,850**
America, cherry, rect top, flaring bead trimmed cornice, pair of single-pan glazed cupboard doors, carved oval paterae and scrolls across top, adjustable shelved int., stepped base with line-incised drawers, bail handles, c1880, 47-1/2" w, 15-1/4" d, 69-1/4" h............... **$1,200**

Empire, crotch mahogany veneers, top section: large architectural type cornice, two large glass doors with cathedral top muttons, three adjustable shelves; base: 11 drawers, oval brass knobs, applied base molding, two panes of glass cracked, 66" w, 83" h.. **$5,500**

Empire style, French, ormolu mounted mahogany, fitted with four tall grill-inset and paneled doors, shelved interior, corners mounted with herm-form pilasters, wreath and paw feet, 19th C, 108" w, 12" d, 84-1/2" h.................................. **$5,900**

Federal
Boston or Salem, Massachusetts, carved mahogany and mahogany veneer, top section with shaped gallery joining square plinths above flat cornice molding, two hinged glazed doors with beaded Gothic arches, four adjustable shelves, projecting base of four cockbeaded short drawers, corners carved with acanthus leaves and fluting, punchwork above vase and ring-turned reeded tapering legs, old refinish, imperfections, c1815-1820, 50" w, 18-1/2" d, 87-1/2" h............... **$9,900**
Southern States, attributed to, mahogany, veneered pediment embellished with inlaid floral vines and leaves above mullioned glazed doors, int. adjustable beaded shelves, lower case as hinged butler's desk with int. of valanced compartments and small drawers outlined with string-

ing, case of three graduated string inlaid drawers, skirt with inlaid vines and leaves, French feet, old refinish, replaced brasses, restored, 1790-1810, 40-1/2" w, 21-1/2" d, 93-1/2" h **$4,700**

George III, inlaid mahogany, dentil-molded cornice above two paneled doors, shelved interior, two candle slides, slant front enclosing fitted interior, two short and three graduated drawers, bracket feet, third quarter 18th C, 37" w, 22" d, 85-1/2" h....**$4,600**

George III-style, with 18th century elements, mahogany, later swan's neck cresting above pair of paneled doors opening to shelves, fitted with candle rests, lower section with slant lid enclosing a fitted int., all above three long drawers, ogee bracket feet, 35" w, 20" d, 95" h..................... **$2,650**

George III style/Edwardian, painted satinwood, breakfront, upper section with four glazed doors; lower section fitted with five drawers on each end, projecting center section with secretaire drawer over pair of cabinet doors, polychrome dec, early 20th C, 75" w, 18" d, 88" h......**$11,750**

Georgian, early 18th C
Inlaid walnut, bureau bookcase, rect cornice, two paneled doors opening to shelves, fitted slant-lid desk, two short over two long drawers, bracket feet, inlaid all over with scrolling vines, 44" w, 22" d, 89" h...... **$10,575**
Mahogany, shaped octagonal cornice over glazed doors, above two cabinet doors, bracket feet **$2,900**

International Movement
Delineator Series, designed by Paul McCobb, manufactured by The Lane Co., retailed by Angelus Furniture Showroom, Los Angeles and San Francisco, walnut, upper cabinet fitted with open shelf over six cubby holes and two drawers, open shelf over pull-out writing surface, lower cabinet fitted with median shelves, one round pull missing, mid-20th C, 36-3/8" w, 15" d, 78" h............... **$600**
Unknown maker, teak, three fully finished modular sections in metal framework, with panel to create right angle, accompanied by magazine illus of unit, c1960, each 35-1/4" w, 17" d, 68-1/2" h....**$2,350**

Louis XV-style, block front, ormolu mounts, floral marquetry, banded inlay, top surface worn, scratches, 56" w, 16" d, 55" h..................... **$2,500**

Box, American, inlaid, hinged lid, stag's head and maple leaves, sides have birds and hearts in variety of woods, mid-19th C, 10-1/4" w x 7" deep, **$425.**

Photo courtesy of Sloans & Kenyon Auctioneers and Appraisers.

Box, lap desk, painted black exterior with polychrome floral decoration, gold trim, unfolds to writing surface, **$95.**

Photo courtesy of Dotta Auction Co., Inc.

Candlebox, Pennsylvania, painted poplar slide lid, retaining yellow and ochre grain, plume decoration, mid 19th C, 8-1/4" h x 17-1/2" l, **$4,600.**

Photo courtesy of Pook & Pook, Inc.

Box, Bucher, lid with central building in a landscape, red green and yellow tulip decoration, sides with similar decoration, 2-3/4" h x 9-1/2" w x 8-1/4" d, **$2,530.**

Photo courtesy of Pook & Pook, Inc.

Regency, late, mahogany, bookcase/breakfront, concave fronted cornice, frieze carved with anthemion, upper section fitted with four arched and glazed doors; lower section fitted with fall front writing surface and fitted int., all above two pedestals fitted with shelves and drawers, early 19th C, 84" w, 26" d, 93" h **$7,475**

Renaissance Revival, American, late 19th C

Carved mahogany, two glass doors, shelved interior, case carved with central portrait bust and scrolling foliage, two columns, gadrooned ball feet, 61" w, 18" d, 64" h **$2,115**

Walnut, rect case carved with foliage and angular flowerheads, two doors, two base drawers, 54" w, 16" d, 57" h **$1,550**

Walnut, rect top, three shaped, foliate, and corbel carved doors, shelved interior, plinth base, 73" w, 13" d, 49" h **$2,350**

Walnut, three tall glazed doors, shelved interior, projecting base with three drawers, 74" w, 20-1/2" d, 90" h **$3,850**

Revolving, American, oak, molded rect top, five compartmentalized shelves with slatted ends, quadruped base with casters, stamped "Danners Revolving Book Case...Ohio," second half 19th C, 24" w, 24" d, 68-1/4" h **$1,200**

Rococo-style, Italian, serpentine front with three shelves, cabriole legs, dec with Chinoiserie scenes, green ground, late 19th C, 38" w, 14" d, 49" h **$690**

Victorian, Globe-Wernicke, barrister type, stacking, three sections, oak, glass fronted drawers, drawer in base, metal bands, orig finish **$900**

Boxes

Artist's, Pennsylvania, fancy inlay, tiger maple, bird's eye maple, and walnut, 1850-70 .... **$950**

Ballot, walnut, eight slide lid compartments, names of election officials and writing under lid, 19th C voting forms from East Berlin, Pennsylvania, last used in 1892, 32-1/2" l, 8-1/4" w, 4-1/4" h **$2,200**

Band, oval

Bucher-type paint dec, black ground, house and trees on center of lid, red/orange, white, and green floral tulip on top and sides, yellow highlights, provenance: Eugene and Dorothy Elgin collection, Conestoga

Auction Co., April 3, 2004, 9-1/4" l, 6-1/8" w, 4-1/2" h................. **$15,950**

Unknown artist, nailed construction, painted light blue with patina turning blue to gray, pencil sgd "Elisha Whipple" under lid, 6-3/4" l, 5" w, 4" h **$2,530**

Bible, chestnut, some curl in lid, molded edges, front panel with punched design, initials and date "L. T. 1705," int. with cov till and single drawer, wrought-iron lock, old dark patina, hasp missing, some edge damage, pulls added to drawer, 27" l **$650**

Book, Pennsylvania, ftd, drawer, top painted with arabesque design, spine with geometric devices in red and gilt, black ground, red borders, mottled mustard painted edges, minor paint war, c1860, 6-3/8" w, 5-1/8" d, 2-5/8" h.......................... **$250**

Bride's, oval, bentwood, overlapping laced scenes, orig painted dec, couple in colonial dress, white, red, brown, and black on brown stained ground, edge damage, German inscription and 1796 in white, 15-7/8" l, 10" w, 6-1/2" h .. **$495**

Candle, hanging

Poplar, orig dry red paint, peaked back two-board back, base board extends beyond lower front and includes six cut-outs for spoons, reeded sides, wire nail construction, small chip on front, 12" w, 7" d, 6" h **$285**

Walnut, poplar secondary wood, dovetailed case, hinged lid, good figure on front and lid, arched backboard, one drawer in lower front with orig turned walnut pull, mellow old finish, minor glued split, 14" w, 7-14" d, 8-3/4" h **$600**

Cheese, pine, circular, incised "E. Temple" on lid, painted blue, America, cracks, paint wear, minor losses, 19th C, 6-1/2" h, 12-1/8" d.......... **$175**

Collar, wallpaper covering, oval, marked "E. Stone No. 116 1/2 William Street, New York," 13" l, 5" h....... **$575**

Cutlery, walnut, dovetailed, int. divided into two compartments, pierced handle, later tapered leg stretcher base, dark finish, 15-5/8" w, 10-1/2" d, 23" h **$300**

Decorated, dovetailed, pine, orig grain painting, rect, dovetailed, conforming hinged lid, ochre ground paint with red putty or vinegar painted seaweed-like designs, orig lock, wallpaper lined int., New England, missing top bail handle, later waxing of surface, 1820s, 14-5/8" w, 7-1/8" d, 6-3/4" h **$690**

Document

Grain painted and gilt stenciled, America, pine, rect, hinged lid, grain painted exterior simulating rosewood with gilt stenciled designs of fruit and foliage on top, gilt stenciled floral designs with green highlights on front and sides, leaf and pendant pinecone motifs on black borders with ovolo corners, minor paint losses, c1825, 18-5/8" w, 8-1/8" d, 6-3/4" h.................**$2,350**

Grain painted, pine, old brown wavy dec over mustard ground, dovetailed, orig internal lock, old padlock on outside, insect damage, 17-1/4" w, 11-3/4" d, 11-1/2" h... **$250**

Pine, gilt stenciled, New York State or New England, hinged dovetail constructed, rect, brass swing handle, top with gilt-stenciled flowers in footed bowl, sides with fruit and flowers, geometric borders, black ground, crack, minor paint wear, c1825, 14-3/4" w, 9-3/8" d, 5-1/4" h.................**$1,000**

Pine, painted, rect, hinged lid, carved and scribed compass stars and rosettes, incised checkerboard, foliate, and heart motifs, painted in shades of red, black, and mustard, wallpaper-lined interior with till, name "Peter Glawson, August 11th, 1863" inscribed on the back, small corner losses, minor paint wear, 13" w, 7-1/8" d, 5-3/4" h........**$5,590**

Federal, America, inlaid mahogany, rect dovetail construction, hinged lid, bracket feet, inlaid oval paterae on top, circular paterae on front, top and sides bordered by string inlay, kite-shaped escutcheon, early 19th C, 11" w, 7-1/2" d, 7" h **$825**

Paint decorated, America, pine, rect, hinged lid, iron latch, vinegar painted graining with dark brown over pinkish-brown base color, c1830, 15" w, 8-1/2" d, 5-5/8" h...........**$600**

Dome-top, paint decorated

America, poplar, dovetailed, orig stenciled black and bittersweet colored vining on front, worn red and black on top, yellow brown ground on ends, some areas of green remain on side, orig iron lock and hasp, age splits, 24" l, 14" d, 12-3/4" h ...**$980**

Dec by Bucher, white ground, red houses and tulips on top and all sides, borders picked out in blue, early 19th C, 9" l.................**$13,500**

Schoharie, New York, pine, painted blue, hinged top with iron latch, decorated with letters "RM" in rectangle and linear borders in black, white, red, yellow, and green, front with flowers and floral border in similar colors, wear, cracks, early 19th C, 27" w, 12-1/4" d, 11" h...........**$1,880**

Worcester County, Massachusetts, paint dec, rect. wire hinged lid, painted black, foliate, swag, and linear embellishments in shades of yellow and red, iron latch and handles, paint wear, crack, early 19th C, 20-1/4" w, 10" d, 7-3/4" h......**$2,235**

Dough, pine and poplar, rect removable top, tapering well, splayed ring-turned legs, ball feet, Pennsylvania, 19th C, 38" w, 19-3/4" w, 29-1/2" h...........**$500**

Grain painted, America, rect, carved from one piece of pine, sliding lid, incised compass, chip-carved dec on top and sides, brass escutcheon on side, old green surface, wear, age crack, early 19th C, 8-3/4" l, 5" w, 1-7/8" h.....**$2,000**

Knife

English, inlaid flame mahogany veneer over pine, bow front, scalloped corners with banded inlay, brass handles on both sides, star inlay on int. of lid, old refinish, contemporary, dovetailed int. lifts out, slotted for letters, hidden compartment below, some sections of inlay missing, age splits in veneer, 9" w, 10" d, 15-3/4" h.........................**$550**

Federal, flamed grained mahogany, serpentine and block front, reeded front columns, fitted int., orig keys, pr, 16" h, 9-3/4" w, 14-1/2" d.. **$2,500**

Mahogany veneer with inlay, edge veneer damage, int. incomplete, inlaid oval on inside of lid, 14-1/2" h **$225**

Letter box, Victorian, English, satinwood veneer, mahogany secondary wood, ebonized moldings, recesses for pens, drop front with divided letter compartments, old finish, two polished glass inkwells, 12-1/2" w, 8-1/2" d, 11-1/4" h.................**$920**

Pantry, America, pine top and bottom, oval, lapped maple sides fastened with copper tacks, painted blue, 19th C, 4-1/4" d, 1-1/2" h **$950**

Pencil box, child's, slide-lid, carved from single pc of cherry, carved heart shaped handle, compass wheel dec, 10" l, 2-1/2" h **$1,045**

Pipe box, hanging, New England, lollipop top, poplar and pine, c1800 ....**$6,250**

Knife box, Federal, American, mahogany, star and line inlay, remains of older inscription inside lid, damage to lid and body, losses to inlay, 19th C, **$350.**
Photo courtesy of David Rago Auctions, Inc.

Knife box, covered, slots for knives, losses to veneer and interior, **$125.**
Photo courtesy of Dotta Auction Co., Inc.

Presentation, walnut, simulated inlay, carved spread wing eagle on lid, presented to Gen George McClellan by Rauch Club, Milwaukee, Nov. 8, 1864 ....**$6,800**

Razor, sailor's, carved cherry, rect, heart-shaped handle, chip carved borders, incised sailing vessel on swivel top, 19th C, 10-3/4" l, 1-3/4" w, 1-1/2" h........**$325**

Salt, hanging, walnut, sq nail construction, base molding, heart shaped wall mounted, hinged lid, paint dec, tan ground, brown highlighted graining, 8-1/2" l, 8-3/4" w, 13-1/8" h **$1,320**

Sewing

America, mahogany inlaid, hinged lid, center inlaid oval reserve with shell motif, ext. with inlaid borders and corners, int. lid centered with diamond motif, lift-out tray with several compartments, minor imperfections, 19th C, 12-1/4" w, 7-1/4" d, 5-5/8" h **$1,000**

Chinese Export, lacquered, Chinoiserie dec, scenic panels surrounded by mosaic patterns, Greek key border, brass bail handles on each end, int. with mirrored lid and fitted compartments, single fitted drawer, containing various sewing implements, minor wear and crackling, 19th C, 17-1/4" w, 11-1/2" d, 5-3/4" h **$475**

Slide lid

America, decorated, pine, bittersweet and white scrolling, initials "A.H.D. 1826" on blue ground, dovetailed corners, reeded lid, mix of orig rose head and later nails in bottom, age splits in base, some rim damage, replaced int. runner, 24-1/2" l, 15-1/2" d, 8-1/2" h **$420**

America, oak, lid with unusual reeded diamond design, dovetailed corners, old dark refinishing, pieced restorations to edges, 19-1/2" w, 12-1/4" d, 10-1/2" h **$250**

America, pine and poplar, orig reddish brown surface, sq cut nails on base, small lock with key inlet in one end, 16" l, 10" d, 10" h **$175**

America, walnut, dovetailed joints, pegged base, paneled lid with gouge carved finger pull, four interior compartments, orig finish, 10-1/4" l, 4-3/4" w, 3" h **$770**

European, pine, dovetailed, comb graining around sides, floral dec and molded edge on lid, European inscription on base with "1815," pieced restorations and touch up to ends, 10-3/4" w, 7-3/8" d, 5-5/8" h **$230**

Pennsylvania, John Drissel, Bucks County, attributed to, pine, pegged construction, gouge-carved edge and finger pull, painted red ground with red, blue, white, and green PA German compass, floral and tulip designs, name on lid "Peter Nehs," German text "I came to a country where I read on the wall be God fearing and don't break what doesn't belong to you," provenance: Eugene and Dorothy Elgin collection, Conestoga Auction Co., April 3, 2004, c1790, 11" l, 6-3/4" w, 4-1/4" h **$82,500**

Spice box

America, pine and poplar, eight drawer, dovetailed, molding at top and base, brass pulls, orig red-brown finish, pencil drawing of man and horse with illegible

name on one drawer side, 13-1/4" l, 10-1/2" w, 12-1/8" h **$1,100**

Pennsylvania, attributed to Mahantongo Valley, slide lid, dovetailed, dusty blue ground, white, salmon, green and yellow tulip dec on four sides and top, c1780, 9" x 5" **$33,000**

Storage

America, pine, painted red, floral and linear dec, int. paper lined, late 19th C, 8-1/2" l, 6-1/2" w, 3-1/2" h ...**$635**

Massachusetts, ochre-painted pine, six board, dovetailed, thumb molded lid dec with flags, shield, and banner inscribed "Mass. Militia 2nd Regt. 1st B. 2nd D," partial paper tag tacked to lid inscribed "...K Rogers Boston," minor imperfections, early 19th C, 18-7/8" l, 8-3/4" h **$1,150**

Sugar box

Amish, pyramid shaped lid, brass knob, black and salmon painted sides, five-point yellow and black star on front, 7" sq...............**$11,500**

Country, fruitwood, single base drawer with holes drilled in interior, wrought iron cane cutter mounted at middle, brass pull on lid, old mellow refinishing, 14" w, 9-3/4" d, 9" h **$250**

Tea bin, dec of gentleman toasting lady, dec by Ralph Cahoon, oil on wood, with certificate of authenticity from Cahoon Museum of American Art, 24-1/8" h, 17-1/2" w, 25" d **$2,530**

Utensil box, poplar, dovetailed, sq nail construction, scrolled sides and handle dividers, worn salmon painted finish, 11-1/2" l, 9" w, 5" h **$1,100**

Vegetable shredding, hanging, orig dry red paint, chestnut and pine, c1850 ....**$3,500**

Wall

America, pine, one drawer, dovetailed, sq nail construction drawer with four-part divider, brass pull, wood hinges, old leather repair, 10-3/4" l, 10" d, 17-3/4" h **$1,045**

America, poplar, early round head nail construction, paint dec, eight drawers, green ground, sponged and fanned graining, yellow and black highlights, green trim around drawers, red base, porcelain drawer pulls, 8-1/8" l, 4" w, 14" h....**$19,800**

Pennsylvania, attributed to Henry Lapp, Lancaster County, PA, sq and early round head nail construction, eight drawers, red ground with comb graining, yellow drawers, por-

celain pulls, one drawer repaired, 8-1/2" l, 3-3/4" d, 14-1/2" h ..**$9,075**

Wallpaper covered, paper and wood construction

Eight-sides, blue, orange, and yellow foliage, 22-3/4" l, 18-1/2" w, 16-1/2" h **$4,675**

Oval, blue ground wallpaper with orange highlights, geometric ad floral dec, int. lined with German and English text newspaper, paper label mkd "Laura May, Jack's Box, Dec 29, 1890," 8" l, 5-1/4" w, 3-3/4" h...**$910**

Oval, eagle, yellow ground, green and pink highlights, int. lined with German text newspaper, 5-1/2" l, 3-3/4" h, 3" h............................**$580**

Oval, green ground, yellow and red highlights, lid lined with Lancaster German text newspaper, mkd "Dr. C. Weaver," 6-1/4" l, 4-1/2" w, 3-1/2" h **$1,540**

Oval, light green ground, maroon, green, and black highlights, bird and floral dec, int. lined with English text PA newspaper, 8-1/4" l, 5-1/8" w, 4-1/8" h.....................**$420**

Rectangular, pink ground, red and white floral dec, int. lined with German text newspaper, 4-1/4" l, 3" w, 1-1/2" h **$715**

Round, pink ground, red and white floral highlights, int. lined with German and English text newspaper, 3" d, 1-7/8" h **$1,650**

Slide lid, pine, nailed construction, red base, green, white, and black wallpaper, minor usage wear, 7" l, 4-1/4" w, 3-1/4" h.....................**$880**

Work, European, marquetry inlaid mahogany veneer, pine secondary wood, slant top lid with pincushion covered in old burgundy velvet, paper lined int., till with lid, engraved strap hinges, old finish, repairs, 12" w, 10-1/2" d, 7-1/4" h **$275**

Writing, English, 20th C

Mahogany, dovetailed case and two drawers, red velvet liners, compartment with lift lid on top, ivory pulls on top drawer, replaced wooden pulls on lower drawer **$230**

Mahogany, old ebonized finish, dovetailed drawer in base with divided interior, open compartment behind roll top, two small int. drawers within top with ivory pulls, sgd under drawer "Sawlish, Sunday, 27th of February, 1820, J. H. Jacob," and religious verse, 14-1/2" w, 10-1/2" d, 6-1/2" h **$200**

Cabinet, display, designed to hold canes, curved oak and glass, round, **$4,200.**

Cellarette, Arts & Crafts, Lifetime, single drawer over cabinet door, stenciled "47.262," remnants of paper label, good orig finish, 29" x 20" x 16", **$1,400.**
Photo courtesy of David Rago Auctions, Inc.

China cabinet, Arts & Crafts, Limbert, No. 1473, three small panes on one large door, side shelves supported by long corbels, branded on back, metal store tag, orig finish, minor scratches on top, 57" x 44" x 15-1/2", **$5,000.**
Photo courtesy of David Rago Auctions, Inc.

Cabinets

Apothecary, pine, yellow grain dec, 29 drawers over two open shelves, cut-out base and sides, bracket feet, open back, 62" l, 12" d, 54" h ...**$1,550**

Bar, Art Deco, walnut, sarcophagus form, two doors, sq top with drop-front cabinet on left, mirrored bar, small drawer on right between two open bays, 48" w, 21" d, 54-1/2" d **$600**

Cellaret, George III, mahogany, serpentine, top enclosing a green baize interior, brass handles at sides, square-section tapering legs, 18" w, 18" d, 25" h **$1,675**

China

Art Moderne, mahogany, double doors, floral-carved relief panels, int. shelves, two drawers below, 45" w, 17" d, 62" h **$2,000**

Arts & Crafts, Limbert, #428, trapezoidal form, two doors, each with four windows at top over one large window, orig copper pulls, sides with two windows over one, refinished, branded, 40" w, 19" d, 63" h **$4,250**

Edwardian-style, curved glass sides, single flat glazed door, illuminated int., mirrored back, 42" w, 16" d, 64" h, pr **$1,675**

International Movement, Gilbert Rhode, manufactured by Herman Miller, glass-sided china cabinet top

Cabinet-on-chest, William and Mary, inlaid burl walnut, two parts, rect molded crown, top has two glazed panel doors, lower body has seven drawers, shaped apron, bun feet , early 18th C, 70-3/4" x 43-1/2" x 20", **$4,500.**
Photo courtesy of Sloans & Kenyon Auctioneers and Appraisers.

over two doors with burled fronts, brushed steel pulls, refinished, glass doors and shelves missing, 36" w, 17" d, 58" h................................**$800**

Victorian, American, c1900, oak, ornate, crest with carved wind god, leaves, and scrolls, curved glass door and side panels, four glass shelves, mirrored back, column supports, claw feet, 51" w, 19" d, 77" h **$2,650**

Chinoiserie, two drawers, double doors, two adjustable int. shelves, walnut veneer with inlay and black lacquer, gilded detail, attached base with turned legs, 20th C, 43" w, 15-1/2" d, 63" h **$625**

Corner

George III style, inlaid mahogany, molded swan's neck cresting, pair of mullioned glass doors, shelved interior, two lower paneled doors, bracket feet, inlaid with fans, 20th C, 45" w, 22" d, 91" h............**$1,410**

Georgian, early, japanned, two part, molded cornice and outset corners above two pairs of doors flanked by solid pilasters, shaped plinth base, decorated overall with Chinoiserie scenes on black ground, 18th C, 35" w, 19" d, 90" h..................**$7,650**

Renaissance Revival, American, walnut, hanging, spindle-inset cornice, two glazed doors and reeded pilasters...**$400**

Cabinet, William and Mary style, walnut veneer, double arched top section over three drawers, scrolled carved cabriole legs, doors missing, interior painted, **$675.**

China cabinet, Arts & Crafts, Lifetime, two doors, three interior shelves, top interior shelf backed by mirror, orig finish, loss of height, 50" x 55" x 15-3/4", **$800.**
Photo courtesy of David Rago Auctions, Inc.

Cabinet, linen press, George III, mahogany veneer, inlaid classical urns, tall bracket feet, damage to front panels, 78" x 49" x 24", **$2,800.**
Photo courtesy of David Rago Auctions, Inc.

Cabinets, Eastlake-style, America, étagère with single cabinet door, gallery shelves, and mirrored back, losses to trim and brackets, 67" x 37" x 13"; music cabinet with gallery top and single lower shelf; 19th C, **$550.**
Photo courtesy of David Rago Auctions, Inc.

Curio, French

Bombé-shaped base, ornate, old gold repaint, carved rococo dec and gesso, beveled glass front, glass side panels, high scrolled feet, scalloped base aprons, 35" w, 15" d, 71-1/2" h **$950**

Serpentine front, flowers around case, courting scene on lower case and door, metallic gold ground, ormolu dec around edges and arched crest, two removable glass shelves, worn red velvet covering bottom shelf, mirrored back, 33-1/2" w, 17" d, 74" h **$850**

Display

Biedermeier-style, poplar and burr-poplar, single door, outset molded cornice, three-pane glazed door flanked by similar stiles and sides, three mirror-backed shelves supporting shaped half shelves, block feet, 41" w, 16" d, 68" h **$800**

Edwardian, rosewood, dentil molded cornice, two glazed doors and projecting lower section fitted with three drawers, sq tapered legs joined by shelf stretcher, late 19th C, 25" w, 15" d, 56" h **$2,415**

Empire-style, gilt metal mounted mahogany, rect case fitted with arched glass door, stemmed bun feet, foliate cast mounts, 33" w, 16" d, 68" h **$1,975**

Queen Anne style, green japanned, pair of shaped and mullioned glass doors, shelved int., cabriole legs, Spanish feet, multicolored chinoiserie scenes, 38" w, 15-1/2" d, 80-1/2" h **$1,530**

Renaissance Revival, oak, foliate and fruit carved borders, shaped feet, glass front and sides, late 19th/early 20th C **$6,500**

Dressing

Art Deco, France, rect curvilinear top, centered mirror over four drawers flanked on each side by full-length curvilinear cabinets, shaped foot skirt, c1925, 68-1/2" w, 19-1/2" d, 66-7/8" h **$1,100**

Fall front

Renaissance Revival, American, ebonized and parcel gilt, angular cresting, fall front enclosing plain interior, trestle base, curved legs, 26" w, 45" h **$900**

Filing, Arts & Crafts

American, golden oak, plain vertical stack, five drawers, orig brass nameplates and pulls, c1910 ... **$650**

Stickley, L. & J. G., Manlius, New York, reissue, two-drawer, rect, hammered copper hardware, branded "Stickley," round yellow and red decal in int. drawer, wear to top finish, 21-3/8" w, 28" l, 31" h **$360**

Hanging

Middle Eastern, inlaid mother-of-pearl, lancet molded cornice, turned shelf supports, spindle inset door above three small open shelves, 20" w, 7-1/2" d, 20" h...............**$425**

Renaissance Revival, American, walnut, spindle-inset gallery, floral incised door and shelved interior, shaped and angular pendant, 26" w, 8" d, 26" h.................................**$765**

Ledger, American, walnut and mixed hardwoods, poplar secondary wood, dovetailed case, single paneled door, int. with divided compartments, later salmon paint, pr, 19th C, 15-1/2" w, 12" d, 24" h....................................**$600**

Sheet music, first half 20th C

Mahogany, rect top over door, opening to 21 doors of graduated sizes, 20" w, 14-1/2" d, 34" h...............**$325**

Mahogany, one door, back rail with beveled mirror, drawer, 18" w, 47" h **$225**

Side

Aesthetic Movement, American, ebonized and parcel gilt, upper section with spindle galleries and mirrored back, lower section with central door with angular foliate designs, flanked by open shelves, angular gilt foliage throughout, 43" w, 14" d, 66" h...............**$3,410**

Arts & Crafts, oak, single door, orig sq copper pull, notched toe-board, refinished, 22" w, 22" d, 38" h..**$700**

Baroque, Dutch, oak, rect case fitted with three paneled doors, borders carved in shallow relief with scrolling tulip vines, stemmed bun feet, 82" w, 20" d, 53" h................**$1,380**

Biedermeier, fruitwood parquetry, rect top, canted corners, pr of cabinet doors enclosing shelves, bracket feet, late 19th C, 55-1/4" w, 24-3/4" d, 40-1/2" h **$1,725**

Empire-style, gilt bronze mounted mahogany, rect marble top, conforming case fitted with cabinet door, pull-out shelves, plinth base, late 19th/early 20th C, 20-3/4" w, 16-1/4" d, 52-1/4" h.................**$750**

Gothic-style, oak, rect case fitted with two doors, upper door carved with gothic tracery, lower with linenfold paneling, sides with linenfold paneling, block feet, late 19th/early 20th C, 22" w, 19" d, 52" h **$450**

Louis XVI, Provincial, oak, paneled door carved with urns, late 18th/early 19th C, 41" w, 18-1/2" d, 73" h **$1,380**

Napoleon III, brass and mother-of-pearl inlaid, ormolu mounts, white

serpentine marble top, conforming case, fitted with door, bracket feet, c1850-70, 35-1/2" w, 16" d, 41" h **$2,645**

Regency, rosewood, shelf with gallery above mirrored back over single drawer above grilled door flanked by columns with maiden terms on squared plinth base, price for pr, early 19th C, 24-1/2" w, 17-1/2" d, 45-1/2" h **$14,160**

Renaissance Revival, attributed to New York, ebonized, marquetry, and parcel-gilt, central elevated cupboard flanked by two similar cupboards, c1865-75, 75" w, 15" d, 64" h **$4,900**

Spice

Counter-type, poplar, old brown sponge dec, vertical stack with four sq nailed drawers with beveled edges, turned wooden pulls, chamfered side moldings, tongue and groove boards on sides of case, one drawer front split, 8-3/8" w, 17-1/2" d, 19-5/8" h.................**$495**

Hanging, rope twist top molding over geometric border flanking eight drawers, inlaid star and heart dec, porcelain knobs, inlaid with ivory and mixed woods, minor losses, second half 20th C, 15" w, 8" d, 18" h **$475**

Vitrine

Biedermeier, part ebonized, triangular pediment and dentilled cornice above two mullioned glazed doors flanked by two columns, block feet, first half 19th C, 47" w, 21" d, 67" h **$4,600**

Biedermeier-style, peaked crest over two glazed doors flanked by ebonized columns, square block feet, price for pr, 45-1/4" w, 18-1/2" d, 73" h.....................**$5,350**

George III-style, mahogany, open swan's neck cresting, glazed doors, lower section with glass top shelf, sq legs joined by stretchers, early 20th C, 22" w, 18-1/2" d, 68" h **$1,495**

Louis XVI-style, giltwood, outset molded rect top, frieze with beribboned floral garlands, front with glazed door with inset corners, flanked by fluted stiles, opening to two shelves, glazed sides, paneled skirt with swags, turned, tapered, and fluted legs with paterae, c1850, 27-1/4" w, 16" d, 61-1/2" h **$1,200**

Candlestands

Adjustable

American, central cherry shaft, turned double adjustable candle arm, ring turned burl base, orig patination, c1780, 29" h........**$9,000**

American, maple, screw-post, traces of orig salmon paint, c1790.......**$4,500**

Chippendale

America, mahogany, round single board top, vase shaped column, cabriole legs, padded snake feet, old finish, well executed repair to one leg, reduced in size, 17-1/2" d, 28-1/4" h...........**$875**

Boston or Salem, Massachusetts, mahogany, carved oval tilt top, vase and ring-turned post, tripod cabriole leg base ending in arris pad feet on platforms, refinished, one leg repaired, late 18th C, 16-1/2" w, 22-3/4" d, 27-1/2" h...............**$1,535**

Massachusetts, mahogany, serpentine molded tilt top, vase and ring-turned post on tripod cabriole leg base, arris pad feet on platforms, old finish, very minor imperfections, late 18th C, 28" w, 27-3/4" d, 28-3/4" h **$4,200**

New England, tilt-top, walnut, circular molded top, vase and ring-turned post and tripod cabriole leg base, arris pad feet, old refinish, imperfections, minor repair, late 18th C, 17" d, 28" h **$2,500**

New Hampshire, attributed to Lt. Samuel Dunlap, old refinish, birch, painted red, imperfections, 16-1/2" w, 16-1/8" d, 26-1/2" h..**$2,950**

Pennsylvania, Chester County, Octorora, walnut, tilt top, molded edge burl top, bird cage support, ball turned pedestal, cabriole legs, well executed carved feet, 6" age crack in top, 24" d top, 29-1/2" h **$4,400**

Chippendale-style, America, inlaid mahogany, round tilt top with small raised edge, circular inlaid center fan, reeded urn shaped column, tripod base, well carved claw and ball feet, orig dark finish, early 20th C, 23-3/4" d top, 28-1/2" h.............**$225**

Country, cherry and maple, southeastern New England, circular top, vase and ring turned post and tripod base, three tapering legs, remnants of old dark green paint, imperfections, late 18th C, 12" d, 25" h.................**$1,150**

Federal

Connecticut, attributed to, cherry inlaid, rect top with string inlaid border, vase and ring-turned chip

Candlestand, Federal, New England, c1820, maple top, tiger maple spider leg base, turned pedestal, refinished, original reddish color, 21-2/3" l, 17" w, 28-3/4" h, **$450.**

Photo courtesy of Alderfer Auction Co.

Candlestand, Chippendale, attributed to England, walnut, circular molded top, vase and ring turned support, tripod cabriole leg base, arris pad feet on platforms, possible height loss, 18th C, 20-3/4" d, 22-1/2" h, **$450.**

Photo courtesy of Skinner, Inc.

Candlestand, George II, c1750, mahogany, circular tilt top, birdcage support, baluster standard, cabriole legs, pad feet, 26-1/2" d, 27-1/2" h, **$800.**

Photo courtesy of Pook & Pook, Inc.

carved post, tripod base of arris cabriole legs, imperfections, c1790, 15" l, 13-3/4" w, 26-3/4" h **$1,120**

Connecticut River Valley, cherry, shaped top with serpentine sides and ovolo corners, vase and ring-turned post, tripod cabriole leg base, arris pad feet, refinished, minor restoration, c1790, 17-3/4" l, 18" w, 26" h **$3,000**

Dunlap School, Antrim, New Hampshire area, painted, octagonal top with shaped underside, turned tapering pedestal ending in turned cap flanked by cabriole leg base ending in pad feet, Victorian polychrome dec with gilt highlight, minor imperfections, late 18th century, 13-5/8" x 13-1/2" top, 26-1/2" h **$25,850**

Massachusetts, inlaid birch and maple, scroll-shaped tilt top centering inlaid oval wavy birch panel, vase and ring-turned and reeded post, tripod shaped tapering legs, refinished, c1820, 15-1/8" w, 21-3/4" d, 29" h **$5,760**

Massachusetts, cherry, sq top with serpentine sides and rounded corners, vase and ring-turned post, tripod cabriole legs, arris feet, refinished, imperfections, note taped to underside of top reads "candlestand Starr-Allen family of Deerfield," late 18th C, 14-3/8" w, 15" d, 26-1/4" h **$950**

Massachusetts, mahogany, oval tilt top, vase and ring-turned post, tripod base with cabriole legs, arris pointed pad feet on platforms, old surface, very minor imperfections, late 18th C, 23-1/4" w, 17-1/4" d, 27" h ...**$8,850**

New England, cherry, serpentine top, vase and ring-turned post, tripod cabriole leg base, pad feet, old refinish, imperfections, c1790, 15-1/2" l, 16" w, 24-3/4" h **$775**

New England, painted, circular top, vase and ring-turned post and tripod cabriole leg base, old black paint over earlier red stain, polychrome floral cluster dec and pin striping, c1800, 16-1/4" d, 26" h **$2,115**

New England, cherry, rect octagonal top with applied cockbeaded edge, swelled ring-turned post, tripod base of arched, shaped, tapering legs ending in plain feet, refinished, imperfections, late 18th/early 19th C, 20-1/2" w, 16-3/4" d, 28-1/4" h ..**$825**

New Hampshire, birch, painted, sq top with rounded corners, urn shaped turned pedestal, high arched cabriole tripod base, pad feet, old red paint, imperfections, early 19th C, 13-3/4" w, 13-1/4" d, 26-1/4" h.. **$7,475**

Rhode Island, cherry, circular top with scratch-beaded edge, ring-turned tapering column, tripod cabriole leg base ending in arris pad feet, old finish, minor imperfections, late 18th century, 17-1/2" d, 27-3/4" h..**$1,100**

Hepplewhite, country, birch and maple, old dark brown surface, round single board top, vase turned column, three serpentine tapered legs, old shims, 18" d, 27-1/2" h **$1,050**

Painted and decorated, Connecticut, cherry, octagonal top with molded edge, turned pedestal with urn shaping over high-arched cabriole leg base ending in pad feet, early black paint with 19th C yellow striping on pedestal and legs, minor imperfections, late 19th C, 15-1/4" w, 15-3/4" d, 29-1/2" h **$4,025**

Primitive, wooden, adjustable candle arm, dark brown patina, early 19th C, 40" h...**$715**

Queen Anne

New England, butternut and maple, octagonal, applied molded edge, baluster turned support, tripod cabriole leg base, old refinish, traces of red paint, imperfections, mid-18th C, 17-1/2" l, 17" w, 29" h **$1,530**

New England, cherry, round top, single double-sided candle drawer below, tapering and ring-turned post, tripod cabriole base, pad feet, old dark stain, alterations and repairs, late 18th C/ early 19th C, 16-1/2" d, 26-1/4" h.................**$850**

Southern New England, cherry, tilt top with molded edge, swelled ring-turned pedestal, cabriole legs, pad feet, refinished, repairs, alterations, late 18th C, 18" w, 18-1/4" d, 27-1/4" h **$1,410**

Regency, English, mahogany, tilt-top, scalloped one board top, boldly turned column, tripod base, saber legs with beaded edges, old refinish, repairs and restoration to top, label underneath "From the summer home (1890-1929) Goshen, NY of Charlotte Beardsley (1852-1914) and George Van Riper (1845-1925), 24" w, 17-1/2" d, 28" h **$595**

Windsor, walnut and curly maple, octagonal top, turned column, octagonal platform base, three turned legs, pegged and wedged construction, old brown finish, 12" w, 11-1/4" d, 24-3/4" h.......................................**$980**

CREST RAIL

BACK SPLAT

STILE

SEAT RAIL

SIDERAIL

STRETCHER   LEGS

Typical Parts of a Chair

Arm chair, carved backsplat with armorial type crest, scrolled arm rests, cabriole legs, paw feet, "H" stretcher, $200.

Arm chair, Arts & Crafts, Limbert, Ebon-oak, geometric inlay, drop-in cushion seat newly decorated in wool Navajo print, branded under arm, refinished, some looseness, 38" x 27" x 23-1/2", $1,400.
Photo courtesy of David Rago Auctions, Inc.

Arm chair, Arts & Crafts, flaring plank back cut out with heart shape, period rush seat, flat curved arms, unmarked, refinished, repegged, break to back of one arm, some looseness, 26-1/4" w, 19-1/2" d, 36" h, $950.
Photo courtesy of David Rago Auctions, Inc.

Chairs
Arm

Adirondack-style, rustic twig construction, including small arms, green paint, roped seat, c1910 .... **$2,300**

Aesthetic Movement, after Philip Webb's Sussex chair for Morris & Co., new natural rush seat, turned spindles, orig black paint, unmarked, c1885, 21-1/4" w, 19" d, 36-1/4" h **$1,045**

Art Deco, France, giltwood, sloping U-form back rail ending in gently swollen reeded arm supports, D-shaped seat upholstered seat cushion, pr, c1925 .... **$15,750**

Art Nouveau, L. Majorelle, France, carved mahogany, horseshoe-shaped back rail, upholstered back, front of arm supports carved with pine cones and needles, continuing to form molded front legs with similar carving, dark green leather upholstery, c1900 .... **$7,000**

Arts & Crafts
Indiana Hickory, twig construction, orig hickory splint seat, weathered finish, branded signature, 26" w, 17" d, 37" h **$50**

Olbrich, Joseph Marie, Jugendstil, mahogany, small back panel inlaid with fruitwood floral pattern, inset upholstered seat, unmarked, good old refinish, 23-1/2" w, 19" d, 41-1/2" h **$1,840**

Stickley, Charles, four back slats, recovered spring cushion seat, orig

Arm chair, Arts & Crafts, Shop-of-the-Crafters, center back panel inlaid in metal and fruitwood, three slats to the floor under broad flat arms, front stretcher mortised through posts with keyed through-tenons, orig finish, cushions missing, paper label on seat deck, 37" x 33" x 26", $2,800.
Photo courtesy of David Rago Auctions, Inc.

finish, remnant of decal, 26" w, 22" d, 41" h **$230**

Stickley, Gustav, Model no. 2604, oak, arched crest rail over three horizontal back slats, shaped flat open arms, prominent front leg posts, offset front, back, and side stretchers, dark brown finish, red decal under arm, c1902, wear, 26-3/4" w, 26" d, 37" h **$1,840**

Stickley, Gustav, Thornden, two horizontal back slats, narrow arms, 1902-04 red decal, replaced seat, orig finish, minor edge wear, 37" x 21" x 21-1/2" **$3,105**

Stickley, Gustav, V-back, vertical back slats, replaced leather seat, orig faceted tacks, good orig finish, red decal, 27" w, 20-1/2" d, 37" h ..**$1,045**

Stickley, L. & J. G., fixed back, drop arm, slats to seat, corbels, replaced drop-in green leather spring seat and back cushion, waxed finish, L & J. G. Stickley Handcraft label, 32-1/2" w, 33" d, 41" h **$5,750**

Stickley, L. & J. G., spindled back, open arms, corbels, seat recovered in leather, refinished, unmarked, 24-1/2" w, 21" d, 38-1/2" h **$690**

Banister-back, New England, mid-18th C, turned maple, yoked crest rail above four molded banisters joining vase and ring-turned stiles, shaped scrolled arms on vase and ring-turned supports continuing to legs, turned feet joined by double sausage-turned stretchers, early splint seat, old refinish,

Library chair, Victorian, upholstered, rolled arms, drop-in seat cushion, turned mahogany legs, losses to one leg, 39-1/2" x 29" x 33", **$500.**
Photo courtesy of David Rago Auctions, Inc.

Morris chair, Aesthetic Movement, in the style of William Morris, mahogany, spindled sides and back, loose tufted pillows, upholstered arms, casters, unmarked, orig finish, minor roughness to leg edges, 42-1/2" x 29" x 31", **$800.**
Photo courtesy of David Rago Auctions, Inc.

Arm chair, New England, c1740, banister back, carved yoke crest, **$575.**
Photo courtesy of Pook & Pook, Inc.

Arm chairs, Louis XVI-style, new frame, price for pr, upholstered in 18th C tapestry, 40-1/2" x 24" x 24", **$2,600.**
Photo courtesy of David Rago Auctions, Inc.

Arm chair, Louis XVI provincial, fruitwood fauteuil, molded-edge medallion back, needlepoint panel, upholstered seat, ball feet, 18th C, 34" x 22-1/4" x 18-3/4", **$750.**
Photo courtesy of Sloans & Kenyon Auctioneers and Appraisers.

imperfections, 14-1/2" h seat, 43" h **$1,175**

Centennial, Colonial Revival, Queen-Anne style, wing back, hardwood cabriole legs, turned stretcher, upholstery removed, old dark finish, 46" h **$900**

Chippendale, English or Irish, walnut, pierced Gothic back splat, scrolled handholds, slip seat cov in cream colored silk upholstery, sq legs, small scalloped returns on front apron, refinished, one foot ended out, 19" h seat, 37" h back **$400**

Chippendale-style, walnut, light green leather upholstery, brass tack borders, shaped arms, sq molded legs, stretcher bases, wear, some splits in leather seats, 18-3/4" h seat, 38-1/4" h, price for six-pc set **$1,200**

Egyptian Revival, American, ebonized and parcel-gilt, upholstered scrolling back and seat, matching upholstered arm pads, sphinx head arm supports, claw feet, c1865, 39-1/2" h **$8,050**

Empire-style, mahogany, rect padded back, padded arms, ormolu-mounted classical busts, bowed padded seat, sq tapering legs with brass caps, white striped upholstery ...**$850**

George III, mahogany, shaped top rail, three pc vertical splat, upholstered seat, tapering sq section legs **$475**

Gothic Revival, America, walnut, old finish, reupholstered in damask, age cracks, 52-1/2" h **$200**

Hepplewhite, birch, pegged construction, eight vertical posts across back, slip seat, tapered legs with broadly shaped stretchers, relief arched fans on front and sides, old mellow refinishing, originally potty seat, base reworked, arms repegged, age splits, 18-1/2" h seat, 37" h back **$450**

Louis XIV, fauteuil, giltwood, serpentine cresting, scrolled and reeded arms, over upholstered seat, scrolled legs joined by stretchers, early 18th C............................. **$2,990**

Louis XIV-style, Baroque, walnut, rect backrest, foliate carved arms and legs, X-form stretcher, late price for pr, 19th C................ **$2,650**

Neoclassical, Italian, walnut, urn and wheat carved splat, downswept arms, raised sq tapering legs, late 18th/ early 19th C, 34-1/4" h..**$1,100**

Chair, Modern, Eero Saarinen for Knoll, bent plywood legs, Knoll Assoc. label, price for set of four, 30-1/2" x 26" x 19", **$500.**
Photo courtesy of David Rago Auctions, Inc.

Queen Anne

Middle Atlantic states, arched crest with square corners, raked stiles, scrolled arms on vasiform supports, trapezoidal seat, frontal cabriole legs ending in pad feet, raked rear legs, imperfections, last half 18th C, 16-1/2" h seat, 49" h **$21,150**

New Hampshire, hardwood with old black repaint, molded and curved back posts with vase splat and carved crest, turned posts support molded and scrolled arms, turned legs, Spanish feet, turned rungs with bulbous front stretcher, old rush seat, some loss to feet, 15-3/8" seat, 41" h................................**$4,125**

Regency

Mahogany, octagonal crest rail over shaped horizontal splat, open arms, shaped padded seat, sq tapering legs..**$600**

Mahogany, rect top rail above horizontal spiral-turned splat and reeded scrolling arms, upholstered seat, ring turned front legs, rear saber legs..**$600**

Regency-style, mahogany, bent reeded crest rail over shaped splat, upholstered seat, tapering turned legs..**$200**

Renaissance Revival, attributed to Pottier & Stymus, New York, walnut, scrolled arms, upholstered back and seed, spherules on seat rail, 1865, 38" h **$1,100**

Rococo Revival, John H. Belter, rosewood, Rosalie pattern, laminated, solid back, crest carved with large rose, fruit, and grape clusters, yellow silk upholstery, tufted back, 42-1/2" h **$3,500**

Rococo-style, Italian, grotto, scallop shell seat, dolphin-shaped arms, rusticated legs, late 19th/early 20th C....................................**$1,725**

Savonarola-style, mahogany, Old Man of the North carved in crest rail **$230**

Shaker, attributed to Canterbury, New Hampshire, birch and pine, concave rect back rail, turned stiles, four spindles, shaped seat, splayed turned tapering legs joined by stretchers, old refinish, traces of red stain, minor imperfections, c1835, 17" h seat, 24-1/2" h **$600**

Victorian, George Huntzinger, New York, patent March 30, 1869, walnut, pierce carved crest, rect upholstered back panel flanked by turned and curved slats and stiles, low upholstered barrel-back, arm frame carved with classical heads, upholstered seat, pierced and scroll-carved front drop under seat connected to turned rung joining carved and turned front legs, ball feet, front leg stamped **$2,100**

Windsor

Bow-back, Pennsylvania, scrolled arms, bamboo turned spindles and legs, later tan and brown swirl paint dec seat, black frame, 16" h seat, 35" h **$470**

Brace-back, continuous arm, B. Green, Connecticut, bowed crest rail continuing to shaped arms above six spindles, vase and ring-turned arm supports, shaped saddle seat, splayed vase and ring-turned legs joined by swelled stretchers, repairs, late 18th C, 16" h seat, 37" h **$950**

Comb-back, attributed to Philadelphia, mixed woods, areas of old dark green paint, arched top with finely scrolled ears, nine back spindles, bentwood arm rain ending in shaped hand rests, D-shaped seat with incised line borders around edges, baluster and ring turned legs, blunt arrow feet, stretcher base, old pegged restoration on arm rail, 23-1/2" w, 17-1/2" h seat, 42" h **$11,275**

Comb-back, old worn red paint over yellow, evidence of earlier paint history, seven spindle back with well shaped crest, bowed arm rain with turned supports, oval seat with incised detailing around spindles, splayed baluster and ring turned legs, "H" stretcher, 17-5/8" h seat, 41-1/4" h back....................**$20,700**

Continuous arm, New England, nine-spindle back, saddle seat, stamped "J Ash," c1815, 36" h..............**$1,100**

Continuous arm, Pennsylvania, nine-spindle back, bamboo turnings, early 19th C, 38" h....................**$275**

Double bow-back, New England, maple, ash, and pine, incised crest rail above seven spindles, applied scrolled arm, writing surface to right, both with bamboo-turned supports on shaped seat, centering drawer mounted on underside, splayed bamboo-turned feet joined by stretchers, orig red-brown stained surface, imperfections, c1800-15, 16" h seat, 45-1/2" h..............**$3,525**

Sack-back, Lancaster County, Pennsylvania, carved knuckles, D-shaped seat, bulbous "H" stretcher, turned splayed legs, blunt arrow feet, worn green-black paint, 16" h seat, 36" h......**$3,025**

Sack-back, Rhode Island, painted maple and ash, arched crest above tapering spindles through crest which continues to shaped handholds above turned arm supports on incised plank seat with pommel on swelled and ring-turned splayed legs joined by swelled stretchers, old black paint, worn surface, imperfections, 1790-1800, 16" h seat, 39-3/4" h......**$2,250**

Slough-back, English, George III, yew and elm, back with turned spindles, center vasiform splat framed by pair of flattened stoles surmounting serpentine crest rail, shaped arm rail on plain spindles, saddle shaped seat, cabriole legs, pad feet, repairs, refinished, late 18th C, 29" w, 15-1/2" d, 46" h......................**$500**

Arm chair, Regency, gilt dec, cane back, scene painted on back splat, 19th C, 34" x 22" x 18", **$275.**
Photo courtesy of David Rago Auctions, Inc.

Chair, Beidemeirer, fruitwood, upholstered seat, price for pr, 19th C, 32-1/2" x 18" x 18", **$500.**
Photo courtesy of David Rago Auctions, Inc.

Corner

Aesthetic Movement, American, possibly by Tisch, rosewood, cushioned and spindle-inset arms, lappet and scroll carved sq tapering legs **$1,650**

Chippendale, walnut, rolled back rest with stepped detail, pierced harp shape splats, serpentine arm supports, scrolled handholds, molded seal frame, slip seat covered in worn upholstery, scalloped aprons, cabriole legs with relief carved shells on knees, claw and ball feet, old dark surface, restorations and replacements.........**$1,870**

Chippendale-style, mahogany, shaped arms, openwork splats, rush slip seat raised on cabriole legs, claw and ball feet, 20th C **$575**

Country, New England, maple, arms with scrolled terminals, shaped

Dining chair, Chippendale style, mahogany, two arm chairs, four side chairs, pierced splats, straight molded legs, cream upholstered seats, **$1,320;** *one shown with red, green, and natural coverlet,* **$125.**
Photo courtesy of Wiederseim Associates, Inc.

Dining chair, set of four, original paint decoration, yellow grand, red and black flowers and bands, 13-1/2" w, 18" h seat, 32-1/2" h, **$2,000.**
Photo courtesy of Alderfer Auction Co.

crest, scrolled horizontal splats attached to swelled and turned baluster forms continuing to turned legs, joined to similar stretchers, old surface, replaced rush seat, minor imperfections, late 18th/early 19th C, 16-3/8" h seat, 30-1/2" h back **$1,610**

Queen Anne, country, old black and gold paint, shaped crest rail with medallion handholds, rose head nails, replaced paper rush seat, turned legs and supports, 16" h seat, 28-1/4" h back................**$520**

William and Mary, New England, shaped backrest and chamfered crest, scrolled handholds, three vase and ring-turned stiles continuing to turned legs, joined to front leg by turned double stretchers, old dark brown paint, replaced wood seat, 18th C, 30" h **$1,380**

Dining

Arts & Crafts

Stickley, Gustav, ladder-back, four slats, cloud-lift aprons, drop-in seats recovered in leather, overcoat finish, roughness to edges, some with red Gustav decal, set of eight, 37" h **$6,300**

Stickley, L. & J.G., arched vertical back slats, drop-in spring seat, covered in new green leather, good new finish, orig labels, price for set of four, 37-1/2" h, 17" w **$3,335**

Assembled set, English, turned ash and alder, open spindle back with two or three tiers of short turnings between flattened stiles, rush seat, tapered round legs, pad feet, bulbous turned front stretcher, plain turned side and rear stretchers, two-arm chairs, 10-side chairs, some with feet ended out, price for set of 12, c1800-60, 19" w, 16" d, 38" h **$1,875**

Biedermeier, fruitwood and part ebonized, black faux-leather upholstery, restorations, set of four, 36" h **$2,500**

Centennial, Colonial Revival, Sheraton-style, mahogany, two arms, eight sides, shield back, reeded front legs, corner posts with carving of urns, needlepoint slip seats, 19-1/2" w, 17-1/4" d, 37-1/2" h................**$3,000**

Chippendale-style, Baker, Connecticut, black lacquer, saber-leg, set of eight, c1960..................**$2,100**

Classical, New England, figured maple, concave crests above vasiform

splats and rails, scrolled and raked stiles, caned seats with serpentine fronts, saber legs joined by stretchers, old refinish, set of six, c1830-40, 17-1/4" h seat, 32" h...................**$950**

Eastlake, American, mahogany, one armchair, six side chairs, fan-carved crest rail, reeded stiles and stretchers, block-carved front legs, minor damage, set of seven, c1870, 35" h.....**$850**

Federal, Rhode Island or Salem, Massachusetts, mahogany carved, set of four side and matching arm chair, shield back with molded crest and stiles above carved kylix with festoons draped from flanking carved rosettes, pierced splat terminating in carved lunette at base above molded rear seat rail, seat with serpentine front rail, sq tapering legs joined by stretchers, over-upholstered seats covered in old black horsehair with scalloped trim, old surface, c1795, 16-1/2" h seat, 37-3/4" h.....................**$23,000**

George III, mahogany, squared inlaid crest, reeded stiles, pierced and inlaid splat, upholstered seat, square tapering legs joined by an H-form stretcher, set of six...**$2,600**

George III-style

Mahogany, foliate carved openwork baluster splat, trapezoidal slip-seat, sq legs joined by stretchers, price for set of 12, two armchairs and 10 side chairs **$9,400**

Mahogany, comprising two armchairs and 10 side chairs, serpentine cresting, pierced vasiform splat, and drop seat, sq legs, price for set of 10, 20th C..............................**$3,525**

International Movement, manufactured by Oda, similar to design by Neils O. Moller, Denmark, two armchairs and four side chairs, teak, new upholstery over original, price for set of six, c1960, 31" h **$1,530**

Louis XVI-style beechwood, incorporating antique elements, comprising two armchairs and 10 side chairs, solid baluster splat, green leather drop-seat, circular fluted and tapered legs, price for set of 12 ....**$2,585**

Regency-style, mahogany and inlay, two armchairs, six side chairs, curved inlaid crest rail, dec horizontal splats, pale blue silk upholstery, Greek key design, late 19th/early 20th C, 33-3/4" h **$10,350**

Renaissance Revival, America, oak, two arm and eight side chairs, each with foliate and beast carved cresting, paneled seat rail and turned legs, set of 10, c1870 .... **$3,105**

Sheraton, one armchair, five side chairs, walnut and mahogany, mahogany flame veneer panels, rect crests with brass line inlay, rope twist carving on back crosspieces, reeded serpentine rear stiles, ring turned front legs, old refinishing, contemporary burgundy upholstered seats, restorations, 17" h seats, 31" h backs **$1,150**

William IV, mahogany, shaped carved crest rail above horizontal splat, trapezoid slip seat, circular fluted tapering legs, set of six: one arm chair, five side chairs, second quarter 19th C **$3,600**

Easy (Wing, Great chair)

Boston, maple, crest continues to shaped wings above outwardly scrolling arms, serpentine shirt joins block and ring-turned front legs connected to sq raking rear legs by similar side stretchers, ring-turned swelled and blocked medial stretcher, old black paint, 20th C cotton show cover, restoration, 1710-1725, 19" h seat, 49" h **$15,275**

Connecticut, attributed to, turned and painted, yoked crest rail above vasiform splat joining turned stiles with canted vase and ring-turned arms ending in knob handholds on vase and ring-turned supports continuing to button feet joined by double bulbous front stretchers and planed side stretchers, painted red/brown over earlier paint, minor imperfections, mid-18th C, 16-1/2" h seat, 48" h **$6,500**

Federal, New England, birch, serpentine crest continues to shaped wings, out scrolled arms, tight seat over sq tapering front legs joined by sq stretchers to rear sq raking legs, floral upholstery, minor imperfections, early 19th C, 14-1/2" h seat, 47-1/4" h **$3,410**

Fauteuil

Louis XV style, beechwood, frames carved with foliage, price for pr **$2,710**

Louis XV style, painted, typical form with foliate carved frames, price for pr **$1,300**

Louis XVI-style, painted, floral and foliate carved top rail, upholstered

back and seat, carved apron, cabriole legs, price for pr **$2,600**

Neoclassical, Continental, possibly Italian, painted green, carved floral crest and oval back, out scrolling arms, fluted tapering legs, painted throughout with flowers, price for pr, early 19th C and later **$4,780**

Neoclassical, Continental, possibly Italian, painted, chapeau de gendarme crest rail above out scrolling arms, fluted tapering legs, blue and gray floral tapestry, price for pr, early 19th C and later **$4,100**

Sheraton-style, English, mahogany, green faux leather upholstery, scrolled and molded arms, balloon shaped seat, turned and reeded legs, matching arm supports, brass tack trim, early to mid-20th C, 17" h seat, 34" h back **$450**

Folding

Austrian, Thonet, bentwood, oval backrest and seat, scrolling arms and legs, late 19th C **$600**

Hall

William IV, octagonal scrolled backrest, center painted crest, shaped seat, turned tapering legs ending in peg feet **$475**

Highchair, child's

New England, attributed to, turned maple and birch, turned tapering stiles with finials joining three arched slats, shaped arms on vase and ring-turned supports, splayed legs joined by double stretchers, old refinish, late 18th C, 20" h seat, 40" h **$1,100**

Shaker-style, ladder back, woven splint seat, turned finials, foot rest, mustard paint, 24" h seat, 38" h back **$880**

Windsor, New England, rect crest above three spindles and outward flaring stiles, turned hand-holds on shaped seat, splayed turned tapering legs joined by stretchers, vestiges of stippled red and black paint, "M.H. Spencer, N.Y." in script on bottom of seat, 1825-40, 22-1/2" h seat, 31-1/2" h **$775**

Ladderback

Child's, woven splint seat, turned finials, red finish, 6-1/2" h seat, 3" h back **$250**

Connecticut, mixed hardwoods, old deep brown finish, bowed arms,

turned supports continue down to medallions on top run of base, back with four arched slats, high finials, replaced woven splint seat, turned posts and stretchers, 14-1/2" h seat, 42" h back **$375**

Pennsylvania, woven splint seat, turned finials, painted red, 13" h seat, 42" h back **$150**

Library

George III, mahogany and caned, pink upholstered loose cushion, c1800, 33-1/2" h **$2,070**

Lolling, Federal

Massachusetts, mahogany, serpentine crest above half serpentine molded shaped arms, concave supports, over-upholstered serpentine seat on sq tapering frontal legs, raked rear legs, casters missing, minor imperfections, 1790-1800, 16-1/2" h seat, 42" h **$4,700**

New England, mahogany, reverse serpentine crest over upholstered back joining shaped arms and molded concave supports on four tapering sq legs, joined by sq stretchers, old refinish, imperfections, c1790, 17" h seat, 43-1/4" h **$6,900**

High chair, Louis XV, fruitwood, crest rail with flower carved cartouche, pierced splat with potted flower, square tapering legs with H stretcher, c1800, **$300.**
Photo courtesy of Pook & Pook, Inc.

Lounge chair, Modern, Charles Eames for Herman Miller, LCW bentwood, Evans Products Co. tag, 26-1/2" x 22" x 23-1/4", **$475.**
Photo courtesy of David Rago Auctions, Inc.

Slipper chair, Victorian, upholstered in brocade fabric, painted gold base, braided rope and tassels dec, 32" x 24" x 33", **$350.**
Photo courtesy of David Rago Auctions, Inc.

Side chair, Hepplewhite, Maryland, mahogany, three-part open work back splat, upholstered seat, c1790, 18" w, 17-1/2" h seat, 35-1/2" h, **$250.**
Photo courtesy of Alderfer Auction Co.

Arts & Crafts chair, Gustav Stickley, Thornden, No. 1299, two horizontal back slats, woven rush seat, early red decal, original finish, some wear, replaced seat, 35" x 18" x 16", **$1,400.**
Photo courtesy of David Rago Auctions, Inc.

Lounge, International Movement

Charles and Ray Eames, MI, molded plywood mahogany seat and legs, purchased c1949, 22" w, 26" h **$1,880**

George Nakashima, New Hope, Pennsylvania, walnut conoid lounge chair, c1975, 31" w, 33-1/3" d, 30-1/2" h chair, 24" w, 24" d, 10-1/4" h ottoman **$4,700**

Hans Wegner, Denmark, teak, reclining upholstered cushion seat, c1960, 29-1/4" w, 48" d, 34-1/2" h chair, 29-1/2" w, 23-1/2" d, 13-1/2" h ottoman **$4,700**

Morris chair, Arts & Crafts

Stickley, Gustav, No. 332, slats to the floor under flat arms, orig brown leather cushions, orig finish, red decal, arms re-pegged and re-glued, 31-1/2" w, 36" d, 37" h **$6,275**

Stickley, L. & J. G., Fayetteville, New York, chair model No. 411, matching model No. 397 footstool, four carved slats on adjustable back, flat open arms with through tenon leg posts and four corbel supports with upholstered spring cushion seat and back, light brown finish, c1915, 29-1/4" w, 35" d, 40-1/4" h; footstool with spring cushion, 20" w, 14" d, 16-1/2" h, both with red and yellow decal "The Work of L. & J. G. Stickley" **$1,725**

Wainscot, Pennsylvania, walnut, pegged construction, shaped crest, raised paneled back, shaped arms, turned legs, stretcher base, 18th C, 24-1/4" w, 19-1/2" d, 17-1/2" h seat, 42" h back **$7,150**

Side Chairs

Arrowback, tan, brown, red, and black dec of cornucopias on crest, leaves on back and front stretcher, incising around seat, brushed detain between, evidence of earlier green, bamboo turned base, 19th C mustard paint, 15-3/4" h seat, 32" h **$935**

Art Deco, Europe, wooden gondola backs, ivory sabots on front legs, cream striped fabric upholstery, pr, 25" h **$2,000**

Arts & Crafts

Stickley, Gustav, H-back, drop-in seat recovered in burgundy leather, red decal, over-coated orig dark finish, roughness to leg edges, 17" w, 16" d, 40" h **$690**

Stickley, L. & J.G., Fayetteville, New York, oak, model No. 940, three vertical slats below crest rail, slip seat, double side stretcher, branded mark, price for set of six, c1916, 35-3/4" h **$2,235**

Banister back

New England, paint dec, shaped crest above four split balusters joining vase and ring-turned stiles, trapezoidal rush seat, vase and ring-turned legs joined to rear legs by turned double stretchers, old surface painted dark brown with gilt stencil and polychrome floral designs, last half 18th C, 17-1/2" h seat, 44" h..............................**$1,100**

New Hampshire, coastal, painted black, flaring fishtail carved crest over three split banisters flanked by vase and ring-turned stiles with ball finials, trapezoidal rush seat over ring-turned frontal legs joined by double turned stretchers, rear legs with old piecing, mid to late 18th C, 17" h seat, 43" h.................**$1,425**

Biedermeier, curved crest rail, central horizontal splat joined by three vertical splats, upholstered seat, squared tapering legs, set of four.........**$1,675**

Centennial, Queen Anne style, European, walnut, pierced and scrolled back splat, serpentine real stiles, balloon shaped slip seat, cabriole legs, scrolled knees, pad feet, old mellow finish, price for pr, 18-1/2" h seat, 41-1/2" h back.................**$600**

Chippendale

America, mahogany, arched crests, interlaced double scroll back splat with piercing, old slip seat cov in black faux leather, sq legs with beaded edges, stretcher base, old dark finish, restorations, price for pr, 19-1/2" h seat, 38" h back......**$1,785**

America, mahogany, serpentine crest with beaded edges, pierced vase shaped back splat, tapered rear stiles, replacement slip seat, sq legs with chamfered backs and beaded corners, stretcher base, old finish, rockers added at one time, now with pieced restorations as it was converted back to chair, 17" h seat, 35-3/4" h.................**$450**

Boston or Salem, Massachusetts area, carved mahogany, serpentine crests end in raked molded ears, center carved shells above owl-shaped splats with carved volutes above slip seats, Marlborough front legs with beaded outer edges, joined by similar sq stretchers to rear raking legs, old refinish, minor imperfections, price for pr, 1755-85, 16-5/8" h seat, 38" h..**$4,200**

Connecticut River Valley, tiger maple, serpentine crest with raked molded terminals above pierced splat, old rush seat, block and vase turned front legs joined by turned stretcher, old refinish, 17-1/4" h seat, 39" h **$900**

Country, maple with some curl, pierced spat and shaped crest with carved ears, sq legs, mortised and pinned stretchers, old mellow refinishing, damage to paper rush seat because of breaks in front seal rail, 39" h **$110**

Massachusetts, cherry, shaped crest rail above pierced splat and raked stiles, upholstered slip seat, sq chamfered legs joined to raking rear legs

by sq stretchers, refinished, repairs, late 18th C, 17-1/2" h, 38" h.....**$600**

Massachusetts, mahogany, shaped crest rail above pierced scroll and diamond splat flanked by raked stiles, trapezoidal upholstered slip seat, beaded straight legs joined to raking rear legs by sq stretchers, imperfections, late 18th C, 18" h seat, 37-1/2" h.................**$500**

New London, CT, carved cherry, serpentine crest rails, pierced splats with C-scrolls and beaded edges, molded shoes, flanked by stiles and rounded backs, molded seat frames and straight legs with beaded edges, pierced brackets joined by sq stretchers, old refinish, set of five, 1760-95, 17" h seat, 39" h ...**$10,350**

New York, carved mahogany, carved crest ending in raked molded terminals above pierced splat with C-scrolls, slip seat, molded seat frame, front carved cabriole legs ending in ball and claw feet, rear raked legs, old surface, imperfections, 1755-65, 18" h seat, 39-1/2" h.............**$2,990**

Pennsylvania, attributed to, carved mahogany, serpentine crest rail with cockbeaded edge and scrolled terminals above pierced shaped splat, molded raking stiles, trapezoidal slip seat, beaded Marlborough front legs joined to raking rear legs by sq stretchers, restored, late 18th C, 17" h seat, 36-1/2" h.............**$1,775**

Rhode Island, mahogany, shaped and carved crest rail, pierced splat, raked stiles, trapezoidal slip seat, molded front legs joined to raked rear legs by sq stretchers, old finish, imperfections, c1765-95, 18" h seat, 38" h **$1,100**

Chippendale-style, country, mixed hardwoods, dark reddish-brown finish, pierced heart and scroll back splat, tapered real stiles, paper rush seat, turned legs and stretchers, Spanish feet, late 19th or early 20th C, 18-1/2" h seat, 40" h back....**$435**

Classical

Baltimore, painted and dec, scrolled crest above inverted vase-shaped splat, cane seat, dec front legs joined by medial stretcher, stencil dec, orig gilt classical motifs on black ground, 34-1/2" h...........**$750**

Boston, MA, attributed to, mahogany veneer, curving crest with the continuous stile and rail construction, shaped splats, bowed veneered

front seat rails, frontal curving legs, rear raking legs, price for set of six, minor imperfections, c1835, 17" h seat, 31" h.............................**$4,350**

New England, carved and turned tiger maple, baluster turned cresting above acanthus carved, pierced splat joining raked stiles above trapezoidal rush seat, vase and ring-turned outward flaring frontal legs and turned stretchers, refinished, imperfections, price for set of six, c1825, 18" h seat, 34-1/2" h..**$1,765**

New York, carved mahogany veneer, scroll back, beaded edges, horizontal splats carved with leafage and other classical motifs, slip seat, curving legs, old surface, set of six, 1810-20, 16-1/2" h seat, 32" h.............**$5,200**

Country, Ohio, painted mustard, black, and gold fruit and leaves, red painted surface in the manner of J. Huey, Zanesville, OH, c1840..**$7,500**

Decorated, attributed to Carlisle, PA, plank seat, orig black over red dec, floral panels surrounded by gold stencils, bordered with salmon and yellow line border dec, carefully cleaned, applied coat of protective varnish, professionally executed slight touch-up, price for set of six, 17" h seat, 31" h...................**$3,650**

Federal

Boston, MA, or Portsmouth, New Hampshire, mahogany, square back with scratch beading enclose three pierced splats above trapezoidal shaped over upholstered seats, sq tapering front legs outlined in stringing and joined by sq stretchers to raked rear legs, refinished, one chair with a pierced rear stile, price for set of four, c1800, 18" h seat, 35-1/2" h............**$1,175**

Massachusetts or Rhode Island, mahogany inlaid, shield back, arched molded crest above 5 molded spindles and inlaid quarter fan, over-upholstered seats with serpentine fronts, molded tapering legs joined by stretchers, c1780, 17-1/2" h seat, 37" h, pr........**$5,475**

New England, attributed to, maple, rush seat, dec with polychrome flowers on yellow ground, price for pr, 18" w, 16" d, 35" h.............**$500**

New Hampshire, Portsmouth, attributed to Langley Boardman, mahogany, sq back, reeded on rest rail, stiles, and stay rail, over upholstered serpentine seat, molded sq tapering front legs, sq stretchers and rakes rear legs,

Side chair, mahogany, wide-shaped back splat over narrow slatted back with applied trim, upholstered seat, shaped skirt, double stretchers, **$65.**
Photo courtesy of Dotta Auction Co., Inc.

Side chair, Queen Anne, English, walnut and mahogany, shaped crest and splat, pad feet, H-stretcher, replaced seat frame, c1760, 18" h seat, 38-1/2" h back, **$425.**
Photo courtesy of Alderfer Auction Co.

refinish, minor imperfections, 1774-1833, 18" h seat, 36" h **$1,035**

George III, mahogany, yoke shaped crest rail, pierced splat carved with wheat sheaves, slip-in padded seat, squared molded legs, price for pr, late 18th C **$650**

Gothic Revival, New York City, mahogany veneer, trefoil pierced splats, curved stay rails, veneered seal rails, curving rococo legs, old refinish, 20th C upholstery, set of eight, 1850s, 16-1/2" h seat, 33-1/2" h **$6,900**

Hepplewhite, American, mahogany, shield back, rush seat **$325**

Hitchcock, Hitchcocksville, Connecticut, rosewood grained surface, orig gilt dec, urn centering cornucopia splat, old rush seats, ring-turned legs, orig surface, price for set of four, 1825-32, 35-1/2" h **$1,265**

International Movement

Designed by Mies van der Rohe, manufactured by Knoll Associates, New York, cantilevered tubular steel frame, green leather padded and upholstered seat, price for pr, 33-1/2" h **$6,450**

Mies van der Rohe Barcelona chairs, attributed to Knoll Associates, New York, black leather cushions on flat bar base, price for pr, 29-1/2" w, 29-1/2" d, 29-1/2" h **$5,590**

Warren McArthur Corporation, machined and tubular anodized aluminum with original upholstery, green decal labels. Height 32 inches .. **$2,150**

Ladderback

Pennsylvania, rush seat, ball turned finials, turned front stretcher, old mustard paint, wear to feet, 14-1/2" h seat, 41" h back **$385**

Pennsylvania, woven splint seat, turned finials, boldly turned front stretcher, turned legs, old brown paint, 14" h seat, 38-1/2" h back **$525**

Pennsylvania, woven splint seat, turned finials, boldly turned front stretcher, reddish-brown finish, 16" h seat, 40" h back **$330**

Pennsylvania, woven splint seat, turned finials, boldly turned front stretcher, old green-black paint, 17" h seat, 40" h back **$385**

Pennsylvania, woven splint seat, turned finials and front stretcher, reddish-brown finish, 16-1/2" h seat, 39-1/2" h back **$360**

Neoclassical, Boston, 1815-20, mahogany, curving carved crests flanked by gadrooning above similar-ly curved horizontal splats enclosing carved elements flanked by reeded curving stiles that continue to half way on front legs and also elaborate front seat rails, curving rear legs and slip seats, upholstered in 20th C green watered moiré fabric, price for pair, 17-1/4" h seat, 33-1/2" h back .. **$1,175**

Plank seat, Pennsylvania, orig paint dec, fruit with green leaves on crest, yellow and white line borders on reddish brown ground, wear, old touch up, set of six, 18-1/2" h seat, 33-1/4" h back **$700**

Queen Anne

American, burl walnut, shaped cresting, serpentine slat, slip-seat raised on shell carved cabriole legs, hoof feet, price for pr, early 18th C **$1,650**

Country, finely alligatored black paint, double arched crest, pierced vase shaped back splat, tapered rear stiles, replaced paper rush seat, pad feet, boldly turned front stretcher, small glued splits on crest, 17" seat, 38-1/2" h back **$375**

English, mahogany, scalloped and scrolled real splat, serpentine rear stiles, later red velvet covering on balloon seat, cabriole legs, relief carved shells on knees, pad feet, old refinishing, two returns replaced, 17" h seat, 39-1/2" back **$1,610**

New England, painted, carved and spooned crest rail above vasiform splat and raking stiles, trapezoidal slip seat, blocked vase and ring-turned legs, carved Spanish feet joined by bulbous turned front stretcher and straight side stretchers, old black paint over earlier paint, imperfections, mid-18th C, 16-1/2" h seat, 41" h back **$600**

Newport, Rhode Island, black walnut, curving crest above vase-shaped pierced splat, compass seat, front and side rail shaping, cabriole front legs joined to rear sq tapering legs by block and vase-swelled side stretchers, swelled and turned medial stretchers, rear feet without chamfering, old refinish, minor repairs, affixed brass plaque reads "Ebenezer Storer 1730-1807," 1750-75, 17" h seat, 38-1/4" h **$2,990**

Regency-style, walnut, five brass rods as back splats, balloon seats with old replaced upholstery, applied ormolu mounts, tapered and fluted legs and rear stiles, old finish, set of four, 17-1/2" h seat, 32" h back **$450**

Rococo Revival, John H. Belter, rosewood, Rosalie without the Grapes pattern, laminated, solid back, crest carved with large rose and fruit, red silk upholstery, casters, pr, 37-1/2" h **$2,550**

Sheraton, walnut, raised medallion crest, rope twist detail on back slats, ring-turned and reeded front legs, rear saber legs, serpentine stiles, old finish, contemporary upholstered seats, restorations, one crest pieced, set of six, 19" h seat, 33" h back .. **$750**

Slat back, Delaware River Valley, turned maple, five reverse graduated concave arched slats joining turned stiles with bulbous finials, rush seat, vase and ring-turned frontal legs joined by bulbous turned front stretcher and side stretchers, old surface, late 18th C, 17" h seat, 45-1/2" h **$4,120**

Victorian, ebonized, lacquered, Wedgwood mounts, openwork backrest, caned seat, turned legs, price for pr **$1,410**

William IV, England, carved rosewood, foliate carved backrest with central diamond-shaped upholstered panel, slip seat, leaf carved circular legs, price for pr, c1835 .... **$700**

Windsor

Bamboo turned, Pennsylvania, grain dec, red, green, and yellow floral, bud, and foliate dec crest rail, 18" h seat, 34" h back **$935**

Birdcage, New England, two horizontal spindles and seven vertical spindles joining bamboo-turned slightly swelled stiles, shaped seats, splayed swelled bamboo-turned legs and stretchers, old worn black paint, price for set of five, 18" h seat, c1810, 35-1/2" h **$3,300**

Bow-back, New England, bowed crest rail above seven spindles and shaped saddle seat, splayed swelled bamboo-turned legs and stretchers, some paint loss to black paint, c1810, 17-1/2" h seat, 39" h **$650**

Bow-back, New England, black painted, molded bowed crest rails above seven spindles and shaped saddle seat on splayed vase and ring-turned legs and swelled stretchers, price for pr, imperfections, late 18th C, 17-1/4" seat, 38-1/4" h **$2,820**

Brace-back, nine spindles bow back, well shaped seat with incised detail

around spindles, vase and ring turned legs, turned "H" stretcher, old mellow refinish, restorations, 17-1/2" h, seat, 36-3/4" h **$385**

Butterfly, Pennsylvania, seven-spindle back, bamboo turnings, poplar seats, hickory legs and spindles, refinished, price for pr, one with crack in top rail **$285**

Clerk's, attributed to New England, ash, shaped concave crest above seven spindles, vase and ring-turned stiles, shaped saddle seat, splayed vase and ring-turned legs joined by turned, swelled stretchers, old refinish, imperfections, c1790, 26" h, 41-1/2" h **$1,430**

Comb-back, mixed woods, arched crest with flared ears, seven-spindle back, turned arms, bentwood arm rail, shield shaped seat, vase and ring turned legs, stretcher base, light refinish, 17" h seat, 38-1/4" h **$800**

Fan-back, Massachusetts, attributed to, shaped crest rail with scroll carved terminals above seven spindles, vase and ring turned stiles and shaped saddle seat, splayed vase and ring turned legs joined by swelled stretchers, old black paint, late 18th C, 18" h seat, 36-1/2" h **$715**

Fan-back, New England, red stained, shaped crest rail above seven spindles, vase and ring-turned stiles, shaped saddle seat, splayed vase and ring-turned legs joined by swelled stretchers, imperfections, late 18th C, 17" h seat, 36" h **$775**

Fan-back, New England, shaped crest rail above seven spindles and vase and ring-turned stiles, shaped saddle seat and splayed vase and ring-turned legs joined by swelled stretchers, old brown paint, late 18th C, 17" h seat, 37" h **$600**

Fan-back, New England, shaped crest rail with scroll-carved terminals above seven spindles and vase and ring-turned stiles, shaped saddle seat and splayed vase and ring-turned legs and swelled stretchers, old black/brown paint over earlier green and red paints, late 18th C, 17" h seat, 36" h **$7,675**

Slipper

Aesthetic Movement, American, walnut, V-shaped cresting, openwork floral and disc carved frieze, angular floral carved legs **$500**

Side chair, Rococo style, carved giltwood, ovoid open foliate carved back above padded seat, carved cabriole legs, scrolled and pegged feet, late 19th C, 37-1/2" x 18" x 17", **$350.**
Photo courtesy of Sloans & Kenyon Auctioneers and Appraisers.

Side chair, Rococo Revival, rosewood, scrolling handgrip crest, serpentine padded and upholstered seat, cabriole legs, scroll toes, peg feet, set of four chairs, 19th century, 33-1/4" x 18-1/4" x 17", **$400.**
Photo courtesy of Sloans & Kenyon Auctioneers and Appraisers.

Arts & Crafts, Gustav Stickley, spindled back, drop-in spring seat recovered in brown leather, orig finish, black decal, 17-3/4" w, 16" d, 37" h **$1,150**

Victorian, rosewood, angular foliate carved backrest with urn form splat, over upholstered seat and circular turned legs, c1875 .... **$300**

Victorian, late, ebonized and bobbin turned needlepoint upholstery, foliate dec seat, c1880 .... **$175**

Typical Parts of a Highboy

Chest of drawers, Arts & Crafts, Gustav Stickley, two-over-three configuration, faceted wooden knobs, swiveling mirror, paneled sides, red box mark, refinished, few stains to top, 33" x 48" x 23", **$5,000.**

Photo courtesy of David Rago Auctions, Inc.

Chest of drawers, Chippendale, walnut, four graduated cockbeaded drawers, reeded corner columns, losses, 41-1/2" w, 22" d, 34" h, **$2,000.**

Photo courtesy of Alderfer Auction Co.

Chests of drawers

Art Deco, Quigley, France, parchment covered, rect top, three tapering drawers, pyramid mirrored stiles, bracket feet, back branded, c1925, 44-1/2" x 35" **$2,750**

Arts & Crafts, English, dresser, orig pivoting mirror with chamberstick shelves, glove boxes, copper repoussé panels, two drawers over one long drawer, orig medium-dark finish, unmarked, split to side, 42-3/4" w, 21-1/2" d, 64" h **$1,725**

Biedermeier, maple, rect case fitted with two drawers, splayed sq legs, c1820, 36" w, 19" d, 31" h **$1,725**

Chippendale

Baltimore, Maryland, mahogany, line inlaid, two split upper drawers, three lower full width graduated cock beaded dovetailed drawers, molded base, ogee bracket feet, 35-1/4" w, 19-1/2" d, 33-1/2" h **$6,050**

Boston, Massachusetts area, carved mahogany, reverse serpentine, shaped mahogany top with veneered edge overhangs case of conforming veneered drawers, cockbeaded drawer separators, molded base, ball and claw feet, old refinish, veneer losses, 1770-80, 38-1/4" w, 20-3/4" d, 34-1/4" h **$3,525**

Connecticut, carved cherry, rect top with molded edge, cockbeaded case of four graduated drawers, gadrooned carved ogee bracket base, replaced brasses, refinished, imperfections, late 18th C, 36-1/2" w, 17" d, 37-1/2" h **$4,450**

English, mahogany, oak secondary wood, molded top with pull-out writing surface, four dovetailed graduated drawers with molded edges, old brass pulls, ogee feet, molded base, old refinishing, old restorations, backboards renailed, 34" w, 18" d, 33-1/4" h **$2,875**

Massachusetts, maple, rect overhanging top, four thumb-molded graduated drawers, ogee bracket feet, replaced brass pulls, old refinish, imperfections, losses, c1780, 32-1/2" w, 17" d, 33" h **$4,700**

Massachusetts, attributed to, maple, flat molded cornice, case of two thumb-molded short drawers and six graduated long drawers,

bracket feet, brasses appear to be orig, old red stained surface, minor imperfections, last half 18th C, 36" w, 18-1/2" d, 57" h **$8,820**

New England, cherry, rect overhanging top, case of five graduated thumb-molded drawers, base with ogee feet, replaced brass, refinished, restored, late 18th C, 36-3/4" w, 17-3/4" d, 34-3/4" h **$2,350**

New England, maple, flat molded cornice, case of two thumb molded short drawers and four graduated long drawers, ogee bracket feet, brasses appear to be original, refinished, minor restoration, late 18th C, 36" w, 18" d, 42" h **$4,200**

New England, maple, molded cornice overhangs case of five thumb-molded graduated drawers, molded bracket base, original brass, refinished, imperfections, late 18th C, 35-1/2" w, 18-1/8" d, 47" h **$3,100**

Pennsylvania, walnut, five drawers, reeded quarter columns, ogee bracket feet, orig varnish, c1780 .... **$12,000**

Rhode Island, carved tiger maple, tall, cornice with dentil molding, case of seven graduated thumb-molded drawers, molded tall bracket base with central drop, top drawer with fan-carving, orig brasses, early surface, late 18th C, 38" w, 18-3/4" d, 63-3/4" h **$27,600**

Southern, walnut, yellow pine secondary wood, orig two-board top with variegated fan inlays in corners, double star in middle, chamfered corners on case, with small urns and line inlay, five dovetailed drawers with banded inlay borders, ogee feet with scalloped returns, molded base, refinished, old replaced brasses, small areas of veneer damage, inlay restorations, minor insect damage, feet are old well-executed replacements, 39" w, 21-1/4" d, 38-1/8" h **$2,645**

Chippendale to Hepplewhite,
transitional, cherry, pine secondary wood, dovetailed case with reeded quarter columns, cove molded cornice, eight dovetailed graduated drawers, French feet with scalloped returns, molding around base, orig oval brasses, old mellow refinishing, 42-1/2" w, 23" d, 63-3/4" h **$5,300**

Chippendale-style, America, black walnut, mahogany, pine secondary wood, two board top, five finely dovetailed drawers with beaded edges, two drawers with divided interiors, bracket base with thin molded edge, brass bale pulls, wire nails, late 19th/early 20th C, 42" w, 20" d, 41-1/2" h **$900**

Classical

New England, bird's eye maple, rect top, case with projecting cockbeaded bird's-eye maple veneered drawers, above three graduated drawers with flanking engaged vase and ring-turned spiral carved columns continuing to turned feet, opalescent pattern glass pulls, refinished, 1825-30, 41" w, 20" d, 47-1/2" h **$1,530**

Ohio, attributed to, tiger and bird's-eye maple, backsplash above overhanging top, case with recessed panel sides, cockbeaded graduated drawers flanked by spiral carved columns and colonettes above dies, turned tapering legs and feet, shaped skirt, refinished, replaced glass pulls, imperfections, 1830s, 46" w, 19-3/4" d, 57-1/4" h **$2,000**

Eastlake, American

Curly walnut, burl veneer, carved detail, scrolled crest, four dovetailed drawers, two handkerchief drawers, well detailed molded panel fronts, refinished, 39" w, 17-1/2" d, 46" h **$750**

Mahogany, five full drawers, two half drawers, carved leaf and branch dec, 38" w, 55" h **$300**

Empire

America, cherry, orig dark red flame graining over salmon ground on façade, worn orig red on sides, maple and poplar secondary woods, two-board top with old chip along back edge, serpentine pilasters on either side of four dovetailed drawers, old clear glass pulls, inset panels on ends, turned feet, age splits in top, c1830, 43" w, 22-5/8" d, 46-3/5" h **$500**

America, tiger maple, rect top, protruding frieze section fitted with single wide drawer over three drawers between applied half-round turnings, vase and ball turned feet, period round brass pulls, c1830, 42-1/2" w, 21-1/2" d, 44-1/2" h **$2,750**

Maine, attributed to, cherry, mahogany veneer, pine secondary wood, two-board top has shaped back splash, four dovetailed drawers with orig brass pulls and key escutcheons, high crisply turned feet, refinished, veneer repairs, pulls cleaned, minor dents, 41-1/4" w, 20" d, 41-1/2" h **$1,100**

Federal

America, bowfront, mahogany, flame mahogany veneer, pine secondary wood, old replaced top with biscuit corners, four dovetailed drawers with applied beading, replaced brass pulls, rope twist carvings on front pilasters, high boldly turned feet, refinished, pierced restorations, one rear foot replaced, 40-1/2" w, 19" d, 36-3/4" h **$770**

Baltimore, Maryland, mahogany veneered and inlaid, serpentine, top with veneered edge overhangs conforming case of four graduated drawers outlined in narrow banding and stringing with ovolo corners, shaped skirt, flaring French feet connected to shaped sides, replaced brasses, old refinish, imperfections, c1810, 45-3/4" w, 22-1/4" d, 38" h **$5,585**

Connecticut, attributed to, cherry, rect overhanging top with string inlaid edge, case with four scratch-beaded graduated drawers, bracket base, replaced brasses, refinished, minor imperfections, c1790-1810, 37-3/4" w, 19-1/2" d, 35" h **$4,415**

Maryland, attributed to, cherry and poplar inlaid, rect top with string inlaid edge, case of four graduated drawers with cockbeaded surrounds flanked by quarter-engaged columns, base with scalloped front skirt and flaring feet, refinished, replaced brass, repairs, 1810-20, 40-1/4" w, 18-5/8" d, 35-1/2" h **$2,115**

Maryland, attributed to, mahogany inlaid, mahogany veneered top with inlaid edge, case of cockbeaded drawers with oval stringing, serpentine veneered skirt flanked by tapering French feet, refinished, old replaced brass, some restoration, early 19th C, 44-1/2" w, 20-1/8" d, 43" h **$1,880**

Massachusetts, cherry, rect top with cross banded edge overhangs conforming case of four graduated scratch beaded drawers, cut-out bracket base, replaced brass, refinished, early 19th C, 40-1/4" w, 20-5/8" d, 35-1/2" h **$2,750**

Chest of drawers, Victorian, English, bow front, mahogany veneer, string inlay, scrolled apron, 42" x 30" x 19", **$2,000.**
Photo courtesy of David Rago Auctions, Inc.

Chest of drawers, cottage style, painted pale green, original painted flowers and foliage on each drawer, arched scrolled back with rectangular mirror, pair of candle shelves, and handkerchief boxes, four drawers, **$295.**
Photo courtesy of Dotta Auction Co., Inc.

Chest of drawers, Hepplewhite, inlay, round brasses, escutcheons, **$500.**
Photo courtesy of Wiederseim Associates, Inc.

Chest of drawers, Sheraton, country, cherry, four drawers with edge beading, flanked by columns, shaped skirt, glass knobs, **$225.**
Photo courtesy of Dotta Auction Co., Inc.

Massachusetts, mahogany veneer, bowed top with cross-banded veneered overhanging edge, conforming case of cockbeaded veneered drawers, molded base with shaped feet, original brass, old refinish, early 19th C, 41-1/4" w, 23-1/2" d, 35" h **$4,125**

Middle Atlantic states, mahogany, mahogany veneer, and cherry, rect, top above case of four graduated, cockbeaded drawers, upper drawer with cross banded mahogany inlay, shaped veneered skirt, slightly flaring French feet, refinished, replaced brasses, restored, 1815-25, 44-1/4" w, 19-7/8" d, 45-1/2" h **$2,115**

New England, inlaid cherry, bow front top with string-inlaid edge overhangs conforming case of inlaid drawers, stringing in outline, quarter fans, and central paterae above shaped skirt flanked by flaring French feet, replaced brass, old refinish, repairs, early 19th C, 42-3/4" w, 21" d, 36-3/4" h **$3,100**

New Hampshire, possibly by the Dunlaps, carved and inlaid wavy birch, rect top with inlaid edge overhangs case of four drawers with stringing in ovolo outline; flanked by quarter-engaged columns wrapped with vine-like stringing, diminutive fan carving above and below columns, molded base with carved geometric shapes, sharply spurred bracket feet, mostly original brass, old refinish, imperfections, early 19th C, 38-1/2" w, 19-1/4" d, 38-1/2" h **$11,200**

Portsmouth or Greenland, New Hampshire, bow front, mahogany and flame birch veneer, bow front mahogany top with inlaid edge overhanging conforming case, four cockbeaded three-paneled drawers, divisions outlined with mahogany cross banded veneer and stringing above skirt, central veneered rect drop panel, high bracket feet joined by shaped side skirts, similar rear feet, turned pulls appear to be orig, old refinish, minor repairs, 1810-14, 40-1/4" w, 21-1/4" d, 39" h .. **$28,750**

Rhode Island, maple, rect top, molded edge, case of four thumb-molded graduated drawers, valanced skirt joining shaped French feet, orig oval brasses, old refinish, imperfections, c1800-10, 42" w, 18-1/4" d, 38-3/4" h **$1,765**

George III, bachelor's, mahogany, rect top over two short and three long drawers, bracket feet, 24-1/2" w, 18-1/2" d, 34" h **$2,600**

George III-style, mahogany, serpentine-front, thumb-molded top above four graduated and cockbeaded drawers, channel-carved bracket feet, 19th C, 43" w, 24" d, 43" h **$4,415**

Grain painted, attributed to Maine or New Hampshire, carved pine, central fan-carved drawer flanked by four small drawers above four long drawers, base with front and side shaping, restoration, late 18th C, 41-1/2" w, 18-3/4" d, 49-1/4" h .. **$4,410**

Hepplewhite

America, mahogany, straight front, four cockbeaded drawers, eagle-punched brasses, plain plant sides, bracket feet, shaped interiors, replaced top band, repairs to feet, lightly refinished, c1800, 42-1/2" w, 21" d, 37" h............................ **$1,550**

America, mahogany, poplar secondary wood, two-board top, four dovetailed drawers with beaded edges, older replaced emb brasses, scalloped fan inlay on lower apron, banding around lower case, French feet, refinished, restorations, replacements, c1810, 39" w, 19-3/4" d, 42-5/8" h **$1,475**

American, bow front, cherry, shaped top, four graduated drawers, flared feet, 19th C, 38-3/4" w, 22" d, 40" h **$3,600**

Country, refinished pine, red stain, solid bird's eye maple drawer fronts with natural finish, 4 dovetailed drawers, cut out feet and apron, old brass knobs, age cracks in front ends, 37-3/4" w, 35-3/4" h **$1,100**

Louis Philippe, walnut, later rect top, conforming case fitted with three drawers, shaped bracket feet, second quarter 19th C, 47" w, 20" d, 31" h **$425**

Queen Anne, Southeastern New England, painted oak, cedar, and yellow pine, rect top with applied edge, case of four drawers each with molded fronts, chamfered mitered borders, separated by applied horizontal moldings, sides with two recessed vertical molded panels above single horizontal panel, base with applied molding, four turned ball feet, old red paint, minor imperfections, c1700, 37-3/4" w, 20-1/2" w, 35" h **$26,450**

Renaissance, Italian, walnut, composed of antique elements, fitted with three long drawers, foliate and shield shaped carved drawer pulls, paw feet, 36" w, 17" d, 37" h......................**$2,450**

Sheraton

Cherry, two-board top with step down and molded edge, case with reeded pilasters and inset side panels, four dovetailed and beaded drawers, turned legs, ball feet, old refinishing, old replaced brass pulls, traces of red wash on front, 41-3/4" w, 21-3/4" d, 40-1/2" h ..**$990**

Cherry, walnut secondary wood, six dovetailed drawers, small variegated sq inlays at upper corners, turned legs with reeding on front two, similar reeding up front posts, paneled ends, refinished, replaced eagle brasses, top reset with small bow-tie shaped splice added below, minor edge restoration to drawers, 42-3/4" w, 18-3/4" w, 44-1/2" h..............................**$1,500**

Transitional, New England, cherry, overhanging rect top, conforming case, four graduated drawers with cockbeaded surrounds, serpentine skirt flanked by flaring veneered French feet, period brasses, refinished, late 18th or early 19th C, 45-3/4" w, 20-3/4" d, 36-1/2" h..................**$1,410**

Chest of drawers, Sheraton, cherry, two deep drawers over three long drawers, c1820, **$650.**

Photo courtesy of Wiederseim Associates, Inc.

Modern pieces with an antique look

Furniture makers have long copied each other's styles, and the 20th century furniture makers are continuing that practice. Collectors should be aware what some of today's well-made replica furniture may sell for. Here are some examples:

Breakfront secretary, Hendredon, Georgian-style, mahogany, shaped cornice over four glazed doors above secretary drawer, over two cabinet doors, flanked on each side by five graduated drawers, 26-1/2" w, 17-1/2" d, 87-1/2" h **$1,770**

Chest of drawers, Hendredon, dark brown, gold sponge dec finish simulating tortoise shell, four drawers, short block feet, flush mounted brass handles on drawers and sides of cases, branded signature inside drawers, price for pr, 28" w, 12-1/2" d, 28-1/4" h **$500**

Chest on chest, Virginia Crafters, walnut, oak and poplar secondary woods, urn and flame finials, broken arch top with carved rosettes, reeded columns, 11 drawers with carved shell on top drawer, ogee feet with scalloped returns, batwing brasses, branded signature on back, 40-1/4" w, 22-1/4" d, 90-1/2" h............**$1,610**

Credenza, Chippendale-style, Kittinger, mahogany and mahogany veneer, oak secondary wood, four dovetailed drawers down left, smaller center drawer with cabinet below, longer drawer over open compartment flanking on right with adjustable shelf, molded edge and base trip, branded label, emb metallic emblem in drawer, 81-1/2" l, 19-1/2" d, 30" h **$900**

Desk, Chippendale-style, Kittinger, mahogany and mahogany veneers, oak secondary wood, four dovetailed drawers on both sides, center drawer, thin applied moldings create decorative panels on sides and front, shaped bracket feet, molding around bases, emb metallic label, 72" w, 36-1/4" d, 30-1/2" h **$1,695**

Dining chairs, Baker, Regency-style, four side and two arm chairs...**$4,250**

Dining table, Regency-style, Baker, 20th C, satinwood cross banded mahogany, rect top, three leaves, double reeded pedestals, downswept legs, casters, 132" l extended, 48" w, 30" h **$2,585**

Settee, Windsor, continuous arm, by Steve, painted by Peter Deen, cherry, scrolled arms, spindle back, turned legs, stretchers, distressed green paint, 56-1/2" l, 17-1/2" d, 17-1/2" h seat, 29" h back................**$2,475**

Sugar chest, Sheraton-style, country, cherry, poplar secondary wood, hand made, two hinged lids, two dovetailed drawers, high turned feet, turned cherry pulls, interior divided into four compartments, small pieced repairs, 47-1/2" w, 20-1/4" d, 34-3/4" h **$900**

Table, lamp, Kittinger, mahogany, concave shaped top, one drawer, shelf in base, branded and metal labels inside dovetailed drawer, tapered legs, casters, 19" w, 18" d, 26" h.................**$250**

Windsor side chairs, set of six, painted red-brown, sgd "R. D. L." (Drew Lausch), painted by Peter Deen, 17-1/2" h seat, 37" h back **$4,675**

Chest on chest, Mid Atlantic Chippendale, walnut, broken arch bonnet over five short drawers, carved center fan, three long drawers, ogee bracket feet, c1770, **$9,200.**

Photo courtesy of Pook & Pook, Inc.

Victorian

American, oak, rect mirror, pair of handkerchief boxes, two small drawers over three graduated long drawers, emb design creates circular decoration on top three drawers, orig brass hardware, 40" w, 68" h **$375**

American, poplar, mahogany veneer facade, serpentine top drawer, two serpentine stepback drawers, five dovetailed drawers, applied beading, worn finish, 40" w, 19-3/4" d, 47" h **$330**

American, walnut, white marble top, 3 drawers, one hidden drawer in base, carved fruit and nut pulls, 39" w, 32" h **$700**

William and Mary

American, burl veneer, bachelor's, five dovetailed drawers, pull-out shelf, worn finish, veneer damage, replaced base molding, turned feet, and backboards, orig brasses, 30" w, 19" d, 35" h **$1,980**

Southern Massachusetts or Rhode Island,

tiger maple, graduated drawer construction, two over four drawers, applied moldings to top and bottom, turned turnip feet, old grunge finish, three escutcheon plates present, rest of hardware missing, some repair, 36-1/4" w, 18-1/4" d, 48" h **$2,950**

Chest of drawers, Victorian, mahogany, five drawers, top one with curved front, carved pilasters, animal foot, **$750.**
Photo courtesy of Dotta Auction Co., Inc.

Chest of drawers, Modern, Frank Lloyd Wright, three long drawers, orig finish, contemporary vintage, 37" x 56" x 20", **$1,400.**
Photo courtesy of David Rago Auctions, Inc.

Chests of drawers, other

Apothecary, painted blue, two drawers, 96" l **$2,900**

Bureau a Cylindre, Louis XV-style, gilt-bronze mounted rosewood and marquetry, rect top with pierced gallery above roll-top enclosing fitted interior, above single drawer, cabriole legs, allover dec with flowers and scrolling foliage, 29-1/2" w, 21" d, 42" h **$1,420**

Campaign, mahogany, pine secondary wood, brass trim, dovetailed case, int. with lift-out tray, one dovetailed drawer, some shrinkage to lid, 30-3/4" w, 18-1/4" d, 19" h **$385**

Chamber, Federal, attributed to the Seymour Workshop, Boston, mahogany inlaid, rect top with inlaid edge overhangs case with single tripartite drawer above six smaller drawers flanking central cabinet on arched inlaid skirt, four turned reeded and tapering legs, similar arched side skirts, upper drawer with oval central stringing reserve, all drawers are outlined in ebonized inlay, missing dressing mirror from int. drawer, minor imperfections, c1915, 44-3/4" w, 19-1/2" d, 34-1/4" h **$42,550**

Chest on chest

Biedermeier, walnut and ebonized, molded plinth cornice, five upper drawers, lower section with two drawers, bun feet, 41" w, 22" d, 64" h **$2,300**

Chippendale, RI, carved tiger maple, scrolled molded top with flame carved side finials, raised paneled faux drawers and six thumb-molded working drawers, lower case of four similar graduated drawers on molded base with ogee feet, some dark mahogany stain, some original brass, central finial is later addition, feet repairs, other imperfections, 1750-1796, 38-1/2" w, 18-7/8" d, 87" h .. **$23,500**

George III

Mahogany, rect cornice with molding and dentil trim, three short drawers over three graduated drawers, lower section with three graduated drawers, bracket feet, 31-1/2" w, 17-1/2" d, 59-1/2" h **$4,720**

Mahogany, rect molded and dentillated cornice above three short drawers, over three graduated drawers, lower section with three graduated drawers supported by bracket feet, 31-1/2" w, 17-1/2" d, 59-1/2" h **$4,720**

Queen Anne

Salem, Massachusetts, attributed to, tiger maple, upper case with molded cornice, five graduated thumb-molded drawers, lower case with one long drawer with two drawer façade, and one long drawer with three short drawer façade, centrally carved fan, four arris cabriole legs with high pad feet on platforms, joined by cyma-curved skirt centering scrolled drops, possibly old brasses, old refinish, minor imperfections, c1740-60, 38-3/4" w, 19-1/2" d, 73-3/4" h **$16,450**

Southern New Hampshire, maple, upper case with cove molded cornice, five graduated thumb-molded drawers, lower case with three graduated drawers, valanced frame joining four short cabriole legs on high pad on platform feet, old refinish, replaced brasses, drawers with chalk and pencil inscriptions, vestiges of old red paint, minor imperfections, late 19th C, 40-1/2" w, 20" d, 80" h **$11,750**

Chest on frame

Queen Anne, Connecticut, painted, flaring cornice with cove molding, case of thumb-molded drawers, arranged in two over four graduating pattern, frame with vigorously scrolling front and side skirts joined to cabriole legs with arris knees, arris disc feet, old red repaint, imperfections, 1740-70, 40" w, 23-1/4" d, 63-1/2" h **$9,200**

Queen Anne-style, English, walnut and burl veneer, mahogany secondary wood, case with four dovetailed drawers, brass teardrop pulls, cabriole legs, duck feet, 20th C, 19-1/4" x 33-1/2" base, 38-1/2" h **$825**

Chest over drawers

Chippendale, New England, painted, molded lift-top above double-arch molded case of two graduated false drawers and two working drawers, turned wooden pulls, high bracket feet centering cut-out pendant, orig red painted surface, 18th C, 37-3/4" w, 18" d, 45-1/2" h **$8,900**

Grain painted, Northern New England, pine, hinged top opens to storage cavity above two thumb-molded drawers, vigorously shaped front and side skirts, faux bois done with ochre and burnt umber, old brasses, minor imperfections, early 19th C, 39-3/4" w, 18-7/8" d, 39-7/8" h **$2,350**

William and Mary, New Jersey, cherry, poplar secondary wood, molded lift-lid, cotter-pin hinges, two faux upper drawer fronts, two full width dovetailed lower drawers, molded base, cut-out feet, incised brass Chinese drop pulls, shaped key escutcheons, replaced hardware, 42-1/2" w, 17-1/4" d, 44-1/2" h **$2,750**

Commode

Baroque, North Italian, walnut, molded rect top above frieze drawer and three long drawers, sides with fielded panels, bracket feet, early 18th C and later, 48" w, 23" d, 35-1/2" h **$5,100**

Biedermeier, birch and ebonized wood, rect top above four drawers flanked by columns, shaped skirt, bracket feet, price for pr, 34-3/4" w, 16-1/2" d, 35-1/2" h **$2,950**

Louis XV, tulipwood and kingwood parquetry inlaid, serpentine front, two short over three long serpentine drawers, flared feet, foliate cast mounts, mid-18th C, 50" w, 24" d, 32" h **$4,700**

Louis XV, Provincial, walnut, serpentine top, case fitted with two short and two long drawers, each carved with rocaille and channel dec, third quarter 18th C, 51" w, 24" d, 31" h..............................**$4,700**

Louis XV-style

Tulipwood and marquetry, gray shaped rect marble top over three graduated drawers, slightly splayed feet ending in gilt metal sabots, 44" d, 19-1/2" d, 34-1/4" h **$2,850**

Tulipwood and marquetry, tan and caramel rect mottled marble top above an apron of intertwined gilt-metal laurel garlands above two drawers, tapering legs ending in floral sabots, price for pr, 40-3/8" w, 18-7/8" d, 33-3/4" h **$21,240**

Louis XV/XVI-style transitional

Ormolu mounted marquetry, inlaid tulipwood, serpentine marble top, conforming case, two drawers and angular legs, floral inlay, 20th C, 36" w, 20" d, 36" h **$1,410**

Parquetry inlaid, reverse breakfronted marble top, conforming case fitted with three drawers, short angular cabriole feet, checkered crossband-

High chest, Chippendale, Pennsylvania, ogee cornice above Greek key molding, nine drawers flanked by fluted quarter columns, spurred ogee bracket feet, c1775, 39" w, 63-3/4" h, **$12,650.**
Photo courtesy of Pook & Pook, Inc.

Chest of drawers, other, lingerie chest, Louis XV-style, book-matched rosewood veneer with doré bronze mounts, bombe top with embossed leather drawer fronts, base with tambour doors, cabriole legs, 1890, 71" x 54" x 18", **$5,000.**
Photo courtesy of David Rago Auctions, Inc.

ing throughout, c1770, 47" w, 20" d, 34" h **$2,530**

Neoclassical, petit, mahogany and marquetry, molded rect top above three drawers decorated with griffins, sphinxes, and rinceaux, tapering square-section feet, 29" w, 18-1/2" d, 33-1/2" h **$2,600**

Regency, French, 18th C

Bronze and brass mounted kingwood parquetry, marble top, three drawers flanked by brass inset and fluted stiles, shaped feet, 30" w, 18" d, 30-1/2" h **$4,600**

Serpentine marble top, conforming kingwood case, brass fluting, two drawers, cabriole legs, 29" w, 19" d, 30" h **$4,700**

Gentleman's dressing chest

Regency, English, mahogany, bow-fronted case fitted with hinged top enclosing mirror, lower case fitted with two long drawers, flared feet, c1820, 36" w, 24" d, 35" h **$1,880**

Highboy

Chippendale, associated with John Goddard and Job Townsend, Newport, RI, carved mahogany, enclosed scrolled pediment centering fluted plinth surrounded by urns and flame finials above two applied plaques over two short and three long graduated thumb-molded drawers, set into lower case of one long and three short drawers above cyma- curved skirt, centered carved shell, frontal cabriole legs ending in ball and claw feet, similar rear legs ending in pad feet, old replaced brasses, refinished, repairs, 1760-80, 39" w, 20-1/2" d, 84" h **$36,550**

Chippendale-style, America, mahogany, broken arch pediment, flame finials, reeded quarter columns at corners, inset panels on either end of top, eight dovetailed drawers with brass pulls, gadrooning around base and edges of base and lower section, cabriole legs with scrolled returns, raised acanthus leaf carvings, claw and ball feet, old reddish brown finish, late 19th/early 20th C, 48-1/2" w, 24-1/4" d, 81" h **$1,200**

Queen Anne

America, cherry, poplar and pine secondary wood, top dovetailed case, circular fan at top, replaced molded cornice, seven graduated drawers on top, four drawers on base, base

with pegged construction, molded trim on dovetailed drawers, carved fan at lower center, scalloped aprons, shaped returns, well shaped cabriole legs, pad feet, mellow refinish, replaced bat wing brasses, pierced restorations to some drawer fronts, replaced returns and waist molding, 35" w top, 40" w base, 22" d, 71-1/2" h **$6,200**

Connecticut, attributed to, cherry and maple, broken arch pediment with three flame finials on fluted plinths, upper case with fan carved thumb-molded short drawer flanked by two shaped short drawers, four graduated long drawers, lower case with long drawer over two short drawers flanking fan carved drawer, carved scrolling skirt joining four cabriole legs, pad feet, replaced brasses and finials, old refinish, repairs and imperfections, c1760-80, 38-1/4" w, 19" d, 86" h **$24,675**

Dunlap School, New Hampshire, carved maple, cove-molded cornice over upper case of five graduated long drawers, lower case of three graduated thumb-molded long drawers, upper and lowermost drawers each fan carved, cyma-curved skirt centering scrolling drops, joining four cabriole legs with shaped returns, pad feet on platforms, dark stained surface, possibly orig brasses, minor imperfections, chalk inscriptions on drawer backs, c1770-80, 39-1/4" w, 21-1/2" d, 78-3/4" h **$14,100**

Massachusetts or southern New Hampshire, tiger maple, flaring cornice above four thumb-molded drawers on lower case of one long drawer and three small drawers, the central one with fan carving above three flat-headed arches, cabriole legs, high pad feet, replaced brasses, refinished, minor imperfections, 1760-80, 37-3/4" w at mid molding, 19-5/8" d at mid molding, 72" h **$16,450**

North Shore, Massachusetts, maple, flaring cove-molded cornice with concealed drawer above four thumb-molded graduated drawers in upper case over mid-molding, two long drawers, lower case visually divided into three drawers centering by carved fan over cyma-curved side skirts, cabriole

legs and high pad feet, old surface, old brasses, imperfections, 18th C, 35-1/2" w, 17-5/8" d, 71" h **$31,050**

Rhode Island, attributed to Abram Utter, tiger maple and cherry, top section with flat molded cornice, case of two thumb-molded short drawers, three long drawers, lower section with projecting molding above case of central thumb-molded short drawer flanked by deeper drawers, four arris cabriole legs, pad feet, all joined to deeply valanced skirt with applied cock beading and two turned drop pendants, replaced brasses, old refinish, minor imperfections, c1730-60, 37" w, 19-1/4" d, 63-3/4" h **$29,375**

William and Mary-style, cross banded walnut, upper section with two short over three long drawers, base with three drawers on trumpet turned legs, 18th C, 40" w, 21" d, 69" h **$1,850**

Linen chest

Georgian, shaped rect cornice over two doors opening to drawers above two short and two long drawers, splayed feet, 48" w, 21" d, 84" h **$3,100**

Hepplewhite, English, two pcs, mahogany and mahogany flame veneer, oak secondary wood, two door to with flame veneer panels, divided int. with five drawers on right side, brass bar and hooks on other, three dovetailed drawers in base with mahogany border inlay with beaded edges, shaped apron, French feet, refinished, old replaced brass pulls, fitted int. top drawer with four small drawers and eleven pigeon holes, pieced restorations, 49" w, 23" d, 83-1/2" h **$1,200**

Liquor chest

Early 19th century, mahogany veneer, chest with brass swing handles opens to reveal compartmented int., 12 blown molded wine and spirit bottles, each with inscribed paper labels and dec with gilt flowers, bowknots, and borders about the neck and shoulders, lift out tray fitted with tumblers, funnel and stemware with similar gilt decoration, one tumbler cracked, some veneer loss, 17" w, 12-1/2" d, 11-1/2" h **$1,410**

Lowboy

Queen Anne, Rhode Island, maple, pine secondary wood, case dovetailed at rear, pegged at sides, old replaced two-board curly maple top, four dovetailed drawers with beaded edges, batwing brasses, scalloped aprons, cabriole legs, slipper feet, refinished, small insect holes, restorations with some alterations, 32-1/2" w, 22-1/2" d, 30-1/4" h **$1,760**

William and Mary style, red japanned, serpentine black marble top, conforming case fitted with five small drawers, shaped kneehole, cabriole legs, pad feet, price for pr, early 20th C, 28-1/2" w, 17" d, 29-1/2" h **$3,400**

Mule chest

New England, poplar, old dark red wash, rect lid, single board ends, two dovetailed drawers in base, well shaped serpentine bracket feet, orig wood pulls, glued split in lid, replaced hinges, added supports, 45-3/4" l, 20-3/4" d, 44" h **$850**

Spice

Ohio, attributed to, walnut, poplar secondary wood, mortised and paneled front door, small brass pull, three drawers with orig turned walnut pulls, turned feet, 14-1/2" w, 12-1/4" d, 18-3/4" h **$2,400**

Pennsylvania, walnut, dovetailed, cove-molded cornice, raised panel hinged door, opens to int. of 11 small drawers, brass pulls, molded base, old surface, 1780-1800, 15-1/2" w, 11" d, 18-1/4" h **$14,950**

Sugar chest

Middle Atlantic states, attributed to, inlaid cherry, hinged lid with molded edge, interior cavity with single (missing) divider over facade with stringing in outline, oval inlaid central reserve and quarter corner inlays, restoration, early 19th C, 32-1/4" w, 16-1/2" d, 34-3/4" h **$12,925**

Tall

Federal, New England, tiger maple, cove molded top, case with six thumb-molded drawers, central fan carved drop pendant flanked by high bracket feet, orig brasses, old refinish, repairs, late 18th C, 41" w, 54-5/8" h **$8,625**

Cradles

Chippendale-style, birch, canted sides, scalloped headboard, turned posts and rails, refinished, 37-1/2" l **$400**

Country

America, tiger maple, dovetailed, heart cut-outs, large rockers, 36" l, 26" w, 16" h **$675**

New England, painted pine, arched hood continuing to shaped and carved dovetailed sides, rockers, old light green paint, old repairs, 18th C, 40" l **$300**

Pennsylvania, dovetailed, refinished curly maple, cut-out hearts, age cracks and shrinkage, late 18th C, 41" l **$550**

Eastlake, walnut, paneled headboard, footboard, and sides, scrolling crest above short turned spindles, platform support, orig finish, dated, 1875 .... **$495**

Rustic, twig construction, rocker base, unsigned, 33" l, 22" d, 22" h **$120**

Windsor, New England, bamboo turned spindles, worn finish, c1800-20 .... **$850**

Victorian, painted wrought wire and cast iron, scrolled trestle base, later int. inset rect marble plaque, 19th C, 40" l, 37" h **$940**

Cupboards

Armoire

Art Deco, France, sycamore and fruitwood, interior fitted with top shelf over divided compartment, hardware fitted for wardrobe, flanked by two shelves, lollipop-shaped key, c1928, 51-1/4" w, 19" d, 71" h **$1,650**

Arts & Crafts, English, single-door, overhanging top supported by corbels, mirror, emb copper panels of stylized flowers, unmarked, refinished, new back and shelves, one corbel missing, 40" w, 18" d, 75" h **$1,050**

Classical, New York, mahogany, bold projecting molded Roman arch cornice, two paneled doors flanked by tapered veneered columns, ogee bracket feet, c1835, 74" w, 31" d, 94" h **$3,200**

Empire-style, Continental, mahogany, shaped cornice above two paneled doors opening to shelves, ribbed lunette-shaped feet, early 19th C, 42" w, 17" d, 74" h **$1,610**

Tall chest, Queen Anne, Chester County, Pennsylvania, Octorara, walnut, molded cornice, three over two over four lipped drawer configuration, original brasses, high removable Spanish feet, c1740, 37" w, 60" h, **$19,800.**
Photo courtesy of Wiederseim Associates, Inc.

Cradle, dovetailed, scrolled rockers, **$350.**
Photo courtesy of Alderfer Auction Co.

Cradle, Victorian, stained pine, 30" x 41" x 20", **$175.**
Photo courtesy of David Rago Auctions, Inc.

Cupboard, corner, Victorian, cherry, three piece, top section with heavy molded cornice, carved squared capitals at corners, single door with carved arches in corners, brass trim, four-shelf interior, mid section with mirrored back, base with pair of cupboard doors with matching arch and brass trim, **$950.**
Photo courtesy of Dotta Auction Co., Inc.

Cupboard, corner, Pennsylvania, walnut, single arched glazed door over two paneled doors, H-hinges, bracket feet, dovetailed case, butterfly shelves, replaced feet, some replaced glass, c1820-35, 31" corner, 82" h, **$2,400.**
Photo courtesy of Alderfer Auction Co.

Armoire, Louis XV provincial, cherry, molded edge crown, cove molding, chamfered corners, recessed panel door, 18th C, 74" x 40" x 36", **$1,900.**
Photo courtesy of Sloans & Kenyon Auctioneers and Appraisers.

Louis XV/XVI-style, transitional, kingwood and parquetry, molded marble top with serpentine sides, pair of doors, each with two shaped and quarter-veneered flush panels, serpentine sides, coated stiles with gilt-brass chutes, sq-section cabriole legs joined by shaped skirt, stamped "Dubreuil," 19th C, 44" w, 18-1/2" d, 59" h...................... **$950**

Restoration, New York, mahogany, flat top with cornice molding, two doors, birds' eye maple lined int., concealed drawer below, ribbed blocked feet, c1830, 56" w, 19-1/2" d, 90" h....................... **$2,800**

Victorian, American, walnut, bold double ogee molded cornice, two arched paneled doors, shelved int., plinth base, ogee bracket feet, c1840, 62" w, 24" d, 89" h...... **$1,400**

Bee keeper's hutch, Canadian, pine, orig red and black painted top panel, paneled door on lower front, door on either end, drop front covers interior workshelf, hinged lid, pegged construction, lid marked "Patent Union, Bee Hive, W. Phelps Pat." 47" w, 19" d, 43-1/4" h **$750**

Chifforobe, Art Deco, herringbone design waterfall veneer, arched center mirror, dropped center section, four deep drawers flanked by tall cupboard doors, shaped apron, 1935............ **$450**

Cupboard, Court, Italian Renaissance revival, upper section with molded cornice over series of small drawers, central prospect drawer resting on lower section, two arched panel cupboard doors, classical figures and lion details, 19th c, 82" h x 44" w, **$6,325.**
Photo courtesy of Pook & Pook, Inc.

Chimney, country, pine, old blue-gray paint, picture frame molding around front of case, single door, beaded panel, brass pull, four int. shelves, age splits, 29" w, 12-1/2" d, 55-1/4" h
.... **$575**

Corner

Blind paneled doors, Kentucky, walnut, bracket feet..................... **$3,000**

One piece, Chippendale, Southern states, pine, heavy projecting cornice molding above arched molded surround, flanking similarly shaped raised panel doors opening to two shelves above two additional fielded panel doors, flanked by fluted pilasters, opening to single serpentine shelf, refinished, hardware replaced, repairs, 1760s, 64" w, 30" d, 93-3/4" h **$7,475**

One piece, paneled pine, New England, flat ogee molded cornice, arched opening flanks three painted scalloped shelves, two fielded panel cupboard doors, single int. shelf, old refinish on ext., old red color on shelves, 19th C, 50" w, 20" d, 88" h
.... **$4,255**

Two pieces, cherry, two doors, orig six wavy glass panes over two doors with four tin panels punch dec with cornflower motif, replacement wooden knobs, repairs, restoration, refinished **$1,425**

Two pieces, Pennsylvania, softwood, molded cornice, reeded stiles, arched top glazed door, serpentine shelves with spoon notches, two dovetailed drawers, two lower paneled doors, molded bracket base, dry blue painted surface, white door, black painted interior, 49" w, 30" d, 89-1/2" h, ex-Elgin....**$29,700**

Court, European, oak, two-pc, mortised construction, top section with two doors and central panel

Incised diamonds and pinwheels, free standing turned pilasters on either side, scrollwork with date "16MIVI" below cornice, two doors with three inset panels each on lower case doors and ends separated by molded T-shaped cross pieces, well executed replaced scrolled wrought iron butterfly hinges, old dark finish, restorations, old alterations, age splits, 63" w, 19-1/4" d, 62-1/2" h.....**$2,950**

Relief flowers, scrolled vining, matching vining below cornice, leaf and arch carvings across center, three inset panels each on lower case doors and ends separated by molded T-shaped cross pieces, well executed replaced scrolled wrought iron butterfly hinges, old dark finish, restorations, old alterations, 49-1/2" w, 20-1/8" d, 67" h....**$1,200**

Desk top, New England, pine, old grain painted dec, two solid doors with relief carved vertical panels, brass hinges, moldings at top and bottom, shaped feet are extensions of case, 10 cubby holes in int., orig green paint on ext. and int., 29" w, 12" d, 27-1/4" h
.....**$1,750**

Dresser, Provincial, English, oak, plate rack with four shelves flanked by architectural uprights, two paneled doors centered by three drawers, bracket feet, 18th C, 83" w, 19" d, 71" h
.....**$4,720**

Hanging

Carlisle, Cumberland, County, Pennsylvania, poplar, molded cornice, raised paneled door, int. shelf, lip molded dovetailed drawer, bold scalloped cut-outs, stained to resemble walnut, restoration to cornice, 27" w, 11-1/2" d, 35" h...**$7,975**

Country, decorated, dovetailed case, painted green, brick red, brown, and white dec on sponged ground, initialed and dated "F.P.S. 1855," molded cornice and base, two dovetailed drawers below two doors, two

int. shelves, pierced restorations, areas of insect damage, 28-3/4" w, 10-3/4" d, 29-3/4" h..............**$750**

English, Chippendale, corner, oak, pine secondary wood, cove molded cornice, dovetailed case, single door with beaded edges, geometric mullions with old wavy glass, molded base, three int. shelves, old brown finish, old repairs, 30-1/4" w, 16-1/2" d, 43" h.....................**$2,530**

Pennsylvania, softwood, painted red, molded cornice, raised carved circular trim, serpentine molded door, interior shelf, lip molded dovetailed drawer, molded base, restoration to door, 27-1/2" w, 14" d, 31-1/4" h
.....**$3,025**

Jelly, country, central Pennsylvania, poplar, old salmon paint, sq nail construction, gallery top, two paneled doors, well-shaped apron, bracket feet, three shelved int., wear, 43-3/4" w, 18-1/2" d, 54" h.....................**$1,380**

Kas, Long Island, New York, cherry, pine, and polar, architectural cornice molding, two raised panel thumb-molded doors flanked by reeded pilasters, applied moldings, single drawer, painted detachable disc and stretcher feet, replaced hardware, refinished, restored, c1730-80, 65-1/2" w, 26-1/4" d, 77-1/4" h.....**$4,500**

Kitchen, orig blue paint, six center drawers with porcelain pulls, two side bins, one bin lid sgd "Ezra Woodside Montare, April 20, 1905," cutting board, continuous scalloped face board covering lower front and feet, back shaped like picket fence, 72" l, 21" d, 54" h.....**$7,200**

Linen press, Federal, Boston, mahogany veneer, three parts, veneered entablature with central rect outlined in stringing above veneered frieze, pair of recessed panel doors which open to five pull-out drawers with shaped sides, lower case with molding and three cockbeaded drawers, flaring high bracket feet, inlaid escutcheons, orig brasses, feet restored, surface imperfections, 1820-25, 48" w, 22-1/4" h, 83-1/2" h
.....**$6,900**

Milk, Pennsylvania, primitive, softwood, molded edge, vertical beaded board door, wrought iron strap hinges with penny ends, cut-out block feet, three interior shelves, red painted surface, 38-1/2" w, 15" d, 58" h
.....**$4,400**

Pewter

Country, one pc, cherry and walnut, beveled cornice with flat top, four shelves flanked by tapered sideboards, notched aprons on ends, two doors in base, old refinishing, originally built-in, edge wear, repairs, 36" w, 16" d, 81-1/2" h.............**$920**

New England, two part, dark maple and cherry, cornice molding above molded sides and plate rails, stepped out surface, three drawers above recessed panel cupboard doors, single shelved interiors, sq feet, straight skirt, turned wooden pulls, restored, 58-3/4" w, 17-1/2" d, 79" h.....**$4,500**

Pennsylvania, walnut, scalloped cornice, three open shelves, lollipop one board side, two cupboard doors with batwing hinges, worn and scrubbed patina, c1780.......**$40,000**

Pie safe

Georgia, pine and cherry, six tin panels, punched sunflower and heart motifs, double door cupboard base
.....**$4,800**

Kentucky, orig red grain paint, pegged construction, six punched tins, punched circular motif, as found condition.....**$1,200**

Southeastern United States, walnut, rect top above along drawer, two hinged cupboard doors each with two pierced tin panels with designs of hearts and initials "J.B." flanked by leafy branches, ends with three conforming decorated panels, sq tapering legs, refinished, minor imperfections, early 19th C, 39-1/2" w, 17" d, 49-1/2" h....**$5,300**

Pie safe, walnut and punched tin, galleried top, two drawers over spread eagle over punched tin doors, turned legs, 19th C, **$1,300.**
Photo courtesy of Wiederseim Associates, Inc.

Cupboard, wall, two-piece, poplar, original red paint, white porcelain knobs, raised paneled upper door, scalloped shelved interior, two drawers and single paneled door in base, feet replaced, early 19th C, 88" h, **$2,350.**
Photo courtesy of Wiederseim Associates, Inc.

Cupboard, wall, New England, mahogany, secretary top with adjustable shelves, two top doors over base with two drawers over two lower doors, replaced hardware, missing return molding on base, c1830-50, 54" w, 18" d, 93-1/2" h, **$1,000.**
Photo courtesy of Alderfer Auction Co.

Tennessee, cherry, 12 tin panels, punched fylfots............**$4,250**

Schrank, Pennsylvania, poplar, decorated, orig paint, sponged brown, salmon, green, and blue, two panels dec with maker's name and date, Philip-Man, 1796-28 Mey (sic), dentil cornice, reeded quarter columns, ogee feet, ex-Clark Garrett, 62" w, 70" h **$300,000**

Slant back, New England, pine, flat molded cornice above beaded canted front flanking shelves, projecting base with single raised panel door, old refinish, doors missing from top, imperfections, late 18th C, 37-1/2" w, 18" d, 73" h **$2,300**

Spice, northern Europe, wall-type, painted, flat molded cornice, hinged cupboard door, molded recessed panel opening, compartmentalized int., molded base, old dark green paint bordered by red, int. drawers missing, imperfections, last half 18th C, 16" w, 8" d, 17" h **$1,500**

Step-back, wall

America, Empire, mahogany and mahogany veneer, molded cornice top, three eight-light doors, adjustable shelves, cabinet base with three cupboard doors, sliding center doors in top and base, c1830, 73-1/2" w, 21" d, 93" h........**$11,100**

Pennsylvania, attributed to, one piece, curly maple, mellow golden color, two mortised and paneled doors on top, one int. shelf, two board top with high pie shelf, five dovetailed drawers in base in three-over-two configuration, turned legs with excellent figure, replaced brass pulls, one glued break on the lower corner of door, 44-1/2" w, 19-1/2" d, 60-1/4" h **$8,525**

Pennsylvania or Ohio, attributed to, painted cherry, flaring cornice molding above fluted frieze, pair of glazed doors open to two-shelf int., flanked by fluting above stepped out surface, two drawers over two recessed panel doors opening to single shelf int., recessed panel sides, four short turned legs, all over red paint, brass pulls, imperfections, 1830-40, 50" w, 21-1/2" d, 88" h..................**$18,400**

Storage, Montgomery County, Pennsylvania, poplar, dovetailed case, molded top, two paneled doors, French bracket feet, int. shelves, scraped finish down to red, replaced

back boards, moldings, 49" w, 18" d, 72" h...**$1,100**

Wall

America, two pieces, pine and walnut, old mustard paint and faint brown grain dec, traces of earlier red in some areas, brown sponging to three curved front drawers and on raised panels of lower doors, cove molded cornice, two-door top with six panes of glass in each door, vertical central panel with three panels, all top panes are tombstone shaped, chamfered corners, turned feet with applied half turned pilasters, blue painted int. with cut-outs for spoons, 61" w, 21" d, 85-3/4" h **$5,500**

Canadian, Hepplewhite, two pieces, pine, beveled and cove molded cornice, two doors in top section with two panes of glass each, two int. shelves with red and white paint, molded waist, five drawers in base with incised beading, turned wooden pulls, well scalloped base, high bracket feet, refinished, evidence of earlier red paint, edge chips, couple of glued splits to feet, 48" w, 23-1/2" d, 78-1/2" h.................**$935**

Federal, New England, second quarter painted, two parts, paneled, cornice molding, chamfered front corners, stepped-out surface with three scratch-beaded drawers above two paneled doors, single shelved int., molded base, bracket feet, orig red surface, turned wood pulls probably original, repairs, 19th C, 57-1/2" w, 23-1/4" d, 85" h.....................**$6,500**

Jacobean, oak and part painted, two parts, upper section with pegs and shelves, projecting lower section with two doors, each with geometric and floral carving, 64" w, 20" d, 80" h **$3,000**

New England, possibly Vermont, hooded, lollipop one board sides, three open shelves on top, single paneled cupboard door in base, dark green paint.................**$11,500**

New York, upstate, painted, flat cornice, case with two hinged doors each with two recessed vertical panels, shelved int., old gray paint, imperfections, early 19th C, 43" w, 18" d, 78" h.............................**$1,000**

Wardrobe

Chippendale, English, mahogany, pine secondary wood, cove molded cornice, two-door front with three raised panels each, three

inset panels on each side, scalloped bracket feet, molded base, brass lock escutcheons, refinished, formerly fitted with shelves and rod, restorations, replacements, 53-3/4" w, 24" d, 78" h..........**$1,500**
French, walnut, walnut veneer applied in herringbone pattern on ends, open pediment crest, double door mirrors with pillars on each side, late 19th C, 50" w, 98-1/2" h **$1,000**

Wardrobe, mahogany, signed "Lejambre," Philadelphia, griffin and floral carved frieze, two mirrored doors, base with two carved drawers, 75" w, 25" d, 102" h, $4,675.
Photo courtesy of Wiederseim Associates, Inc.

Typical Parts of a Desk

Desk, Arts & Crafts, Gustav Stickley, postcard desk, letterholder backsplash, two drawers, paneled back and sides, recessed bookshelf below, original finish, early red decal, 39-1/2" l, 22" d, 36" h, $1,610.
Photo courtesy of David Rago Auctions, Inc.

Desks

Aesthetic Movement, Herter Brothers, Washburn Commission, mahogany, fall front, top section: shelf with gallery top supported by turned and blocked posts, back panel with dec gold threaded material; middle section: slant lid, two supporting pull-out arms, central panel of marquetry inlaid with garland of flowers ending in bows, int. with two drawers, five cubbyholes, supported by two turned front legs, two bottom section with shelf and paneled back, missing orig writing surface, raised panel back, needs restoration, commissioned by Hon. William Drew Washburn for Minnesota Greek Revival house, copy of orig bill of sale, 30" w, 20" w, 53-1/2" h....................................**$9,000**

Art Deco, Leopold Corp, Burlington, Iowa, walnut veneered, semi-oval top over center drawer flanked by pull-out writing surface and two drawers, bronze handles, light brown finish, "Charles S. Nathan Office Equipment New York" distributor's metal tag in drawer, veneer loss, wear, 66-1/8" l, 36-1/8" d, 29" h............**$900**

Arts & Crafts, Stickley, Gustav, Syracuse, New York, lady's, model No. 720, cabinet with four vertical shelves, two small drawers, three horizontal shelves, rect top, two short drawers, paper Craftsman label, c1912, 38" w, 23" d, 37" h................................**$1,725**

Chippendale

Connecticut, mahogany, block front, slant front lid, fitted tiered int. with nine dovetailed drawers, pigeonholes, two pull-out letter drawers with fluted columns, flame-carved

Desk, Arts & Crafts, Gustav Stickley, nine drawers, chamfered sides, bottom mortised through the sides and fastened with keyed through-tenons, old restored finish, 30" x 53" x 30", $3,500.
Photo courtesy of David Rago Auctions, Inc.

finials and door with blocking and fan carving, dovetailed case, four dovetailed drawers, conforming apron, bracket feet, replaced brasses, old refinishing, feet replaced, repairs to case, late 18th C, 41-3/4" w, 21-1/2" d, 42-3/4" h..............**$3,850**
Massachusetts, slant lid, mahogany, lid opens to int. of central fan, concave carved drawer, two conforming drawers flanked by document drawers with half-baluster fronts, four valanced compartments, two drawers, cockbeaded case of four graduated drawers, ogee bracket feet, center drop pendant, old brass bail pulls, refinished, imperfections, c1770-80, 40" w, 20" d, 43" h..**$9,400**
New England, cherry, slant lid opens to an interior of open valanced compartments above small blocked drawers flanking central open compartment, thumb-molded graduated drawers, molded bracket base with central pendant, replaced brass, old refinish, repairs, late 18th C, 38" w, 19-3/4" d, 40-3/4" h................**$2,500**
New England, maple, pine secondary wood, old dark brown surface, slant lid, interior with nine pigeon holes over five small drawers, dovetailed case, four dovetailed graduated drawers with beaded edges, molded base, bracket feet, old replaced batwing brasses, old repairs, late 18th C, 36" w, 17-1/2" d, 41-1/4" h......**$4,900**
North Shore, Massachusetts, mahogany carved oxbow serpentine slant lid, int. of blocked fan-carved prospect door, conformingly curved three-door interior flanked by four valanced compartments and three

Slant front desk, Chippendale, walnut, slant front, document drawer, pigeon holed interior, c1780, 36" w, 41" h, **$2,500.**

Photo courtesy of Wiederseim Associates, Inc.

Slant front desk, Pennsylvania Chippendale, walnut, raised tombstone panel prospect door, bracket feet, c1765, 4-3/4" x 38-1/2" w, **$4,830.**

Photo courtesy of Pook & Pook, Inc.

Slant front desk, Chippendale, mahogany, fall front, fitted interior with central door, six letter slots, six drawers, four graduated drawers, bracket feet, replaced hardware, splits to veneer, **$1,100.**

Photo courtesy of Alderfer Auction Co.

Desk, Arts & Crafts, Gustav Stickley, No. 518, drop-front, chamfered sides and front panel, two lower shelves, iron strap hinges and escutcheon, orig finish with some wear, stain on top, red decal on back, remnants of paper label, **$9,500.**

Photo courtesy of David Rago Auctions, Inc.

Desk, Biedermeier style, matched veneers, fall front over pair of doors, detailed interior, **$950.**

drawers, cockbeaded case of four graduated drawers, carved cabriole legs, claw and ball feet centering shell and scroll carved pendant, replaced brasses, refinished, imperfections, late 18th C, 41" w, 23" d, 44" h **$5,875**

Rhode Island, cherry, slant front, stepped int. of small drawers, central one with shaping, case of beaded graduated drawers, ogee bracket feet, orig brasses, old refinish, restoration, late 18th C, 39" w, 20" d, 43" h **$3,800**

Virginia, attributed to, carved walnut, slant lid opens to stepped interior of six valanced small compartments flanked by pinwheel carved end-drawers above small drawers, case of graduated drawers with cockbeaded surrounds, molded bracket base, brasses appear early, refinished, repairs, late 18th C, 40" h, 19" d, 41-3/4" h **$3,820**

Drop-front, Philadelphia, tiger maple, mahoganized finish, 1830 .... **$6,000**

Eastlake, lady's, walnut, two parts, top section sits on pegs, top: mirror with two columns supported shelves, fancy carving, pressed dec; base section: double hinged writing surface with dec floral carving, writing surface with two panels of green felt, lifts to reveal compartment desk int. with two drawers, one side fitted with two long drawers, gallery shelf in base, dec applied pieces, shoe foot base, metal casters, 31-1/2" w, 19" d, 57" h **$1,150**

Edwardian, kneehole, mahogany, rect cross banded top with central oval medallion, front canted corners, long frieze drawer, two banks of three drawers, center cupboard door, foliate marquetry dec, c1900, 37-1/2" w, 31" h **$600**

Edwardian-style, marquetry inlaid mahogany, U-shaped superstructure fitted with drawers and doors, serpentine case fitted with drawers, sq tapered legs, 20th C, 35" w, 24" d, 37" h **$2,645**

Empire, butler's, cherry and curly maple, poplar secondary wood, scrolled crest with turned rosettes, pull-out desk drawer with arched pigeon holes and three dovetailed drawers, three dovetailed drawers with applied edge beading, turned and carved pilasters, paneled ends, paw feet, old finish, some edge damage, 44-1/2" w, 23" d, 57-3/4" h **$1,925**

Federal

America, butler's, mahogany and mahogany veneer, rect top, case of three cockbeaded short drawers, pull-out desk with cockbeaded drawer façade flanked by wide drawers opening to prospect door over short drawer flanked by document drawer, two short drawers, two compartments, one long drawer, all-over pull-out shelf, three graduated cockbeaded long drawers, cut-out feet joined by shaped skirt, old refinish, 47" w, 19" d, 45-1/2" h **$1,300**

Massachusetts, eastern, tambour, mahogany and mahogany veneer inlaid, upper section with tambour doors flanked by pilasters with chevron inlay enclosing two short drawers over three valanced compartments centering prospect door with inlaid stringing enclosing two short drawers over double valanced compartments, lower section with folding lid over case of two cockbeaded string inlaid long drawers, legs inlaid with bellflowers and stringing tapering to inlaid cuffs, old replaced brasses, old refinish, blue painted int., repairs and imperfections, c1800-10, 38" w, 19-1/4" d, 34-1/2" h............. **$11,750**

Massachusetts, possibly Worcester County, inlaid mahogany and cherry, slant thumb molded lid centering inlaid satinwood diamond panel bordered by rosewood crossbanding and stringing, fitted int. of eight drawers and seven valanced compartments, swelled case of four graduated cockbeaded drawers bordered by crossbanding on inlaid base, flaring French feet, replaced brasses, old refinish, minor imperfections, chalk inscriptions, c1800, 38-3/4" w, 21" d, 44" h........... **$4,450**

New England, mahogany and mahogany veneer inlaid, top section shaped gallery above flat molded cornice, two glazed doors enclosing compartments and drawer, flanking door and small drawer; projecting base with fold-out writing surface, two cockbeaded short drawers, two graduated long drawers, four sq tapering legs, inlaid cross-banding, old refinish, some restoration, inscribed "22 Geo. L. Deblois Sept. 12th 1810," early 19th C, 37-1/8" w, 20" d, 51-1/2"..... **$3,000**

New Hampshire, slant lid, wavy birch, lid opens to two-stepped int. case of drawers with four cockbeaded surrounds, serpentine skirt, tall arched feet, orig brasses, old refinish, repairs, early 19th C, 37-1/2" w, 18-1/4" d, 45" h.... **$2,760**

New York State, mahogany veneer inlaid, slant lid and three graduated drawers outlined in stringing with ovolo corners, int. of veneer and outline stringing on drawers, valanced compartments, prospect door opening to inner compartments and drawers, flanking document drawers, orig brasses, old surface, veneer cracking loss and patching, other surface imperfections, early 19th C, 41-1/2" w, 21-1/2" d, 44" h..................... **$2,550**

Pennsylvania, walnut inlaid, slant front, lid and cockbeaded draw-

ers outlined in stringing, base with band of contrasting veneers, int. of small drawers above valanced compartments, scrolled dividers flanking prospect door which opens to two small drawers, three drawers, old refinish, repairs, early 19th C, 40" w, 20" d, 44-1/2" h.......... **$3,550**

George III, English

Mahogany, oak secondary wood, kneehole, molded top, single cabinet door in center, single long drawer with divided interior over two banks of three dovetailed drawers with beaded edges and old brasses, bracket feet, molded base, old refinishing, some splits, restoration to veneer, 40-1/4" w, 20-1/2" d, 33" h **$2,650**

Mahogany, rect top with partial gallery above a long drawer, kneehole flanked by two short drawers, ring-turned legs, brass casters, 34" w, 20" d, 31" h................................ **$700**

George III-style, pedestal, walnut, gilt-tooled brown leather top, central frieze drawer, two pedestals fitted on both sides with drawers and paneled doors, 65-1/2" w, 35" d, 30" h **$2,585**

Hepplewhite, oxbow slant front, maple and birch, pine secondary wood, int. with ten small drawers with brass knobs, seven pigeon holes, four graduated dovetailed drawers with beaded edges, old replaced oval brasses, high French feet, scalloped returns, band of inlay around base, refinished, restorations to scalloped valances and lid supports, 39-1/2" w, 18" d, 47" h **$2,100**

Louis XV, tulipwood and gilt bronze mounted, top having central writing stand, flanked by two hinged doors opening to storage, central frieze drawer; lower section: black lacquered shaped rect top with Chinoiserie scene, central faux drawer, sides each having single drawer raised on cabriole legs with gilt bronze mounts ending in sabots, stamped "Durand," 25" w, 15-1/2" d, 31-3/8" h **$11,800**

Louis XV-style, parquetry, shaped rect top with inset red leather top, single drawer, cabriole legs, gilt bronze sabots, 23-1/2" w, 20" d, 27-5/8" h **$3,800**

Provincial, English, rect top, central drawer, shaped octagonal standards, H-form stretcher, octagonal block feet, early 19th C...................... **$1,660**

Secretary desk, George III burled walnut, two parts, double dome top, blocked amphitheatered interior, bracket feet, early 18th C, **$12,650.**
Photo courtesy of Pook & Pook, Inc.

Desk, Plantation, American, fold-down front, molded cornice, large ledger shelf, fitted interior with four pigeonholes over larger valanced section, four vertical dividers, single drawer, turned legs, 19th C, **$750.**
Photo courtesy of Dotta Auction Co., Inc.

Desk, Modern, Heywood Wakefield, Wheat finish, stamped label, matching chair and two end tables, price for grouping, 30" x 36" x 21" desk, **$650.**
Photo courtesy of David Rago Auctions, Inc.

Dry sink, Country, pine, dovetailed well top, two drawers over pair of cupboard doors, straight bracket feet, 19th C, **$775.**

Photo courtesy of Wiederseim Associates, Inc.

Dry sink, Pennsylvania, painted, mixed woods, full length hinged lid, two drawers over two scrolled cupboard doors, white porcelain knobs, original cast iron latches, lid raised, **$375.**

Photo courtesy of Dotta Auction Co., Inc.

Dry sink, Pennsylvania, dovetailed well, single door, continuous sides form feet, refinished, c1840, 47" w, 20" d, 34-1/2" h, **$750.**

Photo courtesy of Alderfer Auction Co.

Queen Anne

America, cross banded walnut, slant-lid, rect top, fitted interior of stepped pigeonholes and drawers, split lower case fitted with two short over three long graduated drawers, bracket feet, early 18th C, 35-3/4" w, 23" d, 39-1/2" h.....**$5,885**

Northern Maine, maple, slant front, int. with valanced compartments above small drawers, end drawers separated by scrolled dividers, case of three thumb-molded drawers, molded bracket base with central drop pendant, old darkened surface, 19th C, 35-1/2" w, 17-1/2" d, 40-1/4" h **$5,175**

Vermont, tiger maple and cherry, slant front, int. with central fan-carved drawer, two valanced compartments flanked by molded document drawers, four valanced compartments, three drawers, case with four thumb-molded graduated drawers, bracket feet, replaced brasses, old refinish, imperfections, and repairs, c1750, 36" w, 18" d, 41-1/2" h.............**$3,220**

Regency, English, lady's, cylinder, mahogany, tambour top, fitted int., slide-out writing surface, over two drawers, lyre base, 30" h writing surface, c1850, 35-1/2" w, 20" d, 38" h **$3,000**

Renaissance Revival, American, fall front, turned spindle cresting, paneled fall front and fitted interior, angular trestle base, 26-1/2" w, 16" d, 53" h **$850**

Rococo-style, Italian, painted, slant-lid, fitted interior, serpentine case fitted with three conforming drawers, flared bracket feet, 35" w, 17" d, 40-1/2" h....................................**$4,465**

School master's, Pennsylvania, walnut, interior drawers and compartments, molded lid, dovetailed skirt drawer, tapered legs, early 19th C, 34-1/2" w, 24" d, 37-1/2" h.......**$4,400**

Sheraton

American, stand-up, walnut, slant front, four graduated drawers, turned feet, ivory escutcheons, Sandwich glass pulls, flanked by paint dec columns, simply fitted int. with secret drawers, one pull replaced, repair to lid, hinges replaced, int. refitted, 35" h writing surface, 35" w, 43" h **$1,200**

Country, slant lid, cherry, pine and poplar secondary wood, two dovetailed drawers behind slant lid, two large compartments, three dovetailed drawers in base, turned feet, orig oval brasses with emb pineapple

in basket design, refinished, alternations, restored break on one back leg, 37" w, 19-1/4" d, 38-1/2" h........**$990**

Victorian

Bamboo, lacquered rect top with leather inset over long drawer and four vertical drawers, 35" w, 20" d, 29" h....**$720**

Walnut, hinged rect top, fitted int., single frieze drawer, turned legs, 28" w, 20-1/4" d, 33" h.............**$400**

William and Mary, attributed to CT, tulipwood and oak, fall-front lid with raised panel, int. of four compartments, three drawers, well with sliding closure, double arched molded front, base with long drawer, four turned legs, joined by valanced skirt, shaped flat cross stretchers, turned feet, replaced brasses, old refinish, minor imperfections, early 18th C, 24-3/4" w, 15" d, 42-1/2" h.....**$17,250**

William and Mary-style, American, oak, seven dovetailed drawers, applied moldings, molded edge top, brass tear drop pulls, old finish, turned legs and stretchers, one piece of molding missing from drawer, 20th C, 27-3/4" x 59" x 31" h................................**$500**

Dry sinks

Curly maple, rect well, work surface on right with small drawer, two poplar wood cupboard doors, short bracket feet, hardwood edge stripes, minor repairs, refinished, 55" w, 34-1/2" h...................................**$2,400**

Grain painted, New England, rect well with tin lining, rounded splashboard, two small drawers, two cupboard doors, shelf int., bracket feet, brown and yellow pine graining, 49" w, 38" h.............**$900**

Painted, attributed to Pennsylvania, rect overhanging top, well, cut-out ends with exposed tenons, joined by medial shield fitted with later copper insert, painted red, early 19th C, 44-3/4" w, 18-1/2" d, 32" h **$2,645**

Pine, three drawers on high back, sink with back-curved sides, paneled doors opening to self, stile feet, c1900, 43" w, 18-1/2" d, 33-1/2" h **$900**

Pine and poplar, galleried well, one small dovetailed drawer, two paneled doors, cut-out feet, 46" w, 18-1/4" d, 37-3/4" h.......................................**$600**

Poplar, painted, rect well above pair of paneled cupboard doors, scroll-cut apron continuing to low bracket feet, cast iron thumb latch replaced, layers of old worn green paint, 39-1/2" w, 16-13/4" d, 33" h **$650**

Arts & Crafts, attributed to Charles Rohls, oak, tall sq shaft, two tiers of four wooden hooks, each near the top, half buttresses running up from the cross base on all four sides, sq wafer feet, early 20th C, 64" h **$1,100**

Bavarian, figural carved wood, mountain goat standing before tree branches, base carved with ferns and flowerheads, ovoid umbrella well, late 19th/early 20th C... **$2,250**

Colonial Revival, Baroque-style, American, cherry, shell carved crest over cartouche and griffin carved panel back, lift seat, high arms, mask carved base, paw feet, 1910, 39-1/2" w, 21-1/2" d, 51" h **$700**

Reformed Gothic, American, mahogany, angular superstructure with mirror and pegs, cane well, circular legs, 25" w, 13" d, 84" h **$750**

Renaissance Revival, American, walnut and part ebonized, upper section with arched cornice, rect mirror plate, turned hat pegs; lower section with marble top, curved cane supports, medial drawer, circular fluted legs, base fitted with shell-form cast iron pans, 51" w, 16" d, 89" h.. **$3,200**

Victorian, American, burl walnut, ball finials above paneled and shaped cornice, rect mirror flanked by turned garment holders, marble top drawer supported by turned legs, shaped base, painted metal plant holders, 29" w, 14" d, 93" h **$1,400**

Hat rack

Arts & Crafts, wrought steel, hat and coat style, four sided, double hooks and spindles, unmarked, 21" w, 21" d, 75" h **$865**

International Movement, Charles Eames, "Hang-It-All," manufactured by Tigrett Enterprises, white enameled metal frame, multicolored wooden balls, c1953, 20" w, 6" d, 16" h **$800**

Windsor, American, pine, bamboo turned, six knob-like hooks, orig yellow varnish, black striping, 33-3/4" w **$200**

Stand, Arts & Crafts, coat and umbrella type, wrought steel, cut-out apron, spindles, brass hooks, unmarked, 27" w, 10-1/2" d, 73" h **$850**

Umbrella stand, Black Forest, Germany, carved walnut, figural bear, fierce expression, loose chain around neck, holding tray in raised paw, porcelain base liner, early 20th C, 48" h
.... **$5,750**

Hall chair, Arts & Crafts, Roycroft, tapering legs, tacked-on leather seat, four vertical back slats, carved orb and cross mark, orig finish, leather, and tacks, wear, 41" x 17" x 16-3/4", **$1,300.**
Photo courtesy of David Rago Auctions, Inc.

Hall trees and hat racks
Bench

Gothic Revival, oak, composed of some antique elements, tall backrest inset with foliate and figural panels, lift seat and foliate carved lower panels, 34" w, 73" h **$690**

Gothic-style, oak, tall backrest fitted with three figural, foliate, and seraph carved panels, lift seat, chip-carved sq legs, late 19th C, 60" w, 66-1/2" h **$1,855**

Chair

Arts & Crafts, Limbert, #79, hall chair, unique "bicycle" shape, orig leather back and shaped seat over slab leg with keyed construction, orig finish, branded and numbered, orig leather has been reinforced, 19" w, 20" d, 42" h **$1,100**

Cast iron, Union Army motif, patch boxes on base, belt with buckle carved for cane holder, swords and rifles forming back, topped with Union shield, piece found in Pennsylvania GAR hall **$10,500**

William IV, octagonal scroll worked backrest, center painted crest, shaped seat, turned tapering legs, peg feet **$475**

Hall rack

Art Nouveau, France, mahogany, flaring mahogany panel, five brass curved coat hooks centered by mirror, umbrella stand below, early 20th C, 47" w, 85" h **$1,200**

Hall tree (costumer), Arts & Crafts, Gustav Stickley, tapering post, four iron hooks, orig finish with overcoat, unmarked, 72" h, **$1,200.**
Photo courtesy of David Rago Auctions, Inc.

Mirrors

Adams-style, oval frame, relief molded gesso, urn and feather crest, scrolled foliage and swags, restored split on crest, few chips, 20th C, 23-1/2" w, 42" h............................**$460**

Aesthetic Movement, America, over-mantel, gilt, central cornice supported by two small columns over frieze dec with scene of snake attacking bird in tree, mirror plate highly dec with leaves, orig label of L. Utler, 47 Royal St., New Orleans, c1880, 64" w, 6" d, 84" h............................**$3,600**

Art Deco, France, octagonal mirror in wrought iron frame, rose and leaf dec, 1930, 36" w, 24" h........................**$250**

Arts & Crafts

Boston Society of Arts and Crafts, carved wood, rect, carved and gilded frame, ink mark, initials, orig paper label, 1910, 11-1/4" w, 18-1/2" h....................................**$700**

Limbert, oak, frame with geometric inlaid design over rect cane panel shoe-foot base, recoated orig frame, orig glass, 20" w, 8" d, 22" h.....**$600**

Baroque, Continental, second quarter giltwood, fruit filled cartouche form resting, mirrored borders with grapevines and scrolls, foliate carved pendant, 18th C, 63" h **$5,750**

Biedermeier, walnut, ogee molded cresting, paneled sides, c1830, 26" w, 37" h................................**$350**

Centennial, Chippendale-style, mahogany and mahogany veneer, pine secondary wood, broken arch crest with gilt eagle, gesso liners with orig gilding and rosettes, leaf vining down each side, refinished, restoration and touch up to eagle and areas of gilding, 26-1/4" w, 56-1/2" h....................**$950**

Cheval, German, ebonized, swivel rect mirror, rounded ends, low sq mount, artist sgd, 70" h............................**$425**

Chippendale

America, mahogany and gilt gesso, scrolled frame, molded gilt incised liner enclosing glass, old surface, late 18th C, 21-3/4" w, 44" h..**$3,100**

England or America, mahogany and parcel gilt, scrolled frame, molded and gilt incised liner, old refinish, replaced glass, late 18th C, 20-1/2" w, 36" h........................**$500**

England, walnut and parcel-gilt, gilt-gessoed carved phoenix on leafy branch above scrolled frame with applied gilt leafy floral and fruit

Mirror, Arts & Crafts, Roycroft, provenance: from family of Roycroft artisan, orig hanging chain and board, dark orig finish, broad 6-1/4" moldings, 50" x 30" mirror frame, 50" x 4" hanging board, 5-1/2" chain, **$4,000.**
Photo courtesy of David Rago Auctions, Inc.

devices, gilt incised liner framing beveled glass, restoration, mid-18th C, 20-1/2" w, 44" h................**$6,465**

New England, mahogany and gilt gesso, scrolled frame centering gilt gesso eagle in crest above gilt incised molded liner, imperfections, late 18th C, 18-1/2" w, 40" h **$500**

Pennsylvania, mahogany and gilt gesso, labeled John Elliot & Son, Philadelphia, scrolled frame with pierced cresting centering phoenix above molded gilt incised liner, label affixed to backboard is last one used by the firm, imperfections, repairs, 1804-1810, 19-1/2" w, 34" h..**$950**

Chippendale-style

Cheval, carved mahogany, oval plate, four-legged base carved with foliage, claw and ball feet, late 19th C, 75" h
....**$635**

Table top, carved wood, black lacquer, and polychrome florals, central top figure of Oriental man with umbrella, hinged prop on verso, suspension loop, mid-18th C, 20" w, 29" h **$1,150**

Classical

Dressing, America or England, carved mahogany and mahogany veneer, cylinder top opens to reveal four drawers, centering one door, ivory pulls, above single divided long drawer, restoration, 1810-20, 19" w, 10-5/8" d, 32" h......................**$1,610**

Girandole, America or England, crest with eagle flanked by acanthus leaves, convex glass, ebonized molded liner with affixed candle branches, foliate and floral pendant, imperfections, gilt gesso, 1810-20, 23" w, 35" h
....**$5,175**

Mirror, wall, Biedermeier, burled walnut, rect, early 19th C, 41" x 47" x 5-1/4" **$550.**
Photo courtesy of Sloans & Kenyon Auctioneers and Appraisers.

Mirror, cheval, New York classical mahogany, swiveling mirror, ormolu capitals on formed feet, c1825, 71-1/2" h x 36-1/4" w, **$1,380.**
Photo courtesy of Pook & Pook, Inc.

Mirror, American, tiger maple frame, later mirror, 19th C, 21" x 32", **$2,100.**
Photo courtesy of David Rago Auctions, Inc.

Mirror, Pennyslvania, Federal tiger maple and walnut, panel depicting landscape and cottage, rect glass, c1820, **$3,000.**
Photo courtesy of Pook & Pook, Inc.

Mirror, gesso-over-wood, pierced, scrolling foliate, rect, molded edge fillet, heavily patinated finish, late 19th C, 32" x 27-3/4", **$325.**
Photo courtesy of Sloans & Kenyon Auctioneers and Appraisers.

Overmantel, New England, painted and giltwood, rect mirror frame with sq corner blocks, applied floral bosses joined by vase and ring turned split baluster columns, molded black liner, old gilt surface, replaced mirror glass, surface imperfections, c1820-40, 46" w, 23" h **$920**

Wall, New York, carved and eglomise, entablature overhangs veneered frieze, reverse painted land and waterscape flanked by leaf carved split balusters, orig eglomise and mirror glass, old refinish, minor losses and crazing, 1830s, 38" h **$460**

Courting, wooden frame, reverse painted glass inserts and crest with bird and flowers, orig mirror glass with worn silvering, penciled inscription on back with "restored 1914," touch-up to reverse painting, brass back corner braces, 10-7/8" w, 16-1/2" h **$935**

Eastlake, walnut, carved crest, 29" w, 63" h **$575**

Edwardian, overmantel, boxwood marquetry inlaid, arched cresting inlaid with musical still life and scrolling vines, shaped mirror plate flanked by cross banded stiles, late 19th C, 60" w, 68" h **$900**

Empire, flame mahogany veneer over pine, scalloped crest with scrolled ends, inset oval panel at top, applied half turned pilasters, ogee base, worn silvering, glue repairs at ends of crest, old alligatored varnish finish, 21" w, 51" h **$770**

Federal

America, two parts, orig gilding, black painted on applied half turnings, raised floral corner blocks, orig reverse painting with lady and child on recamier, repainted floral borders, touch up on panel, minor wear, 18-3/4" w, 39-3/4" h **$550**

Architectural, two parts, pine, old alligatored white paint over orig gilding, stepped cornice with applied ball dec, molded pilasters on sides, applied corner blocks at bottom, reverse dec with ribbons, silver, and black leaves on white ground, edge damage, 15-1/4" w, 24-1/4" h **$450**

Massachusetts, gilt gesso and wood, molded cornice with applied spherules above reverse painted tablet showing sea battle, glass below flanked by rope twist molded pilasters, imperfections, c1820, 19" w, 32-1/2" h **$1,300**

Massachusetts, gilt gesso and wood, molded cornice with applied spherules above reverse painted and stenciled tablet showing a cottage and bridge arching a brook, glass flanked by rope twist molded pilasters, minor imperfections, c1875-20, 17" w, 28-1/4" h **$600**

Massachusetts, giltwood and eglomise, turned engaged columns enclose reverse-painted tablet showing woman seated on red and gold neoclassical stool, holding parrot, flanked by red and gold drapery above a mirrored glass, old regilding, replaced mirror glass, early 19th C, 15-3/4" w, 32" h **$500**

New England, mahogany, scrolled frame, rect mitered liner with inlaid contrasting stringing, refinished, c1800, 20-3/4" w, 38" h **$1,000**

New England, mahogany and mahogany veneer, molded cornice above sq and reeded capitals, half engraved vase and ring-turned, acanthus leaf, diamond faceted columns on sq plinths, refinished, replaced glass, imperfections, c1820-25, 18-1/2" w, 40-1/2" h **$355**

New York City, mahogany, swan's neck crest, carved urn, bouquet-type finial with carved florets on wires, veneered frame flanked by wire-bound wood vine work pendants, scrolled apron, heavily reworked, refinished, gold paint, c1780-1800, 21-1/2" w, 53" h **$675**

Tabernacle, attributed to New York or Albany, gilt gesso, molded cornice with pendant spherules over frieze with applied sunflower and wheat sheaf device, flanked by checkered panels over two-part looking glass, flanked by applied double half columns, gilt surface, replaced glass tablet, 1795-1810, 14" w, 30-1/2" h .. **$865**

Wall, giltwood, labeled "Parker and Clover Looking Glass and Picture Frame Makers 180 Fulton St. New York," molded cornice with applied spherules above eglomise table of girl in pasture landscape holding dove, mirror flanked by spiral carved pilasters, 13-3/4" w, 29-1/8" h
.... **$2,875**

Federal, late, attributed to New England, gilt gesso, molded cornice with acorn form drops over frieze centering carved leaf motif flanked by vine and leaf applied devices, two-part mirror glass with grape and leaf designs, flanked by vase, ring, and spiral turned split balusters, old gilt surface, minor imperfections, including replaced mirror glass, c1820-30, 19" w, 37" h **$700**

Federal-style, convex, eagle crest, worn gilding, ebonized liner, eagle with small chain, ball in beak, restorations to wings, late 19th or early 20th C, 16-1/2" w, 24-1/2" h **$700**

Folk Art, America, possibly prisoner made, pine, carved hearts, stars, and various numerals and patterns, year "1902," minor wear, 1902, 29-1/2" x 29-7/8" **$1,410**

George II-style, English, carved gesso and giltwood, C-scroll and shell carved arched crest, serpentine and rect mirror plate, scrolled foliate corner pendants, C-scroll, shell, and acanthus carved shaped apron, 19th C, 29" w, 65-1/2" h **$1,800**

George III, giltwood, crest centered by hoho bird over C-scrolls, flanked by swag-draped urns, frame sides with further C-scrolls, late 18th C, 26-1/2" w, 52" h **$3,100**

Hepplewhite, shaving, mahogany, inlay, two dovetailed drawers, feet, posts, and mirror are old replacements, 17-3/4" h **$225**

Louis XV-style, pier, carved giltwood, large rect mirror topped by crest carved with leafy scrolls and rocaille, marble-topped ovolo 19-1/4" h shelf, flat leaf edge, gilt metal brackets, reeded scrolls with anthemion and female mask terminals, 19th C, 33" w, 73" h **$1,725**

Neoclassical, Trumeau, painted gray, parcel gilt, top with gilt molding over gilt gesso figure of reclining goddess flanked by urns, over rect two-part mirror plate in gilt floral and leaftip surround, continental 19th C, 40" x 98" **$3,820**

Neoclassical-style, pier, gilt wood, crest with roundel with urn issuing foliage flanked by cornucopias, beveled rect plate within surround decorated with garlands of flowers, corners with Greek key motif, 20th C, 35" w, 68" h **$1,200**

Painted, attributed to the work of Nehemiah Partridge, eastern Massachusetts, rect molded frame painted red, intersecting linear designs in black, wear, first quarter 18th C, 7-7/8" w, 9-1/4" h **$4,700**

Queen Anne

American, walnut and pine, old red-dish brown paint, beveled glass, orig hand planed backboard, scrolled crest with replacements and veneer, 12-1/4" w, 23" h **$650**

Scroll, mahogany, old finish, molded frame, detailed scrolled crest, minor split in bottom edge of frame, 9" w, 16-1/4" h **$550**

Walnut, scrolled crest above molded rect frame enclosing beveled mirror glass, backboard inscribed "Capt S Cobb," refinished, glass resilvered, 10-1/2" w, 22-1/2" h **$1,175**

Renaissance Revival, American

Hall, parcel gilt walnut, openwork lappet and floral cresting, shaped plate, frame carved with leaftips, pegs and incised lines, 35" w, 75" h **$950**

Over mantel, parcel gilt walnut, arched mirror plate, carved in high relief with lappets, roundels and architectural motifs, 62" w, 60" h **$750**

Pier, walnut and parcel gilt, molded cornice carved with sawtooth and paterae, long mirror plate flanked by columns, low marble top, turned legs, 27" w, 12" d, 100" h **$500**

Wall, walnut and parcel gilt, sawtooth and spindle cresting, shaped plate, fluted pilasters, 45" w, 31" h **$425**

Rococo

Continental, giltwood, shaped mirror plate, arched top, frame carved with foliage and C-scrolls, third quarter 18th C, 28" w, 54" h **$4,025**

Northern Europe, walnut and gilt gesso, shaped molded cresting with foliate devices enclosing reverse painted tablet showing man in powdered wig above rect molded walnut veneered gilt-lined frame on shaped pierced bracket, imperfections, late 18th C, 14" w, 31" h **$950**

Rococo-style, gilt wood, cartouche form, surround carved with scrolls hung with icicles, plate replaced, possibly re-gilt, c19th C, 47" h **$1,315**

Sheraton, mahogany, spiral turned split columns and bottom rail, inlaid panels of mahogany, rosewood, and cherry, architectural top cornice, split mirror, 24-1/2" w, 47" h **$300**

Victorian, Rococo Revival, giltwood, shaped mirror plate, frame with foliate canopy cresting and mirrored borders, elaborately carved all over in high relief with birds, icicles, columns, and foliage, 19th C, 35" w, 64" h **$1,900**

Mirror, Regency gilt wood bull's-eye, circular molded frame, 16 gilded spheres, convex plate, early 19th C, 20" d, **$700.**
Photo courtesy of Sloans & Kenyon Auctioneers and Appraisers.

Mirror, Venetian, triptych, etched French Bulldogs on side panels, some cracks and losses, early 20th C, 25" x 48", **$450.**
Photo courtesy of David Rago Auctions, Inc.

Mirror, circular convex, gilt gesso frame, scrolling decorations, topped with spread wing eagle clutching arrows, c1920, 26" w, 40" h, **$650.**
Photo courtesy of Alderfer Auction Co.

Rocker, Eastlake style, platform type, reupholstered padded backrest, seat, and head rest, turned spindles, **$250.**
Photo courtesy of Joseph P. Smalley, Jr.

Rocker, Arts & Crafts, Stickley Bros, Morris, long curved arms over three side slats, loose cushions recovered in tan leather, refinished, unmarked, 35" x 31" x 37-1/2", **$550.**
Photo courtesy of David Rago Auctions, Inc.

Rocker, Victorian, carved face on curved back crest rail, shaped back splat, turned spindles, arms, and stretchers, **$135.**
Photo courtesy of Dotta Auction Co., Inc.

Rocker, Arts & Crafts, Gustav Stickley, No. 323, five slats under each arm, curved back and drop-in spring seat, decal inside back stretcher, refinished, 40" x 29" x 30", **$2,300.**
Photo courtesy of David Rago Auctions, Inc.

Rocker, International Movement, Charles Eames for Zenith, yellow fiberglass, rope edge, black wire cat's cradle base, birch runners, Zenith label, one re-glued shock mount, some staining to seat, 27-1/4" x 25" x 27", **$865.**
Photo courtesy of David Rago Auctions, Inc.

Rockers

Art Nouveau, American, oak, fumed finish, carved arms, saddle seat, three splats with floral-type capitals, c1900 .... **$400**

Arts & Crafts

American, oak, four vertical back slats, corbel supports under arms, recovered orig spring cushion, orig finish, 29" w, 34" d, 36" h **$200**

Limbert, #580, oak, T-back design, orig recovered drop-in cushion, recent finish, branded, 24" w, 29" d, 34" h **$150**

Plail, oak, slatted barrel back, D-shaped recovered seat, refinished, unsigned, 26" w, 28" d, 31" h **$2,500**

Stickley Brothers, oak, six vertical back slats, recovered orig spring cushion, worn orig finish, branded, 25" w, 27" d, 35" h **$220**

Bentwood, rustic, hickory and pine, old finish, repairs, 15-3/4" h seat, 37-1/2" h back **$225**

Boston, American, maple, spindle back, 19th C **$200**

Colonial Revival, Windsor-style, Colonial Furniture Co., Grand Rapids, MI, comb back, birch, mahogany finish, turned legs, 21" w, 17" d, 27-1/2" h **$200**

Decorated

America, orig black over red dec, gold stenciled urn of fruit and flowers on crest, shaped seat, scrolled arms, well turned legs, repaired damage to arms, 15" h seat, 40" h **$220**

Pennsylvania, dark green, gold foliate on crest, slats, and seat, traces of red border with yellow line detail, turned legs, shaped medallion stretcher, scrolled arms, repaired break in one arm, 17" h seat, 42" h **$220**

International Movement, Charles Eames, manufactured by Herman Miller, salmon fiberglass zenith shell, rope edge, black wire struts, birch runners, c1950, 25" w, 27" d, 27" h **$1,400**

Ladderback, Pennsylvania, orig rush seat, turned finials, block and turned arm supports, painted green, 15" h seat, 39-1/2" h back **$315**

Wicker, painted white, sq back, basket weave pattern over openwork back, rect armrests with wrapped braces, openwork sides, braided edge on basketweave seat and skirt, X-form stretcher, 32" w, 33" h **$200**

Windsor

American, grain painted, stencil dec, scrolled crest, tail spindle back, shaped seat, bamboo turned legs, box stretcher, c1850 .... **$450**

New England, rect splat stencil dec with grapevines highlighted in freehand yellow fancy work above the raked spindles and stiles, scrolled arms, shaped seat, bamboo-turned legs on rockers, all-over burnt-sienna and black dec, early 19th C, 15" h seat, 43" h **$1,300**

Rocker, Victorian, carved mahogany frame with scrolls and foliage, rose motif needlepoint with maroon background, padded arms, matching footrest, **$350.**
Photo courtesy of Joseph P. Smalley, Jr.

Secretary, Edwardian, two sections, upper section: fan-pierced broken pediment above ribbon-tied foliate spray, two glazed doors with gothic arch mullions, adjustable shelved interior; base with cylinder front, fitted interior of small drawers and pigeon holes, adjustable tooled-leather writing slope, cylinder front inlaid with tassel-and-bead draped urn suspended from ribbon-tied chain within satinwood inlaid oval reserve flanked by foliate-inlaid spandrels, two small drawers inlaid with laurel swags, lion's head circular pulls, square tapering bellflower inlay base, **$7,500.**
Photo courtesy of Sloans & Kenyon Auctioneers and Appraisers.

Pennsylvania, bamboo turnings, cheese cutter rockers, yellow ground paint with smoke dec, red highlights, floral and strawberry dec crest, 17" h seat, 30-1/2" h **$3,300**

Secretaries

Biedermeier-style, inlaid walnut, molded rect top, four drawers, top drawer with fall front, fitted int. with ebonized writing-surface, molded block feet, 50-1/4" w, 23-3/4" d, 35-1/2" h **$1,000**

Centennial, inlay mahogany, two parts: top with four drawers over six cubbyholes center, line inlay door opening to reveal two cubbyholes and large drawer, sliding tambour doors flanked by inlay panels with simulated columns; lower: fold-over line inlay lid, two drawers with line inlay, diamond inlay on legs, some lifting to veneer, replaced cloth writing surface, 37-1/4" w, 19-3/4" d, 46" h

.... **$800**

Chippendale

Connecticut, two pcs, maple and curly maple, pr of panel doors over fall front, fitted int., four drawers, orig pierced brass drop bail hardware

.... **$45,000**

Maryland, attributed to, inlaid walnut, top with molded and pierced swan's-neck cresting with inlaid terminals centering a plinth with cross banded border and urn finial above cross banded frieze, two glazed doors enclosing adjustable shelves, candle slides below on base with fall front opening, central prospect door flanked by string-inlaid document boxes, three drawers and four valanced compartments, case of four cockbeaded graduated drawers, ogee bracket feet, replaced brasses, refinished, restoration, late 18th C, 40" w, 22" d, 95" h **$7,700**

Massachusetts, carved mahogany, scrolled and molded pediment above tympanum with projecting shell and arched raised panel doors flanked by fluted pilasters, candle slides, raised panel slant lid with blocked facade, molded conforming base, bracket feet, int. of upper bookcase divided into open compartments above four small drawers, int. of lower case with two fan-carved blocked drawers, similar prospect door, small blocked and plain drawers, scrolled compart-

ment dividers, replaced brasses, old finish, restored, c1770-90, 39" w, 22" d, 93-1/2" h **$19,550**

New England, block front, two pieces, upper section: flame finial, two blind doors, cyma-carved panels, various-sized open compartments on int., lower section with fur front drawers, plain slant front, fitted int., some later replacements, late 18th C, 91" h **$38,180**

Rhode Island, Providence area, carved cherry, scrolled molded pediment flanks central plinth and finial above applied shell carving atop central fluted and stop-fluted column flanked by raised panel doors, shelved int. enclosed by quarter-engaged fluted and stop-fluted columns, lower case of two stepped int, of serpentine end-blocked drawers with serpentine dividers, valanced compartments, central document drawers with applied columns, above four graduated thumb-molded drawers flanked by fluted and stop-fluted engaged quarter-columns, shaped bracket feet ending in platforms, old surface, some original brasses, presumed owners' names scratched on underside of case: "Abner Lampson, 1743-1797 and Ward Lampson, 1773-1850, Washington N.H." imperfections, 1765-85, 38-1/4" w, 21" d, 80" h **$55,815**

Classical, Boston, secretaire a'abattant, carved mahogany and mahogany veneer, marble top above cove molding, mahogany veneer facade flanked by veneered columns topped by Corinthian capitals, terminating in ebonized ball feet, recessed panel sides, fall front opens to desk int. over two cupboard doors, old refinish, 1820-25, 35" w, 17-1/2" d, 57-1/2" h **$16,100**

Colonial Revival, Colonial Desk Co., Rockford, IL, mahogany, broken arch pediment, center finial, two glazed mullioned doors, fluted columns, center prospect with acanthus carving flanked by columns, four graduated drawers, brass eagle, carved claw and ball feet, c1930, 41" w, 21" d, 87" h **$1,000**

Eastlake, American, burl walnut and mahogany, shaped cornice, pair of glazed cabinet doors, cylinder front, writing surface, two doors in base, shaped apron, 27" w, 22" d, 66" h

.... **$1,500**

Empire, America, mahogany veneer, fall-front, dovetailed construction, two sections, top with two four-light cathedral glass doors, base with fall-front deck, five-drawer int., over three drawers flanked by curved columns, turned feet, c1840, 41-1/2" w, 20" d, 7' 4" h **$1,425**

Empire-style, gilt bronze mounted mahogany, rect top, fall front with fitted int., over pr of recessed cupboard doors, flanked by columns, paw feet, late 19th C, 44-1/4" w, 23-1/2" d, 49-1/4" h **$1,955**

Federal

Massachusetts, Boston or North Shore, mahogany inlaid, top section: central panel of bird's eye maple with cross banded mahogany veneer border and stringing joined to the plinths by a curving gallery above flat molded cornice, glazed beaded doors with Gothic arches and bird's eye maple panels and mahogany cross-banding and stringing enclosing shelves, compartments, and drawers; lower: projecting section with fold-out surface inlaid with oval bird's eye maple panel set in mitered rect with cross banded border and cockbeaded case, two drawers veneered with bird's eye maple panels bordered by mahogany cross-banding and stringing, flanked by inlaid panels continuing to sq double tapered legs, lower edge of case and leg cuffs with lunette inlaid banding, old finish, replaced brasses, imperfections, early 19th, 41" w, 21-3/4" d, 74-1/2" h **$9,775**

Massachusetts, coastal southern, inscribed "Wood" in chalk, mahogany, three pcs, molded cornice with inlaid dentiling above diamond inlaid frieze over two paneled cupboard doors with quarter-fan inlays opening to eight-compartment int., center case with tambour doors centering oval veneered prospect door, flanked by inlaid and reeded applied pilasters, valanced compartments, prospect door opens to single valanced compartment with drawer below, lower case with string inlaid fold-out writing surface, similarly inlaid drawers flanked by stiles, panel inlays, skirt, inlaid dentiling above legs with inlaid bellflowers, line inlay and inlaid cuffs, early surface, replaced pulls, minor veneer loss, c1816,

40" w, 20-1/2" d, 81-3/4" h **$34,500**

New Hampshire, paint decoration, two pieces, pine, old alligatored reddish-brown and yellow dec over earlier red, chamfered corners on dovetailed cases, molded cove cornice, tree dec on two paneled doors, slant front with tree dec, int. with 13 dovetailed drawers with central prospect door, four dovetailed drawers in base with applied beading, slightly shaped bracket feet with applied base molding, replaced wooden pulls, replaced H hinges, touch-up to top doors **$7,425**

George III, last quarter 18th C

Mahogany, molded cornice, two glazed doors, fitted interior with three shelves, rect molded base with pull out secretary drawer, two short and two long graduated drawers, 48" w, 18" d, 98" h **$9,440**

Mahogany, upper section with two mullioned and glazed doors; lower section fitted with secretary drawer over three long drawers, bracket feet...**$1,645**

George III/Early Federal, America, mahogany, two sections, upper: shaped architectural pediment with gilt-metal ball and spike finials, cavetto cornice over cross banded frieze, chequer-banding, front with pair of 13-pane astragal doors, two adjustable shelves; base: outset fall-front opening, fitted int., four graduated cockbeaded oxbow-fronted drawers, conforming molded plinth base, molded and spurred bracket feet, third quarter 18th C, 44-1/4" w, 24-1/4" d, 93-1/2" h **$17,000**

Hepplewhite, North Shore, MA, mahogany, bookcase upper section, slant front desk **$6,250**

International Movement, Gilbert Rhode, manufactured by Herman Miller, upper bookcase with drop front desk over four doors, carved wooden pulls in burl and paldio veneers, refinished, c1940, 66" w, 15" d, 72" h **$2,600**

Louis XV-style, rosewood, bombe form, inset shaped white marble top, fall front, fitted interior, above four aligned drawers, cabriole legs with gilt metal paw feet, 37" w, 19" d, 66-3/4" h **$2,125**

Renaissance Revival, American, walnut, two sections, upper: bookcase section, S-curved pediment with cen-

ter applied grapes and foliage carving, two arched and molded glazed doors, shelved int., three small drawers with applied grapes and foliage carved pulls; lower: fold-out writing surface, two short drawers over two long drawers with oval molding and applied grapes and foliage carved pulls, matching ornamentation on skirt, c1865, 48" w, 21" d, 95" h **$5,000**

Sheraton, New England, mahogany and mahogany flame veneer, cove molded cornice, three drawers across top with oval brasses, two paneled doors in top with fine flame veneer, three interior drawers, four pigeon holes with adjustable shelf, three dovetailed drawers with applied beading, figured book page veneer, reeded legs with ring turnings and molded surround at base of case, refinished, few repaired veneer splits, pierced repairs, stains in bottom, replaced brasses, 42" w, 20" d, 50-1/2" h **$1,760**

Victorian, two pieces, walnut, top: crown molding cornice, two glazed doors with burl and walnut buttons; base: burl cylinder roll with two-drawer walnut int., pigeon holes, slide-out writing surface, base: three long drawers with burl dec, tear drop pulls, refinished, 40" w, 23" d, 86" h **$1,850**

Secretary, Louis XVI style, Provincial, slant front, arched ogee cornice above paneled cupboard doors, fitted interior, two cupboard doors, short scroll legs, 44" w, 19" d, 103-1/2" h, **$3,200.**
Photo courtesy of Sloans & Kenyon Auctioneers and Appraisers.

Settee, Federal, Baltimore, attributed to Renshaw, triple chairback, downward sloping arms with urn-turned supports, bowfront seat supported by turned legs, original overall gilt decoration on black painted ground, c1800, 48" l, 18-1/2" w, 34" h, **$5,750.**
Photo courtesy of Pook & Pook, Inc.

Settee, Federal style, carved mahogany, downcurving reeded arms, reeded tapering legs ending in peg feet, 60-1/2" l, **$850+.**
Photo courtesy of Sloans & Kenyon Auctioneers and Appraisers.

Settee, Louis XVI-style, newer frame, upholstered in 18th C tapestry, 44" x 76" x 31", **$1,200.**
Photo courtesy of David Rago Auctions, Inc.

Settee, Victorian, shell carved crest at back and skirt, tufted back, serpentine front, bracket feet, reupholstered in red velvet, c1880, 48" w, 20" d, 15" h seat, 34" h, **$450.**
Photo courtesy of Alderfer Auction Co.

William III, English, burl walnut veneer, two sections, recessed upper with double-domical crest, pair of domically crested doors mounted with beveled glass mirror panels of conforming upper outline, plain int. of three adjustable wood shelves above pr of candle slides; lower section with canted front, hinged fall-front writing board, shaped desk int. with valanced central cubby hole between two pairs of valanced narrow cubby holes over two shaped drawers each, horizontal sliding door, flanked by two-tier side units with single-drawer bases, straight front of two graduated narrow drawers over two graduated wide drawers, highly figured burl on drawers match writing board and doors, engraved period brasses, later short straight bracket feet, minor veneer damage, c1700-10, 40" w, 23-1/2" d, 84" h
....**$18,750**

Settees

Art Deco, attributed to Warren McArthur, tubular aluminum frame, sheet aluminum seat and back supports, removable vinyl cushions, c1930, 68" l
....**$5,750**

Arts & Crafts
Limbert, #939, oak, 11 back slats, corbels under arm, recovered orig drop-in cushion, branded, refinished, 75" w, 27" d, 40" h..........**$800**
Stickley, Gustav, No. 222, tapering posts, tightly spaced canted slats to back and sides, leather upholstered drop-in seat, fine orig finish, red decal, minor veneer chips, 36" x 80" x 32"....................................**$11,500**
Stickley, L. & J.G., oak, drop-arm form, 12 vertical slats to back and drop-in orig spring cushion, recovered in brown leather, refinished, unsigned, 65" w, 25" d, 36" h **$1,800**
Unknown America maker, even arm, oak, crest rail over nine wide vertical slats, three on each side, joined by sq vertical posts, medium brown finish, replaced seat, joint separation, 20th C, 65" w, 25-3/4" d, 32" h
....**$2,650**
Biedermeier-style, beechwood, curved open back, three vasiform splats, out-curved arms, caned seat raised on six sq-section sabre legs
....**$650**
Classical, American, mahogany, serpentine front, carved crest, transition-

al rococo design elements, c1850, 82" l
....**$600**
Colonial Revival, William and Mary style, American, loose cushions, turned baluster legs and stretcher, c1930, 48" l
....**$750**
Eastlake-style, Confidant, walnut, upholstered scrolling backs with horizontal pierced splats, upholstered seats, tapering square-section legs, 26" w, 26" d, 46" h.......................**$600**
Empire-style, late 19th/early 20th C
Gilt bronze mounted mahogany, settee, pair of side chairs, each with foliate and figural mounts, 80" l settee, price for three pieces ...**$1,725**
Mahogany, two seats, curved backs, each armrest ending on ram's head, hoof-foot feet.......................**$2,100**
French Restauration, New York City, rosewood, arched upholstered back, scrolled arms outlined in satinwood terminating in volutes, rect seat frame with similar inlay, bracket feet, c1840, 80" l, 27" d, 33-1/2" h ...**$1,200**
George II, mahogany, serpentine crest over upholstered back and seat, round reeded, tapering legs **$1,500**
George III, black lacquer and faux bamboo, settee, pair of arm chairs, price for three pieces, early 19th C **$1,265**
Gothic Revival, American, carved walnut, shaped crest rail surmounted by center carved finial, stiles with arched recessed panel and similarly carved finials, upholstered back and seat, open arms with padded armrests and scrolled handholds, carved seat rail, ring turned legs, ball feet, c1850, 67-1/2" w, 23-1/2" d, 49-3/4" h ...**$800**
Louis XVI-style, gilt bronze mounted ebonized maple, Leon Marcotte, New York City, c1860, 55-1/2" l, 25" d, 41-1/2" h.................................**$2,185**
Queen Anne-style, inlaid back flanked by shepherd's crook arms, cabriole legs **$2,250**
Renaissance Revival, America, carved walnut, triple back, each having carved crest and ebonized plaque inlaid with musical instruments, red floral damask upholstery, c1875
....**$1,200**
Rococo Revival
Attributed to John Henry Belter, 65" l settee, pair of lady's chairs, pair of side chairs, each with laminated rose and foliate carved cresting, grapevine openwork sides, cabriole legs, price for three pieces, c1885
....**$14,375**

Attributed to J. & J. Meeks, rose-wood, laminated curved backs, Stanton Hall pattern, rose crest in scrolled foliage and vintage, tufted gold velvet brocade reupholstery, age cracks and some edge damage, 65-1/2" l....................**$5,500**

Victorian, carved rosewood, shaped and padded back, two arched end sections joined by dipped section, each with pierced foliate crest, over upholstered serpentine front seat, flanked by scroll arms, conforming rail continue to cabriole legs, frame leaf carved, c1870 ....**$850**

Wicker, tightly woven rect back, inverted triangle-dec, tightly woven arms, rect seat with woven diamond herringbone pattern, continuous braided edging from crest to front legs, turned spindle apron, 43" w, 36" h...................................**$500**

Windsor, New England, birdcage, maple, ash, and hickory, bamboo turned birdcage crest over 27 turned spindles flanked by stiles joining bamboo-turned arms and supports over bench seat, eight bamboo-turned legs joined by stretchers, old refin-ish, imperfections, early 19th C, 72" l, 14-1/2" h seat, 31-1/2" h **$2,415**

Sideboards

Art Deco, France, walnut and burl book-matched veneer, Bakelite cabinet doors and drawer pulls, c1928, 76" l, 19-1/2" d, 50-5/8" h **$900**

Art Nouveau, Louis Majorelle, oak and mahogany, rect, bowed front, inset marble top, two long draw-ers, undulating brass pulls cast with sheaves of wheat, two cupboard doors with large applied brass sheaves of wheat and undulating leaves, mold-ed apron, four lug feet, 1900, 65" w, 39-1/8" h...................................**$6,000**

Typical Parts of a Sideboard

Arts & Crafts

English, attributed to, with two "V" backsplashes, two drawers with ring pulls, bottom shelf, casters, orig finish, marked "S79FUM90," 42" l, 20" d, 45-1/4" h **$1,150**

Limbert, Charles P., Grand Rapids, Michigan, oak, oblong top, mirrored back above case, three short draw-ers flanked by paneled cupboard doors over long drawer, copper pulls and strap hinges, sq legs, cham-fered tenons, branded mark, c1910, 49-1/2" w, 53-1/2" h **$900**

Stickley Brothers, backsplash, single drawer with hammered brass hard-ware, lower shelf, good orig fin-ish, branded "Stickley Brothers," stenciled "B735," light edge wear, 36" l, 19" d, 37" h **$2,185**

Stickley Brothers, paneled plate rack, four drawers, three panel doors with hammered brass hardware, good orig finish, branded "Stickley Brothers," stenciled "8833," wear to copper patina on iron hardware **$4,025**

Stickley, Gustav, model no. 967, gal-lery top over two short drawers and long drawer, two cupboard doors below, iron strap hinges and door pulls, red decal, imperfections, 1902, 59-3/4" w, 23-3/4" w, 43-3/4" h **$32,300**

Stickley, L. & J.G., Fayetteville, New York, oak, plate rail on rect top, three central drawers flanked by two cabinet doors, over single long drawer, branded mark, c1916, 47" w, 19-3/4" d, 44" h...........**$5,300**

Centennial, Chippendale-style, America, mahogany, block front with shell carving, four drawers, front cab-inet doors, gadrooned apron, cabriole legs, claw and ball feet, late 19th C, 68" w, 24" d, 40" h.......................**$950**

Classical

Mid Atlantic States, carved mahogany and cherry veneer, rect top over mahogany veneered drawer, two recessed panel doors opening to one shelf int., flanked by veneered scrolled supports, veneered base, old refinish, hardware changes, splashboard missing, 1840-45, 40" w, 18-3/4" d, 40-1/8" h **$2,550**

New York, carved mahogany veneer, splashboard with molded edge and four spiral carved and turned columns, topped by urn-shaped finials, rect top overhangs recessed

paneled case, cockbeaded drawers and cupboards outlined with crass banded mahogany veneer, two top drawers with dividers above short drawers, bottle drawers flanked by end recessed panel doors, left one with single shelf int., right one with two-shelf int., flanked by columnar leaf carved supports over frontal carved paw feet, rear feet are heavi-ly turned and tapering, old refinish, imperfections, 1830s, 60-1/4" w, 23-5/8" d, 56-3/4" h..............**$2,760**

Empire

American, carved mahogany and figured veneers, break front, three drawers, four doors across base with inset gothic panels of figured veneer, well carved paw feet, orig brass hardware, old dark finish, 73-1/2" l, 23" d, 42" h **$1,650**

French, gilt bronze mounted mahog-any, shaped mottled green marble top above three frieze drawers deco-rated with palmettes, three cup-board doors decorated with mask in laurel surround and winged maidens, flanked by pilasters with sphinx head capitals, shaped base, gilt bronze feet; top bearing old paper label "BEDEL & CIE/ LE GARDE MEUBLE PUBLIC," late 19th C, 71" w, 23" d, 40" h **$8,400**

French, gilt bronze-mounted mahog-any, shaped mottled green marble top above three frieze drawers decorated with scrollwork and pal-mettes, three cupboard doors deco-rated with portrait medallion, cor-nucopias, and torches, flanked by pilasters with sphinx head capitals, shaped base, late 19th/early 20th C, 78" w, 25" d, 40" h.................**$6,000**

Federal

Baltimore, Maryland, mahogany inlaid, veneered top with ovolo cor-ners and string inlay in outline, case of central drawer and four cup-board doors all embellished with veneered ovals outlined in band-ing and interspersed with maple veneered rectangles, sq tapering legs with stringing in outline and forming five graduated loops above cuff inlays, case with old surface, replaced brass, imperfections, 1790-1810, 75-1/8" w, 25-1/2" d, 39-3/4" h **$14,100**

Massachusetts, Boston, mahoga-ny, maple, and rosewood veneer,

Sideboard, Arts & Crafts, Gustav Stick-ley, two small drawers over single long drawer, chamfered sides, wooden pyra-midal knob-pulls, dark brown original finish, large red decal, c1902, 44-1/2" x 59" x 23-1/2", **$50,000.**
Photo courtesy of David Rago Auctions, Inc.

Sideboard, Empire, American, mahog-any and burl veneer, four carved col-umns and capitals, turned feet, castors, 47-1/2" x 57" x 24", **$1,175.**
Photo courtesy of David Rago Auctions, Inc.

Sideboard, Arts & Crafts, Gustav Stick-ley, plate rack, linen drawer over two small drawers, arched opening, two cup-board doors, red decal in top drawer, orig dark finish with overcoat on top, 45" x 48" x 18", **$3,500.**
Photo courtesy of David Rago Auctions, Inc.

two-tiered case, demilune super-structure, maple inlaid panels surrounded by cross banded rose-wood veneer above cockbeaded end drawers, small central drawer flanked by end cupboards, six ring turned tapering legs, case with concentric turnings, reeding, cock beading, and scenic landscape jointed on underside of arched opening, old surface, replaced pulls, replaced leg, veneer loss, later landscape painting, 1810-20, 74-1/2" l, 24-1/2" d, 44-3/4" h **$9,200**
Massachusetts or Rhode Island, mahogany, cross banded, rect top with ovolo corners and reeded edge overhangs case of cockbead-ed drawers and central cupboards flanked by turned columns con-tinuing to reeding above ring-turned swelled legs, turned feet, refinished, restored, replaced legs, early 19th C, 42-3/4" w, 21-1/2" d, 41-1/4" h **$8,820**
Middle Atlantic States, attributed to, mahogany and cherry inlaid, over-hanging top with canted corners and serpentine front, central cockbead-ed door inlaid with cherry panel with quarter fan inlays and mahog-any mitered border, cockbeaded wine drawer with three-drawer facade at one end, three cockbeaded graduated drawers on other, ends with cherry veneered panels, four sq inlaid tapering legs ending in molded spade feet, lower edge of case with molding, old finish, minor imperfections, c1790, 48-1/2" w, 21-5/8" d, 37" h **$19,950**

New England, mahogany and mahog-any veneer, overhanging top with shaped front, conforming case, central pullout surface, bowed cockbeaded drawers, two cupboard doors flanked by concave drawers and cupboard doors, six sq tapering legs, replaced brasses, old refin-ish, imperfections, c1790, 64" w, 20-1/8" d, 37-1/2" h **$5,500**
Southern States, attributed to Fran-cis Marion Kay, cherry and other hardwoods, yellow pine secondary wood, replaced rest, three draw-ers over two doors, another drawer over prospect door at center, lower doors divided by half turned pilas-ters, six turned legs, one door is restored, hinges replaced, 1816-87, 60-1/4" w, 21-1/4" d, 49" h **$3,410**
Virginia, walnut and yellow pine, molded rect top, cockbeaded case with end drawers, right drawer visually divided into two draw-ers, left with two working draw-ers, central cupboard cockbeaded door, four square tapering legs, old brass pulls, old refinish, repairs, inscription on drawer reads "Vir-ginia Hunt Board, early 19th cent. from family of Admiral Todd, Naval Commander prior to and during the Civil War, Virginia," 1790-1810, 56" w, 22" d, 39" h **$5,520**
Federal-style, Southern States, hunt-board, yellow pine, overhanging rect top, case with three drawers, skirt with central shaping, four sq tapering legs, orig brasses, refinished, 21" w, 19-1/2" h **$1,840**

George III, inlaid mahogany, cross banded and bowfronted top, case fit-ted with four drawers, sq tapered legs, inlaid throughout with stringing and quarter fans, c1790, 79" w, 24" d, 34-1/2" h **$5,875**
George III-style
Mahogany, bow front, shaped top, single drawer flanked by doors, sq tapering legs, spade feet, late 19th C, 54" w, 26-1/2" d, 36" h **$2,000**
Mahogany, inlaid, satinwood cross-banding, serpentine top, conform-ing case fitted with five drawers and two doors, sq tapered legs, late 19th C, 64" w, 22" d, 38-1/4" h **$1,175**
George III/Hepplewhite, mahogany, flame grain mahogany, satinwood, and oak, paterae and shell inlay, 36" h **$11,160**
Gothic, Kimbel & Cabus, New York, design no. 377, walnut, galleried top over two cupboard doors over open self over slant front over central drawer over open well flanked by two cupboard doors, galleried base shelf, bracket feet, c1875, 39-1/4" w, 17-3/4" d, 73" h **$9,775**
Hepplewhite, mahogany and mahog-any veneer with inlay, bowed center section with conforming doors and dovetailed drawer, two flat side doors, sq tapered legs, banding and string-ing with bell flowers on legs, corner fans on doors and drawers, reworked, repairs, replaced brasses, 58-1/4" w, 18-1/2" d, 37-3/4" h **$2,200**
Louis XV, Provincial, oak, rect top and case, fluted frieze, three paneled doors enclosing re-fitted interior of drawers, short cabriole legs, 85" w, 19" d, 40" h **$3,525**

Neoclassical, Boston, mahogany veneer, corner style, paneled and scrolled splashboard over top with veneered molded edge, curving front which overhangs conforming case of three veneered drawers over two recessed paneled doors, single shelved int., similar recessed panel sides above flattened ball feet with brass banding, replaced brass pulls, old surface with some imperfections, 1820-25, 60" w, 35" d, 42" h ...**$55,200**

Queen Anne, converted from highboy base, walnut, pine secondary wood, pegged construction, two dovetailed drawers, one with relief carved shell, scalloped aprons, cabriole legs, pad feet, old dark surface, age splits, replaced returns, 38-1/2" w, 20-1/2" d, 35" h...............**$1,150**

Regency-style, inlaid mahogany, serpentine top, conforming case fitted with three central long drawers, drawer and door at each side, inlaid with quarter fans and checkering, 20th C, 65" w, 21-1/2" d, 40" h **$2,000**

Renaissance Revival, America, cherry, curled mahogany drawer fronts, burled arched panel doors **$900**

Second Empire, French, ebonized wood, scrolled crest with pierte dure florals within gilt metal cartouche, three section mirrored back divided by ebonized brackets, three drawers, center cupboard door flanked by two glazed cupboard doors, shelved int., figural gilt metal mounts, pietre dura floral and bird dec within gilt bronze cartouche, c1870, 67" w, 18" d, 77" h **$4,600**

Sheraton, country, walnut and curly maple, beaded edge top, four dovetailed drawers, scalloped aprons, turned legs, line inlay around apron and drawer fronts, old varnish finish, replaced glass pulls, wear and edge damage, one heart inlay missing, large water stain on top, 69-1/2" w, 21-1/2" d, 43-1/2" h **$5,500**

Southern, Kentucky, walnut and cherry, gallery on three sides of rect top, four drawers over four cupboard doors with punched tin panels dec with quarter fans and fylfots, c1850, 66" l...............**$17,500**

Victorian, American pine, serpentine crest, rect top, four small drawers over two banks of four drawers, center cupboard, late 19th C, 65" w, 19" d, 51-1/2" h...............**$750**

Sofas

Aesthetic Movement, American, walnut, shaped backrest, scrolled end above arcaded apron, circular turned legs, matching bolt of orig fabric, 70" l **$1,200**

Art Nouveau, Carlo Bugatti, ebonzied wood, rect back, mechanical seat, slightly scrolling rect arms, parchment upholstery, painted swallows and leafy branches, hammered brass trim, four block form feet, 1900, 68-3/8" l **$1,900**

Centennial, Chippendale-style, American, mahogany, shaped back, rolled arms, yellow velvet upholstered seat, gadrooned apron, cabriole legs with carved knees, claw and ball feet, late 19th C, 62" l **$1,500**

Chippendale, country, step down back with step down arms, bowed front with large down filled cushions, eight molded carved legs, cup caster feet, reupholstered, 76" w, 32" d, 36" h **$3,000**

Classical

Mid Atlantic States, carved mahogany and bird's eye-maple veneer, Grecian style, scrolled and reeded arm and foot, punctuated with brass rosettes, continuing to similar reeded seat rail with inlaid dies, reeded saber legs flanked by brass flowerettes, brass paw feet on casters, old surface, 1805-20, 75" l, 14-1/2" h seat, 35" h...............**$3,680**

New England, carved mahogany veneer, cylindrical crest ends, leaf carved volutes, upholstered seat and rolled veneer seat rail, leaf carved supports, carved paw feet, 1820-40, 92" w, 16-1/2" h seat, 34-3/4" h **$1,650**

Edwardian-style, Chesterfield, tufted brown leather, flattened bun feet, 81" l **$5,000**

Empire, mahogany and figured mahogany veneer frame, well-detailed carving with sea serpent front legs, turned back legs, lyre arms with relief carved flowers and cornucopia, rope turned crest rail, refinished, reupholstered in floral tapestry on ivory ground, bolster pillows, 107" l **$3,850**

Federal

America, carved mahogany, mahogany veer paneled top crest with scrolled sides, front carved with rosette and leaf dec, carved paw

Sideboard, Hepplewhite, 19th C, mahogany, shaped top, above conforming drawers and doors, square tapered legs with inlay, some losses, $600; bentwood box on top, $125.
Photo courtesy of Wiederseim Associates, Inc.

Sideboard, Georgian-style, serpentine front, crossbanding, inlay detail, center drawer flanked by cupboards, $2,750.
Photo courtesy of Wiederseim Associates, Inc.

Sideboard, Hepplewhite, Pennsylvania, cherry, bowfront top over frieze drawer flanked by two short drawers above two cupboard doors flanked by bottle doors, all with line inlaid edges, square tapering legs with bellflower inlay and banded cuffs, c1810, 67" w, 41" h, $7,475.
Photo courtesy of Pook & Pook, Inc.

Sideboard, International Movement, Heywood-Wakefield, champagne finish, drawers over three cabinet doors, two interior drawers and single shelf, branded mark, 59-3/4" l, 19" d, 32-1/2" h, $500.
Photo courtesy of David Rago Auctions, Inc.

Sofa, Chesterfield-style, tufted, taupe leather upholstery, turned feet, wear and tears to leather, 92" x 36" x 29", **$325.**
Photo courtesy of David Rago Auctions, Inc.

Sofa, Old Hickory, broad overhanging arms, loose cushions, sold as part of a six-piece set, 33" x 85-1/2" x 35" **$3,500 for set.**
Photo courtesy of David Rago Auctions, Inc.

Sofa, International Movement, Charles Eames for Herman Miller, upholstered in original orange and red Alexander Girard fabric, chromed and black enameled flat steel frame, unmarked, 72-1/4" l, 28-1/2" d, 35-3/4" h, **$1,400.**
Photo courtesy of David Rago Auctions, Inc.

Sofa, loveseat, Victorian, rose-colored tufted upholstery, provenance: University of Pennsylvania president's residence, c1880, **$250.**
Photo courtesy of Wiederseim Associates, Inc.

Sofa, Philadelphia or Baltimore Chippendale, arched bck over scrolled arms, serpentine front seat, square legs with stretchers, c1780, 39-1/2" h x 92" w, **$4,370.**
Photo courtesy of Pook & Pook, Inc.

feet with front stylized wings, red flower dec upholstery, 96" w, 19-1/2" d, 32" h **$1,000**
Massachusetts or New Hampshire, mahogany veneer paneled crest topped with reeding that continues on top of arms to reeded arm supports, bird's-eye maple inlaid dies on front swelled and reeded legs, turned feet with sq raked rear legs, old refinish, feet repairs, early 19th C, 32-1/4" h **$2,820**
New Hampshire, carved mahogany, upholstered, straight crest continuing to shaped sides with carved arms on vase and ring reeded and swelled posts and cockbeaded panels, bowed seat rail, vase and ring-turned legs with cockbeaded rect inlaid dies, old finish, minor imperfections, c1815, 78" w, 24" d, 17" h seat, 34" h back **$2,415**

George III-style, English, carved oak, double arched upholstered high backrest, scrolled arms, loose cushion seat, acanthus carved legs, claw and ball feet, 58" l **$1,200**

Louis XV style, recamier
Mahogany, tied ribbon and wheatsheaf carved backrest, scrolled end, foliate carved terminals on gadrooned feet, casters, 91" l **$1,410**
Walnut, high scrolled backrest, carved foliate on armrests and cabriole legs, 90" l **$650**

Neoclassical, Baltic, carved mahogany, paneled cresting, padded arms with lions heads and anthemia, upholstered seat and back, shaped feet, c1825, 68" l **$2,185**

Regency-style, heavily carved, acanthus leaves and claw feet, 89" l, 31-1/2" h **$260**

Renaissance Revival, American, carved walnut, five armchairs in two sizes, angular carved frames, 72" l settee **$2,350**

Rococo Revival, John B. Belter, carved rosewood, triple back, carved central rose and fruit on sides, scroll band underneath, carved segmented scroll, tufted back red silk upholstery, brass caster feet, old restoration to central crest, worn seat fabric, 62" w, 42" h **$4,500**

Sheraton to Empire, transitional, carved mahogany, scrolled arms with molded detail, applied rosettes, relief carved leaf supports, brass caps on turned front legs, relief twist carvings, applied moldings on front panels, casters on base, dark refinish, glued break in one scroll, reupholstered, 70" w, 17-1/2" h seat, 34-1/2" h back **$550**

Victorian, late, American, camel back, reupholstered, turned legs, c1890, 60" l **$750**

Stands

Baker, wrought iron, 48" h, 14-1/2" d, 84" h..**$500**

Basin, Federal, New England, mahogany veneer, scalloped backsplash above basin cut outs, shaped skirt over medial shelf with one working and one faux cockbeaded drawer outlined in cross banded veneer, four reeded legs, turned feet, old surface, replaced brass, minor imperfections, early 19th C, 24" w, 16-1/4" d, 43-1/2" h **$1,300**

Bird cage, wicker, painted white, tightly woven quarter moon-shaped cage holder, wrapped pole standard, tightly woven conical base, 74" h **$225**

Book, Arts & Crafts, oak, four open shelves with cutout sides and through tenons, 45-3/4" h **$500**

Canterbury, Regency, mahogany, drawer with paper label for "G. Ibison Furniture Broker & Appraiser, Cumberland Place, Near the Elephant & Castle," restoration, early 19th C, 19-1/4" l, 14" d, 22-1/2" h.........**$1,380**

Card, Aesthetic Movement, American Marquetry inlaid and parcel gilt, circular top inlaid with floral marquetry, fluted and turned pedestal with turned rod decoration, splayed legs, 17-1/2" d, 33-1/2" h.................**$450**

Polychrome and part gilded walnut, circular top, turned and fluted stem, four turned and splayed legs, 12-1/2" d, 33" h.........................**$530**

Cellarette

Arts & Crafts

Stickley, Gustav, flush top, pull-out copper shelf, single drawer, cabinet door, copper pulls, orig finish, large red decal, veneer lifting on sides and back, 22" w, 16" d, 39-1/2" h **$4,315**

Stickley, L. & J.G., arched backsplash, pull-out copper shelf, two-door cabinet, hammered copper strap hinges, ring pulls, top refinished, orig finish on base, "The Work of ..." decal, 35-1/2" x 32" x 16"...**$13,800**

Federal, attributed to Middle Atlantic states, mahogany inlaid, octagonal top, conforming case, both inlaid with contrasting stringing, interior well with removable lead liner, four sq tapering legs inlaid with bellflowers and stringing, brasses appear to be orig, old refinish, sun faded top, imperfections, c1790-1800, 22-1/4" w, 17-1/4" w, 25-1/4" h **$28,200**

George III, English, mahogany, lozenge form, brass bands, twin loop carry handles, racked chamfered tapering legs, mid-19th C, 24" w, 17-1/2" d, 27-1/2" h..............**$7,500**

Chamber, Federal

New England, painted and dec, dec splashboard above wash stand top with round cut-out for basin, medial shelf with drawer below, orig yellow paint with green and gold stenciling and striping, paint wear, imperfections, early 19th C, 18-1/4" h, 1" d, 39-1/4" h.........**$350**

North Shore, MA, carved mahogany, shaped splashboard, veneered cabinet door flanked by ovolu corners, carved columns of leaves and grapes on punchwork ground, ring

turned tapering legs, brass casters, old replaced brasses, old refinish, minor restoration, c1815-25, 21-1/2" w, 16" d, 35-5/8" h....**$2,300**

Portsmouth, New Hampshire, mahogany inlaid, shaped splashboard with center quarter round shelf, pierced top with bow front, square string inlaid supports continue to outward flaring legs with patterned inlays, medial shelf, satinwood skirt, small center drawer with patterned inlaid lower edge, shaped stretchers with inlaid paterae, old finish, minor imperfections, c1800, 23" w, 16-1/2" d, 41" h......................**$5,750**

Demilune, Hepplewhite, country, pine, salmon paint, dark red fingerline dec, c1800 ....**$10,000**

Dumbwaiter

Georgian, three tiered, mahogany, each graduated dished tier raised on turned standard, three down swept legs, 22-1/2" d largest tier, 38-1/2" h **$600**

Queen-Anne style, walnut, three circular shelves, splayed legs, pad feet, 21" d, 39" h **$300**

Easel

Aesthetic Movement, ash, cresting with stylized scroll, rod and ball design, straight legs and spindle-inset supports, 19th C, 64" h **$275**

Louis XVI-style, mahogany and parcel-gilt, picture support hung with berried laurel swags, trestle-end frame carved with acanthus, imbrications, and dolphins, 25" w, 23-1/2" d, 82" h......................**$950**

Étagère

Classical, New England, mahogany and mahogany veneer, spool turned gallery, ball finials, three shelves with similar supports, two recessed panel cupboard doors, single shelf int., ball turned feet, old refinish, imperfections, 1860s, 35-1/4" w, 15-3/4" d, 66" h........................**$990**

Regency, late, English, six tiers, corner, columnar supports, basal drawer, brass casters, early 19th C, 18" w, 14" d, 62" h..................**$3,000**

Victorian, three rect tiers raised by turned columns over two cabinet doors, ball feet, casters, 20-1/2" w, 16" d, 51-1/2" h......................**$1,180**

Folding, Chippendale

New York State or Pennsylvania, cherry, dished top rotates and titles, birdcage support, swelled and

Magazine stand, Arts & Crafts, Gustav Stickley, No. 514, oak, tongue-and-groove paneled sides, square posts, leather strips tacked to shelf ends, original finish, early red decal under top shelf, wear to top, 35-1/2" x 14-1/4" x 14-1/2", **$8,100.**
Photo courtesy of David Rago Auctions, Inc.

Magazine stand, Arts & Crafts, Gustav Stickley, No. 548, paneled sides, four shelves, unmarked, refinished, 44" x 15-1/4" x 15", **$2,000.**
Photo courtesy of David Rago Auctions, Inc.

Music stand, Arts & Crafts, Gustav Stickley, four shelves, tapered posts, shaped apron, orig finish, decal on leg, paper label, missing small piece from side stretcher, stains, 39" x 22" x 15", **$2,600.**

Photo courtesy of David Rago Auctions, Inc.

Sewing stand, Hepplewhite style, inlaid mahogany, **$250.**

Photo courtesy of Wiederseim Associates, Inc.

Tabouret, Arts & Crafts, L. & J. G. Stickley, legs mortised through top, orig finish, unmarked, 20" x 18" x 18", **$1,200.**

Photo courtesy of David Rago Auctions, Inc.

turned pedestal, cabriole tripod base, pad feet, old refinish, imperfections, 1755-1775, 17-1/2" d, 26" h **$3,220**

Pennsylvania, walnut, molded dish top, inscribed edge tilts, tapering pedestal with suppressed ball, cabriole legs ending in pad feet, imperfections, 1760-80, 22" d, 29" h **$4,600**

Magazine

Arts & Crafts

Stickley, Gustav, Tree of Life, carved sides, four shelves, orig finish and tacks, unmarked, minor edge wear, 14" sq, 43-1/2" h **$1,610**

Stickley, L. & J.G., single broad slat on either side, arched toe board, new finish, "The Work of L. & J. G. Stickley" decal, 36" w, 12" d, 30" h **$2,990**

Eastlake, carved maple, walnut, and bird's eye maple veneer, finely turned posts with ball finials on top corners, turned legs, dovetailed drawer, drop pulls, old finish, old gold paint in carving and turnings, one corner restored, 22" w, 14-1/2" d **$230**

Regency-style, mahogany, four divisions, dipped dividers, frieze drawer, turned legs on casters, late 19th C, 23" w, 16" d, 24" h **$1,775**

Renaissance Revival, mahogany, walnut, parcel-gilt, and ebonized gilt-metal, hanging, back plate with acanthus crest flanked by fleur-de-lis and bellflowers, uprights mounted on top with gilt-metal bust roundels, central hinged magazine folio set with gilt composition oval bust of Mercury, gilt incised detailing, third quarter 19th C, 19-3/4" w, 21-1/2" h **$300**

Victorian, mahogany, burled walnut veneer, turned corner posts and finials with scrolled and pierced panels, short boxed stops which conform to ends, dovetailed drawer with carved pull and applied fretwork, four trumpet turned legs, brass casters, late 19th or early 20th C, 28-1/2" w, 16" d, 21" h **$1,150**

Night, Art Deco, attributed to Maurice Defrene, France, amboyna wood inlaid with stylized flowers in various fruitwoods and mother-of-pearl, price for pr, c1925, 15" w, 18" d, 29-1/2" h **$2,235**

Pedestal

Aesthetic Movement, American

Ebonized, rect top, turned stem, angular supports, four curved legs, 17" w, 14" d, 35-1/2" h **$500**

Gilded and velvet mounted walnut, sq top, gilded lappet corners, sq base, 12" sq, 37-1/2" h **$750**

Renaissance Revival, American, ebonized walnut, sawtooth frieze, turned supports, four-footed circular base, 18" w, 12-1/2" d, 34" h **$450**

Plant

Arts & Crafts

Limbert, ebon-oak line, overhanging top, four caned panels on each side, recent finish, branded signature, 14" w, 14" d, 34" h **$2,100**

Stickley, Gustav, sq top flush with cloud-lift apron, narrow board mortised through corseted stretchers with tenon and key, orig finish, crack in one stretcher, 1902-04 red decal, 14" sq, 27" h **$3,450**

French-style, black lacquered finish, turtle-shaped top with open well, ormolu wreath and quiver designs, acanthus leaves, hoof-shaped caps on feet, 20th C, 19-1/4" w, 14-1/2" d, 30" h **$275**

Folk Art, carved and painted root, America, polychrome painted animal heads radiating from entwined root base, inscribed "MAS 1897," 23" w, 38-1/2" h **$1,725**

Victorian, walnut and pine, three tiers, two top round, larger one octagonal, turned legs, scalloped aprons, old finish, 31" d, 37-1/2" h **$420**

Portfolio, William IV, English, carved rosewood, folding mechanism, c1830 .... **$3,500**

Quilt rack, Renaissance Revival, American, walnut, faceted turned rods on trestle base, 27" w, 35" h **$200**

Reading, Federal, Albany, NY, mahogany, reading stand above ring-turned tapering post on rect shaped canterbury, turned tapering spindles, casters, early 19th C, 22-1/4" w, 14" d, 47-1/2" h **$3,200**

Sewing, Sheraton, country, black walnut, poplar secondary wood, lift top, fitted int. compartment with four int. dovetailed drawers and pigeon holes, single dovetailed drawer with figured front and incised beading, well-turned legs with ring turnings, replaced brass pull, pegged construction, lock missing, one leg with well-executed repair, 20" w, 19-1/2" d, 29" h **$1,155**

Sheet music stand, Aesthetic Movement, American, rosewood, hinged sides, pedestal, four downswept legs, 18" w, 5" d, 36" h **$500**

Single drawer

Country, mahogany and fruitwood, incised monogram on left apron "SC" in script, two board top with gallery, small dovetailed drawer in apron, turned legs and supports, base shelf, old mellow refinishing, insect damage, 16-1/2" w, 16-1/4" d, 28" h **$450**

English, rosewood veneer, mahogany secondary wood, small urn-shaped finials on top, dovetailed center drawer, wooden pulls, three shelves, turned legs, old refinishing, minor edge chips, filled splits, 19th C, 19-1/4" w, 14-1/2" d, 39-1/2" h **$1,050**

Hepplewhite, cherry, pine and poplar secondary wood, two-board top, dovetailed drawer with brass pull, slender legs taper to feet, refinished, old tin patch over knot hole in drawer bottom, 17-3/4" w, 18" d, 27-1/2" h **$500**

Pennsylvania, early, softwood, one molded drawer, deeply beaded skirt, splayed tapered legs, scrubbed top, old tan over red painted base, 21-3/4" w, 21-1/2" d, 30" h **$1,650**

Sheraton, country, curly maple and walnut, poplar secondary wood, two board top, dovetailed drawer, turned legs, old replaced brass pull, old finish, chip on foot ring, 18" w, 17-1/4" d, 28-3/8" h.................**$700**

Sheraton, country, decorated, orig brown sponged dec over bittersweet colored ground, old dry varnish, pine, two board top, sq nail construction in drawer, splayed ring turned legs, ball feet, minor wear, 21" w, 20-3/4" d, 31" h..........**$3,335**

Sheraton, country, walnut and cherry, poplar secondary wood, single board top, well turned legs with raised panels that flank dovetailed beveled edge drawer, orig glass pull, dark refinishing, old repairs, 20-1/2" w, 18" d, 28-3/4" h.......**$500**

Tabouret, Regency-style, carved oak, cushioned top above frame carved with elaborate floral sprays, raised and scrolled toes, 23" w, 19" h **$500**

Tier

Classical Revival, sq onyx top, two tiers, scrolled metal skirt, legs with central leaf tip band, second medial shelf, outward scrolled feet, late 19th C, 31-3/4" h **$360**

English, mahogany, small gallery on top, four shelves, ring-turned columns, half turned moldings resemble bamboo, brass casters, refinished, few trim pcs replaced, putty restorations under shelves, 16" sq, 44-3/4" h **$350**

Federal, New England, mahogany, three trays of diminishing size, molded edges, each rotates on turned urn-shaped shaft, cabriole leg tripod base, arris pad feet, old refinish, minor imperfections, late 18th/early 19th C, largest tier 23-1/4" d, 43-1/4" h...............**$7,650**

Two drawers, Hepplewhite, cherry, pine secondary wood, single board top, two dovetailed and beaded drawers with orig brass pulls, high tapered legs, old mellow finish, 14-3/8" w, 17" d, 28-7/8" h.......**$1,050**

Umbrella, Arts & Crafts, early 20th C, oak, sq form, four posts, top and bottom stretchers with mortise and tenon joinery, one dark brown finish, other medium brown finish, marked "Cedric S. Sweeter Jan 23, 1920," price for pr, 12" w, one 28-3/4" h, other 29" h **$230**

Vitrine, Mahogany, line border inlay, satinwood panels, top with drop front, molded edges, tapered sq legs, brass casters, joined by stretcher base, 21-1/2" w, 16-1/2" d, 28" h **$600**

Wash

Eastlake, walnut and burlwood, three drawers, replaced white marble top, 29" w, 38" h.................**$265**

Empire, figured mahogany veneer, poplar secondary wood, dovetailed gallery fitted with narrow shelf, bowed top with cut-outs for wash bowl and two jars, serpentine front supports, turned rear posts, dovetailed drawer in base with brass pulls, high well turned legs, refinished, edge chips, 18" w, 16" d, 37-3/4" h **$385**

Federal

American, mahogany and figured mahogany veneer, bow front with two small drawers, cutout for bowl, cutout sides, single dovetailed drawer in base, turned legs, worn finish, some water damage, replaced top and two small drawers, 20-1/4" w, 17-1/4" d, 30-1/4" h **$275**

Telephone stand, Arts & Crafts, L. & J. G. Stickley, no. 587, square overhanging top and apron, Handcraft decal inside leg, very good orig finish, minor separation to top, 27" x 16" x 16", **$1,400.** Photo courtesy of David Rago Auctions, Inc.

Tea stand, folding tray, later needlepoint with English storefronts, **$150.** Photo courtesy of Dotta Auction Co., Inc.

Wash stand, cottage style, painted pale green, original painted flowers and foliage on long drawer and pair of cupboard doors, scrolled backsplash, carved foliate pulls, extra painted panel shown on top, **$200.**

Photo courtesy of Dotta Auction Co., Inc.

Stool, hand made, round top, four shaped legs, painted white, **$35.**

Photo courtesy of Joseph P. Smalley, Jr.

Foot stool, attributed to Old Hickory, reed top over spindled sides, overcoated orig finish, unmarked, 13" x 17" x 11-1/2", **$500.**

Photo courtesy of David Rago Auctions, Inc.

Rhode Island, mahogany veneer, top with four shaped corners, canted corners, engaged ring-turned columns ending in reeded legs flanking cockbeaded drawers outlined in cross banded veneer, top two drawers with sections, replaced brasses, old refinish, imperfections, c1790, 20-3/4" w, 15-1/2" d, 28-1/2" h **$4,025**

Hepplewhite, bow front, mahogany and figured veneer, pine and poplar secondary woods, dovetailed gallery, top with cutout for bowl and two cup inserts, dovetailed beaded drawer below door with brass pull, tapered legs with beaded panels on front, restoration to center leg, 24" w, 17" d, 40" h **$600**

Victorian, walnut, white marble top, one drawer, pr lower cupboard doors, carved fruit and nut pulls, 30" w, 30" h **$300**

Whatnot, Corner, Victorian, Chinoiserie bamboo and lacquer, frame set with two diamond-shaped mirrors and shelves, late 19th C, 22" w, 13" d, 56" h **$250**

Work

Classical, carved maple and rosewood veneer, top outlined with rosewood veneer banding above sectional veneered drawer, lower drawer flanked by short columns, tapering pedestal joining four leaf carved legs ending in carved hairy paw feet on castors, old refinish, early 19th C, 20-3/4" w, 18-1/2" d, 28-3/4" h.. **$500**

Federal

Middle Atlantic region, bird's eye maple and oak veneer, top with hinged leaves, two working and two faux string inlaid drawers, top one fitted, ring-turned swelled legs joined by similar double stretchers, curving legs, scrolled feet, old refinish, imperfections, 1815-25, 17-1/4" w, 18" d, 28-1/4" h..... **$2,750**

New England, cherry, rect top with rounded corners, turned and swelled pedestal, outwardly curving legs, refinished, imperfections, early 19th C, 21-3/4" w, 15-7/8" d, 29-1/2" h **$500**

New England, mahogany, rect top, single drawer, turned and reeded legs, old refinish, imperfections, early 19th C, 22" w, 16-3/4" d, 28-1/2" h **$750**

Hepplewhite, New England, cherry inlaid, sq top, outline stringing and quarter fan inlays on ovolo cor-

ners, line inlaid drawer and skirt, line inlaid sq tapering legs, cross banded cuffs, brass drawer pull, refinished, c1810, 19" w, 19" d, 27" h **$2,650**

Renaissance Revival, American, lift top opening to real satinwood interior fitted with compartments, narrow drawer above semi-circular bag drawer, pair of stylized lyre form ends jointed by arched stretcher surmounted by turned finial, c1860 .... **$875**

Sheraton, New England, mahogany, veneered, outset rounded corners, shaped top, pull-out suspended fabric bag below single drawer, ring-turned and reeded round tapering legs ending in ring-turned tapering vasiform feet, old refinish, 1805-15, 16-1/2" w, 18-1/2" d, 28-1/4" h **$3,500**

Steps

Bed, New England, pine and tulipwood, two steps, thumb-molded drawer below bottom one, flanked by shaped sides, demilune base, old color, repaired, early 19th C, 15-1/2" w, 10" d, 17-1/2" h **$575**

Circus, America, painted white stringers, red, yellow, and blue treads, early 20th C, 25" w, 90" d, 27" h **$435**

Library

George III, English, mahogany, rect molded hinged top, eight steps, late 18th C, 49-1/2" w, 53-1/2" h **$2,500**

Regency, English, mahogany, three steps, inset green leather treads, scrolling banister, sq balusters, feet with brass casters, early 19th C, 46" w, 27" w, 56" h **$2,400**

Stools

Cricket, Arts & Crafts, Limbert, #205-1/2", rect top covered with new leather, splayed sides, inverted heart cut-out, single stretcher with through-tenon, replaced keys, orig finish, branded, 20" w, 15" d, 18" h **$950**

Foot

Arts & Crafts, oak

Barber Brothers, oak, nicely replaced leather seat, some color added to orig finish, paper label, 13" w, 13" d, 11" h **$110**

Limbert, cricket, #205-1/2, rect orig leather top and tacks, splayed sides with inverted heart cut-out having single stretcher with through-tenon

Foot stool, oval top with floral needle-point top, **$175.**
Photo courtesy of Joy Luke Auctions.

Stool, hand painted, green ground, country scene with windmill on top, **$125.**
Photo courtesy of Dotta Auction Co., Inc.

Ottoman, Empire, c1830, figured mahogany, serpentine form, shaped supports, wooden casters, green and gold velvet upholstery, 17" w, 13" h, **$480.**
Photo courtesy of Sloans & Kenyon Auctioneers and Appraisers.

construction, orig finish, branded and numbered, 20" w, 15" d, 19" h **$2,000**

Painted, attributed to York County, Pennsylvania, pine, paint dec, man eating oysters in center of top, red ground, scalloped border, inscription "By D. J. Rash for C. F. Rash," stylized leaves on sides and feet, 15-5/8" l, 9-3/4" w, 10-3/4" h **$18,700**

Queen Anne, walnut, rect frieze, 4 cabriole legs each with shell carving on knees, pad feet, slip seat, 18th C, 22-1/2" w, 17" d, 17" h...........**$1,950**

Sheraton, curly and bird's eye maple, old finish, cane top, minor damage to top, 7-3/4" w, 13" l, 6-1/2" h..**$440**

Victorian, carved walnut, short cabriole legs carved at knees with shells, shaped skirting carved with acanthus, velveteen upholstery, late 19th C, 12-3/4" w, 16" l, 11" h **$175**

Windsor, attributed to Maine, early 19th C, rect top, four swelled legs joined by X-form stretchers, orig dark brown grain paint which resembles exotic wood, yellow line accents, paint imperfections, 12" w, 8" d, 7" h **$625**

Joint
Early, oak, old finish, wear and age cracks, 11" w, 16-1/2" l, 17-3/4" h **$990**

Jacobean-style, oak, rect plank top, shaped skirt, block and ring-turned legs joined by box stretcher, 18" w, 11-1/4" d, 21" h.........................**$700**

Milking stool, well turned round wooden seat, splayed bamboo legs and stretchers, old red and yellow graining over cream ground, wear, 10" d, 6-1/4" h **$180**

Ottoman, Classical, attributed to Boston, Massachusetts, mahogany veneer, overstuffed cushions rest inside mitred frame atop molded base, ogee bracket feet, wooden casters, refin-

ished, minor imperfections, price for pr, c1830, 20" w, 18" d, 17-1/2" h **$2,235**

Piano
Louis XVI-style, carved beech, circular, adjustable, close-nailed over stuffed top, petal-carved frieze, leaf-capped turned, tapered, and fluted legs, wavy cross-stretcher, late 19th C **$850**

Renaissance Revival, American, telescopic, X-form, turned wooden screws adjust height, 20" h **$325**

Victorian, mahogany, upholstered, revolving, 20" h, early 19th......**$200**

Seat-type
Country, folk art, attributed to Fredericksburg, PA, painted and dec, octagonal seat, chamfered edge, trimmed with border band of carved hearts, tall splayed and chamfered legs also trimmed with carved hearts and joined by slender rungs, overall polychrome, late 19th/early 20th C **$1,850**

George III, mahogany, gold floral satin upholstered rest seat, sq tapering supports, molded H-form stretchers, pr, late 19th C, 19-1/2" l, 17" h **$1,650**

International Movement
Eames, Charles, manufactured by Herman Miller, Time-Life, walnut, concave seat, 13" d, 15" h......**$1,000**

Platner, Warren, manufactured by Knoll, bronze wire base, peach fabric upholstered seat, 17" d, 21" h **$325**

Renaissance Revival, American, walnut, cushioned and hinged seat opening to well, trestle base with angular supports, 23-1/2" w, 11" d, 19" h **$265**

Windsor, American, oblong plant seat raised on three tall, turned and slightly swelled legs joined by T-stretcher, traces of old green paint, 19th C, 15" w, 24-1/2" h **$200**

Tables
Architect's, George III, English, mahogany, hinged tooled leather work surface above opposing hinged work surface, turned pedestal on three splayed legs, pad feet, some reconstruction, late 19th C, 29" w, 19-1/4" d, 29-1/2" h **$2,300**

Bank, Neoclassical-style, brass and metal, rect glass-inset top above frieze pierced with putti and scrolling foliage, trestle end supports cast as sphinxes, joined by stretcher, black marble block supports, removed from Hyde Park Bank of Chicago, 62" w, 39" d, 40" h **$800**

Breakfast
Chippendale to Hepplewhite, transitional, walnut, one board top, beaded edge apron, sq legs with slight taper, molded corner, and inside chamfer, H stretcher, old finish, stains on top, 19" w, 29-1/4" l, 28-1/4" h **$8,250**

Classical, New York, carved mahogany inlaid, top with brass inlay in outline, stamped brass on edge of shaped leaves, one working and one faux drawers, flanked by drop pendants, four pillar curved platform support, leafage carved legs, carved paw feet, casters, replaced pulls, old finish, repairs, losses, 1820-30, 39" w, 24" d, 28" h.................**$2,450**

Federal
Massachusetts, central, inlaid cherry, rect hinged top with ovolo corners, base with straight skirt, edged with lunette inlay, flanked by sq tapering legs outlined in stringing, topped with icicle inlay, old refinish, c1810, 36" w, 17" d, 29" h.................**$1,150**

Typical Parts of a Table

Card table, Federal, American, tiger maple, reeded legs, 19th C, 30" x 36" x 18", **$4,250.**
Photo courtesy of David Rago Auctions, Inc.

Card table, Massachusetts Federal, mahogany, serpentine top, ovolo corners, satinwood veneer, turned and reeded legs, c1810, 29-1/2" x 35-3/4" **$3,680.**
Photo courtesy of Pook & Pook, Inc.

Massachusetts or New England, mahogany oval top, hinged leaves, flanking two drawers, one working, one faux, both outlined in stringing and have central panel of figured mahogany veneer above chevron-style inlaid banding, reeded, turned, tapering legs, turned feet, old refinish, surface imperfections, 1815, 35-3/8" w, 20-1/4" d, 29-3/4" h **$8,225**

New York City, carved mahogany veneer, rect top, shaped leaves, one working and one faux end drawers, cross banded mahogany veneer, turned acanthus leaf carved pedestal, four acanthus leaf carved legs, brass hairy paw feet, old refinish, repairs, c1815, 25" w closed, 38-1/2" l, 30-1/4" h **$1,725**

Card
Classical

Attributed to firm of Isaac Vine and Isaac Vine Jr., Boston, carved mahogany and mahogany veneer, rect top with beaded edges, skirt with recessed panel, C-scrolls and carved volutes over tapering pedestal accented by carved leafage above serpentine veneered platform with carved and scrolled feet on casters, old refinish, imperfections, 1819-24, 37" w, 17-1/2" d, 28-1/2" h **$1,840**

Attributed to Thomas Astens, New York City, carved mahogany and satinwood, rect swivel top with rounded ends, outlined in cross banded mahogany veneer, satinwood veneered skirt, faceted pineapple-like carving above acanthus leaf carving on pedestal, shaped legs, carved paw feet on casters, old refinish, imperfections, 1822, 36" w, 18-1/4" d, 28" h **$3,335**

New York, carved mahogany, mahogany veneer rect swivel top with rounded front carved corners, leaf carved and shaped shaft, curving platform which joins 4 scrolling leaf carved legs ending in carved paw feet, refinished, minor imperfections, 1820-30, 36" w, 17-1/2" d, 30" h **$1,495**

Federal

Boston or Charlestown, Massachusetts, mahogany inlaid, demilune top with inlaid top edge above undercut lower edge, three-paneled conforming skirt with outline

stringing, interspersed with inlaid dies, string inlaid legs, refinished, top detached, other imperfections, c1800, 35-3/4" w, 17-1/2" d, 30" h **$2,500**

Boston or Charlestown, Massachusetts, mahogany and figured maple inlaid, rect top with ovolo corners and inlaid top edge above undercut lower edge, skirt with figured maple rect panel and inlaid rect dies, sq double tapering legs ending in cuff inlays, old refinish, imperfections, early 19th C, 35-3/4" w, 17" d, 29-1/2" h **$2,235**

North Shore, Massachusetts, mahogany veneer carved, serpentine facade with ovolo front corners, ring-turned leaf and spiral carved legs, turned feet, old refinish, imperfections, c1815, 37-1/2" w, 17-5/8" d, 30-1/4" h **$900**

Philadelphia, mahogany and satinwood veneer, serpentine top, string inlaid skirt flanking rect satinwood center, sq tapering legs outlined in stringing with diamond-shaped die, terminating in cuff inlays, refinished, imperfections, c1800, 36" w, 18-3/8" d, 29-3/4" h **$5,600**

Sheraton

American, pine, old brown flame graining, top with later black paint, finely turned legs with raised acanthus leaf bands below serpentine apron, large raised relief leaf carvings at corners, ball feet, 34-1/2" w, 17-1/2" d, 30" h **$1,725**

English, mahogany, mahogany flame veneer, banded inlay around top, old red felt insert on interior surfaces, inlaid panels and diamonds on aprons, turned legs, relief ring detail, tapered to applied ormolu paw feet, old finish, pieced repair at one hinge, minor edge damage, 36" w, 16-7/8" d, 29-3/4" h **$2,100**

Victorian, rosewood, rounded rect top with red baize surface, quadripartite base, scrolling feet, 36" w, 36" d, 29-1/2" h **$950**

Center
Aesthetic Movement, American

John Jeliff, attributed to, inset white marble top and turret-form corners, paneled frieze with angular pendants, boldly scrolled and fac-

Center table, Eastlake-style, American, ebonized, elaborate polychrome marquetry turtle top shaped apron, turned and carved legs and stretcher, all with burl veneer accents, finial missing ears, 19th C, 30" x 41" x 29-1/2", **$3,750.**
Photo courtesy of David Rago Auctions, Inc.

Conference table, Modern, Jens Rison, veneer top, aluminum base, marked, 29" x 96" x 41", **$1,400.**
Photo courtesy of David Rago Auctions, Inc.

eted trumpet legs joined by and H-form stretcher, delicately carved elongated leaftips, 46-1/2" w, 30-1/2" d, 30-1/2" h **$4,000**
Walnut, white marble top, paneled frieze, four angular legs on scrolled base, 36" w, 24" d, 30" h **$1,650**
Baroque-style, painted, parcel gilt, octagonal marble veined rose colored top above plain frieze, acanthus carved, shaped and tapered legs, late 19th C, 44-1/2" w, 30" h
....**$2,820**
Biedermeier, inlaid walnut, shaped rect top, molded frieze with drawer, canted, sq-section cabriole legs, 25" w, 37" l, 27-3/4" h **$1,100**
Classical
Boston, attributed to, carved mahogany and mahogany veneer, circular top with inset leather surface, cross banded border, conforming base with four drawers, gilt brass lion's head ring pulls, vase and ring-turned spiral carved center support, gadrooned circular platform, four scrolled reeded and paneled legs, gilt brass hairy paw feet and casters, refinished, minor imperfections, c1825, 27-3/4" d, 28" h
....**$12,925**
Philadelphia, carved mahogany veneer, rect top with molded edge, cockbeaded frieze with single central working drawer flanked by faux drawers, turned and carved pedestal ending in gadrooning above stepped, curved pedestal, 4 belted ball feet, old surface, minor imperfections, carving similar to work of Anthony G. Quervelle (1789-1856), Philadelphia, c1827, 45-1/4" w, 20" d, 34-3/4" h **$2,550**

Gothic Revival, attributed to New York State, mahogany veneer, hexagonal top with molded edge overhangs shaped frieze, three faceted columns atop flat base with concave sides on scrolled feet, old refinish, restored, 1935-45, 34-1/4" d, 31" h **$1,120**
International Movement, Wienerwerkstatte, mahogany and brass, circular top with cross banded edge, conforming frieze, sq-section support flanked by four further cylindrical supports, raised on truncated pyramidal base, c1930, 25-1/4" d, 30-1/2" h **$550**
Louis XV-style, mahogany inlaid, ormolu mounted walnut, shaped rect top, one short drawer, opposite faux drawer, cabriole legs, cast sabots, 19th C, 35" w, 22" d, 28" h ..**$600**
Napoleon III, top inset with porcelain plaque depicting Figuros Dining, surrounded by portrait plaques depicting interior scenes, circular carved base mounted with gilt bronze flowers and rams heads, three-sided concave plinth, 35-1/2" d, 34" h **$20,100**
Renaissance Revival, inlaid profile portrait of George Washington, eagle, American flags, images of farming, industry, sailing, and travel, c1876
....**$20,900**
Victorian, bamboo, lacquer octagonal top, four legs joined by a stretcher with medial shelves, 28" w, 20" d, 28" h **$600**
Chair
American, cherry, three-board top, hinged seat lid, scalloped edge sides, apron, shoe feet, black paint on underside of top, old refinishing

on base, minor repairs, late 18th C, 45-1/2" d top, 28-1/2" h **$9,350**
New England, pine and birch, top tilts above plant seat flanked by sq tapering arm supports which continue to chamfered legs, four sq stretchers, old refinish, late 18th C, 40-1/2" w, 42" d, 28-3/4" h
....**$1,100**
New England, pine, maple, and walnut, three-board top tilts above plank seat, walnut arms with turned tapering supports, similar legs terminate in ball and pad feet, old stained red brown surface, repairs, early 19th C, 48-1/4" w, 46-3/4" d, 27-3/4" h **$3,300**
Coach, Georgian, split leather writing surface closing to box form, S-curve legs joined by stretchers, 24-1/4" w, 24-1/4" d, 31-1/4" h **$1,180**
Console
Empire, American, rect white marble top over single drawer, down swept legs joined by medial shelf, mid-19th C, 28-3/4" w, 17" d, 28-1/2" h
....**$1,800**
George III, mahogany, rect banded top over two drawers, square tapering legs, 51-1/2" w, 23-1/2" d, 34" h
....**$1,400**
Neoclassical, attributed to Italy, parcel gilt and painted, inset marble top above frieze painted with rinceaux and scrolling foliage, centered by carved portrait medallion, stop-fluted tapering legs, first half 19th C and later, 38" w, 19-1/2" d, 33" h
....**$3,350**
Neoclassical-style, green painted, parcel gilt, brown marble top above frieze decorated with scrolling foliage, fluted tapering legs, price for

Console table, Modern, Frank Lloyd Wright, broad overhanging top, two central cupboard doors, two side cupboards, long bin-pulls, orig condition, contemporary vintage, 29-1/2" x 87" x 18", **$800.**
Photo courtesy of David Rago Auctions, Inc.

Dining table, Edwardian, burl veneer top, corniced edge supported on barley twist legs, elaborate quatrefoil stretchers, three 24" leaves in original rack, 30-1/2" x 45-1/2" x 66-1/2", **$900.**
Photo courtesy of David Rago Auctions, Inc.

pr, 20th C, 31" w, 14-1/2" d, 35" h **$2,400**
Rococo-style, polychrome painted and parcel gilt, veneered green marble top, heavily carved scrolling legs joined by stretcher surmounted by shell, 45" w, 23" d, 34" h **$4,600**

Dining

Arts & Crafts
Limbert, #403, cut-corner top over intricate base, slab supports with three spindles in an oval cut-out keyed stretchers connecting to a center leg, one leaf, orig finish, numbered, 50" w, 50" d, 30" h **$2,500**
Stickley, Gustav, variant of model 634, oak, oval top, six leaves, sq leg posts with mortise and tenon joinery, c1920, 46" w, 54-3/4" to 120-3/4" d, 30" h **$11,500**
Unknown maker, possibly California, oak, rect board on board top, lower median shelf with through tenons, cutout sides, shoe foot base, deep brown restored finish, c1912, 83-1/2" w, 35-1/4" d, 29" h....**$3,200**
Empire, carved figure mahogany, mahogany veneer, pine secondary wood, two board top, two 14-3/4" d scalloped leaves, pineapple carved column, short turned drops on corners, brass line inlay along aprons, finely carved paw feet and relief hair on legs, refinished, splits in column, repairs, 39" w, 23-1/4" d, 27-3/4" h **$1,560**

Federal
Massachusetts, mahogany, rect top with similar drop leaves, straight skirts, molded tapering legs ending in casters, refinished, repairs, prov-

enance: according to family verbal history, this table belonged to General Benjamin Lincoln, who served in Washington's Army during the American Revolution, and accepted the sword of Cornwallis when the British surrendered, late 18th C, 46-3/4" w, 47-3/4" extended, 28-3/4" h **$1,550**
New England, cherry and bird's eye maple, two parts, two rect ends each with hinged drop-leaf, ring-turned tapering legs ending in ball feet, orig surface, minor surface mars, c1820-25, 82" w, 44-1/2" d, 28-3/4" h **$1,725**
Federal-style, mahogany, three part drop leaf sections, turned, octagonal legs with casters, 19th C, 162" l, 48" d, 29" h **$6,375**
George III, late 19th C
Mahogany, drop leaf, gate leg, 55-1/4" w, 18-1/2" d, 29-1/4" h **$1,770**
Mahogany, rect top with rounded corners and reeded edge, double turned pedestals on paneled and reeded downswept legs, brass cap casters, two leaves, 48" w, 115" l with leaves, 28-3/4" h...........**$9,990**
George III-style
Cross banded mahogany, wide inlaid borders, three turned pedestals, downswept feet, brass cap casters, two leaves, 13' l extended, 53" w, 29" h **$5,875**
Mahogany, D-shaped top with rounded corners and reeded edge, twin pedestal bases of column raised on tripod base, downswept legs, brass toe caps and casters, 120" l, 44" w, 29-1/4" h..........**$2,100**
Mahogany, rect top, rounded cor-

ners, reeded edge, triple turned pedestals, reeded downswept legs, brass cap casters, two additional leaves, 12' 6" l extended, 53-1/2" w, 29-1/2" h **$7,100**
Georgian-style, painted green, rect top, gadrooned edge, plain frieze, shell carved cabriole legs, claw and ball feet, 53" w, 39" d, 28" h **$900**
International Movement, Hans Wegner, c1960, teak, circular top fitted on cross stretcher frame with metal mounts set into four tapered circular legs, 61" d................**$1,880**
Louis XVI-style, walnut, circular top splitting to accommodate eight leaves, plain frieze, circular tapered legs, 54-1/2" w, 30-1/2" h......**$1,175**
Queen Anne
Boston area, c1740-50, inlaid figured walnut, top heavy thumb-molded edge outlined in stringing, hinged leaves flank serpentine shaped skirts above the cabriole legs, pad feet, old surface, imperfections, 42" w, 14-1/4" d, 40-3/4" d extended, 28" h **$11,200**
Virginia or North Carolina, walnut, top with molded edge, hinged demilune leaves flank straight skirts above block and swelled turned straight legs, pad feet, old refinish, imperfections, 1760-70, 50-1/2" w, 18-3/4" d, 57-3/4" extended, 29-1/2" h **$5,600**
Regency, late, inlaid mahogany, three parts, D-shaped ends, rect center section, all cross banded in satinwood, checker cross banded frieze and sq tapered legs ending in spade feet, four leaves, early 19th C, 155" l, 54" w, 29" h................**$5,175**

Regency-style, mahogany, rect top, reeded edge, rounded corners, three ring-turned pedestals, molded cabriole legs, casters, two leaves, late 19th C, 48" w, 177" l, 29" h **$17,250**

Display, Edwardian, inlaid mahogany, shaped rect glazed top on sq tapering legs joined by X-form stretcher **$600**

Dressing

Chippendale, attributed to Pennsylvania, carved mahogany, rect molded top, case of two cockbeaded graduated drawers flanked by reeded stop-fluted lambrequin corners, cabriole legs, pad feet on platforms, all joined by shaped apron, old brasses, refinished, restored, c1760-80, 31" w, 18" d, 29-1/2" h **$5,875**

Classical, New England, grain painted and dec, scrolling crest over two short drawers, projecting top with rounded corners on conforming base, single drawer, ring-turned and incised tapering legs, allover grain paint resembling rosewood, highlighted by stencils of fruit bowls and scrolling leaves and flowers, gold, green, and black line dec, minor imperfections, c1820-40, 30" w, 15-1/4" d, 39" h **$1,550**

Empire, mahogany, small case top with drawer, dovetailed drawer in center, thin molding around lower apron, figured mahogany veneer over pine, high ring turned legs with relief rope twist carvings, small pieced restorations, 35-1/2" w, 17-3/4" d, 36-1/2" h **$1,650**

Federal, New York state, carved mahogany and mahogany veneer, brass inlaid, cockbeaded rect mirror, scrolled acanthus leaf carved supports with brass emb rosettes above three short drawers, projecting case of two short drawers, one long drawer joining four vase and ring-turned acanthus carved legs, casters, refinished, repaired, c1825, 36-1/4" w, 21-1/2" d, 55" h **$1,725**

George I/II, English, walnut veneer, banded rect top with rounded front corners overhanging shallow straight front fitted with five shallow drawers of banded treatment, plain cabriole legs, pad feet, veneer losses, worm damage, c1725, 32" w, 17" d, 30" h **$1,875**

Drop leaf

Chippendale

New England, southern, cherry, oval overhanging drop leaf top, cut-out apron, scrolled returns, four cabriole legs ending in claw and ball feet, imperfections, c1760-80, 44-1/2" l open, 15-1/2" w, 27" h **$4,410**

Pennsylvania, walnut, shaped skirt, molded Marlborough legs, old surface, minor imperfections, late 18th C, 15-1/2" w, 46-3/4" l, 29" h **$550**

Rhode Island, carved mahogany, rect drop leaf top, four sq molded stop fluted legs joined by cut-out apron, repairs, c1780, 47-3/4" w, 38-1/4" d, 29" h **$2,100**

Classical, attributed to New York, carved mahogany and mahogany veneer, rect top, overhanging shaped leaves, conforming base with single drawer, beaded skirt, suspending four circular drops on leaf carved pedestal, four curved scrolling acanthus leaf carved and molded legs, brass paw feet on casters, possibly orig glass drawer pull, old refinish, very minor imperfections, c1820 .... **$1,650**

Federal, New England, mahogany, rect overhanging top, straight skirt, four sq tapering legs, old refinish, imperfections, 1795-1810, 14-1/2" w, 28" l extended, 26-1/2" h **$1,300**

Georgian, oak, shaped rect top opening to round surface, six round tapering legs ending in pad feet two legs swing out to support raised leaves, 42-1/2" w, 47" w open, 29" h **$900**

Hepplewhite, American

Birch, old reddish brown surface, two board top, single board leaves, tapered legs, old split in top, 48" w, 19" d, 29-1/2" h **$750**

Cherry, pegged joints, single board top, scalloped leaves, dovetailed corners on aprons, tapered legs, old mellow finish, old replaced hinges, iron braces added beneath top, 52" l, 19-1/2" d, 18-1/2" leaves, 29" h **$575**

Queen Anne, mahogany, D-shaped leaves, shaped apron, circular tapering legs, pad feet, early 18th C, 54" w, 49-1/2" h, 28" h **$1,765**

Regency, mahogany, oak secondary wood, figured veneer on top and D-

Dressing table, Delaware Valley Queen Anne, walnut, rect molded edge top, 1 long and two short drawers, scalloped apron, cabriole legs, stocking drake feet, c1750, 28-3/4" x 31-1/2" w, **$20,760.**
Photo courtesy of Pook & Pook, Inc.

Drop leaf table, Arts & Crafts, Gustav Stickley, oval top, shoe feet, refinished, paper label, open: 30" x 30" x 32", **$1,600.**
Photo courtesy of David Rago Auctions, Inc.

Game table, Centennial, Hepplewhite-style, mahogany veneer with inlay, gate leg, D-shape front with cockbeading above tapered legs, 35-1/2" w, 17" d closed, 34" d open, 28" h, reinforced with angle brackets, crack on one side of top, **$950.**
Photo courtesy of Alderfer Auction Co.

Lamp table, Arts & Crafts, Limbert, corbels oval top, canted, cut-out sides, rectangular lower shelf with brand mark underneath, cleaned orig finish, 29" x 45" x 29-1/2", **$4,000.**
Photo courtesy of David Rago Auctions, Inc.

Library table, Chippendale, English, oak, rectangular molded top, three drawers, scalloped skirt, square legs, 19th C, 33-1/4" w, 29" h, **$675.**
Photo courtesy of Wiederseim Associates, Inc.

Library table, Louis XVI style, ormolu mounts, tooled green leather top, single drawer, **$1,000.**
Photo courtesy of Wiederseim Associates, Inc.

Library table, Arts & Crafts, Limbert, No. 158, oval, plank legs, cut-out stretchers supporting oval-shaped lower shelf with brand underneath, fine original finish, 28-3/4" x 48" x 37", **$14,000.**
Photo courtesy of David Rago Auctions, Inc.

shaped leaves with banding, single dovetailed drawer on one side with line inlay on front, false drawer on opposite end, urn shaped column with raised rings, tapered saber legs with inlaid ebony dec, brass caps and casters, old refinishing, old restorations, black staining on underneath, 13-1/2" w, 18" d, 27" h **$1,035**

Sheraton, figured birch, single board top, warped single board leaves, one dovetailed beaded edged drawer, well turned legs, band inlay below end aprons, old finish, replaced brass pull, wear, some replaced supports, 41-3/4" w, 18-1/4" d **$700**

Game

Arts & Crafts, Miller Furniture Co., removable circular top, four plank legs inlaid with stylized floral design, paper label, felted gaming surface missing, overcoated top, 36" d, 31" h **$1,150**

Empire, tilt-top, mahogany and mahogany flame veneer, top with ogee aprons on sides, turned drops, carved pineapple column, platform base with scrolled leaf returns to carved paw feet, one drawer on side, old dark finish, 40-1/2" w, 20" d, 30" h **$450**

George III, English, cross banded mahogany, D-shaped, plain frieze, sq tapered and molded legs, c1790, 35" w, 17" d, 28" h **$1,150**

Hepplewhite, American, inlaid cherry, hinged demilune to, conforming apron, sq tapering legs, 19th C **$400**

Phyfe, Duncan, mahogany, top with band of line inlay on edge, urn pedestal, saber legs, top loose, minor veneer loss, c1820, 39" w top open, 29" h **$1,875**

Queen Anne, English, mahogany, hinged two-board top with molded edge, dovetailed drawer, shaped returns, relief carved detail at knees, well shaped cabriole legs, pad feet, rear swing legs, old dark finish, old replaced brass pulls, minor restoration, side returns missing, old splits in top, 35-1/2" w, 16" d, 28-3/4" h **$1,550**

Renaissance Revival, A. Cutler & Son, Buffalo, NY, ebonized and parcel-gilt, drop leaf, orig paper label, wear to baise surface, c1874, 36" w, 13-3/4" d, 28-3/4" h **$700**

Sheraton, mahogany, shaped top, cookie corners, shaped frieze, turned reeded legs, replaced supports under top, 36" w, 30-1/2" h **$1,225**

Victorian, mahogany, rect top, felt playing surface, frieze drawer, Wedgwood mounts, sq tapered legs, late 19th C, 25" w, 15-3/4" d, 30" h **$5,000**

William and Mary-style, with antique elements, seaweed marquetry inlaid walnut, D-shaped top with concave front, frieze similar shaped, frieze drawer, turned legs joined by stretchers, 32" w, 14" d, 30" h **$2,875**

Library

Arts & Crafts

English, overhanging top, arched apron, legs carved with stylized tulips, unmarked, refinished, seam separation to top, minor nicks and edge roughness at feet, 46" w, 27" d, 30" h **$1,955**

Robertson Co., H. P., Jamestown, New Jersey, early 20th C, oak, oval top over single drawer, flanked by side shelves, lower median shelf, imperfections, 48" w, 29-1/4" d, 29-1/4" h **$950**

Stickley, Gustav, three drawers, hammered copper pulls, sq posts, broad lower shelf, red decal, refinished, 66" l, 36" w, 30-1/2" h **$3,775**

Stickley, L. & J. G., Fayetteville, New York, similar to model no. 520, oak, rect top, single drawer, corbel supports, low median shelf with through tenons, red and yellow decal "The Work of L. & J. G. Stickley" on int. drawer, imperfections, 42" w, 28-1/8" d, 29-1/4" h **$1,265**

Classical, attributed to Boston, carved mahogany and mahogany veneer, rect top with rounded corners, conforming skirt with two working drawers and four faux drawers, carved shaped supports with scrolled brackets and applied bosses on platforms, scrolled feet joined by medial vase and ring-turned stretcher, old refinish, minor imperfections, c1825-35, 54-1/2" w, 26-1/2" d, 29-3/4" h **$4,410**

Georgian-style, Morris and Co., mahogany, tooled red leather top and gadrooned edge, two end drawers, boldly carved cabriole legs, claw and ball feet, late 19th/early 20th C, 90" l, 53" d, 30" h **$3,450**

Renaissance Revival, carved oak, rect top, two frieze drawers with mask form pulls, griffin form legs, shaped plinth, third quarter 19th C, 54" w, 28" d, 30" h...................................**$3,910**

Low table, International Movement, triangular glass top with rounded corners, conforming geometric base, mid-20th C, 26-3/4" w, 19-1/4" h **$360**

Night, Louis XV/XVI style, inlaid marquetry, oval, sliding cup rest at side, fitted with three drawers, cabriole legs joined by medial shelf, inlaid allover with flower filled vases, pitchers and table articles, price for pr, 19th C, 12" w, 9-1/2" d, 26-1/2" h **$940**

Occasional

Aesthetic Movement, American, two circular mahogany veneer tiers on stylized tree branch-form legs, 12-1/2" w, 33" h **$500**

Arts & Crafts, Gustav Stickley, circular overhanging top, faceted finial over arched cross-stretchers, very good orig finish, red decal, 24" d, 29" h...........................**$2,185**

Biedermeier, birchwood, solid gallery top, inset petit point needlework panel, plain frieze, turned legs joined by stretchers, casters, inscription underneath reading "J. J. Werner, Paris," early 19th C, 21-1/2" w, 18-1/2" d, 29-3/4" h **$2,760**

International Movement, Mies van der Rohe design, Knoll Associates, NY, circular smoked glass top, tubular metal base, 27-3/8" d, 19-1/2" h **$765**

Refectory, oak, 1-1/2" thick three-board top, two large turned and carved supports, stretcher base, shoe feet, old dark finish, late 19th or early 20th C, 71-1/2" l, 27-1/2" d, 30-1/2" h **$1,550**

Sawbuck, primitive, pine, sq nail construction, two board top, sq legs with chamfered outer corners, old refinishing, old repairs, 48-1/2" l, 34-3/4" w, 28" h...........................**$900**

Serving

Federal, New England, inlaid mahogany, band inlay around top and leaves, large satinwood oval on top, single dovetailed drawer with satinwood band inlay, bowfront top with end-blocking and serpentine sides with string-inlaid edge above conforming base, single

drawer outlined in veneer banding flanked by rect dies above similar banding and string inlaid legs, brasses appear original, old refinish, imperfections, c1800, 34-1/2" w, 17" d, 32" h...........................**$16,450**

George III, Mahogany, slightly bowed top, pair of drawers, sq tapering legs, c1800 ....**$1,725**

Satinwood and marquetry, demilune, later fitted with spring action drawers, restoration, 62-1/4" w, 23-1/2" d, 32-3/4" h.............**$19,550**

Sewing

Federal

Boston, mahogany veneer, mahogany top with outset corners above two veneered cockbeaded drawers, sliding bag frame, flanked by legs with colonettes above reeding, ending in turned tapering feet, old brass, old finish, c1805, 20-3/4" w, 15-3/4" d, 28-1/4" h **$1,610**

New England, mahogany veneer, mahogany top with hinged drop leaves, reeded edge, flanking three veneered drawers, top fitted for writing, bottom with sliding sewing bag frame, ring-turned and spiral carved legs, casters, old refinish, replaced brasses, 18-1/2" w, 18-1/8" d, 29-1/4" h.............**$1,150**

French-style, inlaid mahogany, hinged scalloped top finely inlaid with flowers and scrolled leaves, scalloped aprons, delicate cabriole legs with beaded edging, applied ormolu on apron, knees, and feet, shallow int. compartment, old refinish, some alterations, early 20th C, 25" w, 18-1/2" d, 30-1/2" h **$600**

Sheraton, mahogany, drop leaf, two drawers over one drawer, ring and spiral turned legs, brass cup and caster feet, 20-1/2" closed, 27-3/4" open, 18" d, 28-1/2" h **$1,200**

Side

Baroque, Continental, walnut, rect top, tapered frieze, scalework and scrolling vine carved legs joined by X-form stretcher, 17th C and later, 49-1/2" w, 23-1/2" d, 31" h.......**$600**

Classical, New York, mahogany, rect marble top with rounded corners, conforming ogee molded skirt, pierced and scrolled supports, pillar and scroll bases, applied ripple molding joining scrolled medial shelf, casters, old finish, minor imperfections, 1835-45, 31" w, 18-1/2" d, 31" h.....................**$3,750**

Library table, Arts & Crafts, Stickley Brothers, single drawer, arched rails, slatted sides, Quaint metal tag, 29-1/2" x 40" x 26", **$325.**
Photo courtesy of David Rago Auctions, Inc.

Side table, Victorian, marble top, burl accents, carved urn centered in cross stretchers, 29" x 31" x 21", **$800.**
Photo courtesy of David Rago Auctions, Inc.

Side table, traditional Victorian-Eastlake, marble top, mahogany, rectangular top with cut-away corners, white marble top, fretwork base, c1860, 35" l, 25" d, 29" h, shown with Satsuma vase on top, **$1,295.**
Photo courtesy of Alderfer Auction Co.

Side table, square oak top with inset white veined marble, acanthus carving on skirt and pedestal base, three carved cherubs and claw feet, $250.
Photo courtesy of Dotta Auction Co., Inc.

Side table, Queen Ann, mahogany, single drawer, Queen Anne feet, seam separation on top, 18th C, 27" x 27" x 16", $900.
Photo courtesy of David Rago Auctions, Inc.

Tea table, Arts & Crafts, Gustav Stickley, arched stretchers, splayed legs, mortised top inset with 12 Grueby tiles, old restored finish, unmarked, c1902, 26" x 24-1/2" x 20-1/8", $27,500.
Photo courtesy of David Rago Auctions, Inc.

Federal, attributed to southern New England, mahogany and tiger maple veneer inlay, serpentine top with elliptic ends, conforming base, frieze drawer, inlaid tiger maple veneer panels outlined with crossbanding and stringing, four sq tapering legs with conforming inlay continuing to inlaid cuffs, restored, c1800-10, 23-1/4" w, 17" d, 28-1/4" h **$10,575**

Louis XV, beechwood, demilune, gray and white marble top, plain frieze, sq cabriole legs, third quarter 18th C, 42-1/2" w, 22" d, 27" h **$1,530**

Louis XV-style

Marquetry inlaid mahogany, kidney-shaped top above lower shelf, cabriole legs **$830**

Parquetry inlaid, kidney shaped marble top, three-quarter gallery, sq tapered legs, three drawers, 18" w, 11" d, 30-1/2" h **$950**

Tulipwood, parquetry inlaid, oval marble top, three drawers, sq tapered legs, 18-1/2" w, 12" d, 30-1/2" h **$1,100**

Neoclassical, Italian, fruitwood, inlaid walnut, rect case, two drawers, sq tapered legs, inlaid with leafy vines, price for pr, c1800, 20-1/2" w, 13" d, 29-1/2" h.....................**$3,525**

Regency-style, shaped top inset with needlework, turned standard, tripartite base **$250**

Renaissance Revival, American, walnut, marble top, thumb molded edge, shaped corners, four angular legs with central turned post, mounted with roundels, casters, 28-1/2" w, 20" d, 29" h.............**$750**

Rococo, Italian, walnut, serpentine top and case, foliate carved apron, two drawers, cabriole legs, 19th C, 36" w, 18" d, 34" h **$1,765**

Rococo-style, cross banded fruitwood, serpentine top and case, three drawers, 19th C, 13" w, 10-1/2" d, 29" h........................**$450**

Victorian

Bamboo, octagonal lacquer top over four drop leaves, four legs joined by stretcher with medial shelf, 22" w, 22" d, 28" h **$600**

Mahogany, sq top, frieze with applied branch form carvings, branch form legs, 27" d, 25-3/4" d, 29-3/4" h **$250**

Silver, George III, carved mahogany, galleried tray top, low relief carved

everted lip, repeating border of C-scrolls and foliage, swirling scroll bordered apron, molded sq cabriole supports with trailing acanthus carving at knees, Spanish feet, alternations to top, repairs, c1765, 31-3/4" l, 28-3/4" h **$2,000**

Sofa

Edwardian, painted satinwood, rounded drop leaves, two frieze drawers, trestle supports ending in brass paw casters, c1895, 36" w closed, 26-1/2" d, 28-1/2" h **$8,100**

Regency, cross banded mahogany, wide rect top, drop leaves with canted corners, frieze drawers to both sides, turned trestle bases, inlaid with boxwood and ebony, c1820, 52" w, 36" d, 28-1/2" h **$3,525**

Tavern

Country, Pennsylvania, softwood, circular top, stretcher base, beaded skirt, legs with old orange painted surface, most orig wrought brass and iron tacks, many with remnants of probably orig muslin-like fabric underneath tack head, 28" d, 25-1/2" h **$4,950**

Moravian, Pennsylvania, walnut, pegged construction, pin top, three board thumb molded top, dovetailed drawer, boldly turned legs, horizontal stretchers, turned feet, restoration to feet, 18th C, 61" w, 34" d, 30" h.................**$6,050**

Tea

Art Deco, France, walnut, rect top opens and swivels on U-shaped base, c1928, 44" l open, 22" closed, 35-1/4" w, 28-1/4" h **$1,880**

Chippendale

America, possibly Philadelphia, piecrust tilt top, figured mahogany one-piece circular top, ogee and crescent form carving, birdcage support, fluted column, compressed ball knop, three legs with plain knees, ball and claw feet, 28-1/2" h **$10,575**

Connecticut, cherry, round top tilts and revolves above birdcage mechanism, tapering shaft with suppressed ball and ring turnings, tripod cabriole leg base, pad feet, refinished, imperfections, late 18th C, 36-1/2" d, 28-3/4" h **$3,100**

Country, mahogany, two board dish top and key old replacements, urn shaped column with birdcage, cabriole legs, padded snake feet, old refinishing, shims added, 29-1/4" d, 26-3/4" h **$850**

Chippendale-style, America, mahogany, round tilt-top, well turned column, cabriole legs, snake feet, orig dark finish, minor edge wear, block needs stabilization, 32" d top, 27-1/2" h **$500**

George III, mahogany, circular tilt top, ring turned standard, tripod legs, pad feet, 32-1/4" d, 28-1/2" h **$1,100**

Hepplewhite, tilt top, poplar one board top with cut corners, birch tripod base with spider legs, turned column, old refinishing with painted foliage border designs in shades of gold and black, top replaced, repairs, 15-1/2" w, 23-1/2" l, 28-3/4" h **$440**

Queen Anne

Massachusetts, maple, oval overhanging drop-leaf top, cabriole legs, pad feet on platforms joined by cutout apron, old refinish, repairs, 1740-60, 31" w, 32-1/2" d, 27" h **$30,550**

New England, cherry, circular tilt top, vase and ring-turned post and tripod cabriole leg base, pad feet, refinished, minor imperfections, c1760-80, 34-1/4" d, 27-1/2" h **$1,175**

Victorian, papier-mâché, gilt and mother-of-pearl inlaid, shaped round tilt top, dec with urn of flowers, turned standard, tripartite base, 22" w, 22" d, 29" h **$885**

Tilt-Top

Federal, New England, mahogany inlaid, octagonal top with string inlay in outline, urn shaped pedestal, cabriole legs, arris pad feet on platforms, orig surface, very minor imperfections, 22" w, 14-3/4" d, 29-1/2" h **$3,750**

Georgian, mahogany, plain circular top over turned baluster standard, three cabriole legs ending in shaped pad feet, late 18th C, 32" d, 27-3/8" h **$1,100**

Tray, Edwardian, satinwood and inlay, two oval tiers, removable wood and glass tray, slightly splayed sq tapering legs joined by stretcher, c1900, 36" w, 20-1/4" d, 32" h **$1,150**

Trestle

Country, Pennsylvania, removable sliding scrubbed top, shaped cut-out legs, mortise and tenon stretcher, old green painted surface, 66" l, 16" d, 28-1/2" h **$3,575**

William IV, parquetry inlaid specimen wood, rect top, pendant applied frieze, trestle with turned ends and stretcher, cabriole legs, c1835, 33-1/4" w, 17-1/2" d, 29-1/2" h **$2,000**

Tripod

George III-style, mahogany, tilt-top, piecrust edge, acanthus carved stem and tripod base, slipper feet, 22-1/2" d, 28" h **$825**

Georgian-style, mahogany, silver plated mounts, serpentine reticulated gallery, turned stem, cabriole legs, price for pr, 20th C, 15" d, 22" h **$450**

Work

Biedermeier, walnut and mahogany, rect top with line inlay around center panel, dovetailed drawer with divided interior, beaded aprons, exaggerated serpentine legs, central stretcher, stamped signature "A. Gastaldi" on back of drawer, old refinishing, restorations, 24-1/2" w, 16-3/4" d, 31-1/4" h **$665**

Classical, Boston, mahogany veneer, solid top, hinged rounded drop leaves with beaded edges, flank two convex veneered drawers, top one fitted for writing, lower with replaced fabric sewing fabric bag, turned tapering legs which flank shaped veneered platform, ebonized bun feet, orig stamped brass pulls, imperfections, minor warp in leaf, 1830, 19" w, 19" d, 28-3/4" h **$980**

Federal

Massachusetts, early mahogany veneer, sq top with molded edge, hinged leaves flank two working drawers and bag frame, spiral carved legs, turned feet, casters, original brass, old refinish, 19th C, 18-1/4" w, 17-1/4" d, 29-7/8" h **$1,645**

New England, butternut, birch, and bird's eye maple, overhanging rect top, two drawers, straight skirt, vase and ring-turned legs, old brass pulls, refinished, minor imperfections, c1825, 20" w, 18-3/4" d, 29" h **$1,175**

Federal, late, New York State, tiger maple, shaped hinged top lifts above two drawer facade, upper faux one, lower working one with divided interior, turned pedestal, four incurvate legs ending in tiny ball feet, brasses replaced, refinished, c1820, 22-1/2" w, 15-7/8" d, 32" h **$2,820**

George III, mahogany, rect top, canted corners, fitted int., sq tapered and slightly splayed legs joined by stretchers, early 19th C **$2,380**

Trestle billiard table/settee, Arts & Crafts, Brunswick-Balke-Collenver Co., convertible, lower drawer with cues, rack, and balls, orig finish, new felt and pockets, metal tag, 31-1/4" x 70" x 39", **$15,000.**
Photo courtesy of David Rago Auctions, Inc.

Trestle table, L. & J.G. STICKLEY, shaped feet and a lower shelf mortised through the sides, original finish, light overcoat to top, metal tag under shelf, 39" x 60" x 36", **$2,500.**
Photo courtesy of David Rago Auctions, Inc.

Painted early wooden trunk with iron banding, decorated with flowers and scrolls, with painted names and dates "JTD – 1801" and "Johanes Larssen Roorvig 1853", 39" l, 18" d, 17" h, **$350.**
Photo courtesy of Joy Luke Auctions.

Striped exterior, original hardware,
$95.
Photo courtesy of Dotta Auction Co., Inc.

Trunk, French Provincial, walnut, rect plank top, pierced cartouche escutcheon plate with fitted hinged latch, 17th/18th C, 21-1/2" x 36-3/4" x 15-1/2," **$800.**
Photo courtesy of Sloans & Kenyon Auctioneers and Appraisers.

Trunks

History: Trunks are portable containers that clasp shut and are used for the storage or transportation of personal possessions. Normally "trunk" means the ribbed flat- or domed-top models of the second half of the 19th century.

Early trunks frequently were painted, stenciled, grained, or covered with wallpaper. These are collected for their folk-art qualities and, as such, demand high prices.

Dome top

Arched top with "L G" in scripted yellow paint, nail construction box, all grain painted to simulate mahogany, and outlined in yellow striping with yellow floral device centered under the lock, imperfections and repairs, New England, early 19th C, 28-1/4" l, 13-3/4" w, 13-1/2" h **$235**

Black japanned brass mounts, gilt Chinoisiere dec of figures in garden landscape, side handles, restoration, late 18th/early 19th C, 33-1/4" w, 16-1/4" d, 18-3/4" h **$750**

Fabric on wood, worn painted dec in ivory and green, red border designs and flowers, interior lined with green marbleized paper, worn, 19" l **$425**

Hinged top, dovetailed box, white painted vine, floral and leaf dec over black painted ground, int. papered with early 19th C Boston area broadsides, attributed to Massachusetts, some later paint, 19th C, 44-1/2" w, 22-3/4" d, 19-1/2" h **$1,035**

Paper-covered box green and red sponge dec, blue line and dot patterned paper-lined int., brass ring and iron latch, America, wear, 19th C, 6" l, 3-1/2" w, 2-5/8" h **$265**

Paint dec, black painted ground, central vined pinwheel bordered by meandering floral and arched vines, front with tassel and drape border, central MA, early 19th C, 11-1/2" h, 28" w, 14" d..........**$1,035**

Dovetailed, old dark brown finish, finely painted panels with Chinoiserie vases and planters of flowers in red, tan, and green on front and sides, wrought iron handles on ends, large brass hasp and moon escutcheon on front, 41-3/4" w, 24-3/4" h, 27-1/2" h **$320**

Flat top

Chinese, pigskin, red, painted Oriental maidens and landscapes within quatrefoils, brass loop handles and lock, 19th C, 14" x 8" **$125**

Copper and iron, Arts & Crafts strapwork and pyramidal tack mounts, black paint, hinged slant lid revealing rect box, 30-1/2" w, 16-1/2" d, 17-1/2" h **$200**

Poplar, old black paint, tacks border sides, top, lock, and handles, initials "P.L." on top, leather straps beneath tacks, worn cloth lining, age splits, 24" w, 14" d, 11" h.....................**$150**

Tooled leather on pine, iron straps, brass buttons and lock, lined with worn newspaper dated 1871, hinged replaced, some edge damage, 15-1/4" l...................................**$385**

Military, brass bound camphor wood, hinged rect top, storage well, brass bail handles, English, second half 19th C, 21-3/4" w, 17" d, 12-1/2" h **$200**

Vuitton, Louis, wardrobe, rect, wooden strapping, leather handles on ends, brass corners and clasps, int. with hanger bars, eight Vuitton hangers, early 20th C, 21-1/2" d, 15-1/2" d, 40-1/2" h..................................**$1,100**

Glass

GLASS COLLECTING

Plate, Paden City's Black Forest, black glass, with the rim highlighted with chalk to show the detailed etched pattern.

The world of antique glassware is as fascinating as ever. New discoveries of who made what and when continue to delight collectors. This segment of the marketplace continues to expand and disseminate knowledge because of ongoing scholarship. Museums such as Corning Glass and West Virginia Museum of American Glass have become leaders in the preservation of documentation relating to the glassware industry.

Remembering that glassware was created with high temperatures, many companies suffered terrible losses due to fires. Some rebounded and rebuilt, often glassblowers would travel to a new area or company after a disaster, taking along their formulas and techniques. Because glassware was one of the original American industries, there is a wealth of wonderful antique and collectible glassware available to collectors. Active participation in collector clubs in many aspects of the glassware market, such as carnival and depression glass, also allow collectors to learn more about this fascinating world.

The first glassware made is credited to the early Egyptians, but can be found in other cultures and civilizations. Glass became a good way to store and preserve food, something necessary before the days of refrigeration. Because glassware could be re-used and was trusted to be sanitary, millions of fruit jars, bottles, and other household items were made. As the glass industry geared up to make these mass-produced types of utilitarian items, many other factories, such as Fenton, Fostoria, and Heisey also decided it was a good time to encourage the American consumer to put more glassware on their tables. Early

American Pattern Glass started the trend with beautiful stemware patterns.

The Depression-era glass manufacturers took this trend a step further in their desire to make affordable colorful glassware table settings. Add artists such as Louis Comfort Tiffany and his contemporaries, allowing the glassware industry to bloom with spectacular colors and textures. Companies such as Millersburg and Dugan took the techniques of pressing glass that the Early American Pattern Glass companies had perfected, added color, and finally iridescence to create their versions of carnival glass, which were early attempts to create inexpensive art glass for the masses.

This is an excellent time to buy antique glassware. Many dealers are finding new collectors not coming into the marketplace as fast as old collectors are disposing of their treasures. As with much of the antique marketplace, the high-end quality items are always in demand. The middle market is a little soft, and the low end of the market finds new collectors beginning to look at the market and trying to learn more. It's also a time when tray lots of wonderful vintage pieces of Early American Pattern Glass can be bought for excellent prices. Many of these pieces still have years of useful service in them and can safely be used to set a pretty table.

The very thing that often attracts collectors to glassware, the clarity, the brilliance, or the rich color, can be taken away in a few seconds if the piece is dropped. Antique glassware has been known to crack in cupboards without any warning because of temperature changes, or perhaps, a long hidden internal crack that decided it was

time to let go. Because of this very fragile nature, care must be taken when handling and collecting antique glassware.

The use of cabinets with glass doors is one way to keep dust and pollutants from attacking the surface, but caution must be taken if there is lighting included in the cabinet. Excessive heating and/or exposure to lighting may cause some internal cracking. Exposure to strong ultra violet rays can also alter the chemical formula of glassware. Early American Pattern Glass is particular prone to this problem when it has a high lead content. Long periods of exposure to strong sunlight may cause it to become purple in hue. Some collectors accept this as fine, a way for them to tell the glassware is old. Other collectors aren't so kind and prefer their glassware in as close to original condition as possible.

Opaque glass formulas, such as milk glass, and some of the agate formulas, are very susceptible to heat changes too. Actually it's the newer milk glass, circa 1950s and later, that's more prone to shattering with temperature changes. Apparently the glassblowers who first made milk glass added something to that formula that made it a little more durable. Westmoreland Glass Company offered a guarantee with several of their milk glass patterns and soon regretted the policy as many pieces were returned because of breakage as a result of temperature changes.

To be on the safe side, if purchasing antique glassware on a hot day, wrap it well and leave it cool down before washing it. The same is true for transporting glassware during cold temperatures. Wrap it well and then leave it wrapped and in a quiet state for several hours until it gradually warms up to room temperature.

Repairs to antique glassware can be made, but should be left to the professionals. Some old pieces of Early American Pattern Glass and Victorian Wares can be found with some interesting "make-do" repairs. However, glued on knobs, handles, etc. need to be properly done or the resulting repair shows and can detract from the whole look of a vintage piece. Small chips on the rim or foot of antique glassware can be professionally ground away. This type of professional repair can actually enhance the value of a piece as it will render it useful again. If considering making repairs to antique glassware, ask the restorer to see some examples of their work, discuss what kinds of techniques they would recommend and don't be timid about inquiring how much the work will cost.

Never ever put antique glassware in the dishwasher, the temperatures, chemicals, and rushing water may actually leave tiny surface scratches, something that can never be removed. Some depression-era glassware dealers have taken to the practice of removing aging gilt decoration as they feel it's imperfect nature detracts from the beauty of the piece. Likewise, gilt decoration in excellent condition will add to the value of a piece, so check to see if the decoration appears to be original and not something that's been recently added. Because gilt and other enamel decorations were put onto the surface of the glassware after it was cooled and not refired, it is

relatively easy to remove it. Modern craft paints and even stains are very good and are often used to touch-up missing elements.

Carefully examine any decorated piece and compare the colors, texture, and technique to make sure it is original. If a piece of decorated glassware needs a good cleaning, start with as gentle a process as possible. Fill a plastic dishpan with luke warm water, and then gently try washing the piece. If the surface dirt does not disappear, use Woolite or another gentle type of detergent first. A little experimentation on the back is a good idea. Using common household items, such as vinegar or ammonia, will also make antique glassware sparkle. Again, use a small amount, vinegar will help make it shine, no need to pickle it.

Make sure to carefully rinse and hand dry the object. Using a dishpan and carefully avoiding the facets of a sink are of up-most importance as many a piece of antique glassware has fallen victim to a terrible clink as it hits the sink or plumbing fixtures. Putting an old towel into the bowl of the sink to eliminate hard surfaces may also be a good idea. Better yet, carefully dust antique glassware on a regular basis, so that washing is limited.

If an accident should occur with a piece of antique glassware, carefully note any damage on your personal household inventory. This way, you'll be better informed when selling the piece and can honestly tell the next owner about

it's history. Some items, such as vintage cup plates, are often found in less-than-perfect condition. They were being made in some of the first mass-production settings and quality control wasn't as strict as it is today.

Some molds were simply under or over filled, causing gaps or extra bits of glass on the edges. Collectors often will calculate this type of manufacturing flaw into their valuation of a piece and many do not take too much off because of it. When collecting antique glassware, it's always good to remember that product was one of the first recycled materials known to the young American market. If imperfect pieces were created, they were often just smashed and returned to the cullet mixture where they would re-emerge as a beautiful piece of glassware.

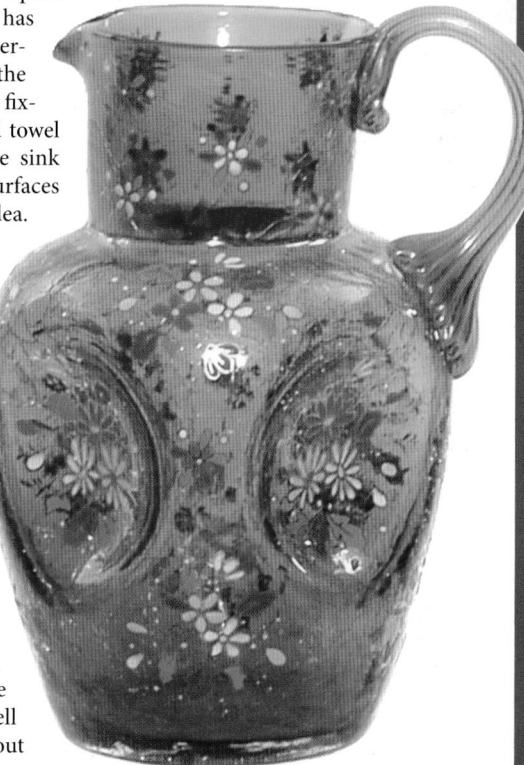

Resources

Magazines

Antique Trader, published by Krause Publications, Iola, WI.

Books

Art Glass Identification & Price Guide, by John A. Shuman, III, Krause Publications, Iola, WI.

Collecting Swarovski, by Dean A. Genth, Krause Publications, Iola, WI.

Early American Pattern Glass, 2nd Ed., by Darryl Reilly & Bill Jenks, Krause Publications, Iola, WI.

Glass A to Z, by David J. Shotwell, Krause Publications, Iola, WI.

Heisey Glass The Early Years 1896-1924, by Shirley Dunbar, Krause Publications, Iola, WI.

Warman´s® Bottles Field Guide, by Michael Polak, Krause Publications, Iola, WI.

Warman´s® Carnival Glass, by Ellen T. Schroy, Krause Publications, Iola, WI.

Warman´s® Depression Glass, 3rd Ed., by Ellen T. Schroy, Krause Publications, Iola, WI.

Warman´s® Depression Glass Field Guide, 2nd Ed., by Ellen T. Schroy, Krause Publications, Iola, WI.

Warman´s® Fenton Glass, by Mark F. Moran, Krause Publications, Iola, WI.

Warman´s® Glass, 4th Ed., by Ellen T. Schroy, Krause Publications, Iola, WI.

Warman´s® Lalique, by Mark F. Moran, Krause Publications, Iola, WI.

Warman´s® Pattern Glass, 2nd Ed., by Ellen T. Schroy, Krause Publications, Iola, WI.

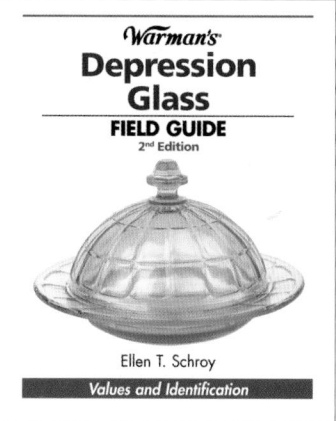

GALLERY

Right: Durand, vase, cylindrical shouldered with flaring rim, iridescent blue, overall white heart and vine design, post-production signature, 8-1/2" h, **$800.**
Photo courtesy of The Early Auction Company, LLC.

Far right: Steuben, Moss Agate, shouldered vase, cylindrical, blue transcluecent glass, yellow, red and white internal mottling, 8-1/2" h, **$2,100.**
Photo courtesy of The Early Auction Company, LLC.

Depression Glass, Avocado, green creamer, ftd, **$40.**

Fenton, mosaic off-hand handled vase mid-1920s, 7" h, **$1,800+.**

Lalique, "Aras," iridescent teal green glass with white patina, molded R. LALIQUE, c1924, 9-3/8" h, **$8,000+.**

Moser, signed amber bowl, oblong paneled, bull elk in forest engraving, firm's stamped signature on base, orig box, 9" l x 3-3/4" h, **$1,000.**
Photo courtesy of The Early Auction Company, LLC.

AGATA GLASS

History: Agata glass was invented in 1887 by Joseph Locke of the New England Glass Company, Cambridge, Massachusetts.

Agata glass was produced by coating a piece of peachblow glass with metallic stain, spattering the surface with alcohol, and firing. The resulting high-gloss, mottled finish looked like oil droplets floating on a watery surface. Shading usually ranged from opaque pink to dark rose, although pieces in a pastel opaque green also exist. A few pieces have been found in a satin finish.

Agata glass, lemonade, loop handle applied, excellent staining, 5" h, **$1,250.**
Photo courtesy of The Early Auction Company, LLC.

Bowl

Crimped rim, Wild Rose shading, strong mineral staining, ex-Maude Feld, 8-1/4" d, 3-1/8" h **$2,250**

Waisted, crimped trefoil rim, overall mineral staining, ex-Maude Feld, 5-1/2" d, 3-1/2" h **$750**

Celery vase, satin, very heavy staining, 6-1/4" h **$8,960**

Cruet, flat bottom, 5-3/4" h **$5,320**

Tankard pitcher, tapering cylindrical body, Wild Rose with strong all over mineral staining, ex-Maude Feld, 8-1/2" h................................... **$5,000**

Toothpick holder, tricorn, gold metallic tracery and mottling... **$645**

Tumbler, gold tracery, peachblow ground, black splotches, 3-3/4" h **$635**

Vase

Bowl shape, mottled blue mineral stain on matte ground, ex-Maude Feld, 5" h **$10,000**

Lily, Wild Rose shading, mineral staining, 7" h........................... **$700**

Lily, shades from salmon pink to cream, ex-Maude Feld, 7-1/4" h........**$1,200**

Morgan, Wild Rose color, overall mineral staining, orig amber griffin holder, orig Maude Feld label, ex-Maude Feld, 10-1/4" h **$5,250**

Water pitcher, amethyst staining framed with perfect gold, 5" crack to body, 7" h **$200**

Agata glass, cruet, New England, Wild Rose color, suppressed circular body and handle, correct stopper, some mineral staining, 6" h, **$1,700.**
Photo courtesy of The Early Auction Company, LLC.

AMBERINA GLASS

History: Joseph Locke developed Amberina glass in 1883 for the New England Glass Works. "Amberina," a trade name, describes a transparent glass that shades from deep ruby to amber. It was made by adding powdered gold to the ingredients for an amber-glass batch. A portion of the glass was reheated later to produce the shading effect. Usually it was the bottom that was reheated to form the deep red; however, reverse examples have been found.

Most early Amberina is flint-quality glass, blown or pattern molded. Patterns include Diamond Quilted, Daisy and Button, Venetian Diamond, Diamond and Star, and Thumbprint.

In addition to the New England Glass Works, the Mount Washington Glass Company of New Bedford, Massachusetts, copied the glass in the 1880s and sold it at first under the Amberina trade name and later as "Rose Amber." It is difficult to distinguish pieces from these two New England factories. Boston and Sandwich Glass Works never produced the glass.

Amberina glass also was made in the 1890s by several Midwest factories, among which was Hobbs, Brockunier & Co. Trade names included "Ruby Amber Ware" and "Watermelon." The Midwest glass shaded from cranberry to amber, and the color resulted from the application of a thin flashing of cranberry to the reheated portion. This created a sharp demarcation between the two colors. This less-expensive version was the death knell for the New England variety.

In 1884, Edward D. Libbey was given the use of the trade name "Amberina" by the New England Glass Works. Production took place during 1900, but ceased shortly thereafter. In the 1920s, Edward Libbey renewed production at his Toledo, Ohio, plant for a short period. The glass was of high quality.

Marks: Amberina made by Edward Libbey in the 1920s is marked "Libbey" in script on the pontil.

Amberina dish, expanded diamond pattern, 5" diameter, **$90.**
Photo courtesy of Joy Luke Auctions.

Amberina basket, New England Glass Works, shading with optical ribs and ornate fold rim, amber handle applied, 6-1/4" h, **$,2,250.**
Photo courtesy of The Early Auction Company, LLC.

Amberina toothpick, square mouth, diamond quilted pattern, 2-1/4" h, **$250.**
Photo courtesy of The Early Auction Company, LLC.

Reproduction Alert. Reproductions abound.

Additional Listings: Libbey, Mount Washington.

Basket, wide flared rim, enameled and gilt dec florals, polished pontil, mounted with finely sculpted gilt bronze dragon form handle, Victorian, 10-1/2" l **$690**

Biscuit jar, Diamond Quilted pattern, polished pontil, lid missing, 5" h **$50**

Bonbon, double reeded handles, 6-1/2" d **$90**

Bottle, Coin Spot pattern, attributed to Libbey, 8" h **$375**

Bowl
  Crimson shading to amber, Diamond Quilted pattern, applied amber peaked overlay extends mid-length, orig Libbey paper label, ex-Maude, 5-1/8" h **$2,100**
  Tricorn, amber base, Mt. Washington, 5" l sides, 2" h **$235**

Celery vase, cylindrical, tightly crimped thumbprint pattern, 6-1/2" h **$575**

Compote, catalog #3017, Libbey acid stamp mark, partial paper label, ex-Maud Feld, 7-1/4" d, 8-3/8" h **$4,000**

Creamer, Thumbprint pattern, polished pontil, Victorian, 4-1/2" h .. **$85**

Cruet
  Inverted Thumbprint pattern, fuchsia trefoil spout, neck, and shoulder, Mt. Washington, 5-1/2" h **$435**
  Inverted Thumbprint pattern, gilt dec, replaced stopper, wear to gilt, 6" h **$90**
  Thumbprint pattern, replaced stopper, Victorian, 6" h **$95**

Decanter, Optic Diamond Quilted pattern, solid amber faceted stopper, 12" h.. **$475**

Demitasse cup, 16 optic panels, applied reeded handle, 2-1/8" h **$185**

Finger bowl, crimped ruffled rim, 5-1/2" d................................... **$200**

Juice glass, Coin Spot pattern, 3-3/4" h **$75**

Lemonade, ribbed, applied amber ring handle, price for set of three, 5" h **$425**

Miniature pitcher, crimson sq mouth extends to amber bulbous body, Inverted Coin Dot pattern, applied reeded handle, 3" h **$400**

Mug, 3-7/8" h............................ **$1,000**

Nappy, handle, enameled dec, polished pontil, Victorian, 6" l **$140**

Punch cup
  Coin Spot pattern, reverse Amberina, 2-3/4" h **$50**
  Optic Diamond Quilted pattern, fuchsia to amber body with 20 panels, applied ribbed handle, New England, 2-1/2" d **$185**
  Optic Ribbed pattern, applied reeded handle, 3-1/2" h **$100**

Shot glass, faint Diamond Quilted pattern, attributed to Brayden Pairpoint, 2-1/4" h............................ **$110**

Spooner, Diamond Quilted pattern, crimped scalloped rim, 4-3/4" h .. **$250**

Sugar, ovoid, Coin Spot pattern, two applied reeded handles, 4-1/4" h .. **$450**

Sweetmeat, Baby Thumbprint pattern, applied colorless florals, feet, and rim, polished pontil, 6" d... **$320**

Syrup pitcher, Hobnail pattern, orig pewter top std "Pat. Jan 29 84," Hobbs, Brockunier & Co., three hobs chipped **$300**

Tankard pitcher, New England, Optic Diamond Quilt pattern, 4-1/4" h .. **$685**

Toothpick holder, sq mouth, 2-1/4" h **$250**

Tumbler
  Coin Spot pattern, ground rim, 3-3/4" h **$125**
  Coin Spot pattern, barrel shape, 4" h **$165**

Vase
  Swirled mold, enameled flowers, gilt scrolling, polished pontil, French, c1890, 8-1/4" h........................ **$150**
  Swirl pattern, applied amber rigaree around crown-form top, applied amber petal feet, polished pontil, Victorian, 8" h **$150**
  Tri-fold lily blossom, 6-3/4" h .. **$250**
  Tri-fold lily blossom, 16 optic ribs, deep fuchsia and honey amber, attributed to Mt. Washington, 9-1/4" h, 4-1/4" w **$485**

Water pitcher
  Bulbous, tricorn mouth shades to amber Coin Spot patterned body, applied reeded amber handle, 8-1/4" h **$295**
  Coin Spot pattern, ftd, applied colorless reeded handle, 7" h **$225**
  Optic Ribbed pattern, applied amber reeded handle, 8" h **$100**
  Ovoid, sq mouth, Thumbprint pattern, faint optic ribbing at rim, applied reeded handle, 5-1/2" h.......... **$175**

Wine, Optic Ribbed pattern, 4-3/4" h **$300**

AMBERINA GLASS, PLATED

History: The New England Glass Company, Cambridge, Massachusetts, first made plated Amberina in 1886; Edward Libbey patented the process for the company in 1889.

Plated Amberina was made by taking a gather of chartreuse or cream opalescent glass, dipping it in Amberina, and working the two, often utilizing a mold. The finished product had a deep amber to deep ruby red shading, a fiery opalescent lining, and often vertical ribbing for enhancement. Designs ranged from simple forms to complex pieces with collars, feet, gilding and etching.

A cased Wheeling glass of similar appearance had an opaque white lining, but is not opalescent and does not have a ribbed body.

Cruet, high color, cut amber faceted stopper, applied amber handle, ex-Maud Feld, 7" h **$9,000**

Finger bowl, ruffled, tightly crimped rim with 12 distinct ribs, 5-1/2" d **$5,750**

Lemonade, applied amber handle, ex-Maude Feld, 5-1/4" h **$2,750**

Pitcher, very rare, one of three known, ex-Maude Feld, 8" h **$37,520**

Toothpick holder, 2-1/4" h . **$15,680**

Tumbler, thin layered bottom with rare citron hue, ex-Maude Feld, 3-3/4" h **$1,600**

Vase
Lily, 8" h **$4,480**
Lily, deep crimson shading to custard yellow, clear amber raised disc base, orig Maude B. Feld label, 9-5/8" h **$6,000**

Water carafe, bulbous body, circular neck, 12 protruding amber ribs, orig New England Glass Works paper label, ex-Maude Feld, 8-1/2" h **$42,000**

Water pitcher, bulbous, deep mahogany extending to cream on lower body, 12 well-defined protruding ribs, trefoil spout, applied amber handle, ex-Maude Feld, 7-1/2" h **$14,000**

Plated amberina bowl, fuchsia shading to cream, amber ribbing, 5" d x 2-1/2" h, **$3,000.**
Photo courtesy of The Early Auction Company, LLC.

BACCARAT GLASS

History: The Sainte-Anne glassworks at Baccarat in Voges, France, was founded in 1764 and produced utilitarian soda glass. In 1816, Aime-Gabriel d'Artiques purchased the glassworks, and a Royal Warrant was issued in 1817 for the opening of Verrerie de Vonâoche éa Baccarat. The firm concentrated on lead-crystal glass products. In 1824, a limited company was created.

From 1823 to 1857, Baccarat and Saint-Louis glassworks had a commercial agreement and used the same outlets. No merger occurred. Baccarat began the production of paperweights in 1846. In the late 19th century, the firm achieved an international reputation for cut glass table services, chandeliers, display vases, centerpieces, and sculptures. Products eventually included all forms of glassware.

Additional Listings: Paperweights.

Bonbon, amberina, swirled mold, pedestal foot, emb "Baccarat," 5-3/4" d **$150**

Candelabra, pr, crystal, four light, diamond-cut baluster standard, four scrolling candle arms terminating urn-form sockets, etched glass globes hung with prisms, 32" h **$2,000**

Cologne bottle, Rose Tiente, matching stopper, price for pr, 6" h **$100**

Decanter, flattened ovoid, scalloped edge, etched flat sides with hunter on horseback, forest animals, scrolling vine, neck with vine etching, similarly shaped and etched stopper, price for pr, 20th C, 11-5/8" h **$550**

Figure, porcupine, clear, trademark on base, 5" l, 3" h **$150**

Finger bowl, ruby ground, gold medallions and flowers dec, 4-3/4" d, 6-3/4" d underplate **$350**

Garniture, five-light candelabrum and four candlesticks, all hung with pendants, 22" h **$2,275**

Lamp, central cut glass urn on short brass stem, two horizontal reeded

Baccarat, 21" x 12-1/4" three-light candelabra with drop prisms, matching candleholder, both red fading to yellow crystal, imprinted "Baccarat" on base, **$1,100.**
Photo courtesy of David Rago Auctions, Inc.

Baccarat, compote, fluted body, clear and frosted glass, scalloped rim, c1873, 4-3/4" h x 7-1/2" d, **$400.**

Photo courtesy of Sloans & Kenyon Auctioneers and Appraisers.

candle arms, fan cut drip pans suspending cut prisms, ovoid glass knop stem, paneled trumpet foot cut with roundels, brass flat leaf base, one with collar at urn for further prisms, other with collars for two etched-glass shades, electrified, price for pr, early 20th C, 19-1/2" l, 24-1/2" h **$2,875**

Liquor set, 10 matching cordials, gilt dec Neoclassical motif, 8-1/2" h decanter.................................... **$450**

Vase, colorless, tapered cylindrical, slightly everted rim, vertical tapered flutes on body, press-cut, 20th C, 9-3/4" h.................................. **$165**

Wash bowl and pitcher, colorless, swirled rib design, pitcher with applied handle and polished base, ground table ring on bowl, polished chip, 12-1/2" h pitcher, 16-1/2" d bowl **$250**

BARBER BOTTLES

History: Barber bottles, colorful glass bottles found on shelves and counters in barber shops, held the liquids barbers used daily. A specific liquid was kept in a specific bottle, which the barber knew by color, design, or lettering. The bulk liquids were kept in utilitarian containers under the counter or in a storage room.

Barber bottles are found in many types of glass—art glass with various decorations, pattern glass, and commercially prepared and labeled bottles.

Note: Prices are for bottles without original stoppers, unless otherwise noted.

Barber bottles, milk glass, opaque white body, green fern decoration, black lettering, one reads "Bay Rum," the other "Toilet Water," worn gold trim, pontil marks, no stoppers, price for pair, **$165.**

Advertising
Koken's Quinine Tonic for the Hair, clear, label under glass, 7-1/2" h **$195**
Lucky Tiger, red, green, yellow, black, and gilt label under glass, emb on reverse **$85**
Vegederma, cylindrical, bulbous, long neck, amethyst, white enamel dec of bust of woman with long flower hair, tooled mouth, pontil scar, 8" h **$130**

Amber, Hobb's Hobnail **$250**

Amethyst, Mary Gregory type dec, white enameled child and flowers, 8" h **$200**

Cobalt blue, cylindrical, bulbous body, long neck, white enamel, traces of gold dec, tooled mouth, pontil scar, 7-1/4" h **$100**

Emerald green, cylindrical bell form, long neck, orange and white enameled floral dec, sheared mouth, pontil scar, some int. haze, 8-1/2" h **$210**

Latticino, cylindrical, bulbous, long neck, clear frosted glass, white, red, and pale green vertical stripes, tooled mouth, pontil scar, 8-1/4" h **$200**

Milk glass, Witch Hazel, painted letters and flowers, 9" h **$115**

Opal glass, squatty, blue and purple pansies dec, Mt Washington, numbered 1039, 7" h **$100**

Opalescent
Coin Spot, blue **$300**
Seaweed, cranberry, bulbous **$465**

Sapphire blue, enameled white and yellow daisies, green leaves, 8-5/8" h **$125**

BISCUIT JARS

History: The biscuit or cracker jar was the forerunner of the cookie jar. Biscuit jars were made of various materials by leading glassworks and potteries of the late 19th and early 20th centuries.

Note: All items listed have silver- plated (SP) mountings unless otherwise noted.

Mt. Washington, Crown Milano, sweetmeat, cream body with peach ribbing, dec with gold ivy, embossed lid, stamped "MW," 5" h, **$550.**

Photo courtesy of The Early Auction Company, LLC.

Burmese glass, raised gold oak leaves and pastel flowers, Mt. Washington, possibly replaced lid, 9" h **$450**

Cranberry glass, two applied clear ring handles, applied clear feet and flower prunt pontil, ribbed finial knob, 9" h, 6-1/4" d **$195**

Glass
Blue, black scenic dec, pewter lid and handle, 9-1/2" h **$175**

Pale yellow ground, green, gold, and rose floral dec, tooled silver-plated cover, handle, and rim, unsigned, Mt. Washington, New Bedford, MA, 8-1/4" h **$150**

Opal glass, shading from white to blue, purple and crimson stemmed flowers, attributed to Wave Crest, 11" h .. **$325**

Satin glass, floral dec, pewter lid and handle, 11" h **$175**

BOHEMIAN GLASS

History: The once independent country of Bohemia, now a part of the Czech Republic, produced a variety of fine glassware: etched, cut, overlay, and colored. Its glassware, which first appeared in America in the early 1820s, continues to be exported to the U.S. today.

Bohemia is known for its "flashed" glass that was produced in the familiar ruby color, as well as in amber, green, blue, and black. Common patterns include Deer and Castle, Deer and Pine Tree, and Vintage.

Most of the Bohemian glass encountered in today's market is from 1875 to 1900. Bohemian-type glass also was made in England, Switzerland, and Germany.

Reproduction Alert.

Basket

Irid green, ruffled, applied reeded handle, gilt dragonfly and fern dec, 6-1/2" h **$175**

Irid green body dec with amethyst straw marks, metal rim and handle, Wilhelm Kralik, 8" d **$150**

Bowl, green ground, random ruby threading, c1910, 6" d **$175**

Candlesticks, set of four, cranberry flashed, cut to clear, wide drip pan cut with guilloche band accented with stars and roundels, similarly cut elongated egg-shaped stem, panel-cut domed foot, late 19th/early 20th C, 10-1/2" h **$1,645**

Compote, irid green, threaded glass trim on bowl, pedestal, and foot, c1900, 9-1/4" h............................ **$175**

Dresser bottle, cut panel body, enameled dec, c1890, 8-1/4" h **$90**

Ewer, ftd, blue cut to clear, horizontal gray panels, dec with cameo carved white and blue grapes and leaves, price for pr, 14" h **$1,050**

Goblet, white and cranberry overlay, thistle form bowl, six teardrop panels alternately enameled with floral bouquets and cut with blocks of diamonds, faceted knob and spreading scalloped foot, gilt trim, 6-3/4" h................ **$600**

Low bowl, ftd, optic ribbed, blue, large enameled roses and foliage, three figural fish form feet, accented with jeweled eyes, and pointillism enamel, Harrach, 8-1/2" d....... **$1,500**

Mantel lusters, pr, trumpet shaped body cased in white, enamel dec floral sprays and gilt moss, cut to ruby flashing, crenellated edge and trumpet foot, hung with long faceted colorless lusters, late 19th C, 12" h **$650**

Mantel urns, cov, pr, amber flashed, tapered octagonal bodies etched with continuous scene of deer in wooded landscape, domed lids with paneled baluster finials, faceted knop, trum-pet foot with scalloped rim, star-cut base, late 19th C, 18-1/2" h **$2,500**

Portrait vase, slender baluster-form cranberry flashed body over-enameled with gilt vines, one side with white cased oval painted with portrait of young lady, late 19th C, 9-1/2" h **$250**

Ramekin, translucent yellow and clear, dec with red, green, yellow, and blue scrolling, white dotted and gold horizontal band, price for set of eight, 3" w.. **$100**

Rose bowl, optic ribbed body, applied ruffled rim, cobalt blue, Harrach, 5" h **$110**

Toothpick holder, tapering body, brass rim, threaded irid body, Pallme-Koening, 2-1/2" h **$115**

Urn, ftd, cranberry, medallion coat of arms, gold encrustations, polychrome floral scrolling, raised glass jewels, two jewels missing, 11" h **$175**

Vase

Baluster, clear, applied snake dec, 7-1/2" h **$75**

Bulbous stick, mottled red, colorful scrolling foliage, Graf Harrach propeller mark, 7-1/2" h **$350**

Bulbous stick, quadra-fold rim, deep amethyst, irid blue oil spot finish, 8-1/4" h **$120**

Bulbous stick, tri-fold rim, cranberry, overall gold oil spot finish, random threading at rim, 8-1/4" h...... **$150**

Cylindrical, shading from amber green to rose, Grenada Line, Rindskopf, 10" h **$175**

Cylindrical tapering body, irid citron, applied irid threading, Pallme-Koenig, 12" h................................ **$400**

Cylindrical, tri-fold inverted rim, irid blue, white draped loops, Rindskopf, 9" h **$150**

Paneled shouldered body, irid dark olive green/ brown, 3-1/4" h......**$35**

Tapering ovoid body, blue cut to clear, notched rims, overlaid circular bases, clear floral pattern cutting, price for pr, 6" h....................... **$200**

Tapered conical body with slightly flared rim, Azure blue, cut with daisy heads between navettes, cut and gilded chinoiserie hunting scenes and florals on smoked ground, paneled foot, early 20th C, 12-1/8" h **$250**

Wide cylindrical, irid green, shades of blue and purple in undulating design, 10-1/2" h **$600**

Water set, 11" h covered water jug, four matching 5" cups, cobalt blue ground, gilt bands, raised pink flowers, mkd "Made in Czecho-Slovakia" **$125**

Wine bottle, ruby flashed, engraved florals, matching stopper, c1890, 10" h **$90**

Bohemian cordial set, decanter with four matching wines, ruby flashed, grape and foliage etched decoration, matching tray, **$375.**

Bohemian vase, glass, reverse trumpet form, iridescent blue with yellow and pink Art Nouveau flowers, attr. To Ferdinand von Poschinger, later Loetz Austria signature, 15" h, **$500.**

BOTTLES, GENERAL

History: Cosmetic bottles held special creams, oils, and cosmetics designed to enhance the beauty of the user. Some also claimed, especially on their colorful labels, to cure or provide relief from common ailments.

A number of household items, e.g., cleaning fluids and polishes, required glass storage containers. Many are collected for their fine lithographed labels.

Mineral water bottles contained water from a natural spring. Spring water was favored by health-conscious people between the 1850s and 1900s.

Nursing bottles, used to feed the young and sickly, were a great help to the housewife because of their graduated measure markings, replaceable nipples, and the ease with which they could be cleaned, sterilized, and reused.

A.M. Bininger & Co. 19 Broad St. N.Y. Distilled In 1848, Old Kentucky Bourbon 1849 Reserve, barrel shape, applied top, tubular open pontil, **$240.**
Photo courtesy of American Bottle Auctions.

Beverage

A. M. Bininger & Co., 338 Broadway, NY, Distilled in 1848, Old Kentucky Bourbon, 1849 Reserve, true green, applied lip, iron pontil.. **$6,000**

Beehive, pattern molded, Midwestern
24 vertical ribs, single roll collar, light green, unusual lip, 7-1/2" d ... **$180**
24 ribs swirled to right, open pontil, wear, light scratches, 9" h **$70**

Empire Soda Works, San Francisco, aqua, 1861-71 .... **$400**

Excelsior Water, eight-sided, iron pontil, dug, uncleaned, some white paint on pontil **$450**

Miller's Extra Old Bourbon, E. Martin & Co., light amber, c1871-75, placed bubbles on front **$12,000**

Napa Soda Natural Mineral Water, sapphire blue, "W" on base, needs int. cleaning, few scratches, wear **$140**

Thos. Taylor & Co., Virginia, Nevada, medium to deep reddish-chocolate color, c1874-80, few scratches . **$4,400**

Union Glass Works Phila Superior Mineral Water, deep cobalt blue, iron pontil, mug base, some int. stain, few scratches............................. **$350**

Williams & Severance San Francisco Calsoda Mineral Waters, light green, orig graphite **$700**

Cosmetic

Kickapoo Sage Hair Tonic, cylindrical, cobalt blue, tooled mouth, matching stopper, smooth base, 5" h **$160**

Kranks Cold Cream, milk glass, 2-3/4" h.......................... **$6.50**

Pompeian Massage Cream, amethyst, 2-3/4" h **$9**

Food and household

Ink, Waterman's, paper label with bottle of ink, wooden bullet-shaped case, orig paper label, 4-1/4" h **$10**

Pickle
Cathedral, pale aqua, sq applied top, sticky ball type pontil, 12" h.. **$190**
W. D. Smith, N.Y., deep aqua, pint, applied lip, graphite pontil, 8-1/2" h **$1,000**

Sewing Machine Oil, Sperm Brand, clear, 5-1/2" h.......................... **$5**

Shoe Polish, Everett & Barron Co., oval, clear, 4-3/4" **$5**

Nursing

Acme, clear, lay-down, emb **$65**

Cala Nurser, oval, clear, emb, ring on neck, 7-1/8" h.......................... **$12**

Empire Nursing Bottle, bent neck, 6-1/2" h.......................... **$50**

Mother's Comfort, clear, turtle type **$25**

Bride's basket, diamond quilted Rubena, blue ruffled rim, silverplate frame with embossed floral sprays, 10" h overall,
$400.
Photo courtesy of The Early Auction Company, LLC.

BRIDE'S BASKETS

History: A ruffled-edge glass bowl in a metal holder was a popular wedding gift between 1880 and 1910, hence the name "bride's basket." These bowls can be found in most glass types of the period. The metal holder was generally silver-plated with a bail handle, thus enhancing the basket image.

Over the years, bowls and bases became separated and married pieces resulted. If the base has been lost, the bowl should be sold separately.

Reproduction Alert. The glass bowls have been reproduced.

Note: Items listed here have a silverplated (SP) holder unless otherwise noted.

Amber, enameled berries and buds, SP holder, 8-1/2" d, 12" h **$1,195**

Blue and white glass bowl, enameled floral dec, SP holder, 6" d, 5-1/2" h **$250**

Bowl only, overlay, heavenly blue, enameled white flowers, green leaves, white underside, ruffled, 10-3/4" d, 3-1/2" h **$215**

Crown Milano, ruffled edge bowl, heavy hand applied gold encrustation on mottled ground, pontil sgd with trademark, 13" l, 5" h **$2,000**

Custard, melon ribbed, enameled daisies, applied Rubena crystal rim, twisted and beaded handle, ftd, emb SP frame, marked "Wilcox," sq, 10" w **$450**

Opalescent Rubena Verde, applied lime stepped flower feet, thorny twist handle, Victorian, 11-1/4" h **$425**

Opaline cased in pink, ruffled amber rim, married plated holder, 9-3/4" h **$150**

Peachblow, bowl only, glossy finish, deep pink shading to pale, 9-7/8" d, 3" h, 3-3/4" base **$250**

Peachblow, cased rose shading to pink ground, applied amber stem, green leaves, amber handle, four applied feet, some losses, 10-1/2" h **$200**

Pink hobnail bowl, blue ruffled rim, SP holder dec with leaves, 10" d, 11" h **$525**

Rubena Verde, sculptured, vaseline shading to pink, yellow and green enameled flowers, Benedict SP holder, 10-1/2" d, 12-1/2" h **$460**

Satin, deep pink ruffled bowl, white ext., marked "Nemasket Silver Co." SP holder, 9-1/2" d, 12" h **$275**

Satin, light beige shading to orange ruffled bowl, hp pink, purple and yellow flowers, green leaves, raised gold outlines, blue int., sgd "Simpson, Hall, Miller Co. Quad Plate" holder, 11" d, 7-1/2" h **$895**

Satin, bowl only, brown shaded to cream overlay, raised dots, dainty gold and silver flowers and leaves dec, ruffled, 11-1/8" d, 3-3/4" h **$250**

White opal basket, cranberry ruffled rim, applied vaseline rope handle, no holder, 9" h **$95**

White opaline, cased in pink, overall colorful enameled dec, emb Middletown plated holder, applied fruit handles, Victorian, minor losses, 12" d, 7-1/2" h **$525**

BRISTOL GLASS

History: Bristol glass is a designation given to a semi-opaque glass, usually decorated with enamel and cased with another color.

Initially, the term referred only to glass made in Bristol, England, in the 17th and 18th centuries. By the Victorian era, firms on the Continent and in America were copying the glass and its forms.

Bowl, light blue, Cupid playing mandolin, gold trim **$45**

Box, cov, oblong, blue, gilt-metal mounts and escutcheon, 4-1/8" l, 2-3/4" d, 3-1/2" h **$550**

Cake stand, celadon green, enameled herons in flight, gold trim **$135**

Candlesticks, pr, soft green, gold band, 7" h **$75**

Decanter, ruffled stopper, enameled flowers and butterfly, 11-1/2" h ...**$75**

Dresser set, two cologne bottles, cov powder jar, white, gilt butterflies dec, clear stoppers **$75**

Ewer, pink ground, fancy gold designs, bands, and leaves, applied handle with gold trim, 6-3/8" h, 2-5/8" d **$135**

Finger bowl, blue, faceted sides, early 20th C, eight-pc set, 4-3/8" d **$500**

Hatpin holder, ftd, blue, enameled jewels, gold dec, 6-1/8" h **$100**

Perfume bottle, squatty, blue, gold band, white enameled flowers and leaves, matching stopper, 3-1/4" h **$100**

Puff box, cov, round, blue, gold dec **$35**

Sugar shaker, white, hp flowers, 4-3/4" h **$65**

Sweetmeat jar, deep pink, enameled flying duck, leaves, blue flower dec,

white lining, SP rim, lid, and bail handle, 3" x 5-1/2" **$110**

Urn, cov, pink opaque, hp bird and branch dec, base mkd "251," 17" h **$150**

Vase, bulbous stick, Delft windmill dec, 11" h **$100**

Bristol cordial compote, deep blue, hand painted polychrome floral decoration, brass hinged mounts, original cordial glasses, wear to gold trim, price for pair, **$275.**

Photo courtesy of Wiederseim Associates, Inc.

Bristol vase, monumental, hp decoration, bird in flowering tree branches, polychrome on white ground, blue footed base, gilt leaf decoration, wooden reeded column base, 24-1/2" h vase, **$450.**

Photo courtesy of Alderfer Auction Co.

CAMBRIDGE GLASS

History: Cambridge Glass Company, Cambridge, Ohio, was incorporated in 1901. Initially, the company made clear tableware, later expanding into colored, etched, and engraved glass. More than 40 different hues were produced in blown and pressed glass.

The plant closed in 1954 and some of the molds were later sold to the Imperial Glass Company, Bellaire, Ohio.

Marks: Five different marks were employed during the production years, but not every piece was marked.

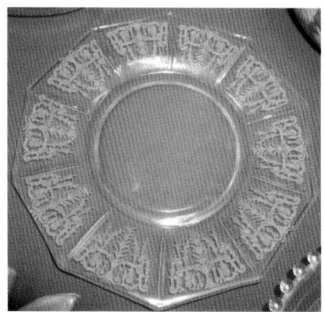

Cambridge dinner plate, Cleo, **$45.**

Cambridge vase, shell shape, Crown Tuscan, Charlton decoration with roses, leaves, gold trim, **$175.**

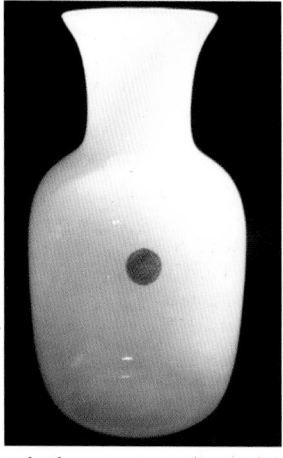

Cambridge vase, opaline, classic baluster shape original paper label, 16" h, **$90.**

Basket, Apple Blossom, crystal, 7" ...**$475**
Bonbon, Chantilly, crystal, Martha blank, two handles, 6" **$35**
Bowl, Wildflower, flared rim, three-ftd, 9-3/8" d **$85**
Butter dish, cov, Gadroon, crystal..**$45**
Candy jar, cov, Rose, green rose-shaped finial, 8" h **$250**
Candlestick
　Caprice, blue, Alpine, #70, prisms, 7" h **$195**
　Doric, black, pr, 9-1/2" h **$160**
　Rose Point, crystal, two-lite, keyhole, pr **$95**
Celery, Gloria, five-part, 12-1/2" l..**$70**
Champagne
　Adonis, crystal, #3500..................**$35**
　Chantilly, crystal **$30**
　Roxbury, crystal............................**$30**
Cocktail
　Apple Blossom, Gold Krystal, #3130 ....**$48**
　Caprice, blue **$55**
　Chantilly, crystal..........................**$42**
Cocktail icer and liner, Adonis, #968 ....**$65**
Cocktail shaker, Chantilly, crystal, glass lid................................... **$250**
Comport, Honeycomb, Rubena, ftd, 9" d, 4-3/4" h **$150**
Cordial
　Caprice, blue **$120**
　Chantilly, crystal..........................**$75**
　Rose Point, #3121.........................**$78**
Corn dish, Rose Point **$88**
Cornucopia vase, Chantilly, 9-1/8" h **$195**
Creamer
　Chantilly, crystal, individual size . **$22**
　Tempo, #1029................................**$15**
Creamer and sugar, tray, Caprice, crystal **$40**
Cream soup, orig liner, Decagon, green **$35**
Cup and saucer
　Caprice, crystal **$14**
　Decagon, pink...............................**$10**
　Martha Washington, amber..........**$12**
Decanter set, decanter, stopper, six-handled 2-1/2 oz tumblers, Tally Ho, amethyst **$195**

Flower frog
　Draped Lady, dark pink, 8-1/2" h **$185**
　Eagle, pink **$365**
　Jay, green **$365**
　Nude, clear, 6-1/2" h, 3-1/4" d .. **$145**
　Rose Lady, amber, 8-1/2" h **$350**
　Seagull...**$85**
　Two Kids, clear **$155**
Fruit bowl, Decagon, pink, 5-1/2"..**$6**
Goblet
　Chantilly, crystal, #3600..............**$45**
　Diane, crystal, #3122....................**$45**
　Roxbury, crystal............................**$30**
　Tempo, #1029/3700.......................**$15**
　Wildflower, gold trim, #3121.......**$45**
Ice bucket
　Chrysanthemum, pink, silver handle **$85**
　Wildflower, #3400/851 .... **$225**
Iced tea tumbler, Chantilly........**$45**
Ivy ball, Nude Stem, Statuesque #3011/2, 9-1/2" h, 4-1/4" h d ruby ball, 4" d base................................. **$500**
Jug
　Gloria, ftd, 9-3/4" h **$325**
　Rose Point, Doulton **$595**
Lemon plate, Caprice, blue, 5" d.**$15**
Marmalade, sterling silver cover, orig spoon, Rose Point, #68.............. **$225**
Mayonnaise set
　Chantilly, divided bowl, underplate, ladle, #3900/111 ....**$95**
　Wildflower, bowl, underplate, #3900/139 ....**$55**
Oyster cocktail, Portia, crystal...**$40**
Pitcher, cov, Forest Green, #3400/107, 1931 .... **$500**
Plate
　Apple Blossom, pink, 8-1/2" d **$20**
　Chantilly, #3900/22, 8" d.............**$18**
　Dianthus, pink, triangle C mark, 7" d **$10**
　Diane, rolled edge, #3900/166, 14" d **$75**
　Rose Point, crystal, ftd, 8" d **$70**
Relish
　Apple Blossom, Gold Krystal, five-part, #3400/67, 12" l.............. **$125**
　Caprice, club, #170, blue **$115**
　Mt. Vernon, crystal, five-part **$35**

Wildflower, three-part, three handles, 8"...**$45**

Salt and pepper shakers, pr, Wildflower, chrome tops, one slightly cloudy....................................**$40**

Seafood cocktail, Seashell, #110, Crown Tuscan, 4-1/2" oz..............**$95**

Server, center handle, Apple Blossom, amber **$30**

Sherbet

Diane, crystal, low **$20**

Tempo, #1029..........................**$12.50**

Sherry, Portia, gold encrusted **$60**

Sugar

Rose Point, gold encrusted, #3900 .**$75**

Tempo, #1029..............................**$15**

Swan, 3-1/2" h

Crown Tuscan **$60**

Crown Tuscan, gold encrusted .**$125**

Crystal **$40**

Torte plate, Rose Point, crystal, three ftd, 13" d.......................................**$95**

Tray, Gloria, four part, center handle, 8-3/4" d......................................**$70**

Tumbler

Adam, yellow, ftd........................**$25**

Carmine, crystal, 12 oz **$25**

Chantilly **$42**

Rose Point, #3500, 10 oz **$35**

Vase

Diane, crystal, keyhole, 12" h ... **$110**

Songbird and Butterfly, #402, blue, 12" h **$375**

Wildflower, #3400, 10-3/4" h.... **$175**

Whiskey, Caprice, blue, 2-1/2 oz **$225**

Wine

Caprice, crystal **$24**

Diane, crystal, 2-1/2 oz **$30**

CAMEO GLASS

History: Cameo glass is a form of cased glass. A shell of glass was prepared, and then one or more layers of glass of a different color(s) was faced to the first. A design was then cut through the outer layer(s), leaving the inner layer(s) exposed.

This type of art glass originated in Alexandria, Egypt, between 100 and 200 a.d. The oldest and most famous example of cameo glass is the Barberini or Portland vase found near Rome in 1582. It contained the ashes of Emperor Alexander Serverus, who was assassinated in 235 a.d.

Emile Gallé is probably one of the best-known cameo-glass artists. He established a factory at Nancy, France, in 1884. Although much of the glass bears his signature, he was primarily the designer. Assistants did the actual work on many pieces, even signing Gallé's name. Other makers of French-cameo glass include D'Argental, Daum Nancy, LeGras, and Delatte.

English-cameo pieces do not have as many layers of glass (colors) and cuttings as do French pieces. The outer layer is usually white, and cuttings are very fine and delicate. Most pieces are not signed. The best-known makers are Thomas Webb & Sons, and Stevens and Williams.

Marks: A star before the name Gallé on a piece by that company indicates that it was made after Gallé's death in 1904.

Reproduction Alert.

Atomizer, amethyst floral cutting on pumpkin orange ground, sgd in cameo "Ciriama," French, 8" h.. **$200**

Basket, textured ground, cameo carved gold highlighted green ferns, metal collar and handle, sgd with ship mark and initials "V.S.," French, 5" h **$250**

Biscuit jar, cov, Webb, white cameo dec, single-petaled blossoms, leafed branch, ruby red ground, silver plate fittings, 6" d, 7-1/4" h **$2,950**

Bowl

Algues pattern, ovoid, three-pointed rim, underwater scene, sgd in cameo "Legras," slight chips to points, 4" d.............................. **$225**

Ftd, four pulled points, pale pink ground, light yellow-green and amber overlay, etched clusters of blossoms on leafy branches, sgd "Galle" among leaves, several bubble bursts and int. wear, 7-3/4" d, 4-1/4" h **$690**

Mottled yellow and amethyst-gray ground, overlaid with vitrified green, red, and yellow powders, cameo cut with stemmed leafy red berries, sgd in cameo "Daum Nancy" with Croix de Lorraine, c1900, 8" d **$2,760**

Olive-green body, heavily etched and engraved Art-Deco swag and drapery design, fire polished, acid-etched "Legras" near base, 10" d, 3-3/4" h **$825**

Box, cov, Triangular form sloping from round opening, cameo cut and etched mountain landscape in blues and greens, sterling silver lid, cameo-etched "Lamartine" on side, int. rim nicks, 3" h.................................. **$360**

Cabinet vase, opal, internally dec with mottled green and amber glass, finely etched dandelion flower heads, fluffy windblown seed pods, gilt highlights, sgd in gilt "Daum Nancy Croix de Lorraine," 3-1/2" h **$2,415**

Cologne bottle

Frosted cylindrical body, cameo

cranberry floral relief, cut faceted stopper, Val St. Lambert, 4-3/8" h **$175**

Lay down, teardrop shaped body, green ground, carved water lily, Webb, 3-3/4" l **$1,900**

Mottled gray to yellow ground, cameo and enameled branching acorns silhouetted against distant forested shoreline, sgd in cameo "Daum Nancy" with Cross of Lorraine, 7" h **$1,550**

Cruet, ruby-red body, textured white enamel meadowland scene, Meadowlark on tall plant stalk, smaller scene on reverse, white rim, trefoil spout, clear frosted handle, teardrop-shaped stopper, pontil mark sgd "59," Florentine Art, 6-1/2" h **$50**

Decanter, flattened oval body, upturned rim, conical stopper, frosted colorless and purple ground, overlaid in deep purple, etched iris, engraved "Cristallerie de Galle Nancy modele et decor deposes" on base, 10-1/4" h **$2,530**

Cameo jardinière, squat, silhouetted lake landscape at dusk, brown, yellow, green, and red, Daum Nancy with Cross of Lorraine mark, 5-1/2" x 9-3/4", $2,100.

Photo courtesy of David Rago Auctions, Inc.

Cameo vase, Legras, square form, shepherd tending flock on rocky landscape, cameo signature, 5-1/2" h, $650.

Cameo vase, French, Richard, oval, brown pinecones and branches acid-etched to orange, 1920s, side signed "Richard," 8-1/2" h, $900.

Photo courtesy of Skinner, Inc.

Epergne, five 6" h etched cameo cylindrical flower holders, stylized naturalistic brass frame, Val St. Lambert, 10-1/2" h **$1,800**

Ewer

Cranberry ground, highlighted in gold, overlaid in deep purple, cameo cut grapevine motif, metal mount flip lid and handle, emb with matching grape dec, sgd in gold "Daum Nancy," c1895, 7-1/2" h **$1,380**

Textured translucent glass, gold highlighted ruby cameo with random trailing flowers, silver-gilt emb collar, handle, and lid with raspberry finial, sgd in gold "Daum Nancy," c1895, 10-1/2" **$1,955**

Flask, tapered cylindrical bottle, translucent colorless body cameo cut with violet blossoms, enameled purple, yellow, orange and white, gilt highlights, inscribed "Daum (cross) Nancy," mounted with bulbed silver cap with emb flower blossoms, engraved "Lola," small cup with raised leaf blade design, emb "SH" in diamond, cap loose, 5-5/8" h **$375**

Floor vase, rose amber ground, overlaid in green, cameo cut towering trees above deep forested lake scene, sgd "Legras" in cameo, c1910, price for pr, 24" h **$4,025**

Incense burner, bell shaped vessel, shading from citron to frosted, wine-red and amethyst floral cameo cutting, lower body sgd in cameo relief "D'Argental," 7" h **$700**

Inkwell, mottled green and purple ground, cameo cut falling oak leaves, five jeweled carved insect and acorn cabochons, sgd "Daum Nancy," c1900, 4-1/4" d, 3-1/2" h **$1,265**

Lamp base

Blue-gray ground, overlaid with cinnamon and orange, cameo cut cascading leafy stemmed fruit, sgd "Galle" in cameo, lamp fittings, 16-3/4" h **$1,330**

Flattened circular body, Prussian blue, detailed white opaque floral cameo relief, butterfly, three frosted feet, English, 4" h, 4-1/2" w ... **$900**

Lamp, table

Mushroom shape, yellow overlaid in dark brown, cut frosted lake scene and oak leaves, French, c1920, 12-1/2" h **$600**

Textured frosted ground, cascading crimson leafy vines, sgd in cameo "Legras," 15" h **$250**

Pitcher, vitrified fall color leaves, mottled earth tone ground, applied gold enameled bug and handle, base engraved with block letters "Mueller Croismare," 7-1/2" h **$2,700**

Tray, triangular, inverted rim, frosted to orange, overlaid and cut large green stemmed oak leaves and acorns, sgd in cameo "Galle," 9" w **$700**

Tumbler, gray ground mottled in yellow and amethyst, cameo cut purple and yellow enameled flowers, green leafy stems, sgd in cameo "Daum Nancy" with Croix de Lorraine, c1900, 3-1/4" h **$1,035**

Vase

Amber glass overlaid in orange and green, cut mountainous lake scene outlined with towering pine trees, sgd in cameo "Daum Nancy" with Croix de Lorraine, c1910, 13" h **$3,115**

Baluster, camellias in polished red and orange, pale ground, sgd "Galle" in cameo, 8" h **$1,300**

Bottle form, martele frosted ground, amethyst gold highlighted cameo stemmed flowers, icicle body, sgd with Burgun Schverer thistle and cross monogram, 9" h **$3,950**

Conical, green ground, bands of stylized flower blossoms on etched and polished surfaces, gilt highlights, inscribed "Daum (cross) Nancy" on base, gilt wear, 4-1/4" h **$325**

Cylindrical citron body, dark crimson and rose colored maple leaves and seed pods, sgd in cameo "D'Argental," 10" h **$900**

Cylindrical, cameo cut trailing vines and flowers in green and brown over frosted ground, Foussin signature at side, 20th C, 14-3/8" h **$500**

Dark amber ground, overlaid in plum and burgundy, cut cascading branches of seed pods and leaves, sgd "D'Argental" in cameo, c1910, 11-3/4" h **$1,610**

Etched colorless body, white and pale yellow overlapping petals emerging from transparent green base, ftd, rolled base rim, rough pontil, sgd "L.C. Tiffany Favrile," numbered "4053D," 5-3/8" h **$11,200**

Ftd, cylindrical matte finish amber body, long stemmed blue flowers and leaves, attributed to Mueller, engraved signature "Crois Mare," 12-1/2" h **$1,500**

Frosted gray ground overlaid in chartreuse and white, cut with trailing leaves and seed pods, sgd "Galle" with star in cameo, c1900, 7-1/2" h **$1,035**

Frosted ground with flecks of orange and green, orange and burgundy orchid, Daum Nancy, signature on side, c1905, 13-3/4" h **$3,525**

Gray and rose mottled ground, overlaid in amethyst, cameo cut shoreline castle between towering trees, distant mountains, sgd "Richard" in cameo, c1915, 22-1/2" h...... **$1,495**

Gray ground, overlaid with amethyst, cameo cut mountainous lake scene and medieval castle, sgd "Richard" in cameo, drilled, c1915, 21-1/2".. **$650**

Gray ground internally dec with amber and frost mottling, cameo carved vitrified leaves, stemmed red bleeding hearts, sgd in cameo "Daum Nancy" with Croix de Lorraine, c1910, 4-1/2" h **$1,100**

Gray ground internally dec with mottled custard, overlaid in variegated orange and brown, cameo cut leafage and buds, inscribed "Degue," c1925, 10-3/4" h **$750**

Lemon yellow ground, cameo cut royal blue thistles, sgd "Richard" in cameo, c1915, 6" h **$320**

Olive green cased to salmon and translucent colorless glass, cameo cut and etched leaves and pendant seed pods, sgd "Galle" in cameo on side, polished pontil, rim possibly ground, base wear, 9-3/4" h ... **$460**

Ovoid cylindrical bulbous mottled green body, seven brown sailing ships, crimson and yellow sky, sgd in cameo "Daum Nancy" with Cross of Lorraine, 5-3/4" h............ **$1,200**

Ovoid, cameo carved red lily on gold Aventurine internally dec ruby and yellow body, sgd "Desiré Christian Meisenthal Loth," 7" h......... **$2,850**

Pale ground, red and orange polished trumpet vines, cameo signature "D'Argental," 12-3/4" h **$1,800**

Pillow shape, scenic, snow covered barren trees against distant gray forest, mottled yellow ground, sgd in cameo "Daum Nancy" with Cross of Lorraine, 4-3/4" h, 5-1/2" w . **$2,450**

Shaded yellow ground, polished dark green blossoming branches, cameo sgd "Galle," 10-1/2" h **$1,500**

Squatty, Prussian blue, cameo carved tropical design, bamboo tree trunks and palms, double banded rim, top band carved with arrow dec, Webb, 5" h **$600**

Swollen elongated neck, flared base, opaque orange glass overlaid in black, cameo cut and etched tall leafy stems, scrolled lower border, cameo-etched "Richard," 11-1/2" h **$300**

Tapering ovoid body, frosted with swirled amethyst, overlaid with detailed summer forest scene, circular base sgd "Lamartine," numbered "327-604," 6-3/4" h **$1,000**

Triangular frosted blue body with blue mottling, cameo carved wisteria blossoms and vines, sgd in cameo "Legras," 8-1/4" h **$675**

Whiskey jug, textured translucent ground, cameo cut and enameled grapevine and leaves, metal lid and handle in form of knight's helmet, lion finial on flip lid, unsigned, c1895, 10-1/2" h.................................... **$815**

Cameo vase, bulbous, white daffodils and green foliage, mottled white and yellow ground, etched "Daum Nancy," 16" x 4-1/2", $6,500.
Photo courtesy of David Rago Auctions, Inc.

CARNIVAL GLASS

History: Carnival glass, an American invention, is colored-pressed glass with a fired-on iridescent finish. It was first manufactured about 1905 and was immensely popular both in America and abroad. More than 1,000 different patterns have been identified. Production of old carnival-glass patterns ended in 1930.

Most of the popular patterns of carnival glass were produced by five companies: Dugan, Fenton, Imperial, Millersburg, and Northwood.

Marks: Northwood patterns frequently are found with the "N" trademark. Dugan used a diamond trademark on several patterns.

Notes: Color is the most important factor in pricing carnival glass. The color of a piece is determined by holding it to the light and looking through it.

Carnival Glass, advertising plate, Fenton, "Eat Paradise Sodas," amethyst, 6", **$500-$800.**

Carnival Glass, advertising plate, North-wood, Dreibus Parfait Sweets, amethyst, rare, 6", $1,100.

Carnival Glass, Big Basketweave, Dugan, vase, ice blue, 11-1/4", $600.

Advertising

Several manufacturers made interesting plates and bowls that were used as promotional giveaway pieces by advertisers. Today these advertising pieces command high prices.

Colors known: amethyst, blue, green, marigold.

Forms: bonbons, bowls, hats, mugs, plates.

Identifying characteristics: Names of advertisers are the predominate characteristic. Many advertisers chose popular patterns of the day to add their names to, such as Heart & Vine or Grape & Cable. Many of these premiums were made in limited quantities. The listing below is a sampling of the current market.

Bonbon, card tray shape, Isaac Benesch & Son's 54th Anniversary, Holly Sprig pattern, Millersburg, marigold ....**$50-$150**

Bowl, ruffled
Compliments of Central Shoe Store, amethyst..........................**Rare-$950**
Driebus Parfait Sweets, light lavender/amethyst.................**$350-$550**
Exchange Bank, amethyst **Rare-$900**
Geo. W. Getts Pianos, amethyst ....**Rare-$1,100**
Gevurtz Bros. Furniture and Clothing, amethyst ....**Rare-$1,600**
Horlacher, Thistle pattern, green ....**$125-$135**
Isaac Benesch & Sons, amethyst ....**$400-$425**
Norris N Smith, amethyst ....**Rare-$1,800**
Ogden Furniture, Carpet Co., amethyst...........................**$600-$700**
Sterling Furniture Co., amethyst ....**$600-$750**

Hat, ruffled, General Furniture, 1910, Peacock Tail pattern, green.. **$55-$75**

Mug, Hotel Vendome, Singing Birds pattern, purple ....**$40-$55**

Plate, hand grip
Braziers Candies, amethyst.**$600-$900**
Campbell & Beesley Co., Millersburg, amethyst..........................**Rare-$750**
Central Shoe Store, amethyst ....**$500-$600**
Davidson Society Chocolates, amethyst............................**Rare-$1,000**
Dreibus Parfait, amethyst ....**Rare-$1,100**
Fern Brand, amethyst........**$850-$950**
Greengard Furniture Co., amethyst ....**Rare-$7,000**

Jockey Club, amethyst ... **Rare-$1,100**
Ogden Furniture, amethyst ....**Rare-$1,100**
Sterling Furniture Co., amethyst ....**Rare-$1,800**
Utah Liquor Co., amethyst ....**Rare-$1,750**

Plate, round
Ballard, 9" d, amethyst .. **Rare-$1,300**
Birmingham Age Herald, 9" d, amethyst.......................**$1,500-$2,600**
Brazier's Candies, 9" d, amethyst ....**Rare-$1,100**
Broeker's Flour, 9" d, amethyst ....**Rare-$3,000**
Central Shoe Store, 9" d, amethyst ....**Rare-$1,300**
Compliments of Spector's Department Store, Heart & Vine pattern, 9" d, marigold................**$750-$900**
Dorsey & Funkenstein, 9" d, amethyst ....**Rare-$2,600**
Eagle Furniture Co., 9" d, amethyst ....**$425-$1,500**
Exchange Bank, 9" d, amethyst ....**Rare-$1,700**
Fern Brand Chocolates, 9" d, amethyst.......................**Rare-$1,850**
Geo. W. Getts Pianos, 9" d, amethyst ....**Rare-$1,300**
J. N. Ledford Company, Cooleemee, NC, Heart & Vine pattern, 9" d, marigold...................**Rare-$9,000**
Jockey Club, 9" d, amethyst ....**Rare-$1,600**
Norris N. Smith, 9" d, amethyst ....**Rare-$1,400**
Old Rose Distilling Co., Stippled Grape & Cable pattern, ribbed back, 9" d, green....................**$600-$750**
Roods Chocolates, 9" d, amethyst ....**Rare-$3,600**
Spectors Department Store, Heart & Vine pattern, 9" d, marigold ....**Rare-$1,100**

Big Basketweave

Made by Dugan-Diamond.

Colors known: amethyst, blue, celeste blue, horehound, ice blue, marigold, peach opalescent, purple, white.

Forms: baskets, bowls, vases.

Identifying characteristics: The pattern is found on the exterior of the forms as they resemble woven wicker items. Produced 1911-1913.

Also known as: Wicker Weave.

Basket, large
Amethyst/purple...............**$135-$165**
Marigold...............................**$45-$75**

Basket, small
Amethyst/purple...................**$40-$60**
Marigold.........................**$15-$20**
Vase, 4" h to 7" h
Amethyst/purple.............**$300-$325**
Celeste blue....................**$350-$475**
Lavender.........................**$200-$300**
Marigold..........................**$95-$125**
Peach opalescent.............**$250-$300**
White................................**$100-$150**
Vase, 8" h to 14" h
Amethyst/purple.............**$150-$200**
Blue.................................**$225-$300**
Celeste blue....................**$375-$425**
Ice blue...........................**$400-$600**
Peach opalescent.............**$325-$425**
Sapphire blue..................**$400-$600**
White...............................**$85-$90**

Blueberry

Made by Fenton.
Colors known: blue, marigold, white.
Forms: water sets.
Identifying characteristics: This pattern has life-like blueberries. The tops of the water pitchers are scalloped and flared out, with handles always applied. Production began in 1912.
Also known as: #1562.

Tumbler
Blue..........................**$45-65**
Marigold.....................**$80-100**
White........................**$90-175**
Water pitcher
Blue.......................**$800-1,400**
Marigold....................**$500-825**

Bushel Basket

Novelty pattern made by Northwood.
Colors known: amethyst, amethyst slag, aqua opalescent, blue, green, ice blue, ice green, lavender, marigold, purple, sapphire blue, smoke, white.
Forms: only two basket forms known, with either a round or octagon shaped base.
Identifying characteristics: As the name implies, this pattern looks like a woven wicker basket, complete with two handles and small feet. Handles are commonly ribbed, but variations with smooth handles and more flare to the top exist. The pattern was made from 1910 to 1921.

Basket, round, ribbed side handles
Amethyst/purple.................**$80-$155**

Amethyst slag ....**$100-$250**
Aqua ....**$325-$425**
Aqua opalescent................**$250-$450**
Blue.................................**$75-$165**
Celeste blue.....................**Rare-$550**
Green ....**$90-$275**
Horehound ....**$400-$600**
Ice blue ....**$250-$450**
Ice green ....**$165-$300**
Lavender...........................**$185-$200**
Marigold............................**$45-$95**
Marigold, dark....................**$65-$95**
Marigold, pastel................**$150-$250**
Sapphire blue ....**$1,350-$2,000**
Smoke..............................**$300-$375**
White................................**$145-$200**
Basket, eight-sided, ribbed side handles
Amethyst/purple..............**$100-$135**
Aqua ....**Rare-$1,500**
Blue.................................**$100-$160**
Green ....**$225-$250**
Horehound ....**Rare-$650**
Ice blue ....**$350-$425**
Ice green ....**$200-$250**
Lavender...........................**$160-$250**
Marigold............................**$95-$125**
Renninger Blue ....**Rare-$550**
White ....**$95-$225**

Captive Rose

Made by Fenton.
Colors known: amethyst, blue, green, marigold.
Forms: bonbons, bowls, calling card trays, compotes, plates.
Identifying characteristics: This detailed pattern has a lacy embroidered motif. Look for the rose in the center as well as the garland of roses. Production began in 1910.
Also known as: Battenburg Lace #2B.

Bonbon, two handles
Amethyst..............................**$65-$95**
Blue.................................**$40-$70**
Green ....**$90-$150**
Marigold............................**$30-$45**
Bowl, CRE, green ....**$130-$135**
Bowl, IC shape, green ....**$70-$80**
Bowl, ruffled or 3-in-1 edge
Amethyst..............................**$35-$40**
Blue.................................**$55-$135**
Green ....**$75-$135**
Marigold............................**$40-$50**
Calling card tray
Amethyst..............................**$65-$95**
Blue.................................**$40-$70**
Green ....**$90-$150**
Marigold............................**$30-$45**

Carnival Glass, Blueberry, Fenton, water pitcher, blue, 10" h, **$1,000-$1,400;** *outstanding condition,* **$4,500.**

Carnival Glass, Bushel Basket, Northwood, pastel marigold, **$50.**

Carnival Glass, Captive Rose, Fenton, flat plate, green, 9", **$800-$950.**

Carnival Glass, Captive Rose, Fenton, flat plate, blue, 9", **$400-$700.**

Carnival Glass, Cherries, Dugan, ruffled bowl, purple, 9", **$325-$350.**

Carnival Glass, Concord, Fenton, ruffled bowl, emerald green, 8-1/2", **$325-$350.**

Compote, ruffled

Amethyst	**$45-$75**
Blue	**$200-$325**
Green	**$65-$110**
Marigold	**$40-$90**
White	**$75-$125**

Plate, 9" d

Amethyst	**$700-$750**
Blue	**$285-$500**
Green	**$800-$950**
Marigold	**$250-$375**

Plate, amethyst, 9-1/2" d ... **$375-$400**

Cherries

Made by Dugan-Diamond.

Colors known: amethyst, electric blue, marigold, peach opalescent, purple.

Forms: banana boat, bowls, plates.

Identifying characteristics: This pattern features clusters of stemmed cherries on leaves and branches. It was made from 1909 until 1914.

Also known as: Cherry.

Banana boat, 3 ftd

Amethyst/purple	**$250-$300**
Electric blue	**$250-$275**
Peach opalescent	**$250-$275**

Bowl, flat, 5" d to 7" d

Amethyst/purple	**$115-$125**
Marigold	**$30-$45**
Peach opalescent	**$50-$65**
White	**$115-$125**

Bowl, collar base, peach opalescent, 9" d ... **$125-$135**

Bowl, IC shape, amethyst/purple, 9" d ... **$40-$45**

Bowl, ruffled, flat, 9" d to 9-1/2" d

Amethyst/purple	**$325-$350**
Marigold	**$80-$100**
Peach opalescent	**$120-$125**
White	**$425-$525**

Bowl, ruffled, ftd, 10" d

Amethyst/purple	**$85-$225**
Marigold	**$35-$45**
Peach opalescent	**$85-$95**

Bowl, tricorn, crimped edge, ftd, amethyst/purple ... **$195-$225**

Plate, 6" d

Amethyst/purple	**$200-$300**
Peach opalescent	**$220-$250**

Concord

Made by Fenton.

Colors known: amethyst, blue, green, marigold, pumpkin marigold.

Forms: bowls, plates.

Identifying characteristics: This pattern features clusters of grapes, vines, and leaves, while the whole background resembles a net.

Bowl, IC shape, ruffled

Amethyst	**$275-$300**
Blue	**$75-$150**
Green	**$325-$350**
Marigold	**$130-$185**
Pumpkin marigold	**$225-$250**

Bowl, 3-in-1 edge

Green, silvery	**$70-$75**
Marigold	**$50-$65**

Plate, 9" d to 10" d

Amethyst	**Rare-$1,400**
Green	**Rare-$3,500**
Marigold	**Rare-$1,100**

Corn

Made by Northwood.

Colors known: amethyst, aqua opalescent, blue, green, ice blue, ice green, lime green, marigold, purple, teal, white.

Forms: vases.

Identifying characteristics: This pattern looks like its name implies, an ear of corn, with the husk forming the base.

Reproduction Alert. A round bowl has been made.

Vase, stalk base

Amethyst/purple	**$300-$650**
Aqua opalescent, cracked 1" from bottom	**Rare-$3,750**
Green	**$350-$375**
Ice blue	**$800-$900**
Ice green	**$270-$325**
Lime green, marigold overlay	**$400-$450**
Marigold, dark	**$800-$900**
Marigold	**$300-$500**
Teal	**Rare-$2,400**
White	**$300-$350**

Carnival Glass, Corn, Northwood, vase, stalk base, aqua, rare, 6-1/2", **$2,200-$3,000.**

Vase, plain base
Amethyst/purple.............**$365-$650**
Aqua ....**$800-$1,000**
Green ....**$400-$900**
Ice green ....**$265-$425**
Marigold......................**$325-$850**
White...........................**$225-$325**

Daisy and Drape
Made by Northwood.
Colors known: amethyst, aqua, aqua opalescent, blue, green, ice blue, ice marigold, white.
Forms: vases.
Identifying characteristics: This pattern features a drape like body with a ring of daisies around the top. Production began in 1912.
Also known as: Daisy Band and Drape.
Vase, turned-in top band
Amethyst ....**$850-$900**
Aqua ....**$450-$550**
Aqua opalescent...............**$375-$625**
Blue............................**$750-$900**
Green ....**Rare-$3,200**
Ice blue ....**$1,800-$2,250**
Ice green ....**Rare-$3,500**
Lavender......................**$500-$700**
Marigold.........................**$375-$400**
Purple ....**$550-$600**
White ....**$185-$260**
Vase, turned-out top band
Amethyst ....**$750-$850**
Aqua ....**$450-$550**
Aqua opalescent...............**$375-$625**
Blue............................**$750-$900**
Marigold.........................**$400-$450**
White ....**$175-$**

Daisy Wreath
Made by Westmoreland.
Colors known: amethyst, aqua opal, blue opal, marigold, marigold on milk glass, peach opalescent.
Forms: bowls, plates, vases.
Identifying characteristics: This pattern features a central daisy surrounded by a wreath border. Production began in 1910.
Also known as: Daisy Bowl.

Bowl, IC shape, marigold on milk glass, 8-1/2" d.....................**$60-$110**
Bowl, ruffled, 8" d to 10" d
Amethyst ....**$200-$250**
Aqua opalescent...............**$200-$300**
Blue opalescent ....**$180-$200**
Marigold.........................**$150-$175**
Marigold on milk glass
....**$80-$90**

Peach opalescent.............**$100-$200**
Plate, blue ....**Rare-$350**
Vase, marigold ....**Rare-$500**

Diamond Points
Made by Northwood.
Colors known: amethyst, aqua opalescent, blue, green, horehound, ice blue, ice green, marigold, sapphire blue, white.
Forms: baskets, rose bowls, vases.
Identifying characteristics: This pattern features squares set on the diagonal, each filled with further criss-cross diamond elements. Production was between 1912 and 1916.

Basket, marigold...............**$850-$900**
Bushel basket
Blue.....................................**$375-$400**
Marigold, dark ....**$2,000-$2,100**
Marigold...........................**$425-$450**
Vase, 6" h to 7-1/2" h, squatty
Amethyst ....**$75-$125**
Green ....**$50-$75**
Ice blue ....**$300-$550**
Ice green ....**$275-$325**
Marigold..........................**$100-$145**
White................................**$175-$350**
Vase, 9-1/2" h to 10" h
Amethyst ....**$50-$85**
Aqua opalescent, butterscotch
....**$600-$650**
Blue...................................**$650-$675**
Ice blue ....**$275-$300**
Sapphire blue ....**$475-$500**
Smoke...............................**$250-$255**
Vase, 10-1/4" h to 10-1/2" h
Aqua opalescent..........**$1,025-$1,650**
Blue...................................**$150-$250**
Vase, 11" h
Green ....**$100-$115**
Ice green ....**$190-$300**
Sapphire blue ....**Rare-$1,700**
White................................**$75-$135**

Diamonds
Made by Millersburg.
Colors known: amethyst, aqua, green, marigold.
Forms: punch bowls, water sets.
Identifying characteristics: This bold diamond pattern features a row of beading inside each diamond. An odd form was made in this pattern when a water pitcher form was created with a handle, but no pouring spout. Production was from 1910 to 1911.

Punch bowl and base
Amethyst ....**Rare-$3,700**

Carnival Glass, Daisy and Drape, Northwood, vase, turned in, ice green, rare **$3,500.**

Carnival Glass, Daisy and Drape, Northwood, vase, aqua opal, **$375-$625.**

Carnival Glass, Daisy Wreath, Westmoreland, bowl, marigold over moonstone, **$80-$90.**

Carnival Glass, Diamond Points, Northwood, vase, aqua opal, pastel, 10-1/2", **$1,025-$1,650.**

Carnival Glass, Diamonds, Millersburg, tumbler, amethyst, 4", **$70-$90.**

Carnival Glass, Dragon and Lotus, Fenton, bowl, ruffled collar, dark red, 8-1/2", **$650-$750.**

Green	**Rare-$2,600**
Marigold	**Rare-$2,800**

Spittoon, whimsy from tumbler mold,
marigold .... **Rare-$7,000**

Tumbler

Amethyst	**$70-$90**
Aqua	**$125-$175**
Green	**$65-$100**
Marigold	**$45-$75**

Water pitcher

Amethyst	**$275-$385**
Aqua	**$450-$550**
Green	**$375-$425**
Marigold	**$150-$275**

Water pitcher, with no spout

Amethyst	**Rare-$600**
Green	**Rare-$600**

Dragon and Lotus

Made by Fenton.

Colors known: amber, amethyst, aqua opalescent, blue, cobalt blue, dark blue, green, marigold, marigold on milk glass, peach opalescent, red, reverse amberina, vaseline opalescent.

Forms: bowls, plates.

Identifying characteristics: This popular pattern shows ovals with a whimsical flying dragon alternating with rose type flowers. A busy inner band is found between the dragons and the lotus flowers in the center. Production started in 1915 and continued until 1920.

Bowl, IC shape

Blue	**$65-$85**
Cherry red	**$1,400-$1,500**
Cobalt blue	**$175-$185**
Marigold	**$40-$45**
Marigold on milk glass, pastel	**$850-$900**
Red	**$650-$700**
Reverse amberina	**$425-$450**

Carnival Glass, Embroidered Mums, Northwood, bowl, blue electric, 9", **$600.**

Bowl, IC shape, spatula ftd

Amethyst	**$40-$45**
Green	**$45-$50**
Marigold	**$45-$70**
Peach opalescent	**$85-$95**

Bowl, ruffled, plain back

Amber	**$115-$120**
Amber with red slag	**$200-$225**
Amethyst	**$145-$150**
Aqua opalescent	**Rare-$2,600**
Blue	**$25-$65**
Dark blue	**$90-$95**
Green	**$35-$55**
Lime green	**$300-$350**
Lime green opalescent	**$350-$375**
Marigold	**$35-$40**
Peach opalescent	**$145-$175**
Red	**$800-$1,200**
Vaseline slag	**$75-$95**

Bowl, 3-in-1 edge

Amethyst, light	**$220-$225**
Marigold	**$65-$85**

Plate, 9-1/2" d

Amethyst	**Rare-$2,500**
Blue	**Rare-$2,200**
Marigold	**Rare-$1,200**
Peach opalescent	**Rare-$2,000**
Red	**Rare-$7,000**

Embroidered Mums

Made by Northwood.

Colors known: amethyst, aqua opalescent, blue, electric blue, green, ice blue, ice green, lavender, lime green opalescent, marigold, peach opalescent, purple, sapphire blue, white.

Forms: bonbons, bowls, plates.

Identifying characteristics: This elegant pattern features a Greek key ring with interspersed chrysanthemums and leaves. An embroidered type star flower is in the center. Production was from 1911 to 1912.

Also known as: Mums and Greek Key.

Carnival Glass, Fashion, Imperial, compote, smoke, **$475-$650.**

Carnival Glass, Fashion, Imperial, rose bowl, purple, 6-1/2" w, **$700-$1,500.**

Carnival Glass, Fisherman's, Dugan, mug, blue, rare, 4", **$400-$650.**

Bonbon, stemmed, two handles, white .... **Rare-$1,000**
Bowl, ruffled, ribbed back, 9" d
  Amethyst .... **$265-$275**
  Aqua .... **Rare-$2,500**
  Aqua opalescent .... **Rare-$3,000**
  Blue .... **$155-$450**
  Electric blue .... **$500-$600**
  Ice blue .... **$600-$900**
  Ice green .... **$1,200-$1,400**
  Horehound .... **Rare-$2,000**
  Lavender .... **$450-$695**
  Marigold .... **$350-$400**
  Sapphire blue .... **Rare-$2,500**
Plate, 9" d
  Blue .... **Rare-$6,500**
  Ice blue .... **$1,000-$1,300**
  Ice green .... **$1,000-$1,100**
  White .... **$1,000-$2,100**

Fashion

Made by Imperial.

Colors known: clambroth, emerald green, helios, horehound, marigold, purple, smoke.

Forms: bowls, breakfast sets, compotes, punch cups, rose bowls, water sets.

Identifying characteristics: Fashion is one of Imperial's imitation cut glass patterns. It's not quite as detailed as most, but includes a hobstar and zippered band as well as fans and diamonds. Production began in 1910.

Also known as: Imperial's #402-1/2.

Reproductions: This pattern never was made in a toothpick holder, but those creating reproductions made one, often found in blue, purple, or red.

Bowl, IC shape, 9" d to 9-1/2" d
  Clambroth .... **$80-$90**
  Marigold .... **$50-$70**
  Smoke .... **$155-$175**
Bowl, ruffled, 9" d

  Marigold .... **$30-$40**
  Smoke .... **$35-$55**
Breakfast creamer
  Emerald green .... **$200-$250**
  Helios .... **$125-$150**
  Marigold .... **$25-$40**
  Purple .... **$145-$200**
  Smoke .... **$80-$100**
Breakfast sugar
  Emerald green .... **$200-$250**
  Helios .... **$125-$150**
  Marigold .... **$25-$40**
  Purple .... **$115-$145**
  Smoke .... **$80-$100**
Compote, smoke .... **$475-$600**
Fruit bowl, ruffled, 12" d, amber
  .... **Rare-$100**
Punch bowl with base
  Marigold .... **$150-$195**
  Purple .... **Rare-$1,750**
  Red .... **Rare-$5,000**
  Smoke .... **Rare-$1,000**
Punch cup
  Marigold .... **$20-$30**
  Purple .... **$30-$40**
  Red .... **$435-$525**
  Smoke .... **$25-$35**
Rose bowl
  Helios .... **$300-$315**
  Marigold .... **$210-$235**
  Purple .... **$700-$1,500**
Tumbler
  Marigold .... **$80-$95**
  Purple .... **$175-$300**
  Smoke .... **$85-$125**
Water pitcher
  Marigold .... **$150-$200**
  Purple .... **$700-$900**
  Smoke .... **$400-$550**

Fisherman's Mug

Made by Dugan/Diamond.

Colors known: amethyst, blue, custard, horehound, lavender, marigold, peach opalescent.

Forms: mug.

Identifying characteristics: This mug must have been designed with a fisherman in mind as it shows a fish, water lilies, and cattails. The design is found only on one side, the other side is blank. Butler Brothers included this pattern in their 1911 catalog. Production continued from 1911 until 1914.

Also known as: Cattails and Fish

> **Reproduction Alert.** Reproductions by L. G. Wright.

Mug, 4"
  Amethyst/purple .... **$90-$120**
  Amethyst, black .... **$90-$135**
  Blue .... **$400-$650**
  Custard, decorated .... **$60-$65**
  Horehound .... **$200-$275**
  Lavender .... **$85-$185**
  Marigold .... **$85-$190**
  Marigold, dark .... **$75-$90**
  Peach opalescent .... **$900-$1,100**

Floral and Grape

Made by Dugan.

Floral and Grape Variant. Made by Fenton.

Colors known: amethyst/purple, blue, horehound, marigold, purple.

Forms: water sets, whimsies.

Identifying characteristics: The designs used by both Fenton and Dugan are remarkably similar. Water pitchers produced by Dugan have ribs in the bands that lean to the left, while the Fenton pitchers have the same element leaning to the right. A raised cable on either side of the ribs distinguishes a tumbler as Dugan rather than Fenton, whose tumblers do not have a cable at all. Production was from 1910 to 1911.

Also known as: Floral and Grapevine.

Carnival Glass, Floral and Grape, Dugan, ruffled-top pitcher, purple, 8-1/2" h, **$165-$295.**

Carnival Glass, Four Flowers, Dugan, eight-ruffled bowl, purple, 10", **$325-$400.**

Carnival Glass, Garden Path Variant, Dugan, chop plate, purple, 11", **$3,000-$13,000.**

Hat, whimsy
Horehound .... **$55-$75**
Marigold .... **$30-$45**
Jack-in-the-pulpit, whimsy, horehound .... **$80-$100**
Tumbler
Amethyst/purple .... **$50-$55**
Blue .... **$30-$45**
Green .... **$75-$100**
Marigold .... **$20-$35**
White .... **$35-$55**
Water pitcher
Amethyst/purple .... **$165-$295**
Blue .... **$300-$350**
Green .... **$200-$300**
Ice green .... **$400-$600**
Marigold .... **$50-$180**
White .... **$225-$325**

Four Flowers

Made by Dugan, Diamond, and possibly Riihimaki.

Colors known: amethyst, green, marigold, peach opalescent, powder blue, smoke.

Forms: bowls, plates.

Identifying characteristics: Four Flowers is a bold pattern with four open flowers alternating with a pointed oval. The design forms a striking geometric design.

Also known as: Posy and Pods; Pods and Posies; Stippled Posy and Pods.

Banana bowl
Amethyst .... **$300-$400**
Peach opalescent .... **$250-$350**
Bowl, 5" d to 7" d
Amethyst .... **$35-$50**
Marigold .... **$30-$45**
Peach opalescent .... **$60-$90**
Bowl, ruffled, 8" d to 10" d

Amber .... **$300-$500**
Amethyst .... **$325-$400**
Green .... **$400-$500**
Marigold .... **$95-$165**
Powder blue .... **$40-$45**
Vaseline .... **$400-$600**
Plate, 6" d to 6-1/2" d
Amethyst .... **$225-$375**
Marigold .... **$115-$165**
Peach opalescent .... **$70-$175**
Plate, 9" d to 10-1/2" d
Amethyst .... **$125-$800**
Green .... **$350-$400**
Marigold .... **$250-$350**
Peach opalescent .... **$400-$650**
Rose bowl
Amethyst .... **$700-$900**
Marigold .... **$350-$500**

Garden Path and Garden Path Variant

Made by Dugan.

Colors known: amethyst/purple, marigold, peach opalecent, white.

Forms: bowls, chop plates, rose bowls.

Identifying characteristics: These two patterns are very similar. Garden Path features a busy field of hearts, fleur-de-lis, and arches. Garden Path Variant has an additional six winged hearts. Values for each pattern are the same.

Bowl, IC shape, 9" d to 10" d
Amethyst/purple .... **Rare-$1,300**
Peach opalescent .... **$375-$850**
White .... **$150-$200**
Bowl, ruffled, 9" d to 10-1/2" d
Amethyst/purple .... **$120-$700**
Marigold .... **$25-$85**
Peach opalescent .... **$200-$400**
White .... **$325-$450**

Chop plate, 11" d
Amethyst/purple .... **$3,000-$13,000**
Marigold .... **$1,500-$1,750**
Peach opalescent .... **$2,000-$2,400**
Plate, 6" d
Amethyst/purple .... **$1,000-$1,575**
Marigold .... **$90-$150**
Peach opalescent .... **$415-$650**
White .... **$300-$600**
Rose bowl, marigold .... **$65-$120**
Sauce, 6" d
Peach opalescent .... **$40-$150**
White .... **$325-$450**

Good Luck

Made by Northwood.

Colors known: amethyst/purple, aqua, aqua opalescent, blue, green, horehound, ice blue, ice blue opalescent, ice green, lavender, lime green, marigold, peach opalescent, Renninger blue, sapphire blue, teal, white.

Forms: bowls, plates.

Identifying characteristics: Look for the traditional good luck sign, a horseshoe and the words "Good Luck" in the center of this design. A riding crop crosses the center of the horseshoe while floral sprays dance around the rest of the design. bowls and plates may have basketweave, ribbed, or stippled features, values are fairly similar. Production began in 1911.

Reproduction Alert. Ruffled bowls have been reproduced by Fenton in light amethyst and contain a modern Fenton logo. Ruffled bowls also are known in blue, green, and marigold, they exhibit a harsh metallic iridescence.

*Carnival Glass, Good Luck, Northwood, plate, Electric blue, rare, 9", **$4,250-$5,500**.*

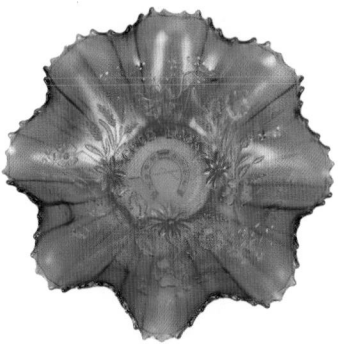

*Carnival Glass, Good Luck, Northwood, bowl, ribbed exterior, ruffled, sapphire, rare, turned out, **$2,000**.*

*Carnival Glass, Grape and Cable, Northwood, cologne, purple, 9", **$155-$355**.*

Bowl, piecrust edge, basketweave, ribbed, or stippled

Amethyst/purple	**$175-$550**
Aqua opalescent	**Rare-$7,000**
Blue	**$350-$650**
Dark blue	**$425-$450**
Green	**$225-$250**
Electric blue	**$475-$495**
Ice blue	**Rare-$2,100**
Lavender	**$375-$475**
Marigold	**$275-$390**
Pastel marigold	**$110-$125**
Renninger Blue, stippled	**Rare-$1,500**

Bowl, ruffled, basketweave, ribbed, or stippled

Amethyst/purple	**$95-$250**
Aqua opalescent, butterscotch	**$1,500-$2,600**
Blue	**$200-$500**
Electric blue	**$450-$1,000**
Green	**$320-$600**
Horehound	**$400-$500**
Ice blue	**Rare-$3,750**
Lavender	**$600-$850**
Lime green	**$825-$975**
Marigold	**$185-$465**
Renninger Blue, stippled	**Rare-$1,200**
Sapphire blue	**Rare-$2,000**

Plate, basketweave or ribbed back, 9" d

Amethyst/purple	**$300-$625**
Blue	**Rare-$4,000**
Electric blue	**Rare-$4,250**
Emerald green	**Rare-$3,000**
Green	**$125-$750**
Horehound	**$500-$950**
Ice blue (ribbed)	**Rare-$3,400**
Marigold	**$375-$900**

Plate, stippled, ribbed back, 9" d

Amethyst/purple	**$900-$1,200**
Blue	**$1,400-$2000**
Marigold	**$600-$1,200**

Grape and Cable

Made by Northwood.

Colors known: amethyst, aqua, aqua opalescent, black amethyst, blue, electric blue, emerald green, green, horehound, ice blue, ice green, lavender, lime green, marigold, pastels, peach opalescent, pearl (custard), purple, sapphire blue, smoke, teal, white.

Forms: extensive pattern, over 30 forms known.

Identifying Characteristics: Grape & Cable represents the largest number of pieces of any carnival glass pattern. Look for delicate grapes, detailed leaves, tendrils, along with a detailed cable running through each form. Both Northwood and Fenton made forms with spatula shaped feet and collar bases. Bowls with piecrust edges are Northwood. Northwood began to produce this ever popular pattern in 1910.

> **Reproduction Alert.** Reproductions include a butter dish made by Mosser in amber, cobalt blue, and ice blue. Fenton is making a variety of shapes and finishes using original Northwood molds for the descendents of the Northwood family. Hatpin holders have also been reproduced.

Banana boat, 4 ftd, 12-1/2" l

Amethyst/purple	**$135-$210**
Blue	**$450-$550**
Green	**$200-$400**
Ice blue	**$350-$600**
Ice green	**$275-$500**
Marigold	**$100-$195**
Pearl	**$200-$350**
Smoky blue	**$300-$350**

White	**$300-$475**

Banana boat, stippled, 4 ftd, 12-1/2"l

Blue	**$400-$600**
Green	**$300-$375**
Marigold	**$150-$275**
Pearl	**$250-$375**
Renninger blue	**$500-$600**

Berry bowl, master, 10" d to 11" d

Amethyst/purple	**$215-$265**
Blue, basketweave ext.	**$225-$275**
Electric blue	**Rare-$1,500**
Green	**$125-$195**
Ice green	**Rare-$1,200**
Marigold	**$65-$100**

Berry bowl, sauce, 5" d to 6" d

Amethyst/purple	**$18-$35**
Green	**$20-$30**
Lavender	**$20-$45**
Marigold	**$20-$30**
Pastel	**$20-$40**
White	**$90-$125**

Bonbon, two handles

Amethyst/purple	**$60-$80**
Blue	**$100-$190**
Green	**$50-$115**
Marigold	**$45-$85**
White	**$135-$175**

Bonbon, two handles, stippled

Amethyst/purple	**$60-$90**
Aqua	**Rare-$1,000**
Aqua opalescent	**$500-$1,000**
Black amethyst	**$100-$165**
Blue	**$120-$250**
Green	**$115-$200**
Marigold	**$65-$125**
Marigold on milk glass	**Rare-$3,000**
Violet	**$375-$450**

Carnival Glass, Grape and Cable, Northwood, hatpin holder, purple, 7", **$175-$300.**

Carnival Glass, Grape and Cable, Northwood, hatpin holder, green, 7", **$245-$400.**

Carnival Glass, Grape and Cable, Northwood, tumbler, lavender, 4", **$15-$40.**

Bowl, 7" d to 7-1/2" d

Amethyst/purple.................**$60-$95**

Aqua opalescent............**Rare-$4,500**

Green, basketweave ext........**$60-$80**

Ice blue................................**$450-$750**

Ice green.............................**$175-$250**

Marigold..................................**$35-$45**

Bowl, IC shape, master, collar base, 10" d to 11" d

Amethyst/purple...............**$250-$425**

Blue....................................**$600-$750**

Green.................................**$100-$200**

Ice blue..........................**Rare-$1,200**

Ice green.........................**Rare-$1,400**

Lavender............................**$275-$325**

Marigold............................**$160-$200**

White..................................**$145-$175**

Bowl, IC shape, individual

Amethyst/purple...............**$115-$135**

Blue....................................**$95-$195**

Ice green............................**$165-$350**

Bowl, piecrust edge, 8" d to 9" d

Amethyst/purple.................**$65-$115**

Aqua opalescent............**Rare-$2,500**

Green.................................**$60-$110**

Emerald green ....**$200-$350**

Ice blue..........................**Rare-$1,200**

Lavender............................**$100-$160**

Marigold..............................**$45-$95**

Bowl, piecrust edge, stippled

Aqua opalescent............**Rare-$2,500**

Electric blue ....**Rare-$1,850**

Ice blue.............................**$600-$750**

Marigold............................**$145-$225**

Bowl, ruffled or round, ftd or collar base, 8" d to 9" d

Amethyst/purple.................**$80-$250**

Aqua opalescent............**Rare-$2,500**

Green..................................**$75-$110**

Ice blue, applied scrolled feet
................................**Rare-$2,100**

Ice green.............................**$200-$450**

Marigold..............................**$45-$70**

Olive green ....**$50-$75**

White..................................**$225-$425**

Bowl, ruffled, stippled, 8" d to 9" d

Aqua..............................**$800-$1,000**

Electric blue..................**$800-$1,400**

Bowl, stippled, 8" d to 9" d

Amethyst/purple...............**$200-$275**

Blue....................................**$200-$310**

Green.................................**$250-$650**

Ice green.........................**Rare-$2,400**

Marigold............................**$145-$265**

Sapphire blue................**$600-$1,200**

Breakfast creamer

Amethyst/purple.................**$95-$165**

Green...................................**$70-$90**

Marigold..............................**$15-$35**

Pastel ....**$80-$100**

Breakfast sugar

Amethyst/purple.................**$95-$165**

Green...................................**$70-$90**

Marigold..............................**$15-$35**

Pastel ....**$80-$100**

Butter dish, cov

Amethyst/purple...............**$175-$250**

Green.................................**$135-$255**

Marigold..............................**$95-$125**

Calling card tray, flat

Amethyst/purple..................**$60-$80**

Blue..................................**$100-$190**

Green ....**$50-$115**

Marigold..............................**$45-$85**

White..................................**$135-$175**

Candle lamp

Amethyst/purple..............**$700-$950**

Green ....**$625-$825**

Marigold............................**$600-$800**

Candlesticks, pr

Amethyst/purple...............**$285-$350**

Green ....**$300-$450**

Marigold............................**$185-$250**

Centerpiece bowl, cupped in

Amethyst/purple...............**$350-$500**

Blue..............................**Rare-$1,250**

Green ....**$300-$550**

Ice blue..........................**Rare-$1,200**

Ice green........................**$750-$1,500**

Marigold............................**$150-$350**

White..................................**$400-$650**

Centerpiece bowl, points straight up

Green ....**$350-$450**

Ice green...........................**$550-$750**

White..................................**$275-$425**

Cologne bottle

Amethyst/purple...............**$155-$355**

Green ....**$200-$300**

Ice blue.............................**$700-$850**

Marigold..............................**$95-$200**

Compote, cov

Amethyst/purple...............**$325-$700**

Marigold.......................**Rare-$1,300**

Compote, open, whimsy, amethyst/purple **400-700**

Cracker jar, cov, two handles

Amethyst/purple...............**$275-$600**

Blue, stippled ....$700-$900
Ice green......................$700-$1,100
Marigold.......................$200-$450
Marigold, stippled ....$300-$500
Smoke.........................$200-$300
White..........................$700-$1,100

Creamer
Amethyst/purple...............$75-$125
Green ....$95-$145
Marigold.........................$50-$75

Cup and saucer
Amethyst/purple.............$170-$250
Green ....$130-$200
Ice blue.........................$500-$575
Ice green.......................$300-$400
Marigold.........................$95-$125
White............................$150-$200

Decanter
Amethyst/purple.............$300-$500
Marigold.......................$200-$475

Dresser tray
Amethyst/purple.............$155-$450
Green ....$400-$650
Ice blue.......................$800-$1,100
Marigold.......................$150-$185
Marigold, stippled ....$200-$300

Fernery
Green ....Rare-$5,000
Ice blue ....$1,700-$2,000
Ice green ....Rare-$16,250
Marigold.......................$485-$900
Purple ....$250-$800
White............................$600-$750

Fruit or orange bowl, ftd
Amethyst/purple.............$200-$375
Blue..............................$600-$800
Green ....$350-$600
Ice green.......................$600-$900
Marigold.......................$100-$190
Olive green ....$200-$250
White............................$400-$750

Fruit bowl, banded, ftd
Blue..............................$250-$450
Blue, stippled ....$450-$650
Marigold.......................$200-$350

Hat, made from tumbler mold
Amethyst...........................$35-$60
Green ....$40-$70
Marigold...........................$35-$60

Hatpin holder
Amethyst/purple.............$175-$300
Amethyst, black ....$185-$325
Aqua opalescent...........Rare-$12,000
Blue..........................$900-$1,200
Emerald green ....Rare-$3,100
Green ....$245-$400
Horehound.....................$450-$550
Ice blue ....Rare-$2,000
Ice green ....Rare-$1,500
Lavender......................Rare-$900
Lime green ....Rare-$2,000

Marigold.........................$160-$325
Pastel ....$45-$75
White ....Rare-$2,000

Hatpin holder, banded
Amethyst/purple.............$250-$450
Blue...........................Rare-$1,200
Marigold.......................$300-$650

Humidor, three-pronged sponge holder in lid
Amethyst/purple.............$325-$450
Blue..............................$500-$600
Blue, stippled ....$700-$1,000
Marigold.......................$200-$375
Marigold, stippled ....$425-$550

Nappy, one handle
Amethyst/purple...............$65-$120
Green ....$65-$120
Ice blue.........................$500-$700
Marigold.........................$40-$65
Pastel ....$45-$75

Perfume bottle (made by Dugan)
Amethyst/purple.............$225-$700
Marigold.......................$250-$400

Pin dish, whimsy, made from punch cup
Amethyst/purple...............$50-$90
Marigold.........................$15-$20

Pin tray
Amethyst/purple.............$185-$300
Blue..............................$200-$400
Green ....$200-$350
Ice blue.........................$600-$875
Marigold.......................$120-$250
Pearl.............................$300-$375

Pin tray, banded
Marigold, stippled............$200-$350
Purple, banded..................$200-$275

Plate, hand grip, 6" d to 8" d
Amethyst/purple...............$80-$150
Green ....$115-$175
Lavender.......................$100-$125
Marigold.........................$75-$100
Smoke...........................$100-$125

Plate, basketweave back, 8-3/4" d to 9" d, amethyst ....$80-$100

Plate, plain back, 7" d to 8" d
Amber ....$75-$125
Amethyst/purple.............$100-$200
Green ....$125-$225
Marigold.......................$165-$900

Plate, plain back, 8-1/2" d to 9" d
Amethyst/purple...............$80-$250
Green ....$95-$265
Marigold.........................$60-$80

Plate, ruffled, stippled, sapphire blue
....Rare-$2,000

Plate, spatula foot, Meander back, 9" d
Amethyst/purple.............$105-$185
Green ....$115-$225
Ice green.......................$400-$600

Marigold.........................$90-$135

Plate, stippled, 9" d
Amethyst/purple.............$375-$575
Blue..........................$700-$1,200
Emerald green ....Rare-$2,500
Green ....$400-$820
Marigold.......................$400-$600
Sapphire blue ....Rare-$2,000

Plate, two sides up, 8" d
Amethyst.......................$115-$125
Green ....$100-$120
Marigold.........................$60-$90

Powder jar, cov
Amethyst/purple.............$125-$200
Blue..............................$650-$850
Green ....$250-$450
Ice green.......................$750-$900
Lavender.......................$300-$500
Marigold.........................$85-$165

Punch bowl and base, master or banquet size
Amethyst/purple.............$750-$900
Blue..........................Rare-$5,500
Marigold.....................Rare-$1,400
White ....Rare-$1,600

Punch bowl and base, midsize
Amethyst/purple.............$750-$950
Blue..........................Rare-$1,600
Emerald green ....Rare-$1,250

Punch bowl and base, small
Amethyst/purple.............$450-$850
Blue..............................$600-$900
Marigold.......................$250-$500

Punch bowl set
Amethyst/purple, midsize, 14 pcs
....Rare-$2,100
Aqua opalescent, small size, 14 pcs
....Rare-$15,000
Blue, master size, 13 pcs Rare-$8,000
Blue, midsize, 8 pcs .... Rare-$2,800
Marigold, master size, 14 pcs
....................................$1,700-$2,300
White, master size, 14 pcs
....................................$3,000-$3,500

Punch cup
Amethyst/purple...............$15-$20
Aqua, stippled ....$150-$250
Aqua opalescent............$700-$1,500
Blue..............................$45-$65
Green ....$25-$35
Ice blue.........................$50-$75
Ice green.......................$40-$60
Lime green ....$45-$65
Marigold.........................$20-$25
White............................$25-$45

Sherbet
Amethyst/purple...............$20-$40
Marigold.........................$15-$30

Shot glass
Amethyst/purple.............$120-$135
Marigold.......................$125-$175

Carnival Glass, Hanging Cherries, Millersburg, green tumbler, **$185-$250;** *water pitcher,* **$1,100-$1,700.**

Spooner

Amethyst/purple	$75-$125
Green	$95-$145
Marigold	$50-$75

Sugar bowl, cov

Amethyst/purple	$75-$125
Green	$125-$175
Marigold	$50-$75

Sweetmeat, cov

Amethyst/purple	$150-$300
Blue	Rare-$3,200
Horehound	$600-$900
Lavender	$200-$290
Marigold	$1,000-$1,750
White	$600-$900

Tumbler, tankard set, 4-1/4" h

Amethyst/purple	$45-$85
Marigold	$50-$95

Tumbler, water set, 4" h

Amethyst/purple	$15-$40
Green	$25-$90
Horehound	$100-$150
Ice green	Rare-$700
Lime green	$125-$225
Marigold	$20-$35
Smoke	$125-$175

Water pitcher, tankard

Amethyst/purple	$550-$900
Green	$400-$475
Ice green	Rare-$4,500
Marigold	$225-$500

Water pitcher, thumbprint base band

Amethyst/purple	$275-$350
Green	$250-$500
Ice green	Rare-$8,000
Marigold	$195-$350
Pumpkin marigold	$600-$700
Smoke	$500-$750

Hanging Cherries

Made by Millersburg.

Colors known: amethyst, blue, green, marigold.

Forms: bowls, chop plates, compotes, table sets, water sets.

Identifying characteristics: Clusters of hanging cherries dominate this popular pattern.

Also known as: Millersburg Cherries.

> **Reproduction Alert.** Fenton made a very similar pattern in 1974. Production was limited to amethyst creamer and sugars.

Bowl, IC shape, 7" d to 9" d

Amethyst	$195-$265
Blue	Rare-$2,450
Green	$250-$400
Green, satin	$75-$200
Marigold	$80-$150
Teal	$250-$350

Bowl, 9" d to 10" d

Amethyst	$150-$300
Aqua	$375-$625
Blue	Rare-$2,750
Green	$300-$350
Marigold	$125-$175

Bowl, 3-in-1 edge, 9" d to 10" d

Blue	Rare-$4,500
Green	$150-$300
Marigold	$125-$175

Butter dish, cov, 6" x 7"

Amethyst	$150-$250
Green	$300-$450
Marigold	$90-$200

Chop plate, 10" d

Amethyst	Rare-$3,500
Green, satin	Rare-$3,700
Marigold	Rare-$2,500

Compote, 7" d, 6-1/4" h

Amethyst	$750-$1,200
Blue	Rare-$4,500
Green	$1,400-$1,650
Marigold	$900-$1,250
Vaseline	Rare-$5,000

Creamer

Amethyst	$75-$190
Aqua	$80-$125
Green	$90-$125
Marigold	$45-$75

Milk pitcher, 6-3/4" h

Amethyst	$600-$1,500
Green	Rare-$1,100
Marigold	$750-$1,500

Plate, 6" d

Marigold	$1,900-$2,600
Marigold, dark, radium	Rare-$3,400

Plate, 7-1/2" d

Amethyst	Rare-3,500
Green	Rare-3,200
Marigold	Rare-2,400

Plate, 8" d

Amethyst	Rare-$2,100
Green	Rare-$4,250

Sauce, round, 5-1/2" d

Amethyst	$95-$125
Blue	Rare-$1,500
Green	$70-$90
Marigold	$60-$80

Spooner

Amethyst	$75-$190
Green	$115-$125
Marigold	$45-$75

Sugar bowl, cov

Amethyst	$75-$190
Green	$115-$125
Marigold	$45-$75

Tumbler

Amethyst	$150-$175
Green	$185-$280
Marigold	$220-$230

Water pitcher

Amethyst	$700-$900
Green	$1,100-$1,700
Marigold	$1,700-$1,800

Hearts and Flowers

Made by Northwood.

Colors known: amethyst, aqua opalescent, blue, blue opalescent, clambroth, electric blue, green, ice blue, ice green, lavender, marigold, pearl (custard), purple, white.

Forms: bowls, compotes, plates.

Identifying characteristics: This

intricate pattern features a circular band of heart shapes. Production began in 1912.

Also known as: Battenburg Lace #1.

Reproduction Alert. Domed 11" ruffled bowls are known in amberina, amethyst, and red and usually have the Fenton logo.

Bowl, PCE, ribbed back, 9" d

Amethyst/purple	**$750-$1,100**
Blue	**$1,200-$2,000**
Electric blue	**Rare-$2,200**
Green	**$1,000-$1,500**
Ice blue	**$750-$1,200**
Ice green	**$1,000-$1,500**
Lime green	**Rare-$2,100**
Marigold	**$475-$1,600**
White	**$350-$475**

Bowl, ruffled, plain back, 9" d

Green	**Rare-$1,300**
Ice blue	**$350-$550**
White	**$200-$215**

Bowl, ruffled, ribbed back, 9" d

Amethyst	**$275-$375**
Aqua	**$900-$1,000**
Aqua opalescent	**$1,200-$1,800**
Blue	**$550-$1,150**
Green	**$1,000-$1,450**
Ice blue	**$250-$525**
Ice green	**$550-$750**
Lavender	**$400-$1,000**
Lime green	**$900-$1,500**
Marigold	**$275-$650**
Pumpkin marigold	**$700-$750**
Purple	**$475-$550**
Renninger blue	**Rare-$3,000**
White	**$200-$400**

Compote, ruffled

Amethyst	**$300-$475**
Aqua opalescent	**$235-$850**
Black amethyst	**$500-$750**
Blue	**$275-$775**
Blue opalescent	**$500-$2,000**
Green	**$1,200-$1,600**
Ice blue	**$300-$800**
Ice green	**$600-$1,200**
Lavender	**$900-$1,200**
Lime green	**Rare-$1,600**
Marigold	**$135-$400**
Pearl	**$4,000-$7,500**
Powder blue opalescent	**Rare-$3,000**
Purple	**$300-$800**
Renninger blue	**$875-$1,800**
White	**$115-$135**

Plate, ribbed back, 9" d

Amethyst	**$800-$1,800**
Green	**$1,000-$3,500**

Ice blue	**$1,100-$1,600**
Ice green, flake on base	**Rare-$950**
Lime green	**$1,900-$3,700**
Marigold	**$650-$1,600**
Marigold, dark	**$850-$1,600**
Purple	**$850-$940**
White	**Rare-$2,500**

Hobnail

Made by Millersburg.

Colors known: amethyst, blue, green, marigold, purple.

Forms: spittoons, rose bowls, table sets, vases, water sets.

Identifying characteristics: As the name implies, this design features pointy hobnails arranged in alternating rows. Most pieces of this interesting pattern have a brilliant radium finish. Production began in 1910 and continued until 1912.

Also known as: Stippled Dots.

Butter dish, cov

Amethyst	**$300-$350**
Blue	**Rare-$1,000**
Green	**$550-$650**
Marigold	**$350-$450**

Creamer

Amethyst	**$275-$375**
Blue	**$400-$600**
Green	**$350-$450**
Marigold	**$200-$275**

Rose bowl

Amethyst	**$185-$350**
Green	**Rare-$1,200**
Marigold	**$125-$225**

Spittoon

Amethyst	**$500-$600**
Green	**Rare-$2,000**
Marigold	**$500-$700**
Purple	**$550-$650**

Sugar bowl, cov

Amethyst	**$375-$475**
Blue	**$600-$750**
Green	**$450-$600**
Marigold	**$275-$400**

Tumbler

Amethyst	**$600-$750**
Blue	**$900-$1,100**
Green	**$1,000-$1,200**
Marigold	**$1,200-$1,700**

Water pitcher

Amethyst	**Rare-$2,500**
Blue	**Rare-$3,000**
Green	**Rare-$4,000**
Marigold	**Rare-$3,000**

Carnival Glass, Hearts and Flowers, Northwood, compote (top view), aqua opal, 6", **$235-$850.**

Carnival Glass, Hobnail, Millersburg, tumbler, marigold, **$1,200-$1,700.**

Inverted Strawberry

Made by Cambridge.

Colors known: amethyst, blue, green, marigold.

Forms: berry sets, candlesticks, celery vases, compotes, milk pitchers, powder jars, spittoons, table sets, water sets.

Identifying characteristics: Cambridge made several exquisite intaglio patterns, including Inverted Strawberry and Inverted Thistle. The strawberries on this pattern are very detailed and are highlighted by strawberry blossoms and leaves. Many, but not all, pieces are marked with the trademark "Near Cut."

Reproduction Alert. Both the tumblers and water pitchers have been reproduced. A miniature punch bowl has been created. The American Carnival Glass Association commissioned a pedestaled creamer in purple slag as their convention souvenir in 1996. Other table set forms and a spittoon were made for other ACGA conventions.

Carnival Glass, Inverted Strawberry, water pitcher and tankard, green, rare, **$1,600.**

Carnival Glass, Leaf and Beads, Northwood, rose bowl, aqua opal, **$200-$300.**

Berry bowl, master
Amethyst .... $75-$95
Marigold .... $55-$75
Berry bowl, small, marigold, 5" d,
.... $25-$35
Bonbon, two handles, whimsy from spooner mold, green ..... **Rare-$1,600**
Bowl, sgd "Near Cut," 10-1/2" d
Amethyst/purple .... $200-$225
Green .... $125-$145
Marigold .... $95-$115
Breakfast creamer and sugar set, pedestal, amethyst .... **Rare-$750**
Butter dish, cov, marigold
.... $500-$850
Candlesticks, pr
Green .... $1,000-$1,200
Marigold .... $350-$450
Celery vase
Blue .... $750-$850
Green .... $700-$900
Purple .... $300-$350
Compote
Amethyst .... $400-$625
Blue .... **Rare-$2,500**
Marigold .... $275-$400
Creamer
Amethyst .... $165-$185
Green .... $400-$450
Marigold .... $300-$400
Milk pitcher, purple ..... **Rare-$5,000**
Powder jar
Green .... $175-$185
Marigold .... $150-$250
Spittoon, sgd "Near Cut," 5-1/2" d, 3" h
Green .... $800-$950
Marigold .... $700-$750
  Spooner, two handles
  Amethyst .... $165-$225
  Marigold .... $65-$90
  Sugar bowl, cov
  Green .... $450-$650
  Marigold .... $375-$425
  Purple .... $450-$650
Tumbler
Amethyst .... $150-$165
Green .... $115-$200
Marigold .... $95-$150
Water pitcher
Green .... **Rare-$1,600**
Purple .... **Rare-$1,900**

Leaf and Beads
Made by Northwood.
Colors known: amethyst, aqu, aqua opalescent, blue, green, ice blue, ice green, lavender, marigold, peach opalescent, purple, Renninger blue, teal, white.
Forms: bowls, candy dishes, nut

bowls, plates, rose bowls.
Identifying characteristics: Rows of vertical beads cascade toward the well defined leaves found at the base or center of this design. Northwood clearly used the same mold to created the rose bowl, then widened it to create the candy dish and nut bowl forms. The interiors of the rose bowls can be plain, rayed, or have a sunflower design.
Also known as: Stippled Leaf & Beads.

Candy dish, purple .... $100-$110
Nut bowl, ftd
Amethyst/purple .... $80-$110
Aqua opalescent .... $800-$1,200
Blue .... $200-$400
Green .... $50-$65
Marigold .... $35-$65
Marigold, dark .... $30-$35
White .... $275-$350
Plate
Green .... $100-$115
Marigold .... $45-$65
Rose bowl
Amethyst .... $95-$150
Aqua .... $200-$275
Aqua opalescent .... $220-$300
Blue .... $85-$200
Electric blue .... $95-$250
Green .... $85-$125
Ice blue .... **Rare-$1,000**
Ice green .... **Rare-$1,500**
Lavender .... $500-$700
Marigold .... $60-$175
Purple .... $80-$95
Renninger blue .... $300-$350
Teal .... $300-$500
White .... $350-$375
Rose bowl, rayed interior
Green .... $65-$100
Purple .... $80-$95
Rose bowl, sunflower interior
Amethyst .... $85-$95
Aqua .... **Rare-$1,200**
Blue .... $500-$700
Green .... $200-$215
Marigold .... $45-$65
Purple .... $85-$95

Many Stars
Made by Millersburg.
Colors known: amethyst, blue, green, marigold.
Forms: bowls, chop plates.
Identifying characteristics: This pattern may remind collectors of starry nights with it's rows of stippled stars and a bright stippled star

Carnival Glass, Many Stars, Millersburg, bowl, 3 in 1, amethyst, 9", **$400-$600.**

Carnival Glass, Orange Tree, Fenton, bowl, collar base, marigold over milk glass, **$500-$600.**

center, which can be either a five-point or six-point star. Production began in 1910.

Bowl, advertising, Bernheimer Bros, ruffled, blue .... **$2,200-$3,000**
Bowl, IC shape, 9" d to 10" d
Amethyst .... **$800-$1,000**
Blue .... **Rare-$3,000**
Green .... **$800-$1,000**
Marigold .... **$1,000-$1,400**
Bowl, ruffled, 9" d to 10" d
Amethyst .... **$400-$600**
Blue .... **Rare-$3,700**
Green .... **$400-$600**
Marigold .... **$275-$375**
Vaseline .... **Rare-$3,000**
Bowl, 3-in-1 edge, marigold
.... **$275-$300**
Bowl, tricorn, amethyst
.... **Rare-$2,500**
Chop plate, marigold .... **Rare-$4,750**

Orange Tree
Made by Fenton

Colors known: amber, amberina, amethyst, aqua, aqua opalescent, blue, chocolate, green, lime green, marigold, marigold on milk glass, peach opalescent, Persian blue, powder blue, red, vaseline, white.

Forms: bowls, breakfast sets, hatpin holders, mugs, plates, punch bowls, shaving mugs, table sets, water sets.

Identifying characteristics: This pattern is one of the most popular Fenton created. The number of items available is extensive as well as the colors available, making it easy to collect and enjoy. The motif is reflected in the name with well designed orange trees, ripe with fruit. Production began in 1911.

Berry bowl, footed, 5-1/2" d
Blue .... **$35-$45**
Green .... **$40-$50**
Marigold .... **$35-$45**
White .... **$80-$100**
Berry bowl, footed, 9" d to 11" d
Blue .... **$100-$125**
Green .... **$150-$175**
Marigold .... **$80-$100**
White .... **$100-$200**
Bowl, collar base, flat, 8" d to 9" d
Amber .... **$170-$190**
Amberina .... **Rare-$1,200**
Amethyst .... **$200-$250**
Blue .... **$85-$95**
Celeste blue .... **Rare-$1,750**
Clambroth .... **$50-$70**
Green .... **$95-$105**
Ice blue .... **Rare-$7,000**
Lavender .... **$225-$275**
Marigold .... **$115-$125**
Marigold over milk glass
.... **$500-$600**
Powder blue .... **$100-$125**
Red .... **Rare-$3,000**
Sapphire blue .... **$300-$350**
Vaseline .... **$225-$275**
White .... **$50-$110**
Berry bowl, footed, 5-1/2" d
Blue .... **$35-$45**
Green .... **$40-$50**
Marigold .... **$35-$45**
White .... **$80-$100**
Bowl, footed, 9" d to 11" d
Blue .... **$100-$125**
Green .... **$150-$175**
Marigold .... **$80-$100**
White .... **$100-$200**
Bowl, IC shape, 8-1/2" d
Blue .... **$65-$75**
Green .... **$155-$350**
Bowl, IC shape, tree trunk center, 7-3/4" d
Blue .... **$75-$90**

Electric blue .... **$200-$250**
White .... **$55-$65**
Bowl, ruffled, 9" d
Blue .... **$85-$95**
Green .... **$95-$105**
Marigold .... **$115-$125**
White .... **$50-$110**
Breakfast set, 2 pc
Blue, repairs .... **$40-$45**
Marigold, damage .... **$70-$75**
Butter dish, cov
Blue .... **$200-$300**
Marigold .... **$225-$325**
White .... **$350-$400**
Centerpiece bowl, ftd, 12" d
Amethyst .... **Rare-$4,000**
Blue .... **Rare-$1,500**
Green .... **Rare-$4,500**
Marigold .... **$800-$900**
Compote, ruffled
Amethyst .... **$55-$75**
Aqua .... **$100-$150**
Blue .... **$60-$80**
Green .... **$70-$90**
Lavender, light .... **$35-$65**
Marigold .... **$40-$50**
Teal .... **$300-$400**
Creamer
Blue .... **$60-$70**
Marigold .... **$40-$45**
White .... **$100-$125**
Creamer, whimsy, made from punch cup, added spout, white ... **$150-$165**
Fruit bowl, scroll feet, 10" d
Amethyst .... **$400-$500**
Blue .... **$185-$200**
Green .... **$800-$1,000**
Marigold .... **$90-$150**
Goblet
Aqua .... **$100-$115**
Blue .... **$40-$80**
Marigold .... **$80-$100**
Vaseline .... **$100-$115**
Hatpin holder
Amethyst .... **$600-$800**
Blue .... **$200-$275**
Chocolate, irid .... **Rare-$2,700**
Green .... **Rare-$2,000**
Marigold .... **$105-$195**
White .... **$600-$700**
Loving Cup
Amethyst .... **$450-$500**
Aqua opalescent .... **Rare-$15,000**
Blue .... **$155-$250**
Green .... **$225-$1,000**
Marigold .... **$150-$275**
White .... **$475-$500**
Mug, 2-1/2" d base, 3-1/2" h
Amber .... **$90-$95**
Amberina .... **$55-$65**
Aqua, dark .... **$130-$225**

Carnival Glass, Paneled Dandelion, Fenton, vase, blue; whimsey, no handle, made from a water pitcher, **$16,000.**

Carnival Glass, Persian Medallion, Fenton, flat plate, marigold, 6", **$55-$150.**

Aqua opalescent	**$80-$85**
Blue	**$65-$185**
Lime green	**$25-$35**
Persian blue	**$45-$60**
Marigold	**$35-$130**
Powder blue	**$130-$150**
Purple	**$150-$165**
Red, amberina base	**$185-$215**
Red	**$95-$125**
Vaseline	**$95-$105**

Plate, 8" d to 9-1/2" d

Amethyst	**Rare-$3,000**
Blue	**$325-$700**
Clambroth	**$100-$135**
Electric blue	**$600-$900**
Green	**Rare-$2,600**
Ice green	**Rare-$7,000**
Marigold	**$350-$425**
Marigold, pastel	**$600-$700**
White	**$175-$250**

Powder jar, cov

Amethyst	**$200-$250**
Blue	**$85-$115**
Green	**$375-$475**
Marigold	**$65-$85**
Vaseline	**$90-$115**
White	**$150-$190**

Punch bowl with base

Blue	**$225-$360**
Green	**$450-$600**
Marigold	**$200-$225**
White	**$400-$500**

Punch cup

Blue	**$30-$35**
Green	**$35-$45**
Marigold	**$15-$35**
White	**$35-$45**

Shaving mug, 3" d base

Amber	**$85-$205**
Amberina	**$200-$225**
Aqua	**$60-$75**
Aqua opalescent	**Rare-$1,100**
Blue	**$90-$150**
Marigold	**$35-$90**
Powder blue	**$90-$135**
Red	**$350-$400**

Spooner

Blue	**$60-$70**
Marigold	**$40-$45**
White	**$100-$125**

Sugar bowl

Blue	**$60-$70**
Marigold	**$45-$60**
White	**$85-$100**

Syrup, made from mug, blue

	Rare-$5,000

Tumbler

Blue	**$50-$65**
Marigold	**$70-$95**
White	**$90-$110**

Water pitcher, ftd

Blue	**$600-$800**
Ice green, spout damage	**Rare-$2,100**
Marigold	**$200-$300**
White	**$300-$400**

Wine

Blue	**$50-$60**
Green	**$95-$200**
Marigold	**$15-$25**
Peach opalescent	**$85-$100**
Vaseline	**$85-$100**

Paneled Dandelion

Made by Fenton.

Colors known: amethyst, blue, green, marigold.

Forms: water sets.

Identifying characteristics: Fenton used a tankard style water pitcher to show off this whimsical pattern that reminds one of all those dandelion puffs that pop up every year and get blown off into the wind. Production began in 1910.

Tumbler

Amethyst	**$50-$55**
Blue	**$30-$50**
Green	**$50-$70**
Marigold	**$30-$50**

Water pitcher

Amethyst	**$300-$400**
Blue	**$500-$650**
Green	**$400-$500**
Marigold	**$200-$300**

Water set, 7 pcs

Amethyst	**$550-$675**
Blue	**$500-$525**
Green	**$650-$750**
Marigold, dark	**$340-$360**

Persian Medallion

Made by Fenton.

Colors known: amber, amethyst, black amethyst, blue, green, lime green, marigold, red, reverse amberina, vaseline, white.

Forms: bonbons, bowls, compotes, hair receivers, plates, rose bowls.

Identifying characteristics: The central motif of this pattern reminds one of elements found in Middle Eastern rugs, along with scrolled borders, and stylized leaves in an outer border. Production began in 1911.

Reproduction Alert. Fenton has issued baskets, bowls, compotes, goblets, plates, and stemmed rose bowls using original molds.

Bonbon, calling card tray
Amber	**$185-$200**
Amethyst	**$95-$225**
Aqua	**$80-$200**
Blue	**$45-$65**
Celeste blue	**Rare-$1,200**
Green	**$215-$235**
Lime green	**$115-$125**
Marigold	**$30-$65**
Red	**$700-$800**
Reverse amberina	**$800-$850**
Vaseline	**$120-$140**

Bowl, IC shape, CE
Amethyst	**$150-$165**
Red	**$600-$675**

Bowl, ruffled, 7" d
Green	**$30-$35**
Marigold	**$65-$75**

Bowl, sauce, IC shape
Blue	**$20-$25**
Red	**$600-$675**
White	**$35-$50**

Bowl, sauce, ruffled
Amethyst	**$35-$50**
Aqua	**$60-$90**
Blue	**$40-$60**
Green	**$40-$60**
Lime green	**$20-$25**
Marigold	**$15-$20**

Bowl, 3-in-1 edge, 8-1/2" d to 10" d
Amethyst	**$55-$140**
Blue	**$160-$175**
Green	**$150-$210**
Lavender	**$275-$315**
Marigold	**$35-$45**
White	**$275-$315**

Chop plate, 10" d, blue | **$225-$750**

Compote, ruffled, large
Amethyst	**$115-$125**
Blue	**$55-$95**
Green	**$250-$300**
Marigold	**$40-$50**
White	**$195-$225**

Compote, ruffled, small
Amethyst	**$125-$195**
Blue	**$65-$185**
Green	**$300-$350**
Marigold	**$85-$125**
White	**$265-$365**

Fruit bowl, ftd, 10" w, 5-1/4" h
Amethyst	**$225-$295**
Blue	**$185-$225**
Green	**$295-$345**
Marigold	**$150-$185**

Hair receiver, sq opening
Amethyst	**$80-$95**
Blue	**$135-$150**
Marigold	**$40-$80**
White	**$110-$130**

Orange bowl, ftd, 11" w, 6-3/4" h
Amethyst	**$350-$425**

Blue	**$290-$335**
Green	**Rare-$2,400**
Marigold	**$260-$315**

Plate, 6" d
Amethyst	**$75-$275**
Black amethyst	**$175-$190**
Blue	**$135-$195**
Clambroth	**$100-$125**
Green	**$115-$200**
Lime green	**$100-$115**
Marigold	**$55-$150**
Purple	**$115-$125**
Vaseline	**$600-$800**

Plate, 7" d
Amethyst	**$275-$350**
Black amethyst	**$190-$250**
Blue	**$195-$265**
Green	**$200-$250**
Marigold	**$150-$190**

Plate, 9-1/2" d to 10" d
Amethyst	**Rare-$3,000**
Blue	**$200-$1,100**
Green	**Rare-$3,000**
Marigold	**$400-$650**
White	**$500-$600**

Punch bowl with base
Amethyst	**$300-$500**
Blue	**$600-$800**
Green	**$400-$600**
Marigold	**$200-$300**

Punch cup
Amethyst	**$20-$40**
Blue	**$30-$50**
Green	**$30-$50**
Marigold	**$20-$40**

Rose bowl, round opening
Amethyst	**$300-$350**
Blue	**$95-$115**
Clambroth	**$65-$95**
Green	**$175-$200**
Marigold	**$55-$75**
Marigold, light	**$20-$40**
White	**$115-$125**

Ripple

Made by Imperial.

Colors known: amber, aqua, blue, clambroth, emerald green, helios, lavender, marigold, olive, powder blue, purple, red, smoke, teal, vaseline, violet, white.

Forms: vases.

Identifying characteristics: This pattern resembles the ripple created when dropping a pebble into a pond. Production was centered in the 1910 until 1912 period.

Also known as: Ripple Threads.

Reproduction Alert. Marigold, pink, and smoke vases known.

Carnival Glass, Ripple, Imperial, funeral vase, marigold, 16", **$105-$120.**

Vase, squatty, 4" to 7"
Amber, 7" h, 2-7/8" base	**$70-$90**
Clambroth, 5" h, 2-1/2" d base	**$40-$60**
Helios, 5" h, 2-1/2" d base	**$185-$200**
Helios, 6-1/2" h, 2-7/8" d base	**$50-$70**
Lavender, 5" h, 2-1/2" d base	**$135-$165**
Marigold, 4-1/2" h, 2-1/2" d base	**$195-$230**
Purple, 6-1/2" h, 2-1/2" d base	**$145-$165**
Purple, 7" h, 3-1/4" d base	**$45-$90**

Vase, standard, 7" h to 12" h
Amber, 7-1/2" h, 2-7/8" d base	**$60-$80**
Amber, 8-1/2" h, 3-3/8" d base	**$80-$120**
Amber, 10-3/4" h, swung	**$100-$120**
Aqua, 10" h, 3-7/8" d base	**$245-$275**
Aqua, 11" h, 2-7/8" d base	**$135-$160**
Clambroth, 10" h, 2-7/8" d base	**$40-$60**
Emerald green	**$200-$250**
Helios, 8-1/2" h, 3-3/8" d base	**$45-$65**
Helios, 10-1/2" h	**$50-$70**
Helios, 11" h, 3-1/4" d base	**$70-$90**
Lavender, 9-1/2" d	**$165-$200**
Lime green, 12" h, 3-3/8" base	**$145-$160**

Carnival Glass, Rose Show, Northwood, plate, pastel marigold, 9", **$1,200-$1,800.**

Marigold, 8-1/2" h, 2-1/2" d base
...................................**$45-$70**
Marigold, 8-1/2" h, 3-3/8" d base
...................................**$55-$95**
Marigold, 9-1/2" h ....**$30-$50**
Olive, 8-1/2" h....................**$145-$185**
Purple, 8" h, 2-1/2" d base ...**$85-$110**
Purple, 8" h, 3-3/8" d base ...**$95-$125**
Pastel, 10-1/2" h.................**$150-$185**
Pastel, 11-1/2" h.................**$165-$190**
Purple, 8-1/2" h, 3-3/8" d base
...................................**$80-$100**
Purple, 10" h, 3-7/8" d base . **$75-$95**
Purple, 12" h ....**$135-$160**
Red.....................................**$600-$750**
Smoke, 11" h, 2-7/8" d base
...................................**$115-$140**
Smoke, 12" h, 3-3/8" d base ...**$75-$95**
Teal, 12" h, 2-7/8" base.........**$70-$90**
Violet, 11-1/2" h..................**$165-$190**
Vase, 12" h to 15" h, mid-size
Amber, 12" h.....................**$220-$225**
Clambroth, 12" h ....**$85-$110**
Helios, 14" h, 3-7/8" base ...**$85-$110**
Lavender, 13" h ....**$300-$350**
Marigold, 12" h, 4-5/8" base. **$90-$120**
Olive green, 13" h, 3-3/8" d base
...................................**$65-$90**
Smoke, 12" h, 3-3/8" d base .**$85-$110**
Teal, 13" h..........................**$400-$450**
Violet, 13" h ....**$300-$350**
Vase, 15" h to 21" h, 3-7/8" d base, funeral
Helios, 16" h......................**$175-$195**
Lime green, 16" h ....**$115-$135**
Marigold, 16" h..................**$105-$120**
Marigold, 17" h..................**$115-$135**
Marigold, 20" h..................**$100-$200**
Purple ....**$350-$385**
Teal ....**4400-$425**

Rose Show
Made by Northwood

Colors known: amber, amethyst, aqua, aqua opalescent, blue, emerald green, green, honey amber, horehound, ice blue, ice green, ice green opalescent, lavender, lime green, lime green opalescent, marigold, purple, Renninger blue, sapphire blue, white.

Forms: bowls, plates.

Identifying characteristics: Northwood designers must have been inspired by beautiful roses when creating this design. The three dimensional flowers and leaves are very life-like as they are clustered in the center of this design. Production began in 1912 and continued until 1914.

Also known as: LaBelle Rose.

Bowl, ruffled, 8-3/4" d to 9" d
Amethyst, chip..............**$900-$1,200**
Aqua ....**$500-$550**
Aqua opalescent............**$850-$2,000**
Blue................................**$550-$1,000**
Emerald green ....**$3,500-$6,000**
Green ....**$900-$1,350**
Honey amber ....**Rare-$4,700**
Horehound..................**$1,000-$2,800**
Ice blue ....**$600-$900**
Ice blue opalescent ....**$800-$1,200**
Ice green ....**$950-$1,500**
Ice green opalescent ...**$3,500-$3,900**
Lavender.......................**500-1,600**
Lime green ....**$800-$2,200**
Lime green opalescent
...................................**$2,000-$3,500**
Marigold........................**$500-$700**
Marigold, dark ....**$400-$1,500**
Renninger blue ....**$800-$1,000**
Sapphire blue ....**$2,400-$3,500**
White ....**$250-$450**
Plate, 9" to 9-1/2" d
Amethyst ....**$700-$1,000**
Blue................................**$600-$1,000**
Custard, dark marigold overlay
...................................**Rare-$16,500**
Electric blue ....**$2,100-$3,000**
Emerald green ....**$3,500-$3,700**
Green ....**$1,500-$3,500**
Ice blue ....**$1,500-$2,100**
Ice green ....**$750-$9,000**
Lavender.......................**$900-$3,100**
Lime green/vaseline ...**$1,900-$2,700**
Marigold........................**$575-$1,600**
Marigold, dark ....**$750-$900**
Marigold, pastel..............**$650-$800**
Purple ....**$1,100-$2,500**
White ....**$325-$565**

Singing Birds
Made by Northwood

Colors known: amber, amethyst, aqua opalescent, blue, emerald green, green, horehound, ice blue, ice green, lavender, marigold, olive green, purple, Renninger blue, sapphire blue, smoke, white.

Forms: berry sets, mugs, table sets, water sets.

Identifying characteristics: This well known pattern features a bird that looks like it's ready to hop off the flowering branch where it's perched. Production was centered in 1911 to 1912.

Reproduction Alert. Tumblers have been reproduced in amethyst, blue, and vaseline.

Berry bowl, master
Green ....**Rare-$2,500**
Marigold...................**Rare-$600**
Purple ....**$150-$250**
Berry bowl, small
Blue ....**$125-$225**
Green ....**$40-$60**
Purple ....**$35-$55**
Butter dish, cov
Green ....**$325-$425**
Marigold....................**$145-$185**
Purple ....**$150-$250**
Creamer
Green ....**$125-$175**
Marigold....................**$100-$150**
Purple ....**$150-$250**
Mug, not stippled, 3-1/2" h
Amber ....**$300-$400**
Amethyst ....**$55-$100**
Aqua opalescent..........**$1,350-$1,600**
Blue ....**$85-$105**
Emerald green ....**$275-$375**
Green ....**$165-$180**
Horehound.................**$300-$550**
Ice blue ....**$550-$580**
Lavender....................**$150-$300**
Marigold.....................**$50-$155**
Purple ....**$55-$100**
Sapphire blue ....**Rare-$1,500**
White ....**$500-$700**
Mug, stippled, 3-1/2" h
Blue ....**$400-$650**
Blue opalescent ....**Rare-$1,450**
Green ....**$375-$475**
Marigold.....................**$80-$160**
Renninger blue ....**$950-$1,500**
Sapphire blue ....**$450-$550**
Spooner
Green ....**$200-$300**
Marigold....................**$125-$225**
Purple ....**$150-$250**

Carnival Glass, Singing Birds, Northwood, mug, aqua opal, **$1,350-$1,600.**

Carnival Glass, Three Fruits, Northwood, bowl, sapphire blue, **$1,200-$1,700.**

Carnival Glass, Three Fruits, Northwood, bowl, pie-crust edge/basketweave, dark marigold, **$60-$95.**

Sugar bowl, covered
Green ....$200-$300
Marigold............................$125-$225
Purple ....$150-$250
Tumbler
Amethyst ....$50-$90
Green ....$35-$135
Lime green ....$150-$175
Marigold.............................$35-$60
Olive green ....$75-$135
Purple ....$90-$135
Water pitcher
Amethyst/purple..............$350-$550
Green ....$450-$1,200
Marigold............................$275-$500

Three Fruits

Made by Northwood.

Colors known: amethyst, aqua, aqua opalescent, black amethyst, blue, clambroth, green, honey amber, horehound, lavender, lime green, marigold, pearlized custard, pumpkin marigold, olive, purple, sapphire blue, smoke, teal, violet, white.

Forms: bowls.

Identifying characteristics: This pattern features a wreath of peaches, cherries, and pears, leaves, and a bunch of plump cherries in the center. Production of this pattern centered between 1915 and 1916.

Bowl, collar base, ribbed back, stippled, white........................$200-$250
Bowl, collar base, ruffled, sapphire blue.............................$750-$950
Bowl, dome ftd, ruffled
Amethyst ....$55-$95
White ....$150-$320
Bowl, spatula ftd, ruffled, 9" d, 3-1/4" h
Amethyst ....$65-$105
Ice green ....$350-$450

Bowl, piecrust edge, basketweave back or plain back, 8" d to 9" d
Amethyst ....$65-$125
Green ....$110-$140
Lime green ....$200-$250
Marigold.............................$60-$95
Purple ....$200-$400
Smoke ....$400-$500
Bowl, piecrust edge, stippled, 8" d to 9" d
Amethyst/purple..............$250-$400
Blue...................................$375-$500
Green ....$400-$600
Horehound ....$250-$350
Ice blue ....**Rare-$8,000**
Lime green, marigold overlay
....................................$800-$1,000
Marigold............................$300-$700
Olive..................................$400-$600
Bowl, ruffled, basketweave, ribbed, or plain back, 8" d to 9" d
Amethyst ....$60-$95
Aqua opalescent...............$500-$800
Green ....$150-$300
Honey amber ....$350-$525
Horehound ....$275-$300
Lavender ....$200-$250
Lime green ....$550-$800
Marigold.............................$80-$225
Pearlized custard ....$350-$450
Pumpkin marigold ....$70-$100
Purple ....$60-$95
Sapphire blue ....$1,200-$1,700
Smoke ....$300-$500
Bowl, ruffled, ribbed back, stippled, 8" d to 9" d
Amethyst ....$200-$300
Aqua ....$1,300-$1,700
Aqua opalescent............$800-$1,600
Blue...................................$300-$500
Green ....$300-$500
Horehound ....$200-$250
Ice blue ....$1,600-$2,600
Lavender ....$200-$250

Lime green ....$400-$575
Marigold...........................$200-4500
Pearlized custard ....$375-$425
Purple ....$100-$200
Sapphire blue ....$1,400-$2,000
White ....$300-$400
Bowl, ruffled, spatula ftd, stippled, 8-1/2" to 9"
Amethyst ....$100-$200
Aqua opalescent............$550-$1,200
Green ....$300-$500
Pumpkin marigold ....$400-$500
Purple ....$110-$210
Plate, basketweave back, 9" d
Amethyst ....$150-$250
Aqua opalescent..........$1,900-$2,500
Black amethyst.................$200-$525
Blue...................................$275-$450
Green ....$105-$210
Horehound ....$350-$500
Lavender ....$200-$300
Marigold.............................$95-$195
Purple ....$150-$250
Plate, plain back, 9" d
Apple green ....**Rare-$650**
Purple ....$165-$300
Plate, stippled, ribbed back, 9" d
Amethyst ....$450-$900
Aqua ....**Rare-$2,000**
Aqua opalescent..........$2,400-$4,500
Black amethyst...............$900-$1,100
Blue.............................$500-$1,300
Clambroth ....$200-$300
Green ....$2,300-$4,000
Honey amber ....$2,000-$2,400
Horehound ....$300-$500
Ice blue ....$4,500-$6,000
Lavender ....$500-$950
Marigold...........................$250-$350
Pumpkin marigold ....$275-$375
Purple ....$375-$500
Sapphire blue ....$1,800-$2,800
Teal ....$1,400-$1,800
Violet ....$400-$1,200

Carnival Glass, Vintage, Fenton, tri-fold, blue, 6", **$100-$150.**

Carnival Glass, Wishbone, Northwood, bowl, pie-crust edge, purple, 9-1/2", **$350-$500.**

Vintage

Made by Fenton.

Colors known: amber, amberina, amethyst, amethyst opalescent, aqua opalescent, blue, celeste blue, green, lime green, marigold, peach opalescent, Persian blue, purple, red, vaseline.

Forms: bonbon, bowls, chop plates, compotes, ferners, pitchers, wine glass,

Identifying characteristics: Detailed grape clusters point towards the center where grape leaves are gathered. Additional grape leaves form a wreath around the grapes. Production began in 1912.

Bonbon

Amethyst	**$30-$50**
Blue	**$20-$40**
Peach opalescent	**$100-$150**

Bowl, 6" d

Amethyst	**$15-$25**
Amethyst opalescent	**$300-$375**
Blue	**$30-$35**
Green	**$20-$25**
Marigold	**$25-$30**

Bowl, 7" d to 8" d

Amethyst	**$30-$50**
Aqua opalescent	**$500-$900**
Blue	**$40-$50**
Green	**$30-$50**
Marigold	**$30-$50**
Persian blue	**$600-$800**
Red	**Rare-$1,000**
Vaseline	**$80-$160**

Bowl, 9" d to 10" d

Amber	**$75-$95**
Amethyst	**$60-$90**
Aqua opalescent	**$1,600-$2,300**
Blue	**$60-$90**

Celeste blue	**$1,700-$3,000**
Green	**$40-$80**
Lime green	**$120-$160**
Marigold	**$30-$50**
Persian blue	**$450-$900**
Red	**$1,500-$3,000**
Vaseline	**$100-$150**

Bowl, 3-in-1 edge, 10" d

Amethyst	**$40-$70**
Blue	**$55-$85**
Green	**$50-$75**
Marigold	**$50-$75**
Red	**Rare-$2,100**

Compote

Amethyst	**$25-$50**
Blue	**$40-$60**
Green	**$30-$50**
Marigold	**$25-$35**
Purple	**$90-$190**

Epergne, 2 pc, large, 6" h

Amethyst	**$200-$300**
Green	**$250-$350**

Epergne, 2 pc, small, 4-3/4" h

Amethyst	**$150-$200**
Blue	**$100-$175**
Green	**$100-$200**
Marigold	**$100-$160**

Ferners

Amber	**$100-$135**
Amberina	**$550-$750**
Amethyst	**$50-$100**
Blue	**$90-$145**
Green	**$60-$80**
Marigold	**$30-$45**
Red	**$300-$500**

Plate, 6" d

Amethyst	**$210-$250**
Green	**$250-$400**
Marigold	**$250-$325**

Plate, 7" d to 8" d

Amethyst	**$125-$225**

Blue	**$100-$200**
Electric blue	**$600-$800**
Green	**$200-$400**
Marigold	**$125-$225**

Plate, 9" d

Amethyst	**$4,000-$4,500**
Blue	**$2,000-$2,750**
Green	**Rare-$4,000**
Marigold	**$550-$750**

Wine glass

Amethyst	**$15-$25**
Marigold	**$10-$15**
Purple	**$20-$30**
Vaseline	**$40-$60**

Wishbone

Made by Northwood.

Colors known: amethyst, aqua opalescent, blue, green, emerald green, ice blue, ice green, marigold, pumpkin marigold, purple, white.

Forms: bowls, chop plates, epergnes, plates.

Identifying characteristics: This pattern is interesting in that wishbone shapes overlap and alternate with exotic looking orchid blossoms. A multi-petaled flower forms the center. Production began about 1911.

Also known as: Melinda.

Bowl, collar base, piecrust edge, 9" d to 10" d

Amethyst/purple	**$350-$500**
Blue	**$1,400-$1,700**
Clambroth	**$400-$450**
Green	**$150-$300**
Lavender	**$400-$500**
Marigold	**$200-$400**
Smoke	**$500-$700**
White	**$300-$400**

Bowl, collar base, ruffled, 9" d to 10" d

Amethyst/purple	**$180-$250**
Emerald green	**$400-$600**
Green	**$200-$300**
Marigold	**$115-$155**
Sapphire blue	**Rare-$3,500**

Bowl, ruffled, ftd, 8" d to 9" d

Amethyst	**$110-$165**
Aqua opalescent	**Rare-$18,000**
Blue	**$465-$665**
Emerald green	**$450-$475**
Green	**$120-$235**
Horehound	**$325-$950**
Ice blue	**$1,000-$1,700**
Ice green	**$800-$1,100**
Lavender	**$110-$200**
Lime green	**1,200-$1,300**
Marigold	**$135-$210**
Pumpkin marigold	**$150-$175**

Purple .... **$120-$165**
White .... **$275-$400**
Bowl, tricorn, ftd
Amethyst .... **$300-$500**
Green .... **$800-$1,000**
Marigold .... **$350-$550**
Chop plate, collar base, 10" d
Amethyst/purple .... **$600-$1,600**
Green .... **$3,000-$3,500**
Marigold .... **$1,200-$2,000**
Pumpkin marigold .... **Rare-$4,000**
Epergne, single lily and base, 2 pc
Amethyst/purple .... **$800-$1,000**
Green .... **$600-$900**
Ice blue .... **$3,750-$4,000**
Ice green .... **Rare-$6,000**
Marigold .... **$350-$550**
White .... **$1,000-$2,500**
Plate, ftd, 8" d to 9" d
Amethyst .... **$250-$400**
Green .... **$450-$675**
Marigold .... **$600-$1,000**
Purple .... **$375-$400**
Tumbler
Amethyst .... **$60-$90**
Green .... **$100-$180**

Marigold .... **$50-$90**
Purple .... **$700-$900**
Water pitcher
Amethyst/purple .... **$600-$800**
Green .... **$650-$1,000**
Marigold .... **$240-$245**

Zig Zag

Made by Millersburg.

Colors known: amethyst, green, marigold.

Forms: bowls,

Identifying characteristics: This interior pattern is striking in that rays resembling lightning bolts start closely in the center and radiate to the edges. The exteriors are plain. Production began in 1911.

Bowl, IC shape
Amethyst .... **$325-$625**
Marigold .... **$225-$425**
Bowl, ruffled or 3-in-1 edge
Amethyst, radium .... **$400-$450**
Amethyst, satin .... **$150-$175**
Green .... **$200-$350**

Marigold .... **$150-$200**
Bowl, square, crimped
Amethyst .... **$800-$1,200**
Green .... **$850-$950**
Marigold .... **$400-$700**
Bowl, tricorn, crimped
Amethyst .... **$700-$1,100**
Green .... **$400-$750**

Carnival Glass, Zig Zag, Millersburg, bowl, amethyst, **$185.**

CONSOLIDATED GLASS COMPANY

History: The Consolidated Lamp and Glass Company was formed as a result of the 1893 merger of the Wallace and McAfee Company, glass and lamp jobbers of Pittsburgh, and the Fostoria Shade & Lamp Company of Fostoria, Ohio. When the Fostoria, Ohio, plant burned down in 1895, Corapolis, Pennsylvania, donated a seven-acre tract of land near the center of town for a new factory. In 1911, the company was the largest lamp, globe, and shade works in the United States, employing more than 400 workers.

In 1925, Reuben Haley, owner of an independent-design firm, convinced John Lewis, president of Consolidated, to enter the giftware field utilizing a series of designs inspired by the 1925 Paris Exposition (l'Exposition Internationale des Arts Décorative et Industriels Modernes) and the work of René Lalique. Initially, the glass was marketed by Howard Selden through his showroom at 225 Fifth Avenue in New York City. The first two lines were Catalonian and Martele.

Additional patterns were added in the late 1920s: Florentine (January 1927), Chintz (January 1927), Ruba Rombic (January 1928), and Line 700 (January 1929). On April 2, 1932, Consolidated closed it doors. Kenneth Harley moved about 40 molds to Phoenix. In March 1936, Consolidated reopened under new management, and the "Harley" molds were returned. During this period, the famous Dancing Nymph line, based on an eight-inch salad plate in the 1926 Martele series, was introduced.

In August 1962, Consolidated was sold to Dietz Brothers. A major fire damaged the plant during a 1963 labor dispute and in 1964, the company permanently closed its doors.

Bonbon, cov, Ruba Rhombic, faceted, smoky topaz, catalog #832, c1931, 8" d **$325**
Bowl, Coronation, Martelé, flared, blue, 5-1/2" d **$75**
Box, cov, Martelé line, Fruit and Leaf pattern, scalloped edge, 7" l, 5" w **$85**
Butter dish, cov, Cosmos, white custard glass, blue, pink, and yellow daisies, 6" h **$250**

Candlesticks, pr, Hummingbird, Martelé line, oval body, jade green, 6-3/4" h **$248**
Cocktail, Dancing Nymph, French Crystal **$90**
Cookie jar, Regent Line, #3758, Florette, rose pink over white opal casing, 6-1/2" h **$370**
Cup and saucer, Dancing Nymph, ruby flashed **$265**
Dinner service, Five Fruits, service

for six, goblet, plate, sherbet, one large serving plate, purple wash, mold imperfections, wear **$375**
Goblet, Dancing Nymph, French Crystal **$90**
Jar, cov, Con-Cora, #3758-9, pine cone dec, irid **$165**
Lamp
Cockatoo, figural, orange and blue, black beak, brown stump, black base, 13" h **$450**

Flower basket, bouquet of roses and poppies, yellows, pinks, green leaves, brown basketweave, black glass base, 8" h **$300**

Mayonnaise comport, Martelé, Iris, green wash **$55**

Miniature lamp, opalescent blue, 10" h... **$380**

Night light, Santa Maria, block base **$450**

Old-fashioned tumbler, Catalonian,

Consolidated sugar shaker, Cone pattern, tall, pink blushed milk glass, 2" d base, 5-1/4" h, **$150.**

yellow, 3-7/8" h **$20**

Perfume bottle, Ruba Rombic, gray frosted body, nick on stopper, 5-1/2" h **$1,420**

Plate
Bird of Paradise, amber wash, 8-1/4" d.................................... **$40**
Catalonian, yellow, 10-1/4" d **$45**
Martelé, Orchid, pink, birds and flowers, 12" d **$115**

Puff box, cov, Lovebirds, blue **$95**

Salt and pepper shakers, pr
Cone, pink................................. **$75**
Cosmos **$115**
Guttate, green **$85**

Sauce dish, Criss-Cross, cranberry opalescent................................... **$55**

Sherbet, ftd, Catalonian, green **$20**

Snack set, Martelé Fruits, pink....**$45**

Sugar bowl, cov, Guttate, cased pink **$120**

Sugar shaker, puff quilted body, pink, brass lid, 3-1/2" d..................... **$150**

Sundae, Martelé, Russet Yellow Fruits **$35**

Syrup, Cone, squatty, pink **$295**

Toothpick holder, Florette, cased pink.. **$75**

Tumbler
Catalonian, ftd, green, 5-1/4" h ...**$30**
Guttate, pink satin **$65**
Katydid, clambroth.................... **$165**

Consolidated vase, Lovebirds, opaque white body, turquoise overlay, **$95.**

Ruba Rhombic, faceted, ftd, silver gray, 6" h **$210**

Umbrella vase, Blackberry **$550**

Vase
Katydid, blue wash, fan-shaped top, 8-1/2" h **$300**
Regent Line, #3758, cased blue stretch over white opal, pinched, 6" h **$175**
Sea foam green, lavender, and tan, floral pattern, 6-1/2" h **$150**

Whiskey glass, Ruba Rhombic, faceted, transparent jungle green, catalog #823, 2-5/8" h........................... **$265**
Duck **$60**

CRANBERRY GLASS

History: Cranberry glass is transparent and named for its color, achieved by adding powdered gold to a molten batch of amber glass and reheating at a low temperature to develop the cranberry or ruby color. The glass color first appeared in the last half of the 17th century, but was not made in American glass factories until the last half of the 19th century.

Cranberry glass was blown, mold blown, or pressed. Examples often are decorated with gold or enamel. Less-expensive cranberry glass, made by substituting copper for gold, can be identified by its bluish-purple tint.

Reproduction Alert. Reproductions abound. These pieces are heavier, off-color, and lack the quality of older examples.

Basket, ruffled edge, petticoat shape, crystal loop handle, c1890, 7" h x 5" w **$250**

Bride's basket, German silver-filigree frame, plain cranberry bowl, 5" h, 3-1/2" d bowl **$115**

Centerpiece, central trumpet-form vase, shallow dish, pedestal foot, gilt Greek-key dec, Victorian, 19-1/2" h **$300**

Cologne bottle, faceted, finely cut faceted stopper, 7" h **$175**

Condiment dish, underplate, scrolling vines and grapes dec, Continental, 6-1/2" h **$175**

Creamer, Optic pattern, fluted to applied clear handle, 5" h, 2-3/4" d **$95**

Cruet, Optic ribbed body, trifold rim, applied clear handled, 9" h **$100**

Decanter, craquelle, bulbous stick form, pinch-sided, crystal collar, oval stopper, 10-1/2" h **$150**

Dresser box, blown out melon ribs, enameled scrolling on bronze feet, French, late 19th C, 5" d........... **$175**

Epergne, five pcs, large ruffled bowl, tall center lily, three jack-in-the-pulpit vases, 19" h, 11" d **$1,200**

Finger bowl, Inverted Thumbprint pattern, deep color **$200**

Garniture, cranberry overlay cut to clear, faceted cut dec, Continental, 14" d bowl, pr 11" h candlesticks.... **$450**

Goblet, acanthus scrolling, clear banded cut stem with polychrome scrolling, foot dec with band of peacock eyes, mkd "Royal Baron," Meyrs Neff crown, Lobmeyer, 6" h **$550**

Lamp, fluid, deep cranberry font connected to sq black base, later electric socket base soldered over early brass collar, brass connector, 1860-75, 8" h **$880**

Nappy, heart shape, tooled crystal feet and handle, English, 5-1/2" d ... **$100**

Pipe, hand blown, tapering-bent neck, bulbous bowl, three bulbs at base, white-enamel dec at outer rim of bowl, 18" l **$250**

Pitcher

Bulbous, ice bladder int., applied clear handle, 10" h, 5" d **$250**

Ripple and Thumbprint pattern, bulbous, round mouth, applied clear handle, 6-1/2" h, 4-1/8" d **$175**

Salt, master, ftd, enameled floral dec **$200**

Sherbet

Ftd, polychrome and acanthus scrolling, various colored dotted peacock eyes, Lobmeyer, 4-1/4" h **$400**

Translucent cranberry, dec with purple, red, yellow, green, and white scrolling flowers on horizontal gilt bands, beaded highlights, Moser, 4-1/2" h **$500**

Sugar shaker, molded fern pattern, 4-1/2" h................................... **$150**

Tankard water pitcher, acanthus scrollwork in shades of purple, red, green, and blue, gilt peacock eyes with various color dots, applied clear handle, Lobmeyer, 11" h **$1,100**

Tumble-up, Inverted Thumbprint pattern **$195**

Tumbler, Inverted Thumbprint pattern **$65**

Vase

Bulbous, white-enameled lilies of the valley dec, cylindrical neck, 8-7/8" h **$150**

Bulbous stick, flaring rim, cranberry, banded gold and silver collar, polychrome scrolling, dots, and florals, Moser, 9" h **$300**

Ribbed body, heavy application of colorless leaves, collar, and scrolled feet, berry pontil, attributed to Harrach, c1890, 5-3/4" h **$100**

Watch stand, figural gilt bronze base with stork, hook for suspending pocket watch, cranberry glass posy vase set in reticulated scroll holder, Austrian or French, c1870, 7" h **$700**

Cranberry finger bowl, delicate painted floral decoration, gilt decoration, **$65.**

Cranberry pitcher, enameled yellow flowers with white centers, white dot enamel trim, worn gold striped design, applied colorless smooth handle, **$250.**

Cranberry crackle pitcher, Moser, pinch sided, medallions of floral sprays, applied, reeded gold highlighted handle, signed, 9" h, **$1,100.**
Photo courtesy of The Early Auction Company, LLC.

CRUETS

History: Cruets are small glass bottles used on the table holding condiments such as oil, vinegar, and wine. The pinnacle of cruet use occurred during the Victorian era, when a myriad of glass manufacturers made cruets in a wide assortment of patterns, colors, and sizes. All cruets had stoppers; most had handles.

Aventurine, applied clear reeded handle, cut faceted stopper, 6-1/2" h **$375**

Bluerina, deep royal blue neck fades to clear at shoulder, optic inverted thumbprint design in body, applied clear glass handle, teardrop-shaped airtrap stopper, in-the-making thin elongated bubble in neck, 7-1/4" h **$500**

Bohemian, amber cut to clear, floral arrangement intaglio carved on ruby flashed ground of three oval panels with carved frames of floral swags,

five cut-to-clear panels at neck, three embellished with gold scrolls, all edged in brilliant gold, 16 decorative panels edged in gold, base and stopper both sgd "4".......................... **$750**

Burmese, Mt. Washington, shiny finish, butter-yellow ribbed body, applied handle, and mushroom stopper, 7" h **$1,250**

Chocolate, opaque, Greentown

Cactus, no stopper..................... **$125**

Leaf Bracket, orig stopper......... **$295**

Cranberry, optic ribbed body, trifold rim, applied clear handle, 9" h . **$100**

Cruet, white spatter over amber ground, applied amber handle, matching amber ball stopper, **$65.**

Custard glass, Wild Bouquet pattern, fired-on dec **$500**

Moser, eight raised cabochon-like ruby gems, deep cut edges of burnished gold, mounted on colorless body, eight alternating panels of brilliant gold squiggles and stylized leaves, handle cut in three sharp edges, six gold dec panels on stopper, each set with ruby cabochon, inside of mouth and base of stopper sgd "4," some loss to gold squiggles, 6" h **$585**

Pattern glass, orig stopper

Amazon, bar-in-hand stopper, 8-1/2" h **$185**

Beveled Star, green **$225**

Croesus, large, green, gold trim . **$395**

Daisy and Button with Crossbars **$75**

Delaware, cranberry, gold trim .. **$295**

Esther, green, gold trim **$465**

Fluted Scrolls, blue dec **$265**

Millard, amber stain................. **$350**

Riverside's Ransom, Vaseline.... **$225**

Tiny Optic, green, dec.............. **$150**

Peachblow, New England, shiny finish, Wild Rose, pink-white handle, orig white stopper **$1,500**

Rubena Verde, Hobbs, Brockunier & Co., Polka Dot No. 308, flashed ruby red trefoil spout and upper half, intense Vaseline base, handle, and stopper, slight flake at tip of stopper, 7" h.. **$585**

Sapphire blue

Hobnail, faceted stopper, applied blue handle, damage to three hobs, 7-1/4" h **$385**

Enameled pink, yellow, and blue flowers, green leaves, applied clear handle and foot, cut clear stopper, 7-1/2" h, 3-1/4" d.................. **$165**

Satin, blue Raindrop MOP, clear frosted reeded handle, clear cut faceted stopper, flake, 7-1/2" h **$385**

CUSTARD GLASS

History: Custard glass was developed in England in the early 1880s. Harry Northwood made the first American custard glass at his Indiana, Pennsylvania, factory in 1898.

From 1898 until 1915, many manufacturers produced custard-glass patterns, e.g., Dugan Glass, Fenton, A. H. Heisey Glass Co., Jefferson Glass, Northwood, Tarentum Glass, and U.S. Glass. Cambridge and McKee continued the production of custard glass into the Depression.

The ivory or creamy yellow-custard color is achieved by adding uranium salts to the molten hot glass. The chemical content makes the glass glow when held under a black light. The more uranium, the more luminous the color. Northwood's custard glass has the smallest amount of uranium, creating an ivory color; Heisey used more, creating a deep yellow color.

Custard glass was made in patterned tableware pieces. It also was made as souvenir items and novelty pieces. Souvenir pieces include a place name or hand-painted decorations, e.g., flowers. Patterns of custard glass often were highlighted in gold, enameled colors, and stains.

Reproduction Alert. L. G. Wright Glass Co. has reproduced pieces in the Argonaut Shell and Grape and Cable patterns. It also introduced new patterns, such as Floral and Grape and Vintage Band. Mosser reproduced toothpicks in Argonaut Shell, Chrysanthemum Sprig, and Inverted Fan & Feather.

Banana stand, Grape and Cable, Northwood, nutmeg stain........ **$315**

Berry bowl, individual size, Chrysanthemum Sprig, blue, slight loss to gold, sgd "Northwood," 5" l x 3-3/4" w, 2-5/8" h...................................... **$165**

Berry bowl, master

Beaded Circle, scalloped top, Northwood, 8-5/8" d, 5" h **$485**

Bonbon, Fruits and Flowers, Northwood, nutmeg stain **$225**

Chrysanthemum Sprig, blue, slight loss to gold, sgd "Northwood," 10-1/2" l x 8" w, 4-7/8" h........ **$385**

Bowl, Grape and Cable, Northwood, basketweave ext., nutmeg stain, 7-1/2" d................................$70

Butter dish, cov

Everglades **$375**

Grape & Cable, Northwood, nutmeg stain.. **$450**

Tiny Thumbprint, Tarentum, rose dec **$300**

Victoria................................... **$300**

Compote, Geneva........................$65

Creamer, Heart with Thumbprint . **$85**

Cruet, Argonaut Shell, orig stopper, minimal loss to gold dec, 6-1/2" h **$985**

Goblet, Grape and Gothic Arches, nutmeg stain.. **$80**

Hair receiver, Winged Scroll **$125**

Jelly compote, Argonaut Shell, gold edge, raised green leaves, gold seashells, 5" h **$235**

Nappy, Northwood Grape.............**$60**

Pitcher, Argonaut Shell **$325**

Plate, Grape and Cable, Northwood **$45**

Punch cup

Diamond with Peg.....................**$40**

Louis XV...................................**$35**

Salt and pepper shakers, pr, Chrysanthemum Sprig **$165**

Spooner

Beaded Circle, Northwood, wear to gold, 4-1/4" h **$195**

Wild Bouquet, Northwood, good floral dec, wear to gold, 4-1/2" h....... **$285**

Sugar, cov

Diamond with Peg..................... **$175**

Georgia Gem, pink floral dec ... **$185**

Tiny Thumbprint, rose dec....... **$185**

Table set, Inverted Fan and Feather, cov butter, creamer, spooner, cov sugar, Northwood, gold dec **$500**

Custard table set, left: sugar, covered; creamer; butter dish, covered; salt shaker; spooner, Chrysanthemum Sprig, blue custard, gold trim, **$800.**
Photo courtesy of Joy Luke.

Tankard pitcher, Diamond with Peg
.... **$275**

Toothpick holder

Chrysanthemum Sprig, blue, gold leaves and blossoms, sgd "Northwood," tiny inside edge base flake, 2-3/4" h **$545**

Chrysanthemum Sprig, custard, gold dec, script sgd "Northwood," 2-3/4" h **$100**

Louis XV **$200**

Tumbler

Beaded Circle, each circle with one blue blossom, and six pink blos-soms and two green leaves, Northwood, worn gold rim trim, 4" h
.... **$165**

Chrysanthemum Sprig, blue, slight loss to gold dec, 3-3/4" h **$185**

Wild Bouquet, Northwood, 3-3/4" h
.... **$285**

CUT GLASS, AMERICAN

History: Glass is cut by grinding decorations into the glass by means of abrasive-carrying metal or stone wheels. A very ancient craft, it was revived in 1600 by Bohemians and spread through Europe to Great Britain and America.

American cut glass came of age at the Centennial Exposition in 1876 and the World Columbian Exposition in 1893. The American public recognized American cut glass to be exceptional in quality and workmanship. America's most significant output of this high-quality glass occurred from 1880 to 1917, a period now known as the Brilliant Period.

Marks: Around 1890, some companies began adding an acid-etched "signature" to their glass. This signature may be the actual company name, its logo, or a chosen symbol. Today, signed pieces command a premium over unsigned pieces since the signature clearly establishes the origin. However, signatures should be carefully verified for authenticity since objects with forged signatures have been in existence for some time. One way to check is to run a fingertip or fingernail lightly over the signature area. As a general rule, a genuine signature cannot be felt; a forged signature has a raised surface.

Many companies never used the acid-etched signature on their glass and may or may not have affixed paper labels to the items originally. Dorflinger Glass and the Meriden Glass Co. made cut glass of the highest quality, yet never used an acid-etched signature. Furthermore, cut glass made before the 1890s was not signed. Many of these wood-polished items, cut on blown blanks, were of excellent quality and often won awards at exhibitions.

Banana bowl, Harvard pattern, hobstar bottom, 11" l, 6-1/2" d **$220**

Basket

Five large hobstars, fancy emb floral silver handle and rim, 9-1/2" h, 11-1/2" d **$225**

Four large hobstars, two fans applied, crystal rope-twisted handle, 7-1/2" h, 8-1/2" d **$350**

Bonbon, Broadway pattern, Huntly, minor flakes, 8" d, 2" h **$135**

Bowl, cov, steeple form finial, flared scalloped rim, ftd, flute, oval, punty and vesica cuts, eastern United States, several edge nicks, repairs, c1840, 17-1/2" h **$215**

Bowl, open

Brilliant cut, cross bars and flowers, scalloped rim, sgd "Libbey" in circle, some grinding to edge, 8" d, 2" h **$175**

Deep-cut buttons, stars, and fans, 10" d **$220**

Hartford, stars with button border, scalloped edge, minor edge flakes, 9" d, 4" h **$125**

Rayed base, diamond point border, sgd "Libbey" in circle, 8" d, 1-1/2" h . **$150**

Rolled-down edge, cut and engraved flowers, leaves, and center thistle, notched-serrated edge, 12" d, 4-1/2" h **$275**

Three brilliant cut thistles surround bowl, flower in center, scalloped edge, etched "Libbey" label, price for pr, 8" d, 4" h **$400**

Box, cov, cut-paneled base, cover cut with large eight-pointed star with hobstar center surrounded by fans, C. F. Monroe, 5" d, 2-3/4" h **$275**

Bread tray, Anita, Libbey in circle mark, 8" x 12" **$535**

Butter dish, cov, Hobstar **$250**

Candlesticks, pr

Adelaide pattern, amber, Pairpoint, 12" h **$250**

Faceted cut knobs, large teardrop stems, ray base, 10" h **$425**

Celery dish, sgd "J. Hoare" **$350**

Centerpiece, wheel cut and etched, molded, fruiting foliage, chips, 10-3/4" d **$490**

Champagne, Kalana Lily pattern, Dorflinger **$75**

Champagne bucket, sgd "Hoare," 7" h, 7" d **$400**

Champagne pitcher, Prism pattern, triple notch handle, monogram sterling silver top, 11" h **$425**

Cheese dish, cov, plate, cobalt blue cut to clear, bull's eye and panel, large miter splints on bottom of plate, 6" h dome, 9" d
.... **$250**

Cider pitcher, hobstars, zippers, fine diamonds, honeycomb-cut handle, 7" h **$225**

Cologne bottle

Hob and Lace pattern, green cased to clear, pattern-cut stopper, Dorflinger, 6" h **$625**

Holland pattern, faceted-cut stopper, 7-1/2" h **$275**

Compote

Deep bowl with trefoil, curved edge, three hobstars, and panels with diamond point, fan, and zipper patterns, short pedestal, round base,

Cut glass, decanters, iris design, sterling silver stoppers, Hawkes, price for pair, **$600.**
Photo courtesy of David Rago Auctions, Inc.

etched maple leaf mark of T. B. Clark & Co., Honesdale, PA, minor grinding to sawtooth edge, 6-3/4" d, 5-1/2" h **$395**

Hobstars on scalloped edge bowl, straight paneled stem with zipper cut edges, minor flakes, 9-1/8" d, 6-1/4" h **$400**

Russian cut, scalloped rim and foot, zipper cut faceted stem teardrop center, minor pinpoints and grinding, 8-1/4" d, 8-3/4" h **$500**

Strawberry and chain pattern, serrated edge, low pedestal base, minor roughness and grinding, 7" d, 4-1/4" h **$95**

Creamer and sugar, pr
Hobstar designs, handles with oval cutting, minor roughness on spout, 3-1/4" h, 3-3/4" h **$250**

Pedestal, geometric cuttings, zippered handles, teardrop full length of handle, sgd "Hawkes," 4-1/2" h **$750**

Pedestal, Carolyn variation, notched handles, 5-1/2" h **$895**

Cruet, round, stars on body, paneled neck with zipper cut edges, scallop cut handle, rayed base, faceted stopper, handle sgd "Tuthill," 6-7/8" h **$250**

Decanter, orig stopper
Pineapple and zipper cut designs, paneled neck with zipper cut designs, diamond pattern on base, faint label of "J. Hoare & Co. Corning 1853," 7-7/8" h **$350**

Quart, triple ring, strawberry diamonds and fans separated by rayed vesicas, flute-cut shoulder and base, polished pontil mark, non-matching cut hollow stopper, Pittsburgh, very minor rim flake, second quarter 19th C, 10-1/2" h **$220**

Russian pattern, pr, 11" h **$600**

Stars, arches, fans, cut neck, star cut mushroom stopper, 11-1/2" h **$125**

Dish
Hobstar, pineapple, palm leaf, 5" d **$45**

Scalloped edge, allover hobstar medallions and hobs, 8" d **$175**

Dresser box, cov, Harvard pattern variation, three-ftd, silver-plated fittings, orig beveled mirror on swivel hinge under lid, cut by Bergen Glass Co., couple of minute flakes, 7" h, 7" w **$750**

Fern dish, round, silver-plate rim, C. F. Monroe, minor roughness to cut pattern, normal wear on base, no liner, 3-3/4" h, 8" w **$200**

Flower center
Etched and wheel cut motif, honeycomb flared neck, some wear, 7-3/4" h, 12" d **$500**

Hobstars, flashed fans, hobstar chain and base, 5" h, 6" d **$325**

Goblet
Buzzstar, pineapple, marked "B & B," 7" h **$40**

Intaglio vintage cut, sgd "Sinclaire," 8-1/2" h **$80**

Humidor, cov
Hobstars, beaded split vesicas, hobstar base, matching cut glass lid with hollow for sponge, 9" h.. **$575**

Middlesex, hollow stopper, sponge holder in lid, Dorflinger, 7-1/2" d **$490**

Ice bucket
Colorless, body cut with vertical flutes, beaded silver-mounted rim with sterling silver swing handle marked for Wilcox Silver Plate Co., early 20th C, 6-5/8" h **$320**

Hobstars and notched prisms, 8" d underplate, double handles, 7" h **$940**

Ice cream tray, Empress pattern variation, sgd "Libbey," 10" x 17-1/2" **$1,000**

Jar, cov, diamond cut finial on stepped lid, ftd ovoid vessel, four Oriental influenced cut medallions, cane and star-cut ground, several nicks, 20th C, 10" h **$260**

Knife rest, 4" l **$95**

Lamp
Cut glass rounded shade with pointed top, inverted trumpet form base, both with etched rose dec, wide borders of geometric design, ring of cut glass prisms, 24" h **$525**

Hobstars, cross-cut diamonds, flashed star cuttings, triangular shaped hanging prisms, 23" h **$1,300**

Loving cup, three handles, sterling top **$350**

Nappy, two handles
Deep-cut arches, pointed sunbursts

and medallions, 9" d **$135**

Hobstar center, intaglio floral, strawberry diamond button border, 6" d
....**$45**

Orange bowl, hobstars and strawberry diamond, 9-3/4" x 6-3/4" x 3-3/4" h
.... **$200**

Perfume bottle

Bulbous, allover cutting, orig stopper, 6-1/2" h **$220**

Cranberry overlay, shaped sides, notched cuts, S. Mordan & Co., silver-mounted cap, 3-1/2" l
.... **$325**

Perfume flask, pistol-form, etched silver-gilt mounts, short chain, spring-action trigger opens lid set with maker's medallion, French, late 19th/ early 20th C, 4-3/4" l **$1,380**

Pickle tray, checkerboard, hobstar, 7" x 3" **$45**

Pitcher

Baluster form body, upper section vertically ribbed and cut, lower section with stylized flowerheads, facet cut handle, silver-plated rim mount with beaded edging, monogrammed, marked "Wilcox Silver Plate Co.," 8-7/8" h **$750**

Baluster, vertical flutes with bead and lozenge cuts, crosshatched and diamond-cut diamonds at base, mounted with sterling bead-edged spout, monogrammed, 14-1/8" h
.... **$250**

Tapered body with quatrefoil flowers, tiny diamond point surface, surrounded by fans and hobstars, paneled neck with zipper cuts, spout with diamonds, cut ridges on applied handle, spout has been reworked on underside, 12-1/2" h
.... **$475**

Plate

Alternating hobstar and pinwheel, 12" d **$100**

Carolyn pattern, J. Hoare, 10" d
.... **$525**

Potpourri jar, baluster shaped cut glass base, silver lid with portrait medallion and floral banding, 6" h
.... **$200**

Punch bowl

Rajah pattern, sgd "Pitkin and Brooks," 13-3/4" d, 15-1/4" h
.... **$2,750**

Round, set into base, cut rim, miter star cut pattern, acid-etched maker's mark for T. G. Hawkes & Co., Corning, NY, on base, 14-3/8" d, 13-1/4" h **$1,880**

Two pcs, Elgin pattern, Quaker City, 11" h, 10" w.............................. **$600**

Punch ladle, silver plated emb shell bowl, cut and notched prism handle, 11-1/2" l **$165**

Relish

Leaf shape, Clear Button Russian pattern, 13" l **$375**

Two handles, divided, Jupiter pattern, Meriden, 8" l **$120**

Salad bowl, Russian pattern........**$90**

Salt, open, Russian pattern, master size
....**$45**

Salt shaker, prism columns........**$30**

Serving dish, two layers, apple and pear branches, grape vine dec, Gravic, 11" d.................................... **$395**

Tankard pitcher

Harvard cut sides, pinwheel top, mini hobnails, thumbprint notched handle, 10-1/4" h **$200**

Hobstar, strawberry diamond, notched prism and fan, flared base with bull's eye, double thumbprint handle, 11" h **$275**

Tobacco humidor, Flute pattern, ornate Whiting sterling lid with sponge holder, 7" h **$650**

Tray

Hobstars, caning, and notched prisms inside vesicas arranged around center star, sgd "Libbey" twice, 12" d
.... **$2,000**

Round, Monarch, sgd "Hoare," 12" d
.... **$975**

Sillsbee pattern, Pairpoint, 14" x 7-1/2"................................ **$335**

Tumbler

Band of strawberry diamonds and fans, plain base edge, polished pontil, Pittsburgh-type, first half 19th C, 3-1/4" h, 3-1/8" d **$150**

Harvard, rayed base **$45**

Hobstars **$40**

Urn, cov, Russian pattern **$175**

Vase

Corset shape, well-cut hobstar, strawberry diamond, prism, flashed star and fan, 16" h **$300**

Fan, amber, engraved grape leaves and vines, round disk base, acid-etched Hawkes mark, small chip on base, 11" h **$300**

Floral and diamond point engraving, sgd "Hawkes," 12-1/2" h, 6-1/2" d
.... **$250**

Lobed rim, alternating vertical cut patterns, star-cut disk base, 20th C, 19-1/2" h **$750**

Monarch pattern, sgd "J. Hoare," 24-1/2" h **$3,750**

Ruffled edge, cut iris dec, Gravic, 14" h **$295**

Squatty body, short flaring neck, scalloped rim, 8" h, 11" d **$550**

Two pcs, trumpet shape, hobstars and paneled ring design, base and top joined with metal post covered with diamond faceted ball, 23-1/4" h **$1,350**

Cut glass, water goblets, iris design, square base, Hawkes, price for set of 12, **$550.**
Photo courtesy of David Rago Auctions, Inc.

DEPRESSION GLASS

History: Depression glass was made from 1920 to 1940. It was an inexpensive machine-made glass and produced by several companies in various patterns and colors. The number of forms made in different patterns also varied.

Depression glass was sold through variety stores, given away as premiums, or packaged with certain products. Movie houses gave it away from 1935 until well into the 1940s.

Like pattern glass, knowing the proper name of a pattern is the key to collecting. Collectors should be prepared to do research.

Reproduction Alert. The number of Depression glass patterns that have been reproduced continues to grow. Reproductions exist in many patterns, forms, and colors. Beware of colors and forms that were not made in the original production of the pattern. Carefully examine every piece that seems questionable and look for loss of details, poor impressions, and slight differences in sizes.

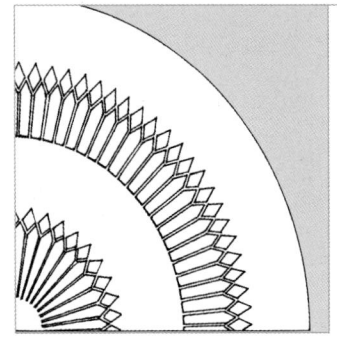

Anniversary

Manufactured by Jeannette Glass Company, Jeannette, Pa., from 1947 to 1949, and late 1960s to mid-1970s.

Made in crystal, iridescent, and pink.

Anniversary, iridescent dinner plate, **$8.**

Item	Crystal	Irid.	Pink
Berry bowl, 4-7/8" d	$3.50	$4.50	$11
Butter dish, cov	25	-	50
Cake plate, 12-3/8" w, square	7	-	16.50
Cake plate, 12-1/2" d, round	8	-	18.50
Cake plate, metal cover	15	-	-
Candlesticks, pr, 4-7/8" h	20	25	-
Candy jar, cov	24	-	45
Compote, open, 3 legs	5	5	16
Compote, ruffled, 3 legs	6.50	-	-
Creamer, ftd	6	6.50	14
Cup	5	4	9
Fruit bowl, 9" d	10	14	24
Pickle dish 9" d	5.50	7.50	12
Plate, 9" d, dinner	5	8	17
Relish dish, 8" d	5.60	7.50	14
Saucer	1	1.50	6
Sherbet, ftd	7	-	10
Soup bowl, 7-3/8" d	8	7.50	18
Sugar, cov	12	10	20
Sugar, open, gold trim	4.50	-	-
Vase, 6-1/2" h	16	-	30
Wine, 2-1/2 oz	10	-	20

Avocado

Avocado, green, preserve bowl, handle, **$32.**

Manufactured by Indiana Glass Company, Dunkirk, Ind., from 1923 to 1933.

Made in crystal, green, pink, and white.

Reproduction Alert. † Creamer, 8" pickle, 64 oz. pitcher, plates, sherbet, sugar, and tumblers. Reproductions can be found in amethyst, blue, dark green, frosted green, frosted pink, pink, red, and yellow, representing several colors not made originally.

Item	Crystal	Green	Pink	White
Bowl, 5-1/4" d, two handles	$12	$38	$27.50	$-
Bowl, 8" d, two handles, oval	17.50	30	25	-
Bowl, 8-1/2" d	20	60	50	-
Bowl, 9-1/2" d, 3-1/4" deep	35	175	150	-
Cake plate, 10-1/4" d, two handles	17.50	60	40	-
Creamer, ftd †	17.50	40	35	-
Cup, ftd	-	36	30	-
Pickle bowl, 8" d, two handles, oval†	17.50	30	25	-

Item	Crystal	Green	Pink	White
Pitcher, 64 oz †	$385	$1,100	$900	$425
Plate, 6-3/8" d, sherbet †	6	22	15	-
Plate, 8-1/4" d, luncheon †	7.50	25	20	-
Preserve bowl, 7" l, handle	10	32	28	-
Relish, 6" d, ftd	10	35	28	-
Salad bowl, 7-1/2" d	9	55	37.50	-
Saucer	6	24	15	-
Sherbet, ftd †	-	75	55	-
Sugar, ftd †	17.50	40	35	-

Beaded Block

Manufactured by Imperial Glass Company, Bellaire, Ohio, from 1927 to the 1930s.

Made in amber, crystal, green, ice blue, iridescent, milk white (1950s), opalescent, pink, red, and Vaseline. Some pieces are still being made in pink and are embossed with the "IG" trademark. The only form known in red is the 4-1/2" lily bowl, valued at $300. The secondary market for milk white is still being established.

Item	Amber	Crystal	Green	Ice Blue
Bowl, 4-1/2" d, lily	$20	$15	$22	$24
Bowl, 4-1/2" d, two handles	18	10	22	28
Bowl, 5-1/2" sq	18	8	20	12
Bowl, 5-1/2" d, 1 handle	18	8	20	12
Bowl, 6" deep	24	12	24	15
Bowl, 6-1/4" d	24	8.50	20	12
Bowl, 6-1/2" d, two handles	24	8.50	20	12
Bowl, 6-3/4" d	28	12	28	14
Bowl, 7-1/4" d, flared	30	12	28	14
Bowl, 7-1/2" d, fluted	30	22	30	24
Bowl, 7-1/2" plain	30	20	30	22
Candy dish, cov, pear shaped	-	-	395	-
Celery, 8-1/4" d	35	18	35	18
Creamer, ftd	25	25	25	24
Jelly, 4-1/2" h, stemmed	20	10	20	12
Jelly, 4-1/2" h, stemmed, flared lid	24	20	24	30
Pitcher, 1 pt, 5-1/4" h	95	115	125	115
Plate, 7-3/4" sq	20	7.50	20	10
Plate, 8-3/4"	30	24	30	30
Sugar, ftd	25	24	30	30
Syrup	-	-	-	-
Vase, 6" h, ftd	25	20	35	35

Additional Colors:

Item	Irid.	Opal	Pink	Vaseline
Bowl, 4-1/2" d, lily	$18	$30	$18	$24
Bowl, 4-1/2" d, two handles	20	30	12	28
Bowl, 5-1/2" sq	10	15	10	12
Bowl, 5 -1/2 d, 1 handle	10	15	20	12
Bowl, 6" deep	12	24	18	15
Bowl, 6-1/4" d	12	18	10	12
Bowl, 6-1/2" d, two handles	12	18	28	12
Bowl, 6-3/4" d	15	20	14	14
Bowl, 7-1/4" d, flared	15	20	14	14
Bowl, 7-1/2" d, fluted	20	24	24	24
Bowl, 7-1/2" plain	24	24	20	22
Candy dish, cov, pear shaped	-	-	-	650
Celery, 8-1/4" d	18	30	16.50	18
Creamer, ftd	24	50	30	24
Jelly, 4-1/2" h, stemmed	12	15	12	12
Jelly, 4-1/2" h, stemmed, flared lid	15	24	15	12
Pitcher, 1 pt, 5-1/4" h	115	125	195	115
Plate, 7-3/4" sq	10	15	8	10
Plate, 8-3/4"	20	24	20	20
Sugar, ftd	20	60	30	20
Syrup	-	-	-	165
Vase, 6" h, ftd	25	110	36	30

Beaded Block, ice blue vase, **$35.**

Reproduction Alert. † Reproductions include: small berry bowl, 8-1/2" d bowl, covered butter dish, cake plate, cereal bowl, cup, pitcher, 6" and 9" plates, divided 13" platter, salt shaker, sandwich tray, saucer, and 3-3/4" and 4-1/2" h ftd tumblers. Reproductions have been made in cobalt blue, Delphite, green, pink, and red. A children's butter dish has also been made, which was never included in the original production.

Children's

Item	Delphite	Pink
Creamer	$50	$50
Cup †	42	42
Plate, 6" d	15	15
Saucer	7.50	7.50
Sugar	50	50

Cherry Blossom

Manufactured by Jeannette Glass Company, Jeannette, Pa., from 1930 to 1939.

Made in Crystal, Delphite, green, jade-ite, pink, and red (production was very limited in crystal, jade-ite and red).

Item	Delphite	Green	Pink
Berry bowl, 4-3/4" d †	$17.50	$25	$22.50
Berry bowl, 8-1/2" d †	55	50	65
Bowl, 9" d, two handles	27.50	95	48
Butter dish, cov †	-	115	75
Cake plate, 10-1/4" d, 3 legs †	-	38	25
Cereal bowl, 5-3/4" d †	-	35	32
Coaster	-	20	15
Creamer	30	35	35
Cup †	28	25	28
Fruit bowl, 10-1/2" d	32	90	90
Juice tumbler, 1 oz, 3-1/2"	-	35	24
Mug, 7 oz	-	195	265
Pitcher, 36 oz, 6-3/4" h, 36 oz †	95	60	72
Pitcher, 36 oz, 8", PAT, ftd	-	65	60
Pitcher, 42 oz, 8", PAT, flat	-	65	60
Plate, 6" d, sherbet †	12.50	10	12
Plate, 7" d, salad	-	27.50	24
Plate, 9" d, dinner †	18	28	35
Plate, 9" d, grill	-	35	32.50
Plate, 10" d, grill	-	32.50	-
Platter, 11" l, oval	40	48	35
Platter, 13" d	-	72	100
Platter, 13" divided †	-	72	75
Salt and pepper shakers, pr, scallop base †	-	995	1,250
Sandwich tray, 10-1/2" d †	20	30	45
Saucer †	6	7.50	6
Sherbet	18	30	19.50
Soup, flat, 7-3/4" d	-	90	80
Sugar, cov	24	37.50	35
Tumbler, 3-3/4" h, AOP, ftd †	-	22	24
Tumbler, 5" h	20	70	72
Tumbler, 8 oz, 4-1/2" h, scalloped ftd base, AOP	-	40	35
Tumbler, 9 oz, 4-1/4" h	-	24	22
Tumbler, 9 oz, 4-1/2" h †	20	30	32
Vegetable bowl, 9" l, oval	45	42	40

Cherry Blossom, delphite berry bowls, 4-3/4" d, each **$17.50.**

Coronation
Banded Fine Rib
Saxon

Manufactured by Hocking Glass Company, Lancaster, Ohio, from 1936 to 1940.

Made in crystal, green, pink, and Royal Ruby.

Item	Crystal	Green	Pink	Royal Ruby
Berry bowl, 4-1/4" d	$-	$50	$8.50	$6.50
Berry bowl, 8" d, handle	-	-	18	20
Berry bowl, 8" d	-	195	-	-
Cup	5	-	6	7.50
Nappy bowl, 6-1/2" d	15	-	7.50	15
Pitcher, 68 oz, 7-3/4" h	-	-	500	-
Plate, 6" d, sherbet	2	-	4.50	-
Plate, 8-1/2" d, luncheon	5	60	12	8.50
Saucer	2	-	4	-
Sherbet	-	85	7	-
Tumbler, 10 oz, 5" h, ftd	-	195	35	-

Coronation, ruby handled berry bowl, **$20.**

Cremax

Manufactured by Macbeth-Evans Division of Corning Glass Works, late 1930s to early 1940s.

Made in Cremax, Cremax with fired-on colors, Delphite, and Robin's Egg Blue. One set is known as Bordette.

Item	Bordette	Cremax	Cremax Fired-On	Delphite	Robin's Egg Blue
Cereal bowl, 5-3/4" d	$5	$6	$9	$10	$10
Creamer	6	6.50	6	11	11
Cup	5	6	8	7	7
Demitasse cup	10	16	18	26	26
Demitasse saucer	6	7	8	12	20
Egg cup, 2-1/4" h	12	-	-	-	-
Plate, 6-1/4" d, bread and butter	4	4.50	5.50	7	7
Plate, 9-3/4" d, dinner	14	7	11	12	12
Sandwich plate, 11-1/2" d	9.50	10	15	17	17
Saucer	3.50	4	4	6	6
Sugar, open	6	6.50	6	11	11
Vegetable bowl, 9" d	10	11	10	20	20

Cremax, dinner plate, Bordette, blue edge, **$11.**

Daisy
No. 620

Manufactured by Indiana Glass Company, Dunkirk, Ind., from late 1930s to 1980s.

Made in amber (1940s), crystal (1933-40), dark green (1960s-80s), fired-on red (late 1930s), and milk glass (1960s-80s).

Item	Amber or Fired On Red	Crystal	Dark Green or Milk White
Berry bowl, 4-1/2" d	$11	$6	$6
Berry bowl, 7-3/8" d, deep	17.50	8.50	9.50
Berry bowl, 9-3/8" d, deep	35	14	14
Cake plate, 11-1/2" d	16.50	14	14
Cereal bowl, 6" d	25	10	10
Cream soup bowl, 4-1/2" d	13.50	7.50	7.50
Creamer, ftd	10	8	8
Cup	8	6	6
Plate, 6" d, sherbet	5	4.50	5
Plate, 7-3/8" d, salad	8.50	8.50	9
Plate, 8-3/8" d, luncheon	10	10	12
Plate, 9-3/8" d, dinner	12	12	15
Plate, 10-3/8" d, grill	15	15	18
Platter, 10-3/4" d	18	11	11
Relish dish, 8-3/8" d, 3 part	24	12	12
Sandwich plate, 11-1/2" d	17.50	14	14
Saucer	2	6	2
Sherbet, ftd	9	5	5
Sugar, ftd	10	8	8
Tumbler, 9 oz, ftd	16	10	10
Tumbler, 12 oz, ftd	40	15	15
Vegetable bowl, 10" l, oval	25	18	18

Daisy, green luncheon plate, **$12.**

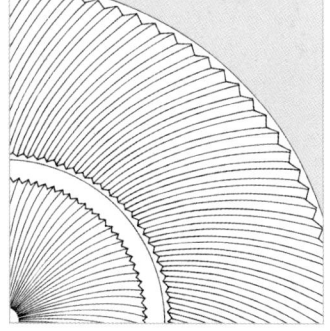

Diana

Manufactured by Federal Glass Company, Columbus, Ohio, from 1937 to 1941.

Made in amber, crystal, and pink.

Item	Amber	Crystal	Pink
Ashtray, 3-1/2" d	$-	$4	$5
Bowl, 12" d, scalloped edge	20	10	32
Candy jar, cov, round	40	18.50	48
Cereal bowl, 5" d	15	6.50	13
Coaster, 3-1/2" d	12	4	7
Console/fruit bowl, 11" d	10	20	44
Cream soup bowl, 5-1/2" d	18	14	24
Creamer, oval	9	4	12.50
Cup	7	4	19
Junior set, six cups and saucers, rack	-	125	300
Plate, 6" d, bread and butter	3.50	3	5.50
Plate, 9-1/2" d, dinner	9	7	18.50
Platter, 12" l, oval	15	12	28
Salad bowl, 9" d	18	15	20
Salt and pepper shakers, pr	100	30	75
Sandwich plate, 11-3/4" d	10	9.50	28
Saucer	2.25	2	6
Sherbet	10	7	12
Sugar, open, oval	10	10	16
Tumbler, 9 oz, 4-1/8" h	27.50	18	45

Diana, pink sherbet, **$12.**

Reproduction Alert. † A 13-1/8" d scalloped pink bowl has been made, which was not original to the pattern.

Doric and Pansy

Manufactured by Jeannette Glass Company, Jeannette, Pa., from 1937 to 1938.

Made in ultramarine, with limited production in pink and crystal.

Item	Crystal	Pink	Ultramarine
Berry bowl, 4-1/2" d	$12	$12	$24
Berry bowl, 8" d	-	24	75
Bowl, 9" d, handle	15	20	35
Butter dish, cov	-	-	600
Candy, cov, three parts	-	-	22.50
Cup	12	14	20
Creamer	72	90	145
Plate, 6" d, sherbet	8	12	14.50
Plate, 7" d, salad	-	-	40
Plate, 9" d, dinner	7.50	8	30
Salt shaker, orig top	-	-	325
Saucer	4.50	4.50	5.50
Sugar, open	80	85	145
Tray, 10" l, handles	45	-	25
Tumbler, 9 oz, 4-1/2" h	-	-	500

Doric and Pansy, pink dinner plate, **$8.**

English Hobnail
Line #555

Manufactured by Westmoreland Glass Company, Grapeville, Pa., from the 1920s to 1983.

Made in amber, cobalt blue, crystal, crystal with various color treatments, green, ice blue, pink, red, and turquoise blue. Values for cobalt blue, red or turquoise blue pieces would be about 25 percent higher than ice blue values. Currently, a turquoise basket is valued at $150; a red basket at $100. Crystal pieces with a color accent would be slightly higher than crystal values.

Item	Amber	Crystal	Green	Ice Blue	Pink
Ashtray, 3" d	$20	$20	$22	$-	$22
Ashtray, 4-1/2" d	9	9	15	24	15
Ashtray, 4-1/2" sq	9.50	9.50	15	-	15
Basket, 5" d, handle	20	20	-	-	-
Basket, 6" d, handle, tall	40	40	-	-	43
Bonbon, 6-1/2" h, handle	15	17.50	30	40	30
Bowl, 7" d, six parts	17.50	17.50	-	-	-
Bowl, 7" d, oblong spoon	17.50	17.50	-	-	-
Bowl, 8" d, ftd	30	30	48	-	48
Bowl, 8" d, hexagonal foot, two handles	38	38	75	115	75
Bowl, 8", 6 pt	24	24	-	-	-
Bowl, 9-1/2" d, round, crimped	30	30	-	-	-
Bowl, 10" d, flared	35	35	40	-	40
Bowl, 10" l, oval, crimped	40	40	-	-	-
Bowl, 11" d, rolled edge	35	35	40	85	40
Bowl, 12" d, flared	32	32	40	-	95
Bowl, 12" l, oval crimped	32	32	-	-	-
Candelabra, two lite	20	20	-	-	-
Candlesticks, pr, 3-1/2" h, round base	24	32	36	-	60
Candlesticks, pr, 5-1/2" h, sq base	30	32	-	-	-
Candlesticks, pr, 9" h, round base	50	40	72	-	125
Candy dish, three feet	45	38	50	-	50
Candy dish, cov, 1/2 lb, cone shape	45	40	55	-	90
Celery, 12" l, oval	24	45	36	-	36

English Hobnail, crystal tumbler, **$10.**

English Hobnail,
continued

Reproduction Alert. † A creamer and sugar with a hexagonal foot have been reproduced, as well as a nut bowl and pickle dish.

Item	Amber	Crystal	Green	Ice Blue	Pink
Celery, 9" d	$18	$20	$32	$-	$32
Champagne, two ball, round foot	8	7	20	-	20
Chandelier, 17" shade, 200 prisms	425	400	-	-	-
Cheese, cov, 6" d	40	42	-	-	-
Cheese, cov, 8-3/4" d	50	48	-	-	-
Cigarette box, cov, 4-1/2" x 2-1/2"	24.50	24.50	30	-	55
Cigarette jar, cov, round	16	18	25	-	65
Claret, 5 oz, round	15	17.50	-	-	-
Coaster, 3"	5	5	-	-	-
Cocktail, 3 oz, round	8.50	12	-	-	37.50
Cocktail, 3-1/2 oz, round, ball	15	17.50	-	-	-
Compote, 5" d, round, round foot	22	20	25	-	25
Compote, 5" d, round, sq foot	24	24	-	-	-
Compote, 5-1/2" d, bell	12	15	-	-	-
Compote, 5-1/2" d, bell, sq foot	20	20	-	-	-
Console bowl, 12" d, flange	30	30	40	-	40
Cordial, 1 oz, round, ball	16.50	17.50	-	-	-
Cordial, 1 oz, round, foot	16.50	16.50	-	-	-
Cream soup bowl, 4-5/8" d	15	15	-	-	-
Cream soup liner, round, 6-1/2" d	5	5	-	-	-
Creamer, hexagonal foot †	20	20	25	-	48
Creamer, low, flat	10	10	-	-	-
Creamer, sq foot	24	24	45	-	45
Cruet, 12 oz	-	25	-	-	-
Cup	8	12	18	-	25
Decanter, 20 oz	55	55	-	-	-
Demitasse cup	17.50	17.50	55	-	55
Dish, 6" d, crimped	15	15	-	-	-
Egg cup	15	15	-	-	-
Finger bowl, 4-1/2" d	7.50	7.50	15	35	15
Finger bowl, 4-1/2" sq, foot	9.50	9.50	18	40	18
Finger bowl liner, 6" sq	6.50	7	20	-	20
Finger bowl liner, 6-1/2" d, round	12	12	10	-	10
Ginger ale tumbler, 5 oz, flat	10	10	18	-	20
Ginger ale tumbler, 5 oz, round foot	10	10	-	-	-
Ginger ale tumbler, 5 oz, sq foot	8	8	32	-	35
Goblet, 8 oz, 6-1/4" h, round, water	12	12	-	50	35
Goblet, 8 oz, sq foot, water	10	10	-	-	50
Grapefruit bowl, 6-1/2" d	12	12	22	-	24
Hat, high	18	18	-	-	-
Hat, low	15	15	-	-	-
Honey compote, 6" d, round foot	18	18	35	-	35
Honey compote, 6" d, sq foot	18	18	-	-	-
Ice tub, 4" h	18	18	50	-	85
Ice tub, 5-1/2" h	36	36	65	-	100
Iced tea tumbler, 10 oz	14	14	30	-	30
Iced tea tumbler, 11 oz, round, ball	12	12	-	-	-
Iced tea tumbler, 11 oz, sq foot	13.50	13.50	-	-	-
Iced tea tumbler, 12-1/2 oz, round foot	14	14	-	-	-
Iced tea tumbler, 12 oz, flat	14	14	32	-	32
Icer, sq base, patterned insert	45	45	-	-	-
Ivy bowl, 6-1/2" d, sq foot, crimp top	35	35	-	-	-
Juice tumbler, 7 oz, round foot	27.50	27.50	-	-	-
Juice tumbler, 7 oz, sq foot	6.50	6.50	-	-	-
Lamp shade, 17" d	175	165	-	-	-
Lamp, 6-1/2" h, electric	45	45	50	-	50
Lamp, 9-1/2" d, electric	45	45	115	-	115
Lamp, candlestick	32	32	-	-	-
Marmalade, cov	40	40	45	-	70
Mayonnaise, 6"	12	12	22	-	22
Mustard, cov, sq, foot	18	18	-	-	-
Nappy, 4-1/2" d, round	8	8	15	30	15
Nappy, 4-1/2" w, sq	8.50	8.50	-	-	-
Nappy, 5" d, round	10	10	15	35	15
Nappy, 5-1/2" d, bell	12	12	-	-	-
Nappy, 6" d, round	10	10	17.50	-	17.50
Nappy, 6" d, sq	10	10	17.50	-	17.50
Nappy, 6-1/2" d, round	12.50	12.50	20	-	20
Nappy, 6-1/2" d, sq	14	14	-	-	-
Nappy, 7" d, round	14	14	24	-	24

English Hobnail, continued

Item	Amber	Crystal	Green	Ice Blue	Pink
Nappy, 7-1/2" d, bell	$15	$15	$-	$-	$-
Nappy, 8" d, cupped	22	22	30	-	30
Nappy, 8" d, round	22	22	35	-	35
Nappy, 9" d, bell	25	25	-	-	-
Nut, individual, ftd †	6	6	14.50	-	14.50
Oil bottle, 2 oz, handle	25	25	-	-	-
Oil bottle, 6 oz, handle	27.50	27.50	-	-	-
Old fashioned tumbler, 5 oz	15	15	-	-	-
Oyster cocktail, 5 oz, sq foot	12	12	17.50	-	17.50
Parfait, round foot	17.50	17.50	-	-	-
Pickle, 8" d †	15	15	-	-	-
Pitcher, 23 oz, rounded	48	48	150	-	165
Pitcher, 32 oz, straight side	50	50	175	-	175
Pitcher, 38 oz, rounded	65	65	215	-	215
Pitcher, 60 oz, rounded	70	70	295	-	295
Pitcher, 64 oz, straight side	75	75	310	-	310
Plate, 5-1/2" d, round	7	7	10	-	10
Plate, 6-1/2" d, round	6.25	6.25	10	-	10
Plate, 6-1/2" d, round, depressed center	6	6	-	-	-
Plate, 8" d, round	9	9	14	-	14
Plate, 8" d, round, ftd	13	13	-	-	-
Plate, 8-1/2" d, plain edge	9	9	-	-	-
Plate, 8-1/2" d, round	7	9	17.50	-	28
Plate, 8-3/4" w, sq	9.25	9.25	-	-	-
Plate, 10" d, round	15	15	45	-	65
Plate, 10" w, sq	15	15	-	-	-
Plate, 10-1/2" d, round, grill	18	18	-	-	-
Plate, 12" w, sq	20	20	-	-	-
Plate, 15" w, sq	28	28	-	-	-
Preserve, 8" d	15	15	-	-	-
Puff box, cov, 6" d, round	20	20	47.50	-	80
Punch bowl and stand	215	215	-	-	-
Relish, 8" d, three parts	18	18	-	-	-
Rose bowl, 4" d	17.50	17.50	48	-	50
Rose bowl, 6" d	20	20	-	-	-
Salt and pepper shakers, pr, round foot	27.50	27.50	150	-	165
Salt and pepper shakers, pr, sq foot	20	20	-	-	-
Saucer, demitasse, round	10	10	15	-	17.50
Saucer, demitasse, sq	10	10	-	-	-
Saucer, round	2	2	6	-	6
Saucer, sq	2	2	-	-	-
Sherbet, high, round foot	7	7	18	-	37.50
Sherbet, high, sq foot	8	8	18	-	-
Sherbet, high, two ball, round foot	10	10	-	-	-
Sherbet, low, one ball, round foot	12	10	-	-	15
Sherbet, low, round foot	12.50	7	-	-	-
Sherbet, low, sq foot	6.50	6	15	-	17.50
Straw jar, 10" h	65	60	-	-	-
Sugar, hexagonal, ftd †	9	9	25	-	48
Sugar, low, flat	8	8	45	-	-
Sugar, sq foot	9	9	48	-	55
Sweetmeat, 5-1/2" d, ball stem	30	30	-	-	-
Sweetmeat, 8" d, ball stem	40	40	60	-	65
Tidbit, two tiers	27.50	27.50	65	85	80
Toilet bottle, 5 oz	25	25	40	65	40
Torte plate, 14" d, round	35	30	48	-	48
Torte plate, 20-1/2" round	55	50	-	-	-
Tumbler, 8 oz, water	10	10	24	-	24
Tumbler, 9 oz, round, ftd water	10	10	-	-	-
Tumbler, 9 oz, sq foot, water	10	10	-	-	-
Urn, cov, 11" h	35	35	350	-	350
Vase, 6-1/2" h, sq foot	24	24	-	-	-
Vase, 7-1/2" h, flip	27.50	27.50	70	-	70
Vase, 7-1/2" h, flip jar with cov	55	55	85	-	85
Vase, 8" h, sq foot	35	35	-	-	-
Vase, 8-1/2" h, flared top	40	40	120	-	235
Whiskey, 3 oz	12	15	-	-	-
Wine, 2 oz, round foot	15	15	-	-	-
Wine, 2 oz, sq ft	24	24	35	-	65
Wine, 2-1/2 oz, ball, foot	20	20	-	-	-

Floragold, iridescent dinner plate, **$40;** *and ruffled berry bowl, 5-1/4" d,* **$16.**

Floragold
Louisa

Manufactured by Jeannette Glass Company, Jeannette, Pa., 1950s.

Made in iridescent. Some large comports were later made in ice blue, crystal, red-yellow, and shell pink.

Item	Iridescent
Ashtray, 4" d	$10
Bowl, 4-1/2" sq	6.50
Bowl, 5-1/4" d, ruffled	16
Bowl, 8-1/2" d, sq	22
Bowl, 8-1/2" d, ruffled	14
Butter dish, cov, 1/4 pound, oblong	30
Butter dish, cov, round, 5-1/2" w sq base	800
Butter dish, cov, round, 6-1/4" w sq base	55
Candlesticks, pr, double branch	60
Candy dish, one handle	16.50
Candy or cheese dish, cov, 6-3/4" d	130
Candy, 5-3/4" l, four feet	12
Celery vase	420
Cereal bowl, 5-1/2" d, round	40
Coaster, 4" d	10
Comport, 5-1/4", plain top	795
Comport, 5-1/4", ruffled top	895
Creamer	21
Cup	8

Item	Iridescent
Fruit bowl, 5-1/2" d, ruffled	$8.50
Fruit bowl, 12" d, ruffled, large	15
Nappy, 5" d, one handle	12
Pitcher, 64 oz	45
Plate, 5-1/4" d, sherbet	15
Plate, 8-1/2" d, dinner	40
Platter, 11-1/4" d	30
Salad bowl, 9-1/2" d, deep	42.50
Salt and pepper shakers, pr, plastic tops	60
Saucer, 5-1/4" d	12
Sherbet, low, ftd	16
Sugar	22
Sugar lid	15
Tidbit, wooden post	35
Tray, 13-1/2" d	75
Tray, 13-1/2" d, with indent	65
Tumbler, 11 oz, ftd	20
Tumbler, 10 oz, ftd	20
Tumbler, 15 oz, ftd	110
Vase	420

Floral and Diamond Band, green luncheon plate, **$40.**

Floral and Diamond Band

Manufactured by U.S. Glass Company, Pittsburgh, Pa., in the late 1920s.

Made in pink and green with limited production in black, crystal, and iridescent.

Item	Green	Pink
Berry bowl, 4-1/2" d	$12	$15
Berry bowl, 8" d	15	18
Butter dish, cov	140	175
Compote, 5-1/2" h	18	17.50
Creamer, 4-3/4"	20	17.50
Iced tea tumbler, 5" h	45	50
Nappy, 5-3/4" d, handle	12	11
Pitcher, 42 oz, 8" h	95	90
Plate, 8" d, luncheon	40	40
Sherbet	8	9.50
Sugar, 5-1/4"	15	15
Tumbler, 4" h, water	25	25

Hobnail

Manufactured by Hocking Glass Company, Lancaster, Ohio, from 1934 to 1936.

Made in crystal, crystal with red trim, and pink.

Item	Crystal	Crystal, red trim	Pink
Cereal bowl, 5-1/2" d	$4.25	$4.25	$-
Cordial, 5 oz, ftd	6	6	-
Creamer, ftd	4	4	-
Cup	5	5	6
Decanter and stopper, 32 oz	27.50	27.50	-
Goblet, 10 oz	7.50	7.50	-
Iced tea goblet, 13 oz	8.50	8.50	-
Iced tea tumbler, 15 oz	8.50	8.50	-
Juice tumbler, 5 oz	4	4	-
Milk pitcher, 18 oz	22	22	-
Pitcher, 67 oz	25	25	-
Plate, 6" d, sherbet	2.50	2.50	3.50
Plate, 8-1/2" d, luncheon	5.50	5.50	7.50
Salad bowl, 7" d	5	5	-
Saucer	2	2	3
Sherbet	4	4	5
Sugar, ftd	4	4	-
Tumbler, 9 oz, 4-3/4" h, flat	5	5	-
Whiskey, 1-1/2 oz	5	5	-
Wine, 3 oz, ftd	6.50	6.50	-

Hobnail, pink sherbet, **$5.**

Laced Edge
Katy Blue

Manufactured by Imperial Glass Company, Bellaire, Ohio, early 1930s.
Made in blue and green with opalescent edges.

Item	Blue	Green
Basket, 9" d	$265	$-
Bowl, 5" d	40	40
Bowl, 5-1/2" d	42	42
Bowl, 5-7/8" d	42	42
Bowl, 11" l, oval	295	285
Bowl, 11" l, oval, divided	165	165
Candlesticks, pr, double lite	175	180
Creamer	45	40
Cup	35	35
Fruit bowl, 4-1/2" d	32	30
Mayonnaise, three pieces	100	125
Plate, 6-1/2" d, bread and butter	24	24
Plate, 8" d, salad	35	35
Plate, 10" d, dinner	95	95
Plate, 12" d, luncheon	90	90
Platter, 13" l	185	165
Saucer	18	15
Soup bowl, 7" d	85	80
Sugar	45	40
Tidbit, two tiers, 8" and 10" plates	110	100
Tumbler, 9 oz	60	60
Vegetable bowl, 9" d	95	95

Laced Edge, blue bowl, 5-1/2" d, **$42.**

Mayfair, amber dinner plate, **$14.**

Mayfair, Federal
Federal

Manufactured by Federal Glass Company, Columbus, Ohio, 1934. Made in amber, crystal, and green.

Item	Amber	Crystal	Green
Cereal bowl, 6" d	$18.50	$15	$22
Cream soup, 5" d	22	12	20
Creamer, ftd	17.50	14	16
Cup	8.50	5	8.50
Plate, 6-3/4" d, salad	7	4.50	8.50
Plate, 9-1/2" d, dinner	14	12	14.50
Plate, 9-1/2" d, grill	17.50	15	17.50
Platter, 12" l, oval	27.50	22	30
Sauce bowl, 5" d	8.50	7	12
Saucer	4.50	2.50	4.50
Sugar, ftd	14	12	14
Tumbler, 9 oz, 4-1/2" h	27.50	16.50	32
Vegetable, 10" l, oval	32	32	32

Mayfair, pink 11 oz tumbler, **$225;** *pink satin-finish covered cookie jar,* **$37.**

Mayfair, Hocking
Open Rose

Manufactured by Hocking Glass Company, Lancaster, Ohio, from 1931 to 1937.

Made in crystal, green, ice blue, pink, pink satin, and yellow.

Item	Crystal	Green	Ice Blue	Pink	Pink Satin	Yellow
Bowl, 11-3/4" l, flat	$-	$35	$75	$65	$70	$195
Butter dish, cov	-	1,295	325	80	95	1,295
Cake plate, 10" d, ftd	-	115	75	40	45	-
Cake plate, 12" d, handles	-	40	95	65	50	-
Candy dish, cov	-	575	325	70	85	475
Celery dish, 9" l, divided	-	155	60	-	-	150
Celery dish, 10" l, divided	-	-	90	295	-	-
Celery dish, 10" l, not divided	-	115	80	55	50	115
Cereal bowl, 5-1/2" d	-	24	48	30	35	75
Claret, 4-1/2 oz, 5-1/4" h	-	950	-	1,150	-	-
Cocktail, 3 oz, 4" h	-	975	-	125	-	-
Console bowl, 9" d, 3-1/8" h, three legs	-	5,000	-	5,000	-	-
Cookie jar, cov †	-	575	295	75	37	860
Cordial, 1 oz, 3-3/4" h	-	950	-	1,100	-	-
Cream soup, 5" d	-	-	-	65	68	-
Creamer, ftd	-	-	-	35	30	-
Cup	-	150	55	24	27.50	150
Decanter, stopper, 32 oz	-	-	-	225	-	-
Fruit bowl, 12" d, scalloped	-	50	125	90	75	215
Goblet, 2-1/2 oz, 4-1/8"	-	950	-	950	-	-
Goblet, 9 oz, 5-3/4" h	-	465	-	90	-	-
Goblet, 9 oz, 7-1/4" h, thin	-	-	225	250	-	-
Iced tea tumbler, 13-1/2 oz, 5-1/4" h	-	-	225	70	-	-
Iced tea tumbler, 15 oz, 6-1/2" h, ftd	-	250	285	65	65	-
Juice pitcher, 37 oz, 6" h †	24.50	525	150	70	65	525
Juice tumbler, 3 oz, 3-1/4" h, ftd	-	-	-	80	-	-
Juice tumbler, 5 oz, 3-1/2" h	-	-	225	80	-	-
Pitcher, 60 oz, 8" h	-	475	195	95	100	425
Pitcher, 80 oz, 8-1/2" h	-	725	295	130	135	725

Item	Crystal	Green	Ice Blue	Pink	Pink Satin	Yellow
Plate, 5-3/4" d	$-	$90	$25	$15	$15	$90
Plate, 6-1/2" d, off-center indent	-	115	42	30	35	-
Plate, 6-1/2" d, sherbet	-	-	24	14.50	-	-
Plate, 8-1/2" d, luncheon	-	85	55	40	35	80
Plate, 9-1/2" d, dinner	-	150	90	65	62	150
Plate, 9-1/2" d, grill	-	75	70	50	35	80
Plate, 11-1/2" d, grill, handles	-	-	-	-	-	100
Platter, 12" l, oval, open handles	17.50	175	60	40	35	115
Platter, 12-1/2" oval, 8" wide, closed handles	-	245	-	-	-	245
Relish, 8-3/8" d, four parts	-	160	65	37.50	37.50	160
Relish, 8-3/8" d, non-partitioned	-	275	-	200	-	275
Salt and pepper shakers, pr, flat †	20	1,000	295	65	70	800
Sandwich server, center handle	-	48	85	65	50	130
Saucer	-	90	30	45	35	140
Sherbet, 2-1/4" flat	-	-	135	185	-	-
Sherbet, 3" ftd	-	-	-	20	-	-
Sherbet, 4-3/4" ftd	-	150	75	75	75	150
Sugar, ftd	-	195	85	35	40	185
Sweet pea vase	-	285	135	250	145	-
Tumbler, 9 oz, 4-1/4" h	-	-	100	30	-	-
Tumbler, 10 oz, 5-1/4" h	-	-	145	65	-	185
Tumbler, 11 oz, 4-3/4" h	-	200	250	225	225	215
Vegetable bowl, 7" d, two handles	-	33	75	65	70	195
Vegetable bowl, 9-1/2" l, oval	-	110	70	40	30	125

Mayfair, Hocking,
continued
Open Rose

Reproduction Alert. † This pattern has been plagued with reproductions since 1977. Items reproduced include cookie jars, salt and pepper shakers, juice pitchers, and whiskey glasses. Reproductions are found in amethyst, blue, cobalt blue, green, pink, and red.

Old Cafe

Manufactured by Hocking Glass Company, Lancaster, Ohio, from 1936 to 1940.

Made in crystal, pink, and royal ruby.

Item	Crystal	Pink	Royal Ruby
Berry bowl, 3-3/4" d	$9.50	$10	$9
Bowl, 6-1/2" d	15	18	-
Bowl, 9" d, closed handles	10	10	15
Candy dish, 8" d, low	18	15	20
Candy jar, 5-1/2" d, crystal with ruby cover	-	-	25
Cereal bowl, 5-1/2" d	30	30	15
Cup	12	12	15
Juice tumbler, 3" h	18	18	20
Lamp	100	100	150
Olive dish, 6" l, oblong	7.50	8.50	-
Pitcher, 36 oz, 6" h	125	145	-
Plate, 6" d, sherbet	5	5	-
Plate, 10" d, dinner	60	65	-
Saucer	5	5	-
Sherbet, low, ftd	15	12	12
Tumbler, 4" h	18	20	18
Vase, 7-1/4" h	40	45	50

Old Café, ruby bowl with handles and original label, **$15.**

Oyster and Pearl

Manufactured by Anchor Hocking Glass Corporation, from 1938 to 1940.

Made in crystal, pink, royal ruby, and white with fired-on green or pink.

Right: Oyster and Pearl, ruby sandwich plate, **$50.**

Item	Crystal	Pink	Royal Ruby	White, Fired-On Green	White, Fired-On Pink
Bowl, 5-1/2" d, handle	$8	$15	$20	$-	$-
Bowl, 5-1/4" w, handle, heart-shape	12	21	-	12	-
Bowl, 6-1/2" d, handle	12	15	28	-	-
Candleholders, pr, 3-1/2" h	35	45	65	25	25
Fruit bowl, 10-1/2" d, deep	20	25	50	30	30
Relish dish, 10-1/4" l, divided	10	35	-	-	-
Sandwich plate, 13-1/2" d	20	40	50	-	-

Pyramid
No. 610

Manufactured by Indiana Glass Company, Dunkirk, Ind., from 1926 to 1932.

Made in crystal, green, pink, white, and yellow. Later production in 1974 to 1975 by Tiara produced black and blue pieces. Production limited in blue and white. Prices for black not firmly established in secondary market at this time.

Item	Crystal	Green	Pink	Yellow
Berry bowl, 4-3/4" d	$20	$35	$35	$55
Berry bowl, 8-1/2" d	30	65	55	75
Bowl, 9-1/2" l, oval	30	45	40	65
Creamer	20	35	35	40
Ice tub	95	145	155	225
Pickle dish, 9-1/2" l, 5-3/4" w	30	35	35	65
Pitcher	395	265	400	550
Relish, four parts, handles	25	65	60	70
Sugar	20	35	35	40
Tray for creamer and sugar	25	30	30	35
Tumbler, 8 oz, ftd	55	50	55	75
Tumbler, 11 oz, ftd	70	75	50	95

Pyramid, green pickle dish, **$35.**

Rosemary
Dutch Rose

Manufactured by Federal Glass Company, Columbus, Ohio, from 1935 to 1937.

Made in amber, green, and pink.

Item	Amber	Green	Pink
Berry bowl, 5" d	$7	$17.50	$17.50
Cereal bowl, 6" d	30	32	35
Cream soup, 5" d	18	25	30
Creamer, ftd	10	16	20
Cup	9	12.50	15
Plate, 6-3/4" d, salad	6.50	12	12.50
Plate, 9-1/2" d, dinner	10	15	22
Plate, 9-1/2" d, grill	12	15	22
Platter, 12" l, oval	18.50	24	35
Saucer	5	8.50	9.50
Sugar, ftd	10	16	20
Tumbler, 9 oz, 4-1/4" h	35	38	50
Vegetable bowl, 10" l, oval	18	40	45

Rosemary, Continued

Rosemary, green platter, **$24.**

Sandwich
Line #41

Manufactured by Duncan & Miller Glass Company, Washington, Pa., from 1924 to 1955.

Made in crystal with limited production in amber, cobalt blue, green, pink, and red. The molds were sold to Lancaster Colony which continues to produce some glass in this pattern, but in newer brighter colors, such as amberina, blue, and green.

Item	Crystal
Almond bowl, 2-1/2" d	$12
Ashtray, 2-1/2" x 3-3/4"	10
Ashtray, 2-3/4" sq	8.50
Basket, 6-1/2", loop handle	135
Basket 10", loop handle, crimped	185
Basket, 10", loop handle, oval	185
Basket, 11-1/2", loop handle	225
Bonbon, 5" w, heart shape	15
Bonbon, 6" w, heart shape, ring handle	20
Bonbon, cov, 7-1/2" d, ftd	45
Bowl, 5-1/2" d, handle	15
Butter, cov, quarter pound	40
Cake stand, 11-1/2" d, ftd	95
Cake stand, 12" d, ftd	115
Cake stand, 13" d, ftd	125
Candelabra, with bobeche and prisms, 10" h, three-lite	200
Candelabra, with bobeche and prisms, 10" h, one-lite	95
Candelabra, with bobeche and prisms, 16" h, three-lite	225
Candlesticks, pr, 4" h	30
Candlesticks, pr, 5" h, three-lite	90
Candy box, cov, 5" d, flat	42
Candy comport, 3-1/4" d, low, ftd or flared	25
Candy dish, 6" sq	375
Candy jar, cov, 8-1/2" d, flat	60
Celery tray, 10" l, oval	30
Champagne, 5 oz	25
Cheese comport, 13" d underplate	60
Cheese dish, cov	125
Cigarette box, cov, 3-1/2"	24
Cigarette holder, 3" d, ftd	30
Coaster, 5" d	12
Cocktail, 3 oz	15
Comport, 2-1/4"	17.50
Comport, 4-1/4" d, ftd	22
Comport, 5" d, low, ftd	22
Comport, 5-1/2" d, ftd, low, crimped	25
Comport, 6" d, low, flared	25
Condiment set, pr cruets, pr salt and pepper shakers, tray	100

Item	Crystal
Console bowl, 12" d	$45
Cracker plate, 13" d	32
Creamer	10
Cup	10
Deviled egg plate, 12" d	65
Epergne, 9" h	125
Epergne, 12" h, three parts	200
Finger bowl, 4" h	12
Finger bowl underplate, 6-1/2" d	8
Flower bowl, 11-1/2" d, crimped	60
Fruit bowl, 5" d	10
Fruit bowl, 10" d	65
Fruit bowl, 11-1/2" d, crimped, ftd	65
Fruit bowl, 12", flared	50
Fruit cup, 6 oz	12
Fruit salad bowl, 6" d	12
Gardenia bowl, 11-1/2" d	48
Goblet, 9 oz, 6" h	18
Grapefruit bowl, 5-1/2" d or 6" d	17.50
Hostess plate, 16" d	100
Ice cream dish 5 oz	12
Ice cream plate, rolled edge, 12" d	60
Ice cream tray, rolled edge, 12" d	45
Iced tea tumbler, 12 or 13 oz, ftd	20
Ivy bowl, ftd, crimped	35
Jelly, 3" d	8
Juice tumbler, 5 oz	12
Lazy Susan, 16" d	115
Lily bowl, 10" d	55
Mayonnaise set, three pcs	35
Mint tray, 6" l or 7" l, rolled edge, ring handle	18
Nappy, 5" d, two parts	15
Nappy, 5" d, ring handle	12
Nappy, 6" d, ring handle	15
Nut bowl, 3-1/2" d	10
Nut bowl, 11" d, cupped	55
Oil bottle, orig stopper	35
Oil and vinegar tray, 8" l	20
Oyster cocktail, 5 oz	18
Parfait, 4 oz, ftd	30
Pickle tray, 7" l, oval	15
Pitcher, 13 oz, metal lip	75

Item	Crystal
Pitcher, 64 oz, ice lip	$125
Plate, 3" d, jelly	5
Plate, 6" d, bread and butter	6
Plate, 7" d, dessert	7.50
Plate, 8" d, salad	10
Plate, 9-1/2" d, dinner	35
Relish, 5-1/2" d, two parts, ring handle	15
Relish, 6" d, two parts, ring handle	18
Relish, 7" d, two parts, oval	20
Relish, 10" d, three parts, rect	27.50
Relish, 10" d, four parts	25
Relish, 10-1/2" l, three parts, rect	27.50
Relish, 12" l, three parts	25
Salad bowl, 10" d, deep	75
Salad bowl, 12" d, shallow	42
Salt and pepper shakers, pr, 2-1/2" h, glass tops	20
Salt and pepper shakers, pr, 2-1/2" h, metal tops	20
Salts and pepper shakers, set, pr 3-3/4" h, metal tops, 6" tray	35
Service plate, 11-1/2" d, handle	50
Service plate, 13" d	55
Sugar shaker	72
Sugar bowl, 5 oz	10
Sugar bowl, 9 oz, 3-1/4" h, ftd	12
Sundae, 5 oz	15
Torte plate, 12" d	48
Tray, 8" l	20
Urn, cov, 12" h, ftd	150
Tumbler, 9 oz, 4-3/4", ftd	15
Vase, 3" h, crimped	18
Vase, 3" h, flared rim	18
Vase, 4" h, hat shape	20
Vase, 4-1/2" h, crimped	25
Vase, 5" h, fan	40
Vase, 5" h, flared or crimped	25
Vase, 10" h, ftd	70
Wine, 3 oz	24

Ships, cobalt blue salad plate, **$27.50.**

Ships
Sailboat
Sportsman Series

Manufactured by Hazel Atlas Glass Company, Clarksburg, W.V., and Zanesville, Ohio, late 1930s.

Made in cobalt blue with white, yellow, and red decoration. Pieces with yellow or red decoration are valued slightly higher than the traditional white decoration.

Item	Cobalt Blue with White Decoration
Ashtray	$60
Ashtray, metal sailboat	120
Box, cov, three parts	250
Cocktail mixer, stirrer	45
Cocktail shaker	45
Cup	15
Ice bowl	45
Iced tea tumbler, 10-1/2 oz, 4-7/8" h	22
Iced tea tumbler, 12 oz	24
Old fashioned tumbler, 8 oz, 3-3/8" h	22
Pitcher, 82 oz, no ice lip	85
Pitcher, 86 oz, ice lip	75
Plate, 5-7/8" d, bread & butter	24
Plate, 8" d, salad	27.50
Plate, 9" d, dinner	32
Saucer	18
Tumbler, 4 oz, 3-1/4" h, heavy bottom	27.50
Tumbler, 9 oz, 3-3/4" h	18
Whiskey, 3-1/2" h	45

Yorktown, yellow relish, **$3.**

Yorktown

Manufactured by Federal Glass Company, in the mid-1950s.

Made in crystal, iridescent, smoke, white, and yellow. Values for all the colors are about the same.

Item	Crystal, etc.
Berry bowl, 5-1/2" d	$4.50
Berry bowl, 9-1/2" d	10
Celery tray, 10" l	10
Creamer	5
Cup	3.50
Fruit bowl, 10" d, ftd	18
Iced tea tumbler, 5-1/4" h, 13 oz	7.50
Juice tumbler, 3-7/8" h, 6 oz	4.50
Mug	15
Plate, 8-1/4" d	4.50
Plate, 11-1/2" d	8.50
Punch bowl set	40
Punch cup	2.50
Relish	3
Sandwich server	4.50
Saucer	1
Sherbet, 7 oz	3.50
Snack cup	2.50
Snack plate with indent	3.50
Sugar	5
Tumbler, 4-3/4" h, 10 oz	6
Vase, 8" h	15

DUNCAN AND MILLER

History: George Duncan, and Harry B. and James B., his sons, and Augustus Heisey, his son-in-law, formed George Duncan & Sons in Pittsburgh, Pennsylvania, in 1865. The factory was located just two blocks from the Monongahela River, providing easy and inexpensive access by barge for materials needed to produce glass. The men, from Pittsburgh's south side, were descendants of generations of skilled glassmakers.

The plant burned to the ground in 1892. James E. Duncan Sr. selected a site for a new factory in Washington, Pennsylvania, where operations began on February 9, 1893. The plant prospered, producing fine glassware and table services for many years.

John E. Miller, one of the stockholders, was responsible for designing many fine patterns, the most famous being Three Face. The firm incorporated and used the name The Duncan and Miller Glass Company until the plant closed in 1955. The company's slogan was, "The Loveliest Glassware in America." The U.S. Glass Co. purchased the molds, equipment, and machinery in 1956.

Additional Listing: Pattern Glass.

Animal
Heron, crystal **$125**
Swan, Sanibel, blue opalescent, 8" h
.... **$165**
Bowl, First Love, crystal, scalloped, 11" d..**$72**
Bud vase, First Love, crystal, 9" h **$75**
Candlestick, Canterbury, orchid carving, 3" h **$68**
Candy box, cov, Canterbury, crystal, three parts, 6" d **$70**
Champagne
Cascade, crystal, #17365, 4-3/4" h..**$25**
Lily of the Valley, crystal.............**$35**

Cocktail
Caribbean, blue, 3-3/4 oz............**$45**
Cascade, crystal, #17365, 4-1/2" h..**$55**
Lily of the Valley, crystal........ **$32.50**
Compote, Spiral Flutes, amber, 6" d
.... **$20**
Console bowl, Rose etch, crystal, 11" d.. **$37.50**
Cordial, Cascade, crystal, #17365.. **$55**
Cornucopia, #121, Swirl, blue opalescent, shape #2, upswept tail........**$75**
Creamer and sugar, Passion Flower, crystal...**$42**
Cup, Sandwich, crystal **$9**

Finger bowl, Astaire, red............**$65**
Fruit bowl, Sanibel, pink opalescent, 6-1/2" l...................................**$40**
Goblet, water
Caribbean, crystal......................**$37**
Cascade, crystal, #17365, 6-1/4" h..**$25**
First Love, crystal, 10 oz **$35**
Lily of the Valley, crystal............**$30**
Plaza, cobalt blue.......................**$40**
Sandwich, crystal.......................**$24**
Iced tea tumbler, Cascade, crystal, #17365, 6" h **$25**
Juice tumbler
Lily of the Valley, crystal............**$28**
Sandwich, crystal, ftd, 3-3/4" h ...**$12**

EARLY AMERICAN GLASS

History: The term "Early American glass" covers glass made in America from the colonial period through the mid-19th century. As such, it includes the early pressed glass and lacy glass made between 1827 and 1840.

Major glass-producing centers prior to 1850 were Massachusetts (New England Glass Company and the Boston and Sandwich Glass Company), South Jersey, Pennsylvania (Stiegel's Manheim factory and many Pittsburgh-area firms), and Ohio (several different companies in Kent, Mantua, and Zanesville).

Early American glass was popular with collectors from 1920 to 1950. It has now regained some of its earlier prominence. Leading auction sources for early American glass include American Bottle Auctions, Garth's, Green Valley Auctions, Heckler & Company, James D. Julia, and Skinner, Inc. A standard reference book used by early collectors as well as collectors today was written by George and Helen McKearin, *American Glass*, Crown Publishers in 1941. Many collectors and dealers refer to the "McKearin" plate numbers when describing early American glass.

Additional Listings: Cup Plates; Flasks; Sandwich Glass; Stiegel-Type Glass.

Bottle, blown, half post case, colorless, copper wheel engraved flowers on all sides, larger two resembling crosshatched tulips, chipped lip, 9-7/8" h... **$200**
Bowl, free-blown, deep
Concave shoulder, folded rim, amber, slightly domed base, rough pontil mark, American, mid-19th C, 5-7/8" d, 1-3/8" h................. **$1,100**
Flaring folded rim, light amber, slightly domed base, rough pontil mark, American, first half 19th C, 5-1/4" d, 2" h.......................... **$525**

Flaring folded rim, amber, slightly domed base, rough pontil mark, American, first half 19th C, 8-1/2" d, 3-3/4" h................. **$1,650**
Slightly concave sides, delicate folded rim, deep muddy black amber, domed base, rough pontil mark, American, first half 19th C, 7" d, 4-1/4" h **$1,980**
Slightly flaring folded rim, light ruby, domed base, rough pontil mark, American, second half 19th C, 6" d, 4" h **$440**
Slightly flaring folded rim, brilliant

emerald green, slightly domed base, rough pontil mark, American, mid-19th C, 6-7/8" d, 3-5/8" h.... **$1,870**
Wide folded rim, aquamarine, slight kick-up, rough pontil mark, New York state, possibly Cleveland Glass Works, mid-19th C, 13" d, 5" h.............. **$880**
Celery vase, Diamond Thumbprint, flint, scalloped rim, bulbous ribbed stem, round base, 9-1/4" h........ **$175**
Compote
Free-blown, colorless, applied blue threading around outside of bowl, applied hollow reverse baluster

stem, high domed circular foot with folded rim, rough pontil mark, American or European, late 18th/ early 19th C, 4-1/8" h, 4-3/8" d rim, 3-3/8" d foot.......................... **$1,155**

Pressed, Diamond Thumbprint, flint, scalloped rim, bulbous ribbed stem, round base, 9" h, 11-1/2" d.... **$230**

Cordial, blown, clear, red, dark green, and cotton twist stem, 4-1/2" h **$175**

Creamer, pressed, Gothic Arch, Palm, and Chain, colorless, lightly scalloped rim, molded handle, circular even scallop foot, Boston & Sandwich and others, chip under spout, 1835-45, 4-1/8" h......................... **$135**

Cream jug, free-blown, deep olive amber with white flecks, crude applied strap-type handle, circular foot, heavy rough pontil mark, possibly Saratoga Glass Works, first half 19th C, 5" h, 3" d rim, 2-5/8" d foot **$1,100**

Decanter

Blown molded, pint, deep olive green, slightly flaring plain lip, rayed base, rough pontil mark, Keene, NH, McKearin GIII-16, 1820-40, 7" h, 3" d base...................... **$825**

Pressed, double Bellflower, ribbed, medium green to olive, second period, 9-5/8" h **$175**

Dish

Gothic Arch and Plume, oval, colorless, center with stippled background, plain table ring, even scallop rim, Midwestern, large shallow rim spall, 1835-45, 6-1/4" x 9-1/4" x 1-5/8" **$235**

Eagle, octagonal, colorless, central design of eagle with American shield surrounded by 13 stars, shoulder with three alternating designs of shields, acanthus leaves and five-point star medallions, plain even scallop rim, possibly Boston & Sandwich, loss of scallops, rim chipping, 1835-45, 7" d, 1-5/8" h $100

Flip, etched, blown, colorless copper wheel engraved borders of crosshatched ovals, wide fluting, 3-7/8" h......................... **$295**

Copper wheel engraved tulip in basket, 4-1/4" h **$350**

Copper wheel engraved border with crosshatched ovals, three-quarter ribbing, 6-1/4" h **$400**

Copper wheel engraved designs of four floral panels, 6-1/2" h **$500**

Hat, blown molded, colorless, inward folded rim, rayed base, rough pontil mark, possibly Boston & Sandwich Glass Co., 1825-35, McKearin GII-18, 2-1/8" h, 2-5/8" d rim, 1-3/4" base................ **$145**

Hurricane shades, pr, blown, colorless, baluster form, medial frosted band with wheel-etched flowering vine, circular folded foot, America, 19th C, 21-3/4" h **$2,235**

Hyacinth vase

Amethyst, good color, minor wear, 8" h **$100**

Amethyst, medium color, added foot with folded rim, minor wear, 8-1/4" h **$575**

Inkwell, blown molded, dark olive amber, 14 diamond base, rough pontil mark, Keene, NH, 1820-1840, McKearin GII-18, top and side wear, 2" h, 2-5/8" d **$160**

Jar, blown molded, olive-green, wide rim, ten panels about shoulder, eastern United States, minor scratches, early 19th C, 8-1/2" h **$2,115**

Milk pan, free-blown, flaring folded rim, deep brilliant teal, slightly domed base, small rough pontil mark, second half 19th C, 7-1/2" d, 2-1/4" h .. **$470**

Nappy, Paneled Diamond, colorless, each panel topped by fan, point, and five scallop rim, possibly Boston & Sandwich, light flaking/mold roughness, 1828-1835, 6-5/8" d, 1-3/8" h................... **$70**

Pan

Free-blown, lily pad dec, flaring folded rim, brilliant light green, slightly domed base, rough pontil mark, New York, probably Redford or Redwood Glass Works, 19th C, 7-5/8" d, 1-3/4" h **$11,000**

Free-blown, slightly flaring folded rim, brilliant amethyst, nearly flat base, polished pontil mark, second half 19th C, 8-7/8" d, 3" h **$330**

Pitcher, free-blown

Ftd, applied reeded handle, cobalt blue, eastern United States, early 19th C, 5" h **$1,200**

Threaded neck, applied strap-type handle, heavy medial rib, aquamarine, kick-up base, rough pontil mark, New York state, possibly Cleveland Glass Works, first half 19th C, 8" h, 6" d rim **$3,300**

Plate, Anchor and Shield, deep olive green, Midwestern, rim chip, 7" d, 1-1/8" d....................................... **$315**

Storage jar, blown, olive green, flared rim, minor scratches, 11-3/4" h $95

Sugar bowl, cov

Pressed, Colonial variant, hexagonal, emerald green, polished finial, base with high scallop rim, rayed and polished underneath, under rim chip on cov, mid-19th C, 4-3/4" h, 4-3/8" d rim **$660**

Free-blown, cobalt blue, domed cov, galleried rim, ftd, eastern United States, early 19th C, 5-3/4" h.. **$1,500**

Translucent blood red bowl and stem, swirled grass green and red foot and cover, bowl slightly compressed bulbous form, galleried rim, wafer attached to hollow knop stem, lower wafer, circular foot with slight red swirls, strongly swirled boldly domed cover with applied mushroom type finial, rough pontil on both base and cov, possibly New England, mid-19th C, rim chip and flake on bowl, 8-1/4" h, 4-1/4" d, rim, 3-3/4" d foot.................... **$880**

Toddy plate, Lee-Rose No. 802, fiery opalescent alabaster, 76 even scallops, rim chip, 1830-45, 4-1/4" d....... **$110**

Tumbler

Blown molded, taper, colorless, rayed base, rough pontil mark, probably Boston & Sandwich Glass Co., McKearin GII-19, 1825-35, 2-1/2" h, 2-3/8" d rim, 1-3/4" d base **$165**

Blown molded, cylindrical, colorless, rayed base, rough pontil mark, probably Boston & Sandwich Glass Co., McKearin GV-4, 1825-35, 3-3/8" h, 2-7/8" d.................... **$275**

Nine-panel, brilliant teal, panels arched at top, American, probably New England, mid-19th C, 3-1/2" h, 3-3/8" d rim **$615**

Eight panel, ftd, translucent light starch blue, alabaster surface, third quarter 19th C, 4-1/2" h............**$80**

Twine holder, Punty, deep red overlay cut to clear, orig metal reinforcement ring, probably New England, c1875, 4-1/4" h, 4" d.............................. **$150**

Vase, free-blown

Bright grass green, opal loopings, Marbrie, baluster, applied circular foot, rough pontil mark, South Jersey, second half 19th C, 7-1/2" h, 3-3/4" d rim, 2-3/4" foot **$550**

Colorless body, opal loopings, Marbrie, rolled over rim, applied triple shoulder ring, colorless applied solid stem, circular foot, rough pontil mark, Pittsburgh or New Jersey, mid-19th C, 11" h, 4" d rim, 4-1/4" d foot......................... **$1,155**

Medium amethyst, trumpet, applied waist ring, solid plain stem, circular foot, faint pontil mark, second half 19th C, 11-1/2" h, 5" d rim, 3-3/4" d foot............................ **$220**

Water jug, blown molded, colorless, applied hollow handle, light horizontal rings, rayed base, rough pontil mark, Boston & Sandwich Glass Co., McKearin GV-17, 1825-35, 8-1/4" h, 5" d rim, 4" d base **$3,100**

Window pane, Gothic Arch, colorless, six individual arches, scrolls, and rosettes above, faintly sgd "Bakewell" on reverse, Pittsburgh Flint Glass Manufactory of Benjamin Bakewell,

broken into two pcs, several edge chips, 1830-45, 4-7/8" x 6-7/8" **$1,100**

Wine glass, blown molded, colorless, button stem, rough pontil mark, possibly Boston & Sandwich Glass Co., 1820-40, McKearin GII-19, small flake, 3-1/4" h, 2" d.................... **$210**

Wine glass, free-blown

Colorless, blown ogee bowl with basal molding, fine enamel twist stem with single white opaque enamel ribbon central twist column, wide conical foot, rough pontil mark, third quarter 18th C, 5-3/4" h **$475**

Colorless, blown twisted bowl, multiple spiral air twist stem, wide conical foot, rough pontil mark, mid-18th C, 6-3/4" h.............. **$500**

Colorless, plain pointed bowl with shoulder, angular knop stem, conical foot with faint pontil mark, mid-18th C, 6" h.................... **$420**

Witch ball and stand, free-blown, aquamarine, trumpet vase form stand with applied threading, circular foot with four point rough pontil mark, ball with rough open pontil mark, mid-19th C, 4-3/4" d ball, 7-1/2" h, 4-7/8" d stand **$450**

FENTON GLASS

History: The Fenton Art Glass company was founded in 1905 and celebrated the centennial of its founding in 2005—a milestone for the American glass-making industry, as Fenton is the oldest continuously running American glass company.

The company produced its first piece of glass in 1907. Early production included carnival, chocolate, custard, and pressed glass, plus mold-blown opalescent glass.

In the 1920s, stretch glass and colors of jade green, ruby, and other art glass were added. In the 1930s, boudoir lamps and slag glass in various colors were produced. The 1940s saw crests of different colors being added to each piece by hand. Hobnail, opalescent, and two-color overlay pieces were popular items.

Handles were added to different shapes to make Fenton baskets, which are identified by the handler's mark at the point where the handle attaches to the basket. Each of these marks is unique to a given Fenton handler, adding to the hand-made charm of these items.

Through the years, Fenton has beautified its glass by decorating it with hand painting, acid etching, and copper-wheel cutting. Today, collectors are especially interested in cranberry opalescent glass, topaz (vaseline) opalescent, Burmese, and Rosalene (an opaque pink glass with colors shaded more deeply toward the edges). Hand-painting on these treatments is especially sought. Items decorated at the factory are usually signed by the painters who worked on them (one means of distinguishing Fenton-decorated pieces from those decorated later by someone outside the company).

Fenton has something for everyone and for every price point, which is one of the factors accounting for its customer loyalty over the last century. People whose purses or living spaces will not accommodate larger pieces have made Fenton's whimsical animal figurines very popular—so much so that these are seldom seen on the secondary market. High-end collectors are particularly interested in items made for the Connoisseur Series, which includes the best—and most expensive—art glass treatments in the Fenton line.

Historically, marks have consisted of various iterations of paper labels, many of which do not permanently adhere. Collectors rely on shapes, glass colors, and decorator signatures to identify older Fenton items. In 1970, the company began to mark its pieces with an embossed company name inside an oval. The numbers 8, 9, and 0 were added under the name for items produced in the decade of the 1980s, 1990s, and 2000s respectively. Burmese and other satin glass doesn't "take" the embossed logo very well and items made in the 70s and later often have the logo barely visible in the glass. Because of this problem, Fenton recently began adding a scripted green "F" stamp to the base of such treatments. The latest sticker mark includes the legend "100 years."

Fenton "seconds" are usually identified by an acid-etched stencil-style "F" on the bottom. This mark can be difficult to see without tilting the item to the proper light. As with many "seconds" produced by companies of quality, it will often be unclear why the piece was rejected as a first-quality item. Nevertheless, these items are considered, for collecting purposes, to be not as valuable as first-quality items.

Adviser: Peggy Whiteneck

Fenton, Amethyst Snow Crest four-horn epergne in Threaded Optic, 1940s, made for L.G. Wright, 17" h, $800.

Fenton, ruby handled bonbon in Hobnail, mid-1970s, 8" d, $35.

Fenton, black (Ebony) fan vase, with thistles in an encrusted pattern done by Lotus Glass Decorating Co., Barnsville, Ohio, 1926, 8" h, $250.

Bell, General Issue

1127se, Magnolia And Berry On Spruce, 1997, 6-1/2" **$40**

1145dx, Trellis On French Opalescent, 1999, 6-1/2" **$45**

3645rn, Red Carnival, 1993, 5-1/2" **$30**

3645rv, Rose Magnolia Hobnail, 1993, 5-1/2" **$25**

3645xc, Persian Blue Opalescent, 1989 .... **$25**

6761ru, Paisley, Ruby, 1997, 7" **$35**

8267bc, Medallion, Bluebirds On Custard, 1977 .... **$45**

8267rc, Medallion, Roses On Custard, 1978 .... **$40**

8267ru, Medallion, White Roses On Ruby, 1979 .... **$40**

8465cb, Threaded Diamond-Optic With Diamond Handle, Colonial Blue, 1977 .... **$30**

8465wt, Threaded Diamond Optic with Diamond Handle, Wisteria, 1977 .... **$45**

8466re, Faberge, Rosalene, 1976 **$55**

8467ch, Patriots In Chocolate Glass (Bicentennial), 1974 .... **$45**

8467ib, Patriots In Independence Blue (Bicentennial), 1974 .... **$45**

8467pr, Patriots In Patriot Red (Bicentennial), 1974 .... **$45**

8467vw, Patriots In Valley Forge White, 1974 .... **$30**

Basket

1925ic, Ivory Crest, 1940, 7", ... **$125**

3834rp, Rose Pastel Hobnail, 1954, 4-1/2" **$55**

3837cr, Cranberry Opalescent Hobnail, 1940, 7" **$110**

3837rp, Rose Pastel Hobnail, 1954 **$75**

3839po, Oval, Plum Opalescent, 1959, 12" **$400**

7237bl, Blue Roses On Blue Satin, 1978, 7" **$65**

7237ec, Ebony Crest, 1968, 7" .. **$175**

7437bc, Bluebirds On Custard, 1977, 8" **$75**

8435re, Threaded, Rosalene, 1976, 7" **$125**

9138ba, Poppy, Blue Satin, 1973, 7" **$65**

9138rs, Poppy, Rose Satin, 1974, 7" **$125**

9235mb, Roses In Blue Marble, 1970, 9" **$75**

Bowl

8520bb, Sculptured Ice Optic, Glacial Blue, 1982, 12" **$50**

9425io, Tibbon Edge, Aqua Blue Carnival, (Made For Levay), 1980, 8" **$85**

K7722kn, Medium Flared, Banded Color (Katja), 1983.................... **$65**

K7724ko, Flame Band (Katja), 1983, 9-3/4" **$75**

R9426ru, Faberge, Ribbed, Ruby (Made For A.L. Randall Co.), 1982 .... **$30**

R9430gs, Water Lily, Green (Made For A.L. Randall Co.), 1982, 6" **$35**

R9430ru, Faberge, Ribbed, Ruby, 1982, 6" **$35**

Box, Hen On Nest

5182cn, Large, Original (Amethyst) Carnival, 1970........................... **$95**

5182mb, Large, Blue Marble, 1971 .... **$125**

5186cn, Original (Amethyst) Carnival, 1970 .... **$65**

5186cu, Custard Satin, 1971 .... **$45**

5186ls, Lime Sherbet Satin, 1973. **$50**

5186mb, Blue Marble, 1971........ **$75**

Candleholder

3870cr, Handled, Cranberry Opalescent Hobnail, 1953 .... **$80 Pr**

3874bo, Cornucopia, Blue Opalescent Hobnail, 1943 .... **$70 Pr**

3971bo, Mini Cornucopia, Blue Opalescent Hobnail, 1943............ **$50 Pr**

Comport

3522dv, Footed, Spanish Lace, Violets In The Snow, 1971.................... **$65**

3522sc, Spanish Lace In Silver Crest, 1975 .... **$45**

3728po, Footed, Plum Opalescent, 1959... **$85**

3731go, Footed, Green Opalescent Hobnail, 1959 .... **$125**

3731mb, Footed, Blue Marble Hobnail, 1978 .... **$75**

3920gp, Footed, Green Pastel Hobnail, 1954 .... **$60**

3920mi, Footed, Milk Glass Hobnail, 1970... **$25**

628bo, Flloted, Blue Opalescent Hobnail, 6" 1941 .... **$50**

7329ab, Low Footed, Apple Blossom On Silver Crest, 1969 .... **$50**

7429dc, Footed, Daisies On Custard, 1970... **$50**

7429eg, Rose Garden On Opal Satin, 1975 .... **$75**

7429sc, Silver Crest, 1961 .... **$40**

7429sf, Strawberries On French Opalescent, 1997 .... **$40**

Creamer

1461bo, Blue Opalescent Coin Dot, 1948, 5" **$55**

1461cr, Cranberry Coin Dot, 1948, 5" **$65**

1924ac, Aqua Crest, 1942, 5" **$50**

1924pc, Peach Crest, 1942, 5" **$50**

1924rc, Rose Crest, 1946, 5" **$50**

1924sc, Silver Crest, 1947, 5" ...**$35**

3901to, Topaz Opalescent Hobnail, 1941 ....**$50**

7261ec, Emerald Crest, 1949 ......**$50**

Cruet With Stopper

3863bo, Round, Blue Opalescent Hobnnail, 1941 .... **$125**

3863cr, Round, Cranberry Opalescent Hobnail, 1941 .... **$145**

3869cr, Oil (Straight Sides), Cranberry Opalescent Hobnail, 1949 .... **$125**

3869fo, Oil (Straight Sides), French Opalescent Hobnail, 1942.........**$40**

3869to, Oil (Straight Sides), Topaz Opalescent Hobnail, 1942.........**$95**

Epergne

1522ic, 1-Horn, 4-Piece (includes base), Ivory Crest, 1940 .... **$175**

1948bo, 3-Horn, Blue Opalescent With Silver Crest, 1948, 12" bowl, ...**$225**

1948fo, 3-Horn, French Opalescent With Aqua Crest, 1948, 12" bowl **$200**

3800mi, 4-Horn, Milk Glass Hobnail, 1954 .... **$150**

3801bo, 3-Horn, Miniature, Blue Opalescent Hobnail, 1949...... **$145**

3801fo, 3-Horn, Miniature, French Opalescent Hobnail, 1949.........**$85**

3801go, 3-Horn, Miniature, Green Opalescent Hobnail, 1959...... **$175**

3801gp, 3-Horn, Miniature, Green Pastel Hobnail, 1954 .... **$125**

3801mi, 3-Horn, Miniature, Milk Glass Hobnail, 1950 ....**$55**

Fairy Light

5108ba, Owl In Blue Satin, 1975 .**$45**

5108cs, Owl In Custard Satin, 1975 ....**$35**

5108ls, Owl In Lime Sherbet Satin, 1975 ....**$40**

5108re, Owl In Rosalene, 1976....**$55**

5406re, Heart In Rosalene, 1976 .**$75**

7300by, Butterflies On White Milk Glass, 1977 ....**$45**

7300cv, Christmas Morn, 1978....**$65**

7300cw, Cardinals In Winter, 1977 ....**$55**

7392db, One-Piece, Autumn Leaves Transfer On Burmese, 1970... **$165**

7492db, Two-Piece, Autumn Leaves Transfer On Burmese, 1972... **$150**

Figurine

Angel

Praying Boy, 5113rn, Berries & Blossoms, 1985 ....**$75**

Praying Girl, 5114ns, Natural Series, 1985..**$65**

Praying Girl, 5114rk, Berries & Blossoms, 1985 ....**$75**

Bird

5163bd, Blue Dogwood On Cameo Satin, 1980 ....**$45**

Happiness, 5197ba, Blue Satin, 1978 ....**$45**

Happiness, 5197bc, Bluebirds On Custard, 1977..............................**$50**

Bunny

5162bd, Blue Dogwood On Cameo Satin, 1980 ....**$55**

5162bj, Pekin Blue, 1980.............**$45**

5162cd, Daisies On Custard, 1978 ....**$45**

5162dv, Violets In The Snow, 1978 ....**$75**

5162ja, Jade Green, 1980.............**$50**

Butterfly On Stand, Wings Open 5171dk, Dusty Rose, 1986 ....**$45**

Cat

5165dv, Violets In The Snow, 1979 ....**$55**

5165ws, White Satin, 1971...........**$55**

Happy 5277br, Burmese (Made In Both Satin And Gloss), 1966 ....**$95**

Doll, "Almost Heaven" Blue Slag (Sold Through Fenton Gift Shop), 1985 ....**$65**

Fawn

5160br, Burmese, 1986.................**$95**

5160ub, Blue Burmese, 1984 .... **$125**

Frog

5166dv, Violets In The Snow, 1979 .... **$175**

5166ls, Lime Sherbet, 1979..........**$65**

Kitten, 5119rk, Berries & Blossoms, 1984 ....**$75**

Mouse, 5148dc, Daisies On Custard, 1978 ....**$40**

Owl, 5158fn, Favrene, 6, 1993. **$125**

Pig, 5220ws, White Satin, 1972..**$65**

Puppies, 5159sp, Cocker Spaniels, Natural Series, 1985 ....**$65**

Rabbit, 5178cn, Original (Amethyst) Carnival, 1971...........................**$75**

Slipper, Cat, 3995bj, Pekin Blue Hobnail, 1968 ....**$25**

Snail, 5135re, Rosalene, 1993.....**$65**

Swan

5161dc, Daisies On Cameo Satin, 1978 ....**$50**

5161ln, Lavender Satin, 1977 ......**$65**

5161py, Pink Blossom On Custard, 1978 ....**$50**

5161re, Rosalene, 1978 ....**$75**

Hat

1492bo, Coin Dot In Blue Opalescent, 1948..**$55**

1492cr, Coin Dot In Cranberry Opalescent, 1948 ....**$65**

1492fo, French Opalescent, 1948 ....**$45**

1492lo, Lime Opalescent, 1952....**$75**

1492xc, Persian Blue Opalescent, 1989..**$35**

1920bo, Stiegel Blue Spiral Optic, 1939, 12" **$325**

1920cr, Cranberry Spiral Optic, 1938, 12" **$400**

1920fo, French Opalescent Spiral Optic, 1939, 12" **$150**

1920go, Green Opalescent Spiral Optic, 1939, 12" **$300**

1920to, Topaz Opalescent Spiral Optic, 1940, 12" **$325**

1921bi, Blue Ridge (Early), 1939, 10" **$250**

1921bo, Stiegel Blue Spiral Optic, 1939, 10" **$250**

1921cr, Cranberry Spiral Optic, 1938, 10" **$350**

1921go, Green Opalescent Spiral Optic, 1939, 10" **$265**

1921go, Green Opalescent Spiral Optic, (Made In Both Crimp And Straight Edge), 1939, 9" **$225**

1923bo, Stiegel Blue Spiral Optic, 1939, 6" **$60**

1923cr, Cranberry Spiral Optic, 1938, 6"..**$95**

1923ic, Ivory Crest, 1940, 6".......**$50**

1923pc, Peach Crest, 1940, 7" **$65**

Jar, Candy

Covered 6688uo, Peaches 'N Cream Opalescent, 1986 ....**$45**

Covered 7380wd, Footed, White Daisies On Ebony, 1973 ....**$75**

Covered 8489bx, Sapphire Blue Opalescent, 1990, 7" **$45**

Pitcher (aka "Jug")

2060cc, Feather In Country Cranberry, 1982, 70 oz. **$150**

2664bi, Blue Ridge, 9" 1985 ...... **$145**

3664cr, With Ice Lip, Cranberry Opalescent Hobnail, 70 oz., 1965 .. **$275**

3664mi, Milk Glass Hobnail, 70 oz., 1987 ....**$55**

3664po, Plum Opalescent with Ice Lip (Made For Levay), 1984, 70 oz **$200**

3762go, Syrup, Green Opalescent Hobnail, 1959 ....**$85**

3764rv, Rose Magnolia Hobnail, 1940, 54 oz. **$250**

3964bo, Blue Opalescent Hobnail, 1941, 4-1/2" **$45**

3965bo, Blue Opalescent Hobnail, 1940, 32 oz...............................**$85**

Plate, Designer Series

7418fv, Down Home On Custard, (Designer: Finn), 1983, 8" **$75**

7418hf, In Season (Hunter), (Designer: Dickinson), 1985, 8" **$95**

7418lt, Lighthouse Point On Custard Satin, (Designer: Dickinson), 1983, 8" **$75**

7618ee, Majestic Flight (Eagle) On White Satin (Designer: Cumberledge), 1984 ....**$85**

7618tl, Smoke And Cinders On White Satin (Designer: Dickinson), 1984 ....**$95**

Fenton, Peach Crest melon-form vase, with Charleton decoration by Abels, Wasserberg of New York, mid-1950s, 5-1/2" h, **$75.**

Fenton, vase, mosaic, two handled, cylindrical, amethyst iridescent glass, amethyst threading, red and yellow oil spots, 1926 catalogue #32006, 11" h, **$2,300.**
Photo courtesy of The Early Auction Company, LLC.

8011le, Sandcarved Statue Of Liberty On Crystal, 1985, 9" **$60**

Punchbowl Set

3712go, 14-Piece, Green Opalescent Hobnail, 1985 ....**$475**

3712xc, 14-Piece, Persian Blue Opalescent Hobnail, 1989 ....**$400**

A3712uo, 14-Piece, Peaches 'N Cream Hobnail, 1988 ....**$325**

Vase

1353xc, Tulip, Fine Dot Optic In Persian Blue Opalescent, 1989, 10" **$75**

1354cr, Cranberry Dot Optic, 1982, 7" **$75**

1824cc, Fern In Country Cranberry, 1982, 4-1/2" **$50**

1850oh, Heritage Green Overlay, 1983, 7-1/2" **$45**

3551dv, Spanish Lace, Violets In The Snow, 1974, 8" **$65**

3752cr, Cranberry Opalescent Hobnail, 1941 ....**$225**

3759go, Swung, Green Opalescent Hobnail, 1959, 18" **$200**

3759mi, Swung, Milk Glass Hobnail, 1959, 18" **$50**

5750dk, Dusty Rose, 1982, 9" **$30**

6854iu, Aurora, Americana With Blue Crest, 7-1/2" (Family Signature, Mike Fenton), 1982 ....**$90**

7051wa, Spiral Ribbed, Rosebuds On Rosalene, 1982, 6" **$125**

7241ba, Blue Satin, 1982, 4-1/2" **$25**

7241vi, Vintage On Cameo Satin, 1980, 4-1/2" **$30**

7252bd, Blue Dogwood On Cameo Satin, 1976, 7" **$45**

7252qh, Raspberry Burmese, (Connoisseur), 1983, 7-1/2" **$175**

7252xa, Clydesdales, (Made For Budweiser), 1977, 7" **$300**

7257bc, Bluebirds On Custard, 1977, 10" **$75**

7554bq, Blue Roses On Custard Satin, 1981, 5" **$45**

7557in, Iris On Bone White, 1982, 9" **$65**

7557ja, Jade, 1980, 10" **$50**

7557pe, Silver Poppies On Ebony, 1981, 9-1/2" **$50**

8251hu, Mandarin, Blue On Cameo Satin, 1982, 9" **$150**

8251ja, Mandarin, Jade Green, 1980 ....**$75**

8252hu, Empress, Blue On Cameo Satin, 1982 ....**$85**

8452re, Fan, Rosalene, 1976 .....**$225**

8455vy, Diamond And Thread, Purple Stretch (Made For Levay), 1981 ..**$60**

8458bo, Bud, Blue Opalescent Hobnail, 1981, 11" **$35**

8956ci, Hanging Hearts In Custard, (Robert Barber Collection), 1976, 6" **$150**

8958ci, Pinch, Hanging Hearts In Custard, (Robert Barber Collection), 1976, 8" **$165**

8958th, Pinch, Hanging Hearts In Turquoise, (Robert Barber), 1975, 8" **$175**

9054ja, Bud, Jade Green, 1980 .....**$25**

9054rd, Bud, Roses On Ruby, 1981 ...**$30**

9055br, Ribbed Burmese, 1971, 5" **$135**

9056bd, Bud, Blue Dogwood On Cameo Satin, 1980 ....**$25**

Water Set (Pitcher With Glasses)

3407io, 7-Piece, Cactus In Aqua Opal Carnival (Made For Levay), 1980 ....**$400**

3407rn, 7-Piece With Goblets, Red Sunset Carnival (Made For Levay), 1982 ....**$350**

FOSTORIA GLASS

History: Fostoria Glass Co. began operations at Fostoria, Ohio, in 1887, and moved to Moundsville, West Virginia, its present location, in 1891. By 1925, Fostoria had five furnaces and a variety of special shops. In 1924, a line of colored tableware was introduced. Fostoria was purchased by Lancaster Colony in 1983.

Ashtray

American, 2-7/8" sq **$7.50**

Coin, crystal **$30**

June, blue **$75**

Baker, June, topaz, oval, 9" **$195**

Bell, Chintz, orig label **$130**

Berry bowl, June, blue, 5" d **$50**

Bonbon, Bridal Wreath, #2630 Century, cut 833, three toes **$75**

Bouillon, Versailles, topaz **$30**

Bowl

American, oval, 10" l **$30**

Baroque, blue, 4" sq, one handle .**$22**

Corsage, flared, 12" d **$110**

Grape Leaf, green, 12" d **$175**

June, 12" d, blue **$125**

Bread and butter plate, Trojan, topaz, 6" d **$10**

Cake salver
Century, crystal............................**$60**
Coin, crystal................................**$98**
Corsage, 10-1/2" d **$32**
Navarre, crystal, handles, 10" d ...**$60**

Candleholders, pr
Baroque, one-lite, silver deposit Vintage dec on base, 4" h, #2496 ...**$75**
Baroque, two-lite, removable bobeche and prisms, 8-1/2" h, 10" w, #2484 ....**$375**
Buttercup, 5-1/2" h, #2594, etch 340 ....**$250**
Coin, red, tall **$150**
Meadow Rose..............................**$185**
Trojan, topaz, 2", #2394, etch 280 **$145**
Trindle, #2594, three-lite, Buttercup etch, 8" h, 6-1/2" w **$250**

Candy dish, cov
Baroque, crystal...........................**$40**
June, yellow **$370**
Navarre, three parts....................**$175**
Versailles, blue, three parts........**$345**

Card tray, Brocaded Daffodil, two handles, pink, gold trim................**$40**

Celery tray, Trojan, topaz **$100**

Cereal bowl, June, rose, 6" d **$85**

Champagne
Bridal Wreath, #6051, cut 833 ....**$35**
Buttercup, #6030, etch 340 ....**$32**
Corsage, #6014, etch 325 ....**$32**
Dolley Madison...........................**$18**
June, saucer, petal stem...............**$27**
Versailles, pink............................**$40**

Cheese and cracker
Chintz **$70**
Colony **$55**

Cigarette box, cov
Cigarette set, Baroque, azure, #2496, five pcs **$450**
Morning Glory etching **$65**
Oriental **$170**

Claret
Bridal Wreath, #6051, cut 833 ....**$38**
Camelia **$30**
June, pink **$175**
Navarre **$80**
Trojan, yellow, 6" h **$100**

Cocktail
Baroque, yellow **$15**
Vesper, amber **$30**

Compote
Baroque, crystal, 6" **$18**
Corsage, #2496 Baroque, etch 325 ....**$75**
Trojan, topaz, #2400, etch 280 ....**$85**

Condiment set, American, pr salt and pepper shakers, pr, cloverleaf tray, pr cruets.........................**$200**

Console set, Baroque, azure, #2496, pr candlesticks, 10-1/2" d bowl........**$300**

Fostoria, American pattern, 8" deep, **$50.**

Cordial, Dolley Madison **$30**
Cosmetic box, cov, American, flake on bottom, 2-1/2" d..................**$900**
Courting lamp, Coin, amber ... **$150**

Creamer, individual size
Bridal Wreath, #2630 Century, cut 833 ....**$30**
Century **$9**
Raleigh **$8**

Creamer, table size
Baroque, azure, #2496..................**$55**
Chintz **$20**
Raleigh **$10**
Trojan, topaz **$22**

Creamer, sugar, tray, individual size
Camelia **$45**
Century **$30**

Cream soup
Colony **$95**
Versailles, pink............................**$65**
Vesper, amber **$30**

Cruet, June, yellow **$700**

Crushed fruit jar, cov, America, c1915-25, 5-7/8" d, 6" h.......... **$1,600**

Cup and saucer
Baroque, blue **$35**
Buttercup....................................**$34**
Camelia **$20**
June, azure **$45**
Minuet, green **$55**
Trojan, topaz, #2375 Fairfax, etch 280 ....**$40**

Decanter, orig stopper, Hermitage, amber, #2449 .... **$125**

Dinner plate
Versailles, pink, slight use............**$75**
Vesper, amber **$30**

Figure
Deer, standing, crystal, 4-1/2" h ...**$45**
Lute and Lotus, ebony, gold highlights, price for pr, 12-1/2" h . **$975**
Mermaid, crystal, 10-3/8" h **$225**

Fruit cocktail, Hermitage, topaz, #2449 ....**$22**

Goblet, water
Baroque, azure, #2496.................**$45**
Bouquet, crystal, #6033, etch 342 **$35**

Fostoria, Coin, red candy dish with cover, **$70.**

Buttercup, #6030, etch 340 ....**$40**
Dolley Madison............................**$20**
Golden Lace, gold trim **$24**
Meadow Rose **$30**
Navarre **$40**
Trojan, topaz **$75**

Grapefruit, Coronet.....................**$9**

Gravy boat, liner, Kasmir, blue **$180**

Ice bucket, Versailles, pink **$155**

Iced-tea tumbler
Bouquet, crystal, #6033, etch 342 **$35**
Navarre, pink **$75**

Jelly, cov
Coin, amber **$30**
Meadow Rose, 7-1/2" d **$90**

Jug
Hermitage, green, #2449, three pints **$145**
Manor, #4020, wisteria foot ... **$1,500**
Trojan, topaz, #5000, etch 280.. **$600**

Juice tumbler, June, topaz, ftd ...**$30**

Lily pond, Buttercup, 12" d **$55**

Marmalade, cov, American **$125**

Mayonnaise
Baroque, azure, #2496.................**$95**
Bouquet, #2360 Century, etch 342 ....**$110**
Buttercup....................................**$90**
Navarre **$90**

Milk pitcher, Century **$60**

Mint, Baroque, azure, #2496, handle, 4" d..**$48**

Nappy, handle
Baroque, azure, #2496.................**$48**
Coin, blue, 5-3/8" d **$30**

Nut cup, Fairfax, amber **$15**

Oil cruet, Versailles, yellow **$550**

Old-fashioned tumbler, Hermitage, azure **$35**

Olive, Hermitage, amber, #2449 ...**$32**

Oyster cocktail, Hermitage, amber, #2449 ....**$18**

Parfait, June, pink...................... **$180**

Pickle castor, American, ornate silver plated frame, 11" h **$900**

Pickle tray, Century, 8-3/4".........**$15**

Pitcher, Lido, ftd.......................**$225**

Plate

Baroque, green, 7-1/2" d **$28**

Century, 9-1/2" d **$30**

Corsage, etch 325, 8" d **$22**

Rose, 9" d **$15**

Platter

June, topaz, oval,12" l **$145**

Trojan, topaz, oval, 12" l **$80**

Punch bowl, ftd, Baroque, crystal, orig label **$425**

Relish dish, cov, Brocaded Summer Gardens, three sections, white **$75**

Relish dish, open

Corsage, three parts, #2496, Baroque, etch 325 .... **$75**

June, topaz, two parts, 8-1/4" l **$40**

Ring holder, American, 4-1/2" l, 3" h **$800**

Rose bowl, American, small **$18**

Salad plate, Buttercup **$12**

Salt and pepper shakers, pr

Bridal Wreath, #2630 Century, cut 833, chrome tops **$95**

Coin, red **$60**

Coronet **$15**

Versailles, topaz, ftd **$200**

Sauce boat, Versailles, pink, matching liner **$300**

Server, center handle, Trojan, topaz, etch 280 .... **$135**

Sherbet

Baroque, azure, #2496 .... **$45**

Buttercup, #6030, etch 340 .... **$32**

Hermitage, green, #2449 .... **$22**

June, azure **$40**

Trojan, topaz, #5099, etch 280 ....**$48**

Snack plate, Century, 8" d **$25**

Sugar, individual size, Baroque, blue **$4**

Sugar, cov, table size, Trojan, topaz **$22**

Syrup, American, Bakelite handle **$200**

Sweetmeat, Baroque, azure, #2496 .... **$58**

Torte plate

Baroque, azure, #2496, 14" d **$125**

Colony, 15" d **$80**

Heather, 13" d **$45**

Tray, Navarre, 8" l **$100**

Tumbler, water

Hermitage, topaz, #2449 .... **$30**

June, ftd **$55**

Trojan, topaz, 5 oz, 4-1/2" h **$30**

Urn, cov, Coin, amber, 12-3/4" h ..**$68**

Vase

Baroque, azure, #2496, 8" h **$225**

Flying Fish, teal, 7" h **$65**

Hermitage, topaz, #2449, 6" h **$45**

Oak Leaf Brocade, c1929-31, 8" h **$240**

Versailles, yellow, flip, 8" h **$395**

Whipped-cream pail, Versailles, blue **$270**

Whiskey, Hermitage, topaz, #2449 .... **$20**

Wine

Buttercup, #6030, etch 340 .... **$45**

Chintz **$40**

Coin, red **$90**

Corsage, #6014, etch 325 .... **$45**

Hermitage, amber, #2449 .... **$20**

FRUIT JARS

Fruit jar, Flaccus Bros., steer's head, amber, matching reproduction lid, RB 1014, **$220.**

Photo courtesy of American Bottle Auctions.

Fruit jar, Star and crescent, self-sealing jar, embossed star and crescent moon, pint, ground lip, **$450.**

Photo courtesy of American Bottle Auctions.

History: Fruit jars are canning jars used to preserve food. Thomas W. Dyott, one of Philadelphia's earliest and most innovative glassmakers, was promoting his glass canning jars in 1829. John Landis Mason patented his screw-type canning jar on November 30, 1858. This date refers to the patent date, not the age of the jar. There are thousands of different jars and a variety of colors, types of closures, sizes, and embossings.

Collectors refer to fruit jars by the numbering system "RB," which was established by Douglas M. Leybourne, Jr. in his book, *The Collector's Guide to Old Fruit Jars, Red Book 9.*

A. & D. H. Chambers Union, quart, yellow, olive green tint, applied groove ring wax sealer, tin lid mkd "A. & D. H. Chambers Pittsburgh, Pa (five-point star in center)," wire yoke, 7-5/8" h, 3-3/4" d base, RB 582 .... **$990**

A. Stone & Co. (arched), Philada Manufactured by Cunningham & Co. Pittsburgh PA" (on five lines), half gallon, aqua, high kick up, bare iron pontil mark, applied lip groove ring wax sealer, 9-3/4" h, 4-1/2" d base, RB 2752 .... **$1,320**

All Right

Half gallon, aqua, reverse mkd "Patd Jan. 28th 1868," base mkd "Pat Nov 26 1867," ground lip, unmarked metal dome shaped lid, wire clamp, two rim chips, 7-1/4" h, 4-1/2" d base, RB 61-3 ....**$90**

Quart, aqua, reverse mkd "Patd Jan 26th 1868," base mkd "PAT Nov 26 1867" and "12" in center, ground lip, unmarked metal dome shaped

lid, wire clamp, 7-3/4" h, 3-3/4" d base, RB 59 .... **$110**

Almy (arched), quart, aqua, base mkd "Patented Dec 25, 1877 (star)" and "B," lid mkd "C," ground lip, Mason shoulder seal, glass screw-on lid, chips on lid, 7-1/8" h, 3-7/8" d base, RB 63 .... **$100**

Banner (encircled by), Patd Feby 9th 1864 Reisd Jan 22D 1867," quart, aqua, ground lip, press-down glass lid, neck indentation in rear, several rim flakes, 7-1/2" h, 3-3/4" d base, RB 403 .... **$135**

Beaver, facing right, chewing log, over word "Beaver," midget pint, Ball blue, base mkd "3," unmarked glass insert and screw band, stippled tail, 5-5/8" h, 3-1/4" d base **$385**

Bloeser Jar, quart, aqua, ground rim, glass lid mkd "Pat Sept 27, 1887," orig wire and metal clamp with necktie wire, rim chip, 8" h, 3-3/4" d, RB 468 ....**$90**

Cohansey Glass Mf'g Co., Pat Mar 20. 77 (on base), half gallon, aqua, barrel shape, base also mkd "3," glass lid mkd "Cohansey Glass Mfg Co., Philada. PA," and "Y" in center, groove ring wax sealer, roughness, bruise on lid rim, 9-1/8" h, 4" d base, RB 633-1 ....**$70**

Cunningham & Co., Pittsburgh (on base), half gallon, deep aqua, bottom push up, bare iron pontil mark, applied lip to receive cork stopper, 9-3/4" h, 4-5/8" d base, RB 721 .. **$310**

Eagle

Half gallon, aqua, unmarked glass lid, iron yoke clamp with six-pointed star-shape thumbscrew, applied lip, 10" h, 4-1/2" d base, RB 872 .. **$110**

Quart, aqua, applied smooth lip, fabricated closure, 7-5/8" h, 3-7/8" d base, RB 871 ....**$90**

F & J Bodine Manufacturers, Philadelphia PA, quart, aqua, unmarked tin lid, soldered wire clamp, small open bubble under base edge, 7-1/8" h, 3-7/8" d base, RB 374 ...**$70**

Fahnestock Albree & Co., quart, dark aqua, pushed up bottom, pontil mark, Willoughby stopple mkd "J. O. Willoughby Patented, January 4, 1859," replaced wing nut, surface wear, 8-1/2" h, 3-3/4" d base, RB 970 .... **$360**

Gem, three gallon, aqua, reverse mkd "Manufactured by The Hero Glass Works, Philadelphia PA," ground lip, glass insert mkd "Pat. Feb 12. 56. Dec 17.61. Nov 4.62. Dec 6.94, June 9.68. Sept 1.68. Sep 8.68. Dec.22.68. Jan 9 69," screw band, 17-5/8" h, 8-3/8" d base, RB 1058.......................... **$3,575**

Glass Pail, one-half pint, teal, base mkd "Glass Pail Pat. Boston Mass June 24. 84," unmarked metal two pc lid with bail handle, 4-1/2" h overall, 3" d base, RB 20 .... **$525**

Globe, quart, red amber, base mkd "65," ground lip, red amber glass lid mkd "Patented May 15 1886," iron clamp and metal band around neck, 8-1/8" h, 3-3/4" d base, RB 1123 .... **$135**

Griffen's, Patent Oct 7 1862 (on lid), quart, amber, ground lip, glass lid with cage-like clamp, rim chip and flake, 7" h, 3-3/4" d base, RB 1154 ....**$70**

Hansee's, (PH monogram) Palace Home Jar, quart, clear, base mkd "Pat. Dec 19 1899," ground lip, monogrammed glass lid, wire clamp and

neck tire wire, edge chips and flakes, 7-1/2" h, 3-3/4" d base, RB 1206 ....**$50**

Johnson & Johnson, New York (vertically), quart, cobalt blue, ground lip, cobalt lid, screw band, 7-1/8" h, 3-3/8" sq base, RB 1344 .... **$360**

Joshua Wright Philada, half gallon, aqua, barrel shape, applied lip, 10-1/2" h, 3-3/4" d base, RB 3036 variant... **$180**

Lafayette (in script, underlined), quart, aqua, base mkd "2," stopper neck finish three-pc glass and metal stopper, mkd "Patented Sept 2 1884 Aug 4 1885," 8-1/2" h, 3-5/8" d, RB 1452... **$110**

Mansfield

Pint, clear, base mkd "Mansfield Knowlton May '03 Pat. Glass W'K'S," and "2" in circle, glass lid, metal screw cap, light 1/4" crack, lid mkd "Mansfield Glass W'ks Knowlton Pat. May .03," 5-1/8" h, 3-1/8" d base, RB 1619 ....**$15**

Quart, clear with light aqua tint, base mkd "Mansfield Knowlton May '03 Pat. Glass W'K'S," glass lid, metal screw cap, lid mkd "Mansfield Glass W'ks Knowlton Pat. May .03," rim flake, 7" h, 3-5/8" d base, RB 1619 ....**$80**

Mansfield Improved Mason, quart, lavender tint, glass insert, screw band, rim flake, 7" h, B 1621 variant.....**$60**

Mason's (cross) Patent Nov. 30th 1858, (erased The Pearl), gallon, dark aqua, ground lip, Mason shoulder seal, plain zinc lid, rim flakes, 12" h, 5-7/8" d base, RB 1943 **$1,100**

Mason's CFJCO Improved, half gallon, amber, base mkd "H43," ground lip, amber insert mkd "P," screw band illegibly mkd, rim chip and flake, 9-1/8" h, 4-1/2" d base, RB 1711.. **$190**

Mason's CFJCO Improved Patent Nov. 30th, 1858, gallon, aqua, base mkd "E122," ground lip, Mason's shoulder seal, metal lid mkd "Trademark Boyd's Porcelain Lined Patd Mar.30.58. June 9.63.Mar.30.69 Extd. Mar.30.72," partially open bubble, rim wear, lid cleaned, 12" h, 6" d, base, RB 1920................. **$2,310**

Mason's Patent Nov. 30th, 1858, half gallon, green, amber swirls, smooth lip, metal "Ball" lid with milk glass insert mkd "Boyd's Genuine Porcelain Lined Cap 18V," 8-3/4" h, 4-3/8" d base, RB 1787............. **$360**

Fruit jar, Mason's Patent Nov. 30th 1858, quart, teal, RB 1787, rough ground lip, **$275.**

Photo courtesy of American Bottle Auctions.

Mason's Patent Nov. 30th, 1858, quart, Ball blue, reverse mkd with Tudor rose emblem, base mkd "A 83," ground lip, disk immerser lid, ext. mkd "TradeMark The Mason Disk Protector Cap Patd. Nov 30 1880," and Tudor rose emblem in center, bottom of disk mkd "Pat. Nov 23.75. Sept 12.76. Nov 30.80, July 20. 1886," 7-1/4" h, 3-3/4" d base, RB 1875 .... **$125**

Millville Atmospheric Fruit Jar, 56 oz, aqua, reverse mkd "Whitall's Patent June 18th 1861," glass lid, squared iron yoke clamp with thumbscrew, 9" h, 4-3/8" d base, RB 2181 ....**$45**

Moore's Patent Dec 3D 1861, quart, aqua, correct but slightly ill-fitting lid, rounded iron yoke clamp with thumbscrew, edge flakes on lid, flakes on interior jar flange, 8-1/8" h, 3-5/8" d base, RB 2204.................**$55**

Owl, pint, milk glass, glass insert emb with daisy rosette, serrated screw band, 6-1/8" h, 2-1/2" d base, RB 3085 .... **$100**

Pansy (superimposed over erased Best), quart, amber, 20 vertical panels, ground lip, glass insert, screw band, rim flaking, 5-1/4" h, 4-1/2" d base, RB 2287............................. **$220**

Patented Oct. 19, 1858 (on lid), quart, aqua, ground lip, glass lid with internal lugs, lugs on neck of jar, 7" h, 3-7/8" d base, RB 1212.................**$45**

PET, half gallon, aqua, correct glass lid, spring wire clamp, lid mkd "Patented Aug 21st 1869. T.G. Otterson," 9-7/8" h, 4-3/8" d base, RB 2359 **$200**

Potter & Bodine Airtight Fruit Jar Philada, half gallon, reverse mkd "Patented April 13th 1858," groove ring wax sealer, patched hole on edge of base, 2-1/4" h crack, 8-1/4" h, 4-1/4" d base, RB 2383 ....**$70**

Safety Valve Patd May 21, 1895 HC, over triangle on base, half gallon, dark aqua, Greek Key design around shoulder and base, glass lid mkd "1," ground lip, metal band clamp with bail handle, 8" h, 5-1/8" d base, RB 2539 ....**$55**

Safety Valve Patd May 21, 1895 HC, over triangle on base, pint, emerald green, partially ground lip, emerald green glass lid, metal band clamp, stamped "Safety Valve Patd May 21, 1895," 5-3/4" h, 3" d base, RB 2538 ....**$210**

Smalley Full Measure AGS (monogram), quart, amber, base mkd "Patented Dec 13 1892 April 7 1896, Dec 1, 1896," 7-1/4" h, 3-5/8" sq base, RB 2648 ....**$90**

Standard (arched), quart, light cobalt blue, reverse heel mkd "W. McC & Co," applied groove ring wax sealer, four-point star under base, tin lid mkd "W. McCully & Co. Glass Pittsburg," 1/2" wide chip on outer rim, 7-1/2" h, 3-3/4" d base, RB 2701-variant. **$880**

Star, emblem encircled by fruit, quart, aqua, ground lip, neck slopes inward to opening, zinc insert and screw band, 7-3/4" h, 3-3/4" d base, RB 2724 ....**$150**

Sun (in circle with radiating lines) Trade Mark, quart, aqua, base mkd "J. P. Barstow," and "4," ground lip, unmarked glass lid, metal yoke clamp, mkd "Monier's Pat April 1 90 Mar 12

95," 7-3/4" h, 3-7/8" d base, RB 2761 ....**$100**

The Empire, quart, aqua, base mkd "Pat Feb 13 1866," ground rim, glass lid, chipping, bruise to ground rim, 8-1/2" h, 3-3/4" d base, RB 927 ...**$80**

The Gem, gallon, aqua, base mkd "H. Brooke Mould Maker NY Pat'd Nov 26th 1868. Patd Dec 17th 1861 Reis' Sept 1st 1868," ground lip, glass insert mkd "Mason's Improved May 10 1870," screw band, loss of lip flange, 12-3/8" h, 5-7/8" d base, RB 1071 ....**$880**

The Hero, half gallon, deep aqua, base mkd "Patd Nov 26 1867" and "5" in center, ground lip, glass insert with "WHA" monogram on interior center, series of patent dates on exterior, screw band, two rim chips, 9" h, 4-1/2" d base, RB 1242 ....**$15**

The Hero, quart, aqua, base mkd "Patd Nov 26 1867. Pat'd Dec 17 '61 Nov 4 '62 Dec 14 '69 Reis's Sept 1 '68 June 9' 69," and "87" in center, ground lip, glass insert with "WHA," monogram on interior center, series of patent dates on exterior, screw band, rim roughness, 7-1/8" h overall, 3-3/4" d base, RB 1244.................**$25**

The Hero, quart, honey amber, base mkd "Pat Nov 26 1867," and "6 (reversed) 7" in center, ground lip, metal lid with partially legible patent dates from 1862 through 1869 including Dec. 22, 1868 and Dec. 14, 1869," 7-1/2" h, 3-3/4" d base, RB 1242 ....**$6,600**

The Heroine, pint, aqua base mkd "22," ground lip, glass inset mkd "Pat. Feb 12.59 Dec. 17.61. Nov 4. 62.Dec 6.64. June 9.68. Jan 1.68. Sep 1.68. Sep 8.68 Dec 22.68," screw band, rim chip with flakes, 6-5/8" h, 3-1/4" d base, RB 1248 ....**$125**

The King, Pat Nov .2, 1869, quart, aqua, base mkd "3," ground lip, glass lid and iron yoke clamp, one half of rim broken out, 7-1/2" h, 3-3/4" d base, RB 1418........................**$125**

The Valve Jar Co., Philadelphia, quart, aqua, base mkd "Patd Mar 1-th 1868," ground lip, glass lid, wire coil clamp, open bubble on edge of base, 7-1/2" h, 4" d base, RB 2873 .....**$385**

The Van Vliet Jar of 1881, half gallon, aqua, base mkd "6," ground lip, glass lid mkd "Pt May 3d 1881," metal yoke clamp with unmarked thumbscrew, attached wire extending vertically around entire jar, bruises, 9-1/4" h, 4-1/2" d base, RB 2878 ...**$525**

Trade Marks Mason's CFJCO Improved, midget pint, aqua, base mkd "C178," ground lip, glass insert mkd "Trade Mark Mason's Improved Registered May 23d 1871" (CFJCo monogram in center) screw band stamped "Consolidated Fruit Jar Co. New York. Trade Mark Mason's Improved Registered May 23 1871," 6" h, 3-1/4" d base, RB 1722........................**$25**

W. Chrysler, Pat. Nov. 21, 1865, quart, aqua, applied lip, three annealing lines, 7-3/4" h, 3-3/4" d base, RB 597-1........................**$1,210**

GOOFUS GLASS

*Goofus bowl, Leaf and Beads, Northwood, c1906-08, opalescent ruffled ring around center design of leafs, center cold painted gold and red, N mark, 9" d, **$55**.*

History: Goofus glass, also known as Mexican ware, hooligan glass, and pickle glass, is a pressed glass with relief designs that were painted either on the back or front. The designs are usually in red and green with a metallic gold ground. It was popular from 1890 to 1920 and was used as a premium at carnivals.

It was produced by several companies: Crescent Glass Company, Wellsburg, West Virginia; Imperial Glass Corporation, Bellaire, Ohio; LaBelle Glass Works, Bridgeport, Ohio; and Northwood Glass Co., Indiana, Pennsylvania, Wheeling, West Virginia, and Bridgeport, Ohio.

Goofus glass lost its popularity when people found that the paint tarnished or scaled off after repeated washings and wear. No record of its manufacture has been found after 1920.

Marks: Goofus glass made by Northwood includes one of the following marks: "N," "N" in one circle, "N" in two circles, or one or two circles without the "N."

Ashtray, red rose dec, emb adv....**$18**

Basket, strawberry dec, 5" h **$50**

Bonbon, Strawberry pattern, gold, red, and green dec, 4" d......................**$40**

Bowl

Cherries, gold leaves, red cherries, 10-1/2" d, 2-1/2" h....................**$35**

Grape and Lattice pattern, red grapes, gold ground, ruffled rim, 6-1/2" d **$45**

Bread plate, Last Supper pattern, red and gold, grapes and foliage border, 7" w, 11" l.......................................**$65**

Candy dish, figure-eight design, serrated rim, dome foot, 8-1/2" d **$60**

Charger, grape and leaves center... **$125**

Coaster, red floral dec, gold ground, 3" d..**$12**

Compote

Grape and Cable pattern, 4" d **$35**

Poppy pattern, red flowers, gold foliage, green ground, sgd "Northwood," 6-1/2" d **$40**

Strawberry pattern, red and green strawberries and foliage, ruffled, 6" d **$40**

Decanter, orig stopper, La Belle Rose **$50**

Dresser tray, Cabbage Rose pattern, red roses dec, gold foliage, clear ground, 6" l **$35**

Jewel box, basketweave, rose dec, 4" d, 2" h.......................................**$50**

Mug, Cabbage Rose pattern, gold ground..**$35**

Nappy, Cherries pattern, red cherries, gold foliage, clear ground, 6-1/2" d **$35**

Perfume bottle, pink tulips dec, 3-1/2" h **$20**

Pickle jar, aqua, molded, gold, blue, and red painted floral design **$50**

Pin dish, oval, red and black florals, 6-1/2" l..**$20**

Plate

Carnations pattern, red carnations, gold ground, 7-3/4" d................**$20**

Cherries, some paint worn off, 11" d **$35**

Sunflower pattern, red dec center, relief molded, 6" d.....................**$20**

Platter, red rose dec, gold ground, 18" l...**$65**

Powder jar, cov, puffy, rose dec, red and gold, 3" d.............................**$40**

Salt and pepper shakers, pr, Grape and Leaf pattern **$45**

Syrup, relief molded, red roses dec, lattice work ground, orig top.......**$85**

Toothpick holder, red rose and foliage dec, gold ground.................**$40**

Tray, red chrysanthemum dec, gold ground, 8-1/4" d, 11" d................**$45**

Tumbler, red rose dec, gold ground, 6" h...**$35**

Vase

Cabbage Rose pattern, red dec, gold ground, 6" h **$45**

Poppies pattern, blue and red dec, gold ground, 9" h.......................**$45**

Goofus bowl, gold and red pears and apples decoration, **$35.**

Goofus plate, gold ground, two bright red roses in center, border with diamond quilting and acanthus scrolling, **$45.**

GREENTOWN GLASS

History: The Indiana Tumbler and Goblet Co., Greentown, Indiana, produced its first clear, pressed glass table and bar wares in late 1894. Initial success led to a doubling of the plant size in 1895 and other subsequent expansions, one in 1897 to allow for the manufacture of colored glass. In 1899, the firm joined the combine known as the National Glass Company.

In 1900, just before arriving in Greentown, Jacob Rosenthal developed an opaque brown glass, called "chocolate," which ranged in color from a dark, rich chocolate to a lighter coffee-with-cream hue. Production of chocolate glass saved the financially pressed Indiana Tumbler and Goblet Works. The Cactus and Leaf Bracket patterns were made almost exclusively in chocolate glass. Other popular chocolate patterns include Austrian, Dewey, Shuttle, and Teardrop and Tassel. In 1902, National Glass Company bought Rosenthal's chocolate glass formula so other plants in the combine could use the color.

In 1902, Rosenthal developed the Golden Agate and Rose Agate colors. All work ceased on June 13, 1903, when a fire of suspicious origin destroyed the Indiana Tumbler and Goblet Company Works.

After the fire, other companies, e.g., McKee and Brothers, produced chocolate glass in the same pattern designs used by Greentown. Later reproductions also have been made, with Cactus among the most heavily copied patterns.

Greentown cat in hamper covered dish, chocolate glass, **$225.**

Reproduction Alert.

Animal-covered dish
Dolphin, chocolate **$225**
Rabbit, dome top, amber **$250**
Bowl, Herringbone Buttress, green, 7-1/4" d................................ **$135**
Butter, cov, Cupid, chocolate **$575**
Celery vase, Beaded Panel, clear **$100**
Compote, Teardrop and Tassel, clear, 5-1/4" d, 5-1/8" h **$50**

Creamer
Cactus, chocolate **$85**
Indian Head, opaque white **$450**
Goblet
Overall Lattice............................. **$40**
Shuttle, chocolate **$500**
Mug, indoor drinking scene, chocolate, 6" w, 8" h.............................. **$400**
Mustard, cov, Daisy, opaque white **$75**
Paperweight, Buffalo, Nile green **$575**
Pitcher, cov, Dewey, chocolate, 5-1/4" h **$115**

Plate, Serenade, chocolate............ **$65**
Relish, Leaf Bracket, oval, chocolate, 8" l.. **$75**
Salt and pepper shakers, pr, Cactus, chocolate **$130**
Sugar, cov, Dewey, cobalt blue .. **$125**
Syrup, Cord Drapery, chocolate, plated lid, 6-3/4" h **$295**
Toothpick holder, Hobnail and Shell, chocolate **$185**
Tumbler
Cactus, chocolate......................... **$60**
Dewey, canary............................. **$65**
Vase, Austrian, 8" h..................... **$55**

HEISEY GLASS

History: The A. H. Heisey Glass Co. began producing glasswares in April 1896, in Newark, Ohio. Heisey, the firm's founder, was not a newcomer to the field, having been associated with the craft since his youth.

Many blown and molded patterns were produced in crystal, colored, milk (opalescent), and Ivorina Verde (custard) glass. Decorative techniques of cutting, etching, and silver deposit were employed. Glass figurines were introduced in 1933 and continued in production until 1957 when the factory closed. All Heisey glass is notable for its clarity.

Marks: Not all pieces have the familiar H-within-a-diamond mark.

1900–58

Reproduction Alert. Some Heisey molds were sold to Imperial Glass of Bellaire, Ohio, and certain items were reissued. These pieces may be mistaken for the original Heisey. Some of the reproductions were produced in colors never made by Heisey and have become collectible in their own right. Examples include: the Colt family in Crystal, Caramel Slag, Ultra Blue, and Horizon Blue; the mallard with wings up in Caramel Slag; Whirlpool (Provincial) in crystal and colors; and Waverly, a seven-inch, oval, footed compote in Caramel Slag.

Animal
Gazelle **$1,450**
Plug horse, Oscar...................... **$115**
Pony, kicking............................. **$175**
Sealyham terrier **$145**
Sparrow **$150**
Ashtray
Old Sandwich, #1404, moongleam, individual size **$68**
Ridgeleigh, #1469, club shape **$10**
Bitters bottle, #5003, tube........ **$165**
Bowl
Plantation Ivy, crystal, 10" d........ **$65**
Queen Anne, light use, 8" d......... **$25**

Buffet plate, Lariat, #1540, 21" ..**$70**
Butter dish, cov, Rose **$200**
Cake plate, Rose, pedestal, 15" d **$325**
Camellia bowl, Lariat, #1540, 9-1/2" d **$40**
Candelabra, crystal, price for pr, 10" w, 16-1/2" h.......................... **$695**
Candlesticks, pr
Flamingo, #112 .... **$150**
Mercury, #122............................. **$70**
New Era, #3877............................ **$90**
Orchid, Trident, two-lite **$155**
Pinwheel, #121............................. **$90**
Regency, two-lite, #1504 .... **$98**
Thumbprint and Panel, #1433.. **$140**
Trophy, #126, flamingo **$275**
Windsor, #22, 7-1/2" h **$140**
Caramel, cov, Lariat, #1540, 7"....**$75**
Celery, Empress, Sahara, 10" l **$45**
Centerpiece bowl, Ridgeleigh, #1469, 11" d **$225**
Champagne, Duquesne, tangerine, saucer **$235**
Cheese dish, cov, Lariat, #1540, ftd **$40**
Cheese plate, Twist, #1252, Kraft, moongleam **$63**
Cigarette holder, Crystolite......**$25**
Claret
Carasonne, Sahara, 4 oz............... **$68**
Orchid, Tyrolean line, 4-1/2 oz **$150**

Coaster
Colonial **$10**
Plantation **$50**
Cocktail
Lariat, #1540, moonglo cut.......... **$12**
Rose Etch.................................. **$33**
Seahorse, crystal **$145**
Cocktail shaker
Cobel, #4225, quart **$55**
Orchid Etch, sterling foot.......... **$200**
Console set, Twist, moongleam, Cattail cutting, 12" oval ftd bowl, pr 2" candles.................................. **$295**
Cordial
Carcassone, #390, Sahara **$115**
Minuet, crystal............................ **$150**
Peerless, crystal......................... **$28**
Creamer and sugar
Twist, #1252, oval, Sahara.......... **$165**
Waverly, #1519, orchid etch......... **$75**
Cream soup, Queen Anne, etching **$20**
Cruet, Greek Key, crystal **$145**
Cup and saucer
Empress, Sahara yellow, round....**$40**
Twist, #1252, flamingo................. **$55**
Custard cup, Queen Anne **$15**
Floral bowl, Orchid, Waverly, crimped, some scratches, 12" d, 4" h .. **$55**
Gardenia bowl, Orchid, Waverly, 13" d................................. **$90**
Goblet
Galaxy, #8005.............................. **$25**

Moonglo, crystal **$35**
Narrow Flute, #393 .... **$29**
Plantation Ivy, crystal.................. **$36**
Provincial, #1506 .... **$15**
Spanish, #3404, cobalt blue **$155**
Tudor **$12**
Honey, Plantation, #1567, ivy etch, 6-1/2" **$80**
Hurricane lamp base, Lariat, #1540, pr. **$85**
Iced-tea tumbler, Moonglo, crystal **$35**
Jug, Old Sandwich, #1404, Sahara, half gallon **$225**
Luster, Ipswich, crystal.............. **$465**
Mayonnaise bowl, Orchid, two-part, Queen Anne **$65**
Mayonnaise ladle, #6, Alexandrite **$245**
Muffin plate, Octagon #1229, moongleam, 12" d **$48**
Nut dish
Empress, #1401, individual, Alexandrite **$175**
Narrow Flute, #393, moongleam **$15**
Oyster cocktail, Pied Piper **$15**
Paperweight, rabbit.................... **$225**
Parfait glass, Orchid, price for set of eight, 5-1/2" h, 2-7/8" d, ... **$480**
Pitcher, Orchid, tankard............. **$625**
Plate
Colonial, 4-3/4" d............................ **$5**
Empress, Moongleam, 7" d **$25**
Minuet, 8" d **$20**
Orchid, Waverly, 8" d.................. **$40**
Ridgeleigh, #1469, 8" d **$10**
Punch bowl set, Crystolite, punch bowl, 12 cups, ladle **$400**

Relish
Normandie etch, star, #1466........ **$95**
Orchid, three-part, three handles, 7-1/4" d **$55**
Provincial, #1506, 12" **$35**
Twist, #1252, flamingo, 13" l **$40**
Waverly, two-part **$25**
Rose bowl, Plateau, #3369, flamingo **$65**
Salt shaker, Old Sandwich, #1404 . **$30**
Sandwich plate, Rose **$220**
Serving tray, center handle, Orchid Etch.. **$150**
Sherbet, Moonglo, cyrstal **$35**
Soda
Coronation, #4054, 10 oz **$10**
Duquesne, #3389, 12 oz, ftd, tangerine.. **$210**
Newton, #2351, 8 oz, Fronetnac etch **$20**
Strawberry dip plate, Narrow Flute, #393, with rim **$195**
Sugar, Crystolite, individual **$18**
Tankard, Orchid, ice lip, 9-1/2" h, 7" w **$480**
Toothpick holder, Fancy Loop, emerald, small base flake, wear to gold trim.. **$120**
Tumbler, Carassone, Sahara, ftd, 2 oz **$72**
Vase
Prison Stripe, #357, cupped, 5" ... **$55**
Ridgeleigh, #1469, Sahara, cylinder, 8" h **$245**
Water bottle, Banded Flute, #150 .... **$125**
Wine
Creole, Alexandrite, 5-1/2" h **$175**
Minuet, crystal, 6" h **$85**

*Heisey Greek Key pattern, creamer in front, **$45**; nappy in back, **$30**.*

*Heisey New Era pattern, sugar and creamer, "H" in diamond mark, **$65**.*

IMPERIAL GLASS

History: Imperial Glass Co., Bellaire, Ohio, was organized in 1901. Its primary product was pattern (pressed) glass. Soon other lines were added, including carnival glass, Nuart, Nucut, and Near Cut. In 1916, the company introduced Free-Hand, a lustered art glass line, and Imperial Jewels, an iridescent stretch glass that carried the Imperial cross trademark. In the 1930s, the company was reorganized into the Imperial Glass Corporation. The firm was sold to Lenox, in 1976, and ceased all operations by 1984.

Imperial acquired the molds and equipment of several other glass companies—Central, Cambridge, and Heisey. Many of the retired molds of these companies are once again in use for a short period of time before Imperial closed.

Marks: The Imperial reissues are marked to distinguish them from the originals.

*Imperial vase, baluster, green heart-shaped leaves and stems, bright white lustered ground, unmarked, minute flecks around rim, 8" x 7-3/4", **$700**.*
Photo courtesy of David Rago Auctions, Inc.

Engraved or hand cut

Bowl, flower and leaf, molded star base, 6-1/2" d $25

Candlesticks, pr, Amelia, 7" h $35

Celery vase, three-side stars, cut star base...$25

Pitcher, tankard, Design No. 110, flowers, foliage, and butterfly cutting...$60

Plate, Design No. 12, 5-1/2" d $15

Jewels

Bowl, purple Pearl Green luster, marked, 6-1/2" d.....................$75

Console set, Golden Green, 1920s, 10-1/2" d bowl, pr 9-1/2" h candlesticks $350

Rose bowl, amethyst, green irid $75

Vase

Bulbous, mustard yellow, orange irid int., shape #1690, 6-1/2" h $100

Cylindrical bud, emerald green, orange irid int., 8-1/2" h $100

Cylindrical, irid marigold, wear at collar, 11" h $75

Lustered (freehand)

Candlestick, slender baluster, cushion foot, clear, white heart and vine dec, tall cylindrical irid dark blue socket, orig paper label, 10" h $440

Hat, ruffled rim, cobalt blue, embedded irid white vines and leaves, 9" w...$120

Ivy ball, Spun, red, crystal foot, 4" h $90

Vase

Bulbous shouldered, irid marigold, price for pr, 6-1/2" h..............$300

Bulbous, strong marigold irid, random blue heart and vine dec, 10" h...$550

Corset shape, irid green, white heart and vine dec, orange int., 10" h $550

Nuart

Ashtray..$20

Lamp shade, marigold.................$50

Vase, bulbous, irid green, 7" h $125

Nucut

Berry bowl, handles, 4-1/2" d......$15

Celery tray, 11" l..........................$18

Imperial bowl, Molly, amber, gold embossed borders, footed bowl, pair of closely related candleholders, sold as set, **$125.**

Creamer...................................$20

Fern dish, brass lining, ftd, 8" l $30

Orange bowl, Rose Marie, 12" d $48

Pressed

Bar bottle, Cape Cod................$150

Basket, Cape Cod, No. 160/73/0 ....$350

Birthday cake plate, Cape Cod $325

Bowl

Cape Cod, 11" l, oval.....................$90

Windmill, amethyst, fluted, 8" d, 3" h..$45

Bread and butter plate, Cape Cod $7

Canapé plate, matching tumbler, #400/36...$36

Center bowl, Cape Cod, No. 160/751, ruffled edge..................................$65

Champagne, Cape Cod, azalea $22

Coaster, Cape Cod, No. 160/76 ....$10

Creamer, #400/30...........................$9

Cruet, orig stopper, Cape Cod, No. 160/119, amber..............................$28

Decanter, orig stopper, Cape Cod, No. 160/163 ....$75

Dish, covered

Dog, caramel slag, ALIG 1982 ....$165

Dove, satin crystal, IG mark.......$75

Lion, amber, from Heisey mold mkd "CG"...$125

Pie wagon, caramel slag, ALIG 1982 ....$225

Figure

Chipmunk, Ultra Blue, ALIG mark $195

Clydesdale, Ultra Blue, ALIG mark $250

Wood Duck, Ultra Blue, IG mark $225

Goblet

Cape Cod, No. 1602, Verde green $20

Traditional...................................$15

Jar, cov

Cathay, Verde Green................. $135

Owl, green and white slag, IG mark $85

Nappy, Quilted Diamond, marigold, ring handle....................................$35

Pitcher, Cape Cod, No. 160/19, ice lip $85

Plate, Windmill, caramel slag, IG mark $75

Relish

Candlewick, two-part, 6-1/2" $25

Cape Cod, three-part....................$35

Rose bowl, Molly, black, silver deposit floral dec, 5" h..........................$45

Salad plate, Cape Cod, use scratches, 8" d $11

Sherbet

Cape Cod.....................................$10

Traditional...................................$10

Sugar, #400/30.................................$9

Tea cup, #400/35..............................$8

Toothpick holder, carnival or milk white, IG mark, 2-1/2" h $30

Tumbler, Georgian, red.................$18

Whiskey set, Cape Cod, No. 160/280, metal rack, clear bottles, raised letters Bourbon, Rye, and Scotch $650

LALIQUE

History: René Lalique (1860-1945) first gained prominence as a jewelry designer. Around 1900, he began experimenting with molded-glass brooches and pendants, often embellishing them with semiprecious stones. By 1905, he was devoting himself exclusively to the manufacture of glass articles.

In 1908, Lalique began designing packaging for the French cosmetic houses. He also produced many objects, especially vases, bowls, and figurines, in the Art Nouveau and Art Deco styles. The full scope of Lalique's genius was seen at the 1925 Paris l'Exposition Internationale des Arts Décorative et Industriels Modernes.

Marks: The mark "R. LALIQUE FRANCE" in block letters is found on pressed articles, tableware, vases, paperweights, and automobile mascots. The script signature, with or without "France," is found on hand-blown objects. Occasionally, a design number is included. The word "France" in any form indicates a piece made after 1926.

The post-1945 mark is generally "Lalique France" without the "R," but there are exceptions.

Reproduction Alert. The Lalique signature has often been forged; the most common fake includes an "R" with the post-1945 mark.

Lalique ashtray, "Chien" in opalescent green glass, engraved R. Lalique France No. 290, 3-7/8" h, **$550-$650.**

Lalique box, "Eglantines" in clear and frosted glass with blue patina, engraved R. Lalique France, c1926, 5-1/3" diameter, **$600-$700.**

Lalique inkwell, "Trois Sirenes" in amber glass, c1921, 9-1/2" diameter, **$5,500.**

Ashtray

Irene, bright green, white patina, stenciled "R. Lalique France," Marcilhac pg 276, no. 304, c1931, 3-3/4" d **$1,100**

Jamaique, clear and frosted, sepia patina, engraved "R. Lalique France," Marcilhac pg 274, no. 296, 5-1/2" d **$225**

Simone, clear and frosted, sepia patina, stenciled "R. Lalique France," Marcilhac pg 275, no. 300, c1929, 4-1/2" d **$300**

Bookends

Bookends, pr, Hirondelles, sgd "Lalique, France," 6-1/4" h **$500**

Bowl

Acacia No. 2, opalescent, stenciled "R. LALIQUE FRANCE," c1928, Marchilhac pg 755, no. 3249, 8-5/8" d **$300**

Cremieu, opalescent, molded "R. LALIQUE FRANCE," engraved No. 400, c1928, Marchilhac pg 297, no.x 400, 11-7/8" d **$550**

Doves, frosted doves with spread wings, oval, etched "Lalique (r in circle) France" in small script, 9" d, 6-1/4" h **$400**

Daisy, deep rim relief dec with band of overlapping daisies, colorless body fluted, brown patina accents, acid-etched mark "Lalique Cristal France," post WWII, 14-1/2" d, 2-3/4" h **$425**

Box, cov

Pommier du Japon, black, whitish patina, molded "R. LALIQUE," Marcilhac pg 227, no. 26, c1919, 3-1/4" d **$1,200**

Quatre Scarabees, black, whitish patina, molded "R. LALIQUE," Marcilhac pg 225, no. 15, c1911, 3-1/4" d **$1,600**

Veronique, black, whitish patina, molded "R. LALIQUE," Marcilhac pg 227, no. 25, c1919, 3-1/4" d **$1,700**

Cane handle, clear and frosted, sepia patina, Marcilhac pg 141, c1905, 3-3/8" l **$900**

Car mascot

No. 1124, Faucon, molded signature "R.Lalique" and etched "France," orig Breves Galleries metal mount, 6-1/4" h **$2,100**

No. 1138, Tete D'Aigle, later example, molded signature "R. LALIQUE" and engraved "Lalique France," 4-1/2" h **$300**

Coupe, Graines d'Asperges No. 2, opalescent, molded DVA mark, Marcilhac pg 751, no. 3221, 8-1/4" **$350**

Figure

Bamara, lion, designed by Marie Claude Lalique, MIB, introduced 1987, 8" h **$1,200**

Black panther, designed by Marie Claude Lalique, introduced 1989, MIB, 14-3/8" l, 4-3/8" h **$1,300**

Cat, crouching, frosted, designed by Rene Lalique, 1932, 4" h **$1,200**

Cheetah, designed by Marie Claude Lalique, MIB, 10" h, 8-1/4" l ...**$2,600**

Hat pin, clear and frosted, sepia patina over gilt metal foil, orig silvered metal mounting and shaft, c1912, 7-3/4" l shaft, 10" l overall

Feuilles, Marchilhac pg 566, no. 1558 ....**$2,800**

Scarabees, Marchilhac pg 566, no. 1559 ....**$1,800**

Inkwell

Biches, clear and frosted, gray patina, engraved "R. Lalique," Marchilhac pg 315, no. 427, c1912, 6" sq base **$2,700**

Cernay, clear and frosted, green patina, molded "R. LALIQUE," Marcilhac pg 318, no. 437, c1924, 3-1/2" x 4" **$5,000**

*Lalique "Je Reviens," a lotion bottle for Worth, in cobalt blue glass, c1931, 4" h, **$2,000**.*

*Lalique vase, "Alicante," triple-cased lime green glass, wheel-cut R. Lalique France in script, c1928, 10-1/4" h, **$15,000**.*

*Lalique vase, "Archers," in cherry red glass with strong white patina, c1921, 10-3/8" h, **$24,000**.*

Mures, clear and frosted, blue patina, engraved "R. Lalique France, No. 431," Marcilhac pg 316, no. 421, c1920, 2" x 6-1/4" **$8,500**

Jewelry

Bracelet, Cerisier, peacock blue, engraved "Lalique," Marchilhac pg 532, no. 1329, small chips, one element reglued, c1928, 12 1-1/8" h elements...................................**$2,000**

Brooch, Trois Anges, clear, sepia patina, gold reflecting foil, gilt metal backing, stamped "Lalique poincon," Marcilhac pg 545, no. 1373, c1912, 1-1/4" d.........................**$800**

Brooch, Chauve-Souris, electric blue, white patina, silver reflecting foil, gilt metal mount, stamped "Lalique poincon," Marcilhac pg 538, no. G.L., c1912, 2-1/8" d **$6,000**

Pendant, Cigognes, clear and frosted, gray patina, molded "LALIQUE," Marchilac pg 581, no. 1663, c1919, 2-1/8" d **$250**

Letter seal, R. Lalique

Rapace, blue, engraved "R. Lalique," Marcilhac pg 257, no. 234, c1931, 2" h **$1,700**

Sauterelle, electric blue, molded "LALIQUE," Marchilhac pg 249, no. 183, c1913, 1-5/8" h **$650**

Statuette Drapee, clear and frosted glass with green patina, early engraved signature, Marcilhac pg 249, no. 181, c1913, 2-1/2" h.........................**$3,000**

Tete D'Aigle, dark amber, engraved "R. Lalique France," Marcilhac pg 248, no. 175, c1911, 3-1/8" h **$1,700**

Paperweight

Bird, Ailes Fermees, clear and frosted, engraved "R. Lalique France," Marcilhac pg 386, no. 1156, 4-1/2"..**$375**

Toby, clear and frosted, stenciled "R. Lalique France," Marcilhac pg 391, no. 1192, c1929, 3-1/2" **$1,200**

Perfume bottle

Bouquet de Faunes, for Guerlain, clear and frosted, gray patina, orig black leather presentation case, unmarked, orig retailer labels on base, c1925, Marchilhac pg 940, no. 1, 3-7/8" h **$1,300**

Camille, electric blue, white patina, molded "R. LALIQUE FRANCE," engraved "R. Lalique France," Marcilhac pg 335, no. 516, c1927, 2-3/8" h **$3,000**

Heart shape, Coeur-Joie, Nina Ricci, 5-7/8" h, 3-3/4" w **$825**

Narkiss, for Roger et Gallet, clear and frosted patina, black enamel, modeled "R.L. FRANCE," Marcilhac pg 947, no. 1, 3-7/8" h................**$2,700**

Vase

Amiens, topaz, whitish patina, stenciled "R. LALIQUE," Marcilhac pg 443, no. 1023, some int. staining, int. flaw in one handle, c1929, 7-1/4" h **$1,200**

Coquillles, clear and frosted, blue patina, molded "R. LALIQUE," Marcilhac pg 424, no. 932, c1920, 7-1/4" h **$1,100**

Dahlias, clear and frosted, sepia patina, black enamel, molded "R LALIQUE," Marcilhac pg 425, no., 938, c1925, 4-7/8" h **$2,300**

Dauphins, opalescent, blue patina, stenciled "R. LALIQUE," engraved "France," Marcilhac pg 464, no. 10-900, 5-3/8" h.....................**$2,200**

Douze Figurines Avec Bouchon, clear and frosted, engraved "R. Lalique France," Marcilhac pg 420, no. 914,

small bruise to base of stopper barrel, c1920, 11-3/8" h **$7,000**

Espalion, electric blue, engraved "R. Lalique, France No. 996," Marcilhac pg 438, no. 996, c1927, 6-7/8" h **$1,300**

Frosted colorless bulbous body, repeating open-petal dahlias with black centers, etched mark "R. Lalique France," Marcilhac no. 3938, model created in 1923, 5" h **$1,410**

Nivernais, bright green, engraved "R. Lalique France, No. 1005," Marcilhac pg 440, no. 1005, c1927, 6-1/2" h **$3,500**

Rampillon, opalescent, stenciled "R. LALIQUE FRANCE," two shallow chips, Marcilhac pg 437, no. 991, c1927, 5" h **$1,100**

Soudan Art, ovoid body, relief dec with three bands of running stags and flowers, sgd "R. Lalique France" on base, Marcilhac no. 1016, design created in 1928, 6-1/2" h.......**$1,120**

Tourterelles, opalescent, blue patina, engraved "R Lalique," Marcilhac pg 431, no. 963, c1925, 11-1/4" h **$14,000**

*Lalique vase, "Montargis," in opaque black glass with white patina, wheel-cut R. Lalique and the style number, 1022, c1930, **$1,500**.*

LIBBEY GLASS

History: Edward Libbey established the Libbey Glass Company in Toledo, Ohio, in 1888 after the New England Glass Works of W. L. Libbey and Son closed in East Cambridge, Massachusetts. The new Libbey company produced quality cut glass, which today is considered to belong to the brilliant period.

In 1930, Libbey's interest in art-glass production was renewed, and A. Douglas Nash was employed as a designer in 1931.

1896–1906

Art glass

Bowl, amberina, crimson shading to amber, Diamond Quilted pattern, applied amber peaked overlay extends mid-length, orig Libbey paper label, ex-Maude Feld, 5-1/8" h..........**$2,100**

Bud vase, shape #3008, amberina, slender neck, wafer base, c1917, 9" h **$1,250**

Center bowl, shape #3019, amberina, pedestal base, pontil sgd with trademark, ex-Maude Feld, c1917, 12" d, 5-3/4" h....................................**$6,250**

Cologne bottle, catalog #3041, amberina, ribbed elongated body shading from fuchsia to amber, raised disk base, blown stopper-dauber with fuchsia amber shading, pontil sgd with trademark, 8-3/4" h **$1,100**

Compote, catalog #3017, amberina, Libbey acid stamp mark, partial paper label, ex-Maude Feld, 7-1/4" d, 8-3/8" h......................................**$4,000**

Creamer and sugar, crystal, blue-green opaque dot trim, dark blue-green glass feet, polished pontil, 5-3/8" h creamer, 3-1/2" h, 4-3/4" d sugar **$475**

Miniature, vase, amberina, flattened oval neck extend to flaring circular body, fuchsia shading to amber, applied rigaree collar, raised dec, ex-Maude Feld, 3-1/4" h..................**$850**

Sugar bowl, open, opaque blue, satin finish, two handles, c1893, 4-1/2" w, 2-3/4" h..**$550**

Toothpick holder

Amberina, crimped bulbous body, deep red to amber, Inverted Baby Thumbprint pattern, ex-Maude Feld, 2-1/4" h **$600**

Amberina, Diamond Quilted pattern, barrel shape, 2-1/2" h...............**$250**

Underplate, amberina, Swirl pattern, scalloped rim, 6-1/4" d................**$150**

Vase

Amberina, Optic Ribbed pattern, acid stamped "Libbey Amberina," ftd, 8" h **$500**

Mushroom shape, clear ribbed glass, allover yellow finish, 7-1/2" d **$120**

Sq mouth, deep crimson extending to graduated double circular body, raised ovals, inverted circular dec, four applied amber shells, ex-Maude Feld, 4-3/4" h.............**$2,100**

Tapering ovoid, circular neck, amberina, shades from very deep ruby to amber, raised and imp dec, orig "Libbey Amberina" label, ex-Maude Feld, 2-7/8" h **$750**

Cut glass

Banana boat, scalloped pedestal base, 24-point hobstar, hobstar, cane, vesica, and fan motifs, sgd, 13" x 7" x 7"..**$1,500**

Bowl, three brilliant cut thistles surround bowl, flower in center, scalloped edge, etched "Libbey" label, price for pr, 8" d, 4" h.................**$400**

Charger, hobstar, cane, and wreath motifs, sgd, 14" d........................**$300**

Miniature lamp, pinwheel design, sgd, 2" sq base, 10-3/8" h............**$425**

Tumble-up, star burst, hobstar, fern, and fan motifs, minor handle check **$725**

Vase, No. 982, Senora pattern, cut glass, ftd, hexed vesicas, deep miter cuts, three 24-point hobstars at top between crossed miter cuts, small stars and trellises, clear knob and stem, scalloped foot cut with extended single star, Libbey over saber mark, some flaws, c1896-1906, 18" h **$2,500**

Libbey rose bowl, Maize pattern, cased, yellow exterior, creamy white interior, **$195.**
Photo courtesy of Alderfer Auction Co.

LOETZ

History: Loetz is a type of iridescent art glass that was made in Austria by J. Loetz Witwe in the late 1890s. The Loetz factory at Klostermule produced items with fine cameos on cased glass, good quality glassware for others to decorate, as well as the iridescent glasswares more commonly associated with the Loetz name.

Marks: Some pieces are signed "Loetz," "Loetz, Austria," or "Austria."

Loetz vase, heart-shaped leaves in yellow, gold luster finish, unmarked, two small abraded areas on body, 11-1/2" x 5", **$1,600.**

Photo courtesy of David Rago Auctions, Inc.

Loetz compote, iridescent gold oval form bowl on iridescent blue pedestal foot, applied blue cabochons, blue lip wrap, signed with acid stamp Czecho-Slovakia, 7" h, **$725.**

Photo courtesy of The Early Auction Company, LLC.

Atomizer, cameo, lemon yellow ground overlaid in blue, cameo cut leafy stemmed cockle shell flowers, sgd "Loetz" in cameo, no stopper, c1910, 7" h **$435**

Bowl
Opalescent, pinched rim, columnar support, triangular foot, engraved with artist cipher for Maria Kirschner, 7" d, 8-1/2" d **$3,585**
Ovoid body, quadrafold pinched rim, irid amber green, undulating irid blue horizontal dec, sgd "Loetz Austria," 5-1/2" h **$1,900**
Ruffled rim, wide body with dimpled shoulder, irid red, gold linear dec, polished pontil, unsigned, 13-1/2" d, 7-1/2" h....................**$825**
Squatty, everted quadrafold rim, irid green, three applied tadpoles, 5" h **$175**
Schaumglas, green and white mottled body, 13" d **$125**
Bud vase, figural flower form, irid, ruffled, crystallized leafy foot, irid gold entwining leafy branch, 8-1/2" h **$1,000**
Cabinet vase, bulbous, tricorn rim, green, overall blue finish, 3" h....**$130**
Candlestick, irid finish, base chip, 15-1/2" h..**$115**
Cup, round bowl, gold and polychrome irid, applied handle, incised "Loetz Austria," 3-3/4" d **$290**
Decanter, Orpheus pattern, irid green, turquoise medallions, controlled threading, slight loss to threading at top, 11-1/4" h **$175**
Low bowl, fold down rim, int. with bluish-gold irid, ext with detailed irid oil spot dec, slight rim roughness, 8-1/2" d, 3" h **$250**
Mantel lamp, Federzeichnung, satin, cased in blue, airtrapped dec, overall gold tracery, enameled dec rim, 11" h **$1,100**
Rose bowl, ruffled purple irid raindrop dec, 6-1/2" d **$265**
Sweetmeat jar, cov, irid silver spider web dec, green ground, sgd, 5" h **$450**

Urn, ovoid, irid, blue oil spot dec, inscribed "Loetz, Austria," 9-1/4" h **$1,600**
Vase
Bulbous stick, deep irid amber, irid blue pulled work dec, gold highlights, 8-1/2" h **$1,300**
Cylindrical, irid opal, applied branch dec, losses, 8" h **$110**
Corset shape, irid gold body cased in pink, sterling silver overlay, 4-1/4" h **$1,000**
Deep red, silver blue irid "Rubin Phanomen" finish, c1890, 12-3/4" h **$3,450**
Emerald green, diamond quilted mother of pearl pattern, overlaid sterling silver florals, trailing vines, inscribed "L" and "Sterling," c1890, 7-1/4" h **$1,850**
Feerzeichnung, flattened bulbous body extends to cylindrical neck, ruffled rim, shading from green to opal, gilt highlights, floral leaf and vine dec, 5-1/2" h **$900**
Figural, fish, gold body, irid Papillion finish, applied green fin feet, 7" h **$700**
Gold colored, irid finish, c1900, 7" h **$250**
Marmorierte Glas, tapered polished marble ground, enameled dec at shoulder and fluted rim, pastel interior, c1890-1910, 7" h..............**$500**
Melon ribbed, everted rim, irid green, blue coin spots, vertical lines, 5" h **$500**
Olive green, wavy silver blue irid stripes, "Loetz Austria" inscribed on pontil, 5-1/4" h **$1,150**
Ovoid, quadrafold pinched rim, irid green graduating to cinnamon, blue oil spots and wavy lines dec, 8" h **$1,200**
Ovoid shouldered, bright lemon yellow, irid blue undulating lines, sgd "Loetz Austria," 6" h **$1,200**
Rusticana, waisted cylindrical, irid blue on green body, 9-1/2" h ...**$250**
Schaumglas, green and white mottled body, orig paper label, 8" h......**$250**
Schaumglas, red and white mottled bulbous body, 6-1/2" h **$315**
Shouldered, irid green textured body, blue thumbprints, undulating lines, 4" h **$1,000**
Squatty stick, irid blue, 4-3/4" h **$200**
Titania, shading from deep ruby to emerald, overall silver irid, 5" h **$2,200**

MCKEE GLASS

History: The McKee Glass Co. was established in 1843 in Pittsburgh, Pennsylvania. In 1852, it opened a factory to produce pattern glass. In 1888, the factory was relocated to Jeannette, Pennsylvania, and began to produce many types of glass kitchenware, including several patterns of Depression glass. The factory continued until 1951, when it was sold to the Thatcher Manufacturing Co.

McKee named its colors Chalaine Blue, Custard, Seville Yellow, and Skokie Green. McKee glass may also be found with painted patterns, e.g., dots and ships. A few items were decaled. Many of the canisters and shakers were lettered in black to show the purpose for which they were intended.

Loetz urn, iridescent blue body, oil spot pattern, two iridescent gold ribbed handles, 9" h, **$1,300.**
Photo courtesy of The Early Auction Company, LLC.

Loetz vase, squat, trefoil rim, dimpled sides, blue swirling bands on gold ground, unmarked, 4" x 4-1/4", **$1,600.**
Photo courtesy of David Rago Auctions, Inc.

Berry set, Hobnail with Fan pattern, blue, master berry and eight sauce dishes **$170**

Candleholder, Rock Crystal, clear, double light, 6-3/4" w, 5-1/2" h **$65**

Candy dish, cov, Rock Crystal, red, 4-1/2" w, 10-1/2" h **$400**

Canister, cov, 10 oz, custard **$75**

Cereal canister, cov, custard, 48 oz **$145**

Child's, butter dish, opaque blue, 5" w base, 3-3/4" h **$55**

Creamer, Aztec, purple carnival **$125**

Egg beater bowl, spout, Ships, black dec on white **$70**

Flour shaker, Seville Yellow **$65**

Grill plate, custard, marked "McK" **$25**

Kitchen bowl, spout, Skokie Green, 7" d **$75**

Measuring cup, four-cup, Seville Yellow **$185**

Mixing bowls, nested set, Ships, red dec on white, 6", 7", 8", 9" **$185**

Pepper shaker, Roman Arch, black, "P" **$40**

Pitcher, Wild Rose and Bowknot, frosted, gilt dec, 8" h **$65**

Reamer, pointed top, Skokie Green . **$45**

Refrigerator dish, cov, Custard, 4" x 9" **$35**

Ring box, cov, Seville Yellow **$20**

Server, center handle, Rock Crystal, red **$140**

Sugar bowl, Aztec, purple carnival **$125**

Sugar shaker, Skokie Green, orig label and top, 2-3/8" sq, 5" h **$115**

Tea canister, custard, 48 oz **$145**

Tom and Jerry punch bowl set, 11-1/2" d, 5" h punch bowl, eight 3-1/2" h mugs, white, black lettering and trim **$95**

Tray, Rock Crystal, red, rolled rim, 13-1/2" l, 6-1/2" w, 2-1/2" h **$120**

Tumbler, Bottoms Up, caramel, 3-1/8" h, 2-3/4" d **$90**

Water cooler, spigot, Vaseline, two pcs, 21" h **$325**

MERCURY GLASS

History: Mercury glass is a light-bodied, double-walled glass that was "silvered" by applying a solution of silver nitrate to the inside of the object through a hole in its base.

F. Hale Thomas of London patented the method in 1849. In 1855, the New England Glass Co. filed a patent for the same type of process. Other American glassmakers soon followed. The glass reached the height of its popularity in the early 20th century.

Loetz vase, taupe ground with some brown inclusions, applied iridescent amethyst loopings, 6" h, **$195.**

Mercury compote, white enameled floral decoration, **$195.**
Photo courtesy of Dotta Auction Co., Inc.

Mercury vases, pair, cobalt blue, 8-1/2" h, **$145.**

Bowl, small plug in bottom, some wear, 8" d...**$120**

Cake stand, pedestal base, emb floral dec, 8" d...**$80**

Candlestick, 10-1/2" h.................**$110**

Cologne bottle, bulbous, flashed amber panel, cut neck, etched grapes and leaves, corked metal stopper, c1840, 4-1/4" x 7-1/2"..................**$160**

Creamer, etched ferns, applied clear handle, attributed to Sandwich, 6-1/2" h..**$140**

Curtain tiebacks, etched grape design, price for pr, 3-1/8" d, 4-1/2" l **$140**

Door knob set, 2-1/4" d.............**$80**

Goblet, gold, white lily of the valley dec, 5" d..**$40**

Pitcher, bulbous, panel cut neck, engraved lacy florals and leaves, applied clear handle, c1840, 5-1/2" x 9-3/4" h...**$225**

Salt, master, circular, ftd, orig base cork, possibly Boston & Sandwich Glass Co., 1860-87, 2-1/4" h, 2-3/4" d...........**$50**

Sugar bowl, cov, low foot, enameled white foliage dec, knob finial, 4-1/4" x 6-1/4"...**$65**

Vase, cylindrical, raised circular foot, everted rim, bright enameled yellow, orange, and blue floral sprays and insects, pr, 9-3/4" h.....................**$225**

MILK GLASS

History: Opaque white glass attained its greatest popularity at the end of the 19th century. American glass manufacturers made opaque white tablewares as a substitute for costly European china and glass. Other opaque colors, e.g., blue and green, also were made. Production of milk-glass novelties came in with the Edwardian era.

The surge of popularity in milk glass subsided after World War I. However, milk glass continues to be made in the 20th century. Some modern products are reissues and reproductions of earlier forms. This presents a significant problem for collectors, although it is partially obviated by patent dates or company markings on the originals and by the telltale signs of age.

Collectors favor milk glass from the pre-World War I era, especially animal-covered dishes. The most prolific manufacturers of these animal covers were Atterbury, Challinor-Taylor, Flaccus, and McKee.

Notes: There are many so-called "McKee" animal-covered dishes. Caution must be exercised in evaluating pieces because some authentic covers were not signed. Furthermore, many factories have made split-rib bases with McKee-like animal covers or with different animal covers.

Animal dish, cov
Cat on drum...................................**$195**
Cat on hamper, green, V mark....**$115**
Chick on sleigh, white.................**$115**
Dolphin..**$145**
Kitten, ribbed base, Westmoreland, white...**$130**
Lion, reclining, white, criss-cross base **$135**
Robin on nest, med blue.............**$165**
Setter dog, blue.............................**$265**
Swan, closed neck, white **$120**
Turkey, amethyst head, white body **$220**
Turkey, white head, dark amethyst body...**$170**
Bowl, Daisy, allover leaves and flower design, open scalloped edge, 8-1/4" d **$85**
Bust, Admiral Dewey, 5-1/2" h....**$300**
Butter dish, cov, Roman Cross pattern, sq, ftd base curves outward toward top, cube-shape finial, 4-7/8" l..**$75**
Calling card receiver, bird, wings extended over fanned tail, head resting on leaf, detailed feather pattern **$150**
Compote, Atlas, lacy edge, blue **$185**
Creamer and sugar, Trumpet Vine, fire painted dec, sgd "SV"...........**$130**
Egg cup, cov, bird, round, fluted, Atterbury, 4-1/4" h **$135**
Hat, Stars and Stripes, black rim ..**$235**
Lamp, Goddess of Liberty, bust, three stepped hexagonal bases, clear and frosted font, brass screw connector, patent date, Atterbury, 11" h.......**$300**
Milk pitcher, Wild Iris, gilt trim, c1825, 8-3/4" h...........................**$125**
Mug, Medallion, c1870, 3-1/4".......**$50**

Plate
Donkey **$50**
Easter, bunny, basket of eggs........**$35**
Fort Necessity, Indian chief, some orig paint, edge chip **$30**
Indian Chief, no paint..................**$70**
Rabbit center, horseshoe and clover border..**$145**
Three dogs and squirrel...............**$65**
Spooner, monkey, scalloped top, 5-1/8" h..**$95**
Sugar shaker, Forget-me-not, green, orig top.......................................**$50**
Syrup, plain, hp red flowers, damage to pewter top.................................**$65**
Tumbler, Royal Oak, orig fired paint, green band **$50**
Vanity box, cov, hand painted enamel floral dec, gold trim, imp "16" on both lid and base, 7" l, 2" w, 2" h **$250**

MILLEFIORI

History: Millefiori (thousand flowers) is an ornamental glass composed of bundles of colored glass rods fused together into canes. The canes were pulled to the desired length while still ductile, sliced, arranged in a pattern, and fused together again. The Egyptians developed this technique in the first century B.C. It was revived in the 1880s.

Reproduction Alert. Many modern companies are making Millefiori items, such as paperweights, cruets, and toothpicks.

Barber bottle, orig top, red, white dec **$350**

Beads, multicolored millefiori beads, blue glass bead spacers, 16" l........**$55**

Bowl, tricorn, scalloped, folded sides, amethyst and silver deposit, 8" d **$125**

Candy dish, light blue, various sized multicolored millefiori flowers, swirled shape, Murano, c1950, 11-1/2" l, 9" w **$85**

Creamer, white and cobalt blue canes, yellow centers, satin finish, 3" x 4-1/2" **$110**

Cruet, bulbous, multicolored canes, applied camphor handle, matching stopper...**$120**

Decanter, deep black ground, allover multicolored flux and canes, including peachblow, and opal, enamel dec, Gundersen, 12" h **$1,450**

Demittase cup and saucer, red and white millefiori, angular applied pink handle, broken pontil scars, Italian **$275**

Door knob, paperweight, New England Glass Co., center cane dated 1852, 2-1/2" d...........................**$395**

Goblet, multicolored canes, clear stem and base, 7-1/2" h **$150**

Lamp, two-pcs, baluster stem, tall mushroom shape shade dec with large and small colorful canes, 16-1/2" h **$850**

Pitcher, multicolored canes, applied candy cane handle, 6-1/2" h **$195**

Slipper, camphor ruffle and heel, 5" l **$125**

Sugar bowl, cov, white canes, yellow centers, satin finish, 4" x 4-1/2" **$125**

Sugar shaker, bulbous, reds and yellows, orig top **$275**

Syrup, pewter top, dark green, browns, blues, applied colorless handle **$295**

Vase

Ftd baluster, large cane dec, 8" h **$150**

Ftd urn shape, small cane dec, 4-1/2" h **$150**

Ftd urn shape, small cane dec, 6" h **$100**

Milk glass, Victorian, painted lamp base, winter scene of farmer and cottage in woods, brass base, 10" h without chimney, **$90.**
Photo courtesy of The Early Auction Company, LLC.

Milk Glass spooner/vase, Westmoreland, Charlton decoration, **$35.**

Millefiori swan, 6" h, **$50;** *rose bowl, 3" h,* **$65;** *and vase, 8" h,* **$45.**
Photo courtesy of Joy Luke Auctions.

MORGANTOWN GLASS WORKS

History: The Morgantown Glass Works, Morgantown, West Virginia, was founded in 1899 and began production in 1901. Reorganized in 1903, it operated as the Economy Tumbler Company for 20 years until, in 1923, the word "Tumbler" was dropped from the corporate title. The firm was then known as The Economy Glass Company until reversion to its original name, Morgantown Glass Works, Inc., in 1929, the name it kept until its first closing in 1937. In 1939, the factory was reopened under the aegis of a guild of glassworkers and operated as the Morgantown Glassware Guild from that time until its final closing. Purchased by Fostoria in 1965, the factory operated as a subsidiary of the Moundsville-based parent company until 1971, when Fostoria opted to terminate production of glass at the Morgantown facility. Today, collectors use the generic term, "Morgantown Glass," to include all periods of production from 1901 to 1971.

Morgantown was a 1920s leader in the manufacture of colorful wares for table and ornamental use in American homes. The company pioneered the processes of iridization on glass, as well as gold and platinum encrustation of patterns. It enhanced Crystal offerings with contrasting handle and foot of India Black, Spanish Red (ruby), and Ritz Blue (cobalt blue), and other intense and pastel colors for which it is also famous. The company conceived the use of contrasting shades of fired enamel to add color to its etchings. It was the only American company to use a chromatic silk-screen printing process on glass, its two most famous and collectible designs being Queen Louise and Manchester Pheasant.

The company is also known for ornamental "open stems" produced during the late 1920s. Open stems separate to form an open design midway between the bowl and foot, e.g., an open square, a "Y," or two diamond-shaped designs. Many of these open stems were purchased and decorated by Dorothy C. Thorpe in her California studio, and her signed open stems command high prices from today's collectors. Morgantown also produced figural stems for commercial clients such as Koscherak Brothers and Marks & Rosenfeld. Chanticleer (rooster) and Mai Tai (Polynesian bis) cocktails are two of the most popular figurals collected today.

Morgantown is best known for the diversity of design in its stemware patterns, as well as for its four patented optics: Festoon, Palm, Peacock, and Pineapple. These optics were used to embellish stems, jugs, bowls, liquor sets, guest sets, salvers, ivy and witch balls, vases, and smoking items.

Most glass collectors recognize two well-known lines of Morgantown Glass today: #758 Sunrise Medallion and #7643 Golf Ball Stem Line. When Economy introduced #758 in 1928, it was originally identified as "Nymph." By 1931, the Morgantown front office had renamed it Sunrise Medallion. Recent publications erred in labeling it "dancing girl." Upon careful study of the medallion, you can see the figure is poised on one tiptoe, musically saluting the dawn with her horn. The second well-known line, #7643 Golf Ball, was patented in 1928; production commenced immediately and continued until the company closed in 1971. More Golf Ball than any other Morgantown product is found on the market today.

Morgantown champagne, Old English pattern, Spanish Red and crystal, **$70.**

Basket

Patrick, #19-4358, Ritz Blue, applied crystal twisted handle, mint leaf prunts, 5" d, 9-3/4" h **$750**

Quilt, crystal, black/amethyst rope-twist handle, leaf form appliqués where handle joins basket, ground pontil **$1,100**

Trindle, #4357, amethyst, applied crystal twisted reed handle, c1930, 9" **$725**

Berry jug, Palm Optic, #37, pink, 8-1/2" w, 9-1/8" h **$235**

Bowl

Fantassia, #67, Bristol Blue, 5-1/2" d **$95**

Janice, Ritz Blue, #4355, 13" d **$475**

Woodsfield, Genova Line, 12-1/2" d, #12-1/2 ....**$565**

Brandy snifter, Golf Ball, #7643, red, crystal base, 4" w, 6-1/4" h **$130**

Candleholders, pr

Golf Ball, #7643, Torch Candle, single, Ritz Blue, 6" h **$300**

Hamilton, #87, Evergreen, 5" h **$65**

Modern, #80, Moss Green, 7-1/2" h ..**$90**

Candle vase, ruby, 5-1/2" h **$55**

Candy jar, cov

Mansfield, #200, burgundy matte, 12" h **$200**

Rachael, crystal, Pandora cutting, 6" h **$395**

Champagne

#7617, ruby bowl **$48**

#7643, Golf Ball, Ritz Blue, 5" **$55**

#7860, Lawton, Azure, Festoon Optic, 5 oz **$50**

Cocktail

Chanticleer, crystal **$30**

Elizabeth, blue, twisted stem, 5-3/4" h **$75**

Filament stem, crystal, ruby filament, 4-1/2" h **$48**

Golf Ball, #7643, crystal, Chateau cutting **$25**

Ruby bowl, #7617 ....**$45**

Venus, #7577, Anna Rose, Palm Optic, 3 oz **$40**

Cocktail set, Deco, black, 7-3/4" h pitcher with weighted base, five 3" w, 3" h cocktail glasses **$65**

Compote, Reverse Twist, #7654, aquamarine, 6-1/2" d, 6-3/4" h **$225**

Console bowl, El Mexicana, #12933, Seaweed, 10" d **$425**

Cordial, 1-1/2 oz
  Brilliant, #7617, Spanish Red **$140**
  Golf Ball, #7643, Ritz Blue **$68**
  Mikado, crystal **$30**

Finger bowl, Art Moderne, #7640, Faun etch, crystal and black, 4-1/2" d, ftd **$150**

Goblet
  Art Moderne, #7640, Faun etch, crystal and black, 7-3/4" h **$125**
  Golf Ball, #7643, Ritz Blue **$60**
  Paragon, #7624, ebony open stem, 10 oz **$215**
  Queen Louise, #7664, 3-1/2" d, 7-1/2" h **$400**

Guest set, Trudy, #23, Bristol Blue, 6-3/8" h..................................**$145**

Iced tea tumbler, Vision, white on white...**$45**

Ice tub, El Mexicana, #1933, Seaweed, 6" d **$225**

Jug
  Kaufmann, #6, Doric star sand blast, 54 oz **$295**
  Melon, #20069, Alabaster, Ritz Blue trim **$1,450**

Measuring cup, adv "Your Credit is Good Pickerings, Furnishings, 10th & Penn, Pittsburgh," clear, 3-1/8" d, 2-7/8" h **$315**

Oyster cup, Sunrise Medallion, blue, 2-3/8" d.....................................**$190**

Pilsner, Floret, etch #796, Lando, 12 oz **$65**

Plate
  Anna Rose, #734 American Beauty etch, 7" d **$65**
  Carlton Madrid, topaz, 6" d **$35**

Sherbet
  Crinkle, #1962, pink, 6 oz.............**$30**
  Golf Ball, #7643, Ritz Blue **$50**

Sophisticate, #7646, Picardy etch, 5-1/2 oz **$55**

Sherry, Golf Ball, #7643, Spanish Red **$43**

Tumbler, water, Owl
  Brown **$60**
  Gold **$65**

Urn, #1160, Bristol Blue, ftd, 6-1/2" h **$650**

Vase
  Catherine, #26, Azure, #758 Sunrise Medallion etch, bud, 10" h **$265**
  Gypsy Fire, orig sticker, 4" h **$68**
  Raindrop pattern, red/orange, yellow base, hobnail design on inside graduating in size down to base, 4-1/2" d, 10" h **$35**

Wine
  #7617, ruby bowl **$65**
  Empress, #7680-1/2, Spanish Red, 3 oz **$90**
  Filament stem, crystal, cobalt blue filament, 4-1/2" h **$65**
  Golf Ball, Ritz Blue, 4-5/8" h........**$58**
  Vision, white on white **$45**

MOSER GLASS

History: Ludwig Moser (1833-1916) founded his polishing and engraving workshop in 1857 in Karlsbad (Karlovy Vary), Czechoslovakia. He employed many famous glass designers, e.g., Johann Hoffmann, Josef Urban, and Rudolf Miller. In 1900, Moser and his sons, Rudolf and Gustav, incorporated Ludwig Moser & Söhne.

Moser art glass included clear pieces with inserted blobs of colored glass, cut colored glass with classical scenes, cameo glass, and intaglio cut items. Many inexpensive enameled pieces also were made.

In 1922, Leo and Richard Moser bought Meyr's Neffe, their biggest Bohemian art glass rival. Moser executed many pieces for the Wiener Werkstätte in the 1920s.

Basket, cranberry, gold encrusted handle, high relief enameled flowers, 7" h...**$450**

Box, cov, amethyst, base dec with band of Amazon warriors, lid with medallion of Spanish galleon, sgd "Moser," 5-1/4" w **$350**

Bowl
  Enameled scrolled foliate dec, cranberry shaded rim, matching underplate, c1900, 7" d **$1,035**
  Horizontal band of cranberry cut to clear, gilt scrolling, pink roses, pr, 7-1/4" w and 9-1/4" w **$200**
  Oblong paneled amber bowl, detailed engraving of bull elk in forest, sgd signature on base, orig lined and fitted box, 9" l, 3-3/4" h.........**$1,000**

Candy dish, cov, green cut to clear, matching lid, acid stamped "Moser Karlsbad," 7-1/2" h.....................**$150**

Cologne bottle, amethyst shaded to clear, deep intaglio cut flowers and leaves, orig stopper, sgd, 7-1/2" h, 3-1/2" d.................................**$695**

Cordial, cranberry bowl, crystal stem, horizontal gilt bands dec with colorful enameled florals and scrolling, price for matched set of six, 4" h **$400**

Cream pitcher, translucent body shading to green, gilt medallions, raised green "jewels," 3-1/4" h....**$350**

Cup and saucer, clear graduating to translucent green, yellow and gold scrolling daffodils, script sgd "Moser"

Moser-style, cut and enameled bowls, band of cranberry cut to clear, gilt and pink roses, 9-1/4" (large); 7-1/4" w (small), **$200.**
Photo courtesy of The Early Auction Company, LLC.

Moser intaglio cut vase, tirangular shape, translucent glass shading to purple, deep cut stem flowers, 4" h, $425.
Photo courtesy of The Early Auction Company, LLC.

in body, price for matched sets, 4-1/2" w, 2-1/2" h **$275**

Decanter, flat sided, green translucent glass, gilt collar dec with overall gold floral scrolling, 8-3/4" h **$325**

Decanter set, 11" h faceted stopper bottle dec with green medallion and fine gold scrolling, six matching 3" h cordials, matching 9-1/2" d tray, chips to stopper finial and cordials **$750**

Dresser box, cov, hinged
Rect, Prussian Blue, multicolored fans and foliage dec, small foot chips, 11" l, 4" h **$375**
Round, translucent green, autumn oak leaves on brown branches, raised acorn jewels, 5" d **$475**

Egg cup, thumbprint patterned translucent colorless ground, red, blue, yellow, and green leaves on brown and yellow vines, chip on foot, 4-1/4" h **$230**

Ewer, cranberry, gilt surface, applied acorns and clear jewels, 10-3/4" h **$2,000**

Finger bowl, underplate
Cranberry, overall gold scrolling and foliate, 6" w, 3" h **$250**
Green, overall gold florals and scrolling, 6" w, 3" h **$175**

Scalloped underplate, clear ground, red, blue, green, and pink acanthus scrollwork, accented with banded peacock eyes, attributed to Lobmeyer, 7" w, 3-1/2" h **$800**

Translucent amethyst, intaglio cut leafy stemmed flowers, 4-1/2" d bowl, 6" d underplate, price for set of four **$850**

Translucent green, gold gilt horizontal bands, pastel scrolling and flowers, 7" w, 3-1/2" h **$600**

Goblet
Enameled scrolled foliage, gilt ground, green tinted rim, price for pr, c1900, 6-3/4" h **$1,265**
Hand painted pastel scrolling flowers on body and foot, gilt bands, rim chip, 7" h **$475**
Shamrock shape, spreading foot, translucent blue body, overall gold flowers and scrolling, gold encrusted stalactite panels with silver scrolling, price for pr, 6-1/4" h **$675**

Juice glass, cranberry, blue and pink flowers, gold scrolling over horizontal gilt bands, set of six, 2-1/2" h **$200**

Pitcher, amberina, IVT, four yellow, red, blue, and green applied glass

beaded bunches of grapes, pinched in sides, three-dimensional bird beneath spout, allover enamel and gold leaves, vines, and tendrils, 6-3/4" h **$3,200**

Portrait vase, woman, gold leaves, light wear, 8-1/2" h **$450**

Rose bowl, cranberry ground, enameled florals and butterfly, applied acorns, c1900, 3-1/2" h **$750**

Sherbet
Enameled scrolled foliage, cranberry shaded rim, price for pr, c1900, 4-1/2" h **$1,100**
Translucent cranberry, dec with purple, red, yellow, green, and white scrolling flowers on horizontal gilt bands, beaded highlights, 4-1/2" h **$500**

Tumbler, enameled dec, c1910, 3-3/4" h
Pale amber **$50**
Pale blue **$50**

Urn, cranberry, two gilt handles, studded with green, blue, clear, and red stones, highly enameled surface, multicolored and gilt Moorish dec, 15-3/4" h **$3,500**

Vase
Bulbous stick, flaring rim, cranberry, banded gold and silver collar, polychrome scrolling, dots, and florals, 9" h **$300**
Faceted cylindrical, clear graduating to translucent green, four gilt and engraved medallion cartouches, blue accents, script sgd "Moser Karlsbad," 5-3/4" h **$150**
Marquetry, ribbed, expanded bowl, tapering stem, intaglio cutting, cinnamon-colored marquetry flowers, pontil sgd "Moser Carlsbad," 13" h **$4,250**
Trumpet, ftd, optic ribbed, clear shading to pumpkin body, blue and yellow flowers, gray and orange scrolling, 16-1/4" h **$500**

Wall vase, conical, crackle body, enameled raised fish, colorful seaweed, 10" h **$900**

Water pitcher, alternating gilt and translucent vertical bands dec with white, blue, and amethyst flowers, 6-3/4" h **$700**

Wine
Elongated gold highlighted faceted stem, overall polychrome enameled scrolling on gold bands, 8" h **$600**
Shamrock shape, trumpet foot, translucent green body, gold scrolling dec, price for pr, 7" h **$125**

MOUNT WASHINGTON GLASS COMPANY

History: In 1837, Deming Jarves, founder of the Boston and Sandwich Glass Company, established for George D. Jarves, his son, the Mount Washington Glass Company in Boston, Massachusetts. In the following years, the leadership and the name of the company changed several times as George Jarves formed different associations.

In the 1860s, the company was owned and operated by Timothy Howe and William L. Libbey. In 1869, Libbey bought a new factory in New Bedford, Massachusetts. The Mount Washington Glass Company began operating again there under its original name. Henry Libbey became associated with the company early in 1871. He resigned in 1874 during the Depression, and the glassworks was closed. William Libbey had resigned in 1872, when he went to work for the New England Glass Company.

The Mount Washington Glass Company opened again in the fall of 1874 under the presidency of A. H. Seabury and the management of Frederick S. Shirley. In 1894, the glassworks became a part of the Pairpoint Manufacturing Company.

Throughout its history, the Mount Washington Glass Company made different types of glass including pressed, blown, art, lava, Napoli, cameo, cut, Albertine, and Verona.

Additional Listings: Burmese, Crown Milano, Peachblow, and Royal Flemish.

Banquet lamp, Colonial Ware (shiny Crown Milano), white ground, sprays of golden roses and single petaled blossoms on globe shaped shade and base, molded-in floral, swag, and geometric dec on base, possibly orig opaque white chimney, burner sgd "Made in United States of America," 23" h.................................**$2,950**

Beverage set, satin, mother-of-pearl, yellow seaweed coralene dec, glossy finish, 9" h, bulbous water pitcher, three spout top, applied reeded shell handle, three matching 4" h tumblers, two blisters on pitcher, three-pc set **$750**

Bowl, Rose amber, fuchsia, blue swirl bands, bell tone flint, 4-1/2" d, 2-3/4" h.......................................**$295**

Collars and cuffs box, opalware, shaped as two collars with big bow in front, cov dec with orange and pink Oriental poppies, silver poppy-shaped finial with gold trim, base with poppies, white ground, gold trim, bright blue bow, white polka dots, buckle on back, sgd "Patent applied for April 10, 1894," #2390/128 ....**$950**

Compote, Napoli, crystal clear ground, ten hp pink full bloom tea roses, green foliage, 6" d bowl, 9-1/2" h **$875**

Condiment set, opaque white salt and pepper shakers, cov mustard, hp floral dec, 6-1/2" h silver plated holder sgd "Wilcox Silverplate Co." **$235**

Cracker jar, opal glass, Egyptian motif, several camels at oasis, distant pyramid and mosque, sgd in lid with Pairpoint Diamond P, #3910, corresponding #3910/530 on jar, 8" h **$2,760**

Cruet, Burmese, shiny finish, butter-yellow body, applied handle, mushroom stopper, each of 30 ribs with hint of pink, color blush intensifies on neck and spout, Mt. Washington, 7" h.................................**$1,250**

Dresser box, portrait of young girl on cov, indigo blue ground, fancy embellishments at collar and other highlights, opaque white body, orig burgundy colors satin lining, sgd "4622/206," 4-3/4" d, 3" h............**$750**

Flower holder, mushroom shape, white ground, blue dot and oak leaf dec, 5-1/4" d, 3-1/2" h **$425**

Fruit bowl, Napoli, solid dark green ground painted on clear glass, outside dec with pale pink and white pond lilies, green and pink leaves and blossoms, int. dec with gold highlight traceries, silver-plated base with pond lily design, two applied loop handles, four buds form feet, base sgd "Pairpoint Mfg. Co. B4704," 10" d, 7-1/2" h.................................**$2,200**

Humidor, hinged silver-plated metalwork rim and edge, blown-out rococo scroll pattern, brilliant blue Delft windmills, ships, and landscape, Pairpoint, 5-1/2" h, 4-1/2" d top **$950**

Jar, cov, peachblow, rim of jar and rim of lid cased in gold metal with raised leaves, 6" w, 5-1/2" h..................**$400**

Jewel box, opalware, Monk drinking glass of red wine on lid, solid shaded green background on cover and base, fancy gold-washed, silver-plated rim and hinge, orig satin lining, artist sgd "Schindler," 4-1/2" d top, 5-1/4" d base, 3-1/4" h **$550**

Jug, satin, Polka Dot, deep peachblow pink, white air traps, DQ, unlined, applied frosted loop handle, 6" h, 4" w **$475**

Lamp, parlor, four dec glass oval insert panels, orig dec white opalware ball shade with deep red carnations, sgd "Pairpoint" base, c1890............**$1,750**

Mt. Washington, Crown Milano, ewer, bulbous body in Nile green to opal, floral and gilt dec, twisted and curled handle, firm's trademark stamp, #559, 10-3/4" h, **$1,900.**
Photo courtesy of The Early Auction Company, LLC.

Mt. Washington, barrel-shaped tooth-pick holder, amethyst and blue stemmed flowers, 2-1/2" h, **$275.**
Photo courtesy of The Early Auction Company, LLC.

Lamp shade, rose amber, ruffled, fuschia shading to deep blue, DQ, 4-1/4" h, 5" d across top, 2" d fitter **$575**

Miniature lamp, banquet style, milk glass, bright blue Delft dec of houses and trees, orig metal fittings, attributed to Frank Guba, 17" h, 4-1/2" d shade **$795**

Mustard pot, ribbed, bright yellow and pink background, painted white and magenta wild roses, orig silver-plated hardware, 4-1/2" h **$185**

Perfume bottle, opalware, dark green and brown glossy ground, red and yellow nasturtiums, green leaves, sprinkler top, 5-1/4" h, 3" d **$375**

Pitcher, satin, DQ, MOP, large frosted camphor shell loop handle, 6" h, 3" w **$325**

Plate, Colonial Ware (shiny Crown Milano), white ground, pink cabbage rose, sprays of blue forget-me-nots, yellow daisies, purple chrysanthemums, dark red tulips, coral nasturtiums, white apple blossoms, white begonias, five raised gold rococo embellishments, sgd, 7" d **$550**

Rose bowl, satin, blue shading to white base, 5" d **$45**

Salt and pepper shakers, pr, Four Lobe shape, white ground, colorful violet nosegays, salt top corroded **$235**

Sugar shaker (muffineer)

Egg shape, white shading to blue ground, pink and gold chrysanthemums, 4-1/4" h **$385**

Egg shape, satin finish, overall green tint shading to pale green at base, vine laden with green leaves, naturalistically colored violet blossoms, 4-1/2" h **$385**

Fig shape, bridal white body, daffodil yellow and pink blossoms, 4" h **$1,950**

Melon ribbed, opaque white ground, daffodil yellow orchid blossoms, two-part metal collar with emb butterfly, dragonfly, and blossom, 3" h, 4" d **$400**

Sweet meat, opaque ground, pseudo Burmese enameling, gilt flowers and leaves, accented with jeweled cabochons, emb bail handle, sgd, lid #P4408, one jewel missing, 5-1/2" d **$815**

Syrup pitcher, Colonial Ware (shiny Crown Milano), white melon ribbed body, 15 sprays of flowers, gold scrollwork, pewter-like collar and lid **$950**

Tumbler, Burmese, shiny finish, thin satin body, soft color blushes from rim to center then shading to pastel yellow base, Mt. Washington **$375**

Vase

Burmese, satin finish, double gourd shape, finely drawn green and coral leafy tendrils, seven nosegays of blossoms, raised blue enamel forget-me-nots, each with pastel center with five coral dots, Mt. Washington, #147, c1885, 7-3/4" h **$985**

Gourd shape, 6" l flaring neck, satin, deep brown shading to gold, white lining, allover enameled seaweed design, 11-1/4" h **$550**

Lava, jet black ground, blue, jade green, gray, white, red, and black chips, small in-the-making blister on one color chip, 5-3/8" h, 4-1/8" d **$2,500**

Stick, Burmese, yellow shading to pink, multicolored flowers dec, remnants of orig paper label, 10-1/4" h **$1,035**

Verona, stylized florals outlined in gold and silver, pastel pink background wash, sgd "Verona 918," 9" h **$1,250**

NASH GLASS

History: Nash glass is a type of art glass attributed to Arthur John Nash and his sons, Leslie H. and A. Douglas. Arthur John Nash, originally employed by Webb in Stourbridge, England, came to America and was employed in 1889 by Tiffany Furnaces at its Corona, Long Island, plant.

While managing the plant for Tiffany, Nash designed and produced iridescent glass. In 1928, A. Douglas Nash purchased the facilities of Tiffany Furnaces. The A. Douglas Nash Corporation remained in operation until 1931.

Bowl, Jewel pattern, gold phantom luster, 7-3/4" x 2-1/2" **$285**

Candlesticks, pr, irid gold, large disc foot and top separated with baluster stem, sgd "650 Nash," 4" h **$350**

Compote, Chintz, transparent aquamarine, wide flat rim of red and gray-green controlled stripe dec, base inscribed "Nash RD89," 7-1/2" d, 4-1/2" h **$865**

Cordial, Chintz, green and blue, 5-1/2" h **$125**

Creamer and sugar, blue-green opaque dots, dark blue-green base, creamer with polished pontil, sugar with waffle pontil, 5-3/8" h creamer, 3-1/2" h sugar **$475**

Goblet, feathered leaf motif, gilt dec, sgd, 6-3/4" h **$295**

Sherbet, bluish-gold texture, ftd, sgd, #417 .... **$275**

Vase

Chintz, pastel, transparent oval, internally striped with pastel orange alternating with yellow chintz dec, 5-1/2" h **$275**

Polka Dot, deep opaque red oval, molded with prominent 16 ribs, dec by spaced white opal dots, base inscribed "Nash GD154," 9" h **$1,100**

OPALESCENT GLASS

History: Opalescent glass, a clear or colored glass with milky white decorations, looks fiery or opalescent when held to light. This effect was achieved by applying bone ash chemicals to designated areas while a piece was still hot and then refiring it at extremely high temperatures.

There are three basic categories of opalescent glass: (1) blown (or mold blown) patterns, e.g., Daisy & Fern and Spanish Lace; (2) novelties, pressed glass patterns made in limited quantity and often in unusual shapes such as corn or a trough; and (3) traditional pattern (pressed) glass forms.

Opalescent glass was produced in England in the 1870s. Northwood began the American production in 1897 at its Indiana, Pennsylvania, plant. Jefferson, National Glass, Hobbs, and Fenton soon followed.

Blown

Basket, cranberry, shading from translucent opalescent to deep rose, crystal handle, 6-3/4" h **$115**

Barber bottle, Raised Swirl, cranberry **$295**

Berry bowl, master, Chrysanthemum Base Swirl, blue, satin **$95**

Biscuit jar, cov, Spanish Lace, Vaseline **$275**

Bride's basket, Poinsettia, ruffled top **$275**

Butter dish, cov, Hobbs Hobnail, vaseline **$250**

Celery vase, Seaweed, cranberry .. **$250**

Creamer
Coin Dot, cranberry **$190**
Windows Swirl, cranberry **$500**

Cruet
Chrysanthemum Base Swirl, white, satin **$175**
Ribbed Opal Lattice, white **$135**

Finger bowl, Hobbs Hobnail, cranberry **$65**

Lamp, oil
Inverted Thumbprint, white, amber fan base **$145**
Snowflake, cranberry **$800**

Pickle castor, Daisy and Fern, blue, emb floral jar, DQ, resilvered frame **$650**

Pitcher
Arabian Nights, white **$450**
Hobbs Hobnail, cranberry **$315**
Seaweed, blue **$525**

Rose bowl, Double Diamond, pink opalescent, gold enameled flowers, 5" h **$90**

Salt shaker, orig top. Ribbed Opal Lattice, cranberry **$95**

Spooner, Reverse Swirl, cranberry . **$175**

Sugar, cov, Reverse Swirl, cranberry **$350**

Sugar shaker
Daisy & Fern, cranberry, 4-1/2" h.... **$230**

Poinsettia, blue, roughness to fitter rim, 5" h **$375**
Spanish Lace, blue, roughness to fitter rim, 4-1/2" h **$200**
Windows, blue, roughness to fitter rim, 4-1/2" h **$250**

Syrup, Coin Spot, cranberry **$175**

Tumbler
Acanthus, blue **$90**
Christmas Snowflake, blue, ribbed **$125**
Maze, swirling, green **$95**
Reverse Swirl, cranberry **$65**

Waste bowl, Hobbs Hobnail, Vaseline **$75**

Novelties

Back bar bottle, robin's egg blue ground, opalescent stripes swirled to the right, 12-1/4" h **$100**

Barber bottle, sq, diamond pattern molded form, light cranberry, white vertical stripes, 8" h **$275**

Bowl, Winter Cabbage, white **$45**

Bushel basket, blue **$75**

Chalice, Maple Leaf, Vaseline **$45**

Hat, Opal Swirl, white, blue edge ... **$95**

Jack-in-the-pulpit vase, green swirl, applied red flower, crystal stem, 6" h **$115**

Whimsy, 9" h trumpet vase with 7-1/2" d bowl in 13" h orig bronzed metal holder, aqua to clear, hp white enamel flowers, vase with ribbed clear stem, Victorian **$850**

Pressed

Berry bowl, master, Tokyo, green **$60**

Butter dish, cov, Water Lily and Cat-tails, blue **$300**

Card receiver, Fluted Scrolls, white **$40**

Cracker jar, cov, Wreath and Shell, Vaseline **$750**

Creamer, Inverted Fan and Feather, blue **$125**

Cruet, Stars and Stripes, cranberry **$575**

Salt and pepper shakers, pr, Jewel and Flower, canary yellow, orig tops **$250**

Spooner, Swag with Brackets, blue **$70**

Toothpick holder, Ribbed Spiral, blue **$90**

Tumbler, Jeweled Heart, blue **$85**

Vase, Northwood Diamond Point, blue **$75**

Opalescent bowl, green, fleur-de-lis design, small spatula feet, **$40**.

Opalescent vase, Corn pattern, blue, **$115**.

Opalescent basket, Vaseline, **$145**.

OPALINE GLASS

History: Opaline glass was a popular mid-to late-19th century European glass. The glass has a certain amount of translucency and often is found decorated with enamel designs and trimmed in gold.

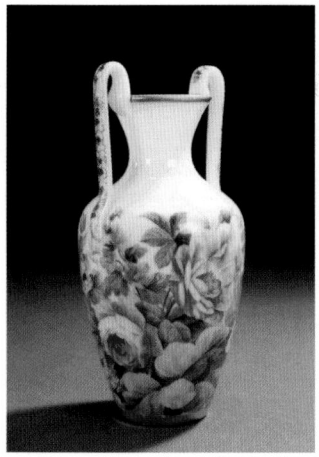

Opaline vase, two handles, multicolored floral decoration, 8-1/4" h, **$450.**
Photo courtesy of Sloans & Kenyon Auctions.

Basket, opaque white ground, applied amber stemmed pink flowers, amber twist handle, 7-1/4" h **$90**

Bouquet holder, blue opaline cornucopia-shaped gilt dec flower holders issuing from bronze stag heads, Belgian black marble base, English, Victorian, pr, early 19th C, 7" h.. **$725**

Box, cov, oblong, green, serpentine scrolled ends, gilt-metal mounts and escutcheon, Continental, mid-19th C, 6" l, 4-3/4" d, 5" h......................... **$920**

Bride's basket, white opaline, cased in pink, overall colorful enameled dec, emb Middletown plated holder, applied fruit handles, Victorian, minor losses, 12" d, 7-1/2" h **$525**

Candelabra, Louis XV style

Two light, gilt bronze and blue opaline, scrolled candle arms and base, late 19th C, 18-1/2" h **$175**

Five-light, gilt metal and blue opaline, 26-1/2" h **$400**

Chalice, white ground, Diamond Point pattern **$35**

Dresser jar, egg shape, blue ground, heavy gold dec, 5-1/2" d............. **$200**

Ewer, white ground, Diamond Point pattern, 13-1/4" h **$135**

Jardinières, gilt bronze and blue opaline, sq, Empire style, tasseled chains, paw feet, pr, early 20th C, 5-1/4" h...................................... **$1,610**

Mantel lusters, blue, gilt dec, slender faceted prisms, Victorian, damage, pr, c1880, 12-3/4" h........................... **$250**

Oil lamp, dolphin-form stepped base, clear glass oil well, frosted glass shade, converted to electric, chips, late 19th C, 24" h **$460**

Oil lamp base, blue, baluster turned standard on circular foot, converted to electric, pr, 20th C, 22" h **$635**

Perfume bottle, baluster form, blue opaline bottle, gilt metal floral overlay, foot, and neck mounts, hinged lid set with shell cameo of young man in feathered cap, French, late 19th/ early 20th C, 4" h **$200**

Salt, boat shaped, blue dec, white enamel garland and scrolling **$75**

Vase

Cased pink ground, colorful enameled flower spray, 6-1/4" h **$225**

Fireglow, gilded banding, price for pr, 13-3/4" h **$115**

Homogenized gray ground, enameled perched birds, price for matched pr, 19th C, 10" h **$175**

Opaque white ground, applied amber stemmed acorn and red leaves, 4-1/2" h **$90**

Pink cased ground, enameled gold day lilies, three rolled over handled rim, Victorian, 9-1/2" h **$125**

Water pitcher, blue, high looped handle, bulbous, early 20th C, 12-1/4" h....................................... **$240**

PADEN CITY GLASS

History: Paden City Glass Manufacturing Co. was founded in 1916 in Paden City, West Virginia. David Fisher, formerly of the New Martinsville Glass Manufacturing Co., operated the company until his death in 1933, at which time his son, Samuel, became president. A management decision in 1949 to expand Paden City's production by acquiring American Glass Company, an automated manufacturer of bottles, ashtrays, and novelties, strained the company's finances, forcing it to close permanently in 1951.

Contrary to popular belief and previously incorrect printed references, the Paden City Glass Manufacturing Company had absolutely no connection with the Paden City Pottery Company, other than its identical locale.

Although Paden City glass is often lumped with mass-produced, machine-made wares into the Depression Glass category, Paden City's wares were, until 1948, all handmade. Its products are better classified as "Elegant Glass" of the era, as it ranks in quality with the wares produced by contemporaries such as Fostoria, New Martinsville, and Morgantown.

Paden City kept a low profile, never advertising in consumer magazines of the day. It never marked its glass in any way because a large portion of its business consisted of sales to decorating companies, mounters, and fitters. The firm also supplied bars, restaurants, and soda fountains with glassware, as evidenced by the wide range of tumblers, ice cream dishes, and institutional products available in several Paden City patterns.

Paden City's decorating shop also etched, cut, hand painted, and applied silver overlay and gold encrustation. However, not every decoration found on Paden City shapes will necessarily have come from the factory. Cupid, Peacock and Rose, and several other etchings depicting birds are among the most sought-after decorations. Pieces with these etchings are commanding higher and higher prices even though they were apparently made in greater quantities than some of the etchings that are less known, but are just as beautiful.

Paden City is noted for its colors: opal (opaque white), ebony, mulberry (amethyst), Cheriglo (delicate pink), yellow, dark green (forest), crystal, amber, blue, and great quantities of ruby (red). The firm also produced transparent green in numerous shades, ranging from yellowish to a distinctive electric green that always alerts knowledgeable collectors to its Paden City origin.

Rising collector interest in Paden City glass has resulted in a sharp spike in prices on some patterns. Currently, pieces with Orchid or Cupid etch are bringing the highest prices. Several truly rare items in these etchings have recently topped the $1,000 mark. Advanced collectors seek out examples with unusual and/or undocumented etchings. Colored pieces, which sport an etching that is not usually found on that particular color, are especially sought after and bring strong prices. In contrast, prices for common items with Peacock and Rose etch remain static, and the prices for dinnerware in ruby Penny Line and pink or green Party Line have inched up only slightly, due to its greater availability.

Adviser: Michael Krumme.

Bowl, nappy
#215 Glades, ruby, 7" x 1-3/4" **$40**
#221 Maya, crimped, ruby, 7" **$50**
#412 Crow's Foot Square, Orchid etch, crystal, 7" **$55**

Bowl, two-handled serving type
#210 Regina, Black Forest etch, green **$125**
#215 Glades, Trumpet Flower etch, crystal **$115**
#220 Largo, ruby **$65**
#411 Mrs. B., Gothic Garden etch, crystal **$45**
#412 Crow's Foot Square, cobalt **$95**
#412 Crow's Foot Square, green **$35**
#412 Crow's Foot Square, Ardith etch, yellow **$50**
#412 Crow's Foot Square, Delilah Bird etch, black **$130**
#412 Crow's Foot Square, Orchid etch, yellow **$150**
#412 Crow's Foot Square, Sasha Bird etch, yellow **$165**
#412 Crow's Foot Square, Trumpet Flower etch, ruby **$165**
#412 Crow's Foot Square, Trumpet Flower etch, yellow **$225**

#881 Gadroon, Rose & Jasmine etch, crystal **$50**

Cake salver, footed
#191 Party Line, high footed, Cheriglo **$65**
#191 Party Line, low, etched & gold encrusted border, crystal **$30**
#210 Regina, Black Forest etch, ebony or green **$75**
#215 Glades, ruby **$45**
#215 Glades, Spring Orchard etch, crystal **$65**
#220 Largo, high footed, crystal ... **$50**
#220 Largo, low footed, ruby **$140**
#300 Archaic, Cupid etch, Cheriglo **$125**
#330 Cavendish, gold encrusted border etch with roses, crystal **$50**
#411 Mrs. B, Ardith etch, green ... **$85**
#412 Crow's Foot Square, cobalt, 8-1/4" w, 4-1/2" h **$125**
#411 Mrs. B, Gothic Garden etch, amber **$40**
#411 Mrs. B, Gothic Garden etch, Cheriglo **$50**
#412 Crow's Foot Square, Ardith etch, ruby **$190**
#412 Crow's Foot Square, Delilah Bird etch, yellow **$85**

Candleholders, pr
#210 Regina, Black Forest etch, ebony **$95**
#220 Largo, light blue **$130**
#220 Largo, Garden Magic etch, light blue **$90**
#300 Archaic, Cupid etch, Cheriglo **$115**
#411 Mrs. B, keyhole style, Ardith etch, ebony **$50**
#411 Mrs. B, keyhole style, Ardith etch, green **$80**
#411 Mrs. B., keyhole style, Gothic Garden etch, yellow **$68.50**
#411 Mrs. B, keyhole style, no etching, ebony **$25**
#412 Crow's Foot Square, mushroom style, no etching, yellow **$30**
#412 Crow's Foot Square, keyhole style, Satin Rose etch, crystal **$45**
#412 Crow's Foot Square, keyhole style, mulberry **$50**
#412 Crow's Foot Square, keyhole style, ruby **$55**
#412 Crow's Foot Square, keyhole style, Orchid etch, crystal **$40**
#881 Gadroon, Irwin etch, crystal **$75**
#890 Crow's Foot Round triple, ruby **$125**
#895 Lucy double, crystal **$145**

Paden City cordial decanter on tray, Ardith etch, Cheriglo, **$250.**
All Paden City photos courtesy of Ken Slater.

Paden City candy dish, covered, flat, #701 Triumph, Ardith etch, **$125.**

Candy box, cov, flat

#215 Glades, ruby $50

#215 Glades, Spring Orchard etch, crystal, filigree base and finial ..$60

#300 Archaic, Cupid etch, Cheriglo $145

#411 Mrs. B, Ardith etch, yellow ..$70

#411 Mrs. B, Ardith etch, black ..$125

#411 Mrs. B, Delilah Bird etch, Cheriglo $240

#412 Crow's Foot Square, Satin Rose etch, crystal $35

Paden City candy dish, covered, flat, #555, heart shape, Utopia etch, **$95.**

Paden City pitcher, #991 Penny Line, ruby, **$125.**

Paden City plate, #220 Largo, forest green, 9" d, **$25.**

#412 Crow's Foot Square, Orchid etch, crystal $60

#412 Crow's Foot Square, Orchid etch, yellow $155

#412 Crow's Foot Square, Orchid etch, Cheriglo $230

#412 Crow's Foot Square, filigree holder, Orchid etch, ruby $275

#412 Crow's Foot Square, filigree holder, Delilah Bird etch, ruby ..$390

#412-1/2, cloverleaf shape, Orchid etch, crystal, filigree holder, ruby $425

#555 heart shaped, Ardith etch, crystal...$45

Candy dish, cov, footed

#191 Party Line, green $40

#210/#503 Black Forest etch, ebony $225

#444 Bridal Wreath etch, ruby $75

#555 footed, light blue $35

#555 footed, ruby $75

#555 footed, wheel cut flowers, ruby $65

#701/#503 base, cutting, green.....$30

Cheese and cracker set

#210 Regina, Black Forest etch, green $100

#210 Regina, Black Forest etch, amber $190

#220 Largo, Garden Magic etch, crystal...$30

#221 Maya, dome lid style, light blue $75

#411 Mrs. B, Ardith etch, Cheriglo $125

#412 Crow's Foot Square, Orchid etch, Cheriglo $200

#777 Comet, domed lid style, cutting, light blue $85

Cigarette box, lid

#191 Party Line, footed jar, etched band of stylized roses, crystal ...$50

#215 Glades, ashtray lid, Spring Orchard etch, crystal...............$125

Cocktail shaker

#156 cobalt..................................$90

#215 Glades, ruby, platinum band dec $75

#901 polished cutting, crystal $40

#901 Utopia etch, crystal $130

Cologne bottle

#191 Party Line, dauber stopper, green...$40

#215 Glades, amber stopper $20

#215 Glades, black stopper $30

#502 dauber stopper, blue.............$50

Comport, footed, open

#210 Regina, Black Forest etch, green, 9-1/2" w $100

#211 Spire, Trumpet Flower etch, crystal..$50

#215 Glades, Forest Green, 6-1/2" w $40

#300 Archaic, turquoise blue $45

#300 Archaic, unusual flared shape, Peacock & Rose etch, green.....$115

#411 Mrs. B, Gothic Garden etch, Cheriglo, 4" h x 6" w.................$60

#411 Mrs. B, Gothic Garden etch, yellow, 7" h x 7" w $35

#412 Crow's Foot Square, low footed, mulberry, 7" w $45

#412 Crow's Foot Square, low footed, Orchid etch, yellow, 7" w $75

#412 Crow's Foot Square, low footed, Ardith etch, ruby, 8" w.............$175

#412 Crow's Foot Square, low footed, Orchid etch, crystal, 10" w.........$50

#412 Crow's Foot Square, cupped sides, two flared sides, Delilah Bird etch, ruby, 5" w $300

#412 Crow's Foot Square, Orchid etch, crystal, 5" h x 9" w...................$185

#881 Gadroon, Irwin etch, ruby, 6-1/2" h x 7" w $150

#890 Crow's F Round, ruby, 6-1/2" h x 7" w................................$40

Nerva, Bridal Wreath, crystal, 9-1/2" w, 6" high $45

Compote, footed, covered, #211 Spire, Loopie etch, crystal, 8-1/2" h $100

Creamer and sugar

#210 Regina, Black Forest, ebony .. $75

#220 Largo, light blue...................$45

#220 Largo, ruby...........................$62

#300 Archaic, Cheriglo.................$20

#411 Mrs. B, amber or ebony $20

#411 Mrs. B, Ardith etch, green.. $165

#411 Mrs. B, Gothic Garden etch, yellow $90

#412 Crow's Foot Square, cobalt ..$35

#412 Crow's Foot Square, mulberry $100

#412 Crow's Foot Square, opal $85

#412 Crow's Foot Square, Ardith etch, ruby $180

#412 Crow's Foot Square, Orchid etch, yellow $135

#701 Triumph, Nora Bird etch, crystal $80

#881 Gadroon, Irwin etch, crystal $40

#881 Gadroon, Irwin etch, ruby...$150

#991 Penny Line, cobalt................$40

Nerva, Rose Cascade etch $65

Cup and saucer

#210 Regina, Black Forest etch, Cheriglo..$180

#210 Regina, Black Forest etch, ebony $100

#210 Regina, Black Forest etch, ebony, gold encrustation $230

#411 Mrs. B, Ardith etch, yellow..**$35**
#881 Gadroon, ruby **$15**
#991 Penny Line, Black Forest etch
....**$100**

Decanter
#191 Party Line, cordial size, green
....**$35**
#210 Regina, Black Forest etch, green
....**$450**
#994 Popeye & Olive, ruby, orig ruby
stopper **$130**

Decanter set
#191 Party Line, five blown whiskeys,
Cheriglo **$75**
Oblong decanter, Ardith etch, six
shots, metal holder, Cheriglo ..**$275**

Egg cup
#210 Regina, Black Forest etch, green
....**$150**
#881 Gadroon, ruby **$75**

Ice bucket, metal bail
#191 Party Line, Peacock & Rose etch,
amber **$120**
#902, Peacock & Rose etch, Cheriglo
....**$165**
#902, Eden Rose etch, green.......**$125**
#902, Cupid etch, Cheriglo **$195**
#902, Lela Bird etch, green **$225**

Ice tub, tab handles
#191 Party Line, Cheriglo **$30**
#300 Archaic, Cupid etch, green
....**$200**
#895 Lucy, Oriental Garden etch,
crystal...**$45**
#991 Penny Line, ruby **$125**
#411 Mrs. B, Ardith etch, yellow, liner
and ladle...**$60**
#412 Crow's Foot Square, Orchid etch,
crystal...**$48**
#412 Crow's Foot Square, Trumpet
Flower etch, yellow...................**$125**
#881 Gadroon, Black Forest etch,
crystal, liner and ladle **$115**

Napkin holder, #210 Regina, green
....**$100**

Night set, pitcher, inverted tumbler,
#210 Regina, Black Forest etch, green
....**$450**

Pitcher, #191 Party Line 74 oz. pitcher,
green..**$75**

Plate
#210 Regina, 8", Black Forest etch,
Cheriglo **$40**
#220 Largo, 9", amber **$10**
#220 Largo, 9", ruby **$25**
#300 Archaic, 8-1/4", Nora Bird etch,
green..**$35**
#411 8" plate, Ardith etch, yellow **$22**
#411 8" plate, Nora Bird etch, crystal
....**$50**
#412 8" plate, Orchid etch, green ...**$45**

#412 10" plate, Orchid etch, cobalt
....**$175**
#881 Gadroon, 8" plate, ruby........**$15**
#890 Crow's Foot Round, 9" mulberry
....**$20**
#890 Crow's Foot Round, 10", Orchid
etch, Cheriglo **$65**

Relish dish, #555 oblong, three parts,
Gazebo etch, light blue.................**$40**

Sugar pourer
#94 Bullet, screw-on metal base,
green...**$145**
#191 Party Line, Cheriglo **$100**

Syrup pitcher
#185, amber **$22.50**
#185, gold encrusted band etch,
amber **$40**
#185, cutting, green......................**$45**
#185, w/underplate, cutting, Cheriglo
....**$85**
#900 Emeraldglo, star cut, metal
underplate......................................**$45**

Tray, two handles
#220 Largo, ruby............................**$25**
#411 Mrs. B Ardith etch green ...**$100**
#412 Crow's Foot Square, hand paint-
ed tulips, opal............................**$195**
#412 Crow's Foot Square, Orchid etch,
crystal...**$40**
#412 Crow's Foot Square, Orchid etch,
ruby **$200**
#412 Crow's Foot Square, Peacock &
Rose etch, yellow......................**$100**

Tumblers and stemware
#191 Party Line, tumbler, Ardith etch,
Cheriglo **$75**
#191 Party Line, banana split, flat,
green..**$25**
#215 Glades, whiskey, Ardith etch,
crystal...**$15**
#890 Crow's Foot Round, tumbler,
amber **$40**
#890 Crow's Foot Round, tumbler,
cobalt..**$70**
#991 Penny Line, whiskey, mulberry
....**$5**
#991 Penny Line, tall stem goblet,
ruby **$20**
#994 Popeye & Olive, goblet, Cheriglo
....**$20**

Vase
#61 hourglass shape, Zinnia & But-
terfly etch, green, 8" **$125**
#61 hourglass shape, Zinnia & But-
terfly etch, Cheriglo, 8" **$175**
#61 hourglass shape, Zinnia & But-
terfly etch, amber, 8"................**$325**
#61 hourglass shape, Zinnia & But-
terfly etch, medium blue, 8"....**$400**
#180 Butterfly & Zinnia etch, green,
12" **$200**

#180 Daisy etch, Cheriglo or green,
12"...**$225**
#180 Daisy etch, gold encrusted
Cosmos etch at top, Cheriglo, 12"
....**$225**
#180 Peacock & Rose etch, Cheriglo,
12"...**$375**
#182 elliptical, ebony, silver overlay,
8" **$65**
#182 elliptical, gold encrusted Utopia
etch, ebony, 8" **$250**
#182-1/2 elliptical, Ardith etch, crys-
tal, 5" **$80**
#182-1/2 elliptical, Frost etch, crystal,
5"..**$40**
#184, bulbous, Gothic Garden etch,
green, 8"......................................**$195**
#184, bulbous, Rose with Jasmine
etch, crystal, 8" **$200**
#184, bulbous, Eden Rose etch, red
and gold encrusted, 10" **$225**
#184, bulbous, Gothic Garden etch,
black, 10".....................................**$125**
#184, bulbous, Orchid etch, ruby, 10"
....**$365**
#191 Party Line, fan shape, Cheriglo
or green..**$35**
#191 Party Line, cuspidor shape,
Ardith etch, black........................**$85**
#191 Party Line, blown, hourglass
shape, crimped top, Cheriglo or
green, 8" **$35**
#210 Regina, squatty, Harvesters etch,
black, 7".......................................**$195**
#210 Regina, cylinder shape, Harvest-
ers etch, ebony, 9"....................**$225**
#210 Regina, Lela Bird etch, ebony,
10" bulbous bottom..................**$110**
#300 Archaic fan vase, Ardith etch,
ebony...**$400**
#411 Gothic Garden etch, black, 9"
....**$125**
#411 Gothic Garden etch, yellow, 9"
....**$165**
#411 Gothic Garden etch, green, 9"
....**$435**
#411 silver deposit dec, crystal, 9"**$50**
#411 Utopia etch, Cheriglo, 9"....**$250**
#412 Crow's Foot Square, ruby, 8"
cupped rim **$50**
#412 Crow's Foot Square, Irwin etch,
8" flared rim..................................**$55**
#503 dome footed fan vase, ruby ..**$95**
#994 Popeye & Olive, 7", ruby **$50**
Unknown #, Frost etch, 8" **$40**
Unknown #, paneled, floral silver
overlay, cobalt, 10-1/2"...............**$90**
Unknown #, paneled, Gothic Garden
etch, green, 10-1/2" **$300**
Unknown #, paneled, silver overlay,
opal, 10-1/2" **$375**

PAIRPOINT

History: The Pairpoint Manufacturing Co. was organized in 1880 as a silver-plating firm in New Bedford, Massachusetts. The company merged with Mount Washington Glass Co. in 1894 and became the Pairpoint Corporation. The new company produced specialty glass items, often accented with metal frames.

Pairpoint Corp. was sold in 1938 and Robert Gunderson became manager. He operated it as the Gunderson Glass Works until his death in 1952. From 1952 until the plant closed in 1956, operations were maintained under the name Gunderson-Pairpoint. Robert Bryden reopened the glass manufacturing business in 1970, moving it back to the New Bedford area.

Pairpoint large cut chalice, bubble knopped baluster-shaped stem, blue cut to clear chalice, 11-1/2" h, **$300.**
Photo courtesy of The Early Auction Company, LLC.

Box, cov, Russian pattern cut glass, silver mountings, sgd "Pairpoint," 7-1/4" d...**$410**

Candlesticks, pr, cobalt blue, controlled bubble sphere...................**$450**

Compote, glass bowl painted with yellow and blue poppies against a rose-colored ground, gilt accents, attributed to Mount Washington Glass Company, Pairpoint ribbed silver plated base with paw feet, sgd "Pairpoint" on base, dent, 7-1/4" d, 5-1/4" h......**$470**

Console set, three-pc set, 12" d bowl, matching 3" h candlesticks, Tavern glass, bouquet of red, white, and green flowers..............................**$575**

Dish, fish shape, teal blue, controlled bubbles dec, late **$275**

Ferner, elongated mold blown oval body, purple and crimson pansies dec, emb metal lid with two ring handles, numbered "5126-211," 8" w..........**$400**

Perfume bottle, amethyst, painted butterfly, teardrop stopper, "P" in diamond mark, 6-3/4" h..................**$375**

Pokal, cov, Chrysopras, dark yellow-green, wheelcut grapes and leaves, finial wheelcut with eight-petaled flower, 14" h **$625**

Vase

Flared colorless crystal trumpet form, bright-cut floral dec, gilt metal foliate molded weighted pedestal base, imp "Pairpoint C1509," 14-1/2" h **$490**

Tavern glass, bulbous, enameled floral dec of vase of flowers, base numbered, 5-1/2" h, 4-1/2" w..........**$225**

PATE-DE-VERRE

History: The term "pate-de-verre" can be translated simply as "glass paste." It is manufactured by grinding lead glass into a powder or crystal form, making it into a paste by adding a two percent or three percent solution of sodium silicate, molding, firing, and carving. The Egyptians discovered the process as early as 1500 B.C.

In the late 19th century, the process was rediscovered by a group of French glassmakers. Almaric Walter, Henri Cros, Georges Despret, and the Daum brothers were leading manufacturers.

Contemporary sculptors are creating a second renaissance, led by the technical research of Jacques Daum.

Bookends, pr, Buddha, yellow amber pressed molded design, seated in lotus position, inscribed "A Walter Nancy," 6-1/2" h..**$2,450**

Center bowl, blue, purple, and green press molded design, seven exotic long-legged birds, central multi-pearl blossom, repeating design on ext., raised pedestal foot, sgd "G. Argy-Rousseau," 10-3/8" d, 3-3/4" h...**$6,750**

Clock, stars within pentagon and tapered sheaves motif, orange and black, molded sgd "G. Argy-Rousseau," clock by J. E. Caldwell, 4-1/2" sq......................**$2,750**

Dagger, frosted blade, relief design, green horse head handle, script sgd "Nancy France," 12" l................**$1,200**

Jewelry, pendant, round plaque, low relief molded rose blossom and branch, shaded rose, brown, and frosted glass, molded "G.A.R," (G. Argy-Rousseau), c1925, 2-1/4" d..........**$700**

Paperweight, large beetle, green leaves, mottled blue ground, intaglio "AW" mark, 3/4" w, 1-1/4" h **$6,800**

Sculpture, crab in sea grasses, lemon yellow, chocolate brown, pale mauve, and sea green, sgd "A. Walter/Nancy" and "Berge/ SC," 9-5/8" l..........**$8,500**

Tray

Molded as large moth, mottled blue, yellow, and emerald green, brown accents, emb "A. Walter," c1910, 5" d **$1,150**

Green to yellow ground, molded school of swimming fish, sgd "A. Walter Nancy, Berge," 6" w ...**$1,450**

Vase, press molded and carved, mottled amethyst and frost ground, three black and green crabs, red eyes, naturalistic seaweed at rim, center imp "G. Argy-Rousseau," base imp "France," 5-1/2" h......................................**$5,500**

Veilleuse, Gabriel Argy-Rousseau, press molded oval lamp shade, frosted mottled gray glass, elaborate purple arches with three teardrop-shaped windows of yellow, center teal-green stylized blossoms on black swirling stems, imp "G. Arty-Rousseau" at lower edge, wrought iron frame, three ball feet centering internal lamp socket, conforming iron cover, 8-1/2" h **$6,900**

PAPERWEIGHTS

History: Although paperweights had their origin in ancient Egypt, it was in the mid-19th century that this art form reached its zenith. The finest paperweights were produced between 1834 and 1855 in France by the Clichy, Baccarat, and Saint Louis factories. Other weights made in England, Italy, and Bohemia during this period rarely match the quality of the French weights.

In the early 1850s, the New England Glass Co. in Cambridge, Massachusetts, and the Boston and Sandwich Glass Co. in Sandwich, Massachusetts, became the first American factories to make paperweights.

Popularity peaked during the classic period (1845-1855) and faded toward the end of the 19th century. Paperweight production was rediscovered nearly a century later in the mid-1900s. Baccarat, Saint Louis, Perthshire, and many studio craftsmen in the U.S. and Europe still make contemporary weights.

Paperweight, Vandermark, red flower, marked "FLC 1980," on lighted base, **$50.**
Photo courtesy of Joy Luke Auctions.

Antique

Baccarat, France, Double Garland, double trefoil garland of red and white canes centered by ring of blue canes, pink white and green cane, minor wear, 19th C, 3" d, 2" h **$490**

Boston & Sandwich Glass Co., second half 19th C

Five large pears, four large leaves, four small vegetables, four small leaves, yellow, red, green, and rose, dew-like air traps, polished concave base, 1-1/2" h, 2-1/4" d **$315**

Flower, 10 bright blue petals with central cane, deep green stem, three leaves, dew-like air traps, polished concave base, 2" h, 2-3/4" d **$550**

Clichy, France, 19th C

Chequer, complex millefiori canes centered by pink and green Clichy rose, all divided by white latticinio twists, 2-3/4" d, 2" h **$1,265**

Millefiori, complex millefiori canes set in colorless crystal, 1-3/4" d, 1-3/8" h **$375**

Swirled, alternating purple and white pinwheels emanating from white, green, and pink pastry mold cane, minor bubbles, 2-5/8" d........**$2,200**

Degenhart, John, window, red crystal cube with yellow and orange upright center lily, one to window, four side windows, bubble in center of flower's stamens, 3-3/16" x 2-1/4" x 2-1/4" **$1,225**

Gillinder, orange turtle with moving appendages in hollow center, pale orange ground, molded dome, 3-1/16" d.....................**$500**

Millville, umbrella pedestal, red, white, green, blue, and yellow int., bubble in sphere center, 3-1/8" d, 3-3/8" h **$800**

New England Glass Co.

Apple form, deep rose to bright yellow, clear circular base, engraved "K. A. Osgood," second half 19th C, 2-1/2" h, 3" d.................**$990**

Pink flower, striated pink five-petal flowers, millefiori cane center, pink bud on deep green leafy stem, white latticino bed, minor wear, 2-1/4" d, 1-3/4" h **$690**

Pinchbeck, pastoral dancing scene, couple dancing before a group of onlookers, 3-3/16" d....................**$650**

Sandwich Glass Co.

Dahlia, red petaled flower, millefiori cane center, bright green leafy stem, highlighted by trapped bubble dec, white latticino ground, c1870, 2-1/2" d, 1-3/4" h......................**$650**

Poinsettia, double, red flower with double tier of petals, green and white Lutz rose, green stem and leaves, bubbles between petals, 3" d **$1,200**

St. Louis, fruit basket, red and green ripening fruits, latticino base basket, central base cane, 3" d, 2-1/2" h **$1,150**

Unknown maker, sulphide, silvery white figure of walking dog, polished base, light scratching and pitting, late 19th or early 20th C, 1-3/8" h, 2-1/8" d **$110**

Val St. Lambert, patterned millefiori, four red, white, blue, pistachio, and turquoise complex canes circlets spaced around central pink, turquoise and cadmium green canes circlet, canes set on stripes of lace encircled by spiraling red and blue torsade, minor blocking crease, 3-1/2" d **$950**

Modern

Ayotte, Rick, yellow finch, perched on branch, faceted, sgd and dated, limited edition, 1979 ....**$750**

Baccarat, Gridel pelican cane surrounded by five concentric rings of yellow, pink, green, and white complex canes, pink canes contain 18 Gridel silhouette canes, lace ground, signature cane, sgd and dated, limited ed. of 350, 1973 date cane, 3-1/16" d **$850**

Banford, Bob, cornflower, blue flower, yellow center, pink and white twisted torsade, "B" cane at stem, 3" d ...**$550**

Bryden Pairpoint Glass Co., red rose, green leaves, cut diamond-point panel base, second half 20th C, 2-1/4" h, 3-1/4" d **$210**

Kaziun, Charles, concentric millefiori, heart, turtle silhouette, shamrocks, six-pointed stars, and floret canes encircled by purple and white torsade, turquoise ground flecked with goldstone, K signature cane, 2-1/16" d **$1,200**

Labino, free form, white, amber, and irid gold flower center, air bubbles, surrounded by green glass, sgd "Labino 1969," 2-1/2" d **$210**

Orient and Flume, red butterfly with blue and white accents, brown and green vines, white millefiori blossoms over dark ground, orig sticker and box, 3-1/2" d, dated 1977............**$235**

Parabelle, tightly packed multicolored millefiori canes, dark blue ground,

Paperweight, Lundberg Studio, butter-fly, 1980, **$65.**
Photo courtesy of Joy Luke Auctions.

Paperweight, Tiffany Studios, gilt-parcel crouching panther, stamped "Tiffany Studios New York," 1-1/2" x 4", **$550.**
Photo courtesy of David Rago Auctions, Inc.

attributed to Gary and Doris Scrutton, signature and date cane, orig paper label, 2-3/4" d **$575**

Perthshire, miniature bouquet, yellow flowers, pink buds, basket of deep blue canes, green and pink millefiori canes cut to form base, orig box and certificate, 2-1/2" d **$160**

Rosenfeld, Ken, Monarch butterfly, leafy stem, red blossom with three buds, R signature cane, inscribed "KR 2001," 1-7/8" h, 2-5/8" h.............**$350**

Salazar, David, compound floral, lavender six-petal poinsettia star blossom, three-leaf stem over green and red wreath, white ground, inscribed "David Salazar/111405/

Lundberg Studios 1991," 3-1/4" d **$225**

Stankard, Paul, morning glory, bee on hive in center of two blue morning glories, three orange berries, two yellow flowers, sandy ground, root figure and word canes "Moist" and "Fertile" beneath, inscribed "Paul J. Stankard V32 '97," 2-3/8" h, 3-1/4" d **$2,875**

Tarsitano, Debbie, pansy, two central blue and yellow pansies flanked by three rose-pink blossoms, three yellow blossoms, green leafy stems, signature cane **$475**

Trabucco, Victor, Buffalo, NY, magnum pansy, purple pansy blos-

som and bud, leaf stem, white lace cushion, inscribed "Trabucco 1998," 2-1/2" h, 3-1/2" d **$635**

Whitefrairs, Star of David, five rows of tightly packed blue and white millefiori canes, 3" d **$395**

Whittemore, Francis, two green and brown acorns on branch with three brown and yellow oak leaves, translucent cobalt blue ground, circular top facet five oval punties on sides, 20-3/8" d......................................**$300**

Ysart, Paul, green fish, yellow eye, yellow and white jasper ground encircled by pink, green, and white complex cane garland, PY signature cane **$550**

PATTERN GLASS

History: Pattern glass is clear or colored glass pressed into one of hundreds of patterns. Deming Jarves of the Boston and Sandwich Glass Co. invented one of the first successful pressing machines in 1828. By the 1860s, glass-pressing machinery had been improved, and mass production of good-quality matched tableware sets began. The idea of a matched glassware table service (including goblets, tumblers, creamers, sugars, compotes, cruets, etc.) quickly caught on in America. Many pattern glass table services had numerous accessory pieces such as banana stands, molasses cans, and water bottles.

Early pattern glass (flint) was made with a lead formula, giving many items a ringing sound when tapped. Lead became too valuable to be used in glass manufacturing during the Civil War, and in 1864, Hobbs, Brockunier & Co., West Virginia, developed a soda lime (non-flint) formula. Pattern glass also was produced in transparent colors, milk glass, opalescent glass, slag glass, and custard glass.

The hundreds of companies that produced pattern glass experienced periods of development, expansions, personnel problems, material and supply demands, fires, and mergers. In 1899, the National Glass Co. was formed as a combination of 19 glass companies in Pennsylvania, Ohio, Indiana, West Virginia, and Maryland. U.S. Glass, another consortium, was founded in 1891. These combines resulted from attempts to save small companies by pooling talents, resources, and patterns. Because of this pooling, the same pattern often can be attributed to several companies.

Additional Listings: Bread Plates, Children's Toy Dishes, Cruets, Custard Glass, Milk Glass, Sugar Shakers, Toothpicks, and specific companies.

Abbreviations

ah	applied handle
GUTDODB	Give Us This Day Our Daily Bread
hs	high standard
ind	individual
ls	low standard
os	original stopper

Pattern Glass, Tree of Life, ice cream tray, green, **$60.**

Reproduction Alert. Pattern glass has been widely reproduced. Items in the listing marked with an * are those for which reproductions are known to exist. Care should be exercised when purchasing such pieces.

Pattern Glass, Thousand Eye, compote, apple green, open, hs, 10" d, **$75.**

Amazon

Sawtooth, Sawtooth Band

Manufactured by Bryce Brothers, Pittsburgh, PA, c1890-91. Reissued by United States Glass Company, Pittsburgh, PA, Factory "B," c1891-1904.

Made in non-flint, clear, with fern and berry etching or plain. Some pieces were made in clear amber, amethyst, blue, canary-yellow, some with ruby stain. Add 20% for those.

Items	Etched	Plain
Banana Stand, hs	$115	$65
Bowl, cov, oval, 6-1/2" l	-	60
Bowl, cov, round, 5" d	30	-
Bowl, cov, round, 6" d	30	-
Bowl, cov, round, 7" d	36	-
Bowl, cov, round, 8" d	36	-
Bowl, cov, round, 9" d	36	30
Bowl, flared, plain rim, 5" d	12	-
Bowl, flared, plain rim, 6" d	18	-
Bowl, flared, plain rim, 7" d	18	-
Bowl, flared, plain rim, 8" d	24	-
Bowl, scalloped, 4" d	-	12
Bowl, scalloped, 4-1/2" d	-	12
Bowl, scalloped, 5" d	-	18
Bowl, scalloped, 6" d	-	18
Bowl, scalloped, 7" d	-	24
Bowl, scalloped, 8" d	-	30
Butter Dish, cov	65	60
Cake Stand, hs, 8" d	-	48
Cake Stand, hs, 9" d	-	48
Cake Stand, hs, 9-1/2" d	-	55
Cake Stand, hs, 10" d	-	60
Celery Vase, flat	42	36
Celery Vase, ftd	42	36
Champagne	-	42
Child's Butter Dish, cov, flat	60	-
Child's Creamer, pedestal	30	-
Child's Spooner, pedestal, sawtooth rim	36	-
Child's Sugar Bowl, cov, pedestal	36	-
Claret	42	36
Compote, cov, hs, 5" d	-	55
Compote, cov, hs, 6" d	-	72
Compote, cov, hs, 7" d	-	55
Compote, cov, hs, 8" d	-	65
Compote, open, flared, scalloped rim, deep bowl, 4-1/2" d	-	30
Compote, open, flared, scalloped rim, deep bowl, 5" d	-	30
Compote, open, flared, scalloped rim, deep bowl, 6" d	-	30

Items	Etched	Plain
Compote, open, flared, scalloped rim, deep bowl, 7" d	$-	$36
Compote, open, flared, scalloped rim, deep bowl, 8" d	-	36
Compote, open, hs, smooth edge, 9-1/2" d	-	55
Compote, open, round, flared bowl, 5" d	-	30
Compote, open, round, flared bowl, 6" d	-	30
Compote, open, round, flared bowl, 7" d	-	36
Compote, open, round, flared bowl, 8" d	-	36
Compote, open, round, flared bowl, 9-1/2" d	-	55
Compote, open, saucer bowl, sawtooth rim, 8" d	-	36
Compote, open, saucer bowl, sawtooth rim, 9" d	-	36
Compote, open, saucer bowl, sawtooth rim, 10" d	-	55
Cordial	48	30
Creamer	36	210
Cruet, ftd, os, fist or Maltese cross stopper	60	55
Dish, cov, oval, flat, lion handles, 6" l	30	-
Dish, cov, oval, flat, lion handles, 7" l	36	-
Dish, cov, oval, flat, lion handles, 8" l	42	-
Dish, open, flat, lion handles, 6" l	12	-
Dish, open, flat, lion handles, 7" l	18	-
Dish, open, flat, lion handles, 8" l	24	-
Dish, open, round, shallow, lion handles, 4-1/2" d	24	-
Dish, open, round, shallow, lion handles, 6" d	24	-
Egg Cup	-	20
Goblet, 4-1/2" h	36	-

Items	Etched	Plain
Goblet, 5" h	$30	-
Goblet, 6" h	36	-
Jelly Compote, cov, 4-1/2" d	48	-
Jelly Compote, open, 4-1/2" d	55	42
Pitcher, water, half gallon	72	55
Relish	210	30
Salt & Pepper Shakers, pr	60	48
Salt, individual	-	18
Salt, master	-	110
Sauce, flat, flared bowl, scalloped rim, 4" d	-	12
Sauce, flat, flared bowl, scalloped rim, 4-1/2" d	-	12
Sauce, flat, flared bowl, scalloped rim, handled, 4-1/2" d	-	18
Sauce, ftd, 4" d	18	18
Sauce, ftd, 4-1/2" d	18	18
Spooner	30	24
Sugar Bowl, cov	55	55
Syrup, orig top	60	50
Tumbler, flat	30	30
Vase, hs, ruffled rim	24	30
Wine	30	24

Reproduction Alert. Goblet, water pitcher, water tray, and tumbler have been found as reproductions, some of which date from the late 1930s.

Basketweave

Unknown maker. Shards have been found at Boston and Sandwich Glass Company, Sandwich, MA, and the Burlington Glass Works, Hamilton, Ontario, Canada. Pattern dates to the mid-1880s.

Made in non-flint, amber, apple green, blue, canary, clear, and vaseline. Some covered pieces have a stippled cat's head finial.

Items	Amber or Canary	Apple	Blue	Clear	Vaseline
Berry Bowl, master	$30	$-	$30	$110	$-
Bread Plate, 11" d	42	-	42	12	-
Butter Dish, cov	42	72	48	36	48
Compote, cov, hs, 7" d	55	75	55	48	66
Compote, cov, ls	55	75	55	48	66
Compote, open, hs	36	55	48	24	42
Compote, open, ls	36	55	48	24	42
Cordial	30	48	210	24	36
Creamer	36	60	42	210	42
Cup and Saucer	42	72	42	36	310
Dish, oval	15	24	18	12	18
Egg Cup	110	36	24	18	30
Finger Bowl	24	42	30	24	30
Goblet	210	60	42	24	36
Mug	30	48	30	18	36
Pickle	110	36	24	110	25
Pitcher, milk	48	72	55	42	60
Pitcher, water	72	75	72	55	85
Plate, 11" d, handles	30	310	30	24	36
Sauce	12	12	15	10	15
Spooner	36	310	36	24	36
Sugar Bowl, cov	42	48	42	36	48
Syrup, orig top	60	75	60	55	55
Tumbler, ftd †	110	36	24	18	24
Waste Bowl	24	42	30	110	30
Water Tray †	42	55	48	36	60
Wine	36	60	36	24	36

Champion

Fan with Cross Bars, McKee's No. 103, Seagrit

Manufactured by McKee & Brothers Glass Company, Pittsburgh, PA, c1894, McKee-Jeannette Glass Company, Jeannette, PA, and National Glass Company, Pittsburgh, PA, from c1894 to c1917. Stained items are believed to have been decorated at the Beaumont Glass Works, Pittsburgh, PA, which also sold them as its own products.

Made in amber, clear, and ruby stained with limited production in emerald green. Pieces are often found with gilt trim.

Item	Amber Stained	Clear	Ruby Stained
Berry Bowl, individual, sq or round	$-	$-	$24
Berry Bowl, master, sq or round	55	-	65
Butter Dish, cov	120	55	120
Cake Stand, hs, 7-1/2" d	120	42	110
Cake Stand, hs, 8-1/2" d	135	48	115
Cake Stand, hs, 10" d	135	55	120
Cake Stand, hs, 11" d	118	60	135
Carafe	142	60	180
Castor Set, 3 bottles, toothpick holder, matching glass holder	-	130	-
Celery Vase	120	48	120
Compote, cov, hs	190	55	240
Compote, open, belled or deep bowl, scalloped, 6" d	155	42	55
Compote, open, belled or deep bowl, scalloped, 7" d	180	48	72
Compote, open belled or deep bowl, scalloped, 8" d	180	48	72
Compote, open, belled or deep bowl, scalloped, 9" d	155	60	85
Creamer, individual	42	24	42
Creamer, table	60	30	72
Cruet, os, 4 or 5 oz	180	36	1115

Item	Amber Stained	Clear	Ruby Stained
Custard Cup	$30	$12	$30
Goblet	65	30	65
Ice Bucket	130	48	-
Jelly Compote, open, belled, deep, or shallow bowl, scalloped, 5" d	65	24	65
Marmalade Jar	110	48	110
Perfume Bottle, orig teardrop stopper, bulbous or squatty	55	30	55
Pickle Dish, 8" l	30	18	30
Pitcher, water, tankard	180	85	190
Plate, 6" d	60	30	90
Plate, 8" d	60	30	90
Plate, 10" d	55	30	95
Punch Bowl, ftd, 14" d	300	120	285
Rose Bowl	55	30	55
Salt and Pepper Shakers, pr	85	36	85
Salt, individual	42	12	42
Sauce, flat, serrated rim, round or sq	24	6	24
Spooner	48	24	55
Sugar Bowl, cov, individual	72	42	90
Sugar Bowl, cov, table	90	48	85
Syrup, orig top, orig top	240	90	240
Toothpick Holder	65	24	85
Tumbler	48	18	55
Water Tray	-	55	-
Wine	55	24	55
Wine Tray	-	55	-

Diamond Thumbprint
Diamond and Concave

Manufacture attributed to Boston and Sandwich Glass Company, Sandwich, MA, and other factories in the 1850s.

Made in flint, clear.

Items	Clear
Ale Glass, 6-1/4" h	$110
Bitters Bottle, orig pewter pourer, applied lip, polished pontil	460
Bowl, cov, 6" d	180
Bowl, cov, 7" d	180
Bowl, cov, 8" d	190
Bowl, open, plain rim, 5" d	65
Bowl, open, plain rim, 6" d	85
Bowl, open, plain rim, 7" d	75
Bowl, open, plain rim, 8" d	85
Bowl, open, scalloped rim, 5" d	65
Bowl, open, scalloped rim, 6" d	85
Bowl, open, scalloped rim, 7" d	75
Bowl, open, scalloped rim, 8" d	75
Butter Dish, cov	240
Cake Stand, hs, 9" d	300
Cake Stand, hs, 10" d	350
Cake Stand, hs, 11" d	400
Cake Stand, hs, 12" d	450
Candlestick, 6-1/2" h	180
Castor Bottle	36
Celery Vase, scalloped top	225
Champagne, large	285
Champagne, small	300
Compote, cov, hs, 6" d	225
Compote, cov, hs, 7" d	250
Compote, cov, hs, 8"	275
Compote, cov, ls, 6" d	240
Compote, cov, ls, 7" d	270
Compote, cov, ls, 8" d	300
Compote, open, hs, scalloped rim, 5" d or 6" d	85

Items	Clear
Compote, open, hs, scalloped rim, 7" d	$95
Compote, open, hs, scalloped rim, 8" d	100
Compote, open, hs, scalloped rim, 9" d	125
Compote, open, hs, scalloped rim, 10" d	150
Compote, open, ls, scalloped rim, 5" d or 6" d	65
Compote, open, ls, scalloped rim, 7" d or 8" d	75
Compote, open, ls, scalloped rim, 9" d	85
Compote, open, ls, scalloped rim, 10" d	110
Cordial, large	330
Cordial, small	360
Creamer, ah, footed	270
Cruet, os	495
Decanter, applied bar lip, pint	190
Decanter, applied bar lip, quart	1115
Decanter, os, pint	190
Decanter, os, quart	270
Dish, oval, flat, 7" l or 8" l	65
Dish, oval, flat, 9" l or 10" l	75
Egg Cup	85
Finger Bowl	120
Goblet	360
Honey Dish, plain or star center	30
Mug, ah	240
Pitcher, milk, ah	460
Pitcher, water, ah	600
Sauce, flat	18
Spooner	85
Sugar Bowl, cov	180
Sweetmeat Jar, cov	300
Tray, rect, 11" l, 7" w	120

Reproduction Alert. Reproduction bitters bottles, celery vases, compotes, sugar bowls, and other pieces were reproduced by Viking Glass Company, New Martinsville, WV, for the Sandwich Glass Museum. Each piece is embossed with the "S. M." trademark. Colors of reproductions include amber, amethyst, blue, clear, peach, ruby, and sterling gray.

Items	Clear
Tumbler, bar	$130
Tumbler, water, flat	85
Waste Bowl	110
Whiskey, applied handle	360
Whiskey, no handle	130
Wine	300
Wine Jug	2,600

Duncan Block

Block, Waffle Variant, Duncan's Pattern Line No. 308 and 309

Manufactured by George Duncan & Sons, Pittsburgh, PA, c1887. The pattern was continuously produced until the merger with United States Glass Company in 1891 until 1904, at Factory "D" and Factory "P."

Made in non-flint, clear. Sometimes found with ruby staining and copper wheel engraving.

Items	Clear
Basket, 7" d	$60
Basket, 8" d	72
Bowl, crimped rim, 8" d	30
Butter Dish, cov, collared base	48
Butter Dish, cov, flat, flanged rim	55
Carafe	60
Catsup Bottle	55
Celery Tray	30
Celery Vase, flat, scalloped rim	42
Celery Vase, footed, scalloped rim	48
Champagne	18
Cheese Dish, cov	60
Cologne Bottle, 1 oz or 2 oz	36
Cologne Bottle, 4 oz, 6 oz, or 8 oz	42
Cologne Bottle, 16 oz	48
Creamer, individual	18
Creamer, table, collared base	30
Creamer, table, flat	30
Cruet, os, round, 1 oz or 2 oz	30
Cruet, os, round, 4 oz or 6 oz	36
Cruet, os, square, 1 oz or 2 oz	36
Cruet, os, square, 4 oz or 6 oz	42
Custard Cup	12
Egg Cup	18
Finger Bowl	15
Goblet	24

Items	Clear
Ice Cream Tray, rect, with or without handles, deep or shallow	$42
Lamp Shade, gas globe, round	42
Lamp Shade, gas globe, ruffled	42
Pitcher, milk, tankard	55
Pitcher, water, bulbous	72
Pitcher, water, tankard	55
Plate, 7" d	12
Plate, 8" d	12
Puff Box, cov, squatty or tall	42
Salad Bowl, crimped rim, 7" d, 8" d, or 9" d	30
Salad Bowl, plain rim, 7" d, 8" d, or 9" d	24
Salt, individual	15
Salt, master	18
Salt Shaker, orig top, 4 styles	42
Sauce, flat, 4" d, 4-1/2" d, or 5" d	12
Sauce, footed, 4" d, 4-1/2" d or 5" d	12
Sherbet Cup	12
Spooner, collared base	30
Spooner, flat base	30
Sugar Bowl, cov, collared base	55
Sugar Bowl, cov, flat base	42
Sugar Shaker, orig top	48
Syrup, orig silver plated top	48
Tray, round, 7" d or 8" d	30
Tumbler	18
Wine	18

Hexagon Block

Manufactured by Hobbs, Brockunier & Company, Wheeling, WV, c1889. Reissued by United States Glass Company, Pittsburgh, PA, after the 1891 merger. Made in non-flint, clear, clear with amber stain, and clear with ruby stain. It is also found plain or etched with the Fern and Berry etching or Bird and Flower etching. Prices below are for plain pieces.

Items	Amber Stained	Clear	Ruby Stained
Bowl, deep or shallow, 7" d	$24	$18	$24
Bowl, deep, 9" d	48	30	48
Bowl, shallow, 9" d	36	30	36
Butter Dish, cov	130	48	142
Celery Vase, ftd	90	42	105
Compote, cov, hs, deep bowl, 7" d	110	55	120
Compote, cov, hs, deep bowl, 8" d	115	60	106
Compote, cov, hs, saucer bowl, 8" d	105	48	115
Compote, cov, hs, saucer bowl, 9" d	110	55	120
Compote, open, hs, deep bowl, 7" d	80	30	90
Compote, open, hs, deep bowl, 8" d	85	36	95
Compote, open, hs, saucer bowl, 8" d	72	24	85
Compote, open, hs, saucer bowl, 9" d	80	30	90
Creamer, ftd, ah	80	48	90
Custard Cup, ftd, ah	30	18	42
Finger Bowl	24	48	36
Goblet	60	42	72
Pickle Jar, cov, ftd	115	55	125
Salt Shaker, ftd, orig top	24	18	30
Sauce, flat, 4" d or 4-1/2" d	24	12	18
Spooner, ftd	55	30	60
Sugar Bowl, cov, ftd	85	55	90
Syrup, orig top, ph	260	60	280
Tumbler	42	18	48

Hickman

La Clede

Manufactured by McKee & Brothers Glass Company, Pittsburgh, PA, c1897. Made in non-flint, clear, and ruby stained. Also documented in light green and two shades of amber.

Items	Clear	Emerald Green
Banana Stand, ftd	$80	$–
Bon Bon, sq, 9" d	18	–
Bowl, round, or with scalloped top, 4" d	15	–
Bowl, round, or with scalloped top, 6" d	18	30
Bowl, round, or with scalloped top, 8" d	24	–
Bowl, square, 7" w	18	110
Butter Dish, cov	42	72
Celery	30	42
Champagne	30	–
Cologne Bottle, faceted stopper	36	–
Compote, cov, hs, 7" d	90	–
Compote, open, hs, 8" d	55	–
Condiment Set, handled tray, cruet, pepper sauce bottle, open salt	105	112
Cordial	30	–
Creamer	30	42
Cruet, os	55	–
Custard Cup	15	–
Dish, sq, 4" w	18	–
Goblet	36	48
Ice Bucket	72	–
Jelly Compote, open, ls, 4-1/2" d	48	55

Items	Clear	Emerald Green
Lemonade	$18	$–
Mustard Jar, underplate, cov	55	–
Nappy, 5" d	12	–
Olive, 4", handle	12	24
Pepper Sauce Bottle	30	–
Pickle	18	24
Pitcher, water	65	–
Plate, 9-1/4" d	155	–
Punch Bowl	190	390
Punch Cup	12	18
Punch Glass, ftd	36	–
Relish	24	18
Rose Bowl	30	36
Salt, individual, flat, sloping sides	12	–
Salt Shaker, single, round, long cut neck	18	–
Salt Shaker, single, round, squat	24	36
Salt Shaker, single, square	24	–
Sauce	10	12
Spooner	35	–
Sugar Bowl, cov	45	60
Sugar Shaker	55	–
Toothpick Holder	55	90
Tumbler	36	–
Vase, 10-1/4" h	15	55
Wine	36	42

Reproduction Alert. The 10" vase and 12" h fan-shaped vase have been reproduced in amberina, clear, and milk white.

Holly

Manufacture attributed to Boston and Sandwich Glass Company, Sandwich, MA, in the late 1860s, and early 1870s. Made in non-flint, clear.

Items	Clear
Bowl, cov, 8" d	$160
Butter Dish, cov	160
Cake Stand, hs, 9 or 11" d	118-130
Celery Vase, pedestal, scalloped rim	112
Compote, cov, hs, 8" d	180
Compote, open, ls, 8-1/2" d	160
Creamer, ah	130
Egg Cup	80
Goblet	120
Pickle, oval	36
Pitcher, water, ah	270
Salt, individual, flat, oval	80
Salt, master, ftd	95
Sauce, flat, 4" d	24
Spooner	72
Sugar Bowl, cov, flat or pedestal	130
Tumbler, flat or footed	130
Wine	130

Jacob's Ladder
Imperial, Maltese, US Glass Pattern Line No. 4,778

Manufactured by Portland Glass Company, Portland, ME, and Bryce, McKee & Company, Pittsburgh, PA, in 1876, by United States Glass Company, Pittsburgh, PA, in 1891, and the Diamond Flint Glass Company, Canada, c1902. The pattern was designed and patented by John Bryce, June 13, 1876, under the name Imperial. Made in non-flint, clear. A few pieces found in amber, yellow, blue, pale blue, and pale green.

Pattern Glass, Jacob's Ladder celery, pale blue, **$55.**

Items	Clear
Berry Bowl, ornate silver plate holder, ftd, 9" d	$130
Bowl, cov, 6" d	42
Bowl, oval, 5-1/2" x 7-3/4"	1,118
Bowl, oval, 7-1/2" x 10-3/4"	24
Bread Tray, oblong	55
Butter Dish, cov	80
Cake Stand, hs, 8" or 12" d	60-72
Castor Bottle	110
Castor Set, 4 bottles	120
Celery Vase	55
Cologne Bottle, Maltese cross stopper, ftd	105
Compote, cov, hs, 6" d	95
Compote, cov, hs, 8-1/2", 9" or 9-1/2" d	105-130
Compote, open, oblong, dolphin stem	360
Compote, open, hs, scalloped, 7", 9", 10-1/2" or 12" d	36-65

Items	Clear
Creamer, pedestal	$42
Cruet, os, ftd	105
Goblet, knob stem	72
Honey Dish, 3-1/2" d	12
Marmalade Jar, cov	90
Mug, ah	120
Pickle Tray, double handles	12
Pitcher, water, ah	160
Plate, 6-1/4" d	24
Relish, 9-1/2" x 5-1/2"	18
Salt, master, ftd	24
Sauce, flat, 4" d, 4-1/2" d, or 5" d	10
Sauce, footed, 4" d, 4-1/2" d, or 5" d	15
Spooner, pedestal	42
Sugar Bowl, cov	95
Syrup, knight's head finial	130
Syrup, plain top	120
Tumbler, bar	105
Wine	42

New Jersey
Loops and Drops

Manufactured by United States Glass Company, Pittsburgh, PA, c1900-08, in States pattern series. Made in non-flint, clear, clear with gilt trim, and ruby stained. Items with perfect gilt trim (gold) are worth more than those with worn gold. An emerald green 11" vase is known (value $90).

Items	Clear with Gilt Trim	Ruby Stained
Bowl, deep or flared bowl, 6", 7" or 8" d	$24-30	$48-60
Bowl, oval, plain or pointed ends, 8", 9" or 10" d	30-36	60-72
Bowl, saucer, 9" d	32	75
Bread Plate	36	–
Butter Dish, cov, flat	90	120
Butter Dish, cov, footed	130	–
Cake Stand, hs, 8" d	75	–
Carafe	72	–
Celery Tray, rect	30	48
Compote, cov, hs, 6", 7" or 8" d	55-75	85-110
Compote, open, hs, 6", 7" or 8" d	36-72	72-90
Compote, open, hs, shallow bowl, 10-1/2" d	75	–
Creamer	42	72
Cruet, os	60	–
Dish, oval, scalloped rim, 6" or 8" l	18-24	–
Dish, oval, scalloped rim, 10" l	30	60
Fruit Bowl, hs, 12-1/2" d	65	100

Items	Clear with Gilt Trim	Ruby Stained
Fruit Plate, 9-1/2", 10-1/2" or 12" d	$24-36	$—
Goblet	48	90
Jelly Compote, cov, hs, 5" d	45	65
Molasses Can	110	–
Olive Dish, pointed ends	18	–
Pickle Dish, rect	18	–
Pitcher, milk, ah	90	175
Pitcher, water, ah, bulbous	95	210
Pitcher, water, ph, straight sides	60	200
Plate, 8" d	36	55
Salt and Pepper Shakers, pr, small or hotel	42-60	65-118
Sauce, flat, 4" d	12	36
Spooner	35	90
Sugar Bowl, cov	72	95
Sweetmeat, cov, 8" d	75	110
Syrup, orig top	110	–
Toothpick Holder	65	230
Tumbler	36	60
Water Bottle	55	110
Wine, flared or straight bowl	48	72

Pressed Leaf
New Pressed Leaf

Manufactured by McKee Brothers, Pittsburgh, PA, c1868, and the Central Glass Company, Wheeling, WV, c1881. Shards have been found at Boston and Sandwich Glass Company, Sandwich, MA. The design was patented by H. S. McKee on Nov. 5, 1867. Made in flint and non-flint, clear.

Items	Non-Flint Clear	Items	Non-Flint Clear
Bowl, oval	$35	Egg Cup, ftd	$30
Butter Dish, cov	60	Goblet	36
Cake Stand, hs	72	Lamp, oil, orig burner and chimney	130
Champagne	55	Pitcher, water, half gallon	120
Compote, cov, hs, 6", 7" or 8" d	65-75	Salt, master, open, ftd	42
Compote, cov, ls, 6", 7" or 8" d	55-65	Sauce, flat, 4" d	12
Compote, open, hs, 6", 7" or 8" d	42-55	Spooner, ftd, scalloped	30
Compote, open, ls, 6", 7" or 8" d	42-55	Sugar Bowl, cov	55
Cordial	60	Wine	48
Creamer, ah	55		

Thistle
Early Thistle, Scotch Thistle

Manufactured by Bryce, Walker & Company, Pittsburgh, PA, in 1872. Shards have been found at Burlington Glass Works, Hamilton, Ontario, Canada. Made in non-flint, clear.

Items	Clear	Items	Clear
Bowl, cov, 8" d	$72	Pitcher, milk, ah, quart	$130
Bowl, open, 8" d	36	Pitcher, water, ah, half gallon	120
Butter Dish, cov	65	Relish Tray, oval	30
Cake Stand, hs, large	90	Salt, master, ftd	45
Compote, cov, hs, 6" or 8" d	75	Sauce, flat, 4" d	15
Compote, cov, ls, 8" d	90	Spooner	45
Cordial	72	Sugar Bowl, cov	75
Creamer, ah	75	Sugar Bowl, open, buttermilk type	48
Egg Cup	48	Syrup, orig top	120
Goblet	55	Tumbler, flat or footed	48-55
Pickle Dish, tapered at one end	30	Wine	60

Reproduction Alert. Reproductions of this pattern are confined to the goblet. These are generally smaller and marked with an "R" within a large shield.

Tree of Life
Portland's

Manufactured by Portland Glass Company, Portland, ME, c1870. Made in flint, and non-flint, in amber, clear, dark blue, green, light blue, purple, and, yellow. Color is rare. A blue finger bowl in a silver plated holder is valued at $190.

Items	Non-Flint	Items	Non-Flint
Bowl, berry, oval	$36	Ice Cream Tray	$60
Butter Dish, cov	65	Lemonade	60
Celery Vase, silver plated frame	65	Mug	60
Cologne Bottle, faceted stopper	55	Pitcher, milk or water, applied handle	115
Champagne	65	Pitcher, milk or water, molded handle	75
Compote, open, hs, 8-1/2" d	130	Plate, 6" d	30
Compote, open, hs, 10" d	112	Sauce, flat, 3-3/4" d	15
Compote, open, ls, 10" d	60	Sauce, leaf shape	18
Creamer, applied handle	85	Spooner	45
Creamer, molded handle	60	Sugar Bowl, cov	85
Creamer, silver plated holder	90	Sugar Bowl, silver plated holder	90
Egg Cup	36	Toothpick Holder, footed, scalloped	60
Epergne, sgd "P.G. Company Patd"	130	Tumbler, ftd	48
Finger Bowl, underplate	72	Vase	60
Fruit Dish, silver plated holder	110	Water Tray	110
Goblet, clear shield on side	60	Wine	65
Goblet, plain	45		
Goblet, regular, sgd "P.G. Flint"	75		

Reproduction Alert. Reproductions of Tree of Life were made by L. G. Wright Glass Company, New Martinsville, WV, 1968. Colors of these reproductions include amber, blue, and clear.

PEACHBLOW

Peachblow finger bow, Mt. Washington, pinched ruffled rim, 5-1/2" d, **$1,800.**
Photo courtesy of The Early Auction Company, LLC.

Peachblow, Wheeling, glossy square mouth vase, 4" h, **$500.**
Photo courtesy of The Early Auction Company, LLC.

History: Peachblow, an art glass which derives its name from a fine Chinese glazed porcelain, resembles a peach or crushed strawberries in color. Three American glass manufacturers and two English firms produced peachblow glass in the late 1880s. A fourth American company resumed the process in the 1950s. The glass from each firm has its own identifying characteristics.

Hobbs, Brockunier & Co., Wheeling peachblow: Opalescent glass, plated or cased with a transparent amber glass; shading from yellow at the base to a deep red at top; glossy or satin finish.

Mt. Washington "Peach Blow": A homogeneous glass, shading from a pale gray-blue to a soft rose color; some pieces enhanced with glass appliqués, enameling, and gilding.

New England Glass Works, New England peachblow (advertised as Wild Rose, but called Peach Blow at the plant): Translucent, shading from rose to white; acid or glossy finish; some pieces enameled and gilded.

Thomas Webb & Sons and Stevens and Williams (English firms): Peachblow-style cased art glass, shading from yellow to red; some pieces with cameo-type relief designs.

Gunderson Glass Co.: Produced peachblow-type art glass to order during the 1950s; shades from an opaque faint tint of pink, which is almost white, to a deep rose.

Marks: Pieces made in England are marked "Peach Blow" or "Peach Bloom."

Bowl

New England, Wild Rose, satin finish, smooth pontil mark, 3-3/4" d, 1-1/4" h **$495**

Acid finished, ftd, shaped trefoil fold down rim, soft pink shades to pale blue on bulbous rubbed body, three vertically ribbed feet, berry pontil, Mt. Washington, ex-Maude Feld, 7-1/2" d, 8" h **$12,000**

Bride's basket, Mount Washington, shades of pink, replated Meriden frame **$650**

Celery vase, New England, sq top, deep raspberry with purple highlights shading to white, 7" h, 4" w **$785**

Claret jug

Shape #322, Hobbs, Brockunier & Co., Wheeling, acid finish, applied reeded amber handle, ex-Maude Feld, 9-1/2" h **$5,500**

Shape #322, Hobbs, Brockunier & Co., Wheeling, shiny finish, applied reeded amber handle, ex-Maude Feld, 10" h **$6,500**

Cologne bottle, Webb, bulbous, raised gold floral branches, silver hallmarked dome top, 5" h **$900**

Cream pitcher

New England, satin finish, 2-3/4" h **$1,120**

Wheeling, applied amber handle, 3-1/4" h **$885**

Hobbs, Brockunier & Co., Wheeling, shiny, applied amber handle, 4-1/4" h, #319 .... **$650**

Cruet

Hobbs, Brockunier & Co., Wheeling, ruby reeded handle, amber faceted stopper, 7-1/4" h **$800**

Wheeling, ball shaped, mahogany colored trefoil spout and neck, paper label from Maude Feld, 6-1/2" h **$2,475**

Wheeling, glossy, petticoat, applied amber handle, cut and faceted stopper, orig Maude Feld label, ex-Maude Feld, 7" h **$850**

Wheeling, satin, teepee shape, applied amber handle, replacement faceted clear glass amber stopper, 7" h **$1,950**

Decanter, Gundersen, Pilgrim Canteen form, acid finish, deep raspberry to white, applied peachblow ribbed handle, deep raspberry stopper, 10" h, 5" w **$950**

Finger bowl, #93, Hobbs, Brockunier & Co., Wheeling, glossy, ovoid, 4-1/2" w, 2-3/4" h **$275**

Goblet, Gundersen, glossy finish, deep color, applied Burmese glass base, 7-1/4" h, 4" d top **$285**

Miniature, pitcher, #319, Hobbs, Brockunier & Co., Wheeling, glossy, sq mouth, orig Maude Feld paper label, ex-Maude Feld, 5" h **$700**

Mustard, cov, Wheeling, SP cov and handle **$475**

Pitcher

Wheeling, Drape, squatty, mahogany shading to lemon yellow, sq mouth, applied clear reeded handle, 5-1/2" h **$350**

Wheeling, glossy finish, sq mouth, applied amber handle, orig Maude Feld label on int. of mouth, ex-Maude Feld, 5-1/2" h **$800**

Wheeling, acid finish, sq mouth, deep mahogany extends to lemon yellow, applied amber handle, orig Maude Feld label, ex-Maude Feld, 5-3/4" h **$1,200**

Wheeling, glossy, rect mouth, applied amber handle, 7" h **$1,050**

Punch cup

Gundersen, acid finish **$275**

Hobbs, Brockunier, 2-1/2" h **$535**

Sugar shaker, Wheeling, 5-1/4" h" **$3,025**

Toothpick holder, Mt. Washington, dec, ex-Maude Feld, 2-1/2" h .. **$15,680**

Tumbler

Gundersen, matte finish, 3-3/4" h **$275**

New England, satin finish, 3-3/4" h **$285**

New England, satin finish, deep raspberry red on upper third shading to creamy white, 3-3/4" h.............**$285**

New England, shiny finish, 3-3/4" h **$285**

Wheeling, matte finish, 3-1/2" h ..**$200**

Wheeling, glossy finish, shading from fuchsia to yellow, 3-7/8" h **$200**

Vase

Mt. Washington, tapering ovoid, raised enameled, Queens design dec, ex-Maude Feld, 9-1/4" h **$20,000**

New England, ovoid, peaked rim, shading from soft pink to cream, camphor tooled base, 7-1/4" h ..**$250**

New England, satin finish, lily, fades to white stem and wafer base, 6-3/4" h **$635**

Wheeling glossy finish, sq mouth, 4" h **$500**

Wheeling, shiny finish, sq mouth, shouldered body, mahogany shading to custard yellow, white opaque liner, 4" h................................**$550**

Wheeling, rare lavender casing, ex-Maude Feld, 4" h, 6" d.........**$15,000**

Wheeling, Morgan, shiny finish, deep red shading to butterscotch, 8" h **$850**

Wheeling, Morgan, shiny finish, three minute-in-the-making rim flakes, 8" h **$1,750**

Webb, cased deep crimson to pink, cascading green leafy branch, gold highlights, 10" h **$1,265**

Wheeling, Morgan, acid finish, shades from mahogany to custard, orig acid finish holder, ex-Maude Feld, 10" h **$3,000**

Peachblow squatty vase, stick neck, Wheeling, glossy finish, 6" h, $1,500. Photo courtesy of The Early Auction Company, LLC.

PERFUME, COLOGNE, AND SCENT BOTTLES

History: The second half of the 19th century was the golden age for decorative bottles made to hold scents. These bottles were made in a variety of shapes and sizes.

An atomizer is a perfume bottle with a spray mechanism. Cologne bottles usually are larger and have stoppers that also may be used as applicators. A perfume bottle has a stopper that often is elongated and designed to be an applicator.

Scent bottles are small bottles used to hold a scent or smelling salts. A vinaigrette is an ornamental box or bottle that has a perforated top and is used to hold aromatic vinegar or smelling salts. Fashionable women of the late 18th and 19th centuries carried them in purses or slipped them into gloves in case of a sudden fainting spell.

Atomizer

Cambridge, stippled gold, opaque jade, orig silk lined box, 6-1/4" h **$140**

Cameo, Gallé, lavender flowers and foliage, shaded yellow and frosted ground, 8" h **$1,250**

Moser, sapphire blue, gold florals, leaves, and swirls, melon ribbed body, orig gold top and bulb, 4-1/2" h **$275**

Cologne

Baccarat, colorless, panel cut, matching stopper, 5-7/8" h **$75**

Cameo glass

Bulbous, crimson satin, opaque white floral cutting, hallmarked British Sterling cap, 3-1/4" h.............**$1,400**

Citrine ground, white shaded star shaped blossoms, sterling mounts, English, very minor nick in foliage, c1900, 4" h **$1,495**

Finely etched ground, citron cameo stemmed flowers, French, attributed to St. Louis, faceted stopper, very minor chips on stopper and rim, 8" h **$300**

Cranberry glass, faceted, finely cut faceted stopper, 7" h **$175**

Cut glass, cranberry cut to colorless, cane cut, matching stopper, 7" h **$250**

Paperweight, double overlay, crimson red over white over colorless squatty bottle, five oval facet windows reveal concentric millefiore cane int., matching stopper, 7" h, 5" d **$460**

Vaseline, vaseline, attributed to New England Glass Co., flint, orig stopper, 4-1/2" h..**$225**

Perfume

Glass

Continental, latticino, tapered ovoid, clear, white, and yellow strands, ext. of bottle with horizontal ribbing, silver gilt floral engraved hinged lid, enclosing glass stopper, early 19th C, 3-7/8" l **$425**

Pink glass perfume bottle, hand-painted scenic panel with castle, matching stopper, 5-1/2" h, $75; Limoges blue porcelain perfume bottle decorated with flowers and gilding, 6-1/2" h, $80.

Perfume bottle, emerald green, woman with arms outstretched embossed on base, Art Deco, original stopper, **$125.**

French, baluster form, blue opaline bottle, gilt metal floral overlay, foot, and neck mounts, hinged lid set with shell cameo of young man in feathered cap, late 19th/early 20th C, 4" h **$200**

Cut glass, colorless, pistol-form, etched silver-gilt mounts, short chain, spring-action trigger opens lid set with maker's medallion, French, late 19th/early 20th C, 4-3/4" l **$1,380**

PHOENIX GLASS

Phoenix vase, pink ground, raised white ferns and grasses, **$250.**

Pair blown glass perfume bottles with gold metal overlay with floral design; dresser tray with lace doily center, amber glass dish with gilt border, 4-1/4" h, **$120.**

Scent

Blown, colorless, cranberry and white stripes, white and gold metallic twist, 4-1/8" h **$95**

Blown molded, sunburst, brilliant sapphire shading to cobalt blue, shield shaped body, plain lip, rough pontil break, early to mid-19th C, 2-3/4" h, 1-1/2" d **$495**

Free-blown, dolphin or mermaid, colorless, opaque white stripes, applied cobalt blue rigaree, plain lip, possibly Boston & Sandwich Glass Co., some losses, 1825-50, 1-3/4" h **$80**

Free-blown, dolphin or mermaid, colorless, applied rigaree, engraved "Eliz-h Richardson" on one side, sprig on other side, American or English, small rough spot on rigaree, mid-19th C, 3" h **$50**

Pattern molded, flattened ovoid, brilliant peacock green, 20 ribs swirled to right, plain rim, rough pontil mark, American or English, early to mid-19th C, 2-1/4" h **$265**

Pattern molded, flattened tapering ovoid, deep brilliant amethyst, 26 ribs swirled to right, plain rim, rough

Perfume, Steuben, gold, melon ribbed, missing stopper, 4" h, **$200.**
Photo courtesy of The Early Auction Company, LLC.

pontil mark, American or English, early to mid-19th C, 2-7/8" h **$200**

Pattern molded, flattened tapering ovoid, teal blue, red swirl, 24 vertical ribs, plain rim, rough pontil mark, American or English, early to mid-19th C, 2-7/8" h **$180**

Pattern molded, flattened tapering ovoid, deep cobalt blue, light iridescence, 24 ribs swirled to right, plain rim, rough pontil mark, American or English, rib flake, pinhead nicks, early to mid-19th C, 3" h **$90**

Pattern molded, flattened tapering ovoid form, pale yellow amber, 26 vertical ribs, plain rim, rough pontil mark, American or English, tiny flake on lip, early to mid-19th C, 3" h **$165**

Vinaigrette

Cranberry glass, rect, allover cutting, enameled tiny pink roses, green leaves, gold dec, hinged lid, stopper, finger chain, 2-1/4" x 1" **$185**

Cut glass, cobalt blue, yellow flashing, sterling silver overlay, emb sterling silver cap, 3-7/8" l **$125**

History: Phoenix Glass Company, Beaver, Pennsylvania, was established in 1880. Known primarily for commercial glassware, the firm also produced a molded, sculptured, cameo-type line from the 1930s until the 1950s.

Ashtray, Phlox, large, white, frosted **$80**

Bowl, nude diving girl, white, 14" d ... **$495**

Creamer and sugar, Catalonia, light green **$45**

Lamp shade, ceiling type, pale pink, emb floral dec, 12" d **$115**

Umbrella stand, Thistle, pearlized blue ground, 18" h **$450**

Vase

Jewel, brown over milk glass,

4-3/4" d, 4-3/4" h **$200**

Daisy, pearlized daisies, light green ground, orig label, 8" h **$360**

Nude Scarf Dancers, light brown ground, cream figures, orig label, 8-1/8" d, 11-3/4" h **$650**

Dogwood, green and white, 10-3/4" h **$600**

Wild rose, blown out, pearlized dec, dark rose ground, orig label, 11" h **$275**

PICKLE CASTORS

History: A pickle castor is a table accessory used to serve pickles. It generally consists of a silver-plated frame fitted with a glass insert, matching silver-plated lid, and matching tongs. Pickle castors were very popular during the Victorian era. Inserts are found in pattern glass and colored art glass.

Amberina, melon ribbed IVT insert, SP lid, ftd frame, lid, tongs, c1875-95 .... **$700**

Colorless, diamond quilted pattern insert, silvered metal frame, 11-3/4" h **$200**

Cranberry, IVT insert, enameled blue and white florals, green leaves, shelf on frame dec with peacocks and other birds **$325**

Crown Milano, cylindrical hobnail insert shades from pink to opal, hand enameled dec, sgd "Pairpoint" silver plate flower emb holder, orig tongs, 8-3/4" h **$2,150**

Double, vaseline, pickle leaves and pieces, resilvered frame **$800**

Mount Washington, opalescent stripes with light and dark pink, Pairpoint #604 frame, 11" h **$850**

Opalescent, cranberry, Daisy & Fern emb apple blossom mold, orig Empire frame, later tongs, Victorian, 11-1/2" h **$500**

Pink, shiny pink Florette pattern insert, white int., bowed out frame **$325**

QUEZAL

History: The Quezal Art Glass Decorating Company, named for the quetzal—a bird with brilliantly colored feathers—was organized in 1901 in Brooklyn, New York, by Martin Bach and Thomas Johnson, two disgruntled Tiffany workers. They soon hired Percy Britton and William Wiedebine, two more Tiffany employees.

The first products, which are unmarked, were exact Tiffany imitations. Quezal pieces differ from Tiffany pieces in that they are more defined and the decorations are more visible and brighter. No new techniques were developed by Quezal.

Johnson left in 1905. T. Conrad Vahlsing, Bach's son-in-law, joined the firm in 1918, but left with Paul Frank in 1920 to form Lustre Art Glass Company, which copied Quezal pieces. Martin Bach died in 1924, and by 1925, Quezal had ceased operations.

Marks: The "Quezal" trademark was first used in 1902 and placed on the base of vases and bowls and the rims of shades. The acid-etched or engraved letters vary in size and may be found in amber, black, or gold. A printed label that includes an illustration of a quetzal was used briefly in 1907.

Quezal lamp shade, iridescent art glass, bell shape, gold zipper pattern, 5-1/2" h, **$145.**
Photo courtesy of The Early Auction Company, LLC.

Bowl, irid gold Calcite ground, stretch rim, pedestal foot, sgd "Quezal," 9-1/2" d **$800**

Candlesticks, pr, irid blue, sgd, 7-3/4" h **$575**

Ceiling lamp shade, drop, radiating irid gold and green leaf dec, domed irid ivory glass shade supported by brass ring suspended from three ball chains, two-socket fixture, shade inscribed "Quezal," Brooklyn, NY, early 20th C, 13-3/4" d, 21-1/2" l **$6,325**

Chandelier, four elaborate gilt metal scroll arms, closed teardrop gold, green, and opal shades, inscribed "Quezal" at collet rim, very minor roughness at rim edge, 14" h **$2,000**

Cologne bottle, irid gold ground, Art Deco design, sgd "Q" and "Melba," 7-1/2" h **$250**

Finger bowl and underplate, gold irid bowl, pontil sgd, ribbed underplate, sgd "Quezal," 4-1/2" d **$300**

Jack-in-the-pulpit vase
Green pulled feather dec tipped in irid gold, alabaster body, shiny gold int., sgd "Quezal," 6-1/2" h **$2,250**
Green pulled feather tipped in irid gold, sgd "Quezal," very minor wear to gold int., 6" h **$1,600**

Lamp, desk, irid gold shade with green and white pulled feather dec, inscribed "Quezal" at rim, gilt metal adjustable crook-neck lamp, 14-1/2" h **$575**

Lamp shade
Aperture, irid gold, cylindrical, ruffled rims, signed, set of three, 4-3/4" h, 1-3/4" d **$235**
Aperture, ribbed bell form, calcite exterior, gold iridescent int., sgd on

Quezal lamp shade, feather-pull glass shade, signed, 5-1/4" h, **$175.**
Photo courtesy of David Rago Auctions, Inc.

rim, 4-1/2" h, 2-3/16" d **$180**

Low bowl, irid gold, ribbed shallow bowl, polished pontil, sgd, 4" d **$450**

Salt, open, shouldered, irid body, protruding ribs, pontil sgd "Quezal," 2-1/2" d, 1-1/4" h **$200**

Sherbet, irid gold body, blue coil dec, sgd "Quezal," 4" h **$700**

Toothpick holder, melon ribbed, pinched sides, irid blue, green, purple and gold, sgd, 2-1/4" h **$200**

Urn, cov, shouldered form, marigold body, overall green King Tut swirl pattern, matching lid, irid gold foot, sgd "Quezal" in silver, 13-1/2" h **$5,500**

Vase
Floriform, folded irid gold rim, green and gold leaf dec, sgd "Quezal S 651," 5-1/4" h **$2,350**
Floriform, wide mouth with stretched ruffled rim, irid gold interior, irid green, gold, and white ext., sgd "Quezal S 594," 6" h **$2,470**
Tri-fold flower form, random wintergreen loops over irid gold pulls, soft velvet gold irid int., sgd "Quezal," 5" h **$1,750**
Tulip-form body, pinched rim, green and gold irid pulled feather dec, circular foot with folded rim, base sgd "Quezal," 10-1/2" h **$18,800**

Whiskey taster, oval, irid gold, four pinched dimples, sgd "Quezal" on base, 2-3/4" h **$200**

REVERSE PAINTING ON GLASS

History: The earliest examples of reverse painting on glass were produced in 13th-century Italy. By the 17th century, the technique had spread to central and eastern Europe. It spread westward as the center of the glassmaking industry moved to Germany in the late 17th century.

The Alsace and Black Forest regions developed a unique portraiture style. The half and three-quarter portraits often were titled below the portrait. Women tend to have generic names, while most males are likenesses of famous men.

The English used a mezzotint, rather than free-style, method to create their reverse paintings. Landscapes and allegorical figures were popular. The Chinese began working in the medium in the 17th century, eventually favoring marine and patriotic scenes.

Most American reverse painting was done by folk artists and is unsigned. Portraits, patriotic and mourning scenes, floral compositions, landscapes, and buildings are the favorite subjects. Known American artists include Benjamin Greenleaf, A. Cranfield, and Rowley Jacobs.

In the late 19th century, commercially produced reverse paintings, often decorated with mother-of-pearl, became popular. Themes included the Statue of Liberty, the capitol in Washington, D.C., and various world's fairs and expositions.

Today craftsmen are reviving this art, using some vintage-looking designs, but usually with brighter colors than their antique counterparts.

Reverse painting portrait of Martha Washington, c1830, 23-1/2" x 19-1/2", **$250.**
Photo courtesy of Pook & Pook, Inc.

Mirrors

Reverse painted panel with fenced house, attributed to John Rupp, Hanover, York County, PA, Federal period, molding and columns, yellow and red grain paint dec frame, 12-1/4" w, 21" h **$3,575**

Reverse painted white house, red and yellow roof, mahogany and mahogany veneer on pine, orig dark finish, reeded lower corner blocks and center divider, applied rope twist pilasters, scalloped cornice, turned acorn drops, orig backboards, some flaking to reverse panel, 13-1/4" w, 22-1/2" h **$260**

Reverse painted panel with two men in boat on lake, cottage in background, attributed to John Rupp, Hanover, York County, PA, Federal period, molding and columns, yellow and red combed grain paint dec frame, 13-1/4" w, 25" h **$1,870**

Federal, primitive orig painting of houses with double chimneys near stream, mahogany frame with old reddish brown varnish, reeded pilasters, cove molded cornice and base, 18-1/4" w, 33-3/4" h **$375**

Reverse painted panel with British naval battle scene, inner walnut veneered surround, giltwood and composition mirror with shaped crest centered by female mask and flanked by scrolls, mid-Georgian-style, 36-5/8" w, 38" h **$4,700**

Portraits

Albert von England, military uniform with medal, sash, and epaulettes, titled in white bottom border, black painted frame, some flaking, damage to one corner, 9-1/4" w, 11-1/2" h **$320**

George Washington, blue coat, ruffles, teal oval background, brown rect, white border, old burl walnut frame, 7-1/4" w, 9" h **$690**

Reverse painting sailing ship, windmill, original oval frame, **$95.**

Reverse painting portraits, left: gentleman in black suit, standing in room with dark green drape, patterned carpet, SRC, "B. F. Ferguson," shaped frame, slight losses, 16-1/4" w, 21-3/8" h, **$200;** *right: woman wearing royal blue gown, hook skirt, holding white fan and lace handkerchief, standing in room with pink drape, patterned carpet, S&DRC, "B. F. Ferguson 1867," shaped frame, stamp on reverse: "B. F. Ferguson Artist, S.W.Cor. 8th & Arch St., Philadelphia," 16-1/4" w, 21-3/8" h,* **$250.**
Photo courtesy of Alderfer Auction Co.

Lafayette, gray hair, blue and red military uniform, fur collared green coat, titled "Lafajetty" in bottom border, orig frame, some flaking, 9" w, 12" h......................................**$825**

Napoleon, military uniform, painted mat, cast plaster frame, 7-1/4" w, 8-1/4" h.....................................**$200**

Woman dressed white, blue shawl, seated outdoors, holding basket of flowers on bounder in front, minor wear with flaking edges, possibly orig backboard, later gilt frame with black repaint, 11-1/2" w, 15-1/2" h.......**$920**

Young woman seated at tea table, holding white rose in hand, yellow skirt, blue jacket, white lace, white border mkd "Morgen," black painted frame, some flaking, corner cracked, 12" w, 15-3/8" h............**$175**

Scenes

Perry's Lake Erie Victory, Sept. 10, 1813, naval battle scene, 7" x 9" ...**$250**

Mount Vernon, river, boat, and trees, old repainted frame, 8-1/4" w, 6-1/4" h **$550**

Country house in winter, gold painted frame, 10-1/2" h, 12-1/2" w........ **$75**

Ohio, side wheeler steamship, poplar frame, 10-1/2" h, 12-1/2" w **$175**

ROSE BOWLS

History: A rose bowl is a decorative open bowl with a crimped, pinched, or petal top which turns in at the top, but does not then turn up or back out again. Rose bowls held fragrant rose petals or potpourri, which served as an air freshener in the late Victorian period. Practically every glass manufacturer made rose bowls in virtually every glass type, pattern, and style, including fine art glass.

Reproduction Alert. Rose bowls have been widely reproduced. Be especially careful of Italian copies of satin, Mother of Pearl satin, peachblow, and Burmese, and recent Czechoslovakian ones with applied flowers.

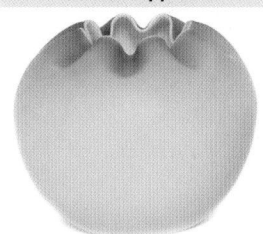

Rose bowl, blue satin, large, ruffle drim, 5-1/2" h, **$100.**
Photo courtesy of The Early Auction Company, LLC.

Amethyst and white leaf design, 5" d..**$90**

Blue and white, shell design, floral dec, 6" d...**$120**

Blue and white, pleated, 5" d......**$95**

Bulbous ruffled top, pastel, frosted and opal vertical bands on body, English, Victorian, 4" h......................**$125**

Cased, blue and white, flowers and leaf dec, 4" d...**$80**

Cased, orange and white satin, 5" d.**$100**

Cased, red and white satin, 5" d ..**$100**

Cased, yellow and white, 4" d **$75**

Diamond quilted, amethyst and white, 3" d **$100**

Green and white opalescent, ruffled rim, 5" d..................................**$95**

Red and white shell design, 5-1/2" d...**$110**

Satin, blue, 4" d **$90**

Rose bowl, Carnival glass, Swirled Hobnail, Millersburg, purple, **$265.**

Rose bowl, Harrach, blue, optic ribbed body, applied ruffled rim, 5" h, **$75.**
Photo courtesy of The Early Auction Company, LLC.

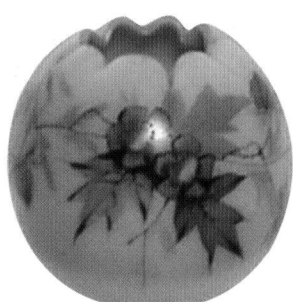

Rose bowl, Webb, Burmese, purple flower on green leaf Hawthorne branch, 2-1/2" h, **$225.**

Satin, blue, ruffled, 5-1/2" h **$100**
Satin, crimped body, shading from medium to light blue, clear applied dec, 3" d, 1-3/4" d **$110**
Satin, diamond quilted mother of pearl, golden brown to golden cream,

3-1/2" d, 3-1/2" h **$495**
Satin, green, 4" d **$75**
Satin, green and white, leaf design, 4-1/2" d **$115**
Satin, green and white, shell design, 5-1/2" d **$125**

Satin, inverted crimped bulbous body shading from deep rose to pink, enamel floral dec, attributed to Thomas Webb & Sons, 3-3/4" h **$100**
Spatter glass, orange and white, 5" d **$90**

SANDWICH GLASS

History: In 1818, Deming Jarves was listed in the Boston Directory as a glass maker. That same year, he was appointed general manager of the newly formed New England Glass Company. In 1824, Jarves toured the glassmaking factories in Pittsburgh, left New England Glass Company, and founded a glass factory in Sandwich.

Originally called the Sandwich Manufacturing Company, it was incorporated in April 1826 as the Boston & Sandwich Glass Company. From 1826 to 1858, Jarves served as general manager. The Boston & Sandwich Glass Company produced a wide variety of wares in differing levels of quality. The factory used the free-blown, blown three mold, and pressed glass manufacturing techniques. Both clear and colored glass were used.

Competition in the American glass industry in the mid-1850s resulted in lower-quality products. Jarves left the Boston & Sandwich company in 1858, founded the Cape Cod Glass Company, and tried to duplicate the high quality of the earlier glass. Meanwhile, at the Boston & Sandwich Glass Company, emphasis was placed on mass production. The development of a lime glass (non-flint) led to lower costs for pressed glass. Some free-blown and blown-and-molded pieces, mostly in color, were made. Most of this Victorian-era glass was enameled, painted, or acid etched.

By the 1880s, the Boston & Sandwich Glass Company was operating at a loss. Labor difficulties finally resulted in the closing of the factory on January 1, 1888.

Bowl, Gothic paneled arches, hexagonal, clambroth............................. **$150**
Butter dish, cov, colorless, flint, Gothic pattern **$225**
Candlesticks, pr, pressed
Yellow, petal form candle cups, columnar shaft, sq stepped base, chips to petals on one, base edge and corner chips on both, c1850-65, 9-1/4" h **$600**
Translucent blue petal socket, clambroth dolphin standard, double-stepped sq base, few minor chips and cracks, c1845-70, 9-7/8" h....... **$1,530**
Translucent light lavender alabaster/clambroth, petal sockets, dolphins, wafer construction, double step base, 1845-70, 10" h **$3,300**

Champagne, Sandwich Star **$850**
Compote, cranberry overlay, oval cuts, enameled birds and flowers on inner surface, c1890, 10-1/2" w, 4-3/4" h **$495**

Creamer
Acanthus Leaf and Shield, colorless, plain rim, molded handle, octagonal even scallop foot, 1835-50, 4-1/4" h **$315**
Heart and Scale, colorless, molded handle, circular foot, 1838-45, 4-1/2" h **$220**
Decanter, blown-molded, quart, colorless, plain base, rough pontil mark, replacement pressed wheel stopper, McKearin GV-17, c1825-35, 11-1/2" h **$625**

Dish
Beaded Medallion and Urn, oval, colorless, shaped plain even scallop rim, chip under rim, 1835-45, 5-7/8" x 8" x 1-3/4" h **$90**
Double Peacock Eye, octagonal oblong, colorless, concave corners, variation with no background stippling on ends, plain cross bars in center, plain even scallop rim with interior beads, some loss to four corners, 1835-50, 9-1/8" x 12-1/4" x 2" h **$360**
Hairpin, colorless, scallop and point rim, near proof, shallow edge flake, 7-3/8" x 7-3/4" x 1-1/4" h, c1830-40 .... **$7,700**
Pipes of Pan, octagonal oblong,

Miscellaneous Sandwich glass: toothpick holder, footed compote, jar, lidded jar, four berry bowls, punch cup, rectangular tray, salt dip, miniature cup (damaged), saucer, creamer and three plates, **$380.** Photo courtesy of Joy Luke Auctions.

Sandwich plate, lacy design, **$115.**

Sandwich lamp base, bright canary yellow, brass collar, wide paneled body, pedestal base, **$200.**

colorless, plain scallop and point rim, rope table ring, corner rim spall, 1930-40, 6-1/4" x 8-1/4" x 1-1/2" h **$310**

Fluid lamp

Bigler pattern, octagonal shaft, sq base, pewter collar, cobalt blue, 1840-65, 10-1/4" h.................**$1,120**

Circle and oval pressed fonts, pressed hexagonal baluster stem and base, clear, brass collars, base flakes, pr, 8-3/4" h **$250**

Colorless, conical font with button stem attached to pressed Lee/Rose No. 32 cup plate base, cork tube whale oil burner, rough pontil mark, minute base chips and flakes, 1828-35, 6-7/8" h.................**$1,980**

Cut overlay font of cobalt blue cut to clear, quatrefoil and punty cuts, brass columnar standard, sq marble base, minor base edge chips, 1840-65, 9-3/4" h **$950**

Sapphire blue, font wafer attached to pressed hexagonal base, early brass #1 collar, 1840-60, top of one loop chipped and later polished, 9-1/2" h **$1,045**

Fruit basket, on stand

Brilliant deep amethyst, basket with 32-point rim, 16 vertical openwork staves, 34-point star in sloping base, wafered to hexagonal knop and foot, possibly in-the-making shallow chip on knop, 1840-55, 8-1/4" d rim, 4-1/2" d foot, 8-1/4" h **$17,600**

Colorless, 32-point rim, 16 vertical openwork staves, 34-point star in sloping base, wafered to hexagonal knop and foot, 1840-55, 8-3/4" d rim, 4-1/2" d foot, 8-1/2" h **$615**

Cut overlay, triple dolphin base, font opaque white cut to colorless, connected to fiery opalescent base,

heavily gilded dec on font, early #2 brass collar, brass connector, kerosene period, 1860-75, 11-3/4" h **$7,150**

Goblet, colorless, flint, Gothic pattern, 12-pc set **$650**

Inkwell, cylindrical-domed form, colorless, pink and white stripes, sheared mouth, applied pewter collar and cap, smooth base, 2-9/16" **$2,300**

Nappy

Crossed Peacock Eye, colorless, rayed center with alternating clear and stippled panels, shaped rim with plain even scallops, loss to several scallops, 1835-50, 9-1/4" d, 1-1/2" h **$150**

Plume and Acorn, medium amethyst, even scallop rim, small rim spall, 4-1/8" d, 1-1/8" h.....................**$100**

Plume and Acorn, fiery opalescent, even scallop rim, minor flaking/mold roughness, 5-1/8" d, 1-1/4" h **$55**

Paperweight, colorless and frosted, portraits of Queen Victoria and Prince Consort, 1851, 3-1/2" w, 1-1/4" h **$220**

Pitcher

Amberina Verde, fluted top, 10" h..**$525**

Electric Blue, enameled floral dec, fluted top, threaded handle, 10" h **$425**

Plate, 6" d, lacy, Shell pattern.......**$175**

Pomade jar, cov

Bear, clambroth, emb "J Hauel & Co., Phila" under base, large chip to back of one ear, flange chips, 1850-87, 5" h **$490**

Bear, deep amethyst, polished around edge of cover and base, 1850-87, 3-3/4" h **$135**

Drum, slightly translucent jade green, plain shield, cover missing, minor rim flake, 3-1/2" h, 2-1/2" d **$360**

Sandwich vase, trumpet, amethyst and colorless, gauffered rim, slightly twisted eight-panel vase, pestle stem fluted on inside, square base, 1840-60, McKearin plate 195, couple minor small base cracks, 10-1/8" h, **$5,000.** Photo courtesy of Skinner, Inc.

Salt, open, pressed, lacy

Shell pattern, red-amethyst, Neal SL 1, minor edge roughness, few base chips, c1825-50, 1-3/4" h **$650**

Beaded Scroll pattern, violet-blue, Neal Bs 3a, edge cracks and chips, c1825-50, 2" h **$360**

Sander, lacy, fiery opalescent, stippled rim with vertical chain of beads on body, rope-edge base, concentric circles under base, pewter cover missing, 2-3/4" x 2-3/4" d rim............**$470**

Spooner/spill, Sandwich Star, slightly translucent electric blue, hexagonal foot, polished pontil mark, 5" h, 3-3/4" d.......................................**$1,265**

Sugar, cov, Star and Punty, colorless, octagonal, short paneled stem, circular foot, finial flake, roughness on rims, 1840-70, 8-3/4" h, 5-1/4" d base **$100**

Toddy, brilliant dark amethyst, lacy, Roman Rosette, edge chips, 5-3/8" d **$330**

Tray, oval, central butterfly and beaded bull's eyes, shoulder with fleur-de-lis, pinwheels, and fans, tiny even scallops on side rims, slight mold roughness, 1835-50, 6-1/8" x 9-1/8" x 1-3/8" h **$235**

Vase

Brilliant deep amethyst, panels continue to peg extension, wafered to octagonal base, 1845-65, 9-3/4" h, 5-1/2" d rim, 4-3/8" d foot....**$4,950**

Elongated loop with bisecting lines, deep fiery opalescent/ opaque, hexagonal foot, polished table ring, 1835-50, 4-3/4" h, 3-1/2" d rim **$1,265**

Elongated loop with bisecting lines, medium brilliant amethyst, hexago-

nal foot, polished table ring, 1835-50, 4-3/4" h, 3-1/2" d rim.........**$990**

Pressed, tulip, amethyst, scalloped rim, paneled oval bowl, octagonal base, minor base chip, 10" h, c1840-60..............................**$2,115**

Pressed, tulip, dark amethyst, octagonal base, mid-19th C, price for pr, small chip on one petal, minor base chips, 10-1/4" h....................**$9,400**

Pressed, tulip, dark amethyst, scalloped rim, octagonal base, very minor edge chips, c1845-65, 9-3/4" h **$4,600**

Ruby stained, acid etched leaves and polished grapes, notch-cut circular foot with polished center, tiny rim flake, 1880-87, 4" h, 3-3/4" d rim, 3-1/8" d foot..........................**$145**

Whiskey taster, cobalt blue, nine panels **$175**

SATIN GLASS

History: Satin glass, produced in the late 19th century, is an opaque art glass with a velvety matte (satin) finish achieved through treatment with hydrofluoric acid. A large majority of the pieces were cased or had a white lining.

While working at the Phoenix Glass Company, Beaver, Pennsylvania, Joseph Webb perfected mother-of-pearl (MOP) satin glass in 1885. Similar to plain satin glass in respect to casing, MOP satin glass has a distinctive surface finish and an integral or indented design, the most well known being diamond quilted (DQ).

The most common colors are yellow, rose, or blue. Rainbow coloring is considered choice.

Additional Listings: Cruets, Fairy Lamps, Miniature Lamps, and Rose Bowls.

Reproduction Alert. Satin glass, in both the plain and mother-of-pearl varieties, has been widely reproduced.

Pair of pink satin glass vases, diamond quilted pattern, 8" h, **$150.**
Photo courtesy of Joy Luke Auctions.

Bowl

DQ, MOP, rainbow, crimped, sgd "Patent," orig Maude B. Feld label, ex-Maude Feld, 4-1/2" d, 2-3/4" h **$1,100**

DQ, MOP, ruffled, shading from white to peach, 6" d, 1-1/2" h **$80**

DQ, MOP, rainbow, int. with fold down ruffled rim, four clear feet (slight roughness), berry pontil, mkd "Patent," ex-Maude Feld, 9-3/4" l, 6-1/4" h, ...**$3,400**

Peacock Eye pattern, MOP, white, painted floral and ladybug dec, gilt highlights, scalloped, 10" d...**$2,000**

Bride's basket, deep rose, enamel swan and floral dec, heavy bronze holder with birds perched at top, 15-1/2" h......................................**$450**

Celery vase, MOP, cased blue, Herringbone pattern, waisted squared body, 5" h **$200**

Center bowl, DQ, MOP, rainbow, cir-

cular ovoid body, alternating bands of multicolored hues, heavily applied clear rigaree collar and thorn handles, clear stylized feet, ex-Maude Feld, 10" d, 9-1/2" h **$7,750**

Cologne bottle, Verre Moire, pulled three-color dec, coral and chartreuse on opaque white body, satin finish, crown-like cap attached to delicate chain to collar, anchor stamps and "cs fs" on collar, 3-1/2" d, 6-1/2" h ...**$750**

Cream pitcher

Blue, DQ, MOP, camphor reeded handle, 3-1/2" h **$200**

Blue, gold lettering "1893 World's Fair," made and dec by Mt. Washington, 2-1/2" h **$435**

Cruet, Rainbow, pastel blue, pink, and yellow swirls from base to trefoil spout, molded-in bulging ribs, polished pontil mark, ribbed applied handle, cut glass stopper, 7" h **$975**

Cup and saucer, Raindrop MOP, pink to white, 3" h cup, 5" d saucer **$385**

Epergne, pink and white, hobnail bowl, resilvered base and lily vase holder, 13-3/4" h, 10" d **$395**

Ewer

DQ, MOP, dusty pink shades to pale pink, air trays cross over 24 vertical ribs of melon shaped body, ruffled and crimped mouth, frosted clear handle with thorns, Victorian, 12" h **$350**

DQ, MOP, pink, fold over ruffled rim, applied rope handle, price for pr, 8-1/4" h **$100**

Glossy blue, tri-fold top, applied crystal twist handle, heat check in handles, price for pr, 9" h **$50**

Fairy lamp, blue shade and base, clear candle base insert, Victorian, 4-1/4" h **$225**

Lamp, white satin body, matching font with air-trapped Flower and Acorn design, enameled Japanese cherry blossoms, bronze ftd base with lions' heads, burner marked "Hinks & Sons Patent" and "Sherwoods Limited," retailer's soldered tag "T. R. Grimes, New Broad St., London," some flakes under font lip, 22" h **$1,260**

Mustard pot, bright yellow, gold prunus dec, SP top, Webb, 2-1/2" h **$450**

Rose bowl

Crimped body, shading from medium to light blue, clear applied dec, 3" h, 1-3/4" d **$110**

DQ, MOP, rainbow, trefoil shaped body, applied clear rigaree collar, berry pontil, three shaped clear feet, mkd "Patent," ex-Maude Feld, 4" h **$1,900**

Herringbone, blue MOP, crimped ruffled rim, 5" h **$50**

Inverted crimped bulbous body shading from deep rose to pink, enamel floral dec, attributed to Thomas Webb & Sons, 3-3/4" h **$100**

Salt shaker, rose shaded to white, MOP, DQ, tapered barrel, orig two-pc lid, 3-1/4" h **$550**

Spill vase, pale green body, hand enameled dec, Victorian, 10-1/8" h **$110**

Sugar shaker, Rainbow MOP, ex-Maude Feld, 5-1/2" h **$4,760**

Tumbler, Rainbow, DQ, enameled floral dec, pr, 3-1/2" h **$375**

Vase

Bulbous, DQ, MOP, pink, ruffled top, gilt design in center, 5-3/4" h **$150**

DQ, MOP, flaring conical body, deep azure shading to pearl, gold prunus dec, applied thorn handles, attributed to Thomas Webb and Sons, 6-1/2" h **$800**

DQ, MOP, blue, shouldered, quadrafold rim, 7" h.............................. **$150**

DQ, MOP, butterscotch shading to pearl, 7" h **$85**

DQ, MOP, rainbow, bulbous, cylindrical neck, crimped fold down rim, 7" h **$800**

DQ, peach MOP, bulbous, tight ruffled crimped rim, 7-1/2" h **$125**

Gourd, DQ, yellow shading to white frost, 10-3/4" h.......................... **$170**

Herringbone, MOP, top ground, 6" h **$50**

Pompeian Swirl, MOP, blue shading to pale blue at base, pale blue cased int., two shiny upward spiraling ribbons, 5-1/2" h **$500**

Ribbed body, flaring ruffled to, shades from mahogany to lemon yellow, acid finish, 4-1/2" h................. **$325**

Stick, MOP, blue, 5" h **$125**

Water pitcher, MOP, cased, shading from rose to pink, Coinspot pattern, applied reeded handle, ground pontil, 8-1/2" h................................. **$425**

Satin glass, rainbow mother-of-pearl ewer, herringbone pattern, frosted handle applied, 8-1/4" h, $1,110.
Photo courtesy of The Early Auction Company, LLC.

Satin glass, lace maker's lamp, pink mold blown shade, two-handled brass oil font holder, 17-1/2" h, $825.
Photo courtesy of The Early Auction Company, LLC.

SCHNEIDER GLASS

History: Brothers Ernest and Charles Schneider founded a glassworks at Epiney-sur-Seine, France, in 1913. Charles, the artistic designer, previously had worked for Daum and Gallé. Robert, son of Charles, assumed art direction in 1948. Schneider moved to Loris in 1962.

Although Schneider made tablewares, stained glass, and lighting fixtures, its best-known product is art glass that exhibits simplicity of design and often has bubbles and streaking in larger pieces. Other styles include cameo-cut and hydrofluoric-acid-etched designs.

Marks: Schneider glass was signed with a variety of script and block signatures, "Le Verre Francais," or "Charder."

Center bowl, rose and caramel-colored spattered glass, flared rim, wafer joined to ftd base with rolled lip, signed "Schneider" on side of base, 13-3/4" d, 7-3/4" h **$900**

Compote, shallow round bowl, pedestal base, mottled rose pink translucent glass with internal bubbles, shading to dark purple, polished pontil, acid etched "Schneider" on base, light edge wear, minor scratches, 8" d, 3-7/8" h **$300**

Ewer, elongated spout, mottled purples, pink, yellow, and orange splashes, applied purple handle, bulbed disk foot, acid stamp "France" on base, c1925, 10-3/4" h......................**$450**

Finger bowl and underplate, mottled red, burnt umber and clear, stamped mark, 4-1/2" d bowl, 7-1/4" d underplate **$350**

Tazza, shallow white bowl rising to mottled amethyst and blue inverted rim, amethyst double-bulbed stem, disk foot, sgd "Schneider," c1920, 7-5/8" h..**$865**

Vase

Cameo dec, orange and mottled green against yellow body, base signature "Verre Francais," later marks "France Ovington New York," 12-1/2" h **$1,120**

Corset shape, internally dec, mottled amethyst and yellow, three amethyst Art Nouveau applied dec, sgd in hourglass in script, 8" h.......**$700**

Gold spattered body, coiled gold threading at shoulder, sgd with a vase and "Schneider," 3-1/8" h **$215**

Mottled orange ground, cameo cut with blue Art Deco design, candy-cane signature, c1920, 4-1/2" h **$490**

Tapering cylindrical, baluster neck, orange overlay, five clusters of pendant grapes, geometric pattern cut foot over yellow mottled ground, inset cane at base, 14" h **$650**

Tapered form, incurvate rim, shaded orange overlaid in mottled brown, cameo-etched and cut cascading fruit and leaves, pedestal foot inscribed "Le Verre Francais," polished pontil, 17-3/4" h **$1,265**

SMITH BROS. GLASS

History: After establishing a decorating department at the Mount Washington Glass Works in 1871, Alfred and Harry Smith struck out on their own in 1875. Their New Bedford, Massachusetts, firm soon became known worldwide for its fine opalescent decorated wares, similar in style to those of Mount Washington.

Marks: Smith Bros. glass often is marked on the base with a red shield enclosing a rampant lion and the word "Trademark."

Reproduction Alert. Beware of examples marked "Smith Bros."

Atomizer, tan shading to cream opaque body, enameled amethyst and pink flowers, painted lion trademark, new hardware, 7" h......................**$260**

Biscuit jar

Green and pastel brown tendrils of ivy wind around melon ribbed body, gold plated fittings, sgd "405," 7" d, 8-1/2" h **$885**

Melon ribbed body shading from white to blue, polychrome enameled flowers, 6" d **$150**

Melon ribbed cream body, fall colored oak leaves, gold acorns, metal lid stamped "S.B.," 7" d, 7-1/4" h ..**$415**

Opaque cream ground, sculptured diagonal swirl pattern, polychrome flower dec, red lion trademark, 7" h **$300**

Bowl

Lobed, pale pink ground, daisies dec, red rampant lion mark, 3" d....**$150**

Melon ribbed, two shades of gold prunus dec, beaded white rim, 6" d, 2-3/4" h **$375**

Melon ribbed, beige ground, pink Moss Rose dec, blue flowers, green leaves, white beaded rim, 9" d, 4" h **$675**

Bride's bowl, opal glass bowl, painted ground, 2" band dec with cranes, fans, vases, and flowers, white and gray dec, fancy silver-plated holder sgd and numbered 2117, 9-1/2" d, 3" h bowl, 16" h overall..................**$1,450**

Creamer and sugar, shaded blue and beige ground, multicolored violet and leaves dec, fancy silverplated metalware, 4" d, 3-3/4" h **$750**

Humidor, cream ground, eight blue pansies, melon-ribbed cov, 6-1/2" h, 4" d..**$850**

Mustard jar, cov, ribbed, gold prunus dec, white ground, 2" h **$300**

Plate, Santa Maria, beige, brown, and pale orange ship, 7-3/4" d **$635**

Ring vase, hand painted floral motif on vase, bamboo and butterfly motif silverplate stand, stamped "Tufts," 9" h..**$75**

Salt and pepper shakers, silverplate napkin ring center on platform base, white shakers with blue floral trim, marked "Rockford #29".....**$750**

SPANGLED GLASS

History: Spangled glass is a blown or blown-molded variegated art glass, similar to spatter glass, with the addition of flakes of mica or metallic aventurine. Many pieces are cased with a white or clear layer of glass. Spangled glass was developed in the late 19th century and still is being manufactured.

Originally, spangled glass was attributed only to the Vasa Murrhina Art Glass Company of Hartford, Connecticut, which distributed the glass for Dr. Flower of the Cape Cod Glassworks, Sandwich, Massachusetts. However, research has shown that many companies in Europe, England, and the United States made spangled glass, and attributing a piece to a specific source is very difficult.

Spatter bowl, tortoise shell pattern, amber ground, brown and black striations, **$450.**
Photo courtesy of Wiederseim Associates, Inc.

Basket, ruffled edge, white int., deep apricot with spangled gold, applied crystal loop handle, slight flake, 7" h, 6" l......................................**$225**

Bride's bowl, ruffled rim, yellow and white mottled ground, overall silver mica flakes, yellow stemmed blue daisies dec, 10-1/2" d **$90**

Candlesticks, pr, pink and white spatter, green aventurine flecks, cased white int., 8-1/8" h......................**$115**

Creamer, bulbous, molded swirled ribs, cylindrical neck, pinched spout, blue ground, swirled mica flecks, applied clear reeded handle, 3-1/4" d, 4-3/4" h..**$225**

Cruet, Leaf Mold pattern, cranberry, mica flakes, white casing, Northwood **$450**

Ewer, raspberry pink ext., white int., mica flecks, twisted applied handle, rough pontil, 9-1/2" h.................**$250**

Jack-in-the-pulpit vase, oxblood, green, and white spatter, mica flakes, c1900, 6-1/4" h............................**$125**

Pitcher, white, and amber cased to clear, mica flakes, applied amber reeded handle, 8-1/2" h...............**$550**

Sugar shaker, cranberry, mica flakes, white casing, Northwood............**$115**

Toothpick holder, alternating crimson and white mottled ground, gold mica, lattice stripes, 2-1/4" h........**$65**

Tumbler, pink, gold, and brown spatter, mica flecks, white lining, 3-3/4" h............................**$90**

Vase
Glossy pink cased satin, silver mica, two applied crystal handles, 6-3/4" h **$75**
Stick, cased satin glass alternating pink and blue panels, overall silver mica, crystal rigaree around neck, 8-3/4" h **$75**

Water set, 9-1/2" h tankard pitcher, Aventurine, pink and white mottled ground, yellow and blue accents, metallic flecks, four matching 3-3/4" h tumblers........................**$350**

SPATTER GLASS

History: Spatter glass is a variegated blown or blown-molded art glass. It originally was called "end-of-day" glass, based on the assumption that it was made from batches of glass leftover at the end of the day. However, spatter glass was found to be a standard production item for many glass factories.

Spatter glass was developed at the end of the 19th century and is still being produced in the United States and Europe.

Reproduction Alert. Many modern examples come from the European area previously called Czechoslovakia.

Spangled Bride's basket, ruffled yellow base with gold spangles, creamy white exterior, applied colorless bark handle, **$145.**

Basket, tortoiseshell, cream, tan, yellow, white, and brown spatter, white lining, rect, tightly crimped edge, colorless thorn handle **$120**

Berry set, master bowl and two sauces, Leaf Mold, cranberry vaseline **$300**

Bowl, amber and brown mottled tortoiseshell, 8-1/2" d **$90**

Box, cov, cranberry ground, white spatter, clear knob finial **$200**

Candlestick, yellow, red, and white streaks, clear overlay, vertical swirled molding, smooth base, flanged socket, 7-1/2" h................................**$60**

Cologne bottle, white spatter, enamel dec, orig stopper applicator, marked "Made in Czechoslovakia," price for pr, 5-1/2" h....................**$115**

Creamer, Leaf Mold, cranberry vaseline...**$250**

Cruet, Aventurine, applied clear reeded handle, cut faceted stopper, 6-1/2" h **$375**

Darning egg, multicolored, attributed to Sandwich Glass...............**$125**

Ewer, yellow ground, white spatter, tri-fold spout, flared applied clear handle, sharp pontil, 8-3/4" h........**$85**

Finger bowl and underplate, tortoiseshell, ruffled, 6" d, 3-1/4" d...**$275**

Jack-in-the-pulpit, Vasa Murrhina, deep pink int., clear ruffled top, 5" h, 3-1/2" d.................................**$115**

Pitcher, burgundy and white spatter, cased in clear, ground pontil, clear reeded handle, 6-1/2" d, 8" h **$395**

Rose bowl

Leaf Mold, cranberry ground, vaseline spatter **$250**

Mt. Washington, pink, blue, and white spatter on colorless ground, white opalescent scalloped top **$135**

Salt, maroon and pink, white spatter, applied clear feet and handle, 3" l **$125**

Sugar shaker, Leaf Umbrella pattern, cranberry.................................**$495**

Toothpick holder, tubular design, crystal rigaree feet, 3" h **$60**

Tumbler, emb Swirl pattern, white, maroon, pink, yellow, and green, white int., 3-3/4" h.........................**$65**

Vase

Aventurine, tapering global body, short cylindrical neck, white opaque lining, 4-3/4" h.........................**$125**

Baluster shape, shades of blue, sgd "Czechoslovakia," 7" h **$50**

Watch holder, dish, ruffled rim, blue spatter, 7" h ormolu metal watch holder, 3-3/4" x 4-1/4" **$175**

STEUBEN GLASS

Steuben Ivrene lamp, urn-shaped body, applied amethyst "M"-shaped handles, shape #8508, 24" h, **$1,100.**

Photo courtesy of The Early Auction Company, LLC.

History: Frederick Carder, an Englishman, and Thomas G. Hawkes of Corning, New York, established the Steuben Glass Works in 1904. In 1918, the Corning Glass Company purchased the Steuben company. Carder remained with the firm and designed many of the pieces bearing the Steuben mark. Probably the most widely recognized wares are Aurene, Verre De Soie, and Rosaline, but many other types were produced.

The firm is still operating, producing glass of exceptional quality.

1903–32

Acid cut back

Lamp, table, ovoid shouldered form, blue Aurene cut to yellow jade, emb metal foot and collar, 22" h......**$2,000**

Vase

Shape #5000, shouldered form, Green Jade over Alabaster, perched songbirds on leafy stems, sgd, 9-1/2" h **$2,000**

Catalog #7391, shouldered form, Green Jade, acid cut stemmed peony flowers and branches cut back to Alabaster, 10" h **$3,250**

Animals

Colorless, NY, 20th C, inscribed "Steuben"

Donkey, standing, 10-1/2" h........**$980**

Dove, on stand, abrasion to side of dove, 12-1/8" h............................**$635**

Eagle, imperfections, 4-3/4" h **$350**

Elephant, raised trunk, script sgd, 8" h **$100**

Frog, sitting, minor base wear, 4-1/4" l **$230**

Preening Goose, #8344, and Gander, #8355, clear, both sgd by artist Lloyd Atkins, orig box and pamphlet, price for pr, 5-1/4" h **$250**

Seal, resting on flippers, 8-1/2" l **$375**

Shore Bird, light scratches to base, 8-3/8" l................................**$115**

Snail, base scratch, 3-5/8" l..........**$115**

Squirrel, 4-1/8" h **$350**

Aurene

Atomizer, amber, gold irid finish, atomizer bulb missing, c1920, 6" h **$415**

Bowl, calcite int., remnants of orig paper label, 10" d........................**$450**

Bud vase, blue, gold highlights, sgd "Steuben Aurene 2556," 3" d base, 10" h..**$700**

Candlesticks, pr, catalog #686, amber, twist stems on applied disc foot, strong gold luster, sgd "Aurene 686," c1920, 10-1/8" h........................**$1,100**

Chandelier, five-light, gold Aurene ribbed bell-shaped shades, burnished bronze metal holder, five chain drop, dec griffin fleur-de-lis, refurbished and rewired, three shades sgd with fleur-de-lis mark, some damage to fitter ring of one, 40" h overall, 17" w **$1,250**

Compote, shape #2604, gold, twist stem, applied cabochons, sgd "Aurene," 7" h **$1,600**

Darner, gold, some nicks and scratches from use, 5-1/2" l, 2-1/4" d **$850**

Goblet

Gold twist, stem, gold irid circular foot, sgd "Aurene 2361," 6" h **$250**

Steuben vase, yellow jade, ovoid form, slight shoulder and collar, shape #6112, 8" h, **$450.**

Photo courtesy of The Early Auction Company, LLC.

Gold, twist stem, sgd "Aurene 2861," 6" h **$250**

Grotesque bowl, 5" h, shape #7276, blue, strong coloring, sgd on bottom of one foot **$1,100**

Lamp base, 8-1/2" h shouldered form insert, pink, dec with gold Aurene random internal threading, acanthus leaf carving at stem, club shaped ftd base, dye stamped "Crest & Co.," 22" h overall **$3,000**

Lamp shade, irid green and gold drag loops, 5" h **$225**

Low bowl, blue, three prunt feet, sgd "Aurene 2586," 12" d **$550**

Perfume, amber, irid gold finish, sgd "Aurene 1818," c1915, 6" h **$650**

Planter, blue, inverted rim, three applied prunt feet, engraved "Aurene 2586," 12" d **$775**

Sherbet, gold, stemmed, sgd "Aurene 2960," 3-1/4" h **$150**

Sherbet and underplate, gold, stemmed, sgd "Aurene 2680," 6" d, 4-1/2" h **$250**

Vase

Shape #599, Style J, gold, leaf, vine, and millefiori dec, inscribed "Aurene" on bottom, 5-3/4" h **$3,750**

Shape #655, rich turquoise irid, dec with striated scrolling lappits, rich amber/pink irid, shouldered ovoid, inscribed "Aurene 655," 5-3/4" h **$17,000**

Shape #727, blue, flaring scalloped rim, sgd "Aurene 727," 6" h **$900**

Shape #2604, gold, corset shape, 7-1/4" h **$350**

Shape #2683, blue, sgd "Steuben Aurene," numbered, shouldered, 10" h **$1,600**

Shape #2683, gold, shouldered, sgd "Steuben," 6" h **$800**

Shape #2683, gold irid, brilliant pink and blue highlights, orig factory aperture filled, shouldered, 10-1/4" h **$950**

Shape #2909, flared rim, conical body, circular foot, rough pontil, gold, sgd "Steuben Aurene 2909," 5-7/8" h **$825**

Shade form, vertical ribbing, blue, sgd, 5" h **$900**

Squatty shouldered form, irid gold over calcite, sgd "Aurene F. Carder," 5-1/2" h **$475**

Calcite

Bowl

Ftd, opal, gold Aurene int., c1915, 8" d **$230**

Ftd, irid gold int., 10" d **$350**

Compote, amber bowl and foot, red and gold irid finish, irid blue rope twisted stem with gold finish, 8" h **$1,880**

Finger bowl and underplate, gold Aurene int., 6" w, 2-1/2" h **$200**

Lamp shade, dome, etched horizontal leaves, 5" h **$125**

Low bowl

Gold irid int., 10" d **$350**

Rolled rim, irid gold int., c1915, 12" d **$460**

Parfait and underplate, gold, partial paper label, 4-1/2" h, 5-1/4" d **$625**

Sherbet and underplate, stemmed, bright blue Aurene int., 6" d **$450**

Celeste Blue

Candlesticks, brilliant blue, applied foliate form bobeche and cups, bulbed shafts, c1920-33, set of four **$2,300**

Center bowl, catalog #112, swirled optic ribbed broad bowl, rolled rim, applied fluted foot, partially polished pontil, c1925, 16-1/4" d, 4-1/4" h **$400**

Finger bowl, underplate, catalog #2889, 5" d flared bowl, 6-1/2" underplate, swirled ribbed design, c1925, set of 12, some chips **$600**

Iced tea goblet, catalog #5192, blue, flared, light ribbon, set of eight, c1918-32, 6-1/2" h **$400**

Juice glass, catalog #5192, blue, flared, light ribbon, set of eight, c1918-32, 4-1/2" h **$375**

Luncheon plate, molded blue body, Kensington pattern variant, engraved border of leaves and dots, set of 12, c1918-32, 8-1/2" d **$550**

Sherbet, optic ribbed body, crystal stem, 4-1/2" h **$95**

Vase, clear glass handles, 10" d, 12-1/4" h **$1,700**

Wine glass, optic ribbed body, crystal stem, 4-3/4" h **$95**

Cluthra

Bowl, squatty shouldered form, pink shading to opal, 5-1/2" h **$600**

Lamp base, ovoid, creamy white cluthra acid-etched Art-Deco flowers, acid-etched fleur-de-lis mark near base, orig gilded foliate bronze lamp fittings, c1925, 12-1/2" **$2,070**

Vase, catalog #2683, rose, acid stamp script mark, 8" h **$2,600**

Wall pocket, half round flared bowl, black and white cluthra, cut and mounted to foliate gilt metal framework, polished pontil, slight corrosion to metal, c1930, 15-1/2" w, 8" h **$490**

Crystal

Bowl, basket shape, form #8079, inscribed "Steuben" on base, orig Steuben sock, 11-1/4" d **$150**

Calyx bowl, floriform oval, solid foot, inscribed "Steuben," 9-1/2" d, 3-3/8" h **$230**

Candlestick, shape #3178, green etched rim, 10" h **$150**

Center bowl, cov, dolphin and wave finial on cov, round bowl, applied wave motif on base, inscribed "Steuben," base scratches, 9" d, 12" h **$690**

Cocktail set, 15" h cocktail shaker, six matching 2-1/2" h glasses, two applied red cherries, wheel-cut leaves, and stems on shaker, ruby stopper, same dec on glasses, some with fleur-de-lis marks, slight damage to stopper **$3,700**

Goblet, flared cylindrical vessel, knobbed stem, sq base, small "S" inscribed on base, designed by Arthur A. Houghton, Jr., Madigan catalog #7846, set of six, two with small chips, 1938, 7-1/16" h **$260**

Paperweight, sphere with randomly imp heart motifs, late 20th C, 2-1/2" d **$115**

Vase, catalog #SP919, flared wing form, pedestal base, inscribed "Steuben" on base, 7-3/8" h **$330**

Grotesque

Bowl, blue jade, Frederick Carder design, minor int. surface wear, fleur-de-lis mark, 11-1/2" l, 6-1/4" h **$3,850**

Vase

Amethyst, catalog #7090, pillar molded floriform body, ruffled rim shaded to colorless crystal at applied disk foot, acid script "Steuben" mark in polished pontil, c1930, 9-1/4" h **$525**

Ftd, cranberry at rim shades to clear, foot chipped, 11" h **$75**

Jade

Bowl, two-line pillar, ftd, alabaster int., fleur-de-lis acid stamp mark, 8" d, 6" h **$800**

Steuben, Aurene blue twist stemcompote, shape #686, signed "Steuben Aurene 686," 6" h, $1,100.
Photo courtesy of The Early Auction Company, LLC

Steuben lamp shade, gold ribbed, inverted urn form, shape #938A, 4-1/4" h, $160.
Photo courtesy of The Early Auction Company, LLC.

Steuben card holder, translucent, pedestal, topaz foot, Pomona green rect holder, 5" h, $150.
Photo courtesy of The Early Auction Company, LLC

Bud vase, green trumpet form vase with ruffled rim, supported on scrolled tripod hammered silver mount over round base, engraved "RAP" monogram, imp "Black Starr & Frost 7050 Sterling" on base, 7-3/4" h **$460**

Candlesticks, pr, No. 2956, jade candle cup and base, alabaster shaft, gold foil labels, 10" h **$550**

Compote, yellow, ftd, 10" h ...**$1,450**

Goblet, alabaster foot, 4-3/4" h **$95**

Lamp base, flared double gourd shaped dark amethyst body cased to alabaster int., overlaid with amethyst, cameo etched in Chinese pattern, double etched with scrolling design, gilt metal fittings with three scroll arms, shallow chip under fixture, 13" h **$1,850**

Parfait, applied alabaster foot, 6" h **$350**

Rose bowl, spherical, smooth jade crystal, 7" d, 7" h **$350**

Vase, catalog #1169, alabaster int., floral design, 3-1/2" d base, 8" h ..**$2,450**

Miscellaneous

Bowl, Old Ivory, catalog #7307, pillar ftd, applied raised foot, c1930, 6-1/2" h **$435**

Candlestick, shape #7564, Ivrene, ruffled collar, sgd "Steuben," 3-1/2" h **$200**

Center bowl, ftd, topaz body, celeste blue rims, eight swirl cabochons, 14" d, 8" h **$375**

Compote, stemmed, translucent body, translucent green rim, etched floral dec, 7" h **$175**

Cordial, optic ribbed body, gray blue, amber twisted stem, price of set of seven, 6" h **$450**

Finger bowl and underplate, optic ribbed amethyst body, turquoise lip wrap, bowls acid etched "Steuben" in block letters with fleur-de-lis mark, price for five matching sets, 7" w **$525**

Goblet
French blue, bubbles and reeding, corkscrewed stem, price for set of five, 8" h **$650**
Translucent, random bubbles, amber threading, 6-1/4" h **$115**

Lamp base, catalog #8023, urn form, swirled purple, blue, and red moss agate, gilt-metal lamp fittings, acanthus leaf dec, purple glass jewel at top, needs rewiring, 10-1/4" h **$2,415**

Paperweight, Excalibur, designed by James Houston, catalog #1000, faceted hand-polished solid crystal embedded with removable sterling silver sword, 18k gold scabbard, base inscribed "Steuben," 1963 .... **$1,955**

Serving plate, catalog #3579, Bristol Yellow, board convex and folded rim, slight optic ribbing, wear scratches, 14-1/4" d, 2" h **$200**

Sherbet and underplate, peach ground, intricately engraved, sgd in block letters, 5-1/2" h **$375**

Vase
Bristol Yellow, swirled, 10" h **$175**
Cintra, ftd ovoid, yellow, fleur-de-lis signature, 6-1/2" h **$850**
Green Silverina, ftd, translucent green, internal diamond quilted silver flecks, 7" h **$325**
Ivrene, flaring ruffled rim, 8" h ..**$425**

Wine glass, colorless, white air twist stems, script sgd, price for pr, 12" h **$300**

Oriental Poppy

Goblet, opalescent foot, 5-3/4" h...**$325**

Wine glass, rose body, opalescent bands, vaseline tinted and opal rimmed foot, unmarked, 5-3/4" h **$320**

Pomona Green

Candlestick, ornamental stem, acid block letters signature, 3-1/2" h ...**$200**

Vase, crystal, faint quilting, Pomona Green threading at top, shape #6980, acid stamped factory signature, 7-1/2" h **$325**

Rosaline

Bowl, one end folded in, other pinched spout, inscribed "F. Carder Steuben 723" on edge of polished pontil, 8" l, 7" w, 3-1/4" h **$350**

Compote, ruffled, alabaster stem and foot, 4" h **$275**

Goblet, crystal foot **$90**

Perfume, catalog #6412, teardrop shape, cloudy pink, applied alabaster glass foot, pr, c1925, 5-3/8" h **$435**

Table setting, four goblets with translucent rose bowl, clambroth foot, 7-1/2" h, four matching plates, 8-1/2" d **$1,260**

Selenium Red

Goblet, ftd, fleur-de-lis framing family crest, 4-1/2" h **$200**

Plate, acid etched factory mark and Carder post-production signature, 8-3/8" d **$200**

Spanish Green

Cordial, lead glass, applied ornamental stem, threading, random bubbles, acid stamped signature, set of six,

one professionally repaired, 5-3/4" h
....**$475**

Pitcher, catalog #6665, slightly ribbed oval, flared mouth, applied angled handle, raised disk foot, acid fleur-de-lis mark, 9" h..............................**$460**

Sherbet, lead glass, applied ornamental stem, threading, random bubbles, acid stamped block letter signature, set of six, 4" h...........................**$225**

Water goblet, lead glass, applied ornamental stem, threading, random bubbles, acid stamped signature, set of four, 7-1/2" h..........................**$325**

Wine, lead glass, applied ornamental stem, threading, random bubbles, acid stamped signature, set of four, 7-1/2" h.......................................**$325**

Verre De Soie

Bonbon, compote form, overall irid surface, swirled celeste blue finial, twisted stem, 6" h **$850**

Finger bowl and underplate, etched floral motif, 6" w, 2-1/2" h **$175**

Steuben shouldered vase, Rose Quartz body, 8-3/4" h, **$1,250.** Photo courtesy of The Early Auction Company, LLC.

Lamp shade, dome shape, price for pr, 3-1/2" d **$80**

Perfume, catalog #1455, ribbed body, celeste blue flame stopper, c1915, 4-1/2" h.......................................**$400**

Vase
Classic form, notched rim, all over floral motif, 10" h **$450**
Ftd, lime green body, Verre de Soie irid finish, 6-3/4" h.................**$250**

STEVENS AND WILLIAMS

History: In 1824, Joseph Silvers and Joseph Stevens leased the Moor Lane Glass House at Briar Lea Hill (Brierley Hill), England, from the Honey-Borne family. In 1847, William Stevens and Samuel Cox Williams took over, giving the firm its present name. In 1870, the company moved to its Stourbridge plant. In the 1880s, the firm employed such renowned glass artisans as Frederick C. Carder, John Northwood, other Northwood family members, James Hill, and Joshua Hodgetts.

19th C

Stevens and Williams made cameo glass. Hodgetts developed a more commercial version using thinner-walled blanks, acid etching, and the engraving wheel. Hodgetts, an amateur botanist, was noted for his brilliant floral designs.

Other glass products and designs manufactured by Stevens and Williams include intaglio ware, Peach Bloom (a form of peachblow), moss agate, threaded ware, "jewell" ware, tapestry ware, and Silveria. Stevens and Williams made glass pieces covering the full range of late Victorian fashion.

After World War I, the firm concentrated on refining the production of lead crystal and achieving new glass colors. In 1932, Keith Murray came to Stevens and Williams as a designer. His work stressed the pure nature of the glass form. Murray stayed with Stevens and Williams until World War II and later followed a career in architecture.

Additional Listings: Cameo Glass.

Basket, tapering ivory body, inverted ruffled rim, appliqué of flowers and leaves, amber twist handle, Victorian, 8-1/2" h.......................................**$175**

Biscuit jar, cov, cream opaque, large amber and green applied ruffled leaves, rich pink int., SP rim, lid, and handle, 7-1/2" h, 5-1/2" d............**$300**

Bonbonniere, matching 4-3/4" d underplate, satin finish, swirling ribbon-like air traps on exterior of bowl and upper side of plate, crimson shading to golden pink at frilly edges, piecrust crimped edge underplate, bowl with robin's egg blue interior, under-plate with oyster white underside, 3-3/4" d, 2" h **$1,485**

Bowl, Osiris, mauve ground, swirling threaded dec, cased, 5" d **$1,430**

Box, cov, hinged, aventurine, green and red spatter, green metallic flakes, white lining, polished pontil, 4-1/2" d, 2-1/2" h.......................................**$250**

Calling card receiver, applied amber handle, rolled edge, translucent opalescent ground, three applied berries, blossoms, and green leaves, three applied amber feet, 10" l **$750**

Ewer, Pompeiian Swirl, deep rose shading to yellow, off white lining, frosted loop handle, all over gold enameled wild roses, ferns, and butterfly, 8-1/2" h, 5" w **$1,500**

Jardinière, pink opalescent, cut back, two spatter flowers and sunflowers, three applied opalescent thorn feet, leaves, and stems, minor damage, 6-1/2" d, 10" h **$350**

STIEGEL-TYPE GLASS

History: Baron Henry Stiegel founded America's first flint-glass factory at Manheim, Pennsylvania, in the 1760s. Although clear glass was the most common color made, amethyst, blue (cobalt), and fiery opalescent pieces also are found. Products included bottles, creamers, flasks, flips, perfumes, salts, tumblers, and whiskeys. Prosperity was short-lived; Stiegel's extravagant lifestyle forced the factory to close.

It is very difficult to identify a Stiegel-made item. As a result, the term "Stiegel-type" is used to identify glass made during the time period of Stiegel's firm and in the same shapes and colors as used by that company.

Enamel-decorated ware also is attributed to Stiegel. True Stiegel pieces are rare; an overwhelming majority is of European origin.

Reproduction Alert. Beware of modern reproductions, especially in enamel wares.

Bottle, blown
Brilliant deep peacock green, 15 diamonds, pot stone in neck, 5-3/8" h **$440**
Flattened octagonal, colorless, bright polychrome dec of deer on obverse, "1763" on reverse, floral dec on sides, flaring polished lip, kick up base, small flake, 6" h **$60**
Hexagonal, colorless, enameled white dove, red rose, scroll work, red, blue, yellow, and white floral designs, flared lip, 5-7/8" h **$175**

Bride's or cordial bottle
Blue, "VIVAT, es leben alle miller 1764," (long live all Miller's) central floral motifs surrounding folklore symbols, 6-1/8" h **$3,100**
Colorless, polychrome enamel floral dec, orig pewter collar with protruding threads, rough pontil mark, late 18th or 19th C, 4-3/4" h, 2-1/8" d x 2-1/2" **$315**

Flip glass, free-blown, polychrome enamel dec, colorless, rough pontil mark, late 18th or 19th C
Bird perched on heart and foliage, 3-1/8" h, 2-1/2" d rim, 1-5/8" d base **$440**
Bird perched on bright blue heart, above "3" and foliage, 3-1/2" h, 3-1/4" d rim, 2-1/8" d base **$385**
Bird perched on heart and foliage, 4-1/2" h, 3-3/4" d rim, 2-1/2" d base **$420**
Building, three tower wings, foliage, 3-1/4" h, 2-3/4" d rim, 1-7/8" d base...**$425**
Front dec with bold tulip, back with stylized flower, 8" h, 6" d rim, 3-3/4" d base **$220**
Two double steeled buildings and

foliage, 4-3/4" h, 3-3/4" d rim, 2-1/2" d base **$315**

Flask
Amethyst diamond and daisy, 4-3/4" h **$495**
Amethyst, globular, 20 molded ribs, minute rim chip, 5" h **$1,380**

Jar, cov, colorless, engraved sunflower and floral motifs, repeating dot and vine dec on cov, applied finial, sheared rim, pontil scar, form similar to McKearin plate 35, #2 and #3, 10-1/2" h.......................................**$750**

Tankard, handle, cylindrical, applied solid reeded handle, flared foot, sheared rim, pontil scar, form similar to McKearin plate 22, #4
Colorless, engraved with bird in elaborate sunburst motif, 5-3/4" h ... **$500**
Milk glass, red, yellow, blue, and green enameled dec of house on mountain with floral motif, old meandering fissure around body of vessel, 5-1/2" h..........................**$150**

Tumbler, colorless, paneled, polychrome enameled flowers, 2-7/8" h **$220**

Stiegel-type salt, master, cobalt blue, molded diamond quilted pattern, double ogee bowl, short stem, circular foot, tooled rim, pontil scars, 3-1/4" h, **$200.**

SUGAR SHAKERS

History: Sugar shakers, sugar castors, or muffineers all served the same purpose: to "sugar" muffins, scones, or toast. They are larger than salt and pepper shakers, were produced in a variety of materials, and were in vogue in the late Victorian era.

Amber, Paneled Daisy, Bryce Bros./US Glass Co., 4-1/4" h **$275**

Amethyst, nine panel, attributed to Northwood Glass Co., 4-1/2" h...**$180**

Apple green, Inverted Thumbprint, tapered, 5-3/4" h.........................**$160**

Blue, Inverted Fern, 5" h...............**$325**

Bristol, tall tapering cylinder, pink, blue flowers and green leaves dec, 6-1/4" h..**$75**

Cobalt blue, Ridge Swirl, 4-3/4" h **$375**

Cranberry glass, molded fern pattern, 4-1/2" h................................**$150**

Custard, Paneled Teardrop, Tarentum Glass Co., 4-3/4" h..................**$110**

Cut glass, Russian pattern alternating with clear panels, orig SS top **$375**

Emerald green, Hobnail, US Glass Co., 4-1/4" h.................................**$170**

Green, four blown molded panels, diamond and cross design, rib between each panel, lid mkd "E. P.," open bubble on surface, 5-3/4" h **$100**

Light blue, Paneled Daisy, Bryce Bros./US Glass Co., 4-1/4" h **$375**

Milk glass

Apple Blossom, Northwood Glass Co., 4-1/2" h **$160**

Quilted Phlox, white, hand painted blue flowers, Northwood Glass Co./ Dugan Glass Co. **$100**

Mt. Washington

Egg shape, yellow ground, blue, yellow, and amethyst mums, sgd, molded patent, 4-1/2" h...........**$200**

Fig shape, opalescent body, pansy dec, orig top, 4" h, 3-1/4" d...**$1,200**

Light blue to white, enameled flowers, Pairpoint metal caddy, paper label from Mt Washington Art Glass Society Annual Convention, 7" h **$950**

Melon ribbed, rose colored hues, raised blue and rust colored berries, emb metal lid, 4" h..........**$300**

Ribbed pillared body, enameled cascading Shasta daisies, emb metal lid, 5-1/2" h **$355**

Tomato shape, cream ground, raised white and blue flowers, 2-3/4" h **$230**

Opalescent glass

Beatty Honeycomb, white, Beatty & Sons, 3-1/2" h **$110**

Bubble Lattice, blue, 4-3/4" h **$325**

Chrysanthemum Base Swirl, blue, Buckeye Glass Co., 4-3/4" h.....**$275**

Coin Spot, bulbous base, blue, Hobbs, Brockunier & Co./Beaumont Glass Co., 4-3/4" h.............................**$160**

Daisy & Fern, cranberry, 4-1/2" h **$230**

Poinsettia pattern, blue, roughness to fitter rim, 5" h..........................**$375**

Reverse Swirl, white, Buckeye Glass Co./Model Flint Glass Co., 4-3/4" h **$120**

Spanish Lace, blue, roughness to fitter rim, 4-1/2" h **$200**

Swirl, cranberry, 5-1/4" h...........**$425**

Windows pattern, blue, roughness to fitter rim, 4-1/2" h...................**$250**

Opalware, Gillinder Melon, light blue shading to white, satin finish, hand painted multicolored floral dec, Gillinder & Sons, 4-1/2" h..........**$180**

Opaque

Acorn, blue, Beaumont Glass Co., 5" h **$230**

Alba, pink, Dithridge & Co., 4-1/2" h **$190**

Challinor's Forget-Me-Not, white, Challinor, Taylor & Co., 3-3/4" h **$90**

Cone, blue, Consolidated Lamp & Glass Co., 5-1/4" h...................**$140**

Little Shrimp, ivory, Dithridge & Co., 3" h **$100**

Parian Swirl, green, hand painted floral dec, Northwood Glass Co., 4-1/2" h...................................**$175**

Quilted Phlox, light green, cased, Northwood Glass Co./Dugan Glass Co., 4-1/2" h............................**$210**

Rings & Ribs, white, hand painted floral dec, 4-1/2" h....................**$50**

Utopia Optic, green, hand painted floral dec, Buckeye Glass Co./ Northwood Glass Co., 4-1/2" h..........**$300**

Satin

Leaf Mold, light blue, Northwood Glass Co., 4" h **$325**

Leaf Umbrella, blue, Northwood Glass Co., 4-1/2" h...................**$425**

Sugar shaker, Mount Washington, ovoid Burmese-colored body, enameled floral decoration, correct cap, 4-1/4" h, **$300.**
Photo courtesy of The Early Auction Company, LLC.

Sugar shaker, Mount Washington, subtle color gradation, enameled daisy decoration, original cap, 4" h, **$200.**
Photo courtesy of The Early Auction Company, LLC.

Slag, Creased Teardrop, brown shading to green, 4-3/4" h.......................**$275**

Smith Bros

Blue body, polychrome flowers, 5" h **$125**

Melon ribbed, enameled flowers, 5" h **$250**

Spatter

Leaf Umbrella, cased cranberry, Northwood Glass Co., 4-1/2" h **$350**

Ring neck, cranberry and white, 4-3/4" h **$140**

Unidentified maker, opal glass body, blue stemmed flowers, Victorian, 4-3/4" h....................................**$100**

Wave Crest, conical, polychrome fern dec, 5" h....................................**$335**

TIFFANY

Tiffany bud vase, Favrile, gold feathers, verre-de-soil ground, etched "L. C. Tiffany Favrile 1502-9507L," 10" x 3", **$1,400.**

Photo courtesy of David Rago Auctions, Inc.

Tiffany covered jar, Favrile, gold, two rows of lappets, jar etched "L.C.T. 1681," lid etched "M 7891," 9-1/2" x 6", **$18,000.**

Photo courtesy of David Rago Auctions, Inc.

History: Louis Comfort Tiffany (1849-1934) established a glass house in 1878 primarily to make stained glass windows. In 1890, in order to utilize surplus materials at the plant, Tiffany began to design and produce "small glass," such as iridescent glass lampshades, vases, stemware, and tableware in the Art Nouveau manner. Commercial production began in 1896.

Tiffany developed a unique type of colored iridescent glass called Favrile, which differs from other art glass in that it was a composition of colored glass worked together while hot. The essential characteristic is that the ornamentation is found within the glass; Favrile was never further decorated. Different effects were achieved by varying the amount and position of colors.

Louis Tiffany and the artists in his studio also are well known for their fine work in other areas— bronzes, pottery, jewelry, silver, and enamels.

Marks: Most Tiffany wares are signed with the name "L. C. Tiffany" or the initials "L.C.T." Some pieces also are marked "Favrile," along with a number. A variety of other marks can be found, e.g., "Tiffany Studios" and "Louis C. Tiffany Furnaces."

Reproduction Alert. Tiffany glass can be found with a variety of marks, but the script signature is often faked or added later. When considering a purchase of Tiffany glass, look first to the shape, the depth of the iridescent coloring, then the signature.

Favrile

Bowl

Flared rim, diamond quilted pattern, aqua, polished pontil, sgd "L.C. Tiffany Favrile," numbered "1926," 8-1/8" d **$1,000**

Irid gold, sgd "L.C.T.," 6" d..........**$100**

Pastel, flattened flaring rim, yellow pastel body, opalescent feathering, stretch border, sgd around pontil "L.C.T. Favrile #1925," 5-3/4" d **$250**

Bowl and flower frog, irid gold, intaglio green lily pad and random green vines, double chain looped flower frog sgd "7127L L.C. Tiffany Favrile," 10" w **$3,900**

Bud vase

Flared rim, tapering cylindrical form, gold favrile, pulled blade dec, rough pontil, sgd "L. C. Tiffany-Favrile, Inc.," numbered "1504," 6" h ...**$825**

Ftd, irid gold, green pulled feather dec, sgd "1501 1980 LC Tiffany Favrile," 8" h..........................**$1,000**

Candle lamp shade, yellow pastel opal, pulled green and silvery irid feather dec, inscribed "L.C.T., N 841," c1900, 5-1/2" h..........................**$1,955**

Candlestick, baluster irid blue, King Tut pattern, gold int., attributed by Christian Revi in *American Art Nouveau Glass* as "blue luster glass candlestick with damascene decoration in gold luster: Tiffany Furnaces, CA 1910," accompanied by book page, 10" h.............................**$1,100**

Carafe, pinched ovoid body, elongated neck, topped with pinched and beaded stopper, ambergris, overall strong gold irid, polished pontil, base sgd "L. C. Tiffany Favrile 430," slight wear to rim, 11" h **$1,035**

Center bowl, deep blue irid swirling ribbed body, sgd "L.C.T. Favrile," orig paper label on pontil, 10" d, 3-3/4" h **$1,700**

Compote, floriform

Gold body, opal overlay, pulled green feathers, irid gold onion skin rim, inscribed "L.C. Tiffany Favrile 2648L," c1917, 4-1/2" h........**$1,495**

Gold body, pinched ruffled rim, sgd "1504C L.C. Tiffany-Favrile," 4-3/4" h **$1,000**

Cordial, cylindrical flaring form, irid gold, sgd "L.C.T.," 3" h................**$300**

Cup, gold, green arrowroot dec around the body, applied handle, sgd "L. C. Tiffany –Favrile," numbered "7246D," 2-1/4" h...**$650**

Decanter set, 11" h decanter with bulbous stopper, irid gold, fine horizontal band of grapes dec, six matching sgd 4-1/4" h cordials **$5,500**

Dish

Extended ruffled rim, round form, blue, inscribed "L. C. Tiffany Favrile 1034-1595m," 5-1/4" d, 1-1/2" h **$490**

Round rim, irid gold, inscribed "L.C.T.," paper label, polished pontil **$215**

Finger bowl, 4-1/4" d, pigtail prunts dec, sgd "L.C.T. T8919," 5-7/8" d **$475**

Finger bowl and undertray, gold favrile

Bowl with ruffled rim sgd "L. C. T.," 5-5/8" d undertray sgd "L. C. T." and numbered "R3491," 4-1/8" d....**$500**

Bright blue hues, pigtail prunts, sgd "L.C.T. M9115," 6" w, 3" h........**$450**

Flower frog, irid blue, two tiers of loops, sgd "L.C. Tiffany Inc. Favrile," numbered "488N," 1-1/2" d **$400**

Goblet, irid gold, sgd "LCT Favrile," 7" h **$550**

Lamp base, bulbous-shaped body, gold Cypriote finish, Doré foot, metal collar, foot die stamped "Cassidy Company Inc. New York," glass body sgd "Louis C. Tiffany Favrile," 25" h **$4,500**

Lamp shade, irid gold, inscribed "L.C.T. Favrile," c1900, 5" h **$575**

Low bowl, fold-over rim, optic ribbed body, irid gold, sgd "1883 L.C. Tiffany Favrile," paper label, 8" d **$550**

Nut dish

Gold swirled rib form, polished pontil, numbered "1401 L.C.T. Favrile," 3" d **$450**

Ruffled rim, irid gold, sgd "L.C.T. Favrile," 2-3/4" d......................**$175**

Punch cup, irid gold, dec with intaglio band of grapes and leaves, applied handle, sgd "L.C. Tiffany Favrile," 2-1/4" h..**$400**

Rondel, circular disk, irid gold glass within metal rope-turned frame with loop handle, polished pontil, unsigned, minor wear, 17-3/8" d **$940**

Rose bowl, 10-ribbed form, ruffled rim, cobalt blue, overall blue irid luster, polished pontil sgd "L. C. Tiffany Favrile 1103-7725K," some scratches, 3-3/4" h..**$865**

Salt, open

Gold, pinched inverted rim, polished pontil, paper label, 2-1/2" d.....**$300**

Gold, ruffled rim, polished pontil, sgd "L.C.T. Favrile," 2-1/2" d **$265**

Irid gold, four pronged feet, sgd "L.C.T.," 3-1/2" h.......................**$450**

Tazza, pastel, aqua bowl, flattened stretch border, opalescent feathering, green tinted translucent stem, raised irid disc, sgd around pontil "L.C.T. Favrile 1702," 5-3/4" d, 6" h **$650**

Toothpick holder

Gold, trailing prunts, sgd "L. C. T.," numbered "D7626," 2-1/4" h ...**$250**

Gold, trailing prunts, sgd "L. C. T.," numbered "-3599," 2-3/8" h.....**$500**

Vase

10-ribbed gourd form, flared and ruffled rim above bulbed top, round disk foot, blue irid, inscribed "L. C. Tiffany Favrile 1089-68201," 10-1/4" h **$1,495**

Bulbous stick, flared rim, irid gold, sgd "2240J L.C. Tiffany Favrile," 4-1/4" h **$450**

Bulbous stick vase, flaring inverted rim, irid gold body dec with undulating white wave and gold zipper pattern, button pontil, sgd "A1493 L.C.T.," 10" h **$1,750**

Cameo, etched colorless body, white and pale yellow overlapping petals emerging from transparent green base, ftd, rolled base rim, rough pontil, sgd "L.C. Tiffany Favrile," numbered "4053D," 5-3/8" h **$11,200**

Colorless, alternating vertical bands of white opal, interior iridized in rich shaded azure blue, inscribed "L.C. Tiffany Favrile 1882," 8-7/8" h **$1,265**

Flared amber Favrile glass oval body, 25 tiny white cane blossoms among emerald green leaf leaves, amber stems, overall irid luster, inscribed "LCT Tiffany Favrile 2889C" around button pontil, 5" h.................**$2,415**

Flared rim, long cylindrical form, irid blue, sgd "L. C. T. Favrile," raised on pair of unsigned brass dolphin-form candlesticks, price for pr, 11-3/4" h **$2,235**

Floriform, blue, white and green hearts and vines dec, foot marked "5090 L. C. Tiffany Favrile," 6" h **$4,800**

Floriform, translucent green and variegated opal, pulled in feather design, slender stem, bell shape foot, inscribed "L.C.T. R 9927," 13" h **$7,130**

Floriform, wide circular opalescent glass cup with irid interior, ruffled edge, exterior dec with green striated leafage continuing to cylindrical stem, amber irid cir-

Tiffany lamp base, Favrile, iridescent, squatty stick form, opal glass, gren pulled feathers with blue iridescent Favrile, signed "56139H L.CV. Tiffany Favrile," 13" h, **$950.**
Photo courtesy of The Early Auction Company, LLC.

Tiffany Favrile vase, shouldered vessel, shading from opal to golden amber iridescence, random green decoration, signed "L.C.T. N 9919," c1900, 5-1/2" h, **$1,850.**
Photo courtesy of The Early Auction Company, LLC.

Tiffany Favrile vase, ovoid form, iridescent gold with random brown vines w/iridescent green leaves, clusters of Millefiori, "4100H L. C. Tiffany Favrile," c1913, 4" h, **$2,750.**
Photo courtesy of The Early Auction Company, LLC.

cular foot, unsgd, Corona period, 13-1/4" h **$3,000**

Floriform, gold int., green pulled feather on alabaster body, sgd "4749G L.C. Tiffany Favrile," 3" crack extends from rim into body, 4-1/2" h **$200**

Gold, high rounded shoulders with irid opal dec, marked "L. C. T. O1105," 7" h **$3,250**

Gourd form, random pulled designs in gold over yellow irid body, wafer pontil inscribed "LCT H1230," 9-1/2" h **$2,500**

Narrow mouth, bulbous body, blue, vertical tone on tone stripes, button pontil, sgd "L.C. Tiffany Favrile 7548H," 5-1/2" h **$1,880**

Ovoid form, irid gold, covered in molded lily pad motif, conical pedestal, sgd "L.C. Tiffany-Favrile," 5-3/4" h **$950**

Ovoid tapering body, cylindrical neck, gold, covered in molded branch and leaf design, raised disc base, mkd "L.C. Tiffany Favrile 1559, 506P," 8-3/8" h **$1,500**

Protruding ribs, scalloped rim, irid gold, sgd "L.C. Tiffany Favrile #N5986," orig paper label on pontil, 8-1/2" h **$1,150**

Ribbed floriform body, ruffled rim, circular foot, irid gold, sgd "L. C. Tiffany Favrile," numbered "66D," 12-3/4" h **$2,710**

Swollen body tapering to bulbed stem, amber, dec with trailing vines and heart leaves, applied dark foot, sgd "L. C. Tiffany-Favrile

5603G," bubbles below surface, 9" h **$1,840**

Tapering, irid gold, intaglio butterfly and insect dec, sgd around pontil "L.C. Tiffany Inc. Favrile 7924N," 4-3/4" h **$750**

Tapering ribbed body, irid waves, special order, sgd "L.C.T. o8136," 3-1/2" h **$1,200**

Translucent green, striking gold drips over rows of cascading irid drops, sgd "L.C.T. A214," 7-1/2" h **$2,500**

Trumpet, knopped stem, elongated irid gold body, flared rim, sgd "1509-9850L L.C. Tiffany-Favrile," 10" h **$1,300**

Wide mouth and shoulder, irid green, lower body shading to purple, polished pontil, sgd "L. C. Tiffany-Favrile," numbered "3525 L" on base, imperfections, 8-1/4" h **$1,880**

Vessel, gold, flared rim and shoulder on ribbed body, raised on circular foot, sgd "L. C. T. 63B," 3-5/8" h **$1,175**

Wine, irid gold, faceted stems, price for set of three, 3-3/4" h **$475**

TIFFIN GLASS

Tiffin lamp, figural, basket of fruit, **$250.**

History: A. J. Beatty & Sons built a glass manufacturing plant in Tiffin, Ohio, in 1888. On January 1, 1892, the firm joined the U. S. Glass Co. and was known as factory R. Fine-quality Depression-era items were made at this high-production factory.

From 1923 to 1936, Tiffin produced a line of black glassware called Black Satin. The company discontinued operation in 1980.

Marks: Beginning in 1916, wares were marked with a paper label.

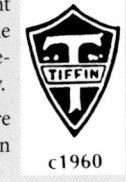

c1960

Bell, June Night, crystal **$65**
Candlestick, June Night, duo, crystal **$75**
Celery, Flanders, pink **$140**
Champagne
  Cherokee Rose, crystal **$20**
  June Night, #17358, crystal **$30**
  Palais Versailles, #17594, gold encrusted **$135**
  Plum, #17762 .... **$35**
Cocktail
  Byzantine, yellow **$15**
  Cerise, crystal **$28**
  Fuchsia, crystal **$20**
  June Night, #17538, crystal **$30**
Compote, cov, #17523, Wisteria, crystal Cellini foot, two minute rim nicks **$395**

Console bowl, Fuchsia, crystal, flared, 12-5/8" d **$135**
Cordial
  Cordelia, crystal **$10**
  Flanders, pink **$150**
  Melrose Gold, #17356, crystal **$125**
  Persian Pheasant, crystal **$45**
  Westchester Gold, #17679, crystal... **$95**
Cornucopia, Copen Blue, 8-1/4" ... **$90**
Creamer, Flanders, pink, flat **$230**
Cup and saucer, Flanders, yellow **$100**
Decanter, Byzantine, crystal **$600**
Goblet
  Cherokee Rose, crystal **$28**
  June Night, #17358, crystal **$35**
  Palais Versailles, #17594, golden-crusted **$150**

Pink Rain, #17477, wisteria **$55**
Plum, #17662 .... **$35**
Iced tea tumbler
Cerise, crystal **$28**
June Night, #17358, crystal **$35**
Pink Rain, #17477, wisteria **$55**
Plum, #17662 .... **$35**
Juice tumbler
Bouquet, gold encrusted, Killarney green **$75**
June Night, #17358, crystal **$30**
Palais Versailles, #17594, gold encrusted **$125**
Lamp, owl, rewired, 8-1/2" h, 5" d **$500**
Martini glass, Shawl Dancer, set of four, 4-1/2" d, 3" h **$150**
Perfume bottle, parrot, slate gray

painted finish, enamel dec, orig label, 4" h **$125**
Pickle, Flanders, yellow **$55**
Plate, Flanders, pink, 8" d **$35**
Rose bowl, Swedish Optic, citron green, mold #17430, c1960, 5-1/2" x 5" **$145**
Salad plate, June Night, crystal, 7-1/2" d **$22**
Seafood cocktail, liner, Palais Versailles, #17594, gold encrusted **$175**
Sherbet
Cherokee Rose, crystal, tall **$24**
Ramblin' Rose, crystal, low **$23**
Sherry
June Night, crystal **$30**
Shawl Dancer, crystal **$55**

Sugar
Cerice, crystal **$25**
La Fleure, yellow **$40**
Vase
Crystal, artist sgd, 7-3/8" d, 14" h .. **$400**
Dahlia, cupped, Reflex Green, allover silver overlay, 8" h **$225**
Dark amethyst satin, poppy like flowers, 8-3/4" h **$200**
Wall pocket, ruby, 9" l, 3-1/4" w .. **$175**
Wine
Byzantine, crystal **$18**
Cherokee Rose, crystal **$40**
Mirabelle, #17361, crystal, 6-1/4" h **$48**
Mystic, #17378, crystal, 5-5/8" h .. **$45**
Palais Versailles, #17594, gold encrusted **$150**

TOOTHPICK HOLDERS

History: Toothpick holders, indispensable table accessories of the Victorian era, are small containers made specifically to hold toothpicks.

They were made in a wide range of materials: china (bisque and porcelain), glass (art, blown, cut, opalescent, pattern, etc.), and metals, especially silver plate. Makers include both American and European firms.

By applying a decal or transfer, a toothpick holder became a souvenir item; by changing the decal or transfer, the same blank could become a memento for any number of locations.

Bisque, skull, blue anchor-shape mark **$65**
China
Royal Bayreuth, elk **$120**
Royal Doulton, Santa scene, green handles **$75**
R. S. Germany, Schlegelmilch, MOP luster **$40**
Mt. Washington
10-lobe, crimson and blue floral dec, 2-1/4" h **$225**
Burmese, flared painted blue rim, mold-in ferns motif, scrolls at base, white blossoms with yellow dot centers, 2-1/2" h **$1,085**
Burmese, sq mouth, matte finish, diamond quilted, yellow rim, 2-3/4" h **$325**
Burmese, sq mouth toothpick holder, orig gilt, white, and yellow daisy dec, silvered plated Victorian frame mkd "James W. Tufts, Boston," 2-1/2" h **$1,000**
Burmese, tri-fold, ruffled rim, diamond quilted body, 1-3/4" h **$200**
Peachblow, sq mouth toothpick holder, shading from soft pink to soft

blue, orig gilt dec and hp yellow daisies, silver plated Victorian holder mkd "James W. Tufts, Boston," 2-1/2" h **$9,500**
Ribbed pillar, blue flowers on leafy stem dec, 2" h **$175**
Pattern glass
Arched Fleur-De-Lis **$45**
Daisy and Button, blue **$75**
Fandango, Heisey **$55**
Hartford, Fostoria **$85**
Jewel with Dewdrop **$55**
Paneled 44, Reverse, platinum stain **$75**
Truncated Cube, ruby stained **$75**
US Coin, colorless, frosted Morgan one dollar coin, c1892 .... **$290**
Satin glass, 2-3/8" h, 3" d at top, 2" d base creamy white diamond quilted mother of pearl satin glass holder with tightly crimped top edge, polished pontil, hallmarked silver plated stand 7-3/4" l, 4" w, 3-1/8" h **$750**
Spatter glass, tubular design, crystal rigaree feet, 3" h **$60**

Three toothpick holders: two peachblow style, one satin glass decorated with ferns and flowers, **$160.**
Photo courtesy of Joy Luke Auctions.

VAL ST.-LAMBERT

History: Val St.-Lambert, a 12th-century Cistercian abbey, was located during different historical periods in France, Netherlands, and Belgium (1930 to present). In 1822, Francois Kemlin and Auguste Lelievre, along with a group of financiers, bought the abbey and opened a glassworks. In 1846, Val St.-Lambert merged with the Socété Anonyme des Manufactures de Glaces, Verres à Vitre, Cristaux et Gobeletaries. The company bought many other glassworks.

Val St.-Lambert developed a reputation for technological progress in the glass industry. In 1879, Val St.-Lambert became an independent company employing 4,000 workers. The firm concentrated on the export market, making table glass, cut, engraved, etched, and molded pieces, and chandeliers. Some pieces were finished in other countries, e.g., silver mounts were added in the United States.

Val St.-Lambert executed many special commissions for the artists of the Art Nouveau and Art Deco periods. The tradition continues. The company also made cameo-etched vases, covered boxes, and bowls. The firm celebrated its 150th anniversary in 1975.

Ashtray, hexagon, colorless crystal, 6" w.................**$35**

Candlesticks, pr, colorless crystal, orig paper labels, 9-1/2" h..........**$250**

Cologne bottle, frosted cylindrical body, cameo cranberry floral relief, cut faceted stopper, 4-3/8" h.......**$175**

Cordial Glasses, set of six, bowls cased in cobalt blue, cut with band of circles over paneled flutes, single knopped stem, spreading foot, 4-5/8" h......**$250**

Epergne, five 6" h etched cameo cylindrical flower holders, stylized naturalistic brass frame, 10-1/2" h.................**$1,800**

Figure, parrot perched on bell, light cranberry, sgd "Val St Lambert, Belgique," 3-1/2" d base, 7-1/4" h.................**$275**

Paperweight, apple, colorless crystal, acid etched script signature, 4" h.................**$85**

Presentation vase, green ground, cameo cut chrysanthemums, maroon enameling, c1900, 14" h..........**$500**

Vase
Cobalt blue ground, overlaid in copper, all over emb rosettes, emb "Val St Lambert Belgique," c1910, 11-1/2" h.................**$575**
Emerald and colorless crystal, 8-3/4" d, 12" h.................**$550**

VALLERYSTHAL GLASS

Two painted Vallerysthal milk glass strawberry-shaped lidded dishes with snail finials, 4-1/2" l, 5-1/2" h, each **$60.**
Photo courtesy of Joy Luke Auctions.

History: Vallerysthal (Lorraine), France, has been a glass-producing center for centuries. In 1872, two major factories, Vallerysthal glassworks and Portieux glassworks, merged and produced art glass until 1898. Later, pressed glass animal-covered dishes were introduced. The factory continues to operate today.

Animal dish, cov
Hen on nest, opaque aqua, sgd.....**$95**
Rabbit, white, frosted...................**$85**
Swan, blue opaque glass.............**$110**

Butter dish, cov, turtle, opaque white, snail finial.................**$120**

Candlesticks, pr, Baroque pattern, amber.................**$75**

Compote, blue opaque glass, 6-1/4" sq.................**$75**

Mustard, cov, swirled ribs, scalloped blue opaque, matching cover with slot for spoon.................**$35**

Plate, Thistle pattern, green, 6" d.................**$65**

Salt, cov, hen on nest, white opal.................**$65**

Sugar, cov, Strawberry pattern, opaque white, gold trim, salamander finial, 5" h.................**$85**

Toothpick holder, hand holding ribbed vessel, opaque blue..........**$30**

Vase, flared folded burgundy red rim, oval pale green body, matching red enamel berry bush on front, inscribed "Vallerysthal" on base, 8" h........**$490**

VENETIAN GLASS

History: Venetian glass has been made on the island of Murano, near Venice, since the 13th century. Most of the wares are thin walled. Many types of decoration have been used: embedded gold dust, lace work, and applied fruits or flowers.

Reproduction Alert. Venetian glass continues to be made today.

Bowl, deep quatraform bowl, applied quatraform rim, blue, clear internal dec, trapped air bubble square, circles, and gold inclusions, c1950, 7-1/2" w, 6-1/8" w **$360**

Candlesticks, pr, white and black glass, formed as coat on twisted stem coat rack on tripod base, black domed foot, 20th C **$275**

Centerpiece set, two 8-1/2" baluster ftd ewers, 8-1/2" ftd compote, red and white latticino stripes with gold flecks, applied clear handles and feet, three-pc set **$150**

Compote, cov, dusty amber body, blue lip wrap, floral finial, 7-1/2" d **$70**

Compote, open, pale green glass body, five gold metallic and colorless glass loop ornaments, price for pr, early 20th C, 7-7/8" h **$600**

Decanter, figural clown, bright red, yellow, black, and white, aventurine swirls, orig stopper, 13" h **$250**

Ewer, pinched sided, alternating green and opal panels, chain dec, 6" h ... **$65**

Goblet, shamrock shape, translucent, dec with pictorial medallions, intaglio cut gilt scrolling and flowers, Lobmeyer, price for pr, 6" h **$275**

Sherry, amber swirled bowls, blue beaded stems, eight-pc set **$495**

Table garniture, two 14-1/4" h clear glass dolphins on white diagonally fluted short pedestals, six 5-3/4" h to 7-3/4" h clear glass turtle, bird, seahorse, dolphin, two bunches of fruit in bowls, figures on similar white pedestals, including 20th C **$550**

Vase, handkerchief shape, pale green and white pulled stripe, applied clear rope base, attributed to Barovier, 1930s, 8" h **$65**

Wine, alternating dec panels, 3-7/8" h **$75**

Venetian glass, vases, swirled, price for pr, 20th C, 7" w, 9-1/2" h, **$300**.
Photo courtesy of David Rago Auctions, Inc.

Six Venetian birds on branch, 17" l, **$225**.
Photo courtesy of Joy Luke Auctions.

WATERFORD

History: Waterford crystal is high-quality flint glass commonly decorated with cuttings. The original factory was established at Waterford, Ireland, in 1729. Glass made before 1830 is darker than the brilliantly clear glass of later production. The factory closed in 1852. One hundred years later it reopened and continues in production today.

Bowl, Kileen pattern, 9-3/4" d **$260**

Cake plate, sunburst center, geometric design, 10" d, 5-1/4" h **$85**

Cake server, cut-glass handle, orig box **$80**

Champagne flute, Coleen pattern, 12-pc set, 6" h **$450**

Christmas ornament, Twelve Days of Christmas Series, crystal, orig box, dated bag, orig sticker, brochure Partridge in Pear Tree, 1982 .... **$450**
Second, two turtle doves, 1985 .... **$250**
Four calling birds, 1987 .... **$200**

Compote, allover diamond cutting above double wafer stem, pr, 5-1/2" h **$400**

Creamer and sugar, Tralee pattern, 4" h creamer, 3-3/4" d sugar **$85**

Decanter, orig stopper, allover diamond cutting, monogram, pr, 12-3/4" h ... **$300**

Lamp, umbrella shade, blunt diamond cutting, Pattern L-1122, 23" h, 13" d **$450**

Napkin ring, 12-pc set, 2" h **$225**

Tumbler, Colleen, set of six, orig box **$400**

Vase, diamond pattern, wreath around center, sgd, 6" h **$225**

Waterford, 5-1/2" d x 13" h vase with scalloped edge with mark; decanter and stopper with mark; open pitcher with mark; covered jar with mark; tall pitcher with long neck and stopper; two small pitchers; two small covered jars, one marked, price for grouping, **$700**.
Photo courtesy of David Rago Auctions, Inc.

WAVE CREST

Wave Crest letter box, decorated with pink flowers, brass trim, 5-1/2" w, 4" h, **$350.**

Photo courtesy of Joy Luke Auctions.

Wave Crest cracker jar, egg crate form, red and yellow roses, CF Monroe, 8" h, **$300.**

Photo courtesy of The Early Auction Company, LLC.

Wave Crest powder box, blue floral dec, bronze mounts, complete with two ivory tipped feather powder puffs, 5-1/2" x 5", **$400.**

Photo courtesy of David Rago Auctions, Inc.

History: The C. F. Monroe Company of Meriden, Connecticut, produced the opal glassware known as Wave Crest from 1898 until World War I. The company bought the opaque, blown-molded glass blanks from the Pairpoint Manufacturing Co. of New Bedford, Massachusetts, and other glassmakers, including European factories. The Monroe company then decorated the blanks, usually with floral patterns. Trade names used were "Wave Crest Ware," "Kelva," and "Nakara."

WAVE CREST WARE
c1892

Biscuit jar, cov, unmarked
Helmschmied swirl opaque white and tan body, red enameled flowers, 6-1/2" d **$460**
Pink and white background, melon ribbed, hp flowers, 5-1/2" d, 5-1/2" h **$250**
White ground, fern dec, 8" h **$200**

Bonbon, Venetian scene, multicolored landscape, dec rim, satin lining missing, 7" h, 6" w **$1,200**

Box, cov
Baroque Shell, Moorish Fantasy design, raised pink-gold rococo scrolls, fancy Arabic designs of pale turquoise and natural opaque white, lace-like network of raised white enamel beads, satin lining missing, 7-1/4" d, 3-3/34" h
.... **$1,250**
Double Scroll, aqua blue tint, hp florals, sgd, no lining, 3" d **$275**
Heart-shape, opaque tan glass body, dec with red and yellow mums, Belle Ware, #4625/10, 6" d
.... **$460**
Ormolu feet and handles, red banner back stamp, c1890, 5-3/4" l **$225**
Pink florals, fancy ormolu fittings, 7" w **$800**

Cigar humidor, blue body, single-petaled pink rose, pink "Cigar" signature, pewter collar, bail, and lid, flame-shaped finial, sgd "Kelva," 8-3/4" h **$685**

Cracker jar, blue and white hp florals, green and brown leaves, white Johnny jump-ups, puffy egg crate mold, 5-1/4" d, 10-1/2" h **$700**

Creamer and sugar, Helmschmeid pattern, pink stemmed flowers, 4-1/2" h **$350**

Dresser box, cov
Enameled violets, red banner back stamp, c1890, 4-1/4" d **$185**
Six-sided form, beaded enameling, unmarked, c1890, 4" d **$250**
Egg crate mold, enameled florals, unmarked, c1890, 5-3/4" l **$245**

Egg crate mold, hp florals, orig lining, red banner back stamp, 6-3/4" sq, 3-3/4" h **$320**
Egg crate mold, hp mums, shaded amber ground, ormolu mounted feet, reticulated shoulder, red banner back stamp, c1890, 6-3/4" w, 6-3/4" h **$2,425**
Florals, blue ground, mkd "Nakara C.F.M. Co.," c1890, 8" d **$900**
Rococo mold, hp florals, orig interior, black block mark, c1890, 7-1/2" h
.... **$525**
Swirl mold, enameled florals, red banner back stamp, hairline in lid, c1890, 7" h **$210**
Swirl mold, hp florals, unmarked, c1890, 7" h **$260**
Swirl mold, enameled florals, red banner back stamp, c1890, 5-3/4" d
.... **$230**

Ewer, lavender, figural woman on handle, ornate base **$225**

Ferner, egg crate mold, enameled blue flowers, four lion emb feet, orig liner, 6-3/4" d **$520**

Mustard jar, cov, spoon, green ground, floral dec, unmarked **$140**

Pin dish, open
Pink and white, swirled, floral dec, unmarked, 3-1/2" d, 1-1/2" h **$35**
Pink and white, eggcrate mold, blue violets dec, marked, 4-1/4" d, 2" h
.... **$80**
White, scrolls, pink floral dec, marked, 5" d, 1-1/2" h **$80**

Plate, reticulated border, pond lily dec, shaded pale blue ground, 7" d
.... **$750**

Portrait box, cov, swirl mold, painted florals and cupid, block mark, c1890, 4-1/4" d **$250**

Salt and pepper shakers, pr
Swirled, light yellow ground, floral dec, unmarked **$75**
Tulip, brown and white ground, birds and floral dec **$70**

Sugar shaker, conical, polychrome fern dec, 5" h **$335**

Syrup pitcher, Helmschmied Swirl, ivory-colored body, blue and white floral dec, smoky-gray leafy branches, SP lid and collar **$485**

Tray, flattened circular form, molded scrolled designs, hp floral dec in reserves, emb collar with openwork handles, sgd, discoloration to metal, 4-1/2" d, 1-3/4" h **$45**

Trinket dish, 1-1/2" x 5", blue and red flowers **$175**

Urn

Egg-shaped body, short pedestal, two ornate handles, centered raised gold, floral bouquet, pale green tinted ground, gold patina on metal fittings, 6-1/2" h **$445**

Horn shape over acorn-shaped body, short pedestal, two ornate handles, centered raised gold, floral bouquet, sea foam green tinted ground, gold patina on metal fittings, 6-1/2" h **$445**

Vase

Rococo mold, hp florals, ormolu ft base, red banner back stamp, c1890, 7-1/2" h **$275**

Swirl mold, ftd ormolu base, red banner back stamp, c1890, 7-1/2" h **$250**

White orchid blossoms with blue-gray shading, cobalt blue ground, gilt ormolu handles, 12-1/2" h **$2,450**

White wild rose blossoms, scattered sprays of gray rose buds, cobalt blue ground, gilt ormolu handles, 12-1/2" h **$2,450**

Vase ornament, light blue, detailed hand enameled dec, fine ormolu mounts, 6-1/4" h **$150**

Wave Crest lamp, opal vase, pink and white mums, amethyst scrolling, four-footed base, two-arm ormolu collar, 10" h vase, 24" overall, **$650.**

WEBB, THOMAS & SONS

History: Thomas Webb & Sons was established in 1837 in Stourbridge, England. The company probably is best known for its very beautiful English cameo glass. However, many other types of colored art glass were produced, including enameled, iridescent, heavily ornamented, and cased.

Biscuit jar, cov, white cameo dec, single petaled blossoms, leafed branch, ruby red ground, silver plate fittings, 6" d, 7-1/4" h **$2,950**

Bowl

Alabaster, ruffled rim, hp silver and gold foliage and butterfly, turquoise int, 5" d................................... **$250**

Burmese, lilac, prunus dec, 2" h **$6,000**

Burmese, silver rim, sgd "Thomas Webb & Sons," 4-1/2" d **$110**

Bride's bowl, hobnail, creamy opal body, rose int., ruffled rim, 10" d **$325**

Cabinet vase, rose ground, cameo carved white flower and butterfly, rim roughness, 2" h **$400**

Cane handle, globular form, cameo carved, intricate Moorish design, 3-1/2" h.................................. **$800**

Cologne bottle, Peachblow, bulbous, blue and white daisies, leafy green branches, two amethyst butterflies in flight, hallmarks on threaded ovoid cap, 5" h **$950**

Cream pitcher

Bulbous, round mouth, brown satin, cream lining, applied frosted handle, 3-3/4" h, 2-1/2" d **$210**

Sepia to pale tan ground, heavy gold burnished prunus blossoms, butterfly on back, gold rim and base, clear glass handle with brushed gold, 3-1/4" h **$385**

Epergne

Burmese, Hawthorne pattern, central post insert and three ruffled rim inserts, metal four-ftd base and holder, small chip, 11-1/2" h ... **$900**

Canary yellow center inverted pyriform vase with everted rim and rigaree collar, flanked by two peachblow apples, four downward curving vaseline leaves with amber stems, shaped mirrored plateau, ex-Maude Feld, 10-3/4" h **$18,000**

Ewer, satin, deep green shading to off-white, gold enameled leaves and branches, three naturalistic applies, applied ivory handle, long spout, numbered base, 9" h, 4" d **$425**

Webb shouldered vase, opaque ivory, blue and pink stemmed floer dec, #16-27359, 10" h, **$100.**

Webb bride's bowl, pink satin, ruffled rim, glossy finish, stemmed gold branch dec, silverplate base, two lions, 11-1/2" h, **$2,450.**
Photo courtesy of The Early Auction Company, LLC.

Figure, pig, solid Burmese body, pink tint to hind quarters, curly tail, four feet, ears, and snout, Webb, 3" l, 1-1/2" h **$750**

Flask, fish shape, lemon yellow glass overlaid in white, wheel carved features, sterling silver fish tail screw lid, cameo carved "Rd. 15711," lid imp "Sterling," hairline and cameo loss at mouth, 11-5/8" h **$9,500**

Lamp, kerosene, Burmese shade and base hand dec in Woodbine pattern, base with stamped trademark, 15" h **$4,250**

Perfume bottle, lay down style, circular, ivory, overall cameo flowers, emb flip lid, orig stopper, 2-3/4" h **$1,700**

Cameo carved leafy ferns and butterfly on reverse, monogrammed silver lid, 10" l **$1,650**

Rose bowl, Burmese, amethyst flowers, green and brown foliage, price for pr, 2-1/4" h, 2-1/2" h **$690**

Salad fork and spoon, ivory ground, cameo carved garden of stemmed flowers, hallmarked "F & Co." with crown and shield, 12" l **$700**

Scent bottle

Burmese, brilliant gold dec, restored gold cap, 3" d, 3-3/4" h **$1,235**

Peacock Eye MOP, pearl white ground, sterling silver fittings, screw-on cap mkd "T. W. & S," hallmarks for 1902, "RD 58374" inscribed in base, minute dents in cap, 3" d, 4" h **$950**

Sociable, Burmese, center crimped rim vase, three round covered dishes, delicate shading and dec, gilt metal ftd base, 8-3/4" h **$9,000**

Sugar shaker, herringbone MOP, tapering ovoid body shades from citron to pearl, British sterling silver cap with hallmark, acid stamped signature on base, 6-1/2" h **$500**

Vase

Alexandrite, honeycomb, 2-3/4" h **$2,700**

Bulbous baluster, gold ground, carved white geraniums, carved white coral bells on reverse, sgd "Webb," 7-1/2" h **$1,750**

Bulbous stick, opal body, cinnamon iced crystal overlay, hand enameled gold flowering vine, numbered "1095-4P5aa," 6-1/4" h **$225**

Bulbous stick, tightly scalloped crimped rim, ivory ground, cascading honeysuckle dec, butterfly on reverse, sgd with half moon "Thos Webb and Sons," 7-3/4" h **$1,000**

Burmese, trumpet, pink petaled rim shades to satin yellow, imp trademark, 8-1/4" h **$350**

Peachblow, tapering body, short everted neck, shades from deep cranberry to satin opal, allover applied coralene dec, 5-1/4" h **$200**

Peachblow, bulbous body extends to knopped conical neck, crimson to pink shading, enameled bird, butterfly, stylized flowers, gilt scrolls, 16" h **$1,200**

Shouldered, body shades from lime green rim to opal base, hp butterfly framed with leafy branch, mkd with registration number 676/5 R167, 7" h **$350**

Shouldered, deep crimson, enameled song birds perched on ginkgo flowering branches, numbered "893/7 P268," slight scratching on reverse, 7-1/2" h **$250**

Tapering ovoid, Prussian blue body, cameo carved opaque white floral cutting, cameo rings at top and base, butterfly on reverse, sgd, 7" h **$1,700**

White blossoms and buds, carved pink folds and veins, frosted clear ground, butterfly on reverse, imp "Thomas Webb & Sons Cameo," 9" h **$3,450**

JEWELRY

ART PLASTIC JEWELRY

by Leigh Leshner

Art plastic jewelry has been a favorite of collectors for decades. Plastic jewelry is often referred to as novelty jewelry because it is fun and whimsical. Plastikos is a Greek word meaning to mold or to form and that is the perfect description for the material we commonly refer to as plastic. Plastic is a material that generally can be shaped and molded under heat and pressure. Plastics come in all colors from clear to vibrant hues of fuchsia, red and orange to more subdued colors of black, brown and avocado.

There are two types of plastics: thermoplastic and thermoset. A thermoset can be reheated and reshaped such as acrylic, gutta percha and polyethylene. A thermoplastic is a plastic that is heated, a chemical reaction occurs, it is shaped into an object and then it permanently hardens and becomes heat resistant. Melamine and Bakelite are thermoplastics.

There are two kinds of plastics: natural and synthetic. Natural plastics are those that have evolved through either the natural biological process or natural materials such as amber, horn, tortoiseshell, gutta-percha and vulcanite. Synthetic plastics are those that are man made with chemicals such as cellulose, Bakelite, casein and Lucite. A variation of this is semi-synthetics which occurs when you modify the chemical composition of natural materials such as casein, celluloid, cellulose acetate, ebonite, Parkisene and vulcanized rubber. When we talk about plastics today, we are generally speaking of man-made synthetic plastics.

Plastics have been used for purposes of all kinds, including jewelry. Manufacturers loved the easily handled material, and the ability to mechanize the production process. Business managers loved the low wholesale price and shoppers smiled at the finished item and happily paid the small bill.

In the 1920s, celluloid, a popular material, was used to create jewelry that used geometric designs, Egyptian motifs, oriental motifs as well as art deco designs that were streamlined and modern. Often the art deco designs were mixed with chrome and rhinestones. Europeans used galalith in their jewelry combining it with chrome, brass, silver and gold plating to create avant-garde and art deco designs.

In the 1930s, Bakelite was used to create whimsical and fun jewelry that incorporated designs of fruits, vegetables, animals, figurals, flowers, cameos and geometric designs.

Because of World War II, the use of pot metal (the tin and lead used in pot metal) was prohibited for use other than for the military. Materials were scarce because of wartime production. However, Bakelite and other plastics were plentiful. Because the material was inexpensive, designers could indulge in their fantasies and create pieces to give life to an outfit for a relatively small price tag. In fact, the pieces were not only found in the high-end department stores like Bergdorf-Goodman and Lord and Taylor but they were abundant in the dime stores as well.

Plastic jewelry has continued to be made throughout the years. Many designers have incorporated plastic elements into their jewelry such as Kenneth Lane, Coro, Trifari, Hobé, Eisenberg, Lisner, and a host of others.

Currently, there are designers who are making wonderful jewelry by designing and carving pieces of jewelry with old materials. This process is a lost art that is now being resurrected by a few select artisans whose work incorporates old methods with a breath of fresh air and design innovation.

Prices of plastic jewelry vary. The handmade modern pieces of jewelry can be expensive because of the amount of intricate work and time needed to produce them. The prices of older pieces vary depending upon scarcity, rarity, condition, quality and popularity. The more detailed and intricately carved, the more expensive it will be.

The first rule of collecting is to collect what you like! Then you need to focus on the condition and the quality. Is the piece well made? Is it cracked, chipped or scratched? Is it deteriorating? Can the piece be repaired and how much will the repair cost?

The quality and the design of the piece are very important. Is it intricate and ornate? Is it handmade or machine made? How is the finish on the piece? The more detail that is involved and the more handwork that is involved will generally make apiece more valuable.

OTHER HELPFUL HINTS:

• Don't buy a piece that is deteriorating.

• Check for scratches, pitting, crazing, cracking, splits, nicks, warping, repairs and glue.

• Check to make sure there are no holes from heat tests.

• Look for signs of age in the hardware to see if the piece is older. Generally the older pieces will use screws and rivets to secure pin-backs while the newer ones will have glued on pin-backs.

• If the piece has hanging charms or beads, check the string that is attaching them.

• You can run your hand over a piece to feel for cracks and nicks.

BIBLIOGRAPHY

Davidov, Corinne and Ginny Redington Dawes. *The Bakelite Jewelry Book.* New York, New York: Abbeville Press, 1988.

Grasso, Tony. *Bakelite Jewelry: A Collector's Guide.* New Jersey: Chartwell Books, 1996.

Katz, Sylvia. *Plastics: Common Objects, Classic Designs.* New York, NY: Harry N. Abrams, 1984.

Kelly, Lyngerda and Nancy Schiffer. *Plastic Jewelry.* West Chester, PA: Schiffer Publishing Co., 1987.

Leshner, Leigh. *Costume Jewelry: A Price and Identification Guide.* Iola, WI: Krause Publications, 2004.

Leshner, Leigh and Christie Romero. *Hidden Treasures: A Collector's Guide To Antique and Vintage Jewelry.* Los Angeles, CA: Venture Entertainment Group, Inc.

McNulty, Lyndi Stewart. *Price Guide to Plastic Collectibles.* Greensboro, NC: Wallace Homestead, 1987.

Parry, Karima. *Bakelite Bangles: A Price and Identification Guide.* Iola, WI: Krause Publications, 1999.

Wasserstrom, Donna and Leslie Pina. *Bakelite Jewelry.* Atglen, PA: Schiffer Publishing Co., 1997.

JEWELRY RESOURCES

100 Years of Vintage Watches, 2nd Ed., by Dean Judy, Krause Publications, Iola, WI.

Answers to Questions About Old Jewelry, 1840-1950, 6th Ed., by C. Jeanenne Bell, G.G., Krause Publications, Iola, WI.

Antique Trader Jewelry Price Guide, by Kyle Husfloen, ed., Marion Cohen contributing ed., Krause Publications, Iola, WI.

Collecting Art Plastic Jewelry, by Leigh Leshner, Krause Publications, Iola, WI.

Collecting Victorian Jewelry, by C. Jeanenne Bell, G.G., Krause Publications, Iola, WI.

Costume Jewelry, by Leigh Leshner, Krause Publications, Iola, WI.

Costume Jewelry Variations, by Marion Cohen, Krause Publications, Iola, WI.

Rhinestone Jewelry, by Leigh Leshner, Krause Publications, Iola, WI.

Vintage Jewelry, 1920-1940s, by Leigh Leshner, Krause Publications, Iola, WI.

Warman's© Antique Jewelry Field Guide, by C. Jeanenne Bell, G.G., Krause Publications, Iola, WI.

Warman's© Jewelry, 3rd Ed., by Christie Romero, Krause Publications, Iola, WI.

Warman's© Jewelry Field Guide, by Leigh Leshner, Krause Publications, Iola, WI.

Warman's© Watches Field Guide, by Dean Judy, Krause Publications, Iola, WI.

GALLERY

Top-carved and reverse-carved and painted applejuice Bakelite and black Bakelite brooch, **$550.**

Nautical brooch, butterscotch Bakelite and wood, **$350.**

Eagle brooch, black Bakelite with rhinestones, **$450.**

Celluloid necklace with celluloid charms, **$325.**

Top: two-tone Bakelite bangle, **$265;** second: carved butterscotch Bakelite bangle: **$150;** third: carved butterscotch Bakelite bangle, **$150;** bottom: carved butterscotch bangle, **$250.**

Jewelry boxes, French, metal mounts, larger: 6" h, polychrome enamel dec with birds and foliage, gilt trim; smaller: gilt and enamel Rocailles decoration, chip to base, price for pair, c1890, **$2,400.**
Photo courtesy of David Rago Auctions, Inc.

Butler and Wilson Galalith bangle, **$500.**

Brooch with intaglio of ship and water, Bakelite, **$235.**

Necklace, butterscotch Bakelite, **$225.**

Bangle with front section made up of individual pieces strung on elastic, Bakelite, **$750.**

JEWELRY

History: Jewelry has been a part of every culture throughout time. It is often reflective of the times as well as social and aesthetic movements with each piece telling its own story through hidden clues that when interpreted will help solve the mysteries surrounding them. The jewelry is at times rich and elegant and at other times ornate yet simple. The pieces range in size and vary from delicate to bold made of both precious and non-precious materials.

Jewelry is generally divided into periods and styles. A circa date is only an approximation. It includes the period of ten years preceding and proceding the circa date. Each period may have several styles with some of the same styles and types of jewelry being made in both precious and non-precious materials. Additionally, there are recurring style revivals which are interpretations of styles from an earlier period. For example, the Egyptian revival that took place in the early and late 1800s, and then again in the 1920s.

Georgian, 1760-1837. Fine jewelry from this period is very desirable but few good quality pieces have found their way to auction in the last few years. Sadly, much jewelry from this period has been lost.

Victorian, 1837-1901. The Victorian period was named after Queen Victoria of England. She ascended the throne in 1837 and remained Queen until her death in 1901. The Victorian period is a long and prolific one; abundant with many styles of jewelry that it warrants being divided into three sub-periods: Early or Romantic period dating from 1837-1860; Mid or Grand period dating from 1860-1880; and Late or Aesthetic period dating from 1880-1901.

Sentiment and romance was a significant factor in Victorian jewelry. Often, symbols within jewelry and clothing represented love and affection with symbolic motifs such as hearts, crosses, hands, flowers, anchors, doves, crowns, knots, stars, thistles, wheat, garlands, horseshoes and moons. The materials of the times were also abundant and varied. They included silver, gold, diamonds, onyx, glass, cameos, paste, carnelian, agate, coral, amber, garnet, emeralds, opals, pearls, peridot, rubies, sapphires, marcasites, cut steel, enameling, tortoise shell, topaz, turquoise, bog oak, ivory, jet, hair, gutta percha and vulcanite.

Sentiments of love were often expressed in miniatures. Miniatures are portraits of a loved one. Sometimes they were representative of deceased persons, but often the miniatures were of the living. Occasionally, the miniatures depicted landscapes, cherubs or religious themes.

Hair jewelry was a popular form of jewelry that was an expression of love and sentiment. The jewelry was a way to keep the loved one near to you. The hair of a loved one was placed in a special compartment in a brooch or a locket or used to form a picture under the glass compartment. Later in the mid-nineteenth century, pieces of jewelry were made completely of woven hair. Individual strands of hair would be woven together to create necklaces, watch chains, brooches, earrings and rings.

In 1861, Prince Albert died causing Victoria to go into mourning for the rest of her life. Victoria required that the royal court wear black. This atmosphere spread to the populace and created a demand for mourning jewelry. Mourning jewelry is another form of sentimentalism. It is a memento to remember a loved one.

Mourning jewelry is typically black. When it first came into fashion, it was made from jet. Jet is a fossilized coal that was mined in Whitby, England. By 1850, there were fifty workshops that used jet to make brooches, lockets, bracelets and necklaces. As the supply of jet dwindled, other materials were used such as vulcanite, gutta percha, bog oak and French jet.

By the 1880s, the dark, gloomy and somber mourning jewelry was losing popularity. Mourning had become relaxed. Fashions had changed. The clothing was simpler and had an air of delicacy. The Industrial Revolution which had begun in the early part of the century was now in full swing and machine manufactured jewelry was affordable to the working class.

Edwardian, 1890-1920. The Edwardian period takes its name from an English Monarch, King Edward VII. Though Edward VII ascended the throne in 1901, he and his wife Alexandria of Denmark exerted influence over the style for the ten year period before and after his ascension. The 1890s was known as La Belle Epoque. This was a time known for ostentation and extravagance. As the years moved on, the lines became simpler. The jewelry became smaller. Instead of wearing one large brooch, women were often found wearing several small lapel pins.

Into the 1900s, extravagance was again in vogue. Luxurious fabrics, sequins, beads and lace were used in clothing. Platinum, diamonds and pearls were prevalent in the jewelry of the wealthy, while paste was being used by the masses to imitate the real thing. The styles were reminiscent of the neo classical and rococo styles. The jewelry was lacy and ornate, feminine and delicate.

Arts and Crafts, 1890-1920. The Arts & Crafts movement was focused on the aesthetic appeal of a piece of jewelry. The heart of the movement was with artisans and handcraftsmanship. There was a simplification of form where the material was secondary to the design and craftsmanship. Guilds of artisans banded together. Some jewelry was mass-produced, but the most highly prized examples of this period are hand made and signed by their makers. The pieces were simple and at times abstract. They were hand made, hand hammered, patinated and acid etched. Common materials were brass, bronze, copper, silver, blister pearls, freshwater pearls, turquoise, agate, opals,

moonstones, coral, horn, ivory, base metals, amber, cabachon cut garnets and amethysts.

Art Nouveau, 1895-1910. In 1895, Samuel Bing opened a shop called "L'Art Nouveau" at 22 Rue de Provence in Paris, France. He is credited with starting the Art Nouveau movement. Art Nouveau was influenced by the aestheticism of the late nineteenth century. The designs of the jewelry were characterized by a sensuality of the designs. Jewelry took on the forms of the female figure, butterflies, dragonflies, peacocks, snakes, wasps, swans, bats, orchids, irises and other exotic flowers. The lines were not angular. Instead, the designers used whiplash curves and exaggerated and stylized lines to create a feeling of lushness and opulence.

1920s-1930s. Costume jewelry was an outgrowth of the desire of the average person to have copies of the real jewelry that had previously been reserved to the wealthy. Costume jewelry began its steady ascent to popularity in the 1920s. Since it was relatively inexpensive to produce, there was mass production. The sizes and designs of the jewelry varied. Often, it was worn a few times, disposed of and then replaced with a new piece. It was thought of as expendable, a cheap throwaway to dress up an outfit. Costume jewelry became so popular that it was sold in both the upscale fine stores as well as the "five and dime."

During the 1920s, the fashion of the times was changing. These fashions were often accompanied by jewelry that drew on the Art Deco movement. The Art Deco movement, 1920—1935, got its beginning in Paris at the Exposition Internationale des Arts Decoratifs et Industriales Modernes. The idea behind this movement was that form follows function. The style was characterized by simple, straight clean lines, stylized motifs, geometric shapes and streamlined curves. Materials often used were chrome, rhodium, pot metal, glass, rhinestones, Bakelite and celluloid.

One designer who played an important role not only in clothing design

but in costume jewelry design was Coco Chanel. She created costume jewelry to decorate her clothing. She knew the true meaning of the complete costume and she began wearing her costume jewelry; jewelry generally reserved for evening wear but Chanel wore it during the day, making it fashionable for millions of other women to do so too.

With the 1930s came the Depression and the advent of World War II. While life was often in turmoil, jewelry was one way to provide a respite. Women could purchase a relatively inexpensive piece of jewelry to spruce up an old outfit to make it look new. Designers began using enameling and brightly colored rhinestones to create wonderful whimsical designs of birds, flowers, circus animals, bows, dogs and just about every other figural you could imagine. Through the use of enameling and colored rhinestones, the jewelry was bright and festive.

Retro Modern, 1939-1950. World War II affected the world of fashion. The exportation of European clothing was down and domestic production was now at the forefront. The jewelry designs of the 1940s were big and bold. The jewelry had a more substantial feel to it and designers began using larger stones to enhance the dramatic pieces. The jewelry was stylized and exaggerated. The designers again indulged in their fantasies. Common motifs included flowing scrolls, bows, ribbons, birds, animals, snakes, flowers and knots.

Due to World War II, the use of pot metal (the tin and lead used in pot metal) was prohibited for use other than for the military. Sterling now became the metal of choice, often dipped in a gold wash known as vermeil. The vermeil was done in yellow, pink and rose gold.

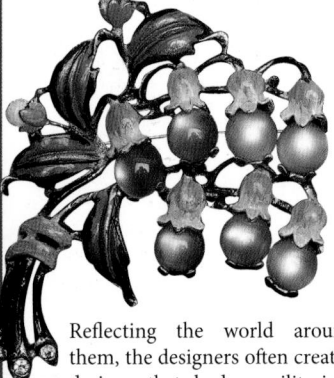

Reflecting the world around them, the designers often created designs that had a militaristic feeling to it. The jewelry had themes of American flags, a v-sign for victory, Uncle Sam's hat, airplanes, anchors and eagles. These creations were made to be worn as a sign of support for the war effort and those involved in the fight for freedom.

Post-War Modern, 1945-1965. This was a movement similar to the arts & crafts movement that emphasized the artistic approach to jewelry making. It is also referred to as mid-century modern. This modernistic approach was occurring at a time when the beat generation was prevalent. These avant-garde designers created jewelry that was handcrafted to illustrate the artist's own concepts and ideas often manifesting itself in abstract and modern designs. The pieces were unusual and abstract. The emphasis was on the design. The materials often used in the jewelry were sterling, gold, copper, brass, enamel, cabochons, wood, quartz and amber.

1950s-1960s. The 1950s saw the rise of jewelry that was made purely of rhinestones. The stones had become the basis of necklaces, bracelets, earrings and pins.

The focus of the early 1960s was on the average woman. Functional clothing was back in style with Jackie Kennedy providing the role model. Clean lines, pill box hats and A-line dresses with short jackets were a mainstay for the conservative woman. The large bold rhinestone pieces were no longer the must have accessory. They were now replaced with smaller, more delicate gold-tone metal and faux pearls with only a hint of rhinestones.

At the other end of the spectrum was the beat collection which consisted of psychedelic colored clothing, Nehru jackets, thigh high mini skirts and go-go boots. These clothes were accessorized with beads, large metal pendants and occasionally big, bold rhinestones. However, times were changing and by the late 1960s, there was the movement back to mother nature and the "hippie" look was born. Ethnic clothing, tie dye, long skirts, fringe and jeans were the prevalent style and the rhinestone had, for the most part, been thrown to the wayside.

There are other areas of jewelry collecting that aren't defined by a period per se, but more by their styles and materials.

Novelty Jewelry is very popular. In the 1920s through the 1960s, new materials to jewelry making were used. Designers used celluloid, Bakelite, Lucite, wood, leather and ceramics to create whimsical figurals, flowers, vegetables, animals, people, western themes and geometric designs.

Mexican Silver: 1930-1970. Mexican silversmiths first made jewelry for tourists. The jewelry had pre-Hispanic and traditional Mexican motifs as well as some abstract modern designs. Artisans used silver, a combination of silver with brass or copper, alpaca, amethysts, malachite, obsidian, sodalite, tiger's eye, turquoise, abalone, ebony, rosewood and enameling to create their original designs. While hundreds of artists set up their shops in the town of Taxco, Mexico in the 30s and 40s creating a silversmith guild, there are only a relatively small number of well-known artisans who gained their reputation for their designs and craftsmanship.

Scandinavian Silver: 1900—1960. Scandinavian jewelry is another silver collectible that consists of jewelry manufactured in Denmark, Norway, Finland and Sweden. The jewelry has a distinct look and is often identified by its use of flowers, foliates, animal, modern, abstract and filigree designs. The materials used included silver, bronze, gold, amber, amethyst, chrysoprase, citrine, crystal, lapis and enamel. The jewelry was generally produced in artist's studios and workshops where the focus was on design and craftsmanship. Import of the jewelry was relatively small with the large manufacturers being the exception.

Value: The value of a piece of jewelry is derived from several criteria, including condition, craftsmanship, scarcity and rarity, age and design. Condition is first and foremost. Don't overlook this. Be conscious of the condition of the piece because it will affect the value. The quality of the piece is also important. Look at the design of the piece. Is it intricate and ornate? Is it handmade or machine made? The more detail that is involved and the more handwork that is involved will generally make a piece more valuable.

While age does play a role in the value of a piece, don't be fooled into believing that antique jewelry has to be over 100 years old to have any value, and that the older the piece the more valuable it is- regardless of the condition.

Design: The factor of the design of the piece is a more subjective personal evaluation, more to do with your own personal taste. However, the design of the piece can help you determine the age of the piece and identify the period and style.

Scarcity and rarity play a role in the price of a piece. Obviously, if a piece is rare and hard to find, the price will reflect it.

The pieces listed here are antique or period and represent fine jewelry (i.e., made from gemstones and/or precious metals). The list contains no new reproduction pieces. Inexpensive and mass-produced costume jewelry is covered in *Warman's Americana & Collectibles*.

Adviser: Leigh Leshner

Note: The images used in this jewelry section are © Leigh Leshner, unless otherwise noted, and are used with permission. Leigh´s images were photographed by Maurice Childs.

FINE JEWELRY

Bar pin

Art Deco

Platinum and diamond, bezel and bead-set with old European and single-cut diamonds, approx. total wt. 2.74 cts.............................**$1,650**

Platinum and diamond, center old European-cut diamond weighing approx. 0.75 cts, further bead and bezel-set with fourteen old European-cut diamonds, millegrain accents, gold pin..................**$1,000**

Sapphires and pearls, A.J. Hedges & Co., alternately set with nine square sapphires and two rows of seed pearls, 14k yg mount, hallmark, 2-1/2" l..**$300**

Edwardian, center line of bezel-set oval rubies, surrounded by 42 old European and full-cut diamonds, approx. total wt. 2.28 cts, platinum topped 14k gold mount, hallmark "AE K," Austrian guarantee mark ...**$3,525**

Etruscan Revival, 14k gold, rose gold arched terminals, applied bead and wirework dec **$260**

Victorian, 14k yg, center carnelian intaglio of three cherubs within wirework frame, applied floral, bead, and ropetwist motifs..........................**$420**

Bracelet

Art Deco

Articulated geometric links bead and bezel-set throughout with 318 old European, square, and single-cut diamonds, approx. total wt. 11.79 cts, millegrain accents and open platinum gallery, French guarantee stamps, 7-3/8" l..................**$18,800**

Articulated links composed of 96 old European-cut and full-cut diamonds, approx. total wt 5.76 cts, channel-set onyx border, millegrain accents, platinum mount, sgd "Tiffany & Co.," one onyx missing, 7-1/8" l................................**$16,450**

Flexible links set with 191 full-and baguette-cut diamonds weighing approx. 5.53 cts, platinum mount, missing one small diamond, 7" l **$8,820**

Line of 40 prong-set old European-cut diamonds, framed by lines of channel-set square-cut emeralds, approx. total diamond wt. 3.98 cts, platinum mount with 18k white gold clasp, engraved gallery, one emerald missing, 7-1/4" l......**$5,400**

Bracelet, Victorian, flexible link, 14K yellow gold chased links, mounted in 14K gold, 31.45 dwt, c 1860-70, 7-1/2", **$500.**
Photo courtesy of Sloans & Kenyon Auctioneers and Appraisers.

Set throughout with old European, single, baguette, and marquise-cut diamonds, platinum mount, approx. total wt. 1.86 cts, 7" l............**$3,000**

Seven center old mine and European-cut diamonds, approx. total wt. 1.75 cts, flanked by rect pierced links, 14k white gold, 7" l................**$1,410**

Seven rect step-cut sapphires alternating with flexible honeycomb of bead-set old European and single-cut diamonds, approx. total wt. 4.64 cts, platinum mount, stamped "MD," French platinum guarantee stamps, 7-1/8" l....................**$16,450**

Art Nouveau, 14k yg, 10 openwork plaques in floral and scroll motif each centering collet-set sapphire, hallmark for Riker Bros., 7" l.........**$4,350**

Arts & Crafts, five bezel-set cushion-cut sapphires alternating with five old European-cut diamonds, approx. total diamond wt. 2.00 cts, joined by oval links, millegrain accents, c1915, 7-3/4" l......................................**$3,645**

Coin, 14k yg, heavy curb link chain suspending 1892 U.S. five dollar coin in a wirework frame, 27.1 dwt., 6" l....**$325**

Edwardian

Bangle, 14k yg, five bezel-set circular-cut sapphires within openwork design, 7" int. circumference...**$400**

Link, center old mine, European, and rose-cut diamonds in pierced and millegrain mount, flanked by knife-edge bar links, platinum-topped 18k gold, 6-1/2" l..................**$1,120**

Etruscan Revival, 18k yg, hinged bypass bangle terminating in two ram's heads, applied bead and wirework dec, 22.5 dwt, hallmark "P," evidence of solder, 6-1/2" int. circumference..**$2,585**

Post-War Modern, Van Gogh, hinged bangle, 14k yg, overlapping textured gold leaves highlighted by prong-set circular-cut ruby, emerald, and sapphire accents, 13.8 dwt, sgd "Van Gogh," c1950 ....**$530**

Retro Modern, double "tubogas"-style bracelet surmounted by bezel and bead-set old European-cut diamonds set in silver flowerheads, stems incorporating initials "H & L," 14k yg, French hallmarks **$425**

Victorian

Bangle, 14k yg, seed pearl buckle motif, black and brown enamel accents, small dents, 6-1/4" d interior circumference............**$550**

Slide, 18k yg, mesh design with adjustable oval slide engraved with scroll and fleur-de-lis motifs, edged with palmettes dec with black tracery enamel, foxtail fringe terminals, 137.8 dwt **$1,200**

Brooch

Art Deco, diamond and platinum

Carved jade plaque depicting scrolling vines and gourds, corners accented by 22 single-cut diamonds, platinum frame, French guarantee stamps and hallmark **$2,585**

Center old European-cut diamond weighing approx. 1.29 cts, frame of 78 French, baguette, and circular-cut diamonds, millegrain accents, platinum frame, sgd "Raymond Yard" **$5,650**

Art Nouveau

Floral spray, white-cream translucent enamel lilies centered by cultured pearls, green enamel leaves, joined by gold coiled cord, 14k polished gold stems................................**$750**

Krementz & Co., light green enamel scrolling leaves centering heart-shape peridot, three old European-cut diamond accents, hallmark **$1,150**

Orchid, light greenish-yellow and purple openwork leaves, baroque pearl and old European-cut diamond highlights, retractable bail, 14k gold................................**$1,265**

Gold brooch, Prince of Wales plumes of hair with seed pearls, c.1840, **$1,850.**

Garnet earrings, c.1900, **$450.**

Lavaliere, pietra dura, polychrome mosaic terminals with geometric pattern in white, blue, pink, green and red, brass frame, **$325.**
Photo courtesy of Sloans & Kenyon Auctioneers and Appraisers.

Pansy, yellow shading to purple enamel leaves edged by seed pearls, center old-European-cut diamond, retractable bail........................**$1,495**

Woman with flowing hair and dolphin with demantoid garnet eye amid waves within chased and engraved scallop shell, old mine-cut diamond moon, 14k yg mount................**$385**

Arts & Crafts, Josephine Hartwell Shaw, 14k yg, center bezel-set oval amethyst surrounded by grapevine motif, sgd **$3,410**

Edwardian

Navette-form openwork brooch set with fancy-cut aquamarine and rose-cut diamonds **$600**

Sword and scabbard, 14k yg, connected by trace link chain, seed pearls, four prong-set old European-cut diamond accents **$235**

Post-War Modern

Robert Altman, 14k yg, seated poodle, prong-set with ruby, emerald, and sapphire highlights, 11.7 dwt, sgd **$470**

Richard Fishman, 24k yg, hand-formed open work abstract circular brooch, sgd "Richard Fishman 1979" **$940**

Renaissance Revival, T.B. Starr, 18k yg, scrolling form, black and white enamel, seven cultured pearl accents, hair compartment en verso, sgd...**$1,645**

Retro Modern

Bow, pink and yellow gold, 14k, sgd "Tiffany & Co.," 5.4 dwt **$360**

Swirl, star and prong-set with full-cut diamond and ruby melee, flexible snake-chain terminals, 14k, 30.8 dwt..**$825**

Victorian

14k yg, boss framed by rope motifs terminating in double tassels star-set with rose-cut diamond melee......**$300**

White gold, amethyst and cultured pearl, single oval amethyst with carved top of lady in profile, faceted bottom, white gold, 22 carats, surrounded by small pearls, 5.80 dwts **$800**

Buckle

Edwardian, rect openwork buckle edged with demantoid garnets spaced by old European-cut diamonds, silver-topped gold mount **$1,380**

Cuff links, pair

Platinum and diamond, geometric design, ten 0.10 carat round brilliant cut diamonds, 14.40 dwts...........**$490**

Platinum, ruby, and blue sapphire, two fine 0.40 carat rubies, two fine oval 0.40 carat blue sapphires, 12.40 dwts **$490**

Dress clips, pair

Art Deco

Platinum, two marquise shaped 1.20 carats diamonds, eighteen baguette cut 1.60 carats total diamonds, two 0.20 carat marquise shape diamonds, numerous small transitional round brilliant cut diamonds

(2.50 carats total), 13.60 dwts **$5,260**

18k yg, WM Wise & Son, 18k yg, shield form, bead and bezel-set with old European-cut and single-cut diamonds, approx. total wt. 0.88 cts, millegrain accents, sgd...**$1,880**

Earrings

Art Deco, pendant-type, each with jadeite cabochon and bead-set single-cut diamonds suspending jadeite drop, platinum mount, later silver screw-back findings, missing one diamond **$1,765**

Etruscan Revival, 14k yg, pendant-type, coach cover, applied bead and wirework accents, later findings **$1,530**

Post-War Modern

Kanaris, 18k yg, dogwood blossoms, sgd "Kanaris," 14.3 dwt...........**$460**

Tiffany & Co., 18k yg, aventurine quartz, carved knot, sgd **$1,000**

Retro Modern, clips, 14k yg, abstracted floral form with circular-cut sapphires and cultured pearls, sgd "Tiffany & Co." **$450**

Victorian, pendant-type, gold, engraved foliate tops suspending two gold balls **$920**

Lavaliere

Edwardian

Amethyst, 14k gold, centered by oval amethyst within openwork scrolled frame surmounted by seed pearl trefoil, suspending similar drop, joined by trace link chain, 15" l **$450**

Platinum, heart-shape aquamarine suspends two collet-set old European-cut diamonds with pear-shape aquamarine terminal, three pearl accents, fine 14k white gold ropetwist chain **$1,410**

Egyptian Revival, 14k gold, centered by amethyst intaglio scarab within shaped lotus flower mount, baroque pearl drop terminal, stylized floral links, amethyst intaglio scarabs set at intervals, 16-1/2" l **$1,380**

Locket

Art Deco, 15k gold, sq black enamel locket unfolding to reveal six pages suspended from black enamel baton and fancy link chain, 28" l **$650**

Art Nouveau, 14k yg, helmeted Roman warrior in center, old European-cut diamond highlight, 4.4 dwt. **$150**

Edwardian

Carrington & Co., circular white enamel and green guilloche enamel locket accented by an old European-cut diamond, platinum trace link chain alternating with green and white enamel baton links, hallmark, some enamel loss to locket, 20" l **$1,590**

French, 18k yg locket with pale blue guilloche enamel, rose and old European-cut diamond surmount, suspended from platinum chain with blue enamel baton links and seed pearls, French guarantee stamp on locket, 20" l **$2,700**

Victorian, 14k yg

Oval, turquoise enamel and five stars with old mine-cut diamond accents, reverse with hair compartment, pendant hook, later trace link chain, evidence of solder **$325**

Pale yellow gold engraved disc surrounded by deeper gold, heavily engraved frame, rose and white gold curb-link chain, 24.7 dwt **$360**

Necklace

Art Nouveau

Butterfly with bezel-set amethysts, seed pearl border, old European-cut diamond highlight, later amethyst drop, suspended later 14k gold and amethyst bead necklace, 16-1/2" l **$1,120**

Three center shaped cartouches designed with florettes and scrolls, joined by baton-shaped fancy links, 18k yg, French guarantee stamp, 6.5 dwt, 16" l **$1,000**

Arts and Crafts, elliptical-shaped jade within conforming enamel scrolled links joined by trace link chains, similarly set pendant suspending three jade drops, 18k gold, sgd "Tiffany & Co.," some enamel loss, 18" l .**$31,050**

Edwardian

Center articulated seed pearl and old European-cut diamond scrolling floral vine, joined by ropetwist chain, 15k gold, 15" l **$940**

Turquoise cabochons joined by delicate trace link chain, 10k gold mount, fringe loss to central tassel, 15" l **$450**

Etruscan Revival, Ivy leaf and berry motif, barrel clasp, 18kt yg, 15-3/8" l **$2,850**

Retro Modern, 14k yg, each link designed as leaf surmounting a ring, convertible to two bracelets, 72.8 dwt, 17" l **$1,120**

Victorian

14k gold and garnet, three floral engraved medallions surmounted by emerald-cut garnets set in ropetwist frames, reverse with plaited hair locket, suspended from snake chain, 16-1/2" l **$420**

18k yg, 18 concave disks centering coral bead within gold wirework frames, joined by oval-shaped links, some replaced beads and links **$1,650**

Negligee

Edwardian

Floral and foliate elements, old European and old mine-cut diamond, seed pearl accents, platinum mounts, one melee missing, later 19-1/2" l 14k white gold fancy link chain **$3,055**

Two rose-cut diamond flower terminals framed by calibre-cut rubies suspended from knife-edge bar links highlighted by bezel-set full and rose-cut diamonds, millegrain accents, platinum and 18k gold mount, orig fitted Parisian jeweler's box, 20" l fancy link chain **$4,935**

Pearls

Bracelet

Caged freshwater pearls interspersed with 18k gold beads with applied

wirework, convertible to necklace with 14k gold rope chain, 8" l .**$425**

Seventy two white cultured pearls with rose overtones, measuring approx. 5.90 to 6.0 mm, 14k white gold bar spacers and clasp with 11 full-cut diamond highlights, 7-1/4" l **$715**

Brooch, Mikimoto, 14k yg, designed as abstract leaf with clusters of cultured pearl flowers, sgd........................**$420**

Earclips, pr

Button pearl suspending chain link button pearl and diamond set cap terminating in teardrop shape pearl, set in 18k white gold, probably natural pearls.................**$3,300**

Elizabeth Locke, center gray pearl within 18k gold frame, hallmark **$1,880**

Necklace

Baroque, 31 South Sea Baroque pearls graduating in size from 10.70mm to 16.20mm, 14k white gold boule with diamond melee, 19-1/2" l **$4,700**

Cultured, David Webb, 31 graduated pearls measuring approx. 9.08 to 12.78 mm, invisible pearl and 14k white gold clasp, 16" l **$1,530**

Cultured, David Webb, 35 graduated pearls measuring approx. 11.02 to 13.12 mm, invisible pearl and 14k white gold clasp, 17" l, together with 3-3/4" l extension **$2,115**

Cultured, one hundred twenty-nine pearls ranging in size from 6.7 to 7.5 mm, 14k gold gem-set clasp, 14-1/2" l **$420**

Pendant

Art Deco

Platinum, numerous small old European cut diamonds (3.70 carats total), 18k white gold chain, 10.90 dwts **$4,185**

Sterling silver, coral and black enamel, Theodore Fahrner, offset by two rect faceted black stone panels (probably onyx), gilt chain mkd "935," pendant stamped "TF (linked) 935"..........................**$1,880**

Art Nouveau

Collet-set sapphires and diamonds set within trefoil open wirework form, accented by rose-cut diamond points, joined by later festoons of fine trace link chain terminating in rose and circular-cut diamonds within triangular frames, later clasp, 18-1/2" l **$1,410**

Sterling pendant on black cord, designed by Björn Weckström, Finland, c1960s, **$900.**

Plique-a-jour enamel, lavender and green irid enamel flowers, green, pink, and white plique-a-jour enamel leaves, rose-cut diamonds and pearl accents, 18k gold mount with later faux pearl chain.... **$1,265**

Cartier, designed as cross composed of eleven rect-cut aquamarines, 18k yg, sgd, provenance: from estate of Reverend Thomas Mary O'Leary (1875-1949), Bishop of Springfield ... **$1,410**

Edwardian
Platinum top, 18k yg, four 3.00 mm pearls, one old European cut diamond, 24 rose-cut diamonds (0.34 carat total) 4.70 dwts **$1,100**
Platinum top, 18k yg, one old European 0.60 carat diamond, 59 rose-cut diamonds (0.70 carat total) suspended from 14k white gold chain, 3.40 dwts
.... **$1,920**

Renaissance Revival, shield form with Renaissance motifs, rose-cut diamonds, rubies, pearls and emerald, cobalt blue enamel highlights, silver-topped 18k gold mount **$885**

Victorian
Circular pendant edged by gold beads and decorated with black tracery enamel, suspending gold bead pendants, fancy double trace link chain, 14k yg, 14.1 dwt., 23-1/2" l **$385**

Pietra dura, rose branch, one open flower, two buds, inlaid in shades of pink, varying shades of green as leaves, 14k rose gold bezel and bale
.... **$400**

Pendant/brooch

Art Deco, platinum, navette set with five old mine and European-cut diamonds weighing approx. 5.33 cts, further surrounded by 142 bead-set old mine and European-cut diamonds weighing approx. 13.32 cts, approx. total wt. for all diamonds, 18.65 cts, provenance: accompanied by orig sketch by designer, Edmond Frisch, 336 Park Ave., New York.......... **$9,900**

Art Nouveau, 14k yg, circular-shaped, profile of classical woman accented by chased gold hair, enameled earring and face **$1,000**

Edwardian, 14k yg, scrolling form set throughout with rose-cut diamonds and pearls, three freshwater pearl and diamond drops **$715**

Victorian, 14k yg
Enameled inverted horseshoe framing three rounded forms, engraved accents, seed pearl highlights, 15.6 dwt, fitted box from Savage & Lyman Jewellers, Montreal **$600**
Openwork scrolling form bezel-set with three oval amethysts, suspending drop with pear-shape amethyst, chain festoons, 18.5 dwt, boxed **$1,000**

Pin

Art Nouveau
Dogwood blossom, center old European-cut diamond weighing approx. 0.50 cts, black enamel, 14k yg, American hallmark **$775**
Lady in profile, 18k yg, rose-cut diamond accent, French guarantee stamps, sgd "TW" **$325**

Edwardian, starburst, center 10.32 x 6.18 mm greenish-brown oval tourmaline, surrounded by sixteen old European-cut diamonds mounted on 14k gold rays, evidence of solder, possibly color change tourmaline, color changes to golden-olive color
.... **$1,175**

Post-War Modern, duckling, 14k gold, freshwater pearl wings, red stone eye, sgd "Ruser" **$390**

Victorian, 18k, tapering silver-topped baton with graduated bead-set rose-cut diamonds, entwined with engraved yellow gold form completed by pearl, French guarantee stamp **$350**

Ring, Lady's

Art Deco, platinum and diamond
Center rect step-cut emerald framed by eight full-cut diamond melee, millegrain accents, open gallery and foliate engraved shoulders **$940**
Rounded form centering bezel-set old European-cut diamond flanked by lines of channel-set sapphires, set throughout with bead-set old European-cut diamonds, approx. total wt. 0.98 cts, millegrain accents
.... **$1,175**

Art Deco, 14k white gold, center bead-set transitional-cut diamond within raised octagonal-shaped mount, openwork gallery with millegrain accents, approx. diamond wt. 0.87 cts
.... **$2,350**

Art Nouveau, 18k yg, shaped rectangular plaque etched with initials "HP" flanked by stylized flowers within open and ribbed shank, inscribed "Vitaline a Hubert, 2 Janv. 1910," size 7-1/2 .... **$355**

Arts & Crafts, 14k yg, three circular-cut pink sapphires, white pearl set among swirling leaves and vines continuing to shoulders, sized .. **$1,175**

Edwardian
Bezel-set fancy-cut aquamarine flanked by single rose-cut diamonds, silver-topped 18k gold mounts
.... **$575**
Intaglio, orange and white carnelian, winged dragon with flower in mouth, 18k yg, 7.20 dwts **$160**

Retro Modern, Birks, platinum, pave-set single-cut diamond buckle motif, channel-set with graduating line of sq step-cut sapphires.................... **$2,000**

Victorian, snake, tri-color gold engraved body, (approx total 0.45 cts) old European-cut diamond, stones missing from eyes...................... **$400**

Stickpin

Art Deco, platinum
Cartier, Y-shaped form, two cultured pearls, bead-set diamond melee, no. 2608, French maker's mark, sgd
.... **$765**
Channel set rubies with diamond melee **$475**
Sugarloaf sapphire cabochon with diamond melee and ruby accents
.... **$425**

Art Nouveau
Crescent moon, 14k yg.................. **$95**
Enameled woman, hallmark for Alling & Co., gold.................... **$400**

Edwardian, nine bead-set old European-cut diamonds, set in platinum, centered by cultured pearl in floret design, 14k gold shank..............**$775**

Egyptian Revival, enameled asps framing turquoise cabochon, 14k yg **$115**

Victorian, flowerhead design centering a round opal framed by 11 old mine-cut diamonds, 14k yg setting **$360**

Suite, Lady's
Brooch and ear pendants

Coral, agate chalcedony, brooch with center coral bead within engraved reserve framed by milky agate chalcedony, ear pendants ensuite **$650**

Coral, each with carved coral rose blossoms and foliage on 14k gold stems, boxed.............................**$235**

Pendant/brooch and earclips, all with circular-cut amethysts and foxtail fringe, 14k yg, brooch sgd "W. & S.B.," boxed, earrings with later screw-back findings, evidence of solder..**$1,175**

Revival-style, bracelet and ring, 14k, hinged flexible braided bangle centering three contiguous balls with wirework and applied bead decoration, ring ensuite, 14.4 dwt, bangle slightly misshapen **$470**

Victorian, demi-parure

Bracelet and earrings, bracelet composed of 15k gold florets with turquoise cabochons; pr earrings each with two 14k gold circles with turquoise cabochons suspending three small drops, 7-3/4" l bracelet **$1,765**

Watches, Pocket

History: Pocket watches can be found in many places—from flea markets to the specialized jewelry auctions. Condition of movement is the first priority; design and detailing of the case is second.

Descriptions of pocket watches may include the size (16/0 to 20), number of jewels in the movement, whether the face is open or closed (hunter), and the composition (gold, gold filled, or some other metal). The movement is the critical element, since cases often were switched. However, an elaborate case, especially if gold, adds significantly to value.

Pocket watches designed to railroad specifications are desirable. They are between 16 and 18 in size, have a minimum of 17 jewels, adjust to at least five positions, and conform to many other specifications. All are open faced.

Study the field thoroughly before buying. There is a vast amount of literature, including books and newsletters from clubs and collectors.

Pocket, Gentleman's

Aurora, Size 18, Roman numeral dial, lever set 15 jewel gilt movement #38691, Grade 3 1/2 Guild, second model, yellow gold-filled hunting case #5161726..............................**$200**

Ball, Size 16, Arabic numeral dial, lever set 17 jewel nickel movement #134015, Official Standard, Waltham model, white gold-filled Illinois hunting case #51032............................**$500**

Borel, Size 19, Roman numeral dial, lever set 20 jewel gilt movement #15110, Minute Repeater, chronograph, 14 karat yellow gold hunting case #6947.............................**$2,650**

Burlington, Size 16, open face Arabic numeral dial, lever set 17 jewel nickel movement #3447536, Illinois, yellow gold-filled case #5001237 ....**$100**

Elgin

Size 6, Roman numeral dial, pendant set 7 jewel nickel movement #10652232, first model, yellow gold-filled Wadsworth hunting case #316391 ....**$120**

Size 12, Arabic numeral dial, pendant set 17 jewel nickel movement #16472602, yellow gold-filled Dueber hunting case #9305829......**$120**

Size 12, open face Arabic numeral dial, pendant set 19 jewel nickel movement #25254082, C.H. Hulburd 431, platinum case #103820 ....**$1,100**

Size 16, open face Arabic numeral dial, lever set 19 jewel nickel movement #21235315, B.W. Raymond, yellow gold-filled case #8048 ..**$215**

English, brass, key-wind, swing-out case, orig paper retailer's label "Thomas Harrison Silver-Smith Danville KY Clock and Watch Maker," iron forged chain and key, early 19th C **$1,700**

Hamilton

Size 16, Arabic numeral dial, lever set 21 jewel nickel movement #776560, Grade 993, yellow gold-filled Illinois engraved hunting case #2922269 ....**$330**

Watch, pocket, Tiffany, hunting case, sterling silver, **$250.**
Photo courtesy of Joy Luke Auctions.

Size 16, open face Arabic numeral dial, lever set 21 jewel nickel movement #324343, Grade 960, model 960, 14k yellow gold-filled case # 5721 ..**$570**

Size 18, open face Arabic dial, lever set 17 jewel nickel movement #8023, Grade 936, silverode Keystone case #9158568, for American Jewelry Co., Leadville, CO. **$180**

Size 18, Roman numeral dial, lever set 17 jewel nickel movement #157179, Grade 925 The Union, yellow gold-filled hunting case....................**$175**

Hampden

Size 16, Arabic numeral dial, lever set 17 jewel nickel movement #1890116, William McKinley, BRDG, in a yellow gold-filled hunting case #6028660 ....**$165**

Size 16, open face Arabic numeral dial, lever set 23 jewel nickel movement #2801029, Grade 104, Bridge model, glass back nickel case..**$350**

Size 18, Roman numeral dial, lever set 17 jewel nickel movement #1332191, Adjusted, silverine Dueber hunting case #2942431........**$90**

Howard

Size 12, open face Arabic numeral dial, pendant set 17 jewel nickel movement #1092624, Series 8, 14 karat yellow gold monogrammed case #121454...........................**$360**

Size 16, open face Arabic numeral dial, lever set 21 jewel nickel movement #1361149, RR Chronometer Ser, white gold-filled Keystone case #1554922..................................**$300**

Illinois

Size 16, open face Arabic numeral dial, pendant set 17 jewel nickel movement #3136048, Texas Special, yellow gold-filled case #6287230...**$120**

Size 18, Roman numeral dial, lever set 11 jewel nickel movement #231676, yellow gold-filled hunting case #143231...............................**$150**

Left and above: Pocket watch, Patek, Philippe & Co., #74501, 18k gold, with watch chain and fob, also signed "Crowell & Hubbard, Cleveland, Ohio," 1885-1890, **$2,600.**
Photo courtesy of Wiederseim Associates, Inc.

Pocket watch, Waltham, hunter cased, 14k gold, 15 jewels, gold-filled chain, **$300.**
Photo courtesy of Wiederseim Associates, Inc.

Watches, pocket, ladies, hunting cases; first designed with decorated circular dial with Roman numerals and "Louis XIV hands," within engraved scenic case set in 18k yellow gold, key, wind and set; second designed with white circular dial with Roman numerals, "spade" hands, set in 14k yellow gold, **$450.**
Photo courtesy of Sloans & Kenyon Auctioneers and Appraisers.

Montgomery Ward

Size 18, open face Roman numeral dial, lever set 21 jewel nickel movement #1448074, Grade 61, sixth model, 10 karat yellow rolled gold plate Illinois case #7769495.....**$175**

Size 18, open face Roman numeral dial, pendant set 11 jewel nickel movement #757650, 20th C, silverine Dueber case #4280...............**$75**

Waltham

Size 14, Roman numeral dial, pendant set 13 jewel nickel movement #3127180, Chronograph, first model, coin silver American hunting case #21280 ....**$150**

Size 16, open face Arabic numeral dial, lever set 21 jewel nickel movement #20142536, Crescent St.U-D, model 1908, with wind indicator, yellow gold-filled case #9308103 ....**$900**

Size 18, open face Arabic numeral dial with 24 hour time, lever set 21 jewel nickel movement #10559638, Crescent St., first model, yellow gold-filled American case #405850 ....**$215**

Pocket, Lady's

Betsy Ross, Size 0, open face Arabic numeral dial, pendant set 7 jewel nickel movement #861180, yellow gold-filled Keystone case #8186017 ....**$100**

Elgin, Size 0, Roman numeral dial, pendant set 15 jewel nickel movement #8773791, first model, yellow gold-filled Wadsworth hunting case #667982 ....**$120**

Meylan, C. H., 18k gold and enamel, openface, white enamel dial with black Arabic numerals, fancy scrolled hands, gray guilloche enamel bezel, cover enameled with gold flowers set with diamonds, suspended from platinum and purple guilloche enamel baton link chain, crystal replaced, minor enamel loss **$850**

Unknown maker, retro, pink gold, hinged rect cover surmounted by rubies and diamonds, similarly set scroll and geometric shoulders, snake link bracelet, 6-1/4" l..................**$750**

Vacheron & Constantin, 18k gold, hunting case, white enamel dial, Roman numerals, gilt bar movement, cylinder escapement, sgd on cuvette, engraved case, 10 size **$350**

Waltham, 14k yg, hunting case, white enamel dial, Arabic numeral indicators, subsidiary seconds dial, Lady Waltham jeweled nickel movement by A.W.W. Co., floral engraved case no. 224709, 0 size, gold ropetwist chain **$300**

Whipperman, A. J., Idaho Falls, Idaho, 14k yg, hunting case, white enamel dial, black Arabic numeral indicators, subsidiary seconds dial, 15 jewel nickel movement by Rode Watch Co., floral engraved case dec with pale pink guilloche enamel, old mine-cut diamond in center, signed Gruen, dust cover inscribed, "Father to Elsie 1914," 0 size, fancy 14k yg curb link and pink enamel baton link chain............. **$180**

Watches, Wrist

History: The definition of a wristwatch is simply "a small watch that is attached to a bracelet or strap and is worn around the wrist." However, a watch on a bracelet is not necessarily a wristwatch. The key is the ability to read the time. A true wristwatch allows you to read the time at a glance, without making any other motions. Early watches on an arm bracelet had the axis of their dials, from 6 to 12, perpendicular to the band. Reading them required some extensive arm movements.

The first true wristwatch appeared about 1850. However, the key date is 1880 when the stylish, decorative wristwatch appeared and almost universal acceptance occurred. The technology to create the wristwatch existed in the early 19th century with Brequet's shock-absorbing "Parachute System" for automatic watches and Ardien Philipe's winding stem.

Gentleman's

Boucheron, dress tank, A250565, white gold, reeded bezel and dial, invisible clasp, black leather Boucheron strap, French hallmarks, orig leather pouch **$2,150**

Bueche-Girod, 18k yg, gold curved dial, black Roman numerals, 17 jewel movement, integrated textural mesh bracelet; dial, movement, case back and clasp all signed "Bueche-Girod," 39.80 dwts **$360**

Cartier, 18k hg, rect convex white dial, black Roman numerals, round gold bezel, black leather strap **$1,380**

Concord, Delirium, 18k gold, round goldtone dial without indicators, flat rect bezel, quartz movement, Swiss hallmarks, orig crocodile band, 9" l..**$1,265**

Garsons, 14k gold, sq goldtone dial with simulated jewel indicators, 17-jewel nickel movement, subsidiary seconds dial, integrated mesh band, 8-1/4" l...**$345**

Hamilton, 18k yg, silverized rect dial, applied Arabic numerals, subsidiary seconds dial, nineteen jewel movement, black leather strap **$180**

Jurgensen, Jules, dress, 14k white gold, Swiss movement, silvertone brushed dial, abstract indicators, diamond-set bevel, black faux alligator strap......**$290**

Le Coultre, Futurematic, goldtone dial, subsidiary seconds dial, power reserve indicator, 10k yg-filled mount, lizard strap, 1950s......................**$425**

Longines, pale green rect dial, applied diamond set platinum Arabic numerals with small round and baguette cut diamonds, fifteen jewel adjusted movement #3731402, case back engraved and dated 1935.........**$2,035**

Nardin, Ulysse, 14k yg, chronometer, goldtone dial, luminescent quarter sections, applied abstract and Arabic numeral indicators, subsidiary seconds dial, lugs with scroll accents, leather strap, discoloration and scratches to dial **$290**

Omega, 18k yg, round cream dial, goldtone Arabic numeral and abstract indicators, heavy mesh bracelet, mild soil to dial, 44.80 dwt.................**$460**

Patek Philippe, 18k yg Round ivory tone dial with stick indi-

cators, later 18k gold band, c1960 ....**$2,700**

Silvertone metal dial with gold abstract numeral indicators joined by curved lugs to brown leather strap, replaced closure **$2,820**

Silvertone metal dial with raised indicators, subsidiary seconds dial, movement #977714, reference # 2470, triple sgd, leather strap, c1949.**$6,230**

Rolex, Oyster Perpetual

14k yg, goldtone dial, abstract indicators, sweep second hand, ostrich strap, slight spotting to dial.....**$850**

Stainless steel, Air King, silvertone dial, applied abstract indicators, sweep second hand, oyster bracelet with deployant clasp, discoloration to dial, scratches to crystal **$575**

Vacheron & Constantin, 18k gold, white round dial, abstract numeral indicators, 17-jewel nickel movements, associated 18k gold brickwork band, 7-1/4" l **$1,495**

Lady's

Bulova, small round dial with Arabic and baton numerals, 17 jewel movement, 14k white gold case and bracelet set with single cut and baguette cut diamonds weighing approx 1.50 carats total.................................**$750**

Cartier, Tank Francaise, 18k yg, rect ivory tone dial with Roman numeral indicators, gold band with integral clasp.......................................**$5,875**

Chanel, 18k yg, black and white dial with Roman numeral indicators, onyx cabochon winding stem, enclosing Swiss quartz movement, adjustable black alligator band and 18k gold clasp, sgd **$1,300**

Elgin, platinum, rect ivory tone dial with Arabic numeral indicators, 17 jewel movement, bezel, lugs, and bracelet set with single-cut and baguette diamonds, 6-1/2" l.....**$1,410**

Gruen, Art Deco, platinum, rect silvertone dial, black Arabic numerals, bezel enhanced with 32 circular-cut diamonds, mesh strap edged by boxset single-cut diamonds, highlighted by diamond-set floret shoulders, 6-1/4" l....................................**$4,225**

Hamilton, platinum, rect ivory tone dial with Arabic numeral indicators, 17 jewel movement, bezel and lugs with single-cut and baguette diamonds, joining cord band. Missing winding stem **$300**

Helbros Watch Co., 17 jewels, Art Deco, combination of old European and single cut diamonds, approx 1 ct, case

hinged to allow better contour when worn, calibre French cut sapphires, curved crystal, platinum setting....**$995**

Movado

18k yg, rect gold tone dial with arabic numeral and dot indicators, 15 jewel movement, 14k gold link band **$765**

Stainless steel, yg, mother-of-pearl dial, diamond set bezel containing thirty-six round brilliant cut diamonds weighing approx 0.72 carat total, quartz movement, deployment buckle **$550**

Patek Philippe & Co., rect gold metallic enamel dial, Arabic and dot numerals, movement #940981, case # 509109; dial, movement, 18k yg, case and bracelet sgd "Patek-Phillipe & Co Geneve," c1940, 46.60 dwt, 8-1/2" l **$3,350**

Rolex, Oyster Perpetual, stainless steel, round blue dial with stick indicators, date aperture, original band with integral clasp, boxed, crystal scratched **$1,530**

Swiss, 18k yg, Swiss movement, manual wind, domed bezel, goldtone dial, black Roman numerals, hallmark, leather strap **$920**

Tiffany & Co., Art Deco, platinum and diamond, rect ivory-tone dial with Arabic numeral indicators, 17 jewel International Watch Company movement, bezel and lugs with bead-set diamond melee, engraved accents, black cord band, case with Krementz hallmark, 7" l **$940**

Watch fob

Art Nouveau

Carter Howe & Co., 14k yg, triple link chain composed of lotus buds and flowers joined by trace links suspending double griffin-head seal, hallmark..................................**$940**

Whiteside & Blank, 14k yg, heartshaped leaves and sinuous vine motifs joined by grosgrain strap, hallmark..................................**$400**

Watch pin

Art Nouveau

Dragon clutching an arrow, 14k yg, partially obliterated American hallmark **$940**

Profile of young woman with flowing hair, encircled by enameled buds, foliage, and emerald-set blossom, 14k yg mount........................**$1,765**

Marbled green Bakelite bangle with rhinestones, **$950.**

Rootbeer and tea Bakelite bangle, **$750.**

Victorian gold-filled wraparound bracelet, **$185.**

Victorian French Jet snake wrap bracelet, **$145.**

Articulated butterfly brooch, green and marbled butterscotch Bakelite, **$1,200.**

Chanel Lily-of-the-valley brooch, pink and green enameling with pink cabochons and rhinestones, 1930s, **$650.**

COSTUME JEWELRY

Bangle/Bracelet

Applejuice Bakelite, carved, hinged bangle with rhinestones **$425**

Cameo bracelet, black Bakelite and celluloid **$350**

Jade, SS, four oval jade plaques pierced and carved with floral motifs, joined by woven foxtail chain bracelet, 7-1/4" l **$175**

Postwar Modern, Hermes, sterling silver, heavy flattened anchor links, sgd, 7-3/4" l **$1,100**

Thermoplastic, yellow, five holes surrounded by aurora borealis rhinestones, hinged bangle **$225**

Hobé carved Bakelite Asian woman brooch with hand painting, **$375.**

Brooch

Art Nouveau, Trout, basse-taille greenish-blue fading to pinkish-white iridescent translucent enamel **$850**

Edwardian, heart-shape form set throughout with seed pearls, highlighted by two bezel-set peridots, English 9k stamp, 10k gold paper clip chain, 16-3/4" l **$500**

Jugendstil, SS, shaped pendant set with two oval green agate, reverse stamped "MiG, TF, 900, depose" for Max Joseph Gradl, Theodor Fahrner **$885**

Leaf brooch, cluster of stemmed leaves, moonglow with rhinestones on foliage **$110**

Turtle brooch, green Bakelite cabochon shell on wooden body **$225**

Enameled bird brooch, pot metal with rhinestones, **$98.**

Micromosaic brooch, black glass with inlaid glass, c.1860, **$165.**

Shell cameo in sterling frame, **$145.**

Hardstone cameo brooch with gold-filled frame, **$195.**

Buckle

Art Nouveau, sterling silver, two repoussé plaques of female faces with flowing hair and flower blossoms, hallmark for William B. Kerr & Co. **$300**

Cameo

Pendant/brooch, Victorian, 14k gold, shell cameo habille bead-set with an old European-cut diamond set within frame, retractable bail, solder to neck-chain on reverse............................**$180**

Pendant necklace, Victorian, 14k gold, hardstone, carnelian agate cameo within oval frame with applied foliate motifs and flexible fringe, pendant bail missing suspended element, suspended from 18" l chain **$450**

Earrings

Bow-shaped, brushed goldtone metal, 1960s...**$15**

Ear cover earrings, paisley shaped, covered with clear rhinestones .**$125**

Round-shaped, red enamel flower at center, surrounded by two rings of faux pearls, followed by a ring of red enamel fleurs-de-lis and a final row of faux pearls, Robert **$125**

Necklace

Handmade pendant, on goldtone chain, green glass, Denmark **$195**

Art Deco, negligee, faux pearl drops, purple enameled links with faux pearl spacers, 1920s **$85**

Victorian, locket on chain, seed pearl cross motif, c.1880.....................**$225**

Earrings with pink and blue glass, clear rhinestones and floral design glass cabochons, c1958, **$95.**

Art Deco earrings, black and coral colored glass beads, c1925, **$175.**

Art Deco earrings, blue glass and rhinestones, c1925, **$125.**

Art Deco, silvertone metal necklace with enameling and beads, **$195.**

Prison ring with image, **$225.**

Applejuice Bakelite necklace, **$225.**

Leather necklace with crystal ball, 1960s, **$75.**

Opera glasses

Lefils, Paris, blue enamel dec with pink and gold floral sprays, mother of pearl eyepieces, engraved name, late 19th C, 4" w..**$360**

Ring, gentleman's

Cameo

Black, white, and brown agate, carved Jesus profile, yellow gold setting, 4.80 dwts, late 19th C..............**$215**

Coral, red, Socrates portrait, 14k yg, 6.30 dwts, mid-19th C **$400**

Medium blue-green beryl, bearded soldier in high relief profile, vg, Victorian, 5.80 dwts................**$575**

Enamel, multicolored, black onyx, portrait of North African gentleman with red and green stripes, yg, Victorian, 5.00 dwts **$250**

Intaglio

Carnelian, Hermes with staff, 14k yg, 8.80 dwts...................................**$275**

Rhodolite garnet, Romulous and Remus in profile, yg, 5.10 dwts **$300**

Seal, black and white agate intaglio, coat of arms, 14k yg, 6.30 dwts ..**$120**

Watch fob chain

Victorian, gentleman's, yg, gold filled locket with black and white onyx cameo of soldier in neoclassical design, chain 12.90 dwts.............**$180**

Sterling pendant on chain, clear rhinestones, c1910, **$165.**

Bakelite dot pendant on French jet beads, **$145.**

Toys

Toys–The State of the Hobby

by Karen O'Brien

Collecting Toys

For more than a century, the materials and production techniques of the post-Industrial Revolution period have been put to good use creating toys. Indeed, the socio-political history of the 20th century can be extrapolated from the material, design, craftsmanship, and production methods employed in the creation of playthings.

Many toys owe their development to the need to make productive use of the scrap materials that were by-products of manufacturing processes. Not a new concept, the "never let anything go to waste" philosophy was put to use famously by the late Henry Ford who contracted engines from the Dodge Brothers and requested that the wooden shipping crates be of a specific size – Ford then used the wood for the floorboards in early Model T production.

Early toy production enjoyed a similar "recycling" mindset. Cast-iron techniques employed to create salesman's samples of real stoves were used to make miniature replicas for children. Early pressed steel toys were produced from recycled sheet steel used in the fledgling automobile industry. Similar stories occur about the tangential creation of toys from companies utilizing tin, wood, rubber, and plastic.

What makes these toys collectible today? Nostalgia. Although experienced collectors appreciate the craftsmanship and

mechanical engineering that qualifies many early toys as works of art, collectors are most often driven by the simple remembrances of childhood's carefree times. Nostalgia develops at its own pace for each generation, and while we gravitate towards the toys of our youths, we also appreciate the artistry of toys from eras other than our own. This appreciation ensures a long life for the toy collecting hobby, no matter what types of toys one prefers.

2006 Perspective

Trends in toy collecting generally occur over long periods of time. Looking back at 2005 and forward to 2006, the hobby is in a period of striking a balance. More collectors have embraced the Internet as a means to buy and sell toys than ever before, creating a new online marketplace and simultaneously creating an interesting niche for toy shows. No longer are shows the only place to obtain toys, and ready access to desired toys shortens the time collectors must wait to obtain them. But ease of acquisition doesn't negate the need to do your homework and stay well-informed about the hobby.

More and more collectors are realizing that a balanced approach to the hobby that embraces Internet participation, toy show attendance, and local networking in addition to reading the hobby's leading print publications yields the most informed collecting decisions.

For additional perspectives on the hobby, I turned to Tom Bartsch, editor of *Toy Shop* magazine, and Merry Dudley, editor of *Toy Cars & Models* magazine.

Toy Shop magazine is a biweekly publication dedicated to toys old and new, and offers collectors a variety of perspectives on the hobby. "Now is a great time to be in the toy hobby, as good-quality classic toys are getting a premium on the secondary market with 1970s and 1980s toys appearing more and more at affordable prices." Bartsch said. "Popeye is on an unbelievable run currently. Look for the demand for character toys to continue, along with a surge in popularity in plastic toys from the 1960s and '70s—ranging from soldiers to space guns."

Toy Cars & Models is a monthly magazine serves the interests of the toy car collector by offering columns on 1:18-, 1:24- and 1:43-scale favorites, die-cast, slot cars, Hot Wheels, promotional models, vintage cars, model kits, and much more. "Expect classic die-cast, such as cars from Corgi and Dinky, to remain popular over the next decade," Dudley said. "Boxed Matchbox cars will likely increase in value, as long as the boxes and cars are kept in great condition. And values for early Hot Wheels, whether in or out of pack, should also increase."

OTHER TRENDS

Another noticeable trend this year is the increasing participation in the farm toy hobby. Replica farm tractors and implements are currently produced with increasing attention to detail in casting and collectors are taking note. Farm toys is one of the fastest growing segments of the hobby, and it is having great success in attracting young participants by including offerings not just in the large 1:16-scale preferred by adults, but by the affordable and well-made 1:64-scale replicas that are finding their way into toy farms across the country and overseas. Frequently, collectors seeking their favorite tractor types obtain the new releases and look back to vintage toys to supplement their collecting tastes. The farm toy segment is doing everything right—there is a healthy interest in vintage toys, new releases, and a promising future.

Grading Condition. The following numbers represent the standard grading system used by dealers, collectors, and auctioneers:

C.10	Mint
C.9	Near Mint
C.8.5	Outstanding
C.8	Excellent
C.7.5	Fine+
C.7	Fine
C.6.5	Fine - (good)
C.6	Poor

RESOURCES

Magazines

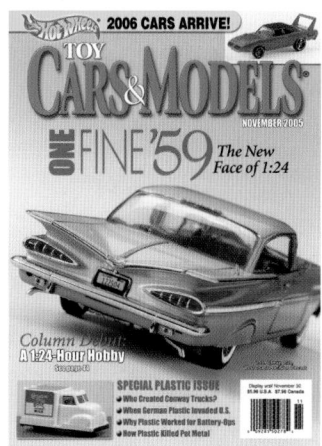

Antique Toy World
Classic Toy Trains
Old Toy Soldier
Toy Cars & Models

Toy Farmer
Toy Shop
Toy Trucker & Contractor
Toy Tractor Times (online-only)

Books

200 Years of Dolls, 3rd Ed., by Dawn Herlocher, Krause Publications, Iola, WI.

Hot Wheels™ Variations The Ultimate Guide, 2nd Ed., by Michael Zarnock, Krause Publications, Iola, WI.

Hot Wheels™ Field Guide, by Michael Zarnock, Tracy Schmidt, ed., Krause Publications, Iola, WI.

Hot Wheels™ The Ultimate Guide, by Michael Zarnock, Krause Publications, Iola, WI.

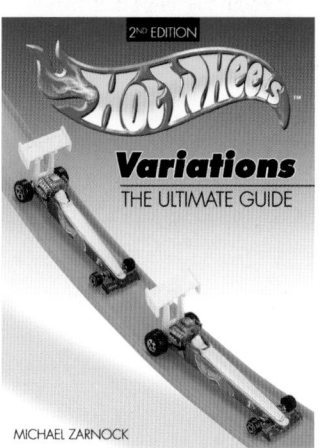

Fisher-Price: Historical, Rarity, and Value Guide 1931-Present, 3rd Ed., by Bruce R. Fox and John J. Murray, Krause Publications, Iola, WI.

O'Brien's Collecting Toys, 11th Ed., Karen O'Brien, ed., Krause Publications, Iola, WI.

O'Brien's Collecting Toy Cars & Trucks, 4th Ed., Karen O'Brien, ed., Krause Publications, Iola, WI.

Official Hake's Price Guide to Character Toys, 5th Ed., by Ted Hake, House of Collectibles

Standard Catalog of® Farm Toys, 2nd Ed., Karen O'Brien, ed., Krause Publications, Iola, WI.

Standard Catalog of Lionel Trains 1900-1942, by David Doyle, Krause Publications, Iola, WI.

Standard Catalog of Lionel Trains 1946-1969, by David Doyle, Krause Publications, Iola, WI.

The Best of Barbie®, by Sharon Korbeck, Krause Publications, Iola, WI.

Warman's® Dolls Antique to Modern, by Mark F. Moran, Krause Publications, Iola, WI.

GALLERY

The Fisher-Price Little Snoopy, #693, 1966, **$25.**

An ARCOR John Deere A manufactured by the Auburn Rubber Co. of Auburn, Ind. in the 1950s, **$30.**

Many pre-WWII games are desired by collectors for their superb box art as evidenced by this early Parker Bros. version of Tiddledy Winks, **$40.**

The Arcade Caterpillar Trac Tractor was released in 1931, and NM is worth **$900.**

Matchbox cars received a new lease-on-life in 1970 with the release of the "Superfast" line. This is the #46 Mercedes 300 SE, **$16.**

Known for its BB Guns, the Daisy Mfg. Co. released the Buck Rogers U-235 Atomic Pistol around 1945, **$500.**

The Sparkling Space Tank was one of the many themes used by Marx for this tin-litho wind-up, 1950s, **$350.**

Unique Art produced this tin wind-up named, G.I. Joe and His Jouncing Jeep in the 1940s, **$325.**

BANKS, MECHANICAL

History: Banks which display some form of action while accepting a coin are considered mechanical banks. Mechanical banks date back to ancient Greece and Rome, but the majority of collectors are interested in those made between 1867 and 1928 in Germany, England, and the United States.

Initial research suggested that approximately 250 to 300 different or variant designs of banks were made in the early period. Today that number has been revised to 2,000-3,000 types and varieties. The field remains ripe for discovery and research.

More than 80 percent of all cast-iron mechanical banks produced between 1869 and 1928 were made by J. E. Stevens Co., Cromwell, Connecticut. Tin banks are usually of German origin.

Reproduction Alert. Reproductions, fakes, and forgeries exist for many banks. Forgeries of some mechanical banks were made as early as 1937, so age alone is not a guarantee of authenticity. In the following price listings, two asterisks indicate banks for which serious forgeries exist, and one asterisk indicates banks for which casual reproductions have been made.

Notes: While rarity is a factor in value, appeal of design, action, quality of manufacture, country of origin, and history of collector interest also are important. Radical price fluctuations may occur when there is an imbalance in these factors. Rare banks may sell for a few hundred dollars, while one of more common design with greater appeal will sell in the thousands.

The mechanical bank market has exploded upward in the last year. Vast sums of money are changing hands daily for high grade examples. Records are falling weekly as more and more new buyers enter the market and compete to previously unheard-of heights to secure superb examples. Both privately and at auction, astonishing amounts of money are being paid. Bargains, however, still remain available for banks with condition problems and those banks with less than 70 percent original paint. My projection for the next year is that superb condition bank prices will move to even more lofty heights , which will make the current numbers seem low. Also, I predict that few bargains in the lesser condition banks will remain available as the supply becomes exhausted by new buyers entering the market, who cannot afford the lofty numbers of the superb examples.

Additionally, there have been large sums of investment money coming onto the mechanical bank market, as of late, specifically directed at purchasing banks in the $20,000 to $100,000 and up levels per bank, causing an upward trend in these higher priced banks. It is my theory that much of this money has been moved into mechanical banks by non-collecting investors who have become fed up with the performance of the stock market and are searching for other directions of investment to protect their capital. I strongly suspect that this trend will continue.

The values listed here accurately represent the selling prices of mechanical banks in the specialized collectors' market. As some banks are hard to find, and the market is quite volatile both up and down in price structure, consultation of a competent specialist in mechanical banks, with up-to-the-moment information, is advised prior to selling any mechanical bank.

The prices listed are for original old mechanical banks with no repairs, in sound operating condition, and with at least 90 percent of the original paint intact. Banks that have touch-ups, flaws, repairs, or less than 90 percent of their original paint sell for much less than these prices. Banks with missing pieces often sell for as little as 10 percent to 20 percent of these prices.

Adviser: James S. Maxwell Jr.

Price note: Prices quoted are for 100 percent original examples with no repairs, no repaint, and which have at least 90 percent bright original paint. An asterisk * indicates casual reproductions; † denotes examples where casual reproductions and serious fakes exist.

Photo note: Photos in the mechanical and still banks sections courtesy Bertoia Auctions unless otherwise noted.

Bank, mechanical, Bad Accident, J & E Stevens Co., patented 9/17/1901, **$1,020.**
Photo courtesy of Pook & Pook, Inc.

Left: Confectionary, Kyser & Rex, 1881, **$15,000;** *middle: Professor Pug Frog's Great Bicycle Feat, J.& E. Stevens, 1886,* **$10,000;** *right: Cupola Bank, J.&E. Stevens, 1874,* **$10,000.**

†Acrobat $3,700
†Afghanistan $1,800
African Bank, black bust, back emb "African Bank" $1,500
American Bank, sewing machine $7,500
*Artillery $900
Atlas, iron, steel, wood, paper $2,500
Automatic Chocolate Vending, tin $450
Automatic Coin Savings, predicts future, tin $150
Automatic Fortune Bank, tin $3,700
Automatic Savings Bank, tin, soldier $400
Automatic Savings Bank, tin, sailor $450
Automatic Surprise Money Box, wood $4,000
†Baby Elephant X-O'clock, lead and wood $15,000
*Bad Accident $2,800
Bambula, black bust, back emb "Bambula" $2,600
Bank Teller, man behind three-sided fancy grillwork $75,000
Bank of Education and Economy, must have orig paper reel $1,200
Barking Dog, wood $2,000
Bear, tin $1,200
†Bear and Tree Stump $1,600
†Bear, slot in chest $320
†Bill E. Grin $900
†Billy Goat Bank $700
Bird in Cage, tin $3,200
Bird on Roof $1,200
Bismarck Bank $7,000
Bonzo, tin $2,500
Book-Keepers Magic Bank, tin $7,500
Bowery Bank, iron, paper, wood $42,000
Bowing Man in Cupola $4,500
†Bowling Alley $125,000

†Boy Robbing Bird's Nest $6,700
†Boy and Bulldog $2,800
†Boy on Trapeze $3,500
†Boys Stealing Watermelons $3,200
Bread Winners $37,000
British Clown, tin $3,500
†Bucking Mule $1,500
*Bulldog, place coin on nose $1,800
†Bull and Bear $45,000
Bull Dog Savings, clockwork $4,500
†Bulldog, standing $1,250
Bureau, wood, Serrill patent $3,200
Bureau, Lewando's, wood $2,500
Bureau, wood, John R. Jennings Patent $14,000
Burnett Postman, tin man with tray $850
†Butting Buffalo $5,550
†Butting Goat $1,200
†Butting Ram $875
*Cabin, black man flips $720
Caller Vending, tin $2,800
†Calamity $25,000
†Called Out $65,000
Calumet, tin and cardboard, with Calumet Kid $200
Calumet, tin and cardboard, with sailor $18,000
Calumet, tin and cardboard, with soldier $20,000
†Camera $5,500
*Cat and Mouse $3,200
†Cat and Mouse, giant cat standing on top $22,000
Chandler's $550
Chandler's with clock $400
Child's Bank, wood $450
Chinaman in Boat, lead $37,000
Chinaman with queue, tin $3,500
Chocolate Menier, tin $950
†Chrysler Pig $750
Cigarette Vending, tin $420

Cigarette Vending, lead $600
Circus, clown on cart in circular ring $7,500
†Circus, ticket collector $950
Clever Dick, tin $400
Clown Bust, iron $4,500
Clown, Chein, tin $45
†Clown on Bar, tin and iron $30,000
*Clown on Globe $2,800
Clown and Dog, tin $950
Clown With Arched Top, tin $150
Clown With Black Face, tin $400
Clown With White Face, tin $200
Clown With White Face, round, tin $2,000
Cockatoo Pelican, tin $280
Coin Registering, many variants .... $25-$1,000
Columbian Magic Savings, iron $150
Columbian Magic Savings, wood and paper $12,000
Coolie Bust, lead $2,000
Cowboy With Tray, Tin $1,600
†Creedmoor $950
Crescent Cash Register $2,000
Cross Legged Minstrel, tin $650
Crowing Rooster, circular base, tin $2,000
Cupid at Piano, pot metal, musical $26,000
Dapper Dan, tin $950
*Darktown Battery $2,800
Darky Fisherman, lead $125,000
†Darky Watermelon, man kicks football at watermelon $450,000
†Dentist $6,500
Dinah, iron $300
Dinah, aluminum $200
Ding Dong Bell, tin, windup $65,000
Dog on Turntable $400
†Dog With Tray $2,000
Domed Vending, tin $1,600
Driver's Service Vending, tin $1,500
Droste Chocolate $900
*Eagle and Eaglettes $950
Electric Safe, steel $1,200
*Elephant and Three Clowns $2,800
*Elephant, locked howdah $260
Elephant, made in Canada $7,500
Elephant, man pops out, wood, cloth, iron $675
†Elephant, no stars $650
*Elephant, pull tail $70

Bank, mechanical, Magician, J & E Stevens Co., patented 9/17/1901, **$2,400.**

Photo courtesy of Pook & Pook, Inc.

Elephant, three stars $400
*Elephant, trunk swings, large ... $210
*Elephant, trunk swings, small .. $200
Elephant, trunk swings, raised coin
　slot $750
†Elephant with tusks, on wheels
　.. $300
Empire Cinema, tin $14,000
English Bulldog, tin $220
Feed the Goose, pot metal $480
5 Cents Adding $1,200
Flip the Frog, tin $2,700
Football, English football $2,800
Fortune Savings, tin, horse race
　.. $7,000
Fortune Teller, Savings, safe ... $1,320
†Fowler $45,000
†Freedman's Bank, wood, lead,
　brass, tin, paper, etc. $375,000
Frog on Arched Track, tin ... $26,000
Frog on Rock $575
Frog on Round Base $950
†Frogs, two frogs $2,200
Fun Producing Savings, tin .. $1,200
*Gem, dog with building $1,000
German Sportsman, lead and iron
　.. $17,000
German Vending, tin $1,200
†Germania Exchange, iron, lead, tin
　.. $32,000
†Giant in Tower $10,500
†Giant, standing by rock $30,000
Girl Feeding Geese, tin, paper, lead
　.. $9,500
†Girl Skipping Rope $32,000
†Girl in Victorian Chair $8,500
Give Me a Penny, wood $4,000
Grenadier $975
Guessing, man's figure, lead, steel, iron
　.. $8,200
Guessing, woman's figure, iron $55,000

Left: Jonah and the Whale, Shepard Hardware, 1890s, **$5,500;** *right: Chief Big Moon, J.&E. Stevens, 1899,* **$420.**

Guessing, woman's figure, lead
　.. $22,000
Gwenda Money Box, tin $1,200
Hall's Excelsior, iron, wood $450
Hall's Liliput, no tray $420
Hall's Liliput, with tray $370
†Harlequin $85,000
Harold Lloyd, tin $3,200
Hartwig and Vogel, vending, tin
　.. $550
Hen and Chick $4,500
Highwayman, tin $12,000
Hillman Coin Target $18,000
*Hindu, bust $2,800
†Hold the Fort, two varieties, each
　.. $8,500
Home, iron $1,200
Home, tin building $570
Hoop-La $2,200
*Horse Race, two varieties, each
　.. $12,000
Humpty Dumpty, aluminum, English
　.. $210
†Humpty Dumpty, bust of clown
　with name on back, iron $1,680
Hunter and Palmers, tin, vending
　.. $700
*I Always Did 'spise a Mule, black
　man on bench $1,200
*I Always Did 'spise a Mule, black
　man on mule $1,200
Ideal Bureau, tin $950
*Indian and Bear $4,000
†Indian Chief, black man bust with
　Indian feathered headdress, aluminum
　.. $28,000
Indiana Paddlewheel Boat ... $14,000
†Initiating Bank, first degree $9,500
Initiating Bank, second degree
　.. $16,000
Japanese Ball Tosser, tin, wood, paper
　.. $90,000
Joe Socko Novelty Bank, tin ... $400
John Bull's Money Box $20,000
**John R. Jennings Trick Drawer
　Money Box**, wood $10,500
Jolly Joe Clown, tin $1,200
*Jolly Nigger, American $390
*Jolly Nigger, English $210

Jolly Nigger, lettering in Greek
　.. $1,200
Jolly Nigger, lettering in Arabic
　.. $1,200
*Jolly Nigger, raises hat, lead $800
*Jolly Nigger, raises hat, iron . $1,320
*Jolly Nigger, stationary ears $150
*Jolly Nigger, stationary eyes $270
*Jolly Nigger, with fez, aluminum
　.. $1,200
Jolly Sambo Bank $1,680
†Jonah and The Whale Bank,
　stands on two ornate legs with rect
　coin box at center $125,000
†Jumbo, elephant on wheels $300
Kick Inn Bank, wood $1,500
Kiltie $390
**Lawrence Steinberg's Bureau
　Bank**, wood $15,000
†Leap Frog $3,200
Lehmann Berlin Tower, tin .. $1,500
Lehmann, London Tower, tin ... $1,500
†Light of Asia $1,600
Lighthouse Bank $2,800
Lion, tin $1,400
Lion Hunter $9,500
†Lion and Two Monkeys $1,800
*Little High Hat $900
Little Jocko, tin $390
*Little Joe Bank $570
Little Moe Bank $210
Lucky Wheel Money Box, tin
　.. $1,200
*Magic Bank, iron house $1,200
Magic Bank, tin $1,200
Magic, safe, tin $270
†Mama Katzenjammer $28,000
†Mammy and Child $5,700
*Mason $4,500
Memorial Money Box $240
*Merry-Go-Round, mechanical, coin
　activates $18,000
†Merry-Go-Round, semi-mechanical, spin by hand $280
Mickey Mouse, tin $30,000
Mikado Bank $60,000
†Milking Cow $6,500
Minstrel, tin $1,200
Model Railroad Drink Dispenser, tin
　.. $3,700
Model Savings Bank, tin, cash register $3,700
*Monkey and Coconut $3,200
Monkey and Parrot, tin $650
†Monkey Bank $650
Monkey, chimpanzee in ornate circular bldg, iron $2,675
Monkey Face, tin with arched top
　.. $1,920
Monkey, pot metal, nods head .. $450
†Monkey, slot in stomach $2,200

Monkey, tin, tips hat $270
Monkey With Tray, tin $570
Mosque $1,450
Motor Bank, coin activates trolley
.... $50,000
Mule Entering Barn $775
Music Bank, tin $225
Musical Church, wood $345
Musical Savings Bank, Regina
.... $12,000
Musical Savings, tin $2,600
Musical Savings, velvet-covered
easel $7,000
Musical Savings, velvet-covered
frame $7,000
Musical Savings, wood house ... $570
National Bank $8,000
National, Your Savings, cash register
.... $1,680
Nestle's Automatic Chocolate,
cardboard, vending $1,200
***New Bank**, lever at center $750
***New Bank**, lever at left $750
†**New Creedmoor Bank** $675
Nodding Clown, pewter and brass
.... $1,800
Nodding Dog, painted tin $7,500
†**North Pole Bank** $18,000
Novelty Bank $1,800
Octagonal Fort Bank $4,500
Old Mother Hubbard, tin $7,500
***Organ Bank**, boy and girl $950
***Organ Bank**, cat and dog $850
***Organ Bank**, medium, only monkey
figure $575
***Organ Bank**, tiny, only monkey fig-
ure $450
Organ Grinder and Dancing Bear
.... $4,500
Owl, slot in book $200
Owl, slot in head $220
***Owl**, turns head $280
***Paddy and the Pig** $4,700
Panorama Bank $22,000
Pascal Chocolate Cigarettes, vend-
ing, tin $1,080
Pay Phone Bank, iron $1,680
Pay Phone Bank, tin $450
†**Peg-Leg Beggar** $1,400
***Pelican**, Arab head pops out ... $1,200
***Pelican**, Mammy head pops out
.... $1,200
***Pelican**, man thumbs nose $1,200
***Pelican**, rabbit pops out $1,200
†**Perfection Registering**, girl and
dog at blackboard $17,000
Piano, musical $1,200
***Picture Gallery** $23,000
Pig in High Chair $950
Pinball Vending, tin $1,320
Pistol Bank, iron $1,400

Bank, mechanical, Reclining Chinaman, E.Stevens Co., c1885, **$2,880.**

Photo courtesy of Pook & Pook, Inc.

Pistol Bank, iron, Uncle Sam figure
pops out $22,000
Pistol Bank, litho, tin $3,700
Pistol Bank, sheet steel $1,120
Policeman, tin $300
Popeye Knockout, tin $950
Post Office Savings, steel $1,200
†**Preacher in the Pulpit** $150,000
†**Presto**, iron building $570
Presto, mouse on roof, wood and
paper $16,000
***Presto**, penny changes optically to
quarter $575
Pump and Bucket $2,000
***Punch and Judy**, iron $2,400
Punch and Judy, iron front, tin back
.... $4,200
Punch and Judy, litho tin, c1910
.... $1,400
Punch and Judy, litho tin, c1930
.... $400
†**Queen Victoria**, bust, brass .. $14,000
†**Queen Victoria**, bust, iron .. $32,000
Rabbit in Cabbage $575
†**Rabbit Standing**, large $1,600
†**Rabbit Standing**, small $950
Reclining Chinaman with Cards
.... $7,500
Record Money Box, tin scales
.... $6,700
†**Red Riding Hood**, iron $55,000
Red Riding Hood, tin, vending ... $700
†**Rival Bank** $65,000
Robot Bank, aluminum $1,500
Robot Bank, iron $3,500
Roller-Skating Bank $37,000
Rooster $1,200
Royal Trick Elephant, tin $5,500
Safe Deposit Bank, tin, elephant
.... $45,000
Safety Locomotive, semi $950
Sailor Face, tin, pointed top ... $1,920
Sailor Money Box, wood $4,000
Saluting Sailor, tin $1,400
Sam Segal's Aim to Save, brass and
wood $15,000
Sam Segal's Aim to Save, iron
.... $22,000
***Santa Claus** $2,800

Upper left: Patronize the Blind Man and His Dog, J.&E. Stevens, 1878, **$8,500;** *lower left: Halls Liliput, J.&E. Stevens, 1877,* **$5,000;** *right: Uncle Sam, Shepard Hardware, 1886,* **$9,200.**

Savo, circular, tin $200
Savo, rectangular, tin $200
†**Schley Bottling Up Cevera**
.... $26,000
Schokolade Automat, tin, vending
.... $1,200
School Teacher, tin and wood, Amer-
ican $15,000
School Teacher, tin, German .. $6,000
Scotchman, tin $650
Seek Him Frisk $55,000
Sentry Bank, tin $375
Sentry Bugler, tin $165
†**Shoot That Hat Bank** $85,000
†**Shoot the Chute Bank** $60,000
Signal Cabin, tin $500
†**Smith X-ray Bank** $3,200
Snake and Frog in Pond, tin . $4,200
***Snap-It Bank** $840
Snow White, tin and lead $8,500
***Speaking Dog** $2,500
Spring Jawed Alligator, pot metal
.... $2,000
Spring Jawed Bonzo, pot metal
.... $2,000
Spring Jawed Bulldog, pot metal
.... $2,000
Spring Jawed Cat, pot metal .. $2,000
Spring Jawed Chinaman, pot metal
.... $3,700
Spring Jawed Donkey, pot metal
.... $2,000
Spring Jawed Felix the Cat, pot
metal $3,700
Spring Jawed Mickey Mouse, pot
metal $22,000
Spring Jawed Monkey, pot metal
.... $1,400
Spring Jawed Parrot, pot metal
.... $1,400
Spring Jawed Penguin, pot metal
.... $1,400

Left: Toy Robbing Bird's Nest, J.&E. Stevens, 1906, **$10,500;** *upper right: Boy Scout Camp, J.&E. Stevens, 1912,* **$6,000;** *lower right: Springing Cat, Charles A. Bailey, 1882,* **$15,000.**

†**Squirrel and Tree Stump** $950
Starkies Aeroplane, aluminum, cardboard **$5,500**
Starkies Aeroplane, aluminum, steel **$8,500**
Stollwerk Bros., large vending, tin **$960**
Stollwerk Bros., Progressive Sampler, tin $330
Stollwerk Bros., two penny, vending, tin $840
Stollwerk Bros., vending, tin $650
Stollwerk Bros., Victoria, sparautomat, tin $570
*****Stump Speaker Bank** $1,200
Sweet Thrift, tin, vending $345
Symphonium Musical Savings, wood $1,200
†**Tabby** $1,200
*****Tammany Bank** $375
Tank and Cannon, aluminum ... $650
Tank and Cannon, iron $1,200
†**Target Bank** $250
†**Target In Vestibule** $5,000
*****Teddy and The Bear** $2,600
Ten Cent Adding Bank $1,200
Thrifty Animal Bank, tin $300
Thrifty Scotchman, wood, paper $1,200
Thrifty Tom's Jigger, tin $1,500
Tid-Bits Money Box, tin $350
Tiger, tin $1,200
Time is Money $750
Time Lock Savings $750

Time Registering Bank $350
*****Toad on Stump** $650
Toilet Bank, tin $300
Tommy Bank $500
Treasure Chest Music Bank $450
*****Trick Dog**, six-part base $875
*****Trick Dog**, solid base $400
*****Trick Pony Bank** $1,200
Trick Savings, wood, end drawer $400
Trick Savings, wood, side drawer $400
Tropical Chocolate Vending, tin $1,800
Try Your Weight, tin, semi $570
Try Your Weight, tin, mechanical $950
†**Turtle Bank** $30,000
Twentieth Century Savings Bank $300
Two Ducks Bank, lead $2,000
U.S. Bank, building $510
†**U.S. and Spain** $5,000
†**Uncle Remus Bank** $4,000
†**Uncle Sam Bank**, standing figure with satchel $1,600
†**Uncle Sam**, bust $1,800
†**Uncle Tom**, no lapels, with star $850
†**Uncle Tom**, lapels, with star $850
†**Uncle Tom**, no star $800
United States Bank, safe $4,000
Viennese soldier $950
Volunteer Bank $750

Watch Bank, blank face, tin $120
Watch Bank, dime disappears, tin $165
Watch Bank, stamped face, tin $90
Watchdog Safe $2,200
Weeden's Plantation, tin, wood .. $950
Weight Lifter, tin $3,000
Whale Bank, pot metal $300
*****William Tell**, iron $775
William Tell, crossbow, Australian, sheet steel, aluminum $875
Wimbledon Bank $750
Winner Savings Bank, tin ... $12,500
Wireless Bank, tin, wood, iron .. $300
Woodpecker Bank, large, tin, c1910 .... $2,800
Woodpecker Bank, small, tin, c1930-1960 .... $50
World's Banker, tin $5,500
*****World's Fair Bank** $2,300
Zentral Sparkasse, steel $750
Zig Zag Bank, iron, tin, papier-mâché $200,000
Zoo $2,300

U.S. and Spain, J.&E. Stevens, 1898, **$NA.**

BANKS, STILL

History: Banks with no mechanical action are known as still banks. The first still banks were made of wood or pottery or from gourds. Redware and stoneware banks, made by America's early potters, are prized possessions of today's collectors.

Still banks reached a golden age with the arrival of the cast-iron bank. Leading manufacturing companies include Arcade Mfg. Co., J. Chein & Co., Hubley, J. & E. Stevens, and A. C. Williams. The banks often were ornately painted to enhance their appeal. During the cast-iron era, banks and other businesses used the still bank as a form of advertising.

The tin lithograph bank, again frequently a tool for advertising, reached its zenith from 1930 to 1955. The tin bank was an important premium, whether a Pabst Blue Ribbon beer can bank or a Gerber's Orange Juice bank. Most tin advertising banks resembled the packaging of the product.

Almost every substance has been used to make a still bank— die-cast white metal, aluminum, brass, plastic, glass, etc. Many of the early glass candy containers also converted to a bank after the candy was eaten. Thousands of varieties of still banks were made, and hundreds of new varieties appear on the market each year.

Brass, beehive, EOS, well detailed, base marked "A. B. Dalames Bank," 4" h, 4-1/2" d..**$385**

Cast iron

Building, Kyser & Rex, Town Hall and Log Cabin, chimney on left side, "Town Hall Bank" painted yellow, c1882, 2-3/4" to 4-3/4" h...**$260**

Bungalow, Grey Iron Ceiling Co., porch, painted, 3-3/4" h...........**$470**

Cab, Arcade, Yellow Cab, painted orange and black, stenciling on doors, seated driver, rubber tires, painted metal wheels, coin slot in roof, 7-3/4" l..............................**$935**

Cat With Ball, A. C. Williams, painted gray, gold ball, 2-1/2" x 5-11/16"...**$190**

Circus Elephant, Hubley, colorfully painted, seated position, 3-7/8" h...**$180**

Coronation, Syndeham & McOustra, England, ornately detailed, emb busts in center, England, c1911, 6-5/8" h..................................**$200**

Duck, Hubley, colorfully painted, outstretched wings, slot on back, 4-3/4" h **$165**

Dutch Boy and Girl, Hubley, colorfully painted, boy on barrel, girl holding flowers, price for pr, c1930, 5-1/4" and 5-1/8" h..................**$260**

Egyptian Tomb, green finish, pharaoh's tomb entrance, hieroglyphics on front panel, 6-1/4" x 5-1/4"...**$275**

Elk, painted gold, full antlers, 9-1/2" h...**$155**

Globe Safe, Kenton, round sphere, claw feet, nickeled combination lock on front hinged door, 5" h..........**$80**

Hall Clock, swinging pendulum visible through panel, 5-3/4" h **$110**

Horseshoe, Arcade, Buster Brown and Tige with horse, painted black and gold, 4-1/4" x 4-3/4"..................**$125**

Husky, Grey Iron Casting Co., painted brown, black eyes, yellow box, repaired, 5" h **$365**

Jewel Chest, ornate casting, ftd bank, brass combination lock on front, top lifts for coin retrieval, crack at corner, 6-1/8" x 4-5/8"................**$90**

Kodak, J & E Stevens, nickeled, highly detailed casting, intricate pattern, emb "Kodak Bank" on front opening panel, c1905, 4-1/4" x 5" w .**$225**

North Pole, nickeled, Grey Iron Casting Co., depicts wooden pole with handle, emb lettering, 4-1/4" h.**$415**

Mailbox, Hubley, painted green, emb "Air Mail," with eagle, standing type, 5-1/2" h **$220**

Maine, Grey Iron Casting Co., japanned, gold highlights, c1900, 4-5/8" l................................**$660**

Mammy, Hubley, hands on hips, colorfully painted, 5-1/4" h **$300**

Pagoda, England, gold trim, c1889, 5" x 3" x 3" **$240**

Pershing, General, Grey Iron Casting Co., full bust, detailed casting, 7-3/4" h.......................................**$65**

Pig, Hubley, laughing, painted brown, trap on bottom, 2-1/2" h, 5-1/4" l **$120**

Professor Pug Frog, A.C. Williams, painted gold, blue jacket, new twist pin, 3-1/4" h..............................**$195**

Radio, Kenton, metal sides and back, painted green, nickeled front panel in Art-Deco style, 4-1/2" h **$445**

Reindeer, A. C. Williams, painted gold, full rack of antlers, replaced screw, 9-1/2" h, 5-1/4" l **$55**

Rumplestiltskin, painted gold, long red hat, base and feet, marked "Do You Know Me," c1910, 6" h......**$210**

Safe, Kyser & Rex, Young America, japanned, intricate casting, emb at top, c1882, 4-3/8" h.................**$275**

Sharecropper, A. C. Williams, painted black, gold, and red, toes visible on one foot, 5-1/2" h.....................**$240**

Spitz, Grey Iron Casting Co., painted gold, repaired, 4-1/4" x 4-1/2" h **$165**

Steamboat, Arcade, painted gold, 7-1/2" l..................................**$190**

Stove, Gem, Abendroth Bros., traces of bronzing, back marked "Gem Heaters Save Money," 4-3/4" h .**$275**

Tank, Ferrosteel, side mounted guns, rear spoke wheels, emb on sides, c1919, 9-1/2" l, 4" w **$385**

U.S. Mail, Kenton, painted silver, gold painted emb eagle, red lettering large trap on back panel, 5-1/8" h **$180**

World Time, Arcade, paper timetables of various cities around the world, 4-1/8" x 2-5/8"............**$315**

Chalk

Cat, seated, stripes, red bow, 11" h **$200**

Winston Churchill, bust, painted green, back etched "Save for Victory," wood base, 5-1/4" h..........**$55**

Glass

Charles Chaplin, Geo Borgfeldt & Co., painted figure standing next to barrel slotted on lid, name emb on base, 3-3/4" h **$220**

Lead

Boxer, Germany, head, painted brown, black facial details, lock on collar, bent in back, 2-5/8" h...............**$130**

Burro, Japan, lock on saddle marked "Plymouth, VT," 3-1/2" x 3-1/2" **$125**

Ocean liner, bronze electroplated, three smoking stacks, hinged trap on deck, small hole, 2-3/4" x 7-5/8" l.......................................**$180**

Pug, Germany, painted, stenciled "Hershey Park" on side, lock on collar, 2-3/4" h **$300**

Pottery

Acorn, redware, paper label reads "Tithing Day/ At The/First Methodist Episcopal Church/Sunday January 2nd 1916/In the Interest of the Improvement Fund," 3-1/2" d, 4" h **$220**

Bulbous, redware, marked with initials "C.R.S.," flakes on base, 3-1/4" h **$220**

Dresser, redware, Empire chest of drawers shape, Philadelphia, PA, loss to feet, roughness on edges, 6-1/2" w, 4" d, 4-1/2" h.............**$220**

Hanging Persimmon, redware, yellow and red paint, 5" x 3" **$90**

House, redware, Georgian style house, brown glazed accents, good detail on windows and doorways, central chimney, Jim Seagreaves, sgd "JCS," 7-1/2" h **$425**

Jug, redware, bulbous, bird atop mouth, green and yellow graffito dev, Jim Seagreaves, sgd "JCS," 7-1/2" h **$515**

Steel

Lifeboat, pressed, painted yellow and blue, boat length decal marked "Contributions for Royal National Life Boat Institution," deck lifts for coin removal, over painted, 14" l.......**$360**

Postal Savings, copper finish, glass view front panel, paper registering strips, emb "U.S.Mail" on sides, top lifts to reveal four coin slots, patent 1902, 4-5/8" h, 5-3/8" w.............**$95**

Stoneware

Dog's Head, white clay, yellow glaze, two-tone brown sponging, shallow flakes, 4" h.................................**$175**

Ovoid, brushed cobalt blue flowers, leaves, and finial, minor flakes at coin slot, 6" h **$6,875**

Pig, sitting, sgd in dark green "Delight M. Caskey Merry Christmas," 6-1/4" l **$3,000**

Tin litho, Keene Savings, Kingsbury, bank building shape, non-working tally wheels, 6-1/2" x 6" x 3" **$70**

White metal

Amish Boy, seated on bale of straw, U.S., painted in bright colors, key lock trap on bottom, 4-3/4" x 3-3/8".......................................**$55**

Cat With Bow, painted white, blue bow, 4-1/8" h............................**$155**

Gorilla, colorfully painted in brown hues, seated position, trap on bottom **$165**

Pig, painted white, decal marked "West Point, N.Y." on belly, 4-3/8" h **$30**

Rabbit, seated, painted brown, painted eyes, trap on bottom, crack in ear, 4-1/2" h **$30**

Spaniel, seated, painted white, black highlights, 4-1/2" h **$470**

Uncle Sam Hat, painted red, white, and blue, stars on brim, slot on top, trap on bottom, 3-1/2" h..........**$135**

Wood

Burlwood inlaid with exotic woods, top dec with geometric banding, front with sailing vessels, end panels with flags, Prisoner of War, late 19th C, imperfections, 5"x 8" x 5-1/4" **$1,150**

Left: Bailey's Centennial Money Bank, 1875; right: City Bank with Chimney, 1870s, **$3,500.**

BARBIE

History: In 1945, Harold Matson (MATT) and Ruth and Elliott (EL) Handler founded Mattel. Initially the company made picture frames but became involved in the toy market when Elliott Handler began to make doll furniture from scrap material. When Harold Matson left the firm, Elliott Handler became chief designer and Ruth Handler principal marketer. In 1955, Mattel advertised its products on "The Mickey Mouse Club," and the company prospered.

In 1958, Mattel patented a fashion doll. The doll was named "Barbie" and reached the toy shelves in 1959. By 1960, Barbie's popularity was assured.

Development of a boyfriend for Barbie, named Ken after the Handlers' son, began in 1960. Over the years, many other dolls were added. Clothing, vehicles, room settings, and other accessories became an integral part of the line.

From September 1961 through July 1972, Mattel published a Barbie magazine. At its peak, the Barbie Fan Club was second only to the Girl Scouts as the largest girls' organization in the United States.

Always remember that a large quantity of Barbie dolls and related material has been manufactured. Because of this easy availability, only objects in excellent to mint condition with original packaging (also in very good or better condition) have significant value. If items show signs of heavy use, their value is probably minimal.

Collectors prefer items from the first decade of production. Learn how to distinguish a Barbie #1 doll from its successors. The Barbie market is one of subtleties.

Recently, many collectors have shifted their focus from the dolls themselves to the accessories. There have been rapid price increases in early clothing and accessories.

Barbie is now a billion-dollar baby, the first toy in history to reach this prestigious mark—that's a billion dollars per year, just in case you're wondering.

Photos excerpted from *The Best of Barbie® Doll* by Sharon Korbeck, published by Krause Publications, Iola WI.

Accessories

Alarm clock, beige plastic, gold clock numbers, gold metal knobs on back, 1964, VG, nonworking **$320**

Autographs book, black vinyl, graphics on cover, white and colored pages, age discolored rect sticker on upper left corner, 1961, NM/VG **$125**

Barbie Teen Dream Bedroom, MIB, discoloration to orig box, dated 1970 .... **$65**

Binder with pencil case, black vinyl covers, metal three-ring binder, Dennison Webster's Notebook Dictionary, Study-Aids in Arithmetic, English Grammar, American History, General Science, NJ, 1962 .... **$400**

Lunch kit, black vinyl, thermos, cardboard insert, plastic handle, metal closure, 1962 .... **$145**

Paper doll book, Whitman, uncut Barbie's Boutique, #1954, dated 1973, NM **$85**

Francie with Growing Pretty Hair, #1982, dated 1973, NM **$35**

Midge, #1962, dated 1963, NM .. **$145**

Play ring, adjustable, side view of Ponytail Barbie head surrounded by 10 clear rhinestones, clear plastic case with blue bottom, cardboard backing, pre-priced at .29, 1962, NRFC **$135**

Snaps n' Scraps, blue vinyl covers, graphics on front cover, nine construction paper-type pages, black

plastic binder with cord ties, 1961, VG **$125**

Transistor radio, Vanity Fair, black vinyl case, Barbie graphics, metal closure, black velveteen liner, peach colored plastic radio, gold front, plastic dials, plastic and metal earphones, matching plastic case, 1962, VG . **$650**

Wallet, red vinyl, graphic of Barbie wearing Enchanted Evening, zipper closure on coin compartment, attached metal bead chain, four clear plastic photo holders, black and white photo of Perry Como and Maureen O'Hara, cream colored plastic change holder, mirror, snap closure, 1962, VG **$120**

Barbie Dolls

American Girl Barbie

Brunette, tan lips, fingernails painted, bendable legs, knit Pak dress, fringe trim, cord belt, pale no box, VG **$300**

Golden blonde, beige lips, nostril paint, fingernails painted, orange one-pc swimsuit, no box, VG .. **$350**

Light blonde hair, peach lips, fingernails painted, bendable legs, Lunch Date, Barbie Pak, sleeveless dress, olive green skirt, green and white bodice no box, VG **$450**

Titian hair, gold lips, fingernails painted, bendable legs, #1665 Here

Comes the Bride outfit, white satin sleeveless gown, white tulle long veil, lace trim on gown and veil, ribbon bow accents, white nylon long gloves, blue nylon garter, white pointed toe shoes, box, VG **$350**

American Girl, first issue, 1965, model #1070, blonde, bendable legs, MIB, **$1,900.**

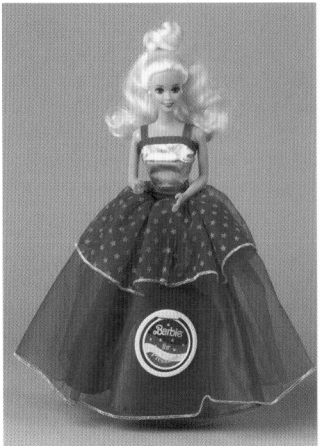

Barbie for President, model #3722, blonde, 1992, MIB, **$65.**

Billions of Dreams Barbie, marked one billionth Barbie sold since 1959, #17641, serial #00305, orig shipping box, box dated 1997, NRFB, box slightly scuffed **$225**

Bob Mackie design series
Goddess of the Sun, 8th in series, #14056, orig shipping box, MIB, bottom box flap insert torn, box dated 1995 .... **$80**
Madame du Barbie, #10 in series, #17934, cardboard shipping box, MIB, top flap insert worn, box dated 1997 .... **$200**

Bubblecut Barbie
Blonde, coral lips, nostril paint, fingernails and toenails painted, straight legs, #1610 Golden Evening outfit, gold knit shirt, matching long skirt with gold glitter, gold belt with buckle, mustard open toe shoes, three-charm bracelet, no box, VG, loss to glitter **$90**
Blonde, white lips with pink tint, white nostril paint, fingernails painted, toenails with faint paint, straight legs, one-pc red nylon swimsuit, red open toe shoes, orig box with gold wire stand, no box, VG **$225**
Brunette, red lips, fingernails and toe-nails painted lightly, straight legs, Pak outfit, red and white striped knit shirt, blue shorts, no box, VG/G, frayed tag **$135**
Light blonde, pink lips, fingernails and toenails painted, straight legs, Best Bow Pak red dress, attached bow, floral print skirt, no box, VG **$125**

Titian hair, coral lips, nostril paint, fingernails and toenails painted, straight legs, black and white striped one-pc swimsuit, pearl ear-rings, black open toe shoes, white rimmed glasses with blue lenses, black white stand, booklet, orig box, VG **$200**

American Beauties Army Barbie, model #3966, blonde, 1989, MIB, **$40.**

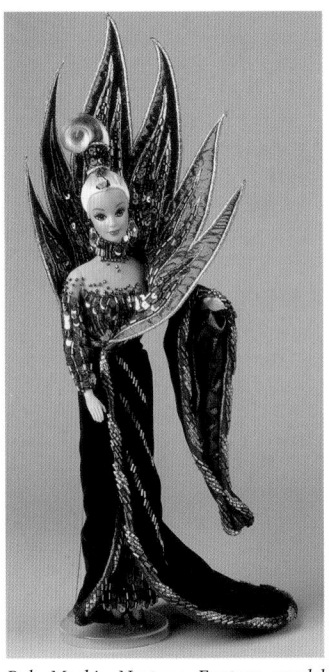

Bob Mackie Neptune Fantasy, model #4248, blonde, MIB, **$750.**

Color Magic Barbie
Lemon yellow hair, blue metal hair barrette, pink lips, cheek blush, fingernails painted, bendable legs, #1692 Patio Party, floral print nylon jumpsuit, blue and green satin over-dress, blue pointed toe shoes, no box, NM **$550**

Bob Mackie Starlight Splendor, model #2704, black hair, MIB, **$500.**

Bubblecut Barbie, second issue, 1962, model #850, blonde, wearing "Busy Morning" sundress, MIB, **$350.**

Red hair, green metal hair barrette, pink lips, fingernails painted, bendable legs, nude, no box, VG **$550**

Red hair, pink lips, cheek blush, fingernails painted, toenails with faint paint, bendable legs, nude, no box, NM/VG......................................**$525**

Busy Barbie, model #3311, gripping hands, blonde, MIB, **$300.**

Hispanic Barbie, model #1292, black hair, 1980, MIB, **$75.**

Fashion Queen, painted brunette hair, blue vinyl headband, pink lips, fingernails and toenails painted, straight legs, gold and white striped swimsuit, matching turban cap, pearl earrings in box with white plastic wig stand with brunette pageboy, blonde bubblecut, and titian side-part wigs, black wire stand, orig box, MIB **$400**

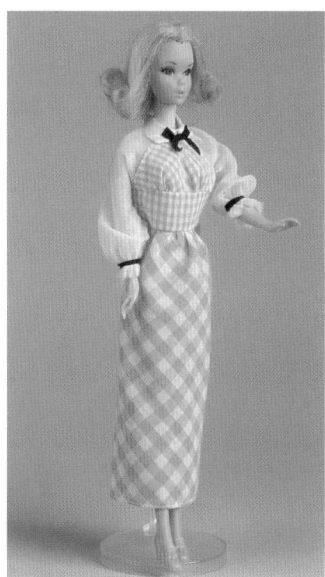

Quick Curl Barbie, model #4220, blonde, curler accessories included, MIB, **$80.**

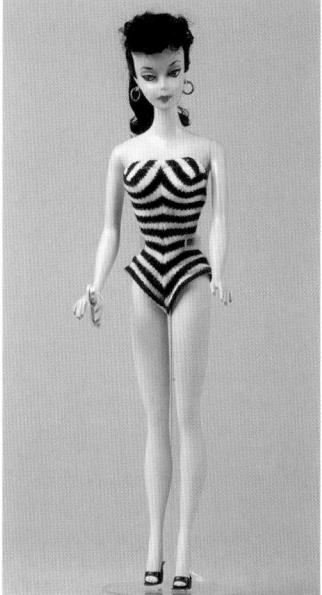

Ponytail #1, model #850, brunette, striped white-striped swimsuit, white sunglasses, red lips and toenails, black shoes, MIB, **$9,000.**

Happy Holidays #7, model #12155, white doll, blonde hair, special 35th anniversary doll, sold exclusively at Walt Disney World, 1994, MIB, **$120.**

Growin' Pretty Hair, blonde, peach lips, cheek blush, rooted eyelashes, bendable legs, pink satin dress, wrist tag, orig box with hair accessories, pink high tongue shoes, orig box, NRFB **$475**

Hair Happenin's, titian hair, pink lips, cheek blush, rooted eyelashes, fingernails painted, bendable legs, nude, titan long hair piece braided with pink ribbon, no box, VG **$225**

Happy Holidays, orig box
1988, #1, NRFB..........................**$230**
1989, plastic window and box scuffed, NRFB......................................**$70**
1990, plastic window and box slightly scuffed, NRFB............................**$75**
1991, box slightly scuffed and discolored, NRFB **$45**
1992, box slightly scuffed and worn, NRFB......................................**$35**

Living Barbie, brunette, pink lips, cheek blush, rooted eyelashes, bendable legs, rotating wrists, orig silver and gold one-pc swimsuit, orange net cover-up with gold trim, booklet, no box, NM ..**$ 75**

Mackie, Bob
Gold Barbie, first in series, #5409, orig shipping box, 1990, NRFB........**$220**
Goddess of the Sun, eighth in series, #14056, certificate, stand, orig shipping box, 1995, NRFB...............**$90**
Madame Du Barbie, tenth in series, #17934, certificate, stand, 1997, MIB..**$145**
Queen of Hearts, seventh in series, #12056, certificate, stand, shipping box, 1994, NRFB **$85**

Ponytail
#1 ponytail
Blonde, red lips, fingernails and toe-

Ponytail #3, model #850, blonde, striped white-striped swimsuit, white sunglasses, red lips and toenails, black shoes, MIB, **$1,300.**

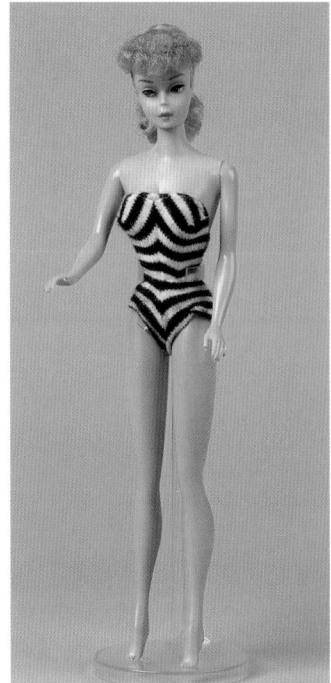

Ponytail #5, model #850, blonde, hollow body, greasy-face plastic, MIB, **$400.**

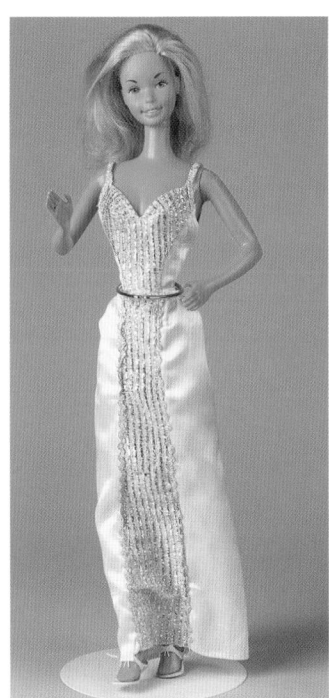

Supersize Barbie, model #9828, blonde, 18" h, MIB, **$200.**

nails painted, straight legs, black and white striped one-pc swimsuit, silver loop earrings, black #1 open-toe shoes with holes, white rimmed glasses with blue lenses, pink cover booklet, reproduction #1 stand, box with replaced insert, VG....... **$3,400**

Blonde, reset in ponytail, red lips, nostril paint, fingernails painted, TL, straight legs, black and white striped one-pc swimsuit, gold hoop earrings, one black #1 open toe shoe with hole (unmarked), white rimmed glasses with blue lenses, pink cov booklet, orig box with partial Marshall Field's sticker, VG **$3,200**

#3 ponytail, brunette, red lips, nostril paint, brown eyeliner, fingernails painted, straight legs, #976 Sweater Girl outfit, orange knit sweater, matching shell, gray skirt, black open toe shoes, pearl earrings, wooden bowl with orange, green and yellow yarn with two needles, metal scissors, *How to Knit* book, black pedestal with plastic base, pink cover booklet, white rimmed glasses with blue lenses, no box, hair and banks no box and fuzzy, VG/G **$475**

#5 ponytail, brunette, orig set, red lips, nostril paint, fingernails and toenails painted, straight legs, Pak outfit, black and white striped knit shirt, red shorts, no box, NM/VG **$225**

#6 ponytail

Brunette, orig ponytail top knot, coral lips, fingernails and toenails painted, straight legs, Japan market silver kimono, lavender lining, black and silver obi tied with silver and purple cord, attached bow, white nylon short gloves, black open toe shoes, silver and white purse with cord handle, VG **$550**

Titian hair, orig top knot, beige lips, fingernails and toenails painted, straight legs, blue two-pc pajamas with lace trim, button accents, no box, VG **$325**

Presidential Porcelain Collection, Royal Splendor, #01078, #10950, 1993, NRFB **$70**

Standard

Brunette, pink lips, cheek blush, fingernails painted, toenails with faint paint, straight legs, orig pink nylon swimsuit bottoms with plastic flower accent, #1804 Knit Hit blue

and pink knit dress, pale blue high tongue shows, no box, VG **$150**

Light brunette, pink lips, cheek blush, fingernails and toenails painted, straight legs, nude, no box, replaced rubber band, VG **$190**

Swirl ponytail

Brunette hair in orig set, coral lips, fingernails and toenails painted, straight legs, #1638 Fraternity Dance gown, pink satin skirt, pink chiffon overskirt, white lacy bodice, blue and green nylon waist scarf, brooch accent, rose colored open toe shoes, single pearl necklace, white nylon long gloves, orig box, VG/G **$450**

Brunette hair in orig set, yellow ribbon, metal hair pin, coral lips, fingernails and toenails painted, straight legs, red nylon one-pc swimsuit, red open toe shoes, pearl earrings, wrist tag, box with gold metal stand, NM **$675**

Platinum hair in orig set, yellow ribbon, metal hair pin, white lips, fingernails painted, straight legs, nude, no box, NM-VG **$475**

Talking, brunette, ribbon bow ties, pink lips, cheek blush, rooted eyelash-

Twist and Turn, model #1160, brunette, MIB, **$500.**

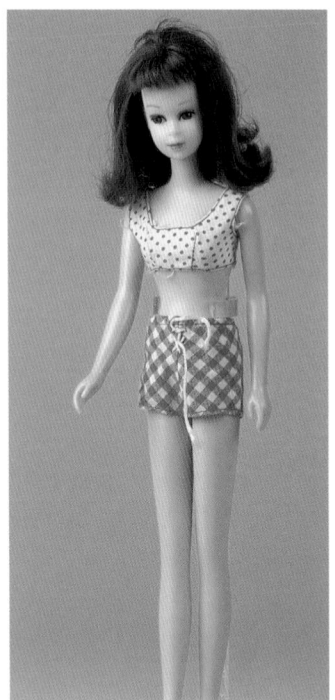

Francie, straight leg, model #1140, brunette, MIB, **$400.**

Busy Francie, model #3313, blonde, MIB, **$425.**

es, bendable legs, red nylon two-pc swimsuit with metal accent on bottoms, white and silver net cover-up with red trim, no box, possible repairs to talker, working condition, VG **$275**

Twist 'n' Turn

Blonde, pink lips, cheek blush, fingernails and toenails painted, bendable legs, multicolored one-pc knit swimsuit, wrist tag, clear plastic stand, booklet, NRFB.............**$425**

Brunette, pink lips, cheek blush, fingernails pain ted, bendable legs, #1485 Gypsy Spirits outfit, pink nylon blouse, aqua suede skirt, matching vest, no box, VG **$125**

Pale blonde, pink lips, cheek blush, rooted eyelashes, fingernails painted, bendable legs, two-pc orange vinyl swimsuit, white net cover-up with orange trim, trade-in program doll, no box, VG **$475**

Friends and family dolls

Allan, painted red hair, pink lips, straight legs, #1409 Goin' Hunting, red plaid shirt, denim pants, red socks, black boots, red plastic cap,

hunting rifle, frayed wrist tag, VG **$65**

Casey, blonde hair, clear plastic headband, peach lips, cheek blush, two-pc hot pink nylon swimsuit, orig clear plastic bag, cardboard hanger, orig price sticker, NRFP......................**$295**

Chris, Color Magic-type titian hair, green metal hair barrette, pink lips, cheek blush, bendable arms and legs, #3617 Birthday Beauties outfit, pink floral dress, white slip, white fishnet tights, white shoes with molded straps, gold wrapped present with white ribbon and pink flower accents, one pink crepe paper party favor with gold glitter, white paper invitation, orig box, VG **$105**

Christie

Talking, red hair, pink lips, cheek blush, rooted eyelashes, bendable legs, wrist tag, clear plastic stand, nonworking, box age discolored, scuffed, and worn, NRFM **$250**

Twist 'n' Turn, red hair, pink lips, cheek blush, rooted eyelashes, bendable legs, #1841 Night Clouds, yellow, orange and pink nylon ruffled nightgown with ribbon straps,

matching yellow nylon robe with ribbon ties and flower accents, no box, VG **$115**

Francie

Brunette, clear plastic headband, peach lips, cheek blush, two-pc yellow nylon swimsuit, orig clear plastic bag, cardboard hanger, orig price sticker, NRFP............................**$250**

Brunette, pink lips, cheek blush, bent legs, ring earrings, Slightly Summery Pak dress, Barbie print top, green pleated skirt, VG **$75**

Malibu, The Sun Set, blonde, pink plastic sunglasses, plastic head cover, peach lips, painted teeth, bendable legs, pink and red nylon swimsuit, yellow vinyl waistband, orange terrycloth towel, box dated 1970, NRFB.............................**$235**

Twist 'n' Turn, blonde, pink lips, cheek blush, rooted eyelashes, bendable legs, orig floral print outfit with lace trim, pink nylon bottoms, no box, VG..**$165**

Jamie, walking, Furry Friends Gift Set, Sears Exclusive, titian hair, pink lips, cheek blush, rooted eyelashes, bendable legs, green, pink, and orange knit dress, orange belt with buckle,

Ken, first issue, blond, flocked hair, model #750, red swimsuit, MIB, **$200.**

Ken, blond, painted hair, 1962 shorter doll, model #750, MIB, **$175.**

Earring Magic Ken, model #2290, painted hair with blond streaks, MIB, **$45.**

orange furry coat with pink vinyl trim, orange boots, gray dot with felt features, pink vinyl dog collar with silver accents, leash, no box, VG **$150**

Julia, talking, red hair, pink lips, cheek blush, rooted eyelashes, bendable legs, gold and silver jumpsuit with belt, wrist tag, clear plastic stand, NRFB, nonworking, box age discolored, scuffed, and worn **$225**

Ken

Brunette flocked hair, beige lips, straight legs, red swim trunks with white stripe, wrist tag, booklet, yellow terrycloth towel, cork sandals in cellophane bag, black white stand, orig box, oily face, worn wrist tag, VG.. **$155**

Brunette flocked hair, beige lips, straight legs, #790 Time for Tennis, white shirt and shorts, white sweater with navy and red trim, white socks and shoes, Tennis Rules book, tennis racquet and two balls, green plastic glasses, no box, NM **$115**

Brunette painted hair, beige lips, straight legs, #0782 Sleeper Set, blue and white striped pajamas,

wax honey bun, metal alarm clock, glass of milk, no box, VG........... **$50**

Painted blond hair, peach lips, straight legs, #799 Touchdown red jersey with felt "7," red pants, white lacing closure, red socks with navy stripe, black cleats, red helmet, brown football, no box, VG **$50**

Painted brunette, peach lips, straight legs, #790 Time for Tennis outfit, white knit shirt, white sweater with blue and red trim, white shorts, socks, and shoes, tennis racquet and ball, no box, VG **$55**

Talking, painted brown hair, peach lips, painted teeth, bendable legs, #1435 Shore Lines outfit, blue nylon jacket with zipper closure, blue shorts, vinyl side stripes, multi-print pants with zipper closure, yellow plastic face mask with elastic head strap, swim fins, no box, non-working, stretched elastic on mask, NM **$75**

Midge

Blonde hair, pink lips, fingernails painted, white satin sleeveless shirt, bolero jacket, wrap skirt, hat with bow accent, white open toe shoes, no box, VG **$85**

Titian hair, ribbon hair band, pink lips, fingernails painted, bendable legs, orig one-pc striped knit swimsuit, aqua open toe shoes, gold wire stand, orig box, VG **$560**

PJ, talking, blonde, beaded tie on left pigtail, replaced rubber-band on right pigtail, attached lavender plastic glasses, pink lips, cheek blush, rooted eyelashes, bendable legs, #1796 Fur Sighted outfit, orange jacket with fur trim, metallic gold tab and button closures, matching pants, zigzag print knit sweater, orange hat with fur trim, metallic gold chin strap, yellow high tongue shoes, no box, non-working, NM/VG.................................... **$155**

Ricky, painted red hair, peach lips, cheek blush, straight legs, striped jacket, blue shorts, cork sandals in bag, black wire stand, orig box with insert, wrist tag torn, NM.......... **$155**

Skipper

Blonde, pink lips, straight legs, #1915 Outdoor Casuals, turquoise knit sweater, matching dickey with button closure, pants, white nylon short gloves, white socks, white flat shoes, red wooden yo-yo, no box, VG.. **$55**

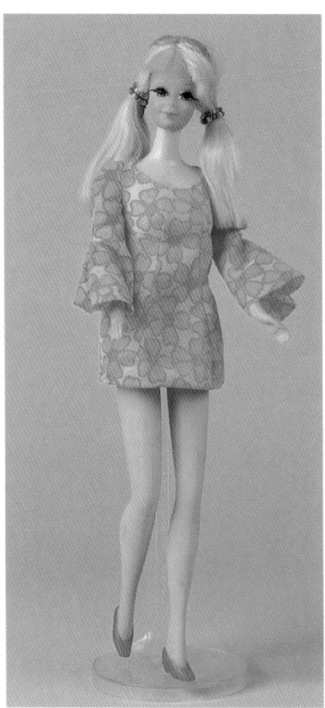

Talking P.J., model #1113, orange flowered dress, blonde, MIB, **$250.**

Skipper, bendable leg, model #1030, brunette, MIB, **$250.**

Skooter, first issue, straight leg, model #1040, blonde, MIB, **$180.**

Color Magic-type dark red hair, pink lips, straight legs, #1902 Silk 'n' Fancy dress, red velvet bodice, white skirt, red lace underskirt, gold braid waistband, white nylon socks, black flat shoes, NM **$90**

Color Magic-type titian hair, pink lips, straight legs, #1926 Chill Chasers, white fur coat, red cap with blue pompon, red flat shoes, no box, NM **$120**

Pose' n Play, blonde, blue ribbon ties, clear plastic headband, pink lips, cheek blush, bendable arms and legs, blue and white outfit with button accents, wrist tag, orig clear plastic bag, cardboard hanger, NRFP **$85**

Quick Curl, blonde hair, blue ribbon bow, pink lips, cheek blush, straight legs, blue and white long dress, orig clear plastic bag, NRFP **$150**

Skooter

Blonde, red ribbon bows, beige lips with tint of pink, cheek blush, straight legs, #1921 School Girl outfit, red jacket with pocket insignia, red and white pleated skirt, white shirt, red felt hat with red

and white band and feather accent, white nylon socks, red flat shoes, brown rimmed glasses, arithmetic, geography, and English books, black book strap, red and natural wooden pencils, orig box, VG **$90**

Brunette, hair in orig set with ribbons, pink lips, cheek blush, straight legs, #1901 Red Sensation dress, gold button accents, white nylon socks, red flat shoes, white nylon short gloves, straw hat with ribbon band and bow accent, NM **$70**

Brunette, retied with red cord, beige lips, cheek blush, straight legs, wearing Best Buy Fashions #9122, red plaid coat, black belt, matching cap with black ribbon accent, #9122 dress with red plaid skirt, black velveteen top, white nylon shirt, no box, VG **$70**

Tutti, Me and My Dog, brunette, red ribbon bow, pink lips, bendable arms and legs, red felt coat, fur trim, white fur hat with ribbon ties, red tights, white flat shoes, white dog with felt features, attached red leash, no box, leash worn and knotted, VG **$75**

Outfits

Barbie

#934 black sleeveless dress, white collar, white hat with black ribbon accent, black open toe shoes, VG **$65**

#957 Knitting Pretty, pink sweater, matching sleeveless shell, pink flannel skirt, pink #1 open toe shoes, metal scissors, How to Knit book, wooden bowl with two needles, yellow, red, and pale pink yarn, VG/G **$160**

#958 Party Date, white satin dress, gold glitter accents, wide gold belt, gold clutch purse, clear open toe shoes, VG **$95**

#968 Roman Holiday, sheath, red and white striped bodice, navy blue skirt, matching red and white striped coat, white open toe #1 shoes, white nylon shirt gloves, red woven hat with bow accent, white vinyl clutch purse, black rimmed glasses, white hankie, pink plastic comb, brass compact, VG **$1,250**

#0873 Guinevere, royal blue velvet gown, embroidered and gold tri, attached chain belt, red and gold

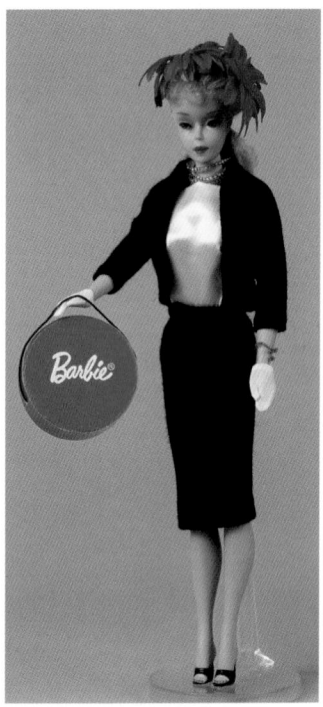

Commuter Set, #916, 1959-1960. This exciting fashion was reproduced in 1999 as part of Mattel's Collectors' Request series, MIP, orig, **$1,500.**

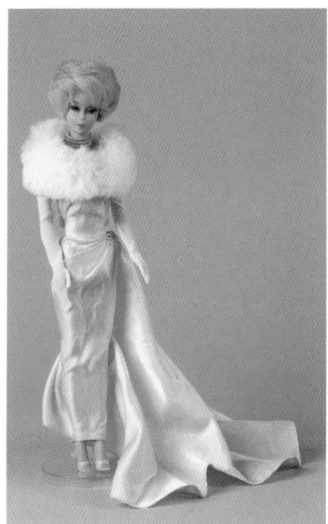

Enchanted Evening, #983, 1960-1963, pictured on a Bubblecut Barbie. This classic formal gown was offered on a collector doll in 1996, MIP, **$385.**

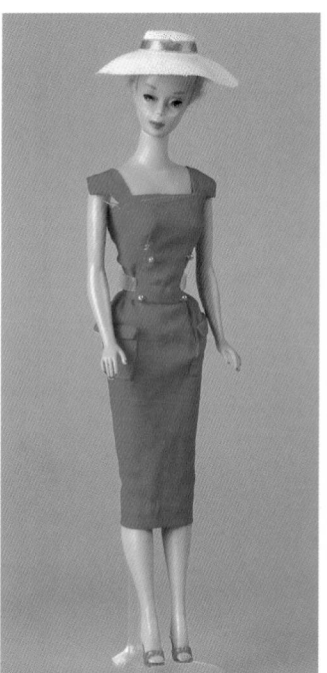

Sheath Sensation, #986, pictured on a Ponytail #3, Sheath Sensation originally came with a white straw hat, (shown) and white gloves and shoes (not pictured), 1961-1964, MIP, **$150.**

brocade slippers, red and gold brocade crown with navy blue and gold trim edging, attached gold nylon snood, red nylon armlets, NM/VG **$105**

#0874 Arabian Night, pink satin blouse, pink chiffon long skirt, matching pink sari with gold trim, gold foil slippers, gold plastic lamp, gold and turquoise beaded necklace, gold drop earrings, gold and turquoise plastic bracelets, paper theater program, VG **$95**

#1452 Now Knit, green, navy blue, and silver dress, matching green furry hat, blue nylon scarf with attached silver thread ring, NM/VG **$50**

#1489 Cloud 9, pale blue nylon short nightie with satin bodice, matching long robe, satin slippers, VG **$55**

#1593 Golden Groove, Sears Exclusive Gift Set, pink and gold lame jacket, matching short skirt, gold thigh-high boots, NM **$145**

#1612 Theatre Date, NRFB **$285**

#1615 Saturday Matinee, NM/VG **$310**

#1617, Midnight Blue, NM/VG **$150**

#1620 Junior Designer, turquoise dress with green design, green pointed toe shoes, metal iron with black handle, *How to Design Your Own Fashion* book, VG **$55**

#1622 Student Teacher, red and white dress, white bodice inset with button accents, red vinyl belt, red pointed toe shoes, black rimmed glasses with clear lenses, plastic globe, wooden pointer stick, geography book, VG/G **$175**

#1629 Skater's Waltz, pink nylon skating suit, pink felt skirt, sheer nylon hose, white skates, pink fur muff, matching mittens, VG **$45**

#1635 Fashion Editor, sheath, turquoise skirt, floral print bodice, glitter accents, matching jacket, green ribbon trim, turquoise cap with flower bud accent and ribbon bow, turquoise pointed toe shoes, plastic camera, NM **$225**

#1637 Outdoor Life, blue and white checked coat, blue and white houndstooth print pants, blue nylon shirt, white hat, tennis shoes, VG **$95**

#1644 On the Avenue, white and gold sheath with textured skirt, gold lame bodice, matching jacket, white nylon short gloves, cream-colored pointed toe shoes, gold clutch purse, jacket tag frayed, P condition belt, NM/VG **$100**

#1645 Golden Glory, gold floral lame long dress, green chiffon waist scarf, matching gold lame long coat with fur trim, white nylon short gloves, green satin clutch purse, VG ... **$120**

#1649 Lunch on the Terrace, green and white checkered dress with polka dot bodice, matching hat with white net cover, VG **$115**

#1650 Outdoor Art Show, VG ... **$145**

#1652, Pretty as a Picture, VG ... **$115**

#1656 Fashion Luncheon, VG/G .. **$225**

#1663, Music Center Matinee, NM/VG **$200**

#1678 Pan American Airways Stewardess, gray-blue jacket, attached metal wings, matching skirt, and cap, white shirt, white nylon short gloves, black pointed toe shoes, black vinyl shoulder bag, VG .. **$700**

#1687 Caribbean Cruise, yellow jumpsuit with halter top, yellow flat soft shoes, NM **$35**

#1695 Evening Enchantment, red taffeta and chiffon long dress, marabou trim, matching chiffon cape, red pointed toe shoes, VG **$135**

#1792 Mood Matchers, paisley print nylon sleeveless blouse, matching pants, aqua nylon shirt, hot pink high tongue shoes, M................. **$65**

#1814 Sparkle Squares, checkerboard pattern coat with ruffle trim, rhinestone buttons, matching dress with pleated white nylon skirt, white sheet stockings, NM................. **$105**

#1848 All That Jazz, satin striped coat, matching dress with pleated skirt, beige sheer stockings, pink shoes with molded bows, VG .. **$140**

#1880 Winter Wedding, cream colored brocade gown with fur trim, brocade and fur trimmed cap with attached metal headband and tulle veil, white pointed-toe shoes, VG **$75**

#3428 The Zig Zag Bag, red and white zig zag pattern knit pants, orange terry cloth sleeveless shirt, zig-zag nylon shirt, red tennis shoes, M. **$185**

#4041 Color Magic Fashion Fun, NM/ VG... **$145**

Dressed Up, Barbie Pak, dress with pale blue satin skirt, gold and white striped bodice, attached belt and buckle accents, pale blue pointed toe shoes, NM/VG **$105**

Gala Abend, foreign market, white brocade gown, matching long coat with pale blue satin lining and fur collar, white nylon long gloves, white pointed toe shoes, VG.... **$700**

Francie

#1216 The Lace Pace, gold lame and pink coat cov with white lace, satin bow, matching dress with satin straps, pink shoes with molded bows, VG **$105**

#1222 Gold Rush, orange satin dress, bright orange open toe shoes, VG **$35**

#1232 Two for the Ball, pink chiffon long coat, black velvet waistband, long dress with pink satin skirt, pink lace overskirt, black velvet bodice, pink soft pumps, coat tag frayed, VG/G **$45**

#3367 Right for Stripes, blue vest, blue and white striped pants, matching midriff top, floral print shoulder bag, aqua sneakers, VG............. **$65**

Pancho Bravo, Francie Pak, blue, pink, green, and white poncho, blue ankle boots, lavender plastic glasses, label, some age discoloration to cardboard backing, orig 99 cent price sticker, NRFP.................... **$40**

The Bridge Bit, white knit sweater, green and blue stitching, royal blue stretch pants with metal accent, pink pillow with flower design, NM **$65**

Ken

#788 Rally Day, NRFB.................. **$60**

#797 Army and Air Force, NRFB **$220**

#799 Touchdown, NRFB, box in F/P condition.................................. **$115**

#0770 Campus Hero, NRFB........ **$130**

#0772 The Prince, green and gold lame coat, lace trim, rhinestone buttons, green velvet cape with gold lining, green nylon tights, green velvet shoes with gold trim, gold velvet hat with emerald, pearl, and feather accents, white collar with lace trim, velvet pillow with gold trim and tassels, paper program, VG **$150**

#0773 King Arthur, silver lame pants, shirt, and cap, red satin surcoat with gold griffin, gray plastic helmet and sword, brown scabbard,

two red plastic spurs, cardboard shield, paper program, VG **$95**

#0779 American Airlines Captain, NRFB............................... **$175**

#1404 Ken in Hawaii, VG............. **$25**

#1416 College Student, VG **$65**

#1417 Rovin' Reporter, red jacket, navy blue pants, white shirt, black socks and shoes, plastic camera, NM/VG **$75**

#1419 TV's Good Tonight, red robe, blue trim, pocket insignia, cork sandals with red straps, brown plastic TV with metal antenna, no tag on robe, VG................................. **$50**

#1425 Best Man, VG-G **$105**

Ricky, #1502 Saturday Show, NRFB **$75**

Skipper

#1738 Fancy Pants, VG **$50**

#1901 Red Sensation, NRFB....... **$135**

#1912 Cookie Time, sleeveless dress, navy blue skirt, attached red belt, red flat shoes, miniature Barbie's Easy-As-Pie Cookbook, metal spoon with red plastic handle, gray bowl, Cookie Mix box, NM **$70**

#1913 Me n' My Doll, pink and white gingham checked dress, ribbon ties, flower embroidered accent, white nylon socks, white flat shoes, miniature plastic Barbie doll with painted features, pink and white checked skirt, VG **$75**

#1936 Sledding Fun, flower print jacket, fur collar, red sleeveless shirt, blue pans with sewn-on red socks, blue hat, one fur mitten, red boots, red and white plastic sled with cord handle, NM................ **$85**

#1972 Drizzle Sizzle, pink and Kelly green knit dress, orange vinyl appliqué flowers, clear plastic raincoat, cap, and boots, VG **$35**

DOLLS

History: Dolls have been children's play toys for centuries. Dolls also have served other functions. From the 14th through 18th centuries, doll making was centered in Europe, mainly in Germany and France. The French dolls produced in this era were representations of adults and dressed in the latest couturier designs. They were not children's toys.

During the mid-19th century, child and baby dolls, made in wax, cloth, bisque, and porcelain, were introduced. Facial features were hand painted, wigs were made of mohair and human hair, and the dolls were dressed in the current fashions for babies or children.

Doll making in the United States began to flourish in the 1900s with companies such as Effanbee, Madame Alexander, and Ideal.

Marks: Marks of the various manufacturers are found on the back of the head or neck or on the doll's back. These marks are very important in identifying a doll and its date of manufacture.

Additional Listings: See *Warman's Americana & Collectibles* for more examples.

Alt, Beck & Gottschalk, bisque shoulder head, blue paperweight eyes, multi-stroke brows, painted upper and lower lashes, closed mouth, molded blonde hair, kid body with pin joints at hips and knees, bisque lower arms, antique white dressing gown, blue coat, new underclothing, marked "998 No. 10" at back bottom of shoulder plate, 23" h **$950**

Amberg

Bottle Babe Twins, solid-dome bisque heads, light blue sleep eyes, softly blues brows, painted upper and lower lashes, open mouths, molded tongues, lightly molded and painted hair, cloth bodies with non-working criers, composition arms, right arms molded to hold celluloid bottles, orig white lace-trimmed baby dresses, slips, crocheted bonnets, diapers, and socks, hold orig celluloid baby bottle, blue and white celluloid rattle, marked "A.M./Germany/341/ 3" on back of heads, "Amberg's/Bottle Babe/Pat. Pending/Amberg Dolls/The World Standard" on dress, both dolls have light rubs on cheeks or hair, cloth bodies are aged, some flaking on arms, paint flaked off right arm of one, price for pr, 12-1/2" h **$500**

New Born Babe, solid dome bisque head, blue sleep eyes, softly blushed brown, painted upper and lower lashes, closed mouth, lightly molded and painted hair, cloth body with composition hands, white lace-trimmed antique baby dress, slip and diaper, light dust in bisque, tiny run on upper lip, left side seam split near bottom of torso, 15" h **$315**

Armand Marseille

990 baby, bisque socket head, brown sleep eyes, feathered brows, painted upper and lower lashes, open mouth, well-accented lips, two upper teeth, antique human-hair wig, composition bent-limb baby body, antique baby dress, slip, diaper, new crocheted sweater, cap and booties, marked "Armand Marseille/ Germany/990/A 12 M" on back of head, heavy French-style body, arms repainted and have rough finish, right big toe missing, other toes repaired and repainted, normal wear at joints, 23" h **$275**

Googly, bisque socket head, large slide glancing blue sleep eyes, single strike brows, closed smiling mouth, dark mohair wig, crude composition five-pc toddler body, lace-trimmed organdy baby dress, matching bonnet, slip, diaper, stockings, crocheted booties, marked "G. 253 B Germany A. 11/0 M" on back of head, repainted body, 6-1/2" h **$675**

Head circumference, Dream Baby, brown bisque socket head, brown sleep eyes, closed mouth, black painted hair, brown bent limb composition baby body, fine lawn christening gown with tucks, ruffles, and lace trim, c1920, 10" l, 9" d **$300**

Arranbee

Nancy Lee, composition head, brown sleep eyes with real lashes, painted lower lashes, single stroke brows, closed mouth, orig human-hair wig in orig set, five-pc composition body, orig brown flannel belted dress, white ruffle trim, orig underwear combination, orig socks and brown suede shoes with fringe tongue, marked "R & B" on back of head, unplayed with condition, 17" h **$300**

Nanette, hard plastic head, blue sleep eyes with real lashes, single-stroke brows, painted lower lashes, closed mouth, saran wig, five-pc hard-plastic walking body, orig red and white striped dress with red organdy sleeves and apron, blue vinyl wide belt with charms attached, wrist tag, curlers on card, comb, marked "R & B" on head, "Nanette/An R & B Quality Doll/R & B Dolly Company New York 3, NY" on label on end of box, "R & B/ Nanette/Walks/ Sits/Stands/ Turns Her Head/R & B Doll Company New York City" on wrist tag, near mint in aged box, lid damaged and repaired, 21" h **$700**

Averill, Georgene

Bonnie Babe, solid dome bisque flange head, brown sleep eyes, softly brushed brows, painted upper and lower lashes, open mouth, two lower teeth, molded tongue, cloth mama doll body, composition lower arms and legs, antique long baby dress, marked "Copr by Georgene Averill 1005 3652 4 Germany" on back of head, body recovered, 20" h **$475**

Solid dome bisque flange head, blue sleep eyes, softly blushed brows, painted upper and lower lashes, open laughing mouth, two lower teeth, molded tongue, deeply molded dimples, lightly molded and painted curly hair, cloth mama-doll body, composition arms and lower legs, non-working crier, dressed in possibly orig white lace-trimmed baby dress, slip, underwear, socks, and knit booties, silk and lace bonnet, marked "Copr by Georgene Averill 1005 3652 3 Germany" on back of head, cloth body aged and lightly soiled, 17" h **$600**

Bahr & Proschild, 300, bisque socket head on bisque shoulder plate, blue set threaded paperweight eyes, feathered brows, painted upper and lower lashes, open mouth, four upper teeth, pierced tongue, orig human-hair wig, kid body with cloth torso, bisque lower arms, gussets at elbows, hips, and knees, antique white dress with lace trim, antique underclothing, orig blue velvet hat with flower trim, marked "300/10" on back of head, inherent red firing line at rim in back, minor wig pulls, tiny rub on right cheek, body aged and discolored, 19" h **$300**

Barrois, E., Poupee, pale bisque swivel head on shoulder plate, set blue eyes with threaded detail, fine multi-stroke brows, painted upper and lower lashes, closed mouth with accented lips, orig blonde mohair wig with orig tortoiseshell comb, kid body with kid-over-wood upper arms, mortise-and-tenon type knee joints, white dotted Swiss dress, possibly orig underclothing, socks, and shoes, marked "E 4 B," at rear edge of bisque shoulder plate, lower bisque arms replaced, 17-1/2" h...............**$1,200**

Bisque

Oriental pair, olive-tone bisque socket heads, dark brown pupilless set eyes, single stroke brows, painted upper and lower lashes, closed mouth, orig black mohair wigs, male with orig queue, five-pc olive-tone bisque bodies jointed at shoulders and hips, Oriental embroidered silk clothing, unmarked, price for pr, 4-1/2" h **$825**

Just Me, painted bisque socket head, blue side-glancing sleep eyes, single stroke brows, closed mouth, orig mohair wig, five-pc composition body jointed at shoulders and hips, orig white dress with orange and green felt trim, orig white cotton socks and white paper shoes with buckles, marked "Just Me/Registered/Germany/A 310/6/0 M" on back of head, needs to be restrung, 10" h **$900**

Miss Liberty, bisque shoulder head, painted blue eyes with molded lids, multi-stroke brows, tiny painted upper and lower lashes, closed mouth, molded earrings, molded and painted blonde hair with copper molded earrings, molded and painted blonde hair with copper tiara, two black ribbons across top of head and lay against left side of neck, molded bun with waterfall effect, cloth body, leather lower arms, red leather boots as part of lower leg, antique ecru wool dress with lace trim, antique underclothing, small holes in dress, 18" h **$1,650**

Bru Jne, bisque socket head, bulbous blue paperweight eyes, heavy feathered brows, painted upper and lower lashes, closed mouth, pierced ears, hand tied mohair wig, kid body with scalloped kid attaching body to shoulder plate, kid-over-wood upper arms, bisque lower arms, wooden lower legs, dressed in outfit made from antique ecru fabric and trims, beige and blue French style hat, French shoes marked "9," marked "Bru Jne/10" on back of head, "Bru" visible above kid on left rear shoulder, "No. 8" visible above kid on right rear shoulder, "Bebe Bru Bte S.G.D.G./Tout Contrefacteur sera saisi et poursuivi conformement a la Loi" on paper label on chest, 1" firing flaw on right forehead at crown, left little finger replaced, 22" h **$7,300**

Century Doll Co., bisque shoulder plate, blue sleep eyes, feathered brows, painted lashes, open mouth, four upper teeth, molded and painted hair, kid body pin jointed at hips and knees, jointed wood and composition arms, composition lower legs, redressed, marked "Made in Germany/Century Doll" on back of shoulder plate, 18" h **$325**

Chase, Martha, black cloth, dark brown painted on eyes, soft brick red painted mouth **$11,165**

China, unmarked

Frozen Charlie, pink tint, painted blue eyes, feathered brows, closed mouth, accent line between lips, painted blond hair with brush strokes around face, unjointed body with arms held in front, hands in fists, fingernails and toenails outlined, antique pink crocheted long dress and matching bonnet, 16" h **$675**

Open mouth, low brow, china shoulder head with turned head, painted blue eyes, red accent line, single-stroke brows, open mouth, molded teeth, molded and painted wavy hair, cloth body, china lower arms and lower legs, painted garters, molded and painted brown shoes with heels, possibly orig beige print dress, underclothing, 18" h **$850**

Cloth, Philadelphia Baby, painted head and shoulders, heavily lidded brown painted eyes, deeply modeled mouth, brown hair, cloth body, painted lower limbs, gray and white striped cotton shift, white undergarments, overall wear, paint rubs and loss, c1900, 21" h **$1,100**

Cochran, Dewees, Cindy, latex socket head, painted blue eyes, multi-stroke brows, painted upper lashes, closed mouth, human hair wig, five-pc latex body jointed at shoulders and hips, faded peach taffeta dress with tan collar and hem, purple velvet trim, marked "Dewees Cochran/Dolls" on torso under left arm, 15" h **$325**

Cuno & Otto Dressel

Bisque head, blue sleep eyes with lashes, open mouth, two upper teeth, replaced auburn mohair wig, fully articulated composition body, blue dress, imp "Cuno & Otto Dressel," some repair to body, early 20th C, 14" h **$200**

Girl, painted bisque socket head, blue sleep eyes with real lashes, feathered brows, shading around eyes, open mouth, four upper teeth, orig human-hair wig, jointed wood and composition teen-age body with high knee joints, orig clothing, short dress, slip, teddy, socks, and leather shoes, marked "Cuno & Otto Dressel/Germany" on back of head, 15-1/2" h **$450**

Demalcol, Googlie, bisque socket head, blue eyes set to side, single-stroke brows, painted upper and lower lash-

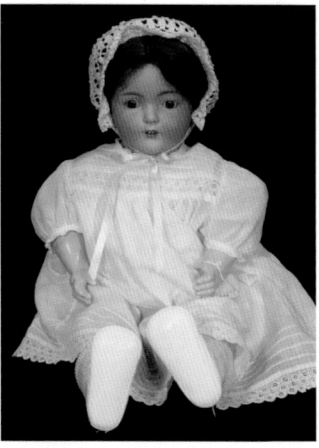

Century Doll Co., bisque head, blue sleep eyes, open mouth, composition arms & legs, cloth body, voice box, marks: Kestner Germany; 24" h, $375.
Photo courtesy of Joy Luke Auctions.

es, closed smiling mouth, human-hair wig, new jointed-composition body, blue and white flowered dress, matching bonnet, new underclothing, socks and shoes, marked "Demalcol/5/0/Germany" on back of head, 9-1/2" h **$525**

Eden Bebe, bisque socket head, blue paperweight eyes, feathered brows, painted upper and lower lashes, open mouth, six upper teeth, pierced ears, replaced mohair wig, jointed wood and composition French body, redressed, pale blue and ecru outfit, blue and beige jacket, antique underclothing, new stockings, and old shoes, marked "Eden Bebe/Paris/7/Depose" on back of neck, "7" on front of neck, light kiln dust on left cheek, flaking at neck socket of body and on both lower legs, normal wear at joints and on hands, 16-1/2" h **$1,200**

Effanbee

American Child Boy, composition head, painted blue eyes, multi-stroke brows, tiny painted upper and lower lashes, closed smiling mouth, orig human-hair wig, five-pc composition child body, orig blue wool two-pc suit, jacket and shorts, white shirt, multicolored tie, orig socks and black leatherette shoes, unmarked, light facial crazing, few light lines of crazing on legs, 17" h **$1,050**

American Child, composition head, blue sleep eyes with real lashes,

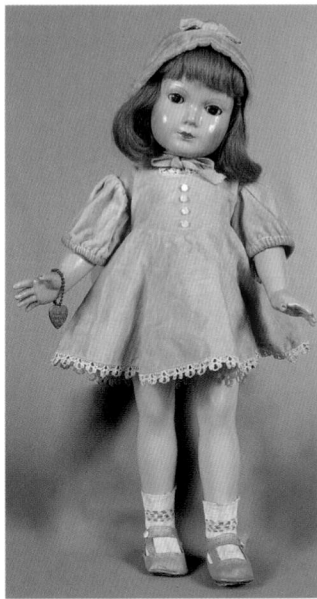

Effanbee Musical American Child, all composition, brown sleep eyes, closed mouth, original human hair wig, working key wind music box, jointed shoulders and hips, marks: Effanbee//American// Children on head, Effanbee//Anne Shirley on back, Effanbee//Durable//Dolls metal heart bracelet; fine general crazing, bottom back of head short composition cracks, aged clothing, 17", **$1,100.**
Photo courtesy of McMasters Harris Auction Co.

Effanbee, "Patsy Ann," composition, blue sleep eyes, molded hair, painted features, jointed body, 19" h, **$100.**
Photo courtesy of Joy Luke Auctions.

multi-stroke brows, painted lower lashes, closed mouth, orig human-hair wig with orig curlers, five-pc composition child body, orig blue and white striped zippered dress, nylon panties, orig white socks with blue trim, blue leatherette tie shoes, marked "Effanbee/American Children" on back of head, "Effanbee/ Anne-Shirley" on back, unplayed with condition, 19-1/2" h......**$1,500**

Grumpy Cowboy, composition shoulder head, painted blue eyes to side, single-stroke brows, closed pouty mouth, molded and painted hair, cloth body, composition arms and feet, cowboy outfit with plaid shirt, gold pants, green bandanna, imitation-leather chaps, holster with gun, replaced felt hat, marked "Effanbee/ Dolls/ Walk Talk Sleep" on back of shoulder plate, light crazing, light wear back of head, few flakes off shoulder plate, wear on edges of feet, 11" h **$475**

Gaultier, Francois

Bebe, bisque socket head, large blue paperweight eyes, feathered brows, painted upper and lower lashes, full-closed mouth, molded tongue, pierced ears, replaced mohair wig, jointed wood and composition body with straight wrists, new blue silk dress with matching bonnet, new underclothing, socks and lace-up boots, marked "F. G. (in scroll)/8" on back of head, fingers touched up, minor repairs, 21" h **$2,200**

Poupee, bisque socket head, bisque shoulder plate, light blue paperweight eyes, feathered brows, painted upper and lower lashes, closed mouth, pierced ears, orig mohair wig, cloth body with kid arms, individually stitched fingers, dressed in probably orig blue and white two-pc outfit with train, marked "2/0" on back of head, "F. G." on right shoulder, illegible mark on left shoulder, some age discoloration to body, one left finger missing, 10-1/2" h **$1,250**

Halbig, Simon

Bisque head, blue sleep eyes, open mouth, four molded teeth, pierced ears, blond mohair wig, chunky straight wrist articulated composition body, orig finish and stringing, new red faille dress, imp "1079 DEP," tiny chip to right ear hole, c1900, 8" h
......**$550**

C M Bergmann bisque head, brown sleep eyes with lashes, open mouth, synthetic auburn wig, jointed composition body, period white lawn dress with lace insertion, sprinkling of pepper spots primarily to the right cheek, early 20th C, 21" h
......**$260**

Oriental, bisque, medium skin tone, dark pupil-less stationary eyes, closed mouth orig black mohair Oriental-style wig, swivel neck, kid-lined neck socket and legs, long black stockings, brick red one-strap shoes, imp "852 3," some mottling/ soil to bisque, late 19th C, 7" h
......**$920**

Hamburger & Co.,

Viola, bisque socket head, blue sleep eyes, feathered brows, painted upper and lower lashes, open mouth, four upper teeth, synthetic wig, jointed wood and composition body, antique dress with lace trim, underclothing, new socks and leather shoes, marked "Made in/Germany/Viola/H & Co./ 7" on back of head, several wig pulls on right side of forehead, light rub on nose, small inherent cut on H in back of head, repairs at neck socket of body, bottom of torso and left upper arm, normal wear at joints, finish of legs slightly different color than rest of body, 22-1/2" h **$300**

Hand sewn

Amish, OH, lavender dress, white apron, purple bonnet, arms and legs made from corn cobs, staining, 15" h
......**$345**

Amish, PA, green dress, black cape and bonnet, 16" h **$690**

Mennonite, PA, red and black checkered dress, black bonnet, fading, holes to cloth, 17-1/2" h
......**$965**

Handwerck,

bisque head, blue sleep eyes, open mouth, pierced ears, orig blonde mohair wig, fully articulated composition body, Alice in Wonderland blue dress and white pinafore, dark brown shoes, imp "109-6 Germany Handwerck," 16" h **$460**

Handwerck, Heinrich

Bisque socket head, blue set eyes with real lashes, fur brows, painted lower lashes, open mouth, four upper teeth, pierced ears, antique human-hair wig, jointed wood and composition Handwerck body, new flowered dress, marked "Germany/Heinrich/ Handwerck/Simon &

Halbig/ 5" on back of head, "Heinrich Handwerch/5" stamped in red, rub on right cheek, minor flake at earring hole, eyes, lashes, and brows replaced, 28" h **$300**
Bisque socket head, blue sleep eyes, molded and feathered brows, painted upper and lower lashes, open mouth, accented lips, four upper teeth, pierced ears, orig human-hair wig, jointed wood and composition Handwerck body with orig finish, antique white child's dress, antique underclothing, cotton socks, black patent leather shoes, marked "Germany/ Handwerck/Simon & Halbig/ 7" on back of head, "Heinrich Handwerck/Germany/7" stamped in red on lower back, finish flaking on lower left arm and knees, left knee ball replaced, 32-1/2" h **$1,025**

Handwerck, Max, bisque head, blue sleep eyes, open mouth, inset teeth, pierced ears, jointed-composition body, orig finish, newly made pink linen dress and hat, imp "421 10 Germany M HANDWERCK 2-1/2", bisque speckling, small chin pit, 21" h **$320**

Harmann, Kurt, bisque head, brown sleep eyes, open mouth, replaced blonde mohair wig, fully articulated composition body, new blue satin and lace dress, worn period blue leather shoes, imp mark "30 5 K (over script H)," early 20th C, white scratch line each cheek, 26" h **$230**

Hertel, Schwab & Co.
140 character, bisque socket head, painted brown eyes, red accent line, feathered brows, closed mouth, accented lips, mohair wig, jointed wood and composition body, straight wrists, white factory chemise, dark green pants, matching cap, cotton socks, and new leather shoes, marked "140/4" on back of head, light rub on right cheek, minor repair at neck socket of body, light flaking on right upper leg,15" h **$4,200**
Bisque socket head, blue paperweight eyes, feathered brows, painted upper and lower lashes, open mouth with accented lips and six upper teeth, pierced ears, replaced human-hair wig, jointed composition body with straight wrists, separate balls at shoulders, elbows, hips and knees, nicely redressed in pale

pink French-style dress, new underclothing, socks and shoes, marks "8/0" on back of head and "Jumeau Medaille d'Or Paris" stamped in blue on lower back, replaced antique paperweight eyes, tiny flake at each earring hole, tiny fleck on upper rim at inside corner of right eye, body has good orig finish with wear at all joints, on toes and heels, 20" h **$1,100**
Head circumference, twin character babies, blue sleep eyes, open mouths, two upper teeth, wispy blond tufts of hair, composition bent-limb bodies, matching period long white baby gown, one with pink, one blue ribbon trim, imp marks "152/2/0," price for pair, early 20th C, 9" l, 7" d **$635**

Heubach, Ernest
399 baby, solid dome painted bisque socket head, brown sleep eyes, single stroke brows, painted upper and lower lashes, closed mouth, lightly molded and painted hair, composition bent-limb baby body, orig multicolored "grass" skirt, marked "Heubach *Koppelsdorf/399*9/0/ Germany" on back of head, 12-1/2" h **$350**
300 baby, bisque socket head, set brown eyes, feathered brows, painted upper and lower lashes, open mouth, accented lips, four upper teeth, replaced wig, composition bent-limb baby body, antique white long baby dress, lace-trimmed antique baby bonnet, underclothing, diaper, and booties, marked "Heubach * Koppelsdorf/300 * 6/Germany" on back of head, arms and legs repainted, cracks in finish under repaint, neck socket touched up, repair on right arm joint and right wrist, 21" h **$275**

Heubach, Gebruder
Bisque shoulder head, blue intaglio eyes, two tone single stroke brows, closed mouth with shaded lips, molded and painted hair, tan oilcloth body with bisque lower arms, pin joints at hips and knees, cloth lower legs, new light blue velvet suit, white lace trimmed shirt, new socks and shoes, marked "8/Germany" on back of head, 22" h character **$350**

Heubach, Koppelsdorf
Screamer, bisque head, painted hair,

Heinrich Handwerk child, bisque socket head, blue sleep eyes, real lash remnants, painted lower lashes, open mouth, original mohair wig, pierced ears, jointed wood and composition body, orig clothing, marks: Germany// Heinrich Handwerk //Simon & Halbig on head, Heinrich Handwerk//Germany on left hip, 2//HH (in heart) on shoe soles; real lashes sparse on both eyes, shoe button missing, 19", **$650.**
Photo courtesy of McMasters Harris Auction Co.

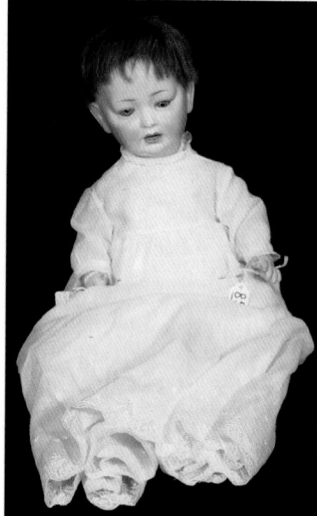

Hertel Schwab, character baby doll, bisque head, blue sleep eyes, open mouth, jointed composition body, marks: 152 L.W. & Co. 10; 17" h, **$275.**
Photo courtesy of Joy Luke Auctions.

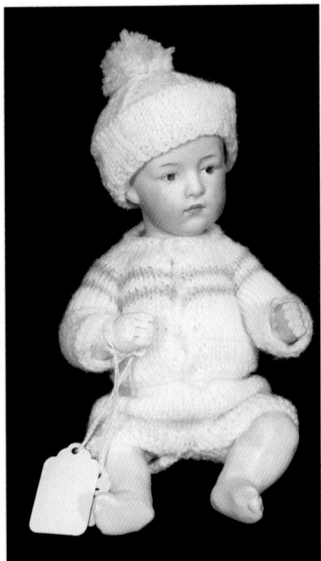

Gebruder Heubach, bisque head, blue painted eyes, closed mouth, molded hair, jointed composition body, marks: sunrise mark, DEP 1 Germany; 9-1/2" h, $250.
Photo courtesy of Joy Luke Auctions

Tete Jumeau, bisque socket head, brown paperweight eyes, open mouth with six upper teeth, pierced ears, cork pate with original mohair wig, jointed wood and composition Jumeau body with jointed wrists, new clothing, marks: Depose// Tete Jumeau//11 on head; body repainted, some flaking 24", $2,000.
Photo courtesy of McMasters Harris Auction Co.

painted blue intaglio eyes, open-closed screaming mouth, furrowed brow, straight-limb composition toddler body, maroon velvet short overalls, white shirt, imp "7684," sunburst mark, 10-1/2" h.........**$690**
Bisque head, blue sleep eyes with lashes, open mouth, brown human-hair wig, fully jointed wood and composition body, period underwear, new print cotton dress, imp mark "312," rub on cheek, early 20th C 24" h **$220**

Horsman, toddler, composition socket head, brown sleep eyes, single stroke brows, painted upper and lower lashes, mohair wig, jointed composition toddler body, straight wrists, diagonal hip joints, old white organdy dress with lace trim, underclothing, socks, high button boots, marked "E.I.H./ Co." on back, 15" h......................**$650**

Ideal

Shirley Temple, composition head, hazel sleep eyes with real lashes, painted lower lashes, feathered brows, open mouth, six upper teeth, orig mohair wig in orig set, five-pc composition body, orig plaid "Bright Eyes" dress, underwear combination, replaced socks, orig shoes, marked "13/Shirley Temple" on head, "Shirley Temple/13" on back, 13" h ..**$700**

Shirley Temple, composition head, hazel sleep eyes, real lashes, painted lower lashes, feathered brows, open mouth, six upper teeth, molded tongue, orig mohair wig in orig set, five-pc composition child body, orig dotted organdy dress with pleats from "Curly Top" movie, orig underwear, combination socks and shoes, marks: "20/Shirley Temple/ Co. Ideal/N & T Co." on back of head, "Shirley Temple/20*" on back, and "Genuine/Shirley Temple/ registered U.S. Pat. Off/Ideal Nov & Toy Co./ Made in U.S.A." on dress tag, 20" h **$500**

Lori Martin, vinyl socket head, blue sleep eyes with real lashes, painted lower lashes, feathered brows, closed smiling mouth, rooted hair vinyl body jointed at waist, shoulders, hips, and ankles, orig tagged clothing, plaid shirt, jeans, vinyl boots with horses, marked "© Metro Goldwyn Mayer Inc./Mfg by/ Ideal Toy Corp/80" on back of head, "© Ideal Toy Corp./6-30-5" on back, "National Velvet's/Lori Martin/© Metro Goldwyn Mayer, Inc./All Rights Reserved" on shirt tag, 28" h **$550**

Jumeau

Bebe, bisque head, brown paper-

weight eyes, mauve eye shadow, closed mouth, pierced applied ears, orig red Jumeau earrings, imp DEPOSE E.9J, cork pate, orig blonde mohair wig, jointed straight wrist, eight-ball composition body marked "Jumeau Medaille d'Or," vintage commercial dress of aqua satin and ecru silk faille, brown leather shoes, marked "E.J., France," tiny red age line side of nose, c1885, 20" h **$5,475**

Bebe Soleil box, bisque socket head, blue paperweight eyes, feathered brows, painted upper and lower lashes, open mouth, accented lips, six upper teeth, human-hair wig, jointed wood and composition French body, dressed in factory chemise pants, "Tete Jumeau" stamped in red, "9" incised on back of head, "Bebe due Bon Marche" partial paper label on lower back, "10700" written upside down on upper back, "S.F.B. J. Paris Bebe Soleil Yeux Mobiles Formes Naturelles Entierement Articule" on label on end of box, 2" hairline on right side of forehead, body finish flaking or loose in places, wear on edges of feet, at joints and on hands, box bottom repaired, lid missing, 23" h Jumeau **$1,400**

K*R, bisque head, blue eyes, open mouth, brown hair, jointed composition body, marks: K*R, Simon & Halbig 126; 20" h, **$450.**
Photo courtesy of Joy Luke Auctions

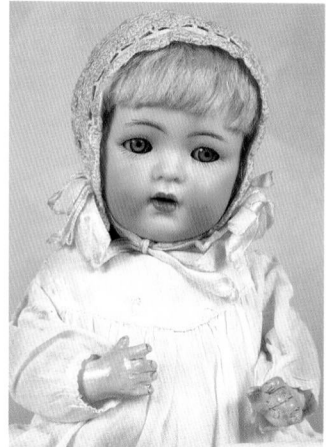

K*R 121 Baby, bisque socket head, blue sleep eyes, deep dimples, open mouth, original mohair wig, composition body, marks: K*R//Simon & Halbig//121 on head; hands repainted, tiny rub on left side of head, 11", **$360.**
Photo courtesy of McMasters Harris Auction Co.

K*R 128 Baby, bisque socket head, brown sleep eyes, open mouth, wobble tongue, composition body, original wig, antique clothing, marks: K*R//Simon & Halbig//128//56 on head; tiny wig pulls, 23", **$700.**
Photo courtesy of McMasters Harris Auction Co.

Bisque socket head, brown paperweight eyes, heavy feathered brows, painted upper and lower lashes, open mouth, six upper teeth, pierced ears, human-hair wig over rock pate, jointed wood and composition French body with jointed wrists, working mama/papa pull strings, old white child's dress, underclothing, socks, black child's shoes, marked "14" on back of head, 35" h **$1,400**

Bisque socket head, paperweight eyes, multi-stroke brows, painted upper and lower lashes, open mouth, four upper teeth, pierced ears, orig mohair wig, orig pate, jointed wood and composition late French bodies, boy and girl doll dressed in orig ethnic costumes of Finistere Department of Brittany, France, marked "4" on back of heads, price for pr, 14" h **$2,000**

Great Ladies series, bisque socket head, blue paperweight eyes, single stroke brows, painted upper and lower lashes, closed mouth, orig mohair wig, five-pc composition body, painted flat black shoes, orig white brocade gown with gold "diamond" jewelry, orig underclothing, marked "221/3/0" on back of head, "fabrication/Jumeau/Paris/ Made in France" on front of paper tag, "Marie-Louise/2, Femme de/

Napoleon Ier/ Epogue 1810" hand written on back of paper tag, 9" h **$475**

Jutta, bisque socket head, brown sleep eyes, feathered brows, painted upper and lower lashes, open mouth, two upper teeth, spring tongue, replaced human-hair wig, composition baby body, navy blue sailor top, hat, shorts, red and white striped socks, leather baby shoes, marked "Jutta/1914/14 1/2" on back of head, cracks on both hands, left little finger missing, 1914 baby, 26" h **$800**

Poupee Peau, bisque socket head on bisque shoulder plate, cobalt blue set eyes, multi-stroke brows, painted upper and lower lashes, closed mouth, pierced ears, orig mohair wig in orig curls, kid lady body with gussets at elbows, hips, and knees, individually stitched fingers, possibly orig clothing, factory chemise as blouse, ecru silk skirt with purple flowers, lavender and white striped under skirt, half slip, pants, socks, and boots with elastic inserts in sides, unmarked, one boot heel missing, 16" h **$3,750**

Kamkins, girl, cloth, molded face with painted features, blue eyes, orig brown mohair wig, cloth body and limbs, blue cotton dress, orig undergarments, purple Kamkins stamp

mark on back of head, some soil and wear on face, early 20th C, 19" h **$1,150**

Kammer & Reinhardt (K*R)

100 baby, solid dome bisque socket head, painted blue eyes, single-stroke brows, open/closed mouth, molded and brush-stroked hair, bent limb composition baby body, possibly orig long baby dress, full slip half slip, diaper, undershirt, knit booties, long fleece coat, matching hat, marked "36/ K*R/100" on back of head, head perfect, orig body finish worn, 14" h **$275**

115A baby, bisque socket head, blue sleep eyes, feathered brows, painted upper and lower lashes, closed mouth, orig mohair wig, five-pc composition baby body, antique-style white baby dress, slip, lace-trimmed panties, eyelet bonnet, marked "1/K*R/Simon & Halbig/ 115A/30" on back of head, wear to orig finish, arms mostly repainted, touch-up around neck socket, on toes, and feet, 10" h **$1,300**

115/A character toddler, bisque head, brown sleep eyes, closed pouty mouth, reddish-blond caracul wig, side-jointed composition toddler body, red and green plush jester's costume, also orig pink gingham outfit, imp "K*R Simon & Halbig 115/A, 48," c1910, 19" h **$4,320**

Kestner 143, bisque socket head, brown sleep eyes, replaced mohair wig, open mouth, jointed wood and composition body, marks: B made in Germany//Germany 6//143 on head, Germany//0 on body; light rubs left cheek and upper lip, right hand and lower arm, thigh replaced, 14", $375.
Photo courtesy of McMasters Harris Auction Co.

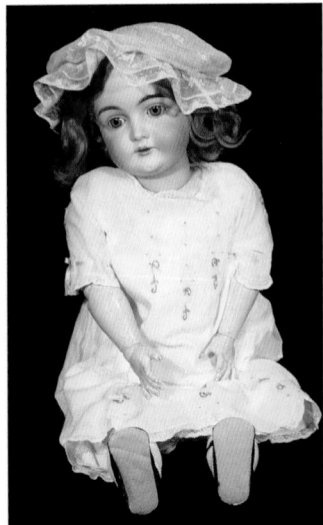

Kestner, bisque head, blue sleep eyes, open mouth, blonde hair, fully jointed composition body, marks: Made in Germany, L 1/2 15-1/2 146.; 30" h, $625.
Photo courtesy of Joy Luke Auctions.

Kestner

161, bisque socket head, brown sleep eyes, feathered brows, painted upper and lower lashes, open mouth, four upper teeth, replaced human-hair wig, orig plaster pate, jointed wood and composition Kestner body, ecru dress with red cross stitch trim, marked "F 1/2 Made in Germany 10 1/2/161" on back of head, "Germany 3" stamped in red on right rear hip, 20-1/2" h **$475**

164, bisque socket head, blue sleep eyes, molded and feathered brows, painted upper and lower lashes, open mouth, shapely accented lips, four upper teeth, skin wig, jointed wood and composition Kestner body, faded dark blue velvet sailor suit, white shirt, old socks and shoes, marked "M1/2 made in Germany 16 1/2/164" on back of head, "Excelsior/Germany/7" stamped in red on right lower back, body has orig finish with light wear, normal wear at joints, right finger repaired, 32" h **$1,200**

208, all bisque, stiff neck, brown sleep eyes, single-stroke brows, painted upper and lower lashes, open/closed mouth, orig mohair wig, all bisque body jointed at shoulders and hips, molded and painted white shirred socks and black one-strap shoes, marked "208/3" on back of head and on arms and legs at joints, "Made in Germany" round red stamp on back, "Baby Rose Germany" on round red label on tummy, orig box, 6" h **$300**

237, Hilda, bisque socket head, blue sleep eyes, feathered brows, painted upper and lower lashes, open mouth, two upper porcelain teeth, orig blond skin wig, composition Kestner baby body, white organdy baby dress, matching bonnet, marked "J Made in Germany 13/JD.K./237 ges gesch/N 1070" on back of head, 16" **$2,000**

257 baby, bisque socket head, brown sleep eyes, feathered brows, painted upper and lower lashes, open mouth, two upper teeth, antique mohair wig on old cardboard pate, composition baby body, new sailor romper, marked "Made in Germany/J.D.K./257/28" on back of head, 11" h **$350**

Kley & Hahn, 525Baby, solid dome bisque socket head, blue sleep eyes, feathered brows, painted upper and lower lashes, open-closed mouth, lightly molded and brush stroked hair, composition baby body, antique baby dress, marked "4/Germany/K&H (in banner)/525" on back of head, repainted, 11-1/2" h **$275**

Knickerbocker, Mickey Mouse, cloth swivel head, white facial, black oil-cloth pie eyes, large black nose, painted open/ closed smiling mouth with accent lines, black felt ears, unjointed black cloth body, orange hands with three fingers and a thumb, red oversized composition feet, black rubber tail, orig shorts with two buttons on front and back, some fading, 11" h **$650**

Konig & Wernicke, Germany, early 20th C

Character baby, bisque head, early 20th century, blue sleep eyes, open mouth, two upper teeth, wobble tongue, orig brown mohair wig, bent limb composition baby body, red circle stamp "K & W," minor wear, 27" l, 16-1/2" d head circumference ... **$815**

Character toddler, bisque head, brown sleep eyes, open mouth, two upper teeth, tongue, orig dark brown mohair wig, fully articulated side hip-joint composition toddler body marked "Made in Germany," period cotton sailor outfit, blue pants, white overblouse, white fabric shoes, imp "Made in Germany 99/7," some wear to finish of limbs, repaint to hands, 17" h **$750**

Kruse, Kathe

Kuhnlenz, Gebruder, 38 Girl, bisque shoulder head, blue threaded paperweight eyes, feathered brows, painted upper and lower lashes, closed mouth, human hair, cloth Goldsmith body, red corset, brown leather lower arms, red lower legs with red kid boots, silver two-pc outfit made from antique fabrics, marked "G.K." on back of head, "38-27.5" at bottom of shoulder plate, 22" h **$250**

Schlenkerchen, all-stockinette, pressed and oil-painted double-seam head, painted features, brown hair, shaded brown painted eyes with eyeliner, light upper lashes, closed mouth in smiling expression, cloth neck ring, stockinette covered, padded armature frame body, mitten hands, rounded feet, unlaundered off-white undergarments, soles stamped "Kathe Kruse, Germany," paint rub tip of nose, soil, c1922, 13" h **$5,475**

Sand Baby, hand painted head, painted blue eyes, single stroke brows, closed mouth, painted hair, stockinette covered body jointed at shoul-

Gebruder Kuhnlenz 34, two dolls, dark brown bisque socket heads, set no pupil dark eyes, open mouths, original curly mohair wigs, crude five piece composition bodies, black molded and painted shoes, orange molded and painted stockings, marks: 34-13 and 34-16 on heads; small doll redressed in antique fabric clothing, large doll may have original dress, light touch up on small doll's legs, 6" (small) 8-1/2" (large), $950.

Photo courtesy of McMasters Harris Auction Co.

Madame Alexander, "Margaret O'Brien" doll, composition, blue sleep eyes, painted features, jointed body, 21" h, $175.

Photo courtesy of Joy Luke Auctions

ders, loose joints at hips, formed navel, "Kathe Kruse" stamped on bottom of left foot, incomplete number stamped on bottom of right foot, 21" h **$550**

Lenci

Girl, pressed felt swivel head, painted brown side-glancing eyes, painted upper lashes, closed mouth with two-tone lips, orig mohair wig, cloth torso, felt limbs, orig pink felt dress with blue trim, blue felt coat with matching hat, orig underclothing, socks, blue felt shoes, marked "2" on bottom of right foot, "Lenci/Made in Italy" on cloth label inside coat, 12" h **$400**

Lady, "Mary Pickford" felt face, light gray-blue painted eyes to right, long nose, closed mouth, long bare felt arms, classic Lenci fingers, white and green organdy summer frock, felt wide-brimmed bonnet, all trimmed with felt flowers and ruffles, silk stockings, pale green felt

shoes with felt flowers, orig Lenci tag sewn to dress, small stain back of skirt, c1930, 28" h **$1,840**

Mascotte, pressed felt swivel head, painted brown "surprise" eyes to side, single-stroke brows, painted upper lashes, open-closed two-tone mouth, orig red mohair wig in braids, cloth body with felt arms and legs, orig blue and white polka dot nylon dress, white felt collar, red felt belt, orig one-pc underwear, red felt sandals, light display soil, front of dress faded, 8" h **$150**

Limbach, character, bisque socket head, blue sleep eyes with real lashes, painted upper and lower lashes, open mouth, accented lips, six upper teeth, human-hair wig, jointed wood and composition body, new white lacy dress, underclothing, new socks and shoes, marked "W/crown/17 72 in shamrock/Limbach" on back of head, two right fingers and three left fingers repaired, finish flaking around neck

socket of body, cracks in finish on side seams of torso, wear at all sockets on torso, 23" h **$625**

Madame Alexander

Marme from the Little Women Series, hard plastic head and body, gray sleep eyes, closed mouth, dark brown wig in snood, gray and pink print dress with orig tags, organdy shawl, shoes and socks, c1955, 14" h **$200**

Special Girl, composition head, composition shoulder plate, blue sleep eyes with real lashes, painted lower lashes, feathered brows, closed mouth, orig human-hair wig in orig set, cloth torso with composition arms and legs, orig pale blue taffeta dress with lace and ribbon trim, attached blue panties, orig socks and center snap shoes, "Madame/Alexander/New York U.S.A." on dress tag, 23" h **$750**

Sweet Violet, hard plastic head, blue sleep eyes with real lashes, painted lower lashes, feathered brows, closed mouth, orig synthetic wig, hard plastic body jointed at shoulders, elbows, wrists, hips, and knees, walking mechanism, orig tagged blue cotton dress, underclothing, flowered bonnet, white gloves, black side-snap shoes, carrying orig pink Alexander hat box, marked "Alexander" on back of head, "Madame Alexander/All Rights Reserved/New York, U.S.A.," unplayed-with condition, comb and curlers missing, c1954, 18" h **$1,700**

Menjou, Adolph, composition shoulder head, painted brown eyes with accent line, molded monocle on right eye, feathered brows, molded and painted mustache, open-closed mouth, seven upper teeth, molded white shirt collar with hole, presumably for a tie, molded and painted hair, excelsior-stuffed cloth body with long limbs, composition white hands as gloves, composition lower legs as socks and shoes, orig black two-pc suit with satin lapels, 32" h **$725**

Motschmann-style, china, flange swivel head, painted blue eyes, single strike brows, closed mouth, molded and painted hair in "Alice" hairstyle, molded hair band, Taufling body, papier-mâché shoulder plate and hip section, china lower arms and legs, molded and painted boots, six painted side buttons, possibly orig homemade white dress, short chemise, leg covers, 14-1/2" h **$2,500**

Parian, untinted bisque shoulder head, painted blue eyes with red accent line, single stroke brows, closed mouth, pierced ears, molded and painted café au lait hair, molded blue tiara trimmed with gold, molded braid across top, on lower sides, and down middle of back of head, old cloth body with red leather boots as part of leg, new arms by Emma Clear, white dotted Swiss and lace dress, antique underclothing, unmarked, old repair to tiara, body aged, 24" h **$1,900**

Petzold, Dora, composition head, painted blue eyes with eye shadow, single-stroke brows, accented nostrils, closed mouth, orig mohair wig, stockinette body stitch-jointed at shoulders and hips, mitten-type hands with stitched fingers, possibly orig white velvet dress with embroidery and lace trim, white teddy, orig socks and marked shoes, marked with girl in circle, "D P/7/7/0" on back of head, girl in circle with "D P" on bottom of shoes, 16-1/2" h **$275**

Poupee Bois, bisque socket head, bisque shoulder plate, pale blue threaded paperweight eyes, feathered brows, painted upper and lower lashes, closed mouth, pierced ears, orig human hair wig, wooden fashion body articulated at shoulders, elbows, wrists, hips, and knees, swivel joint on upper arms and upper legs, nicely redressed with antique fabric and lace, possibly orig stockings and high button boots, marked "4" on back of head, 17-1/2" h **$4,400**

Poupee Raynal, pressed felt swivel head, painted blue eyes, single-stroke brows, painted upper lashes, closed mouth with three-tone lips, orig mohair wig in orig set, five-pc cloth body with stitched fingers, orig light blue organdy dress with pink flower appliqués, matching hat, orig teddy, blue organdy slip, socks, white leather shoes, "Paris" typed on piece of paper pinned to back, unplayed-with condition, 19" h **$725**

Putnam, Grace

Bye-Lo Baby, solid dome bisque swivel head, tiny blue sleep eyes, softly blushed brows, painted upper and lower lashes, closed mouth, lightly molded and painted hair, all bisque baby body jointed at shoulders and

hips, orig knit pink and white two-pc baby outfit with matching cap, marked "Bye-Lo Baby/©/ Germany/G.S. Putnam" on label on chest, "6-20/Copr. By/Grace S. Putnam/Germany" incised on back, "6-20" on hips and right arms, "20" on left arm, chip on right back of neck edge of head, minor firing line behind left ear, 8" h **$525**

Head circumference Bye-Lo Baby, solid dome bisque flange head, blue sleep eyes, softly blushed brows, painted upper and lower lashes, closed mouth, lightly molded and painted hair, cloth body with celluloid hands and "frog" legs, Bye-Lo baby gown, slip, orig flannel undershirt and diaper, cotton stockings, marked "Copr. by/Grace S. Putnam/Made in Germany" on back of head, "Bye-Lo Baby/ Pat Appl'd For/ Copy/by/Grace/ Storey/Putnman" stamped on front of body, 11" h, 10" d **$200**

Head circumference, Bye-Lo Baby, solid dome bisque flange head, blue sleep eyes, softly blushed brows, painted upper and lower lashes, closed mouth, lightly molded and painted hair, cloth body with "frog" legs, celluloid hands, antique baby christening dress, long slip, underskirt, socks and booties, marked "Copr. By/Grace S. Putnam/ Made in Germany" on back of head, partial Bye-Lo Baby stamp on front of torso, body aged and soiled, right hand missing two fingers, 20" h, 16-1/2" d **$250**

Recknagel, character, bisque socket head, tiny painted blue squinty eyes, single-stroke brows, open-closed mouth, five painted upper teeth, four lower teeth, molded tongue, molded and painted short hair with molded pink bow, five-pc chubby composition body, crude unpainted torso, molded and painted socks and shoes, redressed in pink lace-trimmed dress, matching hair ribbon, lace pants, marked "R 57 A/8/0" on back of head, light dust in bisque, light wear on orig body finish, 9" h **$675**

Redmond, Kathy

Eleanor Roosevelt, bisque shoulder head, well modeled painted features, molded and painted hair and necklace, cloth body, bisque arms and lower legs with molded black shoes, orig purple two-pc suit,

marked "Eleanor Roosevelt R (in cat)" on back of shoulder plate, 13" h **$300**

Mary Todd Lincoln, bisque shoulder head, painted blue eyes, painted brows, closed mouth, molded brown hair, molded white roses and green leaves, molded white snood with gold highlights, molded necklace and earrings, molded white bisque ruffle with single rose on shoulder plate, cloth body, bisque lower arms and legs, black silk dress with blue accents, orig underclothing, marked "Mary Lincoln/R (in cat) 17" on back of shoulder plate, 14" h **$175**

S & Q, 201 baby, bisque socket head, set brown eyes, feathered brows, painted upper and lower lashes, open mouth, two upper teeth, molded tongue, mohair wig, composition baby body, navy blue velvet boy's shorts, jacket, and matching hat, white shirt, stockings, white baby shoes, marked "+ 201 SQ" (superimposed) "Germany 14" on back of head, 28" h **$700**

Schmidt, Bruno, 2042, solid dome bisque socket head, painted brown eyes, two-tone single-stroke brows, open-closed mouth, accented lips, brush-stroked hair, jointed composition body, redressed in maroon velour two-pc suit, ecru satin shirt with lace trim, black cotton socks, new black shoes, marked "5/B.S.W. in heart/2042" on back of head, "Handwerck" stamped in red in middle of lower back, 22" h **$1,500**

Schmidt, Franz, 1285 baby, solid dome bisque socket head, blue sleep eyes, softly blushed brows, painted upper and lower lashes, closed mouth, molded and painted hair, composition baby body, smocked baby dress, marked "1285/32/F S & C/Made in Germany" on back of head, 15" h **$575**

Schoenau & Hoffmeister, Masquerade set, bisque socket head, set brown eyes, single stroke brows, painted upper and lower lashes, open mouth, four upper teeth, antique mohair wig, five-pc composition body, walking mechanism, orig pastel dress with pale green ribbon trim, orig gauze-type underclothing, socks, leather shoes with black pompons, marked "4000 5/0/S PB (in star) H 10" on back of head, "F" on back of legs, "Germa-

ny" stamped on bottom of shoes, tied in red cardboard box with two lace-trimmed compartments, blue Pierrot costume brimmed with black, white, and ruffled collar, matching cone-shaped hat, black face mask with lace trim, light rub on nose, 13-1/2" h
....**$525**

Schoenhut

19/308 girl, wooden socket head, brown intaglio eyes, feathered brow, closed mouth with excellent modeling, orig mohair wig, spring-jointed wooden body jointed at shoulders, elbows, wrists, hips, knees, and ankles, white dress with red dots in Schoenhut style, slip, knit union suit, replaced cotton socks and red flocked shoes, marked "Schoenhut Doll/Pat. Jan 17th 1911/ U.S.A." on oval label on back, very light touch up on left cheek, nose, edge of lips, craze lines on front of lower neck, light crazing on right cheek and outer corner of left eye, body has "suntan" color with normal wear at joints and light overall soil, few flakes off ankles, 19" h **$450**

Toddler, wood socket head, painted blue eyes, single-stroke brows, closed mouth, orig mohair wig, wooden body jointed at shoulders, elbows, wrists, hips, knees, and ankles, redressed, marked "Schoenhut/Doll/Pat Jan 17th 1911/USA" on oval label on back, "H. C. Schoenhut/©/ (illegible)" on round label on back of head, light wear on finish of face, rub on nose, wear on toes, 11" h **$425**

Schoenhut & Hoffmeister, character baby, bisque head, blue sleep eyes with lashes, hint of smile, open mouth, two upper teeth, pointy chin, orig dark brown mohair wig, bent-limb composition baby body, white cotton slip, imp "SHPB" in a star, "5, Germany," white spot back of head at rim, early 20th C, 20" h, 13-1/2" d head circumference
....**$325**

S.F.B.J.

236 toddler, bisque socket head, blue sleep eyes, feathered brows, painted lower lashes, open/closed mouth, two upper teeth, orig mohair hair, jointed wood and composition toddler body, antique dark purple satin two pc outfit, matching cap, replaced socks and shoes, marked "S.F.B.J./ 236/Paris/8"

on back of head, cracks in wood on lower half right arm, 18" h
....**$550**

301, bisque socket head, blue sleep eyes with real lashes, open mouth, four painted upper teeth, pierced ears, human-hair wig, jointed wood and composition body, jointed wrists, antique white lace dress and bonnet, marked "S.F.B.J./301/ Paris/1" on back of head, "2" incised between shoulders, "2" on bottom of feet, good original body finish, 11" h
....**$600**

Simon & Halbig

1428, bisque socket head, blue sleep eyes, single stroke brows, tiny painted upper lashes, open/closed mouth, replaced synthetic wig, jointed wood and composition body, new red velvet two pc boy's outfit, socks, new brown boots, marked "1428/4" on back of head, lower leg repainted, 12-1/2" h
....**$1,000**

Schoenhut 19/308, wooden socket head, blue intaglio eyes, closed pouty mouth, replaced mohair wig, fu.lly jointed body with spring joints, original union suit and leather shoes, marks: Schoenhut Doll// Pat. Jan. 17th 1911//U.S.A. on oval label on back; tiny nose flake, light lip rubs, small flake lower lip, 19", **$1,300.**
Photo courtesy of McMasters Harris Auction Co.

Simon & Halbig, 1299, bisque head, blue sleep eyes, missing real lashes, original mohair wig, open mouth, working crier, jointed wood and composition body, antique clothing, marks: 1299// Simon & Halbig//S&H//7 on head, Heinrich Handwerk//Germany//1 oneft hip; flake on left side of head, minor finger damage, 18", **$550.**

Photo courtesy of McMasters Harris Auction Co.

Simon & Halbig, A. Hulls, bisque head, blue sleep eyes, open mouth, jointed composition body, marks: A. HW Germany 156/21/20; 9" h, **$325.**

Photo courtesy of Joy Luke Auctions

1039, bisque socket head, bisque shoulder plate, blue flirty eyes, real lashes, feathered brow, painted lower lashes, open mouth with outlined lips, four upper teeth, pierced ears, orig mohair wig, orig white glass beads at neck joint, kid body, bisque lower arms, gussets at elbows, hips, and knees, cloth lower legs, pink silk two-pc outfit made from old fabric, antique underclothing, new socks and shoes, marked "S.H. 1038/DEP/6/Germany" on back of head, inherent firing line behind right ear, head loose on shoulder plate, normal aging and light soil to body, 18" h **$375**

1039, bisque socket heat, blue flirty eyes, real lashes, molded and feathered brows, painted upper and lower lashes, open mouth with accented lips, four upper teeth, pierced ears, human-hair wig, jointed wood and composition French type body, torso cut for working crier, both arms

with kiss-throwing mechanism, knees jointed, both legs with walking mechanism, rose French-style new dress, antique underclothing, replaced socks and shoes, marked "1039/German/Simon & Halbig/S & H/10-1/2" on back of head, 22" h **$500**

Terri Lee

Buddy Lee, hard plastic head with stiff neck, eyes painted to side, single-stroke brows, painted upper lashes, closed mouth, molded and painted hair, hard plastic body jointed at shoulders only, molded and painted black boots, orig Phillips 66 suit with labeled shirt and pants, black imitation-leather belt, marked "Buddy Lee" on back, "Union Made/Lee/ Sanforized" on label on back of pants, "Phillips/66" on label on front of shirt, 12" h **$215**

Terri Lee, hard plastic head, oversized painted brown eyes, single-stroke brows, long painted upper and lower lashes, closed mouth, synthetic wig, five-pc hard plastic body jointed at shoulders and hips, orig yellow Evening Formal, #3570D orig socks and shoes, long white coat, #3690A, matching hat, marked "Terri Lee" on back, Terri Lee tag on coat, 1954, 16" h **$475**

Connie Lynn, hard plastic head, blue sleep eyes with real lashes, single-stroke brows, painted lower lashes at corners of eyes, closed mouth, orig skin wig, hard plastic baby body, orig two-pc pink baby outfit, plastic panties, orig socks and white baby shoes, Terri Lee Nursery Registration Form and three Admission Cards to Terri Lee Hospital, Connie Lynn tag on clothing, orig box, unplayed with condition, 18" .. **$625**

Unis France, 60, bisque socket head, light blue sleep eyes, single stroke brows, open mouth with 4 upper teeth, orig mohair wig, crude five-pc composition body, dressed in orig ethnic costume of Pont-l'Abbe in Brittany, France, marked "Unis/France/71 60 140/11/0" on back of head, 9-1/2" h **$175**

Vogue

Toddles, Hansel and Gretel, composition heads, painted blue eyes looking to the right, single stroke brows, painted upper lashes, closed mouths, orig mohair wigs, five-pc composition body, orig Tyrolean outfits, marked "Vogue" on back of head, orig clothing labels, orig boxes, price for pr, 7-1/2" h **$500**

Toddles, Nurse, composition, painted blue eyes looking to right, single stroke brows, painted upper lashes, closed mouth, orig mohair wig, body jointed at shoulders and hips, orig white nurse's outfit and hat, oil-cloth snap shoes, marked "Vogue" on head, "Doll Co." on back, orig gold label on dress, 7-1/2" h **$475**

Wax, unmarked, reinforced poured-wax shoulder head, set blue glass eyes, multi-stroke brows, painted upper and lower lashes, closed smiling mouth, pierced ears, orig mohair wig, cloth body, wax-over composition lower arms and lower legs, antique red/white gingham dress, orig underclothing, socks and leather shoes, color worn on lips, eyelashes and brows, minor crack in wax on right front of shoulder plate, cracks on right leg, body is aged, soiled, and repaired, 18" h **$475**

Wislizenus, Adolph, girl, bisque socket head, brown sleep eyes, feathered brows, painted upper and lower lashes, open mouth, accented lips, pierced ears, replaced human-hair wig, jointed composition body with orig finish, possibly orig clothing, white low-waisted dress, antique underclothing, socks and shoes marked "8," blue velvet coat and matching hat with ribbon trim, marked "8/ A.W./ Germany/6" on back of head, "46" stamped in red on bottom of feet, 18" h..**$550**

Simon & Halbig, 1159 Lady, bisque socket head, blue sleep eyes, real lash remnants, painted lower lashes, open mouth, original mohair wig, pierced ears, jointed wood and composition body, original clothing, marked: 1159//S &H//DEP//7 on head, Heinrich Handwerk//Germany//1 on body 1//H.H. (in heart) on shoes; minor wig pulls, 19", **$1,400.**
Photo courtesy of McMasters Harris Auction Co.

GAME BOARDS

History: Wooden game boards have a long history and were some of the first toys early Americans enjoyed. Games such as checkers, chess, and others were easy to play and required only simple markers or playing pieces. Most were handmade, but some machine-made examples exist.

Game boards can be found in interesting color combinations. Some include small drawers to hold the playing pieces. Others have an interesting molding or frame. Look for signs of use from long hours of enjoyment.

Today, game boards are popular with game collectors, folk art collectors, and decorators because of their interesting forms.

Reproduction Alert.

Checkerboard

Blue and white, yellowed varnish, New England, 19th C, 16" sq...**$3,335**

Incised checkerboard under glass, red, lime green, yellow, and black, reverse painted in red, white, and blue, framed, America, minor paint wear, 20th C, 21-1/2" x 17-1/2" **$650**

Oak and mahogany squares, galleried edge with two reserves on sides with sliding lid compartments to hold checkers, two sets of checkers, one round, one square, minor wear, light alligatoring to old black paint on lids and gallery, 14" w, 20-1/4" h **$330**

Checkerboard, America, inlaid wood, rectangle, alternating light and dark wood inlaid squares, contrasting rayed corners and borders, ebony pegged frame with inlaid triangle decoration, age crack, 19th C, 18-1/2" x 24", **$300.**
Photo courtesy of Skinner, Inc.

Painted and gilt dec, molded edge, reverse marked "Saco Lodge No. 2," Saco, Maine, 19th C, 20" w, 18-3/4" h **$5,175**

Painted black and salmon, New England, 19th C, 15-1/4" sq .. **$2,300**

Painted black and white, tan colored ground, sgd "F. Smith," Pennsylvania, c1870, 12-1/2" w, 12-3/4" h **$1,955**

Painted green and white, unfinished, inscribed on reverse, late 19th/early 20th C, 17" w, 16" h **$460**

Painted green and yellow, paint imperfections, late 19th C, 10-1/2" w, 19-1/2" h **$1,955**

Painted hunter green and iron red, black frame, yellow grain paint on reverse, America, minor paint wear, 19th C, 13-7/8" w, 13-3/4" h **$1,380**

Painted red and black, yellow dec, Michigan, c1880, 18" w, 21" h .. **$2,415**

Painted red and white checkerboard, orig cherry frame, Newburyport, Massachusetts, c1850, 16" w, 17-1/2" h **$980**

Painted slate, incised geometric design, hand painted to resemble hardstones, shades of marbleized green and red, solid dark red checks, shaded yellow ground, mottled black border, New England, minor paint wear at margins, late 19th C, 19-1/2" sq **$1,645**

Painted yellow and black, green detailing, c1880, 18-1/2" sq **$5,465**

Pine, breadboard ends, additional strip on one side, old red and black checkerboard slightly off center, varnished, age split, minor edge wear, 17-1/2" x 24" **$200**

Poplar, old dry paint with gold and black blocks surrounded by red borders, black ground, red roundels with gold stars in each corner, reverse side painted red, breadboard ends with wire nails, 25" x 15" **$825**

Double-sided

Mustard and black, 14" sq **$975**

Obverse with Parcheesi, painted red, teal, orange, and green, checkerboard on reverse with orange, black, and yellow paint, paint wear to obverse at edges, c1900, 17" sq **$2,530**

Painted, applied molding, red and black checkerboard outlined in yellow on one side, Ouija board with black stenciled lettering and symbols on reverse, America, late 19th C, 21-1/4" x 21-1/2" **$470**

Painted, one side with Parcheesi game and primitive scene of hunter returning home in center, checkerboard on other side, small plated feet at corners, age split, 18-1/2" sq **$4,485**

Painted apple green, black, and red, checkerboard on obverse, backgammon on reverse, game piece compartments, America, c1870-80, 23" w, 17-1/4" h **$3,750**

Painted apple green, brown, and black, obverse with checkerboard, reverse with snake-motif game, America, mid-19th C, 12-1/4" w, 12" h **$36,800**

Painted black and red, obverse with checkerboard, reverse with Old Mill, applied molded edge, New England, c1850-70, 14-1/4" sq **$4,890**

Painted deep blue-green, red and black, checkerboard on obverse, backgammon on reverse, America, 19th C, 14-7/8" w, 15-7/8" h **$2,530**

Painted mustard, red, and green, checkerboard on obverse, backgammon on reverse, America, 19th C, 15" w, 16" h **$3,335**

Painted pine, brown and black checkerboard on one side, painted brown Old Mill game inscribed on reverse, two sliding panel compartments, New York State, early 19th C, 7-1/4" w, 7" h **$1,150**

Painted wood, sq board with applied frame, one side checkerboard painted yellow, black, green, and red, other side backgammon game in the same colors, America, wear, 19th C, 20-1/8" x 20-1/2" **$1,645**

Folding

Painted avocado green, colorful raised segmented tracks, opens for storage, wear, mid-20th C, 12-1/2" w, 31" h **$575**

Parcheesi

Folding, painted American flag and spade, heart, diamond, and club motifs, Massachusetts, minor paint imperfections, c1870, 18-1/2" sq **$46,000**

Folding, painted green, white, black, and yellow, varied geometric designs on game corners, America, 19th C, 19-1/2" sq **$2,875**

Folding, patriotic red, white, and blue stars and dec, New England, late 19th C, 18" w, 17-3/4" h **$4,350**

Painted, center rosette, bull's eye corners, attributed to Maine, wear, 19th C, 25" w, 24-1/2" h **$4,600**

Painted red, yellow, and green, New England, 1870-80, 27-1/2" w, 27" h **$5,750**

Parcheesi, rectangular, white, red, black, and green polychrome decoration, **$595.**

GAMES

History: Board games have been commercially produced in this country since at least 1822, and card games since the 1780s. However, it was not until the 1840s that large numbers of games were produced that survive to this day. The W. & S. B. Ives Company produced many board and card games in the 1840s and 1850s. Milton Bradley and McLoughlin Brothers became major producers of games starting in the 1860s, followed by Parker Brothers in the 1880s. Other major producers of games in this period were Bliss, Chaffee and Selchow, Selchow and Righter, and Singer.

Today, most games from the 19th century are rare and highly collectible, primarily because of their spectacular lithography. McLoughlin and Bliss command a premium because of the rarity, quality of materials, and the extraordinary art that was created to grace the covers and boards of their games.

In the 20th century, Milton Bradley, Selchow and Righter, and Parker Brothers became the primary manufacturers of boxed games. They have all now been absorbed by toy giant Hasbro Corporation. Other noteworthy producers were All-Fair, Pressman, and Transogram, all of which are no longer in business. Today, the hottest part of the game collecting market is in rare character games from the 1960s. Parker Brothers and All-Fair games from the 1920s to 1940s also have some excellent lithography and are highly collectible.

Additional Listings: See *Warman's Americana & Collectibles.*

Notes: While people collect games for many reasons, it is strong graphic images that bring the highest prices. Games collected because they are fun to play or for nostalgic reasons are still collectible, but will not bring high prices. Also, game collectors are not interested in common and "public domain" games such as checkers, tiddlywinks, Authors, Anagrams, Jackstraws, Rook, Pit, Flinch, and Peter Coodles. The game market today is characterized by fairly stable prices for ordinary items, increasing discrimination for grades of condition, and continually rising prices for rare material in excellent condition. Whether you are a dealer or collector, be careful to buy games in good condition. Avoid games with taped or split corners or other box damage. Games made after about 1950 are difficult to sell unless they are complete and in excellent condition. As games get older, there is a forgiveness factor for condition and completeness that increases with age.

These listings are for games that are complete and in excellent condition. Be sure the game you're looking to price is the same as the one described in the listing. The 19th century makers routinely published the same title on several different versions of the game, varying in size and graphics. Dimensions listed here are rounded to the nearest half inch.

Bull in a China Shop, Milton Bradley, 1937.............................**$100**

Chiromagia Game, McLoughlin, three answer sheets, two question discs, lid missing **$100**

Clue, Parker Brothers, separate board and pieces box, c1949 ....**$25**

Dixie Pollyana, Parker Brothers, all wooden pcs, four orig dice and dice-cups, c1952, 8" x 18"...................**$100**

Elsie and Her Family, Selchow & Righter Co., 1941, 12-1/2" x 14-1/2" x 1-1/2"...**$200**

Fish Pond, McLoughlin Bros., children on cover, c1898, 8" x 18" **$125**

Flying the United States Air Mail Game, Parker Bros, 17" x 27-1/2" playing board, orig playing pcs, deck of cards, 1929 copyright, 1-1/2" x 14-1/2" x 18" box **$55**

Game of Billy Possum, c1910, 8" x 15"...**$600**

Game of Bo Peep, J.H. Singer, 8-1/2" x 14"..**$275**

Game of Snow White and the Seven Dwarfs, The, Milton Bradley, Walt Disney Enterprises, 1937 .....**$100**

Game of the Wizard of Oz, The, Whitman, c1939, 7" x 13-1/2" **$300**

Hi Ho Silhouette Game, 1932 ...**$30**

Limited Mail and Express Game, The, Parker Brothers, metal train playing pieces, c1894, 14" x 21" ..**$250**

Lone Ranger Hi Yo Silver Game, Parker Brothers, 1938..................**$200**

Mansion of Happiness, The, W. & S. B. Ives, c1843 ....**$950**

Mickey Mantle's Big League Baseball Game, Gardner Games **$195**

Monopoly, Parker Brothers, white box edition #9, metal playing pieces and embossed hotels, c1935 ....**$150**

Monopoly, Parker Brothers, separate board and pieces box, 1946 Popular

Edition...**$25**

Motorcycle Game, Milton Bradley, c1905, 9" x 9" **$250**

New Board Game of the American Revolution, Lorenzo Borge, colored scenes and events, 1844, 18-1/2" w opened.......................**$690**

One Two, Button Your Shoe, Master Toy Company, 11" x 12" **$145**

Peter Coddles Trip to New York, Milton Bradley, orig instruction sheet, 6" x 8-1/2"...................................**$65**

Radio Amateur Hour Game, 10" x 13"...**$145**

Strange Game of Forbidden Fruit, Parker Brothers, c1900, 4" x 5-1/2" **$35**

Truth or Consequences, Gabriel, c1955, 14" x 19-1/2"......................**$75**

Uncle Sam's Mail, Milton Bradley, c1910, 16-1/4" x 15" x 1-1/4" **$115**

Young America Target, Parker Bros **$75**

Elsie and Her Family, Selchow & Righter, N.Y. #204, copyright 1941, 12-1/2" x 14" x 1-1/2" deep colorful red box with Elsie, Elmer and Beulah on lid, **$65.**
Photo courtesy of Hake's Americana & Collectibles.

Junior Combination Board, Milton Bradley, c1905, 16-1/2" square two-sided board, **$85.**

Lindy The Flying Game, Parker Bros., "Improved Edition," original box, **$225.**

SPACE TOYS

One of the hottest trends in the toy-collecting hobby surrounds space toys. The children of the *Lost in Space* generation are today's avid collectors—and the demand for extra-terrestrial treasures is being felt at toy shows, flea markets, and even antique malls. The variety of space heroes extends from comic strip favorites Buck Rogers and Flash Gordon to the post-WWII emergence of television and the popularity of characters like Tom Corbett and Buzz Corey. By the 1960s, *Lost in Space* and *Star Trek* captivated youthful imaginations, and we all know what happened to the popularity of space toys with the 1977 release of *Star Wars*!

Toy spaceships, space guns, and space-themed characters are earning devoted followings among toy collectors and their popularity seems to be spreading at "warp speed."

Buck Rogers

25th Century Police Patrol Rocket, tin wind-up, Marx, 1939, 12" l..............................**$950**

***Adventures of Buck Rogers* Book**, Whitman, 1934 ....**$100**

Battle Cruiser Rocket, two grooved wheels run along string, Tootsietoy, 1937 ....**$225**

Chemistry Set, beginners, Gropper, 1937 ....**$775**

***Cut Out Adventure* Book**, Coco-malt premium, 1933................**$3,500**

Figure, cast metal, gray, Tootsietoy, 1937 ....**$150**

Helmet XC-34, leather, Daisy, 1935 ....**$500**

Interplanetary Space Fleet Model Kit, six different kits, 1935.........**$200**

Punching Bag, balloon w/characters, Morton Salt, 1942...........................**$75**

Puzzle, space station scene, Milton Bradley, 1952 ....**$150**

Rubber Band Gun, advertising premium, 1930s **$75**

Satellite Pioneers Button, green or blue, 1958..**$50**

School Bag, suede cloth, 1935 ....**$100**

Sonic Ray Flashlight Gun, black, green, and yellow plastic wi/signal, Norton-Honer, 1955 ....**$150**

Super Scope Telescope, plastic telescope, Norton-Horner, 1955, 9" l .**$70**

Wristwatch, E. Ingraham, 1935..**$750**

XZ-35 Space Gun, blued metal ray gun, produces spark, Daisy, 1934, 7-1/2" l................................**$275**

XZ-44 Liquid Helium Water Gun, red and yellow or copper finish, Daisy, 1936, 7-1/4" l..............................**$500**

Captain Video

Game, Milton Bradley, 1952.........**$150**

Galaxy Spaceship Riding Toy, 1950s.................................**$425**

Rite-O-Lite Flashlight Gun, Power House Candy premium, 1950s, 3" l **$90**

Rocket Tank, Lido, 1952................**$95**

Space Port Play Set, tin, Superior, 1950s.................................**$430**

Flash Gordon

Air Ray Gun, pressed steel, air blaster, Budson, 1950s, 10" l **$350**

Arresting Ray Gun, Marx, 1939, 12" l..**$500**

Book Bag, 1950s, 12" w **$35**

Book, Flash Gordon and the Ape Men of Mor, Dell, 1942.....................**$150**

Hand Puppet, rubber head, 1950s **$145**

Paint Book, 1930s.......................**$125**

Pencil Box, 1951..........................**$150**

Signal Pistol, tin/pressed steel, siren sounds when trigger is pulled, green w/red trim, Marx, 1930s, 7" l **$600**

View-Master Set, viewer, 3 reels "In the Planet Mongo," 1976 ....**$15**

Lost in Space

Costume, silver space suit w/logo, Ben Cooper, 1965 ....**$150**

Helmet and Gun Set, blue and red plastic gun, child-size helmet, Remco, 1967 ....**$530**

Jupiter-2 Model Kit, Marusan/ Japanese, molded in green plastic, 1966, 6" l...............................**$650**

Puzzles, frame tray, Milton Bradley, 1966, 10x14".....................................**$65**

Robot, motorized w/blinking lights, Remco, 19666, 12" h **$365**

Trading Cards, 55 black and white cards, Topps, 1966.....................**$300**

Rocky Jones, Space Ranger

Coloring Book, Whitman, 1951 ....**$50**

Pin, Silvercup Bread premium, 1950s **$20**

Wristwatch, Ingraham, 1954......**$150**

Space Patrol

Atomic Pistol Flashlight Gun, plastic, Marx, 1950s **$160**

Badge, metal oval on card, 1950s..**$400**

Cosmic Glow Ring, red and blue, 1950s.................................**$900**

Cosmic Ray Gun, tin body w/plastic barrel, Ranger Steel Products, 1954, 9" l..............................**$90**

Drink Mixer, boxed, 1950s..........**$100**

Lost in Space 3-D Action Game, Remco, 1966, **$785.**

Interplanetary Space Patrol Credits Coins, different denominations $16

Non-Fall Space Patrol X-16, tin/plastic, blinking lights, Masudaya, 1950s...........$150

Periscope, paper w/mirrors, 1950s.$200

Rocket Lite Flashlight, Rayovac, 1950s...........$250

Space Binoculars, green plastic, logo on sides, Ralston Purina, 1950s.. $190

Wristwatch, w/Terra compass, 1950s $500

Star Trek

Captain Kirk, plastic figure w/cloth costume, Mego, 1975, 8" h $50

Colorforms Set, 1975 ....$20

Communicators, blue plastic walkie talkies, Mego, 1976...........$125

Controlled Space Flight, plastic Enterprise, battery-operated, Remco, 1976 ....$125

Enterprise Model Kit, from Star Trek: The Motion Picture, Mego/Grand Toys, 1980...........$100

Figurine Paint Set, Milton Bradley, 1979 ....$25

Flashlight, from Star Trek: The Motion Picture, Larami, 1979...........$10

Helmet, plastic w/sound and lights, Remco, 1976...........$80

Kirk Costume, Ben Cooper, 1975.. $35

Movie Viewer, red and black plastic, Chemtoy, 1967 ....$16

Needlepoint Kit, "Live Long and Prosper," Arista, 1980...........$23

Paint-By-Numbers Set, Hasbro, 1972 ....$35

Phaser, black plastic, battery operated, Remco, 1975...........$100

Puzzle, 150 pieces, Kirk, Spock, and McCoy, H.G. Toys, 1974...........$8

Spock Bank, plastic, Play Pal, 1975, 12" h $35

Spock Wristwatch, from Star Trek: The Motion Picture, Bradley, 1979 ....$30

Telescreen, plastic, battery operated target game, Mego, 1976...........$100

Tricorder, blue plastic tape recorder, Mego, 1976...........$135

Vulcan Shuttle Model Kit, from Star Trek III, Ertl, 1984 ....$20

Water Pistol, white plastic shaped like the Enterprise, Azarak-Hamway, 1976 ....$30

Star Wars

3-3/4" Figures, 1977-78

Boba Fett $19

C-3PO $11

Chewbacca $13

Darth Vader $14

Death Squad Commander $12

Death Star Droid...........$12

Greedo $20

Hammerhead $15

Han Solo $20

Jawa, cloth cape $20

Jawa, vinyl cape $250

Luke as X-Wing Pilot $15

Luke Skywalker...........$30

Luke w/Telescoping Lightsaber $185

Obi-Wan Kenobi...........$22

Power Droid $11

Princess Leia Organa...........$19

R2-D2 ....$18

R5-D4 ....$17

Sand People $13

Snaggletooth, red body $10

Stormtrooper $30

Walrus Man $15

12" Figures, 1978-79

Boba Fett $135

C-3PO $30

Chewbacca $50

Darth Vader $50

Han Solo $110

Jawa $55

Luke Skywalker...........$70

Obi-Wan Kenobi...........$75

Princess Leia Organa...........$85

R2-D2 ....$45

Stormtrooper $60

Creatures/Play Sets, 1977-78

Creature Cantina $25

Death Star Station $75

Droid Factory...........$50

Land of the Jawas $45

Patrol Dewback...........$25

Vehicles

Darth Vader's TIE Fighter...........$30

Imperial TIE Fighter $27

Imperial Troop Transport $20

Jawa Sandcrawler...........$220

Land Speeder $15

Millennium Falcon $80

X-Wing Fighter $20

Tom Corbett

Atomic Flashlight Pistol, "Tom Corbett Space Cadet" on handgrip, Marx, 1950s $300

Coloring Book, two versions, Saalfield, 1950s $40

Official Sparkling Space Gun, tin litho, Marx, 21" l...........$150

Polaris Wind-Up Spaceship, tin litho, blue and yellow, Marx, 1952, 12" l...........$375

Puzzle, frame tray, Saalfield, 1950s $30

School Bag, plastic/vinyl w/Tom's picture and rocketships on front, 1950s $55

Space Academy Play Set, large, plastic figures and vehicles, tin buildings, #7020, Marx, 1950s...........$550

Space Gun, light blue and black, sparks, 9-1/2" l...........$130

Space Patrol Rocket Lite, Rayovac, 1950s, **$350.**

Luke Skywalker as X-Wing Pilot is one of the original 12 Star Wars figures released by Kenner in 1977-78, **$15.**

TOYS, GENERAL

History: The first cast-iron toys began to appear in America shortly after the Civil War. Leading 19th-century manufacturers include Hubley, Dent, Kenton, and Schoenhut. In the first decades of the 20th century, additional manufacturers joined these earlier firms; Arcade produced quality cast-iron toys, Buddy L and Marx used pressed steel and tin, and Tootsietoy explored die-casting. George Brown and other manufacturers who did not sign or label their work made wooden toys.

Nuremberg, Germany, was the European center for the toy industry from the late 18th through the mid-20th centuries. Companies such as Lehman and Märklin produced high-quality toys.

Today's toy collectors have a wonderful assortment to choose from. Many specialize in one company, time period, or type of toy, etc. Whatever their motivation, collections bring joy. Individual collectors must decide how they feel about the condition of their toys, whether they prefer mint-in-the box or gently played with examples or perhaps even toys that have been played with extensively. Traditionally, the toys in better condition have retained their values more than those in played-with condition. Having the original box, instructions, and/or all the pieces, etc., adds greatly to the collectiblity, and therefore the value.

Toy collectors can find examples to add to their collections at most of the typical antique and collectibles marketplaces, from auctions to flea markets to great antique shows, like Atlantique City, and even shows and auctions that specialize only in toys. For a complete list of toy shows and auctions in your area, consult the Show Calendar section of *Toy Shop* magazine.

Additional Listings: Characters, Disneyana, and Dolls. Also see *Warman's Americana & Collectibles* and *Warman's Flea Market* for more examples. *Toys & Prices 2006* focuses on post-WWII toys, while *O'Brien's Collecting Toys 11th Edition* concentrates primarily on pre-WWII toys.

Notes: Every toy is collectible; the key is condition. Good working order is important when considering mechanical toys. Examples in this listing are considered to be at least in good condition, if not better, unless otherwise specified.

Adviser: Karen O'Brien

Arcade, USA

Auto, cast iron
  Chevrolet, sedan, 1925, 7" l **$650**
  DeSoto, sedan, painted gray, nickeled grill and bumper, decal on trunk reads "Sundial Shoes," rubber tires, 4" l **$325**
  Ford coupe, Model A, No. 106, rumble seat, 1928, 6-3/4" l **$400**
  Pontiac sedan, 1932, 6-1/2" l **$350**
Dump truck, cast iron, International Harvester, painted green, red chassis, yellow pressed steel dump body, 11-1/4" l **$600**
Fire trailer truck, red, blue fireman, detachable trailer, hose reel and ladder turntable, ladders missing, paint loss, 16" l **$450**
Ice truck, cast iron, Mack, railed open-bed body, rear platform, rubber tires, emb sides, painted blue, 6-7/8" l **$275**
Milk truck, cast iron, Borden's, painted green, classic milk bottle design, rubber tires **$1,200**
Pick-up truck, cast iron, "International" decals on door, painted bright yellow, black rubber tires, some rust on left side, 9-1/4" l **$500**
Racer, Bullet, cast iron, classic bullet-shaped body, painted red, nickeled

In 1941, Arcade released the No. 7100 International Dump Truck, **$1,250.**
Photo courtesy Tim Oei.

The Arnold Mac 700 Motorcycle is propelled by a wind-up motor, **$650.**
Photo courtesy Kent M. Comstock.

This Arcade Yellow Cab was released in 1932 and at auction, once brought **$62,000.**
Photo courtesy Bertoia Auctions.

Bing Yellow Taxi c1924, **$2,200.**
Photo courtesy Bob Smith.

The No. 201 "Ratchet" Dump Truck was produced from 1921-30, **$1,250.**
Photo courtesy Joe and Sharon Freed.

On top is the Buddy "L" Baggage Truck No. 203B that was manufactured from 1929-31, **$3,500;** *the bottom truck is the Buddy "L" Auto Wrecker No. 209 released from 1928-31,* **$4,500.**
Photo courtesy Bertoia Auctions.

driver and mechanic, side pipes, and disc wheels, emb "#9" on side **$500**

Stake truck
Chevrolet, 1925, 9" l **$950**
Ford Model T, 1927, 9" l **$700**
Mack, No. 246X, 1929, 12" l **$1,400**

Tank, cast iron, camouflage painting, large metal wheels, 7-1/4" l **$330**

Taxi, cast iron, painted blue, black trim, emb luggage rack, seated driver and passenger, rubber tires, 8-1/4" l
.... **$660**

Thresher, McCormick-Deering, gray and cream wheels, red lining, chromed chute and stacker, 12" l
.... **$320**

Tractor, cast iron
Farmall, "A", No. 7050, 1941, 7-1/2" l
.... **$475**
Fordson, No. 273, 1928, 3-7/8" l
.... **$125**
McCormick-Deering, No. 10-20, 1925, 6-3/4" l **$450**

Trolley, Greyhound, New York World's Fair, blue and orange, nickel driver, decals, three cars with tin-plate canopies, black tires, some chipping and scratching, 16" l
.... **$635**

Wrecker, cast iron
Ford Model T, 1927, 11" l **$750**
Mack, No. 255, 1930, 12-1/2" l .. **$1,900**
Plymouth, No. 1830, 1933, 4-3/4" l
.... **$450**

Arnold, USA

Motorcycle, civilian, litho tin wind-up, mkd "Made in US Zone Germany," tin wheels mkd "Union Cord," C.8+, 7-3/4" l **$450**

Ocean liner, twin funnels, white superstructure, black and red hull, tinplate, clockwork motor, lg, 13"
.... **$475**

Satellite, remote control, tin and plastic, orig box with graphics, C.9, 7" d
.... **$180**

Bing, Gebruder, Germany

Auto, tin, clockwork, center door model, black, seated driver, radiator cap ornament, spare tire on rear, 6-1/4" l **$400**

Garage, litho tin, double doors, extensive graphics, houses sedan and roadster **$800**

Limousine, litho tin wind-up, red, maroon and orange striping, orig driver, c1910, 5-1/4" l **$750**

Open tourer, four seater, litho tinplate, gray-green, black and yellow lining, red button seats, black wings, front steering, orange and gray wheels, twin lamps, windscreen frame, hand-brake operated clockwork motor, chauffeur missing, lamps detached, c1915, 12-1/2" l **$2,400**

Union ferry boat, hand-painted tin, clockwork, red hull, brown open deck, white deck housing, railing on side, window cut-outs on both sides, stack on roof, 12" l **$1,200**

Buddy L, USA

Airmail truck, black front, hood fenders, enc cab, red body and chassis, 1930, 24" l **$875**

Airplane, four-engine transport, monoplane, green wings, yellow fuselage and twin tails, 1949, 27" wingspan **$400**

Auto
Flivver coupe, black, red spoke wheels, aluminum tires, 1924, 11" l .. **$750**
Jr Camaro, metallic blue body, white racing stripes across hood, 1968, 9" l
.... **$75**

Cement mixer truck, red body, white side ladder, water tank, mixing drum, 1965, 15-1/2" l **$75**

Dump truck
Husky, yellow hood, chrome one-pc wraparound bumper, 1969, 14-1/2" l
.... **$100**

Hydraulic Construction, medium blue front, large green dumper, 1967, 15-1/4" l **$150**
Jr Dumper, avocado cab, tiltback dump section, 1969, 7-1/2" l **$35**
Utility, duo-tone slant design, red front, gray chassis, royal blue dump body, yellow seat, 1940, 25-1/2" l **$185**

Electric Emergency Unit wrecker, white pressed steel, rear hoist, paint wear and staining, 16-1/2" l **$245**

Express Line delivery truck, black pressed-steel, front steering and rear doors, 24" l **$750**

Fire truck
Aerial truck, red, nickel ladders, 1925, 39" l **$850**
Extension ladder, rider, duo-tone slant design, white front, red hood top, cab, and frame, red semi-trailer, white ladders, 1949, 32-1/2" l ... **$150**
Ladder truck, red, bright metal grille and headlights, two white ladders, 1939, 24" l **$300**

Greyhound bus, pressed steel, clockwork, bright blue and white, "Greyhound Lines" on sides, rubber tires, 16" l
.... **$325**

Outdoor railroad, No. 1000 4-6-2 locomotive and tender, No. 1001 caboose, No. 1003 tank, No. 1004 stock, No. 1005 coal cars (one with orig decal), 121-1/2" l, repainted
.... **$2,500**

Steam shovel, No. 220, black, red corrugated roof and base, cast wheels, boiler, decal and winch, surface rust, paint crazing on roof, 14" h **$115**

Telephone maintenance truck, No. 450, two-tone green, ladder, two poles, orig maker's box **$350**

Tractor

Husky, bright yellow body, large rear fenders, black engine block, 1966, 13" l **$80**

Ruff-n-Tuff, yellow grille, hood, and frame, black plastic engine block, 1971, 10-1/2" l **$50**

Wrecker, orig condition **$4,500**

This is the Chein Hercules Mack Motor Express Truck, **$1,450.**
Photo courtesy Bob Smith.

This 1974 release from Corgi is a Citroen SM, #284, **$40.**
Photo courtesy Karen O'Brien.

Corgi's 1:43-scale Studebaker Golden Hawk, #211S, was produced from 1960-63, **$180.**
Photo courtesy Dr. Douglas Sadecky.

Cast iron, unknown American makers

Dump truck, green Mack style front, C-cab, red bed with spring lever, spoked nickel wheels, 7-3/4" l **$490**

Gasoline truck, blue, Mack-style front, C-cab, rubber tires, one tire missing. 7" l **$225**

Milk wagon, black cast-iron horse, gilt harness, yellow wheels, blue steel wagon body, 6-3/4" l **$150**

Stake truck, Ford Model A, red, 7" l **$300**

Champion

Auto, cast iron, coupe, painted red, nickeled grill and headlights, rumble seat, rubber tires, spare mounted on trunk, 7" l, repainted **$250**

Gasoline truck, cast iron, painted red, Mack "C" cab, tanker body, emb on sides, rubber tires, 8-1/8" l **$450**

Panel truck, cast iron, enclosed panel van, cast spare tires and headlights, traces of orig blue paint, spoked metal wheels, 7-1/2" l, poor condition **$400**

Racer, cast iron, painted red, silver trim, wind deflector on rear, separately cast driver painted blue, nickeled disc wheels, 8-1/2" l **$650**

Stake truck, cast iron, painted red, Mack "C" cab, stake side body, nickeled spoke wheels, 7" l **$660**

Truck, cast iron, "C" Mack cab, blue body, 7-3/4" l, replaced wheels ... **$250**

Wrecker, cast iron, red C-cab with crane, nickel plated crank and barrel, rubber tires, 8-1/4" l **$600**

Chein

Barnacle Bill, litho tin wind-up, some loss of paint, C.7 .... **$350**

Bass drummer, litho tin wind-up, orig box missing end flap, C.9, 8-3/4" h, ... **$275**

Disneyland ferris wheel, clockwork motor, bell, six gondolas, litho Disney characters and fairgrounds scenes, distortion and paint loss, 16-3/4" h **$400**

Hercules ferris wheel, clockwork motor, bell, six gondolas, litho children and fairground scenes, 16-1/2" l **$325**

Popeye, in barrel, litho tin wind-up, C.8, 7" h **$650**

Roller coaster, litho tin wind-up, orig box, C.8-9, 19" l, 10" h **$525**

Wagon, horse-drawn, "Fine Groceries," tinplate, 12" l **$290**

Converse, USA

Heffield Farms delivery wagon, articulated horse, considerable wear and paint loss, 21-1/2" l **$320**

Klondike Ice Co. delivery wagon, tinplate on wood, two litho horses, paint poor, 17" l **$175**

Trolley, open sides, pressed steel, blue and mustard, stenciled dec, marked "City Hall Park 175" on both ends, reversible benches, large clockwork motor, paint poor, destination boards missing, 16" l **$260**

Corgi

Ambulance, Chevrolet Superior, white body, orange roof, Red Cross decals, 4-3/4" l **$80**

Auto

Buick Riviera, #245, MIB **$75**

Chevrolet Caprice, #325, MIB **$60**

Circus, land rover and animal trailer, #30, MIB **$90**

Citreon DS 19, #210S, MIB **$70**

Ford Consol Saloon, #200M, MIB **$120**

Ford Zephyr Estate Car, light blue, 3-7/8" **$30**

Jeep CJ-5, dark metallic green body **$30**

Mercedes-Benz 220 SE coupe, #230 .... **$60**

Porsche Carrera 6, white body, red or blue trim **$60**

Volkswagen 1200 Driving School .. **$30**

Camera van, Commer Mobile, metallic blue body, black camera on gold tripod, cameraman, 3-1/2" **$60**

Car transporter, Bedford, black diecast cap, 10-1/4" l **$100**

Character cars

Batmobile, glossy black body, gold tow hook **$200**

Captain Marvel Porsche, white body, 4-3/4" l **$20**

At left is Champion's Policeman on motorcycle #2, **$400;** *at right is #3,* **$425.**
Photo courtesy Kent M. Comstock.

This assortment of Dinky vehicles includes, Leyland Cement Wagon, **$250;** *Mighty Antar with Propeller,* **$400;** *Guy Slumberland Van, 1949-52,* **$575.**

David P. Clark founded the Dayton Friction Toy Works after William Scheible purchased Clark's half of the David P. Clark Co. This is his 13-1/4"-long Seven Passenger Touring Car, c.1909, **$300.** Photo courtesy Bob Smith.

Hardy Boys Rolls-Royce, red body, yellow hood **$70**

James Bond Aston Martin, metallic silver body, diecast base, red int., two figures, working roof hatch, ejector seat **$150**

Monkee Mobile, #277, MIB **$450**

Popeye's Paddy Wagon **$195**

Saint's Volvo P-1800, white body, silver trim **$65**

Tank truck, Mack Exxon, white cap and tank, red tank chassis, 10-3/4" l **$15**

Taxi

Austin, London, black, yellow plastic int. **$36**

Thunderbird Bermuda, white body, 4" l **$50**

Tractor, Ford 5000, blue body, yellow scoop arm and controls, chrome scoop, 3-1/8" l **$55**

Dayton Friction Co.

Patrol wagon, pressed metal and wood, friction driven, painted red, stenciled "Police Patrol" on front panel, seated driver on open bench seat, spoke wheels, 10" l **$300**

Touring car, pressed metal, painted red, gold spoke wheels, open sides, friction driver, 12" l **$500**

Dinky

Airplane

Autogyro, gold, blue rotor, 1934-41 **$90**

Bristol Beinhem, 1956-63 .... **$40**

Douglas DC3, silver, #60t, 1937-41 .... **$125**

Lockheed Constellation, #66b, 1940 .... **$85**

Percival Gull, camouflaged, #66c, 1940 .... **$125**

Twin Engine Fighter, silver, #70d/731, 1946-55 .... **$25**

Ambulance

Range Rover, #268, 1974-78 .... **$50**

Superior Criterion, #263, 1962-68 ... **$50**

Auto

Austin Somerset Saloon, #161, MIB **$150**

Cadillac Eldorado, #131, 1956-62 .. **$60**

DeSoto, Diplomat, orange, F545, 1960-63 .... **$85**

Ford Fairlane, pale green, #148, 1962-66 .... **$60**

Jaguar XK 120, white, #157, 1954-62 .... **$120**

Mercury Cougar, #174, MIB **$95**

Plymouth Stockcar, #201, MIB **$40**

Studebaker Commander, F24Y, 1951-61 .... **$75**

Triumph TR-2, gray, #105, 1957-60 .... **$100**

Volkswagen 1300 sedan, #129, 1965-76 .... **$20**

Bulldozer, Blaw Knox, #561 .... **$45**

Bus

Routemaster, #289, 1964-80 .... **$75**

Silver Jubilee, #297, 1977 .... **$25**

Fire truck

Airport fire tender, #276, MIB **$90**

Fire chief's land rover, #195, MIB.. **$50**

Motorcycle

A. A. Motorcycle Patrol, #270/44B, 1946-44 .... **$30**

Police Motorcycle Patrol, #42B, 1946-53 .... **$45**

Police car

Citroen DS19, #F501, 1967-70 .... **$95**

Plymouth, #244, 1977-80 .... **$35**

Taxi

Austin, #40H, 1951-52 .... **$70**

London, #284, MIB **$75**

Plymouth Plaza, #266, 1960-67 .... **$60**

Tractor

David Brown, #305 .... **$60**

Field Marshall, #37N/301 .... **$60**

Massey-Harris, #27A/300 .... **$50**

Truck

Austin Van, Nestle's, #471 .... **$65**

Brink's, #275, MIB **$65**

Coles Hydra, #980, MIB **$100**

Foden Mobilgas tanker, #941 .... **$145**

Leland Tanker, Shell/BP, #944 .... **$125**

The Fisher-Price Donald Duck Drum Major, #400-500, 1946, **$325.**

Fisher-Price's Quacky Family, with felt beaks and wooden dowels between the ducks, 1946, **$185.**

Telephone service van, #261, MIB **$100**

Willeme log truck, #F36A/987 ..... **$75**

Fisher-Price, USA

American Airlines plane, paper litho over wood, bright orange and blue, extensive graphics, two propellers, 20" wingspan **$500**

Chatter Telephone, 1962 .... **$30**

Donald Duck Xylphone, play wear, 1946 .... **$150**

Ducky Cart, 1950 .... **$45**

Easter Bunny, 1936 .... **$125**

Farmer in the Dell TV Radio, 1963 .... **$25**

Gabby Duck, 1952 .... **$55**

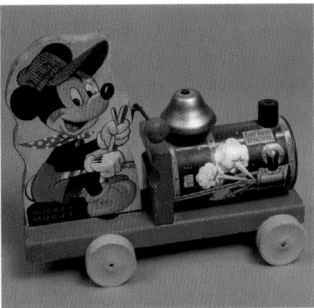

The Mickey Mouse Choo Choo from Fisher-Price, 1949, **$245.**

Jack n Jill TV Radio, #148, 1956 .... **$65**

Junior Circus, 1963 .... **$75**

Katy Kackler, #140, 1954............. **$80**

Lady Bug, 1961 .... **$35**

Merry Mousewife, #473, 1949 .... **$60**

Mickey Mouse Drummer **$250**

Mother Goose Music Cart, #784, 1955 .... **$35**

Nosey Pup, 1956 .... **$25**

Pinky Pig, 1958......................... **$35**

Pony Express, #733, 1941........... **$110**

Pushy Elephant, #525, 1934 ..... **$450**

Rock-A-Bye Baby Cart, #627, 1960 .... **$35**

Sleepy Sue, #632, 1960 .... **$55**

Streamline Express, #215, 1935 .... **$900**

Sunny Fish, #420, 1961 .... **$100**

Talky Parrot, 1963 .... **$145**

Teddy Drummer, #775, 1936 ..... **$300**

This Little Pig, #910, 1963........... **$25**

Uncle Timmy Turtle, #437, 1942 .... **$100**

Wiggily Woofer, #640, 1957 .... **$85**

Ziggy Zilo, #737, 1958 .... **$50**

Hot Wheels, Mattel, MIP

American Hauler, redline, 1976 .. **$70**

American Tipper, redline, 1976 .. **$65**

Baja Bruiser, #8258, orange, 1974 .. **$90**

Beach Bomb, green **$85**

Boss Hoss, #6406, 1971 .... **$250**

Buzz Off, redline, 1973................. **$500**

Captain America, #2879, white, 1979 .... **$175**

Cement Mixer, #6452, 1970....... **$125**

Chevy, '57, Ultra Hots, #47 .... **$100**

Circus Cats, #3303, white, ... **$75**

Classic '36 Ford Coupe, redline, 1969 .... **$125**

Custom Police Cruiser, #6269, 2969 .... **$200**

Datsun 200XS, #3255, maroon, Canada, 1982 .... **$125**

Dune Daddy, #6967, light green, 1975 .... **$75**

Earthmover, #16............................ **$85**

El Rey Special, #8273, light blue, 1974 .... **$1,200**

Emergency Squad, #7650, red, 1975 .... **$65**

Fire Engine, redline, 1970........... **$100**

Flat Out 442, green, Canada, 1984 .... **$150**

Fuel Tanker, #6018, 1971 .... **$200**

Heavy Chevy, #6408, 1970 .... **$200**

Hood, redline **$110**

Hot Heap, #6219, 1968................. **$110**

Ice T, redline, 1971 .... **$200**

Jet Threat, #6179, 1976 .... **$55**

Light My Firebird, redline, 1970 .... **$110**

Lotus Turbine, #6262, 1969.......... **$90**

Mantis, #6423, 1970 .... **$100**

Maxi Taxi, #9184, yellow, blackwall, 1977 .... **$60**

Mongoose Funny Car, redline, 1970 .... **$210**

Moving van, redline, 1970 .... **$125**

Neet Streeter, #9510, chrome, 1976 .... **$40**

Olds 442, #6467, 1971................. **$800**

Poison Pinto, #9240, green, blackwall, 1977 .... **$30**

Police Cruiser, #6963, white, 1973 .... **$550**

Porsche 911, #6972, orange, 1975 .... **$65**

Probe Funny Car, #84, Motorcraft **$30**

Race Ace, #2620, white, 1968........ **$75**

Red Baron, #6963, red, blackwall, 1977 .... **$25**

Rig Wrecker, #45 .... **$225**

Road Roller, #55, yellow **$25**

Rock Buster, #9088, yellow, blackwall, 1977 .... **$15**

Sand Crab, #6403, 1970................ **$60**

Scooper, redline, 1971 .... **$325**

Silhouette, #6209, 1979 .... **$90**

Sir Sidney Roadster, #8261, yellow, 1974 .... **$90**

Snake II, redline, 1971 .... **$275**

Super Van, #9205, chrome, 1976 .... **$40**

Sweet 16, #6422, 1970................. **$75**

Tail Gunner, #29 .... **$75**

Team Trailer, redline, 1971 .... **$225**

Tow Truck, #6450, 1970 .... **$55**

T-Totaller, #9648, brown, blackwall, 1977 .... **$40**

Turbo Streak, #104..................... **$75**

Vega Bomb, #7654, green, 1975 .. **$800**

Volkswagen, #7620, orange, bug on roof, 1974 .... **$60**

Warpath, #7654, white, 1975...... **$110**

Whip Creamer, redline, #1870..... **$60**

Z Whiz, #9639, gray, redline, 1977 .... **$70**

Hubley, Lancaster, PA

Airplane, cast iron

American Eagle, WWII fighter 11" wingspan **$200**

Lindy Glider, painted red, yellow wings, driver seated on front, emb wings, 6-1/2" l...................... **$1,250**

Navy fighter, DC, moving propeller, retractable landing gear, folding wings, orig box, C.9, 8-3/4" **$225**

Sea Plane, orange, and blue, two engines **$75**

Auto, cast iron

Chrysler Airflow, battery operated lights, 1934............................ **$1,250**

Coupe, 1928, 8-1/2" l................. **$600**

Lincoln Zephyr and trailer, painted green, nickeled grill and bumper, 13-1/2" l................................. **$825**

Sedan and trailer, painted red sedan, trailer panted silver and red, rubber tires, factory sample tag, 9-1/2" l **$725**

This 1969 Hot Wheels Redlines Custom Firebird was based on the Pontiac Firebird, **$250.**
KP Photo, Tom Michael collection.

The Hot Wheels Redlines Mantis was released in 1970, car out of pack, **$60.**
KP Photo, Tom Michael collection.

This is the Hot Wheels Paddy Wagon from 1970, **$75.**
KP Photo, Tom Michael collection.

Streamlined Racer, 5" l **$375**

Bell telephone, cast iron

Painted green, silver sides, emb company name, Mack "C" cab, nickeled ladders, long handled shovels, pole carrier, spoked wheels, repainted, 8-1/4" l **$800**

Painted green, winch, auger, nickel water barrel on side, ladders, and pole carrier, fatigued rubber tires, 9-1/4" l **$1,300**

Boat, cast iron, painted red, emb "Static" on sides, sleet form, seated driver, hand on throttle of attached motor, chromed air cleaner, painted orange, three tires, clicker, over painted, 9-1/2" l
.... **$1,650**

Bus, cast iron, new tires, 5-3/4" l .. **$125**

Cement mixer truck, cast iron, red and green, nickel tank, rubber wheels, Mack, restored, 8" l **$1,760**

Delivery truck, Merchants, 1925, 6-1/4" l **$400**

Fire truck, cast iron

Fire Engine, 1930s, 5" l **$75**

Fire Patrol, 7-men, 1912, 5" l ... **$3,575**

Hook and ladder, 1912, 23" l ... **$1,850**

Ladder truck, 5-1/2" l **$70**

Gasoline truck, cast iron, painted silver, red spoked wheels, cast figure, round tank body, rear facets, c1920, 6" l **$495**

Milk truck, cast iron, painted white, emb "Borden's" on side panel, rear opening door, nickeled grill, headlights, and spoke wheels, repaired headlights, 7-1/2" l
.... **$1,980**

Motorcycle, cast iron

Harley-Davidson, 1932, 7-1/2" l. **$500**

Hill Climber, 1936, 6-1/2" l **$450**

Indian Four Cylinder, 1929, 9" l
.... **$1,800**

Motorcycle cop with sidecar **$700**

Patrol Motorcycle, green, 6-1/2" l
.... **$275**

Parcel post, 90% orig paint, 10" l
.... **$2,000**

Panama steam shovel, cast iron, painted red and green, large scale, nickeled shovel, cast people on trailer, dual rubbers on rear, 12" l **$935**

Pull toy, Old Dutch Girl, cast iron, white and blue dress, holding yellow can of cleanser, rubber tires, repaired stick, orig checker floor, c1932, 9" l
.... **$4,100**

Racer, cast iron

Painted blue, painted red articulated pistons, seated driver, black tires, spoked wheels, 10-1/2" l **$1,760**

Painted green, red emb "5" on sides, hood opens on both sides to show extensively cast engine, disc wheels, seated driver, replaced hood doors, 9-1/2" l **$1,500**

Painted red, seated driver, emb "#1" on sides, rubber tires, 7-3/4" l **$400**

Japanese

Haji, car with boat trailer, friction powered, blue Ford convertible, red and cream Speedo motor boat with friction-powered motor, red trailer, orig packing and maker's box, 8" l **$400**

Occupied Japan, Plymouth, litho tin wind-up, nickel trim, orig box, C.8+, 1942, 6" l **$175**

SY, flying man robot, litho tin wind-up, orig box, C.9, 6" x 3" base, 11" h
.... **$375**

T.N.

Dump Truck, friction powered tinplate, red and cream, automatic side dump action, orig maker's box, 11" l **$150**

Great Swanee Paddle Wheeler, friction powered tinplate, whistle mechanism, orig maker's box, 10-1/4" l **$175**

Koko the Sandwich Man, orig box, C.8, 1950s, 7" h **$125**

TPS

Circus parade, tin litho wind-up, clowns and elephants, orig box, C.9, 11" l **$275**

Moon patrol, tin, battery operated, tin astronaut driver, plastic dome, bump-and-go action, C.9, 8" l
.... **$350**

Yone, swinging baby robot, litho tin wind-up, orig box, C.9, 4" x 4" base, 12" h **$350**

Yonezawa

Missile launching tank, litho tin, battery operated, four targets, orig box, C.10, 6" l **$155**

Happy n' sad magic face clown, battery operated, orig box, C.9, 10-1/2" h
.... **$150**

Keystone Mfg. Co., Boston

Air mail plane, olive green, three propellers, 25" **$1,650**

Ambulance, canvas cover and stretcher, 27-1/2" l, C8 .... **$1,400**

Bus, Coast to Coast, blue, 31-1/4" l, C8
.... **$1,900**

Fighter plane, "Ride 'Em," silver pressed-steel, red wings, propeller and seat, 25" l **$720**

Hubley Auto Transport w/2 Cadillacs, plastic, post-WWII, **$160.**
Photo courtesy Terry Sells.

This Hubley Motorcycle with two removable Policemen, cast iron, 9" l, **$1,200.**
Photo courtesy Kent M. Comstock.

This Hubley Packard from 1929 was cast in fifteen different parts and measures 11" l. One of the "Holy Grails" of Hubley collecting, this rarity, at auction, achieved **$16,000.**
Photo courtesy Bertoia Auctions.

Japanese Battery-Operated toys are popular with collectors, like this colorful Batmobile, **$400.**
Photo courtesy Heinz Mueller.

The Keystone Water Tower Pump truck is difficult to find with the water tank free from rust. This one has only minor rusting, **$1,500.**
Photo courtesy Karen O'Brien.

This is the plastic Kilgore Motorcycle,
$750.
Photo courtesy Kent M. Comstock.

Moving van, black cab, red body, rubber tires, 26-1/4" **$1,300**
Packard Ride 'Em water tower, tower, nozzle, tank, and seat, lg. 32" l **$850**
Police patrol truck, decals, 27-1/2" l **$700**
Steam shovel, 20-3/4" l **$250**

Kilgore, Canada

Airplane, cast iron, Seagull, painted red, nickeled wheels and wing mounted propeller, 7-3/4" l **$880**
Auto, open roadster, 1928, cast iron, painted blue, nickeled wheels and driver, decal reads "Kilgore, Made in Canada," 6-1/8" l **$825**
Delivery truck, cast iron, Toy Town, painted red, emb on side panels, gold highlights, silver disc wheels, repainted, 6-1/8" l **$360**
Dump truck, cast iron, painted blue enclosed cab, red dump body, lever to lift, nickeled disc wheels, 8-1/2" l **$450**
Ice cream truck, cast iron, enclosed cab painted blue, orange body, emb "Arctic Ice Cream" on sides, disc wheels, 8" l **$470**

Lehmann, Germany

Beetle, spring motor, crawling movement, flapping wings, maker's box, one leg detached, but present, early Adam trademark **$230**
Catalog, *Patent Lehmann Spielzug,* 1881, 21 pgs, orig order blank, 6" x 9", minor insect damage **$315**
Heinkel-Blitz He 70, tin, orig string, instructions, plane with Nazi swastika, orig box, C.10, 4-1/2" l **$575**
Na-Ob, red and yellow cart, blue eccentric wheels, gray donkey, marked "Lehmann Ehe & Co.," front wheel missing, 6" l **$145**

Top row left to right: Gnom Series BV-Aral Tanker, 4-1/2", **$600;** *Gnom Series Opel Dump Truck, 4-1/2",* **$550;** *bottom row left to right: Gnom Series Racing Car, 4-1/2",* **$650;** *Gnom Series Sedan,* **$500.**
Photo courtesy Bob Smith.

Oh-My Alabama coon jigger, lithograph tinplate, clockwork motor, 10" h **$480**
Sedan, EPL No. 765, litho tin wind-up, some edge and tire wear, C.7+, 5-1/2" l **$150**
Truck, tinplate, cream, red, and yellow, blue driver, fixed steering, clockwork motor, marked "Lehmann Ehe & Co.," 6-3/4" l **$435**
Tut Tut motor car, white suited driver, horn, front steering, bellows, coil springs, paint loss, rust spotting, 6-1/2" l **$650**

Linemar, Japan

Cabin cruiser, litho tin, battery operated, detailed interior, fabric covered seats, orig box, 12" l, C.9 ....**$250**
Clarabell Clown, tin mechanical action, 6-1/2" h, C.8 ....**$210**
Donald Duck, Walt Disney's mechanical tricycle, celluloid Donald Duck riding tin wind-up, box with illus of Mickey riding tricycle, 3-3/4" x 4" x 2-1/2" box **$325**

Feeding birdwatcher, litho tin and plush, battery operated, orig box, C.9, 7-1/2" h **$365**
Mickey Mouse
  Moving van, litho tin friction, wear, 1950s, C.7, 13" l **$350**
  Rocking on Pluto, litho tin wind-up, replaced ears and tail, C.7, 5-1/2" h **$850**
Music box, cowboy dancing to music, tin and plastic, battery operated, orig box, C.9, 5" h **$175**
Prehistoric animal, T-Rex, litho tin wind-up, orig box, 9" l, 6" h **$260**
Rocket express, litho tin wind-up, train and space ship, orig box, C.9, 5-1/2" sq **$575**
Smoking Popeye, tin, battery operated, orig box, C.7+ **$2,500**
Superman tank, tin, battery operated, orig box, © 1958, C.9, 5" h **$3,000**

Lineol, Germany

Armored car, litho tin clockwork, camouflage colors, revolving turret with gun, opening doors, spring lever for gun, wire guard covers vehicle,

The Lineol No. 1218 Bridge Truck is a rare vehicle, **$6,500.**
Photo courtesy Jack Matthews.

This is the battery-operated Marx Combat Tank, "U.S. Tank Division," **$45.**
Photo courtesy Heinz Mueller.

This is the Marx Merchants Transfer truck from 1929, **$700.**
Photo courtesy Bob Smith.

This is the Matchbox Regular Wheels Iron Fairy Crane from 1969-70, **$18.**
KP Photo courtesy George Cuhaj.

rubber tires, symbols repainted, minor paint loss, 10" l **$935**

Cannon, 88mm, litho tin, camouflage colors, stabilizer arms, elevation cranks, four-tire open frame, tow hook, 14-1/2" l **$935**

Motorcycle with side car, composition figures, tin fenders, disc wheels, 4-1/2" l.......................................**$500**

Marx, Louis & Co., NY
Airplane
American Airlines, flagship, pressed steel, wood wheels, 1940, 27" wingspan **$200**

Bomber, metal, wind-up, four propellers, 14-1/2" wingspan **$100**

Floor Zeppelin, 1931, 9-1/2" l.....**$225**

Lucky Stunt Flyer, litho tin wind-up, 1928, 6" l **$175**

Military litho tin wind-up, orig box, mounted to orig insert, 13" l, 18" wing span, C.9 ....**$260**

Pan American, pressed steel, four engines, 1940, 27" wingspan **$90**

Pursuit Plane, one propeller, 1930s, 8" wingspan..................................**$125**

Skybird flyer, litho tin wind-up, plane and zeppelin circling tower, orig box with wear, C.8, 26" w, 10" h........**$350**

Trans-Atlantic Zeppelin, litho tin wind-up, 1930, 10" l.................**$275**

Auto
Army car, battery operated............**$95**

Crazy Dan car, litho tin wind-up, 1930s, 6" l.................................**$375**

Dippy Dumper, celluloid Brutus, litho tin wind-up, 1930s, 9" l...........**$350**

Jalopy, tin driver, friction, 1950s ..**$150**

Leaping Lizzie, litho tin wind-up, 1927, 7" l...................................**$250**

Queen of the Campus, four college students, 1950...........................**$250**

Siren police car, 1930s, 15" l.........**$75**

Speed racer, 1937, 13" l **$250**

Streamline Speedway, two litho tin wind-up racing cars, 1936.......**$175**

Auto transport, plastic cab and cars, orig box, professional repairs, 23" l, C.9..**$225**

Battleship, *U.S.S. Washington,* tin friction, orig box, 14" l, C.9 ....**$275**

Bulldozer/tractor, gold body, rubber treads, plow and farmer driver, blue and red stake wagons, hitch, two discs, plow, corn planter, harvester **$230**

Drummer boy, litho tin wind-up, minor edge wear on drum, C.7+, 7-1/2" h.....................................**$310**

Dumbo, the acrobatic elephant, litho tin wind-up, Disney, orig box, C.9, 1941, 4" h **$725**

Jazzbo Jim, litho tin wind-up, orig box, C.9, 9" h..............................**$575**

Lone Ranger, range rider, litho tin wind-up, C.9, 1938, 11" l, 9" h **$350**

Merrymakers Band, tinplate, one dancer missing............................**$575**

Pluto, litho tin wind-up, Walt Disney Productions, orig box, C.9, 6-1/2" h **$600**

Royal Bus Lines, litho tin wind-up, 1930s, 10-1/4" l..........................**$135**

Set
Bulldog tractor, aluminum, litho wind-up, 1940, 9-1/2" l tractor............**$250**

Sleeping Beauty, Prince Phillip, Samson the Horse, hard plastic, all accessories, orig box, 12" l, C.8+ **$150**

Super Power Tractor and Trailer, litho tin wind-up, 1937, 8-1/2" l tractor **$125**

Truck
Dump truck, yellow cab, blue bumper, red bed, 1950, 18" l...........**$100**

East-West Coast Van, tin litho, ten wheeler, tin balloon tires, adv graphics, orig box, C.9, 18" l....**$320**

Gravel truck, pressed steel cab, red tin dumper, 1930, 10" **$100**

Jalopy pickup, litho tin wind-up, 7" l **$75**

Mack towing truck, dark green cab, wind-up, 1926, 8" l...................**$175**

Pet shop truck, plastic, six compartments with vinyl dogs, 11" l ...**$125**

Royal Oil Co., Mack, dark red cab, medium green tank, wind-up, 1927, 8-1/4" l..................................**$200**

Searchlight, toolbox behind cab, 1930s, 10" l..............................**$150**

Stake bed, pressed steel, wooden wheels, 1936, 7" l......................**$65**

TV and radio station, battery operated, orig box, C.8-9, 27" l, 10" w, 8" h...**$300**

Zippo the climbing monkey, multicolored litho tinplate, pull-string mechanism, 10" l **$60**

Matchbox, England
Austin Taxi, #17, MIB, 1960 ....**$75**

Atlantic Trailer, tan body, six metal wheels, MIB, 1956 ....**$70**

Atlas truck, metallic blue cab, orange dumper, labels on doors, 1975 ....**$7**

Bedford Tipper, #3, gray cap, NM, 1961 ....**$25**

Blue Shark, #61, MIB, 1971 ....**$15**

Caterpillar Tractor, #8, 1955.......**$40**

Chevrolet Impala, taxi, orange, 1965 ....**$30**

Citroen DS19, #66, NM, 1959 ......**$32**

Daimler ambulance, #14, NM, 1955 ....**$25**

Disney car, Donald Duck, 1989....**$45**

Ferrari Berlinetta, metallic green body, NM, 1965 ....**$25**

Fiat 1500, MIB, 1965 ....**$15**

Foden Ready Mix concrete truck, orange body, MIB, 1961 ....**$45**

Ford Customline Station Wagon, #31, yellow body, NM, 1957 ....**$40**

Ford Zephyr 6, #33, MIB, 1963 ....**$33**

Fork Lift Truck, #15, red body, yellow hoist, MIP, 1973 ....**$95**

Harta Tractor Shovel, #69, orange, MIB, 1965.................................**$30**

Honda Motorcycle with Trailer, #38, MIB, 1968.............................**$40**

This Matchbox Regular Wheels Road Roller was released in 1962, **$60.**

This is the Matchbox Models of Yesteryear Y-12 1909 Thomas Runabout that was issued in 1967, **$20.**
Photo courtesy Karen O'Brien.

Here is the Schuco Old Timer 1913 Mercer windup, **$150.**
Photo courtesy Al Kasishke.

This Smith-Miller Dump has a working hand crank that operates the dump bed, **$500.**
KP Photo courtesy Larry Planer.

Horse Drawn Milk Float, #7, orange body, MIB, 1954 .... **$125**
Jaguar XK 140 coupe, #32, MIB, 1957 .... **$70**
Lambretta Motorscooter with Sidecar, #36, metallic green, MIP, 1961 .... **$95**
Land Rover Fire Truck, #57, NM, 1966 .... **$11**
Leyland Royal Tiger Coach, #40, silver-gray, NM, 1961 .... **$10**
London Bus, #5, MIB, 1954 .... **$80**
Mark Ten Jaguar, #28, NM, 1964. **$20**
Maserati 4CLT Racer, NM, 1958.. **$50**
Mercedes Benz Coach, white, 1965 .... **$30**
MGA sports car, #19, MIB, 1969.. **$70**
Military scout car, #61, MIB, 1959 .... **$32**
Morris Minor 1000, dark green, 1958 .... **$20**
Pontiac convertible, #39, MIB, 1962 .... **$65**
Rolls-Royce Phantom V, 1964... **$15**
Scaffolding truck, silver body, green tinted windows, 1969 .... **$5**
Setra Coach, #12, 1970 .... **$5**
Snowtrac Tractor, red body, silver painted grille, 1964 .... **$10**
Swamp Rat, green deck, plastic hull, tan soldier, 1976 .... **$5**
Taxi Cab, Chevrolet Impala, #20, MIB, 1965 .... **$35**
Thames Wreck, red body, 1961, 2-1/2" **$15**
Volkswagon 1500 Saloon, #15, MIB, 1968 .... **$25**
Weatherhill Hydraulic Excavator, decal, 1956 .... **$20**

Pratt & Letchworth

Dray wagon, cast iron, open bed wagon, single slat slides, wooden floor, standing figure, red spoke wheels, one horse, 10-1/4" l **$275**
Hook and ladder truck, cast iron, horse drawn, one red and one white horse, black frame with red detailing, spoked wheels, seated front driver, seated rear driver, two wood ladders and bell, 23" l **$560**
Surrey, cast iron, open carriage, low splash board, two full width seams with arm and back rests, emb upholstering mounted on two prs of spoked wheels, pulled by one horse, c1900, 14" l **$990**

Schuco, trademark of Schreyer and Co., Germany

Acrobat bear, yellow mohair, glass eyes, embroidered nose and mouth, turns somersaults when wound, orig key, 1950s, 5" h **$575**
Ambulance, Mercedes 408 Servo, plastic, orig box, C.7+, 12-1/2" l **$125**
Mercedes Simplex, wind-up, 8-1/2" l **$125**
Monkey bellhops, Yes/No monkey with painted metal face, metal eyes, ginger mohair head and tail, red and black felt outfit and hands, Acrobatic monkey with painted metal face, metal eyes, ginger mohair head, red and black felt outfit and hands, winds by rotating arms, oak Mission style settee, moth damage on both, 1930s, 8-1/2" h.. **$435**
Monkey, tumbling **$110**
Porsche microracer, No. 1037, red, key missing **$100**
Racing kit, BMW Formula 2, tin and plastic, unassembled, orig box, C.10, 10" l **$165**
Set, Highway Patrol, squad car, 1958 .... **$140**
Tank, keywind **$50**
Teddy bear on roller skates, wind-up, beige mohair head, glass eyes, embroidered nose and mouth, cloth and metal body and legs, cotton shirt, felt overalls, hands, and boots, rubber wheels, marked "Schuco, U.S. Zone, Germany," clothes faded, key not orig **$490**
Teddy bear on scooter, friction auction, yellow mohair bear, black steel eyes, embroidered nose and mouth, black felt pants, blue litho scooter, 1920s, 5-3/4" h **$1,100**
Van, battery operated, 4" l **$75**

Smith-Miller

Chevy Ice Truck, c.1945 .... **$350**
GMC Dump Truck, 1950-53, six wheels **$185**
L Mack Aerial Ladder, SMFD, eight wheels **$440**
L Mack P.I.E. truck, fourteen wheels **$450**
MIC House Trailer **$380**

Structo

Bearcat Auto, 16" l, C8, 1919 ..... **$850**
Cement mixer truck, 1950s, 18-1/2" l, C8, 9" h **$150**
Climbing military tank, green, 1929 .... **$500**
Contractor truck, orange dump truck, 1924 .... **$600**
Emergency van, blue and white, 1962 .... **$100**

Fire insurance patrol, 1928, 18" l **$200**

Fire truck, hydraulic hook and ladder, pressed steel, red, 3" l **$200**

Hydraulic dumper **$75**

Lone Eagle airplane, monoplane, spring drive motor, 1928 ....**$675**

Motor dispatch, blue, decals, 1929, 24" **$850**

Sky King airplane, blue, gray wings, 1929 ....**$900**

Tinplate, unknown makers

Clown violinist, stilt-legs, striped trousers, clockwork motor, poor condition, 9" h **$60**

Delivery carriage, litho, black, red, yellow, and pink, flywheel drive, 4-1/4" l **$150**

Horse-drawn omnibus, attributed to Francis, Field and Francis, Philadelphia, two white horses, black painted harnesses, wheel operated trotting, dark green roof with black fleur-de-lis and lining, emb gilt foliate surround, emb rear steps, door surround, driver's rear rest, emb window frames with painted curtains, front, rear upper section, lower half with hand-painted polychrome floral and foliate dec, over blue-gray, ochre int. with ochre vis-a-vis bench seating along sides, wheels, overall paint flaking, wheels detached, one window frame partially detached, 1850s, 23" l **$48,300**

Locomotive, attributed to Fallows, clockwork motor, cast wheels, high wings, cow catcher and bell, old repaint, 10" l **$460**

Locomotive, Victory, red boiler, bell, black and gilt stack, red and blue cab with green roof, silver stenciled windows, yellow chassis, spoked wheels, one wheel damaged, scratches and paint loss, 4-3/4" l **$990**

Porter and trolley, clockwork motor in hinged trunk, blue uniform, red and orange electric-type trolley, 4-1/2" l **$145**

Steamer, three funnels, hand painted, red, cream, and gray hull, cream superstructure, 10" l **$350**

Two-seater tourer, litho, red, yellow, and cream, driver, fly-wheel drive, 3" l **$400**

Tonka

Airlines tractor, set of two baggage carts, C.9, 1963 ....**$150**

Boat transport, 1960, 38" l **$250**

Construction

Bulldozer, #300, 1962 ....**$35**

Dump truck, #180, 1949 ....**$100**

Dump truck and sand loader, #616, 1963 ....**$100**

Hydraulic Dump, #520, 1962........**$75**

Road Grader, #12, 1958................**$75**

Fire truck

Aerial ladder truck, 1957 ....**$250**

Rescue Squad, 1960....................**$100**

Suburban Pumper, #46, 1960 ....**$100**

Mini

Camper, #0070, 1963....................**$35**

Jeep pickup, #50, 1963 ....**$35**

Livestock Van, 1964, 16" l **$50**

Stake truck, #56, 1963..................**$40**

Truck

Air Express, #16, 1959 ....**$350**

Car Carrier, #40, 1960 ....**$100**

Carnation Milk delivery van, #750, 1954 ....**$200**

Deluxe Sportsman, #22, 1961......**$100**

Farm state truck, 1957 ....**$190**

Green Giant Transport semi, 1953 ....**$150**

Minute Maid Orange Juice van, #725, 1955 ....**$275**

Service truck, #01, 1960..............**$100**

Wrecker truck, #18, 1958............**$100**

Tootsietoy

Airplane

Aero-Dawn, 1928..........................**$30**

Beechcraft Bonanza, orange **$15**

Curtis P-40, light green **$120**

Navy Jet, red, 1970s **$10**

P-38, WWII blue props **$225**

Stratocruiser **$30**

Transport plane, orange, 1941 ......**$40**

Auto

Andy Gump Car **$75**

Bluebird Daytona Race Car **$20**

Buick LaSabre, 1951 ....**$25**

Buick Touring Car, HO series, 1960 ....**$30**

Cadillac Coupe, blue and tan........**$40**

Chevrolet Roadster **$20**

Corvette **$15**

Ford Fairlane Convertible, red **$10**

Ford V-8 Hotrod, 1940 ....**$15**

International Station Wagon, red and yellow, 1939 ....**$15**

Lincoln Capri **$20**

Oldsmobile 98, red, 1955 ....**$20**

Packard, white, 1956 ....**$25**

Pontiac Fire Chief, red, 1959 ......**$20**

Boat

Battleship **$10**

Destroyer **$10**

Transport......................................**$15**

Yacht **$10**

This is the Structo Weekender from the 1960s, **$180.**
KP Photo courtesy Ron O'Brien.

This Tonka Suburban Pumper is from the early 1960s and its two-piece grill is indicative of trucks made before 1962, **$350.**
KP Photo courtesy Ron O'Brien.

A 1963 Tonka Wrecker, **$150.**
KP Photo courtesy Karen O'Brien.

The Buck Rogers No. 1033 Attack Ship from Tootsietoy, **$225.**

This 1950s Wyandotte Emergency Auto Service truck has a plastic cab and metal bed with litho graphics, **$145.**
Photo courtesy Brian Seligman.

Doodlebug, die-cast, 4" l, orig paint
Green, C.8 .... **$65**
Red, C.9 .... **$75**
Set, fire department, 1947 Mack pumper, Mack fire trailer, Pontiac fire chief sedan, 1950 Chevy panel truck ambulance, orig box, 1950s, C.9 .... **$250**

Unknown maker, American

Nine-pins, knockdown type, set of Indians, each with different polychrome paint, 9" h to 10-1/2" h **$4,700**
Squeeze type, clown plays tambourine, wood limbs, head loose, 7" l **$375**
Wooden crank, six soldiers on horses, move when handle is turned, orig polychrome paint, 19th C litho paper base, 8-1/2" l **$3,700**

Wyandotte, USA
Airplane
Army bombing plane, 8-1/2" wingspan
.... **$85**
Defense bomber, 9-1/4" l **$75**
Stratoship mystery plane, 4-1/4" l ... **$50**
Ambulance, painted pressed steel, nickeled grill, operating rear door, minor scratches, 11" l **$170**
Car and trailer, painted pressed steel, red, streamlined auto and travel trailer with operating rear door, replaced white rubber tires, paint worn, chips, and scratches, 25" l
.... **$315**
Circus truck and wagon, red and yellow, cardboard animals, 19" l **$650**
Hoky & Poky, litho tin wind-up, play wear, C.7, 6-3/4" l **$225**

Humphrey mobile, litho tinplate, fixed steering, clockwork motor, rear door, moving hat and arm, some scratching, 9" l **$375**
Pan Am clipper, painted pressed steel, red and white, brass engines, nickeled propellers, 9" l **$275**
Streamlined Wagon, rubber wheels, 5-1/4" l **$45**
Zephyr roadster, rubber wheels, 13-3/8" l **$400**

An art-deco influenced Wyandotte Boat-Tail Racer c1934, **$195.**
Photo courtesy Brian Seligman.

TRAINS, TOY

History: Railroading remains an important collecting field to children of all ages, largely because of the "days-gone-by" romance associated with the rail travel and the prominence of toy trains.

The first toy trains were cast iron and tin; wind-up motors added movement. The golden age of toy trains was 1920 to 1955, when electric-powered units and high-quality rolling stock were available and names such as Ives, American Flyer, and Lionel were household words. The advent of plastic in the late 1950s resulted in considerably lower quality.

Toy trains are designated by a model scale or gauge. The most popular are HO, N, O and standard. Narrow gauge was a response to the modern capacity to miniaturize. Today train layouts in gardens are all the rage and those usually feature larger scale trains.

Additional Listings: See *The Standard Catalog of Lionel Trains 1945-69* for more examples.

Notes: Condition of trains is critical when establishing price. Items in fair condition and below (scratched, chipped, dented, rusted, or warped) generally have little value to a collector. Accurate restoration is accepted and may enhance the price by one or two grades. Prices listed are for trains in very good to excellent condition, unless otherwise noted.

Adviser: Karen O'Brien

American Flyer

Boxcar, #33514, HO gauge, Silver Meteor, brown **$45**
Caboose, #935, S gauge, bay window, brown, 1957 .... **$60**
Circus Pullman, #649, S gauge, minor wear to orig box, C.9 .... **$125**

Lionel Trains, Top: No. 2332 Virginian engine, **$900;** *Bottom: No. 2331 Virginian engine (variation),* **$1,500.**
Photo courtesy of Butterfield & Butterfield Auctions.

Flat car, #24558, S gauge, Canadian Pacific, Christmas tree load, 1959-60
.... **$145**
Gondola
#941, S gauge, Frisco, 1953-57 ..... **$12**
#33507, HO gauge, D&H, brown, canister load **$60**
Handcar, #742, S gauge, some wear to orig box and insert, C.8 .... **$75**
Locomotive
#354, S gauge, steam, Silver Bullet, Pacific, 4-6-2, 1954 .... **$200**
#425, decals and paint chipped, 426 tender, decals chipped, C.5 .... **$75**
#435 locomotive, 433A tender, unnatural wear to drivers, C.7-8 .... **$220**
#3020, O gauge, electric, 4-4-4, c1922-25 .... **$375**
#3307 locomotive, 3189 tender, decals chipped, C.5 .... **$100**
#3322 locomotive, 3199 tender, C.4-5
.... **$110**

Set, O gauge
Freight, #476 gondola, #478 boxcar, #480 tank car, #484 caboose.... **$140**
Passenger, Railway Post Office car, Paul Revere coach, Lexington observation, orange **$125**
Set, standard gauge
#12 locomotive, painted cast iron, working clockwork, 120 tender, 1119 cattle car, 1109 gondola, 1111 IC caboose, tunnel, track, switches, C.4-5 ...... **$350**
#20 locomotive, 1131 tender, 1126 hopper, 1113 hopper, two 1223 coaches, C.4-5 .... **$130**
#423 locomotive, 426 tender, 415 searchlight car, 416 wrecker, 410 tank car, 408 box car, 407 gondola, C.5-7
.... **$225**
#434, 282 loco and tender, 500 combine, 501 coach, 502 vista dome, 503 observation, worn orig boxes, C.8-9
.... **$2,000**

#3315 locomotive, 3319 tender, 3380 combine, 3382 observation, C.5-6 .... **$280**

#3322 locomotive, 3189 tender, two 3208 box cars, 3206 lumber car, 3211 caboose, C.5-6 .... **$175**

#4644 locomotive, rewheeled, 4151 coach, 4152 observation, Eagle train, C.6 .... **$350**

#K5364W Silver Rocket, 474 and 475 Rocker AA, three 962 vista domes, 963 observation, orig boxes with some wear, C.6-8 .... **$1,550**

#20305, 21800-355 Baldwin diesel, 702 box of track, orig boxes, C.8-9 .... **$410**

#20740 Defender, 234 logo, 24557 Navy flat with Jeeps, 25056 USM box car and rocket launcher flat car, 24549 searchlight car, 24631 caboose, C.6-8 .... **$950**

Tank car, #24323, Baker's Chocolate, S gauge, gray tank ends, minor wear to orig box, C.8 .... **$350**

Bing, German

Locomotive, O gauge, pre-war Clockwork, cast iron, no tender, head-light missing **$75**

Live steam, 0-4-0, minor fire damage, no tender **$800**

Set, O gauge, passenger, litho, #2395 combine, Winnebago coach, Lakewood observation, green with brown roofs **$175**

Set, #1 gauge, passenger, litho, dark maroon, lettered "Pennsylvania Lines," combine #1250, coach #1207 .... **$435**

Ives

Baggage car

#50, O gauge, four wheels, red litho frame, striped steps, white/silver body, sides marked "Limited Vestibule Express, United States Mail Baggage Co." and "Express Service No. 50," three doors on both sides, one on each end, black roof with celestory, 1908-09 .... **$190**

#70, O gauge, eight wheels, red litho body, simulates steel, tin roof with celestory stripe, sliding center door, marked "The Ives Railway Lines,

Express Baggage Service, 60, U. S. Mail," 1923-25 .... **$75**

Caboose, #67, O gauge, eight wheels, red litho body, sliding door on each side, gray painted tin roof with red cupola, "The Ives Railway Lines," 1918 .... **$85**

Gravel car, #63, O gauge, eight wheels, gray litho, rounded truss rods, marked "63" on sides, 1913-14 .... **$75**

Livestock car, #65, O gauge, eight wheels, orange-yellow litho body, type D trucks, gray painted roof with catwalk, sides marked "Livestock Transportation, Ives RR," c1918 ... **$95**

Locomotive

#19, O gauge, 0-4-0, black cast iron boiler and cab, two arched windows and "IVES No. 19" beneath, cast-iron wheels, NYC & HR No. 17 tender, 1917-25 .... **$225**

#25, O gauge, 4-4-2, black body, boiler tapers towards front, four separate boiler bands, three square windows on both sides of cab, gold frames and stripes, tin pony wheels, four-wheel L.V.E. No. 25 tender, 1906-07 .... **$310**

#3200, O gauge, 0-4-o, cast iron S-type electric center cab, green body, gold trim, cast iron six-spoke wheels, center door flanked by two windows, raised lettering "Ives" and "3200" below windows, 1911 .. **$285**

Lionel

Baggage car, #2602, O gauge, red body and roof, 1938 .... **$100**

Boxcar

#00-44, OO gauge, 1939 .... **$45**

#HO-874, HO gauge, NYC, 1964 .. **$25**

#6464-375 Central of Georgia, unrun, minor wear to orig box, C.7 .... **$120**

Caboose

#217, S gauge, 1926-40, orange and maroon **$250**

#HO-841, HO gauge, 1961, NYC .. **$20**

Cattle car, #213, S gauge, cream body, maroon roof, 1926-40 .... **$425**

Coal loader, #397, coal shield broken, minor wear and tape on orig box, 1948-57, C.6-7 .... **$100**

Derrick, #219, S gauge, C.7 .... **$270**

Dump, #218, S gauge Mojave end plates, minor wear to orig box, C.7 .... **$290**

Hopper, #516, S gauge, coal loads, minor chips, incomplete orig box, 1928-40, C.6-7 .... **$200**

Horse car, #3356, unrun, separate sale orig box, 1956-60 & 1964-66, C.9 .... **$125**

Locomotive

#8, S gauge, rewheeled, replaced head-lights, minor touchup, C.6 .... **$190**

#156, O gauge, electric, 4-4-4, dark green, 1917-23 .... **$465**

#256 locomotive, RS, 1924-30, C.6 .... **$480**

#258 locomotive, 257T tender, wear to paint, 1930-35, C.5-6 .... **$120**

#265E, 265W tender, scratched, black, 1935-40, C.5 .... **$175**

Observation car

#322, S gauge, 1924-27 .... **$100**

#754, O gauge, streamliner, 1936 . **$90**

Pullman

#35, S gauge, orange, c1915 .... **$65**

#607, O gauge, 1926 .... **$60**

Refrigerator car, #214R, Standard gauge, ivory body, peacock roof, 1929-40 .... **$400**

Set, O gauge

Passenger, #252 electric locomotive, #529 coach, #530 observation, olive green, c1926 .... **$225**

Passenger, Union Pacific, #752E power unit, #753 coach, #754 observation, silver, c1934 .... **$375**

Set, S gauge

#8 loco, rewheeled, replaced head-lamps, 337 coach, 338 observation, C.7 .... **$250**

#218 SF Alco AA, dummy with crack, 3428 milk car, 2414 coach, two 2412 vista domes, 2416 observation, C-6 .... **$360**

#225E locomotive, 265W tender, three restored 3659 dump cars, 2657 caboose, C.5-8 .... **$285**

#254E locomotive, replaced headlamps, restored frame, two 610 coaches, 612 observation, C.5 .... **$180**

#380 locomotive, 320 baggage, 319 coach, 322 observation, restored, C.8 ..... **$525**

Lionel Trains, No. 384 locomotive and tender, 1930, **$600.**

Lionel Trains, No. 385E locomotive and tender, 1933, **$500.**

MISCELLANEOUS

ADVERTISING

History: Before the days of mass media, advertisers relied on colorful product labels and advertising giveaways to promote their products. Containers were made to appeal to the buyer through the use of stylish lithographs and bright colors. Many of the illustrations used the product in the advertisement so that even an illiterate buyer could identify a product.

Advertisements were put on almost every household object imaginable and became constant reminders to use the product or visit a certain establishment.

Additional Resources:

Antique Trader® Advertising Price Guide, by Kyle Husfloen, ed., and Rich Penn, contr. ed., Krause Publications, Iola, WI.

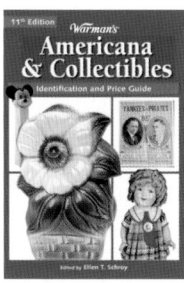

Warman's® Americana & Collectibles, 11th Ed., by Ellen T. Schroy, ed., Krause Publications, Iola, WI.

Ashtray, Buster Brown, glazed china, figural hat, Buster gesturing towards Tige balancing steaming teapot on nose, 4-7/8" l, 1" h **$165**

Bank, figural

Magic Chef, painted vinyl, 7" h **$25**

RCA Nipper, light fuzzy flocked surface over metal, 6-1/4" h, C.8++ **$230**

Blotter, unused

Cotton Overshirts, ivory white and black celluloid cover, bound at each corner by metal mount, two removable cardboard ink blotter ships, image of "Oppenheim, Oberndorf & Co.," 3" x 6" **$28**

Eppens, Smith Co., NY, Coffee and Tea Importer, full-color celluloid, slight use, 1900 seasonal greetings **$15**

Fairbanks Portable Pumping Outfit, graphics of metal vehicle, road paving machinery, 7-1/4" x 9-1/2" **$10**

Booklet, Dutch Boy Paint, 20 pgs, 5" x 6" **$12**

Bookmark, Rally Day, diecut celluloid, Spirit of '76 fife and drummers, large American flag, string tassel, early 1900s **$25**

Box

Proctor & Gamble, 1873, wood **$200**

Weideman Oak Flakes, 14 oz, cardboard, 6-1/4" x 4-1/4" **$120**

Yanks Chewing Gum, counter display box, 20 orig packs of Yanks brand 5¢ Spearmint Chewing Gum, Gum Products Inc., Boston, MA 1" x 3-1/4" x 6-1/2" **$190**

Broom holder, DeLaval Cream Separators, tin litho, black and white, orig adv envelope, 3-1/2" d, C.8 .... **$450**

Calendar

Blue Ribbon Canned Foods, desk, ivory colored celluloid over tin, 1916, 3-1/5" x 4-1/2" **$20**

Nevin's Candy, two-ply cardboard, wall type, 1917, 3-1/4" x 6-1/4" **$15**

Red Goose Shoes, colorful print of mountain goat hunter titled "Getting His Goat," H. C. Edwards, artist, ads for Red Goose Shoes, Friedman-Shelby Shoe Col, Atlantic Shoes, Pacific Shoes, 1924, 8" x 19" wall type **$25**

Candy pail

Novia Kiddie Pops, pail shape, image of pops and children and dog on both sides, 3-3/4" d, 3-1/4" h, C.7.5+ **$675**

Three Pigs, Mayfair Candy Co., NY, tin litho, 3-1/8" x 3-3/8", C.8- **$170**

Cigar box, Pittsburgh's Finest, wood, colorful paper labels with uniformed police officer, 10-7/8" x 7-5/8" x 7-1/2", C.8+ **$275**

Cigar tin, tin litho

Izaak Walton, image of Walton, hunting and fishing scenes in background, 5-3/8" x 5-3/8", C.8 .... **$190**

Bill clip, Priscilla Ware, Speaks for Itself, Leyse Aluminum Co., Kewaunee, WI, litho on aluminum, front with cameo of lady, spring clip on back, **$25.**

Cabinet, Diamond Dyes, oak, tin litho front panel with five children playing with balloon, complete, original Diamond Dye annual and direction booklet, **$2,250.**
Photo courtesy of Dotta Auction Co., Inc.

Child's rocking chair, oak, pressback design of advertising character, the Yellow Kid blowing horn, repair to back support, **$650.**
Photo courtesy of Dotta Auction Co., Inc.

Chair, folding, blue and white enamel plaque on back, "Smoke Piedmont, The Cigarette of Quality," $250.
Photo courtesy of Alderfer Auction Co.

Display, Brown's Jumbo Bread, elephant shape, framed, 19" w, 17" h, $300.
Photo courtesy of Joy Luke Auctions.

Display, tin litho, For Real Satisfaction Smoke a Pipe With This Trademark, WDC, gent smoking pipe and pointing to red triangular trademark, four pipes, easel back, c1918, $145.
Photo courtesy of Dotta Auction Co., Inc.

King Midas, image of king on both sides, 5-1/8" x 6-1/8" x 4-1/8", C.8+ tin, lid fair **$120**

Old Seneca Stogies, W. C. Kildow, colorful graphic Indian image, 5-3/4" x 4-3/8", C.8 .... **$425**

Orcico Cigars, 2 for 5¢, colorful graphic Indian image, 5-1/2" x 6-1/8" x 4-1/8", C.8.5 .... **$550**

Tobacco Girl, detailed image of trademark girl on both sides, 5-1/2" x 6-1/4" x 4-1/4", C.8.5 .... **$3,300**

White Owl Brand, General Cigar Co., blue ground, white owl perched on smoking cigar, 5-3/4" x 5-1/2", C.8+ **$675**

Clicker

Motorcycle Boy, litho tin, boy in yellow motorcycling outfit with goggles and neckerchief, riding red cycle, holding ice-cream cone in one hand, 1930s **$25**

Poll-Parrot Shoes, litho tin, red, yellow, blue parrot, yellow background, red lettering, 1930s **$25**

Twinkie Shoes, litho tin, full-color art of elf character standing on mushroom, dark green background, tiny inscription for "Hamilton-Brown Shoes Co.," 1930s **$30**

Clock

Calumet Baking Powder, Sessions clock, oak, wall-type, gold lettering, 39" x 18" x 5-1/2" **$2,600**

Iroquois Beverages, Buffalo, NY, light-up, double bubble, 16" d **$525**

None Such Mince Meat, Pumpkin-Squash, Like Mother Used to Make,

ribbed cardboard, clock face shaped like pumpkin, tin back shaped like pie plate, easel, hanging hook, clock mechanism not working, 9-1/2" d **$1,150**

Coffee tin

Daisy Fresh Coffee, Euclid Coffee Co., Cleveland, l lb, key wind, 3-5/8" x 5", C.8 .... **$150**

Epicure Coffee, John Sills and Sons, 1 lb, image of butler serving cup of coffee, 6" x 4", C.8+ **$725**

Fairway Coffee, 1 lb, key wind, colorful image of children in field, steaming cup of coffee in background, 4" x 5", C.8.5 .... **$250**

First Pick Coffee, l lb, key wind, 4" x 5", C.8 .... **$350**

Jipco Coffee, Beckers-Prentiss Co., Buffalo, NY, 1 lb, key wind, blue and white, buffalo on front, steaming cup of coffee and blossoms on back, 4" x 5-1/8", C.7 .... **$250**

Loyl Coffee, Rochester Seed & Supply Co., 1 lb, 6-1/4" x 4", C.8.5+ **$120**

Publix Markets Coffee, Lakeland, FL, 1 lb, key wind, grocery store image, 3-5/8" x 5", C.8 .... **$200**

Red Turkey Coffee, Mailby's, Corning, NY, 1 lb, 5-3/4" x 4-1/4", C.8 .... **$375**

Ten Eyck Coffee, Bacon, Stickney & Co., Albany, NY, 1 lb, pry lid, detailed image of Ten Eyck Hotel, 5-1/2" x 4-1/ 4", C.8 .... **$375**

Turkey Coffee, Kasper Co., 1 lb, image of wild turkey on both sides, 5-3/4" x 4-1/4", C.8 .... **$375**

Wake-Em Up Coffee, Anderson-Ryan Coffee Co., Duluth, MN, 10 lb, wooden handle, green and gold, trademark Indian on both sides, 13-1/2" x 9", C.8+ **$475**

Yellow Bonnet Coffee, Springfield Grocer, 1 lb, key wind, white background, 4" x 5", C.7.5+/8- **$325**

Crock, stoneware

Bowers Three Thistles Snuff, cobalt blue lettering, 14" x 9-1/2", few chips **$450**

Heinz, detailed multicolored stone litho label, orig lid and closure, 8" x 4", C.8.5+ **$675**

Diecut, litho cardboard

Colgate talcum powder, two-sided, seated baby in cap and romper, holding product, 1913, price for pr, 14" x 8-1/2", C.8 .... **$675**

Johnson & Johnson talcum powder, baby on back playing with talc container, string hanger, 8-1/8" x 14-1/8", C-7.5 .... **$575**

Larkin Boraxine Laundry Soap, cream-colored cat, red bow at neck, easel back, 12" x 9", C.8.5 .... **$220**

Williard's Candy, 5¢ Nutritious, Wolf Co., Philadelphia Lithographers, blond boy in red sweater, blue shorts, easel back, 17" x 8-3/8" **$400**

Williard's Candy, 5¢ Nutritious, Wolf Co., Philadelphia Lithographers, blonde girl in blue blouse, red romper, easel back, 17" x 8-3/8" **$675**

Display cabinet, countertop

Blue Bird, A Man's Handkerchief, tin litho, hinged top with glass insert, holds four early product boxes, 1920s, 6-3/4" x 11-1/2" x 8", C.8 .... **$450**

Farnam's Famous Kalamazoo Celery and Pepsin Chewing Gum, wood, curved glass, gold lettering, 7-1/2" x 17" x 10" **$5,600**

J & P Coats, thread spools **$1,800**

Nestles, Hazelnut Chocolate Bars, adv labels inside glass lift top, 4-3/4" x 10-1/8" x 7-1/2", C.8 .... **$500**

Tootsie Roll Candies, tin litho, 13" x 8-3/4" x 8-1/4", C.8 .... **$700**

Van Haagen's Fine Toilet Soaps, German silver, curved corners, front glass etched with name, some denting to moldings **$525**

Zeno Gum, wood, emb Zeno marquee with fancy filigree, 18" h, 10-1/2" w, 8" d **$575**

Display

Red Goose Shoes, figural, papier-mâché, glass eyes, 10-1/2" x 9" x 4-1/2", C.7.5 .... **$250**

Tennyson 5¢ Cigars Always Fresh, Mazer Cressman, tin litho, 8" x 5-3/4" x 5-3/4", C.8+ **$400**

Door push

Canada Dry, multicolored bottle and slogan, emb tin litho, 9" x 3" **$210**

Crescent Flour, Voight Milling Co., Grand Rapids, MI, emb tin litho, 9-5/8" x 3-3/4", C.8.5 .... **$300**

Domino Cigarettes, emb tin litho, 14" x 4", C.8.5 .... **$100**

Edgeworth Tobacco, red, white, and blue, emb tin litho, 14" x 4" **$170**

Ex-Lax, multicolored porcelain, 8" x 4" **$375**

Fan, hand held

Alka-Seltzer, cartoon illus, cardboard mounted on wooden rod, late 1930s-40s, 8-1/2" x 9-1/2" **$25**

Planters Peanuts, Mr. Peanut driving peanut shaped car, adv on back, 1940s, 5-1/4" x 8", C.8 .... **$230**

Gauge, Standard Roller Bearing Co., 3" x 3" celluloid covers, diecut openings, inner disk wheels to use in determining precise measurements, requirements, etc. for ball bearings, c1920 .... **$20**

Lapel stud

Alaska Stove Trimmings, brown and white celluloid, metal lapel stud fastener, stove lid lifter illus, plus inscription "Mama! Do You Use

Alaska Stove Trimmings-Always Cold" **$20**

Widow Jones Suits Me, multicolored celluloid on metal, young lady in stylish gray outfit and hat, pale blue to white background, blue lettering, New England clothing store sponsor, 1-1/4" **$40**

Lunch box

Dan Patch Cut Plug, Scotten Dillion Co., tin litho, bale handle, yellow, red, and black, 4-3/8" x 6-7/8" x 4-5/8", tin C.8+, lid C.7+ **$325**

Green Turtle Cigars, Gordon Cigar Co., tin litho, turtle on rock smoking cigar, 5-1/4" x 7-1/2" x 4-1/2", front C.8-, back C.7 .... **$350**

Match safe, Advance Farm Equipment, silvered brass, hinged, celluloid wrapper print in color, one side with medieval figure raising Advance banner on rocky height, opposite side with "Simple Traction Engine," two smaller panels each with lists of offices by city, early 1900s **$115**

Mirror, pocket

Berry Bros Varnishes, celluloid, multicolored, little boy pulling dog in Berry Co. adv wagon, 1-3/4" x 2-3/4" **$200**

I Wear Kleinert's Dress Shields, brown on cream, 2" d **$45**

The Lincoln Savings Bank, blue on white, bright red center stripe surrounding profile of Lincoln above text "Vote for Lincoln As Your Bank," c1940, 2-1/8" d **$30**

Oyster pail, Fresh Oysters, Schneier's Co., Akron, OH, 1 gal, orig lid, 7-3/8" x 6-5/8", C.8+ **$250**

Paperweight, Southern Fruit Julep Co., glass, reverse adv on all four sides, five-year monthly scrolling calendar inside, 1-3/8" x 4" x 2-7/8" **$325**

Peanut butter pail, tin litho

Armour's Veribest Peanut Butter, 2 lb, nursery rhyme characters, yellow ground, 4-5/8" x 4-3/8", C.7.5 .... **$190**

Clark's Peanut Butter, Canadian, 1 lb, sporting images, 3-3/8" x 3-3/4", C.8++ **$875**

Monarch Peanut Butter, Teenie Weenie, 1 lb, colorful image of children and giant peanuts, c1920, 3-3/4" x 3-3/8", C.8++ **$300**

O! Boy Peanut Butter, Stone Ordean Wells Co., Duluth, 1 lb, children eating sandwiches on front, seashore scene on back, 3-3/8" x 3-3/4", C.8+ **$650**

Display cabinet, Shaeffer Fineline, pencils, semi-circular, 27" w, 14" h, **$250**.
Photo courtesy of Joy Luke Auctions.

Promotional items, pair, left: die-cut countertop standee, Donald holding bread loaf, imprint of "Friends", 10" h; right: Simulated bread loaf of waxed paper wrapped around loaf-shaped cardboard insert, pair of attached Donald bread end labels, imprint of "Hardy Baking Co.," light edge wear, small tear, center crease line; both 1950s, pair, **$400**.
Photo courtesy of Hake's Americana & Collectibles.

Display stand, Wise Potato Chips, thin cardboard, image on front of boy and girl at store counter, boy holding up two fingers and smiling as retailer reaches for bags of potato chips from counter display, titled "A Wise Guy," door with logo "Eat Wise Potato Chips," easel back, copyright 1940 Wise Delicatessen Co., Burwick, Va. unused, 17" x 20-1/4", **$50**.
Photo courtesy of Hake's Americana & Collectibles.

Lunch pail, Just Suits Tobacco, P. Lorillard Co., tin, red, gold text accented in black, lid hinged at right, clasp on left, wire handle on top, designed to be reused as lunch pail, bright glossy finish, gold luster, c1900, 7-3/4" l, 5-1/4" w, 4" h, **$150.**

Photo courtesy of Hake's Americana & Collectibles.

Lard pail, Swift's Silver-Leaf Pure Lard Kettle, red, black, and gold label, original handle and lid, some rust, **$25.**

Ring, dark green plastic, brown and white flicker Davy Crockett, Karo Syrup premium,1955, **$85.**

Photo courtesy of Hake's Americana & Collectibles.

Planters High Grade Peanut Butter, 25 lbs, 9-1/4" x 10-1/4", C.7.5 ....**$575**

Squirrel, Canadian, 3 lb, pry lid, squirrel eating peanut, 4-3/4" x 5-1/8", C.8.5 ....**$425**

Pencil clip

Ardee Flour, red, yellow, blue logo, celluloid on brass wire clip, Hubbard Milling Co., Mankato, Minn, sponsor, early 1900s **$25**

Red Man Cigar Leaf, multicolored, tobacco pack mounted on brass wire spring clip, early 1900s **$55**

The Metropolitan, black, white, and red celluloid, mounted on brass wire spring clip, sponsor store designates "Hats" and "Furnishings" **$20**

Pinback button

Cherry-Ripe Ice Cream, two dark red cherries on green, c1940, 3-1/2" d **$20**

Davis OK Baking Powder, multicolored, bottle flanked by slogans, black lettering, back paper, c1896 ....**$20**

Empire Cream Separator, black and white image, blue letters, rim inscription "I Chirp for the Empire because it makes the most dollars for me," clicker hanging from bottom rim **$50**

Farm Boy Bread, red, white, and blue, center bluetone photo of young farm lad posed next to cow and rooster, blue and red lettering, 1930s **$15**

Hessler Rural Mailbox, illus of sample mailbox, "Approved By Postmaster General" **$75**

Kar-A-Van Coffee, multicolored, loaded camel, early 1900s **$20**

Lekko Scouring Powder, multicolored, image of product canister, and housewife on knees scrubbing floor, 1920s **$35**

Mephisto Auger Bits, black and red lettering, white ground **$15**

Metzer's Milk Infant Keeps Them Smiling, tinted flesh-tone face, white background, blue and red lettering, c1930, 1" d **$12**

O.I.C. Hogs, black and white art and inscription, patriotic red, white, blue, and silver outer rim, back paper with lengthy text for "Famous O.I.C. Hogs," c1900 ....**$50**

RCA Micro Mike, ivory white celluloid, red image and title, 3" d **$18**

Stetson Hats Best in the World, multicolored logo, celluloid, oval **$12**

Vote Betty Crocker, red, white, and blue litho, c1960 ....**$12**

Widow Hoffman System-Boys Clothing-Harris Clothing Co., Baltimore, black and white celluloid, young lad in cap and jacket **$15**

Wilbur's Cocoa, multicolored, cherub trademark stirring Wilbur mug, orig back paper, c1896 ....**$20**

Plate, Old Barbee Whiskey, Vienna Art, center with peasants and cabin, tin litho, 10" d, C.8 ....**$400**

Pot scraper, tin litho

MB Flavoring Extracts, Day-Bergwall Co., Milwaukee, Shonk Litho, slight wear, 2-7/8" x 3", C.7+ **$375**

Nesco Royal Graniteware, 3-1/2" x 3", C.8 ....**$500**

Print, Falls City Clothing Co., Imperial Clothes, Louisville, Ky, titled Elsie, sgd B. Tichman, woman in red duster and bonnet, printed by Meek Co., Coshocton, OH, framed, copyright 1908, 30" x 15" **$235**

Rolling pin, Royal Household Flour, Canadian, china body, wooden handles, blue and red printing, mkd "Hand-painted Nippon" on side, 19-1/4" x 3" **$230**

Salesman's sample

Dilworth's Golden Urn Brand Coffee, Pittsburgh, tin litho, 2-1/2" x 2", C.8+ **$150**

Goldsmith & Sons boxing gloves, leather, lace-up, two 4-1/4" x 2-1/2" gloves stamped "GoldSmith 01" in silver, 2-1/2" x 5-1/4" x 5-3/4" orig box **$350**

Home plate, rubber, emb lettering, 4" x 4-1/8" **$180**

Lawnmower, mkd "H. A. Daum, Locksmith" **$3,950**

Toilet, Ariston Silent, Made of Durock, heavy ceramic bowl, orig hardware and seat, spider line to glaze on int., 7-3/4" x 14" x 7" **$825**

Sharpening stone, Pike Mfg. Co., Pike, NH, gold luster finish metal case, pike fish passing through letter "P," rect whetstone, some wear to stone and luster **$45**

Sign

Algo Spearmint Chewing Gum, cardboard, 4-1/2" x 7-3/4", C.8 ....**$160**

Collins Honey Scotch Candy, Minneapolis, emb tin, 7" x 19-1/2" **$210**

Continental Insurance, framed paper in three sections, left panel with Victorian Brooklyn, Continental Insurance Building with signage on front, right panel with New York Continental Insurance Building with multiple horse-drawn carriages in front, center with Indian tribe watching as wild animals run out of burning forest, J. Ottoman litho, some minor staining to orig matting, ©1895, 34-1/2" h, 68-1/2" w **$1,450**

Cracker Jack The More You Eat, The More You Want, F.W. Rueckheim & Bros., Chicago, mother holding child reaching for box, 1900, 14-1/2" x 10-3/4", C.8.5 ....**$5,000**

Dakota Maid Flour, emb tin litho, yellow and blue, 9" x 19-1/2", C.8+ **$120**

De Laval Cream Separators, tin, emb frame **$2,800**

Drink Palmer's Root Beer, It's Better, Palmer Candy Co., Kaufman, TX, heavy porcelain, slightly curved, 14" x 21", C.8+ **$300**

Drink Moxie, emb tin litho, 6-1/4" x 19", C.9 ....**$220**

Elgin Watch, reverse painting on glass, trademark Father Time, gold on black, framed, 23-1/2" h, 17-1/2" w **$500**

Enjoy Hires, it's always pure, emb tin litho, girl in red hat, 9-3/4" x 27-3/4", C.8+ **$475**

Enjoy Hires Healthful Delicious, 9-1/2" x 27-1/2", emb tin litho, C.7.5 ....**$250**

Everybody Likes Popsicle Refreshing Easy to Eat, emb tin litho, red, black, yellow, 9-7/8" x 27-3/4", C.8+ **$325**

Foster Hose Supporters, celluloid, 17" x 9" **$425**

Gail Borden Col's Eagle Brand Condensed Milk, cardboard litho, puppy drinking from sleep baby's glass nursing bottle, 15" x 10-1/2", C.8- **$450**

Georgia Stages, Inc. Ticket Office, Bus Station, porcelain, double-sided, graphics of bus, 1930s **$10,500**

Good Humor Ice Cream, six-color porcelain, 1930s, 18" x 26", C.8+ **$1,200**

John P. Squire & Co., self framed emb tin, pig in center, titled "Squires Arlington, Hams-Bacon-Sausage,"© 1906, 24" h, 20" w **$800**

Jersey Crème The Perfect Drink At Fountains, 5¢ Also in Bottles, two-sided tin litho flange, yellow and black, 6" d, C.9 ....**$725**

Kis-Me-Gum, emb cardboard diecut, lady in diaphanous top, framed, ©1905, 8" h, 13" w **$500**

Korbel California Champagne, tin litho over cardboard, 13" x 19", C.8 ....**$250**

Lee Union-Alls, porcelain **$2,800**

McCormick, The King of the Harvest, stone litho, image of well dressed farmer harvesting in field with team of horses, 15-1/2" x 21-1/2", C.8 ....**$475**

Merry Widow Gum, cardboard, hanging type, 8" x 3", C.8 ....**$375**

Pearl Oil, flanged tin, diecut kerosene can shape **$3,100**

Star Brand Shoes, self framed tin, bust of young lady with flowing hair, advertising "Women's Mayflower Shoe, $2.50," some overall spotting, 26" h, 19" w **$300**

Sterling Super-Bru, Sterling Brewers, Evansville, IN, emb tin, trapezoid, 17-5/8" x 9-3/8", C.8.5+ **$450**

Sunkist Grower, porcelain, black, white, and red, green border, 11-1/2" x 19-1/2" **$375**

Tom Keene Cigar, curved corner type, heavy porcelain, orig Ingram-Richardson paper manufacturer's label on back, 15" x 14-3/4", C.8.5 ....**$575**

United Motor Service, porcelain, double sided **$3,000**

Valentine's Valspar Varnish, It's The Coat That Makes The Boat, hanging, tin litho over cardboard, man varnishing 1920s wooden racing boat, 13" x 19", C.8+ **$3,400**

Wonder Bread, porcelain, dark blue, red, and white, 8-5/8" x 20, C.8 ....**$375**

Woolworth's, fiberboard, diamond-shape, "Woolworth's, Satisfaction Guaranteed, Replacement Or Money Refunded," white and black letters, red and white ground, some paint chipping and flaking **$35**

W W W Rings, tin over cardboard, lady in vintage clothing at college football game, some damage, 9-1/4" h, 6-1/4" l **$100**

Y & S Licorice, figural, pc of black licorice, orig paper label, hanging, 18" x 3-1/2", C.8- **$275**

Zenith Radios, enamel, bright blue and white letters on red field, yellow background, "Long Distance Radio," 60" l, 18" w **$200**

Plate, Season's Greetings, Gately & Fitzgerald Co., Allentown, PA, pretty red haired lady, white dress, red roses decoration, white ground, blue edge trim, **$35.**

Poster, F. H. Ayres Billiard Tables, Bagatelle Boards, scene of family playing billiards, framed, **$145.**

Print, Robert Smith Ale Brewing Co., Spread Eagle Inn, signed "J.P. 1908, Copyright 1909, Robert Smith Ale Brewing Co., original frame, 20" x 17", some staining, **$25.**
Photo courtesy of Michael Ivankovich Auction Co., Inc.

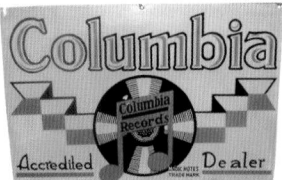

Sign, Columbia Records, litho tin, yellow, red, white, and black, Accredited Dealer, **$125.**

Tins: left: Chicago Assortment, candy; Lady Churchill; Muriel 5 cent; Oceanic Cut Plug, the lot sold for **$130.**

Photo courtesy of Joy Luke Auctions.

Sign, Fatima, A Sensible Cigarette, tin litho, multicolored pack of cigarettes, green background, 12" x 8-1/2", **$165.**

Photo courtesy of Dotta Auction Co., Inc.

Trade card, Metropolitan Life Insurance Co., "The Leading Industrial Insurance Company of America," little girl standing next to chair, branch addresses on other side, scrolling borders, oversized, copyright 1902, **$45.**

Spinner top

Hurd Shoes, black and white celluloid, wooden red spinner dowel, Parisian Novelty Co., maker name on rim curl, 1930s **$20**

Poll-Parrot Shoes, litho tin, wooden spinner dowel, red and yellow parrot striding between black shoes, yellow background, red rim, red star logo, 1930s **$25**

Woodmen of the World, blue lettering on white celluloid, wooden red spinner dowel, Parisian Novelty Co., maker name on rim curl, 1930s **$18**

Store bin, tin litho

Beech Nut Chewing Tobacco, slant front, green ground, white lettering, 6" w, 10" l, 8" h **$400**

Light Sweet Burley Tobacco, Spaulding Merrick, 10-3/4" x 8-1/4", C.8 .... **$210**

Sure Shot Chewing Tobacco, graphic of Indian brave taking aim with bow and arrow, 6-1/2" x 15-1/4" x 10-1/4", C.8++ **$950**

Sweet Cuba Tobacco, slant front, 10" l, 8" w **$365**

Sweet Mist Chewing Tobacco, children in fountain, 11-1/2" x 8-1/4", C.8 .... **$300**

Tiger Chewing Tobacco, Lorrilard Co., round, blue, 11-3/4" h, 8-3/4" d **$850**

Tape measure

Fox's Guernsey Dairy, black lettering on yellow ground, red rim, four red carnations on black ground on reverse **$25**

Sears, Roebuck & Co., white lettering, black ground, lightning bolt-style lettering for "WLS" (World's Largest Store,) red, white, blue, and green stylized floral design on back **$15**

Thermometer

Calumet Baking Powder, wood, black, red, and white, yellow ground, 27" x 7-1/4", C.8+ **$1,100**

Hills Bros. Coffee, porcelain, 1915, 8-3/4" w, 21" h **$825**

Kentucky Club Pure Tobacco, painted metal, 38-1/2" x 8", C.8++ **$200**

Wool Soap, black and white, metal case, glass front, 1895 copyright, 6" d **$600**

Tin, miscellaneous

Busy Biddy Spice, Davies Strass Stauffer Co., red, white, and black, 3-1/8" x 1-3/4" x 1-1/4", C.7.5+ **$120**

Cadette Tooth Powder, figural tin litho soldier, red cap and coat, full, 7-3/8" x 2-1/4" x 1-1/4", C.8 .... **$625**

F. W. Cough Drops, Geo Miller & Co., Phila, "Cured My Cough," detailed graphics, 8" x 5-1/8" x 5-1/8", C.9 .... **$1,400**

Planters Nuts & Chocolate Co., Egyptian design on lid and sides, c1919, 6-1/4" d, 4" h, C.8 .... **$1,050**

Popeye Pop Corn, Purity Mills, Dixon, IL, pry lid, 4-3/4" x 3-1/4" x 2-1/8", C.8++ **$160**

W. Phillips Ltd., London, biscuits, Egyptian images on shaped hinged lid, 6" x 6-3/4" x 3-1/8," C.8- **$90**

Tip tray, Cunard Lines, Aquitania ocean liner, tin litho, 4-5/8" x 6-5/8", C.8+ **$350**

Tobacco tin, tin litho

Bulldog Smoking Tobacco, Lowville Buffington Co., vertical pocket, 4-1/2" x 3" x 7/8", C.8 .... **$675**

Checkers, Weisert Bros, St. Louis, vertical pocket, white, black, and red, 4-1/2" x 3" x 7/8", C.8.5 .... **$525**

C.H.Y.P. Inter-Collegiate Mixture, 2-1/4" x 4-1/2" x 3-3/8", C.8- ... **$160**

Crane's Private Mixture, House of Crane, Indianapolis, vertical pocket, 4-1/4" x 3-3/8" x 1-1/4", C.8 .... **$425**

Dixie Queen, canister, trademark girl in large hat on both sides, 6-1/2" x 4-1/4", C.8.5 .... **$600**

Forest & Stream, Imperial Tobacco Co., Canada, vertical pocket, fisherman in canoe, 4-1/8" x 3" x 7/8", C.8 .... **$475**

Guide Pipe & Cigarette Tobacco, Larus & Bros., vertical pocket, 4-1/4" x 3" x 7/8", C.8+ **$230**

Long Distance, Scotten Dillon Co., pail, multicolored graphics with battleship, 6-1/2" x 5-1/2", C.8+ **$170**

North Pole Tobacco, United States Tobacco Co., hinged box, 3-1/8" x 6-1/8" x 3-7/8", C.8+ **$220**

Pat Hand, Globe Tobacco Co., vertical pocket, full, 2-3/4" x 2-1/2" x 1-3/8", C.8.5 .... **$130**

Paul Jones, shield with Paul Jones on front, image of battleship on back, vertical pocket, 4-1/2" x 3" x 7/8", C.8+ **$1,750**

Pipe Major, Brown & Williamson, vertical pocket, 4-1/2" x 3" x 7/8", C.8+ **$325**

Princeton Mixture, Marburg Bros., paper label, 4-1/2" x 3" x 1-7/8", C.8+ **$400**

Puritan, Phillip Morris, vertical pocket, 4-3/8" x 3" x 7/8", C.8.5 .... **$300**

Seal of North Carolina, Marburg Bros., canister, multicolored graphic trademark on both sides, 6-1/2" x 4-7/8", C.8+ **$375**

Trout-Line, vertical pocket, fly fisherman in stream, 3-3/4" x 3-1/2" x 1-1/8", C.8++ **$675**

Weyman's Cutty Pipe, canister, green ground, red and yellow lettering, 13-1/2" x 10-1/4" x 9-3/8", C.8.5 .... **$1,400**

Whip, Patterson Bros., vertical pocket, rider in red coat, white pants, black boots, brown horse's head, 4-1/2" x 3" x 7/8", C.8- **$850**

White Manor, Penn Tobacco, vertical pocket, 3" x 3-1/2" x 1", C.8++ **$210**

Token, Sambo's Coffee, wooden, printed in red on both sides, one side with patriotic design featuring coffee mug, inscription "What This Country Needs Is A Good 10 Cent Cup of Coffee-Sambo's Has It," reverse inscribed "Sambo's Restaurants Anywhere," late 1970s, 1-1/2" d **$10**

Trade card

8th Wonder or Engle Clock, Capt. J. Reid and his wife standing next to giant mechanical clock built by Hazelton, Pennsylvania, jewelry and watchmaker, c1890, 3" x 5-1/4" **$5**

Ayer's Sarsaparilla, "Ayer's Sarsaparilla Makes the Weak Strong," two gentlemen **$18**

Child's & Staples, Gilbertsville, Maine, young girl chasing butterfly, 2-3/4" x 4-1/2" **$12**

Czar Baking Powder, black woman and boy with giant biscuit **$25**

Granite Iron Ware, three ladies gossiping over tea **$25**

Heinz Apple Butter, diecut, pickle shape **$60**

Hoyt's German Cologne, E.M. Hoyt & Co., mother cat and kittens **$25**

J. & P. Coats, Best Silk Thread, "We Never Fade," black youngster and spool of thread **$18**

New Essay Lawn Mower, scene of Statue of Liberty, New York harbor **$35**

Norton Bros., sign and tin manufacturers, c1870, 2-3/4" x 4" **$575**

Perry Davis, Pain Killer for Wounds, armored man of war ships battle scene **$25**

Reid's Flower Seeds, two high wheeled bicyclers admiring flowers held by three ladies **$25**

Scott's Emulsion of Cod Liver Oil, man with large fish over back, vertical format **$20**

Singer Manufacturing Co., choir of children singing as birds listen **$20**

Solar Tip Shoes, Girard College, Philadelphia, Where Boys Wear Our Solar Tip Shoes **$20**

Thompson's Glove Fitting Corsets, lady and cupids **$35**

White Sewing Machine Co., elves working at sewing machine **$15**

Tray, tin litho

J. Leisy Brewing, Cleveland, OH, multicolored graphic of factory, horse-drawn delivery wagons, oval, 13-5/8" x 16-5/8", C.8+ **$775**

Nova Kola, American Art Works, center graphic of well dressed couple clinging to world while raising glasses together, 13-1/4" x 13-1/4", C.8 .... **$375**

Orange Julep, girl at beach, 1920s, 13-1/4" x 10-1/4" x 1-1/4", C.8+ **$210**

Pabst Brewerys, black ground, gold dec, multicolored graphic of factory, rect, 12-1/4" x 17-1/4", C.8++ **$550**

Robinson's Sons Pilsner Beer, 12" d, C.8 .... **$575**

Stroh's Lager Beer, Detroit, heavy porcelain enamel center insert, 12" d, C.8+ **$1,050**

Watch fob

Corby's Canadian Whiskey, silvered white metal frame, four large flower blossoms surround color insert of pretty woman reclining against stone wall, robe falling open, Whitehead & Hoag **$175**

Savage Arms, emb metal, pointing Indian chief, painted head band, orig patina, 1-5/8" d **$325**

Toy, Oscar Mayer Wienermobile, plastic and vinyl body, bright orange, blue, white, silver, black, and red, **$225.**

Trade card, Jas A Armstrong, Druggist, Camden, NJ, Card No. 20, Design 1, framed, **$15.**

Wall pocket, embossed multicolored stiff paper, woodland scene, text on pocket "Compliments of L. F. Harpel, General Merchandise, Richlandtown, Pa," **$35.**

Trade card, Clark's O.N.T., set of four, multicolored image of pretty blonde girl on front in various activities, light green border, blue promo text on back, 1883, each 3-3/4" x 6-1/2", **$30.**

Stag head, Black Forest carved, mounted on green plaque, 19th C, 17" h, **$475.**
Photo courtesy of Wiederseim Associates, Inc.

Cow, platter, blue and white transfer, marked "Victoria Ironstone," **$125.**

Bull, cast bronze, wooden base, unmarked, break to horns, 20th C, 10", **$475.**
Photo courtesy of David Rago Auctions, Inc.

ANIMAL COLLECTIBLES

History: The representation of animals in fine arts, decorative arts, and on utilitarian products dates back to antiquity. Some religions endowed certain animals with mystical properties. Authors throughout written history used human characteristics when portraying animals.

The formation of collectors' clubs and marketing crazes, e.g., flamingo, pig, and penguin, during the 1970s increased the popularity of this collecting field.

Additional Resources:

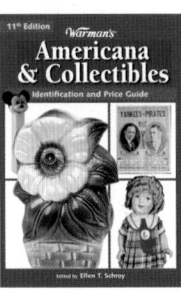

Warman's® Americana & Collectibles, 11th Ed., by Ellen T. Schroy, ed., Krause Publications, Iola, WI.

Barnyard

Carving, folk art, wood
Peep, painted, with stand, c1900, 7" l **$9,545**

Rooster, polychrome red, mustard yellow, and brown, base with indistinct pencil inscription, Pennsylvania, c1840, 9-1/2" l, 2-1/2" w, 8" h **$4,320**

Rooster, old cream-colored paint, 3/4 flat body, stand, 17" l, 15" h **$460**

Chopper, rooster, iron, fanciful silhouette, incised feather detail, mounted on wooden fragment, with stand, lacks wooden handle, late 18th/early 19th C, 12" l, 7-1/2" d, 7-1/4" h **$1,035**

Doorstop, lamb, polychrome glazed molded earthenware, attributed to J Eberly & Co., Strasburg, Virginia **$34,100**

Figure, sewer tile
Frog on log, hand modeled, tooled bark, inscribed initials "H.S." on base, dark brown, slightly metallic glaze, traces of gold on one end of log, 5-1/4" l, 5" h **$425**

Pig, standing, wearing pants, vest, and bow tie, reddish-brown glaze, few spots of wear, 7-7/8" h **$320**

Hooked rug, owl in front of a full moon, oval, late 19th C **$950**

Jar, cov, stoneware, figure of pig eating from trough on lid, German, some damage to base, 6" d, 6-1/2" h **$115**

Lithograph, Prize Poultry, from Cassell's Poultry Book, printed by Vincent, Brooks, Day & Son, each specimen titled including "Mr. Henry Belden's Pair of Golden Spangled Polish," etc., French matted, 21-1/8" x 18-1/2" ebonized and parcel gilt frames, England, price for set of eight, late 19th C, 10" x 7-1/2" **$1,530**

Painting, gouache, 12-1/4" h, 20" w, sheep grazing in hilly pasture, sgd "H. I. Marlatt," (H. Irving Marlatt, Mt. Vernon, New York, 1867-1929, gouache sketch on heavy paper, matted, 22-1/4" h, 29-3/4" w frame, some edge wear **$250**

Painting, oil on canvas, sheep and lamps in stable, nearby chickens, ornate frame with copper and gold repaint, rebacked on board, revarnished, minor touch up, 29-1/8" h, 36-1/2" w **$920**

Pull toy, billy goat, gray fur, papier-mâché horns, leather harness, orig cream painted cart with gold and blue stripes, goat moves with rocking motion, one wheel knob replaced, wear, 23" l..................................**$815**

Tin, Dr. Daniels' Cow Invigorator, 18 oz pry lid tin litho, image of cow on each side, C-8+ **$275**

Birds

Architectural element, Owl, pottery, unglazed, traces of old silver paint, base imp "Owens and Howard, St. Louis, MO," minor hairlines, 18-1/2" h......................................**$550**

Eagle, cast iron, painted, black with white spots, America, late 19th C, 11" l, 5-1/2" d, 3-1/2" h...............**$250**

Figure, sewer tile, horned owl, perched on round pedestal base, orange glaze, 10-1/2" h...................................**$450**

Plaque, Ebonized frame, pietra dura, colorful parrot on perch, Italian, early 20th C, 7" x 4" sight, 11-1/2" x 8-1/2"
....**$250**

Sculpture, eagle, carved wood, standing, spread wings, 15-1/2" wingspan, 20" h......................................**$395**

Trivet, parrot, pastel central figure with intricate flower and vine pattern, eight triangular feet, Rookwood marks, 1929, 5-3/4" sq **$325**

Wall shelf, eagle, carved wood, shaped shelf supported by eagle with spread wings, loss to gilt, 16-1/2" w
....**$475**

Cats

Bank, chalk ware, seated, wearing red bow, minor loss, 11" h.................**$200**

Cane
Carved ivory ball handle with cat face emerging from one side, 1/3" sterling collar with Chester hallmarks for 1903, dark Malacca shaft, 3/4" brass ferrule, 34-1/2" l, 1-3/4" d x 1-3/4" h **$450**

Carved wood head, nicely detailed features, when button on back is pressed, red eyes change to blue, long red tongue shoots out, 1-1/4" dec silver collar, Malacca shaft, 7/8" replaced brass ferrule, German, c1880, 36" l, 2" w x 3-1/2" **$2,020**

Figure
Carved pine, fat cat, incised "E. Sweet," cracks, 20th C, 9-1/2" w, 7" d, 17-1/4" h.............................**$435**

Glass, cast, blue, sgd "Daum France," 20th C, 3-1/4" h **$185**

Glass, cast, colorless, sgd "Baccarat," orig box, 3-7/8" h **$175**

Sewer tile, reclining, hand-tooled eyelashes, white glazed eyes, 9" l
....**$360**

Sewer tile, elongated form, head cocked to one side, curious look, hand tooled eyelashes, metallic glaze, Ohio, 13-1/4" h...............**$660**

Paperweight, hunchback cat, cast iron, adv "Walter A. Zelnicker Supply Co. in St. Louis, U.S.A." on base, rare, excellent, 3-7/8" x 2-1/2"............**$515**

Tip tray, cast iron, figural black kitten's face, "Baker," excellent, 4" x 4"
....**$150**

Painting

Brown Tabby Kitten with a Rose Bow, John Henry Dolph, sgd "JHDolph" lower left, oil on board, framed, scattered retouch, 12" x 9"
....**$4,700**

Gray Tiger Cat with a Blue Bow, sgd "MABrown" lower right, American School, oil on canvas, framed, minor scattered retouch, varnish inconsistencies, 19th C, 17" x 21"
....**$2,000**

Sleepy Tabby, Franklin W. Rogers, sgd "F.W. Roger" lower right, label on reverse, oil on canvas, framed, scattered retouch, varnish inconsistencies, craquelure, 21" x 17"
....**$1,175**

The Sleeping Tabby, monogrammed and dated "JLC 1881" lower left, American School, oil on canvas, framed, scattered retouch, craquelure, 19th C, 9" x 12"
....**$3,300**

Stamp box, carved fruitwood, figural cat lying inside shoe, glass eyes, hinged lid, early 20th C, 4-3/4" l
....**$225**

Dogs

Ashtray, Scottish Terrier, sq, porcelain, center black terrier, images of hounds and rabbits, green and white ground, Hermes............................**$50**

Cane
Carved elephant ivory handle, 3-1/2" l x 1-1/2" h, pug family consisting of father, mother, three pups in line, 1" gold filled collar dec in "C" scrolls, orig owner's elaborate initials, ebony shaft carved with simulated thorns, 1-1/8" burnished brass and iron ferrule, English, c1890, 35" l,
....**$1,570**

*Dog collar, leather, decorated with brass French boxer dog heads, early 20th C, 15" l, **$225**.*
Photo courtesy of Wiederseim Associates, Inc.

*Musical picture, tin figures of adult cat playing fiddle, kittens dancing, tin figures move in conjunction with music box attached to back, German, missing key, losses to frame, 8-3/4" x 12", **$10,450**.*
Photo courtesy of Alderfer Auction Co.

*Portrait of a dog, oil on canvas, later gilt frame, 19th C painting, 11-1/2" x 9-1/4", **$650**.*
Photo courtesy of Wiederseim Associates, Inc.

*Terriers, bronze, designed by M. Kirmse, one seated, one crouched, both signed by artist, Gorham, tallest 1-1/2" x 3/4", **$1,600**.*
Photo courtesy of David Rago Auctions, Inc.

Flock of sheep puzzle, 75 pieces, incomplete, no box, 8-1/4" x 11-1/4", **$50.**

Pug dog, advertising diecut, blue neck ribbon with bell, printed "Compliments of Downing & Welsh, 197 Burnet St, New Brunswick, NJ," back plain, some wear and loss, 11" h, **$20.**

Collie, store display, papier-mâché and synthetic fur, life size, **$850.**

Carved ivory handle, 1-3/4" d x 4-3/4" h, performing poodle, wearing toy soldier's cap, holding toy gun, 3/4" silver collar, tan Malacca shaft, 1" replaced brass ferrule, England, c1890, 35-1/4" l **$1,120**

Elephant ivory handle carved as mastiff emerging from seashell, 2" w x 2-3/4" h brown glass eyes, maccassar ebony shaft, 1-1/2" white metal and iron ferrule, Continental, c1890, 36-7/8" l **$1,680**

Purple quartz handle carved as French bulldog, 2-1/2" w x 2" h, upright ears, dec gold plated collar, ebony shaft, 1" brass and iron ferrule, Continental, c1890, 36-1/2" l **$950**

Figure, bronze, terrier with bone, bronze dog standing possessively over carved ivory bone on ground before him, oblong base, mold incised signature for Friedrich Gornik, founder's monogram AR, 5" l, 3-1/2" h **$900**

Figure, clay

Newcomerstown, Ohio, pottery, seated, unglazed clay, good detail, shallow front chip, 10" h **$3,750**

Ohio white clay, seated, short ears and tail, long jowls, grown glaze, chip on back of base, small flake on ear, 8-1/8" h **$110**

Seated, freestanding front legs, yellow Ohio clay, mottled green glaze on base, brown dec on dog, black eyes, blue ink stamp label "E. Houghton & Co. Dalton, Ohio, 1928," hairline in base, 7" w, 3-1/2" d, 9-1/2" h **$1,450**

Seated, freestanding front legs, gray clay, cream-colored glaze, brown and blue polka dots, long tail with brown, one ear brown, other blue, chips on base, 7-1/4" l, 9-1/4" h **$6,270**

Figure, pearlware, long hair seated dog, white, brown and gold spots, minor flakes on base, short hairline, 2-7/8" l, 3-1/4" h **$520**

Figure, sewer tile

Collie, standing, reddish brown glaze, rect molded base, firing separations, small chips on ears, 10-1/2" l, 5-1/2" w, 11-1/2" h **$935**

Seated, hand modeled, tooled fur and facial features, mat glaze with metallic speckles, traces of white paint, 7-1/2" h **$110**

Seated, molded with hand tooled details on ears and face, long eye-

lashes, glaze varies from light tan to dark reddish brown, Ohio, minor flakes on base, 11" h **$660**

Figure, stoneware, Spaniels, tan and brown speckled matte glaze, glass eyes, oval bases, England, repair to base of one, glaze flakes, price for pr, c1875, 13-1/2" h **$6,465**

Folk art painting, King Charles spaniel and her two pups, 8-7/8" x 11" **$2,800**

Jewelry, brooch

Micromosaic, recumbent King Charles spaniel, gold ropetwist frame, minor lead solder on verso **$900**

Platinum and diamond, terrier, pave setting, green stone eyes **$1,725**

Reverse painted crystal, standing boxer, oval 14k gold frame, sgd "W. F. Marcus" **$920**

Painting, pastel on paper

Naughty puppy worrying a piece of lace, unsigned, American School, molded gilt frame, rippling, 19th C, 13-1/4" x 17-1/4" **$1,295**

Puppy sleeping on green cushion, unsigned, American School, gilt frame, small ear at center right edge, 19th C, 12-1/2" x 17-1/4" **$1,175**

Shaving mug, hp, two hunting dogs, brown background, mkd "St. Louis Electronic Grinding Co., Barber Supplies," some wear to gold trim, crack in ring handle, 4-1/8" x 3-3/4" **$120**

Vase, Lenox, marked "Hunter Arms Co., First Prize, Class A," image of pointer in clearing, sgd "Delan," stamped Lenox logo, 10" h **$3,665**

Watch fob, four graduated round 14k gold plaques depicting dog's heads in repoussé, suspended by trace link chains, monogrammed, swivel clasp, 15.0 dwt **$575**

Horses

Blanket, needlework design of horse, red ground, diamond design in field, black border with cross-stitched multicolored floral design, red yarn fringe, wool backing, reverse stitched with owner's name "Jacob Weber 1871," minor restoration, moth damage in backing, 68" sq **$175**

Book, Rodeo, *A Collection of Tales & Sketches* by R.B. Cunningham Graham, selected by A.F. Tschiffeley, Literary Guild, 1936 .... **$10**

Dog, boot scraper, bronze, dachshund shape, detailed, $115.

Photo courtesy of Dotta Auction Co., Inc.

Hippos, paperweight, crystal, etched marked "Mats Jonasson, Sweden" on original label, $125.

Horse, award, crystal Tiffany vase, engraved "Pennsylvania Horse Breeders Association 1993 Iroquois Award, Pennfield Farms, Inc., breeder of Fleeced," $125.

Cane, 4" l x 2-1/4" h elephant ivory handle carved as two riding horse heads, carved simulated leather tack, 1/2" sterling collar marked "Brigg," London hallmarks for 1897, ebony shaft, 7/8" brass and iron ferrule, 35-3/4" l.....................**$1,350**

Condiment set, electroplate, base formed as horseshoe, spur-form handle, toothpick holder flanked by boot form castor, mustard pot with whip-form spoon, central jockey cap open salt, Elkington & Co., England, late 19th C, 5" l, 3-5/8" h.............**$175**

Figure, carved and painted wood

Articulated circus figure with red textile shoulder girth, riding horse with glass bead eyes, attributed to Connecticut, stand, minor wear, paint imperfections, c1900-10, 10-1/2" l, 14-1/2" h...............**$2,530**

Laminated, stylized form, grommet eyes, orig glossy black paint, America, losses to tail, late 19th C, 7-1/2" h **$1,610**

Figure, porcelain

Man in colonial dress riding white horse, 18" l, 20" h......................**$290**

Painting, oil on canvas, portrait of horse standing in barnyard, sgd and dated "E. Corbet 1881" lower right, identified as Irish race horse by note on reverse, framed, small areas of paint loss, craquelure, varnish inconsistencies, 18-1/4" x 24-1/4" **$2,000**

Woman in colonial dress riding dappled brown horse, 18" l, 20" h **$660**

Pull toy, painted and laminated carved pine, full stride, horsehair

tail, wheeled platform base, America, early 20th C, 11-1/4" l **$635**

Sign, The Stewart Clipping Machine, colorful image of horses in court room jury box, machine in center, cardboard litho, 14" x 20", C.8.5 ....**$475**

Toy, Arabian Trotter, tin and composition wind-up, orig key, orig box **$130**

Watch holder, figural, silver plated metal, detailed jockey and race horse figure, mkd "Reed & Barton," loss to orig silver plate, 10" h, 5-3/8" d **$525**

Weathervane, full-bodied trotting horse, copper, verdigris surface, black metal stand, America, minor dents, late 19th C, 26-1/2" l, 16-1/2" h **$4,325**

Wild animals

Bookends, pr, rabbits, modeled poised on back legs, painted copper over plaster, red square bases, Aesthetic Movement, late 19th/early 20th C, 5" h...**$300**

Cane

Elephant ivory handle carved as American bison, amber glass eyes, finely fashioned features, 1/2" sterling collar with London hallmarks for 1920, heavy ebony shaft, 7/8" brass and iron ferrule, 36" l, 2-1/3" w x 3-1/4" h **$1,120**

Elephant ivory handle carved as six male lions, amber eyes, alternate with mouths open and closed, 1/3" ringed silver collar, thick Malacca shaft, 1-1/2" horn ferrule, English, c1890, 36-1/4" l, 2" d x 3" h **$1,460**

Figure

Carved alabaster, reclining rabbit, full relief, rect base, 9" l, 5" d, 6" h.....**$2,185**

Carved bone, elephant, carved bone, carved wooden armature overlaid with bone tiles in contrasting patterns, India, c1900, 24" l....**$1,610**

Ceramic, white elephant figures, gray and pink enamel detailing, sq bronze bases with gilt rocaille scrollwork to sides, price for pr, early 20th C, 10" w, 5-3/4" d, 10-1/2" h **$2,760**

Kangaroo, Fred Alten, (1872-1945, Wyandotte, Michigan), body with traces of brown stain, red glass eyes, shaped base, with stand, 3-1/4" w, 7-1/4" h **$575**

Polychromed carved wood deer, worn brown paint, white accents on nose and underbelly, green ground stand, America, missing one antler and part of right foreleg, 19th C, 18" l, 3-1/4" d, 17-3/4" h **$3,450**

Sewer tile, recumbent, 15" l **$3,800**

Shooting gallery target, rabbit, Massachusetts, some paint remaining, with stand, c1940, 21" w, 7" d, 31-1/2" h..................................**$815**

Tin, litho

Jumbo Peanut Butter, Frank Tea & Spice Co., one-lb size, 3-3/8" x 3-7/8" **$775**

Red Wolf Coffee, Ridenour-Baker Co., Kansas City, one-lb size, vacuum pack, trademark wolf, 5" d, 4" h **$575**

Tiger Bright Sweet Chewing Tobacco, P. Lorillard Co., vertical pocket size, 3" w, 7/8" d, 2-7/8" h **$275**

ARCHITECTURAL ELEMENTS

History: Architectural elements, many of which are handcrafted, are those items which have been removed or salvaged from buildings, ships, or gardens. Part of their desirability is due to the fact that it would be extremely costly to duplicate the items today.

Beginning about 1840, decorative building styles began to feature carved wood and stone, stained glass, and ornate ironwork. At the same time, builders and manufacturers also began to use fancy doorknobs, doorplates, hinges, bells, window locks, shutter pulls, and other decorative hardware as finishing touches to elaborate new homes and commercial buildings.

Hardware was primarily produced from bronze, brass, and iron, and doorknobs also were made from clear, colored, and cut glass. Highly ornate hardware began appearing in the late 1860s and remained popular through the early 1900s. Figural pieces that featured animals, birds, and heroic and mythological images were very popular, as were ornate and very graphic designs that complimented the many architectural styles that emerged in the late 19th century.

Fraternal groups, government and educational institutions, and individual businesses all ordered special hardware for their buildings. Catalogs from the era show hundreds of patterns, often with a dozen different pieces available in each design.

The current trends of preservation and recycling of architectural elements has led to the establishment and growth of organized salvage operations that specialize in removal and resale of elements. Special auctions are now held to sell architectural elements from churches, mansions, office buildings, etc. Today's decorators often design an entire room around one architectural element, such as a Victorian marble bar or mural, or use several as key accent pieces.

Additional Resources:

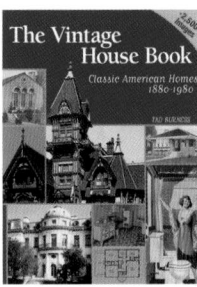

The Vintage House Book, by Tad Burness, Krause Publications, Iola, WI.

Arch, fragmentary, sandstone, carved figures, including Buddha seated on dais, central India, c15th/16th C, 36" l **$1,495**

Bird bath, cast iron, shallow basin, gadrooned rim mounted by two doves, fluted baluster form standard on circular base cast with pierced rose design, 19" d, 33-1/2" h **$300**

Bird cage, house form, grand entrance, front porch, bay windows, dormers, cupola, painted green, trimmed with red painted wooden buttons, knobs, and perches, some paint loss, 21" x 19-1/2" x 18" **$230**

Bracket, carved wood, mermaids, gilded, bifurcated scrolled tails, America, some loss, pr, 19th C, 19-3/4" h, 10-1/2" d, ...**$4,230**

Capitals, galvanized tin, flat tops, raised star and rope twist details, one stripped, other old gray and white paint, wear and split seams, price for pr, 16" w, 10" d, 21" h **$250**

Catalog

Hudson Equipment Co., Chicago, IL, 256 pgs, Hudson Barn Equipment Catalog No. B-31, stalls, stanchions, bull stall, etc., 1940, 6-1/2" x 9-3/4"...**$30**

Morgan Sash & Door Co., Chicago, IL, 180 pgs, Catalog & Price List No. 553, Morgan-Anderson Woodwork, c1953, 8-1/2" x 11" **$35**

Chimneypiece, carved pine, molded shelf above dentilled frieze with central roundel decorated with putto flanked by swags of flowers, jambs decorated with urns above scrolled brackets, acanthus leaves at feet, late Victorian or Edwardian, c1900, 96" w, 7" d, 72" h...............................**$1,800**

Curtain tiebacks, mercury glass, grape dec, pewter collars, price for set of six, some chips, minor wear **$175**

Architectural, eagle, Bellamy-style, gilt carved, inscribed blue banner: "Live and Let Live," 72" wingspan, **$5,500.**
Photo courtesy of David Rago Auctions, Inc.

Architectural, tile frieze, Arts & Crafts, 12 Grueby Pottery tiles modeled with red blossoms and green foliage, banded ochre and red ground, unmarked, few minor nicks, 6" x 6" corners, 5" x 9" rectangles, **$2,600.**
Photo courtesy of David Rago Auctions, Inc.

Architectural, bird or animal cage, wirework interior, ornate building structure with simulated brick and marble decoration, pediment over door, three stories, **$475.**
Photo courtesy of Dotta Auction Co., Inc.

Door

Raised panel, pegged construction, orig red paint, wrought iron thumb latch, old corner chip, 27-1/4" w, 69-1/2" h **$580**

Two molded recessed panels, grain painted to resemble exotic wood, attributed to Maine, very minor surface imperfections, early 19th C, 31-1/2" w, 78-1/2" h **$920**

Doorknob, brown pottery agateware, 2-1/8" d, price for pr.................... **$90**

Door knocker, wrought and hammered copper, tulip shape, monogrammed "IGW," orig dark patina, 4" w, 11-1/4" h.......................... **$175**

Door pull, brass, Arts & Crafts, round, grimacing figure wearing head covering, holding ring in its mouth, 8" d **$270**

Eagle

Carved mahogany, bas-relief carving, perched on arrow, gilt highlights, America, 12-3/4" w, 5" h **$530**

Carved giltwood, perched on carved rockery, Pilot House type, America, old regilding, minor wear, c1875, 26" w, 31" l, 25" h.................. **$2,415**

Gilded tin, outstretched wings, perched on rockery weighted base, holds scales in beak, metal manufacturer M.F. Frand Co., Camden, New Jersey, tag on lower base, imperfections, late 19th C, 32-3/4" w, 19-1/4" h **$1,880**

Finials, pr

Cast stone, cov urn draped with floral swags, fluted socle, sq base, pr, 19th C, 25" h................................. **$1,800**

Molded copper, star and crescent on ball above ring and baluster-form base, all-over verdigris surface, America, purportedly from an Odd Fellows Lodge, minor dents, late 19th/early 20th C, 31" h **$3,525**

Floor vase, alabaster, urn form, scalloped rim, leaftip neck band, vertically fluted body with double leaftip stem, trumpet foot, plinth base, Classical Revival, late 19th C, 28-1/4" h **$325**

Garden bench, cast iron

Openwork vintage design, scrolled seat, worn white paint, price for pr, 36" w, 13-1/2" d, 28" h.............. **$350**

Openwork fern design on back and legs, geometric cast designs on seat, old white repaint, two hairlines, chip near front corner, 43-1/2" w, 15" d, 31" h.............................. **$325**

Garden furniture, cast iron, scrolled medallions on backs, scrolled arms, cast geometric stars on seats, Gothic style aprons, old white paint, price for

two-pc set, 36" h chair, 45" l x 18" d x 37" h settee..................... **$1,495**

Garden ornament

Rabbit, cast iron, seated figure, traces of white, green, and red paint, wear, late 19th C, 10" l, 11-5/8" h **$345**

Urn with flame, carved and painted wood and gesso, painted tan, putty, and white, traces of gilt, 19th C, 16-1/2" l, 29-1/2" h **$2,185**

Garden seat, porcelain, detailed white relief floral and bird dec, dark blue ground, paneled sides with pierced dec on two sides and top, Oriental, 14-1/4" d, 19-1/4" h **$425**

Garden table, cast iron, painted white, ornate detail, openwork inserts on top, high cabriole legs, scrolled feet, foliage returns, one insert missing, 44" w, 26-3/4" d, 30-1/4" h...................................... **$520**

Griffins, winged, stone-cut, English, pr **$4,200**

Hitching post, cast iron, jockey, yellow, red, green, black, and white painted detail, wired for lantern, 31" h................................. **$275**

Joint cap, composition, gilt, shell form, bases with tapering acanthus, Georgian, set of four, 10-1/4" w, 12" l, ... **$900**

Library steps, metamorphic, mahogany, leather top, open position as rect low table, hinged to form four-tread library step, Regency style, 28" w, 17-1/2" d, 17-1/2" h **$900**

Lock, iron, rect plate with male and female silhouettes, key with quatrefoil terminal, stand, minor surface corrosion, 19th C, 8-1/2" w, 11" h **$650**

Obelisks, pr, black slate, parcel gilt, tapered form, front incised with pseudo hieroglyphics on gilt ground, stepped base, gilt metal feet, Egyptian Revival, late 19th C, 13-3/4" h **$940**

Pedestal

Antico-verde marble, round and octagonal tapered revolving top, columnar pedestal carved with band of anthemion between beading, base with further beaded band, sq plinth base, Classical Revival, Italian, late 19th C, 40" h **$2,750**

Burled veneer, applied moldings on columns, stepped molded bases, paper label "Made in Italy," price for pr, 27-1/2" h, 9-1/4" d **$250**

Architectural, fountain, verdigris bronze, nude boy with turtle, signed "H. Gonier," dated 1916, 48" h, **$33,000.**

Photo courtesy of Wiederseim Associates, Inc.

Architectural, fountain, bronze, mermaid and dolphin, wave-form base encrusted with turtle, crab, and shells, 38" d, 85" h, **$3,315.**

Photo courtesy of Sloans & Kenyon Auctioneers and Appraisers.

Architectural, lantern brackets, wrought iron, spiral support and scrolled backplate, set of four, 32" x 42" x 5", **$475.**

Photo courtesy of David Rago Auctions, Inc.

Architectural, fountain, carved alabaster and marble, base with female figure in draped cloth, incised floral decoration, fitted as lamp, chips to base, repairs, turn of the century, 18-1/2" d, 43-1/2" h, **$2,500.**
Photo courtesy of David Rago Auctions, Inc.

Architectural, plaque, rectangle, lacquered floral and butterfly design in gold and black, reverse with black speckled finish, top with rectangular aperture, bottom with two squared hooks, cracking, losses to lacquer, 6" w, 38" l, **$400.**
Photo courtesy of Alderfer Auction Co.

Architectural, pedestal, mottled salmon marble, turned columns, square top and base, scattered chipping, break at base of shorter pedestal, price for pair, 36" and 36-1/4" h, **$375.**
Photo courtesy of Alderfer Auction Co.

Architectural, hanging urns, alabaster, bands of stylized relief caving around rim, chains missing, price for associated pair, 20th C, **$950.**
Photo courtesy of David Rago Auctions, Inc.

Architectural, vault door, center plaque reads "Herring Hall Marvin Safe Co., Hamilton, OH," **$195.**
Photo courtesy of Alderfer Auction Co.

Carved walnut, turned top raised on figure of classical man, turned and bead-carved base, early 20th C, 27-1/2" h **$360**

Copper and brass, twist-turned legs, paw feet, urn finial on base, Renaissance Revival, 31-1/2" h, 14" w sq top **$425**

Mahogany, circular top, turned standard, three paw feet, Victorian, 31" h **$220**

White marble, dark gray striations, circular top, turned rings on column, octagonal base, small edge chips, 40" h, 9-1/4" d top **$450**

Planter, zinc, nautilus shell form, pr, 22" l, 20" h **$2,160**

Staircase and railing, oak, designed for the offices of Charles P. Limbert Co., Holland, Michigan, salvaged from building prior to demolition in 1990 .... **$3,350**

Sundial, lead, circular, alpha numerics, terra cotta base shaped like three gargoyles, shaped plinth, 17" d, 34" h **$850**

Terrarium, walnut and glass, rect body with four chamfered round uprights topped by turned finials, colorless glass sides, base with lead-lined interior, raised on bun feet, Victorian, late 19th C, 17" w, 21-3/8" h **$600**

Topiary form, lyre-shape, wire, conical base, painted green, America, late 19th/early 20th C, 13-1/2" w, 24" h **$150**

Urn, cast iron
Flared rim, shell design on lower reservoir, round stems, painted black, double handles, repairs, price for pr, 14-3/4" h **$200**
Flared rim, sq to round base, double handles, white paint, minor rim chip, 19-1/2" h **$420**
Fluting, relief acanthus leaves, raised cast scroll panels, pedestal base, removable handles, painted white, 37-3/4" h, 30" w **$575**
Ribbed tops and columns, sq base, painted white, price for pr, 20-1/2" h **$120**

Wall plaque, pine, eagle and shield, carved in the manner of John Haley Bellamy, America, painted white, early 20th C, 48-1/4" w, 10-1/2" h **$1,645**

Window frame, arched, mullions in gothic pattern, five small panes remaining, green paint, 20th C, 35-1/2" w, 35" h, ... **$55**

ART DECO

History: The Art-Deco period was named after an exhibition, "l'Exposition Internationale des Arts Déecorative et Industriels Modernes," held in Paris in 1927. Its beginnings succeed those of the Art-Nouveau period, but the two overlap in time, as well as in style.

Art-Deco designs are angular with simple lines. This was the period of skyscrapers, movie idols, and the Cubist works of Picasso and Legras. Art Deco motifs were used for every conceivable object being produced in the 1920s and 1930s (ceramics, furniture, glass, and metals) not only in Europe but in America as well.

Additional Listings: Furniture and Jewelry. Also check glass, pottery, and metal categories.

Aquarium, stepped and paneled molded translucent yellow glass bowl, dec with six panels of stylized flowers, set in bronzed metal tripod stand, three enameled green handles, legs terminating in stylized dolphins, central light fixture, tri-part base, dark patina, chips, wear, c1925, 41-1/2" h...........**$2,415**

Armoire, sycamore and fruitwood, interior fitted with top shelf over divided compartment, hardware fitted for wardrobe, flanked by two shelves, lollipop-shaped key, France, c1928, 51-1/4" w, 19" d, 71" h...........**$1,650**

Ashtray, Frankart, America, second quarter 20th C, white metal striding nude female figure, painted light green, green glazed square pottery ash receptacle on base, raised marks on base "FRANKART. INC. PAT. APPLD FOR," lacking ceramic cigarette box, 12-7/8" h...........**$450**

Bed, single curvilinear bed frame with hanging shelf compartments, France, price for pr, c1930, 82" l...........**$1,410**

Bonbon dish, cov, colorless glass, relief etched dec of three nude mermaids on interior of cover, raised signature, Sabino Glass, Paris, France, wear, 20th C, 6-1/2" d, 1-1/4" h...........**$235**

Bookends, pr, bronze, cast as bust of woman, patinated, unmarked, 8" h...........**$360**

Cabinet, dressing, rect curvilinear top, centered mirror over four drawers flanked on each side by full-length curvilinear cabinets, shaped foot skirt, France, c1925, 68-1/2" w, 19-1/2" d, 66-7/8" h...........**$1,100**

Cabinet, gentleman's, burled veneer cabinet, Bakelite and chrome hardware, England, c1930, 28-1/2" l, 16-1/2" d, 40" h...........**$940**

Center bowl, by Grace Helen Talbot, Roman Bronze Works, fluted bowl, four bronze nude female figures with arms outstretched, dark green-brown patina, signed and dated on base, 1922, 16" d, 3-3/4" h...........**$5,875**

Chair, tub, mahogany frame, upholstered seat, price for pr, 20th C, 27" h...........**$600**

Chandelier, colorless mold-blown and etched glass shade with stylized flowers and leaves, wrought iron frame with vine ornamentation, sgd "Degue 534," France, c1930, 30" h, 19" d...........**$600**

Cigarette case, silver, interior with vermeil wash, engraved "Fran," leather case, 5-3/8" l, 3-1/8" w...........**$100**

Clock, table, Telechron, model 4F65, Ashland, Massachusetts, circular blue glass with Roman numeral dial raised on flat chromed metal bar with curvilinear foot, electric movement, c1935, 7-1/4" w, 6-1/4" h...........**$750**

Coffee set, silver plated, Wilcox, design attributed to Gene Theobald, faceted 10-1/2" h coffeepot, and sugar container with Bakelite finials, matching creamer, 20" l oblong tray, all marked "Wilcox S.P. Co/E.P.N.S./ International S.Co./W. M. Wounts/ 1981N."...........**$1,150**

Credenza, beveled glass cabinet over rect marble top, two drawers over two cabinet doors in burlwood with metal mounts, wear, escutcheon missing, c1930, 61" l, 20-1/2" w, 82" h.....**$600**

Desk

Leopold Corp, Burlington, IA, walnut veneered, semi-oval top over center drawer flanked by pull-out writing surface and two drawers, bronze handles, light brown finish, "Charles S. Nathan Office Equipment New York" distributor's metal tag in drawer, veneer loss, wear, 66-1/8" l, 36-1/8" d, 29" h......**$900**

Plycraft, double pedestal, four drawers on each side, single center drawer, stenciled #331, 30" x 44" x 22-1/2"...........**$350**

Drawings, by Alexander Bronson, pencil drawings of two beds by Paul Frankl, other with pedestal table, sgd, mounted in natural wood frames, price for three-pc set, 13-1/2" x 17"...........**$750**

Dresser box, Egyptian Revival, bentwood Egyptian sarcophagus form, overlaid in emb copper with Egyptian motifs, blue opaque glass scarabs, sides trimmed in tooled leather, silk lining, dark rich patina with verdigris oxidation, c1925, 12" l...........**$460**

End table, mahogany and burlwood, orig marble tops over single drawers, one with two lower shelves, other with shelf and cabinet, raised rosettes on metal hardware, France, price for pr, c1930, 16-1/2" w, 14" d, 29" h...........**$1,400**

Figure, molded opalescent glass, nude female figure, triangular base with raised and etched marks, paper label, Sabino Glass, Paris, France, 20th C, 9-1/2" h...........**$390**

Fireplace screen, wrought iron, diagonal grid with spade elements at intersections, dark patina, attributed to Raymond Subes, France, c1925, 25-1/4" w, 35" h...........**$4,200**

Lamp base, etched brass, silver wash on ovoid brass form, etched nude female figures picking grape clusters from cascading grape vines, weighted round stepped base, France, wear, scattered corrosion, c1925, 21" h...........**$520**

Lamp, boudoir, Danse De Lumiere, molded glass figure of woman with outstretched arms, bearing stylized feather drapery, oval platform base with internal light fixture, molded title and patent mark, mold imperfections, c1930, 11" h...........**$400**

Lamp, floor, domical orange and blue mold-blown shade, wrought iron framework, conforming metal base, France, c1930, 68" h...........**$3,290**

Lamp, hanging, silvered metal, three arms with white etched glass shades attributed to Schneider, France, c1925, 29" l...........**$800**

Lamp, table

Concentric ribbed pink satin shade with stylized rosebud center, shade emb "Vleighe France 1137," nickel-plated brass base with emb geometric designs, minor flakes on shade, 19" h, 11" d...........**$520**

Trefoil etched colorless glass shade, rosette and geometric designs, supported by wrought iron tripod with applied rosette accents and leaf motif, shade sgd "Degue," nicks and chips to shade, 19" h, 13" d shade...........**$920**

Art Deco, Perfume bottles, left: red skyscraper shape, black stepped stopper; right: slender green satin baluster, gold toned top, each **$125.**

Photo courtesy of Joy Luke Auctions.

Art Deco, vase, Rookwood Pottery, squeeze bag decorated by William Hentschel, nude, antelopes, and geese, matte brown and white glaze, flame mark/XXIX/6080/WEH, neatly drilled hole in bottom, 1929, 13-1/2" x 11", **$4,750.**

Photo courtesy of David Rago Auctions, Inc.

Art Deco, lamp, bronzed metal base with two figures, bright orange, white, and blue spatter globe shade, original wiring, **$250.**

Mirror

Cast metal, circular plate supported by two figures with composition faces, stamped "Collection Francaise, made in USA," 10-1/4" h **$360**

Full-length mirror with arched top, asymmetrical rosewood base with geometric ivory inlay, France, c1925, 29" w, 15" d, 70-3/4" h **$1,530**

Octagonal mirror in wrought iron frame, rose and leaf dec, France, 1930, 36" w, 24" h **$250**

Oval beveled glass, wrought metal surround, France, c1928, 36-3/4" h **$1,645**

Nightstand, bird's-eye maple veneer, marble top, France, c1930, 15-1/2" w, 15-1/2" d, 31" h **$300**

Plaque, cast aluminum, Love Birds, sgd "Rene P. Chambllen" lower right, dedicatory inscription verso, c1930, 12" x 9" **$920**

Poufee, floral upholstered round seat in gold, blue-gray, melon, and brown, four reeded legs that taper at base, France, c1925, 23" d, 13-1/2" h **$300**

Punch bowl and cordial set, eight-sided finial on paneled cov, 7-1/2" h, 8-1/2" d bowl dec with silver and red geometric design, six 2-1/2" d paneled cordials with similar dec, 14" d round glass tray with multiple star cuts on base, chrome sides, chrome ladle, imperfections..................... **$290**

Ring, lady's, rounded form bezel and bead-set with old European-cut diamonds, approx. total wt. 1.56 cts, millegrain accents, 18k white gold mount.. **$2,000**

Room divider, four panels, black lacquered arched frames inset with canvas, painted abstract gold and black pattern, slight damage to hinges, each panel 24" w, 71-1/2" h **$1,725**

Salon chair, U-shaped low chair, beige velvet and burlwood, metal tag on bases, "Hotel Le Malandre Modele Depose," price for pr, c1945, 28-1/2" w, 26-1/2" d, 24-1/2" h **$2,185**

Server, stepped rect top, curvilinear ends over fitted cabinet doors, English, c1930, 55" w, 20" d, 36" h **$1,880**

Sideboard, walnut and burl bookmatched veneer, Bakelite cabinet doors and drawer pulls, France, c1928, 76" l, 19-1/2" d, 50-5/8" h **$900**

Stand, amboyna wood inlaid with stylized flowers in various fruitwoods and mother-of-pearl, attributed to Maurice Defrene, France, price for pr, c1925, 15" w, 18" d, 29-1/2" h **$2,235**

Table, dining

Oval top with geometric inlay border with central medallion, angular center support, shaped platform base, US, c1930, 72" l, 43-1/2" w, 29-3/4" h **$1,410**

Burlwood oval top, fine ebony and ash inlay dec, four canted legs, accompanied by two conforming 16" leaves, France, c1930, 79" l, 40" w, 29" h **$1,175**

Table, tea, walnut, rect top opens and swivels on U-shaped base, France, c1928, 44" l open, 22" closed, 35-1/4" w, 28-1/4" h.................**$1,880**

Tea and coffee set, silver, oval tray, coffeepot, teapot, creamer and cov sugar accented by ebonized handles and finials, mkd "835," hallmarked, Germany, creamer handle restored, tray scratches, early 20th C, 18-3/4" d **$1,175**

Torchieres, gilt bronze, skyscraper design raised on four stepped feet, US, price for pr, c1930, 69" h **$2,750**

Tray, rect, two handles, hammered brass, stamped "M. Willig Freising Bavaria," 24" l **$110**

Vase

Cameo glass, black ground, stylized scene of three repeated terriers against bronzed and silvered ground, unsigned, French, c1925, 8-1/2" h **$300**

Ceramic, Boch Frères, extended rim, oval form, stylized light green blossoms, stems, and foliage, gold accents, turquoise ground, glossy glaze, painted "BFK/340," imp "708," minor crazing, minor light scratches, price for pr, 11-3/8" h **$920**

Citrine ground, stylized enameled flowers, sgd "Legras," minor heat check, 8-1/2" h.........................**$200**

Frosted colorless glass angular bulbous body, octagonal rim, ftd, base, incised Sabino signature, France, edge nicks, c1930, 9-1/2" h......**$275**

Mold blown art glass, relief vine and leaf dec, remnants of silvered metal on interior, etched mark on base, France, interior rim ground, c1930, 10-1/4" h **$180**

Molded opalescent glass, Art Deco stylized scene of centaur and panther hunting gazelles, foliage background with blue patina, unmarked, attributed to Sabino, 12-1/2" h **$635**

Art Deco, carpet, pumpkin field, navy blue border, classic Chinese dec, Nicholas, 11' 6" x 9' 1/2", **$1,600.**
Photo courtesy of David Rago Auctions, Inc.

Art Deco, tea set, silver, wood handles, **$495.**
Photo courtesy of Dotta Auction Co., Inc.

Art Deco, wash bowl and pitcher, graniteware, white ground, light brown and blue decoration, chips, **$150.**

Wiener Werkstatte, bulbous, flaring neck, painted white and black geometric pattern, brown ground, stamped "WWW/ Made in Austria/ HB," 12-1/4" h, 5-1/2" d **$125**

Wall hanging, cotton velvet rose-colored curtain with multicolored crewel work design of stylized lanterns and trailing decoration, France, c1925, 63" w, 100" l **$1,470**

Wall sconces, pr, colorless etched shades with vertical bands of flowers supported on bronze Dore mounts, shades signed, by Heiter Vincent, France, c1925, 20" l **$750**

Wrist watch

Concord Watch Co., platinum, ivory tone dial with Arabic numeral indicators, 17 jewel Concord Watch Co. movement, bezel with bead-set single-cut diamond melee, 14k gold band with bead-set diamond accents, 6-1/4" l **$530**

D & L Co., rect ivory tone dial with Arabic numeral indicators, 17 jewel movement, bezel with bead-set single-cut diamonds and channel-set French-cut sapphires, 18k white gold case, adjustable platinum mesh band, case sgd........................ **$1,410**

Lady's Baume & Mercier, center platinum rect dial framed by alternating rows of bead-set single-cut diamonds and channel-set rect sapphires, millegrain accents, 18k mesh band, 14k closure **$1,410**

ART NOUVEAU

History: Art Nouveau is the French term for the "new art," which had its beginning in the early 1890s and continued for the next 40 years. The flowing and sensuous female forms used in this period were popular in Europe and America. Among the most recognized artists of this period were Gallé, Lalique, and Tiffany.

The Art-Nouveau style can be identified by flowing, sensuous lines, florals, insects, and the feminine form. These designs were incorporated into almost everything produced during the period, from art glass to furniture, silver, and personal objects. Later wares demonstrate some of the characteristics of the evolving Art-Deco style.

Additional Listings: Furniture and jewelry. Also check glass, pottery, and metal categories.

Bud vase, glass, deep crimson, cut back to citron, 8-3/4" h **$100**

Candlestick, patinated metal, figural, nymph standing on butterfly, holding flower form candle sconce, flower-form base, early 20th C, 11-3/8" h **$115**

Case, sterling silver, Tiffany & Co., rect, engraved on both sides, monogram "AJC," suspended from silver chain, brown leather interior with two pockets, orig silver retractable pencil, sgd **$215**

Center bowl, purple iridescent threaded glass within green oil spot ground, tooled copper rim, Art Nouveau shaped metalwork sides framing faces, unsgd, Austria, possibly Loetz, early 20th C, 12" d, 9" h **$650**

Clock

Desk, bronze, Chelsea Clock movement, gilt-metal and glass mount, red enamel dec devices, ftd base, circular face with Arabic chapters, imp "Chelsea Clock Co., Boston, USA, 155252" on inside clock works, worn patina, 3-3/4" w, 4-3/8" h **$460**

Figural, enameled cast white metal, relief of woman's head, flowing hair, leaves, thistles, Seth Thomas movement, circular dial with Roman numerals, minor wear, c1900, 12-1/2" h **$300**

Wall, carved walnut, two train movement, floral etched gilt metal dial sgd "Trilla, Barcelona," case topped by bust of young beauty on rocaille shell above iris flower, flanked by poppy roundels, case further carved with stylized florets, writing flower buds at corners, Spanish, early 20th C, 24-1/2" w, 10" d, 38" h................................. **$490**

Art Nouveau, bowl, diamond shaped, green glass, white, yellow, and pink enameled orchids, gold tracery foliage, gold border trim, **$95.**

Photo courtesy of Dotta Auction Co., Inc.

Art Nouveau, thermometer, ornate scrolling Art Nouveau scrolls and flowers, brass, **$125.**

Photo courtesy of Dotta Auction Co., Inc.

Art Nouveau, slipper chair, mother-of-pearl inlay, 32" x 28" x 20", **$300.**

Photo courtesy of David Rago Auctions, Inc.

Desk lamp, two-light bypass fixture, base of colorless glass molded as ocean wave, top with gilt bronze figure of nubile mermaid, flanked by two lidded inkwells formed as fishing trap and whelk shell, flattened feet, early 20th C, 14-1/2" w base **$4,350**

Door pulls, bronze, whiplash handles, orig patina, Belgian, price for pr, 3" w, 15" h..........**$1,150**

Floor vase, glass, gray ground internally dec with streaked orange and mottled blue, blown-out into wrought iron armature with scrolled designs, stylized florals, Muller and Chapelle, glass damaged at base, c1910, 21" h **$1,100**

Garniture, centerpiece with bronze patina, female spelter figure of "L. Historie," flanked by spelter plinth with clock, enameled dial with painted Arabic numbers, sgd "L. Satre-A Pont. Aven," rect molded marble base with center bronze gilt neoclassical mounting, bronze gilded bun feet, pr of bronze patina spelter Louis XVI style urns, ribbons and swags centering figural medallion, sq marble base, bronze gilded feet **$950**

Inkwell, bronze, double inkwells flanking shaped pen tray, raised leaf and berry motif, sgd "C.H. Louchet," 7" x 13" **$460**

Lamp, table, opalescent shell held by arched foliage, supported by female figure in white metal, bronze patina, ruffled water-like base, early 20th C, imperfections, 18-1/4" h **$320**

Notebook, hammered sterling silver, Tiffany & Co., flying bird and branch dec, entwined starfish on reverse, contains celluloid cards with days of week, sgd, additional hallmark for Shiebler..........**$360**

Perfume bottle, paneled slender baluster form bottle painted with blue and gold flowers, gilt-metal hinged lid enclosing glass stopper, lid with short chain, 4-1/4" h..........**$520**

Picture frame

Sterling silver, oval, emb flowers and maiden, Unger Bros., Newark, 4-7/8" h **$175**

Wood, penwork and colored stained dec of stylized fruiting flowers, easel back, 8-1/2" w, 11-3/8" h **$100**

Pitcher, relief wheat dec, mottled blue, brown, and green, imp "Gres Mougin Nancy," by Joseph Victor Xavier, Nancy, France, c1900, 11-3/4" h **$865**

Plaque, 12-3/8" x 9-5/9", Summer Maiden, possibly Limoges, late 19th C, enameled rect plaque depicting profile bust of brunette among sunflowers, bordered by poppy stems, sgd "Dorval," gilt metal frame mounted with flowering branches, maroon velvet surround, 18-3/4" x 15-3/4" **$4,410**

Stove, coal, bronze and iron, shaped structure, pierced bronze plaque with "S"-scroll motifs centering pineapple, applied bronze medallions with female profiles, stamped "Deville Pailliette Forest, No. 17, Charlesville, Ardennes," c1900, 28-1/2" w, 22" d, 36" h..........**$375**

Table, side, scallop-edge rect top inlaid with poppies in exotic woods, fluted legs, cabriole feet, lower shelf with variation of poppy motif, orig finish, inlaid "Galle" signature, 24" w, 17" d, 30" h, ...**$2,100**

Tea kettle, sterling silver, floral repoussé dec, curved handle, marked "J. E. Caldwell & Co., 925, Sterling, 1000, Philadelphia," 47 troy oz, 11" h **$550**

Tumbler, crystal tumbler, acid stamped "WMF," hallmarked silver handled holders, set of four, 4" h **$175**

Urn, conical pottery body, large white and red spring garden flowers, painted blue shiny glazed body, artist sgd, Continental, triple griffin bronze holder base, 17-1/2" h **$475**

Vase

Glass, Bohemian, irid, stylized floral metal frame, 7-1/2" h **$125**

Glass, Bohemian, gray ground internally dec with mottled light and dark blue, blown-out into wrought iron reeded armature, base inscribed "Daum Nancy" and "L Majorelle," c1920, 8-3/4" h **$1,610**

Glass, attributed to Pallme-Koenig, suppressed circular body, extended tapering neck, everted rim, pink, blue, green irid finish, embedded threaded dec, minute rim nicks, 17-1/2" h **$700**

Wine cabinet, carved walnut, panels elaborately carved with nymphs and grapevines, fitted with two pairs of doors and drawer, early 20th C, 46" w, 18" d, 68-1/2" h **$5,550**

Art Nouveau, fruit basket, center majolica-type plate with violet poppies, green leaves, wire work basket, **$350.**

Art Nouveau, jar, cut and etched jar, silver-plated lid, two-handled frame, 8-1/4" h, **$125.**
Photo courtesy of Joy Luke Auctions.

Art Nouveau, collector's cabinet, carved bellflower crown, carved figural panel, etched glass cabinets, mirrored backsplash and inlaid apron, some losses, 90" x 77" x 21-1/2", **$1,400.**
Photo courtesy of David Rago Auctions, Inc.

Art Nouveau, inkwell, double, scrolling foliate design, bronze, faces on ink bottle covers, two dolphins support raised pen rest, **$325.**

Art Nouveau, vase, emerald glass, silver overlay with wild roses and vines, unmarked, 7-3/4" x 5-1/4", **$700.**
Photo courtesy of David Rago Auctions, Inc.

Art Nouveau, candelabra, bronze, four-branch, trumpet flowers on swirling stems attached to free-form organic Art Nouveau base, fine original patina, Jesse Preston, Chicago, 18" x 13", **$9,000.**
Photo courtesy of David Rago Auctions, Inc.

ARTS & CRAFTS MOVEMENT

History: The Arts & Crafts Movement in American decorative arts took place between 1895 and 1920. Leading proponents of the movement were Elbert Hubbard and his Roycrofters, the brothers Stickley, Frank Lloyd Wright, Charles and Henry Greene, George Niedecken, and Lucia and Arthur Mathews.

The movement was marked by individualistic design (although the movement was national in scope) and re-emphasis on handcraftsmanship and appearance. A reform of industrial Society was part of the long-range goal. Most pieces of furniture favored a rectilinear approach and were made of oak.

The Arts & Crafts Movement embraced all aspects of the decorative arts, including metalwork, ceramics, embroidery, woodblock printing, and the crafting of jewelry.

Adviser: David Rago.

Additional Listings: Roycroft, Stickleys, and art pottery categories.

Blanket chest, Greene & Greene, oak and yellow pine, unusually mortised corners fastened with sq dowel pegs, two lift-top doors, good orig finish, from Pratt residence, Ojai, California, 65" l, 23-3/4" w, 18-1/2" h **$22,500**

Bookcase, gallery top, adjustable shelves, small cabinet with leaded glass door, orig finish, Liberty & Co. tag, c1900, 37" w, 10-1/4" d, 47" h **$3,115**

Bookstand, oak, four open shelves with cutout sides and through tenons, 45-3/4" h....................................**$500**

Box

Copper, hammered, riveted handles and strap hinges, Van Erp Workshop, orig patina, open box stamp, few scratches, 2-1/2" x 7" x 3-3/4" **$2,300**

Rect, hinged, enameled plaque of sailboat with marsh grasses and waterscape, Liberty Tudric, imp "Tudric," numbered "083," 6-1/8" l, 4-3/4" w **$940**

Arts & Crafts, chandelier, wrought-iron, monks' head shaft, four pendant lanterns with slag glass panels, 16" x 18" sq chandelier, sold with two matching wall sconces (not shown), **$700.**

Photo courtesy of David Rago Auctions, Inc.

Arts & Crafts, bookends, pr, embossed tall ships on waves, covered in fine curdled matte blue-green glaze, unmarked, glaze chip to one corner, 6" x 5-3/4" x 3-1/4", **$325.**

Photo courtesy of David Rago Auctions, Inc.

Arts & Crafts, candlestick, copper, tulip-shaped, enameled decorated in stylized floral pattern, The Arts Crafts Shop, Buffalo, New York, 8-1/3" x 5-1/4", **$1,000.**

Photo courtesy of David Rago Auctions, Inc.

Silver and enamel rect, hinged lid cov with stylized enamel flowers and leaves in green, rose, blue, and white with applied wire and silver balls, raised artist's initials "EC," for Elizabeth Copeland, Boston, 1915-37, 3-7/8" w, 2-3/4" d, 2" h **$14,100**

Candlesticks, pr
Brass, two-branch, conical holders set in spirals, bright finish, orig bobeches, Omicron, incised "Jarvie," small scratches and dents, 10-3/4" h, 8" d **$6,500**
Cast copper, imp "1797" with double cross, no patina, unmarked, 11-3/4" h, 3-3/4" d **$195**

Chair, dining room, Limbert, side, single broad vertical back slat, tacked-on brown leather, orig finish with heavy overcoat, branded mark, 17" w, 37" h, price for set of four **$1,610**

Chair, side, L. & J. G. Stickley, Fayetteville, New York, oak, model no. 940, three vertical slats below crest rail, slip seat, double side stretcher, branded mark, price for set of six, c1916, 35-3/4" h **$2,235**

Chamberstick, hammered copper, cup-shaped bobeche, riveted angular handle, flaring base, stamped "OMS" for Onondaga Metal Shops, old cleaning and verdigris to patina, 6-1/4" h **$175**

Cigarette box, hammered copper, riveted trim, emb circular medallions, cedar lining, natural patina, unmarked, attributed to England, 2-1/4" x 5" x 4" **$260**

Clock, New Haven, Japanese-style, brass hands, keyed through-tenon sides, amber ripple glass, orig ebonized finish, paper label, 14" w, 4-3/4" d, 21-3/4" h **$490**

Coal scuttle, hammered copper, repoussé floral motif, riveted seams, rolled rim, new patina, some dents to body, some replaced rivets, 15" x 22" **$575**

Coffee and tea service, coffee-pot, teapot, creamer, sugar, and tray, pewter, wicker handles, by Archibald Knox, stamped "Liberty/Tudric," price for five-pc set **$3,115**

Compote, pewter, cluthra green glass liner with opalescent and gold swirls, Liberty Tudric, Archibald Knox, 8" d, 6-3/4" h **$3,115**

Inkwell, faceted copper, curled, riveted feet, enameled green, red, and black, spade pattern, orig patina,

unmarked Arts & Crafts Shop, couple of nicks to dec, 5-1/4" sq, 3-1/2" h **$250**

Lamp, ceiling, polished hammered brass, four arms, flame-shaped opalescent glass shade with green pulled feather pattern, English, 8-1/2" d, 11" h **$1,355**

Lamp, table, shade, eight panels of textured white glass with exterior green paint within bronzed metal strapwork frame, three sockets with acorn pulls on bulbous verdigris base, unsigned, paint wear, 21-1/2" h, 16-1/2" d **$1,060**

Lamp, student, Roycroft brass washed hammered copper base, Stickley Bros. copper and mica shades with silhouetted trees, orig finish, replaced mica, orb and cross mark, 16" h, 13" d **$1,840**

Library table
Double oval, flaring legs, cut-out stretchers, orig finish, branded Limbert mark, 1" cut off legs, 47-1/2" l, 36-1/4" w, 28-1/2" h **$7,475**
Two arched drawers, corbels, one shelf, orig finish, Lifetime Paine Furniture Co. metal tag, 52" l, 24" w, 29-1/2" h **$2,300**

Magazine stand
Gallery top, vertical slats all around, five tiers, fine orig dark finish, branded "CPM," 18-1/4" w, 14" d, 50-1/2" h **$2,415**
Three shelf, two short drawers, arched side rails over slatted sides, light finish, loose joints, 24" w, 12" d, 41-1/2" h **$630**

Music cabinet, attributed to G.M. Ellwood for J.S. Henry, English, mahogany, beveled top, paneled door inlaid with fruitwoods and mother-of-pearl, two drawers, brass hardware, good new finish, c1900, 21-1/2" w, 17" d, 42" h **$2,870**

Nut set, hammered copper, 8-1/2" d master bowl, six 3" d serving bowls, Benedict, some wear to patina, unmarked **$290**

Occasional table, circular top over flaring legs joined by cut-out stretchers, orig finish, branded Limbert mark, wear and stains to top, 30" d, 29-1/2" h **$2,070**

Pagoda table, Limbert, corbels under sq top, flaring sides, arched apron, lower shelf, cut-out base, orig finish, heavy overcoat, paper label under top, 34" sq, 30-1/2" h **$13,800**

Picture frame, hammered sterling silver, emb daisies, English hallmarks, 6" w, 9" h..**$750**

Pillow, embroidered stylized orange and green poppies, beige linen ground, 16" x 25".........................**$490**

Plant stand, Limbert, quarter-round corbels under sq top, flaring sides, ovoid cut-outs, lower shelf, plank base, fine orig factory finish, factory edge repair to top, no visible mark, 20" sq, 29-1/2" h.......................**$6,900**

Room divider, oak, grid-like top, three-panel, each panel cut-out with fern design, replaced linen panels, orig finish, unmarked, some minor chipping to edges, 68" h..........**$1,200**

Server, L. & J.G. Stickley, Fayetteville, New York, oak, rect top over single drawer, lower median shelf, branded mark, c1916, 32" w, 16" d, 33" h **$1,410**

Sideboard, L. & J.G. Stickley, Fayetteville, New York, oak, plate rail on rect top, three central drawers flanked by two cabinet doors, over single long drawer, branded mark, c1916, 47" w, 19-3/4" d, 44" h......................**$5,300**

String holder, sterling on bronze, bell shape, applied silver leaves and vines, orig patina, stamped "HAMS," Heintz, 3-3/4" d, 3-1/2" h **$535**

Tablecloth, circular, linen, embroidered red poppies, green leaves, 39" d.................................**$860**

Table, dining
Limbert, circular, extension, four-sided pedestal base, orig finish with heavy overcoat, 54" d, 27-1/4" h **$2,300**
Unknown maker, California, oak, rect board on board top, lower median shelf with through tenons, cutout sides, shoe foot base, deep brown restored finish, c1912, 83-1/2" w, 35-1/4" d, 29" h......................**$3,200**

Tabouret, Limbert, sq top, box construction, sq cut-outs, top refinished, orig finish on base, branded mark, 16-1/2" sq, 18" h **$2,615**

Trunk, copper and iron, strapwork and pyramidal tack mounts, black paint, hinged slant lid revealing rect box, 30-1/2" l, 16-1/2" d, 17-1/2" h.....**$200**

Vase, bulbous, curtained copper, dimpled and folded sides covered in rare orig red finish, Dirk Van Erp, windmill/ San Francisco mark with partial D'Arcy Gaw visible, 5" h, 6" d **$2,760**

Arts & Crafts, coal bucket, Dirk Van Erp, hammered copper, riveted brass bands, flame shaped brass finial, original dark patina, stamped open box mark, normal wear around rim, 10" d, 17" h, **$4,600.**
Photo courtesy of David Rago Auctions, Inc.

Arts & Crafts, charger, Onodaga Metal Shops, hammered copper, embossed with leaves and pods, stamped "OMS 100," cleaned patina, 20" d, **$1,400.**
Photo courtesy of David Rago Auctions, Inc.

Arts & Crafts, lamp, ceramic, bulbous base, four arms, turtle shade inset with several green slag glass panes, matte green glaze, unmarked, Chicago, restored cracks to arms, 16-1/2" x 11", **$3,335.**
Photo courtesy of David Rago Auctions, Inc.

Arts & Crafts, lantern, hanging, Gustav Stickley, four sided, overhanging vented cap, pierced sides, hammered amber glass, die stamp compass mark, few scratches to original patina, 9" d x 4" h lantern, 21" l chain, **$3,400.**
Photo courtesy of David Rago Auctions, Inc.

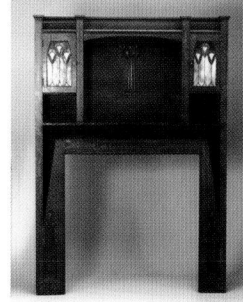

Arts & Crafts, mantel, custom-designed, oak, carved tree of life flanked by stylized floral stained glass cupboard doors, original finish, unmarked, 59" w, 14" d, 82-1/2" h, **$4,100.**
Photo courtesy of David Rago Auctions, Inc.

Arts & Crafts, window, leaded polychrome slag glass, arched top, windmill on hill in front of large puffy clouds, unmarked, wooden frame, from a Michigan home, few minor breaks, 41" w, 78-1/2" h, **$4,025.**
Photo courtesy of David Rago Auctions, Inc.

Wall sconces, pr, 6" d shade, brass, emb stylized poppies, leaded glass period shades, English, 14-1/2" h **$2,530**

AUTOGRAPHS

History: Autographs appear on a wide variety of formats—letters, documents, photographs, books, cards, etc. Most collectors focus on a particular person, country, or category, e.g., signers of the Declaration of Independence.

Abbreviations: The following are used to describe autograph materials.

ADS	Autograph Document Signed
ALS	Autograph Letter Signed
AQS	Autograph Quotation Signed
CS	Card Signed
DS	Document Signed
FDC	First Day Cover
LS	Letter Signed
PS	Photograph Signed
TLS	Typed Letter Signed

Colonial America

Hancock, John, endorsement sgd, as Governor, approving sentences levied by garrison court martial against several convicts held on Castle Island, Boston, three pgs, folds, minor browning, Aug. 3, 1790 .... **$3,910**

Jefferson, Thomas, partially printed vellum DS, sgd as president, granting 327 acres on Northwest Territory to Martha Walker, countersigned by Secretary of State James Madison, small hand colored manuscript map on verso, showing location of plot near junction of Scioto and Whetstone rivers, Washington, minor fading, Feb. 15, 1802, 10" x 12" **$4,370**

Nicolls, Richard, DS, as British colonial governor, confirming Peter Stuyvesant's land grant to Egbert van Borsum, for first Brooklyn ferry house, New York, March 12, 1666, 1-1/2 pgs, separated at folds, some loss, wax seal intact **$2,990**

Foreign

Bonaparte, Napoleon, LS, sgd "Buonparte," to President of Military Council, in French, half pg, small 8vo sheet, General in Chief of the Army of the Interior stationery, c1794 .... **$1,610**

Disraeli, Benjamin, envelope, sgd "Disraeli," addressed to Lady Corneila Guest, matted and framed, 3" x 4" **$80**

Eiffel, Gustave, TLS, Paris, April 19, 1889, sgd "G. Eissel" to E. Hippeau, in French, business stationary, folds, one page, single 8" x 10" sheet **$375**

Peron, Eva, PS, Buenos Aires, Oct. 10, 1950, bust portrait, sgd on mount beneath calligraphic inscription, signature light, framed, 9" x 6-1/2" photo on 13-1/2" x 9-1/2" mount **$620**

General

Einstein, Albert, ALS, to his first wife Mileva, in German, regarding increase in monthly payments for son Tetel, praising his son Albert, acknowledging death of Dr. Zuercher, one page, Dec. 21, 1937 .... **$5,060**

Ford, Henry and Edsel, TLS, congratulating Albert W. Howard as a new dealer, Dearborn, Ford Motor Co. stationery, morocco folder with photograph, Aug. 1, 1939 .... **$1,725**

Freud, Sigmund, newspaper photo sgd, "Sigm. Freud," framed, certificate of authenticity by Charles Hamilton, wax seal on verso of frame, yellowed, 1932, 5-1/2" x 4" **$1,955**

Lindbergh, Charles A., PS, inscribed, large close-up portrait in aviator's cap, Acme Newspictures, 13-1/2" x 19-1/2" **$1,840**

Ruth, Babe

Baseball, graded C.9-9.5 .... **$17,270**
Photo of Babe Ruth with golfer Rudy Jugan, sgd by Ruth **$1,430**

Tiffany, Charles Louis, ALS, sgd "C. L. Tiffany" to George Wilson, NY Chamber of Commerce, sending check for dinner honoring Seth Low, one pg, New York, Oct. 5, 1867 .... **$415**

Vanderbilt, William H., LS, to members of Special Committee of NY Chamber of Commerce, regarding railroad rate legislation, six pgs, New York Central & Hudson River Railroad Co. stationery, New York, Sept. 18, 1879, pin holes, inked stamp on first page **$2,760**

Autograph, ALS, handwritten, written and signed by Abraham Lincoln, dated April 16, 1859, with card supporting authenticity, **$6,800.**
Photo courtesy of Joy Luke Auctions.

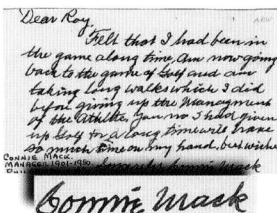

Autograph, ALS, Connie Mack, "...Felt that I had been in the game a long time, am now going back to the game of Golf and am taking long walks which I did before giving up the management of the Athletics. You no [sic] I had given up Golf for a long time will have so much time on my hand...," trimmed, identified in another hand, one page, 5-1/4" x 3", **$290.**
Photo courtesy of Historical Collectibles Auctions.

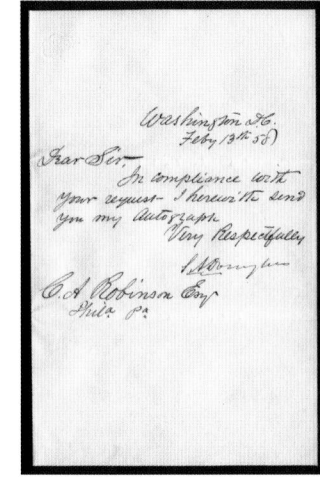

Autograph, Frederick Douglass (abolitionist), addressed to C.A. Robinson, signed, dated Feb. 13, 1858, Washington D.C., **$600.**
Photo courtesy of Sloans & Kenyon Auctioneers and Appraisers.

Wright, Orville and Wilbur, check sgd by both, payable to B.F. Goodrich Co., Winters National Bank, endorsement stamps on verso, cancellation perforation just above Orville's signature, Dayton, Jan. 26, 1911, 3" x 8-1/4" **$4,830**

Literature

Aldrich, Thomas Bailey, poem sgd, titled "Three Flowers," inscribed to Bayard Taylor, 14 lines, one pg, 1876 .... **$260**

Browning Robert, ALS, granting permission to reprint two poems in volume edited by H.W. Dulcken, London, April 8, 1867 .... **$865**

Dickens, Charles, ALS, to J.P. Harley, inviting him for a visit, Twickenham Park, Thursday night, two pgs, toned, soiled, tape repairs, c1838 .... **$1,035**

Frost, Robert, book, *The Best Poems of 1922,* sgd and inscribed by Frost to Carl Bernheimer above poem, The Witch of Coos, page 16, also sgd by Gwendolen Haste on page 57, and Leonora Speyer, page 58, custom slipcase, London, 1923 .... **$690**

Hawthorne, Nathaniel, clipped signature, mounted to another sheet, 1" x 3-3/4" **$290**

Hemingway, Ernest, ALS, sgd "Papa," to Leonard Lyons, graphic letter describing injuries from plane crash and brush fire while on safari in Africa, Venice, two pgs, April 8, 1954 .... **$4,370**

Shaw, George Bernard, ALS, to Bruno E Kohn, declining request, The Hydro Hotel stationery, Torquay, one pg, Oct. 10, 1915 .... **$230**

Stowe, Harriet Beecher, quotation sgd "I know that my redeemer liveth," March 13, 1889, trimmed, 4" x 5" **$230**

Military

Beauregard, Pierre G. T., postcard sgd, thanking General for copies of order, congratulating him, New Orleans, repaired tear, staining on verso from prior mounting, Oct. 27, 1882 .... **$375**

Custer, George Armstrong, ALS, sgd "Armstrong," to his friend John Bulkley, regretting he declined position on Custer's staff, three pgs, orig envelope, Headquarters, 2nd Brigade, 3rd Div Cap Corp A.P., Summer, two minor tape repairs at folds, 1863 .... **$7,475**

Mussolini, Benito, PS, close-up bust portrait, looking downwards, sgd on sheet below image, red wax seal affixed to lower left corner, minor creases in image, emb stamp on lower right corner of image, framed, 11" x 7-1/2" **$520**

Pershing, John J., books, *My Experiences in the World War,* two volumes, publisher's cloth, author's autograph edition, one of 2,100 numbered copies, New York, 1931 .... **$290**

Sherman, William T, PS, sgd "W. T. Sherman, General, New York, Feb. 8, 1889," standing 3/4 portrait, in uniform, image size, matted, framed, 11-1/2" x 7" **$2,300**

Thomas, Lorenzo, PS, "Brig Genl I. Thomas, Adj. Genl U.S.A.," bust portrait carte-de-visite by Frederick Gutekunst, orig photographer's mount, sgd on recto at bottom of image, bit yellowed and soiled, revenue stamp affixed on verso **$260**

Music

Bernstein, Leonard, manuscript sgd, high school exam essay on religion and society, 3-1/2 pgs, April, 1935 .... **$520**

Puccini, Giacomo, clipped signature, framed, March 1916, 1-1/2" x 6-1/2" **$2,30**

Stravinsky, Igor, musical quotation, sgd and inscribed, 20 note tone row from The Flood, Hotel Pierre stationery, New York, framed, May 4, 1962, 7-1/4" x 10-1/4" **$1,035**

Presidents

Cleveland, Grover, ALS, to William Steinway, thanking him for grand piano given as a wedding present, three pgs, Executive Mansion stationery, orig envelope, Washington, Aug. 14, 1886 .... **$490**

Eisenhower, Dwight D., typed quotation sgd, Presidential oath of office, Washington, framed, Jan. 20, 1953, 7" x 5-1/4" **$815**

Grant, Ulysses, partly printed document, four language ship's papers to Captain West Mitchell for whaling voyage of the bark Mount Wollaston, countersigned by Secretary of State Hamilton Fish, Washington, one pg, folio, July 8, 1872 .... **$1,495**

Posters, framed under glass: The Monkees, autographed by Davie Jones, Mickey Dolenz, Peter Tork and Michael Nesmith, 14-1/2" x 18-1/2", **$125**; *Batman movie poster, autographed by Adam West, Burt Ward, Lee Merriweather and Frank Gorshin, 20" x 24",* **$125.**
Photo courtesy of Joy Luke Auctions.

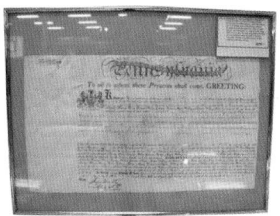

ADS, Thomas McKean, signer of Declaration of Independence, vellum Pennsylvania land warrant for tract of 1099 acre land in Tioga County, signed by McKean as Governor, also signed by James Trimble as Deputy Secretary, 12" x 21", dated June 1, 1806, **$550.**
Photo courtesy of Alderfer Auction Co.

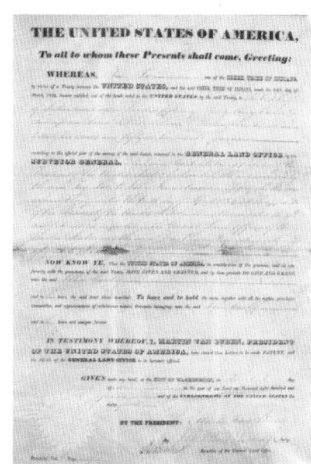

Autograph, President Martin Van Buren, U.S. General Land Office document, Land Offfice seal, signed, printed, and autographed, dated May 20, 1840, 17-1/2" x 11-3/4", **$275.**
Photo courtesy of Sloans & Kenyon Auctioneers and Appraisers.

Hayes, Rutherford B., Remarks of President Hayes, at Celebration of General Garfield's Election, inscribed and sgd "With compliments R. B. Hayes," orig Executive Mansion envelope addressed in Haye's hand to Hon. George K. Forster, postmarked Washington, 2-1/2 pgs, Nov. 17, 1880, ...**$750**

Lincoln, Abraham, partially printed vellum DS, appointing Rowland C. Kellogg a Commissary with rank of Captain, countersigned by Edwin Stanton, Washington, faded, creased, June 8, 1864, 17" x 14-1/2", ...**$4,140**

Nixon, Ford, Carter, Reagan, and Bush, PS, group portrait standing outside behind podium at dedication of Reagan Library, sgd in varying inks below image, Simi Valley, 1991, 7-3/4" x 10-3/4" **$3,450**

Reagan, Ronald, book sgd, *Speaking My Mind*, sgd and dated on front blank, publisher's blue cloth backed boards, dust jacket, New York, 1989 ....**$1,100**

Roosevelt, Theodore, TLS, to Sereno E. Pratt, editor of Wall Street Journal, White House stationery, Washington, thanking him for article, 2-1/4 pgs, March 3, 1906 ....**$21,850**

Wilson, Woodrow, ALS, to W.A. Stein, request for autograph, Princeton, one pg, Feb. 4, 1901 ....**$320**

Show business

Barrymore, John, scrapbook assembled by Barrymore for his daughter, sgd and inscribed to her on front pastedown, hundreds of newspaper and magazine clippings relating to his performance in Hamlet at the Haymarket Theatre, other material, oblong folio, orig morocco, London, some clippings loose, 1925 ......**$1,035**

Holiday, Billie, PS, inscribed "To Norman Stay Happy," souvenir group photo taken in Chicago, showing "Lady Day" with five other people, sgd on mat above image, presentation folder of Garrick Stage Bar, also inscribed by another, inscriptions in pencil, 5" x 7" **$980**

Pavlova, Anna, PS, sgd and inscribed, silver print image by C Mishkin, en pointe, inscribed in blue ink on image, mounted in paper folder, Jan 1907, 7-1/2" x 5-1/2" **$635**

Statesmen

Churchill, Winston, TLS, discussing upcoming General Election, one pg, 28 Hyde Park Gate stationery, London, hole punched in upper left margin, minor toning, Jan. 22, 1950, ...**$2,760**

Roosevelt, Franklin D., TLS, sgd as Acting Secretary of the Navy, on Dept. of Navy letterhead, concerning investigation into collision between USS Lake Tahoe and scow W.T.C. #35, March 27, 1919, 10-1/2" x 8" **$500**

Von Stauffenberg, Count, document of Cavalry Riding School, Hannover, official school handstamp, Aug. 11, 1936, 2-1/4" x 6-3/4" **$1,925**

AUTOMOBILIA

History: Automobilia is a wide-ranging category. It includes just about anything that represents a vehicle, from cookie jars to toys. Car parts are not usually considered automobilia, although there are a few exceptions, like the Lalique radiator ornaments. Most sought after are automobile advertising, especially signs and dealer promotional models. The number of items related to the automobile is endless. Even collectors who do not own an antique car are interested in automobile, bus, truck, and motorcycle advertising memorabilia. Many people collect only items from a certain marque, like Hupmobiles or Mustangs, while others may collect all advertising, like matchbooks or color brochures showing the new models for a certain year. Most material changes hands at automobile swap meets, and specialty auctions held throughout the year. Notably "hot" items on the market are service station and trucking company hat badges.

Additional Resources:

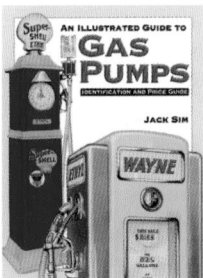

An Illustrated Guide to Gas Pumps, by Jack Sim, Krause Publications, Iola, WI.

PS, Rudolph Valentino (1895-1926) from1924 film "Monsieur Beaucaire," autograph at center bottom "sincerely Rudolph Valentino," silver print, matted, framed, 6" x 8", **$355.**
Photo courtesy of Sloans & Kenyon Auctioneers and Appraisers.

Advertising button

Auto dealership, Butzer Bros, purple on white, early touring car, early 1900s **$25**

Buick Fireball 8, graphic red, white, and blue design, for introduction of high-power engine, 1940s **$45**

Fisk Tires, black, white, and yellow, symbolic youngster ready for bed holding candle and automobile tire, slogan "Time to Re-tire, Get a Fisk," 1930s **$20**

Flying Red Horse, red on white, symbol for Socony-Vacuum, 1940s **$15**

Hyvis Motor Oil, black on white, center red figure for "Automobile Contest" sponsored by Kapisco Oil Co., Shakopee, Minn., 1930s.............**$12**

Nash Airflytes, black inscription on gold, Nash's 50th anniversary year, 1952..**$28**

Pyro-Action Spark Plugs, multicolored image of warrior in armor, orange rim inscribed "Crusade Against Spark Plug Paralysis-Sponsored by Robert Bosch," 1930s **$10**

Advertising tab, Ford Motors Merry Christmas, diecut thin metal tab, two gold lusters, red and green image of Santa in sleigh, red lettering, 1950s, 1-1/4" x 2-1/2"..............................**$50**

Air station, Gilbarco, hose and "Air" sign **$1,100**

Badge, attendant's uniform type
Texaco, inlaid cloisonné enamel, 1-3/4" x 2-1/4" **$425**
Tydol Veedol Gasoline Motor Oil Serviceman, inlaid cloisonné enamel, orange and black on silver, 2-7/8" x 2-1/4" **$675**

Calendar, Harley-Davidson, South Dakota dealer, tin litho, detailed image of 1930s biker on Harley, full 1940 calendar pad, 3" x 5-3/4", C.8 ....**$525**

Catalog
Buick Motor Co., Flint, Michigan, 16 pgs, illus of models, 1916, 5-3/4" x 7-1/2" **$100**
Curtis Aerocar Co., Inc., Coral Gables, Florida, 8 pgs, 1938, 7-1/4" x 11-3/4" **$40**

Compression tester, Hasting's Piston Ring advertising on dial, orig metal storage box **$45**

Dealership sign, Dodge Plymouth, enameled porcelain, neon........**$4,000**

Display cabinet
Auto Lite Spark Plug, painted metal cabinet, glass front, 18-1/2" h, 13" w **$125**
Schrader tire gauge cabinet, figural tire gauge, opens to reveal parts **$350**

Gas pump globe
Atlantic, milk glass **$1,045**
Boron Supreme, plastic **$660**
British Shell, cased glass **$3,410**
White Eagle, eagle-shaped milk glass **$2,750**

Gas pump nozzle, brass **$110**

Island cabinet, Mobil, gargoyle type, orig porcelain signs, replaced globe, restored, 1920s..........................**$1,045**

Key chain fob
Ford Tractors, dark gold plastic, showing key mechanism for "New Ford Select-O-Speed Tractors," reverse with "Greatest tractor advantage since hydraulics" and Ford logo, late 1940s **$12**
Shell Oil, silvered metal emblem, painted on reverse with instructions for return if lost, c1930 ....**$10**

Key ring holder, silvered metal, double ring holder, centered by applied miniature metal 7/8" h figure of smiling and saluting Esso Happy Oil Drop figure finished in porcelain white enamel, copper luster face, Esso logo

on chest in red on silver, blue oval logo, 1960s, 3-1/2" h......................**$25**

Lapel stud, brass, spoked automobile wheel, center engraved "327," tiny inscription on tire wall "Albany Automobile Show, Feb. 15-22," c1922 ....**$15**

Lube tank, double pump, oval, Texaco decals, mounted on wheels, restored, 43" x 17" x 29" h......................**$4,510**

Oil can
Hudson Motor Oil, Kansas City, quart, crimped seal, images of oil tanker, airplanes, and race cars, unopened, 5-1/2" x 4", C.8.5......................**$275**
Sohio Hand Separator Oil, quart, full **$220**

Oil carrier, wire
Esso, eight orig tall quart bottles with labels **$2,100**
Texaco, eight matching quart bottles, labels, restored spouts, restored carrier **$965**

Oil carrier, wood, Casto Penn Motor Oil, 12 matching tall quart bottles, 16" x 12" x 16" **$3,740**

Paperweight, Atlantic Richfield, trapezoid, clear Lucite, small dark amber vial holding liquid "Crude Oil-Prudhoe Bay-North Slope, Alaska," and "Atlantic Richfield Co." with logo in internal blue lettering, 3" x 3" **$15**

Pencil clip, Studebaker, diecut and rolled dark thin brass with name diagonally across image of spoked automobile wheel, early 1900s **$35**

Pocket mirror
Celluloid, Oak Motoring Suits, man wearing suit standing in front of early car, 2-3/4" x 1-3/4" **$240**
Shaded black and white photo, standing man, trees and railing in background, hand on hood of his Ford, license plate "NY 31," 2-1/4" d **$35**

Pump
American Pump Co., octagon body, restored 10-gallon visible pump **$2,640**
Fry Mae West, 10-gallon visible pump, Shell decals, replaced globe, restored **$3,500**
Gilbert & Barker T-8 curbside pump, White Flash decals, restored **$2,475**
Service Station Equipment Corp., Atlantic Richfield decals, twin 10 gallon visible tubes, restored, reproduced globes......................**$10,100**

AAA bumper insignia, White Rose Motor Club, York County, painted black and white, **$35.**

Two 1950s Ford promotional cars: one black, marked on top "EBY Auto Sales, Inc., Wakarusa, IN," one brown with key wind, **$150.**
Photo courtesy of Joy Luke Auctions.

Calendar plate, pretty lady in red touring outfit, driving early auto, seasonal floral sprigs, calendar pages, gold text "W. P. Stellmach, Bottler, Schlitz Beer, Shamokin, PA," 1910, **$65.**
Photo courtesy of Dotta Auction Co., Inc.

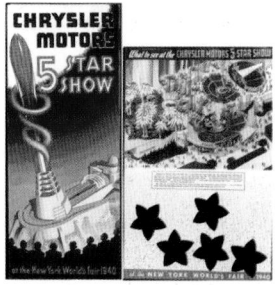

Folder, Chrysler Motors Five Star Show, New York World's Fair, red, white, and blue cover, rocket taking off from stylized rocket port, diagram of exhibit, products, bottom half with diecut stars denoting attractions, 1940, 3-3/4" w, 8-3/4" h, opens to 11-1/4" x 16-3/4", **$30.**
Photo courtesy of Hake's Americana & Collectibles.

Banjo, English, mahogany, broken arch pediment, ivory finial, convex mirror, c1820, 37-3/4" h, **$1,020.**
Photo courtesy of Alderfer Auction Co.

Banjo, English, George III, inlaid mahogany, baluster case inset with shell paterae, silvered thermometer and dial signed "J. Steele, Liverpool," 39" h, **$830.**
Photo courtesy of Sloans & Kenyon Auctioneers and Appraisers.

BAROMETERS

History: A barometer is an instrument that measures atmospheric pressure, which, in turn, aids weather forecasting. Low pressure indicates the coming of rain, snow, or storm; high pressure signifies fair weather.

Most barometers use an evacuated and graduated glass tube that contains a column of mercury. These are classified by the shape of the case. An aneroid barometer has no liquid and works by a needle connected to the top of a metal box in which a partial vacuum is maintained. The movement of the top moves the needle.

Wheel, Aneroid, Swedish, part ebonized, arch top with acorn finials, painted milk glass thermometer between turned uprights, open dial with printed enamel bezel signed "C.L. Malmsjo, Guteborg," within turned frame, acorn pendant finial, late 19th C, 21-1/2" l **$300**

Wheel, Georgian, mahogany, dial sgd "Dolland, London," rounded pediment over thermometer, urn inlaid central roundel line inlay throughout, early 19th C, 26-1/2" h **$1,840**

Wheel, carved oak, foliage and C-scrolls, English, late 19th C, 33" d **$230**

Stick, sgd E. Kendall, N. Lebanon, mahogany, etched steel face, mirrored well cov, 34" l **$550**

Wheel, English, Georgian, mahogany, dial signed "Dolland, London," rounded pediment over thermometer, urn inlaid central roundel, line inlay throughout, early 19th C, 36-1/2" l **$1,840**

Wheel, Scottish, mahogany, swan's neck cresting over later German hygrometer, vertical thermometer, over painted roundel, signature roundel centered by level and sgd "F. Uago, Glasgow," mid-19th C, 38" l **$865**

Banjo, mahogany, dial engraved "P. Nossi & Co. Boston," broken pediment cresting above shaped case with thermometer, circular barometer dial flanked by inlaid patera, 38-3/4" h **$690**

Wheel, English, mahogany, broken pediment centered by finial, round hygrometer dial over vertical thermometer, convex mirror over barometer dial, ending in dial for level, early 20th C, 39" l **$815**

Banjo, shell inlaid, painted black, Kirner Bros., Oxford, Victorian, mid-19th C, 39-3/4" h **$460**

Wheel, rosewood veneer, onion top cornice with hygrometer dial over thermometer over convex mirror, large barometric dial, small level at base, English, mid-19th C, 40" l **$350**

Wheel, rosewood case with thermometer over silvered barometer dial marked for J. Kienzly, Exeter, inlaid throughout with mother-of-pearl, abalone, and brass flowering vines, butterflies, and birds, Victorian, Anglo-Indian, late 19th C, 42-3/8" l **$1,410**

Louis XV-style, gray painted, parcel gilt, case topped by urn flanked by husk swag, floral painted thermometer, barometer dial mkd "Bourgeois, Paris," late 19th C, 42-1/2" h **$940**

Barometer and wall clock, G. V. Mooney, NY, walnut, shaped backboard with molded wood and brass bezel framing paper dial and brass lever movement above printed paper dial "G.V. Mooney's Barometer Patented May 30th 1865—Sold by Arnaboldi & Co. 53 Fulton St. New York," mercury tube extending to the base with a molded wooden boss, 50" h **$1,880**

BASKETS

History: Baskets were invented when man first required containers to gather, store, and transport goods. Today's collectors, influenced by the country look, focus on baskets made of splint, rye straw, or willow. Emphasis is placed on handmade examples. Nails or staples, wide splints that are thin and evenly cut, or a wire bail handle denote factory construction, which can date back to the mid-19th century. Decorated painted or woven baskets rarely are handmade, unless they are American Indian in origin.

Baskets are collected by (a) type— berry, egg, or field; (b) region—Nantucket or Shaker; and (c) composition—splint, rye, or willow.

Reproduction Alert. Modern reproductions abound, made by diverse groups ranging from craft revivalists to foreign manufacturers.

Buttocks, splint, **$200.**

Round, cane and oak splint, raised interior, banded top and base, bentwood handle, 10" d, 12" h, **$220.**
Photo courtesy of Alderfer Auction Co.

Elliptical, two rows of rose-colored weave, flat wooden base, two small handles, 1950s, **$15.**

Half buttocks, woven splint, thick brown paint, bentwood handle, 8" w, 5" h.. **$200**

Miniature

Bushel, painted cream-white over red, America, 19th C, 5-3/4" d, 3-1/4" h **$760**

Woven splint, single handle, painted blue, 1-3/4" d, 2" h.................... **$550**

Nantucket Light Ship, America

Round, carved wooden bail handle, turned wood bottom with incised line dec, America, late 19th/early 20th C, 8-1/8" h **$650**

Round, carved wooden bail handle, turned wood bottom with incised line dec, inscribed "Eldridge" on base, America, losses, late 19th/early 20th C, 6-5/8" h **$700**

Round, carved wooden swing handle, turned wooden bottom with incised lines, America, minor wear, 20th C, 5-1/4" h **$675**

Round, carved wooden swing handle, turned wooden bottom with incised lines, stamped "Nantucket Mass.," paper label "Boyer 4 Federal Street Nantucket MA," minor wear, America, 20th C, 3-5/8" h **$900**

Native American

Covered, woven splint, attributed to New England Algonkian or Iroquois, round domed lid, round to square form, red and green flowering vine motif, side handles, minor wear, fading, early 19th C, 15-1/2" h **$2,000**

Splint, Schaticoke Tribe, CT, rect, two carved handles, decorative bands, polychrome blue, orange, green, and brown splints, 19th C, 13" l, 10-1/4" w, 7" h **$1,725**

Oak

Peach basket shape, initials "CMT," 11-1/2" h, 14" d top **$235**

Sewing, rect, compartments woven into one end, minor cracking, 21" l, 12" d, 6" h.................................. **$250**

Rye straw

Bee skep, ovoid, wood base, 15" h, 15" d **$3,960**

Bulbous, flared rim, 11-1/2" h, 11-1/2" d **$990**

Child's, sewing, attached pin cushion, 1-1/2" h, 4-1/4" d..................... **$250**

Cov, bread rising, round, tapered sides, domed lid, wooden finial, two woven handles, attributed to Pennsylvania maker, 8-1/2" h, 17" d **$3,410**

Cov, hamper style, bulbous, 22" h, 16" d **$1,760**

Cov, hamper style, bulbous, 20" h, 22" d **$2,750**

Cov, hamper, bulbous, fitted lid and base, 12" h, 16-1/2" d **$1,155**

Cov, hamper style, oval, 15-1/2" h, 22" l, 17" w **$1,265**

Cov, oval, carved bentwood handles, attributed to Ephrata, PA, maker, 14-1/4" h, 32-1/2" l, 25" w **$3,850**

Cov, painted salmon dec, wooden knob finial, attributed to unknown maker, Hanover, York County, PA, 12" h, 18" d........................... **$2,970**

Cov, round, bread-rising, tapered sides, wooden finial, 5-1/4" h, 13" d **$3,850**

Hamper style, oval, hidden loss to inner rim, cov, 20" h, 17" d **$770**

Market, oval, pinned bentwood handle, 11-1/4" h, 17" l, 10-1/2" w **$1,980**

Miniature, cov, openwork, woven hinges and latch, 3" h, 4-1/2" d **$1,700**

Miniature, oval, bend handle, wooden base, straw open work weave, Easter egg dated 1925, 3-1/2" h, 3-5/8" l, 2-1/2" w......................... **$385**

Oval, cov, straight sides, 7" h, 12" l, 10-1/2" w................................. **$1,320**

Oval, fruit, two woven handles, looped openwork splint trim, 4-1/2" h, 10" l, 8-3/4" w **$500**

Oval, fruit or table, openwork, base, attributed to unknown maker, Hanover, York County, PA, 4-3/4" h, 11-3/4" l, 7-1/4" w **$3,850**

Oval, market, attached bentwood handle, 9" h, 12" l, 8-1/2" w **$2,750**

Oval, openwork, attributed to unknown maker, Hanover, York County, PA, 4" h, 12-1/2" l, 7-5/8" w **$1,155**

Oval, openwork, two woven handles, attributed to unknown maker, Hanover, York County, PA, 6" h, 13" l, 8" w **$1,045**

Oval, table, painted green, woven handle, 4-5/8" h, 11-1/2" l, 7-3/4" w **$1,320**

Oval, table, tapered sides, two handles, 4" h, 17-1/2" l, 13-1/4" w **$330**

Round, drying, 3" h, 19-1/2" d **$95**

Round, field, bentwood handles, cross supports in base, 10-1/2" h, 23" d **$825**

Round, field, tapered sides, two woven handles, 8-1/2" h, 18" d **$880**

Round, openwork rim, color banding, attributed to Andrew Sheely, Hanover, York County, PA, 4" h, 9-1/4" d **$990**

Round, openwork, Pennsylvania maker, 4-1/2" h, 11" d **$770**

Round basket, high handle, brown stained finish, damage to rim, dry condition, **$20.**

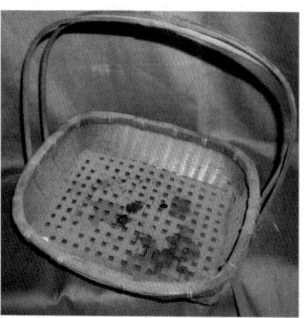

Square basket, high handle, brown stained finish, damage to handle, dry condition, **$35.**

Splint oak, kettle form, fixed handle, 12" d, 12" h, **$150.**
Photo courtesy of Alderfer Auction Co.

Round, openwork, table, 3-1/4" d, 11-1/4" d **$125**

Round, field, tapered sides, attached bentwood handle, 13-1/2" h, 16-1/2" d **$500**

Round, tapered sides, openwork rim, 2" h, 6-1/4" d **$550**

Round, tapered sides, two attached bentwood handles, 8" h, 14-1/2" d **$1,760**

Round triangular openwork rim, single coil base, attributed to Cumberland County, PA, 3" h, 10-1/2" d **$660**

Serving tray, round, two woven handles, 19-1/2" d **$880**

Sewing, applied section for pin cushion, flared base rim, attributed to Hanover, York County, Pennsylvania maker, 7" h, 13" l, 7-3/4" w **$10,725**

Tapered, triple coil base, 10" h, 16" d **$880**

Splint

Oak, D-shape, hanger, rounded head nails, wooden base, 8" h, 5" l, 3-5/8" w **$470**

Oak, rect, market, tapered sides, bentwood handle, pinewood base, round head nails, attributed to Grantville, Dauphin County, PA, maker, 13" h, 16-1/4" l, 10-1/4" h **$990**

Oak, round, tapered sides, pine base, red stained rim and side banding, attributed to maker in Grantville, Dauphin County, PA, 4" h, 8" d **$180**

Oval, market, bentwood handle, pine wood base, attributed to Grantville, Dauphin County, PA, maker, 13-1/2" h, 14" l, 11-1/2" w **$1,210**

Wall pocket, bentwood handle, painted brown, 9-1/2" h, 6-3/4" l, 4" h **$250**

Wooden

Oval, painted green, wood slat and band construction, round head nails, metal support to bentwood handle, 15" h, 15" l, 11-1/2" w **$1,320**

Stave construction, vertical wood staves taper down at base, fixed with wire, dark orig finish over varnish, 13" d, 17" h **$250**

BEATRIX POTTER COLLECTIBLES

History: Helen Beatrix Potter was born in 1864 in London. Her favorite pets were a mouse, rabbit, and a hedgehog. As a child, she loved to sketch these creatures and by 1893, she had created the characters of Flopsy, Mopsy, Cottontail, and Peter Rabbit. By December of 1901, Beatrix published 250 copies of her first book, *The Tale of Peter Rabbit*, which included 41 black and white illustrations. She gave many of these books to friends and family as gifts, but did sell some for a halfpenny each. In 1902, Frederick Warne & Co. publisher the first trade edition of this book and it became an instant bestseller. Beatrix went on to write 23 more tales and each is still in print today and they have been translated into more than 35 languages.

Clearly a clever businesswoman, Beatrix designed and licensed her Peter Rabbit doll in 1903, making him one of the first licensed literary characters. Steiff produced its own version of Peter Rabbit in 1903. Grimwades Pottery, Stoke-on-Trent, England, was granted permission in 1922 to use Potter's illustrations on chlidren's dishes. John Beswick obtained copyrights in 1947 to use Potter's storybook characters as figurines. The first set of nine figures, including Jemima Puddle-Duck, were an instant hit. In 1969, the Royal Doulton Group acquired Beswick and continued to produce the charming characters. Josiah Wedgwood and Sons began to use Peter Rabbit in its designs in the late 1950s.

Backstamps are useful in determining the date of Beatrix Potter figures. A gold circular backstamp is the earliest, dating to the 1940s-50s. Royal Albert backstamps were used only from 1989 to 1998. Some characters, Susan and Old Mr. Pricklepin, and Thomasina Tittlemouse, were produced by Royal Albert for a short six-week period and are much more sought after by collectors.

In 2002, an exhibition to celebrate the 100th anniversary of the first commercial publication was created by the Royal Ontario Museum and it has since traveled to other museums, like the Children's Museum in Indianapolis, delighting children of all ages.

Baby bowl, Peter Rabbit, Grimwades, 1920s-30s **$590**

Barbie, 2002 Peter Rabbit Centenary **$29.95**

Egg-shaped covered jar, Benjamin Bunny on top, Mother Bunny attending at bed on base, **$65.**

Cup, Bunnykins figures, Royal Doulton, **$18.**

Advertising figure, life-size, polychrome papier-mâché, figure posed in seated position, hands poised as if holding newspaper, white hat with red band, dark blue jacket, white shirt, vest, pants, and shoes, red necktie, America, minor paint wear, separations, late 19th/early 20th C, 20" w, 33" d, 48-1/2" h, **$5,900.**
Photo courtesy of Skinner, Inc.

Book

The Roly-Poly Pudding, Frederick Warne, NY, 1908 .... **$80**

The Tailor of Gloucester, Frederick Warne & Co., first US printing, 1903 .... **$130**

The Tale of Peter Rabbit, orig privately printed version, 1901 .... **$110,000**

The Tale of Peter Rabbit, Frederick Warne, first edition, second or third printing, 1902-3 .... **$18,500**

The Tale of Peter Rabbit, American printing, 1904 .... **$450**

Chamber pot, Peter Rabbit, Wedgwood **$200**

Cup and saucer, Peter Rabbit, Wedgwood, 1958 .... **$140**

Dish, Peter Rabbit, jasperware, blue, Wedgwood, 1980s **$200**

Eggcup, Peter Rabbit, Grimwades, 1920s-30s **$400**

Figure

Duchess with Flowers, earthenware 1955-1967 .... **$2,800**

Duchess with Pie, earthenware 1979-1982 .... **$4,255**

Hunca Munca, Beswick, 2-5/8" h, 2-3/4" w **$115**

Jeremy Fisher, Royal Albert, 1st version, 2nd variation, modeled by Arthur Gredington, 3-1/2" h **$135**

Mr Benjamin Bunny, Beswick, brown mark, 4" h, 3-7/8" l **$75**

Mrs Rabbit with basket, F Warne Co., Beswick, England, 4" h **$35**

Mrs Rabbit and bunnies, Beswick, brown mark, 3-5/8" h **$75**

Mrs Ribby and the Patty Pan, Royal Albert, modeled by Martyn Alcock, 3-1/2" h **$50**

Peter Rabbit, Beswick, sky blue jacket, brown shoes, hp "77" on base in brown and "31" in black, 1948, 4-1/4" h **$120**

Pickles, earthenware 1971-1982 .... **$485**

Tailor of Groucester, Royal Albert, 3-1/2" h **$35**

Game, Peter Rabbit's Race Game **$45**

Handkerchiefs, Peter Rabbit, orig package **$385**

Pendant, F. Warne, made in Italy

Knitting bunny in rocking chair, 3-1/4" h **$30**

Moma mouse, babe in her arms, 3-3/4" h **$30**

Mr Pig, cane in hand, 3" h **$32**

Mrs Pig at the market, 3" h **$30**

Print, Squirrel Nutkin from *Tale of Squirrel Nutkin,* published by F. Warne, 1950s **$25**

Tea set, Peter Rabbit, 17 pcs, Grimwades **$5,100**

Watercolor, unpublished, Building a Snowman, 1893 .... **$75,000**

BLACK MEMORABILIA

History: The term "Black memorabilia" refers to a broad range of collectibles that often overlap other collecting fields, e.g., toys and postcards. It also encompasses African artifacts, items created by slaves or related to the slavery era, modern Black cultural contributions to literature, art, etc., and material associated with the Civil Rights Movement and the Black experience throughout history.

The earliest known examples of Black memorabilia include primitive African designs and tribal artifacts. Black Americana dates back to the arrival of African natives upon American shores.

The advent of the 1900s saw an incredible amount and variety of material depicting Blacks, most often in a derogatory and dehumanizing manner that clearly reflected the stereotypical attitude held toward the Black race during this period. The popularity of Black portrayals in this unflattering fashion flourished as the century wore on.

As the growth of the Civil Rights Movement escalated and aroused public awareness to the Black plight, attitudes changed. Public outrage and pressure during the early 1950s eventually put a halt to these offensive stereotypes.

Black representations are still being produced in many forms, but no longer in the demoralizing designs of the past. These modern objects, while not as historically significant

Aunt Jemima, cookie jar, salt and pepper shakers, range shakers, measuring cup, spice shakers, all plastic, **$250.**

as earlier examples, will become the Black memorabilia of tomorrow.

Additional Resources:

Antique Trader® Black Americana Price Guide, 2nd Ed., by Kyle Husfloen, ed., Krause Publications, Iola, WI.

Autograph, Martin Luther King, Jr., photograph, sgd "with best wishes Martin Luther King," 11" x 14" **$3,220**

Baseball cap, Kansas City Black Royals Negro League, white, gray pinstripes, worn black visor, large black "KC" stitched on front, c1920 ....**$930**

Book

George Washington Carver, An American Biography, Rackham Colt, ex-library copy, 1943..........**$5**

Who's Who in Colored America, Volume I, J. Joseph Boris, ed., New York, first edition, portrait plates, small 4to, orig cloth, 1927 ....**$375**

Women of Achievement, Benjamin Brawley, Woman's American Baptist Home Mission Society, portrait plates, small 8vo, orig cloth, 1919 ....**$375**

Bottle opener, cast iron

Alligator and boy with hands up, mkd "John Wright, Inc.," front of base mkd "Souvenir of Tyban Dam, Grafton, W.V.," 3" x 4-1/2"........**$400**

Man's face, indented eyes, Wilton Products, damaged orig box, 4-1/8" x 3-1/2".......................................**$150**

Nickel plated, painted, black caddy, mkd "Pat. #86,603," near mint, 1932, 5-13/16" x 1-7/8" **$1,460**

Cartes-de-visite

Colored Baptist Church, Petersburg, VA, Lazell & McMillin, Petersburg, photographers, ext. view, men and women sitting on front fence, pencil inscription "Church of Petersburg Negroes burned by rebels, given by Lottie, Feb. 9th, 1868," soil, wear, slight crimp, 1966....................**$345**

Frederick Douglas, full-length portrait, erased pencil marks on top border, c1860 ....**$550**

Sojourner Truth, 3/4 view, seated at table, knitting, "I Sell the Shadow to Support the Substance," corners clipped, toning, light browning, 1864..**$660**

Cigar box label, glossy paper label, Booker T., Perfecto Cigars, black and white portrait of Booker T. Wash-

ington, red, pale blue, and dark blue border, white stars, unused, c1930s, 6-1/4" x 10" **$20**

Doll

Golliwog, velveteen face, hands, and feet, applied felt eyes and mouth, inked nose, yellow checked shirt, golden crepe pants, red braid trim, removable gray and white checked wool jacket, some wear and soil, c1930, 20" h **$460**

Mammy, nut head, painted features, looped plush hair, whisk broom body, orig commercial assemblage, pink print dress, twin black babies in green print organdy outfits, early 20th C, 12" h **$635**

Mammy, stuffed cloth, hand-embroidered features, red trimmed dress, blue and white cap, wear, damage, 18" h **$220**

Ephemera

Certificate of Freedom, for Thomas Chambers, resident of New York City, partly printed document, sgd, small folio, docketed on verso, September 1814.......................**$950**

Deposition of Thomas Cook, Shrewsbury, NJ, concerning slave trade and events on the sloop *Fanny*, Jan. 10, 1801, 12-1/2" x 8" **$175**

Depositions concerning slave trade by sloop *Fanny* between Africa and North America, 17 pgs, Oct 8, 1801, 9-1/2" x 7-1/2" **$550**

Plate, advertising, "Chocolate Drops" in gold, center design of Black child, white dress, yellow ribbons, gold rim, **$65.**

Bank, Mammy, cast iron, slot in back, painted red hat, dress, white kerchief and apron, some loss to paint, **$85.**

Sign, tin litho, tan ground, black lettering, red trim, child eating slice of bread with honey, honey pail to right, "Honey, dat's all! Rocky Mountain Honey Co., Producers of Choice Honey, Silver City, New Mexico," red border, some wear, **$195.**
Photo courtesy of Alderfer Auction Co.

Notice, *The Charleston Daily Courier*, regarding issuing of slave badges, giving prices for various trades, Jan. 5, 1858 .... **$1,380**
Receipt, "Negro Apprenticeship 2/6," printed, "Bought of the Anti-Slavery Society, Office, No. 18, Aldermanbury," (England) signed and dated by Francis Wedgwood, Society seal, dated 1838 .... **$490**
Figure, cast iron, painted
Family, 2-1/2" h man, 3-1/4" h woman, two 2-3/8" boys, 2" h girl, Wilton, excellent....................... **$620**
Sitting black boy and girl, Hubley, very good, 1-1/4", price for pr **225**
Swing band, group of six musicians, Hubley, catalog #34, near mint, 2-1/2" x 1-7/8" **$1,680**
Game, Jolly Darkie Ten Pens, McLoughlin Bros, two wooden balls, ten 8" x 2-1/2" diecut cardboard black men figures on wooden bases, orig box, C.8, 14-7/8" x 9-1/2" x 1-1/2" **$1,000**
Nodder, black boy, clockwork, head nods up and down, eyes roll, one arm extended upward, other extended forward in greeting manner, papier-mâché, 30" h **$1,500**
Perfume bottle, Golliwog, stylized faces, black and brown hair covering stoppers, bulbous frosted glass body, painted white collar, black round feet, raised maker's mark for DeVigny, one with partial paper label, price for three-pc set, c1919, 4-3/4" to 6" h **$575**

Pinback button
Baltimore Elite Giants, Negro Leagues, red and white, glossy cello, c1940 .... **$45**
Gold Dust Washing Powder, multicolored trademark of Black twins seated in wash tub, white background, black letters **$60**
Pocket tin, tin litho, vertical pocket type, image of black man smoking pipe on front, mkd "Record Pipe Tobacco" on back, 4-1/4" x 3-3/4" x 7/8" **$625**
Print, litho, *I'm Not to Blame for Being White Sir,* young white child holding out her hand for coins while passing stranger places coins in hands of black child, heavily toned, c1850, 13-1/4" x 9-3/4"...................... **$290**
Puzzle, Darktown Fire Brigade, Parker Bros, heavy cardboard pcs, wear to orig box, c1890s, 7-1/2" x 9-1/2" x 1-1/8" **$425**
Roly poly, Mayo's Roly Poly Tobacco, Mammy, litho tin, two pcs, C-8+, 7" x 5-1/4" **$825**
Slave tag, copper, Charlestown, 1834, 2" sq
Porter, No. 171 .... **$3,065**
Servant No. 205, wear, minor dents **$1,175**
Target game, McLoughlin Bros, image of black man holding musical instruments, C.8.5, 15-1/2" x 8" x 1-5/8" **$500**
Textile, printed, showing Little Black Sambo and tiger, earth tones of red, green, and dark brown, tan linen

ground, folded, sewn seam with red ink label "WPA Handicraft Project #10235, Milwaukee, Wisconsin, Sponsored by Milwaukee County and Milwaukee State Teachers College, c1935-43," 32-1/2" x 42" **$1,350**

BOOKS, EARLY

History: Collecting early books is a popular segment of the antiques marketplace. Collectors of early books are rewarded with interesting titles, exquisite illustrations, as well as fascinating information and stories. The author, printer, and publisher, as well as the date of the printing, can increase the value of an early book. Watch for interesting paintings on the fore-edge of early books. These miniature works of art can greatly add to the value.

Additional Resources:

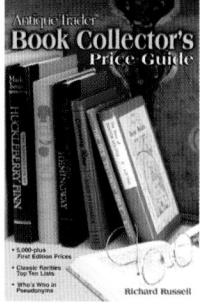

Antique Trader® Book Collector's Price Guide, by Richard Russell, Krause Publications, Iola, WI.

History of Lehigh and Carbon Cos, PA, with Illustrations, 1884, **$225.**
Photo courtesy of Dotta Auction Co., Inc.

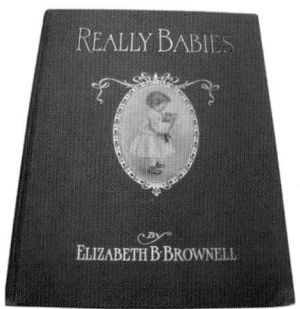

Really Babies, Elizabeth B. Brownell, green cover with gilt trim, oval portrait medallions, **$35.**
Photo courtesy of Alderfer Auction Co.

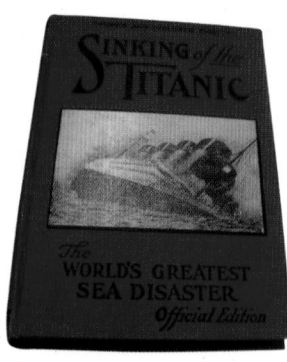

Sinking of the Titanic, The World's Greatest Sea Disaster, Official Edition, red cover, **$75.**
Photo courtesy of Alderfer Auction Co.

Aelianus, Claudis, *Claudis Aelianus His Various History,* translated by Thomas Stanley, London, Thomas Dring, first Stanley edition, small 8vo, modern 1/2 sheep gilt, first blank leaf missing, rubbed, some dampstaining in outer corners, 1665 .... **$130**

Armstrong, John, *The Art of Preserving Health: A Poem,* London, A. Millar, first edition, 134 pgs, 4to, modern 1/4 calf, title browned, 1774
.... **$70**

Bentley, Richard, *The Folly and Unreasonableness of Atheism…In Eight Sermons Preached at the Lecture Founded by the Honourable Robert Boyle, Esquire,* London, J. H. for H. Mortlock, eight parts in one volume, 4to, contemporary mottled sheep, rebacked, 1693 .... **$410**

Bohn, Henry C., *A Catalogue of Books,* London, engraved frontispiece and title page, thick 8vo, contemporary 1/4 road, front cover detached, frontispiece adhere, heavy foxing, 1841 .... **$150**

Burke, Edmund, *Reflections on the Revolution in France,* London, J. Dodsley, second edition, second impression, 356 pgs, 8vo, contemporary calf, rebacked, hinges reinforced, cloth slipcase, 1790 .... **$165**

Burney, Frances, *Evelina or A Young Lady's Entrance into the World,* London, T. Lowndes, second edition, three volumes, 12mo, contemporary sheep, rebacked, 1779 .... **$130**

Dart, John, *Westmonasterium; or, The History and Antiquities of the Abbey Church of St. Peters Westminster,* London, John Coles, engraved titles, 148 of 149 plates, two volumes, folio, contemporary calf gilt, red and green morocco lettering pieces, joints cracked, foxing, 19th C armorial bookplate, c1723 .... **$350**

Dickinson, Emily, *Poems,* FE, 1890
.... **$6,500**

Fairbairn, James, *Fairbairn's Crests of the Families of Great Britain and Ireland, Revised by Laurence Butters,* Edinburgh and London, engraved titles, 148 plates, two volumes, 8vo, contemporary 1/2 levant gilt, rebacked retaining faded orig backstrips, later 19th C **$70**

Fielding, Henry, *Amelia,* London, A. Millar, first edition, integral ad leaf at end of Volume 2, four volumes, 12 mo, modern beige calf gilt with morocco lettering pieces, 1752 .... **$490**

Gay, John, *The Shepherd's Week, In Six Pastorals,* London, Ferd. Burleigh, first edition, seven full-page etched illus by Louis Du Guernier, 8vo, modern 1/2 calf, 1714 .... **$865**

Gibson, Edward, *The History of the Decline and Fall of the Roman*

Empire, London, A. Strahan and T. Cadell, six volumes, three engraved portrait, contemporary calf, map of Constantinople missing, 1782-88
.... **$320**

Godwin, William, *Things as They Are;* or *The Adventures of Caleb Williams,* London, B. Crosby, first edition, three volumes, 12mo, contemporary marbled boards with red morocco lettering, spines darkened, occasional light browning, armorial bookplates and signatures of SC rice planter Charles Izard Manigault (1795-1874), 1794 .... **$1,840**

Howell, William, *An Institution of General History;* or *The History of the World,* second edition with large additions, London, Thomas Bassett, four volumes in three, folio, modern 1/4 Morocco, 1680-80 .... **$435**

Hume, David, *The History of England,* London, A. Millar, six volumes, 4to, contemporary calf gilt with morocco lettering pieces, few joints cracked, 1754-59 .... **$980**

Johnson, Samuel, *Irene, A Tragedy,* London, R. Dodsley and M. Cooper, first edition, 8vo, joints rubbed, 1749
.... **$865**

Knight, Henrietta, Lady Luxborough, *Letters Written by the Late Right Honourable Lady Luxborough to William Shenstone, Esq.,* London, J. Dodsley, first edition, 416 pgs, 8vo, contemporary calf, rebacked, 1775
.... **$375**

Lackington, James, *Memoirs of the First Forty-Five Years of the Life of James Lackington, the Present Bookseller in Chiswell-street, Moorfields, London, Written by Himself,* printed for and sold by the author, first edition, engraved frontispiece portrait, 344 pages, 8vo, modern tree calf gilt, 1791 .... **$215**

Milton, John, *Paradise Lost, Paradise Regain'd,* Birmingham, John Baskerville for J. and R. Tonson, London, together, two volumes, large 8vo, contemporary mottled calf, rebacked, 1760 .... **$575**

Nicolay, John G. and John Hay, *Abraham Lincoln, A History,* two-volume set, 1909 .... **$460**

Priestley, Joseph, *Lectures on History, and General Policy,* London, J. Johnson, 1793, two folding engraved tables, two volumes, 8vo, contemporary calf gilt, joints cracked
.... **$200**

Brass, bowl, reticulated, incised center crest, price for pr, 20th C, 9" d, 6-1/2" h, **$425.**
Photo courtesy of David Rago Auctions, Inc.

Brass, clockwork jack, signed "John Linwood," **$175;** *and brass chamber stick, unmarked,* **$95.**
Photo courtesy of Wiederseim Associates, Inc.

Brass, box, Arts & Crafts, Carence Crafters, pagoda-shape, acid-etched wild roses, pristine copper patina, imp "CC," 7" x 6" x 6", **$1,400.**
Photo courtesy of David Rago Auctions, Inc.

Shakespeare, William, *The Famous History of the Life of King Henry the Eight(h),* extracted from the second folio, London, modern cloth, calf lettering piece, some foxing and minor stains, 18th C owner's signature on last page, 1632 .... **$460**

Thomas, Gabriel, *An Historical Account of the Province and County of Pensilvania and of West-New Jersey in America,* 1698 .... **$27,000**

Unknown author
Confessions of a Medium, FE, London, 1882 .... **$250**
Modern Magic: A Practical Treatise on the Art of Conjuring, FE, London, 1876 .... **$2,000**
The Great Chinese Wizard's Handbook of Magic, Hurst & Co, NY, 1872 .... **$275**

Walpole, Horace, *A Castle of Otranto, A Gothic Story,* London, William Bathoe and Thomas Lownds, second edition, 200 pgs, 8vo, contemporary calf, rebacked endpaper renewed, 1765 .... **$435**

BRASS

History: Brass is a durable, malleable, and ductile metal alloy consisting mainly of copper and zinc. The height of its popularity for utilitarian and decorative art items occurred in the 18th and 19th centuries.

Reproduction Alert. Many modern reproductions are being made of earlier brass forms, especially such items as buckets, fireplace equipment, and kettles.

Additional Listings: Candlesticks, Fireplace Equipment, and Scientific Instruments.

Additional Resources:

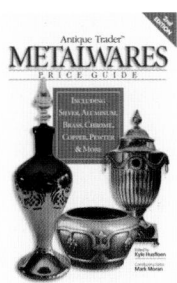

Antique Trader® Metalwares Price Guide, 2nd Ed., by Kyle Husfloen, ed., and Mark Moran, contr. ed., Krause Publications, Iola, WI.

Andirons, pr
Acorn tops, seamed columns, cabriole legs, ball feet, 17-1/2" h **$220**
Ring-turned columns, scalloped cabriole legs, ball feet, 18" h **$360**

Bed warmer
Engraved lid with large central flower surrounded by scrolls, maker's touchmark "ST," turned maple handle with old refinishing, minor damage near hinges, 42-1/2" l **$215**
Engraved lid with central flower surrounded by scrolls, turned wood handle with daubs of brown paint, wear, minor split in ferule, 43-3/4" l **$185**

Candlesticks, pr, pricket, ovoid drip pan on double baluster stem, domed cast foot, Continental, 18th C, 10-1/8" h **$650**

Chandelier, cast, eight scrolled arms with torch shaped ends, each with small electric socket, simulated candle coverings, 20th C, 25" d, 20" h **$250**

Chestnut roaster, oval, pierced hinged lid, long handle, 18-3/4" l **$120**

Chimes, mahogany and rosewood frame, eight brass chimes, turned pilasters on either side, striker missing, 20th C, 18-1/2" w, 27-1/2" h **$220**

Coal bin, brass gallery, applied Wedgwood dec, paterae carved rosewood frieze, tilting bin, splayed legs, Aesthetic Movement, price for pr, c1875, 16-1/2" w, 15-1/2" d, 26" h **$4,410**

Coal grate, Neoclassical-style, back plate cast with scene of figures in revelry, grate with central horizontal bar over guillouche band, uprights with brass urn finials, rear plinth base, front tapered legs, late 19th C, 19-1/2" l, 10-1/4" d, 27" h **$175**

Dresser mirror, French, gilt brass, mirrored glass, scrolls, floral pots, and garlands dec, cracks, loss to silvering 11" w, 18" h **$525**

Easel, A-frame topped by girdled round finial, late 19th/early 20th C, 61-5/8" h **$500**

Figure, Bodhisattva, dark patina, 10 arms, eight faces, single body, walnut block base, 31-1/2" h **$450**

Fireplace fender, pierced grapevines, applied bunches of grapes, rope twist detail, three cast brass paw feet, 47" w, 13" d, 9" h **$350**

Gong, dragons and tokugawa mons designs, Japan, early 20th C, 18" d **$325**

Brass, pipe mold, American, 18th C, 10" l, **$575.**
Photo courtesy of Pook & Pook.

Brass, snuff box, oval, three dials having Roman numerals and arrows for combination, hinged lid, 3-1/2" x 2-1/2", denting, brass button for opening detached, **$175.**
Photo courtesy of Alderfer Auction Co.

Brass, snuff box, top set with blue and white glazed tile of Emperor in profile, marked "Low Tile, Chelsea" and other worn lettering, **$75.**

Brass, foot warmer, hexagonal, wedding presentation type, pierced and embossed body, hearts, flowers, and busts of man and woman, Dutch, 18th C, 8-1/2" d, 7" h, **$2,530.**
Photo courtesy of Pook & Pook.

Ladle, brass bowl attached with copper rivets to wrought iron flattened handle, rattail hanging hook
11-1/4" l...**$300**
16-1/4" l...**$85**

Letter sealer, 2" l brass tube, 23 double-sided brass discs with various sentimental seals for wax, 19th C
....**$100**

Oil lamp, Bouillote, three-light, squat ovoid font with short arms, suspending three tools from chains, spreading foot with ogee shaped rim, black tin frame, 19th C, 19-1/2" h **$420**

Palace jar, chased designs of various deities within scrolled field, India, 20th C, 17" d, 16" h.....................**$420**

Plant stand, old gilding, round top with leaf drops and three scrolls, scrolled supports, leaves, and large flowers, eagle talon feet, lacquered, 14-1/2" d, 35-1/2" h **$450**

Samovar, worn partial marks, illegible from polishing, heavy cast base, replaced burner cover, damage to spout, repair, 19-1/2" h **$150**

Sconces, pr, hammered, gilt carved wooden foo dogs accents, 21" d.....**$360**

Steam whistle, single chime, lever control, 2-1/2" d, 12" h.................**$150**

Sundial, engraved markings, scrolls, and lettering "Merton Londini Anno Dom 1675" and "I stand amid ye Summere flowers To tell ye passinge of ye houres," imp "Made in England," early 20th C, 12-1/2" l, 12" w, 8-3/4" h
....**$265**

Trump indicator, circular flat brass disk, green enamel top, celluloid rotating suit and no trumps indicator
....**$130**

BRONZE

History: Bronze is an alloy of copper, tin, and traces of other metals. It has been used since Biblical times not only for art objects, but also for utilitarian wares. After a slump in the Middle Ages, the use of bronze was revived in the 17th century and continued to be popular until the early 20th century.

Notes: Do not confuse a "bronzed" object with a true bronze. A bronzed item usually is made of white metal and then coated with a reddish-brown material to give it a bronze appearance. A magnet will stick to it but not to anything made of true bronze.

A signed bronze commands a higher market price than an unsigned one. There also are "signed" reproductions on the market. It is very important to know the history of the mold and the background of the foundry.
Additional Resources:

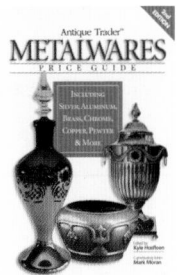

Antique Trader® Metalwares Price Guide, 2nd Ed., by Kyle Husfloen, ed., and Mark Moran, contr. ed., Krause Publications, Iola, WI.

Basket, trompe l'oeil, folded linen form, woven handle, applied florals and insects, Japanese, 19th C, 10-1/4"
....**$350**

Box, chaise lounge form, topped with monkey on pillows, lid lifts to reveal erotic scene of man and woman with carved ivory features, gilt and polychrome dec, marble base, 20th C......................**$1,495**

Bust, Napoleon, Sienna marble column with leaftip surround, plinth base, late 19th/early 20th C, 11-3/8" h......**$1,410**

Candlesticks, pr, figural
Don Quixote standing and holding a lance, 11" h Pancho Sanchez, riding a donkey and holding a staff, each with inverted helmet-formed sconce, both on tripod base, early 20th C, 10" h **$300**
Owl, granite base, 6" h **$225**

Cauldron, four flanges with geometric decoration, two with handles, tripod base, Central Asia, Seljuk period, 15th C, 19" d....................................**$1,100**

Clock, Chelsea Clock Co., Boston, silvered dial, round case, shaped rect base, ball feet, retailed by Tiffany & Co., 8" w, 3" d, 6-1/4" h **$650**

Clock garniture, parcel gilt bronze and slate, 20" h clock with two-train Hersant Freres chiming movement, case topped by griffin-handled urn, front set with female mask, raised front paw feet, pair of three-light candelabra, fruiting vine scrolled candle arms, similarly styled base, French, Renaissance Revival, late 19th C, 18" h **$1,175**

Figure and sculpture

Allegorial Autumn, standing figure holding sheaf of wheat and flowers, holding staff, fluted black slate base, grand tour, late 19th/early 20th C, 15" h **$600**

Cast from model by Vanetti, modeled as warrior in chariot drawn by three horses, rounded rect base, cast signature, 28" l, 13" h **$3,150**

Gentleman reading newspaper, oblong base, indistinct mold incised signature, Continental School, dated 1903, 13-1/2" d **$1,300**

Hockey player, cast, green patina, base sgd "Joe Brown 1956," 11-1/2" h, 12-1/2" w **$1,150**

Little girl covering giggle with her hand as she hides nosegay behind her back, medium brown patina, mold incised signature "Gaudez," (Adrien-Etienne Gaudez, 1845-1902), 23-1/2" h **3,525**

Mythical beast, tail raised, supporting figure sitting on its back, table form base, Southeast Asia, 18th or 19th C, one leg loose, 3-1/4" w, 2-1/2" d, 5-7/8" h **$175**

Napoleon, standing by column, sq base with leaf-tip rim set with gilt eagle, late 19th C, 14" h **$940**

Seated woman with lyre resting on her lap, rect base with mold incised signature, for Georges Van der Straeten, Parisian foundry seal, late 19th C, 20-1/2" h **$1,650**

Shepherdess and her flock, woman in cape, standing with group of sheep by a stream, mold incised signature of Charles (Karl) Korschann, 15" w hexagonal green marble base, 12-1/2" h **$1,410**

Two Arabs, one man drawing water from well, other cooking, under grass roof, cold painted, Viennese, mounted with small electric bulb, early 20th C, 7-3/4" h **$2,350**

Nature Revealing Herself, standing woman in Doré and pewter patinated robe, carved malachite scarab set at bodice, carved ivory bust, arms, and feet, mold incised signature "E. Barrias," Susse Freres foundry seal, slate and onyx base, 2-3/4" h stone base, 22-1/4" h **$11,200**

Young Dionysus, standing, empty wine skin, after the antique, verdigris patination, early 20th C, 14" h **$500**

Garden lantern, jewel finials and eaves decorated with fish finials, pierced fire boxes, bases with cast foo dogs, Japan, price for pr, 19th C, 4" h **$2,115**

Jose stick holder, attendant holding cloth with censer on top, opening in censer to hold joss stick, dark brown patina, China, Ming Dynasty, several holes, 4-3/4" h **$200**

Incense burner, Oriental, circular base with relief birds and foliage, center medallions, applied handles, old clock set into one side which has a loose hand, some damage, soldered restorations, 22" h **$525**

Lamp, designs of birds and flowers in high relief, Japan, Meiji period (1868-1911), 68" h **$1,765**

Lamp base, gilt bronze, candelabra, five flower-form serpentine candle arms, raised on fluted rouge marble stem set with figure of cherub, ovoid base, black painted wood plinth, Louis XVI-style, price for pr, late 19th/early 20th C, electrified, 22" h **$2,235**

Letter holder, Doré, Silvercrest, double tiered, overlay of sailing ship in waves accented by linear decoration, imp mark, numbered "2222," 8-1/2" l, 2" d, 5" h **$300**

Parade helmet, cast

Depicting Hercules battling the hydra with cityscape in background, borders of military motifs and emperors, 19th C, 15-3/8" l, 11-1/4" h **$460**

Gladiator's, Continental-style, China, four-part hinged visor comprising two-piece pierced eye guard, over two-piece face guard cast as figures before prison gates, helmet with high relief battle scene, further Roman-style figures, early 20th C, 18" l **$690**

Pen vase, gilt, cylindrical vessel, flared base, ribbed swirled design, unsigned, attributed to Tiffany Studios, New York, 3-1/2" h **$175**

Plaque

Circular, high relief design of lion's head, early 20th C, 14" d **$1,300**

Flower Maidens, profile busts of long-haired beauties, incised titles "Marguerite" and "Mignon," set in 11-3/4" sq maroon velvet frames, Aesthetic Movement, price for prlate 19th/early 20th C, 5-5/8" sq **$715**

Bronze, censor, foo dog, standing, three-dimensional features, open mouth, removable section in back, 20" l, 21" h, loss to tip of mane, **$715.**
Photo courtesy of Alderfer Auction Co.

Bronze, figure, nomad riding camel, cold-painted, Vienna, mkd "2607" with other indiscernible marks, losses to camel leg, restorations, early 20th C, 8-1/4" x 6-3/4", **$1,100.**
Photo courtesy of David Rago Auctions, Inc.

Bronze, figure sitting on top of tiered pedestal, gilt bronze, red pigment on steps, Southeast Asia, 19th C, overall wear, tip of hair bend, 11-7/8" h, **$350.**

Bronze, ceiling fixture, four arms, matching Fostoria Iris shades, alabaster bodies, gold interior, green heart and vine pattern, shades, 6" h, overall 47" h, **$1,400.**
Photo courtesy of The Early Auction Company, LLC.

Bronze, flower vessel, tightly curled lotus leaf resembling small boat, attached lotus blossoms, seed pods, crabs crawling to top, signed on rectangular reserve, Japanese, carved wooden stand, 19th C, 9-1/2" l, 3-1/4" h, **$2,450.**

Bronze, stags feeding, signed on base "P.J. Mene," Pierre Jules Mene, French, c1810-1879, 7-1/4" h x 9" w, **$1,150.**
Photo courtesy of Pook & Pook, Inc.

Bronze, stag, signed on base "P.J. Mene," Pierre Jules Mene, French, c1810-1879, 11-1/4" h x 11" w, **$575.**
Photo courtesy of Pook & Pook, Inc.

Figural bronze, powder jar, cold painted woman in bonnet, marble base, **$70.**

Bronze, figure, standing peacock with long tail, cold painted, Bergmann, Austrian, 12" l, loss to comb, **$150.**
Photo courtesy of Alderfer Auction Co.

Bronze, dogs, signed on base "P.J. Mene," Pierre Jules Mene, French, c1810-1879, 4-1/2" h x 5-1/2" w, **$980.**
Photo courtesy of Pook & Pook, Inc.

Garden statue, figural, young boy holding lamp, verdigris patina, 20th C, 34" x 24" x 6", **$550.**
Photo courtesy of Sloans & Kenyon Auctioneers and Appraisers.

Scepter, three cast faces, paneled rod, engraved swirled designs, crown finials, Oriental, possible brazed repair on rod, 20-1/2" l.................**$175**

Smoking tray, Doré finish, applied scrolling on ash bowl, cigar rests, matchbox holder, unmarked, c1910, 6-1/4" d.................**$70**

Tray, band of hammered designs, marked "Apollo Studios, New York" c1910, 9" d.................**$45**

Urn, cast, black patinated, everted reeded rim, central band of classical figures, two short handles with male masks, fluted foot, sq black marble base, Classical-style, price for pr, late 19th/early 20th C, 11-3/8" h **$2,530**

Vase, enameled dec of figures in ancient Roman garb, dragons on shoulder, butterflies on rim, mark on underside, possibly Japanese, slight loss to enamel, early 20th C, 13" h **$175**

Wall sconces

Pr, cast, Louis XV-style, two-light, rocaille-shaped candle arms and backplate, floriform drip pans hung with faceted colorless glass lusters, 11-7/8" h **$150**

Set of four, each with two candle sockets on cornucipia-shaped stems bound by ribbons, drapery-like wall plates with rosettes at top, gilded, 21" h **$700**

BUSTS

History: The portrait bust has its origins in pagan and Christian traditions. Greek and Roman heroes dominate the earliest examples. Later, images of Christian saints were used. Busts of the "ordinary man" first appeared during the Renaissance.

During the 18th and 19th centuries, nobility, poets, and other notable people were the most frequent subjects, especially on those busts designed for use in a home library. Because of the large number of these library busts, excellent examples can be found at reasonable prices, depending on artist, subject, and material.

Alabaster, woman in lace headdress and bodice, tapered alabaster socle, early 20th C, 17-1/4" h **$450**

Black basalt, Cicero, waisted circular socle, imp title and Wedgwood & Bentley mark, chips to socle rim, c1775, 10" h...............................**$2,300**

Bronze

Ajax, after the antique, helmet, beard, parcel gilt toga, sq base, dark green patination, 20th C, 16-1/4" h **$865**

Child, modeled as the head of a young child with curly hair, on cylindrical stone base, 20th C, 12-1/2" h **$635**

Cold painted, Bianca Capello, woman wearing classical clothing, Renaissance Revival motifs, sgd "C. Ceribelli," marble plinth, 24" h **$2,100**

Gentleman, Leo F. Nock, brown-green patina, sgd on base "Leo Nock Sc," stamped "Roman Bronze Works, NY," dated 1919, 22" h **$320**

Homer, dark brown patina, French, possibly Barbediene, 19th C, 8-1/2" h **$750**

Mercury, chocolate brown and parcel-gilt patina, short socle, sq base, after the antique, 20th C, 11-1/2" h **$410**

Nubian Princess, Edrmann Encke, Gladenbeck foundry mark, short socle, marble base, 7-1/2" h.....**$415**

Rembrandt, Albert-Ernest Carrier-Belleuse, silvered patination, bronze socle, marble plinth, 20-1/2" h **$2,300**

Virgin, dark brown patina, Leon Pilet, French, sgd, 1836-1916, 9-3/4" h **$575**

Watteau-style woman, tricorn hat, low décolletage, George (Joris) Van Der Straeten, Paris Bronze Society foundry mark, fluted marble socle, reddish brown and black patination, 10-7/8" h.........................**$460**

Winged cherub, seated on broken column, playing hornpipe, pair of doves perched opposite, after Mathurin Moreau, dark brown patination, green marble socle, 9" h **$250**

Bronze and marble, medieval woman, after Patricia by Roger Hart, young woman, sheer headdress, marked "Mino di Tiesole" on ovoid white marble base, 20th C, 11-1/4" h **$575**

Carved marble, Pharaoh's Daughter, John Adams-Acton, snake headdress, beaded necklace, tapered sq section

Bust, marble, classical male, plinth base with natural weathering and wear, late 19th C, 32" x 21" x 10", **$2,700.**
Photo courtesy of David Rago Auctions, Inc.

Bust, marble, classical woman, plinth base with natural weathering and wear, late 19th C, 32" x 21" x 10", **$2,700.**
Photo courtesy of David Rago Auctions, Inc.

base, carved on front with scene of the discovery of Moses and title, 13-3/8" w, 10-3/4" d, 39" h breche d'alep marble tapered sq section pedestal, England, late 19th C, 13-3/4" w, 9-3/4" d, 26" h **$16,100**

Carved marble, Jeanne D'Arc, white marble face and base, pink marble bodice, incised title on front, early 20th C, 15-1/4" w, 6-3/4" d, 15" h **$700**

Gamin, polychromed plaster, Augusta Christine Fells Savage, (American 1892-1962), imp on verse, c1930, 9-1/4" l.................................**$33,350**

Bust, Lord Byron, parian, mounted on waisted circular socle, Copeland, England, c1870, impressed mark, 24" h, **$1,775.**
Photo courtesy of Skinner, Inc.

Bust, marble, woman, Florentine-style, associated marble pedestal, 61" x 17" x 9", **$600.**
Photo courtesy of David Rago Auctions, Inc.

Bust, Enid the Fair, bronze, George Frampton, 1907, signed, titled and dated in the mold, original dark patina, abrasion to nose, 20-1/2" x 9", $7,500.

Photo courtesy of David Rago Auctions, Inc.

Lady, carved facial features, ears, and hair style, stepped base with dentil carving, stamped dec, old surface, America, early 20th C, 8-1/4" h **$650**

Majolica, young boy, French colonial dress, marked "BU 677," 19" h **$900**

Marble, lady with rose, incised "A. Testi," associated partial alabaster pedestal with spiral fluted stem, 20" h **$2,645**

Marble, young pious woman, lace and flower bodice, hair in long braid, matching 6" h marble socle, Italian, late 19th C, 26" h **$7,475**

BUTTER PRINTS

History: There are two types of butter prints: butter molds and butter stamps. Butter molds are generally of three-piece construction—the design, the screw-in handle, and the case. Molds both shape and stamp the butter at the same time. Butter stamps are generally of one-piece construction, but can be of two-piece construction if the handle is from a separate piece of wood. Stamps decorate the top of butter after it is molded.

The earliest prints are one piece and were hand carved, often heavily and deeply. Later prints were factory made with the design forced into the wood by a metal die.

Some of the most common designs are sheaves of wheat, leaves, flowers, and pineapples. Animal designs and Germanic tulips are difficult to find. Prints with designs on both sides are rare, as are those in unusual shapes, such as half-rounded or lollipop.

Butter mold

Pineapple, carved wood, 4-3/8" d **$325**

Roses, carved maple, serrated edges, 5" x 8" **$165**

Sunflower, carved wood, 3-1/2" d **$125**

Butter stamp

Carved fruitwood, strawberry, 2-7/8" d, 4-1/2" l **$50**

Double sided, oval, peony on one side, tulip on other, carved print on handle, age crack, 3-3/4" d.........**$295**

Eagle on laurel branch, star over its head, wavy feathers, one-pc handle, scrubbed surface, 4-1/2" d **$395**

Hexagonal, pineapple print, tall case, pewter straps, orig plunger, 4-1/2" l, 4-3/4" d...**$100**

Lollipop style, carved pinwheel on one side, tulip with leaves on other, 6" l...**$3,900**

Nesting swan, threaded handle, old refinishing, some worm holes, minor edge damage, 4" d.........................**$500**

Pomegranate, concentric circle rim, one-pc handle, dark patina, 4-1/4" d **$100**

Rectangular, backward looking crested peafowl-type bird, sitting on flowering branch, turned inset handle, dark stains, 2-3/8" x 1-3/4".........**$250**

Round, carved primitive eagle, rayed sunbursts, dark patina, worn finish, large one-piece handle, 4-3/8" d **$330**

Round, carved flower, one piece handle, 1-7/8" d **$175**

Round, carved wide-eyed cow and fence, threaded insert handle with chip on end, 3-1/4" d..................**$ 200**

Round, carved tulip, good patina, PA, age cracks, 5" d **$665**

Speckled rooster, leafy foliage, one-piece handle, small chip on handle, 3" d..**$275**

Stylized eagle with shield, natural finish, blue ink stain, 3-3/4" d **$110**

Stylized eagle with shield, concentric circle rim, dry surface, 3-7/8" d..**$110**

Walnut, foliage and flowers, 4-3/4" d, 5-1/2" l................................**$115**

Butter stamp, heart and leaf design, semi-circular form with handle, 6-3/4" l, 4-1/2" h, $935.

Photo courtesy of Alderfer Auction Co.

Butter stamp, Leaf and vine design, round, single handle, $65.

Butter stamp, pineapple carved butter print, round, single handle, age crack, $85.

Photo courtesy of Wiederseim Associates, Inc.

Butter stamp, flowers with center fern leaves, coggled edge, one-piece wooden handle, $90.

CALENDAR PLATES

History: Calendar plates were first made in England in the late 1880s. They became popular in the United States after 1900, the peak years being 1909 to 1915. The majority of the advertising plates were made of porcelain or pottery and the design included a calendar, the name of a store or business, and either a scene, portrait, animal, or flowers. Some also were made of glass or tin.

Additional Resources:

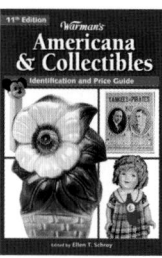

Warman's® Americana & Collectibles, 11th Ed., by Ellen T. Schroy, ed., Krause Publications, Iola, WI.

1906, Compliments of A. K. Clemmer, Kulpsville, Pennsylvia, scattered florals and calendar pages **$60**

1908, hunting dog, Pittstown, Pennsylvania **$40**

1909, Compliments of John U. Francis, Jr., Fancy and Staple Groceries, Oaks, Pennsylvania, multicolored transfer of roses and grapes, calendar pages around rim with holly leaves and berries, worn gold trim, mkd "Iron Stone China, Extra Quality" with lion and shield mark **$35**

1911, Souvenir of Detroit, Michigan, months in center, hen and yellow chicks, gold edge **$30**

1912, Winchester, rifle with grouse, autumn scene **$75**

1913, boy in overalls, mkd "Our Art Dept, 1913" **$65**

1915, black boy eating watermelon, 9" d **$60**

1916, eagle with shield, American flag, 8-1/4" d **$40**

1917, cat center **$35**

1919, ship center **$30**

1920, The Great War, MO **$30**

1921, bluebirds and fruit, 9" d **$35**

1913, holly and roses decoration, William F. Weber, Allentown, Pennsylvania, gold-trimmed edge, **$95.**
Photo courtesy of Dotta Auction Co., Inc.

1922, dog watching rabbit **$35**

1969, Royal China, Currier & Ives, green, 10" d **$40**

CALLING CARD CASES AND RECEIVERS

History: Calling cards, usually carried in specially designed cases, played an important social role in the United States from the Civil War until the end of World War I. When making formal visits, callers left their card in a receiver (card dish) in the front hall. Strict rules of etiquette developed. For example, the lady in a family was expected to make calls of congratulation and condolence and visits to the ill.

The cards themselves were small, embossed or engraved with the caller's name, and often decorated with a floral design. Many handmade examples, especially in Spencerian script, can be found. The cards themselves are considered collectible.

Note: Don't confuse a calling card case with a match safe.

Cases

Ivory, rect, wood inlay, block rows, center framed with diamond design rim band, 4" l **$175**

Leather, sterling silver plaque depicting young woman in Renaissance costume, seed pearl accents, Art Nouveau, French hallmarks **$300**

Silver, American, mid to late 19th C

Coin silver, Albert Coles, engraved dec, monogram **$350**

Coin silver, pointed arched base, engraved dec, monogram **$325**

1906, seasonal floral sprigs, scattered calendar pages, gold lettering "Prince Furniture Co., Complete Home Furnishers, No. 502 Hamilton St, Allentown, Pa," beaded edges, **$90.**
Photo courtesy of Dotta Auction Co., Inc.

1908, pretty girl, calendar pages in center, gold lettering "Compliments of A. A. Eckert, General Merchandise, Packerton, PA," **$55.**
Photo courtesy of Dotta Auction Co., Inc.

1916, pretty girl, calendar pages, blue birds, green ribbon garland on border, gold lettering "E. G. Hassler, Groceries, Dry Goods & Notions, 500 Schuykill Ave, Reading, PA," gold edge, **$80.**
Photo courtesy of Dotta Auction Co., Inc.

1917, pair of grazing deer, calendar pages on border and flags, gold lettering "Compliments of E. D. Reitter, Hoppenville, PA," **$65.**
Photo courtesy of Dotta Auction Co., Inc.

Kodak, Anostigmet f:8.8 lens, original box, **$35.**

Sterling silver, goldwashed, fitted leather case, engine turned dec, monogram **$250**

Sterling silver, Gorham, engraved dec, monogram **$325**

Silver, Chinese Export, rect, all-over hammered appearance, central monogrammed roundel, attributed to Tuck Chang & Co., late 19th/early 20th C, approx four troy oz, 2-7/8" x 3-7/8" **$200**

Silver and ivory, silver filigree work over ivory panels, filigree depicts wild boar hunt on one side, cartouche with monogram framed by filigree border on reverse, engraved brass frame, lid needs regluing, loss to int, 5-1/2" x 3" **$220**

Silver plate, quadruple silver plate, orig chain, Victorian, 3-1/2" x 3-3/4" **$125**

Tortoiseshell with stylized floral plique, hinged metal lid, 19th C, 4" x 3" **$110**

Wood, burl, Victorian, 3" l **$95**

Receivers

Bronze

Figural, bronze, monkey, Victorian, 7" l **$135**

Hammered, ovoid, emb comedy and tragedy masks, orig dark patina, crisp details, Gorham stamp mark, 9-1/2" l, 6" w **$650**

Porcelain, hand painted, roses, foliage, gold handles, 10" l **$45**

Silver plate, marked "Meriden," wear to plating, 7-1/4" l, 5-1/2" h **$60**

Tile, emb monks, gun-metal glaze, raised AETCo medallion for American Encaustic Tiling Co., few edge nicks, 5-1/4" x 6-1/2" **$95**

Kodak, No. 14, Antographic Kodak Junior, original box, **$45.**

CAMERAS

History: Photography became a viable enterprise in the 1840s, but few early cameras have survived. Cameras made before the 1880s are seldom available on the market, and when found, their prices are prohibitive for most collectors.

George Eastman's introduction of the Kodak camera in 1888, the first commercially marketed roll-film camera, put photography in the hands of the public.

Most collectors start with a general interest that becomes more defined. After collecting a broad range of Kodak cameras, a collector may decide to specialize in Retina models. Camera collectors tend to prefer unusual and scarce cameras to the most common models, which were mass-produced by the millions.

Because a surplus exists for many common cameras, such as most Kodak box and folding models, collectors are wise to acquire only examples in excellent condition. Shutters should function properly. Minimal wear is generally acceptable. Avoid cameras that have missing parts, damaged bellows, and major cosmetic problems.

Agfa, Germany, Billy O, vertical folding camera, uses 127 roll film, Solinar f 3.9/75mm lens, Compur shutter, c1932-37 .... **$50**

American Optical Co., New York, Flammang's Patent Revolving Back View Camera, tan and red bellows, mahogany body with brass fittings, Prosh Triplex lens and external shutter, c1886, 5" x 7" **$625**

Eastman Kodak, field type camera, large, front view, **$125.**
Photo courtesy of Dotta Auction Co., Inc.

E. & H.T. Anthony & Co., NY, Anthony view camera, mahogany with nickel and brass fittings, folding bed, original "EA" stamped landscape lens, c1880, 5" x 8" **$350**

Bell & Howell, Chicago, Dial 35, unusually configured half frame camera, spring-powered motor drive, f2.8/28mm Canon lens, molded plastic case, c1968 .... **$35**

Foton, high quality 35mm rangefinder camera with spring-powered motor drive, Cooke Amotal f2/50mm lens, c1948 .... **$850**

Conley Camera Co., Rochester, Minnesota, Conley Folding 3A Kewpie, vertical folding camera with square corners and red bellows, 1916 .... **$40**

Eastman Kodak, Rochester, New York

Kodak Petite, Vest Pocket Kodak Model B, light green, orig faded green bellows (also available in blue, gray, lavender and rose), matching hard case, c1929 .... **$150**

Kodak Cirkut Camera No. 10, Folmer & Schwing Division, large format camera for photographing panoramic pictures on film up to 10" w, outfit includes Turner Reich lens, tripod and gearbox, c1917 .... **$2,700**

No. 4 Folding Pocket Kodak camera, vertical folding camera, 4" x 5" exposures on roll film, red bellows, polished wood insets on bed, c1907-15 .... **$80**

Ordinary Kodak Camera, c1891-95, wooden box camera, loaded with 24, 4" x 5" exposures on roll film, string set shutter **$900**

Franke & Heidecke, Germany, Rolleiflex 3.5F, twin lens reflex camera, Planar f3.5/75mm lens, light meter, excellent condition, c1961 .... **$900**

Heiland Photo Products, Premiere, 35mm non-range-finder camera, made in Germany, Steinheil Cassar f2.8/ 45mm lens, Pronto shutter, c1957 .... **$15**

Ica, Germany, Polyscop, stereo camera with rigid nonfolding body, Tessar f4.5 or 6.3 lenses, c1911-25 .... **$200**

Lionel Manufacturing Co., NY, Linex, cast metal subminiature stereo camera, f8/ 30mm lenses, for taking pairs of 16mm by 20mm exposures on roll film, c1954 .... **$90**

Minolta, Japan, Autocord, twin lens reflex camera, Rokkor f3.5/75mm lens, Seikosha MX 1-500 shutter, non-metered, c1955 .... **$70**

Nippon Kogaku, Japan, Nikon S2, rangefinder camera, Nippon Nikkor f1.4/5cm lens, non-metered, chrome top, excellent condition, c1952 .... **$1,100**

Seneca Camera Co., Rochester, New York, Seneca No. 1, 4" x 5" folding camera, polished wood interior, red bellows, Wollensak Junior brass cased lens, carrying case containing two plate holders................................... **$95**

Spencer Co., Chicago, Falcon Flash Camera, inexpensive plastic miniature camera using 127 roll film, flash attachment, orig box **$15**

Voigtlander, Germany, Vitomatic IIa, 35mm viewfinder camera, outfitted with superior Ultron f2/50mm lens, Prontor 500 SLK-shutter, c1959 .... **$185**

Yamato Koki, Japan, Pax, small 35mm rangefinder camera styled after Leica, Luminor f3.5/45mm lens, YKK shutter, c1952-55 .... **$40**

Yashica, Japan

Electro 35, 35mm rangefinder, Yashinon f1.7/ 45mm lens, screw-on telephoto and wide-angle adaptor lenses, c1974................................ **$50**

Yashica Flash-O-Set, 35mm camera, f4/4cm lens, single-speed leaf shutter, built-in light meter, AG-1 flash unit, c1961 .... **$24**

Zeiss, Germany

Contarex "Bull's-eye," 35mm camera, large round exposure meter window over lens, Tessar f2.8/50mm lens, c1959-66 .... **$425**

Super Ikonta III, folding rangefinder camera, Tessar f3.5/75mm coated lens, Synchro-Compur shutter to 1/500, c1954-1958 .... **$350**

CANDLESTICKS

History: The domestic use of candlesticks is traced to the 14th century. The earliest was a picket type, named for the sharp point used to hold the candle. The socket type was established by the mid-1660s.

From 1700 to the present, candlestick design mirrored furniture design. By the late 17th century, a baluster stem was introduced, replacing the earlier Doric or clustered column stem. After 1730, candlesticks reflected rococo ornateness. Neoclassic styles followed in the 1760s. Each new era produced a new style of candlesticks; however, some styles became universal and remained in production for centuries. Therefore, when attempting to date a candlestick, it is important to try to determine the techniques used to manufacture the piece.

Candelabras are included in this edition to show examples of the many interesting candelabras available in today's antiques marketplace. Check for completeness when purchasing candelabras; most are sold in pairs.

Candelabra

Brass

Baluster stems, scrolled tripod bases, cov with highly detailed cast grape vines, center and two branching arms with cast vines with leaves and bunches of grapes, leaves cover sockets, small dents on one, price for pr, 22-1/4" h **$1,155**

Three scrolled arms, center fruit finial, two Sevres-type blue porcelain pieces with white reserves filled with hand painted polychrome flowers, cast brass base with grape leaves and cherub faces, 14-1/2" h **$300**

Bronze

Bronze and gilt bronze, Victory, winged figure in flowing gown, rising from caramel colored marble plinth, four scrolled arms with candle sockets, later conversion to electric lamp, French Empire, 19th C, 33" h **$980**

Gilt bronze, shafts modeled as quivers rising from acanthus scrolled brackets, rouge marble plinths, columned feet, quiver tops emanating from scrolled arms, fluted candle socket, Napoleon III, French, c1855-70, pr, 27" h **$1,380**

Gilt bronze, ftd base supporting altar from which a column of clouds mounted with winged angels looking up toward five-arm candelabra, French, 19th C, 41" h **$865**

Gilt metal

Five-light candelabra centerpiece with scrolled foliate arms, colorless prisms supported on patinated baluster form shaft with gilt floral and foliate designs on black ground, two matching 16-5/8" h three-light candelabra, all on sq white marble bases, seam separation on shafts, lacking some prisms, 19-3/4" h **$360**

Victorian, Egyptian Revival style, scrolling candle arms supporting five candles, urn-shaped support, black marble plinth, 23" h **$360**

Glass

Deep amethyst base and column with cut panels, cut stars around center, detailed brass castings include four branches, all with scrolled acanthus leaves and sockets, emb "Made in France," wear to silver plating, center finial missing, 11-1/4" h **$550**

Pressed colorless glass, two-light, center faceted prism above drip pan hung with faceted prisms, suspending two chains of prisms to a pair of spiral twisted scrolled arms, flanked by two scrolled candlearms, drip pans hung with further prisms, single knob stem, stepped sq base, late 19th C, bases drilled, 20" h, 14-1/2" w, price for pr **$350**

Candlesticks

Art glass, iridescent gold, large disc foot and top separated with baluster stem, sgd "650 Nash," 4" h **$350**

Brass

Capstan base, damage, soldered repair, 6" h................................. **$215**

Candlesticks, pr, red-brown mottled marble, turned pedestal bases supporting twisted standards, turned candle sockets, bases chipped, 11" h, **$250.**

Photo courtesy of Alderfer Auction Co.

Candlestick, Arts & Crafts, gold-plated hammered copper, fluted candle-holder at top, twisted stem, fluted flower-form base, made by Marie Zimmerman, artist's cipher, 14" x 5-1/4", **$2,000.**

Photo courtesy of David Rago Auctions, Inc.

Candelabra, gilt bronze, urn form supporting five arms with single candle sockets, one central arm with single candle socket, floral foliage, garlands, figural details, 25" h, **$1,760.**

Brass, rectangular base, push-up, ring handle, **$150.**

Photo courtesy of Wiederseim Associates, Inc.

Heavy stem threaded into saucer base, dings and scratches, 5-1/4" h **$320**

Mid-drip pans, baluster stems, round spun base, finely detailed turnings with extractor holes in sockets, Dutch, 19th C copies of earlier style, 9-1/8" h **$230**

Push-rod, round base, 8-3/8" h **$90**

Push-ups, saucer bases, tooled rings around columns, 4-1/2" h, pr **$175**

Removable candlecup, beaded on rim, octagonal, baluster shaft, domed base with ruffled edges, remnants of silver plating, France, early-to mid-18th C, 9-3/4" h **$150**

Removable candlecup, octagonal, baluster shaft, domed base with ruffled edges, remnants of silver plating, France, early-to mid-18th C, 10" h **$150**

Side push-up, threaded into domed base with scalloped edge, 8-3/4" h **$275**

Bronze, patinated bronze, silvered and gilt sconces over rouge marble drip

Candlesticks, pr, Dutch brass, baluster form support on round base, molded edges, 17th C, 8-1/2" h, **$600.**

Photo courtesy of Sloans & Kenyon Auctioneers and Appraisers.

pans, classical male bust, tapered stem, round base, Italian, late 19th C, 10" h **$600**

Cast brass and wrought iron, Gothic Revival, late 19th C, pricket, trefoil-edged drip pan, girdled multi-knopped cast brass standard, wrought-iron trefoil base with serpentine legs, acanthus knees and flowerhead scrolls, price for pr, 61" h **$1,610**

Glass, pressed, early

Alabaster/ clambroth, petal socket, dolphin, single-step base, orig gilt dec shells on base, wafer construction, Boston & Sandwich Glass Co., Sandwich, MA, 1845-70, 10-1/2" h **$1,155**

Canary, hexagonal, large base, wafer construction, Boston & Sandwich Glass Co., Sandwich, MA, socket flake, minor base flakes, 1840-60, 7-1/2" h **$190**

Dark blue-violet, faint white swirls within base, hexagonal socket, circular base, wafer construction, Boston & Sandwich Glass Co., Sandwich, MA, 1835-50, 6-3/4" h **$1,155**

Vaseline, hexagonal sockets, patterned hexagonal base, one pc construction, possibly European, minute socket rim flake, minor base nicks, second half 19th C, price for pr, 8" h **$125**

Gilt bronze

Base of sconce with acanthus, tapered stem with central guilloche band on fish scale ground, ovoid base with leaftip and patera roundels, Empire, French, early 19th C, 10" h **$900**

Candlesticks, pr, continental pewter, circular bases, knopped shaft, 18th century, 8" h, **$400.**
Photo courtesy of Sloans & Kenyon Auctioneers and Appraisers.

Gilt metal, Gothic Revival, hexagonal sconce, drip pan with pierced trefoil rim, hexagonal stem with bulbous shaped knop, loaded floriform base enameled with lion shields and griffins on trefoils, ropetwist foot trim, late 19th C, 11-3/4" h **$1,000**

Marble, Empire-style, late 19th C, engine turned and beaded ormolu nozzles, gray marble columns hung with gilt-metal chains suspending acorns, stepped white marble base with flat leaf and beaded mounts, flattened ball feet, price for pr, 8" h **$350**

Pewter, pricket, wide drip pan, double-baluster stem, shaped-tripartite base, three ball feet, Continental, 18th C, 22-3/4" h **$700**

Porcelain, figural, male and female flower gatherers, against brocage, rocaille base, attributed to Samson, France, late 19th C, price for pr, 10-5/8" h **$450**

Sterling silver, Neoclassical, England, emb gadrooned nozzle, campana-shape stems, foliate festoons and acanthus dec, waisted pedestal base, emb arms and beaded rims, price for pr, first half 19th C, 5-1/2" h **$280**

Tin

Adjustable push-up rod, pie plate base, ring handle, 5-1/2" h, 6" d **$550**

Hog scraper, adjustable push-rod, decorative brass ring, illegible name stamped on push-rod handle, 7-1/4" h, 3-3/4" d **$660**

Pie plate base, ring handle, 4-1/2" h, 7-1/2" d **$1,100**

Wrought iron

Scrolled handle and feet, lip handle, notched push-up, price for pr, 11-1/2" h **$550**

Candlestick, brass, whimsical, decorated with flying owl, bumblebee, and beetle, stamped "BRADLEY & HUBBARD MFG CO. 767," 8-1/2" h, **$200.**
Photo courtesy of David Rago Auctions, Inc.

Spiral, scrolled push-up, turned wood base, 6-7/8" h **$300**

CANDY CONTAINERS

History: In 1876, Croft, Wilbur, and Co. filled small glass Liberty Bells with candy and sold them at the Centennial Exposition in Philadelphia. From that date until the 1960s, glass candy containers remained popular. They reflect historical changes, particularly in transportation.

Jeannette, Pennsylvania, a center for the packaging of candy in containers, was home for J. C. Crosetti, J. H. Millstein, T. H. Stough, and Victory Glass. Other early manufacturers included: George Borgfeldt, New York, New York; Cambridge Glass, Cambridge, Ohio; Eagle Glass, Wheeling, West Virginia; L. E. Smith, Mt. Pleasant, Pennsylvania; and West Brothers, Grapeville, Pennsylvania.

Notes: Candy containers with original paint, candy, and closures command a high premium, but beware of reproduced parts and repainting. The closure is a critical part of each container; if it is missing, the value of the container drops considerably. Small figural perfumes and other miniatures often are sold as candy containers.

Additional Resources:

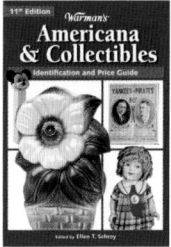

Warman's® Americana & Collectibles, 11th Ed., by Ellen T. Schroy, ed., Krause Publications, Iola, WI.

Airplane, P-38 Lightning, orig wire clip, motors, and ground, no closure **$200**

Auto, coupe, long hood, orig tan snap-on strip, orig gold stamped tin wheels, orig closure **$120**

Barney Google, bank

Orig paint, orig closure **$650**

Repainted, orig closure **$450**

Baseball player, with bat, 50 percent orig paint, orig closure **$500**

Bear, on circus tub, orig tin, orig closure **$500**

Boat, USN Dreadnaught, orig closure **$350**

Bulldog, screw closure, 4-1/4" h **$60**

Bus

Chicago, replaced closure **$275**

New York-San Francisco, orig closure **$375**

Victory Glass Co., replaced closure **$300**

Camera, tripod base, 80 percent paint **$200**

Cannon

Cannon #1, orig carriage, orig closure **$375**

Two-Wheel Mount #1, orig carriage, orig closure **$220**

U. S. Defense Field Gun #17, orig closure **$380**

Cat, papier-mâché, seated, gray and white paint, pink ribbon, glass eyes, touch up and repairs, 3-3/4" h **$375**

Chick, composition, cardboard, base, Germany, 5" h **$20**

Dog, by barrel, 90 percent paint, chip on base, orig closure **$220**

Dog, papier-mâché, gray, painted and molded feathers, stamped "Made in Germany," repair at neck opening **$50**

Candy container, rabbit, papier-mâché, original closure, **$550.**

Elf on rocking horse, pressed glass, no closure, 3-1/2" h **$160**

Felix the Cat, repainted, replaced closure **$550**

Fire truck, with ladders **$45**

George Washington, papier-mâché, with tricorn hat, white ponytail and blue coat, standing beside cardboard cabin with deep roof and chimney, unmarked, 3" h **$195**

Ghost head, papier-mâché, flannel shroud, 3-1/2" h **$150**

Gun, West Specialty Co., 5-3/4" l **$20**

Horse and wagon, pressed glass **$35**

Indian, pressed glass, riding motorcycle with sidecar, no closure, 5" l **$350**

Kettle, pressed glass, clear, T. H. Stough, cardboard closure, 2" h, 2-1/4" d **$50**

Limousine, orig wheels, orig closure, small chip **$600**

Little boy, papier-mâché head and hollow body, large pink nose, closed smiling mouth, painted brown eyes,

molded and painted red vest, green jacket, yellow short pants, purple socks, black shoes, brown tie, 6" h **$210**

Locomotive, Mapother's 1892, orig closure **$125**

Man on motorcycle, side car, repainted, replaced closure **$525**

Mule, pulling two-wheeled barrel with driver, 95 percent paint, orig closure **$85**

Nursing bottle, pressed glass, clear, natural wood nipple closure, T. H. Stough, 1940-50 .... **$20**

Puppy, papier-mâché, painted, white, black muzzle, glass eyes, 2-1/2" h **$35**

Rabbit, glass

Rabbit pushing chick in shell cart, orig closure **$500**

Rabbit with basket on arm, no paint, orig closure **$120**

Rocking horse, small chips on rockers, no closure **$180**

Rooster, papier-mâché, pewter feet, orig polychrome paint, marked "Germany," 6-1/2" h **$225**

Sailor, papier-mâché head and hollow body, large pink nose, closed smiling mouth, protruding lower lip, molded and painted sideburns and hair, molded gray fez, painted blue eyes, molded and painted blue sailor uniform, black belt with knife case and sword, black shoes, unmarked, 6" h **$275**

Santa Claus, by sq chimney, 60 percent paint, replaced closure **$180**

Stop and Go, replaced switch handle, orig closure **$440**

Submarine F6, no periscope or flat, orig super structure, orig closure **$250**

Tank, World War I, traces of orig paint, no closure **$90**

Telephone, small glass receiver **$55**

Turkey, gobbler, small chip under orig closure **$100**

Village bank, with insert, log-cabin roof **$110**

Wagon, orig closure **$90**

Wheelbarrow, orig wheel, no closure **$35**

Windmill, five windows, ruby-flashed orig blades, orig closure **$495**

CANES

History: Canes or walking sticks have existed through the ages, first as staffs or symbols of authority, and then items like religious ceremonial pieces. They eventually evolved to the fashion accessory that is the highly desirable antique prized by today's collector for its beauty and lasting qualities. The best were created with rare materials such as carved ivory, precious metals, jewels, porcelain, and enamel, with many being very high-quality works of art. They were also fashioned of more mundane materials, with some displaying the skill of individual folk artists. Another category of interest to collectors is the gadget canes that contained a myriad of hidden utilitarian objects, from weapons to drinking flasks, telescopes, compasses, and even musical instruments, to cite just a few.

Adviser: Henry A. Taron.

Automata

English, 4-1/3" h x 2-1/4" handle, carved wood full-bodied pug, brown glass eyes, sitting on top of stump, short curly tail swings upward, long red tongue protrudes when button activated, 2/3" smooth gold collar mkd "Brigg, London," mahogany shaft, 7/8" brass ferrule, 36-1/4" l **$3,640**

English, 3-1/2" h x 3-1/2" w carved elephant ivory handle, fierce lion with flowing mane, button at back of neck causes tongue to protrude and eyes change from brown to red, 1/3" silver collar, brown hardwood shaft, 2/3" bone ferrule, c1900, 34-3/4" l **$2,200**

Bamboo, carved, Japanese, 1-1/2" h x 1-1/8" natural root handle, low relief carved shaft with leaves, insects, and moths, dark stained and chip carved background, 1" burnished brass ferrule, c1900, 36" l **$400**

Cameo glass, English, 3-2/3" h x 1-1/3" w pistol handle, cameo carved white palm trees on pale blue blown glass, 3/4" silver collar, rosewood shaft, 1-1/4" dark horn ferrule, c1895, 35-3/4" l **$2,920**

Campaign, American, McKinley, 4-1/4" l x 1-2/3" w tau horn handle, hollow tin, top engraved "Patriotism, Protection, Prosperity," shaft engraved "Pat. Apl'd For, The Winfield Mf'g, Warren, O," oval-shaped tin shaft with multiple small dents, capped end, 1896, 36" l **$450**

Cigarette holder with matchsafe, English, 2" h x 1-1/8" d sterling knob, dec with basketweave pattern, owner's initials on top, hinted lid opens to reveal compartment with central tube for cigarettes, hinged lid scored as striker, matches in crescent box with swing-open lid, London hallmarks, 7/8" horn ferrule, 1884, 37" l **$1,120**

Damascene, English, handle imported from Toledo, Spain, 6-1/2" l steel crook handle with gold damascene of dragons, flowers, geometric designs, ebony shaft, 1" burnished brass ferrule, c1890, 35-3/4" l **$4,370**

Ebony, carved, English, 5-1/4" h x 2" handle, grinning black man, wearing linked silver collar necklace, 1/4" elephant ivory ring collar, ebony shaft, 1-14" ivory ferrule, c1890, 35-1/2" l ....**$785.**

Enamel, Continental, 1-1/2" h x 2-1/2" l duck handle, teal green enamel head, yellow glass eyes, painted yellow beak, 1/3" silver collar, black shaft, 1" horn ferrule, c1890, 36" l **$1,010**

Folk art, American, single piece of hickory, 2-1/3" cylindrical handle, high relief carving of religious and fraternal symbols including bible, all-seeing eyes, IOOF linked chain, bow and arrows, scales of justice, sheaf of wheat, skull and crossbones, caduceus staff, hourglass, heart-in-hand, beehive, coffin, peace dove, urn, crossed writing quills, crossed keys, crossed swords, crossed mallets, three baby bottles, c1895, 36" l **$2,600**

Gadget, English, tape measure, 1-1/2" h x 1-3/4" celluloid handle as Arab with turban, cigarette dangling from mouth, acts as handle for 3 foot cloth tape measure that pulls out of mouth, ringed brass collar, brown hardwood shaft, 1" horn ferrule, c1910, 36" l **$750**

Gold, American, 4-1/2" l x 2-1/4" gold filled handle shaped as finely detailed duck, yellow glass eyes, stepped partridgewood shaft, 7/8" brass ferrule, c1890, 33" l **$425**

Gold, Anglo/Indian, 1-7/8" h x 7/8" d knob, chased and raised owner's initials on top, four standing Hindu gods in relief on side, single pc elephant

ivory carved to simulate thorns, 1-1/4" brass ferrule, c1890, 33-1/2" l **$3,360**

Gun

Belgian, 6" l x 1" d black horn crook handle, 1-1/8" slotted nickel collar hides drop-down trigger, breech opened with quarter turn, 14mm breech with Belgian marks, rosewood veneer shaft, 1" removable ferrule/tampion, very minor crack in horn handle, c1895, 35-3/4" l **$1,200**

Continental, 2-1/2" l "L" handle, black painted metal, opens 4-1/2" down shaft, bayonet type socket for loading pin fire 12 mm cartridge, hammer on top of barrel pulls back with thong, 3/4" removable ferrule/tampion, c1885, 33-1/2" l **$1,100**

Ivory, carved

Continental, 2-3/4" h x 1-7/8" d, high relief carved forest scene with dinosaurs, thick honey-toned Malacca shaft, 1" burnished brass ferrule, c1870, 36" l **$3,810**

Continental, 1-3/4" h x 4-1/3" l handle, semi-nude Cleopatra reclining on fancy divan, scratching dog's back while cat licking her foot, 3/4" silver collar, heavy ebony shaft, 1-1/2" replaced white metal and iron antique ferrule, small chip on divan, c1880, 36" l **$10,640**

English, 3-1/4" h x 1-1/3" ivory handle, pierced in center for cord, 3/4" scalloped and punch dec silver collar, orig thick full bark Malacca shaft, 4" brass ferrule, c1690, 37-1/2" l **3,585**

English, 1-3/4" h x 1-1/3" w hound grasping captured fox by neck, detailed scene with hound trailing fox in woodland setting, punch dec 5/16" gold collar, one-pc ivory shaft, 1" white metal and iron ferrule, c1870, 35-1/2" l **$3,500**

English, 2-1/4" h x 2" handle, covered wicker basket with four puppies, 1/3" silver collar with London hallmarks, Malacca shaft, 7/8" burnished brass ferrule, 1883, 35-1/2" l **$3,100**

English, 1-1/3" h x 2" d whale ivory handle, 1/3" round baleen dot inlaid on top, octagonal with incised lines at sides, thick whalebone shaft carved with rings and 2-1/2" of sawtooth, 5-1/2" of fluting, 7-2/3" of

twist, remainder is tapered, 1-1/2" white metal and iron ferrule, c1845, 34" l **$8,000**

English, 2-1/3" h x 1-2/3" w handle, hand around face of young woman, curly tresses, lace collar, ebony shaft, 2/3" horn ferrule, c1885, 35-1/2" l **$900**

English, 5" h x 2" w octopus handle, long tentacles, yellow glass eyes, ebony shaft, 2-2/3" light horn ferrule, c1885, 36" l **$3,910**

English, 3" h x 2" w handle, cat, articulating mouth, clear glass eyes, bow under chin, spring loaded lever in center of bow opens mouth, red tongue, 1/8" gold gilt collar, black enameled shaft, 1" horn ferrule, c1890, 36-1/2" l **$1,680**

English, 2" h x 3-1/2" l, well carved donkey, brown glass eyes, 3/4" silver collar with London hallmarks for 1896, and button to activate ears and mouth, red tongue, dark bamboo shaft, 1" replaced brass ferrule, attributed to Brigg, 1896, 36" l **$4,190**

English, 1-3/4" d, ball shaped handle carved on one side with winking bulldog and bowtie, other with pointed-eared cat, 1/2" silver collar with braided chain dec, heavy snakewood shaft, 1" horn ferrule, c1905, 37-1/2" l **$1,120**

English, 3-1/4" h x 1-2/3" w handle, hermit crab emerging from spiral shell, 1-1/3" silver collar dec with "C" scrolls and oval cartouche, heavy ebony shaft, 1-1/8" dark horn ferrule, c1910, 37-1/4" l **$2,800**

English, 3-3/4" h x 1-1/4" w handle, full bodied lion on tree stump confronting encircling snake, 1-1/2" gold filled band dec with scrolls and sawtooth edges, inscribed "H. D. Fessen, Jan. 28, 1911," ebony shaft, 1" brass ferrule, c1911, 36" l **$2,500**

French, 2" h x 1" d Napoleon profile shadow handle, 2/3" silver collar, heavy ebony shaft, 1" horn ferrule, c1825, 36-1/4" l **$2,020**

French, 3-1/4" h x 1-1/4" d elephant ivory handle, carved panel on one side with silver lily overlay, 1-1/3" silver collar with French hallmarks, heavy rosewood shaft, 1" black horn ferrule, c1900, 36-1/3" l **$450**

German, 4" h x 2-1/2" handle, bearded troll kneeling on branch of oak tree, hand resting on rock hammer, 3/4" textured silver collar rimmed with two gold rings with gold tree trunk on side, worn Continental hallmark, ebony shaft, 1" replaced ferrule, c1800, 37-1/3" l **$1,800**

German, 7-1/2" h x 2-1/8" w pistol grip handle, carved coat of arms with plumed knight's helmet, detailed shield, inscribed Latin mottos "honestas, equitas, virtus," 1/3" carved ivory ring collar, dark rosewood shaft, 3/4" ivory ferrule, student type, c1885, 36" l **$2,690**

Ivory, hippo, carved, Continental, 4-1/8" h x 1-1/4" d fluted mushroom shaped top, graceful hand with fringed cuff holding ivory top, 3/4" rope turned ivory collar, finely figured thin snakewood shaft, 1-3/4" horn ferrule, c1895, 38" l **$1,010**

Ivory, walrus, carved

Continental, 2-3/4" h x 1-3/4" w, skeleton wearing ruffled collar, holding up bony hands and mask of human face, 1" textured silver collar with two simulated bucks and smooth cartouche, heavy ebony shaft, 1" brass and iron ferrule, c1880, 35-3/4" l **$4,250**

English, 5-1/4" h x 1-3/4" w handle with hunter leaning against tree with propped rifle, dog on hind legs sniffing game bag, hunter lighting pipe, 1" dec sterling collar with 1896 London hallmarks, tightly stepped partridgewood shaft, 7/8" replaced brass ferrule, made in England, imported German handle, 1896, 36-3/4" l **$1,460**

French, 4-1/2" h x 1-7/8" handle carved as young woman wearing fancy hat, blouse revealing breasts, opposite side inscribed "Madamd Plaisir, Orleans," 3/4" rope turned silver collar, smooth partridgewood shaft, 1-1/2" white metal and iron ferrule, c1880, 36" l **$4,480**

Map, American Legion Convention, 6-1/2" wooden crook handle, 3/4" white metal collar with slot, spring-loaded cloth street map of Boston with metal edge and grip, paper label "American Legion Convention 1940," picture of Paul Revere, text "Paul Revere rides again," 2/3" white metal ferrule, 1940, 34-1/2" l **$535**

Marble, English, 4-1/2" h x 3-1/4" l gray opaque L handle, base with diamond overlay fashioned from four graduated pieces of different colored marble, shaft comprised of multicolored marble segments, 3" horn ferrule, c1900, 35-7/8" l **$2,650**

Merchant's measure, English, 2-1/2" h x 1-1/4" d ivory knob handle, rich yellow patina, unscrews to reveal long thing flexible Malacca rod with small round rosewood handle, 1-1/2" brass and iron tip, rod has line of dots to measure in one inch increments, 1" scalloped and punch dec silver collar, worn Malacca shaft, 3" brass ferrule, c1695, 36-1/2" l **$4,700**

Mixed metals, Japanese, fashioned in America, 2-1/2" h x 1" w brass knob with finely detailed standing crane holding plum branch in beak, silver body, copper crest, bamboo shaft with pyrography, sgd in Japanese characters by maker, 1-1/4" white metal and iron ferrule, c1895, 35" l **$1,500**

Mother of pearl, French, 2-2/3" h cylindrical knob handle, 7/8" d top made from 8 diamond shaped pieces that come together at center point, sides with mother-of-pearl bars and vermeil silver overlay with festoons of roses and ribbons at top, center silver ring, chain of laurel leaves at base, French hallmarks and "935," ebony shaft, 1-1/3" white metal and iron ferrule, 36-1/4" l **$1,600**

Music box, Swiss, carved from single pc of hardwood, possibly birch, 3" l, 2" h smooth "L" handle, carved pug dog sitting upright on top of music box on top of shaft, separate winding key, carved shaft with simulated thorns, c1900, 34-3/4" l **$6,440**

Nautical

America, carved whale ivory and whalebone, 2-1/4" h x 1-1/8" d whale ivory mushroom handle, inlaid on top with 1/3" sq piece of baleen with round mother-of-pearl spherule in center, thin baleen separator, fully carved whalebone shaft with section of sawtooth pattern, section of convex fluting, then concave fluting raised stringing turns to left followed by raised piece, uniform yellow patina, c1840, 32-1/4" l............................. **$2,800**

America, whale ivory and carved whalebone, 3" h x 1-1.2" d whale ivory handle, 1/3" round baleen spherule inlaid in flat top, three tin baleen spacers around two 1/4" whale ivory spacers, while whalebone shaft with angled twist carving, some age cracking, spacers cosmetically in-filled, c1850, 35" l **$2,240**

Ophthalmologist, America, 1-1/2" elephant ivory ball handle, 1" brown glass eyes, 7/8" dec collar mkd "sterling," figured rosewood shaft, 1" black horn ferrule, c1890, 36" l **$840**

Phrenology, America, 36-1/3" l, 2-2/3" h x 1-1/4" w handle with markings and clear decoder, yellow patina, 2/3" beaded and lined silver collar, stepped partridgewood shaft, 1" burnished brass and iron ferrule, c1850, 36-1/3" l **$3,360**

Porcelain

English, 1-1/2" d pale blue porcelain ball, painted jockey and horse jumping over water hazard, green wreath of foliage frames scene, 1/4" gold ring collar, heavy ebony shaft, 1" replaced brass ferrule, c1900, 36-3/4" l **$500**

Royal Copenhagen, 2-1/4" h x 7/8" cylindrical handle, hand painted scene with sailboat, pale blue, green, gray, and pink, 1/2" gold wash collar, black enameled shaft, 7/8" horn ferrule, England, 1900 .... **$1,345**

Presentation, America, 18kt gold, double gold quartz inlays, 4" h, 4" l, 1" thick tau handle, inlaid on each end is 1" x 3/4" polished oval gold quartz stone, each matrix with gold flecking in gray/white background, inscribed fancy cartouches on handles, presenter's initials on side, receiver's name on shaft portion, dark tropical wood shaft, 1" white metal and iron ferrule, c1870, 36-1/4" l **$6,160**

Quartz, French, vermeil silver overlay, 2-3/4" h x 7/8" d pale pink rose quartz handle, internal crystalline fissures, two vermeil silver floral rings at top and bottom, three long classical columns topped with ferns, one column with French Minerva hallmark for 950 silver, ebony shaft, 1" burnished brass ferrule, c1900, 37" l **$1,795**

Cane, English, ball and stem, 1-1/3" d polished tiger-eye ball top, gold plated cup mount with seven fingers with round tips, 4" stem with two cylindrical pieces of polished tiger-eye quartz with plated gold simulated strap at mind point, plated gold ring at base, ebony shaft, 1-1/4" ivory ferrule, c1900, 35-7/8" l, **$1,600.**
Photo courtesy of Henry A. Taron.

Cane, American, c1870, 1-1/4" h x 1" d solid gold knob handle, scrolls and flowers dec, "T. Fay, N.Y." on top, octagonal base, tortoiseshell veneer shaft, 3" silver and iron ferrule, 34-3/4" l, **$2,750.**
Photo courtesy of Henry A. Taron.

Cane, America, 1-1/2" h x 1-2/3" w whale ivory handle carved as fist holding a rod, thin baleen separator above 6" of twist and string carving on whalebone shaft, 2-1/2" burnished brass ferrule, c1840, 33-3/4" l, **$3,000.**
Photo courtesy of Henry A. Taron.

Cane, Viennese, silver, 3" h x 1-1/8" d bright green enamel handle, 2/3" circle of light green enamel on top, rimmed in white, enamel over silver with engine-turned guilloche, silver collar, snakewood shaft, 1" horn ferrule, small professional repair to side of handle, c1900, 33-1/4", **$1,000.**
Photo courtesy of Henry A. Taron.

Cane, silver vermeil, rose quartz, pearls and enamel, 3/4" cabochon rose quartz stone on top, 1/2" w white enamel band with guilloche overlaid with festooned floral roping, sides textured with engine-turned guilloche and tiny dots, ring of tiny seed pearls bordered by two laurel leaf chains, mkd "900" and Viennese hallmarks, black enameled hardwood shaft, 1-1/8" black horn ferrule, 36" l, **$1,000.**
Photo courtesy of Henry A. Taron.

Cane, French, Art Nouveau, silver, 6" l x 2-1/4" w handle, flowing chestnut tree theme, openwork loop at top with leaves and hanging fruit, pink copper wash highlights, French hallmarks, maker's mark for Charles Eugene Francois Lefebrve, smooth partridgewood shaft, 7/8" brass ferrule, c1900, 35-1/2" l, **$2,500.**
Photo courtesy of Henry A. Taron.

Cane, Viennese, painted enamel, 2-1/2" h x 1-1/2" d knob handle, hp face of regal lady on top, sides with two 18th C young couples in pastoral setting by castle, two gardeners working in background, ebony shaft, 1-1/3" black horn ferrule, late 19th C, 38" l, $3,000.

Photo courtesy of Henry A. Taron.

Rock crystal

Bavaria, 3" h x 1" d rock crystal handle, top faceted like jewel, fourteen long smooth panels on sides, 2/3" silver collar with blue guilloche enamel, custom 4-1/4" l red leather case mkd "Berthold Fuchs," jewelry from Bad Kissingen, Bavaria, lined with satin and velvet, ebonized hardwood shaft, 1" horn ferrule, c1900, 36" l **$1,345**

French, 36" l, 2-3/4" h x 1" d rock crystal handle, reticulated overlay vermeil silver in diamond and swirled patterns, tiny French hallmarks, brown hardwood shaft, 7/8" horn ferrule, c1900, 36" l **$1,345**

Shooting stick seat, French, birch and bamboo, iron slide fittings, two 6" x 4" folding seat, 3-1/2" pointed ferrule can be inserted into ground for stability, c1900, 34" l **$500**

Silver

2-1/4" l x 1-1/4" d spherical handle of Chinese man with knotted pigtail queue, handle unscrews to reveal water receptacle and long metal siphon, when queue is lifted, man emits strong stream of water from

mouth, maccassar ebony, 1-1/3" horn ferrule, 37-1/8" l **$2,000**

3" l silver dog head with amber glass eyes, mkd "800," partridgewood, 7" crook handle, 1-1/4" brass and iron ferrule, c1895, 36" l **$280**

3-1/4" h x 3-3/4" l "L" handle shaped like golf putter, oval cartouche with owner's initials, dec with fancy scrolls and flowers, mkd "Sterling," opens to gold washed cigarette case, figured snakewood shaft, 1-1/2" burnished brass ferrule, American, c1895, 36" l **$1,120**

Snuff, Austro-Hungarian, 7" h x 1-1/2" d oval vermeil silver handle, engraved C-scrolls, raised spiral chain encrusted with rubies, emeralds, sapphires, garnets, pearls, and shell in raised mounts, shallow gold lined box with curved bottom for snuff under hinged top, ebony shaft, 1-3/4" white metal and iron ferrule, two stones missing, 40-1/2" l **$2,000**

Staghorn, English, 2" h x 4" l polished staghorn handle carved as African elephant, amber glass eyes, 1" gold collar initialed "C.J.W.," dated 1906, hallmarked 12K gold, mkd "Brigg," honey toned bamboo shaft, 3/4" burnished brass ferrule, 1906, 36" l **$840**

Sunday stick, English, tortoiseshell, 1-1/2" h x 3" l handle fashioned like golf driver, faux gold weight on side, inscribed "Good Luck," London hallmarks for 18k and 1905, mkd "Brigg," 7/8" gold collar, inscribed "Sir Louis Nuthsen," stepped partridgewood shelf, 1" burnished bras ferrule, storage bag, 1905, 37-1/4" l **$1,800**

Sword, English, 2-1/2" h x 1-1/4" gold knob handle, ducal stallion engraved on top, engraved with scrolls and flowers, two swimming swans, orig owner's name "E. Barnard" engraved on lower edge, thick Malacca shaft with gold mounts and swing clevis 2-1/2" d down 30" l triangular sword, tight tongue, groove metal fitting, twin blood grooves, minor age pitting, 5-7/8" brass ferrule, c1760, 44-1/4" l **$3,810**

Violin, America, 2-3/4" h x 6-1/2" l mahogany tau handle, 1-1/3" lined nickel collar where handle unscrews, fitted chamber with fitted mahogany horsehair bow, dark horn and ivory

dec, 21" l panel opens for removal, internal ebony seats, maple sounding board, ebony bridge, four tuning pins, separate old clock key for tuning, two other nickel bands secure panel on mahogany shaft for storage, 7/8" nickel and iron ferrule, recently professionally restored, c1860, 34" l **$11,200**

Wood

American, 3-1/2" l x 2-1/2" w carved half crook handle, single pc of ash, carved face of John Brown, revarnished, 2" l iron ferrule, c1860, 36" l **$1,120**

America, 5-1/2" l x 3" d "L" handle, high relief carving of rifle and game shoulder bag with roping, shield with roping at bottom of handle, 2/3" coin silver collar inscribed "F.K. Murray, Captain US Navy, 1868," knobby hickory shaft, 1" brass and iron ferrule, 1868, 34-1/2" l **$360**

Anglo-Indian, carved rosewood, 4-1/4" h x 1-1/3" w stylized bird handle, ivory and ebony eyes, ivory tail, two 1/2" ivory separators and one horn separator, 2-3/4" of reticulated silver at top of rosewood shaft, three more separators, thin ivory ferrule, first half 20th C, 37-1/4" l.................................... **$400**

Bermuda, carved Boer War P.O.W., Bermuda cedar, 2" h x 4-1/4" l "L" handle as horse leg and hoof, bone horseshoe, 1-3/4" tin collar hand cut with six holes for dec, carved raised letters on thin textured ribbon around shaft "C.M.S., P.O.W. Bermuda, 1902," 1-1/4" ferrule made from same soft material as collar with similar dec, 1902, 33-2/3" l.................................... **$840**

English, 2-2/3" h x 2" d dark wood handle carved as detailed monkey wearing collar and tie, when ivory button at back of head engaged, glass eyes roll and change color from blue to yellow, long red tongue shoots out, thin horn collar, dark rosewood shaft, 1" white metal and iron ferrule, c1890, 37-1/3" l **$1,900**

English, made from single piece of hardwood, perhaps birch, 4-3/4" l pistol grip handle carved as brown and white fox, stained dark brown shaft stepped to simulate bamboo, 1" white metal and iron ferrule, c1900, 39-1/2" l...................... **$1,010**

CASTOR SETS

History: A castor set consists of matched condiment bottles held within a frame or holder. The bottles are for condiments such as salt, pepper, oil, vinegar, and mustard. The most commonly found castor sets consist of three, four, or five glass bottles in a silver-plated frame.

Although castor sets were made as early as the 1700s, most of the sets encountered today date from 1870 to 1915, the period when they enjoyed their greatest popularity.

2-bottle, Reed and Barton, Egyptian-style frame, two cranberry glass cruets and matching open salt elevated in center, 18" h $600

3-bottle, Bohemian, three shouldered 14" h decanters, flashed blue, green, and cranberry, cut with circles, etched Greek key band, silver-plated stand with tall central handle above three cylindrical wells, with geometric engine turning, borders with fruiting grapevine, three grapevine feet, late 19th C, 10-1/4" w, 20-1/2" h $865

3-bottle, clear, Daisy-and-Button pattern, toothpick holder center, matching glass holder $125

4-bottle, clear, mold blown, pewter lids and frame, domed based, loop handle, marked "I. Trask," early 19th C, 8" h $320

4-bottle, cranberry bottles and jars, clear pressed-glass frame, silver-plated look handle, two brass caps, one pewter, 9-1/2" h $275

4-bottle, ruby stained, Ruby-Thumbprint pattern, glass frame $360

5-bottle, clear, New England Pineapple, two cruets with orig numbered cut and pressed panel hollow stoppers, two shakers with cut panel necks, period lids, mustard pot with period hinged lid, unmarked Brittania frame, 14-1/4" h, 7" d frame $330

6-bottle, cut, diamond-point panels, rotating sterling-silver frame, all-over flowers, paw feet, loop handle, Gorham Mfg. Co., c1880, 11-1/2" h $2,500

6-bottle, etched designs, revolving silvered metal stand, Victorian $175

Seven-bottle, George III, c1800, Anglo-Irish cut glass shakers, ewers, etc. with silver mounts, fitted oval tray with four feet, 11" h, 8-1/2" l, $1,675.
Photo courtesy of Pook & Pook, Inc.

CATALOGS

History: The first American mail-order catalog was issued by Benjamin Franklin in 1744. This popular advertising tool helped to spread inventions, innovations, fashions, and necessities of life to rural America. Catalogs were profusely illustrated and are studied today to date an object, identify its manufacturer, study its distribution, and determine its historical importance.

Additional Resources:

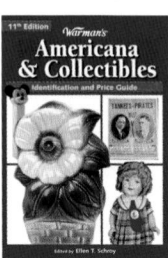

Warman's® Americana & Collectibles, 11th Ed., by Ellen T. Schroy, ed., Krause Publications, Iola, WI.

A. B. See Electric Elev., New York, New York, 24 pgs, stiff wraps, 1908, 8-3/4" x 10" $24

A. Cutler & Son, Buffalo, New York, 86 pgs, Catalog No. 12, early 1900s, 6" x 8" $75

Baraca & Philathea Supply Co., Syracuse, New York, 32 pgs, 1923, 3-1/2" x 6" $21

Bullock & Crenshaw, Philadelphia, Pennsylvania, 60 pgs, 1857, 5-3/4" x 9" $325

Burstein-Applebee Co., Kansas City, Missouri, 114 pgs, wraps, 1948, 8" x 10-1/2" $40

Century Furniture Co., Grand Rapids, Michigan, 145 pgs, hard cover, 1927, 5-1/2" x 8-1/4" $24

Champion Corp, Hammond, Indiana, 39 pgs, vertical fold in center, c1929, 7" x 9-1/2" $35

Crane Co., Chicago, Illinois, 28 pgs, 1927, 3-1/2" x 6-1/4" $15

Crofts & Reed Co., Chicago, Illinois, 148 pgs, Spring & Summer catalog, 1916, 7-3/4" x 10-1/2" $37

Detroit Dental Mfg Co., Detroit, Michigan, 11 pgs, Gilmore Adjustable Attachments, c1924, 5-14" x 8-1/4" $15

Distinctive Weathervane, York, Pennsylvania, 15 pgs, 1930s, 6" x 9-1/4" $80

Eli Lilly & Co, Indianapolis, Indiana, 295 pgs, hard cover, Handbook of Pharmacy & Therapeutics, illus, 1925, 7" x 9-1/4" $48

Erie Engine Works, Erie, Pennsylvania, 48 pgs, 1901, 7-1/2" x 9-3/4" $190

Ernst Heinrich Roth, US, 40 pgs, photos of violins, 1924, 6-1/2" x 9-1/2" $50

Fairbanks, Morse & Co., Chicago, Illinois, 24 pgs, pictorial wraps, 1926, 8-1/2" x 11" $20

Flaig Bros, Pittsburgh, Pennsylvania, 24 pgs, c1930, 6-1/2" x 9" $22

Fuller Brush Co., Hartford, Connecticut, 12 pgs, full color, c1975, 8-1/4" x 11" $10

Geo. Delawrence, Berlin, Wisconsin, 25 pgs, c1929, 4-3/4" x 7" $12

George C. Frys Co., Portland, Maine, 78 pgs, Cat. No. 162, c1928, 8" x 10" $48

Horace Partridge Co., Boston, Massachusetts, 92 pgs, Catalog No. 139, 1932, 6-1/2" x 9-1/2" $85

Howard Tresses, New York, New York, 30 pgs, c1935, 5-3/4" x 9" $16

James B. Clow & Sons, Chicago, Illinois, 52 pgs, c1911, 9-1/4" x 12" $45

James Manufacturing Co., Ft. Atkinson, Wisconsin, 255 pgs, hard cover, 1914, 6-3/4" x 9-3/4" $55

King & Eisele Co., Buffalo, New York, 12 pgs, two pgs illus, order form laid-in, c1928, 9-1/2" x 12-1/4" **$55**

Krafft & Phillips Fashion, Philadelphia, Pennsylvania, 20 pgs, color, 1935, 10-3/4" x 15" **$45**

Liquid Carbonic Co., Chicago, Illinois, 72 pgs, 1914, 6" x 9" **$85**

Louden Machinery Co., Fairfield, Iowa, 50 pgs, illus, 1912, 7-3/4" x 10-3/4" **$42**

Luger Industries Inc., Burnsville, Minnesota, 80 pgs, in mail-out envelope, 1971, 8-1/4" x 11" **$30**

Lyons Band Instrument Co., Chicago, Ilionis, 256 pgs, spiral bound, 1956, 9" x 11" **$40**

Marshall Field & Co., Chicago, Illinois, eight pgs, pocket folder of floor coverings, 1932, 6-1/4" x 8-1/4" **$20**

Norlin Music Inc., Lincolnwood, Illinois, 12 pgs, c1975, 7-1/2" x 11" **$15**

Northfolk Paint & Varnish, Norfolk Downs, Massachusetts, 26 pgs, 1930, 8-1/2" x 11" **$10**

Oakwood Manufacturing Co., Springfield, Ohio, 32 pgs, c1910, 8" x 7-1/2" **$18**

Ohio State Stove & Mfg Co., Columbus, Ohio, 12 pgs, six illus, pages laid-in, c1925, 7-3/4" x 10-1/2" **$26**

Old Town Canoe Co., Old Town, Maine, 48 pgs, 1956, 6" x 8" **$75**

Oskamp, Nolting & Co., Cincinnati, Ohio, 40 pgs, wraps, 8-3/4" x 11-3/4" **$65**

Pan-American Band Instruments, Elkhart, Indiana, 1930s, 3-1/4" x 6-1/4" **$30**

Pass & Seymour Inc., Syracuse, New York, 137 pgs, Catalog No. 25, 1919, 7-1/2" x 10-3/4" **$26**

Richmond Stove Co., Richmond, Virginia, 96 pgs, c1920, 3-1/2" x 6" **$40**

Rock Island Stove Co., Rock Island, Illinois, 63 pgs, Catalog No. 38, 1929, 7-3/4" x 10-1/2" **$32**

Sayre & Fisher Co., New York, New York, c1895, 122 pgs, hard cover, 6-3/4" x 10-1/2" **$32**

Sealed Power Corp, Muskegon, Michigan, 1943, 32 pgs, 8" x 10-1/2" **$14**

Sears, Roebuck & Co., Chicago, Illinois, 34 pgs, automobiles, 1911, 7" x 9-1/2" **$100**

Sears, Roebuck & Co., Chicago, Illinois, 19 pgs, rugs and carpets, 1936, 8-3/4" x 12-3/4" **$20**

Shakespeare Co., Kalamazoo, Michigan, 32 pgs, Angler's Catalog, 1959, 7" x 10" **$24**

Stewart & McGuire, New York, New York, eight pgs, silver gilt highlights, 8-1/4" x 11" **$45**

Stover Mfg & Engine Co., Freeport, Illinois, 24 pgs, folded vertical as issued, c1939, 8" x 9" **$35**

Targ & Dinner, Chicago, Illinois, 472 pgs, bound volume of catalogs, 1967, 9" x 12" **$55**

The Cloak-Drummer Co., Chicago, Illinois, 86 pgs, fall and winter, 1912, 7" x 9-1/2" **$30**

United States Rubber Co., New Orleans, Louisiana, 12 pgs, 1940, 9" x 12" **$32**

Victor Safe & Lock Co., Cincinnati, Ohio, 200 pgs, wear at binding, 1910, 6-1/2" x 9-3/4" **$110**

Weber Lifelike Fly Co., Stevens Point Wisconsin, 96 pgs, No. 19, 1938, 6-1/4" x 9" **$60**

Westinghouse Machine Co., Pittsburgh, Pennsylvania, three pgs, c1895, 6" x 9" **$140**

Whitemore Associates Inc., Boston, Massachusetts, 160 pgs, 1950, 6" x 9" **$30**

Wright & Ditson, Boston, Massachusetts, 112 pgs, Spring & Summer Sports Equipment, 1928, 5-1/2" x 8" **$100**

Wright Co., Inc., Atlanta, Georgia, 212 pgs, kitchen equipment, 1928, 8-1/2" x 11-1/4" **$125**

Yale & Towne Mfg Co., Stamford, Connecticut, 450 pgs, hard cover, Catalog No. 25, 1921, 7-3/4" x 10-3/4" **$110**

CELLULOID ITEMS

History: In 1869, an Albany, New York, printer named John W. Hyatt developed and patented the world's first commercially successful semi-synthetic thermoplastic. The moldable material was made from a combination of camphor, the crystalline resin from the heart of a particular evergreen tree, and collodion, a type of nitrated-cellulose substance (also called Pyroxylin), which was extremely flammable. Hyatt and his brother, Isaiah, called their invention Celluloid, a name they made up by combining the words cellulose and colloid.

By 1873, the Hyatts were successfully producing raw pyroxylin plastic material at the Celluloid Manufacturing Company of Newark, NJ. In the early days of its commercial development, Celluloid was produced exclusively in two colors: flesh tone, for the manufacture of denture-base material, and off white, which was primarily used for utilitarian applications like harness trimmings and knife handles.

However, during the late 1870s, advances in plastics technology brought about a shift in the ways Celluloid could be used. Beautiful imitations of amber, ivory, tortoise shell, jet, and coral were being produced and used in the fabrication of jewelry, fashion accessories, and hair ornaments. Because the faux-luxury materials were so realistic and affordable, Celluloid quickly advanced to the forefront of working and middle class consumerism.

Throughout the 1880s and 1890s, the Celluloid Manufacturing Company experienced stiff competition from a number of newly organized companies that began to aggressively produce their brands of pyroxylin plastic into a variety of products. By the early 20th century, there were four major American manufacturers firmly established as producers of quality pyroxylin plastics. In addition to the Celluloid Company of Newark, New Jersey, there was the Arlington Manufacturing Company of Arlington, New Jersey, which produced Pyralin; Fiberloid Corporation of Indian Orchard, Massachusetts, makers of Fiberloid; and the Viscoloid Company of Leominster, Massachusetts. Even though these companies branded their plastic products with registered trade names, today the word "celluloid" is used in a general sense for all forms of this type of early plastic.

Celluloid was imported into France during the mid 1870s for use in the fabrication of ornamental hair combs and it's success was quickly recognized throughout Europe. By the 1880s it was being manufactured in factories throughout France and Germany. It was the German doll industry that made initial strides in utilizing the material for toys during the late 1890s. The first manufacturing plant for celluloid in Japan was built in 1908 and by the 1920s that country was the world's most prolific manufacturer and fabricator of pyroxylin plastic—due in most part to the island of Formosa's vast natural resources of camphor forests - an essential ingredient in the celluloid recipe.

Cellluloid-type plastics were popular alternatives for costly and elusive natural substances. Within the fashion industry alone, it gained acceptance as a beautiful and affordable substitute for increasingly dwindling supplies of ivory and tortoise shell. However, it should be noted that celluloid's most successful application during the late 19th century was realized in the clothing industry as an imitation of fine-grade linen that was fashioned into stylish waterproof cuffs and collars.

In sheet form, celluloid found many successful applications. Printed political and advertising premiums, pinback buttons, pocket mirrors, and keepsake items from 1890-1920 were turned out by the thousands. In addition, transparent-sheet celluloid was ornately decorated by embossing, reverse painting, and lamination, and then used in the production of decorative boxes, booklets, and albums. The toy industry also capitalized on the used of thin-celluloid sheet for the production of blow-molded dolls, animal toys, and figural novelties.

The development of the motion-picture industry helped celluloid fulfill a unique identity all its own; it was used for reels of camera film, as well as in sheet form by animation artists who drew cartoons. Known as

Post Card, embossed celluloid with horseshoe decorative motif and flocked green shamrock and holly leaves, purple flocking surrounds cream-colored horseshoe, c1910, 5" x 3", **$35.**

animation cels, these are still readily available to the collector for a costly sum, but because of the degredation of old celluloid, many early movies and cels have been lost forever.

By 1930, and the advent of the modern-plastics age, the use of celluloid began to decline dramatically. The introduction of cellulose-acetate plastic replaced the flammable pyroxylin plastic in jewelry and toys, and the development of non-flammable safety film eventually put an end to its use in movies. By 1947, the major manufacturers of celluloid in the United States had ceased production; however, many foreign companies in Germany, France, Denmark, Italy and Japan continued manufacture and produce dolls and toys throughout the post World War II period. Today Japan, Italy and Korea continue to manufacture cellulose-nitrate plastics in small amounts for specialty items such as musical-instrument inlay, knife handles, ping-pong balls, and designer fountain pens.

Beware of celluloid items that show signs of deterioration: oily residue, cracking, discoloration, and crystallization. Take care when cleaning celluloid items; it is best to use mild soap and water, avoiding alcohol- or acetone-based cleansers. Keep celluloid from excessive heat or flame and avoid direct sunlight.

Marks: Viscoloid Co. of Leominster, Massachusetts manufactured a large variety of small hollow animals be-

tween 1914-1930, that ranged in size from two to eight inches. Most of these toys are embossed with one of three trademarks: "Made in USA," an intertwined "VCO," or an eagle with a shield. German and Japanese manufacturers of collectible figural toys numbered in the hundreds. All toys imported into the United States were either embossed with a trademark, and or stamped with country of origin, or carried an export inspection sticker. Many American and German toy designs were copied by the Japanese, particularily the Ando Togoro company, whose trademark resembles a crossed circle.

Adviser: Julie P. Robards.

Advertising and souvenir-keepsake items

Badge, 2-7/8" l shield shaped, on a lanyard, printed with two intertwined American flags, Chaplain Ladies Auxiliary, FOE, thick multiple layered celluloid, fraternal organization for Fraternal Order of Elks, made by Whitehead & Hoag Co., early 1900s, 5-3/4" l, 1-1/4" w............................**$20**

Bookmark, embossed with roses and embroidered, "Greetings" on the long flat surface, pink tassel, c1920 ....**$25**

Card, delicate lacy embossed celluloid printed with floral motif in yellow and pink and the words "Fond Greetings," c1910, 3" x 2" **$30**

Clothing brush, celluloid-laminated photograph showing Pennsylvania State Memorial, Gettysburg, Pennsylvania. Sepia, black and cream. c1920, 3-1/2" d **$75**

Compact, imitation ivory-grained celluloid with gold Elk motif and "Third Annual Ball, BPOE, Leominster Lodge No. 1237, Jan. 26, 1917," produced by the Viscoloid Co. of Leominster, MA, c1917, 1-3/4" d **$65**

Fan, when closed, cream colored celluloid Brise fan, peach colored ribbon, shows the Washington Monument and "Washington D.C." in goldtone paint. Celluloid loop, c1920, 4" h **$40**

Ink blotter, Christmas theme advertising premium. printed celluloid cover with religious imagery of Shepherds and Sheep with Star of Bethlehem. "To our faithful old friends and cherished new friensd we render this greeting. E. Keller & Sons," c1915, 7-3/4" x 3" **$65**

Match safe, souvenir metal safety-match holder, celluloid on cover showing colorized photo of Atlantic City, New Jersey boardwalk, c1920, 2-1/2" x 1" **$45**

Pinback button, printed cream colored celluloid with crossed American and Irish flags with shamrock and lyre motif in the center. "Erin Go Bragh," c1920, 3/4" d **$30**

Pin holder, celluloid disc, metal framework, "F Krupps Steel Works, Thomas Prosser & Son, NY," front shows advertising, back shows small child, engraved ivory-grained celluloid, c1890, 1-3/4" d **$40**

Pocket mirror, topsy-turvy image of a smiling man, "This man trades at Hager's Store, Frostburg, MD," turned upside down, the man is frowning and caption reads, "This man does not. For a satisfied customer see other side," c1900, 1-3/4" d **$110**

Postcard, emb-fan motif with applied fabric and metal-script words, "Many Happy Returns," applied over fabric, c1908, 5-1/2" x 3-1/2" **$35**

Tape measure, pull-out tape, colorful pretty girl with flowers, adv for "The First National Bank of Boswell, The Same Old Bank in its New Home," printed by P.N. Co. (Parisian Novelty

Co. of Chicago), Patent 7-10-17, emb in the side, c1920, 1-1/4" d **$65**

Animals, Toy

Among the most prolific manufacturer of American made celluloid toys was the Viscoloid Co. of Leominster, Massachusetts. This company manufactured a variety of small hollow toy animals, birds, and marine creatures, most of which are embossed with one of these three trade marks: "Made In USA," an intertwined "VCO," or an eagle with shield. A host of foreign countries also mass-produced celluloid toys for export into the United States. Among the most prolific manufacturers were Ando Togoro of Japan, whose toys bear the crossed-circle trademark, and Sekiguchi Co., which used a three-petal flower motif as its logo. Paul Haneaus of Germany used an intertwined PH trademark, and Petticolin of France branded its toys with an eagle head. Japanese- and American-made toys are plentiful, while those manufactured in Germany, England, and France, are more difficult to find.

Alligator, green, white-tail tip, VCO/USA, c1925, 3" **$18**

Animal set, Japanese, six circus animals, garish bright colors, marked "Made In Occupied Japan," elephant, gorilla, giraffe, tiger, lion, and hippo, set, c1945 .... **$85**

Bear, American, cream bear, pink and gray highlights, VCO/USA, c1920, 5" w **$20**

Bison, dark brown, eagle-and-shield trademark, c1920, 3-1/4" l **$18**

Boar, brown, Paul Haneaus of Germany/PH trademark, c1920, 3-1/4" l **$75**

Camel, peach celluloid, pink and black highlights, marked with crossed circle and "Made in Japan," c1930, 3-1/2" x 2-1/2" **$20**

Cat, Japanese, peach, flower trademark, c1935, 3-1/2" l **$30**

Chick, yellow, black eyes and beak, no trademark, c1925, 7/8" **$8**

Chicken, Japanese, metal feet, club trademark w/N, c1935, 1-1/2" **$30**

Cow

Cream-and-orange cow, intertwined VCO/USA, c1925, 4-1/2" **$25**

Nodder, French, realistic design w/ lozenge trademark w/SNF, c1930, rare **$175**

Dog

English Bulldog, spiked neck collar, translucent-green color, rhinestone eyes, intertwined VCO/USA, c1920, 4-3/4" l, 2-1/2" h **$35**

Hound, Japanese. Long tail, peach celluloid, gray highlights, crossed-circle Japan trademark, c1930, 5" **$25**

Scottie, plaster-filled cream-colored celluloid, no detailing, marked JAPAN, c1945, 3-1/4" l **$25**

Donkey, peach celluloid, nodder head, made in Occupied Japan, c1945, 4" l **$55**

Duck, standing, cream-colored celluloid, hand-painted eyes and bill, original paper label, Japan, c1935, 2-1/4" **$20**

Elephant

American Viscoloid gray elephant, tusks, USA, c1920, 6-3/4" x 4-3/4" **$45**

Nodder, trunk down, wide open ears, white, gray highlights, Bird trademark Japan, c1945, 3-3/4" **$45**

Fish

Bright red, USA, c1925, 2-1/4" l **$8**

Yellow with brown highlights, molded scales, intertwined VCO, circle, c1925, 2-7/8" l **$12**

Frog, green or yellow, stripe on back, intertwined VCO/USA, c1920, 1-1/4" **$25**

Giraffe, cream, painted yellow and brown spots, eagle trademark, French, c1940, 7" tall **$85**

Goat, white, curled horns, flower, "N" in circle represents Navy Goat, Japan, c1935, 3" **$35**

Hippopotamus, Japanese, pink, closed mouth, MIOJ, c1945, 3-3/4" **$18**

Horse

Bending to eat grass on base, Occupied Japan, c1945, 5" l **$30**

Cream, purple and pink highlights, USA, 7" l **$18**

Leopard, white, orange highlights, black spots, Occupied Japan, c1945, 4-1/2"...$30

Lion

Japanese, tan, brown highlights, marked TS & Made in Japan, c1930, 3-3/4".....................................$20

Japanese nodder, pink highlights on white celluloid, fierce open mouth, full mane, Japan, c1945, 5-1/4" l
....$65

Lobster, American Viscoloid,bright red, detailed shell, c1925, 1-3/4"
....$65

Penguin, Japanese, Diahachi Kobyashi trademark, nodder, black with red bill and feet, blue eyes, Japan, 4-1/2"
....$65

Pig, pull toy, pink pig on rectangular platform, four celluloid wheels, USA, 4-1/2" animal on 6" base...............$65

Polar Bear, white, USA, c1925, 2-1/4" l...$15

Ram, cream, gray highlights, USA, c1925, 4-1/2"...................................$20

Rhino, German, gray, fine detail, PH trademark, Paul Haneaus, c1920, 5" l
....$65

Seal, gray, balancing red ball, VCO/USA, c1925, 4-1/2" l.....................$70

Squirrel, rare, brown, holding nut, USA, c1925, 2-7/8" h...................$65

Stork, Japanese, standing, white, pink legs, flower mark, Japan, c1950, 6-3/4".....................................$25

Swan, Japanese, multicolored purple, pink, yellow, crossed circle trademark, c1935, 3-3/8".......................$20

Tiger, "P" painted on side for Princeton Mascot; Japanese, c1940, 6 1/2" l
....$35

Turtle, brown top, yellow bottom, USA on foot, c1925, 1-3/8"...................$18

Decorative albums and boxes

Collar box, covered in celluloid coated paper in a green, yellow and brown leaf pattern, embossed edging, c1890, 6" h, 5" w...$85

Hankie box, embossed image of a neoclassical woman petting a small dog, pale green with white embossed fan spray in each corner and garland along sides, c1890, 7" sq, 3" h
....$120

Autograph album, famous print "Giving Thanks" celluloid-coated paper, shows a couple in a field with heads bowed. Autographs inside dated between 1900 and 1906, 6" x 4" **$85.**

Photograph album, Longfellow type, beautiful woman with flowing dress holding flowers across her shoulders, embossed iris motif along bound side. Backed with maroon velour, c1900, 16" x 7"....................................$525

New Testament Booklet, cream colored heavily embossed top with oval celluloid picture of Jesus the Great Shepherd, c1910, 5-1/4" x 4"
....$45

Dolls, rattles and figural toys

English toys, made by Cascelloid marked "Palitoy." The most prolific manufacturer of German dolls was the firm Schildkrott, whose logo was a turtle or a turtle in a diamond.

Baby rattle

Hollow molded pink handle with three heads bobbing on springs at the top, colorful with red and green painted hats, Japan, c1950, 6-1/4" tall...................................$75

At left, teddy bear, Japanese, moveable arms and legs, bright pink, made in Occupied Japan, c1945, 4-1/4", **$30;** *at right, bright red teddy bear, made in Occupied Japan, 6" h,* **$35.**

St. Bernard, tan, black highlights, intertwined VCO/USA, c1925, 3-1/4", **$18.**

Necktie box, brown velour with embossed cream-colored celluloid floral spray attached to top, c1890, 12-1/2" x 4", **$65.**

Whistle, rooster with horn beak, cream celluloid with brown highlights on a green grass base, VCO/USA, 3-1/4" l, 2-1/4" h, **$65.**

England, Cascelloid Company / Palitoy, Round pink sphere on a cream colored handle, very plain, marked Made in England, Palitoy, 6-1/2" t, c1945 .... **$35**

Irwin, small square yellow celluloid block w/ embossed chick, painted white, small thin handle. attached yellow ribbon, c1930 .... **$35**

Irwin, cylinder type chime rattle on a cream colored ring, with printed red and white celluloid coated paper showing toddlers dancing under the word JITTERBUGS, rare, c1935, 5" **$65**

Dolls

American

Marks Brothers, boy doll, molded hair, blue eyes, shoulder plate marked Marks Bros. Co., Boston, Mass, USA, celluloid arms and hands, cloth body and legs, rare, c1920, 18" **$200**

Parsons Jackson, Baby doll with jointed arms and legs, realistic detailing, bald headed, open mouth, trademark of stork on back w/ Parsons Jackson Co. Cleveland, Ohio, USA, c1914 .... **$200**

Louis Sametz, Dutch girl, thin cream colored hollow celluloid, side glancing eyes, hands in pocket of long dress, ring attached to top, rattles, trademarked w/Indian profile on back, c1920 .... **$35**

Viscoloid, figural girl with short dress, hat and side glancing eyes, very well molded hair, socks and shoes, rattles, image of child star Baby Peggy, trademarked w/intertwined VCO/USA, c1925 .... **$45**

Viscoloid, jointed girl doll, naked with well molded shoes and socks, bobbed hair with bow. Marked USA, c1925, 7" tall **$55**

Denmark

Jeris Kofoed, Girl doll with short curly molded hair, naked except for shoes and socks, jointed arms and legs, hair painted blond pearlescent, pink cheeks. Trademarked with scalloped shell trademark, c1940, 4-1/2" tall **$55**

France

Petitcollin Co., Boy doll with jointed arms and legs, dressed as a shepherd. Trademarked with profile of

eagle head, c1930, 8" **$55**

Society Nobel Francaise, realistic toddler doll with brown real hair wig, glass eyes that shift back and forth, flirty smile, fully jointed with socket head, trademarked SNF in lozenge, c1935, 18" tall, rare **$300**

Germany

Buschow & Beck, shoulder plate doll wtih real wig and blue glass eyes, beautifully molded facial features, slightly parted lips, helmet insignia on front of shoulder plate, kid body, composition arms and legs, c1910, 14" tall **$150**

Cellba, chubby girl with curly hair, pink cheeks and pursed lips, jointed arms, fixed legs, dressed in regional costume, trademark with crowned mermaid in shield, c1936, 4-1/2" tall **$45**

Schildkrott fashion doll, young girl with shoulderplate head, real hair wig, glass eyes, fully jointed arms and legs, dressed in blue satin and lace dress, original white leather shoes with fancy buckles, trademarked with turtle. c1920, 14" tall **$250**

Japan

Karl Standfuss Co. Kewpie with top-knot, blue wings, fixed body with moving jointed arms, naked, Grace O'Neill copyright, trademarked JUNO in oval, c1920, 4" rare **$125**

Kewpie knock-off, top knot-no wings, naked with side glancing eyes, jointed legs and arms. Trademark Japan w/ top logo, c1925, 4" **$45**

Royal Company, boy doll "Baby John", fully jointed arms and legs, curley hair, naked with well detailed facial features, toes, fingers, trademarked with Royal & Fleur-de-lies, c1935, 8" **$55**

Sekiguchi Company, Carnival Doll, naked with molded marcel wave hair painted silver, naked with applied colorful feathers around mid section. Jointed arms, holding a cane and wearing a top hat, three lobed flower trademark w/Japan, c1950, 6" **$50**

Roly Poly, Easter related, duckling, peach hat trimmed in flowers, jacket,

necktie, green trim, cream celluloid, VCO trademark, 2-1/2" **$155**

Toy Boat, German ocean liner, gray and red, flag, intertwined PH, 4-1/2" **$50**

Fashion accessories

Bar pin, rect shape, translucent amber bar pin with applied center blue flower. c-clasp, c1920, 2-1/2" l **$30**

Belt, 3/4" x 1-1/2" rect mottled green celluloid slabs linked by chain, applied silver-tone filigree dec, 22" l **$35**

Bracelet, bangle all c1925

Ivory colored, embedded with three rows of aqua blue and clear rhinestones **$75**

Molded imitation coral, imitation ivory, or imitation jade, all-over floral dec, blue-ink stamp "Made in Japan," 3" d.. **$50**

Bracelet, link, 3" d, four oblong two-tone cream and ivory links, attached by smaller round cream links **$65**

Brooch

Photographic image, Gibson girl, twisted gold-tint metal frame, c1900, 2-1/4" oval **$50**

Rect pearlized cream celluloid, black stencil silhouette of man and woman conversing over picket fence, 1-3/4" x 3/4" **$35**

Girl, molded red dress and bandana, 2-1/4" **$30**

Comb and case, c1925

Cream-colored celluloid comb, 3-1/4" x 1" pearlized amber and gray rhinestone-studded case, 3" l **$25**

Folding molded case, emb rose motif, imitation ivory with brown highlights, 2-1/4" l **$30**

Cuff link, toggle back, realistic molded celluloid lion heads, c1896 .... **$125**

Cuff links, pr. c1920

Separable "Kum-a-part" Baer & Wilde Co., 1/4" sq shape divided by purple and black triangular shapes of celluloid, center diamond shape, Art Deco, mid-1920s, orig card **$65**

Dress clips, pr, molded floral motif, semi-translucent cream celluloid, marked "Japan" **$35**

Eyeglasses, Harold Lloyd type, black frames..............$20

Hair ornament, ornamental, imitation ivory filigree hair ornament with single twisted pick for anchoring in upswept hair do, c1900, 6"..............$65

Hair ornament, ornamental, imitation tortoiseshell, double prong, oblong shaped filigree hair ornament for securing upswept hair do, c1900, 6"..............$65

Hair comb, ornamental, imitation tortoiseshell, 24 teeth, applied-metal trim studded with rhinestones and brad fastened Egyptian Revival pink and gold metal floral and beetle dec., 1890, 4" x 5-1/4"..............$145

Hair comb, ornamental, amber celluloid with swirled pearlescent gray overlay, filigree back comb with close set multiple teeth, c1925, 4" w..............$65

Hair comb, ornamental, three prong ornate filigree comb of amber celluloid overlayed with swirled blue green pearlesence and inset with blue rhinestones, c1925, 5-1/2"..............$125

Hat pin, c1910

Elephant head, tusks, black glass eyes, imitation ivory, 4" head on 6" shank..............$100

Filigree-hollow egg, pale-green paint applied over grained celluloid, 10" l..............$85

Hat ornament, c1930

Art Deco, pearlized red and cream half circles, rhinestone trim, 3-1/2" h..............$65

Calla lily, cream-pearlized celluloid, white rhinestones, 1-1/2" l threaded pin with screw-on celluloid point, 4-1/2" h..............$35

Necklace, elegant Art Nouveau filigree pendant, cream celluloid, oval cameo, profile of a beautiful woman, suspended from 20" cream celluloid-beaded necklace, c1910, 2" pendant..............$110

Pendant, c1925

Black, crystal rhinestones, 1-1/2" l..............$35

Cream Celluloid cut out silhouette of dancing couple, 2" l..............$45

Green, rect blue stones, 1-3/4" l...$35

Purse frame

Black pointed horseshoe shape, rhinestones, white molded cameo clasp, 4" l..............$95

Imitation tortoiseshell, crescent shape, molded filigree and center cameo, celluloid push-button latch and linked chain, 6" l..............$110

Purse, basketweave, link celluloid chain, mottled grain ivory and green, 4-1/2" x 4-1/2"..............$200

Stick Pin, lozenge shaped metal frame with black sheet celluloid set w/faux amethyst, 1910, 3-1/2" tall..............$35

Holiday items

Angels, set of three, one holding cross, star, or lantern, Japan, Mt. Fuji trademark, 1-1/2" h..............$35

Christmas decoration, roly poly-type house, opening in back for a small bulb, shows Santa approaching door, red and white, intertwined VCO/USA trademark..............$125

Christmas ornament

Little boy on swing, all celluloid, dark green highlights, holding onto string "ropes" for hanging on tree, 3-3/4"..............$95

Santa, Horn and sack, hole in back for light bulb, trademarked "S" in circle, Japan, 3-3/4"..............$65

Striped green and white Christmas stocking filled with gifts including duck and kitten, crossed-circle trademark, Ando Togoro, 4" l..............$125

Figure

Duck, standing, wearing tails and top hat, red and green paints, 4-3/4" h..............$75

Easter Rabbit, dressed in tails and top hat, holding chicken under arm, cream, pink, and blue highlights, VCO, 7-3/4" h..............$125

Uncle Sam, stars on hat, USA, 8-7/8"..............$150

Halloween favor, orange horn, black witch and trim, intertwined VCO/USA, 4" l..............$150

Rattle, standing black cat, orange bow, intertwined VCO/USA, 3-3/4" l..............$185

Reindeer, white deer, gold glitter, red eyes and mouth, molded ears and antlers, USA, 3-1/2"..............$20

Alligator letter opener w/open mouth bearing teeth, brown and red highlights on cream celluloid, tail molded into blade, Made in Germany, 7-1/4" l, **$75.**

Societe Industrielle de Celluloid, fully jointed baby doll, dressed in vibrant fancy regional costume from Britany region, costume adds height to the doll. Trademarked with SIC in lozenge shape, c1920, 6", **$65.**

Irwin, oval embossed celluloid rattle with Little Red Riding Hood motif, cream on one side painted with red and brown, pink embossed celluloid on reverse, unmarked, c1925, 6-1/2" l, **$55.**

Roly poly, black cat on orange pumpkin, intertwined VCO/USA, 3-1/2" **$235**

Santa

Basket of flowers, fur-trimmed suit, nice detail, VCO/USA trademark, 5" h **$75**

Yellow or mint green translucent celluloid, holding lantern and sack, Japanese, Mt. in circle trademark, 4" **$55**

Toy

Easter rabbit in harness, attached to cart full of eggs, "Made in Japan" on cart, "Pat.15735" on rabbit, 2-7/8" l **$95**

Santa driving house-shaped automobile, white, applied red, yellow, and green painted highlights, VCO/USA trademark, 3-3/8" x 2" **$155**

Paddy, riding pig, movable legs, little boy with dunce cap riding on back, Japan, 4-3/4" h **$200**

Novelty items

Letter opener

Bulldog on long pointed hollow blade, Made in Germany, 7-1/4" l **$75**

Ivory grained, magnifying glass in top, coiled-metal snake, red-glass eyes around the handle, 7-3/8" l **$85**

Pin cushion

Figural hen on weighted base, straight pins stick into holes in base, American VCO/USA, 2-1/4" h **$75**

Figural novelty rabbit with pin cushion baskets, marked "Germany" 2" h **$130**

Tape measure

Billiken, cream celluloid, applied-brown highlights, marked "Japan", 2-1/2" h **$185**

Chariot w/centurian and two rearing horses, imitation bronze, unmarked, 1-3/4" h **$225**

Figural Strawberry, cream w/applied red paint, green stem and hull, no trademark **$200**

Novelty type, basket of flowers, bow on handle, marked "Made in Japan" 2" h **150**

Utilitarian and household items

Bookends, pr, mottled-pink celluloid, emb ornamental gold neoclassic

drape, plaster weighted, no trademark, c1930, 4-1/4" h, 3-1/4" w, 2-1/4" d **$45**

Candle holders, pr, cylindrical, round flared-weighted bases, unmarked, 5-1/4" h **$60**

Clock

German Gothic cathedral design, round face, dark yellow ivory grained celluloid, 5-1/2" x 3" **$45**

New Haven Clock Co., alarm, folding travel case, pearlescent pink laminated over amber celluloid, 3" sq **$30**

Crumb tray set, two dustpan-shaped trays, ivory celluloid, dark blue dec border, monogrammed "T" in center of each tray, c1910 .... **$50**

Cutlery, solid imitation ivory grained-handle utensils, eight forks, eight knives in orig box, Standard Mfg. Co., c1920 .... **$30**

Frame

Pearlized-amber celluloid, diecut floral motif, attached over wood frame, celluloid butterflies in each corner, 5-1/2" x 7" **$35**

Round, ivory grained, easel back, 4" d **$25**

Napkin ring

Basketweave strips of celluloid, 1" w **$15**

Imitation ivory, monogramed, 1-1/2" w **$10**

String holder, round sphere on a weighted base, twist apart, center hole in top for string, imitation-ivory grain, no trademark, c1910 .... **$65**

Vase

Imitation ivory, conical, fluted weighted base, flange around top, c1920, 6" h **$25**

Yellow, bulbous bottom, narrow opening, fluted top, painted pink and blue floral motif, no trademark, c1930, 7" h **$30**

Watch holder, pearlescent blue, green, and amber, wall-hanging banjo-clock style, Wilcox trademark, late 1920s, 6-1/2" l **$25**

Vanity items

Dresser boxes, oval-shaped pearlized peach boxes, dec-shaped lids, marked "Amerith," Lotus Pattern, c1929 pr **$35**

Dresser set

Eight-piece, pearlized yellow-laminated amber celluloid, black trim, mirror, brush, shoe horn, button hook, soap box, nail buffer, toothbrush holder, hair-pin holder, marked "Arch Amereth, Windsor," orig box, c1928 .... **$75**

Seventeen-piece, Fairfax pattern, Fiberloid Company, mottled brown and gold, carved floral trim, comb, brush, mirror, powder box, hair receiver, nail file, scissors, button hook, and clothing brush, c1924 .... **$125**

Dresser tray, pearlized cream color and amber framework, Normandy lace inserted between double-glass bottom, c1925 oval, 7-1/2" l, 5" w **$30**

Hair receiver and powder box set

Pearlized-gray containers, octagonal lids, no trademark, c1925, 3-1/2" d **$30**

Ivory-grained set, scalloped lids laminated in Goldaleur, marked "The Celluloid Co.," c1925, 4" d **$45**

Hatpin holder

Center post, round circular disc on top, circular base, cream celluloid, cranberry-colored velvet cushion, 1910 weighted base, 5" h **$90**

Pale-green celluloid, triangular shape, painted flower, c1920, 5" h **$30**

Manicure set, rolled-up leather pouch fitted with six imitation-tortoiseshell celluloid manicure tools, gold trim, pink-velvet lining **$30**

Trinket box, oval, amber, butterfly, grass and milkweed silk under clear-celluloid lid 5" l, 2" h **$35**

Vanity set, amber, teal-green pearlescent laminate surface, dresser tray, octagonal amber hair-receiver box with pearlized lid, nail buffer, scissors, and button hook, hp-rose motif on all pcs, unmarked, c1930 .... **$45**

CHARACTER AND PERSONALITY ITEMS

History: In many cases, toys and other products using the images of fictional comic, movie, and radio characters occur simultaneously with the origin of the character. The first Dick Tracy toy was manufactured within less than a year after the strip first appeared.

The golden age of character material is the TV era of the mid-1950s through the late 1960s; however, some radio-premium collectors might argue this point. Today, television and movie producers often have their product licensing arranged well in advance of the initial release.

Do not overlook characters created by advertising agencies, e.g., Tony the Tiger. They represent a major collecting sub-category.

Additional Resources:

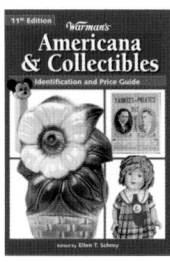

Warman's® Americana & Collectibles, 11th Ed., by Ellen T. Schroy, ed., Krause Publications, Iola, WI.

Character

Andy Gump, pinback button, "Andy Gump For President/I Endorse The Atwater Kent Receiving Set," red, white, blue, and fleshtone, 1-1/4" d **$40**

Betty Boop

Book, Betty Boop Cartoon Lessons, Fleischer Studios, 1935, 12" x 9" **$500**

Marble, Peltier Glass Co., black and white swirl, black transfer of Betty, c1932, 11/16" **$175**

String holder, chalk, head and shoulders, orig paint, 6-1/2" w, 7-1/2" h **$625**

Brownies, Palmer Cox

Book, *The Brownies, Their Book,* Palmer Cox, NY, 1887, first edition, second issue, illus by Cox, 4to, pictorial glazed boards **$230**

Child's fork and spoon, emb Brownies on handles **$18**

Andy, litho tin wind-up, yellow derby, light blue jacket, red and tan striped trousers, Louis Marx & Co., **$320.**
Photo courtesy of Pook & Pook, Inc.

Dolls, stuffed cloth, Uncle Sam, Indian, Highlander, Chinaman, German, Sailor, Soldier, Canadian, Irishman, Policeman, John-Bull, and Dude, each has name stitched on back, colorful-printed outfits, marked "Copyright 1892 by Palmer Cox" on back of each, "Brownie's" on right foot of each, set of 12, 8" dolls **$775**

Buster Brown

Bench, child size bench, four seats divided by diecut animal shapes, one black and white lion, black and white zebra, and orange tiger, red background, detailed illus of Buster and Tige on ends **$6,000**

Children's feeding dish, Buster and Tige, wear to gold trim **$115**

Figure, bisque, red hat and suit, blue bow tie, black shoes, c1920, 2" h **$100**

Sunday comics, St. Paul Daily News, full section, 1914 .... **$20**

Tray, Buster Brown Shoe's, brown grain painting, gold lettering, some wear, 13-3/8" d **$65**

Campbell's Kids

Child's feeding plate, two Campbell kids, one holding doll behind back, Buffalo Pottery **$45**

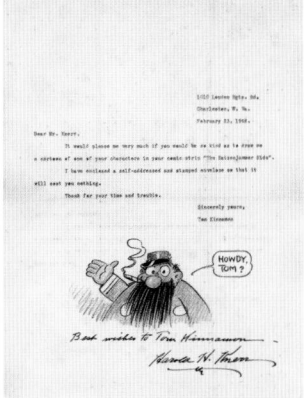

Character and personality, Katzenjammer Kids, original illustration, drawn by Harold H. Knerr, 11" x 8-1/2", **$475.**
Photo courtesy of David Rago Auctions, Inc.

Doll, boy, orig clothing, 1970, 16" h **$35**

String holder, chalk, incised "Copyright Campbell," 6-3/4" h **$395**

Charlie the Tuna

Animation cel, 10-1/2" x 12" clear acetate sheet, centered smiling full-figured 4" image of Charlie gesturing toward 4" image of goldfish holding scissors, 10-1/2" x 12-1/2" white paper sheet with matching blue/lead pencil, 4" tall image of Charlie, c1960 .... **$150**

Wristwatch, bright gold luster bezel, full-color image of Charlie on silver background, ©1971 Star-Kist Foods, grained purple leather band, 1-1/2" d bezel **$60**

Dutch Boy, string holder, diecut tin, Dutch Boy sitting on swing painting the sign for this product, White Lead Paint Bucket houses ball of string, 14-1/2" x 30" **$300**

Elsie the Cow, Borden

Display, mechanical milk carton, cardboard and papier-mâché, figural milk carton rocks back and forth, eyes and mouth move from side to side, made for MN state-fair circuit, 1940s **$500**

Lamp, Elsie and Baby, hollow ceramic figure base, Elsie reading to baby nestled on her lap, brass socket, c1950, 4" x 4" x 10" **$125**

Felix the Cat

Figure, dark copper-colored plastic, loop at top, 1950s, 1" h **$10**

Dionne Quintuplets, booklet, All Aboard for Shut-Eye Time, Dr. Dufoe and Quints on cover, **$25.**
Photo courtesy of Sky Hawk Auctions.

Pinback button, Herald and Examiner, c1930s, 1" d **$45**

Valentine, diecut, jointed cardboard, full color, "Purr Around If You Want To Be My Valentine" inscription, ©Pat Sullivan, c1920 ....**$20**

Happy Hooligan

Figure, 8-1/4" h, bisque, worried expression, tin-can hat, orange, black, blue, and yellow.............**$75**

Stickpin, 2-1/4" l, brass **$25**

Howdy Doody

Belt, suede, emb face....................**$35**

Cake-decorating set, unused **$40**

Pencil case, vinyl, red **$25**

Jiggs and Maggie

Pinback button, The Knoxville Sentinel, black and white image of Jiggs, red bow tie, c1920, 3/4" d **$15**

Salt and pepper shakers, pr, ceramic **$48**

Katzenjammer Kids

Christmas card, copyright King Features Syndicate, 1951, 4-1/4" x 4-1/2" **$18**

Comic strip, Ovaltine ad on back **$15**

Li'l Abner

Bank, Schmoo, blue plastic...........**$50**

Pinback button, Li'l Abner, Saturday Daily News, black litho, cream ground, newspaper name in red, 13/16"..**$20**

Little Annie Rooney, pinback button, comic-strip contest button, serial-number type, c1930, 1-1/4" d **$25**

Little Orphan Annie

Big Little Book, *Little Orphan Annie Secret of the Well,* No. 1417 ....**$85**

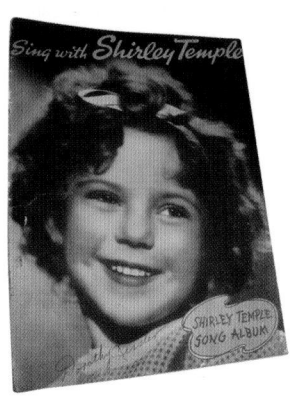

Shirley Temple, Sing with Shirley Temple, song album, **$15.**

Book, *Little Orphan Annie and the Gila Monster Gang,* Harold Gray, Whitman Publishing, © 1944, licensed by Famous Artists Syndicate, 248 pgs, 5" x 8"..................**$12**

Toothbrush holder, bisque, back inscribed "Orphan Annie & Sandy, ©F.A.S., #1565," bottom stamped "Japan," some wear to paint, 4" h **$165**

Mr. Peanut

Ashtray, Golden Jubilee, 50th Anniversary, gold-plated metal, figural, orig attached booklet, orig box, 5" h, 5-3/4" h.........................**$130**

Bank, green, 8-1/4" h **$20**

Booklet, *Mr. Peanuts Guide to Tennis,* 24 illus pgs, ©1960, 6" x 9" **$20**

Mug, green, c1960, 3-3/4" h **$18**

Paint book, Planter's Paint Book No. 2, 32 pgs, ©1929, 7-1/4" x 10-1/2" **$35**

Toy, trailer truck, red cab, yellow and blue plastic trailer, 5-1/2" l **$275**

Mutt & Jeff

Bank, cast iron, orig paint, 4-7/8" h **$125**

Book, *The Mutt & Jeff Cartoon Book,* Bud Fisher, black and white illus by author, Ball Pub. Co., 1911 ....**$100**

Dolls, composition character heads, molded and painted features, molded mustaches, metal ball jointed body, composition hands, orig felt jackets, vests, ties, and pants, molded hat, Bucherer, 6-1/2" h and 8" h, price for pr **$500**

Popeye

Cereal bowl, plastic, white ground, red, blue, and black illus of Popeye and Olive Oyl **$5**

Charm, bright copper-luster plastic figure of Olive Oyl, 1930s, 1" h **$10**

Figure, chalkware, 14" h.............**$150**

Mug, Olive Oyl, figural, 4" h **$20**

Reddy Kilowatt

Hot pad, laminated heat-resistant cardboard, textured top surface with art and verse inscription, "My name is Reddy Kilowatt-I keep things cold. I make things hot. I'm your cheap electric servant. Always ready on the spot," c1940, 6" d **$40**

Pinback button, "Please Don't Litter," blue and white, 1950s **$15**

Stickpin, red enamel and silvered-metal miniature diecut figure, c1950 ....**$30**

Speedy Alka Seltzer, patch, colorful stitched image of smiling Speedy waving his wand, pixie dust accent, 1960s **$35**

Yellow Kid

Cap bomb, cast iron, c1898, 1-1/2" h **$185**

Pinback button, #2, orig paper label, 1894...**$60**

Personality

Amos and Andy

Photograph, framed black and white facsimile signed photograph and brochure.......................................**$95**

Toy, Andy, litho tin wind-up, yellow derby, light blue jacket, red and tan striped trousers, Louis Marx & Co. **$320**

Autry, Gene

Badge, Gene Autry Official Club Badge, black and white, bright orange top rim, c1940, 1-1/4" d **$50**

Child's book, *Gene Autry Makes a New Friend,* Elizabeth Beecher, color illus by Richard Case, Whitman Tell A Tale, 1952 ....**$12**

Watch, orig band **$145**

Ball, Lucille

Magazine, Life, April 6, 1953, five-pg article, full-color cover of Lucy, Desi Arnaz, Desi IV, and Lucy Desiree **$30**

Movie-lobby card, full color, 1949 Columbia Picture "Miss Grant Takes Richmond," 11" x 14" **$40**

Cassidy, Hopalong

Coloring book, large size, 1950 .... **$30**

Tablet, color-photo cov, facsimile signature, unused, 8" x 10" **$24**

Wallet, leather, metal fringe, multicolored cover, made by Top Secret **$35**

Chaplin, Charlie

Candy container, glass, Charlie and barrel, small chip, 3-3/4" h **$100**

Magazine, *Life*, April 1, 1966, Chaplin and Sophia Loren **$10**

Dionne Quintuplets

Advertisement, Quintuplet Bread, Schultz Baking Co., diecut cardboard, loaf of bread, brown crust, bright red and blue letters, named silhouette portraits, text on reverse, 5" x 7" **$70**

Booklet, *All Aboard for Shut-Eye Time*, Dr. Dufoe and Quints on cover **$25**

Doll, Dr. Dufoe, composition, painted blue eyes, single stroke brows, closed smiling mouth, gray mohair wig, jointed at shoulders and hips, orig two-pc doctor's uniform, hat, socks, and shoes, marked "Madame Alexander New York" on clothing tag, doll unmarked, 14" h **$525**

Fan, diecut cardboard, titled, "Sweethearts of the World," full-color-tinted portraits, light-blue ground, funeral director name on reverse, ©1936, 8-1/4" x 8-3/4" **$35**

Garland, Judy

Pinback button, "Judy Garland Doll," black and white photo, used on c1930 Ideal doll, name appears on curl, also "Metro-Goldwyn-Mayer Star" in tiny letters, 1" h **$125**

Sheet music, "On the Atchison, Topeka, and the Sante Fe," 1945 MGM movie, "The Harvey Girls," sepia photo, purple, light pink, and brown cov **$35**

Gleason, Jackie

Magazine, *TV Guide*, May 21, 1955, Philadelphia edition, three-pg article on the Honeymooners.......... **$18**

Pinback button, "Jackie Gleason Fan Club/ And Awa-a-ay We Go!," blue on cream litho, checkered suit, 1950s, 1-5/8" d.................... **$65**

Laurel & Hardy

Movie poster, When Comedy Was King, 20th C Fox, Laurel and Hardy in center **$25**

Salt and pepper shakers, pr **$175**

Lone Ranger

Coloring book, unused.................. **$50**

Game board, target bull's eye **$185**

Ring, Cheerios premium, saddle type, filmstrip missing **$225**

Marx, Groucho, book, *Groucho and Me*, Groucho Marx, Bernard Geis, 1959, 22 photos **$10**

Mix, Tom

Big Little Book, Whitman, *Tom Mix and The Stranger from the Sea*, Pete Daryll, 1936, #1183 .... **$75**

Premium, Tom Mix Ralston Telegraph Set, 1940 .... **$95**

Ring, magnet, 1946 ....**$145**

Scarf, Tom Mix Ralston Straight Shooters **$195**

Our Gang, Little Rascals, display sign, 23-1/4" x 32", heavy diecut cardboard, Felin's Meat Products, c1920, sign and individual 1-1/4" x 3" named figures **$4,700**

Rogers, Roy

Bank, Roy on Trigger, porcelain, sgd "Roy Rogers" and "Trigger" **$200**

Charm, blue plastic frame, black and white glossy paper photo, 1" h **$35**

Ring, litho tin, Post's Raisin Bran premium, Dale Evans, ©1942 .... **$45**

Watch, Roy and Dale.................**$120**

Temple, Shirley

Child's book, *The Shirley Temple Edition of Susannah of the Mounties*, by Muriel Denison, Random House, New York, 1936, reprint orange cover with red and black lettering on front and end cover, orig dust jacket **$20**

Doll, composition, hazel sleep eyes, open mouth, orig mohair wig in orig set, jointed at shoulders and hips, dressed in tagged pajamas from Poor Little Rich Girl, orig shoes, mkd "Shirley Temple, Ideal, N & T Co.," 18" h **$575**

Figure, salt-glazed, 6-1/2" h.......... **$85**

Handkerchief, Little Colonel, boxed set of three **$200**

Magazine tear sheet, Lane Hope Chests adv, 1945 .... **$8**

Pinback button, brown-tone photo, light-pink rim, Ideal Dolls, 1930s, 1-1/4" d **$75**

Three Stooges

Autograph, letter, 4-1/2" x 5-1/2" mailing envelope, two folded 6" x 8" sheets of "Three Stooges" letterhead, personally inked response to fan, sgd "Moe Howard," March 10, 1964 Los Angeles postmark **$200**

Badge, cello, black and white upper face image of Curly-Joe on purple background, Clark Oil employee type, 4" d **$20**

Photo, glossy black and white, facsimile signatures of Curly-Joe, Larry, and Moe, plus personal inscription in blue ink by Moe, 4" x 5" **$95**

Wayne, John

Magazine, *Life*, Jan. 29, 1972 .... **$25**

Magazine tear sheet, "Back to Bataan," black and white, 1945, 10" x 13" **$15**

Movie poster, "McLintock," 1963 .... **$250**

CHILDREN'S BOOKS

History: Because there is a bit of the child in all of us, collectors always have been attracted to children's books. In the 19th century, books were popular gifts for children, with many of the children's classics written and published during this time. These books were treasured and often kept throughout a lifetime.

Developments in printing made it possible to include more attractive black and white illustrations and color plates. The work of artists and illustrators has added value beyond the text itself.

Additional Resources:

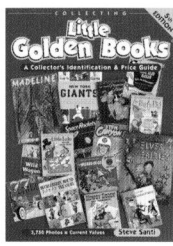

Collecting Little Golden Books®, 5th Ed., by Steve Santi, Krause Publications, Iola, WI.

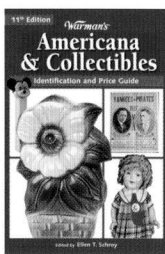

Warman's® Americana & Collectibles, 11th Ed., by Ellen T. Schroy, ed., Krause Publications, Iola, WI.

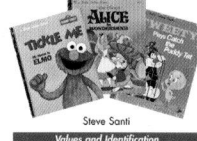

Warman's® Little Golden Books Field Guide, by Steve Santi, Krause Publications, Iola, WI.

Peeps Into Fairy Land, *Ernest Nigler, London, E. P. Dutton, New York, printed in Bavaria,* **$140.**

A Child's Garden of Verses, illus by Myrtle Sheldon, Donahue Pub, 1st ed, 1916 .... **$25**

A Christmas Carol, Charles Dickens, Garden City Pub, color and black and white illus by Everett Shinn, red cover, fancy gold trim, ©1938 ..... **$28**

Adventures of Tom Sawyer, Mark Twain, American Pub. Co., Hartford, Connecticut, blue and gold cover, 1899 .... **$45**

Alice's Adventures in Wonderland in Words of One Syllable, Saalfield, illus by John Tenniel, dj, ©1908 .... **$18**

American Girl Beauty Book, Bobbs-Merrill, New York, illus, 1945 .... **$9**

And To Think That I Saw It On Mulberry Street, Dr. Seuss, Vanguard Pub., 3rd printing, ©1937 .... **$15**

An Old Fashioned Girl, Louisa M. Alcott, Robert Bros. Pub, 1870, 1st ed **$35**

Bobbsey Twins At The County Fair, The, Grossett & Dunlap, 1st ed., dj, 1922 .... **$28**

Book of the Camp Fire Girls, Rev. Ed., paperback, 1954 .... **$6**

Boys Story of Lindbergh, The Lone Eagle, Richard Beamish, John C. Winston Co., dj, 1928 .... **$20**

Bunny Rabbit Concert, Lawrence Welk, illus Carol Bryan, Youth Pub. Sat Evening Post, 2nd printing, 1978 .... **$8**

By the Shores of Silver Lake, Laura Ingalls Wilder, illus Garth Williams, Harper Collins, dj, 1953 .... **$10**

Christmas Eve on Lonesome and Other Stories, John Fox, Jr., Grosset & Dunlap, 1904 .... **$15**

Eric & Sally and Other Stories, Johanna Spyrl, Grosset & Dunlap, 342 pgs, 1932 .... **$7**

Freckles, Grossett & Dunlap, illus by E. Stetson Crawford, 1904 .... **$8**

Girl Scout Handbook, Rev. Ed., 1930 .... **$7**

Hardy Boys, Missing Chums, Franklin Dixon, illus by Walter Rogers, Grossett & Dunlap, 1st ed, 1928 .... **$25**

Helen's Babies, John Habberton, J. H. Sears & Co., colorful illus by Christopher Rule **$10**

How the Grinch Stole Christmas, Dr. Seuss, Random House, Grinch on red and green cover, ©1957 .... **$25**

Little Britches, Father and I Were Ranchers, Ralph Moody, illus Edward Shenton, Peoples Book Club, Chicago, 1950 .... **$8**

Lullaby Land, Eugene Field, Scribner, 1st ed, 1897 .... **$35**

Marcella Stories, Johnny Gruelle, M. A. Donohue Co., color and black and white illus, dj, 1930s **$95**

Metropolitan Mother Goose, Elizabeth Watson, Metropolitan Insurance Co. promo, 1930s, 20 pgs **$18**

Mother Goose and Nursery Rhymes, Anthemum Pub., colored wood engravings by Philip Reed, 1st ed, Mother Goose and gander on orange cover, 1963 .... **$35**

Mother Goose or The Old Nursery Rhymes, Warne, Kate Greenaway illus, pictures on both front and back cov, c1900, 44 rhymes **$45**

Moving Picture Boys and the Flood, The, Victor Appleton, Grossett & Dunlap, pictorial cover, 1914 .... **$15**

Mr. Winkle Goes to War, Theodore Pratt, Duell, Sloan & Pearce, 1st ed, dj, 1943 .... **$8**

Mrs. Appleyard's Year, Louise Andrews Kent, Hough. Mifflin, 195 pgs, rooster on cover, 1941 .... **$9.50**

Mrs. Wiggs of the Cabbage Patch, Alice Hegan Rice, Appleton-Century Co., hardbound, lady in red dress on cover, 1941 .... **$10**

My Very Own Fairy Stories, Johnny Grulle, P. F. Volland Co., 30th ed, color illus, 1917 .... **$65**

Nancy Drew, The Password to Larkspur Lane, illus by Russell Tandy, Grossett & Dunlap, some fading to blue cover, 1933 .... **$65**

Nelly's Silver Mine, Helen Hunt Jackson, Little Brown & Co., illus by Harriet Richards and Henry Pitz, dj, 1924 .... **$20**

Peter Rabbit and the Little Boy, Linda Almond, Platt & Munk, 1935 .... **$15**

Raggedy Ann's Wishing Pebble, Johnny Gruelle, M. A. Donohue Co., color and black and white illus, dj, 1930s **$85**

Riley's Songs O'Cheer, James Whitcomb, Bobbs Merrill Pub, six color illus, black and white illus by Will Vawter, 1905 .... **$35**

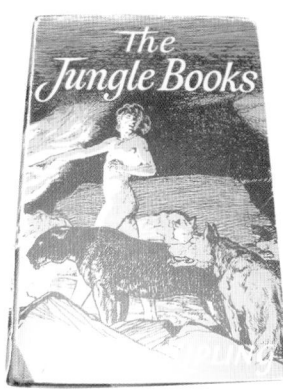

The Jungle Books, *R Kipling*, original orange and black dust jacket, wear, tears, **$45.**

Mother Goose, **$35.**

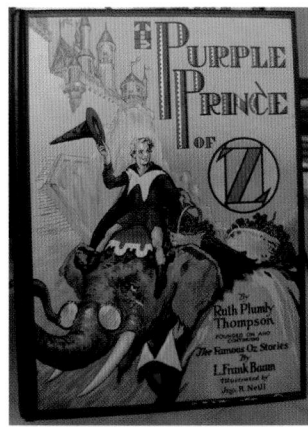

Book, The Purple Prince of Oz, *by Ruth Plumly Thompson, Founded on and Continuing The Famous Oz Stories by Frank L. Baum, Illus by Jno. R. Neill,* **$300.**

Baby plate, rolled rim, decal decoration, verse "Baby Bunting Runs Away, And joins the little pigs at play," wear to gold trim on border, marked "D. E. McNichol, East Liverpool, O, 1218," **$95.**

Six White Horses, Candy Geer, illus Leslie Bennet, M & W Quill Pub, 2nd printing, 1964 .... **$6**

Smoky The Cow Horse, Will James, Aladdin Books **$8**

Swiss Family Robinson, The, Johann Wyss, illus by Lynd Ward, Grosset & Dunlap, Junior Library edition, 1949 .... **$8**

Tarzan and City of the Gold, Edgar Rice Burroughs, Whitman, dj, 1952 .... **$15**

The Cat In The Hat Comes Back, Dr. Seuss, Random House, dj, 1958 .... **$185**

The New Our Friends, Dick and Jane, Scott Foresman, 1951 .... **$38**

The Night Before Christmas, A Little Golden Book, Simon Schuster, illus Cornelius DeWitt, 1946 .... **$45**

Tom Sawyer Detective, Mark Twain, Grossett & Dunlap, 1924 .... **$15**

Uncle Remus His Songs and Sayings, Joel Chandler Harris, 112 illus by A. B. Frost, D. Appleton & Co., 1916 .... **$75**

Uncle Wiggily and the Runaway Cheese, Howard R. Garis, color illus by A. Watson, Platt & Munk, oversize, 1977 .... **$12.50**

When We Were Very Young, A. A. Milne, Dutton, 3rd printing, 1924 .... **$17.50**

CHILDREN'S FEEDING DISHES

History: Unlike toy dishes meant for play, children's feeding dishes are the items actually used in the feeding of a child. Their colorful designs of animals, nursery rhymes, and children's

Buffalo Pottery, Grace Drayton children, worn image, chip on inner rim, **$20.**

activities are meant to appeal to the child and make meal times fun. Many plates have a unit to hold hot water, thus keeping the food warm.

Although glass and porcelain examples from the late 19th and early 20th centuries are most popular, collectors are beginning to seek some of the plastic examples from the 1920s to 1940s, especially those with Disney designs on them.

ABC plate

Aesop's Fables the Leopard and the Fox, black transfer print, pearlware, England, 19th C **$175**

Crusoe Finding the Foot Prints, color enhanced brown transfer, pearlware, England, minor discoloration, 19th C **$125**

Eye of the master will do no more than his hands, multicolored transfer **$145**

Franklin's Provbs, (sic) black transfer print, pearlware, England, 19th C **$175**

Old Mother Hubbard, brown transfer, polychrome enamel trim, alphabet border, marked "Tunstall," 7-1/2" d **$200**

Take Your Time Miss Lucy, black transfer of money and cat, polychrome enamel, titled, molded hops rim, red trim, ironstone, imp "Meakin," 6" d **$125**

Bowl, Sunbonnet girls dec, pale orange band, cream colored ground, marked "Roseville," slight wear, inner rim chip **$200**

Butter pat, "A Present For Ann," blue transfer medallion, 3-1/4" d **$125**

Cereal set, Nursery Rhyme, amber, divided plate, Humpty Dumpty on mug and bowl, Tiara **$125**

Creamer, three yellow ducks, yellow band with black outline, cream-colored ground, marked "R12" **$125**

Cup, Raggedy Ann, Johnny Gruelle, Crooksville China, 1941 .... **$65**

Cup plate, "Constant dropping wears away stones and little strokes fell great oaks," green transfer, polychrome enamel dec, 4-5/8" d **$90**

Feeding dish

Kiddieware, pink, Stangl **$125**

Little Bo Peep, glass, divided, white, red trim **$65**

Nursery Rhyme, green enamelware, marked "Made in Germany" **$40**

Raggedy Ann, Johnny Gruelle, Crooksville China, 1941, 8-3/4" d **$85**

Sunbonnet babies, sweeping, 7-1/4" d **$400**

Mug

Pearlware, black transfer, girl jumping rope, England, early 19th C, 1-7/8" h **$275**

Pearlware, black transfer dec, Dr. Franklin's Maxim's on Industry, England, early 19th C, 2-1/2" h **$345**

Pearlware, black transfer dec, "G is for Giles with weary strides..." with farmer and work horse, int. rim alphabet border, England, early 19th C, 2-1/2" h **$315**

Pearlware, black transfer dec, "Perish Slavery Prosper Freedom, England," early 19th C, 2-1/2" h **$295**

Pearlware, blue transfer dec, "A Present for Charles," vine borders, England, early 19th C, 2-1/2" h **$325**

Pearlware, blue transfer dec, "A Present for Samuel," recumbent cow, England, early 19th C, 2-1/2" h **$275**

Pearlware, blue transfer dec of couple in boat in scene with deer, England, minor rim chip, early 19th C, 2-5/8" h **$195**

Pearlware, brown transfer motto "Better be alone than in bad Company," England, early 19th C, 2-5/8" h **$265**

Pearlware, dark red dec, poem for December, child with dog and cat pulling cart full of toys, England, early 19th C, 2-5/8" h **$295**

Pearlware, green and black transfer dec, "Dr. Franklin's Poor Richard Illustrated," on industry, England, early 19th C, 2-5/8" h **$285**

Pearlware, green transfer dec, "The Orchard," England, early 19th C, 2-5/8" h **$235**

Pearlware, maroon transfer, "Mr. Winkle's Horsemanship," England, early 19th C, 2-7/8" h **$295**

Pearlware, polychrome dec, "Leap Frog," England, early 19th C, 2-3/8" h **$250**

Pearlware, polychrome dec, "Elizabeth," scrolled foliate embellishments, England, early 19th C, 2-3/8" h **$275**

Pearlware, reddish-brown dec, "For loving a book," England, early 19th C, 2-1/2" h **$300**

Plate

Buster Brown, mint center image, 1910, 6" d **$135**

Nursery rhymes, glass, green, 8" d **$40**

"Where Are You Going My Pretty Maid, See Saw Margery Daw," three parts, transparent-green Depression-era glass, 8" d **$45**

CHILDREN'S NURSERY ITEMS

History: The nursery is a place where children live in a miniature world. Things come in two sizes: Child scale designates items actually used for the care, housing, and feeding of the child; toy or doll scale denotes items used by the child in play and for creating a fantasy environment which copies that of an adult or his own.

Cheap labor and building costs during the Victorian era encouraged the popularity of the nursery. Most collectors focus on items from 1880 to 1930.

Additional Listings: Children's Books, Children's Feeding Dishes, Children's Toy Dishes, Dolls, Games, Miniatures, and Toys.

Blocks, boxed set, ABCs, animals, litho of Noah and ark on cov, Victorian **$185**

Boat, play, ice, wood with iron runners, c1900, 24" l **$460**

Bucket, wooden-stave construction, orig yellow paint, blue-painted tin bands, stenciled stars, chick, and eagle, wood and wire bale handle, int. has some crayon marks, bottom band replaced, 5-1/2" d, 4-1/4" h **$660**

Carriage, wicker, brown and white hide-covered horse with glass eyes, leather tack, hair mane, horse-hair tail, two-wheeled vehicle pushed by handle, horse sets between shafts on three-wheeled frame, wire wheels with rubber tread, some damage to hide, wear to paint, late 19th/early 20th C, 53" l, 37" h **$1,380**

Chair

America, pine, shaped crest rail over back splat with keyhole cut-out, shaped seat, splayed ring-turned legs, painted brown with polychrome floral dec on crest and splat, red and black striping, gilt accents, minor paint wear and cracks, 19th C, 9-5/8" h seat, 20-1/8" h back **$265**

Attributed to New England, turned ash, two turned stiles flanking two horizontal and two vertical spindles with turned arms, projecting handholds continuing to slightly tapering legs with stretchers, old refinish, imperfections, late 17th C, 8-1/2" h seat, 21-1/2" h back **$2,820**

High chair, doll size, painted white, play wear, **$25.**

Ladder-back, arms, leather seat, turned finials and legs, old blue-green paint, 6" h, 24" h back **$415**

Chest of drawers, child-size, Hepplewhite-style, curly maple, pine secondary wood, banded inlay around two-board top and base, four graduated dovetailed drawers with dark line inlay, and fans at corners, well-scalloped base, French feet, diamond-shaped escutcheons, emb brasses with cornucopia designs, 27" w, 17" d, 28" h **$1,320**

Crib, refinished birch, tapered high posts with incised line beading along edges, urn-shaped supports on all sides, narrow vertical slats added for stability, 38-3/4" d, 69-1/2" h, orig 48" l rails **$220**

Crib quilt, central diamond, needle-work heart and foliate black bound edges, Amish, Lancaster County, Pennsylvania, 40" x 41" **$4,675**

Desk, Queen Anne, southeastern New England, cherry and poplar, slant lid, int. with four compartments over drawers, sliding panel revealing well, case with single thumb molded drawers, bracket feet, replaced brasses, old refinish, restorations, 18th C, 22-3/4" w, 14-1/4" d, 27" h **$4,120**

Doll bed, Arts & Crafts, oak, rect headboard with two cartoon-like images of baby dolls, footboard with two sq form cut-outs, imperfections, 28-5/8" l, 16" w, 15-3/4" h **$230**

Doll carriage

American, fringed top surrey, original dark green paint, gold stenciling, wooden wheels, platform top, fringe replaced, c1870, 32" l, 28" h **$350**

Heywood Wakefield, woven wicker, natural finish, diamond pattern weave, steel wheels, rubber tires, clamshell hood, maker's label on underside, early 20th C, 30" l, 28" h **$150**

Natural wicker wooden spoked wheels, original button-upholstered back, red cotton parasol on wire hook, late 19th C, 30" l, 28" h **$230**

Doll cradle, pine, sq and "T" head nails, footboard and part of hood are dovetailed, scrolled end rockers, layers of red paint, age cracks, wear,

Child's Windsor arm chair, signed by I. Pugh, Chester County, Pennsylvania, c1810, bamboo turned legs and spindles, 12" w, 8-1/2" h seat, 20-1/2" h overall, **$250.**
Photo courtesy of Alderfer Auction Co.

Doll's ladderback side chair, painted, 3-slat back, rush seat, turned legs with stretchers, 19th C, 12" h, **$374.**
Photo courtesy of Pook & Pook Inc.

one rocker glued, 15" l, 8-1/4" w, 13" h **$150**

Doll crib, poplar, orig reddish-brown painted dec, shaped head and foot-boards, rockers, turned posts with ball finials, edge wear, finial chips, 16-1/2" l, 11-1/2" d, 11" h **$320**

Game, ring toss, green painted wood backplate set with small hooks, each with gold transfer printed number, four leather tossing rings, England, first quarter 20th C, 16" d **$175**

High chair, pillow-back crest rail, rect splat flanked by raked stiles, scrolled arms, turned supports, rush seat, turned legs joined by stretchers, old beige paint, floral polychrome dec, 22" h seat, 33" h back **$1,000**

Horse, pull toy, carved wood, painted white ground, black sponge highlights, horse-hair mane and tail, applied saddle, bridle, and ears, metal wheel base, mid-1800s, 16-1/2" l, 6" w, 16" h **$2,860**

Needlework picture, silk threads and watercolor on silk, titled "The Mother's Hope," young girl in landscape setting, Massachusetts, framed in oval format, minor scattered staining, small areas of fabric loss, replaced tablet, early 19th C **$1,725**

Noah's Ark, painted red, blue, orange, white, and green wood, roof and one side of base open to inner compartments, six carved and painted animals, Noah, two ladies, one glued

leg, some edge wear, 18-1/2" l, 5" d, 11-1/2" h **$750**

Potty chair, Windsor, attributed to New England, orig yellow paint, green and black striping, stenciled front on crest, potty chair hole in seat covered in old brown, green, and white chintz with large bird and foliage design, bamboo turnings, 10" h seat, 22" h back **$250**

Push cart, red and blue, gold stenciled dec, sgd "Wm F. Goodwin's Patents, Jan. 22, 1867 & Aug. 25, 1868," black painted wheels, handles and under-carriage, corner joints need resoldering, 12" l, 5-1/4" h **$250**

Rattle, sterling silver, pink coral handle below knopped body with emb dec, five silver bells, whistle, maker's mark "E.S.B.," Birmingham, England, 19th C, 4" l **$475**

Rocking chair

Plank seat, spindle back, salmon and brown paint, cheese-cutter rockers, 8" h seat, 19" h back **$200**

Shaker, production, Mt. Lebanon, New York, 1880-1930, incised "O" with decal on rocker, old varnished surface, replaced tape seat, minor imperfections, 7-3/4" h seat, 24" h back **$3,300**

Rocking horse, wooden, mortised and dovetailed, tacked leather seat, mustard paint, arched, gouged-carved tail, Adams County, Pennsylvania, use wear, 45" l, 12" w, 26" h **$6,380**

Hobby horse, stuffed hide, wheeled wood platform, 19th C, some damage, **$275.**
Photo courtesy of Wiederseim Associates, Inc.

Paint set, Alice in Wonderland, tin litho box, some original paints, marked "Made in England," **$25.**

Child's table, William and Mary style, oak gate leg, drop leaves, turned legs, trestle base, 19-1/2" h x 23" w, **$800.**
Photo courtesy of Wiederseim Associates, Inc.

Gustav Stickley, Arts & Crafts, 22-1/4" x 36" x 24" trestle table, pair 30" x 37-3/4" x 12-1/2" benches, each with stretcher fastened with keyed through tenons, paper labels, new finish, **$2,800.**
Photo courtesy of David Rago Auctions, Inc.

Rocking horse, carved and painted, base inscribed "E.F. Eggleston & Co. of 3 Fulton St. N.Y.," original red, blue and pumpkin swirl decoration, 46" w, 23-3/4" h, **$1,840.**
Photo courtesy of Pook & Pook, Inc.

Rocking horse, stuffed, red rockers, 19th C, 28" x 42", **$225.**
Photo courtesy of Wiederseim Associates, Inc.

Schoolboy sketchbook, Thomas Stapler, attributed to New England, booklet with pen and ink inscription on cover reading "Thomas Stapler's Book 1803," six pages with pen and ink and watercolor pictures of birds, one titled "The Gull," one page with perspective drawing of a Federal-style building, one page depicting a mathematical problem, toning, light stains, 1803, 6-1/4" x 7-3/4" **$600**

Sled, carved oak and wrought iron, carved horse head, traces of polychrome dec, Pennsylvania, 19th C, 37" l, 12-1/4" w, 20" h **$3,110**

Sleigh, high sides, wooden runners, old repaint with scrollwork and foliage, red ground, yellow line borders, blue int., edge wear, 19" l, 13-1/2" w, 18" h **$385**

Tricycle horse, painted wood horse model, glass eyes, suede saddle, velvet saddle blanket, single front wheel, two rear wheels, chain-driven mechanism, by Jugnet, Lyon, repainted, 39" l, 22-1/2" w, 33" h **$850**

Wheelbarrow, painted red, hand painted scenes with American eagle and flags **$2,700**

CHILDREN'S TOY DISHES

History: Dishes made for children often served a dual purpose— play-

Tea set, partial, porcelain, Buster Brown and girl having tea decoration, mug and two plates shown from 16-piece set, wear, some damage, **$395.**
Photo courtesy of Joy Luke Auctions.

things and a means of learning social graces. Dish sets came in two sizes. The first was for actual use by the child when entertaining friends. The second, a smaller size, was for use with dolls.

Children's dish sets often were made as a sideline to a major manufacturing line, either as a complement to the family service or as a way to use up the last of the day's batch of materials. The artwork of famous illustrators, such as Palmer Cox, Kate Greenaway, and Rose O'Neill, can be found on porcelain children's sets.

Akro Agate

Tea set, octagonal, large, green and white, Little American Maid, orig box, 17 pcs **$225**

Water set, Play Time, pink and blue, orig box, seven pcs **$125**

Bohemian glass, decanter set, ruby flashed, vintage dec, five pcs **$135**

Candlesticks, pr, hexagonal, colorless, tiny socket hole, rough pontil mark, 1850-70, 2" h, 1-3/8" d base **$50**

China

Cheese dish, cov, hunting scene, Royal Bayreuth **$85**

Chocolate pot, Model-T car with passengers **$90**

Cup and saucer, Phoenix Bird **$15**

Dinner set, Willow Ware, blue and white, Japanese **$200**

Tea set, Children playing, cov teapot, creamer, cov sugar, six cups, saucers, and tea plates, German, Victorian **$285**

Tureen, cov, Blue Willow, marked "Made in China," 3-1/2" w **$60**

Decanter, blown molded glass

Colorless, ringed type III base, rough pontil mark, no stopper, Boston & Sandwich Glass Co., 1825-35, 2-3/4" h **$220**

Tea set, original box, white ground, multicolored floral decoration, service for six, Japan, **$90.**

Colorless, rayed and ringed type I base, rough pontil mark, pressed sunburst stopper, Boston & Sandwich Glass Co., 1825-40, quarter pint, 5" h **$450**

Depression glass, 14-pc set

Cherry Blossom, pink **$390**

Laurel, McKee, red trim............ **$355**

Moderntone, turquoise, gold **$210**

Flat iron, light amethyst, Boston & Sandwich Glass Co., tip polished, 1850-70, 7/8" h, 1-5/8" l.............. **$150**

Plate

Lacy Diamond and Scroll with Concentric Rings, amethyst, 49 even scallop rim, rope table ring, Boston & Sandwich Glass Co., loss to one scallop, 1835-50, 2-1/4" d **$440**

Lacy Scroll and Diamond Point, colorless, plain rim, American or possibly Continental, rim spall, minor roughness, 2-5/8" d **$25**

Tumbler

Lacy Pointed Oval, brilliant teal, ten scallop base rayed underneath, faint pontil mark, Boston & Sandwich Glass Co., 1835-50, 1-7/8" h, 1-5/8" d **$525**

Nine-Panel, canary, slightly rough pontil mark, Boston & Sandwich Glass Co., 1845-70, 1-5/8" h, 1-1/2" d **$100**

Nine-Panel, deep translucent starch blue, slightly rough pontil mark, Boston & Sandwich Glass Co., 1845-70, 1-5/8" h, 1-1/2" d **$110**

CHRISTMAS ITEMS

History: The celebration of Christmas dates back to Roman times. Several customs associated with

Tea set, pink Sunderland luster, teapot, lidded sugar, creamer, three cups, three saucers, handle-less cup and saucer, **$350.**
Photo courtesy of Joy Luke.

modern Christmas celebrations are traced back to early pagan rituals.

Father Christmas, believed to have evolved in Europe in the 7th century, was a combination of the pagan god Thor, who judged and punished the good and bad, and St. Nicholas, the generous Bishop of Myra. Kris Kringle originated in Germany and was brought to America by the Germans and Swiss who settled in Pennsylvania in the late 18th century.

In 1822, Clement C. Moore wrote "A Visit From St. Nicholas" and developed the character of Santa Claus into the one we know today. Thomas Nast did a series of drawings for *Harper's Weekly* from 1863 until 1886 and further solidified the character and appearance of Santa Claus.

Reproduction Alert. Almost all holiday decorations, including Christmas, are now being skillfully reproduced. Only by knowing the source of a possible purchase, trusting the dealer, and careful observation can you be sure you are obtaining an antique.

Additional Resources:

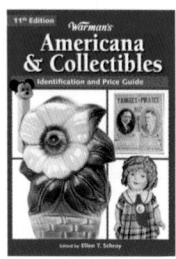

Warman's® Americana & Collectibles, 11th Ed., by Ellen T. Schroy, ed., Krause Publications, Iola, WI.

Advertising

Bank, molded rubber, Santa Claus holding a coin, toys in pack, marked "Christmas Club A. Corp, N.Y. 1972" **$6**

Booklet, *"When All The World Is Kin,"* collection of Christmas stories, Christmas giveaway, Fowler, Dick, and Walker, The Boston Store, Wilkes-Barre, Pennsylvania, 5" x 4" **$7**

Catalog, Boston Store, Milwaukee, WI, 1945, 48 pgs, "For An American Christmas," 8-1/2" x 11"...**$20**

Display, Santa in sleigh with two reindeer, Snow King Baking Powder, diecut cardboard, 16-3/4" x 32" **$675**

Pinback button

American Red Cross, red, green, and white celluloid, Santa carrying toy sack with Red Cross symbol, 1916 .... **$60**

Eagle Tribune, 1991 Santa Fund, red, white, and blue portrait, two green holly sprigs............................... **$25**

Esso, red, white, and blue, centered Santa, 1940.............................. **$45**

Gilmore Brothers Santa, black and white portrait, fleshtone tinted face, red cap, black "Christmas Greetings-Gilmore Brothers," 1940s **$60**

Joske Bros Santason is Here, litho, color design on yellow ground, Santa and child........................ **$60**

Macy's Santa Knows, red and white, 1950s **$35**

National Tuberculosis Assn, Health for All, multicolored litho, Santa, 1936... **$15**

Santa Claus at Schipper & Blocks, multicolored, Santa wearing holly leaf and berry crown, nestled by blond child, pale blue blending to white background, early 1900s **$85**

Santa's Headquarters Namm's New Fulton Street Addition, Whitehead and Hag back paper, c1920, 1-1/4" d **$125**

Spiegel Toyland Santa, multicolored litho, black lettering, 1930s **$50**

Stickpin, diecut thin cello multicolored portrait of Santa on short hanger stickpin, back inscribed, "Meet Me At Bowman's," c1920 .... **$48**

Santa in cardboard candy box chimney, 1-1/4" x 1-3/4" x 2" h red and white cardboard box designed as chimney, wrapped in shiny string, 2-3/4" h composition Santa coming out of top wearing brown wool outfit, red felt arms, waist wrapped in brown string, black fabric legs, Charms Co., Newark, N.J., figure made in Japan, 1920s, **$50.**
Photo courtesy of Hake's Americana & Collectibles.

Christmas Card, slightly textured white paper, full-color Christmas caroling scene of Mickey, Minnie, and Donald standing in front of The Little House, two of Donald's nephews watching them while holding snowballs behind their backs, card opens to reveal two-panel scene of Susie the Little Blue Coupe pulling wheeled wagons containing many Disney characters such as Seven Dwarfs, Gus and Jaq, Bambi, Pinocchio, etc.; each wagon has monthly calendar for 1952, back cover with illustrations of Robin Hood and Peter Pan, title "Coming Soon," 1951, 7" x 8", **$75.**
Photo courtesy of Hake's Americana & Collectibles.

Children's book, Who's There?, **$25.**

Ornament set, 10 wood jointed Jaymar figures, goose, sailor, Betty Boop, Popeye, clown, bear, pig, Ed Wynn, Humpty Dumpty, Little Red Riding Hood, each with hook on top of head, text on lid "Hook These Ornaments Onto Your Christmas Tree. After Christmas, Detach Hook And You Have An Ornamental Gift Or Toy," some wear and loss to original 10-1/2" x 12-1/2" x 1-3/8" deep box, 1935, **$575.**
Photo courtesy of Hake's Americana & Collectibles.

Wall pocket, embossed stiff paper, tan, blue, and rose, Nativity scene, text on pocket "Compliments of E. C. Fritz, Steam Bread and Cake Bakery, 19 S. Hellertown Ave., Quakertown, Pa., Post Office Address: Richland Center, Pa.," **$35.**

Carolers on sled, original boxes, marked "Japan," lot of three, **$30.**

The May Co. Santa, multicolored Santa surrounded by children in winter outfits, holly leaves and berries in background, red lettering "I Am At The May Co." **$95**

Trade card, child holding snowballs, "The White is King of all Sewing Machines, 80,000 now in use," reverse reads "J. Saltzer, Pianos, Organs, and Sewing Machines, Bloomsburg, Pa." **$10**

Candy box

Cardboard, four-sided cornucopia, Merry Christmas, Santa, sleigh, and reindeer over village rooftops, string bail, USA, 8" h **$35**

Cardboard, pocketbook style, tuck-in flap, Merry Christmas, Santa in store window with children outside, marked "USA," 6" x 5" **$15**

Candy pail

Candy pail, tin litho, holiday greetings and adv on front, color graphics of children sledding and skating on back, 2-7/8" x 2-7/8" **$525**

Children's books

A Certain Star, Pearl Buck, Herschel Levit illus, American Weekly, 1957 .... **$10**

How Santa Filled the Christmas Stockings, Carolyn Hodman, color illus by F. W. Stecher, Stecher Litho Co., 1916, 13" x 71" **$85**

Rudolph the Red-Nosed Reindeer, Robert I. May, Maxton Publishers, Inc., 1939 .... **$12**

The Bird's Christmas Carol, Kate Douglas Wiggin, Hough Miffin, dj, 1912 .... **$7.50**

The Fireside Book of Christmas Stories, Edw Wagenknecht, Wallace Morgan illus, Bobbs Merrill 1945, 656 pgs **$8.50**

The Littlest Snowman, Charles Tazewell, Grossett & Dunlap, New York, 1958 .... **$18**

Christmas-tree fence

Cast iron, silver, ornate gold trim, Germany, fifteen 10" l segments with posts **$600**

Wood, folding red and green sections, USA, 48" l **$35**

Feather tree

Green wooden base, 12" h **$95**

Green goose feather-wrapped branches with metal candleholders, painted white with green trim round wooden base, marked "Germany," 4' h **$420**

Red wooden base, 6" h **$35**

Red and green wooden base, 26" h
.... **$225**

Figures

Belsnickle

Chalk, green-hooded coat with clear mica flecks, painted black base, feather tree missing, minor damage to base, 5-1/8" h **$275**

Composition, orig red, white, and black paint, gold mica flecks, green feather tree, blue pipe cleaner trim, minor wear on hood, 8-3/4" h
.... **$980**

Father Christmas

Composition, pink face, red-cloth coat, painted blue pants, black boots, mounted on mica-covered cardboard base, marked "Japan," 7" h **$90**

Papier-mâché, hollow molded, plaster covered, white coat, black boots, sprinkled with mica, 8" h **$300**

Reindeer, pot metal, marked "Germany," 1" h **$20**

Santa Claus

Cotton batting, red, attached to cardboard house, marked "Japan," 3" h
.... **$48**

Celluloid, molded, one-piece Santa, sleigh, and reindeer, 3" l **$35**

Hard plastic, Santa on green plastic skis, USA, 5" h **$120**

Pressed cardboard, red hat and jacket, black boots, 10" h **$90**

Sheep, composition body, carved wooden legs, covered with cloth or wool, glass eyes, 3" h **$40**

Greeting cards

"Sincere Good Wishes," purple pansy with green leaves, greeting inside, Raphael Tuck & Sons, 1892 .... **$12**

"Loving Greetings," flat card, two girls pictured hanging garland, marked "Germany," 1910 .... **$10**

"Merry Christmas," series of six envelopes, decreasing in size, small card in last envelope, American Greeting Publishers, Cleveland, USA, 1933
.... **$12**

House, cardboard

Mica covered, wire loop on top, marked "Czechoslovakia," 2" x 2"
.... **$10**

House and fence, sponge trees, marked "USA," 4" x 5" **$12**

Lantern, four sided, peaked top, wire bail, metal candleholder in base, black cardboard, colored tissue paper scenes, 1940s, 8" h **$25**

Magazine, St. Nicholas, color covers, ads, illus, story, bound edition of 1915 and 1916 .... **$15**

Ornaments

Angel, wax over composition, human-hair wig, spun-glass wings, cloth dress, Germany, 4" h **$60**

Ball, silvered glass, any color, 2" d
.... **$4**

Beads, glass, half-inch multicolored beads, paper label marked "Japan," 72" l **$8**

Bulldog, Dresden, three-dimensional, marked "Germany," 3" h **$250**

Camel, cotton batting, Germany, 4" h
.... **$160**

Cross, beaded, two-sided, silvered, wire hanger, paper label marked "Czechoslovakia," 4" h **$20**

Father Christmas on Donkey, chromolithograph, blue robe, tinsel trim, 10" h **$25**

Kugel, round, deep sapphire blue, brass hanger, 4-1/2" d **$120**

Mandolin, unsilvered glass, wrapped in lametta and tinsel, 5" h **$45**

Parakeet, multicolored glass, spun glass tail, mounted on metal clip, 5" h **$20**

Pear, cotton batting, mica highlights, paper leaf, wire hanger, Japan, 3" h
.... **$15**

Santa Claus in Chimney, glass, Germany, 4" h **$75**

Swan, Dresden, flat, gold with silver, green, and red highlights, 5" x 6"
.... **$150**

Tree top, three spheres stacked with small clear glass balls, silvered, lametta and tinsel trim, attached to blown glass hooks, 11" h **$90**

Postcards, Germany

Christmas bells and snow scene, marked "Made in Germany," used, one-cent stamp, 1911 .... **$20**

"Happy Christmas Wishes," Santa steering ship **$15**

"May Your Christmas Be Merry and Gay," photo card, sepia tones, Father Christmas peeking between two large wooden doors, wearing fur cap
.... **$20**

Toys

Horse and wagon, composition, hand-painted workhorse, gray dappling, remnants of leather harness with brass rosettes, partial paper label, red and yellow painted wagon with sign "St. Claus Dealer in Good Things," wear, wagon fork replaced, 21" l, 9" h **$575**

Jack-in-the-box, "Santa Pops," hard plastic, red-felt hat, orig box, Tigrette Industries, 1956, 9-1/2" h **$30**

Merry-go-round, wind-up, celluloid, green and red base, four white reindeer heads, Santa sitting under umbrella, Santa spins around, stars hanging from umbrella bounce off bobbing deer heads, orig box, Japan
.... **$65**

Santa, battery operated, metal covered with red and white plush suit and hat, soft-plastic face, holding metal wand with white star light, wand moves up and down and lights up while Santa turns head, 10" h **$90**

Tree, brush style, green, mica-covered branches, wooden base, 6" h **$8**

Tree stand, cast iron, old worn green, gold, white, and red paint, relief tree trunk, foliage, and stairway design, 9-3/4" sq, 4" h **$110**

CLOCKS

History: The sundial was the first man-made device for measuring time. Its basic disadvantage is well expressed by the saying: "Do like the sundial, count only the sunny days."

Needing greater dependability, man developed the water clock, oil clock, and sand clock, respectively. All these clocks worked on the same principle— time was measured by the amount of material passing from one container to another.

The wheel clock was the next major step. These clocks can be traced back to the 13th century. Many improvements on the basic wheel clock were made and continue to be made. In 1934, the quartz-crystal movement was introduced.

The first carriage clock was made about 1800 by Abraham Louis Breguet as he tried to develop a clock that would keep accurate time for Napoleon's officers. One special feature of a carriage clock was a device that allowed it to withstand the bumpy ride of a stagecoach. These small clocks usually are easy to carry with their own handle built into a rectangular case.

The recently invented atomic clock, which measures time by radiation frequency, only varies one second in a thousand years.

Notes: Identifying the proper model name for a clock is critical in establishing price. Condition of the works also is a critical factor. Examine the works to see how many original parts remain. If repairs are needed, try to include this in your estimate of purchase price. Few clocks are purchased purely for decorative value.

Additional Resources:

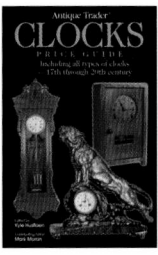

Antique Trader® Clocks Price Guide, by Kyle Husfloen, ed., and Mark F. Moran, contr. ed., Krause Publications, Iola, WI.

Encyclopedia of Antique American Clocks, 2nd Ed., by Robert W. and Harriet Swedberg, Krause Publications, Iola, WI.

Warman's® American Clocks Field Guide, by Robert W. and Harriet Swedberg, Krause Publications, Iola, WI.

Advertising

Chew Friendship Cub Plug, face of man with moving mouth chewing Friendship Tobacco to the tic of the clock, pat'd March 2, 1886, 4" h **$900**

Gruen Watch, Williams Jewelry Co. on marquee at bottom, blue neon around perimeter, 15" x 15" **$600**

Hire's Root Beer, "Drink Hires Root Beer with Root Barks, Herbs," 15" d **$250**

International Tailoring, Chicago, cast iron, emb design, bronzed, orig working clock, 12" w, 2-1/2" d, 16" h, C.8+ **$1,000**

Longine's Watches, "The World's Most Honored Watch," brass, 18-1/2" d.................................... **$300**

None Such Mincemeat, pumpkin face, some wear, 8-1/2" w **$300**

Victrola Records, orig pendulum **$2,100**

Alarm

Attleboro, 36 hours, nickel-plated case, owl dec, 9" h......................... **$75**

Bradley, brass, double bells, Germany **$40**

Champion, 30 hours, American movement, metal frame, ornamental feet, 9" h.. **$75**

New Haven, 30 hours, SP case, perfume-bottle shape, beveled-glass mirror, removable cut-glass scent bottle, beaded handle, c1900.................. **$185**

Bracket

Louis XV, Corne Verte, gilt bronze mounts, bracket stamped "GOTER" and "JME," porcelain dial and backplate signed "F. cois Gilbert A. Paris," five turned pillar movement with silk suspension, recoil escapement with silk suspension, converted from verge escapement, eight-day time and strike movement with vertical striking, count wheel mounted on the back plate, 25-pc porcelain dial mounted on brass dial plate, Roman numeral hours and Arabic five-minute gradations, c1735, 11" w, 6" d, 26" h case, 12" w, 6-3/4" d, 12" h base **$5,500**

Regency, Bennett & Co., Norwich, brass inlaid and gilt bronze mounted mahogany, dial and back plate sgd, oak leaf spandrels, case inlaid with scrolls, gadrooned bun feet, chips, c1810, 17" h.............................. **$4,325**

*Clock, Louis XVI style, marble and bronze, temple style, seated puttti, bronze apron, finial of seated cupid, enamel face dial with Arabic numerals and floral swags, marked "***Renaissance, 49 R(ur) St. Martin, Paris," no pendulum or key, 21" x 9-1/2" x 6-1/2", $850.*
Photo courtesy of Sloans & Kenyon Auctioneers and Appraisers.

Tiffany & Co., bronze, stepped rect-shaped top, four acorn finials, cast foliate frieze, four capitals with reeded columns, shaped and foliate cast base, beveled glass door and panels, circular face dial with Roman numerals, marked "Famiel Marti Medaille...Paris 1900, Tiffany & Co.", 13" h **$600**

Carriage

French, oval, brass, four beveled glass panels, fine cut flowers in border to sides, top oval glass panels initialed "M.E.H.," dial painted with woman and cupid, decorative D-shaped handle on top, 5-1/2" h.................. **$1,150**

Grande Sonnerie, brass, dial marked for "Muiron & Cia., Mexico," phases of the moon, subsidiary day, date, and seconds dial, all enamel, set into brass plate engraved with leafy scrolls and dragons' heads, repeater button, strike/silent quarter strike lever, title on movement engraved in Spanish, made for Mexican market, early 20th C, 7-1/2" h **$7,475**

Bracket clock, Philadelphia, Federal, mahogany, dial inscribed "John J. Parry Philad.," molded arch top over pierced and scrolled sound grills, matchstick molded base, brass ball feet, c1810, **$4,140.**
Photo courtesy of Pook & Pook, Inc.

Japan, 19th C

Brass works and case, floral engraving on rect case, surmounted by bell, stand missing, 6-1/2" h **$3,000**

Brass works, rosewood case, 7" h **$7,100**

New Haven Clock Co., gilded brass case, beveled glass, gold repaint to case, orig pendulum and key, 11-1/2" h **$315**

Tiffany & Co., brass and glass, French half strike repeater movement marked for Souaillet Freres, enamel dial with Arabic numerals and subsidiary seconds dial, early 20th C, 3-3/8" w, 3" d, 7" h **$950**

Desk

American, shaped rect, brass case, white enamel bordering cobalt blue, stylized applied monogram, decorative brass corners, central dial with Arabic numerals, 4-3/4" h **$150**

British United Clock Co., Ltd., Birmingham, England, brass, bracket cut-out edges on diamond-shaped brass clock frame, four pierced diamond patterns, floral, bowknot, and fleur-de-lis punch dec, wire easel stand, printed and imp maker's marks, spotty corrosion, 20th C, 6" w, 4-1/2" h **$260**

Carriage clock, Benrus, eight-day, presentation inscription on top front panel of brass case, marked "Western Germany," **$95.**

Enameled, gilt bronze, tombstone shape, front enameled in translucent emerald green enamel on wavy engine turned ground, c1910, 4-1/4" h **$350**

Mantel

Ansonia, French-style, rococo scroll dec, enameled face sgd "Ansonia," bronze-colored patina on spelter, orig pendulum, missing finial and key, 14-1/2" h **$275**

Birge, Mallory, and Co., Bristol, CT, Classical, mahogany and gilt gesso, scrolled cornice with fruit-filled basket flanked by square plinths, glazed door enclosing white painted and gilt dial, seven-day brass strap weight-driven movement, mirror below, reverse-painted tablet below that, all flanked by gilded engaged and free-standing columns on ball feet, refinished, restoration, imperfections, c1830, 17" w, 5" d, 38" h **$650**

Classical Revival, French, retailed by Theodore B. Starr, New York, two-train half-striking Japy Freres movement, ovoid case with beveled glass sides, dial with colorless paste-set bezel, pendulum centered by portrait miniature on ivory of lady in 18th C dress, double bezel of colorless pastes, early 20th C, 12-1/4" h **$725**

French, Louis XVI-style, patinated metal, figural cherub painter with palette and wreath-draped easel, two-train half-striking movement with Japy Fils Medaille D'Argent

Mantel clock, ogee frame, reverse painted lower tablet with domed gazebo and buildings, **$175.**
Photo courtesy of Dotta Auction Co., Inc.

seal, enamel dial with worn retailer's mark, set into beaded gilt-metal bezel, waisted black marble socle, late 19th C, 17-3/4" w, 7-1/2" d, 22" h **$2,990**

George III, William Stephenson, London, maker, mahogany case, arch top with lifting handle, glass front and rear doors, side frets, brass bracket feet, two-train fusee striking movement, painted dial, c1800, 16-1/2" h **$1,650**

Gothic Revival, French, gilt bronze, two-train half-striking Japy Freres movement with pull repeater, retailed by Bourdin, Paris, case formed as pointed arch Gothic cathedral, central round dial, pierced curved arch revealing red glass panel at back, pair of columns, stacked plinth base, further ebonized wood platform, late 19th C, 20-3/8" h **$2,350**

Jugendstil, oak, retailed by Liberty & Co., exposed bell on top, open sides, copper face emb with violets, purple and yellow slag glass window, orig finish, working condition, unmarked, 9-3/4" w, 14-1/4" h **$1,840**

Leavenworth, Mark, Waterbury, CT, Federal, pillar and scroll, mahogany, scrolled cresting, three brass urn finials on sq plinths above glazed door, eglomise tablet showing house by lake flanked by freestanding columns, wooden dial with gilt dec housing thirty-hour wooden striking movement, cut-out valanced base, refinished, restoration to tablet, c1825, 16-1/2" w, 31-1/4" h **$3,820**

Louis Philippe style, retailed by Hollin, ormolu, figural, Vincenti two-train chiming movement set in bale, topped by hat and bag of coins, figure of boy holding anchor, rect plinth base set with scene of cherub loading ship, another bookkeeping, trumpet feet, late 19th C, 11-3/8" h **$1,880**

Louis XV, gilt bronze mounted, waisted ovoid tulipwood veneered case topped by rocaille urn and trimmed in rocaille C-scrolls, two-train half-striking movement, enamel dial with outer ring of seconds markers, 19" h **$1,175**

Louis XVI style, French, figural, bronze painted white metal figure of classical woman, holding gilt metal and engine-turned orb movement on white metal rod from her upraised hand, onyx plinth base, late 19th C, 26" h **$7,050**

Shreve, Crump & Low, Gothic Revival, carved mahogany, French two-train half-strike movement, engraved silver dial, case formed as Gothic pointed and trefoil arch, paneled turrets, blocked base, late 19th C, 19-1/2" h **$850**

Terry, Samuel, Federal, pillar and scroll, mahogany, scrolled cresting, three brass urn finials on sq plinths above glazed door, eglomise tablet showing building in landscape, flanked by freestanding columns, wooden painted and gilt dial, thirty-day wooden movement, valanced cut-out base, refinished, tablet replaced, c1825, 17" w, 4-1/2" d, 31-1/2" h **$1,530**

Thomas, Seth, Plymouth Hollow, CT, Classical, carved mahogany and mahogany veneer, eagle and shield-carved scroll flanked by square plinths above glazed door with eglomise tablet showing public building with floral stenciled border, opening to wooden painted dial, 36 weight-driven movement, flanked by stencil decorated engaged columns on carved acanthus leaf and hairy paw feet, minor imperfections, c1825, 17" w, 4-3/4" d, 30" h **$775**

Tiffany & Co., marble and patinated metal, two-train half-striking movement sgd by Tiffany & Co., pink marble temple form case, pediment

set with patinated metal plaque of putti with goat, round bezel set to center of case flanked by patinated pilasters, plinth base mounted with central cartouche and laurel branches, late 19th C, 12-1/4" w, 5-7/8" d, 13-1/8" h **$300**

Victorian, black, rect, two-train strike and bell movement, front with breche d'alep marble pilasters flanking round dial, plinth base with breche d'alep band and diamond inlay, gilt incised line dec, late 19th C, 9-3/4" w, 5-3/4" d, 10-3/4" h **$425**

Waterbury, black lacquer, patinated metal scrolled feet, faceplate flanked by marbleized columns with patinated metal mounts, hourly chime, c1900, 15" l, 12" h **$300**

Porcelain

Ansonia, Royal Bonn, shelf, blue and white case dec with flowers, open escapement, time and strike, 9-1/2" w, 15" h **$920**

French, possibly Sevres, architectural stepped-down form, roof with ormolu shell finial, ormolu mounted columns flanking central dial, figural garden scene over scrolled ormolu mounted base, chips, crazing, c1880, 10-1/2" h **$700**

Shelf

Atkins Clock Mfg., Bristol, CT, rosewood, 30-day wagon spring movement (invented by Joseph Ives), case with hinged door, zinc painted dial framed by eglomise tablet above lower mirrored door, iron and brass "patent equalizing lever spring" movement, flanked by canted recessed paneled corners, backboard with maker's label, c1855-58, 13-1/2" w, 4" d, 17-3/4" h

Original, untouched condition **$3,525**

Refinished, dial repaired **$2,235**

Birge and Fuller, Bristol, Connecticut, c1845-50

Gothic, candlestick, double steeple, mahogany, wagon spring, orig painted tablets, painted zinc dial, eight-day time and strike, "J. Ives Patent Accelerating Lever Spring" movement, 13-3/4" w, 4" d, 26" h **$8,225**

Mantel clock, fake graining, yellow ground, black "smoke" type graining, circular dial flanked by two columns on each side, marble base, applied ormolu on sides, no markings, $200.

Gothic, double steeple, wagon spring, case with orig painted tablets, painted zinc dial, 30 hour "J. Ives Patent Accelerating Lever Spring Movement," 11-1/2" w, 4-1/4" d, 24-1/4" h **$3,300**

Brewster and Ingrahams, Bristol, Connecticut, Gothic twin steeple, mahogany, peaked cornice, glazed door, stenciled gilt-green on white table showing love birds, enclosing painted zinc dial, double fusee brass movement, flanked by two turned finials and columns, flat base, dial replaced, minor veneer loss, c1845, 19" h **$1,100**

Forestville Manufacturing Co., J.C. Brown, Bristol, Connecticut, Gothic, acorn, rosewood, shaped laminated case with orig reverse painted tablet, painted zinc dial and eight-day fusee movement, dial attributed to repainted, c1849, 10-1/8" w, 4" d, 20-1/4" h **$6,500**

New Haven, glass door, mirrored side panels, spelter standing cupids, walnut case with drawer at base, 24" h **$490**

North, Norris, Torrington, Connecticut, Classical, mahogany, flat cornice above glazed door, eglomise tablet of young woman flanked by engaged black paint stenciled columns, polychrome and gilt white painted dial, 30-hour wooden weight-driven movement, c1825, 23-3/4" h, 13-1/2" w, 5-1/4" d **$4,900**

Pomeroy, Noah, Bristol, Connecticut, mahogany veneer, movement marked "N. Pomeroy, Bristol, Conn," steeple frame encloses glass tablets, lower one with polychrome beehive imagery, imperfections, 1860s, 14-3/4" h **$1,150**

Terry, Eli and Sons, Plymouth, Connecticut, Federal, paper label "Eli Terry and Sons," mahogany, scrolled pediment, wooden painted dial with gilt spandrels, wooden 30-hour movement, eglomise glass, curving case skirt, French feet, restoration, c1810-15, 31-1/4" h **$1,955**

Thomas, Seth, Plymouth, Connecticut, calendar, double dial, time, and strike, glass door, c1820, 14" w, 27" h **$1,150**

Unidentified, Massachusetts maker, Federal, mahogany, pierced fret over unsigned painted dial, rocking ship and gilt spandrels, red, white, and blue shields, box base on feet, restorations, c1805, 38-1/2" h **$12,650**

Willard, Aaron, Grafton, Massachusetts, mahogany and mahogany veneer, flat rect cornice above hinged square veneered door with mitered corners, brass engraved dial with floral designs, mkd "A. Willard, Grafton," framed by ropetwist bezel with brass weight-driven thirty-hour movement, flanking ball top vase and ring-turned posts above lower section of flat mid molding, central pierced and mitered panel with flanking crossbanding and free standing tapering columns on square plinths and flat base, imperfections, c1775-1825, 9-1/4" w, 3-1/2" d, 18" h **$4,700**

Table

French, gilt bronze and enamel, case finely molded gilt bronze with hooved feet, translucent maroon panel enameled with cherubs and floral sprays, maroon enameled dial with circular florals, gilt numerals, surmounted by matching enameled dome, gilt acorn finial, works stamped "Etienne Maxant, Brevete, Paris made in France," c1900, 14" h **$2,590**

French, gilt bronze and guilloche enamel, round clock, Swiss movement, enameled in translucent azure blue on engraved radiating ground, enameled and gilt chapter ring, gilt bronze case surmounted by petal forms, 19th C, 4" d **$600**

Wendell, "Mr. Clock," sq ribbon-mahogany box, tall verdigris-patinated copper legs, sgd and dated 1988, 24" x 6" **$1,380**

Tall case, dwarf

Gilmanton, Noah Ranlet, New Hampshire, dial sgd "Noah Ranlet Gilmanton 1796," time and strike movement, pine, scrolled solid crest above bonnet that encloses sgd, painted dial, includes side lights, waist door, flanked by quarter-engaged columns above base box, later stenciled eagle dec, pine case with old refinish, replaced crest, other imperfections, 49-1/4" h **$18,400**

French, marble and agate, Egyptian revival style, ormolu anthemion corner pendants, female busts, swans, laurel wreaths, paw feet, 19th C, 52" h **$3,800**

Hingham, J. Wilder, dial face indistinctly sgd, reverse dial reads "J. Wilder Hingham" in period script, painted bowl of fruit in arch, gilt spandrels, eight-day timepiece with drop-off strike, mahogany and mahogany veneer, bonnet flanked by free-standing tapering columns above waist door with applied molding, crossbanded veneer box base, curving skirt and feet, replaced crest, other minor imperfections, c1810-15, 47-1/2" h **$28,750**

Tower, Reuben, Plymouth, Massachusetts, alarm dial sgd "Reuben Tower Kingston," pine, pierced fret above bonnet flanked by free-standing mahogany columns, painted iron dial with spandrels and polychrome painted basket of flowers, fruit, and foliage above waist, box base over curving skirt, ogee feet, refinished case, replaced crest and columns, some height loss, c1820-30, 40-3/4" h **$12,650**

Tall case

Brokaw, Isaac, Federal, mahogany inlaid, dial marked "Isaac Brokaw Bridge Town" (New Jersey), shaped hood with inlaid patera and bookend inlays above glazed door, painted dial, eight-day weight-driven movement, seconds hand, calendar aperture, waist door with serpentine top and elliptical inlay, oval and quarter-fan inlays on lower case, similar embellishments above the bracket feet, refinished, restored, 1800-10, 94-1/2" h.................................**$10,575**

Mantel clock, Black Forest, carved, lamb atop plinth with fox and game, inscribed "Dasson and Godeau, Paris," late 19th C, 13-1/4" h, **$690.**

Shelf clock, Ithaca, painted dial, paneled door, single glass pane, stamped on face, orig finish, veneer lifting on one side, 69" x 18" x 12", **$600.**
Photo courtesy of David Rago Auctions, Inc.

Clocks

C

Caldwell, J. E., Georgian-Revival, mahogany, dial sgd "Caldwell," subsidiary seconds dial, cast scroll and cherub detailing, phases of the moon, two train chiming movement, hood with swan's neck cresting centered by urn, carved scroll detailing, glass front door flanked by tapering and partially reeded circular section columns, case with beveled glass front door flanked by engaged partially reeded columns, paneled plinth base centered by carved shell, front paw feet, rear ogee feet, late 19th/early 20th C, 24" w, 15" d, 95" h **$2,895**

Tall case, Pennsylvania Chippendale, cherry, carved bonnet, pineapple finial, dentil moldings, painted dial, bracket feet, inscribed "Solomon Parke, Philadelpia," ogee bracket feet, c1795, 92-1/2", $17, 250.
Photo courtesy of Pook & Pook, Inc.

English

George III style, works attributed to Elliott of London, retailed by Bigelow, Kennard, three-train movement, quarter striking and chiming, nine tubes, pierced brass spandrels, inlaid mahogany case with swan's neck cresting, three ball and spire finials, mid-case with glass door and engaged columns, inlaid with fan and urn, 91" h **$5,600**

Victorian, dial painted with landscape scenes, sgd "Thompson of Huddersfield," two-train movement, oak case carved all over with flat foliage and lappets, swan's neck cresting, engaged columns, 95" h **$2,350**

Farquharson, Alexander, George III, mahogany, gilt bronze mounts, dial signed "Alexander Farquharson, Edinburgh," etched steel face with date aperture and seconds dial, case with broken pediment cresting, dentil molding, two columnar supports with gilt capitals, shaped long door and bracket feet, 89" h **$2,760**

French, Provincial Renaissance style, quarter strike mobilier, serpentine cresting above glass door, brass face depicting courting couple, single train movement with quarter chiming on two bells, hour strike on one bell, case carved with strap work and mask, 19th C, 94" h **$1,400**

Mulliken, Nathaniel, Lexington, Massachusetts, walnut, hood with molded flat cornice above arched molding, glazed tombstone door with flanking engraved columns, engraved brass dial with brass spandrel, boss in arch engraved "Nath Mulliken LEXINGTON" above chapter ring, seconds indicator, and calendar aperture, waist with thumb-molded door, base with applied thumb-molded panel, bracket feet, refinished, restored, c1760, 87" h **$7,650**

Mulliken, Joseph, Concord, Massachusetts, Federal, cherry, hood with pierced fretwork joining sq plinths and brass ball finials above arched cornice molding, iron painted tombstone dial with bird and floral designs inscribed "J. Mulliken Concord," eight-day weight-driven movement, flanked by free-standing reeded columns, waist with molded rect door flanked by reeded quarter columns on base with inlaid stringing joining corner quarter

fans on flat molding, imperfections, lacks hood door and feet, c1800-10, 88-3/4" h **$4,700**

Mulliken II, Nathaniel, Lexington, Massachusetts, attributed to, mahogany and cherry, hood with broken arched cornice molding, three sq plinths, tombstone glazed door with flanking engaged columns, brass dial with cast spandrels, silvered banner in arch engraved "Nath. Mulliken + Lexington," above the boss with engraved eagle on branch, silvered chapter ring, seconds indicator, calendar aperture, eight-day weight-driven movement, waist with thumb-molded door, molded base, refinished, loss of height, restored, c1770-75, 88" h **$7,650**

Munroe, Daniel, Concord, Massachusetts, Federal, mahogany, hood with pierced fretwork joining three reeded brass stop fluted plinths above arched cornice molding, glazed inlaid tombstone door enclosing polychrome iron moon phase dial with floral spandrels, polychrome indicator, calendar aperture inscribed "Daniel Munroe," eight-day weight-driven movement, flanked by reeded brass stop-fluted columns, rect inlaid waist door flanked by reeded brass stop-fluted quarter columns on inlaid base ending in molding, feet missing, restored fretwork, c1810, 85-1/2" h **$17,625**

Nash, William, Bridge, England, George III, works signed, brass and steel face with date aperture and seconds dial, inlaid mahogany case with swan's neck cresting, columnar supports, cross-banded door inlaid with shell, bracket feet, 85" h **$6,900**

Parke, Soloman, Phila, cherry, replaced dial, late 18th/early 19th C **$7,700**

Read, A., Hepplewhite, country, cherry with old mellow refinishing, bonnet with turned front columns and reeded pilasters in back, broken arch pediment and chip carving on arch, waist with chamfered corners, lamb's tongues and molded edge door, molding between sections, cutout feet and apron, painted wood face labeled "A. Read & Co. Xenia, Ohio," polychrome flowers and vintage dec, wooden works replaced with electric movement, age crack in base, minor pierced repairs, 94-1/2" h **$4,400**

Smith, Benjamin, Provincial, works signed by Benjamin Smith, Leeds, brass face, steel chapter ring, two-train movement, lunar arch, date dial and subsidiary seconds hand, pierced spandrels, inlaid oak case with broken arch cresting, checkered banding, inlaid with shell and fans, bracket feet, 96" h **$7,495**

Taber, Elnathan, Roxbury, Massachusetts , Federal, dial sgd "E. Taber, Roxbury," painted iron dial with calendar aperture, seconds hand, gilt spandrels, two ships, one flying American flag in the arch of dial, eight-day movement, mahogany veneer inlaid case with pierced fretwork, fluted plinths, brass stop fluted free-standing columns flanking bonnet above waist door with applied moldings, flanked by engaged brass stop fluted quarter columns with brass capitals and bases, waist door opens to reveal early 19th C label "Directions for Setting Up a Clock" above box base with inlay in outline, curving skirt, French feet, refinished, imperfections, c1815, 92" h **$48,875**

Unidentified American maker

Federal, Massachusetts, inlaid mahogany, upper case with three spire and ball finials, open fretwork cornice, arched door and painted metal face with flowerhead spandrels and portrait of Washington and flags in the arch, two-train movement and subsidiary seconds dial, mid case with rect door and brass stop-fluted quarter columns, plinth with flared French feet, inlaid checked banding throughout, restorations, c1810-20, 95" h **$9,990**

Hepplewhite, cherry, inlaid, swan neck pediment with carved rosettes, vase finial, barber pole and vine and berry inlay on hood, barber pole, vine inlay, and inlaid oval at waist, 97" h **$15,275**

Weiser, Martin, Northampton, Pennsylvania, Chippendale, softwood, painted red, brown arch pediment, spiral carved finials, carved rosettes, arched side lights, turned and reeded column supports, shaped pendulum door with wrought iron rattail hinges, reeded quarter columns, molded base with raised panel with carved oblong rosette and ogee bracket feet, 30 hour movement, illuminated dial with bird and floral motif, dated register, some minor in-painting on dial, minor repair to bonnet, 92" h **$13,750**

Willard, Benjamin, Lexington, Massachusetts, cherry, brass dial inscribed "Benjamin Willard Lexington," boss inscribed "Tempus fugit," cast brass spandrels, silvered chapter ring, second hand, calendar aperture, eight-day time and strike movement, pagoda style bonnet, fluted plinths above scalloped waist door, molded box base, refinished case, restoration to bonnet, c1771, 82" h **$12,650**

Willard, Simon, Roxbury, Massachusetts, Federal, dial indistinctly sgd, eight-day time and strike movement, mahogany inlaid case with pierced fret on bonnet, American dial with "S+N" on reverse, rocking ship flying two American flags in arch of dial, painted rose spandrels and gilt outline, flanked by brass stop-fluted free-standing columns above waist door with applied molding, cross-banded veneer, boxed inlaid base, sq feet, refinished, height loss, replaced feet, c1800, 93-1/2" h.............. **$37,375**

Wismer, Henry, Plumstead, Bucks County, Pennsylvania, cherry, hood with molded broken-arch resting, carved floral rosettes, three plinths with turned finials, glazed tombstone door, polychrome iron dial, basket of fruit in arch, seashell spandrels, calendar aperture signed "Henry Wismer B.C.," brass weight-driven striking pull-up movement, flanked by turned columns, waist with door flanked by four ring-turned columns, base with canted corners, flaring French feet, old surface, c1820, 95-1/2" h............ **$5,875**

Wood, David, Newburyport, Massachusetts, Federal, cherry and maple, hood with three reeded plinths above arched molding, glazed tombstone door, polychrome and gilt dial with fruit designs, seconds indicator, calendar aperture inscribed "D. Wood," brass weight-driven movement, flanked by reeded columns, cock-beaded waist door flanked by reeded quarter columns, cove molding, base with reeded band and cut-out feet, engraved label affixed to back of door "David Wood, watch and clockmaker," refinished, imperfections, c1800-15, 89" h... **$8,820**

Wall

Automaton movement, Friesland, arched hood, face painted with central landscape scene within chapter ring with hours and seconds, allegorical women in corners, arch with automaton figures of jumping dog, peddler, child on hobby horse, painted bracket case, 39" l................... **$765**

Banjo

Abbott, Samuel, Boston, Massachusetts, attributed to, Federal, mahogany, painted dial, "A"-shaped brass weight-driven eight-day movement, reverse painted throat glass flanked by gilded rope twist and brass side arms, lower eglomise glass depicting in polychrome "Lafayette the Friend of Liberty," restoration, c1815-25, 33-1/2" h.............. **$1,955**

Tall case, English, mahogany, brass face, bracket feet, 19th C, 19-1/2" w, 10" d, 87" h, **$1,700.**
Photo courtesy of David Rago Auctions, Inc.

Cummens, William, Boston, Massachusetts, Federal, dial sgd "warranted by Wm. Cummens," convex painted iron dial enclosed by convex glass and bezel topped by acorn finial, molded mahogany veneer case, T-bridge eight-day weight-driven movement, reverse painted throat glass, flanked by side arms, eglomise tablet marked "Patent" in box base, restoration, c1820, 34" h **$6,325**

Currier, Edmund, Salem, Massachusetts, Federal, dial sgd "E. Currier Salem," eight-day weight-driven movement, throat glass panel reads "Patent," lower reverse painted glass reads "E. Currier Salem" above

Tall case, New Jersey, Federal, mahogany, broken arch bonnet with line and oval inlays, white painted face, signed "Joakim Hill, Flemington," case with arched door flanked by fluted quarter columns over rectangular base, scrolled skirt and bracket feet in overall line, oval, and circular inlays, c1800, 93" h, **$14,950.**
Photo courtesy of Pook & Pook, Inc.

gilt bracket, restoration, c1820, 41-3/4" h **$3,335**

Curtis and Dunning, Concord, Massachusetts, Federal, dial sgd "warranted by Curtis and Dunning," eight-day weight-driven movement, mahogany case with brass bezel and convex glass, tapering throat with reverse painted glass flanked by brass side arms, box base with eglomise panel, rope twist giltwood in outline, period throat glass broken, c1815, 33-1/2" h **$5,175**

Curtis, Lemuel, Concord, Massachusetts, Federal, brass eagle finials, mahogany and gilt gesso case, brass bezel, painted and gilt iron dial inscribed "warranted by L. Curtis," eight-day weight-driven movement, throat glass enclosing thermometer, inscribed "L. Curtis Patent," lower tablet showing figures in farm landscape, both framed by gilt spiral moldings, flanked by brass side arms, restoration, imperfections, c1815, 33-1/4" h **$7,650**

Dyar, J., Concord, Massachusetts, Federal, mahogany, brass eagle finial above brass bezel, painted metal dial, reading "Warranted by J. Dyar," eight-day eight-drive movement, foliate throat glass reading "Patent," flanked by rope twist dec, brass side arms, lower tablet with eglomise naval battle framed by applied rope twist moldings, lower tablet replaced, other imperfections, c1815, 32-3/4" h **$2,820**

Munroe and Whiting, Concord, Massachusetts, Federal, gilt mahogany, acorn-form finial, iron painted dial enclosing eight-day weight-driven movement, foliate throat glass flanked by side arms, lower panel depicting ship battle, both within rope twist dec frames, lower tablet replaced, other imperfections, c1808-17, 33" h **$1,880**

Noyes, L. W., Nashua, New Hampshire, Federal, mahogany, brass belted ball finial, brass bezel, printed dial, eight-day weight-drive movement, throat glass flanked by brass side arms and tablet with foliate and eagle devices framed by half round moldings, restoration including tablets, c1825, 34" h **$1,765**

Sawin, John and John W. Dyer, Boston, Massachusetts, Federal,

giltwood and mahogany, dial sgd "Sawin and Dyer, Boston," acorn finial above convex glass and brass bezel, brass eight-day weight-driven movement, glass throat panel reads "Patent" flanked by brass side arms over lower glass eglomise tablet which depicts seaside hotel, reads "Nahant," minor restoration, c1825, 33" h **$4,025**

Unidentified maker

Concord, Massachusetts, Federal, gilt and mahogany brass ball finial above brass bezel and dial, eight-day weight-driven movement, foliate throat glass reading "PATENT" flanked by brass side arms, lower tablet depicting battle between the Constitution and the Guerriere, both framed by applied rope twist dec, imperfections, c1815, 35" h **$2,475**

Unsigned painted dial, Concord-type eight-day brass weight drive movement, carved wooden eagle finial, throat glass panel reading "Patent," flanked by brass side arms over reverse painted glass panel in box base, restoration, 33-1/2" h **$2,875**

Unidentified Massachusetts maker, Classical, mahogany and mahogany veneer, acorn finial, molded bezel, painted metal dial, brass eight-day weight-driven movement, lyre-form throat, rect pendulum box, both with eglomise tablets, molded bracket with acorn pendant, restored, c1825, 38-3/4" h **$1,300**

Willard, Aaron, Jr., Boston, Massachusetts

Classical, carved mahogany, lyre, urn-turned finial above molded wooden bezel, painted metal dial inscribed "A Willard, Jr., Boston," eight-day weight-driven movement above acanthus leaf scroll-carved throat and pendulum box, both with eglomise tablets, molded bracket, old refinish, old replaced tablets, accompanied by bill of sale dated 1946 for $200, c1825, 40-1/2" h **$10,575**

Federal, mahogany case, molded brass bezel, painted zinc dial, brass eight-day weight-driven movement stamped "A Willard Jr Boston," above half-round molded throat and pendulum and eglomise tablets, imperfections, c1820, 28-1/2" h **$1,645**

Willard, Simon, Roxbury, Massachusetts, Federal, mahogany, unmarked dial, eight-day weight driven T-bridge movement with stepped train, escapement in case with cross-banded veneer, brass side arms, reverse painted throat glass above lower eglomise tablet which reads "S. Willard's Patent," restoration, c1805, 33-1/2" h **$10,350**

Girandole, J. L. Dunning, attributed to, Burlington, Vermont, Classical, carved mahogany, molded wooden bezel, painted iron dial inscribed "..Dunning," brass weight-driven movement above tapering molded throat with mahogany panel flanked by carved scroll side pieces, circular molded door with pierced mahogany panel, scroll carved acanthus leaf bracket, imperfections, c1818-20, 39" h **$62,275**

Lyre, Chandler, Abiel, Concord, New Hampshire, Classical, dial sgd "A. Chandler," striking brass eight-day weight-driven movement, leaf carved mahogany veneer case with bracket, refinished, imperfections, c1825, 43" h **$17,250**

Mirror

Chandler, Abiel, Concord, New Hampshire, gilt gesso and wood, gilt and black painted split baluster door with stencil and painted tablet, mirror below, painted iron dial inscribed "A. Chandler," brass eight-day weight-driven movement, maker's label affixed to backboard, minor imperfections, c1825, 13-3/4" w, 4" d, 29" h **$8,225**

Morrill, Benjamin, Boscawen, New Hampshire, late Federal, dial sgd "B. Morrill Boscawen, N.H.," c1825, eight-day wheelbarrow movement surrounded by gilded spandrels above mirror glass, flanked by gilded and painted split baluster columns, restoration, c1825, 31-3/4" h **$3,740**

Unidentified, attributed to New Hampshire, giltwood and gesso, gilt split baluster framed door with eglomise tablet and mirror below, painted tin dial set into wooden frame enclosing a brass eight-day rack and snail movement, imperfections including replaced

tablet, c1825, 13" w, 4-1/4" d, 29-1/2" h **$1,800**

Spiderweb, Nelson, George, for Howard Miller, wood center, white enameled metal rays, black string, black Howard Miller decal, No. 2214, 18-1/2" h **$1,150**

Watchman, Morrill, Benjamin, Boscawen, New Hampshire, 1860s, rect birch box case, painted iron dial marked "B. Morrill Boscawen," eight-day weight-driven brass movement, imperfections, 54-1/2" h **$2,875**

CLOISONNÉ

History: Cloisonné is the art of enameling on metal. The design is drawn on the metal body, then wires, which follow the design, are glued or soldered on. The cells thus created are packed with enamel and fired; this step is repeated several times until the level of enamel is higher than the wires. A buffing and polishing process brings the level of enamels flush to the surface of the wires.

This art form has been practiced in various countries since 1300 B.C. and in the Orient since the early 15th century. Most cloisonné found today is from the late Victorian era, 1870-1900, and was made in China or Japan.

Box, cov, rounded form, butterflies among flowering branches, turquoise ground, Chinese, 19th C, 4-3/4" d, 2-3/4" h **$345**

Candlesticks, pr, figural, brass, blue mythical animals seated on round dark red base with open-work sides, three feet, each animal holds flower in mouth, red candle socket on back, 7-1/8" h **$200**

Cane, Japanese cloisonné handle, 1-1/3" d x 9-1/2" l, dark blue ground, long scaly three-toed Japanese dragon in shades of white, pale blue, black, and brown, 1/3" gold gilt collar, black hardwood shaft, 7/8" horn ferrule, fashioned in England, c1890, 36" l **$1,460**

Cup, ftd, butterflies and flowers, lappet borders, Chinese, 19th C, 4" h **$100**

Desk set, brush pot, pen, pen tray, blotter, and paper holder, Japanese, price for set **$130**

Figure, Killin, riders atop their backs, one saddle blanket dec with house floating on clouds above waves, other with crane flying above mountainous landscape, Chinese, losses to enamel, pr, late 19th or early 20th C, 11-3/4" h **$800**

Incense burner, globular, three dragon-head feet, high curving handles, scrolling lotus and ancient bronzes motif, openwork lid, dragon finial, raised Quinlong six-character mark, damage, 19-3/4" h **$815**

Jar, cov, ovoid, even green over central band of scrolling flowers, dome lid, ovoid finial, marked "Ando Jubei," 20th C, 6" h **$230**

Jardinière, bronze, bands of cloisonné designs, golden yellow and blue triangles, polychrome geometric designs on dark blue, chrysanthemums on light blue, cast relief scene of water lily, turtle, and flowering branches on int., soldered repair at foot, 13" d, 10" h **$220**

Vase, rectangular form, slender body, four panels profusely decorated with flowers, silver wire, dark blue enamel on shoulder and bottom, Japan, Meiji period, light cracks on shoulder, chip at neck, 7-1/4" h, **$850.**

Planter, quatralobe, classical symbol and scroll dec, blue ground, Chinese, 11" l, pr..**$200**

Scepter, three cloisonné plaques inset with wooden cloud-carved frame, China, early 20th C, 22" l..........**$125**

Tea kettle, multicolored scrolling lotus, medium-blue ground, lappets border, waisted neck with band of raised auspicious symbols between key-fret borders, floral form finial, double handles, Chinese, 19th C, 10-1/2" h................................**$690**

Teapot, central band of flowering chrysanthemums on pink ground, shoulder with shaped cartouches of phoenix and dragon on floral and patterned ground, lower border with chrysanthemum blossom on swirling ground, flat base with three small raised feet, single chrysanthemum design, spout and handle with floral design, lid with two writhing dragons on peach-colored ground, Japanese, late 19th/early 20th C, 4-3/4" d, 3-1/4" h................................**$4,025**

Urn, ovoid, slightly waisted neck, peony dec, black ground, base plaque marked "Takeuchi Chubei," Japanese, Shichi Ho Company, Owari, late 19th C, 23-3/4" h....................**$690**

Vase

Animal head handles, gilt rims and bases, China, 19th C, pr, 3" h **$375**

Lobed form, blue ground, design of phoenix, dragons, and flowers, China, late 18th/early 19th C, 16-1/2" h................................**$1,530**

Surface of minuscule scrolling with scattered chrysanthemums, possibly by Namikawa, unsigned, Japan, Meiji period (1868-1911), 6" h..........**$725**

Two birds taking flight from flowering tree, cluster of plants on back side, gold wire cloisons on dark blue ground, band of shippo designs on mouth rim and base, silver rims, bottom rim mkd "silver," base with Hayashi Kondenji inlaid mark, Japan, Meiji period, 3-3/4" h..............**$3,750**

CLOTHING AND CLOTHING ACCESSORIES

History: While museums and a few private individuals have collected clothing for decades, it is only recently that collecting clothing has achieved a widespread popularity. Clothing reflects the social attitudes of a historical period.

Christening and wedding gowns abound and, hence, are not in large demand. Among the hardest items to find is men's clothing from the 19th and early 20th centuries. The most sought after clothing is by designers, such as Fortuny, Poirret, and Vionnet.

Note: Condition, size, age, and completeness are critical factors in purchasing clothing. Collectors divide into two groups: those collecting for aesthetic and historic value and those desiring to wear the garment. Prices are higher on the West Coast; major auction houses focus on designer clothes and high-fashion items.

Afternoon dress

Dark gray silk, pleated skirt, black lace trim on bodice, c1880 ....**$60**

Pale blue lawn, two-pc, white crocheted buttons, white dotted Swiss detailing on bodice, c1900 ....**$95**

Rust silk, two-pc, train, fitted bodice trimmed with tan silk knotted fringe, silk covered buttons, c1880 ....**$450**

White dotted tulle, two-pc, lace yoke, pin tucks, ruffles, lace cuffs, c1890 ....**$75**

White lawn, white cotton embroidery, filet lace insertion, rows of mother-of-pearl buttons on front, c1910 ....**$225**

White linen, elbow-length sleeves, fitted waistline, crocheted buttons up back of bodice, cotton floral embroidery and trim, c1900 ....**$250**

Beaded dress, black silk crepe and silk chiffon over black taffeta, embroidered all over with black glass beads, black silk chiffon drape from waistline, labeled "Best & Co.," c1940 ....**$200**

Bed jacket, pale blue quilted satin, c1950 ....**$40**

Belt, Hermes, wide beige leather belt, gold tone pyramidal hardware, 31" l **$200**

Blouse

Black dotted net, long sleeves, pin tucks, lace insertion at neckline, c1910 ....**$45**

Cream bobbin lace over net, Battenberg lace yoke, stand-up collar, elbow-length sleeves, c1900 ....**$90**

Ivory silk, gray satin floral embroidery, c1955................................**$35**

White lawn, embroidery and lace insertion, minor edge damage to collar, c1890................................**$30**

Cape

Black velvet, modified Napoleon collar, single button closure, lined with black quilted satin, c1930 ....**$60**

Black wool, black silk lining, rows of black glass beads trim, c1900 ....**$35**

Rose silk velvet, fully lined with pale green silk crepe, wide collar, single button closure, c1920 ....**$195**

Capelet, black, glass beaded trim, open work, fringe, c1890............**$40**

Chemise, linen, ruffles and lace at cuffs, late 18th/early 19th C..........**$25**

Collar

Black net, attached yoke, elaborately embroidered with black glass beads, c1890................................**$30**

Black silk and velvet, steel beading, c1890................................**$25**

Coat, woman's

Black silk velvet, black silk appliqués, cream silk satin lining, black soutache on lapels, red wool appliqué and gold embroidery, labeled "Lazarus Bros, Wilksbarre, PA, c1910 ....**$250**

Black wool cashmere, long sleeves, black satin lining, deep cape of black fur, labeled "Kraeler, Jeannette, Reading, Harrisburg," c1940 ....**$900**

Brown wool, brown silk velvet trim on front, collar, capelet, and cuffs, padded, fully lined in brown silk, c1870................................**$75**

Dress

Black cotton sleeveless, double breasted style, large collar, gray buttons **$30**

Black silk crepe, scallops at sleeves, cream embroidered silk cuffs and collar, wrap style, labeled "Lucille Ltd., New York," c1915 .... **$195**

Burgundy satin brocade, wrap style bodice with frogs, mandarin collar, "Hand Made in Hong Kong, 100% Rayon Brocade," c1955 .... **$90**

Bustle, two-pc, brown silk damask and brown silk, ruching and ruffles on bustle skirt, tan shell buttons on front, later added collar, c1870 .... **$275**

Iridescent mauve and green silk, hand stitched, full skirt gathered at waistline with smocking, pagoda sleeves, rose silk braid and fringe, lace under sleeves, hidden inside pocket, c1850 .... **$65**

Navy blue and white cotton calico wrapper, ruffle at hem, capelet effect at yoke, some old repairs, c1900 .... **$25**

Rust silk crepe, detailed at bodice and hem with cream silk, embroidered with pink, tangerine, aqua, and green satin flowers, labeled "New York, Paris, Claire Gowns, Made by Starr and Herbert," c1920 .... **$120**

Dressing gown, white voile, lace trim, blue and white flowers, c1950 .... **$65**

Frock, tan cotton print, tangerine and blue paisley detailing, brown carved buttons, some old repairs, minor fading, c1880 .... **$65**

Gown

Black velvet, full skirt, silk rose detailing, cream organdy collar, labeled "Trains-Norell," c1950 .... **$75**

Brown lace full-length, brown chenille embroidery on net over brown net, crepe chartreuse velvet sash with brown carved Bakelite buckle, c1930 .... **$125**

Charcoal gray and green silk velvet, pin tucks and smocking on sleeves, deep V-neckline, c1930 .... **$95**

Deep aqua silk chiffon, elaborately embroidered with freeform shapes of clear glass beads, blue, rose, and white glass beaded Art Deco motifs, c1920 .... **$550**

Gold and rust floral printed silk chiffon, cape collar, underpinnings of tan silk crepe, c1930 .... **$85**

*Evening wear and lingerie, left to right: gown, iridescent purple strapless style, ruching from bodice to near hem, purple taffeta lining, cotton floral appliqué, late 1950s, **$65**; evening coat, navy blue silk etched velvet with roses pattern, elbow length sleeves, single button closure, silk satin lining, mid-1950s, **$45**; teddy, pale pink crème, tan fillet lace, silk ribbon appliqué, early 1900s, **$40**.*

Gray and blue woven silk with cream stripe, pagoda sleeves, ruching on bodice, cream braid on sleeves and bodice, bodice lined with cream linen, c1865 .... **$95**

Mauve silk chiffon, sleeveless, elaborately embroidered with lilac satin threads, silver glass beads in Art Deco motif, lilac feather trim at hem, underpinnings of ivory silk chiffon, c1920 .... **$275**

Pale green silk chiffon, trimmed with pale green silk satin, embroidered at scalloped hem with silver and white glass beads, prong-set rhinestones, c1925 .... **$175**

Pale lilac silk, sq cut steel buttons, cream lace collar, bubble-effect skirt, draped back, wear, c1900 .... **$60**

Pumpkin and lilac silk etched velvet, sleeveless, floral design, fur at hem, c1920 .... **$275**

Sheer cream silk in windowpane weave, overprinted with sepia, rose, and blue floral pattern, silk trim at cuffs, bodice lined with cream muslin, c1820 .... **$500**

Tan silk, long sleeves, dropped waistline, button detailing, embroidery, c1920 .... **$75**

Handbag

Alligator, brown, brass clasp, brown leather lining, c1945 .... **$45**

*Bonnet, child's, brown crochet work, silk ribbon ties, mid-1800s, **$65**.*

*Bonnet, sun type, gray denim with stitching, ruffles, and large bow, early 1920s, **$45**.*

*Dresses, left: Lillie Rubin gown, black silk embroidered all over with black glass beads, halter-style neckline, single strap on low back, labeled "Lillie Rubin, 100% silk, Made in China, Size 4," 1970s, **$175**; center: black velvet cape, embroidered on pockets with rhinestones and large black beads, black satin lining, single button closure at neckline, early 1950s, **$95**; right: dress, navy cotton crochet, elbow length sleeves, long fringe, deep scoop neckline, satin fringe hem, mid-1940s, **$115**.*

Black silk faille, embroidered with black glass beads, matching fringe, c1900 .... **$95**

Floral tapestry, rose, green, and blue on cream ground, black border, brass frame with chain handle, c1940, 8-1/2" x 5-1/2" **$30**

Shoes, left: black silk pumps, steel buckles, c1910, $45; right: brown suede pumps with perforations on uppers, brown silk ties, early 1920s, $35.

Hand bags, beaded, left to right: glass beaded with peacock motif on both sides, royal blue and aqua, burgundy flowers, black and yellow geometric shapes, elaborately embossed frame with chain handle, early 1900s, 7" x 8-1/2" plus fringe, $350; glass beaded on both sides in floral design, shades of rose, blue, and green on cream ground, embossed brass frame with chain handle, mauve silk lining, small oval mirror and rosettes, early 1900s, 8" x 11" plus fringe, $300

Hermes, Cabana, large blue leather form, silver tone hardware, two shoulder straps, leather interior with four pockets, 37 cm **$1,765**

Hermes, Constance, rigid red alligator form, gold tone hardware, large "H"-shaped magnetic closure, shoulder strap, leather interior with two pockets, 23 cm **$3,525**

Hermes, Kelly, supple black calfskin form, gold tone hardware, detachable shoulder strap, leather interior with three pockets, 30 cm **$2,350**

Hermes, Kelly, rigid blue alligator form, gold tone hardware, detachable shoulder strap, leather interior with three pockets, boxed, orig felt protection insert, 33 cm **$10,340**

Hermes, Kelly, rigid pebbled brown leather form, gold tone hardware, detachable shoulder strap, leather

interior with three pockets, boxed, orig felt protection insert, 32 cm **$4,820**

Mesh, 10k yg, pierced and scalloped top set with four old mine-cut diamonds, approx 1.12 cts., three oval cabochon turquoise, suspended by trace link chain and gold safety pin, stamped No. "6," European hallmark, c1915, 67.0 dwt..........**$1,120**

Mesh, 14k yg, Edwardian, designed with a floral and scroll frame, the bypass-style thumb piece set with two sugarloaf sapphires joined by a trace link chain, 132.5 dwt. **$1,116.75**

Mesh, 14k yg, Edwardian, pierced, chased, and engraved floral and foliate closure, suspended from a curb link chain, 96.7 dwt........**$835**

Silver and enamel, Birmingham, England, 1938, maker's mark "EJH," oval, lid with lavender basse taille enamel, leather lined interior, silver link chain, monogrammed, 6-1/4" l, 3-7/8" d **$250**

Hat, lady's fashion type

Aqua silk pillbox, aqua veil, colorful beads, embroidery, c1960 ....**$50**

Black velour, wide brim, black feathers, black and white ostrich plumes, c1910 ....**$95**

Wide-brimmed black velvet, under brim of blue velvet, blue ostrich plume, silver stamped on the black silk lining "Dives Pomeroy & Stewart," c1910 ....**$150**

Wide-brimmed natural straw, gold grosgrain ribbon, white cotton daisies, labeled "Jean Allen," c1945 ....**$35**

Hat, man's, top hat, orig box **$85**

Jacket

Battenburg cream lace, long sleeves, gathering at shoulders, c1890 .....**$350**

Lace, cream Irish crochet, borders of elaborate Irish crochet with shamrock motif, V-neckline, four tan crocheted buttons, c1910.........**$325**

Silk velvet, purple, lined with purple silk, fabric covered buttons, patch pockets, c1890 ....**$120**

Wool flannel, black, bolero, black taffeta lining, black fur trim, c1955 ....**$65**

Lingerie dress

White batiste, embroidery and lace insertion on bodice, and skirt,

ruching below waistline, c1910 ....**$45**

White eyelet lace, white lawn, detailed bodice with pin tucks, lace yoke and collar, scalloped hem, c1900 ....**$65**

White lawn, eyelet lace, lace insertion, ruffles at hem, c1790 ....**$375**

Nightgown

Pajamas, leopard print flannel, Dora Lee, unworn, c1950 ....**$35**

Pale pink satin, diminutive roses pattern, cut on bias, c1940.............**$35**

Pants suit, charcoal gray wool flannel, long sleeved tunic top, high collar, straight legged pants, entirely set with prong-set rhinestones, fully lined, labeled "Made In The British Crown Colony of Hong Kong, Best & Co., Fifth Ave, New York," several rhinestones loose, c1960............**$70**

White cotton, embroidered yoke, buttons up front, c1910 ....**$35**

White cotton, lace cutwork yoke, embroidered, matching lace cuffs, c1910 ....**$55**

Petticoat

Cream organdy, pin tucks, lace, ruffles at hem, train, c1890 ....**$35**

White cotton, scalloped eyelet lace hem, front tucked panel, c1880 ....**$40**

Robe, printed green, tan, gray, yellow, and ivory silk, swirls, floral, and feather shapes, c1945 ....**$60**

Scarf, Hermes, silk

Cosmos, blue and white horse-drawn chariots riding upon clouds on light blue and purple background **$250**

Fetes Venitiennes, harlequins and guests at masquerade ball on background of brown, orange and purple...**$200**

Shawl

Cream silk, floral cream satin embroidery, knotted fringe, braided dec, back tassel, c1890 ....**$150**

Ivory silk, floral ivory satin embroidery, knotted satin fringe, Spanish, c1900, 44" sq..............................**$75**

Slip

Ivory silk, net darning trim in floral design, camisole top lace straps, ivory satin embroidery, c1910 ....**$65**

Woven silk taffeta, light gray plaid, rose and green satin flowers, long knotted silk fringe, c1900, 70" sq **$125**

Skirt, lace alternating with voile, black, train, underpinnings of cream silk taffeta, pinking and ruffles, c1870, some minor damage on tulle and lining **$150**

Smoking jacket, man's, silver and black floral design brocade, black silk faille lapels, black silk lining, c1950 .... **$25**

Suit, gray wool tweed, fabric cov buttons, button detailing on jacket pockets, lined with pale gray crepe, flared skirt with gores, "Freiss Orig" label, c1945 .... **$110**

Sweater

Beige cashmere, double lining of beige lace and nylon, long sleeves, rhinestone buttons, rhinestone clasp at waistline, tan mink snap-on collar, some rhinestones missing from clasp, c1955 .... **$40**

Black cashmere, labeled "Made in Scotland for Liberty of London" **$35**

Umbrella

Black silk, silver handle formed as looped snake, Continental, English import hallmarks for London, 1904, 7-1/8" l handle, 36" l overall **$150**

Gold, brown, orange, and yellow paisley ruffle, unused, orig gold and black hang tag for "Made in U.S.A., 100% Nylon," orig Strawbridge & Clothier box, c1955 .... **$45**

Round tapered handle with stamped and engraved vertical bands of leafy scrolls and flowerheads, mother-of-pearl central band, 7-5/8" l handle, 31" l overall **$230**

Vest, white cotton, mother-of-pearl buttons, c1910 .... **$65**

Visiting dress

Dark blue silk, dark blue, bodice and sleeves with light gray silk satin in geometric designs, elaborate embroidery on skirt, underpinnings of lace-trimmed cream silk, embroidered organdy collar, labeled "Rendel, Paris, London, New York," c1900 .... **$100**

Pale pink silk, two-pc, pintucks, lace appliqué, lace cuffs, c1890 .... **$65**

Purple linen, elaborate fabric-covered button detailing, purple silk net trim at neckline and cuffs, minor damage to net, c1910 .... **$40**

Waistcoat, gentleman's, silk, embroidered with floral vines and sprigs, two covered pockets, applied cherub-printed roundels below, England or France, restorations, late 18th C **$250**

Walking suit, wool, silk faille, chestnut brown, brown silk velvet trim, pleats at hem, fabric-covered buttons, lace collar **$325**

COCA-COLA ITEMS

History: The originator of Coca-Cola was John Pemberton, a pharmacist from Atlanta, Georgia. In 1886, Dr. Pemberton introduced a patent medicine to relieve headaches, stomach disorders, and other minor maladies. Unfortunately, his failing health and meager finances forced him to sell his interest.

In 1888, Asa G. Candler became the sole owner of Coca-Cola. Candler improved the formula, increased the advertising budget, and widened the distribution. A "patient" was accidentally given a dose of the syrup mixed with carbonated water instead of still water. The result was a tastier, more refreshing drink.

As sales increased in the 1890s, Candler recognized that the product was more suitable for the soft-drink market and began advertising it as such. From these beginnings, a myriad of advertising items have been issued to invite all to "Drink Coca-Cola."

Notes: Dates of interest: "Coke" was first used in advertising in 1941. The distinctively shaped bottle was registered as a trademark on April 12, 1960.

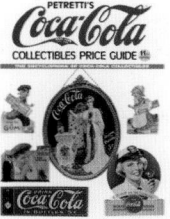

Petretti's Coca-Cola® Collectibles Price Guide, 11th Ed., by Allan Petretti, Krause Publications, Iola, WI.

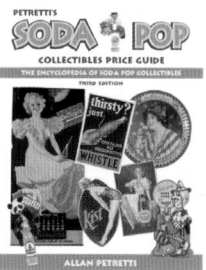

Petretti's Soda Pop Collectibles Price Guide, 3rd Ed., by Allan Petretti, Krause Publications, Iola, WI.

Binder, rigid cardboard, red oilcloth cover, four-ring metal binder to hold advertising sales sheets, no contents, c1950, 13" x 15-1/2" **$48**

Bookmark, Romance of Coca-Cola, 1916 .... **$30**

Bottle

Amber, marked "Lewisburg" **$30**

Christmas, Williamstown, West Virginia **$15**

Commemorative, NASCAR Series, Bill Elliott, Dale Earnhardt, or Bobby Labonte **$5**

Bowl, Vernon Ware, green, artificial ice, C-9.8, 1930s, 10" w **$600**

Calendar, Hamilton King illus, 1913, 13-1/2" x 22-1/2" **$900**

Ceiling globe, milk glass, four logos, C-9.5, 1930s, 14" d **$990**

Clock, octagonal, neon, silhouette girl, C-8.5, 1939, 18" **$1,800**

Cooler, Victor, triple-door, attached counter, mounted jukebox, brass foot rail, three floor-mounted bar stools, restored **$5,775**

Cut-out, 1926, girl under umbrella **$3,995**

Door kick plate, litho tin, scrolling Drink Coca-Cola logo, 11-1/2" x 35"
1923 bottle on left, C-9.9 .... **$1,765**
1942, couple on right, C-9.9 .... **$2,600**

Door pull, plastic and metal, bottle shape, orig instructions and screws, C-9.3-9.5, 8" h **$275**

Dry-server, unused **$5**

Game board, Steps to Health, prepared and distributed by Coca-Cola Co. of Canada, Ltd., orig unmarked brown paper envelope, copyright 1938, 11-1/4" x 26-1/2" **$60**

Mileage meter, originating in Statesville, NC, C-8.4, 10" x 7" **$1,675**

Pin, Hi-Fi Club, gold luster finish, detailed plastic, short metal stickpin, miniature Coke bottle about name in red lettering, phonograph record background inscribed "Sponsored By Your Coca-Cola Bottler," Australian issue, c1950 .... **$40**

Plate, Vienna Art, topless woman **$1,610**

Pocket mirror, oval, celluloid, pretty girl, dark green ground, white and red lettering, 1914, 1-3/4" w, 2-3/4" h **$400**

Poster, two farm girls taking a break, caption "Work Refreshed," 1943 .... **$2,750**

Prize chance card, printed in red and black on white, unused, c1940, 4-1/4" x 5-1/4" **$12**

Radio

Bottle shape, 1930s, C-8.2, 24" h, ... **$8,500**

Cooler shape, red, 1950s **$2,250**

Salesman's sample, cooler, Glasscock **$10,450**

Sandwich plate, white ground, script slogan, bottle and glass in center, Knowles, C-9.8, 7-1/4" d **$750**

Sign, porcelain

Diecut, two-color, script, orig box, attaching instructions, screws, C-10, 6" x 18" **$1,100**

Porcelain, diagonal slash, fountain service, C-9.7, 1934, 23" x 26" **$4,700**

Porcelain, single bottle in center, no slogan, C-9.2, 1950, 24" d **$1,800**

Porcelain, curb-side service, two-sided, green, red, and white, C-9.6, 1933, 60" x 42" **$3,000**

Sign, tin

Drink Coca-Cola, emb tin litho, vertical, C.8.5, c1931, 12-1/4" x 4-1/2" **$625**

Drink Coca-Cola, Ice Cold, Gas To-Day, tin, 1936 .... **$2,700**

Sign, wood, Drink Coca-Cola, fancy metal filigree at top, orig Kay Display label on back, C.8+, c1930, 11-3/8" x 9" **$775**

String holder, two-sided, showing six-lace and logo "Take Home in Cartons," C-9.5, 1940s **$4,000**

Thermometer, round, red and white, c1950, 12" d **$180**

Toy, van, Corgi, 5" l diecast metal and plastic replica, copyright 1978, 2-3/4" x 6" x 3-1/2" color box with display window **$35**

Bingo cards, diecut, lot of three, each 8-1/2" x 9" cardboard card printed on front in red and black, each has 25 diecut windows which reveal different numbers for use in calling Bingo game, text across bottom "Compliments Coca-Cola Bottling Co," issued by Kemper-Thomas, Cincinnati, OH. Some surface dust soil, bit of light wear around edges, right side of bottom of each has original owner's initials in blue ballpoint pen, 1940s, **$25.**
Photo courtesy of Hake's Americana & Collectibles.

Toy, delivery truck, Buddy L, pressed steel, yellow body, red, white, and black decals, no bottles, **$45.**
Photo courtesy of Dotta Auction Co., Inc.

Tray, Springboard Girl, American Art Works, Coshocton, OH, 1939, 13-1/2" x 10-1/2", **$425.**
Photo courtesy of Joy Luke Auctions.

Tray, Roadster, American Art Works, Coshocton, OH, some wear and scratches, 1942, 13-1/4" x 10-1/2", **$88.**
Photo courtesy of Joy Luke Auctions.

Cooler, red, "Drink Coca-Cola, It's The Real Thing," **$1,295.**

Vending machine, red and white, working condition, **$950.**

Tray

Bathing beauty, C-8, 1930 .... **$195**

Girl in convertible being waited on by another girl, C-9.5, 1942 .... **$450**

Madge Evans, C-7.5, 1935 .... **$165**

Oval, girl handing coke to viewer, C-10, 1926, 13" x 19" **$15,250**

Vending machine, Select-O-Matic, Westinghouse, six dial selector, bottle opener set into front, c1960, 23-5/8" x 21-5/8" x 64" h **$3,200**

COFFEE MILLS

History: Coffee mills or grinders are utilitarian objects designed to grind fresh coffee beans. Before the advent of stay-fresh packaging, coffee mills were a necessity.

The first home-size coffee grinders were introduced about 1890. The large commercial grinders designed for use in stores, restaurants, and hotels often bear an earlier patent date.

Arcade, wall type, crystal jar, emb design, marked "Crystal" and "Arcade" orig lid rusted, 17" h **$185**

Wood coffee mill, cast iron grinder and handle, Golden Rule, Columbus, Ohio, **$185.**
Photo courtesy of Dotta Auction Co., Inc.

Crown Coffee Mill, cast iron, mounted on wood base, decal "Crown Coffee Mill Made By Landers, Frary, & Clark, New Britain, Conn, U.S.A.," number 11 emb on top lid **$525**

Enterprise

#00, two wheels, store type, orig paint, orig decals, C8+, 12-1/2" x 7-1/2" x 8-3/4" **$1,450**

#9, orig dec and decals, bright orange/red paint, blue on top of base and edges of wheels, gold detailed lettering, drawer in base stenciled "No. 9," eagle finial, white porcelain knob, minor wear, restored break on lid, 28-1/2" h **$1,200**

Pine, fingered joints, one drawer, iron pull, iron top cup and handle, wooden knob, c1880, 5-3/4" sq, 6" h **$95**

Woodruff Edwards, Elgin, IL, store type, 28" d wheels, eagle finial, repainted, 66" h **$1,800**

COIN-OPERATED ITEMS

History: Coin-operated items include amusement games, pinball machines, jukeboxes, slot machines, vending machines, cash registers, and other items operated by coins.

The first jukebox was developed about 1934 and played 78-RPM records. Jukeboxes were important to teen-agers before the advent of portable radios and television.

The first pinball machine was introduced in 1931 by Gottlieb. Pinball machines continued to be popular until the advent of solid-state games in 1977 and advanced electronic vid-

Cast iron coffee mill, remnants of decorative decals at top, base embossed "Enterprise Mfg Co., Philadelphia, PA," **$500.**

eo games after that.

The first three-reel slot machine, the Liberty Bell, was invented in 1905 by Charles Fey in San Francisco. In 1910, Mills Novelty Company copyrighted the classic fruit symbols. Improvements and advancements have led to the sophisticated machines of today.

Vending machines for candy, gum, and peanuts were popular from 1910 until 1940 and can be found in a wide range of sizes and shapes.

Adviser: Robert Levy.

Notes: Because of the heavy usage these coin-operated items received, many are restored or, at the very least, have been repainted by either the operator or manufacturer. Using reproduced mechanisms to restore pieces is acceptable in many cases, especially when the restored piece will then perform as originally intended.

Additional Resources:

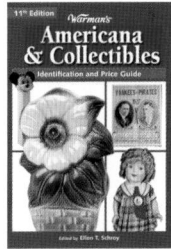

Warman's® Americana & Collectibles, 11th Ed., by Ellen T. Schroy, ed., Krause Publications, Iola, WI.

Slot machine, Mills, 1934, 5 cents, Chevron QT, **$2,200.**

Slot machine, Mills, 1938, 25 cents, Bursting Cherry, **$2,300.**

Slot machine, Mills, 5 cents, Castle, Gold Award, 1938, **$3,000.**

Arcade

Bag Puncher, Mills Novelty, 1926 .... **$4,500**

Big Bronco, Exhibit Supply, 1951 .... **$1,300**

Bowling League, Genco, 1949 .... **$800**

Hunter, Silver King, 1949 .... **$500**

Mutascope, American, 1901.....**$3000**

Slugger, Marvel, 1948................. **$550**

Gum

Big Top, Advance, capsule, 1969 .... **$300**

Cebco Hot Nut, two globes, 1930 .... **$600**

E-Z, Ad-Lee Novelty, gumballs, 1908 .... **$1,500**

Empire Vender, Lawrence, 1935 .... **$600**

Master Novelty, Atlas, 1951...... **$150**

Jukeboxes

AMI, G200, 1950 .... **$700**

Rockola, Deluxe 20, 1939.......... **$1,700**

Seeburg, HF 100R **$3,000**

Seeburg, M100B, 1955.............. **$2,000**

Wurlitzer, 700, 1940................. **$4,500**

Wurlitzer, 1015, 1946................ **$6,000**

Slot machines

Caille, Cadet, 1934 .... **$900**

Caille, Superior, 1928................. **$1,800**

Groetchen, Deluxe Columbia, 1938 .... **$900**

Jennings

Bronze Chief, 1940 .... **$1,600**

Dutchboys, 1928 .... **$1,700**

Sun Chief, 1948........................ **$3,100**

Today Vender, 1928 .... **$2,000**

Victoria Peacock, 1932............. **$3,000**

Mills

Black Cherry, 1946 .... **$1,800**

Diamond Front, 1939................ **$1,600**

Poinsettia, 1930 .... **$1,700**

Token Bell Hightop, 1948.........**$1,800**

Torch Front, 1928 .... **$1,400**

War Eagle, 1931 .... **$2,200**

Watermelon Hightop, 1948......**$2,200**

Pace

All Star Comet, 1936 .... **$1,800**

Bantam, 1930............................ **$1,800**

Deluxe Comet, 1939 .... **$1,400**

Whatling

Bird of Paradise, Rolatop, 1935 .... **$6,000**

Blue Seal, 1929......................... **$1,500**

Treasury, 1939.......................... **$3,000**

Miscellaneous

American Scale, 1937 .... **$200**

Cigarette Machine, Stoner, 1950 .... **$600**

Condom Machine, Advance, 140 .... **$150**

Gillette Razor Blades, 1940 .....**$250**

Jergens Lotion, lotion dispenser, 1937 .... **$350**

Keen Kut Razor Blades, 1940 .... **$200**

Kitco Towels, Kirch, 1936..........**$125**

National Postage, Northwestern, 1950 .... **$125**

Watling Horoscope Scale, 1957 .... **$350**

COINS

History: Coin collecting has long been one of the most respected and honored aspects of the collecting world. Today it still holds its fascination as new collectors come onto the scene every day. And just like the old-time collectors, they should be ready to spend time reading and learning more about this fascinating hobby. The States Quarter Series has spurred many of us to save quarters again and that has encouraged all types of coin collecting.

After the Declaration of Independence, America realized it needed its own coinage. Before that time, foreign coins were used in addition to paper currency. The first real coin of the young America was a copper coin, known as the Fugio Cent. Many of the early states created their own coins until the federal mint was constructed in Philadelphia after 1792. By 1837, the purity of silver was increased from 89.24 to 90 percent with minor adjustments to this weight occurring until 1873. Early dominations included a silver 3-cent piece, a gold $3 piece (1854) $1 and $20 (1849). The coinage law of 1857 eliminated the half-cent, changed the size of some coins, and forbid the use of foreign coins as legal tender. By the time of the Civil War, the two-cent and nickel three-cent pieces and the five-cent nickel were created. The phrase "In God We Trust" was added at this time. From the late 1870s, coins were plentiful. From 1873 to 1918, several laws were passed to force the government to buy silver and strike an abundance of silver dollars. President Theodore Roosevelt is credited with having the Mercury dime, the Walking Liberty half-dollar and the St. Gaudens Double Eagle, and the Buffalo nickel created. Commemorative coins were also becoming very popular at this time. Designs on coins continue to change to reflect events, such as the Bicentennial.

It would be impossible to list values for all types of coins in a general price guide such as *Warman's*, so the following is included to give a general idea of coins. More information about specific coins is available in the various publications, including the *2006 Standard Catalog of World Coins*, published by KP Books.

Grading: The value placed on a coin is highly dependent on its "grade" or condition. The general accepted grades are as follows:

Uncirculated (Unc) (Mint State) (Ms) is known as "Very Good." These coins will show no wear at all, and should appear as though they just came from the mint.

Almost Uncirculated (AU) is known as "Good." An Almost Uncirculated coin describes coins with slight signs of wear.

Extremely Fine (EX) (Extra Fine) (XF) is known as "Fair." Extremely Fine coins exhibit wear that is readily seen, but still has clear details.

Very Fine (VF) is known as "Poor." A "Very Fine" coin will show obvious signs of wear, but still be clear of defects.

Fine (F) is the lowest grade most people would consider collectible. In this grade, about half the design details will show. The wear should be so slight that the viewer requires a magnifying glass to see it. There

are several sub-categories in all these grades.

Very Good (VG). Coins graded at this level will show heavy wear, outlines will be clear.

Good (G). Coins at this grade are considered uncollectible except for novelty purposes.

About Good (AG) and Fair (Fr). These grades are for coins with much wear, often the rims are worn down and the outlines of the design are disappearing.

Poor (Pr) is the lowest grade possible; sometimes the coin will barely be identifiable.

Proof (PF) refers not to a grade, but rather a special way of making coins, usually as presentation pieces. A Proof will usually be double struck with highly polished coins on polished blanks.

> **Reproduction Alert.** Counterfeit coins of all denominations exist.

Additional Resources:

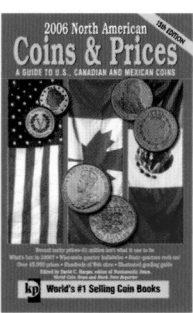

2006 North American Coins & Prices, 15th Ed., by David C. Harper, Krause Publications, Iola, WI.

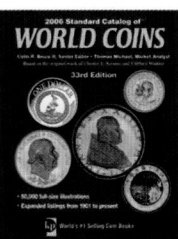

2006 Standard Catalog of® World Coins, 33rd Ed., by Chester L. Krause and Clifford Mishler; Colin R. Bruce, II, senior ed,. Krause Publications, Iola, WI.

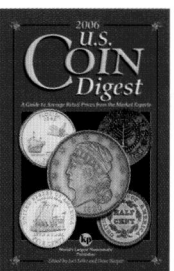

2006 U.S. Coin Digest, 4th Ed., by Joel Edler and Dave Harper, ed., Krause Publications, Iola, WI.

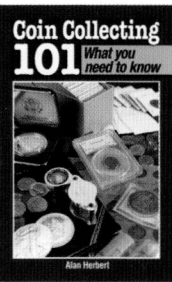

Coin Collecting 101, by Alan Herbert, Krause Publications, Iola, WI.

$2-1/2, gold

1836	**$365**
1925	**$215**
1929	**$200**

$10, 1879, gold ... **$320**

$20, 1927, gold ... **$520**

Barber Half Dollar, 1892-1915, designed by Charles E. Barber.

1892, VG	**$23**
1897S, VF	**$400**
1905, VG	**$19**
1913, VG	**$25**
1915, VF	**$190**

Buffalo Nickel, 1913 to 1938

1913, mound, Unc.	**$32**
1918S, VG	**$32.50**
1936D, VG	**$25**

Double Eagle, $20 gold piece, 1924, modeled by St. Gaudens, walking Liberty verso, eagle in flight with motto recto, 1-5/16" d ... **$470**

Eisenhower Dollar, 1971-1978

1791D, PR	**$3**
1973S, silver, Ms	**$8**
1976S, silver, block letters, PF	**$12**
1978D, PR	**$3.50**
1836, gold	**$325**
1899, gold, half eagle	**$200**

1825 Half Cent with Classic Head, MS63 Brown, **$1,200.**
Photo courtesy of Heritage Numismatics Auctions, Inc.

1907 Liberty Nickel, MS66, **$2,700.**
Photo courtesy of Heritage Numismatics Auctions, Inc.

1881CC Morgan Dollar, MS68, **$25,000.**
Photo courtesy of Heritage Numismatics Auctions, Inc.

Franklin Half Dollar, 1948 to 1963

1948, Ms **$13.75**

1950, XF **$6**

1952, XF **$3**

1961, Ms **$4.25**

Half Cent, production ended in 1859.

Braided hair, proof, 1849 .... **$3,200**

Classic head type, 1810, VG **$140**

Draped bust type, 1804, spiked chin version, VG **$45**

Liberty cap type, 1793, VG **$2,000**

Kennedy Half Dollar, 1964-2001. Obverse d esigned by Gilroy Roberts.

1964, XF **$2**

1965, silver clad, BU **$1.35**

1965-70, XF **$1**

1970S, Proof **$7.75**

1971-date .... **$.50**

1976, Bicentennial reverse, BU **$1.25**

1979, filled "S," Proof **$2.50**

1981S, Proof **$2**

1989D, BU **$1.50**

1996P, BU **$2**

Indian Head Cent, 1859-1909

1860, copper-nickel alloy, F **$37**

1867, bronze, XF **$155**

1909S, F **$300**

Jefferson Nickel, 1938 to present

1938, VG .... **$.05**

1942-1945, silver, VG .... **$.50**

1971S, proof **$1.60**

Large Cents

Classic head type, 1808-1814, 1810, VG **$600**

Coronet type, 1816-1857

1817, 13 stars, VG **$15**

1838, VG **$14**

1847, VG **$19.50**

Draped bust type, 1796 to 1807

1800, VG **$350**

1804, restrike, Unc **$450**

Flowing hair type, 1793, wreath, VG **$1,200**

Liberty cap type, 1793-1796, 1794, VG **$250**

Liberty Nickel, 1883 to 1913

1883, no cents, G **$3.75**

1883-1913, Ms **$60**

Lincoln Cent, 1909-present

1909 to 1958, VG .... **$.05**

1943, VG .... **$.15**

1959-82, Ms .... **$.15**

1982-present .... **$.011**

Mercury Dime, 1916-1945, designed by Adolph Weinman.

1916, VF **$6**

1929, D, Ms **$25**

1940, VG **$1.10**

1944D, Ms **$5.50**

Morgan Dollar, 1878-1921, designed by George T. Morgan.

1878, 8 tail feathers, VG **$20**

1881S, VG **$15**

1887, Ms **$24**

1889CC, VF **$500**

1899, Ms **$100**

1921S, Ms **$26**

Roosevelt Dime, 1946-2001, designed by John R. Sinnock.

1946, BU **$1.05**

1950S, XF **$1.25**

1953S, XF .... **$.65**

1964D, BU .... **$.90**

1970S, proof .... **$.80**

1980P, BU .... **$.40**

1995D, BU .... **$.35**

Seated Liberty Dime, 1837-1891

1837-1838, no stars, G **$30**

1838-1860, Ms **$250**

1860-1891, G **$8.75**

Seated Liberty Dollar, 1840-1873

1840, G **$100**

1846, F **$175**

1853, EF......................................**$575**

1866, G **$100**

Seated Liberty Half Dollar, 1839-1891, designed by Christian Gobrecht, several variations.

1839-1886, G................................**$16**

1840, small reverse letters, VG **$60**

1853, arrows and rays, G..........**$16.50**

1854-55, arrows, G **$16**

1857, arrows removed, VF...........**$45**

1873-74, arrows, G **$16.50**

1866-1891, G................................**$15**

Seated Liberty Quarter, 1838-1891, designed by Christian Gobrecht, several variations.

1840O, VG **$25**

1852, VG..**$145**

1853, arrows at date, VG..............**$20**

1856, arrows removed, VG **$20**

1860S, arrows removed, VG **$50**

1866, motto above eagle, VG **$450**

1873, arrows at date, VG..............**$23**

1876, arrows removed, VG **$17**

Silver Three Cent

1851-1853, G............................**$18.50**

1854-1858, Ms **$240**

1859-1873, G............................**$17.50**

Walking Liberty Half Dollar, 1916-1947. Designed by Adolph Weinman.

1918, F..**$12**

1935, XF...**$6**

1939, XF..**$10**

Washington Quarter, 1932-1998. Designed by John Flanagan.

1932, VG......................................**$7.50**

1941, VG......................................**$1.75**

1946, BU......................................**$3.75**

1957D, BU...................................**$2.50**

1972, BU..**$.75**

COMIC BOOKS

History: Shortly after comics first appeared in newspapers of the 1890s, they were reprinted in book format and often used as promotional giveaways by manufacturers, movie theaters, and candy and stationery stores. The first modern-format comic was issued in 1933.

The magic date in comic collecting is June 1938, when DC issued Action Comics No. 1, marking the first ap-

pearance of Superman. Thus began the Golden Age of comics, which lasted until the mid-1950s and witnessed the birth of the major comic-book publishers, titles, and characters.

In 1954, Fredric Wertham authored *Seduction of the Innocent*, a book that pointed a guilt-laden finger at the comics industry for corrupting youth, causing juvenile delinquency, and undermining American values. Many publishers were forced out of business, while others established a "comics code" to assure parents that their comics were compliant with morality and decency standards upheld by the code authority.

The silver age of comics, mid-1950s through the end of the 1960s, witnessed the revival of many of the characters from the Golden Age in new comic formats. The era began with Showcase No. 4 in October 1956, which marked the origin and first appearance of the Silver-Age Flash.

While comics survived into the 1970s, it was a low point for the genre; but in the early 1980s, a revival occurred. In 1983, comic-book publishers, other than Marvel and DC, issued more titles than had existed in total during the previous 40 years. The mid-and late-1980s were a boom time, a trend that appears to be continuing.

Note: The comics listed here are in near-mint condition, meaning they have a flat, clean, shiny cover that has no wear other than tiny corner creases; no subscription creases, writing, yellowing at margins, or tape repairs; staples are straight and rust free; pages are supple and like new; generally just-off-the-shelf quality.

Additional Resources:

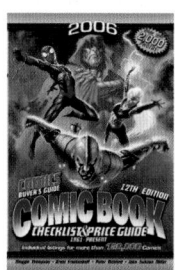

2006 Comic Book Checklist and Price Guide, 12th Ed., by John Jackson Miller, Maggie Thompson, Peter Bickford, and Brent Frankenhoff, Krause Publications, Iola, WI.

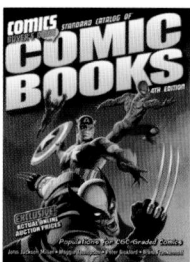

Standard Catalog of® Comic Books, 4th Ed., by John Jackson Miller, Maggie Thompson, Peter Bickford, and Brent Frankenhoff, Krause Publications, Iola, WI.

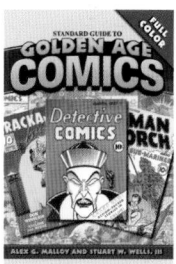

Standard Guide to Golden Age Comics, by Alex G. Mallloy and Stuart W. Wells, III, Krause Publications, Iola, WI.

Warman's® Comic Book Field Guide, by John Jackson Miller and Maggie Thompson, Krause Publications, Iola, WI.

Reproduction Alert. Publishers frequently reprint popular stories, even complete books, so the buyer must pay strict attention to the title, not just the portion printed in oversized letters on the front cover. If there is any doubt, look inside at the fine print on the bottom of the inside cover or first page. The correct title will be printed there in capital letters.

Also pay attention to the dimensions of the comic book. Reprints often differ in size from the original.

Action Comics, #127, Dec 48, © 1938 DC, **$600.**

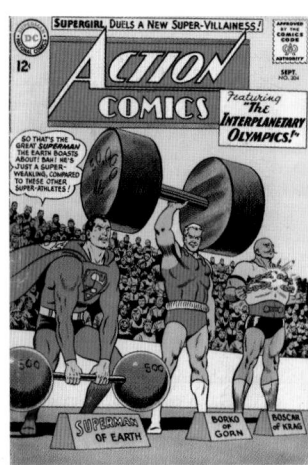

Action Comics, #304, Sep 63, © 1963 DC, **$25.**

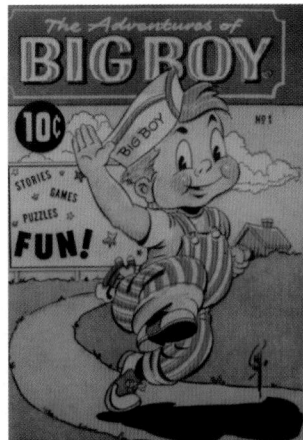

Adventures of the Big Boy, #1, 1956, © 1956 WEBS, **$750.**

Action Comics, DC

#1	**$300,000**
#2	**$28,500**
#3	**$18,400**
#4-5	**$10,250**
#6	**$15,000**
#7	**$15,200**
#8-9	**$6,600**
#10	**$8,000**
#11-12	**$4,100**
13	**$6,100**
#14	**$3,800**
#15	**$6,100**
#16	**$3,100**
#17	**$4,300**
#18	**$3,800**
#19	**$4,000**
#20	**$3,800**
#21-22	**$2,575**
#23	**$7,250**
#24-25	**$2,450**
#26	**$2,050**
#27-30	**$1,700**
#31-33	**$1,280**
#34-40	**$1,150**
#41	**$1,050**
#42	**$2,600**
#43-46	**$980**
#47	**$1,300**
#48-52	**$980**
#53	**$850**
#54-60	**$710**
#61-63	**$630**

#64	**$750**
#65-70	**$630**
#71-99	**$580**
#100	**$1,200**
#101	**$780**
#102-126	**$525**
#127	**$600**
#128-150	**$525**
#151-157	**$480**
#158	**$750**
#159-161	**$450**
#162-180	**$385**
#181-201	**$340**
#202-220	**$290**
#221-240	**$240**
#241	**$250**
#242	**$1,200**
#243-251	**$185**
#252	**$1,100**
#253	**$400**
#254	**$300**
#255	**$225**
#256-261	**$100**
#262	**$90**
#263	**$100**
#264-266	**$80**
#267	**$250**
#268-270	**$80**

Adventures of the Big Boy, WEBS Advertising Group

#1	**$750**
#2	**$300**
#3-5	**$75**

#6-10	**$40**
#11-20	**$20**
#21-50	**$8**
#51-100	**$5**
#101-200	**$4**
#201-300	**$3**
#301-up	**$2**

Amazing Spider-Man Vol. 1, Marvel

#2	**$3,200**
#3	**$2,500**
#4	**$1,900**
#5	**$2,000**
#6	**$1,500**
#7	**$1,100**
#8	**$900**
#9	**$1,000**
#10	**$900**
#11	**$2,000**
#12	**$700**
#13	**$1,200**
#14	**$2,000**
#15	**$1,600**
#16	**$750**
#17	**$700**
#18	**$450**
#19	**$500**
#20	**$425**
#21	**$300**
#22	**$265**
#23	**$440**
#24	**$210**
#25	**$300**

Amazing Spider-Man Vol. 1, #44, Jan 67, © 1967 Marvel, **$125.**

Amazing Spider-Man Vol. 1, #119, Apr 73, © 1973 Marvel, **$40.**

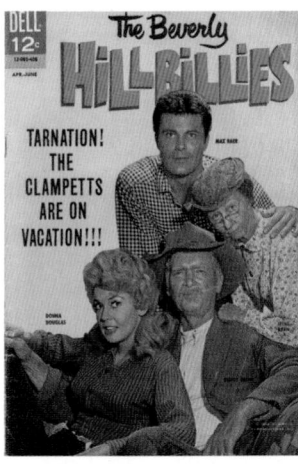

Beverly Hillbillies, #5, Jun 64, © 1964 Filmways, **$25.**

#26	**$285**
#27	**$400**
#28	**$325**
#29	**$200**
#30	**$240**
#31	**$300**
#32-33	**$200**
#34	**$250**
#35	**$150**
#36-38	**$200**
#39-42	**$350**
#42	**$200**
#43-49	**$125**
#50	**$500**
#51	**$175**
#52-57	**$85**
#58-74	**$60**
#75-95	**$60**
#96-98	**$85**
#99	**$50**
#100	**$150**
#101-102	**$80**
#103-115	**$40**
#116-117	**$25**
#118-120	**$40**
#121-122	**$175**
#123-128	**$30**
#129	**$250**
#130-134	**$20**
#134-137	**$40**
#138-151	**$20**
#152-164	**$12**
#165-176	**$8**

#177-179	**$10**
#180-193	**$7**
#194	**$25**
#195	**$10**
#196-199	**$6**
#200	**$10**

Beverly Hillbillies, Dell

1	**$60**
#2	**$38**
#3-5	**$25**
#6-10	**$18**
#11-21	**$15**

Blondie, Charlton

#1	**$245**
#2	**$100**
#3-5	**$75**
#6-10	**$45**
#11-20	**$25**
#21-50	**$16**
#51-80	**$12**
#81-100	**$10**
#101-167	**$8**
#168-222	**$4**

Captain America Vol. 1, Marvel

#100	**$285**
#101	**$55**
#102	**$35**
#103	**$35**
#104	**$35**
#105-110	**$35**
#111	**$60**
#112	**$40**
#113	**$50**

#114	**$30**
#115-116	**$25**
#117	**$80**
#118-120	**$20**
#121	**$10**
#122-136	**$15**
#137-138	**$30**
#139-140	**$15**
#141-142	**$20**
#143-148	**$15**
#149-156	**$20**
#157-158	**$10**
#159-167	**$9**
#168	**$15**
#169-172	**$9**
#173	**$15**
#174	**$9**
#175	**$9**
#176-182	**$6**
#183-191	**$5**
#192-193	**$8**
#194-199	**$5**
#200	**$6**

Captain Marvel Adventures, Fawcett

#1	**$30,000**
#2	**$3,650**
#3	**$2,100**
#4	**$1,500**
#5	**$1,150**
#6	**$1,000**
#7	**$850**
#8	**$800**

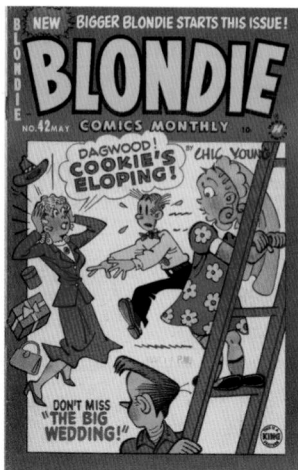

Blondie, #42, May 1952, © 1952 King Features, **$16.**

Captain America Vol. 1, Marvel, #103, Jul 68, © 1968 Marvel, **$35.**

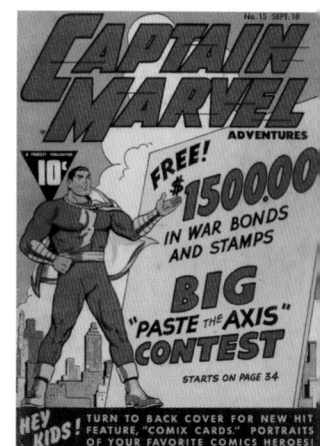

Captain Marvel Adventures, #15, Sep 42, © 1942 Fawcett, **$675.**

#9	$775
#10	$750
#11	$725
#12	$700
#13-15	$675
#16-17	$650
#18	$1,450
#19	$600
#20	$550
#21	$500
#22	$475
#23	$685
#24	$450
#25	$435
#26	$425
#27	$400
#28	$425
#29	$400
#30	$375
#31-35	$350
#36	$360
#37	$340
#38	$300
#39	$330
#40	$325
#41-44	$285
#45-47	$250
#48	$400
#49-50	$250
#51	$240
#52-55	$220
#56-60	$235
#61-65	$230
#66-70	$225

#71-75	$200
#76-80	$190
#81-85	$175
#86-90	$165
#91-120	$150
#121	$240
#122-130	$140
#131-140	$130
#141-150	$125

Wonder Woman Vol. 1, DC

#1	$22,500
#2	$4,100
#3	$2,200
#4	$1,600
#5	$1,525
#6	$1,500
#7	$1,450
#8	$1,500
#9	$1,450
#10	$1,475
#11	$1,200
#12	$1,100
#13	$1,300
#14	$1,200
#15	$1,300
#16	$1,200
#17	$1,100
#18	$1,000
#19	$1,100
#20	$900
#21-25	$750
#26-30	$700
#31-35	$600

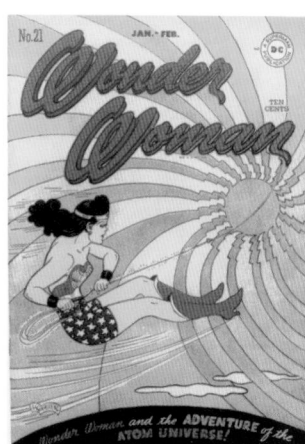

Wonder Woman Vol. 1, #21, Jan 47, © 1947 DC, **$750.**

#36-40	$575
#41-44	$415
#45	$610
#46-50	$415
#51-60	$310
#61-70	$240
#71-79	$190
#80-90	$155
#91-100	$120
#101-104	$90
#105	$600
#106	$110
#107	$100
#108	$90
#109	$85
#110	$80
#111-120	$65

#121-126.................................**$46**

#127-130.................................**$40**

#131-150.................................**$26**

#151-159.................................**$22**

#160-170.................................**$18**

#171-179.................................**$15**

#180 ....**$16**

#181-200.................................**$12**

COPPER

History: Copper objects, such as kettles, teakettles, warming pans, and measures, played an important part in the 19th-century household. Outdoors, the apple-butter kettle and still were the two principal copper items. Copper culinary objects were lined with a thin protective coating of tin to prevent poisoning. They were relined as needed.

Reproduction Alert. Many modern reproductions exist.

Additional Listings: Arts and Crafts Movement and Roycroft.

Notes: Collectors place great emphasis on signed pieces, especially those by American craftsmen. Since copper objects were made abroad as well, it is hard to identify unsigned examples.

Additional Resources:

Antique Trader® Metalwares Price Guide, 2nd Ed., by Kyle Husfloen, ed., and Mark Moran, contr. ed., Krause Publications, Iola, WI.

Breadbox, chamfered oblong rect form, hinged cov, paneled domical form, brass finial raising from lozenge-shaped plaque over brass ring handles, brass bottom, Neoclassical, possibly Dutch, c1800, 12" l x 7-1/2" w x 11" h...............................**$165**

Candy kettle, iron handles, interior worn, 18-1/2" d, **$150.**
Photo courtesy of Joy Luke Auctions.

Carpenter's pot, globular, dovetailed body, raised on three plain strap work iron legs, conforming handle, 11" l x 8" h..............................**$70**

Censer, lobed, carved and pierced lid set with white jade, China, 19th C, 13" d...............................**$1,300**

Charger, hand hammered, emb high relief of owl on branch, naturally forming patina, Liberty paper label, 29-1/2" d..............................**$3,110**

Desk set, hammered blotter, letter holder, bookends, stamp box, each with bone carved cabochon, branch and berry motif, Potter Studio, fine orig patina, die-stamp mark.......**$750**

Fish poacher, cov, oval, rolled rim, iron swing ball handle, 19th C, 20-1/2" l...............................**$350**

Inglenook hood, hammered, emb Glasgow roses, English, small tear at bottom, 30" w, 8" d, 34-1/2" h **$1,610**

Panel, repoussè of Bodhisattva seated on lotus seat, high relief figure, chased detail, traces of red pigment and gilding, Southeast Asia, slight bends, 18th C, 6-3/8" h x 2-7/8" w **$500**

Pot, cov, twin handles, oval, raised on four strap work legs, fitted with tubular end handles, shallow domed cov stamped with shield design, center stationary handle, English, 19th C, 19-1/2" l, 12", 16" h................**$215**

Screen, Arts & Crafts, ruffled edges, repousse design of oak tree, acorns, sun behind it, iron supports with copper coils wrapped around on front, 24" w x 38-1/4" h **$495**

Tea kettle, gooseneck, dovetailed construction, swivel handle, brass finial, stamped "W. Wolfe," 12" h **$3,520**

Tray, Stickley Brothers, hammered copper, loped rim emb with dots, stamped "36" no patina, 13-1/2" d **$800**

Pot, pouring spout, handle, **$85.**

Umbrella stand, hand hammered, flared rim, cylindrical body, two-strap work-loop handles, repoussé medallion, riveted flared foot, c1910, 25" h...............................**$650**

Vase, hammered, ovoid, Dirk Van Erp, fine orig mottled patina, D'Arcy Gaw box mark, small shallow dent on rim, 5-1/2" d x 7" h.........................**$8,100**

Vessel, hammered, ovoid, closed-in rim, orig dark patina, Dirk Van Erp closed box mark, 4" d, 3-1/4" h **$2,300**

Wall sconce, hammered, flame head, riveted Arts & Crafts details, attributed to Dirk Van Erp, cleaned patina, 4-1/2" w x 11" h **$425**

Water urn, copper body, int. with capped warming tube, applied brass ram's head handles, urn finial, brass spout, sq base with four ball feet, unmarked, repairs to lid, 14" h **$125**

Bookends, pr, hammered copper, possibly by Potters Studio, inset large Grueby scarab paperweights, matte brown glaze, orig dark patina, scarabs marked, 5-1/2" x 6", **$2,500.**
Photo courtesy of David Rago Auctions, Inc.

Three ducks, some wear, each **$75-$125.**
Photo courtesy of Wiederseim Associates, Inc.

Canvasback drake, **$275.**
Photo courtesy of Wiederseim Associates, Inc.

DECOYS

History: During the past several years, carved wooden decoys, used to lure ducks and geese to the hunter, have become widely recognized as an indigenous American folk-art form. Many decoys are from 1880 to 1930, when commercial gunners commonly hunted and used rigs of several hundred decoys. Many fine carvers also worked through the 1930s and 1940s. Individuals and commercial decoy makers also carved fish decoys.

Because decoys were both hand made and machine made, and many examples exist, firm pricing is difficult to establish. The skill of the carver, rarity, type of bird, and age all affect the value.

Reproduction Alert.

Notes: A decoy's value is based on several factors: (1) fame of the carver, (2) quality of the carving, (3) species of wild fowl—the most desirable are herons, swans, mergansers, and shorebirds—and (4) condition of the original paint.

The inexperienced collector should be aware of several facts. The age of a decoy, per se, is usually of no importance in determining value. However, age does have some influence when it comes to a rare or important example. Since very few decoys were ever signed, it is quite difficult to attribute most decoys to known carvers. Anyone who has not examined a known carver's work will be hard pressed to determine if the paint on one of his

decoys is indeed original. Repainting severely decreases a decoy's value. In addition, there are many fakes and reproductions on the market and even experienced collectors are occasionally fooled. Decoys represent a subject where dealing with a reputable dealer or auction house is important, especially those who offer a guarantee as to authenticity.

Decoys listed here are of average wear, unless otherwise noted.

Additional Resources:

Collecting Antique Bird Decoys and Duck Calls, An Identification and Price Guide, 3rd Ed., by Carl F. Luckey and Russell E. Lewis, Krause Publications, Iola, WI.

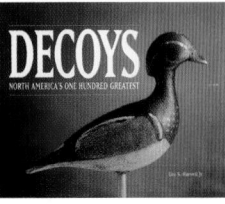

Decoys: North America's One Hundred Greatest, by Loy S. Harrell Jr., Krause Publications, Iola, WI.

Atlantic Brant, Mason, Challenge grade, from the famous Barron rig (Virginia), nearly mint condition, age shrinkage neck crack repair, tight filled factory back crack, c1910 ....**$4,500**

Baldgate Wigeon Drake, miniature, A. Elmer, Crowell, East Harwich, MA, identified in ink, rect stamp on base, 2-1/2" x 4" **$635**

Black Bellied Bustard, miniature, H. Gills, initialed "H. G. 1957," identified in pencil, natural wood base, 3-1/2" x 4"...**$230**

Black Bellied Plover, unknown American 20th C maker, orig paint, glass eyes, mounted on stick on lead base.

Minor paint loss, small chips to beak, 12-1/2" h **$2,530**

Minor paint loss, beak repair, 13-1/2" h **$1,725**

Black Breasted Plover, Harry C. Shourds, orig paint **$2,650**

Black Duck

A. Elmer Crowell, East Harwich, MA, orig paint, glass eyes, stamped mark in oval on base, sleeping, wear, crack, 5-1/4" h **$525**

Ira Hudson, preening, raised wings, outstretched neck, scratch feather paint **$8,500**

Mason, Challenge, hollow, fine orig paint, some neck filler replaced, c1910.................**$3,500**

Mason, Premier, Atlantic Coast, oversized, solid-bodied special order, most desirable snaky head, excellent orig condition, some professional restoration, filled in-the-making back crack, tail chip on one side of crack, neck filler replacement, c1905.............**$4,500**

Carved and painted duck decoy attributed to Bill Shaw, Lacon, Illinois, **$850.**
Photo courtesy of Joy Luke Auctions.

Decoy, Canada goose, carved and painted, mid-20th C, 15" h x 22" w, **$345.**
Photo courtesy of Pook & Pook, Inc.

Mason, Standard, painted eye, dry original paint, all of its original neck filler, invisible professional dry rot repair in the base, c1910 .... **$750**

Unknown maker, carved balsa body, wood head, glass eyes, orig pant, 15-1/2" l **$150**

Wildfowler, CT, inlet head, glass eyes, worn orig paint, green overpaint on bottom on sides, c1900, 13" l **$220**

Black Drake, miniature

A. Elmer Crowell, East Harwich, MA, identified in ink, rect stamp on base, break at neck, reglued, minor paint loss, 3-1/2" x 4-3/4" **$635**

James Lapham, Dennisport, MA, identified in black ink, oval stamp, minor imperfections, 2-1/2" x 4" **$290**

Bluebill Drake, carved by Robert Elliston, painted by wife Catherine Elliston, Illinois River, 19th C **$6,700**

Bluebill Hen, Mason Challenge, hollow, orig paint, c1910 ..... **$3,450**

Blue-Winged Teal Drake and Hen Pair, Davey W. Nichol, Smiths Falls, Ontario, Canada, matched pair, raised wings, scratch feather patterns, sgd on bottom, 1960 .... **$1,650**

Brant, old black, white, and gray paint, glass eyes, age splits on base, minor chips to gesso on back, 14-1/2" l **$115**

Broadbill Drake and Hen Pair, Mason, painted eyes, rare gunning rigmates, untouched original condition, neck filler missing, some shot evidence, hen has small, superficial chip on one side, c1910 .... **$1,450**

Bufflehead Drake

Bob Kerr, carved detail, glass eyes, orig paint, scratch carved signature, c1980, 10-1/2" l **$250**

Harry M. Shrouds, carved, hollow body, painted eyes **$1,800**

James Lagham, Dennisport, MA, identified in ink, oval stamp on base, 3" x 4-1/2" **$345**

Canada Goose

Hurley Conklin, carved, hollow body, swimming position, branded "H. Conklin" on bottom **$600**

Unsigned, carved wood, shaped tin, canvas covering on body, later gray, brown, white, and black paint, glass eyes, restored splits in neck, 22-1/2" l **$100**

Unsigned, gray, black, and white paint, incised carved initials "P.C." on base, carved open bill, relief detail on wings and tail feathers, glass eyes, iron legs, glued break at neck, 27" l, 26-5/8" h **$300**

Canvasback

Chesapeake Bay, carved and painted, glass eyes, metal ring, 12" l, 7-1/2" w, 10-3/4" h **$1,650**

Unknown carver, pine, paint dec, lead weight, metal ring, 8-3/4" l, 6" w, 5" h **$1,210**

Curlew

Dan Leeds, Pleasantville, NJ, carved and painted brown, stand, 1880-1900, 13" l **$2,415**

Harry V. Shrouds, orig paint **$2,000**

Curlew Oyster Eater, Samuel Jester, Tennessee, carved and painted, slight paint wear, age crack in body, stand, c1920, 16" l, 9" h **$1,035**

Elder Duck, old black and white paint, green stripe around head, yellow bill, Maine, unsigned, 17-3/4" l **$250**

Flying Duck, glass-bead eyes, old natural surface, carved pine, attributed to Maine, c1930, 16" l, 11" h **$2,300**

Goldeneye, drake, unknown Maine carver, oversized, classic Maine inletted neck and raised shoulders, worn orig paint with clear patterns, branded "Gigerrish" or "G.I. Gerrish," c1900, 13" l **$1,850**

Great Northern Pike, attributed to Menominee Indian, WI, painted green, glass eyes, ribbed sheet metal fin, tall stand, c1900, 36" l, 9" h **$3,450**

Green Wing Teal Duck, miniature, A. Elmer Crowell, East Harwich, MA, identified in ink, rect stamp on base, 2-1/2" x 4" **$865**

Heron, unknown maker, carved wig and tail, wrought iron legs **$900**

Herring Gull, attributed to Gus Wilson, used as weathervane, traces of old paint, metal feet, weathered and worn, c1910-20, 18-3/4" l **$3,110**

Hooded Merganser Drake, William Clarke, Oakville, Ontario, Canada, transitional plumage, excellent orig condition, minor in-use wear, c1900 .... **$2,450**

Loon, carved and painted, wooden rudder, America, stand, paint wear, 19th C, 27" l **$9,200**

Mallard Drake

Ben Schmidt, Detroit, relief carved, feather stamping, glass eyes, orig paint, orig keep, marked "Mallard drake Benj Schmidt, Detroit 1960," 15-1/4" l **$450**

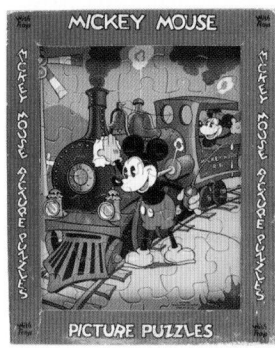

Puzzle set, four puzzles with box and own inner storage trays, each is 9-3/4" x 11-1/4", Marks Brothers Co., box with moderate edge wear, small split at left corner, 3" l surface paper rub w/ lower right split, 1930s, box is 11" x 13-1/2" x 1-3/4", **$1,555.**

Photo courtesy of Hake's Americana & Collectibles.

Bert Graves, carved, hollow body, orig weighted bottom, branded "E. I. Rogers" and "Cleary" **$900**

James Lapham, Dennisport, MA, sgd and identified in ink on bottom, 4" x 5" **$435**

Mason, Challenge, rare hollow model with elaborate Mason Premier style paint patterns, no tail chip, professional repair to some splintering on end of bill, tight neck crack on left side, some shot evidence on right side, c1910 .... **$3,500**

Mason, Premier, hollow snakey head, orig condition, c1900 .... **$6,500**

Robert Elliston, carver, painted by wife Catherine Elliston, Illinois River, 19th C **$6,200**

Mallard Drake and Hen Pair, Mason, glass eyes, gunning rigmates, excellent orig condition, some neck filler replaced, drake has filled factory crack on side, c1905 .... **$1,750**

Mallard Hen

Robert Elliston, carved, hollow body, orig paint **$1,800**

Mason Premier, hollow, excellent orig paint, rich red breast, professional tail chip repair and neck putty restoration, c1905 .... **$3,900**

Merganser Drake, Mason Challenge, Detroit, MI, strong orig paint with no cracks, some shot holes have been filled on one side, branded "C. Simpson," c1910 .... **$7,500**

Owl, carved wood, glass eyes, orig polychrome paint, 20" h **$1,700**

Perch, Heddon, ice-type **$800**

Pintail Duck

Drake, Paw Paw Bait Co., stenciled company name on bottom, c1932-36 .... **$800**

Drake and hen, John H. Baker, Bristol, PA, painted in naturalistic tones, glass eyes, sgd, imp maker's signature, lead ingot affixed to bases stamped "John Baker Bristol, PA," paint flakes on hen, 20th C **$1,100**

Plover, Joe Lincoln, winter plumage, feather painting, orig paint **$800**

Red Breasted Merganser Drake

Amos Wallace, ME, inlet neck, carved crest, detailed feathered paint **$2,000**

George Boyd, NH, carved, orig paint **$8,000**

Redhead Drake, Dan Bartlett, Prince Edward County, Ontario, Canada, hollow, fine orig paint, c1920 .... **$950**

Robin Snipe, Obediah Verity, carved wings and eyes, orig paint **$4,400**

Ruddy Duck, miniature, maker unknown, identified in ink on base, paint loss to bill, 2" x 2-3/4" **$690**

Ruddy Duck Drake, Len Carmeghi, Mt. Clemens, MI, hollow body, glass eyes, orig paint, sgd and dated, 10-3/4" l **$250**

Ruffled Grouse, miniature, A. Elmer Crowell, East Harwich, MA, rect stamp, mounted on natural wood base, 3-1/2" x 4-1/2" **$865**

Sea Gull, weathered surface, used as weathervane, attributed to WI, late 19th/early 20th C, 14" l **$1,840**

Shorebird, carved and painted, mounted on wooden stand, minor wear, America, early 20th C, 6-3/4" l, 9-1/2" h **$775**

Swan, unknown Chesapeake Bay, MD, maker, carved wood, braced neck, white paint, 30" l **$900**

Widgeon, matted pair, Charlie Joiner, MD, sgd on bottom **$800**

Wood Duck, drake, D. W. Nichol, Smiths Falls, Ontario, slightly turned head, 1950s **$2,450**

Yellowlegs, carved and painted, New Jersey, stand, c1890, 11" l **$2,185**

DISNEYANA

History: Walt Disney and the creations of the famous Disney Studios hold a place of fondness and enchantment in the hearts of people throughout the world. The 1928 release of "Steamboat Willie," featuring Mickey Mouse, heralded an entertainment empire.

Walt and his brother, Roy, were shrewd businessmen. From the beginning, they licensed the reproduction of Disney characters on products ranging from wristwatches to clothing.

In 1984, Donald Duck celebrated his 50th birthday, and collectors took a renewed interest in material related to him.

Additional Resources:

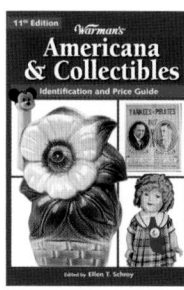

Warman's® Americana & Collectibles, 11th Ed., by Ellen T. Schroy, ed., Krause Publications, Iola, WI.

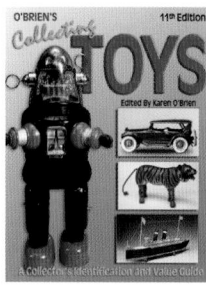

O'Brien's Collecting Toys, 11th Edition, Karen O'Brien, ed., Krause Publications, Iola, WI.

Warman's® Disney Collectibles Field Guide, by Ken Farrell, Krause Publications, Iola, WI.

Adviser: Theodore L. Hake. Author of *Price Guide to Disney Collectibles,* 1st edition, House of Collectibles, 2005, available at Hake's auction site: www.hakes.com.

Bambi

Book, *Bambi,* hardcover, Grosset & Dunlap, copyright 1942, 7" x 8-1/4" **$32**

Charm bracelet, gold luster metal link bracelet, five figural gold luster charms of red/brown Bambi and Faline, blue Thumper, black and white Flower, yellow/green Friend Owl, 1950s, 6" l **$20**

Figure, Goebel, full bee mark, incised "DIS 111," 10950s, orig string tag, 2-1/2" x 6-1/2" x 7" **$65**

Planter, glazed ceramic, Modern Ceramic Pottery, Australian, 1950s, 5" x 7" x 6" **$125**

Studio fan card, stiff buff paper, brown design, Walt Disney facsimile signature, small copyright, 1940s, 7" x 9" **$35**

Cinderella

Costume, two pcs, Ben Copper, copyright Walt Disney Productions, late 1960s, box illus include Spider-Man, Hulk, Thor, and Wonder Woman, wear to box, costume bright, 8-1/4" x 11" x 2-3/4" orig box **$30**

Planter, ceramic, Shaw
Cinderella in serving clothes, 7-1/4" h **$425**

Prince Charming leaning against banister... **$250**

Soaky, soft plastic body, hard plastic head, blue dress, movable arms, 10-1/2" h **$20**

Disney Family

Autograph, Walt Disney, 7" x 8-1/2" glossy photo of Walt standing next to bookcases, wearing tie with symbol ffoor Smoke Tree Ranch, accompanied by letter of authenticity from Hake's Americana & Collectible Auction, 2-3/4" l signature, 11" x 14" cardboard mat................................. **$750**

Autographed photo, Roy E. Disney, glossy photoboldly signed at right corner in black felt tip pen, reverse with sticker, "Roy Disney Vice Chairman The Walt Disney Company," accompanied by letter of authenticity from Hake's Americana & Collectibles Auction **$75**

Disneyland

Book, *A Visit to Disneyland,* Whitman Big Tell-A-Tale, 28 pgs, color photos, copyright 1965, 6" x 8-1/2" **$20**

Game, Disneyland Riverboat Game, Parker Bros, four different colored metal boat playing pcs, copyright 1960, 14-3/4" sq board, 8" x 16" x 1-3/4" deep box **$50**

Key Chain, Mickey head and black text, brass chain, c1960, 1-1/4" d, 3/8" thick transparent plastic disc **$22**

Snow dome, hard plastic, 3-D castle, Tinkerbelle dangling from top, 1960s, 2-1/4" h.................. **$50**

Disney World

Convention badge, black printing, gold background, "110 Club '79/ Disney World," 4" d **$10**

Flicker, I Like Walt Disney World, red metal case, text on reverse including "Vari-Vue" and Walt Disney World logo, black, white, and red image of Mickey wearing blue bow tie, changes to slogan in white on red background **$15**

Donald Duck

Book, Donald's Penguin, hard cover, Garden City Publishing, 24 pgs, copyright, 1940, 8-1/2" x 9-1/2" **$70**

Button, Birthday Club, black & white, inscribed "Member," issued by "Astor Theater, Burwood," (Australia), late 1930s or early 1940s, 13/16" **$115**

Calendar, full color center scene titled "Bedtime," Donald making sure nephews are getting ready for bed, blue and white border with Mickey, Minnie, Pluto, Dumbo, Timothy, Bambi, and Thumper with stars, American Bedding Co., Portland OR, only December calendar remains, 8" x 11" thin cardboard **$145**

Christmas card, image of Donald as Santa, standing on rooftop giving victory symbol, next to sack of war-themed toys, bottom margin reads "Proceeds To The American Woman's Voluntary Services, " card stock, orig plain envelope, World War III era, 6-1/4" x 9".............. **$80**

Doll, Knickerbocker, stuffed, movable head, oilcloth eyes, hat, collar, and jacket buttons held on with safety pins, felt tail, 1930s, 7" x 10" x 17-1/2" h **$425**

Egg Cup, color image of Donald pushing wheelbarrow, brown/iridescent tan, unmarked, 1950s, 2-1/4" x 4" x 3-1/2" **$145**

Fan card, image of angry Donald, clenched fists, card stock, facsimile Walt Disney signature, c1937, 7" x 9".................................... **$200**

Figure, celluloid, plaster filled, metallic blue paint, 1930s, 3" h **$100**

Fun-E-Flex figure, wood body, fabric-covered arms, movable head, near complete decal on front of body, 1930s, 5" h............................ **$1,150**

Juice glass, wrap-around images of Huey, Dewey, and Louie, names 1940s, 3-3/8" h.......................... **$125**

Pail, tin litho, Donald with melons, very glossy, interior surface rust, moderate paint wear and indents on outside, © 1938, 6" h, **$460.**

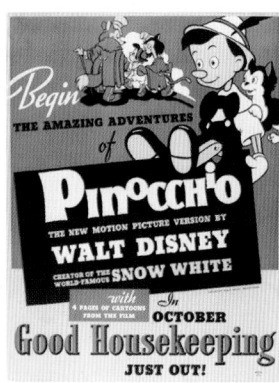

Ad, promoting appearance of four pages of cartoons in the October issue of Good Housekeeping; cardstock, purple and peach color, minor corner tip wear, scattered trace of dust soiling at margins, 1940, 10-1/2" x 13-1/2", **$800.**

Little Golden Book, *Donald Duck in Disneyland*, Golden Press, copyright 1960, 4th printing, 24 pgs **$18**

Pencil Drawing, lead and blue pencil 4" x 4-1/2" image of Donald with green pencil underline, from "Honey Harvester," 1949, 10" x 12" sheet of animation paper **$200**

Fantasia figurine set ceramic, 1985, 2.5" h, **$250.**

Pencil holder, celluloid, designed as lamp, 1" h, 3-D donald figure on base with long bill, shade with images of Mickey and Donald, Disney copyright, mkd "Japan," 1930s, 3-1/4" h **$700**

Pencil sharpener, figural, dark red catalin, full color decal on front, 1-11/16".. **$45**

Toy, Schuco, tin litho and hard plastic, felt hat and collar, wind-up, orig box, 1960s, 6" h **$300**

Dumbo

Bank, cast metal, copyright on back of base, mkd c1941, key missing, 4" h **$250**

Figure, painted and glazed ceramic of newborn Dumbo, red, blue, and silver foil stick-on back, Disney copyright and Modern Ceramic Products PTY Ltd., Sydney," 1940s, 2" x 2-1/2" x 3-1/2" h................ **$185**

Premium button, black, white, red, and gray, "D-X" printed on platform, reverse Kay Kamen back paper includes small image of running Mickey, 1942, 1-1/4" d...... **$24**

Toothbrush holder, painted ceramic, matte finish, three openings for toothbrushes, incised 1942 copyright, 3-1/2" x 5-1/2" x 3-3/4" **$150**

Fantasia

Concept art, watercolor, Dance of the Hours, ominous-looking alligator backing hippopotamus against stone column, reverse with studio backstamp noting artist James Bodrero, sequence #10, sketch #374, July 11, 1939, 10" x 12" sheet of animation paper................ **$2,000**

Figure, painted and glazed ceramic, Vernon Kilns, 1940 Disney copyright

Centaur, incised "31," 10" h **$1,000**

Centaurette, incised "24," 7-1/2" h **$750**

Plate, Flower Ballet, Vernon Kilns, dark maroon, yellow, green, and blue, copyright 1940, 9-1/2" d.............. **$75**

Souvenir movie program, softcover, Western Printing Co., black and white photos of Walt Disney and other contributors, full color plates of scenes from film, from orig 1940 release, 9-1/2" x 12-1/2".................................... **$50**

Goofy

Animation cel, 4" x 5-1/2" image of Sport Goofy, color laser background of stadium, #A-76 from numbered sequence, from 1980s Disney TV show, 10-1/2" x 12-1/2" acetate sheet **$150**

Bank, molded hard vinyl head, Play Pal Plastics, Inc., copyright 1971, red shirt collar, bright yellow hat, trap missing, 5" x 9" 10-1/2" h **$25**

Blotter, Sunoco Oil, Goofy and angry polar bear, broken-down car, unused, copyright 1939, 4" x 7"................ **$40**

Book, *Goofy Best Comics*, Abbeville Press, 184 pgs, title page boldly signed in black felt tip pen, "Very Best to Al, Floyd Gottfredson," hardcover, copyright 1979, 9-3/4" x 13-1/4".. **$75**

Figure, Hagen-Renaker, painted and glazed ceramic, green shirt and hat, tan vest, blue pants, brown shoes, foil sticker missing, 1950s, 2-1/2" h **$135**

Pencil drawing, lead and blue pencil, 4" x 5-1/2" image of Goofy from waist up as porter, #17.5 from "Baggage Buster," 1941, 10" x 12" sheet of animation paper **$250**

Toy, Goofy's Disneyland Stock Car, Linemar, Goofy as Driver, other characters riding, late 1950s, 6" l **$275**

Mickey Mouse

Bank, metal, chest with lightly emb oilcloth fabric, brass plated side panels, text, "Mickey and Minnie At The World's Fair, 1933 Chicago 1934," raised images of Hall of Science, Travel, and Transportation, Federal on front, Zell Products, scattered loss to brass luster, key missing, 2-1/4" x 4-1/4" x 2" h **$200**

Books

Big Little Book, *Mickey Mouse Sails for Treasure Island,* softcover premium for Kolynos Dental Cream Whitman, 1935.............................**$40**

Mickey Mouse Presents Santa's Workshop, hard cover 80 pgs, Collins, c1938, 7-1/4" x 10" **$250**

Mickey Mouse Waddle, Blue Ribbon Books, copyright 1934, orig dust jacket, perforated Waddle pages removed, 7-3/4" x 10-1/4".......**$200**

The Adventures of Mickey Mouse, hard cover, 32 pgs, David McKay Co., copyright 1931, 5-1/2" x 7-3/4" **$85**

The Adventures of Mickey Mouse, softcover, Canadian version, Musson Book Co. Ltd., copyright 1934, 6-1/4" x 8-1/2" **$275**

Candle nightlight holder, ceramic, figural Mickey asleep in chair, 1-1/2" recessed area on front to hold candle, unmarked Crown Devon, 1930s, 2-1/2" x 5-1/2" x 4-1/2" **$215**

Card album, Mickey Mouse Picture, Vol. 2, issued by Gum Inc., for cards #49-96, front cover with Mickey holding open picture card album, mounted cards #77, 87, 90, and 95, 16pgs, 1930s, 6" x 10" **$250**

Car radiator ornament, stamped brass, relief design, dark patina, 1930s, 3" x 5-3/4".....................**$300**

Clock, metal, enameled front with two Mickeys, mkd "Made in Germany," 1930s, 2" x 3"x 3/4" **$800**

Composition book, *Mickey Mouse Composition Book,* by Powers Paper Co., brown, black, and red illus of Mickey and Minnie walking, carrying school books, multiplication tables on back, some penciled school work on pages, dated 1934, 6-3/4" x 8-1/4" **$60**

Demitasse cup, china, highly-stylized image of Mickey on both sides, 1930s, 2-1/4" h..........................**$90**

Dime register bank, tin litho, dark yellow border, top and sides with Mickey, Minnie, and nephews, copyright 1939, 2-1/2" x 2-1/2" x 3/4" **$200**

Doll, Knickerbocker, stuffed cloth, polished cotton face with printed details, separate fabric pants, felt ears, hands, and shoes, 10-1/2" h **$410**

Figure

Bisque, playing accordian, Disney copyright, mkd "Made in Japan," 1930s, 5-1/4" h..........................**$225**

Celluloid, squatty body, oversized head, one arm reaching to back, c1930, 4-3/4" h..........................**$225**

Glass, from 1937 sports set, Mickey as baseball player, 5-1/2" h **$350**

Gum card wrapper, Gum inc., waxed paper, illus of Mickey, Minnie, Pluto, Horace, and Clarabelle, text "Save the Wrappers," 1930s, 5" x 7-1/4" **$90**

Magazine, *Mickey Mouse Magazine,* Vol. 1, #7, 36 pgs, newsprint, Mickey and W.C. Fields dot-to-dot puzzle neatly done in pencil, near mint, April 1937 ....**$475**

Marionette, painted composition head, wood pegs hands and feet, 3-1/2" x 5" x 7" animal fur-covered body, 1930s, 7-1/2" l tail **$165**

Pencil box, carboard, double snap closure front panel, Dixon, #2666, 1934, 5-3/4" x 10-3/4" x 2"......**$250**

Pencil drawing, 3" x 4" lead pencil image of seated Mickey wearing policeman's hat, from "Dognapper," 1934, 9-1/2" x 12" sheet of animation paper...................................**$300**

Pen clip, silvered metal, 9/16" domed metal attachment with colorful Mickey, tiny copyright initials below WDP, Bastian, early 1950s, 1-1/4" h **$35**

Pin, diecut brass, enamel, in boxing gloves, 1940s, 1" **$85**

Plate, china, images of Mickey playing musical instruments, dancing, Minnie wearing hat, mkd "Imperial Ironstoneware N.K.T. Made in Japan," 1930s, 8" d **$100**

Sand pail, tin litho, attached carrying handle, Ohio Art, golf theme, wrap-around illus with Mickey, Donald, Goofy, and black cat, play wear, copyright 1938, 5-3/4" h, 5-3/4" d at top **$300**

Sheet music, *The Wedding Party of Mickey Mouse,* Stasny Music Corp, orig copyright, 1931, 1936 issue, 8 pgs, 9" x 12" **$125**

Space heater, cast-iron front, steel heating element compartment on back, high-relief Mickey on front, hands on either side of center opening, Art Deco-style grills, text "Tabard Mickey Mouse Fire/By Permission of Walt Disney-Mickey Mouse Ltd.," English, 12" x 12" x 5" deep **$2,500**

Mickey and Minnie pair, string tails, moveable arms and heads, Japan, Minnie professionally restrung, slight ear gap where separate ear piece is attached, front bottom of dress has two small hairlines, Mickey has minute hairline between shoes, minor head dents, © 1928, 1930 sticker on bottom of feet, 4.75" tall, **$500.**

Photo courtesy of Hake's Americana & Collectibles.

Mickey Mouse, ring toss game, Spear's box contains complete parts, lid worn, 2" strip missing from side panel, 6-1/2" h die-cutcardboard figure that attaches to stand on box interior, 6 colored rings, dust soiling, ear bend on Mickey, 1930s, box is 6-1/2" x 8-1/2" x 1", **$165.**

Photo courtesy of Hake's Americana & Collectibles.

Pail, tin litho, Mickey on skates and Mickey pulling rabbit from hat, glossy, great color, bottom interior surface has wear/oxidation, outside bends and dents, scattered small paint rubs, Ohio Art, 1930s, 3-1/4" h, **$295.**

Photo courtesy of Hake's Americana & Collectibles.

Disney, toy, Pinocchio, tin, Louis Marx & Co., c1930, 15-1/2" x 11" x 2-1/4", **$300.**

Photo courtesy of David Rago Auctions, Inc.

Toy

Celluloid, Mickey and Donald in rowboat, Disney copyright, mkd "Made in Japan," old repairs, 1930s, 2" x 6" x 2-1/4" h **$350**

Pressed steel, telephone, N. N. Hill Brass Co., rotary dial turns and rings, pop-up cardboard Mickey figure, c1934, 5" x 8" x 4-1/2" h **$300**

Watch fob, silvered brass, loop at top, black accents, reverse "Ingersoll Mickey Mouse Watches & Clocks Copyright Walt Disney," English, 1930s, 1-1/8" **$265**

Wristwatch, Ingersoll, dial with large black, white, and yellow Mickey, hands point to numerals, second wheel with three tiny Mickey images, vintage replacement strap, working order and clean dial, 1933, 1-1/4" d chromed metal case **$325**

Mickey Mouse Club

Australian, dark blue lettering, "New Lyric Theater Mickey Mouse Club," 1" d scrapbook, Whitman, 64 unused pgs, full color cover of Mouseketeers with art supplies, copyright 1957, but actually 1970s printing, 10-3/4" x 14-3/4" **$20**

Minnie Mouse

Bracelet, enameled and incised Mickey and Minnie standing back to back, 1930s, stamped "Sterling" **$200**

Child's feeding dish, divided, color images of Minnie, Mickey, and Salem China Co., 1930s, 8" d, 1-3/4" h **$125**

Cigarette holder, china, Minnie playing piano, mkd "Germany," incised "2885, " 1930s, 3-1/5" x 2-1/4" x 3" h **$200**

Figure

American Pottery, leaning against broom, 6" h **$250**

Shaw, pink outfit, orig label, mkd "Mexico," 4-1/2" h **$275**

Pencil drawing, lead pencil drawing of 2-1/2" x 3" Mickey and 1-1/2" x 2" Minnie, #73 from "Camping Out," 1934, 9-1/2" x 12" sheet of animation paper **$250**

Pull toy, celluloid figure attached to 4" long freewheeling wood scooter, 19" l string, wood knob on end, mkd "Made in Japan," small copyright symbol, 1930s, 3-1/4" h **$320**

Salt and pepper shakers, painted and glazed ceramic, Dan Brechner Exclusive foil sticker, ink stamp copyright, WD-52, standing on top of wood crates which house noisemakers, names on front of base, orig stoppers, 2" x 2"x 5-1/4" **$75**

Sign, Congoleum Gold Seal Rug, diecut cardboard, text "3 Special Prizes Offered By This Store/Ask For A Free Entry Blank," image of Minnie mopping linoleum rug, 1903s, 19-1/2" d **$750**

Teapot, glazed yellow ceramic, full color image of Mickey, Minnie, and Donald, hand-in-hand, text "Ring-A-Ring of Roses," names in blue, roses, unmarked, possibly Wade, 1930s, 3-1/2" x 6" x 3-1/2" h **$90**

Pinocchio

Book, *Pinocchio Linen-Like, #1061,* Whitman, 12 pgs, full color art on each page, copyright 1940, 7" x 7-3/4" **$45**

Candy bar wrapper, Schutter Candy Co., black, white, yellow, and red image of Jiminy and premium "Official Conscience Medal," copyright 1940, 3-1/4" x 8-1/4" **$50**

Figure

Ceramic, Figaro, Goebel, foil sticker, 1950s, 4" h **$125**

Ceramic, Pinocchio and Figaro, Brayton Laguna, company name and "Gepetto Pottery" on underside, 1940s, 4-1/4" h **$950**

Wood, black, white, red, blue, and yellow, separate light blue wood ball hands attached by elastic string, paper label, "Pinocchio," copyright, Geo Borgfeldt Corp., 1940, 4-3/4" h **$95**

Game, Pinocchio Race Game, Chad Valley, scene of Pinocchio and Jiminy Cricket encountering Foulfellow and Gideon leaving Geppetto's workshop on box lid, some fading to box, 14-1/2" sq board, game pcs, c1940, 10" x 15" x 1-3/4" h **$140**

Lamp base, painted and glazed ceramic, donkey and high-relief flowers, Zaccagnini, W72, Disney copyright sticker, wiring missing, 5-1/2" x 4-1/2" **$35**

Planter, painted and glazed ceramic, Figaro dipping paw into aquarium planter, raised image of fish on front, c1940, 3" x 5-1/2" x 4-1/2" **$35**

Soaky, soft plastic body, hard plastic head, Pinocchio sitting on top of tree stump, holding school slate, 1960s, 9-3/4" h.............................**$20**

Toy, walking Pinocchio, litho tin wind-up, Linemar, orig box, 1950s, 5-3/4" h **$750**

Pluto

Drinking glass, glass, small W.D. Ent. Copyright, Pluto with eyes closed, mouth wide open belting out song, music stand in front of him, music notes scattered around front and back, 4-3/4" h...........................**$320**

Pencil drawing, from flip book designed by Art Corner at Disneyland, Ralph Kent artist, 1955, 3-1/2" x 5" image in lead pencil and black crayon on 7-1/4" x 10-1/4" sheet **$100**

Pin, brass, rich yellow enamel, black, white, and red accents, WD copyright, 1930s, 1-1/4".....................**$85**

Push puppet, hard plastic, Kohner, c1960, green base, foil sticker with orange text, 2-1/2" h...................**$25**

Toy drum major windup, Linemar, orig rubber ears, tail missing, 1950s, 6-1/4" h **$175**

Roger Rabbit

Animation cel, pair, one with Jessica Rabbit, other with Weasel, background film scene on high quality Kodak paper, 1988, 7-1/2" x 16-1/2" acetate sheet, 4-1/2" x 7-1/2" certificate of authenticity issued by Walt Disney Co....................................**$200**

Production test cel, set of three, consecutively numbered, each with full figure image in slightly different pose of Roger as gray rabbit, three 11-1/2" x 16-1/2" acetate sheets **$100**

Sleeping Beauty

Book, *Sleeping Beauty,* Whitman, Story Hour series, 32 pgs, copyright 1959, 7-1/2" x 8-1/4" **$18**

Box proof, "Sleeping Beauty Colorforms Dress Designer Kit," full color glossy paper, copyright 1959, 11-1/4" x 16-1/4" **$65**

Figure, Queen, Hagen-Renaker, painted and glazed ceramic, foil sticker, 1950s, 2-3/8" h.............**$600**

Snow White

Birthday card, White & Wyckoff, black, white, red, blue, and green design, front with Doc and Sleepy in front of doorway, opens to Snow White dancing with Doc as others

play instruments, copyright 1938, 4-1/4" x 5-1/2".........................**$30**

Book, *Edgar Bergen's Charlie McCarthy Meets Walt Disney's Snow White,* Whitman Publishing, softcover, 24 pgs, copyright 1938, 9-1/2" x 11-1/2" **$110**

Comic book, full color, 16pgs, copyright 1958 by Western Printing Co., issued as premium by Reynolds Wrap, 5" x 7" **$22**

Figure, celluloid with plaster filling, marked "Foreign" on back, "Celluloid" on underside, some pulling at seams, c1938, 1-1/2" x 2-1/4" x 4-1/2" **$75**

Paper doll, Snow White Magic Doll, mkd "Made in Canada by Somerville Paper Boxes," copyright 1937, storage inside cover for 11" diecut cardboard doll and six different felt outfits, 9" x 13-1/2" cardboard folder **$200**

Pencil sharpener, figural, dark red catalin, full-color decal on front, 1-11/16"...**$65**

Pitcher, Sneezy, painted and glazed, relief and dimensional shape, marked "Wadeheath by Permission Walt Disney England," c1938, 3-3/4" h **$175**

Song folio, *Snow White and the Seven Dwarfs,* 9" x 12", 52 pgs, Bourne Inc. Music Publishers, copyright 1938, 1950s printing...............................**$25**

Song folio, *Snow White and the Seven Dwarfs,* 52 pgs, Bourne Inc. Music Publishers, copyright 1938, 1950s printing, 9" x 12"..............**$25**

Tea set, partial, cake plate with Snow White and Doc, six 4-1/4" d plates for Dopey, Grumpy, Bashful, Sleepy, Doc, and Sneezy; four 1-1/4" h tea cups for Dopey, Sneezy, Grumpy, and Sleepy; three 3-1/4" d saucers for Dopey, Sleepy, and Sneezy; 2-1/4" h creamer with Dopey; and 3" h cov sugar with Happy, mkd "Made in Japan," copyright 1937...........**$200**

Umbrella, red, white, and blue wood handle and shaft, metal frame, white silk like synthetic fabric cover, full color images of Snow White and the Seven Dwarfs, names in black letters, copyright, c1938, 19" l, 24" d open..**$85**

Three Pigs

Game board, Marks Brothers Co., ominous image of Wolf towering over dancing Fiddler and Fifer Pigs, Practical Pig putting fishing touch-

es on brick house, c1934, 16-3/4" sq board **$40**

Plate, white china, full-color center scene of Three Pigs, Little Red Riding Hood, and Grandmother knitting in rocking chair, blue rim trim, marked "Salem China Co./Patriot China," 1930s, 7-1/2" d **$75**

Postcard set, marked "Paris," French text, backs also marked "Disney," each with full color art telling story, sent by soldier to daughter in US, each with typed or handwritten note, sent on consecutive days in April, 1945, set of 12 numbered 3-1/2" x 5-1/5" cards **$150**

Radio, wood, front with 4" opening with pressed wood attachment with three pigs, fabric speaker cover, two pigs play fife and fiddle, while third dances, 5" x 7" x 9-1/4" **$1,000**

Sand pail, tin litho, Ohio Art, Wrapround scene, Spanish version, 1934, 5" h **$300**

Toy, Big Bad Wolf and Three Little Pigs, litho tin windup, Linemar, key-wind, 1960s, each 4-1/2" h..............**$200 ea.**

Zorro

Costume, unused, attached to orig diecut cardboard hanger display, Lindsay, black diecut leatherette mask, black fabric cloak/sash, silver image of Zorro on rearing Toronado, 3-1/4" d Member Lindsay Ranch Club badge, late 1950s, 16" x 37" **$50**

Countertop standee, cardboard, easel on back, printed text on back, "New on TV From Disney Studios Zorro/ABC-TV/Brought To You By Seven-Up, imprint of Channel 6, Thursday 8 P.M.," copyright 1957, 12" x 16" **$50**

Figure, painted and glazed ceramic, Enesco, orig foil sticker, copyright, "WDE.140," attached foil-covered cardboard string tag, replaced metal sword, 3" x 4" x 7" h **$125**

Game, Whitman, 15-1/2" sq board, complete set of picture letter cards, one generic plastic marker missing, copyright 1965, 8" x 15-1/2" x 1-1/2" deep box **$75**

Puzzle, frame tray, , Whitman, full-color Zorro and Captain Ramone sword fighting, copyright 1957, 11-1/2" x 14-1/2" **$25**

School bag, vinyl covered canvas, plastic carrying handle, vinyl carrrying strap, unused store stock, c1958, 3-1/2" x 13" x 10" h...................**$90**

DOLLHOUSES

History: Dollhouses date from the 18th century to modern times. Early dollhouses often were handmade, sometimes with only one room. The most common type was made for a young girl to fill with replicas of furniture scaled especially to fit into a dollhouse. Specially sized dolls also were made for dollhouses. All types of accessories in all types of styles were available, and dollhouses could portray any historical period.

American

Gambrel roof, painted off-white, red pasteboard scalloped shingles, front opening half doors, six rooms, original paper wall and floor coverings, hinged door in rear roof, front steps, orig furniture, bisque dolls, accessories, and rugs, some paint and paper wear, 28-1/4" w, 17-1/4" d, 32-1/2" h **$920**

Ivory-painted gable and center hallway, five large rooms and attic bedroom, attached garage, separate blue shutters and window boxes, most furnishings from same period as house, approx. 40 items, made by John Leonard Plock, NY architect, c1932, 21" w, 43" h **$250**

Victorian, two-story house, modified Federal style, mansard roof with widow's walk, fenced-in front garden, simulated grass and fountains, polychrome details, last quarter 19th C, 21-1/4" l, 28-3/4" h **$400**

Bliss, chromolithograph paper on wood

Two-story, blue litho paper on roof, blue wood on back, red wood chimney and base, two open lower windows and two upper windows, house opens in front, litho wall and floor coverings inside, marked "R. Bliss" on door, some wear, one wall slightly warped, 14" h **$575**

Two-story, front porch with turned columns, working front door, overhanging roof with lattice-work balcony, blue-gray roof with dormer windows, hinged front, int. with two rooms, printed carpeting and wallpaper, celluloid windows with later lace curtains, electric lights, two scratch-built chairs, 16-1/2" h **$1,725**

Two-story, two single windows down, one double window up, remnants of windows and curtains, small porch and balcony on front, marked "R. Bliss" on front door, soiling to paper, cardboard front warped, 12-1/2" h **$525**

Elastolin, Germany, farmyard, house, barn, fencing, trees, and various figures, 29" w **$1,150**

German, Nuremberg Kitchen, dark yellow walls with deep red trim, red and black checkerboard floor, cream stove hood, green furniture, tin stove, tin and copper pots, set of scales, wash boiler, baking pans, utensils, pottery, porcelain, and pewter tableware, some paint wear and imperfections, late 19th C, 35" w, 11-1/4" d, 17" h **$2,300**

McLoughlin, folding house, two rooms, dec int., orig box, 12" x 17" x 16" **$950**

Schoenhut, mansion, two-story, eight rooms, attic, tan brick design, red roof, large dormer, 20 glass windows, orig decal, 1923, 20" x 26" x 30" **$1,750**

Tootsietoy, house, furniture, and accessories, printed Masonite, half-timbered style, two rooms down, two up, removable roof, open back, orchid and pink bedroom sets, orchid bathroom, brown dining room set, flocked sofa and chairs, green and white kitchen pcs, piano, bench, lamps, telephone, cane-back sofa, rocker, some damage and wear to 3/4 scale furniture, 21" w, 10-1/8" d, 16" h **$525**

DOORSTOPS

History: Doorstops became popular in the late 19th century. They are either flat or three-dimensional and were made out of a variety of different materials, such as cast iron, bronze, or wood. Hubley, a leading toy manufacturer, made many examples.

All prices listed are for excellent original paint unless otherwise noted. Original paint and condition greatly influence the price of a doorstop. To get top money, the original paint on a piece must be close to mint condition. Chipping of paint, paint loss, and wear reduce the value. Repainting severely reduces value and eliminates a good deal of the piece's market value, thereby reducing its value. A broken piece has little value to none.

Reproduction Alert. Reproductions are proliferating as prices on genuine doorstops continue to rise. A reproduced piece generally is slightly smaller than the original unless an original mold is used. The overall casting of reproductions is not as smooth as on the originals. Reproductions also lack the detail apparent in originals, including the appearance of the painted areas. Any bright orange rusting is strongly indicative of a new piece. Beware. If it looks too good to be true, it usually is.

Notes: Pieces described contain at least 80 percent or more of the original paint and are in very good condition. Repainting drastically reduces price and desirability. Poor original paint is preferred over repaint.

All listings are cast-iron and flat-back castings unless otherwise noted.

Art Deco woman, wedge sgd "Joe Wagner Realty Co." on front base, very good, 5-1/8" x 4-3/4" **$225**

Bathing beauties, Hubley, sgd "Fish, 240," two Art Deco bathers under bright umbrella, excellent, 10-7/8" x 5-1/4" **$450**

Blue jay, standing in grass with flowers, good, 4-7/8" x 3-3/4" **$500**

Caddy golfer, white caddy, brown plaid knickers, turquoise necktie, excellent, 8" x 5-3/4" **$1,910**

Cape cod, thatched roof, yellow hollyhocks, pink flowering vines, picket fence on side, near mint, 4-3/4" x 7-1/4" **$560**

Cat, sleeping

Hubley, repaint, 8-1/2" x 5-1/4" **$150**

Unknown maker, full figure, painted black, excellent, 5-1/4" x 12-1/4" x 10-1/4" dia **1,460**

Clipper ship, *Charles W. Morgan*, back sgd "P. F. Gay, Dartmouth, Mass. Copyright 1932," ship at dock, flying American flag, near mint, 10-5/8" x 14-7/8" **$1,120**

Cottage, snow capped roofs, yellow clapboards, green trees, excellent, 7-3/4" x 7-1/8" **$4,480**

Elk, attributed to Albany Foundry, standing on rocks, excellent, 9-7/8" x 8-5/8" **$840**

Fawn, sgd "Taylor Cook C 1930, No. 6," Art Deco style, excellent, 9-7/8" x 5-3/4" **$560**

Flower basket, pansies and morning glories, angel-embossed basket, excellent, 11-1/2" x 7" **$280**

Flying ducks, Spencer, realistic paint, near mint, 7-1/2" x 5-1/4" **$1,000**

Fox terrier, Hubley, full standing figure, facing right, near mint, 8-3/4" x 8-1/4" **$450**

Fruit basket, mkd "16," fruit overflowing woven basket, two pcs of fruit lying at base, excellent, 5-1/8" x 5-3/8" **$225**

Heron, Albany Foundry, near mint, 7-1/2" x 5" **$450**

Highland lighthouse, sgd "Highland Light Cape Cod," two pc casting, excellent, 9" x 7-3/4" **$3,360**

Indian maiden, bright colors, excellent, 8-5/8" x 2-7/8" **$340**

John Humphrey house, 3-story saltbox with dormer windows, gray clapboards, green base sgd "The John Humphrey House, Swampscott," excellent, 5-1/8" x 7-1/4" **$1,100**

Medieval Knight in Armor, sgd "I.V.I. Pat Pend.," very good, 13-1/4" x 5-7/8" **$120**

Narcissus, Hubley, flowers in ftd urn, mkd "266," near mint, 7-1/4" x 6-3/4" **$310**

Old mill, Greenblatt Studios, old mill and stone bridge by stream and winding lane, near mint, 9-3/4" x 7-1/4" **$8,400**

Palomino horse, Hubley, near mint, 7-3/4" x 10-3/4" **$260**

Peter Rabbit, Albany or National Foundry, excellent, 8-1/4" x 4-7/8" **$1,120**

Poppies, yellow flowers, slant handled basket, back sgd "C.H.F. CO. E110," excellent, 10-1/2" x 8" **$840**

Puss in Boots, white kitten playing in black boot, sgd "Copyright 1930, Creations Co.," excellent, 8-3/8" x 5-3/4" **$1,910**

Putting golfer, Hubley #34, red coat, gray pinstriped knickers, excellent, 8-3/8" x 7-1/8" **$510**

Rabbit in top hat, blue jacket, red bowtie, plaid vest, National Foundry, #89, near mint, 9-7/8" x 4-5/8" **$1,800**

Doorstop, mansion on top of hill, bronzed, stamped "B&H" (Bradley & Hubbard), 9-1/2" x 8-1/2", **$2,900.**
Photo courtesy of David Rago Auctions, Inc.

Roses in planter, pastel roses, ribbed planter, near mint, 7" x 4-3/4" **$400**

Salt box house, stone fence, attributed to Sarah Symonds, mkd "Appletree, Mass," red clapboard house, stone wall, excellent, 5-7/8" x 9-1/8" **$4,200**

Spanish dancer, Hubley 193, ruffled flowered dress and shawl, holding fan, 8-7/8" x 5" **$200**

Sulgrave manor house

A. M. Greenblatt, sgd "1 Copyright 1925 by A. M. Greenblatt Studios" on back, "Ancestral Home of George Washington" on front base, near mint, 9-1/8" x 10-7/8" **$1,350**

National Foundry, excellent, 5-1/2" x 5-1/16" **$115**

Three kittens, Bradley and Hubbard, sgd "B & H," three kittens seated in open book, orig rubber bumpers, excellent, 5-1/4" x 6-3/8" **$1,100**

Tulips

Albany or National Foundry, mkd "41," multicolored tulips, ridged vase, green 2-tiered base, near mint, 8-1/4" h **340**

Connecticut Foundry, sgd "Conn Fdry Corp 1929," colored tulips in vase, excellent, 10-5/8" x 6-3/4" **$225**

West Wind, CJO, Judd Co., 1253, sgd "The West Wind" on front of base, young girl walking in field of flowers, hair blowing, skirt billowing, rare, near mint, 18" x 8" **$23,250**

Windmill with cottages, post and rail fence, excellent, 9-7/8" x 11-1/2" **$1,100**

Doorstop, swan, brass, English, **$165.**
Photo courtesy of Wiederseim Associates, Inc.

Doorstop, cat, seated, white, green eyes, **$400.**

FAIRY LAMPS

History: Fairy lamps, which originated in England in the 1840s, are candle-burning night lamps. They were used in nurseries, hallways, and dim corners of the home.

Two leading candle manufacturers, the Price Candle Company and the Samuel Clarke Company, promoted fairy lamps as a means to sell candles. Both contracted with glass, porcelain, and metal manufacturers to produce the needed shades and cups. For example, Clarke used Worcester Royal Porcelain Company, Stuart & Sons, and Red House Glass Works in England, plus firms in France and Germany.

Fittings were produced in a wide variety of styles. Shades ranged from pressed to cut glass, from Burmese to Nailsea. Cups are found in glass, porcelain, brass, nickel, and silver plate.

American firms selling fairy lamps included Diamond Candle Company of Brooklyn, Blue Cross Safety Candle Co., and Hobbs-Brockunier of Wheeling, West Virginia.

Two-piece (cup and shade) and three-piece (cup with matching shade and saucer) fairy lamps can be found. Married pieces are common.

Marks: Clarke's trademark was a small fairy with a wand surrounded by the words "Clarke Fairy Pyramid, Trade Mark."

Fairy lamp, Webb, Burmese, four parts, shaded shade and ruffled base, crystal candleholder, underplate marked with Clark's "Cricklite," base has Webb trademark, 6-1/2" d base, 5-1/2" h overall, **$750.**
Photo courtesy of The Early Auction Company, LLC.

Reproduction Alert. Reproductions abound.

Bisque, tri-face baby girl, 3-1/2" **$70**

Blue and white frosted ribbon glass dome top shade, ruffled base, clear marked "S. Clarke" insert, flakes on shade, 6" **$490**

Blue satin mother-of-pearl shade, clear Clarke Fairy pyramid insert, 3-3/4" **$225**

Blue satin swirl shade, matching base, ruffled top and edge, 5" **$325**

Burmese, dec shade, clear Clark's Cricklite base, 4" **$900**

Burmese, egg-shaped shade, crystal insert, colorful porcelain bowl, stamped S. Clark's patent trademark, English trademark backstamp, 8" **$1,380**

Burmese Criklite, dome shaped shade, pleated bowl shaped base, clear glass candle cup sgd "Clarke's Criklite Trade Mark," 7-1/2" d, 5-1/2" h **$1,350**

Clarke Pyramid, light, holder, and white porcelain mug, frosted shade set on finger loop base, sgd "Clarke Food Warmer," adv slogans on mug, 8-1/2" **$125**

Clear molded flame shade, controlled bubbles, clear S. Clarke's Fairy Pyramid base, 4-1/2" **$60**

Figural green glass shade in shape of monk, set on frosted shoulders base, 4-1/2" **$110**

Green Nailsea shade, porcelain Doulton Lamplih dec base, sgd "S. Clarke's Fairy" in center, 5-1/2" **$1,300**

Green opaque shade, gold and blue enamel dec, clear pressed glass pedestal base, 8-3/4" **$275**

Lavender and frosted white shade, matching ruffled base, zigzag design, 5-1/2" **$150**

Metal, colored inset jewels, reticulated shade with bird designs, 4-1/2" **$185**

Ruby red, profuse white loopings, bowl shaped base with eight turned up scallops, clear glass candle cup holder marked "S. Clarke Patent Trade Mark Fairy," 5-3/4" **$1,250**

Ruby red, white loopings, matching piecrust crimped base, inclusion on shade, 4" d, 4-1/2" h **$585**

Ruby red Criklite, white loopings, dome shaped shade, bowl shaped base with 26 pleats, clear glass candle cup sgd "S. Clarke Patent Trade Mark Fairy," 7" d, 6" h **$975**

Ruby red Criklite, white loopings, satin dome shaped shade, clear cup mkd "S. Clarkes Patent Trade Mark," 4" h **$335**

Yellow satin shade, matching ftd base, clear sgd "S. Clarke Fairy" insert, 6-1/4" **$650**

Yellow satin swirl shade, clear S. Clark's Fairy pyramid base, 4" **$150**

Webb, blue shade dec with bird and branch, clear Clarke's Criklite insert, sq blue satin base, 6-1/2" **$1,500**

White and yellow striped shade, clear S. Clarke Fairy insert, nestled on matching white and yellow ruffled base, 6" h **$500**

FIREARM ACCESSORIES

History: Muzzle-loading weapons of the 18th and early 19th centuries varied in caliber and required the owner to carry a variety of equipment, including a powder horn or flask, patches, flints or percussion caps, bullets, and bullet molds. In addition, military personnel were responsible for bayonets, slings, and miscellaneous cleaning equipment and spare parts.

During the French and Indian War, soldiers began to personalize their powder horns with intricate engraving, in addition to the usual name or initial used for identification. Sometimes professional horn smiths were employed to customize these objects, which have been elevated to a form of folk art by some collectors.

In the mid-19th century, cartridge weapons replaced their black-powder ancestors. Collectors seek anything associated with early ammunition—from the cartridges themselves to advertising material. Handling old ammunition can be extremely dangerous because of decomposition of compounds. Seek advice from an experienced collector before becoming involved in this area.

Notes: Military-related firearm accessories generally are worth more than their civilian counterparts.

Calendar, Marble Arms & Mfg Co., artwork by Philip R. Goodwin, top image of two hunters, one with gun raised at animal across river, bottom image of man by campfire, docked canoe, 1918 .... **$5,230**

Canteen, painted, cheese-box style, dark red paint overall, one side painted gold with a large primitive eagle with shield breast, the top of the shield red with cream lettering "No. 37," other side painted in gold letters, "Lt. Rufus Cook," pewter nozzle, sq nail construction, strap loops missing, 7" d, 2-5/8" deep **$1,650**

Cartridge board, 22" x 25", Winchester, New Haven, CT, 1874, showing range of rimfire cartridges, wood frame, some shelf spoiling, corner repair to frame **$12,915**

Cartridge box

Hall and Hubbard, .22 caliber, green and black label "100 No. 1/22-100/ Pistol Cartridges," cov with molded cream and black paper, empty, missing about half green side label, 3-7/8" x 2" x 1" **$300**

Union Metallic Cartridge Co., .32 caliber, cream and black label "Fifth .32 caliber/No. 2/Pistol Cartridges," engraving of Smith & Wesson 1st Model 3rd Issue, checked covering, orange and black side labels, unopened, 4" x 2-1/8" x 1-1/4" **$210**

Catalog

Colt's-The Arm of Law and Order, 42 pgs, black and white illus and specifications of 16 models of Colt revolvers and automatic pistols, 5-3/4" x 7-3/4" **$25**

Savage Arms Corp., Chicopee Falls, MA, 1951, 52 pgs, No. 51, *Component Parts Price List for Savage, Stevens, Fox Shotguns & Rifles*, 8-1/2" x 11" **$35**

Winchester Repeating Arms, New Haven, CT, 215 pgs, Cat No. 81, illus of repeating and single-shot rifles, repeating shotguns, cartridges, shells, primers, percussions caps, shot, 5-1/2" x 8-1/2" **$250**

Firearm accessory, gun cabinet, Arts & Crafts, three doors, mirrored pane over two drawers, 69-1/2" x 44-1/2" x 19", **$2,500.**
Photo courtesy of David Rago Auctions, Inc.

Flask, brass, dead game, emb, stamped "Am. Flask & Cap Co.," 8" l **$200**

Knapsack, painted canvas, flap having American eagle with shield among stars and surrounded by oval cloud border, scrolled banner inscribed "RIFLE CADET," painted in red, white, blue, and gold on black ground, two leather strap and iron buckles, reverse with ink inscription, "Benjamin Pope Bridgewater July 4th 1820," minor paint losses, wooden hanger and twine attached to the back, 13-5/8" x 13-1/4" **$31,725**

Poster, store type, Winchester Rifles, Shotguns and Ammunition For Sale Here, two bear dogs in foreground, bloodhounds in back, 41-1/2" x 32" **$6,300**

Powder horn, engraved

America, incised animal figures, scallop, and linear borders on butt end, inscribed "M RIFLE COMP'Y 1823/ horne" next to the initials "AM," wood plug with applied wire staple for carrying strap, carved wooden stopper, c1823, 10-1/2" h **$450**

"JOB WATERMAN HIS HORN/ CALEB HARRIS/FEB,y THE 10 AD 1758/ PROVIDENCE," Providence, RI, in four circular or lobed reserves, applied silver plated brass mouthpiece, copper band around butt rim, leather band with woven twill strap sewn to neck, c1858, 14-1/8" l **$900**

John Goddard, incised dec, borders of wave-like and compass motifs, scene with figure driving horse and carriage with sun overhead and dog, sgd "JOHN GODDARD," indistinct date 1747 or 1777, butt end with extension lobe pierced for carrying strap, pine plug, late 18th C, 16" l **$1,175**

"Robert Guy's Horn" down side, smaller engraving near spout, dated "1840," domed pine plug, flared end for carrying strap, hole 1" above name, 16-1/2" l **$250**

"Stil not this horn for fear of shame for hear doth stand the oner name jacob lewis 1785, (sic)" two rows of geometric devices round bottom, carved and incised lines at spout, dome-shaped wooden plug, America, small age crack, wear, late 18th C, 18" l **$1,610**

"Wm M. 1799," also "J. M. 1814," surrounded by series of inscribed circles, flat pine plug, 18" l **$1,200**

Primer, engraved, New York scene, primitively engraved men and animals, date "1852" added later, c1800, 7" l **$1,155**

Product leaflet

Western Silvertip Ammunition, glossy paper, color printing, diecut upper corner, one side shows 18 variations of brass cartridges in differing gauges for large game hunting, one panel devoted to three Winchester hunting rifles, 1956, 3-1/2" x 6" closed **$25**

Western-Winchester, full color printing, illus and describes western Super-X and Xpert shotgun shells and cartridges, 1957, 3-1/4" x 6-1/2" closed **$15**

Shotgun box, empty

Austin Cartridge Co., Crack-Shot, 16 gauge, full-color scene of three hunting dogs on front **$2,310**

Chamberlin Cartridge Co., 12 gauge, Blue Rocks **$1,100**

Clinton Cartridge Co., Pointer Brand, 12 ga, smokeless powder, pointer in center with bird in mouth, light blue top and lettering, gold border, red ground, 4-1/8" x 4-1/8" x 2-1/2" **$350**

J. F. Schmelzer & Sons Arms Co., 12 gauge carver cartridges, illus of hunter and pointed on front **$1,750**

Peters Quick Shot, 12 gauge shotgun shells **$5,835**

Robin Hood Eclipse Cartridge, 12 gauge, near smokeless powder shells **$2,550**

Sign, Winchester Guns and Ammo, guns and dead game image by Alexander Pope, tin litho, wood structural backing, dark green background, 36" x 30"..**$1,300**

Tin, Oriental Smokeless Gunpowder, half pound, four litho labels with full-color ducks................................**$1,810**

Tinder box, tin, candle socket, inside damper, flint, and steel, 4-3/8" d **$330**

Tinder lighter, flintlock
Rosewood pistol grip, tooled brass fittings, 5-1/2" l.......................**$750**
Compartment for extra flint, taper holder, 6-1/2" l.........................**$550**

Water keg, wooden, American, oval, flattened bottom, two Shaker-style wide-tongued wooden straps, large hand-forged nail on each end for carrying cord, orig wood stopper, late 18th/ early 19th C, 9" x 7-1/2" x 9" **$400**

FIREARMS

History: The 15th-century Matchlock Arquebus was the forerunner of the modern firearm. The Germans refined the wheelock firing mechanism during the 16th and 17th centuries. English settlers arrived in America with the smoothbore musket; German settlers had rifled arms. Both used the new flintlock firing mechanism.

A major advance was achieved when Whitney introduced interchangeable parts into the manufacturing of rifles. Refinements in firearms continued in the 19th century. The percussion ignition system was developed by the 1840s. Minie, a French military officer, produced a viable projectile. By the end of the 19th century, cartridge weapons dominated the field.

Notes: Two factors control the pricing of firearms—condition and rarity. Variations in these factors can cause a wide range in the value of antique firearms. For instance, a Colt 1849 pocket-model revolver with a five-inch barrel can be priced from $100 to $700, depending on whether all the component parts are original, some are missing, how much of the original finish (bluing) remains on the barrel and frame, how much silver plating remains on the brass

trigger guard and back strap, and the condition and finish of the walnut grips.

Be careful to note a weapon's negative qualities. A Colt Peterson belt revolver in fair condition will command a much higher price than the Colt pocket model in very fine condition. Know the production run of a firearm before buying it.

Laws regarding the sale of firearms have gotten stricter. Be sure to sell and buy firearms through auction houses and dealers properly licensed to transact business in this highly regulated area.

Additional Resources:

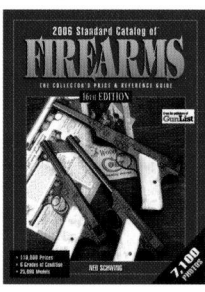

2006 Standard Catalog of® Firearms, 16th Ed., by Ned Schwing, ed., Krause Publications, Iola, WI.

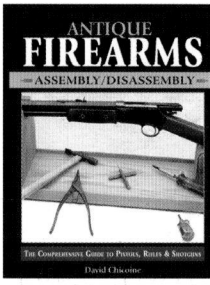

Antique Fireams Assembly/Disassembly, by David Chicoine, Krause Publications, Iola, WI.

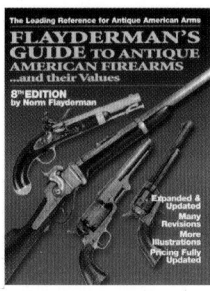

Flayderman's Guide to Antique American Firearms and Their Val-

ues, 8th Ed., by Norm Flayderman, Krause Publications, Iola, WI.

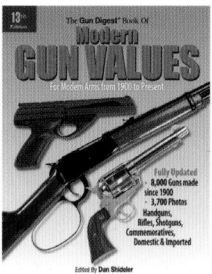

The Gun Digest Book of Modern Gun Values, 13th Ed., by Dan Shideler, ed., Krause Publications, Iola, WI.

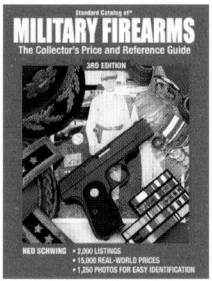

Standard Catalog of® Military Firearms, 3rd Ed., by Ned Schwing, Krause Publications, Iola, WI.

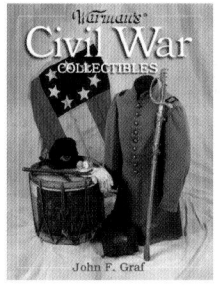

Warman's® Civil War Collectibles, by John F. Graf, Krause Publications, Iola, WI.

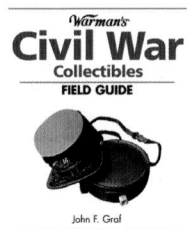

Warman's® Civil War Collectibles Field Guide, by John F. Graf, Krause Publications, Iola, WI.

The .54 caliber, Richmond Sharps carbine (Confederate), is recognized by its brass furniture. **$13,500-$15,500.**

.50 caliber, Maynard carbine, **$900-$1,650.**

Carbine

Hall-North, Model 1843, percussion, .52 caliber, rifled 21" barrel, bold metal stampings, signature and 1849 on receiver, traces of old brown finish, walnut stock with old split between trigger guard and barrel, small repairs near breech, 40" l...........................**$935**

Joslyn Model 1862, .52 caliber, 22" round barrel, walnut stock, clear inspector's markings, brass buttplate, trigger guard and barrel band, stamped signatures on lock and breech block, 38-5/8" l................**$650**

C. S. Richmond, .58 caliber, 25" barrel, all-steel hardware, brass nose cap, buttplate stamped "U.S.," Type 3, humpback lock, "C. S. Richmond, 1864" mark, no sling swivels, 43" l
....**$3,300**

Sharp's New Model 1863, breech loading, walnut stock and forearm, double inspectors markings, 22" blued barrel, areas of very light case coloring on lock, buttplate, hammer, barrel band, and receiver, clear stampings on lock, 34" l.............................**$1,980**

Spencer, Civil War Model, .52 caliber rimfire, 22" round barrel, overall brown finish on all metal surfaces, worn walnut stick, faint inspector's mark, forearm with additional coat of varnish, 39" l............................**$2,100**

Springfield, Model 1884 Trapdoor, saddle ring, mint bore, Buffington sight, stamped "C. Proper," range with inspector's cartouche..................**$825**

Wesson, Frank, 28" octagonal barrel, folding rear peep sight, walnut stock

with orig dark finish, rear open sight missing, 43" l overall **$275**

Dueling pistols, percussion lock

English, London, dolphin hammer, belt clip, engraved scrollwork on frame, checkered burl-wood grip, barrel engraved "London," second quarter 19th C, 8-1/2" l, price for pr
....**$650**

English, Queen-Anne style, London, for J. Wilson, scrolled mask butt, grip set with small monogrammed cartouche, plain stylized dolphin hammer, cannon barrel engraved with cartouches, and maker's mark on underside, late 18th C, 8" l, price for pr..**$500**

Flintlock long arms

Brooks, Cecil, Jager, custom, figured walnut stock with relief carved acanthus leaves on either side of comb, also around cheekpiece and entry pipe, metal surfaces finished bright, good amount of engraving, inlaid signature plate on 25-3/4" l octagonal swamped barrel, sliding lid patch box with ivory inlaid panel, scrimshaw hunting scene, large variegated stray inlay on cheekpiece, 41-1/2" l
....**$4,600**

Buchele, W., Bicentennial, curly maple stock, relief carved bust of George Washington with flag behind cheekpiece along with acanthus leaves on either side of comb, brass hardware including engraved patch box with

eagle finial, applied Liberty Bell, twelve inlays along with brass and nickel silver floral wire inlay, 58-1/2" l
....**$3,500**

Cooper, J, lock sgd "J. Cooper," engraved detail, brass hardware including patch box, curly maple stock with nickel silver escutcheons, thumb piece with faint checkering, 38-1/2" l octagonal barrel turned found for bayonet on last 3" with lug, conversion to flint with pieced repair to forend and other replacements, 54-1/2" l....................................**$950**

French, Model 1766 Charlesville Musket, lock plate only partially legible, matching ramrod, top jaw and top screw period replacements, 44-3/4" l orig barrel length **$1,250**

Golcher, Joseph, Philadelphia, PA, .54 caliber, octagonal barrel, brass patch box, buttplate, trigger guard, carved and brass-fitted pick compartment, brass and silver inlays along tiger maple stock, lock plate marked, barrel initialed, c1800, 54" l, 38-1/2" l
....**$4,750**

Kentucky, R. E. Leman, .38 caliber, small brass front sight and fixed rear sight, top flat in front of chamber area is marked "R.E. LEMAN/ LANCASTER PA/WARRANTED," unmarked flat lock plate, applied grain tiger striped stock, simple brass trigger guard, two-pc patch box with crescent buttplate and dbl. set triggers, ovoid forestock with integral ramrod groove and two small brass guides, dark heavy patina on iron and wood, 37-3/8" oct. bbl
....**$920**

.69 caliber, Model 1842, Harpers Ferry, 3-band musket, **$950-$1,450.**

Hand-fabricated Confederate musket, **$2,500-$2,850.**

Pennsylvania, attributed to W. Haga, Reading School, maple stock, relief carving, incised details, brass hardware with flintlock, some age cracks, glued repair, good patina, replaced patch box lid, 50-1/2" l octagon to round barrel.............................**$1,760**

U. S. Model 1819, Hall, breech loading, second-production type, Harpers Ferry Armory, John Hall's patents, .52 caliber, single shot, three barrel bands, breechblock deeply stamped, 32-5/8" round barrel **$1,200**

Virginia, curly-maple stock with good figure, relief carving, old mellow varnished finish, brass hardware, engraved and pierced patch box, Ketland lock reconverted back to flint, silver thumb piece inlay, barrel and forend shortened slightly, small pierced repair at breech area, top flat engraved "H. B.," 41-1/2" l **$3,300**

Flintlock pistols-single shot
English
Blunderbuss, 14" round iron barrel with Birmingham proofs, fitted with 12-1/2" triangular snap bayonet, walnut full stock with lightly engraved brass furniture, two ramrod pipes, buttplate, trigger guard, small shield-shaped wrist plate, two lock-plate screw escutcheons, attributed to John

Whitehouse, metal parts complete and orig throughout, missing sliver of wood along right side at muzzle, early 19th C, 29-1/2" overall **$1,500**

Tower, .60 caliber, 12" round barrel, full-length military stock, brass trigger guard, butt cap and sidelined, lock plate marked "Tower" behind hammer and crown over "GR" forward of hammer, proofed on left side of barrel at breech, crown on tang behind tang screw, good condition, re-browned and cleaned, replaced front sight, working order **$700**

French, military, 9" round iron barrel, flat beveled lock plate with faceted pan fitted with flat beveled reinforced hammer, brass furniture, unmarked, 16" overall length........................**$800**

Halsbach & Sons, Baltimore, MD, holster pistol, 9" brass part round, part octagon barrel, .65 caliber, lock marked "Halsbach & Sons," large brass butt cap with massive spread wing eagle (primitive) in high relief surrounded by cluster of 13 stars, large relief shell carving around tang of barrel, full walnut stock, pin-fastened, c1785 to early 1800s **$1,750**

Kentucky, T. B. Cherington, octagonal smoothbore barrel, stamped "T. P. Cherington" on barrel and lock plate, .45 caliber, brightly polished iron

parts, walnut stock, 12-1/2" barrel **$2,500**

U. S. Model 1805, iron rib underneath holding ramrod pipe, lockplate marked with spread eagle and shield over "US" and vertically at rear "Harper's Ferry" over "1808," .54 caliber, walnut half stock with brass buttplate and trigger guard, Flayderman 6A-008, 10" round iron barrel **$3,000**

Musket
Colt, Model 1861, .58 caliber, "17th N.Y.V." beneath stock, good signature, date, and stampings on metal, inspector's cartouche on stock, bright gray metal, areas of pitting around bolster and lock, 39" barrel **$1,375**

Enfield, .58 caliber, unmarked, percussion, square base front sight/bayonet lug with 800 meter military sight, lock plate has markings of a crown over "VR" and date "1856," right side of butt stock carries cartouche of circle with broad arrow and date "1856," three bbl bands with sling swivels and slotted head ramrod, upper bbl band and sling loop, as well as sling loop on trigger and ramrod, appear to be recent replacements, bbl retains smooth gray-brown patina with heavy pitting over breech end, light refinish to wood, worn and damaged nipple, dated 1856, 39" bbl.....................**$815**

Confederate, Griswold, .36 caliber, brass-frame revolver, **$22,000-$30,000**.

Cased set, Belgian dueling pistols, **$1,300-$1,700**.

Colt 1851, .36 caliber, Navy revolver, **$750-$1,400**.

Harpers Ferry, Model 1816 Conversion Musket, .69 caliber, standard 1816 Model, makers' name and date 1837 vertically behind hammer, small eagle over "US" in front of hammer on lock plate, top bayonet lug and front sight on rear strap of split front band, iron mounted with three bands and tulip head ramrod, left flat has inspector's initials "JAS," conversion accomplished by mounting nipple at breech end of bbl and filling flash pan cut-out with brass, fine condition, iron retains dark smoky patina with light pitting around nipple area, fine hand-rubbed patina, broken away nipple, 42" bbl.................................**$690**

Parker Snow & Co., Miller conversion, 40" round barrel, bold stampings include signature, eagle, and 1864 on lock, 56" overall **$1,375**

Springfield, Model 1863 Musket, .58 caliber. heavily rusted, deeply pitted except for replacement ramrod, stock is sound, but has some scorching damage, bolster is battered from lack of nipple, lock works, 40" bbl **$815**

Percussion pistol

American, engraved, sgd on lock "P. D. Gwaltney & Co., Norfolk, Va," conversion from flintlock, checkered walnut stock with steel hardware, pineapple finial on trigger guard, swamped octagonal barrel with thin gold band of inlay at breech, small chip, hairline at lock mortise, end cap missing, 15-3/4" l...**$850**

English

Folding bayonet, simple engraving on frame, stands of flags and "Lenning," old hairlines in grip, 4" l barrel, 8-1/2" l **$250**

Single shot, sgd "W. Parker" on lock, "Maker to His Majesty, London" on barrel, finely checkered bag grip, narrow pierced repair just below lock, 8-1/4" l.............................**$715**

Gibbs, Tiffany & Co., Sturbridge, MA, underhammer percussion pistol, 6" cast steel barrel with engraved flower and vine motifs and imp marks: "202," "E HUTCHINGS & CO AGENTS BALTO," "GIBBS TIFFANY & CO. STURBRIDGE MASS.," eagle motif; rosewood grips with geometric mother-of-pearl inlay, silver back strap engraved "Dr. C.A. Cheever;" mahogany hinged case with engraved silver plaque on top "From Eusebius Hutchings of Baltimore, Md. to Charles A. Cheever Portsmouth, New Hampshire," interior contour lined with black velvet, fitted with accessories including copper powder flask, brass bullet mold with mahogany handles marked "202," cleaning rod, ramrod, five small leather ammunition pouches, loss on underhammer, descended from Cheever family, early 19th C, 9-7/8" l pistol, 12-5/8" x 5-5/8" x 2-1/4" case..............................**$3,200**

Remington, New Model, bold inspector's stamp on grips, sub inspector's initials on various other parts, old brown finish with some bluing remaining on cylinder, elevated front sight appears to be early addition, 1858.................................**$980**

Target, figured walnut buttstock, brass buttplate, steel trigger guard, 22-3/4" octagonal barrel stamped 340L at muzzle, single hammer mounted on breech/frame, ramrod missing, narrow pieced repair to stock, 38-1/2" l...**$300**

U. S. Springfield, lock stamped with signature and 1856, eagle on Maynard primer door, 12" barrel dated 1855, brass hardware with iron back strap, walnut shoulder stock, brass hardware, few hairlines, pierced repair on hammer, 28-1/2" l.................**$1,750**

Waters, 8-1/2" round barrel, bright metal, stamped address and "1838" on lock, double inspector markings on stock, 14" l.............................**$660**

Pistol

Colt Model 1911 Army, .45 caliber auto, orig blued finish, checkered walnut grips, good signature and other stampings, 8-1/2" l.....................**$825**

Sharp's Pepperbox, four shot, .22 caliber, 3" barrels, traces of orig bluing, stamped signature, patent information around hammer screw, gutta percha grips with checkered design, 5-1/2" l................................**$220**

Volcanic Lever Action, Navy, .38 caliber, 8" barrel, signature "The Volcanic Repeating Arms Co." on top, walnut grips, brass frame with old patina, minor pitting on one side, tab for magazine tube broken, spring missing, 14-1/2" l.....................**$9,900**

Revolver

Baby Dragoon, .31 caliber, standard 5" oct. bbl without rammer, cylinder has round stop holes, brass grip frame with one-pc wood grips, top flat of bbl is devoid of orig Colt markings, very faintly visible word "Orleans," presumably stamp of New Orleans retailer, medium gray-brown patina on iron, repaired and refinished grip, shoulder repairs on back strap, accompanied by hand-written letter stating that this revolver was owned and used by Confederate Col. Henry C. Kellogg **$4,025**

Colt

Model 1849 Pocket, 4" barrel, .31 caliber, faint New York address, all serial numbers matching, replaced catch **$495**

Model 1860 Army, matching serial numbers, butt signature, New York address, overall light brown to gray surface on metal, brass trigger guard, iron grip straps, 8" barrel, 14" overall, old corner chips on grips, period black leather holster with raised "U. S." design and eight or three over stamped "G" on front flap, worn to grain, 13" l **$675**

Model 1861 Navy, .36 caliber, 7-1/2" round bbl, case color frame with silver-plated trigger guard and back strap, Naval battle cylinder scene with one-pc fine old ivory grips, very deep relief Mexican eagle on left side, accompanied by orig Colt casing containing Colt's patent short angle spout flask and iron bullet mold, packet of Johnston & Dow's skin cartridges, Eley cap tin **$9,500**

Lefaucheux Pin Rimfire, old bright surface on barrel, frame, and cylinder, bold signature and proofmarks, walnut grips finely alligatored varnish, 6-3/8" octagon to round barrel, one Lefaucheux cartridge on mount, 12-1/2" l **$450**

Remington

Beals, 7-3/4" barrel, old dark finish, 13-1/2" l **$825**

Model 1858, .44 caliber, 8" octagonal barrel, good signature with faint inspector's stamp on grips, 14" l **$880**

Model 1861 Navy, 7-3/8" octagon barrel, all-over matte gray finish, signature stamp **$990**

Warner, pocket, .28 caliber, 3-3/4" round bbl, cased with small flask and incorrect accessories, gray-brown patina overall, faint Warner markings on top of frame, light surface rust overall, grips badly chipped at base, gun does not fit partitions in case very well **$920**

Rifle

Allin Conversion Model 1866, 40" round barrel, worn browned finish, three bands, "U. S. Springfield" lock with eagle and 1865 date, walnut stock, in-the-making file marks, 56" l **$250**

Conestoga Rifle Works, half-stock Kentucky, cal. 36, fixed sights, tiger striped stock, pewter nose cap, dbl. set triggers, two-pc patch box, brass furniture, dark brown iron, polished brass, fine dark wood, set trigger won't hold, hammer won't cock, bbl cut to 34-1/4" **$410**

Percussion, half stock

Fordney, Melchoir, Lancaster County, (died 1846), 39-1/4" octagon barrel, sgd "M. Fordney," curly maple stock, old mellow refinishing, checkered wrist, fine engraving on brass hardware, fair border engraving on barrel, chips around lock mortise, some age splits beneath forearm, small putty repair on one side of tang, front portion of triggerguard replaced, 55" l **$1,150**

McComas, Alexander, 1843-75, stamped "A. McComas, Baltimore" on top of barrel, checkered walnut stock with steel hardware, small cap box, beavertail cheekpiece, 34" l octagon barrel, restored stock split behind lock, chip off cap box, 49-1/2" l **$420**

Partial stamped signatures on lock and barrel for J. Henry & Son, 36-3/8" octagon barrel with browned surface, walnut stock, stepped beaver tail, steel buttplate, brass trigger guard, nickel silver inlays, small "U. S." stamp just below trigger guard, 52-1/2" l, orig 8-1/2" l powder horn **$950**

Remington, rolling block

Military, approx .45 caliber, full stock, three barrel bands, 35" tapered round barrel with adjustable rear sight, clear signature on tag, ramrod missing, 50-1/2" l **$220**

Remington signature and address on tang, crown proofs, "G" stamp on buttstock, old dark finish, brass handle bayonet, dents, one band spring mission, 50" l **$330**

Springfield, Model 1873 Trapdoor, 45-70 caliber, cadet model, 29-1/2" round blued barrel, three click tumbler, eagle mark and signature on lock with eagle's head and "V. P." on breech area, minor dents on stock, ramrod, 48-3/4" l **$450**

Winchester, Model 1873 Special Order, cal. 44 WCF, standard grade, 24" oct. bbl, half-nickel front sight, slot blank in rear dovetail, early Lyman tang sight, button magazine with uncheckered wood, straight stock and crescent steel buttplate with trap **$1,610**

Shotgun

European, double barrel, 12 gauge, 30-1/2" damascus barrels, silver band overlay, sgd "R. Baumgarter in Bernburg" on barrel, engraved stag on tang, "Hubertus Geweher," figured walnut stock, horn trigger guard, 47" l **$275**

Fox Sterlingworth, 16 gauge, double barrel, 26" barrel, top lever break-open, hammerless, double trigger, blued, checkered walnut pistol grip stock and forearm **$400**

Parker Brothers, double barrel, "D" grade, Damacus steel barrels, figured walnut stock with checkering, finely engraved #2 frame with skeleton butt plate, 14" pull, extra barrel with own forearm, same serial number on both **$1,495**

San Marco Magnum, Wildfowler, goose gun, 10 gauge, never fired, Dunn's leather and canvas case, 32" over and under full choke barrels **$700**

Stevens, Model 970, 12 gauge, single shot, octagonal breech, top lever break-open, hammerless, automatic shell ejector, automatic safety, blued, case hardened frame, checkered walnut pistol grip stock and forearm, 32" l round barrel **$95**

FIREHOUSE COLLECTIBLES

History: The volunteer fire company has played a vital role in the protection and social growth of many towns and rural areas. Paid professional firemen usually are found only in large metropolitan areas. Each fire company prided itself on equipment

Fire mark, painted cast iron, William Penn in oval center, marked "Leader," **$225.**

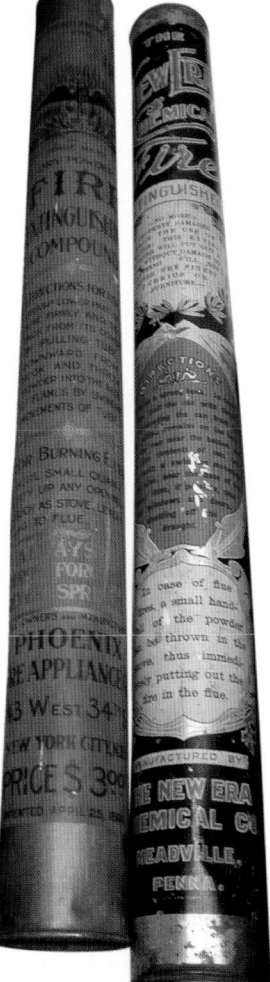

Fire extinguishers, left: Phoenix Dry Powder Fire Extinguisher Compound 22, tin litho container, eagle decoration, dated April 25, 1899, original contents, **$95**; *right: New Era Chemical Fire Extinguisher, tin litho, Meadville, PA, 22" h, original contents,* **$85.**
Photo courtesy of Dotta Auction Co., Inc.

Helmet, leather, white, silvered front plate embossed "Rescue, AFD," crossed ladders motif, brass eagle, original liner, long back, **$225.**

and uniforms. Conventions and parades gave the fire companies a chance to show off their equipment. These events produced a wealth of firehouse-related memorabilia.

Additional Resources:

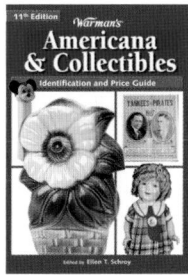

Warman's® Americana & Collectibles, 11th Ed., by Ellen T. Schroy, ed., Krause Publications, Iola, WI.

Advertising button
Baldwin II NO 22 May 26, '97, Williamsport, elderly gentleman, Whitehead & Hoag back paper, 1-1/4" d **$15**
Central NY Volunteer Fireman's Convention, Auspices Seward Tribe Alaska Esquimaus, June 26-28, 1910, Auburn, NY, 1-1/2" d **$20**
Keystone Fire Co. No. 1 Shillington, PA, Dedication May 31, 1924, real photo, man standing by doorway of two story building, Keystone Badge paper, 1-1/4" d **$15**
Marion Fire Co. Stouchsburg, Pa, real photo, truck with ladders and hose reel parked on street in front of house and tree, men standing at left, 1-1/4" d **$15**

Pennsylvania State Firemen's Convention, Allentown, multicolored, fireman in helmet, 1930, 1-1/4" d **$18**
Woodbury Fire Dept., black on gold, center pumper wagon, Friendship No. 1, 1930 event, attached to small red, white, and blue fabric ribbon **$20**

Badge
Columbia PA, arch reads "Centennial of Columbia Fire Co.," pumper, 1896 .... **$40**
Compliments of, diecut fire trumpets and hydrants on hanger, asst chief name, c1890, 2-1/2" h **$35**
15th Annual Convention National Ass'n Fire Engineers, 1887 .... **$45**
Mapleton, Iowa, June 7, '06, multicolored scene of two firemen holding hose at left, larger scene of two fireman using tools against fire bursting thru doorway, Whitehead & Hoag back paper, 1-3/4" h **$40**
Wilmington, DE, 1907, fabric with celluloid pin **$15**
Bell, brass, iron back, 11" **$125**
Belt, red, black, and white, marked "Hampden," 43" l **$85**
Box, cov, oval, wallpaper covering with fire engine scene, blue ground, white and green highlights, inside lined with Der York Democrat 1834 newspaper, 17" l, 13-3/4" w, 14" h **$13,750**

Fire bucket
Leather, stitched seams, nailed strap handle, old black paint, brown painted int., wear, 12-1/2" h **$175**
Leather, leather handle attached with iron rings, old dark green paint over dark red with black painted handle and collar, black lettering "L.TOWER.-3.," in yellow outlined banner, America, alligatored paint surface, early 19th C, 19-1/4" h **$715**
Leather, painted red, black collar, leather handle, gilt lettering "1801. FOUNTAIN NO.2," with black shading, America, losses, handle wear, c1801, 21-1/2" h **$2,280**
Miniature, tin, bail handle, orange paint dec, "Fire Bucket" printed on side, 3" h, 1-7/8" d **$615**

Fire extinguisher
Babcock, American La France Fire Engine Co., Elmire, NY, grenade, amber glass **$500**

Hayward's Hand Fire Grenade, yellow, ground mouth, smooth base, c1870, 6-1/4" h **$85**

Red Comet, red metal canister, red glass bulb **$50**

Fire mark, cast iron, oval,

Black, gold eagle and banner dec, marked "Eagle Ins. Co. Cin O," 8" x 12"............................... **$950**

Polychrome paint, relief molded design, pumper framed by "Fire Department Insurance," 8" x 11-1/2" **$495**

Helmet

Leather, Anderson + Jones, Broad St., NY, emb and ribbed leather, brass trumpetered holder, painted tin front piece lettered "cataract hose 2 j.g.," manufacturer's stamp on underside of brim, repaint, leather losses, 9" x 14-1/4" x 11" **$635**

Stamped aluminum, black enameling, leather front panel marked "Chopmist, F.D.," interior makers label for Cairns & Brothers, Clifton, N.J.,"............................... **$200**

Ink blotter, Fireman's Fund 75th Year, Allendale, CA, fireman with little child, 1938, 4" x 9".................. **$7.50**

Ledger marker, Caisse General Fire Insurance, Statue of Liberty illus, multicolored, tin litho, 12-1/4" l, 3" w **$275**

Medal, Jacksonville Fire Co., silvered brass, firefighting symbols circled by "I.A.F.E.-1917-Jacksonville, Fla.," reverse "Compliments of N. Snellenburg & Co. Uniforms, Philadelphia, Pa," looped ring **$15**

Nozzle, hose, brass, double handle, marked "Akron Brass Mfg. Co., Inc.," 16" l............................... **$165**

Parade hat, painted leather, polychrome dec, green ground, front with eagle and harp, banner above "Hibernia," back inscribed "1752" in gilt, "1" on top, red brim underside, some age cracks, small losses to brim edge, 6-1/2" h............................... **$3,335**

Print, color lithograph, *Engine of the Red Jacket Veteran Fireman's Association...Champion of the New England League, 1894*, printed for the Brooks Bank Note Company, Boston, folio, 22-1/2" x 17-1/4" **$1,410**

Sales sheet, glossy paper, Iron Horse Metal Ware Products, Rochester Can Co., NY, pictures five galvanized red fire pails, 8-1/2" x 11".................. **$20**

Sign, Philadelphia Underwriters, heavy porcelain, detailed graphic image in center with fire mark in upper right corner, made in England, 14" x 20" **$600**

Stickpin, Honor To Our Brave, fireman portrait, red shirt, blue helmet, 1900s, 7/8" celluloid button on 1-3/4" stickpin............................... **$15**

Toy

Arcade, fire pumper, 1941 Ford, cast iron, painted red, emb sides, cast fireman, hose reel on bed, rubber tires, repaired fender, 13" l **$440**

Arcade, ladder truck, cast iron, painted red, two cast fireman, rubber tires, bed contains ladder supports, open frame design, 9-1/4" l............................... **$440**

Hubley, Ahrens Fox fire engine, cast iron, rubber tires, 7-1/2" l........ **$475**

Kenton, fire pumper, cast iron, painted red, gold highlights on boiler, and ball, emb sides, disc wheels with spoke centers.................... **$615**

Kingsbury, horse-drawn ladder wagon, sheet metal, painted red, wire supports, holding yellow wooden ladders, two seated drivers, pulled by two black horses, yellow spoke wheels, bell on frame rings as toy is pulled, 26" l................. **$2,150**

Williams, A. C., fire pumper, cast iron, painted red, gold highlights, cast driver, bell, and boiler, rear platform with railing, rubber tires, 7-1/2" l............................... **$315**

Watch fob, presentation, two sided embossed silver medal with crystal bezels, one side with raised female allegorical figure surrounded by 13 stars, other side with inscriptions "NORTHERN LIBERY FIRE CO. No 1./INSTITUTED MAY 1, 1756./ INCORPORATED MAR 18th 1833.," oval frame with scrolled crest engraved "Retired FROM Service SAM'L ALEXANDER Mar, 15, 1871," America, 19th C, solder repair to crest **$450**

FIREPLACE EQUIPMENT

History: In the colonial home, the fireplace was the gathering point for heat, meals, and social interaction. It maintained its dominant position until the introduction of central heating in the mid-19th century.

Because of the continued popularity of the fireplace, accessories still are manufactured, usually in an early-American motif.

Fire screen, brass, scene of farmer and horses plowing field, **$450.**
Photo courtesy of Joy Luke Auctions.

Fender, gilt bronze, urn and garland motif, French, 20" x 12" x 6-1/2", **$600.**
Photo courtesy of David Rago Auctions, Inc.

Bellows, painted gold fruit, green leaves, red and black decoration, front panel detached at nozzle, wear, 19th C **$90.**
Photo courtesy of Pook & Pook, Inc.

Andirons, pr, ball tops, curled feet, ring pulls joined by heavy chain, orig patina, Gustav Stickley, circular Craftsman stamp, replaced back post on one fire dog, 21" x 13" x 21", **$9,000.**
Photo courtesy of David Rago Auctions, Inc.

Log holder, vertical slats and cut-out pulls, metal Stickley Brothers tag, new finish, some chips, loss of part of one copper strap, 19-1/2" x 20" x 18-1/2", **$1,000.**

Photo courtesy of David Rago Auctions, Inc.

Mantle, Federal, carved pine and plaster, molded and blocked cornice, swag apllique and floral drop sides, late 18th c, **$2,500.**

Photo courtesy of Pook & Pook, Inc.

Fire grate, cast iron and brass, George III, early 19th C, serpentine railed basket above pierced brass frieze centering spread-wing eagle on scrolled supports, vasiform finials, ball feet, 22-1/4" x 21" x 13", **$700.**

Photo courtesy of Sloans & Kenyon Auctioneers and Appraisers.

Reproduction Alert. Modern blacksmiths are reproducing many old iron implements.

Andirons, pr, brass, brass, round ball finials, scrolled spur legs, ball feet, 8-3/4" w, 16" d, 12" h **$385**

Andirons, pr, brass and iron

Belted ball tops, baluster ring-turned shaft, sq stepped base, conforming log stops on curved log supports, America, dents, mid-19th C, 8" w, 27" d, 14-3/4" h, ... **$500**

America, brass urn-tops over iron knife-blade shaft, lower brass shield, arched legs over penny feet, last quarter 18th C, 9-1/2" w, 16-1/2" d, 21-1/2" h **$650**

J. Davis, Boston, Massachusetts, faceted steeples over belted balls, columnar shafts, spurred cabriole legs with slipper feet, conforming steeple-top log stops, signed "J DAVIS BOSTON" on billet bars, 10-5/8" w, 17-3/4" d, 18-1/2" h **$950**

Ball top with concentric ring turnings, shaped columns, cabriole legs, spurred knees, slipper feet, conforming log stops, one imp "BOSTON," losses and cracks near log stops, c1800, 11-1/4" w, 25" d, 16-5/8" h **$600**

New York, beaded belts on double lemon finials, round plinths supported on spurred cabriole legs with ball feet, minor wear, first quarter 19th C, 19" d, 9" h **$775**

Andirons, pr, bronze, ribbon-wrapped torches tapering to leaftip, reeded stem with husk-accented bifurcate base, Louis XVI-style, 19th C, 31" h **$2,400**

Andirons and matching tools, Federal, 24" h brass ring-turned shaft andirons with spurred legs, ball feet, similarly turned fireplace 32" h tongs and 33" h shovel...................... **$1,100**

Bellows, wood and leather, brass tacks, brass wind spout, white ground paint with some dec on back, floral dec on front and handle, good condition leather, 17-3/4" l, 8" w **$550**

Coal grate, George II, brass-mounted iron, bowed central section of four rails over grate, ash drawer between bow front side panels, applied brass starbursts, surmounted with brass urn finials, English, last quarter 19th C, 26" w, 9-1/2" d, 16" h **$200**

Fireboard, wide central raised panel, paint dec to depict seaside village, ships, and houses, surround painted to depict tiles with numerous ships, houses, and trees, America, wear, fading, early 19th C, 36" x 44-3/8" **$7,650**

Fire dogs, pr

Brass, central horizontal reeded orb raised on three reeded legs, reeded horizontal bar on top, Aesthetic Movement, English, third quarter 19th C, 7-1/2" w, 6-1/2" h **$150**

Cast iron, rampant lion bearing twisted horizontal bars, seated on rope twist rounded and octagonal base, late 19th/early 20th C, 15" h **$700**

Gilt bronze, squat urns draped in husks on top, short fluted column with central leaf-scrolled band, large urn opposing berry finial across horizontal cross bar, Louis XVI-style, 19th C, 16-1/4" w, 14" h **$1,300**

Fire fender

Brass rail on serpentine fender, vertical wirework with swag dec, England or America, minor wear to brass rail, loss of one wire, late 18th/early 19th C, 51-1/4" w, 18-1/2" d, 12-1/4" h **$5,600**

Wire and brass, serpentine, brass ball finials, 52" l, 18" d, 12-1/2" h **$1,155**

Fire screen

Walnut, openwork cresting, revolving screen painted with dec scenes, trestle base, Renaissance Revival, American, 26-1/2" w, 44" h...... **$300**

Gilt bronze, cartouche-shaped wire firescreen with central floral stem within rocaille borders, Louis XV-style, together with set of brush, shovel, and tongs in 24" h beaded stand; pair of small 10-3/8" h firedogs formed as rocaille acanthus scrolls, 28-3/4" h **$600**

Wire and brass rail, 30-1/4" h, 36-3/8" l..................................... **$770**

Bamboo, brass mounted, foliate painted panel, turned supports and trestle base, Victorian, 31" w, 40" h **$150**

Leaded glass, tripartite, central square panel and two narrow side panels set with multicolored textured and bull's eye glass pieces, brass surround, griffin-form trestle feet, Renaissance Revival, late 19th/early 20th C, 32-3/4" h **$1,100**

Tubular frame, ormolu scrolling at top, scrolled feet, center oil on canvas with courting scene, French, sgd "G. Jones" on lower right, early 20th C, 33" w, 41-1/4" h **$700**

Fire tools, brass and iron, ball finial on belted ball top, shovel and tongs, minor dents, scattered pitting, 30-7/8" and 31-3/8" l **$420**

Footman, brass, Georgian-style, rect top, turned side handles, pierced apron, cabriole front legs, straight round rear legs, English, 18" w, 15" d, 12" h **$365**

Hearth broom, hardwood handle, bristle holder, carved and painted face of black man, handle end stamped with rocket, inscribed "Forward Biltmore, NC," wear, 8-1/4" w, 22" l **$445**

Hearth toaster, America, wrought iron, toast support embellished with scrolled heart motifs, turned wooden handle with remains of green and red paint, late 18th C, 16-3/8" w, 23" l **$825**

Hearth trivet, wrought iron

Round, flattened handle, hanger hook, three-legged base, rust, 15-1/2" l, 6-1/4" d **$220**

Square grilling surface, flattened handle, circular end, four sun-like stamps, 23-1/2" l, 11-1/2" w **$250**

Kettle shelf, brass and wrought iron, "D" shape with cast top with pierced scrolling, floral medallions around skirt, iron cabriole legs ending in large penny feet, one decorative rosette missing from front, 13" w, 10-1/2" d, 13-1/2" h **$460**

Kettle stand, brass and wrought iron, tripod base, round column, painted black, circular brass top with pierced designs, scalloped edges, 10-3/4" h **$100**

Mantelpiece, faux marble painted, attributed to Vermont, early 19th C

Projecting shelf above molding, rect capitals on pilasters and plinths, orig gray-green paint with white veining, paint wear, 61" w, 6-1/2" d, 49-1/4" h **$1,000**

Rect shelf above cove molding, flanking rect capitals on pilasters and plinths, orig white paint with gray veining, surface wear, 60" w, 6-3/4" d, 48-1/4" h **$715**

Mantle urns, pr, gray marble with white striations, applied ormolu and gilded spelter dec, stamped "P.H. Mourey" around base, minor wear to gilding, 17-1/2" h **$500**

Pole screen

English, candle shield, orig green and mustard paint, table-top **$11,500**

English, mahogany, pole with shaped top, turned tapering urn-shaped pillar, cabriole leg base ending in arris pad feet on platforms, orig needlework panel, gold and blue floral pattern, brown ground, outlined with applied wood moldings, old surface, imperfections, 1760-80 .... **$5,175**

Irish, Chippendale, inlaid walnut and fruitwood veneers, oblong panel with scalloped edges, orig silk needlework of a dragon, saber legs with line border inlay graduate into triangular block with three turned supports, tripod base, short turned feet below applied blocks, some stains on fabric, few veneer chips missing, 53-1/2" h **$470**

Tinder lighter, pistol shape, flintlock striker

Mahogany, brass tinderbox, lyre-shaped front support, small candle socket with drop pan, etched scrollwork on the side, 5-1/8" l **$1,430**

Walnut, steel tinder box, candle socket, simple curved support, front end with compartment for tinder/candles, inscribed "Laurent Gille," 8" l **$935**

FISHING COLLECTIBLES

History: Early man caught fish with crude spears and hooks made of bone, horn, or flint. By the mid-1800s, metal lures with attached hooks were produced in New York State. Later, the metal was curved and glass beads added to make them more attractive. Spinners with painted-wood bodies and glass eyes appeared around 1890. Soon

after, many different makers were producing wood plugs with glass eyes. Patents, which were issued in large numbers around this time, covered the development of hook hangers, body styles, and devices to add movement to the plug as it was drawn through the water. The wood plug era lasted up to the mid-1930s when plugs constructed of plastic were introduced.

With the development of casting plugs, it became necessary to produce fishing reels capable of accomplishing the task with ease. Reels first appeared as a simple device to hold a fishing line. Improvements included multiplying gears, retrieving line levelers, drags, clicks, and a variety of construction materials. The range of quality in reel manufacture varied considerably. Collectors are mainly interested in reels made with high-quality materials and workmanship, or those exhibiting unusual features.

Early fishing rods, which were made of solid wood, were heavy and prone to breakage. By gluing together tapered strips of split bamboo, a rod was fashioned which was light in weight and had greatly improved strength. The early split-bamboo rods were round and wrapped with silk to hold them together. As glue improved, fewer wrappings were needed, and rods became slim and lightweight. Rods were built in various lengths and thicknesses, depending upon the type of fishing and bait used. Rod makers' names and models can usually be found on the metal parts of the handle or on the rod near the handle.

Reproduction Alert. Lures and fish decoys.

Additional Resources:

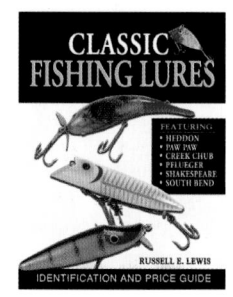

Classic Fishing Lures, by Russell E. Lewis, Krause Publications, Iola, WI.

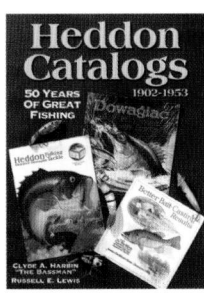

Heddon Catalogs Over 50 Years of Great Fishing, 1902-1953, by Clyde A. Harbin, Sr. and Russell E. Lewis, Krause Publications, Iola, WI.

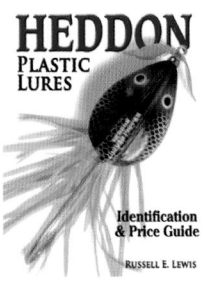

Heddon Plastic Lures, by Russell E. Lewis, Krause Publications, Iola, WI.

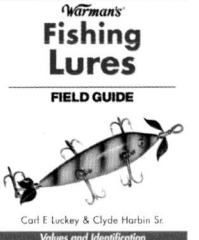

Warman's® Fishing Lures, by Carl F. Luckey and Clyde A. Harbin, Sr., Krause Publications, Iola, WI.

Bait bucket, painted blue, stenciled "Falls City-Magic-Minnow Bucket" **$1,980**

Bait trap, Katch-N-Karry, Glassman Mfg. Co., Jackson, TN, patented 1941, wood, 4" d wire mesh circle, litho of bluegill and roach **$375**

Bank, painted composition, bobbing head, round fisherman in hat and sunglasses, mermaid by side, coin slot in back, felt covering over base, 1960s, 3-1/2" x 4" x 7" h **$30**

Bobber, hand painted
Panfish float, black, red, and white stripes, 5" l **$12**

Pike float, yellow, green, and red stripes, 12" l **$24**

Books

Complete Book of Fresh Water Fishing, P. Allen Parsons, 332 pgs, illus, 1965 ....**$15**

Lures: The Guide to Sport Fishing, Keith C. Schuyler, Stackpole Co., dj, 1955 ....**$20**

The Complete Angler: or Contemplative Man's Recreation: A Discourse on Rivers, Fish-Ponds, Fish & Fishing in 2 Parts, Issac Walton and Charles Cotton, supplementary and explanatory Sir John Hawkins **$125**

Calendar print, Bristol, young couple and their guide getting ready for fishing excursion, cut down and laid down on old style mat board, old frame with wood backing, 1905, 12" x 13" **$330**

Canoe, Old Town Sponson, 16' **$1,430**

Catalog

Creek Chub Bait Co., Garrett, IN, 1934 ....**$330**

Evinrude Motors, Milwaukee, WI, 1961, Catalog of Outboard Motors **$32**

Garcia Fishing Equipment & Supplies, Garcia Corp., Teaneck, NY, c1955, accordion fold large 11-1/4" x 30" sheet **$20**

Hardy Brothers, 1910 ....**$495**

Montague Rod & Reel Co., Montague City, MA, c1949, Catalog No. 49-M **$55**

Orvis, c1900 ....**$330**

Penn Fishing Tackle Mfg., Philadelphia, PA, Catalog No. 17 of Penn Reels, 1952 ....**$32**

Shakespeare Co., Kalamazoo, Catalog No. 27, some pages uncut, 1927 ....**$175**

Wallsten Tackle Co., Chicago, IL, Fishing Tips, Courtesy of Cisco Kid Lures, 1940s **$21**

Weber Lifelike Fly Co., Stevens Point, WI, Catalog No. 22, Flies & Fly Tackle, 1941 ....**$70**

White, E. M. & Co., Old Town, ME, E. M. White Builders of White Canoes, c1922 ....**$40**

Child's kit, Mickey Mouse Fishing Kit, copyrighted "Walt Disney Enterprises," tin litho, C.8+, 1920s, 4-1/2" x 1-1/2" x 7-1/2" **$500**

Cigarette card, King of England deep-sea fishing, New Zealand, 1937 ....**$12**

Clock, mechanical, fish punching hole in side of boat with moving hammer, Hero Clock Co., wind-up, marked "Made in China" **$40**

Creel

Split, reinforced rim on lid, off center hole, orig split splint hinges, wire and loop lid latch, heavy fabric support attached to shoulder strap, 5" x 9" x 9" h **$2,200**

Turtle, bulbous shape, tight rattan weave, full length leather hinge, emb 98" rule, leather worker's stamp "ILHAN New Boulder Colo," leather harness, small mahogany priest attached with leather thong, 7" x 17" **$5,500**

Turtle, leather trimmed, bulbous shape, split reed and cord reinforcing on bottom, orig twisted reed hinges and harness loops, sliding figural turtle lid latch, wood rule on lid, dec cross hatch weaving on front, old leather harness, 5-1/2" x 13" x 7" **$1,210**

Turtle, tight rattan weave, bulbous shape, orig twisted reed hinges and harness loops, split reed and cord reinforcing on bottom, figural turtle latch, wood rule on lid, dec cross hatch weaving on front, leather and web harness, 6" x 15" x 7" h **$1,650**

Decoy, fish, wood

Leroy Howell, gray body, black metal fins, 6-1/2" l **$115**

Ice King, perch, painted, Bear Creek Co., 7" l **$75**

Wood, paint dec, America, minor paint wear and losses, early 20th C, 31-1/2" l **$1,495**

Display, salesman's sample, Pequea, Strasburg, PA

Oilcloth cov box, two panels, lures, 9" x 13" **$1,870**

Oilcloth cov box, 19 round bodied cork floats, 9" x 15" **$1,100**

Oilcloth cov box, eight lures, 18 assorted feathered trebles, large weedless example, 9-1/2" x 13" **$330**

Two-sided, lures and pearl spoons, 9-1/2" x 13" **$1,650**

Two panels, assortment of 58 floats, 18" x 29-1/2" d **$18,700**

Display case, 33 different colorful winders with bobbers, 21" x 21" **$3,410**

Fishing license, for resident use Connecticut, yellow, black, and white, 1935 ....**$65**

Alger, Franklin A., metal lip, grooved head, Getsem external belly weight, stand away hangers, 3-1/4" l, **$200-$400.**

A & I glass-eyed lure, L-rigged hooks mounted on the side, 3-7/8" l, **$20-$40.**

A & I mouse lure, black bead eyes, leather ears and tail, L-rig belly hook hanger and Heddon one-piece short loop tail hanger, 2-3/4" l, **$85-$150.**

Heddon, Jeanette Hawley Mohawk, yellow body, green scale finish, **$15,000-$17,500.**

Lloyd Hunt Lure Company, The Enticer with original box, painted eyes, one-piece-style belly hardware, forward hanger integrated with dive plane, **$5-$10.**

Midget Pikie Minnow, wood, red and white, "Pikie" stamped in gold letters, single line tie, gold eyes, screw hardware, 4" l, **$25-$75.**

Pennsylvania, blue and white, black serial number, 1945 .... **$18**

Flask, pewter, emb on both sides, one side with fisherman landing trout, other side with fisherman netting catch, marked "Alchemy Pewter, Sheffield, England" **$175**

Float, Ideal **$200**

Fly, Carrie Stevens **$440**

Fly fishing display

C. J. Frost, Stevens Point, WI, c1910, 9' l **$3,080**

Painted wood trout replica, fly fishing reel, flies, net, wood case, c1911, 39-3/4" l, 3-3/4" d, 13-1/4" h **$195**

Folk art, wood carving, titled "Two Fish and a Frog," sgd "L. A. Plummer, 1904" in lower right, polychrome dec, minor cracks, 25" h, 40-1/4" l **$17,250**

Ink blotter, Flies and Casts, J. C. Arsenault, New Brunswick, Canada, 3-1/2" x 6-1/4" **$55**

Knife, Marbles Woodcraft **$385**

License holder, paper envelope, Florida Game and Fresh Water Commission, stamped with County Judge's name **$22**

Lure

Al Foss Dixie Wiggler, #13, 1928, metal box, extra hook, pocket catalog, 3-1/2" l **$100**

Allen, Vamp, stripy finish **$550**

Blee, Charles, submarine bait, all metal **$2,000**

Case Bait Co., rotary marvel, c1910 .... **$360**

Creek Chubb Bait Co.

Giant Pike, orig box, 12-1/2" x 2-3/4" **$195**

Glitter beetle, red and white **$615**

Jigger 4100, red side **$140**

Mouse **$470**

Pikie minnow, early orig box **$440**

Plunking dinger, all black **$100**

Red beetle **$315**

Sarasota, #3317, luminous yellow head, c1927-31 .... **$800**

Detroit Glass, minnow tube, fish form, four treble hooks, orig box, c1914 .... **$3,500**

DeWitt, Bil, minnow, orig box with papers **$90**

Dunk's Double Header, black plug, c1931 .... **$125**

Four Brothers, Neverfail Minnow, orig box **$615**

Garland Bros., Plant City, FL, cork head minnow **$315**

Hanson

GE pull-me-slow, two hooks......... **$90**

Muskegon spoon jack minnow, green back, five-hook **$275**

H. Comstock, 1883, Flying Helgramite **$4,400**

Heddon

#175, heavy casting minnow, worn leaping bass box **$420**

#300, Dowagiac surface minnow **$275**

#300, husky minnow, orig box **$660**

#400, bucktail surface minnow **$615**

#450, killer **$175**

#1500, dummy double, unmarked box, orig paper **$360**

Henning, glass minnow tube **$440**

J. A. Holzapfe, Jackson, MI, mushroom, bass, orig box.............. **$660**

Jamison, wig-wag **$95**

K & K, animated minnow **$160**

Like Live Bait Co., Jacksonville, FL, mechanical, patent no. 1,7658,160, orig box **$13, 200**

Manhattan Casting Bait, No. 2, White, orig box.................. **$495**

Moonlight Bay #1, c1904, 4" shallow cup **$400**

Musky

Crazy crawler 2510 mouse.......... **$250**

Giant vamp 7350, jointed, natural scales, c1930 .... **$130**

Surfasser 300, two hooks, rainbow **$150**

Paw-Paw, sucker, perch finish, tack eyes **$30**

Pfleuger

All-in-One.............................. **$470**

Floating monarch minnow, c1906 .... **$90**

Never Fail Minnow, three hooks **$300**

Surprise minnow **$185**

Sam-Bo, bass, pike, pickerel, orig box, 4" l **$215**

Shakespeare

Mouse white and red, thin body, glass eyes, 3-5/8" l **$30**

Underwater minnow, five-hook, c1907 .... **$150**

South Bend Tackle Co.

Panatellia, green crackle-back finish, glass eyes, boxed **$50**

Truck-Oreno, red and white wood **$2.970**

Vacuum Bait, red and white dec **$100**

Souvenir, Lucky Lure, Souv of Indian Lake, OH, nude black female, 3-1/2" l, MOC.................. **$130**

Strike-It-Lure, green, yellow, and red spots, glass eyes **$40**

W. D. Chapman, Theresa, NY, metal minnow and propeller **$2,200**

Winchester

9011, three-hook **$500**

Green plug, repainted by Dale Roberts... **$130**

Minnow bucket, green collapsible canvas, wire bail, orig black painted wooden handle, stamped "No. 08 Mfg for the Planet Co. Patent" **$155**

Net, boat, wooden 32" handle **$90**

Net, trout

Brodin, name branded on wood handle, unused................................. **$50**

English, folding, triangular, alloy and brass construction, rubber grip, belt clip, mkd "Made in Great Britain," unused, 30" handle.................... **$85**

Hardy, collapsible, alloy construction, belt clip, 24" handle.............. **$27.50**

Painting

The Start, A. Von Beust, sgd "AVB" in lower left corner, young Victorian couple with guide getting ready for fishing excursion, used as orig for illus by Bristol Rod Co., 1905, tempera, 19-1/2" x 25" frame with thin mat, 14-1/2" x 19-3/4"........ **$15,400**

Oil on canvas, *Waiting for the Party,* 19th C angler sitting in Windsor chair with his equipment, orig gold frame, unsigned, 17" x 24" **$470**

Patch, Atlantic City Surf Fishing Tournament, 3-3/4" x 5".................... **$12**

Pinback button, Johnsburg Fish & Game Club, red and white, forest safety theme, 1930s **$10**

Poacher's gig, hand forged five pronged rake-type device, long worn wooden handle, from Eastern Shore, MD or VA, 63" l **$145**

Pond boat, sailer, rudder, 30" h, 28" l, 10" w **$200**

Poster

Bristol Fishing Rod Co., colorful scene of young Victorian couple enjoying picnic while lad lifts edge of her dress with rod and line, gold frame, cloth liner, 13-1/2" x 18" **$4,400**

Kingfisher, They Can't Get Away From Kingfisher Lines, E. J. Martin's Sons Kingfisher Brand, Braided Silk Lines, Rockville, Conn, girl ice fishing, matted, 24" x 32" frame, 17" x 24".. **$8,360**

Reel

ABU Ambassador 5000, bait casting, red finish, leather case with spare parts **$125**

A.L. Walker, Y, German silver

Model 100, 4/0, salmon **$1,650**

Model 200, 4/0, salmon **$1,870**

Anson Hatch, side mount C-1866, mkd "Hatch's Patent June 19, 1866" **$5,500**

Army and Navy, English alloy, trout, 2-1/8" d **$220**

Arthur Kovalovsky, No. 64, made for Zane Grey, patented 2,022,204, front plate mkd "Arthur Kovalovsky Hand Made Patented 1,958,919-Hollywood Cal," big game, 8-1/2" d, 6-1/2" w spool, 17 lbs.......... **$20,900**

B. C. Milam, Frankford, KY, #2, casting **$1,760**

B. F. Meek & Sons

#2, casting **$935**

#8, mkd "Hand Made," German silver, bait casting............................ **$6,160**

#33 Bluegrass **$85**

#44, trout, German silver **$5,280**

Bogdan, Model 200, salmon, right hand wind................................. **$825**

Charles M. Clinton, Ithaca, NY, German Silver, c1900 .... **$6,820**

DAM, quick casting, black finish, red agate line guide, orig box.......... **$85**

Dr. Allonzo H. Fowler, Ithaca, NY, hard rubber, Fowler's Improved Gem Fly Reel **$6,600**

Edward R. Hewitt, custom made, initials "M.S.I.," aluminum, raised pillars, trout fly, orig leather case **$13,750**

Edw. Vom Hofe

German silver, tiny upright trout, c1870 .... **$7,810**

Model 621, size 4/0 .... **$250**

Perfection, Model 360, size 2, German silver and hard rubber, trout **$8,820**

Peerless, Model 355, size 3, German silver and hard rubber, trout **$5,280**

Salmon, Cascapedia **$4,290**

Hardy

Cascepedia, salmon, 2/0 size **$12,375**

Princess, trout, German silver reversible line guide **$200**

Uniqua, trout, 3-1/8", flat telephone latch **$275**

Hendryx Safety Reel, trout..... **$995**

H. L. Leonard

Model 50B, wide spool, fly **$1,760**

Patent 1877, upright trout **$3,080**

Heddon, Triple Teaser, Series No. 1000, white and red buck tail, minnow blades stamped, "Heddon Triple Teaser," **$30-$50.**

Horton Mfg.

#3, suede bag **$425**

#7 Blueglass **$880**

#33 Bluegrass Simplex, suede bag **$425**

Julius Vom Hofe

Fly, plain, early size 3 .... **$880**

Freshwater, casting, Pat. Nov. 17, 85, Oct. 8, 1887, torn bag............ **$165**

Meisselbach, #260, featherlight, skeleton, fly, vertical box............. **$330**

Morgan James, side mount, pillbox style, brass, c1860................ **$9,350**

Niangua, casting **$660**

Ocean, 3/0B............................... **$300**

Orvis, presentation

EXR1, trout, right hand wind **$110**

EXR111, trout, spare spool, right hand wind............................. **$110**

Otto Zward, Model 400, multiplying, salmon, 2/0 size.................. **$1,710**

Pflueger

Atlapac, 9/0 size, 5" d **$330**

Hawkeye, bulldog logo, trout, German silver and hard rubber **$350**

Philbrook & Paine, hand made, raised pillar, trout, mkd "Pat Apld For"..................................... **$9,625**

Restigouche

1896 patent **$1,540**

1897 patent **$1,320**

1902 patent **$1,540**

Seamaster

Duel mode, anti-reverse, saltwater fly, all black.................................. **$990**

Mark III, duel mode, anti-reverse, saltwater fly, gold and black **$880**

Shakespeare

Standard **$150**

Standard, professional................ **$150**

Tournament **$110**

South Bend, #1131A, casting, shiny finish, orig box **$18**

Stan Bogdan, hand made, baby trout

Left hand wind, orig pouch, unused, 2-3/4" d, 3/4" w **$1,732**

Spool, hard leather case, 2-3/4" d, 3/4" w **$1,485**

Talbot Star **$385**

Thos. J. Conroy, NY, Wells model, trout, c1889 .... **$3,300**

Union Hardware Co., raised pillar type, nickel and brass **$25**

Unmarked, wood, brass fittings, c1880-1920, 6" d **$85**

Walker, TR-4, fly **$1,210**

Waltonian, Square Stamping Co., Barneveld, NY, casting **$660**

Winchester

Model #2844, raised pillar bay, 3" d, 1-7/8" w spool rest, nickel plated **$275**

Model #2944, raised pillar light salt-water, 3-1/4" d, 1-7/8" w spool, nickel plated **$250**

Wm. H. Talbot Eli, casting **$880**

Rod

C. W. Jenkins, CO, Model GA 70-39, trout, two-pc, two tips, for 4 wt line, orig bag and tube, 7' **$935**

Dickerson, trout, Model 861711, Special 1937, three-pc, two tips, orig bag and tube, 8-1/2' **$2,100**

E. C. Powell

Heavy trout or light salmon, Marys-ville, two-pc, two tips, patent num-bers denoting hollow built configu-ration, orig bag, later tube, 8-1/2' **$910**

Trout, "A" taper, two-pc, two tips, (one replaced), hollow built, orig bag and tube, 8-1/2' **$770**

Trout, B-9, two-pcs, two tips, for 6 wt line, hollow built, profession-ally restored, orig bag and tube, 9' **$825**

Trout, "C" taper, two-pc, two tips, hollow built, orig bag and tube, 8-1/2' **$990**

F. E. Thomas, Bangor, ME

Salmon, two handed, three-pc, two tips, canvas sack, tip tube, several wraps need replacing, 12' **$220**

Trout, Dirigo, three-pc, two tips, orig bag, later tube, 8' **$580**

Trout, Dirigo, three-pc, two tips, orig bag, later tube, varnish roughness, 9' **$165**

Trout, Special, three-pc, two tips, orig bag and tube, restored, 8-1/2' **$385**

Trout, Special, three-pc, two tips, cork spacer on reel seat, orig bag, hang-ing tag, and tube, 9' **$440**

Gary Howells, trout, two-pc, two tips, for 5 wt line, possibly unused, orig bag and tube, 7-1/2' **$2,750**

George Halstead, Danbury, CT, split bamboo, trout, 7-1/2' **$3,410**

Gillum, trout, two-pc, two-tip, light line, orig bag and tube, missing four guides, needs refinishing, 7-1/2' **$3,850**

Goodwin Granger, split bamboo, 7' **$1,100**

Hardy

Centenary set, commemorative, reproduction of 1890s 8' Gold Medal split bamboo rod, blued Houghton Perfect 2-5/8" reel, both numbered "64," of 100 sets made in 1992, rosewood chest with brass plaque **$2,915**

Salmon Deluxe Rod, extra tip, alumi-num case, 9' **$175**

Harold Gillum, Ridgefield, CT, split bamboo, 6-1/2' and 7-1/2' sold as pr **$7,700**

H. L. Leonard

Fly, 6-1/2" **$1,450**

Fly, Leonard Tournament, extra tip, metal case, 9' **$300**

Red wrap, 7-1/2' **$1,925**

Split bamboo, model 50DF, 8' **$880**

#37ACM-6' **$3,025**

#37-6' **$1,925**

Horrocks & Illotson, 9' 3", two tips, split-bamboo fly, maroon wraps **$50**

Montaque, bamboo, two tips, orig case **$135**

Omar Needham, Rangeley, ME, Needham's Special, light salmon, two-pc, two tips, impregnated, screw down-locking reel seat, orig condition, orig bag and tube, 9' **$220**

Orvis

Battenkill, two-pc, two tips, orig bag and tube, 8-1/2' **$425**

Light Spinning, two-pc, one tip, orig bag and tube, 7' **$220**

Model 1882, trout, three-pc, two tip, modern guide replacements, orig bag, 9-1/2' **$110**

Salmon, two-pc, two tips, orig bag and tube, 9-1/2' **$360**

Spinning, two-pc, one tip, superlight, orig bag and tube, 6-1/2' **$250**

Paul H. Young, Perfectionist, trout, two-pc, two tips, orig bag and tube, 1978, 7-1/2' **$2,570**

Payne

Light trout, two-pc, three tips, 1-5/8 oz, orig bag, hanging tag, and tube, 4'4" **$7,975**

Salmon, three-pc, two tips, removable 6" butt extension, orig canvas sack, tip tube, and ferrule plugs, 10-1/2' **$450**

Salmon, dry fly, Model 430, two-pc, two tips, removable 6-3/4" butt extension, 6-1/8 oz, unused, orig bag, tube, and tube cover, 9' **$2,100**

Trolling, three-pc, two tips, restored butt and tip section, orig bag and tube, 9' **$410**

Trout, Model 96, two-pc, two tips, orig bag and tube, 6-1/2' **$3,300**

Trout, Model 98, two-pc, two tips, extra tip, orig bag and tube, 7' **$3,850**

Trout, Model 200, three-pc, two tips, spare unfinished tip, five guides, orig bag and tube, 8' **$3,080**

Trout, Model 204, three-pcs, two tips, screw-up locking over walnut reel seat, poor varnish, Abercrombie & Fitch & Fitch Co. stamp, orig bag and tube, 8-1/2' **$1,870**

Trout, three pcs, two tips, screw up-locking reel seat, orig bag and tube, 9' **$1,760**

R. L. Winston, San Francisco, trout, two-pc, one tip, for 7 wt line, hol-low built, orig bag and tube, 8-1/2' **$525**

Sam Carlson

Light salmon, Four Quad, two-pc, two tips, 3" removable butt exten-sion, orig bag and tube, 8-1/2' **$1,870**

Trout, Four, two-pc, two tips, orig bag and tube, 7-1/2' **$2,530**

Trout, Thomas Special, two-pc, two tips, orig bag and tube, 7' **$1,540**

Shakespeare, Premier Model, three-pc, two tips, split-bamboo fly, red silk wrappings, cloth bag, metal tube, 9' **$75**

Shakespeare Springbrook, fly fish-ing, orig bag **$100**

S. J. Small, split bamboo, three-rod set **$2,640**

Superlight, spinning rod, 5' **$660**

Thomas & Thomas, Caenis, light trout, blued hardware and ferrules, two-pc, two tips, orig bag and tube, 7-1/2' **$1,760**

Union Hardware Co., Kingfisher, saltwater boat rod, split-bamboo fly, dark brown wraps, 7-1/2' **$35**

Walt Carpenter

Trout, Browntone, Model No. 91276, two-pc, two tips, for 4-wt line, unused, orig bag, tube, and tube bag, 7-1/2' **$2,750**

Trout, Browntone Special, three-pc, two tips, dark flamed cane, cap, and ring reel seat, mahogany spacer, blue hardware, wrapper on handle, orig bag and tube, 8'3" ...**$3,300**

Trout, two-pc, two tips, for 5-wt line, blued hardware and ferrules, orig bag and tube, 7'9" **$2,530**

Trout, three-pc, two tips, for 5-wt line, light cane, screw up-locking reel seat, unused, orig bag and tube, 8' **$2,200**

Walton Powell, trout, two-pc, two tips, extra mid section, professionally restored, 9' **$220**

Salesman's sample, cutaway model of Shakespeare Sea Wonder No. 280 Model FB spinning reel.................**$50**

Scale, brass, "Chamllons Improved, New York, Pat. Dec 10 1967".......**$30**

Tackle box, leather......................**$450**

Vise, fly tying

Steel and brass, bolts to table, 7" l, 2-1/2" w....................................**$210**

Cast iron and steel, can be used free standing or bolted down, 7-1/2" l, 6" h **$240**

Wallet, H.L. Leonard, 30 plastic pockets displaying 30 different kinds of poly blend, orig contents, 5-1/2" x 12", opens to 12" x 19" **$40**

FLASKS

History: A flask, which usually has a narrow neck, is a container for liquids. Early American glass companies frequently formed them in molds that left a relief design on the front and/or back. Historical flasks with a portrait, building, scene, or name are the most desirable.

A chestnut is hand-blown, small, and has a flattened bulbous body. The pitkin has a blown globular body with a spiral rib overlay on vertical ribs. Teardrop flasks are gener-

Horse pulling cart/eagle, olive green, pint, pontil, McKearin GV-7a, **$700.** Photo courtesy of American Bottle Auctions.

ally fiddle shaped and have a scroll or geometric design.

Notes: Dimensions can differ for the same flask because of variations in the molding process. Color is important in determining value—aqua and amber are the most common colors; scarcer colors demand more money. Bottles with "sickness," an opalescent scaling that eliminates clarity, are worth much less.

Historical

Baltimore monument, amber upper and lower sections shading to brown center, emb "Corn for The World" and "Baltimore," applied collared lip with ring, slightly domed base, Baltimore Glass Works, quart, lip chipmid-19th C, 8-1/2" h, McKearin GVI-4..............................**$310**

Columbia and eagle B & W, open pontil, pint, McKearin GI-121, slight interior stain keeps **$425**

Columbia, Liberty cap, eagle, Kensington and Union on reverse, pale aqua, bubbles...................**$800**

Eagle-Cornucopia, early Pittsburgh district, 1820-40, light greenish-aquamarine, sheared mouth, pontil scar, pint, McKearin GII-6 ....**$475**

Eagle-Willington/Glass Co., Willington glass Works, West Willington, CT, 1860-72, bright medium yellowish-olive, applied double-collared mouth, smooth base, half pint, McKearin GII-63 ....**$210**

For Pike's Peak, Prospector-Hunter Shooting Deer, attributed to Ravenna Glass Works, Ravenna, OH, 1860-80, aquamarine, applied mouth with ring, smooth base,

Cornucopia/urn, emerald green, pint, pontil, McKearin GIII-17, **$450.** Photo courtesy of American Bottle Auctions.

quart, McKearin GXI-47, 1/4" shallow flake **$325**

Masonic, pale yellow green, emb "Franklin," plain lip, faint rough pontil mark, Monongahela and early Pittsburgh district, 1825-50, pint, 6-3/4" h **$440**

Masonic-Eagle, Zanesville, emb "Zanesville, J. Sheppard & Co.," golden amber, pint, McKearin GIV-32...**$2,975**

Railroad and eagle

Olive green, no inscriptions, pint, 6-5/8" h, McKearin GV-9.........**$450**

Olive green, open pontil, pint, McKearin GV-9 ....**$375**

Railroad, medium blue green, emb "Success to the Railroad" on both side, plain lip, rough pontil mark with straight seam, Lancaster Glass Works, pint, 1825-75, 6-3/4" h, McKearin GV-1 ....**$90**

Union and Wm Frank & Sons, Pitts on one side, cannon on other, aqua, pint, interior blisters, minor residue, flake on base, 7-1/2" h, McKearin GXII-39 ....**$100**

Pattern molded

Emil Larson, NJ, swirled to the right, amethyst, sheared mouth, pontil scar, some exterior high point wear, c1930, 7-3/8" l.................................**$250**

Midwest, 24 ribs swirled to the right, golden amber, sheared mouth, pontil scar, 1800-30, 4-5/8" l.........**$190**

Pictorial

Cornucopia and urn of fruit

Aqua green, pint, McKearin GIII-4, minor int. residue, small pot stone, 7-1/4" h **$250**

Dark olive, pint, 6-1/2" h, McKearin GIII-4...**$125**

Golden amber, half pint, minor surface wear, 5-1/2" h, McKearin GIII-10 .... **$220**

Cornucopia, light green, emb "Lancaster Glass Works, NY," plain lip, iron pontil mark, pint, 1825-50, 6-1/2" h, McKearin GIII-16 .... **$420**

Double eagle, olive amber, pint, roughness inside neck, 7-1/2" h, McKearin GII-85 .... **$250**

Duck, aquamarine, emb "Will You Take A Drink? Will A (duck figure) Swim?" broad flat lip with ring below, smooth base with indented corner, possibly Lockport Glass Works, pint, mid-to late 19th C, 7-3/4" h, McKearin GXIII-29 .... **$235**

Eagle

Deep golden amber, plain lip, rough pontil mark, possibly Coffin & Hay, Hammonton, NJ, section of lip restored, 1825-50, half pint, 5-5/8" h, McKearin GII-56 .... **$235**

Deep olive green, plain lip, rough pontil mark, probably Keene-Marlboro-Street, high spot wear, 1825-50, pint, 6-3/4" h, McKearin GII-73/74 .... **$135**

Flora Temple, deep amber, emb "Floral Temple, Harnes Trot 2.19 3/4," applied plain lip with ring below, plain base, possibly Whitney Glass Works, Glassboro, NJ, mid-to late-19th C, pint, 8-1/2" h, McKearin GXIII-22 .... **$315**

Shield and clasped hands, aquamarine, emb "Waterford," applied double collared lip, rough iron pontil mark, probably Waterford Glass Works, NJ, flake, quart, mid-to late-19th C, 9" h, McKearin GXII-2 .... **$80**

Soldier on horse, yellow, strong olive green overtones, applied double collared lip, rough pontil mark, quart, mid-to late-19th C, 8-1/2" h, McKearin GXIII-16 .... **$880**

Pitkin type

Midwest, ribbed and swirled to the right, 16 ribs, olive green with yellow tone, sheared mouth, pontil scar, some int. stain, 1800-30, 6-1/4" l **$300**

New England, sheared mouth, pontil scar, ribbed and swirled to the left, 36 ribs, light olive yellow, 1783-30, 5-1/4" l **$375**

Pattern molded, flattened ovoid, medium olive amber, 36 rib broken

swirl to right, short neck, plain lip, kick-up base, rough pontil mark, probably New England, pint, early 19th C, 6-3/4" h **$360**

Portrait

Adams-Jefferson, New England, yellow amber, sheared mouth, pontil scar, half pint, 1830-50, McKearin GI-114 .... **$325**

General Jackson, Pittsburgh district, bluish-aquamarine, sheared mouth, pontil scar, pint, 1820-40, McKearin GI-68 .... **$1,500**

General Taylor, pale greenish aquamarine, emb "Genl Taylor Never Surrenders" and "A Little More Grape Capt Bragg," plain lip, rough pontil mark, probably Baltimore Glass Works, pint, 1825-75, 7-1/8" h, McKearin GS-4 .... **$160**

Jenny Lind, Fislerville Glass Works, aqua, calabash, several int. blisters, 9-1/4" h, McKearin GI-107 ...... **$115**

Lafayette-DeWitt Clinton, Coventry Glass Works, Coventry, CT, yellowish-olive, sheared mouth, pontil scar, half pint, 1/2" vertical crack, weakened impression, 1824-25, McKearin GI-82 .... **$2,100**

Rough and Ready Taylor-Eagle, Midwest, aquamarine, sheared mouth, pontil scar, pint, 1830-40, McKearin GI-77 .... **$1,200**

Washington

Deep blue green, plain lip, rough pontil mark, probably Lockport Glass Works, quart, 1825-50, 8" h, McKearin GI-61 .... **$2,860**

Medium blue green, emb "The Father of His Country," applied rounded lip with bevel below, rough pontil mark, possibly Dyottville Glass Works, Philadelphia, quart, 1825-50, 8-1/4" h, McKearin GI-47 .... **$450**

Sapphire blue, violet overtones, emb "The Father of His Country, Dyottville Glass Works Philada, Gen Taylor Never Surrenders," plain lip, rough pontil mark, quart, 1825-75, 8-1/4" h, McKearin GI-37 ..... **$3,850**

Washington and Jackson, light to medium amber, open pontil, pint **$230**

Washington and Taylor

Olive green, pint, some surface wear and minor int. blisters, 6-1/2" h, McKearin GI-31 .... **$260**

Sapphire blue, soda style applied top, open pontil, quart, McKearin GI-54 .... **$2,600**

Majolica, polychrome dec bulldog, landscape, and crest design, Italy, 19th C, 4-1/2" h **$200**

Pewter, Pilgrim, shaped figural handles, moon-shaped body, molded foliage, pierced base, losses, 14" h, 16th C **$345**

Pottery

Pig shape, brown Albany glaze, incised "Brachmann & Moosard, Importers and Dealers in Wines & Liquors, 81 West Third Street, Cincinnati," Anna Pottery, 7" l **$13,500**

Scroll

Aquamarine, flat ring below plain lip, faint large iron pontil mark, quart, 8-1/2" h, McKearin GIX-4, 1825-50 .... **$110**

Greenish aquamarine, plain lip, rough pontil mark, quart, 8-7/8" h, McKearin GIX-2, 1825-50 .... **$90**

Honey amber, pint, minor surface wear, 7" h **$350**

Medium blue green, plain lip, rough pontil mark, quart, 8-3/4" h, McKearin GIX-1, 1825-50 .... **$190**

Sunburst

Deep blue green, tooled lip, rough pontil mark, three-quarter pint, 1825-75, 7" h, McKearin GVIII-29 .... **$220**

Medium green, plain lip, rough pontil mark, New England, pint, early to mid-19th C, 8" h, McKearin GVIII-2 .... **$440**

Medium yellow olive, plain lip, rough pontil mark, Coventry, CT, pint, early to mid-19th C, 7-1/2" h, McKearin GVIII-3 .... **$615**

FOLK ART

History: Exactly what constitutes folk art is a question still being vigorously debated among collectors, dealers, museum curators, and scholars. Some want to confine folk art to non-academic, handmade objects. Others are willing to include manufactured material. The term is used to cover objects ranging from crude drawings by children to academically trained artists' paintings of "common" people and scenery. Some record setting prices for folk art were achieved during the auction of the collection of Eugene and Dorothy Elgin, at Conestoga Auction Company, Inc., in April of 2004 (marked ex-Elgin).

Swan, folk art, painted wooden head, canvas-covered wire framed body, **$700.**

Photo courtesy of David Rago Auctions, Inc.

Cane, folk art, by "Bally Carver," dog's head grip, shaft includes plumed heart, tulip, running horse, stars, buck, birds cows, etc., original varnished surface, 36" h, **$4,830.**

Photo courtesy of Pook & Pook, Inc.

Bald eagle, carved and painted wood, stylized, glass eyes, stippled surface, Ohio, mounted on carved pine base, minor age cracks, attributed to early 20th C, 26-3/8" h **$5,000**

Billfold, beadwork eagle with shield, two stars, crossed American flags, old label: "This pocketbook was made by a Mrs. Davis in the Virginia Colony AD 1758, was found in her son's HB Davis's pocket at the surrender of Lord Cornwallis from George Davis," some deterioration to fabric, some losses, 7-1/2" l **$950**

Bird tree, carved and polychromed, seven stylized birds on wire legs, base made from surface root, PA, c1890-1910, 20" h, 21" w **$17,050**

Birth record, watercolor and ink on paper, Mary Hoyt, born May 6, 1807, two cream, beige, and light brown birds in ovals, flanked by patterned outline and column-like lines, reverse sgd "Henniker May 7, 1829 by Moses Connor," unframed, minor staining, 9" x 7" **$8,225**

Box, cov, carved oak, America, figure of man wearing cap with visor, sitting cross-legged on large dog, both have tails, border of turned finials joined by spiral rails, dovetailed box, leaf-carved drawer, paneled sides, old variegated varnish finish, late 19th/early 20th C, 6" w, 3-1/2" d, 4-1/2" h **$1,265**

Bust, attributed to Albert Abelt, Cumberland County, PA, titled "My Favorite Teacher," carved and painted wood, fabric flowers on hat, soulful eyes, blue dress, ex-Elgin, 6" h **$24,200**

Candle stand, laminated hardwoods, sq top with egg and dart molding, four ladies legs shaped supports with turned drop, old mellow finish, repairs, 16" w, 15-1/2" d, 30-1/4" h **$375**

Carving angel

Bulls' heads, life-size, real horns, glass eyes, old weathered paint, carved by Noah Weiss (1842-1907, Northampton County, PA), dated 1870, price for pr **$38,500**

Pine plank naively carved with face of angel, outstretched wings, radiating layered feathers, remnants of orig polychrome dec, light weathering to gray patina, possibly PA, 19th C, 41" l, 9" h **$900**

Relief carved angel holding star of Bethlehem and scroll, faded inscription begins "Glory to God in the…," right arm with old iron work repair, American, 19th C, 28" l, 17" h **$1,100**

Drawing, pencil, 13-7/8" x 17-1/4", farm scene, detailed two-story house, smaller barns, picket fence, hills and trees in background, stains and foxing, 16-1/2" x 20-3/4" gilt frame **$980**

Drawing, watercolor

American School, two girls standing, each holding red book, wearing applied gold foil brooch, lace collars accented with pinprick designs, framed, tear lower left, repaired tears on edges, 19th C, 9" x 7" **$1,410**

Girl in red dressed flanked by stylized tulip columns, inscribed "Ann Potter's profile drawn by Ruby Devol," verse "Can love for me inspire your tender heart. Dare I to hope and with that hope be blessed. Pursed we shall to us will him virtuous paths and find for time prove more," orig red painted frame, c1840 .... **$20,000**

Man and woman on either side of two handled urn of flowering roses, tulips, and other flowers, inscribed "A Walk in the Garden," Constructed by Michael Palmer, June 14, AD 1838-This is to certify that wife, Sarah B. Abrise, is superior in reciting first class this evening. May 21, 1841," 1841, 14" x 17" **$28,000**

Family record, Elijah and Mary Ann (Blew) Smalley, "Executed by E.S. Van Gleve," attributed to Indiana, pen and ink on paper, recording vital statistics of them and their 11 children, decorated with four columns and foliage, imperfections, c1866, 16-3/4" x 20-7/8" **$300**

Figure, carved and painted wood

Airplane, four engines, tin tail, 44" w wooden wings, propellers, orig red and white paint, some flaking and touch up, 30" l **$250**

Bird on pedestal, pegged articulated head, wings, and body, paper label on base "Done by Stanley Nick Gustwick, Coudersport, Pa," 7-1/2" h, 6-1/2" l, 4-1/2" h **$880**

Crane, carved wood body, neck, and legs, tin tail and wings, tack eyes, painted gray, green and red, aged patina, legs made from turned spindles of old chair, made by Emanuel Myers, York County, PA, broom maker, 20" h, 22" l, 7-1/2" w **$9,350**

Man with drum, Alabama, stand, late 19th/early 20th C, 5" h **$360**

Snake, old dark red paint, yellow polka dots, black, white, and blue eyes, old chip on tail, early 20th C, 25-1/2" l **$575**

Woman, standing, applied extended arms, metal tack eyes and buttons, alligatored surface, America, stand, late 19th C, 6-1/2" h **$600**

Grotesque face jug, stoneware, brown-speckled glaze, found in Ohio, imperfections, 19th C, 5-1/2" h **$14,950**

Hammer, oak and iron, figural, handle surmounted by carved man's head and upper torso, found in PA, 19th C, 13" l **$1,955**

Memorial, incised gilt and ebonized deep recessed shadow box frame, white painted cast iron profile of Lincoln surrounded by wreath of wire stemmed wax silk flowers, grouped with ribbon tied and waxed silk roses and calla lilies, surmounted by white dove with wings spread in flight, c1875, 31" x 23" x 6-1/2" **$700**

Model, Chinese-style side-wheel paddle boat, small horse-drawn cart, two horses powering wheels, carved man, minor breaks, 29" l, 11-1/4" d, 8" h **$115**

Picture frame, painted and incised wood, meandering vine and dot border, corner bosses, one corner boss missing, 12-5/8" w, 15-3/4" h **$920**

Plaque, sun face, carved polychrome, molded edge, America, minor imperfections, stand, early 19th C, 14" d **$16,100**

Scherenschnitte, birth certificate, dated Sept. 5, 1780, for Anna Elizabeth Lauerin, Berks County, PA, Tolpehaden Township, cut-work and painted dec border of flowers, tulips, and hearts attached with vine-work, black ink text, glued down, staining, loss, 11-1/2" x 14-1/2" **$925**

Sculpture, seagull, wood and tin, orig paint, wooden ice fishing decoy in beak, standing on pylon surrounded by fishing related items including netting, lures, eel spear, bobbers, lead sinkers, wear, 34-1/2" h **$450**

Still life, watercolor on paper, American School, 19th C, framed

Fruit and foliage in gray bowl, shades of red, green, and blue, pinprick dec, general toning, tiny scattered stains, 10-3/4" x 9-1/2" **$1,150**

Bouquet of Spring Flowers in a Vase, sgd "Frances Thompson, 1841," tulips, narcissus, and other spring flowers, white handled urn-form vase dec with sea shells, very minor toning, 15" x 13" **$2,715**

Theorem

Lady Liberty feeding eagle, basket of flowers, trees, and flag, on velvet, gilt frame, fading, discoloration to textile, c1790, 12-1/4" w, 15-1/2" h **$3,190**

Basket of flowers, oil and watercolor, sgd "Julia P. Paine," c1840, 12-3/8" x 15" **$12,000**

Basket of fruit still life, watercolor on velvet, unsigned, American School, molded giltwood frame, toning, 19th C, 16-1/2" w, 13-1/2" h **$4,150**

Canton porcelain bowl of fruit, strawberries, pear, blueberries, bird nested in center, sgd "D. Ellinger," orig grain painted frame, 22-1/4" l, 17" h **$4,950**

Tinsel picture, flower arrangement, reverse-painted glass backed with foil and paper, American School, Victorian frame, repaired, late 19th C, 22" x 17" **$180**

Trivet, heart form, single pc carved chestnut, serrated edges, applied legs, wrought iron tacks on top, 11-1/2" l, 4" w, 1-3/4" h **$2,100**

Valentine, pinprick and watercolor on paper, woven, pink paper ribbon border, German verse, woman in pink carrying bottle, soldier in blue uniform on horseback, separated by medallion "Treue Liebe," (True Love) glued down to another pc of paper, some damage, translation included, 12-1/2" h, 8-1/4" w **$500**

Wall hanging, attributed to Noah Weiss, Northampton, Lehigh County, PA, relief carved pine, two hunting dogs and two quail, painted white, black, and brown dogs, green grass, mottled white sky, painted black frame, aged patina, ex-Elgin, 19-1/2" w, 19" h **$8,250**

FRAKTUR

History: Fraktur, the calligraphy associated with the Pennsylvania Germans, is named for the elaborate first letter found in many of the hand-drawn examples. Throughout its history, printed, partially printed/partially hand-drawn, and fully hand-drawn works existed side by side. Schoolteachers or ministers living in rural areas of Pennsylvania, Maryland, and Virginia often made frakturs. Many artists are unknown.

Fraktur exists in several forms— geburts and taufschein (birth and baptismal certificates), vorschrift (writing examples, often with alphabet), haus segen (house blessings), bookplates and bookmarks, rewards of merit, illuminated religious texts, valentines, and drawings. Although collected for decoration, the key element in fraktur is the text.

Notes: Fraktur prices rise and fall along with the American folk-art market. The key marketplaces are Pennsylvania and the Middle Atlantic states.

Alphabet, upper and lower case written in fraktur schrift, orange and black ink, old inlaid frame, minor discoloration and tears, 9-3/4" w, 12" h **$250**

Birth certificate, Geburts and Taufschein

Hand drawn, attributed to Samuel Bentz, Lancaster County, PA, for Susanna Hacker, born 1828, spherical, geometric, and stylized floral and finial dec, old frame, some staining, 6-7/8" w, 9" h **$4,950**

Hand drawn, attributed to Ehre Vater artist, for Margaretha Mayerin, Sept. 28, 1800, Cumberland County, PA, two columns, centralized heart and two birds, tulip and floral dec, illuminated in red, yellow, green, and blue, painted frame, minor folds, tears, small restoration to corner, 10-3/8" w, 17-3/4" h **$8,250**

Hand drawn, attributed to Joseph Lochbaum, for Johannes Schlichter, 1792, ink, illuminated in red, yellow, and green, floral motifs and hearts, two flying eagles, religious text in hearts, black painted frame, 15" w, 12-3/4" h **$4,675**

Hand drawn, Henry Young, watercolor, man in blue frock coat holding glass of wine, inscribed between two red, yellow, and blue eight-point stars, for "Mr. Michael Snyder-A Son of Andrew Snyder and his wife Catherine, born Seysel May 25 AD 1820 in Derry Township Columbia County State of Pennsylvania," 8" w, 11" h **$19,000**

Printed, Daniel May, York, PA, for William Brennemann, 1847, Codorus Township, York County, PA, hand illuminated in blue, green, pink, and yellow, filled by decorator, contemporary marbleized paint dec frame, tears, minor discoloration, 9-1/2" w, 15" h **$180**

Fraktur, ink and watercolor, Southeastern Pennsylvania, central heart, birds and flowers, dated 1788, 12-1/2" x 15", $2,530.
Photo courtesy of Pook & Pook, Inc.

Fraktur, Pennsylvania, watercolor on paper, flowers and angel, dated 1795, 12-3/4" x 15-3/4", $2,760.
Photo courtesy of Pook & Pook, Inc.

Birth and baptismal certificate for Margaretha Sussamans, born Oct. 6, 1796, Marlborough Township, Montgomery County, PA, polychrome decoration in border along with two poems in heart outlines, signed by artist Martin Brechall, 13" x 16", folding, tearing, edge chipping, $1,725.
Photo courtesy of Alderfer Auction Co.

Printed and hand drawn, printed text for Johann Valentine Schuller, hand drawn potted flowers and text attributed to J. Schuller, for Marigreth Schneider, 1789, Pinecreek, Berks County, PA, illuminated in red, yellow, and green, black painted frame, 12-1/2" w, 7-1/2" h **$3,025**

Printed by J. Hartman, 1818, Lebanon County, PA, for Joseph Rudy, 1818, Dauphin County, PA, illuminated in brown and yellows, filled in and signed by Charles Overfield, Hannover, Germany, 1847, framed, 14-1/2" w, 12-1/2" h **$600**

Bookplate
Handwritten, "Jacob Witmeyer's Book, born in 1835," York County, PA, illuminated in yellow, red, green, and blue ink, red ochre painted frame, 6-3/4" l, 4" h **$385**

Watercolor on laid paper, tulips and other flowers, bright red, yellow, and green, yellow and black birds, worn gilt frame, PA origin, 6-1/2" w, 8-1/4" h **$2,990**

Child's Book of Moral Instruction (Metamorphis), watercolor, pen and ink on paper

Dec on both sides of four leaves, when folded reveals different versus and full-page color illus, executed by Sarah Ann Siger, Nazareth, PA, orig string hinges, 6-1/4" x 7" **$575**

Dec on both sides of four leaves, each with upper and lower flaps showing different versus and color illus, unknown illustrator, 5-3/4" x 7-1/2" **$345**

Printed form on paper, hand colored elements, The Great American Metamorphosis, Philadelphia, printed by Benjamin Sands, 1805-06, printed on both sides of four leaves, each with upper and lower flaps, engraved collar illus by Poupard, 6" x 7" **$420**

Christmas card, German text, greeting inside stylized oval, circular border, framed, 6-1/2" w, 4" h **$825**

Confirmation certificate, watercolor, pen and ink on paper, David Schumacher, paired tulips and hearts, for Maria Magdalena Spengler, dated 1780, 6" x 7-3/4" **$4,600**

Copybook, Vorschrift, pen and ink, red watercolor, laid paper, German text with ornate Gothic letters in heading, blocked cut area in lower left unfinished, minor edge damage, 11-3/8" w, 9-1/2" h yellow and red leather covered frame, 8" w, 5-5/8" h
.... **$250**

Drawing
Blue bird within two black snakes climbing poles to arch, decorative name "S. A. Kline," handwritten "A. C. Martin, April 22, 1823," orig frame, 4-1/4" w, 5-3/4" h **$1,980**

House and barn, farm life, cows, horses, rabbit, and snake, buggy and Conestoga wagon, sun with face, pen and green, orange, yellow and brown, dated 1856 in lower right corner, framed, 9-7/8" l, 5-1/8" h
.... **$7,975**

Snow Hill Cloister, Franklin County, PA, potted flowers with compass wheels, tulips, and parrots, decorative border, drawn in red ink, colored in yellow, blue, and green, old painted frame, 8-1/4" w, 10-3/8" h **$6,600**

Ein brief, printed and hand illuminated, printed by King und Baird, Philadelphia, purple, orange, and yellow, ein brief to guard against fired, old frame, 11-1/2" w, 15" h
.... **$315**

Gebruts and Tauf-schein, uncolored, dated 1822, German text, nicely added information, minor edge wear, $275.

Fraktur, Pennsylvania, watercolor on paper, potted tulip, 19th C, 9-1/2" x 6-3/4", $1,725.
Photo courtesy of Pook & Pook, Inc.

Family register, hand drawn, blue-green and red border with stars and flowers in corners, hearts, cherubs, and cross hatch work at center, German names, written in old brown ink, heart and hand medallion with inscription "Orphans Home and Ft. Wayne Hospital, Allen Co., Ind," sgd "John Cornelius Martin," old taped tear near top margin, small piece of corner missing, dates from 1814 to 1870, 19-3/4" w, 16" h **$1,100**

Himmelsbrief, printed, attributed to Stettinius and Leper, text, Hanover, York County, PA, wood blocks of vases and flowers, hand illuminated in red, yellow, and green, old tiger maple frame, water stained, 9-3/4" w, 7-1/2" h.............................**$100**

House blessing (Haus Segen)

Block printed and hand drawn, printed text, dated 1787, hand dec attributed to Arnold Hovelmann, tulip and flowers, border dec, illuminated in red, yellow, green, and brown, old painted frame, 7-1/2" h, 12" w **$10,450**

Printed by Johann Ritter, Reading, hand colored, orange, green, blue, yellow, brown, and black, professionally repaired and rebacked on cloth, 18-1/4" h, 14-3/8" w old stenciled dec frame, 15-1/2" h, 11-3/4" w...............................**$500**

Marriage certificate, watercolor, pen and ink on paper, Daniel Schumacher, paired red, yellow and green birds flanking an arch with crown, for Johannes Haber and Elisabeth Stimmess, Windsor Township, Berks County, PA, dated 1777, 8" x 12-1/2" **$1,035**

Reward of merit, hand drawn, cut-work, attributed to Jacob Botz, Lancaster, PA, floral motif, two birds perched on tulips, cut-work to floral motif, name Salome Schmidin below, red, blue, and green, 3-1/4" w, 4-7/8" h **$3,740**

FRATERNAL ORGANIZATIONS

History: Benevolent and secret societies played an important part in America from the late 18th to the mid-20th centuries. Initially, the societies were organized to aid members and their families in times of distress. They evolved from this purpose into important social clubs by the late 19th century.

In the 1950s, with the arrival of the civil rights movement, an attack occurred on the secretiveness and often-discriminatory practices of these societies. Membership in fraternal organizations, with the exception of the Masonic group, dropped significantly. Many local chapters closed and sold their lodge halls. This resulted in the appearance of many fraternal items in the antiques market.

Benevolent & Protective Order of the Elks, (BPOE)

Book, *National Memorial*, color illus, 1931 ....**$35**

Bookends, pr, bronzed cast iron, elk in high relief....................................**$75**

Pinback button, orange, lavender, and green, white accents, gold rim, brown elk symbol, tiny inscription "Souvenir Elks Convention Los Angeles 1909".......................................**$25**

Shaving mug, pink and white, gold elk head, crossed American flags and floral dec, marked "Germany" on bottom **$90**

Tip tray, Philadelphia, 21st Annual Reunion, July 1907, rect, 4-7/8" x 3-1/4".......................................**$135**

Eastern Star

Demitasse cup and saucer, porcelain...**$25**

Pendant, SP, rhinestones and rubies **$45**

Ring, gold, Past Matron, star-shape stone with diamond in center **$150**

Independent Order of Odd Fellows (I.O.O.F)

Ceremonial staff, polychrome carved wood, reverse tapering staff surmounted by carved open hand in cuffed sleeve holding heart in palm, old red, gold, and black painted surface, mounted on iron base, minor surface imperfections, 3" w, 1-1/2" d, 64" h................................**$2,300**

Gameboard, reverse painted black and gold metallic squares bordered by "I.O.O.F" chain links and other symbols, areas of flaking, black oak frame, 20-1/2" x 20-1/2".............**$350**

Vignette, oil on board, hand beneath three links holding heart and card bearing archery scene, molded gilt gesso frame, flaking, subtle surface grime, 7-3/4" x 14-1/2"................**$920**

Eastern Star, dresser tray, glass top, metal fittings, enameled emblem with gold trim in center, dried flowers under glass top, two handles, **$25.**

Cane, English, silver, 3" h x 1-2/3" unfolding Masonic ball handle, dec with C-scrolls, initialed, June 15th, 1891 on top, sides done in arched panels, four side latches, spreads to six linked pyramids, all engraved with secret symbols, ebony shaft, 2-3/4" horn ferrule, 1891, 35-3/4" l, **$1,900.**
Photo courtesy of Henry A. Taron.

Wall hanging, painted canvas, from Odd Fellows Lodge #4 in Whitehall, NY, several symbols reflecting high ideals, imperfections, 19th C, 75" l, 47-1/2" h.....................................**$2,990**

Watch fob, 94th Anniversary, April 12, 1913 ....**$30**

Knights Templar

Business card, Reynolds, J. P., Columbia Commandery No. 18 (K of P) Sturgis, MI, color logo, c1890 .... **$6**

Loving cup, china, three handles, green and white, gold tracery, Knights Templer insignia and Pittsburgh, 1907, marked "American China Co." **$75**

Magazine, *The Magazine for York Rite Masons*, 12 issues from 1982-83 .... **$18**

Shot glass, bowl supported by three golden swords, dated 1903, Pittsburgh **$25**

Tumbler, emb Indian head, dated 1903, Pittsburgh **$45**

Masonic

Advertising button, Illinois Masonic Hospital, black and white litho, c1920 .... **$10**

Apron, 14" x 12", leather, white, blue silk trim, white embroidery, silver fringe **$35**

Book, *An Inquiry In The Nature & Tendency of Speculative Freemasonry*, John Stearns, 210 pgs, 1829 .... **$65**

Bookends, pr, patinated metal, "appl'd for" on back **$200**

Box, cov, Chinese Export black lacquer, molded top with mother-of-pearl and lacquer Masonic devices, sides with floral dec, top loose, lock mechanism missing, minor lacquer loss, 5" x 16-1/4" x 12-1/2" **$920**

Ceremonial cane, carved lizards, rounded top knop with emblem and eagle, metal top, several age cracks, 33-1/2" l **$350**

Fob, silvered brass, June 14-15, inscription for "Grand Lodge, F & A.M. Wisconson," blank reverse, 1927 event **$18**

Goblet, St. Paul, 1908 .... **$70**

Jug, lusterware, transfer printed and painted polychrome enamels, horseman, inscribed "James Hardman 1823," Masonic dec, royal coat of arms, minor wear, 5-5/8" h **$410**

Match holder, wall type, walnut, pierce carved symbols, 11" h **$75**

Painting, oil on canvas, "Our Motto," framed, retouched, craquelure, 23-1/4" h, 20" w **$2,645**

Pendant, 10k yg, designed as double-headed eagle, set with old European and single-cut diamonds, approx. total wt. 0.78 cts, opening to reveal various enameled emblems, 13.3 dwt, missing two stones **$500**

Pocket watch, Hiram Watch Inc., 14k yg, open face, blue dial with raised gold tone Masonic symbol indicators, case with engraved Masonic scenes and symbols, Hallmark 15 jewel movement, winding stem topped with blue stone cabochon **$2,115**

Ring, 14k rose gold, enameled cross on one side, enameled 32 degrees on other, double eagle head set with 10-point diamond, hand engraved, 1900-20 .... **$175**

Sign, shield shape, polychrome wood, several applied wood Masonic symbols, including All-Seeing Eye, sun, moon, stars, large central "G," pillars, etc., gilt highlights, blue field, red and white stripes below, molded gilt frame, wear and losses, 28-3/4" w, 34" h **$3,055**

Tobacco jar, cast iron, brass, and lead, oval brass finial on domed octagonal cover, fitted onto conforming container plated with lead, sides decorated with various engraved designs: "Daniel Hall" over a foliage-filled pitcher flanked by tobacco pipes and goblets, shield with Masonic symbols encircled with "FRIENDSHIP LOVE AND TRUTH," ship at sea and anchor; the lid and base painted dark red with black, green, and yellow highlights, wear, 4-7/8" l, 3-7/8" w, 7-1/4" h **$1,175**

Shriner

Cup and saucer, Los Angeles, 1906 .... **$70**

Dinnerware, Rajah, partial set, various marks, 52 pcs **$150**

Goblet, St. Paul, ruby stained, pedestal foot, 1908 .... **$70**

Ice-cream mold, pewter, crescent with Egyptian head, marked "E & Co., NY," 4-1/4" d **$30**

Mug, Syria Temple, Pittsburgh, gold figures, 1895 .... **$125**

Shot glass, cranberry and clear, symbols and officers' names, St. Louis, 1909 .... **$300**

Knights Templar, pin tray, Alleghany Commandery, Alleghany, Penna, tan ground, red and gold highlights, **$20.**

Knights Templar, plate, 51st Annual Conclave, Knights Templar, Penna, Gethsemane Commandry, No. 75, York, PA, 1904, blue transfer print, **$65.**

Shriners, fez, Arabia Shrine Temple, Houston, 7-1/8", **$35.**

Print, Grant Wood, "Shriners' Quartet," lithograph, pencil signed lower right, framed, 8" x 12" sight, **$1,800.**
Photo courtesy of David Rago Auctions, Inc.

GAME PLATES

History: Game plates, popular between 1870 and 1915, are specially decorated plates used to serve fish and game. Sets originally included a platter, serving plates, and a sauce or gravy boat. Many sets have been divided. Today, individual plates are often used as wall hangings.

Birds
Plate
Each hand painted with gold trim, light and dark gray corners, center with game birds, gold outlines, mauve circular mark "Carlsbad Mark & Gutherz," price for 11-pc set, 8" sq **$700**

Hp, set of 12 with different center scene of shore birds in natural setting, apple green edge, printed gold scrolled rim dec, artist sgd "B. Albert," Theodore Haviland & Co., France, early 20th C, 9-1/4" d **$865**

Duck, pastel pink, blue, and cream ground, duck flying up from water, yellow flowers and grasses, sgd "Laury," marked "Limoges," not pierced for hanging, 9-1/2" d **$120**

Game bird and pheasant, heavy gold, scalloped emb rococo border, marked "Coronet Limoges, Bussilion," 13-1/4" d **$250**
Platter
Two handles, quail, hp gold trim, Limoges, 16" l **$150**

Flying grouse, scrolled gilt rim, hp, artist sgd "A. Brousselton," mkd "Limoges/Crown/Coronet/France," 18" d **$615**
Set
Fourteen pcs, 20-3/4" platter with strutting tom turkey, 9" gravy boat, twelve 10" d plates with different turkey designs, hp, artist sgd "Gasri," green "LDBC Hambeau Limoges" mark **$700**

Seven pcs, wild game birds, pastoral scene, molded edges, shell dec, Fazent Meheim, Bonn, Germany **$250**

Twelve pcs, 10-1/2" d plates, game birds in natural habitat, sgd "I. Bubedi" **$3,500**

Deer
Plate, buck and doe, forest scene, 9" d **$60**

Set, 13 pcs, platter, 12 plates, deer, bear, and game birds, yellow ground, scalloped border, "Haviland China," sgd "MC Haywood" **$3,200**

Fish
Plate
Bass, scalloped edge, gray-green trim, fern on side of fish, Limoges, 8" d **$65**

Colorful fish swimming on green shaded ground, scalloped border, gold trim, sgd "Lancy," "Bairritz, W. S. or S. W. Co. Limoges, France," pierced for hanging, 8-1/2" d **$50**
Platter
Bass on lure, sgd "RK Beck," 14" l **$125**

Hp, Charoone, Haviland, 23" l **$200**
Set
Seven pcs, platter, six serving plates, each with different fish dec, white ground, gold trim, Italian **$125**

Eight pcs, four plates, platter, sauce boat with attached plate, cov tureen, Rosenthal, 24" l **$425**

Eleven pcs, 10 plates, serving platter, sgd "Limoges" **$360**

Fifteen pcs, 12 9" plates, 24" platter, sauce boat with attached plate, cov tureen, hp, raised gold design edge, artist sgd, Limoges **$800**

GIRANDOLE AND MANTEL LUSTRES

History: A girandole is a very elaborate branched candleholder, often featuring cut glass prisms surrounding the mountings. A mantel lustre is a glass vase with attached cut glass prisms.

Girandoles and mantel lustres usually are found in pairs. It is not uncommon for girandoles to be part of a large garniture set. Girandoles and mantel lustres achieved their greatest popularity in the last half of the 19th century both in the United States and Europe.

Girandoles
Brass, three songbirds on flowering vine, three socket top, cut glass prisms, white alabaster base, worn gilding, old patina, few flakes, 17-1/4" w, 16-1/2" w **$115**

Cast brass, East Indian man dressed in feathered turban, fancy robes, scimitar hanging from chain, white

Pair of blue glass mantel lusters decorated with white flowers, cut glass prisms, 10" h, **$225.**
Photo courtesy of Joy Luke Auctions.

marble base, faceted prisms with cut stars and flowers, minor edge flakes, roughness to prisms, price for pr, 15" h.. **$115**

Cast brass, high relief rococo scrolling and vintage detail, applied flowers on base, columns shaped like large leaves about to burst into blossom, three sockets each with clear cut glass prisms, orig gilding and bobeches, soldered restorations on branches, price for pr, 18" h, 15" w **$990**

Longwy, Aesthetic Movement, two-light, rect, central beveled mirror plate, surrounded by Islamic-inspired tiles in brass frame, scrolled candle arm with two acorn-shaped nozzles, removable bobeches, third quarter 19th C, 9-7/8" w, 17" h **$750**

Pr candlesticks, center 15-1/4" h three-light candelabra, emerald green cut glass prisms, turned and tapered brass columns, white marble bases, worn gilding, 12" h..................... **$575**

Mantel garnitures
Bronze and crystal, three-light candelabra, stylized lyre form garniture hung with cut and pressed glass prisms, above three scrolled candle arms, trefoil base, price for pr, 20-5/8" h...................................... **$980**

Three cov baluster jars and two vases, Hundred Antiques dec, in famille rosé enamels, China, price for five-pc set, 19th C, 14" h, 12" h **$2,185**

Urn form, two short scroll handles, incised on side with Japonesque florals in silver and gold coloration, trumpet foot further dec with Japonesque patterning and insects, sq section marble base, inset to front with mixed metal-style patinated plaque depicting drummer and dancer, Aesthetic Movement, price for pr, third quarter 19th C, 10-1/4" h **$690**

Mantel lusters, pink cased glass, hand-painted floral panel, gilt accents, large hanging prisms, gilt wear, flakes on rim, 14-1/4" h, **$650.**
Photo courtesy of Alderfer Auction Co.

Pan, square, handles, light gray speckle, trademark in center "Ironclad Enameled Ware, (image of submarine titled I.C.M.Co.) The American Standard," some edge wear, **$195.**

Wash basin, aqua and white speckle, stamp mark "Elite Austria Reg. No. (illegible) 26," chip, **$45.**

Mantel lustres

Blown translucent clambroth glass, gauffered rim, rough pontil, seven prisms, price for pr, late 19th C, 10-3/4" h, 5-3/8" d rim **$150**

Cranberry glass, white enamel foliage dec rims, gilt trim, vining floral dec, cut faceted prisms, flakes and roughness to prisms, price for pr, 10" h **$615**

Overlay glass, white cut to pink, enamel flowers, gilt accents, cut glass prisms, Bohemian, price for pr, 9" h **$425**

Ruby glass, overlay and enameled plaques, fluted, heavy gilt, cut glass prisms, France, price for pr, 19th C, 12" h **$2,645**

GRANITEWARE

History: Graniteware is the name commonly given to enamel-coated iron or steel kitchenware.

The first graniteware was made in Germany in the 1830s. Graniteware was not produced in the United States until the 1860s. At the start of World War I, when European companies turned to manufacturing war weapons, American producers took over the market.

Gray and white were the most common graniteware colors, although each company made its own special color in shades of blue, green, brown, violet, cream, or red.

Older graniteware is heavier than the new. Pieces with cast-iron handles date between 1870 to 1890; wood handles between 1900 to 1910. Other dating clues are seams, wooden knobs, and tin lids.

> **Reproduction Alert.** Graniteware still is manufactured in many of the traditional forms and colors.

Additional Resources:

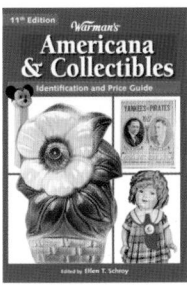

Warman's® Americana & Collectibles, 11th Ed., by Ellen T. Schroy, ed., Krause Publications, Iola, WI.

Berry pail, cov, cobalt blue and white mottled, 7" d, 4-3/4" h **$65**

Bowl, green and white, 11-3/4" d, 3-3/4" h **$50**

Cake pan, robin's egg blue and white marbleized, 7-1/2" d **$45**

Coffeepot, gray, tin handle, spout, and lid, 10" h **$525**

Colander, light blue, pedestal base, 12" d **$45**

Assorted blue spatter pieces, ranging from light blue to cobalt blue, from left: lid, two serving spoons, **$15 each;** *small open berry pail, white interior, wooden bail handle,* **$75;** *small mixing bowl,* **$20;** *coffee boiler, $85; inverted dish pan,* **$35;** *medium size colander,* **$65;** *inverted rectangular roaster with self handle,* **$30;** *inverted medium size dish pan,* **$25;** *inverted shallow pan,* **$25.**

Roaster, covered, long, oval, gray speckled, **$90.**
Photo courtesy of Dotta Auction Co., Inc.

Coffee boiler, **$95;** *on top of inverted large dish pan,* **$35;** *both turquoise and white spatter.*

Shovel, solid white, some usage wear, wooden handle missing, **$35.**

Tea pot, sloping sides, gooseneck spout, original hinged lid and interior pouring strainer, gray and white, **$125.**

Cup, gray, some rust, **$8.**

Dish pan, round, deep sides, two handles, green and white spatter, **$40.**

Dinner plate, dark blue and white spatter, **$30.**

Muffin pan, eight muffins, gray and white, pierced to hang, **$85.**

Cookie sheet, mottled blue and white **$225**
Cup, blue and white medium swirl, black trim and handle, 2-3/4" h ... **$50**
Frying pan, blue and white mottled, white int., 10-1/4" d **$135**
Funnel, cobalt blue and white marbleized, large **$50**
Grater, medium blue **$115**
Kettle, cov, gray mottled, 9" h, 11-1/2" d, ... **$50**
Measure, one cup, gray **$45**
Mixing bowls, red and white, nested set of four, 1930s **$155**
Muffin pan, blue and white mottled, eight cups **$250**
Pie pan, cobalt blue and white marbleized, 6" d **$25**
Pitcher, gray, ice lip, 11" h **$110**
Roaster, emerald green swirl, large **$250**
Skimmer, gray mottled, 10" l **$25**
Teapot, enameled dec, small chips, 9-1/2" w, 5" h **$525**
Tube pan, octagonal, gray mottled .. **$45**
Utensil rack, shaded orange, gray bowls, matching ladle, skimmer, and tasting spoon, 14-1/2" w, 22" h **$400**
Wash basin, blue and white swirl, Blue Diamond Ware, 11-3/4" d **$150**

Wash basin, brown and white speckle, pierced for hanging, chips, **$55.**

Spoon, large, gray, some wear, **$10.**

Roaster, three pieces, oval, green and white spatter, **$45.**

HALLOWEEN

History: There are differing schools of thought as to how the origin of our Halloween celebrations came to be. There are those who believe that it got its beginning thousands of years ago from the beliefs of the Celts as well as those of their religious leaders, the Druids. The Celts were simple people with simplistic convictions. Spirits, whether good or bad, ruled their world and affected the way they lived or died and these convictions even went as far as forecasting the weather and the outcome of crops. The harvest signaled the end of their year while the New Year began with the arrival of winter. This end-of-year celebration was a time of family togetherness and feasting which would include fortune telling and the foretelling of matrimonial prospects. At these family gatherings, the spirits of the "dead" relatives were also welcome for the mortal blood relations believed that these said spirits returned home for the festival of the harvest. The "Veil," which was considered the separation between life and death, was at its thinnest which allowed the ghosts to cross over and join the living, albeit for a short visit. These seasonal rituals would eventually evolve into the Halloween festivities that were celebrated in the early part of the 20th Century.

Contrary to popular belief, Halloween celebrations of the 1910s, 20s and even into the early part of the 1930s were, for the most part, not geared to children but young adults. Trick-or-Treating, as we know it, did not come to the fore until the late 1920s so until then, house parties were the norm. The lucky hostess was one who purchased a Halloween Bogie Book from the Dennison Company and utilized the numerous party topics that included themes, decorating, games, menus and even costumes. As in days of yore, fortune telling once again featured heavily in our All Hallow's Eve celebrations as can be attested by the proliferation of fortune-telling games manufactured by the Beistle Company.

As the years passed, Halloween's popularity grew and with it came an artistic outpouring of seasonal items from the hands of some very talented artists, both here and abroad. Die cuts, lanterns, invitations, place cards, games, noisemakers, paper goods (tablecloths, napkins, table borders, etc.) were just some of the pieces that were fabricated from material such as papier mâché, tin, wood, plastic and the like.

Currently, the pieces that are bringing the highest dividend are those dating from the early 1900s and are of German make. The charm, and, at times, the grotesqueness of these collectibles is evident from the time and genius that was put into each piece. The fact that these German artisans captured the essence of the Halloween holiday is quite extraordinary since Germany, along with most European countries, did not celebrate Halloween.

Many collectors of vintage Halloween pieces wax nostalgic about the 1980s and early 1990s when it was possible to buy up these collectibles at embarrassingly low prices. Many a stellar collection has been started for mere pennies on the dollar. Not so today. With the advent of the Internet, collectors now have the opportunity to peruse hundreds of items that pertain to their collecting category and utilize on-line auction venues. Auction houses throughout the country have realized this growing popularity and have accordingly increased their sales by offering "live auction" options. Now you can bid on your items of interest at an auction house in Minneapolis while you're sitting at your home computer. There is a downside: where once you had the chance of acquiring a choice item and just had the locals to contend with, you now have the world sitting in. However, there are hidden treasures out there waiting to be discovered.

Adviser: Claire M. Lavin.

Additional Resources:

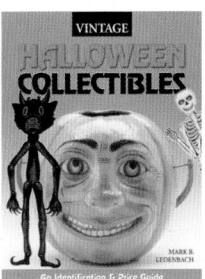

Vintage Halloween Collectibles, by Mark Ledenbach, Krause Publications, Iola, WI.

Bogie book, Dennison
1915 .... **$335**
1928, slight wear **$305**

Candy container
Champagne bucket shape, bottom slides out to place candy inside bucket, German, some wear, 3-1/4" h **$850**
Jol man, sack candy container, Fibro Toy, cardboard, c1940, 6-1/2" h, 6" w **$245**
Witch, glass, wire bail handle, 95% of orig paint, 5" h **$810**

Celluloid
Black Cat, google eyes, Japan, 1930s, 5-3/4" h **$365**
Jack-o-lantern Man, rattle Viscoloid, excellent condition, 4" h **$700**
Owl, witch hat and eyeglasses, Viscoloid, 4" h **$700**

Ceramic, Dept. 56 Snow Village, Halloween Haunted Mansion, 1998, MIB **$1,225**

Composition, lantern, Chinaman (head), German, 1920s **$3,085**

Costume, Grandpa Munster, wear, c1964 .... **$1,510**

Cymbals, tin litho, some dings, minor scratches, price for set, 1920s, 5-1/2" d **$600**

Diecut (paper)
Cat in candle, Dennison, near mint, c1920, 6" h **$230**
Figurines, German, boxed set of eight, orig box, 3-1/4" h **$1,530**
Flying witch, Dennison, few creases, minor surface wear **$165**
Halloween Wumpus, devil lightning monster, Beistle, minor wear **$315**
Lightning Wampus, aka The Halloween Devil, Beistle, c1931, 30" h **$525**

Teapot, 3-1/2" d, 4-1/2" h, **$675;** *2-1/4" d waste bowl,* **$500,** *from 1910-20s tea set, both marked "Germany."*

Jack-o-lantern candy container, "egg crate" or pulp, late 1940s/early 1950s, bottom marked "ATCO Co." (Animal Trap Co.), 5" d, 4-1/2" h, **$65.**

Lantern, layered papier-mâché pumpkin with compo wash, original paper inserts, German, 1908-12, 4-1/2" d, 4" h, **$5,000.**
Halloween photos courtesy of Claire Lavin.

Moon with two black cats, Beistle, 1930s, minor damage, 5-3/5" h **$125**

Puss in Boots, Gerrman, minor loss, 1930s, 8-3/4" h **$570**

Tiara, 1920s, German, 5" h, 9-1/2" w **$800**

Witch, bat-winged, Beistle, some creases, c1925, 18" x 18-1/2" open **$245**

Figure, celluloid
Black cat on Jol, owl on top of moon, pr, c1930 .... **$785**
Squirrel eating acorn while sitting atop pumpkin, tiny dents in bottom, c1930, 3" h **$65**

Game
"I'm a Dumbskull," w/envelope, Beistle, 1920s, some damage **$165**
"Ring the Bell," ring toss game, some wear and tear, 16" h **$710**
"Wheel Witch Fortune," w/fortune card, Beistle, 9" h **$215**
Fortune Teller, litho paper, witch, brownie & black cat in center, 12 Pumpkin ring perimeter, German, c1916 .... **$1,045**
Katzy Party, Selchow, 1920s **$105**

Glass, lantern, jack-o-lantern, glass, US, 90% original paint, 4" h **$350**

Halloween apron, crepe paper, dec with witches, bats, jack-o-lanterns, and black cats, small holes and tears, c1918, 22" h **$120**

Halloween party book, Beistle, c1925 .... **$635**

Jack-o-lantern
Pulp, F. N. Burt, 1950s **$420**
Tin, horn nose, bail handle missing, some minor scratches **$120**

Lantern
Printed on cardboard, transparent eye, nose and mouth with honey-

comb tissue folding sides, Beistle, fitted for electric or candle light, some wear, c1929, 8" d **$800**
Tommy Whiskers, Beistle, c1938, 11" x 11-1/4" **$350**

Nodder, papier-mache, German, slightly soiled, c1920, 8-1/2" h **$1,700**

Paper
Lantern, black cat head, accordian paper, heavy composition, orig wire handle, metal candleholder, German, damage, early 1900s **$1,175**
Lantern, witch, cardboard tab & slot, double-faced, US **$360**
Nut cup, ghoul wearing skull-patterned cape, Beistle **$425**
Tally card, Black-eyed Susan, Beistle, unused condition, 5-3/4" h **$155**

Parade jack-o-lantern, tin, c1908, 7" d **$1,575**

Pennant
Cat head diecut, German, some minor rubbing, c1920, 15-1/2" l **$415**
Jack-o-lantern head diecut, German, c1920, 15-1/2" l **$950**

Plastic, hard
Candy container, witch rocket, pumpkin-shaped wheeels, 1950s, 5-1/2" l, 4" h **$490**
Toy, Pirate Drummer, wheels, 1950s, 7-1/2" h **$665**
Toy, Pirate auto with witch, Rosen/Tico **$300**

Roly poly, witch and broom, celluloid, c1930, 3-1/2" h **$775**

Sugar bowl, cov, German, c1920, 2-1/2" h **$265**

Tambourine, witch on goose flying over city, Chein, light scuff marks,

few scratches, dents, c1920, 7" d **$255**

Teapot, German, c1920, 4" h **$500**

Tin
Jack-o-lantern, US, early 1900s **$1,465**
Toy, jack-o-lantern Drummer, wind-up, German, 8-1/2", C8 .... **$2,130**

HATPINS AND HATPIN HOLDERS

History: When oversized hats were in vogue, around 1850, hatpins became popular. Designers used a variety of materials to decorate the pin ends, including china, crystal, enamel, gem stones, precious metals, and shells. Decorative subjects ranged from commemorative designs to insects.

Hatpin holders, generally placed on a dresser, are porcelain containers that were designed specifically to hold these pins. The holders were produced by major manufacturers, among which were Meissen, Nippon, R. S. Germany, R. S. Prussia, and Wedgwood.

Hatpin
Brass
Child with flowing hair, flanked by sunflowers, Victorian, orig finish, 1-1/2" x 1-3/4", 9" l pin **$125**
Military button, 2" d, 9-1/2" l pin **$125**
Oxidized, four citrine-colored stones in each of four panels, citrine-colored stones on 1/2" bezel, 2-1/4" l **$315**

Tray lot of hairpins and large comb, two smaller decorative combs, $75.

Hatpins, five gold 20mm hat pins; pair of gold ball topped pins by Carter & Gough; citrine cabochon, two jade topped pins by Sloan with two pairs of handy pins, and gypsy mount carnelian ring in celluloid box, price for lot as shown, $275.
Photo courtesy of David Rago Auctions, Inc.

Satsuma, Geisha Girl dec **$245**
Sterling silver
Arts & Crafts motif of ivy leaf in circle, Charles Horner, hallmarks for Chester, England, 1911, 1-1/4" d, 11" l pin **$195**
Elongated tear shape, marked "Horner," 6-1/2" l **$95**

Hatpin holder

Belleek, relief pink and maroon floral dec, green leaves, gold top, marked "Willets Belleek," dated 1911, 5-1/4" h
.... **$125**
Limoges, grapes, pink roses, matte finish, artist sgd **$60**
Nippon, hp blue daisy flowers, marked "E. O. China," 4-7/8" d **$185**
Royal Bayreuth, tapestry, portrait of lady wearing hat, blue mark **$575**
R. S. Germany, pink roses, green foliage, pink luster trim, 4-1/2" d ... **$315**
R. S. Prussia, peach flowers, green foliage, 7" h, 3" d **$180**

HORN

History: For centuries, horns from animals have been used for various items, e.g., drinking cups, spoons, powder horns, and small dishes. Some pieces of horn have designs scratched in them. Around 1880, furniture made from the horns of

Hatpin holder, carnival glass, Grape & Cable pattern, marigold, $200.

Victorian Lady, cameo type profile, round, Victorian, orig finish, 1-1/4" d, 9" l pin **$110**
Enamel, 14k yg, hinged American flag, 5-1/2" l **$275**
Hand-painted china, violets, gold trim **$35**
Glass, 2" l faceted amber glass bead, 13-1/4" l japanned shaft **$125**
Ivory, ball shape, carved design **$65**
Jet, 1-1/4" elongated oval knobby bead, 8" l pin **$200**
Metal, round disk, Art-Nouveau style lady with flowing hair, 9-1/4" l
.... **$125**

Snuff box, rectangular, hinged lid and oval sides, held together with white metal straps and brass nails, marked "L'Auvergnate; Marque Deposee, R.L.," French, late 19th C, 3-1/2" x 1-7/8" x 7/8", $175.
Photo courtesy of Gamal Amer.

Texas longhorn steers was popular in Texas and the southwestern United States.

Ale set, silver plate-mounted cov 9-3/4" h jug, two 5-1/2" h beakers, fitted 17-3/4" l x 15" h plated frame with twisted gallery and upright handle, tripartite circular base with Greek Key border, raised on stepped block feet, English, early 20th C
.... **$850**
Arm chair, steer horn, leather upholstered seat, four pairs of matched horns form base, American, 20th C
.... **$575**
Cane
Dark horn handle, carved as perched eagle, clear and black glass eyes, lighter horn beak, 2/3" woven silver thread collar, blond Malacca shaft, 1-1/2" horn ferrule, Continental, c1895, 35" l, 1-3/4" w, 4" **$490**
Staghorn "L"-shaped handle, high relief carved hunting scene, detailed family crest on top round portion, scene spirals around handle starting at bottom continuing to top, medieval hunt with dogs, men with spears and lances pursing two bears, thin coin silver spacer, Malacca shaft with round silver eyelets, 2-1/4" polished staghorn ferrule, attributed to Germany, c1880, 33-3/4" l, 4" w x 5-1/4" h
.... **$2,800**
Wild boar's tusk handle, pointed silver cap with leaf dec, marked "sterling" on one end, other end with sq cap inscribed "Judge Henry Bank Jr. from KeoKuK Bar Feb. 15, 1919," 1-1/8" dec silver collar, dark briarwood shaft, 1-1/4" white metal and iron ferrule, 34-1/8" l, 7-1/2" l
.... **$1,100**

Cane, all rhino-horn, gold mounts, 3/8" gold collar followed by two oval gold eyelets 3" down shaft, another gold band, gold ferrule dec with C-scrolls, 1-1/3" l x 1-1/4" knob handle, 40" l, **$1,700.**

Photo courtesy of Henry A. Taron.

Case, two part, both sides with tiger underneath pine tree, top with ideogram within circle, written characters on inside flange, cord attached to lower part passes through hole in cover, Korea, cracking and some lifting of horn, 19th C, 6-1/8" l, 2-3/4" h **$150**

Cup, rhinoceros, carved as magnolia flower, base of branch and leaves, carved wood stand, losses, 18th C or earlier, 5" h **$1,100**

Furniture suite, American, 48" w x 25" d x 44" h loveseat, one 38" w x 24" d x 44" h chair, one 32" w x 28" d x 35" h chair, each upholstered, mounted with animal horns, wooden legs, brass casters, from William Wrigley residence, Chicago, IL, late 19th C **$6,375**

Plaque, wall mounted, water buffalo horns, brass caps on ends, engraved dec, 33" l......................................**$275**

Seal, stupa form, carved scene of cranes and flora atop stylized waves, Chinese or Korean, 19th C, 2" h, 1-1/4" d......................................**$100**

Snuff box, rect, carved PA motifs, floral dec, red paint on hinged lid, birds carved on sides, star on bottom, 2" l, 2-3/4" w, 3/4" h **$450**

Tea caddy, cov, Ango-Indian, Vishapatnam, antler veneer, steer horn, ivory, int. cov compartments, etched scrolling vines, restorations, early 19th C, 14-1/2" w, 9" d, 7-1/2" h **$1,850**

Tumbler, silver trim and shield, 4-3/8" h......................................**$195**

Vinaigrette, Victorian, staghorn, 2-1/2" l rough-textured horn mounted with thistle-cast lid, quatrefoil neck band, horn with guilloche strapping, short link chain, late 19th C **$350**

INDIAN ARTIFACTS, AMERICAN

History: During the historic period, there were approximately 350 Indian tribes grouped into the following regions: Eskimo, Northeast and Woodland, Northwest Coast, Plains, and West and Southwest.

American Indian artifacts are quite popular. Currently, the market is stable following a rapid increase in prices during the 1970s.

Additional Resources:

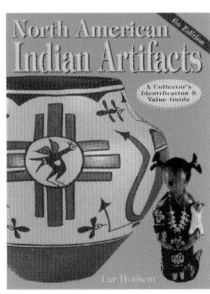

North American Indian Artifacts, 6th Ed., by Lar Hothem, Krause Publications, Iola, WI.

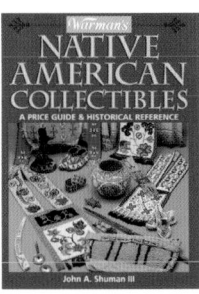

Warman's® Native American Collectibles, by John Shuman, III, Krause Publications, Iola, WI.

Anthropological records, *The 1870 Ghost Dance,* by Cora DuBois, Univ of California Press, Berkley, CA, 1939, paperback, black cloth tape binding **$150**

Awl case, beaded
Attributed to Apache, chevron and scallop, beaded in ruby red, Ute blue, white seed beads, gold, and green, finely beaded leather tassel drops, tassels, 9-1/2" l **$1,150**
Mescalero Apache, chevron beaded, sliding cover, transparent ruby red, green, yellow, navy and

Basket, flat tray form, bands and blocks in dark brown and mustard color, coil formed, dark brown and beige wrapping on edge, loop for hanging, attributed to Papago or Hopi Third Mesa, 10" d, **$75.**
Photo courtesy of Alderfer Auction Co.

white beads, large "white heart" red beads on top leather thongs beaded leather fringe with tin cone tinklers, tassels, late 19th C, 7" l **$575**
Plains, either Central or Southern, Morning Star design, translucent green, greasy orange (pumpkin), blue, and white beads, tassels, wooden needle inside, 10-1/2" l **$920**

Bag
Beaded cloth and hide, Plateau, pictorial beading, eagle, US flag, red, white, and blue banner, shield on orange bead background, eagle with carnival glass body, fringe, 11-1/2" l **$420**
Sioux, beaded graphic flags on one side, geometric design on reverse, sinew sewn beading in rosy red "white hearts," cut metallic, navy, white, medium green, and translucent green, medium blue, and rare pumpkin, beaded throat with quill-wrapped dangle and beaded dangle with tin cone feather tassels, fringe, wear at top, 27" l, 7" w **$2,645**

Basket
California, Pomo, gift, coiled, small compressed form, tightly woven with geometric devices, very fine feather tufts, late 19th C, 3-3/4" d **$1,265**
Northwest Coast, Tlingit, twined polychrome rattle top, lidded jar form, woven with bold false embroidered geometric devices using five colors, 7" l **$2,415**
Belt, Plateau, beaded butterflies, flowers, and leaves, vining stems,

Bowl, Navajo, geometric pattern, 13" d, 3" h, **$1,000.**
Photo courtesy of David Rago Auctions, Inc.

light and dark blue, yellow, light and dark green, orange red and dark red beads on white beaded ground, navy blue stitched cloth border, 40" l **$150**
Basketry tray, Salishan, circular, central imbricated star surrounded by border of diamonds, shaped handles, wear, 16" l **$200**
Birdstone, quartz **$450**
Bonnet, child's, Sioux, cap style, sinew sewn beading, lined with early acid dye calico, geometric bead design in red "white heart," cut metallic and green on white ground, edge beading old yellow and deep blue alternating squares, red silk ribbon lining around face, tie worn and faded pink, c1890, 5-1/2" h **$2,100**
Bowie knife, semi-clip point blade, brass ferrule, stag horn handle, 12" l **$230**
Bowl, basketry
Apache, pictorial, human figures, animals, and geometric devices, 15-1/4" d **$3,500**
Stepped band design in martynia around upper circumference, California Mission, patina, c1910, 8" d, 4" h **$420**
Western Apache, finely patinated Morning Star design radiating from center, willow and martynia, one rim stitch missing, 10-1/4" d, 2-3/8" h **$500**
Bowl, pottery
Acoma Pueblo, polychrome, white slip, avian and curvilinear design around circumference, "Acoma NM" painted in slip on bottom, penciled 3 price, c1930-40, 8" d, 4" h **$150**

Totem, Haida, carved argillite, fish, man with wide and dentated mouth surmounting raven base, some restoration, 20th C, 9" h, **$1,500.**
Photo courtesy of David Rago Auctions, Inc.

Hopi, possibly Nampeyo, rim has extra clay coil forming inner rim, thin and thicker framing band, opposing geometric design elements painted outside, inside faded figural animal with feather, orangish slip, small crack with chip at rim, wear, patina, c1900, 9-1/4" d, 2-1/2" h **$1,495**

Case, Northern Plains, possibly Metis/Sioux or possibly Cree, finely beaded on buckskin, floral and constellations, faceted silver metallic, opalescent green, rose red, and other colors, c1890-1900, 36" h, 12" w **$2,300**

Cradleboard, child size

Ute, Great Basin, girl's, yellow stained ochre leather, wooden base loop, traditional Ute wicker frame, deep sky blue with green, black, and pearly white in floral effect, orig lace inside, hood missing, few loose beads, c1890, 21" h, 8" w **$1,150**

Ute, girl's, yellow ochre staining, two loom beaded ornaments contain initials "M.E.," piece overlapped and sewn shut, beaded flap with clear, red "white hearts," green edged with blue and old yellow, beaded hood and board ornamentation with Ute blue, ruby, yellow, dark blue, and white, tab trim stained/ painted, long leather fringe on back, some bead loss, minor wear, c1880-1895, 31-1/4" l **$4,600**

Ute, Transmontane style, rare flag motifs around curvature of top, stained yellow for a girl, finger-like rows on flap covering laces done on early red and blue strouding with red "white hearts," navy black unstable beads, greasy yellow, and white beads, red stroud trade cloth beaded in black and white at hood edge, cross flap at top of opening geometrically beaded with later cut metallic, orangey red "white hearts" and translucent blue and green beads, attached umbilical fetish bead wrapped in white heart reds and blue with brass bead drops, weasel claw amulet for safety in travel and strength, miniature brass show sole, small Victorian key, fringe at back, replaced laces, provenance: linked to Col. Eugene C. Haynes (1844-1922), Centerville, IA, who gifted cradleboard to C. J. Wilson, further documented by typewritten note, c1875-1890, 39" l **$6,900**

Cradleboard, doll size

Apache, slatted hood, top hoop, muslin baby wrap and hood beaded in green, gold, black, and white, blue and white edging at sides, with doll, c1910, 11-5/8" l **$500**

Chippewa, formed wooden back with heart cutout, curved bow and heart pierced dec on backboard, painted muted green,

beaded cradle wrap finely beaded with floral design in realistic bluebells and wild anemones, faded velvet backing, glued break along middle of board, c1860, 14" l, 6" w **$1,450**

Northern Plains/ Plateau, Blackfoot or Umatilla, geometric beading to head of cradle, ceremonial cloth design with circles of red and green on yellow ochre background, wooden carved doll, c1890, 20-7/8" l **$1,955**

Plateau, possibly Nez Perce, various shades of blue, dark blue, red "white heart" and yellow beads, leather fringe on back, muslin doll with trade cloth hood, late 19th C, 20" l **$2,875**

Cuffs, pr, Yakima, Pendleton Round-up, pictorial beading, cowboy on one, cowgirl on other, American flags on sides with multicolor bead fringe flowing downward, yellow, black, white, sky blue, and clear rose beads, c1900, 6" h **$750**

Cuff gauntlets, pr, Plateau, for wear at Pendleton Roundup, floral beading, graphic roses in blues and red/ orange, long flowing fringe, slight bead loss, 8-1/2" l **$230**

Dispatch bag, 6" twisted fringe, Arapaho, flat, beaded simple geometric design with Southern Cross motifs, commercial leather, attachment handle, green, rose "white heart," white, and black seed beads, cut metallic beads, c1890, 17-7/8" l, 9-3/4" w **$3,450**

Dress, child's, Southern Plains, Southern Arapaho or Kiowa, supple skin, beaded with seed beads around bottom in scallops of red and white, details in deep sky blue and yellow, yellow ochre stained below scallops, one neck band similar to scallops, other band of deep rose beads with blue, white, and yellow, late blue and red clear heart trade beads on decorative tassels, fringed with sq double tab side flaps, c1875-85, 27" l **$6,620**

Fiddle, Apache, one horsehair string, made from century plant flower stalk, incised green and yellow design, patina, 14-1/8" l **$350**

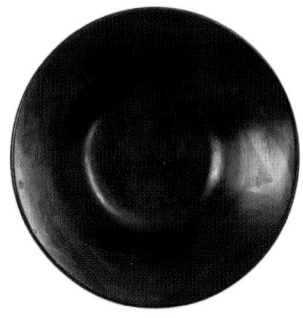

Bowl, Pueblo, San Ildefonso, shallow, black, attributed to Maria, c1920, 13-1/8" d, **$600.**
Photo courtesy of Pook & Pook, Inc.

Beaded jacket, northeast coast, c1890, **$1,600.**
Photo courtesy of Wiederseim Associates, Inc.

Pot, Santa Clara, gourd-shaped, signed by Marie Julian, small chip on top, 7-1/2" x 10", **$3,500.**
Photo courtesy of David Rago Auctions, Inc.

Frog jar, Zuni Pueblo, painted red ochre and black, typical white slip with relief figures of frogs and swirling flower design, c1880-1900, 7-1/2" d, 6" h.......................... **$6,900**

Gauntlets, pr, Plateau, Umatilla, Nez Perce or Yakima, early Pendleton Roundup type wear, cotton homespun cloth interior, tiny seed beads in many shades form lance-shaped finger strips, patriotic flags and shields on hands, bright floral display on cuffs, worn binding, slight insect damage, patch at right thumb, 19th C, 13-1/2" l, 8-1/2" w **$1,495**

Jar, Blackware

San Ildefonso, Marie and Santana, mountain and stepped cloud design around circumference, matte black on black style, highly polished body, sgd "Marie & Santana," slight abrasion, slight haze points, c1943-56, 4" d, 3" h **$865**

Santa Clara Pueblo, Mary Cain Santa Clara, carved blackware, avanyu and arrow design around upper body, sgd "Mary Cain Santa Clara" (aka Blue Rain), minor roughness, 6" d, 6-1/2" h **$700**

Jar, pottery

Pueblo, Acoma or possibly Laguna, polychrome, bottle bottom, lower orange areas heavily smoke smudged, scalloped rim, repaint areas at edge with possible chip repair, 7" d, 6-1/2" h **$815**

Zia Pueblo, polychrome, geometric design and bird, pale slip ground, 3-1/2" d, 2-7/8" h **$200**

Knife sheath

Northern Plains, possibly Blackfoot, sinew sewn, faceted navy, green, red "white hearts," faceted red, and seed white beads, 5-3/4" l **$615**

Northern Plains, sinew sewn, Morning Star design, blue, green, and pink with yellow bead ground, orange quilled, tin cone tipped, 6" dangle, 4-1/4" l **$435**

Plains, Sioux, red, yellow, green beading on white, tin cone and horsehair dangles at tip, 4-1/2" l **$200**

Sioux, blue and yellow beads on white bead background, blue bead edging, red quill wrapped tin cone dangle at tip, tin cones with feather fluff on body, 3-3/4" l, 3" dangle **$300**

Miniature, Parfleche case, folded, made as toy or model in style of Northern Plains or Plateau, 5-1/2" l, 3-1/2" w **$420**

Moccasins, pr

Cheyene, child's, sinew sewn, split back, birds on vamps, orangish red "white hearts," sky blue, bluish white, navy beads, some faceted beads, 6" l **$520**

Child's, blue stripe on vamp, lower areas multicolored, 4-5/8" l .. **$420**

Plains, doll, overall beading in clear green with opalescent white beads, red "white heart" and white beads around top edge, 3-7/8" l **$420**

Plateau (Blackfoot or Crow), child's, yellow, pink, and navy floral dec on bright blue ground, one sole worn much harder, 5" l **$320**

Sioux, child's, beaded in translucent gold, check design in green and white, side and central red bands, 4" l **$460**

Sioux, ceremonial, child size, beaded soles with two shades of blue, white, and red "white heart" accents, uppers with green, gold, old yellow, blue, and white beading, sinew sewn, 5" l **$900**

Sioux, miniature, red "white heart," white, blue, and cut metallic beads, aged stamping on bottom "Ralph Velich Taxidermist, Omaha, Neb," 2" l **$520**

Southern Plains, sinew sewn on buffalo, heel fringe and seam, very tiny red "white hearts," green, old yellow, break to one tie, 7" l **$720**

Southern Plains, Cheyenne, yellow ochre stained hide, heel tassel remnant, line of blue beads up heel seam, varied sky blue, navy, greasy yellow, and red on white beads, some damage to beads, late 19th C, 9" l **$460**

Western Apache, White River area, high style, turned up "noses" dec with metal conchos, loom beaded strips, diagonal red, blue, and white design across vamp, 9" l, 16" h **$575**

Model cradleboard, with doll, Apache, Sunshade hood stained orange, leather cradle stained yellow ochre, beaded in rows of blue, white, and black beads, muslin doll with thread features and stained yellow ochre beaded Western Apache moccasins, two bead rows missing, 21-3/4" h **$2,100**

Blanket, Southwest, light gray, black, red, turquoise, and white geometric motifs, white stripes and fringe, **$600.**

Polychrome pot, Acoma, red, black and orange on cream ground with crosshatching, diamond, floral, and checkerboard decoration, red internal rim, c1890-1900, **$9,775.**
Photo courtesy of Pook & Pook, Inc.

Vase, San Ildefonso, black, matte glaze, decorative geometric band, sgd "Desideria San Ildefonso," 6-1/2" h, **$600.**
Photo courtesy of David Rago Auctions, Inc.

Moose call, Northeast, conical bark, ask ring, binding at horn and mouthpiece, sewn, spring scraped bark with negative figures of moose, birds, and horses, scalloped around horn, late 19th C, 20" l **$250**

Parfleche bonnet case, child's, rawhide, buffalo hook mark, simple line design at ends, 15-1/8" l **$2,415**

Parfleche case, Crow, green, blue, and red geometric design, old tag reads "Indian suitcase, May 1891," remnant tie, staining, 26" l, 12" w **$2,100**

Photo, silver print with sepia tones, by Edward S Curtis, shows Indians riding horses in single file, signature and "L.A." lower right, glued down to thin card backing, 14" x 17" orig brown and black frame, sold with book *Portraits from North American Indian Life*, by Coleman and McLuhan, 13-3/8" l, 10-3/8" h **$1,150**

Pipe, Eastern Woodlands, carved from natural burl, freeform bowl, carved figure of man at right angle below, some old patinated damage, 1830s, 4" x 3" **$300**

Pipe stem, Eastern or Dakota Sioux, spaled maple, tack dec along length, tacks alternate circles with figures of buffalo, turtle, man, and deer or elk, tacks date to 1870, 31" l **$2,300**

Pocket book, Plateau, German silver purse frame, front and back beaded in differing geometric

designs, red, yellow, green, dark blue, and sky blue, white bead background, shell bead handle, two bead fringe loops missing, c1920-35, 11-1/2" x 11-1/2" **$300**

Pouch

Apache, rect, graphic design of outlined "Gaan" on front, blue, black and white bead details, surrounded by border of black and white diagonal beading, bottom border rose "white hearts" with green edging, flap with beaded cross, blue, white, old yellow, and navy, stained yellow ochre, flap covers top of gaan when closed, 4-3/4" l, 4" w **$1,050**

Iroquois, Niagara Falls, crossed American flags on one side, branch of holly with berries on other, large white bead edging, fringe loops, 1919, 5" l, 5-1/4" w **$250**

Southern Plains, beaded in yellow and black on white ground, bordered by transparent, rose, and navy, booth leather, rare lavender rose beads, damaged brass beaded handle, two tabs edged in yellow, white, and navy, center in translucent green and rose, tassels, flap damage, bead loss, 3" l, 2" w **$1,050**

Rug, Navajo

Crystal style, two central stepped diamonds, arrows, and interlocking rectangles in red and natural white, dark brown, and

Stone implements: back, left to right: celt (axe head without grooves), attributed to eastern US, post 1500 A.D., 3-1/2" l, **$320;** *axe head, full groove, attributed to Ohio or Mid-West, believed to be pre-1500, 7" l, incomplete,* **$175;** *center row: mortar, volcanic stone, three feet, Columbia River region, 1,500 to 2,500 years old, 4" d, 2-1/2" h,* **$100;** *axe head, archaic, full groove, pecked hard stone, New England, pre-Columbian, 5" l,* **$100;** *axe head, probably ceremonial, eastern US, pre-Columbian, 5-3/4" l,* **$100;** *front row: axe head, full groove, Mid-West, 2000 to 2500 B.C.,* **$250;** *pestle or seed grinder, Mid-West, 2-7/8" h,* **$90;** *miniature mortar, 2-1/4" d,* **$65;** *full groove axe head, eastern US, probably New York, prehistoric, 1-3/4" l,* **$125.**
Photo courtesy of Alderfer Auction Co.

tan hand-spun wool, natural gray ground, red and natural dark brown stepped border, normal edge wear, 83-1/2" x 51" **$1,850**

Ganado or Klagetoh area, central elongated diamond design, hand carded natural, black, and gray wool, double dye red border design, stains, wear, c1930, 52" x 79" **$1,380**

Inkwell, George Ohr pottery, cottage shape, tile roof, two arches, swinging picket fence, green and amber speckled glaze, mkd "G. E. OHR BILOXI," short firing line to base, 3-1/2" x 6" x 4-1/4", **$5,500.**

Photo courtesy of David Rago Auctions, Inc.

Inkwell, bronze and glass, Tiffany, Grapevine pattern, lined with green slag glass, original bronze patina, stamped "TIFFANY STUDIOS NEW YORK 844," cracks to one glass panel, 4" square, 3-1/2" h, **$875.**

Photo courtesy of David Rago Auctions, Inc.

Inkwell, glass, light blue, pointed lid, brass collar, paneled body, **$45.**

Ganado style, central stepped pattern in red, black and neutral tan, white and dark brown handspun wool, natural gray ground, tan, red and brown border, normal edge wear, 48-1/2" x 75" **$1,725**

Two Gray Hills style, intricate intertwining hook design in black and white, gray carded ground, 26" x 41" **$350**

Shaman basket, cov, round, pocket in lid, 5-1/2" d **$3,600**

Spoon, Sioux, shaped horn, beaded leather handle wrap in dark translucent green, rose "white heart," greasy yellow beads with feather tipped tin dangles, 7" l **$320**

Strike A Light bag, Southern Plains, beaded base, stepped diamond design, medium blue, maraschino red "white hearts," dark navy with white beads, bottom fringe, flap with beaded edging and metal concho with fringe around perimeter, two hairpipe beads, large blue trade beads on twisted handle, boot leather base, c1910, 5-3/4" l, 3-1/2" w **$650**

Tail bag, beaded, Apache, Ute form and style, rose "white heart," red "white heart," black, white, and blue, old yellow, fringe below dangles missing, late 19th C, 19" l **$1,380**

Tapestry weaving, Navaho Yeibechi, finely woven male dancers lead by Talking God, blue, brown, russet, white and black wool, gray wool ground, 25" x 24" **$460**

Tipi bag, Crow, beaded buffalo hide, white, green, red "white hearts," blue and navy design strips, diagonal design alternates with block colors, stroud edged in pony type beads on each side, flap, ties at top, early 19th C, 12" w, 8" h **$2,300**

Tobacco bag, woman's, beaded star or cross, rose, greens, Crow pink, yellow, navy, and white, letter of authenticity included, c1910, 10" l **$700**

Tomahawk, plain brass, handle shows evidence of dec around stem, bead wrapped ornamentation at end with long fringe, 27" l **$2,530**

Trade ax peace pipe, 19th C
Brass head, notched design on handle **$4,000**
Iron forged, tiger maple handle **$36,000**

War club, carved and painted wood, brass tacks, antler, last quarter 19th C, 24" l **$1,150**

War club head, possibly Northern Plains, stone, ram's head, sculptured and colored, tack eyes, beaded strip holds stone, wooden handle broken off, yellow ochre and blue oxide stain, c1880, 4-5/8" h **$420**

INKWELLS

History: Most of the commonly found inkwells were produced in the United States or Europe between the early 1800s and the 1930s. The most popular materials were glass and pottery because these substances resisted the corrosive effects of ink.

Inkwells were a sign of the office or wealth of an individual. The common man tended to dip his ink directly from the bottle. The years between 1870 and 1920 represent the golden age of inkwells when elaborate designs were produced.

Brass, engraved peaked cornice-form backplate cut with central trefoil and flowers, cabochon bloodstone surrounded by four cabochon red stones, rect base with engraved border, central cut glass well flanked by turned pen supports, Gothic Revival style, England, third quarter 19th C, 9-1/4" l, 5-7/8" h **$250**

Bronze
Cast, Victorian, figural, greyhound dog chained to fencepost, two orig glass wells with covers, 12" l **$815**

Central lidded baluster form inkwell, round dish raised on quadripartite leaf-form bronze base, dark green enamel ground, stylized foliate bands with gilt accents, faux jewelling, French, late 19th C, 8" d, 5-1/2" h **$435**

Oval bronze tray, enameled in ivory and jewel dec, pen rest with urn-shaped inkwell, Viennese-style, mid-19th C, 7-1/4" l **$700**

Cast metal, figural, young girl and large dog, bronzed finish, Victorian, c1906, 12" l, 8-1/2" h **$750**

Copper, repoussé, inlays of men, woman, and monkeys, further engraving and gilt, Japan, Meiji period (1868-1911), 3" d **$420**

Glass, crystal, square, four molded rococo feet, 3-1/4" w, 3-1/2" h **$175**

Gilt metal, bronze, French, rococo style, lion's head supporting pen rest above tray with two cov wells, dolphin feet, 14" l **$460**

Paperweight, multicolored concentric millefiori, base with 1848 date canes, Whitefriars, 6-1/4" h, 4-1/2" d **$175**

Pearlware, gilt highlights, imp "By F. Bridges, Phrenologist," and "EM" on base, England, very minor chips, gilt wear, 19th C, 5-1/2" h **$520**

Porcelain, formed as three crested birds, magenta, gilding, white band painted with polychrome flowers, insert and lid, underglaze blue crossed arrows, French, 5" h **$200**

Sterling silver, two bottles, matching pen tray, center sander, Victorian, hallmarked **$1,800**

Stoneware

Brushed cobalt blue on top, imp "C. Crolius. Manhattan-Wells, New York," few chips on base, 3-1/8" d, 1-5/8" h **$3,200**

Incised oval stamp "C. Crolius Stone Ware Manufacturer Manhatten Wells, New York," flat cylindrical form, incised edges, upper one enhanced with cobalt blue slip, center well surrounded by three pen holders, three lower edge chips, 3-1/2" d, 1-1/4" h **$2,990**

Wood, Matthew Bolton, Birmingham, rect, emb silver mounts, gadroon and shell edge, two silver mounted cut glass inkwells in gadrooned holders, four scroll legs, paw feet, c1795, 14" l, 10" w **$1,725**

IRONS

History: Ironing devices have been used for many centuries, with the earliest references dating from 1100. Irons from the medieval, Renaissance, and early industrial eras can be found in Europe, but are rare. Fine engraved brass irons and hand-wrought irons predominated prior to 1850. After 1850, the iron underwent a series of rapid evolutionary changes.

Between 1850 and 1910, irons were heated in four ways: 1) a hot metal slug was inserted into the body, 2) a burning solid, e.g., coal or charcoal, was placed in the body, 3) a liquid or gas, e.g., alcohol, gasoline, or natural gas, was fed from an external tank and burned in the body, or 4) conduction heat, usually drawing heat from a stove top.

Electric irons are just beginning to find favor among iron collectors.

Additional Resources:

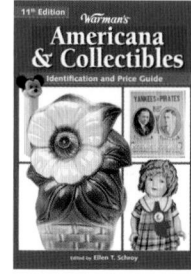

Warman's® Americana & Collectibles, 11th Ed., by Ellen T. Schroy, ed., Krause Publications, Iola, WI.

Advisers: David and Sue Irons.

Reproduction Alert. The highly detailed German charcoal iron known as "dragon chimney" is currently being reproduced in Europe.

There are more reproduction slug irons being hand crafted in Europe. They are well made, so look carefully for wear on handles, and inside parts.

Charcoal

Acme Carbon Iron, 1910 .... **$125**
Cummings & Bless, tall chimney, 1852 .... **$110**
Cutwork sides, wrought, French **$350**
Dragon chimney, highly detailed, German **$450**
Dutch Brass, cutwork sides **$300**
Eclipse, lift off top, 1903 .... **$110**
Improved Progress Iron, 1913 .... **$250**
Junior Carbon Iron, 1911 .... **$200**

Children's

Brass, ox tongue slug, 4" **$180**
Cap, oval, French, "WP," 3-1/2" **$60**
Charcoal, tall chimney, 3-1/2" **$250**
Cross Rib Handle, cast, 2-3/4" **$30**
Dover Sad Iron, No. 812, 4" **$45**
European Ox Tongue, all iron, 3" **$110**
Sensible No. 0, detachable handle, 4" **$120**
Sleeve, with rope handle, cast, 4-1/2" **$50**
Swan, all cast, 2" **$125**
Swan, all cast, 5" **$450**
Swan, original yellow paint with pin striping, 2-1/2" **$300**
The Gem No. 2, wood handle, 4-5/8" **$200**
The Pearl, 3-3/4" **$75**
Tri-bump handle, all cast, 2-3/8" **$40**
Wapak 2, cast, 4" **$50**

Electric

Knapp Monarch, round iron **$200**
Pacific Electric, 1905 .... **$110**
Petipoint Model 410, Art Deco-style fins on sides **$200**

Inkwell, white metal, circular, inkwells concealed under the hinged heads of cast dog figures and a parrot on a stand, revolving lower pen tray, American, 1920s, 9" d, 14-1/4" h, **$375.**
Photo courtesy of David Rago Auctions, Inc.

Flat Iron

Best On Earth, Potts Iron, detachable $60

Czechoslovakia, green, detachable handle **$125**

Double Pointed, cast, 9" **$160**

Dover Sad Iron, detachable **$40**

Enterprise, boxed set of three, detachable handles, wooden box **$350**

Enterprise, boxed set, five irons, three handles, two trivets **$500**

Enterprise, "Star Iron," holes in handle **$70**

Eurpoean, wrought, bell in handle **$80**

French, Le Caiffa, cast, 2-3/4" **$45**

Hoods 1867, soapstone body **$150**

IXL, cast **$20**

LeGaulois, cast, French **$50**

Ober, #6, patent 1912 ...... **$50**

Round back, "L" handle, Belgium **$90**

Sensible, detachable handle, No. 3 ...... **$75**

Weida's Patent 1870, fold-back cold handle **$350**

Fluter, combination type

Eclipse, charcoal with side fluter plate **$200**

Hewitt, revolving, clamp-on side fluter plate **$350**

Knapp, cast, front latch and hinge, Aug. 2, '70 ...... **$150**

Ladies Friend, revoling with slug, 1899 ...... **$600**

Little Giant, fluter at angle **$350**

Street's Magic, three pcs, 1876 ...... **$450**

Fluter, machine type

Eagle, Nov. 2, 1875, American Machine Co. **$100**

English, fine flutes, cast frame **$200**

H. B. Adams, clamp-on **$325**

Manville, cone shape **$400**

Osborne, hand wheel for tension **$450**

The Knox Imperial, good paint **$350**

Fluter, rocker type

Geneva Hand Fluter, 1866 ...... **$80**

Geneva Improved, brass plates **$300**

Howell's Wav Fluter, 1866 ...... **$450**

Iron, charcoal, Dutch brass, mid-1800, IBI 65, 8" l, **$425.**

The Boss **$300**

The Erie Fluter, detachable handle **$250**

The Ladies Friend, 1875 ...... **$160**

Fluter, roller type

American Machine **$90**

American Machine Co., Phila, PA **$125**

Clarks, holes in handle **$180**

Shepard Hardware, 1879 ...... **$130**

Sundry Mfg. Co. **$250**

Goffering Irons

Clamp-on, single barrel, all wrought **$350**

Double barrel, cast base **$500**

Single, brass, ornate "S," oval base **$250**

"S" wire, single barrel, oval base **$75**

Liquid Fuel, gasoline, or kerosene

Coleman 4A, blue **$125**

Coleman 609, black **$120**

Diamond Akron Lamp Co. **$70**

Diamond, Self Heating Iron **$80**

Ellison Bros., revolving, tank in handle **$900**

Montgomery Ward, gasoline iron **$75**

Perfection **$200**

The I mproved Easy Iron **$110**

Liquid Fuel, natural gas

Clarks, Fairy Prince, blue, English **$150**

English, Salter Gas Iron **$160**

European Ox Tongue, gas let "L" handle **$100**

Humphrey **$125**

Nu-Styl, La Rue Gas Iron, removable 2# weight **$500**

Iron, polisher, MAB COOKS, patented Dec. 5, 1848, IBI 271(M), 5" l, **$135.**

Uneedit Gas Iron, 1913 ...... **$100**

Vulcan Gas Iron **$75**

Mangle Board

Horse handle, geometric design, with paint, 1790 ...... **$2,000**

Turned handle, no carving, 1910 ...... **$100**

Miscellaneous

Give-away, Lent Tailor Supplies **$600**

Iron sole plate to attach bottom of iron **$30**

Laundry stove, Prize No. 15, holds nine irons **$450**

Suitcase Iron, Iro-Case, iron is suitcase handle **$350**

Slug Irons

Austrian, brass box, turned posts **$140**

Austrian, ox tongue, brass, L handle **$250**

Bless-Drake, salamander box iron, top lifts off **$250**

Belgium, round back with trivet **$250**

Butters, lift offf top, 1866 ...... **$650**

Danish Brass Box, engraving, 1810 ...... **$450**

Denmark, brass, vine engraving, dated 1810 ...... **$450**

French, hand made, decorative posts, lift gate, c1800 ...... **$700**

Majestic, combination, revolving **$750**

Scottish Box, turned brass posts **$1,200**

Special Purpose

Asbestos, sleeve **$50**

Billiard table iron, London **$300**

Egg iron, hand held **$80**

English

Hot Water iron **$350**

Round bottom polisher, Carron
.... **$75**

Glove form, steam heated, brass
.... **$200**

Hat

Shackle, adjustable edge **$135**

Tolliker, wood, curved shape
.... **$140**

Tolliker, wood, brass base **$150**

Polisher

French, CF, raised pattern on bottom
.... **$200**

Hood's, patent 1867, soapstone body
.... **$400**

Star polisher **$150**

Sleeve iron

Grand Union Tea Co. **$60**

Hub **$50**

Pluto, electric **$200**

IRONWARE

History: Iron, a metallic element that occurs abundantly in combined forms, has been known for centuries. Items made from iron range from the utilitarian to the decorative. Early hand-forged ironwares are of considerable interest to Americana collectors.

Additional Listings: Banks, Doorstops, Fireplace Equipment, Irons, Kitchen Collectibles, Lamps, and Tools.

Additional Resources:

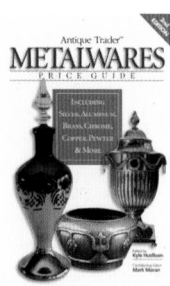

Antique Trader® Metalwares Price Guide, 2nd Ed., by Kyle Husfloen, ed., and Mark Moran, contr. ed., Krause Publications, Iola WI.

Andirons, pr, cast, faceted ball finials, knife blade, arched bases, penny feet, rusted surface, 20" h
.... **$325**

Apple roaster, wrought, hinged apple support, pierced heat end on

Ironware, doorknocker, wrought iron serpent form, 19th C, 11" l, **$460.**
Photo courtesy of Pook & Pook, Inc.

slightly twisted projecting handle, late 18th C, 34-1/4" l **$1,650**

Baker's lamp, cast iron, attached pan, hinged lid, bottom marked "No. 2 B. L.," pitted, 4-1/4" h, 8-1/2" l **$250**

Bill holder, Atlantic Coast Line, cast, c1915, 4" h **$50**

Boot scraper, cast, Scottie Dog, figural side profile, America, minor surface rust, early 20th C, 11-1/2" l, 18-1/2" h **$590**

Bottle openers

Alligator, head up, John Wright Co., near mint, 2-1/2" x 5-1/8" **$200**

Alligator with boy, Wilton Products, excellent, 2-3/4" x 3-7/8"
.... **$450**

Bear head, John Wright Co., wall mount, excellent, 3-3/4" x 3-1/8"
.... **$115**

Beanie Bert, sgd "1988" on front of base, mint, 4" x 2" **$225**

Canada goose, Wilton Products, good, 1-11/16" x 3-5/8" **$85**

Canvasback duck, Wilton Products, near mint, 1-13/16" x 2-7/8"
.... **$225**

Cathy Coed, L & L Favors, repainted, 4-1/2" **$340**

Cocker spaniel, brown, mkd "John Wright Inc., 1947," 2-3/4" x 3-3/4"
.... **$85**

Cowboy holding onto signpost, John Wright, good, some paint loss, 4-1/8" x 2-3/4" **$70**

Cowboy in chaps, Wilton Products, near mint, 4-1/2" x 2-3/4"
.... **$675**

Cowboy with guitar, John Wright Co., near mint, 4-3/4" x 3-1/8"
.... **$115**

Dinky Dan, Gadzik Sales, sgd "Gadzik, Phil, Ivy Weekend 52," excellent, 3-7/8" x 2-1/8" **$310**

English setter, brown and white, mkd "John Wright Inc., 1947," 2-1/4" x 4-1/2" **$85**

Fish, tail up, mkd "John Wright, Inc., 1947," very good, 2-5/16" x 4-5/8"
.... **$200**

Ironware, horse and buggy, cast iron, some original paint, 11" l, **$250.**
Photo courtesy of Joy Luke Auctions.

Freddie Frosh, L & L Favors, front base sgd "Big Game '55," 4" x 2"
.... **$340**

Grass skirt, Greek, Gadzik Sales, sgd "Gadzik Phil." 5" x 1-15/16"
.... **$400**

Reproduction Alert. Use the following checklist to determine if a metal object is a period piece or modern reproduction. This checklist applies to all cast-metal items, from mechanical banks to trivets.

Period cast-iron pieces feature well-defined details carefully fitted pieces, and carefully finished and smooth castings. Reproductions, especially those produced by making a new mold from a period piece, often lack detail in the casting (lines not well defined, surface details blurred) and parts have gaps at the seams and a rough surface. Reproductions from period pieces tend to be slightly smaller in size than the period piece from which they were copied.

Period paint mellows, i.e., softens in tone. Colors look flat. Beware of any cast-iron object whose paint is bright and fresh. Painted period pieces should show wear. Make sure the wear is in the places it is supposed to be.

Period cast-iron pieces develop a surface rust patina that prevents rust. When rust is encountered on a period piece, it generally has a greasy feel and is dark in color. The rust on the artificially aged reproductions is flaky and orange.

Ironware, nutcracker, cast iron, repainted, **$75.**
Photo courtesy of Joy Luke Auctions.

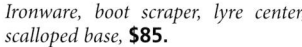

Ironware, boot scraper, lyre center, scalloped base, **$85.**

Mr. Dry, Wilton Products, excellent, 5-1/2" x 3-1/2" **$115**

Monkey, brown paint, mkd "John Wright Inc.," near mint, 2-5/8" x 2-11/16"..................................... **$280**

Paddy the Pledgemaster, Gadzik Sales, sgd "Gadzik Phil, Dinner Dance '57' on front," near mint, 3-7/8" x 2-1/4" **400**

Patty Pep, L & L Favors, Pittston, Pennsylvania, sgd "Women's Weekend '55" on front, excellent, 4" **$675**

Parrot, John Wright Co., near mint, 4-3/4" h **$310**

Parrot on perch, near mint, 4-5/8" x 3-1/4" **$620**

Toucan, John Wright Co., near mint, 3-3/8" x 2-7/8" **$450**

Calipers, pr, wrought

Double, two arms meeting at "Y"-shaped central piece, ring handle with old split, 18-1/2" l **$125**

Ending in delicate ladies legs, stamped "WTI 1863," 18-1/2" l **$115**

Candlestick, wrought, spiral iron stem, curled finger loop and tab, wooden push up, old, cone shaped wooden base with dark patina, 9-3/4" h.......................... **$160**

Carriage fenders, cast, shaped like horse leg, sgd "Fiske, New York," price for pr, c1880 .... **$4,800**

Cleaver, figural-shaped blade with eagle's head, handle terminating in brass boot, stand, minor surface corrosion, 20th C, 11-1/2" l, 4-1/2" h.......................... **$490**

Compote, cast, flower form bowl, shaped and molded star base, America, old rust surface, late 19th C, 10" w, 7" h.................... **$200**

Cookie mold, oval, bird on branch, cast iron, 5-1/4" l.................... **$335**

Door knocker, cast, fox head, ring hangs from mouth, 5-1/2" l **$85**

Embossing wheel, cast iron and bronze, scrolled foliate motif on wheel edge, imp maker's marks for M. W. Baldwin, Philadelphia, handle missing, 4" l, 1-3/4" w, 9-1/4" h...................................... **$460**

Figure, cast, Lady Liberty, Mott Foundry, New York, holding goblet and torch with octagonal marble base, later white wood plinth, c1850, 24-1/4" w, 39" h **$7,425**

Fireback, cast, late Regency-style, arch top flanked by dolphins, central polychrome scene of shepherd with his flock by fountain, beaded surround, scrolling leaf border, 21-1/2" w, 33" h **$300**

Herb grinder, cast, footed trough form, 6" d round disk-shaped crusher with wooden handle through center, late 18th/early 19th C, 16-1/2" l, 4-1/2" w, 4" h **$980**

Hitching post, cast, jockey, yellow, red, green, black, and white painted detail, wired for lantern, 31" h **$275**

Jousting helmet, wrought, cylindrical, tapering vertically at front, narrow eye slits, pierced circular and cruciform breaths, 12th C style, 19th C, 18" h.................. **$1,495**

Kitchen utensils, 9" h hanging rack, wrought, step down crest with scrolled heart, cut out cross bar, three spatulas, two dippers, with tooling and initials, 16" l **$675**

Knife, folding, hand-forged blade with a trigger locking mechanism pivots into iron sheath bound with carved wood handle, held with two iron bands and six pins,

blade illegibly marked, wear, late 18th/early 19th C, 8-1/4" l closed, 15-1/2" l open **$150**

Lamp, floor, arrow-shaped finial on shaft, two sockets, scrolled wrought iron tripod feet, woven striped paneled shades, scattered corrosion, price for pr **$815**

Letter sealer, coat of arms, European, late 18th/early 19th C, 1" d **$40**

Mirror, cast, gilt, rococo scrolled acanthus frame, oval beveled mirror, Victorian, 22" h **$75**

Mold, figural pumpkin, smiling man face, invented by John Czeszczicki, Ohio, used to grow pumpkins in human forms, surface corrosion, later stand, 1930, 7-1/4" w, 8" d, 8" h.. **$635**

Mortar and pestle, urn shape, cast iron, pitted, 10-1/2" d, 8-1/4" h **$50**

Pipe tongs, wrought iron, 18th C, 17-1/4" l................................ **$1,150**

Rush light holder, wrought, twisted detail on stem and arm of counterweight, high tripod feet riveted to disk, traces of black paint, 15-3/4" h **$330**

Shelf brackets, pr, swivel, 5-1/2" h **$20**

Spittoon, cast iron, top hat, Standard Manuf Co., Pittsburgh, Pennsylvania, painted black, glazed porcelain int. **$415**

Sugar nippers, tooled flower at pivot points, 10" l.................... **$600**

Trivet, round, marked "The Griswold Mfg. Co., Eire, PA, USA/8/ Trivet/206," 7-3/4" d **$35**

Umbrella stand, cast, backplate formed as figure of Admiral Nelson, titled at base, stepped base with double shell-form removable drip pan, 30-3/4" h.................. **$750**

Utensil rack, wrought iron, scrolled crest, five hooks with acorn terminals, minor brazed repair, 10-3/4" l............**$770**

Wafer iron, imp with seal of U.S., minor imperfections, c1800, 5-1/4" d, 24" l............**$550**

Wall frame, cast iron, gilt eagle crest, elaborately dec frame, C-scrolls and foliate devices, 19th C, 8-1/2" h, 6" d............**$575**

IVORY

History: Ivory, a yellowish white organic material, comes from the teeth or tusks of animals and lends itself to carving. Many cultures have used it for centuries to make artistic and utilitarian items.

A cross section of elephant ivory will have a reticulated crisscross pattern. Hippopotamus teeth, walrus tusks, whale teeth, narwhal tusks, and boar tusks also are forms of ivory. Vegetable ivory, bone, stag horn, and plastic are ivory substitutes, which often confuse collectors. Vegetable ivory is a term used to describe the nut of a South American palm, which is often carved. Look for a grain that is circular and dull in this softer-than-bone material.

Note: Dealers and collectors should be familiar with The Endangered Species Act of 1973, amended in 1978, which limits the importation and sale of antique ivory and tortoiseshell items.

Ball, carved, three boys forming circle, clothes with traces of paint, China, age cracks, 19th C, 2" d, 3-3/4" with base............**$115**

Box, cov, cylindrical, carved scene of figures in landscape, screw-on lid, China, 19th C, 4-1/2" h ...**$220**

Bridge, carved from hippopotamus tusk, various figures in palace setting, 12" l............**$175**

Brush pot

Incised and stained dec, mountainous landscape with people in foreground, ivory base, inscriptions around foot, China, age cracks, 19th C, 3-5/16" h, 1-7/8" d............**$495**

Incised and stained dec, mountainous landscape with people in foreground, wooden base,

China, age cracks, 19th C, 3-1/8" h, 2" d............**$450**

Relief carving of figures and landscapes, China, 6" h............**$500**

Shaped panels carved with people in landscape, base with openwork dec, China, crack on side of base, 19th C, 3-7/8" h, 1-7/8" d............**$320**

Chess set

16 crimson stained pieces, 15 natural pieces, detailed Chinese figures, lacquered case, gilt dec scenes and mother-of-pearl inlay, Oriental, 20th C, 2-1/2" to 5" h............**$1,100**

Each piece carved in form of Chinese figures, 16 natural color, 16 tea stained, fitted wood case with playing field, Oriental, 20th C, 3-1/2" to 7" h............**$920**

Natural and tea-stained pieces, each carved with Oriental figures standing on mystery ball bases, inlaid box with brass clasp, 3" to 7" h............**$700**

Cup, cov, foliate finial, oval body, carved frieze of putti with hound, mask and acanthus baluster stem, round foot, Continental, early 18th C............**$1,200**

Doctor model, carved, Chinese, 20th C

Embellish with coral and turquoise necklace and bracelets, holding fan, wooden stand, age crack, 13" l............**$850**

Wooden stand, age crack, 10-3/4" l............**$650**

Fan, carved, painted figures amidst courtyard setting, inlaid with painted ivory faces, black lacquer and parcel gilt can, base inscribed in gilt "E. Cardinal's Canton," Chinese export, 19th C, 11" l....**$1,195**

Figure, carved

Ascetic in kneeling position, arms raised, body leaning forward in bowing motion, inlaid eyes, traces of red pigment on skirt, mounted on wooden base, China, right foot replaced, 18th or 19th C, 3-1/8" h............**$260**

Bodhistiva, standing, elaborate dress, two lotus pods flanking head, sinuous tendrils held in each hand, mounted on carved wooden stand, China, 19th C, 13" h............**$1,265**

Gentleman and woman, both carrying peony blossom spray and

Ivory, Japanese, figure of Chinese court lady, 19th C, 9-1/2" h, **$500.**
Photo courtesy of Sloans & Kenyon Auctioneers and Appraisers.

basket, following natural curve of tusk, painted details, China, pr, 20th C, 20" h............**$1,675**

God of longevity, China, 11-3/4" h............**$600**

Guardian, right hand resting on sword with dragon entwined around it, two curved ribbons framing head, wooden stand with cloud designs, well carved and stained detail, China, slight age cracks, missing right dragon whisker, 19th C, 12-3/16" h............**$1,150**

Immortal, frog on left shoulder, black colored hair and shoes, China, 19th C, 5-3/4" h **$850**

Lady, body leaning to right, double gourd bottle on ribbon dangling from her waist, string of beads in her right hand, branch in her left, branch curving and resting behind head, stained details, carved wooden stand, China, age cracks in hand and left arm, 19th C, 5-1/2" h **$1,035**

Lady, holding wine pot, side with sages under pine trees, cov with foo dog, left hand holding handle, long flowing scarf with several joints, elaborate hair contained in phoenix headdress, China, wear to painted surface, age cracks and filled in areas, 18th or 19th C, 12-3/8" h **$1,265**

Ox, recumbent, head turned to right, halter attached to ring through nose, crossing over and resting on blanketed back, inlaid eyes, himotoshi and sgd "Gyokuzan" on base, lightly stained details, Japan, 19th C, 1" h, 1-7/8" l **$300**

Quanyin holding scroll in her left hand, standing on lotus pedestal, stained details, China, age cracks, ivory separated at mouth and reglued, age cracks, 18th C, 7-1/4" h **$460**

Vishnu and his consort, Indian, 7-1/2" h **$300**

Woman in western attire, carrying purse and umbrella, China, 8-3/8" h **$300**

Woman holding a basket and flowers, China, 12-1/2" h **$600**

Jagging wheel, 19th C

Figural, unicorn, inlaid eyes and nostrils, minor losses, 7-1/8" l **$4,600**

Pierced carved, whalebone, minute losses, 5-3/4" l **$2,875**

Letter opener, oblong blade carved to end with writhing dragon, Chinese, early 20th C, 9-3/4" l **$115**

Mask, Jomen carved from one piece of ivory, old man, wrinkled face, deep sinuous curves, raised furrowed brow, locks of hair brought up from side and tied in bow, long beard, back side carved in narrow grooves, ears pierced with hole for hanging wire, unsigned, Japan, Meiji period, minor nick at tip of beard, 8-3/4" l, 4-3/8" w, 2" d **$2,875**

Okimono

Figure of young boy and dog, sgd on bottom, Japan, Meiji period, crack on boy's face, 2-1/8" h **$200**

Man sitting with his left arm resting on small chest, wood grain finely carved and stained, handles of dark horn, sake cup resting on top, holding pipe case in right hand, robes with geometric designs and medallions, part of robe overlapping underside of chest, sgd on base in sq seal, Japan, 19th C, 3" l **$1,000**

Man spilling from his hat cucumbers attached to vine, frog resting on top, details slightly stained, red signature tablet on base, Japan, 19th C, 5-1/2" h **$700**

Samuari holding double gourd sake bottle in his left hand, open fan in right, garment draped over large sword attached to cord over his right shoulder, man keeling beside him holding sake cap in his left hand, gift box wrapped by cord and a bucket lie on foreground, signature on underside of box, Japan, Meiji period, damage to sticks of fan, 6" h **$1,035**

Sectional, marine ivory, man and young boy standing on tree stumps, man playing samisen, small chest with fan on top hangs from his shoulder, child holding fan in left hand, right hand with upside down book with written pages, lightly stained details, sgd on bases, Japan, missing pc from fan, traces of glue, c1900, 9-1/4" h **$250**

Seven gods of good fortune, faces emerging from basket, well carved details, lightly stained, sgd on base, Japan, Meiji period, age cracks, 2" d, 2" h **$300**

Takarabune, seven gods of good future, stained detail, sgd on base, Japan, Meiji period, 4-1/2" l **$375**

Young boy playing with toy model of horse, right hand gripping ribbon attached to horse's mouth, left hand passing under horse, holding drum, sgd on rect reserve, Japan, Meiji period, crack on base, 3-1/8" l, 1-5/8" h **$250**

Ivory, ball, high relief carved flowers, stained details, carved wood stand, Japan, 19th C, 2-1/2" d ball, 4-1/2" h with stand, **$375.**

Ivory, musicians, each on a wooden barrel form stand, highly detailed, set of seven, 19th C, 6-3/4" x 2", **$1,500.**

Photo courtesy of David Rago Auctions, Inc.

Ivory, Chinese, vases, floral motifs, pr, early Republic period, 7-3/4", **$550.**

Photo courtesy of Sloans & Kenyon Auctioneers and Appraisers.

Ivory, Chinese figure of a Meiren, standing, loose robes and high chignon, early 20th C, 11-1/2" h, **$500.**
Photo courtesy of Sloans & Kenyon Auctioneers and Appraisers.

Page turner, Shibiyama, thin blade dec sparrows in flowering tree, gold and pewter colored paint, inlaid with nacre and coral, carved handle with sparrows being chased by rodent, Japanese, one inlay missing, 17" l **$520**

Parasol handle, carved
Monkeys and butterflies feasting on fruit, details partially colored and stained, Japan, crack on side, c1900, 8-3/8" l **$165**
Tapering form with dragons, phoenix, and other birds, blank cartouche with metal divider and tip, stained horn finial on end, China, 19th C, 13" l **$200**

Pickwick, carved, minor losses, repair, 19th C, 3-1/4" h **$210**

Plaque, carved
General (Mad Anthony) Wayne, America, round, relief carved three-quarter view bust length portrait, banner below inscribed with name, houses and foliage in background, age crack, conforming molded wood frame, late 18th/early 19th C, 3-7/8" d **$500**
Low relief carving of figures in garden landscape, letters ARDS on bottom, Chinese, slight staining and age cracks, 18th or 19th C, 4-7/8" l, 3" w **$575**
One side with plants emerging from rock, other side with figures in interior and pine trees in background, stylized wave border, Chinese, slightly curved, age cracks, 18th C, 7-5/8" l, 4-1/8" w **$650**

Puzzle ball, 4" d ball, nine interior balls, outer ball with deep carving of dragons amidst clouds, interior balls with geometric patterns, fountain forms stand with open mouth of dragon on base, stylized wave motif, Chinese, 20th C, 13-1/2" h with stand **$1,450**

JADE

History: Jade is the generic name for two distinct minerals: nephrite and jadeite. Nephrite, an amphibole mineral from Central Asia that was used in pre-18th-century pieces, has a waxy surface and hues that range from white to an almost-black green. Jadeite, a pyroxene mineral found in Burma and used from 1700 to the present, has a glassy appearance and comes in various shades of white, green, yellow-brown, and violet.

Jade cannot be carved because of its hardness. Sawing and grinding with wet abrasives such as quartz, crushed garnets, and carborundum achieve shapes.

Prior to 1800, few items were signed or dated. Stylistic considerations are used to date pieces. The Ch'ien Lung period (1736-1795) is considered the golden age of jade.

Boulder, finely carved interior of Guanyin figure, light green tones, polished amber colored ext., Oriental, 20th C, 13" h **$815**

Box, rect, silver mounted, early 20th C, 3-3/8" l **$320**

Bowl, carved

Two angular handles, carved studs and designs, China, 18th C or earlier, 2-11/16" d, 2-1/4" h **$290**

Russet inclusions, China, internal fissures on base, rim fissure, 19th C, 3-1/4" d, 2" h **$435**

Bracelet, Archaic carved black jade, white inclusions, outside carved with Zhuanshu script, mounted with silver colored metal, internal band with eight straps of different designs, four ending with ruyi heads, China, four old breaks and regluing, 3-3/8" d **$200**

Brush washer, carved

Gray color with russet inclusions on base, carved bat and leafy branch, China, 18th C, 2-1/2" l, 1-3/8" h **$350**

Hollowed out peach form, animal head handle, apple green inclusions, China, filled-in fissure, minor fritting, 18th C or earlier, 3-5/8" l, 2-1/4" w, 1-1/8" h **$200**

Candlesticks, pr, dark green, carved low relief goose with out-spread wings, stands on tortoise, head supports three-tiered pricket, tripod bowl with int. carving, reticulated wood base with carved key scroll motifs and floral scrolls, 12-7/8" h **$550**

Carving

Double gourd and foliage, pale green color stone, China, fitted stand, 18th/19th C, 4" x 2-1/2" ... **$2,250**

Figural woman, pale lavender stone with green and tan accents, China, 6-1/4" h **$360**

Horse, nephrite of celadon color with brown striations, China, 19th/20th C, 7" l **$450**

Pair of birds on nests, long tails, forest green color stone, China, early 20th C, 7" l **$710**

Pair of phoenixes, pale lavender stone with areas of apple green and russet, fitted, carved hardwood stands, repair to one crest, 13" h **$1,000**

Reclining hound, highly translucent green stone, 5" l **$710**

Ceremonial knife, carved, archaic style designs, traces of red pigment, China, 18th C or earlier, 9-3/8" l **$90**

Dish, brownish-celadon, carved in Mughal style, open chrysanthemum flower, China, 19th C, 5-3/4" d **$475**

Figure, carved

Carved yellow-green, dark gray inclusions, four birds perched on tree trunk, carved fitted wood stand, China, one foot missing from stand, 20th C, 7-1/4" to 9-1/4" h **$375**

Celadon, woman, whisk in her right hand, leafy branch in left, branch curving behind her neck and resting on left shoulder, hair styled with large chignon on top of head, russet inclusions on flower and part of garment, China, small fissure at back of head, 19th or 20th C, 10-1/2" h **$200**

Green, dark gray inclusion running vertically, maiden holding flowering branch in right hand and resting on her left shoulder, China, glued to wooden stand, 20th C, 5-3/4" h **$135**

Lotus leaf forming elongated oval bowl with lobed edges, raised from bunch of branches, duck resting on lotus pod, carved and fitted wood stand with lotus design, China, small loss to stand, natural fissure conforming to design, small chips, 18th or 19th C, 4-3/4" h, 10-1/2" l **$650**

Mottled gray and black, Guandi in sitting position, long hair cascading down lower back, hole carved thru right clenched hand, carved wooden base, China, chips to right foot, glued to stand, 19th C, 7-1/8" h, 4-1/2" w **$1,035**

Mottled gray and black, lady holding teapot flanked by phoenix and attendant with fan, carved wood base, China, small chips, base glued on, 20th C, 9-5/8" h **$435**

Jade, bowl, lobed form, sides carved with lotus, two raised handles with carved rings, four scrolled feet, wooden base carved with openwork cash design, China, 19th or 20th C, 11-1/2" l x 7-1/4" w x 4-1/2" h bowl, **$650.**

Mottled, maiden with crane and sacred fungus, China, stand partially rebuilt with plaster, 19th C, 5-5/8" h **$625**

Off-white, mottled celadon, and gray-green color stone, mythical fierce beast with vase on its back, carved fitted wood stand with wire inlay, China, teeth broken, 19th or 20th C, 4-1/8" h, 6" l **$100**

Pale green jade with gray and russet inclusions, two ducks facing opposite directions, each holding lotus sprig in beak, carved fitted wood stand, China, small chip to edge of one leaf, 19th or 20th C, 3-1/4" h, 4-1/4" l **$325**

Turtle, celadon colored flat carapace and head, russet colored lower body and four feet, China, 18th C, 2-1/8" l, 2" w, 3/4" h **$175**

White, apple green inclusions, dark green underfoot, carved duck with fish in its beak, wings carved with tips pointed outwards, China, neck restored, over-painted, 19th C, 4-3/8" h, 4-1/2" l **$260**

White, apple green, russet, and gray inclusions, maiden holding vase, hair combed with large chignon, standing, glued to carved quartz base with flowers on side, hole pierced in base, China, base chipped, 19th or 20th C, 6" h **$135**

White, man with frog resting on his head, Chinese, 19th C, 2-5/8" h **$750**

Flute, light and dark colored cylinders of celadon green tone, wooden frame, India, early 20th C, 22" l **$75**

Inkstone, oval, depression to one side, black and white mottling, incised band, 3-5/8" l **$200**

Letter opener, carved interlocking C scrolls between keyfret bands handle, SS knife, 10-3/4" l **$250**

Libation cup, celadon jade, incised dec, dragon head handles, Chinese, Qing dynasty, price for pr, 5" l **$425**

Palace figure, carved herons, more than 200 pieces of dark green mottled jadeite feathers applied over wooden form, mahogany stained wooden plinth, minor losses, price for pr, 20th C, 76" h **$1,150**

Pendant, carved

Axe shape, white stone, China, 18th C **$215**

Chi dragon, pale mottled green, dark inclusions at base, openwork chi

dragon on crescent, China, small rim chips, 18th or 19th C, 1-3/4" l, 2-1/4" d, 1-1/4" h **$200**

Duck and lotus plants, highly translucent brown color stone, China, 18th C **$300**

Ducks and lotuses, white stone, China, 18th C **$1,000**

Gourd shape, leafy branch, Chinese, 19th C, 1-3/4" l **$200**

Plaque, pale lavender, bright green spots, China, 18th C **$200**

Pi disk, carved

Thick, brown and russet inclusions, deep groove carved on one side near edge, China, 18th C, 2-1/2" d, 3/4" **$100**

Thick, pale green with russet inclusions, coiled fish nose to nose with chi dragon, stylized waves, ruyi designs, fitted stand carved with bats among clouds, areas of pitting, China, small crack on inner circle, old break to stand, small chips, 18th C or earlier, 8-3/8" d, 5/16" **$3,600**

Plaque, carved

Complex design of cranes with entwined lotus plants and tendrils, raised curved shape, back edge with carved holes for attachment, mounted with three silver colored metals on wood base, China, small fissure, 18th C, 3-3/8" w, 3-7/8" l, 5-3/8" h **$435**

Thick, oval, openwork dec, central figure holding flag surrounded by flowers, center with carved quartz cabochon secured with metal pin, China, 20th C, 4-3/4" h, 3-1/2" w, 1/8" **$150**

Saucer, low relief carving of five bats around central longevity emblem, pale green color stone, price for pr, late 19th/early 20th C, 6" d **$650**

Seal, carved

Crouching boy, Chinese, 19th C, 1-1/8" h **$265**

Foo dog, Chinese, 19th C, 1-1/2" h **$245**

Recumbent foo dog, dark green spinach jade, Chinese, 19th or early 20th C, 1-1/8" h **$275**

Snuff bottle, Grayish-white, mottled russet skin on one side, rose quartz stopper **$550**

Tablet, spinach, plain rect shape, carved and recessed wood stand, China, 19th C, 3-3/4" l, 1" h **$520**

Urn, cov, Buddhist figure, open work foliage, lavender and green jadeite,

polished finish, Oriental, 20th C, 11" h **$1,100**

Vase, carved

Celadon, well carved figure riding dragon and chasing flaming pearl, phoenix with figure on back carved on shoulder, rocks emerging around base, well hollowed interior, China, natural fissure, 18th or 19th C, 6-5/8" h **$2,875**

Hu form, stone of celadon color with white striations and brown markings, China, 19th C, 7" h **$1,300**

Vase, cov, carved, spinach, flattened oval form, body carved with archaistic designs, stepped shoulder and plain neck, cov with large oval finial terminating with raised nipple, China, 18th or 19th C, 9-3/4" h **$220**

Water coupe, Mughal-style carving of peach and foliage, pale green color stone, 5" x 4" **$3,000**

Water dropper, celadon, carved wine pot, rat forming handle, leaf and tendril on side, lid and spout of silver metal with pearl and traces of enamel on carved round foot, China, small chip to foot, 18th or 19th C, 2-1/2" h **$290**

JUDAICA

History: Throughout history, Jews have expressed themselves artistically in both the religious and secular spheres. Most Jewish art objects were created as part of the concept of Hiddur Mitzva, i.e., adornment of implements used in performing rituals both in the synagogue and home.

For almost 2,000 years, since the destruction of the Jerusalem Temple in 70 a.d., Jews have lived in many lands. The widely differing environments gave traditional Jewish life and art a multifaceted character. Unlike Greek, Byzantine, or Roman art, which has definite territorial and historical boundaries, Jewish art is found throughout Europe, the Middle East, North Africa, and other areas.

Ceremonial objects incorporated not only liturgical appurtenances, but also ethnographic artifacts such as amulets and ritual costumes. The style of each ceremonial object responded to the artistic and cultural milieu in which it was created. Although diverse stylistically, ceremonial objects, whether for Sabbath, holidays, or the life cycle, still possess a unity of purpose.

Notes: Judaica has been crafted in all media, though silver is the most collectible.

Astrolabe, bronze, finely chased lettering, symbols and foliage, 19th C, 5-1/4" h **$200**

Award of merit badge, silver, Temple Ahawath Chesed Religious School, awarded to Walter R. Herschman, 1892, 2-1/2" h **$265**

Bible, Leviticus, Paris, Robert Estienne, 16 mo, vellum boards, printed in square Hebrew type with vowel points, surrounding Latin commentary in small and neat hand, fifty bound-in pages of theological treatise, 1544-1546 .... **$900**

Box, cov, silver, dec with the Binding of Isaac, hinged lid, Dutch, 18th/19th C, 4" l **$1,650**

Bridal necklace, silver, rows of rect plaques applied with granulation and hung with filigree pendants, Yeminite **$470**

Broadside, Warning to the Inhabitants of the City of Jerusalem, Palestine, sgd R.N. O'Connor, major general, commanding seventh division, text in English, Arabic and Hebrew, 19 October 1938 .... **$210**

Carpet, Bezalel wool, design of Rachel's Tomb, flanked by seven-branch menorahs, stylized Zion lettering, cranberry, gray, green, and blue, sgd "Marvadia, Jerusalem," early 20th C, 19-3/4" x 43" **$3,820**

Charger, majolica, depicting Joseph and his brothers, Italian, 19th C imperfections, 12-1/4" d **$890**

Figure, old Jewish man, Gardiner, Russia, late 19th C, 9" h **$940**

Flagon, stoneware, with incised and blue glazed "Star of David," pewter lid, German, late 19th C, 8" h **$150**

Floor screen, three-panel, sgd G.D. Felice, polychrome dec, ceremonial scenes and fruit and foliage, 1940, 72" h **$1,530**

Folk art, Wedding Feast, carved and painted wood and plaster, sgd J.J. Stark, 11-1/2" x 17-1/4" **$275**

Haftorah scroll, square hand-lettered ink on vellum, cherry wood rollers, probably Germany, late 18th C, 22-1/2" h scroll **$4,120**

Hanukah lamp

Brass, backplate with lions, menorah, and "these lights are holy" in Hebrew, over candleholders, servant lamp to side, Bezalel, Jerusalem, early 20th C, 5-1/2" h **$715**

Havdalah compendium, candleholder with egg and dart and foliate designs, drawer for spices, base formed as full-figured bird, circular base, Czechoslovakian, mark for Prague, c1814-1866, 7" h **$3,055**

Havdalah plate, porcelain, hand painted and transfer dec, M.L. Schwab, Frankfurt a Main, Germany, late 19th C, 8-1/2" d **$235**

Kiddush cup

German silver, neoclassical motif, hand-hammered leaf and berry band at rim, reeded stem, circular foot, German presentation inscription from "Israelitischen kultus-Gemeinde," mkd "800," German, early 20th C, 9-1/2" h **$1,530**

Silver and parcel gilt, beaker form with finely chased scrollwork and cartouche, mkd "800M," Continental, late 19th C, 2-3/4" h **$590**

Silver and silver filigree, applied filigree decoration and three medallions, Bezalel, Jerusalem, early 20th C, 4-3/4" h **$890**

Silver, beaker-form, rim with Hebrew inscription, wide band of foliage and scroll-work, mkd "12," Polish, 19th C, 2" h **$325**

Silver, flared rim over plain tapered body, Hebrew inscription pertaining to circumcision, Dutch, 833 fine, date letter for 1927, 3-1/2" h **$775**

Silver, tapered form, slightly flared foot, intricate acid etched vintage design, palm trees, appropriate Hebrew text, Bezalel, Jerusalem, second quarter 20th C, 3-3/4" h **$940**

Sterling silver, engraved "presented by Cong. Ahavath Achim, Revere, E. Kassoy," Russian-style, 2-1/2" h **$250**

Silver, flared cup with engine-turned detail, slender stem, square foot, Germany or Poland, first half 19th C, 5-1/2" h **$600**

Laver, copper, heavily cast foliate motifs, appropriate Hebrew inscription, Continental, 7" h **$1,120**

Lulav (palm branch) holder, enameled brass, cylindrical form, Hebrew text "Joseph is a fruitful bough...," probably Egyptian, 19th C, 28-1/4" h **$1,530**

Marriage box, pewter, circular, scene of couple, inscribed "Mazel Tov," 19th C, 4-1/4" d **$250**

Matzoh bag, embroidered silk, cream ground, colorful lion, crown, and foliage, Europe, early 20th C **$200**

Matzoh plate, Tepper blue transfer dec, vignettes of the Seder, identified in Hebrew and English, Ridgways, early 20th C, 10" d **$180**

Menorah, cast, **$1,750.**

Circumcision knife, silver, original case, **$300.**

Pillow, red velvet, silver embroidery and bead decoration, **$45.**

Menorah/Candelabra, brass, Modernist design, movable candle arms, domed circular base with Hebrew inscription, 1920s, 19" h **$470**

Mezuzzah

Carved ivory front with lions, crown, and columns, silver rect backplate with scroll-work and cabochon coral, Polish style, 6-1/2" h **$325**

Silver gilt and enamel, foliate motifs, mounted on wooden backing, Russian-style, 6-3/8" h **$325**

New Year's card, lithographed diecut pop-up, Sukkot, Germany, c1890-1910, 6-3/4" h **$150**

Paper cut, rect format, delicate cut work deer and birds amidst foliage, text pertaining to protecting against evil eye, matted, late 19th/early 20th C, 9" x 7-1/2" **$1,000**

Painting, framed

Pondering Rabbi, Josef Johann Suss, sgd lower right, oil on canvas, 11-3/4" x 9" **$1,100**

Rabbi in His Study, Hans Winter, sgd lower right, identified on reverse, oil on board, 5-3/4" x 7-3/4" **$2,350**

Rabbi with Torah, Maria Szanthos, sgd lower right, oil on canvas, 23-1/4" x 19" **$1,000**

Still Life with Pomegranates, Reuven Rubin, sgd "Rubin" in Hebrew and English lower left, oil on canvas board, 7-1/2" x 9-1/2" **$9,990**

Plaque, bronze, mother and child placing money in Tzdaka box, Boris Schatz insignia upper right, Bezalel, Jerusalem, early 20th C, 6-3/8" h **$825**

Plate, white molded ground with brown transfer depicting "Sacred History of Joseph and his Bretheren...," English, chips, early 19th C, 6-1/2" d **$130**

Pocket watch, Waltham, gilt, Hebrew numerals, subsidiary seconds dial, removable nickel silver case **$600**

Postcard album

113 cards, various Jewish personalities, late 19th/early 20th C **$825**

124 cards, New Year and holiday cards **$1,650**

Presentation bowl, sterling silver, shaped rim and foliate motifs, inscribed "presented by the Petoefi Sick & Benevolent Society," Theodore B. Starr, NY, c1910, 9" d **$360**

Purim noisemaker, silver and silver-gilt, applied turquoise, carnelian and paste stones, filigree work, appropriate Hebrew text, Turkmenistan, 11-3/4" h **$1,530**

Sabbath candlestick

Bronze, cast with fox hunt motifs, base with menorah's, Star of David and blessing for candles, France or America, c1875, 10-3/4" h **$235**

Repoussè silver, tulip-form candleholder over foliate cast baluster stem, plain square foot, Abraham Reiner, Warsaw, bobeches replaced, price for pr, c1862-68, 12" h **$1,300**

Silver plated, cast neoclassical motifs, leaf and scroll form feet, removable bobeches, Warsaw, price for pr, late 19th C, 12-3/4" h **$650**

Seder dish, bone china, plate and small dishes for implements of the Seder, illustrations by Eric Tunstall, RI, Royal Cauldon, England, 20th C, 16" d... **$300**

Seder plate, porcelain, transfer dec, center with order of the Seder in tones of rose, yellow and brown, shaped aqua rim with floral sprays, German, late 19th/early 20th C, 9-1/2" d **$590**

Shabbat knife, metal and mother-of-pearl, inscribed in Hebrew "Shabbat Kadosh," Czechoslovakian, early 20th C, 5-1/2" l............................ **$180**

KITCHEN COLLECTIBLES

History: The kitchen was the focal point in a family's environment until the 1960s. Many early kitchen utensils were handmade and prized by their owners. Next came a period of utilitarian products made of tin and other metals. When the housewife no longer wished to work in a sterile environment, enamel and plastic products added color, and their unique design served both aesthetic and functional purposes.

The advent of home electricity changed the type and style of kitchen products. Fads affected many items. High technology already has made inroads into the kitchen, and another revolution seems at hand.

Additional Listings: Baskets, Brass, Butter Prints, Copper, Fruit Jars, Graniteware, Ironware, Tinware, and Woodenware. See *Warman's Americana & Collectibles* for more examples, including electrical appliances.

Additional Resources:

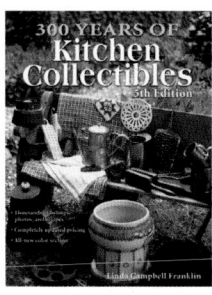

300 Years of Kitchen Collectibles, by Linda Campbell Franklin, Krause Publications, Iola, WI.

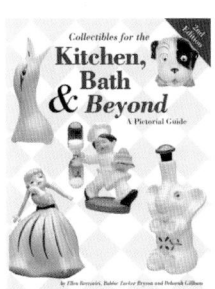

Kitchen, Bath & Beyond, 2nd Ed., by Ellen Bercovici, Bobbie Zucker Bryson and Deborah Gilham, Krause Publications, Iola, WI.

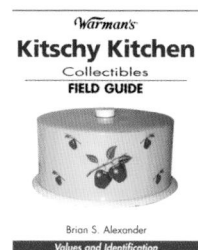

Kitschy Kitchen Collectibles, by Brian S. Alexander, Krause Publications, Iola, WI.

Spiffy Kitchen Collectibles, by Brian S. Alexander, Krause Publications, Iola, WI.

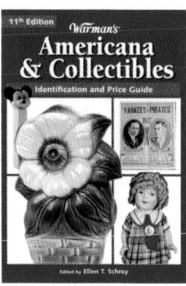

Warman's® Americana & Collectibles, 11th Ed., by Ellen T. Schroy, Krause Publications, Iola, WI.

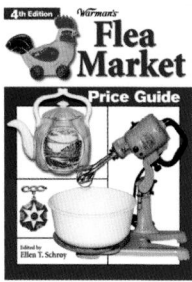

Warman's® Flea Market Price Guide, 4th Ed., by Ellen T. Schroy, Krause Publications, Iola, WI.

Bean pot, cov, Bristol glaze, handle, c1900, 6-1/2" h...............**$25**

Broom holder, Little Polly Brooms, tin litho, image of little girl sweeping floor, 2-1/2" w, 6-1/4" h...........**$425**

Butter churn, old blue paint, America, minor imperfections, 19th C, 49" h..............**$345**

Butter paddle

Burl, dark patina, simple hooked handle, 9-3/4" l..........**$165**

Maple, unusual carved handle resembling bird with open beak, small rim chip, 6-1/4" l.......**$125**

Cheese sieve, plus handle, hand-molded yellow clay, Albany glaze, 10" d, 7" h................**$320**

Colander, stoneware, brown Albany glaze, handled, attributed to Midwest, c1870, 13" h.................**$75**

Cookbook

Mastering the Art of French Cooking, Julia Child, volumes one and two, Knopf, 1971-76, dj...**$27.50**

The Good Housekeeping Illustrated Book of Desserts, Step-by-Step Photographs, Hearst Books, 1991, 5th printing, dj..........**$12**

Cookie mold

Carved woman at well, man and woman near potted plant, few worm holes, 28" l, 3-3/8" w.....**$250**

People and rooster on one side, four animals and two birds on other, minor edge wear, 23-1/2" l, 5-1/4" w
..................**$125**

Cutting board, rect, hardwood, scrolled top edge and handle, minor splits, 13-3/4" w, 27-1/4" l..........**$615**

Dough box, pine and turned poplar, PA, rect removable top, tapering well, splayed ring-turned legs, ball feet, 19th C, 38" w, 19-1/4" d, 29-1/2" h
..................**$425**

Egg beater, Jacquette Scissor, marked "Jacquette, Phila, PA, Patented No. 3," 10-1/2" l.................**$550**

Firkin, cov, wood, painted green, bentwood handle, wooden banding, splits on top, 15" d, 14-1/2" h.............**$990**

Flour sifter, Tilden's Universal, wood, partial intact paper label, 14" h, 12" w.................**$335**

Food chopper, wrought iron, scalloped edge blade, turned wood handle, 7" w.....................**$270**

Fork

Two prongs, bone handle, 6-1/2" l
..................**$65**

Fiesta Kitchen Kraft salad fork, green, **$125-$140.**

Two prongs, wrought iron, flattened handle, heart shaped hanger, 21" l **$550**

Grater
Pierced tin, hanging ring, 4-3/4" h, 2-1/2" w **$50**
Wooden, metal blade, hanger hole, 10-1/4" l, 4" w **$85**

Griddle, cast iron, Griswold, No. 10 ....**$70**

Ice bucket, Frigidaire, frosted green glass **$35**

Kettle, cast iron, Griswold No. 4 ....**$85**

Ladle, brass bowl, wrought iron handle with decorative heart hanger, 20" l, 5-3/8" d..........................**$880**

Lemon squeezer, iron, glass insert, marked "Williams" **$50**

Meat tenderizer, stoneware, orig wood handle, marked "Pat'd Dec. 25, 1877" in relief on bottom, diamond point extensions with some use wear, 9-1/2" h..................................**$90**

Nutmeg grater, Champion, brass and wood, 7" l............................**$635**

Pantry box, cov, oak, bail handle, 11-1/2" d, 6-1/2" h **$175**

Pastry board, wood, three sided **$32**

Pie crimper, carved bone, unicorn with carved fish tail, ball-shaped hooves, front leg glued, late replacement crimper, medium brown stain, 7" l.......................................**$220**

Pie lifter, wrought iron, turned wood handle, 18" l **$95**

Pie safe, hanging, mortised pine case, old thin red wash, door, sides, and back with punched tins with geometric circles and stars, white porcelain door pull, two int. shelves, edge damage, 31" w, 19" d, 31" h **$990**

Potato masher, turned maple, 9" l **$40**

Pot scraper, Sharples Tubular Separator, tin litho, graphic advertising on both sides, 3-1/8" x 2-1/4" **$275**

Rack, rect backplate with arched top, red and white enameled checkerboard pattern, narrow well, single rod suspending two strainer spoons, 20" l **$250**

Reamer
Grapefruit, green, US Glass, cone chips **$575**
Orange, pink, Hazel Atlas **$195**
Orange, Sunkist, blocked pattern, white milk glass, Walker #331b **$125**

Rolling pin
Curly maple, dark color, good patina, 16-1/2" l..................................**$275**
Milk glass, cylindrical, turned wood handles, marked "Imperial Mfg., Co. July 25, 1921," 22" l **$95**
Wooden, turned handle, peg mortised joint, 23-1/2" l, 4-1/2" w **$1,320**

Sausage stuffer, turned wood plunger, 17-1/2" l **$30**

Scoop, rect, carved poplar, round handle, 5-1/2" w, 12-3/4" l..................**$55**

Sieve, brass, wrought iron scrolled handle with rattail hanging hook, 18-1/2" l, 5-1/2" d **$330**

Skillet, cast iron, Griswold, No. 14 ....**$165**

Slaw board
Tombstone shape, 6" w, 11" l **$220**
Two-tier, hickory or ash, old brown surface, pierced detail on either side, steel blade, brass fittings, age splits, one scallop missing, 13" l, 7" d, 7-1/4" h **$100**
Walnut, cut-out heart design, shaped neck on back, semi-circular base, 5-3/4" w, 21-1/4" h **$500**
Walnut, top with stylized heart cut-out, outlined by field of small carved dots, crowned by three six-pointed Germanic carved stars in field of impressed

snowflakes, lower edge gouge carved, molded and dated siderails, hand wrought nut, bottom edge sgd "S.O.A. 1887," York County, PA, 7" w, 16-1/2" h **$2,100**
Walnut, two metal blades, carved star dec, scalloped edges and borders, initialed "F.N.," 7" w, 19" h **$220**

Soap cutting board, wooden, molded sections, use wear, 9" l, 6-1/2" w, 1-1/8" h..........................**$55**

Spatula, iron, D-shape, baluster like turnings on handle, 10" l **$200**

Spice set, Griffiths, set of 16 glass jars with yellow tops, each with spice name, orig rack....................**$160**

Stove, cast iron, chrome, nickel, colorful ceramic tile back................**$6,000**

Sugar shaker, Dutch boy and girl, Tipp City **$22**

Syrup jug, adv, clay inscribed "W. D. Streeter, Richland, NY," Albany glaze, tight hairline on side, c1890, 8" h **$35**

Taster, brass and wrought iron, polished, 7" l.......................................**$150**

Tin
Donovan's Baking Powder, Mt. Morris, NY, 1 lb, paper label, 5-1/4" h, 3" d............................**$475**
Egg-O Brand Baking Powder, paper label, 2-3/4" h, 1-1/4" d...........**$110**
Kavanaugh's Tea, 1 lb, little girl on porch in dress, talking to doll, mother sipping tea in window, cardboard sides, tin top and bottom, 6" h, 4-1/2" w, 4-1/2" d **$500**
Miller's Gold Medal Breakfast Cocoa, red and black, c1890, 2" h, 1-5/8" w, 1-1/8" d **$250**
Opal Powdered Sugar, Hewitt & Sons, Des Moines, 8" h, 4-1/2" w, 3-1/4" d **$180**
Parrot and Monkey Baking Powder, 4 oz, full, 3-1/4" h, 2-1/8" d........**$375**
Sunshine-Oxford Fruit Cake, sq corners, early 1900s.....................**$20**
Towle's Log Cabin Brand Maple Syrup, cabin shaped, woman and girl in doorway, 4" h, 3-3/4" l, 2-1/2" d **$110**

Trivet, lyre form, wrought iron frame and turned handle, brass top, replaced foot, stamped maker's mark, 12" l ..**$45**

Wafer iron, cast iron, octagonal, church with steeple and trees dec on one side, pinwheel with plants and star flowers on reverse, wrought iron handles **$400**

Fiesta Kitchen Kraft cake lifter, yellow, **$140-$150.**

Mixing bowls, nested set, Kitchen Kraft Oven Serve, floral and silver trim, set of three, **$45.**

Fiesta Kitchen Kraft salad spoon, red, **$140-$150.**

Fiesta Ware, cobalt blue, No. 4 mixing bowl, 5" x 7-3/4", **$200-$225.**

LAMP SHADES

History: Lamp shades were made to diffuse the harsh light produced by early gas lighting fixtures. These early shades were made by popular Art Nouveau manufacturers including Durand, Quezal, Steuben, and Tiffany. Many shades are not marked.

Aladdin
Cased, green...............................**$870**
Satin, white, dogwood dec............**$65**
Cameo, gold satin glass cut to clear in acorn and leaves pattern, price for pr, 6-1/2" h...**$225**

Fostoria
Gold, 24 ribs, 4-1/2" h..................**$85**
Iridescent gold, 24 ribs, 4-3/4" h **$90**
Opal, ribbed, gold interior, 4-3/4" h **$100**
Lustre Art, opal, gold ribbon dec, 5" h **$100**
Palme-Koenig, opaline, pink drag loops, 6-3/4" h............................**$110**

Quezal
Chartreuse gold and dark green reverse drape pattern, ribbed, 5" h **$575**
Cylindrical, vertical ribbing, irid calcite, inscribed "Quezal," 6" h **$150**
Egg shape, green and gold pulled feather design, 4-1/2" h............**$200**
Gold snakeskin design, 4-3/4" h **$170**
Green and gold leaf design, gold threading, 4-3/4" h....................**$150**
Irid, bell shaped, gold zipper pattern, 5-1/2" h...**$145**

Lamp shade, Quezal, green and gold pulled feather pattern, egg shape, 4-1/2" h, **$200.**
Photo courtesy of The Early Auction Company, LLC.

Lamp shade, Steuben, green and gold drag loop, ruffled rim, shape # 819S, 5" h, **$225.**
Photo courtesy of The Early Auction Company, LLC.

Irid gold, pulled feathers, 5-1/2" h **$270**
Irid gold, white scaled pattern graduating to irid green rim, sgd "Quezal," 5-1/4" h **$225**
Irid opal, gold pulled feather design, fitter rim chips, 5" h **$75**
Opal, green and gold pulled feather design, 4" h **$375**
Opal ground, irid blue pulled feather dec, tipped in gold, 5" h **$300**
Trumpet shape, dark gold, ribbed, 6-1/2" h **$115**
Slag glass dome, caramel slag, curved, 24" d.............................**$200**

Steuben
Acid etched calcite, scrolling pattern, fleur-de-lis mark, price for set of three, 5" h..................................**$300**
Aurene, gold, ribbed, fleur-de-lis mark, 4-1/4" h **$125**
Bell shape, alabaster body, irid green and gold hooked feather, fleur-de-lis mark, price for pr, 4-1/2" h **$1,200**
Mushroom shape, gold Aurene hooked pulled feather on opal ground, additional zipper dec, 5" w **$350**
Shape #64, gold Aurene, scalloped rim, fleur-de-lis mark, price for matched set of four, 4" h.........**$525**
Shape #672, verre-de-soie, trumpet shape, ribbed, price for pr, 5" h **$125**
Shape #799, tulip shape, green and gold pulled feathers, 1" re-glued chip, 5" h **$65**
Shape #819S, green and gold drag loop design, ruffled rim, 5" h **$225**
Shape #823-1/2, verre-de-soie, engraved hanging flower pattern, 4-3/4" h **$175**

Lamp shades, cameo satin, gold to clear, oak leaves and acorn dec, pr, 6-1/2" h, **$225.**
Photo courtesy of The Early Auction Company, LLC.

Shape #853, verre-de-soie, engraved festoon pattern, ruffled rim, 4-1/8" h **$200**
Shape #938A, gold, inverted urn form, ribbed, 4-1/4" h **$160**
Shape #985, opal, green and gold drag loops, straight rim, 3-1/2" h **$250**
Shape #2268, verre-de-soie, ribbed, 4-1/4" h **$75**
Shape #2327, calcite, acid etched ivy pattern, price for three, 5-1/2" h **$500**
Shape #2354, calcite, acid etched Lumene pattern, 5-1/2" h **$70**
Shape #2533, calcite, acid etched Warwick pattern, 4-1/2" h **$95**
Shape #2533, calcite, acid etched oak leaf and acorn pattern, 4-3/4" h **$90**
Shape #7198, opal, Marbellite, 4-3/4" h **$50**
Tulip shape, gold Aurene, fleur-de-lis mark, price for matched pr, 5" h **$225**
Tulip shape, gold Aurene, unmarked, price for matched pr, 5-1/4" h **$175**

Tiffany
Irid gold, internally dec in coin spot pattern, scalloped rim, price for matched set of four, one with minute fitter rim chip, 3" h **$500**
Ribbed, conical, Favrile, irid, price for matched set of five, two with very minor fitter rim chips, 5-1/4" h **$1,200**

Unidentified American maker
Bulbous, Calcite, price for pr, 5" h **$100**
Irid gold, bell shaped, 4" h............**$80**
Irid gold, bell shaped, 4-1/4" h **$90**

Irid gold, ribbed body, 4-1/4" h **$85**

Irid, gold and white pulled feather, 5-1/2" h **$125**

Irid, opal green pulled feather, 5-1/2" h **$100**

LAMPS AND LIGHTING

History: Lighting devices have evolved from simple stone-age oil lamps to the popular electrified models of today. Aimé Argand patented the first oil lamp in 1784. Around 1850, kerosene became a popular lamp-burning fluid, replacing whale oil and other fluids. In 1879, Thomas A. Edison invented the electric light, causing fluid lamps to lose favor and creating a new field for lamp manufacturers. Companies like Tiffany and Handel became skillful at manufacturing electric lamps, and their decorators produced beautiful bases and shades.

Reproduction Alert.

Additional Resources:

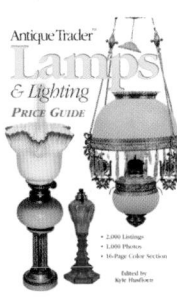

Antique Trader® Lamps & Lighting Price Guide, by Kyle Husfloen, ed., Krause Publications, Iola WI.

Astral

Cornelius & Co., gilt brass weighted base with Gothic detailing, applied prism ring with ovoid frosted etched glass globe with Greek key and floral designs, electrified, flakes on rim, patent 1897, 11" h globe, 26" h overall **$775**

Sq white marble base, ribbed then turned brass column, cut glass prisms, frosted shade with etched flowers and vintage dec, electrified, 22-1/2" h **$250**

Grapevine etched colorless glass shade, gilt metal font, glass prisms, standard with Rococo bronze fittings,

flared, ribbed, blue glass shaft with gilt highlights, white marble base, electrified, imperfections, America, 19th C, 24-5/8" h **$920**

Banquet

Classical Revival, Goldsmiths Co., English, silver plate and cut glass, bowl form cut glass oil font, fluted Corinthian column, tapered sq section loaded base with flower filled urns connected by swags, electrified, early 20th C, 21-3/8" h **$800**

Victorian, cranberry shading to pink satin glass shade, set with amber, red, and green jewels, pink-shaded cased glass font, column fitted on enameled iron base, burner mkd "Kosmos Brenner," c1880, 30-1/2" h **$980**

Boudoir

Aladdin, reverse painted bell shade, pine border, floral molded polychromed metal base, 14-1/2" h, 8" d **$225**

Handel, gilt-finished spelter base, reverse painted etched glass shade with umber harbor scene, orange sky, shade stamped "Handel 6450," Handel Lamps cloth tag on base, chips to patina, 14" h, 7" d **$1,150**

Heintz Art Metal Shop, Buffalo, NY, bronze shade with cut-out Art Nouveau style flowers and foliage, in three sections, similar dec in silver overlay on round bronze base, paper label, two dents, 9-1/4" h, 8-1/2" d **$1,265**

Obverse painted scenic, closed top mushroom-cap glass shade with textured surface mounted on gilt metal handled lamp base, weighted foot, hand-painted silhouetted forested landscape scenes, rim marked "Patented April 29th, 1913," 13-1/2" h **$1,150**

Pittsburgh Lamp, Brass & Co., reverse painted ribbed shade, winter landscape of black barren trees on snowy ground, blue shading to yellow and orange ground, metal base with raised foliage dec, raised "P.I.B. & Co." 2080" on base, 14" h, 7" d shade **$635**

Van Erp, Dirk, hammered copper and mica, four panel shade, single socket, small beanpot base, orig patina, open box mark, 12" x 10-1/2" **$9,000**

Chandelier

Arts & Crafts

Hammered bronze frame with pierced designs, suspending hammered

bronze socket holders with four gold Aurene glass shades, c1910, 18" h, 14-1/2" d **$1,380**

Six panels, red brass, replaced mica panels, three-light cluster, orig dark patina, period chain and ceiling cap, 27" h, 32" d **$2,300**

AVEM, mold blown art glass, six arms terminating in candle lights, alternating with scrolls, silvered metal mounts, wiring restored, c1935, 27-1/2" d **$600**

Degue, colorless mold-blown and etched glass shade with stylized flowers and leaves, wrought iron frame with vine ornamentation, sgd "Degue 534," France, c1930, 30" h, 19" d **$600**

Empire-style, gilt metal and cut glass, six light, top with six outscrolled flat leaves hung with crystals, slender reeded standard with central cut glass orb, flat leaf ring supporting six short serpentine scrolled candle arms offset by pierced ribbon-tied laurel wreaths, strung throughout with crystal strands, end of standard with further crystals, 20th C, 31" l **$1,100**

Lamp, metal newel post base, figural, woman, holding bird, Steuben pulled feather shade with silver fleur-de-lis mark, 21" h, **$450.**

Photo courtesy of The Early Auction Company, LLC.

Desk lamp, orange and white marbleized turtle shaped top panel, blue and white marbleized slag side panels, trophies on sides, acorn on pull chain, **$295.**

Photo courtesy of Dotta Auction Co., Inc.

Chandelier, Neoclassical-style, doré bronze, suspended by six rods terminating in figural mounts which support a bowl-shaped slag work glass shade screened by elaborate scroll work and swans, exterior with six electrified candles supported by acanthus leaf and column detail, all terminating in an acorn-shaped finial, **$6,500.**

Photo courtesy of David Rago Auctions, Inc.

Durand, pair of incense lamps, orig glass shades, Egyptian figural bases, **$1,300.**

Photo courtesy of David Rago Auctions, Inc.

Banquet lamp, cast brass and silvered metal fittings, font, and base, marble pedestal, **$200.**

Photo courtesy of Dotta Auction Co., Inc.

Kerosene lamp, Thomas Webb & Son, Burmese, two parts, lamp, shade and base hand dec "Woodine" pattern, base stamped with trademark, 15" h, **$4,250.**

Photo courtesy of The Early Auction Company, LLC.

Boudoir lamp, Art Deco style skyscraper shape, light blue glass, original wiring, **$300.**

Morreau, gilt and emb iron frame suspending four leaded-glass domed shades, central matching spherical shade, frame emb "The Morreau Co.," 20" h, 20" d................................**$1,100**

Muller Freres, France, five triangular-etched glass shades with geometric designs, wrought iron frame, signed "Muller Freres Luneville," c1930, 31" h, 17-1/2" d....................**$1,060**

Desk

Handel, lobed harp base, swiveling single socket, leaded green slag glass geometric shade, orig dark bronzed patina, base and shade stamped "Handel," 18-1/2" h, 10-1/2" d...........**$2,200**

Steuben, bronze, adjustable, irid hammered glass shade, orig patina, shade sgd "Steuben," 20" h, 7" d..........**$860**

Student, brass frame and adjustable arm, white glass shade, early 20th C, 23-1/2" h......................................**$260**

Tiffany, 13-1/2" h, 7" d swirl dec irid green ribbed dome Damascene shade cased to white, marked "L.C.T" on rim, swivel-socket bronze harp frame, rubbed cushion platform, five ball feet, imp "Tiffany Studios New York 419".......................................**$3,740**

Unknown maker

Brass, ribbed gold irid bell-form shade, unsgd, 20-1/4" h..........**$300**

Frosted blue satin shade with tadpole dec, adjustable brass arm and dome base, 25" h, 4" d.....................**$200**

Early American

Betty lamp, tin, saucer base, weighted column, attached handle, some damage to wick support, 10" h **$150**

Cage lamp, wrought iron, spherical, self righting gyroscope font, two repaired spout burners, 6" d **$500**

Candle holder, wrought iron, hanging type, primitive twisted arms and conical socket, 19" h...................**$385**

Candle stand, wrought iron, double arms, brass candleholders and drip pans, attributed to PA, pitting, losses to drip pans, 18th C, 57-1/4" h, 24-1/2" w..................................**$8,100**

Fluid

Blanc de chine, figural, small boy with heart-shaped medallions around necks, each holds small bowl on his head for lamp oil and small wick, minor rim flakes, price for pr, 5" h **$250**

Blown glass, colorless, ball font, wafer attached to pressed base with extended round corners, possibly Boston & Sandwich Glass Co., Sandwich, MA, minor base chips at low points, 1840-60, 5-1/4" h **$70**

Blown glass, colorless, blown font attached with wafers to pressed lacy base, drop burner, some roughness, edge flakes, 6-1/2" h................**$265**

Blown glass, colorless, blown font with etched swag and tassel design, pressed stepped base, fluid burner, edge flakes, 6-3/4" h.................**$150**

Blown glass, colorless, bulbous font, bladed wafer, pressed paw-foot base, early pewter collar, possibly Boston & Sandwich Glass Co., Sandwich, MA, 1830-45, 10-1/2" h.......**$880**

Blown glass, colorless, bulbous font, ringed wafer attached to pressed base, early pewter collar with correct whale oil burner, possibly Boston & Sandwich Glass Co., Sandwich, MA, minor base chips, slight lean to font, 1830-45, 9-3/4" h......................**$200**

Blown glass, colorless, conical font, applied foot, applied angular handle with thumb rest and medial channel, rough pontil mark, 1820-40, 3-1/2" h......................................**$250**

Blown glass, colorless, conical font, ringed wafer attached to pressed stepped base, possibly Boston & Sandwich Glass Co., Sandwich, MA, base chips, 1840-60, 6-3/4" h **$70**

Blown glass, colorless, flattened font, solid stem, round base, pewter collar, 6" h....................................**$150**

Blown glass, colorless, urn shaped font, disk wafers, pressed sq stepped base with vertical ribbing between extended round corners, pewter collar, correct pewter and tin whale burner, rough pontil mark, possibly Boston & Sandwich Glass Co., Sandwich, MA, chips and flakes to base, 1830-45, 7-1/2" h...........**$145**

Blown glass, colorless, urn shaped font, ringed and disk wafer construction, large blown and hollow ball shaped knop, pressed stepped base, early brass collar, double tube fluid burner with caps and chain, possibly Boston & Sandwich Glass Co., Sandwich, MA, normal flakes under base, 1830-45, 10-1/2" h **$660**

Student lamp, Steuben, double scrolling adjustable arm base, two 10" Aurene shades, iridescent gold and white zigzag border, shades signed with Fleur-de-Lis, 24" h, $5,500.
Photo courtesy of The Early Auction Company, LLC.

Floor lamp, Roycroft, designed and executed by Dard Hunter and Victor Toothaker, gently sloping circular leaded glass shade, stylized pattern of fruit and foliage in yellow and green slag glass, three-socket wrought iron base with twist, in foliate and wood grain patterns, unmarked, few short breaks to glass, 61" x 20", from estate of Miriam Hubbard Roelofs, Elbert and Alice Hubbard's daughter, $22,000.
Photo courtesy of David Rago Auctions, Inc.

Hanging lamp, tin conical shade, embossed brass base, electrified, **$250.**

Blown threaded glass, light cranberry with opposing white spiraling threads, font attached to reeded brass stem, single marble base, early #2 brass collar, probably Joseph Walter & Co. Flint Glass Works or Boston & Sandwich Glass Co., some manuf bubbles at base of font interior causing minor thread distortion, 1860-75, 7-1/2" h **$1,980**

Cut overlay, star and quatrefoil, opaque white cut to colorless font, connected to white alabaster/clambroth Baroque base, early #2 brass collar and connector, probably Boston & Sandwich Glass Co., overlay abrasions, 1860-80, 14-1/2" h **$990**

Pressed glass, colorless, loop font, paneled hexagonal base, pewter collar and cap, minor roughness, price for pr, 11-1/4" h **$200**

White cut to cranberry glass font, brass collar, marble and brass base with lime green glass stem insert, 13-3/4" h **$650**

Grease, tin, brass labels "S.N. & H.C. Ufford, Boston," saucer base with concentric rings, one missing shade brackets and ring carrier, soldered repairs, price for pr, 6-1/2" h **$1,250**

Hanging, wrought iron, "U"-shaped swing hanger with long hook, wick holder with chicken finial, 22-1/2" l, 4-3/4" d **$175**

Lace maker's, colorless, round blown font attached to blown base, hollow stem, 7-3/4" h **$375**

Loom light, wrought iron, candle socket, trammel, 14-3/4" h **$500**

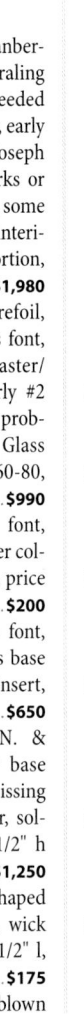

Parlor lamp, pink D.Q.M.O.P., bulbous body, ruffled rim, metal collar and porcelain knobs, four applied rigaree feet, signed "Hinks Duplex Patent," 14" h, **$1,725.**
Photo courtesy of The Early Auction Company, LLC.

Miner's lamp, cast and wrought iron, chicken finial, replaced hanger, 7-3/8" h **$110**

Peg, overlay glass, pink cut to white cut to clear, frosted peg attached with clear wafer, brass collar, 2" d, 4-1/2" l **$450**

Petticoat, tin, round pan base, large ring handle applied to one side of column, small pick and chain attached to handle, 9" h **$260**

Rush light holder, wrought iron, candle socket counter weight, tripod base, penny feet, tooled brass disk at base of stem, simple tooling, 9-1/2" h **$470**

Skater's lamp, brass, clear glass globe marked "Perko Wonder Junior," polished, small splint in top of brass cap, 6-3/4" h **$160**

Student, brass, embossed "MILES PATENT" on whale oil font, adjustable candle holder and pierced shade, removable tin snuffer, brass ring finial, weighted dish base, traces of black paint, England, candle holder loose from drip pan, late 18th/early 19th C, 19" w, 7-1/4" h **$1,650**

Table lamp, four sided metal shade with pink slag glass inserts and pierced work gallery, wick adjuster marked "Made in US of America," square font with pierced floral decoration, waisted pedestal with square base supported on four paw feet, electrified, 22-1/2" h, **$300.**
Photo courtesy of Alderfer Auction Co.

Taper jack, Sheffield silver on copper, old repairs, 5" h **$195**

Floor

Bradley and Hubbard, small domed leaded glass shade, green slag glass, gold key border, open framework adjustable standard, domed circular foot, 56" h, 7" d **$400**

Faries Mfg. Co., Decatur, IL, bright chrome torchere, flaring trumpet shade, diecast mark, 65-1/4" h, 12" d **$150**

Handel

Chipped glass hemispherical reverse painted shade, moonlit tropical scene with tall ship, orig bronze patina, single socket harp, shade mkd "Handel 65-749," cloth label on base, 56-1/2" h, 14" d **$7,000**

Yellow and amber opalescent bent glass paneled shade with faux lead came, green diamond details, five-light, patinated copper columnar base, scrolling feet, marked "HANDEL" on base, 64" h, 24" d **$9,780**

Sarfatti, Gino, manufactured by Arteluce, Italy, three arm, adjustable, steel, wood, and leather, c1950, 74-1/4" h **$3,750**

Table lamp, Handel, reverse painted textured shade with wooded landscape, shade marked "Handel 6159, JB" with three slash marks below, bronze base stamped "Handel," cloth tag sewn to felt on underside, 23" h, **$7,000.**

Photo courtesy of Alderfer Auction Co.

Table lamp, Bigelow and Kennard, leaded glass shade, gothic geometric pattern in white and light green slag glass, three-socket bronze-patinated base, unmarked, 21-1/2" h, 16" d, **$4,025.**

Photo courtesy of David Rago Auctions, Inc.

Table lamp, Gorham, asymmetrically bordered leaded glass shade of white and pink cyclamen blossoms, green leaves, four-socket bronzed foliate base, unmarked, finial appears to be soldered to shade causing separation around top, few short lines to glass, 22-1/2" x 20", **$12,000.**

Photo courtesy of David Rago Auctions, Inc.

Tiffany/Aladdin, reflective white int., marked "Tiffany Studios New York," adjustable bridge lamp base with Arabian Nights motif, orig dark bronze patina, elaborate platform base, stamped "Tiffany Studios New York 576," 50" h, 10" d spun bronze shade.................................... **$2,990**

Unknown maker, black and gold painted metal, topped by three acanthus scrolls, tripartite base with pad feet, Baroque style, electrified, 57-1/4" h...................................... **$765**

Yellin, Samuel, wrought iron, twisted tripod base, conical finial, two socket frame, mkd "Samuel Yellin Phila PA," 61-1/2" h, 17-1/2" d................ **$4,000**

Hanging

American, patinated metal and cut glass, hall type, candle socket, Gothic arches, diamonds and flowerheads dec, 19th C, 18" h **$1,380**

Arts and Crafts

Brass and slag glass shade, linked metal chain suspending shade composed of eight panels of green, caramel, and white bent slag glass panels, dropped apron with emb and cut-out brass border overlay with Dutch windmills, trees, and cottages over band of multicolored slag glass, prisms below, 30" drop, 20-1/2" d **$920**

Four massive iron cross bars, hand hammered and bronzed surface,

support chocolate slag glass shades with brass fleur-de-lis guards, electrified, 17" drop, 22-1/2" d...... **$950**

Handel, Meriden, CT, reverse p ainted, model number 6997, mushroom-shaped glass shade decorated on exterior and interior with exotic blue and gold birds, burgundy and green floral branches and leaves, bronzed metal fittings, stamped "Handel," shade sgd and numbered, early 20th C, 11" d **$3,290**

Morgan, John, and Sons, NY, attributed to, verdigris bronze leaves surrounding ceiling hook suspending four chains supporting six-socket domed shade, similar bronze leaf dec, dropped apron, shade with striated green, amber, and white slag glass segments, round transparent purple "jewels" form grape-type clusters, few cracked segments, 39-1/2" h drop, 25-1/4" d, 11-1/2" h leaded shade **$6,325**

Perzel, chrome, metal, and glass, 40-1/4" d.............................. **$1,225**

Tiffany, attributed to Tiffany Glass and Decorating Co., square green and opalescent diamond-shaped glass jewels arranged as central pendant chandelier drop, twisted wire frame, late 19th C, 18" l, 15" d............ **$2,990**

Unknown maker, brass, slender hanging stem, repaired wiring, 32" h, two 6-1/2" h amber etched shades **$375**

Piano

Handel, gilt leaded lavender and opalescent yellow leaded shade suspended from bronze base, scrolled arm, unmarked, attributed to, c1915, 17" l **$750**

Tiffany, tripartite gold amber glass turtleback shade, framed in bronze, three center gold irid turtleback tiles, single-socket swiveling "dog leg" shaft, shade and weighted base imp "Tiffany Studios New York," 6-3/4" h, 19" l shade **$4,025**

Table

American, early 20th C

20 radiating caramel and white slag glass panels on domed shade, medial geometric green glass border, alternating green and caramel slag glass border, undulating dropped apron, two-socket fixture, ribbed trefoil base with brown/green patina, minor corrosion, some cracked segments, 19-1/4" h, 15-1/2" d **$920**

Reverse painted shade, hemispherical frosted glass shade, int. painted with trees and foliage silhouetted against yellow-orange shaded sky and water, two-socket bronze patinated cast metal base, raised scroll, foliate, and flower motif, base marked "A & R Co.," minor wear, 24-3/4" h, 18" d........................ **$920**

Table lamp, Jefferson, reverse-painted hammered glass shade, branches of red and white flowers, ribbed two-socket patinated base, shade sgd "2369-R," base and shade stamped "Jefferson," 21-1/2" x 16", **$2,300.**
Photo courtesy of David Rago Auctions, Inc.

Table lamp, Arts & Crafts, Heintz, sterling on bronze, helmet shade inset with "jewels," single-socket trumpet base, both with overlay of silver branches with leaves and berries, stamped "Pat. APD 4 1035," some cleaning to patina, 14" x 9", **$1,600.**
Photo courtesy of David Rago Auctions, Inc.

Baccarat, attributed to, blown molded glass, deep emerald green columns and fonts with relief twist designs, black marble bases, brass and brass plated fittings, harp and finial, fittings replaced, pr, 36" h **$1,380**

Bigelow Kennard, Boston, domed leaded shade, opalescent white segments in geometric progression border, brilliant green leaf forms repeat-

ing motif, edge imp "Bigelow Kennard Boston/Bigelow Studios," three socket over Oriental-style bronze base cast with foo dog handles, Japonesque devices, 26" h, 18" d shade **$2,875**

Boston Glass Works, floral and foliate overlay, bronze patina over six radiating striated caramel and white bent slag glass panels, two-socket fixture with similar illuminated base, minor patina wear, few dents, early 20th C, 22" h, 18-1/2" d bent panel slag glass shade **$750**

Bradley and Hubbard, Meriden, CT, early 20th C

Frosted domed shade with stylized floral dec in burgundy, brown, and green, sgd urn form base, 18" h **$750**

Reverse-painted shade with eight lilies in gold and earthtones, shade decorated on exterior with textured brown blades, patinated brown metal strapwork base, maker's stamp on standard, one socket needs repair, 22" h, 15-3/4" d **$2,710**

Duffner and Kimberly, New York, dome leaded glass shade with tuck-under irregular rim, multicolored blossoms with yellow centers, green leaves, long stemmed flowers extending to top on segmented white background, three socket bronze lobed shaft with quatraform shaped base, 26" h, 24-1/2" d shade **$7,435**

Handel, Meriden, CT

Chipped glass reverse painted shade, moonlight forest scene with brook, three socket, four footed Arts & Crafts base with some verdigris to bronze patina, orig cap, Handel 6324, 25" h, 18" d **$6,000**

Chipped glass reverse painted shade, moonlit tropical scene with tall chip painted by John Bailey, three socket bronze base with clefs, orig cap, shade mkd "Handel 6391 John Bailey," base unmarked, 24" h, 18" d **$8,000**

Chipped reverse painted shade, pink and green bouquets of wild roses and butterflies, two socket base, orig pierced cap, some verdigris to bronze patina, shade mkd "Handel 6688," base unsigned, 23" h, 18" d **$9,000**

Conical shade with light green ground and blue gray lower border, segmented by band of pink apple blossoms on branches, stamped "Handel Lamps Pat'd No. 979664," sgd "Handel 6742," three sockets on bronze metal standard, some spotting, 23-1/2" h, 18" d **$3,820**

Reverse painted domical glass shade, band of black eyed susans with orange petals, brown centers, and green leaves against yellow ground, outlined on textured exterior in black, sgd "Handel 6956 BD," three sockets with acorn pulls, bronzed metal vasiform base, 22-1/2" h, 17-1/2" d **$3,290**

Ribbed glass reverse painted shade, tall ships on sea, classical acanthus leaf three-socket base, some verdigris to bronze patina, orig cap, Handel 5887R, base unsigned, small chips to edge of shade, 23-1/4" h, 15" d **$5,500**

Heintz, sterling on bronze, single socket, mushroom shaped shade and flaring base overlaid with delicate sprig pattern, bronze patina, few short scratches, 15" h, 13" d **$1,600**

Jefferson, reverse painted scenic shade with winter scene on textured satin shade, brass candlestick base, unsigned, c1915, 17" h, 12" d **$460**

La Verre Francais, cased glass, frosted ext. over swirled orange, yellow, and cobalt blue, sgd on both shade and base, electrified, replaced shade holder, 19" h **$1,350**

MB Co., paneled shade, conical base, openwork silver-plate grape vine designs, five panels of green and white slag glass, cast leaf finial, engraved leaves on base, base marked "Made and Guaranteed by the MB Co. USA," electrified, five sockets, 20-1/2" h **$1,200**

Muller Fres, frosted domed shade with mottled dec, inscribed "Mueller Fres Luneville," brass tri-support stylized fleur-de-lis base, 20" h **$1,000**

Pairpoint, domed closed top mushroom-cap glass shade, Vienna, coralene yellow int., painted stylized olive green leaves and red berries, gold outline on ext., ball-decorated ring supported by four arms, quatraform base molded with foliate devices, imp "Pairpoint Mfg Co., 3052," 20-1/2" h, 11-1/2" d shade **$2,070**

Pittsburgh Lamp, Brass and Glass Co., Pittsburgh, model no. 1595, domed frosted and textured glass shade, interior painted with mountainous landscape, exterior painted with pine trees, paper manufacturer's label affixed to interior, three-socket patinated metal ribbed standard set into weighted metal base, scroll, shield, floral, and foliate motifs in relief, wear to patina, c1920, 27" h, 17-3/4" d shade **$1,955**

Table lamp, brass, three light, three signed 4-3/4" h Quezal shades, 21" h, **$950.**
Photo courtesy of The Early Auction Company, LLC.

Table lamp, Neoclassical, bronze and ormolu base, each with campana shaped urn with Bacchanalian group at the handles, standing on a plinth dec with alternating bountiful urn and musical instrument medallions, urn 19-3/4" h, 35" h with finial, **$6,000.**
Photo courtesy of David Rago Auctions, Inc.

Steuben, attributed to, jade green long neck vasiform glass standard with white threading spiraling on neck, double socket, leaf-form bronzed metal mounts, 23" h **$420**

Suess Ornamental Glass Co., Chicago, leaded glass shade with stylized yellow, orange, green, and white slag flowers and leaves, brass-washed

Table lamp, Gone With the Wind style, hand painted red, white, and pink morning glories, red beaded fringe trim, electrified, **$200.**
Photo courtesy of Dotta Auction Co., Inc.

base, unmarked, 23" h, 22" d shade **$5,350**

Tiffany Studios, dome shade, layered and striated leaded glass segments designed as tulip blossoms and leaves, red, orange, amber, blue, and green, metal rim tag imp "Tiffany Studios New York 1456," three-socket bronze base with three pronged crutch supporting oval shaft, sq base with mottled brown and green patina, round disk on base imp "Tiffany Studios New York 444," 22-1/2" h, 16" d **$32,220**

Unidentified maker, alabaster, fluted gourd-shaped body with flared top, black marble base, brass paw feet and fittings, tall brass stem, double electric sockets, 52-1/2" h **$300**

Van Erp, Dirk, hammered copper classical base, four paneled mica shade with vented cap, single socket, fine orig patina and mica, open box mark/San Francisco, 17-1/2" h, 13" d **$9,200**

Williamson, Richard, & Co., Chicago, amber slag bordered by red tulips, pink and lavender-blue spring blossoms, green leaf stems, carved glass, mounted on four-socket inte-

grated shaft with stylized tulip blossoms above leafy platform, imp "R. Williamson & Co./Washington & Jefferson Sts./ Chicago, Ill," restored cap at top rim, 25" h, 20" d peaked leaded glass dome **$3,220**

LANTERNS

History: A lantern is an enclosed, portable light source, hand carried or attached to a bracket or pole to illuminate an area. Many lanterns have a protected flame and can be used both indoors and outdoors. Light-producing materials used in early lanterns included candles, kerosene, whale oil, and coal oil, and, later, gasoline, natural gas, and batteries.

Barn, mortised wood frame, four panes of glass, bentwood handle, tin cover over top vent, twisted wire latch, old patina, discolored glass in door, minor damage, make-do repaired split on top, 5-1/4" w, 5-3/4" d, 8-3/4" h **$825**

Candle

Tin, double folding door covering orig glass panel, folding handle in back, brass candle socket with spring loaded push-up in base, traces of black paint, door hinges glued, lid possible replacement, 9-3/8" h **$230**

Tin, octagonal paneled glass globe, punched tin top, ring handle, and font, globe surrounded by wire guards, replaced tin font with candle socket, war, minor damage, traces of japanning on top, 11-1/4" h **$300**

Wood frame, beveled base and top, pegged construction, arched tin deflector on top, wire bale carrier, old refinishing, old pieced restoration on top, one pane cracked, minor insect damage, 12" h **$250**

Dark room, orig black paint, white striping, tin kerosene font and burner "Carbutt's Dry Plate lantern, PA April 25th 1882" label, 17" h **$75**

Folding, tin, glass sides, emb "Stonebridge 1908," 10" h **$75**

Globe, fixed pear-shaped globe, pierced tin frame, ring handle, traces of black paint, America, mid-19th C, 17-1/2" h **$215**

Hall, glass and polychrome, gold painted flat leaf top suspending cut glass drops, joined by curved scrolls, suspending ovoid shade formed by five curved colorless glass panels in metal framework topped by ribbon tied laurel branches, accented with faceted bead trim, bead and glass prism trefoils, Italian, late 19th C, 26" h............................**$2,100**

Japanese, Patterson Bros., Lansing, MI, adv, panes with General U. S. Grant, puppies, young girl, and wilderness scene.............................**$195**

Jeweled, sheet brass, punched designs radiating out from faceted blue, red, green, and pale gold glass jewels, bottom marked "NH Car Trimming Co. New Haven, Conn," ring hanger, 11-1/2" h............................**$250**

Miner, heavy duty iron and brass, threaded brass font and hasp, iron top with brass label "Thomas & Williams, Cambria Type...Aberdare," minor dents, 9-3/4" h.................**$115**

Nautical, masthead, copper and brass, oil fired, orig burner, label reads "Ellerman, Wilson Line, Hull," mid-19th C, 23" h, 11" d.............................**$265**

Painted tin, triangular black painted tin frame with glass panels, int. mirror paneled reflector, small tin kerosene lamp, glass chimney, America, seam separations, late 19th C, 15-3/4" l, 12" d, 19-3/4" h............**$175**

Paul Revere Type, punched tin, circular punching on door and body, cone top, round handle, light overall pitting, 16" h.................**$275**

Railroad, Pennsylvania Railroad, marked "Keystone Lantern Co., Philadelphia," wire ring base, 5" h red globe.............................**$445**

Skater

Brass, grass green globe, 7" h.....**$550**

Tin, amethyst globe, top mkd "Jewel," rust, 7" h.................**$835**

Tin, cobalt blue globe, two scratches, rust, 7" h.................**$520**

Tin, deep amethyst globe, top and globe both mkd "Jewel," rust, 7" h **$1,100**

Tin

Brass base and top with hinged, fluted peak, onion-shaped blown glass globe, wire guards, two wire bale handles, removable tin font held by two wires, burner missing, minor dents, 15" h.............................**$230**

Pear-shaped mold blown glass globe, pierced tin top and base, ring handle, tin oil font with two spring clips, burner missing, soldered repairs, black repaint, 12-1/2" h **$300**

Tin, four panes of glass, hinged door, wire guards, wire bale handle, old worn gold paint, wear, 12" h **$115**

Tin, tin base and top with pierced stars and diamonds, molded glass globe with wire guards, ring handle, removable tin font, brass burner, traces of black paint, 12" h **$200**

Tin, old black paint, clear brown glass insert, applied rings top and bottom, pierced diamonds and stars, make-do candle socket is old glass inkwell, New England, edge dents on base, 16-1/2" h...................**$250**

Hall lantern, Aesthetic Movement, American, pierced bronze banding at top and bottom, four polychrome stained glass panels, each painted with flower, fish, duck, or dove, 19th C, **$2,400.**
Photo courtesy of David Rago Auctions, Inc.

Tin lantern, punched decorated with flower motif, leaded glass panels and hinged door, scalloped back plate, single candle holder, **$85.**

Lantern, Dietz, Acme Inspector Lamp, embossed handle, L.V.R.R., **$395.**
Photo courtesy of Dotta Auction Co., Inc.

Lantern, Dietz, loop handle, large round clear lens, **$225.**
Photo courtesy of Dotta Auction Co., Inc.

MAPS

History: Maps provide one of the best ways to study the growth of a country or region. From the 16th to the early 20th century, maps were both informative and decorative. Engravers provided ornamental detailing, such as ornate calligraphy and scrolling, especially on bird's-eye views and city maps.

Maps generally were published as plates in books. Many of the maps available today are simply single sheets from cut-apart books.

In the last quarter of the 19th century, representatives from firms in Philadelphia, Chicago, and elsewhere traveled the United States preparing county atlases, often with a sheet for each township and each major city or town.

A Map of North America, Edward Wells, London, 1700, double page, engraved, wide margins, 355 x 480 mm **$635**

A Map of the British Empire in America, from the Head of Hudson's Bay to the Southern bounds of Georgia, London, engraved, folding, hand colored and in outline, wide margins, c1750, 265 x 325 mm **$260**

Americae Nova Tabula, Willem Blaeu, Amsterdam, double page, engraved, wide margins, 1633, 365 x 465 mm **$2,990**

A New and Accurate Map of the World, John Overton, London, engraved, folding, double-hemispheric, margins trimmed, 1670, 390 x 515 mm **$8,625**

A New Map of Nova Scotia, Thomas Jeffreys, London, double page, engraved, very wide margins, all edges tissue-backed on verso, 1750, 325 x 415 mm **$220**

A Plan of the Town and Chart of the Harbour of Boston, London, February 1775, engraved, folding, extracted from 1775 issue of *Gentleman's Magazine*, 290 x 350 mm **$220**

Atlas Map of Fulton County, Illinois, 1871 .... **$290**

Asia, Giovanni Botero, Rome, small double page, engraved, trimmed margins, c1595, 205 x 245 mm **$300**

British Dominions in America agreeable to the Treaty of 1763, Thomas Kitchin, Dury, London, double page, engraved, hand colored in outline, wide margins, 1777, 445 x 540 mm **$6,440**

Canada et Louisiane, George Louis Le Rouge, Paris, double page, engraved, wide margins, hand colored in outlined, 1755, 625 x 510 mm **$375**

Capt. James Lane Property, Bedford, Massachusetts, watercolor and ink on paper, shows distances, boundaries, and 223 acres, divided between sons James and Samuel in accordance with last will and testament, "Surveyed and divided by Stephen Davis, Surveyor of Lands," laid down on muslin, creases and separations, tears, fading, staining, 1773, 12-3/4" x 30-1/2" **$150**

Cruchley's New Plan of London, George Frederick Cruchley, London, engraved, 30-section map, hand colored, linen backed, orig board cover with publisher's label, 1836, 460 x 855 mm overall **$175**

Dutch, 7-3/8" x 12-1/4", black on white engraving by O. Lindeman, red, green, brown, and yellow hand coloring showing hemispheres, 2" tear repaired from back, contemporary 13-1/2" x 17-1/2" frame and matting **$250**

Haemisphaerium Stellatum Astrale Antiquum, Andres Cellarius, Amsterdam, double page, engraved celestial map, hand colored, wide margins, clear tear at vertical fold at lower margin just extending into image, 1660, 440 x 515 mm **$2,530**

Jamaica, John Thomson, Edinburgh, double page, engraved, two insets showing harbors of Bluefields and Kingston, wide margins, hand colored in outline, 1817, 440 x 630 mm **$320**

Land Survey Map of Boston Cabinet Maker Stephen Badlam, by Matthew Withington, pen and ink on paper showing parcel of land in Dorchester, Massachusetts, written description and compass star directional highlighted with watercolor, creases, small edge losses, repaired tears, stains, 1786, 20" x 11-1/2" **$650**

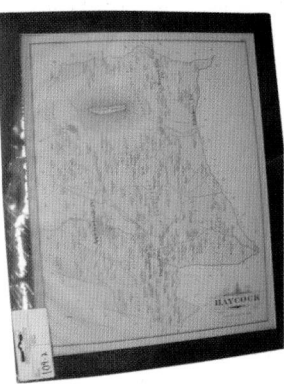

Haycock Township, removed from 1870s, Bucks County atlas, hand colored, **$120.**

Amsterdam, French legend, matted, framed, **$125.**

Philadelphia, hand colored, engraved vignettes, matted, framed, light water damage, **$350.**

Map, sampler, American silk on silk, depicting world map by Skinner, early 19th c, 9-5/8" x 17-1/2", **$3,910.**
Photo courtesy of Pook & Pook, Inc.

Map, New Jersey, geological survey, George Cook cartographer, 1889, sold as suite of 36" x 48" wall charts, index sheet, with original field box, **$300.**
Photo courtesy of David Rago Auctions, Inc.

Map of Oregon and Upper California, John Charles Fremont, Washington, folding, lithographed, hand colored in outline, overall browning, 1848, 905 x 755 mm **$2,185**

Minnesota & All of Unsettled Dakota Territory, Colton, hand colored, 1855, 17" x 14" **$95**

Northern America, including Russian Alaska, entire British Possessions & Danish Iceland, Colton, hand colored, 1857, 17" x 14" **$95**

Ohio, A J. Johnson, New York, with view of capitol building in corner, from *"New Illustrated Family Atlas of the World 1864,"* printed, hand colored, matted, unframed, 23" h, 29" w **$75**

Philadelphia, and Liberties section, set of three, published by John Reed, engraved by James Smithers, vignettes of Pennsylvania Hospital, House of Employment, State house, provenance descended from Gen George Meade family, each with some chipping, tears, foxing, late 18th C, each 31-1/2" x 24" **$9,750**

United States of America, W. and D. Lizars, London, engraved, folding, hand colored, margins trimmed, several folds closed at lower edge with archival tape, c1810, 395 x 460 mm **$260**

Two maps of America, A New and Accurate Map Of America by Thomas Bowen, c1800; "Carte de la Partie Sud des États-Unis," by M. Bonne, c.1790, the larger 11" x 17-1/4", **$300.**
Photo courtesy of Sloans & Kenyon Auctioneers and Appraisers.

MATCH HOLDERS

History: The friction match achieved popularity after 1850. The early matches were packaged and sold in sliding cardboard boxes. To facilitate storage and to eliminate the clumsiness of using the box, match holders were developed.

The first match holders were cast iron or tin, the latter often displaying advertisements. A patent for a wall-hanging match holder was issued in 1849. By 1880, match holders also were being made from glass and china. Match holders began to lose their popularity in the late 1930s, with the advent of gas and electric heat and ranges.

Advertising

Ballard Flour, tin litho, figural obelisk shape, Egyptian hieroglyphics, C.8-, 6-5/8" x 1-7/8", ... **$925**

Buster Brown Bread, tin litho, baker serving bread to Buster Brown and friends, wear to match basket, C.8-, 6-7/8" x 2-1/8" **$475**

Ceresota Prize Bread Flour, figural, diecut, tin litho, boy slicing bread, C.8+, 5-3/8" x 2-1/2" **$300**

Moxie Nerve Food, diecut tin litho, C.8++, 7-1/8" x 2-5/8" **$600**

Vulcan Plow Co., diecut, C.8+, 7-7/8" x 2-3/4" **$825**

Wrigley's Juicy Fruit Gum, tin litho, red, white, and black, C.8, 4-7/8" x 3-3/8" **$400**

Bisque, natural-colored rooster with beige basket, two compartments, round base with pink band, 4" h, 3-5/8" d **$135**

Brass, bear chained to post, cast, orig gilt trim, 3" h **$225**

Bronze, shoe, mouse in toe, 3" h **$125**

Cast iron, figural, high-button shoe, black paint, c1890, 5-1/2" h **$50**

Glass, shaded rose to pink overlay satin, ball-shape, glossy off-white lining, ground pontil, 3" h, 3-1/4" d **$155**

Majolica

Bull dog, striker, large **$440**

Happy Hooligan with suitcase, striker, rim nick to hat **$110**

Monk, striker, hairline in base ... **$140**

Papier-mâché, black lacquer, Oriental dec, 2-3/4" h **$25**

Desk type, upright brass holder with foliate border, square striated marble base with recessed center, felt pads, **$45.**

Hanging type holder, tin, places for matches in back, "Burnt Matches" in front, **$15.**

Hanging type holder, cream painted metal, black silhouette of girl with parasol in garden, **$35.**

Hanging type holder, cast iron, scrolled decoration, **$35.**

Porcelain, seated girl, feeding dog on table, sgd "Elbogen".....................**$125.**

Sterling silver, hinged lid, diecut striking area, cigar cutter on one corner, lid inscription "H. R." and diamond, inside lid inscribed "Made for Tiffany & Co./Pat 12, 09/Sterling," 1-3/4" x 2-1/2"................................**$95.**

Tin, top hat, hinged lid, orig green paint, black band, 2-3/8" h ....**$65.**

Torquay pottery, ship scene, reads "A match for any Man, Shankin," 2" h, 3-1/8" d...**$85.**

MATCH SAFES

History: Pocket match safes are small containers used to safely carry matches in one's pocket. They were first used around the 1840s. Match safes can be found in various sizes and shapes, and were made from numerous materials such as sterling, nickel-plated brass, gold, brass, ivory, and vulcanite. Some of the most interesting and sought after examples are figurals in the shapes of people, animals, and anything else imaginable. Match safes were also a very popular advertising means from 1895-1910, and were used by both large and small businesses. Match safes are known as vesta cases in England.

For more information contact the *International Match Safe Association*, PO Box 791, Malaga, NJ 08328-0791 www.matchsafe.org or email IMSAoc@aol.com

Notes: While not all match safes have a striking surface, this is one test, besides size, to distinguish a match safe from a calling card case or other small period boxes. Values are based on match safes being in excellent condition. All match safe photos courtesy of advisor George Sparacio.

Adviser: George Sparacio

Alligator motif, sterling with gold interior wash, by Watson Mfg. Co., 2-1/2" x 1-1/2"....................**$650-$750**

Anheuser Busch, Pullman car motif, nickel plated, 2-7/8" x 1-1/2"..**$175-$225**

Artillery shell, figural, Compliments Pinchin Johnson & Co., Ltd., made by Wm. H. Haseler, sterling with rose

Reproduction Alert. Copy-cat, reproduction, and fantasy match safes abound. Reproductions include Art Nouveau styles, figural/novelty shapes, nudes, and many others. Fantasy and fakes include Jack Daniel's and Coca-Cola.

A number of sterling reproduction match safes are marked "925" or "Sterling 925." Any match safe so marked requires careful inspection. Many period, American match safes have maker's marks, catalog numbers, 925/1000, or other markings. Period English safes have hallmarks. Beware of English reproduction match safes bearing the "DAB" marking. Always verify the date mark on English safes.

Check enameled safes closely. Today's technology allows for the economic faking of enamel motifs on old match safes. Carefully check condition of enameling for telltale clues.

Numerous reproduction brass match safes are appearing on the market. They are made to resemble original pieces, and do not have any maker marks or numbers to assist in their identification. Some plated brass match safes are also appearing.

gold trim, Birmingham, 1915, Rd. no. 650744, 2-1/4" x 1-1/4" .... **$400-$450**

Athena Riding Pegasus, made by Wm. Kerr, sterling with gold interior wash, catalog no. 19, 2-5/8" x 1-5/8" ....**$275-$325**

Australian bean/Entada Scandens seed, trimmed in 15k gold filigree, 1-3/4" diameter................. **$200-$250**

Bass Ale, figural bottle with cigar cutter, brass, 3" x 1" .... **$100-$125**

Bat, figural, Japanese, brass, 2-1/2" x 1-3/4" ....**$950-$1050**

Brunswick Blake Collendar Co./ Monarch cushions, white highlights, slip top, thermoplastic, 2-3/4" x 1-1/8"...................**$225-$275**

Bowling motif, man smoking cigarette, holding bowling ball, German silver, 2-1/2" x 1-5/8", **$375.**

Bryant & May, oval spring lid type with dog motif, red on gold graphics, 1-1/2" x 2-1/2" .... **$125-$150**

Burt Machine Company, celluloid wrapped, b & w graphics, by Whitehead & Hoag Co., nickel plated ends, 2-7/8" x 1-1/2" .... **$175-$200**

Butterfly and floral motif, G. Silver, 2-3/4" x 1-3/4" .... **$75-$100**

Cardinal Thomas Wolsey, figural, nickel plated brass, hinged at back of head, 2" x 1-3/4" .... **$275-$325**

Champagne bottle with winged nudes, advertising Moet, sterling, made by R. Blackinton & Co., catalog no. 1708, 2-1/2" x 1-3/4" .... **$1000-$1200**

Champagne glass formed from flowers and fruit, sterling with gold interior wash, by Wm. Kerr & Co., catalog no. 479, 2-1/2" x 1-3/4" .... **$200-$250**

Chicago World's Fair, image of Administration Building, litho tin by Bryant & May, 1-1/4" x 1-7/8" .... **$100-$135**

Cigar, bunch of 10, figural, nickel plated brass, 2-3/4" x 1-1/2" .... **$100-$125**

Cigar, burnt stub with brown wrap, figural, brass, 2-1/8" x 5/8" .... **$200-$300**

Cigarette holder and match safe combo, complete with cigarette holder, sterling, made by J. Gloster, Birmingham hallmarks, 2" x 2-1/4" .... **$150-$200**

"Chilly Cherubs," sterling, made by Unger Bros., catalog no. 7040, 2-3/8" x 1-7/8", **$375-$425.**

Clown, legs serves as cigar cutter, figural, brass, 2-3/4" x 1-3/8" .... **$400-$450**

Clown, seated with large nose & single hair curl on head, figural, brass, 2-1/2" x 1-3/8" .... **$350-$450**

Coffee pot, figural, brass, 1-7/8" x 1-3/4" .... **$50-$75**

Columbian World's Fair, 1893, stack of coins, figural, brass, 1-1/2" x-7/8" .... **$125-$150**

Columbian World's Fair, Columbus & Jefferson/applied disk with "Chicago World's Fair 1893," oval cross section type, nickel plated brass, 2-3/4" x 1" .... **$75-$100**

Copper over sterling, oval shaped, made by R. Blackinton & Co., catalog no. 359, 2-1/2" x 1-3/4" .... **$300-$350**

Dog motif in a circle, made by Bristol Mfg. Co., silverine or silveroin, 2-5/8" x 1-5/8" .... **$150-$175**

Dragon holding compass, figural, Japanese, brass, 2-3/4" x 1-7/8" .... **$375-$450**

Eddy Match advertisement, nickel plated brass, made in England, 2-3/8" x 1-1/2" .... **$40-$50**

Eggplant with snail, figural, Japanese, patinated brass, 2-1/2" x 1-5/8" .... **$575-$625**

Erotica, couple copulating, automata type, nickel plated, 2-1/2" x 1-1/2" .... **$3,000-$3,500**

Fireman's Fund Insurance, brass with applied sterling, made by Wm. Shreve, 1915, 2-1/2" x 1-7/8" .... **$400-$450**

Charles Dickens motif-translates to "Bill Stumps, His Mark," sterling, made by Levi & Salaman, English hallmarks, Birmingham, 1904, 1-7/8" x 1-1/2" , **$250-$300.**

Fireman's Fund Insurance, silver-plated, made by Pairpoint Mfg. Co., catalog no. 5002, 2-3/4" x 1-1/2" .... **$225-$275**

Fishing motif, fishermen catching trout, insert type made by August Goertz Co., 2-3/4" x 1-1/2" .. **$75-$100**

Floral motif, one side with hinged rectangular "stand," sterling, made by F. S. Gilbert, 2-3/4" x 1-1/4" .... **$100-$125**

Friar holding wine basket, sterling with gold interior wash, 2-3/4" x 1-3/4" .... **$375-$425**

Frog holding tobacco pouch, figural, Japanese writing that translates to "Take care with fire," Japanese, brass, 2" x 1-1/8" .... **$325-$375**

Golf motif, circular with 9 golfers, sterling, Birmingham hallmarks for 1907, 1-1/2" diameter .... **$450-$550**

Griffin motif, marked "Hand Wrought," made by Gorham Mfg. Co., sterling with gold interior wash, 2-3/8" x 1-5/8" .... **$300-$350**

Gun with cigar cutter, figural, hammer cocks & serves as cutter, nickel plated with wood handles, 4-3/4" x 3-1/8" .... **$350-$400**

Hidden photo made by S. Kind & Son, catalog no. 8280, sterling, 2-7/8" x 1-5/8" .... **$250-$300**

Hobo shoe, figural, advertising on sole, made by Western Aluminum Co., aluminum, 3" x 1-3/8" . **$75-$125**

Holly motif, brass, possibly made by Whiting Mfg. Co., 2-1/2" x 1-5/8" .... **$125-$150**

Home Insurance/3 horse fire engine, made by William Kerr, sterling, 2-1/2" x 1-3/8" .... **$575-$625**

Horseshoe shaped with two men riding horses, hidden photo, made by Battin & Co., sterling, catalog no. 256, 2-3/4" x 2" .... **$650-$750**

Indian chief, sterling, made by Webster Co., 2-1/4" x 1-3/4" ..... **$800-$900**

International Tailoring, pillbox type, nickel plated, made by August Goertz & Co., 1-3/8" x 2-1/2" .... **$30-$40**

King George V & Queen Mary commemorative, book shaped, made by Hamburg Rubber Company, vulcanite, 2" x 1-1/2" .... **$65-$85**

Knife & mechanical pencil combo with vesta compartment, sterling, made by Sampson Mordan & Co., 1888 London hallmarks, 3/4" x 2-1/4" .... **$650-$725**

Knight in armor/castle motif, sterling, 2-1/2" x 1-3/8" .... **$150-$200**

Lady holding cupid with bow and arrow, sterling, made by Gorham Mfg. Co., catalog no. B1280, 2-1/2" x 1-1/2" .... **$350-$400**

Lady of the Light/Louisiana Purchase Monument, brass, 2-1/2" x 1-1/2" .... **$85-$115**

Lady smoking, made by Unger Bros., sterling with gold interior wash, catalog no. 8277, 2-1/2" x 1-1/2" .... **$300-$350**

Lady's head surrounded by butterflies, made by Gorham Mfg. Co., catalog no. B2299, sterling, 2-5/8" x 1-1/2" .... **$750-$850**

Liberty Fire Company, Reading, PA, celluloid wrapped with b & w graphics, made by August Goertz Co., 2-3/4" x 1-1/2" .... **$325-$375**

Lion head motif, sterling with gold interior wash, made by Carter, Howe & Co., 2-1/2" x 1-1/2" .... **$500-$575**

Lion reclining, figural, nickel plated brass, push button lid release, 1" x 1-3/4" .... **$175-$200**

Love's Dream, cherub kissing lady, made by Unger Bros., slant top, curved back, sterling with gold interior wash, catalog no. 2504, 2-5/8" x 1-3/4" .... **$250-$300**

Mail bag, figural, conforms to design patent catalog no. 0586 of March 17, 1891, silver plated, made by E. A. Bliss & Co., 2-3/4" x 1-1/2" .... **$75-$125**

Man smoking pipe, sterling, made by Unger Bros., catalog no. 1628, 2-1/2" x 1-5/8" .... **$750-$850**

Figural boar and whistle combination, brass and plated brass, 3-3/4" x 1-1/2", **$400-$500.**

Figural monkey, Japanese, patinated brass, 2-1/2" x 1-1/2", **$750-$850.**

Lady seated on potty, brass, 2-3/8" x 1", **$350.**

Cobra motif, sterling silver, Gorham Mfg Co., cat. #605, 2-1/2" x 1-3/8", **$2,000.**

Gambling, two counters on one side, hand holding four aces and king on other, silver, soldered, by R. Wallace Co., cat. #051, 2-3/4" x 1-1/2", **$375.**

Stagecoach motif, enamel on sterling, English hallmarks, made by Sampson Mordan, London, 1899, 2-1/4" x 1-1/2", **$1,500-$2,000.**

Tiger clawing rabbit, Japanese, patinated brass, 2-3/4" x 1-5/8", **$1,250.**

Fireman motif, reverse "Good Wishes of Fireman's Fund Insurance," sterling, made by Shreve & Company, 2-3/8" x 1", **$750-$850.**

Three drunks, Gorham Mfg. Co., cat. #605, 2-3/4" x 1-3/4", **$395.**

Mauchline ware, trick-psycho box, 1893 Columbian Expo. transfer, wood, 3" x 1-1/4" .... **$110-$135**

Mixed metal, oriental man holding fan, copper with applied sterling, made by Gorham Mfg. Co., catalog no. 265, 2-1/2" x 1-1/2" ..... **$375-$450**

Moreland Match Co., applied enameled logo on EPNS, made by GHP, 2-1/2" x 1-1/2" .... **$175-$225**

Morgan Tires, gutta percha, slip top lid, 2-3/4" x 1-3/8" .... **$50-$65**

Our Heroes (McKinley, Dewey, Digsbee, Miles, Lee), sterling, made by Whiting Mfg. Co., 2-1/2" x 1-1/2" .... **$400-$500**

Owl on branch, figural, brass, 2-1/4" x 1-1/4" .... **$125-$150**

Owl's face with green glass eyes, figural, brass, 1-5/8" x 2" .... **$135-$150**

Oyster/HMMBA, figural, sterling, made by Gorham Mfg. Co., 1-3/4" x 2-1/2" .... **$400-$500**

Pabst Brewing Co. trademark and advertising, nickel plated brass, 3" x 1-1/2" .... **$50-$75**

Padlock, figural, sterling, made by Arthur & John Zimmerman, Birmingham hallmarks, 2" x 1-3/8" .... **$500-$550**

Pig with applied race horses on back, figural, brass, 1-3/8" x 1-7/8" .... **$90-$110**

President Cleveland, portrait type, figural, nickel plated brass, made by Simon Zinn, 2 5/8" x 1-3/4" .... **$250-$300**

Pug dog begging, figural, brass with glass eyes, 2-1/8" x 1" .... **$125-$150**

Quincy Rock Mine/Copper Country Souvenir, copper, 2-5/8" x 1-1/2" .... **$150-$175**

Risqué, lady urinating in garden, enamel on brass, French, 1-7/8" x 1-3/8" .... **$325-$375**

Scientific American newspaper with enameled postage stamp, figural, sterling with gold interior wash, made by Enos Richardson & Co., conforms to design patent catalog no. 20200 of Oct. 14, 1890, 2-3/8" x 1-1/8" .... **$400-$500**

Sea creatures & shells motif, sterling, made by Wm. Shiebler, catalog no. 22, 2-5/8" x 1-3/8" .... **$800-$900**

Shriners of North America motif, star set with garnet, made by Fairchild, sterling, 2-3/8" x 1-5/8" .... **$175-$225**

Sorrento ware, inlaid decoration of lady, wood, 2-3/4" x 1-1/2" ..... **$85-$100**

Steeplechase motif, silveroin, made by Bristol Mfg. Co., 2-1/2" x 1-1/2" .... **$100-$125**

Suit case, figural, nickel plated brass, 1-3/8" x 1-7/8" .... **$75-$100**

Swimmers in wave, made by Wm. Kerr, catalog no. 941, sterling, 2-3/4" x 1-7/8" .... **$450-$500**

Tavern scene, slide type with German markings, 925 silver, 1-5/8" x 2-1/2" .... **$85-$110**

Teddy bears dancing/advertising on reverse, insert type, nickel plated brass, made by August Goertz Co., 2-3/4" x 1-1/2" .... **$175-$250**

The Times, slide type, sterling, by Goldsmiths & Silversmiths Co., Ltd., London hallmarks, 1926, 1-3/4" x 2-3/8" .... **$225-$275**

Trick, enameled Masonic emblem on front-push to release lid, sterling, made by F. S. Gilbert, 2-1/2" x 1-1/2" .... **$200-$275**

Tunbridge ware, hour-shaped with screw top, 2" x 1-1/2" .... **$150-$175**

Watch, coin holder and match safe combo, made by Wm. Neale, Birmingham, 1887, sterling, 2-1/4" x 1-1/2" .... **$1200-$1400**

Watch, pocket type, converted to match safe, side opening, nickel plated brass with original enameled watch face, 2" diameter .... **$135-$160**

Xmas 1904/Collins & Co, trick type-squeeze edges to open lid, nickel plated, 1-1/2" x 2-1/2" .... **$65-$95**

MEDICAL AND PHARMACEUTICAL ITEMS

History: Modern medicine and medical instruments are well documented. Some instruments are virtually unchanged since their invention; others have changed drastically.

The concept of sterilization phased out decorative handles. Handles on early instruments, which were often carved, were made of materials such as mother-of-pearl, ebony, and ivory. Today's sleek instruments are not as desirable to collectors.

Pharmaceutical items include those things commonly found in a drugstore and used to store or prepare medications.

Advertising

Button, Cloverine Salve Authorized Agent, celluloid, product described in detail, tiny white clover buds on green stems, blue, red, or white rim inscriptions **$45**

Diecut, Johnson & Johnson talcum powder, cardboard litho, baby on back playing with talc container, string hanger, C-7.5, 8-1/8" x 14-1/8" **$575**

Trade card, 13" x 7-1/2", Kidd's Cough Syrup, diecut cardboard, Victorian woman and product advertising **$110**

Amputation knife, Civil War era **$135**

Apothecary chest

Chinese, old black paint, mortised case, shaped aprons with inset panels on sides, six dovetailed drawers with old painted red character labels, ring pulls, and removable dividers, 16-1/2" w, 18" d, 26-1/2" h **$250**

Oriental, old reddish brown finish, mortised case, 45 detailed drawers, some with divided interiors, ring pulls, red and yellow painted labels on front, sq legs, shaped base aprons, restorations, 33" w, 17" d, 46" h **$815**

Apothecary jar, cov, hp dec in burgundy and gold, black lettering on white ground, stenciled signatures on bases "Pouchet Deroche, Paris," acorn-shaped finials, French, wear to gold, 10-3/8" h **$320**

Bifocal spectacles, by McAllister, Philadelphia, silver frame, horseshoe-shaped lenses, sliding temples **$375**

Blood pressure kit, orig manual, 1917 .... **$55**

Book

The Dental Art in Ancient Times, lecture at A.M.A. Meeting, Atlantic City, 1914, map of Atlantic City, New Jersey, and boardwalk layout, cuts of ancient artificial teeth and tools, Burroughs Welcome & Co., London, 216 pgs, 1914, 4" x 6-3/4" **$34**

The People's Common Sense Medical Adviser in Plain English, or Medicine Simplified, Pierce, illus, 100 pgs, 1889 .... **$19.95**

Broadside

Dr Harding's Vegetable Medicines, top text reads "Dr. Harding's Vegetable Medicines; A Cure For Constipation, and Those Diseases…," text details various medicines, some folds, light foxing, minor edge chipping, ink notation on bottom border, mid-19th C, 18" x 9-3/4" **$150**

Drs White & Oatman, top text reads "Stuttering or Stammering Permanently and Easily Cured!" text details accomplishments and details of cure, some folds, mid-19th C, 18" x 8-3/4" **$150**

Cabinet, emb tin insert front, wood cabinet

Munyon's Homeopathic Remedies, 41 orig dovetailed product drawers on

Apothecary bottles, emerald green bottles, original labels and stoppers, price for set of four, 3" d, 7-1/2" h, **$300.**
Photo courtesy of David Rago Auctions, Inc.

back, most labeled, 24" x 18" x 7" **$1,750**

Dr. LeSure's Famous Remedies, 27" x 20-3/4" x 6-3/4" **$5,700**

Dr. Daniels Warranted Veterinary Medicines, orig finish, C.7.5, 28-5/8" x 21-1/2" x 7-3/4" **$2,900**

Pratts Veterinary Remedies, orig finish, stenciling, 30" x 17-1/4" x 7" **$2,200**

Dental cabinet, mahogany, flat top surmounted at rear with long drop-front cabinet raised on stepped base, streamlined main cabinet fitted with tree banks of five stacked short drawers over two banks of two stacked short drawers, over three banks of assorted short drawers above central kneehole franked by two deep short drawers, molded colorless glass drawer pulls, some drawers with porcelain and white glass receptacles and liners, four sq tapering legs, old medium finish, America, early 20th C, 55-3/4" h, 34" w, 12-1/8" h **$1,035**

Dispenser, Alka-Seltzer, blue and white, tin litho adv sign on front, chrome base, orig cobalt blue tumbler, C.8.5, 14-5/8" x 5" **$400**

Electro-medical induction coil, T. Hall, Boston, silvered coil and switches, mahogany base, pair of later handles, 10" h **$1,150**

Field surgeon's set, Lentz & Sons, Philadelphia, all metal instruments, including Rust's pattern bone saw, Liston knife, trephine, bone forceps, etc., metal case with canvas cover case, both marked "2nd Reg. N.G.P.," 10-1/2" w **$350**

Fleam

Two-blade, tortoiseshell on case .. **$60**

Three-blade **$45**

Apothecary chest, table-top type, old blue painted surface, Pennsylvania, late 19th C, 20-3/4" w, 11-1/4" h, **$3,450.**
Photo courtesy of Pook & Pook, Inc.

Apothecary chest, pine and poplar, c1840, 10 dovetailed drawers, mortised case, 40-1/2" w, 10-1/2" d, 13" h, replaced base molding, loss to back of top, **$300.**
Photo courtesy of Alderfer Auction Co.

Druggist's cabinet, oak, mirrored back, small fitted drawers, cabinet door, **$3,650.**

Forceps tooth key, removable bolster/claw, hatched handles, W & H Hutchinson, Sheffield, England, restorations, mid-19th C, 7-1/2" l **$690**

Hour glass, Tartanware, McDuff pattern, half hour, 9-1/2" h **$175**

Jar, orig stopper, Duff's Colic & Diarrhea Remedy, cylindrical glass, recessed reverse painted on glass label, ground stopper matches pattern at base, some minor staining, 10-1/2" h...................................**$250**

Magic lantern slides, set of 195, c1915 ....**$200**

Medical case, Civil War era........**$130**

Optician's trial set, Brown, Philadelphia, retailer's label, oak case, partial set, 21" w **$175**

Optometrist's sample case, mahogany, containing three trays of 20 spectacles each, chart in lid, 20" w **$690**

Photograph

Medical training type, students with skeletons **$80**

Medical training type, human skull **$250**

Unidentified doctor's office interior **$30**

Unidentified doctor with bag **$20**

Phrenological bust, plaster, Fowler, Wells & Co., Boston, labeled cranium, label on back, damaged, 9-1/2" h **$80**

Plugger, Goodman & Shurtler's Patent, mechanical gold foil, sprung, hinged mallet on ebonite body, interchangeable head, 8" l **$460**

Scarificator, brass, 16 blades, sgd "Kolb," European, early 19th C **$215**

Sign

Blackleg Veterinary Medicines, Parke, Davis & Co., diecut cardboard, two cowboys giving shot to calf, C.8++, 17-1/2" x 11-1/8" **$775**

C. F. Hussey Optometrist, zinc, double sided, polychrome and gilt dec, figural eyeglasses, name, and title in banner at base, imperfections, late 19th C, 41" l, 12-1/2" h..........**$2,550**

Surgeon's kit used by Assistant Surgeon Theophilus R. Vankirk, 209th Pennsylvania Infantry. The mahogany case is padded in red velvet and shaped to fit instruments. A second compartment lifts out and is also padded and shaped to hold the gutta-percha-handled instruments. **$4,500.**
KP photo/Wisconsin Veterans Museum collection

Spatula/knife, pearl handle, Remington...**$200**

Surgical knife, from Civil War hospital, 5" l **$40**

Surgeon's kit, ebony handles, velvet lined case, Civil War era **$1,420**

Tin

Blue Ribbon Brand, American Hygienic Co., Baltimore, MD, yellow, white, and red litho with German Shepherd in center, C.8+, 1-7/8" x 2-1/4" x 5/16" **$925**

Cadette Tooth Powder, figural tin litho soldier, green cap and coat, full, C.8, 7-3/8" x 2-1/4" x 1-1/4" **$525**

F. W. Cough Drops, Geo Miller & Co., Phila, "Cured My Cough," detailed graphics, C.9, 8" x 5-1/8" x 5-1/8" **$1,400**

Patent Superior Liquid Latex, yellow and red, C.8.5+, 1-1/2" x 2" x 7/16" **$425**

Town and Country, Nelson Products, NY, C.8++, 1-5/8" x 2-1/8" x 5/16" **$1,750**

Tooth extractor, W. R. Goulding, New York, marked "Baker & Riley patented 1845," removable claw/bolster, cross-hatched handles, 6-3/4" l **$1,380**

Tooth key

Turned horn handle, cranked shaft, adjustable claw, 5" l **$150**

Turned and hatched removable rosewood handle, turned cran-

shaft, adjustable circular bolster and claw, early 19th C, 6-1/2" l **$215**

Wrought-iron handle, cranked and curved octagonal shaft, circular bolster, 10 interchangeable claws, possibly French, 19th C, 5-3/4" l **$635**

Trepan, burnished steel, sgd "Sir Henry a Paris," arrowhead perforator, ivory pivot, ebony handle, five elevators, 18th C, 10-1/4" l.................**$1,725**

MILITARIA

History: Wars have occurred throughout recorded history. Until the mid-19th century, soldiers often had to provide for their own needs, including supplying their own weapons. Even in the 20th century, a soldier's uniform and some of his gear are viewed as his personal property, even though issued by a military agency.

Conquering armed forces made a habit of acquiring souvenirs from their vanquished foes. They also brought their own uniforms and accessories home as badges of triumph and service.

Saving militaria may be one of the oldest collecting traditions. Militaria collectors tend to have their own special shows and view themselves outside the normal antiques channels. However, they haunt small indoor shows and flea markets in hopes of finding additional materials.

Reproduction Alert. Pay careful attention to Civil War and Nazi material.

Additional Resources:

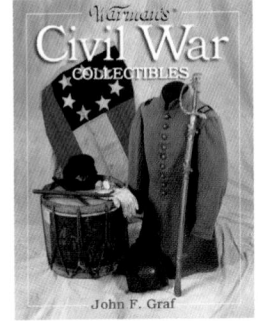

Warman's® Civil War Collectibles, by John F. Graf, Krause Publications, Iola, WI.

Warman's® Civil War Collectibles Field Guide, by John F. Graf, Krause Publications, Iola, WI.

Revolutionary War

Account book, for the Privateer Ship *Chandler,* sailing from Salem, Massachusetts, 70 manuscript pages, names 23 different brigs, sloops, schooners and ships that were supplied during the course Revolutionary war, several named individuals, original calf, scattered foxing and toning, c1779-84 ....**$7,100**

Autograph, document sgd, promotion of First Lieutenant, by Benjamin Harrison, 1783, paper seal, 6" x 8" **$650**

Book

Anthony Haswell, Printer, Patriot, Ballader, J. Spargo, 35 plates, 293 pgs, 1925 ....**$30**

Yale and Her Honor Roll in the American Revolution, H. P. Johnston, privately printed, rebound, 357 pgs, 1888 ....**$40**

Broadsheet

Addressed to the Governor of Massachusetts, published in the *Boston Evening Post,* single folio sheet, double-sided, regarding disturbances in the Colonies, minor restorations, February 1, 1773, 18" x 11-1/2" **$1,880**

Raising troops, requiring all towns to provide full accounting of supplies, bounties and gratuities given any soldier as part of state's proportion of Continental Army, signed by John Hancock in type, originally sent to Tosfield, CT, Oct. 8th, 1779, 13" x 8-1/2" **$2,585**

Inaugural button, George Washington, copper, orig shank attached, American eagle with surrounding date and text design, Albert WI-1-A., c1789 ....**$2,000**

Federal cap box, Confederate factory converted to CS box, **$550-$750.**

Excavated, Enfield combination gun tool, **$85-$95.**

Civil War powder flasks (pair), brass, 8", **$350-$400.**

Map, Seat of War in New York, contained in Nathaniel Low's Almanack, printed by J. Gill, Boston, twenty-four pages, in original wrappers, shows positions of Washington and other troops, 1777 .... **$2,650**

Newspaper, *Thomas's MA Spy: or Worcester Gazette*, May 13th, volume 14, no. 681, folio, printed by Isaiah Thomas, masthead engraved by Paul Revere, four pages, some mentions of the events of the war, 1784, 18" x 11" **$550**

Ordnance report, sent by William Perkins to Samuel Adams as Lt. Governor of Massachusetts, cover letter and ledger sheets describing condition of heavy cannon carriages and platforms in Boston Harbor **$600**

Plaque, General (Mad Anthony) Wayne, America, carved ivory, round, relief carved three-quarter view bust length portrait, banner below inscribed with name, houses and foliage in background, age crack, conforming molded wood frame, late 18th/early 19th C, 3-7/8" d **$500**

Print

Perry's Victory on Lake Erie, Perry in rowboat, eight sailors in midst of battle, steel engraving from painting by Thomas Birch, engraved by A. Lawson, published by William Smith, Philadelphia, Eastlake frame, 24" x 31" **$295**

Washington's Dream, litho by Currier and Ives, New York, Washington, in uniform, sleeping in camp cabin, vignette dream of three women representing Liberty, Plenty, and Justice standing over America, stepping on crown of tyranny, framed, 1857, 25" x 19" **$775**

Snuff box, cov, gutta percha, round, relief scene of battle, ships, coastline, buildings, French inscription "Prise d'Yorck (Taking of Yorktown or Battle of Yorktown)," 1781, 2-7/8" d **$750**

French and Indian War

Marching order, letter addressed to Captain Josiah Thatcher, Yarmouth, his Majesty's Service, Boston, ordering Thatcher to march troops to Springfield to be mustered, sgd by J. Hoar, some fold weakness, June 24, 1761, 8" x 6-1/4" **$185**

Uniform button mold, brass, American, casts six round buttons with central raised letter "I" for infantry, one 25 mm, one 18 mm, four 14.5 mm, each with eyelet, wooden handles missing, 18th C, 9" l **$625**

War of 1812

Broadside, printed calvary orders for the 2nd Brigade 1st Visis, and 7th Reg 2nd Brig 1st Divis, Edmund Fitzgerland Lt. Col. 7th Reg & Cavalry, one sheet, Aug. 18, 1814 .... **$375**

Cartridge box, leather, white cloth strap, very worn, missing plate **$70**

Flag, 13 stars, Naval, hand sewn, 60-1/2" x 110" **$1,100**

Military drum, large eagle painted on sides, red, and blue stripes, one drum head, 22" h, 17" d **$750**

Ship document, British, articles pertaining to private armed ship *Dart* and four carriage guns, six nine-pounders, four swivel guns lying in St. John, New Brunswick, designed to cruise against Americas, details prize division, chain of command, other shipboard administration, right sec-

tion includes signatures and ratings of 44 seamen and officers as crew, some staining, edge chipping, foxing, and fold splitting, Whatman 1808 watermark, dated July 1813, 21" x 29" **$500**

Civil War

Autograph

Davis, Jefferson, partly printed check, Union & Planters Bank, Memphis cancelled, July 22, 1872, 2-1/2" x 8-1/4" **$1,100**

Sherman, William T., ALS, to General Hawley, letter of condolence after death of Hawley's wife, St. Louis, March 10, 1886......................... **$460**

Belt and plate, black leather belt, brass loops, two-piece brass VA state plate, minor wear and splits **$2,350**

Book

Confederate General Robt. E. Lee & His Campaigns in Virginia, 300 pgs, fold-out maps, 1906 .... **$45**

Harper's Pictorial History of the Civil War, four volumes, 1896 .... **$230**

Life of Lincoln, Herndon/Welk, 500 pgs, c1889 ....**$19.95**

Personal Memoir of General Sheridan, limited edition, 2 volumes, faux leather, fold-out maps, 1889 .... **$45**

Personal Memoir of General Wm Tecumseh Sherman, limited edition, 2 volumes, faux leather, 800 pgs, 1876 .... **$45**

The Gettysburg Campaign and the Campaigns of 1864 & 1865 in Virginia by A Lieutenant in Confederate Artillery, Stribling, illus, 308 pgs, 1905 .... **$45**

Broadside

Abraham Lincoln funeral, from Governor Joseph Gilmore of New Hampshire, giving profound and moving instructions to people of New Hampshire to observe and participate in day of mourning, "all of the churches within their jurisdiction to be tolled, and minute guns to be fired...drape their stores and dwelling houses with the appropriate emblems of that grief...," dated April 17th, 1865, 8" x 10" **$950**

Union, Against Morgan's Raiders, issued by Office of Provost Marshall, Lexington, Kentucky, calling upon all citizens to be associated with "Home Guards" against Morgan's Raiders, July 15th, 1862, 6" x 8-1/2" **$2,000**

Union, Condemning U.S. Grant for Battle of Shiloh, large folio, sold by Applegate & Co., Cincinnati, Ohio, recounting events leading up to battle and Grant's action during conflict, c1862, 17-1/2" x 11-1/2" **$750**

Union, recruiting, dated September 12, 1861, Saccarappa, Maine, "Attention Volunteers Seventy-five Men Must be enrolled At Once....," these troops attributed to served in Company C of the 12th ME Volunteers, 12-1/4" x 9-1/2" **$1,175**

Union, recruiting, for M'Call's Division, Reading (Pennsylvania), printed with globe form masthead with "our country" and U.S. flag, dated April 1st, 1862, 13-1/2" x 6" **$1,175**

Union Draft, proclaiming "War Meeting!," Hingham, Massachusetts, black printed on salmon colored paper, light wear , dated 1864, 18-1/2" x 12" **$1,000**

Cane, carved wood, 1-1/2" w x 3" h oval wood knob, relief carved and polychromed shaft with American flag, 24 Union army corps badges, worn red, white, blue, and green polychrome, 1-3/4" brass ferrule, made for veteran, c1880, 35-3/4" l **$350**

Canteen, bull's eye, orig woven cloth strap, pewter spout sgd "Hadden, Porter & Booth, Phila," 7-5/8" d **$325**

Cartridge box, cross belt and eagle plate, "Calhoune New York" maker's stamp on inner flap, tin liners, oval U.S. plate **$900**

Confederate notes, group of $500, $10, and $5, from Richmond, matted and framed, 21-1/2" x 17" **$275**

Coat, Confederate Officer's, double breasted, blue-gray wool, low collar, blue piping along front, 12 large Virginia and North Carolina buttons marked "Scovill Mfg. Waterbury," three small buttons with same markings, two have black velvet coverings, Captain's bars on collar, buttons and insignia removed for previous cleaning, minor moth damage to ext. **$39,600**

Fife, rosewood, nickel silver ends, eight bands, orig dark finish, faint signature "W. Crosby, Boston," 17-1/2" l **$125**

Kepi, 13th Infantry soldier's **$850**

Newspaper, *Cincinnati Gazette*, fold lines and minor damage, group of 19 newspapers, for year of 1863 ......**$150**

Photograph, tintype, cased

Cavalryman, wearing shell jacket with gilt detail on collar and buttons, lightly tinted blue pants, holding cavalry saber, Colt pistol in belt, forage cap with "D2," sixth plate **$770**

Confederate, checked shirt, butternut colored coat, CDV mount **$110**

Infantryman, waist-up portrait, holding Hardee hat with feather, "K," and bugle insignia, wearing epaulettes, cartridge box, holding musket with bayonet, ninth plate **$550**

Soldiers in front of tent, very worn quarter plate tintype, gutta-percha case with relief scene of officers standing at table, scrolled border, minor edge chips **$470**

Pinback button

Battle of Gettysburg 1913 Anniversary, multicolored, blue lettering **$25**

Col. W. C. Johnson, G.A.R., black and white photo, orange ground, black lettering for sponsor "Snellenburg Stores, Philadelphia, Pa.," and "G.A.R. Encampment 1899" **$20**

Shaving mug, hp, US Civil War soldier holding American flag, name Jos. Davis in gold, 3-3/4" x 3-1/2" **$1,500**

Spurs, pr, brass, Confederate, Leech & Rigdon style, 4" h **$115**

Model 1851, Federal eagle, sword belt plate, gilded, officer, stamped brass, **$245-$300.**

Confederate, regulation, tin-drum canteen, **$750-$1,150.**

Confederate, .36 caliber, leather holster, **$650-$795.**

Calendar plate, 1920, The Great World War, 1914-1919, flags and globe in center, coats of arms of countries and calendar pages around border, gold lettering "Compliments of Luther Schoch, Ackermanville, PA," **$35.**

Photo courtesy of Dotta Auction Co., Inc.

Sword, belt rig, non-commissioned officer, NCO sword by Ames Mfg, Chicopee MA, marked on blade, also marked "US, GWC, 1864," marked "GKC" on guard, leather scabbard, NCO sword belt ring, eagle buckle, plated wreath, frog for NCO sword and hangers, some leather deterioration to belt and scabbard **$900**

Textile, printed in black on off-white cloth, "Union-Liberty & Life Without Freedom," poems and images of earlier patriots, New England Chemical Print Company, framed, mid-19th C, 10-1/4" x 10-1/2"........................**$450**

Walking stick, carved wood, dog's head finial with silver collar inscribed "Thos. Thompson Co. H 106 Reg. Pa. Vols. Evacuation of York Town 1862," natural branch carved with dog, squirrel, leafy vine, and reeded and geometric devices, wear, 36-1/4" h
....**$775**

Indian War

Bayonet, Model 1873, 3-1/2" w blade
....**$80**

Belt buckle, Naval officer, brass, stamped "Horstman, Phila".......**$120**

Broadside, Ohio massacre, No. 4, 1791, printed in Boston, foxed, water stained, modern frame, 1792 .....**$900**

Spanish American War

Hat badge, infantry, brass, crossed krag rifles, 2" l...............................**$55**

Cartridge box, U.S. Army **$125**

Pinback button, "Remember the *Maine*," battleship scene, patent 1896
....**$25**

World War I, British recruitment poster: "Britain Needs You At Once," St. George and the Dragon, lithograph with full margins, printed by Spottiswoode & Co., London, 31" x 20," sold with Titanic broadside from Boston Evening Telegram, Friday, April 19, 1912, four full pages, framed, **$375.**
Photo courtesy of David Rago Auctions, Inc.

Spy glass, pocket, brass, Naval, round holder, brown leather grip, 16" l
....**$110**

World War I

American flag, cloth, eight stars and five stripes, made by Prisoner of War, "Arlon Belgium Dec 11th, 1918" written on mat, framed, some losses, discoloration, 6-1/4" x 10-1/4" sight
....**$350**

Bayonet, British, MK II, No. 4, spike, scabbard....................................**$20**

Book, *The Priceless Gift, The Love Letters of Woodrow Wilson and Ellen Axson Wilson*, sgd by Henry Steele Commager, 1962.................**$13**

Buckle, U.S. Balloon Corps, emb hot air balloon....................................**$75**

Flare pistol, Model 1918, French
....**$100**

Gun sling, soft leather, for 03 Springfield, 1917.............................**$17.50**

Helmet, German, Pattern, painted gray/green, 1916...........................**$80**

Overcoat, U.S. Army officers, Melton, olive drab, wool, double breasted, 10 bone buttons...................................**$65**

Trench flashlight and note pad, German, black tin container, orig pad and pencil...................................**$65**

Civil War-period bullet extractor, **$30-$45.**

Brown leather cartridge box with double tin insert attached to leather shoulder strap with brass eagle breastplate attached by leather thong through metal loops. Cartridge box has double closure flaps with inside flapped implement pocket. Main flap is scalloped, no fastener, with oval brass "US" plate on front. Box has horizontal and vertical loops on back, with two buckles on bottom to fit either shoulder or waist belt. The box held 40 rounds of .58 cal. Minié ball paper cartridges. A complete cartridge box like this will sell for **$650-$1,100.**
KP photo/Wisconsin Veterans Museum collection.

Tunic and trousers, gabardine, pinback, Air Corps and U.S. discs **$75**

Watch fob, Federal Seal, U.S. officer **$15**

World War II

Armband, Japan, military police, red lettering, white cotton **$48**

Book

Baa Baa Black Sheep, Pappy Boyington, Marine Corps Pilot Ace with Flying Tigers, 400 pgs, 1958 .... **$38**

Blood and Banquets, Fromm, 350 pgs, photos, 1942 .... **$30**

Bunker's War, The World War II Diary of Colonel Paul D Bunker, 320 pgs **$38**

December 7th, 1941-The Day The Japanese Attacked Pearl Harbor, Prange, 509 pgs, 34 photo plates, 1988 .... **$38**

From Hell to Heaven-Memoirs From Patton's Third Army in WWII, McHugh, 1st ed, 1970 .... **$30**

Semper Fi, Mac-Living Memories of the US Marines in WWII, Berry, 403 pgs, photos **$40**

Cane, Civilian Conservation Corps, fully carved, U-shaped horse-head handle, one piece, carved low relief of trees, bathing beauty, alligator, name of carver's friends, "Middle Creek Camp F34 Co. 997," finish removed around later added date, 1933, 30-3/4" l **$125**

Flag, New Zealand PT boat, printed on blue cotton **$55**

Flyers goggles, Japanese, boxed, gray fur lined cups, yellow lenses **$35**

Gas mask, German, canister style, rubber mask, canvas straps, carrying container **$80**

Helmet, Italian, steel, leather chip strap **$100**

ID tag, U.S. Army, oval pattern, instruction envelope, chain **$25**

Manual, War Department, FM30-30, Military Intelligence, *Aircraft Recognition Pictorial Manual,* Bureau of Aeronautics, Washington, DC, 179 pgs, illus of US, Great Britain, German, Japanese, Italian, Russian, etc. plans, 1943, 6-1/4" x 10" **$40**

Telescope, Australian, MK 1, heavy leather case and carrying straps, 14" l **$45**

MINIATURE PAINTINGS

History: Prior to the advent of the photograph, miniature portraits and silhouettes were the principal way of preserving a person's image. Miniaturists were plentiful, and they often made more than one copy of a drawing. The extras were distributed to family and friends.

Miniaturists worked in watercolors and oil and on surfaces such as paper, vellum, porcelain, and ivory. The miniature paintings were often inserted into jewelry or mounted inside or on the lids of snuff boxes. The artists often supplemented commission work by painting popular figures of the times and copying important works of art.

After careful study, miniature paintings have been divided into schools, and numerous artists are now being researched. Many fine examples may be found in today's antiques marketplace.

Pencil and watercolor on paper, Brigadier General James Miller, Peterboro, New Hampshire, American School, oval frame, toning, sold with accompanying note giving brief history of General's career, early 19th C, 5-3/4" x 4-3/4" **$1,880**

Watercolor and gouache on ivory, two brown-haired, rosy-cheeked children, one wearing a pink dress and holding a tabby kitten in her lap, the other in a purple printed dress, holding a blue ribbon attached to the kitten, unsigned by attributed to Mrs. Moses B. Russell (American, 1809-54), molded giltwood frame, small areas of paint loss on clothing, 3-5/8" x 2-3/4" **$4,120**

Watercolor and pencil on paper

Lady in black, hair comb, reverse inscribed "painted May 12th 1834 by J Sears," oval eglomise mat, framed, scattered small abrasions, toning, 4" x 3-1/4" **$470**

Miss Stevens, Andover, MA, area, half-length profile likeness, precise outlines with delicate drawing, bright blue dress with lace offset, dark upswept hair with tortoise-shell comb, background of blue and orange flanked by black spandrels

at corners, unsigned, attributed to Edwin Plummer (Massachusetts and Maine, 1802-1880), back inscribed in pencil "Stevens, lace, purple," and outline of woman's profile, later black and gilt frame, minor foxing, color loss, some pinpoints, 5" x 3-1/2" **$21,150**

Young man, brown coat, red vest, red paint, bevel edge pine frame, 6-1/4" w, 7-1/2" h **$350**

Watercolor, graphite and ink on paper

Bust-length profile portrait of young woman, Mary L. Amidon, Dudley, Massachusetts, indistinctly signed "Ten—s" on lower sleeve, sitter identified by ink inscription on reverse, mounted in embossed brass mat in poly-resin case, creases, small tear, 2-5/8" d **$775**

Watercolor on ivory

Bust length portrait of Elizabeth Freeman (1786-1815), gold brooch frame with seed pearl border, accompanied by three small notes: one note written in 1888 by her daughter Elizabeth Freeman Duren, concerning birthday gift of brooch to her daughter, another written by great-granddaughter stating it was painted about 1812, last written by friend of the family who mentions the brooch was given to her after she bought a portrait from the great-granddaughter, Bangor, Maine, c1812, 1-7/8" x 1-3/4" **$1,650**

Elizabeth Maderia, sgd "E. B. Taylor," reverse with locket of hair, engraved name and date, oval brass frame, fitted in leatherette case, 1934, 3-1/2" x 2-3/4" **$225**

Gentleman, Anglo/American School, engraved gold pendant frame, reverse centered with en grisaille dec ivory oval medallion depicting dove with ribbon and two hearts suspended in its beak above curved panel inscribed "one mind," surrounded by woven hair, glass cracked, late 18th C, 2" x 1-3/8" **$650**

Gentleman wearing spectacles, sgd "M. B. Katze," brass framed, fitted in leatherette case, 3-1/2" x 2-3/4" **$200**

Gentleman, hand painted on ivory, man wearing powdered wig, white high-collared shirt, yellow vest, brown jacket, signed "Von der Tachlen," 2-1/4" d, **$330.**
Photo courtesy of Alderfer Auction Co.

Gustavis Tuckerman Jr., sgd and dated "Sacro Fratelli 1847" lower right, inscribed on paper within opening on reverse "Gustavis Tuckerman (Jr.,) Born Edgbaston, England, May 15th 1824, Died New York, February 12, 1897," painted in Palermo, Italy, 1847 by Sacro Fratelli, oval engine-turned gilt-metal frame within rect papier-mâché frame inlaid with abalone floral dec, 3" x 2-1/2" **$450**

James L. Small, Camden, Maine, unsigned, American School, mounted in oval metal locket case, cobalt blue and white enameled border, pen and ink inscriptions appear on paper backing including "1818," "TL 20 LWV," conjoined V and W and "1850," conjoined V and W and "1850" also incised into the interior of the frame, 19th C, 2-1/8" d **$1,650**

Julia Clarke Brewster (1796-1826), attributed to John Brewster Jr., painted in the Columbia or Hampton, Connecticut area, orig oval gilded copper locket case within orig red leather hinged case, c1820, 1-7/8" x 2-1/4" **$4,600**

Lady in burgundy, wearing lace bonnet, sgd "G. Harvey" lower right, hinged red leather case with ormolu mat, 3-1/2" x 2-3/4".................**$725**

Military officer wearing a navy blue coat with crimson collar, white braid, and cross belt, silver breast plate, epaulettes, and buttons, unsigned, American School, oval format, ebonized wood frame, 2-3/4" x 2-1/4" **$1,100**

Mme. De St. Marc, hand painted on ivory, woman wearing powdered wig, large bonnet with white veil, blue dress with pink bow decoration, signed "Saintet," 3" x 2-1/4", **$315.**
Photo courtesy of Alderfer Auction Co.

Mother and child Double portrait, dressed in white, blue trim, pearl tiara on mother, child playing with pocket watch, old German typed label on back identifies woman as "Marquise d'Huret-Gonzenbach," ebonized frame, 1803, 5-3/4" w, 6" h **$600**

Napoleonic portrait, tortoiseshell and brass frame, oval format, signature obscured, 3-1/4" x 2-1/2" **$725**

Nobleman in powdered wig, blue sash, medal, holding sheet of paper, oval brass frame, 2-3/4" h **$325**

Richard Wagner, illegible artist's signature, ivory frame, brass liner, nacre inlay, 3-7/8" x 3-1/2" **$250**

Semi-nude slave girl with two cajoling men, unsigned, Continental, giltwood frame, late 19th C, 5" x 3-7/8"...**$750**

Woman with hair in braided ringlets, beaded cap, floral dress, laced bodice, cast brass frame with ram's head corners, 3" x 2-3/4"....................**$325**

Young blond military officer, green and red uniform with epaulettes, sgd "Haberle," oval brass frame with horn, small pc missing, 3-3/8" w, 4-1/2" h **$320**

Young boy, sgd "Jared Sparks Handerson, Baltimore" in pencil on reverse, American School, 19th C, oval format, 2-3/4" x 2-1/4" l **$620**

Young gentleman, black great coat, white waist coat, pleated shirt with stickpin and black neck cloth,

unsigned, Anglo/American School, gilt-metal frame, aperture containing lock of braided hair, fitted leather case, 19th C, 2-3/4" x 2-1/4" **$950**

Young lady, attributed to Jacob Maentel, oval blue ground, lady in blue and white dress, orange ribbon on head covering, orig frame, 6" x 7-1/2"...............**$3,025**

Young woman with curled hair, attributed to Frederick Buck, wearing coral necklace, oval format, late 18th/early 19th C, 3" x 2-1/2" **$825**

Watercolor on paper

Believed to be Commodore Perry, brown curly hair and sideburns, dark blue naval officer's uniform, gold epaulettes, oval ground glued to blue backing, matted with old reeded frame with black paint, some flaking to gold, dark blue alligatored, 5" w, 7-1/8" h **$420**

Gentleman, oval aperture, unsigned, American School, framed, crease, minor foxing. 19th C, 4-1/2" d **$890**

Gentleman, reverse identified as "1825, Eleazar Graves, father of Laura Graves Lincoln," unsigned, attributed to Rufus Porter, America, grain painted frame, laid down, staining in margins, minor toning, c1792-1884, 5-3/4" x 4-3/4" **$445**

Gentleman, wearing black jacket, white vest and stock, seated before window on red upholstered chair before red drapery, penciled inscription "Herbert Lynesey squire Wier," on image, unsigned, Anglo/American, gilt gesso frame, minor foxing, 19th C, 5-1/2" x 4-3/8" **$360**

Lady in blue dress, white cap, brown ribbon, attributed to Edwin Plummer, Boston, c1841-46, oval eglomise mat, framed, laid down, small tear, minor toning, losses, repaint to mat, 4-1/8" x 3-1/2".................**$765**

Woman wearing tortoiseshell comb, sitter identified on reverse as "Mrs. A. Saunders age 18 years," oval eglomise format, molded gilt frame, American School, toning, gilt loss on mat, c1840, 4-3/4" x 3-5/8" **$2,585**

Young brunette seated in lush interior, hair dressed with pearls, lace-trimmed gown and blue wrap, signed to left "J. Isabey," Continental, late 19th C, 6" x 4-7/8" gilt-metal frame, 3-1/8" x 4-1/4" h **$1,725**

Watercolor on porcelain, woman with classical profile, wearing scarf with pearl and gold brooch, brass frame, 4-3/8" h............................**$200**

MINIATURES

History: There are three sizes of miniatures: dollhouse scale (ranging from 1/2 to 1 inch), sample size, and child's size. Since most early material is in museums or extremely expensive, the most common examples in the marketplace today are from the 20th century.

Many mediums were used for miniatures: silver, copper, tin, wood, glass, and ivory. Even books were printed in miniature. Price ranges are broad, influenced by scarcity and quality of workmanship.

The collecting of miniatures dates back to the 18th century. It remains one of the world's leading hobbies.

Child or doll size

Bed, Arts & Crafts, rect headboard with two cartoon-like images of baby dolls, footboard with two sq-form cutouts, imperfections, 28-5/8" l, 16" w, 15-3/4" h.......................................**$230**

Blanket chest, six-board

America, pine, wire hinged top, dovetail and mortise and tenon constructed box, cavity with two compartments, natural surface, early 19th C, 9-3/4" l, 4-1/2" w, 6-3/4" h **$3,650**

America, poplar, dovetailed, sq nail construction, molded lid and base, turned feet, brass hinges, orig red covered by old mustard paint, early 19th C, 11" l, 6" w, 7-1/2" h **$4,400**

Lancaster County, Pennsylvania, dovetailed, bracket feet, molding at lid and bottom, till, red paint dec, old splits in lid, 16-3/4" l, 11" w, 12-1/2" h **$1,760**

New England, blue painted pine, rect hinged top with applied molded

edge, dovetailed case, molded bracket base, wear, early 19th C, 20-3/4" l, 10-3/8" w, 9-5/8" h **$550**

Poplar, dovetailed, old thin red wash, applied moldings around lid and base with worn black paint, dated on back "Mar 6, 1827," restorations to hinge rail, feet missing, 15-3/4" l, 7-1/2" w, 7-3/4" h **$460**

Bookcase, hp, scalloped cornice over four open shelves, base with three drawers, Peter Hunt dec...........**$1,650**

Box on frame, America, grain painted, pine dome-top box with wire hinges, frame with vase and ring-turned legs, int. lined with floral patterned wallpaper, early 19th C, 7" w, 4" d, 5-3/4" h.................................**$2,720**

Bucket, cov, turned wood, two drilled handles, turned lid, orig yellow paint on outside, orange on inside, white, red, black, and blue designs, some wear and varnish flaking, 4-1/2" d, 3-7/8" h.................................**$150**

Buffet, carved wood, dark stained finish, two spindled shelves, lower section with two chip carved front doors, carved and stippled stylized floral dec on sides, Normandy, early 20th C, 9" w, 4-3/4" d, 13-3/4" h **$235**

Chair, arm, New England, carved maple, ball, vase, and ring turnings on banister back, stiles ending in ball finials, finely turned arms, legs, and stretchers, orig upholstered seat, mid-19th C, 7" w, 5-3/4" d, 13-1/2" h **$470**

Chair, side, worn orig light green paint, black striping, gold stenciling, polychrome floral dec, pr, 10-3/4" seat, 22" h.................................**$625**

Chest of drawers

Biedermeier-style, fruitwood veneer, wire nail construction, three drawers, applied half turned pilasters painted black, capped with ormolu trim, tapered sq legs, old refinishing, green velvet lining in drawers, small brass pulls, 14" w, 7-1/2" d, 10-1/4" h **$550**

Carlisle, Cumberland County, Pennsylvania, softwood, paint dec, four drawers, sq nail construction, scrolled ribbon dec on front, wooden pulls, light brown grain paint dec, dark brown highlights to imitate burled walnut, 10" l, 5-1/2" d, 11-1/2" h.................**$990**

Chest of drawers, three drawers, pine, scalloped base, dovetailed, mirror missing, **$225.**

Chest of drawers, oak and chestnut, three long drawers, shaped back with crest, candle shelves, and mirror, simulated bamboo turnings, **$295.**

Miniature, chest of drawers, Georgian-style, salesman's sample, walnut, string inlay, 23" x 23" x 15", **$1,100.**
Photo courtesy of David Rago Auctions, Inc.

Bedroom suite, cottage style, painted green, pink floral decoration, doll size, **$65.**
Photo courtesy of Alderfer Auction Co.

Tea set, silverplated, 4" h tea-pot, covered sugar, creamer, waste bowl, six cups and saucers, and five spoons, fitted box bearing label "Manufactured by James W. Tufts, 33 to 39 Bonker St. Boston," 5" h, 12-3/8" l, **$500.**
Photo courtesy of Pook & Pook, Inc.

Cupboard, step-back

Middle Atlantic States, cherry, flat-molded cornice above cock-beaded case, two cupboard doors with raised panels, two shelves int., arched opening over projecting case with two short drawers with applied molding, two raised-panel cupboard doors, old red-stained surface, mid-19th C, 24" w, 11" d, 37-1/4" h **$1,725**

New England, stained, molded top overhangs case of two drawers opening to two-shelved int., stepped out board overhangs two drawers on legs, side shaping, orig surface, early 19th C, 24-1/2" w, 8-1/8" d, 33" h **$1,265**

Rocker, Empire style, mahogany, vase-shaped splat, rush seat, scrolled arms, 22" h............................ **$225**

Settee, carved wood, dark stained finish, serpentine back, openwork spindled flowerheads and chip-carved and stippled stylized floral dec, hinged lid, Normandy, early 20th C, 7-5/8" l, 7-5/8" w, 4-1/4" h......................... **$145**

Settle bench, PA, orig gold, copper, and silver fruit dec along crest and back slats, mustard yellow ground with areas of wear and touch-up, scrolled arms, plank seat with incised borders, eight turned legs, restoration, 24" l, 6-1/2" w, 6-1/2" h seat **$825**

Spiral staircase, mahogany, dark rosewood grained finials, rect base with demilune cut out in center, late 19th C, 17-5/8" w, 8-5/8" d, 22-1/8" h **$1,500**

Stool

Foot, pine, sq nail construction, D-shape cut-out legs, side skirt, orig natural wood finish with folky diamond and line inlaid wood on top, label "Stool belongs to Hannah C. Raymond," 7-1/2" l, 4-3/4" w, 4-1/2" h **$935**

Dec pine, round top, shaped legs, painted red with yellow and blue star, circular stenciled dec, America, repair, 19th C, 8-5/8" d, 5-1/2" h **$560**

Table, drop leaf, Sheraton, walnut, pine secondary wood, leaves with decoratively cut corners, one dovetailed drawer, turned legs, old finish, minor edge damage, hinges replaced, age crack on top, 23-1/2" l, 12-1/2" w, 10-3/4" l leaves, 19" h **$1,100**

Dollhouse accessories

Bird cage, brass, bird, stand, 7" h **$65**

Carpet sweeper, gilt, Victorian .. **$65**

Christmas tree, decorated **$50**

Coffeepot, brass............................ **$25**

Cup and saucer, china, flower design, c1940 .... **$10**

Decanter, two matching tumblers, Venetian, c1920 .... **$35**

Fireplace, tin, Britannia metal fretwork, draped mantel, carved grate **$85**

Radio, Strombecker, c1930............. **$35**

Refrigerator, Petite Princess **$75**

Silhouettes, Tynietoy, pr, c1930 .... **$25**

Telephone, wall, oak, speaker and bell, German, c1890 .... **$40**

Towel stand, golden oak, turned post **$45**

Umbrella stand, brass, ormolu, sq, emb palm fronds **$60**

Dollhouse furniture

Armoire, tin litho, purple and black **$35**

Bathroom, wood, painted white, Strombecker............................ **$40**

Buffet set, stenciled, three shelves, column supports, Biedermeier, 6" h **$400**

Chair, ormolu, ornate, pr, c1900, 3" h **$75**

Cradle, cast iron, painted green, 2" l **$40**

Desk, Chippendale style, slant front **$60**

Dining room, Edwardian style, dark red stain, extension table, chairs, marble top cupboard, grandfather clock, chandelier, candelabra, 5" h bisque shoulder head maid doll, table service for six, Gebruder Schneerass, Waltershausen, Thuringa, c1915 .... **$1,400**

Kitchen set, litho tin, Modern Kitchen, all parts and pieces, animals, and related items, orig box, Louis Marx **$250**

Living room, Empire-style, sofa, fainting couch, two side chairs, upholstered tapestry, matching drapery **$350**

Piano, grand, wood, eight keys, 5" h **$35**

Sewing table, golden oak, drawer, c1880 .... **$100**

Swiss, marquetry inlaid music box on stand by Bremond, lid with inlaid mother-of-pearl butterfly, case marked "BAB," 11" cylinder, stand with single fitted drawer containing five additional cylinders, turned, fluted and blocked legs joined by stretcher with central finial, 19th C, 26" w, 22-3/4" d, 33" h, **$4,600.**
Photo courtesy of Pook & Pook, Inc.

Swiss music box, single comb, mahogany and satinwood case, inlaid leaf and floral motif on lid, c1900, 5-1/2" x 18-1/2" x 7-1/2", **$600.**
Photo courtesy of David Rago Auctions, Inc.

Table, tin, painted brown, white top, floral design, 1-1/2" x 3/4" h, ornate **$30**

Tea cart, Petite Princess **$25**

Vanity, Biedermeier **$90**

MUSIC BOXES

History: Music boxes, invented in Switzerland around 1825, encompass a broad array of forms, from small boxes to huge circus calliopes.

A cylinder box consists of a comb with teeth that vibrate when striking a pin in the cylinder. The music these boxes produce ranges from light tunes to opera and overtures.

The first disc music box was invented by Paul Lochmann of Leipzig, Germany, in 1886. It used an interchangeable steel disc with pierced holes bent to a point that hit the star-wheel as the disc revolved, and thus produced the tune. Discs were easily stamped out of metal, allowing a single music box to play an endless variety of tunes. Disc boxes reached the height of their popularity from 1890 to 1910, when the phonograph replaced them.

Music boxes also were incorporated in many items, e.g., clocks, sewing and jewelry boxes, steins, plates, toys, perfume bottles, and furniture.

Bremond, interchangeable cylinder, orchestral music, 12 19" cylinders **$82,500**

Cellesta, single-comb ratchet-wind mechanism, walnut case with bone inlaid top and color print in lid, 16 discs, 8-1/4" disc **$980**

Cylinders

Lambert, common, c1900 .... **$225**

Lambert, recording of The Stars & Stripes, pink, 5" d **$2,000**

Criterion, matching cabinet, 15-1/2" disc **$5,200**

Lecoulture, D., plays four airs, plain case, 17" l, 8-1/4" cylinder **$1,100**

Manger, John, large cylinder type **$33,000**

Match striker, gilt cast metal figure of man holding his chamber pot out window, strike-plate activating two-air movement playing "Dixie" and "La Marsille," 9" h **$635**

Mermod Freres, interchangeable cylinder type, three cylinders

Orig finish case **$49,500**

Restored case **$5,500**

Olympia, No. 6566, 20-1/2" upright disc, twin-comb mechanism, disengaged coin slide, manual control, two-piece mahogany cabinet, side disc

storage, 32 discs, sounding boards replaced, 70" h **$6,900**

Polychon, No. 27498, 15-1/2" disc, twin comb movement, coin slide, walnut case with bobbin turned corner columns, paneled and inlaid top, monochrome print in lid, disc storage drawer in plinth, 36 zinc disks, 24" w **$460**

Regina, 15-1/2" disk

Double comb, oak **$3,520**

Style 11 .... **$3,000**

Style 50 .... **$4,000**

Singing bird

Brass, moving head, circular base, 11" h **$420**

Blue enameled case, ivory beak, moving wings and perch, lid with Alpine scene and floral spray, 3-3/4" w **$2,645**

Silver plated, serpentine front and sides, cast with views of country scenes, leather traveling case, bird detached and featherless, 4" w **$815**

Symphonion

Eroica, tall case clock, plays three disks simultaneously, 25 three-disc sets **$46,750**

Eroica, upright, walnut case, 18 three-disc sets, 81" h **$38,500**

Offset double combs, 9" disc **$1,650**

MUSICAL INSTRUMENTS

History: From the first beat of the prehistoric drum to the very latest in electronic music makers, musical instruments have been popular modes of communication and relaxation.

The most popular antique instruments are violins, flutes, oboes, and other instruments associated with the classical music period of 1650 to 1900. Many of the modern instruments, such as trumpets, guitars, and drums, have value on the "used," rather than antiques market.

Collecting musical instruments is in its infancy. The field is growing very rapidly. Investors and speculators have played a role since the 1930s, especially in early string instruments.

Additional Resources:

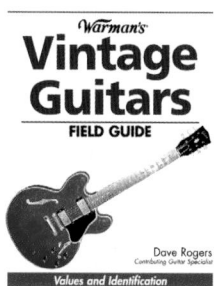

Warman's Vintage Guitar Field Guide, by Dave Rogers, Krause Publications, Iola, WI.

Banjo

Global, with case **$225**

Peerless, with case **$70**

Clarinet, with case

Henry Bouche **$675**

Selmer **$350**

Coronet, English, silver plated, stamped "F. Besson, Brevetee...," with case................................... **$320**

Drum set, Gretsch, three pcs, aqua sides **$600**

Fife, American, Meacham & Co., Albany, maple, brass fittings, case **$320**

Flute, American

Gemeinhardt, with case **$125**

Peloubet, C., five keys, rosewood, round key covers **$550**

Harpsichord, German, labeled "Sperrhake Passau," fruitwood veneer and bird's-eye maple top, possibly replaced legs, 31" x 62" x 25", **$1,000.**
Photo courtesy of David Rago Auctions, Inc.

Phaff, John, Philadelphia, faintly stamped "J. Phaff...," eight keys, rosewood, silver fittings, period case, 19th C............................ **$1,265**

Flute, English

Monzani, London, eight keys, head with turned reeding, silver fittings, round covered keys, 19th C **$200**

Rudall Carte & Co., London, silver, multiple stamps, hallmarks, case **$750**

Wrede, H., London, c1840, four keys, stained boxwood, ivory fittings, silver round cover keys, case **$320**

Guitar, archtop, D'Angelico, John, Model New York, irregular curl maple two-piece back, medium curl sides, medium grain with cross-bracing top, medium curl neck, bound peghead with inlaid pearl D'Angelico logo, bound ebony fingerboard with split-block pearl inlay, stamped internally "D'Angelico, New York, 1808," 1947, 21-7/16" l back, 18-1/2" w bottom bout **$13,800**

Guitar, classical

Bazzolo, Thomas, three-piece rosewood back, similar sides, spruce top of fine grain fully bound, mahogany neck, ebony fingerboard, labeled "Thomas Bazzolo, Luthier #65C24, Lebanon, Connecticut, USA," and sgd, with case,1994, 18-15/16" l back, 14-1/8" w lower bout...... **$750**

Chica, Manuel de la, two-piece Brazilian rosewood back, labeled "Manuel De La Chica, Constructore, De, Violines Y Guitarras, Placeta De La Silleria 8, Granada, Ano De 1966," 19-1/4" l back........................ **$1,725**

Martin, C. F., Style D-35, three-piece Indian rosewood back, similar sides, spruce top of fine to medium grain, mahogany neck with bound ebony fingerboard, inlaid pearl eyes, stamped internally "CF Martin & Co., Nazareth, PA, Made in USA, D-35," 1975.................. **$1,475**

Guitar, flat top, Gibson, flat top, orig case **$900**

Hawaiian guitar, National, New Yorker, with case.................... **$425**

Mandolin, flat back, with case **$175**

Piano, Steinway and Sons, Style VII, sq grand, carved rosewood, c1879 .... **$1,380**

Organ

Band, Arthur Bursens, three-section, drums, symbols, and xylophone **$16,500**

Dance, Arburo, saxophone, accordion, drum, castanets, drums and symbols **$17,600**

Fairground, Limonaire, built in Germany, 1908, plays folding paper books............................... **$24,750**

Recorder, Moeck **$135**

Trumpet, valve type

Buescher...................................... **$125**

Sears & Roebuck........................ **$115**

Ukulele

Aloha Royal, with case **$120**

Giamnini, baritone, with case **$95**

Kkamakall, with case **$250**

Vibraphone **$350**

Viola, no inscription, with orig case, orig bow **$475**

Violin, German, labeled "Thomas Ranik, Lauten and Geigenmacher in Breslau 1731," one-pc maple back, Lupot stamped bow, 19th C fitted rect leather case **$1,150**

Violin, Hungarian, medium curl two-piece back, similar ribs, medium curl scroll, fine grain top, red color varnish, labeled "Janos Spiegel, Budapest, 1907," 358 mm, with case, 14-1/16" l back **$6,620**

Violin, Italian

Attributed to Andrea Postacchini, narrow curl one-piece back, irregular curl ribs, faint curl scroll, fine grain top, golden brown color varnish, labeled "Andreas Postacchini Amieie Filius Fecit Firmi Anno 1819, Opus 11?," 356 mm, with case, accompanied by bill of sale, 14" l back **$17,250**

Bisiach, Leandro, strong medium curl two-piece back, strong narrow curl ribs and scroll, fine grain top, golden brown color varnish, labeled "Leandro Bisiach Da Milano, Fece L'Anno 1942," sgd, 356 mm, with case, undated numbered certificate, 14" l back **$18,400**

Violin, Mittenwald, Klotz School, medium curl two-piece back, similar ribs and scroll, fine grain top, brown color varnish, unlabeled, 353 mm, with case, c1780, 13-7/8" l back **$2,415**

Violin bow, gold mounted

Ouchard, Emile, round stick stamped "Emile Ouchard" at butt, ebony frog with Parisian eye, plain gold adjuster, 63 grams **$4,025**

Seifert, Lothar, octagonal stick stamped "Lothar Seifert" at butt, ebony frog with Parisian eye, gold and ebony adjuster, 61 grams **$1,265**

Unstamped, octagonal stick, later frog engraved "A. Vigneron A Paris 1886," 59 grams **$1,485**

Violin bow, silver mounted

Hill, W. E., round stick stamped "W. E. Hill & Sons" at butt, ebony eye with Parisian eye, plain silver adjuster, 60 grams, baleen wrap **$2,530**

Morizot, Louis, French, round stick stamped "L. Morizot" at butt, ebony frog with Parisian eye, plain silver adjuster, 60.5 grams **$2,300**

Nurnberger, Albert, octagonal stick stamped "Albert Nurnberger" at butt, "Saxony" under plain ebony frog, silver and ebony adjuster, 61 grams **$1,265**

Unstamped, French, Francois-Nicolas Voirin, round stick, ebony frog with pearl eye, later silver and ebony adjuster, 63 grams, c1860 .... **$4,890**

Violoncello

America, Settin, Joseph, strong narrow curl two-piece back, similar ribs and scroll, fine to medium grain top, golden brown color varnish, labeled "Joseph Settin Venetus, Fecit Anno Domani 1953," 748 mm, 29-7/16" l back **$8,100**

Czech, two-piece medium curl back, similar ribs and scroll similar, medium curl top, red color varnish, labeled "CAK Dvorni, A Armadni Dodvatel, Preniceska Tovarna Nastrouju Na Morave, Joseflidil V Brne Zelny Irh 11," 767 mm, 30-3/16" l back **$3,795**

English, James and Henry Banks, narrow curl two-piece back, medium curl ribs, faint curl scroll, fine to medium grain top, red color varnish, sgd internally on table, "James and Henry Banks, Salisbury," c1800, 28-34" l back, 729 mm **$18,400**

French, Thibouville-Lamy, Jerome, narrow curl two-piece back, similar ribs, medium curl scroll, medium to wide grain top, orange color varnish, labeled "Jerome Thibouville-Lamy, 70 Rue Reaumur, Paris, 1938," 756 mm, with case, 29-3/4" l back **$3,795**

German, irregular narrow curl two-piece back, similar ribs, narrow curl scroll, medium to wide grain top, orange color varnish, labeled "Erich Grunert, Penzberg Anno 1976," 756 mm, with case, 29-3/4" l back **$1,150**

Violoncello bow, nickel plated, round stick stamped "L. Bausch, Leipzig," 81 grams **$1,840**

Large bass drum was used by Silas D. Taylor, 3rd Regiment, Wisconsin. The maple rings still have remnants of red paint, **$3,100.**
KP photo/Wisconsin Veterans Museum collection.

Nickel-plated brass E-flat alto horn made by E.G. Wright, a Boston maker of fine instruments. The horn was used by Merrill Sherman, 24th Wisconsin Infantry, **$2,950.**
KP photo/Wisconsin Veterans Museum collection.

NAPKIN RINGS, FIGURAL

History: Gracious home dining during the Victorian era required a personal napkin ring for each household member. Figural napkin rings were first patented in 1869. During the remainder of the 19th century, most plating companies, including Cromwell, Eureka, Meriden, and Reed and Barton, manufactured figural rings, many copying and only slightly varying the designs of other companies.

Notes: Values are determined by the subject matter of the ring, the quality of the workmanship, and the condition. The following examples are all silver-plated.

Barking dog, unknown maker, barking dog jumping over fence, ring rests on back of dog, ring elaborately engraved with floral and basket weave dec, cartouche form panel incised "Leslie '93," scattered spots of wear or discoloration, 2-1/4" w, 2-3/4" h $185

Begging terrier, Hamilton, ring at back, central engraved foliate garland flanked by turned rings and ridged rim on ring, oval base dec with stars and bars, imp "Hamilton & Co., 01541," minor denting to rim of ring, 3" w, 2-1/2" h $100

Bird, Reed & Barton, rect platform with tapered sides with raised leaf and scroll dec, reeded ring topped by bird with outspread wings seated on ball, twisted cord and tassel descend-

Combination napkin ring, open salt, pepper shaker, and butter pat, embossed florals, silver plate, marked "Tufts," **$175.**

ing from ball on one side of ring, imp "Mf'd. and Plated by Reed & Barton, no. 1310," 3-1/8" w, 3-1/4" h $225

Bird in fruit tree, Meriden, bird sitting in branches, ring engraved with birds in branches, circular base with fruit and leaves, imp "Rogers Smith & Co., Meriden, no. 247," minor wear to finish, 2-1/2" w, 3" h $145

Bird on branch, unknown maker, ring having circular base, raised flower and leaf dec, branch rising from base and following curve of ring, bird with wings spread sits atop branch, underside imp "1593," scattered spots of wear to finish, 2-1/2" w, 3-1/2" h $375

Birds and bud vase, Wilcox, ring resting on ftd pedestal, two birds with outstretched wings on ring on either side of central bud vase, flared rim, ring with beaded and ridged detail at edges, imp "Wilcox Silver Plate Co., no. 1899," very minor wear to finish, 2-1/2" w, 5-1/2" h $165

Boy with post, Meriden, boy holding post, shovel on ground beside him, ring with beaded rim details and central engraved band with foliage attached to one side of base, circular base, imp "Meriden Brittannia Company, no. 30," wear, 4" w, 3-1/4" h $75

Bud vase, Reed & Barton, circular base with raised fleur-de-lis motif, ring with floral-decorated rims, ewer-form bud vase with flower inside curved handle, imp "Mf'd. & Plated by Reed & Barton, 1337," discoloration of finish at base of ewer, 2-1/2" w, 4-1/2" h $175

Butterfly and two fans, two Japanese style handled fans supporting ring, butterfly underneath ring, central plain band flanked by two raised curved bands with floral garland motif on ring, sq base with raised floral dec, four ball feet, imp "Meriden Brittannia Company, no. 208," minor wear to finish $75

Butterflies and leaf, unknown maker, ring resting on outspread wings of two butterflies resting on leaf, four ball feet, ring with central band and raised rims, floral motif, scattered spots of wear to finish, 2-1/2" w, 2-1/2" h $225

Chair, unknown maker, ring resting on seat of chair, ring with engraved panel and foliate swag, panel incised "M.A. Hall from Ed. V. Louise," scattered wear to finish, 1-3/4" x 4-1/2" h $180

Cherub

Rogers, ring resting on hips and legs of cherub, arms and head on top of ring, ring having central plain band flanked by bands, engraved floral dec on ridged ground, circular base, imp "Rogers & Bro., no. 224," 3" w, 4" h $385

Unknown maker, seated cherub leaning back against ring with floral dec rims, very minor nicking to rims of ring, 3-1/4" w, 1-3/4" h $550

Cherub with torch, Reed & Barton, cherub with fallen drape, one arm outstretched holding torch, leaning on pedestal and ring, ring with reeded rims, chased bird, and floral motif on center band, circular panel monogrammed "RGM," rect base, imp "Mf'd. & Plated by Reed & Barton, 1285," underside engraved "Aug. 27, 1888," minor loss to finish, 3" w, 4" h $525

Cow and tree, Meriden, oval ring supported by forked branches of tree, cow standing beside, engraved dec of birds on tree branches on ring, circular base, imp "Meriden Brittannia Company, no. 243," wear to finish, 1-3/4" w, 2-3/4" h $100

Crawling child, Rogers, crawling child beside ring, ring with pierced work scrolling dec on edges, imp "Wm. Rogers Mfg. Co., Hartford, Quadruple, 2254," 2-3/4" w, 1-3/4" h $200

Cupid and heart, Rogers, heart-form base with scallop dec at edge, seated cupid with one outstretched arm, arrow resting on base, scalloped dec ring supported by ftd pedestal, engraved "Rudolph, Hearts are Trumps," three ball feet, imp "Rogers & Bro., no. 435," discolored, 2-1/2" w, 2-1/2" h $160

Cupids in canoe, unknown maker, two cupids in canoe using arrows as oars, central ring with incised concentric rings, supporting bud vase with flared neck, canoe rests on two bracket feet, ring inscribed "Geo," wear to finish, 4-3/4" w, 3-1/4" h $385

Cupid, terrier and hearts, Reed & Barton, ring with turned rims supported on back of terrier, cupid facing outward, leaning on ring, two hearts atop ring, oval base with fern dec, imp "Mf'd. & Plated by Reed & Barton, 1315," minor wear to finish, 2-1/4" w, 2-3/4" h $750

Dancing women, Pelton, central foliate engraved ring flanked by two women dancing with tambourines, cartouche form base, four ball feet, imp "Pelton Bros. Silver Plate Co., no. 17," slight nick to one side of ring, 2-1/2" w, 2-1/4" h......................**$100**

Dog and bird, Aurora, dog sitting on hind legs, looking at bird with wings raised seated on top of ring, beaded rim, foliate dec, and "Oscar" engraved on ring, imp "Aurora Silver Plate Co., no. 27," wear to finish, 3" w, 2-1/2" h **$95**

Dog and bud vase, Tufts, dog standing on hind legs, one front paw resting on scroll-engraved ring, vasiform bud vase at other side of ring, cartouche form base, imp "J.W. Tufts, Boston, no. 1582," minor spots of wear to finish, 3-3/4" w, 2-3/4" h.................**$285**

Elephant, unknown maker, ring flanked by elephant with raised trunk, raised dec of elephants on ring, considerable wear to finish, 3" w, 2" h **$130**

Eskimo, Meriden, hooded Eskimo holding pole, standing on ice floe, circular base, ring with central plain band flanked by bands of engraved floral dec on ridged ground, imp "Meriden Brittania Company, no. 220," minor pitting to finish, 2-3/4" w, 2-1/2" h......................**$75**

Girl jumping rope, Wilcox, girl jumping rope, ring behind her resting on pierced scroll and floral motif support, ring with plain center band flanked by flared rims, engraved floral and foliate dec, large circular base with tapered sides, dec with flowers and birds, four feet, imp "Wilcox Silver Plate Co., no. 360," nicks to edges of ring, spots of wear to finish, 5" w, 4-1/2" h......................**$375**

Goat, standing goat figure at one side, ring decorated in engraved floral motif, wear, discoloration to finish, 2-1/2" w, 1-3/4" h......................**$95**

Greenaway girl, ring with engraved dec flanked by large Greenaway girl and lily flower, leaves on long upswept stems, one leaf broken off but present, scattered spots of wear to finish, 3-3/4" w, 7-1/8" h......................**$200**

Horse, unknown maker, horse rearing up on its hind legs, front hooves resting on scroll dec ring supported by ball, oval pierced scroll work base, wear to finish, 3-1/2" w, 2-1/2" h **$135**

Knights in armor, Simpson, Hall, Miller, central ring engraved with floral swags, flanked by figures of knights in armor, rect base, imp "Simpson, Hall, Miller & Co., no. 110," minor wear to finish, 2-1/8" w, 1-5/8" h......................**$215**

Lily pad, Acme, lily pads and flowers form base, stem forms loop handle and ring support, ring rests on ball, engraved wheat sheaf and sunburst dec on ring, imp "Acme Silver Company, Canada, no. 729," some loss to finish, 3-1/2" w, 2" h **$230**

Military band, unknown maker, ring supported by pedestal, flanked by three members of military band and flag bearer, circular base, four pad feet, scattered spots of wear to finish, crack in flag, 3-1/2" w, 3-1/4" h **$160**

Parrot, Rogers, parrot sitting on branch where ring is resting, ring with raised rings, engraved floral and geometric dec, imp on ring "Rogers & Bro., no. 228," denting to edge of ring, 3-1/2" w, 2-1/2" h......................**$185**

Peacock, Meriden, peacock standing on ring, engraved floral dec, rect panel inscribed "Charlie," imp "Meriden Britannia Company, no. 151," wear to finish, 2-1/4" w, 3-1/2" h **$400**

Phoenix birds, Simpson, Hall, Miller, ring resting on ftd pedestal, curved handle descending to two phoenix-type birds on either side of ring, ring engraved with scrolling motif forming panel inscribed "Belle," imp "Simpson, Hall, Miller & Co.," 3-1/4" w, 4" h **$200**

Putto
Simpson, Hall, Miller, seated putto, ring at his back, ring engraved with owls in tree branches, octagonal base with raised scrolling dec, imp "Simpson, Hall, Miller & Co., no. 211," minor spots of wear to finish, 3" w, 2" h **$365**
Webster, putti seated at each end of cartouche form base, ring supported on wings, ring with flared rims and central band with engraved dec, imp "E.G. Webster & Bro., no. 170," denting to one edge of ring, 3" w, 2-1/2" h **$130**
Unknown maker, standing putto leaning back on ring with faintly engraved foliate dec, 3" w, 3" h **$420**

Putto, bird and wishbone, unknown maker, ring with engraved foliate

spray resting on wishbone, flanked by songbird on one side and putto on other, minor wear to finish, 3" w, 2" h **$525**

Rampant lion, unknown maker, rampant lion at one side of ring with raised scrollwork rims, 2-1/2" w, 2" h **$265**

Recumbent lion, Meriden, floral dec ring resting on back of lion, rect base, imp on ring "Meriden Britannia Company, no. 152," small base nick, 2-1/2" w, 2-1/4" h......................**$145**

Squirrel with nut, unknown maker, squirrel alongside ring with scrolling rims, both sitting on branch, ring inscribed "Dudley," imp partially obscured, "143_," spotty wear to finish, 3-1/2" w, 2" h......................**$300**

Terrier, unknown maker, terrier at one side, front paws resting on ring with raised scrollwork rims and engraved scroll dec on band, no maker's mark, minor loss to finish, 2" w, 1-1/2" h **$180**

Terrier and bird, Reed & Barton, terrier barking at bird with outstretched wings atop ring, ring with turned rims with egg and dart type dec, fern dec on oval base, imp "Mf'd. & Plated by Reed & Barton, 1110," minor wear to finish, 3-1/4" w, 2" h...............**$250**

Turtles, unknown maker, plain oval ring resting on two fern leaves, flanked by two turtles, imp "75," 3-1/2" w, 2" h......................**$185**

Two boys
Meriden, two boys facing outward, supporting sq ring standing on corner in back-stretched hands, sq base with raised scrolling foliate dec, four ball feet, imp "Meriden Brittania Company, no. 332," 3" w, 3" h **$200**
Middletown, boy leaning on each side of ring engraved with sunburst and scroll dec, imp "Middletown Plate Co., no. 87," wear to finish, 3" w, 2" h **$100**

Two cherubs, seated cherub on each side of barrel form ring on their backs, imp "Meriden Brittania Company, no. 147," wear to finish, 2-3/4" w, 2-1/4" h...................................**$100**

Two foxes, Meriden, two foxes holding birds on either side of ring with ridged rim, turned rings, and central engraved floral dec, panel engraved "Flora," imp "Meriden Silver Plate Company, no. 217," 2-1/2" w, 2" h **$120**

NAUTICAL ITEMS

History: The seas have fascinated man since time began. The artifacts of sailors have been collected and treasured for years. Because of their environment, merchant and naval items, whether factory or handmade, must be of quality construction and long lasting. Many of these items are aesthetically appealing as well.

Account book, *Bark Arab,* showing purchases and sales from October 1853 to December 1856, 96 pgs, folio, New Bedford or Hawaii, label reads "purchased of John Kehew at his Navigation Store in New Bedford," Kehew's label mounted on front paste down, two volumes **$1,955**

Banner, carved and polychrome painted pine, "Don't Give Up The Ship!," American eagle, attributed to John Hales Bellamy, 26" x 8-1/2" **$24,150**

Book

Allyn, Captain Gurdon L., *Old Sailor's Story, or a Short Account of the Life, Adventures, and Voyages, The,* Norwich, 1879, 111 pgs, 8vo, orig flexible cloth wrappers **$316**

Bligh, William, *Dangerous Voyage of Captain Bligh, in an Open Boat, over 1200 Leagues of the Ocean, in the Year 1789,* Dublin, five full-page woodcut engraved illus, 180 pgs, small 12mo, 1818 .... **$345**

Dexter, Elisha, *Narrative of the Loss of the William and Joseph, of Martha's Vineyard,* Boston, five wood engraved plates, 54 pgs, 8vo, 1842 .... **$1,370**

Box, cov, sailor made, walnut and ivory, rect, dovetail construction, hinged, top and sides with turned and carved pendant ring ivory handles ringed with red and black wax, kite-shaped carved ivory escutcheon, oral history relates that this box came from ship named "Carolus," which operated out of Boston, 19th C, 17-3/4" w, 9-1/4" d, 8-5/8" h **$1,765**

Broadside, issued as circular to mariners at Table Bay, Robben Island, advising of berthing procedures, 1827, 415 x 335 mm **$345**

Cane

Carved from single piece of tooth, 1-3/4" d x 2" h whale ivory handle, carved sailor's Turks-head knot, thin baleen spacer separates whalebone shaft, inlaid at top with four-pointed baleen fingers, white whalebone shaft, tapered with very slight natural bow, American, c1850, 32-7/8" l **$2,800**

Flat brass handle 1-3/4" d x 2/3" h , wide all metal black shaft fashioned with metal nubs all along length, when handle pulled off, hollow exposed to reveal watertight compartment to store nautical charts and documents, 3/4" brass ferrule, English, c1890, 36-1/2" l **$450**

Canoe paddle, painted deep red with black crescent moon and star, America, with stand, late 19th C, 60" l **$375**

Chronometer, Eggert & Son, New York, mahogany brass bound double lidded case, brass cased movement with engraved silver dial inscribed "Eggert & Son, NEW YORK, No 276," applied ivory plaque inscribed "Eggert & Son 276 New York," early 19th C, 7-3/4" h **$3,200**

Clock, brass, Seth Thomas, one-day lever-striking movement, circular case, domed bell mounted below on wooden backboard, late 19th C, 10-1/2" h **$520**

Compass, lifeboat, 8" sq, 7-1/4" h, boxed, 20th C **$175**

Crew list, partly printed, two languages, *Jireh Swift,* lists 13 additional Hawaiian crew members, Lahaina, March 29, 1865 .... **$2,000**

Diorama, three-mast clipper, side-wheel paddle steamer, and smaller vessel, 17 men in black coats and top hats manning vessels, two painted lighthouses and dwelling in background, green-blue sky with white painted clouds, c1850, 40" l shadowbox **$6,500**

Figurehead, carved, Nantucket Island origin, c1830, 30" h **$12,000**

Cane, America, whale ivory snake and whalebone, 5" l x 2-1/3" w whale ivory handle made from single tooth, looped snake with head facing downward, red sealing wax eyes, traces of red in open mouth, brass forked tongue, bottom of handle with sq base inlaid with two rosewood panels, centered with mother-of-pearl diamonds, shaft with multiple pieces of whale ivory and black horn fashioned in rings and angles, smooth taper on whalebone shaft, 1-1/2" burnished brass ferrule, c1890, 35-1/2" l, **$10,500.**
Photo courtesy of Henry A. Taron.

Woolwork, English, depicts frigate, maple frame, 19th C, 14" x 17", **$800.**
Photo courtesy of Wiederseim Associates Inc.

Fishing license, issued to sloop *Kial*, for cod fishing, issued in Newport, RI, some edge chipping, fold splitting, April 23, 1808, 16-1/2" x 10-1/2"..........**$165**

Hourglass, 19th C, 7" h..............**$550**

Inclinometer, brass, cased, bubble type, Kelvin Bottomley & Baird Ltd., 4-1/2" d.........................**$65**

Indenture, document indenturing William McGraa to Isaac Fisher as apprentice mariner for four years, details duties, payment schedule, May 19, 1813, signed by all parties, some foxing, edge chipping, 1810 watermark, 16" x 13-1/2" **$100**

Jewelry chest, sailor-carved walnut and whalebone, America, carved rosette, fan, lapped leaf, pendant, and other designs, front and side drawers, hinged lid opens to mirror which further opens to three oval frames with rope trim, box int. fitted with four compartments with carved lids, carved whalebone drawer and lid handles, 19th C, 18-1/4" l, 12-1/2" d, 10-3/8" h....................**$2,350**

Log book, Ship *Geneva*, George M. Tucker, Master, sailed from Boston, March 4, 1852 towards Richmond, later to San Francisco, then to Calcutta, back to Boston where she docked at Central Wharf on Aug. 13, 1853, worn spine, cover **$1,150**

Masthead, copper and brass, oil fired, complete with burner, 360 degrees, late 19th C, 16" h, 9-1/2" d.........**$200**

Membership certificate, certifying "...That Capt. Green Walden was by a majority of votes regularly admitted a member of the Portland Marine Society at a meeting held the 17th day of September 1839...," certificate dec with reserves depicting various marine scenes, toning, foxing, framed, 12-3/8" x 17-1/2".........................**$530**

Model, cased, Schooner Yacht *Laura*, carved and painted, fully rigged, painted metal sails, painted figures, metal and wood details, hull painted black, carved wood "water," America, imperfections, 19th C, 23-5/8" l, 12" w, 16-1/4" h.........................**$1,550**

Oar, curly maple, well carved, thin broad end, good figure, 57-1/2" l **$420**

Painting, oil on canvas, framed
Two-Masted Schooner *Masconnomet* in Marblehead Harbor, flying American flag, figures on pier in foreground, lighthouse in distance, unsigned, identified beneath image,

Sailor's valentine, orig box, belonging to Samaul Clamer, a merchant marine from Elizabeth, New Jersey, on the USS Minneapolis, 9" d, **$3,500.**
Photo courtesy of David Rago Auctions, Inc.

craquelure, scattered retouch to background sky, 17" x 21".....**$3,525**
Ships Before the Doges Palace, sgd "Ziller" lower left (Leopold Ziller), framed, strip lined, repaired punctures, retouch, surface grime, 21-1/4" x 32" **$3,525**
Two-masted schooner off Vinalhaven, ME, sgd "Coombs" lower left, repaired tear, retouch to upper right sky, 22" x 36".................**$4,250**
Sailing ship flying American flag, several fishing boats in rough seas, high cliffs in background, sgd "RJ Dawson 1882," 22-3/4" w x 14-3/4" h period gilt frame with wear, small areas of touch-up, 20" w x 12" h **$1,610**
William, pictured off Dover with Dover Fort pictured under her bowsprit, sgd "R. B. Spencer" lower left, (Richard Barrett Spencer, c1840-74,) ship identified on bow, scattered retouch, lined, 36" x 22" **$6,450**

Quadrant, ebony, cased, marked "D Booth" and "New Zealand".........**$330**

Sail maker's bench, long canvas cov bench, turned splayed legs, one end with compartments and pierced for tools, suspending two canvas pouches, two canvas sacks with sail maker's tools, America, 19th C, 77" l, 16" w, 15" h.............................**$1,765**

Sailor's razor box, carved cherry, rect, heart-shaped handle, chip carved borders, incised sailing vessel on swivel top, 19th C, 10-3/4" l, 1-3/4" w, 1-1/2" h....................**$325**

Sailor's valentine, various exotic shells, "For My Love," very minor losses, 19th C, 9-5/8" octagonal segmented case **$750**

Sea chest, painted, green, lid painted with flags and pennants centered by Union Jack, name "William Bevan" **$2,760**

Ship anchor, cast, iron ring and chain, mounted on later iron brackets, corrosion, 54" w, 106" h...................**$825**

Diorama, American cruiser, early 20th C, **$250.**
Photo courtesy of Wiederseim Associates, Inc.

Nautical lamps, table, brass, made from lanterns, impressed mark "Perko, Perkins Marine Lamp Home Corp, Brooklyn, NY, USA," red glass lamps marked "Corning," 36" h, **$1,200.**
Photo courtesy of Alderfer Auction Co.

Telescope, brass table top, English, mid-19th C, 35" l, 19" h, **$950.**
Photo courtesy of Pook & Pook, Inc.

Ship's binnacle, Northwest Instrument Co., Seattle, WA, brass stand with two lanterns, plaque with Asian lettering, inscribed "No. 4004," break in one lantern, early 20th C, 42" h, **$395.**
Photo courtesy of Alderfer Auction Co.

Ship bell, cast bronze

Raised linear bands, 14" d, 17" h **$560**

Weathered surface, raised "J. Warner & Sons, London, 1855," 13" d, 13-1/2" h **$1,175**

Ship billethead, scrolled foliate design, painted black, green and gilt highlights, minor loss on scroll, cracks, carved wood, 19th C, 24" l, 7-1/2" w **$715**

Ship billetheads, scrolled foliate design, weathered cracked surface, 19th C, carved wood, one 27-1/2" l x 5-1/2" w, second matching example 23" l x 7-1/4" w **$4,995**

Ship builder's half model, America, 19th C

Alternating laminated mahogany and other wood, mounted on walnut panel, 30" l, 6" h **$1,995**

Natural finished pine, black and gilt trim, loose stempost, 42" l, 10-5/8" h **$9,400**

Pine and other woods, mounted on pine panel, 37-1/2" l, 5" h **$1,300**

Ship license

Issued for ship *Aurora*, 303 tons, armed with 14 guns, two swivel guns, 20 muskets, 20 pistols, 20 cutlasses, 20 pikes, minor edge chipping, Nov. 4, 1912, 12-1/2" x 8" **$135**

Issued to the ship *Nancy* of Newfoundland, two guns weighing 222 tons, issued by High Admiral, masthead scene of allegorical figures and chip, scallop cut top, minor soiling, April 24, 1812, 18" x 11-1/2" ... **$450**

Shipping circular, concerning marine papers lost, stolen, or taken by force on various ships, issued to port collector of Bristol, federal eagle watermark, some chipping, fold splitting, sgd by Clerk of Marine Records of the Treasury Dept, March 31, 1810, 15-1/2" x 9-1/2" **$35**

Ship wheel, various hardwoods, turned spokes, iron reinforced center hub, 48" d **$350**

Stern board, Hesperus, New England, rect form, rounded ends, chamfered edges, chiseled carved letters flanked by star, painted white on black ground, imperfections, 19th C, 7-3/4" h, 66" l **$980**

Telescope, silver plated, one draw, Troughton & Simms, London, orig leather casing, inscription reads "Presented by the British Government, Captain Christopher Crowell, Master of the American Ship 'Highland Light'

of Boston, in acknowledgment of his humanity and kindness to the Master and the Crew of the Barque 'Queen of Sheba' when he rescued from their waterlogged vessel, on the 16th, December 1861," damage to leather, mid-19th C, 32-3/4" l **$980**

Trump indicator, brass and copper, ship's wheel, spinning center orb, 4-1/2" x 3-1/2" **$85**

Walking stick, wood, ivory knop, silver band on shaft engraved "U.S. Frigate Constitution 1797, J.L.S.," brass and iron tip, age cracks on ivory, wear, 35" l **$1,295**

Watercolor on paper

Ship Portrait of the U.S.S. Constitution, unsigned, American School, taken from a ship's log, with Ruse & Turner's watermark, early 19th C, 9-1/2" h, 11-1/4" l **$1,000**

Study of steamboat on desolate river during winter, snow topped mountain in background, light shades of brown and blue, matted with gilt floral frame, minor surface wear, sgd "Mc E. Dun 1899," 14" h, 20" w **$300**

NETSUKES

History: The traditional Japanese kimono has no pockets. Daily necessities, such as money and tobacco supplies, were carried in leather pouches, or inros, which hung from a cord with a netsuke toggle. The word netsuke comes from "ne"—to root—and "tsuke"— to fasten.

Netsukes originated in the 14th century and initially were favored by the middle class. By the mid-18th century, all levels of Japanese society used them. Some of the most famous artists, e.g., Shuzan and Yamada Hojitsu, worked in the netsuke form.

Netsukes average from 1 to 2 inches in length and are made from wood, ivory, bone, ceramics, metal, horn, nutshells, etc. The subject matter is broad based, but always portrayed in a lighthearted, humorous manner. A netsuke must have smooth edges and balance in order to hang correctly on the sash.

Reproduction Alert. Recent reproductions are on the market. Many are carved from African ivory.

Notes: Value depends on artist, region, material, and skill of craftsmanship. Western collectors favor katabori, pieces which represent an identifiable object.

Antler, carved

Foreigner or monk holding trumpet pendant from his right hand, facing upward, hair curling on his back, stained details, himotoshi carved on back, unsigned, Japan, 18th or 19th C, 2-1/2" h **$1,275**

Kwanyu holding halberd in right hand, tugging his beard with his left hand, himotoshi on back, stained details, traces of red pigment on face and vestments, legs carved from separate piece and inserted, good patina and wear, Japan, hole drilled in left foot, small cavity on left leg, 18th C, 3" h **$500**

Corozo nut, carved, basket of flowers, handle at center dividing flowers, small areas of openwork, bottom with attached metal ring himotoshi, Japan, crack along top, 19th C, 1-1/8" h **$125**

Horn, carved, Hannya mask, sgd on back between himotoshi, stained detail, hole at top of head, Japan, 19th C, 2" h **$70**

Ivory, carved

Bearded man holding pumpkin over his left shoulder, flatly carved figure, good patina, worn details, himotoshi on back, unsigned, Japan, age cracks, 18th C, 2-7/8" h **$320**

Boy carrying branch laden with precious things, puppy at left foot, sgd "Tomochikia," Japan, small crack on shoulder, 19th C, 1-1/2" l **$700**

Boy holding rooster, stained details, himotoshi carved on back, Japan, c1900, 1-1/2" h **$200**

Dutchman holding monkey in his arms, details lightly stained, himotoshi spaced wide apart, one hole on back, other carved under his cat, sgd "Takusai" on back, Japan, 18th C, 2-7/8" h **$2,600**

Foo dog, single hole himotoshi, Japan, age cracks, 18th or 19th C, 1-5/8" h **$150**

Frog, sitting on rock with splashing water, turning to right, facing upwards, lightly stained details, himotoshi and sgd on base, mounted as ring with braided gold colored metal wire of varying shapes, Japan, 19th C, 2" h **$300**

Netsuke, wood carving, seated man with bowl over his face, signed, 1" h, **$250.**

Frog, stylized, comical, long thin body, elongated snout, inlaid eyes, himotoshi and signature on base, Japan, age cracks, 19th or 20th C, 3-1/8" h **$125**

Fukurokuju clipping his toenails, child on left side, stained detail, sgd "Gyokko" on rect on base, Japan, Meiji period, crack in face, 1-3/4" h **$460**

Goat, standing, head turned sharply to right, front leg slightly raised, arched back with cascading fleece, left horn conforming to curve of neck, lightly stained, himotoshi carved on back, Japan, repairs to legs, details slightly worn, good patina, small age cracks, 18th C, 2-3/16" h **$5,200**

Horse, grazing, stained detail, himotoshi carved on back, unsigned, Japan, 18th or 19th C **$550**

Manju, rect, carved frog among persimmons and leaves, carved insect damage on leaves, himotoshi formed by interlacing branches, stained detail, Japan, Meiji period, 1-1/2" l **$375**

Man and child with basket of fruit, himotoshi and signature carved on base, Japan, c1900, 1-5/8" h **$200**

Octopus crawling out of large pot, himotoshi and signature on back, Gyokuzan, Japan, 19th C, 1-5/8" h **$300**

Okame, sitting position, stained hair and robe, himotoshi carved at her back, sgd, Japan, early 20th C **$200**

Oni carrying woman on back, stained detail, Japan, Meiji period, 2" h **$375**

Oni embracing drum with inlaid studs, inlaid metal eyes, signature on underside of drum, some staining detail, Japan, Meiji period, 1-1/2" l **$1,265**

Rect, dragon among clouds, large holes forming himotoshi, Japan, 19th C, age cracks **$100**

Netsuke, Masatoshi, Japan, finely carved ebony, wild boar with its young, signed in oval reserve, contemporary, 1" x 2", **$1,700.**
Photo courtesy of David Rago Auctions, Inc.

Three blind men grappling with each other, himotoshi formed as part of design, slightly stained detail, sgd on base, Japan, normal age cracks, Meiji period, 1-1/2" l **$1,495**

Three men wrestling snake, unsigned, Japan, some losses, 19th C, 2-3/4" l **$250**

Tiger, recumbent, body curled to left, fierce expression, sinuous tail resting on back, inlaid eyes, himotoshi and sgd "Tomotada" on base, Japan, 19th C, 2-1/8" h **$400**

Turtle carrying young on its back, sgd on bottom, Japan, damage to back foot, early 20th C, 2" l **$100**

Two figures inside cavern, tengu above, single hole himotoshi, sgd on base, Japan, Meiji period, 1-1/2" h **$750**

Two happy sages, himotoshi carved on back, unsigned, Japan, 18th or 19th C, 2" h **$450**

Ivory and wood, carved, man and child, man with toy in left hand, sgd in small red tablet on base, Japan, Meiji period, 1-1/2" h **$320**

Porcelain, shishimai dancer, child holding lion mask above his head, painted over glaze enamels, himotoshi on back, Japan, possibly Kutani, Meiji period, small chip, 2-1/4" h **$125**

Staghorn, Manju, carved Kinko sennin on carp, 19th C, 2-1/2" d **$200**

Wood, carved

Crouched figure holding basket with peach, homotshi carved on base, good color and patina, Japan, details slightly worn, 19th C, 1" h **$200**

Foreigner, left arm twisted sharply behind his back, supporting child perched on right shoulder, right hand holding trumpet, himotoshi on back, lacquered, unsigned, Japan, areas of wear to lacquer, 18th C, 3-1/4" h **$1,400**

Fox wearing robe with long sleeves, pulling large laden sack, inlaid

Netsuke, Japanese Umimatsu, frog, Iuwami school, 1-1/4" h, **$650.**
Photo courtesy of Sloans & Kenyon Auctioneers and Appraisers.

horn eyes, tail curling underneath to form himotoshi, sgd on base, stained with even brown patination, Japan, Meiji period, 2" l **$920**

NUTTING, WALLACE

History: Wallace Nutting (1861-1941) was America's most famous photographer of the early 20th century. A retired minister, Nutting took more than 50,000 pictures, keeping 10,000 of his best and destroying the rest. His popular and best-selling scenes included "Exterior Scenes," apple blossoms, country lanes, orchards, calm streams, and rural American countrysides; "Interior Scenes," usually featuring a colonial woman working near a hearth; and "Foreign Scenes," typically thatch-roofed cottages. Those pictures that were least popular in his day have become the rarest and most-highly collectible today and are classified as "Miscellaneous Unusual Scenes." This category encompasses such things as animals, architecturals, children, florals, men, seascapes, and snow scenes.

Nutting sold literally millions of his hand-colored platinotype pictures between 1900 and his death in 1941. Starting first in Southbury, Connecticut, and later moving his business to Framingham, Massachusetts, the peak of Wallace Nutting's picture production was 1915 to 1925. During this period, Nutting employed nearly 200 people, including colorists, darkroom staff, salesmen, and assorted office personnel. Wallace Nutting pictures proved to be a huge commercial success and hardly an American household was without one by 1925.

Nutting, Wallace, chair, Windsor, #410, comb back, early paper label, 39" h, **$850.**

Photos courtesy of Michael Ivankovich Auction Co., Inc.

While attempting to seek out the finest and best early-American furniture as props for his colonial Interior Scenes, Nutting became an expert in American antiques. He published nearly 20 books in his lifetime, including his 10-volume State Beautiful series and various other books on furniture, photography, clocks, and his autobiography. He also contributed many photographs published in magazines and books other than his own.

Nutting also became widely known for his reproduction furniture. His furniture shop produced literally hundreds of different furniture forms: clocks, stools, chairs, settles, settees, tables, stands, desks, mirrors, beds, chests of drawers, cabinet pieces, and treenware.

The overall synergy of the Wallace Nutting name, pictures, books, and furniture, has made anything "Wallace Nutting" quite collectible.

Marks: Wallace Nutting furniture is clearly marked with his distinctive paper label, glued directly onto the piece, or with a block or script signature brand, which was literally branded into his furniture.

Notes: "Process Prints" are 1930s' machine-produced reprints of 12 of Nutting's most popular pictures. These have minimal value and can be detected by using a magnifying glass.

Adviser: Michael Ivankovich.

The name Wallace Nutting usually makes folks think of fine hand-colored photographs. However, Mr. Nutting also created wonderful pieces of furniture, many based on the most revered antiques of his day. One such piece, known as the #992 Savery Highboy was sold this year by auctioneer Michael Ivankovich. The mahogany highboy featured interesting intricate carving on both the top and base, a high scrolled pediment, and well proportioned cabriole legs. Created in 1932, the original asking price was $1,230. At Ivankovich's September auction, the highboy offered, with both a branded block signature and original paper label, brought $30,000.

Books

American Windsors	**$50**
England Beautiful, 1st ed.	**$60**
Furniture of the Pilgrim Century, 1st ed.	**$100**
Furniture Treasury, Vol. I	**$100**
Furniture Treasury, Vol. II	**$100**
Furniture Treasury, Vol. III	**$100**
Ireland Beautiful, 2nd ed.	**$40**
Pathways of the Puritans	**$65**
Social Life In Old New England	**$60**

State Beautiful Series

Connecticut Beautiful, 1st ed.	**$45**
Maine Beautiful, 1st ed.	**$45**
Massachusetts Beautiful, 2nd ed.	**$45**
New Hampshire Beautiful, 1st ed.	**$45**
New York Beautiful, 1st ed., 1927, grade 3.5	**$30**
Pennsylvania Beautiful, 1st ed, 1924, grade 4.0	**$45**
Pennsylvania Beautiful, 2nd ed, 1935, grade 4.0	**$35**
Vermont Beautiful, 2nd ed.	**$35**
Virginia Beautiful, 1st ed.	**$50**

Calendar, Webb House interior scene, orig mat and pen signature, period frame with older, but not orig backing paper, grade 4.0, c1915-25, 5" x 7" **$100**

Catalog, Wallace Nutting Reproduction Furniture, final edition, grade 4.0, 1937 .... **$85**

Furniture

Candle Stand, #17, Windsor, tripod base, punched brand, grade 4.0, 14" d, 25" h **$550**

Chair
#410, Windsor, comb back, arm, grade 3.5, 39" h **$850**
#440, Windsor, writing arm, Pennsylvania turnings, drawer beneath seat, block brand **$1,500**
#464, Carver, arm, script brand **$700**
#475, Flemish, arm, block brand **$1,200**
#490/#390, ladderback, two #490 arm chairs, two #390 side chairs, grade 3.75, price for set of four **$1,000**

Cupboard, #923, pine, scrolled **$4,000**

Highboy, #992, Savery, mahogany, block branded signature, paper label **$30,000**

High Chair, liftable food tray, New England turnings, orig light maple finish, block branded signature **$1,500**

Mirror, 8" x 6" orig mat with hand colored untitled interior New England scene, pen signature, c1915-25, 13-1/2" x 22" frame **$275**

Settee, #515, triple bow back, ten legs, New England turnings, knuckle arms, 89" w, 18" d, unmarked, grade 4.0 .... **$1,500**

Stool, #102, Windsor, block brand **$400**

Table
#613, tavern, 36" w, 25-1/2" d, 27-1/2" h, paper label, grade 4.0 .... **$850**
#619, crane bracket **$750**
#628b, Pembroke, mahogany **$1,500**

Greeting card, Mother's Day, hand colored photo of Grandmother's Garden, copyright on back, grade 4.0, c1925-30, 4-1/2" x 5-1/2" **$75**

Ironwork, potato cooker, imp mark on handle **$1,500**

Picture, hand-colored photo, framed
A Barre Brook, orig mat, pen signature, and title, orig frame, orig backing paper mostly intact, grade 4.0, c1915-25, 22" x 15" **$175**
A Birch Grove, orig mat, pen signature and title, new backing paper, grade 4.0, c1915-25, 15" x 13" period frame **$125**

A Bit of Sewing, Southbury, CT, orig mat, pen signature, and title, orig frame, orig baking paper mostly intact, grade 4.0, c1905-10, 13" x 10"..**$175**

A Call For More, orig mat, pen signature and title, grade 4.0, c1915-25, 12" x 10" orig frame having no backing paper **$250**

A Checkered Road, Pennsylvania, orig mat, pen signature and title, grade 3.75, c1930-35, 11" x 9" orig frame with new backing paper **$300**

A Colonial Belle, orig mat, pen signature and title, new backing paper, grade 4.0, c1915-25, framed in 14" x 10" two handled serving tray **$250**

A Colonial Stair, orig mat, pencil signature and title, new backing paper, grade 4.0, c1905-10, 10" x 16" orig frame **$195**

A Delicate Stitch, orig mat, pen signature and title, new backing paper, cropped mat, grade 3.5, c1915-25, 14" x 11" new frame,..................**$80**

Affectionately Yours, orig mat, pen signature and title, no backing paper, grade 4.25, c1915-25, 14" x 11" orig frame..........................**$135**

A Franconia Brook, NH, orig mat, pen signature and title, orig frame, orig backing paper, grade 4.0, c1915-25, 10" x 12".................**$135**

A Garden Enclosed, orig mat, pencil signature and title, older/orig backing paper, slightly dark mat, grade 3.75, c1905-10, 12" x 16" orig frame **$295**

A Garden of Larkspur, England, orig mat, pen signature, and title, orig frame with orig backing paper, grade 4.0, c1915-25, 10" x 12" **$135**

A Golden River, orig mat, pen signature and title, new back paper, grade 3.75, c1915-25, 16" x 13" orig frame **$100**

A Little River, orig mat, pen signature and title, new backing paper, grade 3.75, c1915-25, 17" x 12" orig frame **$75**

A May Drive, orig mat, pen signature, and title, orig frame, newer backing paper, grade 4.0, c1915-25, 17 x 14" **$150**

An Old Back Door, orig mat, pen signature and title, grade 3.75, slightly dark mat, c1915-25, 11" x 14" orig frame..........................**$135**

Nutting, Wallace, Trimming the bonnet, *woman seated by fireplace,* **$65.**

An Old Time Romance, orig mat, pen signature and title, orig backing paper, grade 4.0, c1915-25, 17" x 14" orig frame **$175**

A Patriarch in Bloom, close framed, orig pen signature lower right on image, orig backing paper, orig copyright label, grade 4.0, c1930-35, 19" x 15" orig frame **$175**

A Perkiomen October, orig mat, pen signature and title, orig backing paper, orig copyright label, grade 4.0, c1930-35, 16" x 13" orig frame **$200**

A Pilgrim Daughter, orig mat, pen signature and title, new backing paper, grade 3.5, c1915-25, 15" x 12" orig frame **$125**

A Roadside Brook, orig mat, pen signature, and title, orig frame, newer backing paper, grade 4.0, c1915-25, 11" x 17" **$150**

A Springfield Curve, orig mat, pen signature and title, grade 3.25, c1915-25, 11" x 9" orig frame **$65**

At the Fender, orig mat, pencil signature and title, early orig round Wallace Nutting Southbury label preserved on the back, new backing paper, grade 3.75, c1905-10, 17" x 14" orig frame..........................**$175**

At Paul Revere's Tavern, orig mat, pen signature and title, new backing paper, grade 3.75, c1915-25, 15" x 13" period frame **$250**

A Tufted Shore, orig mat, pen signature and title, grade 4.0, c1915-25, 15" x 12" period frame,...........**$100**

A Tunnel of Bloom, Berkshires, MA, orig mat, pen signature, and title, orig frame, newer backing paper, grade 4.0, c1915-25, 18" x 22" **$175**

A Virginia Reel, orig mat, pen signature and title, grade 3.5, some mat foxing, c1915-25, 16" x 14" orig frame **$90**

Awaiting the Hostess, orig mat, pencil signature and title, new backing

Nutting, Wallace, table, tavern, ball turned legs and stretchers, paper label, 36" w, 25-1/2" d, 27-1/2" h, **$650.**

paper, grade 4.0, c1905-10, 14" x 11" older frame **$150**

A Warm Spring Day, orig mat, pen signature and title, no backing paper, grade 3.5, c1915-25, 30" x 22" orig frame..........................**$130**

A Woodland Cathedral, orig mat, pen signature and title, no backing paper, grade 3.0, cropped mat, c1915-25, 8" x 16" orig frame **$45**

Billows of Blossom, orig mat, pen signature and title, orig backing paper, grade 4.0, c1915-25, 20" x 16" orig frame..........................**$90**

Blossomed Bordered, New England, exterior scene, orig mat, pen signature and title, orig frame with newer backing paper, grade 4.0, c1915-25, 17" x 14"..........................**$185**

Blossom Point, orig mat, pen signature and title, (possibly by Wallace Nutting himself,) grade 3.5, c1915-25, 11" x 9" orig frame **$100**

Broken Lights, orig mat, pen signature and title, new backing paper, grade 3.75, c1905-10, 14" x 20" frame **$70**

California Garden, orig mat, pen signature and title, old backing paper, grade 4.0, c1915-25, 9" x 7" orig frame **$110**

Choosing a Bonnet, orig mat, pencil signature and title, old backing paper, dark mat, grade 3.0, c1905-10, 12" x 14" orig frame **$90**

Comfort and a Cat, orig mat, pencil signature and title, 1new backing paper, grade 3.75, c1905-10, 7" x 14" orig frame **$225**

Coming Out of Rosa, orig mat, pen signature and title, new backing paper, grade 3.0, c1915-25, 17" x 14" orig frame **$65**

Decked as a Bride, Massachusetts, orig mat, pen signature, and title, orig frame with newer backing paper, grade 4.0, c1915-25, 14" x 11"..**$175**

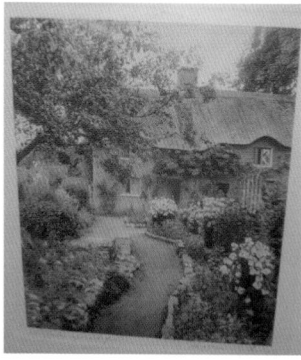

Nutting, Wallace, photo, hand colored, Garden of Larkspur, England, *original mat, pen signature and title, 20" x 24" original frame with original baking paper, c1915-25,* **$165.**

Dell Dale Road, Mystic, CT, orig mat, pen signature, and title, orig frame, no backing paper, grade 4.0, c1915-25, 14" x 11".................**$185**

Dutch Knitting Lesson, orig pen signature lower left on image, orig backing paper, grade 4.0, c1930-35, 3" x 4" orig frame **$120**

Ellicott City, black and white, orig mat, pen signature and title, new backing paper, grade 4.0, c1930, 16" x 13" new frame.......................**$500**

Five O'clock, England, orig mat, pen signature and title, orig backing paper, grade 4.0, c1915-25, 22" x 13" orig frame....................**$130**

Grandmother's Garden, orig mat, pen signature, and title, orig frame, no backing paper, grade 4.0, c1915-25, 12" x 10".......................**$235**

Harbinger's of Spring, orig mat, pen signature and title, orig backing paper with orig copyright label, grade 3.75, c1930-35, 13" x 16" orig frame...........................**$190**

Height of Spring, orig mat, pen signature and title, new backing paper, grade 3.75, c1915-25, 11" x 14" orig frame...........................**$55**

Hollyhock Cottage, England, orig mat, pen signature, and title, orig backing paper, grade 4.0, c1915-25, 17" x 14".........................**$250**

Honeymoon Cottage, pen signature lower right on image, orig copyright label on back, orig backing paper, grade 2.75, minor image flaking, c1930-35, 30" x 20" orig frame **$110**

Honeymoon Stroll, orig mat, pen signature and title, new backing

paper, grade 3.75, c1915-25, 14" x 12" older frame..................**$50**

In Tenderleaf, orig mat, pen signature and title, no backing paper, grade 3.5, c1915-25, 12" x 16" orig frame...........................**$25**

In Upland New England, orig mat, pencil signature and title, new backing paper, grade 4.0, c1905-10, 15" x 10" orig frame,........**$80**

Joy Path, England, orig mat, pen signature and title, orig frame with orig backing paper, grade 4.0, c1930-35, 9" x 11"..................**$175**

Larkspur, orig frame, newer backing paper, grade 4.0, 11" x 14".......**$195**

Life of the Golden Age, orig mat, pen signature and title, no backing paper, grade 4.25, c1915-25, 17" x 13" orig frame.........................**$200**

Mountain Born, High Falls, NY, orig mat, pen signature and title, orig frame with orig backing paper, grade 4.0, c1930-35, 9" x 11"...............................**$175**

Neighborhood News, orig mat, pen signature, and title, period frame, newer backing paper, slightly cropped mat, grade 3.75, c1915-25, 18" x 15".........................**$350**

Old Wentworth Days, orig mat, pen signature and title, new backing paper, grade 3.75, c1915-25, 14" x 17" orig frame **$100**

On the Slope, orig mat, pen signature and title, no backing paper, grade 3.5, c1915-25, 16" x 10" orig frame....................................**$80**

Patti's Favorite Walk, orig mat, pen signature and title, no backing paper, grade 4.0, c1915-25, 12" x 10" orig frame.........................**$80**

Pine Pool, CT, orig mat, pen signature, and title, orig frame with older but not orig backing paper, c1915-25, 14" x 17" **$195**

Purity, Lake Mohonk, NY, exterior scene, orig mat, pen signature and title, orig frame with older (not orig) backing paper,, grade 4.0, c1915-25, 12" x 20"..................**$195**

Shimmering Gold, orig mat, pen signature and title, newer backing paper, grade 4.0, c1915-25, 15" x 12" period frame..................**$70**

Stepping Heavenward, orig mat, pen signature and title, no backing paper, grade 4.5, c1930-35, 16" x 20" orig frame **$600**

Stepping Stones at Bolton Abbey, orig mat, pen signature and title, new backing paper, grade 3.75,

c1915-25, 20" x 14" orig frame **$350**

Sunday Afternoon in the Old Home, 1902 block copyright lower left on image, orig pat, pen signature, new backing paper, cropped mat, grade 3.5, 9" x 7" orig frame **$70**

Sylvan Dell, orig mat, pen signature, and title, orig frame, older but not backing paper, grade 4.0, c1915-25, 10" x 16".........................**$185**

Swirling Seas, close-framed, orig pen signature lower right on image, orig title lower left on image, title, no backing paper, grade 4.0, c1910-20, 40" x 20" orig frame **$100**

Tea at Yorktown Parlor, orig mat, pen signature and title, orig backing paper, grade 4.0, c1915-25, 16" x 10" orig frame **$100**

Tea for Two, Wentworth-Gardiner House, Portsmouth, NH, orig mat, pen signature, and title, orig frame, newer backing paper, grade 4.0, c1915-25, 17" x 14"..................**$295**

The Ancestral Cradle, cat scene, close framed, unsigned, untitled, newer backing paper, grade 2.75, minor image damage, c1915-25, 28" x 18" orig frame..................**$80**

The Bennington Jar, orig signature lower right on image, orig backing paper, orig copyright label, grade 4.0, c1930-35, 8" x 10" orig frame **$375**

The Canal Road, orig mat, pen signature and title, old backing paper, grade 4.0, c1915-25, 14" x 11" orig frame **$120**

The Coming out of Rosa, child holding Mother's hand, orig mat, pen signature, and title, orig backing paper, grade 4.0, c1915-25, 17" x 14".........................**$325**

The Great Wayside Oak, Sudbury, MA, orig mat, pen signature, and title, orig frame, newer backing paper, grade 4.0, c1915-25, 14" x 11".........................**$275**

The Hurrying Saranac, orig mat, pen signature and title, no backing paper, grade 4.0, c1915-25, 10" x 12" orig frame **$50**

The Langdon Door, Portsmouth, NH, orig mat, pencil signature and title, older backing paper, grade 3.5, cropped mat, c1905-10, 11" x 14" orig frame **$70**

The Maple Sugar Cupboard, orig mat, pen signature and title, new backing paper, grade 4.25, c1915-25, 20" x 16" orig frame **$130**

The Meeting of the Ways, orig mat, pen signature and title, newer backing paper, grade 4.0, c1915-25, 17" x 11" orig frame.................. **$100**

The Mills at the Turn, Holland, orig mat, pen signature and title, no backing paper, grade 3.5, c1915-25, 12" x 10" orig frame................. **$80**

The Nashua Asleep, orig mat, pen signature and title, older backing paper, orig copyright label, grade 4.0, c1930-35, 16" x 13" orig frame.................................. **$150**

The Natural Bridge, orig mat, pen signature and title, new backing paper, grade 4.0, c1915-25, 9" x 12" orig frame.............................. **$90**

The Old Sugar Mill Florida, orig mat, pencil signature and title, new backing paper, grade 4.0, c1905-10, 10" x 12" period frame........... **$300**

The Pergola, Amalfi, Italy, orig mat, pen signature and title, new backing paper, grade 3.75, c1915-25, 14" x 12" orig frame............... **$130**

The Saucy Bonnet, orig mat, pen signature and title, orig backing paper, grade 4.0, c1905, 14" x 9" orig frame............................. **$190**

The Settle Nook, orig mat, pen signature (possibly by Wallace Nutting) and title, new backing paper, grade 3.75, c1915-25, 17" x 13" orig frame............................. **$110**

The Spinet Corner, orig mat, pen signature and title, no backing paper, grade 4.0, c1915-25, 14" x 11" orig frame............................. **$90**

The Youth of the Saco, orig mat, pen signature and title, orig backing paper, orig copyright label, grade 4.0, c1930-35, 16" x 13" orig frame.................................. **$160**

Untitled exterior, Connecticut, orig mat, pen signature and title, orig backing paper, grade 4.0, c1915-25, 9" x 7" orig frame.............. **$35**

Untitled exterior, Heart of Maine, orig mat and pen signature, orig backing paper, grade 4.0, c1915-25, 7" x 9" orig frame.......................... **$35**

Untitled exterior, New England, orig mat, pen signature, grade 3.75, c1930-35, 6-1/2" x 8" orig frame.. **$40**

Untitled exterior, New Hampshire, orig backing paper, grade 4.0, c1930-35, 8" x 6-1/2" orig frame.. **$65**

Untitled girls at house, orig mat, pen signature, no backing paper, grade

4.0, c1915-25, 8" x 10" new frame............................... **$45**

Untitled, Honeymoon Windings, MA, orig mat and pen signature, orig frame with orig backing paper, grade 4.0, c1930-35, 8" x 6-1/2".................. **$110**

Untitled interior, Massachusetts, possibly re-signed in pencil, new backing paper, grade 3.0, c1915-25, 10" x 8" orig frame...................... **$25**

Untitled interior, New England, orig frame, newer backing paper, grade 4.0, c1915-25...................... **$25**

Untitled interior, Wentworth-Gardiner House, Portsmouth, NH, new backing paper, grade 4.0, c1915-25, 9" x 8" orig frame...................... **$45**

Untitled, man in red jacket, Vermont, pen "WN" signature, old backing paper, slightly dark mat, minor veneer frame chip, grade 3.75, c1915-25 orig mat, 5" x 7" orig frame.............................. **$110**

Untitled, snow scene, NH, A New Hampshire Roadside,orig mat, pen signature, orig frame with newer backing paper, grade 4.0, c1915-25, 9" x 7".................................. **$475**

Upper Winooski, orig mat, pen signature and title, orig backing paper, grade 4.25, c1915-25, 16" x 10" orig frame........................... **$175**

Watchful Waiting, orig mat, pen signature and title, new backing paper, grade 2.75, overmat and image spot, c1915-25, 17" x 14" orig frame........................... **$50**

Westfield Water, orig mat, pen signature and title, new backing paper, grade 3.75, c1915-25, 15" x 22" period frame........................... **$70**

With Fingers and Toes, black and white, orig mat, pencil signature and title, new backing paper, grade 4.0, c1905, 14" x 11" orig frame............................... **$3,750**

Zinnias, copyright lower right on image, grade 3.0 with over mat, c1930-35, 14" x 18" older frame................................... **$150**

Silhouettes

George and Martha Washington, 3" x 4"............................. **$75**

Girl and Birdcage, copyright lower left, grade 4.0, c1927, 4" x 4" frame............................. **$35**

Girl at Birdbath, grade 4.0, c1927, 4" x 4" new frame................. **$50**

Girl at Vanity Desk, 4" x 4".......... **$50**

Girl by Garden Urn, 4" x 4".......... **$45**

Girl by Spider Web, 5" x 4".......... **$60**

Girl on Fence, new frame, new backing paper, grade 4.0, c1927, 4" x 4"........................... **$35**

Girl Sniffs Flowers, grade 4.0, c1927, 4" x 4" frame............... **$35**

Girl with Flowers, grade 4.0, c1927, 4" x 4" newer frame,............... **$35**

Mary's Lamb, two handled mahogany pin tray, copyright lower left and "EJD" lower right, grade 4.0, c1927, 7" x 8"............................. **$65**

WALLACE NUTTING-LIKE PHOTOGRAPHERS

History: Although Wallace Nutting was widely recognized as the country's leading producer of hand-colored photographs during the early 20th century, he was by no means the only photographer selling this style of picture. Throughout the country literally hundreds of regional photographers were selling hand-colored photographs from their home regions or travels. The subject matter of these photographers was comparable to Nutting's, including Interior, Exterior, Foreign, and Miscellaneous Unusual scenes.

Several photographers operated large businesses, and, although not as large or well known as Wallace Nutting, they sold a substantial volume of pictures which can still be readily found today. The vast majority of their work was photographed in their home regions and sold primarily to local residents or visiting tourists. It should come as little surprise that three of the major Wallace Nutting-like photographers—David Davidson, Fred Thompson, and the Sawyer Art Co.—each had ties to Wallace Nutting.

Hundreds of other smaller local and regional photographers attempted to market hand-colored pictures comparable to Wallace Nutting's during the period of 1900 to the 1930s. Although quite attractive, most were not as appealing to the general public as Wallace Nutting pictures. However, as the price of Wallace Nutting pictures has escalated, the work of these lesser-known Wallace Nutting-like photographers have become increasingly collectible.

A partial listing of some of these minor Wallace Nutting-like photographers includes: Babcock; J. C. Bicknell; Blair; Ralph Blood (Portland, Maine); Bragg; Brehmer; Brooks; Burrowes; Busch; Carlock; Pedro Cacciola; Croft; Currier; Depue Brothers; Derek; Dowly; Eddy; May Farini (hand-colored colonial lithographs); George Forest; Gandara; Gardner (Nantucket, Bermuda, Florida); Gibson; Gideon; Gunn; Bessie Pease Gutmann (hand-colored colonial lithographs); Edward Guy; Harris; C. Hazen; Knoffe; Haynes (Yellowstone Park); Margaret Hennesey; Hodges; Homer; Krabel; Kattleman; La Bushe; Lake; Lamson (Portland, Maine); M. Lightstrum; Machering; Rossiler Mackinae; Merrill; Meyers; William Moehring; Moran; Murrey; Lyman Nelson; J. Robinson Neville (New England); Patterson; Own Perry; Phelps; Phinney; Reynolds; F. Robbins; Royce; Frederick Scheetz (Philadelphia, Pennsylvania); Shelton, Standley (Colorado); Stott; Summers; Esther Svenson; Florence Thompson; Thomas Thompson; M. A. Trott; Sanford Tull; Underhill; Villar; Ward; Wilmot; Edith Wilson; and Wright.

Advisor: Michael Ivankovich.

Notes: The key determinants of value include the collectibility of the particular photographer, subject matter, condition, and size. Exterior Scenes are the most common.

Keep in mind that only the rarest pictures, in the best condition, will bring top prices. Discoloration and/or damage to the picture or matting can reduce value significantly.

Sawyer, Charles, The Swimming Pool, hand-colored photo, original mat, pen signature, and title, 16" x 20" original frame, c1915-25, **$165.**

Photos courtesy of Michael Ivankovich Auction Co., Inc.

David Davidson

Second to Nutting in overall production, Davidson worked primarily in the Rhode and Southern Massachusetts area. While a student at Brown University around 1900, Davidson learned the art of hand-colored photography from Wallace Nutting, who happened to be the Minister at Davidson's church. After Nutting moved to Southbury in 1905, Davidson graduated from Brown and started a successful photography business in Providence, Rhode Island, which he operated until his death in 1967.

A Puritan Lady	$70
A Real D.A.R.	$150
Berkshire Sunset	$60
Christmas Day	$160
Driving Home The Cows	$120

Ebbing Tide, orig mat, pen signature and title, grade 4.0, c1915-25, 11" x 14" orig frame ... **$75**

Heart's Desire	$35
Her House In Order	$75
Old Ironsides	$125
On A News Hunt	$120
Plymouth Elm	$50

Sunset Point, orig mat, pen signature and title, orig gold Davidson paper label, grade 4.0, c1930-35, 5" x 4" orig frame ... **$45**

The Enchanted Window, orig backing, mat discoloration, grade 3.75, c1915-25, 16" x 13" orig frame ... **$45**

The Village Prattlers, New England, grade 4.0, c1910-20, 13" x 16" orig frame ... **$50**

Untitled snow scene, orig mat, pen signature, illegible faded title, new backing paper, two Davidson labels preserved on back, grade 3.75, c1915-25, 7" x 5" orig frame ... **$60**

Sawyer

A father and son team, Charles H. Sawyer and Harold B. Sawyer, operated the very successful Sawyer Art Company from 1903 until the 1970s. Beginning in Maine, the Sawyer Art Company moved to Concord, New Hampshire, in 1920 to be closer to their primary market—New Hampshire's White Mountains. Charles H. Sawyer briefly worked for Nutting from 1902 to 1903 while living in southern Maine. Sawyer's production volume ranks third behind Wallace Nutting and David Davidson.

A February Morning	$175
A New England Sugar Birth	$350
At the Bend of the Road	$35
Crystal Lake	$65
Echo Lake, Franconia Notch	$50
Indian Summer	$35
Lake Morey	$60
Lake Willoughby	$60
Mt. Washington in October	$75
Old Man of the Mountains	$75
Original Dennison Plant	$100

San Juan Capistrano Mission, CA, orig mat, pen signature and title, new backing paper, orig Sawyer label preserved on back, grade 4.0, cropped mat, c1920-30, 6-1/2" x 8-1/2" period frame ... **$150**

The Meadow Stream ... **$75**

The Swimming Pool, orig mat, pen signature and title, no backing paper, grade 4.25, c1915-25, 16" x 20" orig frame ... **$130**

Veil of Tighannock, orig mat, pen signature and title, orig label on back, grade 4.25, c1915-25, 13" x 16" orig frame ... **$80**

Frederick Thompson

Frederick H. Thompson and Frederick M. Thompson, another father and son team, operated the Thompson Art Company (TACO) from 1908 to 1923, working primarily in the Portland, Maine, area. We know that Thompson and Nutting had collaborated because Thompson widely marketed an interior scene he had taken in Nutting's Southbury home. The production volume of the Thompson Art Company ranks fourth behind Nutting, Davidson, and Sawyer.

Apple Tree Road, grade 3.75, c1910-15, 19" x 15" period frame ... **$45**

At the Close of Day, grade 4.0, c1910-15, 17" x 14" orig frame ... **$70**

Blossom Dale	$75
Brook in Winter	$175
Calm of Fall	$60
Fernbank	$69
Fireside Fancy Work	$125

Golden Trail, grade 4.0, c1910-15, 7" x 9" orig frame ... **$60**

High and Dry	$65
Knitting for the Boys	$150
Lombardy Poplar	$75

Miniature exterior, mat stain, c1910-20, 2" x 3" orig frame, grade 3.5 ... **$40**

Miniature interior, close framed, orig Thompson backstamp, hanging calendar missing, grade 3.75, c1915-25, 4" x 3" orig thin metal frame ... **$65**

Mother's Reveries, orig frame, grade 3.5, mat stains, c1910-20, 17" x 14" **$50**

Nature's Carpet **$50**

Neath the Blossoms, orig mat, pencil signature and title, grade 4.0, c1910-15, 11" x 7" orig frame **$150**

Peace River **$35**

Portland Head **$175**

Roadside Brook, orig Thompson stamp on back, grade 3.75, c1910-15, 20" x 16" orig frame **$100**

Six Master **$250**

Sunset on the Suwanee **$65**

The Gossips **$100**

Untitled, girl by house, photocopy of Thompson Stamp on back on new backing paper, grade 4.0, c1910-15, 5" x 9" orig frame **$50**

Untitled, girl by porch door, copyright impressed lower right on image, photocopy of orig label on back of mat preserved on new backing paper, grade 4.0, c1905-10, 5" x 9" orig frame **$60**

Untitled seascape, Maine, orig mat, pencil signature, grade 4.0, c1910-15, 12" x 15" orig frame **$70**

Minor Wallace Nutting-Like Photographers

Generally speaking, prices for works by minor Wallace Nutting-like photographers would break down as follows: smaller pictures (5" x 7" to 10" x 12"), **$10-$75**; medium pictures (11" x 14" to 14" x 17"), **$50-$200**; larger pictures (larger than 14" x 17"), **$75-$200+**.

Barnhill, E. G., Florida, sgd lower left, unframed, grade 4.0, c1910-20, 10" x 13-1/2" **$50**

Bicknell, J. Carleton, closed framed exterior, orig "Bicknell Photos" label on orig backing paper, grade 4.0, c1915-25, 9" x 7" orig frame **$50**

Collier, Paul R., *Country House*, matted, sgd lower left on image, grade 4.0, c1920-30, 16" x 14" orig frame **$20**

Deane, Willis A, *The Flume*, orig mat, pencil signature and title, orig floral wallpaper backing, grade 4.0, c1920-25, 13" x 15" orig frame **$20**

Edson, Norman, *Mount Rainier*, close framed, orig white pen ink signature lower right, grade 4.25, c1920-30, 10" x 8" orig frame **$275**

Farini, *In Her Boudoir* **$30**

Gardiner, H. Marshall, *Bermuda*, orig mat, pencil signature and title, orig backing paper, grade 4.0, c1915-25, 9" x 7" orig frame **$150**

Garrison, J. M., *Tower Pine*, orig brown mat, pencil signature and title, grade 4.0, c1915-25, 20" x 1" orig frame **$75**

Gibson, *Orchard Blossoms*, orig mat, pencil signature and title, grade 4.0, 1915-25, 14" x 11" orig frame **$40**

Harris, *Cocoanut Grove*, Florida, orig backing paper, grade 3.75, c1915-25, 13" x 10" orig frame **$125**

MacAskill, Wallace R, *Margaier Valley*, Nova Scotia, Canada, grade 3.5, mat stains, foxing, c1915-25, 12" x 9-1/2" orig frame **$50**

Northend, Mary Harrod, *Cohassett Garden*, New England, new backing, grade 4.0, c1910-15, 15" x 12" new frame **$125**

Radel, F., *Buckwood Inn*, Shawnee on the Delaware, PA, orig mat, pen signature and title, orig Radel label, grade 3.75, c1910-20, 14" x 11" orig frame **$100**

Standley, Harry Landis, *Long's Peak Estates Park*, Colorado, orig mat, pencil signature and title, grade 4.0, c1915-25, 6" x 12" newer frame **$80**

Wight, Ethel, *Angry Seas*, orig mat, pencil signature and title, grade 4.0, c1920-30, 15" x 12" orig frame **$50**

Thompson, Frederick, Roadside Brook, *hand colored photo, 20" x 16" original frame, original backing paper mostly intact, original Thompson stamp on back, slightly dark mat, c1910-15,* **$100.**

Gutmann, Bessie Pease, Love's Blossom, *signed and titled lower center, 11" x 14" older frame, c1931,* **$70.**

Payne, Elfin Gorge, New York, *hand-colored photo, original mat, pencil signature and title, 8" x 14" original frame, newer backing paper,* **$35.**

ORIENTAL RUGS

History: Oriental rugs or carpets date back to 3,000 B.C., but it was in the 16th century that they became prevalent. The rugs originated in the regions of Central Asia, Iran (Persia), Caucasus, and Anatolia. Early rugs can be classified into basic categories: Iranian, Caucasian, Turkoman, Turkish, and Chinese. Later India, Pakistan, and Iraq produced rugs in the Oriental style.

The pattern name is derived from the tribe that produced the rug, e.g., Iran is the source for Hamadan, Herez, Sarouk, and Tabriz.

Reproduction Alert.
Beware! There are repainted rugs on the market.

Notes: When evaluating an Oriental rug, age, design, color, weave, knots per square inch, and condition determine the final value. Silk rugs and prayer rugs bring higher prices than other types.

Afghan, dark blue and pale salmon, red ground, wear, minor edge damage, 7' 10" x 9' 2"..........................**$350**

Afshar, South Persia, blue and burgundy borders, ivory ground, worn, second quarter 20th C, 3' 9" x 5' 4"................................**$120**

Agra, India, overall design of palmettes, rosettes, and flowering vines in rose, tan, light aubergine, ivory, olive, and blue-green on deep wine red field, wide blue-green border of similar design, small areas of wear, edges, and ends very slightly reduced and machine re-overcast, last quarter 19th C, 8' 6" x 6' 10"...............**$8,625**

Anatolian Kali, two columns of serrated diamonds in red, navy blue, gold, aubergine, and light and dark blue-green on dark brown field, tan eli-belinde motif border, ivory elems, cut and resewn, small repairs, last quarter 19th C, 13' 6" x 5' 9".......**$420**

Armenian Karabagh, South Caucasus, three lightning medallions each inset with quatrefoil floral motifs, navy blue, royal blue, dark red, rose, camel, aubergine, and blue-green on midnight blue field, navy blue rosette border, small replied areas, corner repairs, dated 1911, 8' 10" x 3' 9"......................**$1,265**

Oriental rug, Tabriz, cream and rose red field, blue floral medallion, blue floral border, **$6,000.**
Photo courtesy of David Rago Auctions, Inc.

Caucasian throw, three medallions on red field, ivory border, c1910, 5'1" x 3'5", **$1,150.**
Photo courtesy of Pook & Pook, Inc.

Bahktiari, West Persia, mid/late 20th C

Garden pattern, polychrome colors, trees and peacocks, 5' 4" x 7'
....**$2,875**

Sq grid inset with various animal, bird, tree, and palmette motifs in midnight, slate, and sky blue, red, rose, camel, gold, ivory, and blue-green, red animal combat and palmette border, 12' 10" x 9' 4"
....**$1,175**

Baluch, Northeast Persia, column of 12 flowerheads flanked by stepped motifs in red, ivory, and brown on midnight blue field, wide red "boat" border, areas of wear, creases, last quarter 19th C, 6' x 3' 9"..............**$600**

Belooch, central rect with bands of wavy design, border of floral dec

squares, old reweave, new sides, c1910, 3' 1" x 5' 3".....................**$300**

Bidjar, Northwest Persia, late 19th C

Central light blue medallion on red ground, dark blue floral border, some wear, 7' 2" x 4' 10", c1910.........**$1,725**

Overall design with rows of rosettes, palmettes, and arabesque leaves, red, royal blue, gold, ivory, and blue-green on midnight blue field, red turtle border, areas of wear, small rewoven areas, 18' 2" x 12'.....**$9,990**

Bordjalou Kazak, Southwest Caucasus, prayer rug, rect prayer cartouche inset with concentric gabled sq medallion in navy blue, ivory, and light blue-green on red field, ivory border, small rewoven and replied areas, end fraying, third quarter 19th C, 4' 6" x 3' 7"..............................**$2,235**

Erivan-Kazak, light abrash blue and red borders, medium blue ground, minor wear, 20th C, 5' 1" x 6' 7" **$550**

Ersari, West Turkestan, three columns of six octagonal gulli-gulls in midnight blue and navy blue, apricot and blue-green on red field, multicolored cruciform motif border, moth damage, small holes, several small patches and rewoven areas, last quarter 19th C, 10' 6" x 6' 10" **$1,100**

Feraghan Sarouk

Central black medallion with orange highlights, overall orange and black floral design, c1890, 3' 3" x 4' 9" **$1,150**

Central star-shaped medallion in dark blue and light blue on beige and red ground, dark blue border, c1890, 3' 4" x 5'...**$980**

Hamadan, Northwest Persia, second quarter 20th C

Indented diamond medallion, matching spandrels, overall Herati design in midnight and navy blue, ivory, rose, and dark green on red field, midnight blue turtle border, 7' x 4' 8"..**$650**

Multiple ivory, blue, and tan borders, dark blue spandrels, ivory ground, wear, 4' 1" x 5' 8".....................**$325**

Heriz, Northwest Persia

Azerbejan design, dark blue border, light rust ground, camel and green accents, 9' 4" x 12' 6" **$6,620**

Dark blue border, ivory spandrels, burgundy ground, 9' 1" x 11' 1" **$750**

Large gabled sq medallion with palmette pendants in midnight and navy blue, rose, camel, and blue-green on terra-cotta red field, large ivory spandrels, midnight blue rosette and serrated leaf border, areas of wear, end fraying, late 19th/ early 20th C, 12' x 9' 2" **$2,585**

Large gabled sq medallion surrounded by floral motifs in midnight and royal blue, rose, tan, and dark blue-green on terra-cotta red field, stepped ivory spandrels, midnight blue "turtle" border, small spots of wear, end fraying, early 20th C, 11' 6" x 8' **$1,300**

Light blue central medallion, overall floral ground in shades of red and blue, moth eaten in one corner, c1935, 8' 10" x 11' 9"................**$900**

Three hooked diamond medallions in midnight blue, red, camel, dark brown, ivory, and blue-green on light tan field, ivory floral meander border, slight end fraying, very small edge and corner gouges, early 20th C, 9' 4" x 3' 5" **$1,100**

Wide dark blue border, green and ivory spandrels, tomato red ground, 9' 8" x 12' 9"..........................**$7,475**

Jaf Kurd, Northwest Persia, bagface, diamond lattice of hooked diamonds in midnight and navy blue, red, gold, brown, rust, aubergine, and blue-green, aubergine border, slight brown corrosion, early 20th C, 2' 7" x 2' 7" **$530**

Karabagh, South Caucasus, last quarter 19th C

Bittersweet border, ivory ground, edge wear, small repairs, 3' 5" x 7' **$2,175**

Ivory border, blue abrash ground, wear, 3' 10" x 7'.........................**$500**

Prayer, dated, ivory, orange, and pale blue borders, black abrash ground, minor edge wear, 2' 1" x 4' 5" **$250**

Karaja, central medallion, red, dark blue, and light blue, floral borders, overall wear, c1920, 8' 2" x 10' 7" **$1,495**

Kashan, signature cartouche, midnight blue border, blue and ivory spandrels, deep burgundy ground, 7' 8" x 12' 8" **$1,495**

Konaghend, Northeast Caucasus, characteristic arabesque lattice in ivory, red, rose, royal blue, gold, and blue-green on black field, ivory border, some black corrosion, late 19th/ early 20th C, 6' x 4' 3"...............**$1,295**

Kuba, Northeast Caucasus, three diamond medallions, each radiating four serrated motifs and four small diamonds in red, red-brown, navy blue, ivory, orange, and blue-green, abrashed midnight blue field, navy blue border, areas of minor wear, slight dye runs, black corrosion, some glue to back, late 19th/early 20th C, 4' 10" x 3' 6" **$1,000**

Kurd, Northwest Persia, column of five turkoman-style octagonal turret guls in red, sky blue, gold, aubergine-brown, olive, and blue-green, midnight blue field, dark red border, end fraying, early 20th C, 9' 5" x 3' 9" **$900**

Northwest Persian, red and ivory star and diamond pattern surrounded by polychrome geometric border, 5" 2" x 8" 10", **$350.**
Photo courtesy of David Rago Auctions, Inc.

Persian, vine scroll and floral medallion, crimson, cobalt blue, and ivory, 163" x 118", **$1,200.**
Photo courtesy of David Rago Auctions, Inc.

Sarouk, rust red ground, beige and blue floral designs, c1950, 8'5" x 2'10", **$500.**
Photo courtesy of Alderfer Auction Co.

Sejshour, throw, floral pattern, mustard and navy border, c1900, 7' x 4' 2", $2,760.
Photo courtesy of Pook & Pook, Inc.

Shirvan throw, overall floral design, red field with navy and ivory borders, c1910, 5' 4" x 3' 3", $630.
Photo courtesy of Pook & Pook, Inc.

Oriental throw rug, Lori Pambok, three medallions on blue field, ivory border, late 19th c., 8' 2" x 3' 10", $4,025.
Photo courtesy of Pook & Pook, Inc.

Oriental throw rug, three medallions on red field, ivory border, c1900, 4' 10" x 3' 3", $1,265.
Photo courtesy of Pook & Pook, Inc.

Soumak, flatweave, three cobalt blue and cerulean medallions against ivory and red ground, 5' 9" x 7' 5", $600.
Photo courtesy of David Rago Auctions, Inc.

Yezd, cranberry red floral sprays on cobalt blue ground, cranberry floral border, c1900, 4' 7" x 7' 2", $850.
Photo courtesy of Alderfer Auction Co.

Lenkoran, Southeast Caucasus, three large calyx medallions separated by two large rect medallions in red, navy blue, aubergine, ivory, apricot, light camel, and blue-green on dark brown field, ivory border, brown corrosion, even wear to center, creases, last quarter 19th C, 10' x 4' 4" **$715**

Lesghi, Northeast Caucasus, column of four Lesghi stars in red, sky blue, ivory, tan-gold, and blue-green on navy blue field, two ivory borders, even wear, slight end fraying, last quarter 19th C, 4' 10" x 3' 9" **$1,300**

Luri, Southwest Persia, large gabled and serrated sq medallions flanked by six large rosettes in red, navy blue, apricot, gold, and dark blue-green on midnight blue field, ivory border, even center wear, early 20th C, 7' x 4' 7" **$765**

Malayer, Northwest Persia, overall design of flowerheads and blossoming vines in red, ice blue, camel, and olive on abrashed royal blue field, ivory border, outer guard stripes partially missing from both ends, second quarter 20th C, 4' 10" x 3' 6" **$1,000**

Qashqai, Southwest Persia, large hooked hexagonal medallion inset with blossoming angular vines in red, navy blue, ivory, gold, brown, and blue-green, midnight blue field, brown border, slight wear to center, minor moth damage, small repair, late 19th/early 20th C, 6' 9" x 4' **$1,100**

Sarouk, West Persia, second quarter 20th C

Floral and checkered border with floral spandrels, pink, blues, and ivory on salmon ground, good sheen, 9' 1" x 12' 1" **$2,530**

Overall floral sprays in midnight, navy, and ice blue, red, gold, and light blue-green on rose field, narrow midnight blue floral border, 5' x 3' 4".............................**$500**

Seraband, Northwest Persia, staggered rows of small boteh in midnight blue, apricot, ivory, and blue-green on abrashed terra-cotta red field, three ivory and red floral meander borders, even wear to center, slight end fraying, early 20th C, 19' 6" x 7' 7"
.............................**$3,000**

Shiraz, East Caucasus, Caucasian type design, multiple borders, diagonal stripes in dark blue, red, ivory and gold, late 19th C, 3' x 5'.............**$460**

Shirvan, East Caucasus, late 19th C

Geometric and star designs in blue, burgundy, red, green, gold, and ivory, wear and small splits, 3' 10" x 5' 6".............................**$920**

Three medallions, shades of blue and red, minor border loss at ends, c1890, 5' 10" x 3' 6"...................**$950**

Three columns with stepped diamond and serrated diamond medallions in red, ivory, navy blue, black, gold, and abrashed blue-green on midnight blue field, narrow ivory border, slight moth damage, 9' 6" x 5'
.............................**$2,550**

Soumak, Northeast Caucasus, four elongated diamond medallions flanked by half medallions in midnight blue, black, rose, red, and tan on maroon-brown field, black border, areas of slight wear, late 19th C, 9' 4" x 8' 6"...................**$2,475**

South Caucasian, column of eight radiating hexagonal medallions in navy blue, red, rust, gold, dark brown, and light blue-green on midnight blue field, narrow ivory rosette border, slight dye run in one corner, second quarter 20th C, 13' x 3' 8"...........**$1,175**

Tabriz, silk, tree of life, deer, and floral borders, shades of brown, overall wear, dry areas, missing one end border, c1890, 5' 11" x 4' 5"...........**$1,265**

Tekke Torba, West Turkestan, late 19th/early 20th C

Kejebe design in midnight blue, red, ivory, and dark brown on cochineal field, multiple borders of similar coloration, outer border partially missing from one end, 4' 2" x 1' 4"
.............................**$450**

Multiple borders, overall design, ivory, blue, orange, and red, brown/

brown ground, minor pile wear, 7' 5" x 11' 9" **$1,150**

Ushak, West Anatolia, large crenellated hexagonal medallion and matching spandrels in tan-gold, ivory, and blue-green on red field, red rosette and flowering vine border, areas of wear, edge and end gouges, several patches and rewoven areas, late 19th C, 11' 10" x 8' 2" **$950**

Yomud Chuval, West Turkestan, nine Chuval guls in midnight blue, red, ivory, and blue-green on dark aubergine field, ivory border, plain aubergine elem, small spots of slight wear, re-overcast, last quarter 19th C, 3' 4" x 2' 3" **$825**

ORIENTALIA

History: Orientalia is a term applied to objects made in the Orient, an area which encompasses the Far East, Asia, China, and Japan. The diversity of cultures produced a variety of objects and styles.

Additional Listings: Canton, Celadon, Cloisonné, Fitzhugh, Nanking, Netsukes, Rose Medallion, Japanese Prints, and other related categories.

Additional Resources:

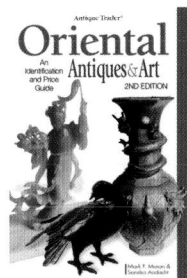

Antique Trader® Oriental Antiques & Art, 2nd Ed., by Mark F. Moran & Sandra Andacht, Krause Publications, Iola WI.

Album, fan paintings, 11 works by various artists including, Ch'en Fang Ting, Hsu Lin Lu (b1916), Shao Ping Chang, Wu Hsi Tsai (1799-1870), Kuo Shang Hsien (1796-1820), Fei Shih Po, Wu Hua Yuan (1893-1972), Wang I Ting, Yang I, Wang I Ting, Hou Pi I (2) **$600**

Altar cabinet, Huang Hua Li wood, moon-shaped brasses, side flanges carved with Chih Lung dragons, Lung Chih fungus, and clouds, China, cracks to top, old repair to back feet,

loss, 18th C, 35-1/2" w, 22" d, 34" h **$2,235**

Architectural element

Capitals, carved wood, foo dogs, gold lacquered surface, China, price for pr, 19th C, 22" l.............**$775**

Finial, bronze, figural dragon, patina with azurite areas, Khmer, 13th C, 4-3/4" h **$850**

Basin, bronze, low relief designs of stylized birds and trees, 18-character grass script poem on the base, Japan, 18th C or possibly earlier, 7" d...................**$300**

Bell, bronze, lid surmounted by two kneeling figures, iron mount with two apsara figures, Burma, 19th C, 19" h
.............................**$400**

Box, cov, lacquer, foliate form, maki-e of a woman with a fan, Raiden inlay, Japan, 19th C, 5" d...................**$2,115**

Bowl

Nephrite, white and pale green, incised and gilt character inscriptions with four character reign mark on base, Qing Dynasty, price for pr, 20th C, 6-1/2" d.............**$920**

Porcelain, dark blue ext. with gilt dragons, clouds, and pearls, white int., China, Ch'ien Lung six-character seal mark, 1736-95, 7-1/2" d **$600**

Brush pot, bamboo, carved in high relief with sages in forest, rosewood base, China, 18th C, 6" h..........**$1,300**

Buddha

Bodhisattva, carved stone, reclining figure, left hand supporting head, right hand resting on bent knee, peaceful expression, Chinese, possibly Tang Dynasty, 16" l, 6" h **$950**

Buddha Amida, lacquered wood, standing with his hands in "abeyance of fear" mudra, gold lacquered robes, eyes inlaid with crystal, Japan, 18th C, 17" h...................**$1,350**

Hardwood figure, seated on lotus throne, numerous coatings of lacquer, China, 18th C, 13" h **$425**

Buddhist bell, Japan, hammered brass with a lacquered design of a dragon and thunder meanders, late 19th/early 20th C, 14" d.............**$450**

Bust

Bronze, Quan Yin, Chinese, Sung or earlier period, losses, 7" h....**$1,200**

Sandstone, head of divinity with jeweled crown, Eastern Thailand, Khmer period, 11th C, 13-1/2" h
.............................**$8,820**

Figure, Kilin, bronze, lying in curved position, some gold splashes, repaired dorsal fin, Chinese, 19th C, 10" l, 5" h, **$925.**

Pair of bronze candlesticks, deer form, each supporting candleholder on back, Chinese, 18th C, 10" h **$600.**

Jar, Korean, dragon jar, baluster form, collar neck, painted under-glaze blue and iron-brown, drag-on chasing flaming pearl among clouds, drilled base, Yi Dynasty, 19th C, 14-1/4" h, **$17,000.**
Photo courtesy of David Rago Auctions, Inc.

Étagère, hardwood, central cupboard covered by hinged doors, flanked by two drawers and open-work carvings, Chinese, 20th C, 38-1/2" x 67" x 14-1/2" h, **$750.**
Photo courtesy of David Rago Auctions, Inc.

Cabinet

Hung Mu wood, two drawers over single gate, moon-shaped brasses, China, 18th/19th C, 56-1/2" l, 20" d, 35" h **$1,560**

Two part, persimmon wood veneer, two long drawers over two smaller drawers each flanked by sq com-partment, ornate iron mounts, Japan, early 20th C, 47-1/2" l, 17" d, 48" h **$1,530**

Cabinet on stand, black lacquer, cabinet with pair of doors, fitted int. of doors and pigeonholes, cen-tral painted oval portrait of a beauty, 27" h square base, cabriole legs, deco-rated all over with gilt scrollwork and foliage, Chinese Export, c1840, 23-1/2" w **$2,500**

Candlesticks, pr, bronze, deer form, each supporting candle holder on back, Chinese, 18th C, 10" h **$600**

Censer, bronze, modeled as capari-soned shishi playing with ball, parcel-gilt accents, Japan, 18th/19th C, 10" l **$1,410**

Chair, side, pr, Huang Hua Li wood with cane seats, China, 18th C or earlier **$18,800**

Charger, hawk design, sgd by member of Li family in red seal characters, China, 19th C, 18" d **$1,175**

Cup, Chinese, porcelain, engraved dragons under egg-yolk yellow color, six-character underglaze blue Kuang Hsu mark, possibly of the period, 1874-1908.................................. **$200**

Deity, gilt bronze, sitting position, robes with chased dec, China, wear to gilding, 17th C, 8-1/2" h **$990**

Dish, Tou Tsai, scalloped edge, design of dragons and flowers in green on yellow ground, six-character Ch'ien Lung seal mark (1735-96), 5-1/4" d
.... **$1,880**

Embroidery, on silk

Courtesan in elaborate costume hold-ing pole with suspended basket of flowers, Chinese, 19th C, 28" x 20"
.... **$345**

Crane by flowering tree, Japanese, Meiji period, 1867-1912, 17" x 13"
.... **$320**

Fan, folding, China, 19th C

Ivory, shaped stays with numer-ous figures in garden scenes, fan painted with harbor scene, other vignettes of idyllic village scenes, black lacquer box with gilt butter-flies and flowers **$490**

Wooden stays with black lacquer and gold dec, fan of paper dec with figures in silk and ivory, reverse magenta with three reserves of country scenes, gold and black lac-quer case **$250**

Fan, folding, Japan, 19th C

All ivory stays dec with shibayama inlay of gold lacquer and semi-pre-cious inlay of birds and flowers, orig box, 11-1/2" l **$4,025**

Carved ivory stays with shibayama inlay, one side dec with landscape, other with children watching fire-works.................................... **$775**

Figure

Carved and painted ivory and horn, maiden holding fan in left hand, basket of flowers in right hand, carved and pierced horn rock beside her with lantern sitting on top, head carved separately and pinned to shoulder, China, wear to paint sur-face, 19th C, 17-3/4" h **$990**

Carved quartz with mauve and white striations, green veining, longevity god or immortal, holding staff in left hand, ruyi scepter in right, fitted wood stand, China, 19th or 20th C, 5-5/8" h **$220**

Carved rose quartz, sitting puppy, head turned slightly to the left, possibly China, 20th C, 2-1/2" h, 2-7/8" d **$100**

Elephant, bronze, sgd on foot, Japan, Meiji period (1868-1911), 15" l **$500**

Goddess, carved stone, gray schist image of Kuan Yin, China, 20th C, 40" h **$285**

Fish bowl, porcelain, blue and white, design of phoenix in garden, scrolling at mouth, Ming period, probably Chia Ching period, 1522-1566, hairline **$1,175**

Flower vessel, bronze, tightly curled lotus leaf resembling small boat, attached lotus flowers, seed pod, and crabs crawling to top, carved wooden stand, sgd on base with rect reserve, Japan, 19th C, 9-1/2" l, 3-1/2" h **$2,225**

Foo Dog, carved wood, surface lacquered in red and gold, China, 19th C, 11" l, 10-1/2" h **$600**

Gong, brass, dragons and tokugawa mons designs, Japan, early 20th C, 18" d **$325**

Guardian figure, standing figure of Nio, bronze, Japan, Meiji period (1868-1911), 9" h **$275**

Hanging scroll, ink and color on silk

Doves and blossoming rose bush, sgd, Japan, mounted on silk, 44-1/2" l, 20" w **$360**

Figure in boat amidst mountainous landscape, China, 37-1/2" h, 19-1/4" h **$360**

Scholar in boat, river landscape, China, 49" l, 25-3/4" w **$540**

Incense box, Komei-style, iron inlaid with gold and silver, Japan, Meiji period (1868-1911), 2" x 2" **$600**

Incense burner, bronze, decorative elements of elephants in handles, tripod base and finial, floral elements, inlaid glass and semi-precious stones, China, 18th C, 15" h **$1,530**

Inro, netsuke, ojime

Gold lacquer, four compartment, each side dec with hawk perched on rail-

ing, sgd "Igawa" lower right, 1-5/8" h carved ivory netsuke in form of shells, one with crab emerging from top, metal ojime with foo dog and peony, stylized signature on side, Japan, Meiji period, 3-1/4" h **$3,750**

Lacquer, three compartment, dragon amidst clouds, unsigned, 1-1/4" d carved wood manju netsuke of dragon with inlaid eyes, agate ojime bead, Japan, some wear and edge losses, crack on neck of netsuke, 19th C, 2-1/4" h, 2-1/8" w **$900**

Inro, Saya type, lacquer, four compartment, dec with Kwannon, moon behind her head, reverse dec with trees and waterfall, removable sheath having small cartouches with dragons, base sgd "Koma Koryu" with kakihan, Japan, slight losses, 19th C, 3-1/2" h **$1,265**

Jar, cov

Baluster, blue and white dec of village by water, foo dog finial, China, 19th C, 25" h **$2,350**

Blue and white, design of cranes, deer, and pine trees, carved hardwood cover, K'ang Hsi period (1662-1722), 11" h **$1,880**

Kogo, silver, chased and repousse dec of two phoenix birds among flowers, applied enamel highlights, silver lined interior sgd on underside, Japan, Meiji period, dent on inside of lid, 3-1/8" d **$1,725**

Libation cup, porcelain, applied Chi dragons in relief, two forming handle, underglaze enamels, Chinese, losses, 18th C, 2" h, 4-1/2" w **$115**

Officials' chairs, pr

Mortised construction, serpentine crests, carved back splats, paneled seats, sq legs, relief carved and scalloped aprons, old red wash, Chinese, restorations, 20" h seat, 43" h back **$650**

Huang Hua Li wood with cane seats, sq sections with inward tapering carving, China, Ming period, ex-James Hightower, 16th/17th C, 20-1/2" h seat, 47" h back, 24-1/2" w, 18-1/2" d **$99,500**

Okimono, ivory study of group of rats and lantern, horn inlay, 19th C, 3" l **$635**

Painting, oil on canvas, Chinese Export School, 19th Century, portrait of American clipper ship, gilt frame

Charger, Chinese, porcelain, blue and white, birds and flowering decoration, 18th C, 12-3/4" h, **$750.**
Photo courtesy of Sloans & Kenyon Auctioneers and Appraisers.

Bottle, porcelain base with diminished neck, underglaze blue decoration, metal fittings, band around foot rim, chain for hanging, Chinese or Japanese, 17th C, 7-1/4" h, neck ground down, **$175.**

The Almeda of Bath, Maine, lined, "Shanghai China 1878, May 8," scattered retouch, craquelure, 20" x 27" **$9,990**

The Charles B. Kenney of New York, handwritten inscription on the stretcher reads "Shanghai China 1878, May 8," lined, scattered retouch, craquelure, 20" x 27" **$9,400**

Painting table, Huang Hua Li Hunah back braces, China, Ming period, 16th/17th C, 70" l, 32-1/2" w, 34" h **$44,650**

Vases, Chinese, porcelain, blue and white dragon, foliage, and mythical beast, **$600.**
Photo courtesy of Sloans & Kenyon Auctioneers and Appraisers.

Plaques, Chinese hard stone, engraved writing, well-figured detail, 19th C, 5" x 3-3/8", 6-3/8" x 4-5/8", 8-1/2" x 4-1/8", price for set of three, **$525.**

Fish bowl, Chinese, porcelain, blue and crackle glaze, riverscape decoration, **$375.**
Photo courtesy of Sloans & Kenyon Auctioneers and Appraisers.

Plate, Chinese-style decoration, green enameled coiled dragon chasing flaming pearl, rose enamel border, Buddhist precious things, back signed in overglaze red "Tashiro," impressed square mark, Japan, c1900, 13-3/4" d, **$550.**

Palace urn, bronze, elaborately dec with scenes of birds, foo dogs, foliage, large applied dragons, rich chocolate brown patina, Chinese, price for pr, c1900, 24" h **$750**

Panel, rosewood, deep relief carving of two peacocks on flowering tree, Chinese, early 20th C, 23" x 16" **$125**

Pitcher, Sumidagawa, monkeys, Japan, loss to one hand, early 20th C, 12" h **$400**

Plaque, bronze, relief dec of Kuan Yin surrounded by attending deities, extensive inscription on back, China, 19th C, 8" x 6" **$135**

Rank badges, pr, K'o ssu work, white egret rank, China, mounted as a tray, 19th C **$380**

Robe

Dragon, China, loose threads, late 19th/early 20th C **$360**

Informal, woman's, black ground, floral embroidery, China, late 19th/early 20th C **$360**

Sagemo, basket cup holder, celadon porcelain netsuke of karako, 19th C **$420**

Scepter, ju-i, carved boxwood, lotus pod with movable seeds and single leaf, sgd, Japan, 19th C, 13" l **$420**

Screen

Six panels, finely detailed Buddhist and Taoist figures, checkered silk border, black lacquered frame, Japanese, accompanied by "Certificate of Antiquity" dated 1971 addressed to US Customs by David Kidd and Y. Morimoto of "Three Dynasties," Ashiya City, Japan, minor losses, c1750, 94" x 18" **$1,450**

"Tagasode-byobu," two-fold, brocade with mounted ink, color, and gold leaf on paper panel showing kimono over rack and accessories, Japan, Meiji period (1868-1912), 67" h, 37" w **$10,755**

Sculpture, bronze

Crayfish, fully articulated, Japan, Meiji period (1868-1911), loose, 17" l **$3,200**

Scene of bull and farmer, carved fitted wood base, sgd, Japan, Meiji period (1868-1911), 24" l **$1,300**

Seal case, four-compartment form with lacquer dec of warrior and courtier, crystal ojime, and netsuke sennin on horse, Japan, 19th C **$775**

Shanxi cupboard, gold and black Chinoiserie dec over dark red ground, mortised construction, paneled ends, two doors with brass hardware, removable int. shelf, wooden rod brackets, pieced restoration to moldings, touch-up, 57" w, 25-1/4" d, 69-1/4" h **$650**

Shrine

Black lacquer case, gilt standing image of Amida Buddha, Japan, 19th C, 7" h **$395**

Black lacquer, gold lacquered figure of Kshitagarba, inlaid eyes, Japan, 18th/19th C, 27" h **$3,200**

Lacquered, structured as temple building, triple roof; ornately carved with shishi, dragons, and flowers, surface lacquered in gold, red, brown, and black, engraved gilt copper metal mounts, Japan, Meiji period (1868-1911), 86" h **$1,250**

Stand, hardwood

Marble insert, round carved openwork sides, China, 19th C, light separation of joints, natural shrinkage, 39-3/4" h, 15" x 16-1/5" top **$520**

Rect, two wooden shelves, red marble insert on top, carved flower and tendrils around top frieze an openwork gallery, ball and claw feet, China, natural fissues in marble, 19th, 31-3/8" h, 16-5/8" x 12" top **$175**

Statues, pr, granite, two officials from spirit way, Korea, Yi period, 18th C or earlier, 53" h **$9,400**

Stool for two, Huang Hua Li wood, humpback stretchers, China, Ming to early Ch'ing dynasty, staining and cracking to top and legs, 40" w, 16" d, 19" h **$9,400**

Stupa, bronze, four makala supports, stupa surmounted by four figures of Buddha, Nepal, 19th C, 6-1/2" h **$550**

Tankard, blue and white, scholar in garden scene, Continental silver mounts with Dutch export hallmarks, China, Transitional period, c1620, 8" h **$3,985**

Table, pr, lacquered, Tzu Tan wood ornately carved with archaic scrolling, inlaid oval pale celadon jade plaques, carved resonance stones and archaic dragons, China, cracks to both tops of both, lacquer wear, 18th C, 47" l, 15-1/4" w, 33" h **$23,500**

Teapot

Globular, Fen tsai palette, design of flowers on brocaded blue ground, ju-i and stylized acanthus leaf borders, gilt accents, four-character seal mark within red square, China, 18th/19th C, 8-1/4" h **$13,000**

Silver, Hira Arare, globular, hailstone pattern, cov surmounted with pierced sphere finial, base marked, Japanese Export, 16.65 oz, 7-1/2" h **$660**

Tonkotsu, wood, applied lacquered ivory and mother-of-pearl dec of sea life, sgd on rect tablet, reddish-brown ojime bead, possibly ceramic, well carved 3-1/4" h netsuke of Ryujin's attendant standing and supporting his left hand on octopus straddling his shoulders, tentacles entwined around each other and the attendant's arms and robes, forming natural himotoshi, attending holding jewel in his right hand, skirt encrusted with shells, inlaid eyes in octopus, Japan, 18th or 19th C, 4" w, 3" h **$46,000**

Vase

Bronze, flared rim, paneled shoulder takers to base with flower petals, detailed peacock sits on flowering tree branch, peahen below, dark patina, peacock's crest missing, 42" h **$3,500**

Bronze, hexagonal body with designs of high relief dragons, Japan, late 19th C, 14" h **$600**

Bronze, relief dec of waves with dragon in round holding glass pearl, sgd "great Japan sei don sai," Japan, Meiji period, 15" h **$1,650**

Stoneware, matte green celadon glaze, Art Deco style, Japan, c1930, 12" h **$450**

Tsun-shape, Wu Tsai ware, birds and flowers dec, China, Transitional period, c1640, 20-1/2" h **$2,000**

Votive plaque, gilt copper and bronze, a central image of the Buddha surrounded by the wheel of law, Japan, late 19th/early 20th C, 7" d **$250**

Wine ewer, Hirado ware, form of Hoi tea, bag of wealth, underglaze blue, yellow, pale green, tan, and black accents, cover missing, 19th C, 6-1/4" h.............................. **$750**

Vase, Chinese, finely painted in black and brown on biscuit ground, dragon among clouds, carp leaping waterfall, Xuande six-character mark on recessed base, 19th or 20th C, **$225.**

Vase, Shibayama, gold lacquer, diamond form, four sides decorated with birds among flowering plants, mother-of-pearl, coral, and stained ivory, unsigned, Japanese, Meiji period, 6" h, several rim and base chips, **$1,950.**

Chinese Kesi, wall hanging textile, woven with warriors on horseback, couched gold thread detail, silk border, 19th C, 74" x 37", **$800.**
Photo courtesy of David Rago Auctions, Inc.

Vase, Chinese, porcelain, blue and white, riverscape on crackled beige ground, late Qing/early Republic period, 14-1/2" h, **$550.**
Photo courtesy of Sloans & Kenyon Auctioneers and Appraisers.

PAIRPOINT

History: The Pairpoint Manufacturing Co. was organized in 1880 as a silver-plating firm in New Bedford, Massachusetts. The company merged with Mount Washington Glass Co. in 1894 and became the Pairpoint Corporation. The new company produced specialty glass items, often accented with metal frames.

Pairpoint Corp. was sold in 1938 and Robert Gunderson became manager. He operated it as the Gunderson Glass Works until his death in 1952. From 1952 until the plant closed in 1956, operations were maintained under the name Gunderson-Pairpoint. Robert Bryden reopened the glass manufacturing business in 1970, moving it back to the New Bedford area.

China

Chocolate pot, cream ground, white floral dec, gold trim and scrolls, sgd "Pairpoint Limoges 2500 114," 10" h **$675**

Gravy boat and underplate, fancy white china with scrolls, Dresden multicolored flowers, elaborate handle, Limoges, two pcs **$175**

Plate, hp harbor scene, artist sgd "L. Tripp," fuchsia tinted rim, gold highlights, back sgd "Pairpoint Limoges," 7-3/8" d..**$550**

Lamp, table

Candlestick type, urn-shaped tops, electric sockets, clear cut columns with diamond designs, octagonal base with fine leaf detail, relief cast signatures on bases "Quadruple Plate," price for pr, 18" h.........................**$550**

Orange Poppy, reverse painted mold blown puffy shade, silvered base, imp "Pairpoint 3085," shade damaged and repaired, 21" h, 14" d **$1,500**

Reverse painted

Dome shade of harbor scene with sailboats in mauve, peach, blue, and gold, sgd "C. Durand," two sockets, wooden vasiform standard with brass mounts, minor nicks at top aperture, 21-3/4" h, 13-3/4" d **$1,645**

Shade dec with three floral and urn-form medallions separated by stylized circular medallions in pink,

blue, and gold against black ground, three sockets, trapped bubble colorless glass standard, hexagonal green stone base, 16-1/2" d **$3,290**

Metal

Lamp base

Patinated metal, quatrefoil wirework supporting shade, ribbed standard with applied foliate handles and feet, bronze patina on white metal, imp "Pairpoint Mfg Co.," "P" in diamond and "30031/2" on base, worn patina, 12" h, 8" d **$400**

Patinated metal, two-socket fixture, four-sided shaft and lobe base, bronze patina on white metal, imp "Pairpoint Mfg Co.," "P" in diamond, and "B3040" on base, patina wear, 15" h **$350**

Trophy, copper, two fancy handles, feather design, plaque inscribed "New Bedford Yacht Club Ocean Race won by Nutmeg for the fastest time, Aug. 5, 1909," base marked "Pairpoint Mfg Co.," "P" in diamond mark, numbered, 7" d, 8-1/2" h **$400**

PAPER EPHEMERA

History: Maurice Rickards, author of *Collecting Paper Ephemera*, suggests that ephemera are the "minor transient documents of everyday life," material destined for the wastebasket but never quite making it. This definition is more fitting than traditional dictionary definitions that emphasize time, e.g., "lasting a very short time." A driver's license, which is used for a year or longer, is as much a piece of ephemera as is a ticket to a sporting event or music concert. The transient nature of the object is the key.

Collecting ephemera has a long and distinguished history. Among the English pioneers were John Seldon (1584-1654), Samuel Pepys (1633-1703), and John Bagford (1650-1716). Large American collections can be found at historical societies and libraries across the country, and museums, e.g., Wadsworth Athenaeum, Hartford, Connecticut, and the Museum of the City of New York.

When used by collectors, "ephemera" usually means paper objects, e.g., billheads and letterheads, book-

plates, documents, labels, stocks and bonds, tickets, and valentines. However, more and more ephemera collectors are recognizing the transient nature of some three-dimensional material, e.g., advertising tins and pinback buttons. Today's specialized paper shows include dealers selling other types of ephemera in both two-and three-dimensional form.

Additional Listings: See Advertising, Catalogs, Comic Books, Photographs, and Sports Cards. Also see Calendars, Catalogs, Magazines, Newspapers, Postcards, and Sheet Music in *Warman's Americana & Collectibles*.

Additional Resources:

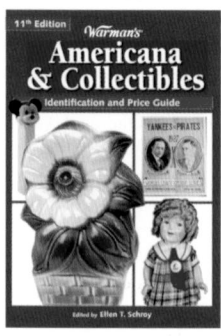

Warman's® Americana & Collectibles, 11th Ed., by Ellen T. Schroy, ed., Krause Publications, Iola, WI.

Calendars

1896, actors and actresses, one per month, sepia and white.............**$125**

1897, pansy, each page with different litho of a pansy, scalloped edges, printed in Bavaria, designed in England, 6" x 4-1/4" **$65**

1906, Christmas Belle, no calendar pad, 14" x 11" **$200**

1908, fish, adv for Spicer & Beasley, Smithshire, IL, 15" x 9" **$180**

1908, woman with red poppies, heavily emb, adv for J.I. Sawyel, General Merchandise, Smithshire, Illinois, full pad, 10" x 14".............................**$270**

1912, Calumet Baking Powder, adv for H. J. Coffey Grocers, LaKemp, Oklahoma, print titled "Firelight," by G. Sether **$220**

1918, Swifts Premium, for January, February, March, Haskell Coffin illus of "The Girl I Leave Behind Me," WWI soldier saying goodbye to pretty girl, 15" x 8-1/4"............................**$90**

1922, lady in car, Hayes Litho Co., Buffalo, NY, 15" x 20-1/2" **$100**

1926, Maxfield Parrish, Fountain of Pirene, orig 6" x 8" box, titled "Sunlit Road Calendar," Dodge Publishing Co., #5895 .... **$125**

1930, Love is Blind, antique cars, service station, 22-1/2" x 14" **$115**

1931, Midland Wood Products, Midland, Ontario, each page is different model home with floor plan on reverse, 9-3/4" x 5-1/2" **$35**

1951, Puzzling Pups, Kinghon, 10" x 17" **$60**

1952, Songbird Families, series 6, Betty Carnes, watercolors by Roger Tory Peterson, published by Barton-Cotton Co. **$12.75**

1960, Look for the Sign of Happy Motoring, Esso Gas, adv for R. Y. Foster, Johnson City, Tennessee, 14-3/4" x 8-1/2" **$48**

Checks

1863, State of Vermont Treasurer's Office, Rutland, state seal at left, brown on white, 2 cent US Internal Revenue bank check stamp, hand and punch canceled **$40**

1865, National Bank of Commerce, New York, issued by Central Railroad Co. of New Jersey, red on white design, orange 2 cent US Internal Revenue Documentary and Proprietary stamp **$20**

1869, First National Bank, New York, New York, bank building vignette, violet on white, orange 2 cent US Internal Revenue Documentary and Proprietary stamp **$15**

1871, Pennsylvania Academy of the Fine Arts, Philadelphia, Pennsylvania, Liberty, eagle, and shield, black on white **$35**

1875, First National Bank of Chicago, issued by the office of Downer & Bemis Brewing Co., vignette of brewery, horse drawn carriages and people in street scene, black printing, olive security paper **$45**

1875, Trenton Banking Co., Trenton, NJ, two vignettes, issued and canceled **$12**

1882, National Park Bank, New York, New York, blue 2 cent US Internal Revenue Documentary and Proprietary stamp at left, "Iron Cliffs Com-

pany" stamped in red above signature line, payable to Third National Bank for $30,000 .... **$20**

1898, Treasurer of Stanton Co., State of Nebraska, locomotive vignette at left, three horse heads at right, brown on sepia, hand stamp canceled **$30**

1903, Pittsburgh Brewing Co., Pittsburgh, Pennsylvania, pale blue, red, gold, and black round logo, hand written, payee endorsement on reverse **$6**

1911, First National Bank, Troutville, Virginia, vignette of bald eagle perched on rock, clutching arrows, olive branch, and US shield, black on orange, issued, canceled, printed by Kennedy Printing Co., Fredonia, Kansas **$10**

1924, Baker Loan & Trust Co., gray vignette of bank entrance **$7.50**

1957, Christmas Club, Anacostia National Bank, Washington, DC, Santa with open book, quill, ink bottle **$7.50**

Cigar box labels

Alfonso Rigos & Co. **$10**

Camel Brand Cigars, Arab man riding camel across desert **$18**

Elektra, red, gold, and white, pretty girl **$15**

Royal Banner, allegorical lion with flag **$15**

Documents

Appointment of administrator of estate, sgd by John Evans, Colonial Gov of Pennsylvania, dated March 24, 1704, wax seal, some fold weakness, 9-1/2" x 15" **$500**

Appointment of Gideon Mumford Deputy Postmaster at East Greenwich, Rhode Island, dated April 19, 1796, foxing, fold weakness, 12-1/2" x 7-1/2" **$75**

Bill of Exchange, written for Robert Robson, London, March 2, 1796, in Charleston, South Carolina, two pgs, concerns exchange for 160 pounds sterling, 8-1/2" x 7" **$50**

Indenture

Vellum, John Penn and Edmund Physick, tract of land in Philadelphia, Pennsylvania, Dec. 27, 1799, framed, 13" x 27-1/2" **$130**

Program, Ringling Bros & Barnum & Bailey circus, 1955, full-color cover, **$15**.

Vellum, between Samuel Jones and wife to John Stillwagon, tract of land in Philadelphia, Pennsylvania, May 10, 1757, sgd on reverse by Charles Brockden, Justice for Pennsylvania, folding, toning, foxing, 15-1/2" x 29" **$60**

Vellum, pre-printed royal seal, between Josiah Winter and wife to William Hambleton, tract of land in Solebury, Pennsylvania, bordering Delaware River, Nov. 9, 1770, folding, slight toning, foxing, 16" x 22" **$85**

Vellum, Jonathon Jones and wife to Samuel Norcross, tract of land in Gloucester Twp, New Jersey, July 23, 1792, small hand drawn map on reverse, sgd by Thomas Rodman, Burlington County Judge, folding, toning, foxing, ink stains, 21" x 24-1/2" **$50**

Legal deposition, involving litigation between Horace Day and Charles Goodyear, Aug. 29, 1851, concerning Indian rubber fabric, attached map of eastern US printed on Indian rubber fabric, reverse marked "Exhibit A4," damaged cover sheet, some soiling to sheets, 13" x 8" **$350**

Ship paper, issued by port of Charleston, South Carolina, for brig *Mary*, March 10, 1812, 8" x 11" **$80**

Greeting cards

Easter Greetings, raised satin fabric with two cloth flowers, red bow, gold lettering, fringed edges, hand writing on back **$25**

Get Well, dachshund, 1950s, 4-1/4" x 4-1/4" **$5**

Happy Birthday to a Sweet Daughter, Raggedy Ann, 4-1/2" x 6-1/2" **$15**

Hawaii Greetings, with orig handkerchief, 1942, 6" x 5" **$18**

Hearty Greeting, diecut, fold-out, emb red roses and dove, verse inside, scalloped edge, made in Germany, 3-1/4" x 4".................................**$25**

Hearty Greeting, male hand and female hand clasping wreath of ivy and forget-me-nots, front panel unfurls to paper card held in place with tasseled cord, "To Greet you and wish you a bright Christmas Day," with poem, published by Davidson Bros, London, printed in Saxony, c1900-10, 5-1/2" x 3-5/8".............**$35**

Pinocchio and Gepetto, mechanical, 1930s...**$35**

Romeo and Juliet, diecut, 3-3/4" x 7-1/2"..**$25**

Miscellaneous

Badge, Red Cross, Official Worker, sgd by Miss L Quinn, 1934, 2-1/2" sq.**$10**

Calling card, First Lady Florence Harding, orig envelope.......................**$95**

Child's diecut book, *Dolly's Adventures,* McLoughlin Bros, heavy stock pages to color, pre-1920..........**$18.50**

Diary, Richard Tregaskis, *Guadal-Canal*, pictorial, 263 pgs, copyright 1945..**$12**

Ink blotter, Lancaster Iron Works, 8-1/2" x 3-1/2"...............................**$8**

Ledger book, Schuylkill Navigation Co., from Aug. 13, 1816 to Feb. 11, 1830, 250 pgs, binding loose, pages dry, spine damage, 9" x 5"...........**$575**

Letterhead, Louisville & Nashville RR Co., typed message, 1913.........**$6.50**

Poster, Kennedy for President, Leadership for the US, red, white, blue, and black, two folds, 28" x 40"..........**$120**

Receipt, M. P. Norris Newspaper, Morristown, New Jersey, Nov 1, 1895...**$12**

Tobacco label, Watson & McGill Tobacco Co., multicolored stone litho, eagle, sailing ships, draped flags, topless woman, 1872 copyright, 14-1/8" x 7-1/4"...**$90**

Tour brochure, Vermont Marble Co., Proctor, Vermont, 27 pgs, 4-1/2" x 6"...**$24**

Postcards

Advertising

Austro Fiat, artist sgd "Wilrab," left side with Austrian ships on Danube

River, sailor and Fiat car, Fiat logo on back, 1920-30........................**$48**

Munich Traffic Exhibition, Deutsche Verkehrsausstellung Muenchen, designed by Eugene O Sporer, man riding bicycle, first day cancellation, 1953....................................**$60**

Art Deco

Blacks, Aint's I yo Honey?, handwritten address, 1907.......................**$40**

Lady smoking cigarette, hand colored, French................................**$32**

Taifun-Wheel, amusement park, sent to Wien, Austria, 1929...............**$28**

Holiday

A Happy New Year 1908, heavily emb holly wreaths and snow, muted icy blue-gray, touch of red, icicles dangle at top, used...........................**$10**

A Merry Christmas, letters outlined in sandy glitter, covered with starlets, black and white, used, 1906 ....**$10**

Humor

Always After New Business, rooster chasing chicken, Lustercomics #151, Tichnor Bros, Inc., Boston, Massachusetts, 3-1/2" x 4-1/2"........................**$12.50**

"An Help Me to Forgive..." Mabel Lucie Attwell, #3696, copyright Valentine and Sons, Ltd., Dundee and London, 1900s, 3-1/2" x 4-1/2" **$15**

"I Work and Worry, Scheme and Plan...," lustercomics #132, Tichnor Bros, Inc., Boston, Massachusetts, 3-1/2" x 4-1/2"..**$12.50**

Let's Grow Old Together, Mabel Lucie Attwell, #3530, copyright Valentine and Sons, Ltd., Dundee and London, 1900s, 3-1/2" x 4-1/2"........**$15**

Old Maid, Lustercomics #143, Tichnor Bros, Inc., Boston, MA, 3-1/2" x 4-1/2" **$12.50**

We're raising a big rumpus, Colourpicture Publication, Boston, Massachusetts, pre-1960....................**$5**

Leather

Disguise our bondage As we will, Tis woman, woman Rules us still, Tom Moore, postmarked Dec. 22, 1906, 5-3/8" x 3-1/4" **$45**

Look before you leap, There are two kinds of women, One that breaks you and one that makes you, hand written personnel message on front,

postmarked April 1908, 5-3/8" x 3-1/4"..**$45**

Political, John F. Kennedy, New York Democratic State Committee, unused, with five Kennedy for President buttons, 1960................................**$80**

Real photo

Geisshuebel, Sauerbrunn, Austria, sent to Union Hotel, Singaore, black and white, 1902.........................**$110**

People digging for gold, black and white, printed in Germany, undivided back, c1910....................**$36**

Roney's Boys Concert Co., Chicago, printed text "Henry B. Roney, Trainer and Manager, 2358 Indiana Ave, Photo by the Root Studio, Chicago, black and white, c1910.....**$15**

Zeynard's Lilliputian Troupe, black and white....................................**$26**

Ship

Cunard *R.M.S. Lusitania-Mauretania,* New York harbor, Statue of Liberty at left, black and white illus, c1910...**$30**

U.S.S. Battleship Virginia, #6507, c1907...**$25**

Silk, WWI, butterfly design formed from flags of the Allies, c1917, 3-1/2" x 5-1/2"...**$95**

World War I, "And You? Sign in for War Bonds" WWI pilot, Germany, unused...**$32**

PAPIER-MÂCHÉ

History: Papier-mâché is a mixture of wood pulp, glue, resin, and fine sand, which is subjected to great pressure and then dried. The finished product is tough, durable, and heat resistant. Various finishing treatments are used, such as enameling, japanning, lacquering, mother-of-pearl inlaying, and painting.

During the Victorian era, papier-mâché articles such as boxes, trays, and tables were in high fashion. Banks, candy containers, masks, toys, and other children's articles were also made of papier-mâché.

Cigar Store Indian, painted, standing on wooden base, holding bundle of cigars in right hand, Indian pipe in decorated bag over left arm, Adams County, Pennsylvania, late 19th C, 8-3/4" l, 8-3/4" w, 42-1/2" h...................**$7,150**

Doll, painted papier-mâché head, wooden arms and legs, stuffed cloth body, orig printed cotton dress, c1860 ....**$5,600**

Fan, demilune, scalloped border, turned wooden handle, one side painted with variety of ferns on ochre ground, black japanning on other side, Victorian, price for pr, late 19th C, 15-1/2" l..................................**$250**

Hat stand, woman's head, painted facial features, sgd "Danjard, Paris," wearing later Amish straw hat, 19th C **$1,300**

Jewel box, painted lid top, fitted int., two doors enclosing small drawers, Victorian, minor restorations, mid-19th, 12" h, 10" w, 10" d, ...**$520**

Lap desk, rect with bombe sides, sloped hinged lid with scalloped edge, painted and mother-of-pearl inlaid center with floral spray within gilt and inlay vines, opening to red velvet-lined writing surface fronted by fitted compartments, and storage, Victorian, late 19th C, 11-5/8" w, 9-1/4" d, 3-3/4" h................................**$325**

Notebook, black lacquered ground, dec with floral arrangement, mother-of-pearl vines, hand painted accents, int. with notebook with some sketches, blank pages, 11-1/2" x 9-1/2" **$295**

Pip-squeak, rooster, orig paint, yellow, orange, and black, recovered wooden bellows, faint squeak, 4-1/4" h **$85**

Plate, painted cat, marked "Patented August 8, 1880," 12" d **$35**

Roly poly, clown, orig white and blue polychrome paint, green ribbon around neck, 4-1/8" h..................**$65**

Snuffbox, round, lid painted with interior genre scene of family with baby, interior lid painted with title "Die Tanzpuppen," painted mark "StabwassersFabrik in Braunschweig," German, late 19th/early 20th C, 3-7/8" d..................................**$460**

Table, tilt-top, hinged 20" d top painted with Continental city view, pedestal painted as stone tower, circular base with maritime scene, Victorian, stamped "J & B/Patent" for Jennens and Bethridge, Birmingham, England, 24" h **$7,475**

Tray, ovoid, ogee rim, painted black, hand painted center scene of children playing, thatched cottage, pigs, ducks,

Papier-mâché match safe with hinged lid, decorated with portrait of Kaiser Wilhelm II, metal push button latch, striker on bottom which shows considerable wear, commemorative piece from coronation, German, 1888, 2-1/2" x 1-7/16" x 9/16", **$250.**
Photo courtesy of Gamal Amer.

and hound, gold painted vine and butterfly surround, back imp "W. & P. Steele, 61 George Street, Edinburgh," Victorian, late 19th C, 32-1/4" w, 25" h..................................**$1,765**

Tray and stand, English

Oval, 30" l, 24" w tray, black ground, large central scene with two scarlet-coated huntsmen, one standing, other seated on bobtail chestnut with black foal on a hill, border with gilt transfer printed guilloche border, Mark Knowles & Son maker, English Registry mark for 1864, burl hardwood 6-1/4" d, 18-3/4" h stand......................................**$1,250**

Rect, 18-1/4" l, 14-1/8" w, black ground, large central scene of white haired gentleman on bobtail chestnut, five hunting dogs in open field, border gold painted with egg and dart design, 7-3/4" w, 4-1/4" d, 9" h mahogany stand..................**$1,100**

Traveling case, lady's, black lacquer and polychrome, hinged front doors dec with portraits of Queen Victoria and Prince Albert, hinged top and sides with scenes from English landscapes, sewing compartment with some orig accoutrements, two doors open to jewelry drawers, fourth drawer with foldout writing desk and ink bottle, Victorian, mid-19th C, 11" w, 9" d, 9-1/2" h..................**$1,150**

Perfume bottle, cameo glass, ivory, circular lay-down type, cameo flowers, embossed flip lid, original stopper, Thomas Webb & Sons, 2-3/4" h, **$1,700.**
Photo courtesy of The Early Auction Company, LLC.

PERFUME, COLOGNE, AND SCENT BOTTLES

History: The second half of the 19th century was the golden age for decorative bottles made to hold scents. These bottles were made in a variety of shapes and sizes.

An atomizer is a perfume bottle with a spray mechanism. Cologne bottles usually are larger and have stoppers that also may be used as applicators. A perfume bottle has a stopper that often is elongated and designed to be an applicator.

Scent bottles are small bottles used to hold a scent or smelling salts. A vinaigrette is an ornamental box or bottle that has a perforated top and is used to hold aromatic vinegar or smelling salts. Fashionable women of the late 18th and 19th centuries carried them in purses or slipped them into gloves in case of a sudden fainting spell.

Cologne

Malachite, Ingrid Line, molded rose garden surrounds artistic medallions, Kurt Schlevogt, c1935, 6-1/2" h **$275**

Perfume

Enamel, pear shape, silvered metal lid with bale, green ground, two central cartouches of courting couples, Continental, late 18th/early 19th C, 3-1/4" l **$215**

Porcelain

Continental, underglaze blue crossed swords mark, leg-form, garter and pale blue shoe, flat metal lid, late 19th C, 2-1/2" l **$250**

Continental, swaddled infant shape, enamel detailing, silvertone domed lid, tapered base, late 18th/19th C, 3-1/4" l **$325**

Meissen, Germany, courting couple, ivy covered tree trunk, enamel and gilt detailing, orig stopper, late 19th C, 2-1/2" l **$635**

Silver gilt, shield shaped, collet-set heart-shaped opal applied to front, surrounded by applied ropetwist, green and yellow enamel dec, back engraved with leafy scrolls, conical screw-in stopper, Hungarian, 20th C, 1-3/4" l **$115**

Silver plate, Victorian, London, bud shape, engraved rim, all over repoussé reeding, glass int., 1885, 2-3/4" l
.... **$190**

Sterling silver

Birmingham, England, hinged heart-shaped case, domed lid, emb angel dec, gilt int. with heart-shaped green glass bottle, monogrammed, 2 troy oz, 1897, 3-1/4" l **$230**

Victorian, London, bud shape, engraved rim, body with all over repoussé reeding, glass int., 1885, 2-3/4" l **$175**

Scent

Silver, Japanese, tear shape, molded dragon dec on stippled ground, attached silver chains, approx 1 troy oz, late 19th/early 20th C, 3-5/8" l
.... **$450**

Ivory, figural, woman holding basket of flowers in one hand, fan in other, polychrome dec, Japan, 3-3/4" h
.... **$90**

Vinaigrette

English, silver

Marker's mark "JT," Birmingham, rect, foliate engraved lid, base with

molded scroll rims, gilt interior with pierced and engraved dec, approx 1 troy oz, c1845, 1" w, 1-1/2" l **$290**

Tooled purse shape, gilded int., John Turner, Birmingham hallmarks, 1792, 7/8" l **$250**

European, silver, shaped as three squashes on vine, engine-turned textured dec, threaded bases, largest with pierced grate to interior, 1 troy oz, late 19th/early 20th C, 3" **$350**

Victorian, staghorn, mounted with thistle-cast lid, quatrefoil neck band, horn with guilloche strapping, short link chain, late 19th C, 2-1/2" l rough-textured horn **$350**

PEWTER

History: Pewter is a metal alloy consisting mostly of tin with small amounts of lead, copper, antimony, and bismuth added to make the shaping of products easier and to increase the hardness of the material. The metal can be cast, formed around a mold, spun, easily cut, and soldered to form a wide variety of utilitarian articles.

Pewter was known to the ancient Chinese, Egyptians, and Romans. England was the primary source of pewter for the American colonies for nearly 150 years until the American Revolution ended the embargo on raw tin, allowing the small American pewter industry to flourish until the Civil War.

Notes: The listings concentrate on the American and English pewter forms most often encountered by the collector.

Additional Resources:

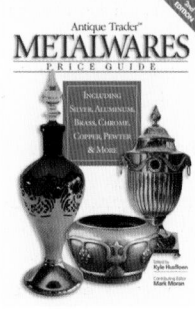

Antique Trader® Metalwares Price Guide, 2nd Ed., by Kyle Husfloen, ed., and Mark Moran, contr. ed., Krause Publications, Iola, WI.

Basin

"Love," attributed to John Andrew Brunstrom, Philadelphia, PA, 1781-93, round, flared sides, single-reed brim, circular mark with facing birds and "LOVE," [Celia Jacobs 16], and "LONDON," minor wear, 10-1/8" d **$650**

Circular mark with facing birds and "LOVE," "LONDON," "X" and crown mark, [Celia Jacobs 16, 17], minor wear, 11-1/2" d..................... **$2,250**

Circular mark with facing birds and "LOVE," "LONDON," and two "X" and crown marks, [Celia Jacobs 16, 17], minor wear, 12-5/8" d
.... **$2,820**

Partial circular mark with facing birds and "LOVE," "LONDON," [Celia Jacobs 16, 17], and "X" and crown mark, 6-11/16" d **$650**

Partial circular mark with facing birds and "LOVE," [Celia Jacobs 16], and "LONDON," 8-1/8" d **$500**

Partial circular mark with facing birds [Celia Jacobs 16], and "LONDON," minor wear, 9-1/8" d **$530**

Basin, quart

Edward Danforth, Middletown and Hartford, Connecticut, 1788-94, circular form, flared sides, single reeded brim, small touch mark with lion and "ED" [Carl Jacobs 82], 7-7/8" d **$650**

Richard Austin, Boston, Massachusetts, round bowl, flared sides, single reed brim, touchmark with dove and lamb, "RICHARD AUSTIN" in shaped oval [Celia Jacobs 230], c1790-1810, 8" d **$750**

Beaker

Boardman & Hart, Hartford, Connecticut, tapered cylindrical body, incised bands, "BOARDMAN & HART" "N-YORK" touchmarks [Carl Jacobs 47], wear, scattered small dents and pitting, second quarter 19th C, 3-1/8" h **$200**

Samuel Danforth, Hartford, Connecticut, tapered cylindrical body, incised bands, "SD," eagle and dagger marks, [Carl Jacobs 105], 1795-1816, 5" h **$1,765**

Timothy Boardman, New York City, tapered cylindrical body, incised bands, molded base, "TB&Co" and "X" quality mark, [Carl Jacobs 49], 1822-24, 5-1/4" h..................... **$900**

Teapot, S. Simpson, baluster form, domed lid, scroll handle, impressed mark, 8-1/2" h, American, mid-19th C, dented, **$185.**

Charger, ringed rim, three indistinct impressed marks, imp "AB," possibly English, scattered pitting and scratching, 16-1/2" d **$320.**

Plate, unmarked, American, 15" d, **$35.**

Bud vase, Secessionist style, orig green glass insert, peacock feather emb, stamped "WMF," 5" d, 10-1/2" h **$865**

Butter plate, American, unmarked, 6" d **$70**

Candlesticks, pr, Freeman Porter, Westbrook, ME, baluster stem, molded round foot, circular mark with "F. PORTER WESTBROOK," and "No. 1," [Laughlin text II p. 110], imperfections, 1835-60, 6-1/4" h **$770**

Charger, Samuel Ellis, London, monogrammed on back "MH," wear, knife, scratches, small rim repairs, 16-3/8" d **$350**

Coffeepot

Rufus Dunham, Westbrook, Maine, conical cover, flared cylindrical body, incised reeding, scrolled black painted handle, marked "R. DUNHAM," [Laughlin text II, p. 100], minor wear, 1837-82, 7-1/4" h **$500**

Issac C. Lewis, Meriden, Connecticut, tapered body, tooled rings around base and rim, worn black paint on scrolled ear handle, interior of base raised, additional touchmark scratched out, touchmark for I.C. Lewis on base, 1834-52, 10-1/2" h **$260**

Freeman Porter, Westbrook, Maine, ovoid, tooled ring at center, flared foot, and rim, domed lid, wafer finial, scrolled ear handle with later black paint, circular touchmark "F. Porter Westbrook No. 1," small hole at base of handle, restored dents, 1835-60, 11" h **$320**

Communion chalice, unmarked American, handles removed, pr, 6-1/4" h **$200**

Creamer, unmarked American, teapot shape, 5-7/8" h **$250**

Deep dish

"Love," attributed to John Andrew Brunstrom, Philadelphia, Pennsylvania, 1781-93, circular, single reed brim, circular mark with facing birds and "LOVE," [Celia Jacobs 16] and "LONDON," 13" d **$1,000**

Round, single reed brim, circular mark with facing birds and "LOVE," crown and "X" quality mark [Celia Jacobs 16, 17] and "LONDON" stamped twice, minor wear, 11" d **$500**

Round, single reed brim, circular mark with facing birds and "LOVE," crown and "X" quality mark [Celia Jacobs 16, 17] and "LONDON" stamped twice, 13" d **$950**

S. Kilbourn, Baltimore, eagle mark, 11" d **$1,045**

Thomas Danforth III, Stepney (Rocky Hill), CT, circular form, rare eagle mark, [Laughlin 370], c1790, 6-1/8" d **$1,650**

Flagon, one quart, Thomas D. and Sherman Boardman, Hartford, Connecticut, disk finial, three domes, molded cover with "chair back" thumb piece above tapered cylindrical body with fillet, scroll handle with bud terminal, molded base, "TD & SB" in rectangle and "X" quality mark, [Celia Jacobs 150], c1815-20, 9" h **$4,700**

Flagon, three quarts

Boardman & Hart, Hartford, Connecticut, domed cover with "chair back" thumb piece, tapered cylindrical form, molded fillet and base, double scrolled handle with bud terminal, "BOARDMAN & HART," "N-YORK" and two round eagle touchmarks, [Carl Jacobs 39, 47], c1825-30, 13" h **$3,100**

Thomas D. and Sherman Boardman, Hartford, Connecticut, urn finial, domed and molded cover with "chair back" thumb piece, tapered cylindrical body with molded fillet and molded base, double scroll handle with bud terminal, marked with "TD & SB," eagle, and "X" quality mark, [Celia Jacobs 64, 150], c1815-20, 14" h **$4,000**

Inkwell, small circular lid, four quill holes surrounding wide flat circular base, replaced glass receptacle, 19th C, 1-3/4" **$225**

Ladle, plain pointed handle, touch mark "WH" in oval, 19th C, 13" l **$65**

Lamp

Plus brass and tin whale oil burner, Putnam touch, James Putnam, Madison, MA, some splits in rim of base, 5-3/4" h **$315**

Plus fluid burner, unmarked American, attributed to Meriden, reeded detail on base, ear handle, light pitting, 7" h **$110**

Plus burner, Yale and Curtis, New York 1 touch, matching fluid burner missing, snuffers and one brass tube loose, 8-1/2" h **$190**

Measure

Assembled set, bellied, English, minor damage, 2-3/8" to 8" h **$550**

John Warne, English, brass rim, battered, old repair, quart, 5-3/4" h **$100**

Mug

Jacob Whitmore, Middletown, Connecticut, flared cylindrical form with fillet, S-scroll handle with bud terminal, molded base, rare rose mark to interior base, round rose touch, [Laughlin 382], mug accompanied by 1997 note from John Carl Thomas commenting on its fine quality and marks, c1750-75, 5-7/8" h **$9,400**

Joseph Danforth Sr., Middletown, Connecticut, quart, flared cylindrical form with molded fillet, S-scroll handle with bud terminal, molded base, "ID" mark near rim and handle, [Celia Jacobs 164], minor wear, 1780-88, 6" h **$4,700**

Robert Palethorp, Jr., Philadelphia (1817-22), 4-1/8" h **$3,800**

Samuel Hamlin, Hartford, Connecticut, quart, flared cylindrical form, everted lip, molded fillet, S-scroll handle with bud terminal, molded base, shaped "SAMUEL HAMLIN" touch, [Carl Jacobs 158], minor wear and pitting, late 18th C, 5-7/8" h **$4,200**

Samuel Hamlin, Hartford, Connecticut, quart, tapered cylindrical form, everted lip, molded banding, S-scroll handle with bud terminal on molded base, shaped "SAMUEL HAMLIN" touch, [Carl Jacobs 158], minor wear, late 18th C, 5-7/8" h **$3,900**

Thomas D. and Sherman Boardman, Hartford, Connecticut, pint, tapered cylindrical form, medial incised banding, S-scroll handle with bud terminal, molded base, "TD & SB" touchmark in rectangle [Celia Jacobs 150], minor wear, small dent on base edge, c1815-20, 4-1/2" h **$1,530**

Unknown maker, Boston, Massachusetts, tapered cylindrical form, everted rim, molded band, scrolled strap handle with shell-like thumb grip, molded base, marked "CM" "S" and "CS" around rim, last half 18th C, 6-1/4" h **$7,100**

Pitcher

Continental, swirl design, hinged lid, angel touch, 6-1/2" h **$85**

Freeman Porter, Westbrook, ME, two quart, 6" h **$225**

Plate

Blakslee Barnes, Philadelphia, Pennsylvania, eagle touchmarks and "BB," [Carl Jacobs #15], knifemarks, dents, some edge damage, set of six, 1812-17, 7-7/8" d **$980**

Richard Austin, Boston, Massachusetts, circular, single reed brim, rare oval shaped touchmark with dove, lamb and "RICHARD AUSTIN," 1792-1817, 7-7/8" d **$250**

Thomas Badger Jr., Boston, Massachusetts, round, single reed brim, arched left facing eagle mark and "BOSTON," [Laughlin 309, 287a], normal wear, price for pr, 1787-1815, 7-7/8" d **$1,000**

Thomas Danforth III, circular, single reed brim, oval lion touchmark with "TI" initials and four hallmarks [Laughlin 363a and 365], normal wear, late 18th C, 7-7/8" d **$650**

John Skinner, Boston, Massachusetts, round, single reed brim and hammered booge, partial lion touchmark and four hallmarks, [Carl Jacobs 249], normal wear, 1760-90, 8" d **$825**

Gershom Jones, Providence, Rhode Island, circular, single reed brim, struck two lions in gateway touch marks, four small hallmarks, [Laughlin 339 and 340], normal wear, 1774-1809, 8-1/4" d **$1,200**

John Skinner, Boston, Massachusetts, round, hammered booge, left facing lion touchmarks, same owner's marks on all, [Laughlin 293], price for set of three, minor wear, 1760-90, 8-1/2" d **$1,880**

Thomas Danforth II, Middletown, Connecticut, round, smooth brim, hammered booge, two lion in gateway touches, four small hallmarks, and "X" quality mark [Carl Jacobs 113], c1760-70, 9-1/2" d **$3,175**

Platter, Townsend and Compton, London, pierced insert, marked "Cotterell," 28-3/4" l **$2,400**

Porringer

Thomas D. and Sherman Boardman, Hartford, Connecticut, round, boss bottom, flowered handle, "TD & SB" in rectangle touchmark [Laughlin 428], c1815-20, 3-1/4" d **$715**

Richard Lee or Richard Lee Jr. Springfield, Vermont or unknown maker, round basin form, boss bottom, openwork handle with crescents and hearts, raised reversed "R" mark on handle back, late 18th C, 3-1/4" d **$600**

Thomas D. and Sherman Boardman, Hartford, Connecticut, circular form, boss bottom, Old English handle, "TD & SB" in rectangle, touchmark [Laughlin 428], 1810-30, 4" d **$470**

William Calder, Providence, Rhode Island, round basin form, boss bottom, openwork handle with partial round eagle touchmark [Carl Jacobs 67], dents, pitting, 1817-56, 4-1/4" d **$360**

Gershom Jones, Providence, Rhode Island, round form, boss bottom, flowered handle, circular lion mark with "GI" initials on handle [Carl Jacobs 176], minor wear, 1774-1809, 4-1/4" d **$2,350**

Samuel Hamlin Jr., Providence, Rhode Island, circular basin form, boss bottom, flowered handle, round mark with eagle and anchor, [Laughlin plate XLIX, fig. 337], 4-1/2" d, 1801-56 .... **$1,100**

Gershom Jones, Providence, Rhode Island, round form, boss bottom, flowered handle, partial circular lion mark [Carl Jacobs 176 or 177], 1774-1809, 5" d **$2,115**

Thomas D. and Sherman Boardman, Hartford, CT, circular form, boss bottom, flowered handle, [Laughlin 428], 1810-30, 5-1/4" d **$900**

Samuel Hamlin Jr., Providence, RI, circular basin form, boss bottom, flowered handle, engraved "LAH" monogram and date "1820" on bottom, round touchmark with eagle and anchor [Laughlin plate XLIX, fig. 337], 1801-56, 5-3/8" d **$1,550**

Soup plate, unmarked Continental, angel touch, 8-7/8" d **$75**

Sugar bowl, Ashril Griswold, Meriden, Connecticut, eagle touch, 6" h **$490**

Tablespoon, rattail handle, heart on back of bowl, marked "L. B.," (Luther Boardman, Massachusetts and Connecticut), set of six **$330**

Teapot

Roswell Gleason, Dorchester, Massachusetts, eagle touch, 6-3/4" h **$495**

Ashbil Griswold, Meriden, Connecticut, eagle touch, some battering and repairs, 6-3/4" h **$200**

Eben Smith, Beverly, Massachusetts, minor pitting and scratches, 1813-56, 7" h **$375**

PHONOGRAPHS

History: Early phonographs were commonly called "talking machines." Thomas A. Edison invented the first successful phonograph in 1877; other manufacturers followed with their variations.

Adviser: Lewis S. Walters.

Angelica, cylinder, duplex horns **$2,100**

Columbia

BN disc player **$1,000**

BQ cylinder player **$1,200**

HG cylinder player **$2,400**

Decca, Junior, portable, leather case and handle **$150**

Edison

Amberola 30 .... **$325**

Army-Navy, c. WW1 .... **$1,200**

Diamond Disc W-19 William & Mary **$500**

Excelsior, coin-op **$2,500**

Fireside-w/original horn **$900**

Gem, maroon, 2-4 minute reproducer **$1,700**

Opera, has moving mandrel & fixed reproducer **$2,500**

S-19 Diamond disc, floor model, oka case **$400**

Standard, Model A, oak case w/metal horn **$550**

Triumph w/cygney horn, mahogany case **$2,500**

Graphone

12.5 oak case, metal horn, retailer's mark, cylinder **$450**

15.0 oak case with columns on corners, nickel-plated platform, metal horn, stenciled cast-iron parts **$725**

Home Grand, oak case, nickel-plated works, #6 spring motor **$1,300**

Kalamazoo, Duplex, reproducer, original horns with decals, pat. date 1904 .... **$3,300**

Odeon Talking Machine Co., table model, crank wind, brass horn, straight tone arm **$500**

RCA-Victor, "45," bakelite record player **$65**

Silvertone (Sears), two reproducers **$500**

Sonora

Gothic Deluxe, walnut case, triple spring, gold-plated parts, automatic stop and storage **$400**

Luzerne, renaissance-style case w/ storage **$200**

Talk-O-Phone, Brooke, table model, oak case rope decorations, steel horn **$200**

Victor

Credenza, crank **$1,100**

Monarch, table model, corner columns bell horn **$1,500**

School House **$2,500**

Victor I, mahogany case, corner columns bell horn **$1,500**

Victor II, oak case, black bell horn **$1,200**

Victrola, VV-XI-244, metal plaque inside, refinished case with two sets of doors, **$575.**

Edison, oak case, **$350.**
Photo courtesy of Dotta Auction Co., Inc.

Edison, brass plaque with name inside top, table-top model, original, **$400.**

Delpheon, mahogany stained case, **$650.**

Victor II, oak case, smooth oak horn
.... **$5,500+**

Victor III w/papier-maché horn
.... **$1,400**

Victor V, oak case, corner columns, no horn **$1,500**

Victor VI, oak case, no horn
.... **$4,000**

PHOTOGRAPHS

History: A vintage print is a positive image developed from the original negative by the photographer or under the photographer's supervision at the time the negative is made. A non-vintage print is a print made from an original negative at a later date. It is quite common for a photographer to make prints from the same negative over several decades. Changes between the original and subsequent prints usually can be identified. Limited edition prints must be clearly labeled.

Additional Resources:

Stereo Views, An Illustrated History & Price Guide, 2nd Ed., by John Waldsmith, Krause Publications, Iola, WI.

Carte de visite of Tom Thumb, **$55-$65.**

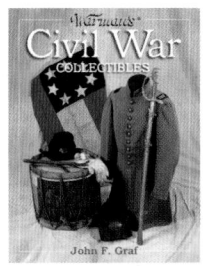

Warman's® Civil War Collectibles, by John F. Graf, Krause Publications, Iola, WI.

Album

"A Souvenir of the Harriman Alaska Expedition, volumes I and II," 251 photographs, more than 100 by Edward Curtin, additional images by Edward H. Harriman, C. Hart Merriam, G. K. Gilbert, D. G. Inverarity, and others, silver prints, various sizes to 6" x 7-1/2", several with handwritten credit and date in negative, others with copyright, album disbound and defective, title pages and map laid in, prints generally in excellent condition, 1899, pr
.... **$21,850**

"Kodak," 104 photographs of Eastern and Midwestern U. S. by Wm Hoblitzell, prints document his train ride across country from Maryland to Missoula, Montana, unposed glimpses of trains and local stations, Missoulan bicyclists and Native-Americans on horseback, handwritten captions and/or dates on mount rectos, mounted four per page recto and verso,

Carte de visite, unidentified Union infantry captain, **$90-$105.**

oblong 4to, gilt-lettered morocco, spine and edges worn, pgs loose, photographer's handstamp on front and rear pastdowns, ties missing, 1890-91 .... **$575**

Albumen print

Lincoln, Abraham **$1,550**

View of the Oswego Harbor, arched top, title, photographer, and date printed on label affixed below image, 1869, 13" x 16-1/2" **$1,380**

Ambrotype, William Gannaway Brownlow, known as Parson Brownlow, the fightin' preacher, half plate
.... **$3,190**

Cabinet card

Early, Gen. Jabal A., sgd, 6-1/4" x 4-1/4" **$1,840**

Garfield, J.A., sgd, 6-1/2" x 4-1/4"
.... **$1,495**

Lincoln, Abraham, lengthy inscription to Lucy Speed, 6-1/2" x 4-1/4"
.... **$1,840**

Sitting Bull, D. F. Barry, titled, copyrighted, dated, and Barry's imprint on recto, Bismarck D. T. imprint on mount verso, 1885, 7" x 5"
.... **$1,495**

Fully octagonal, cased, 1/6-plate tintype Union private with Springfield musket, full belt rig, **$350-$425.**

Wilde, Oscar, age 32, Alfred Ellis & Wallery imprint on mounts recto and verso, period German inscription handwritten on mount verso, 1892, 5" x 4" **$1,100**

CDV, carte de visite

Bill, Buffalo, long dark hair, wide lapel jacket, lighter overcoat with fur collar, light sepia color, 3-3/4" x 2-3/8", minor edge damage **$230**

Lee, Robert E., sgd, large bold signature, 3-3/4" x 2-1/2"...............**$4,025**

Lincoln, Abraham, taken by Matthew Brady, 1864 ....**$1,045**

Mrs. Lincoln, portrait with spirit of Abe behind her, Wm Mumler's Boston imprint on mount verso, c1869 ....**$1,725**

Colotype, 18-1/2" l, 8-1/4" h, by L. A. Huffman, Plains view, several cowboys on horseback rounding up large herd of cattle, professionally matted and framed, 24-1/4" l, 14" h **$750**

Daguerreotype

Northern abolitionists, America, group of men believed to be five Northern abolitionists and a Southern politician, identified left to right as Joshua R. Giddings (1795-1864), John Adams Dix (1798-1879), John Alexander McClernand (1812-1900), Henry Alexander Wise (1806-1876), Levi Coffin (1789-1877), and John Parker Hale (1806-1873), quarter plate, 3-3/4" x 4-5/8" case, mounted in brass mat, black leather covered wood case with red velvet int., case with repaired spine, c1849, 2-1/2" x 3-1/2" plate **$5,000**

Sell, John Todhunter, seated young child, tinted, sixth plate by M. A. Root, Philadelphia, stamped on matt, orig seal, some discoloration to mat, damaged leatherette case, c1840 ....**$475**

Store front, four-story brick building, signage on building, crates piled in front, man with top hat, unknown photographer, quarter-plate, image not sealed, plate marked "Chapman," leatherette case with some damage, c1850.......................**$4,775**

Unknown gentleman, sixth-plate image by Robert Cornelius, orig brass Cornelius frame with repeating diamond pattern, orig seal, affixed yellow paper label on reverse "Daguerreotype Miniatures by R. Cornelius, Eighth Street, above Chestnut, Philadelphia," minor oxidation to image, slight mineral deposits on glass, c1840 ....**$13,200**

Unknown gentleman, seated, sixth-plate image by W & F Langenheim, Philadelphia Exchange, re-sealed image, verdigris on mat, heavy tarnish halo at mat opening, leatherette case with photographer's name on pad, c1840 ....**$425**

Unknown woman, seated, sixth-plate image by W & F Langenheim, Philadelphia Exchange, re-sealed image, verdigris on mat, heavy tarnish halo at mat opening, leatherette case with photographer's name on pad, c1840 ....**$425**

Unknown woman, well dressed in dark taffeta dress, lace collar and cuffs, leather gloves, portrait brooch at neck, slight tint on cheeks, by Collins, 3rd & Chestnut St., Philadelphia, half-plate, orig seal, Collins paper label, full leatherette case, c1840-50...................................**$450**

Magic lantern slides, group of 320 photographic images from 1920s and 1930s, Atlantic City views and events, yachting, fireboats, Mohonk (NY), Duluth (MN), etc. housed in four individual carrying cases, several slides cracked..............................**$230**

Photograph

Aspens, New Mexico, by Ansel Adams, sgd "Ansel Adams" in ink on mount, identified on label from Boston gallery on reverse, framed, 1958, 19-1/2" x 15-1/2" **$6,325**

First Annual Round-Up, sgd in plate "Doubleday Photo, Wichita, Kan, First Annual Round-Up," 47 cowboys, cowgirls, workers, some on horseback, tipping hats, buildings and fences in background with advertising signs, 1920, 33-3/4" l, 8" h, 35-1/2" l x 9-1/2" black frame with worn paint.......................**$550**

Portrait of Albert Einstein, by Lotte Jacobi, sgd "Lotte Jacobi" in pencil lower right, framed, c1938, 9-3/4" x 7"..**$1,265**

Portrait of Marc Chagall and His Daughter in His Studio, by Lotte Jacobi, sgd "Lotte Jacobi" in pencil lower right, 6-3/4" x 5-1/2", framed **$300**

Fully cased, 1/9-plate tintype, **$265-$300.**

Fully cased, 1/6-plate tintype of doubly armed Union infantryman with full belt rig, **$450-$500.**

Ten Mile Creek, detailed scene near mouth of Ten Mile Creek, Powder River, Montana, heard of cattle spread out in the valley, several cowboys on horseback, 20" l, 14-1/2" h, contemporary 21-1/8" l, 16" h frame **$350**

Silver print, sepia tones, by Edward S Curtis, shows Indians riding horses in single file, signature and "L.A." lower right, glued down to thin card backing, 14" x 17" orig brown and black frame, sold with book *Portraits from North American Indian Life*, by Coleman and McLuhan, 13-3/8" l, 10-3/8" h **$1,150**

Tintype

Family, identified on mat "Marshall Kimpton," man wearing military coat, wife wearing elaborate hat, huge bow, daughter stands behind, ninth plate, cased, minor bends, case hinge has old taped repair **$150**

Unidentified Union soldier with rifle and bayonet, 1/6th plate **$360**

POLITICAL ITEMS

History: Since 1800, the American presidency has been a contest between two or more candidates. Initially, souvenirs were issued to celebrate victories. Items issued during a campaign to show support for a candidate were actively being distributed in the William Henry Harrison election of 1840.

There is a wide variety of campaign items—buttons, bandanas, tokens, pins, etc. The only limiting factor has been the promoter's imagination. The advent of television campaigning has reduced the quantity of individual items, and modern campaigns do not seem to have the variety of materials that were issued earlier.

Adviser: Theodore L. Hake.

Reproduction Alert. The reproduction of campaign buttons is rampant. Many originated as promotional sets from companies such as American Oil, Art Fair/Art Forum, Crackerbarrel, Liberty Mint, Kimberly Clark and United States Boraxo. Most reproductions began life properly marked on the curl, i.e. the turned-under surface edge.

Look for evidence of disturbance on the curl where someone might try to scratch out the modern mark. Most of the backs of original buttons were bare metal or had a paper label. Beware of any button with a painted back. Finally, pinback buttons were first made in 1896, and nearly all made between 1896 and 1916 were celluloid covered. Any lithographed tin button from the election of 1916 or earlier is very likely a reproduction or fantasy item.

Additional Resources:

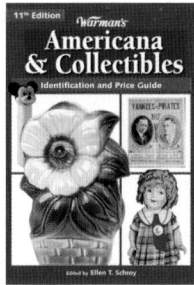

Warman's® Americana & Collectibles, 11th Ed., by Ellen T. Schroy, ed., Krause Publications, Iola, WI.

Arm band, hoover, celluloid, back mkd "Whitehead + Hoag," 1-3/4" x 7-3/4" **$50**

Ashtray, Smoked glass, "Thanks To A Key Leader," facsimile signature "Dick Nixon," 1960, 3-1/2" sq **$15**

Badge, Eisenhower, cardboard pinback changes image when tilted from black and white smiling Ike portrait to red, white, blue and silver design of crossed US flags and "Welcome Mr. President" in black lettering, 1-1/2" x 4-1/2" red fabric ribbon inscribed in gold "Inagural 1953" **$25**

Bandana, George McGovern, red, white, and blue, map, red star on each state capitol, slogans surround map, 30" sq **$20**

Bank, T Roosevelt, cast iron, 3-D bust of T Roosevelt, inscribed "Teddy," gold paint, silver eyeglasses, small red accent on his Spanish-American War hat, 75% orig paint remains, c1898-1904, 5" h **$195**

Banner, Win with Windell L. Willkie, blue-tone photo, 12" x 12" **$50**

Button, McKinley/Roosevelt, Whitehead & Hoag backpaper with moderate soiling, tiny dent in metal collet, slight wear, 2", $85.
Photo courtesy of Hake's Americana & Collectibles.

Button, McKinley, scarce white back version (usually gold) 1900, 2", $190.
Photo courtesy of Hake's Americana & Collectibles.

Button, Theodore Roosevelt, glossy, light surface wear, c1904, 2-3/8", $435.
Photo courtesy of Hake's Americana & Collectibles.

"Rough Rider" Roosevelt button, glossy, three tan dots on upper edge, slight surface wear, tin back with minor oxidation, c1904, 1-1/2", **$380.**
Photo courtesy of Hake's Americana & Collectibles.

Button, Truman with carboard back, raised cello bump, **$306.**
Photo courtesy of Hake's Americana & Collectibles.

Cello with easel, McKinley, sepia, real photo, reverse covered metal back, small center stamp by "J. Abrahams 229 Bowery New York" plus 1896 patent date, two cutout notches holding replacement easel wire. 3-1/2" d, **$290.**
Photo courtesy of Hake's Americana & Collectibles.

Flue cover, US for Ike, red, white, and blue shield with portrait, **$15.**

Bar pin, Hoover, brass lettering, white enamel dec, 3/4" l **$5**

Bookmark, Pres. Roosevelt, diecut aluminum, c1904, 2-14" l **$75**

Brooch, Harrison, brass frame, front with elevated thick piece of glass with beveled edges over hand-colored scene on inserted paper, two tiny figures, red, white, and blue flag, log cabin, hard cider barrel, inscribed "Harrison & Reform", orig bar pin, 1840, 3/4" x 15/16" **$1,500**

Bust, hollow cast metal, Wm McKinley, black patina, reverse stamped "G. B. Haines & Co., Chicago," 7" h **$70**

Campaign poster

Hoover, Herbert, "Republican Candidate for President," 1932, triple matted in 22" x 27" frame, 17" x 22" **$75**

Johnson, Lyndon, red, white, and blue cardboard, for Seante election lost by LBJ to W, Lee O'Daniel, 1941, 11" x 14" **$165**

Roosevelt, Franklin D., notation on bottom "Photo August 1944," 11" x 14-1/2" **$35**

Car attachment, Willkie for President, diecut metal, attachment bracket at bottom, Donaldson Art Sign Co., Covington Kentucky, printed dark blue, red, creamy tan, varnish finish, 3-1/4" x 5" **$85**

Carte de visite, Lincoln family, stiff card, artist retouched sepia protrait of family gathered around Lincoln, holding book on lap, blank reverse, 2-1/2" x 4" **$25**

Charm, FDR, 1-1/4" d **$20**

Christmas card, Adlai E. Stevenson, with letter of authenticity from Hake's Americana and Collectibles, 1960s, 3-1/2" l signature, 4" x 5" **$35**

Coin, US one-cent coin, Liberty head on front, front stamped "Vote the Land Free," reverse lightly struck, date 1838, issued in 1848 for Martin Van Buren, 1-1/8" **$135**

Convention bandana, GOP, Fort Worth, Texas, red, bright white block printing, circle of repeated GOP elephant symbols within 1984 date at each corner, center Lone Star symbol surrounded by text and cowboy boot design, 11-1/2" sq folded, opens to 21-1/2" x 22" **$25**

Convention button, celluloid, 3" d

Carter, yellow, black lettering, Indiana Labor Coalition, name over outline of state of Indiana, 1976 .... **$25**

Reagan, green on white, sponsered by "The other Washington-Reagan Country," used at Rep. Convention-Dallas, Aug 1984 .... **$48**

Dinner program, Ford, slightly textured stiff paper folder, Feb. 15, 1974 annual Republican Douglas County dinner, Omaha Hilton Hotel Ballroom, front cover with black and white photo and id of Ford as Vice President, lists of "Our Republican Family" inside, 7-1/2" x 11" **$25**

Door stop, Teddy Roosevelt, brassplated cast iron, Rough Rider outfit, patent date ono reverse, 1899, 10-1/2" h **$165**

Drinking glass, FDR and Chicago Mayor, Chicago World's Fair, images and names on front, "Chicago's Worlds Fair 1933 with two US flags on back, 1933, 2-1/2" d, 3/4" h" **$65**

Electoral ticket, linen-like fabric, black printed text, cream-colored ground, top reads "National American Fillimore and Donelson Ticket," various elector names, some as-made flaws, archival tape repair, 1856, 10-1/2" x 18" **$300**

Ferrotype pin

Grant, portrait with name, outer edge of diecut circular designs, vertical pin and clasp on back, 7/8" brass frame **$295**

Lincoln & Hamlin, portraits, slogan around front rim, circle of stars, rim hole, 1860, 5/8" **$750**

Hat, Theodore Roosevelt caricature, dark blue felt, stenciled large letters on front "Bull-Moose" under image of TR in tan Rough Rider hat, red bandanna, white eyeglasses and teeth, 1912, roll up brim 2" high in front, 3" h in back, 12" conical shape **$990**

Badge, three metal sections with celluloid inserts, "Reception Committee," b&w illus of waterfall, b&w photo of Taft, few spots on celluloid, 60% silver luster remaining, 3" x 9", **$200.**
Photo courtesy of Hake's Americana & Collectibles.

Top, delegate ticket, 1892, blank reverse, 2-1/2" x 4-1/2", creases and corner chips bottom, pin with 3/4" stud back, 1892, faded red stripes, 1/16" center dent, clean, price for both, **$58.**
Photo courtesy of Hake's Americana & Collectibles.

Horse bridle rosettes, Cleveland and Stevenson, thick glass domes over real photo sepia portraits, gold and silver metal foil borders, silvered brass backs, attachment bar and cases stamped, "Pfluegs Patent U.S. & Canada," 1892, 1-3/4" d price for pr **$700**

Inaugural clothing button, Washington, brass, Linked States design, "GW" in center surrounded by slogan "Long Live The President," 13 oval linked chains with each surrounding initials of one of the original states, 1789, professionally replaced shank, 1-3/8" d..........................**$3,500**

Inauguration program, Kennedy/Johnson, 64 pgs, orig envelope, 8-1/2" x 11"..**$45**

Jugate button

Bryan-Stevenson, black and white photos accented by silver central area, surrounded by red, white, and blue stars and stripes, narrow silver rim, 7/8" d...............................**$65**

Bush, cello, small Bush and Dan Quayle black and white portraits on red, white, and blue double flag symbol, black lettering "On His Way To The White House," 1988, 3-1/2" d **$90**

Coolidge, Republican, back paper from Philadelphia Badge Co., 7/8" d **$65**

FDR-Wallace, litho with photos of both, 1940, 1"...........................**$20**

Kennedy-Johnson, cello, black and white photos, top third with names in white lettering on red, bottom margin with blue arc inscribed in white "America's Men For The 60s," 4" **$70**

Nixon, inagural, 1973, 2-1/4" d **$15**

McKinley-T Roosevelt, black and white photos surrounded by gold beaded circles accented by additional gold scrolls at top center and bottom, dark blue background, W&H backpaper, 1-1/4" **$125**

Reagan-Bush, 1981 inaugural, white cello pinback, black and white jugate photo accented by five tiny blue stars, 5" l red, white, and blue striped fabric ribbon with gold lettering "Presidential Inauguration Wash DC Jan 20, 1981," 1-3/4" **$20**

Roosevelt, T. and Fairbanks, black and white portraits against red, white, and blue shield, Pulver, 1904, 1-1/4".......................................**$265**

Stevenson, black printed names on yellow ribbon panel, red slogan above "Go Forward With Adlai Stevenson," 1952, 1-3/8" color portraits **$40**

Taft-Sherman, wreath, union bug imprint on back, 7/8" d.............**$65**

Jugate poster, McKinly/Hobart, paper, matted, framed, text below each image, Thyer & Jackson Stationary Co., Chicago, copyrright 1896, 14" x 22"..**$65**

Lapel stud

Cleveland, horseshoe, dark red fabric, name in white lettering, dark blue horseshoe, 3/4" **$30**

Harrison, diecut top hat, lapel stud, silver luster, 9/16".......................**$25**

William McKinley, black and white photo in center, dark blue and bright red stars on cream rim **$20**

Letter opener, brass, Roosevelt, diecut and raised FDR image handle, 1930s, 9" l.................................**$45**

Mechanical pencil, Ritepoint, red, white, and blue, black and white photos of Stevenson and Sparkman at top, "Win with Adlai Stevenson and John Sparkman" in blue and red, 5-1/2" l **$35**

Mechanical pin, Taft, Presidential Chair, brass luster back and legs, silver luster seat cover "Who Shall Occupy It," small tab at bottom seat edge pulls and seat flies open to reveal sepia glossy paper real photo of Taft, 1908, 2" h **$150**

Medal

Buchanan, rebus, white metal, "Buchanan and Beckinridge 1856, The Union Must & Shall Be Preserved-United We Stand Divided We Fall," 1856 ....**$1,750**

Fremont, silver lustered white metal, high-relief portrait, "Col. John C. Fremont, Born Jan. 21st, 1813," diemaker's name "Anthony Pacquet" below neck, reverse with wreath and slogan "The Rocky mountains Echo Back Fremont-The People's Choice for 1856," with riboon wrapped around wreath "Free Men/Soil," 2-3/8" d **$200**

Medalet, uncirculated 1" d

Blaine and Logan, brass, front shows both men, reverse with shield at center "Union" on diagonal, surrounded by "The Republicans Have Ruled Since 1860 And With Blaine & Logan Are Good For Another Term," top rim hole, mint luster **$50**

Grant, copper, raised portrait and name on front, designer's name below his shoulder, reverse "Gen US Grant Our Next President May He In Wisdom Rule The Country He Has Saved," 1868, bright copper flashing worn **$85**

Harrison, 1" brass, portrait, name, and 1841 on front, reverse with eagle with ribbons above and below, slogan "Got It Tip-Come It Tyler" **$40**

Miniature

McKinley, glass, full dinner pail, orig swivel handle, removable tin cup lid, bottom reads "Albert Pick & Company, Chicago," 2-1/2" x 4" h, 5-1/2" h with handle raised **$300**

Nixon, alarm clock, Dick Nixon/Peace Time Company, painted metal case, brass accents, c1972, 3" h **$65**

Paperweight, William McKinley, solid brass bust, c1896, 2-1/2" x 3" **$60**

Pennant, inaugural, Eisenhower, brown felt, white letters, fleshtone portrait, pale turquoise suit jacket, gray necktie, yellow-gold felt trim band and streamers, 1953, 12" x 29" **$30**

Pin, plastic, donkey's head, white, Adlai Stevenson printed in blue panel between ears, 7/8" **$15**

Pinback button

Bryan, colored portrait, silver background, brown and white shoulder areas, light fleshtone coloring on face, unusual twisted wire orig pin, 1900, 1-1/4" **$70**

Goldwater, Go-Go Goldwater in '64, gold cello, black printing, small image of elephant as hyphen, tiny union printer symbol, 3-1/2" **$24**

Kennedy, All The Way With Kennedy For President, slogan in blue, white background, name in bright red, 1-3/4" **$75**

"Harrison and Protection 1892," raised dome portrait, tin back reads "American Tinplate Made By Norton Brothers Chicago," horizontal bar pin, five paint dots off and one flake off upper right, 1-5/16", $270.
Photo courtesy of Hake's Americana & Collectibles.

Kennedy, Youth for Kennedy, litho, curl reads "Green Duck, Chicago" 4" d **$150**

McKinley, black and white photo, gold trimdiamond design flanked by red, white, and blue star and stripe motif, bright gold outer motif, 1896, 7/8" d **$30**

Roosevelt, T., Welcome TR, back paper from W. F. Miller Co., NY, 1-1/4" d **$100**

Stevenson, Aldai Likes Me, red, white and blue litho, 1" d **$20**

Truman, For President Harry S. Truman, black on cream, 1-1/4" d **$60**

Postcard, bright red, white, and blue flag design, emb white oval frame at center surrounding browntone image of Teddy Roosevelt, musical notes above "Yankee Doodle" and slogan "Glory to the Union," printed in Germany, undivided back, 3-1/2" x 5-1/2" **$35**

Press photo, glossy sepiatone, President Harding and young Douglas MacArthur, second unnamed individual in civilian cloths, authorization stamp by International Pres service, early 1920s, 6-1/2" x 8-1/2" **$25**

Print, Andrew Jackson, undated, "Andrew Jackson Seventh President of the United States," c1840, 10-3/4" x 13-1/2" stiff paper centered by 8-3/4" x 11" N Currier hand-colored print **$125**

Ulysses S. Grant pin, slightly domed glass, clear sepia cardboard photo in brass shell, tin reverse with vertical pin, tiny amount of luster off right side, glass also has tiny sliver missing from bottom edge, overall near full luster, $275.
Photo courtesy of Hake's Americana & Collectibles.

People's Party jugate ribbon, red, black text "People's Party/Our Standard Bearers/ Omaha, Neb., July 4, 1892/ Equal Rights To All. Special Privileges To Nonoe/Oregon City, Oregon, March 16th and 17th, 1892," with candidates names below their images, center crease, 2-1/2" x 7-1/2", $610.
Photo courtesy of Hake's Americana & Collectibles.

Framed print, "Washington Gives Us Freedom" above Washington, "Lincoln Kept Us United" above Lincoln, "Wilson Fights For America and All Humanity" above Wilson, original glass and 18" x 22" frame, © 1917, 16" x 20" print, **$115.**
Photo courtesy of Hake's Americana & Collectibles.

Ribbon

Cass, Lewis, black on off-white, text above portrait "For President, Lewis Cass, Of Michigan, For Vice President, William O. Butler, Of Kentucky," below portrait "If we are not struck with judicial blindness, we shall cling to this Constitution as the mariner clings to the last plank, when night and the tempest close around him-Lewis Cass," slight folds, 3" x 6-1/2" **$10,000**

Cleveland, Grover, 1885 NY inaugural, purple fabric, gold "New York County Democracy March 4, 1885," top overlaid with brocade like band of woven gold brass thread, stickpin fastener on back, 1" gold luster fringe, 3" x 5" **$65**

Eisenhower/Nixon, blue fabric, gold lettering "Presidential Campaign Kick-Off-Eisenhower-Nixon-Sept. 19, 1956, Whittier, Calif Campaign Committee," 2" x 6-1/2" **$65**

McKinley, William, "Our Standard" platform, black and white, cream ground, brass eagle and flags bar pin hanger at top, 1896, 2-1/2" x 7" **$90**

Taft, William H. Taft for President 1908, woven silk, facsimile signature, portrait and White House, back reads "Patterson Silk Woven Novelty Co.," 2-1/4" x 7"............. **$65**

Washington, George, black on white silk, 2" center inscription, "Washington Association, First In War, First In Peace, First in the Hearts of His Countrymen," oval portrait surrounded by wreath, sword and quill pen, c1832, creases, some missing threads, 12" l, 1-3/4" w............. **$250**

"Sound Money" political ribbon, slight wear, 5/8" celluloid stud, 4" long ribbons, **$50.**
Photo courtesy of Hake's Americana & Collectibles.

Scarf, George McGovern, red, white, and blue repeat pattern of "For President George McGovern," also repeat pattern "Truth, Unity, Peace, Honesty, Togetherness," 13" x 58" **$20**

Sheet music, *Sidewalks of New York,* tan, brown, and white, six pgs, "Complete with Campaign Choruses," image of Al Smith with facsimile signature on cover, 6" x 7-1/2" **$30**

Stickpin

Harrison Morton, 1-3/4" x 1-3/4" metal eagle, wings open to reveal cardboard photos, July 10, 1888 patent date and number, replaced suspended tassel, images faded, 1-1/2" reverse stickpin........................ **$200**

"General Grant Our Next President" ribbon, Made in Switzerland, woven text and image with maker name stitched at bottom, scattered pin dots above eagle, 1868, 1-1/8" w x 4-1/2" l, **$200.**
Photo courtesy of Hake's Americana & Collectibles.

"Union Veterans Solid For Garfield and Arthur" ribbon, light handling wear, horizontal crease, 1880, 2-1/2" x 7", **$285.**
Photo courtesy of Hake's Americana & Collectibles.

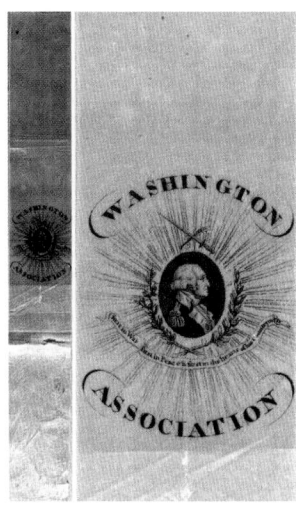

Ribbon, George Washington, black on white silk, "Washington Association," "First In War, First In Peace, First In The Hearts Of His Countrymen," oval portrait surrounded by wreath, burst of black lines, miniature sword and quill pen immediately above portrait, some fold damage, c1832, 12" l, 1-3/4" w, 2" h inscription/portrait area, unlisted in Sullivan-Fischer reference, **$250.**

Photo courtesy of Hake's Americana & Collectibles.

McKinley/Hobart, 3/4" d cello on backstamped "J. H. Shaw Co., Philadelphia," 1-1/2" pin...................... **$25**

Store display, Ilike Ike Sunglasses, cardboard display, six pair of plastic sunglasses with elephants on either side and "Peace/Prosperity," orig generic box, 7-3/4" x 21" **$150**

Stove pipe hole cover, Al Smith, "Smith for President," tin, 1928, 8" d **$50**

Tintype

Lincoln, four levels of elevated ovals surrrounding recessed center, accented by gold oval surrounding slightly domed glass, gutta-percha case, 3" h **$850**

Washington, possibly 1876 Centennial souvenir, 2-1/2" x 4" card with centered 1-1/4" x 1-3/4" x 2" tintype with octagonal edges................ **$150**

Watch fob, 1-3/4", brass, Bull Moose, raised moose image, "National Progressive Party New York State Convention, Syracuse, Sept 5 & 6, 1912," Bastian logo **125.00**

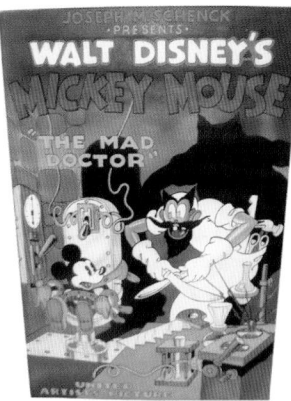

Movie, Walt Disney's Mickey Mouse, "The Mad Doctor," Joseph M. Schenk, United Artists Picture, certificate of authenticity stating it is one of a kind, **$800.**

POSTERS

History: Posters were a critical and extremely effective method of mass communication, especially in the period before 1920. Enormous quantities were produced, helped in part by the propaganda role posters played in World War I.

Print runs of two million were not unknown. Posters were not meant to be saved; they usually were destroyed once they had served their purpose. The paradox of high production and low survival is one of the fascinating aspects of poster history.

The posters of the late 19th and early 20th centuries represent the pinnacle of American lithography. The advertising posters of firms such as Strobridge or Courier are true classics. Philadelphia was one center for the poster industry.

Europeans pioneered posters with high artistic and aesthetic content, and poster art still plays a key role in Europe. Many major artists of the 20th century designed posters.

Advertising

Clarenbach & Herder Ice Skate Manufacturers, Philadelphia, Pennsylvania, large scene of ice skaters on Schuylkill River, Waterworks in background, later archival backing, mid-19th C, 17-1/4" x 23" **$675**

Coffres-Forts Fichet, adv for French bank vaults, c1905, 68" x 23-1/2" **$2,760**

Cycles Clement, Arthur Foache, Bourgerie, Paris, c1900, 53-1/2" x 37" **$5,750**

Ferry's Seeds, full-color image of pretty young lass amid towering hollyhocks, light fold lines, restoration to edges, thin tears, 1925, 21" x 28" **$325**

Fire! Fire! Fire!, "Chicago Lost But J. Dearman of Knoxville, Penna. Continues to Roll Up, Bundle Up, and Box Up As Many Goods As Ever!" red and black, some replacement to border, Oct. 15, 1871, 22" x 27" **$225**

Maggi, Chocolat Menier, Firmin Bouissett, 1895, 54" x 38-1/4" **$4,140**

Richfield Gasoline, race driver in car, c1930, 39" x 53" **$1,100**

Royal Portable Typewriter, dark green detailed manual portable typewriter against leafed red and green ground, c1940, 24" x 36" **$285**

Waterman's Ideal Fountain Pen, paper, Uncle Sam at Treaty of Portsmouth, early 1900s, 41-1/2" x 19-1/2" **$950**

Art Nouveau

La Emeraude, Alphonse Mucha 1900, 26" x 11" **$9,775**

La Topaze, Alphonse Mucha, 1900, 26" x 11".................................... **$9,775**

Leslie Carter, Alphonse Mucha, Strobridge, Cincinnati, 1908, 83" x 31-1/2" **$9,775**

Le Livre de Magda, Paul Berthon, Chaix, Paris, 1898, 25-1/4" x 19" **$2,300**

Les Eglantines, Paul Berthon, Chaix, Paris, 1900, 19-1/2" x 25-1/2" **$815**

Princezna Hyacintha, Alphonse Mucha, V. Neubert, Prague, 1911, 50-1/4" x 35-3/4"................**$18,400**

Vi Slet Vsesokolsky & Lide Cesky! Alphonse Mucha, V. Neubert, Smichov, 1912, 66" x 32"..............**$14,950**

Exhibition

Bals Des Arts, Crane-Howard, Joseph W. Jicha, 1928, 37" x 23"..........**$2,990**

Kunst Im Handwerk, Vereinigte Druckerein und Kunstanstalten, Munich, Bruno Paul, 1901, 34-3/4" x 23-1/2" **$5,635**

Midas, Whatsoever He Touches Might Be Gold, Continental Litho, Cleveland, Joseph W. Jicha, 1927, 37-1/2" x 25" **$2,530**

Magazine

The Chap Book, Stone & Kimball, Chicago, Claude Fayette Bragdon, c1895, 21" x 13-1/2" **$4,140**

The Idler, A. E. Forrest, J. M. Dent & Co, London, 1898, 29-3/4" x 20" **$690**

Movie and theatrical

A Good Man Is Hard To Find, Union Label, New York, Ben Shahn, expertly repaired tears in margins, 1948, 46" x 30-1/4" **$5,750**

Anatomy of a Murder, Columbia, Saul Bass design, 1959, 27" x 41" **$125**

A Trip To Chinatown, Dangerfield Printing Co., London, Beggarstaff Brothers, James Pryde and William Nicholson, 1894, 117" x 89-1/2" **$43,700**

Atlantic City, Republic, Constance Moore, Jerry Colonna in drag, by James Montgomery Flagg, 1941, 14" x 36" **$250**

Bad Boy, James Dunn and Louise Fazenda, Fox, 1934, 27" x 41" **$150**

Bringing Up Father, McManus, "Jiggs, Maggie, Dinty Moore-George McManus's cartoon comedy with music," early newspaper cartoon characters against New York skyline, c1915, 41" x 81" **$425**

Chaussures Caoutchouc, Marque "Au Coq," Gus Bofa (Gustav Blanchot), c1907, 53-1/4" x 37-1/4" **$3,220**

Dr. No, United Artist, Sean Connery, Ursula Andress, 1962, 27" x 41" **$325**

Goodbye Mr. Chips, Robert Donat and Greer Garson, MGM, 1939, 27" x 41" **$450**

Mule Train, Columbia Pictures, Gene Autry, Champion, full-color portraits, 1950, 27" x 41" **$150**

No No Nanette, Tony Gibbons, Theatre Mogador, Paris, European production of American musical, c1925, 15" x 22" **$375**

Smoldering Fires, Pauline Frederick and Laura La Plante, Universal, 1925, 14" x 22" **$125**

Political and patriotic

America Lets Us Worship As We Wish—Attend The Church Of Your Choice, for American Legion sponsored "Americanism Appreciation Month," full-color image of praying Uncle Sam, family at dinner table behind him, c1945, 20" x 26" **$275**

Confidence, large color portrait of Roosevelt over yacht at sea, "Election Day was our salvation/Franklin Roosevelt is the man/Our ship will reach her destination/Under his command…Bring this depression to an end…," c1933, 18" x 25" **$250**

Extra Post. Democratic Salt River Excursion, Incidents of the Annual Voyage to the Old Stamping Ground, Philadelphia, Tuesday, Oct. 10, 1871, comic details of Philadelphia political events, text and 9 vignettes, published by Philadelphia Post, later archival backing, 17-3/4" x 14-1/2" **$200**

Give Us The Faith And Courage of Our Forefathers, dark and somber image of Uncle Sam, Howard Chandler Christy, Recruiting Publicity Bureau, US Army, 1950, 35-1/4" x 24-3/4" **$1,265**

Kennedy for President, Leadership for the 60s, red, white, and blue, photo in center, some restoration, 1960, 42" x 27" **$2,530**

United Nations Day, blue and white U.N. banner waves over airbrushed stylized brown and yellow globe, minor edge crumple, 1947, 22" x 23" **$250**

Transportation

Air France—North Africa, Villemot, stylized imagery of mosques and minarets, lavenders, yellow, and blues against sky blue background, plane and Pegasus logo, c1950, 24" x 39" **$225**

Entertainment, The Golddiggers, Stars of the Dean Martin Show, Boston, real photo of Golddiggers, blue and white ground, **$75.**
Photo courtesy of Gary Sohmers.

Posters, U.S. Navy recruiting, color lithograph, "Your Country Needs You" and "Follow the Flag," 27" x 40-1/2", **$600.**
Photo courtesy of Sloans & Kenyon Auctioneers and Appraisers.

"I Want You for US Army," James Montgomery Flagg, American, 1877-1960, colored lithograph of Uncle Sam, c1917, 40" x 29-7/8", **$4,370.**
Photo courtesy of Pook & Pook, Inc.

A Subway Poster Pulls, Edward McKnight Kauffer, 1947, 45" x 30" **$7,475**

Europe, The SS *United States*, SS *America*, United States Lines, Lester Beall, 30" x 22" **$2,990**

Red Star Line, Antwerpen-Amerika, Henri Cassiers, Couleurs Berger & Wirth, Leipzig, 1899, 43-1/2" x 59-1/4" **$5,060**

Royal Mail Atlantis, Padden, tourists in Royal mail motor launch approaching harbor village, mountains in background, c1923, 25" x 38" **$675**

SS France, Bob Peak, launching of French ocean liner, champagne and confection in front of huge, night-lit bow of ship, 1961, 30" x 46" **$450**

Travel

Boston—New Haven Railroad, Nason, full color, stylized montage of Historic Boston by day and night, faint folio folds, c1938, 28" x 42" **$275**

Come to Ulster, Norman Wilkinson, sailboats and fishermen in front of lighthouse, full color, c1935, 50" x 40" **$450**

Hawaii—United Air Lines, Feher, stylized wahini, island behind her, full color, c1948, 25" x 40" **$650**

Paris, Paul Colin, doves floating above stylized Eiffel tower and Arc de Triumph, 1946, 24" x 39" **$600**

World War I

Call to Duty—Join the Army for Home and Country, Cammilli, recruiting image of Army bugler in front of unfurled banner, 1917, 30" x 40" **$325**

Follow the Flag—Enlist in the Navy, James Daugherty, sailor plants flag on shore, 1917, 27" x 41" **$450**

Gee!! I Wish I Were A Man I'd Join The Navy, Howard Chandler Christy, 1918, 41-1/4" x 27" **$1,955**

Give it Your Best, US Government Printing Office, Charles Coiner, red, white, and blue flag above slogan, 1942, 20" x 28" **$575**

Give Us The Faith And Courage of Our Forefathers, dark and somber image of Uncle Sam, Howard

Chandler Christy, Recruiting Publicity Bureau, US Army, 1950, 35-1/4" x 24-3/4" **$1,265**

I Want You For The Navy, Howard Chandler Christy, Forbes, Boston, 1917, 41" x 26" **$1,265**

Keep Him Free, War Savings Stamps, bald eagle on edge of nest, Charles Livingston Bull, Ketterlinus, Philadelphia, 1918, 30" x 20" **$575**

Put Strength in the Final Blow, Buy War Bonds, Frank Brangwyn, Avenue Press, London, 1916, 60-1/2" x 40" **$815**

Save the Products of the Land, Eat More Fish, Charles Livingston Bull, Heywood Strasser & Voit, New York, c1918, 30" x 20-1/4" **$750**

The Spirit of America, nurse wrapped in American flag calling on people to join Red Cross, Howard Chandler Christy, Forbes, Boston, 1919, 30" x 20" **$1,150**

Treat 'Em Rough—Join The Tanks, A. Hutaf, window card, electric blue-black cat leaping over tanks in fiery battle, white border, c1917, 14" x 22" **$900**

Will You Supply Eyes For The Navy? Gordon Grant, "Navy Ships Need Binoculars and Spy-Glasses... Tag Each Article with Your Name and Address, Mail to Hon. Franklin D. Roosevelt, Asst. Sec'y of Navy,..." image of Naval captain ready with blindfold on stormy deck, gun crew at ready behind him, 1918, 21" x 29" **$625**

Maxfield Parrish, The Knave, 9" x 12" older frame, newer backing paper, c1925, **$100.**

J. Symington, chromolithograph, pencil signed "J. Symington" lower right beneath image, and "J. Symington" lower right within image, 15" x 20" original frame, original backing paper, c1900, **$45.**

John Stewart Curry, "John Brown," lithograph, pencil signed, titled, and dedicated "For Maurice and Connie Liederman with our Best, J. & K. Curry," framed with AAA label verso, 15" x 10-3/4", **$3,750.**

Gustave Baumann, "Windswept Eucalyptus," color woodblock print, no. 22/120, pencil titled, signed, and numbered, matted and mounted in new Arts & Crafts frame, image 9-1/4" x 11", **$7,500.**

PRINTS

History: Prints serve many purposes. They can be a reproduction of an artist's paintings, drawings, or designs, but often are an original art form. Finally, prints can be developed for mass appeal rather than primarily for aesthetic fulfillment. Much of the production of Currier & Ives fits this latter category. Currier & Ives concentrated on genre, urban, patriotic, and nostalgic scenes.

Additional Listings: See Nutting, Wallace.

Reproduction Alert. The reproduction of Maxfield Parrish prints is a continuing process. New reproductions look new, i.e., their surfaces are shiny and the paper crisp and often pure white. The color on older prints develops a mellowing patina. The paper often develops a light brown to dark brown tone, especially if it is acid-based or was placed against wooden boards in the back of a frame.

Size is one of the keys to spotting later reproductions. Learn the correct size for the earliest forms. Be alert to earlier examples that have been trimmed to fit into a frame. Check the dimensions before buying any print.

Carefully examine the edges within the print. Any fuzziness indicates a later copy. Also look at the print through a magnifying glass. If the colors separate into dots this indicates a later version.

Apply the same principles described above for authenticating all prints, especially those attributed to Currier & Ives. Remember, many prints were copied soon after their period introduction. As a result, reproductions can have many of the same aging characteristics as period prints.

Thomas Hart Benton, "In The Ozarks," lithograph, pencil signed "Benton"" lower right, framed, 9-1/2" x 12-3/4", $1,500.
Photo courtesy of David Rago Auctions, Inc.

Arms, John Taylor, *Rodez/The Tower of Notre Dame*, etching on paper, edition of 120 plus six trial proofs, sgd and dated "John Taylor Arms-1927" in pencil lower right, inscribed "Arms 1926" and "Rodez 1926" in the plate, 11-7/8" x 4-7/8", framed **$230**

Atkins & Nightingale, publisher, J. Cartwright, engraver, *Georgetown and Federal City, or City of Washington*, etching with aquatint and hand coloring on paper, framed, few minor scattered stains, light toning, 1801, 16" x 23-1/4" **$17,625**

Barlach, Ernest, Fluchende Alt, woodcut, sgd in pencil lower right, Ferdinand Roten Gallery, Baltimore, on back, 4" x 3" **$920**

Barnet, Will, *Silent Seasons-Summer*, color litho, sgd, titled, and numbered 113/200 in pencil lower margin, 1975, 29" x 22-1/2" **$920**

Bearden, Romare, *Girl in the Garden*, color litho, sgd and numbered 29/150 in pencil, lower margin, 1979, 22-1/8" x 16-1/8"...................... **$5,750**

Benson, Frank Weston, *Geese Alighting*, drypoint on paper, second of two published states, sgd "Frank W. Benson" in pencil lower left, dated in the plate lower left, numbered "44" in pencil lower right, framed, 1916, 9-3/4" x 8" plate size **$1,035**

Benton, Thomas Hart, lithograph, sgd in pencil lower right, published by Associated American Artists, New York, edition of 250
Goin' Home, 1937, 9-1/2" x 12".... **$1,840**
Missouri Farmyard, 1936, 10" x 16" **$2,070**
Old Man Reading, 1941, 10" x 12-1/8"................................... **$2,185**

Boileu, Philip, child, "The Associated Sunday Magazines" cover, Feb. 1, 1914, sgd lower right, grade 4.0, c1914, 16" x 20" frame **$45**

Boydell, John, publisher, image by Benjamin West, engraved by John Hall, *William Penn's Treaty with the Indians, When He Founded the Province of Pennsylvania in North America in 1681*, hand colored engraving, minor repairs to border, c1775, 18-1/2" x 23-1/2"........... **$1,450**

Brundel, Carl Alexander, *Return from the Fields*, color woodcut on cream wove paper, sgd and inscribed "orig Holzchnitt Hand-" in pencil, c1930, 12-1/2" x 15-3/4".............. **$460**

Calder, Alexander, color litho
Composition with Mobile Forms, sgd in ink lower right, numbered 93/100 in pencil lower right, very pale time stain, 19-3/4" x 25-1/4" **$1,840**
Composition with Spirals, sgd in pencil lower right, 26" x 39" **$1,840**

Cassatt, Mary, color drypoint
Margot Wearing a Bonnet, c1902, 9" x 6"................................. **$1,840**
Sara Smiling, c1904, 7-1/4" x 5" **$1,725**

Chagall, Marc

De mauvais Sujets, color aquatint on Japon nacre, sgd and numbered 9/9 in pencil, printed by Lacourière and Frélaut, Paris, published by Les Bibliophiles de l'Union, Francaise, Paris, 1958, 13-5/8" x 10-1/2" **$5,060**

L'Avare qui a perdu son Trésor, aquatint and etching, sgd and numbered 49 in pencil, printed by Maurice Potin, Paris, published by Tériade, Paris, 1927-30, 11-3/4" x 9-5/8"................................... **$1,265**

L'Âne et le Chien, aquatint and etching, sgd and numbered 88/100 in pencil, printed by Maurice Potin, Paris, published by Tériade, Paris, 1927-30, 11-3/4" x 9-1/4"...... **$1,725**

Currier, Nathaniel, publisher, after Arthur Fitzwilliam Tait, *The Cares of a Family 1856*, lithograph with hand coloring heightened by gum Arabic on paper, identified in inscription in the matrix, Conningham, 814, matted, unframed, 22" x 28" **$2,990**

Currier, Nathaniel, publisher, Frances Flora Palmer, lithographer, lithograph with hand coloring on paper, identified in inscription in matrix

American Farm Series No. One, Conningham 134, framed, 1853, 21-3/8" x 28-1/4" **$2,185**

American Forest Scene, Maple Sugaring, Conningham 157, label from Old Print Shop, New York on reverse, framed, 1856, 24-7/8" x 32-5/8" **$19,550**

American Winter Scene, Evening, Conningham 207, unframed, 1854, 20-3/4" x 27" **$8,625**

The American Clipper Ship, Witch of the Wave, undated, Conningham 115, framed, overall toning, scattered staining, fox marks, creases throughout, 13" x 16-1/2" **$865**

Currier and Ives, publishers

A Scene on the Susquehanna, C#5415, farm on one side of river, flock of sheep, damage to modern gilt frame, repaired tears, 21-1/4" w, 18-1/4" h **$175**

Fruit and Flowers No. 2, "Lith & Pub by N. Currier" lower left, "152 Nassau St. Cor. Of Spruce, NY" lower right, framed in 10" x 14" orig frame, grade 3.5, c1848, 8-1/2" x 12-1/2" print **$165**

Meeting of the Waters, orig wooden backing, grade 3.0, 14" x 10" orig frame..**$75**

Scenery of the Upper Mississippi, An Indian Village, C#5422, trimmed, stained, matted, framed, 14" w, 10-1/4" h **$300**

Ensor, James, *La Cathédrale*, etching on imitation Japan paper, sgd and dated in pencil lower right, 1886, 9-1/2" x 7"..................................**$7,475**

Fox, R. Atkinson

A Perfect Melody, pseudonym sgd "DeForest" lower right, title lower center, grade 4.0, c1920-25, 7" x 9" orig frame **$50**

Clipper Ship, grade 2.75, c1920-25, unsigned, 20" x 12" period frame, ...**$40**

Sunset Dreams, sgd "R. Atkinson Fox" lower right, "Copyright Borin Mfg Co., Chicago" lower left, grade 3.75, c1920-25, 18" x 10" orig frame..**$370**

Print, Raphael Soyer, "Waitresses," lithograph, pencil signed lower right, and signed in the plate, framed with AAA label verso, 11-1/2" x 9-1/4" sight, **$800.**
Photo courtesy of David Rago Auctions, Inc.

The Old Mill, unsigned, grade 4.0, c1920-25, 9" x 12" frame...........**$60**

Grimball, Meta M., *The Loving Cup*, sgd lower right, titled lower center, grade 3.0, unusual six-sided double over mat, c1909, 10" x 8" period frame **$165**

Hundertwasser, Friedensreich, *Pacific Steamer*, color woodcut on paper, dated, numbered and inscribed "989/999 ©…868A Auckland 3 March 1986" in ink lower left, sgd with various chops lower right, framed, deckled edges, 1986, 20-1/2" x 15-3/4" image size..................................**$2,875**

Hyde, Helen, *Moon Bridge at Kameido*, color woodcut on paper, sgd "Helen Hyde" in pencil lower right, monogram and clover seals lower left, numbered "67" in pencil lower left, inscribed "Copyright, 1914, by Helen Hyde" in the block lower left, framed, 13-1/4" x 8-7/8"............................**$460**

Icart, Louis, *Sleeping Beauty*, color etching and aquatint, sgd in pencil, artist's blindstamp, 1927, 14-3/4" x 18-1/2" **$1,495**

Kellogg & Co., hand-colored lithograph, *Napoleon*, four stages of life, *Subaltern to Exile*, yellow and orange painted frame, damage, 15" w, 13" h..**$150**

Kent, Rockwell

Diver, wood engraving on paper, edition of 150, sgd "Rockwell Kent" in pencil lower right, 1931, 7-3/4" x 5-1/4" image size, framed, 3/8" margins or more...................**$1,120**

Print, Grant Wood, "In The Spring," lithograph, pencil signed lower right, framed, 9" x 12", **$4,650.**
Photo courtesy of David Rago Auctions, Inc.

Resting, lithograph on paper, edition of 100, sgd "Rockwell Kent" in pencil lower right, 1929, 9-5/8" x 5-7/8" image size, framed, 3/8" margins or more......................................**$1,175**

Knight, Dame Laura Knight, *Gilding the Lily*, etching and aquatint on paper, edition of 35, sgd "Laura Knight" in pencil lower right, 11-1/2" x 7-1/2" plate size, framed, margins over 1"...**$750**

Lindenmuth, Tod, *Low Tide*, color woodcut on paper, sgd "Tod Lindenmuth" in pencil lower right, titled in pencil lower left, framed, 15" x 14" image size................................**$1,600**

Lindner, Richard, *Man's Best Friend*, color lithograph on paper, edition of 250, sgd "R. Lindner" in pencil lower right, numbered "31/250" in pencil lower left on Arches cream paper with watermark, unmatted, unframed, minor handling marks, nicks, creases, c1970, 27-3/4" x 21-1/2" sheet size **$530**

Marin, John, *La Cathedral de Meaux*, 1907, etching on Arches wove paper with watermark, sgd "…de J. Marin" in pencil lower center, sgd and dated within the plate, 8-1/2" x 6-1/8" plate size, matted, deckled edges on two sides...**$350**

Marsh, Reginald

Tattoo-Shave-Haircut, etching and drypoint, tenth state, 1932, 9-7/8" x 9-5/8"..**$9,775**

Three Girls on a Chicken, engraving, sgd in pencil lower right, second state of edition of 20, 1941, 8" x 9-3/4"......................................**$2,185**

Newell, J. P., lithographer and publisher, *Newport, R.I.*, identified in inscription in matrix, lithograph with hand-coloring on paper, framed, tear to margin upper right, toning, stains, foxing..**$1,175**

Parrish, Maxfield

Chancellor and the King, grade 4.0, c1925, orig 9" x 12" frame **$65**

Dinky Bird, grade 4.0, c1915, 5" x 7" frame **$55**

Hilltop, framed in period 9" x 12" blue and gold frame, sgd lower left, titled lower center, "House of Art" lower right, grade 3.75, c1927, 6-1/4" x 10" **$195**

Lady Violetta in the Royal Kitchen, grade 4.0, c1925, 9" x 12" orig frame **$65**

Prince Codadad, orig 11" x 14" mat, orig blue and gold frame, "Copr P. F. Collier & Son" lower left, grade 4.0, c1906, 9" x 11" print **$70**

Rose Bower, unsigned, orig paper label preserved on back, grade 4.0, c1920-25, 10" x 15" period blue and gold frame **$65**

Rubaiyat, "copyright 1917 C. A. Crane Cleveland" lower right, "Reinthal & Newman, New York" imp lower left, grade 4.0, c1917, 28-1/2" x 7" print in 33" x 11" orig brown and gold frame **$250**

The Village Brook, sgd lower right, grade 3.5, c1940, 16" x 20" period frame **$165**

Thy Templed Hills, "Original painting by Maxfield Parrish, of Cornish, NY, courtesy of Brown and Bigelow" lower center, grade 4.0, c1930, 5" x 7" period frame **$65**

Vegetables for the Meal, grade 4.0, c1925, 9" x 4" **$65**

Picasso, Pablo

Deux Femmes Nues, etching on paper, edition of 125, sgd and numbered "34/ 125 Picasso..." in ink beneath image, label from Goodspeed's Book Shop, Boston, on reverse, framed, scattered pale foxing, 1930, 12-1/4" x 8-7/8" plate size **$5,875**

La Guitare Sur la Table, etching with drypoint on paper, reprinted 1961, total edition of 70, stamped signature "Picasso" lower right, numbered "29/50" in pencil lower left, framed, 1922, 3-1/8" x 4-3/4" plate size **$1,100**

Pressler, Gene, *Cinderella*, sgd lower right, titled, grade 4.0, c1920-25, 8" x 11" orig metal frame **$45**

Remington, Frederick, *Indians in Canoe*, sgd lower left, grade 2.75, damaged mat, c1900, 16" x 12" period frame **$35**

Ripley, Aiden Lassell, *Grouse on Pine Bough*, drypoint on paper, sgd "A Lassell Ripley" in pencil lower right, titled in pencil lower left, plate size, framed, unobtrusive mat toning, c1941, 8-3/4" x 11-7/8" **$1,100**

Roth, Ernest David, *Florentine Roofs*, Florentine, etching on laid paper with "G" watermark, sgd and dated "Ernest D. Roth 1912" in pencil lower center, titled dated and inscribed "Trial Proof" in pencil lower left, matted, soiling, breaks to hinges, 10-1/2" x 10-3/8" **$315**

Schille, H., Publisher, American, 19th C, *Panorama of the Catskills*, large folio, lithograph printed in colors with panorama and numerous vignettes, c1870, 21" x 27" **$825**

Sloan, John

McSorley's Backroom, etching and drypoint, sgd, titled and inscribed "100 of 100," third state, 1916, 5-1/4" x 7" **$2,530**

Patience, sgd, titled, inscribed "100 proofs" in pencil, sgd by printer Ernest Roth, in pencil lower left, fourth state, 1925, 5" x 4" **$320**

Soyer, Raphael, *Bust of a Girl*, lithograph in black, red and blue on paper, edition of 300, sgd "Raphael Soyer" in pencil lower right, numbered "86/300" in pencil lower left, image size 18-3/8" x 13-5/8", framed, over 1" margins **$210**

Spence, R. S., publisher, printed by William Robertson, New York, *American Hunting Scene*, four gentlemen with guns, dogs, and boat hunting waterfowl, hand colored lithograph, 22" x 28", framed, some foxing and waterstains at borders **$330**

Prang & Mayer, publishers, J. F.A. Cole, delineator and lithographer, *New Bedford, Massachusetts*, identified in inscriptions in the matrix, hand coloring, framed, repaired tears and punctures, scattered fox marks, staining, light toning, 16" x 32" image size **$865**

Toulouse-Lautrec, Henri

Carnival, color lithograph, fourth state, 1894, 9-7/8" x 6-1/2" **$3,450**

Étude de femme, lithograph, third state, published by Henry Floury, Paris, monogram in stone lower left, 1893, 10-1/2" x 8" **$1,265**

Ward, Lynd, *Giant*, wood engraving on tissue-thin paper, sgd and dated in pencil, 1955, 15-7/8" x 6" **$920**

Warhol, Andy, *Jimmy Carter III*, screenprint, sgd and numbered 14/100 in pencil, printed by Rupert Jasen Smith, New York, published by the Democratic National Committee, Washington, DC, 1977, 28-1/4" x 20-1/2" **$1,725**

Weidenaar, Reynold, *Bridge Builders, Mackinac Straits*, mezzotint, trial proof, sgd and titled in pencil, 1956, 12-7/8" x 6-7/8" **$2,300**

Whistler, James A. M.

Annie, Seated, etching and drypoint on antique cream laid paper, second state, 1858, 5-1/8" x 3-3/4" **$2,070**

Fumette, etching on thin laid paper, fourth state, 1859, 6-3/8" x 4-1/4" **$1,380**

Le Veille aux Loques, etching and drypoint, third state, 1858, 8-1/8" x 5-7/8" **$1,495**

Wood, Grant, lithograph, published by Associated American Artists, New York, *Seed Time and Harvest*, sgd and dated in pencil, edition of 250, 1937, 7-3/8" x 12-1/8" **$4,830**

Zorn, Anders, etching

The New Maid, sgd in pencil, sixth state, 1909, 11-3/4" x 8" **$1,265**

Two Butlers, sgd in pencil lower right, 1910, 6-1/4" x 4" **$1,035**

PRINTS, JAPANESE

History: Buying Japanese woodblock prints requires attention to detail and abundant knowledge of the subject. The quality of the impression (good, moderate, or weak), the color, and condition are critical. Various states and strikes of the same print cause prices to fluctuate.

Knowing the proper publisher's and censor's seals is helpful in identifying an original print.

Most prints were copied and issued in popular versions. These represent the vast majority of the prints found in the marketplace today. These popular versions should be viewed solely as decorative since they have little monetary value.

A novice buyer should seek expert advice before buying. Talk with a specialized dealer, museum curator, or auction division head.

The following terms are used to describe sizes: chuban, 7-1/2 x 10 inches; hosoban, 6 x 12 inches; and oban, 10 x 15 inches. Tat-e is a vertical print; yoko-e a horizontal one.

Chikanobu, framed triptych of women by lake, good impression, somewhat faded, c1890................................**$125**

Chinese, unidentified artist

Landscape, Blue and Green style, numerous seals, 18th/ 19th C, 35" x 19"....................................**$1,880**

Scroll, ink and colors on silk, scene of two monkeys trying to gather honey, Chien Lung cyclical date but probably 19th C, 32" x 19" **$1,530**

Sino Japanese War Poster, fair to good impression, color, and condition, some tears, creases, soiling, losses, framed..**$120**

Eiza, three prints, two kakemono-e of courtesans and one of samurai with a falcon, good impressions, color, stains, toning, fading and creases, framed..**$360**

Goyo, *Portrait of a Beauty,* Dai-oban, excellent impression, toned and matted to within image **$1,100**

Harunobu, pillar print of woman carrying bucket, framed, very good impression, horizontal creases and tears **$345**

Hasui

A Farmer with Wagon in View of Tall Pines and Mt. Fuji, fine color, impression, and condition **$650**

Mt. Fuji from Miho-No-Matsubara, excellent impression, stained and creased **$590**

Nezu Shrine in Snow, excellent impression, color, and condition, framed..**$775**

Rainy Season at Ryoshimachi, Shinagawa, excellent impression, color, and condition, framed **$775**

Hiroaki Takahashi, *Village Below Mt. Fuji at Twilight,* fine impression, color, and condition, framed, c1930 ....**$300**

Hiroshige, *An Island, Lake and Mountains in Rain,* from *Eight Views of Omi,* very good impression, color, and condition, some stains, not examined out of frame, c1850 ....**$360**

Hiroshige II, *Five Views of Edo,* set of five prints, very good impressions, color, and condition, one trimmed to image and laid down, others with soiling, stains, and creases, c1862 ....**$600**

Hiroshige III, *The Port of Yokohama with a Locomotive on a Stone Bridge and Western Steamships in the Harbor,* good impression and color, fading, toning, creases, and staining, framed, c1870................**$825**

Hokusai, *Kajikazawa in Kai Province,* from *Thirty-six Views of Mt. Fuji,* good impression, color, and condition, some staining, soiling, and creases, 20th C **$200**

Japan, unidentified artist, scroll, figure of woman with lines of poetry, very long, 18th C................**$3,525**

Jaquolet, Paul, *An Elegant Chinese Lady Holding a Veil,* matted to image, very good impression, color, and condition, not examined out of frame **$470**

Junichiro Sekino, portrait of actor Kichiemon, "il ne etat," printed signature and seal lower right within the image, pencil sgd, 13/50 in lower margin, 22" x 18" **$920**

Kasamatsu Shiro, *Pagoda in the Rain on a Spring Evening,* fine impression, color, and condition, upper right corner crease **$200**

Kunisada, *Ladies Gathering in Springtime for Music and Poetry,* triptych, good impression, color, and condition, with toning, fading, and stains, framed **$150**

Kunisada II, scene from a legend, good impression, color, and condition, not examined out of frame, framed..**$215**

Hiroshi Yoshida, six color woodblock prints: "Bamboo Wood"; "Kurobe River" (from Twelve Scenes of the Japanese Alps); "Rameido Bridge"; "Temple in the Woods"; "Critemeria Avenue"; and "The Cherry Tree in Kawagoe," pencil signed and titled, artist's chop on the plate, framed, Japanese, 1876-1950, 14-1/2" x 9-1/2", **$2,400.**
Photo courtesy of David Rago Auctions, Inc.

Kiyoshi Saito, color woodcut, Daitoku-Ji, Kyoto, signed lower right, numbered 14/100, dated 1959, sheet size 23-1/2" x 18", **$900.**
Photo courtesy of Sloans & Kenyon Auctioneers and Appraisers.

Kiysoiki Saito, Geisha, color woodcut print, pencil signed and artist's mark lower right, Japanese, 1907-1992, 10" x 15" **$350.**
Photo courtesy of David Rago Auctions, Inc.

Utagawa Kuniyoshi, color woodcut triptych, Ship Battle, signed and sealed, c1837, oban tate-e, Japanese **$1,300.**
Photo courtesy of Sloans & Kenyon Auctioneers and Appraisers.

Kuniyoshi

A Courtesan in Elegant Kimono Holding a Pipe, excellent impression and color with visible wood grain, slight staining and holes **$190**

Ladies Feeding Carp from a Pleasure Boat, triptych, excellent impression, color, and condition, with some fading of the blue, c1840 .... **$950**

Okiie Hashimoto, *Village in the Evening*, sgd in pencil in margin, dated, Hashi seal, good impression, framed, 17" x 21-1/2" **$250**

Shunga, *Couples Engaged in Lovemaking*, two double-page illustrations from album, fine impressions, color, and condition, centerfolds and slight creases, framed, mid-19th C **$420**

Toyokuni, perspective print of busy shopping area and temple grounds, framed, good impression, faded, 1790s.. **$260**

Toyokuni II, *Two Courtesans*, good impression, faded, trimmed, small hole, stains, and creases, c1800 .... **$150**

Toyokuni III, Pentaptcyh of people in boat feeding goldfish, iris garden, framed, very good impression, missing leaf, somewhat faded **$230**

Utamaro, *Woman Washing Her Hair*, good impression, stained, rubbed, and faded, framed **$725**

Utamaro II, three women in an interior, good impression, faded, soiled, c1811 .... **$175**

Yoshida Hiroshi, *Daibutsu Temple Gate*, signed in pencil, with Jizuri seal, excellent impression and color **$490**

PUZZLES

History: The jigsaw puzzle originated in the mid-18th century in Eu-

Parker Brothers, Watching the Yacht Race, *plywood, 423 pcs, orig box, 1936, 19.75" x 11.75",* **$175.**

rope. John Spilsbury, a London mapmaker, was selling dissected-map jigsaw puzzles by the early 1760s. The first jigsaw puzzles in America were English and European imports aimed primarily at children.

Prior to the Civil War, several manufacturers, e.g., Samuel L. Hill, W. and S. B. Ives, and McLoughlin Brothers, included puzzles in their lines. However, it was the post-Civil War period that saw the jigsaw puzzle gain a strong foothold among the children of America.

In the late 1890s, puzzles designed specifically for adults first appeared. Both forms—adult and child—have existed side by side ever since.

Prior to the mid-1920s, the vast majority of jigsaw puzzles were cut out of wood for the adult market and composition material for the children's market. In the 1920s, the die-cut, cardboard jigsaw puzzle evolved and was the dominant medium in the 1930s.

Interest in jigsaw puzzles has cycled between peaks and valleys several times since 1933. Mini-revivals occurred during World War II and in the mid-1960s, when Springbok entered the American market. Internet auction sites are impacting the pricing of puzzles, raising some (Pars, Pastimes, U-Nits, figure pieces), but holding the line or even reducing others (Straus, Victory, strip cut). As with all auctions, final prices tend to vary depending upon the time of year and the activity of at least two interested bidders.

Adviser: Bob Armstrong.

Notes: Prices listed here are for puzzles that are complete or restored, and in good condition. Most puzzles

Rustic England, plywood, 300 pcs, orig box, 1930s, 16" x 12", **$35.**

found in attics do not meet these standards. If evaluating an old puzzle, a discount of 50 percent should be calculated for moderate damage (one to two missing pieces, three to four broken knobs), with greater discounts for major damage or missing original box.

Cardboard, pre-1950
Consolidated Paper Box

A Dangerous Trail, 250 pcs, orig box, 1930s, 10.5" x 13.75"......... **$14**

Moonlight Beauty, 250 pcs, orig box, 1930s, 14" x 10.5" **$15**

Mutual Surprise, 250 pcs, orig box, 1930s, 10" x 13.5" **$14**

Milton Bradley

Grand Canyon, 200 pcs, orig box, 1933, 15" x 11.75" **$12**

Off the Norway Coast, 465 pcs, orig box, 1930s, 26.25" x 18.5" **$14**

Viking MFG

A Dutch Scene, 160 pcs, orig box, 1933, 13.75" x 10"..................... **$15**

The Cardinal Portrait, 184 pcs, orig box, 1933, 13.75" x 10".............. **$14**

Parker Brothers, plywood

Dutch Landing Place, 418 pcs, orig box, 1932, 25.75" x 9"................. **$200**

Fisherfolk at Sunset, 402 pcs, orig box, 1930s, 20.75" x 16" **$165**

Summer Reflections, 755 pcs, orig box, 1930, 28" x 18.5"................. **$330**

The Awakening of Spring, 110 pcs, orig box, 1910s, 13.75" x 5.75" **$45**

Thoroughbreds in Pasture, 307 pcs, replaced box, c1909, 16.5" x 10.5" **$125**

Joseph K. Strauss, plywood

Autumn Along the Seine, 100 pcs, orig box, 1930s, 9.5" x 6.75"........ **$15**

Home for the Holidays, 700 pcs, orig box, 1930s, 22.5" x 15.75" **$110**

Oriental Traders in Venice, 750 pcs, orig box, 1930s, 23.75" x 18" **$85**

Rustic England, 300 pcs, orig box, 1930s, 16" x 12"...............**$35**

Wood and/or handcut, pre-1930

Ayer, Isabel, *Across the Desert*, Picture Puzzle Exchange, solid wood, 240 pcs, orig box, c1909, 14" x 11.5" **$100**

Richardson, Margaret, *In the Meadow Lands*, solid wood, 192 pcs, replaced box, c1909, 11" x 7" **$85**

Tryawhile Puzzle co, The Blue Ribbons, plywood, 268 pcs, orig box, 1920/1930, 10" x 11.75"..............**$100**

Unknown maker

A Winter Day, solid wood, 186 pcs, orig box, 1909, 11.75" x 7.75" **$75**

Happiness, solid wood, 165 pcs, replaced box, 1909, 8.25" x 9.5" **$65**

Katharine and Sylvia, plywood, 364 pcs, replaced box, 1910/20, 14.75" x 19"...............**$120**

Lincoln Training for Greatness, solid wood, 139 pcs, orig box, c1909, 7.5" x 11..............**$50**

Pin Up in a Peck, solid wood, 125 pcs, replaced box, c1909, 5.5" x 8.5" **$50**

Rocky Portal, plywood, 233 pcs, orig box, 1910/20, 12" x 9.75" **$85**

Wood and/or handcut, 1930s-40s, plywood

Allen, P.J./Sparetime, *A Beautiful Garden*, 172 pcs, orig box, 1930s, 11.75" x 8.75" **$35**

Cape Cod Puzzle Co., 1930s

A Good Story But A Bad Shot, 150 pcs, orig box, 10.5" x 7" **$25**

Parker Brothers, Betsy Ross, *plywood, 500 pcs, orig box, 1933, 22" x 14.5"*, **$210.**

Freshening Breeze, 300 pcs, replaced, 11.75" x 13.75" **$60**

Capen, L./Master-Piece, *House and Garden*, 650 pcs, orig box, 1940/50, 19.75" x 15.75" **$150**

Chad Valley, *Lord Mayor's Coachman*, 500 pcs, orig box, 1930/40, 18" x 21"...............**$85**

Hart, Charles L., 1930s

How Grandfather Traveled, 322 pcs, replaced box, 15.25" x 10.25" **$75**

The Fall, 237 pcs, replaced box, 10.25" x 13.5" **$50**

Hayter/Victory Artistic

Bloom Time, 800 pcs, orig box, 1940/50, 22.5" x 19.5" **$135**

Reminiscences, 300 pcs, orig box, 1930/40, 14.5" x 10.75" **$60**

Madmar/Blue Ribbon, *Holland Street Scene*, 102 pcs, orig box, 1930s, 8.5" x 12.5" **$15**

Milton Bradley/Premier

Melody of Love, 301 pcs, orig box, 1930s, 15.75" x 11.5"..................**$90**

Washington at Valley Forge, 312 pcs, orig box, 1930s. 15.5" x 11.75" **$90**

Parker Bros., 1930s

Boston Tea Party, 200 pcs, orig box, 9" x 11.75" **$70**

Lovely Thatched Cottage, 525 pcs, replaced box, 22" x 16.25"........**$170**

Vera, Jouets, *The Fox's Victory*, 1000 pcs, orig box, 1930s, 29.25" x 11.75" **$300**

Winsor, Mrs. Allen P., *Poppies and Delphinium*, 617 pcs, orig box, 1930s, 21" x 16"............................**$220**

Unknown

The Limit of Wind and Sail, 504 pcs, orig box, 1930/40, 20" x 16" **$150**

The Mill Pond Has Gone To Sleep, 665 pcs, replaced box, 1930s, 20" x 16.25"...............**$100**

Wood and/or handcut, post 1950s, plywood

Atlantic/Kingsbridge, *Her Pride*, 300 pcs, orig box, 1950/60 ....**$30**

Browning, James/U-Nit, 1950s

Christening in the New Republic, 210 pcs, orig box, 13.5" x 9.75" **$60**

Leaving Winter Behind, 300 pcs, orig box, 1950s, 15.75" x 11.75" **$80**

The Haywagon, 400 pcs, orig box, 18" x 13.75".............**$130**

Scribner, Louise, 1950/60

Home For Christmas, 340 pcs, orig box, 13.75" x 9.5".....................**$85**

Meet Saeko, 186 pcs, orig box, 9.5" x 12" **$50**

Guardians of Liberty, *plywood, 200 pcs, orig box, 1940s, 8.75" x 11.75"*, **$35.**

Parker Brothers, Village Blacksmith, *plywood, 364 pcs, orig box, 1930s, 18.75" x 12.5"*, **$140.**

Day's Work Done, *plywood, 412 pcs, orig box, 1910s, 20" x 13"*, **$160.**

Ayer, Isabel, The Shrine, *solid wood, 495 pcs, orig box, 1914, 14" x 20.25"*, **$220.**

Parker Brothers, Will You Swap?, *plywood, 309 pcs, orig box, 1933, 11.25" x 15.5"*, **$120.**

Schwartz, F.A.O., Seawitch is Leading, *plywood, 1000 pcs, orig box, 1950/60, 27.75" x 22"*, **$180.**

Foss, Horace, E./Klever Kut, In the Gloaming, *plywood, 225 pcs, orig box, 1930s, 10" x 12"*, **$80.**

Madmar/Blue Ribbon, The Trapper's Cabin, *plywood, 400 pcs, orig box, 1930s, 15.75" x 11.75"*, **$110.**

QUILTS

History: Quilts have been passed down as family heirlooms for many generations. Each one is unique. The same pattern may have hundreds of variations in both color and design. The advent of the sewing machine increased, not decreased, the number of quilts made. Quilts are still being sewn today.

Notes: The key considerations for price are age, condition, aesthetic appeal, and design.

Appliqué

Eagle, red, green, and gold eagles, bordered nine block pattern, white ground, quilted in conforming eagle and geometric pattern, Missouri, 20th C, 83" x 77" **$2,350**

Flower Basket, red, green, and yellow calico, white ground, toning, minor staining, fabric wear, 77-1/2" x 67" **$885**

Grape vines, green and purple vines meandering between quilted stuffed grapes, hand quilted following pattern, minor stains, 66" x 82" **$800**

Nine blocks, each with large red flower, pink and yellow center, blue leaves and vines, red buds, border of blue quarter moons and red stars, white quilted ground, signed with embroidery "Polly Matthias (heart) Lug March 1837," 84" x 84" **$1,750**

Oak leaf, red and green printed fabric vine border, white ground, minor stains, marker lines, late 19th C, 72" x 88" **$300**

Rose of Sharon, pieced scalloped border, red, green, pink, and yellow calico, white ground and backing, red binding, conforming floral pattern quilting, attributed to PA, c1840, 88" x 90" **$1,530**

Tulips

Bright pink and green tulips, white ground, figure eight quilting in border, white back, 80-1/2" x 92" **$300**

Pink and green tulips rising out of blue triangles, white ground with vining stem and leaf design quilted into it, white backing, 74-3/4" sq **$350**

Twenty medallion blocks, blue, green, and red flowers and berries, surrounded by red, and green vining, two with pots of flowers flanking central ground dated "1849" near top, hand quilted, light staining, some damage to appliqué, 82" x 88" **$1,380**

Quilt, appliqué, red and green calico flowers, orange background, 95" x 93", **$630.**
Photo courtesy of Pook & Pook, Inc.

Vine and Blackberry, 16 white blocks, each with appliqued aqua vine with pendant blackberries, separated by aqua grid also forming border, white cotton backing with intricate quilting, America, minor stain, c1920, 82" x 86" **$4,000**

Appliqué and pieced

Album, red plaid separates squares with appliquéd polychrome prints, most are floral, some have deer or birds, two have Eastern scenes with camels and elephants, inked signatures, stains, dates in the 1850s, 64" sq **$1,870**

Embroidered, appliquéd, pieced cotton, 16 white blocks separated by diagonal red grid, each with floral sprigs and blossoms in solid red, yellow, blue and green accented with wool yarn and cotton embroidered buds and leaves, white backing, New England, losses and fading, late 19th C, 80-1/2" x 90" **$1,410**

Nine floral medallions, red, yellow, and green, red and green sawtooth edging, hand quilted, feathering between medallions, scroll work along border, stains, 82" x 83" **$1,430**

Tulips, pink, purple, and orange, green leaves and borders, hand quilted with flowers, feathering, and diamonds, dark black and blue pencil lines, light green edging, 70" x 82" **$770**

Chintz

Printed, overall design of exotic birds drinking from urns hanging from trees, brown on white, printed gold, blue, green, and reddish-brown, brown floral baking, light stains, 94" x 116" **$1,450**

Crazy

Pieced, many embroideries, including chenille goldenrod, owl at center of pin-wheeled fabrics, 1891 .... **$4,500**

Pieced, velvet and satin multicolored fabrics, embroidered seams, many embroidered embellishments, appliquéd flowers, burgundy velvet border, gold cotton backing, wear to binding, 79-1/4" x 81" **$750**

Pieced

Basket, 16 baskets composed of solid white and yellow cotton triangles, white ground with double yellow borders, white cotton backing, quilted with feather medallions, diamond and undulating feather border, possibly Mennonite, c1900, 79" sq **$1,550**

Bow Tie, small green and red triangles, red zig zag border with green sawtooth edging, hand stitched four petal flower quilting, red edging, slight wear and facing, 74" sq **$1,575**

Pennsylvania applique quilt, red and green golden rods, green swag border, c1860, 82" x 84", **$920.**
Photo courtesy of Pook & Pook, Inc.

Broken Star, orange, yellow, green, red, brown, blue, and white printed calico patches, red and white calico Flying Geese border, PA, 19th C, 80" x 76"..**$460**

Cathedral, multicolored diamonds within white circles, hand stitching, 90-1/4" x 105" **$425**

Chinese Lanterns, green, red, blue, yellow, and white printed calico and solid patches, blue and white ground, red border, diamond and rope quilting, PA, minor staining, late 19th C, 82" x 84" **$1,495**

Courthouse Steps, various silk colors, black border, highlighted by decorative embroidery, minor wear, late 19th C, 20" x 26-1/2" **$260**

Diamond blocks, bands of calico alternating with bands of diamond blocks, shades of brown on white ground, scattered staining on front, small hole in backing, 102" x 107" **$750**

Diamonds, polychrome calico bars forming concentric diamonds, white backing, white edge binding, quilting follows bars, 74" sq.....................**$300**

Eagles and sunburst, central teal and red sunburst surrounded by four teal and red eagles and shields, bright yellow ground, leaf motifs in corners, border with band comprised of red and yellow triangles, red band, yellow outer band with red binding, floral motif quilted into yellow ground, pink and yellow broad bands backing, 76" x 81-1/2", some fading on back, small stain................................**$1,400**

Flower Basket in Diamond design, red, yellow, pink, and red calico, 1" tear, 20th C, 89" x 87" **$450**

Four petal flowers, two shades of light yellow and pale green, white ground, border of arches with buds, hand stitched, princess feather medallions, fancy scrolls, and interlacing lines quilting, scalloped edge, light stains, 84" sq **$495**

Irish Chain, pink, green, and peach calico, straight green and pink borders, brown calico backing, embroidered with red "B" in lower left hand corner, very minor staining, 6' 10" x 6' 11" **$225**

Log cabin, silk, satin, and velvet, bright colors, four thin borders surround 20 large blocks, hand and machine stitched, small label attached says "Florida Quilt Heritage, #216 NQG #6, documented Florida quilt, Museum of Florida History," 58" x 74" **$320**

Martha Washington's Flower Garden, calicos and printed fabrics, predominately yellows, red and tan borders, hand stitched, minor wear, 66" x 86" **$300**

Moon and Stars, pieced wool, 49 full and three-quarter circles composed of four pie-shaped wedges, shades or rust and green, tan twill binding, woven wool backing, fading, stains, small holes, 83" x 96" **$770**

Nine Patch, various colors, red grid, hand and machine stitched, backed and bound with red and white printed fabric, minor fading, late 19th/early 20th C, 79" x 71" **$230**

Nine Patch variant

Chintz squares edged with triangles, floral printed border, hand stitched, diamond and floral quilting, orig pencil marks, some stains, 82" x 83"...**$1,540**

Multicolored squares alternating with off-white, arranged diagonally in block and surrounded by red grid, sawtooth border, backed with white, red binding, minor imperfections, 81-1/2" x 75" **$460**

Philadelphia Pavements, blue, red, orange, and white square printed and solid patches, orange and red banded borders with feather and floral fine quilting, PA, late 19th/ early 20th C, 84" x 80" **$825**

Pineapple corner elements with birds, central medallion, golden yellow on red, white green borders, burnt orange calico backing, hand stitched, 92" sq............................**$725**

Pineapple Log Cabin, pieced calico, border of four bands, two yellow, green, and pink, backed with brown figured print, bound with green, Mennonite, Washington, PA, c1880, 96" x 84".............................**$1,175**

Schoolhouse, red, orange, yellow, and tan buildings machine-stitched on white ground, several interesting quilting patterns, scallops, and zigzags on roofs, stars and geometric shapes in gable ends, birds and leaves on sashing, Midwest, late 19th C, 75-1/2" x 73-1/2"..................**$1,060**

Serrated Square, corresponding border, pink and green calico, shell and diamond quilting, 82" x 84"........**$320**

Spider Web, pink, red, blue, purple green, peach, and brown printed calico patches, wide purple calico border, diagonal line quilting, Mennonite, PA, some staining, late 19th C, 82" x 80"..**$825**

Star, large eight-pointed star in pastels, white ground, white backing, repair at corner, 69" sq **$200**

Starbursts inside latticework, eight-pointed starbursts, yellow and green calico blocks and bars form lattice, calico baking, scattered light staining on front, small section of wear, 98" x 101-1/2"....................**$200**

Starbursts with blocks and bars, multicolored starbursts, pink blocks and bars, complex quilting, reverse stamped "M. A. Darby," PA, scattered staining front and back, one star worn through, paper tag states c1865, 82" x 90"..**$350**

Star of Bethlehem, purple, green, red, blue, and pink calico, white ground, toning, minor staining, fabric wear, early 20th C, 82" x 73-1/2" **$650**

Stars, eight-pointed green and pink calico stars, white calico ground, green and pink band on border with figure eight quilting, three broad pink bands on back, two small stains, 72-1/2" x 80" **$200**

Quilt, pair of red and white double Irish chain, Katherine Ann Foltz, Smithburg Maryland, c1880, **$1,350.**
Photo courtesy of Sloans & Kenyon Auctioneers and Appraisers.

Stars, 42 blocks of eight-point stars set on the diagonal in a variety of printed cotton fabrics separated by floral printed blocks, red, yellow, and black, triangle border, edged in same floral pattern, natural woven cotton backing, chevron and concentric diamond quilting stitches, America, minor stains, circa 1870, 80" x 90" **$1,765**

Windmill, yellow, red, green, and blue printed calico patches, wide red calico with swag quilting, PA, late 19th C, 86" x 76" **$690**

RADIOS

History: The radio was invented more than 100 years ago. Marconi was the first to assemble and employ the transmission and reception instruments that permitted the sending of electric messages without the use of direct connections. Between 1905 and the end of World War I, many technical advances affected the "wireless," including the invention of the vacuum tube by DeForest. Technology continued its progress, and radios filled the entertainment needs of the average family in the 1920s.

Changes in design, style, and technology brought the radio from the black boxes of the 1920s to the stylish furniture pieces and console models of the 1930s and 1940s, to midget models of the 1950s, and finally to the high-tech radios of the 1980s.

Additional Resources:

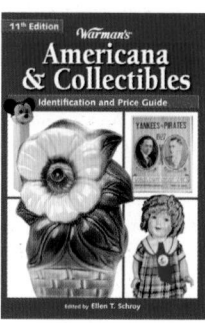

Warman's® Americana & Collectibles, 11th Ed., by Ellen T. Schroy, ed., Krause Publications, Iola, WI.

Adviser: Lewis S. Walters.

Kolster, table model, type 6D, 1920s, **$100.**
Photo courtesy of Dotta Auction Co., Inc.

Ham radios bring in big prices

Outstanding prices were set for ham radios at a January 2004 Ohio auction, during which time the collection of the late Russell Hanselman was sold by Richard Estes.

Chicago Radio Lab Z-nith, receiver, black metal panel, three knobs, c1919-20 .... **$16,000**

DeForest
SP-4 .... **$3,100**
Type MP-100 .... **$3,500**

Marconi Wireless Telegraph Co.
Type 294 receiver, mahogany case, c1918 .... **$19,000**
Type 306 receiver, incomplete **$15,000**

Mignon Wireless RLC2 receiver, pine cabinet finished in dark stain **$11,000**
Norden Hauck receiver **$3,000**
Sodion DR6 receiver **$2,400**

Western Electric
2-A tuner **$2,850**
34-B amplifier **$3,000**
4-C receiver **$3,000**

Wireless Specialty IP-501-A receiver **$8,000**

Admiral
33-35-37 .... **$30**
218 Leatherette **$40**
909 All World **$85**
Imperial **$45**
Transistor 1960s **$15**
Air King, Tombstone, Art Deco **$3,000**
Arvin
Hoppy w/lariatenna **$585**
Mightymite #40 .... **$30**
Rhythm Baby #417 .... **$275**
Rhythm Maid **$215**
Table 444 .... **$100**
522A **$65**
Atwater Kent
Breadboard Style 9A **$55**
Breadboard Style 10 .... **$1,500**
Breadboard Style 10C **$950**
Breadboard Style 12 .... **$950**
Cathedral #80 .... **$200**
Dome #318 .... **$150**
Horn-Type R **$200**
Table-Keil #55 .... **$200**
Bulova
Clock Radio 100 .... **$25**
Clock Radio 110 .... **$25**
Clock Radio 120 .... **$30**
Colonial, New World Radio **$1,000**

Columbia, Table Style Oak **$110**
Crosley
4-28 Battery Set **$120**
10-135 .... **$55**
Ace V **$170**
Bandbox **$80**
Dashboard **$100**
Gemchest **$425**
Litfella **$175**
Pup w/box **$375**
Sheraton-Cathedral **$225**
Showbox **$100**
Sleigh **$125**
Super Buddy Boy **$115**
Dumont, RA346 Table, Fancy **$110**
Emerson
274 Brown Bakelite **$150**
AU-190 Catalin Tombstone **$1,200**
BT-245 .... **$1,100**
Dealer Sign-Porcelain **$150**
Memento 570 .... **$110**
Mickey Mouse 409 .... **$1,200**
Mickey Mouse 411 .... **$1,200**
Patriot **$700**
Portable 640 .... **$30**
Snow White **$1,200**
Vanguard 888 .... **$80**
FADA
43 .... **$250**
53 .... **$200**
60W **$75**
115 Bullet shape **$1,000**
136 .... **$1,000**
252 .... **$575**
625 Rounded end-slide **$700**
652 Butterscotch **$725**
1000 .... **$850**
L56 Maroon & white **$2,600**
Federal
58DX **$500**
110 .... **$550**
General Electric
81, c1934 .... **$150**
400-410-411-414 .... **$30**
515-517 Clock radio **$30**
K-126 .... **$125**
Tombstone **$225**
Grebe
CR-8 .... **$500**
CR-9 .... **$695**
CR-12 .... **$600**
CR-18 .... **$1,000**
MU-1 .... **$250**
Service Manual **$50**
Halicrafters
TW-200 .... **$125**
TW-600 .... **$100**
Majestic
92 .... **$125**

Freshman Masterpiece, three dial set, c1924, speaker not shown, **$95.**
Photo courtesy of Dotta Auction Co., Inc.

381 .... **$225**
Charlie McCarthy **$1,000**
Treasure Chest **$150**

Metrodyne
Super 7 c 1925 .... **$265**

Motorola
68X11Q, Art Deco **$75**
Jet Plane **$25**
Jewel Box **$80**
M Logo **$25**
Pixie **$65**
Plastic Table c 1965 .... **$35**
Ranger 700 .... **$30**
Ranger-portable **$60**

Olympic, radio/phonograph **$60**

Paragon
DA-2 .... **$475**
RD-5 .... **$600**

Philco
17-20-38 Cathedral **$225**
37 table 2 Tone **$60**
37-84 Cathedral **$125**
46-132 Table **$20**
49 Boomerang **$400**
49 Transistone **$35**
52 Transistone **$40**
60 Cathedral **$125**
551 c1928 .... **$165**
T-7 126 Transistor **$50**
T-1000 Clock Radio **$80**

Radiobar
W/glasses & decanter **$1,400**
Tumbler **$50**
Decanter **$75**

Radio Corporation of Amercia RCA
6X7 Table **$25**
8BT-7LE Portable **$35**
LaSiesta **$550**
Radiola 17 .... **$75**
Radiola 18 .... **$95**
Radiola 20 .... **$165**
Radiola 24 .... **$170**
Radiola 28 .... **$200**
Radiola 33 .... **$60**
World's Fair **$1,000**

Silvertone
1 Table **$75**
1582 Wood Cathedral **$200**
1955 Tombstone **$135**

9205 Plastic transistor **$45**
TFM-151 c 1960 .... **$50**
TR-63 c 1958 .... **$125**
Clock Radio-plastic **$15**

Sparton
Blue Bird, Art Deco, original ... **$3,200**
Blue Bird, Art Deco, reproduction
.... **$100**

Stewart-Warner, table-slant **$150**
Stromberg Carlson, 636A console
.... **$125**

Westinghouse, WR-602 .... **$50**

Zenith
6D2615 table w/boomerang dial
.... **$95**
500 Transistor w/owl eye **$55**
500 D Transistor **$55**
750L w/leather case **$40**
Trans-Oceanic **$100**
Zephr-mulit-band **$95**

RAILROAD ITEMS

History: Railroad collectors have existed for decades. The merger of the rail systems and the end of passenger service made many objects available to private collectors. The Pennsylvania Railroad sold its archives at public sale.

Notes: Railroad enthusiasts have organized into regional and local clubs. Join one if you're interested in this collectible field; your local hobby store can probably point you to the right person. The best pieces pass between collectors and rarely enter the general market.

Ashtray, Soo Line, ceramic, track and car design border, "Denver Wright Co." backstamp, 7" d **$25**

Badge pendant, gold luster finish thin metal rim holding color celluloid, showing steam engine during night run, lower center with red, white, and blue logo for Brotherhood of Locomotive Engineers, early 1900s
.... **$20**

Bond
Allegheny & Kinzua Railroad Co., NY & PA, $1000 first mortgage, 5 percent gold bond, train emerging from tunnel, green, Homer Lee Bank Note Co., 30 coupons attached
.... **$95**
Boston, Hartford & Erie Railroad Co., MA, $1,000 7 percent coupon bond, arched fancy "United States of America" over old steam train at station, Columbia, eagle, and shield, green, three printed revenue

stamps, sgd by John S Eldridge, President, National Bank Note Co., 50 coupons attached **$125**
Chicago and North Western Railway Co., $1,000 second mortgage, 4-1/2% convertible income bond series A, vignette Wheel of Progress, olive, American Bank Note Co. **$35**
Cleveland, Cincinnati, Chicago & St. Louis Railway Co., $1,000 refunding and improvement, 4-1/2% mortgage bond, series E, vignette of two steam engines traveling thru tunnel, American Bank Note Co., 10 attached coupons **$20**
West Shore RR, NY, $10,000 bond, brown and black, Hudson River panorama with trains, loading dock, steam ships, distant mountains, second vignette on reverse with bald eagle, canceled, American Bank Note Co. **$15**

Book
1900 Chicago Rock Island & Pacific History, Biographical Publishing Co., 756 pages, CRIP and representative employees, beautiful tooled and gilt engine dec cover, gilt edges, center signatures are loose **$260**
Southern Pacific Color Guide to Freight & Passenger Equipment, Vol. 1, Anthony Thompson, 128 pgs, hardcover **$30**
Western Maryland Diesel Locomotives, P. Salem, hardcover **$35**
Western Pacific Locomotives & Cars, Patrick C. Dorn, hardcover
.... **$35**

Booklet, *Quiz Jr Railroad Questions and Answers*, green and black, printed by Assoc. of American Railroads, 1955 .... **$10**

Brake gauge, Westinghouse, brass, two dial indicators, 140 lbs, 6-1/2" d
.... **$35**

Builders plate
Corps of Engineers U.S. Army 45-ton Diesel Electric Locomotive Manufactured by Vulcan Iron Works, cast bronze, dated 1941, 11" x 6" **$85**
Fairbanks-Morse, stainless steel, etched letters on enamel ground, serial #166-972, 1955, 17" x 8"
.... **$115**

Calendar
New York Central, illustration depicting travel in 1830 and 1920, timetables for various lines in margins, some minor losses, period oak frame, 1922, 18" x 30" **$265**

Plate, Missouri Pacific Lines, state flowers in panels on border, gold rim, **$345.**

Lantern, D. L. & W. R. R., clear globe embossed "D.L. & W.," **$125.**
Photo courtesy of Dotta Auction Co., Inc.

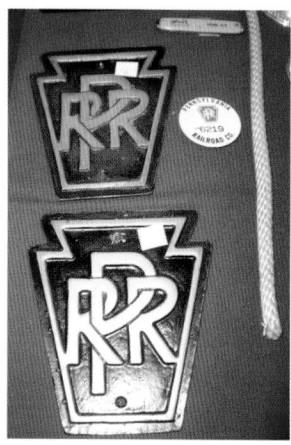

Pennsylvania Railroad items, top: pocket knife, yellow celluloid, **$15;** *two PRR cast iron plaques, each* **$45;** *employee's pinback button, white ground, red logo, black lettering and employee number,* **$35.**

Soo Line, illus, Lake Louise Alberta by R. Atkinson Fox, later oak frame and mat, 1930, overall 34" x 29" **$230**

Calendar plate, Pennsylvania Lines, after a painting by Grif Teller, framed, 1949, 30" x 23" **$35**

Check

Philadelphia & Erie RR Co., Pennsylvania, drawn on Phila National Bank, fancy script bank title, black on white, 1902 .... **$8.50**

Rocky Fork & Cooke City RR, Montana territory, fancy script bank title, hand stamped in blue above bank title, cut cancel, March 1899 .... **$18**

Cap

Agent, Soo Line, pill box style, embroidered "Agent" and "Soo Line," labeled "Marshall Field & Co. Chicago," size 7 .... **$50**

Brakeman's, open-weave crown, missing name plate, labeled "A. G. Meier & Co. Chicago," size 6-3/4 .... **$35**

Railroad Conductors, labeled "A.G. Meier & CO. Chicago," size 7-1/4 .... **$95**

Crimper, railroad seal, nickel plate, dies marked "CNS & M. R. R. Co.," handle emb "Porter Safety Seal Co.," 7" l **$115**

Cuspidor

Missouri Pacific Railroad, white porcelain on metal, black "MOPAC" lettering, minor loss, 7-1/2" d **$150**

Texas & Pacific Railroad, white porcelain on metal, blue lettering, minor loss, 8" d **$260**

Date stamp, Atlantic Coast Line Railroad, c1940, Defiance Stamp Co., 4" h **$35**

Depot clock, electric, oak case, hinged face, marked "Property of the Ball RR Time Service St. Paul, Minn," patent date 1908, 21" sq **$210**

Depot sign, Rock Island System, reverse painted and mother of pearl, Chicago, Rock Island & Pacific 4-4-0 locomotive #476 pulling 11 cars, against tree-lined Midwest route, orig oak ogee frame with gilt liner, c1890, overall 50" x 22" **$23,000**

Directory, *Soo Line Shippers Directory, Vol. III*, softcover, 644 pgs, gilt, ads, illus, two-pg Soo Line map, four color maps of Michigan, Minnesota, North Dakota, Wisconsin, 1918-19 .... **$60**

Fire bucket, Missouri, Kansas & Texas Railroad, orig red paint, stenciled "Fire," emb "MK&T," 12" h **$60**

Flare and flag box, Gulf Mobile & Ohio, tin, stenciled letters, contains flag and fuses, 30" l **$20**

Hollowware

Coffee pot, silver plate, Chicago & Eastern Illinois, 10-oz size, marked "Reed & Barton 086-H, C&E.I.RY. CO" on base, 7" h **$265**

Coffee server, silvered, Nashville, Chattanooga & St. Louis, applied emb "N.C.& St. L" logo on front, gooseneck spout, long wood handle, backstamped "Reed & Barton 482-32 oz, N.C. & St. L" **$520**

Sauce tureen, silvered, Chicago Great Western Railway, two handles, lid. backstamped "C.G.W.R.R.–Reed & Barton," 8" l **$125**

Sugar bowl, silvered, New York Central, imp "NYC" on hinged lid, 3-3/4" h **$50**

Teapot, silvered, Missouri Pacific & Iron Mountain, 10-oz size, front engraved "M.P.I.Mt.RY," backstamped "Missouri Pacific & Iron Mountain R. Wallace 03295," 4-1/2" h **$230**

Illustration, Great Northern Railway, orig illus for cover of travel brochure, scenic marvel of America, Glacier National Park, full-color gouache on paper, detailed study, c1920, 9-1/2" x 14", 1/2" margins **$315**

Jug, Baltimore & Ohio, stoneware, brown cone top, one gal, 11-1/2" **$210**

Kerosene can, Chicago & Northwestern, one gal, oxidized finish, emb "C&NRR," 13" h **$25**

Lantern

Adam & Westlake Co., Adlake Reliable, red 5-1/4" globe with P.R.R. stamped on top, Adlake #300 kero burner, orig wick **$75**

Conger Lantern Co., Twin-Bulb, battery operated, chromed, bulbs missing **$15**

Dietz

Fitzall, Inspectors, clear globe etched "NYC Lines," raised "Dietz Fitzall NYUSA" **$195**

Hi-Top, Vesta, clear globe, raised "US" and "Dietz Vesta" logo, bronze plated, rusted through kero pot **$48**

No. 999, NYC system, red Fresnel globe, Dietz convex kero burner, "NYCS" stamped on top **$95**

Letter opener, Southern Pacific, orig case, 7-3/4" l $30

Locomotive nose plate, Frisco, black, heavy 1/8" stainless steel, 28" l $1,150

Map

Chicago, Iowa, and Nebraska Railroad, color litho, published by J. Sage & Sons, Buffalo, New York, some discoloration and losses, mounted on linen, 1859, 26" x 23" $450

Soo Line, Minneapolis, St. Paul, and Sault Ste. Marie RY, printed by Matthews, Northrup & Co. Buffalo, New York, c1890, 39" x 16" $130

Williams Telegraph and Railroad Map of the New England States, by Alexander Williams, published by Redding & Co. Boston, printed table of construction costs for area railroads, hand-colored state borders, separated folds with later linen backing, some toning, dated 1852, 32" x 30" $60

Name plate, Soo Line, cast aluminum, mounted on walnut back board, 24" l $95

Operation manual, New York Air Brake Co., 1909, 4-1/2" x 7" $5

Paperweight, Adlake Centennial, extruded aluminum, 1857-1957, 5" l $40

Pass, PRR, black and red on blue, 1940 .... $5

Photo

Chicago, Rock Island & Pacific, Rocky Mountains, orig frame, c1910, 7" mat, 53" x 23" $920

Denver & Rio Grande Railroad Depot, Canyon of the Rio Las Animas, Colo, hand colored black and white print, printed logo and title, "Copyright 1900 by Detroit Photographic Co.," orig oak frame, stains in margin, overall 33-1/2" x 27-1/2" $2,645

Machinist Apprentices of the Chicago & Alton R.R., dated Sept. 5th 1908, depicting 34 apprentices posed on C & A R.R. locomotive #605, Stafford B. Cable photo, Bloomington, Illinois, orig frame and mat, 17" x 11" image size $490

Soo Line, Lake Louise, hand-colored black and white print, orig titled mat with Soo Line logo, orig oak frame, early 20th C, overall 25" x 21" $50

Pinback button

Chesapeake & Ohio Railway Veteran Employees Assn, 21st annual meeting, Cincinnati Zoo, June 26, 1937 .... $20

Division 241, American Assn of Street & Electric Railway Employees of America, purple and pink membership button $20

Reading Lines, red image, white logo, green rim, c1930s $20

Poster, Greater Power, The New Haven Railroad, Latham Litho, Long Island City, Sascha Mauer, used to celebrate 50th anniversary and new locomotives, 41-1/2" x 27-1/2" $2,185

Print, *Loco-Erie Watering*, etching, Reginald Marsh, sgd in pencil, 1929, 7" x 10" $1,955

Receipt

Baltimore and Ohio Assoc of Railways Surgeons, for membership dues, 1933 .... $5

Baltimore and Ohio Railroad, freight bill, for shingles, sgd by agent W. L. Gross, 1884 .... $12

Steam whistle, brass

Single chime, lever control, 1884 .... $200

Triple chime, manufactured by Crosby Steam, Gage & Valve Company, Boston, Pat. Jan. 30, 1877, 5-1/2" d, 12" h $720

Step ladder, ST.L.K & N-W Railroad, folding, wooden, four steps, stenciled "St.L.K&N-W" and "Mail Car 103" $270

Step stool, Denver & Rio Grande Western RR, rubber no-skid top, 9" h $260

Stock certificate

Buffalo, Rochester and Pittsburgh Railway Co., New York, train at station at left, miners working at right, 100 shares, common, red-brown design, ornate border, Franklin Bank Note Co., New York $30

Cincinnati and Fort Wayne Railroad, Indiana, small train on left edge, common stock $40

Little Miami Railroad Co., Cincinnati, Ohio, vignette of Tom Thumb engine and cars with passengers and watchers, hole cancel, American Bank Note Co. $22.50

Washington Railway & Electric Co., Washington, DC, vignette of trolley car in busy city, green, 100 shares, Western Bank Note Co., Chicago $24

Ticket

Niagara Gorge RR Co., Great Gorge Route, 1900, 2-1/4" x 1-5/16" $12

Print, framed, Pennsylvania RR, #9604 locomotive, **$125.**
Photo courtesy of Dotta Auction Co., Inc.

Steam whistle, brass and copper, mounted on keystone shaped wooden plaque along with cast iron railroad spike, **$95.**

Lantern, L.V.R.R., Adlake "Reliable" frame, ruby red globe embossed "L.V.R.R.," dated 1931, **$290.**
Photo courtesy of Dotta Auction Co., Inc.

International Railway Co., Buffalo, New York, strip of five employees tickets, engraved title, Security Bank Note Co., Philadelphia, reverse with four digit number and "Not Good for Women or Children," 1903, 1-5/8" l, 11/16" w $18

Ticket cabinet, Soo Line, oak, locking tambour slant front, divided compartments for tickets, timetables, one drawer, stenciled "M.ST.P. & S.S.M.RY" on back, c1914, 21" x 35" x 16" **$460**

Timetable, 4" x 8-1/2"

Atlantic Coast, 1954 ....**$2.50**

Delaware & Hudson, 1951 ....**$2.50**

Lehigh Valley, 1951 ....**$3.50**

New York Central, 1946 ....**$2.50**

Santa Fe, 1959 ....**$2.50**

Seaboard, 1924-25 ....**$5**

Southern Pacific, 1912 ....**$4**

Tray, Soo Line, Montana Success, map of Soo Line Route, tin litho, 10-1/2" x 15" **$200**

Wax sealer

American Exchange Co., El Paso, III, brass die with wood handle, 3" l **$150**

S.W. & B.V. RR, Agent-Bryan, Texas, one-piece brass die and handle, 2-1/2" l **$550**

Toledo, Peoria & Western, Agent-El Paso, III, brass die, wood handle, 4" l **$525**

RECORDS

History: With the advent of the more sophisticated recording materials, such as 33-1/3 RPM long-playing records, 8-track tapes, cassettes, and compact discs, earlier phonograph records became collectors' items. Most have little value. The higher-priced items are rare (limited-production) recordings. Condition is critical.

All records start with a master tape of an artist's or groups' performance. To make a record, mastering agent would play the master tape and feed the sound to a cutting lathe which electronically transcribes the music into the grooves of a circular black lacquer disc, known as an acetate. The acetate was played to determine if the sound quality was correct, to listen for defects or timing errors, order of presentation, etc. The finished acetate was then sprayed with a metal film. Once the film dries, the acetate is peeled away, creating a new "master" with a raised groove pattern. Another metallic compound is sprayed on the new "master" and after this compound is removed, a "mother" disc is created. The "moth-

er" disc is then coated with another metallic compound, and when that is removed, a "stamper" is made. Pertinent production information is often written on the stamper before it is pressed in the production process. Each two-sided record has two stampers, one for each side.

The material used for early 45s and LPs was polyvinyl chloride (PVC), and commonly called "vinyl." To make a record, hot PVC is pressed between the stampers using a compression molding process. Excess vinyl that is trimmed away after the pressing process is recycled. When this re-cycled material is reused, it may result in a record that looks grainy or pockmarked. Each stamper was good for about 1,000 pressings, then the whole process began again. Vinyl is still used for LPs, but polystyrene is now used for 45s. The production process for polystyrene is slightly different in that the base material is more liquid. Application of labels can be made directly to the polystyrene record, eliminating the label stamping process used with vinyl. To tell the difference between vinyl and styrene records, consider the following points:

Vinyl records are thicker and heavier.

7-inch vinyl 45s won't bend.

A label of one color with information "engraved" or spray painted in the center indicates a styrene record.

As with many types of antiques, a grading scale has been developed.

Mint (M): Perfect condition, no flaws, scratches, or scuffs in the grooves. The cardboard jacket will be crisp.

Near Mint (NM) or Mint-Minus (M-): The record will be close to perfect, with no marks in the grooves. The label will be clean, not marked, or scuffed. There will be no ring wear on the record or album cover.

Very Good Plus (VG+): Used for a record that has been played, but well taken care of. Slight scuffle or warps to the grooves is acceptable as long as it does not affect the sound. A faint ring wear discoloration is accept-

able. The jacket may appear slightly worn, especially on the edges.

Very Good (VG): Used to describe a record that has some pronounced defects, as does the cover. The record will still play well. This usually is the lowest grade acceptable to a serious collector. Most records listed in price guides are of this grade.

Good (G): This category of record will be playable, but probably will have loss to the sound quality. Careful inspection of a styrene record in this condition may allow the viewer to see white in the grooves. The cover might be marked or torn.

Poor or Fair (P, F): Record is damaged, may be difficult to play. The cover will be damaged condition, usually marked, dirty, or torn.

Notes: Most records, especially popular recordings, have a value of less than $3 per disc. The records listed here are classic recordings of their type and are in demand by collectors. Picture sleeves will generally increase values, and often have an independent value.

Additional Resources:

Goldmine™ Record Album Price Guide, 4th Ed., by Tim Neely, Krause Publications, Iola, WI.

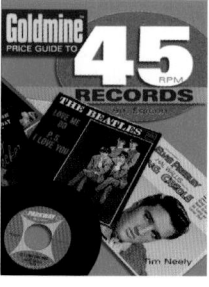

Goldmine™ Price Guide to 45 RPM Records, 5th Ed., by Tim Neely, Krause Publications, Iola, WI.

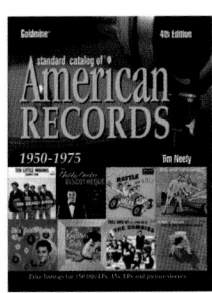

Standard Catalog of® American Records 1950-1975, 4th Ed., by Tim Neely, Krause Publications, Iola, WI.

Warman's® American Records, 2nd Ed., by Chuck Miller, Krause Publications, Iola, WI.

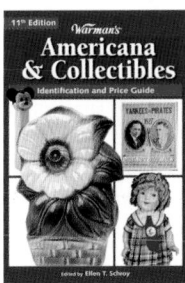

Warman's® Americana & Collectibles, 11th Ed., by Ellen T. Schroy, ed., Krause Publications, Iola, WI.

45s

The Bay City Rollers, Bell
45169, "Keep On Dancing"/"Alright," 1972.......................................**$5-$10**
45618, "All of Me Loves All of You"/"The Bump," 1974 ....**$7.50-$15**

Pat Boone, Mono 45s, Dot
15377, "Ain't That a Shame"/"Tennessee Saturday Night," 1955 ....**$10-$20**
15443, "Tutti Frutti"/"I'll Be Home," 1956 ....**$10-$20**
15472, "I Almost Lost My Mind"/"I'm in Love with You," 1956 ....**$10-$20**

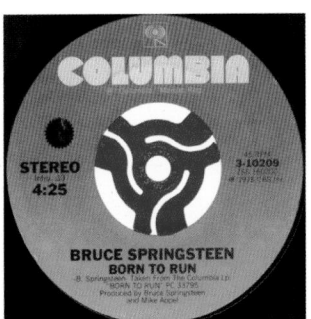

Bruce Springsteen's "Born to Run" 45 was released in its original 4:25 length, NM condition, 1970s, **$20.**

15660, "April Love"/"When the Swallows Come Back to Capistrano," 1957 ....**$7.50-$15**
15955, "Twixt Twelve and Twenty"/"Rock Boll Weevil," 1959 ....**$7.50-$15**
15982, "Fools Hall of Fame"/"The Brightest Wishing Star," 1959 ....**$7.50-$15**
16209, "Moody River"/"A Thousand Years," 1961 ....**$7.50-$15**

David Bowie, RCA Victor
APBO-0001, "Time"/"The Prettiest Star," 1973 ....**$3-$6**
PB-10152, "Young Americans"/"Knock on Wood," 1975..........**$3-$6**
PB-10441, "Golden Years"/"Can You Hear Me," 1975 ....**$2-$4**

The Birds, Columbia
43271, "Mr. Tambourine Man"/"I Knew I'd Want You," 1965 ....**$7.50-$15**
43578, "Eight Miles High"/"Why," 1966......................................**$6-$12**

The Captain and Tennille, Butterscotch Castle 001, "The Way I Want To Touch You"/"Disney Girls" (independent first pressing), 1974 ......**$40-$80**

Creedence Clearwater Revival, Fantasy
617, "I Put A Spell On You"/"Walk on the Water," 1968......................**$4-$8**
619, "Proud Mary"/"Born on the Bayou," 1969 ....**$3-$6**
637, "Travelin' Band"/"Who'll Stop The Rain," 1970 ....**$3-$6**

The 5th Dimension, Soul City
752, "I'll Be Loving You Forever"/"Train, Keep On Moving," 1966 ....**$30-$60**
756, "Up-Up and Away"/"Which Way To Nowhere," 1967 ....**$4-$8**

Fleetwood Mac, Reprise 1345, "Rhiannon (Will You Ever Win)"/"Sugar Daddy," 1976 ....**$2-$4**

Stevie Ray Vaughan picture disc for his LP "Couldn't Stand the Weather," VG+ NM condition, **$100.**

Michael Jackson, Epic
9-50742, "Don't Stop 'Til You Get Enough"/"I Can't Help It," 1979 ....**$2-$4**
34-03509, "Billie Jean"/"Can't Get Outta the Rain," 1983..............**$2-$4**
34-78000, "Scream"/"Childhood," 1995....................................**$1.50-$3**
34-79656, "You Rock My World" (same on both sides), 2001.....**$1-$2**

Billy Joel, Family Productions 0900, "She's Got A Way"/"Everybody Loves You Now," 1971 ....**$12.50-$25**

Kenny Rogers, Carlton 454, Kenneth Rogers, "That Crazy Feeling"/"We'll Always Have Each Other," 1958 ....**$50-$100**

Blues

Jackie Brenston And His Delta Cats, 78s, Chess
1458, "Rocket 88"/"Come Back Where You Belong," 1949 ....**$150-$300**
1472, "Juiced"/"Independent Woman," 1951 ....**$100-$200**

Ida Cox, 78s, Paramount
12053, "Any Woman's Blues"/"Blue Monday Blues," 1923........**$60-$120**
12085,"Mama Doo Shea Blues"/"Worried Mama Blues," 1924 ....**$70-$140**

Lightnin' Hopkins, 45s, Jax
315, "No Good Woman"/"Been a Bad Man" (red vinyl), 1953 ....**$150-$300**
318, "Automobile"/"Organ Blues" (red vinyl), 1953 ....**$150-$300**
321, "Contrary Mary"/"I'm Begging You" (red vinyl), 1953....**$150-$300**

Papa Charlie Jackson, 78s, Paramount
12305, "Mama, Don't You Think I Know?"/"Hot Papa Blues," 1925 ....**$75-$150**

Soundtrack to the TV series The Electric Company, comes with bonus inserts, including a "Crypto-Spectometer," NM condition, **$30.**

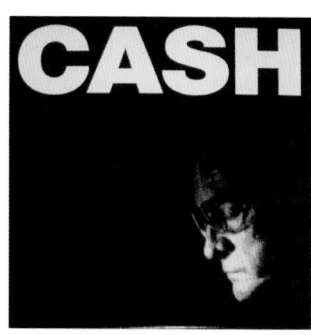

Johnny Cash, American IV: The Man Comes Around, on double-LP vinyl album package, NM condition, **$30.**

Miles Davis Birth of the Cool album, one of the most influential modern jazz albums ever, 1956 pressing, VG+ condition, **$75.**

12320, "All I Want is a Spoonful"/ "Maxwell Street Blues," 1925
.... **$50-$100**
Blind Lemon Jefferson, 78s, Paramount
12347, "Booster Blues"/"Dry Southern Blues," 1926 .... **$500-$1,000**
12493, "Weary Dog Blues"/"Hot Dogs," 1926 .... **$500-$1,000**
12650, "Piney Woods Mama Blues"/ "Low Down Mojo Blues" (label has a portrait of Jefferson, record is designated as "Blind Lemon Jefferson Birthday Record"), 1928
.... **$750-$1,500**
B.B. King, 78s, Bullet
309, "Miss Martha King"/"When Your Baby Packs Up and Goes," 1949
.... **$500-$1,000**
315, "Got the Blues"/"Take a Swing with Me," 1949 .... **$350-$700**
Bessie Smith, 78s, Columbia
13007-D, "Far Away Blues"/"I'm Going Back to My Used To Be," 1924 .... **$60-$120**
14056-D, "Reckless Blues"/"Sobbin' Hearted Blues," 1925 .... **$80-$160**
Stevie Ray Vaughan And Double Trouble, LPs, Epic
BFE 38734, Texas Flood, 1983
.... **$5-$10**
FE 39304, Couldn't Stand the Weather, 1984 .... **$5-$10**

Children's

101 Dalmatians, (original motion picture soundtrack), LPs, Disneyland
ST-1908, mono, 1960 ...... **$12.50-$25**
ST-4903, mono, gatefold cover with pop-up scene in center, 1963
.... **$75-$150**
ST-3931, mono, 1965 .... **$20-$40**
Ray Bolger, 78, Decca CU 102, "The Churkendoose," 1947 .... **$25-$50**

Betty Boop, 7-inch 78, Durotone R-81, Betty Boop in "Peter and Wendy"/ Betty Boop in "She Loves Him Not," 193? .... **$20-$40**
Bozo The Clown, 78s, Capitol
DAS-3046, Bozo Laughs, 1946
.... **$7.50-$15**
BBX65, Bozo and His Rocket Ship, 2 78s with book, 1947 .... **$10-$20**
DBS-84, Bozo Sings, 2 78s in gatefold sleeve, 1948 .... **$10-$20**
DBX-3076, Bozo on the Farm, 2 78s with book, 1950 .... **$10-$20**
The Electric Company, LP, Sesame Street 22052, The Electric Company, 1974 .... **$7.50-$15**
Goldilocks And The Three Bears, 78, Capitol DB-121, Goldilocks and the Three Bears, Margaret O'Brien, narrator, 1948 .... **$5-$10**
Little Nipper Series, 78-RPM records in folio, RCA Victor
Y-383, The Adventures Of Little Black Sambo, 1949 .... **$25-$50**
Y-385, Pinocchio, 1949 .... **$20-$40**
Y-397, Howdy Doody and the Air-O-Doodle, 1949 .... **$25-$50**
Y-414, Howdy Doody's Laughing Circus, 1949 .... **$20-$40**
Y-438, Winnie-the-Pooh No. 1, James Stewart, narrator, 1949 ...... **$30-$60**
Y-446, It's Howdy Doody Time, 1951
.... **$30-$60**

Country, LP

Eddy Arnold, LPs, RCA Victor
LPM-3753, Lonely Again, mono, 1967 .... **$10-$20**
LSP-3753, same title, stereo, 1967
.... **$7.50-$15**
Gene Autry, 78, Banner 32349, "That Silver Haired Daddy of Mine"/ "Mississippi Valley Blues," 1931
.... **$35-$70**

The Carter Family, 78s
"Can the Circle Be Unbroken (By and By)"/"Glory to the Lamb"
(if on Perfect 13155, Oriola 8484, Banner 33465, Romeo 5484, Melotone 13432, or Conqueror 8529, value is equal), 1935 .... **$25-$50**
(if on Vocalion 03027, reissue), 1937
.... **$20-$40**
(if on OKeh 03027, reissue), 1940
.... **$15-$30**
(if on Columbia 37669, reissue), 1947
.... **$10-$20**
(if on Columbia 20268, reissue), 1948
.... **$10-$20**
Wilf Carter, 78s, Bluebird
4966, "My Swiss Moonlight Lullaby"/ "The Capture Of Albert Johnson," 1933 .... **$20-$40**
4600, "My Little Swiss and Me"/"I Long for Old Wyoming," 193??
.... **$15-$30**
4624, "Old Alberta Plains"/"Won't You Be the Same Old Pal," 193??
.... **$15-$30**
Johnny Cash, 45s, Sun
241, "I Walk The Line"/"Get Rhythm," 1956 .... **$20-$40**
283, "Ballad of a Teenage Queen"/"Big River," 1958 .... **$12.50-$25**
Patsy Cline, 45s, Decca
30221, "Walkin' After Midnight"/"A Poor Man's Roses (Or a Rich Man's Gold)," 1957 .... **$10-$20**
31317, "Crazy"/"Who Can I Count On," 1961 .... **$6-$12**
Billy "Crash" Craddock, 45, ABC Dot 17659, "Broken Down in Tiny Pieces"/"Shake It Easy," 1976 .... **$2-$4**
Vernon Dalhart, 78, Victor 19427, "The Prisoner's Song"/"Wreck of the Old '97" (A-side recorded for several different record companies), 1924
.... **$10-$20**

Dale Evans, 78, Majestic 11025, "Under a Texas Moon"/"His Hat Cost More Than Mine," 194?? ... **$10-$20**

The Everly Brothers, 45s, Cadence 1315, "Bye Bye Love"/"I Wonder If I Care As Much," 1957 ... **$12.50-$25**
1337, "Wake Up Little Susie"/"Maybe Tomorrow," 1957 ... **$15-$30**

Merle Haggard, LPs, Capitol ST 638, A Tribute to the Best Damn Fiddle Player in the World (Or, My Salute to Bob Wills), 1970 ... **$12.50-$25**

Emmylou Harris, 45, Jubilee 5679, "I'll Be Your Baby Tonight"/"I'll Never Fall In Love Again," 1969 ... **$10-$20**

Homer And Jethro, LP, RCA Victor LPM-1560, The Worst of Homer and Jethro (RCA Victor LPM-1560), 1958 ... **$25-$50**

Waylon Jennings, 45s Ramco 1997, "My World"/"Another Blue Day," 1968 ... **$6-$12**
RCA PB-10924, "Luckenbach, Texas (Back to the Basics of Love)"/"Belle of the Ball," 1977 ... **$2.50-$5**

Brenda Lee, 45, Decca 31309, "Fool #1"/"Anybody But Me," 1961 ... **$7.50-$15**

Jerry Lee Lewis, LP, Mercury SR-61366, Who's Gonna Play This Old Piano ... (Think About It Darlin'), 1972 ... **$7.50-$15**

Loretta Lynn, 45s, Zero 107, "I'm A Honky Tonk Girl"/"Whispering Sea," 1960 . **$250-$500**
112, "The Darkest Day"/"Gonna Pack My Troubles," 1961 ... **$200-$400**

Willie Nelson, 45s
Belaire 107, "Night Life"/"Rainy Day Blues," 1963 ... **$15-$30**
(if pressed on colored vinyl), 1963 ... **$30-$60**
Sarg 260, "A Storm Has Just Begun"/"When I Sing My Last Hillbilly Song," 196? ... **$25-$50**
Columbia 10176, "Blue Eyes Cryin' in the Rain"/"Bandera," 1975 ... **$2.50-$5**

Dolly Parton, 45s
Gold Band 1086, "Puppy Love"/"Girl Left Alone," 1959 ... **$300-$600**
Monument 982, "Dumb Blonde"/"The Giving and the Taking," 1967 ... **$5-$10**
RCA Victor APBO-0145, "Jolene"/"You're So Beautiful Tonight," 1973 ... **$2.50-$5**

The Sons Of The Pioneers, 78s, Decca
5047, "Tumbling Tumbleweeds"/"Moonlight on the Prairie," 1934 ... **$15-$30**

5939, "Cool Water"/"So Long to the Red River Valley," 1941 ... **$12.50-$25**

Hank Williams, LPs
MGM E-168, Moanin' the Blues (10-inch LP), 1952 ... **$200-$400**
MGM PRO-912, Reflections of Those Who Loved Him (3 LPs) (promo-only box set), 1975 ... **$125-$250**

Jazz

Cannonball Adderly, Stereo LPs, Blue Note
BST-1595, Somethin' Else
(if deep groove pressed into label), 1959 ... **$50-$100**
(if West 63rd Street address on label), 1959 ... **$37.50-$75**
(if New York USA address on label), 1963 ... **$10-$20**

Louis Armstrong, 45s
Decca 29102, "Basin Street Blues" (Pt. 1)/(Pt. 2), 1954 ... **$7.50-$15**
Kapp 573, "Hello Dolly!"/"A Lot Of Lovin' To Do," 1964 ... **$3-$6**
(with picture sleeve, add), 1964* ... **$5-$10**

Count Basie, 10-inch LPs
Clef MCG-120, Count Basie and His Orchestra Collates, 1953 ... **$100-$200**
EmArcy MG-26023, Jazz Royalty, 1954 ... **$35-$70**

Art Blakey And The Jazz Messengers, Mono LPs
Blue Note BLP-1507, At the Café Bohemia, Volume 1
(if "deep groove" indentation on label), 1956 ... **$75-$150**
(if regular version, Lexington Ave. address on label), 1956 ... **$50-$100**
Jubilee JLP-1049, Cu-Bop, 1958 ... **$40-$80**

Clifford Brown, Mono LPs
EmArcy MG-36005, Clifford Brown with Strings, 1955 ... **$60-$120**
Blue Note BLP-1526, Clifford Brown Memorial Album
(if deep groove indentation in label), 1956 ... **$100-$200**
(if regular edition, Lexington Ave. address on label), 1956 ... **$75-$150**
(if "New York, U.S.A." address on label), 196? ... **$12.50-$25**
(if W. 63rd St. address on label), 196? ... **$25-$50**

Dave Brubeck, 45s
Fantasy 524, "Stardust"/"Lulu's Back in Town," 1953 ... **$7.50-$15**

Columbia 41479, "Take Five"/"Blue Rondo A La Turk," 1960 ... **$6-$12**

Cab Calloway, 78s, Brunswick
6209, "Kickin' the Gong Around"/"Between the Devil and the Deep Blue Sea," 1931 ... **$7.50-$15**
6511, "Minnie the Moocher"/"Kickin' the Gong Around," 1931 ... **$10-$20**

John Coltrane, 45s
Impulse! 203, "Easy to Remember"/"Greensleeves," 1961 ... **$5-$10**
Prestige 267, "Stardust"/"Love Thy Neighbor," 1961 ... **$6-$12**

Miles Davis, 45s
Capitol F1221, "Venus de Milo"/"Darn That Dream," 1950 ... **$12.50-$25**
Columbia 42057, "It Ain't Necessarily So"/"All Blues," 1961 ... **$6-$12**
42069, "I Loves You, Porgy"/"It Ain't Necessarily So," 1961 ... **$6-$12**

Kenny Drew, 10-inch LPs
Blue Note BLP-5023, Introducing the Kenny Drew Trio, 1953 ... **$200-$400**
Norgran MGM-29, The Ideation of Kenny Drew, 1954 ... **$125-$250**

Duke Ellington, 45s
RCA Victor 47-2955, "The Sidewalks Of New York"/"Don't Get Around Much Anymore," 1949 ... **$10-$20**
Capitol F2458, "Satin Doll"/"Without A Song," 1953 ... **$6-$12**

Ella Fitzgerald, Stereo LPs
Verve V6-4053, Clap Hands, Here Comes Charley, 1962 ... **$75-$150**
Atlantic SD 1631, Ella Loves Cole, 1972 ... **$6-$12**

Stan Getz, 10-inch LPs
Savoy MG-9004, New Sounds in Modern Music, 1951 ... **$150-$300**
Prestige PRLP-102, Stan Getz and the Tenor Sax Stars, 1951 ... **$100-$200**

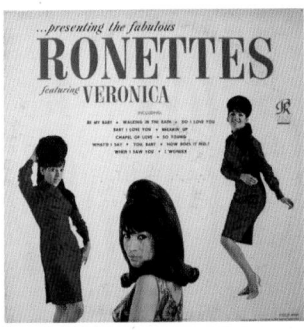

Rare Ronettes album, LP, includes the tracks "Be My Baby," "Baby I Love You," and "Walkin' in the Rain," Good condition, $200.

Roost R-407, Jazz at Storyville, 1952
.... **$75-$150**

Billie Holiday, 10-inch LPs
Columbia CL 6129, Billie Holiday
Sings, 1950 .... **$100-$200**
Decca DL 5345, Lover Man, 1951
.... **$100-$200**

Ma Rainey, 10-inch LPs, Riverside
RLP-1003, Ma Rainey, Vol. 1, 1953
.... **$125-$250**
RLP-1016, Ma Rainey, Vol. 2, 1953
.... **$125-$250**
RLP-1045, Ma Rainey, Vol. 3, 1954
.... **$125-$250**

Rock

Paul Anka, 45s, ABC-Paramount
9831, "Diana"/"Don't Gamble with
Love," 1957 .... **$10-$20**
10082, "Puppy Love"/"Adam and Eve,"
1960 .... **$7.50-$15**

Annette, 45s, Buena Vista
349, "First Name Initial"/"My Heart
Became of Age," 1959 ..... **$7.50-$15**
414, "Teenage Wedding"/"Walkin'
and Talkin'," 1962 .... **$10-$20**
433, "Muscle Beach Party"/"I Dream
About Frankie," 1964 ..... **$7.50-$15**

Frankie Avalon, Stereo LPs, Chancellor
CHLXS 5004, Swingin' on a Rainbow,
1959 .... **$25-$50**
CHLS 5027, You're Mine, 1962
.... **$20-$40**

Chuck Berry, 45s, Chess
1604, "Maybellene"/"Wee Wee Hours,"
1955 .... **$25-$50**
1626, "Roll Over Beethoven"/"Drifting
Heart," 1956 .... **$25-$50**
1671, "Rock & Roll Music"/"Blue
Feeling," 1957 .... **$15-$30**
1691, "Johnny B. Goode"/"Around
and Around," 1958 .... **$15-$30**
1729, "Back in the U.S.A."/"Memphis
Tennessee," 1959 .... **$15-$30**

Chubby Checker, 45s, Parkway
804, "The Class"/"Schooldays, Oh
Schooldays," 1959 .... **$15-$30**
811, "The Twist"/"Toot" (first pressings, white label, blue print), 1960
.... **$15-$30**
811, "The Twist"/"Twistin' U.S.A.,"
1961 .... **$7.50-$15**
824, "Let's Twist Again"/"Everything's
Gonna Be Alright," 1961
.... **$7.50-$15**

Dee Clark, Mono LPs, Abner
LP-2000, Dee Clark, 1959
.... **$60-$120**
LP-2002, How About That, 1960
.... **$40-$80**

Bo Diddley, LPs
Checker LP 1431, Bo Diddley, 1958
.... **$75-$150**
LP 2974, Have Guitar, Will Travel,
1960 .... **$75-$150**
LP 2977, Bo Diddley Is a Gunslinger,
1961 .... **$75-$150**

Fats Domino, 45s, Imperial
45-5058, "The Fat Man"/"Detroit City
Blues" (blue-label "script" logo,
pressed around 1952, counterfeits
exist), 1950 .... **$1,000-$2,000**
45-5209, "How Long"/"Dreaming,"
1952 .... **$40-$80**
(if on red vinyl), 1952 ...... **$150-$300**
X5369, "Poor Me"/"I Can't Go On,"
1955 .... **$12.50-$25**
X5407, "Blueberry Hill"/"Honey
Chile" (black vinyl, red label), 1956
.... **$12.50-$25**
X5417, "Blue Monday"/"What's the
Reason I'm Not Pleasing You," 1957
.... **$12.50-$25**

The Everly Brothers, 45s, Cadence
1337, "Wake Up Little Susie"/"Maybe
Tomorrow," 1957 .... **$15-$30**
1348, "All I Have to Do Is Dream"/
"Claudette," 1958 .... **$12.50-$25**

Fabian, 45s, Chancellor
1033, "Turn Me Loose"/"Stop Thief!,"
1959 .... **$10-$20**
1037, "Tiger"/"Mighty Cold (To
a Warm, Warm Heart)," 1959
.... **$10-$20**

Bill Haley And His Comets,
7-inch EP, Decca ED 2168, Shake,
Rattle and Roll (contains "Shake, Rat-
tle and Roll"/"A.B.C. Boogie"/"(We're
Gonna) Rock Around the Clock"/
"Thirteen Women (And Only One
Man in Town)," value is for record
and jacket), 1954 .... **$60-$120**

Buddy Holly, 45s, Decca
29854, "Blue Days, Black Nights"/
"Love Me" (with star under
"Decca"), 1956 .... **$150-$300**
34034, "That'll Be the Day"/"Rock
Around with Ollie Vee" (with
star under "Decca"), 1957
.... **$125-$250**
62074, "It Doesn't Matter Anymore"/
"Raining in My Heart," 1959
.... **$20-$40**
62134, "Peggy Sue Got Married"/
"Crying, Waiting, Hoping," 1959
.... **$30-$60**
62210, "True Love Ways"/"That
Makes It Tough," 1960 .... **$25-$50**

Roy Orbison, Stereo LPs, Monument
SM-14002, Lonely and Blue, 1961
.... **$300-$600**

SM-14007, Crying, 1962
.... **$300-$600**
SLP-18003, In Dreams (white-rain-
bow label), 1963 .... **$50-$100**

The Ronettes, 45s
Colpix 601, "I Want a Boy"/"Sweet
Sixteen" (as "Ronnie and the Rela-
tives"), 1961 .... **$50-$100**
Philles 116, "Be My Baby"/"Tedesco
and Pittman," 1963 .... **$15-$30**
118, "Baby I Love You"/"Miss Joan
and Mr. Sam," 1963 .... **$15-$30**

RELIGIOUS ITEMS

History: Objects used in worship
or as expressions of man's belief in a
superhuman power are collected by
many people for many reasons.

This category includes icons, since
they are religious mementos, usually
paintings with a brass encasement.
Collecting icons dates from the earliest period of Christianity. Most
antique icons in today's market were
made in the late 19th century.

Reproduction Alert. Icons
are frequently reproduced.

Altar crucifix, wood frame overlaid
with repoussé copper, cabochons,
paste stones, verso with compartment
for relic, 24" h **$550**
Architectural relief of saint, carved
walnut, male figure holding pair of
keys, standing in arched niche, traces
of gilding, Continental, set into velvet
framed open shadow box, late 17th/
early 18th C, 16-1/8" w, 25-5/8" h
.... **$1,650**

Bronze
Amida in appeasement mudra,
bronze, partial gilt, boxed, China,
19th C, 6" h **$2,820**
Amytaus, gilt bronze, China, 18th C,
8" h **$1,410**
Stone, bust, old tan color, 16-1/4" h,
12-1/4" w, 8" d **$415**
Wood, carved, standing image of
Amida, ornate throne, halo at back,
gilt surface, Japan, losses, 19th C,
21" h **$650**
Young features, crane at his feet, Chinese, slight wear to patina, 19th C
.... **$850**

Buddha
Coral, carved, sitting position, base
carved flat and with sedimentary
inclusions, two-character signature,
China, 18th or 19th C **$420**

Bust

Gilded metal Immaculate Heart of Mary and the Sacred Heart of Jesus, onyx pedestal with flared base, French, price for pr, c1920, 10-1/2" h **$320**

Veiled Madonna, hand painted porcelain, Royal Worcester, 1863, 11-1/2" h **$1,495**

Candlestick, Ciborium-form, sil-

ver plated, quatrefoil crown-form sconce, over cathedral-form stem with pointed arches and flying buttresses, square section standard, base with clipped corners and recumbent lion-form feet, conforming marble plinth base, Gothic Revival, C. Nisini, Rome, late 19th C, 38-1/2" h **$650**

Chalice and paten

Engraved and partial gilt sterling, French, c1920, 9" h **$815**

Heavy solid gilded silver, Gothic style, c1922, 9-1/4" h **$1,065**

Partial gilt sterling, c1920, 9-1/2" h **$700**

Sterling, c1920, 9" h **$435**

Chausable, Gothic Revival, silk,

metallic embroidery, and stumpwork, cream silk ground, stitched central Gothic cross, centered by metal purl stumpwork Agnes Dei, flanked by scrolling gilt and gilt embroidered flowering vines, ending in metal spherule mounted grape bunches, metallic ribbon trim, late 19th C, 40-1/2" l **$600**

Corpus, carved wood, polychrome,

gilt, detailed features, hand forged iron spike, European, some repainting, 18th C, 39" h, 23-1/4" w **$2,300**

Crucifix

Finely painted, overlaid with ornate repoussé, chased riza, Russian, 19th C, 14" h **$1,150**

Finely carved, South German, 19th/20th C, 28" x 23" **$520**

Deity

Mahaka, bronze, deity standing on prostrated figure, double lotus base, polychrome highlights, Tibetan, 19th C, 6-3/8" h **$1,315**

Porcelain, seated on lotus pillow, Famille rose enamels, gilt body, Chinese, chips to petals on crown, old repairs around neck, 18th or 19th C, 4-1/2" h **$1,100**

Yamantaka Vajrabhairava, gilt bronze, buffalo-headed deity in yabyum with his consort, trampling pros-

Retablo, Spanish Colonial School, Our Lady of Guadalupe with Juan Diego, paint decoration gesso on hand-adzed wood panel, 19th C, 11" x 7-1/2", **$800.**

Photo courtesy of Skinner, Inc.

trated figures and animals, sealed lotus base with Sanskrit inscription, Tibetan, 18th C, 7" h **$5,260**

Figure

Black Madonna and Child, Pattarino, 18-3/4" h **$3,450**

Christ on the Cross, carved and polychromed wood, clad in loin cloth, blood dripping down body, metal crown of thorns, metal halo inserts, nailed on cross with plaque marked INRI, raised on stepped square base with two carved miniature angels at feet, Spanish, Colonial, 14-1/2" h **$360**

Goddess, Chola-style, bronze, Indian, late 19th C, 7" h **$325**

Image of God of Literature, China, Ming period (1368-1644), bronze, 5-1/2" h **$500**

Lama, seated on double lotus throne, bronze, cold gold paste on the face, inscription on front, 7" h **$3,290**

Madonna and Child, Christ holding rosebud, delivering blessing, Pattarino, 16-1/2" h **$2,990**

Madonna and Child, carved and polychrome gilt wood, Baroque style, South German, 20th C, 21-1/2" h **$815**

Madonna and Child, fully carved in the round, base inscribed "Oberamergare," South German, c1930, 21-1/2" h **$500**

Madonna and Child, finely carved and polychromed, Baroque taste, German, 20th C, 22" h **$575**

Madonna and Child enthroned, Pattarino, 22" h **$3,795**

Madonna and Child, carved polychrome and gilt wood, South German, late 19th/early 20th, 25" h **$1,900**

Alms box, covered, hinged, carved and painted gesso figures, 12-1/2" x 6-1/4" x 10-3/4" h, **$400.**

Photo courtesy of Joy Luke.

Madonna and sleeping Christ, Pattarino, 14-1/2" h **$1,495**

Praying Madonna, Pattarino, 5-1/4" h **$435**

St Christopher carrying Infant Christ, carved and polychrome, glass eyes, silver halo and crown, 20th C, 16" h **$700**

St. Thomas Aquinas, carved and polychrome gilt wood, Spanish-Colonial, 19th C, 12-1/4" **$750**

Wish Bestowing Avalokitesvara, gilt bronze, Korea, possible repair to the feet, 11th C, 15-1/2" **$5,875**

Funerary centerpiece, 45" x 31",

beaded wire construction for casket top, French, c1890-1910............. **$300**

Icon, Buddhist, mandala of Yaman-

takra surrounded by wrathful deities of ancient Bon faith, Tibet, 18th C, 32" x 21" **$1,500**

Icon, Greek

Bishop Saint, carved and polychrome wood, Provincial, French, 17th C, 38" h **$460**

The Evangelist St. Mark, finely painted on gold leafed ground, c1700, 11" x 14" **$980**

The Mother of God, sgd by icongrapher lower right "Georgio Pandi," 18th C, 25-1/2" x 34" **$865**

Icon, Russian

Mandylion, (The Not Made By Hand Image,) c1750, 10-1/2" x 12" **$835**

The Archangel Gabriel, gold leaf and incised ground, c1890, 22-3/4" x 12" **$750**

The Birth of John the Forerunner, c1700, 10" x 12" **$1,265**

The Kazan Mother of God, c1775, 10-1/2" x 12-1/2" **$1,495**

The Korsunskaya Mother of God, c1675-1725, 11" x 13"............ **$1,495**

The Lord Almighty, c1650, 11" x 9-1/4"......**$3,220**

The Sign Mother of God, 32" x 19-1/2".....**$1,610**

Monstrance and lunette, 27-1/2" h Gothic-style gem set gilded silver and enamel monstrance on large sculpted circular base depicting four evangelists with their symbols, octagonal pillar with four sided shelter with column niches, each with saint, Gothic canopy, central exposition window set within open fretwork of scrolling grapevines resting on base set with horizontal row of guillouche enamel and four gilded silver bell drops, flanked by pair of Gothic shrines with spires, 16 individually sculpted saints, each set with champleve enamel, above window baldacchino set with intricate arches and spires, mounted with 82 rose cut garnets and four pearls, bezel surrounding central exposition set with 60 rose cut garnets, 19 diamonds, one synthetic diamond, 10 lbs 2 oz, engraved lunette with 2-1/2" d luna, Madrid, after 1935, custom padded case
......**$9,450**

Mosaic, Madonna and Child, more than 7,000 individually cut and placed colored stones, gilded frame, Byzantine style, early 20th C, 24" x 30"
......**$2,990**

Painting, oil on board, Ernst Christian Pfannschmidt, German 1868-1941, Angels Mourning the Crucified Christ, sgd lower right, dated 1898, 16" x 12"......**$2,070**

Painting, oil on canvas, Charles Bosseron Chambers, American, 1882-1964, Adoration of the Magi, sgd lower left, 32" x 26"......**$6,900**

Pendant, 18k gold rope frame centering two reverse painted images of Virgin Mary holding infant Jesus
......**$265**

Plaque, Duomo from a Distance, pietra dura, showing roof of the Duomo in a distant landscape, with green and gold painted border, Italian, set in gold painted frame, late 19th/early 20th C, 5-1/4" x 4-1/8"......**$275**

Processional candleholders, pr, metal, single light, trumpet shaped, eight trefoil ribs ending in scrolls, band of acanthus, guilloche and trefoil labrequins at waist, candle nozzle set into wood lined interior, Renaissance Revival, Venetian, lacking poles, late 19th C, 15-1/4" d, 19-1/2" l......**$560**

Reliquary

Bronze, relics of cross, apostles, and several saints, 17-1/2" h......**$1,610**

Cross-form, gilded, relic of true cross, 14-1/4"......**$2,875**

Elaborately framed, 18 relics, 15" x 15"......**$1,265**

Gilded filigree and enamel, French, 3-1/4" h **$300**

Ornate gilded filigree, relics of several saints and apostles, 12" h......**$550**

Ornate gilded, paste stones and cabochons, relic of St. Catherine Laboure, 12-3/4" h **$700**

Rosary beads, 18k gold and platinum crucifix, Sloan & Co., black hardstone beads suspending two sided medal, yellow gold crucifix with platinum Christ, 43.1 dwt, hallmark, missing one bead, chain detached, provenance: from estate of Reverend Thomas Mary O'Leary (1875-1949), Bishop of Springfield......**$360**

Santos, carved wood, well dressed shepherd carrying lamb, tin flag, orig red, blue, and yellow paint, trace of gilt, wear, Spanish, 8-1/2" h......**$200**

Still life, 25-3/4" x 29", mosaic, depicting fruit on a tabletop, Vatican Workshops, bearing paper label from the Mosaic Studios at San Pietro in the Vatican, artist name Cassio, early 20th C, 35-3/4" x 29" giltwood frame
......**$7,050**

Tabernacle, gilt bronze, removable dome lid for exposition, c1940, 31" h
......**$980**

Tantric crown, repoussè copper with parcel gilt, coral and turquoise inlays, Tibet or Nepal, 18th C or earlier, 10" h......**$650**

Tapestry fragment, Madonna enthroned, flanked by saints, other biblical scenes, Continental, 17th/18th C, 118" x 81"......**$6,465**

ROCK 'N' ROLL

History: Rock music can be traced back to early rhythm and blues. It progressed until it reached its golden age in the 1950s and 1960s. Most of the memorabilia issued during that period focused on individual singers and groups. The largest quantity of collectible material is connected to Elvis Presley and The Beatles.

In the 1980s, two areas— clothing and guitars—associated with key rock 'n' roll personalities received

special collector attention. Sotheby's and Christie's East regularly feature rock 'n' roll memorabilia as part of their collectibles sales. At the moment, the market is highly speculative and driven by nostalgia.

It is important to identify memorabilia issued during the lifetime of an artist or performing group, as opposed to material issued after they died or disbanded. Objects of the latter type are identified as "fantasy" items and will never achieve the same degree of collectibility as period counterparts.

> **Reproduction Alert.** Records, picture sleeves, and album jackets, especially for The Beatles, have been counterfeited. When compared to the original, sound may be inferior, as may be the printing on labels and picture jackets. Many pieces of memorabilia also have been reproduced, often with some change in size, color, and design.

Additional Resources:

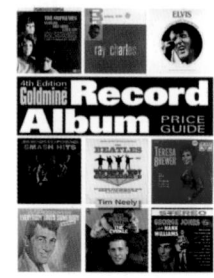

Goldmine™ Record Album Price Guide, 4th Ed., by Tim Neely, Krause Publications, Iola, WI.

Goldmine™ Price Guide to 45 RPM Records, 5th Ed., by Tim Neely, Krause Publications, Iola, WI.

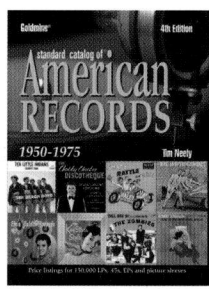

Standard Catalog of® American Records 1950-1975, 4th Ed., by Tim Neely, Krause Publications, Iola, WI.

Warman's® American Records, 2nd Ed., by Chuck Miller, Krause Publications, Iola, WI.

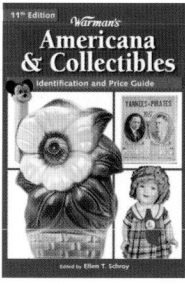

Warman's® Americana & Collectibles, 11th Ed., by Ellen T. Schroy, ed., Krause Publications, Iola, WI.

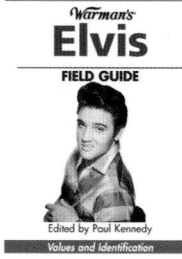

Warman's® Elvis Field Guide, by Paul Kennedy, ed., Krause Publications, Iola, WI.

Autograph, Elvis, poster, **$750.**
Photo courtesy of Gary Sohmers.

Autograph, photo
Chuck Berry.................................**$75**
Mick Jagger...............................**$135**
Harry James...............................**$35**
Madonna.....................................**$195**
Paul McCartney..........................**$275**
Autograph, program, Wayne Newton, 1980s..**$20**
Backstage pass, cloth
Aerosmith, Pump Tour '89, afternoon
....**$10**
Bon Jovi, NJ Guest..........................**$7**
KISS, 10th anniversary, after show, unused...**$7**
Cyndi Lauper, Crew '86-87............**$6**
Rolling Stones, American Tour '81
....**$15**
Book, *The Beatles Authorized Biography,* McGraw-Hill, 32 glossy black and white photos, copyright 1968
....**$25**
Christmas card, The Partridge Family, color photo of family opening presents, Christmas tree, facsimile signatures, matching red envelope, trimmed in dark gold, c1971, 5-3/4" x 8-1/2".......................................**$15**
Counter display, Rolling Stones, "Made In The Shade," 1976, 3-D cardboard, bowed diecut, with four previous LP covers at left and "Rolling Stones & Tongue" logo on silver at top right, 21" x 19"...................**$250**
Drawing, pencil, 2-1/4" x 2-1/2" image of Jeremy the Bobb balancing on one foot, from Beatles Yellow Submarine, production notations, 1968, 12-1/2" x 16" sheet of animation paper......**$150**
Drinking glass, Beatles, clear, images and text in black, 1960s, 6-1/2" h
....**$20**

Poster, Bruce Springsteen, Liberty Hall, blue tone photo, March, 1974, **$750.**
Photo courtesy of Gary Sohmers.

Drumsticks
Alice in Chains.............................**$25**
Black Crows, concerned used, logo
....**$20**
Iron Maiden, 1985........................**$50**
Fan photo, 8" x 10"
Jackson Five, full color, 1970s.......**$10**
James Dean, black and white glossy, c1954...**$15**
Magazine
Lennon Photo Special, Sunshine Publications, copyright 1981, 8" x 11"...**$15**
Life, Rock Stars at Home with Their Parents, Vol. 17, #13, Sept. 14, 1971
....**$5**
Post, Mamas and Papas article, March 25, 1967....................................**$5**
The Rolling Stones Magazine, Straight Arrow Publishers, copyright 1975..................................**$10**
Newsletter, Rolling Stones Fan Club, four pgs, black and white, orig mailing envelope, 5" x 8".................**$15**
Pinback button
Led Zeppelin, group logo in center, blue and white lettering: Summerfest At The Stadium Presents An Evening With Led Zeppelin, Sat, Aug. 6, 1977, Buffalo, NY," 3" d
....**$35**
Hey, Let's Twist, red lettering on white ground, striped peppermint candy design, c1961, 3-1/2" d.............**$20**
Portrait, Elvis Presley, by Ivan Jesse Curtain, wooden frame, 1960s
....**$125**

Two autographed photos: one Yoko Ono, signed "To Billy, Love Yoko, NYC '89" and one black & white photo of Paul McCartney, **$50.**

Photo courtesy of Joy Luke Auctions.

Poster

Beatles, four sheets, each with Richard Avedon stylized portrait, 1968, 79" x 29" **$1,840**

Family Dog, art by Victor Moscoso, second printing, Oct. 6-8, 1967 ....**$35**

Janis Joplin, Neon Rose, Matrix, San Francisco, Jan. 17-22, 1967, 13-3/4" x 20"...**$75**

Press kit, KISS, Casablanca, custom folder, three-page bio, one-page press clipping, five 8" x 10" black and white photos, orig mailing envelope with no writing or postage, 1976 ....**$500**

Scarf, Beatles, glossy fabric, half corner design, marked "The Beatles/Copyright by Ramat & Co., Ltd./London, ECI," c1964, 25" sq......................**$160**

Sheet music

Jackson Five, *Mama's Pearl,* copyright 1971 Jobette Music Co. **$5**

Michael Jackson, *We're Almost There,* browntone photo cover, copyright 1974 Stone Diamond Corp **$5**

Ticket

Beatlefest '82-LA **$10**

Elvis, 9/88................................**$75**

The Beatles Again Movie, 1976, 2-1/4" x 5-1/2"..............................**$20**

Yardbirds/Doors, 1967 ....**$50**

Tour book

Depeche Mode, Devotional Tour 1993/94 ....**$10**

KISS, 10th anniversary, Vinnie V in makeup **$125**

Toy, Beatles car, battery operated tin, 1964 Ford Galaxie, vinyl Beatles-like group, "Los Yes-Yes" lithographed on hood, record inside car is bit garbled, but working, orig Rico (Spain) hang tag, orig box with insert, C.9 ....**$850**

T-shirt, never worn

Bon Jovi, L, Slippery When **$25**

Deep Purple, L, Perfect Str...'85 ....**$25**

Rolling Stones, XL, Steel Wheels **$20**

Watch, Elvis Presley, dial with full-color illus of Elvis in elaborate white jumpsuit, blue background, copyright 1977 Boxcar Enterprises, Unique Time Co., orig blue vinyl straps, 1-1/4" d goldtone metal case **$45**

ROYCROFT

History: Elbert Hubbard founded the Roycrofters in East Aurora, New York, at the turn of the century. Considered a genius in his day, he was an author, lecturer, manufacturer, salesman, and philosopher.

Hubbard established a campus that included a printing plant where he published *The Philistine, The Fra,* and *The Roycrofter.* His most-famous book was *A Message to Garcia,* published in 1899. His "community" also included a furniture manufacturing plant, a metal shop, and a leather shop.

Ali Baba bench, half-log top, flaring plank legs, keyed through tenon stretcher, carved orb and cross mark, minor loss to bark, orig finish, 42-1/2" l, 11" w, 20" h **$16,500**

Billfold, matching change purse, lady's, tooled leather, emb foliate motif, mononngrammed "RK," orig mirror, pencil, and notepad, orb and cross mark, 3-1/2" x 6-3/4" **$425**

Bookcase, slab sides with keyed tenon construction, plate rail top, orig iron hardware, orb mark, refinished, 46" w, 16" d, 71" h **$9,775**

Bookends, pr, 4-1/8" w, 3-1/4" d, 5-1/4" h, model no. 309, hammered copper, rect, riveted center band suspending ring, dark brown patina, imp Roycroft orb, minor wear **$225**

Book

Old John Burroughs, by Elbert Hubbard, full levant, cover and inside covers incised and painted with blossoms, each hand made paper page with watercolor by Clara Schlegel and Richard Kruger, hand painted bookmark, 1901, 8" x 5-1/4" **$4,000**

So Here Then Is The Last Ride, by Robert Browning, half levant and marbleized paper, each page illuminated by Frances June Carmody, sgd and numbered, 1900, 8" x 5-3/4" **$650**

Box

"In" and "Out," from Roycroft Inn, one quarter-sawn oak, stenciled with letter "O," stamped "OF.336. S," other pine, stamped "P501," orig finish, branded orb and cross marks, 3-1/4" x 13" x 10"........**$600**

Tooled leather and suede lined, lid emb with poppy medallion, orb and cross mark, some scuffs and wear to corners, 1-1/2" x 4" x 4" **$475**

Bowl, hammered copper, rolled rim, shouldered bowl, three point feet, red patina, imp mark, traces of brass wash, 10-1/4" d, 4-1/8" h............**$450**

Bud vase, wall hanging, hammered copper, cut-out frame, 10-1/2" l .**$200**

Candle lamp, blue art glass, baluster form, flaring foot, stamped "Roycroft," electrified **$175**

Candle sconce, hammered copper, riveted strap holder, imp backplate, orig dark brown patina, orb and cross mark, few scratches, price for pr, 3-1/2" w, 10" h............**$630**

Candlesticks, pr

Brass washed, good grain, Princess style, double shafts, faceted bases, stamped orb and cross mark, orig patina, 7-1/2" h **$650**

Hammered copper, triple light, curled bands, orig dark patina with some wear, orb and cross marks, 3" x 8-1/4"...**$500**

Hammered copper, double light, wood grain pattern, orb and cross marks, 6" x 6-3/4"......................**$350**

Chair, side, ladderback, three horizontal back slats, leather covered cushions, carved orb and cross mark, refinished, price for pr, 37" x 16-1/2" x 16-1/4".......................................**$460**

Chandelier, from Roycroft Inn, copper, triangular strap support base with cut-out hearts and three pendant fixtures, each with enameled amber glass shade dec in stylized floral motif, triangular ceiling plate, hanging chains, orb and cross mark, 14-1/2" w, 10-3/4" h.................**$1,955**

Desk lamp, Steuben blown glass lustered glass shade, hammered copper, shaft of four curled and riveted bands, stamped orb and cross mark, 14-3/4" h, 7" d **$5,750**

Desk set, hammered copper, blotter corners, inkwell, letter holder, pen tray, perpetual calendar with cards, letter opener, orb and cross marks, orig dark patina **$350**

Dresser, pine and oak, two small drawers over four long drawers, hammered iron hardware, paneled sides, orb and cross die-stamped on each pull, from Roycroft Inn, 62-3/4" x 45" x 21"...............................**$1,500**

Frame, hammered copper, emb with quatrefoils, orb and cross mark, and "Roycroft," orig dark patina, 8" x 5-3/4".................................**$1,100**

Goody box, mahogany, wrought cooper strap hardware, monogrammed "H," orig finish, carved orb and cross on top, 23" l, 13" d, 10" h.............**$630**

High chair, child's, tacked-on leather seat, hand carved name "Silas," orig finish, carved orb and cross front center, seat and tacks replaced, 42" x 16-1/2" x 21-1/2".........................**$950**

Humidor, hammered copper, covered in brass wash, Trillium pattern, stamped orb and cross mark, minor wear to patina, 4-3/4" w, 5-3/4" h **$690**

Kitchen work table, mixed woods, tacked-on zinc counter over two lower shelves, orig finish, unsigned, from Roycroft Inn, 30" x 70" x 18-1/4"..................................**$2,700**

Lamp, boudoir, brass washed hammered copper base, base stamped with orb and cross mark, 10-1/2" d faceted mica shade, wear and flakes to mica..**$350**

Lamp, table

Hammered copper and mica, single socket, riveted heraldic shade, lined with band of mica, orig dark patina, orb and cross mark, 15" h, 10" d **$3,500**

Lime green and purple conical leaded slag glass shade, classical hammered copper base, riveted bands, ring pulls, three sockets, orb and cross mark, replaced cord, 23" h, 18" d **$35,000**

Magazine stand, arched tapering sides, three shelves, orb and cross mark, orig finish, 37-1/2" x 17-3/4" x 15-1/2".................................**$5,550**

Marble bag, laced suede, large orb and cross mark tooled to front panel, 8" l...**$450**

Morris chair, shaped arms and posts, laced leather covered foam cushions, four slats under each arm, carved orb and cross mark on front stretcher, arms refinished, replaced leather and cushions, 39-1/2" x 29-1/2" x 38".......**$3,250**

Motto, orig Roycroft frame, matted

Roycroft bench, Ali Baba, canted, A-shaped sides, lower stretcher mortised through sides and half-log seat, orig finish, carved orb and cross mark, 19-1/4" x 42" x 11", **$7,500.**
Photo courtesy of David Rago Auctions, Inc.

Roycroft table lamp, designed and executed by Dard Hunter, gently sloping circular leaded-glass shade, stylized pattern of fruit and foliage in yellow and green slag glass, ceramic base modeled with salamanders, covered in matte green glaze, base marked "DH," from estate of Miriam Hubbard Roelofs, Elbert and Alice Hubbard's daughter, and the Salon room of the Roycroft Inn, 13" x 17-1/4", **$65,000.**
Photo courtesy of David Rago Auctions, Inc.

"Do Not Keep Your Kindness...," 17-1/4" x 12-1/2" **$350**

"Happiness is a Habit, Cultivate It," 23" x 19" **$350**

Paper folio, six woodblock prints, Roycroft Inn pamphlet with photographs..**$750**

Smoking set, Trillium pattern, hammered copper, humidor, cigarette holder, cylindrical match holder, stacking ashtrays with matchbox holder, 14" x 9" rect tray.............**$500**

Sugar bowl, cov, china, hp by Bertha Hubbard, sgd "B. C. Hubbard".......**$200**

Tray, hexagonal, hammered copper, stitched border, two handles, orb and cross mark, orig dark patina, 14-3/4" d **$475**

Vase, hammered copper cylinder, emb with stylized quatrefoils on tall stems, stamped orb and cross mark and "KK" for Karl Kipp, patina cleaned some time ago, 7" h, 2-1/2" d.............**$1,600**

Roycroft side chair, four vertical back-slats, Mackmurdo feet and replaced leather upholstered seat, original finish, orb and cross mark, 18" w, 17" d, 38" h, **$1,485.**
Photo courtesy of David Rago Auctions, Inc.

Roycroft chair, hand-tooled and embossed leather covered, vertical seat-rail slats, tapered legs, good original finish with minor wear, carved orb and cross mark, from estate of Elbert Hubbard and the salon at the Roycroft Inn, 37-1/2" x 24" x 24", **$27,000.**
Photo courtesy of David Rago Auctions, Inc.

Roycroft child's chair, four vertical back slats, tacked-on replaced vinyl seat, orig finish, carved cross and orb mark, 25" x 13-1/2" x 13-3/4", **$950.**
Photo courtesy of David Rago Auctions, Inc.

Roycroft telephone hammered copper and bakelite, inscribed "PROPERTY OF THE AMERICAN BELL TELE-PHONE COMPANY," original wiring and patina, orb and cross mark, 12", **$8,100.**

Photo courtesy of David Rago Auctions, Inc.

Roycroft vase, hammered copper, cylindrical, incised full-length leaves alternating with buds, verdigris patinated hammered top, orb and cross mark, 8-1/4" x 3", **$1,500.**

Photo courtesy of David Rago Auctions, Inc.

RUSSIAN ITEMS

History: During the late 19th and early 20th centuries, craftsmen skilled in lacquer, silver, and enamel wares worked in Russia. During the Czarist era (1880-1917), Fabergé, known for his exquisite enamel pieces, led a group of master craftsmen located primarily in Moscow. Fabergé also had an establishment in St. Petersburg and enjoyed the patronage of the Russian Imperial family and royalty and nobility throughout Europe.

Almost all enameling was done on silver. The artist and the government assayer sign pieces.

The Russian Revolution in 1917 brought an abrupt end to the century of Russian craftsmanship. The modern Soviet government has exported some inferior enamel and lacquer work, usually lacking in artistic merit. Modern pieces are not collectible.

Enamels

Blood cup, gilt and transfer dec, Imperial double headed eagle, cipher of Czar Nicholas II above date 1896, 4" h **$260**

Bonbonniere, orchid guillouche enamel on silver, cylindrical, cast silver bas-relief applied dec on cov and back, applied relief, monogram of Nicholas II set with precious stones, Henrik Wigstrom, workmaster, St. Petersburg, slight damage, 1908-17, 3-3/8" d, 2-3/16" h **$4,225**

Cane, 4-1/2" l x 3-1/4" tau handle dec with champleve style raised enamel, light blue, dark blue, green, white, and red, worn Russian hallmarks, heavy ebony shaft, 7/8" replaced brass ferrule, c1900, 35" l **$2,350**

Cigarette case, 84 standard, silver gilt, robin's egg blue enamel, feathered guillouche ground, opaque white enamel borders, diamond chips on clasp, gilt in., Ivan Britzin, St. Petersburg, small losses and chips to enamel, 1908-17, 3-1/2" l, 2-1/4" w **$1,200**

Coffee spoon, blue dot border in bowl, stylized polychrome enamel foliage, gilt stippled ground, twisted gilt stem, crown finial, G Tokmakov, c1890 .... **$300**

Cup, silver-gilt and cloisonné enamel, Antip Kuzmichev, Moscow, marked "Made for Tiffany & Co.," price for set of four, dated 1895, 3" w, 2-1/4" h **$4,025**

Egg, silver gilt and shaded enamel ware, two-pc construction, cabochon stone, maker's mark obliterated, ftd, 20th C, 3" h **$700**

Powder box, Russian, lift-off lid, lacquer, miniature of man and woman sitting with priest at a table, dark brown background, interior marked "O.F. Vishnyakov & Sons Workshop, Fedoskino Russia," 1882, 2-1/2" d, 1-1/4" h, **$300.**

Photo courtesy of Gamal Amer.

Cane, Russian, Moscow, silver and enamel champleve, 2-7/8" h x 7/8" d cylindrical handle, two shades of blue, green, red, and white on gold gilt background, Russian hallmarks for 84 zolotnicks, kokshnik marks for 1896-1907, maker marks "M.K." for Michael Koshov, black hardwood shaft, 1-1/4" burnished brass ferrule, 19th C, 35-7/8" l, **$3,250.**

Photo courtesy of Henry A. Taron.

Kovsh, silver-gilt and enamel, probably Moscow, typical shape, notched handle and band of trailing flowering branches in colors, 1895, 4-1/4" l, **$675.**

Photo courtesy of Sloans & Kenyon Auctioneers and Appraisers.

Kovsh, silver, shaded enamel on moss green field, Pan Slavic style, hallmarked Moscow, Cyrillic "Faberge" under Imperial Warrant, 1907, 3" h **$2,875**

Matchbox holder, silver gilt and cloisonné, hallmarked Moscow, indistinguishable makers mark, c1900, 2-1/4" l.....................................**$350**

Napkin ring, enameled green, blue, pink, brown, white, light blue and maroon, Maria Semenova, Moscow, c1890, 1-3/4" x 1" x 1-1/2" **$700**

Spoon

Round bowl, twisted handle ending in crown finial with enamel accents, obverse of bowl dec with hp portrait of woman surrounded by band of blue and green plique-a-jour in geometric design, illegible mark, 7-1/2" d **$1,760**

Silver-gilt and shaded enamel, back with colorful plumed bird on stippled ground, beaded border, Dmitri Nicholiaev, Moscow, c1900, 7-1/4" l **$865**

Sugar shovel, silver gilt and enamel, Antip Kuzmichev, Moscow, 1899, 4-3/4" l.....................................**$500**

Sugar tongs, silver gilt and cloisonné enamel, Moscow, indistinguishable makers mark, 1899, 5-1/4" l **$250**

Vase, champleve enamel, central cartouche on both sides, one with stylized double headed eagle, other side with roosters, Slavonic inscription at base rim, hallmarked Moscow, Cyrillic "P. Ovchinnikov" under Imperial Warrant, dated 1874, 11-1/2" h **$5,750**

Icon

John the Forerunner, c1575, 10-3/4" x 13-1/2"..................**$8,625**

St. Nicholas, cast bronze and champleve enamel, 19th C, 9" x 10" **$635**

Saint Tikhon of Amathus, Moscow workshop, c1890, 35" x 28".....**$2,990**

Icon, St. Nicholas, Moscow, silver-gilt Oklad, richly enameled halo, 1893, 12-1/2" x 10-1/4", **$1,200.**

Photo courtesy of Sloans & Kenyon Auctioneers and Appraisers.

Six Days, c1600, 10-1/2" x 12" **$2,070**

The Apostle John and Prokhorus, 16th C, 15-1/2" x 23-1/2" **$16,100**

The Archangel Mikhail, 19th C, 12" x 14"...................................**$2,645**

The Ascension of the Lord, 19th C, 14-1/4" x 17-1/2"..........................**$920**

The Dormition, 19th C, 10" x 12" **$2,070**

The Entry Into Jerusalem, borders and background gilded and finely incised, c1890, 10-1/2" x 12-1/4" **$2,185**

The Eucharist, c1550-1600, inscribed "Peite Ot Neya Siya Est Krov Moya," 13-1/2" x 15-3/4"....................**$13,800**

The Holy Great Martyr Catherine, 20th C, 12" x 14" **$920**

The Holy Martyr Paraskeva, full-length figure, c1750, 32" x 13-1/2" **$4,370**

The Kazan Mother of God, faux enameled background and borders, c1890, 7" x 5-3/4"........................**$300**

The Lord Almighty, c1700, 10-1/4" x 12"....................................**$2,760**

The Lord Almighty, 18th or 19th C, 12-1/4" x 10-1/4"....................**$1,725**

The Mystical (Last) Supper, 18th C, 17" x 12-1/2".........................**$3,335**

The Not By Hands Made Image of Christ-The Holy Napkin, 10-1/2" x 12-1/4"...................................**$1,725**

The Passion, central panel with elaborate scene of Christ descending into Hades, sixteen separate scenes, c1650, 12-1/2" x 15-1/4".......................**$1,725**

The Resurrection and Descent Into Hades, 1550-1600, attributed to Tver, 9-3/4" x 11-3/4".........**$10,350**

Caviar tub, silver, faux wood grain, vermeil reeded bands, locking cover, glass liner, 1860, 4" d, 10 oz, **$950.**

Photo courtesy of Sloans & Kenyon Auctioneers and Appraisers.

The Smolensk Mother of God, c1775-1825, 10-1/2" x 12-1/4" **$920**

The Smolensk Mother of God, 19th C, 9" x 7" **$1,035**

The Symbol of Faith, second half of 20th C, 28" x 23" **$1,955**

The Terrible Judgment, Strashnuiy Sud, second half 20th C, 31-1/2" x 22" **$2,645**

The Theodore Mother of God, overlaid with custom fitted silvered riza, attached gilded halos, late 18th C, 8-3/4" x 10-1/4" **$1,350**

The Three Handed Mother of God, 19th C, 8-3/4" x 10-3/4" **$435**

The Tikhvin Mother of God, 18th C, 13-1/2" x 11-3/4"....................**$815**

The Tikhvin Mother of God, finely painted, overlaid with finely crafted riza, c1800-50, 9-3/4" x 11-1/2" **$1,380**

The Vladimir Mother of God, c1700-1750, 12-1/2" x 11"........**$1,725**

Metal

Bust, Tsar Alexander Mikhailovich, Cyrillic foundry mark "F. Shopeen," bronze, dated 1867, 10" h **$1,250**

Cross, Palekh or Mstera, recessed edges (kovcheg), painted in classic 16th C style, top with Holy Napkin and Angels, center crossbeam with Mary and Apostle John, center with crucified Christ with implements of the passion, base with skull of Adam, 19th C, 47" x 22" **$4,600**

Samovar

Cylindrical, front and rim stamped with profusion of awards, Kvana Kaprzina, Tula, c1905, 22" h **$575**

Cylindrical, orig bowl and undertray, 19th C, 14" h **$400**

Silver, cigarette case, raised decoration of horse-drawn sleigh with figures, red stone cabochon on latch, gold wash interior, Russian standard marks, 4-3/4" l, 3-1/2" w, **$250.**
Photo courtesy of Alderfer Auction Co.

Cylindrical, paneled body, 19th C, 17-1/2" h **$375**

Sculpture, bronze

Couple being driven in troika, deep brown patina, sgd in base in Cyrillic "Gratchev" (Vasilil Iakovelvich Gratchev, 1831-1905) and "Voerffel Foundry-St Petersburg," 12-1/4" l, 7" w, 7-1/2" h **$2,875**

Mounted Imperial soldier, dark brown patina, indistinguishably signed in Cyrillic on base, c1890, 18-1/2" x 16-1/2" h **$2,300**

Tray, painted and lacquered metal, troika scene, verso sgd in Cyrillic "Lukutin," beneath Imperial Warrant, 19th C, 13-1/2" x 10-1/2" **$690**

Miscellaneous

Box, lacquer and transfer printed papier-mâché, colorful foil backed transfer images of famous Russian scenes on lid, lock and key, price for pr, c1890, 6-1/2" x 4-1/2" **$460**

Card case, nephrite and gold, cabochon thumbpush, hallmarked St Petersburg 1908, standard 56, makers mark "A. A.," 3-1/2" l **$4,890**

Charger, carved in Pan Slavic style, borders carved relief inscription "To Her Imperial Highness Princess Yevheniya Maximiliyanova of Oldenburg," center with Imperial Russian coat of arms and Princess's coat of arms, relief carved "Housewarming from the Chertkov and Sverbeyev families 1887," verso with makers

Russian icon, Madonna and Child, tempera on wood panel, 10-1/2" x 12" x 1-1/4", **$375.**
Photo courtesy of Sloans & Kenyon Auctioneers and Appraisers.

plaque in Cyrillic "F. Schilling, Moscow," 15" d **$850**

Purse, 14k yg, curved frame gypsy-set with 11 old mine-cut and old European-cut diamonds, approx. total wt. 3.00 cts, further set with gypsy-set oval sapphires and circular-cut rubies, mesh body, trace link chain, 95.2 dwt, Russian hallmarks **$200**

Stool, paint dec, geometric strapwork dec on top, turned tapered legs, early 20th C, 13-1/2" w, 9-1/4" d, 8-7/8" h **$125**

Porcelain

Cabinet plate, cobalt blue, green, and red central rosette, gilt ground, 9" d **$275**

Cup and saucer, blue glazed, honoring coronation of Nicholas II, M.S. Kuznetsov, 1878, 4-1/2" h **$250**

Dessert plate, floral rim, magenta ground, Islamic script, printed mark, I. E. Kuznetsov, set of six, 19th C **$265**

Plate, two soldiers, verso with underglaze Cyrillic P.S. beneath crown mark, 8-3/4" d **$750**

Portrait plate, Empress Elizabeth, Safronov, hairline, early 19th C, 8" d **$315**

Tankard, figural, Turk's head, marked "F. Gardner, Moscow," restored, 19th C, 8" h **$1,210**

Tea service, 13 pcs, creamer, sugar, four cov cups, four saucers, two open cups, Kornilov Bros, c1910, 9" w x 5" h cov teapot **$2,415**

Vase, one green with medallion of Olga, other puce with medallion of Vladimir, all-over gilt foliate dec, Gardner, drilled, price for pr, 19th C, 8" h **$250**

SALT AND PEPPER SHAKERS

History: Collecting salt and pepper shakers, whether late 19th-century glass forms or the contemporary figural and souvenir types, is becoming more and more popular. The supply and variety is practically unlimited; the price for most sets is within the budget of cost-conscious collectors. In addition, their size offers an opportunity to display a large collection in a relatively small space.

Specialty collections can be by type, form, or maker. Great glass artisans, such as Joseph Locke and Nicholas Kopp, designed salt and pepper shakers in the normal course of their work.

Additional Resources:

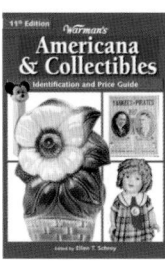

Warman's® Americana & Collectibles, 11th Ed., by Ellen T. Schroy, ed., Krause Publications, Iola, WI.

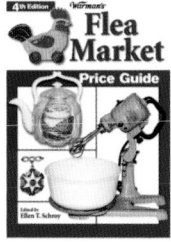

Warman's® Flea Market, 4th Ed., by Ellen T. Schroy, ed., Krause Publications, Iola, WI.

Spiffy Kitchen Collectibles, by Brian S. Alexander, Krause Publications, Iola, WI.

Art glass
(priced individually)
Cranberry, Inverted Thumbprint, sphere **$175**
Hobnail, sapphire blue, Hobbs, Brockunier & Co., one orig metal top, 2-3/4" h..............................**$95**
Mt. Washington
Egg shape, one with pink and blue daisies, other with red mums, 2-1/2" h **$120**
Egg shape, stemmed flower dec, 2-1/2" h **$65**
Pairpoint
Barrel shape, enameled flowers, 3" h **$55**
Mold blown, faceted body, colored flowers, 3" h **$45**
Shell shape, colorless, two purple blossoms, spray of yellow daisies, green leaves..............................**$885**
Wave Crest, Erie Twist body, hp flowers, 2-1/2" h..............................**$185**

Figural and souvenir types (priced by set)
Bride and groom, pigs, nodders, marked "Made in Japan," c1950 ....**$325**
Christmas, barrel shape, amethyst **$165**
Ducks, sitting, glass, clear bodies, blue heads, sgd "Czechoslovakia," 2-1/2" h **$45**
Egg shape, opaque white body, holly dec, 23 red raised enameled berries, Mt. Washington **$175**
Mammy and broom, orig "Norcrest Fine China Japan" foil labels, numbered H424, 4-1/4" h..............................**$395**
Strawberries, flashed amberina glass strawberry-shaped shakers, white metal leaf caps, suspended from emb white metal fancy holder, sgd "Japan," c1921-41, 2-3/4" h strawberries, 5" h stand **$285**

Opalescent glass
(priced individually)
Argonaut Shell, blue..............................**$65**
Fluted Scrolls, vaseline..............................**$65**
Seaweed, Hobbs, cranberry..........**$60**
Windows, Hobbs, blue, pewter top **$55**

Opaque glass
(priced individually)
Bulge Bottom, blue **$25**
Cathedral Panel, white **$20**
Creased Bale, pink..............................**$20**

Salt and pepper shakers, pair of milk cans, cream, blue and red decoration, **$18.**

Salt and pepper, Mt. Washington, Burmese, ribbed pillar, pastel florals, Meridan silverplate caddy, 6-1/2" h, **$500.**
Photo courtesy of The Early Auction Company, LLC.

Fleur de Lis Scrolling, custard **$20**
Heart, blue **$25**
Leaf Clover, blue **$20**
Little Shrimp, white..............................**$20**
Swirl Wide Diagonal, white.......**$20**

Pattern glass
(priced individually)
Block and Fan, colorless, 1891.....**$20**
Francesware, Hobbs, Brockunier Co., c1880, hobnail, frosted, amber stained **$45**
Lobe, squatty **$120**
Tulip **$100**

Silver
Figural, Oriental street merchant pushing cart that contains salt and pepper shakers, toothpick container, hallmarked "90 HM," 5-1/4" l.....**$195**
Spratling, Mexico, domed forms on angular wooden bases, maker's marks, 3-1/2" h..............................**$500**

SALTS, OPEN

History: When salt was first mined, the supply was limited and expensive. The necessity for a receptacle in which to serve the salt resulted in the first open salt, a crude, hand-carved, wooden trencher.

As time passed, salt receptacles were refined in style and materials. In the 1500s, both master and individual salts existed. By the 1700s, firms such as Meissen, Waterford, and Wedgwood were making glass, china, and porcelain salts. Leading glass manufacturers in the 1800s included Libbey, Mount Washington, New England, Smith Bros., Vallerysthal, Wave Crest, and Webb. Many outstanding silversmiths in England, France, and Germany also produced this form.

Open salts were the only means of serving salt until the appearance of the shaker in the late 1800s. The ease of procuring salt from a shaker greatly reduced the use of and need for the open salts.

Notes: Allan B. and Helen B. Smith have authored and published 10 books on open salts beginning with *One Thousand Individual Open Salts Illustrated* (1972) and ending with *1,334 Open Salts Illustrated: The Tenth Book* (1984). The numbers in parentheses refer to plate numbers in the Smiths' books. Another reference book that collectors refer to for salts was written by L. W. & D. B. Neal, *Pressed Glass Salt Dishes of the Lacy Period, 1825-50.*

Condiment sets with open salts

German silver, two castors, two salts, two salt spoons, Renaissance style with swan supports, marked ".800 fine," c1900 .... **$800**

Limoges, double salt and mustard, sgd "J. M. Limoges" (388) **$80**

Metal, coolie pulling rickshaw, salt, pepper, and mustard, blown glass liners, Oriental (461) **$360**

Quimper, double salt and mustard, white, blue, and green floral dec, sgd "Quimper" (388)......................... **$120**

Early American glass

Blown molded, hat shape, brilliant cobalt blue, inward folded rim, rayed type IV base, rough pontil mark, Boston & Sandwich Glass Co., McKearin GIII-23, 1825-35, 2-1/4" h, 2-3/8" x 2-1/2" d rim, 2" d base **$650**

Pressed, lacy

Neal BF-1F, Basket of Flowers, fiery opalescent violet blue, four feet, Boston & Sandwich, unlisted color, extremely rare, slightly warped, small chips, 2" h, 1-3/4" x 3"............. **$1,100**

Neal BS-2, Beaded Scroll & Basket of Flowers, clambroth, Boston & Sandwich Glass Co., 1825-50, 2" h **$375**

Neal BS-2, Beaded Scroll & Basket of Flowers, colorless, Boston & Sandwich Glass Co., 1835-45, flakes on inner rim, 1-7/8" h, 1-7/8" x 3-1/8" **$135**

Neal BS-2, Beaded Scroll & Basket of Flowers, opalescent, Boston & Sandwich Glass Co, 1825-50, 2" h **$400**

Neal BS-3a, Beaded Scroll pattern, violet-blue, Boston & Sandwich Glass Co, edge cracks and chips, c1825-50, 2" h............................ **$360**

Neal BT-2, Pittsburgh Steamboat, colorless, emb on stern, Stourbridge Flint Glass Works, minor rim flakes, 1-1830-45, 1/2" h, 1-7/8" x 3-5/8" **$825**

Neal BT-4D, Lafayet Steamboat, deep cobalt blue, mkd "B & S Glass Co." on stern, "Sandwich" in int. base,

Boston & Sandwich Glass Co., minor inner rim flaking, 1830-45, 1-5/8" h, 1-7/8" x 3-5/8"........ **$2,750**

Neal CT-1, chariot, mottled silvery opaque blue, scallop and point rim, Boston & Sandwich Glass Co., rim corner chip, mold roughness, 1835-50, 1-3/4" h, 2-1/8" x 2-7/8" **$1,265**

Neal EE-3B, fiery opalescent, four feet, Boston & Sandwich Glass Co., near proof, chip on interior of one foot, 1835-45, 2-1/8" h, 2-1/8" x 3-1/4".. **$615**

Neal JY-2, light green, scallop and point rim, emb "Jersey" under base, Jersey Glass Co., c1835-50, 2" h, 2-1/8" x 3" **$880**

Neal NE-6, light green, scallop and point rim, star under base, Jersey Glass Co. or New England Glass Co., two rim chips, 1835-50, 2" h, 2-1/8" x 2-7/8"................................ **$245**

Neal OL-15, Beaded Strawberry Diamond, brilliant deep purple blue, high and low point rim, Boston & Sandwich Glass Co., 1830-50, 1-3/4" h **$495**

Neal OO-2, Octagon, oblong, colorless, c1825-50, 1-1/2" h........... **$195**

Neal OO-9, Octagon, oblong, colorless, flat rim, possibly New England, minor inner flake, 1835-50, 1-3/8" h **$210**

Neal OP-8, Oval Pedestal, amethyst tint, New England, imperfections, c1825-50, 1-7/8" h.................... **$195**

Neal PO-1A, Peacock Eye, oval, colorless, serrated table ring, Boston & Sandwich Glass Co., unlisted color, 1830-50, 1-1/2" h.................. **$275**

Neal PO-4, Peacock Eye, oval, dark blue, rayed base, Boston & Sandwich Glass Co., unlisted color, 1830-45, 1-3/8" h **$2,640**

Neal PO-5, Peacock Eye, oval, colorless, c1825-50, 1-1/2" h........... **$225**

Neal PR-1A, Peacock-Eye, round, violet-blue, Boston & Sandwich Glass Co., 1825-50, 1-1/2" h **$425**

Neal RP-9, Round Pedestal, colorless, imperfections, c1825-50, 1-1/2" h **$165**

Neal SC-5, Scroll, medium blue, c1825-50, 1-7/8" h................... **$365**

Neal SD-7, Strawberry Diamond, medium blue, Boston & Sandwich Glass Co., 1825-50, 2" h **$365**

Neal SL-1, Shell, red-amethyst, Boston & Sandwich Glass Co. minor edge roughness, few base chips, c1825-50, 1-3/4" h **$650**

Salt and pepper shakers with napkin ring combination, loop handle on footed stand, silver plated, **$95.**

Neal SL-4, Shell pattern, dark amber, Pittsburgh area, edge chips, c1830, 1-3/4" h **$350**

Neal SL-11, Shell pattern, peacock blue, Boston & Sandwich Glass Co., 1825-50, 1-3/4" h...................... **$295**

Neal SL-18, Shell pattern, raised scroll pedestal, colorless, Boston & Sandwich Glass Co., edge chips, small base cracks, 1825-50, 2-5/8" h **$715**

Figurals

Basket, coral colored glass, SP basket frame, salt with cut polished facets, 3" h, 2-3/4" d **$55**

Bucket, Bristol glass, turquoise, white, green, and brown enameled bird, butterfly and trees, SP rim and handle, 2-1/2" d, 1-5/8" h **$75**

Sea horse, Belleek, brilliant turquoise, white base, supports shell salt, first black mark (458) **$350**

Individual

Cameo, Daum Nancy, cameo glass, bucket form, two upright handles, frosted colorless ground, cameo etched and enameled black tree lined shore, distant ruins, gilt rim, sgd "Daum (cross) Nancy" in gilt on base, small rim chips, 1-3/8" h **$575**

Cut glass, cut ruby ovals, all-over dainty white enameled scrolls, clear ground, gold trim, scalloped top, 2" d, 1-1/2" h.................................... **$60**

Moser, cobalt blue, pedestal, gold bands, applied flowers sgd (380) **$75**

Mount Washington, blue Johnny Jump-ups, cream ground, raised gold dots on rim **$135**

Pattern glass
Fine Rib, flint............................... **$35**
Pineapple and Fan **$25**
Three Face................................... **$40**

Purple slag, emb shell pattern, 3" d, 1-1/4" h.................................... **$50**

Russian, colorless glass liner, gold finished metal, red and white enamel scallop design, Russian hallmarks, c1940, 1-1/4" h, 1-3/4" d **$110**

Sterling silver, Georg Jensen, Denmark, porringer (238) **$215**

Masters

Coin silver, made by Gorham for retailer Seth E. Brown, Boston, ftd,

China, master salt and six individual oval serving salts, gold floral border and trim, marked "Nippon," **$30.**

gold washed int., monogrammed, pair in fitted case, two coin silver spoons by Jones, Ball & Poor, pr, approx 4 troy oz...................... **$375**

Cranberry, emb ribs, applied crystal ruffed rim, SP holder with emb lions heads, 3" d, 1-3/4" h **$160**

Cut glass, green cut to clear, SP holder, 2" d, 2" h................................. **$115**

Green, light, dark green ruffled top, open pontil (449) **$90**

Mocha, seaweed band, yellow ware ground, 2" h **$250**

Pattern glass
Barberry, pedestal **$40**
Basketweave, sleigh (397)...........**$100**
Portland, branches handle..........**$110**
Snail, ruby stained....................... **$75**
Sunflower, pedestal **$40**

Pearlware
Rounded form, medium blue rim band, vertical ribbed dark brown slip dec on white ground, England, early 19th C, 2-1/2" d.............. **$590**
Rounded form, dark brown banding, dark brown dendritic dec on rust field, narrow green glazed reeded band, cracked, rim chip, early 19th C, 2-3/4" d **$590**

Pewter, pedestal, cobalt blue liner (349) **$65**

Redware, mottled brown alkaline glaze, c1850, 2-1/4" h **$75**

Sterling silver, Stieff Co., chased and emb all-over floral pattern, applied floral rim, three scrolled shell feet, pr, early 20th C, 6 troy oz, 1-3/4" h **$260**

Vaseline, applied crystal trim around middle, SP stand, 3" d, 2-1/4" h **$125**

SAMPLERS

History: Samplers served many purposes. For a young child, they were a practice exercise and permanent reminder of stitches and patterns. For a young woman, they were a means to demonstrate skills in a "gentle" art and a way to record family genealogy. For the mature woman, they were a useful occupation and method of creating gifts or remembrances, e.g., mourning pieces.

Schools for young ladies of the early 19th century prided themselves on the needlework skills they taught. The Westtown School in Chester County, Pennsylvania, and the Young Ladies Seminary in Bethlehem, Pennsylvania, were two institutions. These schools changed their teaching as styles changed. Berlin work was introduced by the mid-19th century.

Examples of samplers date back to the 1700s. The earliest ones were long and narrow, usually done only with the alphabet and numerals. Later examples were square. At the end of the 19th century, the shape tended to be rectangular.

The same motifs were used throughout the country. The name of the person who stitched the piece is a key factor in determining the region.

Abigail A Jenney, Plainfield, New Hampshire, three alphabets, trees, various devices, upper and lower borders, silk threads on linen ground, shades of green, yellow, and brown,

Quaker sampler, silk on linen, New Jersey, Eliza P. Sanger at the Newton Academy, dated 1805, 20" x 21", **$1,380.**

Photo courtesy of Pook & Pook, Inc.

Sampler, silk on linen, Elizabeth Lee Parsons, house and lawn over boy and girl within trailing floral and vinde border, dated 1811, 12" x 11-3/4", **$1,150.**

Photo courtesy of Pook & Pook, Inc.

Sampler, Victorian, wool on linen needlework, wrought by "Rebecca Pursel Age 11," figure and landscape, "We Hope to Meet," 12-1/2" x 12-3/4", **$300.**

Photo courtesy of Pook & Pook, Inc.

4-3/4" x 3-3/4" sight size, 6-3/4" x 5-3/4" frame, 1808 .... **$2,585**

Anne Armstrong, Aged 11 Years Clones 1810, geometric bands in red, pink, green, blue, brown, purple, and yellow, row of trees, alphabets, and vowels, linen ground, verse by "C. Quigley," minor stitch loss, framed, 1810, 19" w, 18-1/4" h **$1,265**

Ann Fuller, "Ann Eliza Fuller wrought in the 12th year of her age 1841," silk threads on linen ground, flowering border surrounding seven rows of alphabet examples, verse and signature, framed, 17" sq, fading, stains, 1841 .... **$300**

Caroline Wills, homespun linen, four alphabets, Roman numerals and house at base, "Paradise Tenant House," sgd "Caroline Elizabeth Wills," tiger maple frame, fading and discoloration, photo on back of maker, undated, 18-1/2" w, 20-3/4" h **$2,530**

Cynthia Taft, Uxbridge, Massachusetts, pink and green floral vine encloses verse worked in pink linen above pictorial lower half with garden, trees, flowers, birds, and grass, pink, green, and red hues, good coloration and condition, reframed, minor imperfections, Late 18th C, 10-5/8" w, 12" h **$4,115**

E. J., homespun linen, vase of flowers, sawtooth border, initialed "E. J. 1826," pulled and frayed edges, red painted frame, 1826, 4" w, 4-1/2" h **$2,090**

Elizabeth Thomas, homespun linen, alphabet and name, "Elizabeth Thomas, April 9, 1812," border by vine and floral motif, grain painted frame of yellow ground, red-brown highlights, 1812, 10-3/4" w, 12-3/4" h **$5,280**

Elizabeth Willits, each corner with different flower in soft pale blue, ivory, and gold, central vining wreath with tulip drop encircles verse, numbers, and "Maidencreek, Elizabeth Willits 1804" all done in dark brown, loosely woven linen ground, modern frame, minor stains, 1804, 13-1/4" x 14" **$2,970**

Fanny Chandler, Born December the 15 1803, silk threads on linen ground, rows of alphabets over pious verse, centered with house flanked by flowering trees and baskets of flowers, grid with the initials of family members, molded wood frame, fading, 1803, 15-1/2" x 19-1/2" **$825**

Frances Croll 1810, England or America, basket of flowers over alphabet panels above pious verse, surrounded by floral dec banner, worked in shades of red, blue, green, yellow, and blue threads, framed, fading, scattered staining, 1810, 16-3/8" x 12-3/4" **$825**

Genealogy, "Wrought by Charlotte Perkins AE t 12 Years Aug. 12 1819," attributed to ME, silk threads on linen ground, listing the vital statistics of Ezekiel Cushing and Frances (McCobb) Cushing and their six children, and Benjamin Perkins and Frances (Cushing) Perkins and their five children, beginning in 1752 and ending in 1808, lower reserve with monument and weeping willow commemorating the deaths of two family members, next to house, figure with sheep and dog, town across the river in the distance, all enclosed by border of flowers, foliage and a bow-

knot, unframed, toning, losses, stains, 1819, 24-1/4" x 21" **$2,585**

Homespun linen, alphabet at top, house scene with dog, bird, fruit, trees, and pump, red, green, blue, and brown, "Work in the year 1854," grain painted frame with yellow ochre ground, red-brown highlights, 1854, 17-1/2" w, 20-1/4" h **$4,620**

Isabella Lunds, work Aged 16 AD 1840, inspirational verse, attached buildings, trees, vines, floral and animal devices surrounded by stylized floral border, toning and fading, 1840, 26-3/4" x 32-1/4" **$2,470**

Jane Harrison Vinnis, "Jane Harrison Vinnis is my name and with My Needle I did work the same that all the World may plainly see what care my Parents took of me, Finished at Mis Tucker Northfleet in Kent November the sixth one thousand eight hundred and five and in the twelve year of my age," floral symbols enclosed in panel above Adam, Eve, the tree, entwined serpent, flanked by various religious, animal, and floral devices, surrounded by stylized floral border, gray blue ground, framed, imperfections, Adam and Eve, England, 1805, 15" x 19" **$1,880**

Lucenda Bingham, Massachusetts, silk threads on woven green and blue Linsey-Woolsey ground, three alphabet panels over pious verse over lettering reading "Lucenda Bingham aged 11 years 1809 born August the 3 1798," floral, star, bird, and tree motifs enclosed in sawtooth border, framed, note on back of frame with family genealogy, several unobtrusive losses to background, 1809, 17-5/8" x 11-1/4" **$2,725**

Lucy Parham, Tyngsboro, Massachusetts, 1822, silk threads on linen ground, centered alphabet panels over inscription "Lucy Parham born October 27, 1811, she wrought this in the 11th year of her age," above verse "When youth's soft season shall be o'er/And seasons of childhood charm no more/My riper year with joy shall see/ This proof of infant industry," flanked by two urns with flowers, wide borders with basket of flowers on top, sides with two urns issuing flowering vines, lower border with house, trees and deer, framed, toning, scattered stains, 1822, 17" x 18" **$27,025**

Lydia Wood's, sample Anno Domini 1799, stylized floral upper border above two alphabet panels over panel of flowering shrubs and birds, black, green, and pink silk threads, unframed, fading, toning, 1799, 15-1/4" x 10-1/2"...........................**$715**

Mary B Kimme, Massachusetts, "Wrought by Mary B Kimme---of Bolton 1823 (?) Aged 12 Years," verse and alphabets, house and floral symbols below, right-hand side appears to be unfinished, unframed, small areas of thread losses, some fabric loss to the linen ground, minor fading, 1823, 17-1/4" x 17-1/2"...........................**$890**

Mary Jane Flint, aged 11 years, April 19, 1850, five alphabet panels, pictorial scene, Federal buildings, trees, bird and inspirational verse, framed, fading, toning, staining, 1850, 22-1/2" x 19-1/2"...................................**$1,175**

Rebecca Myers, homespun linen, three alphabets, name at bottom, sawtooth border, veneered frame with minor paint dec, undated, 11-1/2" w, 14" h..**$1,100**

Sally Clark, Aged 8 Years 1801, inspirational verse flanked by stylized vases of flowers, upper borders above birds on branches, landscape with thatched roof cottages, framed, faded, 21" x 17", 1801 ....**$890**

Sawyer and Ryan families, border of vines and roses surrounding central image of two stylized trees, American, paper panels inscribed in ink with names of Ryan and Sawyer families and dates from 1795 to 1816, 17" sq **$20,000**

SCALES

History: Prior to 1900, the simple balance scale was commonly used for measuring weights. Since then, scales have become more sophisticated in design and more accurate. There are a wide variety of styles and types, including beam, platform, postal, and pharmaceutical.

Advertising, Merchants Metal Spanish Tiles, Star Ventilator, Gothic Shingles, High Grade Roofing Plates, diecut multicolored tin litho, weighs up to 4 oz.....................................**$400**

Apothecary, walnut, fitted ivory dec, 19-1/2" l, 15-3/4" h **$250**

Balance

Cast iron, orig red paint with black and yellow trim, nickel plated brass pans, marked "Henry Troemner, Phila. No. 5B, Baker's," 14" l **$120**

J. L. Brown & Co., 83 Fulton St., New York, circular pans, baluster turned cast iron stand, 26" h **$690**

Gold, Allender's Gold Scale, I. Wilson, New London, Connecticut, cast brass rocker balance, slots and platforms for $1, 2-1/2, 5, 10, and 20, additional weight and instructions in shaped paper box, mid-19th C, 9" l **$490**

Grain, chonodrometer, brass, Fairbanks, arm graduated for "lbs per bush," "lb & oz," and "% of lb," sliding weight, bucket, and suspension ring, 11" l..**$350**

Pamphlet, testimonials, Jones of Binghamton, New York, 32 pgs, illus price list of Jones Scales, cuts of canal weight-lock scale, universal, portable platform, postal, counter, rolling mill, lever, truss scales, etc., c1880, 3" x 5-1/2" **$55**

Platform, Peerless Junior, Peerless Weighing Machine Co., porcelainized steel, tiled platform, gold lettering, 63" h...**$350**

Pocket balance, steel, silvered pans, silver mounted shagreen case, engraved plaque, velvet-lined interior, two fitted circular weights and various others, 18th C, 5-1/2" w **$575**

Postal

Candlestick-style, gilt metal, British, for American market, circular pan with scrolled foliate borders, red enameled stem, trellis work and C-scrolls, rate table with eagle dec, circular foot modeled in high relief with locomotive, steam clipper and farm implements interspersed with cornucopia, 1840s, 7-3/4" h **$275**

Store type, Chatillon's Improved Circular Spring Balance to Weigh 30 lbs by ounces, brass face, some wear, **$165.**

Hanson, white enamel body, red and black logo, measures in pounds, **$40.**
Photo courtesy of Joseph P. Smalley, Jr.

Improved Family Scale, Made in Germany, for household use, cast metal case, paper dial, wear, **$45.**

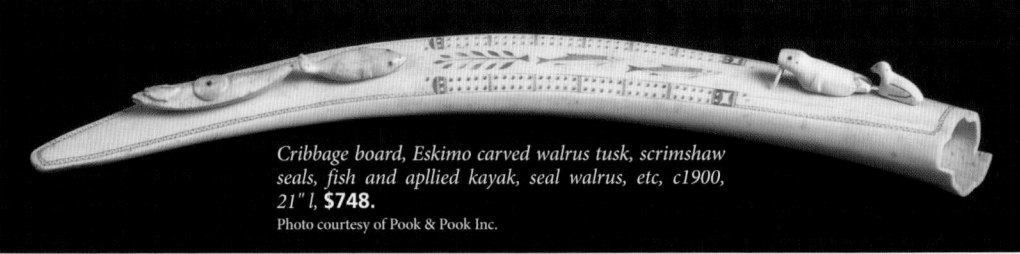

Cribbage board, Eskimo carved walrus tusk, scrimshaw seals, fish and apllied kayak, seal walrus, etc, c1900, 21" l, $748.

Photo courtesy of Pook & Pook Inc.

Health chart, trade stimulator type, black enamel base, tan and red top with chart, $90.

S. Mordan & Co., England, plates with blue and white Wedgwood jasper neoclassical roundels in ropetwist surround, rect base with three weights, 19th C, 4-1/2" h, 6-3/4" l $350

Store

"Computing Scale Co., Dayton, Ohio," 15-1/4" h, 17-1/2" w $225

Hanson Weightmaster, cast iron, gold case with ground, black lettering and indicator, 6" x 14" x 10" $45

SCRIMSHAW

History: Norman Flayderman defined scrimshaw as "the art of carving or otherwise fashioning useful or decorative articles as practiced primarily by whalemen, sailors, or others associated with nautical pursuits." Many collectors expand this to include the work of Eskimos and French POWs from the War of 1812.

Reproduction Alert. The biggest problem in the field is fakes, although there are some clues to spotting them. A very hot needle will penetrate the plastics used in reproductions, but not the authentic material. Ivory will not generate static electricity when rubbed, plastic will. Patina is not a good indicator; it has been faked by applying tea or tobacco juice, and in other ingenious ways. Usually the depth of cutting in an old design will not be consistent since the ship rocked and tools dulled; however, skilled forgers have even copied this characteristic.

Box, circular, engraved and stained, whaling scene, large whale surrounded by compass positions, late 19th C, 2-1/4" d, 2" h $225

Busk

Bone, scratch carved eagle, pinwheels, vining foliage, compass stars, and heart at top, black coloring with red in eagle's shield and one flower, small chip at top, 12-3/8" l $550

Wood, dec with eagle, shield, lovebirds, and ship under sail, heart and foliate devices, inscribed "GC & EW," dated 1840, 13-7/8" l $345

Cane, American, 1-1/3" d x 1-1/8" h whale ivory knob handle, top with

scrimmed spiral sunburst, baleen dot in center, highlighted in red, surrounded by feathery black-inked wreath with red berries, scrimmed around rim "U.S.S. Kearsarge, 1864," with tiny baleen dots, hand fashioned 1/4" ring brass collar on smooth and tapered whalebone shaft with oval brass eyelets, under collar inked scrimshaw "To Capt. John A. Winslow From His Crew," uniform yellow patina, sold with engraved certificate from New York Chamber of Commerce to Captain Winslow and his crew, c1864, 35-1/4" l $15,680

Cribbage board, carved walrus tusk

Carved in relief with Northwest fish and sea life, polychrome dec, late 19th C, 11" l $360

Carved on both sides, obverse, board in floral dec panel flanked by scenes of Northwest animals and fish, reverse with scenes of life in Northwest region, minor age splits, late 19th C, 23" l $475

Domino box, bone and wood, shoe form, pierced carved slide top with star and heart dec, domino playing pcs, Prisoner of War, cracks, minor insect damage, 19th C, 6-7/8" l $520

Game box, bone, pierced carved box with geometric dec, three slide tops, compartmented int., backgammon and other playing pcs, traces of paint dec, Prisoner of War, repair, warping to tops, very minor losses, 19th C, 5-3/4" x 6-1/2" $690

Jagging wheel, dec with building flying American flag, berried vines, very minor losses, 19th C, 7-1/4" l $520

Obelisk, inlaid mahogany, inlaid with various exotic woods, abalone and ivory in geometric and star motifs, minor losses, minute cracks, 19th C, 13-3/8" h.....................................$815

Plaque, sailing ship, pencil inscription "Whale bone found in England by Mrs. Fred Rich," c1800, 14-1/2" l $13,000

Salt horn, engraved "John Snow March…1780 by S. H.," crosshatched borders enclosing reserve of ship, geometric, and foliate devices, insect damage, 5-1/2" l............................ **$460**

Seam rubber, whalebone, geometric designs on handle, traces of orig paint, 19th C, 4" l........................ **$850**

Snuff box, horn, architectural and marine motifs, dated "AD 1853" and "William Sandilands Plumber," English, 5" l............................ **$950**

Swift, all whale bone and ivory, copper pegs, yarn ties, nicely turned detail, pincushion socket on top, age cracks, minor edge damage, possible replaced section, 16" h **$900**

Walrus tusk

Reserves of animals, courting couples, ships under sail, memorials, sailors and armaments, later engraved brass presentation caps, "Presented by George M. Chase to Ike B. Dunlap Jan. 25th 1908," cracks, one restored, pr, 17-3/4" h **$2,530**

Walrus, dec with two eagles, lady, Indian, and vulture, age cracks, 19th C, 18-7/8" l **$1,840**

Watch hutch, bone, pierce carved floral and figural dec, brass backing, polychrome foliate highlights, Prisoner of War, custom-made case, minor cracks, losses, repairs, 19th C, 11-7/8" h............................ **$750**

Whale's tooth, 19th C

Dec with ship, woman resting on anchor holding flag, two potted plants, chips, minor cracks, 19th C, 4-3/8" l............................ **$690**

Historic landmarks, dec on both sides, very minor cracks and chips, 6-5/8" h **$865**

Various ships under sail and young lady, cracks, 6-7/8" h **$1,380**

SEWING ITEMS

History: As recently as 50 years ago, a wide variety of sewing items were found in almost every home in America. Women of every economic and social status were skilled in sewing and dressmaking.

Iron or brass sewing birds, one of the interesting convenience items that developed, was used to hold cloth (in the bird's beak) while sewing. They could be attached to a table or shelf with a screw-type fixture. Later models included a pincushion.

Additional Resources:

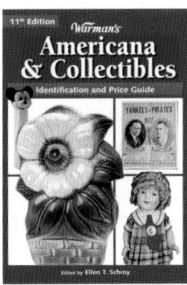

Warman's® Americana & Collectibles, 11th Ed., by Ellen T. Schroy, ed., Krause Publications, Iola, WI.

Bodkins, whalebone and ivory, sealing wax inlaid scribe lines, minor losses, nine-pc set, 19th C **$400**

Book, *Fleisher's Knitting & Crocheting Manual*, S. B. & B. W. Fleisher, Inc., Philadelphia, Pennsylvania, 112 pgs, 21st edition, 1924, 7" x 9-1/2" **$15**

Catalog, E. Butterick & Co., New York, New York, 32 pgs, catalog for fall of women's clothing patterns, 1878, 7-1/2" x 10" **$38**

Folder, 8-3/4" x 14-1/4", Wm. R. Moore Dry Goods Co., Memphis, Tennessee, three pgs, heavy weight, "Guaranteed Fast Color No. 10 Batfast Suitings," 10 tipped-in blue Batfast Suiting swatches, c1937, 19-1/4" x 2" colored swatches tipped in **$28**

Etui, tapered ovoid agate case, ormolu mounts, hinged lid, fitted interior with scissors, knife, pen, ruler, needle, pincers, and spoon, Continental, late 18th/early 19th C, 3-1/2" l **$700**

Hand book, Davis Sewing Machine Co., Watertown, New York, *Centennial Hand Book Presented at the Great Exhibition*, 12 pgs, directions to get around at Exhibition, info on sewing machine, cabinets, etc. **$65**

Instruction book, *Singer Sewing Machines No. 99*, 32 pgs, c1910, 3-1/2" x 5-1/4" **$16**

Magazine, *Home Needlework Magazine*, Florence Publishing Co., Florence, Massachusetts, 176 pgs, Vol. 1, No. 2, April, 1899 .... **$20**

Needle book, Rocket Gold Tipped Needles, cov illus of man and woman riding needle shaped like rocket, nighttime sky background, marked "Made in Japan," 1940s **$10**

Sewing box, original sewing implements, thread, containers with buttons, button hook, lace making implements, fashionable ladies images decoupaged from Godey's or Peterson's Magazine on top, late 1800s, some loss to decoupage, 14" l, 10-1/2" w, 3-1/2" h, **$225.**
Photo courtesy of Alderfer Auction Co.

Hanging cabinet, two drawers, **$100.**
Photo courtesy of Dotta Auction Co., Inc.

Spool cabinet, round, oak case, curved glass, refinished, **$725.**

Needle case, tri-color 18k gold, chase and engraved geometric and floral motifs, European hallmark........**$320**

Pin cushion

Doughnut shape, brown and black cloth on one side, light blue and dark blue cloth on other side, purple hanging loop, 6" d, 1-1/2" h......**$85**

Eight-sided star, brown and red cloth on one side, purple and blue cloth on other side, black ribbon hanging loop, 4" d......**$90**

Felt and yarn cushion strawberry mounted on pattern glass finial, Amish, Lancaster County, Pennsylvania, 9-1/2" h......**$3,080**

Sewing bird shape, brown cloth, foliate pattern, 4" l, 1-1/2" w......**$200**

Woolen, multicolored checkerboard pattern, black edges, brown velvet back, Amish, Centre County, Pennsylvania, price for pr, 6" sq......**$165**

Sewing bird, ivory, four side-mounted spools, geometric and heart exotic wood inlay, inlay loss and replacements, 19th C, 4-1/8" l......**$1,150**

Sewing box, wallpaper covered

Eight-sided, ftd, yellow wallpaper with maroon floral dec, green and blue cloth edging, sgd "Eli Myers, December 1885" in English and German, 5-1/2" d, 5" h......**$3,850**

Round, nine paneled sides, dots and diamonds, orange, blue, green and white polychrome dec, under lid mkd "To Mother Ellin," 6" d, 5-1/2" h......**$1,870**

Sewing box, wood

Inlaid hearts, arrows, diamonds, and circles, one dovetailed drawer, turned pull, worn pin cushion top, minor edge damage at corner, 5-1/2" w, 3-1/2" d, 3-1/4" h......**$275**

Mahogany inlaid, hinged lid, center inlaid oval reserve with shell motif, ext. with inlaid borders and corners, int. lid centered with diamond motif, lift-out tray with several compartments, America, minor imperfections, 19th C, 12-1/4" w, 7-1/4" d, 5-5/8" h......**$998**

Sewing egg, walrus ivory, unscrews to reveal ivory spool, thimble, and needle case, 19th C, 2-1/2" l......**$920**

Spinning wheel

Upright, cherry, mellow refinishing, small ivory buttons, turned legs, tripod base, 9-1/2" d wheel, single flyer, 38" h......**$350**

Upright, hardwoods, turned posts, iron fly wheel, ivory and ebonized wood details, old mellow refinishing, treadle with dec carving, old repair to cord belt, 34-1/2" h......**$450**

Upright, hardwoods, turned posts, wood and wire fly wheel, small turned ivory pegs alternating with wheel spokes, traces of black paint on wheel, base, and legs, German, worm holes, some edge damage, one finial glued, two spokes damaged, 35" h......**$295**

Stand, carved and turned walnut, round, four-tiered, graduated stand, pin cushion mounted on top, two rotating discs, each having six ivory spool holders, four ivory ball feet, New England, mid-19th C, 12-3/4" h......**$300**

Sewing box, lacquered wood, decorated with gilt scrolls and hand-painted flowers, orig fittings, c1840, **$325.**
Photo courtesy of David Rago Auctions, Inc.

Tape loom, standing, floor type, turned wormy maple post, oak step down, cross bar base, loom pegged into post, replacements to loom and base, 39-1/2" h......**$150**

Tape measure, advertising

General Electric Refrigerator, black and white beehive-style refrigerator on dark blue background, light blue rim, black and white name and text for local distributor on back......**$20**

Kiwanis Club, blue and white celluloid canister printed on both sides, one side with international emblem, "We Build" on reverse......**$15**

Lydia E. Pinkham, pale brown and white celluloid canister, sepia portrait of Lydia on one side, reverse with Vegetable Compound Blood Medicine tonics line......**$25**

Parisian Novelty Co., celluloid canister printed in blue, white ground, both sides with text promoting celluloid novelties......**$35**

Pillsbury's Family of Foods, celluloid canister, red, white, and blue flour sack printed on white, blue rim......**$25**

Tape measure, figural, owl, metal, German......**$45**

Thimble, brass, fancy band design......**$15**

Thimble holder, fisherman holding large rod, beautifully detailed large fish on ground, bucket by fish, post in front of fisherman, rect base, marked "Miller Silver Co. Silver Plate," 5-3/4" h......**$350**

Thread and needle holder, turned wood, polychrome paint dec in yellow, red, and green banding, pin cushion on top with metal spool holders, opens to three compartments, 4" d, 7" h......**$2,750**

Thread cabinet

Clarks, white lettering, four drawers, some damage to case......**$100**

Dexter Fine Yarn, oak, four drawers, 18-3/4" h, 18-5/8" w, 16" d......**$650**

Merrick's Spool Cotton, oak, cylindrical, curved glass, 18" d, 22" h......**$725**

Willimantic, four drawers, ornate Eastlake style case, 14-1/4" h......**$550**

Yarn or cord winder, enameled steel and brass works, mahogany platform base, turned feet, signature plate "Goodbrand & Co. Ltd., Makers, Staleybridge," 28" w, 16-1/4" d, 29-1/2" h......**$550**

Shaker, miniature, splint picnic hamper or purse, oval splint form, firm wrapped handle, hinged lids, 19th/20th C, 6" x 5-3/4" x 3", **$450.**
Photo courtesy of David Rago Auctions, Inc.

Herb bentwood box, pine top and base, maple sides, fingered, lift-off lid initialed "BC," mid-19th C, 3-1/2" l, 2" w, 1-1/2" h, **$200.**
Photo courtesy of Gamal Amer.

Trinket box, bentwood, three-finger construction, old red wash surface, late 19th C, 6" l, 2" h, **$865.**
Photo courtesy of Pook & Pook, Inc.

SHAKER

History: The Shakers, so named because of a dance they used in worship, are one of the oldest communal organizations in the United States. Mother Ann Lee, who emigrated from England and established the first Shaker community near Albany, New York, in 1784, founded this religious group. The Shakers reached their peak in 1850, when there were 6,000 members.

Shakers lived celibate and self-sufficient lives. Their philosophy stressed cleanliness, order, simplicity, and economy. Highly inventive and motivated, the Shakers created many utilitarian household forms and objects. Their furniture reflected a striving for quality and purity in design.

In the early 19th century, the Shakers produced many items for commercial purposes. Chairmaking and the packaged herb and seed business thrived. In every endeavor and enterprise, the members followed Mother Ann's advice: "Put your hands to work and give your heart to God."

Apothecary cabinet, stained wood, rect, front fitted with 12 small drawers, molded white glazed porcelain handles, identification labels, drawer sides inscribed with various content titles, New England, 19th C, 66" x 14" **$450**

Basket, finely woven splint, sq shape, two delicate bentwood handles, minor damage, traces of old red stain, 12" x 12" x 4-3/8" h....................**$360**

Blanket chest, New Lebanon, New York, hinged rect breadboard lift top, nail construction well, two long scratch beaded drawers, tapering cut-out feet, all-over later grain paint to simulate exotic wood, old replaced pulls, surface imperfections, 1830-40, 40-1/2" w, 18-1/2" d, 36" h **$1,265**

Bonnet, dark brown palm and straw, black ribbons, Kentucky, 9" flounce **$395**

Book, *How the Shakers Cook & the Noted Cooks of the Country, Feature the Chefs and Their Cooking Recipes*, A. J. White, New York, New York, 50 pgs, bust of men illus, dusted, chips, 1889, 3-3/8" x 6-1/8" **$15**

Bottle, aqua, emb "Shaker Pickles," base labeled "Portland, Maine, E.D.P. & Co.," 9" h....................**$90**

Box, cov, bentwood
Finger construction, two fingers on base, one finger on lid, copper tacks, old green repaint, some wear on lid, 5-1/2" w, 3-1/2" d, 2-1/8" h **$850**
Finger construction, two fingers on base, one finger on lid, brass tacks, old green (black) repaint over traces of earlier green, minor wear, 6-1/8" w, 4" w, 2" h **$690**
Finger construction, two fingers on base, one finger on lid, copper tacks, reddish stain, 7-1/2" w, 5-1/8" d, 2-1/2" h....................**$320**
Finger construction, two fingers on base, one finger on lid, copper

tacks, old blue paint, some wear, 9-1/2" w, 7" d, 3-3/4" h..........**$1,400**
Oval, Harvard lap, copper tacks, mellow natural finish, remnants of paper label on one end, 12" w, 8-3/8" d, 4-3/4" h....................**$440**
Oval, orig light green and cream paint sponged in leaf and feather patterned dec, seven fingers on side, one finger on lid, ex-Elgin, 20" w..................................**$26,000**

Carrier
Oval, maple, three lapped fingers, swing handle, copper tacks, number "5" impressed on base, clear lacquer finish, 9-1/4" l, 6-3/4" w, 8" h **$425**
Round, single stapled finger, bentwood handle, some red stain remains, copy of old Currier & Ives hunting print in center, minor splits, 12-1/2" d, 1" h base, 6" h handle..................................**$250**

Chair, dining, attributed to Canterbury, New Hampshire, birch and pine, concave rect back rail above turned stiles, four spindles, shaped seat, splayed turned tapering legs joined by stretchers, old red stain, missing right side stretcher, c1835, 17" h seat, 25" h back..................................**$825**

Chair, side, maple and hickory, old brick red paint, pegged construction, back with three arched slats, high turned finials, turned and tapered posts with eight rungs each, old striped tape seats, minor variations in turnings, old pieced restoration to one leg, price for set of four, 16" h seat, 37-1/4" h back....................**$700**

Chest of drawers, pine, eight graduated dovetailed drawers arranged in two banks of four, turned pulls, six high feet with semi-curved cut-outs, old mellow refinish, replaced back boards, some pulls replaced, 63" w, 17-1/2" d, 39-1/2" h **$14,300**

Child's rocker, production, Mt. Lebanon, New York, incised "O" with decal on rocker, old varnished surface, replaced tape seat, minor imperfections, 1880-1930, 7-3/4" h seat, 24" h back **$3,300**

Cloak

Adult's, pink wool, labeled "The Dorothy Shakers, East Canterbury, New Hampshire," c1880-1920 ...... **$1,195**

Child's, red wool, labeled "The Dorothy Shakers, East Canterbury, New Hampshire," c1880-1920 ...... **$1,195**

Infant's, white wool, pink silk lining, shattering to lining, c1880-1920 .... **$595**

Dough scraper, wrought iron, 4-1/2" l **$40**

Dry sink, walnut, single double paneled door, shaped feet, Whitewater Shaker Meeting House **$5,500**

Flax wheel, various hardwoods, old dark brown finish, stamped "SR. AL," (Deacon Samuel Ring of Alfred, Maine 1784-1848), two pieces of distaff replaced, 33-1/2" h **$330**

Grain measure, bentwood, stencil label "Shaker Society, Sabbathday Lake, Me," minor edge damage, 7-1/2" d **$160**

Hanger, bentwood, chestnut, 24" w **$65**

Linen cupboard, painted poplar and pine, red, black sponged dec, Whitewater Shaker Meeting House **$21,000**

Mat, braided, plush velvet-like fabric, multiple colors and white, Canterbury, New Hampshire, 24" w **$80**

Recipe book, Laura Sarle, Canterbury, Shaker Village, New Hampshire, inscribed by author, recipes, brief autobiography, short play, housekeeping, records, knitting instructions, pen and ink on paper, mottled orange cardboard cover with black binding, wear to cover, few random annotations by later hand, 1883-87 .... **$5,520**

Rocker

#6, ladderback, old dark brown varnished surface, imp "6" on top slat, four arched back slats, elongated acorn shaped finials, later tan

woven tape seat, curved arms with tapered rear posts, finely turned arm supports, splits at bottom of legs, restoration to one rocker, 15-1/2" h seat, 42" h back **$350**

#7, Mt Lebanon, maple and birch, woven tape seat and back, shaped arms, domed caps, short acorn finials, imp "7" on upper slat, orig label remaining inside one runner, worn surface, 15-1/2" h seat, 42" h back **$500**

Small, Mt. Lebanon, black painted finish, small acorn finials, old woven tape back panel and seat, orig decal label inside one rocker, 14" h seat, 34" h back **$300**

Sewing box, cov, oval, pine lid with maple sides and lid rim, swing handle, five lapped fingers, int. lined with light blue padded silk, repair, wear, 15" l, 11-1/4" w, 11" h including upright handle **$1,880**

Shoe last, wooden, two with removable uppers, one with steel toe and heel, one with leather repair, Canterbury, New Hampshire, provenance: Lewis Noble Wiggins Shaker collection, price for set of four, 9" to 11" l **$150**

Table, maple, drop leaf, rect top, hinged rect leaves, single drawer, sq tapering legs, first half 19th C, 34-3/4" x 35-1/2" x 28" **$6,500**

Table swift, 25" h, maple, 19th C, 29-3/4" d extended **$230**

Tea table, attributed to Mt. Lebanon, NY, birch, circular tilt top with bullnose edge, tilts on platform, tapering turned pedestal, tripod cabriole legs, pad feet, old refinish, c1830, 34-1/4" d, 26-3/4" h **$6,465**

Wash tub, New England, stave and lap fingered hoop construction, two handles, old red paint, imperfections, late 19th C, 24" d, 16-1/2" h **$460**

SHAVING MUGS

History: Shaving mugs, which hold the soap, brush, and hot water used to prepare a beard for shaving, come in a variety of materials including tin, silver, glass, and pottery. One style, which has separate compartments for water and soap, is the scuttle, so called because of its coal-scuttle shape.

Personalized shaving mugs were made exclusively for use in barbershops in the United Sates. They began being produced shortly after the

Civil War and continued to be made into the 1930s.

Unlike shaving mugs that were used at home, these mugs were personalized with the owner's name, usually in gilt. The mug was kept in a rack at the barbershop, and it was used only when the owner came in for a shave. This was done for hygienic purposes, to keep from spreading a type of eczema known as barber's itch.

The mugs were usually made on European porcelain blanks that often contained the mark of "Germany," "France," or "Austria" on the bottom. In later years, a few were made on American-made semi-vitreous blanks. Decorators who worked for major barber supply houses did the artwork on mugs. Occasionally the mark of the barber supply house is also stamped on the bottom of the mug.

After a short time, the mugs became more decorative, including hand-painted floral decorations, as well as birds, butterflies, and a wide variety of nature scenes, etc. These are classified today as "decorative" mugs.

Another category, "fraternal mugs," soon developed. These included the emblem of an organization the owner belonged to, along with his name emblazoned in gold above or below the illustration.

"Occupational mugs" were also very popular. These are mugs that contained a painting of something that illustrated the owner's occupation, such as a butcher, a bartender, or a plumber. The illustration might be a man working at his job, or perhaps the tools of his trade, or a product he made or sold.

Of all these mugs, occupationals are the most prized. Their worth is determined by several factors: rarity (some occupations are rarer than others), size of mug, and size of illustration (the bigger the better), quality of artwork, and condition—although rare mugs with cracks or chips can still be valuable if the damage does not affect the artwork on the mug. Generally speaking, a mug showing a man at work at his job is usually valued higher than that same occupation illustrated with only the tools or finished product.

The invention of the safety razor by King C. Gillette, issued to three and one-half million servicemen during World War I, brought about changes in personal grooming— men began to shave on their own, rather than visiting the barber shop to be shaved. As a result, the need for personalized shaving mugs declined.

Notes: Prices shown are for typical mugs that have no damage and show only moderate wear on the gilt name and decoration.

Fraternal

B.P.O.E., Elks, double emblem, Dr. title **$300**

F.O.E., Fraternal Order of Eagles, eagle holding F.O.E. plaque **$260**

IB of PM, International Brotherhood of Paper Makers, papermaking machine, clasped hands **$275**

I.O.M., International Order of Mechanics, ark ladder **$270**

Loyal Knights of America, eagle, flags, six-pointed star **$275**

Loyal Order of the Moose, gold circle with gray moose head, purple and green floral dec, gilt rim and base, marked "Germany" **$220**

United Mine Workers, clasped hands emblem flanked by crossed picks and shovels, floral dec, rose garland around top, marked "Germany" **$125**

Occupational

Electrician, hand-painted image of electrician wiring inside of electrical box, T & V Limoges, France, wear to gold lettering and trim, 3-5/8" d, 3-5/8" h............................. **$2,500**

Express wagon, hp, man driving horse drawn wagon, word "Express" on side, floral springs, gold rim and name, 4" x 3-3/4" **$400**

Fabric store, colorful hp shop int., owner waiting on well-dressed woman, gold trim and name, 3-5/8" x 4-1/2"..................................... **$700**

General store, pork, flour, and whiskey barrels, Limoges, 4" x 4-3/4" **$650**

Hotel clerk, clerk at desk, guest signing register **$375**

House painter, detailed hand-painted image of man painting side of building, marked "Fred Dole" on bottom, light crack mark around top of

Two shaving mugs, unmarked, left: blue ground, dated 1913; right: pink ground, dated 1902, each **$75-$110.**

handle, wear to gold lettering and trim, 3-1/2" d, 3-1/2" h............... **$350**

Hunting

Duck hunting, hp, duck hunter and dog in boat, 3-1/2" x 3-1/2" **$275**

Ducks, hp, two colorful ducks at water's edge, mkd "J. & C Bavaria," 3-5/8" x 3-5/8" **$100**

Hunting dogs, hp, two hunting dogs, brown background, mkd "St Louis Electronic Grinding Co., Barber Supplies," some wear to gold trim, crack in ring handle, 4-1/8" x 3-3/4" **$120**

Rabbit hunting, hp, large rabbits in foreground, hunter walking thru snow, factory in background, 3-1/2" x 3-1/2".................................... **$120**

Sportsman, hp, caught fish, fishing rod, shot gun, leafy sprigs, scene of men fishing in background, name in scroll, V D Austria, 3-5/8" x 3-5/8" **$130**

Ice man, hp, horse drawn Palmer's Ice Co. delivery wagon, rim and name in gold, T & V France, 3-1/2" x 3-1/2" **$825**

Mail wagon, hp, postal worker driving horse drawn mail wagon, German, repair to top rim on back, gold trim lines redone, 4" x 3-3/4" **$475**

Mover, detailed hand-painted image of two men in moving van, gold name and trim, Royal China Int'l, 3-7/8" d, 3-5/8" **$1,400**

Oil derrick, hp, detailed oil well scene, T & V France, 3-5/8" x 3-5/8" **$220**

Photographer, detailed hand-colored image of portrait photographer, marked "Webb Bros" in gold, wear to gold lettering and trim, 3-5/8" d, 3-1/2" h....................... **$700**

Railroad, detailed hand-painted image of two railway workers on hand car, wear to gold lettering and trim, 3-1/2" d, 3-5/8" h **$650**

Shoemaker, hp, scene of shoemaker in shop, gilt foot and swags around name.................................... **$225**

Soda fountain, hp, serving clerk behind counter of soda fountain, well dressed woman sitting at counter on stool, name in gold, Germany, 3-3/4" x 3-5/8"................................. **$2,500**

Surveyor, hp, detailed land surveying instrument in center, wear to gold name and trim, D & C, 3-1/2" x 3-5/8" **$550**

Tugboat, boat in water, crew and captain.................................... **$750**

Veteran, hp, US Civil War soldier holding American flag, name in gold, 3-3/4" x 3-1/2"...................... **$1,500**

Writer, black desk inkwell with sander, pen, and brass handle **$350**

Other

Drape and flowers, purple drape, pot of flowers, gold name **$85**

Fish shape, scuttle, green and brown **$75**

Skull, white, gray, black, and cream, scuttle, marked "Bavaria" **$135**

Five small-framed silhouettes, three signed "Jean LaTeer," $125.
Photo courtesy of Joy Luke.

SILHOUETTES

History: Silhouettes (shades) are shadow profiles produced by hollow cutting, mechanical tracing, or painting. They were popular in the 18th and 19th centuries.

The name came from Etienne de Silhouette, a French Minister of Finance, who cut "shades" as a pastime. In America, the Peale family was well known for the silhouettes they made.

Silhouette portraiture lost popularity with the introduction of the daguerreotype prior to the Civil War. In the 1920s and 1930s, a brief revival occurred when tourists to Atlantic City and Paris had their profiles cut as souvenirs.

Marks: An impressed stamp marked "PEALE" or "Peale Museum" identifies pieces made by the Peale family.

Boy

Boy under leafy branch, Hollow cut, very faint name underneath, worn gilt frame, fold lines with minor damage, 4-3/8" w, 5-3/4" h **$85**

Cutout, rosewood frame with worn gilt liner, 5" w, 5-3/4" h **$220**

Inked details, wrinkles, stains, partial typed label, pine frame, hollow cut, 4-3/4" w, 5-5/8" h **$200**

Boy and girl, full length, standing facing each other, hollow cut, gilt detail, bird's eye veneer ogee frame, 9-1/2" w, 7-5/8" h **$725**

Girl

Emily and Rosa, two girls playing, hand painted detailing, 1838, 7-1/2" x 10-1/4" **$600**

Girl with flower basket, jumping dog, titled "Miss Montague," 8-1/2" x 7-1/2" **$250**

Man

British officer, ink and watercolor on laid paper, red uniform jacket, gold epaulets and medal, sgd "de Mors," faint inscription on frame "Captain Robert Conig of His Majesty's 40th Regiment of Infantry...," orig

gilt frame with damage, 5-3/4" w, 7-1/2" h **$230**

Cut-out, gold ink details in hair and coat, oval brass liner with convex glass, black painted frame, 5-1/2" h **$175**

Edward Brook, hollow cut, aged 16, wearing top hat, eglomise mat, period gilt frame, wear, repaint, stains, minor edge damage, 5-1/4" w, 5-7/8" h **$435**

Hollow cut, stenciled frock coat, eglomise glass mat with yellow painted designs, black velvet backing, black painted frame with traces of yellow on outer edge, 4-1/2" w, 5-1/2" h **$475**

Man identified in pencil as "Sir Walter Scott" writing at a table, Full length cut-out, attributed to Auguste Edoart, glued to page cut from book, hinged to mat, 12-5/8" w, 13-5/8" h frame, 8" w, 9-7/8" h **$320**

Man, inked hair, scarf, and labels, eglomise mat, period gilt frame, wear, stains, minor edge damage, 4-3/4" w, 5-5/8" h **$435**

Man, painted details, hair, scarf, and lapels, eglomise mat, period gilt frame, wear, repaint, stains, 4-3/4" w, 5-3/4" h **$350**

Man with floral motif around head, cut-work backed with black textile, old typed paper on back "Isaac Darlington, the famous Ice Cream Maker, whose farm overlooked the Brandywine above Jeffrey Bridge. This was cut by a traveling artist who held the scissors with his toes. Bought from Mr. Mark Darlington, May 10, 1927," orig frame, 5-3/4" w, 7-3/4" h **$1,430**

Man and Woman

Hollow cut, ink and watercolor details, framed together, sgd "Doyle," eglomise glass mat with two ovals, gilded frame, 10" w, 6-1/2" h **$425**

Hollow cut, man with high collar, woman with hair comb, black cloth backing, molded gold frame, some foxing of paper, price for pair, 5-1/4" w, 6" h **$440**

Hollow cut and painted, possibly work of William Chamberlain, bust length profile portraits, one of a young woman identified by inscription on reverse as "Pamelia DeWolf, sister of T. K. DeW, born July 16, 1794, D 1862," other young man identified on note as "T. W. DeWolf/Brother," hollow cut head and area below shoulder

Girl with sewing basket, girl wearing long lace-trimmed dress sitting beside sewing basket, Wallace Nutting, 1927, 4" x 5", $40.
Photo courtesy of Michael Ivankovich Auctions.

with black painted detailing of hair, vest, collar, and ruffles, deep blue velvet, matted, molded giltwood frame, toning, stains, small tears, foxing, c1820, 3-1/8" x 2-1/8" **$775**

Man and wife, man with pigtail, wife with bonnet, laid paper, matching grain painted frames with gilt liners, stains, minor wear, 7-1/2" w, 7-1/2" h **$350**

Watercolor, pen and ink, gouache and silk on paper, hollow cut, half-length portraits of woman wearing comb in upswept hair, black dress, ruffled collar set off with blue ribbon, and man with blue best, black jacket, holding red book, black silk lining, unsigned, indistinct penciled inscription on reverse of frame "Dudley, Oct.-1835," emb brass and wood frame, American School, pr, 19th C, 3-1/2" x 2-1/2" **$2,235**

Minister speaking from pulpit, cut-out three-quarters length portrait, wearing spectacles, presentation note "Kings College Cam Apr 30 1836...," backing with notice for "Portrait, _ and Looking Glass Club...H. Flowers, carver and gilder...Southwark," bird's eye maple frame with worn gilt liner, 9-1/4" w, 11-1/4" h **$500**

Woman

Cut-out portrait of matronly woman wearing bonnet, penciled eyelash, reeded frame with black paint and punched brass rosettes, minor edge damage to frame, 3-3/4" w, 5-1/4" h **$220**

Lady with ornate hat, back marked "Mrs. Norman" and "Mrs. Norman, Henley on Thames," black lacquered case with gilded fittings, wear and stain, 4-7/8" w, 5-3/4" h **$200**

Mrs. Rosanna Lamb, full length, sgd and dated "Aug.st Edouart fecit 1842 Boston U.S.," cut-out paper figure laid down on paper, graphite, ink, and watercolor genre scene in background, sitter identified in note affixed to reverse, framed, toning, staining, 10" x 9-3/8"................**$450**

Young woman, hollow cut, cut detail at collar, pencil inscription "Sarah Sage," stains, 5-3/8" w, 6-3/8" h **$200**

SILVER

History: The natural beauty of silver lends itself to the designs of artists and craftsmen. It has been mined and worked into an endless variety of useful and decorative items. Pure silver is too soft to be fashioned into strong, durable, and serviceable utensils. Therefore, a way was found to give silver the required degree of hardness by adding alloys of copper and nickel.

Silversmithing in America goes back to the early 17th century in Boston and New York and the early 18th century in Philadelphia. Boston artisans were influenced by the English styles, New Yorkers by the Dutch.

Additional Resources:

Antique Trader® Metalwares Price Guide, 2nd Ed., by Kyle Husfloen, ed., and Mark Moran, contr. ed., Krause Publications, Iola, WI.

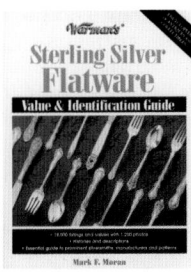

Warman's® Sterling Silver Flatware, by Mark F. Moran, Krause Publications, Iola, WI.

American, Dunham, compote, flower and ball motif, 7" x 11-3/4", **$2,100.**
Photo courtesy of David Rago Auctions, Inc.

American, 1790-1840
Mostly coin

Coin silver is slightly less pure than sterling silver. Coin silver has 900 parts silver to 100 parts alloy. Sterling silver has 925 parts silver. American silversmiths followed the coin standards. Coin silver is also called Pure Coin, Dollar, Standard, or Premium.

Beaker, top and bottom molded rims, engraved, minor dents, Anthony Rasch, Philadelphia, 4 troy oz, 1807, 3" h, 3" d **$490**

Cake server, George C. Shreve, mark partially rubbed, shaped blade engraved with harbor scene within foliate cartouche, unfurling flag, engine-turned ground, fitted case, 3 troy oz, late 19th C, 9-1/8" l.........**$200**

Coffee spoon, John David Jr., Philadelphia, PA, made for Cooch family, monogrammed, one with damage, dents, wear, price for set of eight, 4 troy oz, 1795-99, 5-1/4" l **$1,035**

Creamer, ewer form, beaded detailing, marked "RH," 6" h **$2,750**

Cup, scroll handle, geometric banding at top and bottom, engraved sun motif, inscribed "Awarded by the S.C.A.S. (Southern Central Agriculture Society) & Mechanical Ins of Georgia, Oct 19th, 1852, for the best half dozen pair of Brogan Shoes, marked "Pure Silver Coin, J. E. Caldwell & Co., Phila," 2-1/2" h **$1,320**

Dessert spoon, William Hollingshead, Philadelphia, Pennsylvania, marked "WH" in shaped stamp, twice on each handle, engraved "KIS," wear to bowls, imperfections, price for set of five, 9 troy oz, 1754-85 ....**$490**

Ewer, ftd, repoussé vintage dec, vine form handle extending round shoulder and around base of both pieces, engraved, minor dents, William F.

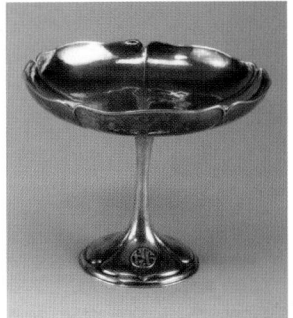

American, compote, Kalo, hammered, floriform, monogram "GSH," stamped "STERLING HAND WROUGHT KALO SHOP CHICAGO, U.S.A., CHRISTMAS 1929," 7" x 9", **$1,100.**
Photo courtesy of David Rago Auctions, Inc.

Ladd, New York City, 1828-45, 12" h **$1,200**

Goblet, Simon Chaundron, Philadelphia, Pennsylvania, marked "Chaundron" in banner, floriform, raised flutes at base of bowls, applied foliate band on bases, price for pr, 16 troy oz, 1812-15, 6-1/2" h and 6-3/4" h......................................**$3,750**

Jug, J. B. Jones & Co. makers, inverted pear-shaped body, scroll handle and stepped neck, round stepped foot, name engraved under spout, 12 troy oz, 2nd quarter 19th C, 7" h **$700**

Mug, John L. Westervelt, Newburgh, New York maker, cylindrical, fine beading to foot and rim, scroll handle, central cartouche engraved with name and dated 1863, engraved Greek key border, allover engine turned ground, 6 troy oz, mid-19th C, 4" h **$200**

Pitcher, bulbous, molded rim above engraved band, body with all-over repoussé strawberries and vines, weighted circular foot with emb dec, inscription on front and foot, mid-19th C, 8" h **$290**

Salt, oval form, four hoofed feet, repoussé floral and wreath dec at knees, gold wash bowls, minor dents, Ball, Black & Co., New York City, 1851-76, 7 troy oz, pr, 1-1/2" x 3-1/2" **$290**

Snuff box, stamped "PP," flattened ovoid form, bottom inscribed "I trust this triffle in thy mind will favor find, 1791," imperfections, 1-1/2" x 3-1/2" x 2-5/8", 2 troy oz **$1,100**

Soup ladle, Simon Chaundron, Philadelphia, Pennsylvania, marked "Chaundron" in banner, English crest dec, 10 troy oz, 1812-15, 14-1/2" l **$920**

American, centerpiece, pierced motif with grape decoration, monogrammed, unmarked, 12" d, **$400.**
Photo courtesy of Wiederseim Associates, Inc.

American, sterling, bread and butter plates, J. E. Caldwell & Co., 1899, repoussé, marked and dated, 26 troy oz, 7" d, **$400.**
Photo courtesy of David Rago Auctions, Inc.

American, Gorham, breakfast set, egg cups in shape of cracked eggs supported on chicken legs, spoons, saucers, and salts, orig fitted case, **$3,250.**
Photo courtesy of David Rago Auctions, Inc.

Sugar bowl, cov, Gorham, squat baluster, stepped foot, wide band of engine-turning, one plain and one engraved cartouche, two serpentine handles, domed lid with flower form finial, 17 troy oz, minor dents, mid-19th C, 8" h **$175**

Tablespoon, front tips, back engraved, bowl with emb scallop shell below short drop handle, minor dents, wear, Samuel Edwards, Boston, 2 troy oz, 1705-62, 8" l **$635**

Tea service, unmarked, 9-1/2" h teapot with hinged lid, creamer, cov sugar, lids with floriform knob finials attached to circle of ribbing, above round form bowl with shaped shoulders having vertical ribbing on lower half of body, raised on round stepped bases, four ball feet, applied tooled banding at neck, shoulder, and base, foliate devices attached to hollow strap handles and spout, 60 troy oz, 19th C **$885**

American, 1840-1920
Mostly sterling

There are two possible sources for the origin of the word *sterling*. The first is that it is a corruption of the name Easterling. Easterlings were German silversmiths who came to England in the Middle Ages. The second is that it is named for the sterling (little star) used to mark much of the early English silver.

Sterling is 92.5 percent per silver. Copper comprises most of the remaining alloy. American manufacturers began to switch to the sterling standard about the time of the Civil War.

Basket, Whiting Mfg Co., reticulated, sides with scrolls and diapering, scroll rim, three scroll feet, fluted base, monogrammed, 11 troy oz, late 19th C, 9" d, 3" h **$460**

Bowl, Arthur Stone, Gardner, Massachusetts, chased decoration on bowl, circular stepped foot, imp mark with initial "H," 5" d, 3-1/4" h **$1,410**

Bread plate, Reed & Barton, banded dec, monogrammed, marked "Sterling 700," set of 12, 50 troy oz, 6-1/2" d **$450**

Butter chip, Gorham, gadrooned border, engraved dragon with crown, monogram for Henredon Family, price for eight-pc set, 3" d **$150**

Castor, S. Kirk & Sons, Baltimore, Egyptian Revival, urn form, domed lid with repoussé leaves, bud form finial, body with three cast loop handles, all-over repoussé foliates, three cast sphinx feet, monogram, 4 troy oz, 1861-1868, 5-3/4" h **$690**

Center bowl, Frank W Smith Silver Co., Inc., retailed by Bigelow, Kennard & Co., ovoid, engraved with quilted style pattern, edges reticulated with engraved leafy scrolls, edge with wide cast border of rocaille shells and C-scrolls, monogrammed center, 31 troy oz, late 19th C, 14-1/2" d **$1,840**

Challis, presentation, engraved "Award by the G & A.A. Society to W. F. Fannin for the best collection of Southern made Plows, Oct 1852," inscription flanked by repoussé wheat sheaves, reverse side with repoussé plow, 7" h, 3-1/2" d at rim **$1,650**

Cigarette case, Reed & Barton, 1" w 14k yg band running entire length and reverse, hinged gate stamped "14kt" and "Sterling R & B," 4.79 troy oz, 4-1/2" h **$300**

Coffee set, Gorham, coffeepot, creamer, cov sugar, 16" tray, 73.05 troy oz **$550**

Compote, Bigelow, Kennard & Co., Etruscan-style, bowl with central roundel of classical man holding grapes, seated woman with baby, dog, beaded surround, engraved anthemion and flowerheads, short stem with single rib to center, trumpet foot, plain flattened loop handles, applied Greek key rim, 22 troy oz, late 19th C, 8-3/4" d, 4-1/2" h **$700**

Dish, Howard & Co., quatrefoil form, filigree sides in fleur-de-lis pattern, applied ornamentation on rim of "C" and "S" scrolls and shells, marked "Howard & Co., New York, Sterling, 1903," 15 troy oz, 8" l **$300**

Dresser set, International Silver Co., Meriden, CT, cut glass powder jar, hair receiver, three dresser jars, all with sterling lids, pair of cut glass perfume bottles with silver mounted stoppers, hair brush, two clothes brushes, mirror, nail buffer, shoehorn, and nail file, all with engraved and banded rims, monograms, early 20th C **$920**

Fish knives, Gorham, Providence, Aesthetic Movement, blades with ornate monograms and bright cut foliates, mixed metal Japanese-style Kozuka handles with molded dec, price for set of 12, late 19th C **$2,300**

Flask

Ovoid, emb foliates on textured ground, domed lid with attached chain, approx two troy oz, late 19th/early 20th C, 4-1/4" l **$175**

Rect, Clarence Vanderbilt, New York, overall textured finish, reeded circular screw cap, approx 10 troy oz, c1909-35, 9" h **$260**

American, punch bowl, retailed by J.E. Caldwell & Co., Philadelphia, molded rim and footed base, approx. 130.6 oz., 13-1/2" d, 7-3/4" h, **$1,850.**
Photo courtesy of Pook & Pook, Inc.

American, serving bowl, Tiffany & Co., Art Deco, footed, marked "23356," approximately 47.10 oz, 12-1/2" d, 4-1/4" h, **$1,150.**
Photo courtesy of Pook & Pook, Inc.

American, Tiffany, vase, three handles, 44 troy oz, 6-1/4 PTS, 6" d, 8-1/2" h, **$1,800.**
Photo courtesy of David Rago Auctions, Inc.

Fruit bowl, Dominick & Haff, retailed by Shreve, Crump & Low, fluted int., wide reticulated edge with realistically modeled chrysanthemums and daisies, 21 troy oz, late 19th/early 20th C, 12-1/2" d **$1,150**

Ice cream slice, George W. Shiebler & Co., hammered finish, handle with Roman style male medallion on end, engraved bands of classical style designs, gold washed blade with further classical style engraving, medallion to lower right, central horizontal band of further small medallions, monogrammed on back of handle, 6 troy oz, late 19th C, 10" l **$4,025**

Ice water pitcher

Jaccard & Co., emb and chased dec, 1870, 12-1/2" h **$210**

Rogers Smith & Co., tilting, pitcher stand, goblet, and tumbler all dec with emb scenic bands of walrus hunters in icy water, enameled lined pitcher, c1872, 16-3/4" h **$550**

Jug, Lewis E. Jenks, Boston, vasiform, shaped lid with cast bird finial, lid and body with all over repoussé foliates, central monogrammed cartouche, spreading circular foot, 17 troy oz, c1875, 10" h **$635**

Kettle-on-stand, bombe repoussé all-over with flowers and leaves on fine stippled ground, hinged cover with similar dec, floral finial, fixed handle, circular base with conforming dec on four paw feet issuing from foliage, marked "S. Kirk & So., #101," burner marked "JI sterling silver," 56 oz, c1903-24, 13" h **$2,500**

Mustard pot, S. Kirk & Son, Baltimore, vegetal finial, glass liner,

7 troy oz, mid-19th C, 4-1/2" d **$150**

Perfume flask, Dominick & Haff, tapered cylindrical, floral chased and emb at lid, neck, and base, wide band of horizontal fluting at center, monogrammed, 5 troy oz, 9" l **$490**

Platter, Dominick & Haff, oval, border repoussé with flowers and leaves on fine matted ground, monogrammed, 16 oz **$475**

Punch bowl, circular stand with shaped rim, interior gold washed, chased and repoussé with garlands, scallop-shells and swags, maker's mark "BSC" on base, 10-1/4" d, 6-1/8" h **$750**

Roast platter, Gorham, Greek key border, early 20th C, 20-5/8" l, 14-1/8" w **$750**

Salad serving set, spoon and fork, Chambord pattern, Reed & Barton, monogrammed, 5 oz, 6 dwt, 9" l **$200**

Salt, open, Black, Starr & Frost, Classical Revival style, ovoid body, hoof feet terminating in lion's heads, red glass liner, 8 troy oz, four-pc set, late 19th C, 3-1/4" l, 1-3/4" h **$450**

Salver, Whiting M.F.G. Co., center chased with crab caught in a fishing net, monogrammed MLI, planished rim, shaped feet, 20.35 oz, 9-3/4" d **$1,195**

Sauce ladle, Wood & Hughes, New York, scalloped bowl, beaded handle with portrait medallion of classical warrior, monogrammed on reverse, 1 troy oz, second half 19th C, 6-3/4" l **$320**

Serving dish, cov, Thomas Kirkpatrick, New York, oval, domed lid with beaded band, cast stag finial, emb key

pattern and beading on underside of rim, base with similar dec, some loses, 59 troy oz, third quarter 19th C, 8-7/8" w, 11-5/8" l **$1,035**

Tazza, Howard & Co., vessel with wide reticulated band and applied scroll rim, center monogram, applied scroll base, reticulated foot, pr, 19 troy oz, dated 1898, 7-1/8" d, 2-1/2" h **$700**

Tea and coffee service, gadrooned border, chased with floral sprays and arabesques, monogrammed A.P.A., 15" h hot water kettle on lampstand, coffeepot, teapot, creamer, cov sugar, double handled waste bowl, all marked; together with silver plate tray, 164.05 oz **$2,400**

Tea service

Ball, Black & Co., tapered ovoid teapot, cov sugar, helmet-shaped open creamer, each with applied profile medallion and anthemion engraving, pendant handles, monogrammed, 36 troy oz, third quarter 19th C **$2,185**

Gorham, made for Blanche M. Halle, Cleveland, Ohio, each pc stamped with her name, panels separated by ribs, dec with repoussé and chased trumpet urns of fruit, lids with carved ivory pineapple finials, 10-1/2" h teapot, 11-1/2" h coffeepot, creamer, cov double handled sugar, waste bowl, 18-1/2" x 30" tray, 276 troy oz **$4,675**

Gorham, Plymouth pattern, coffeepot, teapot, creamer, cov sugar, waste bowl, monogrammed, 55 troy oz, some dents to sugar lid **$875**

Shreve, Stanwood & Co., 16" h hot water urn on stand, creamer, cov sugar, open sugar, and 9" h tea-pot, ovoid, beaded detailing, lids with swan finials, domed stepped foot, urn with presentation inscription on side, burner and one sugar lid missing, 35 troy oz, 1860 .... **$2,185**

Tea tray, Gorham, Providence, shaped molded rim, beaded band, pierced handles, monogrammed, 114 troy oz, 1912, 17-7/8" w, 25-3/4" l **$1,725**

Continental, centerpiece, oval, foliate scroll and shell feet, sides pierced with guilloches, hung with ribbon-tied berried laurel swags between bands of vitruvian scrolls, pierced anthemion, open double scrolls handles, fitted with silver-plated liner, crowned A, crowned P and crowned fleur-de-lis marks, 27 oz, 14" h, **$1,100.**

Photo courtesy of Sloans & Kenyon Auctioneers and Appraisers.

American, water pitcher, presentation type, Tiffany & Co., 1875-91 mark, baluster body, repoussè and chased with Bacchanal couple, medallions framed by scrolling grape vines and acanthus leaf tips, centering presentation tablet inscription 'Monmouth Park, July 12th 1879, Three Quarter Dash, Gentlemen Riders Won By Mr. W. C. Sanford's, Brg. Kadi by Lexington, Owner," *wrapped anthemion-form handle rising from bacchanal mask, 38 oz 4 dwt., 8-3/4" h,* **$5,350.**

Photo courtesy of Sloans & Kenyon Auctioneers and Appraisers.

Tete-a-tete, Gorham, Providence, 4" h teapot, creamer, open sugar, cone shape, ball finial, reeded handles, banded necks, gilt interiors, monogrammed, 16 troy oz, 1880 .... **$320**

Travel clock, Wm Kerr & Co., plain rect case with rounded corners, eight-day movement, oct goldtone engine-turned face, black Roman numerals, silver surround with engine turning, engraved scrolls and floral sprays, monogrammed cover, late 19th C, 3-5/8" l, 3-1/8" w **$200**

Tray, Reed & Barton, Taunton, Massachusetts, rect, shaped molded rim with openwork and engraved band, monogrammed center, 24 troy oz, late 19th/early 20th C, 10-1/4" w, 14-1/4" l **$350**

Trophy pitcher, Whiting, New York, Harvard University, cylindrical, inverted rim, waisted body with inscription on front, circular base with molded scroll dec, 33 troy oz, c1892 .... **$1,380**

Vase

Gorham, flared draped rim, scalloped edge, bulbous base, pedestal foot, engraved scroll, foliage, and floral urn designs, figural accents, monogrammed central cartouche, marked "1083L, Sterling," 99 troy oz, 20-1/2" h **$3,850**

J. E. Caldwell & Co., tapered baluster form with engraved laurel wreath on each side, one with monogram, everted rim with engraved band of lines and circles, trumpet foot with similarly engraved band, 34 troy oz, late 19th/early 20th C, 15-3/4" h **$750**

Water pitcher

Dominick & Haff, New York, vasiform, molded rim, "S" scroll handle, molded base, 22 troy oz, 20th C, 9" h **$375**

Gorham, Providence, paneled vasiform, rim and base with beaded bands, handle with cast acanthus dec, octagonal molded base, monogrammed, 26 troy oz, 1885, 9-1/4" h **$635**

Continental

Generations have enjoyed silver created by Continental silversmiths. Expect to find well-executed forms with interesting elements. Most Continental silver is well marked.

Austria

Candlesticks, pr, Rococo-style, paneled baluster stem and socket, scrolled weighted base, removable bobeche, lacquered, late 19th C, 12-1/2" h **$690**

Casket, rect, lid with cast pear form finial, molded rim and foot, waisted body with silver mount on lock, 14 troy oz, mid/late 19th C, 3-3/8" w, 5-1/4" l **$575**

Order, traces of gilt, inscribed "HM 1929/30," marked, 1.30 oz, 1929-30, 6" l **$120**

Continental

Asparagus server, reticulated handles topped by crowned lion's head, flowerheads and scrolls, standing figure, ending in cherub face above floral basket flanked by cherub herms over reticulation, blades reticulated with C-scrolls and engraved with flowers and further scrolls, monogrammed, 9 troy oz, late 19th C, 11-1/4" l **$230**

Beaker, silver gilt, tapering cylindrical form, circular gadrooned foot, upper body engraved with strapwork enclosing arabesques, base chased with two bands of bosses, 3.35 oz, 17th C **$3,850**

Candelabra, three-light, shaped sq lobed foot with scroll and floral rim rising to fluted stem applied with similar dec, two scrolling foliate branches, central fixed sconce, detachable bobeches, convertible to candlestick, engraved with monogram below crown, weighted base, 21-1/2" h **$900**

Condiment jar, formed as sedan chair, stamped with scrolls and cartouches of dancing couples, hinged lid with quadripartite finial, cobalt blue glass liner, restorations, 5 troy oz, late 19th/early 20th C, 4-3/4" h **$375**

Creamer, figural, horned cow, fly hinged lid, 19th C, 5-1/2" l, 4-1/4" h **$800**

Oil lamp, tapered ovoid form, chased overall with grapes and vines, associated pierced silvered metal shade, 29" h **$720**

Spoon, figural terminal, pear shaped bowl chased on obverse with armorial crest, inscribed "MIS Df HS, ANNO 1642, WER-ALTID LYKLIG," verso inscribed "A," marked, 1.80 oz, possibly 17th C, 6-1/4" l **$420**

Danish

Coffee service, Georg Jensen Silver-smithy, 1933-44, Blossom pattern, 7-1/8" h coffee pot, mkd "no. 2B"; cream jug, mkd "no. 2A"; waste bowl, mkd "no. 2A"; 25.10 oz **$2,650**

Compote, round bowl over round stepped standard, base imp "Denmark 300" at bowl center, price for pr, 6-5/8" d, 5-3/8" h **$290**

Flatware service, Georg Jensen Silversmithy, post 1945, Acorn pattern, 12 each dinner forks, salad forks, oyster forks, dinner spoons, dessert spoons, cream soup spoons, demitasse spoons, dinner knives, butter knives; two serving spoons, one serving fork, 111 pcs, 119.55 oz **$7,200**

Low bowl, circular foot, imp Georg Jensen, "G830s," in beaded oval, signed in script, 7-5/8" d, 2-1/8" h **$1,645**

Water pitcher, tapered egg-shaped body, flared stem with beading to top, stepped foot, spout with curved reeding to underside, wooden handle with stylized floral terminal to top, 20th C, 9-3/4" h................**$750**

Wine coaster, F. Hingelberg, molded rim, twisted wire sides, composition base, price for pr, 20th C, 4-3/4" d **$490**

Dutch

Bowl, .833 fine, Dutch export mark, repoussé, lobed, reserves with chased and emb country scenes, two pierced handles with putto to top, central flowers flanked by putto riding dolphins, 15 troy oz, 19th C, 14-1/4" l, 3" h **$460**

Box, .833 silver, rect, shaped lid with engraved nativity scene within foliates, base with two biblical scenes, banded sides with engraved foliates, 8 troy oz, late 19th C, 2-5/8" w, 5-1/2" l........................**$960**

Chatelaine, cast brooch with scene of putti with goddess, medallion mounted chains supporting two boxes, cylindrical container, pair of scissors, stylized crown, 9 troy oz, c1890, 12-1/8" l........................**$600**

Coffeepot, .833 fine, baluster form pot with all-over scroll and foliage repoussé, windmill vignette on one side, scroll cartouche topped by crown flanked by putto on other side, legs topped by crowned human masks, four ball and claw feet, turned wood handle set at right angle to ram-horned gro-

tesque spout, flattened lid with vertical ribbing, rampant lion finial, 11 troy oz, late 19th C, 8" h **$800**

Pitcher, .833 line, baluster form, neck with band of fluting, repoussé to lower section of foliage, birds and putti, domed foot with vertical ribbing, spout with putto, beaded serpentine handle, lid with vertical reeding, repoussé and vegetal finial, base engraved "Esther Cleveland," 6 troy oz, descended in family of Grover Cleveland, late 19th C, 5-1/2" h **$260**

French, .950 fine

Coffeepot, pear-shaped, cast quad-ripartite scroll embellished serpentine spout and handle, heat stops, domed lid with flower form finial, 22 troy oz, third quarter 19th C, 9-1/4" h **$460**

Dish, cov, undertray, Paris, "C. P." maker's mark, cylindrical body with acanthus and flat leaf handles, rim with beading and flat leaf band, base with band of flat leaves, foot with band of laurel, lid with beaded edge, removable circular handle formed as cornucopia on leaf and flower base, fitted leather case, 30 troy oz, 1819-38....................**$2,615**

Fish serving platter, oval, reeded rim, monogrammed, 66 troy oz, 27-3/4" l, 11-1/2" w **$1,265**

Serving dish, oval, two shell handles, vertical reeded border, 17 troy oz, third quarter 19th C, 11-3/4" l, 2-1/4" h **$490**

Sweetmeat dish, Odiot, Paris, maker, shell form vessel drawn by sea creatures, reins held by two putti, flanking central standing putto poised as Neptune, holding trident-form fork, shaped rect base cast as water, 65 troy oz, pr, late 19th/20th C, 5-1/2" l, 5" h..............**$2,100**

Tureen, cov, sprays of acorns and oak leaves to top, reeded rim, lid with flat leaf rim, stem with reeded shoulder, oval foot, flat leaf band, angular handles with flat leaf to bottom, stylized corn finial about flat leaf and lotus ground, third/fourth quarter 19th C, 12-3/4" l, 10-1/2" h **$1,840**

German, .800 fine

Basket, shaped oval, paneled sides pierced with flowers, garlands, and scrolling foliage centering four vacant cartouches, center repoussé with flowers, foliage, and three putti at play, 15 oz, 8 dwt, 14" l **$200**

Continental, Denmark, Georg Jenson, two sterling hand-hammered bowls, raised on leaf and ball feet, price for pr, 12 t.o., 5" d, 2-3/4" h, **$1,900.**
Photo courtesy of David Rago Auctions, Inc.

Russian, footed basket, mark of Paul Ovchinnikov, turned and cross hatched handle, pierced and draped rim, embossed wreath depicting Moscow, 11-1/2" h x 14-1/2" w, **$8,050.**
Photo courtesy of Pook & Pook, Inc.

Continental, Denmark, Georg Jensen, demitasse spoons, sterling, set of six, **$225.**
Photo courtesy of David Rago Auctions, Inc.

Continental, Denmark, Georg Jensen, pitcher, No. 385, sterling, ivory handle, **$4,250.**
Photo courtesy of David Rago Auctions, Inc.

Beaker, cov, silver gilt, chased with swags and tasseled drapery, highlighted with matting, marked on cover and base, 8.95 oz, 18th C, 7-3/4" h **$2,400**

Box, rect, hinged lid, Roman chariot scene in relief, beaded edge, reeded sides with vine accents, marked "800 Germany," 5-1/4" x 3-1/4" x 1-1/2"..**$200**

Bread tray, repoussé, cartouches of courtship scene, imp German hallmarks and "800," c1920, 15" x 10-1/2"......................................**$920**

Kettle-on-stand, compressed circular with lobed sides, four hoof feet, detachable cover with wooden finial, central swing partial wooden handle, multi-scroll stand with border, 48 oz, 8 dwt, 16" h.............**$325**

Sauceboat, shape of open-mouthed fish, emb and engraved scales, open back with molded rim, tail shape handle, supported by cast fins, glass eyes, 13 troy oz, late 19th/early 20th C, 10-3/4" l **$1,495**

Serving dish, Wilhelm T. Binder, rounded trefoil shape, three handles, repoussé leaf bud and line dec, scalloped, ribbed glass insert, imp "WTB, 800 fine," c1900, 12" d, 3-1/2" h **$1,150**

Tankard, silver gilt, barrel embossed with strapwork enclosing male masks above dentilated band, double scroll handle, cover with baluster finial, marked on footrim

English, sugar caster, **$125.**
Photo courtesy of Dotta Auction Co., Inc.

and cover, 9.45 oz, 17th C, 5-1/4" h **$5,750**

Wedding cup, figural, beaded figure with chased and emb skirt, cup chased and emb with scrolls and grotesques, 15 troy oz, 9" h **$1,955**

Italian

Asparagus tongs, F. Broggi, Milan, individual, plain, tapered form, set of six, 6 troy oz, 20th C, 5-1/4" l **$115**

Punch bowl, repoussé, bowl with band of flat leaves to base below further continuous hunt scene of men attacking various animals, domed foot with band of flat leaves below continuous hunt scene, removable liner, 146 troy oz, late 19th/early 20th C, 12-5/8" d, 10-1/2" h **$4,025**

Portuguese, .833 silver

Bowl, Oporto, molded scroll and shell rim, band of chased dec, molded circular foot, 14 troy oz, 20th C, 11-3/4" d **$230**

Chalice, domed lid with applied openwork foliate band, engraved bands and cruciform finial, bowl with engraved band with Latin inscription, applied gothic style openwork mounts, stem with beaded and engraved knop, stepped circular base, int. gilt, 31 troy oz, 12-1/2" h **$690**

Ewer, maker's mark "S&P," bulbous, molded shaped rim, body with chased stippled dec, emb foliate, scroll, and shell band, cast scroll handle, molded circular foot with emb dec, 33 troy oz, late 19th/early 20th C, 11-3/4" h **$815**

Kettle-on-stand, maker's mark effaced, inverted pear form, domed lid with cased foliates and wood urn finial, upright handle with cast silver acanthus mounts, body with allover chased and engraved foliates and scrolls, circular stand with four scroll legs and shell feet, chased and engraved burner with turned wood handle, 54 troy oz, second half 19th C, 14-1/4" h **$920**

Salver, molded openwork scroll and foliate rim, bright cut foliate dec on face, three cast legs with shell feet, 25 troy oz, 11-5/8" d.................**$350**

Tray, maker's mark "GP," rect, openwork raised rim with molded grape dec, cast foliate handles, face with engraved dec, 85 troy oz, 20th C, 13-1/2" w, 22-5/8" l.................**$1,265**

Swedish

Hot water kettle on lampstand, maker's mark "AH," globular body with gadroon rim and cover, acorn finial, stand raised on s-scroll legs terminating in shell-form feet, marked on kettle base, cover and stand, base and stand with illegible English marks, 49.20 oz, 14-3/4" h **$850**

English

From the 17th century to the mid-19th century, English silversmiths set the styles which inspired the rest of the world. The work from this period exhibits the highest degree of craftsmanship. English silver is actively collected in the American antiques marketplace.

Basting spoon, George I, London, Brittania Standard, rat tail/ Hanoverian pattern, back of terminal inscribed with crest, mkd on back of stem, maker's mark illegible, 5.80 oz, 1714, 13-3/4" l....................................**$2,155**

Basket, J. R. Hennell maker, London, Victorian, reticulated foliate pattern, circular banding, shaped edge with bead and flat leaf rim, four scroll and cylinder feet with husk swags, glass liner, 21 troy oz, pr, 1884, 6" d, 3-1/2" h.....................................**$1,725**

Bowl, W. Comyns & Sons maker, London, Edward VII, shallow bowl emb with shield-shaped panels, hand-hammered surface, low flower form foot, 7 troy oz, 1902, 5-1/4" d, 1-1/2" h **$435**

Candelabra, pr, William Comyns & Son, Edward VII, silver gilt, in Neo-Classical taste, fluted domed base rising to fluted baluster stem hung with floral swags, removable branches with laurel leaf arms supporting candle sockets and vase shaped nozzles, each fully marked on exterior base and detachable nozzle, 232.05 oz, 1908-09, 19" h.................................**$11,360**

Candlesticks, pr, Crichton Brothers, London, Charles II style, quadripartite shell-form base rising to smaller quadripartite shell-form drip pan, vase form standard rising above four open scrolls to fluted columnar sconce with shaped bobeche, each fully marked on base and underside of bobeche, stamped "Crichton Brothers, New York & London," 74.45 oz, 1909-10....................................**$3,700**

Castor, Hester Bateman, London, George III, urn form, engraved pierced lid with cast urn finial, engraved bands at shoulder, waist, and spreading circular foot, 2 troy oz, 1788, 5-3/4" h.................**$690**

Caudle cup, Samuel Wastell maker, London, William III, Brittania Standard, tapered cylindrical body with single applied molded band, cast ear-shaped handles, spreading domed foot, engraved on one side, heraldic device in rococo-style cartouche, 26 troy oz, 1704, 6" h, 10-1/2" l.....**$2,990**

Center bowl, Robert Garrard, London, George III, lobed ovoid body, two short scroll and acanthus handles, gadroon and shell border offset with two scroll details to each side, four cast paw feet topped by group of scrolls, 51 troy oz, 1811, 17" l, 5-1/2" h **$4,325**

Chamberstick, W. Comyns maker, London, Victorian, chased and emb with flowers and scrolls, removable bobeche, handle with monogrammed thumb-piece, 2 troy oz, 1888, 4" l, 1-3/4" h.................**$115**

Charger, Rebecca Emes and Edward Barnard, London, George IV, shaped edge, applied gadroon and shell border, engraved gartered heraldic device on rim, 29 troy oz, 1826, 11-3/4" d.................**$1,380**

Cigarette case, engine turned ext., monogram, 5.29 oz, c1944, 4-1/2" h **$70**

Coaster, "W.H.H." maker's mark, Birmingham, 1904, Edward VII, round, 4 troy oz, pr, inset to center with George III Irish 10-pence bank tokens dated 1905, 4-3/8" d **$115**

Coffeepot, William Grundy maker, London, George III, baluster, spreading foot, scroll handle with ivory heat stops, serpentine spout with rocaille shell to base, flat leaf to spout, engraved monogram within foliate rococo-style cartouche, domed hinged lid with spiral reeded egg-shaped finial, 60 troy oz, 1767, 14-1/2" h.................**$5,750**

Compote, Benjamin Smith maker, London, Victorian, bowl with shaped edge and vertical ribbing, everted rim with applied grapevine dec, tree-trunk form base with twining grapevine, 36 troy oz, 1845, 12-1/2" d, 7" h **$1,150**

Cream jug, Hester Bateman, London, George III, vasiform, chased beaded rim, body with repoussé farm scenes surrounding central cartouche, trumpet foot with spreading rim, 3 troy oz, restoration, 1782, 5-1/4" h.........**$225**

Cup, Samuel Godbeheve, Edward Wigan and J. Bolt makers, London, George III, baluster form, two handles, four drill holes in base, 11 troy oz, 1800, 5-5/8" h.................**$490**

Demitasse spoon, John Wren maker, London, George III, bright cut engraved stem, fluted bowl, 3 troy oz, set of six, 1791, 5" l.................**$260**

Dish cross, "BD" maker's mark, (Burrage Davenport), London, George III, pierced shell form feet and plate supports, burner with gadrooned rim, 15 troy oz, 1772, 12" l.................**$1,265**

Egg cup frame, Henry Nutting maker, London, George III, reeded central handle, four ball feet, six associated Sheffield egg cups, five associated demitasse spoons, 18 troy oz, 1800.................**$550**

Entree dish, cov, "BS" makers mark, London, George IV, lid modified with later band of foliate repoussé and engraved with heraldic crest and monograms, base with gadroon and shell rim, removable leaf and shell handle, 67 troy oz, 1820, 12-1/8" l, 5-3/4" h.................**$1,725**

Epergne, "GJ DF" maker's mark, London, George V, central stem below navette-shaped reticulated basket with applied border, flanked by smaller removable baskets on scrolled arms, ovoid reticulated base with applied scroll and shell border, four scroll feet, 76 troy oz, 1913, 10-1/2" l, 11-3/4" h.................**$6,325**

Fish server, attributed to John Neville, London, George III, reticulated blade with scrolling foliage, stem end with shell, handle, engraved with gadrooned edge, central heraldic device, 4 troy oz, 1770, 11-1/4" l.................**$1,100**

Flatware service, partial, Spaulding-Gorham, London, George VI, six lunch forks, six salad forks, six dinner forks, 18 fish forks, six dinner knives, 18 fish knives, six butter knives, 18 place spoons, six soup spoons, 18 cream soup spoons, 21 teaspoons, 18 five o'clock teaspoons, six demitasse spoons, 12 ice tea spoons, monogrammed MMR, 18 George VI/Elizabeth II fruit knives, maker's mark CWF, 1952, 189 pcs, 221.75 oz, 1938 ....**$3,150**

Flower bowl, George III, Paul Storr, classical design based on Warwick vase, hallmarked London, 1808 ....**$4,700**

Goblet, maker's mark partially obscured (attributed to Henry Greenway), London, George II, beaded collar, tapered round funnel bowl, beaded trumpet foot, engraved coat of arms in roundel, 16 troy oz, pr, 1775, 6-1/2" h.................**$1,955**

Hot water kettle on stand, John Emes maker, London, George III, lid partially reeded with wood finial, pot with ovoid body partially reeded with gadrooned edging, on tapered circular foot, fluted tap, upright silver and wood handle, stand with gadrooned rim with burner and cover, flat leaf legs, four hairy paw feet with wooden ball supports, pot engraved with mottoed coat of arms, small heraldic device on pot lid, burner lid, and burner, 83 troy oz, 1807, 12" h **$2,100**

Jug, cov, "C. W." maker's mark, London, George III, later Victorian adaptations, stamped bands flanking convex band at rim, ovoid body with twisted reeding and fluting to lower section, central cartouche flanked by C-scrolls, serpentine handle, domed foot, short spout, domed hinged lid with Victorian hallmarks, twisted reeding, fluting on urn finial, 18 troy oz, 1769, 7-3/4" h.................**$400**

Marrow scoop, Richard Pargeter, London, George II, back engraved "BWM," mkd, 1.65 oz, 1737-38, 9" l **$500**

Meat skewer, Thomas Whipham & Charles Wright, London, George III, tapering, plain loop terminal, engraved "V," mkd, 3.90 oz, 1761-62, 12-3/4" l.................**$210**

Mirror, "JR SJ" makers, London, Victorian, rect, curved top, reticulated with scrolls and flowers, mask center at base, grotesque beasts on either corner, beveled edge mirror, easel stand on back, 1887, 14-1/4" h, 10" d **$980**

Muffineer, Charles Stuart Harris maker, Brittania standard marks, London, tapered paneled lid with engraving, baluster form finial, paneled baluster form, tiered foot, 14 troy oz, 1899, 8-1/2" h.................**$800**

Mug, Richard Beale, London, George II, cylindrical, cast "S" scroll handle, molded circular foot, engraved crest, 6 troy oz, 1731, 3-3/4" h.................**$980**

English, punch ladle, bearing marks of William Gibson and John Langman, London, c1899, 13" l; together with English silver punch ladle, c1789, bearing mark of "T.S." (Thos. Shephard), 13-1/2" l, **$500.**
Photo courtesy of Pook & Pook, Inc.

Mustard pot, attributed to William Barrett II, George III, circular, disk finial, reeded rim and base, reticulated sides with engraved foliates and urns, associated glass insert, 3 troy oz, 1827, 2-1/2" h **$290**

Porringer, cov, maker's mark II, London, William & Mary, tapered body, engraved armorial within baroque strapwork cartouche below cast scroll handles, raised cov with central fluted dec and baluster finial, mkd only on body, 10.80 oz, 1691, 4-3/4" d, 4" h
....**$1,800**

Salt, open, Walker & Hall, Sheffield, Edward VII, cobalt blue glass liner, mkd, 1902-03, 4" l **$180**

Salver
John Tuite maker, London, George II, shaped molded rim offset with shells, central engraved coat of arms in rococo cartouche, four scrolled leaf feet, 32 troy oz, 1783, 12-3/8" d
....**$2,185**
John Cotton & Thomas Head maker, London, George III, beaded and ribbed border, four beaded and ribbed feet, center engraved with mottoed coat of arms, 64 troy oz, 1813, 16-1/4" d **$3,750**
Mappin & Webb makers, London, shaped edge with bead shell border, four scrolled feet, 60 troy oz, 1946, 17-1/4" d **$1,610**
Robert Abercomby maker, London, George II, shaped edge, engraved with wide band of florals, fruits, shells, scrolls, and diapered cartouches, four paw feet topped by shells, engraved central Chinoiserie-style coat of arms, 156 troy oz, 1750, 22-7/8" h **$4,320**

Sauceboats, pr, maker's mark "T. D. & S.," Birmingham, George III style, oval form, shaped borders, flying scroll handles, hoof feet with fluted

shell headers, marked on bases, 15 oz, 1947, 7-1/4" l **$400**

Sauce ladle, Hester Bateman, London, George III, Old English pattern, mkd on back of terminal, 4.30 oz, 1790, 13" l...**$450**

Sauce tureen, cov, George Smith and Thomas Hayter makers, London, George III, domed lid with urn finial, boat shaped body with ribbed rim, loop handles, pedestal foot, lid and body monogrammed, 33 troy oz, pr, 1804, 9-1/4" l, 5-1/2" h **$2,760**

Serving spoon, William Eley and William Fearn, London, George III, engraved crest, 3 oz, 6 dwt, 1818, 11-3/4" l.......................................**$175**

Soup tureen, cov, William Elliott maker, London, George III, gadrooned rim, acanthus handles, four paw feet terminating in shell and acanthus leaves, lid with two bands of gadrooning and ribbed removable handle, engraved coat of arms on body and lid, 136 troy oz, 1819, 14-1/2" l, 10-1/4" h.................................**$7,475**

Spoon
Illegible marker's mark, London, Henry VIII, maidenhead terminal with traces of gilding, crowned leopard's head mark very worn, 1.00 oz, 1540-41, 6-1/8" l
....**$5,750**
Elizabeth I, London, prick-dot engraved with initials "HRM" to back of bowls, lion Sejant Affronte terminal, traces of gilding, 2.90 oz, worn terminals, pr, 1589-90, 6-5/8" l.................................**$5,750**

Standish, J. C. Vickery maker, London, Edward VII, rect, reeded border, two horizontal pen wells, two tapered inkwells with canted corners and hinged lids, central ovoid covered well, hinged lid fitted with eight-day clock, four ball and claw feet, some restoration needed, 32 troy oz, 1906, 11-3/8" l, 7-1/2" w.................**$2,100**

Sugar basket, Peter & Ann Bateman, London, 1798, George III, navette shape, molded banded rim and swing handle, engraved body with reticulated bands, banded oval foot, monogrammed, cobalt glass insert, 3 troy oz, 5-1/2" l, 3-1/2" w.........**$920**

Sugar bowl, Georgian, marks rubbed, beaded rim, ovoid body with ribbon-tied floral sprays and swags, roundels on each side, heraldic device, spiraled loop handles, trumpet foot with bands

of bright cut engraving, 5 troy oz, 6" l, 5-3/8" h.................................**$350**

Sugar tongs, Georgian, cast with shell, foliage, scrolls engraved with flowers, center vacant cartouche, 1 oz, 2 dwt..**$95**

Sweetmeat dish, R & S Garrard maker, London, 1879, ovoid, flanked by male and female figure, auricular scroll and stylized shell handle, four periwinkle shell feet, 13 troy oz, 9-1/8" l, 5-5/8" w, 2-1/4" h **$1,495**

Tablespoon, William Eley, London, George IV, fiddle pattern, monogrammed, pr, 6 troy oz, 1826, 8-3/4" l...**$200**

Tankard, John Longlands I maker, Newcastle, George III, tapered cylindrical form, plain body with engraved cartouche, serpentine handle with reticulated thumb-piece, gadrooned foot rim, slightly domed lid with gadrooned rim, engraved presentation inscription, lacquered, 26 troy oz, 1769, 7-3/4" h.......................**$1,265**

Taperstick, London, octagonal base with urn-shaped stem rising from circular well to banded campana sconce, base engraved with crest, worn marks, maker's mark appears to be mark for Samuel Margas, 5.10 oz, possibly early 18th C, 4" h
....**$2,160**

Tazza, pr, two-tier, R. & S. Garrard, London, Victorian, in the Renaissance taste, domed base and baluster stem supporting two dishes pierced with shells and chased with interlaced strapwork, top dish engraved with crest, with an inscription reading "Presented to Viscount Cole BY THE TENANTRY OF THE ENNISKILLEN ESTATES, ON THE OCCASION OF HIS MARRIAGE 12th JULY 1869," both marked on underside of base and exterior base of smaller dish with maker's mark, duty mark, lion passant, and date letter, 144.50 oz, 1864-65, 16" h.........................**$9,000**

Teapot
Andrew Fogelberg & Stephen Gilbert, London, George III, oval form, chased with arabesques, floral garlands, cov surmounted with ivory finial, monogrammed, mkd, 14.25 oz, 1786-87, 10-1/2" l, 4-1/4" h **$550**
Attributed to Augustus Le Sage, London, 1771, George III, cylindrical, disc finial, wood ear handle, engraved antelope crest on lid and side, 13 troy oz, 5" h.............**$1,100**

George Smith & Thomas Hayter, London, George III, fluted ovoid, engraved domed lid, bone mushroom finial and handle, engraved foliates and central crest, 15 troy oz, restorations, 1796, 6-1/4" h **$525**

Teapot stand, Robert & David Hennell, London, Georgian, oval with beveled corners, molded rim engraved, face with engraved and bright cut foliate bands, central cartouche, four feet, 5 troy oz, 1795, 4-7/8" w, 7" l **$435**

Tea and coffee service, Rebecca Eames & Edward Barnard, London, George III, coffeepot with gadrooned pedestal, teapot, creamer, open sugar, sq bulbous form, emb lids with cast foliate finials, molded gadrooned rims, bodies with bands of spiral reeding, four ball feet, 73 troy oz, 1814-15, 8-3/4" h **$2,300**

Tea service

Crichton Bros. makers, London, George V, coffee and teapots, kettle on stand, creamer, open sugar, cov sugar, all with ovoid body, arcaded and ribbed banding, teapot and coffeepot with wooden handles topped with silver flat leaves, lion's head roundels, reamer and sugar with curved handles terminating in lion's head roundels, 174 troy oz, 1930, 9" h coffeepot, 16" h kettle on stand **$2,990**

Peter, Ann, and William Bateman makers, London, George III, ovoid teapot, helmet shaped cov creamer with angular handle, cov sugar with angular handles, all with partial vertical lobing, bands of bright cut engraving and engraved heraldic device, wooden pineapple finials, 33 troy oz, 1800, 7-3/4" h teapot **$1,495**

Tea urn, maker's mark "I. R.," London, lid with tapered egg-shaped finial, beaded tape with ivory handle, beaded loop handles, four ball feet with stepped rect base and beaded edge, bright cut engraving throughout with husks, cartouches, and floral swags, 37 troy oz, 1778, 15" h **$2,100**

Tray, "EB" makers mark, London, George IV, rect, gadrooned border, handles with shells and leaves, four paw feet flanked by floral roundels and stylized wings, engraved all-over pattern of flowers and leaves, center with motted crest and later monogram, 120 troy oz, 1822, 25" l, 16-1/4" w **$2,760**

Trefid spoon, stem mkd with arm and sword emerging from crown mark, round terminal, traces of gilding, 3.75 oz, 1686-87, 10-1/8" l **$2,400**

Trump indicator, hallmarked Birmingham, round base, celluloid suit indicators suspended from pair of loops, 2-3/4" x 2-1/4" **$200**

Waxjack, attributed to Augustus Le Sage, London, George III, cast handles, attached snuffer, spindle with spirally reeded bud form finial, domed base with beaded rim, supported by three cast claw and ball feet, inscription on base, 4 troy oz, third quarter 18th C, 6-1/2" h **$980**

Wine coaster, Joseph and John Angel makers, London, Victorian, applied scroll and shell rim, reticulated sides, engraved to base with scrolls, shells, and central heraldic crest, pr, 1846, 5-3/4" d, 2-3/4" h **$5,465**

Irish

Fine examples of Irish silver are becoming popular with collectors.

Candlesticks, pr, George III/IV, Dublin, attributed to John Laughlin, Jr., larger gadrooned knob over gadrooned knob below partially vertically reeded stem with single horizontal beaded band, well with applied stylized wheat or grass fronds, domed gadrooned base, vertically reeded sconce, removable nozzle with gadrooned rim, small heraldic crest engraved on foot and nozzle, 49 troy oz **$7,475**

Caudle cup, cov, Dublin, marked for John Hamilton, domed lid topped by ovoid finial, body with single molded band, crabstock handles, lobed spreading foot, no date mark, 37 troy oz, pr, mid-18th C, 7-1/4" h **$5,175**

Cup, marked for John Letabliere, tapered cylindrical body with leaf cut card work, band of foliate engraving, domed spreading foot, scroll handles topped with flat leaves, engraved on one side with cartouche, no date marks, 44 troy oz, pr, mid-18th C, 4-7/8" h **$5,465**

Ladle, chased floral and scroll designs on silver bowl, Irish hallmarks and maker's mark for Phineas Garde, Corke, baleen handle, minor battering on rim, c1815, 7" l **$320**

Salver, George II/III, Dublin, William Townsend maker, shaped molded

border, engraved center with heraldic crest in rococo cartouche, three pad feet with scroll legs, 8 troy oz, 6-1/2" l **$1,100**

Snuffer tray, George III, Dublin, William Doyle maker, octagonal boat shape, base with bright-cut engraved husk drops, heraldic crest within roundel flanked by leaves, sides reticulated with arcading, paterae, 4 troy oz, 1798 .... **$700**

Scottish

Not to be outdone by their Irish and English neighbors, Scottish silversmiths also created fine objects.

Berry spoon, Edinburgh, George Fenwick maker, 1820 .... **$75**

Punch ladle

Edinburgh, maker's mark "CD," 6 troy oz, 1789, 13-1/2" l **$300**

Edinburgh, maker's mark "AH," ovoid bowl, twisted baleen handle, silver end cap, 1820, 14-1/2" l **$150**

Sheffield, English

Sheffield silver, or Old Sheffield Plate, has a fusion method of silver-plating that was used from the mid-18th century until the mid-1880s, when the process of electroplating silver was introduced.

Sheffield plating was discovered in 1743, when Thomas Boulsover of Sheffield, England, accidentally fused silver and copper. The process consisted of sandwiching a heavy sheet of copper between two thin sheets of silver. The result was a plated sheet of silver, which could be pressed or rolled to a desired thickness. All Sheffield articles are worked from these plated sheets.

Most of the silver-plated items found today marked "Sheffield" are not early Sheffield plate. They are later wares made in Sheffield, England.

Basket, S. Smith & Son, England, second oval, molded foliate rim, emb and reticulated sides, cast foliage handles, oval reticulated and engraved base, cobalt blue glass liner, half 19th C, 7-3/4" w, 13-3/4" l **$460**

Biscuit box, oval, hinged lid, gadrooned trim, lion mask side handles, attached tray base on ball feet, late 19th C, 7" w, 7-1/2" h **$120**

Carving set, fork, knife, and steel, engraved image of Windsor Castle on knife blade, horn handles, silver plated crown finials, leathered case, late 19th C, 16-1/2" l **$350**

Claret jug, cut glass body mounted at neck, hinged cover, baluster finial, multi-scroll foliate handle, c1935, 11" h **$500**

Domed lid, engraved armorial whippet, oval handle, early 19th C, 22" h, 11" l **$575**

Pitcher, finely chased quatrefoil medallions and feathering, Sheffield hallmarks for 1857 by John Fred Fenton, ivory insulators on handle, minor damage, 7-1/4" h **$520**

Plate, circular, gadrooned rim, engraved Carlill crest, George III, price for pr, 9-3/4" d **$175**

Platter and meat cover, oval tree platter, four ball feet, two wooden handles, gadrooned rim, armorials on both sides, dome cover with gadrooned rim, reeded handles, engraved armorials, 26" l **$2,750**

Serving dish, cov, England, rect, gadrooned rim and lid, cast branch and maple leaf handle, engraved coat of arms, first half 19th C, 11-1/2" l, 8-5/8" w **$230**

Tantalus, England, central casket with two engraved hinged lids below handle, sides supporting two cut and pressed glass decanters, pedestal base supported by four column legs, late 19th/early 20th C, 5-3/4" w, 15" l **$490**

Tray, kidney shape, gadrooned rim, pierced gallery of open lattice work, centered engraved lion crest, early 20th C, 18-1/2" x 7-1/2" **$120**

Vegetable dish, cov, plated, shaped rect, applied grapevine, scroll, and foliage handle, monogrammed, 13" l **$250**

Wine bottle holder, wooden base, vintage detail, ivory casters, 16" l **$275**

Silver, plated

Englishmen G. R. and H. Elkington are given credit for being the first to use the electrolytic method of plating silver in 1838.

An electroplated-silver article is completely shaped and formed from a base metal and then coated with a thin layer of silver. In the late 19th century, the base metal was Britannia, an alloy of tin, copper, and antimony. Other bases are copper and brass. Today, the base is nickel silver.

Tea and coffee service, silver plated, five-piece set, **$300.**
Photo courtesy of Dotta Auction Co., Inc.

In 1847, Rogers Bros. of Hartford, Connecticut, introduced the electroplating process in America. By 1855, a number of firms were using the method to produce silver-plated items in large quantities.

The quality of the plating is important. Extensive polishing can cause the base metal to show through. The prices for plated-silver items are low, making them popular items with younger collectors.

Bacon warmer, George III style, rect, dentilated rim, turned wood handle, hinged cover with ivory finial, inscribed crest, 10-1/4" l **$250**

Bun warmer, oval, cover chased with flowers and foliage, beaded rim, paw feet, liner, two reeded handles, 12-1/2" l **$275**

Candelabra, pr, Continental, three-light, tapering stem issuing central urn-form candle-cup and two scrolling branches supporting wax pan and conforming candle-cup, oval foot with reeded border, vertical flutes, 12" h **$150**

Candle lamp shade, Tiffany Studios, Grapevine pattern, domed, pierced grapevine design, imp "Tiffany Studios New York," minor dents, price for four, 6-1/2" d, 2" d fitter rim, 3-3/8" h **$1,265**

Candlesticks, pr, Wurtembergishe Metallwarenfabrik, sq base applied with bow-tie garlands and foliage, rim with stylized leaves and beads rising to Corinthian column stems, detachable bobeches with beaded rims, 7-1/2" h **$375**

Claret jug, eagle-form, textured cranberry glass body with realistic silver plate head and feet, set with glass eyes, hinged at neck, clear draw handle, Continental, early 20th C, 9-1/2" h **$460**

Coffee urn and stand, ovoid body, spout over reeded legs, paw feet joined to X-form stretcher raised on bun feet, cover surmounted with leaf

Dog bowl, Roycroft, silver plated, hammered straight sides, monogrammed ADA, Roycroft orb and cross mark, 2" x 6-1/4", **$1,200.**
Photo courtesy of David Rago Auctions, Inc.

and scroll finial, unmarked, 16" h **$300**

Egg cup, England, stems formed as cast kangaroos resting in circular underplates, price for pr, early 20th C, 2-3/4" h **$100**

Epergne, three pale blue patterned glass vases with central reeded shaft, tripod base, winged sea horses supports, marked "HW & Co.," top insert missing, 13-1/2" h **$450**

Fish set, English, six forks, six knives with engraved blades, mother-of-pearl handles, wood case, late 19th C **$320**

Game platter, English, well and three-platter base with attached hot water pan, raised on four medallion-capped feet, associated domed cov with beaded bands and engraved wide border of entwined circlets, applied open handle surrounded by conforming engraved dec, body with engraved griffin, late 19th C, 16" h, 26-1/2" l **$700**

Garniture, ftd compote with repoussé floral and foliate bands, each side pc with conforming dec, Tiffany & Co., 6-1/4" h **$350**

Hot water kettle on stand, rounded kettle, partially reeded sides, scrolled silver, wood handle, detachable warming stand, marked "Made in England, Hand Chased," 13" h **$150**

Inkwell, England or America, fence form, central fence supporting two urn form candle sconces, ends with three stakes bearing square cut glass inkwells with silver plated lids, 20th C, 11-1/2" h **$195**

Lamp, table, paneled shade, conical base, openwork silverplate grape vine designs, five panels of green and white slag glass, cast leaf finial, engraved leaves on base, base marked "Made and Guaranteed by the MB Co. USA," electrified, five sockets, 20-1/2" h **$1,200**

Monteith cooler, attributed to England, oval, shaped rims and cast loop handles, price for pr, late 19th C, 7-3/4" w, 13" l..............................**$815**

Punch cup, Lavigne, 1881 Rogers..**$25**

Sandwich box, English, rect, loop handle, hinged lid monogrammed, gilt int., leather carrying case, early 20th C, 5-3/4" h, 4-1/8" h..............**$80**

Snuffbox, English, foliate scroll engraved lid, set with central faceted purple stone, cowry shell body, late 19th C, 2-3/4" l............................**$300**

Teapot, Derby Silver Co., emb floral motifs and arabesques, wear, 8" h **$60**

Toast rack, England, oval, central ring handle above cast cricket ball, rack formed as crossed cricket bats, four ball feet, late 19th/early 20th C, 7" l, 2-5/8" w **$90**

Tray, Victorian, oval, field engraved with floral and diaper medallions flanked by foliage with foliate garlands at intervals, beaded and geometrical design border and handles, 32" l..**$350**

Sheffield

Englishmen G. R. Elkington and H. Elkington are given credit for being the first to use the electrolytic method of plating silver in 1838.

Candlesticks, pr, ornate columns with composite capitals, pale blue blown glass hurricane shades with cut floral designs, 24" h................................**$425**

Entree dish, shaped rect, gadrooned rim, detachable handle with gadroon dec, 11" x 8"..................................**$75**

Hot water urn, Philip Ashberry & Sons makers, urn-form body with flat leaf engraving at base, wide central band of engraved anthemion, round domed base with beaded rim, trumpet foot with band of guilloche centered by flowerheads and accented with husks, angular handles terminating in flat leaves, anthemion handle on top, domed lid with flat leaf engraving and foliage baluster finial, inner sleeve, early 19th C, 22-3/4" h **$750**

Sauceboat with underplate, rim applied with grapevines...............**$95**

Soup tureen, ovoid body with applied gadroon and shell border, two fluted handles with leaf terminals, four scroll and flat leaf feet, domed lid

with reeded band, leaf-form finial, body and lid with let-in engraved heraldic device, fitted drop-in liner, restorations, rosing, early 19th C, 16" l, 10-3/4" h **$1,725**

Tankard, Hy Wilkinson & Co. makers, tapered cylindrical form, plain ear handle, gold washed int., fitted leather case, 10 troy oz, 5" h **$235**

Tea and coffee service, baluster shaped coffeepot, teapot, creamer, two handled open sugar, waste bowl, oval with canted corners, angular handles, 12-1/4" h kettle-on-stand **$425**

SILVER OVERLAY

History: Silver overlay is silver applied directly to a finished glass or porcelain object. The overlay is cut and decorated, usually by engraving, prior to being molded around the object.

Glass usually is of high quality and is either crystal or colored. Lenox used silver overlay on some porcelain pieces. Most designs are from the Art Nouveau and Art Deco periods.

Basket, deep cranberry body, all-over floral and lattice design, sterling handle, 5-1/2" l, 6" h **$600**

Decanter, molded, pinched oval bottle, surface bamboo dec overall, base disk imp "Yuan Shun/ Sterling," faceted crystal hollow stopper, 11-1/2" h **$375**

Flask, clear bottle shaped body, scrolling hallmarked silver, hinged cov, 5" h..**$275**

Inkwell, bright green ground, rose, scroll, and lattice overlay, matching cov, monogram, 3-3/4" x 3" **$650**

Jug, colorless glass, tapered baluster form, star-cut base, silver cased applied draw handle, overlay of twining grapes and grape vines, plain cartouche beneath spout, stylized cobweb overlay below, Alvin Mfg Co., late 19th/early 20th C, 9" h **$1,380**

Perfume bottle
Baluster, elongated neck, colorless glass, scrolling foliage overlay, central monogrammed cartouche, 5" h **$225**

Bulbed colorless glass bottle with engraved scrolled foliate silver overlay dec, initial "S" in cartouche,

Bottle, cordial, long neck, matching stopper, Art Nouveau-type foliate silver overlay, **$125.**

silver overlay on ball shaped glass stopper, Continental, wear, some loss to silver, 4" h **$75**

Tea set, Lenox porcelain body, Reed & Barton silver overlay, three-pc set, 8-3/4" h....................................**$325**

Vase
Art Nouveau free-form irid blue body, applied silver overlay in iris pattern, 7" h **$1,100**

Art Nouveau ovoid cranberry glass body, flared rim supported by three applied clear glass handles, silver overlay on rim and body, waterlily and cattails design, marks obscured, minor losses to silver overlay, 13-3/4" h **$1,250**

Baluster porcelain body, cerulean blue ground, painted prunus stems, overlaid with silver detailing, silver neck and foot rims, Aesthetic Movement, French, late 19th C, 9-3/4" h **$470**

Bronze, sterling silver overlay of trees, verdigris patina, Heintz, 5" d, 12-1/4" h **$850**

Bulbous stick, translucent green glass body overlaid with embossed floral Alvin, 8" h **$450**

Vessel, Tiger Ware, bulbous stoneware body with ear handle, narrow neck mounted with strapwork engraved silver collar, engraved monogram "ISA" and date "1594," English, 6-1/8" h....................................**$4,410**

Pitcher, cream-colored porcelain body, scrolling silver overlay, **$125.**

Boudoir lamp, Heintz, silver overlay of daylilies on verdigris patina, topped by pierced flaring shade with new lining, no visible mark, 12" x 11", **$1,600.**
Photo courtesy of David Rago Auctions, Inc.

Vase, Heintz, sterling on bronze, overlaid with poppies on verdigris ground, stamped "HAMS Patent," 1/4" shallow dent to side, 11" x 5-1/4", **$600.**
Photo courtesy of David Rago Auctions, Inc.

SNUFF BOTTLES

History: Tobacco usage spread from America to Europe to China during the 17th century. Europeans and Chinese preferred to grind the dried leaves into a powder and sniff it into their nostrils. The elegant Europeans carried their boxes and took a pinch with their fingertips. The Chinese upper class, because of their lengthy fingernails, found this inconvenient and devised a bottle with a fitted stopper and attached spoon. These utilitarian objects soon became objets d'art.

Snuff bottles were fashioned from precious and semi-precious stones, glass, porcelain and pottery, wood, metals, and ivory. Glass and transparent-stone bottles often were enhanced further with delicate hand paintings, some done on the interior of the bottle.

Agate, carved

Amber, quatrefoil form, each side carved with bat and stylized ruyi design, Chinese, tiny chip and slight wear on rim, slight fissure on shoulder, 19th C, 2-1/4" h **$150**

Flat rect shape, carved sprig of peony, reverse dec with carved ruyi scepter, Chinese, 19th C, 2-3/8" h **$125**

Mottled brown, flattened round form, carved fisherman, reverse with cat looking up at a flying insect, red glass top, orig spoon, Chinese, 19th C, 2-1/2" h **$200**

Mottled gray, flattened oval form, well carved with three men mooring boat, flower, tree dec, Chinese, 19th C, 2-1/2" h **$575**

Amber, landscape and figures, caramel inclusions, conforming id, Chinese, late 19th C, 4" l **$1,265**

Celadon, light jade, flattened ovoid short neck, 2-1/4" h **$200**

Chrysoprase, flattened ovoid, light green, conforming stopper, 3" h **$215**

Cinnabar lacquer, ovoid, continual scene of scholars and boys in a pavilion landscape, dark red, conforming stopper, 3-1/4" h **$230**

Cloisonné, auspicious symbols among clouds, yellow ground, lappet base border, ruyi head neck border, conforming stopper with chrysanthe-

mum design, Qianlong four-character mark **$185**

Coral, carved, tree trunk with foliage, carved flower stopper, China, stopper glued to bottle, 19th or 20th C, 2-1/2" h **$320**

Glass

Clear, flat rect shape, broad oval foot, stone stopper with eye design, Chinese, 19th C, 2-1/4" h **$125**

Interior painted with three horned goats by tree, verso with inscription, sgd "Ma Shaoxian," China, no stopper, 2-1/2" h **$480**

Opaque body, enameled peony blossoms, verso with two birds, three-characters on base, China, 3" h **$175**

Ivory, curved ivory carved with bulrushes and crocodiles, flatleaf cap with ball finial, pebbled gilt-metal lid with glass-inset neck, mounted with short neck chain, Indian, late 19th/early 20th C, 3-3/4" l **$300**

Jade, carved

Flattened oval form, carved sage and pine tree on one side, reverse with man sitting under willow tree, fish on line, Chinese, 19th C, 3" h **$435**

Oval, carved butterfly near flowering branch, amber inclusions on one side, Chinese, design incorporates natural fissure, 18th or 19th C, 2-3/8" h **$875**

Slender oval form, carved basket-weave dec, tiger's eye stopper, Chinese, dark inclusion at base, spoon broken, 18th C, 2-3/8" h **$450**

Lapis lazuli, ovoid, relief carved, figures beneath tree, Chinese, 4" h **$125**

Malachite, carved, gourd, Chinese, 3" h.. **$95**

Opal, carved sage seated before gourd, Ch'ing Dynasty, 3" h **$125**

Overlay glass, seven colors, one side with floral designs in two archaic-form vases, reverse with immortal attending a crane and deer, bats flying above, each side with animal mask and ring handles, green, blue, mauve, coral, brown, and yellow, on white ground, 19th C............................. **$520**

Peking glass, Snowflake

Blue overlay, each side with prancing deer, head turned with a lingchi branch in mouth, 19th C, 2-1/2" h **$490**

Red overlay, flattened ovoid, one side with serpent and tortoise, other with frog sitting under lily pad, 2-1/4" h **$1,265**

Porcelain

Famille Rose dec, vasiform, Chinese, marked, 19th C, 2-1/2" h **$125**

Famille Rose dec, flattened round form, Chinese, marked, 19th C, 2-3/4" h **$125**

Famille Rose dec, raised molded dec, iron-red sacred fungus and bat mark, gilt foot rim, coral stopper, China, small chip, stopper glued to bottle, 18th or 19th C, 3-1/8" h **$95**

Famille Verte dec, Chinese, cap loose, 19th C, 3-3/8" h **$115**

Famille Verte dec, Chinese, 19th C, 3-3/4" h **$150**

Gamboling lions among clouds, ruyi band on shoulder and base, carved wooden stopper and ivory spoon, gilt rims, iron-red Jiaqing four-character mark on base, China, small chips, 19th C, 3-1/4" h **$320**

Rock crystal, carved dec of pine trees in mountainous landscape, inclusions of black crystalline in various lengths, carved coral stopper, Chinese, spoon missing, 19th C, 3-1/2" h **$375**

Rose quartz, flattened ovoid, relief carved leaves and vines, Chinese, 3" h **$45**

Stag horn, flattened ovoid, one side with inset ivory panel with two laughing figures, reserve with inset panel with gold archaic script, 2-1/8" h **$175**

Turquoise, high relief carving of children and prunus trees, China **$235**

SOAPSTONE

History: The mineral steatite, known as soapstone because of its greasy feel, has been used for carving figural groups and designs by the Chinese and others. Utilitarian pieces also were made. Soapstone pieces were very popular during the Victorian era.

Bookends, pr, carved, block form, fu lion resting on top, Chinese, 5" h...................................**$300**

Candlesticks, pr, red tones, flowers and foliage, 5-1/8" h **$85**

Carving

Buddha, seated, praying, carved stone base, 9-1/4" h **$60**

Dog's head, old darkened color, America, chips, with stand, 19th C, 4" w, 4-1/2" d, 3-1/2" h.............**$420**

Even white color, servant kneeling before woman holding fan, China, 19th C, 3" h **$115**

Woman, standing, wearing robe, restoration, 12" h.........................**$120**

Hot plate, 16" l, 8-1/2" w **$75**

Plaque, birds, trees, flowers, and rocks, 9-1/2" h.........................**$125**

Sculpture, kneeling nude young woman, Canadian, 10-1/4" h, 4-1/2" w **$95**

Sealing stamp, carved dec, curved scroll, 5" h, 1" d...........................**$95**

Toothpick holder, two containers with carved birds, animals, and leaves **$85**

Vase

Four openings, red tones, Chinese, c1900, 6-3/4" h, 9-1/2" l...........**$125**

Carved peacock and chrysanthemums, 15-1/2" h......................**$495**

SOUVENIR AND COMMEMORATIVE CHINA AND GLASS

History: Souvenir, commemorative, and historical china and glass includes those items produced to celebrate special events, places, and people.

Collectors particularly favor China plates made by Rowland and Marcellus and Wedgwood. Rowland and Marcellus, Staffordshire, England, made a series of blue-and-white historic plates with a wide rolled edge. Scenes from the Philadelphia Centennial in 1876 through the 1939 New York World's Fair are depicted. In 1910, Wedgwood collaborated with Jones, McDuffee, and Stratton to produce a series of historic dessert-sized plates showing scenes of places throughout the United States.

Many localities issued plates, mugs, glasses, etc., for anniversary celebrations or to honor a local historical event. These items seem to have greater value when sold in the region in which they originated.

Commemorative glass includes several patterns of pressed glass that celebrate people or events. Historical

Soapstone vase, flat back, urn with cascading chrysanthemums, faux bamboo stand as base, **$35.**

glass includes campaign and memorial items.

Ashtray, New York City, china, blue and white transfer, Empire State Building, Statue of Liberty, Rockefeller Center, harbor scene, mkd "Fine Staffordshire Ware, Enco, National, Made in England"........................**$20**

Bust, Gillinder

Lincoln, frosted...........................**$325**

Napoleon, frosted and clear........**$295**

Creamer

New Academy, Truro, multicolored image on white medallion, cobalt blue ground, gold and white dec **$30**

Wadsworth Atheneum, Hartford, CT, multicolored image on white medallion, lustered ground, marked "Wheelock China, Austria," 2" h **$18**

Cup, Entrance to Soldier's Home, Leavenworth, Kansas, multicolored, beaded dec, marked "Germany," slight wear to gold dec, 2-1/2" h **$18**

Cup and saucer

Niagara Falls, cobalt blue ground, gold trim, scene of falls on saucer, marked "Made in Japan," matching wooden display stand, 1-1/4" h x 1-3/4" d, 3-1/2" d saucer **$20**

Souvenir of Edina, Missouri, white ground, rose dec, gold trim, marked "Japan," 2-1/2" h x 3-3/4" w cup, 5-1/2" w saucer........................**$20**

Plate, Souvenir of Plymouth Rock, MA, blue and white, marked "Old English Staffordshire Ware, Made in Staffordshire, (Jonroth England mark) England, Imported for Plymouth Rock Gift Shop, Plymouth, Mass, (Adams mark) Adams, est. 1657," **$20.**

Plate, Valley Forge, 1777-78, Washington's Headquarters in center, vignettes of other signs around border, blue transfer decoration, Rowland & Marcellus Co., Staffordshire, England, with poem by Gus Egolf, Dec. 19, 1910, Norristown, Pennsylvania, **$75.**

Plate, Souvenir of St. Augustine, Florida, Old City Gates in center, vignettes of other sights around border, blue transfer decoration, marked "Usina Brothers King St, St Augustine, Fla, Staffordshire, England," **$60.**

Washington and Lafayette, transfer print portraits on cup of George Washington and Lafayette, saucer with portrait titled "Washington His Country's Father," creamware, England, early 19th C, 1-3/4" h **$490**

Demitasse cup and saucer

My Old Kentucky Home, marked "Handpainted, Made in Japan, NICO," 2" h x 2" w cup, 4" d saucer **$15**

Souvenir of Chicago, Ill, Victorian man and woman on inside of cup, gold trim, marked "Crest O Gold, Sabin, Warranted 22K," 2" h x 2-1/2" w cup **$17.50**

Dish

Beauvoir House, Jefferson Davis House, Biloxi, Mississippi, marked "Made by Adams, England for the Jefferson Davis Shrine," 3-1/4" d **$20**

DeShong Memorial Art Gallery, Lester, Pennsylvania, yellow luster ground, marked "Made in Germany," wear to lettering and gold trim, 3-3/4" x 3-1/4" **$12**

Dish, cov, Remember the *Maine*, green opaque glass **$135**

Figure, souvenir of Atlantic City, two pigs having picture taken, green ground, marked "Germany" **$150**

Goblet

G.A.R., 1887, 21st Encampment **$100**

Mother, Ruby Thumbprint pattern **$35**

Mug, Souvenir of Blairsville, ruby stained, applied clear handle **$25**

Paperweight

Moses in Bulrushes, frosted center **$145**

Plymouth Rock, clear **$95**

Washington, George, round, frosted center **$295**

Pitcher, ironstone, shell molded oval form, wine-red ground, circular paneled sides enamel dec with landscape scenes, gilt trim, titled cartouche below spout "Senator Martin Wyckoff, of Warren County," imp mark "U Pottery," gilt wear, c1885, 10" h **$460**

Plate

Boston department stores, founders in border, blue transfer, white ground, Wedgwood, 9-3/4" d **$35**

Hogg, James Stephen, first native born governor of Texas, brown print, Vernon Kilns, marked "Designed for Daughters of the Republic of Texas" **$25**

Memorial, Garfield center, clear pressed glass, 10" d **$75**

Oklahoma, Agricultural and Mechanical College, Vernon Kilns, marked "Designed especially for Creech's Stillwater, Oklahoma" **$32**

Plymouth Rock, Plymouth, Massachusetts, brown and white, mkd "Old English Staffordshire Ware, Made in England, (Jonroth mark) (Adams mark) Imported Exclusively for Plymouth Rock Gift Shop, Plymouth, Mass" **$25**

Remember the *Maine*, Spanish-American war, c1900, 8-1/2" d **$240**

Sulphur Springs, Delaware, OH, light blue and black transfer, Staffordshire, New York retailer's label, chip on table ring, 10-1/2" d **$200**

Washington, Bellingham, green print, Vernon Kilns **$60**

Tile, Detroit Women's League, multicolored irid glass, 4" d **$135**

Tumbler, etched

Lord's Prayer **$15**

Niagara Falls, Prospect Point, gold rim **$20**

SOUVENIR AND COMMEMORATIVE SPOONS

History: Souvenir and commemorative spoons have been issued for hundreds of years. Early American silversmiths engraved presentation spoons to honor historical personages or mark key events.

In 1881, Myron Kinsley patented a Niagara Falls spoon, and in 1884, Michael Gibney patented a new flatware design. M. W. Galt, Washington, D.C., issued commemorative spoons for George and Martha Washington in 1889. From these beginnings, a collecting craze for souvenir and commemorative spoons developed in the late 19th and early 20th centuries.

Basiwgstoke, red, blue, and orange enameled shield, 5" l **$15**

Boulder, CO, name in bowl, Indian head handle **$40**

B. P. O. E. Elks #896, marked "Reed & Barton Klitzner RI," silverplate, 4-1/2" l **$15**

Cawston Ostrich Farms, marked "Sterling," 3-1/4" l **$15**

Denver, Colorado, sterling, gold washed bowl, acid etched pack mule, stem-end topped with winch with handle that turns, applied pick and shovel, stem entwined with rope, ending in bucket, opposed by modeled rock, 1 troy oz, late 19th C **$85**

Fort Dearborn, marked "Sterling, Hyman Berg," 1803-1857, 6" l **$20**

Golden Gate Bridge, San Francisco, California, marked "Holland 90" and hallmark, 5" l **$15**

Lancaster, city name engraved in bowl, sterling **$30**

Memorial Arch, Brooklyn, New York, round oak stove **$40**

Palm Springs, Aerial Tramway, SP, John Brown, marked "Antico" **$100**

Philadelphia, Independence Hall in bowl, SS **$45**

Prophet, veiled **$135**

Richmond, MO, SS **$30**

Royal Canadian Mounted Police, "Victoria, British Columbia" in bowl, marked "Made in Holland," 4-1/2" l **$30**

Stratford on Avon, yellow enameled shield, mkd "EPNS," 3-5/8" l **$15**

St. Paul, The Tower, Houses of Parliament, West Minister, each marked "L. E. P. A1" on back, set of four in orig box **$42**

Thousand Islands, fish handle, engraved bowl, SS, Watson **$45**

Vista House, Columbia River, Oregon, detailed handle, marked "Sterling" **$32**

SPORTS COLLECTIBLES

History: People have been saving sports-related equipment since the inception of sports. Some was passed down from generation to generation for reuse; the rest was stored in dark spaces in closets, attics, and basements.

Two key trends brought collectors' attention to sports collectibles. First, decorators began using old sports items, especially in restaurant decor. Second, collectors began to discover the thrill of owning the "real" thing. Sports collectibles are more acces-sible than ever before because of on-line auctions and several houses that dedicate themselves to that segment of the hobby. Provenance is extremely important when investing in high-ticket sports collectibles. Being able to know the history of the object may greatly enhance the value, with a premium paid for items secured from the player or directly from their estate.

Additional Resources:

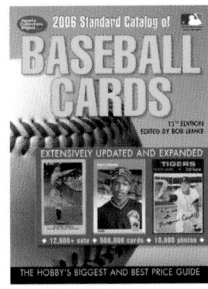

2006 Standard Catalog of Baseball Cards, by Bob Lemke, ed., Krause Publications, Iola, WI.

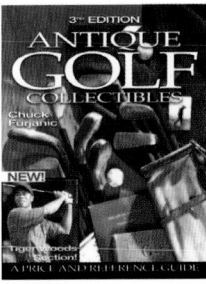

Antique Golf Collectibles, 3rd Ed., by Chuch Furjanic, Krause Publications, Iola, WI.

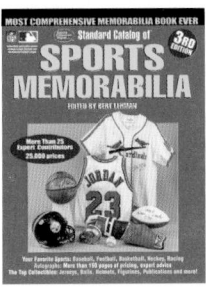

Standard Catalog of ® Sports Memora-bilia, 3rd Ed., by Bert Lehman, ed., Krause Publications, Iola, WI.

Baseball

Annual, *Official Baseball Annual,* Fawcett, color action photo of Los Angeles Dodgers Don Drysdale on cov, 1963 .... **$10**

Autograph

Brett, George, magazine page with full color photo in Kansas City Royals uniform, sgd on shoulder, c1980, 8" x 10-3/4" **$20**

Carew, Rod, four page folio segment from June 29, 1974 issue of Sporting News, bold signature, 11-1/2" x 14-1/2" **$30**

Coveleski, Stanley, Hall of Fame post-card, published for National Baseball Museum, Cooperstown, NY, showing player's bronze plaque, 1969, 3-1/2" x 5-1/2" **$30**

Spahn, Walter, glossy full-color photo, Milwaukee pitcher's uniform, c1953, 8" x 10" **$25**

Bank, All-Stars, bobbing head, painted composition figure, orig string tag, 1960s, 6-1/2" h **$50**

Baseball, autographed, sgd by members of team

American League All-Star Team, Foxx, Gehrig, DiMaggio, 1937 .... **$7,000**

Boston, Herman, Yastrzemski, 1964 .... **$250**

National League All-Star Team, Musial, 1955 .... **$600**

New York, Stengel, Kubek, Maris, Howard, Berra, Ford, 1960 .... **$700**

Oakland, Martin, Henderson, 1981 .... **$200**

Baseball cap, autographed, game used

Bench, Johnny, 1970s Cincinnati Reds **$450**

Jackson, Bo, 1994 California Angels **$95**

Walker, Larry, 1995 Colorado Rockies **$165**

Baseball card, issued by Cracker Jack, Ty Cobb, Detroit Tigers Hall of Fame **$6,400**

Baseball glove

Ashburn, Richie **$45**

Berra, Yogi **$100**

Reese, Pee Wee **$65**

Bobbing head

New York, sq white base, professionally restored, 1961-63, 6-1/2" h **$65**

Painted composition figure, blue cap, painted white initial "M," white shirt trimmed in blue, gold tan trousers, holding yellow bat, mkd "Made In Japan," 3" x 3-1/2" x 6" orig box, 5-1/2" h **$40**

Premier baseball card/gum ball arcade vending machine, made by Oak Mfg, co, inc., red painted cast iron, 1950s, 13" x 13", **$575.**
Photo courtesy of Sloans & Kenyon Auctioneers and Appraisers.

Dixie picture, Bob Feller, Cleveland Indians, four additional action photos on back, plus biography, 8" x 10" photo **$90**

Emblem, white plastic, on orig card
Pirates, black accents, c1950, 4" h
.... **$12**
Reds, red accents, c1950, 4" h
.... **$12**

Exhibit card, sepia tone, facsimile signature
Drysdale, Don, 3-3/8" x 5-3/8"
.... **$25**
Killebrew, Harmon, 3-3/8" x 5-3/8"
.... **$20**
Mayes, Willie, 3-3/8" x 5-3/8" **$35**
Mazeroski, Bill, 3-3/8" x 5-3/8"
.... **$15**

Hartland figure, Roger Maris, 25th anniversary, orig 4" x 6" x 8-1/2" box, 7-1/2" h.. **$70**

Lunch box
Boston Red Sox, Ardee, vinyl, 1960s, 6-1/2" x 8-1/2" x 3-1/2" **$50**
Toronto Blue Jay's, Canadian issue, blue vinyl, late 1980s, 7" x 8-1/2" x 4".. **$25**

Magazine
Baseball Monthly, Vol. 1, #4, June 1962.. **$5**

Complete Baseball Magazine, Sports Life editors, summer issue, 1950
.... **$10**
Life, Aug. 1, black and white cover with close-up photo of Joe DiMaggio, 1949.................................. **$15**
Men Your Goodyear Dealer's Magazine, Mickey Mantle cover, 1957
.... **$45**

Pennant, felt
Brooklyn Dodgers, Ebbert Field, blue, 1940s **$190**
Cooperstown, blue, multicolored Braves style Indian head, 1940s
.... **$75**
Minnesota Twins A. L. Champs World Series, photo, 1965 .... **$125**
New York Yankees, photo "M&M Boys Last Year Together!," 1966
.... **$95**

Photograph, black and white stiff paper, Whiz Kids of 1950, The Fightin' Phillies, shows time lined up on field, holding hats and gloves, newspaper supplement, 10" x 35".................. **$90**

Pinback button
Go-Go Mets, dark orange on navy blue, image of youthful batter in oversized batting helmet, late 1960s, 3-1/2" d **$24**

Minnesota Twins, Western Division Champions, America League, 1987, red, white, and blue, 3-1/2" d
.... **$12**
Ted Williams, black and white photo as youthful Boston Red Sox star, late 1930s, 1-3/4" d............................ **$40**
York White Roses, blue and white celluloid figural baseball suspending blue and white fabric ribbons with miniature plastic baseball, 1940s, 1-1/4" d **$15**

Plate, Base Ball, Caught on the Fly, center transfer print, white glazed ground, c1850, 7-1/4" d **$920**

Pocket tin, Yankee Boy Plug Cut, Scotten, Dillion Co., tin litho, little boy slugger on shield shape, red and white check background, 4-1/8" x 3-1/2" x 1-1/8".. **$625**

Poster, 1930 Chicago Cubs, photo and facsimile signature of each player, adv Blue Ribbon Malt Co., contemporary frame, 11-1/2" x 38" **$250**

Presentation bat, red painted bat, polychrome Odd Fellows symbols, incised in gold "West Lynn 15-3 Kearsarge West Lynn 23 East Lynn 5 Presented by H. W. Eastham, July 21, 1900, Aug. 18, 1900," (MA), with stand, 34" l **$4,025**

Program
All-Star, Philadelphia, 1943 .... **$495**
All-Star, St. Louis, 1948.............. **$325**
New York Yankees, 1937............ **$195**
New York Yankees, 1951 .... **$195**
World Series, 1950, at Philadelphia
.... **$250**

Roster sheet, Pirates, 1927........ **$175**

Score counter, six diecut openings, red and blue printing on white, blank back, c1890, 2" x 3-1/4" cardboard panels **$25**

Tab
Jerome "Dizzy" Dean, St. Louis Cards
.... **$20**
Wally Berger, New York Giants
.... **$15**

Window sign, Mike Higgins Savvy Skipper of the Red Sox, *Saturday Evening Post,* July 21, 1956, 10" x 13-1/2"...................................... **$30**

Yearbook
Famous Slugger, published by Hillerich & Bradsby Co., make of Louisville Slugger bats, 1970, 4-1/2" x 6-1/2" **$10**
Los Angeles Dodgers, 1968, 8-1/2" x 11"... **$15**
Mets, 1965, 8-1/2" x 11" **$20**

Basketball

Autograph, basketball

Archibald, Nate **$100**

Bird, Larry **$200**

Bradley, Bill **$150**

O'Brien, Larry **$125**

Autograph, photograph

McGuire, Dick, 8" x 10" **$20**

Phillip, Andy, 8" x 10" **$20**

Thurmond, Nate, 8" x 10" **$24**

Bobbing head, Seattle Supersonics, painted composition, orig sticker: American Sports Sales Ltd., Made in Korea, late 1970s, 7" h **$25**

Magazine, *Sports Illustrated*, Feb. 1949, Ralph Beard, Kentucky cover **$95**

Pencil holder, high gloss ceramics, All American basketball dribbler, flesh-tone body parts, black hair and shoes, pale blue shirt inscribed "Champ," white shorts, brown basketball hollowed out for pencils, 6-1/2" h, 4-1/4" x 5-1/2" white base **$20**

Pin, Chicago Americans Tournament Championship, brass, 1935 .... **$75**

Program

Basketball Hall of Fame Commemoration Day Program, orig invitation, 1961 .... **$75**

NCAA Final Four Championship, Louisville, Kentucky, 1967 .... **$175**

World Series of Basketball, Harlem Globetrotters and College All-Americans, 1951 .... **$55**

Shoes, pr, game used, autographed

Drexler, Clyde, Avais **$225**

Sikma, Jack, Converse **$100**

Webber, Chris, Nikes **$550**

Souvenir book, *Los Angeles Lakers*, with two records, Jerry West and Elgin Baylor on action cover **$75**

Ticket

NBA Finals Boston Celtics at Los Angeles Lakers, 1963 .... **$95**

San Antonio Spurs ABA Phantom Playoff, 1975, unused **$15**

St. Louis Hawks at San Francisco Warriors, Dec. 17, 1963 .... **$50**

Yearbook

1961-62, Boston Celtics **$150**

1965-66, Boston Celtics **$85**

1969-70, Milwaukee Bucks **$40**

Boxing

Autograph

Baer, Max, 8" x 10" photo **$180**

Foreman, George, upper torso photo in muscular pose, Humble, TX, post office box address, black ink signature, mailed fold creases, 8-1/2" x 11" letterhead **$35**

Badge, Larry Holmes, black and white photo, red and black inscriptions, 1979 copyright Don King Productions, 4" d **$25**

Boxing gloves, 35 readable autographs **$380**

Cabinet card

Corbett, James F., dressed in suit, 4" x 6" **$375**

Ryan, Paddy, full boxing post, dark brown border, 4" x 6" **$395**

Sullivan, John L., dark brown border, "John L. Sullivan, Champion of the World," 4" x 6" **$495**

Dinner program, Boxing Writers Association, January 1968, 6-1/4" x 9" **$20**

Figure, carved fruitwood, fully carved figure throwing right jab, standing on continuation of trunk with tree bark intact, attributed to New Hampshire, c1900, 8" w, 20-1/4" h **$1,955**

Letterhead, white stationery, printed in blue on upper quarter for "International Boxing Club," bluetone photos of Rocky Marcianio-Champion, Joe Walcott-Challenger, James D. Norris-President, designates presentation "For the Heavyweight Championship of the world" schedule for Chicago Stadium, Friday, April 10 (1953), unused, 8-1/2" x 11" **$25**

Magazine

Foreman-Ali Zaire Fight, 52 pgs, Oct. 30, 1974, 8-1/2" x 11" l **$35**

The Ring, cover photo of Emile Griffith, March, 1965, 8-1/4" x 11" **$10**

Plaque, carved pine, polychrome, figure of John L. Sullivan carved in relief against landscape in horseshoe-form, inscribed at base "J. L. Sullivan," old darkened crackled painted surface, New York, late 19th C, 12-1/2" w, 16-3/4" h **$2,185**

Football

Autograph, football

Bergey, Bill **$70**

Ditka, Mike **$125**

Flaherty, Ray **$150**

Green, Roy **$70**

Long, Howie **$75**

Autograph, helmet

Aikman, Troy, Dallas Cowboys **$265**

Dawson, Len, Kansas City Chiefs **$250**

Elway, John, Denver Broncos **$275**

Autograph, photograph,

Bradshaw, Terry, 8" x 10" **$40**

Brown, Jim, 8" x 10" **$30**

Thomas, Thurman, 8" x 10" **$25**

Bank, high gloss black finish ceramic, helmet, orange stripes, white face, orange and black decal "Northampton Area Senior High School/Konkreet Kids," white sponsor decal "First National Bank of Bath," c1960, 4-1/2" h **$20**

Cartoon, 14" x 19" orig sgd art in black ink and pencil by cartoonist Williard Mullin, blue pencil title "Theory vs Practice," blindfolded "All American Selector" attempting to select ideal college team and geographically correct, large center character "Pro Draft" who simply points to smiling footballer while deciding "Me For You," 1950s, 15" x 22" white art sheet **$125**

Drinking glass, National Football Clinic Banquet, Atlantic City, painted football passer, March 23-26, names of Dr. Harry G. Scott, Executive Director and Kenneth McFarland, banquet speaker, reverse lists staff of 14 university football coaches, 6-1/4" h, 3" d **$12**

Media guide, Philadelphia Stars, 1984, 5" x 7-1/2" paperback **$15**

Pennant, felt, A.F.L.

Boston Patriots, white on red, multi-colored Patriot **$75**

Buffalo Bills, white on blue, pink buffaloes **$95**

Houston Oilers, white on light blue **$75**

Pinback button

Gustavus Homecoming, gold and black, cartoon art of Ole and Gus wearing football helmets while tugging at worm between them, 1929 .... **$15**

Hail to Pitt, blue on yellow, cartoon of football player using coal bucket to catch football, inscribed "Scuttle The Lions," c1940 .... **$15**

Philadelphia Eagles, green on white cello, orange suspended miniature football charm, c1950 .... **$15**

Program

Army vs. Duke, at the Polo Grounds, 1946 .... **$40**

Green Bay Packers, 1960 .... **$30**

Cane, wood, etched in ink on top with face of boxer, shaft carved and inked with busts of boxers including J. J. Jeffries (with Champion ribbon), Bob Fitzsimmons, Young Corbett, J. Britt, Bennie Yanger, Eddie Hanlon, Harry Forges, and Jack O'Keefe, background of sparring fighters and training equipment, 1" replaced brass ferrule, c1900, 1-1/4" h x 1-1/2" d knob handle, 34-1/4" l, **$1,800.**

Photo courtesy of Henry A. Taron.

Sports, golf trophy, metal, engraved "NYC," marble base, early 20th C, 6-1/2" h, **$125.**

Photo courtesy of David Rago Auctions, Inc.

Heisman Trophy, John David Crow, 1957 .... **$30**

Rose Bowl, USC vs. Ohio State, 1974 .... **$40**

Soda bottle or can, unopened

Baltimore Colts, RC Cola, late 1970s **$2**

Penn State Championship Season 1986, unopened Coke bottle, 9-1/2" h **$15**

Golf

Autograph, photo, sgd, Tiger Woods **$60**

Drinking glass, USGA Tournament, set of four, clear glass, green inscription "U.S.G.A 56th Open Championship" and "Oak Hill Country Club-Rochester, NY," images of golfers at 18th hole in brown and white, 5" h **$25**

Golf club cane, known as "Sunday Stick," 3" l x 3-1/2" h handle fashioned as early driver, ivory foot held in place with four ebony pins, faux lead weight, marked "Addington" on top of handle, orig owner's initials, two ivory and one ebony separators, oak shaft, 7/8" burnished brass and iron ferrule, c1890, 37-1/2" l **$1,075**

Magazine, *American Golfer*, June 1932 .... **$10**

Noisemaker, litho tin, full-color image of male golfer, marked "Germany" on handle, 1930s, 2-3/4" d, 6-1/2" l **$35**

Print, Charles Crombie, *The Rules of Golf Illustrated*, 24 humorous lithographs of golfers in medieval clothes, London, 1905 .... **$1,265**

Program, Fort Worth Open Golf Championship, Glen Garden Country Club, Ft. Worth, Texas, 1945 ...... **$100**

Tournament badge

Henredon Classic, celluloid, 1987 .... **$12**

PGA Tour, diecut rigid plastic, 1999 .... **$7.50**

21st Bob Hope Desert Classic, Jan. 9-13, diecut rigid plastic, 1980 .... **$9.50**

Hockey

Autograph

Orr, Bobby, photograph, 8" x 10" **$50**

Smith, Clint, photograph, 8" x 10" **$12**

Thompson, Tiny, puck **$50**

Worsley, Gump, sgd 1968-69 Topps card **$15**

Hockey stick, game used, autographed

Beliveau, Jean, 1960s CCM, cracked **$700**

Cashman, Wayne, Sherwood, uncracked **$175**

LeBlanc, J. B., Koho, cracked **$50**

Jersey, game used, Wayne Gretzky, Rangers, autographed **$415**

Magazine, *Sport Revue*, Quebec publication, Feb 1956, Bert Olmstead, Hall of Fame cov **$15**

Program, Boston Bruins, Sports News, 1937-38 .... **$250**

Stick, game used, autographed

Bondra, Peter, Sherwood **$90**

Lindros, Eric, Bauer Supreme **$295**

Tobacco tin, Puck Tobacco, Canadian, tin litho, detailed image of two hockey players on both sides, 4" d, 3-1/4" h **$190**

Tournament badge, 4" d, celluloid, World Hockey Tournament, Canada, red, and white **$8.50**

Hunting

Badge, Western Cartridge Co., plant type, emb metal, pin back, 1-3/4" x 1-3/8" **$100**

Book, *The World of the White-Tailed Deer*, Leonard Lee Rue III, J. B. Lippencott, 134 pgs, black and white illus, dj, 1962 .... **$15**

Box, Peters High Velocity, two-pc cardboard shot gun shells, multicolored graphics, 25 16-gauge shells **$250**

Calendar top, Winchester, paper, man atop rock ledge, hunting rams, artist sgd "Philip R. Goodwin," metal top rim, 20" x 14" **$125**

Manual, *How To Be A Crack Shot*, Remington/Dupont, June 1936 .... **$20**

Print

"Life in the Woods-The Hunters Camp," published by Lyon & Co., printed by J. Rau, NY, five gentlemen in camp, two more fishing in lake, framed, some foxing, center line burn, water stains in borders, 22" x 28" **$150**

"Rabbit Catching-The Trap Sprung," lithographed by Currier and Ives, NY, two boys approaching box trap, winter setting, framed, some toning, water stains at borders, 10" x 13" **$495**

Sign

Paul Jones Whiskey, game-hunting scene, orig gold gilt frame, 43" x 57" $750

Remington UMC, diecut cardboard Oversized shell next to box of ammunition, 15" x 14"..................$200

Nitro Club Shells, English Setter atop pile of Remington Shotgun Shells, 15-1/2" x 9" $100

L. C. Smith Guns, paper, two setters pointing to prey, 14" x 14-3/4" $1,200

Winchester, diecut, cardboard, stand-up, Indian Chief with Winchester shotgun in one hand, additional barrels in other hand, 24" x 60" $200

Trophy, silverplate teapot, engraved in German "2nd Prize of the First Shooting Festival in Cincinnati held the 29th and 30th of September 1867 and won by Julius Lang," Eastlake style, some denting, 10-1/2" h.............$295

Watch fob, Savage Revolver, figural, metal..$110

Olympics

Badge

Enamel on brass, Winter Olympics, Albertville, red and blue on white, colored Olympic rings, 1-3/4" x 2-1/4"....................................$25

Red, white, and blue celluloid, 1966 Central America Games, 4" d ..$10

Brochure, Official Pictorial Souvenir, issued by organizing committee, Los Angeles, stiff paper covers, lightly emb soft green cover design with silver and gold accents, 64 black and white pages, 1932, 9-1/4" x 12-1/2" $40

Cartoon, white art sheet centered by 6-1/4" x 12" orig art cartoon in black ink by Carl Hubenthal, Los Angeles Examiner, art and caption relate to first ever 7' high jump in Olympic trials by US athlete Charlie Dumas, 1956, 8-1/2" x 12-1/2" $45

Key ring tag, metal, finished in pewter silver luster finish, official emblem for 1980 Lake Placid Winter Olympics, 2" x 2-1/2"............................$15

Photo album, 1932 Summer Olympics hosted in Los Angeles, hardcover, printed in Germany, 142 pgs of mounted photos, German text with results and statistics, orig dj, 10" x 12-1/2"....................................$95

Framed stained and leaded glass window decorated with flowers and leaves, blue and red jewels, 24" x 52", **$350.**
Photo courtesy of Joy Luke.

Poster, Lake Placid Winter Olympics, full color, copyright 1978 Amy Schneider, tightly curled, 22" x 30" $20

STAINED AND/OR LEADED GLASS PANELS

History: American architects in the second half of the 19th century and the early 20th century used stained- and leaded-glass panels as a chief decorative element. Skilled glass craftsmen assembled the designs, the best known being Louis C. Tiffany.

The panels are held together with soft lead cames or copper wraps. When purchasing a panel, protect your investment by checking the lead and making any necessary repairs.

Leaded

Door, bench leaded, clear glass, elongated with ornate part beveled glass inserts, 28" w, 78" h..................$1,450

Fire screen, leaded glass, tripartite, central square panel and two narrow side panels set with multicolored textured and bull's eye glass pieces, brass surround, griffin-form trestle feet, Renaissance Revival, late 19th/early 20th C, 32-3/4" h $1,100

Panel, rect, rippled, and opaque glass, turquoise, white, and avocado, clear glass ground, stylized flowering plant motif, six panels, c1910, 96" h, 20" w $6,000

Sketch for leaded glass window

Charcoal on paper, The Crucifixion, America, c1920, 26" d.............$170

Watercolor, garden scene, mother and child before Christ figure, sgd on mat "Louis Comfort Tiffany," 6-3/4" x 4-1/2"....................................$1,725

Triptych, twining grapevines and grape clusters, green slag, textured purple and brown glass, amber border segments, textured colorless glass

Stained and leaded glass panel, water lilies, framed, 23-3/4" x 36", **$250.**
Photo courtesy of Joy Luke Auctions.

background, wood frame, cracks, 34-3/4" h, 17-3/4" w $1,380

Window

Crossed American flag and other fanciful flag, 44" x 33" $875

Henry Belcher, mosaic and chunk jewels, orig frame, 29" h, 93" l $8,400

Outside, bull's eye, beaded gilt-metal frame, octagonal surround, central beveled colorless glass octagon, surrounded by beveled diamonds, price for pr, 17-3/4" d int., 19-1/4" d $1,035

Prairie School, zinc caming, clear, white, green, and violet slag glass, stylized lilies and tulips, set of five, few minor cracks in glass, 36" h, 16-1/4" d $4,250

Stained

Panel

Red, white, green, pink, and blue floral design, two layers of striated and fractured glass, green patinated bronze frame, stamped "Tiffany Studios New York" pr, 24" x 14" ..$2,400

Richard the Lion-Hearted on horseback, 1883, 26" x 21"..............$675

Transom window, arched form, amber, green, and red, later walnut frame, brass plaque "Illinois Traction System Car Number 523," 59" x 17" $260

Window

Fruit and flower design, layered glass in ewer and some fruit, waffle texture ribbon, from west side Buffalo, New York, c1885 home, 36" w, 22" h $4,200

Over entry door type, blue and orange shield and geometric design, c1920, 61" l, 61-1/2" h..........................$490

Rect, arched top, brown glass border, gold glass panels, central stain pained medallion of bush of classical male, sgd "Louis Shuys," scrolled leaf surround, late 19th/early 20th C, 35-1/8" w, 15-1/2" h............$425

Poodle, black, **$75;** *and tan and white cow,* **$45.**

Steiff teddy bear, dark brown mohair, brown glass eyes, beige shaved muzzle, black floss nose and mouth, paws face down, beige shavd feet, beige felt pads on bottom of feet and paws, red leather collar with metal studs and two Steiff button, excelsior stuffed, button in left ear, paper chest tag, bare areas on tops of feet, aged leather collar and tag, hole in left foot pad, 10", **$1,250.**
Photo courtesy of McMasters Harris Auction Co.

Steiff dog, sitting, mohair, brown glass eyes, black floss nose and mouth, three floss claws on feet, excelsior stuffed, Steiff button left ear tip, 8", **$500.**
Photo courtesy of McMasters Harris Auction Co.

STEIFF

History: Margarete Steiff, GmbH, established in Germany in 1880, is known for very fine-quality stuffed animals and dolls, as well as other beautifully made collectible toys. It is still in business, and its products are highly respected.

The company's first products were wool-felt elephants made by Margaret Steiff. In a few years, the animal line was expanded to include a donkey, horse, pig, and camel.

By 1903, the company also was producing a jointed mohair teddy bear, whose production dramatically increased to more than 970,000 units in 1907. Margarete's nephews took over the company at this point.

Newly designed animals were added: Molly and Bully, the dogs, and Fluffy, the cat. Pull toys and kites also were produced, as well as larger animals on which children could ride or play.

Marks: The bear's-head label became the symbol for the firm in about 1907, and the famous "Button in the Ear" round, metal trademark was added.

Notes: Become familiar with genuine Steiff products before purchasing an antique stuffed animal. Plush in old Steiff animals was mohair; trimmings usually were felt or velvet. Unscrupulous individuals have attached the familiar Steiff metal button to animals that are not Steiff.

Bear
Blond mohair
Rattle, no button, black shoe button eyes, fully jointed, embroidered nose and mouth, overall wear, stains, rip on arm, working rattle, excelsior stuffing, no pad style, c1910, 5" h **$415**

Script ear button, glass eyes, embroidered nose, mouth, claws excelsior stuffed, fully jointed, felt feet pads have scattered moth holes, break at sides, mid-19th C, 30" h **$1,955**

Cinnamon, mohair, swivel head, black shoe button eyes, cotton floss stitched nose with vertical stitching, stitched mouth, center seam body and head, no button in earl rig felt pads on paws, 20" h **$9,500**

Golden mohair
Ear button, black embroidered nose and claws, mouth missing, black shoe button eyes, squeaker, fully jointed body, excelsior stuffing, original felt pads, one-inch fabric tear right front arm joint, very minor fur loss, overall soil, c1905, 14" h **$1,955**

One Hundredth Anniversary Bear, ear button, fully jointed, plastic eyes, black embroidered nose, mouth, and claws, peach felt pads, excelsior stuffing, certificate no. 3934, orig box, 17" h **$200**

Shoe button eyes, embroidered nose, mouth, and claws, fully jointed, excelsior stuffing, no pad arms, moth damage to foot pads, c1915, 8-1/2" h **$1,380**

Light apricot mohair, ear button, fully jointed, shoe button eyes, embroidered nose, mouth, and claws, excelsior stuffing, felt pads, fur loss, lower back and back of legs, slight moth damage on pads, c1905, 12-1/2" h **$1,610**

Light golden mohair, underscored ear button, black shoe button eyes, center seam, black embroidered nose, mouth, and claws, fully jointed, tan felt pads, holes in hand pads, c1905, 14" h **$4,890**

Beaver, Nagy, mohair, chest tag, post WWII, 6" l **$95**

Bison, mohair, ear button, chest tag, post WWII, 9-1/2" l **$200**

Boxer, beige mohair coat, black trim, glass eyes, leather collar marked "Steiff," head turns, minor wear, straw stuffing, 16-1/2" l, 15-1/2" h **$165**

Boxer puppy, paper label "Daly," 4-1/4" h................................... **$135**

Cat, pull toy, white mohair coat, gray stripes, glass eyes, worn pink ribbon with bell, pink felt ear linings, button, cast iron wheels, 14" l **$1,980**

Cocker spaniel, sitting, glass eyes, ear button, chest tag, post WWII, 5-3/4" h................................ **$125**

Cocker spaniel puppy, button, 4-3/4" h................................ **$90**

Dalmatian puppy, paper label "Sarras," 4-1/4" h.............................. **$145**

Dog, pull toy, orange and white mohair coat, glass eyes, steel frame, cast iron wheels, one ear missing, button in remaining ear, voice box does not work, 15-1/2" l, 14" h.................. **$280**

Frog, velveteen, glass eyes, green, sitting, button and chest tag, 3-3/4" l **$125**

Goat, ear button, 6-1/2" h............**$150**

Gussy, white and black kitten, glass eyes, ear button, chest tag, post WWII, 6-1/2" l....................**$125**

Horse on wheels, ear button, glass eyes, white and brown, wear and breaks to fabric, on solid metal wheels, non-functioning pull-ring, c1930, 21" l, 17" h.....................**$215**

Kangaroo and joey, both with glass eyes, embroidered nose, and mouth, ear button and tag, 20-3/4" h mohair mother, 4" h velveteen baby **$395**

Koala, glass eyes, ear button, chest tag, post WWII, 7-1/2" h...................**$135**

Lion, pull toy, worn gold mohair coat, glass eyes, worn streaked mane incomplete, no tail, ring pull voice box, steel frame, sheet metal wheels with white rubber treads marked "Steiff," 21" l, 18" h **$500**

Monkey, Jocko, C.8+, 1950s, 7-1/2" h **$100**

Owl, Wittie, glass eyes, ear button, chest tag, post WWII, 4-1/2" h **$95**

Parakeet, Hansi, bright lime green and yellow, airbrushed black details, plastic eyes, button tag, chest tag, plastic beak and feet, 6-1/2" h **$115**

Rabbit, unmarked, wear, 9-1/2" h **$220**

Soldier, slight moth damage, hat and equipment missing, c1913, 14" h **$460**

Turtle, Slo, plastic shell, glass eyes, ear button, chest tag, post WWII, 7" l **$85**

Walrus, Paddy, plastic tusk, glass eyes, ear button, chest tag, post WWII, 6-1/2" l **$145**

STEINS

History: Steins, mugs especially made to hold beer or ale, range in size from the smaller 3/10 and 1/4 liter to the larger 1, 1-1/2, 2, 3, 4, and 5 liters, and in rare cases to 8 liters. A liter is 1.05 liquid quarts.

Master steins or pouring steins hold three to five liters and are called krugs. Most steins are fitted with a metal-hinged lid with thumb lift. The earthenware character-type steins usually are German in origin.

Fox, well loved and played-with condition, $275.

Character

Beethoven, half liter, porcelain, lire on side of body and on porcelain inlaid lid, E. Bohne & Sohn........**$570**

Frederick III, in uniform, 1/2 liter, porcelain, porcelain lid, Schierholz, chips on lid repaired, int. color yellowing..................................**$1,735**

Monk, 1/3 liter, design by Frank Ringer, marked "J. Reinemann, Munchen" on underside of base, inlaid lid, 5" h **$580**

Pug dog, Mettlach, #2018, 1/2 liter, character, pug dog, inlaid lid...**$1,100**

Singing pig, 1/2 liter, porcelain, Schierholz, inlaid lid.....................**$580**

Skull, 1/3 liter, porcelain, large jaw, inlaid lid, E. Bohne & Sohn, pewter slightly bent **$550**

Faience

Thuringen, 1 liter, hp, floral design on front, purple trees on sides, pewter top rim and lid, pewter base ring, tight hairline on side, 18th C, 9-1/2" h **$1,155**

Glass

1 liter, blown, wedding type, hp floral design and verse, pewter lid with earlier date of 1779, pewter brass ring, c1850, 9-1/2" h............................**$925**

Amber, encased in fancy French pewter frame, ram's heads around stein, hinged top lid, 15-1/4" h, 6-1/2" d **$495**

Ivory, c1850-70

Battle scene, elaborately hand carved around entire body, scene with over 100 figures, silver top with repoussé fruit, figural knight finial, man in armor as figural handle, silver base,

with cherub dec, touch marks, discoloation to ivory, 11-1/2" **$6,700**

Hunting scene, elaborately hand carved four men on horseback, 15 dogs, ivory lid with various animals carved around border, man blowing trumpet with dog as 3-1/2" h finial, crowned bare-breasted woman figural handle, dog's head thumb lift, left arm and trumpet missing, 13-1/2" h **$11,550**

Porcelain and pottery

Delft, 1/2 liter, elaborate scene of two people playing lawn tennis, porcelain inlaid lid of sail boat, marked "Delft, Germany".............................**$1,390**

Meissen, 1 liter, hp, scene of three people in forest, floral design around sides, porcelain lid with berry finial and painted flowers, closed hinge, cross swords and "S" mark, strap repoured, c1820, 7" h **$3,100**

Mettlach

#1896, 1/4 liter, maiden on one side, cherub face on other, grape dec, pewter lift handle.....................**$350**

#2007, 1/2 liter, etched, black cat, inlaid lid................................**$660**

#2057, 1/2 liter, etched, festive dancing scene, inlaid lid.................**$325**

#2580, 1/2 liter, etched, Die Kannenburg, conical inlay lid, knight in castle...................................**$695**

#2755, 1/4 liter, cameo and etched, three scenes of people at table, Art Nouveau design between scenes, inlaid lid.................................**$560**

Salt glaze

Blue and brown accent of man and woman drinking at table, thread relief blue accented vine design on back, orig pewter lid, mold mark #6, 11-1/2" h **$180**

Pouring type, imp "Fort Edward Brew Co." along base with blue accents, relief and blue accented man with cane on one side, man and woman reading on opposite side, heavy orig pewter lid, mold mark #3, 11-1/2" h **$1,100**

Relief and blue accented man and woman drinking at table, thread relief blue accented vine design on back, orig pewter lid, gargoyle thumb lift, mold mark #6, 13-1/2" h **$150**

Unknown maker, 1/4 liter, transfer and enameled, color, Ulmer Splatz!, The Bird from the City of Ulm, pewter lid....................................**$115**

Regimental, 1/2 liter, porcelain

2 Schwer. Reit. Regt. Erzh. Fz, Ferd u. Osterr-Este Esk Landshut 1899-02, named to Friedrich Schmidt, two side scenes, lion thumb lift, old tear on lid repaired, minor scruffs, 11-1/2" h **$675**

11 Armee Corps, Mainz 1899, names to Res. Doring, two side scenes, plain thumb lift, strap tear repaired, lines in lithophane, 10" h **$485**

123 Grenadier, Ulm 1908-10, named to Grenadier Schindler, four side scenes, roster, bird thumb lift, open blister on int. base, finial missing **$550**

Wood and pewter, Daubenkrug

1/2 liter, pewter scene of deer, vines and leaves on sides, pewter handle and lid, some separations to pewter, c1820, 6-1/2" h **$925**

1/3 liter, Floral design on sides, oval with crown on front, pewter handle and lid, splints in pewter and wood, 18th C, 5-1/2" h **$1,270**

STEVENGRAPHS

History: Thomas Stevens of Coventry, England, first manufactured woven silk designs in 1854. His first bookmark was produced in 1862, followed by the first Stevengraphs, perhaps in 1874, but definitely by 1879 when they were shown at the York Exhibition. The first portrait Stevengraphs (of Disraeli and Gladstone) were produced in 1886, and the first postcards incorporating the woven silk panels in 1904. Stevens offered many other items with silk panels, including valentines, fans, pincushions, and needle cases.

Stevengraphs are miniature silk pictures, matted in cardboard, and usually having a trade announcement or label affixed to the reverse. Other companies, notably W. H. Grant of Coventry, copied Stevens' technique. Their efforts should not be confused with Stevengraphs.

Collectors in the U.S. favor the Stevengraphs with American-related views, such as "Signing of the Declaration of Independence," "Columbus Leaving Spain," and "Landing of Columbus." Sports-related Stevengraphs such as "The First Innings" (baseball), and "The First Set" (tennis) are also popular, as well as portraits of Buffalo Bill, President and Mrs. Cleveland, George Washington, and President Harrison.

Postcards with very fancy embossing around the aperture in the mount almost always have Stevens' name printed on them. The two most popular embossed postcard series in the U.S. are "Ships" and "Hands across the Sea." The latter set incorporates two crossed flags and two hands shaking. Seventeen flag combinations have been found, but only seven are common. These series generally are not printed with Stevens' name. Stevens also produced silks that were used in cards made by the Alpha Publishing Co.

Stevens' bookmarks are longer than they are wide, have mitered corners at the bottom, and are finished with a tassel. Many times his silks were used as the top or bottom half of regular bookmarks.

Marks: Thomas Stevens' name appears on the mat of the early Stevengraphs, directly under the silk panel. Many of the later portraits and the larger silks (produced initially for calendars) have no identification on the front of the mat other than the phrase "woven in pure silk" and have no label on the back.

Bookmarks originally had Stevens' name woven into the foldover at the top of the silk, but soon the identification was woven into the fold-under mitered corners. Almost every Stevens' bookmark has such identification, except the ones woven at the World's Columbian Exposition in Chicago, 1892 to 1893.

Note: Prices are for pieces in mint or close-to-mint condition.

Bookmarks

Assassination, Abraham Lincoln **$395**

Centennial, USA, 1776-1876, General George Washington, The Father of Our Country, The First in Peace, The First in War, The First in the Hearts of Our Countrymen!, few small stains **$125**

Forget-Me-Not, Godden #441 ....**$350**

I Wish You a Merry Christmas and a Happy New Year **$85**

Lord Have Mercy **$400**

Mail Coach **$225**

Mother and Child, evening prayers, 10-1/2" l, 2" w, 1-1/2" silk tassel **$400**

Mourning, Blessed Are They Who Mourn, 9-1/2" l, 2" w, 2" silk tassel **$450**

My Dear Father, red, green, white, and purple **$200**

Old Armchair **$150**

Prayer Book Set, five orig markers attached with small ivory button, cream-colored tape fastened to orig frame, Communion, Collect, Lesson I, Lesson II, Psalms, gold lettering, gold silk tassels, orig mount, c1880-85 ....**$3,400**

The Old Arm Chair, chair, full text, musical score, four color, 2" w, 11" l **$125**

The Star Spangled Banner, U.S. flag, full text and musical score of song, red tassel, seven color, no maker's mark, 2-1/2" w, 11" l **$185**

To One I Love, Love me little, love me long is the burden of my song, Love that is too hot and strong, burneth soon to waste, Still I would not have thee cold, not too backward or too bold; Love that lasteth till this old fadeth not in haste....................**$175**

Postcard

RMS Arabic, Hands Across the Sea **$465**

RMS Elmina **$225**

RMS Franconia **$225**

RMS Iverina **$215**

USMS Philadelphia **$225**

Stevengraph

Betsy Making the First United States Flag, Anderson Bros., Paterson, New Jersey, 5" x 8-1/2" **$80**

Buffalo Bill, Nate Salsbury, Indian Chief, orig mat and frame, 8" x 7" **$500**

Chateau Frontenac Hotel, Quebec, silver filigree frame **$95**

Coventry, 7-1/4" x 13", framed ...**$100**

Death of Nelson, 7-1/4" x 2-1/2" **$200**

Declaration of Independence **$375**

For Life or Death, fire engine rushing to burning house, orig mat and frame **$350**

Good Old Days, Royal Mail Coach, orig frame, 5-3/4" h, 8-1/2" l, ...**$200**

Stevengraph, Landing of Columbus, framed, **$350.**

Kenilworth Castle, 7-1/4" x 13" framed **$120**
Landing of Columbus **$350**
President Cleveland **$365**
Oxford, Cambridge, Are You Ready, orig frame, 5-3/4" h, 8-1/2" l **$300**
The Water Jump **$195**

STRING HOLDERS

History: The string holder developed as a useful tool to assist the merchant or manufacturer who needed tangle-free string or twine to tie packages. The early holders were made of cast iron, with some patents dating to the 1860s.

When the string holder moved into the household, lighter and more attractive forms developed, many made of chalkware. The string holder remained a key kitchen element until the early 1950s.

Reproduction Alert. As a result of the growing collector interest in string holders, some unscrupulous individuals are hollowing out the backs of 1950s figural-head wall plaques, drilling a hole through the mouth, and passing them off as string holders. A chef, Chinese man, Chinese woman, Indian, masked man, masked woman, and Siamese face are altered forms already found on the market.

Figural wall lamps from the 1950s and 1960s also are being altered. When the lamp hardware is removed, the base can be easily altered. Two forms that have been discovered are a pineapple face and an apple face, both lamp-base conversions.

Advertising

Chase & Sanborn's Coffee, tin, 13-3/4" x 10-1/4" sign, 4" d wire basket string holder insert, hanging chain **$825**
Dutch Boy Paints, diecut tin, Dutch Boy painting door frame, hanging bucket string holder, American Art Sign Co., 13-3/4" x 30" **$2,000**
Es-Ki-Mo Rubbers, tin, cutout center holds string spool, hanging boot moves up and down on sign, 17" x 19-3/4" h **$2,500**
Heinz, diecut tin, pickle, hanging, "57 Varieties," 17" x 14" **$1,650**

Figural

Ball of string, cast iron, figural, hinged, 6-1/2" x 5" h **$100**
Black man and woman, chalkware, matched pair **$275**
Bonzo, blue, chalkware, 6-1/2" h **$185**
Boy, top hat and pipe, chalkware, 9" h **$125**
Bride, ceramic, marked "Made in Japan," 6-1/4" h **$145**
Carrots, chalkware, 10" h **$225**
Cat, red rose on top of face, green bow under chin, chalkware **$165**
Chef, multicolored, chalkware, 7-1/4" h **$165**
Chipmunk, ceramic, 5-1/8" h **$135**
Dog, chalkware, 7" h **$155**
Dutch girl, chalkware, 7" h **$100**
Gourd, green, chalkware, 7-1/2" h **$135**
Indian, chalkware, 10-1/4" h **$295**
Jester, chalkware, 7-1/4" h..........**$195**
Mammy, yellow blouse, blue apron, scissors in pocket, chalkware, 6-1/2" h **$385**
Mammy, white dress, ceramic, 6-1/2" h **$225**
Parrot, chalkware, 9-1/4" h **$235**
Pineapple, face, chalkware, 7" h **$165**
Porter, chalkware, 6-1/2" h **$220**
Rose, red, green leaves, chalkware, 8" h **$175**
Senorita, chalkware, 8" h **$275**
Shirley Temple, chalkware, 6-1/4" w, 6-3/4" h **$395**
Strawberry, chalkware, 6-1/2" h **$115**

Terrier, chalkware, gray and white, 8-1/2" h **$195**
Woody Woodpecker, chalkware, copyright Walter Lantz, 9-1/2" h **$345**

SWORDS

History: The first swords used in America came from Europe. The chief cities for sword manufacturing were Solingen in Germany, Klingenthal in France, and Hounslow and Shotley Bridge in England. Among the American importers of these foreign blades was Horstmann, whose name is found on many military weapons.

New England and Philadelphia were the early centers for American sword manufacturing. By the Franco-Prussian War, the Ames Manufacturing Company of Chicopee, Massachusetts, was exporting American swords to Europe.

Sword collectors concentrate on a variety of styles: commissioned vs. non-commissioned officers' swords, presentation swords, naval weapons, and from a specific military branch, such as cavalry or infantry. The type of sword helped identify a person's military rank and, depending on how he had it customized, his personality as well.

Following the invention of repeating firearms in the mid-19th century, the sword lost its functional importance as a combat weapon and became a military dress accessory.

Note: Condition is key to determining value.

Additional Resources:

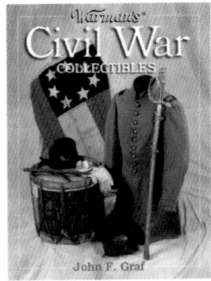

Warman's Civil War Collectibles, by John F. Graf, Krause Publications, Iola, WI.

Warman's® Civil War Collectibles Field Guide, by John F. Graf, Krause Publications, Iola, WI.

Sword

Artillery, Ames, 18-3/4" blade stamped with faint signature, U. S. and inspectors' markings, brass hilt with fish scale design, relief eagle, 25" l **$440**

Artillery officer's saber, 27-1/2" l curved blade, wide fuller, eagle head pommel and hilt show most of orig fire gilding, replaced wooden handle, early 19th C, 33" l **$330**

Calvary saber

Civil War, 35-3/4" blade stamped "Ames Mfg. Chicopee Mas, U.S.J.R. 1857," brass three-branch hilt with good patina, part of wire wrap and most of leather remains, iron scabbard, 41-1/2" l **$700**

Import blade with later date stamp of 1851, brass three branch hilt missing leather and wire wrapping, with scabbard, 41" l, 35-1/2" l **$220**

Model 1860, Emerson & Silver, Trenton, New Jersey, signature on ricasso, inspector's initials and 1863 on other side, brass three branch hilt with good patina, dark leather wrapped handle missing its wire,

browned steel scabbard, 42-3/4" **$825**

Stamped "U. S. 1862," brass three branch hilt with leather and wire wrapped handle, steel scabbard, 1840, 43" l **$660**

European

Broadsword, 31" blade, 1-1/2" wide blade with floral motif, leather covered wooden grip, brass guard, brown pommel cap, provenance descended from Gen George Meade family, early 19th C, some rusting, some dryness to leather, no scabbard, 36" l **$650**

Court type, 33-1/2" blade, thin triangular blade with floral etching, hand engraved steel cross guard, bone grip, provenance descended from Gen George Meade family, some rusting, loss to grip, no scabbard or chain guard, early 19th C, 38-1/2" l **$350**

French, artillery saber, brass single branch hilt, wire and leather cov handle, 32" l curved blade with engraving along top edge, steel scabbard, drag reshaped, 40" l **$350**

Indonesian, long blade carved with figures, scrolling leaf motifs and script, handle carved with figures, bulbous pommel, wooden scabbard, 35" l **$300**

Infantry officer, Model 1850, Ames, 30-1/4" l etched and engraved blade with "Chicopee, Mass" address, cast hilt wash with open work, leather scabbard with brass bands and drag, engraved "Lt. Geo. Trembley, 174th N.Y.S.I.," 36-1/4" l **$1,980**

Japanese

Koto period, No dachi type, mokume grain, choji temper line, single

mekugi ana, silver habaki, scabbard and hilt of negoro lacquer, 34" l blade **$5,600**

Wakizashi, orig scabbard, 20" l **$250**

Officer

Foot officer Model 1850, outstanding blade, 80% bright luster, etched with military motifs, eagle, and "U.S.," proper cast floral design with "U.S.," incorporated into the design, excellent scabbard, plum color steel, adorned with attractive, aged patinia brass mounts, pommel and guard with undisturbed patina, rayskin grip, blade signed on the ricasso, "PDL" **$1,950**

Import, Model 1832, artillery, French made, short sword with matching scabbard, blade marked with maker's cartouche **$395**

Import, 34" blade, sgd "Sargent & Son, Manufacturer to the East India Company," cast brass three-branch hilt with leaf designs, handle retains orig sharkskin and wire wrapping, 19th C, 40" l **$150**

Non-regulation, Civil War, 32" blade with fine etching including "U.S." eagle, and banner on opposite side, steel hilt with pierced "U.S." and detailed eagle with "E. Pluribus Unum," sharkskin cov grip with orig copper wire remaining, steel scabbard with minor pitting, 39" l **$1,200**

Russia, dress, Nicholas II, engraved in Cyrillic lettering on partial basket hilt, further engraved with device of nobility above monogram, leathered sheath, 38-1/4" h **$4,120**

Model 1830, militia officer's sword and scabbard, **$650-$800.**

Model 1850, Union, foot-officer's saber with metal scabbard, **$950-$1,800.**

Nashville Plow Works, Confederate officer's sword and scabbard, **$22,500-$25,000.**

Model 1840, light artillery saber (late model), **$750-$900.**

Model 1840, light artillery saber (early model), **$750-$950.**

TEA CADDIES

History: Tea once was a precious commodity and stored in special boxes or caddies. These containers were made to accommodate different teas and included a special cup for blending.

Around 1700, silver caddies appeared in England. Other materials, such as Sheffield plate, tin, wood, china, and pottery, also were used. Some tea caddies are very ornate.

Famille Rose, Mandarin palette, arched rect form, painted front, figures and pavilion reserve, c1780, 5-1/2" h **$550**

Ivory tusk, formed as section of tusk, silver-plated mountings, flat hinged top with foliate finial, engraved scrolls, beaded and waved rim bands, 19th C, 4-1/4" w, 5" h **$460**

Papier-mâché, Regency Chinoiserie-style, rect case with canted corners, ornately dec with figural reserves within flower blossoms bordered by wide bands of gilding, conforming hinged lid opening to int. fitted with two removable pewter tea canisters with dec chasing, 9-1/4" l, 6-3/4" d, 6" h **$950**

Quillwork, hexagonal, inlaid mahogany frames, blue and gilt quillwork panels covered with glass, floral vintage and leaf designs with crown and "MC 1804," two int. lidded compartments, replaced foil lining, English, 8-3/8" l, 4-3/4" d, 5-1/4" h **$2,750**

Silver, lobed hexagonal form, lobed lid with filigree finial, all-over Eastern style bird and foliate enamel dec, mounted with semi-precious stones, gilt int., approx 17 troy oz, Europe, late 19th/early 20th C, 7" h **$500**

Treen, ovoid, fruitwood, missing finial and internal hasp, late 18th C, 5" h **$1,400**

Wood

Burled veneer, satinwood banding, brass claw and ball feet and ring handles, lion face plates, paneled lid with raised medallion at center, divided interior with two cov containers and well for glass canister, restorations to one foot and back of lid, 12-1/4" w, 6-1/2" d, 7-3/4" h **$635**

Mahogany veneer, banded and string Rosewood, rect box, sloped sides,

Tea caddy, English, mahogany veneer, mahogany drawer fronts, hinged lid opening to interior top compartment, eight interior drawers, wallpaper interior, minor veneer bubbling, 11" w, 6-1/2" d, 12" h, **$750**.
Photo courtesy of Alderfer Auction Co.

inlaid hinged lid and front with brass scrollwork, sides with flush handles, int. fitted with two hinged and inlaid lidded wells flanking area for mixing bowl, int. of lid with velvet ruching, Georgian-style, late 19th C, 12-1/4" w, 6-1/4" d, 6-1/2" h **$450**

Rosewood, ivory escutcheon, sarcophagus shape, two lidded, foil-lined wells, colorless glass mixing bowl, interior of lid lined with ruched velvet, flattened ball feet, Regency, early 19th C, 12-3/8" w, 8" h **$400**

TEDDY BEARS

History: Originally thought of as "Teddy's Bears," in reference to President Theodore Roosevelt, these stuffed toys are believed to have originated in Germany. The first ones to be made in the United States were produced about 1902.

Most of the earliest teddy bears had humps on their backs, elongated muzzles, and jointed limbs. The fabric used was generally mohair; the eyes were either glass with pin backs or black shoe buttons. The stuffing was usually excelsior. Kapok (for softer bears) and wood-wool (for firmer bears) also were used as stuffing materials.

Quality older bears often have elongated limbs, sometimes with curved arms, oversized feet, and felt paws. Noses and mouths are black and embroidered onto the fabric.

The earliest teddy bears are believed to have been made by the original

Tea caddy, mahogany, oblong octagonal form, veneered body with line inlay and monogrammed cartouche, ebonized accents, minor losses to moldings, 6" l, 4" d, 5" h, **$225**.
Photo courtesy of Alderfer Auction Co.

Ideal Toy Corporation in America and by a German company, Margarete Steiff, GmbH. Bears made in the early 1900s by other companies can be difficult to identify because they were all similar in appearance and most identifying tags or labels were lost during childhood play.

Notes: Teddy bears are rapidly increasing as collectibles and their prices are rising proportionately. As in other fields, desirability should depend upon appeal, quality, uniqueness, and condition. One modern bear already has been firmly accepted as a valuable collectible among its antique counterparts: the Steiff teddy put out in 1980 for the company's 100th anniversary. This is a reproduction of that company's first teddy and has a special box, signed certificate, and numbered ear tag; 11,000 of these were sold worldwide.

Blond mohair, fully jointed, excelsior stuffing, black steel eyes, open composition mouth with full set of teeth, fiber wear around mouth and nose, some fur wear at seams, c1908, 11" h **$750**

Brown mohair, brown glass eyes, black cotton floss nose with horizontal stitching, floss mouth, hump on back, excelsior stuffing, brown leather collar with decorative metal studs, wheels mounted on metal housed in mohair covered legs, some mohair missing, 8" h **$325**

Ginger mohair, fully jointed, glass eyes, long arms, shaved muzzle, vertically stitched nose, felt pads, arrow ear button, Bing, excelsior stuffing, very slight fur loss, head disk broken through front of neck, c1907, 16" h **$2,300**

Teddy bear, Steiff, brown glass eyes, swivel head, jointed arms and legs, 17-1/2" h, **$600.**
Photo courtesy of Joy Luke Auctions

Ginger mohair, fully jointed, black steel eyes, black embroidered nose, mouth, and claws, beige felt pads, excelsior stuffing, American, patchy fur loss, felt damage, c1919, 16-1/2" h **$800**

Ginger mohair, fully jointed, black steel eyes, black embroidered nose, mouth, and claws, felt pads, Steiff, blank ear button, spotty fur loss, 10" h **$1,150**

Golden yellow mohair, fully jointed, glass eyes, brown still nose, embroidered mouth, excelsior stuffed, light fur loss, felt pads damaged, probably American, c1920, 16" h **$260**

Light yellow short mohair pile, fully jointed, excelsior stuffing, black steel eyes, embroidered nose, mouth, and claws, felt pads, Ideal, spotty fur and fiber loss, pr, c1905, 10" h ... **$920**

Saffron rayon plush, fully jointed, excelsior stuffing, glass eyes, embroidered nose, mouth, and claws, felt pads, some fur loss, and fiber damage, c1930, 13-1/2" h **$115**

Schuco, perfume, gold mohair, black shoe button eyes, black floss nose and mouth, jointed at shoulders and hips, head lifts off to reveal small bottle for perfume, 5" h **$375**

Unjointed gray mohair, replaced shoe button eyes, black floss nose, vertical stitching, eyes high on head, felt paw pads, mounted on unmarked cast iron wheels, brown leather collar, 8" h **$500**

Yellow mohair, fully jointed, glass eyes, embroidered nose and mouth,

excelsior stuffing, felt pads, Schuco, moth damage, spotty fur loss, early 1920s, 12" h **$350**

TEXTILES

History: Textiles is the generic term for cloth or fabric items, especially anything woven or knitted. Antique textiles that have survived are usually those that were considered the "best" by their original owners, since these were the objects that were used and stored carefully by the housewife.

Textiles are collected for many reasons—to study fabrics, to understand the elegance of a historical period, for decorative purposes, or to use as was originally intended. The renewed interest in antique clothing has sparked a revived interest in period textiles of all forms.

Bedspread

Embroidered candlewick, by Eliza Spink, (1807-77), Auburn, NY, white on white embroidered dec, central cartouche with floral urn, medallion above name and date surrounded by grapevine border, further framed by grapevine and tulip border, central floral urn, 108" x 112", small holes, light staining, repairs **$1,840**

Printed cotton toile, New England, Cupid and several allegorical female figures in scenes of love, hand sewn, pieced and quilted in diamond pattern, backed with white homespun fabric, extended center panel, two pillow gussets, side drops, scalloped border on three sides, white binding, minor repair to backing, late 18th/early 19th C, 109-1/2" l, 52-1/2" w center panel, 31-1/2" l side drops **$1,295**

Braided rug

Oval, multicolored, predominately pink, 28-1/2" l, 23" w **$200**

Round, blue green, and pink, 17-1/2" d **$180**

Round, multicolored, hooked star in center, small repair, 33" d **$660**

Round, shades of green, red, and blue, 36-1/2" d **$125**

Round, blue, red, and green, 39" d **$190**

Child's seat, woven, flame stitch saw tooth pattern, green, pink, and black, 9-1/2" sq **$200**

Coverlet, damask, two pcs, red, blue, and green on white ground, rose and star design, marked "made for P. Matthias by W. H. Gernand Damask Coverlet Manufacturer Westminster Carroll County, MD, 1871," 89" x 90" **$1,125**

Coverlet, jacquard, one pc, Bierderwand, broad loom

Mustard, dark salmon, and navy blue stripes on natural, corner block "William & Rachel Guthrie" with poppy, overall floral designs, tulip-like medallions, added fringe, 84" x 96" **$385**

Natural, dark navy blue, burgundy, and olive, "Latest Improvent P. Warranted M. by H. Stager, Mount Joy" on edge, star medallion with tulip center, surrounded by rose branches, Greek key and rose branch border, corner block with bird in tree branch, worn areas, fringe loss, some edge damage, 69" x 77" **$300**

Coverlet, jacquard, two pcs, Bierderwand

Natural and navy blue, corner block "Daniel Lehr, Dalton, Wayne County, Ohio, 1847," leaf medallions, borders with backwards looking birds with tulips, minor stains and wear, some fringe loss, edge backed with blue cloth, 70" x 76" **$450**

Natural and soft salmon, tan, and gold, corner block "Made by W. Moore 1848," (Newark, OH), rose medallion, grape vine border, another small diamond border, minor wear, fringe loss, some edge damage, two halves don't line up at center seam, 78" x 86" **$250**

Natural, navy blue, and tomato red, corner block "H. Petry, Canton, Stark County, Ohio, 1840," floral medallions with borders of potted tulips, eagles with trees and stars, fringe loss, minor stains, small hole, stitched repairs, 70" x 72" **$425**

Natural, navy blue, red, and golden olive, corner block "T. M. Alexander, Wayne County, S.C.T. Ohio 1845," floral motif, lions and sunbursts, borders of backwards looking birds with roses, grape vines, and diamonds, few stains, fringe loss, small hole, unbound top edge, 72" x 88" **$650**

Natural, navy blue, salmon red, and olive brown stripes, corner block with four oak leaves "Peter Hartman, Wooster, Ohio, 1843," connected mirror images of potted flowers, alternating with bunches of grapes, border with eagles with shields sitting on grape vines and roses, wear, few stains, some repair, fringe loss, 77" x 90" **$300**

Navy blue, red, and olive green stripes, natural ground, corner block labeled "Gabriel Rausher, May 10, Delaware, Ohio, 1854," floral medallions, two vining floral borders, bottom border has backward looking parrots, one rolled edge, minor wear and fringe loss, some stitched repairs, 58" x 86" **$440**

Navy blue, tomato red, and mixed green and yellow stripes with natural, corner block with fancy tulip and "F. Yahraus, Knox County, Ohio 1864," stars with flower and star medallions, one border with backward looking birds and flowers, two borders with grape vines, wear, small repair, edge damage, 74" x 88" **$500**

Tomato red and navy blue bands on foundation of natural threads individually dyed light blue, border labeled "1848 Wove by J.S. for F.L.T.," quatrefoil corner block with bird under tree, diamonds alternating with wavy leaves, double borders of berry vines, worn edges with traces of blue calico binding, 74" x 90" **$385**

Coverlet, jacquard, two pcs, double weave

Blue and white, attributed to Duchess County, New York, unidentified weaver, Agriculture & Manufactures are the Foundations of our Independence, floral medallions bordered by buildings, American eagle flanked by Masonic columns, monkeys, and small human figures, some stains and edge damage, 78" x 82" **$865**

Blue and white, attributed to James Alexander (1770-1870), Orange County, New York, cotton and wool, woven in two lengths with an interior of six large floral medallions on polka dotted background, border designs of Independence Hall flanked by eagles with overhead stars, and eagles with Masonic com-

pass and square and columns, name "PHEBE HULSE OCT. 14 1824" woven in corner blocks, minor toning, stains, second quarter 19th C, 94" x 79" **$3,410**

Blue and white, New York State, central star and floral medallions, side borders of birds, undulating grapevines, and pine trees, lower border with eagles and willow trees over name "DEWITT," corner blocks with flower in vase, flanked by "SA" and "C" over "N.Y. 1841," toning, 1841, 86" x 82" **$500**

Dark tomato red, navy blue, and natural, unusual geometric overshot type pattern, minor fringe loss, 68" x 78" **$425**

Natural, navy blue, and salmon, conch shell corner block for Samel Balantyne, Lafayette, Indiana, flowers in grid, borders of urns and pineapple with internal hearts, fringe missing some wear, edge damage, 1808-1861, 75" x 86" **$365**

Natural, salmon, and navy blue, sunflower corner blocks, thistle medal-

lions surrounded by roses, borders with grape vines, wear, minor stains, 72" x 78" **$600**

Natural, tomato red, and dark green, corner block with pinwheel and "Jas McLD" for James McLeran, Columbiana County, Ohio, flower and leaf medallions on speckled background, pots of strawberries on border, bound edges, few areas of wear, after 1848, 72" x 76" **$425**

White and dark navy blue, geometric pattern, pine tree borders, overall light stains, one edge rebound with blue calico, 76" x 84" **$220**

Coverlet, overshot

One piece, broadloom, intricate optical pattern, natural, purple, and cinnamon, 74" x 106" **$495**

Two piece, optical pattern, natural, pink-red, and navy blue, some fringe trimmed, 68" x 78" **$450**

Two piece, tightly woven, natural, navy blue, and dark red, added red fringe, 80" x 90" **$250**

Coverlet, Pennsylvania, jacquard, inscribed, dated 1847, 94": x 80", **$460.**
Photo courtesy of Pook & Pook, Inc.

Coverlet, single weave, two pc, brick red, navy blue, medium blue, and some green on natural, striped designs, tree borders, most orig fringe, small areas of moth damage, 75" x 93" **$300**

Coverlet, summer/winter, one pc, broad loom

Centennial, red, green, and navy blue stripes on natural, central medallion with star surrounded by flowers and eagles with shields in each corner, bound edge with checkered design, worn areas, fringe loss, 80" x 87" **$125**

Hunter green and tomato red, central floral medallion surrounded by triangles, wide border with capitol building in center flanked by grape vines and flower urns, small stitched repair with minor damage at one of bound ends, 78" x 84" **$450**

Natural, medium green, blue, and tomato red, corner block "Ettinger and Co. Arronsburg, Centre Co., 1865," central acanthus leaf medallion with floral corners, multiple borders including stars, diamonds, and grape vines, minor stains, one end cut down and rebound, 78" x 81" **$350**

Natural, navy blue, red, dark green, corner block "Made by J. Hausman in Lobachsville for John Bechtol 1842," minor wear and stains, 76" x 100" **$400**

Natural, red, blue, and yellow stripes, corner block "Emanuel Ettinger, Aaronsburg, Centre Co. 1846," quatrefoil leaf medallions alternating with stars and diamonds, tulip border, 76" x 91" **$200**

Tomato red and natural, central sunburst surrounded by acorn and oak leaf wreath, eagle corners, wide floral borders with paisley scrolls in corners, minor stains, 76" sq **$230**

Draperies, Fortuny, large green fleur-de-lis patterns on taupe ground, early 20th C, four 19-1/4" w by 54" l panels, three 40" l by 54" l panels **$2,990**

Foot rest, braided, round, padded, hanging loop, multicolored, stuffed with rags, wear, 15" d **$110**

Fragment

Linen and cotton toile, red printed designs on natural white, George

Washington guiding leopard drawn chariot, Franklin, Goddess of Liberty, and soldiers, old but not orig edge binding, stains, torn typewritten paper label stitched to front, 42" x 66" **$320**

Crewel work, wool yarn, colorful bird perched in flowers tree, edges with later stitching, minor stains, 52-1/4" x 49" **$215**

Handkerchief, printed on cotton, Democratic Party, donkeys from Jefferson to Truman, 1949 .... **$230**

Hooked mat

Round, gray, brown, red, and blue turkey on pale green ground, multiple borders, 12" d **$160**

Sailing ship, labeled "Grefell Labrador Industries, Hand Made in Newfoundland & Labrador," minor edge damage, 8" x 8-3/4" **$200**

Hooked rug

Center dog, surrounded by hearts, elves, and geometric designs, multicolored, date "1921" woven into background, repairs, 42-1/2" x 39" **$2,530**

Center gray rabbit, flanked by red tulips in each corner on dark background, scalloped pink-lavender fabric border, 25" x 18" **$690**

Center lying dog, multicolored, hooked crazy quilt background, initialed "E.G.M.," 39" x 30" **$7,150**

Center reclining cat, multicolored, blue ground, black cloth border, 21" x 21-1/2" **$3,300**

Center running horse, surrounded by butterflies and birds, multicolored, 39" x 24" **$1,710**

Central gray dog, flanked by salmon butterflies, red five-pointed stars, two pink sassafras leaves at top, red and green vine with leaves and flowers at bottom, multicolored scalloped border, 41" x 33" **$2,750**

Eagle motif, rope border, 54" x 37" **$1,000**

Full figure red and black Indian holding tomahawk, standing on rock dated 1917, light background, multicolored striped border, 36" x 20" **$5,775**

Multicolored angled line borders, olive green corner blocks, horse's head center, burgundy, red, and brown center ground, mounted to stretcher, areas of loss and wear, 26" x 44-1/2" **$260**

Coverlet, jacquard, red, blue and green, eagle border, made for Elisabeth Rischel, 1836, **$350.**
Photo courtesy of Pook & Pook, Inc.

Hooked rug, American, yellow cat with green eyes, teal balls and blocked border, early 20trh C, 26-1/2" x 32", **$635.**
Photo courtesy of Pook & Pook, Inc.

Hooked rug, New England, reindeer flanking apple trees, 75-1/2" x 39", **$1,380.**
Photo courtesy of Pook & Pook, Inc.

Needlepoint picture, woolwork, rooster and two chickens in landscape, multi-color floral border, America, 19th C, 24-3/8" x 21-3/8", **$275.**

Multicolored, central blue elephant with black legs, eye, ear, and trunk, 35" x 20" **$1,320**

Multicolored, geometric pattern, cloth bound edges, 36" x 22".............**$935**

Rect, center cat with whiskers, multicolored, border, cloth backing, 27" x 11-1/2" **$1,210**

Theorem type, basket of multicolored flowers, black ground, red scalloped border, 31-1/2" x 20" **$1,155**

Three stars surrounded by flowers and concentric diamonds, borders of diamonds and triangles, rect, multicolored, predominantly wool strips hooked onto burlap backing, America, minor imperfections, 19th C, 38-1/2" x 85" **$2,235**

Two central black horses, red background, blue, green, yellow, and red floral vines on top and bottom, vivid orange ground, white panel "M.H." in black script (Mary Hull,) other white panel "1897," later printed cloth backing, provenance: purchased from Hull family estate, Dover, York County, Pennsylvania, 40" x 28" **$7,700**

Welcome, semi-circle, Cape Cod origin...**$1,750**

Mourning picture, framed, silk threads, silk ground, central weeping willow tree, tombstone, obelisk, church in far left ground, never embroidered with names, minor losses, deterioration of silk ground, 16-1/4" x 22" **$600**

Needlework picture

Densely chain and couch stitched allegorical scene of couple espied

Needlework, wool on linen, possible Chester County, Hannah Sharples, three buildings within vine border, 19th C, 17-3/4" x 20-1/4", **$460.**
Photo courtesy of Pook & Pook, Inc.

by nobleman and woman in castle, painted faces, accented with French knots, faux pearls, and gold metal chain, matted, 29-1/2" x 23-1/2" frame, England/ France, mid to late 19th C, 22-5/8" x 17" **$1,300**

Mrs. Saunders and Miss Beach's Academy, Dorchester, Massachusetts, silk threads on silk ground, flowers and fruit in urn, pen and ink inscriptions below reading "Wrought at Mrs. SAUNDER'S & Miss BEACHES Academy Dorchester 1807, by Miss June Withrington," stains, laid down, 1807, 8-1/2" x 7-3/8" **$780**

Silk threads on silk ground, watercolor highlights, shepherdess seated while inscribing the letters "TANCRED" on nearby tree, two sheep in foreground, distant mountain, in an oval enclosed by meandering flowering vine, by "Maria Billings M.E. and A. Sketchley's Boarding School, Poughkeepsie," unframed, thread loss, color runs, couple of tears, 13-5/8" x 13" **$775**

Wool embroidery, allegorical scene of man casting out young woman and boy, French knotted trees, painted silk ground, bird's eye maple frame, Victorian, late 19th C, 17-1/2" x 14-1/4" **$360**

Penny rug

Round discs, black background, yellow, blue, and red, 37" x 23" **$1,210**

Six-sided, appliquéd felt pennies, yellow birds, red berries on stems, green leaves, orange daisies with yellow centers, light background, decorative scalloped border, 57" x 32"...**$2,100**

Shawl, all over paisley design in greens, roses, reds, blues, etc., black center, three sides with short fringe, late 1800s, 70" x 72", **$225.**
Photo courtesy of Alderfer Auction Co.

Pillow, beadwork, central demi-lune beaded panel, white, gray, pink, and blue floral scene, gray velvet ground, blue, gray, and maroon silk trim, late 19th C, 15" h, 14" l **$200**

Pocketbook, America, crewel embroidery, rect containing initials "ZS," various flowers and foliage in shades of red, yellow, green, and gold issuing from urn set against black ground, green twill woven taped edging, blue glazed wool int. lining with two compartments, imperfections, 1740-90, 4-5/8" x 7-5/8" **$10,575**

Rag runner

Blue, rainbow stripes, yellow predominate, Pennsylvania, stains, 2' 10" x 10' 9"...**$125**

Brown, tan, blue, and orange stripes, 3' 1" x 12' 11"................................**$85**

Show towel

Homespun, dark brown finely stitched urns of flowers, one urn is heart shaped, "Betz Huhn 1808," woven decorative bands with pulled work and fringe at end, one end is bound, 19" w, 62" l **$250**

Homespun, pink and two shades of blue cross-stitch needlework, urns of flowers, one with birds, hearts, diamond, and fretwork lines, "Elisabeth Schli 1810," fringed, few small holes, some repaired, 15-3/4" w, 54" l **$440**

Red, pale blue, pink, and yellow yarn crewel work flowers, potted tree, dark blue cross-stitched "ER 1840," decorative woven bands, wear to yarn border, stitch loss, very minor stains, added fringe, 19-1/2" w, 58" l **$385**

Strong blue and dark pink cross-stitch geometric design, "Susanna Johnson 1839," 14-1/2" w, 40" l **$200**

Table cloth, banquet size, damask, banded foliate border with panels of classical subjects, central Portland vase designs, Wedgwood, England, 20th C, 16' 6" **$235**

Table mat, braided

Oval, multicolored, 24" w, 41" l ...**$470**

Oval, tan, maroon, and pink, 21" w, 34-1/2" l....................................**$275**

Round, brown and green, cloth backing, price for pr, 6-3/4" d **$220**

Round, purple, 15" d **$200**

Table runner, homespun linen, brown, white, and blue checkered pattern, frayed ends, price for pr, 19" l, 10-1/4" h **$440**

Tapestry, Aubusson-style, shore bird in landscape of trees and flowering plants, tears and repairs, 60" x 36".........**$2,000**

TIFFANY

History: Louis Comfort Tiffany (1849-1934) established a glass house in 1878 primarily to make stained glass windows. In 1890, in order to utilize surplus materials at the plant, Tiffany began to design and produce "small glass," such as iridescent glass lampshades, vases, stemware, and tableware in the Art Nouveau manner. Commercial production began in 1896.

Tiffany developed a unique type of colored iridescent glass called Favrile, which differs from other art glass in that it was a composition of colored glass worked together while hot. The essential characteristic is that the ornamentation is found within the glass; Favrile was never further decorated. Different effects were achieved by varying the amount and position of colors.

Louis Tiffany and the artists in his studio also are well known for their fine work in other areas— bronzes, pottery, jewelry, silver, and enamels.

Marks: Most Tiffany wares are signed with the name "L. C. Tiffany" or the initials "L.C.T." Some pieces also are marked "Favrile," along with a number. A variety of other marks can be found, e.g., "Tiffany Studios" and "Louis C. Tiffany Furnaces."

Tiffany, bronze, picture frame, Zodiac pattern, verdris and bronze patina, mkd "Tiffany Studios New York 943," 7" x 8", **$1,300.**
Photo courtesy of David Rago Auctions, Inc.

See additional Tiffany listings in the glass section.

Bronze

Bookends, pr, Zodiac, dark brown and green patina, imp "Tiffany Studios New York 1091," 4-3/4" w, 6" h **$490**

Box, cov

Circular, enameled stylized spray flowers in irid gold, blue, and green, on bronze ground, script signature, "Louis C. Tiffany 9151," 2-1/2" h, 5" d **$24,000**

Etched metal grape vine pattern, imp "Tiffany Studios New York 816," three Favrile panels damaged, hinge detached, c1900, 6-1/2" l **$550**

Candelabra

Four bulbous cups with blown green Favrile glass on four curved arms, base with 16 green "jewel" inserts around platform base, imp "TG & D Co., Tiffany Studios New York D 887," corrosion, missing bobeches, 2-1/2" h **$2,100**

Two arms supporting cups with seven green and gold irid glass "jewels," brown and green patina, imp "Tiffany Studios New York," 9-1/8" h **$2,760**

Candlestick, tripod shaft, circular base, prong-set bobeche with flaring rim, orig dark verdigris patina, stamped "Tiffany Studios, New York, 1211," 8" d, 24" h....................**$4,315**

Cigar box, rect hinged box, Zodiac pattern, multicolored enameling to each medallion, partial cedar liner, base stamped "Tiffany Studios New York 1655," 6-1/2" l, 6" d, 2-1/2" h **$1,610**

Tiffany, bronze, playing card holder, Pine Needle pattern, lined in green slag glass, verdigris patina, stamped on divider, 4" x 3" x 2", **$1,600.**
Photo courtesy of David Rago Auctions, Inc.

Tiffany, Favrile, vase, glass and metal flower form, opal glass insert w/green pulled feathers tipped in iridescent gold, "L. C. T.," bronze footed holder stamped "Tiffany Studios New York 1043," 14-1/2" h, **$1,800.**
Photo courtesy of The Early Auction Company, LLC.

Clock, mantle, Pine Needle pattern, sgd "Tiffany Studios New York, #2246," 9" w, 6" d, 13" h **$3,585**

Desk accessories, inkwell, pen holder, stamp box, ten Favrile panels, secret drawer hidden within central drawer, 8-3/4" l, 4-1/2" h **$23,000**

Fountain pen and pencil set, sterling silver, relief decorated with raised putti, floral swags, monogrammed medallion "M. V. P.," impressed "Tiffany & Co. Sterling," minor wear, 7" l, 7-3/4" l, $265.
Photo courtesy of Skinner, Inc.

Tiffany, desk lamp, bronze acid-etched, acanthus leaf motif, adjustable socket, fitted with Arabian-pattern gold and amber Favrile glass shade, shade etched "L.C.T.," base mkd "TIFFANY STUDIOS NEW YORK 637," 13" base, 4-1/2" x 6-3/4" shade, $4,500.
Photo courtesy of David Rago Auctions, Inc.

Desk box, Pine Needle pattern, polished, stamped Tiffany Studios mark and numbered "824," 7-3/4" d, 2-1/2" h

Caramel slag glass **$825**

Green slag glass **$1,000**

Frame, gilt, easel back, cast Heraldic pattern, lower recessed finished in patinated brown, imp mark "Louis C. Tiffany Furnaces Inc. 61," 10-1/4" w, 12" h......................**$1,035**

Glove box, Grapevine pattern, striated green slag glass inserts, ball feet, imp "Tiffany Studios, New York," 13-1/2" l, 4-1/2" d, 3-1/8" h........**$980**

Lamp base, three sockets, hexagonal standard, circular base, base stamped "Tiffany Studios New York 534," 22" h......................**$3,820**

Letter opener, Grapevine pattern, green slag glass **$450**

Letter stand, etched metal grape vine pattern, Favrile panels, brown and mottled verdis gras patina, imp "Tiffany Studios New York, c1910, 6-1/2" l, 5-1/4" h **$1,100**

Magnifying glass, gilt bronze, rosette pattern on handle, imp "Tiffany Studios 1788," imperfections, 8-7/8" l......................**$750**

Paperweight, sphinx, orig patina, some gilt, stamped "Tiffany Studios New York," 1-1/2" h, 2-1/4" l **$275**

Pen tray, Grapevine pattern, green slag glass, numbered "1004" **$650**

Plate, ftd, relief arts and crafts block designs around rim, sgd "Tiffany Studios New York, 1744," 9-3/4" d, 1" h......................**$475**

Stand, circular top centered by medallion relief-decorated with classical figures, three ribbed legs, base accented with scroll and leaf dec, imp Tiffany & Co. mark, and numbered "0297," maker's "7725 M," one ornamental finial missing, 31-1/2" d..........**$1,175**

Thermometer, Grapevine pattern, beaded border, green patina, green slag glass, easel stand, imp "Tiffany Studios New York" on reverse, minor corrosion, 8-3/4" h...................**$1,495**

Tray, circular with extended rim and handles, etched, enameled blue, pink, and green floral cloisonné dec on handles, imp "Louis C. Tiffany Furnaces Inc., Favrile 512" under handle, 9-7/8" d......................**$460**

Twine holder, Bookmark pattern, hexagonal form, hinged lid, reddish patina in lower recesses, imp "Tiffany Studios New York 905," minor spotting, 3" h...................**$1,035**

Lamps

Boudoir, dome shade, restored oviform base, irid gold glass dec with intricate intaglio carved green leaves, trailing budded vines, both sgd "L. C. Tiffany Favrile," shade also marked "5594L," 15-1/2" h......................**$9,775**

Candlestick, 2-1/2" aperture size, quilted blue shade with stretched rim, ribbed and swirled base fitted with green and white pulled feather standard, aperture rim nicks, 12" h, 7-1/2" d shade......................**$2,235**

Desk, bronze, three gold irid ribbed lily shades, each inscribed "L.C.T.," bronze base stamped "Tiffany Studios New York 319," crack and hole in one shade, 13" h......................**$2,500**

Floor, counterbalance, gold Doré finish, base stamped "Tiffany Studios New York 681," unsigned 9-3/4" d shade with four rows of fourteen panels, 52-1/2" h......................**$3,055**

Mantel lamp, slight octagonal form, cream colored glass rising to bulbed top, caramel and gold pulled petal design, fitted gilt bronze and wood base, 8" h......................**$1,150**

Table

Bronze, double branch, each branch with three irid glass shades, central bronze stem hollowed to one side to accept separate candle snuffer (missing), base imp "Tiffany Studios 10456" on each glass shade, sgd "LCT" minor roughness on base of shades, 22" w, 15-1/2" h **$12,500**

Crocus, four inverted clusters of spring green flowers with stems, mottled white ground, lower geometric border, stamped metal tag on shade rim, standard with three sockets, knob with seven cabochon jewels, base plate stamped "S216 437 Tiffany Studios New York," 24" h, 16" d......................**$18,800**

Dragonfly, conical shade, seven blue-bodied dragonflies with red eyes, caramel-gold colored ground with twenty-one oval gold jewels and Doré metalwork, shade stamped "Tiffany Studios New York 1495," three-socket standard base in turtle back design with verdigris Doré finish, base plate stamped "Tiffany Studios New York 587," 24" h, 20" d **$44,650**

Leaded glass globe shade, mottled green geometric slag glass segments progressively arranged, stamped "Tiffany Studios" on rim, four socket bronze standard, domed, stepped, circular base, stamped "Tiffany Studios New York 532" on base, 28-1/2" h, 22-1/2" d **$19,550**

Linenfold, 10 panels of pleated amber glass, doré metalwork, lower edge slightly lipped, stamped "Tiffany Studios New York 1957, PAT APPL'D FOR," three sockets, gold doré standard, base stamped "Tiffany Studios New York 533," 21-1/2" h, 15-5/8" d **$10,575**

Nautilus, adjustable shell-form shade of striated green and white leaded glass segments, supported on bronze standard and cushion base, raised leaf dec, reddish-brown patina, base imp "Tiffany Studios New York 25891" and "Tiffany Glass and Decorating Company" mark, c1892-1902, 12-1/2" h **$8,625**

Silver

After dinner coffeepot, elongated handle and spout, flip lid with leaf finial, ftd, sgd "Tiffany & Co.," 11" h **$300**

Bowl

Ftd, shaped edge with applied flowerhead and fern rim, stylized pad and paw feet with scrolled legs topped by acanthus leaves, center monogram, 1891-1902, 24 troy oz, 9-1/4" h, 4-1/4" h **$1,610**

Incised banding, everted rim, low domed foot, c1907-38, 11 troy oz, 5-3/4" d, 3" h **$200**

Scalloped rim, foot ring marked "Tiffany & Co., Makers Sterling 23844, 26 troy oz, 10-1/4" d **$660**

Bread basket, oval, molded rim, center monogram, 1925-47, approx 12 troy oz, 7" w, 10-3/4" l **$215**

Cake plate, circular, shaped rim with molded foliate edge, face with reticulated and engraved bands, domed circular foot with engraved and reticulated dec, center monogram, c1908-1947, approx 47 troy oz, 13-1/4" d **$1,955**

Candelabra, three-light, cornucopia shoulder and central sconce, flanked by reeded scroll candle arms and further cornucopia sconces, plain columnar stem, foliate cornucopia and shell edge, round floral repoussé foot, removable beaded nozzles, sq base, 1902-07, 26 troy oz, 12-1/4" h **$1,150**

Cigarette case, rect, rounded corners, gold-washed ovoid push button clasp, gold-washed interior, engraved on front with name and date, suspended from silver link chain, c1907-38, 4 troy oz, 3-3/8" x 2-1/4" **$90**

Cocktail set, 6-3/8" h cocktail shaker, six 4-1/8" cordial glasses, tapered ovoid shaker with hammered surface, engraved initials and date in base, glasses with conical bowl, baluster stem, plain foot, monogrammed, c1875-91, 26 troy oz **$865**

Coffee and tea service, coffeepot, creamer, hot water pot on ftd warming stand, cov sugar, waste bowl, each pc chased with band of ivy leaves, circular bases with bracket form feet, pinecone finials, each stamped "Tiffany & Co., 550 Broadway Quality 925-1000, 1375-3139 MM," late 19th C, 171.47 troy oz, 14" h coffeepot **$7,475**

Dresser set, 10 pcs, three brushes, comb, covered jar, receiving jar, hand mirror, shoe horn button hook, rect box, floral and scroll acid etched dec, gold-washed int. on jars and boxes, monogrammed, c1907-38, 23 troy oz **$1,850**

Flower basket, flattened bell shape, flared sides, engraved husk drops and floral swags, reticulated to rim in guillouche pattern, overhead handle engraved with further husks, oval foot, pr, 1907-38, 26 troy oz **$2,645**

Iced tea spoon, Bamboo pattern, molded bamboo form handles, set of four in Tiffany & Co. blue cloth bag in Tiffany box, mid-20th C, 8" l **$175**

Kettle on stand, bulbous, domed lid, reeded bud finial, cast upright handle with leather mount, body with engraved band, circular stand with openwork skirt, three cast scroll legs with shell feet, 1916-47, 59 troy oz, 11-1/2" h **$1,495**

Ladle, Wave Edge, marked "Tiffany & Co., Sterling Pat 1884 M," 6 troy oz, 11" l **$320**

Muffiner, urn form body with bat's wing fluting below applied stylized leaf banding, spiral reeded stem, sq base, screw-in domed lid with paneled ball finial, 1891-1902, 12 troy oz, 7-1/2" h **$635**

Pitcher, repoussé, waisted baluster form, ear handle, short spout, chased and emb all over with flowers and leaves, 1891-1902, 32 troy oz, 8-1/2" h **$3,220**

Serving dish, crenelated banding, lid with ovoid handle flanked by anthemion, c1854-70, 41 troy oz, 11-1/8" l, 5-1/2" h **$1,150**

Strawberry set, 11 strawberry forks, one sugar sifter, all gilt, twisted openwork handles and strawberry finials, early 20th C **$1,800**

Stuffing spoon, Chrysanthemum pattern, monogrammed, 8 troy oz, 12-1/2" l **$750**

Tray, ovoid, reticulated border, emb flowers and shells, sgd "Tiffany & Co.," monogrammed, 11" w **$500**

Vase, cov, flared rims, incised lines, stepped round bases, cov with wafers, elongated tear shaped finials, marked "Tiffany & Co. Makers, Sterling Silver," price for pr, 65 troy oz, 16-3/4" h **$2,55**

TINWARE

History: Beginning in the 1700s, many utilitarian household objects were made of tin. Because it is nontoxic, rust resistant, and fairly durable, tin can be used for storing food; and because it was cheap, tinware and tin-plated wares were in the price range of most people. It often was plated to iron to provide strength.

An early center of tinware manufacture in the United States was Berlin, Connecticut, but almost every small town and hamlet had its own tinsmith, tinner, or whitesmith. Tinsmiths used patterns to cut out the pieces, hammered and shaped them, and soldered the parts. If a piece was to be used with heat, a copper bottom was added because of the low melting point of tin. The industrial revolution brought about machine-made, mass-produced tinware pieces. The handmade era had ended by the late 19th century.

Tinware, ABC plate, alphabet embossed around rim, plain center, use wear, **$30.**

Tin, wall sconce, punched decoration, radiating sun motif in center, cutwork edges and details, **$195.**

Additional Resources:

Antique Trader® Metalwares Price Guide, 2nd Ed., by Kyle Husfloen, ed., and Mark Moran, contr. ed., Krause Publications, Iola, WI.

Anniversary top hat, 19th C, 11" d, 5-3/4" h **$1,150**

Candle lantern

Conical, removable base, circular handle, banded pierce work, Pennsylvania, 10" h, 5-7/8" d **$5,390**

Round removable base, glass panels in sides, cone shaped top with

crimped dec, ring carrier, price for pr, one with pitted surface, 12" h **$400**

Candle mold

Three-tube, handle, 5" h, 4-1/4" w **$715**

12 tube, applied handle, hanger ring, two wick holders, 10" h, 6-1/4" l **$250**

12-tube, round, crimped pie plate top and base, C-shaped handle, 10" h, 6-1/2" d **$990**

72 tubes, sq, applied tin handles, both resoldered, 10-3/4" h..............**$320**

12-tube, round, ring handle and base, 15-3/4" h, 6-1/4" d **$1,650**

Candlestick

Adjustable push-up, scallop grip ring handle, round base, 6" h, 4-1/4" d **$330**

Push-up, scalloped base, adjustable, cone-form sand-filled base with rod for candle adjustment, attributed to William Smith, Dillsburg, York County, Pennsylvania, 18-1/4" h, 6" d **$3,740**

Triangular base, push-up, ring handle, remnants of japanned finish, 3-1/2" h, 5-3/8" w **$580**

Cheese mold, pierced stylized geometric pattern, three tin conical feet, wire hanger, Pennsylvania, 3" h, 7-1/4" w **$2,420**

Coffeepot, conical, gooseneck spout, padded handle, finial, punched birds and flowers, made by William Resser, East Berlin, Adams County, Pennsylvania, early 20th C, 11" h, 8" w **$715**

Cookie cutter, hand made, 19th C

Crowing rooster, mounted on flat back plate with crimped edges, 6" h, 3" w, 1" d..........................**$330**

Eagle on nest, mounted on back plate with raised post for eye, 5-1/4" h, 4-1/2" w, 1" d **$165**

George Washington on his horse, illegible center stamp attributed to Germantown, Pennsylvania maker, 12-1/2" h, 10-1/2" l, 7/8" d................**$13,200**

Indian holding tomahawk, 7" h **$2,700**

Man and woman dancing, 8" h **$3,900**

Man in the moon, mounted on flat back plate, 4-3/4" h, 2-1/2" w, 7/8" w **$385**

Moose, mounted on back plate with crimped edges, 8" h, 10" l, 7/8" d **$1,210**

Parrot, mounted to flat back plate, 8" h, 4" w, 1" d......................**$1,100**

Standing rooster, mounted on flat back plate, 5-5/8" h, 4-3/4" w, 1" d **$1,320**

Swan, mounted to flat back plate, 6" h, 6-1/2" l, 1" d **$880**

Uncle Sam profile, mounted on flat back plate, unusually shaped handle with thumb rest, 8" h, 5" w, 1-1/8" d **$770**

Creamer, polychrome spray of yellow, green, and red flowers beneath spout, attributed to New York, minor paint loss, mid-19th C, 4" h..............**$200**

Dust pan, bell shaped, crimped molding, compass wheel and various stamps, anniversary type, wooden handle, 13-1/2" w, 16-1/2" l **$440**

Foot warmer

Punched panels with heart in circle design, mortised wooden frame with turned posts and incised lines, wire bale handle, refinished, 8-3/4" x 7-3/4" x 6" h **$315**

Punched panels with heart in circle design, mortised wooden frame with turned posts, old red stain, wire bale handle, traces of rust, penciled note inside, 9" x 7-1/2" x 5-5/8" h **$200**

Grater, pierced, tapered sides, reinforced back, 9-1/8" l, 4" w **$310**

Lamp

Grease, colorful glaze, 1-5/8" h **$165**

Petticoat, orig whale oil burner, orig black paint, 4" h......................**$65**

Skater's, light teal-green globe, 6-3/8" h **$225**

Lantern, hanging, old dark green repaint, rococo detail, six panes of glass with reverse painted dec, candle socket in base, attributed to Ohio, one pane with corner missing, 17-1/2" h **$420**

Mold

Heart shape, wire crimped rim, 7-3/4" w, 7" l, 1-3/4" d.............**$300**

Star shape, wire crimped rim, 9-1/2" w, 1-3/4" d....................**$385**

Quilt pattern

Compass wheel in plumed wreath, 9-3/4" d **$990**

Eight-sided star, central hole, 13-1/2" d **$275**

Six-sided star, central hole, names in pencil, 7-3/4" d **$200**

Spice box, dome lid, punched floral dec, molded banding, ring feet, leaf form hasp support, int. spice grater, three compartments **$1,320**

Tea bin, painted red, litho portrait of pretty young lady, stenciled gold dec, America, minor paint loss, price for pr, 19th C, 8-3/4" w, 8" d, 10" h **$750**

Tea kettle, swing handle, copper brackets, straight spout, base finial, 5" h, 5-1/2" h **$525**

Wall sconce

Oval, crimped and scalloped edges, 15" h, 9" w **$990**

Oval, scalloped edges, crimped edge reflector, 11" h, 6-3/4" w **$1,045**

Rect, crimped dec reflector, scalloped roof, crimped band on candleholder base, 12" h, 5" w **$880**

Rect, japanned black, half circle roof, candleholder base, 12-1/4" h, 3-3/4" w **$110**

Rect, scalloped roof, D-shaped base, 12" h, 4" w **$330**

Tapered back, crimped dec, 9" h, 3-1/2" w **$500**

Weather vane pattern

Running horse, 11" h, 15" l **$20**

Running horse, 11" h, 19-1/2" l **$385**

TINWARE, DECORATED

History: The art of decorating sheet iron, tin, and tin-coated sheet iron dates back to the mid-18th century. The Welsh called the practice pontypool; the French, töle peinte. In America, the center for tin-decorated ware in the late 1700s was Berlin, Connecticut.

Several styles of decorating techniques were used: painting, japanning, and stenciling. Both professionals and itinerants did designs. English and Oriental motifs strongly influenced both form and design.

A special type of decoration was the punch work on unpainted tin practiced by the Pennsylvania tinsmiths. Forms included coffeepots, spice boxes, and grease lamps.

Notes: Some record setting prices for decorated toleware were achieved

Toleware, tray, oval, double handles, hand-painted barroom scene with sailors and dancing woman, paint loss, discoloration, 14-1/2" d, 21-3/4" l, **$450.**
Photo courtesy of Alderfer Auction Co.

during the auction of the collection of Eugene and Dorothy Elgin, at Conestoga Auction Company, Inc., in April of 2004. Those items are noted as "ex-Elgin."

Additional Resources:

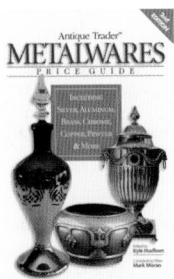

Antique Trader® Metalwares Price Guide, 2nd Ed., by Kyle Husfloen, ed., and Mark Moran, contr. ed., Krause Publications, Iola WI.

Box, cov, dome top, wire and turned wooden handle on lid, yellow scrolled foliate designs, box with red and white swags, yellow leaf embellishments, black ground, America, 19th C, 13-3/4" l, 8-3/4" d, 9" h **$765**

Bun tray, elliptical, pierced handles, off-white rim band dec with yellow, red, green-blue, green, and black flowers, asphaltum ground, crystallized in interior, America, paint losses, late 19th/early 20th C, 12-5/8" d, 3-5/8" h **$500**

Canister, cylindrical, red cherries, green leaves, white border, yellow stylized leaves and swag borders, lid centered with leaf dec, red japanned ground, minor scratches, 6-1/4" h **$400**

Chamberstick, applied handle, japanned ground, polychromed floral dec, yellow, red, green, and white, yellow banding, ex-Elgin, 6-1/4" d, 2" h **$22,000**

Toleware, teapot, from Oliver Filley Tinsmiths, yellow bird and fruit decoration, inscribed on underside "H. Case, April 1824," Pennsylvania, paint loss, 11" h, **$1,725.**
Photo courtesy of Pook & Pook.

Coffeepot, cov

Gooseneck spout, dome top, japanned ground, central medallion, white, orange, red, green, blue, and yellow fruit, floral and foliate dec, ex-Elgin, 10-1/2" h, 6-1/4" d **$38,500**

Gooseneck spout, red ground, central medallion with floral motifs, yellow, black, blue, green, and tan, ex-Elgin, 10-1/2" h, 6-3/8" d, 9-1/2" w **$55,000**

Hooked spout, hinged lid, bands of red and yellow flanking bands of yellow flowers and foliage, asphaltum ground, America, paint wear, minor dents, late 18th/early 19th C, 10-3/4" h **$1,530**

Orig red and yellow pomegranate dec, yellow foliage, brown japanned ground worn and alligatored, orig construction with pieced triangle below handle, wear, 10-1/4" h **$1,495**

Cream pitcher, cov, applied handle, triangular spout, japanned base, yellow floral and band dec, red, yellow, green, and white highlights, ex-Elgin, 3" d, 4" h **$5,500**

Deed box, dome top

Orig dark brown japanning, white band on front panel, green leaves, red cherries, yellow border dec, wire bale handle, tin latch, slight wear, 6-3/4" w, 3-1/8" d, 3-5/8" h **$660**

Black ground, yellow swags and lines, front with fruit, yellow, and green foliate, wire bale handle, tin hasp, minor wear, mostly to lid edges, 8" w, 4" d, 4-3/4" h **$250**

Document box, dome top, brown japanning, red draped swags, yellow leaves, wavy lines, tin hasp, brass bale handle, int. lined with remnants of glue-on leaves, minor touch-up on front of lid and some edges, some wear, 11-1/2" w, 5" d, 6-1/4" h **$990**

Match holder, hanging, scalloped crimped edge, triangular pocket, black base, yellow, orange, and green floral banding, paint flaking, ex-Elgin, 4-3/4" w, 1-5/8" d, 7-1/2" h **$420**

Milk can, black japanning, stenciled red and gold stylized floral design, 8-1/2" h.................................. **$200**

Spice box, round, seven int. containers, worn orig brown japanning, gold stenciled labels, 7-1/4" d **$175**

Sugar bowl, cov, scrolled finial, japanned base, floral polychrome, yellow, green, red, and white band dec, ex-Elgin, 4" d, 3-3/4" h **$11,550**

Tea caddy, dark ground, worn stenciled bronze powder dec, int. lift-out tray fits over two lidded compartments, orig emb brass handle, minor damage, 8-1/4" l **$220**

Toy, dancing man with top hat, arm and leg movement, polychrome dec, wooden handle, 11-1/2" h **$615**

Tray

Eight-sided, black base painted red ground, polychrome floral design, leaves, yellow banding, wire rim edge, minor paint flaking, 8-3/4" l, 6-1/4" w **$990**

Eight-sided, japanned base, polychrome floral banding, crystallized center, yellow banding to sides with white, blue, yellow, orange, and red highlights, wire rim edge, ex-Elgin, 12-1/2" l, 8-3/4" w **$17,050**

Eight-sided, japanned base, crystallized center, yellow, blue, and green floral banding on white ground, wire rim edge, attributed to Adams County, Pennsylvania, ex-Elgin, 12-1/2" l, 8-3/4" w **$9,350**

Oblong, scalloped edge, polychrome paint dec, centered scene of three masted ship, possibly U.S. frigate *Independence,* in coastal waters, enclosed by gilt stenciled leaf and scroll borders, black ground, metal hanging rack, America, imperfections, early 19th C, 29-5/8" l, 24" w **$2,000**

Urn, cov

Slender stem, ovoid foot, gilt florals, birds, and butterflies, pr, 19th C, 13-1/4" h **$1,725**

Two handles, acorn finials, dec with floral sprays and birds, scalloped floral and repeating gilt leaf borders, weighted base, French, some paint loss, minor dents, pr, 19th C
.... **$575**

TOBACCO JARS

History: A tobacco jar is a container for storing tobacco. Tobacco humidors were made of various materials and in many shapes, including figurals. The earliest jars date to the early 17th century; however, most examples seen in the antiques market today were made in the late 19th or early 20th centuries.

Bear with beehive, majolica, Continental, 6-1/2" h................ **$770**

Blackamoor, majolica, marked "DEP" in circle, some restoration, c1900, 6" h.. **$330**

Black boy, red hat with tassel, majolica, repainted, nicks.................... **$275**

Bull dog, porcelain, German **$275**

Creamware, plum colored transfers on side, one titled "Success to the British Fleet," striped orange, blue, and yellow molding, domed lid, 9" h, 6" d.. **$900**

Crystal, hammered copper top, Roman coin dec, sgd "Benedict Studios," 7" h
.... **$250**

Dog's head, with pipe and green hat and collar, majolica **$375**

Dwarf in sack, terra cotta, multicolor dec, marked "JM3478," chips, wear, 8" h.. **$255**

Indian, black, majolica, 5-1/2" h
.... **$330**

Jasperware, raised white Indian chief on cov, Indian regalia on front, green ground.. **$195**

Majolica, barrel shape, cobalt blue, green, gold, and brown, Doulton, Lambeth, England, #8481, artist's initials, 6" h.. **$225**

Mandarin, papier-mâché **$95**

Man with pipe, large bow tie, with match holder and striker, rim chips, hairline.. **$165**

Tobacco jars, Royal Doulton, Walton Ware, 1910; one depicting Battle of Hastings, 7-1/2" h; other street scene, 5-1/2" h, both cream-color earthenware ground, stamped marks, minor wear, **$365.**
Photo courtesy of David Rago Auctions, Inc.

Man with top hat, majolica, Sarreguemines, hairline in base **$165**

Moose, porcelain, Austrian **$200**

Owl, majolica, brown, yellow glass eyes, 11" h **$825**

Royal Winton, hp relief scene, marked "Royal Winton, England".......... **$195**

Stoneware, applied Egyptian motif, brown ground, c1890, 5" d, 6" h
.... **$130**

Treenware, turned and painted poplar, lid with turned finial

Ftd base, incised banding, painted brown, spitting, chips, 4" d, 9-1/2" h
.... **$600**

Finger grained paint dec on yellow base, brown highlights, 8" d, 8" h
.... **$5,500**

Incised banding, red, black, and green polychrome dec, 5-3/4" d, 9-1/4" h
.... **$2,475**

Incised banding, salmon base paint, black banding, 4-3/4" d, 7-1/4" h
.... **$990**

Incised banding, stained in multiple colors, varnished, 5-1/2" d, 7" h
.... **$770**

Wave Crest, white opaque body, SP fittings, 5" sq **$450**

Wood, hand-carved walnut, knotty tree trunk, foreground of foliage, rabbit exiting his lair, flowering trumpet fine encircling vase, side inscribed "Viv Le Vin Lamour et le Tabac 1871," fitted lid with carved branch finial, 7" l, 6-1/2" h **$320**

TOOLS

History: Before the advent of the assembly line and mass production, practically everything required for living was handmade at home or by a local tradesman or craftsman. The cooper, the blacksmith, the cabinetmaker, and the carpenter all had their special tools.

Early examples of these hand tools are collected for their workmanship, ingenuity, place of manufacture, or design. Modern-day craftsman often search out and use old hand tools in order to authentically recreate the manufacture of an object.

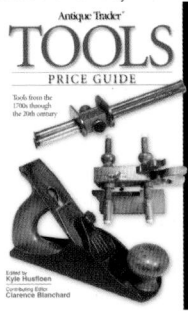

Antique Trader® Tools Price Guide, by Kyle Husfloen, ed. and Clarence Blanchard, contr. ed., Krause Publications, Iola, WI.

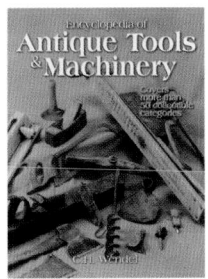

Encyclopedia of Antique Tools & Machinery, by C.H. Wendel, Krause Publications, Iola, WI.

Auger, E. C. Stearns, No. 4, adjustable, hollow, 70% japanning................ **$60**

Axe head, ship builder's, Campbell's, XXX, New Brunswick, 6" w.......... **$55**

Bicycle wrench, Billings & Spencer Co., made for Pope Mfg Co., patent Jan. 15th 1895, adjusting screw on side, 5-1/2".................................... **$95**

Brace

P. S. & W., No. 1202, Samson patent ball bearing chuck, rosewood handle, 1895 patent date, 12" sweep **$40**

Stanley, No. 923-8, 8" sweep **$55**

Yankee, No. 2101-10, 10" sweep **$65**

Chamfer knife, cooper's, L & I. J. White, laminated blade **$65**

Chisel

Buck Bros, 3/8" bevel edge, cast steel **$45**

Stanley, No. 750, 5/8" bevel edge, mkd "Stanley, D, Made in USA," 9-1/4" l **$35**

Clapboard marker, Stanley, No. 88, 80% nickel remains **$25**

Doweling machine, Stanley, No. 77, 3/8 cutter **$375**

Draw knife

C. E. Jennings, pattern maker's type, black egg-shaped handles, 4" **$40**

Whitherby, Winstead, Connecticut, folding handles, 8" **$70**

Fret saw, Miller Falls Co., No. 2, deep throat, extra blades, orig box, 12" l **$175**

Hammer

Claw, Stanley, 7 oz, bell face **$25**

Magnetic tack, Stanley, No. 601, orig decal **$40**

Hand drill

Miller Falls, No. 353, ratchet, three-jaw chuck, solid steel frame, 11" l **$50**

North Bros, Yankee No. 1530A, right and left hand ratchet movement, remnants of orig decal, orig box **$175**

Jeweler's vice, Stevens Patent, c1900, 2" jaws **$175**

Jointer and raker gauge, Simonds, No. 342, adjustable **$30**

Nippers, W. Schollhorn, Bernard's patent, Pat. Oct 24, 90% nickel plating, 1899 .... **$25**

Nut wrench

Boos Tool Corp, Kansas City, Missouri, screw adjust, orig box, 6" l **$85**

Boston Wrench Co., Boston, Massachusetts, quick adjust nut, patent Oct. 2, 1906, 6" l **$195**

Pipe wrench

Balin Tool Co., Los Angeles, California, patent no. 2210274, spring-loaded jaw, 10" **$165**

Eaton, Cole & Burnham, Franklin patent, July 20, 1886 .... **$135**

Machinist's toolbox, Gerstner, walnut, 11 drawers, 26" w, 9" d, 15-1/2" h, $390.
Photo courtesy of Joy Luke Auctions.

Plane

Preston & Sons, miniature, beech, 4" l **$95**

Record, No. 050, "Improved Combo," metallic, Sheffield, England, orig cutters, orig wood box, 9" l **$185**

Stanley, No. 3, made in USA logo, rosewood handle, c1950 .... **$100**

Stanley, No. 4, type 11, three patent dates cast in bed, dark rosewood handle **$115**

Stanley, No. 5, Jack, 1910 patent date cast in bed, dark rosewood handle, tall knob **$135**

Stanley, No. 9-1/2, block, adjustable throat and cutter **$40**

Stanley, No. 20, Circular, locking screw, '92 patent date on cutter **$225**

Stanley, No. 72, chamfer, cast cap screw, brass star-wheel date, rosewood handle and knob, 1886 patent date on cutter **$395**

Stanley, No. 271, router, 3" l **$65**

Pliers, W. Schollhorn, Bernard's patent, parallel jaws, top nippers, blued, 6-1/2" l **$25**

Putty knives, Stanley, Handyman, cocobolo handles, six-pc set, orig box **$95**

Ratchet brace, Stanley No. 2101, Yankee, 14" l **$75**

Rip saw, Henry Disston & Sons, No. 12, London Spring steel, four-screw apple wood handle with early wheat carving, 1896-1917 medallion, 28" l **$145**

Saw jointer, Atkins **$30**

Saw set, Stanley, No. 43, pistol-grip, orig box **$60**

Saw vise, Sears, Roebuck & Co., No. 4920, Dunlap, orig box, 11" l **$55**

Tools, work bench, W. P. Walters & Sons, original drawer and cast metal vice, tapped "W. P. Walters & Sons, Philadelphia," 31-1/2" x 21-1/2" x 42", **$400.**
Photo courtesy of David Rago Auctions, Inc.

Plane, Stanley, cast iron, type 2, circular, No. 113, 10" l, **$70.**
Photo courtesy of Joy Luke Auctions.

Wood clamp, adjustable, **$45.**

Screwdriver, spiral ratchet, North Bros Mfg Co., Philadelphia

Yankee No. 30A, three orig straight bits, orig box **$50**

Yankee No. 35, one orig bit, 12" l **$35**

Ship caulking mallet, oak head, 15-1/2" l **$85**

Shipwright's slick, L. H. Watts, New York, 2-1/2" size, 22-1/2" l **$245**

Slide rule, boxwood, c1800, 24" l **$395**

Socket gouge, Zenith, 1/4", 12-1/2" l **$30**

Spoke pointer, Hargrave, Cincinnati Tool Co., No. 343, 90% enamel remains **$65**

Sweep gouge, J. B. Addis & Sons, No. 9, rosewood handle, 5/8" medium sweep **$30**

Swivel vice, North Bros, Yankee No. 1993, quick adjusting swivel base, cam-action lock, 2-3/4" jaws **$115**

Tap and die set, Greenfield No. AA-4, two-pc adjustable die screw plate **$45**

Yard rule, Stanley, No. 41, maple, 36" l **$45**

Wire gauge, Starrett Co., L. S., Athol, Massachusetts, No. 283, US standard, 3-1/2" l **$15**

TRAMP ART

History: Tramp art was an internationally practiced craft, brought to the United States by European immigrants. Its span of popularity was between the late 1860s to the 1940s. Made with simple tools—usually a pocketknife, and from scrap woods—non-reusable cigar box wood, and crate wood, this folk-art form can be seen in small boxes to large pieces of furniture. Usually identifiable by the composition of thin-layered pieces of wood with chip-carved edges assembled in built-up pyramids, circles, hearts, stars, etc. At times, pieces included velvet, porcelain buttons, brass tacks, glass knobs, shards of china, etc., that the craftsmen used to embellish his work. The pieces were predominantly stained or painted.

Collected as folk art, most of the work was attributed to anonymous makers. A premium is placed on the more whimsical artistic forms, pieces in original painted surfaces, or pieces verified to be from an identified maker.

Bank, secret access to coins, 6" h x 4" w x 4" d **$335**

Box, cov

Hinged cover, dove, heart, and anchor dec, 4-1/4" w, 3" d, 1-3/4" l **$200**

Hinged top, cast brass pull, mounted pincushion on base, two concealed short drawers, painted blue and gold, c1890-1910, 14" l, 7-1/8" d, 8-1/4" h **$815**

Cabinet, building shape, two towers, steeple roofline, small shelves **$3,600**

Chest of drawers, scratch built from crates with four drawers, 10 layers deep, 40" h x 29" w x 20" d **$2,400**

Clock, mantel, red stain with drawers at base, 22" h x 14" w x 7" d **$475**

Comb case, adorned with horseshoes, hearts, birds, two drawers and mirrors, 27" h x 17" w x 4" d **$700**

Crucifix, wooden pedestal base, wooden carved figure, 16" h x 7" w x 4-1/2" d **$195**

Document box, diamond designs, sgd and date, 14" h x 9-1/2" w x 9" d **$375**

Tramp art, spice box, hanging type, painted black, white porcelain knobs, six small drawers over one longer drawer, ornate carved crest, **$250.**

Tramp art, box, covered, carved stag among foliage, cigar box used as base, visible inside, small lock, original key, **$150.**

Frame

Double opening frame with oval opening for photos, 14" h x 24" w $325

Horseshoe shape, light and dark wood, 13" h x 12" w..................$465

Photograph of maker, signed and dated "1906," 9" h, 6-3/4" w $275

Velvet panels and sq corners, 26" h x 24" w...$350

Jewelry box

Covered with hearts painted silver over gold, velvet lined, 6" h x 11" w x 6" d $595

Large, dated "1898," metal lion pulls, 9" h x 11-1/2" w x 7" d $300

Lamp, table, double socket, 24" h, 10" w, 10" d..................................$550

Medicine cabinet, light and dark woods, 22" h x 18" w x 10" d $675

Miniature

Chair, crown of thorns, 8" h x 6" w x 5-1/2" d $245

Chest of drawers, made of cigar boxes, 14" h x 5" w x 4" d $375

Music box, velvet sides, 3" h x 7" w x 6" d...$425

Night stand, dark stain, drawer on top and cabinet on bottom, no losses, 37" h x 22" w x 14" d $1,600

Pedestal

Multi-level, six draws, 14-1/2" h x 12" w x 8" d...............................$675

Polychromed in green and black paint, 16" h x 7" w x 4-1/2" d $950

Plant stand, painted gold, heavily layered, 22" h x 11" w x 11" d $675

Pocket watch holder, ftd, 9" h x 6-1/2" w x 5-1/2" d $375

Sewing box, velvet pin cushion on top, 8-1/2" h x 11-1/2" w x 8-1/2" d $265

Vanity mirror, table top, heart on top and drawer, 26" h, 14" d, 10" d $375

Wall pocket

Painted with hearts and stars, pr, 14" h x 11" w x 7" d $700

Three pockets, hearts on crest, diamond and circle dec, trim and dec painted orig medium blue and goldenrod, 8" w, 3-1/2" d, 14" h......$275

Tramp art, picture frames, left: applied roundels and diamonds, **$45;** *right: carved American eagle, stars, and laurel motif,* **$95.**

Tramp art, frame, crown of thorns, 26-1/2" x 31-1/2", **$150.**
Photo courtesy of David Rago Auctions, Inc.

VALENTINES

History: Early cards were handmade, often containing both handwritten verses and hand-drawn pictures. Many cards also were hand colored and contained cutwork.

Mass production of machine-made cards featuring chromolithography began after 1840. In 1847, Esther Howland of Worcester, Massachusetts, established a company to make valentines that were hand decorated with paper lace and other materials imported from England. They had a small "H" stamped in red in the top left corner. Howland's company eventually became the New England Valentine Company (N.E.V. Co.).

The company George C. Whitney and his brother founded after the Civil War dominated the market from the 1870s through the first decades of the 20th century. They bought out several competitors, one of which was the New England Valentine Company.

Lace paper was invented in 1834. The golden age of lacy cards took place between 1835 and 1860.

Embossed paper was used in England after 1800. Embossed lithographs and woodcuts developed between 1825 and 1840, and early examples were hand colored.

There was a big revival in the 1920s by large companies, like R. Tuck in England, which did lots of beautiful cards for its 75th Diamond Jubilee; 1925 saw changes in card production, especially for children with paper toys of all sorts, all very collectible now. Little girls were in short dresses, boys in short pants, which helps date that era of valentines. There was an endless variety of toy types of paper items, many companies created similar items and many stayed in production until World War II paper shortages stopped production both here and abroad.

Adviser: Evalene Pulati.

Animated, large
 Felix, half tone, German **$30**
 Jumping Jack, Tuck, 1900 .... **$75**
Bank of Love note, England, 1865
 .... **$50**

Bank of Love note, Nister, 1914
 .... **$35**
Charm string
 Brundage, three pcs **$55**
 Four hearts, ribbon **$45**
Comic
 Sheet, McLoughlin Co., USA, 1915, 9" x 14" **$25**
 Sheet, Park, London, 8" x 10" **$25**
 Woodcut, Strong, USA, 1845 .... **$25**
Diecut foldout
 Brundage, flat, cardboard **$25**
 Cherubs, two pcs **$35**
 Clapsaddle, 1911 .... **$50**
Documentary
 Passport, love, 1910 .... **$45**
 Wedding certificate, 1914 .... **$45**
English Fancy, from "Unrequited Love Series"
 Aquatint, couple, wedding, 8" x 10" **$135**
 Aquatint, girl and grandmother, 8" x 10" **$95**
Engraved
 American, verse, 5" x 7" **$35**
 English, hand colored, 8" x 10" sheet **$45**
Handmade
 Calligraphy, envelope, 1885 .... **$145**
 Cutwork, hearts, 1855, 6" x 6" **$250**
 Fraktur, cutwork, 1800 .... **$950**
 Pen and ink loveknot, 1820 .... **$275**
 Puzzle, purse, 1855, 14" x 14" **$450**
 Theorem, c1885, 9" x 14" **$325**
 Woven heart, hand, 1840 .... **$75**
Honeycomb
 American, kids, tunnel of love **$48**
 American, wide-eyed kids, 9" **$35**
 German, white and pink, 1914, 11" **$65**
 Simple, Beistle, 1920, 8" **$15**
Lace paper
American, B & J Cameo Style
 Large **$85**
 Small, 1865 .... **$55**
American, layered
 McLoughlin Co., c1880 .... **$35**
 Cobweb center, c1855 .... **$250**
English, fancy
 3" x 5", 1865 .... **$35**
 5" x 7", 1855 .... **$75**
 8" x 10", 1840 .... **$145**
 Hand layered, scraps, 1855 .... **$65**
Layered, in orig box
 1875, Howland **$75**
 1910, McLoughlin Co. **$45**

Folk art, scherenschnitte, Pennsylvania, 19th C, circular, heart cutouts, 6-3/4" d, **$575.**
Photo courtesy of Pook & Pook, Inc.

 Simple, small pc, 1875 .... **$22.50**
 Whitney, 1875, 5" x 7" **$35**
Novelty, American Fancy, c1900
 Mat, fancy corners, parchment, orig box, 5" x 7-1/2" **$35**
 Oblong, satin, celluloid, orig box, 16" x 10-1/2" **$65**
 Rect, panel with silk, celluloid, orig box, 7-1/2" x 10" **$45**
 Star shape, silk ruching, orig box, 10-1/2" x 10" **$55**
Pulldown, German
 Airplane, 1914, 8" x 14" **$175**
 Auto, 1910, 8" x 11" x 4" **$175**
 Car and kids, 1920s **$35**
 Dollhouse, large, 1935 .... **$45**
 Rowboat, small, honeycomb paper puff **$65**
 Seaplane, 1934, 8" x 9" **$75**
 Tall Ship, 8" x 16" **$175**
Silk fringed
 Prang, double sided, 3" x 5" **$24**
 Triple layers, orig box **$38**
Standup novelty
 Cupid, orig box **$45**
 Hands, heart, without orig box **$35**
 Parchment, violin, large, boxed **$125**
 Parchment, violin, small, boxed **$85**

WEATHER VANES

History: A weather vane indicates wind direction. The earliest known examples were found on late 17th-century structures in the Boston area. The vanes were handcrafted of wood, copper, or tin. By the last half of the 19th century, weather vanes adorned farms and houses throughout the nation. Mass-produced vanes of cast iron, copper, and sheet metal were sold through mail-order catalogs or at country stores.

The champion vane is the rooster—in fact, the name weathercock is synonymous with weather vane—but the styles and patterns are endless. Weathering can affect the same vane differently; for this reason, patina is a critical element in collectible vanes.

Reproduction Alert: Reproductions of early models exist, are being aged, and then sold as originals.

Allen, Ethan, molded and gilded copper, attributed to J. F. Fiske & Co. **$68,500**

Arrow

Copper, spire and belted ball finial, verdigris surface, no stand, dents, several bullet holes, 60" l, 29" h **$950**

Gilt copper, ball finial, weathered gilt surface, no stand, dents, 36" l, 16" h **$360**

Banner

Sheet copper scrolled banner with pierced "1921," cut-out bird perched on end, copper directionals, America, sq white painted wooden plinth, verdigris surface, minor imperfections, c1921, 31-1/4" l, 49-1/2" h **$2,350**

Sheet iron, iron ball finial on shaft above banner, heart and oval cut-outs, weathered black paint, stand, 15-3/4" l, 37" h **$1,645**

Bird and fish, molded metal, full bodied, bird flies with aid of propellers above fish, marble eyes, unpainted weathered gray surface, Illinois, tall stand, early 20th C, 18-1/2" w, 19" h **$1,150**

Cow, full bodied, molded metal **$1,475**

Deer, running, green patinated copper, hollow body, missing one antler, 19th C, 33" l **$32,000**

Eagle

Copper, full bodied, cast zinc feet, wooden base, one foot loose, arrow bent, 21" wing span, 18-1/2" h **$250**

Gilt copper, outstretched wings perched on belted sphere over arrow directional, old gilt-copper verdigris surface, no stand, small loss on arrow feather, 15-1/2" l, 14-3/4" w, 9-1/8" h **$1,100**

Fire wagon, painted copper, two horses, driver, steam fire engine, iron supports on underside, red, black, and gold paint, attributed to I. W. Cushing & Sons, Waltham, MA, including stand, imperfections, late 19th C, 40" l, 29-1/4" h **$15,275**

Fish

Carved and painted wood, salmon orange, chamfered edge, tin reinforced carved bracket, Wakefield, MA, inscribed "this set on a cedar tree near our farm before the Civil War," with stand, 19th C, 27" l, 6" h **$1,150**

Carved wood, full bodied, tail wrapped with lead sheeting, tacked button eyes, Midwestern U.S., remnant of post, minor losses, with stand, late 19th C, 12-3/4" l, 3-1/4" h **$2,645**

Heart and feather, sheet iron, found in New York state, fine rust and overall pitting, with stand, late 18th C, 76-3/4" l, 13-1/4" h **$4,900**

Heron, molded copper **$39,950**

Horse

Prancing, molded copper, weathered gilt surface, vestiges of sizing, with stand, imperfections, 34" l, 25-1/2" h **$4,115**

Running, copper, verdigris patina, traces of gilt, America, includes copper sphere, no stand, dents, small seam separations, late 19th C, 17-3/4" h **$2,350**

Running, copper head, hollow molded full body, no stand, gilt wear, minor dent, 41-1/2" l, 21" h **$4,115**

Running, copper, molded, and cast zinc, verdigris surface, attributed to A. L. Jewell & Co., Waltham, MA, 1850-67, no stand, minor dents, seam separation, 29" l, 14" h **$4,625**

Weather vane, rooster, Hamburg, molded copper, attributed to L.W. Cushing & Sons, Waltham, Massachusetts, flattened full-body figure, verdigris patina with traces of gilt, repairs, bullet holes, dents, late 19th C, 29" l, 28" h, **$25,850.**
Photo courtesy of Skinner, Inc.

Weather vane, New England, full bodied running horse, cast brass head, 19th C, 31" l, **$6,900.**
Photo courtesy of Pook & Pook, Inc.

Weather vane, American, copper full body cow, solid brass head, original directionals, c1900, **$10,925.**
Photo courtesy of Pook & Pook, Inc.

Running, copper, painted, flattened full bodied, older darkened putty painted surface, traces of gilt, no stand, dents, bullet hole repairs, 32" l, 17" h..............**$1,410**

Running, sheet iron, one side with gilt surface, other side gilt with black painted details, including stand, minor wear, late 19th/early 20th C, 38-1/4" l, 24-1/4" h..............**$3,100**

Running, zinc torso, copper ears, legs, and body, corrugated copper tail, attributed to J. Howard & Co., West Bridgewater, MA, old surface with vestiges of gilt, no stand, old repair on one leg, wear, minor dents, third quarter 19th C, 24" l, 18-1/2" h **$7,650**

Horse and jockey, copper, old yellow sizing surface, no stand, minor dents on ears and jockey's head, 31-1/2" l, 22-3/4" h..............**$9,400**

Horse and rider, molded sheet iron, hollow body, orig mustard painted surface, wear, cracks..............**$6,465**

Quill, copper **$4,950**

Pig, molded copper, weathered dark verdigris surface, traces of gilt, stand, imperfections, late 19th C, 32" l, 20-1/4" h..............**$32,300**

Plow, iron and bronze, old surface, no stand, 38-1/4" l, 13-1/2" h........**$3,415**

Pointing hand, sheet iron and wood, two wood finials on iron shaft, hand and sunburst sheet iron motif, no stand, imperfections, 23" l, 35-1/4" h **$2,235**

Rooster

Cast iron, two pc cast iron body, sheet steel tail feathers, old red paint, good detail, on later notched wooden base needs re-welding, 24" w, 23" h **$6,670**

Molded copper, L. W. Cushing & Sons **$41,125**

Sloop, gaff-rigged, molded copper, verdigris surface, America, no stand, early 20th C..............**$4,415**

Stag, leaping

Molded copper, full body, attributed to A. I. Harris & Son, Waltham, MA, including stand, regilded old surface, 55-1/2" l, 41-5/8" h **$12,925**

Molded copper, old regilded surface, mounted on wooden stand, 21-1/2" l, 17-3/4" h..............**$5,290**

WOODENWARE

History: Many utilitarian household objects and farm implements were made of wood. Although they were subjected to heavy use, these implements were made of the strongest woods and well cared for by their owners. Today collectors and decorators treasure their worn lines and patina. Collectors often consider their hand-made wooden items as folk art, elevating what once might have been a common utilitarian item to a place of honor.

Apple tray, pine, dovetailed and sq nail construction, painted yellow ground, green stylized foliate motif, wood separation in base, 10" l, 10" w, 3-1/2" h..............**$6,050**

Bag stamp, pine, relief carved tulip in heart-dec urn, PA, c1750, 5" h **$2,100**

Bank, rect, carved gardenia blossoms and leaves on top and sides, dark blue painted ground, 4-1/2" w, 3-13/16" d, 3-5/8" h..............**$525**

Bas-relief carving

Basket of fruit, repaired, 6-1/8" l, 4-1/8" h **$435**

Woman holding bird, found in Iowa, 5" w, 6-3/4" h **$525**

Basket, carved freeform burl, America, 19th C, 10-3/4" l, 5-3/4" h........**$1,120**

Bowl, cigar box construction, ten paneled cut-out floral and circle designs, cigar label base, painted red ground, yellow, red, and green highlights to cut-outs, 7-1/4" d, 3-1/2" h........**$715**

Bowl, burl

Early red paint, 9-3/8" d........**$11,500**

Dark brown finish, raised band around rim, turned foot, age split, 22-3/4" d, 28-1/2" h..............**$200**

Good figure, dark patina, turned rim and foot, 9" d, 2-1/2" h..........**$1,380**

Box, cov

Book shape, Frisian carved, made from solid piece of wood, sliding lid, overall geometric carving, matching patterns on front and back, hearts and pinwheel on spine, good patina, int. with ivory paint, yellowed varnish, minor edge damage, few worm holes, 6-3/8" w, 3" d, 1-7/8" h **$220**

Wall pocket, Victorian, walnut, carved female head and leaves, 17" w, 22" h, **$195.**
Photo courtesy of Joy Luke Auctions.

Book shape, spruce, inland bands, star, crescent boon, hearts, and leaves, one end with sliding lid, minor alligatoring to varnish, short age cracks, 5-3/4" w, 4" d, 1-3/4" h **$200**

Oval, bentwood, single finger construction with opposite directions on lid and base, iron tacks, old dark green paint shows lighter under lid, minor wear to paint, 5-1/4" d, 3-3/8" h **$2,420**

Oval, bentwood, single finger on lid, overlapping seams on base, steel tacks, old medium blue paint, wear to lid, 8-1/4" w, 6-1/4" d, 4-1/4" h **$495**

Pine and poplar, orig red paint, applied molding on lid, dovetailed case, molded base, int. slotted for divider (missing), 12" w, 6-1/4" d, 5-3/4" h **$550**

Bucket, oak, slat, tapered, metal band, lid with porcelain finial, painted salmon, 9-1/2" d, 10-1/4" h........**$880**

Busk, carved maple, engraved with Indian smoking pipe, chip-carved geometric compass designs, attributed to New England, stand, early 19th C, 12" h **$980**

Butter paddle, figured maple, open heart terminal..............**$2,500**

Candle mold, twenty-four pewter tubes, old brown paint with spattered white, sq cut nail construction, old edge chips and splits, 16" h, 21-1/2" l, 9-1/2" w..............**$590**

Canoe cup, cup with elongated bowl, carved beaver, New England, with stand, 19th C, 5-3/4" l, 2-1/4" h **$520**

Chandelier shaft, turned, acorn finial, painted in dry red and green, never used, 18th C, 20-1/2" l, 2-3/4" d **$385**

Compote, turned, orig painted dec, initials "M.H.D.H." on base, 6" h **$1,500**

Cookie board, walnut, 10" x 12"

Carved man and women in Victorian dress **$3,000**

Carved soldier holding sword, tent, American flag, drum, stack of cannon balls................................**$3,750**

Figure, carved and painted

Frog, pine, applied metal eyes, painted dark green, red mouth, 3-1/4" l, 2-1/4" w, 1-7/8" h.....................**$495**

Seated Doberman with collar, shellacked, aged patina, 2-3/4" l, 1-1/4" w, 3-5/8" h.....................**$495**

Standing bird, white gesso with red and black highlights, 2-3/4" l, 1" w, 3" h **$385**

Standing Scottie terrier, incised lines for fur, painted black, painted black paws, carved "C. S." for Carl Snavely, 4" l, 1-1/4" w, 3-1/2" h **$200**

Firkin

Staved construction, four wooden bands, hand forged iron bail handle, wooden stopper, painted red, America, minor wear, early 19th C, 9" d base, 7" h **$265**

Staved construction, green lapped bands, swing handle fastened with pegs, painted red, "Cassia" inscribed in white letters, matching cover, America, wear, mid-19th C, 12" d, 12-1/2" h **$530**

Flax wheel, upright type, mixed hardwoods, four turned legs, single treadle, double flyers with bobbins, single wheel at top with turned spokes, few replacements, 45" h **$250**

Fruit, grouping of carved, gessoed, and polychromed fruits, grapes, apples, citrus, bananas, and cantaloupe, attributed to Adams County, PA **$6,050**

Fruit bowl, hardwood, sample-type, six-sided, dovetailed, pegged turned feet, painted yellow ground with brown highlighted grain painting, each panel with different graining, rag sponged interior with finger dot pattern, 9-1/2" w, 4" h **$2,860**

Herb drying rack, pine, old brown surface, mortised construction, later added old shoe feet, 29-1/2" w, 48-1/2" h......................................**$115**

Jar, cov

Peaseware, bulbous, shaped finial, incised ring dec on lid and body, low foot, 3-1/2" d, 6" h **$325**

Cage for bird or small animal, rounded top, sliding side opening, original perch and feed containers, **$75.**
Photo courtesy of Dotta Auction Co., Inc.

Treenware, fan shaped sponged vinegar dec in red over mustard, wide sloping rim and base, glued repair, edge damage on lid flange, age crack, 8-3/4" d, 9" h.............**$1,210**

Mask, carved

Divinity, pronounced teeth and eyes, painted white, yellow, red, black, and green, Nepal, 19th C, 14-1/2" l **$825**

Face painted red, early 20th C, 12" l **$715**

Wild boar, red, black, green, white, and orange, 11" l......................**$470**

Measuring device, carved and inlaid shoe-form, carved head of gentleman, ivory inlaid eyes, inlaid metal buckle, two ivory inlaid panels each dec with two engraved shoes, Holland, wear, crack, minor losses, late 18th C **$920**

Mortar and pestle, burl, flame graining, tapered sides, incised ring dec, lignum vitae pedestal, age splits, 7" h..**$375**

Pantry box, round, painted black, top carved with central star within medallion and leafy border, cross hatch swags on side, int. lined with partial advertising lithographs, New England, minor imperfections, mid-19th C, 6-1/4" d, 2-1/4" h...........**$715**

Pewter rack, hanging, oak, dark finish, two shelves, stylized lion finials on tops, wire nail construction, English, 35" w, 3-3/4" d, 29-3/4" h **$150**

Picture frame

Painted pine, black half round frame, meandering fruited vine and plant

Canister and cover, turned and painted wood, yellow and ochre grain decoration, early 19th C, 5-1/2" h x 6" w, **$3,680.**
Photo courtesy of Pook & Pook, Inc.

border, finish alligatored, 19th C, 13-3/4" w, 17-5/8" h **$520**

Rect, reticulated scalloped edge, compass star corner rosettes, painted black, finish alligatored, 19th C, 19-5/16" w, 22" h **$550**

Stenciled and painted, rect, gold floral dec on black ground, remnants of paper label on reverse, 13-3/8" w, 15-1/2" h **$375**

Quilt rack, folding

Three sections, each fitted with three cross pcs mortised into frame, cast iron hinges, old putty colored paint, 108" w, 66" h **$120**

Two sections, pine, old natural finish, three cross pcs mortised into frame, 3/4" w, 64" h **$95**

Saffron cup, Lehnware, blue ground, strawberry motif, blue, green, red, and salmon highlights, minor base chips, 2-1/2" d, 4-7/8" h **$3,080**

Salver, mahogany, molded pie-crust edge, America, staining, edge loss, 19th C, 10-3/4" d **$2,820**

Scoop, carved, America, 19th C, 9-3/4" l **$210**

Scrub box, wall type, pine, painted green, America, wear, 19th C, 7-1/2" w, 11-3/4" h......................**$715**

Shelf, hanging

Softwood, scalloped and scrolled cut-outs, painted black and red, 21-1/2" w, 7-1/2" d, 26-1/2" h **$1,650**

Walnut, four graduated shelves, rope suspended through hole in top of both side supports, 22" w, 6-3/4" d, 29-1/2" h **$990**

Walnut, pine secondary wood, scalloped ends, three graduating shelves with molded edges, brass pulls on two small base drawers, 20-1/2" w, 6-5/8" d, 25-1/4" h **$1,495**

Shoe horn, tiger maple, carved clasped hand terminal, 1826 ... **$4,000**

Slate board, tiger maple frame, slate on both sides, 11-1/4" w, 4-1/2" h **$1,980**

Spoon rack, hanging, butternut or walnut, old faint blue-green graining on black ground, red bird's claw shaped dec, three racks hold six spoons each, pierced arch crest, triangular shaped scalloping across base, nailed splits, one scallop repaired, 10" w, 20" h **$300**

Sugar bucket, cov

Old blue-gray paint over earlier colors, tapered sides, copper tacks in staves, bottom painted green, arched bentwood handle, old chips on lid, 21" h **$490**

Stave construction, copper tacks, bent hickory wood handle, minor wear and edge chips, 13-3/4" h **$460**

Tobacco jar, cov, treenware, turned and painted poplar, round, finger grained paint dec on yellow base, brown highlights, 6-1/2" d, 7-1/2" h **$1,430**

Toddy ladle, carved, notched handle, round bowl, dark brown patina, America, wear, early 19th C, 14-1/4" l **$440**

Trencher, rect, canted sides, rough hewn from pine, good patina, 23" l, 10-3/4" w, 3-1/4" h **$65**

Trivet, pine, wire nails, cut-out feet and ends on apron, old robin's egg blue with red stripes, hand painted decoupaged print of Mt. Vernon on top, minor flaking, multiple nail holes in one area, 4-1/4" x 7-7/8" x 4-3/8" h **$350**

Ventriloquist's head, mounted on later stand, carved pine, natural surface, America, eyes missing, c1930, 5" w, 6" d, 8" h **$375**

Wall shelf, bird's eye maple, carved, shaped and slightly bowed top shelf with incised front on pierced, shaped, scrolling supports, each with three circular bosses joined by incised medial bar, lower shaped shelf, old finish, New England, minor imperfections, mid-19th C, 38-1/2" l, 6-1/2" d, 16" h **$920**

WORLD'S FAIRS AND EXPOSITIONS

History: The Great Exhibition of 1851 in London marked the beginning of the World's Fair and Exposition movement. The fairs generally featured exhibitions from nations around the world displaying the best of their industrial and scientific achievements.

Many important technological advances have been introduced at world's fairs, including the airplane, telephone, and electric lights. Ice cream cones, hot dogs, and iced tea were first sold by vendors at fairs. Art movements often were closely connected to fairs, with the Paris Exhibition of 1900 generally considered to have assembled the best of the works of the Art Nouveau artists.

Centennial, 1876

Bank, still, cast iron, Independence Hall, 9" h x 7" w **$350**

Glass slipper, Gillinder, clear **$35**

Handkerchief, silk, dark golden background, black printed designs of Memorial Hall Art Gallery, Horticultural Hall, Machinery Hall, Agricultural Hall, Main Exhibition Building, large eagle and shield at top with "Fairmount Park, Philadelphia, 1776-1876" at bottom, stitched to cloth covered backing board, framed, small holes and staining, 29-1/2" x 33" **$435**

Medal, wooden, Main Building, 3" d **$60**

Scarf, Memorial Hall, Art Gallery colorful, 19" x 34" **$100**

New Orleans World's Industrial and Cotton Expo, 1885

Program, cover stamped "April 1885" **$45**

Columbian Exposition, 1893

Album, hardcover, gold emb "World's Fair Album of Chicago 1893," 5-3/4" x 9" **$50**

Book, *History of the World's Fair Being A Complete Description of the World's Colombian Exposition from Inception*, Major Ben C. Truman, illus, 592 pgs **$60**

Cup, peachblow glass, double handles, ribbed, shading from pink to white, gilt dec "World's Fair-1893 Chicago," minor crack at handle, 2-1/2" h **$300**

Medal, brass luster finish white metal, bust portrait of Christopher Columbus on one side, other side "400th Anniversary of The Discovery of America," 1492-Oct-1892, 1-1/2" **$20**

Mug, salt glazed stoneware, imp, blue accents "World's Fair Chicago 1893," 4-3/4" h **$165**

Photo booklet **$25**

Souvenir spoon **$25**

Salt and pepper shakers, pr, lay down, verse, Mt Washington, dated 1893, 2-1/2" l **$125**

Sugar bowl, open, peachblow, rose-colored walls, pronounced off-white ribs, satin finish, two applied opaque white glass handles, smooth pontil mark, made by Mt Washington Glass Co., sold by Libbey Glass Co., signature with flourishes, 5-1/2" w, 2-3/4" h **$485**

Ticket **$30**

Watch case opener, Keystone Watch Case Co. **$15**

Pan American, 1901

Cigar case, hinged aluminum 2-1/2" x 5-1/2" **$35**

Frying pan, pictures North and South America, 6" long **$75**

Medallion, bright luster brass, profile of buffalo between "Souvenir" and "1901," reverse marked "Pan-American Exposition/May-November Buffalo, NY" **$15**

Pinback button

Swifts Pig, multicolored plump pig seated in frying pan, tiny inscription "Pan-American Souvenir," black lettering "Swift's Premium Hams and Bacon-Swift & Co., U.S.A." **$25**

Temple of Music, multicolored art view of building exterior **$25**

Plate, frosted glass, three cats painted on dec, 7-1/2" d **$35**

Poster, Pan American Exposition, Buffalo, May 1-November 1, 1901, based on painting "Spirit of Niagara" by Evelyn Rumsey Carey, 47-1/2" x 24-3/4" **$12,650**

St. Louis, 1904

Match safe and cigar cutter, detailed drawing of Palace of Varied Industries on one side, picture of Gardens and Terraces of States on other, tarnished, 2-3/4" w, 1-1/2" h **$150**

Medal, silvered brass, 2-3/4" d **$60**

Photo album, eight pgs, 15 orig photos **$45**

Pinback button, KY home, multicolored exhibit building of Kentucky against upper half gold background, inscribed "Ky. Home World's Fair," bottom margin inscription "It's Part Mine" **$25**

Plate, scene in center, lacy border, 7-1/4" d **$25**

Souvenir mug, bronze, emb scene of Palace of Electricity, 6" h **$115**

Souvenir plate, Festival Hall, Cascade Gardens, 7" d **$55**

Stamp holder, aluminum, 1-1/8" x 1-3/8" **$35**

Tumbler, copper plated base, metal, shows Louisiana Purchase Monument, Cascades, Union Station and Liberal Arts Bldg, 4" h **$35**

Panama-Pacific, 1915

Pocket watch, official, silver plated, 2" **$300**

Postcard **$5**

Century of Progress, Chicago, 1933

Employee badge, round medallion with "A Century of Progress" around perimeter, "International Exposition Chicago 1933" and employee number below **$55**

Menu, Walgreens **$45**

Pinback button, New York Visitor, red, white, and blue **$20**

Playing cards, full deck, showing views of the fair, all different, black and white... **$45**

Ring, adjustable, silvered brass, miniature exhibit building on blue enamel background, inscribed "Chicago, 1934" **$25**

Souvenir key, bright silver luster brass, sponsored by Master Lock Co., "Master Laminated Padlocks Sold All Over the World," opposite side with miniature form image of exhibit buildings and "World's Fair 1933," tiny horseshoe and four-leaf clover, inscribed "Keep Me For Good Luck" **$28**

Toy wagon, red, white wheels, decal of Transportation Bldg in middle approx 3-1/2" l **$175**

Golden Gate, 1939

Bookmark, typical view, 4" l **$20**

Match book, orig matches, pictures Pacifica **$10**

Token, shows Sun Tower and Bridge, 1-1/8" d **$15**

New York, 1939

Bookmark, diecut and silvered thin brass spear page marker and letter opener, applied metal disk with blue and dark orange accents on silver luster "New York Worlds Fair, 1939," plus images of Trylon and Perisphere, 3-3/4" l **$20**

Folder, printed paper, blue, white, and orange, one side with three images of Borden's Elsie, Trylon, and Perisphere, reverse with blue and white printing, pictorial family endorsement, recipe, and text relating to Borden's Chateau cheese, August 1939 publication date, 6-1/4" x 12" **$20**

Pencil sharpener, bakelite **$45**

Pinback button, gold and blue cello, blue fabric ribbon inscribed in gold for May 1, 1939 event, Revolutionary War soldier behind inscription "New Haven Advertising Club, Inc./ Vigilance," outer rim inscribed "New Haven Day-New York World's Fair," 1-1/4" d **$125**

Pocketknife, steel knife based on each side by pearl-like plastic panels, one with tiny blue Trylon and Perisphere, plus inscription "New York World's Fair 1939," two steel blades, 2" l **$40**

Ring, adjustable, silvered brass, inscribed "World's Fair" over "NY," flanked by numeral "19" on one left, "39" on right **$25**

Souvenir spoon, Theme Building on front, "Pat. Pend., Wm Rogers Mfg. Co.," 7" l **$25**

World's Fair, plate, Libbey, enameled, depicts Santa Maria, "World's Fair 1893" verbiage, acid stamped, "Libbey Cut Glass Company," 7-1/2" w, $500.

Photo courtesy of The Early Auction Company, LLC.

Book, The Illustrated Historical Register of the Centennial Exposition, 1876, gold trim on black leather cover, illustrated, $250.

World's Fairs & Expositions, Exposition Universelle at Internationale de Bruxelles, Paris, poster by Eugene Verneau, 1910, framed, 51" x 39-1/2", $1,100.

Photo courtesy of David Rago Auctions, Inc.

YARD-LONG PRINTS

History: In the early 1900s, many yard-long prints could be had for a few cents postage and a given number of wrappers or box tops. Others were premiums for renewing a subscription to a magazine or newspaper. A large number were advertising items created for a store or company and had calendars on the front or back. Many people believe that the only true yard-long print is 36 inches long and titled "A Yard of Kittens," etc. But lately collectors feel that any long and narrow print, horizontal or vertical, can be included in this category. It is a matter of personal opinion.

Values are listed for full-length prints in near-mint condition, nicely framed, and with original glass.

Reproduction Alert. Some prints are being reproduced. Know your dealer.

Notes: Numbers in parentheses below indicate C. G. and J. M. Rhoden and W. D. and M. J. Keagy, *Those Wonderful Yard-Long Prints and More*, Book 1 (1989), Book 2 (1992), Book 3 (1995), book number and page on which the item is illustrated, e.g. (3-52) refers to Book 3, page 52.

Animals

A Yard of Puppies, ten puppies playing, one with foot in feeding dish (Bk 1-50) **$450**

Ducklings, by W. M. Carey, baby ducks playing around a pool of water (Bk 3-22) **$400**

Our Feathered Pets, by Paul DeLongpre, twelve birds sitting on lattice work fence (Bk 3-19) **$400**

Spring is Here, by Cambril, The Gray Litho Co., New York (Bk 2-18), c1907 .... **$325**

Tug of War, seven kittens and seven puppies playing tug of war (Bk 2-28) **$400**

Twenty-one birds, sitting on a wire, (Bk 3-20), c1899 .... **$400**

Yard of Dogs, eight adult dogs, one with bird in mouth, one with bandage on head covering eye (Bk 2-21), copyright 1903 .... **$325**

Yard of Kittens, eleven kittens playing, one climbing on box (Bk 2-23) **$400**

Calendar

1095, Swift's Premium, four beautiful ladies showing four seasons (Bk 3-112) **$400**

1906, Pabst Extract, Indian, by C. W. Henning, "Hiawatha's Wooing" poem on back of print (Bk 2-101) **$575**

1907, Metropolitan Life Ins Co., showing four stages of life (Bk 3-111) **$475**

1915, Seiz Good Shoes, lady and child on swing (Bk 2-102) **$575**

1917, by Knowles Hare Jr., lady in pink hat and dress (Bk 3-88) **$500**

1919, Clay, Robinson & Co., Live Stock Commission, advertising and picture of bull, Merry Monarch, on back (Bk 3-106) **$500**

1925, Seiz Good Shoes, lady with walking stick **$800**

Flowers and fruits

A Yard of Cherries, by Guy Bedford, (Bk 2-69), c1906 .... **$300**

A Yard of Chrysanthemums, by Maud Stumm (Bk 2-33) **$300**

A Yard of Wild Flowers, artist sgd in lower left corner (Bk 3-39) **$300**

Bridal Favors, by Mary E. Hart (Bk 2-65) **$300**

Dogwood and Violets, Paul DeLongpre, sgd (Bk 3-28) **$350**

Lilacs and Lillies, artist sgd in lower right corner (Bk 3-31) **$300**

Study of Sweet Peas, by Grace Barton Allen, (Bk 2-62), copyright 1900 .... **$300**

Yard of Assorted Fruit, basket of cherries, plate of fruit on book (Bk 2-73) **$300**

Long ladies

At the Gate, lady in pink by garden gate (Bk 3-82) **$500**

Beautiful lady, holding vase of red roses (Bk 3-93) **$500**

Beautiful lady, standing by table, holding open basket, vase of yellow roses on table (Bk 2-88) **$700**

Butterick Pattern Lady, copyright 1930 (Bk 3-42) **$600**

Indian Maiden, holding basket of flowers (Bk 3-89) **$500**

The Girl with the Laughing Eyes, by F. Carlyle, lady in long off-shoulder gown, holding paper lantern (Bk 2-92), copyright 1910 .... **$500**

The Girl with the Poppies, by B. Lichtman (Bk 3-125) **$500**

Wynette Lady, standing by large vase of yellow roses (Bk 3-80) **$500**

FAKE AND CONFUSING MARKS ON NEW CHINA, POTTERY

by Mark Chervenka

Historically, collectors have relied on marks to authenticate and date antiques and collectibles. That process is becoming less reliable, though, as more reproductions are appearing with nearly exact copies of original marks.

Some old company names have been legitimately reregistered in America, but most marks on reproductions are deliberately designed to be confusing. In many cases, very slight variations—such as color, whether a mark is raised or impressed, whether the mark includes the country of origin—are all that separate vintage marks from the fakes.

Fake and confusing marks have become so widespread that marks alone should never be used as a single test of age or authenticity. Examine a variety of features on a piece including shape, colors, pattern and decoration before making a conclusion on age. Perhaps the best defense against fake marks is simply a healthy skepticism.

The marks shown here are typical of some of the confusing marks you'll find in the antiques and collectibles market today.

Brush-McCoy Pottery

The original Brush-McCoy Pottery operated between about 1911-1925. In 1925, the name was changed to Brush Pottery. Brush Pottery was among the first American potteries to produce cookie jars it made from 1929 until it closed in 1982.

The pre-1925 company named Brush- McCoy Pottery never made cookie jars; it was Brush Pottery, 1929-1982, which made cookie jars. Yet the market is being flooded with new jars marked Brush-McCoy.

At first, the confusing marks only appeared on reproductions of jars originally made by Brush Pottery. Now the mark also appears on jars by other vintage makers such as Shawnee Pottery and other vintage potteries. Most original Brush Pottery marks were impressed below the surface, not raised. So far, all the new Brush McCoy marks are raised molded marks.

A close up view of the raised molded Brush-McCoy mark found on reproduction cookie jars. No mark like this ever appeared before the late 1990s. It is only found on reproductions.

There are two typical marks of Brush Pottery that appear on vintage cookie jars, ca. 1940s-1982. The closest original Brush Pottery mark to include a paintbrush was the palette mark, left. The "W" in authentic Brush-Pottery marks, right, indicates the jar was designed by Twin Winton Ceramics.

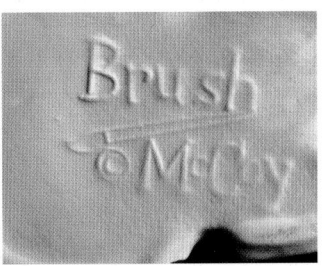

The Brush-McCoy mark on a new Mugsy cookie jar. Original Mugsy cookie jars were made by Shawnee Pottery.

Bauer Pottery

The Bauer Pottery name has been registered again and new pottery is being marked with the Bauer Pottery name. New products, including copies of the popular "ring ware" line, are reproductions of original shapes manufactured in the 1930-1940s using vintage pieces as models.

The new company is hoping to help collectors avoid confusion by adding "2000" to the new marks. However, only about 20 percent of the new shapes include the 2000 mark. Company officials say the 2000 mark will be added to the other shapes as those molds are repaired or replaced.

All vintage Bauer marks are impressed, or incised, into the clay. Most, but not all, marks on new Bauer are raised.

New Bauer ring ware pottery. All pieces are marked Bauer Pottery.

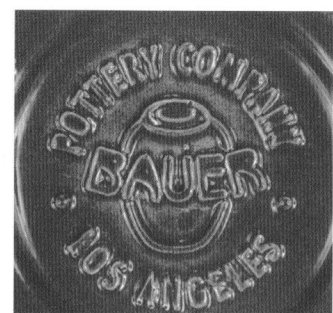

A raised molded mark on new Bauer Pottery. All original Bauer marks are impressed, not raised.

A raised molded mark of new Bauer Pottery with the number 2000. The 2000 appears on many but not all of the new Bauer to help collectors separate old from new.

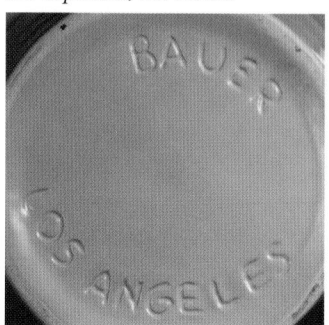

Some pieces of new Bauer Pottery have impressed marks like this example on an 8-inch flower pot. This new mark is similar to incised marks on vintage Bauer

McCoy Pottery

New pottery marked McCoy is one of the most common reproductions in today's market. The new McCoy marks are virtually identical to marks on originals. The marks appear on copies of specific McCoy originals as well as fantasy items never made by McCoy.

Reproductions that copy original McCoy shapes are the most difficult to identify. Since molds used to make the reproductions are taken from authentic samples, new and old shapes are almost impossible to separate. Questionable pieces should be carefully measured and compared to known originals in reference books. The reproductions are one-quarter to three-quarters of an inch smaller than the originals.

This wall vase/planter marked McCoy is a fantasy piece: no original was ever made by McCoy. A piece from another manufacturer was used to make a mold and a fake McCoy mark was added.

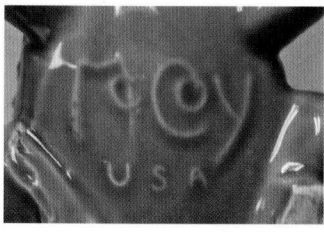

Left: A new frog sprinkler marked McCoy USA. The frog is a direct copy of a McCoy original, but the original McCoy piece was made as a planter only, never as a sprinkler with a handle.
Right: The raised molded "McCoy USA" mark on the bottom of the new frog sprinkler.

Nippon

Fake Nippon marks have appeared on new porcelain since the early 1990s. Although the wreath mark is the most common original mark, many different marks appear on authentic pre- 1921 Nippon. There are now matching fake marks for most of the original variations.

No one rule can be used to detect all the new marks. What may be an indication of a fake in one mark, may not be of help when examining another mark. Most marks need to be examined on a case by case basis. Some of the most common faked marks are shown here.

This is a fake mark: the wreath is closed at the top, and there is a crude hand-painted appearance to the mark.

The wreath is open at the top; the letter "M" in the center. All lines are quite solid and distinct.

This is a fake mark: the wreath is turned upside down, and an hour-glass was never used in the old mark.

This is a fake mark: the wreath is turned upside down, and the letter "K" was never used in old mark. Keep in mind that reproduction wholesalers are using various fake Nippon marks on a wide variety of shapes and forms that have no old counterparts.

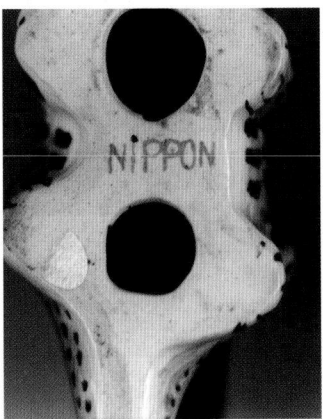

A fake Nippon mark in red block letters. This mark is found on the example shown at right.

A fake RC mark entirely in green. RC is poorly formed and almost unrecognizable as English letters.

The words "Hand Painted" are in red; "RC" and "Nippon" appear in green. Letters RC are distinct.

A new figural marked Nippon in red block letter; also found marked Occupied Japan. No pre-1921 original of this shape was ever marked Nippon.

Red Wing Stoneware

A company named Red Wing Stoneware Company begun in the mid-1980s uses markings similar to those found on vintage collectible stoneware.

Marks of the original Red Wing Stoneware Company established in 1876 never appear as a blue ink oval mark. The original blue oval trademark was not used until ca. 1906 by which time the original Red Wing Stoneware Pottery Company was known as Red Wing UNION Stoneware Company.

The old mark of Red Wing UNION Stone ware Company that appeared with the red wing trademark, ca.1906-1930s.

The mark of the new Red Wing Stoneware Company is easily confused with the mark of the old Red Wing UNION Stoneware Company shown at left.

Roseville Pottery

Roseville Pottery has been reproduced in china since 1996. The majority of reproductions have a fake version of Roseville's Late Period mark, the word Roseville in script above a shape/size number. Original marks include U.S.A. between Roseville" and the shape/size number. The comparable fake mark does not include U.S.A.

On some of the earliest reproductions you may find U.S.A. in very faint weak letters like the examples shown here. In original Late Period marks used 1935-1954, the U.S.A. is the same height and sharpness as Roseville and the shape/size number. The only exceptions are particularly small original shapes where there was no space for U.S.A.

Reproductions of Roseville's pre-1934 patterns have begun appearing with the mark shown here. Although this is a close copy of an authentic pre-1934 Roseville mark, it is easily detected. The original mark is impressed below the surface; the fake mark is molded and raised above the surface.

A typical authentic Roseville mark used during the Late Period, 1935-1954. Note that U.S.A. is the same height and weight as Roseville and the shape/size number. If U.S.A. is missing or very faint in the Late Period mark, it is almost certainly a reproduction.

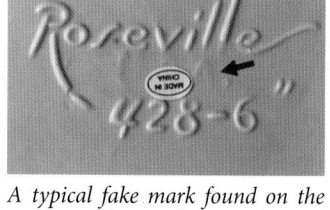

A typical fake mark found on the majority of Roseville reproductions made in China. This example is shown with the removable paper label as it arrives from the reproduction wholesaler. In fake marks, the letters U.S.A. are either missing or, as in this example, very faint.

A fake raised mark used on reproductions of Roseville Middle Period patterns such as Jonquil and Luffa. Original Luffa and Jonquil never had raised marks. Original Luffa and Jonquil usually had paper labels only, never raised molded marks.

INDEX

45s, 686-690

A

Abino Ware, 31

Adams, 57-58, 62, 92, 104, 131, 158-160, 166, 521, 593, 624, 656, 663, 724, 744, 746, 753

Advertising And Souvenir-Keepsake Items, 509

Advertising Button, 482, 565, 579, 621

Advertising Ware, 31

Advertising, 30-31, 66, 112, 132-134, 168, 175, 274, 281-282, 295, 350, 419, 444, 459, 463, 468, 482-483, 487, 489, 497, 507, 509-510, 515, 523, 526, 537, 544, 558, 565, 579, 604, 616-618, 620-621, 654, 656, 663, 669, 703, 706, 733, 753, 755-756

Agata Glass, 271

Agate Ware, 28, 177

Agate, Carved, 408, 722

Amberina Glass, 271-273, 699

Amberina Glass, Plated, 273

American Flyer, 456-457

American Hand-Painted China Jewelry And Buttons, 20

Amphora, 21, 24, 101

Animal Collectibles, 466-469

Animals, Toy, 510

Appliqué, 379, 429, 534-535, 537, 679

Arcade, 413, 419, 446-447, 539-540, 566, 726

Architectural Elements, 470-472

Arnold, USA, 447

Art Deco, 26, 63, 84, 108, 128, 141, 155, 178, 193, 197, 201, 211-212, 215, 220, 224, 231-232, 235, 240, 246-247, 252, 262, 337, 366-367, 374, 386, 392, 397, 399-402, 405, 407, 473-475, 512-513, 535, 556-557, 608, 653, 656, 682-683, 713, 721

Art Glass, 266, 268, 274, 279, 325, 335, 339-340, 345, 348, 364, 367, 369, 372, 374-375, 381-382, 386, 389, 474-475, 499, 607, 694, 699, 741

Art Nouveau, 21, 29, 31, 56, 63-64, 108, 118, 123, 153, 156, 175, 184-185, 188, 197, 201, 215, 239, 243, 247,

249, 275, 337, 374, 382, 386, 397, 399, 401-402, 405-407, 475-477, 497, 505, 513, 606-607, 617, 669, 721, 731, 741, 754

Art Pottery, 16-17, 21-24, 36, 47, 59, 63, 65, 72, 99, 103, 105, 115, 119, 135, 142, 157, 173, 183, 188, 477

Arts & Crafts Movement, 397-398, 477-480

Astral, 56, 607

Atomizer, 24, 279, 340, 365, 374, 376, 657

Austrian Ware, 24, 36

Autographs, 421, 480-482, 511, 727

Automobilia, 482-483

B

Baccarat Glass, 273-274

Bangle/Bracelet, 406

Banks, Mechanical, 414-418

Banks, Still, 419-420

Banquet lamp, 347, 608

Bar Pin, 399-400, 512, 665, 667-668

Barber Bottles, 274

Barbie Dolls, 412, 421-429, 486

Barnyard, 76, 466, 469

Barometers, 484

Baseball, 90-91, 443, 480, 488, 501, 553, 725-726, 732

Basketball, 727

Baskets, 32, 68, 70, 96, 140, 276-277, 282, 285, 296, 325, 484-486, 514, 603, 679, 702, 717

Bavarian China, 25, 36

Beatrix Potter Collectibles, 486-487

Beds, 201-202, 473, 640

Bell, 56, 71, 74-75, 113, 125, 130, 145, 161, 169-170, 177, 186-187, 202, 248, 274, 280, 314-315, 326, 328, 347, 367, 383-384, 386, 393, 415, 448, 451, 454-455, 468, 479, 498, 527-528, 530, 539-540, 561, 565-566, 584, 593, 606-607, 630, 636, 638, 649, 661, 687, 692, 696, 730, 743-744, 747

Belleek, 25-27, 83, 585, 701

Benches, 203-204, 448, 522

Benevolent & Protective Order Of The Elks, (BPOE), 578

Bennington And Bennington-Type Pottery,

28-29, 134

Bentwood, 197, 204, 208, 217, 219-220, 223, 243, 249, 473, 485-486, 603, 613, 707-708, 752, 754

Bing, Gebruder, Germany, 447

Bing, German, 457

Birds, 21, 24, 33-34, 36-37, 40, 43, 45-47, 50-51, 68, 71, 93-94, 97, 100, 109, 114-115, 139-141, 147, 149-150, 152-154, 167, 170, 173, 180, 183, 186, 208, 232, 242, 282, 298-299, 302, 350, 354, 367, 370, 372, 387-388, 390, 395, 397, 465-467, 470, 474, 484, 493, 497, 510, 522, 528, 534, 575-578, 580, 586, 589-590, 592, 598-599, 602-603, 611, 634-635, 649-653, 658-659, 679, 681, 687, 702-703, 705, 708, 715, 722-723, 737-740, 744, 746, 748, 756

Biscuit Jars, 29, 149, 274

Bisque, 30, 73, 83, 93, 110, 116, 119-120, 146, 156, 173, 385, 429-441, 515-516, 553, 556, 558, 616, 630

Black Memorabilia, 487-489

Blanket Chests, 205-206

Bohemian Glass, 275, 522

Bookcases, 195, 206-208, 551

Bookmarks, 576, 732

Books, Early, 489-491

Bottles, General, 276

Boudoir, 325, 473, 607-608, 645, 695, 722, 742

Bow, 38, 46, 83, 94, 120, 124-125, 146, 170, 182, 209, 223, 225-226, 248, 251, 253-254, 347, 364, 400, 419-422, 424, 426-429, 438, 460, 464, 466-467, 503, 506, 512-516, 535, 551, 567, 588, 597, 619, 628, 633, 636-637, 640, 655, 664, 671, 679, 733, 746

Bowl, 21-22, 24-29, 31-34, 36, 38, 40-44, 46-50, 52-63, 65-68, 70-72, 80-85, 93, 98-99, 101-109, 111-114, 118-119, 121-122, 128-132, 135-136, 139-143, 145-153, 155, 157-166, 172, 175, 177-183, 186-188, 209, 253-254, 267, 270-279, 282-330, 332-337, 339-349, 351, 354, 357-364,

366-370, 372-380, 382-385, 387, 389-390, 424, 427, 429, 462, 473-476, 478, 486, 491-492, 494, 516, 519-520, 529, 537, 558, 576, 579, 581, 584, 587, 589-590, 595, 599, 602, 604-605, 607, 609, 630, 639, 649, 651-652, 658, 661, 684, 694-697, 712-721, 724-725, 728, 736, 743, 746, 752-754

Bowl, Burl, 752

Box, Cov, 24, 32-33, 84, 95, 103, 107, 112-113, 117, 122, 141, 145, 155-156, 180-182, 277, 279, 301-302, 305-306, 314-315, 321-323, 329, 337, 341-342, 345-346, 350, 352, 354, 360, 375, 379, 388, 533, 565, 575, 579, 596, 601, 604, 624, 636, 649, 707-708, 741, 745, 748, 752

Boxes, 208-210, 224-225, 228, 239, 244, 386, 395, 410, 441, 456-457, 461, 493, 509, 511, 514, 524, 555-556, 616-617, 627, 631, 656, 682, 715, 722, 736, 743, 745, 748-749

Boxing, 462, 553, 727

Bracelet, 338, 399, 401, 403-406, 422, 432, 512, 551, 554, 599

Bracket, 153, 194, 205-207, 209, 211-213, 224-229, 231-238, 242, 244-246, 248, 255, 303, 333-334, 470, 521, 526-527, 529-533, 613, 629, 634, 640, 665, 743, 751

Bradley Pottery, 46

Brass, 20, 29, 46, 117, 122, 147, 155, 179-180, 194, 202, 205-207, 209-213, 216, 219, 222, 224-235, 237-239, 241, 244, 247-264, 273-275, 277, 280, 302, 336, 342-343, 367, 371, 373, 383, 386, 388, 392, 397-398, 400, 403, 416-417, 419, 427, 456, 461-462, 467-474, 476, 478-480, 483-484, 491-492, 498-507, 515-516, 525-533, 535-537, 547, 551-555, 557-568, 571-573, 579-580, 584-588, 590-596, 601-604, 607-614, 616-620, 622, 624-633, 636-638,

More Pricing & Identification
Expertise from *Warman's*®

Roseville Pottery
A Warman's Companion
by Mark F. Moran

Wherever your collecting takes you a *Warman's*® *Companion* is there! This easy to use and easy to carry guide is packed with 1,100 detailed color to help you easily and accurately identify various Roseville pieces. This handy book contains current and authoritative pricing, offering valuable assistance in maintaining your collection and making savvy purchase decisions.

This must-have reference covers the evolution of Roseville from its humble beginnings to an internationally recognized collectible and popular item at many high-profile auctions. In addition, this book:

• Offers insight on spotting fakes and forgeries in the marketplace, saving you from making costly purchase errors

• Is portable enough to turn to wherever you are, for reliable Roseville details and data.

Softcover • 5 x 8 • 272 pages • 1,100 color photos • **Item# CCRV** • **$17.99**

arman's® Coca-Cola® Collectibles
entification and Price Guide
Allan Petretti

at yourself to the latest collectible Coca-Cola information, pricing and details from leading authority on Coca-Cola. This book covers Coca-Cola collectibles from the 30s to the 1960s, complete with thoroughly researched market pricing, plus details make identifying items easier.

u'll discover 1,500 superb color photos for accurate identification, and simple preciation of this world-famous company. Plus, you'll find brief historical accounts the company's 120-year history. This exhaustive Coca-Cola reference includes:

Calendars and toys

erving trays and posters

ottles and coolers

d More!

Available in June

tcover • 8-1/4 x 10-7/8 • 256 pages • 1,500 color photos • **Item# WCCC** • **$24.99**

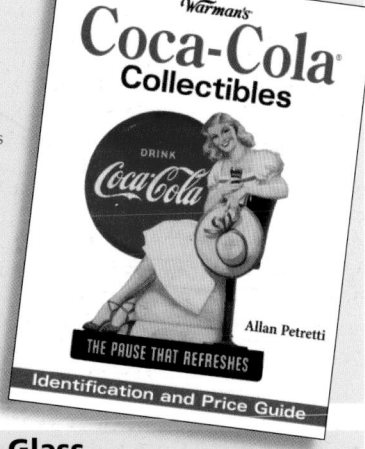

Warman's® Depression Glass
Identification and Value Guide
4th Edition
by Ellen T. Schroy

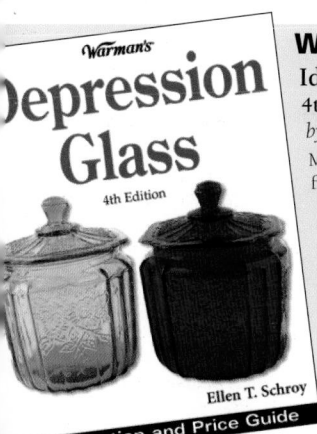

More photos, more details and more expertly researched prices of Depression glass pieces fill the pages of this essential price guide. With current market values for more than 10,000 Depression glass items you get the most up-to-date pricing information for the various Depression glass patterns. The identifying descriptions you'll find in this guide are the most thorough of any Depression glass reference book today.

This comprehensive guide also contains background information about the company, plus a special section showcasing the evolution of Depression glass shapes over the years. With this must-have reference you'll:

• Easily identify patterns through 1,000 detailed color photos and line drawings

• Expand your Depression glass knowledge with expertise from the leading glass authority

Available in June

Softcover • 8-1/4 x 10-7/8 • 320 pages • 1,000 color photos • **Item# WDG04** • **$27.99**

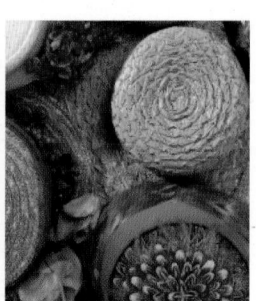